Supplement to Charles Evans'

American Bibliography

Supplement to Charles Evans'

American Bibliography

By Roger P. Bristol

Published for
The Bibliographical Society of America
and
The Bibliographical Society of the University of Virginia

University Press of Virginia
Charlottesville

THE UNIVERSITY PRESS OF VIRGINIA

First published 1970

Standard Book Number: 8139-0287-8
Library of Congress Catalog Card Number: 73-94761
Printed in the United States of America

Preface

Charles Evans, whose name is deeply incised on the slate of American bibliographers, decided at the age of 51 to devote the remainder of his life to the recording in full bibliographical detail of the output of the early American presses, covering the years 1639 to 1820. The reasoning and source of the inspiration behind this dedication and the toil of many years are not revealed, but before his death in 1935 he singlehandedly described 35,854 entries in the 12 volumes of his *American Bibliography*, which appeared over a thirty-year period, 1904–1934. The final volume had brought him through the letter M of the year 1799, close to the year 1800, which his revised goal had become. His work remained unfinished until Clifford K. Shipton published volume 13 in 1955, which completed the entries for 1799 and those for 1800. Richard H. Shoemaker and Ralph R. Shaw subsequently carried the bibliography through the year 1820 in 20 published volumes which appeared between 1958 and 1964. Mr. Shoemaker has, in fact, gone beyond the original terminal date and so far has carried his work through 1823.

In the introduction to his first volume, Charles Evans speaks of the special traits of the bibliographer, and thereby furnishes an autobiographical insight into the ways he approached his material. "To him," he wrote, "a title-page bears the same relation to a book that the face does to the human body. It is the face of the book. It speaks the author's personality. If pleasant spoken, well favored to the sight, instinct with intelligence, direct of purpose, it invites desire for fuller knowledge and better acquaintance, just as a smile and friendly glance welcome to conversation. If coarsely worded, or treating of themes which interest not, it repels. If bold, aggressive, so, too, will be the words, the speech within. If worded quaintly, so will you find the mind within, well stored from books and imitating unconsciously the manners of a past age." It is thus evident that Evans had a very personal approach to the books that passed through his hands in the alembic of his bibliographical research.

No bibliography is ever complete or finally finished, and the *American Bibliography* of Charles Evans is no exception. Evans also had the bad habit of relying all too often on newspaper advertisements and other secondary sources for many of his entries. As a result he produced a fair share of bibliographical ghosts, or nonexistent books. Many of his entries, for other reasons, are inaccurate as to author, title, imprint, or collation and require revision or correction. Corrections became the responsibility of Mr. Shipton, and they will soon be published. As the editor of the microprint edition of "Evans," he was in an ideal position to detect these discrepancies and to make the necessary changes.

About 15 years ago Roger P. Bristol became another worker in the field of Evans' pioneer endeavor. In 1959 he published his index to the pre-1801 imprints. Two years later the Bibliographical Society of the University of Virginia published Mr. Bristol's *Index of Printers, Publishers, and Booksellers Indicated by Charles Evans in His "American Bibliography."* Even before that time Mr. Bristol had become interested in the books and broadsides of this period which had escaped Evans' dragnet. A number of libraries, among them the Henry E. Huntington Library, the Library of Congress, and the New York Public Library, had prepared inventories of their "not-in-Evans" titles. These were grist to Bristol's mill. Similarly many specialized bibliographies, covering in one way or another this early period of American printing, were also sources of other new entries. Mr. Bristol acknowledges the culling of 121 such sources in the foreword to his checking edition of the supplement to Evans which he issued serially between 1962 and 1964. Further lists of supplementary titles were published by the Bibliographical Society of the University of Virginia, as number 52 of the *Secretary's News Sheet* for August 1966 and as number 53 for December 1967. The work of addition and revision continued until 1969 through Mr. Bristol's further checking and through reports of new entries from cooperating libraries to the clearinghouse he maintained in the Alderman Library at the University of Virginia. The final results reveal that this supplement includes more than 11,200 entries which escaped the notice of both Evans and Shipton. This represents an increase of nearly 30 per cent above the Evans-Shipton total of 39,162.

Inevitably new entries will of course continue to turn up from time to time, but it is fair to state that Evans' great work is now virtually finished nearly 70 years after it was begun. A splendid bibliographical tool in its final form is now available to that world of scholarship which is devoted to America's earliest printed books. That world is eternally indebted to the willing and cooperative spirit of the several men who have selflessly given their energy and their special talents to this early period of American bookmaking.

As for the more than 50,000 recorded titles in the Evans-Shipton-Bristol bibliographies, these are the blood and fabric of America's formative years. These books and pamphlets, newspapers and journals, broadsides and other ephemera, are the basic source materials which historians must read and understand if our early history is to be properly appraised and accurately written. I am reminded of an oversimplified but telling phrase of the late Alfred W. Pollard, a former Keeper of Printed Books in the British Museum, who wrote: "The publication of every book which has issued from printing house or Scriptorium is an event in the spiritual history of the country and city in which it appears."

Frederick R. Goff
Chief
Rare Book Division
Library of Congress

April 1969

Contents

Introduction

In 1957 when I began compiling the present *Supplement* to Evans' *American Bibliography*, I naïvely thought that two or three years' work would see it to completion. The push over the brink into twelve years of intermittent work was administered by Frederick R. Goff, who generously offered to supply me with an already prepared typescript of the not-in-Evans (NIE) items at the Library of Congress. Although the list was compiled with unusual completeness and care, a quick check against the 3x5 slips of my index to the 39,162 items described by Evans revealed that some of the items were actually *in* Evans.

Finding duplications even in a list supplied by our national library influenced my later practice. Thereafter I checked every bibliography, every additional item sent me by correspondents, against the index, against Evans' descriptions if the index was not decisive, and ultimately against the microprint reproduction when necessary. If an item was asserted to be in Evans, I accepted it as so, but if the contrary was asserted, it was never taken for granted. I have no figures, absolute or in percentage, to justify my practice, but not-in-Evans items have so often been found *in* Evans that I never considered abandoning it.

I suppose I have learned to trust no bibliographer over 30, not even the most eminent, and especially not myself. For I too have sinned, even to the point of putting the same item in different years under different entries. Such sins of commission have been caught (usually) by friendly bibliographers, right up to May 1969.

Certain other practices were early adopted: to condense every item to what could be typed on a 3x5 card; to add locations when found but not to go looking for them; and especially to describe each item so that a bibliographer could be sure that an item physically in hand was the item described. The success of this last only future bibliographers will be able to evaluate.

Some forty years ago the figure 3.2% was a number to conjure with in certain quarters. If it is not too small beer to suggest it, I should like to propose 3.2% as the maximum error permitted in bibliographies. I hope the *Supplement* has a far smaller percentage of error, perhaps even by an order of magnitude. But to make an error-estimate lower than .0032 would be immodest to the point of absurdity; there are just too many chances for slips of mind or hand between piece and print.

Unfortunately I cannot include among my practices a logical approach to the field as a whole. I worked haphazardly from one available bibliography to another, and I feel confident that some have been overlooked. When unexpected material drifted in (in letters, on cards, on white slips, blue slips, brown slips), I gave it first priority, hoping thus to avoid total submersion. When, for example, in 1957 the Clements Library sent a fat roll of photostats of catalog cards for their NIE items, I postponed work on Alden's *Rhode Island imprints* and the Wroth-Wheeler-Minick trilogy of Maryland imprints until the following spring.

By May 1958 there were 5000 entries, more than I had dreamed existed. But there were many bibliographies still to be checked; Welch's tremendous bibliographical work on children's books was then unknown to me; and I had not yet visited the American Antiquarian Society. Knowing the preëminence of the Society, I tried to prepare myself by putting on cards NIE items from as many printed bibliographies as possible in advance of a visit in the hope of reducing the quantity of new material.

Although entries numbered 7500 by June 1960, I nevertheless spent a frantic fortnight in Worcester with the Society's NIE collection. I added nearly 1200 *new* items to my boxes of cards, and I shall be ever grateful to Clifford K. Shipton for permitting me to stay after hours and to work alone in the building one whole weekend in order to finish going over the uncataloged broadsides. I am grateful also to the staff, who brought me materials *seriatim* and who permitted me to share their expeditious lunchroom.

From the beginning of the project it had been the plan to issue a checking edition when the rate of inclusions had reached a plateau. I am afraid the plateau never became more than a ledge, but at any rate the first 32-page fascicle was issued in late 1962. By the time the body of the checking edition had been issued, in 629 pages, enough material had accumulated for 102 pages more, concluding with a "Supplement to the Appendix to the Supplement." Entries now totaled 10,600, and it was late 1964.

Not as many libraries participated as had been hoped, but even so the decision to issue a checking edition vindicated itself quickly. Information in the returning fascicles resulted in the deletion of several hundred items (mostly duplications of Evans) and the correction of hundreds more; no attempt was made to keep an exact count.

By 1969, however, the deletions had been more than made good by new material. Several new correspondents who learned of the project through the checking edition sent valuable additional items. Bibliographies which included many additional NIE items came to my attention or appeared in print. Nevertheless I feel sure that in many small libraries, in some large libraries, and in private collections NIE items are still tucked away waiting to be discovered. If a plateau has been reached, it is certainly one that slopes upward. I fully expect the present Evans total of nearly 50,400 to increase by another thousand within a decade.

From this historical sketch, I now turn to some of the problems encountered. The arrangement presented the least difficulty. Following Evans' pattern, the entries are arranged alphabetically under each year from 1646 to 1800. Entries generally follow accepted practice for personal or corporate authors, with entry under title when the author is uncertain or pseudonymous, but there are a few deviations. Almanacs are listed under title, not under apparent compiler. And if there are any catalogers who read this and who wonder at some of the corporate entries chosen, I can say only that the project was begun when catalog code revision was winding its weary way through directors and committees. Always anxious to be in the forefront, I followed what seemed to be the wave of the future. When the wave turned out to have considerable backwash, some of my entries were left high and dry. So I left them there.

The problem of preventing duplication in the *Supplement* of an item already described in Evans has been a never-ending one. Let me quote from a July 1960 letter to Mary Isabel Fry of the Huntington Library for a statement of my practice:

> When I know that the Readex microprint edition has used a variant of what Evans said, I fell I should refrain from using the same item as not-in-Evans too. If the printers vary or if the item is reset in a major way, I *do* use it.... Evans was so often incomplete or in error in his description that it is sometimes difficult to say whether a newly described item is or is not his. If he did not see the item and did not locate it, I have decided to give him the benefit of the doubt unless it develops that there is a variant in addition to what he described.

The Readex microprint edition has generally clarified such problems. But occasionally an item has turned up which is what Evans appears to have been describing, but for which the microprint edition uses a variant. In such cases I have usually referred the question to Ted Shipton, who might pencil a note to this effect: "You take it. I can't use it." The alternatives to including it would have been either to replace the item in the microprint edition (an impossibly costly task) or to omit a perfectly valid variant from the total text. A note identifies these few items.

Another problem was that of deciding on a pattern for inclusion or exclusion. Bibliographers on whose works I drew had followed varying practices, sometimes explicit, sometimes not. Some of them may find that perfectly valid pieces of printing are not included because they do not conform to the pattern outlined below.

Before 1700. All types of printing done in this country are included.

1700–1800. Tickets and cards are excluded.
- Newspaper supplements and extras are included, but only if numbered.
- Legal forms (e.g., deeds, indentures) are excluded unless date and printer are *printed* in the text.
- Other forms (e.g., military) are included if they show printer and/or date to the decade.

The inclusion of any forms at all has occasioned some anxiety among a few bibliographers, and perhaps merits somewhat more extended discussion here.

What is a form? To me, a form is a printed broadside which leaves spaces to be filled in by hand. The handwritten portion may be date (whole or in part); person addressed; place; signature; or any combination of these. To quote from a letter of February 1968 to Marcus McCorison,

> The pattern of inclusion/exclusion must be the compiler's view of the importance of a particular item historically or bibliographically. To historians, it may well be that some undated forms (e.g., those issued by the Colonies during the Revolution) are as valuable documents as many dated ones. For bibliographers, it seems to me that the most important determinant is to assemble the available printing of a year or of a printer. I know no way in which to satisfy completely both historians and bibliographers. Since I am interested chiefly in the bibliographical point of view, I am including forms *if* the printer or the date to at least three digits is shown in print (not handwritten).

If there are deviations from the inclusion-exclusion pattern outlined, they are unintentional and, I hope, few.

At a time when the total number of entries still appeared likely to be relatively small, I gave permission (through Shipton) for the Readex Corporation to film the supplementary material and thus bring to a conclusion their project of reproducing in microprint all significant printing (except newspapers) prior to 1801. I have since questioned the wisdom of my decision.

The years went by, the entries grew, the checking edition took longer than anticipated, the pressures mounted. In October 1964 Shipton wrote me that the American Antiquarian Society and the Readex Corporation were caught in a very serious bind by the delay. What would be the chance of getting a quick numbered list of my additions so that they could go to work on the microfilming before costs went completely out of sight?

In reply, I noted difficulties I could foresee and said that I felt sure there would have to be further additions and deletions before the final printing. Nevertheless, I would be glad to make a stab at assigning sequence numbers and to send him a marked set of the fascicles. Would the numbers need to go on the microprint immediately?

I dispatched the fascicles over the next several months, marked 1711-1, 1711-2, 1711-3, and so on. The material was filmed, and microprinting was concluded by the Readex Corporation during 1967.

Not unexpectedly, there were some bibliographic consequences. Not only were there some (not many) items microprinted which have now been discovered to be Evans items and hence excluded from the printed *Supplement*, but more important, the microprinted items number somewhat over 10,000, whereas the *Supplement* includes over 11,200. Well over a thousand new entries were added between 1964 and 1969. The Readex Corporation does not at present have any plans to film these.

This unfortunate bibliographical situation led to the thorniest of all the problems—that of numbering the *Supplement* so as to minimize the possible confusion for future bibliographers who might wish to cite an Evans number beyond 39162. Since Shipton in numbering the microprinted items had preëmpted 39163-49197, the solution ultimately reached (thanks to Fred Goff) was to assign an arbitrary serial number, from B1 to B11204, for each item in the *Supplement*. To provide direct access to the microprint reproduction, each item which has been microprinted bears also the microprint number. Thus a typical item reads:

B7117 U. S. LAWS
An act providing for the actual enumeration ... [Colophon] New-York, Thomas Greenleaf [1789]
4 p. 34 cm. caption title
Brackets in the original except for date
DLC mp. 45702

It is a truism to say that a bibliographer builds on the work of others; but it is a truism of which no one is more conscious than I, for anyone who undertakes the compilation of a work such as a supplement to Evans' *American Bibliography* of necessity depends almost entirely on the efforts of bibliographers past and present.

Perhaps half of the entries were found in one or more of the sources listed in "Bibliographies Cited." To the names of many who are associated with particular sources I should like to add the names of certain others whose work covered areas I might easily have overlooked, or whose work contributed unusual numbers of entries, listing them in a roll call of distinction:

Thomas R. Adams	Douglas C. McMurtrie
John E. Alden	Rachel Minick
Albert C. Bates	Clifford K. Shipton
Clarence S. Brigham	Lewis M. Stark
James B. Childs	James H. Trumbull
Milton Drake	Willard O. Waters
Worthington C. Ford	Oscar Wegelin
Frederick R. Goff	d'Alté A. Welch
Thompson R. Harlow	Joseph T. Wheeler
Thomas J. Holmes	Edwin Wolf 2d
Marcus A. McCorison	Lawrence C. Wroth

My debt to them is great.

I owe much also to uncounted others of the company of bibliographers, from whose work (and works) was derived the remaining fraction (one-fifth? one-fourth?) of the total entries. I have been repeatedly impressed with the readiness of people everywhere, people who are sparetime scholars as well as people who are associated with large institutions, to furnish material and to reply to my inquiries on details which must often have seemed of the greatest insignificance. My profound thanks to them all.

Inevitably there are lacunae and inaccuracies. I hope their presence will stimulate those who discover them to send me corrections and addenda. The ultimate Evans, complete and unflawed, is no doubt unattainable; but the struggle to achieve it, like the struggle to achieve other human ideals, is a measure of man's will to rise out of chaos into light.

Bibliographies Cited

Adams: Pennsylvania Adams, Thomas R. American imprints before 1801 in the University of Pennsylvania Library and not in Evans. *Library chronicle*, 22 (1956): 41-57.

Adams: Plain truth Adams, Thomas R. The authorship and printing of *Plain truth* by "Candidus". *BSA Papers*, 49 (1955): 230-248.

Alden Alden, John E. Rhode Island imprints, 1727-1800. New York, 1949.

Alden: John Mein Alden, John E. John Mein, publisher. *BSA Papers*, 36 (1942): 199-214.

Austin U.S. National Library of Medicine. Early American imprints ... by Robert B. Austin. Washington, 1961.

Bartlett U.S. Library of Congress. Descriptive Cataloging Division. Catalogue of early books on music (before 1800); a supplement ... by Hazel Bartlett. Washington, 1944.

Bates: Connecticut almanacs Bates, Albert C. Check list of Connecticut almanacs, 1709-1850. *AAS Proceedings*, n.s. 24 (1914): 93-215.

Bates: Connecticut laws Bates, Albert C. Early Connecticut laws. *BSA Papers*, 40 (1946): 151-158.

Bates: Connecticut statute laws Bates, Albert C. Connecticut statute laws. Hartford, 1900.

Bausman Bausman, Lottie M. Bibliography of Lancaster County, Pennsylvania, 1745-1912. Philadelphia, 1917. (Pennsylvania county bibliographies, iii).

Bear Bear, James A. A checklist of Virginia almanacs, 1732-1850. Charlottesville, Va., 1962.

Blanck Blanck, Jacob N. Bibliography of American literature. New Haven, 1955–

Brigham Brigham, Clarence S. History and bibliography of American newspapers. Worcester, Mass., 1947.

Brigham: Booksellers Brigham, Clarence S. American booksellers' catalogues, 1734-1800. *In* Essays honoring Lawrence C. Wroth (Portland, Me., 1951), p. 31-67.

Brigham: Robinson Crusoe Brigham, Clarence S. Bibliography of American editions of Robinson Crusoe, to 1830. *AAS Proceedings*, n.s. 67 (1957): 137-183.

Brinley Brinley, George. Catalogue of the American library ... Hartford, 1878-93.

Britton Britton, Allen P. Bibliography of early religious American music, 18th century. Ann Arbor, Mich., 1949.

Chapin Chapin, Howard M. Check list of Rhode Island almanacs, 1643-1850. *AAS Proceedings*, n.s. 25 (1915): 19-54.

Chapin: Calendrier Chapin, Howard M. Calendrier français pour l'année 1781, and the printing press of the French fleet. Providence, 1914.

Chapin: Proxies Chapin, Howard M. Eighteenth century Rhode Island printed proxies. *Americana collector*, 1: 54-59.

Childs: House Childs, James B. "Disappeared in the wings of oblivion": the story of the United States House of Representatives printed documents at the first session of the First Congress, New York, 1789. *BSA Papers*, 58 (1964): 91-132.

Childs: Senate Childs, James B. Story of the United States Senate documents, 1st Congress 1st session, New York, 1789. *BSA Papers*, 56 (1962): 175-194.

Church Church, Elihu D. Catalogue of books relating to ... North and South America. New York, 1907.

Cohen Cohen, Hennig. South Carolina Gazette, 1732-1775. Columbia, S.C., 1953.

Cooley Cooley, Elizabeth F. Vermont imprints before 1800. Montpelier, Vt., 1937.

Curtis Curtis Publishing Company. The collection of Franklin imprints in the museum of the Curtis Publishing Company ... comp. by William J. Campbell. Philadelphia, 1918.

Davis Davis, Katharine M. Check-list of Richmond, Virginia, imprints from 1781 to 1805. Thesis, M.S.L.S. (Catholic Univ., 1956).

DePuy DePuy, Henry F. A bibliography of the English colonial treaties with the American Indian. New York, 1917.

De Renne Wymberley Jones De Renne Georgia Library, Athens, Ga. Catalogue ... vol. 1. Wormsloe, Ga., 1931.

Drake Drake, Milton. Almanacs of the United States. New York, 1962.

Duyckinck Duyckinck, Evert A. Cyclopaedia of American literature. New York, 1856.

Ford Ford, Worthington C. Broadsides, ballads, &c. printed in Massachusetts, 1639-1800. Boston, 1922.

Ford: Bibliographical notes Ford, Paul L. Bibliographical notes on the issues of the Continental Congress. Appended to vol. 1+ of U.S. Continental Congress. Journals. Washington, 1904-37.

Ford: Constitution Ford, Paul L. Pamphlets on the Constitution of the United States ... 1787-1788. Brooklyn, 1888.

Ford: Franklin Ford, Paul L. Franklin bibliography. Brooklyn, 1889.

Ford & Matthews Ford, Worthington C., and Albert Matthews. A bibliography of the laws of the Massachusetts Bay, 1641-1776. Colonial Soc. of Mass. *Publications*, 4 (1910): 291-480.

Gaine Gaine, Hugh. The journals of Hugh Gaine, printer; ed. by Paul Leicester Ford. New York, 1902.

Gaines Gaines, Pierce W. Political works of concealed authorship ... 1789-1809. New Haven, 1959.

Gimbel Gimbel, Richard. Thomas Paine: a bibliographical check list of *Common sense*. New Haven, 1956.

Goff: Georgetown Goff, Frederick R. Early printing in Georgetown (Potomak) 1789-1800. Worcester, Mass., 1958.

Gongaware Gongaware, George J. The history of the German Friendly Society of Charleston, South Carolina, 1766-1916. Richmond, 1935.

Goodman Goodman, Nathan G. Benjamin Rush, physician and citizen, 1746-1813. Philadelphia, 1934.

Gotshall New York. State Library. The Gotshall collection. Albany, 1960. (*Its* Bibliography bulletin 84)

Greely Greely, Adolphus W. Public documents of the first fourteen congresses. Washington, 1900.

Hamilton Hamilton, Sinclair. Early American book illustrators and wood engravers, 1670-1870. Princeton, N.J., 1958.

Hammett Hammett, Charles E. Contribution to the bibliography ... of Newport, R.I. Newport, R.I., 1887.

Hasse Hasse, Adelaide R. Some materials for a bibliography of the official publications of the General Assembly of ... New York, 1692-1775. New York Public Library. *Bulletin*, 7 (1903): 51-79+.

Hawkins Hawkins, Dorothy L. Checklist of Delaware imprints up to and including 1800. Thesis, M.S.L.S. (Columbia Univ., 1928).

Heartman Heartman, Charles F. The New England primer issued prior to 1830. n.p., 1922.

Heartman: Cradle Heartman, Charles F. The cradle of the United States, 1765-1789. Perth Amboy, N.J., 1922.

Heartman: Non-New-England primers Heartman, Charles F. American primers, Indian primers, Royal primers, and ... non-New-England primers issued prior to 1830. Highland Park, N.J., 1935.

Hill Hill, Frank P. American plays, printed 1714-1830. Stanford University, 1934.

Holmes: Cotton Mather Holmes, Thomas J. Cotton Mather, a bibliography of his works. Cambridge, Mass., 1940.

Holmes: Increase Mather Holmes, Thomas J. Increase Mather, a bibliography of his works. Cambridge, Mass., 1931.

Holmes: Minor Mathers Holmes, Thomas J. Minor Mathers. Cambridge, Mass., 1940.

Humphrey Humphrey, Constance H. Check-list of New Jersey imprints to the end of the Revolution. *BSA Papers*, 24 (1930): 43-149.

Huntington Waters, Willard O. American imprints, 1648-1797, in the Huntington Library. Cambridge, Mass., 1933.

Ireland Ireland, Joseph N. Records of the New York stage, from 1750-1860. New York, 1866-67.

James James, Eldon R. List of legal treatises published in America before 1801. *In* Harvard legal essays (Cambridge, Mass., 1934), p. [159]-211.

Karpinski Karpinski, Louis C. Bibliography of mathematical works printed in America through 1850. Ann Arbor, Mich., 1940.

Lapham Newberry Library. Check list of American Revolutionary War pamphlets in the Newberry Library. Chicago, 1922.

McCorison McCorison, Marcus A. Vermont imprints, 1778-1820. Worcester, Mass., 1963.

McCorison: Taylor McCorison, Marcus A. Amos Taylor, a sketch and bibliography. *AAS Proceedings*, n.s. 69 (1959): 37-55.

McCoy McCoy, Mercer G. A check-list of Norfolk, Virginia, imprints from 1774 to 1876. Rochester, N.Y., 1959.

McDade McDade, Thomas M. Annals of murder: a bibliography of books and pamphlets on American murders from Colonial times to 1900. Norman, Okla., 1961.

McKay McKay, George L. American book auction catalogues, 1713-1934. New York, 1937.

McMurtrie: Albany McMurtrie, Douglas C. Check list of eighteenth century Albany imprints. Albany, 1939.

McMurtrie: Georgia Located Georgia imprints of the eighteenth centruy not in the De Renne catalogue. Savannah, 1934.

McMurtrie: Kentucky McMurtrie, Douglas C. Check list of Kentucky imprints, 1787-1810. Louisville, Ky., 1939. (American imprints inventory no. 5)

McMurtrie: Louisiana McMurtrie, Douglas C. Louisiana imprints, 1768-1810. Hattiesburg, Miss., 1942.

McMurtrie: Maine McMurtrie, Douglas C. Maine imprints, 1792-1820. Chicago, 1935.

McMurtrie: Massachusetts McMurtrie, Douglas G. Massachusetts broadsides, 1699-1711. Chicago, 1939.

McMurtrie: Mississippi McMurtrie, Douglas C. Bibliography of Mississippi imprints, 1789-1830. Beauvoir Community, Miss., 1945.

McMurtrie: New Orleans McMurtrie, Douglas C. Early printing in New Orleans, 1762-1810. New Orleans, 1938.

McMurtrie: New York McMurtrie, Douglas C. New York printing MDCXCIII. Chicago, 1928.

McMurtrie: North Carolina McMurtrie, Douglas C. Eighteenth century North Carolina imprints, 1749-1800. Chapel Hill, N.C., 1938.

McMurtrie: Sag Harbor McMurtrie, Douglas C. Check list of the imprints of Sag Harbor, L.I., 1791-1820. Chicago, 1930. (American imprints inventory no. 12)

McMurtrie: Schenectady McMurtrie, Douglas C. Check list of books, pamphlets, and broadsides printed at Schenectady, N.Y., 1795-1830. Chicago, 1938.

McMurtrie: South Carolina McMurtrie, Douglas C. First decade of printing in the Royal Province of South Carolina. *The Library*, 4th ser., 13 (1932/33): 425-452.

McMurtrie: South Carolina 1731 McMurtrie, Douglas C. Four South Carolina imprints of MDCCXXXI. Chicago, 1933.

McMurtrie: South Carolina 1731-1740 McMurtrie, Douglas C. A bibliography of South Carolina imprints, 1731-1740. *South Carolina hist. and gen. magazine*, 34 (1933): 117-137.

McMurtrie: Tennessee McMurtrie, Douglas C. Early printing in Tennessee ... 1793-1830. Chicago, 1933.

Marcus Hebrew Union College–Jewish Institute of Religion. Jewish Americana ... suppl. to ... American Jewish bibliography. Cincinnati, 1954.

Mass. House Journals Massachusetts (Colony) General Court. House of Representatives. Journals. Cambridge, Mass., 1919–

Metzger Metzger, Ethel M. Supplement to Hildeburn's *Century of Printing*, 1685-1775. Thesis, M.S.L.S. (Columbia Univ., 1930).

Minick Minick, Rachel. History of printing in Maryland, 1791-1800. Baltimore, 1949.

Morgan Morgan, Richard P. A preliminary bibliography of South Carolina imprints, 1731-1800. Clemson, S.C. [1965?].

Morrison Morrison, Hugh D. Preliminary check list of American almanacs, 1639-1800. Washington, 1907.

Morsch Morsch, Lucile M. Check list of New Jersey imprints, 1784-1806. Baltimore, 1939. (American imprints inventory no. 9)

Mosimann Mosimann, Jeanne D. A check list of Charleston, South Carolina imprints from 1731 to 1799, with a historical introduction. Thesis, M.S.L.S. (Catholic Univ., 1959).

Nelson Nelson, William. Check-list of the issues of the press of New Jersey, 1723, 1728, 1754-1800. Paterson, N.J., 1899.

New York Public New York. Public Library. Checklist of additions to Evans' *American bibliography* ... comp. by Lewis M. Stark and Maud D. Cole. New York, 1960.

Nichols Nichols, Charles L. Checklist of Maine, New Hampshire and Vermont almanacs. *AAS Proceedings*, n.s. 38 (1929): 63-163.

Nichols: Holy Bible Nichols, Charles L. Thc Holy Bible in verse. *AAS Proceedings*, n.s. 36 (1926): 71-82.

Nichols: Isaiah Thomas Nichols, Charles L. Isaiah Thomas, printer, writer & collector. Boston, 1912.

Nichols: Mass. almanacs Nichols, Charles L. Notes on the almanacs of Massachusetts. *AAS Proceedings*, n.s. 22 (1912): 15-134.

Nolan Nolan, J. B. First decade of printing in Reading, Pennsylvania. Reading, 1930.

Norona Norona, Delf, and Charles Shetler. West Virginia imprints, 1790-1863. Moundsville, W. Va., 1958.

Parsons Parsons, Wilfrid. Early Catholic Americana. New York, 1939.

Phillips Phillips, Philip Lee. A list of maps of America in the Library of Congress. Washington, 1901.

Phillips: Atlases U.S. Library of Congress. Map Division. A list of geographical atlases in the Library of Congress. Washington, 1909–

Porter Porter, Dorothy B. Early American Negro writings: a bibliographical study. *BSA Papers*, 39 (1945): 192-268.

Reichmann Reichmann, Felix. German printing in Maryland, a checklist, 1768-1950. Baltimore, 1950.

Rogers Rogers, Harriet. Books in medicine, botany and chemistry printed in the American colonies and United States before 1801. Thesis, M.S.L.S. (Columbia Univ., 1932).

Rosenbach Rosenbach, A. S. W. American Jewish bibliography. Baltimore, 1926.

Rosenbach-Ch Rosenbach, A. S. W. Early American children's books. Portland, Me., 1933.

Rutherfurd Rutherfurd, Livingston. John Peter Zenger, his press. New York, 1904.

Sabin Sabin, Joseph. A dictionary of books relating to America. New York, 1868-1936.

Scharf Scharf, John T. History of Delaware, 1609-1888. Philadelphia, 1888.

Sealock Sealock, Richard B. Publishing in Pennsylvania, 1785-1790. Thesis, M.S.L.S. (Columbia Univ., 1935).

Seidensticker Seidensticker, Oswald. The first century of German printing in America, 1728-1830. Philadelphia, 1893.

Shearer Shearer, J. F. French and Spanish works printed in Charleston, South Carolina. *BSA Papers*, 34 (1940): 137-170.

Sibley Sibley, John L. Biographical sketches of graduates of Harvard University. Cambridge, 1873–19

Skeel-Carpenter Skeel, Emily E. Bibliography of the writings of Noah Webster ... ed. by Edwin H. Carpenter, Jr. New York, 1958.

Sonneck-Upton Sonneck, Oscar G. T. A bibliography of early secular American music (18th century) ... Rev. and enl. by William Treat Upton. Washington, 1945.

Sowerby U.S. Library of Congress. Jefferson Collection. Catalogue of the library of Thomas Jefferson. Comp. by E. Millicent Sowerby. Washington, 1952-59.

Spear Spear, Dorothy N. Bibliography of American directories through 1860. Worcester, Mass., 1961.

Stanley Stanley, John Henry. Preliminary investigation of military manuals of American imprint prior to 1800. Thesis, M.A. (Brown Univ., 1964).

Starr, Edward C. A Baptist bibliography. Philadelphia, 1947–

Stoddard Stoddard, Roger E. A catalogue of books and pamphlets unrecorded in Oscar Wegelin's *Early American Poetry*, 1650–1820. Providence, 1969.

Tapley Tapley, Harriet S. Salem imprints, 1768-1825. Salem, Mass., 1927.

Taylor Taylor, Edith S. Supplement to Hildeburn's *Century of Printing*, 1776-1784. Thesis, M.S.L.S. (Columbia Univ., 1935).

Torrence Torrence, Clayton. Trial bibliography of colonial Virginia. Virginia. State Library. Dept. of Bibliography. Special report. Richmond, 1908–10.

Trinterud Trinterud, Leonard J. Bibliography of American Presbyterianism during the Colonial Period. Philadelphia, 1968.

Trumbull Trumbull, James H. List of books printed in Connecticut, 1709-1800. Hartford, 1904.

Trumbull: Supplement Bates, Albert C. Supplementary list of books printed in Connecticut, 1709-1800. Hartford, 1938.

Trumbull: Second supplement Bates, Albert C. Second supplementary list of books printed in Connecticut, 1709-1800. Hartford, 1947.

Turnbull Turnbull, Robert J. Bibliography of South Carolina. Vol. I (1563-1814). Charlottesville, Va., 1956.

Vail: Old frontier Vail, R. W. G. Voice of the old frontier. Philadelphia, 1949.

Vail: Patriotic pair Vail, R. W. G. Patriotic pair of peripatetic printers. *In* Essays honoring Lawrence C. Wroth (Portland, Me., 1951), p. 391-422.

Wall Wall, Alexander J. A list of New York almanacs, 1694-1850. New York, 1921.

Walsh Walsh, Michael J. Contemporary broadside editions of the Declaration of Independence. *Harvard Library bulletin*, 3 (1949): 31–43.

Weedon Weedon, M. J. P. Richard Johnson and the successors to John Newbery. *The Library*, 5th ser., 4 (1949/50), 25–63.

Wegelin Wegelin, Oscar. Early American poetry. New York, 1903-7. (Items identified by vol. and page)

Wegelin Wegelin, Oscar. Early American poetry. 2d ed. New York, 1930. (Items identified by serial number)

Welch Welch, d'Alté A. A bibliography of American children's books printed prior to 1821. *AAS Proceedings*, n.s. 73 (1963)–77 (1967).

Wheeler Wheeler, Joseph T. Maryland press, 1777-1790. Baltimore, 1938.

Whittemore Whittemore, Caroline. Checklist of New Hampshire imprints, 1756-1790. Thesis, M.S.L.S. (Columbia Univ., 1929).

Williams Williams College. American imprints before 1801 in the libraries of Williams College not in Evans. Williamstown, Mass., 1957.

Williams: Timothy press Williams, Elizabeth C. The Timothy press. Thesis, M.S.L.S. (Drexel Inst. of Technology, 1950).

Wing Wing, Donald G. Short-title catalogue ... 1641-1700. New York, 1943-51.

Winship Winship, George P. Rhode Island imprints ... between 1727 and 1800. Providence, 1915.

Wolf Wolf, Edwin, 2d. Some unrecorded American Judaica printed before 1851. Cincinnati, 1958.

Wright Wright, Lyle H. American fiction, 1774-1850. San Marino, Calif., 1948.

Wroth Wroth, Lawrence C. History of printing in colonial Maryland, 1686-1776. Baltimore, 1922.

Wroth: William Parks Wroth, Lawrence C. William Parks, printer and journalist ... Richmond, 1926.

Wyatt Wyatt, Edward A. Preliminary checklist for Petersburg, 1786-1876, comp. by various hands and ed. by Edward A. Wyatt, IV. Richmond, 1959.

Key to Library Symbols

CL	Rufus B. KleinSmid Central Library, Los Angeles
CLM	Los Angeles County Medical Association, Los Angeles
CLU	University of California at Los Angeles
CP	Pasadena Public Library
CSmH	Henry E. Huntington Library, San Marino
CSt	Stanford University Libraries, Stanford
CU-B	Bancroft Library, University of California, Berkeley
Ct	Connecticut State Library, Hartford
CtHC	Hartford Seminary Foundation, Hartford
CtHFM	Connecticut Grand Lodge, F. & A. M., Hartford
CtHT-W	Watkinson Library, Trinity College, Hartford
CtHi	Connecticut Historical Society, Hartford
CtLHi	Litchfield Historical Society, Litchfield
CtNhHi	New Haven Colony Historical Society, New Haven
CtNlC	Connecticut College, New London
CtSoP	Pequot Library Association, Southport
CtW	Wesleyan University, Middletown
CtY	Yale University, New Haven
CtY-M	— Medical School Library
DCU	Catholic University of America Library
DFo	Folger Shakespeare Library
DGU	Georgetown University Library
DHEW	U.S. Dept. of Health, Education and Welfare Library
DLC	Library of Congress
DNA	U.S. National Archives Library
DNLM	U.S. National Library of Medicine
DS	U.S. Dept. of State Library
DSC	U.S. Superintendent of Documents Library
De	Delaware State Library Commission, Dover
DeGE	Eleutherian Mills Historical Library, Greenville
DeHi	Historical Society of Delaware
DeWI	Wilmington Institute and the New Castle County Free Library
DeWin	Henry Francis DuPont Winterthur Museum
GHi	Georgia Historical Society, Savannah
GU-De	De Renne Georgia Library, University of Georgia, Athens
ICHi	Chicago Historical Society, Chicago
ICN	Newberry Library, Chicago
ICU	University of Chicago, Chicago
IEG	Garrett Theological Seminary, Evanston
IEN-M	Medical School Library, Northwestern University, Chicago
IU	University of Illinois, Urbana
IaCrM	Iowa Masonic Library, Cedar Rapids
InU	Indiana University, Bloomington
KHi	Kansas State Historical Society, Topeka
KU	University of Kansas, Lawrence
KyHi	Kentucky Historical Society, Frankfurt
KyLo	Louisville Free Public Library
KyLoS	Southern Baptist Theological Seminary, Louisville
KyLx	Lexington Public Library
KyU	University of Kentucky, Lexington
L-Ar	Louisiana State Archives
L-M	Louisiana State Museum Library, New Orleans
LHi	Louisiana Historical Society, New Orleans
LNB	New Orleans Baptist Theological Seminary
LNT	Tulane University Library, New Orleans
M	Massachusetts State Library, Boston
M-Ar	Archives Division, Secretary of State, Boston
MA	Amherst College, Amherst
MAJ	Jones Library, Amherst
MAnP	Phillips Academy, Andover
MAtt	Attleboro Public Library
MB	Boston Public Library
MBAt	Boston Athenaeum, Boston
MBC	American Congregational Association Library, Boston
MBCo	Countway Library of Medicine, Boston
MBFM	Massachusetts Grand Lodge, F. & A. M., Boston
MBNEH	New England Historic Genealogical Society, Boston
MBNMHi	Methodist Historical Society, New England Conference, Boston
MBU	Boston University
MBrZ	Zion Research Library, Brookline
MDedHi	Dedham Historical Society, Dedham
MDeeP	Pocumtuck Valley Memorial Association, Deerfield
MH	Harvard University, Cambridge
MH-AH	— Andover-Harvard Theological Library
MH-BA	— Graduate School of Business Administration Library
MH-L	— Law School Library

MHaHi	Haverhill Historical Society, Haverhill
MHi	Massachusetts Historical Society, Boston
MHolliHi	Holliston Historical Society, Holliston
MMal	Malden Public Library
MMeT-Hi	Universalist Historical Society, Tufts University, Medford
MMidb	Middleborough Public Library
MNBedf	New Bedford Free Public Library
MNF	Forbes Library, Northampton
MNe	Newburyport Public Library
MNtcA	Andover Newton Theological School, Newton Center
MS	City Library, Springfield
MSaE	Essex Institute, Salem
MSaP	Peabody Institute of Salem
MTaHi	Old Colony Historical Society, Taunton
MWA	American Antiquarian Society, Worcester
MWHi	Worcester Historical Society, Worcester
MWM	Worcester Art Museum, Worcester
MWiW-C	Chapin Library, Williams College, Williamstown
MWo	Woburn Public Library
Md	Maryland State Library, Annapolis
MdAA	Hall of Records, Archives, Annapolis
MdAS	Saint John's College, Annapolis
MdBBC	Methodist Historical Society, Baltimore
MdBE	Enoch Pratt Free Library, Baltimore
MdBFM	Maryland Grand Lodge, F. & A.M.
MdBG	Goucher College, Baltimore
MdBJ	Johns Hopkins University, Baltimore
MdBJ-G	— John Work Garrett Library, Baltimore
MdBJ-W	— William H. Welch Medical Library
MdBMA	Baltimore Museum of Art, Baltimore
MdBP	Peabody Institute, Baltimore
MdBS	St. Mary's Seminary and University, Roland Park, Baltimore
MdHi	Maryland Historical Society, Baltimore
MdU-H	Health Sciences Library, University of Maryland, Baltimore
MdW	Woodstock College, Woodstock
MeB	Bowdoin College, Brunswick
MeHi	Maine Historical Society, Portland
MiD-B	Burton Historical Collection, Detroit Public Library
MiGr	Grand Rapids Public Library
MiU	University of Michigan, Ann Arbor
MiU-C	— William L. Clements Library
MnSRM	Ramsey County Medical Society, St. Paul
MnU	University of Minnesota, Minneapolis
MoS	St. Louis Public Library
MoSMed	St. Louis Medical Society Library, St. Louis
MoSpD	Drury College, Springfield
MoU	University of Missouri, Columbia
Ms-Ar	State Department of Archives and History, Jackson
N	New York State Library, Albany
NAll	Albany Institute of History and Art, Albany
NB	Brooklyn Public Library
NBLiHi	Long Island Historical Society, Brooklyn
NBM	Academy of Medicine of Brooklyn, Brooklyn
NBuG	Grosvenor Reference Division, Buffalo and Erie County Public Library, Buffalo
NBuHi	Buffalo Historical Society, Buffalo
NCooHi	New York State Historical Association, Cooperstown
NEh	East Hampton Free Library
NHC	Colgate University, Hamilton
NHi	New-York Historical Society, New York
NIC	Cornell University, Ithaca
NN	New York Public Library
NNB	Association of the Bar of the City of New York, New York
NNC	Columbia University, New York
NNC-L	— Avery Library of Architecture
NNFL	Friends Library, New York
NNFM	Grand Lodge of New York, F. & A. M. Library & Museum, New York
NNFr	Frick Art Reference Library, New York
NNG	General Theological Seminary of the Protestant Episcopal Church, New York
NNHuC	Hunter College, New York
NNMR	Missionary Research Library, New York
NNMer	Mercantile Library Association, New York
NNNAM	New York Academy of Medicine, New York
NNPM	Pierpont Morgan Library, New York
NNRT	Racquet and Tennis Club Library, New York
NNS	New York Society Library, New York
NNU-L	School of Law Library, New York University, New York
NNU-M	Medical Center Library, New York University, New York
NNUT	Union Theological Seminary, New York
NPV	Vassar College, Poughkeepsie
NRAB	Samuel Colgate Baptist Historical Library, Rochester
NRMA	Rochester Museum of Arts and Sciences, Rochester
Nc	North Carolina State Library, Raleigh
Nc-Ar	North Carolina State Department of Archives and History, Raleigh
Nc-SC	North Carolina Supreme Court Library
NcA-S	Sondley Reference Library, Pack Memorial Public Library, Asheville
NcC	Public Library of Charlotte & Mecklenburg County, Charlotte
NcD	Duke University, Durham
NcMHi	Historical Foundation of the Presbyterian and Reformed Churches, Montreat
NcU	University of North Carolina
NcWsM	Moravian Archives, Winston-Salem
NcWsW	Wake Forest College, Winston-Salem
Nh	New Hampshire State Library, Concord
NhD	Dartmouth College, Hanover
NhHi	New Hampshire Historical Society, Concord
NhPlain	Town Clerk's Office, Plainfield
Nj	New Jersey State Library, Trenton

NjHi	New Jersey Historical Society, Newark
NjMoW	Washington Headquarters Library, Morristown
NjP	Princeton University, Princeton
NjPT	Princeton Theological Seminary, Princeton
NjR	Rutgers—The State University, New Brunswick
NjT	Trenton Free Library, Trenton
OC	Public Library of Cincinnati and Hamilton County, Cincinnati
OCHP	Historical and Philosophical Society of Ohio, Cincinnati
OCl	Cleveland Public Library
OClM	Cleveland Medical Library Association, Cleveland
OClW	Western Reserve University, Cleveland
OClWHi	Western Reserve Historical Society, Cleveland
OHi	Ohio State Historical Society, Columbus
OMC	Marietta College, Marietta
OO	Oberlin College, Oberlin
OSW	Wittenberg University, Springfield
OTM	Toledo Museum of Art, Toledo
OU	Ohio State University, Columbus
OWoC	College of Wooster, Wooster
P	Pennsylvania State Library, Harrisburg
PAtM	Muhlenberg College, Allentown
PBL	Lehigh University, Bethlehem
PDoBHi	Bucks County Historical Society, Doylestown
PGC	Gettysburg College, Gettysburg
PGL	Lutheran Theological Seminary, Gettysburg
PHC	Haverford College, Haverford
PHi	Historical Society of Pennsylvania
PLHi	Lancaster Historical Society, Lancaster
PLeB	Bucknell University, Lewisburg
PMA	Allegheny College, Meadville
PNortHi	Historical Society of Montgomery County, Norristown
PP	Free Library of Philadelphia
PPAN	Academy of Natural Sciences, Philadelphia
PPAmP	American Philosophical Society, Philadelphia
PPC	College of Physicians, Philadelphia
PPF	Franklin Institute, Philadelphia
PPFM	Pennsylvania Grand Lodge Library, F. & A. M., Philadelphia
PPG	German Society of Pennsylvania, Philadelphia
PPL	Library Company of Philadelphia
PPLT	Lutheran Theological Seminary, Philadelphia
PPM	Mercantile Library, Philadelphia
PPPH	Pennsylvania Hospital Medical Library
PPPrHi	Presbyterian Historical Society, Philadelphia
PPRF	Rosenbach Foundation, Philadelphia
PPeSchw	Schwenckfelder Historical Library, Pennsburg
PPi	Carnegie Library of Pittsburgh
PPiPT	Pittsburgh Theological Seminary, Pittsburgh
PPiU	University of Pittsburgh, Pittsburgh
PRHi	Historical Society of Berks County, Reading
PSC–Hi	Friends Historical Library, Swarthmore College, Swarthmore
PSt	Pennsylvania State University, University Park
PU	University of Pennsylvania, Philadelphia
PU–V	—— School of Veterinary Medicine Library
PV	Villanova College, Villanova
PWW	Washington & Jefferson College, Washington
R	Rhode Island State Library, Providence
RHi	Rhode Island Historical Society, Providence
RNHi	Newport Historical Society, Newport
RNR	Redwood Library and Athenaeum, Newport
RP	Providence Public Library
RPA	Providence Athenaeum, Providence
RPB	Brown University, Providence
RPE	Elmwood Public Library, Providence
RPJCB	John Carter Brown Library, Providence
RPL	Rhode Island Law Library, Providence
RPM	Rhode Island Medical Society, Providence
RPTP	Town papers, Providence City Hall
RWa	George Hail Free Library, Warren
RWe	Westerly Public Library
Sc–Ar	South Carolina Archives
ScC	Charleston Library Society, Charleston
ScCC	College of Charleston, Charleston
ScCM	Medical College of the State of South Carolina, Charleston
ScGF	Furman University, Greenville
ScHi	South Carolina Historical Society, Charleston
ScSp	Spartanburg Public Library
ScU	University of South Carolina
ScU–S	South Caroliniana Society Library, Columbia
T	Tennessee State Library, Nashville
TKL	Knoxville Public Library System
Vi	Virginia State Library, Richmond
ViHi	Virginia Historical Society, Richmond
ViL	Jones Memorial Library, Lynchburg
ViLxV	Virginia Military Institute, Lexington
ViRU	University of Richmond, Richmond
ViU	University of Virginia, Charlottesville
ViW	College of William and Mary, Williamsburg
ViWC	Colonial Williamsburg, Williamsburg
Vt	Vermont State Library, Montpelier
VtBaHi	Barre Historical Society, Barre
VtBennM	Bennington Museum, Bennington
VtBrt	Brattleboro Free Library
VtHi	Vermont Historical Society, Montpelier
VtMiS	Sheldon Art Museum, Middlebury
VtU	University of Vermont, Burlington
WHi	State Historical Society of Wisconsin
WMMD	Milwaukee-Downer College, Milwaukee
WyHi	State of Wyoming Historical Department, Cheyenne

IMPRINTS

1646

B1 HARVARD UNIVERSITY
Spectatissimis integritate . . . theses . . . Cantabrigiae Nov; Ang; Mens: 5. Die 28. 1646.
broadside 32 X 25 cm.
Ford 5; New York Public 1; Wing H1040
Hunterian Museum, Glasgow. Photostats: MWA; NN
mp. 39163

1653

B2 HARVARD UNIVERSITY
Authoritatis . . . theses hasce . . . Decimo Sextilis Anno Dom: M D C LIII. [Cambridge, 1653]
broadside 28 X 19 cm.
Ford 12; New York Public 3a; Wing H1011
Hunterian Museum, Glasgow. Photostats: MHi; MWA; NN
mp. 39164

B3 HARVARD UNIVERSITY
Clarissimis . . . theses hasce . . . Quint: Id: Sextilis Anno Dom: M D C LIII. [Cambridge, 1653]
broadside 27.5 X 18.5 cm.
Ford 12; New York Public 3; Wing H1015
Hunterian Museum, Glasgow. Photostats: MHi; NN
mp. 39165

B4 HARVARD UNIVERSITY
Qaestiones [sic] in philosophia discutiendae . . . Nono die sextilis M.DC.LIII. [Cambridge, Samuel Green, 1653]
broadside 13.5 X 12 cm.
Ford 11; New York Public 2; Wing H1023
Hunterian Museum, Glasgow. Photostats: MHi; NN
mp. 39166

1654

B5 SHEPARD, THOMAS, 1605-1649
A short catechism familiarly teaching . . . Cambridge, Samuel Green, 1654.
1 p.l., 60 p. 16.5 cm.
New York Public 4; Wing S3117
MWA. Photostats: DLC; MHi; NN; RPJCB mp. 39167

1656

B6 GOOKIN, DANIEL, 1612-1687
To all persons whom these may concern . . . Dated this 25 of March 1656.
broadside 20 X 16 cm.
Ford 14; New York Public 5
Bodleian. Photostats: DLC; MHi; NN mp. 39168

B7 HARVARD UNIVERSITY
Quaestiones in philosophia . . . M. DC. LVI. [Cambridge, 1656]
broadside
Wing H1025
MH mp. 39169

1658

B8 HARVARD UNIVERSITY
Quaestio in philosophia discutienda . . . Decimo die sextilis M.DC.LVIII. [Cambridge, Samuel Green, 1658]
broadside 21 X 16 cm.
Ford 16; New York Public 6; Wing H1026
Hunterian Museum, Glasgow. Photostats: MHi; NN
mp. 39170

1659

B9 HARVARD UNIVERSITY
Quaestiones in philosophia . . . M.DC.LIX. [Cambridge, 1659]
broadside
Wing H1027
MH mp. 39171

1663

B10 HARVARD UNIVERSITY
Quaestiones in philosophia . . . M.DC.LXIII. [Cambridge, 1663]
broadside
MH mp. 39172

1664

B11 MATHER, RICHARD, 1596-1669
[Justification by faith. Cambridge? Samuel Green? before 1664]

Record taken from Increase Mather's ms. catalogue of books in his library in 1664; cf. also Cotton Mather's *Magnalia,* Bk. iii, p. 128
Holmes: Minor Mathers 44
No copy known mp. 39173

1667

B12 VINCENT, THOMAS, 1634-1678
Gods terrible voice . . . Cambridge, Samuel Green [1667]
31 p. 19 cm.
Guerra a-1; Wing V441A
MH mp. 39174

1668

B13 BIBLE. O.T. PSALMS
[Psalms, hymns, and spiritual songs . . . Cambridge, Marmaduke Johnson, 1668]
No. 2 on Marmaduke Johnson's list
Holmes: Minor Mathers 53-C; cf. R. F. Roden: Cambridge press, p. 164
No copy known mp. 39175

B14 MASSACHUSETTS
Whereas the lawes published . . . do require all townes . . . [Cambridge, 1668]
broadside 29 X 18 cm.
Manuscript additions dated Aug. 24, 1668
Ford 37; New York Public 8; Wing M1026
M-Ar. Photostat: NN mp. 39176

B15 MASSACHUSETTS. GENERAL COURT
At a General Court held at Boston, in the year It is ordered . . . that the following order shall be directed . . .

to the constables of the towns . . . [Cambridge, Samuel Green, 1668?]
broadside 23.5 X 16 cm.
Concerns children under family government
Wing M967
MH. Photostat: NN mp. 39177

B16 UPON the death of the virtuous and religious Mrs. Lydia Minot . . . interred January 27, 1667. [Cambridge, Samuel Green, 1668]
broadside 34 X 21 cm.
Ford 33
MHi. Photostat: MWA mp. 39178

1670

B17 DAVENPORT, JOHN, 1597-1670
A sermon preach'd at the election of the governour, at Boston in New-England, May 19th 1669 . . . [Cambridge] Printed in the year, 1670.
16 p. 18.5 cm.
MB. Facsims.: DLC; MHi; NN; RPJCB mp. 39179

B18 WIGGLESWORTH, MICHAEL, 1631-1705
The day of doom . . . Cambridge, Printed by S[amuel]. G[reen]. and M[armaduke]. J[ohnson]. for John Usher at Boston, 1670.
12°
Wing W2104A
CtY mp. 39180

1672

B19 DYER, WILLIAM, 1636-1696
Christs famous titles . . . Cambridge, Printed by M. J. for Edmund Ranger and Joseph Farnham in Boston, 1672.
5 p.l., 244 p. sm. 8vo
Huntington 5; Wing D2937
CSmH mp. 39181

1673

B20 CRADOCK, WALTER, 1606?-1659
Mount Sion: Or the Priviledge and Practice of the Saints Opened and Applied. Cambridge, Printed by M[armaduke]. J[ohnson]., 1673.
[8], 231 p.
MHi. Photostat: MWA mp. 39182

B21 HARVARD UNIVERSITY
Quaestiones in philosophia . . . M.D.C. LXXIII. [Cambridge, 1673]
broadside
MH mp. 39183

1674

B22 HARVARD UNIVERSITY
Johanni Leveretto Armigero . . . [theses?] . . . [Cambridge, 1674]
broadside
Wing H1021
Public Record Off. mp. 39184

B23 MASSACHUSETTS. GENERAL COURT
At a General Court held at Boston, March the eleventh 1673/4 . . . [Cambridge, 1674]
broadside
Appointing March 26 a day of humiliation and prayer
MHi mp. 39185

B24 MASSACHUSETTS. LAWS
Orders, made at a General Court . . . [Cambridge? 1674?]
broadside 27.5 X 18.5 cm.
Wing M1009
MBAt; MHi mp. 39186

B25 THE narrative of the most dreadful tempest, hurricane, or earthquake in Holland . . . the 22 of July last . . . Cambridge, Printed by S[amuel]. G[reen]. for John Ratcliffe of Boston, 1674.
8 p. sm. 4to
MHi mp. 39187

1675

B26 MASSACHUSETTS
At a Council held at Boston, September the seventeenth 1675 . . . The Governour and Council . . . appoint and order the seventh day of next moneth; to be a day of . . . prayer . . . By the [Council, Edward] R[aw]son [Secret.] [Boston, 1675]
broadside 31 X 21 cm.
MHi (mutilated). Photostat: MWA mp. 39188

B27 MASSACHUSETTS
At a Council held at Boston the 25th of June, 1675. The Governour and magistrates being assembled in Council . . . appoint the 29th. day of this instant June . . . a day of humiliation and prayer . . . By the Council, Edward Rawson Secret. [Boston, 1675]
broadside 31 X 20.5 cm.
MHi. Photostat: MWA mp. 39189

B28 MASSACHUSETTS
At a meeting of the Council in Boston . . . March the fourth 1674/5 . . . [Cambridge? 1675]
broadside
Appointing March 25 a Fast Day
MHi mp. 39190

B29 MASSACHUSETTS. GENERAL COURT
At a General Court held at Boston the 11th. of Octob. 1675 . . . This Court doth appoint . . . the ninth day of November next to be a day of solemn thanksgiving . . . By the Court, Edward Rawson Secr. [Boston, 1675]
broadside 28 X 19.5 cm.
MHi; NBuG. Photostat: MWA mp. 39192

B30 MASSACHUSETTS. GENERAL COURT
At a sessions of the General Court held at Boston the 3d. of November 1675 . . . This Court doth appoint . . . the second day of December next . . . a day of solemn humiliation and prayer . . . By the Court, Edward Rawson Secret. [Boston, 1675]
broadside 31 X 20 cm.
MHi. Photostat: MWA mp. 39193

B31 MASSACHUSETTS. LAWS
Severall lawes and ordinances of war past . . . the 26th. October, 1675 . . . [Cambridge, S. Green, 1675]
broadside 31.5 X 18.5 cm.
Wing M1023A
DLC; MH; MHi mp. 39194

1676

B32 A FUNERAL elegy upon the death of that excellent . . . gentleman John Winthrop . . . who deceased April, 1676. [Boston, John Foster, 1676]
broadside
By Stephen Chester?
Ford 51; Wing F2532
MHi. Winthrop (1948) mp. 39195

B33 LAMENTATIONS upon the never enough bewailed death of the Reverend Mr. John Reiner . . . who was gathered to his fathers December, 21. 1676. [Boston? 1676?]
broadside 26.5 X 22.5 cm.
Ford 53; Wing L291
MBAt mp. 39196

B34 LOWLE, PERCIFUL, d. 1665
A funeral elegie (written many years since) on the death of . . . John Winthrope . . . [Boston, J. Foster, 1676]
broadside 31 X 20 cm.
MHi (photostat) mp. 39197

B35 MASSACHUSETTS
The oath of allegiance. [Cambridge, Samuel Green, 1676]
broadside
American Art Assoc. cat. 4079, Jan. 17-18, 1934, item 415
New York Public 11
NN (reduced facsim.) mp. 39200

B36 MASSACHUSETTS. GENERAL COURT
At a General Court held at Boston, February the 21st, 1675 . . . [Boston, 1676]
broadside
Appointing March 2 a Fast Day
MHi mp. 39191

B37 MASSACHUSETTS. GENERAL COURT
At a General Court held at Boston, the eleventh of October, 1676 . . . [Boston, 1676]
broadside
Appointing December 7 a Fast Day
MHi mp. 39198

B38 MASSACHUSETTS. LAWS
At a General Court held at Boston the 3d of May 1676 . . . [Cambridge, S. Green, 1676]
broadside 35.5 X 27.5
Ford 55; New York Public 10; Wing M968 & M968A
MBAt; MH; Salem Court House. Photostats: DLC; NN mp. 39199

B39 MASSACHUSETTS. LAWS
Several laws and orders made at the General Court held at Boston, the 21st of February, 1675 . . . [Cambridge, Samuel Green, 1676]
p. 41-43. fol.
MHi

1677

B40 MASSACHUSETTS
To the constables and select men of According to an order of the General Court held at Boston, May 23. 1677 . . . Boston, June 6. 1677. [Boston, 1677]
broadside 11 X 17.5 cm.
MWA mp. 39202

B41 MASSACHUSETTS. GENERAL COURT
By the General Court held at Boston, October the tenth, 1677 . . . [Boston, 1677]
broadside
Appointing November 15 a day of thanksgiving
Public Record Off. Photostat: MHi mp. 39201

1678

B42 AN Advertisement. Whereas, the lands of Narragansett, and Niantick countryes, and parts adjacent . . . Boston, July 30, 1678. [Boston? 1678?]

Ford 64; Wing A626
MHi. Public Record Off. mp. 39203

B43 A FUNERAL elegy upon the much lamented death of that pretious holy man of God Mr. Thomas Walley . . . of late the reverend pastor of the Church of Christ in Barnstable in New-England, who departed this life . . . March. 24th 167$\frac{7}{8}$ . . . An hearty mourner, J. C. Boston, 1678.
broadside 29 X 21 cm.
In three columns
Mrs. Ed. D. Densmore, Princeton, Mass. (1950). Photostat: MWA mp. 39204

B44 HARVARD UNIVERSITY
Illustrissimis viris . . . theses hasce . . . MDCLXXVIII. [Cambridge, 1678]
broadside
Wing H1020
MHi. Hunterian Museum, Glasgow mp. 39205

B45 MASSACHUSETTS
At a Council held at Boston January the third 1677 . . . [Boston, 1678]
broadside
Appointing Feb. 21 a Fast Day
MHi mp. 39206

B46 MASSACHUSETTS
At a Council held at Boston the 22nd. of August 1678. Whereas Benjamin Wait and Stephen Jennings of Hadley . . . [Boston, John Foster, 1678]
broadside 35.5 X 26 cm.
Ford 68; Wing M966
MHi mp. 39207

B47 MASSACHUSETTS
At a Council held at Boston the 22nd. of August 1678 . . . Boston, John Foster [1678]
broadside
Wing M966A
MH; MHi mp. 39208

B48 MASSACHUSETTS. LAWS
At the second sessions of the General Court held at Boston in New-England. Whereas it hath pleased . . . our Gratious [sic] King . . . it is . . . enacted . . . oath of allegiance . . . be . . . taken by . . . subjects . . . sixteen years of age and upwards . . . [Boston, 1678]
broadside 27.5 X 18 cm.
Wing O69A
MH; MHi mp. 39210

B49 [WILLIAMS, ROGER] 1604?-1683
An answer to a letter sent from Mr. Coddington . . . in what concerns R. W. of Providence. [Boston, J. Foster, 1678]

10 p. 24.5 cm. caption title
Sabin 104330; New York Public 12; Wing W2757
RHi. Photostats: CSmH; DLC; MHi; MWA; NN
mp. 39211

1679

B50 MASSACHUSETTS. TREASURER
To the constables and select men of According to an order of the General Court, October 15. 1679. You are . . . required to collect . . . your towns proportion to one single country rate . . . Dated in Boston, Novemb. 5, 1679. [Boston, 1679]
broadside 7 × 15 cm.
MB mp. 39212

B51 MATHER, INCREASE, 1639-1723
A call from Heaven to the present and succeeding generations . . . Boston, Printed by J. Foster, sold by John Ratcliff, 1679.
[8], 114, [2], 29, [3] p.
Holmes: Increase Mather 19-A^{1}
CSmH (incl. completing photostats); MHi (imperfect); MWA (16, [6], 114, 29 p.); ViU mp. 39212

168-

B52 BOSTON
Custome House, Boston in New England. These may certifie . . . Ed. Randolph. [Boston, 168-]
broadside
Clearance paper
Ford 115; Wing C7704
M-Ar

1680

B53 MASSACHUSETTS
At a Council held at Boston March 8. 16^{79}_{80}. The Governour and Council . . . appoint and order, that the fifteenth day of April next, be set apart for a day of humiliation and prayer . . . Edward Rawson Secr. [Boston, 1680]
broadside 26.5 × 17.5 cm.
NjP. Photostat: MWA mp. 39214

1681

B54 CAPEN, JOSEPH
[A funeral elegy upon the . . . deplorable expiration of the pious . . . Mr. John Foster . . . at Dorcester, Sept. 9th . . . 1681 . . .] [Boston, Sold by John Usher, 1681]
broadside
Advertised in Brattle's *Ephemeris*, 1682, as "There are suitable verses . . . to the memory of . . . John Foster. Price 2d. a single paper."
Ford 79
No copy known mp. 39215

B55 MASSACHUSETTS. COUNCIL
At a General Court held at Boston the 16th of March 1680/1 . . . doth appoint the 21st day of April . . . a day of fasting . . . [Boston, 1681]
broadside
MWA mp. 39216

B56 MASSACHUSETTS. LAWS
. . . Several laws and orders made at a sessions of the General Court held at Boston by adjournment from the 4th. to the 16th. of March, 1680 . . . [Boston, 1681]
p. 83-84
Ford & Matthews p. 308
MB mp. 39217

1682

B57 HARVARD UNIVERSITY
Honoratissimo Simoni Bradstreeto . . . [theses?] . . . [Colophon] Bostonae Nov-Anglorum; die sexto ante ides sextiles. 1682.
broadside
Wing H1017; Wing M1222
MH mp. 39218

B58 MAINE
By Thomas Danforth, Esq; President of the Province of Mayne . . . Octob. 1682 . . . [Boston? 1682]
broadside
Appointing Nov. 23 as a day of thanksgiving
Ford 86
MHi (imperfect) mp. 39219

B59 MATHER, INCREASE, 1639-1723
Heaven's alarm to the world .... The second impression . . . Boston, Printed for Samuel Sewall. And are to be sold by John Browning, 1682.
[8], 38, [2], 32 p. A-E^{8}
Second title: The latter sign discoursed of
Holmes: Increase Mather 62-B^{2}; Wing M1219
ICN; MH; MHi; NjP; ViU. mp. 39220

B60 ROWLANDSON, JOSEPH, 1631-1678
The possibility of Gods forsaking . . . set forth in a sermon . . . Nov. 21, 1678 . . . Cambridge, Samuel Green, 1682.
[6], 22 p. 15.5 cm.
Huntington 9; Sabin 73577; Wing R2092
CSmH; DLC. Photostat: MHi mp. 39221

B61 WESTMINSTER ASSEMBLY
The shorter catechism . . . Cambridge, Printed by Samuel Green, for Samuel Phillips in Boston, 1682.
1p.l., 16+ p. 14.5 cm.
Huntington 11; New York Public 13; Wing W1452
CSmH. Photostat: NN mp. 39222

1683

B62 MASSACHUSETTS. GENERAL COURT
At a General Court on adjournment held at Boston, March 14, 1682/3 . . . [Boston, 1683]
broadside
Appointing May 10 a day of humiliation
Public Record Off. Photostat: MHi mp. 39223

1684

B63 ADVERTISEMENT. These are to give notice to all persons . . . that a servant man belonging to Hannah Bosworth of Hull . . . Matthew Jones . . . a taylor by trade . . . ran away from his mistress the 22d. of February 1682 . . . Whosoever shall bring him to . . . Boston shall have forty shillings . . . [Boston] March 6, 1683 [i.e. 1684]

broadside 11 X 13.5 cm.
Ford 94; Wing A606
MHi mp. 39224

B64 COTTON, JOHN, 1585-1652
Spiritual milk for Boston babes . . . Boston, 1684.
1 p.l., 13 p. 14.5 cm.
New York Public 14; Rosenbach-Ch 2; Wing C6463
PP. Photostats: MHi; NN mp. 39225

B65 GT. BRIT. SOVEREIGNS (JAMES II)
. . . A proclamation [concerning privateers] . . . Boston, Reprinted, 1684.
broadside
Public Record Off. Photostat: MHi mp. 39226

1685

B66 KALENDARIUM Pennsilvaniense; or, America's messenger . . . Philadelphia, Printed and sold by William Bradford, 1685.
8vo
Wing A1303
By Samuel Atkins
PHi mp. 39227

B67 MASSACHUSETTS
The Governour and company of the Massachusetts Bay in New-England. At a General Court held at Boston . . . from the 28th of January to the 18th of March, 1684 . . . [Boston, 1685?]
broadside
An explanation of the law about conveyances
Ford 101; Ford & Matthews p. 312; Wing M1005
MB mp. 39228

1686

B68 ADVERTISEMENT Forasmuch as by His Majesty's gracious care, His immediate government is now settled . . . Boston, June 9th, 1686. [Boston, 1686]
broadside 22.5 X 15 cm.
Ford 103; Wing A611
MHi mp. 39229

B69 . . . AN almanack for the year . . . 1687 . . . Philadelphia, Printed and sold by William Bradford [1686?]
broadside 32.5 X 29 cm.
By Daniel Leeds
cf. Evans 408
MHi (facsim.) mp. 39230

B70 MASSACHUSETTS
By the President and Council of His Majesties territory . . . of New-England . . . Published the 10th of June, 1686 . . . [Boston, 1686]
p. 3-10. B-C^2
An order for the holding of courts and execution of justice
Not Evans 410
MHi (facsim.) mp. 39233

B71 MASSACHUSETTS
A proclamation by the President and Council . . . of New-England . . . The exemplification of a judgment . . . against the governour and company of the Massachusetts Bay . . . May 25, 1686. [Boston, Richard Pierce, 1686]
broadside
Ford 105
CSmH; MHi (photostat). Public Record Off. mp. 39234

B72 MASSACHUSETTS.
[Proclamation of day of thanksgiving, probably celebrated November 1686. Boston, 1686]
broadside?
Known from Richard Pierce's bill for printing (Jeffries papers, v. 1, Mass. Hist. Soc.)
No copy known mp. 39236

B73 MASSACHUSETTS. GOVERNOR, 1686-1687
The Speech of the Honourable Joseph Dudley . . . May 17, 1686. Boston, Printed by Richard Pierce for Samuel Phillips, 1686.
4 p.
Public Record Off. Photostat: MHi mp. 39235

B74 MATHER, INCREASE, 1639-1723
The mystery of Christ opened and applyed . . . [Boston] Printed in the year MDCLXXXVI.
[2], 6, 74, [2], 75-212, [2] p.
Probably printed by Richard Pierce for Joseph Brunning
Holmes: Increase Mather 77^2; Wing M1229
MBAt; MHi; MWA; N; NhD (t.p. imperfect); RPJCB. Brit. Mus. mp. 39231

B75 MATHER, INCREASE, 1639-1723
A sermon occasioned by the execution of a man [James Morgan] found guilty of murder . . . Boston, Printed for John Dunton book-seller, 1686.
[4], 44 p. A-C^8
Holmes: Increase Mather 115-A^1; Wing M1246
NHi; RPJCB mp. 39232

1687

B76 HARVARD UNIVERSITY
Praecellenti et illustrissimo . . . theses hasce . . . Cantabrigia Nov-Anglorum: Anno à Christo nato. MDC.LXXXVII.
broadside 27.5 X 19.5 cm.
Ford 113; New York Public 16; Wing H1022
MH. Photostats: MWA; NN mp. 39237

B77 [THE Indian primer] Prov. 22.6. Nehtupeh peisses ut mayut . . . wunnukkodtumuoon. [Cambridge, Samuel Green, 1687?]
[80] p. A-E^8
Dated by Heartman following Eames
Heartman: Non-New-England 89
MHi mp. 39238

B78 KINGS-COUNTY in the Province of New-Yorke.
These are to certify all whome it may concerne . . . Anno Domini 1687. [Philadelphia, William Bradford, 1687]
broadside obl. 8vo
American Art Assoc. cat., Mar. 5-6, 1918, item 33
Form of certification of oath of allegiance
New York Public 17
NN (facsim.) mp. 39239

B79 MASSACHUSETTS
[Order for the constable to bring in the rates. Boston, Richard Pierce, 1687]

Known from Pierce's bill for printing, Nov. 30, 1686 (Jeffries papers, v. 1, Mass. Hist. Soc.)
No copy known mp. 39241

B80 MASSACHUSETTS
[Order for the price of grain. Boston, Richard Pierce, 1687]

Known from Pierce's bill for printing, Dec. 3, 1687 (Jeffries papers, v. 1, Mass. Hist. Soc.)
No copy known mp. 39242

B81 MASSACHUSETTS
[Order for the rates of a penny a pound. Boston, Richard Pierce, 1687]

Known from Pierce's bill for printing, Dec. 3, 1687 (Jeffries papers, v. 1, Mass. Hist. Soc.)
No copy known mp. 39243

B82 MATHER, INCREASE, 1639-1723
De successu evangelij apud Indos in Nova Anglia epistola . . . Bostoniae Nov-Anglorum Julij 12, 1687. [Boston, 1687]
[1], 6 p. 16mo
MHi mp. 39240

B83 A SMALL testimony of that great honour due to . . . John Alden . . . [Boston?] Printed in the year, MDCLXXXVII.
broadside 33 X 20 cm.
cf. *Mayflower Descendant*, v. 9, no. 3, July 1907
NN (photostat enlarged from facsim.)

B84 WALTER, NEHEMIAH, 1663-1750
An elegiack verse, on the death of . . . Mr. Elijah Corlet . . . deceased . . . Feb. 24, 1687. [Boston? 1687?]
broadside
Ford 114; Wing W651
MH mp. 39244

1688

B85 FRIENDS, SOCIETY OF
Germantown Friends' protest against slavery, 1688. This is to ye Monthly meeting held at Richard Worrell's . . . At our Monthly Meeting at Dublin . . . This . . . was read in our Quarterly Meeting at Philadelphia . . . At a Yearly Meeting held at Burlington the 5th day of the 7th month, 1688 . . . [Philadelphia? 1688]
broadside 34 X 23.5 cm.
PHi. Photostat: MSaE mp. 39245

B86 GT. BRIT.
John Usher Esq; Receiver General of His Majesty's revenues . . . to the commissioner and select-men of the Town of Scittuald . . . [Boston? 1688]
broadside 28.5 X 18 cm.
Notice of tax rates on all male persons, dated Boston, July 14, 1688
NHi mp. 39247

B87 MASSACHUSETTS. GOVERNOR, 1687-1689
By his excellency, a proclamation commanding the setting at liberty His Majesty's subjects lately taken . . . by the Indians . . . October 10, 1688. Boston, Richard Pierce [1688]
broadside
Public Record Off. Photostat: MHi mp. 39246

1689

B88 AN account of the proceedings at New York, 1689. A declaration of the inhabitants and souldiers . . . Boston, Samuel Green, 1689.
[2] p. 27.5 X 17 cm.
New York Public 19; Wing A356A
Public Record Off. Photostats: MHi; NN mp. 39248

B89 THE answer of the subscribers to the declaration given in by the representatives of the several towns . . . publickly declared May 24, 1689. [Boston] Printed for Benj. Harris, 1689.
broadside
Public Record Off. Photostat: MHi mp. 39249

B90 FRIENDS, SOCIETY OF. PHILADELPHIA YEARLY MEETING
To Friends, from a yearly meeting held at Philadelphia, the 4th of the 7th moneth [sic], 1689. Printed by William Bradford at Philadelphia A[nno 1689]
broadside 28 X 27 cm.
Another ed. has title beginning: A loving exhortation to Friends
New York Public 20
NNFL; PHi. Photostat: NN mp. 39250

B91 GT. BRIT. SOVEREIGNS (WILLIAM AND MARY)
The first declaration of His Highness . . . of the reasons . . . [Colophon] Boston, Printed for B. Harris [1689]
4to
Wing W2332A
MH mp. 39251

B92 GT. BRIT. SOVEREIGNS (WILLIAM AND MARY)
His Highness the Prince of Orange, his letter to the Lords . . . at Westminster, in this present convention. Boston, Printed by R. P[ierce] for Benjamin Harris, 1689.
broadside
cf. Ford 145; cf. Evans 501
MB mp. 39252

B93 GT. BRIT. SOVEREIGNS (WILLIAM AND MARY)
His Majesty's most gracious letter to his government . . . Boston, Printed by Richard Pierce for Benjamin Harris, 1689.
broadside 30 X 19 cm.
Ford 146; New York Public 21; Sabin 104147
NN. Photostats: DLC; MHi; MWA mp. 39253

B94 HARVARD UNIVERSITY
Amplissimo ac celeberrimo . . . theses hasce . . . MDCLXXXIX. [Cambridge, 1689]
broadside
MH mp. 39254

B95 KNOW all men by these presents, That holden and firmly bound and obliged unto to be paid unto certain attourney . . . Boston, Printed for John Usher [1689?]
broadside 30 X 21 cm.
Dated in manuscript March 13, 1689/90
DLC

B96 MARYLAND
The address of the representatives of their Majestyes Protestant subjects, in the provinnce [sic] of Mary-Land assembled . . . [Colophon] St. Maryes, August 26th, 1689.
broadside 30.5 X 20.5 cm.
Wroth 1; New York Public 22; Wing A553
Public Record Off. Photostat: NN mp. 39255

B97 MASSACHUSETTS
At a convention of the representatives of the several towns and villages . . . May 24, 1689 . . . Boston, Richard Pierce [1689]
broadside
Public Record Off. Photostat: MHi mp. 39257

B98 MASSACHUSETTS
At the convention of the governour and council, and representatives of the Massachusets Colony . . . June 22, 1689. [Boston, 1689]
broadside
Enjoining obedience to laws of May 12, 1686, still in force
Ford 130; cf. Evans 479; Wing M984
M-Ar mp. 39258

B99 MASSACHUSETTS
Boston 3d December 1689. At the convention of the Governour, and Council, and Representatives of the colony . . . [Boston? 1689]
broadside
Public Record Off. Photostat: MHi mp. 39259

B100 MASSACHUSETTS
[A broadside for subscriptions. September. Boston, S. Green, 1689]
broadside
Known by B. Green's bill, Archives, LVIII. 137.
Ford 135
No copy known mp. 39265

B101 MASSACHUSETTS
By the Council and Representatives of the colony . . . Convened at Boston . . . Dec. 10, 1689. [Boston, 1689]
broadside
Public Record Off. Photostat: MHi mp. 39260

B102 MASSACHUSETTS
[Warrant for a rate and a half. December. Boston, S. Green, 1689]
broadside
Known by B. Green's bill
Ford 140
No copy known mp. 39266

B103 MASSACHUSETTS
[Warrant for 6 rates together. November. Boston, S. Green, 1689]
broadside?
Known by B. Green's bill
Ford 139
No copy known mp. 39267

B104 MASSACHUSETTS
[Warrant for the treasurer. September. Boston, S. Green, 1689]
broadside
Known by B. Green's bill
Ford 137
No copy known mp. 39268

B105 MASSACHUSETTS. CITIZENS
At the town-house in Boston: April 18th. 1689. Sir, Our selves as well as many others the inhabitants of this town and place adjacent . . . judge it necessary that you . . . deliver up the government . . . promising all security from violence to your self . . . To Sr. Edmond Andros . . . Wait Winthrop [and 14 others] Boston, S. Green, 1689.
broadside 29 X 20.5 cm.
M-Ar; MHi. Photostat: MWA mp. 39256

B106 MASSACHUSETTS. GOVERNOR, 1687–1689
By His Excellency, a proclamation. Whereas His Majesty . . . by his royal letter . . . the sixteenth day of October . . . [Jan. 10, 1688] . . . Boston, Richard Pierce [1689]
broadside 38 X 32 cm.
MHi; NNS mp. 39261

B107 MASSACHUSETTS. LAWS
[3 acts of the Council. July. Boston, S. Green, 1689]
broadside?
Known by B. Green's bill, Archives, LVIII. 137
Ford 131
No copy known mp. 39264

B108 MASSACHUSETTS. LAWS
[An act of half a sheet about the militia. July. Boston, S. Green, 1689]
broadside
Known by B. Green's bill
Ford 132
No copy known mp. 39265

B109 MASSACHUSETTS. LAWS
[A sheet of laws both sides. September. Boston, S. Green, 1689]
broadside
Known by B. Green's bill
Ford 136
No copy known mp. 39263

B110 A PREPARATORY sheet, occasioned by the author's being ask'd . . . Shall all that have never heard of Jesus Christ, be eternally damned? [Boston? 1689]
8 p. 8vo
MHi (t.p. lacking) mp. 39269

B111 WESTMINSTER ASSEMBLY OF DIVINES
The shorter catechism . . . Cambridge, Printed and sold by Samuel Green, 1689.
1 p.l., 28 p. 15 cm.
MHi mp. 39270

169-

B112 BOSTON
Naval Office in Boston, in Their Majesties Province of Massachusetts-Bay, in New-England. These are to certifie to whom it doth concern . . . [Boston, 169-]
broadside
Clearance paper
Ford 193; Wing M1007
M-Ar

B113 BOSTON
These are certifie all whom it doth concern . . . [Boston, 169-]
broadside
Clearance paper.
Ford 203
M-Ar

B114 KNOW all men by these presents, that holden and firmly bound unto in the paenal sum of lawful money of the province . . . In witness whereof . . . this day of in the . . . year . . . 169 . . . [New York, 169-]
broadside 29 X 19.5 cm.
RPJCB. Photostat: DLC

B115 TO the constable of You are required . . . forthwith to assemble the freeholders of your town . . . to choose . . . men . . . to serve on the jury of tryals at the next Court of holden at *Boston* . . . Dated in *Boston* this day of Anno Domini *1694*. [Boston, 169-]
broadside 19.5 X 23.5 cm.
Italicized portions in ms.
Ford 205
MHi

B116 TO the constable of You are required . . . forthwith to assemble the freeholders of your town . . . to choose . . . men . . . to serve on the jury of tryals at the next Superiour Court . . . Dated in *Boston* this day of Anno Domini *1694.* [Boston, 169–]
broadside 20 X 24.5 cm.
Italicized portions in ms.
Ford 204
MHi

1690

B117 GT. BRIT. SOVEREIGNS (WILLIAM AND MARY)
[Letter of the King to Henry Compton, Bishop of London. Boston, 1690]
broadside?
"There [Boston] I caused 700 copies . . . to be printed and disperst them . . . according to order." Cuthbert Potter's *Journal*, 1690
Ford 147
No copy known mp. 39271

B118 MASSACHUSETTS
[Warrant for ten rates. April. Boston, S. Green, 1690]
broadside?
Known by B. Green's bill, Archives, LVIII. 137
Ford 161
No copy known mp. 39274

B119 MASSACHUSETTS
[Warrant for 2 rates, a large one. July. Boston, S. Green, 1690]
broadside
Known by B. Green's bill
Ford 165
No copy known mp. 39275

B120 MASSACHUSETTS
[Warrant for rates. August. Boston, S. Green, 1690]
broadside
Known by B. Green's bill
Ford 166
No copy known mp. 39276

B121 MASSACHUSETTS. LAWS
[2 acts of Court on half a sheet of paper 100 of them. July. Boston, S. Green, 1690]
broadside
Known by B. Green's bill
Ford 164
No copy known mp. 39273

B122 MASSACHUSETTS. LAWS
At the General Court . . . of the Massachusetts Bay in New-England, sitting in Boston by adjournment. December 10th. 1690 . . . Cambridge, Samuel Green, 1690.
broadside 27.5 X 15.5 cm.
Act on issuing bills of credit
Ford 170; Wing M986
CSmH; M-Ar; MHi mp. 39272

B123 MATHER, COTTON, 1662–1728
[Serious thoughts in dying times . . . Boston, 1690?]

For the evidence for this printing cf. Holmes: Cotton Mather 348-A
No copy known mp. 39277

B124 MRS. Mehitabel Holt. A person of early piety . . . [Boston, S. Green, 1690?]
broadside 13.5 X 18 cm.
MHi mp. 39278

B125 SECKER, WILLIAM, d. 1681?
A wedding ring for the finger; the salve of divinity [on] the sore of humanity. Directions to those men [who w]ant wives, how to choose . . . [Boston] Printed by S. G. [i.e. Samuel Green] for B. [H., i.e. Benjamin Harris] 1690.
[64] p. 7 cm.
MB (t.p. mutilated; other leaves wanting) mp. 39279

B126 VINCENT, THOMAS, 1634–1678
Christ's certain and sudden appearance to judgment . . . Boston, Printed by Samuel Green for Benjamin Harris, 1690.
[4], 220, [4] p. 14.5 cm.
MWA (imperfect at end) mp. 39280

B127 WILKINS, RICHARD, of Boston
Advertisement. It has been thought proper . . . [Boston, Printed by Benjamin Harris and John Allen, 1690?]
broadside
Wing W2216A
MH mp. 39281

1691

B128 ADVERTISEMENT. Whereas at the instance and request of divers gentlemen and merchants, the Governor and Council . . . have . . . accepted the propositions of the . . . gentlemen . . . to settle and maintain an officer and garrison at Port-Royal . . . Boston, June 5th, 1691. [Boston? 1691]
broadside
Ford 173, 181; Wing A624
M-Ar mp. 39282

B129 FRIENDS, SOCIETY OF
A general testimony from the people of God, Called, Quakers . . . Given forth . . . the 9th of the 7th month, 1691. [Philadelphia, William Bradford, 1691]
broadside 39.5 X 32 cm.
New York Public 23
PHi. Photostat: NN mp. 39283

B130 HARVARD UNIVERSITY
Consultissimo . . . theses hasce . . . M.DC.XCI. [Cambridge, 1691]
broadside
Wing H1016
MH mp. 39284

B131 MASSACHUSETTS
[A large warrant, about 100. June. Boston, B. Green, 1691]
broadside
Known by B. Green's bill, Archives, LVIII. 139
Ford 178
No copy known mp. 39289

B132 MASSACHUSETTS
[Large warrant for deputies. September. Boston, B. Green, 1691]
broadside
Known by B. Green's bill
Ford 182
No copy known mp. 39288

B133 MASSACHUSETTS
[Large warrant to quicken constibles. October. Boston, B. Green, 1691]
broadside
Known by B. Green's bill
Ford 183
No copy known mp. 39286

B134 MASSACHUSETTS
[Warrant. July. Boston, B. Green, 1691]
broadside
Known by B. Green's bill
Ford 179
No copy known mp. 39290

B135 MASSACHUSETTS
[Warrant for commissioners. July. Boston, B. Green, 1691]
broadside
Ford 180
No copy known mp. 39287

B136 MASSACHUSETTS. LAWS
At a General Court for Their Majesties Colony of the Massachusetts-Bay . . . Boston, upon adjournment, December 22th. 1691. Forasmuch as these coasts . . . [Boston, 1691]
broadsheet 31 X 16.5 cm.
Laws for protection against pirates
MHi mp. 39285

B137 MATHER, COTTON, 1662–1728
Ornaments for the daughters of Zion . . . Cambridge, Printed by S[amuel] G[reen] & B[artholomew] G[reen] for Samuel Phillips at Boston, 1691.
104 p., 1 leaf
cf. Holmes: Cotton Mather 266-A[1]
MB; MHi mp. 39291

B138 MULLENAUX, SAMUEL
A journal of the three months royal campaign . . . Boston, Re-printed by R. P. for Benjamin Harris, 1691.
30, [2] p. 19 cm. caption title
DLC mp. 39292

B139 NEW YORK
By his excellency the Governor and Council, and House of Representatives . . . a proclamation . . . [Apr. 17, 1691] [n.p., 1691]
broadside 35 X 44.5 cm.
Concerns the conduct of Jacob Leisler
MHi (photostat) mp. 39293

1692

B140 BOSTON almanack for the year . . . 1692 . . . Boston, Benjamin Harris, and John Allen, 1692.
[20] p. 15 cm.
Not Evans 595; New York Public 24
NN. Photostats: DLC; MWA mp. 39294

B141 FRIENDS, SOCIETY OF. BURLINGTON YEARLY MEETING
From the Yearly meeting at Burlington . . . Seventh month, anno 1691 . . . [Philadelphia, W. Bradford, 1692]
broadside 34 X 26 cm.
PPRF. Photostats: DLC; NN mp. 39295

B142 MASSACHUSETTS
By His Excellency and Council . . . a proclamation [for a day of prayer and fasting, Dec. 29, 1692] . . . [Boston, 1692]
broadside
Public Record Off. Photostat: MHi mp. 39298

B143 MASSACHUSETTS
Naval Office at Boston, in Their Majesties province . . . these are to certifie . . . [Boston, 1692]
broadside
Wing M1007
M-Ar

B144 MASSACHUSETTS
Province of the Massachusetts-Bay, ss. By virtue of an act of the General Assembly . . . for the granting . . . an assessment upon polls and estate; passed the 24th of June, 1692 . . . November , 1692. [Boston? 1692]
broadside
Ford 192; Wing M1015
MSaE mp. 39299

B145 MASSACHUSETTS
A table of the courts. [Boston] Printed & sold by Benja. Harris [1692]
broadside 16 X 11 cm.
Ford 195; Wing T77
MB; MHi mp. 39296

B146 MASSACHUSETTS. GOVERNOR, 1692–1694
By His Excellency the Governour. Whereas it hath been of absolute necessity,that a certain number of men should be impressed . . . July 27, 1692. [Boston] Benjamin Harris, 1692.
broadside
Ford 191; Wing M992
MHi mp. 39297

B147 A TRUE copy of the oaths that are appointed . . . Boston, Printed for, and sold by Benjamin Harris, 1692.
broadside 29 X 21 cm.
DLC; MHi; MSaE mp. 39300

1693

B148 HARVARD UNIVERSITY
Quaestiones pro modulo . . . M DC XC III. [Boston, 1693]
broadside
MH. Photostat: MWA mp. 39301

B149 LANCASTER, WILLIAM
[William] La[nca]ster's Queries to the Quakers, with the [New York, William Bradford, 1693]
[3+] p. 10 cm.
For dating cf. McMurtrie: New York 30; Wing L314
PHi (fragment). Photostats: DLC; MWA mp. 39304

B150 NEW YORK. GOVERNOR, 1692–1695
Benjamin Fletcher, Captain General . . . to all officers and ministers, ecclesiastical & civil . . . New York, William Bradford, 1693.
broadside 32 X 19.5 cm.
Second issue; cf. Evans 669 (first issue)
McMurtrie: New York 12; New York Public 28
PPAmP. Photostats: DLC; MHi; NN mp. 39304

B151 NEW YORK. LAWS
. . . An act passed the 12th of September 1693, for settling a ministry . . . [New York, William Bradford, 1693]
4 p. 32.5 cm.
Photostat: MHi mp. 39305

B152 A TRUE copy of the oaths that are appointed . . . [Boston, Benjamin Harris, 1693]
broadside 34 X 22.5 cm.
Ford 200; Wing T2651
M-Ar; MB; MHi. Photostat: DLC mp. 39306

B153 VAN CORTLANDT, STEPHANUS, 1643-1700
A journal kept by Coll. Stephen Courtland, & Coll. Nich. Beyard . . . in treating with the Indians of the Five Nations, and River Indians of that province . . . June and July, 1693 . . . New-York, Printed and sold by William Bradford, 1693.
15 p. 27 cm.
New York Public 26; Wing C6607
Bibl. Nationale. Photostats: DLC; MWA; NN mp. 39307

B154 [WISWELL, ICHABOD]
Upon the death of that reverend and aged man . . . Samuel Arnold . . . deceased in the 71st year of his age . . . September 1. 1693. [Boston? 1693]
broadside 29.5 X 39 cm.
Ford 197; Wegelin 567
DLC. Photostats: MHi; MWA; NN mp. 39308

1694

B155 BURLING, ELIAS
A call to back-sliding Israel. New-York, Printed and sold by William Bradford, 1694.
22 p. 15 cm. $A\text{-}C^4$
Cambridge University mp. 39309

B156 CONEY, PEREGRINE
[A sermon preaced before His excellency . . . the 26th of September, 1694 . . . St. Mary's City, William Nuthead, 1694]

Wroth 3
No copy known mp. 39310

B157 HARVARD UNIVERSITY
Quaestiones, quas pro modulo . . . M.DC. XC.IV. [Boston, 1694]
broadside
MH. Photostat: MWA mp. 39311

B158 LAWSON, DEODAT
Threnodia, or a mournful remembrance of . . . Anthony Collamore . . . [Dec. 16, 1693] . . . Boston, Barthlomew Green, 1694.
broadside 33 X 26 cm.
MHi (photostat) mp. 39312

1695

B159 HARVARD UNIVERSITY
Quaestiones, quas pro modulo . . . M DC XC V. [Boston, 1695]
broadside
Wing H1038
CtY; MH. Photostat: MWA mp. 39313

B160 KEACH, BENJAMIN, 1640-1704
Instructions for children: or, The child's & youth's delight . . . Written by Benj. Keach. New-York, Printed and sold by Will. Bradford, 1695.
[12], 152+ p. 13.5 cm.
MWA mp. 39314

B161 LEEDS, DANIEL, 1652-1720
The innocent vindicated . . . [New York, W. Bradford] 1695.
24 p. 16 cm.
Huntington 17; Wing L913
CSmH. Photostats: DLC; MWA; NN mp. 39315

B162 NEW YORK. LAWS
An act passed the 12th of September, 1693 . . . [Followed by] Die Veneris. 8 h. A. M. April 12, 1695. A petition of the church-wardens . . . [New York, 1695]
4 p. 31.5 cm. caption title
Public Record Off. Photostats: DLC; NN mp. 39316

1696

B163 BROOK, CHIDLEY
To their excellencys, the Lords Justices of England the humble memorial of Chidley Brook & William Nicolls . . . [New York, William Bradford, 1696]
3 p. 26 cm.
"Given in [sic] May 19th, 1696."
New York Public 31
MHi. Photostat: NN mp. 39317

B164 CONEY, PEREGRINE
[A sermon preached before His Excellency . . . the 7th of May 1696 . . . Annapolis, Dinah Nuthead, 1696]

Wroth 4
No copy known mp. 39318

B165 HARVARD UNIVERSITY
Quaestiones, quas pro modulo . . . M DC XC VI. [Boston, 1696]
broadside
MH. Photostat: MWA mp. 39319

B166 NEW YORK. GOVERNOR, 1692-1695
The speech of . . . Coll. Benjamin Fletcher . . . to the Assembly, the 7th day of April, 1696. [New York, W. Bradford, 1696]
3 p. 24 cm. caption title
Photostats: DLC; MHi mp. 39320

1697

B167 GT. BRIT. TREATIES
An abstract of the treaty of peace . . . at Ryswick . . . Boston, Reprinted by B. Green and J. Allen, 1697.
broadside
MHi mp. 39321

B168 GT. BRIT. TREATIES
Articles of peace . . . William the Third . . . and Lewis the Fourteenth . . . Boston, Reprinted by B. Green & J. Allen, for Samuel Phillips, 1697.
4 p. 27 cm.
MHi mp. 39322

B169 HARVARD UNIVERSITY
Quaestiones quas pro modulo . . . M DC XC VII. [Boston, 1697]
broadside
MH. Photostat: MWA mp. 39323

B170 MASSACHUSETTS
Anno 1697. [Election of councillors] [Boston, 1697]
broadside
Ford 221; Wing M956
M-Ar mp. 39324

B171 [MATHER, COTTON] 1663-1728
Humiliations follow'd with deliverances . . . Boston, B. Green & J. Allen for Samuel Phillips, 1697.
72 p. 13.5 cm.
Holmes: Cotton Mather 178; Huntington 20
CSmH; DLC. Photostats: MHi; MWA; RPJCB mp. 39325

B172 TILLY, WILLIAM
Advertisement. Ran away the 13th of this instant June, from his master, William Tilly of Boston . . . a Carolina Indian manservant, named Tom . . . Boston, June 14th. 1697. [Boston, B. Green and J. Allen, 1697]
broadside 13 X 9 cm.
MB mp. 39326

1698

B173 HARVARD UNIVERSITY
Quaestiones pro modulo . . . M DC XC VIII. [Boston, 1698]
broadside
MH. Photostat: MWA mp. 39327

B174 MASSACHUSETTS. GOVERNOR, 1694-1699
Province of the Massachusetts-Bay in New-England. By the honorable, the Lieut. Governour . . . a proclamation. Whereas the Indians . . . [Feb. 9, 1698] Boston, Bartholomew Green, and John Allen, 1698.
broadside 35 X 19 cm.
DLC mp. 39328

B175 MASSACHUSETTS. GOVERNOR, 1694-1699
Province of the Massachusetts-Bay ss. By the honorable, the Lieutenant Governour . . . a proclamation. For preventing and punishing immorality . . . [June 16, 1698] . . . Boston, Bartholomew Green, and John Allen, 1698.
broadside 37.5 X 28.5 cm.
New York Public 32
MH. Photostats: MWA; NN mp. 39329

B176 [MATHER, COTTON] 1662-1728
[A present] from a farr countrey, [to the] people of New England . . . Boston, Printed by B. Green, and J. Allen, for Michael Perry, 1698.
53, [1] p. 14 cm.
Holmes: Cotton Mather 302
MWA; RPJCB mp. 39330

B177 NEW YORK. GOVERNOR, 1697-1701
By . . . Richard Earl of Bellomont . . . a proclamation. Whereas the acts . . . [Jan. 19, 1698] New York, William Bradford, 1698.
broadside 26 X 20 cm.
Photostat: DLC mp. 39331

B178 TAYLOR, JACOB, d. 1745 or 6
Tenebrae in Or, The Eclip[ses] of th[e] sun & [moon] . . . [By Jacob Taylor] [New York, William Bradford, 1698]
[48] p. 15 cm.
Fragment only, recovered by Wilberforce Eames
New York Public 33
PPRF mp. 39332

B179 THE Turkish fast . . . Boston, B. Green, and J. Allen, 1698.
broadside 30 X 19.5 cm.
Ford 223; Sabin 97458; Wing T3262
MB. Photostats: DLC; MHi; NN mp. 39333

1699

B180 AN almanack for . . . 1699 . . . New-York, Printed and sold by William Bradford, 1699.
[24] p. 14 cm.
By Daniel Leeds
Guerra b-26; NYPL 37; Wall p. 5; Wing A2538
CSmH; CtY; NNPM; PHi (imperfect). A. S. W. Rosenbach (1945) Photostat: NN mp. 39339

B181 ASSOCIATION. Whereas there has been a horrid . . . conspiracy . . . for assassinating His majesties royal person . . . [Boston, 1699?]
broadside 32.5 X 20 cm.
With a number of signatures
Ford 237; Huntington 21; Wing E1236
CSmH; M-Ar. Photostat: DLC mp. 39334

B182 BOND, SAMSON
The sincere milk of the word, for the children of Bermuda . . . [at end] Boston, B. Green, & J. Allen, 1699.
8p. 14.5 cm. caption title
New York Public 35; Wing B3587
RPJCB. Photostat: NN mp. 39335

B183 DANFORTH, JOHN, 1660-1730
A funeral elegy humbly dedicated to the renowned memory of . . . Thomas Danforth, Esq. . . . [Boston, 1699]
broadside
cf. *Harvard Library Bulletin,* v. 1, no. 1, Winter, 1947
New York Public 36
NN (photostat) mp. 39336

B184 HARVARD UNIVERSITY
Quaestiones pro modulo . . . M DC XC IX. [Boston, 1699]
broadside
MH. Photostat: MWA mp. 39337

B185 INDIAN AND AFRICAN COMPANY OF SCOTLAND
Caledonia. The declaration of the council constituted by the Indian and African Company of Scotland for the government . . . of their colonies . . . [Colophon] Boston, May 15th, 1699.
4 p.
Ford 225; Wing C283
MWA; RPJCB mp. 39338

B186 LEEDS, DANIEL, 1652-1720
A trumpet sounded out of the wilderness . . . as a warning . . . to beware of Quakerisme . . . New York, William Bradford; and are to be sold by B. Aylmer and C. Brome, London, 1699.
8 p.l., 151 p. 15 cm.
Consists of the same sheets (with cancel t.p.) as 1697 ed. (New York, W. Bradford). 1699 t.p. probably printed in London
New York Public 38; Sabin 39821; Wing L916
NN. Photostat: RP mp. 39340

B187 MASSACHUSETTS. GOVERNOR, 1694-1699
The address of . . . the Lieutenant Governour Stoughton . . . on the second day of June, 1699. [Colophon] Boston, Bartholomew Green, and John Allen, 1699.
4p. 23 cm. caption title
Ford 233; New York Public 42; Wing S5759
Public Record Off. Photostats: DLC; MHi; MWA; NN
mp. 39346

B188 MASSACHUSETTS. GOVERNOR, 1699-1700
Province of the Massachusetts-Bay. By His Excellency Richard, Earl of Bellomont . . . A proclamation . . . [May 26, 1699] . . . Boston, Printed by Bartholomew Green, and John Allen, 1699.
broadside 33.5 X 26.5 cm.
Ford 230
Photostats: MHi; MWA. Albert D. Bosson, Boston (1921) mp. 39342

B189 MASSACHUSETTS. GOVERNOR, 1699-1700
Province of the Massachusetts-Bay . . . By his excellency, the Earl of Bellomont, a proclamation [proroguing the Assembly to Dec. 6]. Boston, Bartholomew Green and John Allen, 1699.
broadside
Public Record Off. Photostat: MHi mp. 39341

B190 MASSACHUSETTS. GOVERNOR, 1699-1700
His Excellency, the Earl of Bellomont's speech . . . on Fryday the 2d. of June 1699. [Boston, B. Green and J. Allen, 1699]
3 p. 25 cm. caption title
Ford 232; NYPL 39; Wing B1846
Public Record Off. Photostats: DLC; MHi; MWA; NN
mp. 39343

B191 MASSACHUSETTS. HOUSE OF REPRESENTATIVES
The answer of the House . . . to . . . the Earl of Bellomont's speech on Tuesday the 6th. of June, 1699. [Colophon] Boston, Bartholomew Green, and John Allen, 1699.
[2] p. 21.5 cm. caption title
Ford 235; New York Public 40; Wing M958
Public Record Off. Photostats: DLC; MHi; MWA; NN; RPJCB mp. 39344

B192 MASSACHUSETTS. HOUSE OF REPRESENTATIVES
A congratulatory address . . . on Tuesday the 6th of June . . . 1699. [Colophon] Boston, Bartholomew Green, and John Allen, 1699.
2 p. 21 cm. caption title
Ford 234; New York Public 41
Public Record Off. Photostats: DLC; MHi; MWA; NN
mp. 39345

B193 MATHER, COTTON, 1662-1728
[Indian primer . . . Boston, 1699?]

Referred to in Mather's *Diary*, i, 328, Dec.-Jan. 1699-1700; cf. Holmes: Cotton Mather 183
No copy known mp. 39347

B194 NEW HAMPSHIRE. GOVERNOR, 1699-1702
His Excellency, the Earl of Bellomont's speech to the General Assembly . . . convened at New Hampshire . . . on Monday, August 7, 1699 . . . Boston, Bartholomew Green and John Allen, 1699.
broadside
Public Record Off. Photostat: MHI mp. 39348

B195 NEW HAMPSHIRE. HOUSE OF REPRESENTATIVES
The answer of the House of Representatives to . . . the Earl of Bellomont's speech . . . Boston, Bartholomew Green and John Allen, 1699.
broadside
The House convened Aug. 7
Not Ford 235
Public Record Off. Photostat: MHi mp. 39349

B196 NEW HAMPSHIRE. HOUSE OF REPRESENTATIVES
A congratulatory address of the House of Representatives of . . . New Hampshire . . . Boston, Bartholomew Green and John Allen, 1699.
broadside
Public Record Off. Photostat: MHi mp. 39350

B197 NEW YORK. HOUSE OF REPRESENTATIVES
To His Excellency Richard Earl of Bellomont . . . The humble petition and remonstrance of the representatives . . . of New-York . . . in General Assembly. [New York, William Bradford, 1699]
3 p. 24.5 cm.
Dated: 15 May, 1699
cf. *N.Y.P.L. Bulletin,* Nov. 1948
New York Public 43
NN mp. 39351

B198 NEW YORK. LAWS
An ordinance of His excellency and Council for the establishing courts of judicature . . . [May 15, 1699] [New York, W. Bradford, 1699]
4 p. 33 cm.
Title in 7 lines
Huntington 23; cf. Evans 889
CSmH mp. 39352

B199 OATHS appointed to be taken instead of the oaths of allegiance . . . [Boston, 1699?]
broadside 32.5 X 20 cm.
Ford 237; Huntington 22; Wing 081
CSmH; DLC (4 different photostat copies); M-Ar
mp. 39353

B200 STONE, SAMUEL, 1600-1663
A short catechism drawn out of the word of God . . . Boston, Bartholomew Green, and John Allen, for William Gibbons, 1699.
15 p. 14.5 cm.
Sabin 92115; New York Public 44; Wing S5737
RPJCB (lacking beyond p. 12). Photostats: MHi; NN
mp. 39354

B201 STUBBE, HENRY, 1606-1678
Conscience the best friend upon earth . . . Boston, B. Green & J. Allen for Nicholas Buttolph, 1699.
[6], 64 p. [A]-B^4 C-G^6
RPJCB (imperfect) mp. 39355

B202 WESTMINSTER ASSEMBLY OF DIVINES
The shorter catechism . . . Boston, Printed by B. Green, and J. Allen, for Samuel Phillips, 1699.
24? p. 12mo
MWA (lacks p. 17–18, 23+) mp. 39356

1700

B203 [ALMANACK for 1700, by Jacob Taylor. Philadelphia, R. Jansen, 1700?]

PPL (fragment of 1 leaf only) mp. 39369

B204 [DOOLITTLE, THOMAS] 1630-1707
[A call to delaying sinners. Boston, 1700?]
144 p. 14 cm. A-G[12]
MWA copy lacks A1-A3; title taken from running title
MHi; MWA mp. 39357

B205 HARVARD UNIVERSITY
Quaestiones quas pro modulo . . . MDCC. [Boston, 1700]
broadside
Wing H1039
CtY; MH. Photostat: MWA mp. 39358

B206 LYDIUS, JOHANNES, d. 1710
. . . Christelyke religie voorgedyelt . . . [New York, W. Bradford, 1700]
3 p.l., 40, 33-46 p., 1 leaf, 47-96, [2] p. 15.5 cm.
Dedication dated: Albany den 28 October 1700
PHi (t.p. and 5 foll. leaves mutilated; p. 7-8, 17-24 wanting) mp. 39359

B207 MARYLAND. GOVERNOR, 1698-1702
His Excellency's speech, to the honourable the General Assembly Maryland, April the 26th. Anno Domini 1700. [Annapolis, Thomas Reading, 1700]
2 leaves. 34 cm.
On verso: The General Assembly's answer . . . April the 27th. 1700
New York Public 45
NHi. Photostat: NN mp. 39360

B208 MARYLAND. LAWS
[An act for the service of Almighty God and establishment of religion . . . Annapolis, Thomas Reading, 1700]

Ordered printed by Lower House, May 7, 1700
Wroth 6
No copy known mp. 39361

B209 MARYLAND. LAWS
[A complete body of the laws of Maryland. Annapolis, Thomas Reading, 1700]
2 p.l., 118+ p. 33.5 cm.
Wroth 7
DLC (t.p. wanting, and incomplete) mp. 39362

B210 MASSACHUSETTS
Letters of administration. [Boston, 1700]
broadside
Wing M1006
M-Ar mp. 39367

B211 MASSACHUSETTS. GOVERNOR, 1699-1700
Province of the Massachusetts-Bay . . . By his excellency Richard, Earl of Bellomont . . . A proclamation . . . March 14, 1699. Boston, Bartholomew Green and John Allen, 1699 [i.e. 1700]
broadside
Public Record Off. Photostat: MHi mp. 39363

B212 MASSACHUSETTS. GOVERNOR, 1699-1700
Province of the Massachusetts-Bay . . . By his excellency, Richard, Earl of Bellomont . . . A proclamation [for a general fast, Mar. 20, 1699] . . . [Boston, 1700]
broadside
Public Record Off. Photostat: MHi mp. 39364

B213 MASSACHUSETTS. GOVERNOR, 1699-1700
Province of the Massachusetts-Bay . . . By his excellency Richard, Earl of Bellomont . . . A proclamation . . . April 16, 1700. Boston, Bartholomew Green, 1700.
broadside
Dissolving the General Court
Public Record Off. Photostat: MHi mp. 39365

B214 MASSACHUSETTS. GOVERNOR, 1699-1700
Province of the Massachusetts-Bay . . . His Excellency, the Earl of Bellomont's speech . . . Wednesday the 13th of March, 1699 . . . [Boston, 1700]
broadside
Public Record Off. Photostat: MHi mp. 39366

B215 [RUDMAN, ANDREW] 1668-1708
Naogra Andeliga Wisor. [Philadelphia? Reinier Jansen? 1700?]
8 p. 15.5 cm. caption title
New York Public 47
Kungliga Biblioteket, Stockholm. Photostats: MWA; NN mp. 39368

1701

B216 BARBADOS. LAWS
An act to incourage privateers in case of a war . . . [Nov. 18, 1701] [Boston, 1701]
2 p. 25 cm.
Huntington 25; New York Public 48
CSmH. Photostats: MHi; NN mp. 39370

B217 HARVARD UNIVERSITY
Quaestiones pro modulo . . . MDCCI. [Boston, 1701]
broadside
Ford 247
MH; MHi mp. 39371

B218 A LETTER from one in the country, concerning some of the present differences . . . [n.p., 1701?]
[4] p. 21 cm.
Signed: Ireneus Aletheian
Closely trimmed
MWA mp. 39372

B219 MASSACHUSETTS
Province of the Massachusetts-Bay. By the honorable the Council . . . a proclamation for a general fast . . . the death of . . . William Stoughton . . . August 23, 1701. [Boston, 1701]
[2] p. 17 X 11 cm.
Ford 249
MHi; MSaE mp. 39373

B220 MASSACHUSETTS. TREASURER
Province of the Massachusetts-Bay. James Taylor, Gent. treasurer and receiver-general . . . To constable of Boston, the first day of December, 1701. [Boston, 1701]
broadside
Tax warrant
MHi mp. 39374

B221 MATHER, COTTON, 1662-1728
[Certain select passages in certain books about the state of Europe, and the American plantations. Boston, 1701?]

Title from Mather's *Diary*, i, 398, cf. Holmes: Cotton Mather 116
No copy known mp. 39375

B222 [MATHER, COTTON] 1662-1728
A letter concerning the terrible sufferings of our Protestant brethren, on board the French Kings galleys . . . [Boston?] 1701.
8 p. 14 cm.
Dated: 7. d. 3. m. 1701
MWA mp. 39376

B223 WESTMINSTER ASSEMBLY OF DIVINES
The shorter catechism . . . Boston, in New-England, Printed by Bartholomew Green, & John Allen, for Nicholas Buttolph at his shop, 1701.
1 p.l., 46 p. 17 cm.
MB mp. 39377

1702

B224 CLOUGH 1702. The New-England almanack for . . . MDCCII . . . Boston, Printed by B. Green, and J. Allen, for Benj. Eliot, 1702.
[32] p. 15.5 cm.
cf. Evans 970
MWA mp. 39378

B225 CLOUGH, 1702. The New-England almanack for . . . MDCCII . . . Boston: Printed by B. Green, and J. Allen, for N. Buttolph, 1702.
[32] p. 15.5 cm.
Drake 2909
DLC

B226 COPIE of the election made May, 27. 1702. [Boston? 1702]
broadside 29.5 X 19.5 cm.
Ford 254
M-Ar. Photostats: DLC; MWA; NN mp. 39385

B227 CORBYN, SAMUEL, fl. 1677
An awakening call from the eternal God to the unconverted . . . By Samuel Corbin . . . Boston, Re-printed by T. Green, for Nicholas Buttolph, 1702.
59, [1] p. 14 cm.
MWA mp. 39379

B228 GT. BRIT. SOVEREIGNS (ANNE)
Her Majesties most gracious declaration for the incouragement of her ships of war and privateers . . . Boston, Reprinted by Bartholomew Green, and John Allen. Sept. 24th 1702.
broadside 42 X 33 cm.
Ford 252
MHi mp. 39381

B229 HARVARD UNIVERSITY
Quaestiones pro modulo . . . MDCCII. [Boston, 1702]
broadside
MH. Photostat: MWA mp. 39382

B230 J., R.
Dives and Lazarus . . . Delivered in a sermon at Paul's Cross; by R. J. . . . The one and twentieth edition. Boston, Reprinted by T. Green, for Nicholas Buttolph, 1702.
47 p. 14.5 cm.
MWA mp. 39380

B231 THE life & death of our blessed Lord . . . Boston, Printed by T. Green, for Nicholas Boone, 1702.
1 p.l., 5-187, [2] p. 12.5 cm.
DLC (imperfect) mp. 39383

B232 MASSACHUSETTS
To His excellency, Joseph Dudley . . . the address of divers ministers of said province. Boston, Bartholomew Green, and John Allen, 1702.
broadside 29 X 17 cm.
Ford 257
DLC (photostat); MHi (photostat); MWA mp. 39384

B233 MASSACHUSETTS. GOVERNOR, 1702–1715
By His Excellency, Joseph Dudley . . . A proclamation for a general thanksgiving . . . Given at Cambridge the twenty-first day of November, 1702 . . . [Boston, 1702]
broadside
McMurtrie: Mass. broadsides, p. [9]
Reduced photostats: MHi; MWA mp. 39387

B234 MASSACHUSETTS. GOVERNOR, 1702-1715
Province of the Massachusetts-Bay in New-England. By His Excellency, Joseph Dudley . . . A proclamation for a general fast . . . Given at Boston the first day of October, 1702 . . . [Boston, 1702]
broadside
McMurtrie: Mass. broadsides, p. [8]
Reduced photostats: MHi; MWA mp. 39386

B235 MATHER, COTTON, 1663-1728
Magnalia Christi Americana. [Errata. Boston, after August 1702]
[2] leaves, printed on p. [2] and [3]. 29.5 cm.
Page [3] numbered 2
No heading; text begins: THE Holy Bible it self . . . hath been affronted, with Scandalous Errors of the Press-work . . .
Printed in Boston and inserted in some copies of the London-printed edition (1702).—cf. Church 806; Holmes 213A (p. 574); Howes M 391. Analysis by Richard Colles Johnson
ICN; MWA; ViU

B236 STANDFAST, RICHARD
A New-Years-gift for fainting soul. Or, A little handful of cordial comforts . . . By Richard Standfast . . . Boston, Printed by T. Green, for Nicholas Buttolph, 1702.
50+ p. 14 cm. A^6-E^6?
MHi (wanting after p. 48); MWA (wanting after sig. E1) mp. 39388

B237 [WILCOCKS, THOMAS] b. 1622
A guide to eternal glory . . . With several other brief tracts and spiritual hymns. Boston, in N.E. Printed by T. Green, for Nicholas Buttolph, 1702.
108 p. 12mo
cf. Evans 1101
PHi

B238 THE wonder of nature: or Europe's miracle. Being a strange account of one Hen. T'Kent a little boy of seven . . . who hath legible white letters round the ball of his right eye . . . London, Printed by Jer. Wilkins, 1701. Reprinted at Boston, 1702.
8 p. 8vo
"Sold by B. Green."—p. 8
MB mp. 39389

1703

B239 ALLEINE, JOSEPH, 1634-1668
An alarm to unconverted sinners . . . Boston, Printed by B. Green, and J. Allen, for Nicholas Boone, 1703.
1 p.l., [30], 296+ p. 13.5 cm.
DLC (imperfect) mp. 39390

B240 GT. BRIT. LAWS
Anno regni Gulielmi III . . . At the Parliament begun . . . August, 1698 . . . London, Printed by Charles Bill, 1969. Reprinted at Boston for Benj. Eliot, 1703.
8 p.

"An act to prevent the exportation of wool . . . into foreign parts . . ."
Ford 259
MHi mp. 39391

B241 HARVARD UNIVERSITY
Quaestiones in philosophia . . . MDCCIII. [Boston, 1703]
broadside
MH. Photostat: MWA mp. 39392

B242 JANEWAY, JAMES, 1636-1674
Invisibles, realities, demonstrated . . . The third edition. Boston, Printed by T. Green, for Benjamin Eliot, 1703.
177, [2] p. 14.5 cm. A-P^6
DLC; MB; MWA; NN (imperfect); RPJCB mp. 39394

B243 JANEWAY, JAMES, 1636-1674
Invisibles, realities, demonstrated . . . The third edition. Boston, Printed by T. Green, for Nicholas Boone, 1703.
177, [2] p. 14.5 cm.
MB mp. 39393

B244 JULY 14th, 1703. Prices of goods supplyed to the Eastern Indians, by the several truckmasters; and of peltry received . . . [Boston? 1703]
broadside 30 X 21.5 cm.
Ford 263; New York Public 52
M-Ar. Photostats: MWA; NN
mp. 39399

B245 MASSACHUSETTS. GOVERNOR, 1702-1715
By His Excellency Joseph Dudley . . . A proclamation . . . That no trade or commerce whatsoever, be holden with the subjects of the crown of Spain . . . nor supplys . . . to the subjects of the French king . . . Given at Boston the thirteenth day of August, 1703 . . . [Boston, 1703]
broadside
McMurtrie: Mass. broadsides, p. [10]
Reduced photostats: MHi; MWA mp. 39396

B246 MASSACHUSETTS. GOVERNOR, 1702-1715
By His Excellency, Joseph Dudley Esq. . . . A proclamation for a general fast . . . September 7, 1703. [Boston, 1703]
broadside
Ford 264
RHi mp. 39395

B247 MASSACHUSETTS. HOUSE OF REPRESENTATIVES
The answer of the House of Representatives, to . . . Joseph Dudley, Esq. His speech to . . . the Council and House . . . on the 19th of March, 1702. Boston, Printed for and sold by Samuel Phillips, 1702/3.
2 p. 31.5 X 21.5 cm.
Ford 258
MWA mp. 39397

B248 MASSACHUSETTS. TREASURER
Province of the Massachusetts Bay, ss. James Taylor, gent., treasurer and receiver general . . . Given under my hand and seal at Boston, the first day of October, 1703 . . . [Boston, 1703]
broadside 35 X 21 cm.
PPRF mp. 39398

B249 MATHER, COTTON, 1662-1728
Conversion exemplified . . . [Boston, T. Green? 1703?]
6 p. 15 cm. caption title
Dated from Mather's *Diary*, i, 481-482
Holmes: Cotton Mather 73
MWA mp. 39400

B250 THE N. England kalendar, 1703. Or, an almanack for the year . . . 1703 . . . By a lover of astronomy . . . Boston, Printed by B. Green, & J. Allen. Sold at the Printing-House at the south end of the town, 1703.
[16] p. 15 cm.
Not to be confused with Evans 1041
MB mp. 39401

1704

B251 AN account of the behaviour and last dying speeches of the six pirates . . . Boston, Nicholas Boone, 1704.
2 p. 28.5 X 17.5 cm.
Ford 265; New York Public 53
MHi; MiU-C. Photostats: DLC; NN; WHi mp. 39402

B252 COCKSHUTT, THOMAS
[A sermon preached at the opening of St. Anne's Church . . . the 24th of September, 1704 . . . Annapolis, Thomas Reading, 1704]

Wroth 11
No copy known mp. 39403

B253 DYER, WILLIAM, 1636-1696
Christ's famous titles . . . By Will. Dyer . . . Boston, Printed by B. Green, & J. Allen, for Benjamin Eliot, 1704.
[6], 354 p. 14 cm. A-P^{12}
MWA mp. 39405

B254 DYER, WILLIAM, 1636-1696
Christ's famous titles . . . By Will. Dyer . . . Boston, Printed by B. Green, & J. Allen, for Nicholas Boone, 1704.
[6], 354 p. 14 cm. A-P^{12}
MWA mp. 39404

B255 HARVARD UNIVERSITY
Quaestiones pro modulo . . . MDCCIV. [Boston, 1704]
broadside
MH. Photostat: MWA mp. 39406

B256 MARYLAND. LAWS
[The laws of the province of Maryland, . . . passed at a session begun . . . the fifth day of September, 1704. Annapolis, Thomas Reading, 1704]

Wroth 12
No copy known mp. 39407

B257 MARYLAND. LAWS
[The laws of the province of Maryland, . . . passed at a session . . . begun . . . the fifth day of December, 1704. Annapolis, Thomas Reading, 1704]

Wroth 13
No copy known mp. 39408

B258 MASSACHUSETTS. GOVERNOR, 1702-1715
By the honorable Thomas Povey, Esq; Lieutenant Governour . . . for the time being . . . a proclamation [against Quelch and other pirates] . . . May 24, 1704. Boston, Bartholomew Green, 1704.
broadside 36 X 28 cm.
Ford 270
MHi mp. 39411

B259 MASSACHUSETTS. LAWS
. . . An act for punishing of officers and souldiers . . . under pay. [Colophon] Boston, B. Green, 1704.
2 leaves. 30 cm.
At head of caption title: Anno Regni Annae Reginae Tertio. An act, passed by the . . . General Court . . . begun . . . the thirty-first of May, 1704
New York Public 54
NN mp. 39409

B260 MASSACHUSETTS. LAWS
. . . An act of continuation of several acts therein mentioned that are near expiring . . . [Colophon] Boston, Bartholomew Green, 1704.
[2] p. 30.5 cm.
At head of title: An act, passed by the . . . General Court . . . begun . . . the thirty-first of May, 1704
MWA (upper corner wanting) mp. 39410

B261 THE N. England Kalendar, 1704 . . . By a Lover of astronomy. With allowance. Boston, Printed by B. Green, and J. Allen, for Nicholas Buttolph, 1704.
[16] p. 15 cm.
cf. Nichols p. 36 (variant issue)
DLC mp. 39412

B262 THE N. England Kalendar, 1704 . . . By a Lover of astronomy. With allowance. Boston, Printed by B. Green, and J. Allen, for Samuel Phillips, 1704.
[16] p. 15 cm.
MB; MHi; MWA; NhD (imperfect) mp. 39413

B263 NEW JERSEY. GOVERNOR, 1701-1708
By his excellency Edward Viscount Cornbury . . . A proclamation. Whereas there are several quit-rents and arrears of quit-rents . . . New-York, William Bradford, 1704.
broadside 33.5 X 19 cm.
RPJCB mp. 39414

B264 SHERLOCK, RICHARD, 1612-1689
The principles of the holy Christian religion . . . The ninth edition . . . New-York, Re-printed and sold by William Bradford, 1704.
[10], 56+ p. 16 cm. $A\text{-}D^8\ E^{8?}$
MWA mp. 39415

B265 WOOTEN, JAMES
[A sermon preached at the opening of St. Anne's Church . . . the 24th of September, 1704 . . .] [Annapolis, Thomas Reading, 1704]

Wroth 14
No copy known mp. 39416

1705

B266 ALLEN, THOMAS, 1608-1673
[The call of Christ, unto thirsty sinners . . .] preached by . . . Mr. Thomas Allen, late pastor of a church in . . . Norwich, and . . . teacher of the church of Christ at Charlstown in New-England. Boston, Reprinted by T. Green, for Benjamin Eliot, 1705.
96 p. 12mo
"To the reader" (p. 3-6), signed: July 20, 1678, may indicate an earlier edition, now lost
MB (t.p. mutilated) mp. 39418

B267 ALLEN, THOMAS, 1608-1673
The call of Christ, unto thirsty sinners . . . preached by . . . Mr. Thomas Allen, late pastor of a church in . . . Norwich, and . . . teacher of the church of Christ at Charlstown in New-England. Boston, Re-printed by T. Green, for Nicholas Buttolph, 1705.
96 p. 12mo
"To the reader" (p. 3-6), signed: July 20, 1678, may indicate an earlier edition, now lost
Huntington 29
CSmH mp. 39417

B268 . . . AN almanack for the year . . . MDCCV . . . By N[athaniel]. W[hittemore]. . . . Boston: Printed by B. Green. Sold at the Printing House and by E. Phillips, at Charlestown, 1705.
[16] p. 15 cm.
At head of title: 1705
MWA mp. 39436

B269 [ARGUMENTS offered to the inhabitants of New England, and the other neighbouring provinces, to encourage the sowing of hemp. Boston, 1705]
broadside
Advertised in the *Boston News-letter*, July 9, 1705, as "this day printed and to be sold at the post-office, half a sheet, containing several solid Arguments . . ."
Ford 289
No copy known mp. 39419

B270 BIBLE. O.T. PSALMS
The Psalms, hymns, and spiritual songs . . . The twelfth edition. Boston, Printed by B. Green for Benj. Elliot and Nicholas Boone, 1705.
505, [7] p. (music) 10.5 cm. $A\text{-}Q^{16}$
Holmes: Minor Mathers 53-G
ViU (imperfect) mp. 39420

B271 HARVARD UNIVERSITY
Quaestiones pro modulo . . . MDCCV. [Boston, 1705]
broadside
MH mp. 39421

B272 LEEDS, 1705. The American almanack for . . . 1705. By Daniel Leeds . . . New-York, William Bradford [1705]
[32?] p.
Second edition. cf. pref. to Jacob Taylor's almanac (Philadelphia, 1705)
Drake 5539
No copy known

B273 MARYLAND. LAWS
[The laws of the province of Maryland , . . . passed at a session . . . begun . . . the fifteenth day of May, 1705. Annapolis, Thomas Reading, 1705]

Wroth 15
No copy known mp. 39422

B274 MASSACHUSETTS. GOVERNOR, 1702-1715
By His Excellency, Joseph Dudley . . . A proclamation for a general thanksgiving . . . [Dec. 27, 1705] . . . [Boston, 1705]
broadside
cf. McMurtrie: Mass. broadsides (1939)
MWA (reduced facsim.) mp. 39423

B275 MASSACHUSETTS. GOVERNOR, 1702-1715
By His Excellency, Joseph Dudley . . . A proclamation, for an embargo on ships . . . bound to Barbados . . . [Oct. 30, 1705] . . . Boston, Bartholomew Green, 1705.
broadside
cf. McMurtrie: Mass. broadsides (1939)
MWA (reduced facsim.) mp. 39425

B276 MASSACHUSETTS. GOVERNOR, 1702-1715
By His Excellency Joseph Dudley . . . a proclamation. Whereas Her Majesty . . . [Mar. 3, 1704] . . . Boston, Bartholomew Green, 1705.
broadside 30.5 X 20 cm.
Ford 280; New York Public 55
M-Ar; MHi. Photostats: DLC; MWA; NN mp. 39426

B277 MASSACHUSETTS. GOVERNOR, 1702-1715
By His Excellency, Joseph Dudley . . . A proclamation. Whereas there are several seamen . . . [Nov. 9, 1705] . . . Boston, Bartholomew Green, 1705.
broadside
cf. McMurtrie: Mass. broadsides (1939)
MWA (reduced facsim.) mp. 39427

B278 MASSACHUSETTS. GOVERNOR, 1702-1715
Province of the Massachusetts-Bay. By His Excellency, Joseph Dudley . . . A proclamation for a publick thanksgiving . . . [Sept. 20, 1705] . . . [Boston, 1705]
broadside
cf. McMurtrie: Mass. broadsides (1939)
MWA (reduced facsim.) mp. 39424

B279 MATHER, COTTON, 1662-1728
[Family religion . . . Boston, 1705]

Printed in an edition of 1000 copies; cf. Mather's *Diary*, i, 520, under July 27, 1705; cf. Holmes: Cotton Mather 127-A
No copy known mp. 39428

B280 THE N. England Kalendar, 1705 . . . By a Lover of Astronomy . . . Boston, Printed by B. Green, for Nicholas Buttolph, 1705.
[16] p. 15 cm.
MWA mp. 39429

B281 THE N. England Kalendar, 1705 . . . By a Lover of Astronomy . . . Boston, Printed by B. Green, for Samuel Phillips, 1705.
[16] p. 15 cm.
Huntington 31
CSmH; MHi mp. 39430

B282 NEW YORK. LAWS
. . . An act for the better establishment of the maintenance for the minister of the city of New-York . . . [New-York? 1705?]
6 p. 29 cm.
Pagination irregular (1, 222, 223, 4, 5, 6)
p. 223: "An act granting sundry priviledges and powers to the rector and inhabitants . . ."
NHi mp. 39431

B283 PENNSYLVANIA. LAWS
Pensilvania. An act for the better proportioning the rates of money . . . [Philadelphia, 1705]
broadside 31.5 X 43 cm.
DLC mp. 39432

B284 RUSSELL, ROBERT, of Sussex, Eng.
Seven sermons . . . The sixth edition. Boston, Printed by B. Green for N. Buttolph, 1705.
[4], 185 p.
MWA mp. 39433

B285 SECKER, WILLIAM, d. 1681?
A wedding ring, fit for the finger . . . Boston, Printed by T. G[reen]. for N. Boone, 1705.
2 p.l., 3-89, [1] p., 2 l. 8.5 X 5.5 cm. A-E^8 F^7
MWA (lacks p. 83-84, 89-92) mp. 39434

B286 SECKER, WILLIAM, d. 1681?
A wedding ring, fit for the finger . . . Boston, Printed by T. G[reen], for N. Buttolph, 1705.
2 p.l., 3-89, [1] p., 2 l. 8.5 X 5.5 cm. A-E^8 F^7
New York Public 56; Rosenbach-Ch 6
NN (imperfect); PP mp. 39435

1706

B287 BELLINGHAM, RICHARD, d. 1706
A copy of the last will and testament of Richard Bellingham . . . Published by the Reverend Mr. James Allen, one of the executors . . . [Boston, 1706]
[2] p. 29 cm.
Dated from Sewall's note: "Given me . . . Augt. 6. 1706."
Ford 290; New York Public 57
MHi; NHi; NN (photostat) mp. 39437

B288 MARYLAND. LAWS
Maryland ss. At a sessions of assembly begun . . . April the second . . . were enacted these laws following . . . [Annapolis, Thomas Reading, 1706]
10 p. 36.5 cm.
Wroth 16
No *separate* copy known mp. 39438

B289 MASSACHUSETTS. GOVERNOR, 1702-1715
Boston, August 14th, 1706. I do hereby direct you . . . to muster the military company under your command . . . [Boston, 1706]
broadside 15 X 16 cm.
Ford 295
Photostat: MHi

B290 MASSACHUSETTS. GOVERNOR, 1702-1715
By His Excellency, Joseph Dudley . . . A proclamation for a general thanksgiving . . . [Sept. 19, 1706] . . . Boston, Bartholomew Green, 1706.
broadside
cf. McMurtrie: Mass. broadsides (1939)
MWA (reduced facsim.) mp. 39439

B291 MASSACHUSETTS. GOVERNOR, 1702-1715
By His Excellency Joseph Dudley . . . a proclamation for the better regulation of seamen . . . Boston, Bartholomew Green, 1706.
broadside 34 X 24 cm.
Ford 297; New York Public 58
MHi. Photostats: DLC; MH; MWA; NN mp. 39440

B292 MASSACHUSETTS. TREASURER
Province of the Massachusetts-Bay, ss. James Taylor, Gent. Treasurer . . . to the select-men . . . Given under my hand and seal at Boston, the seventeenth day of July, 1706 . . . [Boston, 1706]
broadside 34 X 21 cm.
Ford 298
DLC

B293 THE N. England Kalendar, 1706 . . . By a lover of astronomy. Licensed by authority. Boston, Printed by B. Green, for Nicholas Buttolph, 1706.
[16] p. 14.5 cm.
DLC; MWA mp. 39441

B294 THE N. England Kalendar, 1706 . . . By a Lover of Astronomy. Licensed by authority. Boston, Printed by B. Green, for Samuel Phillips, 1706.
[16] p. 14.5 cm.
MWA mp. 39442

1707

B295 . . . AN almanack of the coelestial motions for . . . 1707 . . . Boston, Printed by Bartholomew Green, for Samuel Phillips, 1707.
[24] p.
cf. Evans 1334
MHi mp. 39457

B296 BRIDGER, JOHN
Informations and directions for the making of tar, and choice of trees for the same . . . [at end] J. Bridger . . . Boston, B. Green, 1707.
[2] p. 31 X 16 cm.
Ford 299
NHi. Photostats: MHi; WHi mp. 39443

B297 A COPY of a letter, written to the souldiers that were at Narragansett in the Army. January 1675 . . . Boston, Printed May 1st, 1707.
broadside 31 X 20 cm.
Signed: T. F.
Matt B. Jones, Boston (1931). Photostats: MH; MWA; NN; RPJCB mp. 39444

B298 DANFORTH, JOHN, 1660-1730
A Pindarick elegy upon the renowned, Mr. Samuel Willard . . . deceased September the 12th. 1707 . . . [Boston, 1707]
broadside 30 X 19.5 cm.
Ford 300
NHi. Photostat: MHi mp. 39445

B299 F[LAVEL], J[OHN] 1630?-1691
A token for mourners: or, The advice of Christ . . . By J. F. . . . Boston, Printed by T. Green, for Benjamin Eliot & Nicholas Boone, 1707.
[10], 154 p. 15 cm. $A\text{–}G^{12}$
Half-title wanting in MWA copy.
MB; MHi (imperfect); MWA (p. 63-64, 81-82 wanting) mp. 39446

B300 HARVARD UNIVERSITY
Quaestiones pro modulo . . . M DCC VII. [Boston, 1707]
broadside
MH mp. 39447

B301 [HILL, JOHN] d. 1732?
The young secretary's guide . . . Collected by B. W. Boston, N.E. Printed by B. Green; for Nicholas Buttolph, & sold at his shop. 1707.
1 p. l., 190 p. 14 cm.
"Errata": p. 179
Editor (B. W.) tentatively identified as Benjamin Wadsworth
Subsequent 1708 issue printed from same setting of type, with altered imprint date
MB; MWA mp. 39448

B302 MARYLAND. LAWS
[Acts of the province of Maryland . . . passed at a session . . . begun . . . the twenty-sixth day of March, 1707. Annapolis, Thomas Reading, 1707]

Wroth 18
No copy known mp. 39450

B303 MARYLAND. LAWS
[All the laws of Maryland now in force . . . Annapolis, Thomas Reading, 1707]
77, [1], 10, 95-114 p. 36.5 cm.
Wroth 17; New York Public 60
MdBP (incomplete); MdHi. Photostat: NN mp. 39449

B304 MASSACHUSETTS. GOVERNOR, 1702-1715
By His Excellency, Joseph Dudley . . . A proclamation for a general fast . . . [July 10, 1707] . . . Boston, Bartholomew Green, 1707.
broadside
cf. McMurtrie: Mass. broadsides (1939)
Reduced facsim.: MHi; MWA mp. 39451

B305 MASSACHUSETTS. GOVERNOR, 1702-1715
By His Excellency, Joseph Dudley . . . A proclamation for a general thanksgiving . . . [Nov. 24, 1707] . . . Boston, B. Green, 1707.
broadside
cf. McMurtrie: Mass. broadsides (1939)
MWA (reduced facsim.) mp. 39452

B306 MASSACHUSETTS. GOVERNOR, 1702-1715
By His Excellency, Joseph Dudley . . . A proclamation to prevent the destruction . . . of Her Majesties woods . . . [Dec. 15, 1707] . . . Boston, B. Green, 1707.
broadside
cf. McMurtrie: Mass. broadsides (1939)
Reduced facsim.: MHi; MWA mp. 39453

B307 MASSACHUSETTS. GOVERNOR, 1702-1715
By His Excellency, Joseph Dudley . . . A proclamation. Whereas divers souldiers . . . [July 21, 1707] . . . Boston, B. Green, 1707.
broadside
cf. McMurtrie: Mass. broadsides (1939)
Reduced facsim.: MHi; MWA mp. 39454

B308 MATHER, COTTON, 1662-1728
[A golden curb for the mouth . . . Boston, 1707]

Holmes: Cotton Mather 145-A
No copy known mp. 39455

B309 NOYES, NICHOLAS, 1647-1717
May 28th. 1706. To my worthy friend, Mr. James Bayley, living (if living) in Roxbury. A poem . . . [Boston, 1707]
broadside 34.5 X 21 cm.
Ford 307
MB; MHi (photostat); NN mp. 39456

B310 WADSWORTH, BENJAMIN, 1669-1737
Now or never the time to be saved . . . The second impression. Boston, Printed by B. Green for Nicholas Buttolph, 1707.
vi, 40 p.
MHi mp. 39458

1708

B311 CONNECTICUT. LAWS
. . . Acts and laws, passed by the General Court . . . of Connecticut . . . [New London, Thomas Short, 1708]
p. 119-142. 27 cm. $Hh\text{-}Nn^2$
Includes laws from May 14, 1702 to Oct. 14, 1708
Continues Evans 1043
PPL mp. 39459

B312 [CROUCH, NATHANIEL] 1632-1725?
Some excellent verses for the education of youth . . . By a Friend. Boston, Bartholomew Green, 1708.

12 p. 14.5 cm.
New York Public 61; Rosenbach-Ch 8
MHi (imperfect); PP. Photostat: NN mp. 39460

B313 CULPEPER, NICHOLAS, 1616–1654
The English physician. Containing, admirable and approved remedies . . . By N. Culpepper . . . Boston, Re-printed for Nicholas Boone, 1708.
94 p. 13.5 cm. A-H^6
Austin 590
MBCo; MWA (photostat of t.p. only); NBM (imperfect); NcD (imperfect) mp. 39461

B314 DIVINE examples of God's severe judgments upon Sabbath breakers . . . Boston, Re-printed and sold in Newbury-Street [1708]
broadside
Ford 311
MWM mp. 39462

B315 GT. BRIT. LAWS
. . . An act for the encouragement of the trade to America. [Boston, B. Green, 1708?]
24 p. 17 cm. caption title
Arms of Queen Anne on p. [1]
MB (p. 9–16 wanting) mp. 39463

B316 GT. BRIT. LAWS
Anno sexto Annae Reginae. An act of Parliament for the encouragement of the trade to America . . . [New York, W. Bradford, 1708]
[6]+ p. fol. caption title
PHi

B317 HARVARD UNIVERSITY
Praeclarissimo . . . theses hasce . . . MDCCVIII. [Boston, 1708]
broadside
MHi mp. 39465

B318 HARVARD UNIVERSITY
Quaestiones pro modulo . . . M DCC VIII. [Boston, 1708]
broadside
MH mp. 39464

B319 [HILL, JOHN]
The young clerk's guide . . . Collected by B. W. Boston, Printed by B. Green for Nicholas Buttolph, 1708.
[2], 188 p. 16 mo
MHi (imperfect) mp. 39476

B320 MARYLAND. GENERAL ASSEMBLY
The Assembly's answer to His excellency's speech. December the 2d 1708. Annapolis, Thomas Reading, 1708.
broadside 29 X 17.5 cm.
Huntington 35a; Wroth 21; New York Pub. 63
CSmH. Photostat: NN mp. 39466

B321 MARYLAND. GOVERNOR, 1703–1709
His excellency's speech to the General assembly. [Nov. 29, 1708] [Annapolis, 1708]
broadside 35 X 20 cm.
Huntington 35b; Wroth 20; New York Pub. 64
CSmH. Photostat: NN mp. 39467

B322 MARYLAND. LAWS
[Acts of the province of Maryland . . . passed at a session . . . begun . . . the twenty-ninth day of November, 1708. Annapolis, Thomas Reading, 1708]

Wroth 19
No copy known mp. 39468

B323 MATHER, INCREASE, 1639–1723
Four sermons, viz. The glorious throne . . . The excellency of a publick spirit . . . The righteous man . . . The morning star . . . Boston, Printed for, and sold by Nich. Boone, 1708.
[2], [97]-122, 38, [2], 41–84 p. [ ]^1 A–B^6 C^1 B–H^6
"The glorious throne" and "The righteous man" have separate title pages, dated 1702
MWA mp. 39469

B324 PEARSE, EDWARD, 1633–1673
The best match: or, The soul's espousal to Christ . . . The tenth edition. Boston, B. Green, for Nicholas Buttolph, 1708.
204 p. 14.5 cm
MB; MWA; RPJCB mp. 39470

B325 [PRINCE, THOMAS] 1687–1758
Carmen miserabile. A solemn lacrymatory for the grave of Jonathan Marsh . . . deceas'd at Harvard . . . June the 10th. 1708 . . . aged eighteen years and ten months. [Boston, 1708]
broadside
Ford 310
MBAt. Photostat: MHi mp. 39471

B326 SHEPARD, THOMAS, 1605–1649
The saints jewel . . . In two sermons preached by Thomas Sheppard . . . Boston, Re-printed by John Allen, for Nicholas Boone, 1708.
[2], 68 p. 11.5 cm.
MWA (p. 15–18, 27–30 wanting) mp. 39473

B327 TO the honourable the committee appointed to receive claims of such as have right and propriety in the Narranganset country . . . Boston, B. Green, 1708.
[2] p. 31.5 X 21.5 cm.
Ford 317; New York Public 62
MHi. Photostats: DLC; MWA; NN mp. 39472

B328 TURNER, THOMAS
Meditations on the uncertainty of mans life . . . To which is added, An alphabet of verses . . . composed for instruction of young persons . . . Boston, Bartholomew Green, 1708.
broadside 42.5 X 33 cm.
Contains also an "Acrostick" on the name Thomas Turner (the author?)
Ford 319
MHi. Photostat: MWA mp. 39474

B329 A USEFUL and necessary companion in two parts . . . To which is added, An appendix, containing useful forms of letters, &c. Boston, Printed for, and sold by Nicholas Boone, 1708.
44 leaves. 12mo A^2 B–H^6
Rosenbach-Ch 9
PPRF mp. 39475

1709

B330 CONNECTICUT. LAWS
[An act for issuance of bills. New London, Thomas Short, 1709]
[3] p.
Sig. mark: an inverted D
Bates: Early Connecticut laws, p. 152
CtY mp. 39477

B331 CONNECTICUT. LAWS
. . . Acts and laws, passed by the General Court . . . Hartford . . . the twelfth, of May, 1709 . . . [Colophon] New London, Thomas Short, 1709.
[4] p. 26.5 cm.
Printed after the June session; cf. Bates: Early Connecticut laws, p. 153
CtY; PPL. Public Record Off. mp. 39478

B332 CONNECTICUT. LAWS
Acts and laws passed by the General Court . . . Hartford . . . the 8th. of June 1709 . . . [Colophon] New London, Thomas Short, 1709
[4] p. A^2
Bates: Early Connecticut Laws, p. 152
CtY; PPL ("B^2"). Public Record Off. mp. 39479

B333 CONNECTICUT. LAWS
. . . Acts and laws passed by the General Court . . . New Haven the thirteenth of October, 1709 . . . [Colophon] New London, Thomas Short, 1709.
[11] p. 26.5 cm. $B–D^2$
Bates: Early Connecticut laws, p. 153
CtY; PPL. Public Record Off. mp. 39480

B334 DOOLITTLE, THOMAS, 1632?–1707
A prospect of eternity . . . Boston, Printed by John Allen, for Nicholas Buttolph, 1709.
[2], 12+ p. 13.5 cm.
MWA (all after p. 12 wanting) mp. 39481

B335 FOX, JOHN, fl. 1676
The door of Heaven opened and shut . . . Boston, Printed by B. Green, for Nicholas Buttolph, 1709.
[4], 138 p. 15 cm.
MWA (poor) mp. 39482

B336 GT. BRIT.
By the honourable Col. Francis Nicholson, and Col. Samuel Vetch, a proclamation. Whereas Her Majesty hath been pleased to intrust us with Her royal commands . . . Given under our hands at Boston, May the ninth, 1709 . . . The aforegoing proclamation . . . let it be made publick. J. Dudley. [Boston, 1709]
broadside 27 X 25.5 cm.
Ford 323; New York Public 65
M-Ar; NHi. Photostats: DLC; MWA; NN mp. 39483

B337 GT. BRIT.
By the honourable Coll. Francis Nicholson & Coll. Samuel Vetch. A proclamation . . . New-York, William Bradford, 1709.
broadside 33 X 21.5 cm.
"Given at New-York, May 26. 1709."
NHi. NN (reduced facsim. from dealer's catalog) mp. 39484

B338 HARVARD UNIVERSITY
Quaestiones pro modulo . . . M DCC IX. [Boston, 1709] broadside
MH mp. 39485

B339 MARYLAND. LAWS
[Acts of the province of Maryland . . . passed at a session . . . begun . . . the twenty-fifth day of October, 1709. Annapolis, Thomas Reading, 1709]

Possibly never printed
Wroth 22
No copy known mp. 39486

B340 MASSACHUSETTS. GOVERNOR, 1702–1715
By his excellency, Joseph Dudley . . . A proclamation for a general fast . . . August 27, 1709. [Boston, 1709]
broadside
Public Record Off. Photostat: MHi mp. 39487

B341 MASSACHUSETTS. GOVERNOR, 1702–1715
By his excellency, Joseph Dudley . . . A proclamation [concerning mariners and seamen] . . . October 20, 1709. [Boston, 1709]
broadside
Public Record Off. Photostat: MHi mp. 39488

B342 MASSACHUSETTS. GOVERNOR, 1702–1715
By his excellency, Joseph Dudley . . . A proclamation [for a general thanksgiving, November 24] . . . November 5, 1709. Boston, Bartholomew Green, 1709.
broadside
Public Record Off. Photostat: MHi mp. 39489

B343 MATHER, COTTON, 1662–1728
[The summ of the matter . . . Boston, 1709?]

For the evidence of printing cf. Holmes: Cotton Mather 378
No copy known mp. 39490

B344 MATHER, INCREASE, 1639–1723
Solemn advice to young men . . . The second edition. Boston, Printed by John Allen, for Nicholas Boone, 1709.
106 p. $A–I^6$
Holmes: Increase Mather 122–B^1
ViU mp. 39491

B345 MIDWEEK, May, 25. 1709. [Boston? 1709]
broadside 34.5 X 21 cm.
Names of candidates for election to the Council
Ford 324
DLC; M–Ar mp. 39492

B346 NEW JERSEY. GOVERNOR, 1709
By the honourable Richard Ingoldesby, Esq; Lieut-Governour . . . of New-Jersey, New-York . . . A proclamation . . . [New York? 1709]
broadside 30 X 19 cm.
Further call for volunteers, dated at Burlington in New-Jersey, June 30, 1709
NHi mp. 39493

B347 NEW YORK. LAWS
. . . An act for an assignment to the Lady Lovelace. New-York, William Bradford, 1709.
[1] p. 30 X 18 cm. caption title preceded by: Anno Regni Octavo Annae Reginae
Inserted between p. 112 and p. 113 of the laws of New York (New York, 1710)
DLC; PPL mp. 39494

B348 RUSSEL, ROBERT, of Wadhurst, Sussex
Seven sermons . . . The sixth edition . . . Boston, Reprinted by J. Allen, for Nicholas Buttolph, 1709.
172 p. 15 cm.
CtHT-W; MWA mp. 39495

B349 [SHERMAN, THOMAS]
Divine breathings: or, A pious soul thirsting after Christ in a hundred pathetical meditations. The tenth edition . . . Boston, [Printed by] B. Green, for Benj. Eliot, 1709.
[4], 75, [5] p. 14 cm.
MHi; MWA mp. 39496

B350 SPRINT, JOHN
The bride-womans counseller. Being a sermon preached at a wedding . . . in Dorcetshire . . . Boston, Re-printed by John Allen, for Eleazer Phillips, 1709.
2 p.l., 20 p. 12.5 cm.
MHi mp. 39497

171-

B351 GT. BRIT. SOVEREIGNS (GEORGE I)
George, by the Grace of God . . . King . . . Know ye that we have . . . appointed . . . to be judge of our county court . . . in . . . Connecticut . . . Witness . . . in Hartford, this twenty-ninth day of May . . . 171 [Hartford? 171-]
broadside 20.5 X 25 cm.
Signed: G. Saltonstall
Earliest known *printed* commission?
CtHi

1710

B352 ALLEN, THOMAS, 1608-1673
The call of Christ unto thirsty sinners . . . The fourth edition. Boston, Printed by J. Allen, for Eleazer Phillips, 1710.
105 p. 12 cm.
MHi; MWA mp. 39498

B353 CONNECTICUT. LAWS
. . . Acts and laws, passed by the General Court . . . Hartford . . . the eleventh, of May . . . 1710 . . . [Colophon] New London, Thomas Short, 1710.
[3] p. 26.5 cm. E^2
Bates: Early Connecticut laws, p. 153
CtY; PPL. Public Record Off. mp. 39499

B354 CONNECTICUT. LAWS
. . . Acts and laws. Passed by the General Court . . . held at New Haven . . . August . . . 1710 . . . [Colophon] New-London, Thomas Short, 1710.
broadsheet 31 X 20 cm.
New York Public 67
MHi; CtY (facsim.); NN (facsim.) mp. 39500

B355 CONNECTICUT. LAWS
[Acts and laws passed by the General Court held at New Haven in October 1710. New London, Thomas Short, 1710]
[3] p. F^2
Bates: Early Connecticut laws, p. 153
CtY. Public Record Off. mp. 39501

B356 DANFORTH, JOHN, 1660-1730
Profit and loss: an elegy upon the decease of Mrs. Mary Gerrish . . . Novemb. 17. 1710 . . . aged 19. years & 20. days . . . [Boston, 1710]
broadside 37 X 22 cm.
Signed: J.D.
Ford 326
MB; MBAt. Photostat: MWA mp. 39502

B357 THE four Indian Kings speech to Her Majesty. London, April 20, 1710. [New York?] Printed in the year. 1710.
broadside
Type surface 26 X 13.5 cm.
Bradford printing suggested by Hasse on basis of paper, printing, and watermark
Hasse 172
Public Record Off. mp. 39503

B358 HARVARD UNIVERSITY
Quaestiones pro modulo . . . M DCC X. [Boston, 1710]
broadside
MH mp. 39504

B359 MASSACHUSETTS. GOVERNOR, 1702-1715
By His Excellency, Joseph Dudley . . . A proclamation for an embargo . . . July 15, 1710. Boston, B. Green, 1710.
broadside
Ford 329
M-Ar mp. 39506

B360 MASSACHUSETTS. GOVERNOR, 1702-1715
By his excellency Joseph Dudley . . . A proclamation [concerning mariners and seamen] . . . August 15, 1710. Boston, B. Green, 1710.
broadside
Public Record Off. Photostat: MHi mp. 39507

B361 MASSACHUSETTS. GOVERNOR, 1702-1715
By his excellency Joseph Dudley . . . A proclamation [concerning Port Royal expedition] . . . July 29, 1710. Boston, B. Green, 1710.
broadside
Public Record Off. Photostat: MHi mp. 39508

B362 MASSACHUSETTS. GOVERNOR, 1702-1715
By his excellency, Joseph Dudley . . . A proclamation for a general fast [Sept. 25] . . . September 12, 1710. Boston, B. Green, 1710.
broadside
Public Record Off. Photostat: MHi mp. 39505

B363 MASSACHUSETTS. GOVERNOR, 1702-1715
By his excellency, Joseph Dudley . . . A proclamation for a general thanksgiving [November 16] . . . October 28, 1710. Boston, B. Green, 1710.
broadside
Public Record Off. Photostat: MHi mp. 39509

B364 MATHER, COTTON, 1662-1728
[Proposals of some consequence . . . Boston, B. Green? 1710]

A tract against rum
Holmes: Cotton Mather 311; cf. Mather's *Diary*, ii, 21
No copy known mp. 39510

B365 MATHER, INCREASE, 1639-1723
Awakening truth's tending to conversion . . . Boston, Printed by B. Green, for Benj. Eliot, 1710.
[2], x, 120 p. $A\text{-}L^6$
Holmes: Increase Mather 11^1
ICN; NN; ViU mp. 39511

B366 MATHER, INCREASE, 1639-1723
A discourse concerning faith and fervency in prayer . . . Boston, Printed by B. Green, for Eleazer Phillips, 1710.
[4], xix, [1], 112, [8] p.
Holmes: Increase Mather $32\text{-}A^5$
DLC mp. 39513

B367 MATHER, INCREASE, 1639-1723
A discourse concerning faith and fervency in prayer . . . Boston, Printed by B. Green, for Nicholas Boone, 1710.
[4], xix, [1], 112, [8] p.

Holmes: Increase Mather 32–A[4]; Huntington 37
CSmH; MHi mp. 39512

B368 [METCALF, JOSEPH]
Tears dropt at the funeral of that eminently pious Christian, Mrs. Elizabeth Hatch . . . of Falmouth . . . May 18th. anno 1710. in the 33d. year of her age . . . [Boston? 1710]
broadside 43.5 X 33.5 cm.
Signed: J. M. (Joseph Metcalf)
MWA. Photostat: MHi mp. 39514

B369 NOYES, NICHOLAS, 1647–1717
Upon the much lamented death of that pious and hopeful young gentlewoman, Mrs. Mary Gerrish . . . daughter of . . . Samuel Sewall . . . November 17th. 1710 . . . Posuit Nicholas Noyes. [Boston, 1710?]
broadside 33.5 X 20 cm.
MB. Photostat: MWA mp. 39515

B370 [PENN, WILLIAM] 1644–1718
A serious expostulation with the inhabitants of Pensilvania in a letter from the Proprietary & Governour. Philadelphia Printed [by Andrew Bradford] 1710.
18 p. 8vo
PHi

B371 A VINDICATING testimonial, of Mr. Hugh Adams (the first and late pastor of the South Church in Brantry:) . . . August 21, 1710. [Boston, 1710]
broadside
Ford 335
MB mp. 39516

B372 THE young man's companion . . . The second edition corrected & enlarged . . . New-York, William and Andrew Bradford, 1710.
8 p.l., 226 p. 14 cm.
Huntington 38; New York Public 68
CSmH (imperfect); MWA (imperfect); MiU–C. Photostat: NN mp. 39517

1711

B373 BIBLE. O.T. PSALMS
The Psalms, hymns, and spiritual songs . . . The fifteenth edition. Boston, B. Green, for Samuel Phillips, 1711.
378, [6] p.
MWA; RPJCB (final leaf lacking) mp. 39518

B374 BOSTON
At a meeting of the freeholders and other inhabitants . . . of Boston, duely qualified . . . [p. 18] being convened . . . the ninth of May, 1711 . . . The two foregoing by-laws . . . approved . . . Boston, August the 14th, 1711. [Boston, 1711]
p. 15–18. 18 cm.
Continuation of Evans 1040
CSmH; MWA; RPJCB mp. 39519

B375 CONDUCTOR generalis; or, A guide for justices of the peace . . . [New York, 1711]

MH-L. Photostat (t.p. only): MWA mp. 39520

B376 CONNECTICUT. LAWS
. . . Acts and laws, passed by the General Court . . . Hartford . . . the 10th day of May 1711 . . . [Colophon] New London, Thomas Short, 1711.
[16] p. 26.5 cm. G–K[2]
Bates: Early Connecticut laws, p. 153
CtY; PPL. Public Record Off. mp. 39521

B377 CONNECTICUT. LAWS
. . . Acts and laws, passed by the General Court . . . New London . . . the 19th day of June 1711 . . . [New London, Thomas Short, 1711]
[4] p.
Sheet mark: inverted triangle of small stars
Bates: Early Connecticut laws, p. 153
CtY; PPL. Public Record Off. mp. 39522

B378 CONNECTICUT. LAWS
. . . Acts and laws passed by the General Court . . . New Haven . . . October 1711. [New London, Thomas Short, 1711]
[3] p. N[2]
Bates: Early Connecticut laws, p. 154
CtY mp. 39523

B379 HARVARD UNIVERSITY
Praestantissimo . . . viro, Josepho Dudleio . . . thèses hasce . . . MDCCXI. [Boston, 1711]
broadside 41 X 28.5 cm.
Ford 337
MHi mp. 39525

B380 HARVARD UNIVERSITY
Quaestiones pro modulo . . . M DCC XI. [Boston, 1711]
broadside 30 X 18.5 cm.
MH; MHi mp. 39524

B381 MASSACHUSETTS
A muster roll of Capt. David Pigeons company of New-England troops, during its being at Annapolis Royal . . . from . . . October 1710 to . . . October 1711. [Boston, 1711]
broadside
Ford 380
M–Ar mp. 39531

B382 MASSACHUSETTS. GENERAL COURT
. . . At a . . . General Court . . . holden at Boston . . . unto Wednesday, March, 14th. 1710. Whereas at the session . . . Boston, B. Green, 1711.
broadside 32 X 21 cm.
At head of title: Anno Regni Annae Reginae Decimo
DLC; M–Ar mp. 35930

B383 MASSACHUSETTS. GOVERNOR, 1702–1715
By His Excellency, Joseph Dudley Esq. . . . A proclamation for a general embargo . . . [June 9, 1711] . . . Boston, B. Green, 1711.
broadside 31 X 19 cm.
Ford 341
MHi mp. 35926

B384 MASSACHUSETTS. GOVERNOR, 1702–1715
By His Excellency the Governour. I hereby command the colonel . . . of the respective regiments within this province to cause this act to be published [on deserters] . . . [July 20, 1711] Boston, B. Green, 1711.
[2] p.
Ford 343
MB mp. 39527

B385 MASSACHUSETTS. GOVERNOR, 1702–1715
By His Excellency the Governour. Upon information from His Excellency General Hill . . . [July 16, 1711] . . . Boston, B. Green [1711]
broadside

cf. McMurtrie: Mass. broadsides (1939)
MWA (reduced facsim.) mp. 39528

B386 MASSACHUSETTS. GOVERNOR, 1702–1715
In the House of representatives, June 12th, 1711. Whereas Her majesty . . . By . . . Joseph Dudley . . . a proclamation . . . Boston, B. Green, 1711.
broadside 42.5 X 32.5 cm.
Ford 342
DLC; MB; MH mp. 39529

B387 MASSACHUSETTS. LAWS
. . . Acts and laws, passed by the . . . General Court . . . begun and held at Boston . . . the thirtieth day of May, 1711. And continued . . . unto Wednesday the seventeenth of October following and then met. [Boston, B. Green, 1711]
p. 363–366. 29.5 cm. caption title
DLC; ICN; MB; NN mp. 39532

B388 MATHER, INCREASE, 1639–1723
Meditations on the glory of the heavenly world . . . Boston, Sold by Timothy Green, 1711.
[2], v, [1], 276, [4] p. 14.5 cm.
Holmes: Increase Mather 73^2
MB; MBAt; NHi; RPJCB; ViU mp. 39533

B389 NEW YORK. LAWS
Acts passed by the General assembly . . . in October and November, 1711 . . . [New York, 1711]
p. 145–150. sm. fol.
Huntington 40
CSmH mp. 39534

B390 [PRIOR, MATTHEW] 1664–1721
To the right honourable, Mr. Harley, wounded by Guiscard. Boston, B. Green, 1711.
broadside
Ford 348
MBAt mp. 39535

1712

B391 BIBLE. O.T. APOCRYPHAL BOOKS. TESTAMENT OF THE TWELVE PATRIARCHS
The Testament of the Twelve Patriarchs translated . . . by Robert Grosthead . . . The three and fortieth edition. New York, Printed and sold by William and Andrew Bradford, 1712.
[11], 122, [3] p. 15.5 cm.
Huntington 42
CSmH; PPRF mp. 39536

B392 CONNECTICUT. LAWS
. . . Acts and laws, passed by the General Court . . . Hartford . . . the eighth day of May 1712 . . . [Colophon] New London, Thomas Short, 1712.
[8] p. 26.5 cm. O-P^2
Bates: Early Connecticut laws, p. 154
CtY; PPL. Public Record Off. mp. 39537

B393 CONNECTICUT. LAWS
Acts and laws, passed by the General Court . . . Hartford . . . the ninth day of October . . . 1712. . . . [Boston? B. Green? 1712]
p. 59–61. 26.5 cm. Q^2
Bates: Early Connecticut laws, p. 154
CtY; PPL mp. 39538

B394 FRIENDS, SOCIETY OF. LONDON YEARLY MEETING
Some advices in the yearly meeting epistle 1709 concerning the education of children: recommended by the yearly meeting 1710 . . . London Printed 1710. Reprinted at Philadelphia [by Jacob Taylor] 1712.
broadside fol.
PPL mp. 39539

B395 HARVARD UNIVERSITY
Quaestiones pro modulo . . . M DCC XII. [Boston, 1712]
broadside
MH; MHi mp. 39540

B396 HAYWARD, JOHN
The precious blood of the Son of God . . . The eighth edition. Boston, J. Allen for N. Boone, 1712.
107 p.
RPJCB mp. 39541

B397 HEIDELBERG CATECHISM
Kort-Begryp der waare Chistelyke Leere, uit den Heidelbergischen Catechismus uitgetrokken . . . 't samengestelt door Gualtherus Dubois . . . Nieuw-York, William Bradford, 1712.
4 p.l., 55 p. 15 cm.
New York Public 70
NN (p. 55 wanting) mp. 39542

B398 HOBART, NEHEMIAH, 1648–1712
Martij 27. 1712. [Boston, S. Sewall, 1712]
broadside 29.5 X 18 cm.
A Latin poem of 33 lines
Ford 351; New York Public 71
DLC; MB; MHi. Photostat: NN mp. 39543

B399 THE husband-man's guide, in four parts . . . The second edition, enlarged. [New-York] Printed [by Will. & Andrew Bradford] for & sold by Elea. Phillips, bookseller, in Boston, 1712.
96 p. 12.5 cm.
Guerra a-25; Karpinski p. 38
RPJCB. Photostats: CtY; MiU-C; NN mp. 39544

B400 MASSACHUSETTS. GOVERNOR, 1702–1715
By His Excellency, Joseph Dudley, Esq; . . . A proclamation for the apprehending of William Hilton . . . [May 1, 1712] . . . Boston, B. Green, 1712.
broadside 32.5 X 20.5 cm.
Ford 353
MB; MeHi mp. 39545

B401 MASSACHUSETTS. LAWS
. . . An act, passed by the . . . General Court . . . begun and held at Boston . . . the twenty-eighth day of May, 1712. An act for reviving . . . [Boston, B. Green, 1712]
p. 377–379. 29.5 cm. caption title
DLC; NN mp. 39548

B402 MASSACHUSETTS. LAWS
. . . An act, passed by the General Court . . . for assessing two taxes on polls and estates pursuant to act of 1709 . . . Boston, B. Green, 1712.
[4] p.
MHi mp. 39546

B403 MASSACHUSETTS. LAWS
. . . Acts and laws, passed by the . . . General Court . . . begun and held at Boston . . . the thirtieth day of May,

1711. And continued . . . unto Wednesday the twelfth of March following, and then met. [Boston, B. Green, 1712]
p. 367–376. 29.5 cm. caption title
DLC; ICN; NN mp. 39547

B404 MASSACHUSETTS. LAWS
. . . Acts and laws, passed by the . . . General Court . . . begun and held at Boston . . . the twenty-eighth of May, 1712. And continued . . . unto Wednesday the twentieth of August following . . . [Boston, B. Green, 1712]
p. 381–383. 29.5 cm. caption title
DLC; ICN; MHi; NN mp. 39549

B405 MASSACHUSETTS. LAWS
. . . Acts and laws, passed by the . . . General Court . . . begun and held at Boston . . . the twenty-eighth of May, 1712. And continued . . . unto Wednesday the twenty-second of October following . . . [Boston, B. Green, 1712]
p. 385–387. 29.5 cm. caption title
DLC; ICN; NN mp. 39550

B406 [MATHER, COTTON] 1662–1728
Pastoral desires . . . Boston, Printed by B. Green, for Timothy Green, 1712.
[2], 116 p. 14.5 cm. A–I^6 Kl–5
Holmes: Cotton Mather 273^1
ViU mp. 39551

B407 MATHER, INCREASE, 1639–1723
Meditations on the sanctification of the Lord's Day . . . Boston, Printed and sold by Timothy Green, 1712.
[2], x, 71, [1]; [2], iv, 51, [1] p.
Holmes: Increase Mather 75^1
CtY mp. 39552

B408 MATHER, INCREASE, 1639–1723
Meditations on the sanctification of the Lord's Day . . . Boston, Printed by T. G. for Daniel Henchman, 1712.
[2], x, 71, [1]; [2], iv, 51, [1] p.
Holmes: Increase Mather 75^4
MB mp. 39553

B409 MATHER, RICHARD, 1596–1669
An answer to two questions . . . I. Whether does the power of church government . . . II. Whether does any church power . . . Published by . . . Increase Mather . . . Boston, B. Green, 1712.
[2], 22 p. 13.5 cm. A^8 B^4
Huntington 41; Holmes: Minor Mathers 35
CSmH; CtY; MB (2 copies); MWA mp. 39554

B410 SMITH, GRACE
The dying mothers legacy, or the good . . . counsel of . . . Mrs. Grace Smith, late widow to Mr. Ralph Smith of Eastham in New-England . . . Boston, Printed and sold by Timothy Green, 1712.
1 p.l., 12 p. 15.5 cm.
MB; NHi mp. 39555

B411 WADSWORTH, BENJAMIN, 1669–1737
The way of life opened . . . Boston, Printed by B. Green, for Samuel Phillips, 1712.
[2], ii, 148, [4] p. 14 cm.
Huntington 43
CSmH; DLC (t.p. lacking); MHi; MWA mp. 39556

1713

B412 . . . AN almanack for the year . . . 1713 . . . By [Nathaniel Whittemore] a Lover of the Mathematicks. [Boston] America: Printed for the year, 1713.
[16] p. 15.5 cm.
At head of title: 1713.
Guerra b-37; Nichols: Mass. almanacs, p. 50
MB; MWA; NN mp. 39582

B413 . . . AN almanack of the coelestial motions for . . . 1713 . . . America, Printed: sold at the booksellers shops, in Boston, 1713.
[16] p. 16 cm.
At head of title: MDCCXIII
By Daniel Travis
cf. Evans 1589
DLC (2 copies, 1 imperfect); MWA; NHi mp. 39584

B414 B-----N, Dec. 8, 1713. To the honourable the Society for propagating . . . [Boston, 1713]
broadside 33 X 21.5 cm.
Ford 357
DLC; MHi mp. 39558

B415 BIBLE. O.T. PSALMS
The Psalms, hymns, and spiritual songs . . . The sixteenth edition. Boston, John Allen, for Samuel Gerrish, 1713.
378, [4?] p. 11.5 cm.
Holmes: Minor Mathers 53K
RPJCB (lacks pages at end) mp. 39557

B416 BURROUGHS, JEREMIAH, 1599-1646
A preparation for judgment. A sermon . . . Boston, Printed by T. Green, for Benjamin Eliot, 1713.
[2], 70 p. 11.5 cm.
CtHT-W; MHi mp. 39559

B417 BURROUGHS, JEREMIAH, 1599-1646
A preparation for judgment. A sermon . . . The second edition. Boston, Printed & sold by T. Green, 1713.
[2], 70 p. 11 cm. A-F^6
MWA mp. 39560

B418 CHEEVER, EZEKIEL, 1617-1708
A short introduction to the Latin tongue . . . The second edition. Boston, B. Green, for Benj. Eliot, 1713.
[2], iv, 50, 7, [1], 16 p.
RPJCB mp. 39561

B419 CONNECTICUT. LAWS
. . . Acts and laws, passed by the General Court . . . Hartford . . . the fourteenth day of May . . . 1713 . . . [Colophon] New London, T. Green, 1713.
p. 63-68. 26 cm. R-S^2 (S2 blank)
Bates: Early Connecticut laws, p. 156
CtY; PPL mp. 39562

B420 CONNECTICUT. LAWS
Acts and laws, passed by the General Court . . . New Haven . . . the eighth day of October 1713. [Colophon] [New London] Printed and sold by T. Green [1713]
p. 69-72. 26.5 cm. T^2
Bates: Early Connecticut laws, p. 156
CtY; PPL mp. 39563

B421 DANFORTH, JOHN, 1660-1730
Honour and vertue elegized: in a poem, upon an honourable . . . mother in our Israel, Madam Elizabeth Hutchinson . . . consort of . . . Col. Elisha Hutchinson . . . She entred into . . . Paradise, Feb. 2. 1712,13. Aetatis suae 71. [Boston, 1713]
broadside 35 X 22 cm.
Ford 358
Signed: J. Danforth
MBAt. Photostat: MWA mp. 39564

B422 DOOLITTLE, THOMAS, 1632?-1707
A treatise concerning the Lord's Supper . . . The five and twentieth edition . . . Boston, Printed by J. Allen, for Samuel Gerrish, 1713.
[8], 168 p. 14 cm.
MHi (imperfect); MWA mp. 39565

B423 [HARDY, SAMUEL] 1636-1691
A guide to Heaven, from the Word . . . Boston, Printed by J. Allen, for Nicholas Boone, 1713.
76 p. 11.5 cm.
MWA mp. 39566

B424 HARVARD UNIVERSITY
Quaestiones pro modulo . . . M DCC XIII. [Boston, 1713]
broadside
MH mp. 39567

B425 HILL, JOHN
The young secretary's guide . . . Fourth edition, by Thomas Hill, gent. Boston, Printed by T. Fleet for S. Phillips, 1713.
4 p.l., 196 p.
RPJCB mp. 39568

B426 LEEDS, 1713. The American almanack for . . . 1713 . . . [New York, W. Bradford] Sold by Elkana Pembrook in Newport 1713.
[24] p. 14.5 cm.
Variant imprint of Evans 1548
Drake 5554; New York Public 77
MWA; NHi; RHi. Photostat: NN mp. 39569

B427 MASSACHUSETTS. GENERAL COURT
Province of the Massachusetts-Bay. At a session . . . held at Boston, October 14, 1713. Resolved that . . . there be some township . . . setled in . . . the County of York, in . . . Mayne . . . Boston, B. Green, 1713.
broadside 25 X 32.5 cm.
DLC (photostat) mp. 39571

B428 MASSACHUSETTS. GOVERNOR, 1702-1715
By his excellency Joseph Dudley . . . A proclamation [concerning return of French prisoners] . . . Boston, B. Green, 1713.
broadside 34 X 21.5 cm.
MHi mp. 39570

B429 MASSACHUSETTS. LAWS
. . . Acts and laws, passed by the . . . General Court . . . begun and held at Boston . . . the twenty-eighth of May, 1712. And continued . . . unto Wednesday the eighteenth of March following . . . [Boston, B. Green, 1713]
p. 389-391. 29.5 cm. caption title
DLC; ICN; NN mp. 39572

B430 MASSACHUSETTS. LAWS
. . . Acts and laws, passed by the . . . General Court . . . May, 1713 . . . [Boston, B. Green, 1713]
p. 393-396. 28.5 cm. caption title
New York Public 79
NN mp. 39573

B431 MASSACHUSETTS. LAWS
. . . An act, passed by the . . . General Court . . . August [1713] . . . [Boston, B. Green, 1713.
p. 397-398, 1 l. 28.5 cm. caption title
Second leaf blank.
New York Public 80
NN mp. 39574

B432 MASSACHUSETTS. LAWS
. . . Acts and laws, passed by the . . . General Court . . . October [1713] . . . [Boston, B. Green, 1713]
p. 399-406. 28.5 cm. caption title
New York Public 81
NN mp. 39575

B433 MASSACHUSETTS. TREASURER
Province of the Massachusetts-Bay, sc. James Taylor, Gent. Treasurer . . . Given under my hand and seal at Boston, the thirtieth day of June, 1713 . . . [Boston, 1713]
broadside 31.5 X 19.5 cm.
DLC; MHi (reduced facsim.) mp. 39576

B434 [MATHER, COTTON] 1662-1728
A letter about a good management under the distemper of the measles . . . Your hearty friend and servant. [Boston, John Allen? 1713?]
4 p. 19.5 cm. caption title
Austin 1229; Guerra a-27; Holmes: Cotton Mather 192-A
MHi; MWA; CtY-M mp. 39577

B435 MATHER, INCREASE, 1639-1723
Now or never is the time . . . Boston, Printed for Benjamin Eliot, 1713.
1 p.l., ii, 113 p. 14 cm.
Variant of Evans 1633
Holmes; Increase Mather 83[1]
CSmH; DLC; MB; MHi mp. 39578

B436 MATHER, INCREASE, 1639-1712
Some remarks on a pretended answer . . . Printed for Nath. Hillier . . . in London: and for the book-sellers in Boston, in New-England. [Boston? Bartholomew Green? 1713]
[2], 36, [2], 10 p. A-E^4 A1-5
Date from second t.p. (on E4); imprint suggested by Holmes on basis of typography
Holmes: Increase Mather 126; Sabin 46747
CSmH; DLC; MB; MBAt; MBC; MH; MHi; MSaE; MWA; NjP; ViU mp. 39579

B437 NEW YORK. GOVERNOR, 1710-1719
By His Excellen[cy Robert] Hunter, Esq; . . . Govern[our in Chief of the] Provinces of New-Jersey, New-York . . . August, in the twelfth year of her Majesties Re[ign]. [New York, William Bradford, 1713]
broadside (fragment)
Appointing day of Thanksgiving
PHi

B438 TO all whom these presents may concern. [Colophon] New York, William Bradford, 1713.
7 p. 30 X 20.5 cm. caption title
Variant of Evans 1641
NHi. Photostat: DLC mp. 39580

1714

B439 ADVERTISEMENT. Whereas there was an advertisement in the . . . *Boston News-Letter* . . . giving notice to subscribers in the Partnership for Circulating Bills or Notes, founded on Land-Security . . . Boston, October 16th 1714. [Boston, 1714]
broadside 18 X 11 cm.
Ford 367
MBAt; MHi mp. 39602

B440 BOSTON
At a meeting of the freeholders and other inhabitants of . . . Boston, duly qualified . . . convened . . . the seventeenth day of May, 1714 . . . At a meeting . . . the fourth of June, 1714 . . . At an adjournment of General Sessions of the Peace . . . the first Monday of August, 1714. The two foregoing orders . . . approved . . . [Boston, 1714]
p. 19-22. 18 cm.
Further continuation of Evans 1040
CSmH; MWA; RPJCB mp. 39583

B441 BOSTON
At a meeting of the freeholders and other inhabitants of . . . Boston, duly qualified . . . assembled . . . the 17th day of May, 1714. For preventing of strangers coming from other places . . . At an adjournment of a Court of General Sessions . . . the last Monday of November . . . 1714. The above order . . . approved . . . [Boston, 1714]
p. 23-24. 18 cm.
Further continuation of Evans 1040
MWA; RPJCB mp. 39584

B442 CONNECTICUT. GOVERNOR, 1708-1725
By the honourable Gurdon Saltonstall . . . A proclamation. Whereas . . . Francis Nicholson Esq. has transmitted . . . copies of the muster roll of Col. William Whiting's company . . . [Aug. 20, 1714] . . . New-London, Timothy Green, 1714.
broadside 30.5 X 18.5 cm.
CtHi mp. 39585

B443 CONNECTICUT. LAWS
. . . Acts and laws, passed by the General Court . . . Hartford . . . the thirteenth day of May . . . 1714. [Colophon] New London: Printed and sold by Timothy Green, 1714.
p. 73-76. 26.5 cm. V^2
Bates: Early Connecticut laws, p. 156
CtY mp. 39586

B444 CONNECTICUT. LAWS
. . . Acts and laws, passed by the General Court . . . New Haven the fourteenth day of October . . . 1714. New London: Printed and sold by Timothy Green, 1714.
p. 77-82. 26.5 cm. $X\text{-}Y^2$ (Y2 blank)
Bates: Early Connecticut laws, p. 156
CtY; PPL mp. 39587

B445 A DIALOGUE between a Boston man and a country man. [Boston] 1714.
2 p. 29 X 19 cm.
Ford 369; New York Public 82
MBAt. Photostats: DLC; MHi; NN mp. 39588

B446 THE farmers almanack for the year 1714. By N. W., a lover of the truth. America: Printed for the author: and are to be sold by N. Boone . . . in Boston, 1714.
[16] p.
Hamilton 8; cf. Evans 1724
MHi; MWA; NjP mp. 39606

B447 GT. BRIT. PARLIAMENT
The humble address of the Right Honourable the Lords . . . and Commons . . . the twenty-fourth day of April, 1714 . . . Boston in N.E. Reprinted by B. Green, by order of the honourable Francis Nicholson Esqr. June 19th. 1714.
broadsheet 29 X 18 cm.
MHi mp. 39589

B448 GT. BRIT. SOVEREIGNS (GEORGE I)
From the *London Gazette* . . . By the King, a proclamation. Declaring . . . [Nov. 22, 1714] Boston, Thomas Fleet and Thomas Crump [1714]
broadside 28.5 X 18.5 cm.
Ford 387; New York Public 88
MBAt. Photostats: DLC; NN mp. 39590

B449 HARVARD UNIVERSITY
Quaestiones pro modulo . . . M DCC XIV [Boston, 1714]
broadside
MH mp. 39591

B450 JAMES, JOHN
On the death of the very learned . . . Gershom Bulkley . . . New London, T. Green, 1714.
broadside 31 X 20 cm.
Signed: Johannes Jamesius Brookfield Decemb. 7, 1713.
New York Public 83
MBAt (mutilated). Photostats: CtHi; MHi; MWA; NN mp. 39592

B451 LONDON GAZETTE
Taken from the *London Gazette* . . . from Saturday July 31 to Tuesday August 3, 1714 . . . Boston, Reprinted and sold by B. Green, 1714.
[2] p.
On the death of Queen Anne
Ford 386
MB; MBAt; MHi mp. 39593

B452 MASSACHUSETTS
By the honourable the Council . . . of the Massachusetts-Bay . . . A declaration. Whereas a printed sheet . . . Boston, B. Green, 1714.
broadside 39.5 X 28.5 cm.
Ford 399; Huntington 46
CSmH; DLC (facsim.); MHi; MWA mp. 39594

B453 MASSACHUSETTS. GENERAL COURT
Province of the Massachusetts-Bay. At a session of the . . . General Court, held at Boston, October 14th. 1713. Resolved, That . . . there be some townships regularly planted . . . in the County of York . . . Boston, B. Green, 1713 [i.e. 1714]
broadside 30 X 20.5 cm.
Includes another resolve dated "February 10th. 1713."
Ford 384; New York Public 84
MBAt. Photostats: DLC; MHi; NN mp. 39597

B454 MASSACHUSETTS. GOVERNOR, 1702-1715
By His Excellency, Joseph Dudley Esq; . . . A proclamation . . . August 16, 1714. Boston, B. Green, 1714.
broadside
Ford 378
MWA mp. 39596

B455 MASSACHUSETTS. GOVERNOR, 1702-1715
By His Excellency, Joseph Dudley . . . a proclamation requiring all persons . . . [October 29, 1714] [Boston, 1714]
broadside 32 X 21.5 cm.
Ford 381
MBAt. Photostats: DLC; MHi mp. 39595

B456 MASSACHUSETTS. LAWS
Acts and laws, passed by the . . . General Court . . . of . . . Massachusetts-Bay . . . [Boston, B. Green, 1714]
p. 249-252
MBAt; MHi mp. 39598

B457 [MATHER, COTTON] 1662-1728
Death approaching . . . Made in a lecture at Boston. 11. d. ix. m. 1714 . . . Boston, B. Green, 1714.
[2], 32 p.
Holmes: Cotton Mather 82
MBC; MHi mp. 39599

B458 MOODY, SAMUEL, 1676-1747
[Judas the traitor hung up in chains . . . Boston, Printed for Nicholas Buttolph? 1714]
[10?], 81, [3] p. 11.5 cm. [A]-H^6
Advertisements at end principally for books printed for Buttolph
MWA (prelim. leaves wanting) mp. 39600

B459 MY son, fear thou the Lord, and the King: and meddle not with them that are given to change . . . Finis. [Boston? 1714?]
broadside ([2] p.) 28.5 cm.
Ford 373; New York Public 85
MBAt. Photostats: MHi; NN mp. 39601

B460 TWO lines of un-accountable characters, found on the perpendicular side of a large rock . . . near the town of Taunton, in New-England. [Boston, 1714]
broadside
Ford 372
CtY mp. 39603

B461 WADSWORTH, BENJAMIN, 1669-1737
Christian advice to the sick and well . . . Boston, Printed by J. Allen for Nicholas Buttolph, 1714.
[4], 107 p. 16mo
MHi (imperfect) mp. 39604

B462 WADSWORTH, BENJAMIN, 1669-1737
Five sermons . . . Boston, Printed by J. Allen for Benj. Eliot, 1714.
xi, [1], 168 p. 13 cm.
Variant of Evans 1721
Sabin 100909
DLC; MB; MH; MHi mp. 39605

1715

B463 . . . AN almanack for the year . . . 1715 . . . By N. W. A Lover of Physick and Astronomy . . . America [Boston]: Printed for the author, 1715.
[16] p.
At head of title: M D C C X V
Drake 2962-63; Huntington 48; Nichols: Mass. almanacs, p. 52
CSmH; DLC; MB; MHi; MWA; NN (t.p. only) mp. 39640

B464 CLAP, NATHANIEL, 1668-1745
Sinners directed to hear & fear . . . Boston, Printed by J. Allen, for N. Boone, 1715.
1 p.l., xix, [1], 56 p. 13 cm.
DLC; MHi; MWA mp. 39607

B465 CONNECTICUT. GOVERNOR, 1708-1725
By the governour, a proclamation. Whereas at the General Court . . . [Oct. 29, 1715] New London, Timothy Green, 1715.
broadside 44 X 25 cm.
MHi. Photostats: DLC; ICN; MWA; NN mp. 39608

B466 CONNECTICUT. LAWS
. . . Acts and laws, passed by the General Court . . . Hartford the twelfth day of May, 1715. [New London, Timothy Green, 1715]
p. 83–87. 26.5 cm. Z^2 Aa^1
Bates: Early Connecticut laws, p. 156
CtY mp. 39609

B467 CONNECTICUT. LAWS
[Acts and laws passed by the General Court . . . New Haven . . . October 1715. New London? T. Green? 1715]
p. 89-94
Bates: Early Connecticut laws, p. 156
No copy known mp. 39610

B468 DOOLITTLE, THOMAS, 1732?-1707
A prospect of eternity . . . Boston, Printed by T. Fleet and T. Crump, for Nicholas Buttolph, 1715.
[2], 105 p. 14 cm. A-I^6
MB (wanting after p. 104); MWA mp. 39611

B469 GT. BRIT. HOUSE OF LORDS
The humble address of the House of Lords to the King, March 23. $17\frac{14}{15}$. With His Majesty's most gracious answer. Boston, Printed by T. Fleet and T. Crump; sold by Nicholas Buttolph and Samuel Gerrish [1715]
broadside 30 X 19.5 cm.
Ford 389
MWA mp. 39612

B470 GT. BRIT. TREATIES
Copy. Of the fifth & sixth articles of the treaty of neutrality in America . . . in the year 1686 . . . Boston, B. Green, 1715.
broadside 29.5 X 21.5 cm.
Ford 390
MBAt. Photostats: DLC; MHi mp. 39613

B471 HARVARD UNIVERSITY
Catalogus eorum qui . . . ad annum 1715 alicujus gradus laurea donati sunt. [Boston, 1715]
broadside 36 X 28.5 cm.
MBAt mp. 39614

B472 HARVARD UNIVERSITY
Quaestiones pro modulo . . . M DCC XV. [Boston, 1715]
broadside
MH mp. 39615

B473 IN luctuosissimum obitum doctissimi . . . Thomae Bridge . . . defuncti, 26 Septrs 1715. Aetatis 59. [Boston, 1715]
broadside
Ford 393
MBAt mp. 39616

B474 [JANEWAY, JAMES] 1636-1674
Three practical discourses . . . Boston, Printed by T. Fleet and T. Crump for Eleazer Phillips in Charles-Town, 1715.
96 p. 13.5 cm.
cf. Evans 1746
MHi mp. 39619

B475 [JANEWAY, JAMES] 1636-1674
Three practical discourses . . . Boston, Printed by T. Fleet and T. Crump, for Nicholas Buttolph, 1715.
96 p. 13.5 cm. [A]-H^6
cf. Evans 1746
MWA; RPJCB mp. 39617

B476 [JANEWAY, JAMES] 1636-1674
Three practical discourses . . . Boston, Printed by T. Fleet and T. Crump, for Samuel Gerrish, 1715.

96 p. 13.5 cm. [A]-H^6
cf. Evans 1746
MWA mp. 39618

B477 LEEDS, 1715. The American almanack for . . . 1715. Philadelphia, Printed, and sold by A. Bradford, 1715.
[28] p. 8vo
PHi

B478 LEEDS, 1716. The American almanack for . . . 1716 . . . New-York, Printed and sold by W. Bradford [1715]
[24] p. 15.5 cm.
New York Public 90; Wall p. 7
CSmH (imperfect); NHi. Photostat: NN
mp. 39620

B479 LONDON
Instructions by the citizens of London, to their representatives for the ensuing Parliament. Boston, Re-printed by Thomas Fleet and Thomas Crump; sold by Samuel Gerrish, 1715.
broadside
Ford 394
MB; MBAt mp. 39621

B480 LONDON. LORD MAYOR
To the King's most excellent Majesty, the humble address of the Lord mayor . . . Boston, Reprinted by B. Green: sold by B. Eliot, 1715.
broadside 30 X 19 cm.
DLC mp. 39622

B481 LOUIS XIV, 1638-1715
An abstract of the French King's will . . . Boston, Reprinted by B. Green: sold by B. Eliot, 1715.
broadside 30 X 19 cm.
DLC mp. 39623

B482 . . . THE Loyal American's almanack for the year 1715 . . . By a new comer into America. Boston, Printed in the Year of Peace, 1715.
[20] p.
At head of title: MDCCXV
MWA; RPJCB (imperfect) mp. 39624

B483 MASSACHUSETTS
By the honourable the Council of . . . Massachusetts-Bay in New-England. A proclamation. Whereas in the royal charter . . . we do require all officers . . . Given at the Council chamber in Boston, the fourth day of February . . . 1714 . . . Boston, B. Green, 1714 [i.e. 1715]
broadside 47.5 X 37 cm.
Ford 397
MHi; MeHi. Photostat: MSaE mp. 39625

B484 MASSACHUSETTS. GOVERNOR, 1702-1715
By His Excellency Joseph Dudley . . . A proclamation against a commerce & trade with the French of Canada . . . March 29, 1715. Boston, B. Green, 1715.
broadside 30 X 20 cm.
Ford 400
MBAt. Photostat: DLC mp. 39626

B485 MASSACHUSETTS. GOVERNOR, 1702-1715
The case of . . . the governour and council of the province . . . truly stated. [Boston, T. Fleet, 1715]
4 p. 30 X 21 cm. caption title
Ford 404; New York Public 86
MBAt; MHi. Photostats: DLC; NN mp. 39627

B486 [MATHER, COTTON] 1662-1728
A monitor for the children of the covenant . . . Boston, Printed by B. Green, for Samuel Gerrish, 1715.
1 p.l., 28+ p. 12.5 cm.
MB (all wanting after p. 28) mp. 39628

B487 MATHER, INCREASE, 1639-1723
Several sermons . . . Boston, Printed by B. Green, for Nicholas Buttolph, 1715.
[2], xi, 126 p. A^8 $B\text{-}F^{12}$ G^4
Holmes: Increase Mather 121[1]
MHi mp. 39629

B488 MATHER, INCREASE, 1639-1723
Several sermons . . . Boston, Printed by B. Green, for Samuel Phillips, 1715.
1 p.l., xi, [1], 126 p. 13 cm.
Holmes: Increase Mather 121[3]
DLC mp. 39630

B489 NEW JERSEY. GOVERNOR, 1710–1719
By His Excellency Robert Hunter . . . A proclamation . . . [New York, William Bradford, 1715]
broadside 30.5 X 19.5 cm.
Concerns offices of register and surveyor
Dated at Perth Amboy, Nov. 7, 1715
New York Public 91
Elmer T. Hutchinson, Elizabeth, N.J. (1932) Photostat: NN mp. 39631

B490 NEW YORK. LAWS
. . . An act passed by the General Assembly of . . . New-York in July, 1715 . . . declaring that all persons of forreign birth . . . shall be . . . esteemed to have been naturalized . . . [New York, William Bradford, 1715]
6 p. 32 cm.
NHi mp. 39632

B491 [SAULT, J.]
The second Spira: being a fearful example of an atheist . . . The sixth edition . . . Boston, T. Fleet & T. Crump, for Benjamin Eliot, 1715.
[11], 1-37, 37-38, 22p.
Author from Wing S733
MWA; RPJCB mp. 39634

B492 SEWALL, SAMUEL, 1652-1730
Province of the Massachusetts-Bay in New-England, December 12, 1715. Samuel Sewall Esq; Judge for the probate of wills . . . purposes . . . to wait upon that business, at his dwelling house in Boston . . . [Boston, 1715]
broadside
Ford 406
MSaE mp. 39635

B493 THE state of the Mohegan fields, lying between the land granted to New-London on the south, and Norwich on the north . . . New London Feb. the 3d. 1714. I have perused the above . . . and allow it to be printed. G. Saltonstall. [New London? 1715]
broadside 22.5 X 15 cm.
CtHi mp. 39633

B494 A SPEECH deliver'd by an Indian chief, in reply to a sermon . . . by a Swedish missionary . . . at an Indian-treaty held at Canastogoe . . . [Philadelphia, A. Bradford, 1715]
broadside 39 X 31 cm.
Huntington 116; Metzger 11
CSmH; PHi mp. 39635a

B495 WADSWORTH, BENJAMIN, 1669-1737
A guide for the doubting, and cordial for the fainting, saint . . . The second impression . . . Boston, Printed by B. Green, for Eleazer Phillips, and sold at his shop in Charlstown, 1715.
[4], 202, [8] p. 15.5 cm. A-S[6]
CtHi (t.p. lacking); MWA (sig. S1 wanting) mp. 39636

B496 WADSWORTH, BENJAMIN, 1669-1737
Invitations to the gospel feast . . . Boston, Printed by B. Green, for Nicholas Buttolph, 1715.
[2], ii, 193, [6] p. 14 cm.
CSmH; MWA mp. 39637

B497 WADSWORTH, BENJAMIN, 1669-1737
Invitations to the gospel feast . . . Boston, Printed by B. Green, for Samuel Phillips, 1715.
[2], ii, 193, [6] p. 14 cm.
MWA mp. 39638

B498 [WATTS, ISAAC] 1674-1748
Honey out of the rock . . . Certain select hymns . . . taken from those of . . . Mr. Isaac Watts . . . Boston, Printed by T. Fleet, and T. Crump, for Samuel Gerrish, 1715.
24 p. 13 cm. A-B[6]
Huntington 47
CSmH. Photostat: MWA mp. 39639

B499 WIGGLESWORTH, MICHAEL, 1631-1705
The day of doom . . . The sixth edition, enlarged with Scripture and marginal notes . . . Boston, Printed by J. Allen, for N. Boone, 1715.
[3]-12, 82 p. 14 cm. A-H[6]
MHi; MWA mp. 39641

B500 WIGGLESWORTH, MICHAEL, 1631-1705
The day of doom . . . The sixth edition, enlarged . . . Boston, Printed by John Allen, for Nicholas Buttolph, 1715.
[3]-12, 82 p. 14 cm.
Huntington 49; cf. Evans 1794
CSmH mp. 39642

1716

B501 ALLEINE, JOSEPH, 1634-1668
An alarm to unconverted sinners . . . Boston, Printed by J. Allen for Nicholas Boone, 1716.
13 p.l., 170, 76 p. 15 cm.
"An epistle to the unconverted reader, by Richard Alleine" precedes the text
MHi (sig. C3 imperfect) mp. 39643

B502 . . . AN almanack of the coelestial motions . . . for the year . . . 1716 . . . By Daniel Travis. Boston, Bartholomew Green, 1716.
[16] p. 16 cm.
At head of title: M D C C X V I
MWA mp. 39657

B503 BLOWERS, THOMAS, 1677-1729
The deaths of eminent men, and excellent friends . . . Set forth in a sermon preacht . . . Decemb. 4. 1715. Occasion'd by the death of . . . Joseph Green . . . Whereunto is annexed a funeral poem . . . by . . . Nicholas Noyes . . . Boston, Printed by B. Green, for Samuel Gerrish, 1716.
1 p.l., iv, 34 p. 15 cm. A-D[4]
"Preface" (p. i-iv) signed: George Curwen
Huntington 50
CSmH; MB. Photostat: MWA mp. 39644

B504 BUNYAN, JOHN, 1628-1682
The heavenly foot-man: or, A description of the man that that gets to Heaven . . . Boston, Re-printed by J. Allen, for N. Boone, 1716.
[10], 72 p. 12mo
MH. Photostats (t.p. only): MHi; MWA mp. 39645

B505 FLYING post. [Boston, Thomas Fleet, 1716]
broadside?
Ford 407
No copy known mp. 39646

B506 GRAILE, EDMUND, 1577?-
The summ of the holy history . . . in meeter . . . By Edmond Graile. The fourth impression . . . Boston, Re-printed by T. Fleet & T. Crump, for John Eliot, 1716.
104 p. 13 cm. A-H[6] I[4]
MB; MWA mp. 39647

B507 GT. BRIT. SOVEREIGNS (GEORGE I)
His Majesties most gracious speech to both Houses of Parliament on the ninth day of January, 1715. [Colophon] Boston, Reprinted by B. Green, 1716.
4 p. 31 cm.
Includes the replies of the House of Lords and the House of Commons
New York Public 92
NN mp. 39648

B508 HARVARD UNIVERSITY
Quaestiones pro modulo . . . M DCC XVI. [Boston, 1716]
broadside
MH; MHi mp. 39649

B509 MASSACHUSETTS. GOVERNOR, 1716-1722
His Excellency Samuel Shute . . . His speech to the honourable Council and House of Representatives . . . the seventh of November, 1716 . . . [Colophon] Boston, B. Green, 1716.
2 p. 29 X 18 cm.
MWA. Photostat: MHi mp. 39650

B510 MASSACHUSETTS. LAWS
. . . An act passed by the . . . General Court . . . begun . . . at Boston . . . the thirtieth of May, 1716. An act for apportioning and assessing a tax of eleven thousand fifty one pounds . . . [at end] Boston, B. Green, 1716.
broadside
M mp. 39650a

B511 MASSACHUSETTS. TREASURER
Province of the Massachusetts-Bay, ss. Jeremiah Allen, Gent. Treasurer . . . To the select-men or assessors of the town or district of Greeting . . . Given . . . at Boston, the second day of July, 1716 . . . [Boston, 1716]
broadside 30.5 X 19 cm.
Tax warrant
MWA mp. 39651

B512 MATHER, COTTON, 1662-1728
[A good evening accommodated with a good employment. Boston, 1716]

Holmes: Cotton Mather 148; cf. Mather's *Diary* for Aug. 13 and 17, 1716.
No copy known mp. 39652

B513 [MATHER, COTTON] 1662-1728
Piety demanded . . . Boston, Printed by T. Fleet and T. Crump, for Daniel Henchman, 1716.
36 p. A-C[6]

Holmes: Cotton Mather 282
Bodleian. Photostat: MWA mp. 39653

B514 [MATHER, COTTON] 1662-1728
Utilia. Real and vital religion served . . . Boston, Printed by T. Fleet & T. Crump, for Samuel Gerrish, 1716.
[2], [5], [1], 288 p. sm. 12mo
Huntington 51; cf. Evans 1834
CSmH mp. 39654

B515 MATHER, INCREASE, 1639-1723
A discourse concerning the existence . . . of God . . . Boston, Printed by John Allen, for Samuel Gerrish, 1716.
[6], 86, [4] p. A-H^6
Holmes: Increase Mather 34[1]
RPJCB mp. 39655

B516 [SMITH, WILLIAM] A. M.
The history of the Holy Jesus . . . The tenth edition . . . Boston, T. Fleet & T. Crump, for Nicholas Buttolph, 1716.
214 p.
Sabin 84553
RPJCB mp. 39656

1717

B517 ALLEINE, JOSEPH, 1634-1668
Remaines of that excellent minister . . . Mr. Joseph Alleine. Being a collection of . . . sermons . . . letters . . . Boston, Printed by John Allen, for Nicholas Boone, 1717.
[4], 235, [1] p. 15 cm.
MWA mp. 39658

B518 BIBLE
The Holy Bible in verse. [Boston, John Allen] 1717.
1 p.l., [60] p. illus. 10 cm.
Versified by Benjamin Harris
Imprint identified by J. C. Wyllie
CLU; MWA; NN; PP. David McKell, Chillicothe, O. (1961); Mrs. Edgar S. Oppenheimer, New York City (1962); d'Alté A. Welch, Cleveland (1962) mp. 39659

B519 BOSTON
[No. 6.] To Your province & county tax. Your town rate . . . The assessors sit . . . in Boston, Frydays . . . 1717 . . . Per George Shore, Constable. [Boston, 1717]
broadside 11 X 15.5 cm.
Ford 426
MHi (photostat)

B520 BUNYAN, JOHN, 1628-1688
Grace abounding to the chief of sinners . . . The eighth edition, corrected . . . Boston, Printed by J. Allen, for Nicholas Boone, 1717.
3 p.l., 144 p. 14 cm.
New York Public 93
MWA; NN (last leaf wanting) mp. 39660

B521 CHARMION, JOHN
AE·M·S· Eximij pietate, eruditione, prudentia viri D. Ebenezrae Pembertoni . . . epitaphium [at end] Posuit Jo. Charmion in literas . . . [Boston, 1717]
broadside
Ford 415; cf. Evans 1871
MHi mp. 39661

B522 DANFORTH, JOHN, 1660-1730
Greatness & goodness elegized, in a poem, upon the . . . decease of . . . Madam Hannah Sewall, late consort of . . . Judge Sewall . . . October 19th . . . 1717. Aetatis suae 60 . . . John Danforth, V.D.M. Dorcestriae. [Boston, 1717]
broadside 33 X 22 cm.
Ford 417; New York Public 94
MB; NN mp. 39662

B523 AN elegy upon the death of several worthy pious persons . . . [Boston? 1717?]
broadside 24 X 13 cm.
DLC; MHi. Photostat: MWA mp. 39663

B524 HARVARD UNIVERSITY
Illustrissimo . . . theses hasce . . . MDCCXVII. [Boston, 1717]
broadside
MHi mp. 39665

B525 HARVARD UNIVERSITY
Quaestiones pro more . . . M.DCC.XVII. [Boston, 1717]
broadside
MH; MHi mp. 39664

B526 HOADLY, BENJAMIN, 1676-1761
The nature of the kingdom, or church, of Christ . . . By . . . Benjamin Lord Bishop of Bangor . . . London, Printed for James Knapton, and Reprinted by William Bradford in New-York, 1717.
18 p. 19 cm.
New York Public 95
MWA. Photostat: NN mp. 39666

B527 LEEDS, 1717. The American almanack for . . . 1717 . . . By Titan Leeds, Philomat. . . . New-York, Printed and sold by W. Bradford [1717]
[24?] p.
Wall p. 7
CSmH ([16] p. only); PHi mp. 39667

B528 NEW YORK. SUPREME COURT
A writ issu'd out from the Supreme Court at New-York to the justices, vestry-men and church-wardens of . . . Jamaica on Nassau-Island . . . [New York? 1717?]
7 p. 32 cm.
NHi mp. 39668

B529 PETER, HUGH, 1599-1660
A dying father's last legacy . . . Boston, B. Green, for Samuel Gerrish, 1717.
[2], ii, 92 p. port. 18mo
CtHi (t.p. and p. 91-2 lacking); MB; MHi; RPJCB mp. 39669

B530 SEWALL, SAMUEL, 1652-1750
A small vial of tears brought from the funeral of John Winthrop . . . [Boston? 1717?]
broadside 15.5 X 10.5 cm.
MHi mp. 39670

B531 WADSWORTH, BENJAMIN, 1670–1737
Acquaintance with God yields peace . . . Boston, Printed by J. Allen, for Daniel Henchman, 1717.
[2], 31, [1] p.
RPJCB mp. 39671

B532 WIGGLESWORTH, MICHAEL, 1631–1705
Meat out of the eater . . . The fifth edition. Boston, Printed by J. Allen, for D. Henchman, 1717.
143 p. 14 cm.
cf. Evans 1938
CtHi mp. 39675

B533 WIGGLESWORTH, MICHAEL, 1631–1705
Meat out of the eater . . . The fifth edition. Boston,

Printed by J. Allen, for N. Boone, 1717.
143 p. 13.5 cm.
cf. Evans 1938
MWA mp. 39672

B534 WIGGLESWORTH, MICHAEL, 1631–1705
Meat out of the eater . . . The fifth edition. Boston, Printed by J. Allen, for Nicholas Buttolph, 1717.
143 p. 13.5 cm.
cf. Evans 1938
MWA (p. 7–8 wanting) mp. 39673

B535 WIGGLESWORTH, MICHAEL, 1631–1705
Meat out of the eater . . . The fifth edition. Boston, Printed by J. Allen, for Robert Starke, 1717.
143 p. 13.5 cm.
cf. Evans 1938
MHi mp. 39676

B536 WIGGLESWORTH, MICHAEL, 1631–1705
Meat out of the eater . . . The fifth edition. Boston, Printed by J. Allen, for Thomas Fleet, 1717.
143 p. 13.5 cm.
cf. Evans 1938
MWA (wanting after p. 140) mp. 39674

B537 WISE, JEREMIAH, d. 1756
A sermon shewing the suitableness . . . Boston, Printed by John Allen, for Nicholas Boone, 1717.
1 p.l., [5], 40 p. 13.5 cm.
DLC. Photostats: MHi; MWA; NN mp. 39677

1718

B538 BIBLE
The Holy Bible in verse. [Boston? John Allen?] 1718.
[64] p. 9 cm.
Copy sold at Amer. Art Galleries, Apr. 8, 1926 (W. G. Schillaber sale)
cf. Nichols, Charles L. The Holy Bible in verse. (In A.A.S. *Proceedings*. n.s. v. 36 (1926) p. 71–82)
No location known mp. 39679

B539 BOONE, NICHOLAS, 1679–1738
Military discipline. The newest way and method of exercising horse & foot . . . Boston, Printed by John Allen, for Nicholas Boone, 1718.
1 p.l., 80 p. 14.5 cm.
DLC mp. 39680

B540 HARVARD UNIVERSITY
Quaestiones pro modulo . . . M.DCC.XVIII. [Boston, 1718]
broadside
MH mp. 39681

B541 [HILL, JOHN]
The young secretary's guide . . . The fifth edition. With large . . . additions. By Thomas Hill, gent. Boston, Reprinted by John Allen, for Benjamin Eliot, 1718.
140, [4] p. 17.5 cm. A–M^6
MWA (p. 3–10 wanting); NHi; NNC mp. 39683

B542 [HILL, JOHN]
The young secretary's guide . . . The fifth edition. With large . . . additions. By Thomas Hill, gent. Boston, Reprinted by John Allen for Benjamin Gray, 1718.
140, [4] p. 17.5 cm. A-M^6
CtHi mp. 39684

B543 [HILL, JOHN]
The young secretary's guide . . . The fifth edition. With large . . . additions. By Thomas Hill, gent. Boston, Reprinted by John Allen for Eleazar Phillips, 1718.
140, [4] p. 17.5 cm.
Karpinski p. 36
DLC; NN mp. 39685

B544 [HILL, JOHN]
The young secretary's guide . . . The fifth edition. With large . . . additions. By Thomas Hill, gent. Boston, Reprinted by John Allen for Nicholas Boone, 1718.
140, [4] p. 17.5 cm.
RPJCB mp. 39682

B545 LEEDS, 1718. The American Almanack for . . . 1718 . . . By Titan Leeds, Philomat. . . . New-York, Printed and sold by William Bradford [1718]
[24] p.
Wall p. 7
NN mp. 39686

B546 MASSACHUSETTS. GOVERNOR, 1716–1722
By . . . Samuel Shute . . . a proclamation. Whereas sundry felons . . . [Nov. 25, 1718] [Boston, 1718]
broadside 32 X 21.5 cm.
Ford 435; New York Public 99
CtHi; PPAmP. Photostats: DLC; NN mp. 39687

B547 MOODEY, SAMUEL, 1676–1747
Smoaking flax inflamed, or, Weary sinners incouraged to go to Christ . . . Boston: Printed by B. Green, for Samuel Gerrish, and sold at his shop, 1718.
1 p.l., 45 p.
MB mp. 39688

B548 PITCHER, NATHANIEL, d. 1723
Words of consolation to Mr. Robert Stetson & Mrs. Mary Stetson . . . on the death of their son Isaac . . . November 7th, 1718. Aged 22 . . . Nathaniel Pitcher. [On same sheet] A sorrowful poem upon that desirable youth Isaac Stetson . . . By a friend. [Boston, 1718]
broadside 25 X 18 cm.
Ford 438; New York Public 100
MSaE. Photostats: MHi; NN mp. 39689

B549 ROGERS, JOHN, 1648–1721
An epistle sent from God to the world, containing the best news that ever the world heard . . . [Colophon] Printed . . . for John Rogers living in New London, 1718.
40 p. 15 cm. caption title
RPJCB mp. 39690

B550 RUSSELL, ROBERT, of Wadhurst, Sussex
Seven sermons . . . The eleveneth edition. Boston, Reprinted by John Allen, for John Eliot, 1718.
178 p. 17.5 cm. A-P^6
MWA mp. 39691

B551 [SMITH, JOHN] writer on agriculture
The husbandman's magazine . . . By J. S. Boston, Reprinted by John Allen, for Nicholas Boone, 1718.
2 p.l., 145, [1] p. illus. 12.5 cm.
Huntington 54; New York Public 101
CSmH; MWA; NN mp. 39692

B552 VINCENT, THOMAS, 1634–1678
Christ's certain and sudden appearance in judgment . . . The tenth edition . . . Boston, Printed by J. Allen, for Benj. Gray, 1718.
234 + p. 15.5 cm.
New York Public 102

MWA (imperfect); NN (all before p. 141 and after p. 234 wanting) mp. 39693

B553 VIRGINIA. GENERAL ASSEMBLY
Some remarkable proceedings in the Assembly of Virginia anno. 1718 . . . The humble address of the House of Burgesses . . . The Lieutenant Governor's speech on the 1st of December 1718 . . . [Philadelphis? Andrew Bradford? 1718?]
[4] p. 28 cm.
cf. Mass. Hist. Soc. *Proceedings* 62:29
MHi; PPAmP. Public Record Office. Photostats: MWA; ViU mp. 39694

B554 WADSWORTH, BENJAMIN, 1669–1737
The sin of pride, described & condemned . . . Boston, Printed by B. Green, for Benj. Eliot, 1718.
1 p.l., 32 p.
MB mp. 39695

B555 YALE UNIVERSITY
Honoratissimo ac insigni virtute . . . Gurdona Saltonstall . . . hasce theses . . . Novi Londini, Timotheus Green, 1718.
broadside 14.5 X 32 cm.
MHi mp. 39696

B556 THE young man's companion . . . The third edition much enlarged . . . Philadelphia, Printed and sold by Andrew Bradford, 1718.
[14], 264 p. 15 cm.
New York Public 103
NN (all after p. 229 [i.e. 228] wanting except for stubs); PHi mp. 39697

1719

B557 BOSTON, N. E. May 27, 1719. Proposals for printing by subscription . . . Samuel Willard's Lectures upon the whole Assemblies Catechism . . . Samuel Phillips Nicholas Buttolph Benjamin Eliot Samuel Gerrish Daniel Henchman Gillam Phillips. Booksellers in Boston, [Boston, 1719]
broadside 31.5 X 20.5 cm.
MH

B558 FRANKLIN, BENJAMIN, 1706–1790
[Ballad on the taking of Teach, or Blackbeard. Boston, 1719?]
broadside?
"My brother . . . put me on composing occasional ballads . . . the taking of Teach . . . the pirate." *Autobiography* (Smyth, I. 239)
No copy known mp. 39698

B559 FRANKLIN, BENJAMIN, 1706–1790
[The lighthouse tragedy. Boston, 1719?]
broadside?
"My brother . . . put me on composing occasional ballads. One . . . contained an account of the drowning of Captain Worthilake . . ." Franklin's *Autobiography* (Smyth, I. 239) Worthilake was drowned Nov. 3, 1718.
Ford 440
No copy known mp. 39699

B560 FRIENDS, SOCIETY OF. LONDON YEARLY MEETING.
An epistle of caution against pride, &c. From the Yearly Meeting on London, 1718. London Printed, and Reprinted by Andrew Bradford in Philadelphia [1719?]
broadside 40 X 31 cm. caption title
RPJCB mp. 39700

B561 GERRISH, SAMUEL, d. 1741
A catalogue of curious and valuable books . . . To be sold by auction . . . Boston . . . October, 1719 . . . [Boston] J. Franklin, 1719.
[2], 18 p. 15.5 cm.
Curtis X5; New York Public 104
NN (photostat); PU mp. 39701

B562 HARVARD UNIVERSITY
Illustrissimo . . . theses hasce . . . MDCCXIX. [Boston, 1719]
broadside
MH; MHi mp. 39703

B563 HARVARD UNIVERSITY
Quaestiones pro modulo . . . M DCC XIX. [Boston,1719]
broadside
MH; MWA mp. 39702

B564 [JANEWAY, JAMES] 1636–1704
Three practical discourses . . . Boston, Reprinted by S. Kneeland, for Eleazer Phillips, in Charlstown, 1719.
[2], 78 p. 12 cm. A-F^6 G^4
MWA mp. 39704

B565 JOSEPHUS, FLAVIUS
The wars of the Jews. In two books . . . The fourth edition. London Printed: Reprinted at Boston by S. Kneeland, for B. Eliot, 1719.
262 p. front. 17.5 cm. A-L^{12}
MWA (sig. A3–10 wanting) mp. 39706

B566 JOSEPHUS, FLAVIUS
The wars of the Jews. In two books . . . The fourth edition. London Printed: Reprinted at Boston by S. Kneeland, for N. Buttolph, 1719.
262 p. front. 17.5 cm. A-L^{12}
Rosenbach 15
A. S. W. Rosenbach (1926) mp. 39705

B567 LEEDS, 1719. The American almanack for . . . 1719 . . . By Titan Leeds, Philomat. . . . New-York, Printed and sold by William Bradford [1719]
[24] p.
Wall p. 7
NN mp. 39707

B568 MARYLAND. GOVERNOR, 1714–1720
His excellency's speech . . . [May 14, 1719] [Philadelphia, A. Bradford, 1719]
10 p. 30.5 cm. caption title
Contains also addresses of both houses to the Governor
Wroth 24
DLC (2 copies); MdBP mp. 39708

B569 MARYLAND. LAWS
The laws of the province of Maryland, at a sessions . . . begun and held . . . the fourteenth day of May . . . Philadelphia, Printed by Andrew Bradford, and are to be sold by Evan Jones at Annapolis, 1719.
[2], 221–248 p. 30.5 cm.
Wroth 25
DLC (2 copies); MdBP 39709

B570 MATHER, COTTON, 1662–1728
An history of seasonable interpositions of Divine Providence . . . [Boston, 1719]
[2], 34 p. A-D^4 E^2
Holmes: Cotton Mather 175
MB mp. 39710

B571 MATHER, INCREASE, 1639–1723
The duty of parents to pray . . . The second impression . . . Boston, Printed by John Allen, for Benjamin Gray, 1719.
vi, 99 p. sm. 12mo
Huntington 55; cf. Evans 2052
CSmH; CtY mp. 39711

B572 NEW YORK. GOVERNOR, 1710–1719
His Excellency Brigadeer [sic] Hunter's speech made to the General Assembly the 24th day of June, 1719. [New York, 1719]
1 leaf 31 X 19.5 cm.
On verso: The humble address of the General Assembly . . .
New York Public 106
NjP. Photostat: NN mp. 39712

B573 [ROBIE, THOMAS] 1689–1729
A letter to a certain gentleman, &c. Boston, J. Franklin, for Daniel Henchman, 1719.
8 p. 14 cm.
Signed at end in Greek: Philos sophias
MWA; RPJCB mp. 39713

172-

B574 MATHER, COTTON, 1662–1728
[The greatest concern in the world . . . n.p., 172–?]

32 p. A-B^4 D-E^4
Holmes: Cotton Mather 165–C
DCU (t.p. and sig. E4 lacking) mp. 39714

B575 WELD, EDMUND
A funeral elegy by way of dialogue . . . Boston, Reprinted & sold by S. Kneeland [172–?]
broadside
MHi (photostat); NHi mp. 39715

1720

B576 BAILEY, NATHAN, d. 1742
English and Latine exercises for schoolboys . . . By N. Bayley . . . The fifth edition newly improv'd and revis'd by several hands. Boston, Printed by T. Fleet, for the booksellers, 1720.
[8], 208 p. 14.5 cm. A-N^8 O^4
MWA mp. 39716

B577 BERNON, GABRIEL
The humble petition of Gabriel Bernon: of New Oxford in New England. [n.p., 1720?]
[2] p.
PHi mp. 39717

B578 BIBLE. O.T. APOCRYPHAL BOOKS. TESTAMENT OF THE TWELVE PATRIARCHS
The Testament of the Twelve Patriarchs . . . Boston, Reprinted by T. Fleet for S. Phillips, N. Buttolph, B. Eliot, & D. Henchman in Boston, and E. Phillips in Charlestown, 1720.
[10], 3–112 p. 12.5 cm. A-K^6
MB (t.p. mutilated; p. 111–112 wanting); MWA; MiU-C; NN. A. S. W. Rosenbach (1933) mp. 39718

B579 [BURT, JONATHAN]
A lamentation occasion'd by the great sickness & lamented deaths . . . Writ, April, 1712. [Boston] 1720.
broadside 28 X 19 cm.
Ford 450; New York Public 109
MHi. Photostats: CSmH; DLC; MWA mp. 39719

B580 COPY of a letter by a gentleman in New-England to his friend . . . containing remarks on a late pamphlet entitled, Some considerations on the French settling colonies on the Mississippi . . . [at end] Boston, 1720.
8 p. caption title
RPJCB mp. 39720

B581 [DANFORTH, JOHN] 1660–1730
The mercies of the year, commemorated: A song for little children in New-England. December 13th 1720. [and] Psalm CVII. last part. Translated by . . . Isaac Watts and by him intitled, A Psalm for New-England. [n.p., 1720?]
broadside 37 X 23.5 cm.
Ford 461; New York Public 112
RPJCB. Facsims.: MHi; MWA; NN; PPAmP mp. 39721

B582 [GERRISH, SAMUEL] d. 1741
[Choice English books. Sold in the house of Andrew Cunningham, Jr. opposite to the north door of the Old Church, Boston. Boston, J. Franklin? 1720]
[2], 32 p.
Title taken from McKay 14
RPJCB (t.p. and possibly last leaf wanting) mp. 39722

B583 HARVARD UNIVERSITY
Illustrissimo . . . theses hasce . . . MDCCXX. [Boston, 1720]
broadside
MH; MHi mp. 39724

B584 HARVARD UNIVERSITY
Quaestiones pro modulo . . . M DCC XX. [Cambridge, 1720]
broadside
MH; MHi; MWA mp. 39723

B585 LEEDS, 1720. The American almanack for . . . 1720 . . . New-York, Printed and sold by William Bradford, 1720.
[24] p. 15 cm.
New York Public 110; Wall p. 7
CsmH. Photostat: NN. A. S. W. Rosenbach (1921) mp. 39725

B586 MARYLAND. LAWS
[Acts of a session . . . begun . . . the eleventh day of October . . . 1720. Annapolis, John Peter Zenger, 1720]

For authorization to print, see L. H. J. Oct. 27, 1720
Wroth 27
No copy known mp. 39727

B587 MARYLAND. LAWS
The laws of the province of Maryland, . . . passed at a session . . . begun . . . the fifth day of April . . . 1720. Annapolis, John Peter Zenger, 1720]

For authorization to print, see L. H. J. Apr. 12, 1720
Wroth 26
No copy known mp. 39726

B588 MASSACHUSETTS. GOVERNOR, 1716–1722
By his excellency Samuel Shute . . . A proclamation to prevent the destruction or spoil of His Majesty's woods . . . Boston, B. Green, 1720.
broadside
Public Record Off. Photostat: MHi mp. 39728

B589 NEW JERSEY. LAWS
Acts passed by the General assembly of . . . New-Jersey . . . 1718. [New York, W. Bradford, 1720]
p. 79–115. 29 cm. caption title
Nelson, William: "Bibliography of the printed acts of the legislature of New Jersey, 1703–1800," *in* First report of the Public Record Commission of New Jersey, 1899, p. 57–58
DLC; NN mp. 39729

B590 NEWS from Robinson Cruso's island: with An appendix relating to Mr. Cook's late pamphlet. [Colophon] Boston: Printed in the year, 1720.
11 p. 4to in half sheets. caption title
Imprint from p. 11
cf. Evans 2153
MB mp. 39730

B591 [SEWALL, SAMUEL] 1652–1730
Upon Mr. Samuel Willard, his first coming into the Assembly . . . May 12th, 1720. [Boston, 1720]
broadside
Ford 462
MHi mp. 39731

B592 [VALENTINE, JOHN] d. 1724
The postscript. [Boston? 1720]
3 p. 18.5 cm.
In reply to Colman's *Distressed state of the town of Boston*. Probably written by John Valentine, attorney general
DLC; MWA. Photostat: MHi mp. 39732

B593 WATTS, ISAAC, 1674–1748
Hymns and spiritual songs . . . Seventh edition. Boston [1720?]
360 p.
MHi (imperfect) mp. 39733

B594 THE waxen doll, The morning air, The primroses, and The tempest of war. [Boston, 1720?]
broadside 33.5 X 19.5 cm.
Four poetical compositions, in two columns
Huntington 58
CSmH mp. 39734

1721

B595 . . . AN almanack . . . for the year . . . 1721. By a Native of New-England [Nathan Bowen] . . . [Boston] Printed for N. Boone, B. Gray, and J. Edwards, 1721.
[16] p. 15.5 cm.
Guerra b-42
MWA mp. 39736

B596 BOSTON
At a publick town meeting of the freeholders . . . of Boston . . . continued to Fryday the eleventh of said month anno 1721 . . . Samuel Checkley, Town-Clerk. Boston: Printed for Benjamin Gray, 1721.
[2] p. 30 X 17 cm.
Ford 465
MBAt; MH. Photostat: MHi mp. 39735

B597 CONGREGATIONAL CHURCHES IN NEW ENGLAND
A letter from the ministers of the Association . . . [n.p., 1721?]
broadside 30.5 X 19.5 cm.
Independent ministers from Conn., Mass., and R.I.
NHi mp. 39737

B598 CONNECTICUT. GOVERNOR, 1708–1724
By the honourable Gurdon Saltonstall . . . A brief . . . New-London, T. Green, 1721.
broadside 30.5 X 20 cm.
Dated June 13, 1721
New York Public 115
CtY. Reduced photo.: CtHi; NN mp. 39738

B599 CONNECTICUT. GOVERNOR, 1708–1724
By the honourable, Gurdon Saltonstall . . . A proclamation [concerning smallpox] . . . N. London, T. Green, 1721.
broadside
Amer. Art Assoc. cat. Feb. 26–27, 1924, item 295
New York Public 116
Dated July 14, 1721
CtHi; NN (reduced facsim.) mp. 39740

B600 CONNECTICUT. GOVERNOR, 1708–1724
By the honourable Gurdon Saltonstall . . . a proclamation for a publick thanksgiving . . . [Oct. 14, 1721] . . . New London, Timothy Green, 1721.
broadside 37 X 24 cm.
MHi. Photostats: CtHi; DLC; MWA; NN mp. 39739

B601 HARVARD UNIVERSITY
Catalogus eorum qui . . . ad annum 1721 alicujus gradus laurea donati sunt. [Boston, 1721]
broadside 36 X 28.5 cm.
MH. Photostats: DLC; MHi mp. 39741

B602 HARVARD UNIVERSITY
Illustrissimo . . . theses hasce . . . MDCCXXI. [Boston, 1721]
broadside
MHi mp. 39742

B603 LEEDS, 1721. The American almanack for . . . 1721 . . . New-York, Printed and sold by William Bradford, 1721.
[24] p. 15 cm.
New York Public 118; Wall p. 7
CSmH (2 leaves wanting). Photostat: NN mp. 39743

B604 MARYLAND. GOVERNOR, 1720–1726
The speech of His excellency Coll. Charles Calvert . . . to both Houses . . . Febr. 20, 1721 . . . [Philadelphia, Andrew Bradford, 1721]?
6+ p. 31.5 cm.
Wroth 29
MdHi (imperfect) mp. 39744

B605 MARYLAND. LAWS
[Acts of a session . . . begun . . . the eighteenth day of July . . . 1721. Annapolis, John Peter Zenger, 1721]

For authorization to print, see L. H. J. Aug. 6, 1721
Wroth 28
No copy known mp. 39745

B606 MASSACHUSETTS
The several votes, orders, & messages pass'd in Council and in the House of Representatives, at the session . . . at Boston, March 15th, 1720 . . . Boston, B. Green, 1721.
3 p.
Concerns logs cut on Province lands in York Co.
Public Record Off. Photostat: MHi mp. 39746

B607 MASSACHUSETTS. TREASURER
Province of the Massachusetts Bay ss. Jeremiah Allen Esqr; treasurer . . . To constable . . . By virtue of

an act . . . the thirty-first day of May 1721 . . . [Boston, 1721?]
broadside 34.5 X 21.5 cm.
MHolliHi; RPJCB

B608 [MATHER, COTTON] 1662–1728
[Elizabeth in her holy retirement . . . Boston? 1721?]

For the evidence for this edition, cf. Holmes: Cotton Mather 108-B
No copy known mp. 39747

B609 MATHER, INCREASE, 1639–1623
Some important truths about conversion . . . The second edition . . . Boston, Reprinted by John Allen, for Nicholas Boone, 1721.
[2], xxii, 260, [1] p.
Holmes: Increase Mather 124–C[1]; Huntington 59
CSmH mp. 39748

B610 PENNSYLVANIA. LAWS
An act for preventing accidents that may happen by fire. Be it enacted by Sir William Keith, Bart. Governor of Pennsylvania . . . Passed August 26, 1721. [Philadelphia, 1721]
broadside 39 X 31 cm.
PHi mp. 39749

B611 RHODE ISLAND. GOVERNOR, 1698–1727
A vindication of the governour and government . . . [Boston, B. Green, 1721]
12 p. 19.5 cm.
Sabin 99808; New York Public 119
Public Record Office. Photostats: DLC; MHi; MWA; NN; RPJCB mp. 39750

B612 ROGERS, JOHN 1648–1721
An answer to a book intituled, The Lords Day proved to be the Christian Sabbath, &c. by B. Wadsworth . . . Boston, Printed for the author, 1721.
[2], 30 p. 16 cm. A-D[4]
MWA mp. 39751

B613 [SEWALL, SAMUEL] 1652–1730
Connecticut's flood, on Merrymak's ebb . . . Anthropos. Extempore, March 10, 1720, 21. [and] Upon the drying up that ancient river, Merrymak . . . S. S. January 15. 1719,20. [n.p., 1721]
broadside 31 X 39 cm.
Ford 480; New York Public 120; Sabin 98058; Wegelin 357
MHi. Photostats: DLC; MWA; NN mp. 39752

B614 SOME funeral verses occasioned by the death of . . . Mr. Jonathan French . . . who departed this life February the 17th. 1720, 21 . . . [n.p., 1721]
broadside 29 X 26.5 cm.
NHi. Photostats: DLC; MWA; NN mp. 39753

B615 [THACHER, THOMAS] 1620–1678
A brief rule to guide the common people of New-England . . . [at end] I am . . . Thomas Thacher. 21 d. 11 m. 1677–8. [Boston? 1721?]
8 p. 19.5 cm. caption title
Rogers 84
DNLM; MHi (photocopy); MWA (photocopy)
mp. 39754

B616 THESES concerning the Sabbath . . . New-London, Printed and sold by T. Green, 1721.
broadside 30.5 X 21 cm.
CtHi mp. 39755

B617 [WALTER, THOMAS] 1696–1725
The Little-Compton scourge . . . By Zechariah Touchstone . . . Boston, Printed and sold by J. Franklin [1721]
broadside 22.5 X 14.5 cm.
cf. Amer. Art Assoc. cat., Dec. 6–7, 1921
Dated: Little-Compton, Aug. 10. 1721
Ford 469; New York Public 122
DLC. Photograph: MHi; NN; PPAmP mp. 39756

B618 WILLIAMS, JOHN, 1664–1729
Several arguments, proving that the inoculating the small-pox is not contained in the law of physick, either natural or divine . . . The second edition. Boston, J. Franklin, 1721.
[4], 20 p.
Sabin 104243; Austin 2059
MH; MHi. Brit. Museum mp. 39757

B619 [WINTHROP, WAIT STILL] 1643–1717
Some meditations concerning our honourable gentlemen . . . By an unfeigned friend . . . N. London, April 4, 1721.
broadside 32.5 X 20 cm.
New York Public 123; Wegelin 464
Photostats: DLC; MWA; NN mp. 39758

B620 [WISE, JOHN] 1652–1725
The freeholder's address to the Honourable House of Representatives. [Colophon] Boston: Printed by J. Franklin, for B. Gray, over against the Brick Church [1721?]
8 p. 15.5 cm. caption title
Signed at end: P. A. March 15. 1720 [i.e. 1721?]
DLC; MB mp. 39759

1722

B621 An almanack of coelestial motions and aspects, for . . . 1722 . . . By Daniel Travis. New London, T. Green, 1722.
[16] p. 16.5 cm.
At head of title: M D C C X X I I
Trumbull: Supplement 1825; Morrison p. 9
DLC mp. 39776

B622 CALEF, JOHN
A poem on the much-lamented death of Mr. Edmund Titcomb . . . May 26, 1722 . . . [Massachusetts, 1722]
broadside 30 X 19 cm.
Ford 482; Wegelin 50; New York Public 124
NHi. Photostats: DLC; MHi; MWA; NN mp. 39760

B623 FOXCROFT, THOMAS, 1697-1769
The day of a godly man's death . . . Boston, Printed by B. Green, and sold by S. Gerrish, 1722.
[2], ii, 196 p. 17.5 cm.
cf. Evans 2336
MWA; NHi mp. 39763

B624 FRIENDS, SOCIETY OF. BURLINGTON YEARLY MEETING
An epistle from our yearly-meeting . . . held by adjournments from the 15th to the 19th day of the seventh month, 1722 . . . [Philadelphia, A. Bradford, 1722]
4 p. 31 cm. caption title
DLC; MWA; PPAmP; RPJCB. Photostat: NN
mp. 39764

B625 HARVARD UNIVERSITY
Illustrissimo . . . viro, D. Samueli Shute . . . theses hasce . . . MDCCXXII. [Boston, 1722]
broadside 42 X 31 cm.
Ford 485
MWA. Photostat: MHi mp. 39766

B626 HARVARD UNIVERSITY
Quaestiones pro modulo . . . M DCC XXII. [Boston, 1722]
broadside
MH; MWA mp. 39765

B627 [JOSEPHUS, FLAVIUS]
The wonderful, and most deplorable history of the later times of the Jews . . . Boston, Re-printed [. . .] for Nicholas Boone, 1718 [1722?]
[16], 332, [7] p. front. 16 cm.
On verso of last leaf is advertised Morton's *New England's Memorial* (Evans 2266) "sold by Nicholas Boone . . . 1722."
Huntington 61
CSmH (lacks part of imprint) mp. 39767

B628 LARNARD, THOMAS
Advertisement. Stole or stray'd from the house of Mr. Thomas Larnard of Watertown . . . a large bay horse . . . Boston, December 3d. 1722. [Boston, 1722]
broadside 15.5 X 10.5 cm.
MB mp. 39768

B629 LEEDS, 1722. The American almanack for . . . 1722 . . . New York, Printed and sold by William Bradford, 1722.
[24] p. 15.5 cm. [A]-C^4
Guerra b-44; New York Public 126
CP; CSmH. Photostats: CtY; MWA; NN mp. 39769

B630 [LOGAN, JAMES] 1674-1751
[Answer of the Commissioners of Property to the charges laid against them by the Hon. William Keith. Philadelphia, William Bradford, 1722]
3? p. fol.
Title an analytic of the contents of p. 3.–E. Wolf
PPL (final leaf only)

B631 LOGAN, JAMES, 1674-1751
A letter from James Logan . . . to Mouns Justis, with the answer . . . New England, 1722.
4 p. 19 cm.
PHi (2 copies) mp. 39770

B632 MASSACHUSETTS. GOVERNOR, 1716-1722
By His Excellency Samuel Shute . . . A declaration against the Eastern Indians . . . July 25, 1722. Boston, B. Green, 1722.
broadside 43 X 34 cm.
Ford 487
NhHi. Photostat: MHi mp. 39771

B633 MIDDLEBOROUGH, MASS.
The confession of faith & church-covenant; solemnly . . . entered into by the Church of Middleborough, December 26, 1694 . . . [Boston, 1722]
13 p. 17.5 cm.
MHi mp. 39772

B634 NEW JERSEY. GOVERNOR, 1720-1728
His Excellency's speech to the General Assembly of New-Jersey . . . May 5. 1722. [New York, William Bradford, 1722]
broadside 29 X 19 cm.
New York Public 127; cf. Evans 2366
NN mp. 39772

B635 NEW SOUTH CHURCH, BOSTON
To Mr. It appearing to the committee appointed to manage the prudential affairs of the New South Meeting-House . . . Boston, February 5th, 1722 . . . [Boston, 1722]
broadside 13 X 11 cm.
MB; MWA mp. 39779

B636 PENNSYLVANIA. GOVERNOR, 1717-1726
By William Keith, Esq; Governor . . . of Pennsylvania . . . A proclamation. Whereas it has been certified to me, That: Robert Moore . . . hath made his escape out of the gaol . . . of New-York . . . Given at Philadelphia . . . [Nov. 5, 1722] . . . [Philadelphia] Andrew Bradford [1722]
broadside 23 X 13 cm.
PHi mp. 39774

B637 THE result of a Council held at Billingsgate in Eastham, November 8, 1720 . . . [at end] Boston, Tho. Fleet [1722]
56 p. 12 mo
MHi mp. 39761

B638 SINGING of Psalms by seven consituted sounds, opened and explained . . . Composed by a council of divines and musicians . . . [Boston?] 1722.
[2], 14 p. 16 cm. A-B^4
"A recommendation from a divine in England" signed by J. Rowe
MWA mp. 39775

B639 [WEBB, JOHN?]
An essay, to make it evident, that the Christian Sabbath begins, in the morning . . . Boston, 1722.
[2], ii, 18 p. 15.5 cm. [A]-C^4
Signed at end: Philadelphus, Jan. 31st 1721,2.
In mss. on p. ii of RPJCB copy: Author Mr. Webb of Brantrey
MWA; RPJCB mp. 39762

1723

B640 [ARNOLD, RICHARD]
A few lines for your consideration . . . This little book written by Richard Arnold . . . [n.p.] 1723.
27 p. 17 cm. A-C^4 D^2 caption title
MWA mp. 39777

B641 BEEBEE, SAMUEL
A three fold cord, or trebble obligation, to love the Lord Jesus Christ . . . [Boston? 1723?]
broadside
Ford 490; New York Public 128
MHi; NHi. Photostat: NN mp. 39778

B642 THE case of Isaac Taylor and Elisha Gatchel, two officers of Pennsylvania, made prisoners by the government of Maryland . . . Printed at Philadelphia, in the year 1723.
[2] p. 32 X 19.5 cm.
DLC; PHi mp. 39779

B643 THE catechism resolved into an easie and useful method . . . Boston, 1723.
1 p.l., v, 82, [1] p.
MHi mp. 39780

B644 ELLIS, CLEMENT, 1630-1700
Christianity in short: or, The way to be a good Christian . . . Boston, Re-printed in the year 1723.
[2], iv, 62+ p. 13.5 cm. A-B^{12} C^{12}?
MWA (imperfect; all wanting after p. 62) mp. 39781

B645 FRIENDS, SOCIETY OF. PHILADELPHIA YEARLY MEETING
An epistle from our yearly meeting held . . . from the fourteenth to the eighteenth day of the seventh month, 1723 . . . [Colophon] Philadelphia, Andrew Bradford, 1723.
4 p. 31 cm. caption title
DLC; PPAmP; PPL; RPJCB Photostat: NN
mp. 39782

B646 A FUNERAL elegy upon the much lamented death of Daniel Rogers . . . who travelling . . . on Saturday, Decemb. 1, 1722 . . . lost his life; his body was found the 14th of January following . . . and was decently interr'd . . . the 16th, in the 56 year of his age . . . J.P. . . . December 10th, 1722. [Boston, 1723]
broadside 31 X 18 cm.
Ford 492
MB. Photostat: MWA mp. 39783

B647 GERRISH, SAMUEL, d. 1741
Catalogue of choice and valuable books . . . [Boston, 1723]
[4], 48 p.
MHi (1st two leaves imperfect) mp. 39784

B648 GT. BRIT. COURT OF VICE-ADMIRALTY
Tryals of thirty-six persons for piracy . . . Boston, Samuel Kneeland, 1723.
1 p.l., 14 p. 25.5 cm.
RHi. Photostats: DLC; MWA; NN; RPJCB mp. 39785

B649 HARVARD UNIVERSITY
Illustrissimo . . . viro, D. Samueli Shute . . . theses hasce . . . MDCCXXIII. [Boston, 1723]
broadside 43 X 30.5 cm.
MWA. Photostat: MHi mp. 39787

B650 HARVARD UNIVERSITY
Quaestiones pro modulo . . . M DCC XXIII. [Boston, 1723]
broadside
MH; MWA mp. 39786

B651 AN help to devotion . . . [Boston, S. Kneeland? 1723?]
1 p.l., 13 p.
MHi mp. 39788

B652 HENRY, MATTHEW, 1662-1714
The communicant's companion . . . The eighth edition, corrected. Boston, Reprinted by S. Kneeland, for D. Henchman, 1723.
[4], 256, [4] p. 17 cm. A-Y^6
cf. Evans 2433
MHi mp. 39791

B653 HENRY, MATTHEW, 1662-1714
The communicant's companion . . . The eighth edition, corrected. Boston, Reprinted by S. Kneeland, for Eleazer Phillips, at his shop in Charlstown, 1723.
[4], 256, [4] p. 17 cm. A-Y^6
cf. Evans 2433
MWA; NhD mp. 39792

B654 HENRY, MATTHEW, 1662-1714
The communicant's companion . . . The eighth edition, corrected. Boston, Reprinted by S. Kneeland, for John Edwards, 1723.
[4], 256, [4] p. 17 cm. A-Y^6
MWA mp. 39790

B655 HENRY, MATTHEW, 1662-1714
The communicant's companion . . . The eighth edition, corrected. Boston, Reprinted by S. Kneeland, for N. Buttolph, 1723.
[4], 256, [4] p. 17 cm.
cf. Evans 2433
MWA mp. 39789

B656 [KEIMER, SAMUEL]
The tripple-plea . . . Philadelphia, S. Keimer [1723?]
broadside 28.5 X 21.5 cm.
Eight 4-line stanzas.
Huntington 67; New York Public 139
CSmH. Photostat: NN mp. 39793

B657 LAID out for Peter Cock senior, a parcel of land called Quessinawomiuck . . . Recorded the 2d of September, A.D. 1723. A true copy of a record remaining in the Office for Recording of Deeds for . . . Philadelphia, per me, Charles Brockden. [Philadelphia, S. Keimer? 1723?]
broadside 19.5 X 15.5 cm.
PHi mp. 39794

B658 A LETTER of Christian advice . . . referring to the terrible . . . hurricane . . . on August 28, 1722. Written by a friend at a distance. [n.p., 1723?]
29 p. 15.5 cm. caption title
At head of title: December 27. 1722
DLC mp. 39795

B659 MASSACHUSETTS. GOVERNOR, 1722-1728
By the honourable William Dummer, Esq; . . . A proclamation. Whereas within some short time past many fires have broke out . . . Boston the fifteenth day of April, 1723 . . . Boston, B. Green, 1723.
broadside 32 X 21 cm.
Ford 498
M-Ar. Photostat: MHi mp. 39797

B660 MASSACHUSETTS. HOUSE OF REPRESENTATIVES
In the House of Representatives. Whereas a difference has arisen about the resolve for the supply of the treasury . . . Resolved . . . Boston, Bartholomew Green and Samuel Kneeland, 1723.
4 p.
Ford 496
MH; MHi mp. 39796

B661 NEW JERSEY. LAWS
Anno regni Georgii . . . decimo, at a session of the General Assembly of . . . New-Jersey, begun the twenty-fourth day of September . . . 1723, and continued . . . to the 30th day of November . . . at which time the following acts were published. New-York, William Bradford, 1723.
32 p. 27 cm.
Humphrey 7 (appendix)
NHi; Nj. Public Record Off. mp. 39798

B662 TAYLOR, JEREMY, 1613-1667
Contemplations of the state of man . . . The ninth edition. Boston, Printed by T. Fleet for J. Edwards, 1723.
3 p.l., 218 p. 16 cm.
MHi mp. 39799

B663 TAYLOR, JEREMY, 1613-1667
Contemplations of the state of man . . . The ninth edition. Boston, Printed by T. Fleet, for J. Eliot, 1723.
[6], 218 p. 15 cm. A-O^8
MWA mp. 39800

1724

B664 AN almanack for the year . . . 1724 . . . By N. Wittemore [sic] Boston, Printed by J. Allen, for the booksellers, 1724.
[16] p. 15.5 cm.
Drake 3004
MB; MHi; MWA; N; NjMoW mp. 39819

B665 . . . THE American almanack for the year . . . 1724 . . . By Titan Leeds . . . New York, William Bradford, 1724.
[24] p. 16 cm.
At head of title: Leeds, 1724
Morrison p. 74; New York Public 134
CSmH; DLC. Photostat: NN mp. 39810

B666 BIBLE
The Holy Bible in verse. [Boston, John Allen] 1724.
[48+] p. illus. 8.5 cm.
Printed from standing type of the 1717 edition, but reset
Gillett Griffin, Princeton Univ. (1962) mp. 39801

B667 BOSTON FIRE SOCIETY
These presents witness, that we the subscribers . . . do mutually agree to the following articles . . . [Boston, 1724]
broadside 37.5 X 30.5 cm.
Ford 502; New York Public 131
MHi. Photostats: DLC; NN mp. 39802

B668 [CHECKLEY, JOHN] 1680-1754
A discourse shewing who is a true pastor of the Church of Christ . . . [Boston? 1724?]
16 p. 21 cm. caption title
MWA mp. 39804

B669 [DANFORTH, JOHN] 1660-1730
The divine name humbly celebrated, on occasion of the translation to Heaven of . . . Madam Susanna Thacher . . . September 4 . . . 1724 . . . [Boston? 1724]
broadside 30.5 X 21 cm.
In verse
Ford 503; New York Public 132
MHi. Photostats: DLC; MWA; NN; WHi mp. 39805

B670 THE farmer's almanack for . . . 1724 . . . By N. W. . . . Boston, T. Fleet [1724]
[16] p.
Drake 3006
MB

B671 HARVARD UNIVERSITY
Catalogus eorum qui . . . ad annum 1724 alicujus gradus laurea donati sunt. [Boston, 1724]
broadside 36 X 28.5 cm.
Christ Church, Oxford. Photostat: MWA mp. 39806

B672 HARVARD UNIVERSITY
Illustrissimo . . . viro, D. Samueli Shute . . . theses hasce . . . MDCCXXIV. [Boston, 1724]
broadside
Christ Church, Oxford. Photostat: MWA mp 39808

B673 HARVARD UNIVERSITY
Quaestiones pro modulo . . . M DCC XXIV. [Boston, 1724]
broadside 42 X 24 cm
MH; RPJCB mp. 39807

B674 [KING George's health. A sacred ode, on the anniversary of His Majesty's coronation, Octob. 20, 1724. Boston, James Franklin, 1724]
broadside?
Advertised in the *New England Courant*, Oct. 19, 1724, as "Tomorrow will be publish'd, and sold by James Franklin."
Ford 514
No copy known mp. 39809

B675 [LE MERCIER, ANDRÉ] 1692-1763
Some observations upon the French tongue . . . Boston, Printed by B. Green, 1724.
[2], ii, 20 p. 16.5 cm. [A]-C^4
Dedication signed: A.L.M.
MWA mp. 39811

B676 MARYLAND. GENERAL ASSEMBLY
[Address and resolves of the Lower House of Assembly at a session begun . . . the tenth day of October. 1722. Philadelphia? Andrew Bradford? 1724?]

For evidence of printing, see L.H.J. Oct. 13, 1724
Wroth 32
No copy known mp. 39812

B677 MASSACHUSETTS. GOVERNOR, 1722-1728
By the honourable William Dummer, Esq; . . . A proclamation for a general thanksgiving [November 5] . . . October 17, 1724. Boston, B. Green, 1724.
broadside
Ford 509
MBAt mp. 39814

B678 MASSACHUSETTS. LAWS
Province of the Massachusetts-Bay . . . November [1724] . . . The following resolve pass'd . . . Boston, B. Green, 1724.
broadside 33 X 20.5 cm.
Concerns providing soldiers with snowshoes
New York Public 135
NN (photostat) mp. 39813

B679 MASSACHUSETTS. TREASURER
Province of the Massachusetts-Bay, ss. Jeremiah Allen, Esq; Treasurer . . . June 24, 1724. [Boston, 1724]
broadside
Tax warrant
Ford 512
MSaE. Photostat: MWA mp. 39815

B680 [THE New-England diary, a sheet almanack wherein all the twelve months are presented to the view at once. By a Native of New-England [Nathan Bowen]. Boston, J. Franklin, 1724]
broadside
Drake 3010; Ford 513
Advertised in the *New England Courant*, Nov. 23, 1724
No copy known mp. 39803

B681 NEW JERSEY. LAWS
An ordinance for regulating courts of judicature in . . . New-Jersey . . . William Burnet, Esq; in council at Perth Amboy, 23th day of April, 1724 . . . New York, Printed by William Bradford, 1724.

10 p. 32 cm.
Humphrey 11 (appendix)
NHi mp. 39816

B682 NEW YORK. LAWS
. . . An act for settling and regulating the militia in this province . . . [New York, W. Bradford, 1724]
p. 269-72, 147, 268, 265, 146; [4] 1.
No sig. marks
Huntington 69
CSmH mp. 39817

B683 THE rebels reward, or, English courage displayed . . . . . . account of the victory . . . over the Indians at Norridgewock . . . by . . . Capt. Johnson Harmon . . . Boston, Printed and sold by J. Franklin, 1724.
broadside
Ford 515; Wegelin II.77
CSmH mp. 39818

1725

B684 [AUBORN, A. D']
The French convert . . . New-York, J. Peter Zenger, 1725.
156 p. 13 cm.
Attributed also to John McGowan
NHi mp. 39820

B685 BELCHER, JOSEPH, 1669–1723
A copy of a letter, found in the study of the Reverend, Mr. Joseph Belcher . . . [Colophon] Boston, Printed & sold by B. Green, 1725.
4 p. 16 cm.
Also attributed to Joseph Eliot
MWA; NHi mp. 39826

B686 BUNYAN, JOHN, 1628–1688
The heavenly foot-man: or, A description of the man that gets to heaven . . . Boston, Re-printed by J. Allen for N. Boone, 1725.
5 p.l., 58 p. 14 cm.
MB mp. 39822

B687 A CONFERENCE between a parish-priest, and a Quaker . . . Philadelphia, Re-printed by Samuel Keimer, 1725.
34, [6] p. 16.5 cm. A-E^4
Huntington 71
CSmH; MWA mp. 39823

B688 EARLE, JABEZ, 1676–1768
Sacramental exercises . . . Boston, Reprinted by T. Fleet for John Phillips, 1725.
1 p.l., iii, 2–116 p. 13.5 cm.
PHi mp. 39824

B689 EDWARDS, JOHN, 1627–1716
The whole concern of man . . . The second edition, with additions. Boston, Reprinted by S. Kneeland, for J. Edwards, 1725.
1 p.l., iv, [2], 346, 64, [6] p. 15 cm.
DLC; MB; MH; MWA; MiU-C; NhHi; RPJCB mp. 39825

B690 FOLGER, PETER, 1618–1690
A looking glass for the times . . . [n.p.] 1725.
16 p. 15 cm. [A]-B^4
MWA mp. 39827

B691 GERRISH, SAMUEL, d. 1741
A catalogue of curious and valuable books, being the greatest part of the libraries of . . . Mr. Rowland Cotton . . . and Mr. Nathanel Rogers . . . To be sold at auction, in the house of Mr. Francis Holmes . . . on Monday, the fourth day of October, 1725 . . . [Boston, 1725]
1 p.l., 18 p. 17 cm.
McKay 22; New York Public 136
MB. Photostat: NN mp. 39828

B692 HALE, SIR MATTHEW, 1609–1676
A New-Year's gift . . . The sum of religion . . . Boston, Reprinted and sold in Newbury Street, January 1st, 1724. [i.e. 1725]
broadside 33 X 21 cm.
Ford 505; Huntington 72; New York Public 133
CSmH; NN (facsim.) mp. 39829

B693 HARVARD UNIVERSITY
Illustrissimo . . . theses hasce . . . MDCCXXV. [Boston, 1725]
broadside
MHi; MWA; RPJCB mp. 39831

B694 HARVARD UNIVERSITY
Quaestiones pro modulo . . . M DCC XXV. [Boston, 1725]
broadside
MH; MWA mp. 39830

B695 MASSACHUSETTS. GENERAL COURT
At a Great and General Court or Assembly . . . begun & held at Boston . . . May 26th. 1725 . . . [Boston, 1725]
broadside
A resolve concerning the salaries of ministers
Ford & Matthews p. 356
MB mp. 39833

B696 MASSACHUSETTS. LAWS
. . . An act passed by the . . . General Court . . . begun . . . at Boston . . . May, 1725 . . . for apportioning and assessing a tax of twenty thousand pounds . . . [at end] Boston, B. Green, 1725.
4 p.
M-Ar mp. 39832a

B697 MASSACHUSETTS. LAWS
. . . An act passed by the . . . General Court . . . begun . . . at Boston . . . May 1725 . . . for apportioning and assessing a tax of forty eight thousand & nineteen pounds . . . [at end] Boston, B. Green, 1725.
[4] p.
M-Ar mp. 39832b

B698 [MATHER, COTTON] 1662–1728
A monitor for the children of the covenant . . . The second edition. Boston, Printed for S. Gerrish, 1725.
[4], 30+ p. A-B^6 Cl-5
Holmes: Cotton Mather 241-B
MH mp. 39834

B699 [MATHER, COTTON] 1662–1728
Repeated admonitions in a monitory letter, about the maintainance of an able and faithful ministry . . . Boston [T. Fleet?] 1725.
[2], iii, 19 p. 15 cm. A-C^4
Holmes: Cotton Mather 243-B^2
MB; MBAt; MH; ViU mp. 39835

B700 . . . THE New-England diary, or almanack for the year . . . 1725 . . . By a native of New England. [Boston] J. Franklin, 1725.

[16] p. 13 cm.
At head of title: M D C C X X V
Drake 3012; Nichols p. 42
DLC; MB; MWA; NjMoW; PHi; RPJCB mp. 39821

B701 QUICK, JOHN, 1636–1706
The young man's claim unto the sacrament of the Lord's Supper . . . Fourth edition. Boston, Re-printed for S. Gerrish, 1725.
[2], viii, 22 p. 24mo
MHi mp. 39836

B702 SEWALL, SAMUEL, 1652–1730
Early piety . . . Third edition . . . Boston, Printed by S. Kneeland for Samuel Gerrish, 1725.
18 p.
MWA

B703 T., T.
A letter to a friend. [Philadelphia, A. Bradford, 1725?]
broadside (4 p.) 27 × 13.5 cm.
Hildeburn 249
PHi mp. 39832

B704 TO the memory of that faithful minister of Christ, Thomas Lightfoot, who fell asleep in Jesus, November 4. 1725 . . . Philadelphia, Printed for the author, and sold by Samuel Keimer [1725]
broadside 39.5 × 31.5 cm.
In verse
New York Public 138
NHi. Photostats: MWA; NN mp. 39837

B705 [THE voluntier's march; being a full and true account of the bloody fight between Capt. Lovewell's company and the Indians at Pigwoket. An excellent new song. Boston, J. Franklin, 1725]
broadside?
Advertised in the *New England Courant*, May 31, 1725, as "Just publish'd and sold by J. Franklin."
Ford 523
No copy known mp. 39838

1726

B706 AN almanack for the year . . . 1727 . . . By John Hughes, philomat . . . Philadelphia, Printed and sold by Andrew Bradford [1726]
[24] p. 16 cm.
PHi mp. 39849

B707 BIBLE. O.T. PSALMS
The Psalms, hymns, and spiritual songs . . . The twenty-first edition. Boston, Printed by S. Kneeland & T. Green, for J. Phillips, 1726.
[2], 10, 309 p. 13 cm.
NN mp. 39841

B708 BIBLE. O.T. PSALMS
The Psalms, hymns, and spiritual songs . . . The twenty-first edition. Boston, Printed by S. Kneeland & T. Green, for N. Buttolph, 1726.
[2], 309 p. 13 cm. A-N^{12}
cf. Holmes: Minor Mathers 53-R
Music (12 tunes): p. 303–309
ViU mp. 39840

B709 [COLDEN, CADWALLADER] 1688–1726
Het voordeel van het land in de oplegginge Van Tollen . . . Niew-York, J. Peter Zenger [1726]
39 p. 15 cm.
Sabin 100770; New York Public 140
MHi; MWA; RPJCB. Photostats: DLC; NN mp. 39842

B710 COOK, EBENEZER
Mors omnibus communis. An elegy on the death of Thomas Bordley . . . Annapolis, Printed and sold by W. Parks [1726]
broadside 33 × 22 cm.
RPJCB. MWA (reduced facsim.); NN (reduced facsim.) mp. 39843

B711 DOOLITTLE, THOMAS, 1632?–1707
A call to delaying sinners . . . The tenth edition. Boston, Re-printed by S. Kneeland and T. Green, for Daniel Henchman, 1726.
[2], xi, [1], 105, [1] p. 14.5 cm. A-K^6
MWA (imperfect) mp. 39844

B712 FLAVEL, JOHN, 1630?–1691
[A saint indeed; or, The great work of a] Christ[ian] open'd and press'd . . . Boston, Printed by S. Kneeland, & T. Green, for Thomas Hancock, 1726.
[2], xiii, [1], 206, [6] p. 13 cm.
MWA (t.p. mutilated; very imperfect) mp. 39845

B713 GRATTON, JOHN, 1641–1712
John Baptist's decreasing . . . Boston, J. Franklin, 1726.
1 p.l., iv, 52 p. 16 cm.
DLC; MHi; RPJCB mp. 39846

B714 GRATTON, JOHN, 1641–1712
A treatise concerning baptism . . . Boston, James Franklin, 1726.
1 p.l., v, 98 p. 16 cm.
DLC; MHi; RPJCB mp. 39847

B715 GREENWOOD, ISAAC, 1702–1745
A course of philosophical lectures, with a great variety of curious experiments . . . [Boston? 1726?]
4 p.
Karpinski p. 41
MH mp. 39848

B716 HARVARD UNIVERSITY
Illustrissimo . . . theses hasce . . . MDCCXXVI. [Boston, 1726]
broadside
MHi; MWA mp. 39851

B717 HARVARD UNIVERSITY
Quaestiones pro modulo . . . M DCC XXVI. [Boston, 1726]
broadside 41 × 24 cm.
Ford 524; New York Public 142
MWA. Photostats: MHi; NN mp. 39850

B718 LEEDS. The American almanack for the year . . . 1726 . . . By Titan Leeds, Philomat. New-York, Printed and sold by William Bradford, 1726.
[24] p. 16 cm.
Huntington 73; Morrison p. 74; New York Public 137
CSmH; PHi; DLC. Photostats: MHi; NN mp. 39852

B719 LEEDS 1727. The American almanack for . . . 1727 . . . New-York, Printed and sold by William Bradford [1726]
[24] p. 14.5 cm.
New York Public 143
CSmH; PHi. Photostat: NN mp. 39839

B720 MASSACHUSETTS. GENERAL COURT. COMMITTEE FOR RESETTLING NORTH YARMOUTH
Advertisement. Whereas the Committee appointed by the . . . General Court . . . for carrying on . . . the re-setling of . . . North Yarmouth in Casco-Bay . . . Boston November 24th. 1726 . . . John Smith Clerk. [Boston, B. Green? 1726]
broadside 19 X 14 cm.
MB; MWA mp. 39853

B721 MORRIS, LEWIS, 1671–1746
The Chief Justice's speech to the General Assembly . . . of New-York the third of May, 1726. [Colophon] New-York, Printed and sold by William Bradford, 1726.
2 p. 29 cm. caption title
New York Public 144
NN. Photostat: DLC mp. 39854

B722 ROGERS, JOHN, 1674–1753
[A brief] account of some of the late suffering[s] of several Baptists . . . Being also a reply to a small pamphlet lately put out by Joseph Backus . . . By John Rogers . . . [New London? 1726]
29 p. 16.5 cm. A-D^4 (D4 wanting)
MWA (closely trimmed) mp. 39855

B723 TUFTS, JOHN, 1689–1750
An introduction to the singing of psalmtunes . . . The fifth edition. Printed from copper-plates, neatly engraven. Boston, Printed for Samuel Gerrish, 1726.
1 p.l., 9, [1] p. 12 plates (music) 13 cm.
Sabin 97422
MB; PPRF. Photostat: MWA mp. 39856

1727

B724 [ALMANACK for 1728. By William Birkett. New York, W. Bradford, 1727]

Advertised in the *New-York Gazette*, Sept. 4, 1727
Drake 5577
No copy known

B725 CHECKLEY, SAMUEL, 1696–1769
The duty of a people to lay to heart . . . The second edition . . . Boston, Printed for Benj. Gray [1727]
2 p.l., 23, [4] p. 18 cm.
CtW; DLC; MB; MHi; MWA; NN; RPJCB; ViU
mp. 39857

B726 DANFORTH, JOHN, 1660–1730
[A poem on the death of Peter Thacher of Milton and Samuel Danforth of Taunton. Boston? 1727?]
broadside?
Ford 530; Wegelin I.21
No copy known mp. 39858

B727 GT. BRIT. SOVEREIGNS (GEORGE II)
London, June 15, 1727. Yesterday arrived an express . . . London printed: Boston, Reprinted [by Samuel Kneeland], 1727.
2 p. 32 X 21 cm.
Ford 535
DLC mp. 39859

B728 HAMMETT, JOHN, 1680?–1773
A letter from John Hammett to John Wright . . . [Colophon] Newport, J. Franklin, 1727.
8 p. 15 cm.
cf. Evans 2877
RHi. Facsims.: MWA; RPJCB mp. 39860

B729 HARVARD UNIVERSITY
Illustrissimo . . . viro, D. Samueli Shute . . . theses hasce . . . MDCCXXVII. [Boston, 1727]
broadside 43.5 X 31 cm.
MWA. Photostats: MHi; NN mp. 39862

B730 HARVARD UNIVERSITY
Quaestiones pro modulo . . . M DCC XXVII. [Boston, 1727]
broadside
MH; MWA mp. 39861

B731 [HILL, JOHN]
The young secretary's guide . . . The sixth edition. With large . . . additions. By Thomas Hill, Gent. Boston, Reprinted for John Phillips, 1727.
116, [4] p.
Karpinski p. 36
N; NHi; NNC mp. 39863

B732 MARYLAND. GENERAL ASSEMBLY
Proceedings of Assembly, of the province of Maryland, containing the speeches . . . Also several messages, debates . . . Collected . . . by John Beale, and Vachel Denton . . . Annapolis, William Parks, 1727.
[2], 33, [1] p. 28.5 cm.
Wroth 40
MdHi mp. 39864

B733 MARYLAND. LAWS
Laws of Maryland, enacted at a session . . . begun . . . Tuesday the tenth day of October . . . 1727. To which are added . . . Annapolis, William Parks, 1727.
[2], 26 p. 28.5 cm.
"Tuesday" identifies this as a variant
Wroth Addenda 1727
MH-L; MHi; MdBP (imperfect); MdBS (imperfect); N (imperfect); NNS (imperfect) mp. 39865

B734 MASSACHUSETTS. GOVERNOR, 1722–1728
By the honourable William Dummer, Esq; Lieut. Governour . . . A proclamation for apprehending John Pittman . . . Boston, the twenty-fourth day of February, 1726 . . . Boston, B. Green, 1726 [i.e. 1727]
broadside 35.5 X 21 cm.
Ford 536; New York Public 146
MHi. Photostats: DLC; MH; NN mp. 39867

B735 MASSACHUSETTS. LAWS
. . . An act . . . for apportioning and assessing a tax of six thousand pounds . . . [Colophon] Boston, B. Green, 1727.
7 p. 34.5 cm. caption title
DLC; M-Ar mp. 39866

B736 MASSACHUSETTS. TREASURER
Province of the Massachusetts Bay, ss. Jeremiah Allen . . . To constable or collector of the town of Greeting, &c. By virtue . . . Given under my hand and seal at Boston, the fifth day of December, 1727 . . . [Boston, 1727]
broadside 29.5 X 18.5 cm.
Ford 540; New York Public 147
NHi; RPJCB. Photostats: DLC; MHi; NN mp. 39868

B737 MASSACHUSETTS. TREASURER
Province of the Massachusetts-Bay, ss. Jeremiah Allen . . . To the select-men or assessors of the town or district of Greeting, &c. In observance of an act . . . Boston, the eighteenth day of October, 1727 . . .[Boston, 1717]
broadside 31 X 19 cm.
NHi mp. 39869

B738 [PARKS, WILLIAM] d. 1750
Advertisement to the reader. In the 237th page of this volume, there is printed by mistake . . . An act for limitation of trespass . . . Annapolis, William Parks, 1727.
broadside 9.5 X 9.5 cm.
Wroth 36a
MdBP; MdHi mp. 39870

B739 PENNSYLVANIA. GENERAL ASSEMBLY
To the right honourable the Lords Commissioners for Trade and Plantations. [Philadelphia, W. Bradford, 1727]
p. 17–19. fol.
Apparently printed during the adjournment of the Assembly, and cancelled when text was included as part of Votes for Apr. 29, 1727.–E. Wolf
PHi

B740 PHILLIPS, CALEB
[New method of shorthand. Boston, 1727]

Advertised in the *Boston News Letter*, Dec. 14, 1727, as "given to the public already in printed papers dispers'd about the town and may be had at . . . Francis Miller's."
No copy known mp. 39871

B741 [SCOUGAL, HENRY] 1650–1678.
The life of God in the soul of man . . . With a preface, by Gilbert Burnet . . . [n.p.] 1727.
[10?], 106, [4] p. 14 cm. $[A]^{12}$ $B\text{-}E^{12}$
MWA (very imperfect) mp. 39872

B742 SERMONS on the death of the Reverend Mr. Waldron. [Boston, Printed for S. Gerrish, S. Kneeland, N. Belknap, and B. Love, 1727]
1 v. 18 cm.
Half-title; volume contains Evans 2848, 2872, 2912, 2971, with half-title added
MWA; RPJCB mp. 39873

B743 [SEWALL, SAMUEL] 1652–1730
In remembrance of Mr. Samuel Hirst . . . died very suddenly . . . January 14, 1726,7. [Boston, 1727]
broadside 14 X 9 cm.
Ford 542; New York Public 148
DLC; MB; MHi. Photostat: NN mp. 39874

B744 TALBOT, ROBERT
A Catalogue of medicines sold by Mr. Robert Talbot at Burlington. [Burlington? Samuel Keimer, 1727?]
broadside
Dated from type and watermarked paper used by Keimer for N. J. Laws printed at Burlington in 1728. cf. Nelson sale cat. (1915)
Humphrey la
NjHi mp. 39875

1728

B745 ADVERTISEMENT. These may certify whom it may concern, that the General Assembly . . . at their session begun . . . the 29th of May 1728, pass'd a resolve for granting lands to soldiers in the Narragansett war. [Boston? 1728]
broadside
Ford 543
M-Ar. Photostat: MHi mp. 39876

B746 [AN almanack for the year 1729 . . . By John Warner . . . Annapolis, William Parks, 1728]

Advertised in the *Maryland Gazette*, Dec. 17, 1728, as "Lately published."
Wroth 48
No copy known mp. 39899

B747 THE ardent desire, and sincere cry, of a true believer . . . Newport, Printed by J. Franklin, for Reuben Packcom, 1728.
broadside 18 X 13.5 cm.
Alden 5
MHi; RHi. Photostat: MWA mp. 39877

B748 BAXTER, RICHARD, 1615–1691
Monthly preparations for the Holy Communion . . . The third edition corrected. Boston, Printed for D. Henchman, 1728.
[8], 166+ p. 14.5 cm. $A\text{-}O^{6}$ $P^{6?}$
MWA (all wanting beyond sig. P3) mp. 39878

B749 [BRADFORD, WILLIAM] 1653–1752
The secretary's guide, or Young man's companion . . . The fourth edition . . . Printed and sold by Andrew Bradford in Philadelphia, 1728.
[10], 192 p.
cf. Evans 2997
CSmH (p. 191–92 wanting)

B750 COOLE, BENJAMIN, d. 1717
Christ the mighty helper of poor helpless man . . . Boston, 1728.
[2], 21 p. 15.5 cm. $[A]\text{-}C^{4}$
MWA; MiU-C mp. 39879

B751 A COVENANT for reformation. Assented in Long-Meadow, in Springfield, August 22d 1728. [Boston, 1728]
broadside 35 X 23 cm.
Ford 545
CtHi; DLC mp. 39880

B752 DULANY, DANIEL, 1685–1753
The right of thf [sic] inhabitants of Maryland, to thf [sic] benefit of the English laws . . . Annapolis, W. Parks, 1728.
4, 31, [1] p. 21 cm.
Wroth 42
MdHi mp. 39881

B753 HART, JOHN, 1682?–1731
The nature and blessedness of trusting in God. A sermon preached . . . May 21, 1727. Occasioned by the death of Mrs. Hannah Meigs, Daughter to Capt. Janna Meigs, who died . . . in the twenty-second year of her age . . . N. London, Printed and sold by T. Green, 1728.
54 p. 14.5 cm.
Trumbull: Supplement 2234
CtHi mp. 39882

B754 HARVARD UNIVERSITY
Honoratissimo . . . theses hasce . . . MDCCXXVIII. [Boston, 1728]
broadside 44 X 34 cm.
CtY; MHi mp. 39884

B755 HARVARD UNIVERSITY
Quaestiones pro modulo . . . M DCC XXVIII. [Boston, 1728]
broadside
MH; MWA mp. 39883

B756 JANEWAY, JAMES, 1636–1674
A token for children . . . Boston, Printed for John Phillips, 1728.

xii, 116 p. 14 cm.
cf. Evans 3042
MWA (mutilated) mp. 39885

B757 MARYLAND. GENERAL ASSEMBLY
To his Excellency Benedict Leonard Calvert . . . the humble address of the Upper House . . . [Annapolis, William Parks, 1728]
[2] p. 31 X 18.5 cm.
Addresses of session Oct. 3-Nov. 2, 1728
Wroth 45
Md mp. 39886

B758 MARYLAND. GENERAL ASSEMBLY
Votes and resolves, of the Lower House . . . [Oct. 3-Nov. 2, 1728] [Annapolis, William Parks, 1728]
[52] p. 31.5 cm.
Wroth 46
Md mp. 39887

B759 MARYLAND. LAWS
Laws of Maryland, enacted . . . 1728 . . . Annapolis, William Parks, 1728.
1 p.l., 30 p. 31 cm.
Huntington 82; Wroth 44
CSmH; DLC; MH; MH-L; MdBP; MdHi; NN (imperfect); NNB; PPL mp. 39888

B760 MASSACHUSETTS
To the selectmen of the town of These are to notifie, that you may proceed to assemble the freeholders . . . Boston, March 1727.8. [Boston, 1728]
broadside 9.5 X 15.5 cm.
MHi mp. 39889

B761 MASSACHUSETTS. GENERAL COURT
The Committee of the General Court appointed the 21st day of February last, to receive and consider any scheme or projection, for retrieving the value of the bills of credit . . . proposed . . . 180,000 Pounds in bills of credit . . . be emitted . . . [41 lines] . . . Per order of the Committee, Nathanael Byfield. Boston, March 15, 1727,8. [Boston, 1728]
broadside 38 X 24 cm.
cf. Ford 555
Cedric L. Robinson, Windsor, Conn. (1965)

B762 MASSACHUSETTS. GOVERNOR, 1722–1728
By the honourable William Dummer . . . A proclamation for a general fast [Mar. 21, 1728] . . . Feb. 22, 1727. Boston, B. Green, 1728.
broadside
Ford 547
MB; MHi mp. 39892

B763 MASSACHUSETTS. GOVERNOR, 1722–1728
. . . By the honourable William Dummer . . . A proclamation for apprehending Henry Phillips . . . [Boston, 1728]
broadside
Dated July 4, 1728
MHi mp. 39893

B764 MASSACHUSETTS. GOVERNOR, 1728–1730
By His Excellency William Burnet, Esq; . . . A proclamation for a general thanksgiving [Nov. 7, 1728] . . . October 15, 1728. Boston, B. Green, 1728.
broadside
Ford 549
MBAt mp. 39890

B765 MASSACHUSETTS. LAWS
. . . An act . . . for apportioning and assessing a tax of eight thousand pounds . . . [Colophon] Boston, B. Green, 1728.
5 [i.e. 7] p. 35 cm. caption title
Paged: 1, 2, 2, 3, 3, 4, 5
DLC; M-Ar (imperfect); MHi mp. 39891

B766 MR. Samuel Gorton's ghost . . . Newport, James Franklin, 1728.
broadside 39 X 31 cm.
Alden 7
MWA; RHi. Photostat: RNHi. mp. 39894

B767 NASH, JOSEPH
An elegy occasioned by the death of the much lamented Doct. Thomas Hastings of Hatfield . . . April 14th, 1728, aged 48 years . . . Josephus Nash. [n.p., 1728]
broadside 37.5 X 22.5 cm.
MB. Photostat: MWA mp. 39895

B768 NEW JERSEY. LAWS
An ordinance for regulating courts of judicature in the province of New-Jersey. [New York, W. Bradford, 1728]
5 p. 32 cm.
Dated Feb. 10, 1728
New York Public 151
NHi. Photostat: NN mp. 39896

B769 SALUS populi . . . [Boston? 1728?]
broadside 31.5 X 17.5 cm.
Ford 556; New York Public 152
WHi. Photostats: MHi; NN mp. 39897

B770 TUFTS, JOHN, 1689-1750
An introduction to the singing of Psalm-tunes . . . Seventh edition. Boston, Gerrish, 1728.
[2], 9, [1] p. 12 plates. 13 cm.
CtY; MWA mp. 39898

B771 WESTMINSTER ASSEMBLY OF DIVINES
The shorter catechism . . . Boston, Printed by Gamaliel Rogers, for Daniel Henchman, 1728.
[2], 46 p. sm. 8vo
Huntington 83
CSmH mp. 39900

B772 WHITE, DANIEL
The true reasons for Mr. Daniel White and Mr. Thomas Byles disposing of their interest . . . Newport, J. Franklin, 1728.
broadside 31 X 20 cm.
Alden 9
RHi mp. 39901

B773 YALE UNIVERSITY
Praeclarissimo summisque ingenii dotibus decorato . . . Josepho Tallcott . . . Theses technologicae . . . theses logicae . . . theses mathematicae . . . Novi-Porti . . . die undecimo Septembris, MDCCXXVIII. Novi-Londini, Timotheus Green [1728]
broadside 43 X 33 cm.
MWA mp. 39902

1729

B774 AN almanack or diary, for the year . . . 1729 . . . By Nathaniel Whittemore. Boston, Printed for N. Boone, 1729.

[16] p.
Drake 3026
MB

B775 THE American almanack for the year . . . 1730 . . . By Titan Leeds . . . [New York, W. Bradford, 1729]
[24] p. 16 cm.
Huntington 84; Morrison p. 74; Wall p. 8
CSmH; DLC; PHi mp. 39915

B776 BEISSEL, JOHANN CONRAD, 1690-1768
Mysterion anomias: the mystery of lawlessness . . . By Cunrad Beysell. Translated out of the High-Dutch, by M. W. [Philadelphia, Andrew Bradford] 1729.
32 p. 21 cm.
Metzger 18
PHi (facsim.) mp. 39903

B777 BIBLE
The Holy Bible in verse . . . [Boston? T. Fleet?] 1729.
[62] p. illus. 9.5 cm.
By Benjamin Harris
Imprint assigned by d'Alté A. Welch on evidence from cuts
CtHi; MWA mp. 39904

B778 BIBLE. O.T. PSALMS.
The Psalms, hymns, and spiritual songs . . . The twenty-second edition. [Bos] ton, Printed for T. Green at New-London, 1729.
1 p.l., 309 p. 13 cm. A-N^{12}
cf. Evans 3134; Holmes: Minor Mathers 53-S
MB (p. 309 wanting; t.p. slightly mutilated); MHi mp. 39905

B779 BOSTON WEEKLY NEWS-LETTER
Postscript to the *Boston Weekly News-Letter.* Numb. 118. Thursday April 3d, 1729. The speech of . . . William Burnett . . . to the . . . General Court . . . met at Salem . . . April 2d, 1729. Boston, Printed and sold by B. Green, 1729.
broadside
Ford 564
MHi

B780 [DUNBAR, DAVID]
Boston, December 2, 1729. Whereas an act of Parliament . . . for the better preservation of His Majestys woods . . . [Boston, 1729]
broadside
Authorship based on ms. annotation in hand of W. C. Ford
Public Record Off. Photostat: MHi mp. 39906

B781 EARLE, JABEZ, 1767?-1768
Sacramental exercises . . . The fifth edition . . . Boston, Re-printed for D. Henchman, 1729.
[4], 92 p. 13.5 cm. A-H^6
MWA mp. 39909

B782 EARLE, JABEZ, 1676?-1768
Sacramental exercises . . . The fifth edition . . . Boston, Re-printed for N. Belknap, 1729.
[4], 92 p. 13.5 cm. A-H^6
MWA; N (imperfect) mp. 39907

B783 EARLE, JABEZ, 1676?-1768
Sacramental exercises . . . The fifth edition . . . Boston, Re-printed for S. Kneeland, 1729.
[4], 92 p. 13.5 cm. A-H^6
MWA mp. 39910

B784 EARLE, JABEZ, 1676?-1768
Sacramental exercises . . . The fifth edition . . . Boston, Re-printed for T. Hancock, 1729.
[4], 92 p. 13.5 cm. A-H^6
MWA mp. 39908

B785 FLAVEL, JOHN, 1630?-1691.
Sacramental meditations . . . Boston, Reprinted for N. Boone, 1729.
[8], 198 p. 13.5 cm. A-R^6 S^2
Sig. A1 blank
MB; MWA mp. 39911

B786 FRIENDS, SOCIETY OF. PHILADELPHIA YEARLY MEETING
An epistle from our yearly meeting held in Philadelphia . . . from the 20th, to the 24th of the 7th month, 1729 . . . [Colophon] Philadelphia, Andrew Bradford, 1729.
3 p. 32 cm. caption title
NHi; PHi; PPAmP; PPL mp. 39912

B787 HARVARD UNIVERSITY
Illustrissimo . . . theses hasce . . . MDCCXXIX. [Boston, 1729]
broadside
CtY mp. 39914

B788 HARVARD UNIVERSITY
Quaestiones pro modulo . . . M DCC XXIX. [Boston, 1729]
broadside
MH mp. 39913

B789 A LETTER from one in the country to his friend in Boston. [Boston, 1729]
[4] p. 30.5 cm.
MHi (photostat) mp. 39918

B790 MARYLAND. GENERAL ASSEMBLY
To His Excellency Benedict Leonard Calvert . . . the humble address of the Upper House . . . [Annapolis, William Parks, 1729]
[2] p. 30 cm.
Wroth 53
NN mp. 39919

B791 MARYLAND. LAWS
Laws of Maryland, enacted at a session . . . begun . . . the tenth day of July . . . 1729 . . . Annapolis, William Parks, 1729.
[2], 37, [1] p. 29 cm.
Huntington 85; Wroth 52
CSmH; DLC; MH; MH-L; Md; MdBP; MdBS; MdHi. Brit. Mus. mp. 39920

B792 MASSACHUSETTS. LAWS
In the House of Representatives, December 20, 1729. A bill entitled, An act for retrieving & ascertaining the value of the bills of credit . . . Boston, Thomas Fleet, 1729.
6 p.
Public Record Off. Photostat: MHi mp. 39921

B793 MASSACHUSETTS. TREASURER
Province of the Massachusetts-Bay, ss. Jeremiah Allen, Esq; Treasurer . . . To constable or collector of the town of Greeting . . . Given . . . at Boston, the eleventh day of November, 1729 . . . [Boston, 1729]
broadside 31.5 X 19 cm.
Ford 567
MB; MWA mp. 39922

B794 NASH, JOSEPH
An elegy upon the much lamented decease of . . . Mr. Solomon Stoddard . . . February 11th . . . 1729 . . . [Boston? 1729]
broadside 32 X 21.5 cm.
MB. Photostats: MHi; MWA mp. 39923

B795 NEW YORK. LAWS
. . . An act for the better clearing . . . high-roads in the city & county of Albany. [New York, W. Bradford, 1729]
p. 401-407. 32 cm. caption title
Hasse 407
DLC mp. 39924

B796 [A PRIMER, containing a most easy way to attain . . . In a catechism compiled by the Assembly of Divines . . . Annapolis? William Parks? 1729?]

Advertised July 1, 1729, as "just publish'd."
Wroth 56
No copy known mp. 39925

B797 [A PRIMER or catechism, set forth agreeable to the Book of Common-prayer . . . Annapolis? William Parks? 1729?]

Advertised July 1, 1729, as "just publish'd."
Wroth 57
No copy known mp. 39926

B798 PRINCE, THOMAS, 1687-1758
Boston, Feb. 20, 1728/9. Reverend Sir, The New England Chronology staying for the remarkables of your place . . . [Boston, 1729]
broadside
MHi mp. 39928

B799 PRINCE, THOMAS, 1687-1758
Boston, April 10, 1729. Reverend sir . . . You are . . . earnestly desired to send your communications . . . The composer Thomas Prince. [Boston, 1729]
broadside 27.5 X 18 cm.
Ford 568
NHi. Facsims.: DLC; MHi; MWA; NN mp. 39927

B800 RHODE ISLAND. LAWS
[An act relating to the small pox . . . Newport, J. Frank J. Franklin, 1729]

A bill under the year 1729 in the R. I. Archives lists the item "To Franklin James for printing of smallpox acts . . .
Alden 12
No copy known mp. 39930

B801 SPIEGEL der Vollkommenheit, worinnen gezeiget wird, wie der Mensch . . . Philadelphia, 1729.
[2], 252 p. 16 cm.
European printing?
Metzger 20
P mp. 39931

B802 STODDARD, SOLOMON, 1643-1729
Some theological conclusions drop'd from the mouth of . . . Solomon Stoddard, gather'd up by an hearer, and . . . here transmitted . . . [Boston? 1729?]
broadside 33.5 X 20.5 cm.
Ford 574
MWA mp. 39932

B803 TITAN'S new almanack for . . . 1729 . . . [New York] Printed and sold by William Bradford, 1729.
[28] p. 17 cm. [A]-[C]^4, D^2
Guerra b-53; New York Public 153; Wall p. 8
DLC; NN (leaves 2-3, 5-6 wanting) mp. 39916

B804 A TOKEN for youth . . . The twenty-fifth edition . . . Boston, Reprinted & sold [by B. Green] at the Printing-house in Newbury-Street, 1729.
[1], iii, 32 p. 15.5 cm. A-C^6
Probably by James Janeway (MWA)
MWA (last leaf wanting) mp. 39929

B805 [THE weeks preparation . . . (Also) The Church of England-man's private devotions . . . Annapolis, W. Parks, 1729]

Advertised May 6, 1729, as "This week will be published."
Wroth 59
No copy known mp. 39933

B806 W[ELFARE], M[ICHAEL]
The naked truth, standing against all painted and disguised lies . . . Or the Lord's seventh-day-Sabbath standing as a mountain immoveable . . . By M. W. [Philadelphia, Andrew Bradford] 1729.
10 p. 21 cm.
Metzger 22
PHi (facsim.) mp. 39934

B807 A WORD or two more from the obscure and remote person; to the late letter-writer in Boston . . . April 7th, 1729. [Boston, 1729]
[2] p.
In ms., "Given me April 16th."
Ford 573
MBAt. Photostat: MHi mp. 39935

173–

B808 AN awakening call to the children of New-England; occasioned by the grievous and mortal sickness that prevails in many parts of this land, whereby great numbers of children . . . have been carried to their long home . . . Boston, Printed and sold at the Heart and Crown in Cornhill [173-?]
broadside 32.5 X 21 cm.
Dr. Josiah C. Trent, Durham, N.C. (1945). MWA (reduced facsim.) mp. 39936

B809 [GREENWOOD, ISAAC] 1702-1745
A course of mathematical lectures and experiments. [Boston, 173-?]
2 leaves. 21 cm.
Identification by L. C. Karpinski; dated by him 1735 or earlier
MiU-C mp. 39937

B810 MASSACHUSETTS
Oaths appointed to be taken instead of the oaths of allegiance & supremacy: and Declaration . . . [Boston, 173-?]
broadside ([2] l.)
Dated in ms.: February 7, 1732
Ford 635
M-Ar. Photostat: MHi mp. 39938

1730

B811 [APPLETON, NATHANIEL] 1693-1784
The Christian's daily practice of piety . . . Boston, Reprinted for John Pemberton, 1730.
8 p. 14 cm.
MWA; NHi; RPJCB mp. 39939

B812 BARBADOS. GENERAL ASSEMBLY
Extract from the votes and proceedings of the . . . Assembly for the island of Barbados. At a meeting . . . the eighteenth day of December 1730 . . . [n.p., 1730?]
8 p. 18.5 cm.
MHi mp. 39940

B813 BEVERIDGE, WILLIAM, 1637-1708
[Private thoughts upon religion. Boston? 1730?]
[20?], 212 p. 16 cm. [A]$^{8?}$ B-O^{8} P^{4}
MWA (t.p. and all matter up to sig. B wanting)
mp. 39941

B814 BIBLE. O.T. PSALMS
The New England Psalter: or Psalms of David . . . Boston, Printed for Thomas Hancock, 1730.
1 p.l., [189] p. 16.5 cm. [A]-M^{8}
RPJCB mp. 39942

B815 BIBLE. O.T. PSALMS
The Psalter or Psalms of David . . . Philadelphia, Printed and sold by Andrew Bradford [1730]
[138] p. 18 cm.
PHi mp. 39943

B816 BOSTON
Boston, N. E., April 1730. Receipt for pew in the South New Brick Meeting House in Marlborough Street . . . [Boston, 1730]
broadside
MHi

B817 A CONFESSION of faith, set forth by many of those Baptists, who own the doctrine of universal redemption. [Colophon] Newport, J. Franklin [1730?]
16 p. 17 cm.
Alden 16
RHi mp. 39944

B818 FLAVEL, JOHN, 1630-1691
A token for mourners . . . Boston, Reprinted by S. Kneeland, and T. Green, 1730.
[10], 134 p. 14 cm. A-M^{6}
MWA; RPJCB mp. 39945

B819 GOOKIN, SAMUEL
Advertisement. Stoln [!] out of the house of Mr. Samuel Gookin of Cambridge, December 7, 1730. [Boston, 1730]
broadside 18 X 12 cm.
PPRF mp. 39946

B820 GT. BRIT. SOVEREIGNS (GEORGE II)
By the King, a proclamation, requiring passes . . . to be returned . . . Boston, B. Green, 1730.
broadside 43 X 33.5 cm.
DLC mp. 39947

B821 HARRISON, FRANCIS
The English and Low-Dutch school-master . . . New-York: Printed and sold by W. Bradford, 1730.
4 p.l., 144 p. 15.5 cm.
Added t.p. in Dutch
NHi; PPRF mp. 39948

B822 HARVARD UNIVERSITY
Quaestiones pro modulo . . . M DCC XXX. [Boston, 1730]
broadside
MH; MWA mp. 39949

B823 HENDERSON, JACOB, 1681-1751
The case of the clergy of Maryland. [Annapolis? William Parks? 1730?]
8 p. 23 cm.
Wroth 62
RPJCB. Photostat: MHi mp. 39950

B824 LEFEVER, MYNDERT
New-York, October 10. 1730. Advertisement, On the second day of November next . . . at publick vendue . . . the plantation . . . of Myndert Lefever . . . [New York, 1730]
broadside 20 X 16 cm.
New York Public 155
MHi. Photostat: NN mp. 39951

B825 A LETTER from one in Boston, to his friend in the country. [Boston, 1730]
[2] p.
In ms., "This half sheet came out March 31st, 1729." It is a reply to the "Second letter from One in the Country."
Ford 572
MBAt. Photostat: MHi mp. 39917

B826 MARYLAND. LAWS
Laws of Maryland, enacted . . . 1730 . . . Annapolis, William Parks, 1730.
1 p.l., 45, [1] p. 31 cm.
Huntington 88; Wroth 62
CSmH; DLC; MH; MH-L; Md; MdBP; MdHi; N; NNB
mp. 39952

B827 MASSACHUSETTS. GOVERNOR, 1728-1730
By the honourable William Dummer, Esq; Lieut. Governour . . . A proclamation for proroguing the General Assembly . . . Given . . . in Boston the twenty-fifth day of February 1729 . . . Boston, B. Green, 1729. [i.e. 1730]
broadside 32 X 20.5 cm.
Ford 582
MHi (photostat); MWA mp. 39956

B828 MASSACHUSETTS. GOVERNOR, 1730-1741
By his excellency Johathan Belcher . . . a proclamation. to prevent the destruction or spoil of His Majesty's woods . . . Boston, B. Green, 1730.
broadside
Public Record Off. Photostat: MHi mp. 39954

B829 MASSACHUSETTS. GOVERNOR, 1730-1741
By his excellency Johathan Belcher . . . a proclamation. Whereas a treaty of peace . . . Boston, B. Green, 1730.
broadside 42 X 33 cm.
DLC mp. 39953

B830 MASSACHUSETTS. GOVERNOR, 1730-1741
By his excellency Jonathan Belcher . . . a proclamation. Whereas His majesty . . . [Dec. 29, 1730] . . . Boston, B. Green, 1730.
broadside 35.5 X 23.5 cm.
DLC mp. 39955

B831 MASSACHUSETTS. TREASURER
Province of the Massachusetts-Bay, ss. Jeremiah Allen, Esq; Treasurer . . . To the sheriff of the County of

. . . Given . . . at Boston this day of 173
[Boston, 1730?]
broadside 30.5 X 18.5 cm.
Filled in for March 22, 1731
MHi

B832 M[ATHER], S[AMUEL] 1706-1785
A country treat upon the second paragraph in His Excellency's speech, Decemb. 17. 1730. [Boston, 1730?]
broadside 32.5 X 17 cm.
Ford 588; Holmes: Minor Mathers 64; New York Public 156; Wegelin 253
NHi. Photostats: DLC; MHi; NN mp. 39957

B833 Deleted.

B834 PENNSYLVANIA. LAWS
At a General Assembly . . . begun . . . October . . . 1729 . . . And from thence continued . . . to the twelvth of January, 1729. Being the second session . . . Philadelphia, Printed and sold by B. Franklin and H. Meredith, 1730.
6 p., 1 l. 32.5 cm.
Separate printing of An act for the better enabling divers inhabitants . . . to hold lands . . .
Adams: Pennsylvania 3; Curtis 13; New York Public 157
PU. Photostat: NN mp. 39958

B835 A PERPETUAL almanack: shewing, the prime, epact, cycle of the sun . . . Newport, Printed by James Franklin, and sold by the author [1730?]
broadside 34.5 X 26 cm.
Alden 14
RHi. Photostats: MHi; MWA; NN mp. 39959

B836 WA[TER baptism,] as it is [practised by the professors of Christianity, proved to be the invention of men. New-York, John Peter Zenger, ca. 1730]
66, [1] p. 4to
Unquestionably Zenger's type; date approximate.— E. Wolf
PHi (lacking all but upper corner of t.p.)

B837 WATTS, ISAAC, 1674-1748
Divine songs attempted in easy language . . . The seventh edition. Boston, Printed by S. Kneeland and T. Green, for D. Henchman, 1730.
[2], iv, 42 p. 13.5 cm.
MWA mp. 39960

B838 WATTS, ISAAC, 1674-1748
To his excellency Jonathan Belcher, esq; in London, appointed by . . . George II. to the government of New-England and now returning home . . . [Colophon] Boston: printed for J. Phillips and T. Hancock. 1730.
iii p.
Advertised in the *Weekly News-Letter*, June 18, 1730
Nat. Lib. of Scotland

1731

B839 BARCKLEY, SIR RICHARD, 1578?-1661
The felicity of man: or, His summum bonum . . . Collected from the historical works of Richard Barkcley [sic] . . . Newport, Printed and sold by J. Franklin, 1731.
[4], 87 p. 15 cm. [A]-M^4 ([A]1-2 blank)
E. A. Frick, Lupton, Arizona (1956) Photostat (t.p. only): MWA mp. 39962

B840 CONGREGATIONAL CHURCHES IN MASSACHUSETTS. CAMBRIDGE SYNOD, 1648
A platform of church-discipline . . . Boston, Printed for D. Henchman, 1731.
xv, 36, [3] p.
Huntington 89; cf. Evans 3401
CSmH mp. 39963

B841 FRELINGHUYSEN, THEODORUS JACOBUS, 1691-1747
A clear demonstration of a righteous and ungodly man . . . New-York, John Peter Zenger, 1731.
1 p.l., ix, [1], 156 p., 1 l. 15.5 cm.
New York Public 159
MWA; NjR. Photostat: NN (p. 31-32, 96-97, 111-112 wanting) mp. 39964

B842 THE genuine Leeds almanack. The American almanack for the year . . . 1732 . . . By Titan Leeds . . . Philadelphia, Andrew Bradford [1731]
[24] p. sm. 8vo
Drake 9551; Huntington 90
CSmH; NN; PDoBHi; PHi mp. 39961

B843 GT. BRIT. SOVEREIGNS (GEORGE II)
South Carolina, George the Second . . . To all to whom these presents shall come Greeting. Know ye, that We . . . do give and grant . . . [37 lines] [Charleston, S.C., Thomas Whitmarsh? 1731?]
broadside 29.5 X 19.5 cm.
Form for the grant of land
Typography similar to Whitmarsh broadside of Nov. 27, 1731
McMurtrie: South Carolina 1731-1740, no. 4
Public Record Off. mp. 39965

B844 HARVARD UNIVERSITY
Quaestiones pro modulo . . . M DCC XXXI. [Boston, 1731]
broadside
MH; MWA mp. 39966

B845 HENRY, MATTHEW, 1662-1714
The communicant's companion: or, Instructions and helps for . . . the Lord's Supper . . . The tenth edition, corrected. Boston, Re-printed for J. Phillips, 1731.
[4], 280, [4] p. 16.5 cm. A-S^8
cf. Evans 3429
MWA mp. 39967

B846 HENRY, MATTHEW, 1662-1714
The communicant's companion . . . The tenth edition, corrected. Boston, Reprinted for N. Procter, 1731.
[4], 280, [4] p. front. (port.) 16.5 cm. A-S^8
cf. Evans 3429
RPJCB mp. 39968

B847 JENKS, WILLIAM
The arguments of . . . William Jenks Esq; and Mr. John Walton . . . against the . . . irregular proceedings of . . . the

Massachusetts-Bay . . . [Colophon] Newport, J. Franklin, 1731.
4 p. 26.5 X 16 cm.
Alden 22
Public Record Off. Photostats: MWA; RHi mp. 39969

B848 LEEDS, 1731. The American almanack for . . . 1731 . . . By Titan Leeds, Philomat. [New York] Printed [by William Bradford] for and sold by Daniel Ayrault and Edward Nearegreas at Newport, 1731.
[24] p.
Wall p. 8
MWA; NHi (imperfect). Roderick Terry, Newport, R.I. (1921) mp. 39970

B849 LEFEVER, MYNDERT
New-York, April 10, 1731. Advertisement, On the second Wednesday of May next . . . at publick vendue . . . the plantation . . . of Myndert Lefever . . . [New York, 1731]
broadside 20 X 17 cm.
New York Public 161
NHi. Photostat: NN mp. 39971

B850 MARYLAND. LAWS
Laws of Maryland, enacted . . . 1731 . . . Annapolis, William Parks, 1731.
1 p.l., 6 p. 31 cm.
Huntington 91; Wroth 71
CSmH; DLC; MH; MH-L; Md; MdBP; MdHi; N; NNB. Brit. Mus. mp. 39972

B851 MARYLAND. LAWS
Laws of Maryland, enacted at a session . . . begun . . . the nineteenth day of August . . . 1731. By authority. Annapolis, William Parks, 1731.
27 p. 31.5 cm.
Huntington 92; Wroth 72
CSmH; DLC; MH; MH-L; Md; MdBB; MdHi; NNB
mp. 39973

B852 MARYLAND GAZETTE (1730/31-1731)
Continued at least through March 1730/31
Wroth 74
No issues known

B853 MASSACHUSETTS. GOVERNOR, 1730-1741
By His Excellency Jonathan Belcher . . . A proclamation [on piracy] . . . April 6, 1731. Boston, B. Green, 1731.
broadside 38.5 X 27.5 cm.
Ford 593; New York Public 162
DLC. Photostat: NN mp. 39974

B854 NEW YORK (CITY) ORDINANCES
City of New-York, ss. A law for regulating Negroes and slaves in the night time. [New York, William Bradford, 1731]
broadside 29 X 19 cm.
Dated April 22, 1731
New York Public 163
NN mp. 39975

B855 Deleted.

B856 A SHORT treatise of the virtues of Dr. Bateman's pectoral drops . . . To be sold only by James Wallace, in New-York, Reprinted by J. Peter Zenger [1731]
4, 36 p. 16.5 cm.
"An abstract of the patent granted . . . the inventor of . . . Dr. Bateman's Pectoral Drops . . . reprinted by John Peter Zenger in New-York, 1731." 4 p. preceding text
New York Public 164; Austin 4
NNNAM. Photostat: NN mp. 39981

B857 SOUTH CAROLINA. AUDITOR GENERAL's OFFICE.
Charlestown, South-Carolina . . . This is . . . to give notice notice, that James St. John . . . auditor general . . . hath now opened his office in Charlestown . . . Charlestown, T. Whitmarsh [1731]
broadside 31.5 X 20 cm.
"Signed . . . this 27th day of November, 1731."
McMurtrie: South Carolina 1731; New York Public 165
NN (facsim.); Public Record Off. (2 copies)
mp. 39976

B858 SOUTH CAROLINA. COUNCIL
. . . At a Council held . . . Tuesday October 19, 1731 . . . [Colophon] Charles Town, George Webb [1731]
6 p. 31.5 cm.
Concerns surveying and granting of land
McMurtrie: South Carolina 1731; New York Public 166
NN (facsim.). Public Record Off. mp. 39977

B859 SOUTH CAROLINA. GOVERNOR, 1730-1735
By His Excellency, Robert Johnson, Esqr; Governor . . . a proclamation . . . [Charlestown, G. Webb, 1731]
broadside 41.5 X 29.5 cm.
Dated: Nov. 4, 1731
Concerns grants of land
McMurtrie: South Carolina 1731; New York Public 167
MWA (photostat); NN (facsim.). Public Record Off.
mp. 39978

B860 THIS indenture made the twenty fifth day of March . . . One thousand seven hundred and thirty one . . . between, the proprietors of a certain tract of land . . . on the western side of the Kenebunk-River . . . [Boston? 1731]
[2] p. 32 X 20.5 cm.
Signed in ms.: Charles Frost
Dated at York, April 12, 1731
MWA mp. 39979

B861 A TOKEN for Children . . . Boston, Printed and sold at the Heart and Crown in Cornhill [1731?]
broadside
Ford 596
MWA mp. 39980

B862 WESTMINSTER ASSEMBLY OF DIVINES
The shorter catechism . . . Boston, Printed by T. Fleet, for the booksellers, 1731.
24 p. 12mo
MB mp. 39982

B863 WILLISON, JOHN, 1680-1750
Looking unto Jesus . . . Boston, Printed for Benjamin Gray, 1731.
[2], 34 p. 14 cm. A-C[6]
CtHi; MWA mp. 39983

1732

B864 BIBLE. O.T. PSALMS
The New-England Psalter: or Psalms of David . . . Boston, Printed by S. Kneeland and T. Green, for T. Hancock, 1732.
[128+] p. 15 cm.
Similar Boston 1740 ed. has [176] p.
MWA (p. [7-10, 23-26] and all after p. [128] wanting) mp. 39984

B865 BECK, ROBERT, 1682-1731
An extract from the manuscripts of . . . Robert Breck . . . Boston, 1732.
1 p.l., 13 p. 14.5 cm.
DLC mp. 39985

B866 THE Catholic remedy . . . [Boston] America, 1732.
broadside 30 X 13 cm.
Ford 598; Wegelin 517
NHi. Photostats: DLC; MHi; NH mp. 39986

B867 THE complete mariner: or, A treatise of navigation . . . Williamsburg: Printed, February the 18th, 1731. [i.e. 1732] E. L. James Hubard.
[56] p. illus. 38 X 24 cm.
T.p. and eight lines on next page printed; remainder in manuscript
ViWC. Photostat: NN mp. 39987

B868 [A DIALOGUE between a subscriber and a non-subscriber . . . The second edition. Charleston, S.C., Thomas Whitmarsh, 1732]

Advertised in the *South-Carolina Gazette*, Jan. 15 and Jan. 22, 1732, and as "Just published" Apr. 29, 1732
McMurtrie: South Carolina 1731-1740, no. 5
No copy known mp. 39988

B869 DULANY, DANIEL, 1685-1753
A letter from Daniel Dulany, Esq; to the Reverend Mr. Jacob Henderson. In answer to Mr. Henderson's . . . letter, dated September 23, 1731 . . . Annapolis, W. Parks, 1732.
[2], ii, 30+ p. 19 cm.
New York Public 169
RPJCB (probably one leaf only lacking). Photostat: NN mp. 39989

B870 FLAVEL, JOHN, 1630?-1691
The cursed death of the Cross described . . . Boston, Printed for Benjamin Gray, 1732.
[2], 20 p. 14 cm.
MWA (poor) mp. 39990

B871 [GOOCH, SIR WILLIAM] 1681-1751
A dialogue between Thomas Sweet-Scented, William Oronoco, planters . . . By a sincere Lover of Virginia. Williamsburg, W. Parks, 1732.
19 p. 20 cm.
Wroth: William Parks 54a (p. 67)
Public Record Off. Photostats: DLC; MHi; MWA; NN; RPJCB mp. 39991

B872 [GOOCH, SIR WILLIAM] 1681-1751
A dialogue between Thomas Sweet-Scented, William Oronoco, planters . . . By a sincere Lover of Virginia. The third edition. Williamsburg, W. Parks, 1732.
19 p. 20 cm.
Wroth: William Parks 55
RPJCB mp. 39992

B873 HARVARD UNIVERSITY
Quaestiones pro modulo . . . M DCC XXXII. [Boston, 1732]
broadside
MH mp. 39993

B874 LEWIS, RICHARD
Carmen seculare, for the year MDCCXXXII . . . [Annapolis, William Parks, 1732]
[4] p. 37.5 cm.
Wroth 76
MdHi mp. 39994

B875 LEWIS, RICHARD, supposed author
March 1, 1731-2 A rhapsody . . . [Annapolis, William Parks, 1732]
[2] p. 37.5 X 24 cm.
Wroth 77
MdHi mp. 39995

B876 LORING, ISRAEL, 1682-1772
It is good to bear the yoke in youth. A sermon preached at Sudbury . . . April, 1732 . . . Boston, Printed by S. Kneeland & T. Green, for J. Phillips, 1732.
2 p.l., 27 p. 19 cm.
NHi mp. 39996

B877 MARYLAND. LAWS
Laws of Maryland, enacted . . . 1732 . . . Annapolis, Williams Parks, and Edmund Hall, 1732.
[2], 46 p. 30 cm.
Huntington 96; Wroth 78
CSmH; DLC; Md; MdHi; N(imperfect) mp. 39997

B878 MASSACHUSETTS. GENERAL COURT
Report of a committee [on Eastern Lands] Boston, Thomas Fleet, 1731/2.
[2], 17 p. fol.
MH-L mp. 39998

B879 MASSACHUSETTS. GOVERNOR, 1730-1741
By His Excellency Jonathan Belcher . . . A proclamation for a general fast . . . Boston, the third day of March 1731 . . . Boston, B. Green, 1732 [sic]
broadside 33.5 X 27 cm.
MHi mp. 39999

B880 MASSACHUSETTS. GOVERNOR, 1730-1741
By his excellency Jonathan Belcher . . . a proclamation. Whereas at a council . . . [Feb. 16, 1732] Boston, J. Draper, 1732.
broadside 43 X 31 cm.
Ford 631
DLC; MB; MHi mp. 40000

B881 A POEM in memory of that pious servant and faithful minister of Jesus Christ, Mr. Isaac Cushman . . . [Boston, 1732]
broadside 33 X 20 cm.
Ford 636
MB. Photostat: MWA mp. 40001

B882 [PROPOSALS for the opening of an insurance office against fire. Charleston, S.C., Thomas Whitmarsh? 1732]

At a meeting at the house of Henry Gignilliat proposals were made which (Jan. 22, 1732, *South-Carolina Gazette*) "will be printed and given Gratis at the aforesaid house, on Monday in the afternoon."
McMurtrie: South Carolina 1731-1740, no. 6
No copy known mp. 40002

B883 [SHEET almanack for . . . 1733. Philadelphia, B. Franklin, 1732?]
broadside
Advertised in the *Pennsylvania Gazette,* Dec. 19, 1732
Drake 9562
No copy known

B884 SIR, The design of these lines . . . [Boston? 1732?]
[3] p.
Signed in ms.: Edw. Goddard
Dated from date of church, and date in ms.
Concerns a church at Framingham, and church government
MHi mp. 40003

B885 SOUTH CAROLINA. LAWS
[The quit-rent roll law. Charleston, S.C., Eleazer Phillips, Jr., 1732]

Copy given to Phillips by an order dated Feb. 11, 1732, "in order that it may be printed;" mentioned in the stock of Eleazer Phillips, Sr., in his notice of intention to "depart the province" published Apr. 5, 1735
McMurtrie: South Carolina 1731-1740, no. 7
No copy known mp. 40004

B886 THE triumphs of justice over unjust judges . . . [Boston, S. Kneeland and T. Green] 1732.
[4], 27 p. 21 cm. A-D^4
Printer identified from type and type ornaments
MHi; MWA mp. 40005

B887 VIRGINIA
The case of the planters of tobacco in Virginia, as represented by themselves, signed by the president of the Council and speaker of the House of burgesses. [Williamsburg, 1732]
4 p. 33 cm.
MdBJ. Photostat: RPJCB mp. 40008

B888 VIRGINIA. GOVERNOR, 1727-1740
The speech of the honourable William Gooch . . . to the General assembly: at a session begun . . . on Thursday the 18th day of may . . . 1732. Williamsburg, W. Parks, 1732.
[4] p.
Wroth: William Parks 64b
Public Record Off. mp. 40006

B889 VIRGINIA. HOUSE OF BURGESSES
The humble address of the House of burgesses, to . . . William Gooch . . . [Williamsburg, W. Parks, 1732]
[2] p.
Dated May 20, 1732
Wroth: William Parks 63b
Public Record Off. mp. 40007

B890 VIRGINIA. LAWS
[Acts passed at a session May 18-July 1, 1732, being the third session. Williamsburg, W. Parks, 1732]
44 p.
Wroth: William Parks 63
Public Record Off. mp. 40010

B891 VIRGINIA. LAWS
At a General assembly . . . held . . . in the city of Williamsburg, the first day of February, in the first year of . . . George II . . . and from thence continued . . . to the eighteenth day of may . . . 1732: being the third session . . . An act to enable the masters of ships . . . [Williamsburg, 1732]
[2] p.
Wroth: William Parks 63a
Public Record Off. mp. 40009

B892 THE Virginia and Maryland almanack . . . for the year . . . 1732 . . . [Williamsburg] William Parks, 1732.
[32] p.
Date in imprint supplied based on 1730 issue (Evans 3374); corner of t.p. missing in RPJCB copy
RPJCB mp. 40011

B893 THE wages of sin . . . a poem; occasioned by the untimely death of Richard Wilson, who was executed . . . the 19th of October, 1732. Boston [1732]
broadside 31.5 X 19 cm.
Ford 619; Wegelin 826
NHi. Photostats: DLC; MHi; NN mp. 40012

B894 WIGHTMAN, VALENTINE, 1681-1747
Some brief remarks on a book, called, tho' unjustly, an impartial account of a debate at Lyme . . . Newport, J. Franklin, 1732.
40 p. 16 cm.
Not used for Evans 3494 in microprint edition
CtHi mp. 40013

1733

B895 ADAMS, ELIPHALET, 1677-1753
A discourse delivered at Colchester, June 13th, 1731. The day after the funeral of . . . John Bulkley . . . New-London, T. Green, 1733.
1 p.l., 46 p.
CtHi; RPJCB (wanting after p. 44) mp. 40014

B896 BOSTON
At a publick town-meeting in Boston, May 9th, 1733 . . . [Boston, 1733]
broadside 34 X 22,5 cm.
Ford 620
DLC; MB. Photostat: MHi mp. 40015

B897 [CROUCH, NATHANIEL] 1632?-1725?
The vanity of the life of man . . . By R. B. Boston, Printed & sold by S. Kneeland & T. Green, 1733.
30 p.
MHi mp. 40016

B898 AN elegy occasioned by the sudden . . . death of Mr. Nathanael Baker . . . the 7th of May, 1733 . . . [Boston ? 1733]
broadside 30.5 X 21 cm.
Ford 624; New York Public 173; Wegelin 557
MDedHi; MWA. Photostats: DLC; MHi; NN mp. 40017

B899 [A FULL and impartial view of Mr. Bowman's visitation sermon in a conference between a Church of England man and a dissenter in South Carolina. Charleston, T. Whitmarsh, 1733]

Advertised in the *South-Carolina Gazette,* Mar. 31, 1733, as "Now in press," and on June 23, 1733, as "On Thursday next will be published . . ."
McMurtrie: South Carolina, p. 438
No copy known mp. 40018

B900 HARVARD UNIVERSITY
Quaestiones pro modulo . . . MDCCXXXIII. [Boston 1733]
broadside
MH; MWA mp. 40019

B901 HEDGES, BETHIAH
A lottery, set forth by Bethiah Hedges of Newport, Rhode-Island . . . Newport, January 18, 1973,3. [Newport, J. Franklin, 1733]
broadside 28.5 X 13 cm.
RNHi. Photostats: MWA; NN; RHi mp. 40020

B902 JULIAN, d. 1733
The last speech and dying advice of poor Julian, who was executed the 22d of March, 1733 for the murder of Mr. John Rogers of Pembroke. Written with his own hand, and delivered to the publisher the day before his execution. Boston, Printed and sold by T. Fleet [1733]
broadside 33 X 21 cm.
Ford 628
MB. Photostats: MHi; MWA mp. 40021

B903 JULIAN, d. 1733
Poor Julleyoun's warnings to children and servants . . . Published at his desire in presence of two witnesses. Boston, Printed for B. Gray, and A. Butler [1733]
broadside 33.5 X 20 cm.
Ford 629
MB. Photostats: MHi; MWA mp. 40022

B904 A LOUD alarm to Annapolis-Royal, in Nova-Scotia . . . [Eclipse of the sun] On May 15, 1733. [The second impression.] [n.p., 1733]
broadside 33.5 X 20 cm.
In verse
New York Public 175
NN (photostat) mp. 40023

B905 MARYLAND. LAWS
Laws of Maryland, enacted . . . 1732 . . . Annapolis, Williams Parrs [sic], 1733.
44 p. 33.5 cm.
Wroth 83
DLC; MH-L; Md; MdHi mp. 40024

B906 MASSACHUSETTS. GOVERNOR, 1730-1741
By His Excellency Jonathan Belcher . . . A proclamation for apprehending Gyles du Lake Tidmarsh . . . November 9, 1733. Boston, J. Draper, 1733.
broadside
Ford 634
MB mp. 40025

B907 NEW JERSEY. GENERAL ASSEMBLY
The votes and proceedings of the General Assembly of . . . Nova-Caesariae, or New-Jersey. Which began at Burlington, the 26th day of April, 1733 . . . [Philadelphia, Andrew Bradford, 1733]
41 p. 30.5 cm.
Metzger 32
Nj mp. 40026

B908 THE pleasant & profitable companion . . . Boston, Printed for J. Edwards, & H. Foster, 1733.
[2], 176 p. front. 14 cm. A-P^6
MWA mp. 40027

B909 A POEM upon the deaths, and in memory of two . . . servants of Christ, viz. the Reverend Mr. Isaac Cushman . . . and Dr. Caleb Loring . . . [Boston, 1733?]
broadside 36.5 X 30 cm.
Cushman died Oct. 21, 1732, Loring Dec. 22, 1732
Ford 637
MB. Photostats: MHi; MWA mp. 40028

B910 POOR Richard, 1734. An almanack for . . . 1734 . . . By Richard Saunders . . . Philadelphia, B. Franklin [1733]
[24] p.
Second edition
Drake 9571
PPAmP

B911 [SCOTTOW, JOSHUA] 1615-1698
Old men's tears for their own declensions . . . Boston: Printed in the year 1691. Reprinted for B. Gray at his shop no. 2. at the head of the town-dock. 1733.
1 p.l., 20 p. 13.5 cm.
MiU-C

B912 SOME considerations against the setting up of a market in this town. With a brief answer to the reasons that are offer'd in behalf of it. [Boston, 1733]
4 p.
Ford 621
MB; MHi mp. 40029

B913 SOME considerations against the setting up of a market in this town. With a brief answer to the reasons that are offer'd in behalf of it. Boston, May 25th, 1733. [Boston, 1733]
4 p.
Ford 622
MB. Photostat: MHi mp. 40030

B914 [SOUTH-Carolina almanack for the year 1733. Charleston, S.C., Thomas Whitmarsh, 1733]

Advertised in the *South-Carolina Gazette,* April 28, 1733
McMurtrie: South Carolina 1731-1740, no. 8
No copy known mp. 40032

B915 T., M.
Some consolatory reflections and lamentations, occasioned by the premature deaths of three of the children of Capt. Joseph and Mrs. Mary Hinckley, of Barnstable . . . M. T. [Boston, 1733?]
broadside 37.5 X 28 cm.
The children died 1732-33
Ford 639
MB. Photostats: MHi; MWA mp. 40031

B916 TRUSDELL, WILLIAM
New-York Mayor's Court. William Trusdell against Francis Harison . . . [Two letters dated Aug. 25, 1733] [New York, 1733]
broadside 30 X 18 cm.
PPRF. Photostats: DLC; MHi; NN mp. 40033

B917 VAUX, G.
Advertisement. Whereas an advertisement was yesterday dispers'd about this town, in order to prejudice Mr. Cox in his business of bookselling here, signed by D. Henchman and T. Hancock, bookbinders in Boston . . . March 31, 1733. [Boston, 1733]
broadside
Ford 640
MB mp. 40034

B918 WANTON, WILLIAM, 1670-1733
A true representation of the conduct of . . . Mr. Richard Ward . . . William Wanton. Newport, on Rhode-Island, 3d. Jan. 1733. [Newport, J. Franklin, 1733]

broadside 31 X 20 cm.
Alden 30; Sabin 101254
RHi. Goodspeed. Photostats: MWA; NN mp. 40035

B919 WESTMINSTER ASSEMBLY OF DIVINES
The shorter catechism . . . Boston, [Printed] by S. Kneeland & T. Green, for [T. Hanco]ck, 1733.
[2], 44 p. 16.5 cm. A-C^8
MWA (mutilated) mp. 40036

B920 WILLISON, JOHN, 1680-1750
Looking unto Jesus . . . Boston, Printed for Benjamin Gray, 1733.
[2], 28 p. 15 cm. A-B^6 C$^{6?}$ (C4-6 wanting)
MWA (poor) mp. 40037

1734

B921 Deleted.

B922 AUCHMUTY, ROBERT
The copy of some queries put to Mr. Auchmuty . . . [at end, p. 2] Robert Auchmuty. Newport, March 30, 1734. [Newport, Ann Franklin, 1734]
2 p. 31 cm.
Contains Auchmuty's opinion on the legal right of Quakers to hold office
Alden 32
Mrs. Townsend Phillips, Newport, R.I. Photostats: MWA; RHi; RNHi mp. 40038

B923 BLACKWELL, EDWARD
A compleat system of fencing . . . Williamsburg, W. Parks, 1734.
x, [2], 91 p.
RPJCB mp. 40039

B924 BURDON, WILLIAM
[The gentleman's pocket farrier. Charleston, S.C., Lewis Timothy, 1734]

Advertised in the *South-Carolina Gazette*, Oct. 19, 1734, as "This little book . . . soon sold for a half a Guinea and a Guinea, altho' the original price was but half a crown."
McMurtrie: South Carolina, p. 444
No copy known mp. 40040

B925 CUSHING, MATTHEW, d. 1734
The declaration & confession of Matthew Cushing . . . [Boston, 1734?]
broadside
Ford 642
MB mp. 40042

B926 AN essay on currency, written in August 1732. Charlestown, Printed and sold by Lewis Timothy, 1734.
24 p. 16 cm.
New York Public 178
ScC. Photostats: MWA; NN; RPJCB mp. 40043

B927 A FEW lines upon the awful execution of John Ormesby & Matth. Cushing, October 17th 1734. One for murder, the other for burglary. [Boston] Printed and sold at the printing house in Queen-street [1734]
broadside
Includes The declaration & confession of Matthew Cushing . . . (Ford 642)
Ford 652
MB. Photostat: MHi mp. 40044

B928 HARVARD UNIVERSITY.
Quaestiones pro modulo . . . M DCC XXXIV. [Boston 1734]
broadside
MH; MWA mp. 40047

B929 LEEDS, 1734. The American almanack for . . . 1734 . . . By Titan Leeds, Philomat. New-York, Printed and sold by William Bradford, 1734.
[24] p. 16.5 cm.
Huntington 99; Wall p. 8
CSmH; DLC (imperfect); NHi; RPJCB mp. 40048

B930 MARYLAND. PROVINCIAL COURT
Maryland ss. Complaint being made to me, Levin Gale, Esq; Chief Justice . . . by Benjamin Tasker, Charles Carrol, and Daniel Dulany . . . that seven men servants ran away . . . Given . . . this third day of July . . . 1734. Levin Gale. [Annapolis? William Parks? 1734]
broadside 15 X 20 cm.
New York Public 179
NN mp. 40049

B931 MASSACHUSETTS
A list of the polls, and of the estates, real and personal of the several . . . inhabitants of the town of in the county of pursuant to an act . . . for inquiring into the rateable estates . . . by the . . . assessors in said town . . . viz. [Boston, 1734]
broadside
Act passed May 1734
Ford 649
MWA mp. 40053

B932 MASSACHUSETTS. GENERAL COURT
The report of the committee of the General court relating to the settlement of North-Yarmouth . . . [Boston, 1734]
[3] p. 37 cm. caption title
Ford 646; Huntington 100
CSmH; M-Ar; MHi. Photostats: DLC; NN mp. 40050

B933 MASSACHUSETTS. GOVERNOR, 1730-1741
By . . . Jonathan Belcher . . . a proclamation for a publick fast . . . Boston, John Draper, 1734.
broadside 39 X 30 cm.
DLC mp. 40051

B934 MASSACHUSETTS. LAWS
. . . An act passed by the . . . General Court . . . begun and held at Boston . . . the twenty-ninth day of May 1734 . . . for apportioning and assessing a tax of sixteen thousand and fifteen pounds and twelve shillings . . . [Colophon] Boston, John Draper, 1734.
[9] p.
Ford & Matthews p. 367
M mp. 40052

B935 A MOURNFUL poem on the death of John Ormsby and Matthew Cushing . . . appointed to be executed on Boston Neck, the 17th of October, 1734. Boston, Sold at the Heart and Crown [by T. Fleet] [1734]
broadside
Ford 653
MB. Photostat: MHi mp. 40054

B936 NEW YORK
At a council held at Fort-George in New-York on the 5th of November, 1734. Present His Excellency William Cosby . . . Governour . . . Whereas several large tracts of . . . land . . . uncultivated . . . Signed . . . Fred. Morris, D. Cl. Conc. New-York, Printed and sold by William Bradford, 1734.
3 p. 26.5 cm.
Vail 380
NHi mp. 40056

B937 NEW YORK (CITY) ORDINANCES, ETC.
. . . A law for preserving the fish in fresh-water pond. [New York, 1734]
broadside 30 X 19 cm.
Huntington 101
Dated May 28, 1734
CSmH mp. 40055

B938 NEW-York, June 3. 1734. On Tuesday last several of the principal merchants . . . New York, William Bradford, 1734.
broadside 32.5 X 19 cm.
DLC (photostat) mp. 40057

B939 ORMSBY, JOHN, d. 1734
The last speech and dying words of John Ormsby . . . appointed to be executed . . . the 17th of October, 1734. Written with his own hand, the day before he was to suffer . . . Boston, Printed and sold by Thomas Fleet, 1734.
broadside
Ford 651
MB. Photostat: MHi mp. 40058

B940 PEED, DEUEL
The door of salvation opened . . . By Dr. Pede. Boston: Re-printed for Alford Butler, 1734.
22, [2] p. 13 cm.
MWA mp. 40059

B941 RANDOLPH, JOHN, 1693-1737
The speech of Sir John Randolph, upon his being elected Speaker . . . Williamsburg, William Parks, 1734.
[4] p. 35 cm. caption title
Wroth: William Parks 75c
DLC (photostat). Public Record Off. mp. 40060

B942 SOUTH CAROLINA. LAWS
[An act for better settling and regulating of pilots, & c. Charleston, S.C., Lewis Timothy, 1734]

Advertised for sale (price 5s) in the *South-Carolina Gazette* of Aug. 24, 1734
McMurtrie: South Carolina 1731-1740, no. 15
No copy known mp. 40061

B943 SOUTH CAROLINA. LAWS
[An act for regulating patrolls in this province. Charleston, S.C., Lewis Timothy, 1734]

Advertised for sale (price 2s 6d) in the *South-Carolina Gazette* of June 29, 1734
McMurtrie: South Carolina 1731-1740, no. 14
No copy known mp. 40062

B944 SOUTH CAROLINA. LAWS
[An act for the better regulating the militia. Charleston, S.C., Lewis Timothy, 1734]

Advertised in the *South-Carolina Gazette,* June 22, 1734, as "Just Published . . . Price 5s."
McMurtrie: South Carolina 1731-1740, no. 13
No copy known mp. 40063

B945 TIMOTHY, LEWIS
[The proposals, together with a specimen of the laws of the Province of South-Carolina. Charleston, S.C., Lewis Timothy, 1734]

Advertised in the *South-Carolina Gazette,* May 11, 1734, as "will be published on Wednesday the 15th inst." and July 13, 1734, as "having been published in one sheet, with a specimen . . . annexed."
McMurtrie: South Carolina 1731-1740, no. 12
No copy known mp. 40064

B946 VIRGINIA. COUNCIL
The humble address of the Council . . . [Williamsburg, W. Parks, 1734]
[2] p. 35 X 21 cm.
In reply to Lieutenant-governor Gooch's address of Aug. 22, 1734
Wroth: William Parks 75b
DLC (photostat) mp. 40065

B947 VIRGINIA. GOVERNOR, 1727-1749
The speech of the honourable William Gooch . . . at a session begun and held . . . the 22d day of August . . . 1734. Williamsburg, William Parks, 1734.
[4] p. 35 cm.
Wroth: William Parks 75a
DLC (photostat) mp. 40066

B948 VIRGINIA. HOUSE OF BURGESSES
Journal of the House of burgesses [Aug. 22-Oct. 4, 1734]. Being the fourth session of this Assembly. [Williamsburg, W. Parks, 1734]
74 p. caption title
Wroth: William Parks 75
Coleman mp. 40067

B949 WALDO, SAMUEL, 1696-1759
Whereas it is industriously reported . . . these are to certifie, that . . . I proposed and drank the said health . . . Tuesday, 7th of May, 1734, at Boston. [Boston, 1734]
broadside 31.5 X 18 cm.
Ford 655
DLC; MB. Photostat: MHi mp. 40068

1735

B949a [ALMANAK voor 1737. New York, 1736]

Drake 5601, following Hildeburn
No copy located

B950 THE American almanack for the year . . . 1735 . . . By Titan Leeds. New-York, Printed and sold by William Bradford, 1735.
[24] p.
Wall p. 9
CtHi ([22] p. only); NN (title-leaf only) mp. 40072

B951 AMERICAN WEEKLY MERCURY, PHILADELPHIA
Yearly verses of the *American Weekly Mercury* . . . [Philadelphia, 1735?]
broadside
Undated, but in original bound file before issue of Jan. 7, 1735 in Amer. Ant. Soc.

1st line: There's not an ear that is not deaf . . .
MWA mp. 40086

B952 BUNYAN, JOHN, 1628-1688, supposed author
Rest for a wearied soul . . . Boston, Printed by S. Kneeland & T. Green for B. Gray, 1735.
21 p. 13.5 cm.
PPRF mp. 40069

B953 COLMAN, BENJAMIN, 1673-1747
Two sermons delivered at Hartford . . . New-London, [Timothy Green] 1735.
[2], 64 p.
Trumbull: Supplement 1989
RPJCB mp. 40070

B954 HARVARD UNIVERSITY
Quaestiones pro modulo . . . MDCCXXXV. [Boston, 1735]
broadside
MH; MHi mp. 40071

B954a CROSS, ROBERT
The danger of perverting the Gospel . . . sermon preach'd . . . April 20th, 1735 . . . New-York, John Peter Zenger, 1735.
vii, 35 p.
Trinterude 86
PPPrHi

B955 A LETTER to a friend, relating to the differences in the First Church in Salem . . . [at end] Boston, T. Fleet, 1735.
31 p. caption title
Printer's device on p. 31
MB

B956 MARYLAND. GENERAL ASSEMBLY
Votes and proceedings of the Lower House . . . [Annapolis, William Parks, 1735]
36 p. 28.5 cm.
Session Mar. 20, 1734/35-Apr. 24, 1735
Wroth 89
Md mp. 40073

B957 MARYLAND. LAWS
Laws of Maryland, enacted . . . 1734 . . . Annapolis, William Parks, 1734 [i.e. 1735]
27, [1] p. 30 cm.
Wroth 88
DLC (2 copies); MH-L; Md; MdBD mp. 40074

B958 MASSACHUSETTS. GOVERNOR, 1730-1741
By His Excellency Jonathan Belcher . . . A proclamation . . . bills or votes of hand emitted by . . . persons in the province of New-Hampshire . . . April 18 [1735] . . . Boston, John Draper [1735]
broadside 37.5 X 30.5 cm.
Ford 658
MHi mp. 40075

B959 MASSACHUSETTS. LAWS
. . . An act, passed by the . . . General Court . . . begun and held at Boston . . . the twenty-eighth day of May 1735 . . . for apportioning and assessing a tax of thirty thousand ninety-nine pounds, fourteen shillings and three pence . . . [Colophon] Boston, John Draper, 1735.
[9] p.
Ford & Mathews p. 369
M-Ar mp. 40076

B960 NEW YORK (CITY) ORDINANCES, ETC.
A law for the better regulating . . . the publick markets . . . of New-York . . . [New York, William Bradford, 1735]
p. 49-44 [i.e. 54] sm. fol.
Includes 2 other laws, whose titles appear on p. 52 and 43 [i.e. 53]
Huntington 105
CSmH mp. 40078

B961 PENNSYLVANIA. RECEIVER-GENERAL'S OFFICE
Advertisement . . . Philad. Dec. 24. 1735. J. Steel, Rec. Gen. [Philadelphia, B. Franklin, 1735]
broadside
Concerns arrears of rent
Curtis 78; New York Public 181
NN (facsim.); PPL mp. 40079

B962 [PENNSYLVANIA 1736. An almanac for the year . . . 1736. Philadelphia, B. Franklin, 1735]

Curtis 95; Hildeburn 525
No copy known mp. 40084

B963 PHILADELPHIA, January 6, 1734/5. Advertisement . . . [Philadelphia, 1735]
broadside 27 X 17.5 cm.
Persons wishing to purchase certain tracts of land should apply to Thomas Lawrence in Philadelphia
PHi mp. 40080

B964 SCHEME of a lottery for one hundred thousand acres of land in the Province of Pennsylvania . . . John Georges, Secr. [Philadelphia, B. Franklin, 1735]
4 p. 31 cm.
Dated July 12, 1735
Metzger 36
PHi mp. 40081

B965 [SHEET almanack for 1736. New York, W. Bradford, 1735]
broadside
Drake 5599
No copy known

B966 SHEPARD, THOMAS, 1605-1648
The sincere convert . . . Newly corrected and amended . . . Boston, Re-printed by John Draper for Daniel Henchman, 1735.
[2], 162+ p. 15 cm. [ ]^{2} B-O^{6} P$^{6?}$
MWA (p. 19–22, 103–106, and all after 162 wanting) mp. 40082

B967 SOUTH CAROLINA. LAWS
[Act of the General Assembly for the better ordering and governing of Negroes and other slaves. Charleston, Lewis Timothy, 1735]

Advertised in the *South-Carolina Gazette*, Apr. 19, 1735, as "Just Published and sold."
McMurtrie: South Carolina, p. 444
No copy known mp. 40083

B968 TENNENT, GILBERT, 1703-1764
The necessity of receiving the truth in love . . . New-York York, John Peter Zenger, 1735.
192 p. sm. 8vo
Huntington 106
CSmH (lacks p. 73-74) mp. 40085

B969 WALDO, SAMUEL, 1696-1759
Boston, May 22d, 1735. Whereas since my return from St. George's River . . . [Boston, 1735]
2 p.
Signed at end: Samuel Waldo
Ford 660
RPJCB mp. 40087

B970 WALDO, SAMUEL, 1696-1759
Samuel Waldo of Boston, merchant . . . hereby notifies all persons . . . 3d. March, 1734 . . . [Boston, 1735]
broadside 24 X 18 cm.
Ford 654
DLC. Photostat: MHi mp. 40088

1736

B971 BOSTON
(No. 13.) To Your province tax. Your town rate.

. . . The assessors sit . . . in Boston, on Thursdays, from 3 to 5 . . . 1736 . . . Stephen Kent, Constable. [Boston, 1736]
broadside 12.5 X 12.5 cm.
Ford 662
MHi mp. 40089

B972 BOSTON. ORDINANCES, ETC.
At a meeting of the freeholders . . . convened . . . the 28th day of April . . . 1736 . . . [Boston, 1736]
3 p. 18.5 cm. caption title
DLC mp. 40090

B973 [DIPPEL, JOHANN CONRAD]
Geistliche Fama, mitbringend einige neuere Nachrichten . . . XX. Stück . . . [n.p.] 1736.
80 p. 16.5 cm. A-E^8
MWA mp. 40091

B974 THE drunkard's looking-glass: or, A short view of their present shames and future misery . . . [Philadelphia? 1736?]
broadside 36 X 21.5 cm.
Original found in 1735-36 volume of Franklin's *Pennsylvania gazette*
NHi. Photostat: MWA mp. 40092

B975 AN elegy upon the much lamented deaths of two desireable brothers . . . sons of Capt. Joshua and Mrs. Comfort Weeks, of Greenland [N.H.] . . . in February 1735,6. [Boston, 1736]
broadside 42 X 30 cm.
Ford 664; Wegelin 570
DLC; NhHi. Photostats: MHi; MWA mp. 40093

B976 GRAY, ANDREW, 1633-1656
An excellent sermon upon the great salvation . . . [Bo]ston, Printed for Benj. Gray, 1736.
[2], 22 p. 14 cm.
cf. Evans 3424
MWA mp. 40094

B977 HARVARD UNIVERSITY
Quaestiones pro modulo . . . MDCCXXXVI. [Boston, 1736]
broadside
MH; MWA (poor) mp. 40095

B978 MARYLAND. LAWS
Laws of Maryland, enacted at a session . . . begun . . . the nineteenth day of March . . . 1735 . . . Annapolis, William Parks, 1736.
[2], 26 p. 31.5 cm.
Wroth 90
Md; MdBB; MdHi. Brit. Mus. mp. 40096

B979 MASSACHUSETTS. COURT OF GENERAL SESSIONS
Essex ss. Anno regni Regis Georgii secundi . . . decimo— At his majesties Court of General Sessions . . . begun and held at Newbury . . . September . . . 1736 . . . Ichabod Tucker, clerk. [n.p., 1736]
broadside 20 X 16.5 cm.
Merrimack River ferry to land at Benjamin Woodbridge's wharf
CtHi mp. 40097

B980 MASSACHUSETTS. GOVERNOR, 1730-1741
By His Excellency Jonathan Belcher . . . A proclamation for a general fast [April 1] . . . February 26, 1735. Boston, J. Draper [1736]
broadside
Ford 670
MWA. Photostat: MHi mp. 40098

B981 MASSACHUSETTS. GOVERNOR, 1730-1741
By His Excellency Jonathan Belcher . . . A proclamation for dissolving the present General Assembly . . . Boston the second day of March, 1736. Boston, J. Draper [1736]
broadside
PHi mp. 40138

B982 MASSACHUSETTS. GOVERNOR, 1730-1741
By His Excellency Jonathan Eelcer . . . A proclamation for proroguing the General Assembly . . . October 4, 1736. Boston, J. Draper [1736]
broadside
Ford 672
MB mp. 40099

B983 THE melancholy state of this province considered, in a letter from a gentleman in Boston to his friend in the country. [Boston] 1736.
14 p.
MWA; RPJCB mp. 40100

B984 MIXER, ELIZABETH
An account of some spiritual experiences and raptures and pious expression of Elizabeth Mixer . . . With a preface by the Rvd. Mr. James Hale. N. London, Printed & sold by T. Green, 1736.
24 p.
"To the reader," signed Ashford June 28, 1736
Trumbull: Supplement 2400
MWA mp. 40101

B985 RHODE ISLAND. GOVERNOR, 1734-1740
[A proclamation for the apprehending of Nathaniel Shelton . . . Newport, Ann Franklin, 1736]
[broadside?]
The June 1736 session of the General Assembly voted to print
Alden 37
No copy known mp. 40102

B986 [TENNENT, JOHN] ca. 1700-ca. 1760
Every man his own doctor; or, The poor planter's physician . . . Third edition, with additions. Williamsburg and Annapolis, W. Parks, 1736.
69, [3] p. 17.5 cm.
Austin 1872
PHi mp. 40103

B987 TUFTS, JOHN, 1689-1750
An introduction to the singing of Psalm-tunes . . . The ninth edition. [Boston?] 1736.

MSaE mp. 40104

B988 USSHER, JAMES, 1581-1656
[Immanuel, or the mystery of the incarnation of the Son of God . . . Williamsburg, W. Parks, 1736]

Wroth: William Parks 81
No copy known mp. 40105

B989 VIRGINIA. COUNCIL
The humble address of the Council . . . [Williamsburg, W. Parks, 1736]
[2] p. 30 X 18 cm.
In reply to Lieutenant-governor Gooch's address of Aug. 5, 1736
Wroth: William Parks 82a
DLC (photostat) mp. 40106

B990 VIRGINIA. GOVERNOR, 1727-1749
The speech of . . . William Gooch . . . on Friday, the sixth day of August . . . 1736 . . . Williamsburg, William Parks, 1736.
[4] p. 30 cm.
Wroth: William Parks 83a
DLC (photostat). Public Record Off. mp. 40107

B991 [WARNER'S almanack, for the year 1737. Williamsburg, W. Parks, 1736]

Advertised in the *Virginia Gazette*, Nov. 26, 1736
Torrence 133; Wroth: William Parks 85
No copy known mp. 40108

B992 WILLIAM AND MARY COLLEGE
The charter, and statutes . . . In Latin and English. Williamsburg, William Parks, 1736.
121, [2] p. 19.5 cm.
Wroth: William Parks 87
DLC; RPJCB mp. 40109

1737

B993 . . . AN almanack for the year . . . 1737 . . . By Titan Leeds . . . New York, William Bradford, 1737.
[20] p. 16 cm.
At head of title: Leeds, 1737
All known copies imperfect
Drake 5603; Morrison p. 75; New York Public 183
DLC; MWA; NHi; RPJCB. Photostat: NN mp. 40119

B994 THE American almanack for . . . 1737 . . . By Titan Leeds . . . New-York, Printed and sold by William Bradford, 1737.
[24] p. 16.5 cm.
Drake 5602; New York Public 182; Wall p. 9
MWA; NBLiHi; PHi. Photostat: NN mp. 40118

B995 APLIN, JOHN
John Walton's religion . . . Newport, Printed by the Widow Franklin, for the author, 1737.
26 p. 16.5 cm.
Alden 39; Huntington 108
CSmH; MHi mp. 40110

B996 BIBLE. O.T. PSALMS
The Psalms, hymns, and spiritual songs . . . The twenty-fourth edition. Boston, Printed by S. Kneeland & T. Green, for S. Eliot, 1737.
1 p.l., 346 p. 13.5 cm.
cf. Evans 4115; Holmes: Minor Mathers 53-U
MB mp. 40111

B997 CHRIST CHURCH, PHILADELPHIA
An account of the births and burials . . . to December 24, 1737. By Charles Hughes, sexton. [Philadelphia, 1737]
broadside 20.5 X 16 cm.
Huntington 109
CSmH mp. 40126

B998 AN elegy on the much lamented death of Sarah Wanton . . . [Newport? Ann Franklin? 1737?]
broadside 34.5 X 33 cm.
Verses in 2 columns
Alden 42
RPB mp. 40112

B999 GT. BRIT. LAWS
An act for maintaining the peace with the Indians, in the province of Georgia, prepared by the . . . trustees, for establishing the colony of Georgia . . . Williamsburg, W. Parks [1737?]
Advertised in the *Virginia Gazette*, Feb. 25, 1736/37 as "Lately printed here."
Wroth: William Parks 88
No copy known mp. 40113

B1000 Deleted.

B1001 HARVARD UNIVERSITY
Quaestiones pro modulo . . . MDCCXXXVII. [Boston, 1737]
broadside
MH; MWA mp. 40115

B1002 HENCHMAN, DANIEL
Boston, March 12, 1736,7. Reverend Sir . . . Your humble servant, D. Henchman . . . [Boston, 1737]
broadside 20 X 15 cm.
An account of the numerous people who died of distemper of the throat in New Hampshire from June 1735 to July 1736
Ford 678
PHi mp. 40116

B1003 MARYLAND. GENERAL ASSEMBLY
Votes and proceedings of the Lower House . . . [Annapolis, William Parks, 1737]
24+ p. 28.5 cm.
Session Apr. 26-May 28, 1737
Wroth 93
Md (imperfect) mp. 40121

B1004 MARYLAND. GOVERNOR, 1735-1742
By his excellency Samuel Ogle . . . a proclamation . . . Whereas . . . two petitions . . . which represented a suit . . . between . . . Maryland and the family of Penns . . . Given . . . twenty first day of November . . . 1737. Philadelphia, Jonas Green, 1737.
broadside 39.5 X 33 cm.
RPJCB. Photostat: NN mp. 40120

B1005 MARYLAND. LAWS
Laws of Maryland, enacted at a session . . . begun . . . the eleventh day of August . . . 1737 . . . Annapolis, William Parks, 1737.
[2], 8 p. 30.5 cm.
Wroth 92
MdBB; MdHi mp. 40122

B1006 MASSACHUSETTS. LAWS
. . . An act passed by the . . . General Court . . . begun and held at Boston . . . the twenty-fifth day of May, 1737 . . . for apportioning and assessing a tax of forty four thousand nine hundred and thirty pounds one shilling and three pence . . . [Colophon] Boston, J. Draper [1737]
[9] p.
Ford & Matthews p. 372
M-Ar mp. 40123

B1007 MASSACHUSETTS. TREASURER
Province of the Massachusetts-Bay, ss. William Foye, Esq; Treasurer . . . November 18, 1737. [Boston, 1737]
broadside
Tax warrant
Ford 688
MSaE mp. 40124

B1008 NEW YORK. LAWS
An ordinance for appointing the times and places for holding the annual circuit courts in the several counties of this province. [New York, John Peter Zenger, 1737]
2 p. 31 cm.
Gotshall 275
N (2 copies) mp. 40125

B1009 RICHARD, ANDREW
On the night following the first of October, instant, Andrew Richard . . . had his shop broken up . . . Norwich, Octob. 3d. 1737. Andrew Richard. [New London? Timothy Green? 1737]
broadside 26 × 15 cm.
MB mp. 40127

B1010 [SHEET almanack for . . . 1737. Philadelphia, A. Bradford, 1737]
broadside
Drake 9589
No copy known

B1011 SOUTH CAROLINA. GENERAL ASSEMBLY
Report of the committee, appointed to examine into the proceedings . . . Charles-Town, Lewis Timothy, 1737.
120 p. 22 cm.
Sabin 87348
DLC; MiU-C; NHi; RPJCB mp. 40128

B1012 [SOUTH-Carolina almanack for the year 1738. Charleston, Printed and sold by Lewis Timothy, 1737]

Advertised in the *South-Carolina Gazette,* Oct. 29, 1737, and thereafter
McMurtrie: South Carolina, p. 446
No copy known mp. 40129

B1013 [WARNER'S almanack, for the year 1738. Williamsburg, W. Parks, 1737]

Advertised in the *Virginia Gazette,* Nov. 25, 1737, as "Just published."
Wroth: William Parks 96
No copy known mp. 40131

B1014 WESTMINSTER ASSEMBLY OF DIVINES
The shorter catechism agreed upon . . . Boston, S. Kneeland & T. Green, 1737.
23, [1] p.
RPJCB mp. 40132

1738

B1014a [ALMANAK voor 1738. New York, 1738]

Drake 5604, following Hildeburn
No copy located

B1015 THE American almanack for . . . 1738 . . . By Titan Leeds . . . New-York, Printed and sold by William Bradford, 1738.
[32] p.
Drake 5606; cf. Evans 4151 ([24] p.)
PHi

B1016 BIBLE. O.T. PSALMS
The New-England Psalter . . . Boston: Published by S. Kneeland & T. Green for N. Procter, 1738.
[176?] p. 14.5 cm.
MHi mp. 40133

B1017 BIRKETT, 1738. An almanack for . . . 1738 . . . New-York, Printed and sold by William Bradford, 1738.
[24?] p. 15.5 cm.
New York Public 185; Wall p. 9
NN (10 leaves only) mp. 40135

B1018 BOSTON. ORDINANCES, ETC.
At a meeting of the freeholders . . . the tenth of May, 1738 . . . [Boston, 1738]
3 p. 18.5 cm. caption title
DLC mp. 40135

B1019 BOSTON, July 21, 1738. Pursuant to an act . . . authorizing and impowring us . . . [Boston, 1738]
4 p. 18.5 cm. caption title
DLC mp. 40136

B1020 BURDON, WILLIAM
[The gentleman's pocket-farrier, shewing how to chuse a good horse . . . Williamsburg, W. Parks, 1738]

Wroth: William Parks 97
No copy known mp. 40137

B1021 CLARKE, GEORGE
Encouragement given for people to remove and settle in the Province of New-York in America . . . New York, William Bradford, 1738.
broadside 29 × 17 cm.
Vail: Old frontier 403
NHi mp. 40138

B1022 DALE, THOMAS
[The case of Miss Mary Roche, more fairly related . . . By Thomas Dale, M.D. Charleston, S.C., Lewis Timothy, 1738]

Advertised in the *South-Carolina Gazette,* Sept. 21, 1738, as "In a few days will be published," and Oct. 19, 1738, as "on Saturday next."

McMurtrie: South Carolina, p. 448
No copy known mp. 40139

B1023 DYCHE, THOMAS, d. 1735
[A guide to the English tongue . . . The twenty fifth edition, corrected. Williamsburg? W. Parks? ca. 1738]

No copy known mp. 40140

B1024 FRIENDS, SOCIETY OF
To the honourable the Governor and Council . . . at Williamsburg. The humble petition of the people called Quakers. . . November 14, 1738. [Williamsburg, W. Parks, 1738]
[2] p. 28 cm. caption title
Wroth: William Parks 100a
G. Coleman mp. 40141

B1025 HARVARD UNIVERSITY
Quaestiones pro modulo . . . MDCCXXXVIII. [Boston, 1738]
broadside 43 X 26.5 cm.
Ford 694; Huntington 112
CSmH; DLC; MH; MHi; MWA mp. 40142

B1026 KENNISON, PHILIP, 1710?-1738
The dying lamentation and advice of Philip Kennison . . . executed at Cambridge . . . the 15th day of September, 1738, in the 28th year of his age . . . Boston, Printed and sold at the Heart and Crown in Cornhill [1738]
broadside 32 X 19 cm.
In verse
New York Public 186
NN mp. 40143

B1027 KILLPATRICK, JAMES
[The case of Miss Mary Roche, who was inoculated June 18, 1738, fairly related . . . Charleston, S.C., Lewis Timothy, 1738]

Advertised in the *South-Carolina Gazette*, Sept. 14, 1738, as "just published"
McMurtrie: South Carolina, p. 447
No copy known

B1028 LAICUS, pseud.
[Letter concerning proper treatment of the smallpox. Charleston, S.C., Lewis Timothy, 1738]

Advertised in the *South-Carolina Gazette,* Sept. 14, 1738, as "the letter of Laicus will be published next week by itself."
Ever printed?
McMurtrie: South Carolina, p. 447
No copy known mp. 40145

B1029 MASSACHUSETTS. GOVERNOR, 1730-1741
By His Excellency Jonathan Belcher . . . A proclamation. Forasmuch as the Island of Sables is not inhabited . . . [Sept. 4, 1738] Boston, J. Draper [1738]
broadside 37 X 31 cm.
Ford 697
MHi mp. 40146

B1030 MASSACHUSETTS. LAWS
. . . An act pass'd by the Great and General Court . . . held at Boston . . . May 1738 . . . An act for erecting a township in the County of York by the name of Brunswick. Boston, John Draper [1738]
broadside 31 X 19.5 cm.
MeHi mp. 40147

B1031 MASSACHUSETTS. TREASURER
Province of the Massachusetts-Bay, ss. William Foye, Esq; Treasurer . . . July 20, 1738. [Boston, 1738]
broadside
Tax warrant
Ford 700
MSaE mp. 40148

B1032 NEW HAMPSHIRE. HOUSE OF REPRESENTATIVES
Appendix (A). To the King's . . . Appendix (B) . . . Boston, June 9, 1738. [Boston, 1738]
4 p. 49.5 cm.
DLC mp. 40149

B1033 PENNSYLVANIA. GOVERNOR, 1738-1747
By the honourable George Thomas, Esq; Lieutenant governor . . . A proclamation [concerning disorders in Pennsylvania and Maryland] . . . Aug. 29, 1738. Philadelphia, B. Franklin, 1738]
broadside
Curtis 121
CtY mp. 40150

B1034 SOUTH CAROLINA. LAWS
[Acts passed by the General Assembly of South-Carolina, at a sessions begun . . . at Charles-Town . . . eleventh year of . . . George the Second . . . continued . . . to . . . one thousand seven hundred and thirty eight. Charleston, Lewis Timothy, 1738]
72 p.
Title supplied by Edwin J. Wolf 2d
PHi (p. 1-6 and 25-26 wanting)

B1035 VIRGINIA. COUNCIL
To the honourable William Gooch . . . The humble address of the council . . . the 4th day of November, 1738 . . . [Williamsburg, William Parks, 1738]
[2] p. 30 X 18 cm.
Wroth: William Parks 100b
DLC (photostat) mp. 40151

B1036 VIRGINIA. GOVERNOR, 1727-1740
The speech of . . . William Gooch . . . [Williamsburg, W. Parks, 1738]
[2] p. 30 X 18 cm.
At the opening of the session Nov. 4, 1738
DLC (photostat) mp. 40152

B1037 VIRGINIA. HOUSE OF BURGESSES
To the honourable William Gooch . . . The humble address of the House of burgesses . . . the 6th day of November, 1738 . . . [Williamsburg, W. Parks, 1738]
[2] p. 30 X 18 cm.
Wroth: William Parks 99a
DLC (photostat) mp. 40153

B1038 WARD, RICHARD
The remonstrance of Richard Ward . . . [Newport, Ann Franklin, 1738]
4 p. 33.5 cm. caption title
"Postscript" dated "February 7, 1737."
Alden 43
RHi. Photostats: DLC; MWA mp. 40130

B1039 [WARNER'S almanack, for the year 1739. Williamsburg, W. Parks, 1738]

Advertised in the *Virginia Gazette,* Dec. 22, 1738
Bear 2; Torrence 151; Wroth: William Parks 102
No copy known mp. 40154

B1040 WATTS, ISAAC, 1674-1748
Divine songs attempted in easy language . . . The eighth edition. Boston: N.E. Re-printed by J. Draper, for T. Hancock in Ann-Street. 1738.
iv, 53 p. 12.5 cm.
CtHi

1739

B1040a [ALMANAK voor 1739. New York, 1739]

Drake 5609, following Hildeburn
No copy located

B1041 B., A.
A brief representation of the case depending between . . . Macsparran, and Mr. Torrey . . . Your humble servant, A. B. Newport, August 29th, 1739. [Newport? Ann Franklin? 1739]
[2] p. 35 X 22.5 cm.
Alden 48; Sabin 96298 (note); NYPL 187
NHi; RPJCB. Photostats: MWA; NN; RNHI
mp. 40156

B1042 BOSTON New England, Nov. 1739. In order to redress the distressing circumstances which the trade of this province is under for want of a medium . . . it is proposed to set up a bank of credit on land security . . . [Boston? 1739]
broadside 33.5 X 20 cm.
Ford 705
MHi; RPJCB mp. 40155

B1043 DALE, THOMAS
[The puff; or, a proper reply to Skimmington's last crudities. Charleston, Lewis Timothy, 1739]

Advertised in the *South-Carolina Gazette,* May 19, 1739, as "just published."
McMurtrie: South Carolina, p. 450
No copy known mp. 40157

B1044 AN earnest expostulation in the name of . . . God with the inhabitants of this land, especially the rising generation . . . [at end] Boston, Printed and sold at the Printing House in Queen–Street over against the prison, 1739.
broadside 28.5 X 20 cm.
MWA. Photostat: MHi mp. 40158

B1045 [FRY, RICHARD]
A scheme for a paper currency for the benefit of the province. [Boston? 1739]
[2], ii, 12, ii p. 31 cm.
Signed "Richard Fry" at end of each section
Dated at end: April 19, 1739
MHi (facsim.); NN (photostat in part); RPJCB
mp. 40159

B1046 HARVARD UNIVERSITY
Quaestiones pro modulo . . . MDCCXXXIX. [Boston, 1739]
broadside
MHi mp. 40160

B1047 HAYWARD, JOHN
The precious blood of the Son of God . . . The twentieth edition. [Williamsburg? W. Parks? ca. 1739]

Advertised by Parks in his 1742 list as "Price bound 1 s. 6 d."
No copy known mp. 40161

B1048 LETTER to B. G. from the members of the Assembly of New-Jersey . . . [Philadelphia, B. Franklin, 1739]
broadside ([2]) p.) fol.
MWA mp. 40162

B1049 LEWIS, JOHN, 1675-1747
The church catechism explain'd . . . Collected by John Lewis, minister of Margate in Kent. [Williamsburg? W. Parks? ca. 1739]

Advertised by Parks in his 1742 list as "Price Stitch'd 10d. bound 1 s. 3d."
No copy known mp. 40163

B1050 THE manual exercise: teaching the military exercise of the firelock. The second edition. [Williamsburg] W. Parks [1739]

Wroth: William Parks 103
No copy known mp. 40164

B1051 MARYLAND. GOVERNOR, 1735-1742
A collection of the governor's several speeches . . . together with several messages and answers thereto . . . at a convention . . . begun the first of May, 1739 . . . [Annapolis, Jonas Green, 1739]
1 p.l., 37, xxxviii-xli, 38-80 p. 30.5 cm.
Wroth 94
DLC; Md mp. 40165

B1052 MASSACHUSETTS. GOVERNOR, 1730-1741
By His Excellency Jonathan Belcher . . . A proclamation for preventing disorders on the Lord's Day . . . Boston, the twenty-fifth day of August 1739 . . . Boston, J. Draper, 1739.
broadside 48 X 37 cm.
MHi mp. 40167

B1053 MASSACHUSETTS. GOVERNOR, 1730-1741
By His Excellency Jonathan Belcher . . . A proclamation [on equipping private ships of war against Spanish vessels] . . . April 10, 1739. Boston, J. Draper [1739]
broadside
Ford 712
MB mp. 40166

B1054 MASSACHUSETTS. LAWS
[Act for regulating the militia, directing how every inlisted foot soldier should be provided with fire arms. Boston, 1739]
broadside
Advertised in the *Boston Evening Post*, Aug. 20, 1739, as "Now printed, and may be had of the publisher of this paper, that paragraph of the Province law."
Ford 720
No copy known mp. 40168

B1055 MASSACHUSETTS. TREASURER
Province of the Massachusetts-Bay, ss. William Foye, Esq; Treasurer . . . July 20, 1739. [Boston, 1739]
broadside
Tax warrant
Ford 716
MSaE mp. 40169

B1056 MASSACHUSETTS. TREASURER
Province of the Massachusetts-Bay, ss. William Foye, Esq; Treasurer . . . to constable or collector of the town of Greeting . . . Given under my hand and

seal at Boston, the twelfth day of November 1739 . . . [Boston, 1739]
broadside 31.5 X 19 cm.
Ford 717; New York Public 190
DLC. Photostats: MWA; NN mp. 40170

B1057 [MATHER, COTTON] 1662-1728
A letter, about a good management under the distemper of the measles . . . [Boston, 1739]
4 p.
MWA (photostat) mp. 40171

B1058 NEW YORK. LAWS
Anno regni Georgii Secundo . . . duodecimo. Acts passed by the General assembly of the colony of New-York in April 1739. [Printed by William Bradford in New-York, 1739.]
[3] p. 31 cm.
Brackets around imprint in original
Gotshall 278
N mp. 40172

B1059 PENNSYLVANIA. GENERAL ASSEMBLY
Anno regni Georgii II . . . duodecimo. At a General Assembly . . . begun . . . the fourteenth day of October . . . 1738. An act for . . . enabling divers inhabitants . . . to trade . . . Philadelphia, Printed and sold by B. Franklin, 1739.
7 p. fol.
Curtis 128
PHi; PPAmP; PU mp. 40173

B1060 PENNSYLVANIA GAZETTE
The yearly verses of the printer's lad . . . Jan. 1, 1739. [Philadelphia, Benjamin Franklin, 1739]
broadside 32 X 9.5 cm.
New York Public 191
MWA. Photostat: NN mp. 40182

B1061 RHODE ISLAND. GOVERNOR, 1734-1740
[A proclamation in regard to counterfeiting . . . Newport, Ann Franklin, 1739]
[broadside?]
At the October 1739 session of the General Assembly the governor was directed to issue a proclamation promising a reward for the discovery of counterfeiting plates
Alden 52
No copy known mp. 40174

B1062 SOUTH CAROLINA. LAWS
Acts passed by the General assembly . . . at a sessions begun . . . [Nov. 10, 1736] . . . and from thence continued . . . to the twenty-fifth day of March . . . 1738. Charles-Town, Lewis Timothy, 1738 [i.e. 1739]
144 p. 29 cm.
The last act included is dated Apr. 11, 1739
Sabin 87565
DLC mp. 40175

B1063 TO the printer. Sir, this minute came to my hands the postscript to the *Boston Gazette* . . . The design of printing the New York paper . . . was not in the least to weaken the hands of those in power . . . Boston, May 2d, 1739. [Boston? 1739]
broadside 18 X 11 cm.
Ford 721
MHi mp. 40176

B1064 [TORREY, JOSEPH] attributed author
A brief representation of the case depending between . . . Mc'Sparran . . . and . . . Torrey . . . July 1739. [Newport? Ann Franklin? 1739]
broadside 30.5 X 20.5 cm.
Presenting Torrey's side of the controversy
Alden 53; Sabin 96298; NYPL 188
MHi; RPJCB. Photostats: MWA; NN; RNHi mp. 40177

B1065 VINCENT, THOMAS
The true Christian's love to the unseen Christ . . . with an appendix [showing] Christ's manifestation of himself to them that love him . . . Boston, Reprinted by J. Draper for D. Henchman, 1739.
[6], 220 p. 12mo
MWA; PPL (all wanting after p. 206) mp. 40178

B1066 [WARNER'S almanack, for the year 1740. Williamsburg, W. Parks, 1739]

Advertised in the *Virginia Gazette*, Nov. 23, 1739
Bear 5; Torrence 150; Wroth: William Parks 106
No copy known mp. 40179

B1067 WHITEFIELD, GEORGE, 1714-1770
The Rev. Mr. Whitefield's answer to the Bishop of London's last pastoral letter. Philadelphia, Andrew and William Bradford [1739]
16 p. 12mo
Huntington 114; cf. Evans 4457
CSmH; MHi mp. 40180

B1068 WHITEFIELD, GEORGE, 1714-1770
The wise and foolish virgins. A sermon preached at Philadelphia, 1739 . . . Philadelphia, Printed and sold by Andrew and William Bradford [1739]
27 p. 19 cm.
cf. Evans 4649
PHi mp. 40181

174–

B1069 ADVERTISEMENT. We do hereby certify, that Mr. Francisco Torres . . . has brought with him some snake stones . . . curing the bites of any venemous or poisonous creatures . . . [Boston? 174–?]
broadside 15 X 14 cm.
Two testimonials, signed "Rhode-Island . . . October 12, 1740. Thomas Saquin . . ." and "Philadelphia, April the 5th, 1743 . . . Anthony Duche."
MB mp. 40185

B1070 FINLEY, SAMUEL, 1715-1766
A letter to a friend . . . [at end] Newport, Printed and sold by the Widdow Franklin [174–[]
16 p. 15 cm. caption title
An attack on George Whitefield
MB mp. 40183

B1071 I do acknowledge to have voluntarily inlisted my self as a private soldier . . . in an expedition against the French settlements at Cape-Breton . . . As witness my hand this day of in the year . . . 174 . [Boston? 174–]
broadside 19.5 X 15 cm.
MWA

B1072 NEW England bravery. Being a full . . . account of the taking of the City of Louisburg . . . on the 17th of June, 1745. Tune of, chivey chase. Boston, Sold at the Heart and Crown in Cornhill [174–?]
broadside
Ford 833
No copy located mp. 40184

B1073 RHODE ISLAND
Custom-house Rhode-Island. Master of the having enter'd the said is permitted to load any goods or merchandize, here lawfully enter'd. Dated this day of 174 To [Newport? 174–]
broadside 7 X 21 cm.
RHi. Photostat: MWA

B1074 WHITEFIELD, GEORGE, 1714-1770
Abraham's offering up his son Isaac. A sermon . . . Philadelphia. Printed and sold by William Bradford [174–?]
30 p., 1 leaf. 16 cm.
Last leaf blank
New York Public 197
NN mp. 40186

1740

B1075 [ADVERTISEMENT. In pursuance of an act of Assembly of this province for encouragement of his Majesty's levies within the same . . . Annapolis, Jonas Green, 1740]
[broadside?]
A recruiting poster
Wroth 99
No copy known mp. 40202

B1076 BIBLE. O.T. PSALMS
The New-England Psalter: or, Psalms of David . . . Boston, Printed by J. Draper for T. Hancock, 1740.
[172] p. 15 cm. A-B^8 C^6 D-L^8
MWA mp. 40187

B1077 Deleted.

B1078 BUNYAN, JOHN, 1628-1688
The pilgrim's progress . . . The twenty fifth edition, with additions of new cuts . . . Boston, Printed by G. Rogers and D. Fowle, for T. Fleet, J. Edwards and H. Foster, 1740.
5 p.l., [1], 12-211, [1] p. 15 cm.
New York Public 192
MWA; NN (fragment only). d'Alté A. Welch, Cleveland (imperfect) mp. 40188

B1079 CONNECTICUT. GOVERNOR, 1724-1741
By the honourable Joseph Talcott Esq; Governour . . . A proclamation . . . New-London, Timothy Green, 1740.
broadside 39 X 30.5 cm.
Call for volunteers in war against Spain, dated at Hartford, May 13, 1740
NHi mp. 40189

B1080 [ERSKINE, RALPH] 1685-1752
The work and contention of Heaven . . . [Boston, 1740]
4 p. 15.5 cm. caption title
Published in *The New England Weekly Journal*, Feb. 12, 1740
MWA mp. 40190

B1081 GARDEN, ALEXANDER, 1685-1756
[Six letters to the Rev. George Whitefield. Charleston, S.C., Lewis Timothy, 1740]

Advertised in the *South-Carolina Gazette*, Aug. 30, 1740, as "Just published and to be sold by the printer."
McMurtrie: South Carolina, p. 451; cf. Evans 4515
No copy known mp. 40191

B1082 H., A.
The Lancaster tragedy: a mournful [e]legy . . . death of the wife [of] Josiah Wilder of Lancaster, and four of his [childr]en . . . burned to death . . . the night following the 23d [Jan]uary, 1739-40 . . . [at end] Boston, Printed and sold at the Heart and Crown in Cornhill [1740?]
leaf 34 X 22.5 cm.
Signed: A. H.
MWA (upper left quadrant lacking) mp. 40194

B1083 HALE, SIR MATTHEW, 1609-1676
The sum of religion . . . Philadelphia, [Printed by B. Franklin and] Sold by Benjamin Lay [1740?]
broadside 30.5 X 19 cm.
cf. Evans 4524
PHi mp. 40192

B1084 HARVARD UNIVERSITY
Quaestiones pro modulo . . . MDCCXL. [Boston, 1740]
broadside 32 X 20.5 cm.
Ford 723
MH; MWA. Photostat: MHi mp. 40193

B1085 A LETTER from a gentleman to his friend in Connecticut. [Boston? John Draper, 1740]
5 p.
Signed at end: Phileleuther. June 23, 1740
Note in contemporary ms. hand: Boston Printed per Mr. Draper came out July 30th 1740
RPJCB. Photostats: MHi; NN mp. 40195

B1086 LORING, ISRAEL, 1682-1772
The nature and necessity of the new-birth . . . delivered in part at the publick lecture in Boston, May 9, 1728 . . . With a preface by the Rev. Mr. Prince. The second edition, Boston, Printed by J. Draper, for D. Henchman, 1740.
[2], 82 p. 15.5 cm. A^4 B-G^6 H^2
CtY; MBC; MWA (sig. B2-5 and H2 mutilated or wanting) mp. 40196

B1087 MANUFACTORY COMPANY
The manufactory scheme. In consequence of the scheme . . . of the Manufactory Company . . . [Dated at end] Suffolk, ss. Boston, December 4th 1740. [Boston, 1740]
[4] p. 37 cm. caption title
Ford 726
DLC; MSaE; MiU-C mp. 40197

B1088 MANUFACTORY COMPANY
Province of the Massachusetts-Bay in New-England. In order to redress the distressing circumstances which the trade of this province labours under . . . its is proposed to set up a bank on land security, no person to be admitted but such as dwell in this province . . . [Boston, 1740]
broadside 39.5 X 32 cm.
Dated at end: March 10th 1739,40
Ford 735
M-Ar; MSaE; RPJCB mp. 40198

B1089 MANUFACTORY COMPANY
Province of the Massachusetts-Bay in New-England. In order to redress the distressing circumstances which the trade of this province labours under . . . it is proposed to set up a bank on land security, no persons to be admitted but such as dwell in this province, and have a real estate therein . . . [Boston, 1740]
broadside 39.5 X 30 cm.
Dated at end: Sept. 9th, 1740
RPJCB mp. 40199

B1090 MANUFACTORY COMPANY
This indenture made the ninth day of September . . . one thousand seven hundred and forty . . . by and between
in the Province of the Massachusetts-Bay . . . and . . . directors of the Manufactory Company . . . [Boston, 1740]
broadside 33.5 X 26 cm.
Ford 745; New York Public 193
MHi. Photostats: DLC; NN

B1091 MARYLAND. GOVERNOR, 1735-1742
The speech of his Excellency Samuel Ogle . . . to both Houses . . . at a session . . . begun . . . the seventh day of July . . . 1740 . . . Annapolis, Jonas Green, 1740.
[4] p. 30.5 cm.
Wroth 101
MH mp. 40200

B1092 MARYLAND. LAWS
An act made and passed at a session . . . begun . . . the twenty third day of April . . . 1740 . . . [Colophon] Annapolis, Jonas Green, 1740.
4 p. 33.5 cm.
Wroth 97
MdBB; MdHi mp. 40201

B1093 MASSACHUSETTS. GOVERNOR, 1730-1741
By His Excellency Jonathan Belcher . . . A proclamation Whereas a scheme for emitting bills or notes by John Colman . . . July 17, 1740. [Boston, 1740]
broadside 31 X 20 cm.
Reprinted from a newspaper
Ford 731
MHi; MSaE; MWA mp. 40203

B1094 NEW JERSEY. GOVERNOR, 1738-1746
The speech of His Excellency Lewis Morris, esq; captain general . . . of New-Jersey . . . Philadelphia, W. and A. Bradford, 1740.
6 p. 32.5 cm.
Metzger 53
Nj mp. 40205

B1095 NEW JERSEY. GOVERNOR, 1738-1746
Speeches made, and a letter wrote by . . . Lewis Morris . . . Philadelphia, Andrew Bradford, 1740.
15 p. 27 cm.
Public Record Off. Photostats: DLC; MHi; MWA; NN; RPJCB mp. 40206

B1096 NEW JERSEY. LAWS
A bill proposed in the Assembly of . . . New-Jersey, entitled, An act to establish two trading companies . . . and enable them to carry on a foreign trade . . . Published for the perusal of the members . . . Philadelphia, Printed and sold by B. Franklin, 1740.
14 p. 30.5 cm.
Metzger 55
Nj mp. 40204

B1097 NEW YORK GAZETTE
A supplement to the *New-York Gazette* of Monday the 14th of April, 1740. [at end] [New York] Printed and sold by William Bradford, 1740.
3 p. 32.5 cm.
Includes letter by Bradford on West Indies expedition
PHi

B1098 PERTH-AMBOY, January 21st 1739-40.
Whereas in a cause of chancery of New-Jersey at the suit of the creditors . . . of Charles Dunstar deceased, against Michael Kearney . . . New-York, John Peter Zenger [1740]
broadside 33 X 21 cm.
NHi mp. 40208

B1099 A SATYRICAL description of commencement.
Calculated to the meridian of Cambridge in New-England. [First printed in the year 1718.] Boston [Thomas Fleet Sr.] [1740?]
broadside 37.5 X 23 cm.
Ford 739; New York Public 196
MWiW-C. Photostats: MHi; NN mp. 40209

B1100 SMITH, JOSIAH, 1704-1781
[A Christmas sermon, preach'd at Charles-Town . . . December 25, 1739, by J. Smith, V.D.M. Charlestown, Lewis Timothy, 1740]

Advertised in the *South-Carolina Gazette*, Dec. 25, 1740, at 5s.
McMurtrie: South Carolina, p. 452
No copy known mp. 40210

B1101 SOUTH CAROLINA. LAWS
[An act for the better ordering and governing Negroes and other slaves in this province. Passed May 10, 1740. Charleston, S.C., Peter Timothy, 1740]

Advertised in the *South-Carolina Gazette*, Nov. 13, 1740, as "Just Published . . . (Price 10s)."
McMurtrie: South Carolina 1731-1740, no. 40
No copy known mp. 40211

B1102 STEBBING, HENRY, 1687-1763
[A caution against religious delusion . . . occasioned by the pretensions of the Methodists. Charleston, S.C., Lewis Timothy, 1740]

Advertised in the *South-Carolina Gazette*, Oct. 23, 1740, "Price 5sh," and "recommended to the inhabitants of South-Carolina by the Rev. Mr. Alex Garden."
McMurtrie: South Carolina, p. 451
No copy known mp. 40212

B1103 TENNENT, JOHN, M.D.
An essay on the pleurisy . . . Williamsburg, W. Parks, 1740.
36 p.
PPAmP mp. 40213

B1104 [THOMSON, JOHN] d. 1753
An essay upon the faith of assurance . . . By a minister of the Gospel . . . Philadelphia, B. Franklin, 1740.
64 p. 16.5 cm.
CtY; DLC mp. 40214

B1105 TO be sold, one moiety or half part of the island of Roanoak . . . six thousand acres . . . surveyed in the year 1718 by William Maule . . . apply . . . to Samuel Swann . . . or to Doct. Belcher Noyes, of Boston . . . the rightful owner thereof. Boston, May 26th, 1740. [Boston? 1740]
broadside 23 X 18 cm.
NcD mp. 40207

B1106 VIRGINIA. COUNCIL
The humble address of the Council . . . [Williamsburg, W. Parks, 1740]
[2] p. 30 X 18 cm.
In reply to the Lieutenant-governor's address of May 22, 1740
DLC (photostat) mp. 40215

B1107 VIRGINIA. COUNCIL
The humble address of the Council . . . [Williamsburg, W. Parks, 1740]
[2] p. 28.5 X 17 cm.
In reply to the Lieutenant-governor's speech Aug. 21, 1740
Wroth: William Parks 109c
DLC (photostat) mp. 40216

B1108 VIRGINIA. GOVERNOR, 1727-1749
The speech of . . . William Gooch . . . [May 22, 1740] [Williamsburg, W. Parks, 1740]
[2] p. 30 X 18 cm.
Wroth: William Parks 111a
DLC (photostat) mp. 40217

B1109 VIRGINIA. GOVERNOR, 1727-1749
The speech of . . . William Gooch . . . [Aug. 21, 1740] [Williamsburg, W. Parks, 1740]
broadside 30 X 18 cm.
Wroth: William Parks 111b
DLC (photostat) mp. 40218

B1110 VIRGINIA. HOUSE OF BURGESSES
The humble address of the House of burgesses . . . [Williamsburg, W. Parks, 1740]
[2] p. 30 X 18 cm.
In reply to Lieutenant-governor Gooch's speech of May 22, 1740
Wroth: William Parks 109a
DLC (photostat) mp. 40219

B1111 VIRGINIA. HOUSE OF BURGESSES
The humble address of the burgesses, met in Assembly . . . [Williamsburg, W. Parks, 1740]
[2] p. 30 X 18 cm.
In reply to the Lieutenant-governor's speech Aug. 21, 1740
Wroth: William Parks 109b
DLC (photostat) mp. 40220

B1112 THE Virginia almanac for the year 1741. [Williamsburg, W. Parks, 1740]
[32] p. 16 cm.
Bear 6; Torrence 163; Wroth: William Parks 112
DLC (lacks t.p. and p. [29-32]) mp. 40221

B1113 WATTS, ISAAC, 1674-1748
[Divine songs attempted in easy language . . . The ninth edition? Boston? S. Draper? 1740?]
50+ p. 11.5 cm.
Tentatively dated by d'Alté A. Welch from comparison of type ornaments of the period
MWA (sig. A^{1-3} and E^{5-6} wanting) mp. 40222

B1114 WHITEFIELD, GEORGE, 1714-1770
The indwelling of the spirit, the common privilege of all believers . . . Williamsburg, W. Parks [1740]

Wroth: William Parks 114
No copy known mp. 40224

B1115 WHITEFIELD, GEORGE, 1714-1770
A journal of a voyage from Gibraltar to Georgia . . . Philadelphia, Printed and sold by B. Franklin, 1740.
45 p. 13.5 cm. $A\text{-}B^{12}$ (B12 wanting)
Second printing of the first section of Whitefield's *Journal*, with sig. A reset.—C. William Miller
Curtis 179
CtY; MB; MWA; N; PHi mp. 40225

B1116 WHITEFIELD, GEORGE, 1714-1770
Journal of a voyage from London to Gibraltar. Sixth edition. Philadelphia, B. Franklin, 1740.
64 p. 24mo
Curtis 178; Hildeburn 676
CtSoP (at CtY); PPL; PPPrHi mp. 40226

B1117 WHITEFIELD, GEORGE, 1714-1770
[A letter from the Reverend Mr. George Whitefield to a friend in London, concerning Archbishop Tillotson. Charleston, S.C., Peter Timothy, 1740]

Advertised in the *South-Carolina Gazette*, Apr. 11, 1740, as "Tomorrow will be published, Price 2s and 6d. Two letters . . . One of which . . . asserted . . . Tillotson knew no more of Christianity than Mahomet . . ."
McMurtrie: South Carolina 1731-1740, p. 21
No copy known mp. 40227

B1118 WHITEFIELD, GEORGE, 1714-1770
A letter from the Reverend Mr. George Whitefield to the inhabitants of Maryland, Virginia, North and South Carolina. [Charleston? 1740?]
4 p. 18 cm.
Dated at end: Savannah, Jan. 23, 1739-40
cf. Evans 4651 (p. 13-16)
ScU

B1119 WHITEFIELD, GEORGE, 1714-1770
The marks of the new-birth . . . Boston, Printed and sold by G. Rogers & D. Fowle, 1740.
16 p. 15.5 cm. $A\text{-}B^4$
MWA mp. 40228

B1120 WHITEFIELD, GEORGE, 1714-1770
A sermon on the eternity of hell-torments . . . Boston, Printed and sold by G. Rogers and D. Fowle, 1740.
16 p. 15 cm. $A\text{-}B^4$
MWA mp. 40229

B1121 WHITEFIELD, GEORGE, 1714-1770
De Wyze en Dwaaze Maagden. Vertoont in een Predicatie . . . Niew-York, Gedrukt en te koop by J. Peter Zenger, en Jacobus Goelet [1740?]
44 p. 17 cm.
cf. Evans 4656-57; New York Public 198
Ownership inscription dated Apr. 22, 1740
NN mp. 40230

B1122 . . . THE wiles of Popery: or, The Popish emissary instructed. A conference 'twixt a famous Roman casuist and an emissary. [Charleston, Peter Timothy, 1740]
15 p. 8vo caption title
At head of title: (Taken from the *South-Carolina Gazette*, Octob. 16, 1740.)
Sabin 103990
No copy located

1741

B1123 [ALMANACK for 1742. By John Nathan Hutchins. New York, 1741]

Drake 5616
No copy known

B1124 BOSTON. ORDINANCES, ETC.
At a meeting of the freeholders and other inhabitants . . . regularly assembled . . . in Boston, on March 10. 1740 . . . [Boston, 1741]

2, [1] p. 18.5 cm. caption title
DLC mp. 40231

B1125 [CHANDLER, WILLIAM]
A journal of the survey of the Narragansett Bay, and parts adjacent . . . May and June, A.D. 1741 . . . [Newport, Ann Franklin, 1741]
broadside 38.5
Alden 56; Wegelin 63
RHi. Photostats: MHi; MWA mp. 40232

B1126 THE condition of this obligation is such, that if above-bounden shall build and finish a dwelling house . . . on a lot . . . in a tract . . . called Bedford . . . and if the said shall dwell in said house three years after the last day of September . . . 1744 . . . [Boston, 1741]
broadside 25 X 20.5 cm.
Ford 741
MHi

B1127 CONNECTICUT. GOVERNOR, 1724-1741
By the honourable Joseph Talcott Esq; Governour . . . A proclamation for a publick fast . . . Given . . . this tenth day of March . . . 1740,41. N. London, T. Green, 1741.
broadside 34.5 X 22.5 cm.
CtHi mp. 40233

B1128 DICKINSON, JONATHAN, 1688-1747
The true scripture-doctrine concerning some important points of Christian faith . . . With a preface by Mr. Foxcroft. Boston, Printed by D. Fowle, for S. Kneeland & T. Green, 1741.
[2], xiii, [1], 253 p. 15.5 cm. A-R^8 (R8 blank and genuine)
CSmH; MHi; MWA (R8 wanting); N; NjP mp. 40234

B1129 HALE, SIR MATTHEW, 1609-1679
Sir Matthew Hale's sum of religion . . . Philadelphia, Printed and sold by B. Franklin, 1741.
16 p. 15.5 cm.
PHi mp. 40236

B1130 HAMILTON, ALEXANDER, of Annapolis
Advertisement. September 29, 1743. The subscriber intending soon for Great-Britain . . . Alexander Hamilton. [Annapolis, Jonas Green, 1741]
broadside 16.5 X 21 cm.
Wroth 109
MdHi mp. 40237

B1131 HARVARD UNIVERSITY
Quaestiones pro modulo discutiendae . . . M D C C X L I. [Cambridge, 1741]
broadside 37.5 X 23.5 cm.
Ford 742
DLC; MH; MHi; MWA mp. 40238

B1132 DER Hoch-Deutsche Americanische Calender auf . . . 1742 . . . Germanton, Christoph Saur [1741]
[30?] p.
Larger issue than Evans 4728
Drake 9632
PDoBHi

B1133 A LAMENTATION on account of disorders and confusions, in two letters to a friend. [Boston, 1741]
broadside
Ms. note: "Came forth May 20th 1741."
Ford 744
MHi mp. 40239

B1134 LIBRARY COMPANY OF PHILADELPHIA
You are hereby notified, that a general meeting of the Library Company of Philadelphia is to be held . . . the 3d of August next . . . July 21, 1741. [Philadelphia, B. Franklin, 1741]
broadside
PPL mp. 40255

B1135 A LIST of men deserted from His Majesty's ship Astrea, Captain James Scott, commander, between the 26th day of April, and the 30th day of May, 1741. [Boston, 1741]
broadside
Ford 749
MHi mp. 40235

B1136 MARYLAND. LAWS
Acts of Assembly . . . passed at a session . . . begun . . . the twenty sixth day of May . . . 1741 . . . Annapolis, Jonas Green, 1741.
[2], 15, [1] p. 32.5 cm.
Wroth 104
Md; MdBB; MdBP; MdHi mp. 40240

B1137 MASSACHUSETTS. GOVERNOR, 1730-1741
By His Excellency Jonathan Belcher . . . A proclamation. Whereas Capt. James Scott . . . hath represented to me . . . [June 8, 1741] . . . Boston, J. Draper, 1741.
broadside 44 X 36.5 cm.
Ford 750
MHi mp. 40241

B1138 MASSACHUSETTS. GOVERNOR, 1730-1741
By His Excellency Jonathan Belcher . . . A proclamation. Whereas . . . the Astraea Capt. James Scott commander . . . [June 9, 1741] Boston, J. Draper, 1741.
broadside 43 X 31 cm.
Ford 751
MHi mp. 40242

B1139 MASSACHUSETTS. GOVERNOR, 1730-1741
Province of the Massachusetts-Bay, by . . . the Governour, a brief. Having lately . . . Boston, J. Draper, 1741.
broadside 43 X 31 cm.
Ford 748; New York Public 199
DLC; MHi. Photostat: NN mp. 40245

B1140 MASSACHUSETTS. GOVERNOR, 1741-1749
By His Excellency William Shirley . . . A proclamation. His Majesty's Royal Commission . . . [Aug. 14, 1741] . . . Boston, J. Draper [1741]
broadside 39 X 31.5 cm.
Continuing officers in their respective offices
Ford 752
MHi mp. 40243

B1141 MASSACHUSETTS. GOVERNOR, 1741-1749
By His Excellency William Shirley . . . A proclamation. Whereas . . . troops are safely landed on . . . Cuba . . . [Oct. 16, 1741] . . . Boston, J. Draper [1741]
broadside 37 X 31.5 cm.
Ford 754
MHi (mutilated) mp. 40244

B1142 MASSACHUSETTS. LAWS
. . . Extract of an act passed . . . November [1736] . . . for supplying the treasury with the sum of eighteen thousand pounds . . . and nine thousand pounds . . . [Colophon] Boston, Printed by J. Draper, 1741.
7 p. 31.5 cm. A-B^2

At head of title: Anno regni Georgij Secundi, Regis, decimo
M; MWA mp. 40246

B1143 MASSACHUSETTS. LAWS
In the House of Representatives, October 8, 1741. Voted, That the Treasurer be directed to apportion the tax . . . upon the several towns . . . In Council, Octo. 8, 1741. Read and concur'd . . . Consented to, W. Shirley . . . [Boston, 1741]
broadside 21 X 15.5 cm.
M; MWA. Photostat: MHi mp. 40247

B1144 [MATHER, COTTON] 1662-1728
Early piety exemplified in Elizabeth Butcher of Boston: who was born July 14th, 1709 and died June 13th, 1718 . . . Fourth edition. Boston: Printed by J. Draper, for C. Harrison, 1741.
[2], iv, 17 p.
CSmH; PPL

B1145 MATHER, COTTON, 1662-1728
Vital Christianity: a brief essay on the life of God in the soul of man . . . Boston, Printed and sold by Rogers and Fowle, 1741.
23, [1] p. 17 cm. A-B^6
MWA (sig. A1-2 photostat); ViU mp. 40248

B1146 MITCHEL, JONATHAN, 1624-1668
The Reverend Mr. Jonathan Mitchel's letter to his friend in New-England. [Colophon] Newport, Re-printed by the widow Franklin, 1741.
16 p. 15.5 cm. caption title
Alden 60
RPJCB mp. 40249

B1147 NEW YORK. LAWS
An act passed in the fifrteenth [sic] year of His Majesty's reign, 1741. An act for the more equal keeping military watches in the city of New-York . . . [Printed by William Bradford in New-York, 1741.]
3 p. 31 cm.
Page numbers changed in ms. to 12-14
Gotshall 282
N mp. 40251

B1148 NEW YORK. LAWS
Anno regni quinquagesimo Georgii Secundo regis. An act for the better fortifying of this colony . . . [New York, William Bradford, 1741]
11 p. 31 cm.
Additions and corrections in ms. in N copy; "quinquagesimo" altered to "quindecimo."
Gotshall 283
N mp. 40250

B1149 ON the Reverend Mr. Gilbert Tennent's powerful and successful preaching in Boston . . . With a few words of advice to awaken'd souls. And of warning to the dispisers of the Gospel offers of salvation.
We bless the man sent by the spirit of grace . . . [Boston, 1741?]
broadside 39 X 24.5 cm.
84 lines of verse in 2 columns
Ford 757
MHi mp. 40252

B1150 PEMBERTON, ISRAEL, AND SON
Copy of part of a letter from Israel Pemberton, and Son . . . to David Barclay, and Son, of London. Philadelphia, B. Franklin, 1741]
broadside 32.5 X 20 cm.
Curtis 157
DLC; PU mp. 40253

B1151 PENNSYLVANIA. CHARTER
The charters of the province of Pensilvania and city of Philadelphia. Philadelphia, Printed and sold by B. Franklin, 1741.
30 p. 21.5 cm.
Curtis 189
PU mp. 40254

B1152 PENNSYLVANIA GAZETTE
The yearly verses of the printer's lad, who carrieth about the *Pennsylvania Gazette* . . . January 1, 1740. [Philadelphia, B. Franklin, 1741]
broadside 32 X 8.5 cm.
Metzger 63
MWA mp. 40269

B1153 PHILADELPHIA, May 7. 1741. Extract of a letter from one of the officers . . . April 3. 1741. [Philadelphia, B. Franklin, 1741]
broadside 33 X 18 cm.
Found in Franklin's copy of the *Pennsylvania Gazette* for 1741
DLC (imperfect); MWA mp. 40256

B1154 A POEM occasion'd by the late powerful and awakening preaching of the Reverend Mr. Gilbert Tennant [sic] by some young lads much affected therewith.
O blessed man! ordained by the great God . . . [Boston, 1741?]
broadside 37.5 X 25.5 cm.
80 lines of verse in 2 columns
Ford 758
MHi mp. 40257

B1155 [SCOUGAL, HENRY] 1650-1678
The life of God in the soul of man . . . Boston, Re-printed by G. Rogers and D. Henchman, 1741.
88 p. 14.5 cm.
PHi mp. 40258

B1156 A SHORT discourse of a life of grace . . . By the author of The spiritual journey temporalized. New-York, William Bradford, 1741.
100 p. sm. 8vo
Huntington 119
CSmH mp. 40259

B1157 SIMS, STEPHEN
A sober reply . . . to a paragraph in Jonathan Edwards's discourse, delivered . . . Sept. 10th. 1741. [New London? Timothy Green? 1741]
broadside 38 X 24 cm.
DLC mp. 40260

B1158 TENNENT, GILBERT, 1703-1764
[The espousals . . . Newport, Ann Franklin, 1741?]
64 p. 16 cm.
Alden 61
Bradford Swan, Providence, R.I. (t.p. lacking)
mp. 40261

B1159 URY, JOHN, d. 1741
The defence of John Ury, made before the Supream Court in New-York, at his tryal for being concerned in the late Negro-Conspiracy . . . [Philadelphia, B. Franklin, 1741]
[2] p. 24 cm. A^2
Includes Ury's dying speech; he was executed at New York, Aug. 29, 1741
Found in the MWA copy of the *Pennsylvania Gazette* for August 1741
MWA mp. 40262; 40263

B1160 Deleted.

B1161 WALTER, NATHANIEL, 1711-1776
The thoughts of the heart the best evidence of a man's spiritual state . . . Boston, Printed and sold by Rogers and Fowle; also sold by N. Procter, 1741.
32 p. 16 cm. A-D^4
MHi; MWA (sig. A1, D4 wanting); N (mutilated)
mp. 40264

B1162 WARNER'S almanack . . . for the year . . . 1742 . . . By John Warner . . . Williamsburg, Wm. Parks [1741]
[26] p. 15.5 cm.
Bear 7; Torrence 168; Wroth: William Parks 168
DLC mp. 40265

B1163 WATTS, ISAAC, 1674-1748
Hymns and spiritual songs . . . The fifteenth edition . . . Philadelphia, B. Franklin, 1741.
xii, [2], 274, [12] p. 13 cm.
Preliminary p. xii misnumbered xiii
cf. Evans 5087
ICN mp. 40266

B1163a WEISS, GEORG MICHAEL, 1770?-
Een getrouwe beschryving der wilden in Noord Amerika . . . [Albany? 1741?]
1 p.l., 97 p. 8vo
Preface dated: Burnetsfield, Albany, N.Y., October 4, 1741
Weiss returned to America in 1731; settled among the Germans in New York (in Dutchess and Schoharie Counties); wrote several pamphlets in German and Dutch, "which have become excessively rare."–Long, J. I. *History of the Reformed Church in the United States* (1899) p. 151
Sabin 102511; cf. Corwin, E. T. *Manual of the Reformed Church in America* (New York, 1902) p. 899
No copy located

B1164 WHITEFIELD, GEORGE, 1714-1770
A brief general account, of the first part of the life of . . . Whitefield . . . Written by himself. Philadelphia, Printed and sold by [William and Andrew Bradford, 1741]
1 p.l., iii, 57 p. 17 cm.
Metzger 72
PHi mp. 40267

B1165 WILLISON, JOHN, 1680-1750
Looking unto Jesus . . . Boston, Printed and sold by S. Kneeland and T. Green, 1741.
1 p.l., 32, [2] p. 15 cm.
"Looking unto Jesus. By another hand": [2] p. at end
DLC; MWA; NN (imperfect); PHi mp. 40268

B1166 WILLISON, JOHN, 1680-1750
Some meditations and materials for prayer . . . Boston, Printed by T. Fleet, for D. Henchman, 1741.
35 p. 17 cm.
CSmH

1742

B1167 [ALMANACK for 1743. By John Nathan Hutchins. New York, 1742]

Drake 5620
No copy known

B1168 BARTLET, MOSES, 1708-1766
Whereas John Rogers yesterday . . . read a printed letter of mine . . . June 8, 1742. Moses Bartlet . . . [Newport, Ann Franklin, 1742]
[3] p. 28 cm.
Alden 62; New York Public 203
RHi. Photostats: MWA; NN mp. 40269

B1169 BOSTON FIRE SOCIETY
Boston, March 8, 1741. These presents witness, That we the subscribers for . . . assistance of each other . . . when in danger by fire, do agree to the following articles, viz. I. That this Society shall consist of a number not exceeding thirty . . . [Boston, 1742]
broadside 43 X 34 cm.
25 members appended in ms.
MHi mp. 40270

B1170 THE case of the inhabitants in Pensilvania. [Philadelphia? 1742?]
broadside (3 p.) 25.5 X 14 cm.
PHi mp. 40271

B1171 CONFESSIO, oder bekantnuss. [Germantown, Christoph Saur, 1742]
20 p. 12mo
Bound at end of Evans 4884
PPL mp. 40272

B1172 CONGREGATIONAL CHURCHES OF NEW ENGLAND
A copy of the resolves of a council of churches, met at Northampton, May 11. 1742. to consider . . . [Colophon] Boston, S. Kneeland and T. Green, 1742.
6 p. 15 cm. caption title
DLC mp. 40283

B1172a FINLEY, SAMUEL, 1715-1766
Christ triumphing, and Satan raging . . . Boston, Printed and sold by Rogers and Fowle, 1742.
32 p.
Trinterud 188
NjPT

B1173 GEORGIA. GOVERNOR, 1733-1752
Order for thanksgiving to Almighty God, for having put an end to the Spanish invasion, a proclamation . . . [July 24, 1742] . . . James Oglethorpe . . . [Colophon] New York, William Bradford [1742]
[2] p. 31 X 19 cm.
DLC mp. 40273

B1174 HARVARD UNIVERSITY
Quaestiones pro modulo . . . MDCCXLII. [Boston, 1742]

broadside 37 X 24 cm.
MH; MHi; MWA mp. 40274

B1175 A LETTER from sundry members belonging to a church . . . in Newport . . . Newport, [Ann Franklin], 1741 [i.e. 1742]
6 p. 18.5 cm.
Dated at end: January 5, 1741,2
Alden 58
RPJCB; RWe mp. 40275

B1176 MARYLAND. LAWS
Acts of Assembly . . . passed at a session . . . begun and held . . . the twenty-first day of September . . . 1742 . . . Annapolis, Jonas Green, 1742.
1 p.l., 56 p. 31 cm.
Wroth 107
DLC; MH-L; Md; MdHi mp. 40276

B1177 MASSACHUSETTS. GOVERNOR, 1741-1749
By His Excellency William Shirley . . . A proclamation for a publick fast . . . [Mar. 4, 1741] . . . [Boston] J. Draper [1742]
broadside 44 X 32 cm.
MWA mp. 40277

B1178 MASSACHUSETTS. GOVERNOR, 1741-1749
By His Excellency William Shirley . . . A proclamation for apprehending Jabez Allen, alias Mead . . . Boston, J. Draper, 1742.
broadside 40 X 30.5 cm.
RPJCB mp. 40278

B1179 MASSACHUSETTS. LAWS
. . . An act. Passed by the . . . General Court . . . begun and held at Boston . . . the twenty-sixth of May, 1742, and continued . . . to Thursday the eighteenth of November following . . . for apportioning and assessing a tax of twenty thousand pounds . . . [Colophon] Boston, J. Draper [1742]
[10] p.
Ford & Matthews p. 381
M-Ar mp. 40279

B1180 MAYLEM, ANN
A short narrative of the unjust proceedings of Mr. George Gardner against Ann Maylem widow . . . of John Maylem late of Newport . . . [Newport, Ann Franklin, 1742?]
broadside 31.5 X 23.5 cm.
Alden 64; New York Public 204
MHi. Photostats: MWA; NN; RHi; RPJCB mp. 40280

B1181 NEW JERSEY. LAWS
[Body of the laws of the Province of New Jersey. Philadelphia, 1742]

Sabin 53076; Humphrey 24 (appendix)
No copy located mp. 40281

B1182 NEW YORK. LAWS
Anno regni quindecimo Georgii II. regis. An act to apply the sum of six hundred and seventeen pounds thirteen shillings and four pence half penny for repairing Fort-George . . . [Published at the City-Hall in the City of New-York the 22th. day of May, 1742. Printed by William Bradford in New-York.]
8-11 p. 31 cm.
Apparently intended to go with Evans 5016, which bears the same date
Gotshall 286
N mp. 40282

B1183 PENNSYLVANIA. GENERAL ASSEMBLY
The Assembly's answer to two messages from the Governor, of the 17th and 23d instant. [Philadelphia, B. Franklin, 1742]
broadside 26 X 20.5 cm.
PHi mp. 40284

B1184 PENNSYLVANIA GAZETTE
The yearly verses of the printer's lad . . . Jan. 1. 1741. [Philadelphia, Benjamin Franklin, 1742]
broadside 33 X 815 cm.
New York Public 200
MWA. Photostat: NN mp. 40296

B1185 PROPOSALS for printing by subscription, A Journal of the proceedings in the detection of the conspiracy . . . white people in conjunction with several Negroes . . . New-York, July 16, 1742. [New York, 1742]
4 p. 38 cm.
NHi mp. 40285

B1186 [RICHARDSON, SAMUEL] 1689-1761
Pamela: or, Virtue rewarded . . . The fifth edition. London, Printed: Philadelphia; Reprinted and sold by B. Franklin. MDCCXLII[-XLIII].
2 v. (xiv, 189; 204 p.) 16.5 cm.
Evans 5486?
MWA

B1187 SOUTH CAROLINA. LAWS
[Acts passed by the General assembly, May 1740–July 1742. Charles-Town, P. Timothy, 1742]
139 p. 30 cm.
Sabin 87566
DLC (t.p. wanting) mp. 40286

B1188 SOUTH CAROLINA. LAWS
[The tax act, passed on the 8th instant, with the estimate thereunto annexed. Charleston, 1742]

Advertised in the *South Carolina Gazette*, Mar. 27, 1742
Mosimann 55
No copy known

B1189 VIRGINIA. COUNCIL
The humble address of the Council . . . [Williamsburg, W. Parks, 1742]
[2] p. 28.5 X 17 cm. caption title
In reply to Lieutenant-governor Gooch's address of May 6, 1742
Wroth: William Parks 119a
DLC mp. 40287

B1190 VIRGINIA. GOVERNOR, 1727-1749
The speech of . . . William Gooch . . . [May 6, 1742] [Williamsburg, W. Parks, 1742]
[2] p. 30 X 18 cm.
Wroth: William Parks 119c
DLC (photostat) mp. 40288

B1191 VIRGINIA. HOUSE OF BURGESSES
The humble address of the House of burgesses . . . [Williamsburg, W. Parks, 1742]
[2] p. 28.5 X 17 cm.
In reply to Lieutenant-governor Gooch's address of May 6, 1742
Wroth: William Parks 119b
DLC mp. 40289

B1192 VIRGINIA. LAWS
. . . At a General assembly, begun . . . the sixth day of May . . . 1742 . . . [Williamsburg, W. Parks, 1742]
58 p. 33 cm. caption title
At head of title: Anno Regni Georgii II . . .
Torrence 171; Wroth: William Parks 118; Sabin 100240
DLC; N; NNB; PHi; RPJCB; Vi mp. 40290

B1193 THE Virginia almanack for the year 1743. [Williamsburg, W. Parks, 1742]
[32] p. 16 cm.
Bear 8; Torrence 170; Wroth: William Parks 120
DLC (lacks t.p. and p. [3-6, 27-32]; ViW (incomplete) mp. 40291

B1194 EIN warhafftiger bericht, von den brüdern in Schweitzerland . . . [Germantown, Christoph Saur, 1742]
46 p. 12mo
Bound at end of Evans 4884
PPL mp. 40292

B1195 WATTS, ISAAC, 1674-1748
Hymns and spiritual songs . . . By I. Watts, D.D. The sixteenth edition . . . Boston, Printed by Rogers & Fowle, for D. Henchman, 1742.
317, [18] p. 14 cm.
"Table": p. [318-332]; "Advertisements concerning the second edition": p. [333-335]
MB mp. 40293

B1196 WHITEFIELD, GEORGE, 1714-1770
The marks of the new birth . . . The fifth edition. Philadelphia, Printed and sold by Andrew and William Bradford [1742?]
24 p. 16 cm.
PHi mp. 40294

B1197 WHITEFIELD, GEORGE, 1714-1770
The prodigal son. A lecture delivered on Boston Common 1740 . . . Boston, Printed and sold by Rogers and Fowle, 1742.
16 p. 18 cm.
Not used for Evans microprint 5089
NHi mp. 40295

1743

B1198 [ALMANACK for 1744. By John Nathan Hutchins. New York, 1743]

Drake 5624
No copy known

B1199 THE American almanack for . . . 1743 . . . By Titan Leeds . . . N. York, Printed and sold by William Bradford, 1743.
[24] p. 16 cm.
New York Public 206; Wall p. 10
MWA; PHi. Photostats: CSmH; NN mp. 40306

B1200 [THE American almanack for . . . 1744. By William Birkett. Philadelphia, A. Bradford [1743]
[24] p.
Drake 9650
MWA? (t.p. lacking)

B1201 A[TKINSON], S[AMUEL]
The interest of New-Jersey considered . . . By S. A. [n.p.] 1743.
20 p. 19.5 cm.
MiU-C mp. 40297

B1202 BISCOE, ROBERT
The merchant's magazine; or, factor's guide . . . Williamsburg, William Parks, 1743.
270, [6] p. 19 cm.
Karpinski p. 56; Sowerby 3576; Wroth: William Parks 121; Huntington 121
CSmH; DLC; NN; PPL; RPJCB mp. 40298

B1203 [BLAIR, SAMUEL] 1712-1751
The reasons of Mr. Alexander Creaghead's receding from the judicatures of this Church, together with its constitution . . . Philadelphia, Printed by B. Franklin, for the author, 1743.
48 p. 16.5 cm.
Curtis 278; Metzger 93
PHi mp. 40299

B1204 BOSTON FIRE SOCIETY
These presents witness, That we the subscribers as neighbours . . . promise to each other as follows, viz. That in case . . . fire . . . Boston, June 2, 1724. Revised and amended, Dec. 7th, 1743 . . . [Boston, 1743]
broadside 46 X 37.5 cm.
17 signers in ms.
Ford 770
MHi mp. 40300

B1205 CONNECTICUT. GOVERNOR, 1741-1750
By the honourable Jonathan Law . . . A proclamation for a day of publick thanksgiving . . . [Oct. 19, 1743] . . . NLondon, T. Green, 1743.
broadside 39.5 X 30.5 cm.
MHi

B1206 CORBET, JOHN, 1620-1680
Self-imployment in secret . . . Left under the handwriting of . . . John Corbet . . . With a prefatory epistle of Mr. John How. The fourth edition. Boston, Re-printed, and sold by J. Draper, 1743.
[2], vi, ii, 42 p. 17 cm. $A\text{-}F^4$ G^2
MWA mp. 40301

B1207 AN elegy, occasion'd by the death of Mrs. Ruth Edson, wife to Mr. Josiah Edson . . . May 31st, 1743, in the 34th year of her age . . . By a friend. Boston, 1743.
broadside 37.5 X 23.5 cm.
Ford 771
MB. Photostat: MWA mp. 40302

B1208 FLEMING, ROBERT, 1630-1694
Fulfilling of the Scripture . . . With a preface by Mr. Foxcroft . . . Boston, Printed by Rogers and Fowle, for Walter McAlpine, 1743.
xxiv, xii, 522p. 17 cm. a^6 aa^6 b^6 $B\text{-}X^{12}$ Y^9
CSmH (sig. Y2 wanting); ICN; MWA (sig. Y3 wanting); NhD mp. 40303

B1209 HARVARD UNIVERSITY
Quaestiones pro modulo . . . MDCCXLIII. [Boston, 1743]
broadside
MH; MHi; MWA mp. 40305

B1210 THE letter to the free-holders of the province of Pennsylvania continued. [Philadelphia? 1743?]
4 p. caption title
Signed at end: T. B.
Continuation of Evans 4988
RPJCB mp. 40307

B1211 MASSACHUSETTS. HOUSE OF REPRESENTATIVES
In the House of Representatives June 2, 1743. [Resolve concerning debts due upon bonds and mortgages] [Boston, 1743]
broadside 30.5 X 17.5 cm.
New York Public 208
NN mp. 40309

B1212 MASSACHUSETTS. LAWS
... An act. Passed by the ... General Court ... begun and held at Boston ... the twenty fifth of May, 1743 ... for apportioning and assessing a tax of twenty thousand pounds ... [Colophon] Boston, J. Draper, 1743.
10 p.
Ford & Matthews p. 384
M-Ar mp. 40310

B1213 MASSACHUSETTS. LAWS
A bill intituled, An act in explanation of sundry acts ... relating to the payment of private debts ... [Boston, 1743]
[3] p. 30.5 cm. caption title
Contains also Gov. Shirley's speech, Apr. 23, 1743, dissolving the General Court
Ford 780; Ford & Matthews p. 382; New York Public 207
MSaE; NN mp. 40308

B1214 MASSACHUSETTS. TREASURER
Province of the Massachusetts-Bay, ss. William Foye, Esq; Treasurer ... In observance of an act ... for apportioning and assessing a tax of twenty thousand pounds ... Given under my hand and seal ... the twelfth day of July 1743 ... [Boston, 1743]
broadside 31.5 X 20 cm.
Ford 779
DLC; MSaE mp. 40311

B1215 NEW JERSEY. GENERAL ASSEMBLY
The votes and proceedings of the General Assembly ... of New-Jersey; held at Amboy ... the tenth of October, 1743. Philadelphia. Printed and sold by William Bradford, 1743.
77 p. 29.5 cm.
New York Public 209; Metzger 92
NN (imperfect); Nj (imperfect) mp. 40312

B1216 NEW JERSEY. GOVERNOR, 1738-1746
The speech of His Excellency Lewis Morris, Esq; Governor ... of New-Jersey, &c. To the Speaker of the House ... the 10th of December, 1743 ... Philadelphia, B. Franklin, 1743.
8 p. 30.5 cm.
Metzger 91
Nj mp. 40313

B1217 NEW YORK. GENERAL ASSEMBLY
Votes of the General Assembly of ... New-York ... [Aug. 2, 1743-Sept. 27, 1743] [New York, J. Parker, 1743]
[2] p. fol.
PHi

B1218 NEW YORK. LAWS
Acts passed in the sixteenth year of His Majesty's reign, 1743. [New York, William Bradford, 1743]
4 p. 31 cm.
Gotshall 288
N mp. 40314

B1219 PENNSYLVANIA. SUPREME COURT
Extract aus der Registratur der Supreem-court zu Philadelphia ... [Philadelphia, Joseph Crellius? 1743]
4 p. 32.5 cm.
DLC mp. 40315

B1220 POOR Richard, 1744. An almanack for the year ... 1744 ... By Richard Saunders, Philom. Philadelphia, Printed and sold by B. Franklin [1743]
[24] p. 15.5 cm.
Curtis 280; not Evans 5189
MWA; PPRF; PU mp. 40304

B1221 PRINCE, THOMAS, 1687-1758
It being earnestly desired by many pious ... people, that ... the revival of religion in every town ... taken and published in The Christian History ... Boston [1743]
broadside 19.5 X 14 cm.
Signed by Thomas Prince, and dated in ms.: April 18, 1743
Ford 781
MWA mp. 40316

B1222 A RIGHT improvement of the righteous judgments of God ... in a few meditations on the ... dreadful storm ... on the 21st of October last ... [Boston? 1743]
broadside 30.5 X 20 cm.
In verse
Huntington 124
CSmH mp. 40317

B1223 SOUTH CAROLINA. LAWS
Acts passed ... at a sessions begun ... the fourteenth day of September ... 1742. And from thence continued ... to the seventh day of May ... 1743. Charles-Town, Peter Timothy, 1743.
40 p. 29 cm.
Sabin 87567
DLC mp. 40318

B1224 THE testimony and advice of an assembly of pastors of churches in New-England, at a meeting in Boston July 7, 1743 ... Boston, S. Kneeland and T. Green, and N. Procter [1743]
51 p. 21.5 cm.
Variant of Evans 5136; 1 line of corrigenda
DLC (2 copies)
Another issue:
6 lines of corrigenda
DLC; ICN
Another issue: 7 lines of corrigenda
NhD

B1225 TO the freeholders of the province of Pennsylvania. [Philadelphia? 1743?]
2 p. 25.5 cm. caption title
Signed at end: A. B.
A reply to Hildeburn 851
RPJCB. Photostat: PHi mp. 40319

B1226 UPON the 24th of May, 1743 ... between Messrs. Penns ... and Lord Baltimore ... [Philadelphia? 1743?]
broadside 14 X 11.5 cm.
PHi mp. 40320

B1227 THE Virginia almanac for the year 1744. [Williamsburg, W. Parks, 1743]
[18+] p. 15.5 cm.
Bear 9; Torrence 174; Wroth: William Parks 122
DLC (lacks t.p. and other leaves) mp. 40321

B1228 WILLISON, JOHN, 1680-1750
Looking to Jesus . . . Boston, Printed for B. Gray, 1743.
[2], 34 p.
From the same setting of type as Evans 5319. Evans collation incorrect, the last 2 pages being included in the pagination
RPJCB mp. 40322

B1229 [ZINZENDORF, NIKOLAUS LUDWIG, GRAF VON] 1700-1760
Mein lieber Mit-Pilger! Da hast du einen Brieff . . . [n.p., 1743]
[4] p. 32 cm.
Metzger 96
DLC; PBMCA mp. 40323

1744

B1230 ADVICE to the inhabitants of the Counties of Hunderton and Morris. As the day of our election draws near to chuse men for our representatives . . . [n.p., 1744?]
2 p. 30.5 cm.
At head of title in an old hand: Benjamin Smith's
Dated by NjR
NjR

B1231 [ALMANACK for 1745. By John Nathan Hutchins. New York, 1744]
Drake 5627
No copy known

B1232 [ALMANACK in Low Dutch for 1745. New-York, W. Bradford, 1744]
Advertised in the *New-York Gazette*, Oct. 29, 1744
Drake 5628
No copy known

B1233 THE American almanack for . . . 1745 . . . By William Birkett. Philadelphia, Andrew Bradford [1744]
Drake 9662
MWA (title leaf only)

B1234 BIBLE. O.T. PSALMS
The Psalms, hymns, and spiritual songs . . . The twenty-sixth edition. Boston, Printed by J. Draper, for S. Kneeland and T. Green, 1744.
[2], 346 p. 13.5 cm. A-O^{12} P^6
Holmes: Minor Mathers 53-W
MWA; ViU mp. 40325

B1235 BIBLE. O.T. PSALMS
The Psalms, hymns, and spiritual songs . . . The twenty sixth edition. Boston, Printed by J. Draper, for T. Hancock, 1744.
[2], 346 p., 12 l. 13.5 cm. A-O^{12} P^6
Holmes: Minor Mathers 53-W; Huntington 126
CSmH (2 issues, differing in contents of 12 l. of music at end) mp. 40324

B1236 BUNYAN, JOHN, 1628-1688
The pilgrim's progress . . . The second part . . . The seventeenth edition, adorn'd with cuts . . . Boston, Printed by John Draper, for Charles Harrison, 1744.
xii, 166 [i.e. 176] p. 15 cm. A-P^6 Q^4
p. 173-176 misnumbered
MHi; MWA; NjP mp. 40326

B1237 COLMAN, BENJAMIN, 1673-1747
[A letter from the Rev. Dr. Colman to Rev. Mr. Williams. Philadelphia? 1744]
Advertised in the *Penn. Gazette*, Oct. 11, 1744, as "Just Published, and to be Sold by B. Franklin." Probably printed in Boston by Rogers & Fowle (Evans 5368). —C. William Miller
No copy known mp. 40327

B1238 CONNECTICUT. GOVERNOR, 1741-1750
By the honourable Jonathan Law, Esq; Governour . . . of Connecticut . . . A proclamation for a day of publick thanksgiving . . . Given . . . in New-Haven, this fifteenth day of October . . . 1744 . . . N. London, T. Green, 1744.
broadside 38.5 X 31.5 cm.
MHi; MWA mp. 40328

B1239 CROSWELL, ANDREW, 1709-1785
The apostle's advice to the jaylor improved . . . Boston, Printed and sold by Rogers and Fowle, 1744. Also sold by B. Gray near the Market.
29, [1] p. 16 cm. A-D^4
MHi; MWA mp. 40329

B1240 FITZ-PARTRICK, EDWARD, d. 1744?
The examination & confession of Edward Fitz-Partrick, after his committing murder on the body of Daniel Campbell at Rutland, on the 8th day of March 1743,4. [Boston] Sold by Benjamin Gray, 1744.
broadside 31 X 19 cm.
McDade 307
MH. Photostat: MHi mp. 40330

B1241 GT. BRIT. SOVEREIGNS (GEORGE II)
A copy of the declaration of war of the King of Great Britain, against the French King. Boston, Printed and sold by T. Fleet [1744]
broadside 30.5 X 21 cm.
Ford 785
MB; MH; MWA mp. 40331

B1242 HARVARD UNIVERSITY
Quaestiones pro modulo . . . MDCCXLIV. [Boston, 1744]
broadside
MH; MHi mp. 40332

B1243 MARYLAND. GENERAL ASSEMBLY
Votes and proceedings of the Lower House . . . at a session begun and held May 1, 1744. [Annapolis, Jonas Green, 1744]
100+ p. 29 cm.
Wroth 112
Md mp. 40333

B1244 MARYLAND. LAWS
Acts of Assembly . . . passed at a session . . . begun . . . the first day of May . . . 1744 . . . Annapolis, Jonas Green [1744]
43, [1] p. 30.5 cm.
Wroth 111
Md; MdBB; MdHi (lacks t.p.) mp. 40334

B1245 MASSACHUSETTS. GOVERNOR, 1741-1749
By His Excellency William Shirley . . . A declaration of war against the Cape-Sable's and St. John's Indians . . . the nineteenth day of October, 1744 . . . Boston, John Draper [1744]
broadside 44 X 29 cm.
Ford 795
MB; MHi (facsim.) mp. 40335

B1246 MASSACHUSETTS. GOVERNOR, 1741-1749
By His Excellency William Shirley . . . A proclamation for proroguing the General Assembly . . . [Sept. 19, 1744] . . . Boston, John Draper, 1744.
broadside 31 X 20.5 cm.
Ford 793
MHi mp. 40336

B1247 MASSACHUSETTS. GOVERNOR, 1741-1749
By His Excellency William Shirley . . . A proclamation for the encouragement of voluntiers to prosecute the war against the St. John's & Cape-Sable's Indians . . . [Nov. 2, 1744] [Boston, 1744]
broadside
New York Public 210
MHi (reduced facsim.); NN (reduced facsim.)
mp. 40337

B1248 MASSACHUSETTS. GOVERNOR, 1741-1749
By His Excellency William Shirley, Esq; . . . A proclamation. Whereas upon Tuesday an heinous riot was committed in . . . Bristol . . . [Oct. 18, 1744] . . . Boston, John Draper [1744]
broadside 40 X 31 cm.
Ford 794
MB; MHi mp. 40338

B1249 MASSACHUSETTS. GOVERNOR, 1741-1749
De la part de Son Excellence Guillaume Shirley . . . Declaration de guerre contre les Indiens du Cap Sable et de Saint Jean . . . October 19, 1744. [Boston, J. Draper, 1744]
broadside
Ford 796
MHi mp. 40339

B1250 MASSACHUSETTS. GOVERNOR, 1741-1749
De la part de Son Excellence Guillaume Shirley . . . Proclamation pour encourager tous volontaires a faire la guerre contre les Indiens . . . [Nov. 2, 1744] . . . [Boston, J. Draper, 1744]
broadside 40 X 31 cm.
Ford 798
MHi mp. 40340

B1251 MASSACHUSETTS. GOVERNOR, 1741-1749
Province of the Massachusetts-Bay. By His Excellency the Governour, I do hereby authorize and impower to beat his drums . . . for the enlisting of voluntiers . . . against the French of Cape-Breton . . . Boston, the day of 1744 . . . [Boston, 1744]
broadside 24 X 19.5 cm.
Signed: W. Shirley
Ford 804
MB; MHi

B1252 MASSACHUSETTS. LAWS
[Act for regulating the militia, relating to fire-arms, &c. Boston, Thomas Fleet, 1744]
broadside
Advertised in the *Boston Evening-Post*, July 30, 1744, as "That paragraph of the province-law . . . may be had ready printed."
Ford 803
No copy known mp. 40341

B1253 MASSACHUSETTS. LAWS
. . . An act passed by the . . . General Court . . . begun and held at Boston . . . the thirtieth day of May 1744 . . . for apportioning and assessing a tax of twenty-five thousand pounds . . . [Colophon] Boston, John Draper, 1744.
[10] p.
Ford & Matthews p. 387
M-Ar mp. 40342

B1254 MASSACHUSETTS. LAWS
An act, passed by the . . . General Court . . . begun and held at Boston . . . the thirtieth day of May 1744 . . . for appropriating a part of the Island called Governour's-Island . . . to the public use of this government . . . Boston, Samuel Kneeland and Timothy Green, 1744.
broadside 20 X 17.5 cm.
MB; MBAt mp. 40343

B1255 MASSACHUSETTS. LAWS
[Temporary.] An act passed by the . . . General Court . . . begun and held at Boston . . . the twenty-fifth day of June 1743, and continued . . . to . . . the eighth day of February following . . . [Boston, 1744]
p. 99-101
A separate edition of chap. vii, the text identical with p. 99-101 of Evans 5430
Ford & Matthews p. 387
MWA; NN mp. 40344

B1256 MASSACHUSETTS. TREASURER
Province of the Massachusetts-Bay, ss. William Foye, Esq; Treasurer . . . [July 10, 1744] . . . [Boston, 1744]
broadside
Tax warrant
Ford 800
MSaE mp. 40345

B1257 MASSACHUSETTS. TREASURER
Province of the Massachusetts-Bay, ss. William Foye, esq; treasurer . . . Boston, the tenth day of November, 1744 . . . [Boston, 1744]
broadside 39 X 31.5 cm.
MiU-C mp. 40346

B1257a NEDERDUYTSCHE almanak voor 1745. New York, William Bradford, 1744.

Advertised in the *New-York Gazette*, Oct. 29, 1744
Drake 5628
No copy known

B1258 A POCKET almanack for the year 1745 . . . By R. Saunders, Phil. Philadelphia, Printed and sold by B. Franklin [1744]
[24] p. 9.5 cm.
Printed throughout in black and red; cf. Evans 5397, in which t.p. is differently aligned and in which items in boldface replace those here printed in red
Drake 9660; Hildeburn 897
CtY; PU

B1259 A PRIMMER for children. Or, An introduction to the true reading of English. [woodcut] N. London, Printed & sold by T. Green, 1744. ⟨13th. edit.⟩
9 X 6 cm.
On recto (serving as cover): The Connecticut Primmer (repeated inverted below woodcut of 3 men in the woods)
MWA (t.p. only) mp. 40347

B1260 RHODE ISLAND. ELECTION PROX.
Richard Ward, Esq; Gov. Samuel Clarke, Esq; Dep. Gov. . . . [Newport, Ann Franklin, 1744?]
broadside 16.5 X 11.5 cm.

Alden 69; Chapin Proxies 1
RHi mp. 40348

B1261 DIE Richtigkeit der Welt und des zeitlichen Lebens . . . . . Kürtzlich beschrieben von einem Englishen Autor, und ins Teutsche übersetzt. Germanton, Christoph Saur, 1744.
17.5 cm.
P

B1262 SHERLOCK, WILLIAM, 1641?-1707
A practical discourse concerning death . . . Williamsburg, William Parks, 1744.
[8], 310 p. 19 cm.
Huntington 127; Sowerby 1603; Wroth: William Parks 123
CSmH; DLC (2 copies); PPL; RPJCB mp. 40349

B1263 [SHOWER, JOHN] 1657-1715
The tryal and character of a real Christian, demonstrated in . . . Henry Gearing . . . who departed this life January 4, 1693,4. Aged sixty one. Collected out of his papers . . . The fourth edition. New-York, Printed and sold by W. Bradford & H. De Foreest, 1744.
xxiv, 118 [i.e. 119] p. 15 cm.
NHi mp. 40350

B1264 SOUTH CAROLINA. LAWS
Acts passed . . . at a session begun . . . the fourteenth of September . . . 1742. And from thence continued . . . to the 29th day of May, 1744. Charles-Town, Peter Timothy, 1744.
60 p. 29 cm.
Sabin 87568
DLC mp. 40351

B1265 STEBBINS, JONATHAN
[An elegy on the death of his first wife, Margaret Bliss, who died in 1744. New London? T. Green? 1744?]
8 p.
They resided in Long Meadow, Mass.
Trumbull: Supplement 2634
CtHi (t.p. lacking) mp. 40352

B1266 VIRGINIA. COUNCIL
The humble address of the Council . . . [Williamsburg, W. Parks, 1744]
2 p. 38 X 23 cm.
In reply to Lieutenant-governor Gooch's address of Sept. 4, 1744
Wroth: William Parks 125a
DLC (photostat) mp. 40353

B1267 VIRGINIA. GOVERNOR, 1727-1749
The speech of the honourable William Gooch . . . to the General assembly: at a session . . . held . . . the fourth day of September . . . 1744. Williamsburg, W. Parks, 1744.
4 p. 38 cm.
Wroth: William Parks 125a [bis];
Sabin 99984
Public Record Off. Photostat: DLC mp. 40354

B1268 VIRGINIA. HOUSE OF BURGESSES
The humble address of the House of burgesses . . . [Williamsburg, W. Parks, 1744]
2 p. 38 X 23 cm.
In reply to Lieutenant-governor Gooch's address of Sept. 4, 1744
Wroth: William Parks 124a
DLC (photostat) mp. 40355

B1269 VIRGINIA. LAWS
Acts of assembly, passed at a General assembly, summoned to be held . . . the sixth day of May . . . and from thence continued . . . to Tuesday the fourth day of September . . . 1744 . . . Williamsburg, William Parks, 1744.
1 p.l., 58 p. 32.5 cm.
Sabin 100241; Torrence 186
DLC; Vi mp. 40356

1745

B1270 ADVERTISEMENT, Perth-Amboy, September 17, 1745. Whereas sundry of the purchasers . . . [New York, John Peter Zenger, 1745]
broadside 15 X 20.5 cm.
This advertisement appeared also in no. 628 (Sept. 30, 1745) of Zenger's *New York Weekly Journal*
Rutherfurd p. 166
DLC; NHi mp. 40357

B1271 [ALMANACK for 1746. By John Nathan Hutchins. New York, 1745]

Drake 5631
No copy known

B1272 THE American country almanack for the year . . . 1746 . . . By Thomas More . . . Philadelphia, B. Franklin [1745]
[20+] p. 16 cm.
Curtis 320; Morrison p. 106
DLC mp. 40381

B1273 [AMERICANSCHE almanak voor 1746. Niew-York, 1745]

Advertised in the *New-York Evening Post*, Dec. 2, 1745
Drake 5633
No copy known

B1274 [CHANLER, ISSAC, 1701–1749]
The state of the church of Christ both militant and triumphant consider'd . . . Occasioned by the death of the Rev. Mr. Tilly . . . Charleston, Peter Timothy? 1745]

Advertised in the *South Carolina Gazette*, July 6, 1745
Mosimann 62
No copy known

B1275 CONNECTICUT. GOVERNOR, 1741–1750
By the honourable Jonathan Law . . . A proclamation for a day of publick thanksgiving . . . the seventh day of November next . . . New-Haven, this sixteenth day of October . . . 1745 . . . N. London, Timothy Green, 1745.
broadside
CtHi mp. 40358

B1276 [ECKERLIN, ISAREL] 1705-
Ein sehr geistreicher Spiegel . . . [Ephrata, 1745]
broadside 28 X 19.5 cm.
PHi (facsim.) mp. 40359

B1277 EDWARDS, JONATHAN, 1703–1758
Boston, May 1. 1745. Proposals for printing by subscription, in one volume, A treatise concerning religious affections . . . [Boston, 1745]
broadside
MH-AH mp. 40360

B1278 THE English soldier encouraged. Rouse heroes, arm, brave captains take the field . . . [Boston? 1745?]
broadside
Ford 808
MSaE. Photostat: MHi mp. 40361

B1279 HARVARD UNIVERSITY
Quaestiones pro modulo . . . M,DCC,XLV. [Boston, 1745]
broadside
MH; MWA mp. 40362

B1280 THE holy life of Armelle Nicolas . . . done out of French . . . Germantown, Chris. Sower Jr., 1745.

PU

B1281 KEACH, BENJAMIN, 1640–1704
The travels of True Godliness . . . Tenth edition . . . Boston, Printed by B. Green and Company for D. Gookin, 1745.
2 p.l., 151 p. front. 14.5 cm.
DLC; MH; RPJCB (wanting p. 1–2, 149–151) mp. 40363

B1282 A LETTER from a gentleman in Salem, to his friend in Boston . . . Salem, October 25, 1745. [Boston? 1745?]
broadside 37.5 X 23.5 cm.
Concerns the settlement of Dudley Leavit over the First Church
Ford 815
MHi (2 copies) mp. 40364

B1283 MARYLAND. LAWS
Acts of Assembly . . . passed at a session . . . begun . . . the fifth day of August . . . 1745 . . . Annapolis, Jonas Green, 1745.
[2], 18 p. 30 cm.
Wroth 114
MH-L; Md; MdBB; MdHi mp. 40365

B1284 MASSACHUSETTS. GENERAL COURT
The following is a perfect list of the establishment of officers and men in the expedition against Louisburg, pass'd the . . . General Court . . . March 1744. [Also] The following further resolve pass'd . . . Sept. 26, 1745. [Boston, 1745?]
broadside 29.5 X 18.5 cm.
MB; MHi mp. 40371

B1285 MASSACHUSETTS. GENERAL COURT
Instructions for masters of transports . . . The foregoing instructions are printed by order of the General court . . . J. Willard, Secr. March 13. 1744. [Boston, 1745]
broadside 31.5 X 20.5 cm.
Ford 831
DLC mp. 40374

B1286 MASSACHUSETTS. GOVERNOR, 1741–1749
Boston, February 3, 1745. Sir, Having received a commission . . . for raising a regiment . . . for the defence and service of Cape-Breton . . . [Boston, J. Draper, 1745]
[2] p. 29 X 19 cm.
Ford 830
MB; MWA mp. 40366

B1287 MASSACHUSETTS. GOVERNOR, 1741–1749
By His Excellency William Shirley . . . A proclamation [on inlisting reinforcements] . . . [June 1, 1745] . . . Boston, J. Draper [1745]
broadside 43 X 31 cm.
Ford 820
MHi; MWA mp. 40370

B1288 MASSACHUSETTS. GOVERNOR, 1741–1749
By His Excellency William Shirley . . . A proclamation. Whereas the Great and General Court . . . [Jan. 26, 1744] . . . Boston, John Draper [1745]
broadside 43 X 31.5 cm.
On inlisting soldiers
Ford 816
MHi mp. 40368

B1289 MASSACHUSETTS. GOVERNOR, 1741–1749
By His Excellency William Shirley . . . A proclamation. Whereas the honourable Peter Warren . . . [May 31, 1745] . . . Boston, J. Draper [1745]
broadside 38 X 31.5 cm.
DLC; MWA mp. 40369

B1290 MASSACHUSETTS. GOVERNOR, 1741–1749
By His Excellency William Shirley . . . A proclamation. Whereas the honourable Peter Warren . . . June 4, 1745. Boston, J. Draper [1745]
broadside 43 X 31.5 cm.
Ford 821
MHi mp. 40367

B1291 MASSACHUSETTS. GOVERNOR, 1741–1749
By the honourable Spencer Phips . . . A declaration of war against the Eastern and Canada Indians . . . [Aug. 23, 1745] . . . Boston, John Draper [1745]
broadside 45 X 31.5 cm.
Ford 823
MHi mp. 40375

B1292 MASSACHUSETTS. GOVERNOR, 1741–1749
By the honourable Spencer Phips . . . A proclamation. Whereas divers persons . . . [Oct. 11, 1745] . . . Boston, John Draper [1745]
broadside 42 X 31 cm.
Ford 826
MHi mp. 40376

B1293 MASSACHUSETTS. GOVERNOR, 1741–1749
By the honourable Spencer Phips . . . A proclamation. Whereas upon Wednesday . . . disorders . . . officers and seamen . . . [Nov. 22, 1745] . . . Boston, John Draper [1745]
broadside 42.5 X 31 cm.
Ford 827
MHi mp. 40377

B1294 MASSACHUSETTS. LAWS
. . . An act passed by the . . . General Court . . . begun and held at Boston . . . the twenty-fifth day of May, 1745 . . . for apportioning and assessing a tax of thirty thousand pounds . . . [Colophon] Boston, John Draper, 1745.
8 [i.e. 12] p.
"Twenty-fifth" is a misprint for "Twenty-ninth."
Ford & Matthews p. 390
M-Ar mp. 40372

B1295 MASSACHUSETTS. LAWS
. . . An act passed . . . December [1745] . . . An act for granting . . . several rates and duties of impost and tunnage of shipping. [Boston, 1745?]
4+ p. 30.5 cm.
New York Public 213
NN (all after p. 4 wanting) mp. 40373

B1296 MASSACHUSETTS. TREASURER
Province of the Massachusetts-Bay, ss. William Foye, Esq; Treasurer . . . July 12, 1745. [Boston, 1745]
broadside
Tax warrant
Ford 832
MB; MSaE; MWA mp. 40378

B1297 MASSACHUSETTS. TREASURER
Province of the Massachusetts-Bay, ss. William Foye, Esq; Treasurer . . . Given . . . the sixth day of November, 1745 . . . [Boston, 1745]
broadside 38.5 X 31 cm.
Tax warrant
MB; MWA mp. 40379

B1298 MOSES pleading with God for Israel . . . [Boston] Sold by Benjamin Gray, 1745.
broadside 31 X 21.5 cm.
In verse
New York Public 214
Original formerly in collection of Matt B. Jones
Photostats: MWA; NN; RPJCB mp. 40382

B1299 NEW-England's Ebenezer . . . Boston, Printed for, and sold by Benjamin Gray, 1745.
broadside 41.5 X 28.5 cm.
In verse
PPRF mp. 40383

B1300 NEW HAMPSHIRE. GOVERNOR, 1741-1767.
By His Excellency Benning Wentworth . . . a proclamation. Whereas I have . . . [Feb. 2, 1744] . . . [Boston, 1745]
broadside 42.5 X 31 cm.
DLC; NhHi. Photostat: NN mp. 40384

B1301 NEW HAMPSHIRE. GOVERNOR, 1741-1767.
By His Excellency Benning Wentworth . . . a proclamation. Whereas the General Assembly . . . have voted a suitable encouragement for the enlistment of . . . voluntiers . . . Given . . . in Portsmouth, the second day of February 1744 . . . [Boston, 1745]
broadside 42.5 X 31 cm.
Concerns the Cape Breton expedition
Ford 817; New York Public 211
DLC; MHi; NhHi. Photostats: MWA: NN mp. 40385

B1302 NEW YORK. GOVERNOR, 1743-1753
By His Excellency, the honourable George Clinton . . . A proclamation, prohibiting all traffick and correspondence . . . all Indians in league with the French . . . [New York, 1745]
broadside 30.5 X 20.5 cm.
Dated at New-York, Sept. 5, 1745
NHi mp. 40386

B1303 NEW-YORK WEEKLY POST-BOY
The yearly verse of the printer's lad . . . [New York, James Parker, 1745]
broadside 21 X 13.5 cm.
Dated in ms.: Jan 1745
New York Public 215
NN mp. 40393

B1304 PENNSYLVANIA GAZETTE.
Supplement to the *Pennsylvania Gazette*, no. 867. July 25, 1745. Monday evening the General Assembly . . . met . . . called by the Governor, who the next morning sent them the following message . . . [Philadelphia, 1745]
broadside 31 X 19 cm.
DLC

B1305 PHILADELPHIA. ORDINANCES
An ordinance for establishing a market in the District of Southwark. [Philadelphia] D. Humphreys [1745]
broadside 24.5 X 11.5 cm.
PHi mp. 40387

B1306 POOR Will's almanack for . . . 1746 . . . By William Birkitt [sic] Philadelphia, W. Bradford [1745]
[24] p.
Drake 9674
InU (imperfect); MWA; PHi

B1307 PRAYERS and thanksgivings for a family or private person. [Boston, J. Draper, 1745]
1 p.l., 5 p. 19.5 cm.
"Taken from the publick prayers of the Church of England:" p. 1
DLC mp. 40388

B1308 SOUTH CAROLINA. LAWS
Acts passed by the General assembly . . . Charles-Town, Peter Timothy, 1745.
40 p. 29 cm.
Sabin 87571
DLC mp. 40389

B1309 [THE Virginia almanack, for the year . . . 1746. Williamsburg, W. Parks, 1745]

Advertised in the *Virginia Gazette*, Oct. 10, 1745, as "Just published."
Wroth: William Parks 126b
No copy known mp. 40390

B1310 WATTS, ISAAC, 1674-1748
The first set of catechisms and prayers . . . The ninth edition. Boston, Printed for J. Blancard, 1745.
16 p. 16.5 cm. A^8
MWA mp. 40391

B1311 WESTMINSTER ASSEMBLY OF DIVINES
The larger catechism . . . Boston, Reprinted by J. Draper, for W. McAlpine, 1745.
88 p. 15 cm. $A\text{–}L^4$
MWA mp. 40392

1746

B1312 [AN almanac for 1747, by Thomas More. Philadelphia, B. Franklin, 1746]

Curtis 338; Hildeburn 981
No copy known mp. 40413

B1312a BLAIR, SAMUEL, 1712-1751
A sermon preach'd at George's–Town . . . at the funeral of . . . William Robinson . . . who departed . . . August 3d. 1746 . . . Philadelphia, William Bradford [1746?]
30 p.
Trinterud 26
NjPT

B1313 BURGH, JAMES, 1714-1775
Britain's remembrancer . . . Williamsburg, W. Parks [1746]
50 p. 17.5 cm.
Wroth: William Parks 128a
ViHi (t.p. wanting) mp. 40394

B1314 [DELONEY, THOMAS]
Fai[r Rosamond] Ga[? . . .] . . . Newport, Widow Franklin, 1746.

8? p. 14.5 cm.
Alden 74; cf. Catalogue of English and American chapbooks . . . (Cambridge, 1905) p. 47
MWA (mutilated mp. 40395

B1315 HARRISON, GEORGE
Philadelphia, July 14, 1746. Advertisement. At the Marble Shop . . . in Arch Street, Philadelphia . . . [Philadelphia, B. Franklin, 1746]
broadside 19 X 16 cm.
Monuments, fonts, tombstones, for sale by George Harrison
Curtis 326; Hildeburn 4622
PHi mp. 40396

B1316 HARVARD UNIVERSITY
Quaestiones pro modulo . . . MDCCXLVI. [Boston, 1746]
broadside
MHi; MWA mp. 40397

B1317 THE HISTORY of the Holy Jesus . . . The third edition. Boston, Printed for B. Gray, 1746.
[48] p. illus. 9.5 cm.
New York Public 215a
MSaE. Facsims: MHi; MWA(also fragment); NN
mp. 40398

B1318 [INSTRUMENT of a voluntary association for defence. Philadelphia, B. Franklin, 1746]
[2] p. 39 cm.
Begins: We whose names are hereunto subscribed . . . provide ourselves . . . firelock, cartouch box . . .
PHi mp. 40399

B1319 MACPHERSON, CAPT. JAMES
The history of the present rebellion in Scotland . . . Boston, Re-printed for D. Henchman, 1746.
31 p. 17 cm. A–D^4
MWA(sig. Al wanting); N mp. 40400

B1320 MARYLAND. GENERAL ASSEMBLY
Votes and proceedings of the Lower House . . . at a session begun . . . March 12, 1745,6. [Colophon] Annapolis, Jonas Green, 1746.
23, [1] p. 29 cm.
Wroth 119
Md mp. 40401

B1321 MARYLAND. GENERAL ASSEMBLY
Votes and proceedings of the Lower House . . . [Colophon] Annapolis, Jonas Green [1746]
42 p. 29 cm.
Session June 17-July 8, 1746
Wroth 120
Md mp. 40402

B1322 MARYLAND. LAWS
Acts of Assembly . . . passed at a session . . . begun . . . the seventeenth day of June . . . 1746 . . . Annapolis, Jonas Green, 1746.
22 p. 29.5 cm.
Wroth 118
MH-L; Md; MdBB; MdHi mp. 40403

B1323 MASSACHUSETTS. GOVERNOR, 1741-1749
By His Excellency William Shirley . . . A proclamation. Whereas Captain Richard Farrish . . . [July 12, 1746] . . . Boston, John Draper [1746]
broadside 43 X 31 cm.
Ford 846; Huntington 133
CSmH; MHi mp. 40407

B1324 MASSACHUSETTS. GOVERNOR, 1741-1749
By His Excellency William Shirley . . . A proclamation. Whereas His Majesty . . . [June 2, 1746] . . . Boston, John Draper [1746]
broadside 23 X 17 cm.
Concerns volunteers for the Louisburg expedition
Ford 844; New York Public 216
NN (reduced facsim.) mp. 40408

B1325 MASSACHUSETTS. GOVERNOR, 1741-1749
By His Excellency William Shirley . . . A proclamation. Whereas I have lately received advice . . . [Sept. 16, 1746] . . . Boston, John Draper [1746]
broadside 43 X 31 cm.
Ford 848
MHi mp. 40409

B1326 MASSACHUSETTS. GOVERNOR, 1741-1749
By His Excellency William Shirley . . . A proclamation. Whereas it is of great importance . . . [May 14, 1746] . . . Boston, John Draper [1746]
broadside 42.5 X 31 cm.
Ford 843
MHi mp. 40406

B1327 MASSACHUSETTS. GOVERNOR, 1741-1749
By His Excellency William Shirley . . . A proclamation. Whereas the soldiers . . . deserted from Castle William . . . [Feb. 10, 1745] . . . Boston, J. Draper [1746]
broadside 42 X 31 cm.
Ford 840
MHi mp. 40404

B1328 MASSACHUSETTS. GOVERNOR, 1741-1749
By His Excellency William Shirley . . . A proclamation. Whereas the soldiers . . . deserted from the Hospital [April 26, 1746] . . . Boston, John Draper [1746]
broadside 42.5 X 31 cm.
Ford 842
MHi mp. 40405

B1329 MASSACHUSETTS. LAWS
. . . An act passed by the . . . General Court . . . begun and held at Boston . . . the twenty-eighth day of May 1746 . . . for apportioning and assessing a tax of twenty-eight thousand four hundred and ninety-nine pounds seven shillings and six pence . . . [Colophon] Boston, J. Draper [1746]
7 [i.e. 11] p.
Ford & Matthews p. 393
M-Ar mp. 40410

B1330 MASSACHUSETTS. LAWS
. . . An act passed by the . . . General Court . . . begun and held at Boston . . . the twenty-eighth day of May 1746 . . . more effectually to prevent profane cursing . . . Boston, S. Kneeland and T. Green, 1746.
broadside 43 X 31 cm.
Ford 839
DLC; MHi mp. 40411

B1331 MASSACHUSETTS. TREASURER
Province of the Massachusetts-Bay, ss. William Foye, Esq; Treasurer . . . [Nov. 4, 1746] . . . [Boston, 1746]
broadside 38.5 X 31 cm.
Tax warrant
Ford 852
MSaE; MWA; MeHi mp. 40412

B1332 NEW HAMPSHIRE. GOVERNOR, 1741-1767
By . . . Benning Wentworth . . . a proclamation. Whereas His majesty . . . [June 5, 1746] . . . Boston, Thomas Fleet [1746]
broadside 44 X 31.5 cm.
Ford 855; New York Public 217
DLC; NhHi. Photostat: NN mp. 40414

B1333 PENNSYLVANIA. GOVERNOR, 1738-1747
By the Honourable George Thomas, esq; Lieutenant Governor . . . A proclamation . . . [June 9, 1746] . . . Philadelphia, Printed [sic] by B. Franklin [1746]
broadside 52 X 40 cm.
For raising troops for the reduction of Canada
MB mp. 40415

B1334 TAYLOR'S successor: a new almanack and ephemeris for . . . 1747. By Zach. Butcher . . . Philadelphia: Printed for the author [1746]
[26+] p.
Drake 9685
PHi (imperfect)

B1335 TOWNSEND, JONATHAN, 1697-1762
God's terrible doings are to be observed. A sermon preach'd at Needham, and occasion'd by the sudden and awful death of Mr. Thomas Gardner, jun. . . . kill'd by lightning on Friday April 4, 1746 . . . Boston, Printed by S. Kneeland and T. Green, 1746.
23 p. 16 cm.
Sabin 96386
DLC; MH; OClW mp. 40416

B1336 VIRGINIA. COUNCIL
To . . . William Gooch . . . the humble address of the Council . . . [Williamsburg, W. Parks, 1746]
[2] p. 32 X 21 cm.
In reply to Lieutenant-governor Gooch's speech of Feb. 20, 1745/6
Wroth: William Parks 133a
DLC (photostat) mp. 40417

B1337 VIRGINIA. HOUSE OF BURGESSES
To . . . William Gooch . . . the humble address of the House of burgesses . . . [Williamsburg, W. Parks, 1746]
[2] p. 31 X 20 cm.
In reply to the Lieutenant-governor's speech of Feb. 20, 1745/6
Wroth: William Parks 134b
DLC (photostat) mp. 40418

B1338 VIRGINIA. LAWS
Acts of assembly, passed at a General Assembly, summoned to be held . . . the sixth day of May . . . and from thence continued . . . to Thursday the twentieth day of February . . . 1745 . . . Williamsburg, William Parks, 1746.
1 p.l., 55 p. 32.5 cm.
Sabin 100242; Torrence 181; Wroth: William Parks 131
DLC; Vi. Public Record Off. mp. 40419

B1339 VIRGINIA. LAWS
. . . At a General Assembly . . . [July 11-16, 1746] . . . being the fourth session . . . [Williamsburg, W. Parks, 1746]
[4] p. 30 cm. caption title
Torrence 182; Wroth: William Parks 132
Vi mp. 40420

B1340 THE Virginia almanack, for the year . . . 1747 . . . Williamsburg, William Parks [1746]
[32] p. 17 cm.
Bear 11; Drake 13746
ViWC

1747

B1341 BOSTON
Boston ss. At a meeting of the selectmen February 21, 1746. Whereas the small pox . . . hath prevail'd in the neighbouring governments . . . An act . . . the spreading of the small-pox . . . and to prevent the concealing of the same . . . Ezekiel Goldthwait, Town Clerk. [Boston, 1747]
broadside 44 X 33 cm.
Austin 257; Ford 835
MHi mp. 40422

B1342 CALDWELL, JOHN, fl. 1742
An impartial trial of the spirit . . . Williamsburg, Reprinted by William Parks, 1747.
xvi, 28 p. 20.5 cm.
Sabin 9905; Wroth: William Parks 129; cf. Evans 5750 (dated 1746)
DLC mp. 40423

B1343 DILWORTH, THOMAS, d. 1780
A new guide to the English tongue . . . Eighth edition. Philadelphia, B. Franklin, 1747.
ix, [4], 154 p. 17 cm.
Curtis 354
MWA (photostat t.p. and p. 139 only); NNC mp. 40424

B1344 HARVARD UNIVERSITY
Quaestiones pro modulo . . . MDCCXLVII. [Boston, 1747]
broadside
MH; MHi; MWA mp. 40425

B1345 A LATE letter from a solicitous mother, to her only son, both living in New-England. Boston, Printed and sold by S. Kneeland and T. Green, 1747.
15 p. 16 cm. A-B[4]
MWA mp. 40426

B1346 MARYLAND. LAWS
An act of Assembly . . . passed at a session . . . begun . . . the 6th day of November . . . 1746. An act for issuing . . . nine hundred pounds current money, in bills of credit . . . [Annapolis, Jonas Green, 1747]
4 p. 30.5 cm.
Wroth 123
Md; MdBB mp. 40427

B1347 MARYLAND. LAWS
An act to remedy some defects in an indenture of bargain and sale . . . executed by Michael Curtis . . . to Charles Carroll . . . [Annapolis, Jonas Green, 1747]
broadside 33 X 21 cm.
Wroth 124
MdHi mp. 40428

B1348 MARYLAND. LAWS
Acts . . . passed at a session of Assembly, begun and held . . . the sixteenth day of May . . . 1747 . . . Annapolis, Jonas Green, 1747.
57 p. 30 cm.
Wroth 125
DLC; MH-L; Md; MdHi; N mp. 40429

B1349 MASSACHUSETTS. GOVERNOR, 1741-1749
By His Excellency William Shirley . . . A proclamation. Whereas the Great and General Court . . . [July 22, 1747] . . . Boston, John Draper [1747]
broadside 37 X 25 cm.
Ford 862
MHi mp. 40430

B1350 MASSACHUSETTS. TREASURER
Province of the Massachusetts-Bay, ss. William Foye, Esq; Treasurer . . . to constable or collector of the town of Greeting, &c. By virtue . . . [Nov. 10, 1747] [Boston, 1747]
broadside 38 X 31.5 cm.
Ford 868; not Evans 4039
DLC; MSaE; MWA mp. 40431

B1351 MERCER, JOHN, 1704-1768
To the worshipful, the speaker and gentlemen of the House of Burgesses, the case and petition of John Mercer . . . [Williamsburg, W. Parks, 1747]
[4] p. 28 cm. caption title
Wroth: William Parks 137; Torrence 183
Coleman mp. 40432

B1352 Deleted.

B1353 NEW JERSEY. PROPRIETORS OF THE EASTERN DIVISION
Bill in the Chancery of New-Jersey, at the suit of John Earl of Stair, and others, Proprietors of the Eastern-Division of New-Jersey; against Benjamin Bond . . . New-York, J. Parker, 1747.
124 p. 3 maps
cf. Evans 6021
NjR mp. 40421

B1354 NEW JERSEY. SURVEYOR GENERAL
General instructions by the Surveyor General, to the deputy surveyors of the Eastern Division of New-Jersey. [Philadelphia? B. Franklin? 1747]
5, [1] p. 36 cm. caption title
Attributed also to James Parker's press in New York
Humphrey 3; Huntington 137; Sabin 53111?
CSmH; DLC; NN; NjR; PHi; PU; RPJCB mp. 40434

B1355 NEW JERSEY. SURVEYOR GENERAL
General instructions by the Surveyor General, to the deputy surveyors of the Western Division of New-Jersey. [Philadelphia? B. Franklin? 1747]
5, [1] p. 36 cm. caption title
Attributed also to James Parker's press in New York
Metzger 117
PHi; PU mp. 40435

B1356 PENNSYLVANIA
[Proclamation for a general fast, 1747. Philadelphia, G. Armbrüster? 1747]
broadside?
In German; cf. Autobiography, 265: "translated into German, printed in both languages."
Probably not printed by Franklin, who had no fraktur letter and would not have printed this in roman unless Armbrüster had refused the job.—C. William Miller
No copy known mp. 40436

B1357 A PLAIN and serious address to the inhabitants of the Massachusetts Province, relating to the choice of their representatives . . . Philo Patriae. [Boston, 1747?]
broadside 31.5 X 21.5 cm.
Ford 869
MHi mp. 40437

B1358 POOR Richard improved: being an almanack . . . for . . . 1748. By Richard Saunders . . . Philadelphia, B. Franklin [1747]
[36] p.
Verso sig. Fl: Court calendar for Virginia, North-Carolina . . .
Drake 9695
CSmH; DLC; PHi

B1359 POOR Richard improved: being an almanack . . . for . . . 1748. By Richard Saunders . . . Philadelphia, B. Franklin [1747]
[36] p.
Verso sig. Fl: List of governors of Pennsylvania . . .
Drake 9693
CSmH; DLC; MB (t.p. lacking); NN (imperfect); PPAmP (imperfect); PPL; PPRF (imperfect); PU

B1360 POOR Robin's spare hours, employ'd in calculating a diary, or almanack, for . . . 1747. Philadelphia: Printed and sold by W. Bradford [1747]
36 p. 12mo
PHi

B1361 A SECOND letter to . . . George Whitefield . . . From his friend Publicola . . . Charles-Town, Peter Timothy, 1747.
16 p. 18.5 cm.
Cohen: South Carolina Gazette p. 170
DLC mp. 40438

B1362 SOME remarks on the settlement of the line, and removal of the courts from Bristol to Taunton. [n.p., 1747?]
broadside 29 X 18 cm.
In verse
New York Public 219
RHi. Photostat: NN mp. 40439

B1363 SOUTH CAROLINA. LAWS
[An act for the tryal . . . of the small and mean causes and for repealing the several acts . . . recovery of small debts. Charleston, P. Timothy, 1747]

Advertised in the *South Carolina Gazette*, July 6, 1747
Mosimann 76
No copy known

B1364 SOUTH CAROLINA. LAWS
[An act, to empower two justices and three freeholders . . . to determine . . . debts . . . exceed twenty pounds current money . . . Charleston, 1747]

Advertised in the *South Carolina Gazette*, July 6, 1747
Mosimann 77
No copy known

B1365 SOUTH CAROLINA. LAWS
Acts passed . . . at a sessions begun . . . the tenth day of September . . . 1745. And from thence continued . . . to the twenty-third day of January, 1745 6. Charles-Town, Peter Timothy, 1747.
43 p. 29.5 cm.
Sabin 87572
DLC mp. 40440

B1366 SOUTH CAROLINA. LAWS
Acts passed . . . at a sessions begun . . . the tenth day of September . . . And from thence continued . . . to the 13th day of June, 1747. Charles-Town, Peter Timothy, 1747.
60, [1] p. 29 cm.
Sabin 87574
DLC; NNB mp. 40441

B1367 SOUTH CAROLINA. LAWS
. . . At a General assembly begun . . . the tenth day of September . . . And from thence continued . . . to the

thirteenth day of June, 1747. Charles-Town, Peter Timothy, 1747.
23 p. 29 cm.
Tax act
Sabin 87575
DLC mp. 40442

B1368 SWIFT, JONATHAN, 1667-1745
Three sermons . . . Williamsburg, W. Parks, 1747.
39 p. 17.5 cm.
ViHi mp. 40443

B1369 TODD, JONATHAN, 1713-1791
The soldier waxing strong . . . N. London, T. Green, 1747.
[4], 46 p. 15 cm.
Huntington 139; Trumbull: Supplement 2679
CSmH; CtHi; DLC mp. 40444

B1370 VIRGINIA. COUNCIL
To . . . William Gooch . . . the humble address of the Council . . . [Williamsburg, W. Parks, 1747]
[2] p. 31 X 21 cm.
In reply to Lieutenant-governor Gooch's address of Mar. 30, 1747
Wroth: William Parks 140b
DLC (photostat) mp. 40445

B1371 VIRGINIA. HOUSE OF BURGESSES
To . . . William Gooch . . . the humble address of the House of burgesses . . . [Williamsburg, W. Parks, 1747]
[2] p. 31 X 21 cm.
In reply to Lieutenant-governor Gooch's address of Apr. 1, 1747
Wroth: William Parks 140c
DLC (photostat) mp. 40446

B1372 VIRGINIA. LAWS
. . . At a General assembly . . . [Mar. 30-Apr. 18, 1747] . . . being the fifth session . . . [Williamsburg, W. Parks, 1747]
[4] p. fol. caption title
Sabin 100244; Wroth: William Parks 139
Coleman mp. 40447

B1373 THE Virginia almanack, for the year . . . 1748 . . . Williamsburg, William Parks [1747]
[32] p. 17 cm.
Bear 12
ViWC (C1, D3 wanting) mp. 40448

1748

B1374 [AN almanac for 1749, by T. More. Philadelphia, B. Franklin, 1748]

Curtis 388; Hildeburn 1083
No copy known mp. 40470

B1375 APPLETON, NATHANIEL, 1693-1784
The cry of oppression where judgment is looked for . . . Boston, J. Draper, 1748.
51 p.
Half title: Mr. Appleton's fast sermons . . . The second edition
MHi; MWA; RPJCB mp. 40449

B1376 AN astronomical diary, Or, An almanack for . . . 1749 . . . Boston: Printed for the booksellers [1748]
[16] p.
Drake 3082; Nichols: Mass. almanacs, p. 60
MB. E. S. Phelps (1912) mp. 40450

B1377 BRIEF instruction in the principles of Christian religion, agreeable to the Confession of Faith . . . The sixth edition, corrected. Philadelphia, B. Franklin and D. Hall, 1748
49 p. 15.5 cm.
By Abel Morgan?
Curtis 376; Metzger 121
N; PHi; PU mp. 40451

B1378 CONNECTICUT. GOVERNOR, 1741-1750
By . . . Jonathan Law, Governour . . . A proclamation for a day of publick thanksgiving . . . Given under my hand . . . [Oct. 19, 1748] New London, Timothy Green, 1748.
broadside 39 X 26 cm.
CtHi mp. 40452

B1379 CRANE, EZEKIEL
A table of board measure, whereby the contents of any board may be readily known, from 7 to 36 feet in length, and from 4 to 30 inches in breadth. Done at the desire of several. By Ezekiel Crane. New-York: Printed by James Parker, at the New Printing Office, in Beaver-Street, 1748.
[12] p. 12.5 cm.
NjR

B1380 Deleted.

B1381 DAVIES, SAMUEL, 1723-1761
The impartial trial, impartially tried . . . Williamsburg, W. Parks, 1748.
59, 15 p. 19 cm.
Torrence 188 (59 p.); Wroth: William Parks 141 (60 p.)
DLC; PHi (59 p.) mp. 40453

B1382 ERSKINE, RALPH, 1685-1752
The fountain-head of all blessings: or, The great store-house opened. A sermon preached . . . August 10th 1740 . . . Boston, Re-printed and sold opposite the prison in Queen-Street, 1748.
39 p. 15.5 cm. A-E^8
MWA (sig. B wanting; replaced by duplicate sig. D); N mp. 40454

B1383 ERSKINE, RALPH, 1685-1752
The harmony of the divine attributes displayed . . . Boston, Re-printed and sold by S. Kneeland and T. Green in Queenstreet, 1748.
63 p. 16 cm. A-H^4
MWA mp. 40455

B1384 GIDDINGE, DANIEL
Whereas the subscriber, one of the brethren that left Mr. Pickering's church being in Boston, and perceiving that the answer to the Aggrieved's Plain Narrative is dispersed . . . Boston, Febr. 12. 1747,8. Daniel Giddinge. [Boston, 1748]
broadside 20 X 14.5 cm.
MWA. Photostat: MHi mp. 40456

B1385 GT. BRIT.
By the Lords Justices, a proclamation . . . Whereas preliminaries for . . . peace were signed at Aix-la-Chapelle . . . Philadelphia, B. Franklin, 1748.
broadside 42.5 X 17 cm.
Metzger 128
CtY mp. 40457

B1386 THE great honor of a valiant London prentice, being an account of his . . . brave adventures . . . Boston, Printed and sold at the Heart and Crown [by T. Fleet] [1748?]
broadside 30 X 21.5 cm.
Printed on the back of one of the Spanish indulgences bought and re-sold by Fleet in 1748, as advertised in the *Boston Evening-Post,* Nov. 7, 1748
Ford 875
NHi mp. 40458

B1387 HARRIS, HOWELL, 1714-1773
Copy of a letter from Mr. Howell Harris an eminently pious and successful preacher in Wales, to the Society at the Tabernacle, London. [Boston? S. Kneeland? 1748?]
7, [1] p. 15.5m caption title A^4
In ms.: Isaac Backus:s book 1748
MWA mp. 40459

B1388 HARVARD UNIVERSITY
Quaestiones pro modulo . . . MDCCXLVIII. [Boston, 1748]
broadside
Ford 877
MB; MH; MHi; MWA mp. 40460

B1389 HENCHMAN, DANIEL, 1689-1761
Boston, June 23. 1748. Proposals for printing by subscription, an account of the life of . . . David Brainard . . . Daniel Henchman. [Boston, 1748]
[2] p. 21.5 cm.
Ms. list of Attleborough subscribers on p. [3-4]
MWA mp. 40461

B1390 HOW, NEHEMIAH, 1693-1747
A narrative of the captivity of Nehemiah How, who was taken by the Indians . . . October 11th 1745 . . . Boston, Printed and sold opposite to the Prison in Queen-Street, 1748.
23 p. 16 cm.
First issue, with obituary of How on p. 23 and without list of subscribers
Vail: Old frontier 437; cf. Evans 6162
ICN; MB; MWA; PP mp. 40462

B1391 MARYLAND. LAWS
Acts . . . made and passed at a session of Assembly, begun . . . the tenth day of May . . . 1748 . . . Annapolis, Jonas Green, 1748.
32 p. 31.5 cm.
Wroth 128
DLC; MH-L; Md; MdHi mp. 40463

B1392 MARYLAND, the 1748. Exchange for £ Sterling. Pursuant to an act of Assembly . . . . . . for emitting . . . ninety thousand pounds current money . . . Annapolis, Jonas Green [1748]
broadside 11.5 X 24.5 cm.
Bill of exchange with imprint traversing left end
Wroth 131
MdHi mp. 40541

B1393 MASSACHUSETTS. GOVERNOR, 1741-1749
By His Excellency William Shirley . . . A proclamation for proroguing the General Assembly [to Oct. 5] . . . August 31, 1748. Boston, John Draper, 1748.
broadside 31.5 X 21.5 cm.
Ford 884
MHi mp. 40464

B1394 MASSACHUSETTS. GOVERNOR, 1741-1749
By His Excellency William Shirley . . . A proclamation for proroguing the General Assembly [to Oct. 26] . . . [Sept. 21, 1748] . . . Boston, John Draper, 1748.
broadside 31.5 X 22 cm.
Ford 885
MHi mp. 40465

B1395 MASSACHUSETTS. LAWS
. . . An act passed by the . . . General Court . . . begun . . . the twenty-fifth day of May 1748 . . . for apportioning and assessing a tax of ninety-one thousand pounds . . . [Colophon] Boston, John Draper, 1748.
9 [i.e. 12] p.
Ford & Matthews p. 398
M mp. 40466

B1396 MASSACHUSETTS. LAWS
At a Great and General Court or Assembly for the Province of the Massachusetts-Bay, begun and held at Boston the The 27th day of May 1747 . . . March 2d. 1747 . . . [Boston, 1748]
broadside 21 X 16 cm.
On provision by churches for their ministers
Ford 880; New York Public 221
MB; MHi; MWA. Photostat: NN mp. 40467

B1397 MASSACHUSETTS. LAWS
Forasmuch as there have been many disputes . . . concerning the titles . . . it is therefore apprehended, that the printing . . . of extracts and collections of those acts . . . will be of considerable service . . . [Boston? 1748?]
4 p. 21 cm. caption title
DLC; MH mp. 40468

B1398 MASSACHUSETTS. TREASURER
Province of the Massachusetts-Bay. William Foye, Esq; Treasurer . . . July 20, 1748. [Boston, 1748]
broadside
Tax warrant
Ford 891
MSaE mp. 40469

B1399 NEW JERSEY. LAWS
Anno regni Georgii II . . . vigesimo primo. At a General Assembly . . . of New-Jersey . . . holden at Burlington, November the 17th, 1747, and continued to February 18, 1747. On which day the following act was passed . . . Philadelphia, William Bradford [1748]
18 p. 28 cm.
Humphrey 32 (appendix)
Nj mp. 40471

B1400 A NEW-Year's gift, or A brief account . . . of the Lord's Supper . . . Philadelphia, William Bradford, 1748.
viii, 26 p. 8vo
Huntington 140
CSmH mp. 40472

B1401 PENNSYLVANIA. COUNCIL
By the honourable the President and Council of . . . Pennsylvania. A proclamation. Whereas divers insults, captures and depredations . . . [Apr. 11, 1748] . . . Philadelphia, B. Franklin [1748]

broadside 41 X 30 cm.
Curtis 392
MB mp. 40473

B1402 PRINCE George's county is so very large . . . [Annapolis, Jonas Green, 1748]
broadside 33.5 X 21 cm.
Wroth 133
MdHi mp. 40474

B1403 RHODE ISLAND. LAWS
At the General assembly . . . begun . . . on the last Monday in February . . . [Newport, Ann Franklin, 1748]
12 p. 34 cm. caption title
Alden 81; Sabin 70516 (note); Winship p. 12
Ct; DLC (facsim.); MH-L; MWA; NNB; RHi; RPB; RPJCB; RPL mp. 40476

B1404 RHODE ISLAND. LAWS
At the General assembly . . . begun . . . the last Wednesday of October . . . [Newport, Ann and James Franklin, 1748]
p. 37-44. 34 cm. caption title
Alden 84; Sabin 70516 (note); Winship p. 12
DLC (facsim.); MH-L; RHi; RPB; RPJCB; RPL mp. 40477

B1405 SCHEME of a lottery at Rariton-Landing, in Piscataway, consisting of 2000 tickets at fourteen shillings each . . . Rariton Landing, September 23, 1748. [n.p. 1748]
broadside 32 X 21 cm.
NjR

B1406 DIE Schule der Weisheit oder Theil in Poesie, als das Hoch-Teutsche A. B. C. von Schuler und Meister in Israel. [Ephrata] 1748
12mo
Metzger 131; cf. Evans 6602
No copy located mp. 40478

B1407 THE situation of Frederick-Town. [Annapolis, Jonas Green, 1748]
broadside 17 X 21 cm.
Wroth 134
MdHi mp. 40479

B1408 SOUTH CAROLINA. ASSEMBLY
[Votes of the Commons House of Assembly, with respect to guarding the coasts . . . Charleston, P. Timothy, 1748]

Advertised in the *South Carolina Gazette*, May 2, 1948
Mosimann 80
No copy known

B1409 SOUTH CAROLINA. LAWS
Acts passed . . . at a sessions begun . . . the tenth day of September . . . and from thence continued . . . to the seventeenth day of February, 1746. Charles-Town, Peter Timothy, 1748.
7 p. 29 cm.
Sabin 87573
DLC; NNB mp. 40480

B1410 [THE South-Carolina almanack for . . . 1749. By John Tobler. Charles-Town, Peter Timothy [1748]]

Advertised in the *South Carolina Gazette*, Nov. 14, 1748
Drake 13071
No copy known

B1411 VIRGINIA. COUNCIL
To . . . William Gooch . . . the humble address of the Council . . . [Williamsburg, W. Parks, 1748]
[2] p. 28.5 X 17 cm.
In reply to the Lieutenant-governor's address of Oct. 17, 1748
Wroth: William Parks 142a
DLC (photostat). Coleman mp. 40481

B1412 VIRGINIA. GOVERNOR, 1727-1749
By the honourable Sir William Gooch . . . a proclamation. Proroguing the General assembly . . . twenty-sixth day of August . . . [1748] [Williamsburg, W. Parks, 1748]
broadside
Wroth: William Parks 142; Torrence 190
ViHi mp. 40482

B1413 VIRGINIA. GOVERNOR, 1727-1749
The speech of . . . William Gooch, Bart. [Williamsburg, W. Parks, 1748]
4 p. 31 cm.
Speech delivered Oct. 27, 1948
Wroth: William Parks 142b; Sabin 99988
Public Record Off. Photostat: DLC mp. 40484

B1414 VIRGINIA. GOVERNOR, 1727-1749
The speech of . . . William Gooch . . . on Monday the thirtieth day of March . . . 1747. Williamsburg, William Parks, 1748.
4 p. 31 cm.
Sabin 99986; Wroth: William Parks 140a
Public Record Off. Photostat: DLC mp. 40483

B1415 VIRGINIA. HOUSE OF BURGESSES
To . . . William Gooch . . . the humble address of the House of burgesses . . . [Williamsburg, W. Parks, 1748]
broadside 36 X 22 cm.
In reply to Lieutenant-governor Gooch's address of Oct. Oct. 27, 1748
Wroth: William Parks 142c
DLC (photostat) mp. 40485

B1416 VIRGINIA. LAWS
Acts of Assembly, passed at a General Assembly, begun . . . Williamsburg . . . the twenty seventh day of October . . . 1748. Examined and corrected, by the Clerk of the House of Burgesses. Williamsburg: Printed by William Parks, M M,DCC,XLVIII.
[2], 41 p. 30 cm.
Oak Spring Library, Upperville, Va. (1966) mp. 40565

B1417 THE Virginia almanack, for the year . . . 1749 . . . Williamsburg, W. Parks [1748]
[32] p. 16 cm.
Bear 12a; Drake 13748
CSmH (last 2 leaves wanting); ViWC (13 l.) mp. 40486

B1418 WALDO, JOSEPH AND DANIEL
Imported from London & sold by wholesale or retail at the cheapest rates by Joseph and Daniel Waldo at the sign of the elephant . . . in King Street Boston New England. [Boston, 1748]
broadside
An engraved advertisement by James Turner
Ford 892
MHi (photostat) mp. 40487

B1419 [WATTS, ISAAC] 1674-1748
An essay toward the proof of a separate state of souls . . . From the second edition, enlarged . . . Boston, Printed and sold by Rogers and Fowle in Queen-Street, 1748.

[9]-189 p. 20 cm. B-M^8 N^4
MWA mp. 40488

1749

B1420 [ALMANACK for 1750. By Joseph Grover. Charles-Town, John Remington [1749?]]

Advertised in the *South Carolina Gazette*, Jan. 8, 1750
Drake 13072
No copy known

B1421 [ALMANACK in Dutch for 1750. New York, 1749]

Advertised in the *New-York Gazette Revived in the Weekly Post Boy,* Nov. 13, 1749
Drake 5653
No copy known

B1422 THE American almanack. For the year . . . 1750 . . . By W. Jones, Philomath. . . . New-York, Printed and sold by Henry De Foreest [1749]
[24] p.
Drake 5654; Wall p. 11
NHi; NBLiHi mp. 40497

B1423 THE American country almanac for the year . . . 1750. By Thomas More. Philadelphia, Printed and sold by B. Franklin and D. Hall [1749]
[24] p. 16.5 cm.
Curtis 425; Hildeburn 1140
PHi mp. 40506

B1424 BAPTIST CHURCH, BOSTON
A summary declaration of the faith and practice of the Baptist-Church of Christ, in Boston . . . Read and assented to, at the admission of members . . . [at end] Boston [Philip Freeman] 1749.
broadside 53 X 52.5 cm.
MWA (mutilated) mp. 40491

B1425 BIBLE. O.T. PSALMS
The Psalms of David, imitated . . . The eighteenth edition . . . Boston, Printed by Rogers and Fowle, for J. Edwards, 1749.
vii, 320, [7] p. 13.5 cm.
MWA mp. 40524

B1426 BOLLES, JOHN
[Answer to an election sermon preached by Nathaniel Eels. Newport, 1749]

Alden 86; Brinton 19
No copy known; description from Brinton mp. 40489

B1427 BOLLES, JOHN
[Good news from a far country. Newport, 1749]

Alden 87; Brinton 18
No copy known mp. 40490

B1428 CONNECTICUT. GOVERNOR, 1741-1750
By the honourable Jonathan Law Esq; Governour . . . A proclamation for a day of publick thanksgiving . . . Given under my hand . . . [Oct. 17, 1749] New-London, Timothy Green, 1749.
broadside 34.5 X 29 cm.
CtHi mp. 40492

B1429 CONNECTICUT. LAWS
. . . An act passed by the General Court . . . begun . . . on the second Thursday of May . . . 1749. [Colophon] N. London, Timothy Green, 1749.
p. 571-574. 30.5 cm. caption title
DLC (facsim.); NN (facsim.) mp. 40493

B1430 ENGLISH PRESBYTERIAN SOCIETY
To all charitably disposed persons greeting. The petition of the English Presberterian [sic] . . . Society, (who have . . . worshiped in a large house in . . . Philadelphia . . .) . . . Signed . . . December 28, 1749-50 . . . [Philadelphia, William Bradford? 1749]
broadside 29 X 19 cm.
In the phrase "1749-50" the "50" has been effaced in manuscript
MB mp. 40512

B1431 [DER Fama. Philadelphia, B. Francklin und Johannes Boehm, 1749]

Hildeburn 1127; Curtis 416
No copy known mp. 40494

B1432 HARVARD UNIVERSITY
Quaestiones pro modulo . . . M,DCC,XLIX. [Boston, 1749]
broadside
MH; MHi; MWA mp. 40495

B1433 HEYWOOD, HENRY, d. 1755
Two catechisms by way of questions and answer . . . South-Carolina: Charles-Town, P. Timothy, 1749.
xxi, 83 p. 18.5 cm.
KyLoS; MWA (t.p. photostat only); RPJCB mp. 40496

B1434 A LETTER to the freeholders, and qualified voters, relating to the ensuing election . . . Boston, Rogers and Fowle, 1749.
12 p.
Sabin 40475
MHi; RPJCB mp. 40498

B1435 LUTHER, MARTIN, 1483-1546
The shorter catechism, of D. Martin Luther . . . Now published in English chiefly for the use . . . of the Lutheran Congregations in America . . . Philadelphia: Printed by John Behm, MDCCXLIX.
p. 13 cm.
NN (photostat t.p. only of unknown original)

B1436 M., S.
The triumphs of faith manifested to the world or, Abraham offering up his son Isaac . . . [New London] Printed & sold by T. Green, 1749.
broadside 31.5 X 22 cm.
In three columns
Signed at end: [S.M.]
CtHi mp. 40519

B1437 MARYLAND. LAWS
Acts . . . made and passed at a session . . . begun . . . the twenty-fourth of May . . . 1749 . . . Annapolis, Jonas Green, 1749.
20 p. 29.5 cm.
Wroth 136
DLC; Md; MdHi; PPL mp. 40499

B1438 MASSACHUSETTS. GOVERNOR, 1741-1749
By His Excellency William Shirley . . . A proclamation. Whereas discovery has lately been made in . . . Connecticut . . . [Mar. 15, 1748] . . . Boston, John Draper [1749]
broadside 42.5 X 31 cm.
Counterfeiting ring
Ford 896
MHi mp. 40500

B1439 MASSACHUSETTS. GOVERNOR, 1749-1753
By His Excellency Spencer Phips . . . A proclamation. Whereas information . . . that Samuel Ball and Benjamin Ledyke . . . [Dec. 28, 1749] . . . [Boston, 1749]
broadside 42.5 X 31 cm.
Ford 901
MHi mp. 40502

B1440 MASSACHUSETTS. LAWS
Province of the Massachusetts-Bay, Extract of two clauses . . . from An act passed by the . . . General Court . . . begun . . . the twenty-fifth day of May 1748, and continued . . . to . . . the twenty-first day of December following . . . for drawing in the bills of credit . . . [Colophon] Boston, John Draper [1749]
4 p. 28.5 cm. caption title
Ford & Matthews p. 400
M-Ar; PHi mp. 40501

B1441 MASSACHUSETTS. TREASURER
Province of the Massachusetts-Bay, ss. William Foye, Esq; Treasurer . . . [June 28, 1749] [Boston, 1749]
broadside
Tax warrant
MWA mp. 40504

B1442 MASSACHUSETTS. TREASURER
Province of the Massachusetts-Bay, ss. William Foye, Esq; Treasurer . . . [Nov. 4, 1749] [Boston, 1749]
broadside
Tax warrant
Ford 903
MSaE mp. 40503

B1443 [MONSIEUR Ragoo; or, A squib for the late F-RE W-RKS; in humorous verse. Boston, T. Fleet, 1749]
broadside?
Advertised in the *Boston Evening-Post,* Sept. 4, 1749
Ford 905
No copy known mp. 40505

B1444 NEW BRUNSWICK CHURCH LOTTERY
A list of the numbers that came up prizes in the New-Brunswick church lottery drawn April, 1749. [n.p., 1749]
broadside 26 X 16 cm.
PHi mp. 40507

B1445 THE New-England primer further improved . . . Boston, Rogers and Fowle, 1749.
40 leaves. 16 mo A-E^8
Rosenbach-Ch 36
A. S. W. Rosenbach (1933) (sig. A1, E8 lacking)
mp. 40508

B1446 NOBLE, WILLIAM
A terror to some lawyers, or a light to the people . . . And a collection of some of the laws of this province, wrote and ordered to be printed by a Lover of his Country, William Noble . . . [Philadelphia? B. Franklin?] 1749.
p. 15.5 cm.
J. Dryden Hess, Baltimore, Md. (1936). Photostat (t.p. and sig. A2 only): MWA mp. 40509

B1447 NORTH CAROLINA. HOUSE OF BURGESSES
The journal of the House of Burgesses, of . . . North-Carolina . . . Newbern [June 12, 1746–Sept. 26, 1749] . . . Being the seventh session of this present General Assembly. Newbern, Printed and sold by James Davis, 1749.
14 p. 31 cm.
McMurtrie: North Carolina 1
Public Record Off. mp. 40510

B1448 PENNSYLVANIA. GENERAL ASSEMBLY
Anno regni Georgii II . . . vigesimo tertio. At a General Assembly . . . begun . . . at Philadelphia, the fourteenth day of October . . . 1748 . . . And . . . continued . . . to the seventh day of August, 1749. Philadelphia: Printed by B. Franklin, 1749.
19 p. 8 vo A-B^4 C^2
Curtis 408
PPeSchw; PU mp. 40511

B1449 Deleted.

B1450 RHODE ISLAND. LAWS
At the General assembly . . . held at Providence . . . on the first Tuesday of January . . . [Newport, Ann and James Franklin, 1749]
p. 45-61. 35 cm. caption title
Alden 90; Sabin 70516 (note); Winship p. 12
DLC (facsim.); RHi; RPB; RPJCB; RPL mp. 40513

B1451 RINGEWALD, BARTHOL
Neue Zetung and wahre Prophezeyung haus frummens . . . in liebliche Reimen verfasset durch Barthol Ringewald. Ephrata, Verlegt von mich, M, 1749.

Metzger 136
No copy located mp. 40514

B1452 ROGERS & FOWLE, firm, Boston
Boston, Nov. 9, 1749. Whereas Mr. Moses Dickinson hath prepared . . . a defence of his brother the late Mr. Jonathan Dickinson's Second Vindication . . . we the subscribers . . . promise to pay to Messi. [sic] Rogers and Fowle . . . for the number of books annexed to our names . . . [Boston, Rogers and Fowle, 1749]
broadside 11.5 X 14.5 cm.
MHi mp. 40515

B1453 SOUTH CAROLINA. LAWS
Acts passed . . . at a sessions begun . . . the nineteenth day of January . . . 1747. Charles-Town, Peter Timothy, 1749.
1 p.l., 25 p. 29 cm.
Sabin 87576
DLC mp. 40516

B1454 SOUTH CAROLINA. LAWS
. . . At a General assembly, begun . . . the 28th of March . . . 1749. And from thence continued . . . to the 1st day of June, 1749. Charles-Town, Peter Timothy, 1749.
1 p.l., 25 p. 29 cm.
Half-title: The tax act . . .
Sabin 87577
DLC mp. 40517

B1455 TENNENT, GILBERT, 1703-1764
Several discourses upon important subjects . . . Philadelphia, Printed and sold by W. Bradford, 1749.

3 p.l., 5-40, 27, 10 p. 18.5 cm.
Metzger 137; cf. Evans 6425-28
DLC mp. 40518

B1456 TURELL, EBENEZER, 1702-1778
The life and character of . . . Benjamin Colman . . . Boston, Printed and sold by Rogers and Fowle, 1749.
[16], iv, 238, [1] p. 18.5 cm.
Variant issue of Evans 6434
Sabin 97450 (pt. 2)
DLC; ICN; MH; NjP mp. 40520

B1457 TURELL, EBENEZER, 1702-1778
The life and character of . . . Benjamin Colman . . . To which is added, the doctor's Discourses on the Parable of the Ten Virgins. Boston, Printed and sold by Rogers and Fowle, and by J. Edwards, 1749.
238, [2], vi, 344 p. 18.5 cm.
cf. Evans 6434 and 1602
MWA mp. 40521

B1458 VIRGINIA. LAWS
. . . At a General Assembly . . . [Oct. 27, 1748-May 11, 1749] [Williamsburg, W. Parks, 1749]
40+ p. 33 cm.
Sabin 100245; Swem 22553; Torrence 192; Wroth: William Parks 144
Vi(imperfect) mp. 40522

B1459 THE Virginia almanack, for the year . . . 1750 . . . Williamsburg, William Parks [1749]
[32] p. 17 cm.
Bear 12b; Torrence 195; Wroth: William Parks 146
DLC (t.p. and 2 following leaves wanting).
T. Randolph Buck, Richmond (C1, C4, D1-4 wanting)
mp. 40523

175-

B1460 [THE advantages of employing a man to sweep the pavements in Philadelphia, twice a week, at a cost of 6 pence per month to each property holder. Philadelphia, B. Franklin and D. Hall, 175-]
broadside?
Curtis 549; Ford: Franklin 103; Metzger 185
No copy known mp. 40525

B1461 CHURCH OF ENGLAND. LITURGY
Prayers and thanksgivings for a family or private person. [Boston? 175-?]
[2], 5 p. 19.5 cm. A^4
"Taken from the publick prayers of the Church of England."
MWA mp. 40526

B1462 AN elogy on death of Mr. Nathaniel Burt . . . who was killed . . . Sept. 8, 1755, in the 45th year of his age. [New England? 175-?]
broadside 41.5 X 26.5 cm.
Ford 1006; Wegelin 571
Not the same poem as Evans 7855
MWiW-C. Photostats: MHi; MWA; N; NN mp. 40527

B1463 KENNEBECK PROPRIETORS
To all to whom these presents shall come, Greeting. Whereas his late Majesty King James the first . . . Know ye, that we the heirs and assigns of the said Antipas Boyes . . . in all said lands on Kenebeck River . . . at our meeting held at Boston, this day of A.D. 17 . . . have voted, granted and assigned to . . . [Boston? 175-]
broadside ([2] p.) 36.5 X 22 cm.
MWA; RPJCB mp. 40531

B1464 MASSACHUSETTS. MILITIA
175 Received of the several species of provisions, ammunition & slop-cloathing as mentioned in these columns, Bread Pork Rum . . . [Boston? 175-]
broadside 23 X 38.5 cm.
Ford 927
MHi

B1465 MITCHELL, JOHATHAN, 1624-1668
Mr. Mitchel's letter to his brother [from Harvard College, May 19, 1649. To which is added] The life of faith, in a letter wrote by the Rev. Mr. John [Joseph] Elliott of Guilford, decreased . . . Being an answer to . . . How to live in this world, so as to live in Heaven. New-London, Printed and sold by T. Green [175-?]
[24] p. 17 cm.
CtHi; MWA (lacks p. 21-24) mp. 40528

B1466 A NEW Year's gift for children. Delightful and entertaining stories for little masters and misses .... [at end] Boston, Printed & sold by Fowle in Ann-street [175-]
broadside 46 X 31 cm.
Fowle was at this address from 1735-56
MWA mp. 40529

B1467 A PACK of cards chang'd into a compleat almanac and prayer-book . . . Boston, Printed and sold at the Printing-Office in Back-Street [175-?]
8 p. 16 cm.
MWA mp. 40530

B1468 PENNSYLVANIA
Pennsylvania ss. By the Proprietaries. Whereas of the County of hath requested . . . acres of land . . . agrees to pay . . . rate of fifteen pounds ten shillings . . . for hundred acres . . . Seal of the Land-Office . . . this day of Anno Domini, 175 To Nicholas Scull, Surveyor General. [Philadelphia, 175-]
broadside 19.5 X 32 cm.
Filled in for Oct. 24, 1752
PU

B1469 RHODE ISLAND
Custom-House, Rhode-Island. In pursuance of . . . An act for the better encouragement of the trade to his Majesty's sugar colonies in America. An account of the names, ages . . . of the men belonging to the whereof is master . . . Given . . . this day of . . . One Thousand seven hundred and fifty [Newport? 175-]
broadside 38 X 20 cm.
RHi. Photostat: MWA

B1470 SHEWING the harmony of the divine attributes, in the way of man's salvation . . . [Boston? 175-?]
broadside 44 X 29 cm.
27 4-verse stanzas, in 2 columns
Ford 928
MHi mp. 40532

B1471 WELD, EDMUND
A funeral elegy by way of dialogue . . . composed by Edmund Weld . . . Boston, Reprinted and sold by S. Kneeland, in Queen Street [175-?]
broadside 33 X 20.5 cm.
Kneeland printed in Queen Street from 1751 to 1765
Ford 948; NYPL 114; Sabin 102529
NHi. Photostats: MHi; NN mp. 40533

1750

B1472 ADVERTISEMENT. Whereas the Plymouth Proprietors (so called) have impowered John North . . . and Samuel Goodwin . . . to survey large tracts of lands . . . In order to prevent such mean . . . constructions for the future . . . March 7, 1950, Voted, That an extract of the patent of the Plymouth Proprietors be herewith printed . . . James Halsey Clerk . . . [Boston, 1750]
broadside 33 X 20 cm.
MHi; MWA mp. 40562

B1473 [ALMANACK for 1751. By Joseph Grover. Charles-Town, John Remington [1750]]

Advertised in the *South Carolina Gazette*, Nov. 19, 1750
Drake 13073
No copy known

B1474 [THE American almanackfor 1751. By W. Jones New-York, Henry De Foreest, 1750]

Title from a contemporary note about authors of almanacs in NBLiHi copy of Sherman's almanac for 1751
Drake 5662
No copy known

B1475 THE American country almanack for . . . 1751 . . . By Thomas More . . . New York, J. Parker [1750]
[24] p.
cf. Evans 6553; but type completely reset.—L. H. Wright
Drake 5663
CSmH. Milton Drake, NYC (1964)

B1476 BALTIMORE, FREDERICK CALVERT, 7th baron, 1731-1771, defendant
Penn against Ld. Baltimore. In Chancery. Copy of minutes on hearing . . . Tuesday, May 15, 1750. [Philadelphia, Franklin and Hall, 1750]
15 p. 42.5 cm. caption title
Metzger 140
DLC; PHi, PPL mp. 40534

B1477 BOSTON, April 2, 1750. A song on the remarkable resurrection of above one hundred and fifty thousand pounds sterling . . . bury'd for many months . . . [Boston, Rogers and Fowle, 1750]
broadside 32 X 21 cm.
At foot: Rogers & Fowle's announcement of their *Exact table* (Evans 6495)
Ford 913
MSaE mp. 40565

B1478 [CHEEVER, EZEKIEL] 1615-1708
A short introduction to the Latin tongue . . . The sixth edition . . . Boston, Printed for D. Henchman, 1750.
72 p.
RPJCB mp. 40535

B1479 A CORRECT table to bring old tenor into lawful money . . . Boston, Rogers and Fowle, 1750.
[12] p. 10 cm.
Evans 6496 (note)
DLC; MHi; MWA mp. 40536

B1480 A DISCOURSE on government and religion, calculated for the meridian of the thirtieth of January. By an Independent . . . Boston: Printed and sold by D. Fowle in Queen Street, and by D. Gookin in Marlborough-Street. 1750.
56 p. 21 cm.
cf. Evans 6484 (also at CtHi)
CtHi

B1481 DYCHE, THOMAS, fl. 1719
A guide to the English tongue . . . The thirty-seventh edition, corrected. New York, James Parker, 1750.
4 p.l., 86+ p. 16 cm.
DLC (all after p. 86 wanting) mp. 40537

B1482 THE dying speech of Old Tenor, on the 31st day of March 1750; being the day appointed for his execution . . . [Boston] Sold next to the prison in Queen-Street [by S. Kneeland] [1750]
broadside 35.5 X 23.5 cm.
Ford 912; New York Public 224
MSaE; PPRF. Photostats: MHi; NN mp. 40538

B1483 AN exact table to bring old tenor into lawful money . . . Boston, Printed and sold by Rogers and Fowle, 1750.
5, [7] p. incl. tables. 10.5 cm.
New York Public 225
MB; MHi; NWA; NN; RPJCB mp. 40539

B1484 AN exact table to bring old tenor into lawful money . . . Second edition. Boston, Printed and sold by Rogers and Fowle, 1750.
12 p. incl. tables. 10 cm.
New York Public 225a
MB; MWA; PPRF; RPJCB. Photostats: MHi; NN mp. 40540

B1485 GORDON, JOHN
Brotherly love explain'd and enforc'd . . . Annapolis, Jonas Green, 1750.
[4], 27 p. 19 cm.
Wroth 141
RPJCB mp. 40541

B1486 HAND-IN-HAND FIRE CLUB, NEWPORT, R.I.
The Hand-in-hand fire club. These presents witness, that we the subscribers . . . do hereby severally promise . . . [Dec. 30, 1749] . . . [Newport, James Franklin, 1750]
broadside 38.5 X 31 cm.
Alden 97; New York Public 223
RNHi. Photostats: MWA; NN; RHi mp. 40558

B1487 HAND-IN-HAND FIRE CLUB, NEWPORT, R.I.
These presents witness, that we the subscribers . . . do hereby severally promise . . . [Nov. 10, 1726] Re-printed in October, 1750. [Newport, James Franklin, 1750]
broadside 41.5 X 31 cm.
Alden 98
NHi; RHi. Photostats: DLC; MWA mp. 40559

B1488 HARVARD UNIVERSITY
Quaestiones pro modulo . . . MDCCL. [Boston, 1750]
broadside 38 X 25 cm.
MWA. Photostat: NN mp. 40542

B1489 [HOOKE, ELLIS]
The spirit of the martyrs revived . . . [London] Printed in the year 1682. [New London?] Re-printed in the year 1750.
[8], 283 p. sm. 4to
Huntington 145; Trumbull: Supplement 2272
CSmH; RPJCB mp. 40543

B1490 A LETTER to the freemen and freeholders of the province of New-York . . . New-York, 1750.

12 p. 19 cm.
Signed: Tribunus populi
Church 973; Huntington 152; Sabin 96961
CSmH; DLC. Photostat: NN mp. 40544

B1491 MARYLAND. LAWS
Acts of Assembly . . . passed at a session . . . begun . . . the eighth day of May . . . 1750 . . . Annapolis, Jonas Green, 1750.
34 [i.e. 36] p. 30.5 cm.
Wroth 142
Md; MdBB; MdHi mp. 40545

B1492 [THE Maryland almanack for the year . . . 1751 . . . Annapolis, Jonas Green, 1750]

Advertised in the *Maryland Gazette*, Dec. 19, 1750, as "Just Published."
Wroth 144
No copy known mp. 40546

B1493 MASSACHUSETTS. GOVERNOR, 1749-1753
By the honourable Spencer Phips . . . A proclamation for proroguing the General Assembly [to Sept. 26] . . . [Aug. 13, 1750] . . . Boston, John Draper, 1750.
broadside 34.5 X 26 cm.
Ford 920
MHi mp. 40549

B1494 MASSACHUSETTS. GOVERNOR, 1749-1753
By the honourable Spencer Phips . . . A proclamation for proroguing the General Assembly [to Dec. 19, 1750] . . . [Nov. 16, 1750] . . . Boston, John Draper, 1750.
broadside 39 X 25.5 cm.
Ford 922
MHi mp. 40550

B1495 MASSACHUSETTS. GOVERNOR, 1749-1753
By His Excellency Spencer Phips . . . A proclamation for proroguing the General Assembly [to Jan. 9] . . . [Dec. 7, 1750] . . . Boston, John Draper, 1750.
broadside
Ford 923
MHi mp. 40551

B1496 MASSACHUSETTS. LAWS
. . . An act for granting . . . rates and duties . . . Boston, J. Draper, 1750.
7 p.
MWA mp. 40547

B1497 MASSACHUSETTS. LAWS
Province of the Massachusetts-Bay in New-England. In pursuance of an act of Parliament . . . passed in the 7th and 8th years of . . . William the Third . . . for preventing fraud . . . Jurat. [Boston, 1750?]
broadside
Ford 925
MHi mp. 40548

B1498 NASSAU STREET THEATRE, NEW YORK
New York, March 1750. By His Excellency's permission; at the theatre in Nassau-Street, on Monday evening next . . . The Orphan . . . [New York, James Parker? 1750]
broadside 28.5 X 21.5 cm.
New York Public 227
MH (imperfect); NN (facsim.) mp. 40557

B1499 THE New-England primer further improved . . . Boston, Printed for the booksellers, 1750.
[80] p. [A]-E^8
Heartman 7
R. Terry (1922) mp. 40553

B1500 THE New-England primer improved . . . Boston, John Green, 1750.
[80] p. [A]-E^8
Heartman 8
CtY (CtSoP copy) mp. 40554

B1501 A NEW gift for children . . . Boston, D. Fowle [1750?]
30 p. illus. 10 cm.
Printed covers
Huntington 149
CSmH mp. 40555

B1502 NEW HAMPSHIRE. GOVERNOR, 1741-1767
Province of New-Hampshire. By his excellency Benning Wentworth . . . A proclamation for a general thanksgiving . . . 25th day of November . . . [Portsmouth? 1750]
broadside 39 X 32 cm.
DLC mp. 40556

B1503 NEW-YORK GAZETTE
Monday, December 31. The yearly verses of the printer's lads, who carry the *New-York Gazette* reviv'd . . . [New York, 1750?]
broadside
1st line: To wish you happy thro' the coming year . . .
NHi. Photostat: NN mp. 40552

B1504 NORTH CAROLINA. HOUSE OF BURGESSES
The journal of the House of Burgesses . . . [Newbern, James Davis, 1750]
4 p. 30.5 cm. caption title
Session July 5-July 10, 1750, prorogued to the last Tuesday in September
McMurtrie: North Carolina 2
Public Record Off. mp. 40560

B1505 A PLAIN answer from a gentleman in Queen's County, to a familiar letter from a citizen of New-York . . . [Aug. 21, 1750] [New York? 1750]
2 p. 30 cm.
New York Public 228
Original in collection of Morton Pennypacker, 1931
NHi. Photostat: NN mp. 40561

B1506 PRICHARD, SAMUEL
Masonry dissected: being an universal and genuine description of all its branches . . . By Samuel Prichard, late member of a constituted lodge. Re-printed in the year M,DCC,XLIX. [Newport? Ann and James Franklin? 1750?]
32 p. 16 cm.
Alden 89
MBFM mp. 40563

B1507 RHODE ISLAND. LAWS
At the General assembly . . . begun and held at Newport . . . the first day of May . . . [Newport, Ann and James Franklin, 1750]
18 p. 34 cm. caption title
Alden 100 (first part); Sabin 70516 (note); Winship p. 13
DLC (facsim.); MH-L; MWA; NNB; RHi; RPB; RPJCB; RPL mp. 40564

B1508 RHODE ISLAND. LAWS
At the General assembly . . . begun and held at Newport . . . on the second Monday in June . . . [Newport, Ann and James Franklin, 1750]
p. 19-32. 34 cm.
Alden 100 (first part); Sabin 70516 (note); Winship p. 13
DLC (facsim.); MH-L; MWA; NNB; RHi; RPB; RPJCB; RPL mp. 40567

B1509 RHODE ISLAND. LAWS
At the General assembly . . . begun . . . at Newport, the third Monday of August . . . [Newport, Ann and James Franklin, 1750]
p. 33-60. 34 cm. caption title
Alden 101; Sabin 70516 (note); Winship p. 13
DLC (facsim.); MWA mp. 40568

B1510 RHODE ISLAND. SECOND BANK
Mortgage deeds laid by in the office, without bonds, of the Second bank, with indorsements on them. [Newport, Ann and James Franklin, 1750]
16 p. 19 cm. caption title
Alden 102
RHi mp. 40566

B1511 ROCHE, MATHEW
[A modest reply to His Excellency the governor's written answer to the affadavit of Charles M'Naire & Mathew Roche . . . late revolt of the Chactaw nation . . . Charleston, 1750]

Advertised in the *South Carolina Gazette*, Feb. 26, 1750
Mosimann 86
No copy known

B1512 SHERLOCK, THOMAS, 1678-1761
A letter . . . to the clergy and people of London . . . Williamsburg, W. Hunter, 1750.
20 p. 18.5 cm.
DLC mp. 40569

B1513 SOUTH CAROLINA. COMMITTEE OF CONFERENCE
Report from the Committee of Conference, appointed to take into consideration . . . state of the paper currency in . . . South-Carolina. [Charleston, 1750?]
broadside 41.5 cm.
Text mentions retirement of 6,000 in currency in 1749
Mosimann 87
Public Record Off.

B1514 SOUTH CAROLINA. LAWS
Acts passed . . . at a sessions begun . . . the twenty-eighth of March . . . 1749. Charles-Town, Peter Timothy, 1750.
1 p.l., 41, [1] p. 29 cm.
Half-title: Laws passed . . . in June 1749, and May 1750
Sabin 87578
DLC; NNB mp. 40570

B1515 A TABLE, shewing how provisions ought to be sold when the dollars pass for six shillings a-piece . . . Boston, Thomas Fleet [1750]
broadside 26 X 20.5 cm.
Ford 911
NHi; RPJCB mp. 40571

B1515a TENNENT, GILBERT, 1703-1764
The Gospel a mystery. A sermon preach'd at Philadelphia, December 1749 . . . Philadelphia, William Bradford [1750]
20 p.
Trinterud 396
PPPrHi

B1516 VIRGINIA
. . . Thomas Lee . . . commander in chief . . . Whereas Low Jackson . . . silver-smith . . . is charged . . . with coining . . . [Aug. 15, 1750] . . . [Williamsburg, 1750]
broadside 37 X 21.5 cm.
Huntington 154
CSmH mp. 40572

B1517 THE Virginia almanack, for the year . . . 1751 . . . Williamsburg, William Hunter [1750]
[32] p. 15.5 cm.
Bear 13; Morrison p. 154; Torrence 196
DLC; ViHi mp. 40573

B1518 WATTS, ISAAC, 1674-1748
Divine songs, attempted in easy language . . . The twelfth edition . . . Philadelphia, Re-printed and sold by B. Franklin, and D. Hall, 1750.
vi, 41 p. 13.5 cm.
Curtis 457; Metzger 143
PHi mp. 40574

B1519 WIR endes unterscheibene [sic] sämtliche Einwohner der gegend Broad-Bay gennant, in dem Ostteil der Provintz Neu-Engelland in America . . . den lsten May 1750 . . . [Philadelphia? 1750?]
broadside 33 X 22.5 cm.
Metzger 144
DLC mp. 40575

1751

B1520 [AN almanack for 1752. By John Nathan Hutchins. New York, 1751]

Drake 5669
No copy known

B1521 ANNAPOLIS, MD. ORDINANCES, ETC.
[The bye-laws of the city of Annapolis . . . Annapolis, Jonas Green, 1751]

Advertised Feb. 13, 1751, as "Just Published."
Wroth 146
No copy known mp. 40576

B1522 BARD, JOHN
A letter to the proprietors of the Great-Nine-Partners-Tract . . . New-York, Printed and sold by J. Parker, 1751.
22+ p., 2 l. incl. map. 18 cm.
New York Public 230; Huntington 155
CSmH (incomplete). Photostat: NN (incomplete) mp. 40577

B1523 BAYARD, STEPHEN
New-York, August 10, 1751. Advertisement. The ferry and farm call'd Wehaken . . . belonging to Stephen Bayard, will be let to the highest bidder . . . [New York, 1751]
broadside 15 X 21 cm.
New York Public 231
Original owned by E. H. Sauer, 1923
NN (photostat) mp. 40578

B1524 BOSTON
(No. 8.) To
Your province tax, lawful money. Your town and country rate, lawful money . . . The assessors sit at Faneuil-

Hall . . . Thursdays from three to five . . . 1751 . . . John Ruddock, Collector. [Boston, 1751]
broadside 12 X 19.5 cm.
Ford 930
MHi

B1525 BRUNSWICK PROPRIETORS
Advertisement. At a meeting of the proprietors of the township of Brunswick . . . May 15th, 1751, the following vote was passed. Whereas in order to . . . undeceive those persons . . . unwarily led to take up . . . lands in Kenebeck River . . . [Boston, 1751]
broadside
Ford 931
MHi; MSaE. Photostat: RPJCB mp. 40579

B1526 CLAYPOOLE, DEBORAH
Philadelphia, June 9, 1751. Advertisement. To be sold by Deborah Claypoole, William Coleman, and John Swift, executors of Abraham Claypoole . . . tracts of land . . . [Philadelphia, 1751]
broadside 25.5 X 16 cm.
PHi mp. 40580

B1527 GODFREY, BENJAMIN, fl. 1751
Zeugnisse etlicher Persohnen die vermittelst Doctor Benjamin Godfreys Allgemeinen Herzstärkung von der Rothen Ruhr curiret worden . . . [Philadelphia, 1751?]
broadside 37 X 25.5 cm.
With translation from German text
PHi mp. 40608a

B1528 GT. BRIT. LAWS
[The act of Parliament, passed the last session . . . for the more effectual securing the duties upon tobacco. Annapolis, Jonas Green, 1751]
24 p. fol.
Advertised Nov. 6, 1751, as "Just Published (Containing 24 pages in folio . . .) . . . "
Wroth 147
No copy known mp. 40581

B1529 GT. BRIT. LAWS
[An extract of a law relating to tobacco; which . . . lay before the House of Lords in June last. Annapolis, Jonas Green, 1751]

Advertised Sept. 18, 1751, as "Just Published."
Wroth 148
No copy known mp. 40582

B1530 HARVARD UNIVERSITY
Quaestiones pro modulo . . . MDCCLI. [Boston, 1751]
broadside
MH; MHi mp. 40583

B1531 MARYLAND. CHARTER
[The charter of the province of Maryland . . . Annapolis, Jonas Green, 1751]

Advertised May 15, 1751, as "Just Published."
Wroth 152
No copy known mp. 40584

B1532 MARYLAND. LAWS
Acts of Assembly . . . passed at a session . . . begun . . . the fourteenth day of May . . . 1751 . . . Annapolis, Jonas Green, 1751
30 p. 30 cm.
"Erratum" on p. 28
Wroth 149
DLC; Md; MdBP mp. 40586

B1533 MARYLAND. LAWS
Acts of Assembly . . . passed at a session . . . begun . . . the fifteenth day of May . . . 1751 . . . Annapolis, Jonas Green, 1751.
28, [1] p. 30 cm.
Wroth 150
MH–L; MdBB; MdHi mp. 40587

B1534 MARYLAND. LAWS
Acts of Assembly . . . passed at a session . . . begun . . . the seventh day of December . . . 1751 . . . Annapolis, Jonas Green, 1751.
[2], 6 p. 28.5 cm.
Wroth 151
MH–L; Md; MdBB; MdBP (imperfect); MdHi mp. 40588

B1535 MARYLAND. LAWS
[A collection of all the laws of this province, relating to the inspection of tobacco . . . passed in the years, 1747, 1748, 1749 and 1750 . . . Annapolis, Jonas Green, 1751]
80 p. lg. 4to
Advertised Apr. 17, 1751, as "Just Published."
Wroth 153
No copy known mp. 40585

B1536 [THE MARYLAND almanac for the year . . . 1752 . . . Annapolis, Jonas Green, 1751]

Advertised in the *Maryland Gazette* Nov. 27, 1751, as "Just Published."
Wroth 155
No copy known mp. 40589

B1537 MASSACHUSETTS. GOVERNOR, 1749-1753
By the honourable Spencer Phips . . . A proclamation for proroguing the General Assembly [to Dec. 26] . . . [Nov. 19, 1751] . . . Boston, John Draper, 1751.
broadside 35.5 X 21.5 cm.
Ford 941
MHi mp. 40593

B1538 MASSACHUSETTS. GOVERNOR, 1749-1753
By the honourable Spencer Phips . . . A proclamation. Whereas the Indians of the Penobscot tribe . . . [Sept. 3, 1751] . . . Boston, John Draper, 1751.
broadside 42.5 X 31 cm.
Ford 939
MHi mp. 40594

B1539 MASSACHUSETTS. GOVERNOR, 1749-1753
By . . . Spencer Phips . . . a proclamation. Whereas there has been lately published . . . [Apr. 18, 1751] . . . Boston, John Draper, 1751.
broadside 41 X 30.5 cm.
Ford 938
DLC (photostat); M–Ar; MHi mp. 40595

B1540 MASSACHUSETTS. LAWS
. . . An act for granting . . . rates and duties of impost on tonnage . . . Boston, J. Draper, 1751.
7 p.
MWA mp. 40590

B1541 MASSACHUSETTS. LAWS
. . . An act passed by the . . . General Court . . . begun . . . the twenty-ninth day of May, 1751 . . . for apportioning and and assessing a tax of thirty thousand three hundred and ninety-four pounds eight shillings and eight pence . . . [Colophon] [Boston] New–[ ], John Draper, 1751
7 [i.e. 11] p. 32 cm.
Ford & Matthews p. 407
M–Ar (mutilated) mp. 40591

B1542 MASSACHUSETTS. LAWS
... The following order passed the General court ... June 22, 1751 ... the assessors ... are required ... to make out the ... assessments ... [Boston, 1751]
broadside 25.5 X 22 cm.
Huntington 157
CSmH; MHi; MWA mp. 40592

B1543 MASSACHUSETTS. LAWS
Province of the Massachusetts-Bay, In the House of Representatives, April 24, 1751 ... In Council, April 25, 1751. Read and concurr'd, F. Willard, Sec'y. Consented to, S. Phips ... [Boston, 1751]
broadside 32.5 X 20.5 cm.
Assessing towns for repairing the Old State House after the fire of 1747.
Mass. Bar Assoc.

B1544 MASSACHUSETTS. TREASURER
Province of the Massachusetts-Bay, ss. William Foye, Esq; Treasurer ... To the selectmen ... Boston, the twelfth day of July 1751 ... [Boston, 1751]
broadside 37 X 22.5 cm.
Tax warrant
Ford 945
MHi; RPJCB mp. 40596

B1545 MASSACHUSETTS. TREASURER
Province of the Massachusetts-Bay, ss. William Foye, Esq; Treasurer ... [Nov. 1, 1751] ... [Boston, 1751]
broadside 39 X 31.5 cm.
DLC; MWA mp. 40597

B1546 NORTH CAROLINA. HOUSE OF BURGESSES
The journal of the House of Burgesses ... [Newbern, James Davis, 1751]
p. 3–20. 33 cm. caption title
Session Sept. 26, 1751-Oct. 12, 1751; prorogued to second Tuesday in February, 1752
McMurtrie: North Carolina 3
Public Record Off. (t.p. wanting?) mp. 40598

B1547 NOYES, BELCHER, d. 1785
Advertisement. Province of the Massachusetts-Bay. ss. Pursuant to a warrant to me directed by ... Samuel Danforth ... these are to advertise the proprietors of a certain tract of land ... County of York ... to assemble ... at the Sun Tavern in Corn-hill Boston ... Belcher Noyes. Boston, November 13th 1751. [Boston, 1751]
broadside 32.5 X 19.5 cm.
MHi mp. 40599

B1548 PLYMOUTH COMPANY
Advertisement. Whereas by some late advertisements, it may be understood that Lieutenant John North, and Mr. Samuel Goodwin ... have exceeded the limits ... May 1, 1751. [Boston, 1751]
broadside
Ford 929
MWA mp. 40600

B1549 RHODE ISLAND. GOVERNOR, 1748-1755
By the honourable William Greene ... Whereas, upon occasion of the death of ... Frederick, Prince of Wales ... [June 19, 1751] ... [Newport, Ann and James Franklin, 1751]
broadside 21 X 33 cm.
Alden 105; Winship p. 13
NjR; RHi. Photostat: MWA mp. 40601

B1550 RHODE ISLAND. GOVERNOR, 1748-1755
[Proclamation occasioned by His Majesty's creating Prince George, Prince of Wales. Newport, Ann and James Franklin, 1751]
[broadside?]
Authorized at the October session of the General assembly
Alden 106
No copy known; description conjectured mp. 40602

B1551 RHODE ISLAND. LAWS
At the General assembly ... begun ... at Providence, the first Monday of December ... [Newport, Ann and James Franklin, 1751]
p. 60 [i. e. 61]-70. 34 cm. caption title
Alden 107; Sabin 70516 (note); Winship p. 13
DLC; MH-L; MWA; NNB; RHi; RPB; RPJCB; RPL
mp. 40603

B1552 RHODE ISLAND. LAWS
At the General assembly ... begun ... on the third Monday of March ... [Newport, Ann and James Franklin, 1751]
p. 71-97. 29.5 cm. caption title
Alden 108; Sabin 70516 (note); Winship p. 13
DLC; MH-L; MWA; N; NNB; RHi; RPB; RPJCB; RPL
mp. 40604

B1553 SOUTH CAROLINA. LAWS
Acts passed ... at a sessions begun ... the twenty-eighth day of March ... 1749. And from thence continued ... to the 24th day of April, 1751. Charles-Town, Peter Timothy, 1751.
71, [1] p. 29. cm.
Sabin 87579
DLC (2 copies); MH-L mp. 40605

B1554 [THE South-Carolina almanack for ... 1752. By John Tabler. Charles-Town, Peter Timothy [1751]]

Advertised in the *South Carolina Gazette*, Dec. 6, 1751
Drake 13074
No copy known

B1555 STODDARD, SOLOMON, 1643-1729
An appeal to the learned ... The second edition ... New-York, Reprinted by James Parker, 1751.
[4], iii-vi, 83 p. 14 cm. $[\,]^{1}$ $A\text{-}C^{12}$ D^{9}
MWA mp. 40606

B1556 STODDARD, SOLOMON, 1643-1729.
A guide to Christ ... With an epistle prefixed, by ... Increase Mather. The second edition. New-York, James Parker, 1751.
[20], 97, [2] p. 14.cm. $A\text{-}E^{12}$
MWA mp. 40607

B1557 [TENNENT, JOHN] M.D.
Every man his own doctor: or, the poor planter's physician ... The fourth edition, with additions. Williamsburg, Printed and sold by William Hunter, 1751.
47, [1] p. 17.5 cm. $A\text{-}C^{6}$
MWA mp. 40608

1752

B1558 [BADGER, JONATHAN, comp.]?
[A collection of the best psalm and hymn tunes, to be

sold by the subscriber at his house, near Col. Brewton's . . . Charleston, P. Timothy? 1752]

Advertised in the *South Carolina Gazette*, Nov. 6, 1752
Mosimann 92
No copy known

B1559 BUFFIN, ANN (WOOLMAN) 1694-1750
A few words concerning that pious youth . . . Thomas Scattergood . . . [Colophon] Philadelphia, James Chattin [1752?]
8 p. 16.5 cm. caption title
Signed: Ann Buffin
Huntington 161; New York Public 233
CSmH. Photostats: DLC; MHi; MWA; NN mp. 40609

B1560 COALMAN, JOSEPH
[An] Elegy [on the d]eath of the Reverend [Jonath]an Colt [on of] Hebron; [who departed this life May t[he 7th, 1752 (as he was returning from [London . . .] to preach . . . to a parish of [Hebron in Connecticut, in New England [in the 27th] year of his age . . . [n.p., 1752]
broadside 35.5 X 27.5 cm.
CtHi (mutilated) mp. 40610

B1561 DIVES and Lazarus, or, the rich glutton, and the poor beggar . . . N. London, Printed and sold by T. Green, 1752.
broadside 39 X 32 cm.
CtHi mp. 40611

B1562 FELLOWSHIP CLUB, BOSTON, MASS.
Rules and orders to be observed by a . . . friendly society, called, the Fellowship Club; began at Boston . . . June 1, 1742. Boston, May 5, 1752. [Boston, 1752]
[2] p.
Ford 952
M-Ar mp. 40612

B1563 FELLOWSHIP CLUB, NEWPORT, R.I.
To be observed by a friendly society . . . began at Newport . . . December 5, 1752 . . . List of members . . . [Newport, James Franklin, 1752?]
broadside 32 X 27.5 cm.
Alden 119; Winship p. 13
RNHi. Photostats: MHi; MWA; RHi mp. 40613

B1564 FRIENDS, SOCIETY OF. LONDON YEARLY MEETING
The epistle from the Yearly-Meeting, held in London . . . the 18th of the fifth month, 1752 . . . [Philadelphia? 1752]
4 p.
MWA mp. 40614

B1565 [GRAVES, J.]
A letter of advice from one clergyman to another . . . Newport, J. Franklin, 1752.
7 p. 21 cm.
Signed at end: J. Graves. Clapham, Jan. 8. 1750-1
Alden 116
MB mp. 40615

B1566 GT. BRIT. LAWS
. . . At the Parliament begun . . . at Westminster, the tenth day of November . . . 1747 . . . An act for regulating the commencement of the year; and for correcting the calendar . . . New London, Reprinted by Timothy Green, 1752.
[2], 6, [24] p.
Trumbull: Supplement no. 2200
RPJCB mp. 40616

1567 GT. BRIT. LAWS
The two first clauses of an act for the more effectual securing the duties upon tobacco . . . [n.p., 1752?]
broadside
MWA mp. 40617

B1568 H., J.
A lamentation on occasion of the sickness of mortality in East-Guilford . . . 1751. By J. H. N. London, Printed & sold by T. Green, 1752.
broadside 37.5 X 31.5 cm.
In verse
New York Public 232; cf. CtHi *Bull.* XXIII, 3 (Jy 1958)
CtHi; NHi (imperfect). Photostats: MWA (imperfect); NN (imperfect) mp. 40621

B1569 HAND-IN-HAND FIRE CLUB, NEWPORT, R.I.
These presents witness, that we the subscribers . . . [Sept. 26, 1752] . . . [Newport, James Franklin, 1752?]
broadside 28.5 X 28 cm.
Alden 120; New York Public 237
RHi; RNHi. Photostats: MWA; NN mp. 40633

B1570 JANEWAY, JAMES, 1636?-1674
A token for children . . . Boston, Printed and sold by S. Kneeland, 1752.
1 p.l., x, 33 p.; 2 leaves, 46, ii, 38+ p. 14 cm.
P. E. Clapp, New York (1947) seen by NN mp. 40618

B1571 [KENNEDY, ARCHIBALD] 1685?-1763
An essay on the government of the colonies . . . New York, J. Parker, 1752.
42 p. 17.5 cm.
For authorship cf. Wroth: *An American bookshelf, 1755*, p. 29-31, 118-19, 122-26
RPJCB. Photostats: DLC; MHi; MWA; NN mp. 40619

B1572 KINNERSLEY, EBENEZER, 1711-1778
Newport, March 16, 1752. Notice is hereby given . . . A course of experiments, on the . . . electrical fire . . . By Ebenezer Kinnersley . . . [Newport, J. Franklin, 1752]
broadside 32 X 22.5 cm.
Alden 117; Winship p. 13
RPB; PPRF. Photostats: MWA; NN; RHi mp. 40620

B1573 MARYLAND. LAWS
Acts of Assembly . . . begun and held . . . the third day of June . . . 1752 . . . Annapolis, Jonas Green, 1752.
19, [1] p. 29 cm.
Wroth 157
DLC; MH-L; Md; MdBP; MdHi mp. 40622

B1574 [THE Maryland almanack, for the year 1753. Annapolis, Jonas Green, 1752]

Advertised in the *Maryland Gazette* Dec. 14, 1752, as "Just Published."
Wroth 161
No copy known mp. 40623

B1575 MASSACHUSETTS. GOVERNOR, 1749-1753
By the honourable Spencer Phips . . . A proclamation [on attempt to communicate the small-pox to the family of Benjamin Lynde] . . . May 28, 1752. Boston, John Draper, 1752.
broadside 39 X 30.5 cm.
Austin 1215; Ford 956
MHi mp. 40626

B1576 MASSACHUSETTS. GOVERNOR, 1749-1753
By the honourable Spencer Phips . . . A proclamation for proroguing the General Assembly [to Nov. 22] . . . [Aug. 28, 1752] . . . Boston, John Draper, 1752.
broadside 36 X 25.5 cm.
Ford 959
MHi mp. 40627

B1577 MASSACHUSETTS. LAWS
. . . An act for granting to His Majesty several rates and duties . . . Published June 16, 1752. Boston, John Draper, 1752.
8 p.
MWA mp. 40624

B1578 MASSACHUSETTS. LAWS
. . . An act passed by the . . . General Court . . . begun . . . the twenty-seventh day of May, 1752 . . . for the supply of the Treasury with eight thousand one hundred and forty-two pounds, four shillings . . . [Colophon] Boston, John Draper, 1752.
8 [i.e. 12] p. 32 cm.
Ford & Matthews p. 410
M-Ar; MWA mp. 40625

B1579 MASSACIIUSETTS. TREASURER
Province of the Massachusetts-Bay, ss. William Foye, Esq; Treasurer . . . November 27, 1752. [Boston, 1752]
broadside
Tax warrant
Ford 961
MSaE mp. 40628

B1580 NASSAU STREET THEATRE, NEW YORK
For the benefit of Mrs. Upton . . . at the theatre in Nassau-Street, on Thursday of 20th of February, will be acted . . . Venice Preserv'd . . . [New York, 1752]
broadside
cf. *American collector*, v. 2, no. 2, May 1926
New York Public 236
NN (reduced facsim.) mp. 40631

B1581 THE New-England primer enlarged . . . To which is added, the Assembly's catechism. Boston, Printed and sold by S. Kneeland, and T. Green, 1752.
[80] p. 10 cm.
MWA mp. 40629

B1582 A NEW song, on the alteration of the stile . . . [n.p., 1752?]
broadside fol.
MWA mp. 40630

B1583 NEW YORK. RECEIVER-GENERAL
New-York, May 22, 1752. Advertisement. All persons indebted to his Majesty for quit-rent of lands, in the County of Albany, are hereby notified to pay the same forthwith . . . [New York? 1752]
broadside 15 X 21.5 cm.
NHi mp. 40632

B1584 OLD Ireland's misery at an an [sic] end . . . inchanted lady, who appeared the 5th day of June, 1752, in the form of a mermaid . . . Newport, [Ann and James Franklin?] [1752?]
8? p. illus. 15.5 cm.
Alden 121
MWA (all after p. 6 lacking) mp. 40634

B585 PAINE, SOLOMON, 1698-1754
A short view of the difference between the church of Christ, and the established churches . . . in Connecticut . . . Newport, James Franklin, 1752.
13, [2], 74 p. 20.5 cm.
Alden 122; Winship p. 13
CtHi; CtY; MBC; MNtCA (imperfect); MWA; NN; NNPM; RPB; RPJCB mp. 40635

B1586 PENNSYLVANIA. HOUSE OF REPRESENTATIVES
Votes and proceedings of the House of Representatives . . . met at Philadelphia . . . October . . . 1751, and continued by adjournments. Philadelphia, Printed and sold by B. Franklin, 1752.
62 p. 24.5 cm.
Curtis 498; Hildeburn 1283
PU mp. 40636

B1587 PENNSYLVANIA HOSPITAL
Rules agreed to by the managers of the Pennsylvania Hospital, for the admission and discharge of patients . . . [Jan. 23, 1752] . . . B F Clerk of the Hospital Managers. [Philadelphia, 1752]
[2] p.
PPPH mp. 40637

B1588 PENNSYLVANIA HOSPITAL
This is to certify, that of the hath contributed the sum of to the Pennsylvania Hospital, and is hereby become one of the Corporation . . . Witness my hand, this day of 175 Treasurer. [Philadelphia, B. Franklin and D. Hall, 1752?]
broadside 15.5 X 19 cm.
Filled in for Aug. 29, 1754
CtY; PHi; PPPH; PU (2 copies)

B1589 PHILADELPHIA lottery accounts. Philadelphia, B. Franklin and D. Hall, 1752.
16 p. 12mo
Curtis 494
CtY. Photostats: PPAmP; PPRF mp. 40638

B1590 PLYMOUTH PROPRIETORS
Advertisement. This is to notify . . . September the 1st day, 1752. [Boston, 1752]
broadside 27 X 19.5 cm.
Meeting at the house of Robert Stone in Kingstreet, Boston, on October 17
Ford 950
MWA mp. 40639

B1591 [POOR Roger's almanack for . . . 1753. By Roger More. New-York, J. Parker [1752]]

Drake 5680
No copy known

B1592 PRINCETON UNIVERSITY
A general account of the rise and state of the college lately established in . . . New-Jersey . . . Published by order of the trustees . . . New-York, Printed by James Parker, 1752.
8 p. 31.5 cm.
New York Public 239
MH; NjP. Photostat: NN mp. 40640

B1593 RHODE ISLAND. LAWS
[At the General assembly . . . begun and held at Newport . . . An act to prevent the small-pox . . . Newport, Ann and James Franklin, 1752]

Printing ordered by the May 1752 session of the General assembly; billed Aug. 19, 1752
Alden 127; Winship p. 13
No copy known mp. 40641

B1594 SOUTH CAROLINA. LAWS
... At a General assembly, begun ... the fourteenth day of November ... 1751. And from thence continued ... to the 16th day of May, 1752. Charles-Town, Peter Timothy, 1752.
27 p. 29 cm.
Tax act
Sabin 87582
DLC mp. 40642

B1595 [THE South Carolina almanack for 1753. Charleston, P. Timothy, 1752]

Advertised in the *South Carolina Gazette*, Mar. 26, 1753
Mosimann 91
No copy known

B1596 [WELD, EDMUND] 1736-1816
A funeral elegy, by way of dialogue; between Death, Soul, Body, World, and Jesus Christ. [n.p., 1752?]
broadside 41.5 X 23.5 cm.
Dated from an endorsement in an old hand, possibly contemporary
Ford 947
PHi. Photostat: MWA mp. 40643

B1597 THE worlds vanity ... N. London, Printed & sold by T. Green [1752?]
broadside 31 X 14.5 cm.
32 lines of verse
"Dated 1752 in a book catalogue."–Note by A. C. Bates
CtHi mp. 40644

B1598 THE youth's instructor ... Boston, Printed by Z. Fowle for J. Edwards and T. Leverett, 1752.
192 p.
Karpinski p. 50
NNC mp. 40645

1753

B1599 AN astronomical diary, or, an almanack for ... 1754 ... Boston, D. Fowle [1753]
[16] p.
By George Wheaton [Wheten], 1728-1803
Drake 3096; Nichols: Mass. almanacs, p. 61
MB mp. 40679

B1600 BACON, THOMAS
[A sermon, preached ... in June last ... Annapolis, Jonas Green, 1753]

Advertised Oct. 11, 1753, as "Just Published."
Wroth 163
No copy traced mp. 40646

B1601 BRUNSWICK PROPRIETORS
At a meeting of the proprietors of the township of Brunswick ... on January 4th, 1753; the following vote was passed ... [Boston, 1753]
broadside 35 cm.
Reissue of the vote of 1751, with Thomas Johnson's map attached
Ford 966
MHi; MWA. Photostat: RPJCB mp. 40647

B1602 CONGREGATIONAL CHURCHES
The result of a late ecclesiastical council ... An ecclesiastical council of seven churches ... convened December 5th, 1752, in ... Braintree, at the house of Deacon John Adams ... at the request of ... aggrieved persons ... [Boston, 1753]
7 p. 4to
Samuel Niles, moderator
MHi

B1603 [DODSLEY, ROBERT] 1703-1764
The oeconomy of human life. Part the second ... Boston, Re-printed and sold by D. Fowle [1753]
44+ p. 18 cm.
MHi; MWA (all wanting after p. 44) mp. 40648

B1604 GT. BRIT . POST OFFICE
Instructions given by Benjamin Franklin, and William Hunter ... His Majesty's Deputy Post-masters General ... to their deputy post-master, for the stage of in the province of [Philadelphia, Franklin & Hall, 1753?]
broadside 56 X 43.5 cm.
Curtis 503
PU

B1605 HARVARD UNIVERSITY
Quaestiones pro modulo ... MDCCLIII. [Boston, 1753]
broadside
MH mp. 40649

B1606 THE HISTORY of Don Alonzo, from the private memoirs of a noble family in Spain ... New-York, Printed and sold by Hugh Gaine, 1753.
vi, 14 p. 19 cm.
NHi mp. 40650

B1607 JEFFRYS, JOHN
A serious address to the people of the Church of England ... Philadelphia: Reprinted and sold by James Chattin, 1753.
69, [2] p. 8vo
Not Evans 7028 (also at PHi)
PHi; PPL

B1608 MARYLAND. LAWS
An act to repeal ... an act for the confirmation of the lands therein mentioned ... [Annapolis, Jonas Green, 1753]
2 leaves. 32.5 cm.
Dated Nov. 16, 1753
Wroth 165
MdHi mp. 40651

B1609 MASSACHUSETTS. GOVERNOR, 1749-1753
By ... Spencer Phips ... a proclamation for proroguing ... [Aug. 1, 1753] ... Boston, John Draper, 1753.
broadside 37.5 X 25 cm.
DLC mp. 40657

B1610 MASSACHUSETTS. GOVERNOR, 1749-1753
By the honourable Spencer Phips ... A proclamation. Whereas the Great and General Court ... [April 13, 1753] ... Boston, John Draper, 1753.
broadside 40 X 31.5 cm.
Prohibiting hunting of beaver east of the Saco River
Ford 972
MHi mp. 40656

B1611 MASSACHUSETTS. GOVERNOR, 1753-1756
By His Excellency William Shirley ... A proclamation. Whereas the Great and General Court ... [Aug. 10, 1753] ... Boston, John Draper, 1753.
broadside 42 X 25.5 cm.
General Court to meet Sept. 5 as appointed
Ford 973
MHi mp. 40652

B1612 MASSACHUSETTS. GOVERNOR, 1753-1756
By His Excellency William Shirley . . . A proclamation for proroguing the General Assembly [to Nov. 6] . . . [Oct. 5, 1753] . . . Boston, John Draper, 1753.
broadside 42 X 26.5 cm.
Ford 974
MHi mp. 40653

B1613 MASSACHUSETTS. GOVERNOR, 1753-1756.
By His Excellency William Shirley . . . A proclamation for proroguing the General Assembly [to Dec. 4] . . . [Oct. 18, 1753] . . . Boston, John Draper, 1753.
broadside 37 X 24 cm.
Ford 976
MHi mp. 40654

B1614 MASSACHUSETTS. LAWS
. . . An act in addition to an act . . . directing how meetings of proprietors of lands lying in common may be called. Boston, Kneeland & Green, 1753.
p. 439–440.
Separate printing from the session laws
MWA mp. 40654a

B1615 MASSACHUSETTS. LAWS
. . . An act passed by the . . . General Court . . . begun . . . the thirtieth day of May, 1753 . . . Boston, John Draper, 1753.
8 p.
Impost tax
MWA mp. 40655

B1616 MASSACHUSETTS. TREASURER
Province of the Massachusetts-Bay, ss. Harrison Gray, Esq; Treasurer . . . [Boston, 1753]
broadside 38.5 X 24.5 cm.
Ford 982
DLC; MSaE mp. 40658

B1617 MASSACHUSETTS. TREASURER
Province of the Massachusetts-Bay, ss. Harrison Gray, Esq; Treasurer . . . Given . . . at Boston, the first day of November 1753 . . . [Boston, 1753]
broadside 38 X 31 cm.
MWA mp. 40659

B1618 NASSAU STREET THEATRE, NEW YORK
For the benefit of the poor. Thursday, December 20, 1753. At the New Theatre in Nassau-Street. This evening . . . Love for love . . . [New York, 1753]
broadside 31 X 19 cm.
Original formerly in the collection of George P. Elder, Brooklyn, N.Y.
NN (photostat) mp. 40660

B1619 NEW YORK. GOVERNOR, 1743-1753
By His Excellency the honourable George Clinton . . . A proclamation. Whereas several incroachments . . . by the inhabitants of . . . Massachusetts-Bay and New-Hampshire . . . [New York, 1753]
broadside 40.5 X 32 cm.
Dated at Fort-George, New York, July 28, 1753
NHi mp. 40661

B1620 NORTH CAROLINA. HOUSE OF BURGESSES
The journal of the House of Burgesses, of . . . North-Carolina: At a General Assembly . . . Newbern [June 12, 1747—Mar. 31, 1752] . . . Being the eleventh session of this present General Assembly. Newbern, James Davis,
16 p. 31 cm.
Session Mar. 31–Apr. 15, 1752; prorogued to "the second Tuesday in October next."
McMurtrie: North Carolina 9
Public Record Off. mp. 40662

B1621 NORTH CAROLINA. HOUSE OF BURGESSES
The journal of the House of Burgesses . . . [Newbern, James Davis, 1753]
p. 3–18. 32.5 cm. caption title
Session Mar. 28–Apr. 12, 1753; prorogued to the fourth Tuesday in September
McMurtrie: North Carolina 10
Public Record Off. (t.p. wanting?) mp. 40663

B1622 PENNSYLVANIA. LAWS
Eine im herbst 26sten jahrs der regierung George des Zweyten . . . gemachte acte oder landsgesetz . . . der provinz Pennsylvanien . . . [at end] Germantown, Christoph Sauer, 1753.
24 p. caption title
RPJCB mp. 40664

B1623 [PENNSYLVANIA town and country man's almanack for 1754. By John Tobler. Philadelphia, 1753]
[32] p. 16.5 cm.
InU (fragment); MWA (t.p. wanting); PNortHi
mp. 40675

B1624 PLYMOUTH COMPANY, 1749-1816
At a meeting of the proprietors of the Kenebeck Purchase . . . voted, That the following votes be printed . . . [Boston, 1753]
broadside 31.5 X 19 cm.
Ford 964
MH; MWA; RPJCB mp. 40665

B1625 PLYMOUTH COMPANY, 1749-1816
Forasmuch as there have been many disputes and controversies for a long time, concerning the titles to . . . lands in the eastern parts of this province . . . the printing . . . of extracts . . . acts, laws and orders . . . down to the present times, will be of considerable service . . . viz. . . . [Boston? 1753?]
4 p. 23 cm.
Ford 968
MB; MHi; MWA (2 issues) mp. 40666-67

B1626 PREISS, JOHANNES
Geistliche u. andächtige Lieder. Aufgesetzt von Br. Johannes Preiss . . . [Germantown, Christoph Saur, 1753]
16, 8 p. 16.5 cm. caption title
Kleiner Anhang: 8 p. at end
PHi mp. 40668

B1627 PROPRIETORS OF THE EASTERN DIVISION OF NEW JERSEY
To His Excellency Johathan Belcher . . . The memorial of the Council of Proprietors of the eastern division of New-Jersey . . . Perth-Amboy, November 20, 1753. [n.p., 1753?]
12 p. 31 cm.
Humphrey 44 (appendix)
DLC; PHi mp. 40669

B1628 [SMITH, WILLIAM] 1726-1803
Ode on the New-Year, 1753 . . . New-York, J. Parker [1753]
16 p. 21 cm.
Huntington 169
CSmH; PHi mp. 40670

B1629 SOCIETY FOR ENCOURAGING INDUSTRY AND EMPLOYING THE POOR, BOSTON
Advertisement. Boston, January 15. 1752. For the encouragement of the raising and well-curing and dressing of

flax within this province, a praemium . . . is hereby offered . . . The claims of the several persons to the four last praemiums to be determined at the Manufactory-House in Boston, on the first Thursday in April 1753 . . . [Boston, 1753]
broadside 27 X 21 cm.
Ford 949; New York Public 240
DLC; MHi. Photostats: MH; MWA; NN mp. 40671

B1630 SOCIETY FOR ENCOURAGING INDUSTRY AND EMPLOYING THE POOR, BOSTON
The report of the committee to the Society for Encouraging Industry . . . at their quarterly meeting . . . February, A.D. 1752 . . . By the report . . . in the looms, nine hundred and fifty yards of linen . . . Boston, February the 12th. 1752. [Boston, 1753]
broadside 31 X 21 cm.
NHi mp. 40672

B1631 SOUTH CAROLINA. LAWS
Acts passed . . . at a sessions begun . . . the fourteenth day of November . . . 1751. And from thence continued . . . to the 16th day of May, 1752. Charles-Town, Peter Timothy, 1753.
1 p.l., 36, [1] p. 29 cm.
Half-title: Acts passed . . . on the 7th and 16th days of May, 1752
Sabin 87580
DLC; NNB mp. 40673

B1632 SOUTH CAROLINA. LAWS
Acts passed . . . at a sessions begun . . . the fourteenth day of November . . . 1751. And from thence continued . . . to the 7th day of October, 1752. Charles-Town, Peter Timothy, 1753.
7 p. 29 cm.
Sabin 87581
DLC; NNB mp. 40674

B1633 [THE SOUTH-Carolina almanack for . . . 1754. By John Tobler. Charles-Town, Peter Timothy [1753]]

Advertised in the *South Carolina Gazette*, Oct. 22, 1753
Drake 13075
No copy known

B1634 TUBBS, THOMAS
Advertisement. Ran away yesterday morning from the house of Mrs Clough . . . an Irish fellow named William Haly . . . Thomas Tubbs . . . Boston, March 22. 1753. [Boston, 1753]
broadside 18.5 X 10.5 cm.
MB mp. 40676

B1635 VIRGINIA. LAWS
Acts of Assembly, now in force, in Virginia. Occasioned by the repeal of sundry acts made . . . in the year . . . 1748. [Williamsburg, W. Hunter, 1753]
58 p. 34.5 cm. caption title
Huntington 170; Sabin 100389; Torrence 191; New York Public 241
CSmH; DLC; NN; NNB; Vi. Brit. Mus. mp. 40677

B1636 VIRGINIA
Anno regni Georgii II . . . vicesimo septimo. At a General Assembly . . . 27th day of February . . . 1752, and from thence . . . to . . . 1st day of November, 1753 . . . being the second session . . . [Williamsburg, W. Hunter, 1753]
46 p. fol.
PHi

B1637 WARRINGTON, THOMAS
The love of God, benevolence, and selflove, considered together . . . Williamsburg, W. Hunter, 1753.
24 p. 18 cm.
RPJCB mp. 40678

1754

B1638 [ANCOURT, ABBÉ D']
The lady's preceptor . . . Woodbridge, J. Parker, 1754.
12mo
According to Amer. Book Prices Current copy sold by S. V. Henkels June 11, 1929
No copy located

B1639 [AN astronomical diary . . . for . . . 1755. Boston, 1754]
[16] p. 16 cm.
By George Wheaton [Wheten], 1728-1803
MWA (t.p. wanting) mp. 40732

B1640 BIBLE. O.T. PSALMS
A new version of the Psalms of David . . . By N. Brady . . . and N. Tate . . . Boston, Re-printed and sold by J. Draper, 1754.
385, [1] p. 14.5 cm.
MWA mp. 40680

B1641 BIBLE. O.T. PSALMS
A new version of the Psalms of David . . . By N. Brady . . . and N. Tate . . . Boston, Re-printed by J. Draper, for T. Leverett, 1754.
320 p. 14.5 cm.
MB; MWA mp. 40681

B1642 BOSTON
(No. 8.) To Your province tax. Lawful money. Your town and county rate. Lawful money . . . The assessors sit at Faneuil Hall . . . Thursdays, from 3 to 5 . . . 1754 . . . John Ruddock, Collector. [Boston, 1754]
broadside 12 X 15.5 cm.
Ford 985
MHi

B1643 [BRIANT, TIMOTHY]
A receipt from Middleborough in . . . Massachusetts-Bay, concerning the canker, or throat-distemper. Boston, Printed and sold by D. Fowle, in Ann-Street [1754]
8 p. 16 cm.
Dated Middleborough, Jan. 3, 1754, and signed Timothy Briant
Austin 273; Rogers 87
MBCo; MHi mp. 40682

B1644 CONNECTICUT. GOVERNOR, 1750-1754
By the honourable Roger Wolcott . . . A proclamation for a day of public fasting and prayer . . . [Apr. 10, 1754] . . . New-London, March the 25th, 1754. Printed by Timothy Green . . .
broadside 36 X 31 cm.
CtHi

B1645 CONNECTICUT. GOVERNOR, 1754-1756
By the honorable Thomas Fitch . . . A proclamation for a public thanksgiving . . . [Nov. 13, 1754] . . . N. London, March [October?] the 21st 1754, Printed by Timothy Green . . .
broadside 42.5 X 33 cm.
CtHi

B1646 ELIOT, JOSEPH, 1630-1694
A copy of a letter, found in the study of the Reverend Mr. Joseph Belcher . . . since his decease . . . [Boston] Printed and sold at the Printing-Office in Back Street [by Zachariah Fowle] [ca. 1754]
broadside
Fowle printed in Back Street from 1751 to 1754
Ford 987
PHi mp. 40684

B1647 Deleted.

B1648 GARDEN, ALEXANDER, 1685-1756
A farewell sermon, preached in the parish church of St. Philip . . . the 31st day of March 1754 . . . Charles-Town, Peter Timothy, 1754.
25 p. 18.5 cm.
NcD

B1649 HALL, DAVID, 1714-1772
Imported in the last ships from London, and to be sold by David Hall, at the New-Printing-Office, in Market-street, Philadelphia, the following books . . . [Philadelphia, 1754?]
broadside 38 X 24 cm.
MWA copy from *Pennsylvania Gazette* after June 27, 1754
MWA mp. 40686

B1650 HAMMETT, JOHN, 1680?-1773
John Hammett's confession of faith . . . Newport, J. Franklin, 1754.
23 [i.e. 22] p. 16.5 cm.
Alden 141
MWA mp. 40687

B1651 HARVARD UNIVERSITY
Catalogus eorum qui . . . ab anno 1642, ad annum 1754 alicujus gradus laurea donati sunt. Cantabrigiae, Nov-Anglorum, M,DCC,LIV. [Boston, 1754]
broadside 43 X 15 cm.
Ford 988; New York Public 243
CtHi. Photostats: MHi; NN mp. 40688

B1652 HARVARD UNIVERSITY
Quaestiones pro modulo . . . MDCCLIV. [Boston, 1754]
broadside
MH; MHi; MWA mp. 40689

B1653 INDEPENDENT REFLECTOR, NEW YORK
New-York, February 29, 1754. Advertisement. Just published, and to be sold by Robert Mc.Alpine, bookbinder . . . a Preface to the *Independent Reflector* . . . The whole containing thirty-two pages in folio. [New York, 1754]
broadside 29 cm.
New York Public 244
NN mp. 40690

B1654 A LETTER from Quebeck . . . Newport, J. Franklin, 1754.
13 p. 17 cm.
Signed on p. 13: De Roche
Alden 149; Winship p. 14
DLC mp. 40683

B1655 LIFE and death of riches and poverty; or, The ready way to true contentment. Philadelphia, W. Bradford, 1754.
12mo
Metzger 167
No copy located mp. 40691

B1656 MARYLAND. LAWS
Acts of the province . . . made and passed at a session . . . begun . . . the seventeenth day of July . . . 1754 . . . Annapolis, Jonas Green, 1754.
[2], 13, [1] p. 28.5 cm.
Wroth 169
MH–L; MdBB; MdBP mp. 40693

B1657 MARYLAND. LAWS
Acts of the province . . . made and passed at two sessions . . . Annapolis, Jonas Green, 1754.
11 p. 29 cm.
Wroth 168
DLC; MH–L; MdBB; MdBP; MdHi mp. 40692

B1658 [THE Maryland almanack, for the year 1754. Annapolis, Jonas Green, 1754]

Advertised Jan. 17, 1754, in the *Maryland Gazette*
Wroth 174
No copy known mp. 40694

B1659 MASSACHUSETTS. GOVERNOR, 1753-1756
By His Excellency William Shirley . . . A proclamation. Whereas it is apprehended . . . [April 19, 1754] . . . Boston, John Draper, 1754.
broadside 39.5 X 30.5 cm
Defence of the eastern frontiers
Ford 993
MHi (mutilated) mp. 40696

B1660 MASSACHUSETTS. GOVERNOR, 1753-1776
By His Excellency William Shirley . . . A proclamation. Whereas it is of great importance . . . [June 21, 1754] . . . Boston, John Draper, 1754.
broadside 39 X 31 cm.
Ford 994
MHi; MMal mp. 40697

B1661 MASSACHUSETTS. HOUSE OF REPRESENTATIVES
Province of the Massachusetts-Bay. In the House of Representatives, Nov. 19, 1754. Ordered, That . . . the exact number of Negro slaves . . . [Boston, 1754]
broadside
MB mp. 40700

B1662 MASSACHUSETTS. LAWS
. . . An act passed by the . . . General Court . . . begun . . . the twenty-ninth day of May 1754 . . . for the supply of the Treasury with the sum of nine thousand four hundred fifty-six pounds seven shillings and eight pence . . . [Colophon] Boston, John Draper, 1754.
8 [i.e. 12] p. 32 cm.
Ford & Matthews p. 416
M–Ar mp. 40699

B1663 MASSACHUSETTS. LAWS
. . . An act passed by the . . . General Court . . . begun . . . the twenty-ninth day of May 1754 . . . tunnage of shipping . . . [at end] Published, June 20, 1754. Boston, John Draper, 1754.
8 p.
Impost law
MWA mp. 40698

B1664 MASSACHUSETTS. LAWS
Anno Regni Regis Georgii Secundi Vicesimo Septimo. A

bill for further ascertaining the descent of real estates of persons dying intestate without issue . . . [Boston, 1754]
broadside
Ford 996; cf. Evans 7055
M–Ar; MHi. Photostat: DLC mp. 40695

B1665 MASSACHUSETTS. TREASURER
Province of the Massachusetts-Bay, ss. Harrison Gray, Esq; Treasurer . . . . July 3, 1754. [Boston, 1754]
broadside
Tax warrant
Ford 997
MB; MSaE mp. 40701

B1666 [MOODY, ELEAZAR]
The school of good manners . . . The fifth edition. New-London, Printed & sold by T. & J. Green, 1754.
[2], ii. 80 p. $A\text{–}G^6$
Rosenbach–Ch 41; Trumbull: Supplement 2404
CtY; PP mp. 40702

B1667 THE New-England primer further improved . . .
Boston, Printed for the booksellers, 1754.

Heartman 12
E. M. Kidder (1922) mp. 40703

B1668 NEW HAMPSHIRE. LAWS
. . . An act for preventing and suppressing riots . . . 23d April 1754 . . . An act for the suppressing of lotteries . . . B. Wentworth . . . 7th May 1754 . . . [n.p., 1754?]
9 p.
MWA mp. 40704

B1669 NEW JERSEY. GOVERNOR, 1747-1757
By His Excellency, Jonathan Belcher . . . governor . . . over . . . Nova-Caesarea or New-Jersey . . . A proclamation . . . [Feb. 7, 1754] Philadelphia, W. Bradford, 1754.
broadside 39 X 30 cm.
Concerns a riot in the County of Hunterdon
Humphrey 46 (appendix)
NHi (2 copies) mp. 40705

B1670 NEW-YORK LIBRARY
A list of the subscribers to the New-York Library. [New-York, 1754]
broadside 31 X 18 cm.
"The subscribers are to meet . . . the 29th of April, inst."
New York Public 245
NN mp. 40706

B1671 NEW-YORK LIBRARY
Whereas a publick library would be very useful . . . we . . . do promise to pay five pounds New-York currency, each . . . [New York, 1754]
broadside 32.5 X 25.5 cm.
Dated: April 2d, 1754
New York Public 246
NN mp. 40707

B1672 NORTH CAROLINA. HOUSE OF BURGESSES
The journal of the House of Burgesses, of . . . North-Carolina . . . Newbern [June 12, 1747–Feb. 1754] and then held at Wilmington: Being the thirteenth session of this present General Assembly. Newbern, James Davis, 1754.
16 p. 30.5 cm.
McMurtrie: North Carolina 13
Public Record Off. mp. 40709

B1673 NORTH CAROLINA. LAWS
A draught of an act proposed to the Assembly of North-Carolina, for establishing a paper credit, for 80,000 pounds, currency, upon a new plan. Newbern, James Davis, 1754.
15 p. 26 cm.
McMurtrie: North Carolina 15
Public Record Off. mp. 40708

B1674 A PLAIN scriptural description of Jesus Christ . . .
Newport, J. Franklin, 1754.
8 p. 17 cm.
Signed: Joseph Tillinghast [and others]
Alden 151; Winship p. 14
MWA; RHi mp. 40711

B1675 PLYMOUTH COMPANY, 1749-1816
Advertisement. Whereas the proprietors of the Kennebeck Purchase . . . are making divers settlements on Kennebeck-River . . . Boston, Jan. 2, 1754. Robert Temple, Sylvester Gardiner [etc.] [Boston, 1754?]
broadside 29 X 19 cm.
Ford 984
MWA; RPJCB mp. 40712

B1676 A POCKET almanack, for . . . 1755 . . . By Jesse Parsons . . . New York, Printed and sold by H. De Foreest [1754]
[24] p.
Wall p. 13
NHi mp. 40710

B1677 A POEM, on the joyful news of the Rev. Mr. Whitefield's visit to Boston . . . Boston, 1754.
broadside 35 X 18.5 cm.
Huntington 172; Ford 1000
CSmH; RPJCB. Photostats: MHi; MiU–C; NN; WHi
mp. 40713

B1678 [QUINCY, JOSIAH] 1709-1784
A letter to the inhabitants of Braintree, relating to the excise bill now depending . . . [Boston? 1754]
7 p. 20.5 cm. caption title
Signed: Jos[a]. Quincy
Dated: Braintree, August 22, 1754
DLC mp. 40714

B1679 RHODE ISLAND. LAWS
An act for the relief of insolvent debtors . . . [Newport, Ann and James Franklin, 1754]
5 p. 31.5 cm. caption title
Bill paid to the Franklins Nov. 2, 1754, in the Rhode Island Archives
Alden 148; Winship p. 14 (also 74)
RHi; RPB mp. 40716

B1680 RHODE ISLAND. LAWS
At the General assembly . . . of Rhode-Island . . . begun . . . on the last Wednesday of October . . . An act for assessing and levying a tax of thirty-five thousand pounds . . . [Newport, Ann and James Franklin, 1754]
3 p. 31.5 cm. caption title
Alden 147; Winship p. 14
RHi mp. 40715

B1681 SOCIETY FOR ENCOURAGING INDUSTRY AND EMPLOYING THE POOR, BOSTON
At the quarterly meeting of the Society . . . Wednesday May 8th 1754. Voted, That there be a dinner provided at the annual meeting . . . On receipt of this, pay four shillings, and bring this ticket with you. Boston, July 1754 . . . [Boston, 1754]
broadside 19.5 X 15 cm.
MWA mp. 40717

B1682 SOUTH CAROLINA. LAWS
Acts passed . . . at a sessions begun . . . the fourteenth day of November . . . 1751. And from thence continued . . . to the 21st day of April, 1753. Charles-Town, Peter Timothy, 1754.
19, [1] p. 29 cm.
Sabin 87583
DLC; MH–L; NNB mp.40718

B1683 SOUTH CAROLINA. LAWS
. . . At a General assembly begun . . . the fourteenth day of November . . . 1751. And from thence continued . . . to the 11th day of May, 1754. Charles-Town, Peter Timothy, 1754.
27 p. 29 cm.
Tax act
Sabin 87585
DLC mp. 40719

B1684 THE South Carolina almanack, for the year . . . 1755 . . . Germantown, Christopher Saur [1754] and sold in Charles-Town South Carolina by Jacob Viart.
[24] p. 16.5 cm.
Metzger 174
NHi mp. 40720

B1685 VIRGINIA. COUNCIL
February 16th, 1754. To the honourable Robert Dinwiddie . . . the humble address of the Council. [also] . . . the following answer . . . [Williamsburg, William Hunter, 1754]
broadside 27 X 20 cm.
Sabin 99903
PHi mp. 40721

B1686 VIRGINIA. GOVERNOR, 1751-1758
. . . By . . . Robert Dinwiddie . . . lieutenant-governor . . . A proclamation, for encouraging men to enlist . . . [Feb. 19, 1754] [Williamsburg, William Hunter, 1754]
broadside 28.5 X 32.5 cm.
Huntington 178
CSmH; PHi mp. 40722

B1687 VIRGINIA. GOVERNOR, 1751-1758
September 5th, 1754. The speech of the honourable Robert Dinwiddie . . . at the prorogation of the General Assembly . . . [Williamsburg, William Hunter, 1754]
broadside ([2] p.) 28 X 19 cm.
PHi mp. 40723

B1688 VIRGINIA. GOVERNOR, 1751-1758
The speech of the honourable Robert Dinwiddie . . . to the General Assembly . . . [Feb. 27, 1954] . . . Williamsburg, William Hunter, 1754.
4 p. 28 cm.
Sabin 99942
PHi mp. 40724

B1689 VIRGINIA. LAWS
Acts of Assembly, passed at a General assembly, begun . . . the twenty seventh day of February . . . And from thence continued . . . to Thursday the first day of November . . . being the second session . . . Williamsburg, William Hunter, 1754.
1 p.l., 46 p. 34.5 cm.
Huntington 174; Sabin 100247; Torrence 219; New York Public 248
CSmH; DLC (2 copies); NN; NNB; Vi mp. 40725

B1690 VIRGINIA. LAWS
. . . At a General assembly, begun . . . on Thursday the 27th day of February . . . And from thence continued . . . to Thursday the 14th day of February . . . 1754 . . . being the third session of this Assembly. [Williamsburg, W. Hunter, 1754]
4 p. 33.5 cm. caption title
Huntington 175; Sabin 100248; Torrence 221
CSmH; DLC (2 copies); MH–L; NN; NNB; PHi; Vi mp. 40726

B1691 VIRGINIA. LAWS
. . . At a General assembly, begun . . . on Thursday the twenty seventh day of February . . . And from thence continued . . . to Thursday the twenty second day of August . . . being the fourth session . . . [Williamsburg, W. Hunter, 1754]
6 p. 33.5 cm. caption title
Huntington 176; Sabin 100249; Torrence 222
CSmH; DLC; MH–L; NN; NNB; Vi mp. 40727

B1692 VIRGINIA. LAWS
. . . At a General assembly, begun . . . on Thursday the twenty seventh day of February . . . And from thence continued . . . to Thursday the seventeenth day of October . . . being the fifth session of this Assembly. [Williamsburg, W. Hunter, 1754]
11 p. 33.5 cm. caption title
Huntington 177; Sabin 100250; Torrence 223
CSmH; DLC mp. 40728

B1693 WADSWORTH, EBENEZER
To His Excellency William Shirley . . . The representation and petition of Ebenezer Wadsworth of Grafton, and Samuel Robinson of Hardwick, in the County of Worcester, and Richard Seaver of Roxbury, in the County of Suffolk . . . [Boston, 1754]
broadside
Dated in print for the General Court of May, 1754, but changed by pen to Oct. 17, 1754
Ford 1002; Sabin 100928
DLC; M–Ar mp. 40729

B1694 A WARNING to young & old: in the execution of William Wieer, at Boston, the 21st of November, 1754, for the murder of William Chism . . . [Boston? 1754?]
broadside 31 X 24 cm.
Ford 1003
NN (reduced facism.); RPJCB mp. 40730

B1695 WESTMINSTER ASSEMBLY OF DIVINES
The shorter catechism agreed upon . . . New-London, T. Green, 1754.
[24] p.
RPJCB mp. 40731

B1696 WOODMASON, CHARLES
A letter from a gentleman of South-Carolina, on the cultivation of indigo . . . [at end] Charles-Town, South-Carolina, October 1st, 1754. [Charleston, 1754]
25 p. 17 cm.
Caption title from p. 3
NNC (p. 1–2 lacking)

B1697 EIN Wort für allerley Sünder die der Busse bedurffen . . . Philadelphia, Anton Armbruster, 1754.
96 p. 15 cm.
PHi mp. 40733

1755

B1698 ARISTOTLE'S compleat master piece . . . To which is added, A treasure of health . . . The twenty-

sixth edition. [n.p.] Printed and sold by the booksellers, 1755.
142+ p. 15.5 cm. A–$E^{12}F^{11}$
MWA (sig. A5–8 wanting) mp. 40735

B1699 AN astronomical diary . . . for the year . . . 1756 . . . By Nathaniel Ames . . . [Boston] New England: Printed for the booksellers [1755]
[16] p.
Drake 3102
MWA; MiU–C; NhD; PHi; RPB mp. 40734

B1700 BIBLE. O.T. PSALMS
A new version of the Psalms of David . . . By N. Brady and N. Tate. Boston, Re-printed by B. Edes and J. Gill, 1755.
332 p. 17 cm.
cf. Evans 7358
DLC; MHi; NNUT mp. 40736

B1701 BILES ISLAND LOTTERY
A list of the numbers that came up prizes in Biles'-Island Lottery, for the benefit of a place of worship in Bordentown . . . [Philadelphia, B. Franklin and D. Hall, 1755]
broadside fol.
PPL mp. 40737

B1702 BLAKENEY, WILLIAM, 1672-1761
The new manual exercise . . . To which is added, The evolutions of the foot, by General Bland, corrected with additions. Philadelphia, William Bradford, 1755.
22, [2] p. 20.5 cm. A–C^4
MWA (sig. A4 wanting); PPL (sig. C3–4 wanting) mp. 40738

B1703 BOSTON
Boston, ss. Whereas at a meeting of the freeholders and other inhabitants . . . the 16th of May last . . . the inhabitants . . . to give or bring in to the assessors a just list of their polls . . . Ezekiel Goldthwait, Town-Clerk. Boston, June 10th 1755. [Boston, 1755]
broadside 10.5 X 15.5 cm.
MHi mp. 40739

B1704 BRICE, JOHN
[The case between Philip Hammond and the late Vachel Denton, stated: By John Brice. Annapolis, Jonas Green, 1755]

Advertised Nov. 20, 1755, as "Lately Published, and to be sold by the printer hereof . . . "
Wroth 176
No copy known mp. 40740

B1705 BROGDEN, WILLIAM
Popish zeal inconvenient to mankind . . . A sermon, preached . . . the fifth of November, 1754 . . . Annapolis, Printed and sold by Jonas Green, 1755.
47 p. 19 cm. [A]–F^4
Wroth 177
MdHi mp. 40741

B1706 CALVERT, BENEDICT
Advertisement. July 23, 1755. Ran away, yesterday morning . . . Benedict Calvert. [Annapolis, Jonas Green, 1755]
broadside 16.5 X 20 cm.
Wroth 178
PPL. Photostat: MdHi mp. 40742

B1707 CHANDLER, SAMUEL, 1713-1775
Ezekiel's parable of the boiling pot. Considered in a discourse preached . . . March 20th, 1755 . . . Boston, D. Fowle [1755]
32 p. 19 cm.
Half-title on printed wrapper with advertisement on back
MHi; MSaE; MWA; RPJCB mp.40743

B1708 CONNECTICUT. GOVERNOR, 1754-1766
By the honourable Thomas Fitch . . . A proclamation for a day of public fasting and prayer . . . ninth day of July . . . New-London, Timothy Green, 1755.
broadside 37.5 X 27.5 cm.
CtHi

B1709 CONNECTICUT. GOVERNOR, 1754-1766
By the honourable Thomas Fitch . . . A proclamation, for a public thanksgiving . . . [Oct. 27, 1755] . . . [New London? 1755]
broadside 40 X 27.5 cm.
MHi

B1710 FAMILY-RELIGION revived . . . New-Haven Printed and sold by James Parker, 1755.
107, [1] p. 15 cm.
Huntington 179; Trumbull: Supp. 2126
CSmH; CtY; DLC; MB; MWA (p. 71–72, 75–82, 91–94 wanting); NN mp. 40744

B1711 FRANKLIN, BENJAMIN, 1706-1790
Advertisement. Lancaster, April 26, 1755. Whereas 150 waggons, with 4 horses to each waggon, and 1500 saddle or packhorses are wanted . . . [Lancaster? William Dunlap? 1755]
broadside 31 X 19 cm.
MB mp. 40745

B1712 FRANKLIN, BENJAMIN, 1706-1790
[Franklin's Plan of union. Newbern, James Davis, 1755]

The House of Burgesses, on Dec. 24, 1754, "Resolved that the . . . said plan be referred to the next session . . . and that in the meantime the printer print the same." (*Colonial Records of North Carolina*, vol. 5, p. 251.)
McMurtrie: North Carolina 16
No copy known mp. 40746

B1713 A FUNERAL sermon, on Michael Morin . . . [Colophon] New York, Parker and Weyman, 1755.
8 p. 16 cm. caption title
DLC mp. 40747

B1714 GT. BRIT. LAWS
An act to regulate and restrain paperbills of credit . . . [Newport, Ann and James Franklin, 1755]
3 p. 31.5 cm. caption title
Bill for printing this item submitted by the Franklins Jan. 25, 1755
Alden 154A; Winship p. 13 (1751) and p. 15 (1755); New York Public 251
MWA; RHi (2 copies); RPB; RPJCB. Photostat: NN mp. 40748

B1715 HARVARD UNIVERSITY
Quaestiones pro modulo . . . MDCCLV. [Boston, 1755]
broadside
MH; MHi; MWA mp. 40749

B1716 [HAZARD, SAMUEL]
Scheme for the settlement of a new colony to the westward of Pennsylvania . . . [Philadelphia, 1755]
[2] p. 33 X 20.5 cm.
Hazard personally petitioned the Connecticut Assembly on May 8, 1755

Vail: Old frontier 485; Wroth: *American bookshelf*, 1755 (p. 172)
Ct mp. 40750

B1717 [HAZARD, SAMUEL]
Scheme for the settlement of a new colony to the westward of Pennsylvania . . . Dated at Philadelphia, July 24th, 1755. [Philadelphia, 1755]
[2] p. 37.5 X 21 cm. caption title
Metzger 188; Vail: Old frontier 486
Ct; MHi. Photostats: DLC; NN; RPJCB mp. 40751

B1718 THE heavenly damsel . . . [Newport? Ann and James Franklin? 1755?]
8 p. 15.5 cm.
Alden 155
MWA mp. 40752

B1719 HEIDELBERG CATECHISM
Catechismus, oder kurtzer unterricht . . . Germantown, Christoph Saur [1755?]
94, [1] p. 12mo
PPL mp. 40753

B1720 HOFF, CHARLES
Nothing but the love of truth could have prevailed with me . . . [Philadelphia, 1755]
broadside 34 X 21.5 cm.
Huntington 180
CSmH mp. 40754

B1721 [HUSKE, ELLIS] 1700-1755, supposed author
The present state of North-America . . . two editions already this year in England, and this is the second edition in Boston . . . Boston, Re-printed and sold by D. Fowle, and by Z. Fowle, 1755.
[2], 64, [1] p. 18.5 cm.
Huntington 181; cf. Evans 7434
CSmH; ICN; MHi; MWA; NHi; NN mp. 40755

B1722 . . . ICH kehrete erliche unter euch um . . . auf Mennachten . . . [n.p., 1755?]
broadside 33 X 21.5 cm.
At head of title: Amos. 4, 11. cap. 8. 10. cap. 4. 12.
Metzger 175
DLC (not traced) mp. 40756

B1723 THE invitation. It has been observed by the best writers of government, That an unsuccessful attempt to deprive a free people of their liberties . . . [at end] January, 6, 1755. [n.p., 1755]
4 p. 16 cm.
DLC; MWA mp. 40757

B1724 JOHNSON, SIR WILLIAM, 1715-1774
Camp on Lake George, Sept. 9, 1755. To the governors . . . Wm. Johnson. Newport, Sept. 20, 1755. We have intelligence from a person who left the camp the 12th instant . . . [Newport, James Franklin, 1755]
3 p. 18.5 cm.
Alden 157; Winship p. 14; cf. Evans 7441 (without mention of the Newport postscripts)
MHi; RPJCB. Photostats: MiU-C; NN mp. 40758

B1725 LAMB, ANTHONY
Anthony Lamb mathematical instrumentmaker at Sr. Isaac Newton's Head. New York. [New York, 1755?]
broadside 31 X 21 cm.
NHi mp. 40759

B1726 MARK (NEGRO)
The last & dying words of Mark, aged about 30 years, a negro man who belonged to the late Captain John Codman, of Charlestown; who was executed at Cambridge, the 18th of September, 1755, for poysoning his abovesaid master . . . [Boston] Sold next to the prison in Queen-street. [1755]
broadside 42.5 X 31 cm.
In three columns
Phillis, his wife, was burned at the stake
MHi mp. 40760

B1727 MARYLAND. LAWS
Act of Assembly passed in December, 1754 . . . An act for taking and detaining . . . Annapolis, Jonas Green [1755]
2 p. 31.5 X 19 cm.
Huntington 183; Wroth 179
CSmH; DLC; MH-L; MdBB; MdHi; N mp. 40761

B1728 MARYLAND. LAWS
Acts of the province . . . passed at a session . . . begun . . . the twenty third of June . . . 1755 . . . Annapolis, Jonas Green, 1755.
12 p. 31.5 cm.
Wroth 181
MH-L; MdBB; MdHi mp. 40762

B1729 MASSACHUSETTS. GOVERNOR, 1753-1756
By His Excellency William Shirley . . . A proclamation . . . February 22, 1755. Boston, John Draper [1755]
broadside
Concerns an embargo on vessels outward bound
Ford 1013
MB; MHi mp. 40765

B1730 MASSACHUSETTS. GOVERNOR, 1753-1756
By His Excellency William Shirley . . . A proclamation . . . [Feb. 27, 1755] Boston, John Draper, 1755.
broadside
Proclaiming a general fast March 20
Ford 1014; New York Public 256
MB; MBAt; NN (reduced facism.) mp. 40766

B1731 MASSACHUSETTS. GOVERNOR, 1753-1756
By His Excellency William Shirley . . . A proclamation. Whereas the several governments . . . [Mar. 26, 1755] . . . Boston, John Draper, 1755.
broadside 39 X 32 cm.
Articles of the expedition against the French
Ford 1016
MHi mp. 40767

B1732 MASSACHUSETTS. GOVERNOR, 1753-1756
By His Excellency William Shirley . . . A proclamation. Whereas the General Court . . . the twenty-ninth day of March 1755 . . . Boston, J. Draper, 1755.
broadside 31 X 19 cm.
Concerns pay on the expedition against Crown Point
Ford 1017
MB; MHi mp. 40768

B1733 MASSACHUSETTS. GOVERNOR, 1753-1756
By His Excellency William Shirley . . . A proclamation . . . [June 12, 1755] Boston, John Draper, 1755.
broadside 39 X 31 cm.
Declaring the Norridgewock Indians and others to be enemies
Ford 1020; New York Public 255
MHi; MWA (reduced facism.); MWiW-C (imperfect); NN (reduced facism.) mp. 40770

B1734 MASSACHUSETTS. GOVERNOR, 1753-1756
By His Excellency William Shirley . . . A proclamation. Whereas the Great and General Court . . . [June 18, 1755.] . . . Boston, John Draper, 1755.

broadside 38.5 × 31.5 cm.
Encouragement to penetrate the Indian country and kill enemy Indians
Ford 1021
MHi mp. 40769

B1735 MASSACHUSETTS. GOVERNOR, 1753-1756
By His Excellency William Shirley . . . To Sir, As you have receiv'd beating-orders . . . Given under my hand at Boston, the day of 1755 . . . [Boston, 1755]
broadside 32 × 19.5 cm.
Ford 1032; New York Public 257
DLC; MB; MHi (printer's proof); NHi. Photostats: MWA; NN mp. 40771

B1736 MASSACHUSETTS. GOVERNOR, 1753-1756
By His Honour Spencer Phips . . . A proclamation. Whereas the tribe of Penobscot Indians . . . [Nov. 3, 1755] . . . Boston, John Draper, 1755.
broadside
Ford 1027
MHi; MWA mp. 40783

B1737 MASSACHUSETTS. GOVERNOR, 1753-1756
By the honourable Spencer Phips . . . A proclamation. Whereas the Great and General Court . . . [Apr. 25, 1755] . . . Boston, John Draper, 1755.
broadside 31.5 × 19 cm.
Encouragement to inlist on the Crown Point expedition
Ford 1018; New York Public 259
MHi; NN (reduced facsim.) mp. 40777

B1738 MASSACHUSETTS. GOVERNOR, 1753-1756
By the honourable Spencer Phips . . . A proclamation . . . [Apr. 28, 1755] . . . Boston, John Draper, 1755.
broadside 33 × 28 cm.
£100 reward for the murders of William Race
N mp. 40778

B1739 MASSACHUSETTS. GOVERNOR, 1753-1756
By the honourable Spencer Phips . . . A proclamation . . . [Aug. 22, 1755] . . . Boston, John Draper, 1755.
broadside
Proroguing the General Court to Sept. 24
Ford 1023
MHi mp. 40779

B1740 MASSACHUSETTS. GOVERNOR, 1753-1756
By the honourable Spencer Phips . . . A proclamation . . . [Sept. 1, 1755] . . . Boston, John Draper, 1755.
broadside
Convening the General Court
Ford 1024
MeHi mp. 40780

B1741 MASSACHUSETTS. GOVERNOR, 1753-1756
By the honourable Spencer Phips . . . A proclamation . . . [Sept. 9, 1755] . . . Boston, John Draper, 1755.
broadside 32 × 19.5 cm.
Encouragement to inlist in expedition against Crown Point
Ford 1025
MB; MHi; MWA mp. 40784

B1742 MASSACHUSETTS. GOVERNOR, 1753-1756
By the honourable Spencer Phips . . . A proclamation for His Majesty's service . . . [Oct. 29, 1755] . . . Boston, John Draper, 1755.
broadside 31.5 × 19 cm.
Requiring all serving in the Crown Point expedition to repair to the army
Ford 1026
MHi; MWA mp. 40782

B1743 MASSACHUSETTS. GOVERNOR, 1753-1756
By the honourable Spencer Phips . . . A proclamation. Whereas in the proclamation . . . [Nov. 3, 1755] . . . Boston, John Draper, 1755.
broadside 39 × 32 cm.
Reward for captives or scalps of Penobscot Indians
Ford 1029
MHi

B1744 MASSACHUSETTS. GOVERNOR, 1753-1756
By the honourable Spencer Phips . . . A proclamation . . . [Nov. 28, 1755] . . . Boston, John Draper, 1755.
broadside
Embargo on export of provisions or warlike stores
Ford 1030
MHi mp. 40781

B1745 MASSACHUSETTS. GOVERNOR, 1753-1756
Notice is hereby given to such persons as have received beating-orders . . . Boston, March 7, 1755. [Boston, 1755]
broadside 13 × 16 cm.
DLC mp. 40772

B1746 MASSACHUSETTS. GOVERNOR, 1753-1756
Province of the Massachusetts-Bay. By His Honour Spencer Phips, Esq; . . . Whereas the . . . General Court . . . have . . . voted (for reinforcing the army destined to Crown-Point) . . . You are . . . hereby required . . . Given under my hand at the day of September A.D. 1755 . . . [Boston, 1755]
broadside 38 × 23.5 cm.
Ford 1035
MHi

B1747 MASSACHUSETTS. GOVERNOR, 1753-1756
Province of the Massachusetts-Bay. By His Honour the Lieutenant Governour. To Greeting. Whereas the . . . General Court . . . have . . . desired me to give orders to impress a sufficient number of men . . . September 19, 1755. [Boston, 1755]
broadside
Ford 1036
MB

B1748 MASSACHUSETTS. HOUSE OF REPRESENTATIVES
Extract from the votes of the House of Representatives, April 25th, 1755 . . . [Boston, 1755]
broadside 32 × 20 cm.
Concerns pay for Crown Point expedition
Original in collection of Matt B. Jones, 1931
New York Public 258
NN (photostat) mp. 40764

B1749 MASSACHUSETTS. LAWS
. . . An act, passed . . . May 1755. Chap. I. An act for the more effectual prevention of supplies of provisions, and warlike store to the French . . . [Boston, 1755]
p. 167-168. 31 cm.
"Published June 14, 1755."
New York Public 260
NN mp. 40774

B1750 MASSACHUSETTS. LAWS
. . . An act passed by the . ... General Court . . . begun . . . the twenty-eighth day of May, 1755 . . . Boston, John Draper, 1755.
9 p.
Impost law
MWA mp. 40773

B1751 MASSACHUSETTS. LAWS
... An act passed by the ... General Court ... specially convened ... the fifth day of September 1755 ... for apportioning and assessing a tax of eighteen thousand pounds ... [Colophon] Boston, John Draper, 1755.
5 p. caption title
Ford & Matthews p. 421
M-Ar; PHi mp. 40775

B1752 MASSACHUSETTS. LAWS
... An act passed by the ... General Court ... specially convened ... the fifth day of September 1755 ... for the more speedy levying of soldiers for the expedition gainst Crown-Point ... [Colophon] Boston, S. Kneeland, 1755.
p. 177-178. 33.5 cm.
Ford & Matthews p. 421; New York Public 261
NN mp. 40776

B1753 MASSACHUSETTS. LAWS
In the House of Representatives, December 27. 1755. Whereas ... the inhabitants of Nova-Scotia arrived here the 26th instant ... In Council ... read and concur'd ... Consented to S. Phips ... Boston, December 29th 1755 ... [Boston, 1755]
broadside 32 X 19 cm.
Concerns resettlement of refugees
MWA mp. 40763

B1754 MASSACHUSETTS. TREASURER
Province of the Massachusetts-Bay, ss. Harrison Gray, Esq; Treasurer ... To the Select-Men ... of the town or district of Boston, the eighth day of July, 1755 ... [Boston, 1755]
broadside
MWA mp. 40785

B1755 MASSACHUSETTS. TREASURER
Province of the Massachusetts-Bay, ss. Harrison Gray, Esq; Treasurer ... September 12, [1755] [Boston, 1755]
broadside
Tax warrant
Ford 1037
MSaE mp. 40786

B1756 NEW YORK. GOVERNOR, 1753-1755
By ... James De Lancey ... a proclamation. Whereas several desertions ... [May 13, 1755] ... [New York, J. Parker, 1755]
broadside 31.5 X 21.5 cm.
DLC mp. 40787

B1757 NEWLAND, JEREMIAH
Verses occasioned by the earthquakes in the month of November, 1755. By Jeremiah Newland. [Boston, 1755]
broadside
Confused by Evans with Ford 1007
Ford 1042
MHi mp. 40788

B1758 NORTH CAROLINA. HOUSE OF BURGESSES
The journal of the House of Burgesses ... [Newbern, James Davis, 1755?]
14+ p. 30 cm. caption title
Session Dec. 13, 1754–Jan. 15, 1755
Only known copy covers the session only through Dec. 23
McMurtrie: North Carolina 17
Public Record Off. (t.p. and all after p. 14 wanting)
mp. 40789

B1759 NORTH CAROLINA. LAWS
An act, for erecting that part of Rowan county called Wachovia, into a distinct parish. [Newbern, James Davis, 1755?]
broadside 20 X 21 cm.
A separate printing of chap. XIII, 1755 North Carolina laws
NcU mp. 40790

B1760 PENNSYLVANIA. GOVERNOR, 1754-1756
By the honourable Robert Hunter Morris, Esq; Lieutenant Governor ... A proclamation. Whereas ... the nineteenth day of June, to be observed ... as a day of ... fasting and prayer ... Philadelphia, B. Branklin, and D. Hall, 1755.
broadside fol.
PPL mp. 40791

B1761 PETERS, RICHARD, ca. 1704-1776
Lancaster, May 30th, 1755. To the inhabitants of the County of Berks ... We having been with ... General Braddock ... [Lancaster, William Dunlap, 1755]
broadside 33 X 21 cm.
Signed: Richard Peters, William Franklin
cf. Parke-Bernet cat. 1385, Nov. 25-26, 1952, item 64
New York Public 262
NN (reduced facsim.); MWA (reduced facsim.); PPAmP
mp. 40792

B1762 POOR Roger, 1756. The American country almanack for ... 1756 ... By Roger More. Philadelphia, B. Franklin, and D. Hall [1755]
[24] p.
Drake 9778
NjR (photocopy)

B1763 PRINCETON UNIVERSITY
To his Excellency Jonathan Belcher ... Governor ... of ... New-Jersey ... An address from the trustees of the College of New-Jersey. [New York? 1755]
broadside 38 X 24.5 cm.
Dated: Newark, Sept. 24, 1755
New York Public 263
NjP. Photostats: NN; NjR mp. 40793

B1764 RHODE ISLAND. CENSUS, 1755
Account of the people in the colony of Rhode-Island, whites and blacks, together with the quantity of arms ... [n.p., n.d.]
broadside 21 X 33 cm.
This printing of the census, dated Dec. 24, 1755, was apparently produced in the 19th century
Alden 159A
RHi. Photostat: MWA mp. 40794

B1765 RHODE ISLAND. LAWS
November 1, 1755. To the House of magistrates. Gentlemen, Resolved ... And that the Secretary send a copy of this act in print, to each town clerk ... within twenty days ... [Newport, Ann and James Franklin, 1755]
2 p. 33 cm.
Bill paid Dec. 22, 1755
Alden 167; Winship p. 15
RHi; RNHi (mutilated); RPB mp. 40795

B1766 ROCKHILL, JOHN
Forasmuch as the judicious readers of the paper published by Charles Hoff, Junior, in answer to John Rockhill's *State of the controversy* ... [Philadelphia? 1755]
broadside 34 X 20.5 cm.

Huntington 184
CSmH mp. 40796

B1767 ROCKHILL, JOHN
The state of a controversy between Charles Hoff, Junior, and John Rockhill . . . at Bethlehem, in the Jerseys . . . [Philadelphia? 1755]
broadside 38.5 X 24.5 cm.
Huntington 185
CSmH mp. 40797

B1768 [SERVICE for the Pennsylvania German congregations, occasioned by the defeat of General Braddock, 1755. n.p., 1755?]
broadside
Metzger 189
No copy located mp. 40798

B1769 A SHORT reply to Mr. Stephen Hopkins's vindication . . . [Newport, James Franklin, 1755]
6 p. 32.5 cm. caption title
Dated and signed at end: April 10, 1755 . . . Philolethes
Hammett p. 63 (note); Alden 158; Winship p. 14
RNHi; RPB; RPJCB mp. 40799

B1770 Deleted.

B1771 SOUTH CAROLINA. LAWS
[The act for trial of small and mean causes, &c. Charleston, P. Timothy, 1755]

Advertised in the *South Carolina Gazette*, May 29, 1755
Mosimann 104
No copy known

B1772 SOUTH CAROLINA. LAWS
Acts passed . . . at a sessions begun . . . the fourteenth day of November . . . 1751. And from thence continued . . . to the 8th and 11th days of May, 1754. Charles-Town, Peter Timothy, 1755.
41, [2] p. 29 cm.
Sabin 87584
DLC mp. 40802

B1773 SOUTH CAROLINA. LAWS
Acts passed . . . at a sessions begun . . . the twelfth day of November . . . 1754. And from thence continued . . . to the first of February, and 12th of April, 1755. Charles-Town, Peter Timothy, 1755.
7 p. 29.5 cm.
Sabin 87586
DLC mp. 40803

B1774 SOUTH CAROLINA. LAWS
An additional act, to an act, entitled, An act for the better regulating taverns and punch houses. Passed the 8th day of March 1741-2. Charles-Town, Peter Timothy, 1755.
8 p. fol.
MH-L

B1775 SOUTH CAROLINA. LAWS
. . . At a General assembly begun . . . the twelfth day of November . . . 1754. And from thence continued . . . to the 20th day of May, 1755. Charles-Town, Peter Timothy, 1755.
31 p. 29 cm.
Tax act
Sabin 87588
DLC mp. 40801

B1776 SOUTH CAROLINA. LAWS
[The executor's act. Charleston, P. Timothy, 1755]

Advertised in the *South Carolina Gazette*, May 29, 1755
Mosimann 108
No copy known

B1777 SOUTH CAROLINA. LAWS
[The militia act. Charleston, P. Timothy, 1755]

Advertised in the *South Carolina Gazette*, July 3, 1755
Mosimann 109
No copy known

B1778 SOUTH CAROLINA. LAWS
[The patrol act. Charleston, P. Timothy, 1755]

Advertised in the *South Carolina Gazette*, May 29, 1755
Mosimann 110
No copy known

B1779 THE South Carolina almanack, for the year . . . 1756 . . . By John Tobler. Germantown, Printed by Christopher Sower [1755] and sold in Charles-Town, South-Carolina, by Jacob Viart.
[24] p. 17.5 cm.
Guerra b-100; Metzger 193
NN (photostat); ScHi mp. 40804

B1780 TO the freemen of Pennsylvania, and more especially to those of the city and county of Philadelphia. [Philadelphia, 1755?]
broadside 37 X 16.5 cm.
PHi mp. 40805

B1781 TUESDAY CLUB, ANNAPOLIS, MD.
By Permission of . . . the president, of the Tuesday Club . . . [Notice from Jonas Green that there would be no meeting that week] . . . Annapolis, July 15, 1755. [Annapolis, Jonas Green, 1755]
broadside 17 X 13 cm.
Printed on green paper
Wroth 187
DLC mp. 40806

B1782 TUESDAY CLUB, ANNAPOLIS, MD.
Sir, I hope I shall have the honour of your company, at the Tuesday club . . . this evening . . . Jonas Green, H.S. Annapolis, December 2, 1755. [Annapolis, Jonas Green, 1755]
broadside 4 X 7 cm.
Wroth 188
DLC mp. 40807

B1783 VIRGINIA. GOVERNOR, 1751-1758.
The speech of . . . Robert Dinwiddie . . . to the General assembly, summoned to be held . . . the 27th day of February . . . 1752. And from thence continued . . . to Thursday the 1st day of May . . . 1755 . . . being the sixth session . . . Williamsburg, William Hunter, 1755.
[4] p. 30 cm.
DLC mp. 40808

B1784 VIRGINIA. LAWS
. . . At a General assembly, begun . . . the 27th day of February . . . 1752. And from thence continued . . . to

Thursday the 1st day of May . . . 1755 . . . being the sixth session . . . [Williamsburg, W. Hunter, 1755]
35 p. 34.5 cm. caption title
Huntington 187; New York Public 265; Sabin 100251; Torrence 231
CSmH; DLC; NN; Vi mp. 40809

B1785 VIRGINIA. LAWS
. . . At a General assembly, begun . . . the 27th day of February . . . 1752. And from thence continued . . . to Tuesday the 5th day of August . . . 1755 . . . being the seventh session . . . [Williamsburg, W. Hunter, 1755]
22 p. 34.5 cm. caption title
Huntington 188; New York Public 266; Sabin 100252; Torrence 232
CSmH; DLC (2 copies); NN; NNB; PHi; Vi mp. 40810

B1786 VIRGINIA. LAWS
. . . At a General assembly, begun . . . the 27th day of February . . . 1752. And from thence continued . . . to Monday the 27th day of October . . . 1755 . . . being the eighth session . . . [Williamsburg, W. Hunter, 1755]
8 p. 35 cm. caption title
Huntington 189; Sabin 100253; Torrence 233; New York Public 267
CSmH; DLC (2 copies); NN; NNB; PHi; Vi mp. 40811

B1787 THE Virginia almanack for the year . . . 1755 . . . Williamsburg, W. Hunter, 1755.
[32] p. 15 cm.
Vi mp. 40812

B1788 WOODWARD, JOSIAH
A disswasive from the sin of drunkenness . . . Lancaster, W. Dunlap, 1755.
22 p., 1 l. 14 cm.
Huntington 190; New York Public 268
CSmH; MHi. Photostats: DLC; MWA; NN; RPJCB
mp. 40813

B1789 WOODWARD, JOSIAH
An earnest persuasive to the serious observation of the Lord's day . . . Lancaster, Printed and sold by W. Dunlap, 1755.
14 p. 15 cm.
PHi mp. 40814

1756

B1790 AN account of the late dreadful earthquake and fire, which destroyed the city of Lisbon . . . The third edition. Boston, Re-printed and sold by Green & Russell, 1756.
23 p. 20 cm. A-C^4
MWA mp. 40815

B1791 AN astronomical diary; or, an almanack for . . . 1757 . . . By George Wheten . . . Boston, Edes and Gill [1756]
[16] p. 16 cm.
Drake 3106; Nichols p. 49; Huntington 204
CSmH; DLC; MB; MWA (2 varieties); MiD-B; RHi
mp. 40869

B1792 AN astronomical diary: or, an almanack for . . . 1757 . . . By Nathaniel Ames . . . New-England: Printed for the booksellers. [1756]
[16] p. 17.5 cm.
DLC; MB; MWA; PHi; RPJCB mp. 40816

B1793 BEISSEL, JOHANN CONRAD, 1690-1768
Die Kirche Gottes. Geschrieben von Johann Conrad Beissel, an Peter Becker. Ephrata deu [sic] 20ten des 3ten Monats 1756 . . . [Ephrata? 1756?]
broadside 19.5 X 9.5 cm.
MWA mp. 40817

B1794 BOSTON, May 13, 1756. To be seen (for a short time) at the house of Mr. William Fletcher . . . the Microcosm, or the World in Miniature . . . [Boston] Edes and Gill [1756]
broadside
Ford 1044
MWA mp. 40825

B1795 CHURCH OF ENGLAND
A form of prayer used on the late general fast in England, now reprinted for . . . this city . . . New-York, Printed and sold by J. Parker and W. Weyman, 1756.
11 p. 20 cm.
NHi mp. 40818

B1796 CONNECTICUT. GOVERNOR, 1754-1766
By . . . Thomas Fitch . . . a proclamation for a day of public fasting . . . [Feb. 25, 1756] . . . New London, Timothy Green [1756]
broadside 40 X 32 cm.
DLC mp. 40819

B1797 DICKINSON, JONATHAN, 1663-1722
Die Göttliche Beschützung ist der Menschen gewisseste Hülffe . . . Die 4th Edition. Zu Philadelphia gedruckt, und nun zum zweyten mal in Teutsch heraus gegeben. Germanton, Gedruckt und zu haben bey Christoph Saur, 1756.
98 p. 16.5 cm. A-F^8 [ ]^1
MWA mp. 40820

B1798 EARLE, JABEZ, 1676?-1768
Sacramental exercises . . . Boston, Reprinted by D. Fowle, and Z. Fowle, for D. Henchman [1756?]
103, [1] p. 14 cm. A-H^6 I^4
MWA mp. 40821

B1799 AN endeavour to animate and incourage our soldiers, for the present expedition . . . M. B. Boston, Green and Russell [1756?]
broadside 29 X 22.5 cm.
By Mather Byles?
Ford 1045
PHi. Photostat: MHi mp. 40822

B1800 EXACT tables of the value of gold and silver . . . Boston, 1756.
[7] p. 15 cm.
CtY; DLC; MWA (mutilated); PPRF; RPJCB. Photostat: NN mp. 40823

B1801 FLEMING, WILLIAM
Eine Erzehlung von den trübsalen . . . so geschehen an William Fleming . . . Zweite Edition. ZuLäncester gedruckt von W. Dunlap und ins Teutsche übersetzt, und gedruckt zu Germanton bey Christoph Saur, 1756. Auch zu haben bey David Däschler zu Philad.
29, [1] p. 16.5 cm.
Vail: Old frontier 509; cf. Evans 7663
MWA; PPL mp. 40824

B1802 FULLER, SAMUEL, d. 1736?
Some principles and precepts of the Christian religion . . . New-York, Printed and sold by H. Gaine, 1756.

1 p.l., iv, 22 p., 2 l. 14.5 cm.
New York Public 270
NN mp. 40826

B1803 HARVARD UNIVERSITY
Quaestiones pro modulo . . . MDCCLVI. [Boston, 1756]
broadside
MH; MWA mp. 40827

B1804 IMRIE, DAVID
A letter from the Reverend Mr. David Imrie . . . to a gentleman in the City of Edinburgh . . . Boston, Re-printed and sold next to the prison in Queen-Street [by Edes & Gill], 1756.
16 p. 20 cm. A-B^4
MHi; MWA mp. 40828

B1805 JONES, THOMAS, of Southwark, Eng.
A sermon preached at the visitation of . . . Dr. Thackeray . . . on Tuesday, September 16, 1755 . . . New-York, Re-printed, and sold by H. Gaine, 1756.
[4]. 16 p. 17.5 cm. A-B^4 C^2
Huntington 193
CSmH; MWA mp. 40829

B1806 KINGS County in rouw: wegens het zalig afsterven . . . Antonius Curtenius . . . leeraar der . . . Nederduytse Gereformeerde-Kerk op 't Lange-Eyland . . . zynde op den 19de October, 1756 . . . in 't 59ste jaar zyne levens . . . [New York, 1756]
[2] p. X 16 cm.
NjR (bottom third (?) missing)

B1807 MARYLAND. LAWS
Acts of the province . . . made and passed at a session . . . begun . . . the twenty third day of February . . . 1756 . . . Annapolis, Jonas Green, 1756.
33, [1] p. 29.5 cm.
Wroth 190
DLC; MH-L; MdBP; MdHi mp. 40832

B1808 MARYLAND. LAWS
[At a session of Assembly begun. . . the 23d day of February 1756, the following law was enacted . . . granting a supply of forty thousand pounds . . . Annapolis, Jonas Green, 1756]

Advertised Aug. 12, 1756, as "Just Published."
Wroth 191
No copy known mp. 40831

B1809 MARYLAND. LAWS
The following bill (which did not pass into a law . . .) is published . . . for the perusal of their constituents. An act for regulating the militia . . . [Colophon] Annapolis, Printed and sold by Jonas Green, 1756.
11, [1] p. 31 cm.
Wroth 192
Md; PPRF mp. 40830

B1810 [THE Maryland almanack for the year 1756. Annapolis, Jonas Green, 1756]

Advertised in the *Maryland Gazette*, Jan. 15, 1756, as "Lately Published."
Wroth 193
No copy known mp. 40833

B1811 [THE Maryland almanack for the year . . . 1757 . . . Annapolis, Jonas Green, 1756]

Advertised in the *Maryland Gazette*, Dec. 30, 1756, as "Just Published."
Wroth 194
No copy known mp. 40834

B1812 MASSACHUSETTS. GOVERNOR, 1753-1756
By His Excellency William Shirley . . . A proclamation. Whereas a number of soldiers . . . [Feb. 12, 1756] . . . Boston, John Draper, 1756.
broadside 39 X 31 cm.
Concerns deserters from the Fiftieth Regiment
Ford 1052
MHi mp. 40835

B1813 MASSACHUSETTS. GOVERNOR, 1753-1756
By His Excellency William Shirley . . . A proclamation. Whereas the governments . . . [Feb. 18, 1756] . . . Boston, John Draper, 1756.
broadside 40 X 31 cm.
Encouragement to inlist in service against the French
Ford 1053
MB; MHi mp. 40837

B1814 MASSACHUSETTS. GOVERNOR, 1753-1756
By His Excellency William Shirley . . . Whereas a number of battoe-men will be wanted . . . I have thought fit . . . New-York. January 19, 1756. [Boston? 1756]
broadside 31.5 X 21.5 cm.
Ford 1061; Huntington 192
CSmH; MHi mp. 40838

B1815 MASSACHUSETTS. GOVERNOR, 1753-1756
By the honourable Spencer Phips . . . A proclamation for proroguing the General Court [to Jan. 6] . . . [Dec. 6, 1756] . . . Boston, John Draper [1756]
broadside 37 X 24.5 cm.
Ford 1060
MHi mp. 40848

B1816 MASSACHUSETTS. GOVERNOR, 1753-1756
By the honourable Spencer Phips . . . A proclamation. Whereas an act was made . . . [Jan. 20, 1756] . . . Boston, John Draper, 1756.
broadside 39.5 X 32 cm.
Prohibiting the export of provisions and warlike stores
Ford 1051
MHi; MWA mp. 40849

B1817 MASSACHUSETTS. GOVERNOR, 1753-1756
By the honourable Spencer Phips . . . A proclamation . . . [June 9, 1756] . . . Boston, John Draper, 1756.
broadside 39.5 X 32 cm.
Prohibiting the export of provisions or warlike stores until after Sept. 20
Ford 1056
MWA mp. 40850

B1818 MASSACHUSETTS. GOVERNOR, 1753-1756
Province of the Massachusetts-Bay. By His Excellency William Shirley . . . Whereas the quota of men . . . was . . . determined to be three thousand five hundred . . . August 1756. [Boston, 1756]
broadside
Ford 1065
MHi mp. 40839

B1819 MASSACHUSETTS. GOVERNOR, 1753-1756
Province of the Massachusetts-Bay. By His Honour the Lieut. Governour . . . You are hereby required to cause all the military companies . . . to be mustered on the third Wednesday of June next . . . May 28, 1756. [Boston, 1756]

broadside
Ford 1063
MB; MHi mp. 40847

B1820 MASSACHUSETTS. GOVERNOR, 1753-1756
Spencer Phips, Esq; Lieutenant-Governor . . . To Greeting. Whereas . ... repeated orders . . . there is a deficiency in the . . . men ordered to be raised for . . . the Crown-Point expedition . . . Given . . . at Boston, the eighth day of July, One thousand seven hundred and fifty-six . . . [Boston, 1756]
broadside 32.5 X 20.5 cm.
MHi. Photostat: MWA mp. 40851

B1821 MASSACHUSETTS. LAWS
. . . An act, passed by the . . . General Court . . . begun . . . the twenty-eighth day of May, 1755, and continued . . . to the fourteenth day of January following . . . An act for reviving . . . several rates and duties . . . Boston, S. Kneeland, 1756.
broadside (p. 211)
Impost law
MWA mp. 40841

B1822 MASSACHUSETTS. LAWS
. . . An act passed by the . . . General Court . . . begun . . . the twenty-eighth day of May 1755, and continued . . . to . . . the thirtieth day of March following . . . An act for granting unto His Majesty several rates and duties of impost . . . [Colophon] Boston, John Draper, 1756.
9 p. 32 cm. caption title
Ford & Matthews p. 425; New York Public 273
MWA; NN mp. 40840

B1823 MASSACHUSETTS. LAWS
. . . An act, passed by the . . . General Court . . . begun . . . the twenty-eighth day of May, 1755. And continued . . . to . . . the thirtieth day of March following . . . An act for the government of the forces . . . against Crown-Point. Boston, S. Kneeland, 1756.
broadside 30.5 X 21 cm.
Huntington 194
CSmH mp. 40842

B1824 MASSACHUSETTS. LAWS
. . . An act, passed by the . . . General Court . . . begun . . . the twenty-eighth day of May, 1755. And continued . . . to . . . the thirtieth day of March following . . . An act for the more speedy levying of soldiers . . . against Crown-Point. [Colophon] Boston, S. Kneeland, 1756.
p. 195-196. 31.5 cm.
Huntington 195; New York Public 275
CSmH; NN mp. 40843

B1825 MASSACHUSETTS. LAWS
. . . An act, passed by the . . . General Court . . . begun . . . the twenty-eighth day of May, 1755. And continued . . . to . . . the thirtieth day of March following . . . Chap. XXIII. An act in addition to an act intitled, An act for regulating the militia. [Colophon] Boston, S. Kneeland, 1756.
p. 199-200. 32 cm.
"Published April 16th 1756."
New York Public 274
NN mp. 40844

B1826 MASSACHUSETTS. LAWS
. . . An act passed by the . . . General Court . . . begun . . . the twenty-sixth day of May 1756 . . . for the supply of the Treasury with the sum of three thousand and six pound pounds . . . [Colophon] Boston, John Draper, 1756.
7 [i.e. 11] p. 32 cm.
Ford & Matthews p. 425; Huntington 196
CSmH; M-Ar; MHi mp. 40845

B1827 MASSACHUSETTS. LAWS
A bill concerning bankrupts, and for the relief of creditors . . . [Boston, 1756]
4 p. 32 cm.
On August 25 the bill was ordered to be printed
New York Public 276
NN mp. 40836

B1828 MASSACHUSETTS. LAWS
Province of the Massachusetts-Bay. In the House of representatives, February 26. 1756. Voted, That the following . . . wages . . . for the officers . . . Consented to, W. Shirley. [Boston, 1756]
2 p. 30.5 X 19.5 cm.
Ford 1050; Huntington 197; NYPL 271
CSmH; DLC; MHi; MWA (mutilated). Photostat: NN mp. 40846

B1829 MASSACHUSETTS. MILITIA
Mr. You being a training soldier . . . are hereby required . . . April. 1756. [n.p., 1756]
broadside 9 X 13 cm.
MiU-C; NHi. Photostat: DLC

B1830 MASSACHUSETTS. TREASURER
Province of the Massachusetts-Bay, ss. Harrison Gray, Esq; Treasurer . . . July 1, 1756. [Boston, 1756]
broadside
Tax warrant
Ford 1071
MSaE mp. 40852

B1831 MASSACHUSETTS. TREASURER
Province of the Massachusetts-Bay, ss. Harrison Gray, Esq; Treasurer . . . To constable or collector for the town of Greeting . . . Boston, the second day of November 1756 . . . [Boston, 1756]
broadside 47.5 X 38.5 cm.
Ford 1072
MHi mp. 40853

B1832 THE New-England primer improved . . . Boston, Printed for the booksellers, 1756
[26+] p. 10 cm. A-B^6 C^{1+}
MWA (sig. A2, B2-5, and all after C1 wanting) mp. 40854

B1833 NEW JERSEY. GOVERNOR, 1747-1757
By His Excellency Jonathan Belcher . . . a proclamation . . . [June 2, 1756] . . . [Woodbridge? 1756]
broadside 28.5 X 22.5 cm.
Humphrey 10; Huntington 198
CSmH mp. 40855

B1834 NEW JERSEY, GOVERNOR, 1747-1757
By His Excellency Jonathan Belcher . . . a proclamation . . . [July 1, 1756]. . . [Woodbridge? 1756]
broadside 31 X 19 cm.
Humphrey 11; Huntington 199
CSmH mp. 40856

B1835 NEW JERSEY. GOVERNOR, 1747-1757
By His Excellency Jonathan Belcher . . . a proclamation . . . [July 23, 1756] . . . [Woodbridge? 1756]
broadside 23.5 X 17.5 cm.
Humphrey 12; Huntington 200
CSmH mp. 40857

B1836 ON Philemon Robbins . . . who died, a member of Yale-College, Sept. 6th, A.D. 1756. AEtat. 19. An acrostick . . . [New Haven? 1756]
broadside 19.5 X 15.5 cm.
CtHi mp. 40858

B1837 PECK, ABIEZER
On the proceedings of the English and . . . French in North America . . . Rehoboth, Feb. 2, 1756 . . . [n.p., 1756]
3 p.
MWA (photostat) mp. 40859

B1838 PECK, ABIEZER
On the valiant New-England general. [19 stanzas in 2 columns] Rehoboth, April 5, 1756. Abiezer Peck. [Boston?] 1756]
broadside 33.5 X 20.5 cm.
Ford 1073; New York Public 277
RPJCB. Photostats: DLC; MHi; MWA; NN mp. 40860

B1839 PENNSYLVANIA. LAWS
An act for the better ordering and regulating such as are willing . . . to be united for military purposes . . . [Philadelphia, B. Franklin and D. Hall, 1756]
broadside (3 p.) 28.5 X 15.5 cm.
PHi (2 copies) mp. 40861

B1840 SCHEME of a lottery to raise £10,000 old-tenor, for . . . fortifications for the defense of . . . Rhode-Island. [Providence? 1756]
broadside 26 X 20 cm.
PHi mp. 40862

B1841 SOUTH CAROLINA. LAWS
. . . At a General assembly begun . . . the 12th day of November . . . 1754; and from thence continued . . . to the 6th day of July, 1756. Charles-Town, Peter Timothy, 1746 [i.e., 1756]
27 p. 29 cm.
Sabin 87589
Tax act
DLC mp. 40863

B1842 THE South-Carolina almanack, for . . . 1757 . . . By John Tobler . . . Germantown, Christopher Sower [1756] and sold in Charles-Town, South-Carolina, by Jacob Viart.
[24] p. 16 cm. $[A]^8$ B^4
Guerra b-105; Metzger 204
ScHi mp. 40864

B1843 VIRGINIA. COUNCIL
September 22d, 1756. To the honorable Robert Dinwiddie . . . the humble address of the Council . . . [Williamsburg, W. Parks, 1756]
[2] p. on 2 leaves. 31 X 21.5 cm.
On verso of second leaf: . . . The humble address of the House of burgesses . . .
Huntington 202; Sabin 99904
CSmH. Photostat: DLC mp. 40865

B1844 VIRGINIA. GOVERNOR, 1751-1758
The speech of . . . Robert Dinwiddie . . . to the General assembly, summoned to be held . . . the 25th day of March . . . 1756: and from thence continued . . . to Monday, the 20th day of September, 1756 . . . being the second session . . . Williamsburg, William Hunter, 1756.
4 p.
Huntington 203; Sabin 99993
CSmH. Photostat: DLC mp. 40866

B1845 WEBSTER, JACOB
Jacob Webster, of Windsor, in Connecticut, being taken blind, did thereupon compose the following verses. A.D. 1756 . . . [n.p., 1756?]
broadside 34.5 X 20 cm.
MWA mp. 40867

B1846 WESLEY, JOHN, 1702-1791
Hymns and spiritual songs . . . Fourth edition. Philadelphia, 1756.
132, [4] p. 14.5 cm.
MH mp. 40868

B1847 WHITEFIELD, GEORGE, 1714-1770
A short address to persons of all denominations . . . New York, Reprinted by H. Gaine, 1756.
8 p. 20 cm.
Sabin 103592
DLC mp. 40870

B1848 WILLISON, JOHN, 1680-1750
Some dying words of the late Reverend John Willison . . . To which is added, some of his dying ejaculations . . . Boston, Printed and sold by Z. Fowle in Ann-Street [1756]
8 p. 16.5 cm.
MWA mp. 40871

1757

B1849 THE agonies of a soul departing out of time into eternity. A few lines occasioned by the untimely end of John Harrington, who is to be executed . . . this day . . . for the murder of Paul Learnard, the 1st of September last. [Boston, 1757]
broadside
Ford 1078
MHi mp. 40872

B1850 AN astronomical diary: or, an almanack for the year . . . 1758 . . . By Nathaniel Ames . . . Boston, Edes and Gill [1757]
[16] p. 17 cm.
cf. Evans 7820
DLC; MB; MBAt; MHi (imperfect); PHi; RHi mp. 40873

B1851 AN astronomical diary: or, An almanack for the year . . . 1758 . . . [Boston] New-England, Printed for the booksellers [1757]
[16] p. 16 cm.
"The third pirated edition."—Nichols: Mass. almanacs, p. 50
Drake 3107; New York Public 278
MH; MWA; NN (last leaf wanting); PHi; RPJCB
mp. 40874

B1852 AN astronomical diary . . . for the year . . . 1758 . . . Calculated for the meridian of Portsmouth . . . Portsmouth, Printed and sold by Daniel Fowle [1757]
[16] p.
By David Sewall, 1735-1825
Drake 4613
DLC; MH; MHi; MWA; N; NHi; NN; Nh; NhHi
mp. 40938

B1853 BIBLE. O.T. PSALMS
The New-England Psalter; or, Psalms of David . . . Boston, Printed and sold by Green and Russell, 1757.
191, [1] p. 15 cm.
MB mp. 40876

B1854 BIBLE. O.T. PSALMS
A new version of the Psalms of David . . . By N. Brady and N. Tate . . . Boston, Reprinted by Green & Russell for J. Edwards, 1757.
276, 6, 60 p.
MWA (lacking after p. 54 at end); RPJCB mp. 40877

B1855 BILES-ISLAND LOTTERY
Scheme of a lottery erected, and to be drawn on Biles'-Island . . . [n.p., 1757]
broadside 35 X 22 cm.
Dated, New-Jersey, June 28, 1757
NHi mp. 40878

B1856 BOWERS, ARCHIBALD
A discovery of some of the inhuman practices . . . of the Holy Inquisition . . . Being, a remarkable account given by Mr. Archibald Bowers, an English gentleman . . . New-Haven, Printed and sold by J. Parker, 1757.
27 p.
Trumbull: Supplement 1938
CtY mp. 40879

B1857 [CHAPLIN, JOHN]
A journal containing some remarks upon the spiritual operations, beginning about the year . . . 1740, or 1741 . . . [n.p.] Printed, 1757.
11 p. 17 cm.
MWA mp. 40880

B1858 CHARLESTON. PARISH OF ST. PHILIP
Births and burials, in the Parish of St. Philip. Charles-Town . . . 1755, to Dec. 25th, 1756. By George Sheed . . . [Charleston, 1757?]
broadside 31 X 19.5 cm.
cf. Waring: *Hist. of Medicine in South Carolina*, p. 64
MiU-C

B1859 CHATTIN, JAMES
Philadelphia, January 29, 1757. Proposals for printing by subscrption [sic], the translation of three French volumes [by J. N. Moreau] . . . [Philadelphia, J. Chattin, 1757]
broadside 32 X 20 cm.
Published with title: A memorial, containing A summary view of facts . . . Translated from the French . . . Philadelphia, J. Chattin, 1757.
MB; MBAt mp. 40881

B1860 CONNECTICUT. GENERAL ASSEMBLY
. . . At a General Assembly of the Governor and Company . . . of Connecticut . . . holden at Hartford . . . February . . . 1757 . . . This Assembly . . . do hereby resolve . . . that there be a public contribution . . . New-London, Timothy Green, 1757.
broadside 32 X 20 cm.
CtHi mp. 40882

B1861 CONNECTICUT. GOVERNOR, 1754-1766
By the honourable Thomas Fitch . . . A proclamation for a day of public fasting and prayer . . . Given under my hand . . . in Hartford . . . [Aug. 19] . . . New-London: Printed by John Green, 1757.
broadside 38.5 X 30 cm.
CtHi mp. 40883

B1862 CONNECTICUT. GOVERNOR, 1754-1766
By the honourable Thomas Fitch . . . A proclamation, for a publick thanksgiving . . . Given under my hand . . . in New-Haven . . . [Oct. 29, 1757] . . . New-Haven, James Parker [1757]
broadside 39 X 32.5 cm.
MHi

B1863 CONNECTICUT. GOVERNOR, 1754-1766
By the honourable Thomas Fitch . . . A proclamation, for a publick thanksgiving . . . [Nov. 16, 1757] . . . New-Haven, James Parker [1757]
broadside 38 X 29 cm.
CtHi

B1864 CONNECTICUT. GOVERNOR, 1754-1766
By the honourable Thomas Fitch . . . A proclamation. Whereas the General Assembly . . . Given under my hand in Norwalk . . . [Dec. 5, 1757] . . . Printed at the Printing-Office in New-London, MDCCLVII.
broadside 43 X 31 cm.
MHi

B1865 A DISCRIPTION of fox-like teachers . . . By a layman . . . Boston, 1757.
15 p. 16 cm.
DLC; MBAt mp. 40884

B1866 FREE AMERICAN FIRE CLUB, BOSTON
Rules and orders, agreed to be observed by the Free American Fire-Club, instituted at Boston, N. E. the 12th day of July, A.D. 1757 . . . [Boston, 1757?]
broadside 41.5 X 33 cm.
MH

B1867 Deleted.

B1868 GEORGIA. LAWS
An act for the better settling the province of Georgia. Passed the 19th of July, 1757. [Charleston? P. Timothy? 1757?]
3 p. 25 cm.
De Renne, p. 148; New York Public 279
GHi; NNB. Photostats: DLC; NN; RPJCB mp. 40886

B1869 GT. BRIT. ADJUTANT-GENERAL'S OFFICE
A new exercise to be observed by his Majesty's troops . . . Boston, Re-printed, and sold by Green & Russell, 1757.
8 p. 32 cm. A-B^2
MWA mp. 40887

B1870 GT. BRIT. TREATIES
A treaty with the Shawanese and Delaware Indians . . . negotiated . . . by . . . Sir William Johnson . . . New York, J. Parker and W. Weyman, 1757.
10 p. fol.
Huntington 206; DePuy p. 38; cf. Evans 7925
CSmH; ICN; MH; PPL mp. 40888

B1871 HARRINGTON, JOHN, 1713?–1757
The last words and dying speech of John Harrington . . . executed at Cambridge, March 17, 1757, for the murder of Paul Learned. [Boston] Sold next to the prison, in Queen-Street, 1757.
broadside 38 X 21.5 cm.
Ford 1977
MHi mp. 40889

B1872 JACOB, ELIZABETH HEAD, 1674-1739
An epistle in true love containing a farewell exhortation ... [at end] Boston, J. Draper, 1757.
12 p. caption title
Signed at end: Elizabeth Jacob ... the 5th of the 9th month, 1712
RPJCB mp. 40890

B1873 JOHNSON, JOHN, 1706-1791
The advantages and disadvantages of the marriage-state ... The Third edition. Boston, Re-printed and sold by Green and Russell, and by P. Freeman, 1757.
[2], 26 p.
RPJCB mp. 40891

B1874 [THE Maryland almanack, for the year 1758. Annapolis, Jonas Green, 1757]

Advertised in the *Maryland Gazette*, Dec. 8, 1757, as "Just Published."
Wroth 201
No copy known mp. 40892

B1875 MASSACHUSETTS. COUNCIL
Province of the Massachusetts-Bay. By the honourable His Majesty's Council ... A proclamation ... April 5, 1757. Boston, John Draper, 1757.
broadside
Confirming all military commissions not heretofore revoked
Ford 1085
MHi mp. 40899

B1876 MASSACHUSETTS. COUNCIL
By the honourable His Majesty's Council ... A proclamation ... April 7, 1757. Boston, John Draper, 1757.
broadside
Embargo on ships until April 20
Ford 1086; New York Public 280
MHi; MWA (reduced facsim.); NN (reduced facsim.)
mp. 40900

B1877 MASSACHUSETTS. COUNCIL
By the honourable His Majesty's Council ... A proclamation ... [Apr. 18, 1757] ... Boston, John Draper, 1757.
broadside 40 X 32.5 cm.
Embargo on fishing vessels until May 10
Ford 1987
MB; MHi; MWA; MiU-C mp. 40901

B1878 MASSACHUSETTS. COUNCIL
By the honourable His Majesty's Council ... A proclamation ... [May 9, 1757] ... Boston, John Draper, 1757.
broadside 39.5 X 30.5 cm.
Embargo on ships until May 20
Ford 1088
MHi mp. 40898

B1879 MASSACHUSETTS. COUNCIL
By the honourable His Majesty's Council ... A proclamation for proroguing the General Court [to July 21] ... [June 28, 1757] ... Boston, John Draper, 1757.
broadside 33 X 21 cm.
Ford 1090
MHi mp. 40894

B1880 MASSACHUSETTS. COUNCIL
By the honourable His Majesty's Council ... A proclamation for proroguing the General Court [to Aug. 4] ... [July 12, 1757] ... Boston, John Draper, 1757.
broadside 33 X 20.5 cm.
Ford 1091
MHi mp. 40895

B1881 MASSACHUSETTS. COUNCIL
By the honourable His Majesty's Council ... A proclamation for proroguing the General Court [to Aug. 16] ... [July 26, 1757] ... Boston, John Draper, 1757.
broadside 33 X 21.5 cm.
Ford 1092
DLC; MHi mp. 40896

B1882 MASSACHUSETTS. COUNCIL
By the honourable His Majesty's Council ... A proclamation for proroguing the General Court [to Oct. 19] ... [Sept. 26, 1757] ... Boston, John Draper, 1757.
broadside 33 X 20.5 cm.
Ford 1095
MHi mp. 40897

B1883 MASSACHUSETTS. GOVERNOR, 1756-1757
By the honourable Spencer Phips ... A proclamation. It having been signified ... [Jan. 11, 1757] Boston, John Draper [1757]
broadside 39 X 30 cm.
Concerns sending provisions to the French by way of the West Indies
Ford 1081
MHi; MWA mp. 40920

B1884 MASSACHUSETTS. GOVERNOR, 1756-1757
By the honourable Spencer Phips ... Whereas ... eighteen hundred men ... are to be raised out of the several regiments in this province ... and to be put under ... the Earl of Loudon ... Boston, the twenty-first day of February 1757 ... [Boston, 1757]
broadside 38.5 X 25.5 cm.
Ford 1101
MHi mp. 40921

B1885 MASSACHUSETTS. GOVERNOR, 1756-1757
By the honourable Spencer Phips ... a proclamation. For the encouragement of persons ... [Feb. 25, 1757] ... Boston, John Draper [1757]
broadside 39 X 31 cm.
Ford 1082; Huntington 209
CSmH; DLC; MB; MHi mp. 40919

B1886 MASSACHUSETTS. GOVERNOR, 1756-1757
By the honourable Spencer Phips ... A proclamation, His Majesty's service requiring ... [Mar. 9, 1757] ... Boston, John Draper [1757]
broadside 39.5 X 30.5 cm.
Embargo on vessels until April 10
Ford 1083; Huntington 210
CSmH; MHi mp. 40917

B1887 MASSACHUSETTS. GOVERNOR, 1756-1757
By the honourable Spencer Phips ... A proclamation ... [Nov. 19, 1757] ... Boston, John Draper [1757]
broadside
Embargo on export of provisions or war-like stores
Ford 1099
MHi mp. 40918

B1888 MASSACHUSETTS. GOVERNOR, 1757-1760
By His Excellency Thomas Pownall ... A proclamation ... [Aug. 3, 1757] ... Boston, John Draper, 1757.
broadside
Continuing officers in the exercise of their trusts
Ford 1093
MHi mp. 40904

B1889 MASSACHUSETTS. GOVERNOR, 1757-1760
By His Excellency Thomas Pownall . . . A proclamation for proroguing the General Court [to Oct. 5] . . . [Sept. 10, 1757] . . . Boston, John Draper, 1757.
broadside 33 X 20.5 cm.
Ford 1094
MHi mp. 40905

B1890 MASSACHUSETTS. GOVERNOR, 1757-1760
By His Excellency Thomas Pownall . . . A proclamation for proroguing the General Court [to Nov. 2] . . . [Oct. 8, 1757] . . . Boston, John Draper, 1757.
broadside 33.5 X 21 cm.
Ford 1096
DLC; MHi; NhHi mp. 40906

B1891 MASSACHUSETTS. GOVERNOR, 1757-1760
By His Excellency Thomas Pownall . . . A proclamation for proroguing the General Court [to Nov. 23] . . . [Oct. 20, 1757] . . . Boston, John Draper, 1757.
broadside 33.5 X 21 cm.
Ford 1097
MHi mp. 40907

B1892 MASSACHUSETTS. GOVERNOR, 1757-1760
By His Excellency Thomas Pownall . . . A proclamation. Whereas it has been represented . . . [Dec. 5, 1757] . . . Boston, John Draper, 1757.
broadside 34 X 20.5 cm.
Concerns mutiny on the ship George
Ford 1100
MHi mp. 40908

B1893 MASSACHUSETTS. GOVERNOR, 1757-1760
Province of the Massachusetts-Bay, by His Excellency the Governour, To . . . Having received certain intelligence, that . . . the French and Indian enemy have invested Fort William-Henry . . . Boston this eighth day of August, 1757 . . . [Boston, 1757]
broadside 39.5 X 25 cm.
Ford 1102
CSmH; MHi mp. 40903

B1894 MASSACHUSETTS. HOUSE OF REPRESENTATIVES
In the House of Representatives, January 27, 1757. Voted, That the arms and accoutrements . . . be returned into the Commisary General's Office. [Boston, 1757]
broadside
Ford 1080
MB mp. 40902

B1895 MASSACHUSETTS. LAWS
. . . An act passed by the . . . General Court . . . May 1756 . . . continued . . . sixth day of January [1757] . . . Boston, J. Draper, 1757.
7 p.
Impost law
MWA mp. 40911

B1896 MASSACHUSETTS. LAWS
. . . An act passed by the . . . General Court . . . October [1756] . . . Chap. I. An act for the better regulating the choice of petit jurors . . . [Boston, 1757]
p. 251-254. 34 cm.
"Published October 19. 1756."
New York Public 281
NN mp. 40913

B1897 MASSACHUSETTS. LAWS
. . . An act passed by the . . . General Court . . . January [1757] . . . Chap. XIV. An act for the better regulating the fishery . . . [at end] Boston, S. Kneeland, 1757.
p. 251. 34 cm. caption title
MWA mp. 40914

B1898 MASSACHUSETTS. LAWS
. . . An act passed by the . . . General Court . . . January [1757] . . . Chap. XVII. An act for the more speedy levying eighteen hundred men . . . [Colophon] Boston, S. Kneeland [1757]
p. 261-263. 32 cm. caption title
Typographically different from New York Public 282
Huntington 207
CSmH

B1899 MASSACHUSETTS. LAWS
. . . An act passed by the . . . General Court . . . January [1757] . . . Chap. XVII. An act for the more speedy levying eighteen hundred men . . . [Colophon] Boston, S. Kneeland [1757]
p. 259-261. 32 cm. caption title
New York Public 282
NN mp. 40915

B1900 MASSACHUSETTS. LAWS
. . . An act passed by the . . . General Court . . . January [1757] . . . Chap. XVIII. An act for preventing the exportation of provisions and war-like stores out of this province . . . [Colophon] Boston, S. Kneeland, 1757.
p. 265-266. 34 cm. caption title
MWA mp. 40912

B1901 MASSACHUSETTS. LAWS
. . . An act passed by the . . . General Court . . . March [1757] . . . Chap. XXVII. An act for enquiring into the rateable estates of the province . . . [Boston, 1757]
p. 289-290. 29 cm.
New York Public 283
NN mp. 40910

B1902 MASSACHUSETTS. LAWS
. . . An act passed by the . . . General Court . . . March [1757] . . . Chap. XXIX. An act to prevent the desertion of soldiers during the present war . . . [Boston, 1757]
p. 286-287. 31 cm.
"Published April 8th. 1757."
New York Public 284
NN mp. 40916

B1903 MASSACHUSETTS. LAWS
. . . An act passed by the . . . General Court . . . May, 1757 . . . Boston, J. Draper, 1757.
7 [i.e. 11] p.
For apportioning and assessing £81,000
MWA mp. 40909

B1904 MASSACHUSETTS. TREASURER
Province of the Massachusetts-Bay, ss. Harrison Gray, Esq; Treasurer . . . July 1, 1757. [Boston, 1757]
broadside
Tax warrant
Ford 1106
MHi; MSaE; MWA mp. 40922

B1905 NEW HAMPSHIRE. GOVERNOR, 1741-1767
Province of New-Hampshire by . . . Benning Wentworth . . . To Whereas in order to put a stop . . . Given . . .

this day of in the 30th year of His majesty's reign . . . 1757 . . . [Portsmouth? D. Fowle? 1757]
broadside 32 X 18 cm.
DLC

B1906 NEW HAMPSHIRE. GOVERNOR, 1741-1767
Province of New-Hampshire. By . . . Benning Wentworth . . . A proclamation [for raising 350 men] . . . Feb. 28, 1757 . . . [Portsmouth? D. Fowle? 1757]
broadside 38 X 31 cm.
DLC; NhHi mp. 40924

B1907 NEW HAMPSHIRE. GOVERNOR, 1741-1767
Province of New-Hampshire By . . . Benning Wentworth . . . a proclamation for a general thanksgiving . . . Given . . . in Portsmouth the 16th day of November, in the 30th year of His majesty's reign . . . 1756 [i.e., 1757] . . . [Portsmouth, 1757]
broadside 38.5 X 32 cm.
DLC mp. 40923

B1908 NEW YORK. GOVERNOR, 1753-1757
By the honourable James De Lancey . . . Lieutenant-Governor . . . A proclamation [warning rioters off Livingston Manor] . . . [New York, 1757]
broadside 39.5 X 26.5 cm.
Dated June 8, 1757
New York Public 285
NN (reduced facsim. from James G. Wilson: *Memorial history of New York*, 1893); PHi mp. 40926

B1909 NEW YORK. GOVERNOR, 1753-1757
By the honourable James De Lancey . . . Lieutenant-Governor . . . A proclamation . . . [June 21, 1757] . . . [New York, 1757]
broadside 42 X 29 cm.
Declaring July 13 a day of prayer and fasting
PHi mp. 40925

B1910 NEW-YORK, February 25, 1757. Scheme of a lottery, to be drawn at Brookhaven, in the County of Suffolk . . . New-York . . . intended to convert into money, the real estate of Mr. Humphrey Avery . . . to pay his debts . . . [New York, 1757]
broadside 39 X 25 cm.
N mp. 40875

B1911 NORTH CAROLINA. GOVERNOR, 1754-1765
North-Carolina. His Excellency Arthur Dobbs . . . A proclamation. Whereas, The Honorable James Murray and John Rutherford . . . issued a great number of notes for money . . . Given . . . at Newbern [Dec. 5, 1757] Arthur Dobbs . . . Richard Fenner, Dep. Sec. . . . [Newbern, James Davis, 1757]
broadside 19 X 31 cm.
McMurtrie: North Carolina 22
Public Record Off. mp. 40927

B1912 PLYMOUTH COMPANY, DEFENDANT
The proprietors holding under Lake & Clark, plaintiffs, against proprietors from Plymouth-Colony, defendant . . . [Boston? 1757?]
7 p. 33 cm. caption title $A\text{-}B^2$
MWA mp. 40928

B1913 POPISH cruelty displayed: being a full and true account of the massacre of the Protestants in Ireland . . . Portsmouth, Daniel Fowle, 1757.
24 p. 17.5 cm.
Whittemore 14
NHi; NhHi mp. 40929

B1914 RHODE ISLAND. GOVERNOR, 1755-1757
[By the honorable Stephen Hopkins . . . A proclamation . . . for raising, cloathing and paying four hundred and fifty men . . . Newport, James Franklin, 1757]
broadside?
Alden 180; Winship p. 15
No copy known mp. 40931

B1915 RHODE ISLAND. LAWS
At the General assembly . . . holden at Newport . . . the tenth of August, 1757 . . . An act for raising one sixth part of the militia . . . [Newport, J. Franklin, 1757]
4 p. 31 cm. caption title
Alden 188; Winship p. 15
RHi. Photostats: DLC; MWA; NHi mp. 40934

B1916 RHODE ISLAND. LAWS
At the General assembly . . . holden at South-Kingstown . . . on the last Wednesday of October . . . An act for assessing . . . a rate or tax of four thousand pounds . . . [Newport, Ann and James Franklin, 1757]
3 p. 32 cm.
Alden 190; Winship p. 15
RHi; RPB mp. 40933

B1917 RHODE ISLAND. LAWS
[At the General assembly . . . holden at South-Kingstown . . . on the last Wednesday of October . . . An act for the more . . . speedy payment of the charges of the late expedition . . . Newport, Ann and James Franklin, 1757?]

Billed by the Franklins in 1758
Alden 191; Winship p. 15
No copy known mp. 40937

B1918 RHODE ISLAND. LAWS
At the General assembly . . . holden . . . on Monday the thirteenth of June . . . An act for proportioning the rate . . . upon the several towns . . . [Newport, Ann and James Franklin, 1757]
2 p. 32 cm.
Billed by James Franklin Sept. 19, 1757
Alden 187; Winship p. 15
RHi; RPB mp. 40932

B1919 RHODE ISLAND. LAWS
At the General assembly . . . holden . . . on Monday the nineteenth of September . . . An act for supplying the general treasury . . . by a rate or tax . . . [Newport, Ann and James Franklin, 1757]
3 p. 32 cm.
Alden 189
RHi; RP; RPB mp. 40935

B1920 RHODE ISLAND. LAWS
At the General assembly . . . holden . . . on the third Monday of November . . . Be it . . . enacted . . . that the said rates, shall be . . . proportion'd unto the several towns as followeth . . . [Newport, James Franklin, 1757]
5 p. 31 cm. caption title
Bill submitted Mar. 10, 1757
Alden 192; Winship p. 15
RHi; RPB (lacks p. 5) mp. 40930

B1921 RHODE ISLAND. LAWS
At the General assembly . . . holden . . . on Tuesday the first of February . . . An act for taking a true account of all rateable estates . . . Newport, James Franklin, 1757]
[4 p.?]
Billed Mar. 10, 1757, by James Franklin
Alden 186; Winship p. 15
No copy known mp. 40936

B1922 SOME inquiries with thoughts on religious subjects. Partly collected from several books . . . to be set on the walls of a room in frames, and cover'd with glass . . . New York] Printed, 1757.
3 p.l., 3-27, [1] p. 20 cm.
Place of printing supplied by Hildeburn
Sabin 86654
Ms. note: By Mr. Joseph Brown
NHi; PHi mp. 40939

B1923 SOUTH CAROLINA. LAWS
. . . At a General assembly begun . . . the twelfth day of November . . . 1754. And from thence continued . . . to the 21st day of May 1757. Charles-Town, Peter Timothy, 1757.
27 p. 29.5 cm.
Tax act
Sabin 87590
DLC; NNB mp. 40940

B1924 THE South-Carolina almanack, for the year . . . 1758 . . . By John Tobler . . . Germantown, Christopher Sower [1757] And sold in Charles-Town, South-Carolina, by Jacob Viart.
[32] p. 16.5 cm. [A]-B^8
Guerra b-108; Metzger 208
NHi; ScHi mp. 40941

B1925 DIE Teutscher Kriegsartikel. Philadelphia, B. Franklin und A. Armbruester, 1757.

Curtis 609; Hildeburn 1564
No copy known mp. 40942

B1926 VIRGINIA. COUNCIL
April 16th, 1757. To . . . Robert Dinwiddie . . . the humble address of the Council . . . [Williamsburg, W. Hunter, 1757]
broadside 32 X 18 cm.
Huntington 211; Sabin 99905
CSmH. Photostat: DLC mp. 40943

B1927 VIRGINIA. GOVERNOR, 1751-1758
The speech of . . . Robert Dinwiddie . . . to the General assembly, summoned to be held . . . the 25th day of March . . . 1756: and from thence continued . . . to Thursday, the 14th of April, 1757 . . . being the third session . . . Williamsburg, William Hunter, 1757.
[4] p. 32.5 cm.
Huntington 213; Sabin 99994
CSmH. Photostat: DLC mp. 40945

B1928 VIRGINIA. HOUSE OF BURGESSES
April 18th, 1757. To . . . Robert Dinwiddie . . . the humble address of the House of burgesses . . . [Williamsburg, 1757]
broadside 31.5 X 19 cm.
Huntington 212
CSmH mp. 40944

B1929 VOLLSTÄNDIGES Marburger Gesang-buch . . . Germanton, Christoph Saur, 1757.
[12], 527, [16], 14 p. front. sm. 8vo
With this is bound, as issued, Evangelia und Episteln (1758)
Huntington 214
CSmH (mutilated) mp. 40893

1758

B1930 ALBANY, N. Y.
Whereas a publick library, would be very useful . . . We . . . do promise to pay five pounds New-York currency, each . . . City of Albany, November 30, 1758 . . . [New York? 1758?]
broadside 40 X 31 cm.
New York Public 286; Sabin 103244
NN mp. 40946

B1931 THE American ephemeris; or, an Almanack for . . . 1759 . . . New-Haven, J. Parker [1758]
[16] p. 16.5 cm.
By Jesse Parsons
Advertised in the *Connecticut Gazette*, Dec. 23, 1758, as "Just published and to be sold at the Printing-Office."
Bates: Conn. almanacs p. 115
CtY; MWA mp. 40999

B1932 AN astronomical diary . . . for 1759 . . . [n.p., 1758]
[16] p. 17 cm.
By Nathaniel Ames
MWA; N mp. 40947

B1933 AN astronomical diary . . . for 1759 . . . Boston, Edes and Gill [1758]
[16] p. 15.5 cm.
By John Eddy
MWA mp. 40955

B1934 [AUBORN, A. D']
The French convert . . . The twelfth edition. Philadelphia, Printed and sold by W. Dunlap, 1758.
[6], 134 p. 13.5 cm. A-L^6 M^4
Huntington 218
CSmH; MWA mp. 40948

B1935 BIBLE. O.T. PSALMS
The New-England Psalter . . . Boston, Printed and sold by Edes & Gill, 1758.
[161] p. 15.5 cm.
MB (sig. G7, L2, L3 wanting) mp. 40949

B1936 BIBLE. O.T. PSALMS
The New-England Psalter . . . Boston, Printed and sold by Benjamin Mecom, 1758.
[132] p. 16 cm.
MWA (60 leaves only) mp. 40950

B1937 BIBLE. O.T. PSALMS
The Psalms, hymns, & spiritual songs . . . faithfully translated . . . Boston, D. Henchman, and S. Kneeland, 1758.
1 p.l., vi, 360 p. 16 cm.
Variant of Evans 8082. Pages in sig. D do not follow in sequence due to error in imposition
DLC; NBuG

B1938 BIBLE. O.T. PSALMS
The Psalms of David, imitated . . . by I. Watts, D. D. The nineteenth edition . . . New-York, Printed and sold by Garrat Noel, 1758.
[8], 320, [24], [2], iii, [3], [30], 2 p. 14 cm.
A-U^8 X-Y^8 Z^4
MWA (sig. F8, G1, H-K, and L1 wanting) mp. 41048

B1939 BOWLER, CHARLES, 1700?-1768
Reflections on the conduct and principles of the Quakers ... [Newport, James Franklin, 1758]
3 p. 33 cm. caption title
Signed at end: Charles Bowler. Portsmouth, September, 1758
Alden 194; Winship p. 16
RHi. Photostats: MWA; NN mp. 40951

B1940 BOWLER, CHARLES, 1700?-1768
Reflections on the conduct of the people who call themselves Friends ... Charles Bowler. Rhode-Island, May 5. 1758. [Newport, James Franklin, 1758]
broadside 32 X 19.5 cm.
Alden 195; Winship p. 16
RHi (mutilated). Photostats: MWA; NN mp. 40952

B1941 CAMP at 1758. Sir, Please to deliver to of my company, in Col. Regiment to the value of lawful money ... for which this shall be your voucher. [Boston, 1758]
broadside
Ford 1147
MHi

B1942 CONNECTICUT. GOVERNOR, 1754-1766
By the honourable Thomas Fitch ... A proclamation ... day of public [thanksgiving?] ... [ ]y of November ... [New-London] Timothy Green, 1758.
broadside 35.5 X 26 cm.
CtHi

B1943 CONNECTICUT. GOVERNOR, 1754-1766
Thomas Fitch, Esq; Governor ... To the forces raised by the colony foresaid ... New-London, Timothy Green, 1758.
broadside 37.5 X 29.5 cm.
Dated at Hartford, June 7, 1758
NHi mp. 40954

B1944 AN endeavour to animate and incourage our soldiers, for the present expedition. Made, and fitted to the tune of George's Coronation ... Boston: Printed and sold by Green and Russell, in Queen-street [1758?]
broadside 32 X 19 cm.
Green & Russell at this address 1755-1774; probably for Louisburg Expedition
PHi. Photostat: MHi mp. 40956

B1945 EVANGELIA und episteln auf alle Sonntage ... Germanton, Christoph Saur, 1758.
94 p. sm. 8vo
Issued with continuous signatures with Vollständiges Marburger Gesang-buch (1757)
Huntington 217
CSmH mp. 40957

B1946 FATHER Abraham's almanack ... for the year ... 1759 ... By Abraham Weatherwise ... Philadelphia, Printed by William Dunlap, for Daniel Henchman [1958]
[42] p.
Drake 9801
MHi

B1947 FATHER Abraham's almanack ... Fitted for the latitude of Cape-Breton. For the year ... 1759 ... By Abraham Weatherwise, gent. Philadelphia: Printed and sold by W. Dunlap [1758]
[40] p. front., fold. port., plan. 17.5 cm.
MB (imperfect) mp. 41019

B1948 FATHER Abraham's almanack ... Fitted for the latitude of Nevis. For the year ... 1759 ... Philadelphia, Printed by William Dunlap, for the author [1758]
[32] p. fold. port., plan. 17.5 cm.
By A. Weatherwise
Huntington 224; cf. Evans 8280-81
CSmH; MHi; MWA mp. 40958

B1949 GT. BRIT. ARMY
Articles of agreement made ... by and between ... and Colonel Henry Bouquet in behalf of the King ... to furnish ... General Forbes ... [Lancaster? 1758]
broadside
New York Public 287
NN mp. 40959

B1950 GT. BRIT. ARMY
By order of General Forbes. Notice ... that a number of waggons will be wanted ... [Philadelphia, 1758]
broadside 33.5 X 21.5 cm.
New York Public 290
NN (reduced facsim.); MWA (reduced facsim.); PPAmP mp. 40960

B1951 HARVARD UNIVERSITY
Quaestiones pro modulo ... MDCCLVIII. [Boston, 1758]
broadside
MH; MHi; MWA mp. 40962

B1952 HAYNES, JOSEPH, 1714?-1801
A reply to a vindication of an association, &c. and Mr. S. Bacheller, appendix writer. Also Mr. H. True's Dialogue ... Portsmouth, Printed and sold by D. Fowle, 1758.
82, [1] p. 23 cm. A-K^4 L^2
MWA (t.p. photostat); NHi; NhHi mp. 40963

B1953 IMPORTANT [news of the taking of Louisburg] 1758 by Admiral Bosc[awen] ... [n.p., 1758?]
broadside 54 X 41 cm.
RPJCB. Photostat: MWA mp. 40964

B1954 KEN, THOMAS, 1637-1711
The retired Christian, exercised in divine thoughts, and heavenly meditations, for the closet ... The fifth edition. New-York, Printed and sold by Garrat Noel, 1758.
[4], 86, [2] p. 14 cm. [ ]^2 A-E^8 F^4
MWA mp. 40965

B1955 MARYLAND. LAWS
Acts of the province ... passed at a session ... begun ... the twenty-eighth of September ... 1757 ... Annapolis, Jonas Green, 1758.
[2], 10, [2] p. 30 cm.
Wroth 203; Huntington 220
CSmH; MH-L; MdBB; MdBP; MdHi (imperfect) mp. 40966

B1956 MARYLAND. LAWS
Acts of the province ... passed at a session ... begun ... the twenty-eighth of March ... 1758 ... Annapolis, Jonas Green, 1758.
[2], 8 p. 30 cm.
Wroth 204; Huntington 221
CSmH; MH-L; MdBP; MdHi mp. 40967

B1957 MARYLAND. LAWS
Acts of the province of Maryland ... passed at a session ... begun ... the twenty-second day of November ... 1758. Annapolis, Jonas Green, 1758.

8 p. 30 cm.
Wroth 205
DLC; MH-L; MdBP; MdHi mp. 40968

B1958 MASSACHUSETTS
Province of the Massachusetts-Bay. Establishment of thc forces on the intended expedition against Canada. To each ablebodied effective man . . . Boston, March 17, 1758 . . . Tho's Clarke, Dept'y Secr'y. [Boston, 1758]
broadside 38 X 20.5 cm.
Ford 1135
MHi mp. 40988

B1959 MASSACHUSETTS
A return of the men inlisted and impressed for . . . the intended expedition against Canada, April 1758. [Boston, 1758]
broadside
Ford 1137
MHi mp. 40969

B1960 MASSACHUSETTS. GOVERNOR, 1757-1760
By His Excellency Thomas Pownall . . . A proclamation for proroguing the General Court [to Aug. 16] . . . [July 15, 1758] . . . Boston, John Draper, 1758.
broadside 33.5 X 20 cm.
Ford 1124
MHi mp. 40973

B1961 MASSACHUSETTS. GOVERNOR, 1757-1760
By His Excellency Thomas Pownall . . . A proclamation for proroguing the General Court [to Sept. 20] . . . [Aug. 29, 1758] . . . Boston, John Draper, 1758.
broadside 33.5 X 19.5 cm.
Ford 1128
MHi mp. 40974

B1962 MASSACHUSETTS. GOVERNOR, 1757-1760
By His Excellency Thomas Pownall . . . A proclamation for proroguing the General Court [to Dec. 13] . . . [Nov. 18, 1758] . . . Boston, John Draper, 1758.
broadside 33.5 X 21 cm.
Ford 1131
MHi mp. 40975

B1963 MASSACHUSETTS. GOVERNOR, 1757-1760
By His Excellency Thomas Pownall . . . A proclamation for proroguing the General Court [to Dec. 29] . . . [Dec. 5, 1758] . . . Boston, John Draper, 1758.
broadside 33.5 X 20.5 cm.
Ford 1133
MHi mp. 40976

B1964 MASSACHUSETTS. GOVERNOR, 1757-1760
By His Excellency Thomas Pownall . . . A proclamation for the encouragement of piety and virtue . . . [Feb. 14, 1758] . . . Boston, John Draper, 1758.
broadside 42 X 31.5 cm.
Ford 1120
MHi mp. 40972

B1965 MASSACHUSETTS. GOVERNOR, 1757-1760
By His Excellency Thomas Pownall . . . A proclamation. Having on the twenty-third day . . . [Apr. 22, 1758] . . . Boston, John Draper, 1758.
broadside 41.5 X 32 cm.
Encouragements to men to inlist in the invasion of Canada
Ford 1123
MHi mp. 40977

B1966 MASSACHUSETTS. GOVERNOR, 1757-1760
By His Excellency Thomas Pownall . . . A proclamation. His Majesty feeling for the miseries . . . [Mar. 23, 1758] . . . Boston, John Draper, 1758.
broadside 43 X 34 cm.
Ford 1122
MHi; MSaE mp. 40978

B1967 MASSACHUSETTS. GOVERNOR, 1757-1760
By His Excellency Thomas Pownall . . . A proclamation. Whereas in and by an act . . . [Dec. 5, 1758] . . . Boston, John Draper, 1758.
broadside 41 X 33.5 cm.
Concerns billeting the King's troops
Ford 1132
MHi mp. 40970

B1968 MASSACHUSETTS. GOVERNOR, 1757-1760
By His Excellency Thomas Pownall . . . A proclamation. Whereas it has been represented . . . [July 25, 1758] . . . Boston, John Draper, 1758.
broadside 52 X 42 cm.
Concerns desertion
Ford 1125
MHi mp. 40971

B1969 MASSACHUSETTS. GOVERNOR, 1757-1760
Province of the Massachusetts-Bay. By His Excellency the Governor. I do hereby authorize and impower to beat his drums . . . Given under my hand at Boston, the day of 1758 . . . [Boston, 1758]
broadside 19 X 16 cm.
Ford 1138; New York Public 291
DLC; MHi; MWA. Photostat: NN

B1970 MASSACHUSETTS. GOVERNOR, 1757-1760
Province of the Massachusetts-Bay. By His Excellency Thomas Pownall . . . To Colonel . . . You are required, to do . . . what in you lies for the speedy inlistment of . . . men . . . for the invasion of Canada. March 25, 1758. [Boston, 1758]
broadside
Ford 1136
MHi mp. 40797

B1971 MASSACHUSETTS. GOVERNOR, 1757-1760
Province of the Massachusetts-Bay, by His Excellency Thomas Pownall . . . you are hereby required . . . to use your utmost endeavours . . . in the intended expedition against Canada . . . Boston this 22d of April 1758 . . . [Boston, 1758]
broadside 37.5 X 21.5 cm.
Ford 1139
MHi mp. 40980

B1972 MASSACHUSETTS. LAWS
. . . An act passed by the . . . General Court . . . begun . . . the twenty-fifth day of May . . . 1757, and continued . . . to . . . the twenty-third day of November following . . . An act in addition to the several acts . . . for regulating the militia . . . [Boston, S. Kneeland? 1758]
4 p. 34 cm. caption title
"Published January 26. 1758."
Ford & Matthews p. 433; New York Pub. 292
NN mp. 40985

B1973 MASSACHUSETTS. LAWS
. . . An act passed by the . . . General Court . . . begun . . . the twenty-fifth day of May 1757. And continued . . .

to Thursday the second day of March following . . . An act for laying an embargo upon ships . . . [Colophon] Boston, S. Kneeland, 1758.
broadside 32 cm. caption title
Ford & Matthews p. 434; New York Pub. 293
NN mp. 40986

B1974 MASSACHUSETTS. LAWS
An act passed by the . . . General court . . . begun . . . the twenty-fifth day of May 1757. And continued . . . to Tuesday the eighteenth day of April following . . . Boston, S. Kneeland [1758]
2 p. 31.5 X 18.5 cm.
At head of title: . . . Levying of soldiers
Ford 1118; New York Public 294
MHi. Photostats: DLC; NN; WHi mp. 40987

B1975 MASSACHUSETTS. LAWS
. . . An act passed by the . . . General Court . . . begun . . . the thirty-first day of May 1758 . . . for apportioning and assessing the sum of eighty-two thousand and thirteen pounds six shillings and eight pence . . . [Colophon] Boston, John Draper, 1758.
[7] p. 32 cm. caption title
Ford & Matthews p. 435
M-Ar; MWA mp. 40982

B1976 MASSACHUSETTS. LAWS
An act passed by the . . . General Court . . . in addition to an act . . . passed this present year . . . for the speedy levying of soldiers for an intended expedition. [Colophon] Boston, Samuel Kneeland, 1758.
2 p.
Ford 1119
MHi mp. 40984

B1977 MASSACHUSETTS. MILITIA
The exercise for the militia . . . of the Massachusetts-Bay . . . Boston, Printed and sold by John Draper; sold also by Green & Russell, 1758.
13 p. 33.5 cm.
MH; MWA; MWiW-C; RPJCB mp. 40981

B1978 MASSASHUSETTS. MILITIA
Mr. You being a training soldier in the company of militia, under the command of are hereby required . . . to appear at your colours . . . the 2d of May next . . . April 17, 1758. [Boston, 1758]
broadside
Ford 1154
MWA

B1979 MASSACHUSETTS. TREASURER
Province of the Massachusetts-Bay, ss. Harrison Gray, Esq; Treasurer . . . [July 3, 1758] [Boston, 1758]
broadside 34 X 21 cm.
Tax warrant
Ford 1140
MHi; MSaE; MWA mp. 40989

B1980 MASSACHUSETTS. TREASURER
Province of the Massachusetts-Bay, ss. Harrison Gray, Esq; Treasurer . . . November 2, 1758. [Boston, 1758]
broadside
Tax warrant
Ford 1141
MSaE mp. 40990

B1981 NEW HAMPSHIRE. GOVERNOR, 1741-1767
By . . . Benning Wentworth . . . a proclamation. Forasmuch as our dependance . . . [Mar. 28, 1758] . . . Portsmouth, Daniel Fowle, 1758.
broadside 38.5 X 31.5 cm.
DLC; NhHi. Photostat: MHi mp. 40992

B1982 NEW HAMPSHIRE. GOVERNOR, 1741-1767
By . . . Benning Wentworth . . . a proclamation. His majesty having nothing more at heart . . . [Apr. 1, 1758] . . . Portsmouth, Daniel Fowle, 1758.
broadside 38.5 X 31.5 cm.
DLC; NhHi. Photostat: MHi mp. 40993

B1983 Deleted

B1984 NEW JERSEY. GOVERNOR, 1758-1760
By His Excellency Francis Bernard . . . A proclamation . . . [n.p., 1758]
broadside 31 X 19 cm.
Dated at Perth-Amboy, Mar. 9, 1758
Appointing March 30 a day of humiliation
Humphrey 30
NHi mp. 40991; 40994

B1985 NEW JERSEY. LAWS
Anno regni Georgii II . . . tricesimo secundo. At a session of the General Assembly of . . . New-Jersey, began . . . March 23, 1758, and continued . . . to the 12th of August following; at which time the six following acts were passed. Woodbridge, James Parker, 1758.
3-60 p. 30 cm.
Humphrey 29
Nj. Public Record Off. mp. 40995

B1986 NEW YORK. GOVERNOR, 1753-1757
By the honourable James DeLancey . . . Lieutenant Governor . . . A proclamation . . . Given under my hand . . . at Fort-George . . . [Apr. 14, 1758] . . . Geo. Banyar, Depy. Secry. . . . [New York, 1758]
broadside 40 X 34 cm.
Setting aside May 12 as a day of fasting
PHi mp. 40996

B1987 NEW-YORK MERCURY
The carrier of the *New-York Mercury* . . . sends the following occasional piece: Greeting. Printing-Office . . . Jan. 2, 1758. [New York, 1758]
broadside
1st line: Awake, O! drooping muse . . .
NjHi mp. 40953

B1988 NORTH CAROLINA. GOVERNOR, 1754-1765
North-Carolina. By his Excellency Arthur Dobbs . . . A proclamation . . . [Apr. 29, 1758] . . . Richard Fenner, Dep. Sec. . . . [Newbern, James Davis, 1758]
broadside 30.5 X 31.5 cm.
Appoints "the Seventh of June next" as day of fasting and humiliation
McMurtrie: North Carolina 26
Public Record Off. mp. 40997

B1989 ON the landing of the troops in Boston, 1758, September 13th. Their march out Sept. 16th . . . To which is added, The present state of Europe. [Boston] Sold at the Printing-office [by John Draper, 1758]
broadside 37.5 X 24.5 cm.
Ford 1151
MWA mp. 40998

B1990 PENNSYLVANIA. GOVERNOR, 1756-1759
By . . . William Denny, Esq; Lieutenant-governor . . . a

proclamation. Whereas constant experience . . . [Sept. 22, 1758] . . . Philadelphia, B. Franklin, and D. Hall, 1758.
broadside 41.5 X 33 cm.
DLC mp. 41000

B1991 POLLEN, THOMAS
The duty of defending our countrymen recommended. A sermon preached . . . the 12th day of March, 1758 . . . Newport, J. Franklin, 1758.
9 p. 25 cm.
Alden 196; Winship p. 16
NHI; NNG; RHi; RNHi; RP mp. 41001

B1992 PRESBYTERIAN CHURCH
The plan of union between the synods of New-York and Philadelphia. Agreed upon May 29th, 1758. Philadelphia, W. Dunlap [1758]
2 p.l., [3]-13, [1] p. sm. 8vo
Huntington 222
CSmH mp. 41002

B1993 [PRIME, BANJAMIN YOUNG] 1733-1791.
The unfortunate hero; a Pindaric ode . . . New York, Parker and Weyman, 1758.
15 p. 20 cm.
Huntington 223; Sabin 97745; Wegelin 814
CSmH; NHi. Photostats: DLC; MWA; NN mp. 41003

B1994 [THE PRODIGAL DAUGHTER . . .] [Colophon] Boston, Sold at the new Printing-Office, over-against the old Brick Meeting, near the Court House, in Cornhill [1758?]
fragment: [3] leaves 15.5 cm.
MWA mp. 41004

B1995 REFORMED GERMAN CHURCH
Lutherisches A. B. C. und Namen Büchlein für Kinder welche anfangen zu lernen. Germantown, Christoph Saur, 1758.
12mo
Metzger 210
No copy located mp. 41005

B1996 RHODE ISLAND. ELECTION PROX.
Hon. Stephen Hopkins, Esq; Gov. Hon. John Gardner, Esq; Dep. Gov. . . . [Newport, Ann and James Franklin, 1758?]
broadside 20 X 13 cm.
Alden 198; Chapin Proxies 2
RHi mp. 41006

B1997 RHODE ISLAND. GOVERNOR, 1758-1762
[Proclamation calling for the enlistment of 1000 men. Newport, J. Franklin, 1758]
[broadside?]
Payment for printing authorized Aug. 22, 1758
Alden 199; Winship p. 16
No copy known mp. 41007

B1998 RHODE ISLAND. GOVERNOR, 1758-1762
[Proclamation comanding deserters to give themselves up. Newport, J. Franklin, 1758]
[broadside?]
Bill sumitted by James Franklin Dec. 18, 1758
Alden 200; Winship p. 16
No copy known mp. 41008

B1999 RHODE ISLAND. GOVERNOR, 1758-1762
[Proclamation laying an embargo on shipping and navigation . . . Newport, Ann and James Franklin, 1758]
[broadside?]
cf. Schedules for the May, 1758, session of the General assembly
Alden 201
No copy known mp. 41009

B2000 RHODE ISLAND. LAWS
At the General assembly . . . holden . . . on Monday the twelfth of June . . . An act for assessing and levying . . . a rate or tax of six thousand pounds . . . a rate or tax of six thousand pounds . . . [Newport, J. Franklin, 1758]
2 p. 30.5 cm. caption title
Alden 206; Winship p. 16
RHi mp. 41010

B2001 SOUTH CAROLINA. LAWS
. . . At a General assembly begun . . . the sixth day of October . . . 1757; and from thence continued . . . to the nineteenth day of May, 1758. Charles-Town, Peter Timothy, 1758.
35 p. 29 cm.
Tax act
Sabin 87591
DLC mp. 41011

B2002 THE South-Carolina almanack for the year . . . 1759 . . . By John Tobler, Esq; Charles-Town, Peter Timothy [1758]
[32] p. 17.5 cm.
Guerra b-114; Cohen: The South Carolina gazette p. 174
DLC; ScHi mp. 41012

B2003 VIRGINIA. COUNCIL
September 18, 1758. To . . . Francis Fauquier . . . the humble address of the Council . . . [Williamsburg, W. Hunter, 1758]
broadside 32 X 18 cm.
Sabin 99906
DLC (photostat) mp. 41013

B2004 VIRGINIA. HOUSE OF BURGESSES
September 18, 1758. To . . . Francis Fauquier . . . the humble address of the House of burgesses . . . [Williamsburg, W. Hunter, 1758]
broadside 33 X 19 cm.
Sabin 99924
DLC (photostat) mp. 41014

B2005 VIRGINIA. LAWS
. . . At a General assembly, begun . . . the twenty-fifth day of March . . . 1756, and from thence continued . . . to Thursday the thirtieth of March . . . 1758; being the fourth session . . . [Williamsburg, W. Hunter, 1758]
5 p. 34 cm. caption title
Sabin 100257; Torrence 262
DLC; NNB; PHi; Vi mp. 41015

B2006 VIRGINIA. LAWS
. . . At a General assembly, begun . . . the fourteenth day of September . . . 1758; being the first session . . . [Williamsburg, W. Hunter, 1758]
34 p. 34.5 cm. caption title
Sabin 100258; Torrence 263
DLC; NNB; PHi; Vi mp. 41016

B2007 [WARD, SAMUEL] 1725-1776
To the freemen of the colony of Rhode-Island. Gentlemen, I last year appeared . . . [Newport, J. Franklin, 1758]
6 p. 31 cm. caption title
Signed at end: Newport, April 11, 1758. S. Ward
Alden 207; Bartlett p. 268; Sabin 101334; Winship p. 16
MWA (lacks final leaf); MiU-C; RHi. Photostat: NN
mp. 41017

1759

B2008 AN astronomical diary, or, an almanack for the year . . . 1760 . . . By Nathaniel Ames . . . Portsmouth, D. Fowle [1759]
[24] p. 18 cm.
Drake 4617; Morrison p. 67
DLC; MWA; Nh mp. 41021

B2009 BIBLE. O.T. PSALMS
The Psalms of David, imitated . . . by I. Watts, D.D. From the London nineteenth edition . . . Boston, Printed by S. Kneeland for T. Leverett, 1759.
vi, 304, [26] p. 14.5 cm. A-N^{12} O-P^{6}
MWA mp. 41091

B2010 BIBLE. O.T. PSALMS
Der Psalter des Königs . . . Davids . . . Germanton, Christoph Saur, 1759.
229 [i.e., 252] p. 13.5 cm.
p. 146-68 repeated in numbering
DLC; MWA mp. 41023

B2011 BIRD, SAMUEL
The importance of the divine Presence with our Host. A sermon, delivered in New-Haven, April 27th, 1759. To Col. David Wooster, and his company . . . [New Haven] Printed by James Parker, and Company: Sold by John Hotchkiss, in New-Haven, 1759.
24 p. 17 cm.
cf. Evans 8299
CtHi

B2012 BLAND, RICHARD, 1710-1776
A letter to the clergy of Virginia . . . Williamsburg, W. Hunter, 1759.
vi, 20 p.
Entry from Brinley catalogue, no. 3723
Evans 8551?
No copy known mp. 41024

B2013 BOSTON. ORDINANCES, ETC.
Boston, ss. At a meeting of the select-men, February 7th 1759. Whereas by means of the neglect of the inhabitants . . . Ordered, that the following clause of . . . An act relating to the admission of town inhabitants, be printed and dispers'd, viz. . . . Ezekiel Goldthwait, Town Clerk. [Boston, 1759]
broadside 34.5 X 22 cm.
MWA mp. 41025

B2014 [BROWN, ELISHA]
Reftections [sic] upon the present state of affairs in this colony . . . [Newport, J. Franklin, 1759]
5 p. 31.5 cm. caption title
"Sworn in Providence the 20th day of September, A.D. 1759." Signed at end: Elisha Brown
Alden 209; Winship p. 16
MWA; RHi (2 copies). Photostat: NN mp. 41026

B2015 CANADA subjected. A new song. [n.p., 1759?]
broadside 33 X 20.5 cm.
16 4-line stanzas in double columns
MWA mp. 41027

B2016 CARTER, LANDON, 1710-1778
A letter to the right reverend father in God, the Lord B. . . . p of L. . . . n . . . From Virginia. [Williamsburg, W. Hunter, 1759?]
1 p.l., 56 p. 22 cm.
Torrence 268
Vi mp. 41028

B2017 CONNECTICUT. Governor, 1754-1766.
By the honourable Thomas Fitch . . . A proclamation. Whereas His Majesty . . . has nothing so much at heart . . . New-Haven, James Parker, 1759.
broadside 49.5 X 31.5 cm.
3600 men to be raised for military service
CtHi mp. 41029

B2018 CONNECTICUT. MILITIA
To Captain of the military Company, in the Regiment in the Colony of Connecticut, Greeting. You are hereby required . . . Dated at the day of . . . 1759. [New London? 1759]
broadside 25.5 X 20.5 cm.
CtHi

B2019 CORBYN, SAMUEL
Advice to sinners under convictions . . . Boston, Reprinted and sold by S. Kneeland, 1759.
36 p. 10.5 cm.
Huntington 225
CSmH; MWA; RPJCB mp. 41030

B2020 DEWEY, ISRAEL, 1713-1773
Israel Dewey's letters to . . . Samuel Hopkins . . . [Sheffield, Mass.? 1759?]
16 p. 18 cm.
Final letter dated: Sheffield, Jan. 9, 1759
Trumbull 2056
CtHi; DLC mp. 41031

B2021 Deleted.

B2022 GIBERNE, WILLIAM
The duty of living peaceably with all men . . . Williamsburg, W. Hunter, 1759.
16 p. 19.5 cm.
Huntington 226
CSmH mp. 41033

B2023 HALE, MATTHEW, 1609-1676
Some necessary and important considerations . . . Twelfth edition . . . Woodbridge, James Parker, 1759.
16 p. 18.5 cm.
cf. Evans 8361
DLC mp. 41035

B2024 [HALES, STEPHEN]
The pernicious practice of dram-drinking . . . Woodbridge, James Parker, MCCLIX [i.e. 1759]
1 p.l., 8 p. 20 cm.
New York Public 299; Humphrey 35
NN mp. 41036

B2025 [HARDY, SAMUEL] 1636-1691
A guide to Heaven . . . The twelfth edition. Boston, Reprinted and sold by S. Kneeland, 1759.
48 p. 13 cm. A-C^{8}
MHi; MWA mp. 41037

B2026 HARVARD UNIVERSITY.
Quaestiones pro modulo . . . MDCCLIX. [Boston, 1759]
broadside 44 X 28 cm.

Ford 1162
DLC; MH; MHi; MSaE; MWA mp. 41038

B2027 HERVEY, JAMES, 1714-1758
A serious and affectionate address . . . London: Printed. 1759. Boston, Re-printed by Fowle and Draper. [1759?]
12 p. 17 cm.
DLC mp. 41039

B2028 JOHNSON, JOHN, 1706-1791
The advantages and disadvantages of the marriage-state . . . The fourth edition . . . Boston, Re-printed, and sold by S. Kneeland, 1759.
24 p. 14.5 cm. A-C^4
MWA mp. 41040

B2029 JONES, DANIEL
To all who intend to engage in this year's expedition against Canada, notice is hereby given, that treasurer's bounty-notes will be taken without discount . . . by Daniel Jones . . . Boston, March, 1759. [Boston, 1759]
broadside
Ford 1165
MB mp. 41041

B2030 MARTYN, CHARLES
[A discourse of mutual love and benevolence, delivered to a society of Masons in South-Carolina, on the 27th of December last . . . Charleston, 1759]

Advertised in the *South Carolina Gazette,* July 14, 1759
Mosimann 119
No copy known

B2031 [THE Maryland almanack for the year 1760 . . . Also a receipt, by which meat, ever so stinking, may be made . . . wholesome . . . Annapolis, Jonas Green, 1759]

Advertised in the *Maryland Gazette,* Nov. 29, 1759, as "Just Published."
Guerra b-117; Wroth 214
No copy known mp. 41020

B2032 MASSACHUSETTS. GOVERNOR, 1757-1760
April 2, 1759. To Col. Sir, Inclosed you receive the bounty notes . . . in proportion to your quota of the levies . . . [Boston, 1759]
broadside 18.5 X 23 cm.
Signed in ms.: T. Pownall
Ford 1186
MHi mp. 41043

B2033 MASSACHUSETTS. GOVERNOR, 1757-1760
By His Excellency Thomas Pownall . . . A proclamation for proroguing the General Court [to Aug. 1] . . . [July 6, 1759] . . . Boston, John Draper, 1759.
broadside 35 X 22 cm.
Ford 1174
MHi mp. 41044

B2034 MASSACHUSETTS. GOVERNOR, 1757-1760
By His Excellency Thomas Pownall . . . A proclamation for proroguing the General Court [to Aug. 15] . . . [July 20, 1759] . . . Boston, John Draper, 1759.
broadside 34.5 X 20 cm.
Ford 1175
MHi mp. 41045

B2035 MASSACHUSETTS. GOVERNOR, 1757-1760
By His Excellency Thomas Pownall . . . A proclamation for proroguing the General Court [to Aug. 29] . . . [Aug. 4, 1759] . . . Boston, John Draper, 1759.
broadside 35 X 20.5 cm.
Ford 1176
MHi mp. 41046

B2036 MASSACHUSETTS. GOVERNOR, 1757-1760
By His Excellency Thomas Pownall . . . A proclamation for proroguing the General Court [to Sept. 19] . . . [Aug. 18, 1759] . . . Boston, John Draper, 1759.
broadside 35 X 21.5 cm.
Ford 1177
MHi mp. 41047

B2037 MASSACHUSETTS. GOVERNOR, 1757-1760
By His Excellency Thomas Pownall . . . A proclamation for proroguing the General Court [to Oct. 3] . . . [Sept. 3, 1759] . . . Boston, John Draper, 1759.
broadside 34 X 22 cm.
Ford 1178
MHi mp. 41048

B2038 MASSACHUSETTS. GOVERNOR, 1757-1760
By His Excellency Thomas Pownall, . . . A proclamation. Whereas the Great and General Court . . . [Mar. 29, 1759] . . . Boston, Green & Russell [1759]
broadside 34.5 X 23.5 cm.
Concerns rank and pay of American forces against the French
Ford 1171; New York Public 300
MB; MHi; MSaE. Photostat: NN mp. 41049

B2039 MASSACHUSETTS. GOVERNOR, 1757-1760
By His Excellency Thomas Pownall, . . . A proclamation. Whereas the Great and General Court . . . [Mar. 29, 1759] . . . Boston, Green & Russell [1759]
[2] p. 39 X 31 cm.
Concerns inducements to enter the sea service
On verso is the form for signing up
Ford 1172
MHi mp. 41050

B2040 MASSACHUSETTS. GOVERNOR, 1757-1760
Province of Massachusetts-Bay, 1759. By His Excellency the Governor. This doth certify, that the bearer was by my order enlisted . . . as a seaman . . . until the first of November next . . . [Boston, 1759]
broadside
Ford 1182
MHi

B2041 MASSACHUSETTS. GOVERNOR, 1757-1760
Province of the Massachusetts-Bay, by His Excellency Thomas Pownall . . . To Colonel . . . You are hereby required . . . that able-bodied effective men be inlisted . . . against Canada . . . Boston, this sixteenth day of March, A.D. 1759 . . . [Boston, 1759]
broadside 38 X 22.5 cm.
Ford 1181
MHi mp. 41053

B2042 MASSACHUSETTS. GOVERNOR, 1757-1760
Province of the Massachusetts-Bay, To Colonel of a regiment . . . The Adjutant-General . . . has sent you your . . . number of men to be raised in your regiment . . . Given under my hand this 19th of March, 1759 . . . [Boston, 1759]
broadside 38 X 20.5 cm.
MHi mp. 41052

B2043 MASSACHUSETTS. GOVERNOR, 1757-1760
To captain of the military foot company in greeting . . . Given under my hand and seal at this day of . . . 1759. [Boston, 1759]

broadside 25.5 X 19 cm.
Ford 1185
DLC

B2044 MASSACHUSETTS. LAWS
. . . An act passed by the . . . General Court . . . begun . . . May 1758, and continued . . . to the twenty-eighth day of Feb. 1759 . . . for granting . . . several rates and duties of import . . . Boston, John Draper, 1759.
7 p.
Impost law
MWA mp. 41054

B2045 MASSACHUSETTS. LAWS
. . . An act passed by the . . . General Court . . . begun . . . the thirtieth day of May 1759 . . . for apportioning and assessing the sum of ninety-four thousand seven hundred and eighty pounds three shillins and two pence . . . [Colophon] Boston, John Draper, 1759.
7 [i.e. 11] p. 32 cm. caption title
Ford & Matthews p. 438
M-Ar; MWA mp. 41055

B2046 MASSACHUSETTS. LAWS
. . . An act passed . . . Chap. I. An act for the speedy levying of soldiers . . . [Colophon] Boston, S. Kneeland, 1759.
4 p. 29.5 cm. caption title
At head of title: . . . Levying soldiers
Ford 1167; New York Public 301
MHi. Photostats: DLC; NN; WHi mp. 41046

B2047 MASSACHUSETTS. LAWS
In the House of Representatives, March 23d. 1759. Voted, That the following establishment be made for the officers . . . In Council March 23. 1759. Read and concur'd . . . Consented to T. Pownall. [Boston, 1759]
broadside 25.5 X 19.5 cm.
Ford 1168
MWA mp. 41057

B2048 MASSACHUSETTS. MILITIA
Return of the men inlisted or impressed . . . to be put under the . . . command of . . . Jefery [sic] Amherst . . . for the invasion of Canada. [Boston, 1759?]
broadside
Ford 1188
MHi mp. 41058

B2049 MASSACHUSETTS. MILITIA
Return of the men inlisted or impressed . . . to be put under the . . . command of . . . Jeffry Amherst . . . for the invasion of Canada. [Boston] 1759.
broadside
MB mp. 41059

B2050 MASSACHUSETTS. TREASURER
Province of the Massachusetts-Bay ss. Harrison Gray, Esq; Treasurer . . . July 3, 1759. [Boston, 1759]
broadside
Tax warrant
Ford 1184
MWA mp. 41061

B2051 MASSACHUSETTS. TREASURER
Province of the Massachusetts-Bay, ss. Harrison Gray, Esq. Treasurer . . . [Nov. 1, 1759] . . . [Boston, 1759]
broadside 38 X 31.5 cm.
Tax warrant
MeHi mp. 41060

B2052 THE memorable year 1759
Come my brave jolly Britons, no longer complain,
Britannia, Britannia, once more rules the main . . .
[Boston, 1759]
broadside 42 X 11.5 cm.
Ford 1190
MWA mp. 41062

B2053 NEU-eingerichteter Americanischer Geschichts– und Haus-Calender auf . . . 1760 . . . Philadelphia, Peter Müller [1759]
[44] p.
Drake 9816
MWA (18 l.); PPeSchw

B2054 NEW HAMPSHIRE. GOVERNOR, 1741-1767
By his excellency Benning Wentworth . . . A proclamation for a general thanksgiving [Nov. 10, 1759] for the success of his Majesty's arms . . . [Colophon] Portsmouth, Daniel Fowle [1759]
broadside 32.5 X 20 cm.
Whittemore 32
NhHi mp. 41063

B2055 NEW JERSEY, LAWS
An act for the further preservation of timber within the colony of New-Jersey . . . [Mar. 17, 1759] . . . [Woodbridge? James Parker?] 1759.
broadside 17.5 X 9.5 cm.
Amer. Art Assoc. cat., Apr. 5-7, 1916, item 789
Humphrey 38; New York Public 303
NN (reduced facsim.); NjR (reduced facsim.) mp. 41064

B2056 NEW JERSEY. LAWS
Anno regni Georgii II . . . trigesimo secundo. At a session of General Assembly, at Perth-Amboy, began March 8th, 1759, and continued till the 17th . . . during which time the following laws were passed. Woodbridge, James Parker, 1759.
41 p. 30 cm.
Humphrey 39
Nj. Public Record Off. mp. 41065

B2057 NEWPORT MERCURY
[The reduction of Quebec to the obedience of His Majesty, in a letter from a gentleman in Boston. Newport, 1759]
broadside
Supplement to no. 69
cf. Anderson Galleries, Terry sale, May 2-3, 1934, item no. 357
No copy located mp. 41066

B2058 NORTH CAROLINA. COUNCIL
To his excellency Arthur Dobbs . . . The humble address of the Council . . . [n.p., 1759?]
broadside 36 X 24 cm.
A reply to Dobbs' speech of May 8, 1759
MiU-C mp. 41067

B2059 NORTH CAROLINA. GENERAL ASSEMBLY
To his excellency Arthur Dobbs . . . The humble address of the Assembly . . . [n.p., 1759?]
broadside 36.5 X 23.5 cm.
A reply to Dobbs' speech of May 8, 1759
MiU-C mp. 41068

B2060 NORTH CAROLINA. GOVERNOR, 1754-1765
The speech of . . . Arthur Dobbs . . . to the General assembly . . . at a session held at Newbern the 8th day of May, 1759 . . . [n.p., 1759?]

broadside 35 X 22 cm.
MiU-C mp. 41069

B2061 NOVA SCOTIA. GOVERNOR, 1756?-1760
Province of Nova-Scotia, by . . . Charles Lawrence . . . a proclamation. Whereas since the issuing . . . [Jan. 11, 1759] . . . Boston, John Draper, 1759.
broadside 46 X 30.5 cm.
Ford 1191; New York Public 304
MHi; N. Photostats: DLC; NN mp. 41070

B2062 PARKER, JAMES, 1714-1770
An appeal to the public of New-York. [at end] Woodbridge, N.J., James Parker, 1759.
2 p. 28 X 17 cm.
PPL. Photostat: MWA mp. 41071

B2063 PARKER, JAMES, 1714-1770
A letter to a gentleman in the City of New-York: shewing the unreasonableness of the present stamp-duty upon newspapers, and . . . upon the printers. [New York, James Parker, 1759]
4 p. caption title
PPL mp. 41042

B2064 PERTH-AMBOY, March 26, 1759. Scheme of a lottery, for raising 1920 dollars . . . to be applied towards paying the Indians for their claims to all land in the said Province . . . [n.p., 1759]
broadside 23.5 X 15 cm.
NjR (mutilated)

B2065 PLYMOUTH PROPRIETORS
Advertisement. The Proprietors of the Kennebeck-Purchase from the late Colony of New-Plymouth hereby give notice . . . Boston, May 9th, 1759. [Boston, 1759]
broadside 25.5 X 19.5 cm.
MHi mp. 41051

B2066 QUESTIONS & answers, to the prophetic numbers of Daniel & John . . . Boston, Green & Russell, and Edes & Gill, 1759.
16 p. 17.5 cm.
DLC; MHi mp. 41072

B2067 RHODE ISLAND. GOVERNOR, 1758-1762
By the honorable Stephen Hopkins . . . A proclamation. It having pleased . . . [Nov. 2, 1759] . . . [Newport, James Franklin, 1759]
broadside 35 X 28.5 cm.
Alden 213; New York Public 305
RHi. Photostats: MHi; NN mp. 41073

B2068 RHODE ISLAND. LAWS
At the General assembly . . . holden . . . on Monday the eleventh of June . . . An act apportioning . . . the rate or tax lately ordered to be assessed . . . [Newport, J. Franklin, 1759]
2 p. 31.5 cm.
Alden 218; Winship p. 16
RHi (2 copies); RPJCB mp. 41074

B2069 RHODE ISLAND. LAWS
At the General Assembly . . . holden . . . on Monday the twentieth of August . . . [at end] Printed at Boston, New-England, by Richard Draper, in Newbury-Street. [1759]
[17] p. 29 cm. caption title
RHi mp. 41075

B2070 A SERIOUS call to baptized children. The third edition. Boston, S. Kneeland, 1759.
22 p. 14.5 cm.
DLC mp. 41076

B2070a A SHORT account of the life, death and character of Esther Hayden, the wife of Samuel Hayden, of Braintree. Who died, February 14. 1758. In the forty-fifth year of her age. Boston: Printed by Fowle and Draper, M,DCC,LIX.
12 p. 15.5 cm. A^6
Stoddard 221
RPB

B2071 ["A SMALL pamphlet with a preface by . . . Whitefield, wherein the cruelties of the Russians to the Prussians are fully displayed . . ."]

Advertised in the *South Carolina Gazette,* Aug. 4, 1759
Mosimann 120
No copy known

B2072 SMITH, JOSIAH, 1704-1781
[Two sermons preach'd at Charles-Town in the years 1739 & 1741 . . . Charleston, 1759]

Advertised in the *South Carolina Gazette,* Apr. 7, 1759
Mosimann 121
No copy known

B2073 SOME thoughts on the duration of the torments . . . Charlestown, Printed by Robert Wells: Sold by John Edwards, 1759.
1 p.l., 37 p. 20 cm.
By John Martin?
Sabin 86774
DLC (2 copies); MMeT-Hi mp. 41077

B2074 SORGE,
Extracts of two letters, wrote originally in German, from . . . Mr. Sorge . . . Boston, Reprinted and sold at Fowle and Draper's, 1759.
23, [1] p. 17 cm.
[1] p. at end: "Books lately published"
Huntington 227; Sabin 87146
CSmH; DLC; MHi; MWA; RPJCB mp. 41078

B2075 SOUTH CAROLINA. LAWS
Acts passed . . . in the years 1755, 1756, 1757, and 1758. Charles-Town, Peter Timothy, 1758.
83, [1] p. 29.5 cm.
Sabin 87587
DLC mp. 41080

B2076 SOUTH CAROLINA. LAWS
Acts of the General assembly . . . passed the 7th of April, 1759. Charles-Town, Peter Timothy, 1759.
56 [i.e., 58], [1] p. 29.5 cm.
Sabin 87592
DLC; NNB mp. 41081

B2077 SOUTH CAROLINA. LAWS
. . . At a General assembly begun . . . the sixth day of October . . . 1757: and from thence continued . . . to the 7th day of April, 1759. Charles-Town, Peter Timothy, 1759.
28 p. 29.5 cm.
Tax act
Sabin 87593
DLC mp. 41079

B2078 THE South Carolina almanack and register for . . . 1760 . . . By George Andrews, Esq; Charlestown, Printed and sold by Robert Wells [1759]
[50] p. 16 cm. $[\ ]^1$ $A\text{-}F^4$
Guerra b-116
MWA (t.p. lacking); NHi; ScC; ScHi mp. 41022

B2079 THE South Carolina and Georgia almanack for the year . . . 1760 . . . By John Tobler . . . Charles-Town, Printed and sold by Peter Timothy [1759]
[32] p. 17 cm. [A]-D^4
Cohen, p. 174; Guerra b-124
DLC (imperfect) mp. 41083

B2080 STANWIX, JOHN, 1690?-1766
By Brigadier General Stanwix, commanding His Majesty's forces . . . Whereas a number of the King's horses . . . were lost, or stolen . . . [Philadelphia, 1759]
broadside 32 X 18 cm.
New York Public 306
PHi. Facsims.: MWA; NN mp. 41034

B2081 THE surprizing appearance of a ghost, with the message he brought . . . being a brief paraphrase and improvement . . . on the 4th chap. of Job . . . Boston, Fowle and Draper, 1759.
23 p. 12mo
In verse
Huntington 228
CSmH mp. 41082

B2082 THROOP, BENJAMIN, 1712-1755
The rest in reserve for the righteous, worth striving for. A sermon deliver'd in Norwich Second Society, September 5th, 1758, at the funeral of . . . Henry Willes . . . New-London, Printed and sold by T. Green, 1759.
25 p. 16.5 cm. [A]-C^4 $[\ ]^2$
Half-title: Mr. Throop's funeral sermon, on the death of the Reverend Mr. Henry Willes
CtHi; MWA; NHi mp. 41084

B2083 VIRGINIA. COUNCIL
February 24th, 1759. To . . . Francis Fauquier . . . the humble address of the Council . . . [Williamsburg, W. Hunter, 1759]
broadside 32.5 X 19 cm.
DLC (photostat) mp. 41085

B2084 VIRGINIA. GOVERNOR, 1758-1768
The speech of . . . Francis Fauquier . . . to the General Assembly, summoned to be held . . . the fourteenth day of September . . . 1758; and from thence continued . . . to Thursday the twenty-second day of February . . . 1759 . . . being the third session . . . Williamsburg, William Hunter, 1759.
4 p. 33 cm.
DLC (photostat) mp. 41087

B2085 VIRGINIA. GOVERNOR, 1758-1768
The speech, &c. Gentlemen of the Council . . . [Mar. 5, 1759] [Williamsburg, W. Hunter, 1759]
broadside 32 X 19 cm.
DLC (photostat) mp. 41086

B2086 VIRGINIA. HOUSE OF BURGESSES
February 27th, 1759. To . . . Francis Fauquier . . . the humble address of the House of burgesses . . . [Williamsburg, W. Hunter, 1759]
broadside 32 X 18 cm.
DLC (photostat) mp. 41088

B2087 VIRGINIA. HOUSE OF BURGESSES
March 6th, 1759. To . . . Francis Fauquier . . . the humble address of the House of burgesses . . . [Williamsburg, W. Hunter, 1759]
broadside 32 X 19 cm.
DLC (photostat) mp. 41089

B2088 WATTS, ISAAC, 1674-1748
Divine songs attempted in easy language . . . The eleventh edition. Boston, Reprinted and sold by Z. Fowle and S. Draper, 1759.
[2], iv, 48 p. 14 cm.
MWA (lacking after p. 42) mp. 41090

B2089 WHITEFIELD'S almanack for the year . . . 1760 . . . By Nathaniel Whitefield. Newport, James Franklin [1759]
[24] p. 18 cm.
Alden 208; Guerra b-126
DLC; MWA; RHi; RNHi mp. 41092

B2090 WILLISON, JOHN, 1680-1750
Looking to Jesus . . . Boston, Printed and sold by S. Kneeland, 1759.
[2], 46 p. 14 cm. A-C^6
MHi; MWA mp. 41093

B2090a WORCESTER, FRANCIS, 1698-1783
The rise and travels of death are here set forth . . . [Bost] on; Printed and sold by Fowle and [Drap] er, 1759.
111 p. 15 cm.
Sabin 105228; Stoddard 259
MB (t.p. mutilated; sig. A4 lacking)

176-

B2091 BASS, ROBERT
Doctor Keyser's famous pills, imported and warranted genuine, by Robert Bass, apothecary . . . Philadelphia . . . Particular directions for using Keyser's pills . . . [Philadelphia, 176-]
broadside
RPJCB mp. 41094

B2092 BLACK ey'd Susan's lamentation for the departure of her sweet William, who was impresse'd to go to sea . . . Sold [by T. and J. Fleet] at the Heart and Crown, in Cornhill, Boston [176-?]
broadside 33 X 21 cm.
CtHi mp. 41095

B2093 [THE Brave Grenadier . . .] and The Year 1759. Now take up your muskets, and gird on your swords . . . The Year 1759 Come my brave jolly Britons, no longer complain . . . Printed and sold in New-London [176-?]
broadside 31 X 11 cm.
RPB (left half torn off)

B2094 CHESTER CO., PA.
To the honourable the representatives of the freemen of the Province of Pennsylvania, in General Assembly met; the petition of divers of the inhabitants of the County of Chester, respectfully sheweth . . . the want of a sufficient medium of circulating cash . . . well aware of the Act of Parliament which prohibits our paper money . . . being a legal tender . . . [Philadelphia? 176-]
broadside 48 X 38.5 cm.
MWA mp. 41096

B2095 DEBORAH; a bee. I. A. bee is a laborious, diligent creature: so is the Christian . . . [Boston] Sold by Kneeland and [Adam]s in Queenstreet [176-?]
broadside 34 X 20.5 cm.
CtHi mp. 41097

B2096 FIRE CLUB, HAVERHILL, MASS.
Rules and orders, agreed upon to be observed by the Fire-Club at New-England . . . [Boston? 176-?]

broadside 39 X 32 cm.
Blank form filled in for Haverhill, Feb. 22, 1768, with 31 signers
MWA mp. 41101

B2097 GODDARD, WILLIAM, 1739-1817
Printing in all its various branches, correctly and expeditiously performed by William Goddard, at his office in Marketstreet, near the post-office . . . [Philadelphia, W. Goddard, 176-]
broadside 38 X 23.5 cm.
Metzger 296
NHi mp. 41099

B2098 GT. BRIT. ARMY
By His Excellency the honourable Thomas Gage, major general, and commander-in-chief . . . forces in North-America, &c. &c. Rules and directions, for the . . . troops . . . [New York? 176-?]
broadside 56 X 43.5 cm.
Gage was major general and commander 1764-1770
MiU-C mp. 41100

B2099 KNOW all men by these presents, that *I Isaac Zane . . . now of the County of Frederick in the province of Virginia . . . am* held and firmly bound unto in the sum of . . . the day of One Thousand Seven Hundred and *Seventy* . . . Philadelphia, William Goddard [176-]
broadside 33 X 20.5 cm.
Parts italicized in ms.
RPJCB

B2100 MARYLAND. GOVERNOR, 1753-1769
By His Excellency Horatio Sharpe . . . A proclamation . . . Given at Annapolis, this day of in the year . . . 176 Signed per order . . . [Annapolis, Jonas Green, 176-?]
broadside 26 X 18.5 cm.
Form for prorogation of the Assembly
Wroth 223
MdHi mp. 41102

B2101 A NEW method of ejectment; being a compendious and easy way . . . recommended to young practitioners in the law, especially in N.-C-r-l-na. Charles-Town, Printed for J. S. [176-?]
broadside 25 X 15.5 cm.
New York Public 313
NN mp. 41103

B2102 NORTH CAROLINA
North-Carolina. A table of the number of taxables in this Province from the year 1748 inclusive, with the taxes laid for each year, and an account of the sums that should arise by the sinking tax yearly to . . . 1770 . . . [n.p., 176-?]
[2] leaves. 37.5 cm.
Text in 24 columns separated by crude rules; the two leaves overlap to make a continuous reading
MHi mp. 41104

B2103 ROBINSON, NATHANIEL
Some mournful reflections on the death of Mr. Isaac Finch, who . . . in the year 1758 . . . was killed by a British soldier . . . Mr. Nathaniel Robinson, being confined in Albany Goal, wrote the following lines . . . [n.p., 176-?]
broadside 34.5 X 20.5 cm.
cf. Trumbull: Supplement 2571, dated 1769
MH

B2104 SALISBURY, S. AND S.
Hard-ware goods. S. and S. Salisbury, continue importing from London, Bristol, Birmingham and Sheffield, . . . assortment of hard-ware goods, which they sell very cheap . . . at Boston . . . and at their shop at Worcester . . . [Boston? 176-]
broadside 31.5 X 19 cm.
Probably printed about 1767
MWA mp. 41105

B2105 WILLIAM Crotty. To which are added, Five other new songs . . . [Philadelphia] Printed and sold by Andrew Steuart in Second-Street [176-]
8 p.
Steuart printed at this address from 1759 to 1769
Hamilton 51a
NjP mp. 41106

B2106 WORTHY example of a married daughter: who fed her father with her own milk . . . Boston, Sold at the Bible & Heart [176-?]
broadside 32.5 X 22 cm.
In verse
New York Public 316
NN mp. 41107

1760

B2107 . . . AN account of the success of His Majesty's army, under General Amherst, in the river St. Lawrence. [New York, 1760]
broadside 20.5 X 14.5 cm.
Dated New York, September 4
PHi mp. 41108

B2108 AMES 1761. An astronomical diary, or an almanack for . . . 1761 . . . In the first year of the reign of King George III . . . By Nathaniel Ames. Boston, John Draper; Richard Draper; Green & Russell, & Edes & Gill and Thomas & John Fleet [1760]
[24] p. 18 cm.
Drake 3127; cf. Evans 8529
N; NN; PHi

B2109 AMES, 1761. An astronomical diary, or an almanack for . . . 1761 . . . By Nathaniel Ames . . . Portsmouth, Printed and sold by D. Fowle [1760]
[24] p.
Guerra b-132; Nichols p. 85
MB; MWA; NN; Nh; NhHi mp. 41109

B2110 BIBLE
Verbum sempiternum. The seventh edition with amendments. New-York, Printed for S. P. [1760?]
275 p. 5 cm.
John Taylor's Thumb Bible
"S.P." probably stands for Samuel Parker
MH; NN; PP mp. 41171

B2111 BIBLE. O.T. PSALMS
The New-England Psalter . . . Boston, Printed and sold by S. Kneeland, 1760.
[156] p. 14.5 cm.
MWA mp. 41110

B2112 BIBLE. O.T. PSALMS
A new version of the Psalms of David . . . Boston, Printed by D. & J. Kneeland, for J. Winter, 1760.

276, 86, 16 p.
cf. Evans 8544
CtHC; DLC; MHi; NN; NNS; NNUT; RPB mp. 41112

B2113 BIBLE. O.T. PSALMS
A new version of the Psalms of David . . . Boston, Reprinted by D. & J. Kneeland, for Samuel Webb [1760?]
276, 86 p.
CtHC mp. 41111

B2114 BIBLE. O.T. PSALMS
The Psalms of David, imitated . . . By I. Watts . . . Philadelphia, Printed by W. Dunlap, for G. Noel, book-seller, in New-York, 1760.
viii, 308, 28 p., 12 numb. leaves (music) 15.5 cm.
PHi mp. 41175

B2115 BOSTON
(No. 9.) To Your province tax. Lawful money. Your town and county rate. Lawful money . . . The assessors sit at the Town-House . . . on Thursdays, from 3 to 5 . . . 1760 [?] . . . John Grant, Collector. [Boston, 1760]
broadside 12.5 × 14 cm.
Ford 1261
MHi

B2116 BOSTON POST BOY
A New-Year's wish, from the lad, who carries the *Post-Boy & Advertiser* . . . Boston, January 1, 1760. [Boston, 1760]
broadside 24 × 16.5 cm.
PHi mp. 41156

B2117 BROWN, THOMAS, 1740–
A plain narrative of the uncommon sufferings, and remarkable deliverance of Thomas Brown, of Charlestown, in New-England . . . The third edition. Boston, Printed and sold by Fowle and Draper, 1760.
24 p. 16.5 cm. $[A]^2\ a^4\ B^2\ b^4$
ICN; MWA (sig. [A] photostat); NjP mp. 41114

B2118 CHURCH OF ENGLAND. LITURGY
A form of prayer with thanksgiving proper to be used in the churches . . . on Thursday the twenty-third day of October . . . New-York, W. Weyman, 1760.
8 p. cm.
Mosimann 127?
MWiW-C mp. 41115

B2119 A CONGRATULATORY address &c. to all the faithful ministers of the gospel of all denominations . . . [at end] Boston, S. Kneeland, 1760.
4 p. 21.5 cm. caption title
RPJCB. Photostat: MWA mp. 41116

B2120 CONNECTICUT. GENERAL ASSEMBLY
At a General assembly . . . holden . . . on the second Thursday of May . . . 1760 . . . This Assembly . . . judge it to be a duty incumbent on the people . . . to extend their liberality . . . New London, Timothy Green, 1760.
broadside 30.5 × 19.5 cm.
DLC mp. 41118

B2121 CONNECTICUT. GOVERNOR, 1754-1766
By the honourable Thomas Fitch . . . a proclamation. Whereas the General assembly . . . [Mar. 18, 1760] . . . New London, Timothy Green, 1760.
broadside 37.5 × 29 cm.
DLC mp. 41117

B2122 ERSKINE, RALPH, 1685-1752
Gospel sonnets; or, Spiritual songs . . . The ninth edition . . . Philadelphia, Reprinted by W. Dunlap for John Murdoch, who is sole proprietor of this edition, 1760.
22, 363 p. 17 cm.
cf. Evans 8593
MWA mp. 41119

B2123 FATHER Abraham's almanac for . . . 1761. By Abr. Weatherwise . . . Philadelphia, Printed by W. Dunlap, for the Author [1760]
[24] p.
Drake 9824; cf. Evans 8766
NHi

B2124 FIRE CLUB, BOSTON
[Rules and orders of the Fire Club. Boston, R. Draper, 1760]
broadside?
The financial records of the club, in manuscript at Boston Public Library, record payment of one pound 20 May 1760 for printing the above
No copy known mp. 41113

B2125 [FOTHERGILL, SAMUEL] 1715-1772
To Friends of the Island of Tortola. [Philadelphia? 1760?]
8 p. 27.5 cm. caption title
Sabin 25273
PHi mp. 41120

B2126 [FRANKLIN, BENJAMIN] 1706-1790
The beauties of Poor Richard's almanack for the year 1760: being short essays . . . interspersed with moral hints, wise sayings and entertaining remarks. Philadelphia, Printed: Boston, Re-printed by Benjamin Mecom [1760?]
23, [1] p. 17 cm. $[A]^4\ B^2\ C^4\ D^2$
MWA. Photostat: MHi mp. 41121

B2127 [FRANKLIN, BENJAMIN] 1706-1790
Father Abraham's speech to a great number of people . . . introduced to the publick by Poor Richard . . . Printed and Sold by Benjamin Mecom, at the New Printing Office, near the Town-House, in Boston. [1760]
16 p. fold. front. 19.5 cm. $[A]\text{-}B^4$
Evans 8131 (microprint ed.) contains "seven curious pieces" not found here
CtHi; CtY (lacks front.); MB; MHi (mutilated); MWA (photostat front.); NN mp. 41122

B2128 [FRANKLIN, BENJAMIN] 1706-1790
Father Abraham's speech to a great number of people . . . introduced to the publick by Poor Richard . . . New-London, Printed and sold by T. Green [1760?]
24 p.
Contains two of the "seven curious pieces" included in Evans 8131, but not in the foregoing Mecom 1760 ed.
Trumbull: Supplement 2158
CtHi; CtY mp. 41123

B2129 FRANKLIN, SAMUEL
Samuel Franklin, rasor-maker from London; living at the sign of the Rasor and Crown . . . Boston: makes and grinds, rasors, lancets, scissars, penknives, scaits . . . all sorts of instruments for drawing teeth, and sundry other sorts of cutlary . . . [Boston, 1760?]
broadside 21 × 15.5 cm.
Dated [ca. 1760?] by John E. Alden
MWo mp. 41098

B2130 Deleted.

B2131 GAINE, HUGH, 1726-1807
[Catalogue, shewing the books which were sent to America before the Revolutionary War. New York, 1760]
22+ p. 21 cm.
DLC (imperfect; p; 5-22 only) mp. 41125

B2132 GEORGE the II reigns. Pitt is Secretary of State. Amherst goes on conquering . . . A new song on the success of the year past . . . Portsmouth, Sold at the printing office [by D. Fowle] [1760]
broadside 57 X 44 cm.
Whittemore 37
MWA (mutilated) mp. 41126

B2133 GORDON, JOHN, 1700-1788
A supplement to the Mathematical traverse tables in epitome, intitled A sure guide to . . . mariners . . . gentlemen that deals in land . . . [Colophon (p. [6])] Philadelphia, Printed by W. Dunlap, and to be sold by him, and the author John Gordon . . . in New-Jersey [1760]
[48] p. 2 plates. 16 X 8 cm.
Dedication on t.p. dated: New-Jersey, June 20, 1760
Revised traverse tables, p. [25-48], untitled; directions on p. [47-48] begin: "The second edition, with the Supplement . . ."
NN (p. [1-24] only); NjR (lacks plates); PPAmP (p. [1-24] only) mp. 41127

B2134 GT. BRIT. ARMY
Copy of a letter from His Excellency General Amherst, to . . . Governor Wentworth. Camp at Montreal, September 9, 1760. [Boston? 1760?]
broadside
Ford 1193
MB mp. 41128

B2135 HAMMON, JUPITER
An evening thought. Salvation by Christ with penitential cries . . . [n.p., 1760?]
broadside 27 X 20 cm.
Dated, Dec. 25, 1760
NHi mp. 41129

B2136 HARVARD UNIVERSITY
Quaestiones pro modulo . . . MDCCLX. [Boston, 1760]
broadside
MH mp. 41130

B2137 JANEWAY, JAMES, 1636-1674
Heaven upon earth; or, The best friend in the worst times . . . From the third edition. Corrected. Boston, Sold by Benjamin Mecom, 1760.
260 p. 8vo
cf. Evans 8625
MB; MHi mp. 41131

B2138 JANEWAY, JAMES, 1636-1674
A seasonable and earnest address to the citizens of London, soon after the dreadful fire . . . Together with a particular relation of the great fire of Boston . . . March 20, 1760. Boston, Printed and sold by Fowle and Draper, 1760.
55 p. 16 cm.
cf. Evans 8626
MiU-C mp. 41282

B2139 JEWETT, JEDIDIAH, 1705?-1774
A sermon, preached in the audience of the First Church . . . in Rowley . . . after the death of Mr. John Noyes . . . died . . . Aug. 13th 1759 . . . Boston, D. and J. Kneeland, 1760.
2 p.l., 17 p., 1 leaf. 19 cm. [A]-C^4
MWA (half-title and blank sig. C4 wanting); NN (imperfect); NhHi; RPJCB (same as MWA). Brit. Mus. mp. 41132

B2140 JEWS. LITURGY AND RITUAL
The form of prayer, which was performed at the Jews Synagogue, in . . . New-York . . . October 23, 1760 . . . Composed by D. R. Joseph Yesurun Pinto, in the Hebrew Language; and translated into English, by a Friend to Truth. New-York, Printed and sold by W. Weyman, 1760.
7 p. 21 cm.
Rosenbach 39
PHi mp. 41133

B2141 MARYLAND. GOVERNOR, 1753-1769
By his Excellency Horatio Sharpe . . . A brief. It having been represented to me . . . that on the 20th of March last, a fire broke out in . . . Boston . . . [May 6, 1760] . . . [Annapolis, Jonas Green, 1760]
broadside 38 X 30.5 cm.
Wroth 222; Huntington 232
CSmH; MB; MdBP; MdHi mp. 41134

B2142 MARYLAND. HOUSE OF DELEGATES
At a session . . . began [sic] . . . the 22d day of March, 1760 . . . it was ordered by the . . . Lower house, that the follwing three bills which did not pass . . . be printed . . . [Colophon] Annapolis, Jonas Green, 1760.
58 p. 28.5 cm.
Wroth 221
Md mp. 41135

B2143 MARYLAND. LAWS
Acts of the province . . . passed at a session . . . begun . . . the twenty-second day of March . . . 1760 . . . Annapolis, Jonas Green, 1760.
6 p. 29.5 cm.
Wroth 219
MH-L; MdBP; MdHi mp. 41136

B2144 MARYLAND. LAWS
Acts of the province . . . passed at a session . . . begun . . . the twenty sixth day of September . . . 1760 . . . Annapolis, Jonas Green, 1760.
8 p. 29.5 cm.
Wroth 220
MH-L; MdBP; MdHi mp. 41137

B2145 THE Maryland almanack, for the year . . . 1761 . . . Annapolis, Jonas Green, 1760.
[20] p.
Advertised in the *Maryland Gazette*, Dec. 24, 1760, as "Just Published."
Drake 2168; Wroth 226
PU mp. 41138

B2146 MASSACHUSETTS. GOVERNOR, 1757-1760
By His Excellency Thomas Pownall . . . a brief. It having pleased Almighty God to permit a fire . . . [Mar. 24, 1760] . . . Boston, John Draper, 1760.
broadside 41.5 X 31.5 cm.
Ford 1212; New York Public 310
DLC; MB; MHi; MeHi; NN (photo.) mp. 41140

B2147 MASSACHUSETTS. GOVERNOR, 1757-1760
By His Excellency Thomas Pownall . . . a proclamation for a general fast . . . [Mar. 6, 1760] . . . Boston, John Draper, 1760.
broadside 42 X 33.5 cm.
Ford 1202
DLC; MB mp. 41141

B2148 MASSACHUSETTS. GOVERNOR, 1757-1760
Province of the Massachusetts-Bay, by . . . the governor, to I do hereby authorize . . . Given under my hand, and seal, at Boston, this day of 1760. [Boston, 1760]
broadside 30.5 X 18.5 cm.
Ford 1213; New York Public 311
DLC; MHi. Photostat: NN mp. 41139

B2149 MASSACHUSETTS. GOVERNOR, 1757-1760
Province of Massachusetts-Bay, June 6, 1760. By the nonorable Thomas Hutchinson, Esq; Lieutenant Governor . . . Wm. Brattle, Adjt.-General. [Boston, 1760]
broadside 20.5 X 16.5 cm.
Offering a bonus for enlisting
MHi mp. 41143

B2150 MASSACHUSETTS. LAWS
. . . An act passed by the . . . General Court . . . begun . . . the thirtieth day of May 1759 . . . continued . . . to the second day of January following . . . Boston, John Draper, 1760.
7 p.
Impost law
MWA mp. 41142

B2151 MASSACHUSETTS. MILITIA
Province of the Massachusetts-Bay, 1760. I do hereby inlist . . . the ensuing campaign . . . I have received of five dollars, part of the bounty-money. [Boston, 1760]
broadside
Ford 1216
M-Ar; MWA

B2152 MASSACHUSETTS. TREASURER
Province of the Massachusetts-Bay, ss. Harrison Gray, Esq; Treasurer . . . [July 2, 1760] . . . [Boston, 1760]
broadside 31.5 X 20 cm.
Ford 1223; New York Public 312
MB; MSaE. Photostats: DLC; NN mp. 41144

B2153 MASSACHUSETTS. TREASURER
Province of the Massachusetts-Bay, ss. Harrison Gray, Esq; Treasurer . . . [Nov. 3, 1760] . . . [Boston, 1760]
broadside 52.5 X 32 cm.
MWA mp. 41145

B2154 MR. Weatherwise's pocket-almanac . . . for 1761 . . . By A. Weatherwise, Gent. Philadelphia, Printed and sold by W. Dunlap [1760]
[24] p. 12.5 cm.
DLC; PHi mp. 41176

B2155 NEU eingerichtet A B C Buchstabir- und Lese-Büchlein . . . herausgegeben im Jahr 1743 . . . Wieder aufgelegt, Philadelphia, 1760.
44 p. 16.5 cm.
PHi mp. 41146

B2156 THE New-England primer enlarged . . . Philadelphia, B. Franklin and D. Hall, 1760.
[52] p. 9.5 cm.
Metzger 228
PPeSchw mp. 41147

B2157 NEW HAMPSHIRE. GOVERNOR, 1741-1767
By his excellency Benning Wentworth . . . A brief. The great God having permitted a fire to lay waste . . . part . . . of Boston . . . collection for the . . . sufferers . . . Portsmouth, April 8, 1760. [Colophon] Portsmouth, Daniel Fowle, 1760.
broadside 38.5 X 31 cm.
Whittemore 44
MHi mp. 41148

B2158 NEW HAMPSHIRE. GOVERNOR, 1741-1767
By his excellency Benning Wentworth . . . I have therefore thought fit to cause . . . said proclamation to be herewith printed . . . [Feb. 28, 1760] . . . By the King. A proclamation for a public thanksgiving . . . [Oct. 23, 1759] [Colophon] Portsmouth, Daniel Fowle [1760]
broadside 38.5 X 31.5 cm.
Whittemore 43
DLC. Photostat: NhHi mp. 41149

B2159 NEW HAMPSHIRE. LAWS
An act . . . Feb. 9th, 1760. An act in addition to . . . an act, for the better regulating high ways. [Portsmouth, 1760]
4 p. 29 cm.
Whittemore 41
NhHi mp. 41150

B2160 NEW HAMPSHIRE. LAWS
An act for regulating the admeasurement of lumber, the gaging of oak, the making and size of bricks. [Portsmouth, 1760]
4 p.
Whittemore 42
MWA mp. 41151

B2161 NEW HAMPSHIRE. TREASURER
Province of New-Hampshire. To the select-men of in the province . . . for the current year 1760 . . . [Portsmouth, Daniel Fowle, 1760]
[2] p. 32 X 19.5 cm.
DLC; NhHi mp. 41152

B2162 NEW JERSEY. LAWS
Anno regni, Georgii II . . . trigesimo tertio. At a session of General Assembly, at Perth-Amboy, began March 11th, 1760, and continued till the 26th . . . during which time the following law was passed. Woodbridge, James Parker, 1760.
24 p. 30 cm.
An act for raising 1000 volunteers
Humphrey 44
Nj. Public Record Off. mp. 41153

B2163 A NEW Pilgrims Progress: shewing the many discoveries which Christian had in the town of Formality . . . Boston, 1760.
24+ p.
RPJCB (imperfect) mp. 41154

B2164 A NEW th[anksgiving] song revised, enlarged and adapted [to] the glorious conquest of Canada. Fitted to . . . the Grenadiers March . . . Boston, Sold at the new printing-office, near the Town House [1760]
broadside 48 X 36.5 cm.
Ford 1225
MWA mp. 41155

B2165 NEW YORK
By the honourable Cadwellader Colden, Esq; President of

His Majesty's Council . . . A proclamation . . . [New York, 1769]
broadside 39.5 X 26.5 cm.
Concerns the apprehension of sailors and officers who fired on the Winchester
Dated at Fort-George, Aug. 20, 1760
NHi mp. 41158

B2166 NEW YORK
By the honourable Cadwallader Colden, Esq; President of His Majesty's Council . . . A proclamation. Given . . . at Fort-George, in the City of New-York, the first day of October, 1760 . . . [New York, 1760]
broadside 41.5 X 33 cm.
Proclaiming a day of thanksgiving
PHi mp. 41157, 41159

B2167 NEW YORK. GOVERNOR, 1757-1760
By the honourable James De Lancey . . . Lieutenant Governor . . . [New York, 1760]
broadside 32.5 X 19 cm.
Orders for recruiting in Orange County, dated at Fort-George, New York City, May 9, 1960
NHi mp. 41161

B2168 NEW YORK. LAWS
Extract of an act of the General-Assembly . . . of New-York. Published the 22d of March, 1760. Entitled, An act for levying . . . two thousand six hundred and eighty effective men . . . New-York, Printed and sold by W. Weyman [1760]
16 p. 21 cm.
NHi mp. 41160

B2169 PENNSYLVANIA. GOVERNOR, 1759-1763
By the honourable James Hamilton Esq.; Lieutenant-Governor . . . To These are to authorize you, by beat of drum . . . to raise many volunteers . . . [Philadelphia, B. Franklin and D. Hall, 1760]
broadside
Adams: Pennsylvania 18
PU

B2170 PLYMOUTH PROPRIETORS
Advertisement. The proprietors of the Kennebeck Purchase from the late Colony of New-Plymouth . . . Boston, February 16, 1760.
broadside 40 X 25 cm.
DLC; MB mp. 41162

B2171 PRINCETON UNIVERSITY
Viro praeclarissimo ingenuis artibus . . . theses hasce . . . [at end] Philadelphia, Ex typis Andreae Steuart [1760]
broadside 53 X 36 cm.
NHi; NjP mp. 41163

B2172 RHODE ISLAND. GOVERNOR, 1758-1762
By the honorable Stephen Hopkins . . . A proclamation for a general thanksgiving . . . [Nov. 5, 1760] . . . [Newport, James Franklin, 1760]
broadside 37 X 32 cm.
Alden 219; Winship p. 17
RHi mp. 41164

B2173 RHODE ISLAND. GOVERNOR, 1758-1762
[Proclamation prohibiting the inhabitants of the colony . . . from trading . . . with the subjects of the French king . . . Newport, Ann and James Franklin, 1760]
[broadside?]
Alden 220; Winship p. 17
No copy known; description conjectured from the Schedules for the October 1760 session
mp. 41165

B2174 RHODE ISLAND. GOVERNOR, 1758-1762
[Proclamation recommending unto every congregation of Christians the relieving the distressed persons who have suffered by the late fire in Boston . . . Newport, Ann and James Franklin, 1760]
[broadside?]
Alden 221; Winship p. 16
No copy known; description conjectured from the Schedules for the May 1760 session
mp. 41166

B2175 RHODE ISLAND. LAWS
[An act for a rate of £15,547 in bills of credit. June session, 1760. Newport, James Franklin, 1760]
[broadside?]
Payment for printing authorized at the August 1760 session
Alden 227; Winship p. 16
No copy known mp. 41167

B2176 RIVINGTON, JAMES, 1724-1802
A catalogue of books, lately imported, and sold by James Rivington . . . at his store . . . in Hanover-Square, New-York. And also at his store . . . in Front-street, Philadelphia . . . New-York, H. Gaine, 1760.
64 p. 18.5 cm.
T.p. conjunct with sig. H1, and wrapped around intervening signatures
DeWin

B2177 SOUTH CAROLINA. LAWS
. . . At a General assembly, begun . . . the sixth day of October . . . and from thence continued . . . to the thirty-first day of July One Thousand Seven Hundred and Sixty. Charles-Town, Peter Timothy, 1760.
1 p.l., 29 p. 29.5 cm.
Tax act
Sabin 87595
DLC mp. 41169

B2178 A STATE of the trade carried on with the French on the island of Hispaniola . . . under colour of flags of truce . . . By a merchant of London . . . New-York, H. Gaine, 1760
15 p. 18.5 cm.
Huntington 233
CSmH; RPJCB mp. 41170

B2179 TURNER, JAMES
To His Excellency Edwd Cornwallis . . . this map of . . . Nova Scotia and parts adjacent is humbly presented . . . 2d. edition. Philadelphia, Andrew Hook, 1760.
map 33.5 X 46.5 cm.
Huntington 234
CSmH mp. 41172

B2180 EINE Unterweisung von der Richtigkeit des menschlichen Lebens . . . [Ephrata, 1760?]
broadside fol.
PPL mp. 41173

B2181 WATTS, ISAAC, 1674-1748
Appendix, containing a number of hymns, taken chiefly from Dr. Watts's scriptural collection . . . Boston, Printed for T. Leverett, 1760.
84 p. music (16 p.) 15 cm.
MB; MWA mp. 41174

B2182 WELD, EDMUND, 1631-1668
A funeral elegy by way of dialogue between Death, Soul, Body and Jesus Christ. Boston, Re-printed and sold by S. Kneeland [1706?]
broadside 34 X 20.5 cm.
NHi mp. 41177

B2183 WELD, EDMUND, 1631-1668
A funeral elegy . . . composed by Edmund Weld, formerly of Harvard . . . Boston, Reprinted by D. and J. Kneeland, for J. Winter [1760?]
broadside 36 X 23 cm.
Earliest Evans imprint for D. and J. Kneeland, 1759; latest Evans imprint for Jonathan Winter, 1761
DLC; MH; NHi mp. 41178

B2184 WORCESTER, FRANCIS, 1698-1783
A bridle for sinners and a spur for saints . . . The second edition. Boston, 1760.
35 p.
Sabin 105225
MB; RPJCB (imperfect) mp. 41179

B2185 THE youth's instructor . . . Boston, Printed by Daniel and John Kneeland, 1760.
149 p.
Karpinski p. 50; cf. Evans 8582
MB; MH mp. 41180

1761

B2186 AN account of the voyages and cruizes of Capt. Walker . . . Boston, B. Mecom, 1761.
42, [2] p. 17.5 cm.
MHi; MiU-C. Photostats: DLC; MWA; NN; RPJCB mp. 41181

B2187 ALL you that come this curious art to see,
From handling any thing must cautious be . . .
And if this art be pleasing to your eye,
Then let the artists find your generosity.
Boston, June 5, 1761. [Boston, 1761]
broadside 12.5 X 16.5 cm.
Verse in couplets
Ford 1226
PHi mp. 41182

B2188 THE American almanac, for the year . . . 1762 . . . By John Jerman . . . Philadelphia, W. Dunlap [1761]
[24] p. 16 cm.
DLC mp. 40205

B2189 AN astronomical diary: or, almanack for the year . . . 1762 . . . By Nathaniel Ames . . . Portsmouth, D. Fowle [1761]
[24] p. 17 cm.
DLC; MWA; NHi; NhHi mp. 41183

B2190 BIBLE. O.T. PSALMS
The Psalms of David, imitated . . . The twentythird edition . . . Boston, Re-printed by D. and J. Kneeland, for J. Wharton and N. Bowes, 1761.
vi, 304, [5] p. 14 cm.
MWA; NNUT mp. 41250

B2191 BIBLE. N.T. APOCRYPHAL BOOKS. EPISTLE OF JESUS CHRIST
The copy of a letter written by our blessed Lord and Saviour Jesus Christ . . . To which is added An hymn of praise to the name of Jesus . . . by the late . . . Mrs. Rowe. Philadelphia, Andrew Steuart, 1761.
8 p. 16.5 cm.
MWA (imperfect) mp. 41189

B2192 BOSTON. ASSESSORS
Boston, April 13, 1761. Whereas an act was pass'd . . . in January 1761, for enquiring into the rateable estate of the said province; the assessors of the Town of Boston, in conformity . . . [Boston, 1761]
broadside 34.5 X 21.5 cm.
Ford 1228
MHi mp. 41185

B2193 BOSTON NEWS-LETTER
A New-Years present from the lad that carries the *Boston News-Letter* . . . January 1, 1761. [Boston, John Draper, 1761]
broadside 17 X 13 cm.
Ford 1259
PHi mp. 41231

B2194 BOSTON POST-BOY
A New Years wish, from the lad, who carries the *Post-Boy & Advertiser*. Boston, January 1, 1760. [Boston, Green & Russell, 1761]
broadside
Ford 1260
Year printed 1760, changed by pen to 1761
PHi mp. 41232

B2195 CONNECTICUT. GOVERNOR, 1754-1766
By the honourable Thomas Fitch . . . A proclamation . . . [Jan. 22, 1761] . . . New-London, Timothy Green, 1761.
broadside 32 X 19 cm.
Concerns rewording the prayer for the royal family
CtHi mp. 41186

B2196 CONNECTICUT. GOVERNOR, 1754-1766
By the honourable Thomas Fitch . . . a proclamation . . . [April 29, 1761] . . . New-London, Timothy Green, 1761.
broadside 40 X 33 cm.
CtHi; DLC mp. 41187

B2197 CONNECTICUT. GOVERNOR, 1754-1766
By the honourable Thomas Fitch . . . A proclamation . . . [Dec. 14, 1761] . . . New-London, Timothy Green [1761]
broadside 32 X 19 cm.
Concerns adding Queen Charlotte's name to prayer for the royal family
NHi mp. 41188

B2198 DAVIES, SAMUEL, 1724-1761
Little children invited to Jesus Christ. A sermon preached in Hanover County Virginia, May 8, 1758 . . . The third edition. Boston, Printed and sold by Fowle & Draper, 1761.
12 leaves. 12mo A-B^6
Rosenbach-Ch 45
A. S. W. Rosenbach (1933) mp. 41190

B2199 DAVIES, SAMUEL, 1724-1761
A sermon delivered . . . January 14, 1761 . . . The second edition . . . New York, J. Parker, 1761.
2 p.l., x, 3-20 p. 20 cm.
DLC; MH; MHi; NjP; PHi; PPAmP mp. 41191

B2200 DILWORTH, W. H.
Lord Anson's voyage round the world . . . Boston, B. Mecom. 1761.

104 p. 8vo
Huntington 235; cf. Evans 8534
CSmH; MB mp. 41192

B2201 [AN enquiry into the value of Canada and Guadaloupe . . . By a British gentleman. Philadelphia? J. Rivington? 1761]
1 p.l., 40 [i.e., 41], iv p. 19.5 cm.
Page 41 wrongly numbered 40
Hildeburn 1730
DLC (imperfect; t.p. wanting) mp. 41193

B2202 ERSKINE, RALPH, 1685-1752
The great ruin, and the great relief . . . A sermon . . . preached . . . March 22, 1738 . . . Boston, Printed by D. and J. Kneeland for W. McAlpine, 1761.
72 p. 16 cm.
MWA; RPJCB mp. 41194

B2203 AN example of sincere love, in a letter to a gentleman in France, from his sister . . . Boston, Printed, and sold at Fowle and Draper's Office, 1761.
12 p. 18 cm.
MWA mp. 41195

B2204 FATHER Abraham's almanac for . . . 1762 . . . By Abraham Weatherwise . . . Philadelphia, W. Dunlap [1761]
[40] p.
"Fitted for the latitude of New-York."
Drake 9835; cf. Evans 9037 (microprint)
PHi

B2205 [FISK, JOSEPH] b. 1701?
A few lines on the happy reduction of Canada . . . Some lines, on the remarkable providence of God in the year 1761 . . . Written the same year. [n.p.] 1761.
16 p. 16 cm.
Acrostic, with author's name, p. 16
New York Public 318
MWA. Photostats: MHi; NN mp. 41196

B2206 FRIENDS, SOCIETY OF
To George the Third . . . The humble address of his Protestant subjects, the people called Quakers . . . London, the first day of the twelfth month, 1760 . . . London, printed: And, Philadelphia, re-printed by Andrew Steuart [1761?]
broadside 33 X 20 cm.
MB mp. 41197

B2207 Deleted.

B2208 GT. BRIT. ARMY
A list of His Majesty's land forces in North-America . . . Carefully corrected to April, 1761. New-York, Printed by James Parker for James Rivington, 1761.
1 p.l., 36 p. 8vo
Huntington 236; cf. Evans 8866
CSmH mp. 41199

B2209 HARVARD UNIVERSITY
Quaestiones pro modulo . . . MDCCLXI. [Boston, 1761]
broadside 43 X 27.5 cm.
Ford 1231; New York Public 1231
DLC; MH; MHi; MSaE; MWA; NN; NhHi mp. 41200

B2210 HAVEN, JASON, 1733-1803
A sermon delivered at a private meeting in Framingham; on Thursday, October 8. 1761 . . . Boston, Printed by D. and J. Kneeland for J. Winter, 1761.
22 p. cm.
Huntington 237
CSmH; MWA; MWiW mp. 41201

B2211 HOW, URIAH, 1738-1758
A discourse, written by Uriah How of Canaan . . . killed, in the year 1758. [New Haven?] Printed in the year MDCCLXI.
15 p. 19.5 cm.
MWA mp. 41202

B2212 IMRIE, DAVID
The letters of Mr. David Imrie . . . Philadelphia, Andrew Steuart, 1761.
16 p. 17 cm.
DLC mp. 41203

B2213 JANEWAY, JAMES, 1636-1674
Heaven upon earth: or, The best friend in the worst of times . . . The fourth edition, corrected. Boston, Sold by Benjamin Mecom, at the New Printing-Office [1761?]
260 p. 8vo
A re-issue, with cancel t.p., of Evans 8625
MB; MHi mp. 41204

B2214 [KENRICK, WILLIAM] 1725?-1779
The whole duty of woman . . . By a Lady. . . . The second edition . . . Boston, Reprinted, and sold by Fowle & Draper, 1761.
44+ p. 20 cm. A-E^4 F^4?
MWA (ends with sig. F2) mp. 41206

B2215 Deleted

B2216 MARYLAND. HOUSE OF DELEGATES
To his Excellency Horatio Sharpe . . . the humble address of the House of delegates . . . April 14, 1761 . . . Annapolis, Jonas Green [1761]
broadside 31.5 X 19 cm.
Wroth 229
MdHi mp. 41208

B2217 MARYLAND. SENATE
To his Excellency Horatio Sharpe . . . the humble address of the Upper house . . . April 15, 1761 . . . Annapolis, Jonas Green [1761]
broadside 31.5 X 19 cm.
Wroth 230
MdHi mp. 41209

B2218 THE Maryland almanack, for the year . . . 1762 . . . Annapolis, Printed and sold by Jonas Green [1761]
[24] p. 16 cm. [A]-C^4
Guerra b-146; Wroth 232
DLC mp. 41210

B2219 MASSACHUSETTS. GOVERNOR, 1760-1769
By His Excellency Francis Bernard . . . A proclamation . . . [April 21, 1761] Boston, John Draper, 1761.
broadside 41 X 33 cm.
Concerns raising 3000 men to be under the command of General Amherst
Ford 1238
MWA mp. 41211

B2220 MASSACHUSETTS. GOVERNOR, 1760-1769
Province of Massachusetts-Bay. By His Excellency the Captain-General . . . April 21, 1761. [Boston, 1761]

broadside 31.5 X 19 cm.
Returns to be made of enlistments within three weeks after beating orders are received
Ford 1254; Ford 1286?
MWA mp. 41212

B2221 MASSACHUSETTS. LAWS
. . . An act passed by the . . . General Court . . . begun . . . the eleventh day of December 1760 . . . Boston, John Draper, 1761.
7 p.
Impost tax
MWA mp. 41214

B2222 MASSACHUSETTS. LAWS
. . . An act, passed by the . . . General Court . . . December [1760] . . . Chap. I. An act for enquiring into the rateable estates of this province . . . [Boston, S. Kneeland, 1761]
2 p. 32 X 18 cm.
At head of title: Valuation
Ford 1234
MWA; PPRF mp. 41213

B2223 MASSACHUSETTS. LAWS
. . . An act, passed . . . December [1760] . . . Chap. I. An act for repealing the several laws . . . which relate to the observation of the Lord's-Day . . . [Colophon] Boston, S. Kneeland, 1761.
4 p. 32 cm.
New York Public 320
NN mp. 41215

B2224 MASSACHUSETTS. LAWS
. . . An act, passed . . . March [1761] . . . Chap. XX. An act in addition to an act . . . intituled An act for enquiring into the rateable estates of this province. [Colophon] Boston, S. Kneeland, 1761.
p. 493-494. 29 cm.
New York Public 321
NN mp. 41216

B2225 MASSACHUSETTS. LAWS
. . . An act passed . . . May 1761 . . . for apportioning and assessing the sum of seventy-five thousand pounds . . . [Colophon] Boston, John Draper, 1761.
7 [i.e. 11] p. 32 cm. caption title
Ford & Matthews p. 446
M-Ar mp. 41217

B2226 MASSACHUSETTS. MILITIA
Province of the Massachusetts-Bay. 1761. I do hereby inlist . . . in one of the regiments raised in this Province, to provide for the . . . security of His Majesty's dominions in North-America . . . 1761. [Boston, 1761]
broadside 16.5 X 21 cm.
Ford 1253
MHi; MWA mp. 41218

B2227 MASSACHUSETTS. MILITIA
Return of men inlisted for His Majesty's service for the protection . . . of His Majesty's dominions and conquests in North-America, 1761. [Boston, 1761]
broadside
Ford 1256
MHi; MWA mp. 41219

B2228 MASSACHUSETTS. TREASURER
Province of the Massachusetts-Bay. Harrison Gray, Esq; Treasurer . . . July 20, 1761. [Boston, 1761]
broadside
Tax warrant
Ford 1250
MB mp. 41220

B2229 MASSACHUSETTS. TREASURER
Province of the Massachusetts-Bay ss. Harrison Gray, Esq; treasurer . . . Second day of December 1761 . . . [Boston, 1761]
broadside 39 X 29.5 cm.
Tax warrant
MB mp. 41221

B2230 MERRY Andrew's almanac . . . for the year . . . 1762 . . . Philadelphia, Andrew Steuart [1761]
[24] p. 15.5 cm.
DLC; MWA mp. 41222

B2231 MILTON, ABRAHAM
The farmer's companion . . . Annapolis, 1761.
34 p. fold. plate. sm. 4to
Wroth 234
Privately owned mp. 41223

B2232 NAMEN-BUCHLEIN samt den fünff Haupt-Stücken, vor Kinder, welche anfangen zu lernen. Philadelphia, gedruckt und zu haben bey Peter Müller, 1761.
[16] p. 8vo
Adams: Pennsylvania 19
PU

B2233 [THE New-England primer. Boston? 1761?]
[80] p. sm. 32mo
Church Catalogue 1035; Huntington 239; *not* Evans 8941
CSmH (lacks first 2 leaves)

B2234 NEW HAMPSHIRE. GOVERNOR, 1741-1767
By his excellency Benning Wentworth . . . A proclamation. Almighty God having . . . [Nov. 24, 1761] . . . [Colophon] Portsmouth, D. Fowle [1761]
broadside 38 X 30.5 cm.
Whittemore 31
DLC. Photostat: NhHi mp. 41225

B2235 NEW HAMPSHIRE. HOUSE OF REPRESENTATIVES
Province of New-Hampshire. In the House of Representatives, January 28th, 1761. Whereas by the change in circumstances . . . In council, Feb. 9, 1761 . . . consented to, B. Wentworth . . . [Portsmouth, D. Fowle, 1761]
broadside
Concerns levying a new province tax
Whittemore 53
NhHi. Photostat: MWA mp. 41226

B2236 NEW JERSEY. LAWS
Anno regni, Georgii III . . . primo. At a session of General Assembly, at Burlington . . . July 4th, 1761 . . . till the 8th day of the same month . . . the following law was passed. Woodbridge, James Parker, 1761.
11 p. 30 cm.
Humphrey 57
Nj mp. 41228

B2237 NEW JERSEY. LAWS
Anno regni, Georgii III . . . primo. At a session of General Assembly, at Perth-Amboy . . . March 27th, 1761 . . . till the 7th day of April following . . . the following laws were passed. Woodbridge, James Parker, 1761.
28 p. 30 cm.

Humphrey 56
Nj. Public Record Off. mp. 41227

B2238 NEW JERSEY. LAWS
Anno regni, Georgii III . . . primo. At a session of General Assembly of . . . New-Jersey . . . Burlington, October 27th 1760 . . . to the 5th of December . . . the twenty-two following acts were passed. Woodbridge, James Parker, 1761.
80 p. 30 cm.
Humphrey 55
Nj (chap. xx (part) and xxi-xxii wanting) mp. 41229

B2239 NEW JERSEY. LAWS
Anno regni, Georgii III . . . secundo. At a session of General Assembly, of . . . New-Jersey . . . Perth-Amboy, November 30, 1761 . . . to the 12th of December . . . the seven following acts were passed. Woodbridge, James Parker, 1761.
20 p. 30 cm.
Humphrey 58
Nj mp. 41230

B2240 NEW YORK. LAWS
An act of the General-Assembly of . . . New-York, published the 4th of April, 1761 . . . for raising, paying, and cloathing, Seventeen Hundred and Eighty Seven effective men . . . New-York: Printed and sold by W. Weyman [1761]
16 p. 22 cm.
NHi mp. 41233

B2241 NEW-YORK GAZETTE
For the *New-York Gazette*, Jan. 1, 1761. To all gentlefolks in town, and every, and any, The petition of Lawrence, or Bloody-news Swinny . . . Lawrencius Swinny. [New York, 1761]
broadside 27 X 13 cm.
PHi mp. 41248

B2242 NEWBURY FIRE SOCIETY
These presents witness, that we the subscribers . . . do mutually agree to the following articles . . . December 8, 1761, at Newbury . . . [Newburyport? 1761]
broadside 40 X 32 cm.
Ford 1258
MSaE mp. 41234

B2243 NILES, SAMUEL, 1674-1762
A pressing memorial . . . Braintree, June 23, 1761. [Boston, 1761]
4 p. 18 cm. caption title
DLC (facsim.) Photostats: MHi; NN mp. 41235

B2244 PETERS, RICHARD
Philadelphia, January 29, 1761. Advertisement . . . Richard Peters, Richard Hockley. [Philadelphia, 1761]
broadside 19 X 15.5 cm.
PHi mp. 41236

B2244a THE plan of agreement between the Corporation for the Relief . . . of Ministers . . . and the annual contributors. Philadelphia, Andrew Steuart, 1761.
broadside
Trinterud 502
PPPrHi

B2245 PLYMOUTH PROPRIETORS
Advertisement. The Proprietors of the Kennebeck purchase from the late colony of New-Plymouth, hereby inform the publick . . . Boston, 20th February, 1761. [Boston, 1761]
broadside 24.5 X 20 cm.
Ford 1233
MWA mp. 41237

B2246 POOR Roger, 1762. The American country almanack, for . . . 1762 . . . By Roger Moore . . . New-York, Printed and sold by James Parker [1761]
[36] p. 16 cm.
Wall p. 16; cf. Evans 8934
DLC; MWA; NHi; NN (fragment of 5 leaves) mp. 41224

B2247 REFORMED CHURCH IN AMERICA
Den Nederduytse Gereformeerde Kerkenraden en Gemeeten in onsen lande wenscht . . . Aldus gedaan te N—— Brunswyk den 6 October 1761 . . . [Philadelphia? 1761]
broadside 39 X 26 cm.
New York Public 325
NjR. Photostat: NN mp. 41239

B2248 RHODE ISLAND
The following is a list of all the mortgage deeds . . . now in the Grand committee's office, belonging to the county of Kent . . . [Newport, J. Franklin, 1761?]
broadside 31 X 21 cm.
Bill submitted by James Franklin Feb. 18, 1761
Alden 229; Winship p. 17
RHi (mutilated) mp. 41241

B2249 RHODE ISLAND
[The following is a list of all the mortgage deeds . . . now in the Grand committee's office, belonging to the county of Kings county . . . Newport, J. Franklin, 1761?]
[broadside?]
Bill submitted by James Franklin Feb. 18, 1761
Alden 230
No copy known mp. 41240

B2250 RHODE ISLAND
[The following is a list of all the mortgate deeds . . . now in the Grand committee's office, belonging to the county of Providence . . . Newport, James Franklin, 1761?]
[broadside?]
Bill submitted by James Franklin Feb. 18, 1761
Alden 231
No copy known mp. 41242

B2251 RHODE ISLAND. LAWS
[An act for enquiring into the value of rateable estates in this colony . . . Newport, J. Franklin, 1761]
[broadside?]
Alden 240; Winship p. 17
No copy known; description conjectured from the June 1761 session Schedules
mp. 41244

B2252 RHODE ISLAND. LAWS
At the General assembly . . . begun . . . at Newport . . . in October . . . One Thousand Seven Hundred and Sixty-one . . . An act for apportioning . . . the rate of tax . . . [Newport, J. Franklin, 1761]
3 p. 33 cm. caption title
Alden 241
DLC; RHi; RPB; RPJCB mp. 41243

B2252a RITZEMA, JOHANNES
Ware vryheyt tot vrede beantwoort . . . van het boekje van Do. Johannes Leydt . . . Niew-York: Gedrukt by H. Gaine, 1761.
40 p. 19 cm.
cf. Evans 9158
NHi mp. 41207

B2253 THE royal convert: or, The force of truth . . . Written in French by the Messieurs of Port-Royal, and now newly translated into English. Boston, Printed and sold by D. and J. Kneeland, 1761.
[2], ii, [5]-95 p. 15.5 cm. A-F^8
MWA mp. 41238

B2254 SENTENTIAE pueriles; or, Sentences for children . . . Philadelphia, William Dunlap, 1761.
36 leaves. 12mo A-D^6 a-b^6
English and Latin on opposite pages
Rosenbach-Ch 46
A. S. W. Rosenbach (1933) mp. 41245

B2255 SMITH, WILLIAM, 1727-1803
An exercise, consisting of a dialogue and ode . . . Philadelphia, Printed and sold by Andrew Stewart . . . and by Hugh Gaine, in New-York [1761?]
8 p. 8vo
Sabin 84607; reprint of Evans 8882; Adams: Pennsylvania 20
PU

B2256 SOME thoughts occasioned by the earthquake . . . March 12th, 1761 . . . Portsmouth, D. Fowle [1761]
12 p.
Sabin 86771
RPJCB mp. 41246

B2257 SOUTH CAROLINA. LAWS
Acts of the General assembly . . . 1761. Charles-Town, Peter Timothy, 1761.
25, [1] p. 29 cm.
Sabin 87596
DLC mp. 41247

B2258 THE South-Carolina almanack . . . for the year . . . 1762 . . . By George Andrews . . . Charlestown, Robert Wells [1761]
[32] p. 16 cm.
Sabin 87748
DLC (2 copies); MWA (t.p. lacking); ScHi mp. 41184

B2259 [THE South-Carolina and Georgia almanack for . . . 1762. By John Tobler. Charles-Town, Peter Timothy [1761?]]

Advertised in the *South Carolina Gazette*, Jan. 16, 1762
Drake 13085
No copy known

B2260 THOMAS, 1762: being an almanac . . . for the year . . . 1762 . . . By Thomas Thomas . . . Philadelphia, W. Dunlap [1761]
[32] p. 16.5 cm.
DLC mp. 41249

B2261 WING reviv'd: being an almanack . . . for the year . . . . . 1762 . . . New-York, Printed and sold by Samuel Brown [1761]
[32] p. 17 cm. [A]-D^4
Guerra b-153
CtHi; NHi mp. 41251

B2262 THE youth's instructor in the English tongue: or The art of spelling improved . . . Collected from Dixon, Bailey, Owen, Dilworth, Strong and Watts. Boston, Thomas and John Fleet, 1761.
146, [1] p. 16 cm. A-I^8 K^2
MB; MWA mp. 41252

1762

B2263 AN account of the remarkable conversion of a little boy and girl. Boston, Printed and sold by Fowle and Draper, 1762.
24 p. 16 cm. A-B^6
Rosenbach-Ch 47
MB; MWA (t.p. and p. 5-8 lacking); PP mp. 41253

B2264 BIBLE. O.T. PSALMS
A new version of the Psalms of David . . . By N. Brady . . . and N. Tate . . . Boston, Re-printed by D. and J. Kneeland, for J. Edwards, 1762.
276, 84, xiv p. 15.5 cm.
cf. Evans 9068-69
MWA mp. 41255

B2265 BIBLE. O.T. PSALMS
A new version of the Psalms of David . . . By N. Brady . . . and N. Tate . . . Boston, Re-printed by D. and J. Kneeland for John Perkins, 1762.
276, 84, xiv p. 15.5 cm.
Huntington 241; cf. Evans 9068-69
CSmH; MH mp. 41256

B2266 BIBLE. O.T. PSALMS
The Psalms of David, imitated in the language of the New Testament . . . By I. Watts, D. D. The twentieth edition. Portsmouth, Printed and sold by Daniel Fowle, 1762.
viii, 336 p. 15.5 cm.
Whittemore 58
MB; MWA; NhHi mp. 41324

B2267 BOSTON POST-BOY
A New Year's wish, from the carrier of the *Post-Boy & Advertiser*. Boston, January 1, 1762. [Boston, Green & Russell, 1762]
broadside
Ford 1288
PHi. Photostat: MWA mp. 41293

B2268 COCKINGS, GEORGE, d. 1802
War: an heroic poem . . . Portsmouth, Daniel Fowle, 1762.
1 p.l., ii, 28 p. 29 cm.
Sabin 14110; Wegelin 78 (note)
DLC; MWA mp. 41257

B2269 CONNECTICUT. GOVERNOR, 1754-1766
By the honourable Thomas Fitch Esq. Governor . . . A proclamation . . . New-Haven, this twelfth day of March . . . 1762 . . . [New Haven ? 1762]
broadside 35 X 24 cm.
Appointing April 7 as a day of fasting
CtHi mp. 41258

B2270 DAVIES, SAMUEL, 1723-1761
Little children invited to Jesus Christ . . . 4th edition. Boston, T. and J. Fleet, 1762.
24 p. 16.5 cm.
MWA; NjP mp. 41259

B2271 DELAWARE. HOUSE OF REPRESENTATIVES
Votes and proceedings of the House of Representatives . . . twentieth day of October, 1762. Wilmington, James Adams, 1762.
27 p. fol.
PHi

B2272 DILWORTH, THOMAS, d. 1780
New guide to the English tongue . . . The twenty-third edition . . . Philadelphia, Re-printed, by W. Dunlap, 1762.

164 p. illus. 17 cm.
CtHi mp. 41259a

B2273 DRAPER, RICHARD, 1727-1774
To . . . Francis Bernard . . . The petition of Richard Draper, printer . . . [Boston, 1762]
broadside 38 X 21.5 cm.
Dated in manuscript: December 1st 1762
Ford 1264; New York Public 326
M-Ar; MHi. Photostats: DLC; NN mp. 41260

B2274 AN elegy on the death of that worthy Friend Priscilla Coleman, deceased, widow of John Coleman . . . who departed this life on the 14th day of the third month. 1762. Boston, Zechariah Fowle & Samuel Draper, 1762.
broadside 30.5 X 23.5 cm.
Ford 1265
MB (mutilated). Photostats: MHi; MWA mp. 41261

B2275 FARRAND, DANIEL, 1722-1803
A sermon delivered at the funeral of Mrs. Elizabeth Lee . . . February 23, 1762 . . . New-Haven, James Parker [1762]
19 p. 8vo
Huntington 244
CSmH mp. 41262

B2276 Deleted.

B2277 GODDARD, WILLIAM, 1739-1817
Printing-office, Providence, August 31, 1762. To the publick . . . I purpose to carry on the printing business in this town . . . William Goddard. [Providence, William Goddard, 1762]
broadside 34.5 X 26 cm.
Alden 246; Winship p. 18; Winship Addenda p. 92
RHi; RPJCB. Photostat: MWA mp. 41264

B2278 GREEN, JONAS
[A letter to his Excellency Horatio Sharpe . . . from Jonas Green, printer. Annapolis, J. Green, 1762]

Wroth 236
No copy known mp. 41265

B2279 GREEN, JONAS
To his Excellency Horatio Sharpe . . . the petition of Jonas Green, printer . . . [Annapolis, Jonas Green, 1762]
broadside 46.5 X 37.5 cm.
Wroth 237
MdHi mp. 41266

B2280 GROSVENOR, BENJAMIN, 1676-1758
Health. An essay on it's nature, value . . . The third edition. Boston, Printed by D. and J. Kneeland, for John Perkins, 1762.
[12], 223 p. 16 cm. A^6 B-F^{12} G-P^6
MWA; N mp. 41267

B2281 HARVARD UNIVERSITY
Quaestiones pro modulo . . . MDCCLXII. [Boston, 1762]
broadside 41 X 24.5 cm.
Ford 1266
MH; MWA; NN (photostat) mp. 41268

B2282 HEIDELBERG CATECHISM
Der kleine catechismus . . . Philadelphia, Anton Armbrüster, 1762.
94, [2] p. 13 cm.
DLC; P mp. 41269

B2283 THE history of the Holy Jesus . . . By a Lover of their precious souls. The eighth edition, with some additions. Boston, Printed and sold by Fowle & Draper, 1762.
[32] p. illus. 12.5 cm. [A]-B^8
MWA mp. 41270

B2284 HOPKINS, ESEK
To the public. A brief reply to a paper signed by George Taylor . . . Esek Hopkins. Providence, April 18, 1762. [Newport, Ann and James Franklin, 1762]
broadside 16.5 X 16.5 cm.
Alden 247; Winship p. 17
RHi mp. 41271

B2285 HOPKINS, STEPHEN, 1707-1785
Governor Hopkins's Vindication of his conduct, in relation to the sugars . . . Providence, April 6, 1762. [Newport, Ann and James Franklin, 1762]
3 p. 33 cm. caption title
Alden 248; Winship p. 17
PPL; RHi. Photostats: MHi; MWA; NN mp. 41272

B2286 [HOPKINS, STEPHEN] 1707-1785
In memory of Obadiah Brown . . . [Providence? William Goddard? 1762?]
broadside 33.5 X 21 cm.
Alden 249; Winship p. 18
MWA; RHi. Photostats: MHi; NN mp. 41273

B2287 HUDSON, SETH
The humble confession of that notorious cheat, Doctor Seth Hudson. 1762. [Boston, 1762]
broadside
Ford 1269
PHi mp. 41274

B2288 IMPORTANT news. Portsmouth, in New Hampshire, September 7, 1762. Yesterday arrived at Newbury Captain James Hutson . . . [Portsmouth, 1762]
broadside 20 X 11 cm.
Whittemore 61
NhHi mp. 41275

B2289 LITCHFIELD, August 2, 1762. Advertisement. A post having begun to ride from New-York, to Hartford, comes through Litchfield, and brings the *New-York Gazette* . . . All persons . . . send in their names to William Stanton, in Litchfield, with whom the papers will be lodged . . . [Hartford? 1762]
broadside 20 X 17 cm.
CtHi mp. 41314

B2290 MARTINICO. Number II. Philadelphia, February 25. By Captain White, from Barbados, we have the following advices, relatinng [sic] to our army at Martinico, &c. . . . [New York] Printed by S. Farley [1762]
broadside 39 X 24 cm.
In two columns
New York Public 330
NN mp. 41276

B2291 MARYLAND. LAWS
Acts of the province . . . made and passed at a session . . .

begun and held . . . the seventeenth day of March . . . 1762 . . . Annapolis, Jonas Green, 1762.
16 p. 31.5 cm.
Wroth 238
DLC; MH-L; MdHi mp. 41277

B2292 THE Maryland almanack, for the year . . . 1763 . . . Annapolis, Jonas Green [1762]
[20] p. 17 cm.
Wroth 241
MH; MHi mp. 41278

B2293 MASSACHUSETTS. GOVERNOR, 1760-1769
By . . . Francis Bernard . . . a proclamation for a general fast . . . [Mar. 24, 1762] . . . Boston, John Draper, 1762.
broadside 40.5 X 33 cm.
Ford 1273
DLC mp. 41279

B2294 MASSACHUSETTS. LAWS
. . . An act passed by the . . . General Court . . . begun . . . the twenty-seventh day of May, 1761 . . . Boston, John Draper, 1762.
7 p.
MWA mp. 41280

B2295 MASSACHUSETTS. LAWS
Province of the Massachusetts-Bay. An act for rendering more effectual the laws already made relating to shingles . . . [Pass'd the . . . General Court . . . June 1762.] . . . [This act published June 12th 1762.] [Boston, 1762]
broadside 37 X 25 cm.
Ford 1270
MHi; MWA; PHi mp. 41281

B2296 MASSACHUSETTS. MILITIA
Province of Massachusetts-Bay, I aged years, do . . . inlist . . . in one of the regiments raised in this Province, to provide for the . . . security of His Majesty's dominions in North-America. 1762. [Boston, 1762]
broadside
Ford 1285
MHi

B2297 MASSACHUSETTS. MILITIA
Return of men inlisted for His Majesty's service for the protection . . . of His Majesty's dominions and conquests in North-America, 1762. [Boston, 1762]
broadside
Ford 1287
MHi; MWA mp. 41282

B2298 MASSACHUSETTS. TREASURER
Province of the Massachusetts-Bay, ss. Harrison Gray, Esq; Treasurer . . . To constable or collector of Greeting, &c. By virtue of an act . . . [Dec. 3, 1762] . . . [Boston, 1762]
broadside 39 X 31.5 cm.
DLC; MB mp. 41283

B2299 MATHER, WILLIAM, fl. 1695.
[The young man's companion . . . The twenty first edition, with large additions . . . by Dr. J. Barrow. New York, Garrat Noel, 1762]

Advertised in the *New York Gazette*, Feb. 1, 1762, as "Also this day is published by said Garrat Noel."
Guerra a-330
No copy located mp. 41284

B2300 MR. FRANKLIN, I have lately been favor'd with the perusal of a narrative . . . entitled, "A dialogue between the governor . . . and a Freeman . . ." . . . [at end] A Freeman of the Colony. [Newport, Ann and James Franklin, 1762]
2 p. 32 cm.
Alden 244; Winship p. 17
RHi. Photostats: MWA; NN mp. 41285

B2301 MR. WEATHERWISE's pocket almanac . . . for 1763 . . . Philadelphia, W. Dunlap [1762]
[24] p. 12.5 cm.
MWA mp. 41325

B2302 MOORE, EDWARD, 1712-1757
Fables for the female sex . . . A new edition. Dedicated to the ladies of these provinces. Philadelphia: Printed by Andrew Stewart, 1762.
[1], [i]-ii, [1], 75 [5] p. 12mo
PPL

B2303 [MORRO Castle taken by storm . . . Providence, William Goddard, 1762]
broadside
Alden 250; Winship p. 18
No copy known mp. 41286

B2304 A MOST unaccountable relation of one Miss Sarah Green, a widow, living at Beesly, in the County of Worcester . . . practice of witchcraft . . . [n.p.] Printed in the year M.DCC.LXII.
8 p. 19.5 cm.
MWA mp. 41287

B2305 NEW HAMPSHIRE
Province of New-Hampshire. To the selectmen . . . for the year current 1762 . . . [Portsmouth, 1762]
broadside 38 X 30 cm.
Whittemore 64
NhHi mp. 41289

B2306 NEW HAMPSHIRE. GOVERNOR, 1741-1767
George the Third . . . to our trusty and well-beloved Theodore Atkinson [and 96 others] Greeting . . . Witness, Benning Wentworth . . . [Feb. 8, 1762] . . . [Portsmouth, D. Fowle, 1762]
broadside 49.5 X 39 cm.
DLC. Photostat: NhHi mp. 41288

B2307 NEW JERSEY. LAWS
Anno regni, Georgii III . . . secundo. At a session of General Assembly, at Burlington . . . March 3, 1762 . . . till the 10th day of the same month . . . the following laws were passed. Woodbridge, James Parker, 1762.
33, [1] p. 30 cm.
Humphrey 54
Nj. Public Record Off. mp. 41291

B2308 NEW JERSEY. LAWS
Anno regni, Georgii III . . . secundo. At a session of General Assembly, at Burlington . . . September 14, 1762 . . . till the 25th . . . the following laws were passed. Woodbridge, James Parker, 1762.
36 p. 30 cm.
Humphrey 66
Nj; NjHi. Public Record Off. mp. 41292

B2309 NEW JERSEY. LAWS
Anno regni Georgii III . . . secundo. At a session of General Assembly, at Perth-Amboy, began April 26, 1762; and continued till the 28th . . . during which time the two following laws were passed. [Colophon] Woodbridge, James Parker, 1762.

4 p. 32 cm. caption title
Humphrey 65; New York Public 332
NN; Nj mp. 41290

B2310 NEW YORK. GOVERNOR, 1761-1765
By the honourable Cadwallader Colden . . . Lieutenant Governor . . . [New York, 1762]
broadside 29 X 30 cm.
Details to recruiting officers, dated at Fort-George May 21, 1762
NHi mp. 41295

B2311 NEW YORK. GOVERNOR, 1761-1765
By the honourable Cadwallader Colden . . . Lieutenant-Governor . . . A proclamation. Whereas it appearing that certain persons . . . had entered into a combination to dispossess Robert Livingston, jr. . . . [New York, 1762]
broadside 30.5 X 19 cm.
Dated at Fort-George, Mar. 31, 1762
NHi mp. 41294

B2312 NEW YORK. LAWS
[Laws of New York. Passed Dec. 11, 1762. New York, W. Weyman, 1762]
p. 269-308. 35.5 cm.
Running title: Laws of New-York. The honourable Robert Monckton, governor
DLC; NNS mp. 41296

B2313 NEWBURYPORT, Sept. 30, 1762. Captain Moses Rolfe of this town, sailed from hence . . . the 28th of last May, in a brig . . . His body was brought to this town, and buried last Monday evening . . . [Salem? 1762]
broadside 30 X 19 cm.
One paragraph, surrounded by an ornamental border
MSaE

B2314 NORTH CAROLINA. HOUSE OF ASSEMBLY
The journal of the House of Assembly. North-Carolina, ss. At an Assembly . . . Wilmington [Apr. 13, 1762] . . . Being the first meeting of this present Assembly. [Newbern, James Davis, 1762]
28 p. 26 cm. caption title
McMurtrie: North Carolina 38
Public Record Off. mp. 41297

B2315 NORTH CAROLINA. LAWS
Anno regni Georgii III . . . tertio. At an Assembly, begun . . . at Newbern, the third day of November . . . [1762], being the first session of this present Assembly. [Newbern, James Davis, 1762]
28+ p. 26 cm. caption title
Running head between rules at top of page: Laws of North-Carolina 40
NcU (all wanting after p. 28) mp. 41298

B2316 PARNELL, THOMAS, 1679-1717
A vision . . . New York, James Parker, 1762.
10 p. 14.5 cm.
DLC mp. 41299

B2317 REFLECTIONS on Gov. Hopkins's vindication of his conduct in relation to the sugars. [at end] Newport . . . April 17, 1762. A Freeman. [Newport, Ann and James Franklin, 1762]
4 p. 33.5 cm.
Alden 245; Winship Addenda p. 87
MiU–C; RHi. Photostat: NN mp. 41302

B2318 REMARKS on a late performance, sign'd, A freeman of the colony, in answer to a Dialogue . . . [at end] Newport, March 22, 1762. [Newport, Ann Franklin and Samuel Hall, 1762]
3 p. 31 cm.
Alden 251; Winship p. 17
MWA; RHi; RPJCB. Photostats: MHi; NN mp. 41303

B2319 RHODE ISLAND. GOVERNOR, 1762-1763
By the honourable Samuel Ward . . . A proclamation. Almighty God . . . [Nov. 5, 1762] . . . Providence, William Goddard [1762]
broadside 41 X 32 cm.
Bill submitted by Goddard Nov. 9, 1762
Alden 253
MWA; PPL; RHi (2 copies); RPJCB. Mrs. H. F. Holbrook. Photostat: MHi mp. 41304

B2320 RHODE ISLAND. GOVERNOR, 1762-1763
By the honourable Samuel Ward . . . A proclamation prohibiting the exportation of provisions from this colony . . . [Newport, Ann Franklin and Samuel Hall, 1762]
[broadside?]
Billed August 1762 by Ann Franklin and Hall
Alden 252
No copy known mp. 41305

B2321 RHODE ISLAND. LAWS
An act, in addition to an act . . . providing in case of fire . . . in the town of Newport . . . [Newport, Ann Franklin, 1762]
broadside 30.5 X 18 cm.
Passed at the June 1762 session of the Assembly
Alden 261; Winship p. 17
R mp. 41307

B2322 RHODE ISLAND. LAWS
At the General assembly . . . holden . . . the twenty-first day of September . . . An act for supplying the general treasury . . . Published . . . the thirtieth of September, 1762 . . . [Newport, Ann Franklin and Samuel Hall, 1762]
3 p. 30 cm.
Alden 262; Winship p. 17
RHi; RPB; RPJCB mp. 41306

B2323 RHODE ISLAND. LAWS
[At the General assembly . . . holden . . . the twenty-first day of September . . . An act, in addition to several acts, regulating the manner of admitting freemen . . . Newport, Ann Franklin and Samuel Hall, 1762]
[4?] p. [folio?]
Alden 263; Winship Addenda p. 87
No copy known mp. 41308

B2324 ST. JAMES'S CHURCH, PHILADELPHIA
And this stone which I have set as a pillar, shall be God's house: . . . in the year . . . MDCCLXII. . . . this foundation was laid for . . . St. James's Church . . . Philadelphia, Henry Miller [1762]
broadside oblong 8vo
PPL mp. 41300

B2325 A SERIOUS-comical dialogue between the famous Dr. Seth Hudson, and the noted Joshua How . . . convicted of counterfeiting . . . Boston, Printed and sold by Benjamin Mecom, 1762.
28+ p. 21.5 cm. [A]-C^4 $D^{4?}$
MWA (lacks half-title, p. 9-10, and all after p. 28)
mp. 41309

B2326 SMITH, CALEB, 1723-1762
The various branches of ministerial duty . . . Woodbridge, James Parker, 1762.
1 p. l., 26 p. 19.5 cm.
DLC mp. 41310

B2327 SOUTH CAROLINA. LAWS
Acts of the General assembly . . . passed in the year 1762. Charles-Town, Peter Timothy, 1762.
1 p. l., 49, [1] p. 29 cm.
Sabin 87597
DLC mp. 41312

B2328 SOUTH CAROLINA. LAWS
. . . At a General assembly, begun . . . the sixth day of February . . . Charles-Town, Peter Timothy, 1762.
1 p. l., 30 p. 29 cm.
Half-title: The Tax-act, passed the 29th of May, 1762. With the estimate
Sabin 87598
DLC mp. 40311

B2329 THE South-Carolina almanack . . . for . . . 1763 . . . Charles-Town, Robert Wells [1762]
[48] p. 16.5 cm.
By George Andrews
Sabin 87749
MWA (lacks sig. A2 and F8); ScHi mp. 41254

B2330 [THE South-Carolina and Georgia almanack and register for 1763. Charles-Town, Peter Timothy [1762]]

Advertised in the *South Carolina Gazette*, Nov. 20, 1762
Drake 13087
No copy known

B2331 [THE South-Carolina sheet almanack for . . . 1763. By John Tobler. Charles-Town, Peter Timothy [1762]]
broadside
Advertised in the *South Carolina Gazette*, Nov. 20, 1762
Drake 13088
No copy known

B2332 SPECIMEN of a surprizing performance shortly to be sent to the press: being a scene from a new play call'd the Bully . . . Jethro Plainheart, a Quaker, Tom Swagger. . . . [Boston? John Draper? 1752?]
8 p. 19 cm.
Imprint and date assigned by Clarence S. Brigham
Trumbull 2885
MHi (facsim.); MWA mp. 41313

B2333 [A THEATRICAL playbill for the local theatre. Providence, William Goddard, 1762]
broadside
Evidence from Isaiah Thomas. cf. Alden 265; Winship p. 18
No copy known mp. 41301

B2334 THE triumphant Christian . . . The fifteenth edition. New York, S. Farley, 1762.
40 p. 19.5 cm.
DLC; NN mp. 41315

B2335 TUCKE, JOHN, 1702-1773
The ministers of Christ should be strong in the grace . . . A sermon at the ordination, of . . . John Tucke . . . in Epsom, September 23d, 1761. By his father . . . To which is annexed, the charge by his father, and the right hand of fellowship by the Rev. Mr. Whittemore. Portsmouth, Daniel Fowle [1762]
47 p.
cf. Sibley, VII, 263-265
NHi; NhHi (imperfect); RPJCB mp. 41316

B2336 UNIVERSITY OF PENNSYLVANIA
Viris praecellentissimis, Thomae Penn ac Richardo Penn . . . Catalogus eorum qui . . . in Collegio Philadelphiensi admissi fuerunt . . . [Philadelphia] Typis Henrici Miller [1762]
broadside 55 X 44.5 cm.
PU mp. 41317

B2337 VIRGINIA, COUNCIL
April 1, 1762. To . . . Francis Fauquier . . . the humble address of the Council . . . [Williamsburg, J. Royle, 1762]
broadside 31 X 19.5 cm.
DLC (photostat) mp. 41318

B2338 VIRGINIA. GOVERNOR, 1758-1768
The speech of . . . Francis Fauquier . . . to the General-assembly, summoned to be held . . . the 26th of May . . . 1761, and from thence continued . . . to Tuesday the 2d of November 1762 . . . being the fourth session . . . Williamsburg, Joseph Royle, 1762.
4 p. 26.5 cm.
Sabin 99998
DLC mp. 41319

B2339 VIRGINIA. HOUSE OF BURGESSES
April 1, 1762. To . . . Francis Fauquier . . . the humble address of the House of burgesses . . . [Williamsburg, J. Royle, 1762]
broadside 31 X 19.5 cm.
DLC (photostat) mp. 41320

B2340 A VOICE from the tombs . . . By two eminent authors . . . New York, James Parker, 1762.
12 p. 14.5 cm.
DLC mp. 41321

B2341 WATTS, ISAAC, 1674-1748
The first set of catechisms and prayers . . . The twelfth edition. Boston, S. Kneeland, 1762.
16 p. 16 cm.
DLC; MWA mp. 41322

B2342 WATTS, ISAAC, 1674-1748
Hymns and spititual songs . . . The twentieth edition . . . Boston, Re-printed and sold by Z. Fowle and S. Draper, 1762.
xxiv, 312 p. 15 cm.
MB; MWA mp. 41323

B2343 WE the subscribers, owners, and possessors of wharf in this city . . . [Philadelphia? 1762]
broadside 24 X 21 cm.
Comprises regulations
Dated Feb. 7, 1762
PHi mp. 41326

B2344 WESTMINSTER ASSEMBLY OF DIVINES
The shorter catechism . . . Boston, 1762.
24 p. 14 cm.
New York Public 336
NN mp. 41327

1763

B2345 THE American calendar; or an almanack for . . . 1764 . . . By Philo Copernicus. Philadelphia, Printed and sold by William and Thomas Bradford [1763]
25 p. 17.5 cm.
PHi mp. 41328

B2346 AN astronomical diary: or, Almanack for . . . 1764 . . . By Nathaniel Ames . . . Portsmouth, D. Fowle [1763]
[24] p. 17 cm.
Drake 4621; Nichols p. 85
MB; MWA; NHi; NN; NhHi; VtHi mp. 41329

B2347 AN astronomical diary: or, Almanack for . . . 1764

. . . By Nathaniel Low . . . Boston, R. and S. Draper; Edes & Gill; and Green & Russell; and T. & J. Fleet [1763]
[24] p.
Drake 3140; Nichols: Mass. almanacs, p. 64
ICN; MB; MBAt; MH mp. 41393

B2348 BAPTISTS. PENNSYLVANIA. PHILADELPHIA ASSOCIATION
The original state of thirty Baptist churches whose messengers annually meet in association at Philadelphia . . . The publisher will give a small premium . . . error corrected in this historical table . . . [Philadelphia, 1763]
broadside
Latest date in table: Oct. 11, 1763
cf. Evans 9590
MWA (photostat) mp. 41329a

B2349 BIBLE. O.T. PSALMS
A new version of the Psalms of David . . . By N. Brady . . . and N. Tate . . . Boston, Printed by D. and J. Kneeland, for J. Edwards, 1763.
276, 84 p. 14.5 cm.
MWA; NBuG mp. 41330

B2350 BIBLE. O.T. PSALMS
A new version of the Psalms of David . . . By N. Brady . . . and N. Tate . . . Boston, Printed by D. and J. Kneeland, for Samuel Webb, 1763.
276, 84 p. 14.5 cm.
DLC mp. 41331

B2351 BIBLE. O.T. PSALMS
The Psalms of David, imitated . . . By I. Watts, D.D. The twentyfourth edition. Boston, Printed by D. and J. Kneeland, for Thomas Leverett, 1763.
vi, 304, [25], 22 p. 15 cm.
cf. Evans 9346
MB; MWA (very imperfect) mp. 41423

B2352 BIBLE. O.T. PSALMS
The Psalms of David, imitated . . . By I. Watts, D. D. The twenty-fourth edition. Boston, Printed by D. & J. Kneeland for Wharton and Bowes, 1763.
1 p.l., 304, [23] p. 16 cm.
PHi mp. 41424

B2353 BIBLE. N.T. APOCRYPHAL BOOKS. GOSPEL OF NICODEMUS
Evangelischer Bericht von dem Leben Jesu Christi, welches Nicodemus . . . beschrieben . . . Tubingen, Gedruckt im Jahr 1748, und nun auf Schesnot Hüll [Chestnut-Hill, Nicholas Hasselbach] 1763.
94 p. 16 cm.
MWA

B2354 THE childrens Bible: or, An history of the Holy Scriptures . . . Philadelphia, Reprinted and sold by A Steuart, 1763.
xiv, [15]-224 p. illus. 12 X 10 cm.
"The principles of the Christian religion," p. [129]-158, and "An history of the New Testament," p. [161]-224, have independent title-pages
New York Public 338; Rosenbach-Ch 53
DLC; NN (2 copies, imperfect); PP mp. 41333

B2355 THE child's new play-thing . . . Philadelphia, W. Dunlap, 1763.
136 p. 13 cm.
DLC mp. 41334

B2356 CONCERNING a mother-in-law, blinding her husband, to the undoing of his S[on] in Norton, in the Y[ear] [1]760 . . . Boston, Printed in the year 1763.
broadside 42 X 32.5 cm.
Ballad in 3 columns
MH mp. 41335

B2357 CONNECTICUT. LAWS
At a General Assembly . . . holden at Hartford . . . on the second Thursday of May . . . 1763. On the memorial of the Rev'd Mr. Eleazar Wheelock . . . New London, T. Green [1763]
broadside 33.5 cm.
New York Public 339
NN (facsim.) mp. 41336

2358 DELAWARE. LAWS
Laws of the government of New-Castle, Kent and Sussex, upon Delaware. Vol. I. Wilmington, James Adams, 1763.
363, xvii p. 29.5 cm.
Evans 9375 (Vol. II through p. 81) bound at end
MdBP mp. 41337

B2359 THE fall of Samuel the Squomicutite . . . Tropwen: Printed by desire of the Pumkinites. [Newport? Samuel Hall? 1763]
broadside 29.5 X 18 cm.
Alden 274; Winship p. 19
MB; RHi. Photostats: MWA; NN; RNHi mp. 41339

B2360 THE fall of Samuel the Squomicutite . . . Made public at Tropwen, as a memorial of the deliverance of the Pumkinites. [Providence? William Goddard? 1763?]
broadside 28 X 16.5 cm.
Alden 275; Winship p. 19
RHi; RPJCB. Photostats: MWA; NN mp. 41338

B2361 THE fine bay horse True Briton: six years old . . . belonging to Anthony Waters, covers mares . . . at Capt. Heard's, in Woodbridge . . . [New York, William Weyman? 1763]
broadside 32 X 22 cm.
Originally bound with *Weyman's New York Gazette*, Apr. 18, 1763
New York Public 342
NN mp. 41340

B2362 FORBES, ELI, 1726-1804
Mr. Forbes's two sermons, I. The support of pious parents . . . II. The kingdom of God . . . [Boston, S. Kneeland, 1763]
[4], 27, 27 p.
Each sermon has separate t.p., but collective half-title indicates they were issued together
RPJCB mp. 41341

B2363 FRANKLIN, BENJAMIN, 1706-1790
Tables of the post of all single letters, carried by post in North-America . . . Woodbridge, James Parker, by order of the Post-Master General . . . [1763]
broadside
American Art Assoc. cat. 4125, Nov. 7-8, 1934, item 98
New York Public 343
Signed: B. Franklin. J. Foxcroft
N; Hi; NN (reduced facsim.) mp. 41342

B2364 Deleted.

B2365 GEORGIA. GOVERNOR, 1760-1776
By Governor and Commander in Chief of . . .

Georgia . . . To . . . Given under my hand and seal this By his command. [Savannah, James Johnston, 1763]
broadside 33 X 20.5 cm.
Dated in Johnston's first year of printing from Gov. James Wright's ms. note on Pub. Rec. Office copy
McMurtrie: Georgia 1
Public Record Off.

B2366 GEORGIA. GOVERNOR, 1760-1776
By Governor and Commander in Chief of . . . Georgia . . . Instructions for that in all places . . . you are direct [sic] the Indians to be honest . . . Given under my hand and seal this By his Command. [Savannah, James Johnston, 1763?]
broadside 33 X 19 cm.
Instructions to accompany trading license with Indians (cf. McMurtrie: Georgia 1)
McMurtrie: Georgia 2
Public Record Off.

B2367 GEORGIA. LAWS
. . . An act declaring it high treason to counterfeit . . . March the 7th, 1755. [Savannah, J. Johnston, 1763]
broadside 25.5 X 19 cm.
De Renne p. 149
DLC; GU-De; RPJCB mp. 41344

B2368 GEORGIA. LAWS
. . . An act for amending an act, intituled, An act for the better regulating the town of Savannah . . . the 9th day of June 1761. Assented to, Ja. Wright. [Savannah, J. Johnston, 1763]
2 p. 25.5 cm. caption title
De Renne p. 160
DLC; GU-De; RPJCB mp. 41372

B2369 GEORGIA. LAWS
. . . An act for ascertaining the qualifications of jurors . . . April the 24th, 1760. Assented to, Henry Ellis. [Savannah, J. Johnston, 1763]
6 p. 25.5 cm. caption title
De Renne p. 156
DLC; GU-De; RPJCB mp. 41363

B2370 GEORGIA. LAWS
. . . An act for better regulating the market . . . the 15th day of March, 1758. [Savannah, J. Johnston, 1763]
5 p. 25.5 cm. caption title
De Renne p. 150
DLC; GU-De; RPJCB mp. 41352

B2371 GEORGIA. LAWS
. . . An act for confirming sales of land . . . Feb. the 8th, 1757. [Savannah, J. Johnston, 1763]
broadside 25.5 X 19 cm.
De Renne p. 150
DLC; GU-De; RPJCB mp. 41347

B2372 GEORGIA. LAWS
. . . An act for constituting and dividing . . . the 15th day of March, 1758. [Savannah, J. Johnston, 1763]
7 p. 25.5 cm. caption title
De Renne p. 151
DLC; GU-De; RPJCB mp. 41350

B2373 GEORGIA. LAWS
. . . An act for empowering trustees . . . 24th day of April, 1760. Assented to, Henry Ellis. [Savannah, J. Johnston, 1763]
2 p. 25.5 X 19 cm. caption title
De Renne p. 157
DLC; GU-De; RPJCB mp. 41364

B2374 GEORGIA. LAWS
. . . An act for establishing and regulating of patrols . . . 28th July, 1757. Henry Ellis. [Savannah, J. Johnston, 1763]
5 p. 25.3 cm. caption title
De Renne p. 149
DLC; GU-De; RPJCB mp. 41348

B2375 GEORGIA. LAWS
. . . An act for establishing the method . . . 27th March, 1739. Assented to, Henry Ellis. [Savannah, J. Johnston, 1763]
4 p. 25.5 cm. caption title
De Renne p. 154
DLC; GU-De; RPJCB mp. 41354

B2376 GEORGIA. LAWS
. . . An act for limiting the time . . . the 15th day of March, 1758. [Savannah, J. Johnston, 1763]
3 p. 25.5 cm.
De Renne p. 151
DLC; GU-De; RPJCB mp. 41351

B2377 GEORGIA. LAWS
. . . An act for raising a publick store . . . December the 14th, 1756. [Savannah, J. Johnston, 1763]
broadside 25.5 X 19 cm.
De Renne p. 149
DLC; GU-De; RPJCB mp. 41346

B2378 GEORGIA. LAWS
. . . An act for raising and granting . . . the 9th day of June, 1761. Assented to, Ja. Wright. [Savannah, J. Johnston, 1763]
4 p. 25.5 cm. caption title
De Renne p. 159
DLC; GU-De; RPJCB

B2379 GEORGIA. LAWS
. . . An act for raising and granting . . . 19th December, 1761. Assented to, James Wright. [Savannah, J. Johnston, 1763]
7 p. 25.5 cm. caption title
De Renne p. 160
DLC (facsim.); GU-De; RPJCB mp. 41373

B2380 GEORGIA. LAWS
. . . An act for raising and granting . . . March the 4th, 1762. Assented to, James Wright. [Savannah, J. Johnston, 1763]
3 p. 25.5 cm. caption title
De Renne p. 162
DLC (facsim.); GU-De; RPJCB mp. 41376

B2381 GEORGIA. LAWS
. . . An act for reducing the interest . . . 27th March, 1759. Henry Ellis. [Savannah, J. Johnston, 1763]
broadside 25.5 X 19 cm.
De Renne p. 155
DLC; GU-De; RPJCB mp. 41355

B2382 GEORGIA. LAWS
. . . An act for regulating the assize of bread . . . 12th December, 1758. Henry Ellis. [Savannah, J. Johnston, 1763]
4 p. 25.5 cm. caption title
De Renne p. 152
DLC; GU-De; RPJCB mp. 41356

B2383 GEORGIA. LAWS
. . . An act for stamping . . . the 1st day of May, 1760. Assented to, Henry Ellis. [Savannah, J. Johnston, 1763]

9, [1] p. 25.5 cm. caption title
De Renne p. 157
DLC; GU-De; RPJCB mp. 41365

B2384 GEORGIA. LAWS
. . . An act for subjecting and making liable . . . 9th June, 1761. Assented to, James Wright. [Savannah, J. Johnston, 1763]
6 p. 25.5 cm. caption title
De Renne p. 159
DLC; GU-De; RPJCB mp. 41374

B2385 GEORGIA. LAWS
. . . An act for the better regulating fences . . . 27th day of March, 1759. Henry Ellis. [Savannah, J. Johnston, 1763]
2 p. 25.5 X 19 cm. caption title
De Renne p. 153
DLC; GU-De; RPJCB mp. 41357

B2386 GEORGIA. LAWS
. . . An act for the better regulating taverns, punch-houses, and retailers of spirituous liquors . . . Assented to the 27th day of March 1759. Henry Ellis. [Savannah, James Johnston, 1763]
4 p. 25.5 cm. caption title
De Renne p. 153; Huntington 248; New York Public 365
CSmH; DLC; GU-De; NN (photostat); RPJCB
mp. 41358

B2387 GEORGIA. LAWS
. . . An act for the better regulating the town of Savannah . . . the 1st day of May, 1760. Assented to, Henry Ellis. [Savannah, J. Johnston, 1763]
3 p. 25.5 cm. caption title
De Renne p. 158
DLC; GU-De; RPJCB mp. 41366

B2388 GEORGIA. LAWS
. . . An act for the more easy and speedy recovery of small debts . . . 24th day of April, 1760. Assented to, Henry Ellis. [Savannah, J. Johnston, 1763]
7 p. 25.5 cm. caption title
De Renne p. 156
DLC; GU-De; RPJCB mp. 41367

B2389 GEORGIA. LAWS
. . . An act for the repairing of Christ-Church in Savannah . . . Assented to the 27th day of March, 1759. Henry Ellis. [Savannah, J. Johnston, 1763]
4 p. 25.5 cm. caption title
"An act to prevent the building wooden chimnies:" p. 2–4
De Renne p. 154–155
DLC; GU-De; RPJCB mp. 41359

B2390 GEORGIA. LAWS
. . . An act inflicting and imposing penalties . . . Council-chamber, 17th Feb. 1755. [Savannah, J. Johnston, 1763]
broadside 25.5 X 19.5 cm.
De Renne p. 148
DLC; GU-De; RPJCB mp. 41345

B2391 GEORGIA. LAWS
. . . An act intituled, An act to oblige the male white persons . . . 28th July, 1757. Henry Ellis. [Savannah, J. Johnston, 1763]
broadside 25.5 X 19 cm.
De Renne p. 150
DLC; GU-De; RPJCB mp. 41349

B2392 GEORGIA. LAWS
. . . An act to amend an act, intituled, An act to prevent masters . . . the 1st day of May, 1760. Assented to, Henry Ellis. [Savannah, J. Johnston, 1763]
broadside 25.5 X 19 cm.
De Renne p. 158
DLC; GU-De; RPJCB mp. 41368

B2393 GEORGIA. LAWS
. . . An act to amend and continue an act, intituled, An act for establishing and regulating of controls . . . the 1st day of May, 1760. Assented to, Henry Ellis. [Savannah, J. Johnston, 1763]
broadside 25.5 X 19 cm.
De Renne p. 158
DLC; GU-De; RPJCB mp. 41369

B2394 GEORGIA. LAWS
. . . An act to ascertain the manner and form of electing . . . the 9th day of June, 1761. Assented to, James Wright. [Savannah, J. Johnston, 1763]
4 p. 25.5 cm. caption title
De Renne p. 160
DLC; GU-De; RPJCB mp. 41375

B2395 GEORGIA. LAWS
. . . An act to enable feme coverts to convey . . . 24th April, 1760. Assented to, Henry Ellis. [Savannah, J. Johnston, 1763]
2 p. 25.5 X 19 cm. caption title
De Renne p. 156
DLC; GU-De; RPJCB mp. 41370

B2396 GEORGIA. LAWS
. . . An act to explain and amend an act, intituled, An act for better regulating the market . . . the 27th day of March, 1759. Henry Ellis. [Savannah, J. Johnston, 1763]
broadside 25.5 X 19 cm.
De Renne p. 152
DLC; GU-De; RPJCB mp. 41360

B2397 GEORGIA. LAWS
. . . An act to explain and amend an act, intituled, An act for the more easy . . . 4th March, 1762. Assented to, James Wright. [Savannah, J. Johnston, 1763]
2 p. 25.5 X 19 cm. caption title
De Renne p. 162
DLC; GU-De; RPJCB mp. 41377

B2398 GEORGIA. LAWS
. . . An act to oblige ships . . . 24th April, 1760. Assented to, Henry Ellis. [Savannah, J. Johnston, 1763]
3 p. 25.5 cm. caption title
De Renne p. 155; Guerra a-339
DLC (facsim.); GU-De; RPJCB mp. 41371

B2399 GEORGIA. LAWS
. . . An act to prevent masters of vessels . . . 27th March, 1759. Henry Ellis. [Savannah, J. Johnston, 1763]
4 p. 25.5 cm. caption title
De Renne p. 154
DLC; GU-De; RPJCB mp. 41362

B2400 GEORGIA. LAWS
. . . An act to prevent private persons . . . 15th February, 1758. [Savannah, J. Johnston, 1763]
2 p. 25.5 X 19 cm. caption title
De Renne p. 151
DLC; GU-De; RPJCB mp. 41353

B2401 GEORGIA. LAWS
. . . An act to prevent stealing . . . the 27th day of March, 1759. Henry Ellis. [Savannah, J. Johnston, 1763]
4 p. 25.5 cm. caption title
De Renne p. 152
DLC; GU-De; RPJCB mp. 41361

B2402 GEORGIA. LAWS
Acts passed . . . at a session begun . . . the 11th day of November . . . 1761 . . . and from thence continued . . . to the 4th day of March, 1762, being the second session . . . Savannah, James Johnston [1763]
18 p. 25.5 cm.
De Renne p. 161
DLC; GU-De; RPJCB mp. 41381

B2403 GEORGIA. LAWS
Acts passed . . . at a session begun . . . the 11th day of November . . . 1761 . . . and from thence continued . . . to the 7th day of April, 1763, being the second session . . . Savannah, James Johnston [1763]
1 p.l., 23, [1] p. 25.5 cm.
De Renne p. 163; Guerra a-341
DLC; GU-De; RPJCB mp. 41382

B2404 GEORGIA. LAWS
. . . A bill, intituled, An Act for granting . . . April the 7th, 1763. Assented to, James Wright. [Savannah, J. Johnston, 1763]
8 p. 25.5 cm.
De Renne p. 165
DLC (facsim.); GU-De; RPJCB mp. 41379

B2405 GEORGIA. LAWS
A bill intituled an act to empower commissioners to sell . . . [Savannah, J. Johnston, 1763]
broadside 29 X 19.5 cm. caption title
DLC (facsim.) mp. 41380

B2406 GEORGIA. LAWS
[Bill to impower commissioners to lay out lots . . . at the west end . . . of Savan]nah and to dispose thereof, and pay the money . . . into the hands of the public treasurer . . . [Savannah] Printed by order of the Honourable the Commons House of Assembly. [1763]
broadside 27.5 X 19 cm.
Introduced Mar. 16, 1763, and defeated Mar. 30 on the third reading
GHi (imperfect)

B2407 THE Georgia and South-Carolina almanack for . . . 1764 . . . Savannah, James Johnston [1763]
[22+] p.
By John Tobler
Drake 1551
MHi

B2408 GOFFE, JOHN
Province of New-Hampshire. Whereas application hath this day been made to me the subscriber, one of His Majesty's justices of the peace . . . This is therefore to notify . . . the owners and proprietors . . . to meet . . . the twenty six day of April . . . Bedford, April 2d 1763. John Goffe . . . [n.p., 1763]
broadside 9.5 X 9.5 cm.
MWA mp. 41383

B2409 GT. BRIT. SOVEREIGNS (GEORGE III)
By the King, a proclamation, declaring the cessation of arms . . . [Colophon] London, Mark Baskett, 1762; Annapolis, Reprinted by Jonas Green, 1763.
broadside 24.5 X 14.5 cm.
Huntington 249; Wroth 244
CSmH; Md (not traced) mp. 41384

B2410 GT. BRIT. SOVEREIGNS (GEORGE III)
His Majesty's instructions to all the governours of his provinces in America . . . [Charleston, S.C., 1763]
broadside 25 X 31.5 cm.
Concerns observance of Indian treaties
Dated at Charlestown, July 4, 1763
New York Public 344
NN (photostat) mp 41385

B2411 HALL, DAVID, 1714-1772
Imported in the last vessels from Europe, and sold by David Hall . . . Philadelphia, the following books, &c. [Philadelphia, D. Hall, 1763]
[2] p. 33 cm. caption title
In two columns
Originally bound in 1763 vol. of the *Pennsylvania Gazette*, after the issue for Nov. 23
New York Public 345
NN mp. 41386

B2412 HARVARD UNIVERSITY
Quaestiones pro modulo . . . MDCCLXIII. [Boston] R. & S. Draper [1763]
broadside
MHi; MWA mp. 41387

B2413 HOPKINS, ESEK
To the public. Injustice, under whatever form . . . Providence, April 2, 1763. Esek Hopkins . . . [Providence, 1763]
broadside 34.5 X 15 cm.
Alden 278; Winship p. 19
RHi. Photostats: MWA; NN mp. 41388

B2414 HOPKINS, STEPHEN, 1707-1785
To the freemen of the colony. Gentlemen, Mr. Ward and his friends . . . Stephen Hopkins. Providence, April 19, 1763. [Providence, William Goddard, 1763]
broadside 22.5 X 17 cm.
Alden 279; Winship p. 19
RHi. Photostats: MWA; NN mp. 41389

B2415 [HOPKINSON, FRANCIS] 1737-1791
A second edition [with necessary improvements, which now render the sense entirely plain] of The lawfulness . . . of instrumental music, in the public worship of God . . . Philadelphia, Andrew Steuart, 1763.
16 p. 15.5 cm.
Bartlett p. 99
DLC; NHi mp. 41390

B2416 [INGLIS, JOHN]
The little book open . . . predicting and declaring the coming of the expected Redeemer . . . Philadelphia, Printed [by William Dunlap] for the author, 1763.
3 p.l., L [i.e., xlvi], 281 [i.e. 285], [1] p. folded plate. 21.5 cm.
DLC; MWA; PPL mp. 41391

B2417 A LETTER from a solicitous mother, to her only son, both living in New-England. Boston, Re-printed, and sold by D. & J. Kneeland, 1763.
12 p. 16.5 cm. A^6
MWA mp. 41392

B2418 MARYLAND. GOVERNOR, 1753-1769
By His Excellency Horatio Sharpe . . . A proclamation.

Whereas His Majesty's royal commands . . . [Feb. 11, 1763] . . . [Annapolis, Jonas Green, 1763]
broadside 24.5 X 14.5 cm.
Huntington 250; Wroth 245
CSmH; Md (not traced) mp. 41394

B2419 MASSACHUSETTS. GOVERNOR, 1760-1769
By His Excellency Francis Bernard . . . A proclamation for proroguing the General Court [to Nov. 23] . . . [Sept. 10, 1763] . . . Boston, Richard Draper, 1763.
broadside 30 X 18.5 cm.
Ford 1301
MSaE mp. 41395

B2420 MASSACHUSETTS. LAWS
. . . An act passed . . . for granting . . . duties . . . [May 26, 1762] . . . Boston, R. Draper, 1763.
7 p.
MWA mp. 41396

B2421 MASSACHUSETTS. LAWS
. . . Acts and laws, passed by the . . . General Court . . . begun and held . . . the twenty-sixth day of May, 1762, and continued . . . to Wednesday the twelfth of January following . . . [Colophon] Boston, S. Kneeland, 1763.
p. 551-561. 28.5 cm. caption title
DLC; MH. Photostat: NN mp. 41397

B2422 MASSACHUSETTS. TREASURER
(No. 5.) To Your province tax. Lawful money. Your town and county rate. Lawful money . . . 1763. [Boston, 1763]
broadside
Ford 1307
Private collection

B2423 MASSACHUSETTS. TREASURER
Province of the Massachusetts-Bay. The honourable Harrison Gray, Esq; Treasurer . . . November 21, 1763. [Boston, 1763]
broadside
Tax warrant
Ford 1304
MSaE mp. 41398

B2424 MOODY, SAMUEL, 1676-1747.
Mr. Moody's discourse to little children. The third edition. Boston, Printed and sold by S. Kneeland, 1763.
22, [1] p. 12 cm. A^8B^4
MWA mp. 41399

B2425 NEW HAMPSHIRE. GOVERNOR, 1741-1767
By . . . Benning Wentworth . . . a proclamation, for a general thanksgiving . . . [July 28, 1763] . . . [Portsmouth, D. Fowle, 1763]
broadside 38.5 X 32 cm.
DLC. Photostat: NhHi mp. 41400

B2426 NEW HAMPSHIRE. GOVERNOR, 1741-1767
By . . . Benning Wentworth . . . a proclamation, for a general thanksgiving . . . [November 9, 1763] . . . Portsmouth, D. Fowle [1763]
broadside 37.5 X 30 cm.
DLC. Photostat: NhHi mp. 41401

B2427 NEW HAMPSHIRE. TREASURER
Treasurer's warrant. Province of New-Hampshire. To the select-men of in the province of New-Hampshire, for the year current, A.D. 1763 . . . [Portsmouth, D. Fowle, 1763]
broadside 38 X 31.5 cm.
DLC; NhHi. Photostat: MHi mp. 41402

B2428 NEW JERSEY. LAWS
Anno regni, Georgii III . . . tertio. At a session of General Assembly . . . Perth-Amboy, May 25, 1763 . . . till the third day of June following. Being the seventh session of the twentieth assembly . . . Woodbridge, James Parker, 1763.
19, [1] p. 30 cm.
Humphrey 70
Nj; NjHi. Public Record Off. mp. 41403

B2429 THE new universal pocket almanack for . . . 1764 . . . New-York, W. Weyman [1763]

Advertised in the *New-York Gazette,* Nov. 28, 1763
Drake 5754
No copy known

B2430 NEW YORK. GOVERNOR, 1763-1765
By . . . Cadwallader Colden . . . To You are hereby authorized and impowered . . . December, 1763. [New York, W. Weyman, 1763]
broadside 32 X 21 cm.
DLC mp. 41404

B2431 PENNSYLVANIA. GOVERNOR, 1763-1777
By the honourable John Penn . . . a proclamation. Whereas I have received information . . . [Dec. 22, 1763] . . . Philadelphia, B. Franklin, and D. Hall [1763]
broadside 41.5 X 32.5 cm.
Adams: Pennsylvania 21
DLC; PU mp. 41405

B2432 THE Pennsylvania town and country-man's almanack, for the year . . . 1764 . . . By John Tobler, Esq; Germantown, C. Sower; to be had in Philadelphia of William Willson, also of Jonathan Zane [1763]
[36] p. 16 cm.
DLC mp. 41416

B2433 THE pleasures of a single life . . . Philadelphia, Andrew Steuart, 1763.
16 p. 15.5 cm.
DLC mp. 41406

B2434 PLYMOUTH PROPRIETORS
Advertisement. The proprietors of the Kennebeck Purchase from the late Colony of New-Plymouth . . . May 18, 1763 . . . David Jeffries, Proprietors clerk. [Boston, 1763]
broadside 33.5 X 21.5 cm.
Ford 1294
MWA; PHi mp. 41407

B2435 REFORMED CHURCH IN THE U.S.
Catechismus, oder kurtzer Unterricht Christlicher Lehre . . . Heydelberg, Gedruckt im Jahr 1751. Und nun suf Schesnot-Hill [Chestnut-Hill, Nicolaus Hasselbach] 1763.
[96] p. $A\text{-}H^6$
Metzger 246; Rosenbach-Ch 52
PP mp. 41409

B2436 RHODE ISLAND. ELECTION PROX.
Honorable Samuel Ward, Esq; Governor. Honorable Elisha Brown, Esq; Dep. Governor . . . [Newport? Samuel Hall? 1763?]
broadside 23 X 13 cm.
Alden 284; Chapin Proxies 3
RHi mp. 41409

B2437 RHODE ISLAND. GOVERNOR, 1763-1765
By the honorable Stephen Hopkins . . . A proclamation. The burthens and calamities . . . [Aug. 8, 1763] . . . Providence, William Goddard [1763]

broadside 33 X 22 cm.
Alden 285; Winship p. 19
PPL; RHi. Photostats: MWA; NN mp. 41410

B2438 RHODE ISLAND. LAWS
At the General assembly . . . holden . . . the first Monday in August . . . An act for assessing . . . a rate or tax of twelve twelve thousand pounds . . . Newport, S. Hall [1763]
3 p. 30 cm.
Alden 292; Winship p. 18
RHi mp. 41411

B2439 RUSSEL, ROBERT, of Wadhurst, Sussex
Seven sermons . . . The fifty-first edition. Philadelphia, Printed and sold by Andrew Steuart, 1763.
164, [4] p. 13.5 cm. [A]-G^{12}
MWA mp. 41412

B2440 THE South-Carolina and Georgia almanack, for the year . . . 1764 . . . By John Tobler, Esq; . . . Savannah, James Johnston [1763]
[24] p. 16.5 cm.
De Renne p. 166; Drake 1552
DLC; GU-De mp. 41417

B2441 A TABLE of the value of the following lawful money bills . . . Providence, William Goddard [ca. 1763]
broadside 33 X 20.5 cm.
Date assigned by Lawrence C. Wroth
Alden 294; Winship p. 19; Winship Addenda p. 87
RHi; RPJCB. Photostats: MWA; NN mp. 41413

B2442 TAYLOR, GEORGE
To the freeholders of the county of Providence. Though, in a legal sense . . . Geo. Taylor. Providence, April 11, 1763. [Providence, William Goddard, 1763]
broadside 36.5 X 24 cm.
Alden 295
RPJCB. Photostat: MWA mp. 41414

B2443 THOMPSON, JOHN
The lost and undone son of perdition . . . Boston, Printed and sold at the Printing Office, in Marlboro-Street [Z. Fowle], 1763.
20, [2] p.
RPJCB mp. 41415

B2444 VIRGINIA. COUNCIL
May 20, 1763. To . . . Francis Fauquier . . . the humble address of the Council . . . [Williamsburg, J. Royle, 1763]
broadside 31 X 18 cm.
DLC (photostat) mp. 41418

B2445 VIRGINIA. GOVERNOR, 1758-1768
The speech of . . . Francis Fauquier . . . to the General-assembly, summoned to be held . . . the 26 of May . . . 1761, and from thence continued . . . to Thursday the 19th of May, 1763 . . . being the fifth session . . . Williamsburg, Joseph Royle, 1763.
4 p. 31 cm.
DLC (photostat) mp. 41419

B2446 VIRGINIA. HOUSE OF BURGESSES
May 21, 1763. To . . . Francis Fauquier . . . the humble address of the House of burgesses . . . [Williamsburg, J. Royle, 1763]
2 p. 31 X 18 cm.
DLC (photostat) mp. 41420

B2447 VIRGINIA. LAWS
. . . At a General assembly, begun . . . the 26th of May . . . 1761, and from thence continued . . . to Thursday the 19th of May, 1763 . . . being the fifth session . . . [Williamsburg, William Hunter, 1763]
9 p. 34.5 cm. caption title
NYPL 352; Sabin 100270; Torrence 308
DLC; NN; NNB; PHi mp. 41421

B2448 [WANTON, JOSEPH]
Observations and reflections on the present state of . . . Rhode-Island . . . [Newport, Samuel Hall, 1763]
4 p. 29 cm. caption title
Signed at end: Joseph Wanton. Newport, April 15, 1763
Alden 296
MHi; RHi; PPL mp. 41422

B2449 WELD, EDMUND, 1631-1668
A dialogue between Death, Soul, Body and Jesus Christ. Composed by Edmund Weld . . . [at end] Boston, Printed and sold by Z. Fowle, 1763.
broadside 34.5 X 21.5 cm.
MWA mp. 41425

B2450 WING, improv'd. An almanack; for . . . 1764. By W. Wing. New-York, Samuel Brown [1763]
[40] p. 15.5 cm.
Drake 5760
MWA mp. 41426

1764

B2451 ADDRESS to the voters of Philadelphia, Oct. 1, 1764. [Philadelphia, 1764]
8vo
Metzger 259; Sabin 61442
No copy located mp. 41427

B2452 ADVICE to youths, to which is added a short sketch, and a warning to scolding wives: written by a young woman in Philadelphia, for the good of such sex. [Philadelphia] Printed by Anthony Armbruster, 1764.
8 p. 8vo
Imprint is part of caption title
Adams: Pennsylvania 22
PU

B2453 AMERICAN mock-bird, or songster's delight . . . New-York, Printed by S. Brown, and sold by Garret Noel, 1764.
216, viii p.
MWA mp. 41428

B2454 [APPLETON, NATHANIEL] 1693-1784
The Crhistian's daily practice of piety . . . Hartford [1764]
8 p.
RPJCB mp. 41429

B2455 BIBLE. O.T. PSALMS
The New-England Psalter: or, Psalms of David . . . Boston, Printed by D. and J. Kneeland, for S. Webb, 1764.
158 p. 15.5 cm.
cf. Evans 9603
MB mp. 41430

B2456 BIBLE. N.T.
Das Neue Testament . . . verteutscht von D. Martin Luther . . . Fünfte auflage. Germantown, Christoph Saur, 1764.
529, [5] p. 16.5 cm.
Huntington 253
CSmH; MdBP; PHi mp. 41431

B2457 [BLAND, RICHARD] 1710-1776
The Colonel dismounted . . . By Common Sense . . . [Williamsburg, J. Royle, 1764]
1 p.l., 30, xxvii p. 18.5 cm. [A]-G^4
Adams 1
DLC; MWA mp. 41432

B2458 BOSTON EVENING POST.
The news-boy's Christmas and New-Year's verses . . . December 31, 1764 . . . [Boston, T. & J. Fleet, 1764]
broadside 29.5 X 17.5 cm.
Wegelin 681
DLC mp. 41477

B2459 BRADFORD, WILLIAM, 1719-1791
William Bradford, printer, bookseller, and stationer, at his store adjoining the London Coffee-House, has imported a collection of books . . . [Philadelphia, 1764?]
broadside 36 X 23.5 cm.
1764 earliest date at above address
NN mp. 41433

B2460 BUELL, SAMUEL, 1716-1798
A copy of a letter from the Rev. Mr. Buell . . . to the Rev. Mr. Barber, of Groton in Connecticut . . . [at end Mar. 17, 1764. [New London? 1764]
8 p. 15 cm.
Huntington 255
CSmH; CtHi; MWA mp. 41434

B2461 BUY the truth, and sell it not . . . Providence, [William Goddard?] 1764.
broadside 36 X 25.5 cm.
Alden 300; Winship p. 20
RHi. Photostats: MHi; MWA; NN mp. 41435

B2462 CATÉCHISME pour la Province de la Loüisianne . . . rédigé par le R. F. Hilaire . . . Supérieur Général de la Mission des Capucins . . . vû par nous . . . Commandant Général . . . permettons que l'impression en soit faite . . . Nlle. Orléans [Dec. 24, 1764] Signé Dabbadie. [New Orleans, 1764?]

Title taken from order of council suppressing the book
McMurtrie: New Orleans 2
No copy known mp. 41436

B2463 CHURCH'S COVE LOTTERY
Scheme of the second class of a lottery, granted by the General Assembly . . . of Rhode-Island . . . February, A.D. 1763, for raising six thousand pounds . . . for the building a wharf at . . . Church's Cove, in Little-Compton . . . [Newport? 1764]
broadside 21 X 17 cm.
MWA (photostat). Philip G. Nordell, Ambler, Pa. (1960) mp. 41437

B2464 CUNNINGHAM, WADDEL, defendant
The report of an action of assault, battery and wounding, tried in the Supreme Court of Judicature for . . . New-York, in the term of October 1764, between Thomas Forsey, plaintiff, and Waddel Cunningham, defendant. New-York, John Holt, 1764.
68 p.
cf. Evans 9660 (23 p.)
CSmH mp. 41438

B2465 DAVYS, P.
Adminiculum puerile . . . Dublin Printed: Philadelphia Re-printed by W. Dunlap, 1764.
[9], 105, [45] p.
PPL mp. 41439

B2466 DILWORTH, THOMAS, d. 1780
A new guide to the English tongue . . . Boston, Printed by D. and J. Kneeland, for Samuel Webb, 1764.
xii, [6], 160+ p. 16 cm. A^8 $B^{8?}$ C-L^8 $M^{8?}$
MWA (sig. B3-6, L2-7, and all after M1 wanting) mp. 41440

B2467 ELWOOD, THOMAS, 1639-1713
Davideis: the life of David, king of Israel . . . The seventh edition, corrected . . . Wilmington, Reprinted and sold by James Adams, 1764.
vi, 160 p., 1 l. 17.5 cm.
New York Public 354
MWA; NN (imperfect) mp. 41441

B2468 FRANCE. SOVEREIGNS (LOUIS XV)
Extrait de la lettre du roi, a M. Dabbadie . . . commandant . . . a La Louisianne. [Nouvelle Orléans] Denis Braud [1764]
broadside 42 X 28 cm.
Dated: le 21. Avril 1764
McMurtrie: New Orleans 1; New York Public 355
CU-B. Photostat: NN. Facsims.: MWA: PHi mp. 41442

B2469 Deleted.

B2470 GEORGIA. LAWS
. . . An act for granting . . . 29th February, 1764. Assented to, James Wright. [Savannah, J. Johnston, 1764]
8 p. 25.5 cm. caption title
De Renne p. 169
DLC (facsim.); GU-De; RPJCB mp. 41444

B2471 GEORGIA. LAWS
Acts passed by the General assembly . . . at a session begun . . . the 21st day of November . . . 1763 . . . and from thence continued . . . to the 29th day of February 1764, being the third session . . . Savannah, James Johnston [1764]
28 p. 25.5 cm.
De Renne p. 168
DLC; GU-De; RPJCB mp. 41445

B2472 GEORGIA. LAWS
Acts passed . . . at a session begun . . . the 26th day of May . . . 1764 . . . and from thence continued . . . to the 29th day of May 1764, being the fourth session . . . Savannah, James Johnston [1764]
5 p. 25.5 cm.
De Renne p. 170
DLC; GU-De; RPJCB mp. 41446

B2473 GESSNER, SALOMON, 1730-1787
The death of Abel . . . Attempted from the German of Mr. Gessner. Boston, Printed for, and sold by John Perkins, 1764.
129 p. 16.5 cm. A-L^6
CtHi; MWA mp. 41447

B2474 GODDARD, WILLIAM, 1739-1817
Providence, (Tuesday morning) September 25, 1764. Madam . . . I take the liberty to request you to make one at a petticoat frisk . . . William Goddard. [Providence, W. Goodard, 1764]

broadside 27 X 19.5 cm.
Alden 301
RHi. Photostat: MWA mp. 41448

B2475 GT. BRIT. LAWS
. . . At the Parliament begun . . . the nineteenth day of May . . . 1761 . . . and from thence continued . . . to the fifteenth day of November 1763 . . . Charlestown, Robert Wells [1764]
[24] p. 25 cm.
DLC mp. 41449

B2476 THE history of the Holy Jesus . . . By a lover of their precious souls. The tenth edition, with addition [sic]. Boston, Printed and sold by Z. Fowle, 1764.
[48] p. 10.5 cm. [A]-C^8
MWA (t.p. and end leaves wanting). d'Alté A. Welch, Cleveland (1964) ([A]1, C8 and covers wanting)
mp. 41450

B2477 HOPKINS, STEPHEN, 1707-1785
The importance of the following intelligence . . . Your Majesty's most humble petitioners. Thus stand the facts . . . Stephen Hopkins. Providence, April 12, 1764. [Providence, April 12, 1764. [Providence? William Goddard? 1764]
broadside 31 X 21.5 cm.
Alden 303; Winship Addenda p. 87
PPL mp. 4145

B2478 INHUMAN cruelty or villany detected. Being a true relation of the . . . intended murder of a bastard child belonging to John and Ann Richardson, of Boston . . . for which crime . . . both . . . sentenc'd to set on the gallows . . . [n.p., 1764]
broadside 37 X 23.5 cm.
Winslow 43
PHi

B2479 JOHNES, TIMOTHY, 1717-1794
The following is the copy of a letter from the Reverend Mr. Johnes of Morris-Town . . . to the Rev. Mr. Barber of Groton . . . dated November 25th, 1764 . . . [n.p., 1764?]
3 p. 16.5 cm.
CtHi; MWA mp. 41452

B2480 A JUST and impartial representation of a very illegal procedure of Mr. Henry Ward . . . A Lover of Justice. Wickford, N. Kingstown, April 11, 1764. [Providence, William Goddard, 1764]
broadside 40 X 26 cm.
Alden 303A
RHi mp. 41453

B2481 [KINNERSLEY, EBENEZER] 1711-1778
A course of experiments in . . . electricity; accompanied with lectures on electric fire. By William Johnson [pseud.]. New-York, H. Gaine, 1764.
8 p.
RPJCB mp. 41454

B2482 LETTRE d'un officier de la Louisiane a M*** commissaire de la marine a ***. Nouvelle Orleans [Denis Braud?] 1764.
45 leaves 8vo [ ]^1 A-E^8 F^4
cf. H. V. Jones cat., *Adventures in Americana,* 1928, no. 176
MWA (t.p. only, photostat) mp. 41455

B2483 LUTHER, MARTIN, 1483-1546
Der kleine Catechismus . . . Fünfte und vermehrete Auflage. Philadelphia, Gedruckt und zu haben bey Anton Armbruster, 1764.
[4], 139, [1] p. 12mo
PPL mp. 41456

B2484 MARYLAND. LAWS
Acts of Assembly . . . passed at a session . . . begun . . . the fourth day of October . . . 1763 . . . Annapolis, Jonas Green [1764]
[74] p. 34.5 cm.
Wroth 249
MdBP; MdHi mp. 41457

B2485 MARYLAND. LAWS
13 Frederick Lord Baltimore. At a session . . . held . . . the fourth day of October . . . 1763, and ended the 26th November, the following laws were enacted . . . [Colophon] Annapolis, Jonas Green [1764]
[50] p. 33.5 cm.
Wroth 250
MdHi mp. 41458

B2486 THE Maryland almanack, for the year . . . 1765 . . . Annapolis, Jonas Green [1764]
[20] p. 19 cm.
Wroth 252
DLC mp. 41459

B2487 MASON, JOHN, 1706-1763
Serious advice to youth . . . Recommended by the Rev. I. Watts, D.D. Boston, Printed and sold by Fowle at his Printing-Office in Back-Street, 176[4?]
16 p. 16 cm. [A]-B^4
MWA mp. 41460

B2488 MASSACHUSETTS. HOUSE OF REPRESENTATIVES
A journal of the honourable House of Representatives . . . begun . . . at Boston . . . Wednesday the twenty-fifth day of May . . . 1763 [-4 Feb. 1764] . . . [Boston, Green and Russell, 1764]
p. 117-164, 157-275. fol. caption title
Not Evans 9438, but expanded text with duplicate pagination
PHi

B2489 MASSACHUSETTS. LAWS
. . . An act, passed . . . by the . . . General Court . . . begun . . . [May 25, 1763] . . . [Colophon] Boston, Richard Draper, 1764.
8 p.
Import act
cf. Evans 9433
MWA mp. 41461

B2490 MASSACHUSETTS. LAWS
A bill, now pending in the House of Representatives, and published by their order, . . . intituled, An act for regulating the whale fishery . . . [Boston, 1764]
[3] p. 34 cm.
cf. H.R. Journal, Nov. 3, 1764
Ford 1317
MHi mp. 41461

B2491 MASSACHUSETTS. TREASURER
Province of Massachusetts-Bay, ss. The honourable Harrison Gray, Esq; Treasurer . . . [Nov. 1, 1764] . . . [Boston, 1764]
broadside 38.5 X 31.5 cm.
Tax warrant
MHi mp. 41463

B2492 MR. Weatherwise's pocket alamanack for . . . 1765. By A. Weatherwise. Philadelphia, W. Dunlap [1764]

[24] p.
Drake 9874
Milton Drake, NYC (1964)

B2493 MURRAY, JOHN, 1742-1793
An extract of a letter from Mr. John Murray . . . at New-York, to the Rev. Mr. Moorhead, in Boston; dated June 6, 1764 . . . [Boston? 1764?]
3 p. 16 cm. B^2
CtHi; MHi; MWA mp. 41464

B2494 THE New-England primer enlarged . . . Germantown, Printed and sold by Christopher Sower, 1764.
10+ p.
Heartman 20; Metzger 265
Hetrich (1922; Heartman) mp. 41466

B2495 THE New-England primer enlarged . . . Philadelphia, Printed and sold by B. Franklin and D. Hall, 1764.
[78] p.
Curtis 696; Heartman 19
CtY mp. 41467

B2496 THE New-England primer improved . . . Boston, Printed for Wharton & Bowes, 1764.
[80] p. [A]-E^8
Heartman 18; Huntington 257
CSmH mp. 41465

B2497 NEW HAMPSHIRE. GOVERNOR, 1741-1767.
By his excellency Benning Wentworth . . . A proclamation . . . [Mar. 13, 1764] . . . [Colophon] Portsmouth, Daniel Fowle [1764]
broadside
Concerns the western boundary of New Hampshire
Whittemore 78
NhHi. Photostat: MWA mp. 41470

B2498 NEW HAMPSHIRE. GOVERNOR, 1741-1767
By his excellency Benning Wentworth . . . a proclamation for a general fast . . . [Mar. 31, 1764] . . . Portsmouth, Daniel Fowle [1764]
broadside 37.5 X 30.5 cm.
DLC; NhHi mp. 41468

B2499 NEW HAMPSHIRE. GOVERNOR, 1741-1767
By his excellency Benning Wentworth . . . A proclamation for a general thanksgiving [Nov. 8, 1764] . . . [Oct. 29, 1764] . . . [Portsmouth, 1764]
broadside 36.5 X 30 cm.
Whittemore 80
NhHi mp. 41469

B2500 NEW HAMPSHIRE. TREASURER
Treasurer's warrant. Province of New-Hampshire. To the select-men of in the Province of New-Hampshire, for the year . . . 1764 . . . Dated at Portsmouth . . . the day of May . . . 1764 . . . [Portsmouth, 1764]
broadside 37.5 X 31 cm.
MWA mp. 41471

B2501 NEW JERSEY. LAWS
Anno regni Georgii III . . . quarto. At a session of General Assembly, began at Burlington, November 15, 1763 . . . till the 7th day of December following. Being the eighth session of the twentieth assembly . . . Woodbridge, James Parker, 1764.
74, [2] p. 30 cm.
Humphrey 73
Nj. Public Record Off. mp. 41472

B2502 NEW JERSEY. LAWS
Anno regni, Georgii III . . . quarto. At two sessions of General Assembly . . . Perth-Amboy, February 14, 1764 . . . till the 23d . . . Being the ninth and tenth sessions of the twentieth assembly . . . Woodbridge, James Parker, 1764.
40 p. 30 cm.
Humphrey 74
Nj. Public Record Off. mp. 41473

B2503 A NEW Year's wish, a Happy Year to my generous customers. Boston, January 1, 1764. [Boston, 1764]
broadside
Ford 1333
PHi mp. 41474

B2504 NEW YORK. LAWS
. . . [Laws of New York] The twenty-first assembly. Fourth session. [Colophon] New York, W. Weyman, 1764.
p. 309-353 [i.e., 357 35.5 cm. caption title
Running title: Laws of New-York . . .
DLC; NNS mp. 41475

B2505 NEW YORK. LAWS
[Laws of New York. Passed Oct. 20, 1764. New York, W. Weyman, 1764]
p. 359-407. 35.5 cm.
Running title: Laws of New York . . .
DLC; NNS mp. 41476

B2506 [OSBORNE, SARAH (HAGGAR)] 1714-1796
The nature, certainty, and evidence of true Christianity: in a letter from a gentlewoman in New-England . . . Newport, S. Hall, MDCCLIV [i.e. 1764?]
15 p. 18 cm.
Samuel Hall started printing in Newport in 1763
Alden 305; Winship Addenda p. 96
RHi; RNHi mp. 41478

B2507 PARKER, JAMES, 1714-1770
Conductor generalis: or, the office, duty and authority of justices of the peace . . . Woodbridge, in New-Jersey: Printed and sold by James Parker: Sold also by John Holt, printer in New-York. M.DCC.LXIV.
ivi, 592 p. 19 cm.
James 22; Sabin 58682; cf. Evans 9775
MH-L; NHi; NjP. Pierce Gaines, Fairfield, Conn. (1963) mp. 41479

B2508 PEJEPSCOTT PROPRIETORS
Province of the Massachusetts-Bay. To the Proprietors of a tract of land . . . known by the name of Pejepscott Purchase . . . Belcher Noyes, Propr's clerk. Boston, Dec. 31, 1764. [Boston, Edes and Gill, 1764]
broadside 27.5 X 11.5 cm.
DLC; MWA mp. 41480

B2509 PENNSYLVANIA. CITIZENS
. . . An Seine Königliche Mäjestat, in Dero Rath. Die Bittschrift der Erblehenleute und Einwohner der Provinz Pennsylvanien . . . [Philadelphia, Anton Armbruster? 1764]
broadside 32 X 19.5 cm.
New York Public 356
Public Record Off. Photostat: NN mp. 41481

B2510 PENNSYLVANIA. GENERAL ASSEMBLY
Resolves of the Assembly of Pennsylvania, March 24, 1764. [Philadelphia, B. Franklin and D. Hall, 1764]

broadside 13 X 16.5 cm.
PHi mp. 41483

B2511 THE Pennsylvania town and countryman's almanack for the year . . . 1765. Germantown, C. Sower, and to be had in Philadelphia of William Wilson [1764]
40 p.
Prepared by John Tobler
cf. Evans 9856
PPL mp. 41493

B2512 A PROTEST presented to the House of Assembly . . . concerning the sending Mr. Franklin as an assistant to our agent at the Court of Great-Britain. [Philadelphia, William Bradford, 1764]
broadside 28.5 X 16.5 cm.
Dated Oct. 26, 1764
PHi mp. 41484

B2513 RHODE ISLAND. ELECTION PROX.
Honorable Stephen Hopkins, Esq; Governor. Honorable Joseph Wanton, Jun. Esq; Dep. Gov. . . . [Newport, Samuel Hall, 1764]
broadside 20 X 13 cm.
Alden 306; Chapin Proxies 4
RHi mp. 41485

B2514 RHODE ISLAND. LAWS
At the General assembly . . . holden . . . the second Monday in September . . . An act for assessing . . . a rate or tax of twelve thousand pounds . . . Newport, S. Hall [1764]
3 p. 33 cm.
Bill submitted Sept. 20, 1764
Alden 316; Winship p. 19
RHi; RPB mp. 41486

B2515 SHEARMAN, JOHN, d. 1764
The last words and dying speech of John Shearman, executed at Newport . . . the sixteenth day of November, 1764, for burgulary . . . Boston: Printed and sold by R. and S. Draper's Printing-office in Newbury-street, and at Green and Russell's in Queen-street. 1764.
broadside 33 X 23 cm.
Ford 1335
PHi

B2516 SHEARMAN, JOHN, d. 1764
[bottom of col. 1] . . . And as I am now about resigning this transitory life, by way of expiation to offended justice, I ardently . . . May all . . . take warning by the awful spectacle which this body of mine will exhibit, when suspended in the place destined for its suffering . . . John Shearman. Boston, Printed and sold by Z. Fowle, 1764.
broadside X 30.5 cm.
MWA (top half wanting) mp. 41487

B2517 SOME serious thoughts on the frowns of Divine Providence in the year 1764 . . . [n.p., 1764?]
broadside 35.5 X 21.5 cm.
35 4-line stanzas in double columns
MWA mp. 41488

B2518 SOUTH CAROLINA. LAWS
. . . At a General assembly, begun . . . the twenty-fifth day of October . . . 1762; and from thence continued . . . to the 6th day of October . . . 1764. Charles-Town, Peter Timothy, 1764.
36 p. 29 cm.
Sabin 87601
DLC mp. 41489

B2519 [THE South-Carolina almanack and register for . . . 1765. By George Andrews. Charles-Town, Robert Wells [1764]]
[52] p.
Drake 13091
ScC (t.p. lacking)

B2520 THE squabble, a pastoral eclogue. By Agricola. [Philadelphia] Printed [by A. Armbruster] in the year MDCCLXIV.
8 p. 4to
cf. Evans 9564 (2nd ed.)
PHi

B2521 A TABLE to bring old tenor into lawful money, at twenty-three and one third for one . . . Newport, Samuel Hall [1764]
broadside 33 X 21 cm.
Advertised Jan. 23, 1764, as "This day . . . published."
Alden 317; Winship p. 18
RHi; RPB. Photostats: MHi; MWA; NN mp. 41490

B2522 A TABLE to bring old tenor into lawful money, from six pence to ten thousand pounds . . . Providence, William Goddard, January 1, 1764.
broadside 40 X 27 cm.
Alden 318
RPJCB. Photostat: MWA mp. 41491

B2523 THE ten year's almanack . . . 1765. By Joseph Fisk. Portsmouth, Daniel Fowle [1764?]

Drake 4622
PPRF

B2524 . . . THIS Indenture made the day of *May* in the year . . . one thousand seven hundred and *sixty four* between John Miller . . . and Elizabeth his wife . . . Ephratae, Typis Societatis per P. M. [1764]
broadside
Underlined words in ms.; date assigned from year printed in text
Imprint at head of title
T and I of This Indenture floral capitals
Ephrata Cloister Museum

B2525 THOMSON, JAMES, 1708-1748
The seasons . . . [Boston?] Printed in the year MDCCLXIV.
xxvii, 206+ p. 17 cm. [ ]^2 a-b^6 B-S^6 T^2
MWA (sig. T2 wanting) mp. 41492

B2526 A TOUCH on the times. A new song . . . [Philadelphia? 1764]
4 p. 16.5 cm. caption title
A reply to Dove's "The Quaker unmask'd."
New York Public 359; Sabin 96322
T.W. Schreiner (1929). Photostat: NN mp. 41494

B2527 A TRUE and wonderful narrative of two intire [sic] particular phoenomena, which were seen in the sky in Germany . . . Philadelphia, Anthony Armbruster, 1764.
4 p. 20.5 cm.
RPJCB mp. 41495

B2528 VIRGINIA. COUNCIL
January 14, 1764. To . . . Francis Fauquier . . . the humble address of the Council . . . [Williamsburg, J. Royle, 1764]

broadside 31 X 18 cm.
DLC (photostat) mp. 41496

B2529 VIRGINIA. COUNCIL
October 31, 1764. To . . . Francis Fauquier . . . the humble address of the Council . . . [Williamsburg, J. Royle, 1764]
broadside 31 X 18 cm.
DLC (photostat) mp. 41497

B2530 VIRGINIA. GOVERNOR, 1758-1768
The speech of . . . Francis Fauquier . . . to the General-assembly, summoned to be held . . . the 26th of May . . . 1761, and from thence continued . . . to Thursday the 12th of January, 1764 . . . being the sixth session . . . Williamsburg, Joseph Royle, 1764.
4 p. 31 cm.
Torrence 313
DLC (photostat); MHi mp. 41498

B2531 VIRGINIA. GOVERNOR, 1758-1768
The speech of . . . Francis Fauquier . . . to the General assembly, summoned to be held . . . the 26th of May . . . 1761; and from thence continued . . . to Tuesday the 30th of October, 1764 . . . being the seventh session . . . Williamsburg, Joseph Royle, 1764.
4 p. 31 cm.
DLC (photostat) mp. 41499

B2532 VIRGINIA. HOUSE OF BURGESSES
January 16, 1764. To . . . Francis Fauquier . . . the humble address of the House of burgesses . . . [Williamsburg, J. Royle, 1764]
broadside 31 X 18 cm.
DLC (photostat) mp. 40500

B2533 VIRGINIA. HOUSE OF BURGESSES
January 19, 1764. To . . . Francis Fauquier . . . the humble address of the House of burgesses . . . [Williamsburg, J. Royle, 1764]
broadside 31 X 18 cm.
DLC (photostat) mp. 40501

B2534 VIRGINIA. HOUSE OF BURGESSES
November 2, 1764. To . . . Francis Fauquier . . . the humble address of the House of burgesses . . . [Williamsburg, J. Royle, 1764]
broadside 31 X 18 cm.
DLC (photostat) mp. 40502

B2535 VIRGINIA. LAWS
. . . At a General-assembly, begun . . . the 26th of May . . . 1761, and from thence continued . . . to Thursday the 12th of January, 1764 . . . being the sixth session . . . [Williamsburg, J. Royle, 1764]
10 p. 38 cm. caption title
Sabin 100271; Torrence 317
DLC; NN mp. 40503

B2536 WALTER, THOMAS, 1696-1725
The grounds and rules of musick explained . . . Boston, Printed for, and sold by Thomas Johnston, 1764.
1 p.l., 25 p., 24 leaves (music) 11 X 17 cm.
Sabin 101196
CtY; DLC; MH; MWA; RPJCB mp. 40504

B2537 THE wandering young gentlewoman: or Catskin's garland, in five parts. To which is addded [sic], Nancy Dawson. [Philadelphia] Andrew Steuart, 1764.

RPJCB (has photostat of t.p. only) mp. 40505

B2538 WARD, HENRY, 1732-1797
Peter Mumford, post-rider, doth, upon oath, declare . . . Henry Ward. Newport, August 9th, 1764. [Newport, S. Hall, 1764]
broadside 30.5 X 18 cm.
Alden 319; Winship Addenda p. 87
PPL. Photostat: Mhi mp. 40506

B2539 WARD, SAMUEL, 1725-1776
To the public. Governor Hopkins having published a piece in the *Providence Gazette* . . . Samuel Ward. Newport, 10th April, 1764. [Newport, S. Hall, 1764]
4 p. 21 cm. caption title
Alden 320; Winship p. 19
MWA; RHi; RPB mp. 40507

B2540 WARD, SAMUEL, 1725-1776
To the public. I must confess that I am not a little surprised . . . Samuel Ward. Newport, 16th April, 1764. [Newport, Solomon Southwick, 1764]
[2] p. 31 X 21 cm.
Alden 321; Winship Addenda p. 87
MWA; RHi mp. 40508

B2541 WATTS, ISAAC, 1674-1748
Divine songs attempted in easy language . . . The fifteenth edition. Portsmouth, Daniel & Robert Fowle, 1764.
32 p. 17 cm.
MWA mp. 40509

B2542 [WIELAND, CHRISTOPH MARTIN] 1733-1813
The trial of Abraham, in four cantos. Translated from the German. [Boston] Printed [and sold by John Perkins] 1764.
vi, 70 p. 16 cm. A-F^6 G^2
MHi; MWA mp. 40510

B2543 [WIELAND, CHRISTOPH MARTIN] 1733-1813
The trial of Abraham. In four cantos. Translated from the German. [Boston?] Printed, [and sold by John Perkins] 1764.
vi, 70, 4 p. cm.
cf. *Modern language notes,* April 1950, p. 246-47
MWiW-C mp. 41511

B2544 WRIGHT, JOHN, fl. 1720-1730
Spiritual songs for children: or Poems on several subjects and occasions . . . The fourth edition. Boston, Printed and sold by Z. Fowle, 1764.
64 p. 11 cm. [A]-D^8
MWA mp. 41512

1765

B2545 AMES'S almanack revived and improved . . . for the year . . . 1766 . . . By a late student at Harvard-College. Boston: Printed and sold by R. & S. Draper, Edes & Gill, T. & J. Fleet, S. Hall in Rhode Island. Printed for and sold also by T. Leverett, Wharton & Bowes, J. Perkins, B. Emerson [1765]
[24] p. 19 cm.
Morrison p. 51; Nichols p. 52
CSmH; DLC (2 copies); MH; MHi; MWA; NN mp. 41013

B2546 AMORY, JONATHAN AND JOHN
Jonathan & John Amory, in King-Street, Boston, and at Salem, in the house where . . . Timothy Lindall . . . lately dwelt, near the Friends-Meeting . . . [Boston? 1765?]

broadside 11 X 19.5 cm.
Lindell died in 1765
Ford 1339
MSaE mp. 41514

B2546a AN answer with advice to the author of the base quarto-pamphlet . . . Sold at the printing-office in Back-Street. [Boston? ca. 1765?]
12 p. 18.5 cm. $[A]^4$ B^2
Dedication signed: Z. B.
Stoddard 6
RPB

B2547 ANTI-STAMP FIRE SOCIETY, BOSTON
Rules and orders to be observed by the Anti-Stamp Fire Society, instituted in Boston, October 1763. [Boston, 1765?]
5, [1] p., 2 l. 15.5 cm.
Imprint date suggested by John Alden
Huntington 246; New York Public 337
CSmH. Photostat: NN mp. 41332

B2548 ARNOLD, BENEDICT, 1741-1801
Benedict Arnold, has just imported . . . and sells at his store in New-Haven . . . assortment of drugs . . . with the following books . . . [New Haven, 1765?]
broadside
In three columns
New York Public 362
MB; OTM. Photostats: CtY; MWA; NN mp. 41515

B2549 BARCLAY, ANDREW, 1738–1823
A catalogue of books, lately imported from Britain; and to be sold by A. Barclay . . . Corn-hill Boston . . . [Boston, 1765?]
broadside
3 columns of about 135 titles
Brigham: Booksellers, p. 40; Ford 1340
MWA mp. 41516

B2250 BARROLL, WILLIAM
A sermon preached at St. Stephen's Church at the funeral of Mr. James Louttit. Philadelphia, B. Franklin and D. Hall, 1765.
12 p. 16.5 cm.
Curtis 710
PHi mp. 41517

B2551 BAYLEY, DANIEL
A new and compleat introudction to the grounds and rules of music . . . Newbury-Port, Printed for and sold by D. Bayley, 1765.
24, 28, 11 p. 9.5 X 15.5 cm.
MBAt; MHi mp. 41518

B2552 BIBLE. O.T. PSALMS
A new version of the Psalms of David . . . Boston, Printed for, and sold by, A. Barclay, 1765.
2 v. in 1.
MB mp. 41519

B2553 BIBLE. O.T. PSALMS
A new version of the Psalms of David . . . . By N. Brady . . . and N. Tate . . . Boston, Printed by J. Kneeland, and S. Adams, for J. Edwards, 1765.
276 p. 15.5 cm.
MWA mp. 41520

B2554 BIBLE. O.T. PSALMS
A new version of the Psalms of David . . . By N. Brady . . . and N. Tate . . . Boston, Printed by J. Kneeland, and S. Adams, for S. Webb, 1765.
276 p. 15.5 cm.
CtHi; DLC mp. 41521

B2555 BIBLE. O.T. PSALMS
A new version of the Psalms of David . . . By N. Brady . . . and N. Tate . . . Boston, Printed by W. M'Alpine and J. Fleeming, for J. Hodgson, 1765.
246 p. 15.5 cm.
MWA mp. 41522

B2556 BOSTON EVENING POST
Extract from the *Boston Evening-Post*, of September 2, 1765. By His Excellency Francis Bernard . . . Governor . . . A proclamation. Whereas yesterday . . . [n.p., 1765]
7 p. 30 cm.
NHi mp. 41564

B2557 BOSTON GAZETTE
A New-Year's address, to the customers, of the *Boston Gazette*, &c. for January 1765. [Boston, 1765]
broadside
Ford 1365
PHi mp. 41573

B2558 BOSTON NEWS-LETTER
A New-Year's address, which the carrier of the *Boston News-Letter*, &c. humbly presents . . . January, 1765. [Boston, 1765]
broadside 23 X 14 cm.
Ford 1366
PHi mp. 41574

B2559 BROWN UNIVERSITY
Whereas the Governor and company of the . . . colony of Rhode-Island . . . incorporated certain persons . . . and granted them full power . . . to found . . . a college . . . we therefore, the subscribers . . . [Newport, S. Hall, 1765]
[3] p. 18.5 cm. caption title
Record of payment in Brown Univ. Arch. dated Oct. 11, 1765
Alden 340A; Winship p. 19
RHi; RPB (3 copies). Photostat: MWA mp. 41524

B2560 BUNYAN, JOHN, 1628-1688
Rest for a wearied soul . . . being the last legacy of John Bunyan . . . New-London, Re-printed and sold by T. Green [1765?]
23 p.
Trumbull: Supplement 1950
CtHi; MWA (t.p. only, photostat); NjP mp. 41525

B2561 [A CARICATURA, being a representation of the tree of liberty, and the distresses of the present day. Boston, Sold by N. Hurd near the Exchange, 1765]
broadside?
Advertised in the *Massachusetts Gazette*, Oct. 31, 1765
Ford 1344
No copy known mp. 41526

B2562 CHARITABLE IRISH SOCIETY
Articles agreed upon by the Charitable Irish Society, in Boston . . . Boston, W. M'Alpine and J. Fleeming, 1765.
broadside 39 X 33 cm.
Ford 1343
MHi mp. 41527

B2563 THE child's plain path-way to eternal life . . . New-London, T. Green, 1765.
8 leaves
RPJCB mp. 41528

B2564 [CHURCH, BENJAMIN] 1734-1776
Liberty and property vindicated . . . By a friend to the liberty of his country. Boston, 1765.
15 p. 18.5 cm.
DLC; MWA. Photostat: NhD mp. 41529

B2565 COLLECTION of verses. Applied to November 1, 1765, etc. including a prediction that the S—p A—t shall not take place in North America . . . New Haven [1765?]
24 p.
Trumbull: Supplement 1988; Wegelin v. 1, p. 63
Ghost of Evans 10085?
No copy located mp. 41530

B2566 THE conversation of two persons under a window on Monday evening the 23d of March. [Boston, 1765?]
broadside
Endorsed in ms. "R. Tyler who was a Councillor. A conversation about him."
Ford 1345
MHi mp. 41531

B2567 DAVIES, SAMUEL, 1724-1761
Little children invited to Jesus . . . The fifth edition. Boston, T. and J. Fleet, 1765.
24 p. 16.5 cm.
DLC mp. 41532

B2568 DAVIES, SAMUEL, 1724-1761
Little children invited to Jesus . . . Fifth edition. Hartford, Printed and sold by T. Green, 1765.
24 p. 14.5 cm.
CtHi mp. 41533

B2569 DOUGLASS, D
To the publick. A sense of past favours . . . my motives for planning an entertainment this winter . . . not . . . unworthy the attention of . . . the ladies and gentlemen of Carolina . . . I shall proceed with the utmost dispatch to refit the Theatre . . . to receive an audience on Monday the 11th . . . D. Douglass. Charlestown, Nov. 4, 1765. [Charleston, 1765]
broadside 40 X 26.5 cm.
MWA mp. 41534

B2570 [DULANY, DANIEL] 1721-1797
Considerations on the propriety of imposing taxes . . . [Annapolis?] North-America, Printed by a North-American [Jonas Green?], 1765.
90 p. 8vo A-L^4 M^1
"N. B." by an unknown editor (p. 32)
Adams 11b; Wroth 258
Mrs. W. Howard White, Baltimore. RPJCB (microfilm)
mp. 41535

B2571 AN exact table, to bring old tenor into lawful money . . . [Colophon] Portsmouth, Printed and sold by Daniel and Robert Fowle, 1765.
broadside 31 X 21 cm.
Whittemore 83
NhHi mp. 41536

B2572 EXTRACTS from several authors, to discourage evil-speaking one of another . . . [n.p., ca. 1765?]
broadside 36.5 X 15 cm.
Probably printed in America.—C. William Miller
PPL mp. 41537

B2573 [FISK, JOSEPH] fl. 1765
The ten year's almanack, or A poetical attempt made . . . ending with the year 1764 . . . [n.p.] 1765.
3, 160 p. 17 cm.
Acrostics, with the author's name, Joseph Fisk, on t.p., p. 27, p. 37
New York Public 364
NN (photostat) mp. 41538

B2574 Deleted.

B2575 GEORGIA. LAWS
. . . An act for granting . . . 25th March, 1765. Assented to, James Wright. [Savannah, J. Johnston, 1765]
8 p. 25.5 cm. caption title
cf. De Renne p. 174
DLC; GHi; NNB; RPJCB mp. 41540

B2576 GEORGIA. LAWS
Acts passed . . . at a session begun . . . the 20th day of November . . . 1764 . . . and from thence continued . . . to the 25th day of March 1765, being the first session . . . Savannah, James Johnston [1765]
1 p.l., 71, [1] p. 25.5 cm. A-S^2
De Renne p. 172; Guerra a-361
DLC (facsim.); GU-De mp. 41541

B2577 GILLILAND, JAMES
New-York 176[5] Bought of James Gilliland, at his Earthen and Glass Ware-House on Cannon's Dock . . . Bills will be taken in payment . . . [New York, 1765]
broadside 21 X 19 cm.
5 added to 176 in pencil. "Cannon's Dock" deleted and "Crugar's Wharf" added, in ink, in a contemporary hand
DLC. Photostat: ICN mp. 41717

B2578 A GOLDEN chain of four links . . . Boston, Printed and sold by Zechariah Fowle, at his Printing-Office, in Back-Street [1765?]
22, [1] p. 15 cm. A-B^6
Page 7 omitted in numbering
Dated by Clarence S. Brigham from internal evidence
MWA mp. 41542

B2579 GT. BRIT. LAWS
Anno regni Georgii III . . . quinto. At the Parliament . . . the nineteenth day of May . . . 1761 . . . to the tenth day of January, 1765 . . . New-York, Re-printed by H. Gaine, and sold at his Book-store, 1765.
24 p. 21.5 cm.
Caption title, p. 3: Chap. XII. An act for granting and applying certain stamp duties . . .
New York Public 367
MHi. E. H. Sauer (1932). Photostat: NN mp. 41543

B2580 GT. BRIT. LAWS
. . . Stamp act. Anno quinto Georgii III. Regis. Chap. I. An act for granting . . . certain stamp duties . . . in the British colonies . . . [Boston, Richard and Samuel Draper, and Green and Russell, 1765]
499-520 p. 33 cm. caption title
This appears to be a separate printing. Printers assigned from Evans 10323, which has similar typography and cut of royal arms
MHi; MWiW-C; NN mp. 41544

B2581 [HARDY, SAMUEL] 1636-1699
A guide to heaven from the world . . . And especially rules for the strict and due observation of the Lord's Day . . . [New London?] Printed [by Timothy Green?] for, and sold by James Larrabe of Norwich, 1765.
48 p. 16mo
Trumbull: Supplement 2229
CtHi mp. 41546

B2582 HARVARD UNIVERSITY
Quaestiones pro modulo . . . MDCCLXV. [Boston, 1765]
broadside
MB; MH; MHi; MSaE; MWA mp. 41547

B2583 HOBBY, WILLIAM, 1708-1765
Mr. Hobby's advice to his people, from the grave . . . [Boston? 1765?]
8 p. 19 cm. caption title
cf. Sibley VII, 537
ICN; MWA mp. 41549

B2584 HOBBY, WILLIAM, 1708-1765
Mr. Hobby's advice to his people from the grave. Boston, Printed and sold by Z. Fowle, at his Printing-Office in Back-Street [1765?]
8 p. 15 cm.
MHi; MWA; NHi (t.p. lacking) mp. 41550

B2585 THE indictment and trial of Sir Richard Rum, at a court held at Punch-Hall . . . Portsmouth, D. & R. Fowle, 1765.
23 p. 16 cm.
Whittemore 84
NhHi mp. 41551

B2586 JENNINGS, SAMUEL, d. 1764
A narrative of the wonderful deliverance of Samuel Jennings, Esq; . . . [n.p.] 1765.
7 p. 21 cm.
MWA mp. 41552

B2587 [JOHNSON, JOHN] 1706-1791
The advantages and disadvantages of the marriage state . . . The sixth edition. Newport, S. Hall, 1765.
19 p. 20.5 cm.
"Advertisement" (p. 2) signed: J. Johnson. Liverpool, June 1. 1758
Alden 330; Winship p. 20
RHi mp. 41553

B2588 [JOHNSON, JOHN] 1706-1791
The advantages and disadvantages of the marriage state . . . The sixth edition. Newport, S. Hall [ca. 1765]
21 p. 17.5 cm.
"Advertisement" (p. [2]) signed: Liverpool, June 1, 1758. J. Johnson
Alden 331
RNHi mp. 41554

B2589 LIBERTY, property, and no excise. A poem, compos'd on occasion of the sight seen on the great trees . . . in Boston . . . on the 14th of August, 1765. [Boston, 1765]
broadside
Ford 1348; New York Public 368
MB. Photostat: MHi; NN mp. 41555

B2590 LIGHTLY, JOSEPH, d. 1765
The last words and dying speech of Joseph Lightly . . . executed at Cambridge, November 21, 1765. For the murder of Elizabeth Post, at a place called Ware. [Boston, 1765]
broadside
Ford 1349
MHi mp. 41556

B2591 LOUISIANA. CONSEIL SUPÉRIEUR
Extrait des régistres, des audiances du Conseil supérieur . . . du 7. May 1765 . . . [New Orleans, Denis Braud, 1765]
4 p. 36.5 cm. caption title
McMurtrie: New Orleans 3
DLC; NN (photostat) mp. 41557

B2592 LOUISIANA. CONSEIL SUPÉRIEUR
Extrait des registres des audiances du Conseil supérieur . . . . . du 1er. Juin 1765 . . . [New Orleans, Denis Braud, 1765]
3 p. 32 cm.
cf. BSA *Papers*, v. LXII (1968) p. 252
CU-B

B2593 MANCHESTER, JOB
Advertisement. Stolen out of the pasture of Mr. Matthew Manchester . . . a dark bay horse . . . a reward of eight dollars . . . shall be paid . . . by Job Manchester, Cranston, July 15, 1765. [Providence, 1765]
broadside 23 × 16.5 cm.
Alden 333; Winship p. 21
RPJCB. Photostats: MHi; MWA; NN; RHi mp. 41558

B2594 MASON, DAVID
A course of experiments in that instructive and entertaining branch of natural philosophy, called Elictricity . . . [Boston, 1765]
broadside 23.5 × 18 cm.
MB mp. 41559

B2595 [MASON, JOHN] 1646?-1694
Spiritual songs: or, Songs of praise . . . The seventeenth edition, corrected. Boston, Printed and sold by Z. Fowle, 1765.
[8], 151 p.
MWA; NN mp. 41560

B2596 MASSACHUSETTS. GOVERNOR, 1760-1770
By His Excellency Francis Bernard . . . A proclamation. Whereas towards evening on the 26th day of August instant, a great number . . . riotously assembled . . . and did . . . attack the dwelling-house of William Story . . . [Aug. 28, 1765] . . . [Boston, 1765]
broadside 30 × 22 cm.
Ford 1356
MiU-C mp. 41562

B2597 MASSACHUSETTS. GOVERNOR, 1760-1770
By His Excellency Francis Bernard . . . A proclamation. Whereas yesterday, towards evening, a great number . . . riotously assembled . . . and . . . pulled down a new-erected building . . . [Aug. 15, 1765] . . . [Boston, Richard Draper? 1765]
broadside 25.5 × 18.5 cm.
Ford 1355
MiU-C mp. 41563

B2598 MASSACHUSETTS. HOUSE OF REPRESENTATIVES
Advertisement. In the House of Representatives, Feb. 21, 1765 . . . March 1, 1765. [Boston, 1765]
broadside
Appointing a committee to prepare an alphabetical list of all officers and soldiers serving in the several expeditions since the first Louisburg expedition in 1745

Ford 1361
MB mp. 41561

B2599 MASSACHUSETTS. TREASURER
Province of Massachusetts-Bay. The honourable Harrison Gray, Esq; Treasurer . . . the twenty-eighth day of October, 1765. [Boston, 1765]
broadside 39.5 X 30.5 cm.
Ford 1364
MMidb; MWA; RPJCB mp. 41566

B2600 MONSANTO & CIE., plaintiffs
Réponse du Sieur Monsanto & Compagnie . . . demandeur. Au mémoire du Sieur Radolt . . . deffendeur. [at end] A la Nlle. Orleans, le 16 juillet 1765 . . . Monsanto & Compagnie. Doucet. Avocat. [New Orleans] Denis Braud [1765]
20 p. 28 cm.
McMurtrie: New Orleans 4
LHi. Edward A. Parsons, New Orleans (1942) mp. 41568

B2601 MORGAN, JOHN, 1735-1789
Apology for attempting to introduce the regular practice of physic in Philadelphia . . . Philadelphia, William Bradford, 1765.
[2], 26 p. 19 cm. $[\ ]^1$ $A\text{-}C^4$ D^1
Guerra a-368
PPL mp. 41569

B2601a NEDERLANDSCH HERVORMDE KERK. CLASSIS AMSTERDAM
Brief van de Wel-Eerwaarde Classis van Amsterdam . . . New York, J. Holt, 1765.
15 p. 12mo
Introduction by Ritzema dated Oct. 11, 1765. Published in 400 English and 600 Dutch copies.—cf. *Ecclesiastical Records of the State of New York*, p. 3991
cf. Evans 10029 (in English)
No copy traced

B2602 NEW HAMPSHIRE. GOVERNOR, 1741-1767
By his excellency Benning Wentworth . . . A proclamation for a general fast [Apr. 5, 1765] . . . [Mar. 14, 1765] . . . [Colophon] Portsmouth, Daniel Fowle, 1765.
broadside 38 X 31 cm.
Whittemore 89
NhHi mp. 41570

B2603 NEW HAMPSHIRE. GOVERNOR, 1741-1767
By his excellency Benning Wentworth . . . A proclamation for a general thanksgiving [Nov. 14, 1765] . . . [Oct. 29, 1765] . . . [Colophon] Portsmouth, Daniel and Robert Fowle [1765]
broadside 37 X 31 cm.
Whittemore 90
NhD; NhHi mp. 41571

B2604 NEW JERSEY. LAWS
Anno regni, Georgii . . . quinto. At a session of General Assembly . . . Burlington, May 21, 1765 . . . till the 20th day of June following. Being the eleventh session of the twentieth assembly . . . Woodbridge, James Parker, 1765.
87, [1] p. 30 cm.
Humphrey 83
Nj; NjHi. Public Record Off. mp. 41572

B2605 A NEW Year's wish. 1765. [Boston, 1765]
broadside
"Europe still partakes the joys of Peace . . ."
Ford 1367
PHi mp. 41575

B2606 NEW YORK. LAWS
. . . [Laws of New York] The twenth-first assembly. [Passed Dec. 23, 1765] [Colophon] New-York, W. Weyman [1765]
p. 409-440. 35.5 cm. caption title
Running title: Laws of New-York . . .
DLC; NNS mp. 41577

B2607 NEW YORK. MERCHANTS
A patriotic advertisement. City of New-York, October 31, 1765, at a general meeting of the merchants . . . [New York, Hugh Gaine? 1765]
broadside fol.
PPL mp. 41576

B2608 NEW YORK GAZETTE
The news-boy's verses, for January 1, 1765 . . . [New York, W. Weyman, 1765]
broadside 42 X 16 cm.
DLC. Photostat: ICN mp. 41578

B2609 NORTH CAROLINA. HOUSE OF ASSEMBLY
[The journal of the House of Assembly . . . Wilmington [Feb. 3, 1764–May 3, 1765] . . . being the third session . . . Newbern, James Davis, 1765]

On May 6, 1765, "Mr. Montfort moved that the Clerk furnish James Davis . . . a copy of the journal . . . daily, and . . . direct him to print the same & dispense the copys so printed . . ." (*Colonial Records*, VII, 64.)
McMurtrie: North Carolina 47
No copy known mp. 41579

B2610 NORTH CAROLINA. LAWS
A collection of all the acts of Assembly, of . . . North Carolina, now in force . . . [Newbern] James Davis, 1765.
2 v. in 1 (xvi, 176; 393, [21] p.) 24 cm.
McMurtrie: North Carolina 50
NN; NNB; Nc-SC; NcU. Brit. Mus. mp. 41580

B2611 PENNSYLVANIA. GENERAL ASSEMBLY
Weil am 18ten jetztlaufenden Septembers zu Germantown eine Schrift . . . unterzeichnet Christoph Saur . . . mit einem Mischmasch von Unwahrheit und Wahrheit . . . so hat die Assembly dieser Provinz verordnet, folgende Ihre Schlüsse denen Deutschen durch den Druck bekannt zu machen . . . [Colophon] Philadelphia, Henrich Miller [1765]
[2] p. 35 X 22 cm.
MWA mp. 41581

B2612 PENNSYLVANIA. GOVERNOR, 1763-1777
By the honourable John Penn . . . A proclamation [concerning licences to trade with the Indians] . . . June 4, 1765. Philadelphia, B. Franklin and D. Hall [1765]
broadside 37.5 X 22.5 cm.
Curtis 721; Metzger 279
CtY; PHi; PU mp. 41582

B2613 PENNSYLVANIA. GOVERNOR, 1763-1777
By the Honorable John Penn, esquire, Lieutenant Governour . . . Whereas prayed my licence to trade with the . . . Indians . . . Given under my hand . . . at Philadelphia, the day of 1765 . . . [Philadelphia, B. Franklin? 1765]
broadside 20 X 32.5 cm.
MB mp. 41583

B2614 PHILADELPHIA. MERCHANTS
The merchants and traders of the city of Philadelphia, taking into consideration the melancholy state of the

North-American commerce . . . [Philadelphia, W. Bradford? 1765]
broadside fol.
Non-importation agreement
PPL mp. 41584

B2615 [POOR Thomas improved: being More's country almanack for . . . 1766 . . . New-York, W. Weyman, 1765]
[32] p.
In his 1767 almanac More states: "The last year your kindness was so great, as to oblige me to print my Almanack twice: the first [Evans 10081] had the substance of the Stamp Act in it; and the 2d an Act to enable you to get money . . ."
Drake 5776; Wall p. 18
NjR

B2616 READING made easy, in some Scripture instructions for children . . . Philadelphia, W. Dunlap, 1765.
[2], 78 p. 16 cm. [A]-K^4
MWA (sig. K1, K4 wanting); RPJCB mp. 41585

B2617 RHODE ISLAND. GOVERNOR, 1765-1767
By the honorable Samuel Ward . . . A proclamation . . . [Nov. 11, 1765] . . . Newport, Samuel Hall [1765]
broadside 35 X 25 cm.
Bill submitted Nov. 14, 1765
Alden 334; Winship p. 20
MWA; RHi. Photostats: MHi; NN mp. 41586

B2618 RHODE ISLAND. LAWS
At the General assembly . . . holden . . . the last Wednesday in October . . . An act for assessing . . . a rate or tax of twelve thousand four hundred and sixty-eight pounds . . . Newport, S. Hall [1765]
[3] p. 32 cm.
Bill submitted Nov. 6, 1765
Alden 340; Winship p. 20
RHi mp. 41587

B2619 Deleted.

B2619a SMITH, SAMUEL, 1720-1776
The history of the Colony of Nova-Caesaria, or New-Jersey . . . Burlington, in New-Jersey: Printed and Sold by James Parker: Sold also be David Hall, in Philadelphia. M,DCC,LXV.
x, 573 [1] p.
cf. Evans 10166, with different setting of type (mp. 10166 has MDCCLXV)
CSmH

B2620 SOUTH CAROLINA. HOUSE OF ASSEMBLY
South-Carolina. In the Commons House of Assembly, the 29th. day of November 1765. This House . . . esteem it their indispensable duty . . . to come to the following resolutions . . . by reason of several late acts of Parliament . . . [at end] Charles-Town, Peter Timothy [1765]
broadside
Signed: Peter Manigault, Speaker
Sabin 87354
DLC (not traced). Public Record Off. mp. 41589

B2620a SYNOD OF NORTH HOLLAND, EDAM, 1763
Extract uit de Handelingen van het . . . Synode, van Noord-Holland, gehouden te Edam, van den 26th July tot den 4 Augustus, 1763. Met een . . . voor afspraah . . . door Johannes Ritzema. New York, 1765.
16 p. 12mo
cf. Corwin, E. T. *Manual of the Reformed Church in America* (New York, 1902) p. 570
Sage Library, Theol. Seminary, New Brunswick, N. J. (not traced 1969)

B2621 A TABLE of simple interest at 6 per cent. for any sum . . . Haverhill, July 10, 1765. An explanation of the table . . . Boston, W. McAlpine and J. Fleeming, 1765.
broadside 45 X 54.5 cm.
MHaHi mp. 41591

B2622 TENNENT, JOHN, ca. 1700-ca. 1760
[Every man his own doctor . . . Fifth edition. Charles-Town: Reprinted and sold by Peter Timothy. MDCCLXV]

Advertised in the *South Carolina Gazette*, May 25, 1765
Mosimann 161
No copy located

B2623 TO the public. I congratulate my countrymen on the near and certain prospect of the repeal of the Stamp-Act . . . A son of liberty. [New York, 1765]
broadside fol.
PPL mp. 41592

B2624 TO the publick of Connecticut. Perhaps there never was a more unpromising time for the encouragement of another newspaper in this colony . . . [New Haven] B. Mecom [1765]
[2] p. 34 X 21 cm.
Probably refers to the *Connecticut Courant*, revived July 5, 1765
DLC; MWA mp. 41567

B2625 TRUE SONS OF LIBERTY
Boston, (Hanover-Square,) Dec. 18, 1765. Messieurs Drapers, Your inserting the following letter, sent . . . to the Honourable Andrew Oliver . . . will oblige the True Sons of Liberty. [Boston, 1765]
[2] p. 34 cm. caption title
Ford 1368; New York Public 372
NN mp. 41523

B2626 TRUE SONS OF LIBERTY
St—p! st—p! st—p! No: Tuesday-Morning, December 17, 1765. The True-born Sons of Liberty, are desired to meet under Liberty-Tree, at XII o'clock, this day, to hear the the [sic] public resignation . . . of Andrew Oliver . . . [Boston, 1765]
broadside 19 X 12 cm.
MHi mp. 41590

B2627 VIRGINIA, sc. I do hereby certify that George Mercer . . . declared before me . . . that he did not bring with him . . . any stamps, particularly for the use of the officers of the customs . . . [Williamsburg, J. Royle, 1765?]
broadside 15 X 17 cm.
DLC (photostat) mp. 41595

B2628 VIRGINIA. GOVERNOR, 1758-1768
Virginia sc. By . . . Francis Fauquier . . . a proclamation. Whereas a party of Cherokees . . . [May 13, 1765] . . . [Williamsburg, J. Royle, 1765]
broadside 31 X 35 cm.
DLC (photostat) mp. 41593

B2629 VIRGINIA. LAWS
. . . At a General assembly, begun . . . the 26th of May . . . 1761, and from thence continued . . . to Tuesday the

30th of October, 1764 . . . being the seventh session . . . [Williamsburg, J. Royle, 1765]
73 p. 32 cm. caption title
Sabin 100272; Torrence 324
DLC; MH-L (imperfect); NN; NNB mp. 41594

B2630 VON der Richtigkeit des menschlichen Lebens . . . [Ephrata, 1765?]
broadside fol.
PPL mp. 41596

B2631 WATKINSON, EDWARD
An essay upon oeconomy. The fourth edition . . . Providence, William Goddard, 1765.
35 p. 18 cm.
Alden 343
NjP; RHi mp. 41597

B2632 WATTS, ISAAC, 1674–1748
Divine songs, attempted in easy language . . . The fifteenth edition. Boston, Reprinted by D. & J. Kneeland for Thomas Leverett, 1765.
36 p. 14 cm.
MWA mp. 41598

B2633 WHITAKER, NATHANIEL, 1710-1795
A sermon preached at the ordination of . . . Isaac Foster, at Stafford Second Society, in . . . Connecticut; on the 31st day of October, 1764 . . . Hartford, T. Green, 1765.
64 p. 15.5 cm.
Trumbull: Supplement 2785
CtHi (p. 57+ lacking) mp. 41599

B2634 WÖCHENTLICHE PHILADELPHISCHE STAATSBOTE
Des Herumträgers des *Staatsboten* Neujahrs-Verse, sein resp. Geehrten Kundleuten überreicht den lten Jenner, 1765 . . . [Philadelphia, Henrich Miller, 1765]
broadside 32.5 X 14.5 cm.
Hildeburn 4658
PHi mp. 41548

B2635 THE wood-lark, or a choice collection of the newest and most favourite English songs . . . sung at the public theatres and gardens. Philadelphia, Reprinted by William Bradford [1765?]
[2], xiv, 190, 194 p. 12mo
PPL (top of t.p. defective) mp. 41600

1766

B2636 AMBROSE, ISAAC, 1604-1664
Christ in the clouds coming to judgment . . . [Bos]ton, Re-printed and sold by Kneeland [and A]dams, 1766.
16 p. 17 cm. [A]-B^4
MWA mp. 41601

B2637 ARISTOTLE'S compleat masterpiece . . . The twenty-eighth edition. [n.p.] Printed, and sold by the booksellers, 1766.
124+ p. 16 cm. A-K^6 L$^{6?}$
MWA (sig. H2-3, I4-5, K1-3, and all after L2 wanting) mp. 41602

B2638 AN astronomical diary; or, Almanack for . . . 1767. By Nathaniel Ames. Boston, William McAlpine [1766]
[24] p.
Second edition
Drake 3151
Phelps

B2639 AN astronomical diary; or, Almanack for 1767. By Nathaniel Ames . . . New Haven, The Printers [1766]
[24] p.
Drake 244
CtHi

B2640 AN astronomical diary; Or, Almanack for 1767. By Nathaniel Ames . . . New-London, Timothy Green [1766]
[24] p.
Drake 245
CtNlC

B2641 AN astronomical diary; or Almanack for . . . 1767. By Nathaniel Low. Boston, Printed by Kneeland and Adams, for the booksellers [1766]
[24] p.
Drake 3155
MWA

B2642 [AUBORN, A. D']
The French convert . . . Boston, Printed and sold by Z. Fowle, 1766.
78 p. 18 cm. A-K^4
MWA mp. 41603

B2643 BIBLE. O.T. PSALMS
The New-England Psalter: or, Psalms of David . . . New-York, Printed and sold by H. Gaine, 1766.
132 p. 16 cm.
PPRF mp. 41604

B2644 BIBLE. O.T. PSALMS
The Psalms of David, imitated . . . The twenty-first edition . . . Boston, William M'Alpine, 1766.
328, [8] p. 16 plates. 14.5 cm.
MWA mp. 41672

B2645 BIBLE. O.T. PSALMS
The Psalms of David, imitated . . . The twenty-first edition . . . Boston, Printed by William M'Alpine, for Thomas Ran, 1766.
328 p. 16 cm.
MB (t.p. and other leaves wanting); MWA mp. 41673

B2646 BOSTON, September 30. 1766. On Monday, the 13th of October next, will be offered to sale . . . a valuable collection of books . . . [Boston, 1766]
broadside
American Art Assoc. cat., May 3-4, 1923, item 74
In three columns
New York Public 374
NN (reduced facsim.) mp. 41605

B2647 BOSTON EVENING POST
Vox populi. Liberty, property, and no stamps. The news-boy who carries the *Boston Evening-Post*, with the greatest submission begs leave to present the following lines . . . [Boston, T. & J. Fleet, 1766?]
broadside 27 X 12 cm.
Ford 1395
PHi. Photostat: MWA mp. 41670

B2648 BOSTON GAZETTE
January 1766. The carrier of the *Boston-Gazette*, to his customers. A New-Year's wish. [Boston, Edes & Gill, 1766]
broadside 29 X 12 cm.
Ford 1393
PHi. Photostat: MWA mp. 41631

B2649 BOSTON POST-BOY
New-Year's wish from the carrier of the *Boston Post-Boy*, &c. [Boston, Green & Russell, 1766]
broadside 16.5 X 13 cm.
Ford 1394
PHi. Photostat: MWA mp. 41647

B2650 [BROOKE, FRANCES (MOORE)] 1724-1789
The history of Lady Julia Mandeville. In two volumes. By the translator of Lady Catesby's letters. The fourth edition ... Philadelphia, Re-printed, by William Bradford, 1766.
2 v. in 1 ([2], 175; 142 p.) 16.5 cm.
MWA mp. 41606

B2651 A BUNDLE of myrrh, or Rules for a Christian's daily meditation and practice ... Boston, Re-printed and sold, opposite the Probate-Office in Queen-Street, 1766.
32 p. 10 cm. [A]-B^8
MWA mp. 41607

B2652 COUNTY, ss. March 1766
Whereas the shutting up all the public offices of this province ... is an obstruction to justice ... [Annapolis, Jonas Green, 1766]
broadside 12.5 X 35 cm.
Calls on the principal gentlemen of each county to repair to Annapolis
Wroth 264
NHi mp. 41608

B2653 DEN Herren lobt und benedeyt, Der von der Stämpel-Act uns hat befreyt. Eine Herrliche Beylage zum 226ten Stück des *Philadelphischen Staatsboten* ... [Philadelphia, 1766]
broadside 34 X 22 cm.
Dated May 19, 1766
New York Public 375
PPAmP. Rosenbach Company (1922). Photostat: NN mp. 41611

B2654 [DODSLEY, ROBERT] 1703-1764
The oeconomy of human life ... Philadelphia, Andrew Steuart, 1766.
2 pts. in 1 v. 13.5 cm.
MWA; MiU-C mp. 41609

B2655 A DREAM or, Vision of the night ... New-London, Printed and sold by T. Green, 1766.
10 p. 19 cm. $[A]^4$ B^2
MWA mp. 41610

B2656 [FLAGG, JOSIAH]
Sixteen anthems, collected from Tans'ur, Williams ... Engraved and printed by Josiah Flagg, and sold by him at his house ... in Boston ... [1766]
60, [10] p. 12.5 X 22 cm.
Britton p. 541
DLC; MWA mp. 41612

B2657 THE following thoughts came from a youth scarce 15. [Also] The following lines (wrote by a youth aet. 16.) were designed for the consolation of the late Rev. Dr. Mayhew's spouse. [Boston, R. and S. Draper, 1766?]
broadside 24 X 15.5 cm.
The first poem is dated July 11, 1766
Ford 1372
DLC. Photostat: MWA mp. 41613

B2658 FORBES, ELI, 1726-1804
The evangelical preacher's determination – a sermon preached at the ordination of ... Asaph Rice ... at Westminster, October 16, 1765 ... Boston, Edes and Gill, 1766.
22 p. 20 cm. [A]-C^4
MB; MHi; MWA; RPJCB (half-title wanting?) mp. 41614

B2659 GEORGIA. LAWS
... An act for granting ... one thousand nine hundred ... pounds ... 6th March, 1766. Assented to, Ja. Wright. [Savanah, J. Johnston, 1766]
8 p. 25.5 cm. caption title
De Renne p. 180
DLC (facsim.); GU-De; RPJCB mp. 41615

B2660 GEORGIA. LAWS
An act for the establishing and regulating patrols ... Council-Chamber, 18th Nov. 1765. Assented to, Ja. Wright. [Savannah, J. Johnston, 1766?]
7 p. 25.5 cm.
Distinguished from the session printing by a tail-piece below the Act on p. 7
De Renne p. 177
GU–De mp. 41616

B2661 GEORGIA. LAWS
Acts passed ... at a session begun ... the 24th day of October ... 1765 ... and from thence continued ... to the 6th day of March 1766, being the second session ... Savannah, James Johnston [1766]
1 p.l., 41, [1] p. 25.5 cm.
De Renne p. 178
DLC; GU–De; RPJCB mp. 41617

B2662 GERMAN FRIENDLY SOCIETY
Charles:Town So:Carolina. This is to certify ... member of the German Friendly Society ... *July* Anno Domini *1766* ... President Secretary
broadside 23 X 21 cm.
Engraved certificate of membership, in elaborate floral and pictorial border
Reproduced in Gongaware, p. 8
Italicized portions in manuscript
German Friendly Society

B2663 GERMAN FRIENDLY SOCIETY
South-Carolina. These a[re] to certify, That was regularly [adm]itted a member of the German Friend [ly S]ociety ... Given ... this day of *August* 1766. *M [Ka]lteisen* President ... [Charlestown, 1766]
broadside 32.5 X 20.5 cm.
Italicized portions in manuscript; the Society was formed in 1766
Reproduced in Gongaware, p. 6
German Friendly Society

B2664 GLORIOUS news. Constitutional liberty revives! New-Haven, Monday-morning, May 19, 1766 ... New Haven, B. Mecom [1766]
broadside 34.5 X 22.5 cm.
DLC mp. 41618

B2665 GLORIOUS news, just received from Boston, brought by Mr. Jonathan Lowder. Boston, Friday 11 o'clock, 16th May, 1766. This instant arrived here the Brig Harrison ... New-London, Timothy Green [1766]
broadside 39.5 X 26 cm.
Stamp Act repeal
cf. Evans 10317
CtHi mp. 41619

B2666 GT. BRIT. ARMY. 9TH REGIMENT OF FOOT
Standing regimental orders for the IXth Regiment of

Foot . . . together with the standing orders of the Army. Charlestown, Robert Wells, 1766.
61 p. 18 cm.
New York Public 376
NN (partly interleaved, with ms. additions) mp. 41621

B2667 GT. BRIT. COLONIAL OFFICE
By . . . the honourable Thomas Gage . . . rules and directions . . . for procuring and issuing fuel to the troops . . . [New York, 1766]
broadside 57 X 43 cm.
Dated in manuscript: New York 25th April, 1766
DLC (photostat) mp. 41620

B2668 GT. BRIT. LAWS
Anno regni Georgii III . . . sexto . . . An act for opening and establishing certain ports in . . . Jamaica and Dominica . . . New-York, Reprinted by W. Weyman [1766]
6 p. 33 cm. caption title
New York Public 377
Morton Pennypacker (1941). Photostat: NN
mp. 41622

B2669 GROVE, HENRY, 1684-1738
A discourse concerning the nature and design . . . The eighth edition . . . Boston, 1766.
179, [1] p. 16.5 cm.
Huntington 268
CSmH; DLC; MB; MHi; MWA; MWiW; MeB; N; RPJCB
mp. 41623

B2670 HARVARD UNIVERSITY
Quaestiones pro modulo . . . MDCCLXVI. [Boston] R. et S. Draper [1766]
broadside
Ford 1374
MH; MHi; MWA mp. 41624

B2671 HENRY, WILLIAM
[Account of the captivity of William Henry in 1755, and of his residence among the Senneka Indians six years and seven months. Boston, 1766]
160 p. 4to
Title from the *London Chronicle*, June 23, 1768, p. 601
Vail: Old frontier, 570
No copy known mp. 41625

B2672 THE history of the Holy Jesus . . . By a Lover of their precious souls. The eighth edition. New-London, Printed and sold by Timothy Green, 1766.
[48] p. 15 illus. 10.5 cm. $[A]^8$ B^8 $[C]^8$
MWA (front. wanting) mp. 41627

B2673 THE history of the Holy Jesus . . . By a Lover of their precious souls. The eleventh edition. Boston, Printed and sold by Z. Fowle, 1766.
[24] leaves. 11 cm. $[A]^8$ B^{10} C^6
MWA mp. 41626

B2674 HYMNS and spiritual songs, collected from the works of several authors . . . New-York, Printed by Samuel Hall and sold by William Rogers and Charles Brown, 1766.
[6], 178 p. 14.5 cm.
NNC mp. 41629

B2675 JAMES Davis, Sen. was born the 21st of October . . . MDCCXXI. Prudence Davis, was born the 22d of November, MDCCXXV . . . [Newbern, James Davis, 1766]
broadside 19 X 13 cm.
Lists also birth dates of seven Davis children
T. L. Davis, Wilson, N.C. Photocopy: NcU
mp. 41630

B2676 LITERARY SOCIETY, N. Y.
For the encouragement of learning, in King's-College, New-York. Several gentlemen having thought proper to form themselves into . . . the Literary Society . . . met on the eleventh of November, 1766, in the evening; and agreed to subscribe . . . three pounds, yearly . . . [New York, 1766]
broadside 30.5 X 18.5 cm.
NHi mp. 41632

B2677 LITERARY SOCIETY, N. Y.
Subscribers names who have agreed to pay three pounds yearly, for five years, commencing November the ninth, 1766, for the encouragement of learning, in King's-College, New-York . . . Disbursements by Dr. Clossey . . . [New York, 1766]
broadside 29.5 X 19 cm.
Text in 2 columns
NHi mp. 41633

B2678 MASSACHUSETTS
The proceedings of the Governor, Council, and House of representatives . . . concerning an indemnification for the sufferers by the riots . . . from JAugust 27, 1765, to June 28, 1766. [Boston, 1766]
4p., 1 leaf. fol.
Ford 1389; Huntington 270
CSmH mp. 41634

B2679 MASSACHUSETTS. GOVERNOR, 1760-1769
By His Excellency Francis Bernard . . . A proclamation . . . April 30, 1766. Boston, Richard Draper, 1766.
broadside
For the discovery of the murderers of Noodogawwerret and his wife of the Norridgewock Tribe
Ford 1379
M–Ar mp. 41637

B2680 MASSACHUSETTS. HOUSE OF REPRESENTATIVES
Boston, January 23, 1766. Tuesday last a committee of the honorable House . . . waited on . . . the Governour, with the following message . . . [Boston, 1766]
[4] p. 33 cm.
Printed only on p. [1]
Ford 1388
MHi mp. 41635

B2681 MASSACHUSETTS. HOUSE OF REPRESENTATIVES
Extract from the votes of the Hon. House of Representatives of . . . Massachusetts-Bay. Veneris, 17 die Januarii, A. D. 1766. The Committee appointed to . . . answer . . . speech of the 8th of November last . . . reported . . . [Boston, 1766]
[3] p. 33 cm.
MHi mp. 41636

B2682 MASSACHUSETTS. LAWS
. . . An act passed . . . for apportioning and assessing a tax of forty thousand pounds . . . [Boston, 1766]
8 [i.e. 13] p. 33 cm. caption title
cf. Evans 10378
MWA mp. 41638

B2683 MASSACHUSETTS. LAWS
. . . An act passed . . . impost and tunnage . . . 1766 . . . [Boston, 1766]
p. 309-315.
MWA mp. 41639

B2684 MASSACHUSETTS. TREASURER
Province of Massachusetts-Bay. The honorable Harrison

Gray . . . to constable or collector of Greeting, &c. . . . [Nov. 4, 1766] . . . [Boston, 1766]
broadside 38 X 30.5 cm.
Ford 1391
DLC mp. 41640

B2685 MASSACHUSETTS. TREASURER
Province of Massachusetts-Bay. The honorable Harrison Gray, Esq; Treasurer . . . To the select-men or assessors of the town or district of Greeting, &c. . . . Given . . . at Boston, the thirtieth day of July, 1766 . . . [Boston, 1766]
broadside 34 X 21 cm.
MBB; MWA mp. 41641

B2686 MEIN, JOHN
A catalogue of curious and valuable books. To be sold at the London Book-Store . . . [Colophon] John Mein. [Boston, William McAlpine, 1766]
51, [1] p. 18 cm. A–F^4 G^2
Advertised in the *Boston Evening Post*, May 19, 1766
1741 numbered titles
Brigham: Booksellers, p. 38; Guerra a-384
MWA mp. 41642

B2687 MEIN AND FLEEMING
Boston New-England. Specimen of Mein and Fleeming's printing types. [Boston, 1766?]
broadside 28 X 20 cm.
Printed after Fleeming's return from Scotland with types purchased there. – J. E. Alden
Ford 1440; New York Public 395
Photostats: MHi; NN; RPJCB mp. 41643

B2688 [MONTAGU, LADY MARY PIERREPONT WORTLEY]
Letters of the right honourable Lady M——y W——y M——e . . . The fourth edition. Providence, Sarah Goddard, 1766.
ix, [2], 204 p. 17 cm.
Alden 352; Guerra a-386; Winship p. 21
CtHi; CtY; MWA (imperfect); NN; RPB mp. 41644

B2689 NEDERLANDSCH HERVORMDE KERK. CLASSIS AMSTERDAM
A letter from the reverend Classis of Amsterdam, to the . . . ministers . . . of New-York and New-Jersey, who call themselves the Coetus. New-York, John Holt, 1766.
2 p.l., 21 p., 1 leaf. 18 cm.
New York Public 379
NHi; NN (photostat) mp. 41645

B2690 A NEW and true relation, of a little girl . . . supposed to be bewitch'd in March 1763 . . . Boston [J. Kneeland] 1766.
broadside 36 X 21.5 cm.
Ford 1392; New York Public 380
PHi. Photostats: DLC; MHi: MWA; NN mp. 41646

B2691 THE New-England almanack or, Lady's and gentleman's diary, for the year . . . 1767 . . . By Benjamin West . . . Boston, Printed and sold by the printers and booksellers [1766]
[12] leaves. 17 cm.
Morrison, p. 51
MWA; MiU–C mp. 41677

B2692 [THE New Hampshire almanack for 1767 . . . By David Sewall. Portsmouth, D. & R. Fowle, 1766]

Advertised in the *Portsmouth Gazette*, Dec. 5, 1766
Whittemore 103
No copy known mp. 41658

B2692a NEW-York, 1766 Proposals, for printing by subscription . . . a select collection of practical discourses . . . by . . . Samuel Finley . . . We the subscribers agree to take the number of sets affixed to our names . . . [New York, 1766]
broadside 35 X 16 cm.
PPPrHi

B2693 NEW YORK. LAWS
. . . [Laws of New York] The twenty-first Assembly. [Passed July 3, 1766] [Colophon] New-York, W. Weyman [1766]
p. 441-444. 35.5 cm. caption title
Running title: Laws of New-York . . .
DLC; NNS mp. 41649

B2694 NEW YORK. LIBRARY
A catalogue of the library, belonging to the Corporation of the City of New-York. New-York, John Holt, 1766.
48 p. 20 cm. A–F^4
Guerra a-388; Huntington 271
CSmH; NN (photostat) mp. 41648

B2695 NEW-YORK, May 16, 1766. By the post from Philadelphia . . . we have the following . . . Great and glorious news to America . . . [New York, H. Gaine, 1766]
broadside 34.5 X 20 cm.
DLC (photostat) mp. 41650

B2696 NEW YORK GAZETTE
New Year's ode for the year 1766 . . . [New York, 1766]
broadside 28 X 8.5 cm.
Distributed by Lawrence Swinney
PHi mp. 41663

B2697 NORTH CAROLINA. HOUSE OF ASSEMBLY
The journal of the House of Assembly. North Carolina. At an assembly begun and held at Wilmington [Feb. 3, 1764-May 3, 1765] . . . Being the third session . . . Newbern, James Davis, 1766.
18 p. 29 cm.
McMurtrie: North Carolina 47
NcU mp. 41651

B2698 NORTH CAROLINA. HOUSE OF ASSEMBLY
[Journal of the House. Nov. 20-24, 1766] [Newbern, J. Davis, 1766?]
25 cm.
DLC (p. 37-44 only) mp. 41652

B2699 NORTH CAROLINA. LAWS
Anno regni Georgii III . . . septimo. At an Assembly . . . Newbern [Nov. 3, 1766]: being the first session of this present Assembly. [Newbern, James Davis, 1766]
p. 395-438. 28 cm. F5–$Q5^2$ Caption title
McMurtrie: North Carolina 51
NNB; NcU; NcWsM mp. 41653

B2700 [ORTON, JOB] 1717-1783
Memoirs of the life, character and writings of . . . Philip Doddridge . . . London: Printed in the year MDCCLXVI. [Boston, Mein and Fleeming, 1766]
265, [3] p. 17.5 cm.
Alden: John Mein 4
MH; MWA mp. 41654

B2701 PARKER, JAMES, 1714-1770
An humble address to the publick . . . [New York, J. Parker, 1766?]
[2] p.
PPAmP mp. 41655

B2702 PENNSYLVANIA JOURNAL
Supplement to the *Pennsylvania Journal*, extraordinary. Philadelphia, May 19, 1766. This morning arrived Capt. Wise, in a brig from Pool . . . [Philadelphia, 1766]
broadside 35 X 22 cm.
Huntington 274
CSmH; PHi; PPL

B2703 REFORMED CHURCH IN THE U.S.
Hoch-deutsch reformirtes A B C and Namen Büchlein für Kinder . . . Germantown, Christoph Saur, 1766.
16mo
Metzger 298
No copy located mp. 41628

B2704 RUSH, BENJAMIN, 1745-1813
Philadelphia 1766. Sir, I am desired to inform you, that your . . . brother departed this life this morning . . . Benjamin Rush. [p. [4]] The sayings of [Mrs.] Ann Campbell, immediately previous to her death, taken verbatim . . . Letter from Doctor Benjamin Rush . . . to Mr. Finly of York County Pennsylvania . . . [Philadelphia? 1766?]
[4] p. 34 X 19.5 cm.
Pages [2-3] blank
MWA mp. 41657

B2705 SONS OF LIBERTY
The proceedings of the Sons of liberty, March 1, 1766. The Sons of liberty of Baltimore County and Anne-Arundel County . . . [Annapolis, Jonas Green, 1766]
broadside 34.5 X 22 cm.
Wroth 274
NHi mp. 41656

B2706 SOUTH CAROLINA. GOVERNOR, 1764-1766
. . . By the Honourable William Bull, esq; Lieutenant-Governor . . . Whereas Mr. Caleb Lloyd . . . Distributor of Stamped-Papers . . . has signified . . . not to issue any Stamped Papers . . . I DO . . . certify . . . that no Stamped Papers are now to be had . . . Given . . . at Charles-Town this day of 1766. [Charleston, 1766]
broadside 20 X 23 cm.
Clearance for Brig Polly, dated Apr. 2, 1766
MHi

B2707 SOUTH CAROLINA. HOUSE OF COMMONS
South-Carolina. In the Commons House of Assembly, the 28th day of January, 1766. Ordered . . . that the message of this house . . . be printed . . . [at end] Charles-Town, Peter Timothy [1766]
[4] p. 32 cm.
CtHi. Public Record Off. Photostat: MWA
mp. 41659

B2708 SOUTH CAROLINA. HOUSE OF COMMONS
South-Carolina. In the Commons House of Assembly, the 3d of February, 1766. Ordered, that the petition of the merchants, owners . . . be printed and made public . . . [at end] Charles-Town, Peter Timothy [1766]
[8] p. 31 cm. $[A]-B^4$
CtHi. Photostat: MWA mp. 41660

B2709 SOUTH CAROLINA. HOUSE OF COMMONS
Votes of the Commons House of Assembly of South Carolina from the twenty-eighth of April to the seventh of May 1766 . . . Charles-Town printed by Peter Timothy who begs leave to fill up this vacant space of the sheet with his congratulations to the Province . . . TOTAL repeal of the American Stamp Act . . . May 7, 1766.
14 p.
Williams: Timothy press, p. 37
PPAmP. Public Record Off. mp. 41661

B2710 THE Stamp-Act repealed, the 8th of February, 1766. Hartford, April 11, 1766. — XII. o'Clock. Just now come to town, a gentleman from New-Haven, who bro't the following in writing . . . [Hartford, 1766]
broadside 18 X 11 cm.
CtHi mp. 41662

B2711 THIS morning the Duke of Cumberland packet, Capt. Goodridge, arrived here from Falmouth . . . New York, April 26, 1766. [New York, H. Gaine, 1766]
broadside 25 X 17.5 cm.
DLC (photostat) mp. 41664

B2712 VIRGINIA. COUNCIL
November 7, 1766. To . . . Francis Fauquier . . . the humble address of the Council . . . [Williamsburg, Purdie and Dixon, 1766]
broadside 29 X 19 cm.
DLC (photostat) mp. 41665

B2713 VIRGINIA. GOVERNOR, 1758-1768
The speech of . . . Francis Fauquier . . . to the General assembly, summoned to be held . . . on Thursday the 6th of November . . . Williamsburg, Purdie and Dixon, 1766.
4 p. 37 cm.
DLC (photostat) mp. 41666

B2714 VIRGINIA. GOVERNOR, 1758-1768
The speech of . . . Francis Fauquier . . . to the General assembly, summoned to be held . . . on Thursday the 6th day of November . . . Williamsburg, William Rind [1766]
broadside 42 X 30 cm.
DLC (photostat) mp. 41667

B2715 VIRGINIA. HOUSE OF BURGESSES
The journal of the House of burgesses. [Nov. 6–Dec. 16, 1766] [Williamsburg, W. Rind, 1766]
p. 3-77. 32-34 cm. caption title
Sabin 99966; Torrence 332
DLC (t.p. wanting); Vi. Public Record Off.
mp. 41668

B2716 VIRGINIA. HOUSE OF BURGESSES
November 14, 1766. To . . . Francis Fauquier . . . the humble address of the House of burgesses . . . [Williamsburg, Purdie and Dixon, 1766]
[2] p. 30 X 18.5 cm.
DLC (photostat) mp. 41669

B2717 THE Virginia almanack for . . . 1767 . . . By Theophilus Wreg . . . Williamsburg, Purdie and Dixon [1766]
[24] p. 12mo
Bear 30; Huntington 267
CSmH (lacks last leaf) mp. 41679

B2718 WATTS, ISAAC, 1674-1748
Hymns and spiritual songs . . . The twenty-first edition. Boston, Printed [by William M'Alpine] for and sold by J. Mein, 1766.
xxiv, 264+ p. 15.5 cm.
Inverted q's used as b's point to M'Alpine's shop as printer. — cf. J. E. Alden
MB (all wanting after p. 264) mp. 41671

B2719 WATTS, ISAAC, 1674-1748
A wonderful dream . . . [Colophon] Printed and sold in New-London. [1766]

12 p. 16 cm. caption title
Trumbull 1570
DLC; MWA mp. 41674

B2720 WATTS, ISAAC, 1674-1748
A wonderful dream . . . [Colophon] Sold at the Printing-Office in New-London. [1766?]
12 p. illus. 15.5 cm. caption title
New York Public 381
Morton Pennypacker (1934). Photostat: NN
mp. 41675

B2721 WATTS, ISAAC, 1674-1748
A wonderful dream, by Doct. Watts . . . [Colophon] Sold at the Printing-Office in Hartford [1766]
12 p. illus. 15 cm. caption title
CtHi; MWA mp. 41676

B2722 WO des Verächters Netz uns Weg and Pfad bestrickte, Die wehen Knorr'n am Fuss die uns der Stiefel drückte . . . Philadelphia den 19ten May 1766. Heute Morgen wurden wir durch ein Freuden-Geläut . . . gemacht . . . [Philadelphia, 1766]
broadside 36 X 26.5 cm.
PHi mp. 41680

B2723 WÖCHENTLICHE PHILADELPHISCHE STAATSBOTE
Des Herumträgers des *Staatsboten* Neujahrs-Verse, bey seinen resp. Geehrten Kundleuten abgelegt den 6ten Jenner, 1766 . . . [Philadelphia, 1766]
broadside 23 X 14 cm.
Stamp Act theme
PHi mp. 41681

1767

B2724 AN address to the freeholders and electors of the County of New-Castle . . . By a lover of his country . . . [Wilmington, James Adams, 1767]
4 p. 33.5 cm.
Dated: October 1st, 1757
Signed on p. 4: A freeholder of New-Castle County
Hawkins 2
Richard S. Rodney, Newcastle, Del. mp. 41682

B2725 ADVERTISEMENT. Twenty pounds reward.
Run away last night, William Burns . . . Whoever takes up the said Burns, and will deliver him to Capt. Fuser, in Charlestown, shall have twenty pounds, South-Carolina currency reward . . . New-Barracks, near Charlestown, November 24th, 1767. [Charleston, 1767]
broadside 19.5 X 15.5 cm.
MWA mp. 41683

B2726 ALLEINE, JOSEPH, 1634-1668
An alarm to unconverted sinners . . . By Joseph Alliene [sic] . . . Boston, Reprinted by D. Kneeland, for T. White [1767?]
[2], xxii, [25]-311, [1] p. 15.5 cm.
A^6 a^6 $B–Z^6$ $Aa–Bb^6$
Identical with Evans 10538 except for absence of date; MWA has Evans 10538 also
MWA mp. 41684

B2727 ALLEN, JOLLEY
Just imported from London, by Jolley Allen, at his shop . . . almost opposite the Heart and Crown in Cornhill, Boston. [Boston, 1767?]
broadside
Bears endorsement of a tea transaction dated Jan. 3, 1767.
Ford 1400
MB mp. 41685

B2728 DIE alte und neue Wahrheit . . . [n.p.] Gedruckt im Jahr Christi 1767.
350, [18] p. 18.5 cm. $A–U^8$ $X–Z^8$
MWA mp. 41686

B2729 [AMBROSE, ISAAC] 1604-1664
Christ in the clouds, coming to judgment . . . Being the substance of a sermon preached by . . . Dr. Bates. Hartford, Printed and sold by Thomas Green [1767]
16 p. 17 cm.
CtHi; MWA (top closely trimmed) mp. 41687

B2730 [AMBROSE, ISAAC] 1604-1664
Christ in the clouds, coming to judgment . . . Being the substance of a sermon preached by . . . Dr. Bates. New-London, Printed and sold by Timothy Green [1767?]
16 p. 17 cm.
MWA (t.p. mutilated) mp. 41688

B2731 AN astronomical diary . . . for . . . 1768 . . . New-London, T. Green [1767]
[24] p. 16.5 cm.
By Nathaniel Ames
Drake 250
CtHi; CtY; MB; MWA; NHi mp. 41689

B2732 BARR, JOHN
Advertisement. Lancaster the 17th of August 1767. [Lancaster, 1767]
broadside 10 X 20.5 cm.
Notice of auction in English and German, signed: John Barr Sheriff
cf. *Midland notes*, no. 69, 1957, item 433
New York Public 382
NN (photostat of facsim.) mp. 41727

B2733 BAYLEY, DANIEL, 1725?-1792
The Psalm-singer's assistant . . . Boston, Printed for, and sold by the author in Newbury-Port, 1767.
8 p.; 16 numb. leaves (music) 15 cm.
NhD mp. 41692

B2734 BAYLEY, DANIEL, 1725?-1792
The Psalm-singer's assistant . . . Boston, Printed by W. M'Alpine, for the author in Newbury-Port, 1767.
8 p.; 16 numb. leaves (music) 15 cm.
MWA; MiU–C mp. 41691

B2735 BENEZET, ANTHONY, 1713-1784, ed.
Collection of religious tracts, viz. On the spirit of prayer . . . Christian piety . . . Daily conversation with God . . . Philadelphia, Henry Miller [1767]
[2], 48, 30, 26, [4], 52 p. 16.5 cm.
Consists of Evans 10352, 10505, 10455, 10659, 10555, with separate title pages
PPL mp. 41702

B2736 BIBLE. O.T. PSALMS
A new version of the Psalms of David . . . by N. Brady . . . and N. Tate . . . Boston, Wm. M'Alpine, 1767.
246 p. 15.5 cm.
Second title
Watts, Isaac, 1674-1748
A collection of hymns . . . Boston, 1767.
74 p. 15.5 cm.

cf. Evans 10558
DLC (2 copies); MB; MWA mp. 41693

B2737 BIBLE. O.T. PSALMS
The Psalms of David, imitated . . . [Boston] Printed by Kneeland & Adams, for Thomas Leverett, 1767.
304 p.
CtHC mp. 41777

B2738 BOSTON
At a meeting of the freeholders and other inhabitants of the Town of Boston . . . the 31st day of March, A.D. 1767 . . . [Boston, 1767]
broadside
Concerns shutting up a part of the Town's land adjoining Faneuil-Hall Market
Ford 1401
MB mp. 41697

B2739 BOSTON. MERCHANTS
Whereas this Province labours under a heavy debt . . . we the subscribers . . . do promise . . . that we will encourage the use . . . of all articles manufactured . . . in this Province . . . Boston, 28 October, 1767. [Boston, 1767]
broadside 19.5 X 25 cm.
Ford 1425
MWA mp. 41695

B2740 BOSTON. SELECTMEN
Boston, October 31, 1767. Gentlemen. In compliance with the orders of the Town it is our honour to serve, we inclose you their votes past the 28th instant . . . [Boston, 1767]
broadside 15 X 17.5 cm.
Ford 1404
MB; MWA mp. 41696

B2741 BOSTON EVENING-POST
The boy who carries the *Boston Evening-Post*, presents his compliments . . . on the commencement of the year 1767. [Boston, T. & J. Fleet, 1767]
broadside 28 X 17.5 cm.
Ford 1420
PHi. Photostat: MWA mp. 41698

B2742 BOSTON POST BOY
A New Year's wish from the carrier of the *Post-Boy & Advertiser.*
Suffer my muse with soft address,
In humble rhime,
To point the time
Which crown'd America's happiness.
[Boston, Green & Russell, 1767]
broadside 17 X 12 cm.
Ford 1422
PHi. Photostat: MWA mp. 41744

B2743 BRADFORD, WILLIAM, 1719-1791
William and Thomas Bradford, printers, booksellers and stationers . . . have for sale, the following books and stationary . . . [Philadelphia, 1767?]
broadside 40 X 25 cm.
In four columns
Bound originally in a volume of the *Pennsylvania Journal* for 1767
New York Public 383
NN mp. 41699

B2744 Deleted

B2745 BYRD, WILLIAM, 1674-1744
This shall entitle the owner to such prize . . . 1767. [n.p., 1767]
broadside 5.5 X 6.5 cm.
DLC mp. 41701

B2746 CHRIST CHURCH, PHILADELPHIA
Of the rules of the United Episcopal Churches of Christ and St. Peter's, concerning the letting of the pews and seats in both churches. [Philadelphia, 1767]
broadside 9 X 14 cm.
PHi mp. 41753

B2747 CONNECTICUT. GOVERNOR, 1766-1769
By the honourable William Pitkin . . . A proclamation . . . Given under my hand . . . in New-Haven . . . [Oct. 17, 1767] . . . [New London? 1767]
broadside 39.5 X 31.5 cm.
Appointing Nov. 19, 1767, a day of public thanksgiving
MHi

B2748 CONNECTICUT GAZETTE, NEW HAVEN
New-Year's verses for the lad who carries the *Connecticut Gazette* to its encouragers in New-Haven. A.D. 1767. [New Haven, 1767]
broadside
1st line: It is a point will be agreed . . .
PHi mp. 41742

B2749 DELL, WILLIAM, d. 1664
The trial of spirits, both in teachers and hearers . . . New-London, Timothy Green, 1767.
48 p. 17.5 cm.
Huntington 278
CSmH; CtHi mp. 41703

B2750 DUNCAN, ELLIOT
Elliot Duncan, at his shop, the east side of Second-street . . . has . . . both wet and dry-goods, and sells them . . . wholesale and retail. Philadelphia, Andrew Steuart [1767]
broadside 32 X 19.5 cm.
Metzger 305
PHi mp. 41704

B2751 EXTRACT of a letter, wrote by a pious person, describing the progress of the soul . . . [Philadelphia, 1767?]
8 p.
PHi mp. 41705

B2752 A FEW lines on Magnus Mode, Richard Hodges . . . who are sentenc'd . . . [Boston, Z. Fowle, 1767]
broadside 26 X 20 cm.
Ford 1407; Wegelin 587
PHi. Photostats: DLC; MHi; NN mp. 41706

B2753 FIRE CLUB, BOSTON
[Notification form for meetings. Boston, 1767]
broadside
The financial records of the Club, in manuscript at the Boston Public Library, record payment of 15 shillings on 6 May 1767 for printing the above
No copy known mp. 41694

B2754 FORDYCE, JAMES, 1720-1796
Sermons to young women: in two volumes. By the Reverend Dr. Fordyce. Volume I[-II]. [Boston] Printed [by Mein and Fleeming, for sale by John Mein] in MDCC-LXVII.

2 v. 15.5 cm.
Attributed to Mein and Fleeming by John Alden on basis of distinctive type face
Alden: John Mein 5
MB mp. 41707

B2755 FORDYCE, JAMES, 1720-1796
Sermons to young women . . . A new edition, corrected and enlarged. Volume I. Boston, Printed by Mein and Fleeming, and sold by John Mein, 1767.
viii, 180 p. 15.5 cm.
Page iv misnumbered vi
cf. Alden: John Mein 5 note
CtHC; MWA (v. 1 only) mp. 41708

B2756 FORDYCE, JAMES, 1720-1796
Two sermons to young women: I. On female devotion and good works. II. On female meekness . . . Boston, Printed by Mein and Fleeming, and sold by John Mein, 1767.
2 p.l., [127]-227 p. 15 cm.
Sheets from an edition printed by Mein and Fleeming without their name on t.p., here issued separately with special t.p. cf. BSA *Papers* 36 (1942) no. 3
MB; RPJCB (p. 129-130 wanting) mp. 41709

B2757 [FREEMAN'S New York royal sheet almanac for 1768. New York, 1767]
broadside
Advertised in *Holt's New-York Journal*, Nov. 5, 1767
Drake 5789
No copy known

B2758 THE friar and boy . . . Boston, Printed for, and sold by A. Barclay, 1767.
24 p. 15 cm. [A]-B^6
Rosenbach-Ch 59
PP mp. 41710

B2759 FRIENDLY SOCIETY OF TRADESMEN
Articles and regulations of the Friendly Society . . . agreed upon the 10th day of March . . . 1767 . . . [XX regulations] [New York, 1767]
broadside 53 X 44 cm.
NN. Photostats: DLC; MHi mp. 41711

B2760 FRIENDSHIP SOCIETY, BOSTON
Rules and orders, agreed to be observed, by the Friendship Society, instituted at Boston, the twenty-fifth day of May, A. D. 1767. We the subscribers for the more speedy . . . assistance of each other . . . when in danger of fire . . . [Boston, 1767?]
broadside
Ford 1408
MB mp. 41712

B2761 GAY, EBENEZER, 1718-1796
The sovereignty of God . . . illustrated and improved, in a sermon preached . . . May 22d 1766. at the funeral of three young men . . . killed by lightning . . . Hartford, Printed by Thomas Green, 1767.
24 p. 20 cm. [A]-C^4
CtHi; MWA; RPJCB mp. 41713

B2762 GEORGIA. LAWS
An act for granting . . . the sum . . . for the use and support of the government of Georgia . . . Council-chamber, 26th March, 1767 . . . [Savannah, James Johnston, 1767]
8 p. 25.5 cm. caption title
cf. De Renne p. 185
DLC (facsim.); RPJCB mp. 41714

B2763 GEORGIA. LAWS
Acts passed . . . at a session begun . . . on Monday the 16th day of June . . . 1766 . . . and from thence continued . . . to the 26th day of March 1767 . . . Savannah, James Johnston [1767]
1 p.l., 39, [1] p. 25.5 cm. A-K^2
De Renne p. 183; Guerra a-400
DLC; GU-De; RPJCB mp. 41715

B2764 GOLDSMITH, OLIVER, 1728-1774
[The vicar of Wakefield. Boston, Printed by Mein & Fleeming, for J. Mein, 1767]

Alden: John Mein 6
No copy known mp. 41716

B2765 GT. BRIT. SOVEREIGNS (GEORGE III)
George the Third, by the grace of God . . . To our trusty and well-beloved Henry Hulton, John Temple, William Burch . . . September 15, 1767. [Boston, 1767]
7 p.
Ford 1409; also pt. 2 of Evans 9682
MHi; MWA mp. 41718

B2766 GT. BRIT. SOVEREIGNS (GEORGE III)
The Governor's commission of vice-admiral. George the Third . . . to . . . John Wentworth . . . governor . . . of New-Hampshire . . . Greeting . . . [Portsmouth, 1767]
5 p. sm. fol.
Dated Aug. 9, 1766
Huntington 279
CSmH mp. 41717

B2767 HALL, DAVID, 1714-1772
Imported in the last vessels from England, and to be sold by David Hall, at the New Printing-Office, in Market-street, Philadelphia, the following books, &c. Horsman's and Bridgman's conveyancer . . . [Philadelphia, 1767?]
[2] p. 35.5 X 21 cm. caption title
Bound in *Pennsylvania Gazette*, after Nov. 26, 1767
MWA mp. 41719

B2768 THE happy child . . . Boston, Printed and sold [by T. and J. Fleet] at the Heart and Crown in Cornhill, 1767.
8 p. 11.5 cm.
In verse
MDedHi. Photostat: d'Alté A. Welch, Cleveland (1962) mp. 41720

B2769 HARVARD UNIVERSITY
Quaestiones pro modulo . . . MDCCLXVII. [Boston] Draper [1767]
broadside
MH; MHi; MWA mp. 41722

B2770 THE history of the Holy Jesus . . . By a Lover of their precious souls. The fifteenth edition. Boston, Printed by I. Thomas, for Z. Fowle [1767?]
[48] p. 18 illus. 11 cm. [A]-C^8
Dated by d'Alté A. Welch
CtHi; MWA. d'Alté A. Welch, Cleveland mp. 41723

B2771 INTERESTING hints to the inhabitants of **** **** . . . Y. Z. [Philadelphia, A. Armbruster, 1767]
4 p. 4to caption title
PPL mp. 41724

B2772 [JACOB, ELIZABETH HEAD] 1674-1739
An epistle in true love . . . [At end] Elizabeth Jacob, written in the city of Worcester, the 5th of the 9th month, 1712. Wilmington, James Adams, 1767.

12 p. 18.5 cm. caption title
Hawkins 3
DeWI mp. 41725

B2773 JONES, ANDREW
The black book of conscience . . . The twenty-seventh edition. Hartford, Thomas Green, 1767.
16 p. 19 cm.
CtHi; MWA mp. 41726

B2774 LAW, WILLIAM, 1686-1761
Auszüge aus den Schriften William Laws . . . Aus dem Englischen übersetzt. Philadelphia, Henrich Miller, 1767.
16 p. 17 cm.
Metzger 308
PPeSchw mp. 41728

B2775 [LEE, ARTHUR] 1740-1792
Extract from an address in the *Virginia Gazette*, of March 19, 1767. [Philadelphia, D. Hall and W. Sellers, 1767]
4 p. 17 cm. caption title
On p. 1, line 1 of last paragraph ends with "who favor sla-"
For authority for authorship, cf. Brookes: *Friend Anthony Benezet*. Philadelphia, 1937
DLC (2 copies); RPJCB

B2776 [LEE, ARTHUR] 1740-1792
Extract from an address, in the *Virginia Gazette*, of March 19, 1767. Mr. Rind, Permit me in your paper . . . [Philadelphia? 1767?]
4 p. 15.5 cm.
Probably earlier than the following edition; line 16, p. 4 has "probale" for "probable;" p. 2 has "unfortunate and detestable people."
NN

B2777 [LEE, ARTHUR] 1740-1792
Extract from an address in the *Virginia Gazette*, of March 19, 1767. Mr. Rind, Permit me, in your paper . . . [Philadelphia? 1767?]
4 p. 16 cm.
Not Evans 11651
Probably later than the preceding edition; line 16, p. 4 has "probable" correctly spelled; p. 2 has "unfortunate ******** people."
NN

B2778 LOUISIANA. CONSEIL SUPÉRIEUR
Extrait, des régistres des audiances du Conseil Supérieur . . . du 7. Mars 1767 . . . [New Orleans, Denis Braud, 1767]
broadside 47 X 35 cm.
cf. BSA *Papers*, LXII (1968) p. 253
CU-B

B2779 MARCH, EDMUND, 1703-1791
Specialities relative to the kingdom of God in the latter days . . . Boston, Printed by W. M'Alpine in Marlborough-Street, sold by him and B. Emerson in Newbury-Port, 1767.
12, 6+ p.
MHi (lacking after p. 6) mp. 41729

B2780 MASSACHUSETTS. GOVERNOR, 1760-1769
By His Excellency Francis Bernard . . . A brief . . . [Mar. 18, 1767] . . . Boston, Richard Draper, 1767.
broadside 40.5 X 32.5 cm.
Ford 1414
M-Ar; MWA mp. 41731

B2781 MASSACHUSETTS. GOVERNOR, 1760-1769
By His Excellency Francis Bernard . . . A proclamation [for discovering the murderers of four Indians] . . . [Sept. 10, 1767] . . . Boston, Richard Draper, 1767.
broadside
Ford 1416
M-Ar mp. 41732

B2782 MASSACHUSETTS. GOVERNOR, 1760-1769
By His Excellency Francis Bernard . . . A proclamation, for proroguing the General Court . . . Given at Boston, the twenty-third day of September 1767 . . . Boston: Printed by Richard Draper, 1767.
broadside fol.
PHi

B2783 MASSACHUSETTS. GOVERNOR, 1760-1769
By His Excellency Francis Bernard . . . a proclamation. Whereas His Majesty . . . [July 22, 1767] . . . Boston, Richard Draper, 1767.
broadside 41 X 33 cm.
DLC mp. 41733

B2784 MASSACHUSETTS. LAWS
. . . An act passed by the . . . General Court . . . begun . . . May, 1767 . . . for apportioning and assessing a tax . . . [Colophon] Boston, Richard Draper and Green & Russell, 1767.
10 [i.e. 14] p. 35 cm.
Huntington 280; New York Public 386
CSmH; M; MH; MWA; NN mp. 41734

B2785 MASSACHUSETTS. LAWS
. . . Province of Massachusetts-Bay. June 23, 1767. The following bill is printed by order of the two houses . . . An act incorporating a Society for relieving the widows and orphans of the ministers of the Congregational Churches . . . Boston, Richard Draper [1767]
[4] p. 33.5 cm.
Ford 1413
MHi mp. 41730

B2786 MATHER, COTTON, 1662-1728
The everlasting gospel . . . Second edition. Philadelphia, Henry Miller, 1767.
59 p. A-G^4 H^2
Holmes: Cotton Mather 115-B
RPJCB mp. 41735

B2787 MEIN AND FLEEMING, FIRM
Boston, October 22d, 1767. Proposals for printing . . . *The Boston Chronicle* . . . [Boston] Mein and Fleeming [1767]
broadside (2 p.) 27 X 21.5 cm.
Ford 1418
DLC; MB; MHi; MWA mp. 41736

B2788 MEIN AND FLEEMING, FIRM
Boston, November 19th, 1767. Proposals for printing . . . the *Boston Chronicle* . . . [Boston, Mein and Fleeming, 1767]
[2] p.
MWA mp. 41737

B2789 MILLER, HENRICH
Henrich Miller, Buchdrucker in der Zweiten-Strasse . . . hat folgende Bücher zu verkaufen . . . Calender auf das Jahr 1768 . . . [Philadelphia, H. Miller, 1767]
broadside 22.5 X 19.5 cm.
PHi mp. 41738

B2790 THE new book of knowledge . . . Boston, Printed for A. Barclay, 1767.

172 p. 16 cm. [A]-O^6 P^2
MB; MHi (imperfect); MWA mp. 41739

B2791 THE New-England primer improved . . . Boston, Printed for, and sold by John Perkins, 1767.
[80] p. [A]-E^8
Heartman 24; Huntington 282
CSmH mp. 41740

B2792 NEW HAMPSHIRE. HOUSE OF REPRESENTATIVES
The news-boy, who now carries the *New-Hampshire* Oct. 1767] . . . [Portsmouth, 1767]
31 p.
MWA mp. 41741

B2793 NEW HAMPSHIRE GAZETTE
The news-boy, who now carries the *New-Hampshire Gazette* . . . of the year 1767 . . . [Portsmouth, 1767]
broadside
MWA mp. 41748

B2794 A NEW-YEARS WISH
Once more my friends I do appear,
With liberty from the press,
And all my grateful wishes now
To you I shall address.
[n.p., 1767?]
broadside
Dated from an endorsement in an old hand, possibly contemporary
Ford 1396
PHi. Photostat: MWA mp. 41745

B2795 NEW YORK. LAWS
[Laws of New York passed Dec. 19, 1766-June 6, 1767] [New York, W. Weyman, 1767]
p. 445-469. 35.5 cm.
Running title: Laws of New-York. Sir Henry Moore, Baronet, Governor
DLC; NNS mp. 41746

B2796 NEW-YORK GAZETTE
New-Year's verses made and carried about to the customers of the *New-York Gazette*, by Lawrence Swinney, alias (for the present) Bloody-News, but on the prospect of the approaching peace, for the future, Lawrence White-Flagg . . . [New York, 1767?]
broadside
1st line: For breaking faith, and eating frogs . . .
NjHi mp. 41767

B2797 NEWBURYPORT, MASS. FIRE SOCIETY
These presents witnesseth; That we the subscribers . . . do mutually agree to the following articles . . . Newburyport, February 23, 1767. [Boston? 1767]
broadside 42 X 33 cm.
Ford 1419
MWA mp. 41747

B2798 NORTH CAROLINA. COUNCIL
To His Excellency William Tryon . . . the humble address of his Majesty's Council . . . [Newbern, James Davis, 1767]
broadside 32 X 19 cm.
McMurtrie: North Carolina 52
Public Record Off. mp. 41749

B2799 NORTH CAROLINA. GOVERNOR, 1765-1771
The speech of his Excellency William Tryon . . . To the General Assembly, held at Newbern [Dec. 5, 1767] . . . [Newbern, James Davis, 1767]
[3] p. 32 cm. caption title
McMurtrie: North Carolina 53
Public Record Off. mp. 41751

B2800 NORTH CAROLINA. HOUSE OF ASSEMBLY
To his Excellency William Tryon . . . the humble address of the House of Assembly . . . [Newbern, James Davis, 1767]
2 p. 31 cm. caption title
McMurtrie: North Carolina 54
Public Record Off. mp. 41750

B2801 PENNSYLVANIA. TREATIES
A treaty with the Shawnese and Delaware Indians . . . Negociated at Fort-Johnson . . . in the province of New-York, by . . . Sir William Johnson . . . New-York, Printed and sold by J. Parker and W. Weyman, 1767.
10 p. 33 cm.
DePuy 38
PHi mp. 41752

B2802 THE prodigal daughter: being a strange and wonder [sic] relation of the young lady in Bristol . . . Boston, Printed and sold in Back-street [by Z. Fowle?] [1767?]
[15] p.
Title cut has initials "I.T." [Isaiah Thomas?]
Fowle printed in Back-street from 1763 to 1771
Hamilton 45
MWA [1770?]; NjP mp. 41754

B2803 PROVIDENCE, December 2, 1767. Luxury and extravagance . . . having of late greatly increased . . . we the subscribers . . . promise each other, that we will not . . . import . . . the following articles . . . [Providence, 1767]
broadside 15.5 X 20 cm.
Alden 365; Winship p. 22
RHi mp. 41755

B2804 [REGISTER of New-Hampshire, and almanack for 1768 . . . [n.p., 1767?]
[6+] p.
Drake 4627
ICN [3 1.]

B2805 REMINGTON, E
A short account of three men . . . killed by lightning . . . Samuel Remington, James Bagg, Jonathan Bagg . . . New London, Timothy Green, 1767.
broadside
Hamilton 46
NjP mp. 41756

B2706 RHODE ISLAND. CHARTER
The charter, granted by . . . Charles II. to the Governor and company . . . Newport, Samuel Hall, 1767.
15 p. 29.5 cm.
Usually bound, as issued, preceding the 1767 *Acts and laws* (Evans 10749) mp. 41757

B2807 RHODE ISLAND. ELECTION PROX
Seekers of peace. Honorable Stephen Hopkins, Esq;

Gov. Honorable Joseph Wanton, jun. Esq; Dep. Gov. . . . [Newport? Samuel Hall? 1767?]
broadside 20 X 13 cm.
Alden 366; Chapin Proxies 6
RPJCB. Photostat: MWA mp. 41758

B2808 RHODE ISLAND. GOVERNOR, 1767-1768
By the honorable Stephen Hopkins . . . A proclamation. Whereas the General assembly . . . [June 15, 1767] . . . [Newport, Samuel Hall [1767]
broadside 33 X 25.5 cm.
Bill submitted June 22, 1767
Alden 367; Winship p. 22
RWe mp. 41759

B2809 RHODE ISLAND. LAWS
At the General assembly . . . begun and held . . . on the second Monday in June . . . An act for taking a just estimate . . . [Newport, S. Hall, 1767]
4 p. 33 cm. caption title
Alden 375; Winship p. 22
DLC; RHi; RPB (2 copies) mp. 41761

B2810 RHODE ISLAND. LAWS
[At the General assembly . . . begun and holden . . . on the first Monday in December . . . An act for assessing . . . a rate or tax of six thousand pounds . . . Newport, S. Hall [1767].]
[3?] p. [folio?]
Bill submitted by Hall at the May, 1767, session
Alden 375A
No copy known mp. 41760

B2811 [RIDLEY, JAMES] 1736-1765
The adventures of Urad . . . Boston, Printed by Mein and Fleeming, and to be sold by John Mein, 1767.
2 p.l., 58 p. 11 cm. [A-B]-D^8
Rosenbach-Ch 58
MB; MH (wanting through p. 10); MWA; PP mp. 47162

B2812 ROME, GEORGE
Copy of a letter returned . . . Narragansett, 22d. December 1767. [n.p., 1767]
broadside 41 X 31.5 cm.
Ford 1423; New York Public 387
MHi. Photostats: DLC; NN mp. 47163

B2813 RUSTON, THOMAS
An essay on inoculation for the small pox. Wherein the nature of the disease is explained, the various methods . . . practised in America are critically examined . . . Philadelphia, W. and T. Bradford, 1767.

Advertised as "Just published" in the *Pennsylvania Journal*, Sept. 3, 1767
Guerra a-407; Rogers 109; Sabin 74428
No copy located mp. 47164

B2814 SCHABALIE, JAN PHILIPSEN
Die wandlende seele . . . Germantown, Gedruckt und zu finden bey Christoph Saur, 1767.
[8], 463, [25] p. 8vo
MWA; PPL mp. 47165

B2815 SOUTH-CAROLINA GAZETTE, CHARLESTON
New-Year's verses, of the printer's boys, who carry about the *South-Carolina Gazette, and Country Journal* . . . Thursday, January 1, 1767. [Charleston, 1767]
broadside 28.5 X 17 cm.
1st line: May honour'd patrons . . .
PHi mp. 41743

B2816 [STEVENS, GEORGE ALEXANDER] 1710-1784
The celebrated lecture on heads . . . New York, John Holt, 1767.
32 p. 15.5 cm.
Sabin 91498
DLC mp. 41766

B2817 TANS'UR, WILLIAM, 1699-1783
The royal melody complete . . . The third edition, with additions . . . Boston, W. M'Alpine; also sold by D. Bayley at Newbury-Port, and M. Williams at Salem, 1767.
13, [2], 14, [2], 112 p. sm. obl. 4to
Huntington 283; cf. Evans 10782
CSmH

B2818 THIS is unto all GENTLEMEN who shoes here,
I wish you a merry Christmas, a happy New-Year:
For shoeing your horses, and trimming their locks,
Please to remember my New-Years BOX.
[n.p., 1767?]
broadside
Dated from an endorsement in an old hand, possibly contemporary
Ford 1397
PHi. Photostat: MWA mp. 41768

B2819 THOMPSON, JOHN
The lost and undone son of perdition . . . Judas Iscariot . . . Hartford, Printed and sold [by Thomas Green] [1767?]
15 p. 19 cm.
Trumbull: Supplement 2670
CtHi mp. 41769

B2820 THOMPSON, JOHN
The lost and undone son of perdition . . . Judas Iscariot . . . New-London, Printed and sold by T. Green [1767?]
23, [1] p.
MWA mp. 41770

B2821 TIFFANY, CONSIDER, 1733-1796
Relation of the melancholy death of six young persons who were kill'd by lightning . . . June, 1767, viz. . . . By Consider Tiffany, of Hartland, in Connecticut . . . Hartland, July, 17[67?] [n.p., 1767]
broadside 38 X 24 cm.
42 4-line stanzas in three columns
CtHi. Photostat: MWA mp. 41771

B2822 TISSOT, SAMUEL AUGUSTE ANDRÉ DAVID, 1728-1797
Advice to the people in general, with regard to their health . . . Translated from the French edition . . . By J. Kirkpatrick . . . London [i.e. Boston, Mein and Fleeming] Printed in Year MDCCLXVII.

2 v.
Alden: John Mein 8
CtY; DNLM; MA; MBCo; MH; MeB; NhD (v. 2); RPJCB (v. 1) mp. 41772

B2823 VIRGINIA. HOUSE OF BURGESSES
The journal of the House of burgesses. [Mar. 12-Apr. 11, 1767] [Williamsburg, W. Rind, 1767]
p. 78-136. 33.5 cm. caption title
Sabin 99966; Torrence 340
DLC; Vi mp. 41774

B2824 WARD, SAMUEL, 1725-1776
Newport, April 7, 1767. To enable the freemen . . . Samuel Ward . . . [Newport, S. Hall, 1767]
[2] p. 31 X 18.5 cm.
Alden 378; Winship p. 22
RWe mp. 41775

B2736 WATTS, ISAAC, 1674-1748
A collection of hymns . . . Boston, Wm. M'Alpine, 1767.
74 p. 15.5 cm.
Second title of Bible. O.T. Psalms *supra* mp. 41693

B2825 WATTS, ISAAC, 1674-1748
Hymns and spiritual songs . . . The twenty-first edition . . . Boston, Printed by Kneeland and Adams for John Perkins, 1767.
xxiv, 312 p. 22 plates. 16 cm.
MB; MWA mp. 41776

B2826 WELLS'S Register of the Southern British American Provinces, together with an almanack [for 1768] by George Andrews. Charles-Town, Printed and sold by Robert Wells [1767?]
[52] p.
Drake 13097; Sabin 87753
MWA mp. 41690

B2827 WHIPPLE, LEVI
I Levi Whipple, of Cranston . . . depose and say, That I heard Elisha Brown . . . Deposition, April 13th, 1767, before me, Samuel Chace . . . [Providence, Sarah Goddard, 1767]
broadside 16 X 21.5 cm.
Alden 379; Winship p. 22
RPJCB. Photostats: MHi; MWA; NN; RHi mp. 41778

B2828 WILLIS, LYDIA (FISH) 1709-1767
Rachel's sepulchre; or, A memorial of Mrs. Lydia Willis, taken, chiefly, from her letters to friends . . . [Boston? N. Coverly? 1767?]
39 p. 17.5 cm. [A]-E^4
MWA mp. 41779

B2829 WOODWARD, JOSIAH
The young man's monitor . . . By Josiah Woodward, D. D. . . . From the fourth London edition. Philadelphia, Printed and sold by Henry Miller, 1767.
60 p. 25.5 cm.
Metzger 313
PHi mp. 41780

B2830 THE youth's instructor in the English tongue . . . Boston, W. M'Alpine, 1767.
148+ p.
MWA (all lacking after p. 148) mp. 41781

1768

B2831 ALLEN, BENNET
[Advertisement. Baltimore, Nicholas Hasselbach? 1768]

Reprinted in *Maryland Gazette*, Sept. 22, 1768, where it is stated that it was printed in Baltimore
Wroth 278
No copy known mp. 41785

B2832 ALLEN, BENNET
To the public. November 9, 1768. Mr. Wolstenholme having, in his hand-bill of this day, vindicated his conduct . . . Bennet Allen . . . [Annapolis, Anne Catharine and William Green, 1768]
broadside 44 X 27.5 cm.
Wroth 279
MdHi mp. 41786

B2833 AN almanack agreeable to the new-stile . . . For the year . . . 1769 . . . By William Ball, Philomath. Charles-Town, Printed and sold by Charles Crouch [1768]
[36] p.
Advertised in the *South Carolina Gazette and Country Journal*, Nov. 29, 1768
Drake 13098; Guerra b-220
MHi mp. 41789

B2834 ANDREWS'S almanack for the year . . . 1769. January begins on Sunday, hath 31 days . . . Charleston: Printed and sold by Robert Wells [1768]
broadside 42 X 33 cm.
Drake 13099; Sabin 87754
MWA mp. 41787

B2835 AN astronomical diary . . . for . . . 1769 . . . By Nathaniel Ames . . . Boston, Printed [by William M'Alpine[for D. & R. Fowle [1768]
[24] p. 16.5 cm.
Drake 3168
DLC; MHi; MWA mp. 41788

B2836 AN astronomical diary . . . for . . . 1769 . . . By Nathaniel Ames . . . Boston, Printed for Daniel Bayley, Newbury-port [1768]
[14] p.
Drake 3167
MHi

B2837 AN astronomical diary . . . for . . . 1769. By Nathaniel Ames. Hartford, Green & Watson [1768]
[24] p.
Drake 253
CtHi; DLC; NN (imperfect)

B2838 AUBRY, CHARLES PHILIPPE
Je proteste contre l'arrêt du Conseil, qui renvoye . . .

Wlloa [sic] de cette colonie . . . 29. Octobre 1768. Signé Aubry . . . [New Orleans, Denis Braud, 1768]
broadside
McMurtrie: Louisiana 2; cf. Marc de Villiers du Terrage: *Les dernières années de la Louisiane française* (Paris [1903?]), p. 260
Archives Nationales, Paris mp. 41788a

B2839 THE Ballator. Proposal for election of members in General assembly . . . New-York, March 7, 1768 . . . [New York, 1768]
broadside 31 X 19.5 cm.
DLC. Photostat: MWA mp. 41791

B2840 BALTIMORE COUNTY. CITIZENS
To His Excellency Horatio Sharpe . . . the petition of the subscribers, inhabitants of Baltimore County . . . [Baltimore, Nicholas Hasselbach, 1768]?
broadside 44 X 28 cm.
Wroth 285
MdHi mp. 41792

B2841 BALTIMORE COUNTY. CITIZENS
To His Excellency Horatio Sharpe . . . the petition of the subscribers, inhabitants of Baltimore County . . . [Baltimore, Nicholas Hasselbach, 1768]?
broadside 51.5 X 39.5 cm.
Wroth 286
MdHi mp. 41793

B2842 BALTIMORE COUNTY. CITIZENS
To His Excellency Horatio Sharpe . . . the petition of the subscribers, inhabitants of Baltimore County . . . An seine Excellenz Horatio Scharpe . . . die Bittschrift der unterschriebenen . . . [Baltimore, Nicholas Hasselbach, 1768]?
[2] p. 44 X 28 cm.
Wroth 287
MdHi mp. 41794

B2843 BARD, JOHN
New-York, May 12, 1768. Advertisement. To be sold by the subscriber, living in New-York, either all together, or in distinct farms . . . [New York, 1768]
broadside 18 X 20 cm.
NHi mp. 41795

B2844 BIBLE
Verbum sempiternum. The seventh edition with amendments. Boston, Mein & Fleeming [1768?]
[12], 275 p. 4.5 cm.
John Taylor's Thumb Bible
New Testament portion also issued separately
MB (imperfect); MH (imperfect). Ruth Adomeit, Cleveland (p. 274-275 wanting) mp. 41889

B2845 BIBLE. O.T. PSALMS
The New-England Psalter . . . Boston, Printed by Edes and Gill, for John Perkins, 1768.
[168] p. 16 cm.
MB mp. 41797

B2846 BIBLE. O.T. PSALMS
The Psalms of David imitated . . . By I. Watts, D.D. The twenty-sixth edition . . . Boston: Printed by Mein and Fleeming, and to be sold by William Appleton at Portsmouth in New-Hampshire, 1768.
xxx, 346, [2] p.
MHi; RPJCB mp. 41895

B2847 BIBLE. N.T.
The history of the New-Testament. Boston, Mein & Fleeming [1768?]
[151]-275 p. 4.5 cm.
The New Testament portion of John Taylor's Thumb Bible, issued separately
MWA (p. 263-275 wanting) mp. 41889

B2848 BICKERSTAFF'S Boston almanack, for . . . 1769 . . . Second edition. Boston, Mein and Fleeming [1768]
[44] p. 16.5 cm.
By Benjamin West
Drake 3175
MB; MHi; MWA mp. 41898

B2849 BLAY, RUTH, d. 1768
The declaration and confession of Ruth Blay who was tried . . . In Portsmouth, New-Hampshire, September 21st, 1768 for concealing the birth of her infant, which was found dead; and is to be executed the 30th day of December 1768 . . . [Portsmouth, 1768]
broadside 36.5 X 14 cm.
MSaE

B2850 BOSTON. CITIZENS
At a meeting of the freeholders and other inhabitants of Boston . . . Monday the 12th of September, A.D. 1768 . . . [Boston, 1768]
broadside
Concerns a report that three regiments were to garrison the town
Ford 1429
MB; MBB; MHi; PPRF mp. 41804

B2851 BOSTON. SELECTMEN
Boston, September 14, 1768. Gentlemen, You are already too well acquainted with the melancholly . . . circumstances . . . [Boston, 1768]
broadside 32 X 19.5 cm.
Circular letter from the selectmen
Ford 1430
MB; MHi; NHi. Photostat: MWA mp. 41799

B2852 BOSTON. SELECTMEN
The freeholders and other inhabitants of the town of Boston . . . By order of the select-men, Boston, March 5. 1768 . . . [Boston, 1768]
broadside 19.5 X 16 cm.
DLC mp. 41800

B2853 BOSTON. SELECTMEN
Notification. The freeholders and other inhabitants of the town . . . Boston, March 17th, 1768. [Boston, 1768]
broadside 13.5 X 11 cm.
DLC mp. 41801

B2854 BOSTON. SELECTMEN
Notification. The freeholders and other inhabitants of the town . . . Boston, May 19, 1768 . . . [Boston, 1768]
broadside 11 X 13.5 cm.
DLC mp. 41802

B2855 BOSTON. SELECTMEN
Notification. The freeholders and other inhabitants of

the town . . . to meet at Faneuil-Hall on Monday the 12th day of September currant [sic] . . . Boston, September 10, 1768. [Boston, 1768]
broadside
New York Public 390
NN (facsim.) mp. 41803

B2856 BOSTON EVENING POST
New-Year's Day, 1768. The news boy's verses who carries the *Boston Evening-Post*. [Boston, T. & J. Fleet, 1768]
broadside 26.5 X 13 cm.
Ford 1461
PHi mp. 41855

B2857 BOSTON GAZETTE
A New-Year's wish.
This years begun my humble muse
Attempt to greet you on the news.
[Boston, Edes & Gill, 1768]
broadside
With a new engraving of the cut used on their 1766 New Year's greeting
Ford 1460
PHi. Photostat: MWA mp. 41859

B2858 BOSTON NEWS LETTER
Postscript to the *Boston News-Letter*, August 25, 1768. Account of the celebration of the anniversary of the Fourteenth of August by the Sons of Liberty . . . [Boston, 1768]
broadside
Ford 1465
MWA mp. 41866

B2859 BOSTON POST BOY
A New Year's wish, from the carrier of the *Post Boy and Advertiser*. 1768. I. The course of time . . . [Boston, Green & Russell, 1768]
broadside 17 X 13.5 cm.
Ford 1458
PHi. Photostat: MWA mp. 41857

B2860 BROWN, ELISHA
Boston, December 1768. Proposals for printing by subscription, The miser . . . By William Clarke . . . Subscriptions are taken in by Elisha Brown . . . [Boston, 1768]
broadside 17 X 10.5 cm.
Ford 1433; New York Public 384
MHi. Photostats: DLC; NN mp. 41700; 41809

B2861 BROWN, JEREMIAH, 1723?-1793
Christ's example, and the fashion of the world; or, A ticket looking-glass . . . Here is Jeremiah Brown's roll . . . New-England, Printed for the author, MDCCLXVIII.
16 p. 19 cm. $A\text{-}B^4$
In verse
Criticizing (probably) the Warren, R.I., Baptist Church lottery in 1767.
RPB. Miss Alvaretta Tupper, Providence, R.I. Photostat: MWA mp. 41805

B2862 BURNS, GEORGE, d. 1768
The confession and declaration of George Burns, now a prisoner in Charles-Town goal . . . which he voluntarily makes . . . this 9th day of February, 1768 . . . George Burns . . . The unhappy person, who made the above declaration, was executed . . . the 10th of February inst. . . . Charles-Town, John-Hugar Van Huerin [1768]
[2] p. 31.5 X 19.5 cm.
MWA mp. 41806

B2863 BYRD LOTTERY
A list of the numbers which have come up prizes in the honourable W. Byrd's lottery . . . [Philadelphia? 1768]
broadside 24.5 X 19 cm.
PHi mp. 41807

B2864 THE children in the woods . . . Providence [John Waterman, 1768?]
broadside 34 X 23 cm.
Text in 3 columns of verse
Dated 1768 on the basis of other Waterman imprints
Alden 381
Bradford Swan, Providence, R.I. mp. 41808

B2865 [COWPER, WILLIAM] 1731-1800
The diverting history of John Gilpin . . . Sold at the Bible and Heart, Salem [1768?]
broadside 34.5 X 21.5 cm.
Text in 3 columns
Ms. note on verso: "Printed the year a press was established here."
Ford 3032
MSaE

B2866 DEBLOIS, GILBERT
Gilbert Deblois, at his shop opposite School-Street . . . Boston, imports from London, Bristol, and Scotland . . . all sorts English, India & Scotch goods . . . Boston, April 15. 1768. [Boston, 1768]
broadside oblong 8vo
PPL mp. 41810

B2867 DILWORTH, THOMAS, d. 1780
A new guide to the English tongue . . . Boston, Printed by Kneeland and Adams, for R. Draper, 1768.
xii, [2], 168 p.
MWA mp. 41811

B2868 DILWORTH, THOMAS, d. 1780
A new guide to the English tongue . . . Philadelphia, Printed and sold by D. Hall, and W. Sellers, 1768.
[14], 152+ p. front. 17.5 cm. $A\text{-}O^6$
MWA (sig. O6 wanting) mp. 41812

B2869 DYER, WILLIAM, 1636-1696
A cabinet of jewels: or, A glimpse of Sion's glory. Written by William Dyer . . . New-London, Timothy Green, 1768.
38 p. 17 cm.
Trumbull: Supplement 2092
CtHi mp. 41813

B2870 DYER, WILLIAM, 1636-1696
Christ's voice to London . . . New-London, Re-printed and sold by Timothy Green, 1768.
38, [1] p. 17.5 cm.
Trumbull: Supplement 2093
CtHi; NhD (final p. wanting) mp. 41814

B2871 DYER, WILLIAM, 1636-1696
Follow the Lamb . . . taken from . . . A believer's golden chain. New-London, Timothy Green, 1768.
56 p. 17.5 cm.
CtHi; MWA (p. 3-4 mutilated); RPJCB (imperfect) mp. 41815

B2872 THE famous Tommy Thumb's little storybook . . . Boston, Printed and sold by W. M'Alpine, 1768.
31 p. illus. 10 cm.
Scalloped marbled paper covers
NjP (p. 23-26, 31 wanting) mp. 41890

B2873 FANEUIL HALL LOTTERY
Faneuil-Hall lottery. Boston, January, 1768. [Boston, 1768]
broadside
Ford 1432
MHi mp. 41816

B2874 A FEW thoughts on the death of Mr. Luke Rich of Western, who was killed on Coy's hill by his cart wheels, April, 1768, in the 23d year of his age . . . [n.p., 1768]
broadside 27.5 X 22 cm.
MWA mp. 41817

B2875 FIRE CLUB, HAVERHILL
Rules and orders, agreed upon the to be observed by the Fire-Club at New-England. [Boston, 1768?]
broadside 39 X 32 cm.
Filled in for Haverhill, Feb. 22, 1768
MWA mp. 41101

B2876 FOOT, JOHN, 1742-1813
Death a welcome messenger to the true Christian. A sermon, occasioned by the . . . death, of Doctor John Hull . . . May 25th, 1768 . . . New-Haven, Thomas and Samuel Green, 1768.
22 p.
CtHi; CtY; RPJCB mp. 41818

B2877 [FOTHERGILL, SAMUEL] 1715-1772
Two discourses, and a prayer, publickly delivered . . . at the Quakers Year Meeting . . . in Bristol . . . New-York, Reprinted and sold by James Parker, 1768.
27 p. 18 cm. $[A]^2$ $B-D^4$
MWA; RPJCB (p. 27 wanting) mp. 41820

B2878 [FOTHERGILL, SAMUEL] 1715-1772
Two discourses, and a prayer, publickly delivered . . . at the Quakers Yearly Meeting . . . in Bristol . . . New-York, Re-printed and sold by James Parker [1768?]
23 p.
cf. Evans 10615-16
RPJCB (date removed by trimming) mp. 41819

B2879 FRASIER, ISAAC, 1740-1768
A brief account of the life, and abominable thefts, of the notorious Isaac Frasier . . . penned from his own mouth, and signed by him, a few days before his execution. New Haven, Printed & sold by T. & S. Green [1768?]
16 p. 20 cm.
Black borders and cut on t.p.
CtHi; MWA; RPJCB mp. 41822

B2880 FRASIER, ISAAC, 1740-1768
A brife [sic] account of the life, and abominable thefts, of . . . Isaac Frasier . . . penned from his own mouth . . . With his dying speech. New Haven, T. & S. Green [1768]
15 p. 17 cm.
Imprint supplied from Trumbull 732
New York Public 391; cf. Evans 10808
NN (mutilated) mp. 41823

B2881 FRIENDS, SOCIETY OF
Advice and caution from the Monthly meeting . . . the twenty-third day of the ninth month. 1768 . . . Philadelphia, D. Hall, and W. Sellers [1768]
broadside 35 X 21 cm.
DLC; PHi mp. 41824

B2882 FROM the Boston papers, October 24, 1764. Last week the Lady of the Honorable John Temple . . From the *New-York Journal*, Nov. 10th, 1768 . . . [Philadelphia, 1768]
broadside 18 X 7.5 cm.
PHi mp. 41825

B2883 GEORGIA. LAWS
. . . An act for granting . . . the sum of three thousand . . . Council-chamber, 11th April, 1767 [i.e., 1768, corrected in manuscript in the original] [Savannah, J. Johnston, 1768]
7 p. 29 cm. caption title
De Renne p. 188
DLC (photostat); GU-De; RPJCB mp. 41826

B2884 GEORGIA. LAWS
Acts passed . . . [Oct. 26, 1767-Apr. 11, 1768] Savannah, James Johnston [1768]
1 p.l., 34, [1] p. 25.5 cm. $[\ ]^1$ $A-T^2$
De Renne p. 186; Guerra a-413
DLC (t.p. in facsim.); GU-De; RPJCB mp. 41827

B2885 GESSNER, SALOMON, 1730-1787
The death of Abel . . . Attempted from the German of Mr. Gessner. Boston, Printed and sold by Z. Fowle and N. Coverly, 1768.
92 p. illus. 20 cm.
Dedication signed: Mary Collyer
Hamilton 48
MB; MWA; NjP; RPJCB mp. 41828

B2886 A GOLDEN chain of four links . . . Boston, Printed and sold by Z. Fowle, 1768.
16 p. 17 cm. $[A]-B^4$
MWA (t.p. mutilated) mp. 41829

B2887 GT. BRIT. SOVEREIGNS (GEORGE III)
Copy of the commission of Jared Ingersoll, Esq; Judge of the High Court of Admiralty at Philadelphia. Also, A letter directed to the said judge . . . [at end] Russel. The above is taken from the *Pennsylvania Journal*. [Philadelphia? 1768?]
broadside 59 X 48 cm.
In five columns
New York Public 392
MWA; NN (mutilated) mp. 41830

B2888 GREEN, WILLIAM
To the public. Annapolis, May 28, 1768. Whereas a controversy has been published . . . a Bystander, and his opponents . . . [Annapolis, Anne Catharine and William Green, 1768]
broadside 29.5 X 20 cm.
Wroth 280
MdHi mp. 41831

B2889 HALDIMAND, SIR FREDERICK, 1718-1791
By Frederick Haldimand Esqr., Brigadier General . . . commanding the Southern district . . . English deserters in the Province of Louisiana . . . [New Orleans, Denis Braud, 1768]
broadside 48 X 39.5 cm.
Dated at Pensacola, Jan. 14, 1768
MiU-C; NN (facsim. by McMurtrie (Chicago, 1941))
mp. 41832

B2890 HALE, SIR MATTHEW, 1609-1676
A New-Year's gift. By Sir Matthew Hale, Knight . . . New-London: Printed and sold by Timothy Green, 1768.
broadside 39.5 X 24.5 cm.
MH

B2891 HALL, DAVID, 1714-1772
Imported in the last vessels from England, and to be sold by David Hall, at the New Printing-Office, in Market-street, Philadelphia, the following books, &c. Steuart's enquiry

into the principles of political economy . . . [Philadelphia, 1768?]
[2] p. 35.5 X 21 cm. caption title
Bound in *Pennsylvania Gazette* after Aug. 18, 1768
MWA; PPL mp. 41833

B2892 HALL, SAMUEL, 1740-1807
Proposals for printing a weekly publick paper to be entitled, *The Essex Gazette* . . . Printing-Office, Salem, July 5, 1768 . . . Subscriptions are taken in by all those gentlemen, who are possessed of these proposals, and by . . . Samuel Hall. [Salem, 1768]
broadside
Tapley p. 303
MSaE mp. 41834

B2893 AN happy New Year.
Revolving scenes attend revolving years;
To us a strange fatality appears . . .
But Wisdom does their destin'd courses know – [n.p., 1768?]
broadside 24 X 15 cm.
Dated from an endorsement in an old hand. possibly contemporary
Ford 1464; New York Public 394
PHi. Photostats: MHi; MWA; NN mp. 41835

B2894 HARVARD UNIVERSITY
Quaestiones pro modulo . . . MDCCLXVIII. [Boston] R. Draper [1768]
broadside
CtY; MH; MHi; MSaE; MWA mp. 41836

B2895 IZARD, JOHN
Advertisement. South-Carolina, October, 1768. Seventy dollars reward. Strayed or stolen from my plantation . . . three mares with foal . . . John Izard. [Charleston? 1768]
broadside 32 X 19 cm.
MWA mp. 41837

B2896 KING'S CHAPEL, BOSTON
At the anniversary meeting of the proprietors of King's Chapel, on Easter Monday April 4. 1768. at XI o'clock in the forenoon . . . [Boston, 1768]
[2] p. 19.5 cm.
MHi mp. 41798

B2897 A LETTER from a Gentleman at a Distance to his friend at court. Dear Sir, Since you are pleased to enquire . . . my sentiments respecting the right of the British Parliament to lay taxes on the colonies . . . the best answer . . . is by way of reference to the . . . letters, signed a Farmer . . . But how can you, Sir, in New-England, join the other colonies in complaining . . . of such a taxation, when . . . you are . . . persecuting one another, in matters of much greater importance . . . April 26, 1768. A Dissenter. [n.p., 1768]
broadside ([2] p.) 35 X 20.5 cm.
MWA mp. 41838

B2898 LOUISIANA. CITIZENS
Mémoire des habitans & négocians de la Louysiane, sur l'événement du 29 octobre 1768. [Nouvelle Orléans, Denis Braud, 1768]
90 p. 21 cm. caption title
DLC; MiU-C mp. 41839

B2899 LOUISIANA. CITIZENS
Mémoire, des habitans et négocians de la Louisianne, sur l'événement du 29. Octobre 1768. [at end] Nlle. Orléans, Denis Braud, 1768.
21 p. 30 cm. caption title
McMurtrie: New Orleans 6; N. Y. Pub. 396
Archivo general de Indias, Seville; Bibliothèque nationale. Photostats: MWA; NN mp. 41840

B2900 LOUISIANA. CONSEIL SUPÉRIEUR
[Arrêt du Conseil sous la date de 29 Octobre 1768. New Orleans, 1768]

Title taken from a letter of Governor O'Reilly demanding the name of the writer and the authority by which it was printed
McMurtrie: New Orleans 5
No copy known mp. 41841

B2901 LOUISIANA. CONSEIL SUPÉRIEUR
Extrait des régistres du Conseil Supérieur de . . . la Louisianne. Du 31 Octobre 1768. Vu . . . la protestation faite par Mr. Aubry . . . à l'arrêt de la Cour . . . contre Mr. Wlloa [sic] . . . [New Orleans, Denis Braud, 1768]
broadside
McMurtrie: Louisiana 3; cf. Marc de Villiers du Terrage: *Les dernières années de la Louisiane française* (Paris [1903?]), p. 265
Archives nationales, Paris mp. 41842

B2902 MASSACHUSETTS. GOVERNOR, 1760-1769
By . . . Francis Bernard . . . a brief. Whereas on the eleventh day of April last . . . [July 9, 1768] [Boston, Richard Draper, 1768.
broadside 41.5 X 31.5 cm.
Ford 1448
DLC; MHi; MWA mp. 41844

B2903 MASSACHUSETTS. GOVERNOR, 1760-1769
Province of the Massachusetts-Bay. Boston, June 30, 1768. On Tuesday . . . the Governor sent the following message to the . . . House . . . [Boston, 1768]
broadside 31.5 X 19 cm.
Ford 1446
MB; MHi mp. 41843

B2904 MASSACHUSETTS. HOUSE OF REPRESENTATIVES
The following resolves pass'd the Hon. House . . . on Friday last. In the House of Representatives February 26, 1768. Whereas the happiness . . . [Boston, 1768]
broadside 37 X 16.5 cm.
Ford 1442
MWA mp. 41845

B2905 MASSACHUSETTS. LAWS
. . . An act . . . for enquiring into the rateable estates of this province . . . [Colophon] Boston, Printed by Richard Draper, and Green & Russell, 1768.
3 p. 35 cm.
MHi; PPRF mp. 41846

B2906 MASSACHUSETTS GAZETTE
An address from the carrier of the *Massachusetts-Gazette*, to his respectable customers. Boston, January 1st, 1768. [Boston, Richard Draper, 1768]
broadside 16 X 12 cm.
Ford 1459
PHi. Photostat: MWA mp. 41782

B2907 MAXWELL, JAMES, 1720-1800
Hymns and spiritual songs . . . New-York, Re-printed and sold by Samuel Brown, 1768.
[2], v, 179 [i.e. 189], [8] p. 15.5 cm.
MWA; MdBP; RPJCB mp. 41847

B2908 MOUNT HOLLY, N. J. LIBRARY COMPANY
A catalogue of books, belonging to the Library Company of Bridge-Town, (commonly called Mount-Holly) in New-Jersey. Philadelphia, William Goddard, 1768.
xxxv, 11 p. 19 cm. [A]-F^4
Guerra a-417; New York Public 397
NN (p. xvii-xxiv wanting) mp. 41849

B2909 A MOURNFUL elegy, on the death of Martin Willcocks and James Rois, of Goshen in Connecticut . . . kill'd with lightening, on the 6th of June, 1767 . . . [Hartford? Thomas Green?] 1768.
[8] p. 17.5 cm.
MWA mp. 41850

B2910 [MURRAY, JAMES] 1732-1782
Sermons to asses. [Boston, Mein and Fleeming] 1768.
135 p. 15.5 cm. A-L^6 M^2
Alden: John Mein 13
CtY; CU; DLC; MWA; MiU-C; MnU; NHi; PPL
mp. 41851

B2911 NAMES of the subscribers. [New York? 1768?]
lvi p. 20.5 cm.
This list of American subscribers which appears in the 1768 [London] edition of Churchill's *Poems* was probably printed in New York for Rivington. cf. his advertisement in Gaine's *New York Gazette*, Nov. 21, 1768
MWA; NN mp. 41875

B2912 THE New-England almanack; or Lady's and gentleman's diary for . . . 1769. By Benjamin West. Providence, John Carter [1768]
[32] p.
Drake 12822
CLU

B2913 THE New-England primer improved . . . Boston, Printed by Kneeland and Adams, for T. Leverett, 1768.

Heartman 29
Samuel A. Green (1904) mp. 41852

B2914 THE New-England town and country almanack for . . . 1769. By Abraham Weatherwise . . . Providence, Sarah Goddard and John Carter [1768]
[32] p.
Second edition; advertised in the *Providence Gazette*
Drake 12825; cf. Alden 380
No copy known

B2915 THE New-England town and country almanack for . . . 1769. By Abraham Weatherwise . . . Providence, Sarah Goddard and John Carter [1768]
[32] p.
Third edition; advertised in the *Providence Gazette*
Drake 12826; cf. Alden 380
No copy known

B2916 NEW HAMPSHIRE. TREASURER
Province of New-Hampshire. George Jaffrey, esq; treasurer . . . To the select-men of These are in His Majesty's name, to will and require you . . . to assess the polls and estates within said [n.p., 1768?]
broadside 31 X 19.5 cm.
Dated Nov. 15, 1768
MiU-C

B2917 NEW HAMPSHIRE GAZETTE
Portsmouth, January 1st, 1768. To the customers of the *New-Hampshire Gazette*. Getlemen [sic] and ladies . . . [Portsmouth, 1768]
broadside 32 X 19 cm.
Poem in eight stanzas, containing New Year's greeting and requests for subscriptions
Whittemore 120
NHi. Photostat: NN mp. 41821

B2918 A NEW song, address'd to the Sons of Liberty . . . particularly to the . . . ninety-two of Boston . . . A son of Liberty. [Boston, Green & Russell, 1768]
broadside 31 X 17.5 cm.
Reprinted in the *Essex Gazette*, Aug. 16, 1768
Ford 1457
PHi mp. 41853

B2919 A NEW-YEARS address, which your obedient servant the young shaver humbly presents to all his generous customers. [n.p., 1768?]
broadside
Dated from an endorsement in an old hand, possibly contemporary
Ford 1521
PHi. Photostat: MWA mp. 41854

B2920 A NEW Year's wish, from the baker's boy. Boston, January 1, 1768. [Boston, 1768]
broadside 15.5 X 12.5 cm.
Ford 1462
PHi. Photostat: MWA mp. 41856

B2921 A NEW-YEAR'S wish.
My honour'd patrons, and my friends,
Your humble farrier now pretends . . .
To wish you all a happy year.
[Boston, 1768]
broadside
Ms. note: Boston, Jany. 1, 1768
Ford 1463
PHi. Photostat: MWA mp. 41858

B2922 NEW York, March 2, 1768. Advertisement. To be sold by public vendue, on Thursday the 14th of April . . . [New York, 1768]
broadside 17 X 17 cm.
DLC. Photostat: ICN

B2923 NORTH CAROLINA. GOVERNOR, 1765-1771
North-Carolina, ss. George the Third . . . A proclamation [enjoining public officers to post tables of fees] . . . William Tryon . . . Benj. Heron, Secretary . . . [Newbern, James Davis, 1768]
broadside 30 X 35 cm.
Dated at Brunswick, July 21, 1768
McMurtrie: North Carolina 56
Public Record Off. mp. 41860

B2924 [THE North-Carolina almanack for the year 1769. Williamsburg, William Rind, 1768]

Advertised in the *Virginia Gazette*, Aug. 25, 1768, as "Just published, and to be sold by the printer hereof . . . this almanack, in any quantity, by applying to Mr. Williams Scarbrough in Edenton."
No copy known mp. 41861

B2925 OBSERVATIONS and propositions for an accommodation between Great Britain and her colonies . . . Tenth edition . . . [New York? 1768]
3 p.
MWA mp. 41862

B2926 [THE parody parodized, or the Massachusetts song of liberty.

Come, swallow your bumpers, ye
Tories, and roar . . .]
[Boston, 1768?]
broadside
A parody on a Tory poem appearing in the supplement to the *Boston Gazette*, Sept. 26, 1768. cf. Duyckinck, I. 452
Ford 1456
No copy known mp. 41863

B2927 PENNSYLVANIA. GOVERNOR, 1767-1771
By . . . John Penn . . . a procalamation. Whereas it appears by a deposition . . . [Jan. 19, 1768] . . . Philadelphia, D. Hall, and W. Sellers, 1768.
broadside 42.5 X 34.5 cm.
DLC mp. 41864

B2928 PENNSYLVANIA. LAWS
An act to remove the persons now settled, and to prevent others from settling on any lands . . . not purchased from the Indians. [Philadelphia, D. Hall and W. Sellers, 1768]
broadside 34.5 X 19 cm.
Passed Feb. 3, 1768
PHi mp. 41865

B2929 PENNSYLVANIA CHRONICLE.
To William Goddard, Dr. To the *Pennsylvania Chronicle*, &c. one year beginning at N° and ending at N° . . . Philadelphia [William Goddard] 1768.
broadside 19.5 X 15.5 cm.
Metzger 316
RPJCB

B2930 POOR Roger's Universal pocket almanack, for . . . 1769. By Roger More, Philodespot. New-York, Printed and sold by J. Parker [1768]
[36] p.
Wall p. 19
NjR mp. 41848

B2931 THE prodigal daughter . . . Boston, Printed and sold at the Heart and Crown [1768?]
[16] p. 17.5 cm.
Dated by d'Alté A. Welch
cf. Hamilton 51 (1)
NjP mp. 41867

B2932 THE prodigal daughter . . . Providence, [John Waterman, 1768?]
16 p. 19.5 cm.
In verse
Dated 1768 on the basis of other Waterman imprints
Alden 386; Winship p. 23
MWA; RHi mp. 41868

B2933 REFLECTIONS on the evil consequences of tea drinking . . . [n.p.] Printed in the year, 1768.
24 p. 15 cm.
Signed (p. 19): Manly Plain-dealing
"Verses, by another hand": p. 21-24
NHi mp. 41869

B2934 RELIGIOUS SOCIETY, CHARLESTON, S. C.
The constitutional rules of the Religious Society; revised and finally ratified the third day of May, one thousand seven hundred and sixty-eight . . . Charles-Town, Printed by Charles Crouch, for the Society. MDCCLXVIII.
v, 15 p. 20.5 cm.
Turnbull p. 166
NPV; ScGrvF

B2935 THE renowned history of Giles Gingerbread, a little boy who lived upon learning . . . Boston, Printed by Mein and Fleeming, and to be sold by John Mein, 1768.
34, [2] p. illus. 12 cm.
Hamilton 49
CtHi; NjP. Photostat: MWA mp. 41870

B2936 [THE renowned history of Giles Gingerbread. Providence, John Waterman [1768?].]
29, [1] p. 16 woodcuts. 14 cm.
Alden 388
RPB (p. 5-[30] only); RWe (t.p. and p. 29 wanting) mp. 41871

B2937 THE result of a council, conven'd at Barrington, September 6, 1768 . . . Samuel Macclintock, moderator . . . [Boston? 1768]
broadside 34 X 21 cm.
Concerns difficulties between the Barrington Church and the Rev. Joseph Prince
Ford 1466
MB; MHi mp. 41796

B2938 RHODE ISLAND
A summary of the amount of the estimation . . . of Rhode-Island . . . Newport, May 6th, 1768. Nathaniel Mumford, James Angell . . . [Newport, Solomon Southwick, 1768]
broadside 38.5 X 31 cm.
Bill submitted Sept. 17, 1768
Alden 389; Winship p. 23
MWA; RHi mp. 41872

B2939 RHODE ISLAND. GOVERNOR, 1768-1769
[By the honorable Josias Lyndon . . . A proclamation . . . for the apprehending Melchisedeck Kinsman . . . [Newport, Solomon Southwick, 1768]
[broadside?]
Bill submitted Sept. 19, 1768
Alden 390
No copy known mp. 41873

B2940 RHODE ISLAND. LAWS
The table. [Newport, Solomon Southwick, 1768]
46 p. 29.5 cm. caption title
The index to the 1767 edition of the *Acts and Laws* (Evans 10749), advertised Dec. 5-12, 1768, as "Just published," and billed by Southwick Jan. 16, 1769
Alden 396
CSmH; Ct; CtY; DLC; M; MH-L; MHi; MdBB; NN; PPAmP; R; RHi; RNR; RP; RPJCB; RPL; WHi mp. 41874

B2941 THE royal primer . . . Boston, Printed and sold by W. M'Alpine, 1768.
[56?] p.
Heartman: Non-New-England 162; Rosenbach-Ch 61
A. S. W. Rosenbach (1933) (wanting after p. 44) mp. 41876

B2942 ST. JOHN, PETER
A dialogue between Flesh and Spirit: composed upon the decease of Mr. Abijah Abbot . . . 1768 . . . [New York? 1768?]
broadside 25.5 X 20 cm.
Signed: By Peter St. John, of Norwalk
In two columns
New York Public 399
NN mp. 41877

B2943 [SAULT, RICHARD]
The second Spira: being a fearful example of an atheist . . . By J. S. . . . Newport, Solomon Southwick, 1768.

37 p. 17 cm.
Alden 397; Winship p. 22
MWA; RHi mp. 41878

B2944 SCHENECTADY, N.Y. CITIZENS
A brief state of the case of Ryer Shermerhorn, John Glen . . . and others . . . of the Township of Schenectady . . . submitted to . . . the Representatives of . . . New-York, convened in General Assembly, in support of . . . a bill for the division of the common lands . . . [New York, Hugh Gaine, 1768?]
6 p. 30.5 cm. caption title
New York Public 400
NHi; NN mp. 41879

B2945 SECOND edition of Edes & Gill's North-American almanack for . . . 1769. Boston, Edes & Gill [1768]
[16], 21, [3] p. front. 16.5 cm.
By Samuel Stearns
Drake 3177; Nichols p. 54
DLC; MB; MH; MWA mp. 41885

B2946 SONGS, composed for the use and edification of such as love the truth . . . Providence, Waterman & Russell; sold also by Benoni Pearce [1768?]
36 p. 16 cm.
The firm was dissolved before July 1768
Alden 398; Winship p. 23 (also p. 75)
RPB mp. 41880

B2947 SOUTH CAROLINA. LAWS
[An act for establishing circuit courts . . . Charleston, P. Timothy? 1768]

Advertised in the *South Carolina Gazette*, Aug. 22, 1768
Mosimann 184-A
No copy known

B2948 SOUTH CAROLINA. LAWS
[An act for establishing courts, building gaols . . . Charleston, P. Timothy, 1768]

Advertised in the *South Carolina Gazette*, Apr. 25, 1768
Mosimann 186
No copy known

B2949 SOUTH CAROLINA. LAWS
An act for regulating and ascertaining the rates of wharfage . . . Charles-Town, South-Carolina, Peter Timothy, 1768.
1 p.l., 13 p. 29 cm.
Sabin 87607
DLC; ScHi mp. 41881

B2950 SOUTH CAROLINA. LAWS
[An act to direct executors and administrators . . . Charleston, P. Timothy? 1768]

Advertised in the *South Carolina Gazette*, Aug. 22, 1768
Mosimann 186
No copy known

B2951 SOUTH CAROLINA. LAWS
[An act to prevent the stealing of horses . . . Charleston, P. Timothy, 1768]

Advertised in the *South Carolina Gazette*, Aug. 22, 1768
Mosimann 187
No copy known

B2952 SOUTH CAROLINA. LAWS
. . . At a General assembly begun . . . on Monday the twenty-eighth day of October . . . and from thence continued . . . to the twenty-eighth day of May 1767. Charles-Town, South-Carolina, Peter Timothy, 1768.
31 p. 29 cm.
Tax act
Sabin 87605
DLC mp. 41882

B2953 SOUTH-CAROLINA & AMERICAN GENERAL GAZETTE
To the readers of the *South-Carolina & American General Gazette*, January 1, 1768. [Charleston, 1768]
broadside 30.5 X 16 cm.
Signed: Nathan B. Child
NHi mp. 41897

B2954 SOUTH End forever. North End forever. Extraordinary verses on Pope-Night . . . Sold by the printers boys in Boston. [1768?]
broadside 37 X 24 cm.
Ford 1467; Wegelin 785
DLC. Photostat: MHi mp. 41883

B2955 STANLY, JOHN WRIGHT
A state of the accounts and disputes . . . Philadelphia, Henry Miller, 1768.
20 p. 23 cm.
Sabin 90353
DLC mp. 41884

B2956 A STATE of the Earl of Stirling's title, to that part of New-England, now commonly called Sagadahook. [Woodbridge? James Parker? 1768]
broadside 30 X 17 cm.
New York Public 40; Sabin 90611
M–Ar. Photostats: DLC; MHi; MWA; NN
mp. 41783

B2957 [STERNE, LAURENCE] 1713-1768
A sentimental journey through France and Italy. By Mr. Yorick . . . [Boston, Mein and Fleeming] MDCCLXVIII.
2 v. $A–H^6$; $A–H^6$ $[I]^2$
Alden: John Mein 15
MH mp. 41886

B2958 THE substance of two letters, concerning communion . . . Newport [Solomon Southwick] 1768.
23 p. 18.5 cm.
Alden 400; Sabin 93378; Winship p. 23
RHi; RNHi mp. 41887

B2959 TO be sold, a tract of land of one hundred thousand acres, situate on the east side of Penboscot-River . . . [Woodbridge? James Parker? 1768]
broadside 39 X 19 cm.
Dated July 20, 1768
New York Public 423; Sabin 90611, note
M–Ar. Photostats: DLC; MHi; MWA; NN mp. 41784

B2960 TO the freeholders and freemen of the city and county of New-York. This vindication . . . is humbly submitted . . . The Querist. [New York, 1768]
4 p. 39.5 cm. caption title
DLC; MWA; NN; NNS mp. 41892

B2961 TOM Thumb's play book to teach children their letters . . . Providence, John Waterman, 1768.

30, [2] p. illus. 8 X 5 cm.
Alden 402; Hamilton 50
MWA; NjP mp. 41891

B2962 VIRGINIA. HOUSE OF BURGESSES
[Journal of the House of burgesses . . . Williamsburg, W. Rind, 1768]

Covers session Mar. 31–Apr. 16, 1768
Advertised in *Rind's Gazette*, June 9, 1768, as "Just published and to be sold by . . . William Rind."
Torrence 347
No copy known mp. 41894

B2963 VIRGINIA. HOUSE OF BURGESSES
To his excellency the right honourable Norborne, baron de Botetourt . . . the humble address of the House of burgesses . . . [Williamsburg, 1768]
broadside
ViW mp. 41893

B2964 WELLS, ROBERT
Charlestown, February 3d, 1768. The sale of Negroes belonging to Mr. John Miles . . . is put off to . . . the 5th inst. when the said Negroes . . . will be sold by publick outcry at Mr. Nightingall's . . . Robert Wells, Vendue-Master . . . [Charleston, 1768]
broadside 20.5 X 17 cm.
MWA mp. 41896

B2965 WHILE gasping Freedom wails her future Fate,
And Commerce sickens with the sick'ning State . . .
[Boston, 1768?]
broadside 25 X 23.5 cm.
Also lists "The Seventeen Proselytes to His Excellency's Doctrinal Faith of Submission."
Ford 1469
MHi. Photostat: MWA mp. 41899

B2966 WHITEFIELD, GEORGE, 1714-1770
A collection of hymns for social worship . . . The thirteenth edition. Philadelphia, Re-printed and sold by David Hall, 1768.
xi, 182 p. 16 cm.
Metzger 324; cf. Evans 11116
PHi mp. 41900

B2967 WOLSTENHOLME, DANIEL
To the public. As Mr. Allen, in two hand-bills . . . has endeavoured to bring me in as a principal . . . [Affidavit signed Nov. 9, 1768] . . . [Annapolis, Anne Catharine and William Green, 1768]
broadside 44 X 27 cm.
Wroth 288
MdHi mp. 41901

B2968 THE youth's instructor in the English tongue or, The art of spelling improved . . . Collected from Dixon, Bailey, Owen, Strong and Watts. Boston, Printed by Daniel Kneeland for Thomas Leverett, 1768.
159 p. incl. tables. 16 cm.
New York Public 403; Karpinski p. 50
MB; NN (mutilated) mp. 41902

B2969 ZUM 29ten August 1768. [Philadelphia, Henrich Miller, 1768]
[8] p. 17.5 cm. caption title
PHi mp. 41903

1769

B2970 ADVERTISEMENT. A certain Jonathan Mayhew . . . some time ago published a saucy performance against the Church of England . . . [Boston, 1769?]
broadside
Ford 1472
MBAt; MHi mp. 41905

B2971 ADVERTISEMENT. As the agreements entered into by the merchants and traders of the town of Boston . . . we the masters of the ships and subscribers . . . Boston, August 23d, 1769 . . . [Boston, 1769]
2 p. 32.5 X 21 cm. broadside
Ford 1473
DLC; MB mp. 41906

B2972 ANDREW, JONATHAN
To be sold by Jonathan Andrew, tanner, fronting the training-field in Salem, choice hemlock tann'd sole-leather . . . Salem, Sept. 4, 1769. [Salem, 1769]
broadside
Ford 1496; Tapley p. 306
MSaE mp. 41907

B2973 AN astronomical diary, or, almanack for the year of our Lord Christ 1769 . . . By Nathaniel Ames . . . Hartford, Green & Watson, 1769.
[24] p. 16 cm.
Bates: Conn. almanacs 1763
CtHi; DLC mp. 41908

B2974 BELLAMY, JOSEPH, 1719-1790
The half-way covenant, a dialogue. By Joseph Bellamy, D. D. . . . New-London: Printed and sold by Timothy Green [1769]
16 p. 17 cm.
CtHi mp. 41910

B2975 BIBLE
Verbum sempiternum. Philadelphia, A. Steuart [1769?]
272, [8] p. 5 cm.
Taylor's Thumb Bible
Dated by Welch from owner's inscription
CLU; DLC; PP. d'Alté A. Welch, Cleveland (1963)

B2976 [BLACK bird songbook. Philadelphia, Sold by William Woodhouse, 1769]

Advertised July 13, 1769, as "for sale."
Sonneck-Upton, p. 43.
No copy known mp. 41914

B2977 BOSTON. SELECTMEN
Notification. The freeholders and other inhabitants of the Town of Boston . . . are hereby notified . . . Boston, May 1, 1769. [Boston, 1769]
broadside 11.5 X 15.5 cm.
DLC mp. 41916

B2978 BOSTON. SELECTMEN
The select-men of the town of Boston having received from William Bolton . . . do hereby notify the freeholders . . . to assembly . . . the fourth day of October . . . Boston, Sept. 28, 1769 . . . [Boston, 1769]
broadside 10 X 17.5 cm.
MiU–C mp. 41917

B2979 BOSTON, January 25, 1769. A dialogue between Sir George Cornwell . . . and Mr. Flint . . . London, and Boston, Printed: Charles-Town [S. C.], Re-printed 1769.

14 p. 20 cm. $A–B^4$
MWA mp. 41924

B2980 BOSTON, March 28, 1769. To the owner of pew No. in Christ Church . . . We have . . . valued your pew, and laid a tax upon it of . . . [Boston, 1769]
broadside 10 × 13 cm.
RPJCB mp. 41915

B2981 BOSTON EVENING POST
To all his kind customers, the boy who carries the *Evening-Post*, wishes a Happy New-Year. 1769. [Boston, T. & J. Fleet, 1769]
broadside
Ford 1495
PHi. Photostat: MWA mp. 42010

B2982 BOSTON GAZETTE
A New-Year's wish for the public, for the year 1769 . . . [Boston, Edes & Gill, 1769]
broadside
Ford 1497
PHi. Photostat: MWA mp. 41981

B2983 BOSTON, Tuesday, January 10, 1769. Important advices! New-York, January 3. Last night the snow Mercury, Captain Kemble, arrived here . . . [Boston, 1769]
broadside
Gives the King's speech of Nov. 8, 1768
Ford 1483
MHi mp. 41938

B2984 BRITANNIA'S intercession for the deliverance of John Wilkes . . . The seventh edition. London: Printed. Boston: Re-printed [by Daniel Kneeland? 1769?]
24 p. 21 cm. $A^4\ B^2\ C^4\ D^2$
MWA mp. 41918

B2985 BROWN UNIVERSITY
Newport, September 11. On Thursday . . . was celebrated . . . the first Commencement . . . [Newport] Solomon Southwick [1769]
broadside 29.5 × 23 cm.
Alden 428; Winship p. 24
MWA; RPB; RPJCB. Photostats: MHi; NN; RHi
mp. 42919

B2986 BYLES, MATHER, 1707-1788
A sermon on the nature and necessity of conversion . . . Boston, Edes and Gill, 1769.
15, [1] p. 21 cm.
Huntington 286
CSmH; DLC; MH; MHi; MWA; NHi; RPJCB; ViRU
mp. 41920

B2987 CHAPMAN, JOHN, & CO.
Charlestown, April 27, 1769. To be sold, on Wednesday the tenth day of May next, a choice cargo of two hundred & fifty negroes . . . [Charleston, S. C., 1769]
broadside 30.5 × 18.5 cm.
New York Public 407
MWA. Photostat: NN mp. 41921

B2988 COLEY, SIMEON
To the public . . . New-York, 21st July, 1769. Afternoon, 2 o'clock. [New York, 1769]
broadside 20 × 22.5 cm.
DLC mp. 41922

B2989 COMPENDIÖSE Hand-Bibliothek, für Liebhaber Jesu und seines Leidens, zur täglichen Seelen-Weide. Enthaltend einen Kern des Heil. Evangelien-Buchs . . . Alles kurz beysammen. [Philadelphia, H. Miller, 1769]
1 v.
Includes Die Geschichte der Tage (Evans 11273); Thomae Wilcocks köstlicher Honig-Tropfen (Leipzig und Ebersdorf, 1758); and Anhang der übrigen Brüder-Lieder seit 1749 (n.p., ca. 1755)
PPL mp. 41923

B2990 [CRISP, STEPHEN] 1628–1692
A new book for children to learn in . . . By S. C. Newport, Solomon Southwick, 1769.
96 p. 10 cm.
Alden 408; Winship p. 24
RHi (p. 1–12 missing) mp. 41925

B2991 DEAS, DAVID & JOHN, firm, Charleston
Charles-Town, July 24th, 1769. To be sold, on Thursday the third day of August next, a cargo of ninety-four . . . Negroes . . . [Charleston, 1769]
broadside 31 × 19.5 cm.
MWA mp. 41926

B2992 DESCRIPTION of the Pope, 1769. Toasts on the front of a large lanthorn. Love and unity. – The American Whig . . . [Boston? 1769]
broadside 27 × 13.5 cm.
Contains an acrostic on John Mein
Ford 1502; New York Public 408
NHi. Photostats: MHi; NN mp. 41927

B2993 EDDIS, JOSEPH
Joseph Eddis, shoemaker, at the sign of the boot, in Cannon-Street . . . [Philadelphia, 1769]
broadside 9 × 14 cm.
PHi mp. 41928

B2994 ESSEX GAZETTE
On the commencement of the year 1769 . . . Job Weeden, Salem news-boy, begs leave . . . to present the following lines to the gentlemen and ladies to whom he carries the *Essex Gazette* . . . [Salem, Samuel Hall, 1769]
broadside
Ford 1498; Tapley p. 305
PHi. Photostat: MWA mp. 42023

B2995 EVERY man his own lawyer . . . Philadelphia, John Dunlap, 1769.

Hildeburn 2438; James 28
No copy located mp. 41929

B2996 FANEUIL HALL LOTTERY
Faneuil-Hall lottery, Letter E . . . February, 1769. [Boston, 1769]
broadside
Ford 1482
MB; MWA

B2997 FREEMAN'S New-York pocket almanack for . . . 1770 . . . By Frank Freeman. [New York] John Holt [1769]
[48] p.
Wall p. 20
NHi mp. 41930

B2998 FRESH advices. Philadelphia, March 7, 1769 . . . [Colophon] Philadelphia, W. Goddard [1769]
[2] p. 40 × 23.5 cm.
Extra of *Pennsylvania Chronicle*, Mar. 7, 1769
MWA mp. 41931

B2999 THE friendly instructor: or, A companion for young ladies and gentlemen . . . With a recommendatory

preface by . . . Doddridge. London, Printed: New-York; Re-printed by J. Holt. 1769.
xii, 79 p. 14 cm.
CtHi mp. 41932

B3000 GEMINIANI, FRANCESCO, 1680–1762
An abstract of Geminiani's Art of playing on the violin, and of another book of instructions for playing . . . the violin, German flute, violoncello . . . Boston, John Boyles, 1769.
14 p.
RPJCB mp. 41933

B3001 THE gentleman and citizen's pocket almanack for . . . 1770. By Andrew Steuart . . . [Philadelphia] William Evitt [1769]
[24] p.
Drake 9929
DLC; MWA

B3002 GEORGIA. LAWS
. . . An act for granting to his Majesty the sum of three thousand and forty-six pounds sixteen shillings and eight-pence . . . Council-Chamber, 24th December, 1768. Assented to, Ja. Wright. [Savannah, J. Johnston, 1769]
8 p. 25.5 cm.
Orders payments to James Johnston
De Renne p. 191
GU-De mp. 41934

B3003 GEORGIA. LAWS
Acts passed by the General Assembly of Georgia, at a session begun and holden at Savannah, on Monday the 7th day of November . . . to the 24th day of December 1768 . . . Savannah, James Johnston [1769]
1 p.l., 12, [1] p. 25.5 cm.
Five acts and table
De Renne p. 190
DLC (t.p. in facsim.); GU-De; RPJCB mp. 41935

B3004 GERMAN FRIENDLY SOCIETY
[Rules, in German. Philadelphia, 1769?]

On Mar. 22, 1769, it was "agreed . . . each member . . . shall pay . . . One Pound, 6 Shillings and 7 Pence for the Rules translated and printed from the English in the German language. An order . . . 50 pounds . . . paid to the printer at Philadelphia for translating and printing . . ."—cf. Gongaware, p. 7
No copy known

B3005 GESSNER, SALOMON, 1730–1787
The death of Abel . . . attempted from the German of Mr. Gessner. The ninth edition. [n.p.] Printed in the year, M,DCC,LXIX.
156 p. 14 cm. A-N^6
MWA mp. 41936

B3006 GILL, JOHN, 1697–1771
Infant-baptism, a part and pillar of Popery . . . Third edition. Boston, Reprinted for, and sold by Philip Freeman, 1769.
32 p. 18.5 cm. [A]-D^4
MWA; RPJCB mp. 41937

B3007 HALL, EBENEZER
To the customers of the *Newport Mercury*. Gentlemen and ladies . . . Eben Hall . . . [Newport, S. Southwick? 1769?]
broadside 26.5 X 12.5 cm.
Date ascribed from a contemporary ms. annotation
Alden 414; New York Public 409
RNHi. Photostats: MWA; NN mp. 41940

B3008 HAMILTON, THOMAS, JR.
Some account of the small-pox . . . [n.p.] 1769.
7 p. 18.5 cm.
New York Public 410; Sabin 86584
DLC. Photostat: NN mp. 41941

B3009 HARVARD UNIVERSITY
Quaestiones pro modulo . . . MDCCLXIX. [Boston] R. Draper [1769]
broadside
Ford 1484
MH; MHi; MSaE; MWA mp. 41943

B3010 THE history of the Holy Jesus . . . By a Lover of their precious souls . . . The tenth edition. New-London, Printed and sold by T. Green, 1769.
[48] p. 16 illus. 11.5 cm.
CtY. Mrs. Arthur M. Greenwood, Marlborough, Mass. (1962) mp. 41944

B3011 HOPKINS, JOSEPH
A line to the modern ladies: found among the writings of Joseph Hopkins, late of Farmington, deceased . . . [n.p.] Printed in the year 1769.
broadside 31 X 19.5 cm.
MWA (imperfect) mp. 41945

B3012 HOPKINS, JOSEPH
A line to the modern ladies: found among the writings of Joseph Hopkins, late of Farmington, deceased . . . [n.p., 1769?]
broadside 33.5 X 20 cm.
Ford 3171
PHi. Photostats: MHi; MWA mp. 41946

B3013 HUME, SOPHIA, 1701-1774
The justly celebrated Mrs. Sophia Hume's advice and warning . . . Newport, Solomon Southwick [1769?]
broadside 41 X 31 cm.
Alden 415; Winship p. 74; Winship Addenda p. 95
RHi. Photostat: MWA mp. 41947

B3014 [LAURENS, HENRY] 1724-1792
An appendix to the Extracts from the proceedings of the High Court of Vice-Admiralty in Charlestown, South-Carolina, &c. containing stricutres [sic] upon and proper answers to a pamphlet entitled The man unmasked . . . Charlestown, David Bruce, 1769.
64 p.
PPAmP; ScHi mp. 41949

B3015 [LAURENS, HENRY] 1724-1792
Extracts from the proceedings of the High Court of Vice-Admiralty, in Charlestown, South-Carolina . . . in the years 1767 and 1768 . . . Charlestown, David Bruce, 1769.
iv, 42, 4, 5 p. 32 cm.
Adams 57b; New York Public 411; cf. Evans 11307 (2nd ed.)
CSmH; MHi; MWA; NN; PPAmP; RPJCB mp. 41950

B3016 LIBERTY and property, without oppression . . . [n.p. 1769]
23 p. 19.5 cm.
Published in the interests of the antilawyer agitation of 1769
Sabin 40939
DLC mp. 41951

B3017 LIBRARY COMPANY OF PHILADELPHIA
Whereas a law was passed the thirteenth day of March . . by the Library Company of Philadelphia, enabling the

directors . . . to admit the members of the Union Library Company . . . is hereby admitted . . . this day of 1769 . . . [Philadelphia, 1769]
broadside 32.5 X 20 cm.
PPL; PU; RPJCB mp. 41975

B3018 LOUISIANA. COMMANDANT (CHARLES PHILIPPE AURBY)
De par le Roi. Charles Philippe Aubry . . . Commandant pour le Roi, a la Louisianne. En vertu des pouvoirs que . . . Alexandre OReilly . . . nous a communique pour prendre possession au nom du Roi d'Espangne . . . 16. Août 1769. [New Orleans, Denis Braud, 1769]
broadside 41 X 30 cm.
McMurtrie: Louisiana 4
Edward A. Parsons, New Orleans (1942) mp. 41952

B3019 LOUISIANA. CONSEIL SUPERIEUR
Extrait, des régistres des audiances du Conseil Supérieur de . . . la Louisianne. Du ll Fevrier 1769. Entre Mr. Olivier Duvezin . . . demandeur. Contre le Sr. Her . . . défendeur. [at end] [New Orleans] Denis Braud [1769]
7 p. 30 cm.
McMurtrie: New Orleans 8
L-Ar mp. 41953

B3020 LOUISIANA. GOVERNOR, 1769-1770
De par le roi, Don Alexandre O Reilly . . . Gouverneur . . . En vertu des ordres & pouvoirs . . . [Nouvelle Orléans, D. Braud, 1769]
broadside 28 X 29 cm.
Dated Aug. 21, 1769
McMurtrie: New Orleans 9; New York Public 412
CU-B. Archivo general de Indias, Seville. Photostat: NN mp. 41954

B3021 LOUISIANA. GOVERNOR, 1769-1770
Don Alexandro O Reilly . . . Capitania General . . . [at end] Nueva Orleans [Nov. 25, 1769] Don Alexandro O Reilly . . . Francisco Xavier Rodriguez, escribano . . . [New Orleans, Denis Braud, 1769]
42 p. 20 cm.
McMurtrie: New Orleans 12
LNT mp. 41956

B3022 LOUISIANA. GOVERNOR 1769-1770
Don Alexandre O Reilly . . . Gouverneur . . . Aucune chose n'exige plus l'attention . . . Lu, publié & affiché le 7 septembre mil sept cent soixante-neuf. [Nouvelle-Orléans, Denis Braud, 1769]
broadside 27 X 19.5 cm.
McMurtrie: Louisiana 5
Archivo general de Indias, Seville. Photostat: DLC mp. 41955

B3023 LOUISIANA. GOVERNOR, 1769-1770
Don Alexandre O Reilly . . . Gouverneur . . . Le procès qui a été fait à cause du soulévement . . . [Nouvelle Orléans, D. Braud, 1769]
32 p. 23.5 cm.
Dated Nov. 25, 1769
McMurtrie: New Orleans 14; New York Public 414
CU-B. Photostat: NN mp. 41957

B3024 LOUISIANA. GOVERNOR, 1769-1770
Don Alexandre O Reilly . . . Gouverneur . . . Le procés qui a été fait à cause du soulévement . . . [Nouvelle Orléans, D. Braud, 1769]
broadside 41.5 X 30.5 cm.
Dated Dec. 21, 1769
McMurtrie: New Orleans 17; New York Public 415
Archivo general de Indias, Seville. Photostat: NN mp. 41958

B3025 LOUISIANA. GOVERNOR, 1769-1770
Don Alexandre O Reilly . . . Nous faisons sçavoir à toutes les personnes de cette ville . . . [Nouvelle Orléans, D. Braud, 1769]
broadside 40 X 30 cm.
Dated Aug. 23, 1769
New York Public 413
Archivo general de Indias, Seville. Photostat: NN mp. 41959

B3026 LOUISIANA. GOVERNOR, 1769-1770
Don Alexandre O Reilly . . . Gouverneur . . . On fait sçavoir à tous les habitants . . . que les . . . loix de Sa Majesté . . . [at end] Donné . . . à la Nouevelle Orléans. le 7. Decembre, 1769. [New Orleans, 1769]
broadside 48 X 39 cm.
McMurtrie: New Orleans 16
L–M mp. 41960

B3027 LOUISIANA. GOVERNOR, 1769-1770
Don Alexandre O Reilly . . . Gouverneur . . . Plusieurs habitans nous ayant représenté . . . [New Orleans, Denis Braud, 1769]
broadside 39 X 30 cm.
Dated Aug. 24, 1769
cf. BSA *Papers*, LXII (1968) p. 253
CU–B

B3028 LOUISIANA. GOVERNOR, 1769-1770
Don Alexandre O Reilly . . . Gouverneur . . . Pour remedier aux grands inconveniens qui resultent . . . de la facilité avec laquelle s' introduiserent les etrangers . . . [at end] Donné . . . à la Nouvelle Orléans, le 11 Septembre, 1769. [New Orleans, Denis Braud, 1769]
broadside 41 X 33 cm.
McMurtrie: New Orleans 10
L–M mp. 41961

B3029 LOUISIANA. GOVERNOR, 1769-1770
Don Alexandre O Reilly . . . Gouverneur . . . Rien n'étant plus essentiel . . . que le maintien des loix . . . [Nouvelle Orléans, D. Braud, 1769]
broadside 42 X 31 cm.
Dated Aug. 27, 1769
New York Public 416
Archivo general de Indias, Seville. Photostat: NN mp. 41962

B3030 LOUISIANA. GOVERNOR, 1769-1770
Don Alexandre O Reilly . . . Gouverneur . . . Sur ce qui nous a été representé qu'une des principales causes du désordre . . . multiplicité des auberges, billards & carabets . . . [New Orleans, Denis Bruad, 1769]
broadside 41 X 33 cm.
Dated Sept. 21, 1769
McMurtrie: New Orleans 11
L–M mp. 41963

B3031 LOUISIANA. GOVERNOR, 1769-1770
Don Alexandre O Reilly . . . Gouverneur . . . Sur l'exposé qui nous auroit été fait par Mr. le Medécin du Roi en cette colonie . . . [Nouvelle Orléans, D. Braud, 1769]
broadside 41 X 30.5 cm.
Dated Aug. 29, 1769
New York Public 417
Archivo general de Indias, Seville. Photostat: NN mp. 41964

B3032 LOUISIANA. GOVERNOR, 1769-1770
Instructions sur la maniere de former . . . les procès civils & criminels . . . redigées & mises en ordre par . . . Manuel Joseph de Urrustia, & . . . Felix Rey, par ordre de . . . Alexandre O Reilly . . . [at end] A la Nouvelle Orléans [Nov. 25, 1769] Don Alexandre O Reilly . . . [New Orleans, 1769]
4 p. 22 cm.
McMurtrie: New Orleans 15
Edward A. Parsons, New Orleans (1942); T. P. Thompson (1942) mp. 41965

B3033 LOUISIANA. GOVERNOR, 1769-1770
Réglement. Pour servir d'instructions aux aubergistes, cabaretiers . . . et le maitre limonadier. Du 8. Octobre 1769. [New Orleans] Denis Braud [1769]
11 p. 25 cm. caption title
McMurtrie: Louisiana 6
Ms-Ar. Archivo general de Indias, Seville. mp. 41966

B3034 MCKESSON, JOHN
New York, *June 16th, 1769* As civil and religious liberty is justly esteemed amongst the greatest of human blessings . . . [New York, 1769]
2 p.
Form letter urging formation of other societies of non-episcopal churches.
Part italicized in ms.
RPJCB mp. 41967

B3035 [MACLAURIN, JOHN, LORD DREGHORN] 1734-1796
[The Keekeiad, a poem. Williamsburg? Purdie and Dixon? 1769?]

Referred to by Thomas Jefferson in an unpublished account book (Apr. 17, 1769) as: "pd. towards printing poem I never saw or ever wish to see 2/–".
Advertised in *Purdie & Dixon's Gazette*, Apr. 20, 1769, as "Now in the press and will be published by the end of this month."
Authorship ascribed from Brit. Mus. Catalog (1760 ed.)
No copy known mp. 41948

B3036 MASSACHUSETTS. COURT OF SESSIONS
The Court of Sessions have appointed Thursday . . . to grant licences on spirituous liquors . . . [Boston, 1769]
broadside
Ford 1677
MHi mp. 41968

B3037 MASSACHUSETTS. COURT OF SESSIONS
To The Court of Sessions have appointed . . . the third and fourth day of August . . . to grant licences on spirituous liquors . . . Boston, July 17, 1769. [Boston, 1769]
broadside 13 X 11 cm.
Ford 1481
MHi mp. 41969

B3038 MASSACHUSETTS. GOVERNOR, 1760-1769
Copies of letters from Governor Bernard, &c. to the Earl of Hillsborough. [Boston, Edes and Gill, 1769]
[4] p. 40 cm. caption title $[A]^2$
In three columns
Probably issued as supplement to the *Boston Evening-Post*, Apr. 10, 1769
Adams 68a; Ford 1477
MBAt; MHi; NjR (variant); RPJCB mp. 41911

B3039 MASSACHUSETTS. GOVERNOR, 1760-1769
Copies of letters from Governor Bernard, &c to the Earl of Hillsborough. [No. 1.] [Philadelphia, William & Thomas Bradford, 1769]
[2] p. 41 X 26 cm. caption title
In three columns
Bound originally in 1769 volume of the *Pennsylvania Journal*, following Apr. 27
New York Public 405
MHi; NN mp. 41912

B3040 MASSACHUSETTS. GOVERNOR, 1760-1769
Letters to the ministry from Governor Bernard, General Gage, and Commodore Hood . . . Salem, Re-printed and sold by Samuel Hall, 1769.
24 p. 20 cm. $[A]^4$ B^4 B^4
"[The remainder of these letters are now in the press, the second part . . . published . . . Friday next . . . Salem, Sept. 22, 1769.]"
Adams 69c
CtY; MH; MHi; MWA (t.p. photostat); NHi; RPJCB mp. 41913

B3041 MASSACHUSETTS. TREASURER
The following is the apportion of £92500 laid upon the several towns, districts and parishes, by Harrison Gray . . . passed at their session in June 1769 . . . [Boston, 1769]
4 p. 42 cm.
MHi mp. 41970

B3042 MASSACHUSETTS. TREASURER
Province of Massachusetts-Bay. The honorable Harrison Gray, Esq; Treasurer . . . To the select-men or assessors of the town or district of Greeting, &c. . . . Given under my hand and seal at Boston, the first day of August, 1769 . . . [Boston, 1769]
broadside 33.5 X 21 cm.
Tax warrant
Ford 1491
DLC; MSaE mp. 41971

B3043 MASSACHUSETTS GAZETTE
An happy New-Year to the worthy customers of the *Massachusetts-Gazette* . . . Boston, January 1769 . . . [Boston, Richard Draper, 1769]
broadside 17 X 13 cm.
Ford 1499
PHi. Photostat: MWA mp. 41942

B3044 [Mémoire contre les Républicains. New Orleans, Denis Braud, 1769]

Title assumed from reports of its publication
McMurtrie: New Orleans 7
No copy known mp. 41972

B3045 MOODY, SAMUEL, 1676-1747
Mr. Moody's discourse to little children. Boston: Printed. New-London: Re-printed and sold by Timothy Green [1769?]
16 p. 18 cm.
CtHi; MWA mp. 41973

B3046 THE New-England primer enlarged . . . Philadelphia, Printed and sold by D. Hall, and W. Sellers, 1769.
[80] p. $[A]–E^8$
Heartman 31; Rosenbach–Ch 63
A. S. W. Rosenbach (1933) (sig. A8 lacking) mp. 41976

B3047 NEW HAMPSHIRE. HOUSE OF REPRESENTATIVES
A journal of the House of representatives . . . conven'd the 17th day of May 1768 . . . Portsmouth, Daniel and Robert Fowle, 1769.
[2], 63-124 p. 31.5 cm.
DLC; MWA (p. 97-124 only); NhHi (p. [61]-96 only) mp. 41977

B3048 NEW HAMPSHIRE. TREASURER
Province of New-Hampshire. George Jaffrey . . . To the selectmen . . . [Portsmouth, 1769]
broadside
Warrant for collecting taxes, May, 1769
Whittemore 129
NhHi mp. 41978

B3049 NEW JERSEY
To / the Honourable, / the / Commissioners / "appointed . . . for ascertaining, set- / "tling, adjusting . . . the boundary, or partiti- / "on line, between . . . New York, and Nova Cae- / "sarea or New Jersey." [New York, James Parker, 1769]
9 p. 32 cm. caption title
Dated July 18, 1769
New York Public 418; Sabin 95936
DLC; MH; NN; PPL; RPJCB mp. 42011

B3050 NEW JERSEY
To / the Honourable , / the / Commissioners, / "appointed . . . for ascertaining, set– / "tling, adjusting . . . the boundary, or partition / "line, between . . . New-York, and Nova-Caesarea, / "or New-Jersey." [New York, James Parker, 1769]
9 p. 31 cm.
Dated July 18, 1769
New York Public 419
DLC. Photostat: NN mp. 42012

B3051 NEW JERSEY. LAWS
Anno regni, Georgii III . . . decimo. At a session of General Assembly, began at Burlington, October 10, 1769, and continued till the 6th of December following. Being the first session of the twenty-first assembly . . . Woodbridge, James Parker, 1769.
123 p. 30 cm.
The first six acts passed Nov. 16; the remaining twenty passed Dec. 6, 1769
Humphrey 101
Nj. Public Record Off. mp. 41979

B3052 THE New-Jersey almanack, agreeable to the New-Stile, and on an entire New-Plan. For . . . 1770 . . . By William Ball, Weather-Guesser. New-York, Printed and sold by James Parker [1769]
[36] p. 18 cm.
Wall p. 20
PHi mp. 41909

B3053 A NEW-Year's wish, from the baker's lad. Boston, January 1769. [Boston, 1769]
broadside 17 X 14.5 cm.
Ford 1501
PHi. Photostat: MWA mp. 41982

B3054 A NEW-Year's wish, from the farrier's lad. Boston, January 1769. [Boston, 1769]
broadside 16.5 X 12 cm.
Ford 1500
PHi. Photostat: MWA mp. 41983

B3055 NEW YORK (CITY). ELECTION PROX.
[Election ticket for 1769] Philip Livingston, Peter Van Brugh Livingston . . . [New York, 1769]
broadside 9.5 X 17.5 cm.
DLC mp. 41984

B3056 NEW York, January 6, 1769. Advertisement, for summoning the freeholders and freemen, of . . . New-York, to nominate and elect four representatives to . . . the next General Assembly . . . [New York, J. Holt, 1769]
broadside 25.5 X 20 cm.
NHi mp. 41987

B3057 NEW York, [*April 3^d^ 1769*] Gentlemen, Boston and this place, having considered and adopted; and Philadelphia having also acceded to . . . restricting the importation of goods from Great-Britain . . . [New York, 1769]
broadside
Dated and signed in ms. by Isaac Sears and others
American Art Assoc. cat. 3381, Jan. 14, 1931, item 253
New York Public 422
NN (reduced facsim.) mp. 41985

B3058 NEW-York, July 1769. Mr. Printer, I send you the inclosed copy of a printed circular letter, and the Articles of a certain Society of Dissenters in this city . . . [New York, 1769]
broadside 36 X 27.5 cm.
NHi mp. 41988

B3059 NEW YORK GAZETTE.
Printing office, in Hanover-Square, Jan. 1, 1769. The printer's lads . . . [New York, 1769]
broadside
MWA (bound in newspaper) mp. 41995

B3060 NEWPORT MERCURY
New Year's verses . . . January 1, 1769. [Newport, 1769]
broadside
MWA mp. 41980

B3061 NORTH CAROLINA. GOVERNOR, 1765-1771
The speech of his Excellency William Tryon . . . To the General Assembly, met at Newbern [Oct. 23, 1769] . . . [Newbern, James Davis, 1769]
[3] p. 26 cm. caption title
McMurtrie: North Carolina 57
Public Record Off. mp. 41989

B3062 NORTH CAROLINA. HOUSE OF ASSEMBLY
The journal of the House of Assembly . . . At an Assembly . . . held at Newbern . . . Being the first session of this present Assembly . . . [Newbern, James Davis, 1769]
20 p. 31.5 cm. caption title
Session Oct. 23-Nov. 6, 1769
McMurtrie: North Carolina 58
NcWsM mp. 41990

B3063 PENNSYLVANIA. GOVERNOR, 1763-1771
By the honourable John Penn, esquire, lieutenant-governor . . . a proclamation. Whereas by an act of General Assembly . . . [Oct. 7, 1769] Philadelphia, D. Hall and W. Sellers, 1769.
broadside 52 X 42 cm.
Metzger 330
DLC; PHi mp. 41991

B3064 PICTET, BÉNÉDICT, 1655-1724
[The affections of the mind. Williamsburg? 1769?]
52 p. 19 cm. $A–F^4\ G^2$
A summary of bk. 8 of Pictet's *La morale chrétienne*
MWA (t.p. wanting) mp. 41992

B3065 [A POEM on winter, printed for the benefit of a poor child. Williamsburg? W. Rind? 1769?]

Advertised in *Rind's Virginia Gazette*, Feb. 16, 1769, as "Lately published and to be sold at the New printing-office in Williamsburg."
No copy known mp. 41993

B3066 A POEM, wrote upon the execution of a man . . . at Fairfield, for burglary, the first day of March . . . 1769 . . . [n. p., 1769]
broadside 23.5 X 17 cm.
In verse in two columns
CtHi mp. 41994

B3067 POOR Thomas improved: being More's country almanack, for . . . 1770 . . . By Thomas More, Philodespot. New-York, Printed and sold by Alexander and James Robertson [1769]
[40] p. 17 cm.
Guerra b-248; Sabin 64089
MWA mp. 41974

B3068 POOR Will's pocket almanack for . . . 1770 . . . Philadelphia, Joseph Crunkshank [1769]
[32] p.
Drake 9939
DLC (t.p. wanting); InU; MWA; PHi

B3069 THE prodigal daughter . . . Boston, Sold at the Heart and Crown, in Cornhill [by Thomas Fleet] [1769?]
16 p. illus. 18.5 cm.
Ownership inscription (Greenaway copy): Moses Sargent Morell his book. 1769
Hamilton 51 (2)
NjP (p. 15-16 wanting). Emerson Greenway, Philadelphia (1962) mp. 41996

B3070 READ, MARY
An account of the remarkable recovery of Mrs. Mary Read, of Rehoboth . . . [Providence? 1769?]
broadside 22.5 X 16.5 cm.
Dated 1769 from internal evidence
Alden 416; Ford 1471; NYPL 404
MWA. Photostats: CSmH; DLC; MHi; MiU–C; NN mp. 41904

B3071 REMER LOTTERY
Scheme of a lottery consisting of three classes . . . Peter Perrine, John Roy, Alexander Linn . . . November 3, 1769. [New York, James Parker? 1769]
broadside fol.
Lottery to make up the deficiencies of George Remer as sheriff
PPL mp. 41997

B3072 RHODE ISLAND. ELECTION PROX.
American liberty. Honourable Joseph Wanton, Esq; Governor. Honourable Darius Sessions, Esq; Dep. Governor . . . [Providence? 1769?]
broadside 20 X 13.5 cm.
Alden 417; Chapin Proxies 7
RHi mp. 41998

B3073 RHODE ISLAND. GOVERNOR, 1768-1769
[By the honorable Josias Lyndon . . . A proclamation . . . relating the seizure of a sloop . . . Newport, S. Southwick, 1769]
[broadside?] [folio?]
Bill submitted Jan. 17, 1769
Alden 418
No copy known mp. 41999

B3074 RHODE ISLAND. LAWS
[An act for the relief of insolvent debtors . . . Newport, S. Southwick, 1769]

Bill submitted Jan. 23, 1769
Alden 424
No copy known mp. 42000

B3075 ROBINSON, NATHANIEL
Verses composed by Nathaniel Robinson, when he was in Albany goal. New-London, Timothy Green, 1769.
36 p.
Trumbull: Supplement 2571
CtHi (lacks bottom of t.p. and all after p. 22); CtY (lacks sig. C); NN mp. 42001

B3076 SALEM, Thursday, January 12, 1769. Important advices! New-York, January 3. Last night, the snow Mercury Captain Kemble arrived here from London . . . [Salem, 1769]
broadside
Contains His Majesty's speech to both Houses
Tapley p. 305
MSaE mp. 41939

B3077 SALEM, Wednesday, January 18, 1769. [Salem, 1769]
broadside 38 X 23.5 cm.
Contains the addresses made to the King Nov. 8, 1768, brought by Capt. Scott
Ford 1504
MSaE; MWA mp. 42002

B3078 SECHS neue politische Lieder, das erste: Trau, schau, wem du thust vertrauen &c. . . . das sechste: Es sterben zwey Brüder in einem Tag. [n.p.] Gedruckt 1769.
8 p.
PPL mp. 42003

B3079 SMITH, THOMAS-LOUGHTON, & ROGER, firm
Charles-Town, [ ] To be sold on Wednesday the 29th instant, a cargo of two hundred and ninety [ ] slaves . . . Charles-Town, March 18, 1769. To be sold . . . a cargo of one hundred and thirty-eight slaves . . . Thomas-Loughton & Roger Smith. [Charleston] Printed at Timothy's Office [1769]
broadside 33 X 21 cm.
MWA (mutilated) mp. 42004

B3080 SOUTH CAROLINA. GOVERNOR, 1768-1769
South-Carolina By His Excellency the right honourable Lord Charles-Greville Montagu . . . A proclamation: Whereas the present General Assembly . . . stood prorogued . . . hereby further proroguing the same to . . . the twenty-sixth day of June . . . Given . . . 16th day of June . . . C. G. Montagu . . . Charlestown, Robert Wells [1769]
broadside 31.5 X 18.5 cm.
Sabin 87358
MWA mp. 42005

B3081 SOUTH CAROLINA. LAWS
Acts of the General Assembly . . . passed in the year 1769. Charles-Town, South Carolina, Peter Timothy, 1769.
1 p.l., 48 [1] p. 29 cm.
Sabin 87608
DLC mp. 42006

B3082 SOUTH CAROLINA. LAWS
[Tax act and estimate. Charleston, 1769]
[2], 33 p.

Sabin 87609; Turnbull p. 172
ScC (t.p. lacking)

B3083 THE spelling-book, and child's plaything. Calculated for the instruction and amusement of children. New-London, Printed and sold by Timothy Green, 1769.
118 p. 14 cm. A–K[6]
MWA (sig. A2, A5 wanting) mp. 42007

B3084 THE Tom Cod-Catcher. On the departure of an infamous B r t.
Go B[ernard], thou minion! – to thy country go,
For Boston, loud proclaims you, Freedom's foe . . .
[Boston? 1769]
broadside
Ford 1505
MWA; NHi mp. 42013

B3085 TRAILL, ROBERT
To the impartial publick. Although private disputes afford but little entertainment to the public . . . necessity to vindicate myself . . . Robert Traill. Portsmouth, June 6th, 1769. [Portsmouth, 1769]
[2] p. 32 cm.
Found in MHi file of [Portsmouth] *New Hampshire Gazette* between June 2 and 9, 1769
MHi mp. 42014

B3086 THE unfortunate lovers: a short, beautiful poem . . . Newport, S. Southwick, 1769.
8 p. 17 cm.
Alden 432
MHi mp. 42015

B3087 URRUTIA, MANUEL JOSEPH DE
Ynstruccion del modo de substanciar, y determinar las causas civiles, criminales . . . óbra hecha por el Doctor Don Manuel Joseph de Urrutia, y el abogado don Feliz Rey de orden . . . O'Reilly . . . [at end] Nueva Orleans [Nov. 25, 1769] Don Alexandro O'Reilly . . . Francisco Xavier Rodriguez, escribano . . . [New Orleans, Denis Braud, 1769]
51 p. 22 cm.
McMurtrie: New Orleans 13
Archivo general de Indias, Seville mp. 42016

B3088 A VERSE, occasioned by seeing the North-Spinning, in Boton [sic]. Boston, behold the pretty spinners here . . . Boston, Printed and sold 1769.
broadside 20 X 16.5 cm.
MHi. Photostat: MWA mp. 42017

B3089 VIRGINIA. GOVERNOR, 1768-1770
The speech of his excellency . . . Norborne Baron de Botetourt . . . the 7th day of November, 1769. [Williamsburg, 1769]
broadside 37 X 23 cm.
DLC (photostat) mp. 42020

B3090 VIRGINIA. GOVERNOR, 1768-1770
Virginia, sc. By his excellency . . . Norborne Baron de Botetourt . . . a proclamation. Whereas I have received information . . . [Oct. 19, 1769] [Williamsburg, 1769]
broadside 42 X 28 cm.
DLC (photostat) mp. 42019

B3091 VIRGINIA. HOUSE OF BURGESSES
Journal of the House of burgesses . . . begun and held . . . on Monday the eighth day of May . . . 1769. [Colophon] Williamsburg, William Rind, 1769.
42 p. 28.5 cm. caption title
Sabin 99968; Torrence 360
DLC; ViWC mp. 42021

B3092 VIRGINIA. HOUSE OF BURGESSES
To his excellency the right honourable Norborne Baron de Botetourt . . . the humble address of the House of burgesses . . . [Williamsburg, 1769]
broadside 33 X 20 cm.
Speech of May 10, 1769
DLC (photostat) mp. 42018

B3093 VIRGINIA GAZETTE
Supplement to *Purdie & Dixon's Virginia Gazette.* May 11, 1769 . . . On Monday last . . . Norborne Baron de Botetourt . . . delivered the following speech to the General Assembly . . . [Williamsburg, 1769]
4 p. 43 cm.
Contains also foreign news, the humble address of the House of Burgesses, etc.
ViU

B3094 [VIRGINIA revived: or, A plan to bring in cash, and make money circulate without paper currency . . . By one who has seen the world. Williamsburg, W. Rind, 1769?]

Advertised in *Rind's Virginia Gazette*, Mar. 16, 1769, as "On the 15th of next month, will be published and sold at the New printing-office."
No copy known mp. 42022

B3095 WESLEY, JOHN, 1702-1791
Hymns for the nativity of Our Lord . . . Philadelphia, John Dunlap, 1769.
24 p. 17.5 cm.
Metzger 327
MH; PHi mp. 42024

B3096 WESTMINSTER ASSEMBLY OF DIVINES
The shorter catechism, agreed upon by the reverend Assembly of Divines . . . New-London, Printed and sold by T. Green, 1769.
34+ p.
Trumbull: Supplement 2610
CtHi (wanting beyond p. 34) mp. 42025

B3097 WHEREAS it is of the utmost importance for the . . . denominations in this country, not belonging to the Church . . . to unite . . . to form a Society of Non-Episcopal Churches . . . [New York? 1769?]
4 p.
Blank notice of meeting and election of Moderator [Peter V. B. Livingston] and Secretary [John McKesson]
RPJCB mp. 41986

B3098 A WHIP for the American Whig by Timothy Tickle Esqr. [No. LXIII]. [New York, 1769]
[2] p. 37.5 cm.
NHi mp. 42026

B3099 [WINDHAM, WILLIAM] 1717-1761
Plan of exercise, for the militia of the Colony of Connecticut . . . New-London: Printed and sold by Timothy Green [1769]
103 p. 17.5 cm.
Advertised in the *New London Gazette*, Aug. 4, 1769, as "Just publish'd and to be sold by T. Green."
Trumbull 1251
CtHi

B3100 THE youth's instructor in the English tongue . . . Collected from Dixon, Bailey, Owen, Strong and Watts. Boston, Printed by D. Kneeland fro J. Perkins, 1769.
159 p. 16 cm.
Karpinski p. 50
MH mp. 42027

177-

B3101 BAPTIST SOCIETY, PROVIDENCE
To all persons to whom these presents shall come: Know ye, That we the subscribers, Treasurer of the Baptist Society, and Treasurer of the Charitable Baptist Society, in the town of Providence, and colony of Rhode-Island . . . do assign . . . a pew . . . in the New Baptist Meeting-House . . . this day of in the year . . . [Providence, 177-?]
broadside 40 X 25.5 cm.
Filled in for June 9, 1777; "colony" struck out and "state" substituted
MWA mp. 42040

B3102 BOSTON. SELECTMEN
Boston, ss. 177 At a meeting of the select-men, ordered, That the assize of bread . . . be as follows, viz. . . . [Boston, 177-]
broadside 19 X 15.5 cm.
Dated Jan. 26, 1774
RPJCB

B3103 BOSTON EVENING POST
A New Year's wish, of the printer's boy who carries the *Boston Evening-Post.*
Old Time again has run the circling year . . .
[Boston, 177-]
broadside 17.5 X 12 cm.
PHi mp. 42038

B3104 BOSTON, 177 . Mr. You are hereby warned to attend the working of the engine called the Hancock, on the first Mondays of the seven following months. [Boston, 177-]
broadside 12.5 X 10.5 cm.
Ford 1508
MWA mp. 42028

B3105 BROWN UNIVERSITY
Subscriptions for the Rhode-Island College . . . [Newport, 177-]
broadside 19.5 X 16 cm.
RHi. Photostat: RPJCB mp. 42028

B3106 THE children in the woods . . . [Boston] Sold at the Heart & Crown in Cornhill [by T. and J. Fleet, 177-?]
broadside
In three columns
Rosenbach–Ch 64
A. S. W. Rosenbach (1933) mp. 42030

B3107 [COZINE, JOHN]
Dick Twiss. A poem. [n.p., 177-?]
8 p. 18 cm.
Ms. note on t.p.: Written by John Cozine sometime during . . . the American Revolutionary War
New York Public 428; Sabin 17320
NHi. Photostats: MHi; MWA; NN mp. 42031

B3108 DABNEY, NATHANIEL
Dr. Stoughton's Elixir Magnum Stomachicum . . . faithfully prepar'd and sold by Nathaniel Dabney, at his shop nearly opposite the Town House and directly opposite Rev'd Mr. Barnard's Meeting House in Salem. [Salem, 177-?]
broadside
References to Dabney as an apothecary 1771-1774; his shop burned in 1774, and he is thereafter mentioned as a bookseller
MSaE mp. 42032

B3109 A DIALOGUE between death and a lady. Very suitable in these times. Boston, Sold at the Heart and Crown [177-?]
broadside 31.5 X 21.5 cm.
In verse
Ford 3057; New York Public 429
MWA. Photostats: MHi; NN mp. 42033

B3110 ESSENTIA euphragiae. A specific remedy for weakness of sight . . . prepared by directions of Dr. Hill, and sold by Mr. Jackson . . . London, and by Dr. John Sparhawk of Philadelphia in Pennsylvania . . . [Philadelphia? 177-?]
broadside 15 X 18 cm.
MWA mp. 42044

B3111 THE famous and remarkable history of Sir Richard Whittington . . . Boston: Printed [by T. and J. Fleet] and sold at the Heart & Crown [177-?]
16 p. 20 cm.
Earlier editions signed "T. H." [Thomas Heywood?]
T. and J. Fleet printed at the Heart & Crown 1731-1776
MB mp. 42049

B3112 THE farmer and his son's return from a visit to camp; together with The rose tree. [n.p., 177-?]
broadside
Ford 1941
Photostats: MHi; RPJCB mp. 42034

B3113 [FRANKLIN, BENJAMIN] 1706-1790
[Father Abraham's speech . . . New Haven? 177-?]
16 p. 14 cm.
Caption on p. [3] same as caption on same page of Evans 8131 and 10619; but ornamental type border at top of p. [3] differs. Similar ornaments not found in other Mecom or T. & S. Green New Haven publications
CtY (lacks t.p.)

B3114 AN Indian gazette. [cuts] Explanation of the above gazette engraved from an authentic copy, drawn by a French engineer from the original. 1760 . . . [Ph]iladelphia, Printed by John Dunlap, at the Newest Printing-Office, in Market Street [177-?]
broadside 40 X 19 cm.
Dunlap was at this address 1768-1778
MWA (closely trimmed) mp. 42035

B3115 MASSACHUSETTS. TREASURER
State of the Massachusetts-Bay, the honorable Henry Gardner, Esq; treasurer . . . To the sheriff of . . . 177 . [Boston, 177-]
broadside
Used in the years 1777-1781
Ford 2159
M–Ar

B3116 MIDDLESEX, C. To the select-men of the town of Gentlemen, This contains the names of the persons licenced in your town the last year, viz. The time for renewing licences for this present year will be on Tuesday the day of September . . . Cambridge, May 177 [Boston, 177-]
broadside
MWA (photostat) mp. 42036

B3117 THE New-England primer improved . . . Salem, S. and E. Hall [177-]
[80] p. illus. 10 cm.
Heartman 386 (1934 ed.); Tapley p. 311

Press of Samuel and Ebenezer Hall located at Salem 1772-1775
DLC mp. 42037

B3118 PENNSYLVANIA
By the proprietaries. Pennsylvania, ss. Whereas of the county of hath requested . . . acres of land . . . seal of the Land-office to be affixed at Philadelphia, this day of One Thousand Seven Hundred and Seventy To John Lukens, Surveyor-general. [Philadelphia, 177-]
broadside 21 X 33.5 cm.
MiU–C copy dated in ms. Feb. 16, 1773
DLC; MiU–C.

B3119 PENNSYLVANIA. GENERAL ASSEMBLY
Sir, Pay to Esquire . . . the sum of for his wages as a member of Assembly for days . . . In General Assembly at Philadelphia, the day of 177 To David Rittenhouse State Treasurer. [Philadelphia, 177-]
broadside 22.5 X 19 cm.
Dated in ms. Dec. 6, 1778
Taylor 166
NN

B3120 PROVIDENCE, 177 These may certify, that the bearer permitted to depart the hospital, being sufficiently freed from . . . the small-pox. [Providence, 177-]
broadside 9.5 X 16.5 cm.
Filled in for Oct. 24, 1776
RPJCB

B3121 RETURN of the battalion of foot, North-Carolina, whereof esquire, is Colonel. 177 Philadelphia, John Dunlap [177-]
broadside 40.5 X 33.5 cm.
Form not filled in
RPJCB

B3122 [SMITH, WILLIAM]
Advertisement. To all farmers, desirous to remove back from the . . . sea coasts, for the better establishment of their families, upon Hudson's and Connecticut-Rivers . . . The subscriber has for sale . . . [page ends] New-York, [New York? 177-]
[2?] p. 33.5 cm.
Second page of what appears to be a broadsheet is lacking
Mrs. Nathan Haskell, Amherst, Mass. (1939).
MWA (photostat) mp. 42041

B3123 SMITH, WILLIAM
New lands to be sold, upon very moderate and easy terms, in the great patent of Queensborough, or Kayaderosseres, in the County of Albany . . . William Smith, Abraham Lott. [New York? 177-]
broadside 42 X 32.5 cm.
Mrs. Nelson Haskell, Amherst, Mass. (1939).
Photostat: MWA mp. 42042

B3124 SMITH, WILLIAM
To farmers inclining to purchase new lands in the province of New-York, at a cheap rate . . . Dated at New-York, the day of William Smith, on behalf of all the proprietors. [New York, 177-]
broadside 37.5 X 21 cm.
Mrs. Nelson Haskell, Amherst, Mass. (1939).
MWA (photostat) mp. 42043

B3125 SOUTH-CAROLINA Price-current. Charles-Town, the day of 177 . By the hundred . . . [Charles-Town] Printed for Crouch & Gray [177-]
broadside 15.5 X 43 cm.
Filled in in manuscript for July 30, 1774
DLC; RPJCB

B3126 STICKNEY, JOHN, 1742–1826
The gentleman and lady's musical companion. Newbury-Port [177-?]
[8], 212 p. 13 X 20 cm.
Printed between 1774 and 1783
DLC; MWA; NN mp. 42045

B3127 TAXATION of America . . . [n.p., 177-?]
broadside
While I rehearse my story, Americans give ear . . .
Attributed to Samuel St. John, or to Peter St. John
Ford 2121
NHi mp. 42046

B3128 THIS evening, March 27th, will be presented, the celebrated tragedy . . . David and Goliah . . . [Philadelphia, 177-?]
broadside 11 X 9 cm.
New York Public 452
NN mp. 42039

B3129 U. S. ARMY. CONTINENTAL ARMY
Protection. All officers, soldiers or followers of the army, are hereby strictly forbid to molest or injure inhabitant of county . . . Given at this day of 177 By order of the commander in chief. [n.p., 177-]
broadside 13.5 X 31 cm.
DLC

B3130 U. S. ARMY. CONTINENTAL ARMY
Provision return for the regiment of foot, commanded by Colonel 177 [Philadelphia] John Dunlap [177-]
broadside 21 X 33 cm.
Dated in ms. Dec. 24, 1776. Form not filled in
RPJCB

B3131 U. S. ARMY. CONTINENTAL ARMY
Return of the sick and wounded, in the General Hospital, belonging to the army under . . . George Washington . . . from to the 177 [n.p., 177-]
broadside
Ford 1904
MHi

B3132 THE vanity of war and riches, compair'd with the pleasures of a retir'd . . . life. A poem, composed to the tune of Dr. Watts's Indian philosopher. [n.p., 177-?]
broadside 40 X 15 cm.
Eleven six-line stanzas
New York Public 454
NN mp. 42047

B3133 VIRGINIA
The Commonwealth of Virginia To Gentlemen, You are hereby . . . appointed inspectors of tobacco at the warehouses . . . in the county of and you are hereby empowered . . . Witness Patrick Henry, Esq; Governour . . . the day of in the year of Commonwealth . . . 177 [Williamsburg, 177-]
broadside 19 X 13 cm.
DLC

B3134 WESLEY, CHARLES, 1707–1788
To the Reverend Mr. George Whitefield: By Mr. Charles Wesley. [38 lines] A poem by the Reveren[d] Mr. Whitefiel[d] [36 lines] Printed and sold over against the South-East corner of the Town House in Boston. [177-?]
broadside 32.5 X 21.5 cm.
MBB (mutilated) mp. 42048

1770

B3135 [AN account of the remarkable conversion of Zachial Heishel from the Jewish to the Christian religion . . . Savannah, 1770]
32 p. 8vo
De Renne p. 264; Rosenbach 51
No copy located mp. 42051

B3136 [ALLEN, BENNET]
A reply to the Church of England planter's first letter respecting the clergy. Annapolis, Anne Catharine Green, 1770.
22 p. 21.5 cm.
Wroth 295
MdHi mp. 42052

B3137 ANDREWS, SAMUEL, 1737–1818
A discourse, delivered in St. Paul's-Church, at Wallingford, before the . . . Masons, on the 26th day of June, 1770 . . . New-Haven, Printed by T. and S. Green [1770]
16 p. 19 cm. $[A]-B^4$
CtHi; MWA mp. 42056

B3138 AN astronomical diary, or, almanack for the year of our Lord Christ 1771 . . . By Nathaniel Ames . . . [Boston, 1770]
[24] p. 17.5 cm.
Drake 263
CtHi; DLC (2 copies); MWA; NhD; NjP mp. 42053

B3139 AN astronomical diary: or almanack, for . . . 1771 . . . By Nathaniel Ames . . . New-Haven. Reprinted by T. and S. Green [1770]
[24] p. 19 cm.
Guerra b-260; Trumbull: Supplement 1811
CtHi; CtY; MBCo; MWA mp. 42054

B3140 AN astronomical diary, or, almanack, for the year of our Lord Christ, 1771 . . . By Nathaniel Ames . . . Newport [S. Southwick, 1770]
[24] p. 17.5 cm.
Alden 435; Guerra b-262
DLC; MWA; NN mp. 42055

B3141 AN astronomical diary; or Almanack for . . . 1771. By Nathaniel Ames . . . Portsmouth: Printed and sold by D. & R. Fowle; sold also by William Appleton [1770]
[24] p.
Drake 4630
MB; MHi; MWA; NHi; NN (imperfect); Nh; NhHi

B3142 AUSTIN, SAMUEL
Samuel Austin in Union-street, Boston, near the sign of the Corn-Fields, imports and sells . . . [Boston, 1770?]
broadside
Ford 1506
MHi mp. 42058

B3143 BELL, ROBERT, 1731–1784
A catalogue of new and old books consisting of history, divinity, biography, surgery . . . Sold at a house upon Hunter's Quay . . . New York. [New York, 1770]

Advertised in the *New York Gazette*, Feb. 5, 1770, as ". . . Just published, and to be had gratis."
Guerra a-444
No copy located mp. 42059

B3144 BELL, ROBERT, 1731–1784
A catalogue of new and old books, which will be exhibited by auction, by Robert Bell, bookseller and auctioner, on Wednesday the 4th of July, 1770 . . . Kingstreet, in the Town of Boston. [Boston, 1770]
[2] p. 39 cm.
Ford 1507; Guerra a-445
MHi mp. 42060

B3145 BIBLE. O.T. PSALMS
The New-England Psalter . . . Boston, Printed and sold by William M'Alpine, 1770.
194 p. $A-Q^6R^2$ (R2 wanting)
cf. Evans 11568 (with Nicene creed at end)
DLC (mutilated) mp. 42062

B3146 BIBLE. O.T. PSALMS
The New-England Psalter . . . Boston, Printed by D. Kneeland, for Nicholas Bowes, 1770.
[176] p.
PMA mp. 42061

B3147 BIBLE. O.T. PSALMS
A new version of the Psalms of David . . . By N. Brady . . . and N. Tate . . . Boston, Printed [by Mein and Fleeming] for, and sold by A. Barclay, 1770.
261, [1], 78, 8, 16 p.
cf. Evans 11570
MWA mp. 42063

B3148 BIBLE. O.T. PSALMS
The Psalms of David imitated . . . by I. Watts, D.D. The twenty-sixth edition . . . Boston, Printed by D. Kneeland, for Thomas Leverett, 1770.
xxxi, 372 p. 15 cm.
cf. Evans 11571
MB mp. 42084

B3149 BOSTON
A short narrative of the horrid massacre in Boston . . . [Boston] Printed by order of the town of Boston, and sold by Edes and Gill, and T. & J. Fleet, 1770.
48, 88 p. plate. 8vo
Adams 75d; Huntington 297
CSmH; CtHt-W; CtY; DLC; InU; MB; MHi; MWA; MWiW-C; MeB; MiU-C; NHi; NjP; PPL. Brit. Mus.

B3150 BOSTON
A short narrative of the horrid massacre in Boston . . . [Boston] Printed by order of the Town of Boston, and sold by Edes and Gill . . . and T. & J. Fleet . . . 1770.
35, 80, 79–81 p. 8vo $[A]-P^4$
Textual differences from Evans 11581.–T. R. Adams
Adams 75a
MBAt

B3151 BOSTON
A short narrative of the horrid massacre in Boston . . . Boston, Printed, by order of the Town, by Messirs. [sic] Edes and Gill; and reprinted for W. Bingley . . . London, MDCCLXX.

3 p.l., [5]-48, 83 p.
"Printed by Edes and Gill in imitation of the London edition."—T. R. Adams
Adams 75e
CSmH; CtY; DLC; MB; MBAt; MH

B3152 BOSTON. SELECTMEN
Notification; the freeholders and other inhabitants . . . are hereby notified to meet at Faneuil Hall on Monday next . . . Boston, August 10. 1770. [Boston, 1770]
broadside
MB mp. 42067

B3153 BOSTON, Sept. 11, 1770. Sir, On Friday last at a meeting of the body at Faneuil-Hall, a committee of ten persons were appointed . . . Gibbins Sharp, Chairman of said Committee. [Boston, 1770]
broadside 15 X 12 cm.
MHi mp. 42068

B3154 BOSTON CHRONICLE
A New-Year's wish, for the year 1770. By the carrier of the *Boston Chronicle*. [Boston, 1770]
broadside
Ford 1561
PHi. Photostat: MWA mp. 42138

B3155 BOSTON EVENING POST
January 1, 1770. A New Year's address of the printer's boy who carries the *Boston Evening-Post*. [Boston, 1770]
broadside 23 X 12 cm.
Ford 1562
PHi. Photostat: MWA mp. 42109

B3156 BOSTON GAZETTE
An account of a late military massacre at Boston . . . taken from the *Boston-Gazette*, of March 12, 1770. [Boston, 1770]
broadside 50 X 40 cm.
Illustration has imprint: Engrav'd printed & sold by Paul Revere Boston
Brigham: Paul Revere, p. 46, pl. 16; New York Public 424
NHi. Photostats: MWA; NN mp. 42050

B3157 BOSTON GAZETTE
An ode for the year 1770. From the carrier of the *Boston-Gazette* . . . [Boston, 1770]
broadside 16.5 X 12 cm.
Ford 1564
PHi. Photostat: MWA mp. 42142

B3158 BROWN UNIVERSITY
Advertisement. Providence, Monday, February 5, 1770. The inhabitants . . . are desired to meet . . . this afternoon . . . Providence, John Carter [1770]
broadside 20 X 26 cm.
Alden 453; Winship p. 26
RHi; RPJCB. Photostats: MHi; MWA; NN mp. 42069

B3159 BROWN UNIVERSITY
Viro ornatissimo . . . Jacobo Manning . . . Haec philosophemata . . . A.D. MDCCLXX. Providentiae, J. Carter [1770]
broadside 51.5 X 39.5 cm.
Alden 454; Winship p. 26
RPB. Photostats: MHi; MWA; NN; RHi mp. 42071

B3160 BROWN UNIVERSITY
Whereas the Governor . . . incorporated certain persons . . . we therefore . . . engage to give . . . unto Job Bennett . . . [Providence, J. Carter? ca. 1770?]
broadside 31 X 37.5 cm.
Bennett was College treasurer from 1767 to 1775
Alden 454A; Sabin 103255; Winship p. 24
RPB. Photostats: NN; RHi mp. 42070

B3161 [BURGWIN, JOHN] 1731–1803
North-Carolina. A table of the number of taxables . . . and an account of the sums that should arise by the sinking tax yearly to the year 1770. [n.p., 1770?]
2 fold. tables 37 X 41.5 cm.
15 copies made from the original in the Mass. Hist. Society
MHi. Photostats: DLC; MWA; NN [etc.] mp. 42072

B3162 CAZNEAU, JAMES & WILLIAM, firm, Boston
Imported from London and Bristol, by James & William Cazneau, and are to be sold . . . at their shop in . . . Boston, a large assortment of goods . . . [Boston, 1770?]
broadside 20 X 16 cm.
Huntington 298
CSmH; PPL mp. 42073

B3163 [CHAMBERLAIN, THOMAS] d. 1784
England's timely remembrancer: or, The minister preaching his own funeral sermon . . . Newport: Re-printed, 1770.
[16] p. 13 cm.
MWA mp. 42088

B3164 THE character and death of the late Rev. George Whitefield . . . About fifteen thousand persons attended his funeral. [Portsmouth] D. and R. Fowle. [1770]
broadside 39 X 31.5 cm.
DLC; NN (reduced facsim.); NhHi mp. 42074

B3165 CHARACTER of the celebrated Dr. Robertson, author of the History of Scotland . . . [Philadelphia, R. Bell, 1770]
4 p. 8vo caption title
PPL mp. 42075

B3166 CHARLESTON LIBRARY SOCIETY, CHARLESTON, S.C.
The rules and by-laws of the Charlestown Library Society . . . The third edition. Charlestown, Robert Wells, 1770.
26 p. 21.5 cm.
DLC mp. 42076

B3167 COOKE, ____
Cooke's speech from the pillory. [Boston, Z. Fowle] Sold at the Printing-Office in Back Street [1770]
broadside
In verse
Ford 1514
PHi mp. 42077

B3168 COT-ER'S speech from the pillory. [Boston, Z. Fowle, 1770]
broadside
The cut is the same as that on *Cooke's speech*
In verse
Ford 1515
PHi mp. 42078

B3169 [CRISP, STEPHEN] 1628–1692
A short history of a long travel from Babylon to Bethel . . . Newport, S. Southwick, 1770.
22 p. 18 cm.
Signed on p. 22: S. C.
Alden 439; Winship p. 26
RHi mp. 42079

B3170 THE cruel parents: or Bedlam garland. [Boston] Printed and sold at the Printing Office in Milk-Street, 1770.
broadside 31.5 X 19.5 cm.
On the same sheet: Scornful Celia
Ford 1515a, 3034a
MHi (imperfect) mp. 42080

B3171 DELAWARE. HOUSE OF REPRESENTATIVES
Votes and proceedings of the House of representatives . . . [Oct. 21, 1765–Mat. 24, 1770] Wilmington, James Adams, 1770.
233 p. 33.5 cm.
Each section has caption title
Hawkins 4
DeHi; PHi. Photostat: DLC mp. 42081

B3172 A DETEST against the common scheme of arbitration; likewise an account of an instance of the ill consequence of it . . . [Boston? 1770?]
broadside
A clue to an unknown specific event occurs in:
"As Justice did F——S——forsake
In pity I his part did take".
Ford 1516
NHi mp. 42082

B3173 [A DIALOGUE between Jockey and Maggy [or] How to court a country girl. Philadelphia, R. Aitken, 1770]

cf. Spawn, W. and C.: *R. Aitken, colonial printer of Philadelphia*. (In *Graphic arts review*, Jan.-Feb. 1961)
No copy located mp. 42083

B3174 DILWORTH, THOMAS, d. 1780
A new guide to the English tongue . . . Boston, Printed for, and sold by J. Perkins, 1770.
xi, [1], 154 p. illus. 16 cm.
New York Public 430
NN (imperfect); NNC mp. 42084

B3174a AN elegiac poem sacred to the memory of the Rev. George Whitefield . . . Boston, Printed: Sold by Zechariah Fowle, in Back-Street, MDCCLXX.
8 p. 17.5 cm.
Porter 261; Sabin 103619; Stoddard 81b
MWA; NHi mp. 42197

B3175 AN elegy, &c. Mourn, O ye saints, since Whitefield's dead . . . [n.p., 1770?]
[2] p. 20.5 cm.
In double columns, separated by heavy rule
NjR

B3176 AN elegy on the death of the Rev. Mr. George Whitefield . . . [New York, J. Holt, 1770]
broadside 23.5 X 19.5 cm.
Text in 2 columns divided by heavy rule
PHi mp. 42085

B3177 AN elegy on the much lamented death of the Reverend Mr. George Whitefield . . . [n.p., 1770]
broadside 33.5 X 19 cm.
Ford 1548
RPJCB. Photostats: DLC; MHi; MWA mp. 42086

B3178 ERSKINE, RALPH, 1685–1752
Christ the people's covenant, a sermon . . . Boston, Printed and sold by William M'Alpine, 1770.
86, [1] p. 16 cm. $A\text{-}G^6 H^2$
MHi; MWA mp. 42087

B3179 AN exercise, containing a dialogue and two odes . . . Philadelphia, J. Crukshank and I. Collins [1770]
8 p. 4to
By Provost William Smith??
Adams: Pennsylvania 24; Sabin 84610 note
PU

B3180 A FEW thoughts compos'd on the sudden & awful death of Mrs. Fessenden . . . who was shot May 30, 1770 . . . Boston, Printed and sold in Milk-Street, 1770.
broadside 34 X 20 cm.
Ford 1518; New York Public 431
MHi. Photostats: DLC; MWA; NN mp. 42091

B3181 FISHER, GEORGE
The American instructor: or, Young man's best companion . . . The fourteenth edition, revised and corrected. New-York: Printed and sold by H. Gaine, 1770.
v, 390 p. front., fold. pl. 17 cm. $[\ ]^1 A\text{-}Q^{12} R^6$
Guerra a-449; New York Public 432
DLC; MH; MWA; MiU-C; NHi; NN; NhD; NjP; PHi; RPJCB (p. 261–84 lacking) mp. 42090

B3182 FLEEMING, JOHN
The first Bible ever printed in America. Proposals for printing by subscription . . . The Holy Bible . . . and a table of the Scripture promises. By the late Rev. Samuel Clark . . . Subscriptions are taken in by John Fleeming, at his Printing-Office . . . [Boston, J. Fleeming, 1770?]
[4] p. folder 49 X 32 cm.
Dated by John E. Alden
Pages [3–4]: Genesis I:1–26
MHi mp. 42091

B3183 THE following lines were occasioned by the death of Richard Brown, Samuel Brown, John King & Peter Brown who . . . all drowned . . . attempting a passage from East-Hampton, to the Oyster-Ponds, March 9th, 1770 . . . Easthampton . . . March 20th, 1770. Printed and sold in New-London [1770]
broadside 37.5 X 25 cm.
NjP mp. 42092

B3184 FREEMAN'S New-York almanac for . . . 1771. By Frank Freeman. [New York] John Holt [1770]
[72] p.
Drake 5816
Private collection

B3185 FRIENDS, SOCIETY OF. LONDON YEARLY MEETING
An epistle from our yearly-meeting . . . from the 4th of the sixth month, 1770 to the 9th of the same . . . [Colophon] Philadelphia, Joseph Crukshank [1770]
4 p. 33 cm. caption title
Metzger 335
DLC; MWA mp. 42093

B3186 FROM the *New-York Gazettes*, August 13, & 27. Mr. Gaine, A publication having made its appearance in your last paper . . . [New York, 1770]
broadsheet 35 X 20.5 cm.
Text in 2 columns, continued in right margin of recto and left margin of verso, at right angles to main text
Two letters to "Mr. Gaine," one signed: Coriolanus
New York Public 433
MHi; NN

B3187 FROM the *New-York Journal, or, the General Advertiser*, of August 30th, 1770. Mr. Holt, New-York, August 28, 1770. As you published the proceedings of a late meeting at Faneuil Hall . . . you will no doubt . . . insert the following letter in your next Journal . . . To Messrs.

Thomas Cushing, John Hancock . . . [New York, John Holt, 1770]
broadside
Heartman: Cradle 175
Charles F. Heartman (1922) mp. 42094

B3188 A FUNERAL elegy on the Rev. and renowned George Whitefield . . . who departed this life . . . the 30th of September, 1770. [Boston? 1770]
broadside
Ford 1553
MB mp. 42095

B3189 A FUNERAL elegy, on the Rev'd and renowned George Whitefield . . . who departed this life . . . the 30th day of September, 1770. [Boston? 1770]
broadside 34.5 X 20 cm.
Ford 1550; Sabin 103624
PHi. Photostats: MHi; RPJCB mp. 42096

B3190 GEORGIA. LAWS
Acts passed by the General Assembly of Georgia, at a session begun . . . on Monday the 30th day of October . . . 1769 . . . and continued . . . to the 10th day of May 1770 . . . Savannah, James Johnston [1770]
1 pl., 52, [1] p. 25.5 cm.
Seventeen acts, and table
De Renne p. 195; Guerra a-451
DLC; GU-De; RPJCB mp. 42097

B3191 GESSNER, SALOMON, 1730–1788
The death of Abel . . . Attempted from the German of Mr. Gessner. New-London, Printed and sold by Timothy Green, 1770.
88 p. 20 cm. [A]-L^4
CtHi; MWA mp. 42098

B3192 GESSNER, SALOMON, 1730–1788
The death of Abel. In five books. Attempted from the German of Mr. Gessner. Philadelphia, Re-printed and sold by John Dunlap [1770?]
106 p. 16.5 cm.
New York Public 433a; cf. Evans 11667
NN; PPL mp. 42099

B3193 GODDARD, WILLIAM, 1739–1817
Advertisement. July 19, 1770 . . . [Philadelphia, W. Goddard, 1770]
broadside 18 X 15.5 cm.
Metzger 338
PPL mp. 42101

B3194 GODDARD, WILLIAM, 1739–1817
Advertisement. I have the satisfaction to acquaint the public, that on the first inst. . . . Mr. Galloway . . . fled to Bucks County, and . . . obtruded himself upon that county as a representative . . . William Goddard. Philadelphia, October 8, 1770. [Philadelphia, 1770]
broadside 19.5 X 11.5 cm.
CSmH; RPJCB. Photostat: MWA mp. 42100

B3195 GT. BRIT. LAWS
Anno regni Georgii III . . . quinto At the Parliament . . . May . . . 1761 . . . to the tenth day of January, 1765 . . . An act to amend and render more effectual . . . in America . . . An act for punishing mutiny and desertion . . . New-York, Re-printed by H. Gaine, 1770.
1 p.l., 3–21 p. 27 cm.
New York Public 434
Photostat: NN mp. 42102

B3196 GT. BRIT. SURVEYOR-GENERAL OF THE KING'S WOODS
Province of New-Hampshire. By the surveyor-general of the King's woods in North America . . . Notice is hereby given, that all white pine logs cut . . . will be seized . . . Portsmouth, 1st January 1770. [Portsmouth, 1770]
broadside 31.5 X 17 cm.
New York Public 441; Whitemore 135
NHi. Photostats: DLC; NN mp. 42103

B3197 [Green, Jacob] 1722–1790
A vision of Hell . . . by Theodorus Van Shemain . . . New Haven, 1770.
24 p.
NHi mp. 42104

B3198 HAND-IN-HAND FIRE CLUB, NEWPORT, R.I.
These presents witness, that we the subscribers . . . do hereby severally promise . . . [Newport] Reprinted [by Solomon Southwick] in May, 1770.
broadside 38.5 X 31 cm.
Alden 444A
RNHi. Photostat: MWA mp. 42139

B3199 HARTFORD, June 6, 1770. At a meeting of the principal merchants and traders . . . of Connecticut . . . Voted . . . we will not have any . . . dealing with the inhabitants . . . of New-Port . . . [Hartford, 1770]
broadside 20? X 15? cm.
CtHi mp. 42106

B3200 HARVARD UNIVERSITY
Quaestiones pro modulo . . . MDCCLXX. Boston, Draper, 1770.
broadside
Ford 1521
CtY; MH; MHi mp. 42107

B3201 [THE history of Jack and the giant . . . Newport? S. Southwick? ca. 1770?]
24 p. 15 cm.
Date assigned from a ms. inscription in MWA copy
Alden 441
MWA (lacks p. 1–6) mp. 42108

B3202 [HOPKINS, STEPHEN] 1705-1785
Rare observations . . . By S. H. . . . Providence, John Carter, 1770.
76 p. 20 cm.
Alden 442; Winship p. 26
MWA; RHi; RPB (imperfect) mp. 42111

B3203 [HUSBANDS, HERMAN] d. 1795
A continuation of the Impartial relation . . . of the recent differences, in publick affairs, in the province of North-Carolina, &c. Second part. [Newbern?] Printed for the author, 1770.
39 p. 16 cm.
Huntington 299; McMurtrie: North Carolina 60
CSmH mp. 42112

B3204 THE K * * *'s answer to Junius. Taken from an English paper. [Boston? John Fleeming] 1770.
8 p. 20 cm.
MWA mp. 42113

B3205 LINSEY, WILLIAM, d. 1770
The dying speech and confession of William Linsey, to be executed at Worcester, October 25th, 1770 . . . Worcester-Goal, Oct. 18, 1770. Boston, 1770.

broadside 35 X 42 cm.
Ford 1525
MHi (imperfect); MWA; NHi mp. 42114

B3206 [LIVINGSTON, WILLIAM] 1732–1790
A soliloquy. The second edition. [New York] [S. Inslee and A. Car] 1770.
1 p.l., 15 p. 21.5 cm.
A satire on Lieutenant-Governor Colden
cf. Evans 11702–703; Sabin 41651
DLC; RPJCB mp. 42115

B3207 LOUISIANA. GOVERNOR, 1769–1770
Don Alexandre O Reilly . . . Capitaine Géneral de cette Province . . . La loy 2 titre 15 livre 5 de la recopilation de Castille prescrit . . . [Nouvelle Orléans, D. Braud? 1770]
3 p. 31.5 cm.
Dated Feb. 12, 1770
McMurtrie: New Orleans 18; New York Public 435
Archivo general de Indias, Seville. Photostat: NN
mp. 42116

B3208 LOUISIANA. GOVERNOR, 1769–1770
Don Alexandre O Reilly . . . Capitaine Général de cette Province . . . Le premier soin d'un gouvernement sage . . . [Nouvelle Orléans, D. Braud? 1770]
4 p. 34.5 cm.
Dated Feb. 12, 1770
Guerra a-453; McMurtrie: Louisiana 7; New York Public 437
Archivo general de Indias, Seville. Photostats: DLC; NN
mp. 42117

B3209 LOUISIANA. GOVERNOR, 1769–1770
Don Alexandre O Reilly . . . Capitaine Général de cette Province . . . Plusieurs plaintes & requêtes . . . par les habitans des Opeloussas . . . [Nouvelle Orléans, D. Braud? 1770]
3 p. 29 cm.
Dated Feb. 18, 1770
McMurtrie: New Orleans 20; New York Public 436
Archivo general de Indias, Seville. Photostat: NN
mp. 42118

B3210 LOUISIANA. GOVERNOR, 1769–1770
Instructions a laquelle doivent se conformer les lieutenants . . . établis par nous . . . [Nouvelle Orléans, D. Braud? 1770]
5 p. 30 cm. caption title
Dated at New Orleans, Feb. 12, 1770, and signed in ms.: O'Reilly
McMurtrie: New Orleans 19; New York Public 438
Archivo general de Indias, Seville. Photostat: NN
mp. 42119

B3211 MADAN, MARTIN, 1726–1790
An account of the triumphant death of F—S—, a converted prostitute, who died in April, 1763, aged twenty-six years. By the Reverend Martin Maden, Esq. . . . Salem, Printed and sold by S. Hall [1770?]
8 p.
Tapley p. 307
MSaE mp. 42120

B3212 MANSON, DAVID
A new primer, or child's best guide . . . By David Manson, schoolmaster in Belfast. Philadelphia, John Dunlap [1770?]
62, [2] p. 10 cm. [A]-D^8
Heartman: Non-New-England 104; Metzger 342
PHi mp. 42121

B3213 MARMONTEL, JEAN FRANÇOIS, 1723–1799
The history of Belisarius . . . [Burlington] America: Printed [by Isaac Collins] for R. Bell, 1770.
viii, 135 p. 17.5 cm.
PHi mp. 42122

B3214 MARMONTEL, JEAN FRANÇOIS, 1723–1799
The history of Belisarius . . . A new translation from the French . . . Burlington: Printed and sold by Isaac Collins, 1770.
viii, 135 p. 17.5 cm.
Humphrey 103a
CtY; NHi; PHi mp. 42123

B3215 MARMONTEL, JEAN FRANÇOIS, 1723–1799
The history of Belisarius . . . Philadelphia, Printed and sold by J. Dunlap, 1770.
viii, 135 p. 16.5 cm.
Forrest Bowe, New York (1964) mp. 42124

B3216 [THE Maryland almanack, for . . . 1771 . . . Annapolis, Anne Catherine Green [1770]

Advertised in the *Maryland Gazette*, Nov. 8, 1770, as "Just Published."
Wroth 301
No copy known

B3217 MASSACHUSETTS. GENERAL COURT. HOUSE OF REPRESENTATIVES
Copy of the complaint of the House . . . against Sir Francis Bernard . . . [Boston, 1770]
16 p. 4to A-B^4
"Report of the Lords . . . March 7. 1770:" p. 16
Adams 81c
DLC; MBAt

B3218 MASSACHUSETTS. GOVERNOR, 1769–1771
By the honorable Thomas Hutchinson . . . a brief. Whereas Jeremiah Lee . . . Boston, Richard Draper, 1770.
broadside 42.5 X 33.5 cm.
Ford 1530; New York Public 439
DLC; MWA; PPL. Photostats: MHi; NN mp. 42125

B3219 MASSACHUSETTS. LAWS
. . . An act . . . for superceeding and repealing the two last paragraphs in an act . . . intitled, "An act for supplying the Treasury . . . " [Colophon] Boston, Richard Draper, and Green & Russell, 1770.
10 [i.e. 15] p. 33.5 cm. caption title
DLC; M-Ar; MHi mp. 42127

B3220 MASSACHUSETTS. LAWS
. . . Acts and laws, passed . . . the thirty-first day of May [1770] . . . Chap. II. An act for effectually preventing the currency . . . of Connecticut, New-Hampshire and Rhode-Island, within this province. . . . Boston, Richard Draper, and Green and Russell [1770]
[2] p. 36 X 21 cm.
New York Public 440
MeHi; NN (cropped at bottom); PPRF mp. 42126

B3221 MASSACHUSETTS. TREASURER
[Province of Massachusetts-Bay. The honorable Harrison Gray, Esq; Treasurer . . . [June 30, 1770] . . . Boston, 1770]
broadside

Referred to in tax warrant of Nov. 26, 1770 in these terms: N.B. The warrant that I sent to you dated the thirtieth of June, 1770, being superseded . . . you are not to act upon it . . .
No copy known

B3222 MASSACHUSETTS. TREASURER
Province of Massachusetts-Bay. The honorable Harrison Gray, Esq; Treasurer . . . Given . . . at Boston, the twenty-sixth day of November, 1770 . . . [Boston, 1770]
broadside 38 X 30 cm.
MWA mp. 42128

B3223 MASSACHUSETTS GAZETTE
An happy New-Year from the carrier of the *Massachusetts-Gazette and Boston News-Letter*, to all his generous customers, January, 1770. [Boston, 1770]
broadside
Ford 1565
PHi. Photostat: MWA mp. 42105

B3224 MASSACHUSETTS GAZETTE
January 1, 1770. New Year's verses, from the lad who carries the *Massachusetts-Gazette & Boston Post-Boy*. [Boston, 1770]
broadside 22 X 12 cm.
Ford 1563
PHi. Photostat: MWA mp. 42110

B3225 THE merchants, and all others, who are any ways concerned in . . . trade, are desired to meet at Faneuil-Hall to-morrow . . . to receive the report of the Committee of Inspection . . . April 19, 1770. [Boston, 1770]
broadside 24.5 X 19.5 cm.
Ford 1543
MHi mp. 42065

B3226 THE merchants of this town, and all others connected with trade . . . are hereby notified that the committee appointed at their late meeting . . . to strengthen the union of the Colonies . . . Boston, Tuesday, September 4, 1770 . . . [Boston, 1770]
broadside 21 X 14 cm.
MHi mp. 42066

B3227 THE most delightful history of the king and the cobler . . . Boston, Sold at the Heart and Crown in Cornhill [by T. and J. Fleet, 1770?]
8 leaves. $A\text{-}B^4$
Rosenbach-Ch 66
PP mp. 42130

B3228 THE most delightful history of the king and the cobler . . . [Boston] John Boyle [1770?]
16 p. illus. 18.5 cm.
Dated by d'Alté A. Welch
MWA (poor); MiU-C. d'Alté A. Welch, Cleveland (p. 15-16 wanting) mp. 42129

B3229 NAZRO, JOHN
John Nazro, at his shop, the corner of Queen-street . . . imports and sells . . . a great variety of linnen . . . [Boston, 1770?]
broadside 11 X 17.5 cm.
Receipt in ms. on verso dated June 13, 1771
MB mp. 42131

B3230 THE New-England primer enlarged . . . Boston, T. and J. Fleet, 1770.
[80] p. $[A]\text{-}E^8$
CtSoP; MWA mp. 42132

B3231 NEW HAMPSHIRE. GOVERNOR, 1767–1775
Province of New-Hampshire. By his excellency John Wentworth . . . A proclamation for a general thanksgiving [Dec. 6, 1770] . . . [Nov. 6, 1770] . . . [Portsmouth, 1770]
broadside 38.5 X 31 cm.
Whittemore 134
NhHi mp. 42133

B3232 NEW JERSEY. GOVERNOR, 1763-1776
. . . A proclamation [by William Franklin] . . . Burlington, Isaac Collins [1770]
broadside 34 X 16.5 cm.
Concerns apprehension of certain persons
PHi mp. 42134

B3233 THE new Massachusetts liberty song . . . [7 stanzas] [Boston, 1770]
broadside 34.5 X 21 cm.
Written parody on verso, dated April 1770
Ford 1544; New York Public 442
DLC; PHi. Photostats: MHi; NN mp. 42135

B3234 NEW-YORK, February 27th, 1770. Forasmuch as it is manifest, that there is a . . . pernicious conspiracy . . . [New York, 1770]
broadsheet ([2] p.) 32.5 X 20.5 cm.
A proposal to form an association to support "the Rights of America."
RPJCB mp. 42136

B3235 NEWPORT MERCURY
New-Year's verses, addressed to the customers of the *Newport Mercury* . . . [Newport, Solomon Southwick, 1770]
broadside 22 X 14.5 cm.
Alden 445
RNHi mp. 42137

B3236 NORTH CAROLINA. GOVERNOR, 1765–1771
[A plan for keeping the public accounts. Newbern, James Davis, 1770]

On Dec. 14, 1770, the Governor said in a message to the House of Assembly: "I herewith send you a printed copy of a plan laid before the last Assembly . . ." (*Colonial Records*, VIII, 317.)
McMurtrie: North Carolina 61
No copy known

B3237 NORTH CAROLINA. LAWS
[An act for authorizing Presbyterian ministers to solemnize the rites of matrimony. Newbern, James Davis, 1770]

On July 2, 1771, the Rev. James Reed wrote the Soc. for the Propagation of the Gospel: ". . . I have sent you a printed copy of the act." (*Colonial Records*, IX, 5, 6.)
McMurtrie: North Carolina 62
No copy known mp. 42140

B3238 NORTH CAROLINA. LAWS
[Laws of North Carolina] [n.p., 1770]
p. 29–64 only 16.5 cm.
DLC mp. 42141

B3239 ON the death of five young men who was murthered, March 5th 1770 . . . [6 stanzas] [Boston? 1770]
broadside 32 X 14 cm.
NHi. Photostats: DLC; MHi; MWA; NN mp. 42143

B3240 PALMER, JOSEPH, & CO.
Sperma-ceti candles warranted pure; are made by Joseph Palmer & Co. at Germantown near Boston, & to be sold at their store in Boston . . . [Boston, 1770?]
broadside
A card in French and English engraved by Nathaniel Hurd
Ford 1545
MHi mp. 42144

B3241 A PARTICULAR account of the most barbarous and horrid massacre! Committed . . . March 5, 1770 . . . [Boston? 1770]
broadside 55 X 39 cm.
Four columns within mourning borders with woodcut of five coffins at head
MH; MHi (imperfect); MWA (imperfect); RPJCB. Photostat: NN mp. 42145

B3242 A PARTICULAR account of the most barbarous and horrid massacre! Committed . . . March 5, 1770 . . . [within mourning border] [Boston] Typis Johannes Boyles, MDCCLXX.
broadside 55 X 39 cm.
Four columns within mourning borders with woodcut of five coffins at head
PPL mp. 42146

B3243 PAYNE & INCHES, firm
Messieurs Payne & Inches. In the *Evening Post* of March 5th . . . [at end] Boston, March 15th, 1770. [Boston, 1770]
8 p. 20 cm.
Typographically the same as Evans 10622–10627.–T. R. Adams
MWA. Bodleian Lib. mp. 42147

B3244 PENNSYLVANIA. GOVERNOR, 1763–1771
By the honourable John Penn . . . a proclamation. Whereas a number of persons . . . [June 28, 1770] Philadelphia, D. Hall, and W. Sellers, 1770.
broadside 44.5 X 35 cm.
DLC mp. 42148

B3245 PENNSYLVANIA. GOVERNOR, 1763–1771
By the honorable John Penn . . . a proclamation. Whereas information hath been made . . . [Oct. 1, 1770] Philadelphia, D. Hall, and W. Sellers, 1770.
broadside 44.5 X 35 cm.
For apprehending the murderer of Isaac Meyer
Metzger 348
DLC; PU mp. 42149

B3246 PENNSYLVANIA. GOVERNOR, 1763–1771
By the honourable John Penn . . . a proclamation. Whereas it appears . . . [Oct. 3, 1770] Philadelphia, D. Hall, and W. Sellers, 1770.
broadside 44 X 35 cm.
DLC mp. 42150

B3247 PENNSYLVANIA. LAWS
An act for incorporating the Society for the relief of poor, aged and infirm masters of ships . . . in Philadelphia . . . Passed February 24, 1770 . . . [Philadelphia, 1770]
8 p. 27.5 cm.
Huntington 303
CSmH; PHi mp. 42151

B3248 PHILADELPHIA, Thursday, Sept. 27, 1770.
Many respectable freeholders and inhabitants of this city, justly alarmed . . . In consequence of the above advertisement, which was published in the papers and dispersed in handbills . . . a large body of . . . inhabitants assembled . . . and . . . came to the following resolutions . . . [Philadelphia, 1770]
broadside 17 X 20.5 cm.
MWA (photostat) mp. 42153

B3249 PITT, WILLIAM, EARL OF CHATHAM, 1708–1778
The speech of Lord C----------m, (Mr. P**t.) London, Dec. 6. He who has ears to hear, let him hear . . . It is proposed, that public prayers in all the religious assemblies in America, be every Lord's Day . . . offer'd up . . . for the preservation of the . . . life of the Earl of Chatham. [n.p., 1770?]
broadside 39 X 32.5 cm.
MWA mp. 42154

B3250 A PLAN of union, by admitting representatives from the American Colonies, and from Ireland into the British Parliament. [Philadelphia, 1770?]
3 p. 26.5 cm.
Sabin 63299
PHi; PPL mp. 42155

B3251 A POEM, in memory of the (never to be forgotten) fifth of March, 1770 . . . [Boston] Printed and sold next to the Writing-School, in Queen-Street [1770]
broadside 33.5 X 20.5 cm.
New York Public 445
Matt B. Jones (1931). Photostats: MHi; MWA; NN mp. 42156

B3252 [POOR Will's pocket almanack . . . for . . . 1771. Philadelphia, Printed by Joseph Crukshank for Isaac Collins in Burlington, 1770]
[36] p. 11 cm.
MWA (imperfect) mp. 42157

B3253 [POWNALL, THOMAS] 1722-1805
March 5th 1770. Mr S––r. I did, last sessions, endeavor to move this house, to come to . . . taking off the duties, payable in America . . . [Boston? 1770?]
10 p. 31 cm.
Speech in the House of Commons, attributed to Pownall by *Cobbett's parliamentary history*, London, 1806-20, v. 16, p. 855
London imprint?–L. M. Stark
New York Public 446
MHi; NN mp. 42157

B3254 THE prodigal daughter: or, a strange and wonderful relation . . . Newport [S. Southwick] 1770.
16 p. 17.5 cm.
In verse
Alden 446; Winship Addenda p. 88
RHi mp. 42158

B3255 RELLY, JOHN
Written on hearing of the much-lamented death of . . . George Whitefield . . . Philadelphia, John Dunlap [1770?]
broadside 44 X 28 cm.
In verse
MB mp. 42159

B3256 REMARKS upon a late paper of instructions, calculated for the meridian of four counties . . . of New-York . . . New-York, John Holt, 1770.
1 p.l., 22 p. 8vo
MWiW-C mp. 42160

B3257 REVERE, PAUL, 1733-1818
The bloody massacre perpetrated . . . on March 5th 1770 . . . Engrav'd printed & sold by Paul Revere Boston [1770]
engraving 28.5 X 24 cm.
Church 1081A
CSmH; DLC; MB; MHi; MSaE. Photostat: MH
mp. 42161

B3258 RHODE ISLAND. GOVERNOR, 1769-1775
[By the honourable Joseph Wanton . . . A proclamation . . . [Nov. 7, 1770] . . . Providence, John Carter [1770].]
[broadside]
Offering a reward for the apprehension of certain criminals
Bill submitted Nov. 8, 1770
Alden 447
No copy known mp. 42162

B3259 RHODE ISLAND. GOVERNOR, 1769-1775
Colony of Rhode Island. To the freemen and freeholders . . . Gentlemen, You were pleased the last year . . . to place me in the chief seat of government . . . Joseph Wanton. Newport, April 9, 1770 . . . [Newport, S. Southwick, 1770]
broadside 22.5 X 18 cm.
Alden 459; New York Public 447
RHi (multilated); RPJCB (mutilated. Photostats: MHi; MWA; NN mp. 42183

B3260 RHODE ISLAND. LAWS
At the General assembly . . . holden . . . on the second Monday in September . . . An act for assessing . . . a rate or tax of twelve thousand pounds . . . [Newport, S. Southwick, 1770]
4 p. 29 cm. caption title
Bill submitted September, 1770
Alden 452; Winship p. 26; Huntington 304
CSmH; RHi; RPB mp. 42163

B3261 ROBERTSON, WILLIAM, 1721-1793
The history of the reign of Charles the Fifth . . . In two volumes . . . Philadelphia, Sold by Robert Bell, 1770.
2 v. 21.5 cm.
MWA; PLeB mp. 42164

B3261a ROBINSON, NATHANIEL
Verses composed by Nathaniel Robinson, when he was in Albany goal. The second edition. New-London: Printed for and sold by George Wolcott, 1770.
24 p.
Stoddard 206
RPB

B3262 ROWLANDSON, MARY (WHITE) 1635?-1678?
A narative [sic] of the captivity . . . Boston, Nathaniel Coverly, 1770.
48 p. 16 cm.
Brinley 486; Vail: Old frontier 604; cf. Evans 11841
DLC; MH mp. 42165

B3263 THE royal primer. Or, An easy and pleasant guide to the art of reading . . . Boston, Printed and sold by William M'Alpine, 1770.
52 [i.e. 56] p.
MHi

B3264 THE royal primer. Or, An easy and pleasant guide to the art of reading . . . Boston, Printed [by William McAlpine] for and sold by John Boyles, 1770.
52 [i.e. 56] p.
Hamilton 54; Heartman: Non-New-England 163
MB; NjP mp. 42166

B3265 [RUSH, BENJAMIN] 1745-1813
Syllabus of a course of lectures in chemistry . . . Philadelphia, 1770.
48 p. 18.5 cm. A-F^4
Guerra a-460; Metzger 352
PHi; PU mp. 42167

B3266 RUTGERS UNIVERSITY
Charter of a college to be erected in New-Jersey, by the name of Queen's College . . . New-York, John Holt, 1770.
8 p. 25.5 cm.
New York Public 448
NjR; N (facsim.); NN (facsim.) mp. 42168

B3267 SEVEN hints for all who will take them: by a Church of England-man. When the balance of power is duly fixed in a state . . . J. S. [n.p., 1770?]
broadside 27.5 X 22 cm.
Dated in ms.: July 17th, 1770
MWA (photostat) mp. 42170

B3268 A SHORT poem, on the death of the Rev'd. Mr. George Whitefield. Who departed this life . . . Sept. 30th, 1770, in the 56th year of his age. [n.p., 1770]
broadside 28 X 12.5 cm.
Ford 1554; Sabin 103650
MH; PHi mp. 42171

B3269 SOME thoughts on religion. By a youth. Providence [John Carter] 1770.
24 p. 17 cm.
Alden 456; Sabin 86772
MWA mp. 42172

B3270 SOUTH CAROLINA. LAWS
Acts of the General Assembly . . . Charlestown, South Carolina, David Bruce, 1770.
1 p.l., 48, [1] p. 29 cm.
Sabin 87610
DLC; ScC (imperfect) mp. 42173

B3271 THE South-Carolina and Georgia almanack, for . . . 1771 . . . Charlestown, Printed for the editor [John Tobler]: Sold; in South-Carolina, by Robert Wells . . . in Charlestown; in Georgia, by James Johnston . . . Savannah [1770]
[32] p. 16 cm.
Drake 13106; New York Public 453
InU; MWA (2 leaves lacking); NHi. Photostat: NN
mp. 42177

B3272 SOUTH CAROLINA SOCIETY
The constitutional and additional rules of the South-Carolina Society, established . . . Sept. 1, 1737 . . . The fifth edition. Charles-Town, Peter Timothy, 1770.
iv, 4, 65 p.
Sabin 88033
RPJCB mp. 42174

B3273 A STATE of importations from Great-Britain . . . from the beginning of January, 1770: taken from the dockets and manifests . . . Boston: Printed [by John Fleeming?] in the year, MDCCLXX.
51 p. A-D^4 E-I^2
Adams 83a; of. Evans 11744
MH (p. 49-51 wanting)

B3274 A STATE of importations from Great-Britain . . . from the beginning of January 1770. To which is added, An account of such of these goods . . . Boston, Printed [by John Fleeming?] in the year 1770.

59 p. A-D^4 E-L^2
Adams 83b; cf. Evans 11744
PHi (p. 53–59 wanting)

B3275 [STERNE, LAURENCE] 1713-1768
A sentimental journey . . . By Mr. Yorick . . . [Philadelphia] Printed for R. Bell, 1770.
2 v. in 1 (paged continuously) 16.5 cm.
MWA; MiU-C; NHi; NN mp. 42175

B3276 TO the freeholders, and freemen, of the City and Province of New-York. Gentlemen, The method of taking the suffrages . . . [New York, 1770?]
broadside ([2] p.) 38.5 X 25 cm.
NHi mp. 42176

B3277 TOWNE, BENJAMIN
A defence of Messrs. Galloway and Wharton, late printers of the *Pennsylvania Chronicle*, humbly offered to the public. [Philadelphia, 1770]
broadside fol.
PPL mp. 42178

B3278 UNION FIRE CLUB
Rules and orders, agreed to be observed by the Union Fire Club, instituted at Salem, the 13th day of September, A.D. 1770. [Salem, 1770?]
broadside
Tapley p. 307
MSaE mp. 42169

B3279 UNIVERSITY OF PENNSYLVANIA
An exercise, containing a dialogue and two odes, performed at the commencement in the College of Philadelphia, June 5th, 1770. Philadelphia, J. Crukshank and I. Collins [1770]
8 p. 22.5 cm.
Hill 106
PU mp. 52152

B3280 A VERSE occasioned by the late horrid massacre in King-Street. You True Sons of Liberty . . . [Boston, 1770?]
broadside 35 X 21 cm.
MHi (photostat). Staley W. Smith (1939) mp. 42179

B3281 VINCENT, THOMAS, 1634-1678
God's terrible voice . . . New-London, Seth White, 1770
28 p.
cf. Evans 11908
CtHi mp. 42179a

B3282 VIRGINIA. GOVERNOR, 1770-1771
Virginia, sc. By the honourable William Nelson, Esq; President of His Majesty's Council . . . A proclamation. Whereas by the death of . . . Norborne Baron de Botetourt . . . [Williamsburg, 1770]
broadside 32 X 40 cm.
In both upper corners, in black borders: "The Gentlemen appointed to conduct the funeral . . . beg . . . attendance at the Palace at two o'clock on Friday next . . ."
ViW mp. 42180

B3283 WALSH, THOMAS, 1730-1759
The great salvation . . . A sermon on Hebrews ii. 3 . . . Wilmington [Del.], James Adams, 1770.
20 p. sm. 8vo
Huntington 306
CSmH mp. 42181

B3284 WALSH, THOMAS, 1730-1759
The whole armour of God . . . Wilmington [Del.], James Adams, 1770.
1 p.l., 28 p. sm. 8vo
Huntington 307
CSmH mp. 42182

B3285 WATTS, ISAAC, 1674-1748
A guide to prayer . . . By I. Watts, D.D. . . . Philadelphia: Printed by Thomas and William Bradford . . . No. 8, South Front Street [ca. 1770?]
1 p.l., ix, [13]-228 p. 17 cm.
"Contents": p. 227-228 appears incomplete; additional page lacking in MiU-C copy?
MiU-C

B3286 WE observe in one of the South-Carolina newspapers an advertisement, dated the 19th of June, 1770, published by the General Committee . . . declare the whole colony of Georgia infamous. [54 lines] Georgians. July 1770. [Savannah, James Johnston, 1770]
broadside 26 X 12.5 cm.
Reprint from a newspaper [*Georgia Gazette*]
McMurtrie: Georgia 9
Public Record Off. mp. 42185

B3287 [WESLEY, CHARLES] 1707-1788
A funeral hymn, composed by . . . the late . . . George Whitefield . . . [n.p., 1770?]
broadside 34 X 18.5 cm.
By Charles Wesley, though attributed to Whitefield.—John E. Alden
Ford 1555; New York Public 456
MWA. Photostat: NN mp. 42186

B3288 [WESLEY, CHARLES] 1707-1788
A funeral hymn, composed by . . . the late . . . George Whitefield . . . [Boston] Printed and sold at Green & Russell's [1770?]
broadside
By Charles Wesley, though attributed to Whitefield.—John E. Alden
Ford 1556
MB; MHi mp. 42187

B3289 [WESLEY, CHARLES] 1707-1788
A funeral hymn, composed by . . . the late . . . George Whitefield . . . Portsmouth, Printed and sold by D. and R. Fowle [1770]
broadside 36.5 X 30 cm.
In three columns
By Charles Wesley, though attributed to Whitefield.—John E. Alden
Whittemore 138; New York Public 457
NN (reduced facsim.); NhHi mp. 42188

B3290 [WESLEY, CHARLES] 1707-1788
A hymn, composed by the Reverend Mr. George Whitefield, said to be designed to have been sung over his own corps by the orphans belonging to his tabernacle in London . . . [Boston? 1770?]
broadside 33.5 X 20.5 cm.
Woodcut illustration at top right
By Charles Wesley, though attributed to Whitefield.—John E. Alden
Sabin 103527
PPRF mp. 42189

B3291 [WESLEY, CHARLES] 1707-1788
A hymn, composed by the Reverend Mr. Whitefield, to be sung over his own corps. Taken from the original, May 1, 1764. [Boston, 1770?]
broadside 36 X 21.5 cm.

By Charles Wesley, though attributed to Whitefield.—John E. Alden
Ford 1557; Sabin 103528
MHi; PHi. Photostat: MWA mp. 42190

B3292 WESLEY, CHARLES, 1707-1788
A sermon preached . . . April 4, 1742 . . . The nineteenth edition. Wilmington [Del.], James Adams, 1770.
12 p. 8vo
Hawkins 5; Huntington 308
CSmH mp. 42191

B3293 WESLEY, JOHN, 1702-1791
Hymns and spiritual songs . . . The fourteenth edition. Bristol, printed; and, Philadelphia, re-printed by John Dunlap, 1770.
132, [4], 4 p. 17 cm.
Metzger 355
PHi mp. 42192

B3294 WESLEY, JOHN, 1702-1791
Hymns and spiritual songs . . . Philadelphia, Melchior Steiner, 1770.
iv, 132, [4] p. 17 cm.
PHi mp. 42193

B3295 WESLEY, JOHN, 1702-1791
Salvation by faith, a sermon . . . [Philadelphia? J. Dunlap? 1770?]

Referred to in Stevens' *History of the M.E. Church*, I, 193, as "One of Robert Williams's cheap publications—". Williams received payments from New York and Philadelphia churches 1769-1771, and preached in Virginia and North Carolina in 1772. cf. Stevens I, 87, 165
No copy known

B3296 [WEST'S Sheet almanack, for the year 1771. Providence, John Carter, 1770]
broadside
Alden 437; Chapin p. 35; Winship p. 26 (on basis of advertisement in *Providence Gazette*)
No copy known mp. 42194

B3297 WHEATLEY, PHILLIS, 1754-1784
An elegiac poem, on the death of . . . George Whitefield . . . Newport, S. Southwick [1770]
broadside 38 X 25 cm.
Porter 255; Sabin 103127
PHi mp. 42195

B3298 WHEATLEY, PHILLIS, 1754–1784
An elegiac poem. On the death of . . . George Whitefield . . . Newport, S. Southwick [1770?]
8 p. 20 cm.
Alden 460; Sabin 103130; Winship Addenda p. 92
RNHi mp. 42196

B3299 Deleted

B3300 WHEATLEY, PHILLIS, 1754-1784
Phillis's poem on the death of Mr. Whitefield. [Boston, 1770]
broadside 33.5 X 24.5 cm.
New York Public 455; Porter 268; Sabin 103135
MWA. Photostat: NN mp. 42198

B3301 WHITEFIELD, GEORGE, 1714-1770
A true copy of the last will and testament of the late Rev. George Whitefield. [Boston, 1770?]
broadside 34.5 X 21 cm.
Ford 1559; Sabin 103600
PHi. Photostat: MWA mp. 42199

B3302 WHITEFIELD, GEORGE, 1714-1770
Two funeral hymns, composed by . . . the late . . . George Whitefield . . . who departed this life . . . the thirtieth of September, 1770, at 6 o'clock in the morning . . . [Boston] Sold by E. Russell, and by J. Boyles [1770]
broadside 35.5 X 18.5 cm.
Ford 1560
MHi; PHi mp. 42200

B3303 WILLIAM & Mary College, March 20, 1770 . . . On the 15th of August . . . the medals will be publickly presented . . . [Williamsburg, 1770]
broadside 33 X 20.5 cm.
DLC mp. 42201

B3304 THE youth's instructor in the English tongue . . . Boston, Mein and Fleeming, 1770.
151 p.
Karpinski p. 50
MH; MHi; MWA; MiU; NNC mp. 42202

B3305 YOUTH'S warning piece: the tragical history of George Barnwell, who was undone by a strumpet . . . Printed and sold at the Printing-Office in New-London [1770?]
15, [1] p. port. 17 cm.
Trumbull: Supplement 2815
CtHi mp. 42203

B3306 ZUBLY, JOHANN JOACHIM, 1724-1781
A letter to the Reverend Samuel Frink . . . rector of Christ Church Parish in Georgia . . . [Savannah? 1770?]
[8] p. 20 cm.
Huntington 310; McMurtrie: Georgia 8
CSmH; MHi mp. 42204

B3307 ZUBLY, JOHANN JOACHIM, 1724-1781
The wise shining as the brightness of the firmament . . . A funeral sermon, preached at Savannah . . . November 11, 1770, on the . . . death of the Rev. George Whitefield . . . Savannah, Printed and to be sold by James Johnston, also to be had of Mr. John Edwards, merchant in Charlestown, 1770.
[2], 34+ p. 8vo
PPL mp. 42205

1771

B3308 AN almanack for the year . . . 1772. [Boston, Isaiah Thomas, 1771]
broadside
Ford 1566; Nicholas: Mass. almanacs 11
MWA mp. 42206

B3308a [ALMANAK voor 1772. New York, H. Gaine? 1771?]

Advertised in the *South Carolina Gazette*, Jan. 21, 1772 as "More's Dutch almanack for 1772."
Drake 5824
No copy known

B3309 AN astronomical diary; or Almanack, for the year . . . 1771 . . . By Nathaniel Ames . . . Portsmouth, Printed and sold by D. &. R. Fowle, 1771. Sold also by William Appleton.
[24] p. 19 cm.
Nichols, p. 86
MB; MHi; MWA; NHi; NN mp. 42210

B3310 AN astronomical diary; or Almanack for the year 1772. [n.p., 1771]
[24] p.
Drake 268
Ct; CtHi; DLC; MWA (imperfect)

B3311 AN astronomical diary; or almanack, for the year . . . 1772 . . . By Joseph Perry. New-Haven, Thomas and Samuel Green [1771]
[28] p.
Bates: Connecticut almanacs p. 125
CtHi; CtY; MWA mp. 42268

B3312 AN astronomical diary; or almanack for the year . . . 1772 . . . By Nathaniel Ames . . . Boston, Printed for and sold by Ezekiel Russell [1771]
[24] p. 12 mo.
Publisher's announcement and advt. of Daniel Jones on final page
Huntington 311; cf. Evans 11962 (without publisher's announcement)
CSmH; MHi; NhD

B3313 AN astronomical diary, or almanack for the year . . . 1772 . . . By Nathaniel Ames. New-Haven, T. & S. Green [1771]
[24] p. 17.5 cm.
CtHi; CtY; MWA mp. 42207

B3314 AN astronomical diary, or almanack for the year . . . 1772 . . . By Nathaniel Ames. [New London, T. Green, 1771] Price 2s 8d. per dozen.
[24] p. 17 cm.
cf. Bates: Connecticut almanacs p. 124
CtHi; DLC; MBCo; MWA mp. 42208

B3315 AN astronomical diary, or almanack for the year . . . 1772 . . . By Nathaniel Ames . . . New-London, Timothy Green [1771]
[24] p. 17 cm.
Advertised in the *New London Gazette*, Dec. 27, 1771, as "To-Morrow, will be published and sold by T. Green . . ."
Bates: Connecticut almanacs p. 124
CtW mp. 42209

B3316 AN astronomical diary: Or, Almanack for the year . . . 1772. By Samuel Ellsworth. Hartford, Ebenezer Watson [1771]
[16] p.
Drake 272
CtHi; NHi

B3317 AUSTIN, SAMUEL, fl. 1771
Samuel Austin in Union-street, Boston, near the Sign of the Corn-Fields, imports and sells at the cheapest rates . . . English and India goods, of the newest fashion. [Boston, 1771?]
broadside 17? X 14? cm.
Handwritten memo on recto: "Mrs. Austin invoice June 28, 1771"
Ford 1506
MHi (trimmed) mp. 42211

B3318 BALDWIN, MOSES, 1732-1813
The ungodly condemned in judgment. A sermon preached . . . December 13th 1770. on occasion of the execution of William Shaw, for murder . . . New-London, Printed and sold by T. Green, 1771.
14 p. 19.5 cm. [A]-C^2 [ ]^1
CtHi; MWA mp. 42212

B3319 BELL, ROBERT, d. 1784
[Proposals for printing] Commentaries on the laws of England. By William Blackstone . . . America: Printed for the subscribers, MDCCLXXI. [Philadelphia, R. Bell, 1771]
8 p. 23.5 cm.
On verse of t.p.: "Conditions," and at bottom: "Subscriptions . . . gratefully received by the publisher Robert Bell."
PHi; PPL mp. 42213

B3320 BIBLE. O.T. PSALMS
The New England Psalter; or, Psalms of David . . . Boston, Printed and sold by D. Kneeland, 1771.
[176] p. 16 cm.
NhD mp. 42214

B3321 BIBLE. O.T. PSALMS
The Psalms of David, imitated . . . By I. Watts, D.D. The twenty-fifth edition . . . Boston, Printed [by W. M'Alpine] for, and sold by J. Perkins, 1771.
328 p. 15 cm.
MWA mp. 42298

B3322 BIBLE. O.T. PSALMS
The Psalms of David, imitated . . . By I. Watts, D.D. The twenty-fifth edition . . . Boston, Printed and sold by William M'Alpine, 1771.
328 p. 15.5 cm.
MBC; MWA mp. 42297

B3323 BIBLE. O.T. PSALMS
The Psalms of David, imitated . . . By I. Watts, D.D. The twenty-seventh edition. Boston, Printed for J. Mein, 1771.
xxiv, 298, [20] p.
NNUT mp. 42299

B3324 BLAND, PRISCILLA, plaintiff
A bill in the chancery of New-Jersey, at a suit of Priscilla Bland, John Mann and Mercy his wife; against Redford Ashfield, and others. [n.p.] 1771.
25 p. 32 cm.
Humphrey 110
NHi; PHi mp. 42215

B3325 BOSTON. ASSESSOR
Prov[ince of] the Massachusetts-Bay. Pursuant to an Act . . . for enquiring into the ratable estates of this Province . . . Office, Boston, August 1, 1771. [Boston, 1771]
broadside 25 X 19 cm.
WHi mp. 42216

B3326 BOSTON. SELECTMEN
Notification. The freeholders and other inhabitants of the Town of Boston . . . notified to meet at Faneuil-Hall . . . the 7th day of May . . . William Cooper, Town-Clerk. Boston, May 2, 1771 . . . [Boston, 1771]
broadside 12 X 16 cm.
MWA mp. 42217

B3327 BOYLSTON, WARD NICHOLAS
Ward Nicholas Boylston, imports from London and Bristol, and sells at his store in . . . Boston, a variety of goods . . . [Boston, 1771?]
broadside 26 X 20 cm.
Huntington 312
CSmH mp. 42218

B3328 BRIDGHAM, EBENEZER
Ebenezer Bridgham, at the Stratfordshire and Liverpool ware house in King-Street Boston: imports directly . . . all kinds of china, glass, and earthen ware . . . [Boston, 1771?]
broadside 35 X 22 cm.
Ford 1569
MHi mp. 42219

B3329 BROWN UNIVERSITY
Viro ornatissimo . . . Stephano Hopkins . . . Haec philosophemata . . . habita . . . Septembris, A.D. M,DCC,LXXI. [Providence] J. Carter [1771]
broadside 51 X 38.5 cm.
Alden 479; Winship p. 27; NYPL 458
RHi; RPB. Photostats: MHi; MWA; NN mp. 42220

B3330 BUCHAN, WILLIAM, 1729-1805
Domestic medicine . . . Philadelphia, Printed for and sold by R. Aitken [1771]
viii, [3], 368 p. 19.5 cm.
DLC; DNLM; MWA mp. 42221

B3331 BYLES, MATHER, 1707-1788
A sermon on the nature and necessity of conversion . . . The third edition. Boston, Thomas and John Fleet, 1771]
15, [1] p. 21 cm. [A]-B^4
Sabin 9717
MWA; RPJCB mp. 42222

B3332 CARPENTER, WILLIAM, fl. 1770
A poem, on the execution of William Shaw, at Springfield, December 13th 1770, for the murder of Edward East . . . [Salem? Samuel Hall? 1771]
broadside 35 X 21 cm.
Ford 1511; New York Public 459; cf. Evans 12200
PHi. Photostats: MWA; NN mp. 42223

B3333 CATALOGUS medicinarum . . . Philadelphia, John Dunlap, 1771.
31 p. 19.5 cm. A-D^4
DLC mp. 42224

B3334 [CHEEVER, EZEKIEL] 1615-1708
A short introduction to the Latin tongue . . . The fifteenth edition. Boston, Printed by Isaiah Thomas, for John Perkins, 1771.
72 p. 16.5 cm. [A]-I^4
MHi; MWA mp. 42225

B3335 COLUMBIA UNIVERSITY
Order of commencement, in King's College, New York, May 21, 1771. Prayers. Ds. Copp, Salutory oration . . . Mr. Moore, Valedictory oration . . . [New York, 1771]
broadside 32.5 X 20.5 cm.
MH; NNC mp. 42226

B3336 CONNECTICUT. CITIZENS
To the honorable the General Assembly of . . . Connecticut, to be held at Hartford . . . May 1771. Whereas it appears from authentic records . . . We the subscribers, inhabitants of this Colony, (not being proprietors in . . . the Susquehannah Purchase) pray . . . Dated in this 7th day of March, 1771. [Hartford? 1771]
broadside 34 X 21 cm.
CtHi mp. 42227

B3337 THE Connecticut almanack, for the year . . . 1772 . . . By Edmund Freebetter . . . New-London, Printed and sold by T. Green [1771]
[24] p. 17.5 cm.
Bates: Connecticut almanacs p. 125; Guerra b-289
CtHi; DLC; MWA; NN mp. 42234

B3338 DEBLOIS, GILBERT
Gilbert Deblois at his shop opposite School-Street . . . imports from London, Bristol, Scotland and Holland . . . all sorts . . . goods . . . Boston, November 1771 . . . [Boston, 1771]
broadside 15.5 X 20 cm.
MWA mp. 42228

B3339 DODDRIDGE, PHILIP, 1702-1751
The rise and progress of religion in the soul . . . The tenth edition. Boston, Printed by D. Kneeland, for Thomas Leverett, 1771.
xii, [4], 184 [i.e. 284] p. 18 cm. A-R^8 S^4 T^8 U^2
Pages 280, 282-284 misnumbered
MB; MWA (sig. C3-8 wanting); NjP; RPJCB mp. 42229

B3340 [DODSLEY, ROBERT] 1703-1764
The oeconomy of human life . . . Burlington, Printed and sold by Isaac Collins, 1771.
xii p., 1 l., 54, iv, 70 p. 12.5 cm.
In two parts, each with separate t.p.
Humphrey 117
MWA; NjT; PHi mp. 42230

B3341 DUNLAP, JOHN, 1747-1812
Just published, and to be sold by John Dunlap, at the Newest Printing-Office . . . Philadelphia, Father Abraham's Almanack, for the year 1772 . . . [Philadelphia, 1771]
broadside 43.5 N 27 cm.
MWA mp. 42231

B3342 DUNLAP, JOHN, 1747-1812
Propos[al] for printing by subsc[ription] a weekly newspaper, [called] the *Pennsylvania Pack[et] and General Advertiser*. [Philadelphia, J. Dunlap, 1771]
broadside 38 X 22.5 cm.
PHi (imperfect) mp. 42232

B3343 FISH, JOSEPH, 1707-1781
Ready for the press, The examiner examined . . . By Joseph Fish, A.M. The above performance will be committed to press, so soon as a number of subscribers appear . . . Subscriptions . . . at the Printing-Office in New-London . . . [New London, T. Green, 1771?]
broadside 31 X 20.5 cm.
Right half of broadside blank, for subscribers
cf. Evans 12042
CtHi mp. 42233

B3344 FRESH and important advices . . . Burlington, Isaac Collins [1771]
broadside 37.5 X 24 cm.
DLC. Photostat: NjR mp. 42235

B3345 FRIENDS, SOCIETY OF. PHILADELPHIA MEETING FOR SUFFERINGS
From our Meeting for Sufferings, held . . . the 23d day of the Third month, 1771 . . . [Philadelphia, 1771]
broadside 27.5 X 18 cm.
DLC mp. 42236

B3346 GAINE, HUGH, 1726-1807
Just imported in the last vessels from London, and to be sold, by Hugh Gaine . . . [New York, H. Gaine, 1771?]
broadside 50 cm.
Dated from document on back of MWA copy, dated July 23, 1771
Brigham: Booksellers, p. 40; Guerra a-473
MWA mp. 42237

B3347 GARDINER AND JEPSON, firm
A true state of the copartnership of Gardiner and Jepson, taken from their books and settlements from time to time under Dr. Jepson's own hand . . . Boston, May 1, 1771. [Boston, 1771]
4 p.
William Jepson was the partner
Ford 1572
MHi mp. 42238

B3348 GILMAN, JOHN W.
A new introduction to psalmody . . . The whole engrav'd on copper-plates . . . Engrav'd printed & sold by John W[d] Gilman. Exeter, 1771.
22 p. 15 cm.
Huntington 314; New York Public 461
CSmH. Photostat: NN mp. 42240

B3349 GREEN, JACOB, 1722-1790
A small help, offered to heads of families, for instructing children and servants. By J. G. . . . New-York, H. Gaine, 1771.
16 p. 20 cm.
New York Public 466
NN; RPJCB mp. 42241

B3350 HARVARD UNIVERSITY
Quaestiones pro modulo . . . MDCCLXXI . . . Bostoniae, R. Draper, 1771.
broadside 49.5 X 35.5 cm.
Ford 1573
MH; MHi; MSaE mp. 42242

B3351 HAY, JOHN
Advertisement. Whereas the Honourable Thomas Penn . . . did assure unto Martin Frey 250 acres of land . . . Lancaster, Francis Bailey and Stewart Herbert [1771?]
broadside 23 X 12 cm.
New York Public 462
NN (photostat) mp. 42243

B3352 THE history of the Holy Jesus . . . By a Lover of their precious souls. Eleventh edition. New-Haven, T. & S. Green, 1771.
48 p. 10.5 cm.
NjP mp. 42244

B3353 THE history of the Holy Jesus . . . By a Lover of their precious souls. The twenty-fourth edition. Boston, Printed and sold by N. Coverly, 1771.
46, [1] p. 16 illus. 10 cm. [A]-C^8
MWA (sig. A1, C7-8 wanting) mp. 42246

B3354 THE history of the Holy Jesus . . . By a Lover of their precious souls. The twenty-fourth edition. Boston, Printed for, and sold by Isaiah Thomas, 1771.
46, [1] p. 16 illus. 10 cm.
MWA (wanting after p. 42); RPB (p. [2] and [47] wanting) mp. 42247

B3355 THE history of the Holy Jesus . . . By a Lover of their precious souls. The twenty-fourth edition. Boston, Printed for, and sold by J. Boyles, 1771.
46, [1] p. 16 illus. 10.5 cm. [A]-C^8
CtHi; MWA (back cover lacking); NRU mp. 42245

B3356 THE history of the Holy Jesus . . . By a Lover of their precious souls. The twenty-fourth edition. Boston, Printed for, and sold by J. Perkins, 1771.
32 p.
B. Tighe

B3357 KING'S-BRIDGE LOTTERY
A list of the fortunate numbers that drew prizes in the King's-Bridge Lottery . . . the 13th September, 1771 . . . [n.p., 1771]
broadside 40 X 25.5 cm.
CtHi mp. 42248

B3358 MARYLAND. LAWS
A bill, entitled, An act to redress the evils arising from the variation of the compass in surveying lands . . . [Annapolis, Anne Catharine Green, 1771]
[3] p. 32.5 cm.
Issued with the Votes and proceedings of the third and fourth sessions of the 1770 Lower House
Wroth 304
RPJCB mp. 42249

B3359 MASSACHUSETTS. COURT OF SESSIONS
To The Court of Sessions have appointed Wednesday the first day of July . . . to grant licences on spirituous liquors . . . Boston, July 13, 1771. [Boston, 1771]
broadside 12 X 9.5 cm.
Ford 1589
MB; MHi mp. 42250

B3360 MASSACHUSETTS. GOVERNOR, 1769-1771
Massachusetts-Bay. By the Governor. A proclamation. Whereas His Majesty's pleasure has been signified to me by the . . . Earl of Hillsborough . . . augmentation of the King's troops . . . Boston, Richard Draper, 1771.
broadside 38.5 X 26 cm.
MHolliHi mp. 42252

B3361 MASSACHUSETTS. GOVERNOR, 1771-1774
Massachusetts-Bay. By the Governor. A proclamation for proroguing the General Court . . . [Dec. 28, 1771] Boston, Richard Draper, 1771.
broadside 34 X 20.5 cm.
Ford 1588; New York Public 463
Photostats: DLC; MHi; NN mp. 42251

B3362 MAURY, JAMES
To Christians of every denomination . . . an address: enforcing an inquiry into . . . the pretensions of the . . . Anabaptists . . . Annapolis, Anne Catharine Green, 1771.
45 p. 21 cm.
Wroth 311
MdHi mp. 42253

B3363 MESSRS Green and Russell, I was in hopes of seeing in your last *Gazette* some solution of the difficulties started by Scrutator . . . A Real Freethinker. [Boston] 1771.
broadside 39.5 X 23.5 cm.
Ford 1590
RPJCB mp. 42254

B3364 A NEW ballad upon a new occasion, to the tune of A cobbler there was &c. . . . [Philadelphia, 1771]
broadside
Concerns the excise law
Heartman, C. F.: Cradle 840; Metzger 362
NHi. Photostats: MB; MHi mp. 42255

B3365 NEW England harmony. Boston, J. Fleeming, 1771.
15 cm.
MWA (t.p. only) mp. 42256

B3366 THE New-England primer enlarged . . . Germantown: Printed and sold by Christopher Sower, 1771.
[79] p. 16mo A-E^8
Rosenbach-Ch 69
PP; PPL mp. 42257

B3367 THE New-England primer improved . . . Boston, Printed for and sold by John Perkins, 1771.
[80] p. [A]-E^8
Hurst sale, No. 684, Nov. 28, 1904
Heartman 42
George J. Smith (1904) mp. 42258

B3368 NEW-YORK, March 13, 1771. Advertisement
To be sold at public vendue, at the house of Richard Cartwright, in . . . Albany . . . the 14th day of May next, by the executors of Elizabeth Hamilton, deceased . . . [New York, 1771]
broadside 29 X 19 cm.
Describes the number of acres in each parcel of land
PHi mp. 42259

B3369 NORTH CAROLINA. GRAND JURY
[Presentment of the Grand Jury, approving the proposal by Governor Tryon to go in person to suppress the insurgents. Newbern, James Davis, 1771]

Gov. Tryon wrote on Apr. 12, 1771, to Earl Hillsborough: "Printed coppies of these have been circulated through the Province." See *Colonial Records*, VIII, 547
McMurtrie: North Carolina 64
No copy known mp. 42260

B3370 NORTH CAROLINA. HOUSE OF ASSEMBLY
The journal of the House of Assembly. North-Carolina, sc. At an Assembly . . . Newbern [Dec. 5, 1770]; being the first session of this present Assembly. [Newbern, James Davis, 1771]
74 p. 32.5 cm. caption title
Session ended Jan. 26, 1771
McMurtrie: North Carolina 66
NcU; NcWsM (p. 21-74 only) mp. 42261

B3371 NORTH CAROLINA. HOUSE OF ASSEMBLY
The journal of the House of Assembly. North Carolina, ss. At an Assembly . . . Newbern [Dec. 5, 1770]; being the first session of this present Assembly. [Newbern, James Davis, 1771]
24+? p. 32 cm. caption title
In NcWsM copy, the text is consecutive, but p. 24 is followed by p. 21-74 of the preceding item. The caption titles differ typographically
McMurtrie: North Carolina 65
NcWsM mp. 42262

B3372 OLD England's triumph: sung at the second anniversary meeting of the Sons of St. George, in New-York, April 23d, 1771 . . . [New York, 1771]
broadside 41.5 X 27.5 cm.
MWA mp. 42263

B3373 PENNSYLVANIA. GOVERNOR, 1767-1771
By the honorable John Penn, esq; President, and the Council of the Province of Pennsylvania. A proclamation . . . Philadelphia, D. Hall and W. Sellers, 1771.
broadside 41 X 26 cm.
Concerns continuance of officers
Metzger 363
DLC mp. 42266

B3374 PENNSYLVANIA. LAWS
An act for preventing tumults . . . February 9, 1771. [Philadelphia, 1771]
broadside 38.5 X 21 cm.
MHi. Photostats: DLC; MWA; NN mp. 42267

B3375 PENNSYLVANIA. PRESIDENT, 1771
By the honourable James Hamilton . . . a proclamation. Whereas a number of persons . . . [July 10, 1771] . . . Philadelphia, D. Hall and W. Sellers, 1771.
broadside 44.5 X 34.5 cm.
Huntington 315
CSmH; DLC; PHi; RPJCB mp. 42264

B3376 PENNSYLVANIA. PRESIDENT, 1771
By the honourable James Hamilton . . . a proclamation. Whereas the honourable John Penn . . . [May 6, 1771] Philadelphia, D. Hall, and W. Sellers, 1771.
broadside 41 X 26 cm.
Adams: Pennsylvania 27
DLC; PU mp. 42265

B3377 A POEM
One God there is, of Wisdom, Might:
One truth there is, to guide our Souls aright . . .
Medford: Printed & Sold, 1771.
broadside 23 X 20 cm.
Ford 1591
MHi mp. 42270

B3378 A POEM occasioned by the late sudden and awful death, of a young woman, who was found drowned, in Medford-River, July 14th, 1771. Medford, Printed and sold, 1771.
broadside 24 X 18 cm.
Ford 1593; New York Public 465
MHi; MSaE. Photostat: NN mp. 42269

B3379 [POOR Robert improved: being an almanack and ephemeris for . . . 1772. By Robert Cockburn . . . Annapolis, Anne Catherine Green [1771]]

Advertised in the *Maryland Gazette*, Nov. 7, 1771, as "Just Published."
Wroth 303
No copy known

B3380 PROVIDENCE
At a town-meeting held at Providence . . . the committee appointed to draw up such rules . . . as are necessary . . . in case of fire . . . April 17, 1771. [Providence] John Carter [1771]
broadside 35.5 X 23 cm.
Alden 469; Winship Addenda p. 88
Stephen Hopkins House, Providence mp. 42273

B3381 PROVIDENCE
Scheme of a lottery, granted by the General assembly . . . for purchasing a parsonage . . . Providence, John Carter, 1771.
broadside 38 X 25.5 cm.
Alden 470; Winship p. 27
RHi mp. 42272

B3382 THE renowned history of Giles Gingerbread . . . Newport, Re-printed and sold by S. Southwick, 1771.
30, [1] p. illus. 16mo
Alden 473
Miss Elizabeth Ball, New York City (1962) mp. 42239

B3383 RHODE ISLAND. LAWS
At the General assembly . . . holden . . . on the third Monday in August . . . An act for assessing . . . a rate or tax of twelve thousand pounds . . . [Newport, S. Southwick, 1771]
4 p. 32 cm.
Bill submitted Sept. 2, 1771
Alden 478; Winship p. 27
RHi mp. 42274

B3384 [ROGER More's Americaanse almanack for . . . 1772. New-York, 1771]

Advertised in the *South Carolina Gazette*, Jan. 21, 1772
Drake 5824
No copy known

B3385 THE Scourge. 4th. edition. Numb. 1. . . . Boston, Re-printed and sold by I. Thomas [1771]
broadside 43 X 34 cm.
Ford 1595
MHi; MWA mp. 42275

B3386 SEARLE, JOHN, 1721-1787
A funeral sermon delivered at Newbury-Port, Dec. 30, 1770. Occasioned by the death of Mrs. Phebe Parsons, consort of . . . Jonathan Parsons . . . in the 55th year of her age. By John Searl . . . Boston, Thomas and John Fleet, 1771.
54 p.
cf. Evans 12223
MWA mp. 42274a

B3387 SMITH, JOSIAH, 1704-1781
Death the end of all men: a sermon, sacred to the memory of the Reverend Mr. John Thomas . . . who died at New-York, September 29th, 1771. AEtat. 26 . . . Charlestown: Printed for the authour, by Robert Wells. MDCCLXXI.
16 p. 19 cm.
Evans 12228 (not used for microprint ed.)
NHi mp. 42277

B3388 SOUTH CAROLINA. LAWS
Acts of the General Assembly . . . the 20th of March, 1771. Charlestown, South-Carolina, David Bruce, 1771.
1 p.l., 17, [1] p. 29 cm.
Sabin 87611
DLC mp. 42278

B3389 SPARHAWK, JOHN
A table of the several chapters and principal contents of . . . Dr. Tissot's Advice to the people in general, with regard to their health . . . The London edition is sold at fifteen shillings. ___ It is now reprinted for, and sold by, John Sparhawk, at the London book-store . . . Philadelphia . . . [Philadelphia, 1771]
broadside 36.5 X 24 cm.
Guerra a-484
MWA mp. 42279

B3390 STILLMAN, SAMUEL, 1738-1807
Young people called upon to consider . . . In a sermon . . . May 8, 1771 . . . Boston, John Boyles, 1771.
31 p. 20 cm. [A]-D^4
Not Evans 12238; completely reset from p. 5 on
MBAt; MWA mp. 42280

B3391 THE sum of religion . . . Providence [John Carter] 1771.
broadside 36 X 24 cm.
Alden 480; Winship Addenda p. 88
RNHi mp. 42281

B3392 [SYMONDS, FRANCIS] OF DANVERS
To the printer in Essex. As I have met with what I call hard treatment . . . by a deputy-sheriff . . . [Salem? 1771]
[2] p.
Signed: An Enemy to Unfaithfulness and Deceit
Ford 1599
MHi mp. 42282

B3393 TEALL, BENJAMIN
The following song composed on the lamented death of Michael Griswould, Junior, of Killingworth . . . in the year 1771 . . . [Boston? 1771]
broadside 38.5 X 24 cm.
Ford 1598
MH mp. 42283

B3394 TEMPLETON AND STEWART, firm, New York
[A large and elegant assortment of new books, on divinity, law, history, physic . . . New York, 1771]

Advertised in *The New-York Gazette*, May 27, 1771, as ". . . Catalogues of which may be seen."
Guerra a-482
No copy known mp. 42284

B3395 THIS evening, the tenth of December, at six o'clock, the new organ, at King's Church, will be play'd on by Mr. Flagg . . . A sermon . . . will be preached by the Reverend John Graves . . . [Providence, J. Carter, 1771]
broadside 22.5 cm.
Alden 472; New York Public 467
RPJCB. Photostats: MWA; NN; RHi mp. 42271

B3396 THOMAS, ISAIAH, 1749-1831
Just published, embellished with four plates, neatly engraved, viz. The Boston Massacre . . . Printed on much larger paper than almanacks commonly are, The Massachusetts calendar . . . for the year . . . 1772 . . . Boston, Printed and sold by Isaiah Thomas [1771]
broadside 39 X 24 cm.
Ford 1575
MHi (imperfect); MWA mp. 42285

B3397 THOMPSON, JOHN
The lost and undone son of perdition . . . Judas Iscariot . . . Boston, Printed by John Boyles, 1771.
15 p. 20 cm.
MWA mp. 42286

B3398 TISSOT, SAMUEL AUGUSTE ANDRÉ DAVID, 1728-1797
Advice to the people in general with regard to their health . . . with all the notes in the former English editions, and a few corrected . . . London, Printed; Philadelphia, Reprinted for John Sparhawk, 1771.
xviii, [4], 307 p. 20.5 cm.
Austin 1915
DLC; MdBJ-W; NNNAM; PHi; PPF mp. 42287

B3399 TO the honourable the General assembly of . . . Connecticut, to be convened . . . the second Thursday of October, 1771 . . . [n.p., 1771]
broadside 36.5 X 22 cm.
Dated Sept. 5, 1771
Huntington 317
CSmH mp. 42288

B3400 TO the honorable the General assembly of . . . Connecticut, to be held . . . the second Thursday in May, 1771 . . . [Hartford? 1771]
[2] leaves, second blank
Petition to assert claim to the Susquehannah Purchase
RPJCB mp. 42289

B3401 TOWNSEND, ——
Alderman Townsend's speech in defence of the Lord Mayor. [Boston? 1771?]
broadside 43 X 10.5 cm.
Ford 1600
MWA mp. 42290

B3402 THE trial of Atticus before Justice Beau for a rape . . . Boston, Printed and sold by Isaiah Thomas, for the author, 1771.
55 p. 20 cm.
Apparently laid in Braintree, Mass.

Hill 305; Huntington 318; New York Public 468
CSmH; DLC; MWA; NN mp. 42291

B3403 UNION LIBRARY SOCIETY OF NEW YORK
Articles of the Union Library Society of New York . . . [New York] Printed by S. Inslee, and A. Car, 1771.
12 p. 19 cm.
Sabin 97809
NNS

B3404 VIRGINIA. COUNCIL
To the honourable William Nelson . . . The address of the Council . . . [Williamsburg, W. Rind, 1771]
2 p. 32 X 16.5 cm.
Speech of July 12, 1771
DLC (photostat) mp. 42292

B3405 VIRGINIA. HOUSE OF BURGESSES
Journal of the House of Burgesses . . . [Colophon] Williamsburg, William Rind, 1771.
24 p. 29 cm. caption title
Torrence 383
Vi. Photostat: DLC mp. 42293

B3406 WATTS, ISAAC, 1674-1748
Hymns and spiritual songs . . . Philadelphia, Re-printed and sold by John Dunlap, 1771.
xxvi, 326, [2] p. 15.5 cm.
RPJCB mp. 42296

B3407 WATTS, ISAAC, 1674-1748
Hymns and spiritual songs . . . Twenty-second edition . . . Boston, Printed by Daniel Kneeland for John Perkins, 1771.
xxiv, 312? p. 15 cm.
cf. Evans 12273
MWA (lacking after p. 264) mp. 42295

B3408 WATTS, ISAAC, 1674-1748
Hymns and spiritual songs . . . The twenty-second edition . . . Boston, Printed by Daniel Kneeland, for Nicholas Bowes, 1771.
xxiv, 312? p.
cf. Evans 12273
RPJCB (lacks all after p. 240) mp. 42294

B3409 WESLEY, JOHN, 1703–1791
A sermon on the death of the Rev. Mr. George Whitefield . . . New-York, Re-printed by John Holt, 1771.
28 p. 20 cm. [A]-C^4 D^2
MWA mp. 42300

B3410 [WEST'S Sheet almanack, for the year 1772. Providence, John Carter, 1771]
broadside
Advertised in the *Providence Gazette*, Nov. 9, 1771, as "Just published."
Alden 465; Chapin p. 36; Winship p. 27
No copy known mp. 42301

B3411 WHEATLEY, PHILLIS, 1754-1784
To Mrs. Leonard, on the death of her husband . . . [Boston, 1771]
broadside 33 X 20.5 cm.
Porter 280; Sabin 103140
PHi. Photostat: MHi mp. 42302

B3412 WHITE, JOHN
To the honourable the Senate, and House of Representatives . . . assembled. The petition of John White, baker, and other . . . inhabitants of said Commonwealth. [Boston, 1771?]
broadside
Against the assize of bread passed in the 6th year of George I
Ford 1602
MWA mp. 42303

B3413 WHITEFIELD, GEORGE, 1714-1770
A true copy of the last will and testament of the late Rev. George Whitefield . . . Boston, Printed and sold by Nathaniel Coverly, 1771.
broadside 38.5 X 24.5 cm.
Ford 1603
MWA; NhD mp. 42304

B3414 [WINDHAM, WILLIAM] 1717-1761
For promoting military discipline, this plan of exercise . . . practiced by Norfolk Militia, is presented to   of the regiment of militia, by the province of New-Hampshire. Portsmouth, Printed and sold by D. and R. Fowle, 1771.
91 p. 19.5 cm.
Attributed to Windham by MWA
Whittemore 144
CtHi; MWA; NhD mp. 42305

B3415 A WORD of Council and warning . . . Written by ——— ——— . . . Providence [John Carter] 1771.
23, [1] p. 20 cm.
Alden 483; Winship Addenda p. 88
NN (imperfect); RHi (mutilated) mp. 42306

B3416 THE youth's instructor in the English tongue . . . Boston, Printed for and sold by J. Perkins, 1771.
159 p.
Karpinski p. 50
MH mp. 42307

B3417 ZUM 29sten August 1771. [Philadelphia, Henrich Miller, 1771]
[7] p. 17 cm. caption title
PHi

B3418 ZUM 7ten September, 1771. [Philadelphia, H. Miller, 1771]
[7] p. 8vo caption title
PHi

1772

B3419 . . .AN account of the execution of Bryan Sheehen, . . . this day executed in Salem . . . for committing a rape upon the wife of Benjamin Hollow[ell] . . . [Salem? 1772]
broadside 34.5 X 21.5 cm.
The execution took place Jan. 16, 1772
Ford 1634; Tapley p. 310
MSaE (mutilated) mp. 42309

B3420 AN address to the true-born Sons of Liberty in the government of the Massachusetts-Bay. [Signed] A Countryman. [n.p., ca. 1772]
broadside 39 X 24 cm.
Ford 1338, 1605; New York Public 470
DLC; MWA. Photostats: MHi; NN mp. 42310

B3421 AN astronomical diary or almanack, for . . . 1773 . . . By Joseph Perry . . . New-Haven, Printed and sold by Thomas & Samuel Green [1772]
[28] p. 18 cm. [A]-C^4 D^2
Bates: Conn. almanacs p. 126; Drake 281; Guerra b-317
Ct; CtHi; CtY mp. 42365

B3422 AN astronomical diary: or Almanack, for . . . 1773 . . . By Nathaniel Ames . . . New-Haven, T. & S. Green [1772]
[16] p.
Drake 278; Trumbull: Supplement 1813
CtHi; CtY mp. 42311

B3423 BAPTISTS. PENNSYLVANIA. PHILADELPHIAN ASSOCIATION
Minutes of the Philadelphian Association met at New-York, October 13th, 14th & 15th 1772 . . . [Philadelphia? 1772?]
8 p. caption title
RPJCB. Photostat; MWA mp. 42312

B3424 BASS, ROBERT
Doctor Keyser's famous pills, imported and warranted genuine, by Robert Bass, apothecary in . . . Philadelphia . . . [Philadelphia, William and Thomas Bradford, 1772]
broadside 49 X 39.5 cm.
Printer, date, and author established from letter sent the Bradfords by Rivington Oct. 30, 1772
Guerra a-509
RPJCB mp. 42313

B3425 BIBLE. N.T. APOCRYPHAL BOOKS. EPISTLE OF JESUS CHRIST
A copy of a letter written by our blessed Lord and Saviour, Jesus Christ . . . Boston, Reprinted and sold by I. Thomas [1772?]
8 p. 15.5 cm.
MWA (mutilated) mp. 42335

B3426 BLACKSTONE, SIR WILLIAM, 1723-1780
The law of crimes and misdemeanors. With the means of their prevention and punishment . . . Being the complete book of the . . . Commentaries on public wrongs. Philadelphia: Printed and sold by Robert Bell, 1772.
[9?], 436, vii, [3] p. 24 cm.
Vol. 4 of the Commentaries, with list of subscribers omitted and t.p. added
Hildeburn 2751; James 36
MH-L mp. 42314

B3427 BOATE, GERSHON, 1648?-1704
A father's advice to his child: or the maiden's best adorning . . . [at end] Gershon Boat. Philadelphia, William Evitt [1772?]
4 p. 18 cm.
MWA mp. 42315

B3428 BOSTON
Boston, November 20, 1772. Gentlemen, We the freeholders and other inhabitants of Boston . . . apprehending there is abundant reason to be alarmed . . . [Boston, 1772]
broadside 36.5 X 38 cm.
Ford 1608; New York Public 472
MB; MBAt; MHi; MWA; NN (reduced facsim.); PPRF mp. 42317

B3429 BOSTON. SELECTMEN
Notification. The town having at a late meeting appointed a Committee of Correspondence . . . Boston, November 16, 1772 . . . William Cooper, Town-Clerk. [Boston, 1772]
broadside 11.5 X 13.5 cm.
Ford 1607; New York Public 471
MB; MHaHi; NN mp. 42316

B3430 THE Boston almanack, for the year of our Lord God 1772. Boston, Isaiah Thomas [1772]
broadside
Advertised Jan. 4, 1773, in the *Boston Gazette* as "Very Useful for Merchants . . . to paste or hang up . . . "
Ford 1610
MWA mp. 42320

B3431 A BRIEF relation of a murder committed by Elizabeth Shaw, who was executed at Windham, on the 18th of Nov. 1744, for the murder of her child . . . New-London: Printed in the Year 1772.
broadside 27.5 X 16.5 cm.
CtHi; ICN mp. 42321

B3432 BROWN UNIVERSITY
Catalogus eorum qui in Collegii . . . ab anno 1769 ad annum 1772 . . . [Providence] Typis Johannis Carter [1772]
broadside 38 X 28 cm.
Alden 502
RPB mp. 42322

B3433 BROWN UNIVERSITY
Viro honoratissimo . . . Stephano Hopkins . . . Haec philosophemata . . . habita . . . Sept. A.D. M,DCC,LXXII. [Providence] Typis Johannis Carter [1772]
broadside 52 X 35.5 cm.
Alden 503; Winship p. 28; NYPL 473
RPB. Photostats: MHi; MWA; NN; RHi mp. 42323

B3434 CADOGAN, WILLIAM, 1711-1797
A dissertation on the gout, and all chronic diseases . . . The tenth edition . . . Boston, Re-printed by J. Boyles, 1772.
76, [3] p. 22 cm. [A]-H^4 K^2
[3] p. at end: a list of books sold by Henry Knox
Guerra a-490; Rogers 134; cf. Evans 12341
CSmH; MBCo; RPM mp. 42324

B3435 [CHAPTERS of Isaac the Scribe. New York, John Holt, 1772]

Advertised in the *New York Journal*, Dec. 10, 1772, as "lately published in this paper . . . republished in a small pamphlet, and may be had of the printer of this paper."
Rosenbach 53
No copy known mp. 42326

B3436 CHARLESTON LIBRARY SOCIETY, CHARLESTON, S.C.
Appendix to the Catalogue of books . . . Charlestown, Robert Wells, 1772.
11 p. 21.5 cm.
With its Catalogue. 1770
DLC mp. 42327

B3437 CHARLESTON LIBRARY SOCIETY, CHARLESTON, S.C.
A catalogue of books, given . . . by John MacKenzie . . . Charlestown, Robert Wells, 1772.
24 p. 21.5 cm. [A]-C^4
With its Catalogue. 1770
DLC; ScC mp. 42328

B3438 [DER Christliche Kalender auf . . . 1773. Ephrata [1772]]

Drake 9973, from Bausman
No copy known

B3438a COCKINGS, GEORGE, d. 1802
The conquest of Canada . . . Baltimore, Hodge and Shober Press, 1772.
73 p. 16 cm.
Second book printed in Baltimore
DLC; RPB

B3439 CONNECTICUT. GOVERNOR, 1769-1776
By the honorable Jonathan Trumbull . . . a proclamation . . . [May 18, 1772] [New London?, 1772]
broadside 36.5 X 23 cm.
Photostats: DLC; ICN; MH; MHi; NN mp. 42332

B3440 CONNECTICUT. GOVERNOR, 1769-1776
By the honorable Jonathan Trumbull . . . A proclamation . . . [New London? 1772]
broadside 39.5 X 24 cm.
Dated at Hartford, May 26, 1772
Concerns changing form and order of the Book of Prayer
NHi mp. 42329

B3441 CONNECTICUT. GOVERNOR, 1769-1776
By the honorable Jonathan Trumbull . . . a proclamation . . . [June 29, 1772] . . . New-London, Timothy Green, 1772.
broadside 36 X 22.5 cm.
Concerns prohibition of exportation of wheat, corn, flour, etc.
New York Public 475
Photostats: DLC; ICN; MH; MHi; NN mp. 42330

B3442 CONNECTICUT. GOVERNOR, 1769-1776
By the honorable Jonathan Trumbull . . . a proclamation. As it is the will of God . . . [Oct. 13, 1772] . . . New-Haven, Thomas and Samuel Green [1772]
broadside 44.5 X 27.5 cm.
MHi; MiU-C mp. 42331

B3443 THE Connecticut almanack, for the year . . . 1773 . . . By Nathan Daboll, Philomath. New-London, T. Green [1772]
[24] p. 18 cm.
Bates: Connecticut almanacs p. 126; Drake 283
CtHi; DLC; MWA; NHi; NjMoW; OClWHi mp. 42337

B3444 COOKE, GEORGE
The complete English farmer . . . Boston, Re-printed by Daniel Kneeland, for Henry Knox [1772?]
142 p. 17 cm. A-M^6
MWA mp. 42333

B3445 COOKE, GEORGE
The complete English farmer . . . Boston, Re-printed by Daniel Kneeland, for Thomas Leverett [1772?]
142 p. 17.5 cm. A-M^6
Ms. date on p. 10: June 2, 1772; cf. Evans 11612
DLC mp. 42334

B3446 COX & BERRY, firm, booksellers, Boston
A catalogue of a very large assortment of the most esteemed books in . . . literature, arts and sciences . . . Which are to be sold by Cox & Berry . . . [Boston, 1772?]
44 p. 23 cm. A-E^4 F^2
Brigham: Booksellers p. 41; Guerra a-500; New York Public 475a
MWA; NN mp. 42336

B3447 DILWORTH, THOMAS, d. 1780
A new guide to the English tongue . . . Boston, Printed for Thomas Leverett, 1772.
7 p.l., 152 [1] p. 15 cm. A-K^8 L^4
MWA mp. 42338

B3448 EDWARDS, JONATHAN, 1703-1758
Sinners in the hands of an angry God . . . The third edition . . . Boston, J. Kneeland, 1772.
27 p. 19.5 cm. [A]-C^4 D^2
MHi; MWA; RPJCB (lacks half-title) mp. 42339

B3449 ESSEX GAZETTE
Job Weeden, Salem news-boy . . . carries the *Essex Gazette* . . . Jan. 1, 1772. [Salem, 1772]
broadside 17.5 X 15 cm.
MWA mp. 42389

B3450 THE exhibitor of the lectures on heads, having received an advertisement signed W, X, Y, Z; admonitioning him to omit the Tabernacle harrangue . . . [Philadelphia, 1772]
broadside 26 X 17 cm.
Sabin 91499 note
RPJCB copy has note in contemporary ms.: 27th July 1772, Phi.
RPJCB mp. 42340

B3451 FOTHERGILL, SAMUEL, 1715-1772
1772. The substance of a few expressions delivered by Samuel Fothergill to some of his relations . . . Philadelphia: Re-printed by J. Crukshank [1772]
broadside 28 X 15 cm.
Date at top in large type
MBrZ (trimmed) mp. 42341

B3452 GEORGIA. GOVERNOR, 1769-1772
Georgia. By His Honour James Habersham, Esquire, President and Commander in Chief of . . . Georgia . . . a proclamation . . . Given under my hand . . . [Aug. 4, 1772] . . . [Savannah, James Johnston, 1772]
broadside 32 X 17.5 cm.
McMurtrie: Georgia 13
Public Record Off. mp. 42342

B3453 GOODWIN, SOLOMON, d. 1772
[The last words and dying speech of Solomon Goodwin, lately executed at Falmouth, Casco-Bay, for the murder of David Wilson . . . Salem, 1772]
broadside?
Advertised in the *Essex Gazette*, Dec. 15, 1772, as "may be had at the Printing-Office."
Ford 1613; Tapley p. 310
No copy known mp. 42343

B3454 GRAY, ANDREW, 1633-1656
An excellent sermon, upon the great salvation . . . New-London, Re-printed by T. Green, 1772.
23 p. 17 cm. $[A]^4$ B^2 C^4 D^2
CtHi; MWA mp. 42344

B3455 GT. BRIT. SOVEREIGNS (GEORGE III)
George R. By the King. A proclamation: for the discovering and apprehending the persons . . . [Aug. 26, 1772] . . . [Newport] Solomon Southwick [1772]
broadside 43 X 28 cm.
Bill submitted Dec. 21, 1772
Alden 489; Winship p. 28
RHi. Photostat: RPJCB mp. 42345

B3456 GREEN, JACOB, 1722-1790
A vision of Hell . . . By Theodorus Van Shemain . . . The third edition. New London, 1772.
36 p.
CtHi mp. 42346

B3457 HALL, SAMUEL, 1740-1807
Salem, May 6, 1772. The subscriber, original publisher of the *Essex Gazette*, having lately admitted a partner . . . [Salem, 1772]
broadside 17 X 10 cm.
Ford 1614
MSaE mp. 42347

B3458 HARVARD UNIVERSITY
Quaestiones pro modulo . . . MDCCLXXII. Bostoniae, R. Draper, 1772.
broadside 49 X 33.5 cm.
Ford 1615
DLC; MH; MHi; MSaE; MWA mp. 42348

B3459 HERZLICHER zuruf an die ledigen Brüder zu ihrem Chor-Feste, den 29ten August 1772. [Philadelphia, Henrich Miller, 1772]
14 p. 19 cm.
PHi mp. 42349

B3460 JANEWAY, JAMES, 1636?-1674
A token for children . . . Burlington, Isaac Collins, 1772.
5 p.l., 34 p., 3 leaves, 44 p. 16.5 cm. $[A]^{4?}$ $B\text{-}H^{6}$
MWA (sig. A2-3, B2-5, D1-6 wanting); NjP (t.p. of pt. I missing); PHi mp. 42350

B3461 JOHNSON, GUY, 1740?-1788
Manual exercise . . . to be observed . . . by the militia of . . . New-York . . . Albany, Alexander and James Robertson, 1772.
23, [1] p. illus. 18.5 cm.
MWA; MiU-C mp. 42351

B3462 MARINE SOCIETY, NEWBURYPORT
Laws of the Marine Society at Newbury Port, New-England, commencing the thirteenth day of November, 1772. [Salem? 1772?]
broadside 39.5 X 31.5 cm.
Ford 1628
CtHi; MWA mp. 42352

B3463 MASSACHUSETTS. HOUSE OF REPRESENTATIVES
Boston. From the votes of the honorable House . . . 13 die Julii, A.D. 1772 . . . [Boston, 1772]
broadside 36 X 21.5 cm.
Ford 1618; New York Public 476
MeHi. Photostats: DLC; MHi; NN mp. 42354

B3464 MASSACHUSETTS SPY
The carrier of the *Massachusetts Spy*, wishes all his kind customers a Merry Christmas, and a Happy New Year; . . . January 1, 1772. [Boston, 1772]
broadside 28.5 X 12.5 cm.
Ford 1639
MB; MWA; PHi mp. 42325

B3465 MAY 20, 1772. Philadelphia, New-Castle, and Baltimore stages, for the conveyance of passengers and goods . . . [Philadelphia? 1772]
broadside 34.5 X 21 cm.
NHi mp. 42355

B3466 NEW-CASTLE lottery . . . for raising the sum . . . towards purchasing a lot of ground, and erecting a Presbyterian church, in . . . Philadelphia. [Philadelphia, 1772]
broadside 32.5 X 21 cm.
PHi mp. 42356

B3467 NEW HAMPSHIRE. TREASURER
Province of New Hampshire, George Jaffrey, esq; treasurer . . . To the selectmen . . . [Portsmouth, 1772?]
broadside 28.5 X 18 cm.
Tax warrant dated July 4, 1772
Whittemore 151
NhHi mp. 42357

B3468 NEW-HAVEN, September 2, 1772. A short account of the life of Moses Paul, (an Indian) who is this day to be executed . . . for the murder of Mr. Moses Cook . . . [New Haven, 1772]
broadside 42.5 X 19 cm.
NHi mp. 42358

B3469 NEW JERSEY. GENERAL ASSEMBLY
Votes and proceedings . . . [Aug. 19-Sept. 26, 1772] Being the first session of the twenty-second Assembly of New-Jersey. Burlington, Isaac Collins, 1772.
105 p. 32 cm.
Humphrey 122; New York Public 477
NHi; NN; Nj; NjHi (p. 93–105 wanting). Public Record Off. mp. 42359

B3470 NEW JERSEY. LAWS
Anno regni, Georgii III . . . duodecimo. At a session began at Perth-Amboy . . . [Aug. 19-Sept. 26, 1772]. Being the first session of the twenty-second assembly of New-Jersey. Burlington, Isaac Collins, 1772.
67, [1] p. 30 cm.
Humphrey 119
Nj; NjHi mp. 42360

B3471 A NEW song, called the Gaspee. 'Twas in the reign . . . Providence [1772?]
broadside 36 X 23.5 cm.
The Gaspee incident occurred June 10, 1772
Alden 491; Winship p. 28
RHi (mutilated) mp. 42361

B3472 A NUMBER of Englishmen have heretofore arrived in this province, unacquainted with the country, and having conceived expectations, in which they found themselves disappointed . . . [Philadelphia, 1772]
broadside 15.5 X 15.5 cm.
Metzger 372
NN mp. 42362

B3473 OCCOM, SAMSON, 1723-1792
Mr. Occom's Address to his Indian brethren. On the day that Moses Paul, an Indian, was executed at New-Haven, on the 2d of September, 1772, for the murder of Moses Cook . . . [n.p., 1772?]
broadside 34 X 21 cm.
cf. Evans 12911
MWA mp. 42362a

B3474 PENNSYLVANIA. ELECTION PROX.
Assembly. John Dickenson, Michael Milligas . . . Burgesses. Samuel Shoemaker, Thomas Mifflin. Fellow citizens, and countrymen . . . Philadelphia, October 1, 1772.
broadside 23 X 21 cm.
PHi mp. 42363

B3475 PENNSYLVANIA. GOVERNOR, 1771-1773
By the honourable Richard Penn . . . a proclamation. Whereas I have received . . . [June 22, 1772] Philadelphia, D. Hall, and W. Sellers, 1772.
broadside 44 X 35.5 cm.
DLC. Photostat: MHi mp. 42364

B3476 PETTIE'S ISLAND LOTTERY
A list of the numbers, that came up prizes in the Pettie's Island Jewellry and Plate Lottery, viz. . . . [Philadelphia, J. Dunlap, 1772]
broadside fol.
PPL. Photostat: MWA mp. 42366

B3477 PHILADELPHIA, March 12th, 1772. The author of the Complete Surveyor, to the public in general, and

to the subscribers in particular . . . Philadelphia, John Dunlap [1772]
broadside 37 X 27.5 cm.
PHi mp. 42367

B3478 POOR Tom revived: being More's almanack for . . . 1773. By Thomas More . . . Charles-Town, Charles Crouch [1772]
[24] p.
Drake 13109; Sabin 87759
No copy known

B3479 PROVIDENCE
Scheme of a lottery, granted by the honourable General assembly . . . for building a market-house in Providence . . . April 28, 1772. Providence, John Carter [1772]
broadside 37 X 25 cm.
Alden 493; Winship p. 28
RPTP mp. 42353

B3480 REFLECTIONS of a saint, under a view of the presence of . . . God. By Philomuse. Boston, Printed and sold by J. Kneeland, 1772.
8 p. 17 cm.
MWA mp. 42368

B3481 REFORMED GERMAN CHURCH
Verbessertes Hochdeutsch-Reformirtes Namen-Büchlein . . . für die Kinder . . . Philadelphia: Gedruckt und zu finden bey Henrich Miller, 1772.
[16] p. 8vo
PPL

B3482 A REMARKABLE relation . . . Sold at the Printing-Office in Hartford, 1772.
broadside 34.5 X 21 cm.
Three columns of verse
MWA mp. 42369

B3483 REMARKS. The common rates of land carriage . . . Philadelphia, January 20, 1772. [Philadelphia, 1772]
broadside fol.
Concerns the use of the Susquehanna River for transportation
With engraved map
PPL mp. 42370

B3484 RHODE ISLAND. GOVERNOR, 1769-1775
By the honorable Joseph Wanton . . . A proclamation. Whereas on Tuesday . . . [June 12, 1772] . . . [Newport, S. Southwick, 1772]
broadside 33.5 X 21 cm.
Bill submitted June 13, 1772
Alden 494; Winship p. 28
NN; R; RHi mp. 42371

B3485 RHODE ISLAND. LAWS
At the General assembly . . . holden . . . on the third Monday in August . . . An act for assessing . . . a rate or tax of twelve thousand pounds . . . [Newport, S. Southwick, 1772]
4 p. 31 cm.
Bill submitted Aug. 26, 1772
Alden 501; Winship p. 28
RHi; RPB (imperfect) mp. 42372

B3486 RICHARDSON, EBENEZER
The life, and humble confession, of Richardson, the informer . . . [Boston? 1772?]
broadside 30 X 18 cm.
Ford 1630
PHi mp. 42373

B3487 THE second Spira . . . Boston, Re-printed and sold at the Heart & Crown [by Thomas Fleet, 1772?]
8 p. 17 cm.
MWA mp. 42374

B3488 [A SHEET almanack for . . . 1773. Charles-Town, T. Powell & Co. [1772]]
broadside
Advertised in the *South Carolina Gazette*, Dec. 31, 1772
Drake 13110
No copy known

B3488a SMITH, ROBERT, 1723-1793
The bruised reed bound up . . . Wilmington, James Adams, 1772.
60 p.
Trinterud 357
NjPT

B3489 SWEASEY, RICHARD
To be sold at private sale, the following plantations, lying in . . . Morris . . . New-Jersey, viz. One plantation . . . now occupied by the proprietor Richard Sweasey. Also one other plantation . . . belonging to Samuel Sweasey. [n.p., 1772]
broadside 14 X 21 cm.
Dated by Rutgers
NjR

B3490 TEA, destroyed by Indians. [Cut] Ye glorious sons of Freedom . . . [Boston? 1772]
broadside
Ford 1635
No copy known mp. 42375

B3491 TEALL, BENJAMIN
. . . Discourse to his scholars, after catechising . . . New-Haven, T. and S. Green [1772]
11, [1] p. 16.5 cm.
Hymn on p. [12]
CtHi mp. 42376

B3492 THE 25th of the 3d Month, 1772. From the Weekly Meeting in G-n-h, to the Monthly Meeting in S-m. Dear Friends, We think it incumbent on us . . . to communicate to you . . . the wise schemes we have laid, and the favourable reception . . . at our late election . . . Signed, by order of the meeting, Z. O. Cl. . . . [n.p., 1772]
broadside 41 X 26.5 cm.
NjR

B3493 UNION FIRE CLUB, BOSTON
Rules and orders agreed to be observed by the Union Fire-Club, instituted at Boston, September 1st, 1772 . . . [Boston, 1772?]
broadside 39.5 X 25.5 cm.
On lower half the names, shops and places of abode of 18 members, printed, with others in manuscript
MHi mp. 42318

B3494 UNION SOCIETY, BOSTON
Rules and orders to be observed by the Union Society, founded in Boston, the twenty-fifth of November, MDCCLXXII. [Boston, 1772?]
broadside 47.5 X 39 cm.
Ford 1636
MB; MWA mp. 42319

B3495 UPON the enlargement of the infamous Ebenezer Richardson, convicted of wilful-murder. [Salem? 1772?]
broadside
Ford 1632
MHi; MSaE mp. 42377

B3496 THE vade mecum . . . Boston, T. and J. Fleet, 1772.
1 p.l., ii, [36] p. 17 cm.
Sabin 98275
DLC; MH; RPJCB mp. 42378

B3497 VERPLANCK, ISAAC
Advertisement [regarding lots in Wall St.] Isaac Verplanck. Albany, Sept. 2, 1772. [Albany, 1772]
broadside 20 X 17 cm.
McMurtrie: Albany 2; New York Public 478; Sabin 99279
NN mp. 42379

B3498 VIRGINIA. COUNCIL
To his excellency the right honourable John Earl of Dunmore . . . the humble address of the Council . . . [Williamsburg, W. Rind, 1772]
broadside 29 X 16.5 cm.
Speech of Feb. 10, 1772
DLC (photostat) mp. 42380

B3499 VIRGINIA. GOVERNOR, 1771-1775
The speech of . . . John Earl of Dunmore . . . on Monday the 10th day of February, 1772. [Williamsburg, W. Rind, 1772]
broadside 31 X 17 cm.
DLC (photostat) mp. 42382

B3500 VIRGINIA. HOUSE OF BURGESSES
To his excellency . . . John Earl of Dunmore . . . the humble address of the House of burgesses . . . [Williamsburg, W. Rind, 1772]
broadside 31 X 17 cm.
Speech of Feb. 11, 1772
Photostats: DLC; MHi mp. 42383

B3501 VIRGINIA. LAWS
Acts of the General assembly, 12 Geo. III. with an index. Williamsburg, W. Rind, 1772.
59 p. 32.5 cm.
cf. Evans 12591 (51 p.)
DLC; NN mp. 42384

B3502 VIRGINIA. LAWS
Saturday, the 28th of March, 12 George III. 1772 . . . Ordered, that the bill . . . be printed. A bill for the more easy . . . administration of justice. [Williamsburg, W. Rind, 1772]
6 p. 31 cm. caption title
DLC (photostat) mp. 42381

B3503 THE Virginia almanack for the year . . . 1773 . . . Williamsburg, William Rind [1772]
[36] p. 16 cm.
Bear 41; Drake 13780
DLC; ViHi (t.p. lacking) mp. 42385

B3504 WATTS, ISAAC, 1674-1748
Divine songs attempted in easy language . . . The sixteenth edition. New-London, Printed and sold by T. Green, 177[2?]
35, [1] p. 14.5 cm.
Trumbull: Supplement 2733
CtY (mutilated) mp. 42386

B3505 WATTS, ISAAC, 1674-1748
Horae lyricae . . . The twelvth edition, corrected . . . Boston, Printed by Daniel Kneeland, for Nicholas Bowes, 1772.
[32], 250 p. 17.5 cm.
Not used for Readex microprint edition of Evans 12604
MB; MWA; NBu mp. 42387

B3506 WATTS, ISAAC, 1674-1748
Hymns and spiritual songs . . . The twenty-fourth edition . . . Philadelphia, D. Hall and W. Sellers, 1772.
xiii, [1], 281, [4] p. 13.5 cm.
MHi; MWA mp. 42388

B3507 WHEELOCK, ELEAZAR, 1711-1779
A continuation of the narrative of the Indian charity school . . . [Portsmouth?] New-Hampshire, 1772.
40 p. 20 cm.
Sabin 103209
CtHi; ICN; MWA; NhHi; RPJCB mp. 42390

B3508 W[ILCOCKS], T[HOMAS] b. 1622
A choice drop of honey, from the rock Christ . . . The seventh edition. New-London, Timothy Green, 1772.
24 p.
Trumbull: Supplement 2790
No copy located mp. 42391

B3509 WILCOCKS, THOMAS, b. 1622
A choice drop of honey from the rock Christ . . . Newport, Printed [by Solomon Southwick] for Eldad Hunter, 1772.
23 p. 18 cm.
Alden 505
MWA mp. 42392

B3510 [ZUBLY, JOHN JOACHIM] 1724-1781.
Calm and respectful thoughts . . . occasioned by some publications . . . of May and June 1772 . . . By a freeman. [Savannah? J. Johnston? 1772]
24 p. 21 cm. caption title
Adams 89; McMurtrie: Georgia 12; Sabin 106383
DLC; MWiW-C; NjP mp. 42393

B3511 ZUM 29sten August, 1772. [Philadelphia, Henrich Miller, 1772]
[4] p. 22.5 cm. caption title
PHi mp. 42394

1773

B3512 AN account stated on the manumission of slaves, shewing that . . . certain sums paid at several periods of manumission, will amply secure the publick . . . [Burlington, Isaac Collins, 1773]
8 p. 8vo caption title
PPL; RPJCB mp. 42395

B3513 AN address to the inhabitants of Boston . . . occasioned by the execution of Levi Ames . . . He was tried . . . on the 7th of September . . . [Boston, 1773]
broadside 36 X 21.5 cm.
Ford 1640; Wegelin 477B; NYPL 479
PHi; RPJCB. Photostats: DLC; MHi; MWA; NN
mp. 42396

B3514 THE alarm, number IV. My dear fellow citizens . . . [New York, 1773]
[2] p. 33 X 21 cm.
Dated: New York, October 19th, 1773
New York Public 496; cf. Evans 12802 (dated Oct. 27, 1773)
NN. Photostat: MHi mp. 42397

B3515 [ALLEN, JOHN] fl. 1764
An oration, upon the beauties of liberty . . . The third edition, carefully corrected . . . By a British Bostonian. Boston, Printed and sold by E. Russell, 1773.
80 p. [A]-K^4

Advertised in the *Boston Evening Post*, May 17, 1773
Adams 91c
MBAt; MH; MWA; RPJCB

B3516 AMBROSE, ISAAC, 1604-1664
Christ in the clouds coming to judgment . . . Boston, Isaiah Thomas, 1773.
16 p. 17.5 cm. [A]-B[4]
MWA mp. 42398

B3517 AMES, LEVI, 1751-1773
Boston, October 21, 1773. The dying penitent; or, the affecting speech of Levi Ames, taken from his own mouth, as delivered by him at the goal in Boston the morning of his execution . . . [Boston] Sold opposite the Court-House in Queen-Street. [1773]
broadside 34.5 X 21.5 cm.
In verse
MHi mp. 42399

B3518 AMES, LEVI, 1751-1773
The dying groans of Levi Ames . . . executed at Boston, the 21st of October, 1773, for burglary . . . [Boston, 1773]
broadside 36 X 21.5 cm.
Ford 1641; New York Public 490
PHi. Photostats: DLC; MHi; MWA; NN mp. 42400

B3519 AMES, LEVI, 1751-1773
The last words and dying speech of Levi Ames, who was executed . . . on Thursday the 21st day of October 1773 . . . Boston [1773]
broadside 49.5 X 37.5 cm.
Ford 1644; Evans 12642 (without imprint)
DLC; MHi; MWA; MiU-C; NHi mp. 42401

B3520 ANDERSON improved: being an almanack . . . for the year . . . 1774 . . . By John Anderson, Philom. The second edition. Newport, Solomon Southwick [1773]
[32] p. 17.5 cm.
Alden 507; Chapin p. 37; Winship p. 30
RHi (imperfect); RNHi mp. 42403

B3521 APPLETON, JOHN, 1739-1817
Imported in the last ships from London . . . a fine assortment of English and India goods . . . [Salem, 1773]
broadside
MWA mp. 42404

B3522 AN astronomical diary; or an almanack for . . . 1774 . . . By Nathaniel Ames. New-Haven, T. & S. Green [1773]
[16] p. 17.5 cm.
MWA mp. 42402

B3523 BATES,
Horsemanship, by Mr. Bates, the original, who has had the honor of performing before the Emperor of Germany . . . On Tuesday next the 28th. of September instant . . . at the bottom of the Mall, in Boston . . . [Boston, 1773]
broadside 25 X 19 cm.
Advertised in the *Boston Evening Post*, Sept. 27, 1773
MWA mp. 42405

B3524 BIBLE. O.T. PSALMS
The New England Psalter; or Psalms of David: with the Proverbs of Solomon, and Christ's Sermon on the Mount . . . Boston: Printed by John Boyles, for John Perkins, 1773.
58, [59] p. 15.5 cm.
cf. Evans 12672
d'Alté A. Welch, Cleveland (1962) (t.p. mutilated)
mp. 42407

B3525 BIBLE. O.T. PSALMS
A new version of the Psalms of David . . . By N. Brady . . . and N. Tate . . . Boston, Printed for, and sold by Andrew Barclay, 1773.
276, 60+ p. 15.5 cm.
MWA mp. 42406

B3526 BIBLE. O.T. PSALMS
The Psalms of David imitated . . . By I. Watts, D.D. The twenty-seventh edition . . . Boston, Printed and sold by William M'Alpine, 1773.
312 p. 15 cm.
Not Evans 12679
CtHC; MWA (mutilated); RPJCB mp. 42536

B3527 BIBLE. O.T. PSALMS
The Psalms of David, imitated . . . By I. Watts, D.D. The thirty-seventh edition . . . Boston, Printed for Mills and Hicks, 1773.
299 p. 16 cm.
MWA mp. 42538

B3528 BIBLE. O.T. PSALMS
The Psalms of David, imitated . . . With . . . an enquiry into the right way of fitting the . . . Psalms for Christian worship, and notes By I. Watts, D.D. . . . The thirty-seventh edition. Boston, Printed for A. Ellison, 1773.
[2], xxx, 346 p. 15.5 cm.
MWA mp. 42537

B3529 BLAND, RICHARD, 1710-1776
To the clergy of Virginia . . . I take the liberty to communicate to you, through Mrs. Rind's press, my opinion of the governor's power to exercise ecclesiastical jurisdiction . . . [Williamsburg, Clementina Rind, 1773?]
4 p. 31 cm. caption title
New York Public 481; Torrence 397
NHi. Photostat: NN mp. 42408

B3530 BOSTON. COMMITTEE OF CORRESPONDENCE
Boston, September 21, 1773. Gentlemen, The state of publick affairs . . . demands the greatest wisdom . . . [Boston, 1773]
broadside 30.5 cm.
Ford 1653; New York Public 482
MB; MHi; MWA; NN. Middendorf Collection
mp. 42411

B3531 BOSTON. COMMITTEE OF CORRESPONDENCE
Boston, December 1, 1773. Gentlemen, the Committee of Correspondence . . . [Boston, 1773]
broadside 31 X 19 cm.
Ford 1655; New York Public 483
DLC; MB; MHi; NN. Middendorf Collection
mp. 42412

B3532 BOSTON. SELECTMEN
Notification: The freeholders and other inhabitants . . . of Boston . . . are hereby notified to meet at Faneuil-Hall, on Friday the 5th day of November . . . Boston. Nov. 4, 1773. [Boston, 1773]
broadside
Concerns shipment of tea
MB mp. 42414

B3533 BOSTON. SELECTMEN
Notification. The town being greatly alarmed . . . Inhabitants . . . to meet at Faneuil-Hall tomorrow . . . Boston. Nov. 17. 1773. [Boston, 1773]

broadside
MB mp. 42415

B3534 BOSTON, April 20th, 1773. Sir. The efforts made by the legislative . . . Peter Bestes, Sambo Freeman, Felix Holbrook, Chester Joie . . . [Boston, 1773]
broadside 25.5 X 18.4 cm.
Ford 1649; Porter 48; New York Public 480
MB; NHi. Photostats: DLC; MHi; NN; WHi mp. 42416

B3535 BOSTON, December 17, 1773. At a meeting of the people of Boston, and the neighboring towns at the Old South meeting house . . . [Boston, Edes and Gill, 1773]
broadside 34 X 21 cm.
PPRF mp. 42417

B3536 BOSTON FIRE SOCIETY
Nos conserva, Deus; nam tibi confidimus. These presents witness that we . . . do promise as neighbours . . . in case . . . the breaking out of fire, in Boston . . . N.B. . . . the Articles corrected and revised, March 4th, 1773. [Boston, 1773?]
broadside 31? X 29.5 cm.
Ford 1660
MWA mp. 42413

B3537 THE Boston sheet almanack, for the year . . . 1774 . . . Boston, I. Thomas, and Mills and Hicks [1773]
broadside 55 X 45 cm.
Ford 1662; Nichols p. 57; Nichols: Isaiah Thomas printer, 32
DLC; MB; MWA mp. 42418

B3538 BOSTWICK, DAVID, 1720-1763
A fair or rational vindication of the rights of infants to the ordinance . . . Williamsburg, A. Purdie and J. Dixon, 1773.
24 p. 20 cm.
NcU mp. 42419

B3539 BRATTLE, WILLIAM, 1702-1776
Sundry rules and directions for drawing up a regiment . . . Boston, Mills and Hicks, 1773.
24 p. 17 cm.
CtHi; CtY; DLC; MHi; MWA; NN mp. 42420

B3540 BRATTLE STREET CHURCH, BOSTON
Notice is hereby given, that there will be a meeting of the Society . . . on Friday next . . . Boston, July 6, 1773. [Boston, 1773]
broadside 12 X 20.5 cm.
Ford 1659
MHi mp. 42410

B3541 BROWN, WILLIAM, of Georgia
An aggregate and valuation of exports . . . of Georgia . . . from the year 1754 to 1773 . . . Savannah, James Johnston [1773?]
broadside 26.5 X 42 cm.
RPJCB mp. 42421

B3542 BROWN UNIVERSITY
Viro honoratissimo . . . haec philosophemata . . . Providentiae, Typis Johannis Carter, 1773.
broadside 48 X 38 cm.
Alden 526; New York Public 485
DLC; RHi; RPB. Photostats: MHi; MWA; NN
mp. 42422

B3543 BY permission of his Excellency the Governour. Mr. Wall, comedian, will exhibit at Mr. Hull's great room . . . the twenty-first of July, 1773, a new lecture . . . [New York, 1773]
broadside 26 X 21.5 cm.
NHi mp. 42423

B3544 [CHEEVER, EZEKIEL] 1615-1708
A short introduction to the Latin tongue . . . The sixteenth edition. Boston, Printed for, and sold by Henry Knox, 1773.
72 p. 15.5 cm. [A]-I^4
MWA mp. 42424

B3545 CHURCH, BENJAMIN, 1734-1776
An oration delivered March 5th, 1773 . . . to commemorate the bloody tragedy of the Fifth of March, 1770 . . . The fourth edition. Salem, Re-printed by Samuel and Ebenezer Hall, 1773.
16 p. 20.5 cm. [A]-B^4
Adams 94d
MHi; MWA; NHi; ViU mp. 42426

B3546 CLEVELAND, EBENEZER, 1725-1805
Sinners persisting in sin . . . two discourses, preached . . . October 10th, 1773 . . . Newburyport, I. Thomas and H. W. Tinges [1773]
52 p. 19 cm.
New York Public 486
MNe; MWA. Photostat: NN mp. 42427

B3547 CONNECTICUT. ELECTION PROX.
Nomination for election in May, 1774. The gentlemen nominated . . . to stand for election in May next, as sent in to the General Assembly . . . October, A.D. 1773, are as follow [sic] . . . [New Haven? 1773]
broadside 33 X 20 cm.
New York Public 522
Photostats: DLC; ICN; MH; MHi; NN mp. 42428

B3548 CONNECTICUT. GENERAL ASSEMBLY
At a General assembly . . . holden at New-Haven . . . on the second Thursday of October, A.D. 1773. Resolved . . . account of all the persons . . . [n.p., 1773]
broadside 33 X 21 cm.
DLC; MHi; MWA. Photostats: ICN; MWA mp. 42429

B3549 CUMBERLAND, RICHARD, 1732-1811
The fashionable lover . . . Philadelphia, Printed for William LaPlain, 1773.
72 p. 18 cm. A-F^6
MWA mp. 42430

B3550 DEBLOIS, GILBERT
Gilbert Deblois at his shop . . . near the late Rev. Dr. Sewall's Meeting-House, Boston, imports from London . . . Boston, 1773.
broadside 17 X 21 cm.
Ford 1663
MH; MHi; MWA mp. 42431

B3551 [DEFOE, DANIEL] 1661-1731
The dreadful visitation: in a short account . . . of the plague . . . in the City of London, in the year 1665 . . . New-Haven [1773?]
8 p. 21 cm.
Abridged from Defoe's *Journal of the plague year*
Guerra a-517; New York Public 488
NN; NNC (photocopy) mp. 42432

B3552 DELAWARE. HOUSE OF REPRESENTATIVES
[Votes and proceedings . . . Wilmington, J. Adams, 1773?]
33+ p. 33.5 cm.
Hawkins 6

Richard S. Rodney, Newcastle, Del. (imperfect: p. 25-33 only, covering Apr. 6-10, 1773) mp. 42433

B3553 A DIALOGUE between Elizabeth Smith, and John Sennet, who were convicted . . . Elizabeth Smith for thievery, and John Sennet for beastiality! . . . [Boston, Draper, 1753?]
broadside
Ford 1692
PHi mp. 42502

B3554 DILWORTH, THOMAS, d. 1780
A new guide to the English tongue . . . Boston, Printed by J. Kneeland for A. Ellison, 1773.
xi, [1], 152 p. illus. 16 cm.
New York Public 489
NN mp. 42434

B3555 DILWORTH, THOMAS, d. 1780
A new guide to the English tongue . . . Boston, Printed by J. Kneeland for John Perkins, 1773.
xi, [1], 152 p. illus. 16cm.
Hamilton 64
NjP mp. 42435

B3556 DODDRIDGE, PHILIP, 1702-1751
The family expositor . . . Sixth edition. Charles-Town: Printed and sold by Robert Wells, 1773.
6 v. 22 cm.
Probably printed in England
Mosimann 228
MWA. St. Stephen's Church, Charleston (not located 1959) (v. 4 only)

B3557 ESSEX GAZETTE
The lad who carries the *Essex Gazette* . . . January 1, 1773. [Salem, 1773]
broadside
MWA mp. 42456

B3558 AN exhortation to young and old to be cautious of small crimes . . . Occasioned by the unhappy case of Levi Ames, executed . . . October 21st, 1773, for the crime of burglary . . . [Boston, 1773]
broadside 29 X 16 cm.
Ford 1642
PHi. Photostat: MHi mp. 42436

B3559 FENNING, DANIEL
[The universal spelling book . . .] The fifteenth edition, with additions . . . Providence, Re-printed and sold by John Carter, 1773.
[12], 152, [4] p. 17 cm. [A]-X^4
MWA (mutilated) mp. 42437

B3560 A FEW lines wrote upon the intended execution of Levi Ames . . . and being sent to him for his improvement, are now published at his desire . . . [Boston, 1773]
broadside
Ford 1643
PHi mp. 42438

B3561 FLETCHER, BRIDGET (RICHARDSON) 1726-1770
Hymns and spiritual songs. Composed by . . . the wife of Timothy Fletcher, late of Wesford, deceased. Boston, I. Thomas, 1773.
70 p. 15 cm.
MWA (imperfect) mp. 42439

B3562 THE following circumstances relating to the famous Ansell Nickerson . . . Also, the testimony of two men . . . robbed by a topsail schooner . . . on the fourteenth of November: To which is added, the declaration of a justice of the peace, respecting Mr. Nickerson's innocence of the murder and robbery . . . [Boston? 1773?]
broadside 35.5 X 19.5 cm.
Ford 1678
PHi mp. 42475

B3563 [FRANKLIN, BENJAMIN] 1706-1790
The way to wealth, as clearly shewn in the preface of an old Pennsylvania almanack, intitled, Poor Richard improved. Philadelphia, Printed and sold by B. Franklin, 1758 [i.e., Philadelphia, Hall & Sellers, 1773]
16 p. 18.5 cm.
Imprint assigned from information from Yale Univ. Lib. (1945)
CtY. Photostat (t.p. only): MWA mp. 42440

B3564 FRIENDS, SOCIETY OF. PHILADELPHIA MONTHLY MEETING
An epistle from the Monthly meeting . . . held the 27th of the 8th month, 1773 . . . [Baltimore, W. Goddard, 1773]
Imprint assigned by Edwin Wolf 2d
3 p. 29.5 cm. caption title
DLC; NN; PHC; RPJCB mp. 42441

B3565 A FUNERAL elegy, occasioned by the tragedy, at Salem . . . the seventeenth of June, 1773, at which time the ten following persons . . . were drowned, having been out on a party of pleasure . . . [Boston] Printed and sold by E. Russell [1773]
broadside
RPB. Geo. R. Curwen (1875). 1875 facsim.: MHi; MWA mp. 42442

B3566 GEORGIA. GOVERNOR, 1772-1776
Georgia. By His Excellency Sir James Wright . . . Governor, and Commander in Chief . . . a proclamation. Whereas I have received information that two Cherokee Indians have been . . . murdered . . . [23 lines] Given under my hand . . . [July 22, 1773] . . . Ja. Wright . . . [Savannah, J. Johnston, 1773]
broadside 36 X 21 cm.
McMurtrie: Georgia 14
Public Record Off. mp. 42443

B3567 THE Georgia and South-Carolina almanack, for . . . 1774 . . . By John Tobler . . . Charlestown: Printed for the Editor. Sold in Georgia, by James Johnston . . . in Savannah. Sold in South Carolina, by Robert Wells . . . in Charlestown [1773]
[32] p. 17 cm. A-D^4
Drake 13114; Guerra b-342
NHi; ScHi mp. 42524

B3568 [GILL, JOHN] 1697-1771
Perseverance, a poem . . . Boston, I. Thomas, 1773.
13 p. 22 cm.
Nichols: Isaiah Thomas 36
DLC; MBAt (pref. intact; poem missing); MHi; NN mp. 42444

B3569 GOODHUE, SARAH (WHIPPLE) 1641-1681
The copy of a valedictory, and monitory writing, left by Sarah Goodhue, wife of Joseph Goodhue . . . New-London, Reprinted by the desire of David Kimball, of Preston, grandson to said Sarah Goodhue, 1773.
7 p. 18.5 cm.
CtHi mp. 42444a

B3570 GRATZ, BARNARD
To be sold, the following lands, situate, lying, and being on the south side of the Mohawk's-River, in the County of

Tryon, viz. . . . an indisputable title will be given, by the subscriber. Barnard Gratz. Albany May 25, 1773. [Albany, 1773]
broadside 4to
New York Public 494; Rosenbach 54
A. S. W. Rosenbach (1926). NN (reduced facsim.)
mp. 42445

B3571 GT. BRIT. ADJUTANT GENERAL'S OFFICE
The manual exercise as ordered by His Majesty in 1764 . . . Boston: Printed by T. and J. Fleet, at the Heart and Crown, in Cornhill. [1773]
39 p. fold. plate. 21.5 cm.
On verso of t.p.: "Position of a soldier under arms," followed by 14 lines of text
Dated from inscription in InU copy: " . . . Dorchester May 13th 1773."
InU; RPJCB mp. 42446

B3572 [GREGORY, FRANCIS]
Nomenclatura brevis. Anglo-Latino in usum scholarum. Together with examples of the five declensions . . . Boston, Printed and sold at the New Pringing-Office, in Hanover, Street, 1773.
83 p. 16 cm.
MB (imperfect) mp. 42448

B3573 HALIFAX, VT. CITIZENS
A petition of the people of Halifax. We the inhabitants . . . Signed by us at a legal town-meeting, November 11th, 1773 . . . [n.p., 1773]
broadside 31 X 19 cm.
Ford 1683; New York Public 495
MHi; RPJCB. Photostats: DLC; NN mp. 42449

B3574 HARVARD UNIVERSITY
Quaestiones pro modulo . . . MDCCLXXIII. Boston, R. Draper, 1773.
broadside 45 X 33 cm.
MH; MWA mp. 42450

B3575 HUTCHIN'S improved: being an almanack . . . for the year . . . 1774 . . . The second edition. By John Nathan Hutchins, Philom. New-York, Hugh Gaine [1773]
[36] p. 16 cm.
Gaine v.l, p. 131-32; Morrison p. 86; Wall p. 21
CtHi; CtW; DLC; MSaE; MWA; NHi; NN mp. 42451

B3576 HUTCHINSON, THOMAS, 1711-1780
Copy of letters sent to Great-Britain, by . . . Thomas Hutchinson . . . and several other persons . . . Boston, Edes and Gill, 1773.
40 p. 20 cm.
cf. Evans 12818; lacks the errata on p. 40, and additional pages 41-51
Huntington 328; Sabin 34071
CSmH; DLC (2 copies); ICN (2 copies); MB; MHi (t.p. lacking); MWA; MWiW-C; MiU-C; NHi; NN; NcD; NhD; PHi; PPL; PU; RPJCB; ViU

B3576a HYMN to the God of Abraham. Philadelphia, 1773.
8 p.
PHi mp. 42452

B3577 HYMNS and spiritual songs. [Boston?] 1773.
102 p. 14 cm.
Preface signed: Rehoboth [i.e. Elkanah Ingalls]
MBC mp. 42453

B3578 INHUMAN cruelty: or villany detected. Being a true relation of the . . . intended murder of a bastard child belonging to John and Ann Richardson, of Boston, . . . for which crime they were . . . sentenc'd to set on the gallows . . . [Boston, Draper? 1773]
broadside
Ford 1686
PHi mp. 42454

B3579 [JAMES, PHILIP]
A dialogue between a blind-man and Death. Boston, Printed and sold at John Boyle's Printing-Office, 1773.
16 p. 18.5 cm.
Hamilton 63b
MB; MWA; NjP mp. 42511

B3580 JOSEPHUS, FLAVIUS
The works of Flavius Josephus . . . The seventh edition. New-York, Printed for Hugh Gaine, 1773.
3 v. 8vo
Probably printed in Glasgow (Eames)
New York Public 497; Rosenbach 56
NN

B3581 JOSEPHUS, FLAVIUS
The works of Flavius Josephus . . . The seventh edition. New-York, Printed for Samuel Lowdon [sic], 1773.
3 v. 8vo
Probably printed in Glasgow (Eames)
New York Public 498; Rosenbach 57
A. S. W. Rosenbach (1926). NN (v. 1 only)
mp. 42455

B3582 A LETTER from the country, to a gentleman in Philadelphia. My dear friend, I am very sorry for the piece of intelligence . . . Five ships, loaded with tea, on their way to America! . . . I am, with sincere affection, your's, Rusticus. Fairview, Nov. 27, 1773. [Philadelphia? 1773]
broadside 36 X 22.5 cm.
MWA mp. 42457

B3583 A LIST of the gentlemen invited to commemorate St. Tammany, on the first of May, 1773. [Philadelphia, 1773]
broadside 32 X 21 cm.
New York Public 500
Elmer T. Hutchinson (1934). Photostat: NN
mp. 42458

B3584 LOVEY, JOHN WALL, d. 1773
The last speech, confession and dying words, of John Wall Lovey. Who was executed at Albany . . . the 2d of April, 1733 for counterfeiting the currency of . . . New-York . . . [New York? 1773]
broadside 35 X 21 cm.
CtHi mp. 42531

B3585 M'ALPINE, WILLIAM
Proposals for printing by subscription, the Fort-Royal of the Scriptures . . . containing an hundred heads of Scripture . . . By an Admirer of the Word . . . Subscriptions are taken in by William M'Alpine . . . printer . . . [Boston, 1733?]
broadside 34 X 12 cm.
Ford 1684; New York Public 501
NN mp. 42459

B3586 [MACGOWAN, JOHN] 1726-1780
Priestcraft defended . . . The twelfth edition . . . New-London, Re-printed and sold by Timothy Green, 1773.
iv, [1], 6-24 p. 19 cm.
New York Public 502; Trumbull: Supplement 2366
CtHi; MWA; NN mp. 42460

B3587 MARVELL, ANDREW
To my fellow citizens, friends to liberty, and enemies to despotism . . . [Philadelphia, 1773]
broadside 38 X 20 cm.
Signed: Andrew Marvell
Dated: Philadelphia, June 10, 1773
Hildeburn 2901
PHi mp. 42461

B3588 MASSACHUSETTS. HOUSE OF REPRESENTATIVES
The committee appointed to consider certain letters laid before the House . . . reported the following resolves. Tuesday, June 15, 1773 . . . [Boston, Edes and Gill, 1773]
8 p. 17.5 cm. caption title
cf. Adams 96b
MWA; RPJCB mp. 42462

B3589 MASSACHUSETTS. HOUSE OF REPRESENTATIVES
On Tuesday, June 16, 1773, the House of Representatives . . . came into the following resolves, upon the letters . . . laid before them on Wednesday the second of the same month . . . [Boston, Edes and Gill, 1773]
8 p. 19 cm.
Huntington 330; cf. Adams 96b
CSmH; MWA; RPJCB mp. 42463

B3590 MASSACHUSETTS. HOUSE OF REPRESENTATIVES
On Wednesday, June 16, 1773, the House of Representatives . . . came into the following resolves, upon the letters . . . laid before them on Wednesday the second of the same month . . . [Boston, Edes and Gill, 1773]
8 p. 19 cm.
cf. Adams 96b
MWA; RPJCB mp. 42464

B3591 MASSACHUSETTS. TREASURER
(No. 2.) Your Province tax for the year 1773. Your town and county rate . . . The assessors sit at the Turk's-Head in Dorchester . . . Philip Withington. [Boston, 1773]
broadside
Ford 1664
MHi

B3592 MASSACHUSETTS. TREASURER
Province of Massachusetts-Bay. The honorable Harrison Gray . . . Boston, the second day of August, 1773 . . . [Boston, 1773]
broadside 39.5 X 26 cm.
MHi mp. 42465

B3593 THE Massachusetts calendar; or an almanack for . . . 1774. By Ezra Gleason . . . Boston, Isaiah Thomas [1773]
[32] p.
Second edition
Drake 3233
MWA

B3594 MASSACHUSETTS GAZETTE
New-Year's verses, addressed to the customers of the *Massachusetts-gazette* . . . [Boston, 1773]
broadside 18.5 X 10 cm.
Ford 1696; Huntington 331
CSmH; PHi mp. 42469

B3595 THE mathamatician's [sic] glory, astronomy and New-England almanack for . . . 1774. By Elisha Stimson. [Boston] Printed for the author [1773]
Drake 3234
MWA (11 1.)

B3596 [MORGAN, ABEL] 1713-1785
A brief instruction in the principles of the Christian religion . . . The eighth edition, corrected . . . New-York, John Anderson, 1773.
sm. 4to
Huntington 332
CSmH

B3597 A NEW collection of hymns, on various subjects . . . Newport, Solomon Southwick, 1773.
56 p. 16.5 cm.
Alden 516; Winship p. 30
MB; RPB mp. 42466

B3598 THE New-England primer enlarged . . . Philadelphia, Printed and sold by D. Hall, and W. Sellers, 1773.
[80] p. $[A]-E^8$
Heartman 45; Huntington 333; Metzger 390
CSmH mp. 42468

B3599 THE New-England primer improved . . . Boston, Printed for, and sold by John Perkins [1773]
[80] p.
cf. Evans 12877
MWA mp. 42467

B3600 NEW HAMPSHIRE. HOUSE OF REPRESENTATIVES
Province of New-Hampshire, January 14, 1773. In the House of Representatives. Whereas . . . in several places that pay a province tax a new proportion is necessary . . . [Portsmouth, 1773]
broadside 31 X 18.5 cm.
Whittemore 138
NhHi mp. 42470

B3601 NEW HAMPSHIRE. LAWS
[Acts and laws, 1771-1773] [Portsmouth, 1773?]
p. 273?-286
Continuation of Acts and laws published 1771 (Evans 12146)
New York Public 503; Whittemore 155
MWA; NBuG; NN; Nh; NhHi

B3602 NEW-HAMPSHIRE GAZETTE
On the New-Year 1773. To all the worthy customers of the *New-Hampshire Gazette*, the following lines . . . by . . . The Printers Boys . . . [Portsmouth, Daniel and Robert Fowle, 1773]
broadside 37 X 13 cm.
NHi mp. 42481

B3603 NEW-HAVEN, February 26, 1773. Proposals for re-printing by subscription, The venerable Mr. Stoddard on the nature of conversion . . . Subscriptions to be sent to the Printing-Office in New-Haven. [New-Haven, 1773]
broadside 19.5 X 16 cm.
DLC mp. 42447

B3604 NEW JERSEY. LAWS
A supplement to the act, intituled, "An act for running and ascertaining the line of partition or division between the eastern and western divisions of the province of New-Jersey . . . [Burlington, I. Collins, 1773]
broadside 40.5 X 50.5 cm.
DLC; NN (reduced facsim.); NjR; PPRF; RPJCB
mp. 42471

B3604a NEW JERSEY. TREASURER
A bill in the chancery of New-Jersey, at the suit of Samuel Smith, esq. one of the treasurers of New-Jersey, against Archibald Kennedy . . . Burlington, Isaac Collins, 1773.
11 p. 34 cm.
Humphrey 129
DLC; NN mp. 42472

B3605 NEW YORK (CITY)
City of New-York, ss. Personally appeared, Moses Sherwood and William Bennet, . . . Sworn before me, this 7th day of October, 1773. George Brewerton . . . [New York, 1773]
broadside 27 X 20.5 cm.
MHi; NN; PHi; WHi. Photostat: DLC mp. 42473

B3606 NEW YORK. GOVERNOR, 1771-1777
By his excellency William Tryon . . . To any Protestant minister of the gospel. Whereas there is a mutual purpose of marriage . . . [New York, Hugh Gaine? 1773?]
broadside 42 X 33 cm.
PPRF mp. 42474

B3607 THE New-York almanac, for . . . 1774 . . . By Mark Time . . . New-York, John Holt [1773]
48 p. 16.5 cm.
New York Public 506
MWA; NN (photostat) mp. 42519

B3608 NORTH CAROLINA. HOUSE OF ASSEMBLY
The journal of the House of Assembly. North Carolina, ss. At an Assembly, begun . . . at Newbern [Jan. 25, 1773]; being the first session of this present Assembly. [Newbern, James Davis, 1773]
67 p. 3].5 cm. caption title
Session until Mar. 6, 1773
McMurtrie: North Carolina 67
NcWsM mp. 42476

B3609 NORTH CAROLINA. HOUSE OF ASSEMBLY
The journal of the House of Assembly, of . . . North Carolina. At an Assembly, begun . . . at Newbern [Dec. 4, 1773]; being the first session of this present Assembly. Newbern, James Davis, 1773.
8+ p. 28.5 cm.
Session until Dec. 21, 1773
McMurtrie: North Carolina 68
NcWsM (wanting after p. 8) mp. 42477

B3610 OCCOM, SAMSON, 1723-1792
A sermon, preached at the execution of Moses Paul, an Indian . . . executed . . . for the murder of Mr. Moses Cook . . . Boston, Printed and sold by John Boyles, next door to the Three Doves in Marlborough-Street, 1773.
31, [1] p. 19 cm. [A]-D^4
Variant t.p. has imprint: Printed and sold by John Boyles, in Marlborough-Street, 1773.
MHi (imperfect); MWA mp. 42478

B3611 OCCOM, SAMSON, 1723-1792
A sermon, preached at the execution of Moses Paul, an Indian . . . executed . . . for the murder of Mr. Moses Cook . . . Boston, Printed and sold by Richard Draper, 1773.
31, [1] p. 19.5 cm.
CSmH; MWA (photostat, t.p. only) mp. 42479

B3612 OLIVERS, THOMAS, 1725-1799
A hymn to the God of Abraham . . . The sixth edition . . . Philadelphia: Reprinted by Henry Miller, in the year MDCCLXXIII.
8 p. 17 cm.
PHi mp. 42480

B3613 PEIRCE, JOSEPH
Joseph Peirce, at his shop . . . fronting the west end of the Town-House, Boston . . . [Boston] Mills and Hicks [1773?]
broadside
Ford 1682
MB mp. 42482

B3614 PENNSYLVANIA. HOUSE OF REPRESENTATIVES
Votes of the House of Representatives. Monday, January 4, 1773 [-Saturday, February 6, 1773] [Colophon] Philadelphia: Printed by Henry Miller [1773]
25 p. fol. caption title
PHi

B3615 PENNSYLVANIA. HOUSE OF REPRESENTATIVES
Votes of the House of Representatives, from Monday, February 8, to Saturday, February 13, 1773. [Colophon] Philadelphia: Printed by Henry Miller [1773]
p. 27-31. fol. caption title
PHi

B3616 PENNSYLVANIA. HOUSE OF REPRESENTATIVES
Votes of the House of Representatives, from Monday, February 15, to Saturday, February 20, 1773 [-February 26] [Colophon] Philadelphia: Printed by Henry Miller [1773]
p. 33–41. fol. caption title
cf. Evans 12922
PHi

B3617 PENNSYLVANIA GAZETTE.
Postscript to the *Pennsylvania Gazette*. Friday evening . . . December 24, 1773 . . . [Philadelphia, 1773]
broadside
Concerns the Boston Tea Party
MB mp. 42484

B3618 PENNSYLVANIA JOURNAL
Christmas-box for the customers of the *Pennsylvania Journal*. Friday . . . Dec. 24, 1773. [Philadelphia, 1773]
broadside 32 X 18 cm.
New York Public 507
MB. Facsims.: MWA; NN mp. 42425

B3619 PERSONEL, FRANCIS BURDETT, 1747-1773
An authentic and particular account of the life of Francis Burdett Personel . . . [n.p., 1733?]
[23?] p.
Title taken from caption title (p. [3])
Title-leaf fragmentary; all lacking after p. 22
Differs from following item and from Evans 12936.-- D. Sinclair
NjR

B3620 PERSONEL, FRANCIS BURDETT, 1747-1773
An authentic & particular account of the life of Francis Burdett Personel, written by himself . . . New-Haven [1773]
23 p. 16.5 cm.
McDade 741; New York Public 508
CtHi; NN mp. 42483

B3621 PHILADELPHIA, 9th of December, 1773. By the medium of the curious numerical machine, invented by the ingenious Mr. Cox, are to be dsposed [!] of the follow-

ing two hundred and fifty lots of . . . plated goods, just imported by Samuel Bogle . . . [Philadelphia, 1773]
broadside 41 X 25 cm.
PPL mp. 42409

B3622 A PROSPECTIVE view of death: being, a solemn warning to inconsiderate youth, occasioned by the trial . . . of Levi Ames . . . to be executed on Thursday the fourteenth day of October next . . . Boston, Printed and sold by E. Russell [1773]
broadside 42 X 36 cm.
MWA mp. 42485

B3623 [PROUT, TIMOTHY]
Diana's shrines turned into ready money . . . Being remarks on the Northern Priest's pamphlet . . . In a letter to the author. <Numb. I.> . . . New-York: Printed [by Hugh Gaine] in the year MDCC,LXXIII.
23 p. 8vo [A]-C^4
Distinguished from Evans 12965 by <Numb. I.> on t.p.; sig. B typographically different
Adams 99a
MBAt

B3624 REFLECTIONS of a saint, under a view of the pretence of an infinitely holy, and all-seeing God. Norwich, Printed and sold by Green & Spooner [1773?]
8p. 15 cm.
MWA mp. 42486

B3625 RELIEF SOCIETY, BOSTON
Rules and orders for the Relief Society, instituted at Boston, March 5th, . . . 1773. [Boston] J. Boyles [1773?]
broadside 56 X 33 cm.
Ford 1685
MB mp. 42487

B3626 [RELLY, JAMES] 1720-1778
A short specimen of apostolick preaching . . . Burlington, Isaac Collins, 1773.
19 p. 19 cm.
Humphrey 130; Huntington 335
CSmH; DLC; MH; NHi mp. 42488

B3627 RHODE ISLAND. ELECTION PROX.
Colony of Rhode-Island, 1773. The honorable Joseph Wanton, Esq; Gov. The honorable Darius Sessions, Esq; Deputy-Gov. . . . [Newport? 1773]
broadside 19.5 X 13 cm.
Alden 518; Chapin Proxies 8
RHi mp. 42489

B3628 RHODE ISLAND. ELECTION PROX.
The honorable Joseph Wanton, Esq; Governor. The honorable Darius Sessions, Esq; Dep. Governor . . . [Newport? 1773]
broadside 19 X 12 cm.
Alden 519; Chapin Proxies 9
RHi mp. 42490a

B3629 RHODE ISLAND. ELECTION PROX.
The honorable Joseph Wanton, Esq; Gov. The honorable Darius Sessions, Esq; Dep. Gov. . . . [Newport? 1773]
broadside 17 X 11 cm.
Alden 520; Chapin Proxies 10a, 10b
RHi (variants) mp. 42490

B3630 RHODE ISLAND. LAWS
At the General assembly . . . holden . . . on the third Monday in August . . . An act for assessing . . . a rate or tax of four thousand pounds . . . [Newport, Solomon Southwick, 1773]
3 p. 32 cm.
Bill submitted Aug. 25, 1773
Alden 525; Winship p. 30
RHi mp. 42491

B3631 ROBINSON, NATHANIEL
Verses upon fourteen different occasions . . . The third edition. Boston, Printed and sold by William McAlpine, 1773.
24 p. 16.5 cm. [A]-B^6
MBAt; MWA; NHi; RPB mp. 42492

B3632 ROMANS, BERNARD, 1720-1784
Philadelphia, August 5, 1773. Proposals for printing by subscription, three very elegant and large maps of the navigation, to . . . the new ceded countries . . . the Mississippi . . . East-Florida . . . The curious may see the originals . . . by applying to Messrs. William and Thomas Bradford. [Philadelphia, W. and T. Bradford, 1773]
broadside 42 X 25.5 cm.
RPJCB. Photostats: MWA; NN mp. 42493

B3633 ROWE, ELIZABETH SINGER, 1674-1737
[The history of Joseph and his brethren. Philadelphia, Printed for Daniel Lawrence, 33 N 4th Street, 1773?]
16 p. 16mo
Imprint from the bookseller's catalogue
Marcus 1
No copy known mp. 42494

B3634 ROXBURY, MASS.
An address of freeholders of the first precinct in Roxbury in relation to being set off to the third precinct . . . [Boston, 1773?]
broadside
Ford 1687
MWA mp. 42495

B3635 ROXBURY, MASS.
Whereas the Great and General Court were pleased at their last session to appoint a committee, to whom they referr'd the petition of several who had petitioned to be set off from the first to the third precinct in Roxbury . . . [Boston, 1773]
broadside 50 X 39.5 cm.
Presented Jan. 12, 1773
Ford 1688
MWA mp. 42496

B3636 RUSSELL, EZEKIEL, 1743-1796
This day is published. Sold by E. Russell, next the Cornfield . . . Diana's shrines turned into ready money, by priestly magic . . . [Boston, 1773?]
broadside 19 X 11.5 cm.
MWA mp. 42497

B3637 SALEM HOSPITAL
Rules for regulating Salem Hospital. Rules approved of and voted by the town . . . [Salem, 1773]
8 p. 22 cm.
Advertised in the *Essex Gazette*, Dec. 21, 1773, as "Just published, and to be sold by the printers of this paper."
Austin 1700; Ford 1689; Rogers 391
MHi; MWA mp. 42498

B3638 SALEM, June 25, 1773. Verses on the sudden and awful death of Mrs. Rebecca Giles, Mr. Paul Kimball and his wife . . . and Mrs. Sarah Becket, all of Salem, who were drowned . . . on the 17th day of June, 1773. Boston, Printed and sold in Milk-Street [by John Kneeland, 1773]
broadside 35 X 23 cm.

Ford 1690, 1691; Tapley p. 314
MHi; MSaE; MWA (imperfect): PHi mp. 42525

B3639 SALISBURY, S. AND S., FIRM
Hard-ware goods. S. and S. Salisbury, continue importing from London, Bristol, Birmingham and Sheffield, a large . . . assortment of hard-ware goods, which they sell . . . at their shop at Boston, two doors southward of Dr. Silvester Gardner's . . . and at their shop at Worcester . . . [Boston, 1773?]
broadside 32 X 20 cm.
Dated from internal evidence by Clarence Brigham
MWA mp. 42599

B3640 SAYBROOK BAR LOTTERY
Say-Brook Barr Lottery, to raise the sum of five hundred and thirty seven pounds . . . fixing buoys and other marks . . . mouth of Connecticut River . . . Hartford, June 5, 1773. [Hartford, 1773]
broadside 32 X 18.5 cm.
CtHi mp. 42500

B3641 THE second Spira . . . Boston, Re-printed and sold [by I. Thomas?] at the Printing Office near the Mill-Bridge [1773?]
8 p. 16.5 cm.
MWA mp. 42501

B3642 SMITH, JOSIAH, 1704-1781
The broken heart relieved: a sermon preached at Charlestown, South-Carolina, March the 27th, 1763 . . . The second edition. Charlestown, Robert Wells, 1773.
14 p. 16.5 cm.
Sabin 8354 (note)
DLC; NcMHi; NjP mp. 42503

B3643 SMITH, JOSIAH, 1704-1781
A sermon, preached at Charlestown, South-Carolina, in the year 1739 . . . The second edition. Charlestown, Robert Wells, 1773.
25 p. 8vo
Huntington 338; Sabin 83447
CSmH; NcMHi. Photostat: NN mp. 42504

B3644 SMITH & COIT, firm, Hartford
Hartford, 5th July, 1773. Just imported from London . . . a universal assortment of drugs . . . together with the following books . . . [Hartford, 1773]
broadside 38.5 X 34 cm.
Huntington 339
CSmH mp. 42505

B3645 A SOLEMN farewell to Levi Ames, being a poem written a few days before his execution . . . Oct. 21, 1772 [sic] Boston, Printed and sold at Draper's Printing-Office [1773]
broadside 32 X 20 cm.
Ford 1645
PHi mp. 42506

B3646 SPARHAWK, JOHN, of Philadelphia
A catalogue of books, &c. to be sold by John Sparhawk, at the London Bookstore, in Philadelphia. [Philadelphia, 1773?]
44 p. 17 cm.
RPB mp. 42507

B3647 THE speech of death to Levi Ames. Who was executed on Boston-Neck, October 21, 1773 . . . [Boston, 1773]
broadside 31 X 19 cm.
Ford 1647; Huntington 340
CSmH; PHi. Photostat: MHi mp. 42508

B3648 SPENCER, ARTHUR
To the public. Mr. Arthur Spencer, at present an inhabitant of Boston, formerly surgeon's mate of His Majesty's ship Glasgow . . . [Boston, 1773?]
broadside 36 X 21.5 cm.
Ford 1693
MH; MHi; MWA mp. 42509

B3649 [STANDFAST, RICHARD]
A dialogue between a blindman and death . . . Boston, Printed and sold at John Boyle's, 1773.
14 p.
MWA mp. 42511

B3650 [STANDFAST, RICHARD]
Dialogue between a blind man and death. To which is added a poem on death. Extracted from Mr. John Peck's Description of the last judgment . . . [Boston, 1773?]
16 p. 18.5 cm.
CtHi mp. 42510

B3651 STEDMAN, STEIGEL AND CO
. . . There are likewise to be sold by Stedman Steigel and Company, several valuable tracts of land and plantations . . . Lancaster, Printed by Francis Bailey, in King's-street . . . [1773?]
broadside 23 X 24 cm.
Metzger 393
PHi (fragment) mp. 42512

B3652 STILLMAN, SAMUEL, 1738-1807
Two sermons: the first . . . delivered . . . before the execution of Levi Ames . . . The second . . . preached . . . after his execution . . . The second edition. Boston, Printed and sold by E. Russell; sold also by A. Ellison, 1773.
31 p. 20 cm. [A]-D^4
MWA mp. 42513

B3653 STILLMAN, SAMUEL, 1738-1807
Two sermons: the first . . . delivered . . . before the execution of Levi Ames . . . The second . . . preached . . . after his execution . . . The fourth edition. Boston, Printed and sold by E. Russell; sold also by A. Ellison, 1773.
31, [1] p. 22 cm. [A]-D^4
MHi; MWA mp. 42514

B3654 SUPPLEMENT extraordinary. June 10, 1773.
On Friday last the Chamber of Commerce of this city, waited on . . . General Gage . . . [New York, 1773]
broadside 44.5 X 26.5 cm.
NHi mp. 42515

B3655 TAMMANY SOCIETY
Sir, as all nations have for seven centuries past, adopted some great personage . . . as their tutular saint . . . [Philadelphia, R. Aitken, 1773]
card 12mo
Invitation to the meeting of May 1
PPL mp. 42516

B3656 TEA, destroyed by Indians. Ye glorious sons of freedom, brave and bold . . . [Boston, 1773?]
broadside 32 X 20.5 cm.
26 lines of verse on the Boston Tea Party
MHi mp. 42517

B3657 THEFT and murder! A poem on the execution of Levi Ames, which is to be on Thursday . . . for robbing the house of Mr. Martin Bicker . . . [Boston] Sold near the

Mill-Bridge: and at the Printing Office near the Market [1773]
broadside
Ford 1648
MH mp. 42518

B3658 TO be sold by public vendue, on Wednesday the first of December next . . . at the house of Capt. Nathaniel Little, innholder in Kingston . . . real estate of Charlotte Tyler, a minor . . . Samuel-Phillips Savage, her guardian . . . Boston, October 26, 1773. [Boston, 1773]
broadside 21.5 X 18 cm.
Sale of real estate
MHi mp. 42520

B3659 TO the commissioners appointed by the East-India Company, for the sale of tea, in America. [New York? 1773]
broadside 32.5 X 21 cm.
In three columns
New York Public 510; cf. Evans 12999 (in two columns)
NN; PPL. Photostat: MHi mp. 42521

B3660 TO the inhabitants of Pennsylvania. Friends, countrymen, and fellow citizens . . . [Philadelphia? 1773?]
broadside
Signed at end: Cives
A reply to Publicus on the matter of the excise
Adams: Pennsylvania 28
PU

B3661 TO the inhabitants of Pennsylvania. A very dangerous attempt to render ineffectual your virtuous exertions . . . Wednesday, October 13, 1773. [Philadelphia, 1773]
broadside 16.5 X 7.5 cm.
A call to prevent the landing of a large quantity of tea
PHi (closely trimmed) mp. 42522

B3662 TO the public. Civis avows himself to be the person . . . alluded to in the publications of Titus Ironicus . . . Civis. [Philadelphia, 1773]
broadside fol.
PPL mp. 42523

B3663 TO the public. The following letters between Mr. William Neilson, of this city, merchant, and Mr. Josiah Holt, of Newbern, North-Carolina, merchant, are published at the . . . request of . . . Josiah Holt. [New York, 1773?]
broadside
Letters written in April 1773 and attested to Oct. 29, 1773
NNS

B3664 VIRGINIA. COUNCIL
To his excellency . . . John Earl of Dunmore . . . the humble address of the Council . . . [Williamsburg, W. Rind, 1773]
broadside 32 X 15 cm.
Reply to his speech of Mar. 4, 1773
DLC (photostat) mp. 42526

B3665 VIRGINIA. GOVERNOR, 1771-1775
The speech of . . . the right honourable John Earl of Dunmore . . . on Thursday the 4th of March, 1773. [Williamsburg, W. Rind, 1773]
broadside 32 X 16 cm.
DLC (photostat) mp. 42527

B3666 VIRGINIA. HOUSE OF BURGESSES
By the Upper House . . . October 28, 1773. Gentlemen, we return the bill . . . [Williamsburg, C. Rind, 1773]
broadside 23 X 17.5 cm.
DLC mp. 42528

B3667 VIRGINIA. HOUSE OF BURGESSES
To his excellency . . . John Earl of Dunmore . . . the humble address . . . [Williamsburg, W. Rind, 1773]
broadside 32 X 16 cm.
Speech of Mar. 13, 1773
DLC (photostat) mp. 42530

B3668 WASHINGTON, GEORGE, 1732-1799
Mount Vernon, July 15 1773. The subscriber, having obtained patents for upwards of 20,000 acres of land, on the Ohio and great Kanhawa . . . George Washington. [Williamsburg? 1773]
broadside 29.5 X 19 cm.
Half of broadside printed parallel to narrow dimension; remainder used for letter by Washington
InU mp. 42532

B3669 WATTS, ISAAC, 1674-1748
Divine songs, attempted in easy language . . . The fifteenth edition. Boston, Printed and sold by T. and J. Fleet, 1773.
[2], 44, [2] p. 16 cm.
MWA mp. 42534

B3670 WATTS, ISAAC, 1674-1748
Divine songs, attempted in easy language . . . The fifteenth edition, corrected. Boston, Printed for and sold by Nicholas Bowes, 1773.
v, 42 p. 14.5 cm.
MHi (imperfect); MWA mp. 42533

B3671 WATTS, ISAAC, 1674-1748
Divine songs, attempted in easy language . . . The fifteenth edition, corrected. Boston, Printed for and sold by Thomas Leverett, 1773.
v, 42 p. 15 cm.
MWA mp. 42535

B3672 WESTMINSTER ASSEMBLY OF DIVINES
The larger catechism agreed upon by the Assembly of Divines at Westminster . . . Boston, Printed by Mills and Hicks, and sold at their Printing-Office, 1773.
47 p. 17 cm. $A\text{-}D^6$
MB; MWA mp. 42539

B3673 WHEATLEY, PHILLIS, 1754-1784
An elegy, to Miss Mary Moorhead, on the death of her father . . . [Boston] William M'Alpine, 1773.
broadside 40.5 X 30 cm.
New York Public 512; Porter 263; Sabin 103132
MHi. Photostats: MWA; NN mp. 42540

B3674 WHEATLEY, PHILLIS, 1754-1784
To the Hon'ble Thomas Hubbard, Esq; on the death of Mrs. Thankfull Leonard . . . Boston, January 2, 1773. [Boston, 1773]
broadside 33 X 20.5 cm.
Ford 1637; Porter 281; Sabin 103141
PHi. Photostats: MHi; MWA mp. 42541

B3675 WHEELOCK, ELEAZAR, 1711-1779
A continuation of the narrative of the Indian charity school . . . [Portsmouth] New-Hampshire, Printed in the year 1773.
40 p. 20 cm.
The third of the author's five "continuations"

Huntington 342; Sabin 103210
CSmH; CtHi; DLC (2 copies); ICN; MHi; MWA; MiU-C; NHi; NN; NhHi; RPJCB mp. 42542

B3676 WILLIAM AND MARY COLLEGE
To all to whom these present shall come, greeting: Know ye, that we the President and masters . . . do constitute and appoint surveyor of during pleasure . . . in the year . . . one thousand seven hundred and seventy three. [Williamsburg, 1773]
broadside 18.5 X 15 cm.
DLC

B3677 WINCHELL, JACOB, b. 1739
A short treatise, in favour of the Baptists: in a letter to Mr. Israel Holly . . . Hartford, Eben. Watson [1773]
27 p. 18 cm.
"To the reader" dated: Springfield, July 20, 1773
New York Public 514; Sabin 104716
NN; RPJCB (imperfect) mp. 42543

B3678 WINCHESTER, ELHANAN, 1751-1797
[cut] The execution hymn, composed on Levi Ames, who is to be executed . . . this day, the 21st of October, 1773 . . . To which is annexed . . . dying soliloquy . . . of Levi Ames . . . By Elhanan Winchester . . . author of the Execution hymn . . . [Boston] Sold by E. Russell [1773]
broadside 36.5 X 24 cm.
MHi mp. 42544

1774

B3679 ACCOUNT of the number of inhabitants in the town of on the first of January, 1774, taken and certified by the subscribers, select-men of said town . . . [n.p., 1774]
broadside 21 X 33 cm.
CtHi mp. 42576

B3680 AN address to New-England: written by A Daughter of Liberty. [Boston, Nathanael Coverly, 1774]
broadside 35.5 X 19 cm.
In verse
Ford 1697
PHi mp. 42545

B3681 ADDRESSES &c. to the late Governor Hutchinson. Boston, May 30. 1774 . . . [Boston, T. & J. Fleet, 1774]
broadside 38.5 X 23 cm.
Ford 1698
MHi mp. 42546

B3682 AN astronomical diary, or almanack, for . . . 1775 . . . New-Haven, Thomas & Samuel Green [1774]
[20] p. 19 cm.
By Joseph Perry
Bates: Connecticut almanacs p. 128
CtHi; CtY; MWA mp. 42665

B3683 AT a meeting of delegates of the towns . . . Norwich, Judah P. Spooner [1774]
broadside 30 X 17.5 cm.
CtHi; MWA. Photostats: DLC; ICN; MHi; NHi
mp. 42660

B3684 AN attempt to confute error, and establish truth . . . Presented unto Mr. Jirah Sweft, jun. of Dartmouth, &c. Providence, John Carter, 1774.
2 p.l., [3]-18 p. 17 cm.
Alden 531; Winship p. 31
MHi (imperfect); RHi; RPB mp. 42548

B3685 BAPTISTS. PENNSYLVANIA. PHILADELPHIAN ASSOCIATION
Minutes of the Philadelphian Association, held at New-York, the 25th of May, MDCCLXXIV. [New-York? 1774?]
5 p. caption title
RPJCB mp. 42551

B3686 BAPTISTS. SOUTH CAROLINA. CHARLESTON ASSOCIATION
A confession of faith, put forth by the elders and brethren of many congregations . . . Adopted by the Baptist Association in Charlestown, South-Carolina . . . Charlestown, David Bruce, 1774.
viii, 88 p., 3 l., 50 p., 1 l. 15 cm.
New York Public 517; Sabin 87794
NN mp. 42552

B3687 BAPTISTS. SOUTH CAROLINA. CHARLESTON ASSOCIATION
Minutes of the Charlestown Association, met in Charlestown, South-Carolina, February 7, 1774 . . . [Charleston, 1774]
4 p.
MWA (photostat) mp. 42553

B3688 BELL, ROBERT, d. 1784
Proposals for printing by subscription, A dissent from the Church of England, fully justified . . . Philadelphia, Robert Bell, 1774.
[4] p. 16 cm.
Metzger 399
MWA; NN; PHi; PPL mp. 42554

B3689 [BENEZET, ANTHONY] 1713-1784
The mighty destroyed displayed . . . By a Lover of Mankind . . . Philadelphia, Joseph Crunkshank, 1774.
48 p. 16 cm.
Also as second title of The potent enemies of America . . . Philadelphia [1774]
CSmH; DLC; ICN; MWA; N; PBL mp. 42555

B3690 BENGEL, JOHANN ALBRECHT, 1687-1752
Die Hauptsache der Offenbarung Johannis . . . aus den . . . Schriften . . . Bengels . . . Philadelphia, Zu finden bey Ernst Ludwig Baisch, 1774.
[6], 118 p. 19.5 cm. $[\ ]^4$ A-G^8 H^4
MWA mp. 42556

B3691 BEVERSTOCK, GEORGE
The silver-key . . . shewing the benefit of money, and the contempt of the poor . . . Boston [1774?]
broadside 34.5 X 21.5 cm.
Huntington 344
CSmH mp. 42557

B3692 BIBLE. O.T. PSALMS
The New-England Psalter . . . Boston, Printed for, and sold by John Boyle, 1774.
159, [1] p. 16.5 cm.
d'Alté A. Welch, Cleveland (1962) mp. 42558

B3693 BIBLE. O.T. PSALMS
The New-England Psalter . . . Boston, Printed for, and sold by John Perkins, 1774.
159, [1] p. 16.5 cm.
cf. Evans 13148; Sabin 52737
DLC; N (mutilated); NN; RPJCB (p. 3-14 lacking).
d'Alté A. Welch, Cleveland (1962) mp. 42559

B3694 BIBLE. O.T. PSALMS
The Psalms of David, imitated . . . The thirty-seventh edition . . . Boston, John Boyles, 1774.
299 p. 14.5 cm.
Probably issued with thc 37th ed. (Boston, 1774) of Watts' Hymns and spiritual songs
MWA; RPJCB mp. 42747

B3695 [BICKERSTAFF'S New-England almanack for 1775. Norwich, Robertsons and Trumbull, 1774]

Drake 297, following Bates
No copy known

B3696 BILLS pending before Parliament concerning Mass. Bay . . . Boston, June 3, 1774. Salem, S. and E. Hall [1774]
broadside
Tapley p. 315
MSaE mp. 42617

B3697 BLACKSTONE, SIR WILLIAM, 1723-1780
Commentaries on the laws of England . . . Philadelphia: Printed and sold by Robert Bell, 1774.
[4], ii, [2], 485 p.
Vol. I only, reprint of 1771 ed.
PHi

B3698 BLACKWELL, THOMAS, 1660?-1728
Forma sacra, or, A sacred platform of natural and revealed religion . . . To which is now added, an introduction . . . by Simon Williams . . . Boston, Printed and sold by William M'Alpine for the Rev. Mr. Williams, of Windham, 1774.
xvii, [1], xviii, 339 [1] p. 16.5 cm.
Not used for microprint of Evans 13155
MHi; MWA mp. 42561

B3699 BOSTON. CARPENTERS
The carpenters rules of work, in the town of Boston. Boston, Mills and Hicks, 1774.
11 p. 16.5 cm.
NHi. Photostat: MWA mp. 42561

B3700 BOSTON. COMMITTEE OF CORRESPONDENCE
Boston, May 12, 1774. Gentlemen, by the last advices from London we learn that an act has been passed . . . for blocking up the harbour of Boston . . . [Boston, 1774]
broadside 21 X 19 cm.
Ford 1706; Huntington 346; NYPL 518
CSmH; MHi; MiU-C; NHi; NN. Photostat: DLC mp. 42562

B3701 BOSTON. COMMITTEE OF CORRESPONDENCE
Gentlemen, The evils which we have long foreseen . . . [Boston, 1774]
[3] p. 31.5 cm.
Varies in punctuation and in wording of 3rd linc from end, from Evans 13157 (and Ford 1707-1708)
p. [3]: "We the subscribers, inhabitants of the town of having taken into our serious consideration . . ." (50-line issue of Evans 13163, 13427)
MHi (p. [3] only); MWA (p. [3] only); MiU-C (4-page folder enclosed by Gage to Dartmouth)

B3702 BOSTON. SELECTMEN
Notification. Agreeable to the order of the town . . . the freeholders . . . are hereby notified, to meet at Faneuil-Hall . . . the 26th of July instant . . . Boston, July 23d, 1774 . . . [Boston, 1774]
broadside 17.5 X 21.5 cm.
MiU-C (2 copies) mp. 42563

B3703 BOSTON EVENING POST
Supplement to the *Boston Evening Post*, (No. 2016.) Monday, May 16, 1774. The act of Parliament . . . [Boston] Thomas and John Fleet [1774]
[2] p. 35 X 23.5 cm.
Summary of the Boston Port Bill
PHi mp. 42615

B3704 [BOUCHER, JONATHAN] 1738-1804
A letter from a Virginian to the members of the Congress to be held at Philadelphia on the first of September, 1774. Boston, Re-printed and sold by Mills and Hicks, and Cox and Berry, 1774.
32 p. 17.5 cm. [A]-D^4
cf. Evans 13168
MHi (imperfect); MWA; NjP mp. 42565

B3705 BRAINERD, DAVID, 1718-1747
To the foregoing testimonies of the happiness of a life spent in the service of God, may be added that of . . . David Brainard . . . [Philadelphia, 1774]
16 p. 8vo caption title
cf. Evans 13145
PPL mp. 42566

B3706 BRATTLE, WILLIAM, 1706-1776
To the public. Boston, September 2, 1774. I think it but justice to myself to give an account of my conduct, for which I am blamed . . . W. Brattle. [Boston, 1774]
broadside 27 X 18.5 cm.
Ford 1717
MHi; MWA mp. 42567

B3707 BRIDEWELL LOTTERY
Advertisement. Notice is hereby given, that the tickets of the Bridewell lottery are now rolling up . . . New-York, John Holt [1774]
broadside 24 X 19 cm.
Dated Apr. 13, 1774
New York Public 515
Elmer T. Hutchinson (1933). Photostat: NN mp. 42568

B3708 BROWN UNIVERSITY
Viro honoratissimo . . . Stephano Hopkins . . . Haec philosophemata . . . habita . . . Septembris, A.D. MDCCLXXIV. [Providence] Johannis Carter [1774]
broadside 52 X 39 cm.
Alden 560; Winship p. 31
RPB (mutilated). Photostats: MHi; MWA; NN; RHi mp. 42569

B3709 CARTER, JOHN
The young surveyor's instructor . . . Philadelphia, W. and T. Bradford, 1774.
iv, 64 p. 13.5 cm.
DLC mp. 42570

B3710 CARTWRIGHT, EDMUND, 1743-1823
Armine and Elvira . . . Philadelphia, Reprinted by James Humphreys, 1774.
30, [1] p. 8vo
Third title of Evans 13449
MWA; NHi; PPL mp. 42571

B3711 [CHANDLER, THOMAS BRADBURY] 1726-1790
The American querist . . . By a North-American. The eleventh edition. New-York, James Rivington, 1774.
32 p. 18 cm. [A]-D^4
Adams 106c; Huntington 347;
CSmH; DLC; ICN; MBAt; MiU-C; N; PPL mp. 42572

B3712 CLARK, CHRISTOPHER
A confession of faith held by a Society of Friends called Separates . . . Christopher Clark. Williamsburg, Clementina Rind, 1774.
17 p. 15 cm.
NN (mutilated) mp. 42573

B3713 COLLES, CHRISTOPHER, 1738-1816
As the several inhabitants of this city are particularly interested . . . Copy of a proposal of Christopher Colles. For furnishing . . . New-York with . . . fresh water . . . New-York, Hugh Gaine [1774]
broadside 38 X 24 cm.
MWiW-C. Photostat: NN mp. 42574

B3714 CONGREGATIONAL CHURCHES OF CONNECTICUT
The general Association of the pastors of the Consociated Church . . . of Connecticut, convened . . . June 22, 1774 . . . settlements now forming to the westward . . . destitute of a preached Gospel . . . Norwich, Robertsons and Trumbull [1774]
broadside 31 X 19.5 cm.
CtHi mp. 42575

B3715 CONNECTICUT. CITIZENS
At a meeting of the committees of twenty-three towns in this colony at Middletown, on the 30th of March 1774, appointed . . . to confer . . . alarming situation . . . respecting Susquehannah matters . . . Adam Babcock, Clerk. To the honorable, the General Assembly . . . [Hartford? 1774]
[2] p. 33.5 X 22 cm.
MHi

B3716 CONNECTICUT. CITIZENS
To the honorable General Assembly of the Colony of Connecticut, to be holden at Hartford . . . May next. The memorial of the subscribers, freemen and inhabitants of said Colony, humbly sheweth . . . Dated the 10th day of March, A.D. 1774. Hartford, Eben. Watson [1774]
broadside 30.5 X 19 cm.
CtHi mp. 42577

B3717 CONNECTICUT. HOUSE OF REPRESENTATIVES
In the House of Representatives. The report of the delegates of this Colony in the late Continental Congress . . . Resolved, That the Association entered into . . . be printed . . . and dispersed . . . Association, & c. We his Majesty's . . . Philadelphia, October 20, 1774 . . . [at end] New-Haven, Thomas and Samuel Green [1774]
[2] p. 33.5 cm.
CtHi mp. 42578

B3718 CONNECTICUT. TREASURER
. . . Colony of Connecticut, in New-England. To constable of and collector of the Colony tax . . . for . . . 1774, Greeting . . . Dated at Hartford, the 20th day of June . . . 1774 . . . Treasurer . . . [Hartford, 1774]
broadside 31 X 19.5 cm.
CtHi mp. 42579

B3719 COOK, JAMES, 1728-1779
A new journal of a voyage around the world, performed in His Majesty's ship Endeavour, in the years 1768, 1769, 1770, and 1771 . . . To which is added, A concise vocabulary of the language of the Otahitee . . . London Printed; Philadelphia Re-printed, by James Humphreys, junr. for John Douglas M'Dougall, bookbinder, 1774.
iv, 139, [7] p. front. 12 cm.
Evans 13218, but not filmed for microprint ed.
MWA mp. 42580

B3720 CROUCH & GRAY
Gentlemen, Our Mr. John Gray, has entered into copartnership with Mr. Henry Crouch, a Carolinian, and we have formed a house for the purpose that Mr. Gray left his friends in New-England . . . Crouch & Gray. [Charles-Town, 1774]
broadside 23.5 X 19 cm.
RPJCB mp. 42581

B3721 [DEFOE, DANIEL] 1659?-1731
The wonderful life, and surprizing adventures of . . . Robinson Crusoe . . . New York, H. Gaine, 1774.
138, [4] p.
Brigham 1
CtY; MWA (imperfect); PP mp. 42582

B3722 DELAWARE. HOUSE OF REPRESENTATIVES
Votes and proceedings of the House of Representatives . . . met at New-Castle . . . October 20, 1773. Wilmington, James Adams, 1774.
46 p. 32 cm.
Hawkins 7
DLC mp. 42583

B3723 DELAWARE LOTTERY
Delaware Lottery. For the sale of lands belonging to the Earl of Stirling. The scheme. New-York, H. Gaine [1774?]
broadside 40 X 34.5 cm.
PHi mp. 42584

B3724 DELAWARE LOTTERY
List of the numbers that came up prizes in the Delaware Lottery, for the use of New-Jersey College . . . which began drawing . . . May 23, and ended on Thursday, June 9, 1774 . . . [Philadelphia, 1774]
[4] p. 42 cm.
Note on enclosing folder: "Pennsylvania Journal probably supplement. June 15, 1774."
Not Evans 13243
MH mp. 42585

B3725 DERBY, RICHARD
Advertisement. Ran-away from the subscriber [Richard Derby] last Saturday, a Negro man, named Obed. Salem, February 28, 1774. [Salem, 1774]
broadside 15 X 11 cm.
Tapley p. 315
MSaE mp. 42586

B3726 A DIALOGUE between a renowned Rhode-Island colonel and one of his . . . lackeys J---- R-----n [Jacob Richardson?] [Newport? S. Southwick? ca. 1774?]
12 p. 18.5 cm. caption title
Alden 534A
MWA; RP (mutilated); RPJCB mp. 42587

B3727 DOD, JOHN, 1549?-1645
Old Mr. Dod's sayings . . . The ninth edition. New-London, Printed and sold by T. Green [1774?]

23, [1] p. port. 17 cm. [$]^4 B^6 D^2$
CtHi; MWA mp. 42588

B3728 DUKETT, VALENTINE, d. 1774
The life, last words, and dying speech of Valentine Dukett: who was shot for desertion . . . Sept. 9, 1774 . . . Boston Camp (at mid-night) 9th Sept. 1774. [Boston] Sold at the Printing-Office in School-street [1774]
broadside 49 X 35 cm.
Ford 1722
MWA mp. 42589

B3729 AN elegy, occasioned by the melancholly catastrophe . . . the night of the 10th of August, 1774: in which . . . perished in the unrelenting flames . . . Mrs. Murphy and her two small children, Mrs. Fling and Mrs. Whitemore . . . [Boston] Sold at the Printing-Office in Milk-Street [by John Kneeland] [1774]
broadside 35.5 X 22.5 cm.
Ford 1723
PHi. Photostats: MHi; MWA mp. 42590

B3730 AN elegy on the death of the Reverend John Ogilvie . . . the 26th of November, 1774. By a Young Gentleman of this City . . . [New York, 1774]
broadside 19 X 13 cm.
NHi mp. 42591

B3731 AN elegy, on the much lamented death of Lamson Mitchel, the eldest son of Mr. Peter Mitchel of Woodbury, and . . . a member of Yale-College, . . . March 1, 1774 . . . [New Haven? 1774]
broadside 40 X 26 cm.
CtHi mp. 42592

B3732 . . .THE examination of Mr. Meseres, late attorney general of Quebec . . . and of Mr. Hey . . . at the bar of Parliament, on the 3d of June, 1774. [at top of p. [1]] [Philadelphia] Sold by James Humphreys [1774]
4 p. 8vo caption title
MWA; PPL mp. 42593

B3733 FERRIS, EBENEZER
A reply to the general arguments brought in favour of infant baptism . . . New-York, John Anderson, 1774.
107 p. 18.5 cm.
MWA; RPJCB mp. 42594

B3734 THE first book of the American chronicles of the times. Chap. I . . . [Boston, J. Boyle, 1774]
8 p. sm. 4to
Huntington 349; cf. Evans 13105
CSmH mp. 42596

B3735 THE first book of the American chronicles of the times. Chap. I . . . [at end] [Boston] Sold by D. Kneeland [1774]
8 p. 19 cm. caption title
MHi (imperfect); MWA; RPJCB mp. 42598

B3736 THE first book of the American chronicles of the times. Chap. I . . . [at end] [Boston] Sold by Edes and Gill [1774]
8 p. 19.5 cm. caption title
MWA mp. 42597

B3737 THE first book of the American chronicles of the times. Chap. I. [Newport, S. Southwick, 1774]
10 p. 19 cm. caption title
Imprint assigned by H. M. Chapin
Alden 535; Winship Addenda p. 88
RHi mp. 42600

B3738 THE first book of the American chronicles of the times. Chap. I. [n.p., 1774?]
10 p. 19 cm. $[A]^4 B^1$
MWA mp. 42595

B3739 THE first book of the American chronicles of the times. Chap. I . . . [at end] Providence, John Carter [1774]
8 p. 20.5 cm. caption title
Alden 536
MWA; RHi mp. 42601

B3740 THE first book of the American chronicles of the times . . . Chap. I[-II] . . . [at end] New-York, John Anderson [1774?]
22 p. 20 cm.
Printer given at the end of each chapter
CtHi; NHi mp. 42599

B3741 THE first book of the American chronicles of the times. Chap. II . . . [at end] Providence, John Carter [1774?]
[9]-15 p. 20.5 cm. caption title
Alden 537; Winship p. 31
MHi; MWA; RHi mp. 42602

B3742 THE following is a copy of a bill which was stuck up at Richmond, on Saturday the 4th of June, 1774, close to the playbill for that day . . . [Richmond? 1774?]
broadside 45 X 28 cm.
Denouncing gay and vain amusements
"Apparently an early reprint of E13182." "Probably English printing." —C. K. Shipton
MWA mp. 42603

B3743 GAINE, HUGH, 1726-1807
Gaine's new memorandum book, or The merchant's and tradesman's daily pocket journal for the year 1774 . . . New-York, H. Gaine, 1774.
[4], [96], 41 p. 15.5 cm.
MWA mp. 42605

B3744 GENTLEMEN, The evils which we have long foreseen are now come upon this town and province . . . June 8, 1774. [Boston, 1774]
[2] p.
Ford 1708; cf. Evans 13157
NN mp. 42606

B3745 GEORGIA. GOVERNOR, 1772-1776
Georgia. By His Excellency Sir James Wright . . . Governor, and Commander in Chief . . . of Georgia . . . a proclamation. Whereas I have received information that a certain Indian, named . . . the Mad Turkey . . . was . . . murdered . . . [23 lines] Given under my hand . . . [Mar. 28, 1774] . . . Ja. Wright . . . [Savannah, J. Johnston, 1774]
broadside 30 X 20.5 cm.
McMurtrie: Georgia 15
Public Record Off. mp. 42608

B3746 GEORGIA. GOVERNOR, 1772-1776
Georgia. By His Excellency Sir James Wright . . . Governor, and Commander in Chief . . . of Georgia . . . a proclamation. [18 lines] Given under my hand . . . [Aug. 5, 1774] Ja. Wright . . . [Savannah, James Johnston, 1774]
broadside 31 X 21.5 cm.
Declares the proposed August 10 meeting illegal
McMurtrie: Georgia 21
Public Record Off. (2 copies) mp. 42607

B3747 THE Georgia and South-Carolina almanack, for . . . 1775 . . . By John Tobler . . . Charleston: Printed for the Editor. Sold in Georgia, by James Johnston . . . in Savannah. Sold in South-Carolina, by Robert Wells . . . in Charleston [1774]
[32] p. 17 cm.
Guerra b-361
MWA mp. 42723

B3748 [GODDARD, WILLIAM] 1739-1817
The plan for establishing a new American post-office. [Boston? 1774]
broadside 51.5 X 40 cm.
Huntington 350
CSmH; RPJCB mp. 42609

B3749 GT. BRIT. ADJUTANT GENERAL
The manual exercise as ordered by His Majesty in 1764 . . . Boston, New-England: Printed by T. and J. Fleet, at the Heart and Crown in Cornhill. [1774]
39, [1] p. fold. plate. 21.5 cm.
Page [1] at end: "A method of sizing a company."
Page 39 ends with "finis."
Stanley 73
MH

B3750 GT. BRIT. ADJUTANT GENERAL
The manual exercise as ordered by His Majesty in 1764 . . . Boston: Printed by T. and J. Fleet, at the Heart and Crown in Cornhill. [1774]
39 p. fold. plate. 21.5 cm.
On verso of t.p.: "In Provincial Congress, at Cambridge, October 29, 1774."
Stanley 72
MH

B3751 GT. BRIT. ADJUTANT-GENERAL
The manual exercise, as ordered by His Majesty, in the year MDCCLXIV . . . Norwich, J. P. Spooner [1774]
31 p. 8vo
Huntington 351; cf. Evans 13322
CSmH mp. 42621

B3752 GT. BRIT. ADJUTANT-GENERAL
The manual exercise, as ordered by His Majesty in MDCCLXIV. Now adopted in Connecticut, Rhode-Island . . . Norwich, Robertsons and Trumbull [1774]
23 p. 19 cm. A-C[4]
CtHi (final leaf photostat); MWA mp. 42620

B3753 GT. BRIT. LAWS
Act for blocking up the harbour of Boston . . . An act to discontinue, in such manner, for such time as is therein mentioned, the landing and discharging . . . of goods . . . [Newport, S. Southwick, 1774]
broadside 35 X 20.5 cm.
Published as supplement to no. 822 or 823 of the *Newport Mercury*
MiU-C mp. 42610

B3754 GT. BRIT. LAWS
An act to block up Boston Harbour . . . [Boston] Sold at the Printing-Office in School-street [1774]
broadside 37.5 X 24 cm.
Ford 1733
MHi; NHi mp. 42611

B3755 GT. BRIT. LAWS
An act to block up the harbour of Boston . . . [Boston] Sold at the printing-office, near the Court-House [1774]
broadside 41.5 X 26.5 cm.
Huntington 352
CSmH mp. 42612

B3756 GT. BRIT. LAWS
The Boston Port Bill, together with Governor Johnsone's speech in the House of Commons on the same . . . [Boston? 1774]
[2] p.
Ford 1731
MHi mp. 42613

B3757 GT. BRIT. LAWS
The following is the act of Parliament, assented to . . . on the 30th of March, 1774. . . . Williamsburg, Clementina Rind [1774]
broadside ([2] p.) 32.5 X 25 cm.
DLC; ViW mp. 42614

B3758 GT. BRIT. PRIVY COUNCIL
Proceedings of his Majesty's Privy-Council on the address of the Assembly of Massachusetts-Bay, to remove his Governor . . . with the substance of Mr. Wedderburn's speech relative to said address . . . [Boston] Sold at the Printing-Office in School-street [1774?]
4 p.
Ford 1727
MHi mp. 42618

B3759 THE happy child . . . [Colophon] Boston, Sold at the Heart & Crown in Cornhill [by T. and J. Fleet, 1774?]
[8] p. 10.5 cm. caption title
In verse
New York Public 523; Rosenbach-Ch 78
PP. d'Alté A. Welch, Cleveland (1962). Photostat: NN mp. 42619

B3760 HAWKESWORTH, JOHN, 1715?-1773.
A new voyage, round the world . . . performed by, Captain James Cook . . . drawn up from his own journal, and from the papers of Joseph Banks . . . Vol. I. [-II.] New-York: Printed for William Aikman . . . at Annapolis, 1774.
2 v. fronts., fold. map. 19.5 cm.
Lehman-Haupt: *Book in America* p. 54; cf. Evans 13324 for an edition with differing imprint
DGU (v. 2); DLC; MWA; RPJCB mp. 42622

B3761 HERVEY, JAMES, 1714-1758
Contemplations on the night . . . The thirty-third edition. New York, James Rivington, 1774.
6, vii-viii, 75, [1] p. 16 cm.
DLC; MWA; NN; PHi mp. 42623

B3762 HERVEY, JAMES, 1714-1758
Meditations among the tombs . . . The thirty third edition. [New York?] Printed by James Rivington and sold by Henry Knox and James Lockwood, 1774.
72 p. 16 cm.
MiU-C; NBuG; NN mp. 42624

B3763 THE history of the Holy Jesus . . . By a lover of their precious souls. The twenty-fifth edition. Boston, Printed and sold by John Boyle, 1774.
[44] p. illus., port. 10 cm.
Hamilton 68; Rosenbach-Ch 79
CSmH; DLC (2 copies); ICN; MB; MWA; NjP; PP. d'Alté A. Welch, Cleveland (1962) mp. 42625

B3764 HOLLY, ISRAEL
A second letter to Mr. Isaac Backus, upon the controversy concerning the subjects of baptism . . . with a remark

upon Mr. Winchell's piece . . . Hartford, Eben. Watson, 1774.
51 p. 19.5 cm.
Trumbull: Supplement 2264
CtHi; MWA (t.p. wanting, and all after sig. F3); RPJCB
mp. 42626

B3765 HUMPHREYS, JAMES, 3d
Hymns and spiritual songs on the principal doctrines of the Gospel of Jesus. Boston, J. Kneeland, 1774.
32 p. 17 cm.
RPB
mp. 42627

B3766 HUMPHREYS, JAMES, 1748-1810
Philadelphia, 1774. Just published, and to be sold, by James Humphreys . . . The search after happiness . . . by Miss Hannah More . . . [Philadelphia, J. Humphreys, 1774]
broadside fol.
PPL
mp. 42629

B3767 HUMPHREYS, JAMES, 1748-1810
Philadelphia, April 22, 1774. Just published, and ready to be delivered to the subscribers by James Humphreys, junior . . . The first volume of Sterne's Works . . . [Philadelphia, J. Humphreys, 1774]
broadside 42.5 X 26.5 cm.
Offered (1962) by Richard Wormser, Bethel, Conn. (cat. 259)
No copy located
mp. 42628

B3768 IN memory of Capt. John Crawford, of Providence, who sailed . . . December 11, 1746, and was lost at sea. Aetat. 28. . . . In memory also of Abijah Crawford, his wife . . . She departed this life September 23, 1774. Aetat. 55 . . . [Providence, 1774?]
broadside 30 X 23 cm.
Alden 533; Winship Addenda p. 95
MWA (photostat); RHi
mp. 42630

B3769 KAST, PHILIP GODFRID
Drugs and medicines. Philip Godfrid Kast takes the pleasure to acquaint his friends . . . that he . . . is now opening at his Apothecary Store . . . in King-Street, Salem . . . [Salem? 1774?]
broadside 25 X 20 cm.
Ford 1739; Guerra a-349; Tapley p. 315
MSaE
mp. 42631

B3770 THE Lancaster almanack, (improved) being a prognosticator, for the year . . . 1775 . . . A Country-man. Lancaster, Printed and sold by Stewart Herbert [1774]
[18] p. illus. 18 cm.
Bausman p. 12
PHi
mp. 42632

B3771 LORD North's soliloquy. A plague take that Boston port act . . . New-York, John Anderson [1774]
broadside 32.5 X 28 cm.
New York Public 526
NHi. Photostats: MHi; NN
mp. 42633

B3772 LOUDON, SAMUEL, 1727?-1813
This day is published. At Samuel Loudon's . . . a new book, printed and sold by R. Aitken . . . Essay on the Character . . . of women . . . from the French of Mr. Thomas . . . [New York, S. Loudon, 1774]
broadside 28 X 20.5 cm.
cf. Evans 13650
RPJCB
mp. 42634

B3773 MARINE SOCIETY, BOSTON, MASS.
Laws of the Marine Society, at Boston in New-England, incorporated . . . February 2, 1754. [Boston, 1774]
[2] p. 38 X 31.5 cm.
On verso: List of the members' names, and the time of entrance
Dated 1774 by MHi
Ford 986
MHi
mp. 42635

B3774 MARYLAND
At a meeting of the deputies appointed by the several counties . . . on the 8th day of December, 1774 . . . [Annapolis, Anne Catharine Green, 1774]
[2] p. 35.5 X 23 cm. [With Maryland. Convention. Proceedings, June 22, 1774-27 July 1775]
Wroth 329
DLC; MdHi
mp. 42547

B3774a [MASON, JOHN] 1646-1694
Spiritual songs . . . Sixteenth edition corrected. Boston, Printed and sold by T. & J. Fleet, 1774.
2 p.l., 124 p.
NBuG

B3775 MASSACHUSETTS
Province of Massachusetts-Bay. In observance of His Majesty's writ to me directed . . . freeholders . . . to assemble . . . to elect . . . to serve . . . General Court . . . Given . . . at *Worcester* the *12th* day of *September* . . . 1774 . . . Sheriff of the County of *Worcester*. [Boston, 1774]
broadside
Italicized portions in manuscript
MBAt
mp. 42636

B3776 MASSACHUSETTS GAZETTE
Supplement to the *Massachusetts Gazette* . . . [Boston, 1774?]
broadside 21 X 13 cm.
Ford 1783
PHi. Photostat: MWA
mp. 42647

B3777 MASSACHUSETTS GAZETTE
Supplement to the *Massachusetts Gazette, and Boston Post-Boy*. Monday, May 16, 1774 . . . [Boston] Mills and Hicks [1774]
[2] p. 35 X 26.5 cm.
The Boston Port Bill
MWA; PHi
mp. 42616

B3778 THE mathematicians glory of astronomy and New-England almanack for . . . 1774. [n.p.] Printed for the author, 1774.
[22] p. 17.5 cm.
By Elisha Stimson
MWA
mp. 42709

B3779 MATHER, ALLYN, 1747-1784
The blessedness of the saints described. A sermon, delivered at Fairhaven Meeting-House, in New-Haven . . . Succeeding the decease of Mrs. Esther Potter . . . December 21, 1773, in the LXIVth year of her age . . . By Allyn Mather . . . New-Haven, T. and S. Green [1774?]
17 p.
Trumbull: Supplement 2391
CtHi
mp. 42637

B3780 [MORISON, JAMES] OF NORHAM, ENG.
An attempt to vindicate, explain and enforce the important duty . . . Lancaster, Francis Bailey, 1774.
vii, [1], 222 p. 16.5 cm.
Prefatory letter signed: James Morison
MiU-C; PPL
mp. 42638

B3781 A NARRATIVE of the late disturbances at Marblehead. [Salem, Samuel and Ebenezer Hall, 1774]
[4] p. 39 cm.
Statement issued May 2, 1774 relative to the Essex Hospital
Ford 1769; Tapley p. 316
DLC; MHi; MSaE mp. 42639

B3782 NEW BERN, N. C. CITIZENS
Newbern, August 9, 1774. To the freeholders of Craven County. Gentlemen, This day . . . the inhabitants of Newbern met at the Court-House . . . [Newbern, James Davis, 1774]
broadside 14 X 14 cm. (lower portion cut away)
Among the 9 names printed at the end, that of James Davis is first
McMurtrie: North Carolina 72
Public Record Off. mp. 42657

B3783 NEW HAMPSHIRE
Province of New-Hampshire. To the selectmen of the Gentlemen, as we were appointed . . . there should be a convention of deputies . . . held at Exeter, the 17th day of May next . . . [Portsmouth, 1774]
broadside 22.5 X 14 cm.
DLC mp. 42641

B3784 NEW HAMPSHIRE
Whereas the American Continental Congress have recommended another . . . Nov. 30, 1774 . . . J. Wentworth, Chairman. [Portsmouth? 1774]
broadside 21 X 17 cm.
Towns to appoint deputies to meet at Exeter Jan. 25, 1775
Whittemore 170
NHi; NhD; NhHi mp. 42643

B3785 NEW HAMPSHIRE
Whereas the colonies in general, upon this continent . . . [Portsmouth? 1774]
broadside 34 X 21.5 cm.
Concerns subscriptions to send delegates to a general Congress
Whittemore 171
MWA; NhHi mp. 42644

B3786 NEW HAMPSHIRE. GOVERNOR, 1767-1775
Province of New Hampshire. A proclamation, by the Governor. Whereas several bodies of men did, in the day time of the 14th . . . attack . . . His Majesty's Castle . . . [Portsmouth, 1774]
broadside 40 X 30 cm.
Dated Dec. 26, 1774
New York Public 527; Whittemore 167
PPRF. Photostats: NN; NhHi mp. 42642

B3787 Deleted

B3788 NEW HAVEN. SELECTMEN
New-Haven, March 11, 1774. At a meeting of the select-men . . . [New Haven, 1774]
broadside 24 X 16.5 cm.
NHi. Photostats: DLC; MH; MHi; NN; WHi mp. 42645

B3789 NEW JERSEY. GOVERNOR, 1763-1776
Burlington, June 25, 1774. Sir, I have it in command . . . that you cause to be taken . . . an account of the number of births and burials . . . from the 1st day of July 1773 to the 1st day of July 1774 . . . [Burlington, I. Collins, 1774]
broadside 33.5 X 21 cm.
DLC mp. 42646

B3790 NEW YORK. COMMITTEE OF CORRESPONDENCE
New-York, July 29, 1774. Gentlemen, We should have answered your letter sooner . . . By order of the committee, Isaac Low, chairman. [New York, 1774]
broadside 24.5 X 20.5 cm.
New York Public 530
NN mp. 42648

B3791 NEW YORK. COMMITTEE OF CORRESPONDENCE
New-York, Aug. 9, 1774. Gentlemen, The distresses of the poor . . . of Boston . . . call aloud for our . . . compassionate concern . . . By order of the committee, Isaac Low, chairman. [New York, 1774]
broadside 25 X 20.5 cm.
New York Public 531
NN mp. 42649

B3792 NEW YORK. COMMITTEE OF CORRESPONDENCE
Notice. The committee appointed in New-York to correspond with the sister colonies . . . are desired to meet . . . on this day . . . New-York, 23 July, 1774. [New York, 1774]
broadside 7.5 X 20 cm.
NHi mp. 42650

B3793 NEW YORK. COMMITTEE OF CORRESPONDENCE
To the inhabitants of the city and county of New-York. My friends and fellow citizens . . . fifty-one gentlemen were by this city appointed, to be a Committee, to correspond with the committees of our sister-colonies . . . An American. July 5, 1774. [New York, 1774]
broadside 34.5 X 22.5 cm.
NNS. Photostat: MWA mp. 42651

B3794 NEW YORK. ELECTION PROX.
To the inhabitants of the City and County of New-York; My friends and fellow-citizens . . . [New York, 1774]
broadside 35.5 X 22.5 cm.
Supporting the election of Isaac Low, John Alsop, John Jay, and others
Dated July 5, 1774
NHi mp. 42652

B3795 NEW-YORK, September 28, 1774. To the public. An application having been made to the merchants of Philadelphia, by the agents of the British Ministry for supplying the troops now in . . . Boston . . . [New York, 1774]
broadside 21 X 20 cm.
Expressing strong opposition
NHi mp. 42656

B3796 NEW-YORK, November 13, 1774. The mechanicks of this city, are earnestly requested to meet at five o'clock in the afternoon . . . [New York, 1774]
broadside 11 X 15.5 cm.
NHi mp. 42653

B3797 NORTH CAROLINA. GOVERNOR, 1771-1776
Advertisement. Whereas it appears that many persons . . . . . Newbern, May 3, 1774. Jo. Martin. [Newbern, James Davis, 1774]
broadside 22 X 19 cm.
NcU mp. 42658

B3798 NORTH CAROLINA. HOUSE OF ASSEMBLY
[The journal of the House of Assembly. Mar. 2-Mar. 25, 1774. Newbern, James Davis, 1774]

49 p. 31.5 cm.
No imprint at end
McMurtrie: North Carolina 73
NcWsM (p. 21-49 only) mp. 42659

B3799 NOW ready for the press, and to be printed by subscription . . . the Deputy commissary's guide within the province of Maryland . . . By Elie Vallette . ... [Annapolis, Anne Catharine Green, 1774]
broadside 18.5 X 15.5 cm.
Wroth 339
MdHi mp. 42737

B3800 PEMBROKE, MASS.
A list of the training soldiers jn the first military foot companey jn pembrke under the command of captain seth hatch, taken october ye 17, ad 1774 . . . [Pembroke, Mass., 1774]
[3] p. fol.
Apparently locally and crudely printed, with a single size type
PPL mp. 42662

B3801 PENNSYLVANIA. CONVENTION, 1774
Resolutions . . . July 15, 1774 . . . [Philadelphia, 1774]
8, [v-vi], 9-126 p. 21 cm. caption title
DLC mp. 42663

B3802 PENNSYLVANIA. LAWS
An act for preventing tumults . . . January 22, 1774. [Philadelphia, 1774]
broadside 41.5 X 24 cm.
DLC (photostat) mp. 42664

B3803 PENNSYLVANIA PACKET
From the *Pennsylvania Packet*. Philadelphia, October 3. Extract of a letter from a gentleman in Bristol, to his friend in this city, dated July 20, 1774 . . . [Philadelphia, 1774]
broadside 32 X 19.5 cm.
MWA mp. 42604

B3804 PHILADELPHIA. CITIZENS
At a very large and respectable meeting of the freeholders and freemen of the city and county of Philadelphia, on Saturday, June 18, 1774. Thomas Willing, John Dickinson, esquires, chairmen . . . [Philadelphia, 1774]
broadside 23.5 X 21.5 cm.
6 resolutions adopted in sympathy with Boston
PHi mp. 42666

B3805 PHILADELPHIA. ELECTION PROX.
Committee. 1 John Dickinson. 2 Thomas Mifflin . . . [Philadelphia, 1774]
broadside 8vo
PPL mp. 42667

B3806 PHILADELPHIA. ELECTION PROX.
Committee. 1 Thomas Mifflin. 2 Robert Morris . . . [Philadelphia, 1774]
broadside 8vo
PPL mp. 42668

B3807 PHILADELPHIA, May 4. (Reprinted in New-York.) Yesterday, about 3 o'clock in the afternoon, the effigies of Alexander Wedderbourne . . . [New York, 1774]
broadside 31 X 19 cm.
NHi mp. 42669

B3808 PHILADELPHIA, (Saturday) June 18, 1774. The inhabitants of the city and county qualified by law to vote for representatives, are desired to attend . . . the State-House . . . this afternoon . . . [Philadelphia, 1774]
broadside 19 X 8 cm.
PHi mp. 42670

B3809 PICKERING, TIMOTHY, 1745-1829
Salem, September 27th, 1774. To the freeholders of the County of Essex. Gentlemen, Colonel Higginson . . . being dead . . . I am, Gentlemen, Your humble servant, *Tim. Pickering jun.* [Salem, 1774]
broadside 25 X 20 cm.
Signature handwritten
MHi

B3810 PITT, WILLIAM, 1707-1778
The speech of . . . the Earl of Chatham . . . on Friday, the 17th June, 1774. [Boston, 1774]
[2] p. 39 X 26 cm.
Ford 1771; New York Public 532
DLC; NN. Photostat: MHi mp. 42671

B3811 THE plan for establishing a new American post-office . . . 1. That subscriptions be opened . . . 2. That the subscribers, in each Colony . . . 8. That whatever balances remain . . . enlargement of the present institution within their respective provinces . . . We the subscribers . . . promise to pay the several sums annexed to our names . . . Boston, April 30, 1774. [Boston, 1774]
broadside 24.5 X 38 cm.
MHi mp. 42672

B3812 A POEM, occasioned by the sudden and surprising death of Mr. Asa Burt . . . the 28th of January, 1774, in the 37th year of his age . . . Sold at the Printing-Office in Hartford [1774]
broadside 33 X 20.5 cm.
CtHi mp. 42673

B3813 PORTSMOUTH, N. H. COMMITTEE OF CORRESPONDENCE
Gentlemen, we presume you are not unacquainted with the very alarming situation . . . Signed by order, and in behalf of the Committee of Correspondence for Portsmouth. [Portsmouth, 1774]
broadside 31 X 22 cm.
Concerns aid for the inhabitants of Boston
Whittemore 173
NhHi mp. 42674

B3814 THE potent enemies of America laid open . . . Philadelphia, Joseph Crukshank [1774]
1 p. l., 48, 83 p. 16 cm.
Second title
[Benezet, Anthony] 1713-1784
The mighty destroyer displayed . . . Philadelphia, J. Crukshank, 1774.
Third title
Wesley, John, 1703-1791
Thoughts upon slavery . . . Philadelphia, J. Crukshank, 1774.
Huntington 356; cf. Evans 13146
CSmH; DLC; ICN mp. 42675

B3815 PROVIDENCE GAZETTE
Supplement to the *Providence Gazette*. No. 565. List of the fortunate numbers in the second class of the Baptist Meeting-House lottery . . . [Providence, 1774]
broadside 38.5 X 24.5 cm.
RPJCB. Photostat: MWA mp. 42550

B3816 PTOLOMY, PSEUD.
The new and true Egyptian fortune-teller; discovering to young men, maids and widows, their good or bad fortunes

. . . [Boston] Sold [by John Boyle?] at the Printing-Office in Marlborough Street, MDCCLXXIV.
23 p. 17.5 cm.
MB mp. 42640

B3817 [PUTNAM, ARCHELAUS] 1743-1800
To the public. The dispute that has lately arisen . . . [and] To the public. When I wrote my last address I designed not again to solicit the attention . . . A Lover of Truth . . . Salem, April 9th, 1774. [Salem, 1774]
[2] p. 36 cm.
Ford 1774; Guerra a-556; Tapley p. 317
MWA mp. 42676

B3818 [RANDOLPH, JOHN] 1727-1784, supposed author
Considerations on the present state of Virginia. [Williamsburg] 1774.
24 p. 20.5 cm. [A]-C^4
Adams 133; New York Public 533; Torrence 409
NHi; NN; NjP; PPAmP. Public Record Off.
Photostats: MHi; MWA mp. 42677

B3819 Deleted

B3820 REFLECTIONS of a saint, under a view of the presence of an . . . all-seeing God. Norwich, Printed and sold by Green & Spooner [1774?]
8 p.
Inscription dated 1776
Trumbull: Second supplement 2880
MWA mp. 42678

B3821 REFORMED CHURCH IN THE U.S.
A collection of the psalm and hymn tunes, used by the Reformed Protestant Dutch Church . . . of New-York . . . New-York, Hodge and Shober, 1774.
1 p.l., [5], 54, [2] p. 19 cm.
Opposite pages numbered in duplicate: p. 1-54
Huntington 345
CSmH; NHi mp. 42679

B3822 REMARKS, &c. on some late laws passed in New-York . . . for . . . apprehending and imprisoning . . . Ethan Allen, Seth Warner, Remember Baker . . . Dated at Bennington, April 15th, 1774 . . . [n.p., 1774]
broadside 39 X 32 cm.
MHi (photostat) mp. 42680

B3823 RHODE ISLAND
We, a part of the electors . . . of Rhode-Island . . . will not vote for a Tory . . . [Providence? 1774]
broadside 32 X 21 cm.
Alden 546; Winship p. 31
RHi mp. 42684

B3824 RHODE ISLAND. ELECTION PROX.
Colony of Rhode-Island, 1774. The honorable Joseph Wanton, Esq; Gov. The honorable Darius Sessions, Esq; Deputy-Gov. . . . [Newport? 1774]
broadside 20.5 X 13 cm.
Alden 547; Chapin Proxies 12
RHi mp. 42681

B3825 RHODE ISLAND. ELECTION PROX.
For the privilege of trials by juries; no demurs . . . The honorable Darius Sessions, Esq; Deputy-Gov. . . . [Providence? 1774]
broadside 10 X 13 cm.
Alden 548; Chapin Proxies 11
RHi; RPJCB mp. 42682

B3826 RHODE ISLAND. ELECTION PROX.
The honorable Joseph Wanton, Esq; Gov. The honorable Darius Sessions, Esq; Dept. Gov . . . [Newport? S. Southwick? 1774]
broadside 19 X 11.5 cm.
Alden 549
RHi mp. 42683

B3827 RHODE ISLAND. GOVERNOR, 1769–1775
[A proclamation for apprehending Daniel Wilson . . . Providence, J. Carter, 1774]
[broadside?]
Bill for printing submitted Apr. 16, 1774 by Carter
Alden 551
No copy known; description conjectured mp. 42685

B3828 RHODE ISLAND. LAWS
[At the General assembly . . . holden . . . on the first Wednesday in May . . . It is voted and resolved, that the number of families and persons in the colony be taken . . . Newport, S. Southwick, 1774]
[broadside?]
Bill submitted for printing May 10, 1774
No copy known; description conjectured from the Schedules for the May 1774 session mp. 42688

B3829 RHODE ISLAND. LAWS
At the General assembly . . . holden . . . on the last Wednesday in October . . . An act for assessing . . . a rate or tax of four thousand pounds . . . [Newport, S. Southwick, 1774]
3 p. 33 cm.
Bill submitted Nov. 3, 1774
Alden 558
RHi. Photostat: MHi mp. 42686

B3830 RHODE ISLAND. LAWS
At the General assembly . . . holden . . . on the first Monday in December . . . Whereas the Hon. Stephen Hopkins . . . [Newport, S. Southwick, 1774]
broadside 31 X 19 cm.
Bill submitted by Southwick Dec. 26, 1774
Alden 559; Winship p. 31
MWA; RHi; RPB mp. 42687

B3831 DIE Richtigkeit der Welt und des zeitlichen Lebens . . . Kurtzlich beschrieben von einem Englischen Autor, und ins Teutsche übersetzt. Germanton, Christoph Saur, 1774.
30 p. 18 cm.
Metzger 408
P mp. 42689

B3832 RIVINGTON, JAMES, 1724–1802
Whosoever would purchase the English edition of the . . . voyage . . . by Captain Cook . . . must give three guineas . . . which excessive price has engaged James Rivington's proposing . . . a complete edition of that work . . . [New York, J. Rivington, 1774]
broadside 32 X 19 cm.
Dated at end: Mar. 16, 1774
RPJCB mp. 42690

B3833 RIVINGTON'S NEW-YORK GAZETTEER
Ode on the New Year 1774. Delivered by Hugh Duncan, one of the carriers of *Rivington's New-York Gazetteer.* [New York, J. Rivington, 1774]
broadside 30 X 17 cm.
New York Public 534
NN mp. 42661

B3834 ROBIN HOOD SOCIETY, N.Y.
Debates at the Robin-Hood Society, in . . . New-York, on Monday night 19th of July, 1774. New-York: Printed [by John Holt] by order of the Robin-Hood Society. [1774]
14 p. 20 cm.
Ends on p. 14; text set differently from Evans 13486 except last page
NHi mp. 42691

B3835 ROBINSON, NATHANIEL
Verses composed by Nathaniel Robinson, when he was in Albany goal, in the year 1758. The third edition. Norwich: Printed and sold by Green & Spooner, 1774.
30+ p. 16.5 cm.
NBuG (mutilated, wanting after p. 30)

B3836 RUSH, BENJAMIN, 1745-1813
A syllabus of a course of lectures on chemistry . . . Philadelphia, Printed for, and sold by R. Aitken [1774]
40 p. fold. table. 17.5 cm. $A-C^6 D^2$
cf. p. 15 of the introd. to the 1954 facsim. reprint of his Syllabus (1770 ed.)
PU mp. 42692

B3837 [RUSH, JACOB]
Copy of the commission of Jared Ingersoll, Esq; Judge of the High Court of Admiralty at Philadelphia. Also, A letter directed to the said Judge. [Philadelphia, William and Thomas Bradford, 1774]
broadside fol.
Signed: Russel
PPL

B3838 SALEM. COMMITTEE OF CORRESPONDENCE
The Committee of Correspondence desire the merchants, freeholders and other inhabitants . . . to meet . . . to appoint five or more deputies, to meet at Ipswich . . . Salem, August 19, 1774. [Salem, 1774]
broadside 16.5 X 13.5 cm.
Ford 1775?
MHi

B3839 SALEM. SELECTMEN
Salem, September 27th, 1774. To the freeholders of the County of Essex. Gentlemen, As by the death of Colonel Higginson, a vacancy has taken place . . . Capt. Timothy Pickering, jun. . . . will . . . have the votes of the freeholders . . . Selectmen of the Town of Salem: Committee of Correspondence for the Town of Salem. [Salem, 1774]
broadside 27 X 20 cm.
MHi

B3840 SAVANNAH. CONVENTION
The critical situation to which the British Colonies in America are likely to be reduced, from the alarming . . . imposition of the late acts of the British Parliament respecting . . . Boston . . . It is therefore requested, That all persons . . . attend at Savannah . . . the 27th instant . . . Savannah, July 14, 1774. [Savannah, 1774]
broadside 29.5 X 16.5 cm.
McMurtrie: Georgia 16
Public Record Off. mp. 42694

B3841 SAVANNAH. CONVENTION
Resolutions entered into at Savannah in Georgia . . . the 10th day of August, 1774, at a general meeting of the inhabitants . . . [Savannah, James Johnston, 1774]
broadside 30.5 X 17 cm.
Printed from the same setting of type in the *Georgia Gazette*, Aug. 17, 1774
McMurtrie: Georgia 22
Public Record Off. mp. 42695

B3842 SAY, THOMAS, 1709-1796
The visions of a certain Tho. Say, of the City of Philadelphia, which he saw in a trance. Philadelphia: Printed and sold by William Mentz [1774]
8 p. 8vo
cf. Evans 13598
PHi

B3843 [SCOTT, SARAH (ROBINSON)] 1723-1795
The man of real sensibility . . . Philadelphia, James Humphreys, Junr., 1774.
2 p.l., [3]-84, [1] p. 17.5 cm.
Hildeburn 3102; Huntington 358; Sabin 78356
CSmH; DLC; MWA; MiU-C; PHi; PPAmP; RPJCB
mp. 42696

B3844 [SEABURY, SAMUEL] 1729-1796
Free thoughts, on the proceedings of the Continental Congress . . . Sept. 5, 1774 . . . [New York] Printed [by James Rivington] in the year M,DCC,LXXIV.
29 [i.e. 31] p. 18 cm. $[A]-D^4$
Adams 136a; Huntington 359
CSmH; CtHt-W; DLC; MH; MHi; ViU

B3845 [SEABURY, SAMUEL] 1729-1796
Free thoughts, on the proceedings of the Continental Congress . . . Sept. 5, 1774 . . . [New York] Printed [by James Rivington] in the year M.DCC.LXXIV.
31 p. 18 cm. $[A]-D^4$
Adams 136b
MBAt; MWA mp. 42697

B3846 [A SERMON on tea. Charleston, S.C., C. Crouch, 1774]

Advertised in the *South Carolina Gazette*, Aug. 30, 1774, as "now in the press and speedily will be published;" and Sept. 13, 1774, as "just published at C. Crouch's Printing Office."
No copy known mp. 42698

B3847 SHIPLEY, JONATHAN, 1714-1788
A speech intended to have been spoken on the bill of altering the charters . . . of Massachusetts Bay . . . Williamsburg, John Pinkney, 1774.
15 p. 22 cm. $[A]-B^4$
Adams 141o; Huntington 361
CSmH; RPJCB mp. 42699

B3848 THE silver-key. Or, A fancy of truth, and a warning to youth. Shewing the benefits of money, and the contempt of the poor . . . From your servant, poor George Beverstock. Boston: Printed and sold in Milk-Street [1774?]
broadside 21.5 X 34 cm.
2 columns of verse
CSmH

B3849 THE silver-key. Or, A fancy of truth, and a warning to youth. Shewing the benefits of money, and the contempt of the poor . . . From your servant, poor George Beverstock. Printed and sold in New-London [1774?]
broadside 32 X 23 cm.
3 columns of verse.
CtHi

B3850 [THE singular and very affecting case of the Marquis d'Aubarede . . . Williamsburg, Purdie & Dixon, 1774]

Advertised in Purdie & Dixon's *Virginia Gazette*, June 2, 1774, as "Just published."
No copy known

B3851 SINNERS invited to come to Jesus . . . Boston, Printed and sold in Milk-Street [by John Kneeland] 1774.
broadside 30.5 X 17.5 cm.
Ford 1776
PHi' mp. 42700

B3852 SINNERS invited to come to Jesus . . . Providence: Printed and sold at the Paper-Mills [John Waterman] [1774]
broadside 36 X 23 cm.
Probably printed after the opening of Waterman's second paper mill in 1773
Alden 563; New York Public 535
RHi. Photostats: MWA; NN mp. 42701

B3853 SMITH, JOSIAH, 1704–1781
St. Paul's victory and triumph . . . Charlestown [S.C.], Printed for the authour by Robert Wells, 1774.
73 p. 17.5 cm. [A]-I⁴ [ ]²
MWA mp. 42701a

B3854 SMITH, WILLIAM, 1728–1793
An examination of the Connecticut claim to lands in Pennsylvania. With an appendix, containing extracts and copies taken from original sources. Philadelphia, Joseph Crukshank, 1774.
[2], 93, 32 p. fold. map. 8vo
Sabin 84604; Vail: Old frontier 633; cf. Evans 13629 (which collates [2], 94, 32 p.)
DLC; NHi; PPL; RPJCB; WHi mp. 42702

B3855 SOCIAL FIRE COMPANY, SALEM, MASS.
Articles agreed to be observed by the Social Fire Company, in Salem. Associated October 21, 1774 . . . Salem, S. and E. Hall [1774?]
7 p.
Contains list of members
Tapley p. 318
MSaE mp. 42693

B3856 SOUTH CAROLINA
Charles-town, November 10th, 1774. Gentlemen, The delegates, who were sent by this province to the . . . Congress at Philadelphia, being returned, we take the earliest opportunity of transmitting to you . . . [Charleston, 1774]
2 leaves, [2], 8 p. 21.5 cm. caption title
PPRF mp. 42703

B3857 THE South-Carolina almanack . . . for . . . 1775 . . . Charles-Town, Charles Crouch [1774]
[24] p. 18.5 cm.
By Benjamin West
MWA mp. 42750

B3858 STACKHOUSE, THOMAS, 1677–1752
. . . Lehrbegriff der ganzen christlichen Religion . . . Aus der engländischen Sprache übersetzet . . . von Friedrich Eberhard Rambach . . . Philadelphia, Ernst Ludwig Baisch, 1774.
7 v. 20 cm.
MWA (v. 1, 3, 5–6 only); N (v. 2 only) mp. 42704

B3859 STEDMAN, STEIGEL AND CO.
There are likewise to be sold by Stedman Steigel and Company, several valuable tracts of land . . . Lancaster, Francis Bailey [1774]
broadside 20.5 X 19 cm.
Metzger 393
PHi mp. 42705

B3860 STERNE, LAURENCE, 1713-1768
The works of Laurence Sterne . . . With the life of the author. In six volumes. . . . Philadelphia, Re-printed; by James Humphreys, 1774.
6 v. 17 cm.
cf. Huntington 363
MWA (v. 1–5 only) mp. 42706

B3861 STICKNEY, JOHN, 1742–1826
The gentleman and lady's musical companion . . . Newbury-Port, Daniel Bayley; sold also by John Boyle, Henry Knox, John Langdon, Nicholas Bowes, Thomas Leverett, and Cox and Berry in Boston, Mascoll Williams in Salem, Smith and Coit in Hartford, 1774.
12, 212 p. sm. obl. 4to
[21] p. ms. music at end
Huntington 364; cf. Evans 13642
CSmH; MHi mp. 42707

B3862 [STILES, EZRA] 1727–1795
To the candid public. In Hartford and New-Haven papers . . . New-London, Timothy Green, 1774.
broadside 38.5 X 25 cm.
Trumbull 1420
DLC; MHi mp. 42708

B3863 SUBSCRIPTION paper for the Deputy commissary's guide. [Annapolis, Anne Catharine Green, 1774]
broadside 36.5 X 31 cm.
Wroth 340
MdHi mp. 42738

B3864 [SWEFT, JIRAH]
Infant baptism, considered in a letter, 1773 . . . Newport, S. Southwick, 1774.
16 p. 18.5 cm.
Alden 565
CtY; DLC; MHi; RHi mp. 42710

B3865 THOMAS'S Boston almanac, for the year . . . 1775. Boston, Isaiah Thomas [1774]
broadside
Ford 1777
MWA mp. 42711

B3866 TO the freeholders and gentlemen, of Baltimore County. Gentlemen, On Tuesday last we received . . . a letter from the Committee of Correspondence at Philadelphia . . . May 27, 1774. Baltimore, Enoch Story [1774]
broadside 35.5 X 21 cm.
New York Public 516
MdHi. Photostat: NN mp. 42549

B3867 TO the gentlemen, freeholders and others in the County of New Castle, upon Delaware . . . [Rehearsing grievances and calling a meeting to procure relief for Boston] . . . A Freeman. [Wilmington, J. Adams, 1774]
broadside?
Hawkins: List C 6; Scharf: *History of Delaware* 1:216
No copy known mp. 42712

B3868 TO the inhabitants of the City and County of New-York. Gentlemen, The five deputies nominated by the Committee of Correspondence . . . not being all approved of . . . [New York, 1774]
broadside 14 X 17 cm.
Dated July 7, 1774
NHi mp. 42713

B3869 Deleted

B3870 TO the printer. [6 lines, quotations] Sir, It was a custom among the Lacedemonians . . . [Savannah, James Johnston, 1774]
broadside 34.5 X 22 cm.
Found following the Aug. 24, 1774, issue of the *Georgia Gazette*
McMurtrie: Georgia 23
GHi mp. 42714

B3871 TO the public. An advertisement having appeared at the Coffee-House . . . alarming advices . . . from England . . . the merchants to meet at the house of Mr. Samuel Francis . . . New-York, Wednesday, May 18, 1774. To the public. The mechanicks . . . requested to meet this afternoon . . . [New York, 1774]
broadside 19.5 X 14.5 cm.
DLC mp. 42654

B3872 TO the public. Audi et alteram partem. [Boston? 1774]
[4] p. fol. caption title
Signed at end: Candor. Portsmouth, New-Hampshire, April 19th, 1774
A reply to an attack (in the Feb. 14 *Boston Gazette*) on Capt. Mowat of HMS Canceaux for his capture of the brigantine Brothers
MHi; RPJCB mp. 42715

B3873 TO the public. The printer not being able to publish Capt. Sweet's answer to Col. Wanton's address . . . Newport, April 19, 1774 . . . A friend to liberty and justice . . . [Newport, S. Southwick, 1774]
[2] p. 35.5 X 20.5 cm.
Alden 567; Sabin 95980
RNHi; RPJCB. Photostats: MWA; RHi mp. 42716

B3874 TO the publick. In consequence of the unhappy dispute at present subsisting between Great-Britain and her colonies, many of the Northern Provinces have entered into resolutions . . . [Savannah, James Johnston, 1774]
broadside 37 X 23.5 cm.
The writer urges Georgia not to become involved in the Boston dispute
McMurtrie: Georgia 18
GHi mp. 42717

B3875 TO the publick. [7 lines, quotation] It must be an unpleasing reflection to every lover of peace and moderation . . . A Friend to Moderation. Savannah, August 3, 1774. [Savannah, James Johnston, 1774]
broadside 37 X 23.5 cm.
McMurtrie: Georgia 20
GHi mp. 42718

B3876 TO the publick. The ship Lady Gage . . . New-York, Dec. 15th, 1774.
broadside 16.5 X 20.5 cm.
DLC. Photostat: MWA mp. 42719

B3877 TO the representatives of the Province of Pennsylvania, now met in this city . . . A Freeman. [Philadelphia, 1774]
broadside
PPL mp. 42720

B3878 TO the worthy freeholders and others, inhabitants of the Province of Georgia. Savannah, July 25, 1774. Gentlemen, As I presume many of you intend to meet here, pursuant to the summonses . . . in hand-bills . . . [Savannah, James Johnston, 1774]
broadside 37 X 23.5 cm.
Signed at end: A Friend to Georgia
McMurtrie: Georgia 17
GHi mp. 42721

B3879 TO the worthy freeholders and others, inhabitants of the Province of Georgia. Savannah, July 30, 1774. Gentlemen, Impelled by the most pure . . . desire . . . [Savannah, James Johnston, 1774]
broadside 37 X 23.5 cm.
Signed at end: A Friend to Georgia
McMurtrie: Georgia 19
GHi mp. 42722

B3880 U. S. CONTINENTAL CONGRESS, 1774
The association, agreed upon by the Grand American Continental Congress . . . October, 1774. Boston, Edes & Gill [1774]
broadside 39.5 X 26.5 cm.
Ford 1720
MHi; MWA mp. 42724

B3881 U. S. CONTINENTAL CONGRESS, 1774
The association entered into by the American Continental Congress . . . In Congress, Philadelphia, October 20, 1774 . . . [Philadelphia, 1774]
broadside 33.5 X 32.5 cm.
DLC mp. 42725

B3882 U. S. CONTINENTAL CONGRESS, 1774
Continental Congress. Proceedings . . . In Congress Philadelphia October 20, 1774. . . . Sold at the printing-office in Portsmouth [1774]
broadside 39 X 24.5 cm.
DLC (photostat) mp. 42734

B3883 U. S. CONTINENTAL CONGRESS, 1774
Extracts from the votes and proceedings of the American Continental Congress . . . [n.p., 1774?]
[2], 16 p.
Text in double columns
RPJCB mp. 42726

B3884 U. S. CONTINENTAL CONGRESS, 1774
[Extracts from the votes and proceedings of the American Continental Congress. Albany? A. and J. Robertson? 1774?]
12, 8, 33, 11, 3, 5 p. 15 cm. $[A]\text{-}I^4$
MWA (t.p. wanting) mp. 42727

B3885 U. S. CONTINENTAL CONGRESS, 1774
Extracts from the votes and proceedings of the American Continental Congress . . . Boston, Re-printed by Edes and Gill, and T. and J. Fleet, 1774.
40 p. 19 cm. $[A]\text{-}E^4$
Huntington 366; cf. Evans 13719
CSmH; MWA; RPJCB mp. 42728

B3886 U. S. CONTINENTAL CONGRESS, 1774
Extracts from the votes and proceedings of the American Continental Congress . . . Boston, Re-printed by Edes and Gill, and T. and J. Fleet, 1774.
41 p. 18.5 cm. $[A]\text{-}E^4\ [\ ]^1$
cf. Evans 13719

Pages 29–40 of preceding entry reset
MWA mp. 42729

B3887 U. S. CONTINENTAL CONGRESS, 1774
Extracts from the votes and proceedings of the American Continental Congress . . . Lancaster, Stewart Herbert, 1774.
14 p. 17 cm.
MWA mp. 42730

B3888 U. S. CONTINENTAL CONGRESS, 1774
Grand American Congress . . . [Resolutions of Oct. 8, 10, &11, 1774] Salem, S. & E. Hall [1774]
broadside 25.5 X 19.5 cm.
DLC mp. 42731

B3889 U. S. CONTINENTAL CONGRESS, 1774
A letter to the inhabitants of the province of Quebec . . . Philadelphia, William and Thomas Bradford, 1774.
[2], 37–50 p. 20.5 cm.
Ford: Bibliographical notes 18; *not* Evans 13726
CSmH; DLC (2 copies); ICN; MB; MH; MdHi; MiD-B; MiU-C; NjHi; PHi (2 copies); PPAmP; PPL; RPJCB
mp. 42732

B3890 U. S. CONTINENTAL CONGRESS, 1774
Philadelphia. In Congress, Thursday, September 22, 1774 . . . [Philadelphia, W. and T. Bradford, 1774]
broadside 10.5 X 17.5 cm.
Variant of Evans 13702, without imprint
DLC. Photostat: NN mp. 42733

B3891 U. S. CONTINENTAL CONGRESS, 1774
Proceedings of the Grand American Continental Congress at Philadelphia, September 5, 1774. Association, &c. . . . [Colophon] Portsmouth, D. Fowle [1774]
broadside ([2] p.) 37 X 23 cm.
Extra of the *New Hampshire Gazette*
MWA mp. 42735

B3892 U.S. CONTINENTAL CONGRESS, 1774
To the printer of the *Pennsylvania Packet*. Sir, Please to insert in your paper, the following extract from the minutes of the Congress now sitting at Philadelphia . . . Charles Thomson, Secretary. In Congress, Saturday Sept. 17, 1774 . . . Resolved unanimously . . . [Philadelphia, 1774]
broadside 53 X 33 cm.
MHi mp. 42736

B3893 VIRGINIA
At a very full meeting of delegates . . . begun . . . the first day of August . . . 1774, and continued . . . to Saturday the 6th . . . [Williamsburg, Clementina Rind, 1774]
broadside 33 X 19 cm.
DLC (photostat) mp. 42739

B3894 VIRGINIA. COUNCIL
To his excellency . . . John Earl of Dunmore . . . the humble address of the Council. [In reply to his speech of May 6, 1774] . . . [Williamsburg, Clementina Rind, 1774]
broadside 19 X 17 cm.
DLC (photostat) mp. 42740

B3895 VIRGINIA. GOVERNOR, 1771-1775
The speech of . . . the right honourable John Earl of Dunmore . . . the 5th of May, 1774. [Williamsburg, 1774]
broadside 31 X 17 cm.
DLC (photostat) mp. 42741

B3896 VIRGINIA. GOVERNOR, 1771-1775
Whereas I have reason to apprehend . . . Given under my hand . . . this 25th day of April 1774 . . . Dunmore . . . [Williamsburg, Clementina Rind, 1774]
broadside 32 X 18 cm.
DLC (photostat) mp. 42742

B3897 VIRGINIA. HOUSE OF BURGESSES
To . . . John Earl of Dunmore . . . the humble address of the House of burgesses. [In reply to his address of May 6, 1774] . . . [Williamsburg, Clementina Rind, 1774]
broadside 30 X 17 cm.
DLC (photostat) mp. 42743

B3898 THE Virginia almanack for . . . 1775 . . . Williamsburg, Purdie & Dixon [1774]
[48] p.
Drake 13784
ViWC

B3899 WANTON, JOSEPH, JUNIOR
Postscript to the *Newport Mercury*. To the freemen of the town of Newport . . . [at end] Joseph Wanton, jun. [Newport, S. Southwick, 1774]
3 p. 42 cm.
Alden 571
RPB (mutilated) mp. 42744

B3900 WATTS, ISAAC, 1674-1748
Divine songs, attempted in easy language . . . The fourteenth edition. Boston, Printed and sold at Greenleaf's Printing-Office, 1774.
44 p. 14.5 cm. A–E^4 F^2
Rosenbach–Ch 80
PP. d'Alté A. Welch, Cleveland (1962) mp. 42745

B3901 WATTS, ISAAC, 1674-1748
Hymns and spiritual songs . . . The thirty-seventh edition . . . Boston, John Boyle, 1774.
237, [1] p.
ICN (p. 229-230 lacking); MHi; MWA; NN; RPJCB
mp. 42746

B3902 WE the subscribers . . . for blocking up the harbour of Boston . . . [Portsmouth? 1774]
broadside 31 X 19.5 cm.
Non-importation agreement
Whittemore 169
NhHi mp. 42748

B3903 WESLEY, JOHN, 1703-1791
A dialogue between a predestinarian and his friend . . . The fifth edition . . . Newport, S. Southwick, 1774.
15 p. 17.5 cm.
Alden 572; Winship p. 31
DLC; MWA; RHi mp. 42749

B3904 WIGGLESWORTH, MICHAEL, 1631-1705
The day of doom . . . Norwich, Re-printed by Judah P. Spooner, 1774.
36 p. 17.5 cm. $[A]^4$ $[B]^2$ C^4 D^2 E^4 F^2
MHi; MWA mp. 42751

B3905 WILCOCKS, THOMAS, 1622-1687
A choice drop of honey . . . To which is added, The holy and sure way of faith . . . Translated from the German of . . . August Herman Franke . . . Philadelphia, Printed and sold by Henry Miller, 1774.
32 p. 19 cm.
cf. Sabin 10396; cf. Evans 13771
NHi (p. 31-32 lacking); PHi mp. 42752

B3906 WILLIAMSBURG, May 31, 1774. Gentlemen, Last Sunday morning several letters were received from Boston, Philadelphia, and Maryland, on the . . . important subject of American grievances . . . [Williamsburg, 1774]

broadside 23.5 X 18 cm.
Printed on first page of a folder
Signed by Peyton Randolph and others
DLC mp. 42753

B3907 WILMINGTON, N.C. COMMITTEE OF CORRESPONDENCE
Gentlemen, At this conjuncture of British politics when the liberty and property of North-American subjects are at stake . . . [22 lines] [Wilmington, Adam Boyd, 1774]
broadside 19 X 14.5 cm.
Circular letter sent out by the committee appointed at the meeting on July 21, 1774
McMurtrie: North Carolina 76
Public Record Off. mp. 42754

B3908 WILMINGTON, N.C. INHABITANTS
At a general meeting of the inhabitants of the district of Wilmington in . . . North-Carolina, held at . . . Wilmington July 21st, 1774. William Hooper, Esq; Chairman. Resolved . . . [Wilmington, Adam Boyd, 1774]
broadside 19 X 15 cm.
Resolutions appointing a committee to prepare a circular letter to the other counties
McMurtrie: North Carolina 75
Public Record Off. mp. 42755

B3909 WORCESTER. COMMITTEE OF CORRESPONDENCE
Worcester June 13th. 1774. Gentlemen. Many persons in this county conceiving that an agreement not to purchase the goods . . . imported . . . We are of opinion, that the enclosed covenant is by no means inconsistent . . . [Worcester, 1774]
broadside 26 X 19.5 cm.
cf. Evans 13158
MHi; MWA; MiU-C mp. 42756

B3910 YORK FIRE CLUB, BOSTON
[Notification form for meetings. Boston, 1774]
broadside
"York Fire Club" adopted as name of the Club on 1 Feb. 1769
The financial records of the Club, in manuscript at the Boston Public Library, record payment for printing; 12 shillings on 2 Feb. 1774
No copy known mp. 42564

B3911 ZUM 29sten August, 1774. [Philadelphia, Henrich Miller, 1774]
[6] p. 16.5 cm. caption title
PHi mp. 42757

1775

B3912 ACCOUNT of the battle between the Provincials and Regulars . . . [Portsmouth? 1775]
broadside 28 X 21 cm.
Battle of Chelsea Creek
Dated: Portsmouth, May 29, 1775; probably printed as a newspaper extra
Matt B. Jones (1934). Photostat: NN mp. 42758

B3913 AN account of the bloody battle on Bunker-Hill.
An elegiac poem, composed on the never-to-be-forgotten . . . battle . . . on Bunker-Hill, now justly call'd (by the regulars) Bloody Hill . . . [Boston, 1775]
broadside 43 X 33 cm.
Row of 20 coffins at top
Text in 2 columns of 31 lines each, poem in four columns
G. A. Baker and Co. cat. 28, no. 329
No copy located mp. 42759

B3914 ADVERTISEMENT. Perquimans County, Feb. 11, 1775. The respective counties and towns . . . are requested to elect delegates . . . to meet at . . . Newbern . . . the 3d day of April next. John Harvey, moderator. [Newbern, James Davis, 1775]
broadside 10 X 15 cm.
McMurtrie: North Carolina 81
Public Record Off. mp. 42761

B3915 ADVICES from St. John's. Cambridge, November 15. Yesterday a courier arrived here from the Continental Army in Canada . . . [Cambridge? 1775]
broadside 30.5 X 21.5 cm.
New York Public 544
Jones (1934) Photostats: MWA; NN mp. 42762

B3916 ALEXANDER, WILLIAM, CALLED LORD STIRLING, 1726-1783
On the 24th of November, 1773, the Earl of Stirling made the following motion in the Council of New-Jersey . . . [Burlington, Isaac Collins, 1775]
26 p. 25 cm. caption title
Humphrey 139; Huntington 343; New York Public 545
CSmH; MH; NN (p. 9-26 photostat) mp. 42763

B3917 THE American crisis. Let God and the world judge between us . . . Hartford, Eben. Watson [1775]
broadside 32 X 21 cm.
Dated: "America, May 1, 1775."
Huntington 368
CSmH mp. 42764

B3918 AMERICAN liberty, a new song. [n.p., 1775?]
broadside 34.5 X 21.5 cm.
18-stanza poem in 2 columns, beginning: Awake, awake Americans, / Put cheerful courage on, . . .
Woodcuts of ships over each column
RPJCB mp. 42765

B3919 AMERICANS to arms. Sung to the tune of, Britons to arms. America's sons yourselves prepare . . . [Salem, E. Russell, 1775]
broadside 35 X 15 cm.
Woodcut portrait of Gen. Warren at head
Ford 1788
PPRF mp. 42766

B3920 THE association of company in Lancaster, county of In order to make ourselves perfect . . . we have hereunto set our hands, the day of 1775. [n.p., 1775]
broadside 34.5 X 21.5 cm.
DLC

B3921 . . . AN astronomical diary, or, almanack for the year . . . 1775 . . . By Isaac Warren . . . Woburn, Printed and sold by the author, 1775.
[20] p. 15.5 cm.
Nichols p. 59
DLC; MWA mp. 42979

B3922 BAPTISTS. SOUTH CAROLINA. CHARLESTON ASSOCIATION
Minutes of the Charleston Association. Charlestown, Feb. 6, 1775 . . . [Charleston, 1775]
4 p. 21.5 cm. caption title
KyLoS; ScGF mp. 42767

B3923 BELL, ROBERT, d. 1784
. . . Proposals, for printing . . . A collection of designs in architecture . . . by Abraham Swan. [Philadelphia, R. Bell, 1775]
broadside 31 X 15.5 cm.
Dated June 26, 1775
cf. Evans 14481
PHi mp. 42768

B3924 BERGEN CO., N.J. CITIZENS
Being fully convinced that the preservation of the rights and privileges of the British Colonies in America, now depends on the firm union of their inhabitants . . . we the freeholders and inhabitants of the County of Bergen . . . will not submit . . . taxes on us without our consent . . . May 12, 1775. [n.p., 1775]
broadside 25.5 X 21 cm.
In English and Dutch
NjR

B3925 BIBLE. O.T. PSALMS
A new version of the Psalms of David . . . By N. Brady . . . and N. Tate . . . Boston, Edes and Gill, 1775.
324 p.
MB mp. 42769

B3926 BIBLE. N.T.
Das Neue Testament Unsers Herrn Jesu Christi, nach der deutschen Uebersetzung D. Martin Luthers . . . Sechste Auflage. Germantown, gedruckt und zu finden bey Christoph Saur, 1775.
529, [3] p.
PPL mp. 42770

B3927 BICKERSTAFF'S Albany almanack, for the year . . . 1776 . . . Fitting New-York, Connecticut, Rhode-Island, Massachusetts-Bay, and New-Hampshire . . . Albany, Alexr. and James Robertson [1775]
[24] p. 16.5 cm.
MWA mp. 42771

B3928 A BLOODY butchery, by the British troops . . . Philadelphia, Reprinted by Henry Barber [1775]
broadside 51 X 40 cm.
Metzger 424
PHi mp. 42773

B3929 BLOODY butchery, by the British troops; or the runaway fight of the regulars . . . To which is annexed a funeral elegy . . . and extracts from E. Russell's *Gazette* . . . [Salem? E. Russell? 1775]
broadside 57 X 47 cm.
Similar to microprint of Evans 13839 but different typographically
MHi; MWA; RPJCB mp. 42772

B3930 BOIES AND CLARK, firm, Milton, Mass.
Paper mills, in compliance with the recommendation of the late Provincial Congress, and to encourage the paper manufactory, we now propose to give one shilling . . . per pound, for all white linnen . . . Boies and Clark . . . Milton, January 10th, 1775. [Boston, 1775]
broadside 29 X 19 cm.
Amos Hollingsworth (1949). Photostat: MWA
mp. 42774

B3931 BOSTON. CITIZENS
An address of the gentlemen and principal inhabitants of the Town of Boston, to . . . Governor Gage. [on 2nd leaf] The address of His Majesty's Council . . . [Boston, 1775]
[2] p. 39 cm.
Pages 2 & 3 of 4-page folder printed
Ford 1784
MHi mp. 42775

B3932 BOSTON. COMMITTEE TO RECEIVE DONATIONS
Boston, May 1775. The bearer Mr. and family removing out of . . . Boston recommended to the charity and assistance of our . . . sympathizing brethren . . . [Boston, 1775]
broadside 10 X 19 cm.
Ford 1798; New York Public 546
MB; NN; PPRF. Photostat: MWA mp. 42776

B3933 BOSTON. COMMITTEE TO RECEIVE DONATIONS
To the publick. The committee appointed by the Town of Boston to receive . . . donations for . . . the sufferers by means of the act of Parliament . . . January 20, 1775 . . . Samuel Adams. [Boston, 1775]
broadside 24 X 18.5 cm.
Ford 1796
MWA mp. 42777

B3934 BRADISH, EBENEZER
Whereas Ebenezer Bradish, jun. . . . has been represented . . . unfriendly . . . Therefore . . . to do justice . . . we the subscribers . . . are satisfied that Mr. Bradish, had no desire . . . to do any injury to his country . . . N.B. . . . I am certain my house was . . . plundered by the Regulars. May 11, 1775. Ebenezer Bradish. [Watertown? 1775]
broadside 22 X 18.5 cm.
MWA mp. 42778

B3935 BRUFF, CHARLES OLIVER
All those gentlemen . . . forming themselves into companies . . . that are not provided with swords, may be suited therewith by applying to . . . In Maiden Lane . . . [New York, 1775?]
broadside 21.5 X 19.5 cm.
For date cf. Gottesman: *Arts and crafts in New York*, p. 35
RPJCB. Photostat: NN mp. 42779

B3936 [BUEL, SAMUEL] 1716-1798
Youth's triumph: a poem or vision. [New London, 1775]
13 p.
At end: Ex meo museo, East-Hampton, Jan. 20, 1775
Part of Evans 13849
NHi mp. 42780

B3937 BUNKER'S Hill. A new song. [Boston? 1775]
broadside 22 X 18 cm.
New York Public 548
Matt B. Jones, Boston (1934). Photostats: NHi; NN
mp. 42781

B3938 BURGOYNE, SIR JOHN, 1722-1792
Copy of Gen. Burgoyne's answer (dated July 8, 1775) to Gen. Lee's letter of June 7, 1775. [n.p., 1775]
broadside 48.5 X 30 cm.
In four columns
At end: A copy of General Lee's letter . . .
RPJCB mp. 42783

B3939 [BURGOYNE, SIR JOHN] 1722-1792
The speech of a general officer in the House of Commons, February 20th, 1775. [Boston? 1775?]
8 p. $[A]^4$
A printing of this speech was advertised June 1, 1775, in the *Boston Evening Post*, while Burgoyne was in the city

Adsms 155b; Sabin 9254
MHi; RPJCB mp. 42784

B3940 BY a packet, arrived at New-York, and Capt. Spain . . . from England, we have the following interesting advices . . . Providence, John Carter [1775]
broadside 27.5 X 21 cm.
Alden 577A
CtHi; RHi mp. 42785

B3941 BY the Lion & Unicorn . . . Whereas I have been informed . . . that a certain Patrick Henry . . . Given, &c. this 6th day of May, 1775 . . . [Williamsburg, A. Purdie, 1775]
broadside 16 X 19.5 cm.
DLC mp. 42786

B3942 CAMBRIDGE, April 24, 1775. Whereas you have this day received orders for inlisting 86 soldiers . . . [Watertown? 1775]
broadside
Ford 1890
MB mp. 42787

B3943 CAMDEN, CHARLES PRATT, EARL OF, 1714-1794
Lord Camden's speech on the New-England fishery bill . . . Newport, S. Southwick [1775]
broadside 36 X 23 cm.
Alden 578; Winship p. 32
DLC; RNHi mp. 42788

B3943a CHESTERFIELD, PHILIP DORMER STANHOPE, EARL, 1694-1773
Letters written . . . to his son . . . In four volumes. The fifth edition. Vol. I. New-York: Printed by J. Rivington and H. Gaine, 1775
[4], 204 p.
PPL (v. 1 only)

B3944 THE child's plain path-way to eternal life . . . New Haven, Printed and sold by T. & S. Green [1775?]
8 p. 19 cm.
Trumbull: Supplement 1976
CtHi mp. 42790

B3945 CHRISTIE, JAMES, JR.
Baltimore, July 18. At a special meeting . . . Thursday the 13th July, 1775 . . . A letter from James Christie, jun. merchant, of this town, directed to Lieut. Col. Gabriel Christie . . . [Baltimore, M. K. Goddard, 1775]
broadside 42.5 X 26 cm.
Wroth 347
MdHi mp. 42791

B3946 CHRISTLICHES buss-lied, gestellt auf den 20th Julius 1775 . . . [n.p., 1775]
broadside 39 X 24 cm.
11 stanzas in 2 columns
DLC mp. 42792

B3947 CONNECTICUT. ELECTION PROX.
Nomination for election in May, 1776 . . . The gentlemen, nominated by the votes of the freemen, to stand for election in May next, as sent in to the General assembly, holden . . . October, 1775 . . . [New London, T. Green, 1775]
broadside 33.5 X 21 cm.
CtHi; DLC. Photostat: MWA mp. 42793

B3948 CONNECTICUT. GENERAL ASSEMBLY
At a General Assembly . . . holden at Hartford . . . on the 26th day of April . . . 1775. Resolved, that the three thousand stands of arms . . . be of the following dimensions . . . [Hartford? 1775]
broadside 20.5 X 17 cm.
New York Public 552
Matt B. Jones, Boston (1933). Photostat: NN
mp. 42799

B3949 CONNECTICUT. GENERAL ASSEMBLY
At a General Assembly . . . holden at Hartford . . . on the 26th day of April . . . 1775. Resolved, that the three thou- . . . it is resolved . . . that each inlisted inhabitant . . . [New London, T. Green, 1775]
broadside 29 X 17 cm.
Photostats: DLC; ICN; MH; MHi; NHi; NN; WHi
mp. 42798

B3950 CONNECTICUT. GENERAL ASSEMBLY
At a General Assembly . . . holden at New-Haven . . . on the fourteenth day of December . . . 1775. Whereas the non-commissioned officers and soldiers . . . stand liable . . . to pay taxes . . . New-London, T. Green [1775]
broadside 31 X 19 cm.
MWA (photo.) mp. 42800

B3951 CONNECTICUT. GOVERNOR, 1769-1776
By the honorable Jonathan Trumbull . . . A proclamation . . . Given under my hand at Hartford . . . [Apr. 27, 1775] . . . Hartford, Ebenezer Watson, 1775.
broadside 30.5 X 18 cm.
Embargo on foodstuffs and live cattle
MHi

B3952 CONNECTICUT. GOVERNOR, 1769-1776
By the Honorable Jonathan Trumbull . . . a proclamation . . . New-London, Timothy Green [1775]
broadside
Dated at Lebanon, Aug. 17, 1775
Embargo on foodstuffs
New York Public 549
NN (reduced facsim.) mp. 42794

B3953 CONNECTICUT. GOVERNOR, 1769-1776
By the honorable Jonathan Trumbull . . . a proclamation. Whereas it is resolved . . . that an embargo . . . [Oct. 19, 1775] . . . [New London, T. Green, 1775]
broadside 34.5 X 21.5 cm.
DLC; MHi. Photostats: NHi; NN mp. 42795

B3954 CONNECTICUT. GOVERNOR, 1769-1776
Copy of a letter to . . . Gen. Gage, from . . . Jonathan Trumbull . . . Hartford, April 28th, 1775. [Boston? 1775]
[3] p. 33 cm. caption title
Huntington 371; New York Public 551
CSmH; MHi; MiU-C; NN mp. 42796

B3955 CONNECTICUT. LAWS
. . . An act and law, made and passed by the General court . . . holden . . . on . . . the second day of March . . . 1775 . . . for regulating naval officers . . . [New London, 1775]
broadside 29 X 17 cm. (p. 407)
Huntington 370
CSmH mp. 42797

B3956 CONNECTICUT. MILITIA
To Captain, or to the chief officer of the company in the regiment in this colony. Greeting. In pursuance . . . of an act . . . passed in December, 1775 . . . Given . . . at the day of A.D. 177 . . . Form of an inlistment, viz. We the subscribers . . . January, 1776. [n.p., 1775?]
broadside 30 X 16.5 cm.

MWA copy filled in for Jan. 2, 1776, at New Haven
CtHi; NHi; MWA (lower half wanting). Photostat: MWA

B3957 CONSTITUTIONAL GAZETTE
The *Constitutional Gazette*. Wednesday August 2, 1775. By Capt. Spain, arrived at Philadelphia, from Bristol . . . The following noble lords . . . Cambridge . . . July 21. Last Tuesday morning . . . orders . . . by Major General Putnam . . . [Philadelphia, 1775]
broadside 35 X 21.5 cm.
NHi

B3958 COOMBE, THOMAS, 1758-1822
A sermon, preached before the congregations of Christ Church and St. Peter's, Philadelphia . . . July 20, 1775 . . . Baltimore, John Dunlap, 1775.
[2], [2], 29 p. 8vo
Huntington 372; cf. Evans 13892
CSmH mp. 42801

B3959 COOPER, ROBERT, A.M.
Courage in a good cause . . . A sermon preached near Shippensburgh . . . 31st of August, 1775 . . . Lancaster, Francis Bailey, 1775.
30 p.
RPJCB mp. 42802

B3960 THE Crisis Number I [and II]. London: Printed [Philadelphia reprinted?], 1775.
12 p. 8vo
Imprint suggested by Edwin Wolf 2d
Unlike other editions, these two parts are a single entity
PPL

B3961 THE Crisis, number III. Thy name, O Chatham . . . To the King. Sir, . . . [Newport, S. Southwick, 1775]
17-24 p. 22 cm. caption title
Alden 582; Sabin 17517 (note); Hammett p. 42; Winship p. 32; cf. Evans 13919
CtY; DLC; NHi; RHi; RNHi mp. 42803

B3962 DABOLL'S New-England almanack for . . . 1775. The second edition. New-London, T. Green [1775]
[32?] p.
Advertised in the *Connecticut Gazette*, Jan. 6, 1775, as "The second edition . . . is now in the press, and will be ready for sale tomorrow."
Drake 299
No copy known

B3963 DELAWARE. HOUSE OF REPRESENTATIVES
Votes and proceedings of the House of Representatives . . . from October sessions 1774, 'till the end of August sessions 1775. Wilmington: Printed and sold by James Adams, 1775.
74+ p.
PHi (lacking beyond p. 74)

B3964 A DESCANT on the command, Mat. xxviii. 19, 20 . . . By a Wellwisher to truth . . . Wilmington, Printed by James Adams, for the author, 1775.
31 p. 19.5 cm. [A]-D^4
MWA mp. 42804

B3965 DILWORTH, THOMAS, d. 1780
A new guide to the English tongue . . . Boston: Printed and sold by John Boyle, 1775.
152 p.
MWA

B3966 A DISSERTATION on disputes between Great Britain and her colonies . . . 10th October 1775 . . . Analysis A.P. [n.p., 1775]
broadside 33.5 X 25 cm.
NHi mp. 42805

B3967 DOSE for the Tories. Ireland Printed: America Re-Printed, 1775.
broadside 27 X 20 cm.
Ford 1808; New York Public 554
MHi; MWA. Photostat: NN mp. 42806

B3968 DRAYTON, WILLIAM HENRY, 1742-1779
South-Carolina, Ninety-six District. By the honourable William Henry Drayton, Esquire. Whereas, by commission from the . . . Council of Safety . . . I am upon a progress . . . Snow-Hill . . . this 30th of August, 1775 . . . [n.p., 1775]
broadside 28 X 18.5 cm.
PHi mp. 42807

B3969 AN elegiac poem, composed on the . . . battle fought . . . on Bunker Hill . . . Salem, Printed and sold by E. Russell, 1775.
broadside 50 X 38.5 cm.
New York Public 555; Tapley p. 319
CSmH; MHi; PPRF. Photostats: MWA (mutilated); NN
mp. 42809

B3970 AN elegy, occasion'd by the death of Major-General Joseph Warren, who fell . . . on the memorable 17th day of June, 1775 . . . Printed and sold in Watertown, 1775.
broadside 35 X 21.5 cm.
24 stanzas in double columns
Ford 1809; Wegelin 555; New York Public 556
DLC; NHi; PHi. Photostats: MHi; MWA; NN
mp. 42810

B3971 ELLERY, WILLIAM, 1727-1820
To the freemen of the colony of Rhode-Island. Gentlemen . . . William Ellery. Providence, April 17, 1775. [Providence, J. Carter? 1775]
broadside 32 X 21 cm.
Concerns the removal of Gov. Wanton from office
Alden 590; Winship p. 32
RHi. Photostats: MHi; MWA; NN mp. 42811

B3972 EMERY, THOMAS J.
T. J. Emery, gives this public notice to his friends and customers . . .just imported . . . complete assortment of European goods . . . at his new store in Newbern . . . [Newbern? 1775?]
broadside 44.5 X 28 cm.
In four columns
New York Public 558
NN (2 copies) mp. 42812

B3973 AN essay on public speaking . . . Collected from various authors . . . Providence, John Carter, 1775.
15 p. 22 cm.
Alden 591; Winship p. 32
Nj; RHi; RPB mp. 42813

B3974 THE farmer and his son's return from a visit to the camp. [Boston? 1775?]
broadside 28.5 X 17.5 cm.
5 woodcuts of soldiers at head
With refrain: Yankee Doodle . . .
PPRF. Photostat: MHi mp. 42814

B3975 FATHER Hutchin's New-York, New-Jersey, and Connecticut almanack . . . for . . . 1776. New-York, Printed for the booksellers and storekeepers [1775]

[36] p.
Drake 5856
DLC; NRMA. Milton Drake, NYC (1964)

B3976 THE first book of the American "chronicles of the times. Chap. II . . . [Colophon] [Boston] Printed and sold by D. Kneeland [1775?]
p. [9]-16. 20 cm. caption title
New York Public 559
MHi; MWA; NN; RPJCB mp. 42815

B3977 THE first book of the American chronicles of the times. Chap. III. [Colophon] [Boston] Printed and sold by D. Kneeland [1775?]
p. [17]-24. 19 cm. caption title
New York Public 560
MHi; NN mp. 42816

B3978 THE first book of the American chronicles of the times. Chap. III . . . [at end] [Boston] Sold by Edes and Gill, in Queen-Street [1775]
p. [17]-24. 19.5 cm.
MWA mp. 42817

B3979 THE first book of the American chronicles of the times. Chap. III . . . [at end] Providence, John Carter [1775]
[17]-23 p. 20.5 cm. caption title
Alden 592
MWA mp. 42818

B3980 THE first book of the American chronicles of the times . . . Chap. III[-VI] . . . [at end] New-York, John Anderson [1775?]
13–70 p. 20 cm.
Printer given at end of each chapter
Ends with (To be continued), like Evans 13808
CtHi; NHi mp. 42819

B3981 THE first book of the American chronicles of the times. Chap. IV . . . [Colophon] [Boston] Printed and sold by D. Kneeland [1775?]
[8] p. 19 cm. caption title
New York Public 561
MHi; NN mp. 42820

B3982 THE first book of the American chronicles of the times. Chap. IV . . . [at end] [Boston] Sold opposite the Court-House, in Queen-Street [1775]
p. [25]–32. 20 cm.
MWA mp. 42821

B3983 THE first book of the American chronicles of the times. Chap. IV . . . [at end] Providence, John Carter [1775]
[25]–32 p. 20.5 cm. caption title
Alden 593
MWA mp. 42822

B3984 THE following is a copy of a letter which was wrote by a Lady of this City, to Capt. S---s . . . [3 lines] A friend of Justice and Humanity. Gentlemen . . . [43 lines] New-York, March 20, 1775. Your Afflicted Friend. [New York, 1775]
broadside 27 X 21 cm.
A plea to prevent the "unspeakable distress" of banishment from "my native country."
NHi mp. 42823

B3985 THE following was received by a vessel . . . Newport, Sept. 12, 1775. Printed by S. Southwick.
broadside 31 X 18 cm.
Alden 608; Winship Addenda p. 88
NHi; RHi. Photostat: DLC mp. 42824

B3986 FRANKLIN, BENJAMIN, 1706-1790
An eulogium sacred to the memory of Major General Warren, who fell bravely fighting . . . on Bunker's Hill . . . June 17, 1775 . . . [Boston? 1775]
broadside 50.5 X 39 cm.
MHi mp. 42825

B3987 FRESH advices. Baltimore (Maryland) Dec. 13. By a gentleman arrived last night from Virginia . . . [Providence] John Carter [1775]
broadside 26 X 20 cm.
Alden 594; New York Public 563
NN mp. 42826

B3988 FRESH advices from London. By a packet, arrived at New-York, and Capt. Spain . . . [Providence, John Carter? 1775]
broadside 26.5 X 20 cm.
Extracts from letters written in London, the latest dated March 16
Alden 595
MWA; NhHi. Photostat: RHi mp. 42827

B3989 FRESH news. Just arrived an express from the Provincial-camp near Boston . . . New-York, John Anderson [1775]
broadside ([2] p.) 26.5 cm X 22 cm.
Photostats: DLC; MWA; NN. William Randolph Hearst (1926); Middendorf Collection (1969) mp. 42828

B3990 FRESHEST advices, foreign and domestic. Newport, Nov. 13, 1775. [Newport] Solomon Southwick [1775]
[2] p. 42 X 26 cm.
Alden 597; Winship p. 32
RNHi mp. 42829

B3991 FRESHEST advices, foreign and domestic. Newport, Nov. 20, 1775. [Newport] Solomon Southwick [1775]
[2] p. 42 X 26 cm.
Alden 598; Winship p. 32
RNHi mp. 42830

B3992 FRESHEST advices, foreign and domestic. Newport, Nov. 27, 1775. [Newport] Solomon Southwick [1775]
[2] p. 42 X 26 cm.
Alden 599; Winship p. 32
RNHi mp. 42831

B3993 FRIENDS and Fellow Citizens, In these distracted days, when the politics of the times has almost unhinged every mode of government . . . An American. [n.p.,1775?]
broadside 37.5 X 22.5 cm.
Dated from internal evidence by NNS
NNS

B3994 FRIENDS, SOCIETY OF
Ein einklärung-zeugniss der sogenannten Quäker, ausgesetzt in einer versammlung der vorsteher besagter gemeinen in Pennsylvanien und Neu-Jersey, welche zu Philadelphia gehalten worden den 24sten tag des ersten monats, 1775. Germantown, Christoph Saur, 1775.
8 p. 8vo
PPL mp. 42832

B3995 FRIENDS, SOCIETY OF
. . . To our friends and brethren in Pennsylvania and New Jersey . . . 1775. John Pemberton, clerk. [Philadelphia, 1775]
broadside
Heartman: Cradle 950; Metzger 436
No copy located mp. 42834

B3996 FRIENDS, SOCIETY OF
We the subscribers, in consideration of the distresses . . . of our fellow-subjects . . . promise to pay the sums by us respectively subscribed . . . unto John Reynell . . . or Samuel Smith . . . Treasurers of the Yearly-Meeting of Friends in Pennsylvania, and New-Jersey . . . Witness our hands the day of the month, 1775. [Philadelphia? 1775]
broadside 17 X 21 cm.
MWA (not traced 1966)

B3997 FRIENDS, SOCIETY OF. LONDON YEARLY MEETING
From our Yearly-Meeting held in London by adjournments, from the 5th of the 6th month 1775, to the 10th of the same . . . To our friends and brethren in America. [Philadelphia, 1775]
2 p. 33 X 21 cm. caption title
Not Evans 14051
MB mp. 42833

B3998 GEORGIA. COUNCIL OF SAFETY
Georgia. In the Council of Safety. Savannah, 21st December, 1775. Whereas it was resolved, by the late Provincial Congress . . . By order of the Council of Safety, George Walton, President . . . [Savannah, James Johnston, 1775]
broadside 31.5 X 18 cm.
McMurtrie: Georgia 25
Public Record Off. mp. 42836

B3999 GEORGIA. COUNCIL OF SAFETY
In the Council of Safety, Savannah, 27th July, 1775. Resolved . . . [Savannah, J. Johnston, 1775]
broadside 24.5 X 13 cm.
Concerns military regulations
PHi mp. 42837

B4000 GEORGIA. PROVINCIAL CONGRESS
Savannah, 17th July, 1775. In Provincial Congress. Whereas . . . Sir James Wright . . . hath been pleased to appoint . . . the 19th instant as a day of fasting . . . [Savannah, 1775]
broadside 31.5 X 19.5 cm.
Huntington 375; McMurtrie: Georgia 24
CSmH mp. 42835

B4001 GLOUCESTER COUNTY, N.J.
The inhabitants of the county of Gloucester, in New-Jersey, May 18th, 1775 . . . [n.p., 1775]
broadside 42.5 X 27 cm.
DLC mp. 42838

B4002 GORDON, WILLIAM, 1728-1807
A discourse preached December 15th 1774 . . . and afterwards at the Boston lecture . . . The second edition. Boston: Printed for, and sold by Thomas Leverett, 1775.
32 p., 1 l. 8vo [A]-D^4 $[E]^1$
Adams 167b
CtHi; DLC; NHi; PPL

B4003 GT. BRIT.
Head-quarters, Boston, 18th December, 1775. The bearer hereof having voluntarily engaged to serve . . . in the Royal Regiment of Highland Emigrants . . . [Boston, 1775]
broadside
Ford 1829
MHi mp. 42839

B4004 GT. BRIT. SOVEREIGNS (GEORGE III)
New-York, January 31, 1775. This day arrived here the Lord Hyde packet, Capt. Jefferies . . . by whom we have His Majesty's . . . speech . . . November 30, 1774. [New York] H. Gaine [1775]
broadside 31 X 20 cm.
New York Public 565
NN mp. 42841

B4005 GREGORY, JOHN, 1724-1773
A father's legacy to his daughters . . . New-York, Shober and Loudoun, 1775.
v, [6]-45 p. 19.5 cm. A-E^4 F^3
MiU-C; N mp. 42842

B4006 THE happy ship-carpenter, You loyal lovers far and near . . . Providence, [John Waterman] [ca. 1775?]
broadside 37 X 20 cm.
Alden 604
MWA (mutilated and photostat) mp. 42843

B4007 HAY, JOHN, of Lancaster, Pa.
Advertisement. Whereas the Honourable Thomas Penn by his warrant . . . the 30th day of October 1736 . . . [Lancaster, Printed by Francis Bailey and Stewart Herbert [ca. 1775]
broadside 23 X 18 cm.
Signed at end: John Hay
PPRF mp. 42844

B4008 HOW, SAMUEL
Simplicity of the gospel defended . . . Norwich, Printed by Alexander Robertson, James Robertson, and John Trumbull, 1775.
43 p. 19.5 cm.
CtHi; NjR (final page lacking) mp. 42845

B4009 HOWE, WILLIAM HOWE, 5TH VISCOUNT, 1729-1814
Howe's proclamation, versified . . . By William Howe, whose high command, Extends o'er all this western land . . . [Boston? 1775]
broadside 35 X 14 cm.
Ford 1827
MWA mp. 42846

B4010 HOWE, WILLIAM HOWE, 5TH VISCOUNT, 1729-1814
A proclamation. By His Excellency, the honorable William Howe . . . Whereas many inconveniences and abuses have arisen . . . this harbour of Boston . . . Boston, this first day of November, 1775. [Boston, 1775]
broadside 30.5 X 18 cm.
Ford 1825
MHi mp. 42840

B4011 AN humble intercession for the distressed Town of Boston . . . By a Young Lady, who was lately a resident . . . Salem, E. Russell, 1775.
broadside
Ford 1837; Tapley p. 320
MB mp. 42847

B4012 INDEPENDENT COMPANY OF FREE CITIZENS
New-York 1775. Sir, the Independant company . . . are to meet this day . . . [New York, 1775]

broadside 10.5 X 19 cm.
DLC mp. 42897

B4013 INTELLIGENCE extraordinary from Boston. Narrative of the Battle on the 19th of July, at Roxborough . . . Boston . . . July 22, 1775 . . . [n.p., 1775?]
[2] p. 25.5 cm.
New York Public 567
MHi; RHi. Photostat: NN mp. 42849

B4014 INTERESTING intelligence. Norwich, April 22, 1775, 10 o'clock, P.M. . . . [Norwich] Printed by Robertson and Trumbull [1775]
broadside
cf. Stan V. Henkels cat. 1238, June 26, 1919, item 103
New York Public 568
PPRF. Facsims.: MHi; MWA; NN mp. 42848

B4015 ISH, CHRISTIAN
Six dollars reward. March 27th, 1775. Ran away yesterday from the subscriber . . . Christian Ish . . . Lancaster, Francis Bailey [1775]
broadside
NHi mp. 42850

B4016 JEMMY and Nancy. Or, A tragical relation of the death of five persons. Norwich, Printed at Spooner's Printing-Office [ca. 1775]
broadside 36 X 26.5 cm.
In verse, in three columns
New York Public 569
NN. Photostat: MHi mp. 42851

B4017 JONES, JOHN, 1729-1791
Plain concise practical remarks, on the treatment of wounds and fractures . . . New-York, John Holt, 1775.
viii, 92 p. 21.5 cm.
NhD; OClW mp. 42852

B4018 LANCASTER, PA.
Bey einer versammlung von der committee . . . den 11ten July, 1775. [Lancaster, 1775]
broadside 13 X 21 cm.
DLC (lower part of page wanting) mp. 42853

B4019 THE Lancaster almanack for . . . 1776. By Anthony Sharp . . . Lancaster, Francis Bailey [1775]
[40] p.
"Tables of interest" and "Roads westward" on final two leaves
Drake 10022
RPA

B4020 LAST Sunday the schooner Hawke . . . arrived at Marblehead . . . Newport, April 5, Printed by S. Southwick [1775]
broadside 30.5 X 18 cm.
Alden 600
DLC (photostat); RHi mp. 42854

B4021 LATE advices from England, brought by a vessel arrived at the eastward . . . February 20, 1775 . . . Providence, J. Carter [1775]
broadside 32.5 X 18.5 cm.
Alden 601; Winship p. 33
RHi. Photostats: MHi; MWA; NN mp. 42855

B4022 LATE advices from London . . . February 20, 1775. Boston, Thomas & John Fleet [1775]
broadside 22.5 X 18 cm.
Ford 1838; New York Public 571
MHi. Photostats: DLC; NN mp. 42856

B4023 LATE and important intelligence from England. Boston, April 3, 1775. Yesterday the Schooner Hawke, Captain Andrews, arrived at Marblehead from Falmouth . . . a London print of the 11th of February, from which . . . the following important advices . . . [New York? 1775]
[2] p.
NNS (mutilated and trimmed)

B4024 LEE, CHARLES, 1731-1782
General Lee's resignation. To . . . Lord Viscount Barrington, His Majesty's secretary at war. Philadelphia, June 22, 1775. My Lord, Although I can by no means subscribe . . . New-York, Printed by John Anderson at Beekman-Slip [1775]
broadside 27.5 X 20.5 cm.
NHi; PPRF; RPJCB. Photostat: MHi mp. 42857

B4025 LEE, CHARLES, 1731-1782
A letter from General Lee, to General Burgoyne, dated June 7, 1775; received at Boston, July 5. Printed from the *New York Gazetteer*, July 6 . . . [Boston, 1775]
broadside 44 X 38 cm.
Ford 1839; New York Public 572; cf. Evans 14149
DLC; MB; MWA; MiU-C; NN; PPRF mp. 42858

B4026 [LEE, CHARLES] 1731-1782
Strictures on a pamphlet, intituled, "A friendly address . . ." . . . Philadelphia, Printed: Providence, Reprinted and sold by John Carter, 1775.
15 p. 20 cm.
Adams 125E; Alden 607; Sabin 92831
NHi; RPJCB mp. 42859

B4027 LEE, CHARLES, 1731-1782
The true spirit of a brave and honest Englishman . . . A genuine copy of General Lee's letter to General Burgoyne . . . Philadelphia, June 7, 1775 . . . [Philadelphia? 1775]
broadside 30 X 18.5 cm.
MiU-C mp. 42860

B4028 EIN Lied gegen das unrechte Verfahren des Königs, gegen America. Nach der Weis, Ich kann recht sorglos leben . . . [Philadelphia? Henrich Miller, 1775?]
[2] p. 34 X 21 cm.
21 8-line stanzas
MWA mp. 42861

B4029 LONDON
The address, petition, and remonstrance, of the City of London, to the King, in favour of the Americans, and their resolves, presented to his Majesty, July 5, 1775. [Boston, 1775]
broadside 38.5 X 24 cm.
Ford 1785; New York Public 574
MHi. Photostat: NN mp. 42862

B4030 LONDON
The address, petition, and remonstrance of the city of London . . . in favour of the Americans . . . presented . . . July 5, 1775 . . . Watertown [1775]
broadside 34.5 X 20.5 cm.
Huntington 379; Ford 1785a; New York Public 573
CSmH; NN (reduced facsim.) mp. 42863

B4031 MASSACHUSETTS
Chamber of supplies, Watertown, 1775. Sir, Pay to the sum of and charge the same to the Colony . . . [Watertown, 1775]
broadside
Ford 1909
M-Ar; MB

B4032 MASSACHUSETTS
Chamber of supplies, Watertown, June 18, 1775 . . . David Cheever, per order of Committee of supplies. [n.p., 1775]
broadside 19.5 X 23 cm.
Ford 1910
MB; MHi. Photostat: DLC mp. 42870

B4033 MASSACHUSETTS
Colony of the Massachusetts-Bay. In observance of the foregoing resolve of the honorable Continental Congress now sitting at Philadelphia . . . June 19th, 1775. [Boston? 1775]
[2] p.
MWA mp. 42872

B4034 MASSACHUSETTS
Colony of the Massachusetts-Bay. To field officers of the regiment of militia . . . Given under our hands . . . this day of A.D. 1775 . . . [Boston? 1775]
broadside 24.5 X 17 cm.
Ford 1888
MB; MHi. Photostat: DLC

B4035 MASSACHUSETTS
The day of 1775. Received of firelock to the use of the colony . . . [n.p., 1775]
broadside 12 X 22 cm.
Ford 1906
MHi. Photostat: DLC

B4036 MASSACHUSETTS
Supply Chamber Watertown, May 25th, 1775. Gentlemen, The quantity of bread daily expended . . . is very large . . . David Cheever, per order . . . [Watertown? 1775]
broadside
cf. *The month at Goodspeed's*, v. 1, no. 9, June 1930
New York Public 576
NN (reduced facsim.). Photostat: MWA mp. 42880

B4037 MASSACHUSETTS
Watertown, July 8th, 1775. Gentlemen, In obedience to the order of Congress we have proportioned thirteen thousand coats . . . [Watertown, B. Edes, 1775]
broadside 13.5 X 19 cm.
MWA mp. 42882

B4038 MASSACHUSETTS
Watertown, November 18, 1775. You have hereunder . . . [Watertown, B. Edes, 1775]
broadside 21.5 X 34.5 cm.
Ford 1877; Huntington 382
CSmH; MHi; MWA. Photostats: DLC; NN mp. 42869

B4039 MASSACHUSETTS. COMMITTEE OF SAFETY
Cambridge, May 8, 1775. Whereas you have this day received orders for inlisting 56 soldiers . . . By order of the Committee of Safety. [Watertown? 1775]
broadside 20 X 13 cm.
PHi mp. 42864

B4040 MASSACHUSETTS. GOVERNOR, 1774-1775
Boston, May , 1775. Permit together with his family . . . to pass between sunrise and sunset. By order of . . . the Governor . . . No arms or ammunition is allowed to pass. [Boston, 1775]
broadside 8.5 X 21 cm.
Ford 1834
MHi

B4040a MASSACHUSETTS. GOVERNOR, 1774-1775
By His Excellency the Hon. Thomas Gage . . . Governor . . . A proclamation. Whereas the infatuated multitudes . . . have at length proceeded to avowed rebellion . . . Given at Boston the 12th day of June . . . 1775 . . . [Boston, 1775]
broadside 36 X 24.5 cm.
Small royal arms at top; text uncolumned
Variant of Ford 1814
Middendorf Collection, New York City (1970)

B4041 MASSACHUSETTS. GOVERNOR, 1774-1775
By the Governor. A proclamation . . . [June 19, 1775] [Boston, 1775]
broadside
Concerns delivery of fire arms
Ford 1817
MHi; MWA (reduced facsim.) mp. 42865

B4042 MASSACHUSETTS. HOUSE OF REPRESENTATIVES
In the House of Representatives, October 14, 1775. Ordered, That Col. Freeman, Col. Orne . . . be a committee to make suitable provision . . . for the committee expected from the . . . Continental Congress . . . Watertown, October 16, 1775. [Watertown, 1775]
broadside
MB mp. 42866

B4043 MASSACHUSETTS. HOUSE OF REPRESENTATIVES
In the House of Representatives, December 2, 1775. Whereas the supply of the article of wood . . . [Watertown, B. Edes, 1775]
broadside 21 X 14 cm.
Ford 1879
MHi. Photostat: DLC mp. 42867

B4044 MASSACHUSETTS. HOUSE OF REPRESENTATIVES
In the House of Representatives, December 11, 1775. Resolved . . . [Watertown, B. Edes, 1775]
broadside 19 X 23 cm.
Ford 1881
MHi. Photostat: DLC mp. 42868

B4045 MASSACHUSETTS. PROVINCIAL CONGRESS
In Congress, at Watertown, April 30, 1775. Gentlemen, the barbarous murders . . . [Watertown, B. Edes, 1775]
broadside 24 X 18.5 cm.
Ford 1848; Huntington 380
CSmH; MHi. Photostat: DLC mp. 42871

B4046 MASSACHUSETTS. PROVINCIAL CONGRESS
In Provincial Congress, Watertown, May 5, 1775. Whereas the term for which this present Congress was chosen, expires on the thirtieth instant . . . [Salem? 1775]
broadside 25.5 X 20.5 cm.
In different type from Evans 14226, and without imprint
Ford 1852
MHi; MiU-C mp. 42874

B4047 MASSACHUSETTS. PROVINCIAL CONGRESS
In Provincial Congress, Watertown, May 25, 1775. Resolved, That there be draughted out of the town stock of powder . . . [Watertown? 1775]
broadside
Ford 1856
M-Ar mp. 42875

B4048 MASSACHUSETTS. PROVINCIAL CONGRESS
In Provincial Congress, Watertown, June 10, 1775. Resolved, That each soldier in the Massachusetts Army, shall have the following allowance per day, viz. Article 1. One pound of bread . . . Joseph Warren, President. Attest. Samuel Freeman, Secr'y. [Watertown, 1775]
broadside
MB mp. 42876

B4049 MASSACHUSETTS. PROVINCIAL CONGRESS
In provincial Congress, Watertown, June 15, 1775. Whereas some of the inhabitants . . . have inlisted . . . [Watertown, 1775]
broadside 35 X 22 cm.
[Endorsement] 200 of these
Ford 1859
MHi mp. 42877

B4050 MASSACHUSETTS. PROVINCIAL CONGRESS
In Provincial Congress, Watertown, July 1st, 1775. Resolved, That all offences committed by any of the forces . . . shall be tried by a court-martial . . . [Watertown, 1775]
broadside
Ford 1867
MHi mp. 42878

B4051 MASSACHUSETTS. PROVINCIAL CONGRESS
Rules and regulations for the Massachusetts army. Published by order. Cambridge, Printed by Samuel and Ebenezer Hall, 1775.
15 p. 20.5 cm. [A]-B^4
cf. Evans 14244
MB; MWA mp. 42879

B4052 MASSACHUSETTS. PROVINCIAL CONGRESS
To the military officers, select-men, and Committee of Correspondence in the town of Gentlemen, You are . . . requested to procure the execution of the subsequent resolve with the greatest possible expedition. In Provincial Congress, Watertown, July 12, 1775 . . . By order of Congress . . . [Watertown, 1775]
broadside 32 X 19 cm.
MWA mp. 42881

B4053 MASSACHUSETTS. PROVINCIAL CONGRESS
Watertown, 1775. To the select-men of the persons here named viz are ordered to your town by the Provincial Congress . . . [Watertown, 1775]
broadside
Ford 1907
MWA

B4054 MASSACHUSETTS. TREASURER
Colony of Massachusetts-Bay. Henry Gardner, esquire; treasurer . . . Given under my hand . . . the twentieth day of December, 1775. [Watertown, B. Edes, 1775]
broadside 42 X 33 cm.
Ford 1885
DLC; MHi; MWA mp. 42883

B4055 MASSACHUSETTS. TREASURER
Receiver-General's Office. 1775. Received of being of the province tax set on the town of . . . [Watertown? 1775]
broadside
Ford 1886
MWA

B4056 MASSACHUSETTS. TREASURER
Watertown, 1775. Received of Moses Gill Esq; Treasurer . . . [Watertown, B. Edes, 1775]
broadside 17 X 21 cm.
Ford 1797
MHi. Photostat: DLC

B4057 MASSACHUSETTS GAZETTE.
Carrier of the *Massachusetts-Gazette* . . . to all his generous customers. 1775. [Boston, Margaret Draper, 1775]
broadside 26 X 13 cm.
Ford 1942; Wegelin 513
PHi. Photostats: DLC; MHi; NN mp. 42789

B4058 MAYLEM, JOHN, 1695-1742
The conquest of Louisburg. A poem. By John Maylem, Philo-Bellum. [Newport, S. Southwick, 1775]
10 p. 20.5 cm. caption title
Attributed to Southwick's press by Lawrence C. Wroth
Alden 609; Winship p. 32
MH; PHi; RHi; RPB. Rosenbach mp. 42884

B4059 [THE modern veni, vidi, vici.
We came, we saw, but could not beat,
And so—we sounded a retreat; . . .
[n.p., 1775?]
broadside
Appeared on a large handbill (Moore: *Ballad history*, 74)
Ford 1914
No copy located mp. 42885

B4060 [MOODY, ELEAZAR]
The school of good manners . . . Boston, Printed and sold by John Boyle, 1775.
79, [1] p. 14 cm.
CtY (p. 79-[80] wanting); MB; MWA (p. 79-[80] wanting). David McKell, Chillicothe, O. (p. 77-[80] wanting)
mp. 42886

B4061 MORGAN, GEORGE, 1743-1810
Orders. Thursday, July 27, 1775 . . . George Morgan. [Philadelphia, 1775]
broadside 11 X 17 cm.
DLC mp. 42887

B4062 NEW BERN, N.C.
At a meeting of the Committee for the County of Craven, and town of Newbern, on the 4th day of March, 1775. Resolved, that at this critical juncture . . . [Newbern, James Davis, 1775]
broadside 30 X 18 cm.
McMurtrie: North Carolina 77
Public Record Off. mp. 42909

B4063 NEW BERN, N.C.
Proceedings of the Committee for the town of Newbern, and County of Craven, May 31, 1775. Circular letter to the several committees of this Province. [Newbern, James Davis, 1775]
4 p. 31 cm. caption title
McMurtrie: North Carolina 78; NYPL 578
NcWsM; NN (facsim.) mp. 42910

B4064 THE New-England primer improved; for the more easy attaining . . . Providence, John Carter, 1775.
[72] p. 10 cm.
Alden 611; Heartman 56; Winship p. 32
CSmH; RHi mp. 42888

B4065 NEW HAMPSHIRE
Province of New-Hampshire. To the selectmen of the . . . As we were appointed by the late provincial convention a committee to call another . . . [Portsmouth? 1775]
broadside 21 X 17 cm.

To convene at Exeter May 17
Whittemore 175
NhHi mp. 42889

B4066 NEW HAMPSHIRE. PROVINCIAL CONGRESS
Colony of New-Hampshire. In Congress at Exeter, the 4th day of November, 1775. Voted, that it be recommended to the several taverners and retailers . . . [Exeter? Robert Fowle? 1775]
broadside 14.5 X 19 cm.
Whittemore 180
NhD; NhHi mp. 42891

B4067 NEW HAMPSHIRE. PROVINCIAL CONGRESS
In Congress at Exeter, November 16th, 1775. Voted, that the Committees of Safety . . . transmit . . . the names . . . persons . . . any ways enimical [sic] to this country . . . [Exeter? Robert Fowle? 1775]
broadside 30.5 X 13 cm.
Whittemore 182
NhD; NhHi mp. 42890

B4068 NEW HAMPSHIRE. PROVINCIAL CONGRESS
In Congress at Exeter, December 27th, 1775. Whereas a vote of this Congress hath excused all . . . soldiers, who served in the summer past . . . [Exeter? Robert Fowle? 1775?]
broadside 13 X 15.5 cm.
Whittemore 190
NhD; NhHi mp. 42892

B4069 NEW HAMPSHIRE. PROVINCIAL CONGRESS
In Provincial Congress, Exeter, June 2, 1775. To the inhabitants of the colony . . . a very affecting and alarming cricis [sic] . . . [Exeter? Robert Fowle? 1775]
broadside 36 X 24.5 cm.
Whittemore 176
MHi; NhD; NhHi mp. 42893

B4070 NEW HAMPSHIRE. PROVINCIAL CONGRESS
In Provincial Congress, New Hampshire, August 25th, 1775. Whereas it is necessary that an exact account of all the inhabitants . . . be taken . . . Matthew Thornton, President. [Exeter? Robert Fowle? 1775]
broadside 43 X 22 cm.
DLC; MB; NhD; NhHi mp. 42894

B4071 NEW JERSEY. COUNCIL
A message to the Governor from the Council. [Burlington, 1775]
broadside 32 X 21 cm.
Dated: Council-Chamber, Dec. 4, 1775
Humphrey 149; New York Public 579
NN mp. 42895

B4072 NEW JERSEY. GOVERNOR, 1763-1776
A message to the Council [from the governor, William Franklin] . . . [Dec. 6, 1775] [Burlington, Isaac Collins, 1775]
broadside 31.5 X 20.5 cm.
Humphrey 148; New York Public 580
NN mp. 42896

B4073 A NEW liberty song, composed at the camp on Prospect Hill, August, 1775. By a Son of Liberty. Salem, E. Russell [1775]
broadside
Ford 1915; Tapley p. 322
MB mp. 42897

B4074 NEW YORK. COMMITTEE OF OBSERVATION
The following persons were mentioned in the Committee of Observation, as proper to be elected for a general committee . . . [100 names] . . . The following are the names of persons mentioned . . . as deputies . . . in Provincial Congress . . . [20 names] . . . Isaac Low, Chairman. New-York, April 28, 1775. [New York, John Holt, 1775]
broadside 46 X 31 cm.
Facsims.: DLC; MWA; NHi mp. 42898

B4075 NEW YORK. COMMITTEE OF SAFETY
In Committee of Safety for the Colony of New-York, the day of 1775. To Greeting . . . [New York, 1775]
broadside 21.5 X 33 cm.
NHi mp. 42901

B4076 NEW YORK. ELECTION PROX.
The following are the names of the gentlemen nominated, as deputies . . . for whom the Friends of Liberty are requested to give their votes: Isaac Low [and 10 others] [New York, 1775]
broadside 6 X 10 cm.
New York Public 562; *not* Evans 13485
NN mp. 42902

B4077 NEW YORK. GENERAL ASSEMBLY
Extract of the votes and proceedings of the General Assembly . . . of New-York. January 26, 1775 . . . [on verso] To the public. The following proceedings of the General Committee, for the City of New-York, confirm the assurances given on the other side . . . New-York, 31st January, 1775 . . . [New York, 1775]
[2] p. 30.5 cm.
CtHi mp. 42903

B4078 NEW YORK. GOVERNOR, 1771-1780
Letters which lately passed between His Excellency Governor Tryon, and Whitehead Hicks . . . Mayor . . . of New-York. New-York, James Rivington, 1775.
8 p. 18.5 cm.
New York Public 581; Sabin 97291
NHi. Photostat: NN mp. 42904

B4079 NEW YORK. MILITIA
Instructions for the inlisting of men. First, You are not to inlist any man . . . not able-bodied . . . In Provincial Congress at New-York, June 1775 . . . [New York, 1775]
broadside 42 X 25 cm.
NHi mp. 42906

B4080 NEW YORK. PROVINCIAL CONGRESS
In Provincial Congress, New-York, Dec. 13, 1775. Whereas this Congress has received information that . . . disaffected persons . . . have been supplied . . . from . . . the Asia ship of war . . . [New York, 1775]
broadside 16.5 X 21 cm.
NHi mp. 42905

B4081 NEW YORK. PROVINCIAL CONGRESS
The Provincial Congress at their meeting, having unanimously chosen . . . gentlemen, to represent this Colony at the general Congress . . . at Philadelphia . . . have thought proper that an ox should be roasted . . . on Monday next . . . New-York, April 22, 1775. [New York, 1775]
broadside 20 X 12.5 cm.
NHi mp. 42907

B4082 NEW-YORK, April 28, 1775. To the public . . . [New York, 1775]
broadside 12.5 X 20.5 cm.
DLC mp. 42908

B4083 [NILES, NATHANIEL] 1741-1828
The American hero. Made on the battle of Bunker-Hill, and the burning of Charlestown . . . [n.p., 1775?]
broadside 25 X 21 cm.
Ford 1787; Huntington 384; Wegelin I. 60
CSmH mp. 42911

B4084 NORD-AMERICANISCHE Calender des . . . 1776. Von Gottlieb Himmels-Bewunderer . . . Lancaster, Franz Bailey [1775]
[44] p.
Drake 10024
NHi

B4085 THE North-American almanack for . . . 1776 . . . Boston, Printed and sold in Queen-Street [1775]
[16] p. 15.5 cm.
By Samuel Stearns
MWA mp. 42943

B4086 NORTH CAROLINA. CONVENTION, 1775
At a general meeting of delegates of the inhabitants of this province . . . [Journal, Apr. 3-7, 1775] [Newbern, James Davis, 1775]
4 p. 30.5 cm. caption title
NcU. Mrs. J. G. Wood, Edenton, N.C. mp. 42913

B4087 NORTH CAROLINA. CONVENTION, 1775
North-Carolina. At a convention . . . held at Newbern the 6th day of April, 1775, Mr. Thomas Macknight . . . withdrew himself . . . We . . . Samuel Jarvis, Solomon Perkins, and Nathan Poyner, late representatives for . . . Currituck . . . having found ourselves under the necessity of withdrawing . . . [Newbern, James Davis? 1775]
broadside 35.5 X 23 cm.
In two columns
NcU. Mrs. J. G. Wood, Edenton, N.C. mp. 42912

B4088 NORTH CAROLINA. GOVERNOR, 1771-1776
North-Carolina. By His Excellency Josiah Martin . . . A proclamation. Whereas . . . sundry ill-disposed persons have been . . . propagating . . . scandalous reports . . . [June 16, 1775] . . . Alexander Maclean pro James Biggleston, D. Secretary . . . [Newbern, James Davis, 1775]
broadside 43 X 18 cm.
In two columns
McMurtrie: North Carolina 83; NYPL 582
NN. Public Record Off. mp. 42915

B4089 NORTH CAROLINA. GOVERNOR, 1771-1776
North-Carolina, ss. By his Excellency Josiah Martin . . . A proclamation . . . [Feb. 10, 1775] . . . James Parratt, D. Sec. [Newbern, James Davis, 1775]
broadside 44 X 32 cm.
Forbidding Richard Henderson to establish a colony for undesirable citizens
McMurtrie: North Carolina 82
MiU-C. Public Record Off. mp. 42914

B4090 AN occasional paper, containing the most important . . . advices. Newport, Monday, Nov. 6, 1775. [Newport, S. Southwick, 1775]
broadside 40 X 26 cm.
Alden 612; Winship p. 32
RNHi mp. 42916

B4091 OGDEN, SAMUEL
A plain narrative of a certain dispute between the Earl of Stirling & Samuel Ogden . . . [n.p.] Printed for the author, 1775.
56 p. 21.5 cm.
NjR; PPAmP mp. 42917

B4092 PALMER, JOSEPH, & CO.
Sperma-ceti candles warranted pure; are made by Joseph Palmer & Co. at Germantown near Boston, & to be sold at their store in Boston, New England . . . Nat. Hurd, sculp. [Boston? 1775?]
broadside 15.5 X 18.5 cm.
Engraved, with text mostly in script, upper portion in English, lower portion in French. Whale in center oval
Ford 1545
MHi

B4093 A PARAPHRASE on the second epistle of John, the Round-head, to James, Prolocutor of the Rump-Parliament, in a liberal manner . . . [Boston? Mills and Hicks? 1775]
broadside 39 X 25 cm.
Text of an actual letter from John Adams to James Warren, July 24, 1775, with satirical commentary
MB (imperfect). Photostat: DLC mp. 42918

B4094 PHILADELPHIA. ELECTION PROX.
Committee for the City of Philadelphia and Northern Liberties, to continue for six months. Doctor Franklin, Thomas Mifflin . . . [Philadelphia, 1775]
broadside
Not Evans 14385
Dated by Du Simitiere Aug. 16, 1775
PPL mp. 42919

B4095 PHILADELPHIA. ELECTION PROX.
Committee, for the city of Philadelphia, district of Southwark and Northern Liberties. Doctor Franklin. Thomas Mifflin . . . [Philadelphia, 1775]
broadside 4to
Dated by Du Simitiere Aug. 16, 1775
PPL mp. 42920

B4096 PITT, WILLIAM, EARL OF CHATHAM, 1708-1778
An authentic copy of Lord Chatham's proposed bill, entitled A provisional act . . . Annapolis, Frederick Green, 1775.
16 p. 8vo [1]-2^4
Adams 190Ab; Lapham 412
ICN

B4097 PITT, WILLIAM, EARL OF CHATHAM, 1708-1778
[The speech of the Earl of Chatham, January 20, 1775, on a motion for an address to his Majesty, for removing his troops from Boston. Newbern, James Davis, 1775]

Advertised in the *North-Carolina Gazette,* June 30, 1775, as "just published, and to be sold at the Printing Office," and "From that [Philadelphia] Copy the same is now published here."
McMurtrie: North Carolina 85
No copy known mp. 42922

B4098 [THE progress of Methodism, or, the itinerant's sure guide. Charleston, 1775]

Title from *South Carolina Gazette and Country Journal,* Apr. 19, 1775
Mosimann 249
No copy known

B4099 PROPOSALS for printing by subscription, The conquest of Canaan [by Timothy Dwight] . . . [Boston? 1775?]
broadside 38 X 15 cm.

MWA copy filled in with subscribers' names in Massachusetts
MWA mp. 42808

B4100 PROVIDENCE
Providence beacon. The town of Providence to the inhabitants of the towns adjacent . . . August 10, 1775. [Providence, J. Carter? 1775]
broadside 18 X 12.5 cm.
Alden 613; Winship p. 32
Henry R. Drowne, New York. Photostat: NHi mp. 42923

B4101 THE recantations of Jacob Fowle, Benjamin Marston, John Gallison, Robert Hooper, Tertius, Nathan Bowen, Samuel White, and Thomas Lewis . . . May 2, 1775. In Committee of safety, Cambridge. [Watertown? 1775]
broadside ([2] p.) 38 X 24.5 cm.
Ford 1918
MHi; MWA mp. 42925

B4102 THE recantations of Robert Hooper, John Pedrick . . . Cambridge, May 4, 1775 . . . [Boston] Printed and sold in Queen-Street. [1775]
broadside 23.5 X 14 cm.
Ford 1919; cf. Evans 14194
DLC; MHi. Photostat: NHi mp. 42926

B4103 THE recantations of Robert Hooper, John Pedrick . . . May 4, 1775. Salem, E. Russell [1775]
broadside 38.5 X 24.5 cm.
Ford 1920
MWA. Photostat: NHi mp. 42927

B4104 RHODE ISLAND. ELECTION PROX.
Liberty, and no Tories. The honorable William Greene, Esq; Gov. The honorable Darius Sessions, Esq; Deputy-Gov. . . . [Providence? 1775]
broadside 18 X 12 cm.
Alden 614; Chapin Proxies 16
MWA; RHi mp. 42930

B4105 RHODE ISLAND. GENERAL ASSEMBLY
[At the General assembly . . . holden . . . the twenty-eighth day of June . . . It is voted and resolved, that messieurs Jabez Champlin . . . Providence, J. Carter, 1775]
[broadside?]
Billed by Carter July 4, 1775
Alden 620B
No copy known mp. 42932

B4106 RHODE ISLAND. GOVERNOR, 1769-1775
To the freemen of the Colony of Rhode-Island. Gentlemen, permit me . . . Your . . . servant, J. Wanton. Newport, April 12, 1775. [Newport, S. Southwick, 1775]
broadside 32 X 20 cm.
Alden 629; NYPL 583; Sabin 101253
RHi; RPJCB. Photostats: MHi; MWA; NN mp. 42978

B4107 RHODE ISLAND. GOVERNOR, 1775-1778
[By the honorable Nicholas Cooke, Esq; Deputy-Governor . . . A proclamation [for a day of public fasting] . . . [June 22, 1775] . . . Providence, J. Carter [1775].]
[broadside?]
Bill submitted by Carter June 24, 1775
Alden 613A
No copy known mp. 42929

B4108 RHODE ISLAND. GOVERNOR, 1775-1778
[By the honorable Nicholas Cooke . . . A proclamation for a day of thanksgiving . . . [Nov. 16, 1775] . . . Providence, John Carter [1775].]
[broadside?]
Bill submitted by Carter Nov. 15, 1775
No copy known mp. 42928

B4109 RHODE ISLAND. LAWS
[At the General assembly . . . holden . . . the twenty-eighth day of June . . . An act for inlisting one fourth part of the militia . . . as minute-men . . . Providence, J. Carter, 1775]
[broadside?]
Bill submitted by Carter July 4, 1775
Alden 620A
No copy known mp. 42931

B4110 RHODE ISLAND. MILITIA
Rules and regulations for the Rhode-Island army . . . Newport, S. Southwick, 1775.
16 p. 18 cm.
Alden 620C; Winship p. 32
MHi (imperfect); RHi mp. 42933

B4111 RICH, ELISHA, 1740-1804?
Poetical dialogues . . . Boston, Printed, by Nathaniel Coverly, for the author, 1775.
36 p. 17.5 cm. $[A]\text{-}D^4\ E^2$
Wegelin 324
MWA; PU; RPJCB mp. 42934

B4112 SALEM. THIRD CHURCH
Rev. Sir, Our destitute state earnestly bespeaks your compassion . . . March 6, 1775 . . . Nathaniel Whitaker. [Salem, 1775]
broadside 32.5 X 19 cm.
Ford 1924
MWA mp. 42935

B4113 SALEM, Tuesday, July 19, 1775. This day at noon, Captain John Derby . . . arrived here . . . from London . . . Salem, E. Russel [1775]
broadside 35.5 X 22 cm.
Ford 1926; Tapley p. 323
MHi mp. 42936

B4114 SESSIONS, DARIUS
To the freemen of the colony of Rhode-Island . . . Your . . . servant, Darius Sessions. Providence, April 15, 1775. [Providence, 1775]
broadside 35 X 23 cm.
Alden 622; New York Public 584
NN; RHi; RPJCB mp. 42937

B4115 SESSIONS, DARIUS
To the freemen of the colony of Rhode-Island . . . Your . . . servant, Darius Sessions. Providence, April 15, 1775. [Newport? 1775]
broadside 31 X 17 cm.
In this edition the title occupies a single line, with "Rhode Island" in roman type
Alden 623
RHi

B4116 SMITH, WILLIAM, 1727-1803
A / sermon / on the present situation of / American affairs / . . . Philadelphia, Printed and sold by James Humphrays Junior . . . MDCCLXXV.
2 p.l., iv, 32 p. 8vo $[-]^4$ $A\text{-}D^4$
Entirely different setting from Evans 14459
Adams 196b
CSmH; CtHi; CtY; InU; MB; MBAt; MWA; MWiW-C; NjP; PP; PPAmP; PU; RPB; RPJCB

B4117 A SONG, composed by the British butchers, after the fight at Bunker-Hill . . . [Chelmsford? Nathaniel Coverly? 1775?]

broadside 35 X 22 cm.
Woodcut (4¾" X 7½") at head of sheet
Ford 1933; cf. Evans 14465
MWiW-C; NN mp. 42940

B4118 A SONG. Composed by the British butchers, after the fight at Bunker-Hill on the 17th of June 1775. Boston, Sold at the Bible and Heart in Cornhill [1775]
broadside 28.5 X 18.5 cm.
Ford 1930; New York Public 586
MHi; NHi. Photostat: NN mp. 42941

B4119 A SONG, composed by the British soldiers, after the battle at Bunker-Hill, on the 17th of June, 1775. [n.p., 1775]
broadside
Ford 1934; Wegelin I. 61?
MB; RPB mp. 42939

B4120 A SONG. American triumphant: or, Old England's downfali [!]. This world is like a whirligig . . . Printed and sold [by B. Edes] in Watertown, 1775.
broadside 33 X 21 cm.
PPRF

B4121 SOUTH CAROLINA. PROVINCIAL CONGRESS
Rules and articles for the government of the military forces of South-Carolina. Published by order of the Congress. Charles-Town, Peter Timothy, 1775.
36 p.
ScU

B4122 SOUTH-Carolina. The actual commencement of hostilities against this continent . . . [Charleston? 1775]
broadside 13 X 23.5 cm.
Resolution concerning defence of the colonies
New York Public 587
NN mp. 42942

B4123 SPENCER, ELIHU
To cover, at Ezekiel Ball's, at three dollars the season, or ten shillings a leap, the beautiful bay colt Spark . . . bought . . . in April 1775, is rising four years . . . Elihu Spencer. Grass for mares, at 2s. 6d. per week . . . by Ezekiel Ball, at Newark Farms. [Newark? 1775]
broadside 25.5 X 21 cm.
NjR (mutilated)

B4124 SWAN, ABRAHAM
The British architect . . . Philadelphia, Printed by R. Bell for John Norman, 1775.
3 p.l., vi, 17, [2] p. 60 plates. 42 cm.
DLC (3 copies); DeWin; MWA; MiU-C; N; NHi; PPF; RPJCB mp. 42944

B4125 SWAN, AMOS
Will cover the ensuing season, the fine black horse Victory . . . at the house of the subscriber, inn-keeper at the Scotch Plains, in the borough of Elizabeth . . . Amos Swan . . . March 8, 1775. [Elizabeth? 1775]
broadside 27 X 20 cm.
NjR

B4126 TEN minutes advice to every gentleman going to purchase a horse . . . Philadelphia, Printed by Joseph Crukshank, for W. Aikman, bookseller, in Annapolis, 1775.
[6], 49, iv, 70 p. 13 cm. A-K^6 (K6 wanting)
Pages 30-35 omitted in numbering
Second t.p. (sig. E2): The gentleman's pocket-farrier . . . by William Burdon. Philadelphia, Printed by Joseph Crukshank, for W. Aikman, 1775.
MWA mp. 42782

B4127 THURSDAY last (25th May) Capt. Chads arrived here from England in the Cerberus frigate, and has brought papers to the 18th of April . . . . [Boston] Mills and Hicks [1775]
broadside 39 X 26 cm.
MHi mp. 42950

B4128 TO Mr. Isaac Low Veritas presents his compliments . . . New-York, March 16th, 1775. [New York, 1775]
broadside 25 X 21 cm.
NHi; PPL. Photostat: MWA mp. 42945

B4129 TO the committees of the several towns and counties of . . . North-Carolina, appointed for . . . carrying into execution the resolves of the Continental Congress. Gentlemen, When the liberties . . . [Newbern? 1775]
[2] p. 29 cm.
Signed: William Hooper, Joseph Hewes, Richard Caswell, Philadelphia, June 19, 1775
McMurtrie: North Carolina 88
Public Record Off. mp. 42946

B4130 TO the inhabitants of the city and county of New-York. The wisest men in all ages . . . A Citizen. New-York, March 4, 1775. [New York, 1775]
2 p. 43 X 25 cm.
Stan Henkels (1931). Photostat: MWA mp. 42947

B4131 TO the public. By the following letters, these facts appear unquestionable, viz. That the Committee of fifty-one . . . Remembrancer. New-York, January 18, 1775. The first letter wrote by the Committee of Fifty-one to Boston . . . The second letter wrote . . . [New York, 1775]
[2] p. 43 X 24.5 cm.
NNS. Photostat: MWA mp. 42948

B4132 TO the worthy inhabitants of the city of New-York. Friends and fellow citizens, At a time so truly critical and alarming . . . Signed by order of the Committee of Inspection, William Flanagan, Chairman. New-York, February 16, 1775. [New York, 1775]
broadside
Concerns second choice of delegates to the Continental Congress
NNS

B4133 TRINITY CHURCH, N.Y.
An hymn, to be sung by the children of the Charity-School, of . . . Trinity Church, on Sunday the 3d December, 1775 . . . [New York, 1775]
broadside 36.5 X 23.5 cm.
NHi (2 copies) mp. 42900

B4134 TWO favorite songs of the American camp. Exhortation to the freemen of America . . . The American Liberty song. [Boston, 1775?]
broadside 34.5 X 19 cm.
Ford 2402; Sabin 97557
PHi mp. 42949

B4135 U.S.
Naval pay list . . . extract from the minutes . . . [Philadelphia? 1775?]
broadside 17 X 15 cm.
Text in 2 columns
Rates for those of 1775
RPJCB mp. 42967

B4136 U.S. ARMY. CONTINENTAL ARMY
Cambridge, 21st August, 1775. Wanted for the Continental army . . . [Watertown? B. Edes? 1775]

broadside 13.5 X 18 cm.
Ford 1802
MHi; MWA. Photostat: DLC mp. 42951

B4137 U.S. ARMY. CONTINENTAL ARMY
Headquarters. Cambridge, 27 August, 1775. His Excellency General Washington has been informed that great quantities of new cyder . . . [Watertown? B. Edes? 1775]
broadside
MB mp. 42952

B4138 U.S. ARMY. CONTINENTAL ARMY
A return of cloathing, &c. wanting in Col. regiment, September 1775. [Watertown? B. Edes? 1775]
broadside
Ford 1905
MHi mp. 42953

B4139 U.S. ARMY. CONTINENTAL ARMY
A return of the regiment in the service of the United Colonies of North-America, commanded by July 1, 1775. [Watertown? B. Edes? 1775]
broadside
Ford 1901
MHi mp. 42954

B4140 U.S. ARMY. CONTINENTAL ARMY
A return of the regiment in the service of the United Colonies of North-America, commanded by Colonel July 1, 1775. [Watertown? B. Edes? 1775]
broadside 38.5 X 34 cm.
Ford 1900
MWA mp. 42955

B4141 U.S. ARMY. CONTINENTAL ARMY
We whose names are hereunto subscribed, being determined to . . . defend our country . . . have . . . inlisted as soldiers in the Continental Army . . . from the last day of December next . . . October , 1775. [Watertown? B. Edes? 1775]
broadside 5? X 15.5 cm.
Ford 1895
MHi; MWA mp. 42956

B4142 U.S. CONTINENTAL CONGRESS, 1774
Auszüge aus den stimmungen . . . und die schlüsse der im Jenner 1775 gehaltenen Provinzial-Convention von Pennsylvanien. Philadelphia, Henrich Miller, 1775.
66 p. 19 cm.
cf. Evans 13735
DLC mp. 42957

B4143 U.S. CONTINENTAL CONGRESS, 1774
[Extracts from the votes and proceedings of the American Continental Congress, held at Philadelphia, on the fifth day of September, 1774 . . . Also the letter to the inhabitants of Quebec . . . Newbern, James Davis, 1775]

Advertised in the *North-Carolina Gazette*, Feb. 24, 1775, as "just published, and to be sold at the Printing Office, in Newbern."
McMurtrie: North Carolina 87
No copy known mp. 42960

B4144 U.S. CONTINENTAL CONGRESS, 1775
A declaration by the representatives of the United Colonies . . . setting forth the causes . . . of their taking up arms. Newbury-port, 1775.
8 p. 20 cm.
Huntington 390
CSmH; MWA mp. 42958

B4145 U.S. CONTINENTAL CONGRESS, 1775
A declaration by the representatives of the United Colonies . . . setting forth the causes . . . of their taking up arms. Salem, Re-printed, and sold by E. Russell, 1775.
8 p. 17.5 cm.
MWA mp. 41959

B4146 U.S. CONTINENTAL CONGRESS, 1775
The humble petition of the Twelve United Colonies, by their delegates in Congress, to the King. Philadelphia, William and Thomas Bradford, 1775.
8 p. 19.5 cm.
Huntington 391; Metzger 461
CSmH; PPL; RPJCB mp. 42961

B4147 U.S. CONTINENTAL CONGRESS, 1775
In Congress, Monday, June 12, 1775. As the great governor of the world . . . [n.p., 1775]
broadside 43 X 33.5 cm.
cf. Evans 14563
DLC; PHi mp. 42962

B4148 U.S. CONTINENTAL CONGRESS, 1775
In Congress, Saturday, July 15, 1775. Whereas the government of Great Britain hath prohibited the exportation of arms . . . Charles Thomson, Secretary. [Philadelphia, 1775]
broadside 23 X 20 cm.
PHi

B4149 U.S. CONTINENTAL CONGRESS, 1775
In Congress, Thursday, June 22, 1775. Resolved, That a sum not exceeding two millions . . . [n.p., 1775]
broadside 35.5 X 16 cm.
Contains other resolves of June 23, July 21, 25 & 29, 1775
CtHi; DLC mp. 42963

B4150 U.S. CONTINENTAL CONGRESS, 1775
Philadelphia, in Congress, June 12, 1775. A proclamation for a continental public fast . . . Charles Thomson, Secretary. [Philadelphia, 1775]
broadside 38 X 25.5 cm.
MHi mp. 42964

B4150a U.S. CONTINENTAL CONGRESS, 1775
Philadelphia. In Congress, December 6, 1775. We the delegates . . . [Philadelphia? 1775]
broadside
In three columns
New York Public 588; cf. Evans 14567-68; cf. Stan V. Henkels cat. 809 (Supplement), Mar. 25, 1898, item 9
NN (reduced facsim.) mp. 42965

B4151 U.S. CONTINENTAL CONGRESS, 1775
The twelve united colonies, by their delegates in Congress, to the inhabitants of Great-Britain. Friends, countrymen, and brethren . . . Philadelphia, July 8th, 1775. [Colophon] Portsmouth, Sold at the Printing-office, 1775.
broadside 42.5 X 26.5 cm.
Whittemore 185
NhHi mp. 42966

B4152 VERMONT. CONVENTION, 1774
The proceedings of the convention . . . of the New-Hampshire settlers . . . Hartford, Ebenezer Watson, 1775
17 p. 33.5 cm.
Sabin 98998; New York Public 589
DLC (2 copies); Vt; VtU; NN (facsim.) mp. 42968

B4153 VIRGINIA. COMMITTEE OF SAFETY
Williamsburg, October 26. Whereas Lord Dunmore, not contented with having involved the affairs of this colony . . . Baltimore, John Dunlap [1775]
broadside 27.5 X 19.5 cm.
Wroth 368
MdHi mp. 42969

B4154 VIRGINIA. COUNCIL
To all the good people of Virginia. We . . . can no longer forbear to express our abhorrence . . . of that licentious and ungovernable spirit . . . John Blair, C. C. [Williamsburg, Dixon and Hunter, 1775]
broadside 26.5 X 17 cm.
DLC (photostat) mp. 42970

B4155 VIRGINIA. COUNCIL
To . . . the right hon. John Earl of Dunmore . . . the humble address of the Council. [In reply to his address of June 1, 1775] [Williamsburg, Dixon and Hunter, 1775]
broadside 31 X 18 cm.
DLC (photostat) mp. 42971

B4156 VIRGINIA. GOVERNOR, 1771-1775
At a council held at the palace May 2, 1775. Present . . . the governor, Thomas Nelson, Richard Corbin . . . The governor was pleased to address himself to the board . . . Williamsburg, John Pinkney [1775]
broadside 32 cm.
Public Record Off. Photostat: Vi mp. 42972

B4157 VIRGINIA. GOVERNOR, 1771-1775
By . . . the right honourable John Earl of Dunmore . . . a proclamation. Virginia, to wit . . . Given under my hand . . . this 21st day of March . . . [Williamsburg, Dixon and Hunter, 1775]
broadside 40 X 32 cm.
DLC (photostat) mp. 42974

B4158 VIRGINIA. GOVERNOR, 1771-1775
By . . . the right honourable John Earl of Dunmore . . . a proclamation. Virginia, to wit . . . Given under my hand . . . this 28th day of March . . . [Williamsburg, Dixon and Hunter, 1775]
broadside 31 X 18 cm.
DLC (photostat) mp. 42975

B4159 VIRGINIA. GOVERNOR, 1771-1775
By . . . the right hon. John Earl of Dunmore . . . a proclamation. Virginia, to wit, Whereas I have been informed . . . Given under my hand . . . this 6th day of May, 1775 . . . [Williamsburg, John Dixon and William Hunter, 1775]
broadside 31 X 18 cm.
Public Record Off. Photostats: DLC; Vi mp. 42976

B4160 VIRGINIA. GOVERNOR, 1771-1775
By . . . the right honourable John Earl of Dunmore . . . a proclamation. As I have ever entertained hopes . . . Given under my hand, on board the ship William, off Norfolk, the 7th day of November . . . [Williamsburg, Alexander Purdie, 1775]
broadside 31 X 19.5 cm.
Evans 14592 was printed at Norfolk; cf. *Amer. notes and queries* Feb. 1947, p. 163-4
DLC; ViU mp. 42973

B4161 VIRGINIA. HOUSE OF BURGESSES
Journal of the House of burgesses . . . begun . . . the first day of June . . . 1775. [Williamsburg, A. Purdie? 1775]
[4] p. 31.5 cm. caption title
NN mp. 42977

B4162 VIRGINIA GAZETTE
Williamsburgh, Friday evening, eight o'clock. Our paper was entirely prepared for the press; but . . . the arrival . . . of the snow Martin . . . Williamsburgh, John Pinkney [1775]
broadside 17 X 20.5 cm.
MWiW-C mp. 42921

B4163 WATTS, ISAAC, 1674-1748
Divine songs, attempted in easy language . . . The fourteenth edition. Boston, Printed and sold by N. Coverly, 1775.
47 p. illus. 14.5 cm.
MWA mp. 42981

B4164 WATTS, ISAAC, 1674-1748
Divine songs, attempted in easy language . . . The fourteenth edition. Boston, Printed for and sold by A. Barclay, 1775.
47 p. illus. 13.5 cm.
MB; MBC mp. 42980

B4165 WE, freeholders and inhabitants of Queen's County, feeling in common with our fellow subjects, the deepest anxiety . . . [Dec. 6, 1775] . . . [New York 1775]
broadside 30.5 X 25 cm.
Tories defend their action
NHi mp. 42924

B4166 WESTMINSTER ASSEMBLY OF DIVINES
The larger catechism . . . Philadelphia, Printed and sold by Robert Aitken, 1775.
40 p. 18 cm. A-C^6 [D]^2
MWA mp. 42982

B4167 [WHARTON, SAMUEL] 1732-1800
View of the title to Indiana . . . [Philadelphia? 1775]
24 p. 21 cm.
cf. Alvord, C. W. *The Mississippi Valley in British politics*, v. 2, p. 317
Huntington 394; Sabin 99584
CSmH; DLC; NjP; RPJCB; WHi. Photostat: NN mp. 42983

B4168 WHEELOCK, ELEAZAR, 1711-1779
A continuation of the narrative of the Indian charity-school . . . Hartford, Ebenezer Watson, 1775.
31 p.
Stitched and uncut copy indicates this was issued without p. 33-54 of Evans 14623
Sabin 103212
CSmH; NhD; RPJCB

B4169 WHEREAS it is the prevailing rage of the present times . . . to form associations . . . a military congress be immediately formed . . . to take cognizance . . . of the proceedings of the Provincial Congress now sitting at Concord . . . [n.p., 1775]
broadside 23.5 X 18 cm.
Ford 1938; New York Public 592
DLC; MHi. Photostat: NN mp. 42984

B4170 WHOEVER has candidly traced the rapid growth of these colonies from their little beginnings . . . The Watchman. Memorandums, for a report [on the garrisoning of Boston] . . . [Boston, Edes and Gill? 1775?]
broadside
MB; MHi mp. 42985

B4171 WILLIAMS, WILLIAM, 1731-1811
Advertisement. Any gun-smith or lockmaker, within the County of Windham . . . June 1st, 1775. Wm Williams . . .

William Hillhouse, Esq; is a committee for the same purpose in New London County. [New London? 1775]
broadside 15 X 11 cm.
CtHi mp. 42760

B4172 WILLIAMSBURG, (Virginia) Sept. 9, The shocking accounts of damage done by the rains . . . [Baltimore] John Dunlap [1775]
broadside 26.5 X 21 cm.
Wroth 369
MdHi mp. 42986

B4173 WORCESTER COUNTY.
[At a convention of committees for the County of Worcester, convened . . . January 27, 1775, the following resolve (among others) passed, viz.] Resolved, That it be recom[mended that all those citizens] that have not signed this or a similar covenant . . . do it as soon as may be . . . Witness our hands this 17th day of January 1775 . . . [Worcester? 1775]
broadside
Ford 1939
MWA (mutilated) mp. 42987

B4174 WORCESTER COUNTY
At a convention of committees for the County of Worcester, convened . . . January 27, 1775, the following resolves (among others) passed, viz. Whereas Isaac Jones of Weston . . . has . . . manifested a disposition inimical to the rights . . . of his countrymen . . . [Worcester? 1775]
broadside 21.5 X 18 cm.
Ford 1790
MWA mp. 42988

B4175 ZUM 7ten September, 1775. [Philadelphia? Henrich Miller, 1775?]
[7] p. 17 cm.
PHi mp. 42989

1776

B4176 THE American crisis. When I consider the late speech of the king . . . [Colophon] Williamsburg, Printed by Alex. Purdie, at the Constitutional Post Office [1776]
21 p. 22 cm. [ ]^4 C-D^4 (D4 blank)
MWA mp. 42990

B4177 THE American primer, improved . . . To which is added, The Assembly of Divine's Catechism. Boston, Printed by Nathaniel Coverly, for James Gardner, of Providence, 1776.
[64] p. [A]-D^8
Heartman: Non-New-England 3
CtY (Pequot copy) mp. 42991

B4178 AMERICANISCHE Reichs-Staats-Kriegs- und Geschichts-Calendar auf . . . 1777. . . Lancaster, Matthias Bartgis, 1776.

Bausman p. 13
No copy known mp. 42992

B4179 AT a meeting of the Committee of Correspondence, &c. of the towns of Mendon, Uxbridge, and Douglass, on the 29th day of May, 1776 . . . [n.p., 1776]
broadside 22 X 9 cm.
Ford 2028
MWA mp. 43066

B4180 BELL, ROBERT, d. 1784
Philadelphia, May 6th, 1776. Just printed, published, and now selling by R. Bell . . . The diseases incident to armies . . . The military guide for young officers . . . Political pamphlets; either for, or against independency . . . [Philadelphia, R. Bell, 1776]
broadside 26 X 22 cm.
Taylor 1
DLC mp. 42993

B4181 BENEZET, ANTHONY, 1713-1784
The Pennsylvania spelling-book . . . compiled by Anthony Benezet. Philadelphia, Joseph Crukshank, 1776.
160 p. 12mo
PPL mp. 42994

B4182 BIBLE. N.T. APOCRYPHAL BOOKS. EPISTLE OF JESUS CHRIST
A copy of a letter written by Our Blessed Lord and Savior Jesus Christ . . . To which is added, King Agbarus's letter to our Saviour . . . London, Printed: Salem, Reprinted and sold by E. Russell, 1776. Sold also by S. Richardson, travelling-trader, in Woburn.
8 p.
Tapley p. 326
MSaE mp. 43015

B4183 BICKERSTAFF'S Boston almanack, for the year . . . 1777 . . . [Danvers? 1776]
[26] p.
Contains a full-face portrait of John Hancock
Hamilton 78; cf. Evans 14777
N (cropped); NjP mp. 43029

B4184 BOSTON. CITIZENS
At a meeting of the freeholders and other inhabitants of Boston, on Monday the 18th of November inst. . . .
[Boston, 1776]
broadside 36 X 22 cm.
Ford 1795, 1945; New York Public 593
MHi; MWA. Photostats: DLC; NN mp. 42996

B4185 BOSTON. POST OFFICE
The officers of the Army and Navy, and others in the Town of Boston to whom the following list of letters now at Cambridge belong, are desired to send the postage . . . the Post-Office in Boston Saturday next . . . Jonathan Hastings, Post-Master. [Boston, 1776]
broadside 45.5 X 24.5 cm.
Ford 2032
MHi mp. 42995

B4186 BUCKS County, den 14ten December, 1776, Der Fortgang der Brittischen und Hessischen Truppen durch Neu-Jersey ist mit solcher Verwüstung . . . begleitet gewesen . . . [n.p., 1776]
broadside 24.5 X 18.5 cm.
Taylor 3
PHi mp. 42997

B4187 CAMDEN, CHARLES PRATT, EARL OF, 1714-1794
The speeches of the Right Honorable Lords Camden and Abingdon in favor of America. Spoken in the House of Lords, March sixteenth, one thousand seven hundred and seventy-five, during the interesting debates on the New-England fishery-bill . . . they will serve to shew we have some friends in England . . . Salem: Printed by E. Russell, next to John Turner [1776?]
broadside 38.5 X 26.5 cm.
Mass. Bar Assoc.

B4188 [CHALMERS, JAMES] d. 1806
Additions to Plain truth; addressed to the inhabitants of America . . . Written by the author of Plain truth. Philadelphia, R. Bell, 1776.
[2], [97]-135 p. 19.5 cm.
With Plain truth. Philadelphia, R. Bell, 1776
DLC mp. 42998

B4189 [CHALMERS, JAMES] d. 1806
Plain truth; addressed to the inhabitants of America . . . By Candidus . . . Philadelphia: Printed, and sold, by R. Bell . . . MDCCLXXVI.
84 [i.e. 94], [2] p. 19.5 cm. [A]-K^4 L^3 M^4
[2] p. at end: advertisements
This issue has several incorrectly paged variants
Adams 308b
CtHT-W, DLC; MH; MHi; MWA; PHi; PPAmP; PPL; PU
mp. 42999

B4190 [CHALMERS, JAMES] d. 1806
Plain truth; addressed to the inhabitants of America . . . written by Candidus. Philadelphia, R. Bell, 1776.
96, [8], [97]-135 p. 19.5 cm.
A reissue of the first edition, differing in collation, etc.
Huntington 409; Sabin 84642; Sowerby III 3120
CSmH; DLC mp. 43000

B4191 [CHALMERS, JAMES] d. 1806
Plain truth; addressed to the inhabitants of America . . . written by Candidus. Philadelphia, R. Bell, 1776.
96, [8], [97]-136 p. 20.5 cm.
A reissue of the first edition, differing in collation, etc., and containing additions
DLC (2 copies; copy 2 has Additions . . . printed in part on blue paper); MWA mp. 43001

B4192 [CHALMERS, JAMES] d. 1806
Plain truth; addressed to the inhabitants of America . . . written by Candidus. Philadelphia, R. Bell, 1776.
96, [8], [97]-135, [136] blank, [137-138] p. 19.5 cm.
Pages [137-138]: "The Printer to the Public [on the liberty of the press]" and an advertisement
ICN mp. 43002

B4193 CONNECTICUT. GENERAL ASSEMBLY
At a General assembly . . . on the second Thrusday of May 1776. Whereas the General assembly . . . have at this session . . . [New London, T. Green, 1776]
broadside 26 X 21 cm.
MHi. Photostats: DLC; ICN; MH; MWA; NN
mp. 43013

B4194 CONNECTICUT. GOVERNOR, 1769-1776
By the honorable Jonathan Trumbull . . . a proclamation, for an embargo . . . [May 16, 1776] [New London, T. Green, 1776]
broadside 32.5 X 20 cm.
Photostats: DLC; MHi; NHi; NN mp. 43003

B4195 CONNECTICUT. GOVERNOR, 1769-1776
By the honorable Jonathan Trumbull . . . A proclamation. The race of mankind . . . [June 18, 1776] . . . [New London, T. Green, 1776]
broadside 43 X 25 cm.
Huntington 399; New York Public 597
CSmH; CtHi; MHi; NhHi. Photostats: DLC; MH; MWA; NHi; NN mp. 43006

B4196 CONNECTICUT. GOVERNOR, 1769-1776
By the honorable Jonathan Trumbull . . . a proclamation. Whereas it is resolved . . . embargo be laid upon the exportation out of this Colony by water . . . Hartford, this [ ] day of June, 1776 . . . [Hartford? 1776]
broadside 34 X 21.5 cm.
CtHi. Photostat: RPJCB mp. 43009

B4197 CONNECTICUT. GOVERNOR, 1769-1776
By the honorable Jonathan Trumbull, Esq; Governor . . . Whereas the General Assembly . . . on the fourteenth day of June . . . enacted, That seven battalions . . . . raised by voluntary enlistment . . . Given . . . at Hartford, the 18th day of June, A.D. 1776. Jonathan Trumbull. [Hartford, 1776]
broadside 36 X 23.5 cm.
CtHi. Photostat: MWA mp. 43011

B4198 CONNECTICUT. GOVERNOR, 1769-1776
By the honorable Jonathan Trumbull . . . a proclamation. Whereas the honorable Continental Congress have resolved, that eight battalions of troops be raised within this state . . . Hartford, the 26th day of November . . . 1776. Jonathan Trumbull. [Hartford, 1776]
broadside 34.5 X 21 cm.
CtHi; NHi mp. 43010

B4199 CONNECTICUT. GOVERNOR, 1769-1776
By the honorable Jonathan Trumbull . . . a proclamation . . . New-Haven, November 6, 1776 . . . [New Haven? 1776]
broadside 32.5 X 21 cm.
Regular bounty to immediate volunteers to the eight battalions being raised
NHi mp. 43005

B4200 CONNECTICUT. GOVERNOR, 1769-1776
Colony Connecticut, ss. By the Governor. Whereas I have authentic intelligence . . . Lebanon . . . the 18th day of January . . . 1776 . . . [New London, 1776]
broadside
Goodspeed's Bookstore (1940) mp. 43012

B4201 CONNECTICUT. GOVERNOR, 1769-1776
Colony of Connecticut. By the Governor, a proclamation. Whereas I have received advice . . . [Jan. 20, 1776] [New London, T. Green, 1776]
broadside 31 X 18.5 cm.
CtHi. Photostats: DLC; MHi. NHi; NN mp. 43008

B4202 CONNECTICUT. GOVERNOR, 1769-1776
Colony of Connecticut. By the Governor. A proclamation . . . [Jan. 27, 1776] . . . [New London? 1776]
broadside 35 X 21 cm.
Huntington 398
CSmH mp. 43004

B4203 CONNECTICUT. GOVERNOR, 1769-1776
Connecticut. By the Governor, proclamation. Whereas I am desired by Major-General Schuyler . . . to issue a proclamation of pardon to . . . deserters . . . Lebanon, the 16th day of July . . . 1776. Jonathan Trumbull. [Hartford? 1776]
broadside 34 X 21 cm.
CtHi mp. 43007

B4204 CONNECTICUT. LAWS
At a General Assembly . . . at New-Haven . . . December, 1775. Resolved . . . selectmen . . . inspectors of . . . salt-petre . . . At a General Assembly . . . at Hartford . . . May, 1776. An act . . . carrying into execution . . . making of salt-petre . . . within this colony. [New London? 1776]
3 p. 33 cm.
New York Public 599
NN mp. 43014

B4205 CONNECTICUT. MILITIA
To Captain of the Company in the regiment of militia . . . of Connecticut. Whereas the General Assembly have enacted . . . Given under my hand, in the day of June . . . 1776 . . . [n.p., 1776]
broadside 41 × 26.5 cm.
CtHi (2 copies)

B4206 [CRISP, STEPHEN] 1628-1692
A short history of a long travel . . . The ninth edition. Philadelphia, Printed and sold by Joseph Crukshank, 1776.
24 p. 18.5 cm.
New York Public 601
MWA; NN; PHi mp. 43016

B4207 CROSBY, B OF CHELMSFORD
A discourse on the condemn'd state of sinners . . . Chelmsford, Printed by Nathaniel Coverly, for the author, 1776.
28 p. 19 cm.
MB mp. 43017

B4208 DELAWARE. CONVENTION, 1776
Proceedings of the convention . . . held . . . the twenty-seventh of August, 1776. Wilmington, James Adams, 1776.
35 p. 31 cm.
Hawkins 8; New York Public 602
DLC; NN; NNB; NcD. Richard S. Rodney, Newcastle, Del. mp. 43018

B4209 AN essay on the culture and management of hemp . . . By a farmer. [Baltimore, M. K. Goddard, 1776?]

Advertised Jan. 10, 1776, as "Published and sold at the Printing-Office."
Wroth 351; cf. Evans 14022
No copy known

B4210 EXTRACT of a letter from London, dated Feb. 13, 1776. [And] Extract of a letter from Bristol, Feb. 1, 1776. [Boston? 1776]
broadside
Ford 1959
MHi mp. 43021

B4211 EXTRACT of a letter from New York, dated Aug. 28, 1776. Yesterday morning the enemy . . . [Annapolis, Frederick Green, 1776]
broadside 26.5 × 21.5 cm.
Wroth 371
Howard Sill, Baltimore. Photostats: MWA; RPJCB mp. 43022

B4212 FATHER Hutchin's New-York, New-Jersey, and Connecticut almanack . . . for the year . . . 1776. New-York, 1776.
[36] p. 17.5 cm.
DLC mp. 43023

B4213 FRESH advices received by the northern post . . . Baltimore, Feb. 15, Extract of a letter from Philadelphia, dated February 12th, 1776 . . . [Philadelphia] John Dunlap [1776]
broadside 17.5 × 20.5 cm.
MWA mp. 43024

B4214 FRIENDS, SOCIETY OF. PHILADELPHIA MEETING FOR SUFFERINGS
An epistle from the Meeting for sufferings . . . held at Philadelphia, for Pennsylvania and New-Jersey . . . Signed . . . the 20th day of the twelfth month 1776 . . . [Philadelphia, 1776]
2 p. 34.5 cm.
MiU-C mp. 43025

B4215 FRIENDS, SOCIETY OF. PHILADELPHIA YEARLY MEETING
The testimony of the people called Quakers, given forth by a meeting . . . held at Philadelphia the twenty-fourth of the first month, 1775 . . . [Philadelphia, 1776]
4 p. 33.5 cm. caption title
On verso is printed Evans 14765, signed " . . . the 20th day of the first month 1776."
MiU-C; RPJCB

B4216 GAGE'S folly: or, The tall fox out-witted. An excellent new song . . . By a farmer, in the county of Worcester. Salem, E. Russell; sold also by G. Allen, in Concord [1776]
broadside 32.5 × 22 cm.
Huntington 400
CSmH mp. 43026

B4217 GENTLEMEN and fellow-citizens. The time is now arrived . . . [Philadelphia, 1776]
broadside 12.5 × 16 cm.
Anti-Loyalist propaganda
PHi mp. 43027

B4218 GOOD news for America. Salem, Tuesday, April 16, 1776. We have just received . . . account of the success of the continental fleet under . . . Admiral Hopkins . . . Salem, Printed and sold by E. Russell [1776]
broadside 39 × 25 cm.
New York Public 603
MHi; MSaE; NN (reduced facsim.) mp. 43030

B4219 GOVERNMENT scheme. 1. Let the people choose as usual . . . a representative body . . . [seven-point plan] . . . [Boston? 1776-1777?]
broadside 16 × 10 cm.
Place and date of printing based on evaluation of internal evidence by Elisha P. Douglas
MWiW-C mp. 43031

B4220 GT. BRIT. ARMY
By his Excellency Henry Clinton . . . Whereas, for the better supply . . . Newport, Dec. 23, 1776. H. Clinton, L.G. . . . [Newport, John Howe, 1776]
broadside 33.5 × 19.5 cm.
Alden 633; Winship p. 33
RNHi; RPB. Photostat: RHi mp. 43032

B4221 GT. BRIT. ARMY. 16TH REGIMENT
God and a soldier all men doth adore, In time of war, and not before . . . Whereas an uncommon . . . disturbance prevails throughout this city, by some . . . who stile themselves the S___s of L____y, but . . . more properly . . . enemies to society . . . Signed by the 16th Regiment of Foot. [New York? 1776]
broadside 21 × 20 cm.
NHi mp. 43033

B4222 GT. BRIT. COLONIAL OFFICE
By Richard Viscount Howe, of the Kingdom of Ireland, and William Howe . . . the King's Commissioners for restoring peace . . . Declaration. Whereas by an act passed . . . to prohibit all trade . . . with . . . New-Hampshire, Massachuset's-Bay . . . Given at Staten-Island, the fourteenth day of July, 1776 . . . [New York, 1776]
broadside 30.5 × 19.5 cm.
MHi mp. 43035

B4223 GT. BRIT. SOVEREIGNS (GEORGE III)
His Majesty's most gracious speech to both Houses . . . October 27, 1775 . . . [New York] H. Gaine [1776]

broadside 30.5 X 25 cm.
Printed also in the *New-York Gazette*, Jan. 8, 1776, p. [2]
New York Public 604
NHi; PPRF. Reduced facsims: MWA; NN mp. 43036

B4224 GT. BRIT. SOVEREIGNS (GEORGE III)
His Majesty's most gracious speech to both Houses . . . October 31, 1776. My Lords and Gentlemen . . . [at end] Philadelphia, Wm. & Thos. Bradford [1776]
broadside 21 X 12.5 cm.
CtHi mp. 43037

B4225 GT. BRIT. SOVEREIGNS (GEORGE III)
The King of Great-Britain's speech to both houses of Parliament, on Thursday, October 31, 1776. [n.p., 1776]
broadside 18.5 X 15 cm.
Ford 1962; New York Public 605
MHi. Photostat: NN mp. 43038

B4226 GREEN, JACOB, 1722-1790
Observations, on the Reconciliation . . . Philadelphia, 1776.
40 p.
cf. Evans 14791
CSmH; CtY; DLC; MHi mp. 43040

B4227 GROSCH, DAVID
Der Lebenslauf von T. Jefferson und J. Adams, zwey ausgezeichnete Patrioten, und Helden von 1776 . . . Lancaster, 1776.
53 p. 16mo
Bausman p. 14
PHi mp. 43041

B4228 HALL, SAMUEL, 1740-1807
Advertisement. The extreme difficulty of collecting pay for news-papers . . . has determined the subscriber to discontinue . . . the *New-England Chronicle* . . . Boston, May 13, 1776. [Boston, 1776]
broadside 19 X 16 cm.
New York Public 606
NN mp. 43042

B4229 THE happy man: or, The true gentleman . . . Salem, Printed and sold at E. Russell's Printing-Office [1776?]
broadside 24 X 17.5 cm.
MWA mp. 43044

B4230 THE happy man: or, The true gentleman . . . Salem: Printed by desire of R. Napier, 1776. Sold at John Rogers Printing-Office.
broadside 24.5 X 19 cm.
Ford 1963; Tapley p. 328
RPJCB. Photostat: MHi mp. 43043

B4231 HARVEY, JAMES, 1714-1758
The way of holiness . . . New-York, Samuel Loudon, 1776.
30 p. 19 cm.
MWA; MWiW; NHi; NN mp. 43045

B4232 HICKEY, THOMAS, 1749-1776
The last speech, and dying words of Thomas Hickey . . . who was executed . . . June 28, 1776 . . . By a vessel yesterday . . . Newport, July 4, 1776. [Newport, S. Southwick, 1776]
broadside 35 X 23 cm.
Alden 634
RNHi. Photostat: MWA mp. 43046

B4233 HISTORY of Giles Gingerbread . . . Boston, Printed and sold by Edes & Gill; sold also by Cox & Berry [1776?]
32 p. 10 cm. A–B^8
Ownership date of 1778 inside front cover
MWA (very poor) mp. 43028

B4234 HOLLY, ISRAEL
Boanerges: or Christ's ministers are sons of thunder. The substance of a sermon . . . at the ordination of Robert Campbell . . . June 13, 1776 . . . New-Haven, T. and S. Green [1776?]
36 p. 17.5 cm.
CtHi mp. 43047

B4235 HUDSON, BARZILLAI, fl. 1776-1815
One hundred and twenty dollars reward. Major Christopher French, Ens. Joseph Moland, and the infamous Gurdon Whitmore, broke goal . . . this evening . . . Barz. Hudson, goaler. December 27th, 1776. [Hartford? 1776]
broadside 20 X 16 cm.
New York Public 608
Photostats: DLC; MH; NHi; NN mp. 43048

B4236 IN observance of the Colony-writ to me directed, these are in the name of the government of the Massachusetts-Bay . . . to cause the freeholders and other inhabitants . . . Given . . . at the day of in the year . . . one thousand seven hundred and seventy-six . . . [n.p., 1776]
broadside 28.5 X 21 cm.
Filled in for Pittsfield, Israel Dickinson sherriff
M–Ar. Photostats: MHi; NHi

B4237 INDIANA PROPRIETORS
William Trent, Robert Callender, David Franks, Joseph Simons, Levy Andrew Levy . . . Proprietors of a certain tract . . . called . . . Indiana. To all unto whom these presents shall come, Greeting . . . [Philadelphia, 1776]
broadside fol.
Rosenbach 68
A. S. W. Rosenbach (1926) mp. 43049

B4238 [INGLIS, CHARLES] BP. OF NOVA SCOTIA, 1734-1816
The deceiver unmasked; or, Loyalty and interest united . . . By a loyal American . . . New-York, Samuel Loudon, 1776.
87 p. 19 cm. A–G^6 H^2
Adams 219a; New York Public 610
NHi; PPAmP. Photostat: NN mp. 43050

B4239 JONES, JOHN, 1729-1791
Plain concise practical remarks, on the treatment of wounds and fractures . . . Philadelphia, Robert Bell, 1776.
114, [1] p. 20 cm.
Austin 1084; cf. Evans 14814
CLM; CSmH; CtY–M; DLC; DNLM; IEN–M; MBCo; NNNAM; PHi; PPL; PU; RPJCB mp. 43051

B4239a LANCASTER COUNTY
In Committee, Lancaster, February 10th, 1776. Whereas it is represented . . . that many of the soldiers, prisoners of war here . . . Geo. Ross, Chairman. [Lancaster, F. Bailey, 1776]
broadside fol.
PHi

B4239b LANCASTER COUNTY
In Committee, Lancaster, July 25, 1776. Gentlemen, The Committee of Safety of this Province, by their resolve of the 15th of July instant . . . [Lancaster, F. Bailey, 1776]

broadside 4to
PHi

B4239c LANCASTER COUNTY
In der Committee von Lancaster Caunty, den 29sten Februarius, 1776. Nachdem eine Bittschrift . . . [J.] Yates, Chairman. [Lancaster, 1776]
broadside fol.
PHi

B4240 LANCASTER COUNTY
Lancaster, the 14th July, 1776. In committee. Gentlemen, the committee have received orders . . . To the members of the committee, in Township, and the officers of the militia there. [Lancaster, F. Bailey, 1776]
broadside 34 X 21.5 cm.
Text in German at bottom of page
DLC mp. 43052

B4241 LONG Island, 1776. You are hereby ordered to preserve for the King's use, loads of hay, of wheat . . . and not to dispose of the same, but to an order in writing, from Major John Morrison, Commissary for Forage . . . [New York? 1776]
broadside 14 X 21.5 cm.
MWA; PHi mp. 43034

B4242 [MCGREGORE, DAVID] 1710-1777
The voice of the prophets considered in a discourse or sermon . . . [Hartford?] Printed in the year M,DCC,LXXVI.
15 p. 18 cm.
CtHi mp. 43055

B4243 MCLEAN, HUGH, AND CO.
In the House of Representatives, February 16, 1776. Whereas the colony cannot be supplied with . . . paper . . . Paper-mills, at the slitting-mill, in Milton. In compliance with the foregoing resolve, and to encourage the paper-manufacture . . . Hugh McLean and Co. . . . Salem, E. Russell [1776]
broadside 39.5 X 25.5 cm.
MWA mp. 43056

B4244 MANLY. A favorite new song, in the American fleet . . . Salem, Printed and sold by [E. Russell] [1776?]
broadside 40 X 15.5 cm.
In 10 stanzas
MSaP. Photostats: MHi; MWA mp. 43057

B4245 MARYLAND. CONSTITUTION
The constitution and form of government proposed for the consideration of the delegates . . . [Annapolis, F. Green, 1776]
10 p. 21.5 cm.
Wroth 373
PHi mp. 43058

B4246 MARYLAND. CONSTITUTION
The declaration and charter of rights. [Annapolis, F. Green, 1776]
[2] p. 39 X 21.5 cm.
Wroth 374
PHi. Photostat: RPJCB mp. 43059

B4247 MARYLAND. CONSTITUTION
The declaration of rights, and the constitution . . . Annapolis, Frederick Green [1776]
1 p. l., 26 p. 29 cm.
Wroth 376
DLC; PHi. Photostat: RPJCB mp. 43060

B4248 MARYLAND. CONVENTION, 1776
By the convention of Maryland, June 25, 1776. You are empowered to enroll effective freemen . . . Matthew Tilghman . . . [Annapolis, Frederick Green, 1776]
broadside 12 X 17.5 cm.
Wroth 372a
MdHi mp. 43061

B4249 MARYLAND. CONVENTION, 1776
Proceedings of the convention . . . held at . . . Annapolis . . . the fourteenth of August, 1776. Annapolis, Frederick Green [1776]
[2], 30 p.
Not Evans 14835, but a preliminary issue ending Sept. 17
RPJCB mp. 43062

B4250 MASSACHUSETTS
Advertisement. Watertown, January 26, 1776. Ran away from the custody . . . of the General Court . . . [Watertown, B. Edes, 1776]
broadside 21 X 13 cm.
Ford 1943; New York Public 612
DLC; MHi. Photostat: NN mp. 43065

B4251 MASSACHUSETTS
Colony of Massachusett's-Bay, 1776. We the subscribers, do . . . declare . . . that the war, resistance and opposition . . . is . . . just and necessary . . . [Watertown? 1776]
broadside X 21 cm.
MWA (lower half wanting; also facsim. of perfect copy) mp. 43064

B4252 MASSACHUSETTS
To Sir, You are hereby impowered . . . Watertown, January 4, 1776. [Watertown, B. Edes, 1776]
broadside 18.5 X 20 cm.
Ford 2017
MHi. Photostat: DLC mp. 43063

B4253 MASSACHUSETTS
To You are hereby impowered immediately to inlist a company . . . to continue . . . 'till the end of the present war . . . day of 1776 . . . State of Massachusetts-Bay, October 19, 1776. The following are extracts from the resolves of Congress . . . [Watertown? 1776]
broadside 22.5 X 21.5 cm.
Ford 2018, 2019, 2020
M-Ar; MHi; MWA mp. 43067

B4254 MASSACHUSETTS. COUNCIL
In Council, June 6, 1776 . . . [Watertown, 1776]
broadside
Printed copy of the instructions by the Continental Congress, Apr. 3, 1776, for commanders having letters of marque, adapted by ms. changes to vessels of Massachusetts
Ford 1987
M-Ar mp. 43069

B4255 MASSACHUSETTS. COUNCIL
State of Massachusetts-Bay. Council-Chamber, December 10, 1776. Whereas an embargo was laid . . . on all vessels, excepting such . . .fitted out by order of the United States . . . [Watertown, 1776]
broadside
Ford 2006
M-Ar mp. 43068

B4256 MASSACHUSETTS. COUNCIL
Watertown, July 3, 1776. In Council. Ordered . . . [Watertown, B. Edes, 1776]

broadside 21.5 X 17 cm.
Ford 1992
MHi. Photostat: DLC mp. 43070

B4257 MASSACHUSETTS. HOUSE OF REPRESENTATIVES
In the House of Representatives, January 9, 1776. Whereas it appears to this Court, that . . . the militia of this Colony now in the American army . . . Perez Morton, Dep. Sec'y. [Watertown, B. Edes, 1776]
broadside 34 X 19 cm.
DLC mp. 43074

B4258 MASSACHUSETTS. HOUSE OF REPRESENTATIVES
In the House of Representatives, January 16, 1776. The committee appointed to consider . . . further measures . . . for furnishing hay for the army, reported . . . [Watertown, 1776]
broadside 35 X 22 cm.
Ford 1969
MHi mp. 43075

B4259 MASSACHUSETTS. HOUSE OF REPRESENTATIVES
In the House of Representatives, January 21, 1776. Whereas it is of . . . importance to . . . the inhabitants of Canada . . . that the advantages gained . . . under the American arms . . . Charles Chauncy. [Watertown, B. Edes, 1776]
broadside 41.5 X 16.5 cm.
DLC mp. 43076

B4260 MASSACHUSETTS. HOUSE OF REPRESENTATIVES
In the House of Representatives, February 13, 1776. Whereas it appears . . . [Watertown, B. Edes, 1776]
broadside 24 X 18 cm.
Ford 1977
M-Ar; MHi; MWA (mutilated). Photostat: DLC
mp. 43085

B4261 MASSACHUSETTS. HOUSE OF REPRESENTATIVES
In the House of Representatives, Feb. 15, 1776. Resolved, That the plantations . . . [Watertown, B. Edes, 1776]
broadside 22 X 18 cm.
Ford 1980
MHi. Photostat: DLC mp. 43077

B4262 MASSACHUSETTS. HOUSE OF REPRESENTATIVES
In the House of Representatives, April 9, 1776. Whereas it is of the greatest importance . . . [Watertown, B. Edes, 1776]
broadside 43 X 17.5 cm.
Ford 1982
MHi. Photostat: DLC mp. 43078

B4263 MASSACHUSETTS. HOUSE OF REPRESENTATIVES
In the House of Representatives, April 11, 1776. The House voted . . . [Watertown, B. Edes, 1776]
[2] p. 33.5 X 21 cm.
Ford 1984
MHi. Photostat: DLC mp. 43079

B4264 MASSACHUSETTS. HOUSE OF REPRESENTATIVES
In the House of Representatives, May 7, 1776. Resolved, That a regiment . . . [Watertown, B. Edes, 1776]
broadside 24 X 10.5 cm.
Ford 1986
MHi. Photostat: DLC mp. 43080

B4265 MASSACHUSETTS. HOUSE OF REPRESENTATIVES
In the House of Representatives, June 7th, 1776. A resolve . . . passed on the 10th of May . . . [Watertown, B. Edes, 1776]
broadside 23 X 19 cm.
Ford 1988
MHi. Photostat: DLC mp. 43081

B4266 MASSACHUSETTS. HOUSE OF REPRESENTATIVES
In the House of Representatives, June 26, 1776. Whereas repeated applications have been made by . . . Congress to this Court, to procure . . . hard money, to be sent into Canada . . . It is therefore resolved . . . Timothy Danielson, Speaker, Pro. Tem. In Council, June 27, 1776. Read and concurr'd . . . [Watertown, 1776]
broadside 32.5 X 16.5 cm.
NHi mp. 43086

B4267 MASSACHUSETTS. HOUSE OF REPRESENTATIVES
In the House of Representatives, September 17th, 1776. Resolved, That it be recommended . . . [Watertown, B. Edes, 1776]
broadside 28 X 21 cm.
Ford 1997; cf. Evans 14867
DLC; M-Ar; MB; MWA mp. 43082

B4268 MASSACHUSETTS. HOUSE OF REPRESENTATIVES
In the House of Representatives, September 17th, 1776. Whereas doubts may arise . . . Resolved, That all those persons who shall march out on this exigence . . . J. Warren, Speaker. In Council, September 17, 1776. Read and concurred . . . [Watertown, 1776]
broadside 27 X 20 cm.
NHi; RPJCB mp. 43087

B4269 MASSACHUSETTS. HOUSE OF REPRESENTATIVES
A list or return on oath of the householders dwelling . . . February 16, 1776 . . . [Boston, 1776]
broadside
MWA mp. 43073

B4270 MASSACHUSETTS. HOUSE OF REPRESENTATIVES
A list or return on oath, of the names of the householders in the town of in the county of in the colony of the Massachusetts-Bay . . . including inmates and boarders . . . In the House of Representatives, February 16, 1776 . . . two hundred and sixty lists of the forms aforesaid, be printed and sent . . . as soon as may be . . . [Boston, 1776]
broadside 42 X 33.5 cm.
Ford 2014
DLC; MHi; MWA mp. 43072

B4271 MASSACHUSETTS. HOUSE OF REPRESENTATIVES
State of Massachusetts-Bay. In the House of Representatives, December 28, 1776. Resolved, That the following persons . . . are appointed to muster the men that have inlisted . . . [Watertown, 1776]
broadside
Ford 2008
MHi mp. 43083

B4272 MASSACHUSETTS. HOUSE OF REPRESENTATIVES
Whereas it has been represented to the General Court of this state, by the . . . governor of . . . Connecticut . . . September 12, 1776. [Watertown? 1776]
broadside ([2] p.) 32.5 X 19 cm.
Ford 1996
MHi; MWA mp. 43088

B4273 MASSACHUSETTS. LAWS
Falmouth, February 1776. Whereas . . . [Watertown, B. Edes, 1776]
broadside ([2] p.) 32.5 X 19 cm.
Ford 1974
MHi. Photostat: DLC mp. 43084

B4274 MASSACHUSETTS. LAWS
In the sixteenth year of the reign of George the Third . . . 1776. Militia. Acts and laws, pased by the . . . General Court . . . begun . . . Watertown . . . nineteenth day of July . . . 1775. [Colophon] Watertown, Benjamin Edes, 1776.
p. 15-59
PHi

B4275 MASSACHUSETTS. MILITIA
All male persons from sixteen to sixty-five . . . belonging to the training-band and alarm lists . . . of militia in this town . . . warned to appear . . . on Monday next . . . at nine o'clock . . . for . . . chusing one clerk, four serjeants . . . Salem, July 18, 1776 . . . [Salem, 1776]
broadside 17.5 X 10.5 cm.
MHi

B4276 MASSACHUSETTS. MILITIA
A return of troops in the pay of the state of Massachusetts, in the year 1776, stationed at [Watertown? 1776]
broadside 21 X 34 cm.
Ford 2026
MWA mp. 43089

B4277 MASSACHUSETTS. TREASURER
Province of Massachusetts-Bay. Henry Gardner, Esq; treasurer . . . November 20, in the sixteenth year of . . . George the Third . . . [Watertown, 1776]
broadside
Ford 2012
MSaE mp. 43091

B4278 MEEKER, OBADIAH
[. . .] The beautiful and [J]ersey Farmer, fifteen hands and an half high, eight years old . . . Good pasture will be provided for mares . . . by Obadiah Meeker. New-York, April 29, 1776.—Printed by Hugh Gaine, in Hanover-Square.
broadside X 24 cm.
NjR (top lines torn off)

B4279 MOLLINEAUX, MARY (SOUTHWORTH) 1651?-1695
Fruits of retirement . . . By Mary Mollineux . . . The seventh edition. Philadelphia, Re-printed by Joseph Crukshank, 1776.
[32], 142, [2] p. 17 cm. a-c^6 A-M^6
MWA; N; NHi; P; PHi mp. 43092

B4280 [MORGAN, JOHN] 1735-1789
Recommendatory preface . . . [Boston, J. Gill, 1776?]
16 p. 18 cm. A-B^4 caption title
Same as Evans 14891, without title and with pagination changed. Probably printed to accompany projected Boston ed. of Dimsdale's "The present method of inoculating for the small-pox," probably not published on account of the war
MWA mp. 43093

B4281 NEW HAMPSHIRE. HOUSE OF REPRESENTATIVES
Exeter, July 4, 1776. In the House of Representatives July 4, 1776. Voted that three hundred hand bills be . . . printed . . . exert every nerve . . . to repel the army coming against us from Canada . . . Exeter, Printed at the new printing-office [1776]
broadside 22 X 12 cm.
Whittemore 196
NhHi mp. 43094

B4282 NEW HAMPSHIRE. PROVINCIAL CONGRESS
In Congress at Exeter, January 5th, 1776. We the members . . . [Portsmouth, D. Fowle, 1776]
broadside ([2] p.) 31 X 20 cm.
cf. Evans 14901, but without the imprint and the resolution of the House of Representatives
DLC (2 copies); RPJCB. Photostats: NHi; NN mp. 43095

B4283 NEW HAMPSHIRE. TREASURER
State of New-Hampshie [sic] Nicholas Gilman, esq; treasurer . . . [Exeter? 1776]
broadside 26 X 19.5 cm.
Tax warrant dated 1776
Whittemore 200
NhD (2 copies); NhHi mp. 43096

B4284 NEW JERSEY. CONVENTION, 1776
In convention of the state of New Jersey, Brunswick, August 11, 1776 . . . [Burlington, Isaac Collins, 1776]
[2] p. fol.
Resolution organizing the militia
PPL mp. 43097

B4285 NEW JERSEY. LAWS
An act to punish traitors and disaffected persons. Passed at Princeton the fourth of October 1776 . . . [Burlington] 1776.
broadside 36.5 X 24 cm.
NjP

B4286 NEW JERSEY. PROVINCIAL CONGRESS
In Provincial Congress, New Jersey, Burlington, June 14, 1776 . . . Resolved . . . five battalions, consisting of eight companies . . . in readiness and marched to New-York . . . By order of Congress, Samuel Tucker, president. [Burlington, 1776]
broadside 39 X 22 cm.
Humphrey 161
NjHi mp. 43098

B4287 A NEW primer. Norwich, Printed by John Trumbull; bound and sold by Henry Spencer at East-Greenwich, in Rhode-Island, 1776.
[64] p. [A]-D^8
Heartman: Non-New-England 105
CtHi; RPJCB mp. 43099

B4288 A NEW song, for the Sons of Liberty, to the tune of King John, and the Abbot of Canterbury . . .
But the total defeat of those heroes I sing
That would fix a Republic, in lieu of a K- - - . . .
[New York? 1776?]
broadside
NNS

B4289 NEW YORK. COMMITTEE OF SAFETY
Gentlemen, Although a certain day is fixed for the session of Congress . . . the first of February . . . we adjure you . . . that you meet punctually . . . Signed . . . in behalf of the Committee of Safety. Pierre Van Cortlandt, Chairman. To the members of the Provincial Congress of the Colony of New-York. [New York, 1776]
broadside 22 X 17 cm.
Dated in ms.: Jan: 9th, 1776
NHi mp. 43101

B4290 NEW YORK. COMMITTEE OF SAFETY
In Committee of Safety, for the State of New-York. Fish-Kills, Oct. 9, 1776 . . . Robert Benson, Sec'ry. [Fish-Kill, Samuel Loudon, 1776]
broadside 24 X 20.5 cm.
Concerns the purchase of coarse woolen cloth
Vail: Patriotic pair, p. 395
N; NHi; RPJCB. Photostat: NN mp. 43100

B4291 NEW YORK. COMMITTEE OF SAFETY
In Committee of safety, for the state . . . Nov. 12, 1776. Resolved, That notice be given . . . [Fish-Kill, S. Loudon, 1776]
broadside 19 X 19 cm.
Vail: Patriotic pair, p. 395
DLC. Photostat: NN mp. 43103

B4292 NEW YORK. COMMITTEE OF SAFETY
In Committee of Safety, New-York, January 27, 1776. Instructions to the colonels . . . for inlistment of four new battalions . . . for the defence . . . of New York . . . [New York, 1776]
broadside 42 X 34.5 cm.
NHi mp. 43102

B4293 NEW YORK. COMMITTEE OF SAFETY
Sir, By virtue of the authority vested in us by certain resolutions of the Congress of the colony . . . in the year . . . 1776 . . . we . . . summon you to appear before us . . . [Fish-Kill, S. Loudon, 1776]
broadside 28.5 X 17 cm.
DLC; NHi (2 copies). Photostat: NN mp. 43104

B4294 NEW YORK. COMMITTEE OF SAFETY
To the inhabitants of the Colony of New-York . . . By order of the Committee, Pierre Van Cortlandt, chairman. Jan. 9, 1776 . . . [at end] New-York, Printed by John Holt [1776]
8 p. 24.5 cm.
Huntington 402, pt. 2 (pt. 1 is Evans 15146)
MWA; N; NHi mp. 43105

B4295 NEW YORK. CONVENTION
In convention of the representatives of the state . . . [Fish-Kill, S. Loudon, 1776]
broadside 24 X 17 cm.
Vail: Patriotic pair, p. 396; cf. Evans 14931 (also at DLC)
DLC mp. 43106

B4296 NEW-YORK, October 18, 1776. To the public. Considerations on the present revolted state of America . . . Camillus. [New York] Printed [by M'Donald & Cameron] in Water-Street [1776]
broadside 36 X 19.5 cm.
New York Public 594
DLC; MH; MHi. Photostat: NN mp. 43108

B4297 NEW-YORK, October 30, 1776. To the King's Most Excellent Majesty. The humble address of the high sheriff . . . and freeholders . . . of Devonshire, England . . . [New York] Printed [by M'Donald and Cameron] in Water-Street [1776]
broadside 41.5 X 23 cm.
NHi mp. 43019

B4298 NEW York, Dec. 13, 1776. To the public. Considerations on the present revolted state of America . . . Camillus. [New York] Printed by M'Donald & Cameron [1776]
broadside 33.5 X 20 cm.
DLC; NHi mp. 43107

B4299 NO Provincial convention. Let us act for ourselves . . . Vote against the eleven deputies. [Philadelphia, 1776]
broadside 10.5 X 12.5 cm.
cf. Evans 14350; Taylor 21
DLC mp. 43109

B4300 NOW fitting for a privateer, in the harbour of Beverly, the brigantine Washington . . . Beverly, September 17th, 1776. [n.p., 1776]
broadside 25 X 20 cm.
Ford 2029
MWA mp. 43020

B4301 O'BEIRNE, THOMAS LEWIS, 1748-1823
A sermon preached at St. Paul's, New York, September 22, 1776 . . . [New York? H. Gaine? 1776?]
15 p. 18 cm. $A^4 B^4$ caption title
NN. John Howell, San Francisco (1959) mp. 43110

B4302 O'BEIRNE, THOMAS LEWIS, 1748-1823
A sermon preached at St. Paul's, New-York, September 22, 1776 . . . New-York, Hugh Gaine, 1776.
20 p. 18.5 cm.
New York Public 617; cf. Evans 14952
MBAt; NHi. Photostat: NN mp. 43111

B4303 [OBSERVATIONS on the practicability of independency . . . Charleston, David Bruce, 1776]

Advertised in the *South Carolina and American General Gazette*, Aug. 2, 1776
Mosimann 263
No copy known

B4304 ON the death of Beulah Worfield, who departed this life September 26, 1776, aged 17. [n.p., 1776?]
broadside 35 X 21.5 cm.
Ford 2033
MWA mp. 43112

B4305 ON the evacuation of Boston by the British troops, March 17th, 1776 . . . [n.p., 1776?]
broadside
Bostonian Society. MWA (1926 reproduction)
mp. 43113

B4306 [PAINE, THOMAS] 1737-1809
The American Crisis. (No. 1.) By the author of Common sense. [Boston] Sold opposite the Court-House, Queen-Street. [1776]
broadside 24 X 16 cm.
Ford 2036
MHi. Photostat: DLC mp. 43114

B4307 [PAINE, THOMAS] 1737-1809
The American Crisis. Number 1. By the author of Common Sense. Norwich, John Trumbull [1776]
11 p.
Imprint in colophon
Trumbull 1212
CtHi; RPJCB mp. 43115

B4308 [PAINE, THOMAS] 1737-1809
Common sense; addressed to the inhabitants of America . . . Newport, Printed and sold by Solomon Southwick, 1776.
2 p. l., 16 p., blank leaf, [3]-31 p. 20.5 cm.
$[A]\text{-}B^4 C^2 [A]^3 B\text{-}D^4$
Adams 222 p; Alden 639; Gimbel CS-46; Sabin 58214; Winship p. 33
DLC; MB; MHi; MWA; NHi; RPB. Brit. Mus. mp. 43118

B4309 [PAINE, THOMAS] 1737-1809
Common sense: addressed to the inhabitants of America . . . Philadelphia, R. Bell, 1776.
77 p. 20.5 cm.
Adams 222d; Gimbel CS-8; New York Public 619
CSmH; CtY; MHi; MWA; NHi; NN; PU; RPJCB
mp. 43120

B4310 [PAINE, THOMAS] 1737-1809
Common sense; addressed to the inhabitants of America . . . Philadelphia, W. and T. Bradford, 1776.
99 p. 20 cm.
Printed in Dublin?
Adams 222g; Gimbel CS-14-15; Huntington 403; Sabin 58214
CSmH; CtY; DLC; InU; MHi; MWA; MdBJ; MiU-C; NN; NNS; PHi; PPM; PU; RPJCB. Brit. Mus. mp. 43121

B4311 [PAINE, THOMAS] 1737-1809
Common sense; addressed to the inhabitants of America . . . N.B. The new addition . . . increases the work upwards of one third . . . Hartford, Re-printed, and sold by Eben. Watson [1776]
59 p. 18 cm. $[A]^4$ $B\text{-}E^6$ $[F]^2$
Adams 222k; Gimbel CS-22
MWA (half-title wanting) mp. 43116

B4312 [PAINE, THOMAS] 1737-1809
Common sense; addressed to the inhabitants of America . . . N.B. The new addition . . . increases the work upwards of one third. Philadelphia printed: Newbury-Port, Re-printed, [by Mycall] for Samuel Phillips, jun. of Andover [1776]
61, [1] p. 19.5 cm. $[A]\text{-}H^4$ (H4 blank)
The American patriot's prayer: [1] p. at end
Adams 222h; Gimbel CS-22
DLC; MH; MHi; MWA; MiU; MiU-C; NHi; NN; PHi; RPJCB mp. 43117

B4313 [PAINE, THOMAS] 1737-1809
Common sense; addressed to the inhabitants of America . . . N.B. The new addition . . . increases the work upwards of one third . . . Philadelphia: Printed. Norwich: Re-printed and sold by Judah P. Spooner, and by T. Green, in New-London [1776]
64 p. 20.5 cm. $[A]\text{-}H^4$
Advertised in the New London *Connecticut Gazette*, Apr. 12, 1776, as "just published."
Adams 222i; Gimbel CS-50
CtHi; MWA; MiU-C; RPJCB mp. 43119

B4314 PAINE, THOMAS, 1737-1809
Common sense; addressed to the inhabitants of America . . . A new edition, with several additions in the body of the work. To which is added an appendix . . . [n.p.] Printed for the perusal of the inhabitants of the Thirteen United Colonies, 1776.
44 p. 8vo $[A]\text{-}E^4$
Adams 222w; Gimbel CS-56
PPL mp. 43122

B4315 [PAINE, THOMAS] 1737-1809
Common sense; addressed to the inhabitants of America . . . Philadelphia; Printed and sold by R. Bell . . . and re-printed and sold in Charlestown, South Carolina, by David Bruce, MDCCLXXVI.
2 p. l., 68 p. 8vo $[A]^2$ $B\text{-}I^4$
Adams 222j; Gimbel CS-20
Bodleian

B4316 [PAINE, THOMAS] 1737-1809
Common sense: addressed to the inhabitants of America . . . Philadelphia printed [by B. Towne]. And sold by W. and T. Bradford [1776]
3 p. l., 50 p. 20.5 cm.
Plain rule above and below half title
Gimbel CS-11, CS-12, CS-13
No locations given

B4317 [PAINE, THOMAS] 1737-1809
Common sense; addressed to the inhabitants of America . . . Philadelphia printed [by Steiner and Cist]. And sold by W. and T. bradford [1776]
3 p. l., 50 p. 20.5 cm.
Row of type ornaments above and below half title
Gimbel CS-10
No locations given

B4318 [PAINE, THOMAS] 1737-1809
Common sense; addressed to the inhabitants of America . . . The second edition. Philadelphia printed; New-York, Reprinted and sold by John Anderson [1776]
2 p.l., 56 p. 8vo $[A]\text{-}G^4$ H^2
Adams 222n; Gimbel CS-41
CtY; NN

B4319 [PAINE, THOMAS] 1737-1809
Common sense; addressed to the inhabitants of America . . . The sixth edition. Philadelphia, Printed: Providence, Re-printed and sold by John Carter, 1776.
45, [1] p. 22.5 cm. $[A]\text{-}D^4$ $[\text{-}]^1$ $E\text{-}G^2$
Adams 222t; Alden 637; Gimbel CS-51 & 52
DLC; PU; RPB

B4320 [PAINE, THOMAS] 1737-1809
Common sense; addressed to the inhabitants of America . . . The tenth edition. Providence, John Carter, 1776.
33 p. 20.5 cm.
Adams 222u; Alden 638; Gimbel CS-53; Winship p. 34; Winship Addenda p. 93
CtY; DLC; MWA; NhD; RHi; RNHi; RP; RPJCB
mp. 43123

B4321 [PAINE, THOMAS] 1737-1809
Large additions to Common sense . . . Printed and sold [by Edes & Gill] at the Printing-Office in Queen-Street, Boston, 1776.
43, [1] p. 18 cm. $[A]\text{-}E^4$ F^2
Adams 223b; Gimbel CS-19; Huntington 404
CSmH; DLC; MB; MH; MHi; MWA; MiU-C; NN; RPJCB
mp. 43053

B4322 [PAINE, THOMAS] 1737-1809
Large additions to Common sense . . . The twelfth edition, with an addition of two parts . . . Vol. II . . . Salem, Printed, and sold by E. Russell, 1776.
23, [1] p. 20 cm. $[A]^2$ $B\text{-}C^4$ D^2
MWA mp. 43054

B4323 [PAINE, THOMAS] 1737-1809
N° 1. The American Crisis. By the author of Common Sense. [Fish-Kill, S. Loudon, 1776?]
8 p. 18.5 cm. caption title

Unsigned at end; dated: Dec. 23, 1776
Huntington 405; Vail: Patriotic pair 397
CSmH; DLC; MH

B4324 PENN, WILLIAM, 1644-1718
Fruits of a father's love . . . The sixth edition. Philadelphia, Printed and sold by Joseph Crukshank, 1776.
60 p. 15 cm.
Taylor 18
P mp. 43124

B4325 PENN, WILLIAM, 1644-1718
. . . To the children of light in this generation, called of God to be partakers of eternal life in Jesus Christ . . . [Philadelphia? 1776?]
4 p. 33 cm.
cf. Evans 14968 (quarto ed.)
MB mp. 43125

B4326 PENNSYLVANIA
Pennsylvania ss. 1776. We reposing especial trust and confidence in your patriotism . . . appoint you to be in the service of this Province . . . Signed by order of the Assembly. [Philadelphia? 1776]
broadside 33.5 X 20 cm.
Taylor 24
RPJCB

B4327 PENNSYLVANIA. CONVENTION, 1776
In convention for the state of Pennsylvania. Philadelphia, August 13, 1776. [Philadelphia, Henry Miller, 1776]
broadside 4to
Setting the county quotas to make up the Flying Camp
PPL mp. 43126

B4327a PENNSYLVANIA. CONVENTION, 1776
An ordinance of the convention of the State of Pennsylvania. Whereas the non-associators . . . Philadelphia, July 20, 1776. [Philadelphia] Printed by John Dunlap [1776]
broadside fol.
PHi

B4328 PENNSYLVANIA. CONVENTION, 1776
To the several Committees of Correspondence for the Counties of Philadelphia, Bucks, Chester . . . Gentlemen, You are required by the Convention now sitting to forward . . . the following letter to the respective colonels . . . In Convention, Philadelphia, July 19, 1776 . . . [Philadelphia, 1776]
[2] p. 18 cm.
Pages 1 and 4 printed of 4-page fold.
PHi mp. 43127

B4329 PENNSYLVANIA. COUNCIL OF SAFETY
In Congress, December 9, 1776. Whereas General Washington . . . immediate reinforcement . . . In Council of Safety, Philadelphia, December 9, 1776. Fellow countrymen . . . join General Washington's army . . . agreeable to the above resolve of Congress . . . By order of Council, Thomas Wharton, jun. President. [Philadelphia, 1776]
broadside 26 X 21 cm.
Taylor 71
DLC mp. 43128

B4330 PENNSYLVANIA. COUNCIL OF SAFETY
In Council of Safety, December 5, 1776. Resolved, That Messieurs Robert Baily, Samuel Penrose, John Hart . . . Philadelphia, John Dunlap [1776]
broadside 25.5 X 21 cm.
DLC mp. 43129

B4331 PENNSYLVANIA. COUNCIL OF SAFETY
In Council of Safety, Philadelphia, November 16th, 1776. Sir, The fleet . . . [Philadelphia, 1776]
broadside 25.5 X 20 cm.
DLC; PHi mp. 43130

B4332 PENNSYLVANIA. COUNCIL OF SAFETY
Philadelphia, September 2, 1776. In compliance with Sir, The army . . . [Philadelphia, 1776]
broadside 20 X 16.5 cm.
DLC mp. 43131

B4333 PENNSYLVANIA. COUNCIL OF SAFETY
In Council of Safety, Philadelphia, December 7, 1776. Whereas the safety and security of every state . . . Resolved. That no excuse . . . sufficient against marching with the militia . . . Jacob S. Howell, Secretary. [Philadelphia] John Dunlap [1776]
broadside 24 X 15 cm.
Taylor 30
PHi mp. 43132

B4334 PENNSYLVANIA. HOUSE OF REPRESENTATIVES
Instructions for inlisting rifle-men, in the service of Pennsylvania . . . [Philadelphia? 1776]
[4] p. 33 cm.
Dated and signed in ms.: March 14th 1776—Signed by order of the House John Morton Speaker
New York Public 621; Taylor 20
PHi (mutilated). Photostat: NN mp. 43133

B4335 PENNSYLVANIA LEDGER
Postscript extraordinary to the *Pennsylvanis Ledger*, January 8, 1776. His Majesty's most gracious speech to . . . Parliament. London, October 28 . . . [Philadelphia] James Humphreys [1776]
broadside 35.5 X 24.5 cm.
PHi mp. 43039

B4336 THE people the best governors: or A plan of government founded on the just principles of natural freedom . . . [n.p.] 1776.
13 p. 12.5 cm.
Huntington 406
CSmH; CtHi; N. Photostat: MWA (t.p. only) mp. 43134

B4337 PHILADELPHIA
Bey einer Versammlung einer Anzahl Philadelphischer Bürger, gehalten . . . den 8ten November, 1776, unter Vorsitz Herrn Peter Chevalier, wurde einmüthig beschlossen . . . [Philadelphia, John Dunlap, 1776]
broadside 35.5 X 23.5 cm.
Taylor 2
DLC mp. 43135

B4338 PHILADELPHIA
Philadelphia, September 2, 1776. In compliance with the resolves of Convention of the 24th and 28th of August last, empowering the Committee of the City and Liberties of Philadelphia to distribute salt, belonging to Joshua Fisher and Jos Sewell . . . [Colophon] Snyder [sic] and Cist, Philadelphia [1776]
broadside
Taylor 34
No copy located mp. 43137

B4339 PHILADELPHIA. COMMITTEE OF INSPECTION
In Committee of inspection and observation. Philadelphia, May 21, 1776 . . . [Philadelphia, 1776]

broadside ([2] p.) 38.5 X 24.5 cm.
DLC; PHi mp. 43136

B4340 PHILADELPHIA. ELECTION PROX.
Committee for the city of Philadelphia, to be and continue until the sixteenth day of August, A.D. 1776, and no longer. 1 Samuel Meredith, 2 Samuel Massey . . . [Philadelphia, 1776]
broadside 4to
PPL mp. 43138

B4341 PHILADELPHIA, January 16, 1776. Williamsburg (Virginia) Jan. 6. Extract of a letter from Col. Howe . . . Thursday the 21st ult. in Lancaster county, a negroe fellow was . . . found guilty of sheep-stealing . . . [Philadelphia] John Dunlap [1776]
broadside 39.5 X 13.5 cm.
DLC; MWA mp. 43139

B4342 PHILADELPHIA, July 20, 1776. By an express arrived yesterday from South-Carolina, we have the following important intelligence. Extract of a letter from Fort Johnson, South-Carolina, July 2, 1776 . . . [Philadelphia, 1776]
broadside 35 X 21.5 cm.
In two columns
NHi mp. 43140

B4343 PICKERING, TIMOTHY, 1745-1829
An easy plan of discipline for a militia . . . The second edition . . . Boston, Printed and sold by S. Hall, 1776.
24, 154, 2 p. 12 plates, part fold. 21 cm.
MHi; MWA mp. 43141

B4344 A PLAN of the attack of Fort Sullivan the key of Charlestown in South Carolina on the 28th of June 1776 . . . . . By an officer on the spot. Philadelphia, Printed for Daniel Humphreys, by Styner and Cist [1776?]
map 32.5 X 39.5 cm. on sheet 57 X 44 cm.
Huntington 407
CSmH mp. 42142

B4345 POPE, ALEXANDER, 1688-1744
An essay on man . . . Providence, J. Douglass McDougall, 1776.
viii, 48 p. 17.5 cm.
Alden 642; Winship p. 34
MH; NN; NjP; RHi mp. 42143

B4346 THE prodigal daughter: or, a strange and wonderful relation . . . Danvers: Printed and sold by E. Russell [1776?]
16 p. 17.5 cm.
NjP mp. 43144

B4347 [PROVIDENCE, December 7, 1776 . . . Providence, John Carter [1776?]]
[broadside?]
Bill submitted by John Carter Dec. 7, 1776, for printing handbills relative to the appearance of the enemy's fleet
Alden 642A
No copy known mp. 43151

B4348 Deleted

B4349 QUEENS COUNTY, N.Y. CITIZENS
To the Right Honorable Richard, Lord Viscount Howe . . . and . . . William Howe . . . The humble representation and petition of the . . . inhabitants of Queen's County . . . [New York] Printed [by M'Donald and Cameron] in Water-Street [1776]
broadside 38.5 X 22 cm.
New York Public 623
MH. Photostats: DLC; NHi; NN mp. 43145

B4350 RHODE ISLAND. ELECTION PROX.
For the preservation of the liberties of America. The honorable Nicholas Cooke, Esq; Governor . . . [Newport? S. Southwick, 1776?]
broadside 21 X 13.5 cm.
Contains officers elected in May, 1776
Alden 642B; Chapin Proxies 13
NHi; RHi; RNHi mp. 43146

B4351 RHODE ISLAND. GENERAL ASSEMBLY
[At the General assembly . . . holden . . . on the last Monday in February . . . This Assembly taking into consideration a resolution of . . . the Continental Congress . . . for procuring gold and silver coin . . . Providence, John Carter [1776]]
[broadside?]
Bill submitted by Carter Mar. 4, 1776
Alden 659
No copy known mp. 43147

B4352 RHODE ISLAND. GENERAL ASSEMBLY
State of Rhode-Island and Providence Plantations. At a meeting of the general committee, appointed to act in recess of the General Assembly, convened . . . the 11th day of December, A.D. 1776. [Providence, J. Carter, 1776]
20 p. 17.5 cm. caption title
Alden 643; Winship p. 35
MWA; RHi; RP; RPJCB mp. 43148

B4353 RHODE ISLAND. GOVERNOR, 1775-1778
By the honorable Nicholas Cooke . . . A proclamation . . . [for a day of fasting] . . . [May 6, 1776] . . . Providence, John Carter [1776]
broadside 38.5 X 32 cm.
Alden 644; Winship p. 34
RHi. Mrs. H. F. Holbrook. Photostats: MWA; NN; RNHi mp. 43150

B4354 RHODE ISLAND. GOVERNOR, 1775-1778
By the honorable Nicholas Cooke . . . A proclamation. Whereas it is the duty . . . [Nov. 4, 1776] . . . Providence, John Carter [1776]
broadside 40 X 31.5 cm.
Bill submitted Nov. 9, 1776
Alden 645; Winship p. 34
RHi. Mrs. H. F. Holbrook mp. 43149

B4355 RHODE ISLAND. LAWS
At the General assembly . . . holden . . . on Thursday the twenty-first day of November . . . Be it enacted . . . that one regiment be forthwith raised . . . Providence, John Carter [1776]
broadside 19.5 X 16.5 cm.
Bill submitted Nov. 26, 1776
Alden 664; Winship p. 34
RHi; RPJCB mp. 43152

B4356 RHODE ISLAND. LAWS
At the General assembly . . . holden . . . on Thursday the twenty-first day of November . . . It is voted and resolved, that each captain . . . Providence, John Carter [1776]
broadside 19.5 X 16.5 cm.
Bill submitted Nov. 26, 1776
Alden 665; Winship p. 34
RHi mp. 43153

B4357 RHODE ISLAND. LAWS
Rules and regulations for the forces raised, by the Colony of Rhode-Island . . . Newport, S. Southwick, 1776.

23 p. 21.5 cm. [A]-C4
Alden 671
MH; MWA (uncut); RHi mp. 43156

B4358 RHODE ISLAND. LAWS
State of Rhode-Island and Providence Plantations. In General assembly, December session, A.D. 1776. It is voted and resolved, that all male persons . . . [Providence, J. Carter, 1776]
broadside 23 X 18 cm.
Alden 666; Winship p. 35
NHi; Nh; NhHi; RHi; RPJCB mp. 43155

B4359 RHODE ISLAND. LAWS
State of Rhode-Island and Providence Plantations. In General assembly, December 2d session, 1776. Whereas the act made . . . directing the alarm list . . . [Providence, J. Carter, 1776]
broadside 23 X 17.5 cm.
Alden 667; Winship p. 35
R; RHi; RPJCB mp. 43154

B4360 RICH, ELISHA
A sermon on ecclesiastical liberty . . . Concord, Nathaniel Coverly, 1776.
40 p. 18 cm.
DLC; MH mp. 43157

B4361 [SEWALL, JONATHAN MITCHELL] 1748-1808
Gen. Washington, a new favourite song, at the American camp. To the tune of the British Grenadiers. [n.p., 1776]
broadside 32.5 X 19.5 cm.
Same verses as Evans 14918
Ford 2038; New York Public 625
NHi. Photostats: MWA; NN mp. 43158

B4362 A SHORT account of the trouble and dangers our forefathers met with to obtain this land . . . Now published as highly necessary . . . Danvers, E. Russell [1776]

Two woodcuts at top, one of the battle of Lexington
Anderson Galleries auction catalog no. 1797, Jan. 21-22, 1924
Tapley p. 329
No copy traced mp. 43159

B4363 SOME poetical thoughts on the difficulties our fore-fathers endured in planting religious and civil liberty, in this western world . . . [New Haven? 1776?]
broadside 39.5 X 28 cm.
Text in 4 columns, beginning: "When our forefathers were oppressed . . ."
New York Public 536; Sabin 86714; Trumbull 1402; Wegelin 775
RPJCB. Photostats: MHi; MWA; NN mp. 43160

B4364 SOUTH CAROLINA. LAWS
An act for the more effectual prevention of the desertion . . . Passed April 9th, 1776. [Charles-Town, P. Timothy, 1776]
5 p. 28.5 cm.
Half-title only
Sabin 87618
DLC mp. 43161

B4365 SOUTH CAROLINA. LAWS
An act to empower the Court of admiralty . . . Passed April 11th, 1776. [Charles-Town, P. Timothy, 1776]
9 p. 29 cm.
Half-title only
Sabin 87622
DLC mp. 43162

B4366 SOUTH CAROLINA. LAWS
An act to increase the number of firemasters in Charles-town . . . Passed the 9th day of April 1776. [Charles-Town, P. Timothy, 1776]
4 p. 28 cm.
Half-title only
Sabin 87616
DLC mp. 43163

B4367 SOUTH CAROLINA. LAWS
An act to prevent sedition . . . Passed April 11th, 1776. [Charles-Town, P. Timothy, 1776]
7 p. 29 cm.
Half-title only
Sabin 87621
DLC mp. 43164

B4368 SOUTH CAROLINA. LAWS
An act to punish those who shall counterfeit . . . Passed the 9th day of April 1776. [Charles-Town, P. Timothy, 1776]
4 p. 28 cm.
Half-title only
Sabin 87617
DLC (2 copies) mp. 43165

B4369 SOUTH CAROLINA. LAWS
An act to revive and continue . . . Passed the 11th day of April 1776. [Charles-Town, P. Timothy, 1776]
7 p. 29 cm.
Half-title only
Sabin 87623
DLC mp. 43166

B4370 SOUTH CAROLINA. LAWS
Acts . . . passed in September and October, 1776. Charles-Town, Peter Timothy [1776]
1 p.l., 20, [1] p. 29 cm.
Sabin 87624
DLC mp. 43172

B4371 SOUTH CAROLINA. LAWS
An ordinance for altering the time . . . Passed April 11th, 1776. [Charles-Town, P. Timothy, 1776]
5 p. 28.5 cm.
Half-title only
Sabin 87619
DLC mp. 43167

B4372 SOUTH CAROLINA. LAWS
An ordinance for establishing an oath of office . . . passed the 6th day of April 1776. [Charles-Town, P. Timothy, 1776]
4 p. 28.5 cm.
Half-title only
Sabin 87613
DLC mp. 43168

B4373 SOUTH CAROLINA. LAWS
An ordinance for making disposition of monies . . . passed the 6th day of April 1776. [Charles-Town, P. Timothy, 1776]
4 p. 28 cm.
Half-title only
Sabin 87614
DLC mp. 43169

B4374 SOUTH CAROLINA. LAWS
An ordinance to ascertain the duties . . . passed the 11th day of April 1776. [Charles-Town, P. Timothy, 1776]
4 p. 28.5 cm.
Half-title only

Sabin 87620
DLC mp. 43170

B4375 SOUTH CAROLINA. LAWS
An ordinance to repeal part of an ordinance . . . Passed the 9th day of April 1776. [Charles-Town, P. Timothy, 1776]
4 p. 28 cm.
Half-title only
Sabin 87615
DLC mp. 43171

B4376 TO all gentlemen volunteers, who . . . are free and willing to . . . learn the noble art of gunnery, in the Massachusetts state train of artillery . . . [Boston, 1776]
broadside 22.5 X 17.5 cm.
NHi. Photostat: DLC mp. 43090

B4377 TO all persons whom it may concern. New-York 1776 Permit the bearer to pass, he having leave to go to [New York, 1776]
broadside 7 X 17 cm.
Signed by Henry Wilmot, D. Chair~ of the Genl. Committee
NNS

B4378 TO the General Assembly of the State of South Carolina the petition and memorial of the underwritten Protestants of the said State . . . [n.p., 1776]
broadside 38 X 32 cm. caption title
In ms.: Briton's Neck, Nov. 25, 1776
Methodist Pub. House, Nashville

B4379 TO the honourable magistrates, and worthy electors of King's County . . . New-York. January 23, 1776. Gentlemen, It is with . . . singular pleasure . . . A Freeholder. [New York, 1776]
broadside 35.5 X 23 cm.
NHi mp. 43173

B4380 TO the inhabitants of the city and county of New-York. Fellow citizens, Be not deceived by sounds . . . A foe to dissention. [New York, 1776?]
broadside 20.5 X 20 cm.
DLC mp. 43174

B4381 TO the public. The commissioners appointed to examine . . . the public accounts . . . Albany, 1776]
broadside 18 X 12.5 cm.
McMurtrie: Albany 8
NHi mp. 43175

B4382 TO the public. The Provincial Congress of New-York yesterday passed a resolve . . . [New York, 1776]
broadside 42.5 X 23.5 cm.
Attack on the resolution, with an answer by the Provincial Congress, June 9, 1776
NHi mp. 43176

B4383 TUCKER, JOSIAH, 1711-1799
The true interest of Britain . . . Philadelphia, Robert Bell, 1776.
66, [4], [2] p.
Not Evans 15119 (statement of Tucker's authorship omitted on t.p.)
CSmH; MHi; NRU; RPJCB mp. 43177

B4384 TWO favorite new songs at the American camp. Exhortation to the freemenof America . . . The American liberty song . . . [n.p., 1776?]
broadside
Ford 2042
PHi. Photostat: MHi mp. 43178

B4385 TWO favorite songs, made on the evacuation of the Town of Boston, by the British troops, on the 17th of March, 1776. [n.p., 1776?]
broadside 44.5 X 27 cm.
Ford 2040
MHi; MSaE mp. 43179

B4386 TWO favorite songs made on the evacuation of the town of Boston by the Britons, March 17th, 1776. [Boston? 1776?]
broadside 34 X 19 cm.
Ford 2041
RPJCB mp. 43180

B4387 TWO new songs: On the disgraceful flight of the ministerial fleet & army . . . on March 17, 1776 . . . Sold at the Bible & Heart in Cornhill, Boston [1776?]
broadside 30 X 21.5 cm.
Wegelin 808
MiU-C mp. 43181

B4388 TWO songs on the brave General Montgomery, and others, who fell within the walls of Quebec, Dec. 31, 1775 . . . Danvers, Printed and sold next the Bell-Tavern [1776]
broadside
Ford 2043; Tapley p. 329
MSaE mp. 43182

B4389 UNITED COMPANY
To the honorable General assembly of the colony of Connecticut, to be holden at Hartford in May 1776. The memorial and petition of . . . the United Company. [Norwich? 1776]
8 p. caption title
Trumbull: Second supplement 2887
RPJCB mp. 43183

B4390 U.S.
the 1776. Sir, Please to deliver for the armed vessel under my command, rations . . . and rum Captain. To Mr. John Mitchell. Rations . . . Philadelphia, the 1776 . . . [Philadelphia, 1776]
[2] p. 16.5 X 10.5 cm.
On verso: Philadelphia, the 1776. Received of Mr. John Mitchell . . .
Dated in ms.: Feb. 14, 1777
Taylor 117
DLC

B4391 U.S.
Warrant. The Marine committee appointed by Congress, to equip . . . the fleet of the United Colonies, having . . . John Hancock, Presidt. [Philadelphia? 1776]
broadside 16.5 X 21.5 cm.
RPJCB mp. 43195

B4392 U.S. ARMY. CONTINENTAL ARMY
By His Excellency George Washington, Esq; . . . commander in chief of the forces of the thirteen United Colonies. Whereas the ministerial army have abandoned . . . Boston . . . Given . . . in Cambridge, this twenty-first day of March, 1776. George Washington. [Boston, 1776]
broadside
cf. Anderson sale, Nov. 9, 1927, no. 221
MWA (reduced facsim.) J. Scopes (1927) mp. 43184

B4393 U. S. ARMY. CONTINENTAL ARMY
Head-Quarters, New-York, April 8th, 1776. The general informs the inhabitants . . . that all communication, be-

tween the ministerial fleet and shore, should be immediately stopped . . . Israel Putnam. [New York, 1776]
broadside 20 X 16 cm.
New York Public 622
NHi; NN mp. 43185

B4394 U. S. ARMY. CONTINENTAL ARMY
Instruction to the officers appointed to recruit in New York, for the service of the United States of America . . . [Fish-Kill, S. Loudon, 1776]
broadside 37.5 X 24 cm.
Vail: Patriotic pair, p. 397
NHi mp. 43186

B4395 U.S. CONTINENTAL CONGRESS, 1776
Extracts of letters, &c. Published by order of Congress. Charles-Town, Peter Timothy, 1776.
25 p.
Half-title: Copies of extracts from intercepted and other letters, from John Stuart, Esq; Major Furlong . . . Also of an original letter from Moses Kirkland to Col. Laurens
Sabin 87364; cf. Evans 15126
Hist. Commission of S.C. mp. 43187

B4396 U.S. CONTINENTAL CONGRESS, 1776
In Congress, January 30, 1776. Resolved, That it be recommended to the several assemblies in New-England, to assist the General in procuring arms . . . Extract from the minutes, Charles Thomson, Sec'ry. [Watertown? B. Edes? 1776]
broadside 17.5 X 7 cm.
Ford 1948
MB; MHi. Photostat: DLC mp. 43188

B4397 U.S. CONTINENTAL CONGRESS, 1776
In Congress, July 19, 1776. Resolved, That a copy of the circular letters and of the declarations they enclosed from Lord Howe . . . be published in the several Gazettes . . . [Boston? 1776]
broadside
With Boston items of July 27 and 29
Ford 1956, 1957
MHi (2 variants) mp. 43189

B4398 U.S. CONTINENTAL CONGRESS, 1776
In Congress, Wednesday, April 3, 1776. Instructions to the commanders of private ships or vessels of war . . . President. [Philadelphia? 1776]
broadside 34.5 X 22.5 cm.
Signed in ms. by John Hancock
Variant of Evans 15137
RPJCB mp. 43190

B4399 U.S. CONTINENTAL CONGRESS, 1776
Philadelphia, July 4th, 1776. Gentlemen, The Congress this morning . . . To the Convention of associators . . . at Lancaster. [Philadelphia, John Dunlap, 1776]
broadside 35.5 X 21 cm.
DLC; PHi mp. 43191

B4400 U.S. CONTINENTAL CONGRESS, 1776
A proclamation for a Continental Fast. In Congress, Saturday, March 16, 1776. In times of impending calamity . . . [Philadelphia? 1776]
broadside 31 X 18 cm.
Different issue from Evans 15132 (microprint)
RPJCB mp. 43192

B4401 U.S. CONTINENTAL CONGRESS, 1776
Resolves of the Hon. Continental Congress. Published by order of the general committee for the city and county of Albany. [Albany, 1776]
broadside 31 X 19 cm.
McMurtrie: Albany 9; cf. Evans 13147
NHi mp. 43193

B4402 U.S. CONTINENTAL CONGRESS, 1776
Rules and articles for the better government of the troops raised . . . at the expence of the United States of America. Philadelphia, Printed: Fish-Kill, Re-printed by S. Loudon, 1776.
31 p. 18.5 cm.
Vail: Patriotic pair, p. 398
Cty; NHi mp. 43194

B4403 U.S. DECLARATION OF INDEPENDENCE
In Congress, July 4, 1776. A declaration by the representatives of the United States of America, in general Congress assembled . . . New-York, Hugh Gaine [1776]
broadside
Walsh: 4
NHi. Photostat: MWA mp. 43203

B4404 U.S. DECLARATION OF INDEPENDENCE
In Congress, July 4, 1776. A declaration by the representatives of the United States of America, in general Congress assembled . . . [n.p., 1776]
broadside
2 columns, with 70 lines in the first
Walsh: 5
NHi mp. 43196

B4405 U.S. DECLARATION OF INDEPENDENCE
In Congress, July 4, 1776. A declaration by the representatives of the United States of America, in general Congress assembled . . . [n.p., 1776]
broadside 37.5 X 22 cm.
2 columns, with 65 lines in the first
Walsh: 6
NHi mp. 43197

B4406 U.S. DECLARATION OF INDEPENDENCE
In Congress, July 4, 1776. A declaration by the representatives of the United States of America, in general Congress assembled . . . [n.p., 1776]
broadside 37 X 22 cm.
2 columns, with a line of 65 type ornaments between
Walsh: 11
MB mp. 43198

B4407 U.S. DECLARATION OF INDEPENDENCE
In Congress, July 4, 1776. Declaration by the representatives . . . [n.p., 1776]
broadside
2 columns, with 58 lines in the first
Walsh: 14
CtY; MWA (2 copies) mp. 43199

B4408 U.S. DECLARATION OF INDEPENDENCE
In Congress, July 4, 1776. Declaration by the representatives . . . [Exeter, R. L. Fowle, 1776]
Broadside 48.5 X 38 cm.
Walsh: 15; cf. *Lib. of Cong. Quarterly journal of current acquisitions* 5:1
DLC; MWA; NhHi mp. 43201

B4409 U.S. DECLARATION OF INDEPENDENCE
In Congress, July 4, 1776. Declaration, by the representatives . . . [n.p., 1776]
broadside (2 pages, double folio)
Title from Libbie auction catalogue of May 12-21, 1903, lot 72
Walsh: 16
No copy traced mp. 43200

B4410 U.S. DECLARATION OF INDEPENDENCE
[Engraved oval portrait of John Hancock, framed by crossed palms and topped by a liberty cap] In Congress, July 4, 1776. A declaration by the representatives of the United States of America, in general Congress assembled . . . [n.p., 1776]
broadside
2 columns with 58 lines in the first
Printed in London?
Walsh: 17
RPJCB. Photostat: MWA mp. 43202

B4411 Deleted

B4412 THE Universal calendar, and the North-American almanack for . . . 1777. By Isaac Warren. Worcester, W. Stearns and D. Bigelow [1776]
[24] p.
Drake 3270
MB

B4413 VIRGINIA
[Continental and provincial articles of war. Williamsburg, A. Purdie, 1776]

cf. *Purdie's Virginia Gazette*, Aug. 30, 1776
No copy known mp. 43210

B4414 VIRGINIA. CONVENTION, 1776
The following declaration was reported to the Convention by the committee appointed to prepare the same . . . A Declaration of Rights made by the representatives of the good people of Virginia . . . [Williamsburg, Alexander Purdie, 1776]
[2] p. 34 cm.
From minor differences in wording, probably a proof copy of the Declaration, preceding its appearance in the *Virginia Gazette* of June 14, 1776
ViHi. Photostat: RPJCB mp. 43205

B4415 VIRGINIA. CONVENTION, 1776
Friday, June 14, 1776. Postscript. No. 72. In convention. June 12, 1776. A Declaration of Rights made by the representatives of . . . Virginia . . . Edmund Pendleton, President . . . [Williamsburg, 1776]
4 p. 22.5 cm.
DLC (2 copies) mp. 43206

B4416 VIRGINIA. CONVENTION, 1776
In a general convention . . . on Monday the sixth day of May . . . [Williamsburg, A. Purdie, 1776]
broadside ([2] p.) 40 X 24.5 cm.
DLC; PPL mp. 43207

B4417 VIRGINIA. COUNCIL
Williamsburg, August 20, 1776. Sir, As we have . . . Given under my hand, this 20th of August, 1776 . . . [Williamsburg, A. Purdie, 1776]
broadside 20 X 16 cm.
DLC mp. 43208

B4418 VIRGINIA. GENERAL ASSEMBLY
A plan of government. Laid before the committee of the House . . . [Williamsburg, A. Purdie, 1776]
[2] p. 35.5 X 22.5 cm.
DLC mp. 43209

B4419 THE voice of the prophets considered . . . [n.p.] Printed in the year M, DCC, LXXVI.
15 p. 19 cm. [A]-B^4
MWA mp. 43211

B4420 WATERTOWN, September, 1776. Received of . . . pounds weight of salt-petre, valued at [Watertown? 1776]
broadside
Ford 2016
M-Ar

B4421 WE the subscribers do hereby severally inlist ourselves . . . to continue in that service 'till the end of the present war with Britain . . . October 19. [n.p., 1776]
broadside
Ford 2023
M-Ar; MHi mp. 43212

B4422 WORCESTER, MASS. COMMITTEE OF CORRESPONDENCE
In Committee chamber, Worcester, Nov. 18, 1776. As expedients . . . [Worcester, 1776]
broadside 27 X 21 cm.
Ford 2046; New York Public 627
MWA. Photostats: DLC; NHi; NN mp. 43213

B4423 WORCESTER CO.
At a Court of General Sessions of the Peace, within and for the County of Worcester, held . . . the first Tuesday of September, 1776. Ordered, that the following rules and regulations be printed on hand bills. Signed, Joseph Allen, Clerk. [Worcester? 1776]
broadside 38 X 24.5 cm.
Austin 2089; Ford 2047
MWA; NNNAM mp. 43071

B4424 YALE UNIVERSITY
Two dialogues, on different subjects, being exercises, delivered on a Quarter-Day, in the chapel of Yale-College . . . March 28, 1776 . . . Hartford, E. Watson, 1776.
31 p. 23 cm.
Sabin 97555; Trumbull 1535; Wegelin 750
CtHi; DLC; MWA; NHi; RPB mp. 43214

1777

B4425 THE American primer improved . . . Boston, Printed by Edward Draper & sold by John Boyle, 1777.
[80] p. [A]-E^8
Heartman: Non-New-England 5
No copy located mp. 43215

B4426 ANNAPOLIS, June 27, 1777. Extract of a letter, dated Camp at Middlebrook, June 21, 1777. "Our army is on a very respectable footing . . ." . . . [Annapolis, F. Green, 1777]
broadside 27 X 19 cm.
MdHi. Photostats: MWA; RPJCB mp. 43216

B4427 ANNAPOLIS, October 18, 1777. By a letter from Thomas Jones . . . to . . . the governor . . . we have the following important intelligence. . . . [Annapolis, F. Green, 1777]
broadside 20 X 13.5 cm.
Describes the wounding of Benedict Arnold
MdHi. Photostats: MWA; RPJCB mp. 43217

B4428 ANNAPOLIS, October 21, 1777. Extract of a letter . . . to the president of the Council of . . . New-York. Albany, 15th October, 1777 . . . [Annapolis, Frederick Green, 1777]
broadside 21 X 18 cm.
Capitulation of Burgoyne
MdHi. Photostats: MWA; RPJCB mp. 43218

B4429 ANNAPOLIS, November 2. Extract of a letter from William Smith . . . to . . . the governor, dated York-Town, October 31, 1777 . . . Articles of convention between . . . Burgoyne and . . . Gates . . . [Annapolis, F. Green, 1777]
broadside 27 X 20.5 cm.
MdHi. Photostats: MWA; RPJCB mp. 43219

B4430 ANNAPOLIS, December 1. Extract of a letter from York, dated Nov. 22, 1777 . . . [Annapolis, F. Green, 1777]
broadside 27 X 21 cm.
Foreign intelligence; peace proposals of Lord Howe
MdHi. Photostats: MWA; RPJCB mp. 43220

B4431 ARTICLES of agreement, made and concluded upon, in on the 1777 between the owners, captain, officers and mariners . . . bound from on a CRUIZE for months against the enemies of the United States . . . These articles we . . . engage faithfully to keep . . . of Pennsylvania . . . [Philadelphia? 1777]
broadside 52.5 X 42.5 cm.
DLC; NHi

B4432 BALTIMORE, October 8, 1777. Extract of a letter from York-Town . . . Baltimore, M. K. Goddard [1777]
broadside 17 X 20.5 cm.
Battle of Germantown
MdHi. Photostats: MWA; RPJCB mp. 43221

B4433 BALTIMORE, November 2, 1777. Fresh important intelligence . . . This moment . . . dispatches . . . of the capitulation of Gen. Burgoyne . . . A new song . . . [Baltimore] John Dunlap [1777]
broadside 40.5 X 16.5 cm.
Wheeler 22
MdBE mp. 43222

B4434 BAPTISTS. SOUTH CAROLINA. CHARLESTON ASSOCIATION
Minutes of the Charlestown Association. Charlestown, Feb. 3, 1777 . . . [Charleston, 1777]
4 p. 21.5 cm. caption title
ScGF. Photostat: MWA mp. 43223

B4435 [BECCARIA, CESARE BONESANA, MARCHESE DI] 1738-1794
An essay on crimes and punishments . . . Charlestown [S.C.], Printed and sold by David Bruce, 1777.
xii, 155 p. 19 cm.
Huntington 410; James 51
CSmH; MH-L; MWA mp. 43224

B4436 BELL, ROBERT, 1731?-1784
Books in physick, surgery, and chemistry, now selling at Bell's Book-Store . . . Philadelphia [Robert Bell, 1777]
[4] p. 21 cm.
58 books listed
Guerra a-598
NNNAM mp. 43225

B4437 BICKERSTAFF'S New-York almanack, for the year . . . 1778 . . . New-York, Mills and Hicks [1777]
[24] p. 17.5 cm.
Wall p. 22
DLC; MH; PHi; WHi (imperfect) mp. 43226

B4438 BOSTON. COMMITTEE OF CORRESPONDENCE
Boston, February 27, 1777. Gentlemen, At a time when degenerate Brittons . . . [Boston, 1777]
[4] p. 25 X 20 cm.
Signed in ms.: Jona. Williams, Chairman
Ford 2054; New York Public 628
MHi; MWA; NN mp. 43227

B4439 BOSTON. COMMITTEE OF INSPECTION AND SAFETY
Boston, 1777. Permit to pass to the town of with his waggon, containing . . . Chairman of the Committee of Inspection and Safety . . . of Boston. [Boston, 1777]
broadside
Ford 2051
MWA

B4440 BOSTON, Feb. 19th, 1777. In pursuance of an act of the General Assembly . . . the Select-men and Committee of Correspondence of this town have . . . affixed the following prices . . . [Boston, 1777]
broadside 38 X 15 cm.
Ford 2055; New York Public 630
MWA. Photostat: NN mp. 43228

B4441 BOSTON, September 26, 1777. Last evening a gentleman arrived here from Providence . . . with the following, fresh advices from the Northern Army . . . [Boston, 1777]
broadside 34 X 14 cm.
Ford 2055; New York Public 630
MWA. Photostat: NN mp. 43229

B4442 BRITISH taxation of North-America. [n.p., 1777?]
broadside
In verse
New York Public 631
MWA (reduced facsim.); NN (reduced facsim.); RPJCB mp. 43230

B4443 CLARK, JONAS, 1730-1805
The fate of blood-thirsty oppressors . . . A sermon . . . April 19, 1776 . . . Boston, Powars and Willis, 1777.
31, 8 p. 8vo
Huntington 411; cf. Evans 14679
CSmH; MHi mp. 43231

B4444 CONNECTICUT. GENERAL ASSEMBLY
At a General Assembly of the Governor and Company . . . of Connecticut, holden at Hartford . . . 13th day of August . . . 1777 . . . Resolved . . . Hartford, Ebenezer Watson [1777]
broadside 35 X 20.5 cm.
Resolutions for the raising of troops
NHi mp. 43237

B4445 CONNECTICUT. GENERAL ASSEMBLY
At a General Assembly of the Governor and Company . . . of Connecticut, holden at Hartford . . . 11th day of October . . . 1777. Whereas his Excellency . . . it is Resolved by this Assembly . . . quota of soldiers . . . George Wyllys, Secretary. [Hartford, 1777]
broadside 30.5 X 17 cm.
CtHi mp. 43239

B4446 CONNECTICUT. GOVERNOR, 1776-1784
By His Excellency Jonathan Trumbull . . . A proclamation for a fast . . . [Aug. 14, 1777] . . . Hartford, Ebenezer Watson [1777]
broadside 41 X 25.5 cm.
Appointing Sept. 3 a day of fasting
cf. Evans 15270
MHi

B4447 CONNECTICUT. GOVERNOR, 1776-1784
By His Excellency Jonathan Trumbull . . . A proclamation. Whereas the multitude of our iniquities . . . I . . . earnestly exhort all persons . . . to abstain from oppression, injustice and every vice . . . Hartford, the 5th day of November . . . 1777. Jonathan Trumbull. New-London, T. Green [1777]
broadside 34.5 X 21 cm.
CtHi mp. 43235

B4448 CONNECTICUT. GOVERNOR, 1776-1784
By the honourable Jonathan Trumbull . . . a proclamation for a day of fasting . . . [Mar. 29, 1777] . . . New-London, Timothy Green [1777]
broadside 36.5 X 29 cm.
cf. Evans 15268
MHi; MiU-C mp. 43233

B4449 CONNECTICUT. GOVERNOR, 1776-1784
By the hon. Jonathan Trumbull . . . A proclamation. Whereas I am informed . . . that inoculation . . . [Feb. 1, 1777] . . . [New London? 1777]
broadside 33 X 19.5 cm.
CtHi; MHi; MiU-C mp. 43236

B4450 CONNECTICUT. GOVERNOR, 1776-1784
By the honourable Jonathan Trumbull . . . to the commanding officer of the regiment of militia . . . should any apprehend danger of taking the small-pox . . . none who have had it shall march further than Peck's-Kill . . . Lebanon, in said state, the 17th day of March, A.D. 1777. [New London, T. Green, 1777]
broadside 33 X 21 cm.
Guerra a-600
NNNAM mp. 43234

B4451 CONNECTICUT. LAWS
At a General Assembly of the Governor and Company . . . of Connecticut, holden at Hartford . . . 11th day of October . . . 1777. An act in addition to the law injoining an oath of fidelity . . . [Hartford ? 1777]
broadside ([2] p.) 29.5 X 19 cm.
Includes four other acts
CtHi mp. 43238

B4452 CORDIER, MATHURIN, 1479-1564
Corderii colloquiorum centuria selecta . . . with an English translation . . . By John Clarke . . . The twenty-second edition. Philadelphia, Printed and sold by Joseph Crukshank, 1777.
vii, 170 p. 16.5 cm.
MWA mp. 43240

B4453 DELAWARE. HOUSE OF ASSEMBLY
[Votes and proceedings of the House of Assembly . . . (Oct. 28, 1776-Jun. 7, 1777) Wilmington, James Adams, 1777.]
155 p. fol.
Title supplied by Edwin Wolf 2d
PHi (t.p. lacking)

B4454 DELAWARE. LAWS
. . . At a General assembly . . . continued by adjournment to the twenty-second day of February 1777 . . . [Wilmington, J. Adams, 1777]
p. 339-369 [i.e. 359-389] 30 cm. caption title
Hawkins 9
DLC; MdBP; NNB; PPL mp. 43241

B4455 LE dieu et les nayades du fleuve St. Louis. A Don. Bernard de Galvez . . . Sur sa convalescence. Poeme. [Colophon] À la Nouvelle Orléans, Antoine Boudousquié, 1777.
[4] p. 25 cm. caption title
Attributed to Julien Poydras de Lalande
McMurtrie: New Orleans 24; New York Public 633
NN. Photostat: MWA mp. 43343

B4456 DILWORTH, THOMAS, d. 1780
A new guide to the English tongue . . . [A new edition, with some improvements.] Boston, T. and J. Fleet, 1777.
[3], vii, [1], 160 p. front. 17 cm. A-L^8 (L8 wanting)
MWA (p. 5-16 wanting) mp. 43242

B4457 A DISCOURSE on Daniel vii. 27 . . . Also a short improvement of the subject. [Norwich?] Printed in the year M,DCC,LXXVII.
22 p. 17.5 cm. [A]-C^4 (C4 wanting)
Signed: A hearty friend to all the colonies
Trumbull: Supplement 2067; cf. Evans 14737
MWA. L. A. Welles (1928) mp. 43243

B4458 A DISCOURSE on the times . . . The third edition, with an addition. Norwich: Printed by J. Trumbull, for the author, 1777.
22 p. 17 cm.
Signed: A hearty friend to all the colonies
Attributed to Jabez Huntington, 1738-1782
Sabin 20244
CtHi; NHi mp. 43244

B4459 DORCHESTER, MASS.
To Your Province tax. 1776 Your town rate. (Assessors sit February 27, 1777.) [Boston? 1777]
broadside
Ford 2057
MHi

B4460 DUNBAR, MOSES, d. 1777
[The last speech and dying words of Moses Dunbar who was executed at Hartford . . . the 19th day of March 1777 for high treason against the State of Connecticut. Hartford? 1777?]

Reprinted with above title in "The Calendar," Aug. 22, 1846, where it is called "a little pamphlet."
Trumbull: Supplement 2090; cf. Evans 15607
No copy known mp. 43245

B4461 ÉPITRE à D$^{on.}$ Bernard de Galvez . . . [Colophon] À la Nouvelle Orléans, Antoine Boudousquié, 1777.
[4] p. 24.5 cm. caption title
In verse
Attributed to Julien Poydras de Lalande
McMurtrie: New Orleans 23; New York Public 634
NN. Photostat: MWA mp. 43344

B4462 THE following is given to the public from good authority . . . New york, James Rivington [1777]
broadside 53 X 43.5 cm.
Describes the capture of Forts Clinton and Montgomery by the British, Oct. 6, 1777
MiU-C mp. 43246

B4463 THE following messages, &c. passed between Major General Gates and Lieutenant General Burgoyne, previous to the Convention of Saratoga . . . [Colophon] York-Town, Hall and Sellers, 1777.
[4] p. 25 cm. caption title
New York Public 636
NN (photostat) mp. 43247

B4464 FOSTER, DANIEL, 1751-1795
Dust thou art and unto dust shalt thou return. A funeral oration . . . delivered at Dartmouth-Hall, January 30th, 1776 . . . Hartford, Ebenezer Watson, 1777.
10 p.
RPJCB mp. 43248

B4465 FOSTER, ISAAC, 1725-1807
A discourse upon extortion . . . Hartford, Ebenezer Watson, 1777.
16+ p. 21 cm.
In August "expected soon to be published." Ordered to be seized by the sheriff of Hartford County
Trumbull: Supplement 2070
MWA (wanting after p. 16) mp. 43249

B4466 THE freeman's remonstrance against an ecclesiastical establishment . . . by a Freeman of Virginia . . . Williamsburg, John Dixon and William Hunter, 1777.
13 p. 16 cm.
Huntington 413
CSmH mp. 43250

B4467 FRESH advices from the northern army. Danvers, Friday, September 27 . . . [Danvers, 1777]
broadside 32 X 10.5 cm.
Ford 2059
MSaP. Photostats: DLC; MSaE
mp. 43251

B4468 FRESH advices from the northern army. Providence, September 25, 1777. The following intelligence was last night received . . . [Providence, J. Carter, 1777]
broadside 26.5 X 14 cm. (to torn edge)
Alden 676; Winship p. 35
RHi (mutilated). Photostats: MWA; NN mp. 43252

B4469 FRESH advices from the northern army. Providence, October 14. The following is extracted . . . [Providence, John Carter, 1777]
broadside 38.5 X 12.5 cm.
Alden 677; Winship p. 35; NYPL 638
MWA; RHi. Photostat: NN mp. 43253

B4470 FRESH and important news! Jan. 12, 1777. This morning an express . . . from . . . Governor Trumbull, of Connecticut . . . [Boston] Powars & Willis [1777]
broadside 36 X 22 cm.
Concerns the Battle of Princeton
Ford 2060
MB; MWA mp. 43254

B4471 FRIENDS, SOCIETY OF
. . . The testimony of the people called Quakers, given . . . at Philadelphia the twenty-fourth day of the first month, 1775 [and subsequent documents, 1776-77] [Colophon] [Philadelphia] Printed by John Dunlap [1777]
sheet 40 X 24 cm.
From same setting of type as p. 2-3 of Dunlap's *Pennsylvania Packet*, Sept. 9, 1777
DLC

B4472 FROM the *Pennsylvania Evening Post*, of July 17, 1777. Extract of a letter . . . [New York] Printed by H. Gaine [1777]
broadside 41 X 23.5 cm.
DLC (photostat) mp.43255

B4473 GAINE'S Universal register, or, American and British kalendar, for the year 1777. New-York, H. Gaine [1777]
[17], 17-35, 37-143, [1] p. fold. map. 12.5 cm.
[A]-F24
Advertised in the *New-York Gazette* Feb. 17, 1777, as "just published."
Guerra b-386; New York Public 639
NHi; NN (map wanting); RPJCB mp. 43256

B4474 GRAND news. Salem, January 12, 1777. This afternoon arrived here one Mr. Haistie from New-York . . . and says . . . an express arrived there from . . . Princeton . . . and that their army was entirely routed . . . of the 17th Regiment (British) only 18 men left alive...... [Salem, 1777]
broadside 17.5 X 15 cm.
MHi

B4475 GT. BRIT. ARMY
By His Excellency John Burgoyne . . . lieutenant-general . . . The forces entrusted to my command are designed to act in concert . . . Camp at the River Bongret [i.e. Bouquet], June 23, 1777 . . . [Newport? John Howe? 1777]
broadside 32 X 20 cm.
Alden 678; Winship p. 35
MiU-C mp. 43257

B4476 GT. BRIT. ARMY
By His Excellency Sir Henry Clinton . . . Proclamation. Whereas it is consonant not only to the common principles of humanity . . . [New York] James Rivington [1777]
broadside 40 X 32.5 cm.
Dated Dec. 20, 1777
Concerns prices of grain
New York Public 632
NHi; NNMer. Photostat: NN mp. 43258

B4477 GT. BRIT. ARMY
By his excellency Sir William Howe . . . Declaration. Sir William Howe, regretting the calamities . . . doth . . . promise a free and general pardon to all such officers and private men . . . [Aug. 27, 1777] . . . [n.p., 1777]
broadside 34 X 20 cm.
Printed on board ship or in camp?
MiU-C; PHi mp. 43259

B4478 GT. BRIT. ARMY
By His Excellency Sir William Howe . . . Proclamation. Whereas, by my proclamation bearing date the fourth day of this instant, all masters of merchant ships . . . 18th day of December, 1777 . . . [Philadelphia, J. Humphreys, jun., 1777]
broadside fol.
Not Evans 15334, but different printing of same text.—Edwin Wolf 2d
PPL

B4479 GT. BRIT. ARMY
By His Excellency Sir William Howe . . . Proclamation. Whereas complaints have been made . . . 7th day of November . . . [Philadelphia, J. Humphreys, jun., 1777]
broadside fol.
Not Evans 15329, but different printing of same text.—Edwin Wolf 2d
PPL

B4480 GT. BRIT. ARMY
No. 7. State of the troops, British and German, under the command of General Sir William Howe, encamped at Philadelphia, Dec. 14, 1777 . . . J. Paterson, Adjutant-General, North-America . . . [n.p., 1777]

broadside 49.5 X 39.5 cm.
NHi mp. 43260

B4481 GT. BRIT. ARMY
No. 8. State of the troops, British and German, under the command of . . . Sir Henry Clinton, at New-York . . . October 1, 1777 . . . J. Paterson, Adjutant-General, North-America . . . [n.p., 1777]
broadside 49.5 X 37 cm.
NHi mp. 43261

B4482 GT. BRIT. SOVEREIGNS (GEORGE III)
Baltimore, Feb. 4, 1777. The speech of George the Third . . . delivered October 31, 1776. Baltimore, M. K. Goddard [1777]
broadside 18 X 15.5 cm.
PHi mp. 43263

B4483 GRUNDRISS der Erdbeschreibung. Nach der zweyten Ausgabe des fürstlichen Waysenhauses zu Arnstadt . . . Philadelphia, Gedruckt und zu haben bey Henrich Miller, 1777.
68 p. 16.5 cm.
PHi; PPL mp. 43264

B4484 HARRISON, ROBERT HANSON, 1745-1790
Hartford, September 17. The following intelligence was received in town last night by express. Chad's Ford, Sept. 11, 1777 . . . [Hartford, Hudson & Goodwin? 1777]
broadside 29 X 20 cm.
Contains also a letter of Washington from Chester, describing the battle
MB

B4485 DER Hoch-Deutsch-Americanische Calender auf . . . 1778 . . . Philadelphia, Johann Dunlap [1777]
[32] p.
Drake 10056
MWA; PHi; PPG

B4486 . . . HUTCHIN'S almanack: containing the kalendar . . . for the year . . . M.DCC.LXXVII . . . Fish-Kill, S. Loudon [1777]
[24] p. 15.5 cm.
At head of title: 1777
Advertised in Loudon's *New-York Packet*, Fish-Kill, Feb. 6 and 13, 1777, as "In the press . . . The day of its publication will be mentioned in our next."
Vail: Patriotic pair, p. 398
MWA (lacks last 4p.); N mp. 43265

B4487 IMPORTANT intelligence. Providence, August 23, 1777 . . . [Providence, J. Carter, 1777]
broadside 37.5 X 24 cm.
Alden 679; New York Public 640
DLC; RHi. Photostats: MHi; NN mp. 43266

B4488 IMPORTANT news. Boston . . . Friday, August 22. The following letter from Major-General Lincoln . . . [Boston, 1777]
broadside 24 X 10.5 cm.
Ford 2064
MHi; NhHi. Photostat: DLC mp. 43267

B4489 INTELLIGENCE from Red Bank . . . Lancaster, Francis Bailey [1777]
broadside 28.5 X 20.5 cm.
Consists of three letters addressed to Washington from John Hazelwood, Samuel Ward, and Robert Ballard dated "Red Bank Oct. 23d 1777"
RPJCB mp. 43402

B4490 KINGSTON, Tuesday, 9 o'clock, A.M. 23 Sept.
Last night arrived here, an express . . . from the secretary of the Committee of Albany . . . Kingston, John Holt [1777]
broadside 25 X 17 cm.
Capture of Ticonderoga
MB mp. 43268

B4490a LANCASTER COUNTY
Das Verbündniss von den freyen Lehnshalter und Einwohner von Lancaster Caunty . . . [Lancaster, Francis Bailey, 1777]
broadside fol.
PHi

B4490b LEARNED, LYDIA, 1703-1792
[A poem on the death of Mr. Abraham Rice, aged 80, and Mr. John Cloyes, aged 41 . . . struck with lightning, June 3, 1777] in Framingham . . . Boston: Printed at the Bible & Heart in Cornhill. [by T. and J. Fleet, 1777]
10 p. 16 cm.
Stoddard 136
RPB (top of title-leaf lacking)

B4491 LOUISIANA. GOVERNOR, 1777-1785
Don Bernard de Galvez . . . Donné . . . à la Nouvelle Orléans, le 3 mars 1777 . . . [New Orleans] Antoine Boudousquié, 1777.
broadside 41 X 33 cm.
McMurtrie: New Orleans 21
DLC; RPJCB. Bibliotheca Parsoniana mp. 43269

B4492 LOUISIANA. GOVERNOR, 1777-1785
Don Bernard de Galvez . . . Donné . . . à la Nouvelle Orléans, le 13 avril 1777 . . . [New Orleans] Antoine Boudousquié, 1777.
broadside 41 X 30.5 cm.
McMurtrie: Louisiana 8
G. William Nott, New Orleans (1942) mp. 43270

B4493 LOUISIANA. GOVERNOR, 1777-1785
Don Bernard de Galvez . . . Donné . . . à la Nouvelle Orléans, le 14 octobre 1777 . . . [Nouvelle Orléans] Antoine Boudousquié, 1777.
broadside 48 X 32.5 cm.
McMurtrie: New Orleans 25; New York Public 641
NN (photostat) mp. 43271

B4494 LOUISIANA. GOVERNOR, 1777-1785
Prix fixé pour le tabac . . . le 15 juin 1777 . . . [New Orleans] Antoine Boudousquié, 1777.
[4] p. 18.5 cm.
McMurtrie: New Orleans 22; New York Public 642
CU-B. Photostats: DLC; NN mp. 43272

B4495 MARYLAND. HOUSE OF DELEGATES
By the General assembly of Maryland. A proclamation . . . [Feb. 13, 1777] [Annapolis, F. Green, 1777]
broadside 26.5 X 18 cm.
DLC (photostat) mp. 43273

B4496 MARYLAND. HOUSE OF DELEGATES
Votes and proceedings . . . February session, 1777. [Annapolis, Frederick Green, 1777]
108 p. 30 cm.
Wheeler 13
DGU; MdHi (2 copies); RPJCB mp. 43275

B4497 MARYLAND. HOUSE OF DELEGATES
Votes and proceedings . . . June session, 1777. [Annapolis, F. Green, 1777]

p. [109]-133. 33.5 cm. caption title
Wheeler 15
DGU; DLC (2 copies); MdBP; MdHi mp. 43274

B4498 MARYLAND. LAWS
An act to prevent desertion . . . An act to promote the recruiting service. [Annapolis, F. Green, 1777]?
[4] p. 32 X 20 cm.
Chap. II-III, Maryland Laws, Feb. sess. 1777
MdHi. Photostat: MWA mp. 43276

B4499 MARYLAND. SENATE
Votes and proceedings . . . June session, 1777. [Annapolis, F. Green, 1777]
p. 65-81. 29 cm. caption title
Wheeler 16
DLC; MdBP; MdHi mp. 43277

B4500 THE Maryland almanack, for the year . . . 1778 . . . By a gentleman of observation. Frederick-Town, Matthias Bartgis [1777]
[20] p. 17 cm.
Wheeler 17
MWA mp. 43278

B4501 MASON'S Lodge, September 9th, 1777 . . . [Philadelphia, 1777]
2 p.
MWA (photostat) mp. 43279

B4502 MASSACHUSETTS
The government and people of the Massachusetts-Bay. To all unto whom these presents shall come, Greeting . . . Boston, July 25, 1777. [Boston, 1777?]
broadside
Commission of justice of peace
Ford 2111
MHi mp. 43281

B4503 MASSACHUSETTS. CONSTITUTIONAL CONVENTION
A report of a Committee of convention, of a form of government for the State of Massachusetts-Bay . . . [Boston, 1777]
8 p. 33 cm.
Ford 2068
DLC; M-Ar; MWA (p. 5-8 wanting) mp. 43280

B4504 MASSACHUSETTS. COUNCIL
State of Massachusetts-Bay. In Council, January 1, 1777. Whereas a considerable number of men . . . have inlisted into the service of the United States . . . [Boston, 1777]
broadside
Ford 2070
M-Ar mp. 43282

B4505 MASSACHUSETTS. COUNCIL
State of Massachusetts-Bay. In Council, January 9, 1777. Whereas by a resolve . . . [Boston, 1777]
broadside 28.5 X 20 cm.
Ford 2071; New York Public 643
M-Ar. Photostats: DLC; MHi; NHi; NN mp. 43283

B4506 MASSACHUSETTS. COUNCIL
State of Massachusetts-Bay. In Council, July 7, 1777. Resolved, That all such men as may inlist . . . [Boston, 1777]
broadside 19 X 16 cm.
Ford 2088
MB; MHi. Photostat: DLC mp. 43284

B4507 MASSACHUSETTS. GENERAL ASSEMBLY
Resolves of the General Assembly . . . of Massachusetts-Bay. Begun and held at Watertown . . . the 29th day of May . . . 1776, and thence continued . . . to Wednesday the 5th day of March following, and then met at Boston . . . [Boston, B. Edes, 1777]
51, 15 p. 36 cm. A^1 $B\text{-}R^4$ S^1
Guerra a-603
MBAt; NN mp. 43289

B4508 MASSACHUSETTS. GENERAL COURT
State of Massachusetts-Bay. Resolved, That it be recommended to the two regiments . . . now doing duty in . . . Rhode-Island . . . whose time of service will expire on the first day of January next . . . A true extract of a resolve passed the General Court, December 13, 1777 . . . [on verso] We the subscribers do . . . inlist . . . until the first day of January, 1779 . . . [Boston, 1777]
broadside 32 X 19.5 cm.
Ford 2069, 2098
MWA mp. 43293

B4509 MASSACHUSETTS. HOUSE OF REPRESENTATIVES
State of Massachusetts Bay. In the House of Representatives, February 5, 1777. Resolved, That when any waggon-master . . . [Boston, 1777]
broadside 17.5 X 22.5 cm.
Ford 2078
MB; MWA mp. 43292

B4510 MASSACHUSETTS. HOUSE OF REPRESENTATIVES
State of Massachusetts-Bay. In the House of Representatives, February 6, 1777. Whereas there may be . . . an omission . . . [Boston, 1777]
broadside 20.5 X 17.5 cm.
Ford 2079
MHi; NHi mp. 43285

B4511 MASSACHUSETTS. HOUSE OF REPRESENTATIVES
State of Massachusetts-Bay. In the House of Representatives, April 19th, 1777. Whereas this Court have voted to raise a number of men for the defence of this State . . . [Boston, 1777]
broadside
Ford 2084
M-Ar mp. 43286

B4512 MASSACHUSETTS. HOUSE OF REPRESENTATIVES
State of Massachusetts-Bay. In the House of Representatives, October 8, 1777. Whereas by information from the commanding officer . . . a number of drafted men for the secret expedition have not joined . . . [Boston, 1777]
broadside 21 X 17.5 cm.
Ford 2095
MHi mp. 43287

B4513 MASSACHUSETTS. LAWS
State of Massachusetts-Bay. In the year . . . [1777]. An act for apportioning and assessing a tax of three hundred and five thousand . . . pounds . . . [Boston, 1777]
8 leaves. 35.5 cm.
MWA mp. 43290

B4514 MASSACHUSETTS. LAWS
State of Massachusetts-Bay. In the year . . . 1777. An act for securing this and the other United States against the danger to which they are exposed by the internal enemies thereof. [Boston, 1777]

broadside
Ford 2100
M-Ar mp. 43291

B4515 MASSACHUSETTS. TREASURER
State of Massachusetts-Bay. The honorable Henry Gardner . . . Greeting . . . the seventh day of February . . . 1777. [Boston, 1777]
broadside 42.5 X 33.5 cm.
MHi; MeHi mp. 43294

B4516 MASSACHUSETTS. TREASURER
State of Massachusetts-Bay. The honorable Henry Gardner . . . To constable or collector of Greeting . . . Given under my hand . . . the twenty first day of February, 1777. [Boston, 1777]
broadside 41.5 X 24 cm.
Ford 2104
DLC; MB; MBB; MSaE; MWA mp. 43295

B4517 MASSACHUSETTS. TREASURER
State of Massachusetts-Bay. The honorable Henry Gardner . . . To the selectmen or assessors of the town of Greeting . . . Given under my hand . . . the twenty ninth day of October . . . 1777. [Boston, 1777]
broadside 42 X 33 cm.
DLC mp. 43296

B4518 MASSACHUSETTS. TREASURER
State of Massachusetts-Bay. The honorable Henry Gardner . . . Greeting . . . the first day of December, 1777. [Boston, 1777]
broadside 41.5 X 33 cm.
Ford 2105
MWA; NHi mp. 43297

B4519 MASSACHUSETTS. WAR BOARD
State of Massachusetts-Bay. *Samuel Phillips Savage* . . . in the county of and state aforesaid, maketh oath, that the *sloop Republick* . . . was built *at Swanzey* . . . and that no subject of the king . . . hath any share . . . Dated at this day of . . . 1777. [Boston? 1777?]
broadside 33 X 24.5 cm.
Italicized portions in ms.
MiU-C (facsim.)

B4520 MASSACHUSETTS. WAR BOARD
War-Office, Boston, February 3, 1777. To the selectmen of As the articles herein enumerated, are absolutely necessary for the ensuing campaign . . . By order of the Board, Samuel P. Savage, President . . . [Boston, 1777]
broadside 21.5 X 18 cm.
MWA mp. 43298

B4521 MORGAN, JOHN, 1735-1789
A vindication of his public character in the station of director-general of the military hospitals . . . Boston, Powars and Willis, 1777.
xxxii p. 21 cm.
Consists of preface only
PPL

B4522 NEW HAMPSHIRE. COUNCIL
State of New-Hampshire. Whereas . . . in the several places in this state paying taxes, the last proportion is become unequal . . . By order of the Council .... March 31, 1777. [Exeter? 1777]
broadside 42.5 X 31 cm.
Whittemore 211
NhHi mp. 43299

B4523 NEW HAMPSHIRE. HOUSE OF REPRESENTATIVES
State of New-Hampshire. In the House of Representatives, June 7th, 1777. Voted, that all military officers of . . . places, who are delinquent, in raising their quota . . . [Exeter? 1777]
broadside 14.5 X 17 cm.
Whittemore 212
NhHi mp. 43300

B4524 NEW HAMPSHIRE. LAWS
[Acts and laws, 1777] [Colophon] Exeter, Sold at the Printing-office, 1777.
p. 43-46. 32 cm.
Continuation of Acts and laws published 1776
Whittemore 204
NhHi. Photostat: MWA mp. 43302

B4525 NEW HAMPSHIRE. LAWS
[Acts and laws, 1777] [Colophon] Portsmouth, Sold at the Printing-office, 1777.
p. 47-54. 33 cm.
Continuation of Acts and laws published 1776
Whittemore 205
NhHi. Photostat: MWA mp. 43303

B4526 NEW HAMPSHIRE. LAWS
[Acts and laws, 1777] [Colophon] Exeter, Printed and sold at the Printing-office, 1777.
p. 55-58. 30.5 cm.
Continuation of Acts and laws published 1776
Whittemore 206
MH. Photostats: MWA; NhHi mp. 43304

B4527 NEW HAMPSHIRE. LAWS
[Acts and laws, 1777] [Exeter? 1777] p. 59
p.59-86. 33 cm.
Continuation of Acts and laws published 1776
New York Public 644; Whittemore 207
NhHi (partly photostat); NN (p. 67-70, 83-86). Photostat: MWA mp. 43305

B4528 NEW HAMPSHIRE. PROVINCIAL CONGRESS
State of New-Hampshire. Exeter, January 14th, 1777. Whereas orders have issured [sic] to several recruiting officers . . . Extract from the votes of council and assembly . . . [Exeter? 1777]
broadside 35 X 11 cm.
Whittemore 208
NhHi mp. 43301

B4529 NEW JERSEY. GOVERNOR, 1776-1790
By his excellency, William Livingston . . . A proclamation. Whereas by a certain act . . . Given . . . at Morris-town, [Aug. 14, 1777] [Burlington, Isaac Collins, 1777]
broadside 43 X 31 cm.
Humphrey 174
DLC mp. 43306

B4530 NEW JERSEY. LAWS
An act to explain and amend an act, intitled, An act for the better regulating the militia . . . [Burlington, 1777]
[2] p. 40 cm.
Passed Sept. 1777
NjR

B4531 NEW JERSEY. LAWS
[Law of New Jersey for purchasing clothes for New Jersey regiments. Nov. 27, 1777. n.p., 1777?]

"Fifty copies only printed" (Sabin)

Humphrey 177, from Sabin 53142
No copy known mp. 43307

B4532 NEW JERSEY. SENATE
A journal of the proceedings of the Legislative-Council of . . . New-Jersey . . . [Aug. 27, 1776-June 7, 1777] Burlington, Issac Collins, 1777.
95 p. 32 cm.
Humphrey 175; New York Public 645
NHi; NN; Nj mp. 43308

B4533 NEW JERSEY GAZETTE
Burlington, Nov. 14, 1777. Proposals for printing . . . the *New-Jersey Gazette* . . . [Burlington, I. Collins, 1777]
broadside 37 X 24 cm.
"Subscriptions will be taken in . . .": 5 lines
DLC mp. 43232

B4533a NEW JERSEY GAZETTE
Burlington, Nov. 14, 1777. Proposals for printing . . . the *New-Jersey Gazette* . . . [Burlington, I. Collins, 1777]
broadside 37 X 24 cm.
"Subscriptions will be taken in . . .": 15 lines
DLC

B4534 NEW LONDON, CONN.
At a meeting of the authority, selectmen, &c. in New-London, 21st January, 1777. Voted, That the undermentioned articles . . . be sold at the prices annexed thereto . . . [New London, 1777]
broadside 26 X 17.5 cm.
CtHi mp. 43309

B4535 A NEW privateering song: concluding with some remarks upon the cruelty . . . upon our poor prisoners in New-York. [n.p., 1777?]
broadside 41.5 X 21 cm.
34 4-line stanzas, in two columns
New York Public 646
NN mp. 43310

B4536 NEW YORK. COMMITTEE OF SAFETY
In committee of Safety for the State of New-York, Fish-Kill, Jan. 6, 1777. Whereas it appears . . . that fines have been levied . . . Robert Benson, Sec'ry. [Fish-kill? 1777]
broadside 23 X 20 cm.
NHi mp. 43315

B4537 NEW YORK. COMMITTEE OF SAFETY
In Committee of Safety for the State of New-York. Fish-Kill, Jan. 22, 1777. Several matters of the utmost importance . . . Call of the Convention . . . punctually to attend . . . 3d day of February next . . . Robert Benson, Sec'ry . . . [Fish-Kill, Samuel Loudon, 1777]
broadside 16.5 X 14 cm.
Vail: Patriotic pair, p. 399
DLC; N; NHi (photostat) mp. 43316

B4538 NEW YORK. CONVENTION, 1776-1777
Fish-Kill, December 12, 1776. An address of the convention of the representatives of the state of New-York to their constituents. [Annapolis, Frederick Green, 1777]
[4] p. 26 cm. caption title
Printed in the Annapolis *Maryland Gazette* in successive issues, Feb. 20, Feb. 27, and Mar. 6, 1777, from the same setting of type
MdHi mp. 43311

B4539 NEW YORK. CONVENTION, 1776-1777
In Convention of the representatives of the state . . . March 7, 1777. Whereas divers persons . . . [Fish-Kill, S. Loudon, 1777]
broadside 27 X 15 cm.
Vail: Patriotic pair, p. 399
CSmH; MHi; MWA; MiU-C; NN; WHi. Photostats: DLC; NHi; RPJCB mp. 43312

B4540 NEW YORK. CONVENTION, 1776-1777
In Convention of the representatives of the state . . . April 1, 1777 . . . [Fish-Kill, Samuel Loudon, 1777]
broadside 10 X 14.5 cm.
New York Public 648; Vail: Patriotic pair, p. 401
MH-L; N; NHi. Matt B. Jones (1932). Photostat: NN mp. 43313

B4541 NEW YORK. CONVENTION, 1776-1777
In Convention of the representatives of the state . . . May 5, 1777 . . . [Fish-Kill, Samuel Loudon, 1777]
broadside 21 X 18 cm.
New York Public 649; Vail: Patriotic pair, p. 401
CtY; NN mp. 43314

B4542 NEW YORK. COUNCIL OF SAFETY
In Council of Safety for the State of New York, July 30, 1777, a proclamation [declaring George Clinton elected governor] . . . Kingston, John Holt [1777]
broadside 31 X 17.5 cm.
New York Public 650-651
MiU-C; NHi; NN (2 variants) mp. 43317

B4543 NEW YORK. COUNCIL OF SAFETY
In Council o[f Safety for the] State of New [York] Kingston, July 21, 1777 Whereas it hath pleased Almighty God . . . Resolved, That upon any future draught from the militia . . . John M'Kesson, Sec'ry. Kingston, John Holt [1777]
broadside 28 X 20.5 cm.
Vail: Patriotic pair, p. 402
N (3 copies). Photostat: NHi mp. 43318

B4544 NEW YORK. COUNCIL OF SAFETY
In Council of Safety, for the State of New-York, Kingston, August 13, 1777. Whereas many people . . . benefit of the late act of grace . . . Kingston, John Holt [1777]
broadside 16.5 X 21 cm.
New York Public 652; Vail: Patriotic pair, p. 402
NHi. Photostat: NN mp. 43319

B4545 NEW YORK. COUNCIL OF SAFETY
In Council of Safety for the State of New-York, Marble-Town, Nov. 11, 1777. Whereas this Council has . . . information, that . . . vast quantities of flour have been purchased . . . for the use of the enemy . . . By order, Evert Bancker, President pro tem. [Fish-Kill, Samuel Loudon, 1777]
broadside 41.5 X 25.5 cm.
Vail: Patriotic pair, p. 403
N. Photostat: NHi mp. 43320

B4546 NEW YORK. GOVERNOR, 1777-1795
By His Excellency George Clinton . . . A proclamation . . . The honourable the Congress, having by sundry resolutions . . . Given . . . at Poughkeepsie . . . the fifte [sic] . . . December . . . one thousand seven hundred and seventy [mutilated] . . . [Fish-Kill, S. Loudon? 1777?]
broadside 16.5 X 13 cm.
Vail: Patriotic pair, p. 403
N (mutilated). Photostat: NHi mp. 43321

B4547 NEW YORK. MAYOR
I do hereby certify, that has, in my presence . . . taken an oath . . . true allegiance to His Majesty . . . this day of in the seventeenth year of His Majes-

ty's reign, Anno. Dom. 1777. mayor of the city of New-York. [New York, 1777]
broadside 19 X 11 cm.
Signed by D. Mathews
MiU-C (5 copies)

B4548 NEW-YORK, April 23, 1777. Song for St. George's Day. Tune, Hail England, Old England . . . [New York? 1777]
broadside 39 X 16 cm.
NHi mp. 43322

B4549 NEWBURYPORT, MASS.
In pursuance of an act from the . . . General Court . . . the selectmen and committee of the town of Newburyport, have set . . . the following prices .... Newbury-Port, John Mycall, 1777.
broadside 43 X 35.5 cm.
MWA mp. 43323

B4550 NORTH CAROLINA. LAWS
An act for confiscating the property . . . December 28, 1777 . . . [Newbern, J. Davis, 1777]
broadside 33 X 23 cm.
DLC (photostat) mp. 43324

B4551 [PAINE, THOMAS] 1737-1809
The American crisis. Number I[-III]. By the author of Common sense . . . [at end] Philadelphia, April 19, 1777 . . . [Philadelphia? 1777]
54 p. 18.5 cm. [A]-G[4]
Separately issued as unit? – Edwin Wolf 2d
MHi; MWA; RPJCB mp. 43325

B4552 [PAINE, THOMAS] 1737-1809
The American crisis. Number II. To Lord Howe . . . [Colophon] Norwich, J. Trumbull [1777]
[13]-32 p. 16 cm.
Advertised in the Norwich *Packet*, Feb. 24, 1777, as "just published."
MWA (closely trimmed) mp. 43326

B4553 [PAINE, THOMAS] 1737-1809
N° II. The American Crisis. By the author of Common sense. To Lord Howe. [Fish-Kill, S. Loudon, 1777]
p. 9-24. 19 cm. caption title
Huntington 416; Vail: Patriotic pair, p. 403
CSmH; DLC (2 copies); MH; MWA mp. 43327

B4554 [PAINE, THOMAS] 1737-1809
N° III. The American Crisis. By the Author of Common Sense . . . [Fish-Kill, S. Loudon, 1777]
p. [25]-54, [1] 18 cm. caption title
Signed and dated at end: Philadelphia, April 19, 1777
Huntington 417 & 419; Vail: Patriotic pair, p. 404
CSmH; MH; MWA; NHi mp. 43328

B4555 [PAINE, THOMAS] 1737-1809
N° IV. The American Crisis. By the Author of Common Sense . . . [Fish-Kill, S. Loudon, 1777]
p. [57]-60. 19 cm. caption title
Signed and dated at end: Philadelphia, Sept. 12 at Noon [1777]
Vail: Patriotic pair, p. 404
NHi mp. 43329

B4556 PEMBERTON, ISRAEL, 1715-1779
An address to the inhabitants of Pennsylvania, by those freemen . . . now confined in the Mason's Lodge . . . By the Vice President of the Council of Pennsylvania. [Philadelphia] Robert Bell, 1777.
36 p. 19 cm.
"Seven o'clock P.M. We presented another remonstrance . . . we shall endeavor to hand to the Public To-morrow" (p. 36)
Taylor 96; cf. Evans 15496
NHi; PPL; RPJCB mp. 43330

B4557 PENNSYLVANIA
Philadelphia, June 1777. Sir, You being drawn in the class of Captain Company, and Colonel Bradford's Battalion; you . . . are . . . desired to parade at your Captain's quarters at drum beat . . . with your arms . . . agreeable to the militia law of this State . . . William Henry, C.P. [Philadelphia, 1777]
broadside 6 X 12 cm.
Taylor 110
PPL

B4558 PENNSYLVANIA. COUNCIL OF SAFETY
In Council, June 13, 1777. Major General Mifflin, Quarter-Master General . . . having occasion for a number of waggons . . . You are . . . requested to exert yourself in procuring . . . waggons with four horses . . . Thomas Wharton jun. President. To Lieutenant of the County of [Philadelphia? 1777]
broadside 16.5 X 20 cm.
Taylor 105
PHi mp. 43331

B4559 PENNSYLVANIA. COUNCIL OF SAFETY
In Council of safety. Lancaster, 25th October, 1777. An ordinance for appointing . . . sub-lieutenants . . . Lancaster, Francis Bailey [1777]
broadside 33 X 21 cm.
DLC mp. 43332

B4560 PENNSYLVANIA. COUNCIL OF SAFETY
In Council of safety. Lancaster, 25th October, 1777. An ordinance for the more effectual levying . . . Lancaster, Francis Bailey [1777]
broadside 32 X 20.5 cm.
DLC mp. 43333

B4560a PENNSYLVANIA. COUNCIL OF SAFETY
In Council of Safety, Philadelphia, January 31, 1777. Sir, The militia of this state . . . have generally been supplied with public arms . . . [Philadelphia, Henry Miller, 1777]
broadside fol.
PHi

B4561 PENNSYLVANIA. COUNCIL OF SAFETY
In Council, Philadelphia, July 31, 1777. Sir, I wrote you on the 28th instant, and ordered . . . [Philadelphia, John Dunlap, 1777]
broadside 34 X 21 cm.
Circular letter ordering militia to the defence of Philadelphia
Heartman: Cradle 770; Taylor 106
NHi mp. 43334

B4562 PENNSYLVANIA. COUNCIL OF SAFETY
Sir, The opinion which General Washington and all the General Officers of our Army entertain of the designs of General Howe against this State [i.e., Pennsylvania] . . . Philadelphia, April 16, 1777. [Philadelphia, 1777]
broadside 34 X 21 cm.
NHi mp. 43335

B4563 PENNSYLVANIA. COUNCIL OF SAFETY
To the inhabitants of Pennsylvania. In Council of safety. Lancaster, 23d October, 1777 . . . Lancaster, Francis Bailey [1777]

broadside 33 X 20 cm.
DLC mp. 43336

B4564 PENNSYLVANIA. GENERAL ASSEMBLY
In General assembly of the state of Pennsylvania, Tuesday, June 17, 1777. The House resumed the consideration of the report of a committee appointed to prepare an address . . . [Philadelphia, John Dunlap, 1777]
[4] p. 8vo
PPL mp. 43337

B4565 PENNSYLVANIA. GENERAL ASSEMBLY
Lancaster, 1777. Sir, Pay to Esquire, for his wages for service in the General Assembly . . . Speaker. To David Rittenhouse, Esq; Treasurer. [n.p., 1777]
broadside 16 X 20 cm.
Signed by John Bayard, Speaker
MiU-C

B4566 PENNSYLVANIA. GENERAL ASSEMBLY
Minutes of the General assembly of Pennsylvania, commencing at their sitting at Philadelphia, September 30 . . . [Colophon] Lancaster, Francis Bailey [1777]
[85]-100 p. fol.
PPL mp. 43338

B4567 PENNSYLVANIA. GENERAL ASSEMBLY
Philadelphia, 1777. Sir, Pay to Esquire, for his wages for service in the General Assembly . . . Speaker. To David Rittenhouse, Esq; Treasurer. [Philadelphia, 1777]
broadside 16.5 X 20.5 cm.
Signed by John Bayard, Speaker
Taylor 104
MiU-C; NN

B4568 PENNSYLVANIA. LAWS
An act obliging the male white inhabitants of this state to give assurances of allegiance . . . [at end] Philadelphia, John Dunlap [1777]
7 p. 19.5 cm. caption title
Signed at end: Enacted into law, June 13, 1777
RPJCB mp. 43339

B4569 PHILADELPHIA, June 18, 1777. Sir, You are desired to take notice, that you are rated in the tax on non-associators . . . [Philadelphia, 1777]
broadside 18.5 X 10.5 cm.
PPL mp. 43340

B4570 PHILADELPHIA, August 22, 1777. By an express arrived last evening from General Schuyler to Congress, we have the following . . . intelligence . . . Annapolis, August 25, 1777. The Governor is informed . . . [Annapolis, F. Green, 1777]
broadside 27 X 20.5 cm.
Battle of Bennington
MdHi. Photostats: MWA; RPJCB mp. 43341

B4571 POTTER, ELAM, 1742-1794
A warning to America . . . Hartford, Eben. Watson, 1777.
8 p.
Trumbull: Supplement 2509
CSmH; CtY mp. 43342

B4572 PROVIDENCE. CONVENTION, 1776-1777
Extract from the minutes of the committees appointed by the states . . . convened at Providence . . . by adjournments to the 2d of January, one thousand seven hundred and seventy-seven. [n.p., 1777]
10 p. 21 cm. caption title
MHi. Photostats: DLC; MWA; NN mp. 43346

B4573 PROVIDENCE, January 5, 1777. Fresh advices from the westward . . . Providence, J. Carter [1777]
broadside 23 X 18 cm.
Alden 680; Winship p. 35
MWA; RHi. Photostat: NN mp. 43345

B4574 RHODE ISLAND. COUNCIL OF WAR
State of Rhode-Island and Providence Plantations. In Council of war, April 8, 1777. This Council having received intelligence . . . [Providence, J. Carter, 1777]
broadside 26.5 X 21.5 cm.
Alden 697; Winship p. 36
RHi mp. 43347

B4575 RHODE ISLAND. COUNCIL OF WAR
State of Rhode-Island and Providence Plantations. In Council of war, July 1, 1777. Whereas blankets are wanted . . . [Providence, J. Carter, 1777]
broadside 21.5 X 26.5 cm.
Alden 705; Winship p. 36
NHi; RHi mp. 43348

B4576 RHODE ISLAND. ELECTION PROX.
Defenders of American rights. The honorable Josiah Arnold, Esq; Governor. The honorable William West, Esq; Dep. Governor . . . [Providence? 1777]
broadside 21.5 X 14 cm.
Alden 681; Chapin Proxies 18a
RHi mp. 43349

B4577 RHODE ISLAND. ELECTION PROX.
Defenders of American rights. The honorable Josiah Arnold, Esq; Governor. The honorable William West Esq; Dep. Gov. . . . [Providence? 1777]
broadside 21.5 X 14 cm.
For another edition, see the preceding
Alden 682; Chapin Proxies 18b
RHi mp. 43701

B4578 RHODE ISLAND. ELECTION PROX.
For the safety of the people. The honorable Nicholas Cooke, Esq; Governor. The honorable William Bradford, Esq; Dep. Gov. [Providence? J. Carter? 1777]
broadside 21 X 13.5 cm.
Alden 683; Chapin Proxies 17
RHi mp. 43350

B4579 RHODE ISLAND. GENERAL ASSEMBLY
State of Rhode-Island and Providence Plantations. In General assembly, March Second session, A.D. 1771. Resolved, That each of the three divisions of the militia . . . [Providence, J. Carter, 1777]
broadside 38.5 X 25.5 cm.
Alden 696; Winship p. 36
RHi mp. 43354

B4580 RHODE ISLAND. GENERAL ASSEMBLY
State of Rhode-Island and Providence Planatations. In General assembly, March session, A.D. 1777. This Assembly being under great concern . . . do resolve . . . [Providence, J. Carter, 1777]
broadside 36 X 21.5 cm.
Alden 693; Winship p. 35
DLC; RHi mp. 43352

B4581 RHODE ISLAND. GENERAL ASSEMBLY
State of Rhode-Island and Providence Plantations. In General assembly, April 21, 1777. It is voted and resolved, That the first division . . . [Providence, J. Carter, 1777]
broadside 21.5 X 24.5 cm.
Alden 700; Winship p. 36
RHi mp. 43357

B4582 RHODE ISLAND. GENERAL ASSEMBLY
State of Rhode-Island and Providence Plantations. In General assembly, May session, 1777. This Assembly taking into consideration . . . [Providence, J. Carter, 1777]
broadside 21.5 X 18 cm.
Alden 701; Winship p. 36
RHi; RPJCB. Photostat: MWA mp. 43358

B4583 RHODE ISLAND. GENERAL ASSEMBLY
State of Rhode-Island and Providence Plantations. In General assembly, May session, 1777. Whereas by an act . . . passed at the last session, five hundred men . . . [Providence, J. Carter, 1777]
broadside 21.5 X 18 cm.
Alden 702; Winship p. 36
RHi; RPJCB mp. 43359

B4584 RHODE ISLAND. GENERAL ASSEMBLY
State of Rhode-Island and Providence Plantations. In General assembly, July 9, 1777. Resolved, that one of the divisions . . . be immediately called . . . [Providence, J. Carter, 1777]
broadside 27 X 21.5 cm.
Alden 706; Winship p. 36
RHi mp. 43362

B4585 RHODE ISLAND. GENERAL ASSEMBLY
State of Rhode-Island and Providence Plantations. In General assembly, August session, 1777. It is voted and resolved, that the Continental officers . . . [Providence, J. Carter, 1777]
broadside 39 X 25.5 cm.
Alden 707; Winship p. 36
RHi; RPJCB mp. 43363

B4586 RHODE ISLAND. GENERAL ASSEMBLY
State of Rhode-Island and Providence Plantations. In General assembly, September session, A.D. 1777. Resolved, that one half of the militia . . . [Providence, J. carter, 1777]
broadside 31 X 17 cm.
Alden 709; Winship Addenda p. 88
RHi; RPB mp. 43365

B4587 RHODE ISLAND. GENERAL ASSEMBLY
State of Rhode-Island and Providence Plantations. In General assembly, October session, A.D. 1777. Whereas, by a resolve of this Assembly, the families of officers . . . [Providence, J. Carter, 1777]
broadside 25 X 18.5 cm.
Alden 710; Winship p. 36
RPJCB. Photostat: MWA mp. 43366

B4588 RHODE ISLAND. GENERAL ASSEMBLY
State of Rhode-Island and Providence Plantations. In General assembly, October session, A.D. 1777. Whereas, owing to divers causes . . . [Providence, J. Carter, 1777]
broadside 21 X 27.5 cm.
Alden 711; Winship Addenda p. 88
R mp. 43367

B4589 RHODE ISLAND. GOVERNOR, 1775-1778
State of Rhode-Island, &c. Providence, July 21, 1777. By an express . . . this morning . . . Nicholas Cooke, Gov. To all brigadiers . . . [Providence, J. Carter, 1777]
broadside 17 X 19.5 cm.
Alden 684; Winship Addenda p. 88
RHi. Photostat: MHi mp. 43351

B4590 RHODE ISLAND. LAWS
State of Rhode-Island and Providence Plantations. In General assembly, March Second session, 1777. An act for numbering all persons . . . [Providence, J. Carter, 1777]
broadside 34 X 21 cm.
Alden 695; Winship Addenda p. 88
MHi; RHi. Photostats: MWA; RNHi mp. 43353

B4591 RHODE ISLAND. LAWS
State of Rhode-Island and Providence Plantations. In General assembly, April 19, 1777. Be it enacted . . . that five hundred effective men . . . [Providence, J. Carter, 1777]
[2] p. 35.5 X 21.5 cm.
Alden 698; Winship p. 36
R; RHi; RPJCB. Photostat: MWA mp. 43355

B4592 RHODE ISLAND. LAWS
State of Rhode-Island and Providence Plantations. In General assembly, April 21, 1777. An act in addition to an act . . . for the relief of persons of tender consciences . . . [Providence, J. Carter, 1777]
broadside 35 X 21.5 cm.
Alden 699; Winship p. 36
MWA; R (2 copies); RHi; RPJCB mp. 43356

B4593 RHODE ISLAND. LAWS
State of Rhode-Island and Providence Plantations. In General assembly, May 2d session, 1777. An act to prevent monopoly . . . [Providence, J. Carter, 1777]
15 p. 17.5 cm. caption title
Advertised June 21, 1777, as "now in the press."
Alden 703; Sabin 70505; Winship p. 36
MHi; MWA; NN; RHi; RP; RPB; RPJCB mp. 43360

B4594 RHODE ISLAND. LAWS
State of Rhode-Island and Providence Plantations. In General assembly, June session, 1777. An act establishing and regulating fees. [Providence, J. Carter, 1777]
7 p. 18 cm. caption title
Alden 704; Winship p. 36
MWA; RHi mp. 43361

B4595 RHODE ISLAND. LAWS
State of Rhode-Island and Providence Plantations. In General assembly, August 23d, 1777. An act assessing . . . a rate or tax of thirty-two thousand pounds . . . [Providence, J. Carter, 1777]
[2] p. 31 X 19.5 cm.
Alden 708; Winship p. 36
NNC. Photostat: RHi mp. 43364

B4596 RHODE ISLAND. LAWS
State of Rhode-Island and Providence Plantations. In General assembly, December 4, 1777. An act assessing . . . a rate or tax of forty-eight thousand pounds . . . [Providence, J. Carter, 1777]
broadside 35 X 23 cm.
Alden 712; Winship p. 36; Winship Addenda p. 93
R; RPJCB mp. 43368

B4597 RHODE ISLAND. MILITIA
Return of the second battalion in the state of Rhode-Island, commanded by Col. Israel Angell . . . [Providence? J. Carter? ca. 1777]
broadside 50.5 X 18 cm.
Alden 713
RHi mp. 43369

B4598 ROBERTSON, JAMES, 1720?-1788
Proclamation. By Major General James Robertson . . . [New York, 1777]
broadside 32 cm.
Concerns watches to prevent fires
New York Public 657
NN mp. 43262

B4599 [RUSH, BENJAMIN] 1745-1813
Directions for preserving the health of soldiers recommended to the consideration of the officers in the Army of the United States . . . [n.p., 1777?]
broadside 41.5 X 25.5 cm.
CtHi mp. 43370

B4600 THE second edition of Lord Howes, & General Howes proclamation with notes, and emendations . . . A Norvician. Norwich, Jan. 1, 1777. [Norwich, 1777]
broadside 35 X 21 cm.
In verse
CtHi mp. 43371

B4601 [SEWALL, JONATHAN MITCHELL] 1748-1808
A new epilogue to Cato. Spoken at a late performance of that tragedy. [And] From an Irish paper . . . Janus. [n.p., 1777?]
broadside ([2] p.) 33 X 21 cm.
Ford 2113
MWA mp. 43372

B4602 SOUTH CAROLINA. GENERAL ASSEMBLY
South-Carolina. At a General Assembly . . . holden at Charles-Town . . . [Dec. 6, 1776-Feb. 13, 1777] . . . An ordinance for establishing an oath of abjuration . . . [Charleston, P. Timothy? 1777]
[2] p. 30 cm.
Mosimann 290; Sabin 87625A
MBAt

B4603 SOUTH CAROLINA. LAWS
Acts of the General assembly . . . Passed the 22d and 23d of August, 1777. [Charles-Town, Peter Edes, 1777]
1 p.l., 11, 4 p. 29 cm.
Half-title only
Sabin 87626
DLC mp. 43375

B4604 SOUTH CAROLINA. LAWS
The tax act. Passed in January, 1777. [Charles-Town, Peter Timothy, 1777]
1 p.l., 13 p. 29 cm.
Half-title only
Sabin 87625
DLC mp. 43374

B4605 STANTON, PHINEAS
A brief historical view, of the several cases and trials . . . between Mr. Adam Babcock, merchant, at New-Haven . . . and Phineas Stanton, Junior, of Stonington . . . By Phineas Stanton, Junior . . . Norwich, John Trumbull, 1777.
121, 47 p. 19 cm.
cf. Evans 14655
CtHi; NHi mp. 43376

B4606 SYNOD OF NEW YORK AND PHILADELPHIA
A list of the ministers & congregations belonging to the Reverend Synod of New-York & Philadelphia, together with the money collected . . . by said Synod for propagating Christian knowledge . . . [Philadelphia, 1777?]
6 p. 18 cm.
Taylor 93
PHi mp. 43377

B4607 TO all gentlemen volunteers, who prefer liberty to slavery . . . who are . . . willing to serve this state . . . and learn . . . gunnery, in the Massachusetts State Train of Artillery . . . now stationed in . . . Boston . . . [Boston, 1777?]
broadside 23 X 17.5 cm.
Printed also as an advertisement in the *Independent Chronicle*, Dec. 19, 1777, and later
MHi (facsim.); NHi. Photostat: MWA mp. 43288

B4608 TO satisfy the impatience of the public . . . the printer has been desired to publish the following accounts of the glorious victory.. . . New-York, James Rivington [1777]
broadside 41.5 cm. X 32.5 cm.
Concerns the battle of Germantown, Oct. 4, 1777
MiU-C; NHi. Photostat: NN mp. 43378

B4609 TO the independent citizens of Exeter. Gentlemen, the unhappy contest . . . is a circumstance that must give every man . . . feelings . . . to petition His Majesty . . . A Citizen. Exeter, Dec. 15, 1777. [Exeter, 1777]
broadside 9.5 X 16 cm.
Whittemore 216
MWA mp. 43379

B4610 U. S. ARMY. CONTINENTAL ARMY
By the Honorable Major-General Putnam, commander of the forces . . . near the White-Plains. A proclamation . . . Given . . . at Head-Quarters, this 17th of November . . . 1777. Israel Putnam. [Fish-Kill, S. Loudon? 1777]
broadside 27.5 X 19 cm.
NYPL 755; Vail: Patriotic pair, p. 404
NHi; RPJCB. Photostat: NN mp. 43380

B4611 U. S. ARMY. CONTINENTAL ARMY
Extract of a letter from General Gates, dated . . . November 25, 1777. . . [at end] York-Town, Hall and Sellers, 1777.
[2] p. 33.5 cm. caption title
New York Public 635; Taylor 85
MHi; NN mp. 43381

B4612 U. S. ARMY. CONTINENTAL ARMY
Good news from the Northern Army. Boston, October 13th, 1777. This morning . . . an express . . . with the following letter, viz. Camp three miles above Stillwater, October 9th, 1777 . . . John Glover, Major-General . . . Exeter, 1777.
broadside 32.5 X 20 cm.
DLC mp. 43382

B4613 U. S. ARMY. CONTINENTAL ARMY
Good news from the Northern Army. Boston, October 13, 1777. This morning . . . an express . . . with the following letter . . . John Glover, Major-General . . . Portsmouth, Printed [1777]
broadside 25.5 X 18 cm.
RPJCB mp. 43383

B4614 U. S. ARMY. CONTINENTAL ARMY
Head Quarters, August 25, 1777. Sir, A messenger is just arrived with the inclosed letters from General Arnold and Colonel Gansevoort . . . Horatio Gates . . . Philadelphia, John Dunlap [1777]
broadside 39 X 24.5 cm.
CtHi mp. 43384

B4615 U. S. ARMY. CONTINENTAL ARMY
Head Quarters, Peeks-Kill, General orders for the army under . . . Brigadier General M'Dougall . . . Instructions for soldiers . . . concerning the means of preserving health . . . W. [Fish-Kill, Samuel Loudon, 1777]
broadside 42.5 X 27 cm.
Vail: Patriotic pair, p. 404
MH; NHi mp. 43385

B4616 U. S. ARMY. CONTINENTAL ARMY
Important and fresh intelligence. Exeter, August 26th, 1777. Sunday evening an express arrived in this town . . . intelligence from General Stark at Bennington . . . [Exeter, 1777]

broadsheet ([2] p.) 34 X 19 cm.
In double columns
Contains also a letter from Burgoyne to Baum
ICN mp. 43386

B4617 U. S. ARMY. CONTINENTAL ARMY
Recruiting instructions for Thomas Hartley, Esq; You are hereby authorized to enlist . . . all such able-bodied freemen as are willing . . . G. Washington. Morris-Town, January 12, 1777 . . . Baltimore, M. K. Goddard [1777]
broadside 34 X 21 cm.
Wheeler 32a
RPJCB mp. 43387

B4618 U. S. ARTICLES OF CONFEDERATION
Articles of confederation and perpetual union. [Providence, J. Carter, 1777]
8 p. 18 cm. caption title
Printing attributed to Carter by Lawrence C. Wroth
Alden 714; NYPL 660; Winship p. 36
MH; MWA; RHi; RPJCB. Photostat: NN mp. 43388

B4619 U. S. CONTINENTAL CONGRESS, 1776
Congress, December 27, 1776. Resolved, That the Council of Safety of Pennsylvania be requested to take . . . measures for punishing all . . . refuse Continental currency . . . In Council of Safety, Philadelphia, January 1, 1777 . . . Philadelphia, John Dunlap [1777]
broadside 39 X 23 cm.
PHi mp. 43390

B4620 U. S. CONTINENTAL CONGRESS, 1776
Rules and articles for the better government of the troops raised . . . at the expence of the United States . . . Hartford, Re-printed by Eben. Watson, 1777.
26+ p. 23 cm. [A]-C^4 D^4?
Page [3]: . . . In Congress, September 20, 1776. Resolved . . .
MWA (all wanting after sig. D1) mp. 43391

B4621 U. S. CONTINENTAL CONGRESS, 1777
Bey dem Congres, den 8ten October, 1777. [Philadelphia? 1777?]
broadside 33.5 X 21 cm.
German translation of Evans 15677?
RPJCB. Photostat: NN mp. 43392

B4622 U. S. CONTINENTAL CONGRESS, 1777
Extract of a letter from General Gates, dated . . . October 18, 1777 . . . In Congress, Nov. 1, 1777 . . . Burlington, Isaac Collins [1777]
broadside 37.5 X 24 cm.
DLC mp. 43393

B4623 U. S. CONTINENTAL CONGRESS, 1777
Extract of a letter from General Gates . . . October 18, 1777 . . . In Congress, Nov. 1, 1777. Forasmuch as it is the indispensible duty . . . It is . . . recommended . . . to set apart Thursday, the 18th day of December . . . for solemn thanksgiving . . . Lancaster, Francis Bailey [1777]
[2] p. 32.5 X 20 cm.
Taylor 86
MiU-C; PHi mp. 43394

B4624 U. S. CONTINENTAL CONGRESS, 1777
In Congress, April 4, 1777. Resolved, 1. That there be one commissary-general . . . Philadelphia, John Dunlap [1777]
broadside 33 X 19.5 cm.
cf. Evans 15659; Taylor 130
DLC mp. 43395

B4625 U. S. CONTINENTAL CONGRESS, 1777
In Congress, April 14, 1777. Resolved, That from and after the publication hereof . . . the rules and articles for the better government of the troops . . . Extracts from the minutes. Charles Thomson, Secretary. Philadelphia, John Dunlap [1777]
broadside
Contains resolves of May 27 and June 17
Heartman: Cradle 231; cf. Evans 15662
CSmH; MHi; MWA. Charles F. Heartman (1922) mp. 43396

B4626 U. S. CONTINENTAL CONGRESS, 1777
In Congress, June 10, 1777. Resolved, I. That for supplying the army . . . Poughkeepsie, John Holt [1777]
4 p. 40.5 cm.
Ford: Bibliographical notes 172; Vail: Patriotic pair, p. 405
CtY; DLC. Photostat: MWA mp. 43397

B4627 U. S. CONTINENTAL CONGRESS, 1777
In Congress, June 20, 1777. Resolved, That a suitable person be appointed commissary, to receive all raw hides . . . October 11, 1777. Resolved, That the commissary of hides be supplied with money . . . Extract from the minutes, Charles Thomson, secretary. [Colophon] York-Town, Hall and Sellers [1777]
broadside 39 X 24 cm.
PHi; PPL mp. 43398

B4628 U. S. CONTINENTAL CONGRESS, 1777
In Congress, October 4, 1777. Congress resumed the consideration of the report . . . on the . . . Commissary General's department . . . Poughkeepsie, John Holt [1777]
broadside
Vail: Patriotic pair, p. 405
CtY; N mp. 43399

B4629 U. S. CONTINENTAL CONGRESS, 1777
In Congress, October 8th, 1777. Whereas it is of essential consequence . . . Lancaster, Francis Bailey [1777]
broadside
American Art Assoc. cat., Apr. 22, 1919, item 53
New York Public 662
NN (reduced facsim.) mp. 43400

B4630 U. S. CONTINENTAL CONGRESS, 1777
In Congress, November 22, 1777. Pursued by the injustice . . . of Great-Britain . . . [Providence, J. Carter, 1777]
broadside 38 X 25 cm.
Text in 3 columns
Alden 715; Taylor 151; Winship p. 36
RHi; RPJCB mp. 43401

B4631 U. S. TREASURY DEPT.
Treasury-Office, Philadelphia, September 6, 1777. Additional instructions from the Board of Treasury to the Commissioners of Accounts . . . By order of the Board. [Philadelphia, 1777]
broadside 33 X 21 cm.
Taylor 154
CtHi; PHi mp. 43389

B4632 VERMONT. COUNCIL OF SAFETY
Providence, Aug. 21. The following was received last night . . . from Hartford. Hartford, August 18 . . . This moment an express arrived . . . State of Vermont. In Council of safety, Bennington, August 16, 1777 . . . [Providence, J. Carter, 1777]
broadside 19 X 10 cm.

Alden 716
DLC. Photostat: RHi mp. 43403

B4633 VIRGINIA. GOVERNOR, 1776-1779
Williamsburg, December 13, 1777. The following resolution of the General Assembly, received by me this day, is of so important a nature to the welfare of our soldiery . . . [signed in manuscript] P. Henry. In General Assembly, November 27, 1777. Resolved, that the Governour . . . [Williamsburg, A. Purdie, 1777]
broadside 19 X 16 cm.
WHi mp. 43404

B4634 WATTS, ISAAC, 1674-1748
Divine songs, attempted in easy language . . . The seventeenth edition. Norwich, Green & Spooner, 1777.
36 p. 16.5 cm.
Gillett Griffin, Princeton Univ. (1962) mp. 43405

B4635 WATTS, ISAAC, 1674-1748
The young child's catechism . . . New-Haven, Thomas and Samuel Green [1777?]
24 p. 17 cm. $[A]^4$ B^2 C^4 D^2
CtHi; MWA mp. 43406

B4636 WESTMINSTER ASSEMBLY OF DIVINES
The shorter catechism . . . Norwich, Printed and sold by Green & Spooner, 1777.
32 p. 19 cm. $[A]$-D^4
CtHi; MWA mp. 43407

B4637 WHEELOCK, JOHN, d. 1817
A concise narrative of my proceedings in raising men . . . Kingston, September 3, 1777. [Fish-Kill, Samuel Loudon? 1777]
broadside 25.5 X 20.5 cm.
Vail: Patriotic pair, p. 406
MA; NhD. Photostats: DLC; MWA mp. 43408

B4638 WIGGLESWORTH, MICHAEL, 1631-1705
The day of doom . . . Norwich, Green & Spooner, 1777.
36 p. 17 cm.
CtHi; ICN; MWA. Photostat: MHi mp. 43409

B4639 WILLETT, MARINUS, 1740-1830
Hartford, August 21, 1777. The following is a narrative . . . of the transactions . . . near Fort Stanwix . . . given . . . by Lieutenant-Colonel Willet . . . [Hartford, 1777]
broadside 39.5 X 25 cm.
New York Public 663
CSmH; NN. Photostats: DLC; ICN; MH; MHi; NHi mp. 43410

B4640 YOUNG, EDWARD, 1683-1765
Resignation; in two parts, and a postscript . . . Philadelphia, Joseph James, 1777.
54 p.
RPJCB mp. 43411

1778

B4641 BAPTISTS. SOUTH CAROLINA. CHARLESTON ASSOCIATION
Minutes of the Charlestown Association. Charlestown, Feb. 2, 1778 . . . [Charleston, 1778]
4 p. 21 cm. caption title
ScGF. Photostat: MWA mp. 43412

B4642 BAPTISTS. SOUTH CAROLINA. CHARLESTON ASSOCIATION
Minutes of the Charlestown Association. High Hills of Santee, Oct. 19th, 1778 . . . [Charleston, 1778]
4 p.
NRAB. Photostat: MWA mp. 43413

B4643 BELL, ROBERT, d. 1784
Robert Bell, bookseller, provedore to the sentimentalists, and professor of book-auctioniering . . . is just arrived from Philadelphia; with a small collection of . . . books, which he will exhibit by auction . . . [Philadelphia? 1778]
broadside 35 X 21.5 cm.
MWA mp. 43414

B4644 BICKERSTAFF'S New-York almanac for the year . . . 1779 . . . New York, Mills and Hicks [1778]
[24] p. 18 cm.
Wall p. 22
DLC; PHi; RPJCB; WHi mp. 43415

B4645 BILLINGS, WILLIAM, 1746-1800
The singing master's assistant . . . Boston, Draper and Folsom, 1778.
29, [1], 104 p. 11 X 19.5 cm.
cf. Evans 15744, which differs typographically
DLC; MHi mp. 43416

B4646 BOOTH, BENJAMIN
A meeting of the inhabitants having been called . . . Thursday evening, Nov. 19, 1778. [n.p., 1778]
broadside 24 X 20 cm.
DLC mp. 43418

B4647 BOSTON
Your state tax. Lawful money. Your town tax . . . The assessors sit . . . at the east end of Faneuil-Hall Market . . . till the 23d of April 1778 . . . [Boston, 1778]
broadside
Ford 2126
MHi

B4648 BOSTON, April 20. The following articles of intelligence . . . was received by the Prigate [sic] L'Sensible . . . at Falmouth, Casco-Bay, on Monday last . . . and came to hand last evening . . . General Burgoyne's defeat . . . the treaty with France . . . [n.p., 1778]
broadside 25 X 18.5 cm.
MWA mp. 43419

B4649 BOSTON, April 27, 1778. The following bills . . . [Boston, 1778]
broadside 24 X 19 cm.
Ford 2128; Huntington 428
CSmH; MHi. Photostat: DLC mp. 43420

B4650 THE British downfall. Come all ye heroes . . . [n.p., 1778?]
broadside 28 X 22.5 cm.
Three woodcuts above title
MiU-C mp. 43421

B4651 BUCHANAN, JAMES, d. 1778
The dying declaration of James Buchanan, Ezra Ross and William Brooks, who were executed at Worcester, on Thursday July the 2d, 1778, for the murder of Mr. Jashua [sic] Spooner. [Worcester, Isaiah Thomas, 1778]
broadside 42.5 X 33 cm.
McDade 898; New York Public 664; Sabin 105350
MWHi; NHi. Photostats: MWA; NN mp. 43422

B4652 BUCHANAN, JAMES, d. 1778
The dying declaration of James Buchanan, Ezra Ross, and William Brooks, who were executed at Worcester, July 2, 1778 for the murder of Mr. Joshua Spooner. [Worcester? Isaiah Thomas? 1778?]
8 p. 23 p. caption title
Thomas M. McDade, Purchase, N.Y. (1960) mp. 43423

B4653 BUCHANAN, JAMES, d. 1778
The last words and dying speech of James Buchanan, Ezra Ross and William Brooks, who are executed this day at Worcester, for the murder of Mr. Joshua Spooner. Boston, Draper and Folsom [1778]
broadside 41 X 31 cm.
NjP mp. 43427

B4654 BUCHANAN, JAMES, d. 1778
The last words and dying speech of James Buchanan, Ezra Ross, and William Brooks, who were executed at Worcester, for the murder of Mr. Joshua Spooner. [Boston? 1778?]
broadside 41.5 X 36 cm.
Ford 2129; New York Public 665
NN. Photostat: MWA mp. 43426

B4655 [BURDON, WILLIAM]
The gentleman's pocket-farrier . . . Boston, N. Coverly, 1778.
48 p. 12.5 cm. [A]-C^8
MWA; RPJCB mp. 43428

B4656 BURROUGHS, EDEN, 1738-1813
A sincere regard to righetousness and piety . . . Illustrated in a sermon preached . . . in the state of Vermont, October 8th, A.D. 1778 . . . Dresden, J. P. & A. Spooner [1778]
30 p. 18.5 cm.
McCorison 2
NhD; RPJCB (half-title lacking); VtU-W. Photostats: NHi; NN mp. 43429

B4657 CAMP, ABRAHAM
A short discourse delivered by Mr. Abraham Camp, at the funeral of Amasa Tinkham . . . called to officiate in the holy ministry at Middleborough . . . This pious . . . young gentleman died in full assurance of faith . . . [n.p.,] Printed for Jon. Hallowell, trader, in Bridgwater [1778?]
broadside
Ford 2130
MHi (facsim.) mp. 43430

B4658 CONNECTICUT. GOVERNOR, 1776-1784
By . . . Jonathan Trumbull . . . a proclamation. Whereas the General assembly . . . [June 19, 1778] . . . New London, T. Green [1778]
broadside 33.5 X 18.5 cm.
DLC. Photostat: MWA mp. 43431

B4659 CONNECTICUT. GOVERNOR, 1776-1784
By the Governor. An address and proclamation . . . [Dec. 2, 1778] New London, T. Green [1778]
broadside 48.5 X 37.5 cm.
CtHi. Photostats: DLC; NN mp. 43432

B4660 CONNECTICUT. GOVERNOR, 1776-1784
State of Connecticut. By the Governor. Whereas his Most Christian Majesty . . . Given . . . at Lebanon, the first day of August, A.D. 1778. Jonathan Trumbull. [New London, 1778]
broadside 30 X 19.5 cm.
CtHi. Photostat: MWA mp. 43433

B4661 CONNECTICUT. LAWS
At a General Assembly of the Governor and Company . . . of Connecticut, holden at Hartford . . . 2d Thursday of January . . . 1778. An act [regarding the raising of the battalion] . . . [Hartford? 1778]
broadside 33.5 X 18.5 cm.
NHi mp. 43434

B4662 CONNECTICUT. LAWS
At a General Assembly of the Governor and Company . . . of Connecticut, holden at Hartford . . . 12th day of February . . . 1778. An act for raising two brigades . . . [Hartford? 1778]
broadside 35 X 20 cm.
NHi mp. 43435

B4663 CONNECTICUT. LAWS
At a General Assembly of the Governor and Company of . . . Connecticut, holden at Hartford . . . May . . . 1778. An act in addition to . . . an Act . . . for raising two brigades . . . Hartford, Watson and Goodwin [1778]
broadside 36 X 20 cm.
CtHi mp. 43436

B4664 CONNECTICUT. LAWS
At a General Assembly of the Governor and Company . . . of Connecticut, holden at Hartford . . . May . . . 1778. Be it enacted . . . that two regiments, to consist of seven hundred and twenty-eight men each . . . George Wyllys, Sec'ry. Hartford, Bevil Webster [1778]
broadside 36 X 18.5 cm.
CtHi mp. 43437

B4665 CONNECTICUT. MILITIA
Articles, rules, and regulations, for preserving order . . . and discipline, among the militia . . . of this state . . . Hartford, Watson and Goodwin, 1778.
15 p. 20 cm.
CtHi; MWiW-C mp. 43438

B4666 DEANE, SILAS, 1737-1789
To the free and virtuous citizens of America. Friends and countrymen, The happiness or misfortunes . . . of an individual, have generally no claim to the public attention . . . S. Dean. Philadelphia, November, 1778. [Philadelphia, 1778]
broadside 42 X 24.5 cm.
CtHi mp. 43439

B4667 DELAWARE. LAWS
. . . An act for the further security . . . [Colophon] Lancaster, Francis Bailey [1778]
4 p. 30 cm. caption title
At end: Passed May 18, 1778
Hawkins p. 40 (note); Taylor 156
DLC; NNB; PPL mp. 43441

B4668 DELAWARE. LAWS
An act of the General assembly . . . for establishing a militia . . . Lancaster, Francis Bailey, 1778.
15 p. 30 cm.
Hawkins p. 40 (note); Taylor 155
DLC; MdBP; PPL. Photostat: RPJCB mp. 43443

B4669 DELAWARE. LAWS
. . . An act to prevent the inhabitants of this state . . . [Lancaster, Francis Bailey, 1778]
5 p. 30 cm. caption title
At end: Passed May 20, 1778
Hawkins p. 40 (note)
DLC; MdBP; NNB; PPL mp. 43444

B4670 DELAWARE. LAWS
Anno Millesimo Septingentesimo Septuagesimo Octavo. At a General Assembly begun at Dover . . . the first day of December . . . 1777 . . . An act for regulating . . . June 26, 1778. [Wilmington, James Adams, 1778]
5 p. fol. caption title
PPL mp. 43440

B4671 DELAWARE. LAWS
. . . At a General assembly begun at Dover . . . the first day of December . . . 1777, and continued . . . till the 4th of April 1778, the following act was passed . . . [Wilmington, J. Adams, 1778]
4 p. 30 cm. caption title
At end: Passed April 4, 1778
Hawkins 10
DLC; MiU-C; NNB; PPL mp. 43445

B4672 DELAWARE. LAWS
. . . At a General assembly begun at Dover . . . the first day of December . . . 1777, and continued . . . till the 26th day of June 1778, the following act was passed . . . an act of free pardon . . . [Wilmington, James Adams, 1778]
8 p. 30 cm. caption title
At end: Passed June 26, 1778
Hawkins 12
DLC; MiU-C; NNB; PPL mp. 43442

B4673 DELAWARE. LAWS
. . . At a General assembly begun at Dover . . . the first day of December . . . 1777, and continued . . . till the 26th day of June 1778, the following acts were passed . . . [Wilmington, J. Adams, 1778]
5 p. 30 cm. caption title
At end: Passed June 26, 1778
Hawkins 11
DLC; NNB mp. 43448

B4674 DELAWARE. LAWS
. . . Rules and articles, for the better regulating of the militia . . . [Lancaster, F. Bailey, 1778]
4 p. 30 cm. caption title
At end: Passed May 15, 1778
Hawkins p. 40 (note)
DLC; NNB; PPL mp. 43446

B4675 DELAWARE. PRESIDENT, 1778-1781
By . . . Caesar Rodney . . . a proclamation. Whereas the honorable the Congress . . . [Dec. 7, 1778] . . . Wilmington, James Adams [1778]
broadside 34.5 X 21 cm.
Hawkins: List C 8
DLC mp. 43447

B4676 A DISCOURSE on Daniel vii. 27 . . . The second edition, with considerable additions. Norwich, J. Trumbull, 1778.
32 p. 17.5 cm. [A]-D^4
Signed: A hearty friend to all the colonies
MWA; RPJCB mp. 43449

B4677 DODDRIDGE, PHILIP, 1702-1751
A plain and serious address . . . Hartford, Watson and Goodwin, 1778.
31 p. 19 cm.
Huntington 422; Trumbull 605
CSmH; CtHi; CtY; DLC; ICN; MWA; NHi; NN; PPL; RPJCB mp. 43450

B4678 DORCHESTER, MASS.
Your Province tax. 1777. Your town rate. (Assessors sit in February, 1778.) [Boston? 1778]
broadside
Ford 2134
MHi

B4679 DORCHESTER, MASS.
Your state tax. 1778. Your town tax. (Assessors sit in July.) [Boston? 1778]
broadside
Ford 2135
MHi

B4680 [DRAYTON, WILLIAM HENRY] 1742-1779
The genuine spirit of tyranny, exemplified in the conduct of the Commissioners, sent . . . to bully, delude or bribe . . . [Colophon] Poughkeepsie, John Holt [1778]
6 p. 23 cm. caption title
Signed at end: W. H. D. Philadelphia, September 4, 1778
In double columns
Huntington 423; Vail: Patriotic pair, p. 406
CSmH; NHi mp. 43451

B4681 [ESTAING, CHARLES HENRI, COMTE D'] 1729-1794
Déclaration adressée au nom du Roi a tous les anciens francois . . . [Colophon] A bord du Languedoc, de l'Imprimerie de F. P. Demauge [1778]
3 p. 29 cm. caption title
Chapin p. [8]; New York Public 670
DLC; MiU-C; NN; RPJCB; ViU. Photostats: MHi; MWA mp. 43452

B4682 FISKE, NATHAN, 1733-1799
A sermon, preached at Brookfield, March 6, 1778. On the day of the interment . . . Norwich, Green & Spooner, 1778.
16 p. 18 cm.
Trumbull: Second supplement 2148
DLC; MWA; RPJCB mp. 43453

B4683 FISKE, NATHAN, 1733-1799
A sermon preached at Brookfield, March 6, 1778; on the day of the interment . . . The third edition. Danvers, E. Russell, 1778.
16 p. 17.5 cm.
DLC; MSaE; NN mp. 43454

B4684 THE following return of the prisoners, taken at Forts Montgomery and Clinton, are published for the satisfaction of the public, and particularly for the benefit of their relations . . . [n. p., 1778]
broadside 29.5 X 19.5 cm.
NHi mp. 43455

B4685 FOSTER, ISAAC, 1740-1781
The faithful preacher of the gospel described. A sermon preached at the ordination of . . . Emerson Foster . . . the 22d day of January, 1778. By his father . . . To which is added . . . the right-hand of fellowship, by the Rev'd Mr. Russel . . . New-London, T. Green, 1778.
22 p. 18 cm.
Trumbull 726
MWA; RPJCB mp. 43456

B4686 DER Gantz neue verbesserte Nord-Americanische Calender auf . . . 1778. Von Anthony Sharp. Lancaster, Franz Bailey [1778]
[44?] p.
Second edition
Advertised in the *Pennsylvanische Zeitungs-Blatt*, Feb. 11, 1778
Drake 10052
No copy known

B4687 GEORGIA. LAWS
An act for opening and regulating the superior courts . . . Savannah, March 1, 1778. Savannah, Wm. Lancaster, 1778.
7 p. fol.
De Renne p. 214
GU-De mp. 43458

B4688 GOSS, THOMAS, 1733?-1778?
The last words and dying speech of Thomas Goss, in a private conference, previous to his execution. [n.p., 1778?]
broadside 48 X 27.5 cm.
McDade 368; New York Public 672
NN mp. 43459

B4689 GT. BRIT. ARMY
. . . A list of the general and staff officers . . . New-York, James Rivington, 1778.
68 p. 19 cm.
At head of title: [By permission.]
DLC; PHi mp. 43460

B4690 GT. BRIT. ARMY
Quarter-master-general's office, Newport, the 23d May 1778. Advertisement . . . [Newport, John Howe, 1778]
broadside 16.5 X 20 cm.
Alden 719; Winship p. 36
RPB. Photostat: RHi mp. 43461

B4691 GT. BRIT. COLONIAL OFFICE
Emmerick's chasseurs, to all gentlemen volunteers. By virtue of a warrant . . . bearing date the 30th of April, 1778 . . . [n.p., 1778]
broadside 30 X 18.5 cm.
DLC mp. 43462

B4692 GT. BRIT. LAWS
. . . At the Parliament begun and holden at Westminster . . . November . . . 1774 . . . continued . . . to the twentieth day of November, 1777. An act for removing all doubts and apprehensions concerning taxation by the Parliament . . . in . . . the colonies . . . in North America . . . New-York: Re-printed by James Rivington, 1778.
4 p. 34 cm.
NHi mp. 43463

B4693 GT. BRIT. PARLIAMENT
Draft of a bill for declaring the intentions of the Parliament . . . Given under my hand at Newport . . . this 22d day of April, 1778. Robert Pigot . . . [Newport? John Howe? 1778]
4 p. 32.5 X 19 cm.
Alden 720
MWA mp. 43464

B4694 GT. BRIT. SOVEREIGNS (GEORGE III)
Baltimore, February 4th, 1778, By Captain Thomas Moore . . . we have received a copy of his Britannic Majesty's speech . . . London, November 20th, 1777 . . . Baltimore, John Dunlap [1778]
broadside 35 X 18.5 cm.
Wheeler 36
MdBE mp. 43467

B4695 GT. BRIT. SOVEREIGNS (GEORGE III)
[Speech] to both Houses of Parliament, Nov. 20, 1777 . . . [New York] James Rivington [1778?]
broadside X 30 cm.
MWA (top half apparently wanting) mp. 43468

B4696 GREENLEAF, WILLIAM
Two hundred dollars reward. Broke goal, in Worcester . . . Nathan Davis . . . William Mosman . . . William Greenleaf, Sheriff. Worcester, October 25, 1778. [Worcester, 1778]
broadside 22 X 17.5 cm.
MWA mp. 43596

B4697 GROTON, CONN.
The civil authority and select-men of the town of Groton, met agreeable to the direction of an act of the General Assembly . . . passed at Hartford, 12th Feb. 1778, for regulating the price of labour . . . within said town . . . viz. Men's common labour . . . [n.p., 1778?]
broadsheet 35.5 X 21 cm.
NHi

B4698 HAMMON, JUPITER
Hartford, August 4, 1778. An address to Miss Phillis Wheatly, Ethiopian poetess . . . Composed by Jupiter Hammon . . . [Hartford? 17; 8?]
broadside 22 X 15 cm.
Porter 108
CtHi mp. 43470

B4699 HERVEY, JAMES, 1714-1758
Meditations and contemplations . . . By James Hervey . . . The eighth edition . . . Boston, Printed for, and sold by Martha Leverett, 1778.
2 v. in 1 (xiv p., 1 l., 200; xiv, 198, [2] p.) 16 cm.
Vol. 2 has imprint: Boston, Printed and sold by Daniel Fowle, and by Daniel Gookin, 1750.
A re-issue of the 1750 Fowle edition, with p. [i]-[xvi] cancelled (or reset)
MB; MWA mp. 43471

B4700 HOLLY, ISRAEL
An appeal to the impartial. The censured memorial made publick . . . Norwich, Green & Spooner, 1778.
24 p.
CtW mp. 43472

B4701 IMPORTANT intelligence from Europe. From Humphrey's Philadelphia paper, of May 9. By the Porcupine frigate . . . we are favored with the following advices . . . Parliamentary proceedings . . . Baltimore, M. K. Goddard, 1778.
[2] p. 32 X 21.5 cm.
Wheeler 54
MdBE mp. 43473

B4702 IMPORTANT intelligence, just received by express. Baltimore, May 4. York Town, May 3, 1778 . . . Copy of a letter from the . . . Virginia delegates at Congress to . . . the Governour. York Town, May 3, 1778. [Williamsburg, Dixon & Hunter, 1778]
[2] p. 24 X 19 cm.
DLC (photostat) mp. 43474

B4703 IN pursuance of a law passed by the State of New-York, dated . . . 6th of March, 1778, impowering me to export one thousand barrels of flour out of that state to Boston . . . [n.p., 1778]
broadside
Ford 2136
M-Ar mp. 43475

B4704 INTELLIGENCE of current events, May 4, 1778 . . . Lancaster, John Dunlap, 1778.
broadside 21.5 X 17.5 cm.
Taylor 92; Bausman p. 18
PHi mp. 43476

B4705 AN intercepted letter, to General Sullivan . . . Newport, John Howe, 1778.
8 p. 19 cm.
Signed: Nat. Northwester
Photostat: RHi mp. 43477

B4706 KEYSER,
Mr. Keyser's method of administering his pills, in venereal complaints . . . Translated from the French. New-York, H. Gaine, 1778.

[8], 23, [1] p. 17.5 cm.
Rogers 168
NHi mp. 43478

B4707 LATHROP, JOHN
A discourse preached on March the fifth 1778 . . . Boston, Printed by Draper and Folsom, 1778.
24 p.
cf. Evans 15866
MWA; NjP mp. 43479

B4708 LEARNED, LYDIA
A letter to a worthy officer of the American army . . .
From your unfeigned friend it came,
And so I write my worthless name.
Lydia Learned. Framingham, March 17, 1778. [Worcester? 1778]
broadside 34 X 20.5 cm.
MWA mp. 43480

B4709 LETTERS from General Washington, to several of his friends in the year 1776. In which are set forth, a . . . view of American politics . . . [New York] Printed [by J. Rivington] in the year 1778.
1 p.l., 52 [i.e. 53] p. 15.5 cm.
Page 48 repeated in numbering
Sabin 101740; cf. Evans 15868
ICN; MiU-C; NhD mp. 43591

B4710 LOUISIANA. GOVERNOR, 1777-1785
Dn. Bernard de Galvez . . . Sa Majesté que Dieu garde, ayant été . . . informée . . . [Nouvelle-Orléans, Antoine Boudousquié, 1778]
broadside 42 X 33 cm.
Dated Oct. 26, 1778
New York Public 673; McMurtrie: Louisiana 9
ICHi. Photostats: MWA; NN mp. 43481

B4711 LOUISIANA. GOVERNOR, 1777-1785
Dn. Bernard de Galvez . . . Sa Majesté que Dieu garde, donnant toujours ses attentions à l'augmentation . . . du commerce . . . [Nouvelle-Orléans, Antoine Boudousquié, 1778]
broadside 51.5 X 37 cm.
Dated Oct. 27, 1778
New York Public 674
NN (photostat) mp. 43482

B4712 LOUISIANA. LAWS
Code noir ou loi municipale, servant de reglement pour . . . la Louisianne, entreprit par délidération [sic] du Cabildo . . . [Colophon] A la Nlle. Orleans. De l'imprimerie d'Antoine Boudousquié, 1778.
16 p. 19 cm.
McMurtrie: New Orleans 26
DLC. Edward A. Parsons, New Orleans (1942)
mp. 43483

B4713 LUTHER, MARTIN, 1483-1546
Der kleine Catechismus . . . Nebst einem Anhang der sieben Buss-Psalmen . . . Lancaster, Gedruckt und zu haben bey Francis Bailey, 1778.
[4], 139, [1] p. 13.5 cm.
MWA mp. 43484

B4714 MACCARTY, THADDEUS, 1721-1784
The Rev. Mr. Maccarthy's account of the behaviour of Mrs. Spooner after . . . the murder of her husband at Brookfield, March 1. 1778. [n.p., 1778?]
4 p. 17.5 cm. caption title
McDade 902
DLC; MWA mp. 43485

B4715 [MACDOUGALL, ALEXANDER] 1732-1786
To the supporters and defenders of American freedom and independence . . . New-York, May 20, 1778 . . . [at end] Pro patria. [New York, 1778]
10 p. 20 cm. $[A]^4$ B^2
MWA; RPJCB mp. 43558

B4716 MARSH, JOSEPH, fl. 1778
Remarks on the proceedings of the General Assembly . . . October, A.D. 1778. Containing an explanatory comment . . . By a committee of the protesting members . . . Joseph Marsh, chairman . . . [Dresden, J. P. & A. Spooner, 1778]
[4] p. 32.5 cm. caption title
Dated at Windsor, Oct. 23d 1778
McCorison 5; New York Public 687; Sabin 99001
VtBrt; VtHi. Photostat: NN mp. 43486

B4717 MARY K. Goddard's Pennsylvania, Delaware, Maryland . . . almanack . . . for . . . 1779 . . . Baltimore, Mary K. Goddard [1778]
[36] p. 17 cm.
Guerra b-415
MWA (t.p. lacking) mp. 43487

B4718 MARYLAND. HOUSE OF DELEGATES
By the state of Maryland. A declaration . . . December 15, 1778 . . . [Annapolis, F. Green, 1778]
broadside 41 X 24.5 cm.
New York Public 675; Wheeler 39
Ct; M-Ar; MHi. Photostats: DLC; MWA; NN; RPJCB
mp. 43488

B4719 MASSACHUSETTS. CONSTITUTION
A constitution and form of government for the state . . . February 28, 1778 . . . Danvers, E. Russell, 1778.
16 p. woodcut
RPJCB mp. 43489

B4720 MASSACHUSETTS. COUNCIL
By the Council of the State of Massachusetts-Bay. A proclamation. Whereas this Council have received information of a high-handed affray . . . last evening . . . [Sept. 9, 1778] . . . [Boston, 1778]
broadside 35.5 X 20 cm.
Ford 2150
MHi mp. 43490

B4721 MASSACHUSETTS. HOUSE OF REPRESENTATIVES
State of Massachusetts-Bay. In the House of Representatives, February 19, 1778. Gentlemen, The exertions lately made . . . to put the currency of the United States . . . [Boston, 1778]
broadside
Ford 2142
MB mp. 43491

B4722 MASSACHUSETTS. HOUSE OF REPRESENTATIVES
State of Massachusetts-Bay. In the House of Representatives, April 20, 1778. Resolve for filling up . . . fifteen battalions . . . [Boston, 1778]
[4] p. 35 cm.
4-page folder
cf. Ford 2146
MSaE; MeHi mp. 43492

B4723 MASSACHUSETTS. HOUSE OF REPRESENTATIVES
State of Massachusetts-Bay. In the House of Representa-

tives, April 20, 1778. Resolve for filling up . . . [Colophon] Boston, Powars and Willis, 1778.
6 p. 32 cm. caption title
Ford 2146
DLC; MHi mp. 43493

B4724 MASSACHUSETTS. HOUSE OF REPRESENTATIVES
State of Massachusetts-Bay. In the House of Representatives, April 23, 1778. Whereas, by a resolve of the General Court . . . the several towns are ordered to raise 2000 men . . . [Boston, 1778]
broadside 16.5 X 21 cm.
Ford 2147
MHi. Middendorf Collection, New York City (1970) mp. 43494

B4725 MASSACHUSETTS. HOUSE OF REPRESENTATIVES
State of Massachusetts-Bay. In the House of Representatives, October 5th, 1778. Whereas by a late law . . . the assessors . . . [Boston, 1778]
broadside 21 X 17.5 cm.
Ford 2152; New York Public 676
MHi; NN mp. 43496

B4726 MASSACHUSETTS. HOUSE OF REPRESENTATIVES
State of Massachusetts-Bay. In the House of Representatives, October 10, 1778. Whereas the . . . General Court . . . on the 13th day of March . . . did make a resolve . . . [Boston, 1778]
broadside ([2] p.) 35 X 21.5 cm.
Ford 2153
MHi; MSaE; MWA mp. 43497

B4727 MASSACHUSETTS. TREASURER
State of Massachusetts-Bay. The honorable Henry Gardner . . . Greeting . . . the twenty-ninth day of March . . . 1778. [Boston, 1778]
broadside 42.5 X 34 cm.
Ford 2159
MHi mp. 43498

B4728 MASSACHUSETTS. TREASURER
State of Massachusetts-Bay. The honorable Henry Gardner . . . Greeting . . . [July 4, 1778] [Boston, 1778]
broadside
Tax warrant
MB mp. 43499

B4729 MASSACHUSETTS STATE LOTTERY
The General Assembly having passed a resolve . . . money, not exceeding 750,000 dollars, for the benefit of those officers . . . appointed Oliver Wendall . . . directors of a lottery for that purpose . . . The following scheme is . . . offered . . . [Sept. 26, 1778] [Boston, 1778]
broadside 42.5 X 27.5 cm.
Ford 2154
MHi mp. 43500

B4730 A MOURNFUL poem: occasioned by sentence of death . . . upon William Brooks, James Buchanan, Ezra Ross and Bathsheba Spooner . . . all executed . . . the 2d day of July 1778 . . . Boston, Printed and [sold by 1778]
broadside 33.5 X 21.5 cm.
MWA (imprint mutilated) mp. 43501

B4731 NEW HAMPSHIRE
Advertisement. This is to give notice to all . . . soldiers . . . whose furloughs are expired . . . Enoch Poor, Brigadier-General. Valley-Forge-Camp . . . January 21st, 1778. State of New-Hampshire, February 17th 1778. These are to give notice . . . Exeter . . . place of rendezvous . . . [Exeter? 1778]
broadside 13.5 X 17.5 cm.
Whittemore 227
NhHi mp. 43559

B4732 NEW HAMPSHIRE. COUNCIL
A proclamation . . . 30th day of December next . . . thanksgiving and praise . . . In Council, December 18th, 1778 . . . E. Thompson, secretary. [Colophon] Exeter, Zechariah Fowle, 1778.
broadside 41 X 35 cm.
Sabin 52897; Whittemore 233
Photostat: NN mp. 43502

B4733 NEW HAMPSHIRE. GOVERNOR, 1776-1785
State of New-Hampshire. A proclamation. Whereas many persons . . . have basely deserted . . . reward will be paid . . . M. Weare, president . . . [Exeter? 1778]
broadside 21 X 18.5 cm.
Whittemore 228
NhD; NhHi mp. 43505

B4734 NEW HAMPSHIRE. HOUSE OF REPRESENTATIVES
State of New-Hampshire. In the House of representatives, February 17th, 1778. Voted, That one suitable person . . . [Exeter, 1778]
broadside 30.5 X 19.5 cm.
DLC; NhHi. Photostats: MWA; NN mp. 43503

B4735 NEW HAMPSHIRE. HOUSE OF REPRESENTATIVES
State of New-Hampshire. In the House of representatives, February 26th, 1778. Whereas the present situation . . . [Mar. 4, 1778] . . . Exeter [1778]
broadside 30 X 20 cm.
DLC; NhHi. Photostat: NN mp. 43504

B4736 NEW HAMPSHIRE. LAWS
[Acts and laws, 1778] [Exeter? 1778]
p. 87-104
Continuation of Acts and laws published 1776
Whittemore 225
MWA; NhHi (mostly photostats) mp. 43506

B4737 NEW JERSEY. GOVERNOR, 1776-1790
Lancaster, June 11, 1778. Extracts from . . . Governor Livingston's message . . . Princeton, May 29, 1778. Lancaster, John Dunlap [1778]
broadside 39.5 X 25 cm.
DLC mp. 43507

B4738 NEW JERSEY. LAWS
An act for recovering the arrears of certain taxes . . . Trenton, December 7, 1778. Caleb Camp, Speaker pro temp. [n.p., 1778?]
broadside 40 X 24 cm.
Humphrey 182
NjHi mp. 43508

B4739 NEW JERSEY. LAWS
. . . An act for taking charge of . . . the real estates, and for forfeiting the personal estates of certain fugitives . . . [Apr. 18, 1778] . . . [Trenton, 1778]
[4] p. fol.
Huntington 425
CSmH mp. 43509

B4740 NEW JERSEY. LAWS
. . . An act for the speedy and effectual recruiting of the four New-Jersey regiments . . . Trenton, April 3, 1778 . . . John Hart, Speaker . . . [Trenton? I. Collins? 1778?]
2 leaves. 36 cm. caption title
NN

B4741 NEW JERSEY. PROPRIETORS OF THE EASTERN DIVISION
Advertisement. The general proprietors of the Eastern Division of New-Jersey, will attend at the Court-house in Freehold . . . the twelfth day of August, to dispose of rights to locate vacant lands . . . July 24, 1778. [n.p., 1778]
broadside 18 X 15 cm.
Humphrey 187
NHi mp. 43417

B4742 NEW LONDON, CONN.
New-London County, ss. New-London, April 1, 1778. Agreeable to an act of assembly . . . for regulating the prices of labour . . . the undermentioned articles at the following prices, in said New-London . . . [New London, 1778]
broadside 36 X 21.5 cm.
CtHi mp. 43510

B4743 A NEW touch on the times. Well adapted to the distressing situation of every seaport town. By a Daughter of Liberty, living in Marblehead. [Salem? 1778?]
broadside
Ford 2161; Tapley p. 332
NHi mp. 43511

B4744 NEW YORK. CITIZENS
New-York, November 25, 1778. At a late meeting of the merchants of this city . . . To . . . the Earl of Carlisle, Sir Henry Clinton, and William Eden . . . The address of the inhabitants of the City . . . [New York, James Rivington, 1778]
3 p.
cf. Heartman's cat. 59, Sept. 27, 1916, item 140; Harper's cat. 166 (1943) item 857?
NN (reduced facsim., p. 1 only) mp. 43512

B4745 NEW YORK. GOVERNOR, 1771-1780
By His Excellency William Tryon . . . A proclamation . . . [New York? 1778]
[4] p. 33 cm.
Concerns pardon to persons serving in the colonies
Dated: 24th day of December, 1778
New York Public 679
NN (photostat) mp. 43514

B4746 NEW YORK. LAWS
State of New-York, An act for raising monies . . . Passed the 28th of March, 1778. Poughkeepsie, John Holt [1778]
[2] p. 41 X 26 cm.
Vail: Patriotic pair, p. 408
MH; MHi; MiU-C. Photostats: DLC; NN mp. 43515

B4747 NEW YORK. MERCHANTS AND TRADERS
To their Excellencies the Earl of Carlisle, Sir Henry Clinton, and William Eden . . . The petition of the Merchants and Traders of the city of New-York . . . [New York? James Rivington? 1778?]
[3] p. 22 cm.
NHi mp. 43513

B4748 NEW YORK PACKET.
Postscript to the *New-York Packet*, of May 14, 1778. York-Town, May 13. From a Philadelphia paper, of May 9, 1778 . . . the following . . . London, March 17. Parliamentary proceedings . . . Fish-Kill, S. Loudon, 1778.
broadside 26 X 21 cm.
NHi (margins trimmed) mp. 43465

B4749 NEWBURYPORT, MASS.
County of Essex, and State of Massachusetts-Bay. Gentlemen. The inhabitants of the town of Newburyport in town meeting assembled have adverted to the constitution . . . March 31, 1778. [Salem? 1778]
broadside 44 X 27 cm.
MHi mp. 43516

B4750 NEWCASTLE COUNTY, DEL.
New-castle County, ss. In August sessions, 1778. Ordered by the court, that the keepers of public houses . . . shall receive . . . the prices herein after mentioned . . . Wilmington, J. Adams [1778]
broadside 21 X 17 cm.
Hawkins: List C 7
De mp. 43517

B4751 THE Newport Gazette. Published weekly. Thursday, January 1, 1778[-November 19, 1778] Newport, John Howe [1778]

Brigham p. 995
DLC (photostat)

B4752 NORTH, FREDERICK, EARL OF GUILFORD, 1732-1792
Lord North's speech. House of Commons. Tuesday, February 17. [Boston? 1778]
broadside
Ford 2137
MHi mp. 43466

B4753 NORTH CAROLINA. HOUSE OF COMMONS
The journal of the House of commons. State of North-Carolina. At a General assembly, begun . . . the 14th day of April . . . 1778 . . . being the first session of this Assembly. [Newbern, James Davis, 1778]
36+ p. 30 cm. caption title
McMurtrie: North Carolina 96
DLC (lacking after p. 36) mp. 43518

B4754 NORTH CAROLINA. HOUSE OF COMMONS
The journal of the House of Commons. State of North-Carolina. At a General Assembly, begun . . . at Hillsborough on the 8th day of August . . . 1778 . . . Being the second session of this Assembly. [Newbern, James Davis, 1778]
24+ p. 28 cm. caption title
McMurtrie: North Carolina 97
NcU (lacking after p. 24) mp. 43519

B4755 NORTH CAROLINA. LAWS
An act for confiscating the property of all . . . as are inimical to the United States . . . [Newbern, James Davis, 1778]
broadside 33 X 25 cm.
A separate printing of chap. XVII of the session laws; the printed volume appeared in March 1778
Public Record Off. mp. 43520

B4756 NORWICH, CONN.
An account of the prices of articles as stated by the civil authority and select-men, of . . . Norwich, March, 1778 . . . [at end] [Norwich] Printed at Green & Spooner's Printing-Office [1778]
[2] p. 34 cm.
CtHi mp. 43521

B4757 [PAINE, THOMAS] 1737-1809
The American crisis. Number V. Or, Two letters, one addressed to General Sir William Howe, the other, to the inhabitants of America. Charles-Town, Timothy's office, 1778.
[1], 22, [2] p. 18.5 cm.
NcD

B4758 PAINE, THOMAS, 1737-1809
To the public. By the Goddess of Plain Truth, a manifesto and proclamation . . . [Philadelphia, B. Towne, 1778]
broadside 31 X 15.5 cm.
In verse
Hildeburn 3765; cf. Evans 14967
PHi mp. 43522

B4759 PENNSYLVANIA. COUNCIL OF SAFETY
In Council, Lancaster, May 29, 1778. Instructions to the agents . . . [Colophon] [Lancaster] Francis Bailey [1778?]
2 p.
Heartman: Cradle 772; Taylor 163
PPAmP mp. 43523

B4760 PENNSYLVANIA. COUNCIL OF SAFETY
In Council. Philadelphia, July 9th, 1778. Sir, As it is of great importance to the reputation of this State . . . By order of Council, To Esquire one of the Commissioners for the County of [Philadelphia, 1778]
broadside 31 X 19 cm.
Concerns reports of estates confiscated
Taylor 164
NHi mp. 43524

B4761 PENNSYLVANIA. GENERAL ASSEMBLY
In der General Assembly von Pennsylvanien, Samstag. Philadelphia, Steiner and Cist [1778]
broadside 32.5 X 23 cm.
Concerns calling of a constitutional convention
Taylor 165
PHi mp. 43525

B4762 PENNSYLVANIA. GENERAL ASSEMBLY
In General Assembly of Pennsylvania, Saturday, November 28, 1778 . . . John Morris Junior, Clerk of the General Assembly. Philadelphia, John Dunlap [1778]
broadside
Initial "W" at beginning of text
Concerns calling of a constitutional convention
PHi mp. 43526

B4763 PENNSYLVANIA. LAWS
An act for raising a regiment of horse . . . [Philadelphia, 1778?]
broadside 30.5 X 17.5 cm.
PHi mp. 43527

B4764 PENNSYLVANIA. LAWS
An act to prohibit for a limited time the making of whiskey and other spirits from wheat, rye . . . [Nov. 27, 1778] Philadelphia, John Dunlap [1778]
broadside 34.5 X 18 cm.
Signed by John Bayard, Speaker
PHi mp. 43528

B4765 PENNSYLVANIA. LAWS
A farther supplement to the Act entitled "An act to regulate the militia . . . of Pennsylvania." Lancaster, John Dunlap, 1778.
8 p.
Bausman p. 17
No copy known mp. 43529

B4766 PENNSYLVANIA GAZETTE
Philadelphia, December 12, 1778. To the public. The *Pennsylvania Gazette* will be published . . . Gentlemen, who choose to subscribe . . . [Philadelphia, Hall and Sellers, 1778]
broadside 22 X 17 cm.
DLC mp. 43469

B4767 PENNSYLVANIA GAZETTE
Postscript to the *Pennsylvania Gazette* of May 2, 1778. York-Town, May 4 . . . [York] Hall and Sellers [1778
broadside
Treaty of alliance with France
MB mp. 43584

B4768 [PERRY, JOSEPH] 1731-1783
Died at East-Windsor, the 28th of August, 1778, in the 47th year of her age, Mrs. Sarah Perry, consort of the Rev. Joseph Perry . . . [n.p., 1778?]
broadside 25.5 X 19 cm.
Reproduced in Groton Historical Series, II, 455
CtHi mp. 43530

B4769 POOR Job. An almanack for . . . 1779 . . .
Charles-Town, Nicholas Boden [1778]
[24] p.
Drake 13122
ScU-S

B4770 RHODE ISLAND. COUNCIL OF WAR
State of Rhode-Island and Providence Plantations. In Council of war, January 4, 1778. Resolved, that the following orders . . . [Providence, 1778]
broadside 27 X 21 cm.
Alden 729
RHi. Photostats: CSmH; MWA mp. 43531

B4771 RHODE ISLAND. COUNCIL OF WAR
State of Rhode-Island and Providence Plantations. In Council of war, July 29, 1778. Whereas . . . the Continental Congress . . . [Providence, 1778]
broadside 41 X 25 cm.
Alden 746; Winship p. 37
MB; RHi mp. 43532

B4772 RHODE ISLAND. ELECTION PROX.
His excellency William Greene, Esquire, Governor. Hon. Jabez Bowen, Esq; Dep. Gov. . . . [Providence? 1778]
broadside 20.5 X 12 cm.
Alden 722; Chapin Proxies 20
RHi mp. 43533

B4773 RHODE ISLAND. ELECTION PROX.
Independence, liberty, and safety. The honorable William Bradford, Esq; Governor. The honorable William Greene, Esq; Dep. Governor . . . [Providence] J. Carter [1778?]
broadside 20.5 X 13 cm.
Alden 722A; Chapin Proxies 19
RHi. Bradford Swan, Providence, R.I. mp. 43534

B4774 RHODE ISLAND. GENERAL ASSEMBLY
State of Rhode-Island and Providence Plantations. In General assembly, March session, 1778. It is voted and resolved, That the colonels . . . Greeting. You are hereby required . . . this eighteenth day of March, A.D. 1778. [Providence, 1778]
broadside 26.5 X 21.5 cm.
Alden 734; Winship p. 37
RHi mp. 43537

B4775 RHODE ISLAND. GENERAL ASSEMBLY
State of Rhode-Island and Providence Plantations. In General assembly, May session 1778. It is voted and resolved, That any person . . . [Providence, 1778]
broadside 20 X 25 cm.
Alden 736; Winship p. 37
RHi; RPJCB mp. 43538

B4776 RHODE ISLAND. GENERAL ASSEMBLY
State of Rhode-Island and Providence Plantations. In General assembly, May second session, A.D. 1778. Resolved, That a committee . . . [Providence, 1778]
broadside 18.5 X 25 cm.
Alden 738
RHi. Photostat: MWA mp. 43540

B4777 RHODE ISLAND. GENERAL ASSEMBLY
State of Rhode-Island and Providence Plantations. In General assembly, May second session, A.D. 1778. Resolved, That all persons . . . [Providence, 1778]
broadside 25 X 19.5 cm.
Alden 739; Winship Addenda p. 88
RHi. Photostat: MHi mp. 43541

B4778 RHODE ISLAND. GENERAL ASSEMBLY
State of Rhode-Island and Providence Plantations. In General Assembly, May second session, A.D. 1778. Resolved, That eight hundred and thirty-nine effective men . . . [Providence, 1778]
broadside 38 X 26.5 cm.
Alden 740; Winship p. 57
RHi; RPJCB; RWe mp. 43542

B4779 RHODE ISLAND. GENERAL ASSEMBLY
State of Rhode Island and Providence Plantations. In General assembly, May second session, A.D. 1778. Resolved, That it be recommended to . . . Major-general Sullivan . . . [Providence, 1778]
broadside 17 X 18 cm.
Alden 741; Winship p. 37
RHi mp. 43543

B4780 RHODE ISLAND. GENERAL ASSEMBLY
State of Rhode-Island and Providence Plantations. In General assembly, May second session, A.D. 1778. Resolved, That the act permitting inoculation . . . [Providence, 1778]
broadside 19 X 24.5 cm.
Alden 742; Austin 1600; Winship p. 37
DNLM; R; RHi mp. 43544

B4781 RHODE ISLAND. GENERAL ASSEMBLY
State of Rhode-Island and Providence Plantations. In General assembly, September session, A.D. 1778. Whereas by reason of the late expedition against the enemy . . . [Providence, 1778]
broadside 39 X 13 cm.
Alden 749; Winship p. 38
RHi; RPJCB. Photostat: MWA mp. 43545

B4782 RHODE ISLAND. GENERAL ASSEMBLY
[State of Rhode-Island and Providence Plantations. In General Assembly, September session, A.D. 1778. Whereas it hath happened . . . Providence? 1778]
[broadside?]
The Schedules for the September, 1778, session state that "the several Town-Councils shall be furnished . . . with copies hereof."
Alden 750; Winship p. 38
No copy known mp. 43546

B4783 RHODE ISLAND. GENERAL ASSEMBLY
State of Rhode-Island and Providence Plantations. In General assembly, December session, 1778. Whereas great difficulties have arisen . . . [Providence, 1778]
broadside 24 X 20 cm.
Alden 755; Winship p. 38
RHi; RPJCB mp. 43550

B4784 RHODE ISLAND. GOVERNOR, 1778-1786
By His excellency William Greene . . . A proclamation . . . [Dec. 8, 1778] . . . [Providence, 1778]
broadside 33 X 25 cm.
Alden 723; Winship Addenda p. 88
R mp. 43535

B4785 RHODE ISLAND. LAWS
State of Rhode-Island and Providence Plantations. In General assembly, February 16, 1778. An act assessing . . . a rate or tax of thirty-two thousand pounds . . . [Providence, 1778]
broadside 43 X 17 cm.
Alden 732; Winship p. 37
R; RHi mp. 43536

B4786 RHODE ISLAND. LAWS
State of Rhode-Island and Providence Plantations. In General assembly, May second session, A.D. 1778. An act for calling and sinking . . . [Providence, 1778]
broadside 38.5 X 26.5 cm.
Alden 737; Winship p. 37
NNC; RHi mp. 43539

B4787 RHODE ISLAND. LAWS
[State of Rhode-Island and Providence Plantations. In General assembly, October session, A.D. 1778. An act assessing . . . a rate or tax of thirty thousand pounds . . . [Providence? 1778]
[broadside?]
Alden 751; Winship p. 38
No copy known mp. 43547

B4788 RHODE ISLAND. LAWS
[State of Rhode-Island and Providence Plantations. In General assembly, Oct. session, A.D. 1778. An act establishing and regulating fees. [Providence, 1778]
8 p. 20 cm. caption title
Alden 752; Winship p. 38
R; RHi mp. 43548

B4789 RHODE ISLAND. LAWS
State of Rhode-Island and Providence Plantations. In General assembly, October session, A.D. 1778. An act for enquiring into the rateable property . . . [Providence, 1778]
broadside 39 X 25.5 cm.
Alden 753; Winship p. 38
RHi mp. 43549

B4790 RIPLEY, SYLVANUS, 1749-1787
[title unknown. Dresden, J. P. & A. Spooner, 1778]

Mentioned by Ripley in a letter dated Oct. 30, 1778
McCorison: Vermont 3
No copy known

B4791 [ROMANS, BERNARD] 1720-1784
The townships or grants east of Lake Champlain are laid down as granted by the state of New Hampshire . . . [New Haven, 1778]
map 51 X 64 cm.
Title above taken from text in upper left corner. cf. Phillips p. 88-91

Huntington 426
CSmH mp. 43551

B4792 ROSS, EZRA, d. 1778
The last words and dying speech of Ezra Ross, James Buchanan and William Brooks, who were executed at Worcester on Thursday the 2d day of July 1778, for the murder of Mr. Joshua Spooner, of Brookfield. Bathsheba Spooner . . . accessary to the murder . . . was also executed . . . [n.p., 1778]
broadside 43 X 33 cm.
MWA mp. 43424

B4793 ROSS, EZRA, d. 1778
The lives, last words, and dying speech of Ezra Ross, James Buchanan, and William Brooks, who were executed at Worcester, on Thursday the 2d day of July, 1778, for the murder of Mr. Joshua Spooner, of Brookfield. Bathsheba Spooner . . . accessary to the murder, was also executed . . . [Worcester? 1778?]
7, [1] p. 18.5 cm.
McDade 901
MWA mp. 43425

B4794 SONG of Washington. [n.p., 1778?]
broadside 23.5 X 12 cm.
Huntington 427
CSmH mp. 43552

B4795 SOUTH CAROLINA. LAWS
Acts and ordinances . . . passed in the year 1778. [Charles-Town, P. Timothy 1778]
1 v. 28.5 cm.
Half-title only
Sabin 87627
DLC (contains pts. [1]-[12] of Sabin 87627, and Sabin 87628); ScC mp. 43553

B4796 SPAIN. CONSEJO DE LAS INDIAS
Traduction d'une lettre de D. Joseph de Galves, ministre & secretaire d'etat, ayant le Départment des Indes . . . Je suis véritablement sensible . . . [at end] St. Ydelphonse ce 6 Aoust 1778. Signé Joseph De Galvez. [New Orleans, Antoine Boudousquié, 1778]
broadside 30 X 21 cm.
McMurtrie: New Orleans 28; New York Public 671
Simon J. Schwartz, New Orleans (1942) Photostat: NN mp. 43554

B4797 SPAIN. SOVEREIGNS (CHARLES III)
Traduction d'une lettre du roi . . . [New Orleans] Antoine Boudousquié [1778]
2 p. 30 cm.
McMurtrie: New Orleans 27; New York Public 682
RPJCB. Photostat: NN mp. 43555

B4798 STAFFORD'S Connecticut almanack, for the year . . . 1779 . . . By Hosea Stafford, Philomathes. Hartford: Printed and sold by B. Webster [1778]
[20] p.
Drake 325
MB; NBLiHi

B4799 A TABLE shewing the value of any number of dollars . . . [Philadelphia] Zachariah Poulson, 1778.
broadside 38 X 23 cm.
DLC mp. 43556

B4800 THOMAS'S Massachusetts, New-Hampshire, and Connecticut almanack for . . . 1779. By Philomathes. Worcester, Isaiah Thomas [1778]
[24] p.
Second edition
Drake 3284
MWA

B4801 THOMAS'S Massachusetts, New-Hampshire, and Connecticut almanack for . . . 1779. By Philomathes. Worcester, Isaiah Thomas [1778]
[24] p.
Third edition
Drake 3285
NjR

B4802 THOMPSON, JOHN
The lost and undone son of perdition . . . Norwich, Printed and sold by Green & Spooner [1778?]
19 p. 17.5 cm. $[A]$-B^4 C^2
MWA mp. 43557

B4802a The trial and establishment of American independence . . . By a Nova-Scotia refugee . . . Norwich, John Trumbull, 1778.
20 p. 17 cm. $[A]$–B^4 C^2
Stoddard 242
RPB

B4803 U. S.
The following state of facts, is taken from the papers now lying on the table . . . [Philadelphia, 1778?]
broadside 33 X 20 cm.
6 items, concerning Arthur Lee, Stephen Sayre, Randolph, and consuls. Letter from Lee dated Paris, Nov. 27, 1777
MWA mp. 43568

B4804 U. S.
A proclamation. It having pleased Almighty God . . . State of Massachusetts-Bay . . . December 5th, 1778 . . . [declaring Dec. 13, 1778, as a day of thanksgiving] [Boston? 1778?]
broadside 42 X 34 cm.
Ford 2157; reprint of Evans 16134 & 15899
MWiW-C; MWA mp. 43582

B4805 U. S. ARMY. CONTINENTAL ARMY
By the honorable William Heath, Esq; Major-General in the Army of the United States . . . A proclamation. Whereas the . . . General Assembly . . . of Massachusetts-Bay, were pleased on the 30th day of April last to pass the following resolve . . . [July 10, 1778] . . . [Boston, 1778]
broadside 43.5 X 35 cm.
Ford 2140
MBB; MHi mp. 43560

B4806 U. S. ARMY. CONTINENTAL ARMY
Head Quarters, Peeks-Kill, General Orders for the army under the command of Brigadier General M'Dougall . . . Instructions for soldiers . . . concerning the means of preserving health . . . [Poughkeepsie? 1778]
broadside 42.5 X 27 cm.
NHi mp. 43561

B4807 U. S. ARMY. CONTINENTAL ARMY
Rules and articles for the better government of the troops, raised . . . at the expence of the United States of America. Poughkeepsie, Re-printed by John Holt, 1778.
26 p.
Anderson Galleries auction cat. 2016, Dec. 9, 1925, no. 16
Vail: Patriotic pair, p. 408
No copy located mp. 43562

B4808 U. S. ARMY. CONTINENTAL ARMY
Standing orders for the garrison of Philadelphia, July 7, 1778. The guards and sentries having been . . . negligent . . . it is ordered . . . By order of . . . General Arnold, Lewis Nicola, Town Major. [Philadelphia, 1778]
broadside 28.5 X 20.5 cm.
Taylor 167
PHi mp. 43563

B4809 U. S. ARMY. CONTINENTAL ARMY
This is to certify, that hath enlisted himself as a waggoner . . . In witness whereof the said and . . . have . . . set their hands this day of 1778. [Philadelphia? 1778]
broadside 13.5 X 17 cm.
Taylor 192
DLC

B4810 U. S. BOARD OF TREASURY
Treasury office, York-Town, April 15, 1778 . . . [n.p., 1778]
broadside 34 X 20.5 cm.
DLC; NhHi mp. 43564

B4811 U. S. CONTINENTAL CONGRESS, 1777
In Congress, June 10, 1777. Resolved, That to supply the army of the United States with provisions . . . [Colophon] Yorktown, Hall and Sellers [1778?]
4 p. fol.
cf. Evans 15672
PPAmP mp. 43565

B4812 U. S. CONTINENTAL CONGRESS, 1778
An address of the Congress to the inhabitants of the United States . . . Three years have now passed . . . In Congress May 9, 1778. Resolved . . . Baltimore, J. Dunlap [1778]
broadside 40.5 X 24 cm.
Wheeler 52
MdBE (mutilated) mp. 43566

B4813 U. S. CONTINENTAL CONGRESS, 1778
[An address] of the Congress to the inhabitants of the United States of America . . . Boston, Printed and sold by White and Adams [1778]
broadside 39 X 30 cm.
Used as a folder for "State, Town and County taxes, 1781" on verso; "An address" and other margins apparently removed in opening
MWA mp. 43567

B4814 U. S. CONTINENTAL CONGRESS, 1778
In Congress, February 5, 1778. Resolved that the Captain . . . February 6. Whereas it hath been found . . . February 9. Resolved, That it be recommended . . .Charles Thomson, Secretary. [Philadelphia, 1778]
broadside 39.5 X 26 cm.
RPJCB. Photostat: NN mp. 43569

B4815 U. S. CONTINENTAL CONGRESS, 1778
In Congress, February 6, 1778. For the better regulating the hospitals . . . [Philadelphia, 1778]
broadside 33.5 X 22 cm.
DLC mp. 43570

B4816 U. S. CONTINENTAL CONGRESS, 1778
In Congress, February 11, 1778. Resolved, That there shall be . . . [Philadelphia, 1778]
broadside 36 X 19 cm.
DLC mp. 43571

B4817 U. S. CONTINENTAL CONGRESS, 1778
In Congress, February 27, 1778. Resolved, That a company of bakers . . . [Philadelphia, 1778]
broadside 22 X 17 cm.
Ford 2131
DLC; MHi mp. 43572

B4818 U. S. CONTINENTAL CONGRESS, 1778
In Congress, March 13, 1778. Congress resumed the consideration of the report of the Committee appointed to revise the System of the Commissary's Department . . . Extract from the minutes, Charles Thomson, Secretary. [York, Pa., 1778]
broadside 27.5 X 21.5 cm.
MHi mp. 43573

B4819 U. S. CONTINENTAL CONGRESS, 1778
In Congress, April 14th, 1778. Resolved, That the Commissary general . . . have full power to appoint and remove . . . In Congress, April 16th, 1778. Resolved, That nothing . . . be construed to make the commissary general liable for the misapplication of money . . . by any inferior officer . . . Extract from the minutes, Charles Thomson, Secretary. [Philadelphia, 1778]
broadside 35 X 20.5 cm.
Taylor 176
CtHi; NHi mp. 43574

B4820 U. S. CONTINENTAL CONGRESS, 1778
In Congress, 16th April, 1778. Resolved, That nothing contained in the system for the commissary-general's department . . . 1st September. Resolved, That where accounts of back rations are presented . . . Charles Thomson, secretary. Philadelphia, John Dunlap [1778]
broadside fol.
PPL mp. 43575

B4821 U. S. CONTINENTAL CONGRESS, 1778
In Congress, May 6, 1778. Whereas Congress have received, from their commissioners at the Court of France, copies of a treaty of amity and commerce, and of a treaty of alliance . . . to the end that the said treaty may be well . . . performed . . . Resolved, That all captains . . . do govern themselves strictly . . . Extract from the minutes, Charles Thomson, Secretary. [Philadelphia, 1778]
broadside 44 X 26 cm.
MWA mp. 43576

B4822 U. S. CONTINENTAL CONGRESS, 1778
In Congress, June 9, 1778. Whereas doubts have arisen, as to the sum which shall be paid for the rations . . . Resolved, That the value of the rations due . . . be estimated at One Third of a Dollar . . . Extract from the minutes, Charles Thomson, Secretary. York-Town, Hall and Sellers [1778]
broadside 27.5 X 22 cm.
Taylor 185
CtHi; NHi mp. 43577

B4823 U. S. CONTINENTAL CONGRESS, 1778
In Congress, July 20, 1778. The Committee, to whom were referred the letter . . . from Ebenezer Hazard . . . report . . . [Philadelphia, 1778]
broadside 23.5 X 18.5 cm.
MHi mp. 43578

B4824 U. S. CONTINENTAL CONGRESS, 1778
In Congress, July 25, 1778. 1. Resolved, that the expedition against the fortress . . . [Philadelphia, 1778]

broadside 19.5 X 23.5 cm.
DLC; WHi mp. 43579

B4825 U. S. CONTINENTAL CONGRESS, 1778
Mr. Dunlap, Be pleased to print the following letters from . . . General Washington, together with the return of killed, wounded . . . Henry Laurence, President of Congress. Philadelphia, July 4, 1778. Philadelphia, John Dunlap [1778]
broadside
Heartman: Cradle p. 836; Taylor 189
No copy located mp. 43580

B4826 U. S. CONTINENTAL CONGRESS, 1778
Paris, May 18, 1778. Gentlemen, Certain intelligence . . . that eleven British ships of war . . . are in the Road of St. Hellens . . . bound for North-America . . . B. Franklin, John Adams . . . Reading in Congress, July 8, 1778, and ordered to be published. Charles Thomson, Secretary. [Philadelphia, 1778]
broadside 34.5 X 20.5 cm.
NHi mp. 43581

B4827 U. S. CONTINENTAL CONGRESS, 1778
York-Town. In Congress, May 6, 1778. Whereas Congress have received . . . copies of a treaty of amity . . . Annapolis, Frederick Green [1778]
broadside 31.5 X 20.5 cm.
Wheeler 55
MdAA mp. 43583

B4828 U. S. TREATIES, ETC.
Treaties between the Thirteen United States of American and His Most Christian Majesty. Treaty of amity and commerce . . . Done at Paris . . . [1778] C. A. Gerard. B. Franklin . . . [n.p., 1778?]
broadside 69.5 c 48.5 cm.
NHi mp. 43585

B4829 U. S. TREATIES, ETC.
Treaties, of amity and commerce, and of alliance eventual and defensive . . . Boston, Re-printed and sold by Draper and Folsom, 1778.
[2], 6, [2], 7–9, [2], [10]–23 p.
Sabin 96566
MWA; RPJCB mp. 43457

B4830 VERMONT. CONVENTION, 1778
[Handbill of the Committee of the Cornish convention. Dresden, 1778?]

Convention held at Cornish Dec. 9, 1778
Whittemore 247
No copy known

B4831 VERMONT. GENERAL ASSEMBLY
Outlines of a plan agreed by the General Assembly . . . of Vermont . . . in October, A.D. 1778, to be pursued for the establishment of the state . . . [Dresden, J. P. & A. Spooner, 1778.
broadside 29 X 20.5 cm.
McCorison 4; Sabin 99024
NhPlain mp. 43586

B4832 VERMONT. GOVERNOR, 1778–1789
By his excellency Thomas Chittenden . . . A proclamation. Amid the many private and public distresses . . . Windsor, this 18th day of October . . . 1778. Thos. Chittenden. [Dresden, J. P. & A. Spooner, 1778]
broadside 41 X 33 cm.
Whittemore 240; New York Public 688
NhD. Photostats: MHi, NN mp. 43587

B4833 VIRGINIA. GOVERNOR, 1776–1779
Williamsburg, August 6, 1778. Sir, By the resolutions of Congress . . . I am, Sir, your must humble servant, [Signed in manuscript] P. Henry. [Williamsburg, A. Purdie, 1778]
broadside 23.5 X 19.5 cm.
DLC; PHi mp. 43589

B4834 VIRGINIA. SENATE
Journal of the Senate. Williamsburg, John Dixon & William Hunter, 1778.
20 p. 31 cm.
Session May 4–June 1, 1778
Sabin 100111 (50 p.)
DLC; RPJCB; ViL mp. 43590

B4835 WATTS, ISAAC, 1674–1748
Divine songs attempted in easy language . . . Boston, Nathaniel Coverly, 1778.
48 p. 14.5 cm.
Hamilton 85
MWA; NjP. d'Alté A. Welch, Cleveland (variant without cut and with differing type) mp. 43593

B4836 WATTS, ISAAC, 1674–1748
Divine songs attempted in easy language . . . Boston, Nathaniel Coverly [1778?]
48 p. 14.5 cm.
MWA mp. 43592

B4837 WEST, SAMUEL, 1730–1807
An anniversary sermon, preached at Plymouth, December 22d, 1777 . . . Boston, Draper and Folsom [1778?]
79 p. 20 cm. [A]-K^4
cf. Evans 16169
MHi; MWA; RPJCB mp. 43594

B4838 [WITHERSPOON, JOHN] 1723–1794
Recantation of Benjamin Towne. The following was printed in *Loudon's New-York Packet*, published at Fishkill, October 1st, 1778 . . . [Fishkill? 1778?]
[5] p. 19 cm.
Pagination possibly removed by trimming
MWA mp. 43595

B4839 WRIGHT, ELIPHALET
The difference between those called standing churches, and . . . Congregationalists illustrated . . . at the ordination of Mr. Emerson Foster . . . January 22, 1778 . . . Norwich, Printed by John Trumbull, M,DCC,LXXV [sic] [1778]
24 p. 16.5 cm.
CtHi. F. H. Curtiss (1939) mp. 43597

B4840 YALE UNIVERSITY
Catalogus recentium . . . M,DCC,LXXVIII. [New Haven, 1778]
broadside
CtY; MHi mp. 43598

1779

B4841 ALLEN, IRA, 1751–1814
To the inhabitants of the State of Vermont. Friends and fellow-countrymen. Pursuant to instructions . . . to wait on the . . . Assembly of . . . New-Hampshire . . . I waited on them; and . . . now publish a short . . . account . . . Norwich, April 19th, 1779 . . . [Dresden, J. P. & A. Spooner, 1779]

2 p. 33 cm.
350 copies printed
McCorison 11
MHi mp. 43599

B4842 ALLEN, IRA, 1751–1814
To the inhabitants of the state of Vermont. Friends . . . I waited on the General Court of New-Hampshire . . . Ira Allen. Norwich, July 13, 1779 . . . [Dresden, J. P. & A. Spooner, 1779]
[2] p. 38 cm. caption title
McCorison 10; New York Public 689; Whittemore 243; Sabin 99005
VtBrt. Photostats: DLC; MHi; NHi; NN mp. 43600

B4843 [ARMSTRONG, JOHN] 1709–1779
The oeconomy of love: a poetical essay. Philadelphia, Printed for William Mentz, 1779.
24 p. 17.5 cm.
DLC; MWA mp. 43601

B4844 AN astronomical diary, or almanack for . . . 1780. By Nathaniel Low. Boston, Printed by John Gill, and T. & J. Fleet [1779]
[24] p.
Second edition
Drake 3288
MH

B4845 BAPTISTS. SOUTH CAROLINA. CHARLESTON ASSOCIATION
Minutes of the Charlestown Association. Charlestown, South-Carolina, November 8, 1779 . . . [Charleston, 1779]
4 p. 21 cm. caption title
ScGf

B4846 BELKNAP, JEREMY, 1744–1798
Jesus Christ, the only foundation. A sermon . . . June 29, 1779 . . . Portsmouth, Daniel Fowle, 1779.
32 p. 18.5 cm.
New York Public 690; Whittemore 245
MWA; NN mp. 43604

B4847 BIBLE. N.T.
The New Testament . . . Trenton, Printed and sold by Isaac Collins, 1779.
368 p. 17 cm.
PHi mp. 43605

B4848 BOSTON, Aug. 3d, 1779. Sir, As it is necessary for the committee appointed by the town to regulate the prices of labour and the wares of the different tradesmen, to know the rates . . . [Boston, 1779]
broadside 15.5 × 17 cm.
Ford 2170
MHi mp. 43607

B4849 BOYLE, JOHN, 1746–1819
Boston, April 22, 1779. Now in the press . . . a new edition . . . of Letters written by the . . . Earl of Chesterfield . . . Boston, Printed for John Boyle, and John Douglass M'Dougall, 1779.
viii p. 17.5 cm.
MWA mp. 43608

B4850 BY the commandant of New-York, &c. No.
Permission is hereby given to to pass to
Given at New-York, the day of One Thousand Seven Hundred and Seventy Nine . . . [New York, 1779]
broadside 17 × 16.5 cm.
DLC (facsim.)

B4851 A CHOROGRAPHICAL map of the Northern Department of North America drawn from the latest and most accurate observations. New Haven, Engraved printed and sold [by Amos Doolittle] [1779]

A map of the New Hampshire grants in Vermont
Trumbull: Supplement 2377
CtHT-W mp. 43609

B4852 CONCORD, MASS. CONVENTION, 1779
Boston, July 21st, 1779. Gentlemen, Inclosed you have a copy of the proceedings . . . [Boston, 1779]
broadside 20.5 × 16 cm.
Ford 2174
MHi. Photostat: DLC mp. 43610

B4853 CONNECTICUT. GENERAL ASSEMBLY
An address of the General Assembly of . . . Connecticut, to the freemen and other inhabitants of the same . . . The army of the United States raised for three years or during the war, is greatly reduced . . . Sir Henry Clinton . . . flushed with . . . success, is returned to New-York and meditates new designs . . . [Hartford? 1779?]
broadside 36 × 25 cm.
CtHi mp. 43611

B4854 CONNECTICUT. GENERAL ASSEMBLY
At a General Assembly of the Governor and Company . . . of Connecticut, holden at Hartford . . . May, 1779. Resolved, That Mr. Elijah Hubbard . . . is hereby appointed sub or State Cloathier for this State . . . Hartford, Hudson and Goodwin [1779]
broadside 38.5 × 25.5 cm.
cf. Evans 16240
NHi mp. 43612

B4855 CONNECTICUT. GOVERNOR, 1776–1784
By His Excellency Jonathan Trumbull . . . A proclamation. Whereas it hath pleased . . . Lebanon . . . the 5th day of August . . . 1779. Jon. Trumbull. [Hartford? 1779]
broadside 36 ×21 cm.
CtHi mp. 43613

B4856 CONNECTICUT. GOVERNOR, 1776–1784
By His Excellency Jonathan Trumbull . . . A proclamation. Whereas the General Assembly at their present session, in consequence of a requisition from Congress . . . inlistment, six hundred effective men . . . [Apr. 19, 1779] . . . Hartford, Hudson and Goodwin [1779]
broadside 38.5 × 25 cm.
Middendorf Collection, New York City (1970)
mp. 43614

B4857 CONNECTICUT. GOVERNOR, 1776–1784
State of Connecticut. By the Captain-General. Whereas His Excellency General Washington . . . expects the arrival of . . . Count D'Estaing . . . Given under my hand in Lebanon . . . the ninth day of October, A.D. 1779. [New London? 1779]
broadside 33.5 × 21 cm.
Signed: Jonathan Trumbull
CtHi; RPJCB mp. 43615

B4858 CONNECTICUT. LAWS
At a General Assembly . . . holden at Hartford . . . May . . . 1779. An act for providing for the families of the officers and soldiers . . . George Wyllys, Secretary. [Hartford, 1779]
broadside 38 × 28 cm.
CtHi mp. 43616

B4859 CONNECTICUT. LAWS
At a General assembly . . . holden . . . the 2d Thursday of May, 1779. An act for raising two regiments . . . Hartford, Hudson and Goodwin [1779]
broadside 32 X 19 cm.
MHi Photostats: DLC; MH; MWA; NHi; NN
mp. 43617

B4860 CONNECTICUT. TREASURER
State of Connecticut in America. To constable of and collector of the state tax for . . . 1779, Greeting . . . Dated at Hartford, the 1st day of March . . . 1779. Treasurer. . . . [Hartford, 1779]
broadside 34 X 21.5 cm.
CtHi mp. 43618

B4861 CONSIDERATIONS on the mode and terms of a treaty of peace with America . . . Charles-Town: Reprinted and sold by John Wells, MDCCLXXIX.

ScCC

B4862 THE continental pocket almanac, for . . . 1780 . . . By Anthony Sharp, Philom. Philadelphia, Francis Bailey [1779]
[24] p. 10.5 cm.
Drake 10087
NHi; NN

B4863 COPY of an illiberal and disrespectful letter founded on party prejudice; with a candid . . . answer . . . To the printer of the *Public Advertiser* . . . [New York? 1779]
broadside 34.5 X 21 cm.
NHi mp. 43619

B4864 DEANE, SILAS, 1737–1789
To the free and virtuous citizens of America. Friends and countrymen, The happiness or misfortunes . . . of an individual have generally no claim to the public attention . . . S. Dean. Philadelphia, November, 1778. [Philadelphia, 1779]
broadside 41.5 X 27 cm.
In mss. on verso: 4th Jany. 1779 Date of the Letter inclosed
Taylor 171
DLC mp. 43620

B4865 DEFOE, DANIEL, 1659?–1731
The wonderful life, and surprising adventures of . . . Robinson Crusoe . . . Boston, N. Coveely [sic] [ca. 1779]
32 p. 10.5 cm.
Printed between 1779 and 1787
Brigham: Robinson Crusoe 4, 5
MWA (also a variant issue, with "Coverly") mp. 43621

B4866 DELAWARE. PRESIDENT, 1778–1781
By . . . Caesar Rodney . . . a proclamation. Whereas by an act . . . [May 3, 1779] . . . Wilmington, James Adams [1779]
broadside 34.5 X 21 cm.
Hawkins: List C 10; Huntington 431
CSmH; DLC; MWA; PHi mp. 43622

B4867 DELAWARE. PRESIDENT, 1778–1781
By . . . Caesar Rodney . . . a proclamation. Whereas the honourable the Congress . . . [Mar. 30, 1779] . . . Wilmington, James Adams [1779]
broadside 34.5 X 21.5 cm.
Hawkins: List C11
DLC mp. 43623

B4868 A DIALOGUE between A and B , on a subject of the last importance . . . New-England, Printed for the author, 1779.
44 p. 20.5 cm.
MWA; NN; RPJCB mp. 43624

B4869 . . . DISCOURSE, shewing the difference between Whigandus and Torybandus. By a Friend to Peace . . . [n.p.] Printed in the year 1779.
9 p. 19.5 cm.
CtHi mp. 43625

B4870 DORCHESTER, MASS.
To Your state tax. Your town rate. The assessors sit at the house of Mr. John Champney, in Dorchester, the two last Thursdays in January, 1779 . . . [Boston, 1779]
broadside
Ford 2171
MHi

B4871 DORCHESTER, MASS.
To Your state tax. Your town rate. The assessors sit at the house of Mr. John Champney, in Dorchester, the two first Thursdays in June . . . [Boston, 1779]
broadside
Ford 2172
MHi

B4872 DORCHESTER, MASS.
To Your state tax. Your town rate. The assessors sit at the house of Mr. John Champney, in Dorchester, the second and third Thursdays of November, 1779. [Boston, 1779]
broadside
Ford 2172a
MHi

B4873 DRESDEN MERCURY, AND THE UNIVERSAL INTELLIGENCER
[Proposals for printing a newspaper. Dresden, J. P. & A. Spooner, 1779]

Referred to by Sgt. Maj. John Hawkins in his journal, located at PHi
McCorison 16
No copy known mp. 43707

B4874 AN entertaining story book for little boys and girls . . . Adorn'd with cuts. Boston, Printed and sold by N. Coverly, 1779. Price five shillings.
31, [1] p. illus. 9.5 cm.
MWA mp. 43626

B4875 AN entertaining story book for little boys and girl's . . . Adorned with cuts. Boston, Printed and sold by N. Coverly, 1779. Price six shillings.
26, [6] p. illus. 10 cm.
MWA (p. 29-30 wanting) mp. 43627

B4876 EVANS, ISRAEL, 1747-1807
A discourse, delivered at Easton, on the 17th of October, 1779 . . . Lancaster, 1779.

Sabin 23160; Vail: Old frontier 662
No copy located mp. 43628

B4877 FRANCE, MINISTÈRE DE LA MARINE
Signaux de l'escadre du roi . . . A bord du Languedoc, De l'imprimerie de F. P. Demauge, 1779.
2 p.l., 113 p. 21.5 cm.
Photostats: DLC; MHi; RPJCB [and 8 more]
mp. 43629

B4878 FRESH intelligence. London, August 30. Fifteen thousand Hanoverians . . . New-London, Dec. 15. . . . Boston, Dec. 20. There are letters . . . Newport, J. Weeden [1779]
broadside 34 X 23.5 cm.
Alden 767; Winship Addenda p. 89
RNHi. Photostat: MWA mp. 43630

B4879 FRIENDS, SOCIETY OF. DUBLIN HALF-YEAR'S MEETING
At a Meeting for Sufferings held in Philadelphia, the fifteenth of the fourth month, 1779 . . . An epistle from the National Half-Year's Meeting, held in Dublin . . . 1778 . . . [Philadelphia, 1779]
4 p. 27 cm.
MB; NjR; PHi; RPJCB mp. 43631

B4880 GT. BRIT. ARMY
Army list of the general and staff officers, and of the officers in the several . . . regiments, serving in North-America, under . . . General Sir Henry Clinton, K.B. . . . New-York, Macdonald & Cameron, 1779.

cf. Lathrop C. Harper cat. no. 166 (May 1943), item 705
No copy located mp. 43632

B4881 GT. BRIT. COLONIAL OFFICE
By Archibald Campbell . . . in Georgia. A proclamation. Whereas information . . . [Jan. 11, 1779] . . . [Savannah, John Daniel Hammerer, 1779]
broadside 31 X 19.5 cm.
DLC (photostat) mp. 43634

B4882 GT. BRIT. COLONIAL OFFICE
By His Excellency Sir Henry Clinton . . . Proclamation. Whereas there are several deserters . . . [Feb. 23, 1779] . . . [New York] Macdonald & Cameron [1779]
broadside 31.5 X 18.5 cm.
MH; NHi. Photostats: DLC; NN; WHi mp. 43633

B4883 GT. BRIT. COLONIAL OFFICE
By Hyde Parker . . . a proclamation. Whereas the blessings of peace . . . [Jan. 4, 1779] . . . [Savannah, John Daniel Hammerer, 1779]
broadside 32.5 X 19 cm.
DLC (photostat) mp. 43635

B4884 GT. BRIT. COLONIAL OFFICE
I do solemnly swear , that I will bear true and faithful allegiance . . . Given at Savannah this day of , One Thousand Seven Hundred and Seventy-nine . . . [Savannah, John Daniel Hammerer, 1779]
broadside 18.5 X 19.5 cm.
DLC (photostat)

B4885 GT. BRIT. NAVY
By Commodore Sir George Collier . . . Address, To the inhabitants of Connecticut .. Given on board . . . Camilla . . . July 4th, 1779 . . . New-York, Macdonald and Cameron [1779]
broadside 32 X 19 cm.
Evans 16291 (with differing imprint)
DLC mp. 43637

B4886 GT. BRIT. NAVY
By Commodore Sir George Collier . . . Address. To the inhabitants of Connecticut . . . Given on board . . . Camilla . . . July 4th, 1779 . . . Newport, July 5, This moment arrived . . . the Otter . . . [Newport] John Howe [1779]
broadside 32 X 17 cm.
Alden 769; New York Public 695
NHi; PHi. Photostats: DLC; NN mp. 43636

B4887 GT. BRIT. NAVY
Pursuant to His Excellency Sir William Howe's proclamation of the 17th July, 1777. Permission is hereby given to . . . New-York, Superintendent's-Office, 1779. To the officers attending. [New York, 1779]
broadside 21 X 16.5 cm.
Permission to put stores aboard the schooner Eagle, signed by Andrew Elliot super[t]:
MiU-C

B4888 GT. BRIT. SOVEREIGNS (GEORGE III)
Baltimore, February 4, 1779. Captain Marvin . . . is just arrived at Annapolis . . . From the *London General advertiser* . . . of the 27th of November . . . his Britannic Majesty's speech . . . to his Parliament . . . Baltimore, M. K. Goddard [1779]
broadside 34.5 X 16.5 cm.
Wheeler 59
MdBE mp. 43638

B4889 GT. BRIT. SOVEREIGNS (GEORGE III)
His Majesty's most gracious speech, to both Houses of Parliament. House of Lords, Nov. 26 . . . [The above speech . . . from the *New-Jersey Gazette* . . . 10th of February.] [New York] Published by James Rivington [1779]
broadside 42 X 31 cm.
MWA (photostat) mp. 43639

B4890 HAND, STEPHEN
[Verses on the sixth, seventh and eighth chapters of Genesis. Chatham? Shepard Kollock? 1779]

Advertised in the *New Jersey Journal*, June 8, 1779, as "Just published and to be sold by Foster Horton, in Chatham and John Dixon at Settle Hill." The Horton shop was opposite Kollock's printing office
Humphrey 194
No copy known

B4891 THE history of the Holy Jesus . . . The twenty-sixth edition. Boston, Printed for John Boyle, 1779.
[48] p. front. 10.5 cm.
Hamilton 88; Rosenbach-Ch 88
CtHi; CtY; MHi (imperfect); MWA; NjP mp. 43640

B4892 [DER Hoch-Deutsch-Americanische Calendar auf . . . 1780. Germantown [1779]]
[24] p.
Drake 10091
MWA (t.p. lacking)

B4893 LANCASTER MERCURY
Supplement to the *Lancaster Mercury*, no. 26. Philadelphia. In General Assembly . . . March 17, 1779. The bill entitled, "An act for supplying the army . . ." Timothy Matlack, Secretary. Philadelphia, March 29, 1779 . . . [Philadelphia, 1779]
broadsheet 33.5 X 21.5 cm.
In 2 columns
PHi mp. 43679

B4894 LOUISIANA. GOVERNOR, 1777–1785
D$^{n.}$ Bernardo de Galves . . . Hazemos saver que Su Majestad . . . nos a hecho llegar . . . [Nueva Orleans, Antoine Boudousquié, 1779]
broadside 43.5 X 33 cm.
Dated Mar. 20, 1779
In Spanish and French
McMurtrie: Louisiana 10; New York Public 696
ICHi. Photostats: MWA; NN mp. 43642

B4895 LOUISIANA. GOVERNOR, 1777–1785
D$^{n.}$ Bernardo de Galvez . . . Su Real Majestad . . . haviendo reparado que del modo arbitrario . . . [Nueva Orleans, Antoine Boudousquié, 1779]
broadside 42 X 31 cm.
Dated June, 1779
In Spanish and French
McMurtrie: Louisiana 11; New York Public 697
ICHi. Photostats: MWA; NN mp. 43643

B4896 LOUISIANA. GOVERNOR, 1777–1785
D$^{n.}$ Bernardo de Galvez . . . Su Real Majested . . . por su real cedula feche . . . à 24 de enero ultimo proximo passado . . . [Nueva Orleans, Antoine Boudousquié, 1779]
broadside 42 X 33 cm.
Dated June, 1779
In Spanish and French
McMurtrie: New Orleans 29; New York Public 698
NN (photostat) mp. 43644

B4897 M'ALPINE, JAMES
The deposition of Captain James M'Alpine . . . Sworn this 17th day of June, 1779, before me, D. Mathews, Mayor. [New York, 1779]
broadside 23 X 17.5 cm.
MHi; MiU-C. Photostats: DLC; NHi; NN mp. 43645

B4898 MARTIN, LUTHER, 1748–1826
An address to Robert Lemmon . . . Baltimore, M. K. Goddard, 1779.
19 p. 19.5 cm.
Wheeler 63
MdHi mp. 43646

B4899 MARYLAND. LAWS
An act of the General assembly . . . passed October session, 1778 . . . to raise the supplies for the year . . . Annapolis, Frederick Green [1779]
27 p. 17 cm.
Wheeler 66
MdHi mp. 43647

B4899a MARYLAND. LAWS
A bill, entitled, An act for the relief of certain non-jurors . . . [Annapolis, F. Green, 1779]
[2] p. fol. caption title
PHi

B4900 THE Maryland Gazette, and Annapolis Advertiser. [Apr. 3- , 1779, being Nos. 1 to of Vol. I]. Annapolis, James Hayes.
1 v. 41 cm.
Brigham v. 1, p. 223; Wheeler 77
DLC (July 9)

B4901 MASSACHUSETTS
State of Massachusetts-Bay. Town of the day of 1779 . . . agreeable to a resolve of the General court passed June 29, 1779. [Boston, 1779]
broadside 13 X 16.5 cm.
DLC mp. 43648

B4902 MASSACHUSETTS. CONSTITUTIONAL CONVENTION
The report of a constitution . . . agreed upon . . . to be laid before the convention . . . assembled at Cambridge . . . Boston, Benjamin Edes & Sons, 1779.
15 p. 22 cm.
cf. Evans 16352 ([50] p.)
DLC; MHi mp. 43649

B4903 MASSACHUSETTS. COUNCIL
By the Honourable the Council of the State of Massachusetts-Bay. A proclamation. Whereas the inveterate enemies of the United States of America have for some time past invaded the Eastern parts of this State . . . [Boston, 1779]
broadside 34.5 X 22 cm.
Dated Boston, Aug. 19, 1779
MB; MeHi mp. 43650

B4904 MASSACHUSETTS. HOUSE OF REPRESENTATIVES
In the House of Representatives, April 16, 1779. Resolved, That one regiment of light infantry be raised . . . [Boston, 1779]
broadside
Ford 2187
M-Ar mp. 43651

B4905 MASSACHUSETTS. HOUSE OF REPRESENTATIVES
State of Massachusetts-Bay. In the House of Representatives. June 9, 1779. Whereas a requisition . . . In Council, June 9, 1779 . . . [Boston, 1779]
[2] p. 50.5 X 38.5 cm.
On verso: The Schedule
Ford 2190
DLC; MHi; MWA mp. 43657

B4906 MASSACHUSETTS. HOUSE OF REPRESENTATIVES
State of Massachusetts-Bay. In the House of Representatives. June 18, 1779. Resolved, That the resolution of the 16th of April last . . . [Boston, 1779]
broadside
Ford 2193
MB mp. 43652

B4907 MASSACHUSETTS. HOUSE OF REPRESENTATIVES
State of Massachusetts-Bay. In the House of Representatives, June 29, 1779. Whereas it is of importance . . . [Boston, 1779]
broadside 25 X 20 cm.
Ford 2195
MHi. Photostat: DLC mp. 43653

B4908 MASSACHUSETTS. HOUSE OF REPRESENTATIVES
State of Massachusetts-Bay. In the House of Representatives, November 18, 1779. Resolved, That Capt. Ezra Lunt . . . [Boston, 1779]
broadside ([2] p.) 33 X 19.5 cm.
Ford 2202
MHi mp. 43654

B4909 MASSACHUSETTS. HOUSE OF REPRESENTATIVES
State of Massachusetts-Bay. To the selectmen of the Town of Boston. These are to will and require you . . . to . . . elect . . . a person . . . to serve . . . in the . . . General Court . . . Boston [Sept. 8, 1779] . . . John Hancock, Speaker. [Boston, 1779]
broadside
MB mp. 43655

B4910 MASSACHUSETTS. LAWS
State of Massachusetts-Bay . . . . An act to prevent sundry articles being exported . . . September 23, 1779 . . . [Boston, 1779]
broadside 24 X 15.5 cm.
Ford 2182
MHi. Photostat: DLC mp. 43656

B4911 MASSACHUSETTS. TREASURER
State of Massachusetts-Bay. The honorable Henry Gardner . . . Greeting . . . Boston, the thirteenth day of March . . . 1779. [Boston, 1779]
broadside 40 X 31.5 cm.
CSmH; MHi mp. 43658

B4912 MASSACHUSETTS. TREASURER
State of Massachusetts-Bay. The honorable Henry Gardner, Esq; treasurer . . . [April 15, 1779] [Boston, 1779]
broadside
Tax warrant
Ford 2203
MSaE mp. 43659

B4913 MASSACHUSETTS. TREASURER
State of Massachusetts-Bay. The honorable Henry Gardner, Esq; treasurer . . . [Sept. 15, 1779] [Boston, 1779]
broadside
Tax warrant
Ford 2204
MSaE mp. 43660

B4914 MASSACHUSETTS. TREASURER
State of Massachusetts-Bay. The honorable Henry Gardner . . . Greeting . . . Boston, the thirteenth day of December . . . 1779. [Boston, 1779]
broadside 39 X 30.5 cm.
Tax warrant
MHi mp. 43661

B4915 THE New-England primer improved . . . Boston, Printed and sold by N. Coverly, 1779.
[80] p. [A]-E^8
Heartman 56
MWHi mp. 43662

B4916 NEW HAMPSHIRE
State of New-Hampshire. The government and people . . . to the selectmen of in said state . . . By order of the Council and Assembly . . . Exeter, October 23, 1779. [Exeter, 1779]
broadside 33.5 X 21 cm.
Whittemore 262
NhHi mp. 43665

B4917 NEW HAMPSHIRE. COMMITTEE OF SAFETY
A list of the soldiers who have deserted from the three New-Hampshire battalions . . . State of New-Hampshire . . . Exeter, July 23, 1779 . . . M. Weare, president. [Exeter, 1779]
broadside
New York Public 702; Whittemore 257
MWA; NN (reduced facsim.) mp. 43664

B4918 NEW HAMPSHIRE. COMMITTEE OF SAFETY
State of New-Hampshire. In Committee of safety, Exeter, September 24th, 1779. Whereas General Washington lately wrote . . . [Exeter, 1779]
broadside 24.5 X 20 cm.
Concerns supplies for the army
Huntington 436
CSmH; NhD; NhHi mp. 43663

B4919 NEW HAMPSHIRE. HOUSE OF REPRESENTATIVES
. . . In the House of representatives, Nov. 8, 1779. Voted, that the proclamation for a general thanksgiving . . . be forthwith printed . . . [Exeter, 1779]
broadside 33 X 20.5 cm.
Huntington 437
CSmH mp. 43666

B4920 NEW HAMPSHIRE. LAWS
State of New-Hampshire. In the year . . . [1779] An act to prevent monopoly of corn . . . [Exeter? 1779]
broadside 34.5 X 21.5 cm.
Passed Apr. 3, 1779
Whittemore 259
MWA mp. 43667

B4921 NEW JERSEY
Gentlemen, the Legislative-Council and General assembly . . . beg leave to congratulate you . . . September 29, 1799 . . . [Trenton, 1779]
broadside 26 X 16.5 cm.
Humphrey 199; Huntington 438
CSmH mp. 43670

B4922 NEW JERSEY. LAWS
State of New-Jersey. An act for procuring provisions for the use of the army . . . and for settling the publick accounts . . . [Trenton, 1779?]
[2] p. 36 cm. caption title
"Passed at Mountholly, December 25, 1779."
Humphrey 195; New York Public 703
Ct. Photostats: MHi; NN; RPJCB
mp. 43668; 43849

B4923 NEW JERSEY. LAWS
State of New-Jersey. An act to procure a supply of flour for the use of the army . . . Caleb Camp, Speaker. Passed at Trenton, Sept. 27, 1779. [Trenton, 1779]
broadside 34.5 X 21 cm.
CtHi mp. 43669

B4924 A NEW touch on the times. Well adapted to the distressing situation of every sea-port town. By a Daughter of Liberty, living in Marblehead . . . [n.p., 1779]
broadside 32.5 X 21 cm.
NHi mp. 43671

B4925 NEW YORK. GOVERNOR, 1771-1780
By his Excellency William Tryon . . . Convinced by experience, of the beneficial tendency of the assurances, lately given . . . against the impressing of certain persons . . . [New York, 1779]
broadside 51 X 24 cm.
Dated at Kingsbridge Out-Post, Mar. 8, 1779
New York Public 704
Photostats: DLC; MH; NHi; NN mp. 43672

B4926 NEW YORK. SENATE
Votes and proceedings of the Senate . . . of New-York; at their third session, held at Kingston . . . Commencing, August 24, 1779. Fish-Kill, Samuel Loudon, 1779[-80]
107 p. 30.5 cm.
New York Public 705; Vail: Patriotic pair, p. 418
NHi; NIC; NN; NNS; PHi mp. 43673

B4927 NEW YORK (CITY) SUPERINTENDENT OF POLICE
By Andrew Elliot, Superintendent-General of the Police, Permission is given to Given under my hand, in the City of New-York, the day of in the nineteenth year of His Majesty's reign, 1779 . . . [New York, 1779]
broadside 15.5 X 13 cm.
Signed by Peter Dubois, for August 2
NNS

B4928 NEW-YORK, March 27, 1779. A list of the fortunate numbers in the . . . lottery, 1779 . . . [New York, H. Gaine, 1779]
broadside 37.5 X 23 cm.
Gaine p. 150
DLC (photostat) mp. 43674

B4929 THE New-York almanack, for . . . 1780 . . . By Isaac Bickerstaff . . . New-York, Printed and sold by Mills and Hicks [1779]
[24] p. 19.5 cm.
Guerra b-435; New York Public 691
NN mp. 43606

B4930 THE Newport Gazette: published weekly. Newport, John Howe [1779]
31.5 cm.
Brigham p. 995
DLC (photostat) mp. 43641

B4931 NORTH CAROLINA. HOUSE OF COMMONS
The journal of the House of Commons . . . At a General assembly, begun . . . the third day of May . . . 1779 . . . being the first session . . . [Newbern, James Davis, 1779]
33 p. 19.5 cm. caption title
McMurtrie: North Carolina 103
DLC mp. 43675

B4932 NORWICH, August 26. The following interesting intelligence, we received yesterday, by a gentleman . . . from Boston . . . Norwich, J. Trumbull [1779]
broadside 38 X 23.5 cm.
New York Public 706
MHi. Photostat: NN mp. 43676

B4933 ON friendship . . . [Hartford] Printed by Hudson & Goodwin [1779?]
broadside 32 X 23.5 cm.
Printers' names within elaborate printers' ornaments
Dated from ms. note: 1779 (in contemporary hand)
CtHi mp. 43677

B4934 ON this day of renown, All joys shower down . . . New-York, April 23, 1779. [New York, 1779]
broadside 25.5 X 22.5 cm.
NHi mp. 43678

B4935 PENNSYLVANIA. LAWS
An act to regulate the militia of the Commonwealth of Pennsylvania. Philadelphia, F. Bailey, 1779.
67 p. 8vo
PHi

B4936 PHILADELPHIA, July 23, 1779. To the public. Fortunately we have preserved . . . James Roney, Chairman. [Philadelphia, 1779]
broadside 32.5 X 20 cm.
DLC mp. 43680

B4937 THE Philadelphia almanack for the year 1780 . . . calculated for Pensilvania and its neighbouring states . . . [Philadelphia, Engraved by J. Norman, 1779]
[36] p. 15.5 cm.
Engraver noted on an inside page
Drake 10097
NjR

B4938 PHILADELPHIA almanack for the year . . . 1780 . . . [Philadelphia] Engraved printed and sold by Norman and Bedwell in Front Street [1779]
broadside 26.5 X 19.5 cm.
Drake 10098
NjR

B4939 PORTSMOUTH, N.H.
Regulation of sundry articles, at the town-meeting at Portsmouth, October 1st, 1779. [Portsmouth, 1779]
broadside 32.5 X 16 cm.
M-Ar. Photostats: DLC; MHi; NN mp. 43681

B4940 POUGHKEEPSIE, N.Y.
State of New-York. Instructions proposed for the consideration of the inhabitants of Poughkeepsie Precinct . . . [at end] Poughkeepsie, July 24th, 1779. [Poughkeepsie, John Holt, 1779]
broadside 31.5 X 21.5 cm.
Vail: Patriotic pair, p. 409
NHi mp. 43682

B4941 [POYDRAS, JULIEN] 1746-1824
La prise du morne du Baton Rouge par Monseigneur de Galvez . . . Nouvelle Orléans, Antoine Boudousquié, M.DCC.LXXIX.
[7] p. 22 cm.
McMurtrie: New Orleans 30; Stoddard 196
LNT mp. 43683

B4942 PROVIDENCE, R.I. COMMITTEE OF CORRESPONDENCE
Providence, July 26, 1779. Sir; By the annexed vote . . . Theodore Foster, Town-clerk. Providence, John Carter [1779]
broadside 27 X 20.5 cm.
Alden 772; Winship p. 39
DLC; NHi; RHi; RPJCB. Photostats: MWA; NN
mp. 43684

B4943 RHODE ISLAND. COUNCIL OF WAR
State of Rhode-Island and Providence Plantations. In Council of war, March 8, 1779. Resolved, That the following orders be given . . . Providence, John Carter [1779]
broadside 26 X 19.5 cm.
Alden 790; Winship p. 39
MWA; RHi mp. 43685

B4944 RHODE ISLAND. ELECTION PROX.
Freedom in elections! His Excellency William Greene, Esq; Governor. The honorable Jabez Bowen, Esq; Dep. Gov. . . . [Providence] Southwick and Wheeler [1779]
broadside 21 X 13 cm.
Alden 773; Chapin Proxies 23
RHi mp. 43686

B4945 RHODE ISLAND. ELECTION PROX.
His Excellency William Greene, Esq; Governor. The

honorable Jabez Bowen, Esq; Dep. Governor . . . [Providence] John Carter [1779]
broadside 20 X 13 cm.
Alden 774; Chapin Proxies 22
RHi mp. 43687

B4946 RHODE ISLAND. ELECTION PROX.
Let us and our constituents remain free from slavery. His Excellency William Greene, Esq; Governor . . . [Providence] John Carter [1779]
broadside 18.5 X 12.5 cm.
Alden 775; Chapin Proxies 21
RHi mp. 43688

B4947 RHODE ISLAND. GENERAL ASSEMBLY
[General assembly. March 20, 1779. Attack on Rhode Island. Providence, 1779]
[broadside?]
Alden 776; Winship Addenda p. 88
RHi (not traced) mp. 43689

B4948 RHODE ISLAND. GENERAL ASSEMBLY
State of Rhode-Island and Providence Plantations. In General assembly, May session, 1779. Whereas it is necessary . . . Providence, John Carter [1779]
broadside 27 X 21 cm.
Alden 793; Winship p. 39
MWA; RHi mp. 43693

B4949 RHODE ISLAND. GENERAL ASSEMBLY
State of Rhode-Island and Providence Plantations. In General assembly, August session, 1779 . . . Resolved, That the inlistments of the non-commissioned officers . . . [Providence, 1779]
broadside 13 X 19 cm.
Alden 797; Winship p. 40
DLC; MWA; RHi mp. 43697

B4950 RHODE ISLAND. GOVERNOR, 1778-1786
By his Excellency [William Greene] . . . Instructions to the commanders of private ships or vessels of war . . . authorising them to make captures of British vessels . . . [Providence, 1779?]
broadside 35 X 22.5 cm.
Governor's name in ms.; dated in ms. June 28, 1779
New York Public 709
RPJCB. Photostats: MWA; NN mp. 43690

B4951 RHODE ISLAND. LAWS
[An act to raise the sum of one hundred thousand pounds . . . Providence, John Carter, 1779]

The schedules for the September, 1779, session state "that the Secretary cause Copies of this Act to be transmitted to the several Town-Clerks . . . within two days . . ."
Alden 798; Winship p. 40
No copy known mp. 43691

B4952 RHODE ISLAND. LAWS
State of Rhode-Island and Providence Plantations. In General assembly, February session, 1779. An act for enforcing an act . . . obliging persons delinquent in military duty . . . Providence, John Carter [1779]
broadside 25 X 20.5 cm.
Alden 789
RPB mp. 43692

B4953 RHODE ISLAND. LAWS
State of Rhode-Island and Providence Plantations. In General assembly, June session, 1779. An act assessing . . . a tax of sixty thousand pounds . . . Providence, Southwick and Wheeler [1779]
broadside 38 X 26.5 cm.
Alden 794; Winship p. 40
RHi mp. 43694

B4954 RHODE ISLAND. LAWS
State of Rhode-Island and Providence Plantations. In General assembly, June session, 1779. An act assessing . . . a tax of two hundred and twenty-five thousand pounds . . . Providence, John Carter [1779]
broadside 43 X 17 cm.
Alden 795; Winship p. 40
RHi mp. 43695

B4955 RHODE ISLAND. LAWS
State of Rhode-Island and Providence Plantations. In General assembly, June session, 1779. An act for the better forming . . . the military force . . . Providence, John Carter [1779]
[2] p. 38 X 26 cm.
Text in 3 columns
Alden 796; Winship p. 40
R; RHi. Photostat: MWA mp. 43696

B4956 RHODE ISLAND. LAWS
State of Rhode-Island and Providence Plantations. In General Assembly, October session, 1779. An act for the better forming . . . the military force . . . [Providence] John Carter [1779]
2 p. 38 X 26 cm.
Text in 3 columns
Alden 800; Winship p. 40
DLC; RHi. Photostat: MWA mp. 43698

B4957 RHODE ISLAND. LAWS
State of Rhode Island and Providence Plantations. In General assembly, December session, 1779. An act establishing and regulating fees. [Providence, J. Carter, 1779]
8 p. 19 cm. caption title
Alden 801; Winship p. 40
RHi; RPB mp. 43699

B4958 RHODE ISLAND. LAWS
State of Rhode-Island and Providence Plantations. In General assembly, December session, A.D. 1779. An act for assessing . . . [Providence, 1779]
broadside 52.5 X 19 cm.
Alden 802; Winship p. 20
DLC; R; RHi mp. 43700

B4959 ROCKINGHAM, N.H.
State of New-Hampshire, Rockingham, ss. At a public town meeting . . . July 29th, 1779 . . . [n.p., 1779]
broadside 26.5 X 19.5 cm.
Whittemore 269
NhHi mp. 43701

B4960 THE salvation of American liberty. To the public. No period since the glorious . . . Revolution has been so alarming . . . New-York, May 15, 1779. A Son of Liberty. [New York, 1779]
broadside 39 X 24 cm.
NHi mp. 43702

B4961 SAVANNAH, GA. TOWN GUARD
The friends of constitutional liberty, who would wish for an opportunity of manifesting their loyalty to the King . . . John Milner, Maj: com. of the Savannah town guard. [Savannah, 1779]

broadside 16 X 20 cm.
PPRF mp. 43703

B4962 SOUTH CAROLINA. LAWS
An ordinance for printing . . . one million of dollars . . . Ratified by the General assembly . . . the eighth day of February, 1779 . . . [Charles-Town, P. Timothy, 1779]
1 p.l., 4 p. 29 cm.
Half-title only
Sabin 87629
DLC mp. 43705

B4963 SOUTH CAROLINA. LAWS
State of South Carolina. At the General Assembly begun . . . at Charlestown . . . the 4th day of January . . . 1779, and . . . continued . . . to the thirteenth day of February . . . 1779 . . . [Charles-Town, Peter Timothy, 1779]
4 p. fol.
Concerns regulation of the militia
Heartman: Cradle 441; Mosimann 338
CtY mp. 43706

B4964 TABLE of rates . . . The above rates to commence from the first of April next, and be charged to travellers and townsmen, if they bespeak a bed . . . Baltimore, March 30, 1779. Baltimore, M. K. Goddard [1779]
broadside 29.5 X 17 cm.
Wheeler 550
Henry A. Rowland collection mp. 43603

B4965 TO further in some degree, the service of our most gracious sovereign . . . the commander in chief has, at the request of . . . loyal refugees, permitted them to associate . . . and to retaliate upon . . . the inhabitants . . . Signed at Newport, the 30th of March, 1779 . . . [Newport? John Howe? 1779?]
broadside 38 X 28 cm.
Alden 763
Mrs. E. J. Guthrie Nicholson, Newport, R.I. Photostats: MWA; MiU-C; RHi; RPJCB mp. 43602

B4966 TO Robert Lemmon and Luther Martin . . . who have been stimulated . . . into a controversy . . . Cineas. Baltimore, Nov. 17, 1779. [Baltimore, 1779]
broadside
Wheeler 63
MdHi mp. 43708

B4967 TO the freemen of Pennsylvania. By the thirty-fifth section of the Constitution . . . the writer . . . takes the liberty of animadverting upon two acts of Assembly . . . for reverting the attainders of Reynold Keen and Albertson Walton . . . A Whig Citizen. [Philadelphia, John Dunlap, 1779]
broadside 44.5 X 34 cm.
Taylor 208
PHi mp. 43709

B4968 U.S. ARMY. CONTINENTAL ARMY
. . . An estimate of the average prices of the different articles of cloathing allowed the soldiery . . . [Nov. 16, 1779] . . . Philadelphia, James Hayes, Jun. [1779]
broadside 30 X 16.5 cm.
Huntington 440; Taylor 216
CSmH mp. 43710

B4969 U.S. BOARD OF TREASURY
Instructions from the Board of treasury to the respective commissioners . . . January 12, 1779 . . . [Philadelphia, 1779]
broadside 33 X 20.5 cm.
Ford: Bibliographical notes 240
DLC; NN mp. 43711

B4970 U.S. CONTINENTAL CONGRESS, 1778
In Congress, August 14, 1778. Resolved, That the resolution . . . of the 9th of June last, authorizing the Deputy-Director-General . . . to superintend the medical affairs . . . be repealed . . . Extract from the minutes, Charles Thomson, Secretary. [Philadelphia] Hall and Sellers, 1779.
broadside
Austin 1958
NNNAM mp. 43713

B4971 U.S. CONTINENTAL CONGRESS, 1779
A circular letter from the Congress . . . to their constituents . . . Philadelphia, John Dunlap [1779]
12 p. 20.5 cm.
Signed: Philadelphia, Sept. 13, 1779
cf. Evans 16558
MHi; MiU-C mp. 43712

B4972 U.S. CONTINENTAL CONGRESS, 1779
In Congress, March 16, 1779. Whereas discontent, loss of discipline, and diminution . . . [Philadelphia] Hall and Sellers [1779]
broadside 26.5 X 21 cm.
MHi mp. 43716

B4973 U.S. CONTINENTAL CONGRESS, 1779
In Congress, August 16, 1779. Resolved, That the cloathier general estimate . . . Philadelphia, David C. Claypoole [1779]
broadside 32.5 X 20.5 cm.
CtHi; DLC; NjR mp. 43714

B4974 U.S. CONTINENTAL CONGRESS, 1779
In Congress, Friday, June 11, 1779. Resolved, That twenty millions of dollars . . . be borrowed . . . Notice is hereby given that . . . the following . . . are duly authorized . . . to receive subscriptions . . . James Booth, secretary. Wilmington, James Adams [1779]
broadside 33.5 X 21 cm.
Hawkins: List C9
DLC mp. 43715

B4975 U.S. CONTINENTAL CONGRESS, 1779
Supplement to the *Maryland Gazette* . . . June 4, 1779. To the inhabitants of the United States of America . . . [May 26, 1779] . . . [Annapolis, F. and S. Green, 1779]
[2] p. fol.
Huntington 441; cf. Wheeler 61
CSmH mp. 43717

B4976 U.S. CONTINENTAL CONGRESS, 1779
To the inhabitants of the United States . . . The present situation . . . demands . . . attention . . . John Jay, President . . . Annapolis, Frederick and Samuel Green [1779]
broadside 30.5 X 18.5 cm.
Wheeler 61
MdAA mp. 43718

B4977 U.S. INSPECTOR-GENERAL'S OFFICE
Regulations for the order and discipline of the troops of the United States. Part I. Hartford, Nathaniel Patten [1779]
107, [1] p. 8 fold. plates. 16mo
cf. Evans 16628
DLC

B4978 U.S. TREASURY OFFICE
Treasury-Office, March 12, 1779. Ordered, That the several commissioners . . . make return . . . the first of June next, of . . . the counterfeit bills . . . destroyed. Extract from the minutes, [Philadelphia, 1779]
broadside 33 X 20.5 cm.
CtHi mp. 43719

B4979 U.S. TREASURY OFFICE
Treasury-Office, Philadelphia, February 5, 1779. Sir, I am directed by the Board of Treasury to inform you, that Congress have ordered a supply of Loan-Office Certificates to be forthwith struck . . . To the Commissioner of the Continental Loan-Office in the State of [Philadelphia, 1779]
broadside 33 X 20.5 cm.
CtHi mp. 43720

B4980 THE United States almanack, for the year . . . 1780 . . . Chatham, Printed and sold by Shepard Kollock [1779]
[32] p. 16 cm.
Drake 5118; Humphrey 211
MWA ([28] p.); NjHi; NjR mp. 43721

B4981 VARNUM, JAMES MITCHELL, 1748-1789
An oration: delivered before a lodge of . . . Masons . . . the twenty-eighth day of December, 1778 . . . Providence, John Carter [1779]
11 p. 18 cm.
Advertised Jan. 9, 1779, as "Just published."
Alden 805; Sabin 98640; Winship p. 39
MBFM; MWA; PPFM; RHi; RPJCB mp. 43722

B4982 VERMONT
[Scheme of a lottery. Dresden, J. P. & A. Spooner, 1779]

Printer's bill for 50 copies dated Apr. 15, 1779
McCorison 18
No copy known mp. 43726

B4983 VERMONT. CONVENTION, 1778
To the inhabitants of the town of on the New-Hampshire Grants. The committee appointed by the convention held at Cornish . . . Dresden, April 23d, 1779 . . . Dresden, 1779]
broadside 34.5 X 21 cm.
McCorison 22; Sabin 99003
DLC; NhPlain. Photostats: MWA; VtU-W mp. 43723

B4984 VERMONT. GENERAL ASSEMBLY
[Letters. Dresden, J. P. & A. Spooner, 1779]

Printer's bill for 150 copies dated Mar. 5, 1779
McCorison 20
No copy known mp. 43724

B4985 VERMONT. GENERAL ASSEMBLY
[Votes of Assembly. Dresden, 1779]

Whittemore 283
No copy known mp. 43727

B4986 VERMONT. GOVERNOR, 1779-1781
[Proclamation for a general fast day, April 1779. Dresden, 1779]
broadside?
70 copies printed
McCorison 25; Whittemore 281
No copy known mp. 43725

B4987 VIRGINIA. GOVERNOR, 1776-1779
Williamsburg, April 12, 1779. Sir, The season is now come when the enemy will take the field, and perhaps . . . overrun and ravage a great extent of country . . . [signed in ms.] P[atrick] He[nry]. [Williamsburg, A. Purdie, 1779]
broadside 24 X 19.5 cm.
MHi mp. 43588

B4988 VIRGINIA. GOVERNOR, 1779-1781
Port To all the faithful in Christ . . . I Thomas Jefferson . . . greet you well . . . Seeing the good called the now at Norfolk . . . is now ready to sail . . . for and other foreign ports . . . One Thousand Seven Hundred and Seventy Nine . . . [Williamsburg, 1779]
broadside 19.5 X 15.5 cm.
DLC

B4989 VIRGINIA. GOVERNOR, 1779-1781
Williamsburg, June 18, 1779. Sir, You are desired to give notice to such recruits . . . as may not yet have marched from your county . . . [signed in ms.] Th. Jefferson. [Williamsburg, 1779]
broadside 19 X 10 cm.
WHi mp. 43728

B4990 VIRGINIA. LAWS
A bill, entitled, An act for the relief of certain nonjurors . . . By the House of Delegates, March 22, 1779: . . . "By order, J. Duckett, cl. H. Del." [Williamsburg, John Dixon and Thomas Nicolson, 1779]
2 p.
PPL mp. 43729

B4991 VIRGINIA. WAR OFFICE
War Office (Williamsburg) August 17, 1779. Sir, It is a matter of no small moment to the salvation of this country . . . [Williamsburg, 1779]
broadside 23.5 X 21.5 cm.
NHi mp. 43730

B4992 WETENHALL, EDWARD, 1636-1713
A short introduction to grammar . . . being a new edition of Whittenhall's Latin grammar . . . The third edition. Philadelphia, Joseph Crukshank, 1779.
v, 145 p. 15.5 cm.
Taylor 243
DLC; PU mp. 43731

B4993 [WHARTON, SAMUEL] 1732-1800
View of the title to Indiana, a tract of country on the River Ohio, containing Indian conferences . . . in May, 1765; the deed of the Six Nations to the proprietors of Indiana . . . Williamsburg, J. Dixon & T. Nicolson, 1779.
8 p.
Sabin 99584
RPJCB mp. 43732

B4994 WHEATLEY, PHYLLIS, 1754-1784
[Poems. 1st American ed. Albany, 1779]

Title from N. R. Campbell & Co. catalogue (summer 1929) p. 22, described as "on vellum and possibly unique."
McMurtrie: Albany 10
No copy located mp. 43733

B4995 [WOOD, SAMUEL] 1752-1836
An oration on early education . . . Dresden, Alden Spooner, 1779.
14 p. 15.5 cm.
On original ms. (NhHi) in hand of John Farmer: By Samuel Wood

New York Public 711; Whittemore 284
MWA; NHD; OC. Photostat: NN mp. 43734

B4996 WOODRUFF, HEZEKIAH S 1754-1844
To the publick . . . Were all men faithful in discharging their duties . . . [Trenton, Isaac Collins, 1779]
broadside 35 cm.
Reply to Dr. Aaron Craig's accusation that Joseph Costner died because of Woodruff's medications. Testimonials dated Dec. 29 and 31, 1778
Guerra a-662
NNNAM; NjR mp. 43735

B4997 WORCESTER, MASS. CONVENTION, 1779
Proceedings of the convention, began and held at Worcester . . . the 3d day of August, 1779 . . . [Worcester, 1779]
broadside 41.5 X 33 cm.
Ford 2210; New York Public 712
MWA. Photostats: DLC; MHi; NN mp. 43736

B4998 YORK, 18th June, 1779. A meeting of the inhabitants of this town . . . for putting a stop to . . . the depreciation of the Continental currency, it was agreed . . . to draw up resolves . . . Lancaster, Francis Bailey [1779]
[4] p. 31.5 cm.
Taylor 247
NHi mp. 43737

B4999 YOUNG, ROBERT, d. 1779
The dying criminal: poem, by Robert Young, on his own execution, which is to be on this day, November 11th, 1779, for rape . . . at Brookfield, in the County of Worcester . . . [Worcester, Isaiah Thomas, 1779]
broadside 37 X 20.5 cm.
Ford 2211; New York Pub. 713; Sabin 106090
NHi (mutilated). Photostats: MWA; NN mp. 43738

B5000 YOUNG, ROBERT, d. 1779
The dying criminal: a poem. By Robert Young, on his own execution . . . Thursday last, November 11th, 1779, for a rape . . . at Brookfield, in the County of Worcester . . . Sold at the Printing-Office, New-London [1779]
broadside 24 X 37 cm.
Huntington 443
CSmH; RPB. Photostats: MHi; MWA mp. 43739

178–

B5001 THE above mentioned having signed a parole . . . has permission to pass from hence to Elizabeth-Town, in New-Jersey, and . . . by flag, to New-York . . . Given under my hand at Philadelphia, this day of 178 [Philadelphia? 178-]
broadside 7.5 X 16 cm.
Taylor 430
PHi

B5002 AN account of the wonderful old hermit's death, and burial. Sometime in June, 1786 . . . Doctor Samuel Brake . . . [n.p., 178-?]
broadside 36.5 X 30.5 cm.
Colored woodcut
cf. Ford 2458, with note
MWA mp. 43740

B5003 ADVERTISEMENT! To the several printers in Hartford, New-Haven, New-London and Norwich. Pray print the following immediately! . . . March 19. Sancho Panca . . . [n.p., 178-?]
broadside 25 X 20 cm.
CtHi; PPRF mp. 43750

B5003a [CHANDLER, DAVID]
. . . Verses composed on the burning of the meeting-house in Elizabeth Town by the enemy; the 25th of January . . . 1780 . . . [n.p., 178-?]
8 p. 18.5 cm. caption title
Includes: On the sudden death of the Rev. Mr. James Caldwell . . .
Stoddard 44
NjMo

B5004 [CLARKE, SAMUEL] 1721?-
The strange and remarkable Swansey vision . . . Boston, Sold at the Bible and Heart [178-?]
4 p. sm. 8vo
Huntington 579; cf. Evans 14680
CSmH mp. 43741

B5005 CONSTANT Charley: together with the Banks of the Dee, and The Answer . . . [Boston] Sold [by Thomas Fleet] at the Bible and Heart [178-]
broadside
Three poems in 2 columns
Adams: Pennsylvania 39
PU

B5006 DEATH and the lady . . . Philadelphia, for Henry Green [178-?]
4 leaves. 12mo
In verse
On t.p. autograph signature of Adam Boyd, 1790
Rosenbach-Ch 146
A. S. W. Rosenbach (1933) mp. 43742

B5007 AN elegy on the death of . . . Alexander Scammel, who was killed at the taking of Lord Corn Wallis . . . [Portsmouth, N.H.? 178-?]
broadside 24 X 18 cm.
MB mp. 43743

B5008 ESSENTIA amara. Diese bittere Magen-Essens, ist in Verschleimung des Magens und der Gedärme eine bewährte Medicin . . . [Philadelphia? 178-?]
broadside
Dated ca. 1780 by Edwin Wolf 2d
PPL mp. 43744

B5009 [FRENEAU, PHILIP MORIN] 1752-1832
Description of the sufferings of those who were on board the Jersey . . . in the harbour of New-York . . . [n.p., 178-?]
broadside 45 X 26.5 cm.
Huntington 576
CSmH mp. 43745

B5010 GAIFER
The conversion of a Mehometan . . . described in a letter from Gaifer . . . to Aly-Ben-Hayton . . . The sixteenth edition. Hartford, B. Webster [178-?]
20+ p.
Trumbull: Supplement 2020
CtHi mp. 43746

B5011 INGRAHAM, DUNCAN, JR.
Price current at Philadelphia . . . Philadelphia, 178 . Duncan Ingraham, junr. [Philadelphia, 178-]
broadside 23 X 19.5 cm.
Text in 2 columns. Duties on imports at bottom in single column

Filled in for Feb. 8, 1785
RPJCB

B5012 A JOURNAL of the practice of medicine, surgery, and pharmacy in the military hospitals of France . . . Reviewed and digested by M. de Horne . . . Translated from the Frency by Joseph Browne. Volume I. New-York, J. M'Lean [178–?]
120 p. 19 cm.
Rogers 188
DNLM; NNNAM (photostat of t.p.) mp. 43747

B5013 LUSHINGTON AND KIRK, firm, Charleston, S.C.
Price current, from Lushington and Kirk. Charlestown, South Carolina 178 [Charleston, 178-]
broadside 24 X 20 cm.
Text in 2 columns
Filled in for 4 mo. 5th, 1786
RPJCB

B5014 MASSACHUSETTS. TREASURER
Commonwealth of Massachusetts. Thomas Ivers . . . to the sheriff of the county of . . . greeting . . . Given . . . this *6th* day of *January* one thousand seven hundred and eighty *six* . . . [n.p., 178-]
broadside 32.5 X 20.5 cm.
Italicized portions in ms.
MiU-C

B5015 MIDDLESEX CO., MASS.
You of in the county of Middlesex, are permitted to sell . . . Given under my hand, this day of 178 . . . You cannot purchase above ten gallons of liquors . . . [n.p., 178-]
broadside 15.5 X 19.5 cm.
Dated in manuscript: Jan. 1789
DLC

B5016 THE most delightful history of the King and the Cobler . . . Boston, Printed and sold at the Bible & Heart in Cornhill [178-]
16 p. 17.5 cm.
Hamilton 48
NjP. Photostat: MWA (t.p. only) mp. 43748

B5017 THE New-England primer (enlarged and much improved) for the more easy attaining the true reading of English . . . Philadelphia, W. Spotswood, and T. Seddon [178-]
[80] p. 16mo
PPL mp. 43749

B5018 PENNSYLVANIA. SUPREME EXECUTIVE COUNCIL
For £ In Council. Philadelphia, 178
Sir, Pay to . . . [Philadelphia, 178-]
broadside 17 X 20 cm.
Dated in manuscript: November 1, 1787
DLC; MiU-C

B5019 PRICE current Boston, 178 [Boston? 178-]
broadside 23.5 X 19 cm.
Text in 3 columns
Filled in for May 29, 1786
RPJCB

B5020 PRICE current. Dollars Rials . . . N.B. 7 rials is a dollar, and an arobe 27 lb. Havana, 178 [Salem? 178-]
broadside 25.5 X 10.5 cm.
Filled in for Jan. 23, 1783; filed with a letter from Joseph and Joshua Grafton to Mr. Joshua Huntington dated "Salem 12th March '83," beginning "Permit us to transmit you the enclos'd Price Current."
MHi

B5021 PRICE current Philadelphia, 178
[Philadelphia, 178-]
broadside 23 X 19 cm.
Text in three columns
Filled in for June 29, 1785, on earliest RPJCB copy
RPJCB (6 copies)

B5022 PRICES current:—Charleston, 178
[Charleston? 178-]
broadside 14.5 X 17 cm.
Text in 2 columns
Filled in for June 29, 1789
RPJCB

B5023 PRICES current, in Baltimore [at top]
Baltimore, William Goddard [178-]
broadside 39 X 23.5 cm.
Text in 3 columns
Filled in for Jan. 1, 1785
Signed: Sam & Thos Blanchard
RPJCB

B5024 THE prodigal daughter . . . Boston, Printed and sold [by T. and J. Fleet] at the Bible and Heart [178–?]
16 p. 19.5 cm. [A]-B^4
MWA mp. 43751

B5025 PROVIDENCE, R. I.
State of Rhode-Island, and Providence-Plantations. Providence, sc. The Town-Council of . . . Providence . . . Whereas of said Providence, hath requested a licence to keep a tavern . . . Given at a Town-Council . . . on the day of A.D. 178 [Providence, 178-]
broadside 32.5 X 18.5 cm.
RPJCB. Photostat: MWA

B5026 RELLY, JAMES, 1722?-1778
Union: or, a treatise of the consanguinity and affinity . . . Boston, Printed by Edes for Benjamin Larkin [178-?]
xxxiv, 174 p. 17 cm.
DLC; MHi mp. 43752

B5027 RHODE ISLAND
State of Rhode-Island and Providence Plantations. In conformity to an act . . . passed . . . 1776 . . . maketh oath, That the of which is at present master . . . the sole owner thereof . . . Given . . . this day of in the year . . . One Thousand Seven Hundred and Eighty and in the year of independence. [Providence, 178-]
broadside 34 X 20.5 cm.
RPJCB. Photostat: MWA

B5028 SWETLAND, LUKE, 1729-1823
A very remarkable narrative of Luke Swetland . . . taken captive four times in . . . fifteen months . . . Written by himself. Hartford, Printed for the author [178-]
16 p. 18 cm.
Trumbull: Supplement 2661; Vail: Old frontier 739
CtY. Photostats: CtHi; MWA mp. 43753

B5029 TEALL, BENJAMIN
Benjamin Teall's Discourse, to his scholars, after catechising . . . New-Haven, T. and S. Green [178-?]
12 p.
Trumbull: Supplement 2666
CtHi mp. 43754

B5030 TO Esquire, Receiver of Continental taxes for the state of At sight pay to Esquire, Treasurer of the United States . . . Given under my hand and the seal of the Treasury . . . 178 [n.p., 178-]
broadside 34 X 21 cm.
Filled in for Sept. 13, 1787, for New-Hampshire
CtHi

B5031 TOM Thumb's folio, for little giants . . . Boston, Sold [by T. and J. Fleet] at the Bible and Heart [178-?]
32 p. illus. 10 cm.
Thomas and John Fleet were at The Bible and Heart 1780-1795
Rosenbach-Ch 91
CtHi; MWA (poor); PP mp. 43755

B5032 TURNER, JOHN, & CO.
European and Indian goods, by John Turner, jun. and Co. Who have imported in the last vessels from . . . E[ngland,] Scotland, Ireland, France and Holland . . . the following articles in great variety . . . [New York] Printed by Morton and Horner, No. 22, Water-St. [178-]
broadside 41.5 X 25.5 cm.
Morton and Horner in partnership 1782-1785
NHi mp. 43756

B5033 EINE wahre und approbirte Kunst in Feuers-Brünsten und Pestilentz-Zeit nützlich zu gebrauchen. [n.p., 178-]
broadside
PPL mp. 43757

B5034 WATERHOUSE, BENJAMIN, 1754-1846
Heads of a course of lectures intended as an introduction to natural history. By B. Waterhouse . . . Providence, Bennett Wheeler [178-?]
broadside
Rogers 204
MH (dated 1794 in ms.). Photostat: PPC mp. 43758

B5035 THE young man's dream: together with The young maiden's dream, and A damsel's moan for her dear Jemmy. Sold at the Bible and Heart in Cornhill, Boston. [178-?]
broadside 35 X 21 cm.
New York Public 735
NN mp. 43759

1780

B5036 ACCOUNT of the siege of Savannah; chiefly extracted from the *Royal Georgia Gazette*. Savannah, James Johnston, 1780.
8 p. 18.5 cm.
De Renne p. 220
GU-De mp. 43760

B5037 DER allerneuste, verbesserte- und zuverläszige Americanische . . . Calender, auf das Jahr . . . 1781 . . . Friedrich-Stadt, Gedruckt und zu finden bey Matthias Bartgis [1780]
[24] p. 21 cm.
Cover title: Marylandischer calender auf das jahr 1781
Drake 2186; Wheeler 105
Booksellers in seven other towns listed
DLC ([22] p.); N ([22] p.) mp. 43761

B5038 [ALMANACK for 1781. By John Anderson. Newport, Southwick & Barber, 1780]
[24] p. 18 cm.
Alden 809; Chapin p. 39; Winship p. 40
RNHi (t.p. lacking) mp. 43762

B5039 ANNAPOLIS-ROYAL. [n.p., 1780?]
7 p. 18.5 cm. caption title
In verse
New York Public 714; Sabin 99539
MB. Photostat: NN mp. 43763

B5040 [AN astronomical diary; or almanack, for the year . . . 1781. By Daniel Sewall. Portsmouth, 1780]

Advertised in the Portsmouth *Gazette*, November 1780
Nichols p. 87
No copy known mp. 43894

B5041 ASSOCIATED LOYALISTS
Articles of the Associated Loyalists . . . His Majesty . . . pleased to approve of a plan for . . . employing the zeal of his faithful subjects . . . [n.p., 1780?]
broadside 38 X 22.5 cm.
New York Public 715
MHi. Photostats: MWA; NN mp. 43764

B5042 AUCKLAND, WILLIAM EDEN, BARON, 1774-1814
Four letters to the Earl of Carlisle, from William Eden . . . The third edition. New-York, James Rivington, 1780.
122 p. 15 cm.
DLC mp. 43765

B5043 [BACKUS, ISAAC] 1724-1806
An appeal to the people of the Massachusetts State against arbitrary power . . . Boston, Printed and sold by Benjamin Edes and Sons; sold also by Philip Freeman, 1780.
8 p. 20 cm.
New York Public 716
MHi; NN; PPAmP; RPJCB mp. 43766

B5044 BARBER, HENRY
Newport, October 30, 1780. Just published, and now selling, by Henry Barber . . . the North-American calendar . . . for the year . . . 1781 . . . By Benjamin West . . . [Newport, Henry Barber, 1780]
broadside 35 X 22.5 cm.
Alden 816; Winship Addenda p. 89
RHi. Photostats: DLC; ICN; MHi; MWA mp. 43767

B5045 BARKLEY, ANDREW
Blonde, New-York, August 10, 1780. Admiral Arbuthnot, having signified to me his desire to engage seamen . . . A rendezvous will be opened . . . at the house of John Aymer . . . Andrew Barkley. [n.p., 1780]
broadside 19 X 20 cm.
DLC mp. 43768

B5046 BEVERLY, JOHN
Two hundred silver dollars reward . . . Broke gaol, this evening, George Howell . . . John Beverly, Sheriff. Providence, Nov. 19, 1780. Providence, John Carter [1780]
broadside 15.5 X 4.5 cm.
Alden 817; Winship p. 42
RPB mp. 43870

B5047 BIBLE. N.T.
The New Testament . . . Boston, Thomas & John Fleet, 1780.
[397] p. 17 cm. A-Z^8 Aa-Bb^8 (Bb8 blank)
MB (Bb8 wanting) mp. 43769

B5048 BIBLE. N.T. GOSPELS
The New Testament . . . Philadelphia, Printed and sold by Francis Bailey, 1780.

161 p. 16 cm.
Contains the Gospels only
New York Public 717
NN mp. 43770

B5049 [BICKERSTAFF'S New-England almanack for 1781. Hartford, Sold by Nathaniel Patten, 1780]

Advertised in the *Connecticut Courant*, Oct. 10, 1780, as "Just printed, and to be sold, wholesale or retail, by Nathaniel Patten, book-binder . . . Hartford."
Drake 333
No copy known

B5050 BOSTON
Boston, December 15, 1780. At a legal meeting of the inhabitants . . . of Boston, on the 13th instant, —— it was voted, That a committee of three . . . [Boston, 1780]
broadside 11 X 22 cm.
Ford 2219
MHi mp. 43772

B5051 BOSTON
Notification. The freeholders and other inhabitants of the Town of Boston, qualified as the law directs, are hereby notified to meet . . . the 13th day of March current . . . March 8th, 1780. [Boston, 1780]
broadside 13 X 17.5 cm.
Ford 2218
MHi mp. 43773

B5052 BOSTON
Notification. The male inhabitants of the Town of Boston, of the age of twenty-one years and upwards, are hereby notified to meet at Faneuil-Hall . . . the 3d day of May next . . . Boston, April 24, 1780. [Boston, 1780]
broadside 12 X 18 cm.
MHi (photostat) mp. 43774

B5053 BOSTON
To Your state tax, in gold or silver. Your town tax, in Continental currency . . . Boston, July 1780. [Boston, 1780]
broadside
Ford 2217
MHi

B5054 BOSTON
To Your state tax. Your town and county tax. Errors excepted. *Josiah Torrey* Collector. Boston, July 1780. [Boston, 1780]
broadside 13 X 16 cm.
Portion italicized in ms.
Ford 2116
MHi

B5055 BOSTON. TREASURER
Boston, 1780. I promise to pay to or order pounds out of the next tax . . . Town-Treasurer. [Boston, 1780]
broadside 8 X 16.5 cm.
Printed form filled out in ms., to supply £200,000 "for . . . carrying on the war."
MB

B5056 BOSTON. TREASURER
Boston, 1780. In pursuance of a vote of the town, passed the 16th of October, 1780, borrowed and received of the sum of of the new emission . . . which sum I promise to repay . . . in three months . . . Town Treasurer. [Boston, 1780]
broadside 14 X 18 cm.
MWA mp. 43775

B5057 CHAMBERLAIN, THOMAS, d. 1784
The minister preaching his own funeral sermon. Hartford, Printed and sold [by Hudson & Goodwin, 1780?]
14 p.
Trumbull: Supplement 1965
Ct mp. 43776

B5058 CHESTER the 7th day of April, 1780. "D. Sir, At a meeting . . . to consider the necessary steps preparitory to the next election . . ." [n.p., 1780]
broadside 16 X 14.5 cm.
NHi mp. 43777

B5059 COCK Robin's death and funeral. Boston [1780]
32 p. 9.5 cm.
DLC; MWA (p. 29-30 wanting; t.p. and p. 2 photocopy) mp. 43778

B5060 COMPOSED by a British officer.
Hail, sovereign love, that first began,
The scheme to rescue fallen man! [Boston? 1780?]
broadside
Ford 2227
MWA mp. 43779

B5061 CONNECTICUT
At a meeting of the Governor and Council, convened at Hartford, the second day of November . . . 1780. Whereas Gideon Comas, Elijah Wimpty, and others . . . Resolved that the memorialists have liberty . . . to ask the charitable contributions . . . William Pitkin, Clerk. [Hartford, 1780]
broadside 33 X 19.5 cm.
CtHi mp. 43781

B5062 CONNECTICUT. GENERAL ASSEMBLY
At a General Assembly . . . holden . . . on the second Thursday of May . . . 1780. Whereas it is necessary that the two regiments ordered to be raised . . . be immediately compleated . . . [Hartford, 1780]
broadside 31 X 20 cm.
CtHi (mutilated) mp. 43783

B5063 CONNECTICUT. GENERAL ASSEMBLY
At a General assembly . . . holden . . . on the second Thursday of October, 1780. Resolved . . . That the several towns . . . Hartford, Hudson and Goodwin [1780]
broadside 32 X 19 cm.
Attached, as issued, to Evans 16741
DLC mp. 43788

B5064 CONNECTICUT. GENERAL ASSEMBLY
At a General Assembly of the Governor and Company . . . of Connecticut, holden at Hartford . . . November . . . 1780. Resolved . . . That for the defence of the posts of Horseneck . . . Hartford, Hudson & Goodwin [1780]
broadside 34 X 21 cm.
CtHi mp. 43789

B5065 CONNECTICUT. GOVERNOR, 1776-1784
By . . . Jonathan Trumbull . . . a proclamation . . . [Aug. 25, 1780] . . . New-London, Timothy Green [1780]
broadside 37 X 23.5 cm.
Huntington 446; New York Public 718
CSmH; MHi; MWA; NN (reduced facsim.); NhHi mp. 43782

B5066 CONNECTICUT. LAWS
At a General Assembly of the Governor and Company . . . of Connecticut holden at Hartford . . . April . . . 1780. An act for the establishment of public credit . . . [Hartford? 1780]
2 p. 37 cm.
CtHi (mutilated) mp. 43783

B5066a CONNECTICUT. LAWS
At a General Assembly of the Governor and Company . . . of Connecticut, holden at Hartford . . . May, 1780. An act for filling up the Connecticut battalions in the Continental Army . . . [Hartford, 1780]
broadside 33.5 X 21.5 cm.
CtHi; CtY. Middendorf Collection, New York City (1970)

B5067 CONNECTICUT. LAWS
At a General assembly . . . holden . . . on the second Thursday of October, 1780. An act for collecting and storing a quantity of provisions . . . Hartford, Hudson and Goodwin [1780]
broadside 30 X 18.5 cm.
CtHi; DLC; MHi mp. 43785

B5068 CONNECTICUT. LAWS
At a General assembly . . . holden . . . on the second Thursday of October, 1780. An act for suppling [sic] the Treasury . . . Hartford, Hudson and Goodwin [1780]
broadside 33 X 20.5 cm.
Huntington 445
CSmH; MHi mp. 43786

B5069 CONNECTICUT. LAWS
At a General Assembly . . . holden . . . on the second Thursday of October, A.D. 1780. An act to ascertain the current value of continental bills of credit . . . [Hartford, 1780]
broadside 33.5 X 20 cm.
New York Public 719
CtHi; NN mp. 43787

B5070 CONNECTICUT. TREASURER
State of Connecticut, in America. To constable of and collector of the state tax for said town, for . . . 1780, Greeting . . . Dated at Hartford, the 21st day of June . . . 1780. Treasurer . . . [Hartford, 1780]
broadside 34 X 21 cm.
MWA; NHi mp. 43790

B5071 [COZINE, JOHN]
Dick Twiss, a poem . . . [New York? 17801]
8 p. 20 cm.
Sabin 17320
NHi mp. 43791

B5072 D., T. C.
Remarks on a law of Maryland enacted in July, 1779. [n. p., 1780]
9 p. 8vo caption title
Dated by Edwin Wolf 2d
PHi

B5073 DAVENPORT, BARNETT, 1760-1780
A brief narrative of the life and confession . . . [at end] Barnet Davenport. Litchfield Goal April 29th, 1780. [Hartford? 1780?]
14 p. 20 cm.
MWA (lacks imprint and very poor) mp. 43792

B5074 [DEFOE, DANIEL] 1661-1731
The life, death & misfortunes of the famous Moll Flanders . . . Written from her own memorandums . . . [Boston] Printed and sold at the printing-office in Marlborough-Street [1780?]
8 p. 16 cm.
MB

B5075 DELAWARE. HOUSE OF ASSEMBLY
[Votes and proceedings of the House of Assembly . . . (Oct. 20, 1779-June 21, 1780) Wilmington, James Adams, 1780.]
149 p. fol.
Title supplied by Edwin Wolf 2d
PHi (t.p. lacking)

B5076 DELAWARE. LAWS
Acts of the General assembly . . . at a session begun at Dover on the twentieth day of October 1779 . . . Being their fourth session. Wilmington, James Adams, 1780.
67 p. 29 cm.
Includes Evans 16757, 16758
Hawkins 14
MdBP; NNB; PPL mp. 43793

B5077 DILWORTH, THOMAS, d. 1780
A new guide to the English tongue . . . Boston, Printed for John Boyle, 1780.
144 p. 18.5 cm. $A\text{-}M^6$
MWA mp. 43794

B5078 DORCHESTER, MASS.
Your state tax 1780. [Boston, 1780]
broadside
Ford 2223
MHi

B5079 DORCHESTER, MASS.
Your state tax, 1780. Your county and town rate. 1780. [Boston, 1780]
broadside
Ford 2224
MHi

B5080 DORCHESTER, MASS.
Your state tax, 1780. Your town rate, 1780. [Boston, 1780]
broadside
Ford 2225
MHi

B5081 DORCHESTER, MASS.
Your state tax, 1780. To be paid in specie or grain, &c. Your town rate, 1780. Payable in the currency of the United States of America. [Boston, 1780]
broadside
Ford 2226
MHi

B5082 AN elegy upon the death of several worthy pious persons. [n.p., 1780?]
broadside 24 X 13 cm.
Ford 2228; New York Public 720
NN (photostat) mp. 43795

B5083 AN extaact [sic] of a letter from an officer of the 71st regiment . . . [n.p., 1780]
broadside 31 X 21 cm.
Dated in manuscript: June 20th 1780
DLC mp. 43796

B5084 THE famous and remarkable history of Sir Richard Whittington . . . Sold at the Bible and Heart in Cornhill, Boston, [ca. 1780]
16 p. illus. 15.5 cm.
Wm. M. Fitzhugh, Jr., Pebble Beach, Cal. (1964)
mp. 43917

B5085 A FEW lines composed on the Dark Day, May 19, 1780. [n.p., 1780?]
broadside 26 X 17 cm.
New York Public 721; *not* Ford 2268
MWA. Photostat: NN mp. 43798

B5086 A FEW lines composed on the Dark Day of May 19, 1780. [n.p., 1780]

broadside 33 X 19 cm.
Woodcut in upper left; 22 verses, unnumbered
MWA mp. 43799

B5087 A FEW lines composed on the Dark Day, of May 19, 1780. [n.p., 1780]
broadside 35 X 21.5 cm.
Verses numbered I. to XXII.
Ford 2268
MB; MWA; NHi. Photostat: MHi mp. 43800

B5088 FISHER, JOHN, of Lancaster, Pa.
John Fisher, brush-maker, at the Sign of the Seven Brushes . . . An apprentice lad to the said trade . . . is wanted . . . Lancaster, Francis Bailey [1780?]
broadside 25 X 21 cm.
Taylor 250
PHi mp. 43801

B5089 FISHER, JOHN, of Lancaster, Pa.
John Fisher, Bürsten-Macher, in der Königstrasse . . . Man verlangt einen Lehrjungen . . . Lancaster, Francis Bailey [1780?]
broadside 25 X 21 cm.
Taylor 251
PHi mp. 43802

B5090 THE following is a list of the names of the men claimed by the several towns in the state, now serving in the Connecticut line of the Continental Army. Those mark'd thus (a) are returned from the army. [n.p., 1780?]
53 p. 17 cm.
Trumbull: Supplement 2151
CtHi mp. 43780

B5091 FREEMASONS. PENNSYLVANIA GRAND LODGE
Grand Lodge, Philadelphia, March 15, 1780. To the Master and Brethren of Lodge No. . . . [Philadelphia, 1780]
4 p. 18 cm.
Huntington 447; Taylor 249
CSmH mp. 43803

B5092 FRIENDS, SOCIETY OF. LONDON YEARLY MEETING
An epistle from the Yearly-Meeting held in London . . . from the 15th of the 5th month 1780, to the 20th of the same . . . To friends and brethren, at their next Yearly-Meeting to be held in Philadelphia . . . [Philadelphia, 1780]
3, [1] p. 33 cm. caption title
Not Evans 19412; Taylor 317
DLC; MB; MWA; PPL mp. 43804

B5093 GAIFER
The conversion of a Mehometan . . . The eighth edition . . . Boston, Re-printed by E. Draper, for Phillip Freeman [1780?]
16 p. 17 cm.
NHi mp. 43805

B5094 GT. BRIT. ARMY
By His Excellency Sir Henry Clinton . . . A proclamation . . . Given . . . at Head Quarters, on James Island, the third day of March . . . [1780] . . . [South Carolina: Printed by Robertson, Macdonald & Cameron? 1780]
broadside 28.5 X 21 cm.
Public Record Off. mp. 43806

B5095 GT. BRIT. ARMY
Head-quarters, Charles-Town Neck, June 1, 1780. Orders, The Commander in chief congratulates the army on the success . . . in the back country under . . . Cornwallis . . . [Charleston? 1780]
broadside 19 X 14.5 cm.
NHi

B5096 GT. BRIT. ARMY
Head-quarters, Charles-Town Neck, June 1, 1780. . . New-York, Reprinted by James Rivington [1780]
broadside 31 X 19.5 cm.
DLC mp. 43807

B5097 GT. BRIT. ARMY
North-Carolina. By the Right Honourable Charles Earl Cornwallis . . . A proclamation. Whereas the enemies . . . have . . . propagated a belief . . . that the King's army indiscriminately makes war . . . Given . . . at Head-Quarters in Charlotte-Town . . . [Sept. 27, 1780] . . . Charlestown: Printed at Wells's office [1780]
broadside 38 X 32.5 cm.
MiU-C mp. 43808

B5098 GT. BRIT. ARMY
South-Carolina. By His Excellency Sir Henry Clinton . . . Proclamation. Whereas notwithstanding the gracious offers . . . some wicked and desperate men . . . are still endeavouring to support . . . rebellion . . . Given under my hand . . . [May 22, 1780] . . . Charles-Town: Printed by Robertson, Macdonald & Cameron [1780]
broadside 33.5 X 21 cm.
MiU-C mp. 43809

B5099 GT. BRIT. ARMY
When the Royal army arrived in South-Carolina, the Commander in Chief avoided . . . every measure . . . But Charles-Town . . . being now reduced . . . the time is come . . . duty of every good man to be in readiness to join the King's troops . . . [Charleston? 1780]
broadside 39 X 32 cm.
Printed probably between May 12 (capitulation of Charleston) and June 4, when Clinton sent the message to Germain
MiU–C mp. 43810

B5100 GT. BRIT. COLONIAL OFFICE
By his Excellency James Robertson . . . Governor . . . A proclamation. The King having been graciously pleased . . . [Apr. 15, 1780] . . . [New York] James Rivington [1780]
broadside 41.5 X 31.5 cm.
New York Public 730
MWA (defective). Photostats: DLC; NN mp. 43854

B5101 GT. BRIT. COLONIAL OFFICE
By James Pattison . . . Proclamation. Whereas in all well regulated societies . . . [Jan. 20, 1780] . . . [New York, 1780]
broadside 31 X 17.5 cm.
DLC (photostat) mp. 43811

B5102 GT. BRIT. COLONIAL OFFICE
By James Pattison . . . Whereas the several captains . . . [Jan. 24, 1780] . . . [New York, 1780]
broadside 31 X 17.5 cm.
DLC (photostat) mp. 43812

B5103 GT. BRIT. COLONIAL OFFICE
A narrative of Sir Henry Clinton's cooperations with Sir Peter Parker, on the attack of Sullivan's Island . . . 1776. And with Vice-Admiral Arbuthnot . . . at Rhode-Island, in 1780 . . . [New York? J. Rivington? 1780?]
39 p.

Sabin 13752; Lathrop C. Harper cat. no. 165 (Nov. 1942), item 522
N (burned in 1911 fire) mp. 43813

B5104 GREEN, JACOB, 1722-1796
A sermon on persons possessing the iniquities of their youth in after life . . . Chatham, Shepard Kollock, 1780.
16 p. 16.5 cm.
Humphrey 213
NjHi; RPJCB mp. 43814

B5105 HART, WILLIAM, JR.
To the public. As a member of this state . . . I think it my duty to publish . . . That William Worthington . . . was so lost to all sense of right . . . Wm. Hart, Jun. Hartford, 14th February, 1780. [Hartford, 1780]
broadside 14 X 16 cm.
CtHi mp. 43815

B5106 HUTCHINS revived: an almanack . . . for . . . 1781 . . . Fish-Kill, Printed and sold by Samuel Loudon [1780]
[24] p. 17 cm.
New York Public 723; Vail: Patriotic pair, p. 411; Wall p. 23
MWA; NHi; NN; NPV mp. 43816

B5107 INVENTORY of Ship Mars, as she is to be sold on the 13th April instant . . . [Boston, 1780]
broadside 34 X 20 cm.
She was bought by the Board of War of Massachusetts
Ford 2230; New York Public 724
M-Ar. Photostats: MHi; NN mp. 43817

B5108 [LANCASTER almanack for . . . 1781 . . . Lancaster, F. Bailey? 1780]
[32] p.
Drake 10113
WHi (t.p. lacking)

B5109 LOUISIANA. INTENDANT (MARTIN NOVARRO)
Carta l los habitantes de la provincia de la Luisiana. De 29 de agosto de 1780. Mui señores mios: Haviendo dado quenta . . . del uracan . . . [Aug. 18, 1779] . . . Martin Novarro. [New Orleans, Antoine Boudousquié, 1780]
broadside 33 X 20 cm.
McMurtrie: Louisiana 13
G. William Nott, New Orleans (1942) mp. 43818

B5110 LOUISIANA. INTENDANT (MARTIN NOVARRO)
Lettre aux habitants de la province de la Louisianne. Du 29 Aoust 1780. Messieurs, Après avoir rendue compte . . . de l'ouragon desastreux . . . [Aug. 18, 1779] . . . Martin Novarro. [New Orleans, Antoine Boudousquié, 1780]
broadside 33 X 20 cm.
McMurtrie: New Orleans 31a; McMurtrie: Louisiana 12
G. William Nott, New Orleans (1942) mp. 43819

B5111 MAJOR Andre, written while he was a prisoner in the American camp.
Ah! Delia, see the fatal hour . . . [Boston? 1780?]
broadside
Ford 2233
MB. Photostat: MHi mp. 43820

B5112 MARYLAND. GENERAL ASSEMBLY
Messages between the two Houses . . . on the subject of confiscation of British property. Annapolis, Frederick Green [1780]
37 p. 15.5 cm.
Wheeler 94
MdHi mp. 43821

B5113 MARYLAND. LAWS
An act for recruiting this state's quota of troops to serve in the Continental Army . . . [Annapolis, F. Green, 1780]
4 p. 33 cm.
NHi mp. 43822

B5114 MARYLAND. LAWS
An act of the General assembly . . . passed November session, 1779 . . . for the assessment of property . . . Annapolis, Frederick Green [1780]
28 p. 16 cm.
Wheeler 90
MdHi mp. 43823

B5115 MARYLAND. LAWS
An act to procure a supply of salt meat for the use of the army . . . [n.p., 1780]
broadside 31.5 X 20 cm.
The Maryland General Assembly is named in the text
DLC mp. 43824

B5116 MARYLAND. LAWS
An act to procure an extra supply of provisions of the bread kind, also waggons and horses, for . . . the Continental Army. Whereas the state hath been called upon . . . by General Washington . . . [Philadelphia, 1780]
2 p. 32 cm.
Passed in July 1780
Two pages printed of a 4-page folder
The Maryland General Assembly is named in the text
DLC mp. 43825

B5117 MASSACHUSETTS. COUNCIL
By the major part of the Council of the State of Massachusetts-Bay. A proclamation for convening the . . . General Court . . . Given at the Council-Chamber . . . this twenty-ninth day of August, A. D. 1780 . . . [Boston, 1780]
broadside
M-Ar

B5118 MASSACHUSETTS. GENERAL COURT
Boston, January 20, 1780. The committee appointed by the Great and General Court . . . to . . . settle the public accounts . . . [Boston, 1780]
broadside 26.5 X 22 cm.
Ford 2220
MHi (2 copies); MWA mp. 43827

B5119 MASSACHUSETTS. GENERAL COURT
Resolves of the General Assembly . . . begun . . . the thirty-first day of May . . . 1780. Boston, Nathaniel Willis, 1780.
111 p. 37 cm.
Through the October 4 session
DLC; MB; MHi; PHi mp. 43834

B5120 MASSACHUSETTS. HOUSE OF REPRESENTATIVES
Commonwealth of Massachusetts. In the House of Representatives, Dec. 4th, 1780. Whereas by the resolutions . . . [Boston, 1780]
3 p. 35 cm.
Ford 2255; Heartman: Cradle 91
DLC; MSaE mp. 43833

B5121 MASSACHUSETTS. HOUSE OF REPRESENTATIVES
State of Massachusetts-Bay. In the House of Representatives, Mar. 23, 1780. Resolved, That Major-General Heath ... [Boston, 1780]
broadside 22.5 X 17.5 cm.
Ford 2240
MHi mp. 43828

B5122 MASSACHUSETTS. HOUSE OF REPRESENTATIVES
State of Massachusetts-Bay in the House of Representatives, April 21st, 1780. As justice and humanity ... [Boston, 1780]
[6] p. 38 cm.
Ford 2241; New York Public 727
DLC; MWA; NN mp. 43829

B5123 MASSACHUSETTS. HOUSE OF REPRESENTATIVES
State of Massachusetts-Bay. In the House of Representatives, May 5th, 1780. Resolved, That the selectmen ... [Boston, 1780]
broadside 24 X 18.5 cm.
Ford 2242; Huntington 451
CSmH; MHi. Photostat: DLC mp. 43830

B5124 MASSACHUSETTS. HOUSE OF REPRESENTATIVES
State of Massachusetts-Bay In the House of Representatives, June 14, 1780. Whereas the Congress ... have called for an immediate supply of money ... [Boston, B. Edes, 1780]
broadside 33 X 19 cm.
On verso: ... June 24, 1780. Resolved, That commissioners be appointed ...
DLC mp. 43831

B5125 MASSACHUSETTS. HOUSE OF REPRESENTATIVES
State of Massachusetts-Bay. In the House of Representatives, June 14, 1780. Whereas the Congress ... have called for an immediate supply of money ... [Boston, B. Edes, 1780]
broadside 33 X 19 cm.
Verso blank
MB mp. 43832

B5126 MASSACHUSETTS. LAWS
State of Massachusetts-Bay. In the year ... One Thousand seven Hundred and Eighty. An act making provision for calling in ... [This act passed May 5th, 1780.] ... [Boston, 1780]
broadside 45 X 34 cm.
Ford 2236, 2238; New York Public 728
MHi. Photostats: DLC; MH; NHi; NN mp. 43835

B5127 MASSACHUSETTS. TREASURER
State of Massachusetts-Bay. The honorable Henry Gardner, Esq; treasurer ... January 5, 1780. [Boston, 1780]
broadside
Tax warrant
Ford 2260
MSaE mp. 43836

B5128 MASSACHUSETTS. TREASURER
State of Massachusetts-Bay. The honorable Henry Gardner ... To the selectmen or assessors of the town of Greeting ... [May 18, 1780] [Boston, 1780]
broadside 42 X 34 cm.
DLC mp. 43837

B5129 MASSACHUSETTS. TREASURER
State of Massachusetts-Bay. The honorable Henry Gardner, Esq; treasurer ... June 25, 1780. [Boston, 1780]
broadside
Tax warrant
Ford 2261
MSaE mp. 43838

B5130 MASSACHUSETTS. TREASURER
State of Massachusetts-Bay. The honorable Henry Gardner, Esq; treasurer ... July 18, 1780. [Boston, 1780]
broadside
Tax warrant
Ford 2262
M-Ar mp. 43839

B5131 MESSIEURS Edes. By inserting the following address, you will oblige a constant reader. My fellow countrymen. It is now upwards of five years ... A Military Countryman. [Boston, 1780]
broadside
Ford 2267
MHi mp. 43840

B5132 A MOHAWK song and dance ... A tune to an Indian drum ... [n.p.] Printed for little Master Caldwell, 1780.
broadside 8.5 X 11 cm.
New York Public 729
NhD. Photostat: NN mp. 43841

B5133 MUCKARSIE, JOHN
The children's catechism ... Philadelphia, R. Aitken, 1780.
[24] p. 16.5 cm. A–B[6]
In double columns
Rosenbach–Ch 89; Taylor 252
PPL mp. 43842

B5134 THE New-England almanack ... for the year ... 1781 ... By Isaac Bickerstaff, Esq; Philom. Providence, John Carter [1780]
32 p. 16.5 cm.
Alden 813; Sabin 52650
NHi; RNHi mp. 43771

B5135 THE New-England primer. For the more easy attaining the true reading of English. Philadelphia, R. Aitken, 1780.
[48] p. 9.5 cm. A^4 B–C^8 D^4
Rosenbach–Ch 90; Taylor 253
A. S. W. Rosenbach (1933) mp. 43843

B5136 NEW HAMPSHIRE. GENERAL COURT
State of New-Hampshire. The government and people of said state. To the selectmen of in the county of in said state, Greeting ... Portsmouth, October 20, 1780 ... [Exeter, Z. Fowle, 1780]
broadside 30 X 19 cm.
DLC; NhD; NhHi mp. 43844

B5137 NEW HAMPSHIRE. LAWS
State of New-Hampshire. In the year ... [1780] An act to prevent the transportation of live cattle ... out of this state. [Exeter? 1780]
broadside ([2] p.)
Whittemore 290
MWA mp. 43845

B5138 NEW HAVEN BRIDGE LOTTERY
New-Haven Lottery, for building a bridge over East-

River. Class first . . . Second class . . . New-Haven, July 31, 1780. [New Haven, 1780]
broadside 41 X 17.5 cm.
CtHi mp. 43846

B5139 NEW JERSEY. LAWS
State of New-Jersey. An act for compleating the quota of troops . . . March 11, 1780 . . . [Trenton, 1780]
broadside 39 X 25 cm.
Humphrey 226
DLC mp. 43848

B5140 NEW JERSEY. LAWS
State of New-Jersey. An act for compleating and keeping up the quota . . . December 26, 1780 . . . [Trenton, I. Collins, 1780]
[2] p. 37 X 25 cm.
Humphrey 227
DLC mp. 43847

B5141 Deleted

B5142 NEW JERSEY. LAWS
State of New-Jersey. An act to compleat the three regiments . . . June 14th, 1780 . . . Trenton, Isaac Collins [1780]
broadside 38.5 X 23.5 cm.
Humphrey 307
DLC mp. 43850

B5143 NEW JERSEY. LAWS
State of New-Jersey. An act to raise and embody . . . six hundred and twenty-four men . . . [Trenton, I. Collins, 1780]
[4] p. 37 cm. caption title
Humphrey 228
DLC (imperfect; p. [3-4] wanting) mp. 43851

B5144 NEW JERSEY. LAWS
State of New-Jersey. A supplemental act to the Act, intituled, An act for procuring provisions . . . March 18, 1780 . . . [Trenton, I. Collins, 1780]
2 p. 45.5 X 39 cm.
Humphrey 308
DLC; Nj mp. 43852

B5145 NEW YORK. ASSEMBLY
The votes and proceedings of the Assembly, &c. . . . [Fish-Kill, Samuel Loudon, 1780]
p. [87]-156. 33 cm. caption title
Third session, second meeting, Jan. 27-Mar. 14, 1780
New York Public 731; Vail: Patriotic pair . . . p. 420; Huntington 453
CSmH; NN; DLC; MH; NHi; NIC; PHi mp. 43853

B5146 NEW YORK. GOVERNOR, 1777-1795
By His excellency George Clinton . . . To Whereas, the emergency . . . requires the same, These are, therefore in pursuance of an act of the legislature . . . ". . . to grant warrants of impress", . . . Given under my hand . . . [July 1, 1780] Geo. Clinton. [Poughkeepsie, J. Holt? 1780]
broadside 18.5 X 23.5 cm.
Printer and date assigned by R.W.G.Vail
MWiW-C

B5147 NEW YORK. GOVERNOR, 1777-1795
State of New-York. Head-Quarters, Poughkeepsie, November 1780. General orders. His Excellency the Governor . . . has assigned . . . the following quotas . . . [Poughkeepsie, John Holt? 1780]
broadside 22 X 22 cm.
Vail: Patriotic pair, p. 412
MH. Photostat: NHi mp. 43855

B5148 NEW YORK. LAWS
An act for regulating the militia of the State of New-York, passed at Albany, in the third session . . . Poughkeepsie, John Holt, 1780.
26 p. 19 cm.
Vail: Patriotic pair, p. 411
NHi mp. 43856

B5149 NEW York, Saturday, July 15, 1780. The Admiral having requested a number of seamen volunteers . . . [New York? 1780]
broadside 31 X 20 cm.
RPJCB mp. 43857

B5150 NORWICH, CONN.
At a town-meeting, held in Norwich the twenty-fourth day of June, one thousand seven hundred and eighty, Voted . . . that a committee of fifty . . . be appointed to engage fifty . . . soldiers . . . [Norwich? 1780?]
broadside 21.5 X 17.5 cm.
RPJCB mp. 43858

B5151 N° 1.[-7.] Gazette françoise. Du vendredi 17 novembre 1780 [-Du mardi 2 Janvier 1781] [Colophon] A Newport, De l'imprimerie royale de l'escadre [1780-81]
8 no. in 1 v. 34 cm. caption title
Chapin: *Calendrier français* . . . p. [8]
RHi. Photostats: DLC; MHi mp. 44275

B5152 ON the Dark Day, May nineteenth, 1780. [Boston? 1780]
broadside 29 X 19 cm.
Ford 2269
MSaE; MWA mp. 43859

B5153 ON the Dark Day May 19th 1780. [n.p., 1780]
broadside 24.5 X 22 cm.
MWA mp. 43860

B5154 PENNSYLVANIA. COUNCIL
In Council, Philadelphia, June 1, 1780. Sir, The Continental Army . . . reduced to great distress . . . To Esq; Commissioner for securing supplies for the army. [Philadelphia, 1780]
broadside 25 X 19 cm.
Signed in ms. by Joseph Reed
PHi mp. 43862

B5155 PENNSYLVANIA. LAWS
An act for confirming and amending the charter of the German Lutheran Congregation in . . . Philadelphia . . . Enacted into a law . . . the third of March, Anno Domini, one thousand seven hundred and eighty . . . Thomas Paine, Clerk . . . [Philadelphia, 1780]
broadside 44 X 27 cm.
Taylor 248
PHi mp. 43864

B5156 PENNSYLVANIA. PRESIDENT, 1778-1781
By . . . Joseph Reed . . . a proclamation. To all justices of the peace . . . [July 25, 1780] . . . [Philadelphia, 1780]
broadside 42.5 X 32 cm.
DLC mp. 43865

B5157 PENNSYLVANIA. PRESIDENT, 1778-1781
By . . . Joseph Reed . . . a proclamation. Whereas divers of the inhabitants . . . [Mar. 25, 1780] . . . [Philadelphia] Hall and Sellers, 1780.
broadside 40.5 X 31 cm.
DLC mp. 43866

B5158 PENNSYLVANIA. SUPREME EXECUTIVE COUNCIL
An address . . . to the inhabitants of Pennsylvania . . . Council chamber, August 7, 1780. [Philadelphia, 1780]
broadside 41.5 X 26 cm.
DLC mp. 43867

B5159 PENNSYLVANIA. SUPREME EXECUTIVE COUNCIL
To the merchants and traders of the city of Philadelphia. Gentlemen, the subject of this address is too interesting not to claim your attention . . . [Philadelphia, 1780?]
broadside 35.5 X 22 cm.
PPRF mp. 43868

B5160 [PRATT, SAMUEL JACKSON] 1749-1814
The pupil of pleasure. By Courtney Melmoth. A new edition, corrected and improved . . . Boston, Re-printed by John D. M'Dougall, 1780.
2 v. in 1. 16.5 cm.
MWA mp. 43869

B5160a PRESBYTERY OF NEW CASTLE
A serious address of the reverend Presbytery of New-Castle, to the congregations under their care. Lancaster, Francis Bailey, 1779.
32 p.
Trinterud 504
NjPT

B5161 RÉPONSE a la lettre circulaire de Monsieur Dn. Martin Novarro, intendant . . . Du 29 Aoust, 1780 . . . [at end] [New Orleans] Antoine Boudousquié, 1780.
[2] p. 28 X 19 cm.
McMurtrie: New Orleans 31b
Edward A. Parsons, New Orleans (1929); T. P. Thompson Library mp. 43871

B5162 RHODE ISLAND. ELECTION PROX.
A.D. 1780. The happiness of the community . . . His Excellency William Greene Esq; Governor. The honorable Jabez Bowen, Esq; Dept. Governor . . . [Providence] John Carter [1780]
broadside 13 X 19.5 cm.
Alden 823; Chapin Proxies 24
MWA; RHi; RPB mp. 43872

B5163 RHODE ISLAND. ELECTION PROX.
Friends to America and Gen. Washington. His Excellency William Greene, Esq; Governor. The honorable William West, Esq; Deputy-governor . . . [Providence? 1780]
broadside 18 X 13 cm.
Alden 824; Chapin Proxies 27a, 27b
MWA; RHi (2 variant issues) mp. 43873

B5164 RHODE ISLAND. ELECTION PROX.
His Excellency William Greene, Esq; Governor. The honorable Jabez Bowen, Esq; Dep. Governor . . . [Providence] John Carter [1780]
broadside 20 X 13 cm.
Alden 825; Chapin Proxies 25
RHi mp. 43874

B5165 RHODE ISLAND. ELECTION PROX.
Real friends to liberty, Washington . . . His Excellency William Greene, Esq; Governor. The honorable Jabez Bowen, Esq; Deputy-governor . . . [Providence? 1780]
broadside 18.5 X 12.5 cm.
Alden 826; Chapin Proxies 28
RHi mp. 43875

B5166 RHODE ISLAND. GENERAL ASSEMBLY
[A list of deputies of the February session, 1780 . . . Providence, Bennett Wheeler, 1780]
[broadside]
Bill submitted by Wheeler Apr. 23, 1785
Alden 827
No copy known mp. 43888

B5167 RHODE ISLAND. GENERAL ASSEMBLY
State of Rhode-Island, &c. In General assembly, February session, 1780. Whereas it will be necessary . . . [Providence] John Carter [1780]
broadside 19 X 13 cm.
Alden 830; Winship p. 41
RHi; RPJCB mp. 43877

B5168 RHODE ISLAND. LAWS
State of Rhode-Island and Providence Plantations. In General assembly, February session, 1780. An act for assessing . . . a rate or tax of one hundred and eighty thousand pounds . . . Providence, John Carter [1780]
broadside 46 X 17 cm.
Alden 829; Winship p. 41
R; RHi mp. 43876

B5169 RHODE ISLAND. LAWS
State of Rhode-Island and Providence Plantations. In General assembly, June session, 1780. An act for raising . . . six hundred and ten men . . . [Providence] John Carter [1780]
broadside 32 X 20.5 cm.
Alden 833; New York Public 732; Winship p. 41
MHi; NN; RHi mp. 43879

B5170 RHODE ISLAND. LAWS
State of Rhode Island and Providence Plantations. In General assembly, July 7, 1780. Whereas . . . six hundred and ten effective men were ordered . . . Be it therefore enacted . . . [Providence] Bennett Wheeler [1780]
broadside 55 X 27 cm.
Bill submitted July 7, 1780
Alden 836; Winship p.42
RHi; RPB; RPJCB mp. 43885

B5171 RHODE ISLAND. LAWS
State of Rhode-Island and Providence Plantations. In General assembly, July session, 1780. An act for assessing and apportioning a rate or tax of four hundred thousand pounds . . . Providence, John Carter [1780]
broadside 34 X 25 cm.
Alden 834; Winship p. 41; Winship Addenda p. 93
CtY; R mp. 43880

B5172 RHODE ISLAND. LAWS
[State of Rhode-Island and Providence Plantations. In General assembly, July session, 1780. It is voted and resolved, That six hundred and ten blankets . . . Providence, Bennett Wheeler, 1780]
[broadside?]
Bill submitted by Wheeler July 6, 1780
Alden 835
No copy known mp. 43882

B5173 RHODE ISLAND. LAWS
State of Rhode Island and Providence Plantations. In General assembly, July session, 1780. An act to prevent certain persons . . . from being admitted within this state . . . Providence, Bennett Wheeler [1780]
broadside 37.5 X 26 cm.
Bill submitted July 12, 1780

Alden 837; Winship p. 41
MWA; NHi; RHi mp. 43881

B5174 RHODE ISLAND. LAWS
State of Rhode Island and Providence Plantations. In General assembly, July second session, 1780. An act for assessing . . . a rate or tax of ten thousand pounds . . . Providence, Bennett Wheeler [1780]
broadside 38 X 18 cm.
Bill submitted July 28, 1780
Alden 838; Winship p. 41; Winship Addenda p. 93
CtY mp. 43883

B5175 RHODE ISLAND. LAWS
State of Rhode-Island and Providence Plantations. In General assembly, July 2d session, 1780. Whereas notwithstanding the provision . . . for bringing six hundred and ten men into the field . . . [Providence] John Carter [1780]
broadside 17.5 X 23 cm.
Alden 841; Winship p. 41
RHi; RPJCB mp. 43884

B5176 RHODE ISLAND. LAWS
State of Rhode Island and Providence Plantations. In General assembly, November session, 1780. An act for assessing . . . a rate or tax of one million of pounds . . . [Providence] Bennett Wheeler [1780]
broadside 36 X 16.5 cm.
Alden 842; Winship p. 42
R; RHi mp. 43886

B5177 RHODE ISLAND. LAWS
State of Rhode-Island and Providence Plantations. In general assembly, November session, 1780. An act for granting . . . a tax of sixteen thousand pounds . . . [Providence] Bennett Wheeler [1780]
broadside 40.5 X 19 cm.
Alden 844; Winship p. 42
R; RHi mp. 43887

B5178 RHODE ISLAND. LAWS
"And whereas there is a very large sum of money due . . . to the militia . . ." The preceding is a true extract form [sic] an act passed . . . at November session, 1780 . . . [Providence] Bennett Wheeler [1780?]
broadside 26.5 X 19.5 cm.
Alden 845; Winship p. 42
RHi mp. 43878

B5179 RHODE ISLAND. MILITIA
I the subscriber do hereby solemnly . . . inlist myself . . . in the battalion of . . . Rhode-Island . . . agreeable to an act . . . passed at November session, 1780 . . . [Providence? 1780]
broadside 11.5 X 18 cm.
Form not filled in
RHi. Photostat: MWA mp. 43889

B5180 RHODE ISLAND. MILITIA
We the subscribers do hereby solemnly . . . inlist ourselves . . . in the battalion ordered to be raised by the General Assembly of . . . Rhode-Island . . . held at Newport . . . in July, 1780 . . . [Providence? 1780]
broadside 23 X 18 cm.
Form not filled in
NHi; RPJCB mp. 43890

B5181 RHODE ISLAND. TREASURER
State of Rhode-Island and Providence Plantations, ss. To the sheriff of the county of or to his lawful deputy, Greeting . . . [November, 1780] [Providence, 1780]
broadside 35.5 X 22.5 cm.
DLC mp. 43891

B5182 . . . SAINT George's Day. Verses. For a believer, when looking on a watch . . . [Philadelphia] Zachariah Poulson, Jun. April twenty-third, 1780. 1780 [centered]
broadside 22 X 14 cm.
At head of title: 1780
NHi mp. 43892

B5183 EIN schön geistlich Lied. Mel. Wo bleiben meine Sinne? Lancaster, Francis Bailey [1780?]
broadside 22.5 X 20.5 cm.
Taylor 268
PHi mp. 43893

B5184 SMITH, BENJAMIN, of South Carolina
South-Carolina, May 11, 1780. Copy of an intercepted letter from B. Smith, to Mrs. Benjamin Smith, dated Charles-Town, 30th April, 1780 . . . in the hands of the printers . . . on board the . . . ship Palliser . . . South-Carolina: Printed by Robertson, Macdonald & Cameron [1780]
broadside 36 X 22.5 cm.
Brit. Mus. mp. 43895

B5185 SOUTH CAROLINA. GOVERNOR, 1779-1782
By . . . John Rutledge . . . a proclamation: Whereas the enemy have invaded . . . [Mar. 2, 1780] . . . [Charleston, 1780]
broadside 34 X 20 cm.
Sabin 87535
DLC mp. 43896

B5186 THE South-Carolina and Georgia almanack, for the year . . . 1781 . . . By William Rider . . . Charles-town: Printed and sold by Mills and Hicks [1780]
[22+] p. 18.5 cm.
Drake 13125
NcD (lacking after p. [22])

B5187 [SOWER, CHRISTOPHER] 1754-1799
Zuschrift an die Teutschen in Pennsylvanien, und benachbarten Provinzen . . . [New York, 1780]
16 p. 23 cm. A-B[4]
cf. AAS *Proceedings*, v. 41, p. 246
Public Record Off. Photostats: MWA; MiU-C
mp. 43897

B5188 TO the Americans in general, but to the citizens of South-Carolina in particular: this small tract is dedicated . . . by . . . A Black Whig. [n.p., 1780?]
11 p. 21 cm.
Turnbull p. 230 (v. 1)
NHi mp. 43898

B5189 TO the honorable the justices of the Inferior Court of Common Pleas, holden at *Boston* . . . One Thousand Seven Hundred and Eighty, be it remembered, That complains . . . that said . . . levied war, and conspired to levy war . . . [Boston, 1780]
broadside
Word italicized in ms.
Ford 2274
MHi mp. 43899

B5190 TO the representatives of the freemen of the Commonwealth of Pennsylvania, in General Assembly met, the representation and petition of the subscribers, citizens of Pennsylvania . . . Your petitioners . . . request

. . . such additions to the said law, as shall effectually put a stop to the slave trade . . . in this Commonwealth . . . [Philadelphia, 1780?]
broadside 34 X 27.5 cm.
Richard Gimbel. Photostat: MWA mp. 43861

B5191 TRENTON, July 4, 1780. The ladies of Trenton . . . emulating their patriotic sisters of Pennsylvania . . . appointed . . . a committee . . . to open subscriptions . . . transmitted by Mrs. (Moore) Furman . . . to . . . the Commander in Chief . . . [Trenton? 1780]
broadside 33.5 X 20 cm.
NjR (facsim.; original in private hands)

B5192 U. S. ARMY. CONTINENTAL ARMY
L'amour paternel qui a toujours animé le coeur du Roy pour les habitans du Canada . . . Fait au quartier General, de Sur la Riviere de Connecticut, le mille sept ceus [sic] quatre vingts. Signé La Fayette . . . [Philadelphia, 1780]
broadside 33.5 X 20.5 cm.
MBAt; MWA (photostat) mp. 43900

B5193 U. S. ARMY. CONTINENTAL ARMY
Boston, June 12, 1780. The inhabitants of the town (ministers of the Gospel only excepted) are hereby notified to meet . . . at their usual place of parade, on Thursday next . . . then by draft, lot, or voluntary inlistment, to procure their quota of men for the Continental Army . . . Edward Procter, Col. of Boston Regiment. [Boston, 1780]
broadside 9.5 X 13 cm.
MHi mp. 43901

B5194 U. S. ARMY. CONTINENTAL ARMY
By Horatio Gates . . . a proclamation. The patriotick exertions . . . Given at headquarters, on the river Peedee, in South Carolina . . . [Aug. 4, 1780] . . . [n.p., 1780]
broadside 30.5 X 20 cm.
DLC mp. 43902

B5195 U. S. ARMY. CONTINENTAL ARMY
Proceedings of a board of general officers held by order of . . . Gen. Washington . . . Respecting Major John Andre . . . September 29, 1780. Fish-Kill, Samuel Loudon, 1780.
23 p. 19.5 cm. A^4 B^2 C^4 D^2
Vail: Patriotic pair, p. 412
NHi; NjP; RPJCB mp. 43903

B5196 U. S. ARMY. CONTINENTAL ARMY
[Proceedings of a board of general officers, held by order of . . . General Washington . . . respecting Major John André . . . September 29, 1780 . . . New-London, Reprinted by T. Green, 1780]
16+ p.
Trumbull: Supplement 2517
No copy located mp. 43904

B5197 U. S. ARMY. CONTINENTAL ARMY
Proceedings of a board of general officers, held by order of . . . Gen. Washington . . . respecting the trial of Major John André . . . Sept. 29, 1780 . . . Norwich, John Trumbull, 1780.

Trumbull: Supplement 2518
MH-L mp. 43905

B5198 U. S. ARMY. CONTINENTAL ARMY
Proceedings of a Board of General Officers, held by order of . . . General Washington . . . respecting Major John André . . . Philadelphia, Francis Bailey [1780]
32 p. 8vo
cf. Evans 17043
PHi

B5199 U. S. ARMY. CONTINENTAL ARMY
[Proceedings of a Board of Rebel Officers, held by order of General Washington . . . respecting Major Andre . . . September 29th, 1780. Charleston? James Robertson, Donald McDonald, and Alexander Cameron? 1780]

Advertised in the *Royal South-Carolina Gazette*, Dec. 8, 1780
Mosimann 347
No copy known

B5200 U. S. ARMY. CONTINENTAL ARMY
To the medical officers of the general and flying hospitals in the army of the United States, Philadelphia, January 20, 1780 . . . W. Brown, Phys. Gen. M.D. [Philadelphia, 1780]
broadside
Austin 1946
PPC mp. 43906

B5201 U. S. CONTINENTAL CONGRESS
Journals of Congress . . . from January 1st, 1779, to January 1st, 1780 . . . Volume V. Philadelphia, David C. Claypoole [1780?]
54+ p. 18 cm.
New York Public 733
NN (Jan. 1779 only) mp. 43907

B5202 U. S. CONTINENTAL CONGRESS, 1780
Plan for conducting the Quartermaster General's Department, agreed to in Congress, July 15th, 1780. Philadelphia, Printed by David Claypoole, 1780.
16 p. 20.5 cm.
cf. Evans 17042
MWA mp. 43908

B5203 U. S. INSPECTOR-GENERAL'S OFFICE
Rules and articles for the better government of the troops, raised . . . at the expence of the United States . . . Charlestown [S.C.], John Wells, 1780.
35 p. 22 cm.
Turnbull p. 228 (v. 1)
MiU-C

B5204 VERMONT. GOVERNOR, 1778-1789
[Thanksgiving day proclamation for Dec. 1780. Westminster, J. P. Spooner & T. Green, 1780]
broadside
Printer's bill for 80 copies dated Nov. 24, 1780
McCorison 32
No copy known mp. 43909

B5205 VERMONT. LAWS
Acts and laws, passed by the General Assembly of the representatives of the freemen . . . at their session at Bennington, October, 1780. [Westminster, Spooner and Green, 1780]
[6] p. 32 cm. caption title
Cooley 1; Sabin 99078
MH-L. Photostats: MHi; NN; VtU. Mrs. Geo. M. Powers, Burlington, Vt. (1963) mp. 43910

B5206 VIRGINIA. LAWS
An act for speedily recruiting the quota of this State for the Continental Army. Whereas the General Assembly hath received authentick intelligence . . . [Richmond? 1780]

[2] p. 32.5 X 20 cm.
Act passed July (?) 1780
DLC mp. 43911

B5207 VIRGINIA. LAWS
An act more effectually to prevent and punish desertion . . . [Williamsburg, 1780]
broadsheet ([2] p.) 36 X 21 cm.
DLC mp. 43912

B5208 WALPOLE CONVENTION
At a convention of delegates from . . . towns in the county of Cheshire . . . held at Walpole . . . 15th day of November . . . [1780] [Westminster, Vt., J. P. Spooner & T. Green, 1780]
broadside 35 X 22 cm.
McCorison 31; Whittemore 297
NhHi; NhPlain mp. 43913

B5209 WATTS, ISAAC, 1674–1748
Divine songs, attempted in easy language . . . The twentieth edition, corrected. [imprint cut off] [1780?]
46 p. 14 cm.
Dated by d'Alté A. Welch
MWA mp. 43914

B5210 WEBSTER, SAMUEL, 1719–1796
Young children and infants declared by Christ members . . . Two discourses delivered September 20th, 1772 . . . Boston, T. and J. Fleet, 1780.
36 p. 22 cm.
cf. Evans 17066 (3rd ed., 1780)
DLC; ICN; MBAt; MH; MHi; MWA; MiU-C; RPJCB
mp. 43915

B5211 WEST, BENJAMIN, 1730–1813
Newport, October 30, 1780. Just published, and now selling . . . the North-American calendar . . . for the year . . . 1781 . . . [Newport, H. Barber, 1780]
broadside 35 X 22 cm.
Alden 816; Winship Addenda p. 89
RHi. Photostats: DLC; MHi mp. 43916

B5212 THE world turned upside down or the comical metamorphoses . . . Decorated with 34 copper plates . . . engraved . . . Boston, Printed and sold by John D. M'Dougall [1780?]
2 p.l., 64 p. illus. 12 cm.
John M'Dougall & Co. were printing only in 1780–81.
cf. MWA printers' file
OO. Photostat: MWA mp. 43918

B5213 ZANE, ISAAC
[Memorials to the Committee of grievances of Pennsylvania. February 3, and May 17, 1780] [Colophon] [Philadelphia] John Dunlap [1780]
p. 294–303. 32.5 cm.
Manuscript note (p. 294): Left out in the pamphlet delivered out by the printers
DLC mp. 43919

1781

B5214 AN accurate table, ascertaining the progressive depreciation of the paper-currency in the province of South-Carolina . . . Charlestown, John Wells, 1781.
[2], 34 p.
RPJCB mp. 43919a

B5215 THE alarm. Or a plan of pacification with America. [New York? 1781?]
64 p. 16 cm. caption title
Signed (p. 8): Cassanrda [sic]
"The New-York Freeholder. Number I[-VII]": p. 9–64
Huntington 470; New York Public 736; Sabin v. 1, p. 72
CSmH; MB; MHi; MWA; NN (No. IV wanting); RPJCB
mp. 43920

B5216 ALLERNEUSTE, verbesserte- und zuverlässige Americanische . . . Calender, für . . . 1782 . . . Friedrich-Stadt, Matthias Bartigis [1781]
[28] p. 20.5 cm.
Drake 2188
MWA mp. 43921

B5217 AN almanack for the year of Our Lord 1782. [Worcester, Isaiah Thomas, 1781]
broadside
Ford 2276
MWA mp. 43922

B5218 AMERICAN Independent; an oratorial entertainment. [Philadelphia, 1781]
broadside 40.5 X 25 cm.
Manuscript notation: Performed at the Chev[r] De la Luzerne, Minister of France, March 21, 1781
DLC mp. 43923

B5219 ANNAPOLIS THEATRE
By permission. Friday September 14th, 1781. This evening . . . a medley of theatrical trifles . . . [Annapolis, F. Green, 1781]
broadside 33 X 20.5 cm.
Wheeler 109
Randall Collection (Baltimore) mp. 43924

B5220 ANNAPOLIS THEATRE
By permission. On Friday evening, being the 17th of August, 1781 . . . a medley of theatrical trifles . . . [Annapolis, F. Green, 1781]
broadside 33 X 20.5 cm.
Wheeler 107
MdHi. Randall Collection mp. 43925

B5221 ANNAPOLIS THEATRE
By permission. On Monday evening, the 19th of November, 1781 . . . A medley of theatrical entertainments . . . [Annapolis, F. Green, 1781]
broadside
Wheeler 114
Randall Collection mp. 43926

B5222 ANNAPOLIS THEATRE
By permission. On Saturday the 25th of August, 1781 . . . a farrago of theatrical amusements . . . [Annapolis, F. Green, 1781]
broadside 33 X 20.5 cm.
Wheeler 108
Randall Collection mp. 43927

B5223 ANNAPOLIS THEATRE
By permission. On Thursday evening, the 14th of June, 1781 . . . a medley of theatrical trifles . . . [Annapolis, F. Green, 1781]
broadside 33 X 18.5 cm.
Wheeler 106
Randall Collection mp. 43928

B5224 ANNAPOLIS THEATRE
By permission. On Wednesday evening, the 14th of

November, 1781 . . . a medley of theatrical entertainments . . . [Annapolis, F. Green, 1781]
broadside
Wheeler 113
Randall Collection mp. 43929

B5225 ANNAPOLIS THEATRE
By permission. Saturday September 15th, 1781. This evening . . . a farrago of theatrical amusements . . . [Annapolis, F. Green, 1781]
broadside 33 X 20.5 cm.
Wheeler 110
Randall Collection mp. 43930

B5226 ANNAPOLIS THEATRE
By permission. Thursday September 20th, 1781. This evening . . . a medley of theatrical amusements . . . [Annapolis, F. Green, 1781]
broadside
Wheeler 112
MdHi. Randall Collection mp. 43931

B5227 ANNAPOLIS THEATRE
By permission. Tuesday September 18th, 1781. This evening . . . a farrago of theatrical amusements . . . [Annapolis, Frederick Green, 1781]
broadside 33 X 20.5 cm.
Wheeler 111
MdHi. Randall Collection mp. 43932

B5228 ASSOCIATED LOYALISTS
Articles of the Associated Loyalists . . . His Majesty having been graciously pleased to approve of a plan for . . . employing the zeal of his faithful subjects . . . in annoying the sea coasts . . . [New York? 1781?]
4 p.
Certificate signed by Wm Franklin in ms. and dated New York, July 26, 1781
NHi mp. 43933

B5229 BALTIMORE THEATRE
By permission. Mr. Wall . . . will present, on Friday evening the 28th of September, 1781 . . . a farrago of theatrical amusements . . . Baltimore, M. K. Goddard [1781]
broadside 34.5 X 20.5 cm.
Wheeler 120
MdHi. Randall Collection mp. 43934

B5230 BALTIMORE THEATRE
By permission. Mr. Wall, comedian . . . will present, on Monday evening, the 1st of October 1781 . . . a medley of theatrical amusements . . . Baltimore, M. K. Goddard [1781]
broadside 33.5 X 19 cm.
Wheeler 121
MdHi. Randall Collection mp. 43935

B5231 BALTIMORE THEATRE
By permission. On Friday the twenty-second of June, Mr. Wall . . . will present . . . a new lecture on heads . . . Baltimore, June 21, 1781. Baltimore, M. K. Goddard [1781]
broadside 33 X 19 cm.
Wheeler 116
MdHi. Randall Collection mp. 43936

B5232 BALTIMORE THEATRE
By permission. On Thursday evening, the fifth of July, 1781, Mr. Wall . . . will present . . . a new lecture on heads . . . Baltimore, July 4, 1781. Baltimore, M. K. Goddard [1781]
broadside 33.5 X 24 cm.
Wheeler 119
MdHi. Randall Collection mp. 43937

B5233 BALTIMORE THEATRE
By permission. On Thursday the twenty-eighth of June, 1781 . . . the old lecture on heads . . . Baltimore, June 27, 1781. Baltimore, M. K. Goddard [1781]
broadside 32 X 19 cm.
Wheeler 117
Randall Collection mp. 43938

B5234 BALTIMORE THEATRE
By permission. On Tuesday the third of July, 1781 . . . the old lecture on heads . . . Baltimore, July 2, 1781. Baltimore, M. K. Goddard [1781]
broadside 33.5 X 20 cm.
Wheeler 118
MdHi. Randall Collection mp. 43939

B5235 BALTIMORE THEATRE
By permission. On Wednesday evening the 3d of October 1781 . . . a medley of theatrical amusements . . . Baltimore, M. K. Goddard [1781]
broadside 34 X 19 cm.
Wheeler 122
MdHi. Randall Collection mp. 43940

B5236 BIBLE. O.T. PSALMS
The Psalms of David, imitated . . . Hartford, Bavil Webster, 1781.
337, [10] p.
CtHC mp. 44085

B5237 BIBLE. O.T. PSALMS
The Psalter: or Psalms of David . . . Boston, T. and J. Fleet, 1781.
157, [1] p. 16 cm.
MWA mp. 43941

B5238 BICKERSTAFF'S New-England almanack, for . . . 1782 . . . Hartford, Bavil Webster [1781]
[24] p. 16 cm.
MWA mp. 43942

B5239 BILLINGS, WILLIAM, 1746–1800
The singing master's assistant . . . (The third edition.) . . . Boston, Draper and Folsom, 1781.
32, 104 p. sm. obl. 8vo
Huntington 460
CSmH; ICN (imperfect); MHi; MWA; N (mutilated); RPJCB mp. 43943

B5240 BOSTON
Notification. In obedience to the order of the town, the Committee for inlisting men, hereby inform you . . . Boston, April 28, 1781 . . . [Boston, 1781]
broadside 10.5 X 18 cm.
DLC mp. 43944

B5241 BOSTON
Your commonwealth tax. Your town and county tax. Your beef tax. . . . Boston, August, 1781. [Boston, 1781]
broadside
Ford 2279
MHi

B5242 BOSTON
Your state tax. Old emission. Your town tax. New emission. [Boston, 1781?]
broadside

Ford 2278
MHi

B5243 BOSTON, October 26. This morning arrived here a gentleman from Providence . . . with the following glorious intelligence . . . Salem, S. Hall [1781]
broadside 27 X 21.5 cm.
Concerns the surrender of Cornwallis
Ford 2282
MSaE mp. 43946

B5244 THE Boston almanack 1782. The Boston pocket almanack for the year . . . 1782 . . . [Boston, John Norman, 1781]
broadside 29 X 22 cm.
Line engraving
Ascribed to Norman on basis of plate 50 in Brigham's *Paul Revere's engravings*, plus DAB account of Norman in 1781
RPJCB (lower half of last 4 months lacking) mp. 43945

B5245 [BOUDIER DE VILLEMERT, PIERRE JOSEPH] 1716–1800
The ladies friend . . . Philadelphia, Printed and sold by R. Aitken, 1781.
103, [4] p. 13 cm. A-I^{6}
Taylor 284
MWA; PHi mp. 43947

B5246 THE British and American register, with an almanack for . . . 1782 . . . New-York, Printed by Robertsons, Mills and Hicks, and sold at their office in Queen-Street; and by Berry and Rogers [1781]
139, [1] p.
Wall p. 23
MB; NHi mp. 43948

B5247 CHAMBERLAIN, THOMAS, d. 1784
The minister preaching his own funeral sermon . . . To which is added, The deathbed discourse, of Mr. Phinehas Burnham, of East-Hartford, (in Connecticut,) who died December 27th, 1776. In the 24th year of his age. [Hartford?] Re-printed 1781.
23, [1] p. 17 cm.
Trumbull: Supplement 1966
CtHi mp. 43950

B5248 CHARLESTOWN CONVENTION, 1781
At a convention of members from forty-three towns on the New-Hampshire Grants . . . held at Charlestown, January 16th, 1781 . . . Beza. Woodward, Clerk. [Westminster, J. P. Spooner & T. Green, 1781]
[2] p. 33 X 21 cm. caption title
McCorison 34
NhPlain mp. 43951

B5249 CIRCULAR. Under cover, we transmit you the plan of a bank devised by Mr. Morris . . . [Philadelphia? 1781]
broadside 31 X 20 cm.
Dated: Philadelphia, May 31, 1781
New York Public 739
NN mp. 43952

B5250 CLINTON, SIR HENRY, 1738?–1795
Correspondence between . . . Sir Henry Clinton, K. B. and . . . Cornwallis. [New York, 1781]
70 p. 22 cm.
Leaf bearing a letter from Clinton dated Sept. 30, 1781, inserted after p. 54
DLC (4 copies); RPJCB mp. 43953

B5251 CLINTON, SIR HENRY, 1738?–1795
Correspondence between . . . Sir Henry Clinton, K. B. and . . . Cornwallis. [New York, 1781]
76 p. 19.5 cm.
Leaf bearing a letter from Clinton dated Sept. 30, 1781, inserted after p. 54
DLC (7 copies); MWA; MiU; N; NHi; RPJCB
mp. 43954

B5252 CONNECTICUT. COUNCIL OF SAFETY
At a meeting of the Governor and Council of Safety, holden . . . the 19th day of June . . . 1781. Whereas since the rising . . . Hartford, Hudson & Goodwin [1781]
broadside 31.5 X 21 cm.
CtHi; DLC; NHi; RPJCB (facsim.) mp. 43955

B5253 CONNECTICUT. COUNCIL OF SAFETY
State of Connecticut. At a meeting of the Governor and Council of Safety, at Lebanon, July 26, 1781 . . . William Williams, Clerk. [n.p., 1781]
broadside 24 X 17 cm.
CtHi. Photostats: DLC; ICN; MH; MHi; NHi; WHi
mp. 43956

B5254 CONNECTICUT. GENERAL ASSEMBLY
At a General Assembly . . . holden at Hartford . . . February, A.D. 1781. It being of importance, towards filling up this State's quota . . . Resolved . . . That a committee of five judicious persons . . . [Hartford? 1781]
broadside 33 X 20.5 cm.
CtHi; MHi

B5255 CONNECTICUT. GENERAL ASSEMBLY
At a General Assembly . . . holden at Hartford . . . February, A.D. 1781. Resolved, by this Assembly, that Jeremiah Wadsworth, late Commissary-General, be . . . requested . . . account of the sums . . . [Hartford, Hudson and Goodwin, 1781]
broadside 28 X 19 cm.
CtHi

B5256 CONNECTICUT. GENERAL ASSEMBLY
At a General Assembly . . . holden at Hartford . . . February, A.D. 1781. Whereas, many disputes have arisen . . . quotas of recruits . . . [Hartford, Hudson and Goodwin, 1781]
broadside 28 X 19 cm.
CtHi

B5257 CONNECTICUT. GENERAL ASSEMBLY
At a General Assembly . . . holden at Hartford . . . February, A.D. 1781. Whereas the General Assembly . . . Resolved . . . that the receivers of provisions for public use . . . [Hartford? 1781]
broadside 33 X 20.5 cm.
CtHi; MHi

B5258 CONNECTICUT. GENERAL ASSEMBLY
At a General Assembly . . . holden at Hartford . . . May, A.D. 1781. A return of the several towns . . . their quota . . . Resolved . . . That a list of the deficiencies . . . Hartford, Hudson and Goodwin [1781]
broadside 33 X 20.5 cm.
CtHi; MHi mp. 43957

B5259 CONNECTICUT. GENERAL ASSEMBLY
At a General Assembly . . . holden at Hartford . . . October . . . 1781. Resolved . . . That the Treasurer receive French guineas in all payments . . . Hartford, Hudson & Goodwin [1781]
broadside 32.5 X 20.5 cm.
CtHi; MHi

B5260 CONNECTICUT. GENERAL ASSEMBLY
At a General Assembly . . . holden . . . the second Thursday of May, 1781. His Excellency General Washington, having represented the necessity of having fifteen hundred men . . . Resolved . . . that the two State Regiments . . . Hartford, Hudson and Goodwin [1781]
broadside 32.5 X 19.5 cm.
New York Public 742
CtHi; RPJCB. Photostats: DLC; MHi; NHi; NN
mp. 43958

B5261 CONNECTICUT. GOVERNOR, 1776–1784
By His Excellency Jonathan Trumbull . . . a declaration. In the beginning of the unhappy contest with the King . . . [Hartford? 1781]
broadside 36 X 23 cm.
Dated at Hartford, Mar. 8, 1781
New York Public 740
Photostats: DLC; MH; MHi; NHi; NN; RPJCB; WHi
mp. 43959

B5262 CONNECTICUT. GOVERNOR, 1776–1784
State of Connecticut, by the Governor. Whereas by the act . . . passed in November last, laying a tax of one penny half-penny . . . [Mar. 28, 1781] . . . [Hartford, 1781]
broadside 20.5 X 15 cm.
Photostats: DLC; MH; MHi; NHi; NN; RPJCB
mp. 43960

B5263 CONNECTICUT. LAWS
At a General Assembly . . . holden at Hartford . . . February . . . 1781. An act for the more effectually preventing inimical persons . . . George Wyllys, Sec'ry. [Hartford? 1781]
broadside 34 X 21 cm.
CtHi; MHi mp. 43961

B5264 CONNECTICUT. LAWS
At a General Assembly . . . holden at Hartford . . . February . . . 1781. An act in addition to a law . . . for the punishment of high treason . . . Hartford, Hudson and Goodwin [1781]
broadside 33 X 22 cm.
MHi

B5265 CONNECTICUT. LAWS
At a General Assembly . . . holden at Hartford . . . February . . . 1781. An act, in addition to an act . . . for filling up and compleating this state's quota . . . Hartford, Hudson and Goodwin [1781]
broadside 34 X 20 cm.
CtHi mp. 43962

B5266 CONNECTICUT. LAWS
At a General Assembly . . . holden at Hartford . . . Febuary . . . 1781. An act, in addition to an act . . . for securing the balances . . . due to the officers and soldiers . . . Hartford, Hudson and Goodwin [1781]
broadside 33 X 19.5 cm.
Huntington 461
CSmH; CtHi; MHi mp. 43963

B5267 CONNECTICUT. LAWS
At a General Assembly . . . holden . . . the second Thursday of May, 1781. An act for raising supplies . . . [New London, T. Green, 1781]
broadside 32.5 X 20.5 cm.
CtHi; DLC; NHi mp. 43964

B5268 CONWAY, HENRY SEYMOUR, 1721–1795
General Conway's speech, for quieting the troubles in America . . . May 17th, 1781 . . . New York, Tuesday, May 22, 1781. [New York] J. Rivington [1781]
broadside 39.5 X 30 cm.
DLC; PPL mp. 43965

B5269 CORNWALLIS taken! Boston, (Friday) October 26, 1781. This morning an express arrived . . . [Boston] B. Edes [1781]
broadside 24 X 18.5 cm.
MWiW-C; NN (reduced facsim.) mp. 43966

B5270 DAVID'S victory over Goliath . . . [Boston] Sold at E. Russell's Office, near the Stump [1781]
broadside
Ford 2284
MSaE mp. 43967

B5271 DILWORTH, THOMAS, d. 1780
A new guide, to the English tongue . . . Norwich, John Trumbull, 1781.
iv, [5]-141 p. incl. front. (port.) illus. 16 cm.
New York Public 744
NN mp. 43967

B5272 DILWORTH, THOMAS, d. 1780
New guide to the English tongue . . . Philadelphia, Joseph Crukshank, 1781.
viii, 158 p. 17.5 cm.
CtHi mp. 43969

B5273 DIRECTIONS for ploughing, harrowing, sowing . . . grassing, and full management of white flax . . . Hartford, Hudson and Goodwin, 1781.
7 p. 18.5 cm.
New York Public 745
NN mp. 43970

B5274 DORCHESTER, MASS.
Your state tax for 1781. Your town rate. To be paid in gold or silver. [Boston, 1781]
broadside
Ford 2286
MHi

B5275 DORCHESTER, MASS.
Your state tax. 1781. To be paid in gold or silver, or bills of credit equivalent . . . Your town rate. 1781. To be paid in gold or silver . . . [Boston, 1781]
broadside
Ford 2287
MHi

B5276 DORCHESTER, MASS.
Your town tax, for hiring soldiers, 1781. To be paid in specie or paper . . . Your town rate, for purchasing beef, 1781, in the old currency . . . [Boston, 1781]
broadside
Ford 2285
MHi

B5277 ESCADRE commandée par M. le Compte de Barras. A le 178 pour la somme de tournois. Monsieur a trente jours de vue . . . [Newport, De l'Imprimerie Royal de l'Escadre, 1781]
broadside 15 X 24.5 cm.
Filled in for July 18, 1781, at Newport
RPJCB. Photostat: MWA

B5278 ESCADRE commandée par M. Destouches. A le 178 pour la somme de tournois. Monsieur a trente jours de vue . . . [Newport, De l'Imprimerie Royal de l'Escadre, 1781]

broadside 12.5 X 24.5 cm.
Filled in at Newport, Apr. 18, 1781
RPJCB. Photostat: MWA

B5279 THE Extraordinary Intelligencer. (To be continued occasionally.) Tuesday, October 2, 1781. Providence. We are happy to announce . . . Providence, Printed and sold by Bennett Wheeler [1781]
broadside 26 X 17 cm.
Battle of Yorktown
NHi mp. 43971

B5280 FRANCE. ARMY
Articles de la capitulation . . . Fait á York en Virginie, le 19 Octobre 1781. [Newport, De l'Imprimerie Royale de l'Escadre, 1781]
7 p.
Chapin p. [8]
RPJCB mp. 43972

B5281 FREEMAN'S JOURNAL
Postscript to the *Freeman's Journal*, Oct. 24. . . . the official account of the surrender of the army under Lord Cornwallis . . . Philadelphia, Francis Bailey, 1781.
broadside 42 X 33 cm.
NHi

B5282 FRESH advices from Virginia. Providence, Feb. 26, 1781. It is with pleasure . . . [Providence] J. Carter [1781].
broadside 23 X 9 cm.
Alden 855; New York Public 746; Winship p. 43
RHi. Photostats: MHi; MWA; NN mp. 43973

B5283 FRIENDS, SOCIETY OF. LONDON YEARLY MEETING
The epistle from the Yearly-Meeting in London, held by adjournments, from the 4th of the sixth month 1781, to the 9th of the same, inclusive . . . [Philadelphia, 1781]
4 p. fol.
Not Evans 19413
MWA; PPL mp. 43974

B5284 GAINE, HUGH
Just published, and may be had at the Book Store and Printing-Office in Hanover-Square, Gaine's Universal Register, or American and British Kalendar, for the year 1782 . . . [New York, Hugh Gaine, 1781]
broadside 59 X 41 cm.
CtHi mp. 43975

B5285 GLORIOUS intelligence! Norwich, October 26, 1781. Friday evening, six o'clock. By a gentleman this moment from New-London we are favoured with the following handbill . . . Norwich, John Trumbull [1781]
broadside 31 X 22 cm.
Announcing the surrender at Yorktown
RPJCB mp. 43976

B5286 GT. BRIT. ARMY
Whereas in pursuance of adquate powers . . . June 22d, 1781. Charlestown, Mills and Hicks [1781]
broadside 32 X 20 cm.
DLC mp. 43977

B5287 GT. BRIT. COLONIAL OFFICE
By their Excellencies, Sir Henry Clinton . . . and Mariot Arbuthnot . . . A declaration to the inhabitants . . . Given . . . this twenty ninth day of December, in the twenty first year of his Majesty's reign . . . [New York, 1781]
broadside 42 X 25.5 cm.
DLC (photostat) mp. 43978

B5288 GREENE, NATHANAEL, 1742–1786
Providence, February 20, 1781. This afternoon an express arrived . . . [Providence] John Carter [1781]
broadside 36.5 X 29 cm.
Alden 857
MWA; RHi mp. 44035

B5289 GUILFORD, VT.
At a town meeting holden in Guilford, this day of March [1782] Voted . . . there is a treaty entered into with the British . . . Voted . . . the New Hampshire Grants, justly owe their allegiance to . . . New York. Voted . . . to withdraw all allegiance . . . from . . . Vermont . . . [Westminster? J. P. Spooner, 1781?]
broadside 19 X 9 cm.
McCorison 35
VtHi mp. 43979

B5290 HEART-IN-HAND FIRE COMPANY, NEW YORK
Rules and orders to be ovserved by the Heart-in-hand Fire Company, instituted at New-York, January 1781. New-York, James Rivington, 1781.
11 p., 2 leaves.
RPJCB mp. 44010

B5291 HUNTINGTON, JONATHAN
The duty of all, when they marry, to invite Jesus to the wedding. A sermon, preached at the marriage of Mr. John Buck, and Miss Esther Clark . . . June 6, 1780 . . . Hartford, Hudson and Goodwin, 1781.
14 p. 19 cm.
Trumbull: Supplement 2283
CtHi mp. 43980

B5292 HUTCHINS, THOMAS, 1730–1789
Proposals for publishing by subscription, a map of the coast of West-Florida . . . By Thomas Hutchins, . . . has determined the author to fix the price of the map and pamphlet at three Spanish dollars . . . Mr. Robert Aitken . . . authorized to receive the subscription money. Philadelphia, October 15th, 1781.
broadside 34 X 20.5 cm.
Vail: Old frontier, 706
NHi mp. 43981

B5293 IMPORTANT intelligence! Boston, Friday, September 14, 1781 . . . [Boston] Willis's Office, Court-Street [1781]
broadside 25 X 19 cm.
Concerns action of General Greene in Carolina
Ford 2291
MHi; MSaE mp. 43982

B5294 INFLUENCE du depotisme de l'Angleterre . . . Prix, trente-six sols. Boston [1781]
145 p. 20 cm.
Doubtful American imprint
cf. Sabin 4177
DLC; MiU-C; NjP mp. 43983

B5295 INTELLIGENCE from the South. Major Giles, aid-de-camp to General Morgan, passed through this place yesterday morning, on his way to Congress, with the followieg [sic] intelligence . . . Richmond, February 3, 1781. [Richmond? 1781]
broadside 21.5 X 17 cm.
Tarleton's defeat at Cowpens
MiU-C mp. 43984

B5296 JANEWAY, JAMES, 1636?–1674
A token for children . . . With new additions. Boston, Printed and sold by Thomas and John Fleet, 1781.

[3], v, 26, [2], 37, [1], 38 p. 16 cm.
CLU; MH; MWA; N; PU. d'Alté A. Welch, Cleveland (1962); Miss Elizabeth Ball, Muncie, Ind. (1962)
mp. 43985

B5297 LAMSON, EBENEZER
Mene, tekel: or, A sermon; on the balances . . . The substance by Ebenezer Lamson . . . Hartford, Bavil Webster [1781?]
16 p. 17 cm. [A]-B^4
Trumbull: Supplement 2310
CtHi; MWA mp. 43987

B5298 LANCASTER, MASS.
Your proportion of the tax assessed *Sept. 10* 178*1*, is as follows, viz. State tax. Town and county rate. [n.p., 1781?]
broadside
Parts italicized are in ms.
Ford 2292
MHi

B5299 LYON, JOHN
The touchstone: a philosophical controversy, interspersed with satire and raillery . . . Annapolis, Frederick Green, 1781.
66, [2] p. 17 cm.
MdBP mp. 43988

B5300 [MCNUTT, ALEXANDER] 1725?–1811?
Considerations on the sovereignty, independence, trade and fisheries of New-Ireland . . . [Philadelphia? R. Aitken? 1781?]
24 p. 17 cm.
Contains over 3 p. not in Evans 16825, in a letter dated October 19, 1781, beginning on p. 12
MWA mp. 43989

B5301 MARINE SOCIETY, SALEM
Laws of the Marine Society, at Salem, in New-England. March 25, 1766 . . . [on verso] List of the member's names, and the time of entrance. N. B. From 1766 to inclusively . . . Simon Forrester, January 25, 1781. . . . Ephraim Emerton, March 29 . . . [Salem, 1781]
[2] p. 32.5 X 26.5 cm.
MHi; MSaE. Photostat: MWA mp. 44052

B5302 MARYLAND. COURT OF OYER AND TERMINER
Sentence of death for high treason. At a special court of Oyer and Terminer . . . at Frederick Town . . . July, 1781. Peter Sueman, Nicolaus Andrews, Jost Blecher, John George Grafes, Henry Schnell and Caspar Fritchie . . . indicted for high treason and convicted . . . [Philadelphia, Melchior Steiner, 1781]
broadside 18 X 14 cm.
In English and German
PHi mp. 43990

B5303 THE Maryland and Virginia almanack . . . for the year . . . 1782 . . . Baltimore, M. K. Goddard [1781]
[48] p. 17 cm.
Wheeler 130
MWA mp. 43991

B5304 MASSACHUSETTS. COURT OF GENERAL SESSIONS
Commonwealth of Massachusetts. Worcester ss. At a Court of General Sessions of the Peace . . . held at Worcester . . . the first Tuesday of December, A.D. 1781 . . . [Worcester, Isaiah Thomas, 1781]
broadside 32.5 X 19.5 cm.
MWA mp. 43992

B5305 MASSACHUSETTS. GOVERNOR, 1780–1785
By His Excellency John Hancock . . . a brief. Whereas the United States . . . have recommended . . . [Nov. 14, 1781] . . . [Boston, B. Edes, 1781]
broadside 37 X 25 cm.
DLC; MHi; MSaE (3 copies); PPRF mp. 43993

B5306 MASSACHUSETTS. HOUSE OF REPRESENTATIVES
Commonwealth of Massachusetts. In the House of Representatives, March 3, 1781. On the petition of Cols. Putnam, Jackson, and Brooks a committee from the army . . . liberty to purchase confiscated estates . . . [March 6, 1781] . . . [Boston, B. Edes, 1781?]
broadside 20 X 17 cm.
Date assigned from ms. note
MHi mp. 43994

B5307 MASSACHUSETTS. HOUSE OF REPRESENTATIVES
Commonwealth of Massachusetts. In the House of Representatives, June 16, 1781. Whereas it is of great consequence that provision be made for the defence of . . . Rhode-Island . . . [Boston, 1781]
broadside 51 X 19.5 cm.
MHi mp. 43995

B5308 MASSACHUSETTS. HOUSE OF REPRESENTATIVES
Commonwelath of Massachusetts. In the House of Representatives, June 22, 1781. Whereas it is necessary . . . [Boston, 1781]
4 p. folder. 35 cm.
Ford 2297
DLC; MHaHi; MHi; MWA mp. 43996

B5309 MASSACHUSETTS. HOUSE OF REPRESENTATIVES
Commonwealth of Massachusetts. In the House of Representatives, June 23, 1781. Whereas a number of soldiers . . . were rejected . . . as unfit . . . [Boston, 1781]
broadside 25 X 19.5 cm.
MWo mp. 43997

B5310 MASSACHUSETTS. TREASURER
Commonwealth of Massachusetts. The honorable Henry Gardner . . . To the selectmen or assessors of the town of Greeting . . . [Nov. 8, 1781] . . . [Boston, 1781]
broadside 41.5 X 33 cm.
DLC mp. 43998

B5311 MORRIS, ROBERT, 1734–1806
To the public. On the 17th day of May, 1781, the following plan was submitted to . . . congress assembled: Plan for a national bank . . . [Philadelphia, 1781]
broadside 42 X 34 cm.
Signed and dated: Robert Morris. Philadelphia, May 28, 1781
New York Public 747; Taylor 307
NHi; NN (reduced facsim.); PPAmP; PU
mp. 43999; 44060

5312 A MOURNFUL lamentation on the untimely death of paper money . . . died . . . in . . . 1781 . . . [Boston?] Printed by Sam. Adams, in the 10th, year of his age, and 1st month of his apprenticeship, 1781.
broadside
In verse

New York Public 748
NN (photograph) mp. 44000

B5313 NEW HAMPSHIRE
State of New-Hampshire. Exeter, November 22, 1781. Pursuant to an order of the General Court, will be farmed at public vendue . . . [Colophon] Exeter [1781]
broadside 34 X 21 cm.
Excise on spirituous liquors
Whittemore 301
NhHi mp. 44001

B5314 NEW HAMPSHIRE. HOUSE OF REPRESENTATIVES
State of New-Hampshire. In the House of Representatives, January 27, 1781. Resolved, that the selectmen . . . are directed to bring in their accounts of supplies . . . [Exeter, 1781]
broadside 17 X 17 cm.
Whittemore 302
NhHi

B5315 NEW HAMPSHIRE. HOUSE OF REPRESENTATIVES
State of New-Hampshire. In the House of representatives, July 3, 1781. The committee to form a table or scale . . . [Exeter, Z. Fowle, 1781]
broadside 31.5 X 20 cm.
DLC; NhD; NhHi mp. 44003

B5316 NEW HAMPSHIRE. HOUSE OF REPRESENTATIVES
State of New-Hampshire. In the House of Representatives, August 24th, 1781. The committee to consider . . . those towns who are deficient in . . . Continental Soldiers, reported . . . [Exeter, 1781]
broadside 25 X 18 cm.
NhHi mp. 44004

B5317 NEW HAMPSHIRE. HOUSE OF REPRESENTATIVES
State of New-Hampshire. In the House of Representatives: November 20th, 1781. Resolved, That the several towns . . . make out their accounts for supplies . . . [Exeter, Zechariah Fowle, 1781]
broadside 22 X 17.5 cm.
Lewis M. Stark, New York (1963) Photostat: NN
mp. 44005

B5318 NEW HAMPSHIRE. LAWS
. . . An act for making gold and silver a tender for all debts . . . [Sept. 1, 1781] . . . [Exeter? 1781]
broadside 34.5 X 22.5 cm.
Huntington 467
CSmH mp. 44006

B5319 NEW HAMPSHIRE. LAWS
State of New-Hampshire. In the year . . . One Thousand Seven Hundred and Eighty-one. An act for the raising & compleating . . . January 12th, 1781 . . . [Exeter, Z. Fowle, 1781]
[2] p. 49.5 X 19 cm.
DLC mp. 44007

B5320 NEW HAMPSHIRE. PRESIDENT
State of New-Hampshire. The government and people of said State. To the selectmen of in the County of Rockingham, in said State. Greeting . . . Exeter, the 27th of January, 1781. M. Weare, President. [Exeter, 1781]
broadside
To choose replacement for George Atkinson, resigned Council member
NhHi mp. 44002

B5321 NEW HAVEN BRIDGE LOTTERY
A list of the fortunate numbers in the first class of New-Haven Bridge Lottery . . . [New Haven? 1781]
broadside 35.5 X 21 cm.
NHi mp. 44009

B5322 NEW JERSEY. LAWS
An act for the regulating, training, and arraying of the militia . . . Passed at Trenton, January 8, 1781. Trenton, Isaac Collins [1781]
p. 20.5 cm.
NjR (t.p. only)

B5323 NEW JERSEY. TREASURER
No. The State of New-Jersey is indebted unto in the sum of being the fourth part of the sum allowed for the depreciation of his pay . . . Witness my hand this day of one thousand seven hundred and eighty-one . . . [n.p., 1781?]
broadside 11.5 X 21.5 cm.
MiU-C

B5324 NEW YORK. ASSEMBLY
Votes and proceedings of the Assembly, &c. Poughkeepsie . . . October 24th, 10 o'clock, A.M. [-Nov. 23, 1781] [Poughkeepsie, John Holt, 1781?]
47 p. 30.5 cm. caption title
Vail: Patriotic pair, p. 420
N; NHi; NNS mp. 44011

B5325 NEW YORK. GOVERNOR, 1777–1795
By His excellency George Clinton . . . Proclamation [convening state legislature] . . . Poughkeepsie [J. Holt?] Sept. 6, 1781.
broadside 12 X 8 cm.
MB; MWA mp. 44012

B5326 NEW YORK. GOVERNOR, 1777–1795
By His Excellency George Clinton . . . To Greeting. Pursuant to the authority in me vested . . . "An act for raising two regiments for the defence . . ." Given at Poughkeepsie, this Day of 1781. [Poughkeepsie. 1781]
broadside 21.5 X 26.5 cm.
New York Public 749; Vail: Patriotic pair, p. 412
NHi; NNMer (formerly). Photostat: NN

B5327 NEW YORK. GOVERNOR, 1777–1795
State of New-York. Head-Quarters, Poughkeepsie, July 1st, 1781. General orders. . . . [Poughkeepsie, John Holt, 1781]
broadside 25.5 X 19.5 cm.
Proclamation for raising of troops
Vail: Patriotic pair, p. 413
NHi mp. 44013

B5328 NEWPORT, October 25, 1781. Glorious intelligence! Yesterday afternoon arrived . . . New-London, T. Green [1781]
broadside 31.5 X 17 cm.
MHi. Photostats: DLC; MWA; MiU-C; NN mp. 44014

B5329 [NEWPORT, October 25, 1781. Yesterday afternoon arrived . . . Capt. Lovett . . . and brought us the glorious news of the surrender of Lord Cornwallis . . . Newport, Southwick and Barber? 1781]
[broadside?]

Alden 861; Winship p. 42
No copy known mp. 44015

B5330 NORTH CAROLINA. MILITIA
Rules and regulations for the well-governing the loyal militia . . . of North-Carolina . . . Head-quarters, Wilmington, 25th September, 1781. [Wilmington? 1781]
broadside 30.5 X 18 cm.
14 rules plus a concluding paragraph
NcU mp. 44016

B5331 OFFICIAL intelligence from Virginia. Providence, November 8, 1781. This morning a flag of truce . . . Providence, John Carter [1781]
broadside 47 X 36 cm.
Alden 862; Winship 43
DLC; RHi mp. 44017

B5332 PENNSYLVANIA
Pennsylvania, ss. The Supreme Executive Council of . . . Pennsylvania . . . Whereas requested permission to go into . . . New-York not to return again . . . Given by order of the Council . . . this day of 1781 [Philadelphia, 1781]
broadside 22 X 30 cm.
Permit signed by Timothy Matlack, dated Aug. 3, 1781
Taylor 291
NN

B5333 PENNSYLVANIA. COMMISSIONERS
Gentlemen, Agreeable to a late act . . . passed the 25th of June 1781 . . . You are required to enlist . . . one able bodied recruit . . . [Philadelphia, 1781]
broadside 33 X 20 cm.
DLC mp. 44018

B5334 PENNSYLVANIA. COUNCIL
Council-chamber, Philadelphia, 1781. Instructions for recruiting . . . Joseph Reed, President . . . [Philadelphia, 1781]
broadside 31 X 19 cm.
DLC; NHi mp. 44019

B5335 PENNSYLVANIA. COUNCIL
Im Rath. Philadelphia, den 26sten Jenner, 1781. Da das Militz-Gesetz dieses Staats erfordert, dass die Sub-Leutenants . . . Auszug aus dem Protocoll, T. Matlack, Secretär. [Philadelphia, 1781]
broadside 26 X 20.5 cm.
Taylor 287
PHi mp. 44020

B5336 PENNSYLVANIA. COUNCIL
In Council. Philadelphia, January 26th, 1781. Whereas the Militia Law of this State, requires, that the Sub-lieutenants . . . Extract from the minutes, T. Matlack, Secretary. [Philadelphia, 1781]
broadside 25.5 X 21 cm.
Taylor 288
PHi. Goodspeed's (1965) mp. 44021

B5337 PENNSYLVANIA. COUNCIL
In Council, Philadelphia, June 15, 1781. Whereas . . . Congress, have required of this State, three troops of militia cavalry . . . Resolved, That the Lieutenants of each County . . . Extract from the minutes, T. Matlack, Secretary. [Philadelphia] Francis Bailey [1781]
broadside 33 X 21 cm.
Taylor 290
PHi mp. 44022

B5338 PENNSYLVANIA. COUNCIL
To the commissioners and assessors of the county of Gentlemen, Herewith we send you a law passed at the last session . . . [In manuscript] Jos: Reed President. In Council Philad[a] June 30th 1781. [Philadelphia, 1781]
broadside 33 X 20 cm.
DLC mp. 44024

B5339 PENNSYLVANIA. LAWS
An act for the gradual abolition of slavery. [Philadelphia, 1781?]
16 p. 19.5 cm.
Taylor 285
DLC (not traced 1964) mp. 44027

B5340 PENNSYLVANIA. LAWS
The acts of the General Assembly . . . And an appendix, containing the laws now in force . . . Philadelphia, Francis Bailey, 1781.
2 p.l., xxxi, [1], 527, viii p. 30 cm.
Taylor 286; cf. Evans 17656
CtY; DLC; MWA; PPAmP mp. 44029

B5341 PENNSYLVANIA. LAWS
Postscript to the *Pennsylvania Packet*. State of Pennsylvania. In General assembly, Thursday, June 14, 1781 . . . [Philadelphia, David C. Claypoole, 1781]
[2] p. 36 X 24 cm.
DLC mp. 44030

B5342 PENNSYLVANIA. LAWS
State of Pennsylvania. / An act for recruiting the Pennsylvania Line in / the Army of the United States. / . . . [at end] Enacted into a law at Philadelphia, on / Monday the 25th of June, in the / year 1781. / S. Sterrett, clerk of the General Assembly. [n.p., 1781]
[2] p. 31 cm.
DLC mp. 44025

B5343 PENNSYLVANIA. LAWS
State of Pennsylvania. / An act for recruiting the Pennsylvania line in / the Army of the United States / . . . [at end] Enacted into a law at Philadelphia, on Monday / the twenty-fifth day of June, in the year / One thousand seven hundred and eighty and one. / Samuel Sterrett, Clerk of the General Assembly. / [Philadelphia, Thomas Bradford, 1781]
[2] p. 43 X 26 cm.
Taylor 293
DLC; PHi mp. 44026

B5344 PENNSYLVANIA. LAWS
State of Pennsylvania. An act to raise effective supplies for the year one thousand seven hundred and eighty one. [Philadelphia, 1781]
[4] p. 43 X 26 cm. caption title
Dated June 21, 1781
New York Public 751; Taylor 294
NN mp. 44028

B5345 THE Pennsylvania, Maryland, and Virginia almanack and ephemeris, for . . . 1782 . . . Baltimore, Printed and sold by M. K. Goddard [1781]
[48] p. [A]-F^4
Wheeler 134
MdHi. J. W. Garrett, Baltimore (1938)

B5346 PHILADELPHIA, January 22, 1781. Extract of a letter from Trenton, dated Jan. 20, 1781. Military systems, in general . . . [Philadelphia, 1781]

broadside 34.5 X 19.5 cm.
Cites blunders in British strategy
PHi mp. 44031

B5347 PHILADELPHIA, February 8, 1781. This morning arrived from the southward, Major Giles . . . with dispatches to Congress . . . [Philadelphia] David C. Claypoole [1781]
broadside 34.5 X 17 cm.
Text in 2 columns
Report of the battle of Cowpens
RPJCB mp. 44032

B5348 PRO bono [publico] Ascot-Heath, second meeting. By permission, three days sport. [New York] Printed by A. Robertson [1781]
broadside 35 X 26.5 cm.
Dated May 8th, 1781
New York Public 752
MWA (mutilated). Photostat: NN mp. 44033

B5349 PROPOSALS made to the non-commissioned officers and soldiers of the Pennsylvania Line, at Trenton January 7, 1781. [n.p., 1781]
broadside 28 X 18 cm.
DLC mp. 44034

B5350 PROVIDENCE, October 25, 1781 . . . This moment an express arrived . . . Providence, John Carter [1781]
broadside 22 X 16 cm.
Alden 863; Winship Addenda p. 89
Ct; MHi; RHi. Photostats: DLC; MWA; NN
mp. 44036

B5351 RELATION de la sortie de l'escadre francais . . . [Newport, 1781]
4 p. 24 X 20 cm.
March 16 [1781] is the latest date given in the text
Alden 865; New York Public 754
MWA. Photostats: NN; NjP; RPJCB
mp. 44037

B5352 RHODE ISLAND. ELECTION PROX.
Gentlemen landholders, who pay a heavy tax . . . look out for yourselves. His Excellency William Greene, Esq; Governor. The honorable Jabez Bowen, Esq; Deputy-governor . . . [Providence? 1781]
broadside 23 X 13.5 cm.
Alden 866; Chapin Proxies 31a, 31b
RHi (2 variants) mp. 44038

B5353 RHODE ISLAND. ELECTION PROX.
His Excellency William Greene, Esq; Governor. The honorable Jabez Bowen, Esq; Deputy governor . . . [Providence? 1781]
broadside 20 X 13 cm.
Alden 867; Chapin Proxies 29a, 29b
RHi (2 variants) mp. 44039

B5354 RHODE ISLAND. ELECTION PROX.
His Excellency William Greene, Esq; Governor. The honorable Jabez Bowen, Esq; Dep. Governor . . . [Providence] John Carter [1781]
broadside 20.5 X 12.5 cm.
Alden 868; Chapin Proxies 30
MWA; RHi mp. 44040

B5355 RHODE ISLAND. GENERAL ASSEMBLY
State of Rhode-Island and Providence Planatations. In General assembly, March session, 1781. Whereas by an act . . . passed . . . in January last, for apportioning . . . and for collecting fresh beef . . . [Providence] Bennett Wheeler [1781]
broadside 38 X 26 cm.
Alden 877; Winship p. 44
RHi (mutilated) mp. 44041

B5356 RHODE ISLAND. GENERAL ASSEMBLY
State of Rhode-Island and Providence Plantations. In General assembly, May session, 1781. Whereas the legislature . . . Providence, John Carter [1781]
broadside 36 X 23.5 cm.
Alden 879; Winship p. 44
DLC; RHi mp. 44042

B5357 RHODE ISLAND. GENERAL ASSEMBLY
State of Rhode-Island and Providence Plantations. In General Assembly, July session, 1781. Whereas five hundred men . . . [Providence, J. Carter, 1781]
broadside 34 X 23.5 cm.
Printed in a Scotch type used by Carter
Alden 885
MWA; RHi mp. 44047

B5358 RHODE ISLAND. GENERAL ASSEMBLY
State of Rhode-Island and Providence Plantations. In General Assembly, July session, 1781. Whereas from the neglect of the collectors . . . [Providence, 1781]
broadside 26.5 X 17.5 cm.
Alden 886
NNC; R; RHi; RPB mp. 44048

B5359 RHODE ISLAND. GENERAL ASSEMBLY
State of Rhode-Island and Providence Plantations. In General assembly, August session, 1781. Whereas it is necessary that measures be taken . . . [Providence, J. Carter, 1781]
broadside 38 X 26 cm.
Set in a Scotch type used by Carter
Alden 891; Winship p. 44
MWA; RHi; RPJCB; RWe mp. 44050

B5360 RHODE ISLAND. LAWS
State of Rhode-Island and Providence Plantations. In General assembly, May second session, 1781. An act for granting . . . a tax of six thousand pounds . . . Providence, John Carter [1781]
broadside 32.5 X 23 cm.
Alden 880; Winship p. 44
CtY; R; RHi mp. 44043

B5361 RHODE ISLAND. LAWS
State of Rhode-Island and Providence Plantations. In General assembly, May second session, 1781. An act for granting . . . a tax of twenty thousand pounds . . . Providence, John Carter [1781]
broadside 39 X 26.5 cm.
Alden 881; Winship p. 44
R; RHi; RWe mp. 44044

B5362 RHODE ISLAND. LAWS
State of Rhode-Island and Providence Plantations. In General Assembly, May second session, 1781. An act for incorporating and bring into the field five hundred . . . men . . . [Providence, John Carter, 1781]
broadside 43 X 20 cm.
Printed in a Scotch type used by Carter
Alden 882; Winship p. 44
MWA; R; RHi mp. 44045

B5363 RHODE ISLAND. LAWS
State of Rhode-Island and Providence Plantations. In General assembly, July session, 1781. An act for proportioning . . . supplies of beef . . . [Providence] Bennett Wheeler [1781]
broadside 43 X 16 cm.
Alden 884; Winship p. 44
RHi (2 copies); RPJCB; RWe mp. 44046

B5364 RHODE ISLAND. LAWS
State of Rhode-Island and Providence Plantations. In General assembly, August session, 1781. An act for mitigating of penalties . . . Providence, John Carter [1781]
broadside 30.5 X 19.5 cm.
Alden 889; Winship p. 44
MWA; RHi; RPJCB mp. 44049

B5365 [ROCHAMBEAU, JEAN BAPTISTE DONATIEN DE VIMEUR, COMTE DE] 1725–1807
Relation, ou journal des opérations du Corps Francais sous le commandement du Comte de Rochambeau . . . depuis le 15 d'août . . . [Colophon] A Philadelphie, De l'imprimerie de Guillaume Hampton [1781]
15 p. 27 cm.
National Archives, Paris. Photostats: MHi; MWA
mp. 44051

B5366 SANDS, COMFORT, AND CO.
Fish-Kill, December 22, 1781. The subscribers inform the gentlemen of the army . . . [Fishkill, 1781]
broadside 33 X 20.5 cm.
Huntington 468; Vail: Patriotic pair, p. 413
CSmH mp. 44053

B5367 SCALE of depreciation, agreeable to an act of the (now) Commonwealth of Massachusetts, passed September 29, 1780. [Boston, 1781]
broadside 24 X 9 cm.
Ford 2309
MWA mp. 44054

B5368 SCALE of depreciation . . . to be observed as a rule for settling the rate of depreciation on all contracts . . . From April 1st, 1780, to April 20th, one Spanish milled dollar was equal to forty of the old emission . . . February 27th, 1781, 75 [Boston, 1781]
broadside 35 X 21 cm.
Ford 2310; New York Public 755
MWA; RPJCB. Photostat: NN mp. 44055

B5369 SCALE of depreciation . . . to be observed as a rule for settling the rate of depreciation on all contracts . . . From April 1st, 1780, to April 20th, one Spanish milled dollar was equal to forty of the old emission . . . February 27th, 1781 75 . . . From the 15th of June to the 1st of October, four of the new emission were equal to one in specie. [Boston, 1781]
broadside 35 X 21 cm.
MHi; MWA mp. 44056

B5370 SCALES, WILLIAM, 1742–1799
Priestcraft exposed from its foundation . . . Danvers, near Salem, Printed and sold by E. Russell, 1781.
16 p. 18 cm. [A]-B^4
MSaE; MWA mp. 44057

B5371 SOUTH CAROLINA
Instructions for the office established to receive the pay of Negroes employed in the different departments. [Charleston? 1781?]
broadside fol.
Turnbull p. 232 (v.1)
NN

B5372 THE South-Carolina and Georgia almanack for . . . 1782. By John Tobler. Charles-Town, R. Wells; Savannah, David Zubly [1781]
[32] p.
Drake 13129
ScC

B5373 TABLES shewing the amount of any number of dollars . . . in the currencies of all the United States . . . Rules for reducing the currency of either of the states to that of any other of them . . . [New England? 1781?]
broadside 44.5 X 20.5 cm.
In ms. on back: A table shewing the value of a dollar . . . Jany 1781
RPJCB mp. 44058

B5374 TO the commissioners of forfeitures of the Western District . . . Whereas by an act . . . passed the 4th October, 1780 . . . [New York, 1781?]
broadside 20 X 16 cm.
Blank form dated in manuscript: 3. August 1782
DLC mp. 44059

B5375 TO the public. A number of merchants, traders and others in New-Haven, conceive that some transactions passed yesterday . . . We declare . . . that we are not . . . concern'd in . . . illicit trade . . . New-Haven, August 31st, 1781. [New Haven, 1781]
broadside 36 X 20.5 cm.
CtHi mp. 44008

B5376 Deleted

B5377 U. S. ARMY. CONTINENTAL ARMY
Orders for regulating the drawing and issuing of provision . . . [Newburgh? 1781]
broadside 33 X 19.5 cm.
DLC mp. 44061

B5378 U. S. CONTINENTAL CONGRESS, 1781
By a gentleman from Philadelphia we are favour'd with the *Pennsylvania Packet* of the 18th instant . . . the late important action . . . near Charlestown, the 8th ultimo. Philadelphia, October 18, 1781 . . . Published by order of Congress . . . [Boston?] Printed and sold opposite the Court-House [1781]
broadside
Amer. Art Assoc. catalog, Feb. 8, 1917, item 85
New York Public 738; Taylor 297
NN (reduced facsim.) mp. 44063

B5379 U. S. CONTINENTAL CONGRESS, 1781
By the United States in Congress assembled. August 7th, 1781. Whereas the state of New-Hampshire and New-York have submitted to Congress the decision of the disputes between them and . . . the New-Hampshire Grants . . . State of New-Hampshire . . . Exeter, Sept. 27th, 1781 . . . [Exeter, 1781]
broadside 29 X 19 cm.
Whittemore 314
NhHi. Photostat: NhD mp. 44064

B5380 U. S. CONTINENTAL CONGRESS, 1781
(Circular.) Philadelphia, February 8, 1781. Sir, Your Excellency . . . Providence, John Carter [1781]
broadside 28 X 19 cm.

Alden 897; Winship p. 44
R; RHi mp. 44065

B5381 U. S. CONTINENTAL CONGRESS, 1781
An ordinance, relative to the capture and condemnation of prizes . . . [Mar. 27, 1781] Philadelphia, David C. Claypoole [1781]
broadside 39 X 20.5 cm.
DLC; MB mp. 44066

B5382 U. S. CONTINENTAL CONGRESS, 1781
The United States in Congress assembled. September 7, 1781. The following form of the exequatur, is recommended to . . . the several states. To all to whom it may concern: having been recognized by the United States . . . [Philadelphia? 1781]
broadside 26 X 20 cm.
Taylor 308
NN mp. 44067

B5383 U. S. INSPECTOR-GENERAL'S OFFICE
Regulations for the order and discipline of the troops of the United States. Part I. Boston, Printed by T. and J. Fleet, 1781.
110+ p. 20 cm. [A]-F^8 $G^{8?}$
MWA (wanting after p. 110) mp. 44068

B5384 U. S. OFFICE OF FINANCE
Office of finance, Philadelphia, 12th December, 1781. Proposals will be received . . . for the following contracts . . . [Philadelphia, 1781]
broadside 24.5 X 19.5 cm.
DLC mp. 44069

B5385 VERMONT. GENERAL ASSEMBLY
[Claim to the New-Hampshire Grants. Westminster, J. P. Spooner & T. Green, 1781]
broadside
Printer's bill dated Mar. 17, 1781
McCorison 38
No copy known mp. 44070

B5386 VERMONT. GOVERNOR, 1778–1789
[Fast day proclamation for April, 1781. Westminster, J. P. Spooner & T. Green, 1781]
broadside
Printer's bill dated July 16, 1783
No copy known mp. 44071

B5387 VERMONT. LAWS
An act for levying a tax of six-pence on the pound, on the polls and rateable estate of the inhabitants . . . Passed October 27, 1781. Westminster, Judah P. Spooner [1781]
broadside 28 cm.
Cooley 10; Sabin 99086
MWA. Photostat: VtU mp. 44072

B5388 VERMONT. LAWS
[An act for the purpose of procuring provision for the troops. Westminster, Judah P. Spooner, 1781]
broadside
Cooley 3; Sabin 99085
No copy known mp. 44073

B5389 VERMONT. LAWS
[An act regulating the militia of the State of Vermont, passed February 1781. Westminster, J. P. Spooner & T. Green, 1781]

Printer's bill dated Mar. 30, 1781
McCorison 43
No copy known mp. 44074

B5390 VERMONT. LAWS
[Acts and laws, passed at Windsor, April, 1781. Westminster, J. P. Spooner & T. Green, 1781]
2 p.
Printer's bill dated Apr. 23, 1781
McCorison 46; Sabin 99081
No copy known mp. 44075

B5391 VERMONT. LAWS
Acts and laws, passed by the General Assembly of the representatives . . . at their session at Bennington, October, 1780. [Westminster, Spooner and Green, 1781]
125-128 p. 32 cm.
Cooley 4; New York Public 756; Sabin 99079
MH-L; PHi; Vt. Photostats: MHi; NN; VtU
mp. 44076

B5392 VERMONT. TREATIES
Articles of Union, agreed upon between the Committee of the Legislature of . . . Vermont, and the Committee of the Convention of the New-Hampshire Grants, at Windsor, in February, 1781 . . . [Westminster, J. P. Spooner & T. Green, 1781]
3 p. 33 cm. caption title
McCorison 37
NhPlain; RPJCB mp. 44077

B5393 VIRGINIA. COUNCIL
In Council, March 30, 1781. Sir. The act of October 1780, for recruiting this state's quota of troops . . . [Richmond, John Dixon and Thomas Nicolson? 1781]
broadside 20.5 X 16 cm.
DLC mp. 44078

B5394 VIRGINIA. COUNCIL
In Council, April 12, 1781. Sir, Having received an application from the commanding officer . . . [n.p., 1781]
broadside 33 X 20 cm.
DLC mp. 44079

B5395 VIRGINIA. GOVERNOR, 1779-1781
By His Excellency Thomas Jefferson, Esq; Governour . . . I have thought fit . . . to issue this my proclamation . . . Richmond, this *19th* day of January . . . [1781] . . . [Richmond, 1781]
broadside 21 X 16 cm.
DLC; MiU-C; NHi mp. 44080

B5396 VIRGINIA. LAWS
An act for enlisting soldiers . . . June 21, 1781. Charlottesville, Dunlap and Hayes [1781]
broadside 29 X 19 cm.
DLC mp. 44081

B5397 VIRGINIA. LAWS
An act for recruiting this State's quota of troops to serve in the Continental Army . . . [Richmond? 1781]
[4] p. 33 cm. caption title
DLC mp. 44082

B5398 VIRGINIA. LAWS
An act for supplying the army with clothes, provisions and waggons . . . [Richmond? 1781]
2 p.
Enclosed with a letter from Benjamin Harrison dated Feb. 16, 1781, to Washington
DLC mp. 44083

B5399 THE Virginia almanack for . . . 1782 . . . By Robert Andrews . . . Richmond, Printed and sold by J. Dixon, & T. Nicolson [1781]

[24] p. 13 cm.
Bear 53; Drake 13793
MWA; NN

B5400 WATTS, ISAAC, 1674-1748
Hymns and spiritual songs . . . Hartford, Bavil Webster, 1781.
289, [1] p. 15 cm.
CtHi; MWA (imperfect) mp. 44084

1782

B5401 AITKEN, ROBERT, 1734-1802
Philadelphia, 11 August, 1782. Sir, Various inducements have led me to print . . . the Bible . . . for sale by the beginning of October . . . R. Aitken . . . [Philadelphia, 1782]
[4] p. 24 cm.
Pages 2 and 4 blank; p. 3 has sample passage
MHi mp. 44086

B5402 [DER allerneuste, verbesserte- und zuverlassige Americanische Reichs-Staats- Siegs- und Geschichts-Calender auf . . . 1783. Friedrich-Stadt, Matthias Bartgis [1782]]

Drake 2192; Reichmann
No copy located

B5403 ANNAPOLIS THEATRE
Annapolis, October 5, 1782. Mr. Lindsay . . . intends opening the theatre . . . on the 23d instant . . . [Annapolis, F. Green, 1782]
broadside 12 X 17 cm.
Wheeler 136
NHi mp. 44087

B5404 ANNAPOLIS THEATRE
By permission. At the Theatre in Annapolis . . . on Tuesday, the 29th of October, 1782 . . . the Merchant of Venice . . . To conclude with a hornpipe by Mr. Patterson . . . [Annapolis, F. Green, 1782]
broadside 34 X 17 cm.
Wheeler 138
NHi mp. 44088

B5405 ANNAPOLIS THEATRE
By permission. On Friday evening, the 25th of October, 1782 . . . the tragedy of Douglass . . . [Annapolis, F. Green, 1782]
broadside 33.5 X 17 cm.
Wheeler 137
NHi mp. 44089

B5406 ANNAPOLIS THEATRE
By permission. On Friday, the 1st of November, 1782 . . . The Fair Penitent . . . To conclude with a hornpipe by Mr. Patterson . . . [Annapolis, F. Green, 1782]
broadside 33.5 X 20 cm.
Wheeler 141
NHi mp. 44090

B5407 ANNAPOLIS THEATRE
By permission. On Saturday, the 2d of November, 1782 . . . Venice preserved . . . [Annapolis, F. Green, 1782]
broadside 33.5 X 21 cm.
Wheeler 142
NHi mp. 44091

B5408 ANNAPOLIS THEATRE
By permission. On Thursday, the 31st of October, 1782 . . . The London merchant . . . [Annapolis, F. Green, 1782]
broadside 33.5 X 17 cm.
Wheeler 140
NHi mp. 44092

B5409 ANNAPOLIS THEATRE
By permission. On Wednesday evening, the 6th of November, 1782 . . . The Beaux Stratagem . . . [Annapolis, F. Green, 1782]
broadside 34 X 21 cm.
Wheeler 143
NHi mp. 44093

B5410 ANNAPOLIS THEATRE
By permission. On Wednesday, the 30th of October, 1782 . . . The Revenge . . . [Annapolis, F. Green, 1782]
broadside 33.5 X 17 cm.
Wheeler 139
NHi mp. 44094

B5411 ASHE, SAMUEL, 1725-1813
A charge given to the Grand-Jury at Wilmington, Nov. 30, 1782, by the Hon. Samuel Ashe Esq; one of the judges of the Superior Courts. [n.p., 1782]
broadside 29.5 X 38 cm.
In two columns
McMurtrie: North Carolina 111
NcU mp. 44095

B5412 ASSOCIATE PRESBYTERY OF PENNSYLVANIA
Act of the Associate Presbytery of Pennsylvania, for a fast. At Philadelphia, October 21st, 1782 . . . [Philadelphia] Robert Aitken [1782]
broadside 26.5 X 21.5 cm.
MHi; MWA mp. 44096

B5413 AT the sign of the Indian King, in Baltimore, in a large room fitted up in a theatrical manner, on Monday evening, the 2d day of December . . . the noted Bayly will exhibit his grand medley of entertainments . . . Baltimore, M. K. Goddard [1782]
broadside 34.5 X 20.5 cm.
Wheeler 209
NHi mp. 44175

B5414 AUSBUND geistlicher Lieder, gestellt in der Gemeinde an Antitum. [Ephrata] Gedruckt Anno 1782.
[16] p. 16 cm.
Taylor 313
PHi mp. 44097

B5415 BALTIMORE THEATRE
By particular desire. At the Theatre . . . the 24th of September, 1782 . . . the tragedy of Jane Shore . . . Baltimore, M. K. Goddard [1782]
broadside 34.5 X 21.5 cm.
Wheeler 196
NHi mp. 44132

B5416 BALTIMORE THEATRE
By permission. At the new Theatre . . . the 18th of January, 1782 . . . King Richard III . . . [Baltimore, M. K. Goddard, 1782]
broadside 33.5 X 21 cm.
Wheeler 146
Randall Collection, Baltimore mp. 44098

B5417 BALTIMORE THEATRE
By permission. At the new Theatre . . . the 25th of January, 1782 . . . the tragedy of the Orphan . . . Baltimore, M. K. Goddard [1782]

broadside 33.5 X 21 cm.
Wheeler 147
Randall Collection mp. 44099

B5418 BALTIMORE THEATRE
By permission. At the new Theatre . . . the 29th of January, 1782 . . . the tragedy of the Orphan . . . Baltimore, M. K. Goddard [1782]
broadside 33.5 X 21 cm.
Wheeler 148
Randall Collection mp. 44100

B5419 BALTIMORE THEATRE
By permission. At the new Theatre . . . the 8th of February, 1782 . . . the Beaux Stratagem . . . Baltimore, M. K. Goddard [1782]
broadside 33.5 X 21 cm.
Wheeler 150
Randall Collection mp. 44101

B5420 BALTIMORE THEATRE
By permission. At the new Theatre . . . the 22d of February, 1782 . . . the Gamester . . . Baltimore, M. K. Goddard [1782]
broadside 33.5 X 21 cm.
Wheeler 153
Randall Collection mp. 44102

B5421 BALTIMORE THEATRE
By permission. At the new Theatre . . . the 1st of March, 1782 . . . The Busy Body . . . Baltimore, M. K. Goddard [1782]
broadside 33.5 X 21 cm.
Wheeler 154
Randall Collection mp. 44103

B5422 BALTIMORE THEATRE
By permission. At the new Theatre . . . the 5th of March, 1782 . . . Venice Preserv'd . . . Baltimore, M. K. Goddard [1782]
broadside 33.5 X 21 cm.
Wheeler 155
Randall Collection mp. 44104

B5423 BALTIMORE THEATRE
By permission. At the new Theatre . . . the 8th of March, 1782 . . . the Beaux Stratagem . . . Baltimore, M. K. Goddard [1782]
broadside 33.5 X 21 cm.
Wheeler 156
Randall Collection mp. 44105

B5424 BALTIMORE THEATRE
By permission. At the new Theatre . . . the 13th of March, 1782 . . . The Busy Body . . . Baltimore, M. K. Goddard [1782]
broadside 33.5 X 21 cm.
Wheeler 158
Randall Collection mp. 44106

B5425 BALTIMORE THEATRE
By permission. At the new Theatre . . . the 15th of March, 1782 . . . the Fair Penitent . . . Baltimore, M. K. Goddard [1782]
broadside 33.5 X 21 cm.
Wheeler 159
Randall Collection mp. 44107

B5426 BALTIMORE THEATRE
By permission. At the new Theatre . . . the 19th of March, 1782 . . . Venice preserv'd . . . Baltimore, M. K. Goddard [1782]
broadside 33.5 X 21 cm.
Wheeler 160
Randall Collection mp. 44108

B5427 BALTIMORE THEATRE
By permission. At the new Theatre . . . the 22d of March, 1782 . . . the Fair Penitent . . . Baltimore, M. K. Goddard [1782]
broadside 33.5 X 21 cm.
Wheeler 161
Randall Collection mp. 44109

B5428 BALTIMORE THEATRE
By permission. At the new Theatre . . . the 26th of March, 1782 . . . the tragedy of Jane Shore . . . Baltimore, M. K. Goddard [1782]
broadside 33.5 X 21 cm.
Wheeler 161a
Randall Collection mp. 44110

B5429 BALTIMORE THEATRE
By permission. At the new Theatre . . . the 1st of April, 1782 . . . the London Merchant . . . Baltimore, M. K. Goddard [1782]
broadside 31 X 20 cm.
Wheeler 162
Randall Collection mp. 44111

B5430 BALTIMORE THEATRE
By permission. At the new Theatre . . . the 2d of April, 1782 . . . The Busy Body . . . Baltimore, M. K. Goddard [1782]
broadside 33.5 X 20.5 cm.
Wheeler 162a
Randall Collection mp. 44112

B5431 BALTIMORE THEATRE
By permission. At the new Theatre . . . the 4th of April, 1782 . . . the Fair Penitent . . . Baltimore, M. K. Goddard [1782]
broadside 34 X 21 cm.
Wheeler 163
Randall Collection mp. 44113

B5432 BALTIMORE THEATRE
By permission. At the new Theatre . . . the 9th of April, 1782 . . . the comedy . . . A Woman keeps a Secret . . . Baltimore, M. K. Goddard [1782]
broadside 34 X 18.5 cm.
Wheeler 164
Randall Collection mp. 44114

B5433 BALTIMORE THEATRE
By permission. At the new Theatre . . . the 12th of April, 1782 . . . the comedy . . . A Woman keeps a Secret . . . Baltimore, M. K. Goddard [1782]
broadside 33.5 X 18.5 cm.
Wheeler 165
Randall Collection mp. 44115

B5434 BALTIMORE THEATRE
By permission. At the new Theatre . . . the 16th of April, 1782 . . . the tragedy of Zara . . . Baltimore, M. K. Goddard [1782]
broadside 34 X 19 cm.
Wheeler 166
Randall Collection mp. 44116

B5435 BALTIMORE THEATRE
By permission. At the new Theatre . . . the 19th of April, 1782 . . . the tragedy of Zara . . . Baltimore, M. K. Goddard [1782]

broadside 34 X 20.5 cm.
Wheeler 167
Randall Collection mp. 44117

B5436 BALTIMORE THEATRE
By permission. At the new Theatre . . . thc 23d of April, 1782 . . . She Stoops to Conquer . . . Baltimore, M. K. Goddard [1782]
broadside 33.5 X 19 cm.
Wheeler 168
Randall Collection mp. 44118

B5437 BALTIMORE THEATRE
By permission. At the new Theatre . . . the 26th of April, 1782 . . . She Stoops to Conquer . . . Baltimore, M. K. Goddard [1782]
broadside 34 X 19 cm.
Wheeler 169
Randall Collection mp. 44119

B5438 BALTIMORE THEATRE
By permission. At the new Theatre . . . the 30th of April, 1782 . . . the tragedy of Zara . . . Baltimore, M. K. Goddard [1782]
broadside 33.5 X 19.5 cm.
Wheeler 170
Randall Collection mp. 44120

B5439 BALTIMORE THEATRE
By permission. At the new Theatre . . . the 7th of May, 1782 . . . the tragedy of the Revenge . . . Baltimore, M. K. Goddard [1782]
broadside 33 X 19 cm.
Wheeler 172
Randall Collection mp. 44121

B5440 BALTIMORE THEATRE
By permission. At the new Theatre . . . the 10th of May, 1782 . . . the tragedy of the Revenge . . . Baltimore, M. K. Goddard [1782]
broadside 33 X 18 cm.
Wheeler 173
Randall Collection mp. 44122

B5441 BALTIMORE THEATRE
By particular desire. At the new Theatre . . . the 14th of May, 1782 . . . Venice Preserv'd . . . Baltimore, M. K. Goddard [1782]
broadside 32 X 19 cm.
Wheeler 174
Randall Collection mp. 44123

B5442 BALTIMORE THEATRE
By permission. At the new Theatre . . . the 21st of May, 1782 . . . the Foundling . . . Baltimore, M. K. Goddard [1782]
broadside 32.5 X 19 cm.
Wheeler 176
Randall Collection mp. 44124

B5443 BALTIMORE THEATRE
By permission. At the new Theatre . . . the 24th of May, 1782 . . . King Lear . . . Baltimore, M. K. Goddard [1782]
broadside 30.5 X 19 cm.
Wheeler 177
Randall Collection mp. 44125

B5444 BALTIMORE THEATRE
By permission. At the new Theatre . . . the 4th of June, 1782 . . . All in the Wrong . . . Baltimore, M. K. Goddard [1782]
broadside 33.5 X 19 cm.
Wheeler 180
Randall Collection mp. 44126

B5445 BALTIMORE THEATRE
By permission. At the new Theatre . . . the 6th of June, 1782 . . . A Woman keeps a Secret . . . Baltimore, M. K. Goddard [1782]
broadside 34 X 19.5 cm.
Wheeler 182
Randall Collection mp. 44127

B5446 BALTIMORE THEATRE
By permission. At the new Theatre . . . the 7th of June, 1782 . . . the Fair Penitent . . . Baltimore, M. K. Goddard [1782]
broadside 34 X 19.5 cm.
Wheeler 183
Randall Collection mp. 44128

B5447 BALTIMORE THEATRE
By permission. At the new Theatre . . . the 8th of June, 1782 . . . the tragedy of the Revenge . . . Baltimore, M. K. Goddard [1782]
broadside 33.5 X 19.5 cm.
Wheeler 184
Randall Collection mp. 44129

B5448 BALTIMORE THEATRE
By permission. At the new Theatre . . . the 14th of June, 1782 . . . All in the Wrong . . . Baltimore, M. K. Goddard [1782]
broadside 34 X 20.5 cm.
Wheeler 187
Randall Collection mp. 44130

B5449 BALTIMORE THEATRE
By permission. At the Theatre in Baltimore . . . the 20th of September, 1782 . . . the tragedy of Douglas . . . Baltimore, M. K. Goddard [1782]
broadside 34 X 21.5 cm.
Wheeler 195
NHi mp. 44131

B5450 BALTIMORE THEATRE
By permission. At the Theatre . . . the 27th of September, 1782 . . . the tragedy of the Revenge . . . Baltimore, M. K. Goddard [1782]
broadside 34.5 X 21 cm.
Wheeler 197
NHi mp. 44133

B5451 BALTIMORE THEATRE
By permission. At the Theatre . . . the 1st of October, 1782 . . . the tragedy of Mahomet . . . Baltimore, M. K. Goddard [1782]
broadside 34.5 X 19 cm.
Wheeler 198
NHi mp. 44134

B5452 BALTIMORE THEATRE
By permission. At the Theatre . . . the 4th of October, 1782 . . . the London Merchant . . . Baltimore, M. K. Goddard [1782]
broadside 34 X 20.5 cm.
Wheeler 199
NHi mp. 44135

B5453 BALTIMORE THEATRE
By permission. At the Theatre . . . the 8th of October, 1782 . . . the tragedy of Douglas . . . Baltimore, M. K. Goddard [1782]

broadside 33.5 × 20.5 cm.
Wheeler 200
NHi mp. 44136

B5454 BALTIMORE THEATRE
By permission. At the Theatre . . . the 11th of October, 1782 . . . King Henry IVth . . . Baltimore, M. K. Goddard [1782]
broadside 35 × 20.5 cm.
Wheeler 201
NHi mp. 44137

B5455 BALTIMORE THEATRE
By permission. At the Theatre . . . the 15th of October, 1782 . . . the tragedy of Mahomet . . . Baltimore, M. K. Goddard [1782]
broadside 33 × 19 cm.
Wheeler 202
NHi mp. 44138

B5456 BALTIMORE THEATRE
By permission. At the Theatre . . . the 18th of October, 1782 . . . Romeo and Juliet . . . Baltimore, M. K. Goddard [1782]
broadside 33 × 19.5 cm.
Wheeler 203
NHi mp. 44139

B5457 BALTIMORE THEATRE
By permission. At the Theatre . . . the 26th of December, 1782 . . . the tragedy of Zara . . . Baltimore, M. K. Goddard [1782]
broadside 33 × 20.5 cm.
Wheeler 216
NHi mp. 44140

B5458 BALTIMORE THEATRE
By permission. By particular desire. At the new Theatre . . . the 5th of February, 1782 . . . the tragedy of the Orphan . . . Baltimore, M. K. Goddard [1782]
broadside 33.5 × 21 cm.
Wheeler 149
Randall Collection mp. 44141

B5459 BALTIMORE THEATRE
By permission. February 11, 1782. New Theatre, Baltimore . . . Friday, the 15th inst. . . . the Beaux Stratagem will be performed . . . Baltimore, M. K. Goddard [1782]
broadside 33.5 × 21 cm.
Wheeler 151
Randall Collection mp. 44142

B5460 BALTIMORE THEATRE
By permission. February 15, 1782. New Theatre, Baltimore . . . the Beaux Stratagem is obliged to be deferred; and in its stead will be presented . . . the 19th of February, 1782 . . . the Gamester . . . Baltimore, M. K. Goddard [1782]
broadside 33.5 × 21 cm.
Wheeler 152
Randall Collection mp. 44143

B5461 BALTIMORE THEATRE
By permission. On account of particular scenery that cannot be finished . . . Mahomet is obliged to be deferr'd, and . . . the 17th of September, 1782, the Baltimore Theatre, will be open'd, with . . . the Drummer . . . Baltimore, M. K. Goddard [1782]
broadside 34.5 × 23 cm.
Wheeler 194
NHi mp. 44144

B5462 BALTIMORE THEATRE
By permission. The new Theatre . . . will open . . . the 15th of January, 1782, with . . . King Richard III . . . Baltimore, M. K. Goddard [1782]
broadside 33.5 × 21 cm.
Wheeler 145
Randall Collection mp. 44145

B5463 BALTIMORE THEATRE
For the benefit of Miss Wall. By permission. At the Theatre . . . the 6th of December, 1782 . . . King John . . . Baltimore, M. K. Goddard [1782]
broadside 33 × 20.5 cm.
Wheeler 211
NHi mp. 44146

B5464 BALTIMORE THEATRE
For the benefit of Mr. Heard. By permission. At the new Theatre . . . the 17th of May, 1782 . . . King Lear . . . Baltimore, M. K. Goddard [1782]
broadside 33.5 × 19 cm.
Wheeler 175
Randall Collection mp. 44147

B5465 BALTIMORE THEATRE
For the benefit of Mr. Lewis. By permission. At the new Theatre . . . the 11th of June, 1782 . . . Tamerlane the Great . . . Baltimore, M. K. Goddard [1782]
broadside 34 × 20.5 cm.
Wheeler 186
Randall Collection mp. 44148

B5466 BALTIMORE THEATRE
For the benefit of Mr. Ryan. At the Theatre . . . the 15th of November, 1782 . . . Hamlet . . . Baltimore, M. K. Goddard [1782]
broadside 33 × 20.5 cm.
Wheeler 204
NHi mp. 44149

B5467 BALTIMORE THEATRE
For the benefit of Mr. Shakespear. By permission. At the Theatre . . . the 29th of November, 1782 . . . The Moor of Venice . . . Baltimore, M. K. Goddard [1782]
broadside 34 × 19.5 cm.
Wheeler 208
NHi mp. 44150

B5468 BALTIMORE THEATRE
For the benefit of Mr. Smith. By permission. At the Theatre . . . the 27th of December, 1782 . . . Richard III . . . Baltimore, M. K. Goddard [1782]
broadside 34 × 20.5 cm.
Wheeler 217
NHi mp. 44151

B5469 BALTIMORE THEATRE
For the benefit of Mr. Street. By permission. At the Theatre . . . the 22d of November, 1782 . . . the West-Indian . . . Baltimore, M. K. Goddard [1782]
broadside 34.5 × 20.5 cm.
Wheeler 206
NHi mp. 44152

B5470 BALTIMORE THEATRE
For the benefit of Mr. Tilyard. At the Theatre . . . the 31st of December, 1782 . . . Hamlet . . . Baltimore, M. K. Goddard [1782]
broadside 33 × 20 cm.
Wheeler 218
NHi mp. 44153

B5471 BALTIMORE THEATRE
For the benefit of Mr. Tilyard. By permission. At the Theatre . . . the 3d of December, 1782 . . . the tragedy of Cato . . . Baltimore, M. K. Goddard [1782]
broadside 34.5 X 20.5 cm.
Wheeler 210
NHi mp. 44154

B5472 BALTIMORE THEATRE
For the benefit of Mr. Willis. At the Theatre . . . the 19th of November, 1782 . . . Romeo and Juliet . . . Baltimore, M. K. Goddard [1782]
broadside 34 X 19 cm.
Wheeler 205
NHi mp. 44155

B5473 BALTIMORE THEATRE
For the benefit of Mrs. Bartholomew. By permission. At the new Theatre . . . the 18th of June, 1782 . . . Gustavus Vasa . . . Baltimore, M. K. Goddard [1782]
broadside 34 X 20 cm.
Wheeler 188
Randall Collection mp. 44156

B5474 BALTIMORE THEATRE
For the benefit of Mrs. Bartholomew. New Theatre, June 18, 1782. The managers being desirous to have . . . Gustavus Vasa . . . perfect, have postponed the performance of it till Friday, the 21st instant. Baltimore, M. K. Goddard [1782]
broadside 16.5 X 19 cm.
Wheeler 189
Randall Collection mp. 44157

B5475 BALTIMORE THEATRE
For the benefit of Mrs. Elm. By permission. At the Theatre . . . the 26th of November, 1782 . . . the Recruiting Officer . . . Baltimore, M. K. Goddard [1782]
broadside 33 X 21.5 cm.
Wheeler 207
NHi mp. 44158

B5476 BALTIMORE THEATRE
For the benefit of Mrs. Robinson. By permission. At the Theatre . . . the 17th of December, 1782 . . . the Merchant of Venice . . . Baltimore, M. K. Goddard [1782]
broadside 31.5 X 20.5 cm.
Wheeler 214
NHi mp. 44159

B5477 BALTIMORE THEATRE
For the Benefit of Mrs. Robinson. Theatre, December 16, 1782. On account of the inclemency of the weather . . . the Merchant of Venice . . . postponed till Friday the 20th instant. Baltimore, M. K. Goddard [1782]
broadside 14 X 18 cm.
Wheeler 215
NHi mp. 44160

B5478 BALTIMORE THEATRE
For the benefit of Mrs. Wall. By permission. At the new Theatre . . . the 28th of May, 1782 . . . All in the Wrong . . . Baltimore, M. K. Goddard [1782]
broadside 33 X 20 cm.
Wheeler 178
Randall Collection mp. 44161

B5479 BALTIMORE THEATRE
For the benefit of Mrs. Wall. On account of the sudden indisposition of a performer, the play is . . . deferred till . . . the 31st of May . . . Baltimore, M. K. Goddard [1782]
broadside 20.5 X 19 cm.
Wheeler 179
Randall Collection mp. 44162

B5480 BALTIMORE THEATRE
The last night but one of performing this season. At the new Theatre . . . the 8th of July, 1782 . . . the Clandestine Marriage . . . Baltimore, M. K. Goddard [1782]
broadside 33.5 X 20 cm.
Wheeler 191
Randall Collection mp. 44163

B5481 BALTIMORE THEATRE
The last night of performing this season. At the new Theatre . . . the 9th of July, 1782 . . . the Orphan . . . [Baltimore, M. K. Goddard, [1782]
broadside 33.5 X 20 cm.
Wheeler 192
Randall Collection mp. 44164

B5482 BALTIMORE THEATRE
New Theatre, Baltimore, March 8th, 1782. On account of the rainy weather, the play is postponed till to-morrow. [Baltimore, M. K. Goddard, 1782]
broadside 33.5 X 21 cm.
Wheeler 157
Randall Collection mp. 44165

B5483 BALTIMORE THEATRE
New Theatre, Baltimore, May 2, 1782. The tragedy of the Revenge . . . is deferred till Tuesday . . . [Baltimore, M. K. Goddard, 1782]
broadside 18 X 19 cm.
Wheeler 171
Randall Collection mp. 44166

B5484 BALTIMORE THEATRE
New Theatre, Baltimore, June 5, 1782. Mr. Lewis's benefit is postpon'd till Tuesday, June 11. [Baltimore, M. K. Goddard, 1782]
broadside 15 X 16.5 cm.
Wheeler 181
Randall Collection mp. 44167

B5485 BALTIMORE THEATRE
On account of the celebration of the birth-day of the dauphin . . . the play is postponed till . . . the 28th of June, 1782 . . . Baltimore, M. K. Goddard [1782]
broadside 33.5 X 20 cm.
Wheeler 190
Randall Collection mp. 44168

B5486 BALTIMORE THEATRE
[On Friday evening, the 12th of December, 1782 . . . a comedy called A Bold Stroke for a Wife . . . Baltimore, M. K. Goddard, 1782]

Performance announced in the *Maryland Journal* Dec. 10, 1782
Wheeler 213
No copy known mp. 44169

B5487 BALTIMORE THEATRE
[On Friday the 13th of September, 1782 the Theatre in Baltimore will open for the ensuing season, with the tragedy of Mahomet . . . Baltimore, M. K. Goddard, 1782]

Performance announced in the *Maryland Journal* Sept. 3, 1782
Wheeler 193
No copy known mp. 44170

B5488 BALTIMORE THEATRE
Theatre, December 5, 1782. Miss Wall's benefit is obliged to be postponed till . . . the 10th inst. on account of Mr. Wall's . . . hoarseness . . . Baltimore, M. K. Goddard [1782]
broadside 15.5 X 19.5 cm.
Wheeler 212
NHi mp. 44171

B5489 BAPTIST ASSOCIATION, PHILADELPHIA
The following is a copy of a circular letter sent by the several Baptist churches, met in association, at Philadelphia, October 22, 1782. Albany, Solomon Balentine [1782]
16 p. caption title
Imprint in colophon
RPJCB mp. 44172

B5490 BAUMAN, SEBASTIAN
To His excellency Gen[l] Washington . . . This plan of the investment of York . . . R. Scot sculp. Philad. 1782.
map 65.5 X 47.5 cm.
Phillips p. 1133
DLC; MB; PPL mp. 44173

B5491 BIBLE. O.T. PSALMS
A new version of the Psalms of David . . . by N. Brady . . . and N. Tate . . . Boston, Thomas and John Fleet, 1782.
1 p.l., 276 [i.e., 274] p. 16 cm.
Without music
DLC (72 p. at end); MWA (162 p. of hymns at end= Evans 17848) mp. 44178

B5492 BIBLE. O.T. PSALMS
The Psalms of David, imitated . . . By I. Watts, D.D. The thirty-ninth edition . . . Boston, Thomas and John Fleet, 1782.
[26], [3]-300 p. 15 cm.
MB; MWA mp. 44288

B5493 [BICKERSTAFFE, ISAAC] d. 1812?, supposed author
The life, and strange, unparallel'd and unheard of voyages and adventures of Ambrose Gwinett . . . Boston, E. Russell, 1782. Sold also by Hopestill Capen . . .
38 p. 17 cm.
DLC; MH; PPM mp. 44179

B5494 BICKERSTAFF'S almanack for . . . 1783. By Isaac Bickerstaff. Boston, Nathaniel Coverly [1782]
[24] p.
Drake 3317
Ct; ICHi; MS (10 l.)

B5495 BICKERSTAFF'S Boston almanack for . . . 1783. Boston, E. Russell [1782]
[24] p.
Third edition
Drake 3320
MH; MWA; N

B5496 BOSTON
At a legal meeting of the freeholders . . . May 14, 1782 . . . Voted, That the selectmen be directed to publish in handbills . . . [Boston, 1782]
broadside 19 X 16 cm.
Ford 2315
MHi. Photostat: DLC mp. 44181

B5497 BOSTON
Commonwealth of Massachusetts. Boston, March 15, 1782. Whereas the General Court . . . did resolve, "That eighty-five men . . . immediately raised within the Town of Boston . . ." the assessors . . . have fixed upon the under-written persons to compose one class, viz. . . . [Boston, 1782]
broadside 36 X 22 cm.
MB; MWA mp. 44180

B5498 BOSTON
Your Commonwealth tax. Your town and county tax. Boston, February , 1782. [Boston, 1782]
broadside
Ford 2313
MHi mp. 44181

B5499 BOSTON
Your Commonwealth tax. Your town tax. Boston, July 1782. [Boston, 1782]
broadside
Ford 2314
MHi mp. 44182

B5500 BOSTON, October 3, 1782. The Alarm & Train-band Muster. Sir, You are hereby legally notified to appear at the parade . . . Monday the 7th instant . . . compleat in arms and accoutrements . . . [Boston, 1782]
broadside 10.5 X 12.5 cm.
MHi mp. 44220

B5501 [CADWALADER, JOHN] 1742-1786
To the public. It may appear somewhat extraordinary . . . [relative to the conduct of Samuel Chase while a member of Congress, in 1778] [Annapolis? F. Green? 1782]
24 p. 17 cm. caption title
Authorship attribution by PHi
Brinley 4174; Wheeler 234
MdHi; PHi mp. 44182

B5502 CONGREGATIONAL CHURCHES IN MASSACHUSETTS
Charlestown, November 14, 1782. Sir, This accompanies a brief, issued by his Excellency . . . [Boston, 1782]
broadside 28.5 X 19 cm.
Circular letter
PPRF (addressed in ms. to Isaac Backus, of Middleborough) mp. 44183

B5503 CIRCULAR letter. Friends and fellow citizens, Being appointed by the legislature of this Commonwealth, to make application to you for relief . . . [Boston, 1782]
broadside ([2] p.)
Dated in ms.: July 18, 1782
Ford 2317
MB; MHi mp. 44215

B5504 CONNECTICUT
A return of the number of inhabitants in the state of Connecticut, February 1, 1782 . . . [n.p., 1782]
broadside 17 X 21 cm.
#84 in Heartman's Catalog 63 (11/17/16)
MHi. Photostats: DLC; ICN; MiU-C; NN mp. 44184

B5505 CONNECTICUT. GENERAL ASSEMBLY
At a General Assembly . . . holden . . . on the 10th day of January, Anno Dommini [sic] 1782. The gentlemen nominated . . . to stand for election in May next, delegates in Congress . . . as sent to this Assembly, are as follows . . . Hartford, Hudson & Goodwin [1782]
broadside 34 X 21 cm.
CtHi; DLC; MHi mp. 44185

B5506 CONNECTICUT. GENERAL ASSEMBLY
At a General Assembly . . . holden . . . on the second Thursday of May, 1782. Resolved . . . That a list of the deficient numbers of recruits . . . [n.p., 1782]
broadside 25 X 17.5 vm.
Photostats: DLC; ICN; MH; MHi; NHi; WHi mp. 44186

B5507 CONNECTICUT. GOVERNOR, 1776-1784
By His Excellency Jonathan Trumbull . . . A proclamation . . . [June 20, 1782] . . . [Hartford? 1782]
[2] p. 34 X 21 cm.
Huntington 473
CSmH; CtHi; MHi; MWA mp. 44187

B5508 CONNECTICUT. LAWS
At a General Assembly . . . holden . . . on the second Thursday of May . . . 1782. An act for forming, regulating and conducting the military force . . . [Hartford, 1782]
27 p. 16.5 cm. caption title
CtHi; DLC mp. 44188

B5509 CONNECTICUT. TREASURER
State of Connecticut, in America. To constable of and collector of the state tax for said town, for the year 1782, Greeting . . . Dated at Hartford, the 20th day of June . . . 1782. Treasurer. [Hartford, 1782]
broadside 31 X 20.5 cm.
Hamilton 97
CtHi; NjP mp. 44189

B5509a CONNECTICUT. TREASURER
State of Connecticut, in America. To constable of and collector of the state tax for said town, for the year 1782, Greeting . . . Dated at Hartford, the 24th day of October . . . 1782. Treasurer. [Hartford, 1782]
broadside 33.5 X 21 cm.
Middendorf Collection, New York City (1970)

B5510 [A CURIOUS ornamental piece, to be sold by Simeon Jocelyn, & Amos Doolittle, in New-Haven.— Price nine pence. New Haven, 1782]

"Now printing, (Neatly engraven on Copperplate,) for the use of writing schools."
Trumbull: Supplement 2030
No copy known

B5511 DELAWARE. GOVERNOR, 1778-1782
By the President of the Delaware State, a proclamation . . . [Apr. 19, 1782] John Dickinson . . . [Wilmington, James Adams, 1782]
broadside fol.
Concerns setting aside rewards for the capture of prisoners
PPL mp. 44195

B5512 DELAWARE. LAWS
. . . An act for increasing the powers of the justices . . . [Wilmington, J. Adams, 1782]
4 p. 30 cm. caption title
At end: Passed at Dover, February 5, 1782
Hawkins 17
DLC; MdBP; NNB; PPL mp. 44190

B5513 DELAWARE. LAWS
An act for inflicting penalties . . . [Wilmington, James Adams, 1782]
8 p. 30 cm. caption title
DLC (not available for examination) mp. 44191

B5514 DELAWARE. LAWS
. . . An act for the protection of the trade . . . [Wilmington, J. Adams, 1782]
4 p. 30 cm. caption title
At end: Passed at Dover, February 5, 1782
Hawkins 16
DLC; MdBP; NNB mp. 44192

B5515 DELAWARE. LAWS
. . . An act to remedy defects that have arisen in the execution of an act . . . for embodying a number of the militia . . . [Wilmington, James Adams, 1782]
6 p. fol.
PPL mp. 44193

B5516 DELAWARE. LAWS
. . . An act to vest in the Congress of the United States a power to levy duties . . . [Wilmington, James Adams, 1782]
p. 17-22. fol.
PPL mp. 44194

B5517 DEUTSCHE GESELLSCHAFT, PHILADELPHIA
Regeln der Deutschen Gesellschaft zur Unterstützung bedrängter Deutschen . . . Philadelphia, Melchior Steiner, 1782.
1 p.l., [15]-30 p. 19.5 cm.
PHi mp. 44202

B5518 DILWORTH, THOMAS, d. 1780
New guide to the English tongue . . . Boston, Printed and sold by Robert Hodge, 1782.
154 p.
MWA mp. 44196

B5519 DORCHESTER, MASS.
Your state tax. 1782. Your town & county rate, to be paid in specie. 1782. [Boston, 1782]
broadside
Ford 2318
MHi

B5520 AN essay on the education of youth. (Written by an approved School-Master.) Humbly offered to the . . . consideration of the parents of such children in Newbury-port, as are entrusted to . . . the school-masters, in said town. [Newburyport? J. Mycall? 1782]
8 p. 17.5 cm.
Signed at end; Newbury-port, August 23, 1782
MB mp. 44197

B5521 A FEW more numbers belonging to the gentleman's very valuable library, which will be sold by auction, at the City Vendue Store . . . the 26th of October, 1782 . . . John Bayard, Auctionier. Now selling at Bell's Book-Store . . . History of Emma Corbett . . . [Philadelphia, 1782]
fragment (broadside) 28 X 24 cm.
Taylor 315
PHi mp. 44174

B5522 FORDYCE, JAMES, 1720-1796
Addresses to young men . . . Boston, Robert Hodge, for William Green [1782]
2 v. (352 p.) 17 cm.
DLC; MB; MBAt; MH; MWA; MnU; RPJCB; ViU mp. 44199

B5523 THE friendly instructor . . . Philadelphia, Re-printed, by Joseph Crukshank, 1782.
xi, [1], 87, [1] p. 13 cm. [A]-H^6 I^2
MWA; PHi mp. 44200

B5524 FRIENDS, SOCIETY OF
Philadelphia, Ninth Month 7th, 1782. The following memorial and address was presented to the Assembly . . . entered on the journals of the House in the Second Month last; a recent attack of Isaac Howell and White Matlack . . . makes it necessary to be more extensively published. To the General Assembly of Pennsylvania. An addres [sic] and memorial . . . [Philadelphia, 1782]
4 p. 35.5 cm.
NjR

B5525 FRIENDS, SOCIETY OF
To the General Assembly of Pennsylvania. An address and memorial on behalf of the people called Quakers . . . 18th 1st month, 1782. John Drinker, clerk. [Philadelphia, J. Crukshank, 1782]
4 p. 33.5 cm.
PPL mp. 44201

B5526 GT. BRIT. ARMY
By Samuel Birch . . . commandant of New-York, &c. Whereas the safety of the city . . . 23d January, 1782. New-York, William Lewis [1782]
broadside 40 X 31.5 cm.
Huntington 478
CSmH mp. 44203

B5527 GT. BRIT. ARMY
New-York, August 6, 1782. Copy of a letter from Sir Guy Carleton . . . to Gen. Washington . . . Newport, Henry Barber [1782]
broadside 20 X 15.5 cm.
Alden 908; Winship Addenda p. 89
RPJCB mp. 44204

B5528 GUILFORD, VT.
At a town meeting holden in Guilford . . . [13th] day of March [1782] . . . [n.p., 1782]
broadside 19 X 9 cm.
VtHi mp. 44205

B5529 HEIDELBERG CATECHISM
The Heidelberg catechism . . . Translated for the use of the Reformed Protestant Dutch Churches, in the State of New-York. The third edition. Albany, Balentine and Webster, 1782.
64 p. 15.5 cm.
Second t.p. (p. 49): A compendium of the Christian religion . . . Albany, Printed and sold by Balentine and Webster, 1782.
McMurtrie: Albany 13a
N mp. 44206

B5530 HOCH-DEUTSCHES Evangelisch-Lutherisches
A B C- und Namen-Büchlein, für Kinder . . . Philadelphia, Melchior Steiner, 1782.
[24] p. illus. 16 cm.
Printed illustrated covers; first and last leaves pasted to covers
New York Public 760
NN mp. 44207

B5531 [KELLOGG, EZEKIEL] 1732-1785
A A [sic] poem, on the unsuccessful measures, taken ay [sic] the British army: in order to . . . destroy the United States . . . [n.p.] Printed 1782.
16 p. 14.5 cm. [A]-B^4
New York Public 764; Wegelin 732
MWA; PPRF. Photostat: NN mp. 44208

B5532 [LATHROP, BARNABAS]
. . . Poem, on the absurdity and sinfulness of wearing high rolls. [n.p., 1782]
8 p. 17 cm. caption title
Signed at end: Barnabas Lathrop
DLC mp. 44209

B5533 LOUISIANA
[Tarifa ejecutada por el intendente de la Luisiana para la exacción de 6 por ciento sobre los efectos de importación que vengan á este rio desde los puertos de Francia . . . Nueva Orleans, 10 de mayo de 1782.]
22 p.
Title from Luis Martino Pérez: *Guide to the materials for American history in Cuban archives* (Washington, 1907), no. 366
McMurtrie: Louisiana 14
Archivo Nacional, Havana mp. 44210

B5534 LUTHER, MARTIN, 1483-1546
Der kleine Catechismus . . . Lancaster, Gedruckt und zu haben bey Francis Bailey, 1782.
[4], 139, [1] p. 13.5 cm. A-M^6
MWA mp. 44211

B5535 MARYLAND
Office for confiscated estates, Annapolis, January 26, 1782. Pursuant to an act . . . will be sold . . . the following property . . . [Annapolis, F. Green, 1782]
broadside 32.5 X 21 cm.
Huntington 479; Wheeler 223
CSmH mp. 44214

B5536 MARYLAND. HOUSE OF DELEGATES
House of Delegates. Friday, January 11, 1782. General Cadwalader having made the following motion . . . [Annapolis, Frederick Green, 1782]
broadside fol.
Concerns charge of breach of trust by Samuel Chase
PPL mp. 44212

B5537 MARYLAND. LAWS
An act for founding a college at Chester . . . [Colophon] [Philadelphia] John Dunlap [1782]
4 p. 44 cm. caption title
DLC; MdHi mp. 44213

B5538 MASSACHUSETTS
Commonwealth of Massachusetts. Suffolk ss. Boston, 1782 . . . [Boston, 1782]
broadside
Certificate of commissioners' report on claims against estate of absentee
Ford 2332
M-Ar

B5539 MASSACHUSETTS
Commonwealth of Massachusetts. Worcester ss. 1782 . . . [Worcester? 1782]
broadside 17.5 X 29 cm.
Certificate of commissioners' report on claims against estate of absentee
Ford 2343
M-Ar. Photostat: MWA

B5540 MASSACHUSETTS. GOVERNOR, 1780-1785
By His Excellency John Hancock . . . A brief. Whereas the hostile forces of Great-Britain . . . Given . . . in Boston, the twelfth day of November . . . One Thousand Seven Hundred and Eighty-Two . . . [Boston, 1782]

broadside 36 X 21 cm.
Concerns aid to meeting-house in Charlestown
Ford 2326
MB; PPRF. Photostats: MHi; MWA mp. 44216

B5541 MASSACHUSETTS. HOUSE OF REPRESENTATIVES
Commonwealth of Massachusetts. In the House of representatives, March 1, 1782. Whereas it appears . . . [Boston, 1782]
5 p. 32.5 cm. caption title
Ford 2322
DLC; MHi; MWA (p. 5 wanting) mp. 44219

B5542 MASSACHUSETTS. LAWS
. . . An act for apportioning and assessing a tax of two hundred thousand pounds . . . Boston, Benjamin Edes and Sons, 1782.
11 p. 35 cm.
cf. Evans 17597
MHi mp. 44217

B5543 MASSACHUSETTS. LAWS
. . . An act to repeal a certain clause in an act . . . entitled, An act for apportioning and assessing a tax . . . In Senate, July 5, 1782 . . . [Boston, 1782]
broadside 39.5 X 25 cm.
DLC; MHi mp. 44218

B5544 MASSACHUSETTS. TREASURER
Commonwealth of Massachusetts. The honorable Henry Gardner . . . January 1782. [Boston, 1782]
broadside
Warrant to collect unpaid taxes
Ford 2327
M-Ar mp. 44221

B5545 MASSACHUSETTS. TREASURER
Commonwealth of Massachusetts. The honorable Henry Gardner . . . To the selectmen or assessors of the town of Greeting . . . [March 18, 1782] [Boston, 1782]
broadside 47 X 36.5 cm.
DLC; MHi; RPJCB mp. 44222

B5546 MASSACHUSETTS. TREASURER
Commonwealth of Massachusetts. Thomas Ivers, Esq; Treasurer . . . [Dec. 12, 1782] . . . [Boston, 1782]
broadside 37 X 23.5 cm.
MHi; MWA mp. 44223

B5547 MYCALL, JOHN, 1750–1833
Newbury-Port, Feb. 19, 1782. Sir, On behalf of the gentlemen concerned in the publication of *The Temple*, I am directed to trouble you . . . John Mycall. [Newburyport, 1782]
broadside 20.5 X 16 cm.
Ford 2336
MHi mp. 44224

B5548 MYCALL, JOHN, 1750–1833
To the public. The interests of liberty are inseparable from those of learning and virtue . . . John Mycall. Newbury-Port, February 19th, 1782 . . . [Newburyport, 1782]
broadside 40 X 37 cm.
Proposals by John Mycall for a weekly paper, *The Temple*, never issued
Ford 2337
MHi mp. 44225

B5549 DER neue, verbessert- und zuverlässige Americanische calender, auf das 1783ste Jahr Christi . . . Philadelphia, Theophilus Cossart [1782]
[40] p. 20 cm. [A]-E^4
MWA; PPeSchw mp. 44226

B5550 THE new American almanac for the year . . . 1783 . . . Frederick-Town, Matihias [sic] Bartgis [1782]
[32] p. 17 cm.
Wheeler 231
MWA mp. 44227

B5551 THE New-England primer. Philadelphia, Charles Cist, 1782.
[80] p. 10 cm.
Heartman 71; Rosenbach-Ch 93; Taylor 320
A. S. W. Rosenbach (1933) mp. 44229

B5552 THE New England primer improved . . . Exeter, 1782.
[80] p.
MWA (last 7 leaves lacking) mp. 44228

B5553 NEW HAMPSHIRE. COMMITTEE OF SAFETY
State of New-Hampshire. In Committee of Safety, April 12th, 1782 . . . A proclamation . . . Done by the United States in Congress assembled . . . [Mar. 19, 1782] . . . Exeter, 1782.
broadside 41.5 X 30 cm.
Whittemore 330
NhHi mp. 44230

B5554 NEW HAMPSHIRE. HOUSE OF REPRESENTATIVES
State of New Hampshire. In the House of Representatives, June 13th, 1782. Resolved, that the time of returning the extents issued by the treasurer . . . [Exeter, 1782]
broadside 26.5 X 20 cm.
Whittemore 323
NhHi mp. 44232

B5555 NEW HAMPSHIRE. LAWS
[Acts and laws, 1782] [Exeter, 1782]
p. 273–295. 28.5 cm.
Continuation of Acts and laws published 1780; included in Evans 16877 (microprint)
Whittemore 321
MWA; NN; Nh; NhD (p. 273–286, 289–295); NhHi

B5556 NEW HAMPSHIRE. LAWS
State of New-Hampshire . . . An act for raising and compleating this state's quota . . . March 21st, 1782 . . . Exeter [1782]
3 p. 28 cm. caption title
DLC; NhHi mp. 44231

B5557 NEW-JERSEY pocket almanack, for the year, 1783. Trenton, Printed and sold by Isaac Collins [1782]
[24] p. 10.5 cm.
Interleaved with blank leaves
Drake 5127; Humphrey 280
DLC; NHi; NjHi; RPJCB mp. 44233

B5558 NEW YORK. ASSEMBLY
Votes and proceedings of the Assembly, &c. Poughkeepsie . . . February 21st, 1782 [-Apr. 14, 1782] Poughkeepsie, John Holt, 1782]
p. [49]-100 [sic 104] 30.5 cm. caption title
Huntington 480; Vail; Patriotic pair, p. 421
CSmH; CtY; N; NHi; NNS mp. 44234

B5559 NEW YORK. ASSEMBLY
Votes and proceedings of the Assembly, & c. at the first meeting of the sixth session. Poughkeepsie . . . July 11th, 1782 [-July 25, 1782] [Poughkeepsie, John Holt, 1782]

p. [105]-122 [six 128] 30.5 cm. caption title
Vail: Patriotic pair, p. 421
N; NHi; NNS mp. 44235

B5560 NEW YORK. GOVERNOR, 1777-1795
General orders. Poughkeepsie, 25th March, 1782. His Excellency the Governor thinks proper to inform the officers . . . on bounties of unappropriated lands . . . [Poughkeepsie, John Holt, 1782]
broadside 20 X 13.5 cm.
Vail: Patriotic pair, p. 413
N. Photostat: NHi mp. 44236

B5561 NEW YORK. SENATE
The votes and proceedings of the Senate . . . of New-York, beginning with the fifth session, at Poughkeepsie . . . the first day of October, 1781. Vol. II. Poughkeepsie, John Holt, 1782.
35 p. 35 cm.
5th session, 1st meeting, Oct. 10-Nov. 23, 1781
New York Public 761; Vail: Patriotic pair, p. 418
N; NHi; NN; NNS mp. 44237

B5562 NEW YORK. SENATE
Votes and proceedings of the Senate, &c. [Poughkeepsie, John Holt, 1782]
p. [37]-77. 35 cm. caption title
5th session, 2nd meeting, Feb. 23-April 14, 1782
New York Public 762; Vail: Patriotic pair, p. 419
N; NHi; NN; NNS mp. 44238

B5563 NEW YORK. SENATE
Votes and proceedings of the Senate, &c. at the first meeting of the sixth session. [July 3-25, 1782] [Poughkeepsie, John Holt, 1782]
p. [79]-96. 35 cm. caption title
New York Public 763; Vail: Patriotic pair, p. 419
N; NHi; NN; NNS mp. 44239

B5564 NEWPORT, May 15, 1782. By the arrival of the eastern post last evening . . . [Newport, Henry Barber, 1782]
broadside 39.5 X 20 cm.
Alden 911
DLC (photostat) mp. 44240

B5565 THE news-carriers address to his customers. January 1st, 1782. [n.p., 1782]
broadside 35.5 X 14 cm.
NHi mp. 44241

B5566 OBSERVATIONS and prognostications on the urine . . . [n.p.] 1782.
2 p.l., 33, [4] p., 1 leaf. 20 cm.
Label mounted on fly leaf: . . . To be had at Philadelphia . . . Yorktown . . . Fredericks-Town . . .
DLC mp. 44242

B5567 PEARCE, BENONI
One hundred pounds reward. Escaped last night . . . William Prentice . . . Benoni Pearce, sheriff. Providence, September 7, 1782. [Providence, 1782]
broadside 10.5 X 16 cm.
Alden 912; Winship p. 45
RPTP mp. 44249

B5567a PENNSYLVANIA. GENERAL ASSEMBLY
Minutes of the third session of the sixth General Assembly . . . of Pennsylvania . . . [Aug. 2-Sept. 21, 1782] [Philadelphia, J. Dunlap, 1782]
pp. [651]-712. fol.
PHi; PPL

B5568 PENNSYLVANIA. GENERAL ASSEMBLY
Report of the Committee of Assembly, on the state of the public accounts . . . for the year 1781 . . . [Philadelphia] John Dunlap [1782]
51 p. 31 cm.
Taylor 325
P; PPL mp. 44244

B5569 PENNSYLVANIA. GENERAL ASSEMBLY
State of Pennsylvania. In General Assembly, Tuesday, February 26, 1782. P.M. . . . To the public . . . Plan for establishing a national bank, for the United States of North America . . . Robert Morris. Philadelphia, May 28, 1781. [Philadelphia] Hall & Sellers [1782]
broadside fol.
PPL mp. 44243

B5570 PHILADELPHIA, May 25, 1782. A gentleman from the eastward . . . Philadelphia, Hall and Sellers [1782]
broadside 28 X 21 cm.
DLC mp. 44245

B5571 A POEM occasioned by the most shocking and cruel murder that ever was represented on the stage . . . [Hartford, B. Webster, 1782]
broadside 42 X 33.5 cm.
Winslow 51
MiU-C mp. 44246

B5572 A POEM, spoken extempore, by a young lady, on hearing the guns firing . . . on account of . . . the surrender of York-Town . . . His Lordship humbled: or, Cornwallis's lamentation . . . [Boston] Printed and sold by E. Russell, near Liberty-Stump [1782]
broadside 35 X 21 cm.
In two columns, one poem to each
Includes text of a broadside printed at Providence (Alden 863) on October 25
MB (slightly mutilated); MWA mp. 44247

B5573 POOR Ned's Albany almanack, for the year . . . 1783 . . . by Ned Foresight . . . Albany, Printed and sold by Balentine and Webster [1782]
[26+] p. 16.5 cm.
Huntington 477; McMurtrie: Albany 11
CSmH (lacks all after leaf C4); MWA (imperfect); N; NHi; NRMA mp. 44198

B5574 PORTSMOUTH, N.H.
To your Continental, state, county and town tax, is in lawful money . . . Gershom Flagg, collector. September 1782. [Portsmouth, 1782]
broadside 14.5 X 10 cm.
Whittemore 327
MHi

B5575 A PRESENT to children. Consisting of several new divine hymns and moral songs. New-London, T. Green [1782?]
[16] p. 12 cm.
Signature of Eber Chapman on t.p. of PP and CtY copies, dated 1783
New York Public 785; Rosenbach-Ch 94
CtY; PP. Photostat: NN mp. 44248

B5576 PROVIDENCE, July 20. Extract of a letter from Newport . . . to a gentleman in this town . . . [Providence, 1782]
broadside 29 X 19 cm.
Alden 913; New York Public 765
RWa. Photostat: MWA; NN mp. 44250

B5577 RHODE ISLAND. ELECTION PROX.
His Excellency William Greene, Esquire, Governor. Hon. Jabez Bowen, Esq; Dep. Gov. . . . [Providence? 1782]
broadside 20.5 X 12 cm.
Alden 915; Chapin Proxies 34
RHi mp. 44251

B5578 RHODE ISLAND. ELECTION PROX.
Independent landholders—The friends of the people—and the patrons of their liberties. His Excellency William Greene, Esq; Governor . . . [Providence] John Carter [1782]
broadside 20 X 13 cm.
Alden 916; Chapin Proxies 32
RHi mp. 44252

B5579 RHODE ISLAND. ELECTION PROX.
Under such rulers we hope for justice! His Excellency William Greene, Esquire, Governor. Hom. Jabez Bowen, Esq; Dep. Gov. . . . [Providence] Bennett Wheeler [1782]
broadside 20.5 X 12 cm.
Alden 917; Chapin Proxies 33
RHi mp. 44253

B5580 RHODE ISLAND. GOVERNOR, 1779–1786
By . . . William Greene . . . a proclamation. Whereas the most honorable the Congress . . . [April 13, 1782] . . . Providence, John Carter [1782]
broadside 45.5 X 36 cm.
Alden 918
DLC; RHi mp. 44254

B5581 RHODE ISLAND. GOVERNOR, 1779–1786
[By . . . William Greene . . . a proclamation . . . [Nov. 4, 1782] . . . Providence, J. Carter, 1782]
[broadside?]
Proclaiming Nov. 28 a day of Thanksgiving
Bill submitted by Carter Nov. 7, 1782
Alden 919
No copy known mp. 44255

B5582 RHODE ISLAND. LAWS
State of Rhode-Island and Providence Plantations. In General assembly, January session, 1782. An act for granting . . . a tax of six thousand pounds . . . Providence, John Carter [1782]
broadside 34.5 X 21 cm.
Alden 928; Winship p. 46
RWe mp. 44256

B5583 RHODE ISLAND. LAWS
State of Rhode-Island and Providence Plantations. In General assembly, January session, 1782. It is voted and resolved, That an account of the number of families and persons . . . [Providence, J. Carter? 1782]
broadside 29 X 23 cm.
Alden 930; Winship p. 46; Winship Addenda p. 93
CtY; R mp. 44257

B5584 RHODE ISLAND. LAWS
State of Rhode-Island and Providence Plantations. In General assembly, February session, A.D. 1782. An act for granting . . . a tax of six thousand pounds . . . Providence, Bennett Wheeler [1782]
broadside 34.5 X 12.5 cm.
Alden 931; Winship p. 46; Winship Addenda p. 93
R; RWe mp. 44258

B5585 RHODE ISLAND. LAWS
State of Rhode-Island and Providence Plantations. In General assembly, March 1, 1782. An act for raising two hundred and fifty-nine men . . . Providence, John Carter [1782]
broadside 45.5 X 34 cm.
Alden 934; Winship p. 46
DLC; RHi; RPJCB mp. 44259

B5586 RHODE ISLAND. LAWS
State of Rhode-Island and Providence Plantations. In General assembly, June session, 1782. An act for granting . . . a tax of twelve thousand pounds . . . [Providence, 1782]
broadside 33.5 X 16.5 cm.
Alden 935; Winship p. 46
RWe mp. 44260

B5587 RHODE ISLAND. TREASURER
State of Rhode-Island and Providence Plantations, ss. To the sheriff of the County of . . . Greeting. Whereas the General Assembly . . . passed an act . . . apportioning a tax of six thousand pounds . . . Given . . . in Providence . . . this day of September, A.D. 1782 . . . [Providence, 1782]
broadside 35 X 23 cm.
Signed in ms.: Jos Clarke
MWA (photostat) mp. 44261

B5588 ROUSSEL,—
M. Roussel, dancing-master, lately from Philadelphia . . . intends to open a dancing-school in Baltimore, on Monday next . . . Roussel. Baltimore, June 12, 1782. Baltimore, M. K. Goddard [1782]
broadside 18 X 19 cm.
Wheeler 185
Randall Collection mp. 44262

B5589 THE Royal South-Carolina gazette. Charles-Town, James Robertson [1782]

Brigham, p. 1035
DLC (issues for March 5, Supplement, March 28, September 12)

B5590 SALEM, MASS.
Salem, December 10, 1782. Gentlemen, A bill has passed the House . . . [Salem, 1782]
broadside 20.5 X 16 cm.
Ford 2339; Tapley p. 338
DLC mp. 44263

B5591 A SHORT account of the life and death of William Adams, a youth of Virginia. Drawn up by a friend, personally acquainted with the deceased . . . Philadelphia, Melchior Steiner, 1782.
34 p. 19 cm.
MWA; NN; RPJCB mp. 44264

B5592 SOUTH CAROLINA. COMMISSIONERS OF FORFEITED ESTATES
Advertisement. The Commissioners of Forfeited Estates give notice, that a sale . . . at George Town on the 1st day of August next . . . June 11th, 1782. By order of the Board. By Benjamin Waring, Clerk. [Charleston, 1782]
broadside 22 X 27 cm.
Sc-Ar

B5593 SOUTH CAROLINA. GOVERNOR, 1779–1782
The speech of His Excellency John Rutledge . . . to the General Assembly, met at Jacksonburgh . . . the 18th day of January, 1782. [Jacksonburgh, David Rogers, 1782]
12 p.

Imprint assigned on basis of similarity to laws printed by Rogers in 1782
ScU. Photostat: RPJCB mp. 44266

B5594 SOUTH CAROLINA. GOVERNOR, 1779–1782
State of South Carolina. By His Excellency John Mathews . . . A proclamation. Whereas such measures only . . . March 14, 1782. [Jacksonburgh, David Rogers, 1782]
3 p.
Imprint assigned on basis of similarity to laws printed by Rogers in 1782
ScU. Photostat: RPJCB mp. 44265

B5595 SOUTH CAROLINA. LAWS
An act for disposing of certain estates and banishing certain persons therin mentioned . . . [Halifax? Thomas Davis? 1782?]
8 p.
Imprint assigned on basis of similarity of type and style to other Davis printing. Mr. Inabinett (ScU) suggests [Charleston: J. Miller]
Sabin 87634 (credits to Jacksonburgh)
RPJCB mp. 44267

B5596 SOUTH CAROLINA. LAWS
An act for inflicting penalties on and confiscating the estates of such persons as are declared guilty of treason . . . [May 4, 1782] [Charleston, 1782]
8 p. fol.
Title from Libbie's sale catalogue, May 2, 1906, lot 424
No copy known

B5597 SOUTH CAROLINA. LAWS
Extracts from an act to procure recruits . . . February 26, 1782. Jacksonburgh, David Rogers [1782]
3 p. 20 cm. caption title
DLC mp. 44268

B5598 SOUTH CAROLINA. LAWS
Jacksonburgh, March 1, 1782. We have the pleasure of informing the good citizens . . . that the General Assembly . . . for six weeks sitting in this village was on Tuesday last adjourned to . . . the 5th day of August . . . having passed the following weighty . . . laws . . . Jacksonburgh, David Rogers, 1782.
4 p.
Imprint in colophon
ScU. Photostat: RPJCB mp. 44269

B5599 SPAIN. SOVEREIGNS (CHARLES III)
Real cedula, concediendo nuevas gracias para fomento del comercio de la Luisiana. 1782. De orden S. M. . . . [New Orleans, 1782]
15 p. 26 cm.
In Spanish and French
Signed at end: Es copia del original, Galvez
McMurtrie: New Orleans 32
CU-B mp. 44270

B5600 TIT for tat . . . [Boston] Edes [1782]
broadside 23.5 X 15 cm.
Ford 2341; Wegelin 15
DLC; MHi; MWA mp. 44271

B5601 TO the electors of the State of New-York. Friends and fellow-citizens, We should not again have addressed you . . . They state . . . that Mr. Jay . . . intends to wait for the ratification of the treaty, in mere surmise . . . [New York? 1782?]
broadside 27.5 X 21 cm.
NHi mp. 44272

B5602 TO the General Assembly of Maryland. An individual . . . presumes to offer his sentiments . . . Aratus. Maryland, November 9, 1782. Baltimore, M. K. Goddard [1782]
[2] p. 41 X 24 cm.
Wheeler 144
MdBE mp. 44273

B5603 TO the honorable the speakers of the two houses of the General Assembly . . . of Virginia . . . now sitting . . . [Alexandria? 1782?]
broadside 35.5 X 33.5 cm.
A petition with manuscript signatures of citizens of Fairfax County, presented May 27, 1782
Vi mp. 44274

B5604 U. S. CONTINENTAL CONGRESS, 1782
By the United States in Congress assembled. February 23, 1782 . . . [Philadelphia, D. C. Claypoole, 1782]
broadside
Concerns refusal to exchange Cornwallis; parole of Henry Laurens; maintenance of British prisoners
Ford: Bibliographical notes . . . 380
No copy known mp. 44275

B5605 U. S. CONTINENTAL CONGRESS, 1782
By the United States in Congress assembled, July 23d, 1782. Resolved, That in conducting the business . . . [Philadelphia, David C. Claypoole, 1782]
broadside 41 X 31 cm.
Ford: Bibliographical notes . . . 384
DLC; PHi mp. 44276

B5606 U. S. CONTINENTAL CONGRESS, 1782
A system on which provisions are to be issued. [Philadelphia, David C. Claypoole, 1782]
broadside 34.5 X 46 cm.
Second title: . . . April 22, 1782. Resolved, That from and after the first day of May . . .
Taylor 335
DLC; MHi; NHi; PHi mp. 44277

B5607 U. S. INSPECTOR-GENERAL'S OFFICE
Regulations for the order and discipline of the troops of the United States . . . By Baron Stuben [!] . . . Boston, T. and J. Fleet, 1782.
112 p. 18.5 cm.
MBU mp. 44278

B5608 U. S. INSPECTOR-GENERAL'S OFFICE
Regulations for the order and discipline of the troops of the United States. Part I. Hartford, Hudson and Goodwin [1782?]
138 p., 3 leaves. 8 fold. pl. 16.5 cm.
New York Public 767
CtHi; MB; MHi; N; NN mp. 44279

B5609 U. S. TREATIES, ETC.
By the United States in Congress assembled. A proclamation . . . Done at the Hague, the 8th day of October, 1782. [n.p., 1782?]
broadside 43.5 X 56 cm.
Text in four columns
Treaty of amity and commerce between the U. S. and the Netherlands
NHi mp. 44280

B5610 THE United-States almanack, for . . . 1783 . . . Hartford, Nathaniel Patten [1782]
[24] p. 17 cm.
By Andrew Beers
CtHi (imperfect); MWA mp. 44176

B5611 THE United-States almanack, for . . . 1783 . . . Hartford, Bavil Webster [1782]
[24] p. 17 cm.
By Andrew Beers
Half-title: An Almanack, for 1783
Bates: Conn. almanace p. 134; cf. Evans 17467 for variant
CtHi; MWA mp. 44177

B5612 VARNUM, JAMES MITCHELL, 1748–1789
An oration: delivered in the Episcopal Church in Providence . . . before the . . . Masons . . . December 27, 1782 . . . Providence, John Carter [1782]
10 p. 18 cm.
Alden 971; Winship Addenda p. 89
DLC; MWA; RHi mp. 44281

B5613 VERMONT
[Gazetteer with list of officers. Westminster, J. P. Spooner, 1782]

Printer's bill for 200 copies dated Jan. 14, 1782
McCorison 55
No copy known mp. 44282

B5614 VERMONT. LAWS
An act for the puspose of raising three hundred able bodied effective men for the ensuing campaign. Passed Feb. 1782. [Westminster, J. P. Spooner, 1782]
[2] p. 29 cm. caption title
McCorison 57; Sabin 99088
MWA (p. [2] only); Vt mp. 44283

B5615 VERMONT. TREASURER
The treasurer's address to the legislature, in June last . . . Sunderland, August 15, 1781. Westminster, Judah P. Spooner, 1782.
12 p. 19.5 cm.
McCorison 58; Sabin 99133
DLC. H. P. McCullough, Bennington (1963). Photostat: NN mp. 44284

B5616 VERSES made on the sudden death of six young women . . . drowned July 13, 1782 . . . Newport, Henry Barber [1782?]
broadside 36.5 X 25.5 cm.
Alden 939; Winship p. 45
RP (mutilated) mp. 44285

B5617 WARREN revived. An astronomical diary: or almanack, for . . . 1783 . . . Norwich, John Trumbull [1782]
[24] p. 18 cm.
By Lemuel Warren
CtHi; CtNlC; MWA mp. 44286

B5618 WASHINGTON COLLEGE
To the inhabitants of the Eastern Shore . . . Gentlemen, By the foregoing act for founding a college among yourselves . . . [Annapolis? F. Green? 1782]
broadside 54.5 X 35.5 cm.
Wheeler 235
MdHi mp. 44287

B5619 YALE UNIVERSITY
Catalogus recentium in Collegio Yalensi, M,DCC,LXXXII . . . [New Haven? Thomas and Samuel Green? 1782]
broadside 32 X 18 cm.
MWA mp. 44289

1783

B5620 AN account of Colonel James Cary's land, in South Carolina, and of whom purchased, viz. Acres. 650 On the Wateree River, of John Milhous. 2 On ditto of Zebulon Gaunt . . . The above 1032 acres of land . . . confiscated and sold . . . on account of the Colonel's . . . zeal for the British Government . . . Anno. Dom. 1783. [n.p., 1783]
broadside 11 X 16 cm.
NcD

B5621 ALLEN, WALTER
Twenty pounds reward. Lost on the 17th of October . . . a large black . . . pocketbook . . . Walter Allen . . . Decemb. 10th, 1783. Newbern, R. Keith [1783]
broadside 21 X 27 cm.
McMurtrie: North Carolina 113; New York Public 769
DLC; NN (reduced facsim.) mp. 44290

B5622 [ALMANACK for . . . 1784. Newbern, R. Keith, 1783]

Advertised in imprint of broadside (DLC) headed "Twenty pounds reward," dated Dec. 10, 1783
Drake 8869
No copy known

B5623 AMERICANISCHE Hinckende Bot, Calender auf . . . 1784 . . . Friedrich-Stadt, Matthias Bartgis [1783]
[20] p.
Drake 2195
PHi

B5624 ANNAPOLIS THEATRE
Annapolis Theatre. Dennis Ryan . . . intends opening . . . this Theatre, on the 19th of April next, with . . . the Grecian Daughter . . . March 24, 1783. [Annapolis, F. Green, 1783]
broadside 15 X 20.5 cm.
Wheeler 238
NHi mp. 44291

B5625 ANNAPOLIS THEATRE
By authority. At the Theatre in Annapolis . . . April 19, 1783. By the American Company . . . The Grecian Daughter . . . [Annapolis, F. Green, 1783]
broadside 34.5 X 21 cm.
Wheeler 239
NHi mp. 44293

B5626 ANNAPOLIS THEATRE
By authority. At the Theatre . . . A Bold Stroke for a Wife . . . [Annapolis, F. Green, 1783]
broadside 34.5 X 21 cm.
Wheeler 240
NHi mp. 44292

B5627 ANNAPOLIS THEATRE
By authority. At the Theatre . . . April 23, 1783. . . . The Fatal Discovery . . . [Annapolis, F. Green, 1783]
broadside 34.5 X 21 cm.
Wheeler 241
NHi mp. 44294

B5628 ANNAPOLIS THEATRE
By authority. At the Theatre . . . April 25, 1783 . . . a tragedy, called Douglas . . . [Annapolis, F. Green, 1783]
broadside 34.5 X 21 cm.
Wheeler 242
NHi mp. 44295

B5629 ANNAPOLIS THEATRE
The last night of performing. By authority. At the Theatre . . . April 26, 1783 . . . The West-Indian . . . [Annapolis, F. Green, 1783]
broadside 34.5 X 21 cm.
Wheeler 243
NHi mp. 44296

B5630 AS the public had had much writing and . . . falsehoods laid before them, concerning Mr. Temple; the following plain statement . . . will enable that public to form a right judgment . . . Narrator. [Boston, 1783]
[3] p. 45 cm.
Ford 2344
MHi mp. 44297

B5631 ASH, JOHN, 1724?-1779
Grammatical institutes . . . A new edition, revised and corrected by the author. Chatham, S. Kollock, 1783.
143, [1] p. 13 cm. [A]-D^{18}
cf. Humphrey 284
MWA (very imperfect). George C. Rockefeller, Madison, N.J. (1969) mp. 44298

B5632 ASSOCIATE REFORMED PRESBYTERIAN CHURCH
The constitution of the Associate-Reformed Synod . . . Philadelphia, Francis Bailey, 1783.
28 p. 21.5 cm.
DLC; MWA; NHi; OWoC; PPiPT; RPJCB mp. 44299

B5633 AN astronomical diary, or Almanack and ephemeris for . . . 1784 . . . By Jonas Sidrophel . . . Hartford, B. Webster [1783]
[14+] p.
Eben W. Judd in his almanac for 1785 calls himself the "Author of Sidrophel's Almanack."
Bates: Conn. almanacs p. 136; Trumbull: Supplement 1786
CtHi mp. 44453

B5634 AN astronomical diary; or, Almanack, for . . . 1784 . . . By Ned Foresight, Gent. . . . Albany, Printed and sold by S. Balentine [1783]
[24] p. 16.5 cm.
McMurtrie: Albany 15; cf. Evans 1791
DLC. Photostat: NN mp. 44366

B5635 [AN astronomical diary or almanack, for . . . 1784. Calculated for the meridian of Rutland. Bennington, Haswell & Russell, 1783]

Advertised in the *Vermont Gazette* as published on Dec. 20, 1783
McCorison 59
No copy known mp. 44300

B5636 AN astronomical diary, or Almanack, for . . . 1784 . . . New-Haven, T. [& S. Green] [1783]
[16] p. 18 cm.
By Joseph Perry
Advertised in the *Connecticut Journal*, Dec. 31, 1783, as "To-Morrow will be published, Dr. Perry's Almanack."
Bates: Conn. almanacs p. 136
CtHi (imprint torn) mp. 44438

B5637 AT a general meeting of the Committee of Mechanicks, at Mrs. Van Dyke's, the 27th December, 1783 . . . New-York, S. Kollock [1783]
broadside 26 X 21 cm.
Names offered as candidates for state elections
NHi mp. 44301

B5638 BAILEY'S pocket almanac, being an American register, for . . . 1784 . . . Philadelphia, Printed and sold by Francis Bailey [1783]
[80] p. 9 cm.
Drake 10159
NHi; NjR; PHC

B5639 BAKER, JOHN, 1732?-1796
Dr. Baker's Albion-essence, and antiscorbutic dentifrice . . . Sold, wholesale and retail, at his house, No. 45, Second Street, Philadelphia. [Philadelphia, Thomas Bradford, 1783]
broadside 31 cm.
Guerra a-707
Francisco Guerra, New Haven (1962) (photostat)
mp. 44302

B5640 BALTIMORE THEATRE
Advertisement. Baltimore . . . June 7, 1783. The play of the Orphan . . . postpon'd . . . will be presented this evening . . . Baltimore, M. K. Goddard [1783]
broadside 23 X 18 cm.
Wheeler 280
NHi mp. 44303

B5641 BALTIMORE THEATRE
By authority. At the Theatre . . . the 2d of April, 1783 . . . Theodosius . . . Baltimore, M. K. Goddard [1783]
broadside 34.5 X 21 cm.
NHi mp. 44304

B5642 BALTIMORE THEATRE
By authority. At the Theatre . . . the 8th of April, 1783 . . . The Inconstant . . . Baltimore, M. K. Goddard [1783]
broadside 34.5 X 21 cm.
Wheeler 270
NHi mp. 44305

B5643 BALTIMORE THEATRE
By authority. At the Theatre . . . the 13th of May, 1783 . . . The Roman Father . . . Baltimore, M. K. Goddard [1783]
broadside 33.5 X 18.5 cm.
Wheeler 272
NHi mp. 44306

B5644 BALTIMORE THEATRE
By authority. At the Theatre . . . the 16th of May, 1783 . . . a tragedy, called Douglas . . . Baltimore, M. K. Goddard [1783]
broadside 33 X 18.5 cm.
Wheeler 273
NHi mp. 44307

B5645 BALTIMORE THEATRE
By authority. At the Theatre . . . the 23d of May, 1783 . . . The Fair Penitent . . . Baltimroe, M. K. Goddard [1783]
broadside 33.5 X 19 cm.
Wheeler 274
NHi (mutilated) mp. 44308

B5646 BALTIMORE THEATRE
By authority. At the Theatre . . . the 29th of May, 1783 . . . Isabella . . . Baltimore, M. K. Goddard [1783]
broadside 33 X 18.5 cm.

Wheeler 275
NHi mp. 44309

B5647 BALTIMORE THEATRE
By authority. At the Theatre . . . the 30th of May, 1783 . . . George Barnwell . . . Baltimore, M. K. Goddard [1783]
broadside 33 X 19 cm.
Wheeler 277
NHi mp. 44310

B5648 BALTIMORE THEATRE
By authority. At the Theatre . . . the 3d of June, 1783 . . . The Fatal Discovery . . . Baltimore, M. K. Goddard [1783]
broadside 33 X 21 cm.
Wheeler 278
NHi mp. 44311

B5649 BALTIMORE THEATRE
By authority. By particular desire, being . . . the last night of performance . . . At the Theatre . . . the 9th of June, 1783 . . . Isabella . . . Baltimore, M. K. Goddard [1783]
broadside 32.5 X 18.5 cm.
Wheeler 281
NHi mp. 44312

B5650 BALTIMORE THEATRE
By authority. The last night, but one, of the performance here . . . At the Theatre . . . the 11th of April, 1783 . . . The Roman Father . . . Baltimore, M. K. Goddard [1783]
broadside 34.5 X 21 cm.
Wheeler 271
NHi mp. 44313

B5651 BALTIMORE THEATRE
By authority. The last night of performance here this season. At the Theatre . . . the 6th of June, 1783 . . . The Orphan . . . Baltimore, M. K. Goddard [1783]
broadside 33.5 X 21 cm.
Wheeler 279
NHi mp. 44314

B5652 BALTIMORE THEATRE
By particular desire. At the Theatre . . . the 7th of February, 1783 . . . the Grecian Daughter . . . Baltimore, M. K. Goddard [1783]
broadside 34 X 19 cm.
Wheeler 255
NHi mp. 44315

B5653 BALTIMORE THEATRE
By permission. At the Theatre . . . the 14th of January, 1783 . . . the tragedy of Cato . . . Baltimore, M. K. Goddard [1783]
broadside 33 X 20.5 cm.
Wheeler 248
NHi mp. 44316

B5654 BALTIMORE THEATRE
By permission. At the Theatre . . . the 17th of January, 1783 . . . Venice Preserv'd . . . Baltimore, M. K. Goddard [1783]
broadside 34 X 20.5 cm.
Wheeler 249
NHi mp. 44317

B5655 BALTIMORE THEATRE
By permission. At the Theatre . . . the 21st of January, 1783 . . . the Grecian Daughter . . . Baltimore, M. K. Goddard [1783]
broadside 34 X 20.5 cm.
Wheeler 250
NHi mp. 44318

B5656 BALTIMORE THEATRE
By permission. At the Theatre . . . the 24th of January, 1783 . . . the Beggars Opera . . . Baltimore, M. K. Goddard [1783]
broadside 33.5 X 19 cm.
Wheeler 251
NHi mp. 44319

B5657 BALTIMORE THEATRE
By permission. At the Theatre . . . the 28th of January, 1783 . . . the Grecian Daughter . . . Baltimore, M. K. Goddard [1783]
broadside 34.5 X 20.5 cm.
Wheeler 252
NHi mp. 44320

B5658 BALTIMORE THEATRE
By permission. At the Theatre . . . the 31st of January, 1783 . . . the comedy of the Busy Body . . . Baltimore, M. K. Goddard [1783]
broadside 32 X 20.5 cm.
Wheeler 253
NHi mp. 44321

B5659 BALTIMORE THEATRE
By permission. At the Theatre . . . the 4th of February, 1783 . . . Richard III . . . Baltimore, M. K. Goddard [1783]
broadside 36.5 X 21 cm.
Wheeler 254
NHi mp. 44322

B5660 BALTIMORE THEATRE
By permission. At the Theatre . . . the 11th of February, 1783 . . . A Bold Stroke for a Wife . . . Baltimore, M. K. Goddard [1783]
broadside 34.5 X 21 cm.
Wheeler 256
NHi mp. 44323

B5661 BALTIMORE THEATRE
By permission. At the Theatre . . . the 14th of February, 1783 . . . the London Merchant . . . Baltimore, M. K. Goddard [1783]
broadside 34.5 X 21 cm.
Wheeler 257
NHi mp. 44324

B5662 BALTIMORE THEATRE
By permission. At the Theatre . . . the 18th of February, 1783 . . . the West-Indian . . . Baltimore, M. K. Goddard [1783]
broadside 34.5 X 21 cm.
Wheeler 258
NHi mp. 44325

B5663 BALTIMORE THEATRE
By permission. At the Theatre . . . the 21st of February, 1783 . . . the Fair Penitent . . . Baltimore, M. K. Goddard [1783]
broadside 34.5 X 21 cm.
Wheeler 259
NHi mp. 44326

B5664 BALTIMORE THEATRE
By permission. At the Theatre . . . the 25th of February, 1783 . . . the West-Indian . . . Baltimore, M. K. Goddard [1783]

broadside 34.5 X 21 cm.
Wheeler 260
NHi mp. 44327

B5665 BALTIMORE THEATRE
By permission. At the Theatre . . . the 28th of February, 1783 . . . the Fatal Discovery . . . Baltimore, M. K. Goddard [1783]
broadside 34.5 X 21 cm.
Wheeler 261
NHi mp. 44328

B5666 BALTIMORE THEATRE
[By permission. At the Theatre . . . the 4th of March, 1783 . . . Romeo and Juliet . . . Baltimore, M. K. Goddard, 1783]
broadside?
Described from page of sale catalogue preserved at MdBE
Wheeler 261a
No copy known mp. 44329

B5667 BALTIMORE THEATRE
By permission. At the Theatre . . . the 7th of March, 1783 . . . the tragedy of Theodosius . . . Baltimore, M. K. Goddard [1783]
broadside 34.5 X 21 cm.
Wheeler 262
NHi mp. 44330

B5668 BALTIMORE THEATRE
By permission. At the Theatre . . . the 14th of March, 1783 . . . The Fatal Discovery . . . Baltimore, M. K. Goddard [1783]
broadside 34.5 X 21 cm.
Wheeler 264
NHi mp. 44331

B5669 BALTIMORE THEATRE
By permission. At the Theatre . . . the 21st of March, 1783 . . . The Revenge . . . Baltimore, M. K. Goddard [1783]
broadside 34.5 X 21 cm.
Wheeler 266
NHi mp. 44332

B5670 BALTIMORE THEATRE
By permission. At the Theatre . . . the 28th of March, 1783 . . . The Roman Father . . . Baltimore, M. K. Goddard [1783]
broadside 34.5 X 21 cm.
Wheeler 267
NHi mp. 44333

B5671 BALTIMORE THEATRE
For the benefit of Mr. Heard. At the Theatre . . . the 11th of March, 1783 . . . The Provok'd Husband . . . Baltimore, M. K. Goddard [1783]
broadside 34.5 X 21 cm.
Wheeler 263
NHi mp. 44334

B5672 BALTIMORE THEATRE
For the benefit of Mr. Wall. At the Theatre . . . the 3d of January, 1783 . . . the comedy of the Constant Couple . . . Baltimore, M. K. Goddard [1783]
broadside 35 X 19.5 cm.
Wheeler 245
NHi mp. 44335

B5673 BALTIMORE THEATRE
For the benefit of Mrs. Ryan. At the Theatre . . . the 7th of January , 1783 . . . Tamerlane . . . Baltimore, M. K. Goddard [1783]
broadside 33 X 19.5 cm.
Wheeler 246
NHi mp. 44336

B5674 BALTIMORE THEATRE
For the benefit of Mrs. Ryan. At the Theatre . . . the 18th of March, 1783 . . . The Grecian Daughter . . . Baltimore, M. K. Goddard [1783]
broadside 34.5 X 21 cm.
Wheeler 265
NHi mp. 44337

B5675 BALTIMORE THEATRE
For the benefit of the bridge. At the Theatre . . . the 31st of March, 1783 . . . The Siege of Damascus . . . Baltimore, M. K. Goddard [1783]
broadside 34.5 X 21 cm.
Wheeler 268
NHi mp. 44338

B5676 BALTIMORE, March 26, 1783. (Five o'clock A.M.) By an express, on his way to the southward . . . The principal articles of the preliminaries of the peace, of the 20th of January , 1783 . . . Baltimore, John Hayes [1783]
broadside
Amer. Art Assoc. cat., May 14, 1917, item 30
New York Public 770; Wheeler 244
NN (reduced facsim.) mp. 44340

B5677 BALTIMORE, April 12. Wednesday last an officer arrived . . . with letters from sir Guy Charleton and admiral Digby . . . Baltimore, John Hayes [1783]
broadside 35 X 13.5 cm.
Wheeler 283
Photostat: DLC mp. 44339

B5678 BANKS, JOHN
[Statement by John Banks regarding General Nathaniel Greene, beginning] Whatever opinions prevail with the public . . . [n.p., 1783]
broadside 36 X 19.5 cm.
Dated in manuscript at end: Feb. 15, 1783
DLC; RPJCB mp. 44341

B5679 BARTON, BENJAMIN SMITH, 1766-1815
An inquiry into the question, whether the Apis Mellifica . . . is a native of America. [Philadelphia, Robert Aitken, 1783]
21 p. 4to caption title
Separate from Am. Phil. Soc. *Transactions*
PPL mp. 44342

B5680 BATES, WILLIAM, 1625-1699
Christ in the clouds . . . [Hartford] Printed [by Hudson & Goodwin] for, and sold by Shem Chapin, 1783.
16+ p. 20 cm.
Trumbull: Supplement 1894
CtHi (wanting after p. 16); MiU-C (15 p.) mp. 44343

B5681 BENEZET, ANTHONY, 1713-1784
The plainness and innocent simplicity of the Christian religion . . . Philadelphia, Joseph Crukshank, 1783.
48 17 cm.
MWA; N; NBLiHi; NNUT; PHi; PPL; RPJCB
mp. 44345

B5682 BENNEVILLE, GEORGES DE, 1703-1793
[A true and remarkable account of the life and

trance of Dr. . . . Benneville . . . Translated from the French of his own manuscript. Philadelphia? 1783?]

The editor of the 1890 Germantown reprint obtained biographical data and the "original MS" from Benneville's granddaughter. The publisher of the reprint stated that soon after Benneville wrote his MS in 1782, it was given "to the American public by the translator."–Forrest Bowe
No copy known

B5683 BIBLE. O.T. PSALMS
A new version of the Psalms of David . . . By N. Brady . . . and N. Tate . . . Boston, D. & J. Kneeland, 1783.
276, 84 p.
MB mp. 44346

B5684 BIBLE. O. T. PSALMS
The Psalter; or, Psalms of David . . . Boston, T. and J. Fleet, 1783.
157, [1] p.
MHi; MWA (p. 157 numbered 175); RPJCB mp. 44347

B5685 BICKERSTAFF'S Boston almanack for . . . 1784 . . . Boston, Printed and sold by E. Russell; sold also by Adams and Nourse [1783]
[24] p.
cf. sig. B: "2d edit. corrected"
Drake 3332; cf. Evans 18304
Milton Drake, NYC (1964)

B5686 BOSTON. CITIZENS
Boston, April 10, 1783. At a meeting of the freeholders . . . April 7, 1783. [Boston, 1783]
broadside 33 X 42 cm.
Resolve against the return of the refugees and absentees
PPRF; RPJCB mp. 44350

B5687 BOSTON. COMMITTEE OF CORRESPONDENCE
Boston, April 17, 1783. Gentlemen, By the inclosed resolve [of Apr. 10, 1783], transmitted to you . . . you may form some judgement of their sentiments respecting the absentees . . . [Boston, 1783]
broadside 33.5 X 21 cm.
M-Ar mp. 44348

B5688 BOSTON. FIRE CLUB
Rules and orders to be observed by a Fire-Club instituted . . . March 5th, 1783. [Boston, 1783?]
4, [1] p.
MWA mp. 44349

B5689 BOSTON. TREASURER
Your Commonwealth tax. Your county tax . . . Boston, July 1783. [Boston, 1783]
broadside
Ford 2347
MHi mp. 44350

B5690 BOSTON. TREASURER
Your Commonwealth tax. Your county tax . . . Boston, March 1783. [Boston, 1783]
broadside
Ford 2346
MHi

B5691 BRADFORD, CORNELIUS
New-York Coffee-house. All masters of vessels in this port . . . [Concerning registration of ships and delivery of letters] [New York, 1783]
broadside 14 X 11 cm.
Dated Nov. 20, 1783
cf. *New York History*, v. 17, no. 4, Oct. 1936
New York Public 771
NN (facsim.) mp. 44351

B5692 CAREY, JAMES, AND CO.
Baltimore, 1st June, 1783. We beg leave to inform you of our establishment of . . . the firm of James Cary and Co. . . . [Baltimore, 1783]
broadside 31 X 19 cm.
Wheeler 282
RPJCB mp. 44352

B5693 CARTER, JOHN, 1745-1814
Just imported from London, and to be sold by John Carter . . . an assortment of books . . . [Providence, J. Carter, 1783]
broadside 44 X 19 cm.
Alden 947
RHi. Photostat: MWA mp. 44353

B5694 CHAPONE, HESTER (MULSO) 1727-1801
Letters on the improvement of the mind . . . Boston, Printed by Robert Hodge, for William Green [1783]
2 v. in 1 ([8], 13-254 p.) 17.5 cm.
Advertised in the *Independent Chronicle*, Feb. 6, 1783, as "Just published."
Huntington 471; New York Public 757
CSmH; MWA; MdBP; NN; RPJCB mp. 44354

B5695 CHAPONE, HESTER (MULSO) 1727-1801
Letters on the improvement of the mind . . . Boston, Printed for Isaiah Thomas, at Worcester [by Robert Hodge], 1783.
2 v. in 1 ([9], 14-254 p.) 17 cm.
MWA mp. 44355

B5696 CHARLESTON. HARBOUR-MASTER
Charleston, October 4, 1783. No. 3 Broad-Street. By virtue of the powers . . . vested in me, by an ordinance . . . ". . . duties of the Harbour-Master . . . of Charleston" I . . . order and direct the pilots . . . Robert Cochran, Harbour-Master. [Charleston] N. Childs [1783]
broadside 30 X 20 cm.
Turnbull p. 239 (v.1)
CtY

B5697 CHURCHILL, MEHETABLE, 1756-
A remarkable instance of the interposition of the spirit of grace . . . Written by herself . . . [Springfield? Mass.] Printed for, and sold by Joseph Warriner, 1783.
16 p. 16 cm.
Type ornaments exactly like those used by John W. Folsom in 1784
MWA mp. 44356

B5698 COMMONWEALTH of Massachusetts. Boston, 25th of May, 1783. The candid public will recollect that when the two houses . . . in September last, were about to come to a final resolution, upon the integrity . . . of Mr. Temple's conduct towards his country; James Sullivan, Esq; . . . wrote a letter . . . [Boston, 1783]
[3] p. 38.5 cm.
A refutation
MHi mp. 44357

B5699 THE commutation, or half pay: a Hudibrastic poem. By a Centinel . . . America, 1783.
8 p. 18 cm.
RPJCB mp. 44358

B5700 CONNECTICUT. GENERAL ASSEMBLY
At a General Assembly . . . holden . . . on the eighth day of January . . . 1783. The gentlemen nominated . . . to stand for election in May next, for delegates in Congress . . . as sent into the present Assembly, are as follows . . . Hartford, Hudson and Goodwin [1783]
broadside 34 X 14.5 cm.
CtHi

B5701 CONNECTICUT. GOVERNOR, 1776-1784
By His Excellency, Jonathan Trumbull, Governor . . . of Connecticut. A proclamation . . . public thanksgiving on November 20th . . . All servile labour is forbidden on said day. Given . . . this 29th day of October, 1783. Gov. Trumbull . . . [New Haven, Printed for Thos. and Samuel Green [1783]
broadside
Heartman: Cradle 64; cf. Evans 17887
MHi. Charles F. Heartman (1922) mp. 44359

B5702 CULLEN, WILLIAM, 1710-1790
Synopsis nosologiae methodicae . . . Ad normam novissimae editionis edita atque emendata. Americae [New York?] Abrah. Hodge, 1783.
392 p. 22 cm.
Running title: Genera morborum Culleni
DNLM; MBM; MWA (p. 75-78 wanting); OClM
mp. 44362

B5703 DELAWARE. LAWS
Laws enacted by the General Assembly . . . in the year . . . One Thousand Seven Hundred and Eighty-three. [Wilmington, James Adams, 1783]
4 p. 30 cm. caption title
DLC; PPL mp. 44364

B5704 DORCHESTER, MASS.
Your continental tax. 1783. Your town and county rate, to be paid in specie. 1783. [Boston, 1783]
broadside
Assessors to sit in February
Ford 2354
MHi

B5705 DORCHESTER, MASS.
Your continental tax. 1783. Your town and county rate, to be paid in specie. 1783 . . . [Boston, 1783]
broadside
Assessors to sit in August
Ford 2355
MHi

B5706 THE East-Florida gazette. St. Augustine, Printed by Charles Wright for John Welles [1783]

Brigham p. 109
DLC (photostat; issues for Mar. 1, May 3 & 17, 1783)

B5707 FLAVEL, JOHN, 1630-1691
A discourse, showing that Christ's tender care of his Mother is an excellent pattern . . . [Hartford?] Printed [by Hudson & Goodwin?] for, and sold by Shem Chapen [sic] 1783.
16 p.
Trumbull: Supplement 2149
CtHi; MWA ([Springfield, Mass.?]) mp. 44365

B5708 FRIENDS, SOCIETY OF. LONDON YEARLY MEETING
The epistle from our Yearly Meeting, held in London . . . sixth month 1783 . . . To the Quarterly and Monthly Meetings . . . in Great-Britain, Ireland, and elsewhere . . . [Philadelphia, 1783]
4 p.
MWA mp. 44367

B5709 GEORGIA. COMMISSIONERS OF CONFISCATED ESTATES
State of Georgia. Savannah, 11th October, 1783. Notice is hereby given by the Commissioners . . . Hugh Lawson, Hepworth Carter, Abraham Ravot, Com'rs. [Savannah] James Johnston [1783]
broadside 43 X 34 cm.
De Renne p. 228
GU-De mp. 44368

B5710 GEORGIA. GENERAL ASSEMBLY
Georgia. House of assembly, 15th July 1783. Ordered, That . . . the Governor . . . In Council, Savannah, 19th August, 1783 . . . [Savannah, J. Johnston, 1783]
broadside 42 X 25 cm.
De Renne p. 228; New York Public 772
GU-De; NcD. Photostats: DLC; NN mp. 44374

B5711 GEORGIA. GOVERNOR, 1783-1784
Georgia. By the Honourable Lyman Hall . . . A proclamation. Whereas, in order to preserve peace . . . June 13, 1783. [Savannah? 1783]
broadside
MWA mp. 44369

B5712 GEORGIA. LAWS
An act for the laying out the reserve land in the town of Augusta into acre lots . . . Augusta, 31st July, 1783. [Savannah, James Johnston, 1783]
3 p. fol. caption title
De Renne p. 228
GU-De mp. 44370

B5713 GEORGIA. LAWS
An act to ascertain the various periods of depreciation . . . Savannah, February 17, 1783 . . . [Savannah, James Johnston, 1783]
13 p. fol. caption title
De Renne p. 227; cf. Evans 27041
GU-De mp. 44371

B5714 GEORGIA. LAWS
An act to continue the several laws of this state near expiring . . . Savannah, James Johnston, 1783.
4 p. fol.
De Renne p. 227
GU-De mp. 44372

B5715 GEORGIA. LAWS
An act to empower certain commissioners . . . to regulate the hire of porters . . . in . . . Savannah . . . Augusta, 31st July, 1783. [Savannah, James Johnston, 1783]
3 p. fol. caption title
De Renne p. 228
GU-De mp. 44373

B5716 GT. BRIT. ADJUTANT-GENERAL'S OFFICE
Head-Quarters, New-York, April 15, 1783. Orders . . . Ol. De Lancey, Adjutant-General. [New York, 1783]
broadside 28 X 17 cm.
DLC mp. 44375

B5717 GT. BRIT. SOVEREIGNS (GEORGE III)
The British King's speech. New-York, February 10. By the brigantine Peggy . . . we have received the following

copy of his Majesty's . . . speech . . . Decemb. 5, 1782 . . . [New York, 1783]
broadside 36.5 X 25 cm.
DLC mp. 44376

B5718 GT. BRIT. SOVEREIGNS (GEORGE III)
Important intelligence. Providence, Feb. 24, 1783. . . . the British King's speech . . . on the 5th of December . . . [Providence] John Carter [1783]
broadside 25 X 17.5 cm.
Alden 950; Winship Addenda p. 89
RHi. Photostats: MHi; MWA; NN mp. 44377

B5719 GT. BRIT. SOVEREIGNS (GEORGE III)
Philadelphia, February 13. By a gentleman just arrived . . . New-York, February 9, 1783 . . . [Philadelphia] E. Oswald [1783]
broadside 32 X 21.5 cm.
Taylor 372
DLC; MiU-C; PHi mp. 44378

B5720 GT. BRIT. SOVEREIGNS (GEORGE III)
Salem, February 22, 1783. Capt. George Williams . . . has favoured us . . . The speech of the King of Great-Britain . . . [Salem] S. Hall [1783]
broadside 38.5 X 25 cm.
Ford 2379; Tapley p. 339
DLC mp. 44379

B5721 GT. BRIT. TREATIES
. . . Translation of the preliminary articles of peace, between His Britannic Majesty and the Most Christian King; signed at Versailles the 20th of January, 1783 . . . Baltimore, John Hayes [1783]
broadside 44 X 25.5 cm.
PPRF mp. 44380

B5722 THE happy man, and true gentleman. [n.p., 1783]
broadside 32 X 20 cm.
cf. Evans 18520
DLC mp. 44381

B5723 HELLENBROEK, ABRAHAM, 1658-1731
A specimen of divine truths . . . Translated from the Dutch. Philadelphia, Robert Aitken, 1783.
86, [2] p. 15 cm.
DLC; PPAmP mp. 44382

B5724 HENNINGER, JACOB
By authority. At the next door to the New-England Coffee-house, in Fell's-Point . . . on evening, the The noted Jacob Henninger will exhibit his grand medley of entertainments . . . Baltimore, M. K. Goddard, 1783.
broadside 32.5 X 19.5 cm.
Wheeler 276
NHi mp. 44383

B5725 HENNINGER, JACOB
By permission. At the sign of St. Patrick, Fell's-Point, in a large room fitted up in a theatrical manner . . . the noted old artist will exhibit his grand medley of entertainments . . . Baltimore, M. K. Goddard [1783]
broadside 34.5 X 20.5 cm.
Wheeler 247
NHi mp. 44384

B5726 HERE Bickerstaff from ev'ry star pulls his predictions down . . . Predictions for the year 1783 . . . [Boston] Sold at the Printing Office in Essex-Street, near Liberty-Stump. [1783]
broadside 33 X 24 cm.
Ford 2377
MHi (photostat) mp. 44385

B5727 THE history of Little Goody Two-Shoes . . . Boston: Printed and sold by Nathaniel Coverly, 1783.
62, [2] p. illus. 9 cm.
CtHi (imperfect); CLU (imperfect); NjP. Oppenheimer (imperfect) mp. 44386

B5728 AN hymn to be sung by the charity scholars, on . . . the 12th of October, 1783, at St. George's Chapel, after the charity sermon . . . New-York, October 11, 1783. [New York, 1783]
broadside 32 X 18.5 cm.
NHi mp. 44387

B5729 AN hymn to be sung by the charity scholars . . . the 19th of October, 1783 . . . New-York, October 16, 1783. [New York, 1783]
broadside 33 X 21 cm.
DLC; NHi mp. 44388

B5730 IMPORTANT intelligence of peace! Between America and Great-Britain . . . New-York, March 26. A general peace . . . Worcester, April 1, 5 o'clock, P.M. 1783. We have this moment received the above . . . by a gentleman directly from Boston . . . [Worcester, 1783]
broadside 30 X 22.5 cm.
MWA mp. 44389

B5731 INGLIS, CHARLES, 1734-1816
A sermon preached before the Grand Lodge . . . in New-York . . . New-York, Printed by Robertsons, Mills and Hicks, 1783.
31 p. 18.5 cm. $[A]\text{-}D^4$
MWA mp. 44390

B5732 JOHNSON, JOHONNOTT AND CO.
Baltimore, 1783. We have established a house in Baltimore . . . under the firm of Johnson, Johonnott, and Co. . . . Baltimore, 1783.
broadside 23 X 18.5 cm.
Wheeler 289
RPJCB (2 copies) mp. 44391

B5733 KENT COUNTY, DEL.
At a meeting of deputies . . . of Kent County . . . the first day of September 1783 . . . Resolved, That . . . the people . . . [Ticket headed by] Councellor: Caesar Rodney . . . [Wilmington? James Adams? 1783]
broadside 21 X 17 cm.
Only Adams was then printing in Delaware
Hawkins: List C 12
DLC mp. 44392

B5734 MACPHERSON, MARY ANN
Mrs. MacPherson's most respectful compliments . . . Monday morning, June 16, 1783 . . . [Philadelphia, 1783]
broadside 27 X 22.5 cm.
DLC mp. 44393

B5735 MARYLAND. LAWS
An act to raise the supplies for the year seventeen hundred and eighty-three. Annapolis, Frederick Green [1783]
35 p. 17 cm.
750 copies of this act were ordered to be printed and distributed before Jan. 10, 1783
Wheeler 290
MdHi (lacks t.p.) mp. 44394

B5736 MARYLANDISCHER calender auf das jahr 1784. Friederich-stadt, Matthias Bartgis [1783]

[20] p. 21.5 cm.
Wheeler 300a
PHi mp. 44395

B5737 MASSACHUSETTS
Lands for sale. Commonwealth of Massachusetts . . . John Ashley, jun., Jonathan Smith, Nathaniel Kingsley, Committee . . . September 18, 1783. [Boston, 1783]
broadside
Ford 2361
M-Ar mp. 44396

B5738 MASSACHUSETTS. GENERAL COURT
Commonwealth of Massachusetts. In the House of Representatives, July 11, 1783. Whereas it is necessary . . . account of all bounties paid to soldiers . . . In Senate, October 4, 1783. Read and concurred . . . Council-Chamber, Boston, October 17, 1783 . . . I have collected the . . . resolves . . . and orders . . . for raising . . . men to serve in . . . the army . . . John Avery, Sec'y. [Boston, 1783]
[2] p. 36 X 21.5 cm.
Huntington 488
CSmH; MHi; MWA; MeHi mp. 44401

B5739 MASSACHUSETTS. HOUSE OF REPRESENTATIVES
Commonwealth of Massachusetts. In the House of Representatives, November 27, 1783. [Boston, 1783]
broadside
Ford 2367
MWA mp. 44402

B5740 MASSACHUSETTS. LAWS
An act in addition to, and for altering and amending . . . "An act for forming and regulating the militia within . . . . Massachusetts . . ." Published by order of the General Assembly. Boston, T. and J. Fleet, 1783.
1 p.l., 8 p., 1 l. 21 cm.
Last leaf blank
New York Public 775; Sabin 45560
MHi; MWA; NN mp. 44398

B5741 MASSACHUSETTS. LAWS
An act, laying duties of impost and excise, on certain goods . . . Boston, Adams and Nourse, 1783.
20 p. 20 cm. [A]-B^4 C^2
MBAt; MHi; MWA mp. 44399

B5742 MASSACHUSETTS. LAWS
An act to prevent impositions on the inhabitants of any town . . . in the sale of fire-wood . . . Vote of town meeting of Newbury-Port, March 26, 1783 . . . Newbury-Port, 31st December, 1783. [Newburyport, 1783]
broadside
Ford 2364
MSaE mp. 44400

B5743 MASSACHUSETTS. SENATE
Commonwealth of Massachusetts. In Senate, June 18, 1783. Resolved, That the commissioners . . . [Boston, 1783]
broadside 29.5 X 22 cm.
Ford 2365
DLC mp. 44397

B5744 MASSACHUSETTS. TREASURER
Commonwealth of Massachusetts. Continental tax no. 2. Thomas Ivers, Esq; Treasurer . . . Boston, the day of in the year . . . one thousand seven hundred and eighty three. [Boston, 1783]
broadside
Ford 2370
MBB; MSaE mp. 44403

B5745 MASSACHUSETTS. TREASURER
Commonwealth of Massachusetts. (Tax no. 3.) Thomas Ivers, Esq; Treasurer . . . Boston, the day of in the year . . . one thousand seven hundred and eighty three. [Boston, 1783]
broadside 40 X 25.5 cm.
Ford 2372
MHi; MWA (2 copies) mp. 44404

B5746 MASSACHUSETTS. TREASURER
Tax no. 3. Commonwealth of Massachusetts. Thomas Ivers, Esq; Treasurer . . . [Boston, 1783]
broadside
Different printing from B5745; "Tax no. 3" at left
MHi

B5747 MERCER, SILAS
Tyranny exposed . . . Halifax, Thomas Davis, 1783.
70, [1] p. 15.5 cm.
Sabin 47907
DLC mp. 44405

B5748 MILL-LOTTERY. Boston, (State of Massachusetts.) According to an act of the General Assembly, passed February twenty-sixth, 1783 . . . [Boston, 1783]
broadside
Ford 2374
MB mp. 44406

B5749 MORRIS, THOMAS & CO.
Charlestown, We beg leave to acquaint you that we have established a house of business . . . [Charlestown, 1783?]
broadside 20.5 X 18.5 cm.
RPJCB mp. 44407

B5750 [MURRAY, JAMES] 1732-1782
An impartial history of the war in America . . . The second edition. Vol. I. Boston, Robert Hodge, 1783.
445 p. ports., map. 8vo
Huntington 484; cf. Evans 17241
CSmH mp. 44408

B5751 EIN neu Trauer-Lied, wie man vernommen von einem Menschen der nach dem Todt ist wieder kommen. Die Melodey thut so anfangen . . . [n.p.] MDCCLXXXIII.
broadside 39.5 X 53 cm.
cf. Evans 18041
NHi mp. 44409

B5752 THE New England primer (enlarged and much improved) . . . Philadelphia, Joseph Crukshank, 1783.
80 p. [A]-E^8
Heartman 72; Taylor 361
L. Spring (1922) mp. 44411

B5753 THE New-England primer, improved . . . To which is added, The Assembly of Divines catechism. Hartford, Hudson & Goodwin, 1783.
[80] p.
Trumbull: Second supplement 2865
Ct mp. 44410

B5754 NEW HAMPSHIRE
State of New Hampshire. The committee to consider what method . . . for proportioning future taxes . . . In council, February 21, 1783 . . . M. Weare, president. [Exeter, 1783]
broadside 38.5 X 31 cm.

Whittemore 339
MHi; NhHi mp. 44412

B5755 NEW HAMPSHIRE. LAWS
[Acts and laws, 1782-83] [Exeter, 1783]
p. 297-304.
Continuation of Acts and laws published 1780
Whittemore 335
MWA (p. 297-298); Nh; NhHi mp. 44413

B5756 NEW JERSEY. GENERAL ASSEMBLY
[Minutes and proceedings of the joint meeting of the Council and General Assembly June 17, 1780–Dec. 20, 1783. Trenton? Isaac Collins? 1783?]
p. 41-60. 32 cm.
Humphrey 299
Nj (t.p. wanting) mp. 44414

B5757 NEW JERSEY. GOVERNOR, 1776-1790
By . . . William Livingston . . . Proclamation . . . [Nov. 11, 1783] . . . Trenton, Isaac Collins [1783]
broadside 41.5 X 26 cm.
Huntington 489; New York Public 776
CSmH; NN (reduced facsim.) mp. 44415

B5758 NEW YORK. ASSEMBLY
Votes and proceedings of the Assembly, &c. at the [third] last meeting of the third session. [Poughkeepsie, John Holt, 1783]
p. [157]-192. 31 cm. caption title
Third meeting: May 25-July 2, 1780
Vail: Patriotic pair, p. 420
NHi; NNS mp. 44417

B5759 NEW YORK. ASSEMBLY
Votes and proceedings of the Assembly, &c. at the first meeting of the fourth session. [Poughkeepsie, John Holt, 1783]
43 p. 31 cm. caption title
First meeting: Sept. 7-Oct. 10, 1780
Vail: Patriotic pair, p. 420
NHi; NNS mp. 44418

B5760 NEW YORK. ASSEMBLY
Votes and proceedings of the Assembly, &c. at the [third] last meeting of the fourth session. [Poughkeepsie, John Holt, 1783]
[23] p. 31 cm. caption title
Third meeting: June 16-July 1, 1781
Vail: Patriotic pair, p. 420
N; NHi; NNS mp. 44419

B5761 NEW YORK. ASSEMBLY
Votes and proceedings of the Assembly, &c. at the second meeting of the sixth session. Kingston, Ulster County, 27th January, 1783 [-Mar. 28, 1783] [Poughkeepsie, John Holt, 1783]
p. [97]-179 p. 30.5 cm. caption title
Vail: Patriotic pair, p. 421
MH (p. 101-179); N; NHi; NNS mp. 44420

B5762 NEW YORK. LAWS
Haerlem, November 21, 1783. State of New-York, ss. By the Council appointed by the act . . . entitled, "An act to provide for the temporary government . . ." New-York, Samuel Loudon [1783]
broadside 24.5 X 15.5 cm.
DLC; RPJCB mp. 44421

B5763 NEW YORK. SENATE
Votes and proceedings of the Senate, &c. at the [third] last meeting of the third session. [Poughkeepsie, John Holt, 1783]
p. [109]-134. 30.5 cm. caption title
Third meeting: May 23-July 2, 1780
Vail: Patriotic pair, p. 418
NHi; NIC; NNS mp. 44422

B5764 NEW YORK. SENATE
Votes and proceedings of the Senate, &c. At the first meeting of the fourth session. [Sept. 7-Oct. 10, 1780] [Poughkeepsie, John Holt, 1783]
p. [3]-34. 30.5 cm. caption title
New York Public 778; Vail: Patriotic pair, p. 418
N (fire-damaged); NHi; NN; NNS mp. 44423

B5765 NEW YORK. SENATE
Votes and proceedings of the Senate, &c. at the second [-last] meeting of the fourth session. [Poughkeepsie, John Holt, 1783]
p. [35]-114. 30 cm. caption title
Second meeting: Jan. 31-Mar. 31, 1781; last meeting, June 15-July 1, 1781
New York Public 779; Vail: Patriotic pair, p. 418
N (fire-damaged); NHi; NN; NNS mp. 44424

B5766 NEW YORK. SENATE
Votes and proceedings of the Senate, &c. at the second meeting of the sixth session. [Jan. 27-Mar. 28, 1783] [Poughkeepsie, John Holt, 1783]
p. [97]-165. 35 cm. caption title
New York Public 780; Vail: Patriotic pair, p. 419
N; NHi; NN; NNS; PHi mp. 44425

B5767 NEW-YORK, Nov. 24, 1783. The committee appointed to conduct the order of receiving their excellencies Governor Clinton and General Washington . . . Order of procession . . . New-York, Samuel Loudon [1783]
broadside 34 X 23 cm.
Original formerly in collection of Elmer T. Hutchinson
New York Public 777; Sabin 101860
MiU-C (facsim.); N; RPJCB. Photostat: NN
mp. 44426

B5768 NEW-YORK GAZETTEER
Supplement to the *New-York Gazetteer* No. 44. Peace! Liberty! and Independence! Philadelphia, March 24, 1783. [Philadelphia, 1783]
broadside 20.5 X 17 cm.
NHi mp. 44462

B5769 NEWPORT, October 27, 1783. By the brig ———, Captain Coffin, arrived last evening . . . the printer has received papers . . . Copy of a letter . . . C.J. Fox . . . [Newport] Henry Barber [1783]
broadside 26 X 20 cm.
Alden 949; Winship p. 46
RHi mp. 44429

B5770 THE news-carrier's address to his customers. Hartford, January 1, 1783. [Hartford, 1783]
broadside
First line begins: In England, where the poets scribble . . .
MWA mp. 44430

B5771 THE North-American calendar, or, The Rhode-Island almanack, for the year . . . 1784 . . . Newport, Solomon Southwick [1783]
[24] p. 16.5 cm.
Alden 942; Winship p. 46; Chapin p. 40
CtY; InU; MWA; N; NHi; NN; RHi; RNHi; RPE
mp. 44498

B5772 NORTH CAROLINA. HOUSE OF COMMONS
The journal of the House of Commons. At a General Assembly begun . . . at Hillsborough . . . Being the first session of this Assembly . . . [at end] Halifax, Thomas Davis [1783]
67 p. 22 cm. caption title
Huntington 491; McMurtrie: North Carolina 114
CSmH mp. 44431

B5773 OCTOBER 17, 1783. Monsieur Stephen Regne, a French gentleman, lately from the West-Indies, died this morning . . . [Philadelphia, 1783]
card 16mo
PPL

B5774 OFFICIAL intelligence of peace. Published by the authority of the minister of France at Philadelphia. [Worcester, Isaiah Thomas, 1783]
broadside 22 X 20 cm.
Ford 2375; Nichols: Isaiah Thomas 103
DLC mp. 44433

B5775 ORDER of exhibition of the fire-works, on Monday evening the first of December, 1783. [New York] Printed at the State Printing-Office [by John Holt] 1783.
broadside 41 X 26 cm.
New York Public 781
NN mp. 44434

B5776 PEACE. Salem, February 21, 1783. By Captain John Osgood in twenty-nine days from Martinico . . . interesting intelligence relative to peace. [Salem, 1783]
broadside 34 X 20.5 cm.
Ford 2376; Tapley p. 339
NHi (photostat) mp. 44435

B5777 PENNSYLVANIA
By the President and the Supreme Executive Council of the Commonwealth of Pennsylvanis, a proclamation . . . Given in Council . . . this thirteenth day of September . . . one thousand seven hundred and eighty three. John Dickinson. [Philadelphia] Francis Bailey [1783]
broadside fol.
PPL mp. 44437

B5778 PENNSYLVANIA. COUNCIL
For specie. In Council, Philadelphia 1783. Sir, Pay to . . . To David Rittenhouse, Esquire, Treasurer. [Philadelphia, 1783]
broadside 19 X 22 cm.
DLC; MiU-C

B5779 PENNSYLVANIA. GENERAL ASSEMBLY
State of Pennsylvania. In General Assembly, Saturday, February 1, 1783. The bill entituled "An act for extending the provision made in the seventh section . . . was read the second time . . . Ordered to be transcribed for a third reading . . . Peter Z. Lloyd, Clerk . . . [Philadelphia] Hall and Sellers [1783]
2 p. 35.5 X 22.5 cm.
Taylor 368
PHi mp. 44436

B5780 PENNSYLVANIA GAZETTE
The New-Year verses of the printers lads, who carry about the *Pennsylvania Gazette* . . . January 1, 1783. [Philadelphia, Hall and Sellers, 1783]
broadside 35.5 X 15 cm.
New York Public 782
NN mp. 44416

B5781 PENNSYLVANIA PACKET
Supplement to the *Pennsylvania Packet*. Wednesday, April 9, 1783. The printer takes the earliest opportunity . . . Authentic copy of the preliminary articles of peace . . . Philadelphia, David C. Claypoole [1783]
broadside 50.5 X 37 cm.
Text in 3 columns
MiU-C mp. 44486

B5782 PHILADELPHIA COUNTY
State of the accounts of William Crispin, Esq. late collector of excise, for the city and county of Philadelphia, from July 1, 1781, to July 1, 1782 . . . Philadelphia, T. Bradford, 1783.
[10] p. 8vo
PPL mp. 44439

B5783 PHILANDER and Rosabella. "Philander, Since Rosabella my true love consents to be Philander's bride . . ." Printed & sold in New-London [1783?]
broadside 33.5 X 22 cm.
In three columns
In ms. on verso: . . . Bought of Mr. Aaron Baxter of Hebron. Glastenbury February 14th 1783
MWA (mutilated) mp. 44440

B5784 PICKERING AND HODGDON, firm, Philadelphia
Philadelphia May 1783. Sir, the publick services in which so many years . . . [Philadelphia, 1783]
Folder ([1] p.) 23.5 X 19 cm.
Circular letter to business correspondents with identifying signatures for firm in autograph of both Timothy Pickering and Samuel Hodgdon
MB

B5785 PIERCE, WHITE, & CALL, firm, Savannah
Savannah, (in Georgia) May 25th, 1783. We having opened a house in Savannah . . . request the indulgence of such consignments as you may . . . make to this port . . . Wm. Pierce, A. W. White, Richard Call. [Savannah, 1783]
broadside 23.5 X 19.5 cm.
NjR

B5786 A POEM composed July 4, 1783, being a day of general rejoicing, for . . . independence to the United States of America. [n.p., 1783]
broadside 29 X 16 cm.
Swann Auction Galleries sale no. 483, Dec. 5, 1957, item 72; New York Public 783
NN (photostat) mp. 44441

B5787 A POEM occasioned by the horrid crime of William Beadle late of Wethersfield, in Connecticut, who on the 11th of December 1782, . . . murdered his wife . . . [n.p., 1783?]
broadside 37.5 X 25 cm.
14 verses of 4 lines each
MAJ

B5788 POOR Richard's almanack for . . . 1784 . . . New-York, Printed and sold by Morton and Horner [1783]
[32] p.
Wall p. 24
NHi mp. 44442

B5789 [PRATT, SAMUEL JACKSON] 1749-1814
Emma Corbett: exhibiting Henry and Emma, the faithful modern lovers . . . Published by Courtney Melmoth . . . Philadelphia, Printed and sold by Robert Bell, 1783.
3 v. 20 cm.
MWA mp. 44443

B5790 PREDICTIONS for the year 1783. [Boston] Sold at the Printing-Office in Essex-Street, near Liberty-Stump [1783]
broadside 33.5 X 24 cm.
Ford 2377; Wegelin 748; New York Public 784
RPJCB. Photostats: DLC; MHi; NN mp. 44444

B5791 PRESBYTERIAN CHURCH IN THE U.S. SYNOD OF NEW YORK AND PHILADELPHIA
A pastoral letter from the Synod . . . Philadelphia, May 24, 1783 . . . Philadelphia, Francis Bailey [1783]
broadside 31 X 17 cm.
DLC mp. 44445

B5792 A PRESENT to children . . . New-London, T. Green, 1783.
16 p. 12 cm.
CtY mp. 44446

B5793 RHODE ISLAND. ELECTION PROX.
His Excellency William Greene, Esq; Governor. The honorable Jabez Bowen, Esq; Dep. Governor . . . [Providence] John Carter [1783]
broadside 20.5 X 13 cm.
Alden 953; Chapin Proxies 35
RHi mp. 44447

B5794 RHODE ISLAND. GOVERNOR, 1779-1786
[By . . . William Greene, Esq; Governor . . . A proclamation . . . [Nov. 14, 1783] . . . Providence, J. Carter, 1783]
[broadside?]
Bill submitted April, 1784, with item dated Nov. 18, 1783
Alden 954
No copy known mp. 44449

B5795 RHODE ISLAND. GOVERNOR, 1779-1786
[By . . . William Greene, Esq; Governor . . . A proclamation . . . [Nov. 17, 1783] . . . Providence, J. Carter, 1783]
[broadside?]
Bill submitted April, 1784, with item dated Oct. 18, 1783
Alden 955
No copy known mp. 44448

B5796 RHODE ISLAND. LAWS
State of Rhode-Island and Providence-Plantations. In General assembly, February session, 1783. An act to disqualify persons . . . [Providence, Bennett Wheeler, 1783]
broadside 20 X 15.5 cm.
Bill submitted by Wheeler Mar. 20, 1783
Alden 959; Winship p. 47
MWA; RHi mp. 44450

B5797 RHODE ISLAND. LAWS
State of Rhode Island and Providence Plantations. In General assembly, June session, 1783. An act for granting . . . a tax of twenty thousand pounds . . . [Providence, J. Carter, 1783]
broadside 52 X 19 cm.
Bill submitted by Carter in April, 1784, with item dated July 2, 1783
Alden 960; Winship p. 47
RHi mp. 44451

B5798 RICHMOND, April 17th, 1783. By a gentleman who arrived last night . . . the following intelligence . . . Richmond, James Hayes [1783]
broadside 28 X 16 cm.
Letters of General Carleton and Admiral Digby concerning the treaty of peace
Davis 2
NcD mp. 44452

B5799 [SMITH, MERIWETHER]
Observations on the fourth and fifth articles of the preliminaries for a peace . . . Richmond, Dixon & Holt [1783]
28 p. 18 cm.
Ms. note on t.p.: "By Merryweather Smith Esq. Published 20th July 1783."
Davis 3; Sabin 83609
RPJCB mp. 44454

B5800 SMITH, WILLIAM, 1727-1803
A sermon preached in Christ-Church, Philadelphia, [for the benefit of the poor] by appointment . . . before the . . . Masons . . . of Pennsylvania . . . December 28, 1778 . . . Philadelphia, Re-printed by Hall and Sellers, 1783.
[2], 149-166 p. 19.5 cm.
Brackets are in the text
Taylor 376; cf. Evans 17915
PHi mp. 44455

B5801 SOUTH CAROLINA. COMMISSIONERS OF FORFEITED ESTATES
Advertisement. The Commissioners of Forfeited Estates give notice . . . 16th day of June next . . . will be sold . . . houses, lands, &c. in and near Charlestown . . . James O'Hear, Clk. Charlestown, April 14, 1783. [Charleston] E. Boden [1783]
broadside 36 X 30.5 cm.
Sc-Ar (2 copies)

B5802 SOUTH CAROLINA. COMMISSIONERS OF FORFEITED ESTATES
Advertisement. The Commissioners of Forfeited Estates give notice . . . 17th day of December next . . . will be sold . . . the following houses, lands, &c. . . . James O'Hear, Clk. Charleston, October 17, 1783. [Charleston] Printed for A. Timothy [1783]
broadside 45 X 36.5 cm.
Sc-Ar

B5803 SOUTH CAROLINA. COMMISSIONERS OF FORFEITED ESTATES
Advertisement. Will be sold at public auction . . . by the Commissioners of Forfeited Estates, the 30th day of June . . . the following lands . . . James O'Hear, Clk. Charlestown, April 9th, 1783. [Charleston] Elizabeth Boden [1783]
broadside 30.5 X 18.5 cm.
Sc-Ar (2 copies)

B5804 SOUTH CAROLINA. COMMISSIONERS OF FORFEITED ESTATES
Advertisement. Will be sold at public auction, by the Commissioners of Forfeited Estates . . . the 8th day of July next, at Ninety-Six, the following valuable tracts of land . . . James O'Hear, Clk. Ninety-Six, May 6th, 1783. [Charleston? 1783]
broadside 43 X 30.5 cm.
PHi; Sc-Ar (mutilated)

B5805 SOUTH CAROLINA. COMMISSIONERS OF FORFEITED ESTATES
Advertisement. Will be sold at public auction by the Commissioners . . . the 15th of November next, at Orangeburgh, the following tracts of land . . . [and] the 8th day of December next, at Ninety-Six, the following tracts . . . James O'Hear, Clk. Charlestown, 10th September, 1783. [Charleston, 1783]

broadside 31.5 X 22 cm.
PHi; Sc–Ar mp. 44456

B5806 SOUTH CAROLINA. COURT OF GENERAL SESSIONS
State of South-Carolina! At the Courts of General Sessions . . . for the districts of Cheraws and Camden, the 15th and 26th of November, 1783, before . . . Judge Grimke . . . [Charleston? 1783]
[4] p. 27.5 cm.
MHi mp. 44457

B5807 SOUTH CAROLINA. GOVERNOR, 1783-1785
By his Excellency Benjamin Guerard, Esq; Governor . . . Whereas in and by an ordinance . . . to oblige all persons nominated as magistrates . . . to qualify . . . Given . . . at Charlestown, this day of and in the year . . . one thousand seven hundred and eighty and in the year of the independence . . . [Charleston, 1783?]
broadside 38.5 X 30.5 cm.
MWA mp. 44458

B5808 SOUTH CAROLINA. LAWS
An act for levying and collecting certain duties . . . in aid of the public revenue. [n.p., 1783]
6 p. 30 cm.
Dated at end: In the Senate House, the 13th day of August, 1783 . . .
DLC mp. 44459

B5809 SOUTH CAROLINA. LAWS
An act to incorporate Charleston. [Aug. 13, 1783] [Charleston, 1783]
6 p. fol. caption title
Same setting of type as Evans 18190, but issued separately
Sabin 87637
ScC

B5810 THE South-Carolina and Georgia almanack for . . . 1784. By John Tobler. Charles-Town, J. Miller [1783]
[24] p.
Drake 13134
ScC

B5811 [SOUTHWICK, SOLOMON] fl. 1760-1785
Newport, April 17, 1783. Proposals for printing . . . An inquiry concerning the future punishment . . . By Samuel Hopkins . . . [Newport, S. Southwick, 1783]
broadside 26 X 19 cm.
Southwick subsequently printed the work
Alden 963
NHi mp. 44460

B5812 SPRING, SAMUEL, 1746-1819
Three sermons to little children . . . Newbury-Port, John Mycall, 1783.
72, [11] p. 13 cm. A–G^6
Rosenbach-Ch 95
MWA (sig. F3–4 wanting). A. S. W. Rosenbach (1933) mp. 44461

B5813 TILLINGHAST, JOHN
Thirty dollars reward. Broke open, last evening, the dwelling-house of the subscriber . . . John Tillinghast. Providence, Aug. 12, 1783. Providence, John Carter [1783]
broadside 18.5 X 15 cm.
Alden 965
RPJCB. Photostat: RHi mp. 44463

B5814 TO all adherents to the British government and followers of the British army . . . within . . . New-York. Messiuers Tories . . . Poughkeepsie, August 15, 1783. [New York] Morton and Horner [1783]
broadside 42 X 25.5 cm.
Signed: Brutus
NHi mp. 44464

B5815 TO the electors of the City of New-York. Friends and fellow-citizens, That the acts of the Legislature may faithfully correspond . . . New-York, December 26, 1783. New-York, Samuel Loudon [1783]
broadside 30.5 X25 cm.
Candidates offered for election
NHi mp. 44465

B5816 TO the electors of this city at large. Fellow-Citizens! There is a tide in the affairs of men . . . New-York, December 23, 1783. New-York, Samuel Loudon [1783]
broadside 27 X 22 cm.
Election broadside calling for consideration of candidates' experience
Signed: Cincinnatus
NHi mp. 44466

B5817 TO the mechanicks and free electors of the city and county of New-York. Gentlemen . . . Juvenis . . . New-York, December 23, 1783. [New York] Samuel Loudon [1783]
broadside 29.5 X 24 cm.
NHi mp. 44467

B5818 TO the Whig mechanicks of the City and County of New-York. My friends and fellow-citizens! . . . New-York, Dec. 27, 1783. [New York] Published at the State Printing-Office [1783]
broadside 23.5 X 16.5 cm.
NHi mp. 44468

B5819 TO the worthy and industrious mechanicks of this state. Fellow-Citizens!!! In all countries . . . New-York, Samuel Loudon [1783]
broadside 29.5 X 24 cm.
NHi (2 copies) mp. 44469

B5820 TOM Thumb's folio, or a new play-thing for little boys and girls . . . Boston, Printed and sold by Nathaniel Coverly, 1783.
32 p. 10.5 cm.
MWA mp. 44470

B5821 THE town and country almanack for . . . 1784. By Leander Harvy. New-York, Samuel Loudon [1783]
[38+] p.
Drake 5914
CtY. Milton Drake, New York (1964) (19 1.)

B5822 UNITED FIRE CLUB, NEWPORT, R. I.
Articles of the United Fire club, instituted February 6, 1783 . . . if it shall please God to permit fire to break out in Newport . . . [Newport, 1783?]
broadside 33.5 X 27 cm.
Alden 952; Winship p. 46
RHi; RP; RPJCB mp. 44427

B5823 U. S. CONTINENTAL CONGRESS, 1783
By the United States in Congress assembled, a proclamation . . . Baltimore, Hayes and Killen [1783]
broadside fol.
Concerns the treaty of amity and commerce with Sweden
PPL mp. 44473

B5824 U. S. CONTINENTAL CONGRESS, 1783
By the United States in Congress assembled. A proclamation . . . Philadelphia, David C. Claypoole [1783]
broadside
Concerns Indian lands
Dated by Ford Sept. 22, 1783
Ford: Bibliographical notes . . . 414
No copy located mp. 44472

B5825 U. S. CONTINENTAL CONGRESS, 1783
By the United States in Congress assembled. A proclamation, declaring the cessation of arms . . . Done in Congress, at Philadelphia, this eleventh day of April . . . [Philadelphia, David C. Claypoole, 1783]
broadside
Autograph signatures of Elias Boudinot and Charles Thomson
Ford: Bibliographical notes . . . 400; cf. Evans 18238 (also in PPL)
MHi; PPL mp. 44471

B5826 U. S. CONTINENTAL CONGRESS, 1783
By the United States of America, in Congress assembled, March 22d, 1783. [Philadelphia? 1783?]
broadside 42.5 X 14 cm.
Amendment of resolution of Oct. 21, 1780, giving 5 years full pay instead of half pay for life
NHi (2 copies); RPJCB mp. 44474

B5827 U. S. CONTINENTAL CONGRESS, 1783
[By the United States in Congress assembled, October 15, 1783.] [Philadelphia? 1783?]
broadside 43 X 30 cm.
Text begins: The Committee, consisting of Mr. Duane, Mr. Peters . . .
Proof-sheet, with many manuscript corrections and additions; heading also in manuscript
Concerns instructions for a treaty with the Indians
ICN mp. 44475

B5828 U. S. LAWS
An ordinance, to amend an ordinance, entitled, "An ordinance for establishing courts . . ." . . . [Mar. 4, 1783] . . . Elias Boudinot. Charles Thomson, Secretary. [Philadelphia, 1783]
broadside 22.5 X 12.5 cm.
Ford: Bibliographical notes . . . 396; Taylor 396
RPJCB. Photostat: DLC mp. 44476

B5829 U. S. MARINE OFFICE
[To all captains, commanders . . . of armed vessels . . . I do hereby recall all armed vessels . . . Robert Morris . . . Providence, April 14, 1783 . . . Providence, John Carter, 1783]
[broadside?]
Bill submitted by Carter Apr. 14, 1783
Alden 967
No copy known mp. 44477

B5830 U. S. TREATIES, ETC.
Declaration of the American ministers. Providence, April 7, 1783. By a gentleman . . . from Boston, we have received a handbill . . . of which the following is a copy . . . Given at Paris, the twentieth day of February . . . Providence, John Carter [1783]
broadside 17.5 X 15 cm.
Statement of armistice terms
Alden 968; Winship p. 47
CtY; RHi. Photostats: Ct; MWA mp. 44478

B5831 U. S. TREATIES, ETC.
Definite treaty of peace. Providence, December 1, 1783. By the brig Don Galvez, Capt. Silas Jones . . . Providence, John Carter [1783]
broadside 37 X 25.5 cm.
Text in 2 columns
Alden 969; Winship p. 47
CtY; RHi. Photostats: Ct; MWA mp. 44479

B5832 U. S. TREATIES, ETC.
Definitive treaty. Sunday evening arrived the Lord Hyde packet . . . with the definitive treaty . . . signed at Paris . . . September, 1783. New-York, W. Ross, 1783.
broadside 45.5 X 39.5 cm.
New York Public 773
NN (photostat) mp. 44480

B5833 U. S. TREATIES, ETC.
The following is a correct transcript of the treaty between France and the United States . . . Whereas, Benjamin Franklin . . . has made . . . concluded and signed a contract . . . Elias Boudinot, President, this 22d of January . . . 1783 . . . [Philadelphia, 1783]
broadside 48.5 X 34 cm.
Taylor 391
NHi mp. 44481

B5834 U. S. TREATIES, ETC.
A general peace! New-York, March 26 . . . Salem, B. Hall [1783]
broadside
Ford 2357
MSaE mp. 44482

B5835 U. S. TREATIES, ETC.
A general peace. Providence, March 31, 1783. Last evening a flag of truce . . . Providence, John Carter [1783]
broadside 37 X 24.5 cm.
Alden 970; Winship p. 47
RHi (2 copies) mp. 44483

B5836 U. S. TREATIES, ETC.
Philadelphia, March 19. Articles agreed upon by and between Richard Oswald . . . for the treating of peace . . . [Philadelphia? 1783]
broadside 44 X 18 cm.
In double columns
Ford: Bibliographical notes . . . 399
MHi; RPJCB mp. 44484

B5837 U. S. TREATIES, ETC.
Salem, April 5. By the ship Astrea, Captain John Derby . . . we have received a printed copy of a declaration . . . By the ministers plenipotentiary . . . A declaration of the cessation of arms . . . agreed upon between the King . . . and the United States . . . Salem, Printed and sold by S. Hall [1783]
broadside 34 X 22 cm.
Ford 2350; Tapley p. 340
MB; MSaE mp. 44485

B5838 THE United States almanack, for . . . 1784 . . .
Hartford, B. Webster [1783]
[24] p. 16 cm.
By Andrew Beers
CtHi; MWA mp. 44344

B5839 VERMONT. LAWS
. . . Acts and laws, passed by the General assembly . . . [Colophon] Windsor, George Hough and Alden Spooner, 1783.

12 p. 28 cm. caption title
Sabin 99089; Cooley 24; NYPL 787
MWA; Vt (lacks final leaf). Photostats: DLC; MHi; NN
mp. 44488

B5840 VERMONT. LAWS
An act directing the Treasurer to issue state notes ... An act empowering the ... Select Men ... [Colophon] Bennington, Haswell & Russell, 1783.
3 p. 28.5 cm. caption title
Cooley 23; New York Public 788; Sabin 99092
MWA; NHi; VtU-W. Photostats: DLC; MHi; NN
mp. 44487

B5841 VERMONT. TREASURER
The Treasurer takes this method to inform the public, that ... he shall ... make a tour through the counties of Windham, Windsor and Orange ... Ira Allen, Treasurer ... Sunderland, May 27, 1783. Notice is hereby given to the ... soldiers ... who served ... 1780 and 1781 ... Thomas Tolman, Paymaster ... Arlington, June 3, 1783 ... [Windsor? Hough and Spooner? 1783]
broadside 30.5 X 20 cm.
McCorison 68; Sabin 99134
NHi mp. 44489

B5842 [THE vocal magazine of new songs. Philadelphia, For sale at Bell's bookstore, 1783]

Advertised Oct. 1, 1783, as "now for sale."
Sonneck-Upton, p. 445
No copy known mp. 44490

B5843 EINE Warnung an erweckte Seelen von einem Mitglied der Reformirten Kirche. Philadelphia, Melchior Steiner, 1783.
52 p. 21 cm.
PHi; PPL mp. 44491

B5844 WASHINGTON, GEORGE, 1732-1799
His Excellency George Washington's last legacy. A circular letter ... dated June 11, 1783 ... [Philadelphia? 1783]
broadside 49 X 34 cm.
In the opinion of Clarence S. Brigham not printed in Newport or Providence
Alden 973; Sabin 101538 (with imprint [Newport? 1783])
MBNEH; MWA; RPJCB. Photostats: CSmH; NN
mp. 44492

B5845 WASHINGTON, GEORGE, 1732-1799
A letter from His Excellency George Washington ... to ... Benjamin Harrison ... Richmond, Nicolson and Prentis, 1783.
16 p. 18 cm.
Davis 5; Sabin 101706; New York Public 790
MiU-C. Photostat: NN mp. 44493

B5846 WATTS, ISAAC, 1674-1748
Divine songs attempted in easy language ... Hartford, Hudson & Goodwin, 1783.
60 p. 13 cm.
MWA mp. 44494

B5847 WEATHERWISE'S town and country almanack for ... 1784. By Abraham Weatherwise. Boston, Edmund Freeman [1783]
[24] p.
Drake 3336
MHi (imperfect); MWA

B5848 WEBSTER'S New-York almanack, for the year ... 1784 ... New-York, Charles Webster [1783]
[26] p. 16.5 cm.
Wall p. 24
DLC mp. 44495

B5849 WESLEY, JOHN, 1703-1791
The works of the Rev. John Wesley ... Volume I ... Philadelphia, Re-printed by Melchier Steiner, 1783.
[v]-xiv, [15]-296, [4] p. 16.5 cm.
MWA mp. 44496

B5850 WESLEY, JOHN, 1703-1791
The works of the Rev. John Wesley ... Volume III ... Philadelphia, Re-printed by Melchior Steiner, 1783.
296, [4] p. 16 cm.
Taylor 397
PHi mp. 44497

B5851 WHEELER, BENNETT
Proposals for printing a new weekly paper, entitled the *United States Chronicle* ... Bennett Wheeler. Providence, November 26, 1783.
broadside 35.5 X 19 cm.
Alden 974; Winship Addenda p. 89
Henry R. Drowne. Photostat: MWA mp. 44499

B5852 WIDOWS FUND, PHILADELPHIA
At a meeting of the Corporation of the Widows Fund, at the First Presbyterian Church in ... Philadelphia, May 23, 1783. Whereas by a standing rule ... A true copy, extracted from the minutes ... May 23, 1784 ... James Sproat, Secty. [Philadelphia, 1784]
broadside 26 X 22 cm.
Taylor 400
PHi mp. 44360

1784

B5853 THE A, B, C. With the Church catechism, and several hymns, and prayers for youth. Frederick-town: Printed & sold, by Matthias Bartgis, 1784.
[16] p. 16 cm.
Cover title
PPRF mp. 44500

B5854 [AN almanack for ... 1785. By Daniel George. Boston, 1784[

Advertised in *Bickerstaff's Boston almanack* for 1785 (Evans 18875)
Drake 3339
No copy known

B5855 AMBROSE, ISAAC, 1604-1664
[Christ in the clouds coming to judgment ... Bennington, Haswell & Russell, 1784]

Advertised in the *Vermont Gazette*, June 7, 1784
McCorison 72
No copy known mp. 44501

B5856 AMERICAN ACADEMY OF ARTS AND SCIENCES
Boston, January 29, 1784. Sir, I am requested by the Academy to forward the enclosed proposals, and desire

you to procure as many subscriptions to them as possible . . . [Boston, 1784]
broadside 34 X 21 cm.
MSaE; MWA mp. 44502

B5857 THE American bloody register . . . Boston, E. Russell, 1784.
31–56 p.
No. II of the American bloody register; for No. I cf. Evans 18324
MH

B5858 AMERICAN lands, and funds . . . Land-office, in Boston, April, 1784. Boston, E. Russell [1784]
broadside 21 X 17 cm.
DLC; RPJCB mp. 44503

B5859 ANDERSON, JOHN
Observations on the constitution of the Association reformed synod . . . Lancaster, Jacob Bailey, 1784.
2 p.l., 82 p. 16.5 cm.
MiU–C mp. 44504

B5860 AN astronomical diary or almanack, for . . . 1785 . . . Calculated for the meridian of Bennington . . . By Samuel Ellsworth . . . Bennington, Haswell & Russell [1784]
[24] p. 18 cm.
Cooley 34; Drake 13468
CSmH; MWA (p. [21-24] lacking); Vt; VtU
mp. 44527

B5861 BAILEY, FRANCIS
A descriptive catalogue of pictures, painted by Robert Edge Pine. 1784. Philadelphia, Francis Bailey [1784]
[2], 6, [2] p. 20 cm.
Taylor 405
PPL mp. 44505

B5862 BANK OF NORTH AMERICA
For the information of persons transacting business . . . December 1, 1784. [Philadelphia] Hall and Sellers [1784]
broadside 23.5 X 20 cm.
DLC mp. 44506

B5863 BANK OF PENNSYLVANIA
Proposals for establishing another bank in . . . Philadelphia, by the name of the Bank of Pennsylvania . . . Witness our hands, January [19th] 1784. [Philadelphia, 1784]
broadside
PPL mp. 44507

B5864 BANK OF RHODE ISLAND
Proposals for establishing a bank, at Providence . . . We the subscribers . . . engage to take . . . shares . . . upon the following plan . . . Providence, March 8, 1784.
[2] p. 45.5 X 16.5 cm.
RHi. Photostat: MWA mp. 44508

B5865 BELCHER, JOSEPH, 1669-1723
The life of faith, exemplified and recommended, in a letter found in the study of the Rev. Mr. Joseph Belcher, late of Dedham . . . [n.p.] 1784.
12 p. 12mo.
Attributed also to Joseph Eliot, 1638-1694
PPL mp. 44526

B5866 BELL, ROBERT, 1732?-1784
To the honorable the representatives of the freemen . . . February 28th. 1784. Robert Bell. [Philadelphia, 1784]
[2] p. 32.5 cm.
cf. Evans 17836
Photostats: DLC; MHi mp. 44510

B5867 BIBLE. O.T. PSALMS
The Psalter: or, Psalms of David, with the Proverbs of Solomon . . . Being an introduction for children . . . Worcester, Printed by Isaiah Thomas, for Ebenezer Battelle, in Boston, 1784.
160 p. 16.5 cm.
DLC; MHi; MWA mp. 44512

B5868 [BICKERSTAFFE, ISAAC] d. 1812? supposed author
[The life and adventures of Ambrose Gwinett . . .] [Philadelphia, Robert Bell, 1784]?
16 p. 22 cm. [A]–B[4]
Title supplied from Evans 18505. Dated from advt. at end: The Sorrows . . . of Werter . . . "just published and now selling at Bell's Book-Store . . . Complete in two Volumes." Cf. Evans 18501
MdBP (lacks t.p.)

B5869 BICKERSTAFF'S New-England almanack, for the year . . . 1785 . . . Hartford, Nath. Patten [1784]
[24] p. 17 cm.
Bates: Connecticut almanacs p. 136; New York Public 792
Ct (imperfect); CtHi; DLC; InU; NN mp. 44513

B5870 BOSTON. ASSESSORS
Boston, September 1, 1784. Ward no. 11 To You are requested to fill up this list as your valuation . . . [Boston, 1784]
broadside 51.5 X 14.5 cm.
MBB

B5871 BOSTON. TREASURER
Your Commonwealth tax. Boston, December 31, 1784. [Boston, 1784]
broadside
Ford 2383
MHi

B5872 BOSTON. TREASURER
Your town and county tax. Boston, August 1784. [Boston, 1784]
broadside
Ford 2382
MHi

B5873 BOSTON MAGAZINE
Proposals for printing by subscription the *Boston Magazine* . . . Norman, White & Freeman . . . [Boston, Norman, White and Freeman, 1784]
broadside 21 X 16 cm.
Ford 2378
DLC mp. 44576

B5874 BOSTON POST BOY
A New-Year's wish, from the carrier of the *Post-Boy and Advertiser*. [Boston, 1784?]
broadside
To scenes of blood, and dreadful deeds of arms
Inur'd too long—kind patrons! shall I bring . . .
Ford 2400
PHi mp. 44570

B5875 BOTTLER, JOHANN GEORG, 1754-1816
Eine kurzgefasste einfältige Betrachtung vom und hertzliche Aufforderung zum wahren Hertzens-Gebät . . . Pathenopoli [i.e. Ephrata]: Typis Societatis MDCCLXXXIV.
46 p. 20 cm.
PGL

B5876 BURGWIN, HOOPER, AND ALEXANDER, firm
Charleston, 1784. We take the liberty of requesting your attention, whilst we give . . . account of the connection in trade which we have lately entered into . . . [Charleston, S. C., 1784]
broadside 24.5 X 19 cm.
RPJCB mp. 44511

B5877 BURROUGHS, EDEN, 1738-1813
The profession and practice of Christians . . . Windsor, Hough and Spooner, 1784.
72 p. 22 cm.
McCorison 73
DLC; VtHi (2 copies); VtU mp. 44516

B5878 CAMPBELL, JOHN
Falls of Ohio. Proposals for laying off a town at the Lower Falls . . . Jan. 2d, 1784 . . . [n.p., 1784]
broadside sm. fol.
PPL

B5879 [CARTWRIGHT, EDMUND] 1743-1823
Armine and Elvira. A legendary tale. Boston, Warden and Russell, 1784.
32 p. 20 cm.
In verse
Huntington 496; New York Public 793
CSmH; MB; NN (p. 3-4 mutilated) mp. 44517

B5880 [CHAMBERLAIN, THOMAS] d. 1784
The minister preaching his own funeral sermon . . . To which is added, [The] death-bed discourse, [of Mr.] Phineas Burnham, of East-Hartford . . . who died December 27th, 1776 . . . [n.p.] Reprinted 1784.
20 p. 18.5 cm. $[A]–B^4\ C^2$
MWA; NHi mp. 44518

B5881 COLMAN, GEORGE, 1762-1836
Inkle & Yarico, an opera . . . Philadelphia, Printed and sold at E. Story's office, 1784.
66 p. 16 cm.
Hildeburn 4590; cf. Evans 24200
PHi (p. 65-66 wanting) mp. 44519

B5881a CONNECTICUT. GENERAL ASSEMBLY
At a General Assembly of the Governor and Company . . . of Connecticut, holden at New-Haven . . . the eighth day of January . . . 1784. The gentlemen nominated by the votes of the freemen . . . for election in May next . . . are as follow, viz. Jedidiah Strong, Esq. . . . New-Haven, Thomas and Samuel Green [1784]
broadside 32 X 15 cm.
CtHi. Middendorf Collection, New York City (1970)

B5882 CONNECTICUT. GENERAL ASSEMBLY
At a General Assembly of the Governor and Company . . . of Connecticut, holden at New-Haven . . . the eighth day of January . . . 1784. The gentlemen nominated for election in May next . . . are as follow, viz. Hon. Jabez Hamlin . . . New-Haven, Thomas and Samuel Green [1784]
broadside 34.5 X 14.5 cm.
CtHi. Middendorf Collection, New York City (1970
mp. 44521

B5883 CONNECTICUT. GENERAL ASSEMBLY
At a General Assembly of the States of Connecticut, holden at New-Haven . . . October, A.D. 1784. The gentlemen nominated by the votes of the freemen . . . to stand for election in May next . . . are as follow, viz. Hon. Stephen Mix Mitchel . . . [New Haven? 1784]
broadside 34 X 14.5 cm.
CtHi mp. 44520

B5884 COXE AND FRAZIER, firm
Duties in the port of Philadelphia. Madeira wines–per gallon, 4d. and on val. 1½ per cent . . . Coxe and Frazier. Philadelphia, March 26, 1784. [Philadelphia 1784]
broadside 18.5 X 11 cm.
NHi mp. 44522

B5885 CRAFTS, WILLIAM, & CO.
Charleston, South-Carolina, January 1, 1784. We take the liberty to advise you . . . of our establishment in this city in the mercantile line . . .[Charleston? 1784]
broadside 24 X 19 cm.
RPJCB mp. 44523

B5886 CRUKSHANK, JOSEPH
Lately re-printed, and to be sold by Joseph Crukshank, on the North-Side of Market-Street, between Second and Third Streets, Philadelphia, an Account of the life of . . . John Richardson . . . Meeting for Sufferings, 2d month, 19th, 1784. [Philadelphia, Joseph Crukshank, 1784]
broadside 33.5 X 21 cm.
Taylor 398
DLC mp. 44361

B5887 CUMBERLAND CO., PA.
State of the accounts of the lieutenants and sub-lieutenants of Cumberland County . . . Philadelphia, F. Bailey, MDCCLXXIV [i.e. 1784]
68 p. 21.5 cm.
NN; PPL mp. 44581

B5888 DAY, THOMAS, 1748-1789
Fragment of an original letter on the slavery, of the Negroes . . . Philadelphia, Francis Bailey, 1784.
8 p. 18 cm.
cf. Evans 18437 (describing a 1784 broadside edition)
CtY; DLC; MH-BA; PHi; RP; RPJCB mp. 44524

B5889 DELAWARE State, November 15, 1784. Public notice. Whereas . . . the Continental Congress . . . have called upon this state . . . In conformity thereto, this state have passed a law . . . auhorizing [sic] three collectors . . . Wilmington, James Adams [1784]
broadside fol.
Hawkins: List C 13; Heartman 662
No copy known mp. 44363

B5890 EFFUSIONS of female fancy. By a young lady, native of America: consisting of elegies, and other original essays in poetry. New York, Printed for the author, and sold . . . in York, Baltimore and Philadelphia, 1784.
59, [1], [2] p. 20 cm.
MB; MWA; PPL; RPB. Photostat: NN mp. 44525

B5891 FACTS and observations, justifying the claims of the Prince of Luxembourg, against the State of South Carolina, and against Alexander Dillon, Esq. late commodore of the navy of the said state. [Charleston, 1784]
52 p. 8vo
PPL mp. 44528

B5892 FENNING, DANIEL, d. 1767
The universal spelling-book . . . The seventeenth edition, with additions . . . Providence, John Carter, 1784.
x, 150, [4] p. frontispiece. 16.5 cm.
Postscripts: [4] p. at end
Alden 982; Winship p. 48
MWA; RHi mp. 44529

B5893 FOR the benefit of the poor in spirit. By command of the Supreme Governor of the World, at the desire of all who "love his appearance." Philadelphia: to be sold by William Woodhouse [1784]
broadside fol.
A mystical imitation of a playbill
PPL

B5894 FREEMAN, NATHANIEL
Sandwich, Sir. My son I have lately settled in the business of printing, with Messieurs Norman & White . . . Among other business, they will continue the monthly publication of the *Boston Magazine* . . . [Boston, 1784]
broadside 21 X 16 cm.
DLC mp. 44530

B5895 FRIENDS, SOCIETY OF
On the 3rd of the Second Month, 1784, a number of . . . Quakers, resident in Philadelphia, attended the General Assembly and presented the following . . . [Philadelphia, 1784]
[2] p. 37 cm.
PHi mp. 44533

B5896 FRIENDS, SOCIETY OF. LONDON YEARLY MEETING
The epistle from the Yearly-Meeting held in London, by adjournments, from the 31st day of the fifth month 1784, to the 5th day of the sixth month inclusive . . . [Philadelphia, 1784]
4 p. 34 cm.
Taylor 408
CSmH; DLC (3 copies); MWA mp. 44531

B5897 FRIENDS, SOCIETY OF. LONDON YEARLY MEETING
The following petition was presented to the Parliament . . . by a deputation from the Yearly-Meeting . . . Philadelphia, 16th of the 9th month, 1784. John Drinker, clerk. [Philadelphia, 1784]
[1], [1] p. 8vo
PPL mp. 44532

B5898 GARCELLI, CASSUMO, d. 1784
The life, last words, and dying speech of Cassumo Garcelli, who was this day (Thursday, January 15, 1784,) executed, for the . . . murder of Mr. John Johnson . . . Boston, January 15, 1784 . . . [Boston] Printed and sold at the Printing-Office in Marlborough-Street [1784]
broadside 43.5 X 35 cm.
MWA (imperfect) mp. 44534

B5899 GEOGRAPHICAL gazetteer of the towns in the commonwealth of Massachusetts. [Boston, Greenleaf and Freeman, 1784-85]
98+ p. fold. plan. 20.5 cm. caption title
Issued in parts, appended to the monthly numbers of the *Boston Magazine*, Oct. 1784-Dec. 1785
DLC; MWA; NN mp. 44535

B5900 GEORGIA. LAWS
An act for settling and ascertaining the fees to be taken by . . . publick officers . . . Savannah, February 25th, 1784. [at end] Savannah, James Johnston, 1784.
11 p. fol. caption title
De Renne p. 231
GU–De mp. 44537

B5901 GEORGIA. LAWS
An act for the fixing and establishing court-houses and gaols . . . Savannah, 26th February, 1784. [Savannah, James Johnston, 1784]
2 p. fol. caption title
De Renne p. 231
GU–De mp. 44536

B5902 GEORGIA. LAWS
An act to compel persons who . . . may receive publick money . . . Savannah, 25th February, 1784. [Savannah, J. Johnston, 1784]
4 p. fol. caption title
"An act for reviving and enforcing certain laws:" p. 3-4
De Renne p. 231
GU–De mp. 44538

B5903 GEORGIA. LAWS
An act to empower the Governor and the Executive Council to issue special commissions of oyer and terminer to the Chief Justice . . . Savannah, 24th February, 1784. [Savannah, James Johnston, 1784]
2 p. fol. caption title
De Renne p. 230
GU–De mp. 44539

B5904 GOLDSMITH, OLIVER, 1728-1774
The deserted village, a poem . . . Providence, Bennett Wheeler, 1784.
16 p. 20 cm.
Alden 983; Winship Addenda p. 89
MWA; NN; RHi mp. 44540

B5905 GRAVESANDE, WILLEM JAKOB VAN S'
Physices elementa mathematica, experimentis confirmata . . . Editio quarta duplo auctior. Philadelphia, Boinod & Gaillard, 1784.
2 v. (1074 p.) 127 tables. 26 cm.
Taylor 409
NNS mp. 44541

B5906 GREENLEAF AND FREEMAN, firm
Boston, September 1st, 1784. Proposals for collecting, and publishing in a series of numbers of the *Boston Magazine*, a complete geographical gazetteer of all the towns in the Commonwealth. [Boston, Greenleaf and Freeman, 1784]
broadside 33.5 X 21 cm.
Advertisement for Greenleaf and Freeman at bottom
MHi; RPJCB mp. 44542

B5907 GROUT, DIRICK, 1748?-1784
The life, last words and dying speech of Dirick Grout . . . aged 36; and Francis Coven . . . aged 22; who were executed this day . . . for the crime of burglary . . . October 28, 1784. [n.p., 1784]
broadside 50 X 35 cm.
Ford 2385
NHi mp. 44543

B5908 HEART-IN-HAND FIRE COMPANY, NEW YORK
Rules and orders to be observed by the Heart-in-Hand Fire Company, instituted at New-York, January 1781. New-York, Samuel Loudon, 1784.
12 p. 18 cm.
NHi mp. 44572

B5909 HEIDELBERG CATECHISM
Catechismus, oder kurzer Unterricht . . . Germantown, Gedruckt und zu finden bey Leibert und Billmeyer. 1784.
94 p., 1 leaf, 95-118 p. 14 cm. $A–E^{12}$
Taylor 403
MWA mp. 44544

B5910 HELLENBROEK, ABRAHAM, 1658-1731
Specimen of divine truths . . . New-York, Samuel Loudon, 1784.

74 p., 1 l. 18.5 cm.
New York Public 797
NN mp. 44545

B5911 HENNING, FRIEDERICH
Abdruck der Copien zweyer Memoriale, welche an Se. . . . Majestät in Wien von Friederich Henning übergaben worden . . . 1784. [Colophon] Philadelphia, zuhaben bey Georg Reinhold [1784]
16 p. 18 cm.
New York Public 798
NN mp. 44546

B5912 HENRY, JOHN
The life and conversion of William Chester, of the City of London. Taken from the original papers of the said Chester . . . By John Henry . . . London, Printed. Bennington, re-printed by Haswell & Russell, 1784.
16 p. 16.5 cm.
McCorison 75
VtBennM mp. 44547

B5913 AN hymn, to be sung by the charity scholars, the 12th and 19th of December, 1784, at St. Paul's and St. George's Chapels, after the charity sermon . . . [New York, 1784]
broadside 32 X 19 cm.
NHi (2 copies) mp. 44548

B5914 [JERNINGHAM, EDWARD]
Yarico to Inkle, an epistle. Springfield, Elisha Babcock, 1784.
24 p. 18.5 cm.
Sabin 105981
CtY; DLC; MWA mp. 44637

B5915 LOUDON'S almanack . . . for the year . . . 1785 . . . By Andrew Beers, Philom. New-York, Samuel Loudon [1784]
[36] p. 15.5 cm.
Drake 5921; Wall p. 24
DLC; MWA; MiD-B; N; NHi; RPJCB; WHi mp. 44509

B5916 LUDLOW & GOOLD, firm
New-York, . . . 1784. Permit us to congratulate you on the return of peace . . . [New York? 1784?]
broadside 23 X 18.5 cm.
Announces formation of partnership
RPJCB mp. 44549

B5917 LUTHER, MARTIN, 1483-1546
Der kleine Catechismus . . . Philadelphia, Gedruckt und zu haben bey Carl Cist, 1784.
2 p.l., 139, [1] p. 13.5 cm.
PHi mp. 44550

B5918 MARY K. Goddard's Pennsylvania, Delaware, Maryland, and Virginia almanack . . . for the year . . . 1785 . . . Baltimore, M. K. Goddard [1784]
[40] p. 16.5 cm.
Wheeler 320
MWA; MdHi mp. 44552

B5919 MARYLAND. LAWS
An act of the General assembly . . . for making the river Susquehanna navigable . . . to tide water. Annapolis, Frederick Green [1784]
17 p. 16.5 cm.
Wheeler 322
MdBJ-G mp. 44553

B5920 MASSACHUSETTS. LAWS
An act to prevent impositions on the inhabitants of any town within this state in the sale of fire-wood and bark . . . Newbury-Port, 31st. December, 1783. Printed by J. Mycall in Newbury-Port, 1784.
broadside 33.5 X 22 cm.
MSaE

B5921 MASSACHUSETTS. LAWS
Commonwealth of Massachusetts . . . An act to enable the inhabitants . . . In Senate, March 23, 1784 . . . [Boston, Adams and Nourse, 1784]
broadside 35 X 21 cm.
Ford 2389
DLC; MB mp. 44555

B5921a MASSACHUSETTS. LAWS
Commonwealth of Massachusetts. An act to enable the inhabitants . . . [Passed March 23, 1784] . . . [Boston? 1784]
broadside 22 X 18.5 cm.
cf. Ford 2389
RPJCB mp. 44554

B5922 MASSACHUSETTS. LAWS
Commonwealth of Massachusetts. In the year . . . [1784]. An act describing the power of justices of the peace . . . In Senate, March 11th, 1784 . . . [Boston, 1784]
broadside 44.5 X 18.5 cm.
MH

B5923 MASSACHUSETTS. TREASURER
Commonwealth of Massachusetts. In the year . . . [1784] Thomas Ivers, Esq; Treasurer . . . To the selectmen or assessors of the town of Greeting . . . Boston, this eighteenth day of May . . . 1784. [Boston, 1784]
broadside 37.5 X 31 cm.
MHi mp. 44558

B5924 MASSACHUSETTS. TREASURER
Commonwealth of Massachusetts, Tax No. 4. Thomas Ivers, Esq; Treasurer . . . to constable or collector of By virtue of an act of the General Court . . . [Boston, 1784]
broadside 37 X 30.5 cm.
Dated at end: Boston, September 20th 1784
Not Evans 18597
MWA; RPJCB mp. 44556

B5925 MASSACHUSETTS. TREASURER
(Tax No. 4.) Commonwealth of Massachusetts . . . 1784. Thomas Ivers, Esq; Treasurer . . . [Boston, 1784]
7 p.
MWA mp. 44557

B5926 MOUNT SION SOCIETY, CHARLESTON
Rules of the Mount Sion Society established at Charleston . . . 1777, and incorporated . . . February 13, 1777 . . . Charleston: Printed for the Society by Nathan Childs & Co. MDCCLXXXIV.
18 p. 4to
Turnbull p. 247 (v.1)
MH

B5927 MOYES, HENRY
Heads of a course of lectures on the natural history of the celestial bodies . . . The course will consist of eighteen lectures . . . [Boston? 1784?]
15 p. 21.5 cm.
MBAt; MHi; MWA; PPL; RPJCB mp. 44559

B5928 MOYES, HENRY
Heads of a course of lectures on the philosophy of

chemistry and natural history . . . The course will consist of twenty-one lectures . . . [Boston? 1784]
15 p. 20 cm.
On cover in a contemporary hand: Doct. Mayes's Lectures 1784 Commenced June
MHi; MWA; PPAmP; PPL; RPJCB mp. 44560

B5929 DER neue, verbessert- und zuverlässige Americanische calender, auf das 1785ste Jahr Christi . . . Philadelphia, Joseph Crukschank [1784]
[40] p. 20 cm.
Cover title: Philadelphischer calender auf das jahr 1785
DLC; MWA mp. 44561

B5930 THE New-England almanack, and gentleman's and ladies diary for 1785. By Edmund Freebetter. Norwich, John Trumbull [1784]

Drake 374, from an auction catalog
No copy known

B5931 THE New-England primer improved . . . Boston, Printed and sold by Benjamin Edes and Sons, 1784.
[80] p. [A]-E8
Heartman 75
CtY mp. 44562

B5932 THE New-England primer, or the first step to the true reading the English tongue . . . Boston, Warden and Russell, 1784.
[78?] p.
Heartman 74
MH (imperfect) mp. 44563

B5933 NEW HAMPSHIRE
State of New-Hampshire. A proclamation. Whereas, by the Constitution . . . it is provided . . . [Nov. 24, 1784] [Exeter, 1784]
broadside 19.5 X 15.5 cm.
Whittemore 359
NhHi mp. 44564

B5934 NEW HAMPSHIRE. GENERAL COURT
The state of New-Hampshire, To the selectmen of in the county of Greeting. You are hereby required . . . Concord, 1784. [Exeter? 1784]
broadside 32 X 20 cm.
Warrant for election of state president and senators
DLC; NhHi mp. 44565

B5935 NEW HAMPSHIRE. GENERAL COURT
The state of New-Hampshire. To the selectmen of in the county of Greeting. You are hereby required . . . Concord, January, 1784. [Exeter? 1784]
broadside 29 X 18 cm.
Warrant for election of representatives to a general assembly
Whittemore 363
NhHi

B5936 NEW HAMPSHIRE. HOUSE OF REPRESENTATIVES
A journal of the proceedings of the Hon. House . . . at their second session . . . began and held . . . on the third Wednesday in October . . . [Exeter, Melcher and Osborne, 1784]
p. [27]-68. 28.5 cm. caption title
DLC; NN mp. 44566

B5937 NEW HAMPSHIRE. SENATE
State of New-Hampshire. In Senate, June 15, 1784. Resolved, that the soldiers who enlisted . . . shall be fully recompensed . . . M. Weare, president . . . Exeter, Melcher and Osborne, 1784.
broadside 32 X 17.5 cm.
Whittemore 358
MHi mp. 44567

B5938 NEW HAMPSHIRE. TREASURER
State of New-Hampshire. John Taylor Gilman . . . Treasurer . . . To the selectmen of Greeting . . . [June 30, 1784] . . . Exeter, Melcher and Osborne, 1784.
broadside 33 X 21 cm.
DLC; NhD mp. 44568

B5939 NEW HAVEN, CONN.
The charter of the city of New-Haven; granted by the General Assembly . . . of Connecticut . . . January, 1784. New-Haven, Thomas and Samuel Green [1784]
16 p.
Trumbull: Supplement 1973
CtY mp. 44569

B5940 NEW YORK (CITY). CITIZENS
At a meeting of a number of inhabitants at Cape's Tavern, on Friday evening the twenty-third instant, the following address . . . was agreed to. Isaac Roosevelt . . . in the chair . . . New-York, Samuel Loudon [1784?]
broadside 43 X 27.5 cm.
New York Public 800
Roosevelt House (1928). Photostat: NN mp. 44571

B5941 NEW YORK. ASSEMBLY
Journal of the Assembly of the State of New-York, at their first meeting of the seventh session . . . the sixth day of January, 1784. New-York, E. Holt, 1784.
168 p. fol.
PHi

B5942 NEW YORK. GOVERNOR, 1777-1795
New-York, October 18, 1784. The speech of . . . the Governor, delivered this morning to the Legislature . . . [New York] E. Holt [1784]
broadside 32 X 19.5 cm.
NHi mp. 44573

B5943 NEW YORK. LAWS
An act imposing duties on the importation of certain goods, wares and merchandize. Passed the 22d day of March, 1784. [New York, 1784]
broadside fol.
PPL mp. 44574

B5944 NEWHALLS TAVERN
Newhalls Tavern, Lynn. Breakfast . . . 1784. [n.p., 1784]
broadside
Of 22 items printed 14 were drinks
Ford 2397
No copy located mp. 44551

B5945 THE news-carriers address to his customers. Hartford, January 1, 1784 . . . [Hartford, 1784]
broadside 37 X 13 cm.
1st line: I'm come (you'll all expect) . . .
NHi mp. 44575

B5946 [THE North-American calendar: or, the Rhode-Island almanack, for the year . . . 1785 . . . By Copernicus Partridge . . . Providence, B. Wheeler [1748].]
[24?] p.
Alden 977; Chapin p. 40; Winship p. 48 (locating a copy not now found)
No copy known mp. 44580

B5947 NORTH CAROLINA. HOUSE OF COMMONS
The journal of the House of commons. At a General assembly begun . . . the nineteenth day of April . . . being the first session . . . [Colophon] Halifax, Thomas Davis, 1784.
71 p. 25.5 cm. caption title
McMurtrie: North Carolina 117
DLC; N mp. 44577

B5948 NORTH CAROLINA. SENATE
The journal of the Senate. At a General assembly begun . . . the nineteenth day of April . . . being the first session . . . [Colophon] Halifax, Thomas Davis, 1784.
52 p. 26 cm. caption title
McMurtrie: North Carolina 118
DLC mp. 44578

B5949 OBSERVATIONS on a late pamphlet entitled "Considerations on the Society or Order of the Cincinnati," . . . By an Obscure Individual . . . Hartford: Reprinted by Bavil Webster, M,DCCC,LXXXIV.
22 p.
cf. Evans 18665
CtHi mp. 44579

B5950 OLDEN, DAVID
Confiscated property. New-Jersey, Middlesex County. By virtue of sundry precepts to me directed . . . Court of Common Pleas . . . expose at publick sale . . . David Olden, Agent. March 20, 1784. [n.p., 1784]
broadside 41.5 X 26 cm.
NjR

B5951 PENNSYLVANIA
Philadelphia County, ss. The Commonwealth of Pennsylvania to the Sheriff of the County of Philadelphia. Greeting. We command you, that you summon so that he be . . . at our County Court of Common Pleas . . . Philadelphia, the day of in the year . . . One Thousand Seven Hundred and Eighty-four. J. B. Smith . . . [Philadelphia, 1784]
broadside 36.5 X 21.5 cm.
Taylor 419
PHi

B5952 PENNSYLVANIA. CONSTITUTION
We, the people of the Commonwealth of Pennsylvania ordain and establish the Constitution for its government . . . [Philadelphia, 1784]
3 p.
Heartman: Cradle 987; Taylor 421
No copy located mp. 44583

B5953 PENNSYLVANIA. GOVERNOR, 1782-1785
By the President and the Supreme Executive Council of the Commonwealth of Pennsylvania, a proclamation . . . [June 4, 1784] [Philadelphia, Francis Bailey, 1784]
broadside 4to
Concerns a reward for the capture of Charles Julian de Longchamps
PPL mp. 44589

B5954 PENNSYLVANIA. GOVERNOR, 1782-1785
Pennsylvania, ss. By the President and the Supreme Executive Council of the Commonwealth of Pennsylvania, a proclamation . . . [Oct. 5, 1784] [Philadelphia, Francis Bailey, 1784]
broadside fol.
Concerns a reward for apprehending marauders in Wyoming
PPL mp. 44590

B5955 PENNSYLVANIA. LAWS
An act of the General Assembly, of the State of Pennsylvania. An act for opening the land-office, for granting and disposing of the unappropriated lands . . . [Philadelphia, T. Bradford, 1784]
4 p. fol.
PPL mp. 44586

B5956 PENNSYLVANIA. LAWS
An act of the General Assembly, of the State of Pennsylvania. An act to remedy the defects of the several acts of Assembly heretofore made for regulating the election of the justices of the peace . . . [Philadelphia, Thomas Bradford, 1784]
8 p. fol.
PPL mp. 44588

B5957 PENNSYLVANIA. LAWS
An act 1784 for the further regulation of the port of Philadelphia . . . [Colophon] Enacted into a law at Philadelphia . . . [Apr. 1, 1784] Peter Z. Lloyd, Clerk . . . [Philadelphia, Thomas Bradford, 1784]
8 p. 34 cm.
Taylor 413
PHi mp. 44587

B5958 PENNSYLVANIA. LAWS
State of Pennsylvania. In General Assembly. Monday, September 27, 1784. The bill entitled "A further supplement to the Test Laws" was read the second time, and debated by paragraphs . . . Extract from the minutes, Peter Z. Lloyd, Clerk . . . [Philadelphia, 1784]
broadside 36.5 X 21.5 cm.
Taylor 419
PHi mp. 44584

B5959 PENNSYLVANIA. LAWS
State of Pennsylvania in General Assembly. Tuesday, March 16, 1784, A.M. The bill entitled "An act for opening the land-office . . ." was read the second time, and debated by paragraphs . . . [Philadelphia] Thomas Bradford [1784]
4 p. fol.
PPL mp. 44585

B5960 THE Pennsylvania, Delaware, Maryland and Virginia almanack . . . for the year . . . 1785 . . . Baltimore, M. K. Goddard [1784]
[36] p. 16.5 cm. $[A]^4\ B^2\ C^4\ D^2\ F^4\ G^2$
Wheeler 332
MdBJ-G

B5961 PHILADELPHIA. CITIZENS
To the honorable the representatives of the freemen . . . the petition of the subscribers . . . to extend the arch over the common sewer . . . [Philadelphia, 1784]
broadside 25 X 33 cm.
DLC mp. 44591

B5962 PHILADELPHIA. WARDENS OFFICE
Philadelphia, February 1, 1784. Wardens Office. Whereas by an act . . . to prevent infectious diseases being brought into this state . . . [Philadelphia, 1784]
broadside 44.5 X 26 cm.
PU (2 copies, joined) mp. 44592

B5963 PHILADELPHIA 1784. The independence of the United States . . . opens a new . . . field of business . . . [Philadelphia, 1784]
broadside 23 X 18 cm.
Blank form (not filled in) announcing the formation of a firm
RPJCB

B5964 PRICES current:—Charleston, 1784. [Charleston, 1784]
broadside 32 X 20.5 cm.
Text in 2 columns
At bottom (full width): Duties on importation
RPJCB (2 copies) mp. 44593

B5965 PROTESTANT EPISCOPAL CHURCH IN THE U. S. A. MARYLAND (DIOCESE)
At a convention of the clergy and lay-delegates . . . in the state of Maryland, held at Chester . . . October 1784 . . . [Baltimore, William Goddard, 1784]
broadside 19.5 X 11.5 cm.
Huntington 501; Wheeler 335
CSmH; MdBP; PPL mp. 44594

B5966 PUBLICK concert. At Concert-Hall, on Wednesday next . . . will be performed, a concert of instrumental musick . . . Tickets may be had at the Hall, at 4s. each. Salem, April 2, 1784. [Salem, 1784]
broadside 17.5 X 15 cm.
MSaE

B5967 RHODE ISLAND. ELECTION PROX.
1784. His Excellency William Greene, Esq; Governor. The honorable Jabez Bowen, Esq; Dep. Governor . . . Providence, Bennett Wheeler [1784]
broadside 18 X 12.5 cm.
Alden 988; Chapin Proxies 36
RHi mp. 44595

B5968 RHODE ISLAND. LAWS
State of Rhode-Island and Providence-Plantations. In General assembly, February session, A. D. 1784. An act repealing the act, commonly called the Test-Act . . . Providence, Bennett Wheeler [1784]
broadside 26 X 19 cm.
Bill submitted Mar. 5, 1784
Alden 997; Winship p. 48
RHi mp. 44596

B5969 ROSS, ROBERT, 1726-1799
[A new primer, or Little boy and girl's spelling-book. Bennington, Haswell & Russell, 1784]

Advertised in the *Vermont Gazette*, Jan. 31, 1784, as "to be sold at the printing-office, Bennington for clean cotton or linen rags."
McCorison 78
No copy known mp. 44598

B5970 SMITH, MOORE, & CO.
At the Medical Pillar . . . Smith, Moore & Co. have for sale, a general collection of the materia medica, botanical chymical and Galenical . . . New-York, Samuel Loudon [1784]
broadside 30 X 18.5 cm.
Advertised in the same wording in the *New York Packet*, Oct. 11, 1784
NjR mp. 44599

B5971 SOUTH CAROLINA. COMMISSIONERS OF FORFEITED ESTATES
Advertisement. Will be sold at public auction . . . the 18th of October next . . . in Charleston . . . valuable lands . . . about fifty Negroes, and stock . . . C. H. Simmons, Clerk. Charleston, August 16, 1784. [Charleston] J. V. Burd and E. Boden [1784]
broadside 53.5 X 41.5 cm.
Sc-Ar

B5972 STENSON, WILLIAM
William Stenson . . . in Market-Street, Baltimore, has for sale . . . liquors . . . with an . . . assortment of groceries . . . Baltimore, William Goddard [1784]
broadside 20.5 X 16 cm.
Huntington 502; Wheeler 338
CSmH mp. 44600

B5973 STEUBEN, FRIEDRICH WILHELM AUGUST, FREIHERR VON, 1730-1794
A letter on the subject of an established militia . . . by Baron De Steuben . . . New-York, J. M'Lean [1784?]
[4], 16 p. 20 cm. [ ]^2 A-B^4
MHi; MWA; N mp. 44601

B5974 TO the real patriots and supporters of American independence. Friends and countrymen! . . . An Independent Patriot. July 10, 1784. The following sentiments were intended for a public paper . . . A Spectator. July 1784. [Philadelphia, 1784]
broadside 4to
cf. Evans 18807, also at PPL
PPL mp. 44602

B5975 U. S. CONTINENTAL CONGRESS, 1784
By the United States in Congress assembled, January 14, 1784. Resolved unanimously . . . [Annapolis, J. Dunlap, 1784]
broadside 27 X 22 cm.
Ford: Bibliographical notes . . . 425; Huntington 503; Wheeler 341
CSmH; DLC; MHi; MWA; PPAmP mp. 44603

B5976 U. S. CONTINENTAL CONGRESS, 1784
The Committee consisting of to whom was referred a motion, submit the following report [concerning negotiation of certificates] [Annapolis? John Dunlap? 1784?]
broadside 43 X 26 cm.
New York Public 801
NN mp. 44604

B5977 U. S. CONTINENTAL CONGRESS, 1784
The United States in Congress assembled, April 27, 1784. Congress resumed the consideration of the report of the Grand Committee . . . Charles Thomson, Sec'ry. [n.p., 1784]
broadside 42 X 35 cm.
Signature printed
Different typesetting from Evans 18845
CtHi mp. 44605

B5978 U. S. CONTINENTAL CONGRESS, 1784
The United States in Congress assembled, April 27, 1784. Congress resumed the consideration of the report of the Grand Committee . . . on the national debt . . . [Philadelphia? 1784]
4 p. 33 cm.
cf. Evans 18845
MWA; RPJCB mp. 44606

B5979 THE United States almanac, for . . . 1785 . . . By Anthony Sharp . . . New York, Kollock [1784]
[36] p. 16.5 cm.
By David Rittenhouse
MWA mp. 44597

B5980 UNITED STATES BANK
For the information of persons transacting business with

the Bank. The following rules are made known . .. Bank, December 1, 1784. [Philadelphia] Hall and Sellers [1784]
broadside 23.5 X 19.5 cm.
Taylor 426
DLC mp. 44607

B5981 UNIVERSITY OF PENNSYLVANIA
Rules for the good government and discipline of the schools in the University of Pennsylvania . . . Copied from the minutes of the Board . . . August 4, 1784 . . . Philadelphia, Francis Bailey [1784]
broadside 42.5 X 27 cm.
PPAmP; PU mp. 44608

B5982 VERMONT. GENERAL ASSEMBLY
[Doings of the Assembly for the consideration of the people. Bennington, Haswell & Russell, 1784]
4 p.
Printer's bill dated Mar. 8, 1784
McCorison 79
No copy known mp. 44609

B5983 VERMONT. GOVERNOR, 1778–1789
By his Excellency Thomas Chittenden . . . A proclamation . . . Given under my hand . . . at Rutland . . . [Oct. 18, 1784] . . . [Windsor? Hough & Spooner? 1784]
broadside 32.5 X 20 cm.
Thanksgiving day proclamation
Advertised for sale by C. E. Tuttle Co., July 1941
McCorison 82
MWA (photostat) mp. 44610

B5984 VERMONT. GOVERNOR, 1778-1789
[Fast day proclamation. Bennington, Haswell & Russell, 1784]
broadside?
Printer's bill dated Mar. 6, 1784
McCorison 81
No copy known mp. 44611

B5985 VERMONT. LAWS
An act for the limitation of actions. [Windsor, Hough and Spooner, 1784]
broadside 28.5 cm.
McCorison 83; New York Public 802; Sabin 99018
VtU-W. Photostats: M; MHi; MWA; NN mp. 44612

B5986 VERMONT. LAWS
Acts and laws. [Oct. 1783] [Colophon] Windsor, Hough and Spooner, 1784.
p. 39-47. 28 cm.
McCorison 84; New York Public 803; Sabin 99094
MH-L; MHi; MWA; VtU. Photostat: NN mp. 44615

B5987 VERMONT. LAWS
Acts and laws . . . [March 1784] [Colophon] Windsor, Hough and Spooner, 1784.
p. 49-54. 28 cm.
McCorison 85; New York Public 804; Sabin 99096
Continuation of Evans 18275
MWA. Photostats: MHi; NN; VtU mp. 44618

B5988 VERMONT. LAWS
State of Vermont. An act regulating the choice of a Council of Censors. [Windsor? Hough and Spooner? 1784]
[2] p. 34 cm. caption title
McCorison 90; Sabin 99018
VtU-W mp. 44613

B5989 VERMONT. LAWS
State of Vermont. An act to enable persons who have . . . made improvements on lands . . . to recover the value of what the estate is made better . . . from the legal owners . . . and to direct the manners of process therein. [Windsor, Hough and Spooner, 1784]
[3] p. 34.5 cm. caption title
McCorison 87; Sabin 99020
VtU-W mp. 44614

B5990 VERMONT. LAWS
State of Vermont. Bennington, March 1, 1784. An act to enable persons who have . . . made improvements on lands . . . who shall be driven out . . . to recover the value . . . [Windsor? Hough and Spooner? 1784]
[2] p. 33 cm. caption title
McCorison 88; New York Public 805; Sabin 99019
VtU-W. Mrs. George M. Powers, Burlington, Vt. (1959). Photostat: NN mp. 44616

B5991 VERMONT. LAWS
State of Vermont. Bennington, March 1, 1784. Extract from a proposed act for the limitation of actions. [Windsor? Hough and Spooner? 1784]
broadside 20.5 X 17 cm.
McCorison 89; Sabin 99022
VtU-W mp. 44617

B5992 VIRGINIA. GENERAL ASSEMBLY. HOUSE OF DELEGATES
In the House of Delegates, Friday, the 24th of December, 1784. A motion was made . . . that the third reading of the engrossed Bill establishing a provision for the teaching of the Christian religion, be postponed . . . [Richmond, 1784]
[2] p. 32 X 24 cm. caption title
Includes the text of the proposed bill
DLC mp. 44619

B5993 VIRGINIA. GENERAL ASSEMBLY. HOUSE OF DELEGATES
In the House of Delegates, Tuesday the 28th of December, 1784. Mr. Ronald reported, from the Committee appointed to examine into the state of the public accounts . . . [Richmond, 1784]
4 p. 36 cm.
Pages 3–4: "Wednesday, the 29th of December, 1784. Mr. Pendleton reported . . ."
DLC mp. 44620

B5994 VIRGINIA. LAWS
An act for regulating pilot fees. [Richmond? 1784?]
broadside 37 X 23 cm.
DLC (mutilated) mp. 44621

B5995 [THE Virginia almanack for the year . . . 1785. Richmond? 1784]
[20+] p. 15 cm.
Contents includes: Of Scandal. Of Treason.
ViHi (t.p. missing) mp. 44622

B5996 WALLIS, GEORGE
From the *United States Chronicle*, Thursday, February 19, 1784. In this paper last week a clear confutation . . . the subject is now concluded with the sentiments of . . . George Wallis . . . Providence, Bennett Wheeler [1784]
broadside 26 X 20.5 cm.
Alden 1000
RHi. Photostat: MWA mp. 44623

B5997 WASHINGTON, GEORGE, 1732–1799
General Washington's Resignation. The United States, in

Congress assembled, December 23d, 1783, at Annapolis . . . [Newburyport] John Mycall, 1784.
broadside 40 X 32 cm.
RPJCB mp. 44624

B5998 WASHINGTON, GEORGE, 1732–1799
Mount-Vernon, April 2, 1784. The subscriber would lease about 30,000 acres of land on the Ohio and Great Kanhawa . . . Alexandria, G. Richards [1784]
broadside 27.5 X 16 cm.
In two columns
New York Public 806; Sabin 101745
NN mp. 44625

B5999 WATTS, ISAAC, 1674–1748
Divine songs, attempted in easy language . . . Newbury-Port, Printed and sold by John Mycall, 1784.
54 p. 11.5 cm.
CtHi; DLC; MSaE (wanting after p. 36); MWA. d'Alté A. Welch, Cleveland (1962) mp. 44627

B6000 WATTS, ISAAC, 1674–1748
Divine songs attempted in easy language . . . The seventeenth edition. Philadelphia, Printed and sold by Joseph Crukshank, 1784.
24 p. 13 cm.
Taylor 427
MWA; P mp. 44628

B6001 WATTS, ISAAC, 1674–1748
Divine songs, attempted in easy language . . . The twenty-fifth edition. With some additional composures. Hartford: Printed and sold by Z. Webster [1784?]
48 p. 14.5 cm.
Webster printed in Hartford in 1784.—cf. Evans 18482
CtHi; CtHT-W (wanting after p. 46) mp. 44626

B6002 WEBSTER, SAMUEL, 1719–1796
The nature and importance of being always ready for Our Lord's coming . . . A discourse occasioned by the sudden death of two young men . . . drowned May 12, 1784 . . . Newbury-Port, John Mycall, 1784.
32 p. 18.5 cm.
New York Public 807; Sabin 102422
MB; MHi; MWA; N; NN mp. 44629

B6003 WESLEY, JOHN, 1702–1791
Thoughts upon slavery . . . Philadelphia, Re-printed by Enoch Story, 1784.
87 p. 14.5 cm.
Taylor 428
Aldine Book Co. (1935?; text as far as p. 11 missing)
mp. 44630

B6004 WHARTON, CHARLES HENRY
[A letter to the Roman Catholics of the city of Worcester . . . Annapolis, F. Green, 1784]
56+ p.
Wheeler 361
RPJCB (p. 51–56 only) mp. 44631

B6005 WHIG SOCIETY
At a meeting of the Whig Society, at the long room . . . the 3d of May, 1784 . . . The question proposed . . . to be debated this evening, was read . . . [New York, 1784]
broadside 28.5 X 22.5 cm.
NHi mp. 44632

B6006 WHITE, ALEXANDER, 1762–1784
The life, last words and dying speeches of Alexander White, and John Sullivan, who were be [!] executed this day . . . [Boston] E. Russell [1784]
broadside 44.5 X 37.5 cm.
PPRF mp. 44633

B6007 [WINTER displayed, describing the season in all its various stages and vicissitudes . . .]

Prospectus for printing this poem in *Maryland Journal* for Feb. 20, 1784. It was to be published in octavo "containing between eighty and ninety pages."
Wheeler 333; cf. Evans 18562
No copy known

B6008 WORDS for a funeral anthem . . . to be performed at the funeral of . . . Samuel Cooper, on Friday, Jan. 2, 1784. [Boston, 1784]
broadside 23 X 19 cm.
DLC; MHi; MWA mp. 44634

B6009 WRIGHT, JOHN, fl. ca. 1720–1730
Spiritual songs for children . . . By J. Wright. The seventh edition . . . Boston, Re-printed by Nathaniel Coverly, 1784.
47 p. 19.5 cm. $A\text{-}D^6$
MSaE (final leaf wanting); MWA (t.p. and p. 3–6 wanting)
mp. 44635

B6010 YALE UNIVERSITY
Catalogue recentium . . . M,DCC,LXXIV. New-Haven, Meigs, Bowen & Dana [1784]
broadside
CtY mp. 44636

B6011 YORK CO., PA.
State of the accounts of the lieutenants & sub-lieutenants of York County. Philadelphia, F. Bailey, 1784.
56 p. 22 cm. $A\text{-}C^4\ D^2\ E\text{-}G^4\ H^2$
MWA mp. 44582

1785

B6012 AN account of Count D'Artois . . . Litchfield, Collier and Copp [1785]
33 p. 18 cm.
Entered for copyright July 29, 1785
DLC (photostat). Samuel H. Fisher mp. 44638

B6013 ADGATE, ANDREW, d. 1793
Philadelphia, June 1, 1785. Plan of Mr. Adgate's Institution for Diffusing more generally the Knowledge of Vocal Music . . . October 1, 1785 . . . The regulations of the school are as follows . . . Philadelphia, B. Towne [1785]
broadside 26 X 21.5 cm.
MHi mp. 44639

B6014 ADVERTISEMENT. Whereas many of the general Proprietors of East New-Jersey, considerable for their numbers and the shares they hold . . . March 2, 1785 . . . Trenton, Isaac Collins [1785]
broadside 24 X 18.5 cm.
NHi mp. 44640

B6015 AMBROSE, SAMUEL
A brief account of the life and conversion of Peggy Walker, who died at Parristown . . . New-Hampshire . . . May, 13, 1784 . . . Norwich, J. Trumbull, 1785.
16 p. 16 cm. $[A]\text{-}B^4$
MWA mp. 44641

B6016 AMERICAN HERALD
The carrier of the *American Herald's* congratulation to

his customers, presenting the following balloon wish! Boston, January 1 [torn] [Boston, 1785?]
broadside
Ford 2430
PHi. Photostat: MWA mp. 44656

B6017 AMERICAN MERCURY
The carrier of the *American Mercury* wishes his customers . . . [Hartford, 1785]
broadside
Probably by Joel Barlow, the editor
MWA mp. 44646

B6018 AMICABLE FIRE SOCIETY, PROVIDENCE, R.I.
Articles of the Amicable fire society . . . In witness whereof, we have . . . set our hands, in Providence, this twenty-second day of December, A.D. 1785 . . . Providence, John Carter [1785?]
broadside 43 X 34 cm.
Alden 1017; Winship p. 49
MWA; RHi mp. 44782

B6019 ASH, JOHN, 1724–1779
Grammatical institutes: or, an easy introduction to Dr. Lowth's English grammar . . . A new edition. Revised, corrected, and enlarged . . . Philadelphia, Re-printed and sold by Joseph Crukshank, 1785.
174 p., 3 leaves. 13.5 cm.
Sealock 1
PU mp. 44642

B6020 AN astronomical diary or almanack for . . . 1786. By Nathan Ben Salomon. New-Haven, Meigs, Bowen and Dana [1785]
[24] p. fold. map.
Drake 384
CtHi; CtY; DLC; MWA

B6021 AUSBUND geistreicher Lieder. Ephrata, 1785.
[8] p. 8vo
PPL mp. 44643

B6022 BAPTISTS. PENNSYLVANIA. PHILADELPHIA ASSOCIATION
Minutes of the Baptist Association, held in Philadelphia, October, 1785. [Colophon] Philadelphia, Robert Aitken [1785]
8 p. 20.5 cm. caption title
DLC; NHC; NHi; RPJCB. Photostat: MWA
mp. 44645

B6023 BAXTER, RICHARD, 1615–1691
Baxter's Directions to slave-holders, revived . . . To which is subjoined, A letter from . . . Anthony Benezet . . . deceased, to . . . Raynal, with his answer . . . Philadelphia, Francis Bailey, 1785.
16 p. 15 cm. [A]-B^4
"The case of the oppressed Africans": p. [11]-16
Huntington 504; cf. Evans 22330
CSmH; ICN; MB; MWA; NjP; PHi mp. 44647

B6024 [BENEZET, ANTHONY] 1713–1784
Short observations on slavery, introductory to some extracts from . . . Raynal . . . [Colophon] Philadelphia, Enoch Story [1785?]
12 p. 16 cm. A^6 caption title
cf. Evans 17096
MB mp. 44648

B6025 BIBLE. O.T. PSALMS
The Psalter; or, Psalms of David, after the translation of the Great Bible. Philadelphia, Printed and sold by Joseph Crukshank, 1785.
115 p. 16 cm.
In double columns
New York Public 808
NN mp. 44649

B6026 BICKERSTAFF'S North-Carolina almanack for . . . 1786 . . . Plymouth, Nathaniel Coverly [1785]
[24] p.
Drake 3361
MHi; MTaHi

B6027 BOSTON. SELECTMEN
Notification. The freeholders and other inhabitants . . . to meet at Faneuil-Hall, on Wednesday 26th of Octob. . . . Boston, Octob. 22, 1785. [Boston, 1785]
broadside 8.5 X 15 cm.
MHi mp. 44514

B6028 BOSTON, April 18, 1785. The minds of the people being greatly and justly agitated by the . . . intention . . . to deprive the industrious trade . . . [Boston] Peter Edes [1785]
broadside 24 X 19 cm.
Ford 2405; New York Public 809
MHi; MWA. Photostats: DLC; NN mp. 44652

B6029 BRECKENRIDGE, JOHN, 1760–1806
To the freeholders and inhabitants of the counties of Botetourt and Montgomery . . . John Breckenridge. Archibald Stuart. [n.p., 1785]
broadside 19.5 X 25 cm.
Dated in manuscript: January 5th 1785
DLC mp. 44653

B6030 BUCKS CO., PA.
State of the accounts of Gerardus Wynkoop . . . to 21st Nov. 1784. Philadelphia, John Steele, 1785.
9 p. 22 cm.
DLC mp. 44762

B6031 CAMPBELL, ISAAC, d. 1784
A rational enquiry into the origin, foundation, nature and civil government . . . In four volumes. By the Rev. Isaac Campbell . . . Vol. I. Annapolis: Printed by Frederick Green [1785?]
230+ p. 21.5 cm.
Date supplied by Edward G. Howard
MdHi (mutilated; lacking after p. 230)

B6031a CAREY, MATHEW, 1760–1839
Sir From the very flattering encouragement . . . *Pennsylvania Evening Herald*, I . . . solicit your patronage . . . Mathew Carey. Philadelphia, February 22, 1785. [Philadelphia, M. Carey, 1785]
broadside 22.5 X 18 cm.
PHi

B6032 CARTER, JOHN, 1745–1814
A list of the names of the sons and daughters, of the family of John Carter . . . [Providence, J. Carter? 1785?]
broadside 31.5 X 19.5 cm.
Latest date in text is Nov. 9, 1785
Alden 1006; Winship p. 75; Winship Addenda p. 95; New York Public 810
PHi; RPB. Photostats: MWA; NN; RNHi mp. 44658

B6033 CASSON, HENRY, d. ante 1795
[Antipriestian observations; prose and poetry . . . Philadelphia, Robert Aitken, 1785]

"From Robert Aitken's Waste Book, p. 418:
May 18 Mr. Henry Casson D[r]. . . . To print-
1785 ing 10½ Sheets Antipriestian Observations . . ." (communication from Will-
man Spawn)
No copy known mp. 44659

B6034 CENSOR
Censor The carrier of the *Censor*, wishes all happiness to his generous customers.
What means this clamour? why this strife?
To poison all the joys of life . . .
[Boston? 1785?]
broadside
Ford 2429
PHi mp. 44660

B6035 CHAMBER OF COMMERCE, N.Y.
Chamber of Commerce, New-York, March 1, 1785. Upon a motion of Mr. Constable's, Resolved . . . to draw up a memorial to the Legislature . . . counteract the late restrictions . . . by foreign nations . . . [New York, 1785]
broadside 23 X 19 cm.
CtHi mp. 44744

B6036 CHAMBERLAIN, THOMAS, d. 1784
England's timely remembrancer; or, The minister's preaching his own funeral sermon . . . Litchfield, Collier and Copp [1785]
8 p.
Trumbull: Supplement 1967
CtY mp. 44661

B6037 CHARLES RIVER BRIDGE COMPANY
Charles River Bridge. At a meeting of the proprietors . . . [Boston? 1785?]
8, [6] p. 16mo
"Subscribers names" [6] p. at end
MB; MWA (8 p. only) mp. 44662

B6038 CHARLES RIVER BRIDGE COMPANY
Charles River Bridge. Boston, July 12, 1785. Voted . . . [Boston? 1785?]
broadside
MHi; MWA mp. 44663

B6039 CHESTER CO., PA.
State of the account of Robert Smith . . . from the 1st of April, 1783, to 1st of April, 1785. Philadelphia, John Steele, 1785.
4 p. 22 cm.
Sealock 8
PHi mp. 44764

B6040 CHESTER CO., PA.
State of the accounts of Robert Wilson . . . From the time of his appointment, April 8, 1778, to the 11th August 1779. Philadelphia, F. Bailey, 1785.
4 p. 21.5 cm.
Sealock 9
PHi mp. 44765

B6041 CHRIST CHURCH, PHILADELPHIA
At a meeting of the congregations of Christ Church and St. Peter's . . . the 15th August, 1785 . . . revenues of the churches . . . repairs of both churches . . . [Philadelphia] Hall and Sellers [1785]
broadside 23 X 18 cm.
Huntington 514; Sealock 34
CSmH; PHi mp. 44770

B6042 [CIRCULAR.] At a meeting of a number of respectable inhabitants of the counties of York, Cumberland, and Lincoln . . . in Falmouth, on the fifth of October . . . Voted . . . to send delegates . . . separate state . . . [Falmouth, T. B. Waitt, 1785]
broadside 19 X 24 cm.
Ford 2407; New York Public 811
MHi; NN (reduced facsim.) mp. 44715

B6043 [COKE, THOMAS] 1747-1814
A plan for erecting a college, intended to advance religion in America . . . [Baltimore, 1785]
8 p. 8vo
PHi

B6044 COKE, THOMAS, 1747-1814
The substance of a sermon on the godhead of Christ. Preached at Baltimore . . . the 26th day of December, 1784 . . . New-York, Shepard Kollcok, 1785.
22 p. 21 cm. [A]-C4 (C4 blank)
Huntington 506
CSmH; MWA (poor) mp. 44664

B6045 COLLES, CHRISTOPHER, 1738-1821
Sir, Your company is requested at the Coffee-House . . . the 19th inst. . . . to determine . . . mode of laying the design of the Mohawk navigation before the Legislature . . . Christopher Colles. New-York, December 15, 1785. [New York, 1785]
broadside 20.5 X 14.5 cm.
NHi mp. 44665

B6046 [A COMPLEAT gamut, or scale of music, for the instruction of youths in that delightful study, psalmody. Bennington, Haswell & Russell, 1785]

Advertised in the *Vermont Gazette*, Dec. 12, 1785; earliest Evans edition dated 1788
McCorison 92
No copy known mp. 44667

B6047 THE complete counting house companion.
Philadelphia: Printed weekly by Carey, Talbot, and Spotswood, and delivered gratis to the subscribers to the *Pennsylvania Evening Herald* [1785]

NHi (has May 21, 1785)

B6048 CONNECTICUT. GENERAL ASSEMBLY
At a General Assembly . . . holden at New-Haven . . . October . . . 1785. An account of what is by law made receivable by the several collectors . . . [at end] New-Haven, Meigs, Bowen and Dana [1785]
[2] p. 35 cm.
CtHi mp. 44668

B6049 CONNECTICUT. GOVERNOR, 1784-1786
By His Excellency Matthew Griswold . . . a proclamation . . . Hartford . . . [March 2, 1785] . . . New-London, Timothy Green, 1785.
broadside 45.5 X 28 cm.
Appointing April 20 a day of humiliation
NHi mp. 44669

B6050 CONSTANT Charley: together with The banks of the Dee, and The answer. Three excellent songs . . . [Boston? Ezekiel Russell?] Sold at the office in Essex-Street, 1785.
broadside 35.5 X 24.5 cm.
New York Public 812
NN mp. 44670

B6051 COXE & FRAZIER, firm
Philadelphia, 1785. The present crisis . . . Your most respectful servants, Coxe & Frazier . . . [Philadelphia, 1785]
[2] p. 38 X 23 cm.
On verso: France. Arret of the King's Council . . . Paris the 31st August, 1784 . . .
Evans 19010 (second title only)
DLC

B6052 CULLEN, WILLIAM, 1712–1790
First lines of the practice of physic, for the use of students . . . Part III. Philadelphia, Charles Cist, 1785.
iv, 155 p. 8vo
PPL; PPPH mp. 44671

B6053 CUSHMAN, ROBERT, 1579?–1625
The sin and danger of self-love . . . Plymouth, Re-printed by Nathaniel Coverly, M,DCCLXXXVIII [i.e. 1785]
viii, 30 p. 21 cm.
cf. Evans 18981, of which this is a state with incorrect date
MWA (ownership inscription dated Feb. 23, 1786); PPL (ownership inscription dated 1785) mp. 44672

B6054 DARTMOUTH COLLEGE
Catalogus eorum qui in Collegio-Dartmouthensi . . . ab anno M.DCC.LXXI, ad annum M.DCC.LXXXV, alicujus gradus laurea donati sunt. [n.p., 1785?]
broadside 54 X 45.5 cm.
NhD; RPJCB mp. 44673

B6055 DEARBORN, BENJAMIN, 1755–1838
A schedule for reducing the science of music to a more simple state . . . calculated . . . by Benjamin Dearborn. Portsmouth, New-Hampshire, 1785.
16 p. 20 X 9.5 cm.
NHi mp. 44674

B6056 DELAWARE. PRESIDENT, 1783–1786
Delaware State, ss. His Excellency the President having received the following act . . . orders that the same be made public . . . James Booth, secretary . . . May 5, 1785 . . . Wilmington, Jacob A. Killen [1785]
broadside 42.5 X 26.5 cm.
Hawkins: List C 14
DLC; MWA mp. 44675

B6057 DILWORTH, THOMAS, d. 1780
A new guide to the English tongue . . . Philadelphia, Printed and sold by Young, Stewart, and M'Culloch, 1785.
148 p. 17.5 cm.
MWA mp. 44676

B6058 DIRECTIONS for sailing in and out of Plymouth Harbor . . . in July 1768.
[Boston, 1785]
broadside
Reissued by the Commonwealth
Ford 2408
MB mp. 44677

B6059 DODD, WILLIAM, 1729–1777
Reflections on death . . . The sixth edition. Boston, B. Edes, 1785.
129, [3] p. 18 cm.
DLC; MWA; NN mp. 44678

B6060 DOLL, J
Ein schoñes Lied, welches auf Noten ist, in J. Dolls deutschem Notenbuch, Pagia 66 . . . [Ephrata, 1785?]
broadside 16.5 X 19 cm.
Ornamental borders
PHi mp. 44679

B6061 DORCHESTER, MASS.
Your state tax 1785. County £. s. d. [Boston, 1785]
broadside
Ford 2409
MHi

B6062 FALMOUTH February 2, 1785. Sir, This is to inform you, that a meeting of the proprietors of the township number one, situated in the county of Lincoln . . . is to be holden at the house of Mrs. Mary Parker . . . [n.p., 1785]
broadside
Ford 2410
MHi mp. 44680

B6063 FATHER Tammany's pocket almanac, for 1786 . . . By a son of Tammany. Philadelphia, Printed and sold by Young, Stewart, and M'Culloch [1785]
[40] p. 12 cm.
New York Public 815
MWA; NN; PPiU mp. 44681

B6064 FENNING, DANIEL, d. 1767
The ready reckoner . . . The sixth edition . . . Boston, Re-printed, by John W. Folsom, for J. Boyle and E. Battelle & B. Larkin [1785?]
2 p.l., 166 p. 17.5 cm.
New York Public 816
MB (p. 43–48 wanting); MWA; NN mp. 44682

B6065 [FIELD, MISS]
The glory of the heavenly city . . . manifested in a vision to a young lady of Bristol . . . 1781. As related by herself. Philadelphia, Re-printed by Joseph Crukshank, 1785.
36 p. 16.5 cm. A-C^6
MWA; NHi; PPL mp. 44683

B6066 FRANKLIN, BENJAMIN, 1706–1790
Advice to a young tradesman . . . Philadelphia, Printed by Daniel Humphreys, at the new printing-office, in Spruce-street, near the Drawbridge [1785]
broadside 20.5 X 11.5 cm.
Humphreys at the above address only in 1785
cf. *The Bibliographer*, v. 1, no. 3, Mar. 1902
New York Public 817
NN (reduced facsim.); PHi mp. 44684

B6067 FREEMAN'S JOURNAL
Postscript to the *Freeman's Journal*, (no. 132.) Wednesday, September 28, 1785. Mr. Bailey, Sir . . . Harlequin. [New York, 1785]
broadside 42 X 27 cm.
NHi

B6068 FREEMASONS. MASSACHUSETTS
At a convention of delegates from the following lodges . . . holden at . . . Charlestown . . . Massachusetts . . . 26 May, 5785 . . . [Charlestown? 1785]
7 p. 20 cm.
NN mp. 44685

B6069 FREEMASONS. NEW YORK. GRAND LODGE
The constitutions of the Ancient and Honourable Fraternity of . . . Masons, in the State of New-York, collected . . . by order of the Grand Lodge . . . New-York, Shepard Kollock, 1785.
116, [8?] p.

MWA (typescript and photostat t.p.); N; NNFM
mp. 44686

B6070 FRIENDS, SOCIETY OF. LONDON YEARLY MEETING
The epistle from our Yearly-Meeting, held in London . . . from the 16th of the fifth month 1785, to the 23d of the same . . . To Friends at their ensuing Yearly-Meeting in Philadelphia . . . [Philadelphia, 1785]
3, [1] p. 33 cm. caption title
MB; NjP; PPL; RPJCB mp. 44687

B6071 GEORGIA. LAWS
An act for laying out a district . . . situate on the River Mississippi, and within the limits of this state, into a county, to be called Bourbon . . . Savannah, Georgia, February 7, 1785. [Savannah? 1785]
[2] p. 32 cm.
No copy located mp. 44688

B6072 GILL, SARAH (PRINCE) 1728–1771
[Devotional papers . . . Bennington, Haswell & Russell, 1785]

Advertised in the *Vermont Gazette*, Feb. 14, 1785
McCorison 93
No copy known mp. 44689

B6073 THE Golden Age; or, Future glory of North America discovered by an angel to Celadon, in several entertaining visions . . . [n.p.] 1785.
16 p.
Text begins: In one of our American states . . . Other textual references strongly indicate its American production
Sabin 27701; Wright 500
DLC mp. 44690

B6074 GREEN, FREDERICK
Annapolis, May, 1785. Sir, I have undertaken to print . . . a few copies of all the laws . . . Frederick Green. [Annapolis, F. Green, 1785]
broadside 34.5 X 26 cm.
Wheeler 369
Photostats: MdHi; RPJCB mp. 44691

B6075 GREEN, FREDERICK
Annapolis, May 4, 1785. Frederick Green, printer to the state, having undertaken . . . to print . . . one hundred copies of all the laws now in force . . . [Annapolis, F. Green, 1785]
broadside 30.5 X 18.5 cm.
Wheeler 370
Photostats: MdHi; RPJCB mp. 44692

B6076 GREGORY, JOHN, 1724–1773
A father's legacy to his daughters . . . London, Printed: Philadelphia: Re-printed for William Aikman in Annapolis. M,DCC,LXXV.
viii, [2], 132 p. 8vo
DGU mp 44693

B6077 THE happy man, and true gentleman. The happy man was born in the city of regeneration . . . New-York, Samuel Loudon [1785?]
broadside 34 X 21 cm.
NHi mp. 44694

B6078 HAWEIS, THOMAS, 1734–1820
The communicant's spiritual companion . . . The eighth edition. New-York, Samuel Loudon, 1785.
viii, 116 p. 20.5 cm. [A]-Q^4 (Q3-4 blank)
CSmH; MWA (mutilated); N mp. 44695

B6079 HILLIARD, TIMOTHY, 1746–1790
Paradise promosed . . . A sermon delivered . . . the eighteenth of November . . . preceding the execution of Alexander White . . . Newbury-port, John Mycall for Joseph Hilliard of Kensington [1785]
32 p. 20 cm.
DLC; NhHi mp. 44696

B6080 THE history of Dr. John Faustus . . . [Norwich? John Trumbull? 1785?]
15, [1] p. 13 cm. [A]-B^4
Imprint and date assumed from dating of advertisements at end
MWA (t.p. wanting) mp. 44697

B6081 HOCH-DEUTSCHES reformirtes A B C und Namen Büchlein für Kinder, welche anfangen zu lernen. Germantoun, Gedruckt und zu finden bey Leibert, und Billmeyer, 1785.
[32] p. 8vo
PPL mp. 44698

B6082 HOLLINGSWORTH, LEVI
Philadelphia, September 10, 1785. A robbery. Fifty dollars reward. Last night a store . . . Paid by Levi Hollingsworth. Philadelphia, Dunlap & Claypoole [1785]
broadside 31 X 24.5 cm.
PHi mp. 44699

B6083 [HOPKINS, WILLIAM] 1706–1786
A friendly dialogue, between a Scripturian and an Athanasian . . . [Philadelphia? Charles Cist?] M.DCC.LXXXV.
36 p. 19.5 cm.
". . . now reprinted from a London copy published in 1784 . . . The notes signed B. are the present editor's. February 11th, 1785."—p. iv
Edited by John Beale Bordley?
MB

B6084 THE horror of murder, blasphemy, and sacrilege . . . committed on the body of the Rev. Father Moor . . . in Ireland. Frederick-Town, M. Bartgis, 1785.
8 p. 15 cm.
Wheeler 371
MdHi mp. 44700

B6085 HYMN on St. John the Evangelist's day, 1785. New-York, Shepard Kollock [1785]
broadside 33 X 21 cm.
DLC; NHi; RPJCB mp. 44701

B6086 AN hymn, to be sung by the charity scholars, the 27th of November 1785, at St. Paul's . . . after the charity sermon, for the benefit of the school. [New York, 1785]
broadside 35 X 20.5 cm.
NHi mp. 44702

B6087 INDEPENDENT LEDGER
The carrier of the *Independent Ledger*, &c. wishes his kind customers a Merry Christmas & Happy New-Year, and presents the following . . . January 1, 1785. [Boston, 1785]
broadside
Ford 2428
PHi. Photostat: MWA mp. 44657

B6088 JENYNS, SOAME, 1704–1787
A view of the internal evidence of the Christian religion . . . The ninth edition, corrected. Richmond, Dixon and Holt, 1785.
40 p. 19 cm.

Davis 8
NHi; Vi mp. 44703

B6089 KAYADEROSSERAS PATENT
. . . Verkoop van de onderstaande onbebouwde Loten Landen in de Patent van Kayadarosseras, in de County van Albany, New-York . . . [at end] Philadelphia, F. Bailey [1785]
broadside 42.5 X 30 cm.
At head of title; 1785
Sabin 98089; Vail: Old frontier 729
NHi mp. 44706; 44820

B6090 LATHROP, BARNABAS
Poetical meditations . . . Norwich, J. Trumbull, 1785.
43 p. 17.5 cm.
Trumbull: Supplement 2314
DLC mp. 44707

B6091 [LAVOISIER, ANTOINE LAURENT] 1743–1794
The art of manufacturing alkaline salts and potashes . . . Translated from the French by Charles Williamos [!] . . . [Philadelphia, 1785?]
vi, 50 p. 4 fold. plates, tables. 18.5 cm.
Dated by Forrest Bowe
A Paris imprint?—F. R. Goff
Shaw 20528
DLC; MB; PPAmP mp. 44708

B6092 [LE ROY, PETR LUDOVICK] 1699–1774
A narrative of the extraordinary adventures of four Russian sailors . . . Norwich, Printed and sold by John Trumbull, 1785.
16 p. 18 cm. [A]-B^4
MWA mp. 44709

B6093 A LETTER, written by an Universalist to his friend, with his friend's answer . . . Providence, Printed by B. Wheeler for Enoch Hunt [1785]
1 p.l., 29 p. 20.5 cm.
Alden 1011
RPJCB. Bradford Swan, Providence, R.I. mp. 44710

B6094 LOCKWOOD, BLANCHARD & CO.
Mr. Thomas Russell, one of the house of Lockwood, Blanchard & Russel, having removed from this city . . . in future the business will be conducted under the firm of Lockwood, Blanchard & Co. . . . Philadelphia, [June 25, 1785] [Philadelphia, 1785]
broadside 23 X 18.5 cm.
RPJCB mp. 44711

B6095 LUTHER, MARTIN, 1483–1546
Der kleine Catschismus . . . Erste Auflage. Germanton, Leibert und Billmeyer, 1785.
[4], 127, [1] p. 14 cm. $[\ ]^2$A-J^6 K^4 L^6
MWA mp. 44712

B6096 LUTHER, MARTIN, 1483–1546
The rudiments of the shorter catechism . . . Philadelphia, M. Steiner, 1785.
15, [1] p. 15.5 cm.
cf. Evans 19055
DLC; PPLT mp. 44713

B6097 MCLAURIN, JOHN, 1693–1754
Glorying in the cross of Christ: a sermon . . . Philadelphia, Young, Stewart, & M'Cullough, 1785.
34, [1] p. 16.5 cm.
Imprint at head of title
cf. Evans 19765
MWA; PPL mp. 44714

B6098 MARY, JOHN
A new grammar, English and French . . . The second edition . . . Boston, Printed for and sold by the author, and by J. Norman, 1785.
141 p., 11 l., 120 [i.e. 121] p., 1 l. 20.5 cm.
Last leaf blank
Huntington 509; New York Public 818
CSmH; MWA; NN mp. 44716

B6099 MARYLAND. ELECTION PROX.
Federal ticket . . . Electors . . . [Annapolis, Fr. Green, 1785]
broadside 21.5 X 13 cm.
Wheeler 366
MdHi (2 copies) mp. 44717

B6100 MARYLAND. ELECTION PROX.
Federal ticket . . . Electors . . . [Baltimore, John Hayes? 1785]
broadside 19 X 11.5 cm.
Wheeler 367
MdHi (2 copies) mp. 44718

B6101 MARYLAND. HOUSE OF DELEGATES
By the House of delegates, January 12, 1785. Resolved, That the bill to lay a general tax . . . [Annapolis, F. Green, 1785]
[3] p. 34 cm.
Wheeler 373
DLC mp. 44719

B6102 MARYLAND. INTENDANT OF THE REVENUE
Intendant's-office, July 11, 1785. Confiscated property for sale . . . on Wednesday the 10th day of August next . . . [Annapolis, F. Green, 1785]
broadside 31 X 19.5 cm.
Wheeler 374
MdAA mp. 44720

B6103 MARYLAND. INTENDANT OF THE REVENUE
The report of the intendant of the revenue to . . . the General assembly . . . [Annapolis, F. Green, 1785]
7 p. 32 cm.
Wheeler 376
DLC; MdHi mp. 44721

B6104 MASSACHUSETTS
Commonwealth of Massachusetts. Lands for sale. To be sold . . . in behalf of the Commonwealth, seven townships . . . in the Passamaquoddy country . . . from a report made by Rufus Putnam . . . [Boston? 1785?]
broadside 34.5 X 21 cm.
Signed at end: Boston, 10th, February 1785
RPJCB mp. 44723

B6105 MASSACHUSETTS
Commonwealth of Massachusetts. Worcester ss. To the select-men, or assessors of the town of in the County of Worcester, Greeting . . . require you to assess the sum of upon the inhabitants . . . [Worcester? 1785]
broadside 32.5 X 19.5 cm.
Dated at Worcester, Sept. 7, 1785
MWA mp. 44722

B6106 MASSACHUSETTS. HOUSE OF REPRESENTATIVES
Commonwealth of Massachusetts. In the House of Representatives, March 18, 1785. Whereas it is represented to this court, that sundry persons . . . [Boston, 1785]
broadside
Ford 2416
MHi mp. 44724

B6107 MILLS, JOHN
The vision of John Mills. In Bedford County, at Virginia, in the year 1785. [n.p., 1785?]
broadside 28 X 20 cm.
New York Public 821; Sabin 100601
MWA; NN mp. 44727

B6108 MIRABEAU, HONORÉ GABRIEL RIQUETTI, COMTE DE, 1747-1791
Considerations on the order of Cincinnatus . . . tr. from the French. [Philadelphia? 1785?]
vi, 82 p. 22 cm.
Sabin 49395
MHi; MdBP; NjP; PPL mp. 44728

B6109 MORE, HANNAH, 1745-1833
Poems by Miss Hannah More . . . Philadelphia, Young, Stewart, and M'Culloch, 1785.
24 p. 12mo
PPL mp. 44729

B6110 MURRAY, J
[The author of the following piece intended it for publication in the *Salem Gazette*, of November 1, 1785—but . . . the reader will consider this half sheet as a supplement . . .] Boston, October 29, 1785 . . . J. Murray. [Boston, 1785]
broadsheet 45.5 X 28 cm.
Text in 3 columns
MHi mp. 44730

B6111 EIN neu Trauer-Lied, wie man vernommen, von einem Menschen, der nach dem Tod ist wieder kommen. Diese Begebenheit . . . vor nicht langer Zeit zehn Meilen von Carlisle zugetragen . . . [Carlisle] Neu verfasset und gedruckt für Georg Hohman [1785?]
broadside 38 X 30 cm.
PHi mp. 44731

B6112 DER neue, verbessert- und zuverlässige Americanische calender, auf des 1786ste Jahr Christi . . . Philadelphia, Joseph Crukschank [1785]
[38+] p. 20 cm.
MWA mp. 44732

B6113 THE New-England almanack, and gentlemen and ladies diary for 1786. By Edmund Freebetter. Norwich, John Trumbull [1785]

Drake 390, from an auction catalog
No copy known

B6114 THE New-England almanack . . . for . . . 1786 . . . Hartford, Barlow & Babcock [1785]
[24] p. 15.5 cm.
By Isaac Bickerstaff
Ct; CtHi; MWA mp. 44650

B6115 THE New-England almanack, for . . . 1786 . . . By Isaac Bickerstaff . . . Hartford, Elisha Babcock [1785]
[24] p. 15.5 cm.
Bates: Connecticut almanacs p. 138
CtHi; NN mp. 44651

B6116 THE New England primer improved . . . Hartford, Nath. Patten, 1785.
[80] p.
MWA (imperfect) mp. 44733

B6117 THE New England primer improved . . . New London, T. Green, 1785.
[80] p.
MWA (imperfect) mp. 44734

B6118 THE New-England primer improved . . . Plymouth, Printed and sold by Nathaniel Coverly, 1785.
[64] p. [A]-E^8
Heartman 79
No copy located mp. 44735

B6119 THE New-England primer, improved . . . Providence, John Carter, 1785.
[80] p. illus. 11 cm.
Alden 1012; Winship p. 49; Heartman 78
MH; MWA (lacks A1); RHi mp. 44736

B6120 NEW HAMPSHIRE. GOVERNOR, 1776-1785
State of New-Hampshire. To [list of 99 names, some in manuscript] Greeting . . . [Exeter] Melcher & Osborne, 1785.
broadside 41 X 32.5 cm.
Appointments as justices of the peace
Whittemore 379
DLC. Photostat: NhHi mp. 44737

B6121 NEW HAMPSHIRE. HOUSE OF REPRESENTATIVES
A journal of the proceedings of the . . . House of representatives . . . at the first session of the second court . . . [June 1-24, 1785] Portsmouth, Robert Gerrish, 1785.
54 p. 28.5 cm.
Huntington 511; New York Public 822
CSmH; DLC; MWA; NN; NhD; NhHi; RPJCB
mp. 44739

B6122 NEW HAMPSHIRE. HOUSE OF REPRESENTATIVES
State of New-Hampshire in America. A journal of the proceedings of the . . . House of representatives . . . at their third session . . . [Feb. 9-24, 1785] [Colophon] Portsmouth, Robert Gerrish, 1785.
p. 69-104. 28.5 cm. caption title
Huntington 510; New York Public 821a
CsmH; DLC; MWA; NN; Nh; NhD; NhHi mp. 44738

B6123 NEW HAMPSHIRE. SENATE
A journal of the proceedings . . . at the first session of the second court . . . begun . . . the first Wednesday in June . . . [June 1-23, 1785] Portsmouth, Robert Gerrish, 1785.
29 p. 31 cm.
New York Public 824; Whittemore 377
MWA; NN; NhD; NhHi; RPJCB mp. 44740

B6124 NEW HAMPSHIRE. SENATE
State of New Hampshire. At a session of the General Court . . . [Oct. 19-Nov. 10, 1785] [Colophon] Portsmouth, Daniel Fowle [1785]
p. 31-50. 32 cm. caption title
New York Public 825; Whittemore 402
MWA; N; NN; NhD; NhHi mp. 44741

B6125 NEW HAMPSHIRE. TREASURER
State of New-Hampshire. John Taylor Gilman, Treasurer . . . To the selectmen of Greeting . . . [Mar. 25, 1785] [Exeter] Melcher & Osborne, 1785.
broadside 32 X 19 cm.
DLC; NhD mp. 44742

B6126 NEW YORK (CITY)
Ordinances, rules and bye-laws, for the government of the Alms-House . . . of the City of New-York. New-York, Samuel Loudon [1785?]

broadside 53 X 39 cm.
New York Public 826
NN mp. 44745

B6127 THE news-carrier's address to his customers. Hartford, January 1, 1785 . . . [Hartford, 1785]
broadside 42 X 13 cm.
1st line: Old customs teach ('tis said m[!]y many . . .
NHi; RPJCB (on deposit at RPB) mp. 44747

B6128 NORCOTT, JOHN, d. 1676
[Baptism discovered plainly and faithfully] being a clear and distinct investigation of the important doctrine . . . The twentieth edition. Bennington, Haswell & Russell, 1785.
36 p. 22 cm.
Cooley 52
Vt (t.p. partly missing) mp. 44748

B6129 NORMAN, JOHN
Boston, May 5th, 1785. Rev. Sir, By the advice of . . . gentlemen of the first character . . . we take the liberty to commit to the . . . patronage of the reverend ministers . . . the following subscription address . . . for an accurate map of the four New-England states. [Boston, 1785]
broadside
Address by Norman and Coles
Ford 2422
MHi mp. 44749

B6130 NOTICE is hereby given to the Surveyor-General and deputy surveyors of the several districts within the last Indian purchase . . . Thomas Clifford, John Abrams denormandie, Miers Fisher, and Charles Hurst. Philadelphia, May 17, 1785. [Philadelphia, 1785]
broadside 21 X 19 cm.
MB (2 copies) mp. 44750

B6131 OBSERVATIONS on the slavery of the Negroes, in the southern states, particularly intended for the citizens of Virginia, by Juvenis. New-York, W. Ross, 1785.
23 p.
RPJCB mp. 44751

B6132 OBSERVER
The *Observer*, extra. Friday, April 15, 1785. Exertion or ruin . . . [Boston, 1785]
broadside 24 X 17 cm.
Ford 2423; Huntington 512
CSmH; DLC; MHi mp. 44752

B6133 OSBORNE, HENRY
An English grammar, adapted to the capacities of children. Charleston, Burd and Boden for the author [1785]
33 leaves. 16 mo [-] A-H^4
Rosenbach-Ch 105
A. S. W. Rosenbach (1933) Photostat: NN
mp. 44753

B6134 OTTO, HENRICH
Eine grausame geschichte, oder ein lied von einem mörder, Philip Bebel, welcher . . . hat ausgangs Aprils, 1785, seine frau . . . mit einer axt erschlagen . . . [Philadelphia? 1785?]
broadside 39.5 X 29 cm.
Wheeler 383
DLC mp. 44754

B6135 OTTO, HENRICH
Eine unerhörte that von einem mörder, genannt Philip Beppel . . . In ein lied verfasset von Henrich Otto . . . [Philadelphia? 1785?]
broadside 42 X 35.5 cm.
Wheeler 384
PPRF mp. 44755

B6136 OUTLINES of a plan for the establishment of a mint . . . [Colophon] Philadelphia, Charles Cist [1785]
[4] p. 34 cm.
Dated at end: Philadelphia, August 22, 1785
DLC mp. 44756

B6137 PAEDAGOGIUM, NAZARETH, PA.
Regulations of the Paedagogium or boarding school, established by the United Brethern, at Nazareth . . . in Pennsylvania. [Philadelphia, ca. 1785]
2 p. 20 cm.
Founded in 1785
New York Public 827
NN mp. 44757

B6138 PENN, WILLIAM, 1644–1718
A letter from William Penn, to his wife and children, written a short time before his first voyage to America. Lancaster: Printed by A. Busher. M,DCC,LXXXV.
16 p. 18.5 cm.
PHi mp. 44758

B6139 PENNSYLVANIA
Pennsylvania, ss. By the Vice-President and the Supreme Executive Council . . . a proclamation . . . [Philadelphia? 1785?]
broadside 42 X 33 cm.
Concerns a reward for apprehension of persons "taking off the said Timothy Pickering."
Lower half in German
Sealock 29
RPJCB mp. 44768

B6140 PENNSYLVANIA. CITIZENS
To the honourable the representatives of the freemen . . . of Pennsylvania . . . the remonstrance and petition of the subscribers . . . affected by the shad and other fisheries on the river Schuylkill. [Philadelphia, 1785]
[3] p. 34 cm.
PHi mp. 44760

B6141 PENNSYLVANIA. LAWS
Port of Philadelphia. Wardens Office, Philadelphia, 30th of April, 1785 . . . [Philadelphia] Hall and Sellers [1785]
broadside 41 X 33.5 cm.
DLC mp. 44579

B6142 PENNSYLVANIA. SUPREME EXECUTIVE COUNCIL
The Supreme Executive Council of the Commonwealth of Pennsylvania. To all . . . greeting: Know ye, that . . . services . . . in the late army . . . granted . . . tract of land . . . the day of in the year . . . one thousand seven hundred and eighty . . . [n.p., 1785?]
broadside 31 X 40 cm.
Printed on vellum; filled in for Nov. 16, 1786
MiU-C

B6143 THE Pennsylvania, Delaware, Maryland, and Virginia almanack . . . for the year . . . 1786 . . . Baltimore, M. K. Goddard [1785]
[40] p. 18 cm.
Wheeler 385
MdHi mp. 44769

B6144 THE Pennsylvania Evening Post, and Daily Advertiser. Philadelphia, B. Towne [1785]

Brigham, p. 931
DLC (issues for Mar. 22–27, Apr. 19–20, May 24, June 5, 8, 11, 16, 18, 25, 28, July 19, 24, Aug. 4, 10, Sept. 20, 25, Oct. 26)

B6145 PENNSYLVANIA GAZETTE
New-Year verses, for those who carry the *Pennsylvania Gazette* to the customers. January 1, 1785. [Philadelphia, Hall and Sellers, 1785]
broadside 36 X 13.5 cm.
New York Public 828
MWA; NN mp. 44743

B6146 PHILADELPHIA, 1st February, 1785. You have probably heard before now, of my being under the disagreeable necessity of stopping payment on the 29th November last . . . [Philadelphia? 1785]
[3] p. 36 cm.
Form letter announcing continuance of business, signed by Geo. Meade
Sealock 23
PHi mp. 44725

B6147 THE Philadelphia price current . . . [Philadelphia, 1785]
fol.
Huntington 515
CSmH (14 issues, [2] p. each)

B6148 PHILADELPHIA SOCIETY FOR PROMOTING AGRICULTURE
Laws of the Philadelphia Society . . . Philadelphia, Hall and Sellers, 1785.
8 p. 22 cm.
MWA mp. 44773

B6149 . . .A PLAN for liquidating certain debts of the state of Pennsylvania . . . [Philadelphia] R. Aitken [1785 or 1786]
[6] p. 31 cm. caption title
At head of title: By permission . . . The second edition, price 1 s.
cf. Evans 16954
DLC mp. 44774

B6150 A PLAN for the payment of the national debt, by means of a National Bank. Philadelphia, 1785.
16 p. 19 cm.
Signed: Philadelphus
Sealock 36
PHi mp. 44775

B6151 POLLOCK, CARLISLE
I request the favour of your attendance at the Coffee-House, to-morrow . . . scheme of an institution for a Fire Insurance Society . . . Carlisle Pollock, Commercial Insurance Office. New-York, April 7, 1785. [New York, 1785]
broadside 20.5 X 16 cm.
NHi mp. 44776

B6152 [POOR Robin's almanack, for the year . . . 1786 . . . Frederick-Town, M. Bartgis, 1785]

Announced as just published in *Maryland Chronicle*, Jan. 18, 1786
Wheeler 386
No copy known mp. 44777

B6153 POOR Will improved: or, The town and country almanack for . . . 1786 . . . By William Meanwell, Philom. New-York, Printed and sold by W. Ross [1785]
[36] p. 16.5 cm.
New York Public 819
NN mp. 44726

B6154 PRICE, RICHARD, 1723–1791
Observations on the importance of the American Revolution . . . Hartford, Reprinted by Barlow and Babcock, 1785.
60 p. 20 cm. A-E^6
MWA mp. 44778

B6155 PRICE, RICHARD, 1723–1791
Observations on the importance of the American Revolution . . . Philadelphia, Printed by M. Carey and Co. for Spotswood and Rice; and T. Seddon, 1785.
60, [2] p. 21.5 cm.
MWA; NjP mp. 44779

B6156 PRICES current:—Charleston, 1785.
[Charleston, 1785]
broadside 38 X 23 cm.
Text in 2 columns
Duties on importations at bottom
RPJCB (6 copies)

B6157 PROCTER, THOMAS
Philadelphia, September 22, 1785. On Monday, the third of October next . . . will be sold . . . the household-goods . . . taken in execution as the property of said Caleb Hughes, by Thomas Procter, Sheriff . . . [Philadelphia, 1785]
broadside 25 X 21.5 cm.
In English and German
MWA mp. 44771

B6158 PROTESTANT EPISCOPAL CHURCH IN THE U.S.A. PENNSYLVANIA (DIOCESE)
An act of association of the clergy and congregation of the Protestant Episcopal Church in . . . Pennsylvania. [Philadelphia? 1785?]
3 p. 32.5 cm.
NHi mp. 44780

B6159 PROTESTANT EPISCOPAL CHURCH IN THE U.S.A. VIRGINIA (DIOCESE)
Journal of a convention of the clergy and laity of the Protestant Episcopal Church of Virginia, begun . . . in . . . Richmond . . . May 18, 1785. Richmond, Dixon and Holt, 1785.
23 p. 21 cm.
New York Public 829; Sabin 100513
NN mp. 44781

B6160 RATHBUN, DANIEL
A letter, from Daniel Rathbun . . . to James Whittacor, cheif elder of the . . . Shakers. [n.p., 1785?]
120 p. 20 cm. [ ]^2 a-i^6 k^4
cf. Evans 19212
MWA; OClW mp. 44783

B6161 A REMEMBERABLE account, of the death of Stephen Fisk, of Brinfield. [n.p., 1785?]
broadside 33 X 21 cm.
Six stanzas in two columns
Fisk's death occurred "August last, the year of eighty-five."
New York Public 830
NN mp. 44784

B6162 RHODE ISLAND. ELECTION PROX.
1785. His Excellency William Greene, Esq; Governor.

The honorable Jabez Bowen, Dep. Governor . . . Providence, Bennett Wheeler [1785]
broadside 21.5 X 14 cm.
Alden 1018; Chapin Proxies 37
RHi (2 copies); RPB; RWe (2 copies) mp. 44785

B6163 RHODE ISLAND. GOVERNOR, 1779-1786
By . . . William Greene . . . A proclamation . . . [Nov. 10, 1785] . . . Providence, John Carter [1785]
broadside 41 X 33 cm.
Bill submitted Nov. 14, 1785
Alden 1019; Winship p. 49
RHi. Photostats: MWA; NN mp. 44786

B6164 RHODE ISLAND. LAWS
State of Rhode-Island and Providence Plantations. In General assembly, February session, 1785. Whereas certain classes . . . did not procure the recruits . . . Providence, John Carter [1785]
broadside 36 X 25 cm.
Bill submitted Mar. 7, 1785
Alden 1028; Winship Addenda p. 89
NHi; RNHi mp. 44787

B6165 RHODE ISLAND. LAWS
State of Rhode-Island and Providence Plantations. In General assembly, August session, A.D. 1785. An act for granting . . . [Providence, 1785]
broadside 51 X 19 cm.
Alden 1029; Winship p. 49
DLC; RHi mp. 44788

B6166 ROOTS, BENAJAH, 1725-1787
The true church of Christ described; in a sermon delivered at Rutland . . . October 20th A. D. 1783 . . . Bennington, Haswell & Russell [1785]
38 p. 16 cm.
McCorison 98
Advertised in *Vermont Gazette*, Feb. 14, 1785
MWA mp. 44789

B6167 ST. ANDREW'S SOCIETY
Rules for the St. Andrew's Society, of the State of New York. New-York, John M'Lean, 1785.
14 p. 19.5 cm.
p. 11-14: "A List of the Officers and Resident Members . . . August 31, 1785."
cf. Evans 19135
NN; PPRF

B6168 ST. JOHN'S COLLEGE
The following is the draught of a proposed act . . . for founding a college on the western shore of this state . . . [Annapolis, F. Green, 1785]
broadside
Wheeler 387
MdAS mp. 44791

B6169 [SHEET almanac for 1786] February hath XXVIII days . . . Vulgar notes for 1786 . . . Norwich: Printed and sold by J. [Trumbull] [1785]
broadside 46? X 43 cm.
Drake 391
MWA (first part missing)

B6170 EIN '76ger lied. [n.p., 1785?]
broadside 39 X 24 cm.
31 stanzas of German verse
Huntington 516
CSmH mp. 44792

B6171 SMITH, ABRAHAM
The attack made on Mr. B. Livingston . . . the 5th of October instant, I consider one of the most unfortunate incidents of my life . . . New-York, October 7, 1785. Abraham Smith. [New York, 1785]
broadside 17 X 13 cm.
Affidavits exonerating himself from the attack
NHi mp. 44793

B6172 SOME brief remarks on the nature of gospel ministry, and the qualification of ministers, in an affectionate address, to Christian societies . . . in the State of Maryland, or elsewhere. Baltimore, Goddard and Langworthy, 1785.
11 p. 8vo
PPL mp. 44794

B6173 SOUTH CAROLINA. COMMISSIONERS OF FORFEITED ESTATES
Advertisement. Will be sold at public auction . . . the 3d day of October next . . . valuable lands . . . about sixty Negroes . . . Charles H. Simmons, C. C. F. E. Charleston, August 1, 1785. [Charleston] Childs, M'Iver & Co. [1785]
broadside 55.5 X 44 cm.
Sc-Ar (3 copies)

B6174 SOUTH CAROLINA. LAWS
An act for establishing county courts, and for regulating the proceedings therein. Charleston, A. Timothy [1785]
35 p. 29.5 cm.
Passed Mar. 17, 1785
New York Public 831; Sabin 87640
NN mp. 44795

B6175 STAR FIRE SOCIETY, NEWPORT, R.I.
Articles of the Star fire society . . . concluded the ninth day of June, 1785 . . . [Newport, 1785]
broadside 33.5 X 27 cm.
Alden 1015; Winship p. 48; Sabin 90487
RNHi. Photostats: MWA; NN; RHi mp. 44746

B6176 A SYNOPSIS of geography, with the use of the terrestrial globe . . . Wilmington, James Adams, 1785.
58 p. 16.5 cm.
Hawkins 19
DeWI; MWA mp. 44796

B6177 [THACHER, THOMAS] 1756-1812
[Funeral sermon for Jotham Gay and Theodore Gay, of Dedham. Boston, Benjamin Edes, 1785]
24 p. 4to
Attribution of author and printer by MBAt
MBAt (p. 1-2 lacking)

B6178 TIVERTON. CONGREGATIONAL SOCIETY
Scheme of a lottery . . . for raising 1500 dollars . . . towards repairing the meeting and parsonage houses . . . Tiverton, May 20, 1785. Providence, Bennett Wheeler [1785]
broadside 24 X 18.5 cm.
Alden 1031; Winship p. 89
RHi; RPJCB. Photostat: MWA mp. 44797

B6179 TO perpetuate the memory of peace The triumphal arch, and looking glass, or The Continental mirror . . . [Philadelphia, 1785?]
8 p. 20.5 cm.
In verse
New York Public 813; Wegelin 798
NN (photostat) mp. 44798

B6180 TO the honest electors of this day. Be cool, my friends, be exceedingly wary . . . [Boston, 1785]
broadside
In favor of James Bowdoin
Ford 2426
MHi mp. 44799

B6181 TO the honourable the General Assembly of Maryland. The petition of the subscribers . . . humbly sheweth . . . [Annapolis, F. Green, 1785?]
4 p. 39.5 cm.
A proposal for the creation of a new county to be called Paca after the then governor
Wheeler 388
MdHi (2 copies) mp. 44800

B6182 TO the inhabitants, particularly the farmers and planters of the state of Maryland. Planter. Worcester County, Feb. 1, 1785. [n.p., 1785]
broadside 34.5 X 21 cm.
DLC (mutilated) mp. 44801

B6183 TO the public. Pursuant to an act of the General assembly . . . for . . . extending the navigation of Potowmack River . . . Jacquelin Ambler, John Beckley, managers [n.p., 1785?]
broadside 33.5 X 33 cm.
A report of the Commissioners of Virginia and Maryland
DLC (not traced 1963) mp. 44666

B6184 U. S. BOARD OF TREASURY
Board of Treasury, June 6, 1785. The Board of Treasury to whom was referred the petition of John Allan, Esquire, late Superintendant of Indians Affairs for the Eastern Department. Report . . . [Philadelphia, 1785]
broadside 36 X 21 cm.
The last paragraph records action of Congress taken September 29
Ford: Bibliographical notes . . . 499
DLC (2 copies) mp. 44802

B6185 U. S. BOARD OF TREASURY
The Board of treasury, on the motion of . . . Mr. Howell, of the 8th July instant . . . [Philadelphia, J. Dunlap, 1785]
[2] p. 42.5 X 26.5 cm.
Ford: Bibliographical notes . . . 486
DLC mp. 44803

B6186 U. S. BOARD OF TREASURY
The Board of treasury to whom was referred on the 7th July inst. a paper from le Sieur Marbois . . . [Philadelphia, J. Dunlap, 1785]
[2] p. 44.5 X 27 cm.
Dated at end: . . . 30th July, 1785
Ford: Bibliographical notes . . . 489
DLC mp. 44804

B6187 U. S. CONTINENTAL CONGRESS, 1784
By the United States in Congress assembled. April 23, 1784. Resolved, That so much of the territory . . . May 20, 1785. An ordinance for ascertaining the mode . . . [Colophon] Hartford, Hudson and Goodwin [1785]
[4] p. 33.5 cm.
Trumbull: Supplement 1959; cf. Evans 19283
CtHi; DLC; MHi mp. 44805

B6188 U. S. CONTINENTAL CONGRESS, 1785
By the United States in Congress assembled. March 17th, 1785. Whereas it must conduce . . . [Philadelphia, J. Dunlap, 1785]
broadside 42.5 X 26 cm.
Ford: Bibliographical notes . . . 460
DLC mp. 44806

B6189 U. S. CONTINENTAL CONGRESS, 1785
The Committee appointed to revise the system of the War-Office . . . beg leave to submit the following draft of an ordinance . . . [New York? 1785]
broadside 35.5 X 25.5 cm.
Setting salary and duties of the Secretary of War
NHi mp. 44807

B6190 U. S. CONTINENTAL CONGRESS, 1785
The committee consisting of to whom was referred a motion, submit the following report. To enable the commissioners . . . [New York, 1785]
broadside 43 X 27 cm.
Ford: Bibliographical notes . . . 447
DLC (4 copies) mp. 44808

B6191 U. S. CONTINENTAL CONGRESS, 1785
The committee consisting of Mr. Gerry, Mr. Ellery and Mr. Wilson, to whom was referred a petition . . . of Mr. Oliver Pollock . . . [Philadelphia, J. Dunlap, 1785]
broadside 36 X 21.5 cm.
Ford: Bibliographical notes . . . 484
DLC; MHi mp. 44809

B6192 U. S. CONTINENTAL CONGRESS, 1785
The committee consisting of Mr. Pinckney, Mr. R. R. Livingston . . . to whom were referred a letter of the of December . . . [Philadelphia, J. Dunlap, 1785]
broadside 42.5 X 26.5 cm.
Ford: Bibliographical notes . . . 479
DLC mp. 44810

B6193 U. S. CONTINENTAL CONGRESS, 1785
The committee of qualifications report, That the confederation . . . That Mr. Howell . . . continued in Congress until January 5, 1783 . . . [Philadelphia, J. Dunlap, 1785]
broadside 44.5 X 28 cm.
Alden 1032; Ford: Bibliographical notes . . . 441 & 494
DLC (2 copies); RHi. Photostat: MWA mp. 44811

B6194 U. S. CONTINENTAL CONGRESS, 1785
The committee to whom were referred a letter of the of December from . . . Cyrus Griffin and John Lowell . . . [Philadelphia, J. Dunlap, 1785]
broadside 42.5 X 26.5 cm.
Ford: Bibliographical notes . . . 466
DLC; MWA mp. 44813

B6195 U. S. CONTINENTAL CONGRESS, 1785
The committee to whom were referred the petition of the inhabitants of the Kaskaskies . . . [Philadelphia, J. Dunlap, 1785]
broadside 43 X 27 cm.
Ford: Bibliographical notes . . . 458
DLC; MHi mp. 44814

B6196 U. S. CONTINENTAL CONGRESS, 1785
Motion of Mr. Gerry, seconded by Mr. Howell. Whereas it is indispensibly . . . [Philadelphia, J. Dunlap, 1785]
broadside 36 X 22 cm.
Ford: Bibliographical notes . . . 502
DLC mp. 44815

B6197 U. S. CONTINENTAL CONGRESS, 1785
That upon supplies furnished by impressment . . . [New York, Francis Childs, 1785]
broadside 33 X 20 cm.
Ford: Bibliographical notes . . . 482
DLC mp. 44816

B6198 U. S. CONTINENTAL CONGRESS, 1785
An ordinance for ascertaining the mode of disposing of lands in the Western Territory. [Philadelphia, J. Dunlap, lap, 1785]
broadside 43 X 26 cm.
In double columns
The form in which the ordinance passed the 1st reading
Ford: Bibliographical notes . . . 454
DLC mp. 44817

B6199 U. S. CONTINENTAL CONGRESS, 1785
An ordinance for ascertaining the mode of disposing of lands in the Western Territory. [Philadelphia, J. Dunlap, 1785]
[2] p. 44 X 27 cm.
In double columns
Apparently the form in which the ordinance passed the 2d reading
Ford: Bibliographical notes . . . 459
DLC mp. 44818

B6200 U. S. CONTINENTAL CONGRESS, 1785
An ordinance for ascertaining the mode of disposing of lands in the Western Territory. [Philadelphia, J. Dunlap, 1785]
broadside 42.5 X 27 cm.
In double columns
Ford: Bibliographical notes . . . 468; cf. Evans 19326
DLC (2 copies)

B6201 U. S. CONTINENTAL CONGRESS, 1785
An ordinance for ascertaining the mode of disposing of lands in the Western Territory. [Philadelphia, J. Dunlap, 1785]
[2] p. 41.5 X 25.5 cm.
In double columns
The 3d reading
Ford: Bibliographical notes . . . 477
DLC (3 copies)

B6202 U. S. TREASURY DEPT.
General account of receipts and expenditures of the United States, from the 1st of November, 1784, to the 1st of November, 1785 . . . Register's office, New-York, Nov. 1, 1785. Joseph Nourse, Register. [New York, 1785]
broadside 34.5 X 42 cm.
RPJCB mp. 44819

B6203 THE United States almanack, for the year . . . 1786 . . . By Eben. W. Judd . . . Elizabeth-Town, Shepard Kollock [1785]
[40] p. 16.5 cm.
Drake 5134; Morsch 23
DLC; MWA; NHi mp. 44704

B6204 THE United States almanack, for the year . . . 1786 . . . By Eben W. Judd . . . New York, Printed and sold by Shepard Kollock [1785]
[40] p. 17.5 cm.
Drake 5933
MWA; N (imperfect); NjHi; PHi; WHi (18.1.) mp. 44705

B6205 Deleted

B6206 VERMONT, GOVERNOR, 1778-1789
By His Excellency Thomas Chittenien . . . A proclamation . . . I . . . do hereby appoint Wednesday, the twenty-seventh day of April next . . . as a day of public fasting . . . [Mar. 24, 1785] . . . [Windsor, Hough and Spooner, 1785]
broadside 44 X 18 cm.
Cooley 59; McCorison 102; Sabin 99057
VtBrt mp. 44821

B6207 VERMONT. GOVERNOR, 1778–1789
[Thanksgiving day proclamation, Nov. ? 1785. Windsor, Hough & Spooner, 1785]
broadside
200 copies ordered printed Oct. 20, 1785
McCorison 103
No copy known mp. 44822

B6208 VERMONT. LAWS
State of Vermont. An act for the purpose of levying the taxes therein contained . . . passed by the Legislature . . . 16th June instant . . . [Windsor? Hough & Spooner? 1785]
broadside 34 X 22 cm.
McCorison 106
George A. Russell, Arlington, Vt. (1963) mp. 44823

B6209 [THE Vermont primer, or Young child's guide to the English language. Containing . . . a greater [amount] of spelling, than any book of the kind extant. Bennington, Haswell & Russell, 1785]

Advertised in the *Vermont Gazette*, Nov. 28, 1785, as "For sale, cheap for cash, or country produce."
McCorison 108
No copy known mp. 44824

B6210 VIRGINIA. COUNCIL
Council chamber, October 20, 1785. Gentlemen, The act . . . [Richmond, 1785]
broadside 21 X 17 cm.
DLC (mutilated) mp. 44825

B6211 VIRGINIA. GENERAL ASSEMBLY
In the House of delegates, Thursday, the 30th of December, 1784 . . . Wednesday, the 5th of January, 1785 . . . [Richmond, J. Dunlap and J. Hayes, 1785]
4 p. 40 cm. caption title
Davis 10
ViU. Brit. Mus. mp. 44826

B6212 VIRGINIA. HIGH COURT OF CHANCERY
Virginia. At a High Court of Chancery held in Richmond, the 8th day of May, 1785. John Hite, Isaac Hite . . . plaintiffs, against the executors . . . of Thomas Lord Fairfax . . . defendants . . . John Brown, C.H.C.C. [Richmond? 1785?]
broadside 30.5 X 18 cm.
Ms. note on verso dated July 1786
WHi (not traced 1964) mp. 44827

B6213 WASHINGTON CO., PA.
State of the accounts of James Marshall, Esq. lieutenant of Washington County. Philadelphia, John Steele, 1785.
3 p. 22.5 cm.
MWA; PHi mp. 44763

B6214 WATTS, ISAAC, 1674–1748
Divine songs attempted in easy language, for the use of children . . . The seventy eighth edition. Bennington, Haswell & Russell, 1785.
24 p. 16 cm.
Cooley 66; McCorison 109
MWA mp. 44828

B6215 WATTS, ISAAC, 1674–1748
First set of catechisms . . . The eighth edition. Portsmouth, Melcher and Osborne, 1785.
36, 26, 34 p. 17 cm. A-H[6]
CtHi; NhD mp. 44829

B6216 WEATHERWISE'S Boston almanack, for the year . . . 1786 . . . Plymouth, Nathaniel Coverly [1785]

[24] p. 17.5 cm.
Ct; DLC mp. 44830

B6217 WEATHERWISE'S Plymouth almanack, for the year . . . 1786 . . . Plymouth, Nathaniel Coverly [1785]
[24] p. 17.5 cm.
Nichols p. 65; New York Public 833
DLC; MB; MHi (imperfect); MWA; N; NN mp. 44831

B6218 WEATHERWISE'S Town and country almanac for . . . 1786 . . . Boston, Edmund Freeman [1785]
[24] p.
Drake 3370
DLC; MHi; MWA (imperfect); N mp. 44832

B6219 WEBSTER, NOAH, 1758-1843
A grammatical institute of the English language . . . In three parts. Part III . . . The second edition . . . Hartford, Hudson and Goodwin [1785?]
188 p.
RPJCB mp. 44833

B6220 WESTMORELAND CO., PA.
State of the accounts of Edward Cook . . . From 1st April 1783, to 1st June 1784. Philadelphia, John Steel, 1785.
4 p. 22 cm.
DLC; PHi mp. 44761

B6221 WHITE, WILLIAM, 1748-1836
The character of the Evangelist St. John, in a charity sermon, preached . . . before the . . . Masons . . . Philadelphia, Hall and Sellers, 1785.
24, [3] p. 19 cm. $[A]\text{-}C^4 \; [\;]^2$
MWA; NjP mp. 44834

B6222 WILLISON, JOHN, 1680-1750
The mother's catechism, enlarged and improved . . . The second edition, with some additional questions. Philadelphia, John Steele, 1785.
48 p. 17 cm.
RPJCB mp. 44835

B6223 YORK CO., PA.
State of the accounts of Thomas Armor . . . From the 31st May, 1781, to 28th January, 1783. Philadelphia, John Steele, 1785.
6 p. 23 cm.
MWA; P; PHi mp. 44766

B6224 YORK CO., PA.
State of the accounts of William Scott . . . from the 1st of April, 1783 to 1st of November, 1784. Philadelphia, John Steele, 1785.
6 p. 22 cm.
Sealock 43
MWA; PHi mp. 44767

B6225 YOUNG, EDWARD, 1683-1765
Resignation, in two parts, and a Postscript, to Mrs. B****** . . . Philadelphia, Re-printed by Enoch Story, 1785.
48 p. 20 cm.
New York Public 834
MB; MWA; NN; PPL (imperfect) mp. 44836

B6226 ZUR Freude der Eltern und Kinder, am Christage, den 25sten December, 1785 . . . [n.p., 1785]
broadside 10.5 X 17.5 cm.
In German and English
MWA mp. 44837

1786

B6227 THE A, B, C. With the shorter catechism . . . Philadelphia, Peter Stewart, 1786.
16 p. 17.5 cm.
PHi mp. 44838

B6228 THE A, B, C. with the shorter catechism . . . Philadelphia, Young and M'Culloch, 1786.
[16] p. 17 cm.
MWA mp. 44839

B6229 ADDISON, JOSEPH, 1672-1719
Cato. A tragedy . . . [Philadelphia] MDCCLXXXVI. Printed for, and sold by the booksellers.
59, [1] p. 17.5 cm.
PHi mp. 44840

B6230 ADOPTED SONS OF PENNSYLVANIA
Principles, articles, and regulations . . . of "The Adopted Sons of Pennsylvania," . . . the 2d day of January 1786 . . . Philadelphia, F. Bailey [1786]
broadside 43.5 X 31.5 cm.
New York Public 836
NAll. Photostats: DLC; NN mp. 44841

B6231 ALLINE, HENRY, 1748-1784
Hymns, and spiritual songs . . . Boston, Peter Edes, 1786.
[2], iii, [1], 381 p.
RPJCB mp. 44842

B6232 AMERICAN ACADEMY OF ARTS AND SCIENCES
Boston, March16, 1786. At a meeting of the Academy . . . on the 6th of November 1785, the following vote was passed . . . [Boston, 1786]
broadside 46 X 29 cm.
Ford 2431; New York Public 835
MB; MBAt; NN mp. 44843

B6233 AMERICAN MERCURY, HARTFORD
The carrier of the *American Mercury* wishes his customers a Happy New-Year, and presents the following . . . January 1, 1786. [Hartford, Elisha Babcock, 1786]
broadside 23.5 X 14 cm.
Blanck 863
MH; NHi. Photostat: CtY mp. 44868

B6234 AS the piece dedicated to the young gentlemen has met with a kind reception, the author would address her own sex in the following manner; hoping it will have . . . acceptance with the young ladies . . . more especially in the Town of Boston. Composed June 10, 1786. [Boston] Sold next Liberty-Pole, 1786.
broadside
Ford 2432
MBAt mp. 44847

B6235 AN astronomical diary . . . for the year . . . 1787 . . . By Daniel Sewall . . . Portsmouth, Robert Gerrish; sold also by Lamson & Ranlet, at Exeter [1786] [Second edition]
[24] p. 17.5 cm.
DLC; ICN mp. 44965

B6236 AN astronomical diary, or almanack, for . . . 1787. By Nehemiah Strong . . . New-Haven, Meigs & Dana [1786]
[24] p.
Bates: Connecticut almanacs p. 141; Drake 397
CtHi; MB (imperfect) mp. 44973

B6237 BAPTISTS. PENNSYLVANIA. PHILADELPHIA ASSOCIATION
Minutes of the Baptist Association . . . October, 1786. [Colophon] Philadelphia, Robert Aitken [1786]
8 p. 23 cm. caption title
DLC (2 copies); MWA; NHC mp. 44848

B6238 BAPTISTS. U. S.
The Baptist catechism . . . Philadelphia, Robert Aitken, 1786.
23, [1] p. 18.5 cm.
DLC mp. 44849

B6239 BARRETT, NAT
Boston, August 1, 1786. Being just . . . embarking for France . . . connection with Messrs. Le Couteulx and Co, merchants in Boston and bankers in Paris . . . [Boston, 1786]
broadside 24 X 19 cm.
RPJCB mp. 44850

B6240 BE merry and wise . . . By Tommy Trapwit, Esq. . . . The first Worcester edition. Worcester, Printed by Isaiah Thomas, and sold at his book store. Sold also by E. Battelle, Boston, 1786.
128 p. incl. front. 10 cm.
Not used for Evans 20028 microprint ed.
MWA mp. 44851

B6241 BEDFORD CO., PA.
State of the account of Thomas Urie . . . from April 1st, 1772, till 17th Oct. 1775 . . . Philadelphia, Robert Aitken, 1786.
[2], 1 p. 20 cm.
DLC; MWA; NHi; NN; PHi mp. 44944

B6242 BEERS, ISAAC, 1740?-1813
A catalogue of books, stationery and other articles, sold by Isaac Beers, at his Book-store in New-Haven. New-Haven, Meigs & Dana, 1786.
27 p.
Trumbull: Supplement 1902
No copy located mp. 44852

B6243 BIBLE
The Holy Bible abridged . . . The first Worcester edition. Worcester, Printed by Isaiah Thomas, and sold at his book-store, 1786.
176 p. illus. 10 cm.
Ruth Adomeit, Cleveland (imperfect); d'Alté A. Welch, Cleveland (most of sigs. A and C wanting)
mp. 44853

B6244 BIBLE
The verbum sempiternum. The twelvth [sic] edition with amendments. Boston, 1786.
vii, v [i.e. iv], 148; vi, 107, iv, iv p.
John Taylor's Thumb Bible
MB (imperfect, and all after p. 148 wanting); MH (imperfect); MWA (lacks p. 19-20); MiD. Ruth Adomeit, Cleveland (1962); d'Alté A. Welch, Cleveland (1962)
mp. 44974

B6245 THE big puzzling-cap: a choice collection of riddles . . . The first Worcester edition. Worcester, Isaiah Thomas, 1786.
90, [2] p. 10 cm. [A]-E^8 F$^{6?}$
MWA (back cover wanting) mp. 44855

B6246 BICKERSTAFF'S Boston almanack for . . . 1787. Boston, E. Russell [1786]
[24] p.
Drake 3377
MHi

B6247 BICKERSTAFF'S New-England almanack for . . . 1787 . . . Boston, Printed for Ebenezer Battelle, and William Green [1786]
[24] p.
Drake 3381
NjR

B6248 BLAGRAVE, J
Laws for regulating bills of exchange, inland and foreign . . . The fourth edition . . . New-York, Re-printed by S. & J. Loudon, 1786.
36 p. 15 cm. [A]-D^4 E^2
MWA; NhD mp. 44856

B6249 BLAIR, ROBERT, 1699-1746
The grave . . . Philadelphia, Robert Aitken, 1786.
31 p. 15 cm.
Interleaved
MWA; MiU-C; PPL mp. 44857

B6250 BOSTON
Gentlemen, The selectmen . . . have directed me to inclose . . . Sept. 11, 1786. [Boston, 1786]
broadside 45 X 28 cm.
In three columns
DLC. Photostat: MHi mp. 44858

B6251 BOSTON, March 13, 1786. To the public.
Whereas Mr. John de Neufville, by a libellous paper, published . . . the 5th day of September last (which he has extensively circulated) has endeavoured to wound the reputation of the subscribers . . . [Boston, 1786]
broadsheet 33.5 X 21 cm.
Signed in ms.: D. Leertouwer James Huyman
Ford 2441
MHi mp. 44860

B6252 BRITISH lamentation, together with Bunker-Hill ode . . . Ode composed by T. Dawes, jun Esq.—Sung on Bunker-Hill, June 17th, 1786, at the opening of Charles River Bridge . . . [Boston, 1786?]
broadside 35 X 20 cm.
Ford 2433
MWA mp. 44861

B6253 BROWN UNIVERSITY
Honoratissimo Jabez Bowen . . . habita in solennibus academicis comitiis A.D. M,DCC,LXXXVI. [Providence] Typis Johannis Carter [1786]
broadside 33.5 X 24.5 cm.
Alden 1059; New York Public 838; Winship p. 50
M; MWA; RHi; RPB. Photostat: NN mp. 44862

B6254 [BUCKLAND, JAMES]
A wonderful discovery of a hermit! Who lived upwards of 200 years. [n.p., 1786?]
broadside
The hermit was discovered in 1785
Hamilton 110
NjP mp. 44863

B6255 [BUCKLAND, JAMES]
A wonderful discovery of a hermit, who lived upwards of 200 years. Printed at Springfield, 1786.
12 p. 15 cm.
MWA mp. 44864

B6256 [BUCKLAND, JAMES]
A wonderful discovery of a hermit, who lived upwards of two hundred years. Worcester, 1786.
6 leaves. 12mo
Rosenbach-Ch 107
A. S. W. Rosenbach (1933) mp. 44865

B6257 BUCKS CO., PA.
State of the accounts of Gerardus Wyncoop . . . from November the 21st, 1784, till the 21st November, 1785. Philadelphia, Robert Aitken, 1786.
6 p. 21 cm.
DLC; MWA; NN; PHi mp. 44942

B6258 BURGH, JAMES, 1714–1775
The art of speaking . . . Philadelphia, Printed by Charles Cist, 1786.
[2], 326, [18] p. 12mo
cf. Evans 19535
OU; PPL. Forrest Bowe, NYC (1967) mp. 44866

B6259 CAREY, MATHEW, 1760–1839
The plagi-scurriliad: a Hudibrastic poem. Dedicated to Colonel Eleazer Oswald . . . By Mathew Carey. Philadelphia: Printed and sold by the author. January 16, M.DCC.LXXXVI.
xvi, 17–50 p. port. 20.5 cm.
Second edition; 1st ed. (Evans 19540) iv, 30 p.
MiU-C; RPB

B6260 CARPENTERS' COMPANY OF PHILADELPHIA
Articles . . . Philadelphia, Hall and Sellers, 1786.
xv, 47 p. 37 plates. 8vo
MWiW-C; P mp. 44867

B6261 CHANNING, HENRY, 1760?–1840
God admonishing his people of their duty . . . preached at New-London, December 20th, 1786. Occasioned by the execution of Hannah Ocuish . . . for the murder of Eunice Bolles . . . The second edition . . . New-London, T. Green, 1786.
30 p.
Not Evans 20264 (also at NHi)
NHi mp. 44869

B6262 CHASE, SAMUEL, 1741–1811
To the voters of Anne-Arundel County . . . Annapolis. Oct. 25, 1786. Samuel Chase. [Annapolis, Frederick Green, 1786]
broadside 56 X 44 cm.
Wheeler 397
DLC mp. 44870

B6263 CHESTER CO., PA.
State of the accounts of John Christie, Esquire, collector of excise, for the County of Chester. Philadelphia, Robert Aitken, 1786.
5 p. 22 cm.
MWA; PHi mp. 44943

B6264 CHURCHMAN, JOHN
To the American Philosophical Society this map of the peninsula . . . is inscribed by John Churchman. [Philadelphia, T. Dobson, 1786]
map 59.5 X 44.5 cm.
Phillips p. 228; not used for Evans 20272 microprint edition
DLC (2 copies) mp. 44871

B6265 CIRCULAR memorial, To His excellency James Bowdoin . . . Your devoted moralist . . . September 28, year of independence eleven. [Concord, 1786]
broadside 30.5 X 18.5 cm.
Signed: David Hoar
Ford 2495
DLC mp. 44872

B6266 CLIO HALL, BENNINGTON, VT.
Know all men by these presents that we the President and Trustees of Clio Hall, in Bennington . . . [Bennington, Haswell & Russell, 1786?]
broadside 32 X 20 cm.
Bond of Clio Hall to Aaron Hubbel for £25, dated Oct. 23, 1786
McCorison 112
VtU-W

B6267 COLE, ROBERT
The Deist reclaimed . . . Bennington, Haswell and Russell, 1786.
8 p. 17 cm.
MB mp. 44873

B6268 COLUMBIAN HERALD, CHARLESTON, S.C.
New Year's verses, for 1786; addressed to the customers of the *Columbian Herald*, by the printers lads who carry it . . . Charleston, T. B. Bowen & J. Markland [1786]
broadside 32 X 17.5 cm.
By Philip Freneau
1st line: Old Eighty-Five is past . . .
NHi; PHi mp. 44889

B6269 COLUMBIAN MAGAZINE
Philadelphia Sir, Your reputation in the literary world, us to take the liberty of enclosing you a sketch of the plan of a Magazine, which we mean to publish in this city . . . [Philadelphia, 1786]
broadside 23.5 X 19.5 cm.
Letter to accompany prospectus of the *Columbian Magazine*
Sealock 58
PHi

B6270 COLUMBIAN MAGAZINE
To the citizens of the United States of North-America. Encouraged by the promised assistance of a number of gentlemen . . . the subscribers have agreed to publish . . . the *Columbian Magazine* . . . [Philadelphia, 1786]
broadside 38.5 X 22.5 cm.
Signed by Thomas Seddon, Mathew Carey, William Spotswood, Charles Cist, James Trenchard
Sealock 59
PHi mp. 44874

B6271 COMPANY FOR OPENING INLAND NAVIGATION
Rules of the company for opening the inland navigation, between the Santee and Cooper rivers, agreed to on March the 23d, 1786 . . . Charleston, Bowen and Markland, 1786.
[16] p. 16.5 cm.
New York Public 840
NN (photostat of original in private collection, 1934) mp. 44875

B6272 CONNECTICUT. GENERAL ASSEMBLY
At a General Assembly . . . holden at New-Haven . . . October, A.D. 1786. The gentlemen nominated . . . to stand for election in May next, as sent in to this present General Assembly, are as follow, viz. His Excellency Samuel Huntington [and 19 others] . . . New-Haven, Thomas and Samuel Green [1786]
broadside 33 X 19 cm.
CtHi mp. 44876

B6273 CONNECTICUT. GENERAL ASSEMBLY
At a General Assembly . . . holden at New-Haven . . . October, A.D. 1786. The gentlemen nominated . . . to stand for election in May next, delegates in Congress . . . as sent in to this present General Assembly, are as follow, viz. William Samuel Johnson [and 11 others] . . . New-Haven, Thomas and Samuel Green [1786]
broadside 32 X 19 cm.
CtHi mp. 44877

B6274 DARTMOUTH COLLEGE
Catalogus eorum qui in Collegio-Dartmuthensi . . . ab anno M.DCC.LXXI, ad annum M.DCC.LXXXVI, alicujus gradus laurea donati sunt. [Hanover, 1786]
broadside 42 X 31.5 cm.
Whittemore 389
NhD; NhHi mp. 44878

B6275 [DEUTSCHE zeitung. Friederich-Stadt, M. Bartgis, 1786]

Wheeler 398; Seidensticker pp. 117–118
No copy known

B6276 DILWORTH, THOMAS, d. 1780
A new guide to the English tongue . . . Printed by Thomas Collier, in Litchfield, for E. Babcock, in Hartford, 1786.
[iv]-vii, 136+ p.
MWA (wanting after p. 136)

B6277 Deleted

B6278 A FAITHFUL narrative of Elizabeth Wilson . . . executed at Chester, Jan. 3, 1786. Charged with the murder of her twin infants . . . Drawn up at the request of a friend unconnected with the deceased. Printed in Hudson, by Ashbel Stoddard, M.DCC.LXXXVI.
16 p. 16 cm.
cf. Evans 19637 ff.
NHi mp. 44881

B6279 A FAITHFUL narrative of Elizabeth Wilson . . . executed at Chester, Jan. 3, 1786. Charged with the murder of her twin infants . . . New-Haven: Reprinted in the year 1786.
12 p.
CtY mp. 44882

B6280 FALMOUTH, ME. CONVENTION, 1786
At a convention of delegates from a number of towns in the counties of York, Cumberland and Lincoln, held at Falmouth . . . January, 1786:—The Hon. William Gorham . . . chosen President, Mr. Stephen Longfellow, jun. Clerk. [n.p., 1786]
broadside 31.5 X 19 cm.
Ford 2434
MHi mp. 44883

B6281 FENNING, DANIEL, d. 1767
The ready reckoner . . . Newbury-Port, Re-printed correctly from the fifth London edition, by John Mycall, 1786.
[4], 166 p. 18 X 7.5 cm.
MWA mp. 44884

B6282 FLETCHER, MARY (BOSANQUET) 1739–1815
An account of the death of the Rev. Mr. Fletcher, vicar of Madeley . . . Bristol: printed. Philadelphia: re-printed by Joseph Crukshank . . . MDCCLXXXVI.
16 p.
MdBBC

B6283 THE following extracts from the writings of pious men . . . are recommended to . . . all who profess Christianity . . . New-York, Francis Childs [1786]
32 p. 16 cm.
Dated from owner's autograph in PU copy, with date July 7, 1786
Adams 41; New York Public 888; cf. Smith, Joseph: *Descriptive catalogue of Friends' books*, v. 1, p. 281
NN; PU mp. 44886

B6284 FRANKLAND (STATE)
A declaration of rights, also the constitution or form of government agreed to . . . by the representatives . . . of the State of Frankland . . . in convention . . . at Greeneville, the 14th of November, 1785. Philadelphia, Francis Bailey, 1786.
23 p. 16.5 cm.
New York Public 842; Sabin 94720
MWA; NN mp. 44887

B6285 FRANKLIN, BENJAMIN, 1706–1790
Maritime observations: in a letter . . . to Mr. Alphonsus Le Roy . . . Philadelphia, Robert Aitken, 1786.
[1], 294–329 p. fold. plate, fold. map. 26 cm.
From the *Transactions* of the Amer. Phil. Soc., v. 2, with added title
DLC; MB; MWA; MiU-C; PPAmP mp. 44888

B6286 FREDERICKSBURG, March 25, 1786. Sir, Being about to settle in *Liverpool* with a view of establishing a commercial connexion . . . Either . . . afternamed gentleman will . . . receive tobacco . . . and ship it . . . to my address . . . Your . . . servant, *James Maury* Mr. Josiah Watson, Alexandria . . . Mr. Richard Morris, Louisa. [Alexandria? 1786]
[4] p. 30 cm.
Printing only on p. [1]
Italicized words in manuscript
ViW. Photostat: ViU

B6287 GAIFER
The conversion of a Mahometan to the Christian religion, described in a letter from Gaifer . . . to Aly-Ben Hayton . . . The ninth edition. New-York, Kollock, Carroll & Paterson, 1786.
16 p.
RPJCB mp. 44890

B6288 GEORGIA. GENERAL ASSEMBLY
In General Assembly, August 11, 1786. Ordered, That the executive be directed . . . to cause five hundred copies of the law . . . small debts . . . printed . . . Augusta, Reprinted by John E. Smith [1786]
8 p. fol. [A]-B^2 caption title
"An act for the more speedy recovery . . . April, 1760:" p. [2]-8
De Renne p. 239
GU-De mp. 44898

B6289 GEORGIA. LAWS
An act to continue an act to authorize the auditor to liquidate . . . claims against the confiscated estates . . . Augusta, 13th February, 1786. [Savannah? J. Johnston? 1786]
4 p. fol. caption title
"An act to authorize the delegates;" p. 3–4
De Renne p. 238; cf. Evans 16676
GU-De mp. 44893

B6290 GEORGIA. LAWS
An act to improve the navigation of Brier Creek . . .

Augusta, 30th January, 1786. [Savannah? J. Johnston? 1786]
4 p. fol. caption title
"An act for improving the navigation of Savannah River:" p. 2–4
De Renne p. 238
GU-De mp. 44894

B6291 GEORGIA. LAWS
[Acts of the General Assembly, passed at Augusta in January, 1786. Augusta? 1786]
4 p. fol. caption title
3 acts, the first beginning: An ordinance for empowering commissioners to fix on . . . a seat of government."
De Renne p. 236
GU-De mp. 44899

B6292 GEORGIA. LAWS
[Acts of the General Assembly, passed at Augusta in January and February, 1786. Augusta? 1786]
4 p. fol. caption title
4 acts, the first beginning: "An act to regulate the toll to be taken at mills."
De Renne p. 236
GU-De mp. 44896

B6293 GEORGIA. LAWS
[Acts of the General Assembly, passed at Augusta in February, 1786. Savannah? James Johnston? 1786]
4 p. fol. caption title
3 acts, the first beginning: "An act to authorize Zachariah Lamar, Esquire, to lay out a town."
De Renne p. 237
GU-De mp. 44892

B6294 GEORGIA. LAWS
[Acts of the General Assembly, passed at Augusta in February 1786. Savannah? J. Johnston? 1786]
4 p. fol. caption title
4 acts, the first beginning: "An act to make provision for officers . . . disabled in the service of the United States."
De Renne p. 238
GU-De mp. 44895

B6295 GEORGIA. LAWS
[Acts of the General Assembly, passed at Augusta in February, 1786. Savannah? James Johnston? 1786]
8 p. fol. caption title
4 acts, the first beginning: "An act to revise and amend an Act for regulating the trade."
De Renne p. 237
GU-De mp. 44897

B6296 GEORGIA. LAWS
[Acts of the General Assembly, passed at Augusta in August 1786. Augusta? John E. Smith? 1786]
12 p. fol. [A]–C^2 caption title
7 acts, the first beginning: "An act for regulating the militia . . . August 15, 1786."
De Renne p. 239
GU-De mp. 44891

B6296a [GRAHAM, WILLIAM]
An essay on government. By a citizen of Frankland. Philadelphia, Francis Bailey, 1786.
37 p.
New York Public 841; Trinterud 214
NN; PPPrHi mp. 44880

B6297 HEIDELBERG CATECHISM
Catechismus, oder Kurzer Unterricht Christlicher Lehre . . . Germantaun, Gedruckt und zu finden bey Leibert und Billmeyer, 1786.
138 p. 13.5 cm.
p. [95]–138: "Kurze und einfältige Kinderlehr . . . Germantaun: Gedruckt bey Michael Billmeyer, 1788."
New York Public 843
NN mp. 44900

B6298 HENRY, MATTHEW, 1662–1714
Prayers in scripture expressions . . . Wilmington, James Adams, 1786.
204 p. 17 cm.
Hawkins 20
DLC; DeWI mp. 44901

B6299 H[OECKER], L[UDWIG]
Kurz gefasztes nützliches Schul-Büchlein . . . Zweyte Auflage. Ephrata, Gedruckt und zu bekommen bey dem Schulmeister, Drucker und Buchbinder, 1786.
48, [1] p.
Karpinski p. 87
MiU-C mp. 44902

B6300 HOLKER, JOHN
Correspondence between John Holker . . . Inspector General of Trade and Manufactures, and . . . Robert Morris . . . late Superintendant of the Finances of the United States . . . Philadelphia, Charles Cist, 1786.
[2], 45 p. 4to
PPL mp. 44903

B6301 HUGHES, JAMES
To be sold, on Monday the 19th day of June instant . . . by James Hughes, master in chancery. A lease of seven lots of land . . . [New York] Francis Childs [1786]
broadside 37.5 X 23.5 cm.
NHi mp. 44904

B6302 HUMANE SOCIETY OF MASSACHUSETTS
The institution of the Humane Society of the commonwealth of Massachusetts. [Boston? 1786?]
15 p. 19 cm. caption title
The first meeting of the Society took place in December, 1785
MBM; MHi; MWA; NHi; RPJCB mp. 44905

B6303 HUNTER, WILLIAM
For London, the ship Charlotte, Captain William Lambert, now lying at this port, will sail . . . July . . . Alexandriz, George Richards [1786]
broadside 25 X 16.5 cm.
Signed and dated: William Hunter, jun. Alexandria, July 6, 1786
NN mp. 44906

B6304 AN hymn to be sung by the charity scholars . . . the 19th of November, 1786, at St. Paul's Church, after the charity sermon . . . [New York, 1786]
broadside 37.5 X 23.5 cm.
NHi mp. 44907

B6305 INSTRUCTIONS to representatives of the county of in the commonwealth of Virginia . . . Baltimore, William Goddard [1786]
19 p. 17 cm.
Wheeler 402
MdBJ-G

B6306 JAY, JOHN, 1745–1829
Letters, being the whole of the correspondence between . . . Jay . . . and . . . Littlepage . . . A new and correct edition . . . New-York, F. Childs, 1786.

102 p. 19.5 cm.
DLC; MB; MBAt; MWA; NHi; NN; PPL; RPJCB
mp. 44908

B6307 LAW, WILLIAM, 1686–1761
An extract from a letter written by the late William Law, to J---- R-----, of Northampton . . . [Philadelphia, Joseph Crukshank, 1786]
3 p. 8vo caption title
PHi

B6308 LEVY, AARON
To the public. The subscriber begs leave to inform the public, that he hath laid out a town, called Aaronsburgh . . . Plans of the town to be seen . . . at Philadelphia . . . and of the subscriber, at the town of Northumberland aforesaid. Aaron Levy. May 23, 1786. [Philadelphia? 1786]
broadside fol.
New York Public 846; Rosenbach 75
A. S. W. Rosenbach (1926); NN (reduced facsim.)

B6309 LOUDON'S New-York pocket almanack for . . . 1787. New-York, S. Loudon [1786]
[32] p.
Drake 5941
Private collection

B6310 LUX, GEORGE
To the electors of Baltimore county. During the last election . . . George Lux. Chatsworth, April 15, 1786. Baltimore, William Goddard [1786]
broadside 30 X 20 cm.
Wheeler 405
MdBE mp. 44913

B6311 MARINE SOCIETY, NEWPORT
[Charter and by-laws . . . Newport, 1786]
8vo?
Alden 1046; Sabin 55038 (possibly in error for the 1785 edition)
No copy known mp. 44936

B6312 MARTIN'S CIRCULATING LIBRARY
Catalogue of Martin's Circulating Library, at No. 45, Main-Street, Boston. [Boston] Edmund Freeman, 1786.
16 p.
RPJCB mp. 44915

B6313 MARYLAND. HOUSE OF DELEGATES
An address of the House of delegates . . . to their constituents. [Annapolis, F. Green, 1786]
[3] p. 42 cm. caption title
Wheeler 406
DLC mp. 44916

B6314 MARYLAND. HOUSE OF DELEGATES
By the House of delegates, January 6, 1786. Ordered, that the memorial of Henry Harford . . . be published . . . and that the printer strike two hundred copies . . . [Annapolis, F. Green, 1786]
5 p. 33 cm.
Wheeler 407
MdHi mp. 44917

B6315 MARYLAND. LAWS
Several acts of the General assembly . . . respecting Saint John's College. Annapolis, Frederick Green [1786]
35 p. 16.5 cm.
New York Public 848; Wheeler 410
DLC; DHEW; MdAS; MdHi; NN mp. 44918

B6316 MARYLAND GAZETTE
Verses of the printer's boy . . . January 1, 1786 . . . [Baltimore, James Hayes, 1786]
broadside 33 X 20.5 cm.
New York Public 849; Wheeler 416
NN mp. 45008

B6317 MASSACHUSETTS. GOVERNOR, 1785–1787
Commonwealth of Massachusetts. Boston, November 25, 1786. The Commander in Chief has received information, That insurgents . . . obstruct the course of law . . . [Boston, 1786]
broadside 33 X 20 cm.
MHi mp. 44919

B6318 MASSACHUSETTS. GOVERNOR, 1785–1787
Commonwealth of Massachusetts. By His Excellency James Bowdoin . . . Public orders respecting the militia . . . August 14, 1786. [Boston, 1786]
broadside
Ford 2451
MB mp. 44920

B6319 MASSACHUSETTS. LAWS
Commonwealth of Massachusetts. In Senate, March 24, 1786. Whereas by a law . . . In the House . . . March 24th, 1786. Read and concurred . . . [Boston, Adams and Nourse, 1786]
broadside 37 X 23 cm.
DLC; MHi; MWA mp. 44921

B6320 MASSACHUSETTS. MILITIA
General orders for the second division . . . [Dec. 1, 1786] . . . Newbury-Port, John Mycall [1786]
broadside 41.5 X 27 cm.
Ford 2452; New York Public 854
MHi. Photostats: DLC; NN mp. 44922

B6321 MASTER, LEGH
To the worthy electors of Frederick-County. Gentlemen, I beg leave to offer myself as a candidate . . . Legh Master. Legh-Furnace, Pipe-Creek, Sept. 22, 1786. Frederick-Town, Matthias Bartgis [1786]
broadside 22 X 20.5 cm.
Wheeler 418
G. R. Geahr, Westminster, Md. Photostat: MdHi
mp. 44923

B6322 METEOROLOGICAL observations made at Springmill, 13 miles N N W. of Philadelphia . . . November, 1786 . . . [Philadelphia? 1786]
broadside 21.5 X 22 cm.
Sealock 66; cf. Evans 21960
PHi mp. 44924

B6323 METHODIST EPISCOPAL CHURCH
A pocket hymn book, designed as a constant companion for the pious . . . Fifth edition. New-York, W. Ross, 1786.
224, [8] p. 14 cm.
MWA; MdBP mp. 44949

B6324 [A NEW and valuable collection of religious poems, and devout productions. ⟨Never before published in a pamphlet⟩ Bennington, Haswell & Russell, 1786]

Advertised in the *Vermont Gazette*, Dec. 18, 1786, as "This day published, and now ready for sale, at this office."
McCorison 117
No copy known mp. 44925

B6325 THE New-England primer, improved . . . Norwich, J. Trumbull, 1786.

[64] p. sm. 16mo
Huntington 523
CSmH mp. 44926

B6326 NEW HAMPSHIRE. HOUSE OF REPRESENTATIVES
State of New-Hampshire. A journal of the proceedings of the . . . House of Representatives . . . at their session, began . . . the nineteenth day of October, A.D. one thousand seven hundred and eighty-five . . . [Colophon] [Portsmouth] R. Gerrish [1786?]
p. 55–97. 30 cm. caption title
New York Public 823; Whittemore 400
MWA; NN; NhD; NhHi mp. 44927

B6327 NEW HAMPSHIRE. TREASURER
Treasury-office, state of New-Hampshire: John Taylor Gilman, treasurer . . . Portsmouth, John Melcher, 1786.
broadside 41.5 X 33.5 cm.
Tax warrant for March 1786
Whittemore 406
NhD; NhHi mp. 44928

B6328 NEW HAMPSHIRE. TREASURER
Treasury-office, state of New-Hampshire, John Taylor Gilman, treasurer . . . Exeter, Lamson and Ranlet [1786]
broadside 32 X 19 cm.
Tax warrant for Sept. 1786
Whittemore 407
NhD; NhHi mp. 44929

B6329 [THE New-Haven sheet almanack for 1787. New-Haven, Meigs & Dana, 1786]
broadside
Advertised in the *New-Haven Gazette*, Jan. 12, 1787, as "The New-Haven Sheet Almanack for 1787 to be sold at this Office."
Probably by Nehemiah Strong
Bates: Connecticut almanacs p. 141
No copy known mp. 44930

B6330 A NEW primer, or little boy and girls spelling-book . . . Springfield, [Mass.] Printed . . . for the author [1786?]
1 leaf, [78] p.
MWA mp. 44931

B6331 NEW sentiments, different from any yet published . . . By Adelos . . . Providence, Bennett Wheeler, 1786.
64 p. 22 cm.
The "Appendix" occupies p. 63–64
Alden 1033; Winship p. 50; cf. Evans 19452 (68 p.)
CtY; MBAt; MWA; NHi; NN; RHi; RPB; RPJCB. Brit. Mus. mp. 44932

B6332 A NEW set of geographical cards, for the agreeable improvement of gentlemen . . . [Philadelphia, T. Dobson, 1786]
63 cards 8 X 6 cm.
Advertised in the *Pennsylvania Gazette* of July 25, 1786
DLC mp. 44933

B6333 NEW set of round hand writing copies: Engrav'd, Printed and Sold by Beach & Sanford . . . Hartford. 1786.
8 leaves. 7 X 21 cm.
Engraved throughout
cf. Nash, R. *American writing masters and copybooks* (Boston, 1959) p. 50–51
ICN

B6334 NEW YORK (CITY)
The citizens of New-York are informed . . . Monday, March 27, 1786. [New York, 1786]
broadside 17.5 X 21 cm.
DLC mp. 44934

B6335 NEW YORK. COMMISSIONERS OF FORFEITURE
By the Commissioners of Forfeiture, for the Eastern District . . . the following lands . . . forfeited . . . will be sold at public vendue . . . Albany, Commissioner's Office, July 27, 1786. [Albany, 1786]
broadside 36.5 X 19 cm.
NHi mp. 44935

B6336 NEW-YORK PACKET
Anniversary address of the printers carriers of the *New-York Packet*. For the year 1786. [New York, 1786]
broadside
1st line: All hail! cry we heralds . . .
DLC mp. 44846

B6337 NICHOLS, JAMES, 1748–1824
A sermon, delivered at Manchester . . . the 27th of December 1785 . . . Bennington, Haswell & Russell, 1786.
21 p. 20.5 cm.
Signatured to Evans 19450
DLC; MBFM; MiU-C mp. 44938

B6338 NORTH CAROLINA. COMPTROLLER
Abstract of the army accounts of the North-Carolina line, settled by the commissioners at Halifax [Sept. 1, 1784–Feb. 1, 1785]; and at Warrenton in the year 1786 . . . J. Craven, Comptroller. [n.p., 1786?]
224 p. 22.5 cm. caption title
McMurtrie: North Carolina 122
NcU (2 copies, one lacking p. 1–4, and 223–224) mp. 44939

B6339 ORDER of Procession, for November 4, 1786 . . . Philadelphia, Eleazer Oswald [1786]
broadside 26.5 X 19 cm.
PHi mp. 44914

B6340 A PACK of cards changed into a compleat almanac and prayer-book . . . Boston, Printing-Office in Marlborough-Street [1786?]
4 leaves. 8vo
Rosenbach-Ch 110
A. S. W. Rosenbach (1933) mp. 44940

B6341 PEALE, CHARLES WILLSON, 1741–1827
A descriptive catalogue of Mr. Peale's exhibition of perspective views . . . Tickets . . . may be had at Messrs. Charles and James Peale's in Lombard-Street; Messrs. Dunlap and Claypoole, and of Mr. Francis Bailey, printers, in Market-Street . . . [Philadelphia, 1786]
broadside 31 X 20 cm.
MHi; PPAmP mp. 44941

B6342 PENNSYLVANIA
I do certify, that of hath voluntarily taken . . . the of allegiance . . . as directed by an act . . . passed the fourth day of March . . . 1786. Witness my hand and seal, the day of . . . 178 [Philadelphia] Francis Bailey, Printer [1786?]
broadside 21.5 X 16 cm.
Repeated on lower half of paper on opposite side
Sealock 70
PHi

B6343 PENNSYLVANIA. CONSTITUTION
The constitution of the commonwealth . . . Philadelphia, Daniel Humphreys, 1786.
16 p. 8vo
Verso of t.p. bears resolution of General Assembly
Huntington 524; cf. Evans 19883 (verso of t.p. blank)
CSmH

B6344 PENNSYLVANIA. GENERAL ASSEMBLY
In General Assembly, December 26th, 1785. Resolved, That all officers . . . intitled to salary . . . do make true return . . . Philadelphia, M. Carey and Co., 1786.
broadside 4to
PPL mp. 44946

B6345 PENNSYLVANIA. GENERAL ASSEMBLY
Minutes of the first session of the eleventh General Assembly . . . [Oct. 23, 1786–Dec. 30, 1786] . . . [Philadelphia, Hall and Sellers, 1786]
114 p. 33 cm.
DLC; NN; PPL mp. 44947

B6346 PENNSYLVANIA. LAWS
. . . Bill entitled, An act for incorporating the city of Philadelphia and for other purposes therein mentioned . . . [Philadelphia, T. Bradford, 1786]
14 p. fol.
Dated: Thursday, April 6, 1786
PPAmP mp. 44945

B6347 PENNSYLVANIA. PAYMASTER
State of the accounts of John M. Nesbitt, Esquire, late paymaster of the land and naval forces of Pennsylvania . . . Philadelphia, Robert Aitken, 1786.
138 p. 22 cm.
Sealock 74
PHi mp. 44948

B6348 PHILADELPHIA
Philadelphia, ss. Whereas collector of the taxes in . . . has made return to me, that . . . has been delinquent in paying the sum of his assessment in the funding tax of the year 1785 . . . [Philadelphia, 1786]
broadside 16.5 X 20 cm.
DLC

B6349 POOL,
Mr. Pool, the first American that ever exhibited . . . feats of horsemanship on the Continent, intends performing on Saturday afternoon next . . . Providence, August 23, 1786. Providence, John Carter [1786]
broadside 33.5 X 20.5 cm.
Alden 1047; Winship Addenda p. 89
RHi. Photostats: MHi; NN mp. 44950

B6350 POOR Robin's almanack, for the year . . . 1787 . . . Frederick-Town, Printed and sold by Matthias Bartgis [1786]
[32] p. 16 cm.
Advertised as published Nov. 29, 1786
Drake 2207; Wheeler 419
NjP mp. 44951

B6351 PORTLAND, ME. CONVENTION, 1786
Proceedings of the convention, held at Portland, September 6, 1786, at a convention of delegates from a number of towns and plantations, in the three counties of York, Cumberland and Lincoln . . . for . . . considering the grievances . . . [Portland? 1786]
broadside 43 X 34 cm.
Ford 2456
MHi mp. 44952

B6352 PRESBYTERIAN CHURCH IN THE U.S.A. PRESBYTERY OF PENNSYLVANIA
Formula of questions, to be put to elders at their ordination; agreed to at Pequea, April 13, 1785, by the Associate presbytery . . . [Philadelphia? Young, Stewart and M'Culloch? 1786?]
4 p. 16.5 cm. caption title
MiU-C mp. 44953

B6353 A PRETTY New-Year's gift . . . By Solomon Sobersides . . . Worcester, Printed by Isaiah Thomas, and sold at his book store. Sold also by E. Battelle, Boston, 1786.
152, [4] p. illus. 10.5 cm.
MWA; NjP mp. 44967

B6354 PRINTING-OFFICE in Newbury-port . . . March 22d, 1786. Proposals, for publishing A complete system of arithmetic . . . by Nicholas Pike . . . [Newburyport, 1786]
broadside 39 X 39 cm.
DLC mp. 44954

B6355 PROTESTANT EPISCOPAL CHURCH IN THE U.S.A. VIRGINIA (DIOCESE)
Journal of a convention . . . begun . . . in . . . Richmond . . . the twenty fourth of May, 1786. Richmond, Thomas Nicolson [1786]
16 p. 22 cm.
New York Public 851
NN mp. 44955

B6356 READ, DANIEL, 1757-1836
The American singing book; or A new and easy guide to the art of psalmody . . . Composed by Daniel Read . . . The second edition, corrected. New-Haven, Printed for and sold by the author, 1786.
72 p., 1 l. 11.5 X 18.5 cm.
Pages 25-72 printed from engraved plates
CtHT-W; MB (imperfect) mp. 44957

B6357 RHODE ISLAND. ELECTION PROX.
To relieve the distressed. His Excellency John Collins, Esq; Governor. The honorable Daniel Owen, Esq; Deputy-Governor . . . [Providence? 1786]
broadside 20 X 13 cm.
Alden 1050; Chapin Proxies 38
RHi; RNHi; RPB. Henry R. Drowne mp. 44958

B6358 RHODE ISLAND. GENERAL ASSEMBLY
Newport, (Rhode-Island) October 9, 1786 . . . The following draught of an act . . . My fellow-citizens . . . A well-wisher to the state. [Newport] Southwick and Barber [1786]
broadside 34 X 20 cm.
Alden 1051; Winship p. 49
RHi; RNHi. Photostats: MWA; NN mp. 44937

B6359 RHODE ISLAND. LAWS
An act to stimulate and give efficacy to the paper bills . . . October session, A.D. 1786 . . . Providence, Bennett Wheeler [1786]
broadside 38.5 X 18 cm.
Alden 1057; Winship p. 50
DLC; MWA; R; RHi; RNHi mp. 44959

B6360 RHODE ISLAND. LAWS
An act for granting . . . a tax of twenty thousand pounds . . . [Providence, B. Wheeler, 1786]
broadside 34.5 X 20 cm.
Bill submitted by Wheeler, dated July 20, 1786
Alden 1055; Winship p. 50; Winship Addenda p. 94
R. André de Coppet. Photostat: MWA mp. 44960

B6361 RHODE ISLAND. LAWS
[State of Rhode-Island and Providence Plantations. In General assembly, May session, A.D. 1786. An act for emitting one hundred thousand pounds . . . Providence, B. Wheeler, 1786]
[broadside?]
Bill submitted by Wheeler, dated May 11, 1786
Alden 1054; Winship Addenda p. 89
R (not found); title conjectured mp. 44961

B6362 ROWE, ELIZABETH (SINGER) 1674-1737
Friendship in death . . . New-York, Robert Hodge, 1786.
[iii]-xiv, [2], [17]-264 p. 17 cm.
MWA mp. 44962

B6363 RUSH, BENJAMIN, 1745-1813
An enquiry into the effects of spirituous liquors upon the human body . . . Philadelphia, Thomas Bradford [1786]
11 p. 17 cm.
Austin 1636; Sealock 79; cf. Evans 20690
DNLM mp. 44963

B6364 [RUSSELL, EZEKIEL]
. . . [torn] Elegy, etc. Fair Daughters of America, and eke of Britain's Isle . . . [Boston, E. Russell, 1786?]
broadside 30 X 22 cm.
Authorship and imprint assigned by MWA
Concerns Elizabeth Wilson, who murdered her two children
MWA mp. 44964

B6365 SCOTCH PRESBYTERIAN CHURCH, PHILADELPHIA
To the representatives of the freemen of Pennsylvania, in General Assembly met. The petition of Peter January, John Purdon, Robert Aitken . . . members . . . the Scotch Presbyterian Church in Philadelphia . . . [at end] February 22, 1786. [Philadelphia, Robert Aitken? 1786]
broadside
Adams: Pennsylvania 42
PU

B6366 [A SHORT compendium of English grammer. Collected from a variety of authors . . . Bennington, Haswell & Russell, 1786]

Advertised in the *Vermont Gazette*, Feb. 6, 1786
McCorison 120
No copy known mp. 44966

B6367 SOCIETY OF THE CINCINNATI
In the Society of the Cincinnati, established in . . . South-Carolina: additional rules . . . ratified the 4th day of July, 1786 . . . Charleston, Bowen, Vandle, and Andrews [1786]
broadside 34 X 18.5 cm.
DLC mp. 44968

B6368 SOCIETY OF THE FRIENDLY SONS OF ST. PATRICK
Rules to be observed by the Society . . . in the State of New-York. New-York, Hugh Gaine, 1786.
8 p. 21.5 cm.
New York Public 853; Sabin 86145
NN mp. 44969

B6369 SOUTH CAROLINA. COMMISSIONERS OF FORFEITED ESTATES
Advertisement. Will be sold at public auction . . . the 1st day of November next . . . valuable lands . . and a few Negroes . . . Robert Dewar, Clerk. Charleston, September, 1st, 1786. [Charleston] Childs, Haswell, & M'Iver [1786]
broadside 42 X 25.5 cm.
Sc-Ar

B6370 SOUTH CAROLINA. GENERAL ASSEMBLY. COMMITTEE OF WAYS AND MEANS
Second report . . . [Charleston, 1786]
[3] p. 30.5 cm. caption title
Dated at end: February 15, 1786
Sabin 87498
DLC mp. 44970

B6371 THE Southern States ephemeris: or, the North and South-Carolina, and Georgia almanac for . . . 1787 . . . Charleston, Bowen and Co.; Burd and Co. [1786]
[44] p.
Drake 13141; not used for Evans 20001 (microprint ed.)
Vi

B6372 STATE of New-Hampshire, in the year . . . One Thousand Seven Hundred and Eighty-four . . . [n.p., ca. 1786]
16 p. caption title
A collection of laws passed by each of the 13 colonies to enable Congress to lay import duties
RPJCB mp. 44971

B6373 [STEBBINS, JONATHAN]
An elegy on the death of Mrs. Margaret Stebbins, who died June 16, 1744, in her 29th year . . . Springfield, Stebbins and Russell, MDCLXXXVI [i.e. 1786]
8 p. 20 cm.
CtHi (title-leaf lacking); MWA; NHi mp. 44972

B6374 THOMAS, ISAIAH, 1749-1831
To the customers for Thomas's *Massachusetts Spy*. Kind patrons . . . Worcester, April 3d, 1786 . . . [Worcester, Isaiah Thomas, 1786]
broadside 33 X 21.5 cm.
DLC; MHi mp. 44975

B6375 . . . THOMAS'S Massachusetts, Connecticut . . . almanack . . . for the year . . . 1787 . . . Worcester, Isaiah Thomas [1786]
[48] p. 19 cm.
By Ezra Gleason
At head of title: Second edition
Nichols p. 67; Nichols: Isaiah Thomas 133
DLC; NhD ([42] p.; t.p. wanting) mp. 45021

B6376 THOUGHTS on general safety; addressed to the youth and others . . . especially the inhabitants of Maryland, Printed in Baltimore, 1786 . . . [Baltimore? 1786?]
4 p. 17 cm. caption title
RPJCB mp. 44977

B6377 THOUGHTS on general safety. Addressed to the youth and others . . . By a lover of his country and a friend to all . . . Baltimore, William Goddard [1786]
broadside 33 X 19 cm.
Wheeler 420
MdBE mp. 44976

B6378 TO the honourable the members of the Senate . . . Justice and humanity call the attention . . . Baltimore-town, February 22, 1786. [Baltimore, W. Goddard, 1786]

broadside 23 X 19.5 cm.
Wheeler 421
MdHi mp. 44978

B6379 TO the public. Albany, Charles R. Webster [1786]
16 p. 15.5 cm. caption title
Imprint at head of title
Signed at end: A Republican, and dated: October 7, 1786
Concerns the need for Federal revenue
McMurtrie: Albany 23a
MB (trimmed) mp. 44979

B6380 TO the voters of Ann-Arundel County. On Monday, the second day of next month . . . A friend to paper money. Elk-Ridge, September 23, 1786. [Annapolis, F. Green, 1786]
broadside ([2] p.) 34.5 X 21.5 cm.
Wheeler 422
MdHi mp. 44980

B6381 TO the worthy inhabitants of Baltimore-Town. At this juncture . . . An independent mechanick. Baltimore, September 2, 1786. [Baltimore, William Goddard, 1786]
broadside 30 X 20.5 cm.
Wheeler 401
MdBE mp. 44981

B6382 TOM Bolin: together with Collin and Phebe. A couple of excellent new songs; with good tunes . . . [Boston] Sold next Liberty Pole, 1786.
broadside 34 X 20 cm.
Ford 2457
MWA (imperfect) mp. 44982

B6383 THE town and country almanack, for the year . . . 1787 . . . By Abraham Weatherwise . . . Boston, John W. Folsom [1786]
[24] p. sm. 4to
Drake 3385; Huntington 529
CLU; CSmH; InU (imperfect); MHi; MWA (poor); NHi; NhD; NjR; OMC (imperfect) mp. 45017

B6384 TRINITY CHURCH, BOSTON
[The Parker Psalter. A selection of Psalms and hymns, compiled by Samuel Parker for the use of Trinity Church. Boston, B. Edes, 1786]
[112] p. 18 cm.
Published without t.p.
Benton, J. H. *The Book of Common Prayer.* 2d ed. (Boston, Priv. print. 1914) no. 512
MB mp. 44859

B6385 THE true policy of New-Jersey defined: or, Our great strength led to exertion, in the improvement of agriculture . . . By a Fellow Citizen. Elizabeth-Town: Printed for the author, and sold by Shepard Kollock, at the White House. M.DCC.LXXXVI.
40 p. 18 cm.
NjR

B6386 TSCHERNING, VALERIUS
Catechismus, oder kurzer unterricht . . . mitgetheilt von Valerius Tscherning . . . Philadelphia, C. Ludw. Baisch, 1786.
8 p.l., 392 p. 16 cm.
DLC mp. 44983

B6387 UNITED FIRE SOCIETY, PROVIDENCE, R. I.
The constitution of the United fire society, formed in Providence, March 2d, 1786 . . . [Providence] Bennett Wheeler [1786]
broadside 40 X 34 cm.
Alden 1049; Winship p. 50
MWA; RHi mp. 44956

B6388 U. S. BOARD OF TREASURY
The Board of treasury, to whom it was referred to revise the system . . . [Philadelphia, J. Dunlap, 1786]
broadside 34 X 20 cm.
Dated at end: January 12, 1786
Ford: Bibliographical notes . . . 512
DLC; MWA mp. 44984

B6389 U. S. BOARD OF TREASURY
Estimate of the annual expenditure of the civil departments . . . [Philadelphia, J. Dunlap, 1786]
13 p. 31 cm. caption title
Dated at end: February 20, 1786
Ford: Bibliographical notes . . . 517
DLC mp. 44985

B6390 U. S. CONTINENTAL CONGRESS, 1785
Whereas doubts have arose with some of the commissioners . . . whether the resolution of the 3d of June, 1784 . . . [Philadelphia, J. Dunlap, 1786]
broadside 36 X 21 cm.
Monroe's motion on accounts of Dec. 30, 1785
Ford: Bibliographical notes . . . 509
DLC; MHi mp. 44986

B6391 U. S. CONTINENTAL CONGRESS, 1786
[Address from the United States in Congress assembled to the legislatures of several states . . . Philadelphia, John Dunlap, 1786]

60 copies printed, probably between August 31 and September 4
Not Evans 20039
Ford: Bibliographical notes . . . 553
No copy known mp. 44987

B6392 U. S. CONTINENTAL CONGRESS, 1786
By the United States in Congress assembled. October 10, 1786. The committee consisting of Mr. Pettit, Mr. Lee, Mr. Pinckney, Mr. Henry and Mr. Smith, to whom was referred the letter from the War Office . . . [Philadelphia, 1786]
broadside 28 X 19 cm.
PHi mp. 44988

B6393 U. S. CONTINENTAL CONGRESS, 1786
By the United States in Congress assembled. Wednesday, May 31, 1786. [New York, 1786]
8 p.
Articles of war and courts-martial
RPJCB mp. 44989

B6394 U. S. CONTINENTAL CONGRESS, 1786
The committee consisting of Mr. Johnson, Mr. Pinckney, and Mr. Pettit, to whom was referred a motion of Mr. Pinckney: Report . . . [Philadelphia, J. Dunlap, 1786]
broadside 33 X 20.5 cm.
Ford: Bibliographical notes . . . 551
DLC; DNA mp. 44990

B6395 U. S. CONTINENTAL CONGRESS, 1786
The committee consisting of Mr. King, Mr. Johnson . . . to whom was referred an act . . . of New-York . . . [Philadelphia, J. Dunlap, 1786]
broadside 43 X 27 cm.
Ford: Bibliographical notes . . . 539
DLC mp. 44991

B6396 U. S. CONTINENTAL CONGRESS, 1786
The Committee consisting of Mr. Pinckney, Mr. King, Mr. Johnson, Mr. Grayson and Mr. Hindman, to whom were referred several memorials and petitions from persons claiming vessels in the Courts of Admiralty . . . [Philadelphia, John Dunlap, 1786]
broadside 32 X 18.5 cm.
An edition of 60 copies
Ford: Bibliographical notes . . . 534
DLC mp. 44992

B6397 U. S. CONTINENTAL CONGRESS, 1786
The committee, to whom a motion of Mr. Dane was referred for considering . . . [Philadelphia, J. Dunlap, 1786]
[2] p. 43 X 27.5 cm.
Ford: Bibliographical notes . . . 532
DLC mp. 44993

B6398 U. S. CONTINENTAL CONGRESS, 1786
The committee to whom was referred the letter of Governor Henry, report . . . [Philadelphia, J. Dunlap, 1786]
broadside 32.5 X 20.5 cm.
Ford: Bibliographical notes . . . 536
DLC (2 copies); MHi mp. 44994

B6399 U. S. CONTINENTAL CONGRESS, 1786
The grand committee, consisting of to whom were . . . referred a motion of Mr. Monroe, respecting the cessions . . . of western lands . . . report . . . [Philadelphia, J. Dunlap, 1786]
broadside 33 X 20.5 cm.
Ford: Bibliographical notes . . . 524
DLC; MHi; MiU-C mp. 44995

B6400 U. S. CONTINENTAL CONGRESS, 1786
The grand committee, consisting of Mr. Livermore, Mr. Dane . . . appointed to report such amendments . . . and such resolutions . . . [Philadelphia, J. Dunlap, 1886]
[2] p. 42.5 X 27 cm.
Ford: Bibliographical notes . . . 549
DLC; MHi mp. 44996

B6401 U. S. CONTINENTAL CONGRESS, 1786
The grand committee, to whom were referred a motion of Mr. Monroe, upon the subject . . . [Philadelphia, J. Dunlap, 1786]
broadside 33 X 20.5 cm.
Ford: Bibliographical notes . . . 523
DLC; MiU-C mp. 44997

B6402 U. S. CONTINENTAL CONGRESS, 1786
Impressed with a sense of the sacred trust . . . the United States in Congress assembled, have . . . pointed out the dangerous situation of this nation, for want of funds . . . [Philadelphia, J. Dunlap, 1786]
broadside 42.5 X 27 cm.
Ford: Bibliographical notes . . . 563
DLC (4 copies); MHi; MiU-C mp. 44998

B6403 U. S. CONTINENTAL CONGRESS, 1786
An ordinance for establishing a board to liquidate . . . [Philadelphia, J. Dunlap, 1786]
broadside 32.5 X 20 cm.
Ford: Bibliographical notes . . . 560; cf. Evans 20072 (Ford 561)
DLC (3 copies on one sheet); MHi mp. 45001

B6404 U. S. CONTINENTAL CONGRESS, 1786
[Resolved, that the Court of Appeals . . . Philadelphia, John Dunlap, 1786]
Concerns the case of the sloop Chester
Ordered published July 24; 50 copies printed
Ford: Bibliographical notes . . . 545
No copy known mp. 44999

B6405 U. S. PAY DEPT.
Register of the certificates, issued by John Pierce . . . Paymaster-general . . . Volume the First. [-Fourth.] New York, Francis Childs, 1786.
4 v. (252, 231, 300, 147 p.) 20 X 32 cm.
93,843 entries, from July 11, 1783 to Mar. 2, 1786
DLC (2 copies)

B6406 U. S. TREATIES, ETC.
Articles of a treaty concluded at Hopewell, on the Keowee . . . [Jan. 10, 1786] between . . . the United States . . . and . . . the Chickasaw Nation . . . [Philadelphia, J. Dunlap, 1786]
[4] p. 31.5 cm.
An edition of 100 copies
Ford: Bibliographical notes . . . 526; Huntington 527
CSmH: DNA mp. 45003

B6407 U. S. TREATIES, ETC.
Articles of a treaty, concluded at the mouth of the Great Miami . . . [Jan. 31, 1786] between the . . . United States . . . and the . . . Shawnoe Nations . . . [Philadelphia, J. Dunlap, 1786]
[4] p. 32 cm.
An edition of 100 copies
Two treaties: the second, Nov. 28, 1785, with the Cherokees
Ford: Bibliographical notes . . . 529; Huntington 528; cf. Evans 20041
CSmH; DLC; MHi; Sc-Ar mp. 45004

B6408 THE United States almanack for the year . . . 1787 . . . By Eben. W. Judd . . . Elizabeth Town, Shepard Kollock [1786]
[32] p. 16.5 cm.
Drake 38; Morsch 38
CLU; DLC; MWA; MoU; NHi; NjR mp. 44909

B6409 THE United States almanack for the year . . . 1787 . . . By Eben. W. Judd . . . New-York, Printed for Robert Hodge [1786]
[32] p. 15.5 cm.
Drake 5943; New York Public 845
NN (imperfect): OMC mp. 44910

B6410 THE United States almanack for the year . . . 1787 . . . By Eben. W. Judd . . . New-York, Shepard Kollock, No. 32 Maiden Lane [1786]
[32] p. 16.5 cm.
Drake 5944; Wall p. 25
WHi mp. 44911

B6411 VERMONT. GOVERNOR, 1778-1789
[Fast day proclamation. Bennington, Haswell & Russell, 1786]
broadside?
Printer's bill dated Apr. 10, 1786
McCorison 125
No copy known mp. 45005

B6412 VERMONT. LAWS
Acts and laws, of the State of Vermont. Passed at the session of the General Assembly, holden in Rutland, in October, 1786. Bennington, Haswell & Russell, 1786.
[12] p. 23 cm.
Cooley 72; Sabin 99102; New York Public 855

MHi. Photostats: CSmH; MWA; NN; NhD; RPJCB; VtU. Mrs. Geo. M. Powers, Burlington (1963)
mp. 45006

B6413 VERMONT. LAWS
Acts and laws, passed by the General Assembly of the State of Vermont, at their stated session, at Rutland, in October 1786. [Windsor, Hough and Spooner, 1786]
20 p. 26 cm.
McCorison 126; New York Public 856; Sabin 99101
DLC; Vt. (P. 1-4, 19-20 photostat): VtU-W. Photostats: CSmH; MHi; MWA; NN mp. 45007

B6414 VIRGINIA. COUNCIL
In Council, February 20, 1786. Gentlemen, I am under the necessity . . . [Richmond, 1786]
broadside 28 X 21 cm.
Signed in manuscript: P. Henry
DLC mp. 45010

B6415 VIRGINIA. COUNCIL
In Council, December 27, 1786. The Board taking into consideration the . . . "act to . . . reduce into one act the several laws for . . . the militia . . ." advise . . . Archibald Blair, C.C. In Council, December 29, 1786. Sir, I seriously intreat [sic] you . . . [Richmond, 1786?]
broadside 29.5 X 18 cm.
WHi mp. 45009

B6416 VIRGINIA. COUNCIL
To prevent impositions, the board advise . . . [Richmond, 1786]
broadside 30 X 19.5 cm.
In ms.: In Council Dec. 4, 1786
DLC mp. 45011

B6417 VIRGINIA. GENERAL ASSEMBLY
Virginia. In the House of Delegates, January 13, 1786. Resolved, that the damages on foreign bills of exchange . . . ought to be the same in this state and . . . Maryland . . . John Beckley, C.H.D., teste. Agreed to by the Senate, H. Brooke, C.S. [Richmond, Dixon and Holt, 1786]
broadside 25 X 21 cm.
MB; MWA; RPJCB mp. 45012

B6418 VIRGINIA. LAWS
An act concerning the erection of the District of Kentucky into an independent state . . . Jan. 6, 1786. Passed the House of delegates . . . [Richmond? 1786?]
broadside 40.5 X 28 cm.
MiU-C (facsim.); N. T. W. Streeter (1964) mp. 45013

B6419 VIRGINIA. LAWS
An act to enable the citizens . . . to discharge certain taxes . . . [Richmond, 1786]
broadside 22 X 18.5 cm.
For date see Virginia House *Journal* for Nov. 16, 1786
DLC mp. 45014

B6420 VIRGINIA. TREASURY OFFICE
Revenue taxes . . . J. Ambler. Treasury-Office, October 30, 1786. [Richmond, 1786]
[2] p. 35.5 X 22 cm. caption title
Tabular accounts of tax receipts for 1782-1785
DLC mp. 45015

B6421 THE Virginia almanack for the year . . . 1787 . . . By Robert Andrews . . . Richmond, Dixon & Holt [1786]
[24] p. 12 cm.
Bear 63; Drake 13805; Huntington 519
CSmH; ViU mp. 44844

B6422 THE Virginia almanack for the year . . . 1787 . . . By Robert Andrews . . . Richmond, Thomas Nicolson [1786]
[24] p. 14 cm.
Bear 65; Drake 13806
MWA; ViW ([20] p.); ViWC mp. 44845

B6423 WATTS, ISAAC, 1674-1748
Hymns and spiritual songs . . . The first Worcester edition . . . Worcester, Isaiah Thomas, 1786.
[2], 123-224, [1] p. 18 cm.
Second part of Evans 19509, with t.p. added
MWA mp. 45016

B6424 WEBSTER, NOAH, 1758-1843
A grammatical institute of the English language . . . Part I. Containing a new and accurate standard of pronunciation . . . Boston, Peter Edes [1786?]
138? p. 15 cm.
New York Public 857; Skeel-Carpenter 5
NN (lacks all after p. 134) mp. 45018

B6425 WEBSTER, NOAH, 1758-1843
A grammatical institute of the English language . . . Part III. Containing the necessary rules of reading and speaking . . . The second edition . . . Hartford, Hudson and Goodwin [1786]
188 p. 17 cm.
New York Public 858; Sabin 102357 (note); Skeel-Carpenter 451; cf. Evans 19365
CtHT-W; CtY; DFo; DLC; MH; MNF; MWA; NBLiHi; NN; NjR; RPJCB mp. 45019

B6426 WEBSTER, NOAH, 1758-1843
A syllabus of Mr. Webster's Lectures on the English language and on education . . . New-Haven, June 15, 1786.
broadside 33 X 20 cm.
Sabin 102400; Skeel-Carpenter 737
CtNhHi; CtY. Photostat: NN mp. 45020

B6427 WEBSTER'S Connecticut pocket almanack, for . . . 1787. By Isaac Bickerstaff, Jun. Hartford, Zephaniah Webster [1786]
[32] p. 10.5 cm.
MWA mp. 44854

B6428 WEST, WILLIAM
Scheme of a lottery. Granted . . . at October session, A.D. 1785, to William West . . . for the disposal of certain lands and stock . . . 7th day of January, 1786 . . . [Providence? 1786]
broadside 36 X 18 cm.
Alden 1060
RHi (slightly mutilated). Photostat: MWA mp. 45022

B6429 WINN, RICHARD
Pursuant to an ordinance of Congress of the 7th of August, 1786, I give this public notice, that none but citizens . . . will be permitted . . . to reside among or trade with any Indian nation whatever, southward of the River Ohio . . . Richard Winn, Superintendant [sic] Charleston, Markland & M'Iver [1786?]
broadside 26.5 X 21.5 cm.
WHi mp. 45002

B6430 YALE UNIVERSITY
Catalogus recentium in Collegium Yalense admissorum, M.DCC.LXXXVI . . . Novi-Portus: E typis Meigs at Danae [1786]
broadside 24 X 18.5 cm.

Text in two columns
MHi

B6431 YALE UNIVERSITY
Freshman laws . . . New-Haven, Daniel Bowen [1786?]
broadside 36 X 20.5 cm.
New York Public 860
CtY; NN (facsim.) mp. 45023

B6432 YORK ACADEMY
The order for morning and evening prayer, as used in York Academy: to which are added, a collection of Psalms. Philadelphia, Young, Stewart, and M'Culloch, 1786.
23 p. 15.5 cm.
Sealock 82
P mp. 45024

1787

B6433 AN account of the wonderful old hermit's death, and burial. [n.p., 1787?]
broadside
Describes Dr. Samuel Brake's visit to the hermit in 1786
Hamilton 111
NjP mp. 45025

B6434 AN address of the subscribers members of the late House of Representatives of . . . Pennsylvania to their constituents. [Philadelphia, 1787]
3 p. 38 cm. caption title
In ms. at end: Published & sold Oct. 2, 1787
Signed by James M'Calmont [and 15 others]
New York Public 871; Sealock 83?
DLC. Photostats: CSmH; MHi; MWA; NN mp. 45026

B6435 ADGATE, ANDREW, d. 1793
Uranian instructions. Philadelphia, Young and Mc-Culloch, 1787.
12 p. 11 X 23 cm.
ICN (t.p. lacking) mp. 45027

B6436 ALEXANDRIA SOCIETY FOR THE PROMOTION OF USEFUL KNOWLEDGE
Constitution of the Alexandria Society . . . [Alexandria, Hanson and Bond, 1787]
broadside fol.
PPL mp. 45028

B6437 AN almanack, for the year . . . 1788 . . . By Abraham Weatherwise . . . Boston, John W. Folsom [1787]
[32] p. 16.5 cm.
Drake 3391; Nichols p. 68
CLU; DLC; MH; MHi (imperfect); MWA (imperfect); N; NHi; NjP mp. 45199

B6438 AMERICAN MERCURY, HARTFORD
The carrier of the *American Mercruy* presents the following to his customers, wishing them a Happy New-Year . . . Hartford, January 1, 1787. [Hartford, Elisha Babcock, 1787]
broadside 42.5 X 28 cm.
1st line: Some miles above the milky way . . .
MSaE; NHi mp. 45049

B6439 THE American musical magazine. Jan.-Sept. 1787. New-Haven, Published by Amos Doolittle and Daniel Read [1787]
1 v. 25 cm.
cf. Evans 19945 (1786)
ICN (Jan.-Apr.); CtHi (copy 1 38 p.; copy 2 48, [1] p.); MH

B6440 AN das deutsche Publicum, Freunde und Landsleute . . . Lancaster, 1787.

Bausman p. 23
Frank R. Diffenderfer (1916) mp. 45029

B6441 AN astronomical diary, kalendar, or almanack for 1788. By Isaac Bickerstaff. Hartford, Sold by Nathaniel Patten [1787]
[24] p.
Drake 412
CLU

B6442 AN astronomical ephemeris, calendar, or almanack for 1788. By N. Strong. Hartford, Hudson & Goodwin [1787]
[24] p.
Drake 414
MB

B6443 ATTENTION! Awake, my fellow citizens, or ye may soon become the servants of Tories . . . By Hosea . . . [Boston, 1787]
broadside 28.5 X 23 cm.
Huntington 536
CSmH mp. 45031

B6444 AUF den Tod des entschlafenen Vater Mühlenbergs. [Philadelphia? Melchior Steiner? 1787?]
broadside 16 X 20.5 cm.
In verse; probably printed to be sung at Mühlenberg's funeral in 1787
New York Public 861
NN mp. 45032

B6445 BABBITT, CHRISTOPHER
To his Excellency John Hancock, Esquire, Governor of the State of Massachusetts. Being impressed upon the mind, being a beggar . . . I declare unto you rulers . . . going to the French, hiring money . . . enlisting soldiers, and cheating of them with your States notes . . . Christopher Babbitt, of Lanesborough, in the county of Berkshire . . . [n.p., 1787?]
broadside 39.5 X 27 cm.
Babbitt was an insurgent in Shay's Rebellion
MWA

B6446 BEERS, ISAAC
Appendix. To Beers's Catalogue of books. August, 1787. [New Haven, Meigs & Dana, 1787]
7 p.
Trumbull: Supplement 1901
No copy located mp. 45035

B6447 BELKNAP, ABRAHAM
Stop thief! On Thursday night the house of the subscriber was broken open . . . Abraham Belknap. Johnston, May 25, 1787. Providence, Bennett Wheeler [1787]
broadside 24.5 X 18 cm.
Alden 1068; Winship p. 51
RPTP mp. 45036

B6448 BIBLE
Concise history of the Holy Bible . . . [Philadelphia] Printed [by D. Humphreys] for H. Stead, in Philadelphia, 1787.
119, 16 p. illus. 5 cm.
Second title (p. [69]) has: Printed by D. Humphreys
PHi; PP; PPL mp. 45053

B6449 BIBLE. O.T. PSALMS
Doctor Watts's Imitation of the Psalms of David, corrected and enlarged, by Joel Barlow . . . The third edition. [Hartford] Hudson and Goodwin [1787?]
356 p. 16mo
cf. Evans 23188; Trumbull: Supplement 2718
CSmH mp. 45034

B6450 BIBLE. O.T. PSALMS
Psalms carefully suited . . . Philadelphia, Printed and sold by Francis Bailey, 1787.
275 p.
cf. Evans 20230 (which MWA has also)
MWA mp. 45037

B6451 BIBLE. N.T.
The New Testament . . . Pennsylvania: Printed by F. Bailey, J. Steele, and J. Bailey; and sold by F. Bailey, Philadelphia, J. Bailey, Lancaster, and J. Steele, at the printing-office Octorara [1787?]
[298] p. 18 cm.
Steele was in Octorara 1786-1789
PHi mp. 45038

B6452 BIBLE. N.T.
The New Testament . . . Wilmington, James Adams, 1787.
[335] p. 15.5 cm.
Hawkins 21
DeWI mp. 45039

B6453 BIBLE. N.T. APOCRYPHAL BOOKS. EPISTLE OF JESUS CHRIST
A copy of a letter written by . . . Jesus Christ . . . [Middleborough] County of Plymouth, Printed and sold by Nathaniel Coverly, 1787.
8 p. 14.5 cm.
Huntington 533; New York Public 862; cf. Evans 19586
CSmH. Photostat: NN mp. 45055

B6454 BICKERSTAFF'S Boston almanack, or The federal calendar, for . . . 1788 . . . Fourth edition. [Boston, E. Russell, 1787]
[24] p. 18 cm.
Drake 3397; New York Public 863
MWA; NN (imperfect) mp. 45040

B6455 BLAIR, ROBERT, 1699-1746
The grave. A poem . . . To which is added, An elegy, written in a country churchyard. By Mr. Gray. Philadelphia, Printed for Thomas Dobson, 1787.
31, [1] p. 16.5 cm.
Huntington 530
CSmH; MB; PHi; PPAmP; PPL; PU mp. 45041

B6456 THE book of knowledge: treating of the wisdom of the ancients . . . Written by Erra Pater . . . Made English by W. Lilly . . . To which is added, The true form of all sorts of bills . . . Boston, Sold by John W. Folsom, and Benjamin Larkin [1787]
107 p. front., illus. 15.5 cm.
New York Public 868
MWA; NN mp. 45063

B6457 BOSTON, 1787. This is to certify, that a load of hay weighed this day . . . [Boston, 1787]
broadside
Ford 2459
MHi

B6458 BOSTON, THOMAS, 1677-1732
Human nature in its fourfold state . . . A new edition . . . [n.p.] Printed for the booksellers, 1787.
344 p. 20 cm.
MWA mp. 45042

B6459 [BRIGGS, ISAAC]
Dedication. To Messrs. Charles Wharton, Richard Vaux, Samuel Baker, and Arthur Collins. Gentlemen, To you I dedicate these letters . . . [Augusta, John Erdman Smith, 1788]
42 p. 4to
PHi

B6460 BROWN UNIVERSITY
Honoratissimo Jabez Bowen . . . Theses technologicae. Theses metaphysicae. Theses mathematicae . . . Nonis Septembris, A.D., M,DCC,LXXXVII . . . Providentiae, Bennett Wheeler [1787]
broadside 53 a 42 cm.
Alden 1102
NHi. Photostats: MWA; RPB mp. 45044

B6461 [BRYAN, SAMUEL]
Centinel, To the people of Pennsylvania . . . Timoleon. New-York, October 24, 1787. [New York, 1787]
[2] p. 54.5 X 40.5 cm.
New York Public 864
DLC; N; NHi; R. Photostats: MWA; NN mp. 45045

B6462 [BRYAN, SAMUEL]
From the *Independent Gazetteer*, &c. Centinel No. V. To the people of Pennsylvania. Friends, Countrymen, and Fellow-Citizens . . . Centinel. Philadelphia, Nov. 30, 1787. [Philadelphia, Eleazer Oswald, 1787]
broadside 32 X 27.5 cm.
MWA mp. 45046

B6463 [BUCKLAND, JAMES]
A wonderful discovery of a hermit, who lived upwards of 200 years. Printed at Hartford, 1787.
12 p. 16.5 cm.
MWA mp. 45047

B6464 BUCKS CO., PA.
State of the account of Gerardus Wyncoop . . . Bucks County . . . until . . . October 26th, 1786. Philadelphia, Robert Aitken, 1787.
6 p. 21.5 cm.
DLC; NN; PHi mp. 45120

B6465 CAREY, MATHEW, 1760-1839
Sir, Give me leave respectfully to solicit your patronage . . . for the *American Museum* . . . Philadelphia [M. Carey] May 14, 1787.
broadside 24 X 19.5 cm.
Sealock 91
PHi mp. 45048

B6465a CAREY, MATHEW, 1760-1839
Sir, Having been enabled by the patronage . . . solicit your name to . . . subscribers . . . September 7, 1787. [Philadelphia, M. Carey, 1787]
broadside 39 X 16.5 cm.
Information from Charles Hollenbeck
NHi

B6466 CARGILL, WILLIAM
Thirty dollars reward. Stolen out of the store of the subscriber . . . by one Ezra Holbrook, a large quantity of merchandize . . . Dudley, December 30, 1783. [Worcester? 1787?]

broadside 13.5 X 22 cm.
Date altered with pen to read 1787; 1783 typographical error
Huntington 505
CSmH mp. 44655

B6467 CENTINEL
Parks, carrier of the *Centinel*, begs permission to present the generous patrons of that publication the following . . . [Boston, 1787]
broadside
MWA mp. 45119

B6468 CHARLESTON, S. C.
General exports from the port of Charleston . . . from November 1786, to November 1787 . . . [Charleston, 1787]
broadside 37 X 21 cm.
DLC mp. 45050

B6469 [A CHILD'S address to Christ for grace. Bennington, Haswell & Russell, 1787]

Advertised in the *Vermont Gazette*, Mar. 19, 1787
McCorison 129
No copy known mp. 45051

B6470 [CLARKE, SAMUEL] b. 1728
The strange and remarkable Swansey vision: Or a dream, that was dreamed about 44 years ago, which exactly fortells [!] . . . calamities . . . now come to pass . . . Norwich: Printed and sold, 1787.
7 p. 17 cm.
RPJCB

B6471 COLLEY, THOMAS, 1742-1812
A discourse, publicly delivered, on third day morning, the eighth day of the fifth month 1787, at a public meeting of . . . Quakers . . . By Thomas Colley. Carefully taken down in short hand. Philadelphia, Printed and sold by Enoch Story [1787]
28 p. 17.5 cm.
Sealock 92; cf. Evans 21003 (2nd ed.)
NHi; PHi (wanting after p. 24) mp. 45052

B6472 COLUMBIAN HERALD
New-Year's address, of the boys, who carry the *Columbian Herald* . . . January 1, 1787 . . . [Charleston, 1787]
broadside 31 X 14 cm.
NHi

B6473 CONNECTICUT. GENERAL ASSEMBLY
At a General Assembly of the state of Connecticut, holden at New-Haven . . . October . . . 1787. The gentlemen nominated by the votes of the freemen of this state, to stand for election in May next . . . James Hillhouse, Esq. . . . New-Haven, Thomas and Samuel Green [1787]
broadside 35 X 21 cm.
CtHi mp. 45054

B6474 COWPER, WILLIAM, 1731-1800
The task. A poem . . . A new edition. Philadelphia, Printed for Thomas Dobson, 1787.
2 p.l., 186, [2] p. 15.5 cm.
DLC; MWA; PPL; RPJCB mp. 45056

B6475 CRAWFORD, DUGALD
A sermon, preached before the Cape-Fear Union Lodge of . . . Masons . . . Assembled at Fayetteville on December 7, 1786 . . . By the Reverend Dugald Crawford . . . minister at Fayetteville. Fayetteville, Hodge & Blanchard, 1787.
18 p. 17 cm.
McMurtrie: North Carolina 126
NcU mp. 45057

B6476 CUMBERLAND CO., PA.
State of the accounts of the taxes, of Cumberland County. Philadelphia, Robert Aitken, 1787.
47 p. 21.5 cm.
P; PPL; PPiU; RPJCB mp. 45122

B6477 THE curiosities of London, and Westminster described; containing a description of Black Friars Bridge . . . Boston, Printed by Henry G. Jenks, 1787.
9 p. incl. front. 10 cm.
Title page and perhaps frontispiece printed or from copper plate; text probably hand-lettered, stopping in the middle of sentence
MWA

B6478 CURTENIUS, PETER T., AND CO.
New-York Air Furnace. Peter T. Curtenius, and Co. have repaired the New-York Air-Furnace, and have procured the best workmen . . . manufacture of cast-iron . . . New-York, J. M'Lean [1787]
broadside 33 X 21 cm.
Advertised in the *New-York Packet*, Oct. 23, 1787
New York Public 866
NHi; NN (photo.) mp. 45058

B6479 DAUPHIN CO., PA.
State of the accounts of Andrew Forrest . . . Dauphin County . . . till the 26th of September 1786. Philadelphia, Robert Aitken, 1787.
5 p. 21.5 cm.
DLC; NN mp. 45123

B6480 DEFOE, DANIEL, 1659?-1731
The wonderful life, and surprising adventures of . . . Robinson Crusoe . . . Philadelphia, C. Cist, 1787.
[164] p.
Pages lacking at end
Brigham: Robinson Crusoe 7
PHi mp. 45059

B6481 DISADVANTAGES of federalism, upon the new plan. 1. The trade of Boston transferred to Philadelphia; and the Boston tradesmen starving . . . Truth. [Boston, 1787?]
broadside
Ford 2462
MHi mp. 45060

B6482 ELLICOTT, ANDREW, 1754-1820
The right ascension and declination of . . . Bootes adapted to the beginning of the year, 1787 . . . [n.p., 1787?]
broadside nar. fol.
PPAmP mp. 45061

B6482a ELLSWORTH, SAMUEL
There shall be wars . . . [Bennington, Vt.] Printed and sold by Haswell & Russell for the author, in the year M D CCLXXXVII.
10+ p. 17 cm.
Stoddard 85b; cf. Evans 20343 (microprint)
RPJCB (mutilated; all lacking after p. 10)

B6483 ENTERTAINING fables for the instruction of children . . . To which is added, The trial of an ox for

killing a man. Philadelphia, Printed by Young and M'Culloch, 1787.
[3]-28, [2] p. 24°
Mrs. Arthur M. Greenwood, Marlborough, Mass. (1962) mp. 45062

B6484 AN excellent pair of verses, composed on the pious life and death of the late . . . Sarah Thayer, the virtuous consort of the late . . . Ephraim Thayer, of Braintree . . . Now re-published . . . Boston, Printed and sold by E. Russell, 1787.
broadside 31 X 25.5 cm.
MHi; MWA mp. 45064

B6485 EXTRACT from an address to the people . . . [Followed by] A sermon on the slave trade . . . [n.p., 1787]
broadside 39 X 22.5 cm.
DLC. Photostat: MHi mp. 45065

B6486 FATHER Tammany's pocket almanac, for the year 1788 . . . Philadelphia, Printed for W. Young and J. M'Culloch [1787]
[36] p. 11 cm.
PHi mp. 44066

B6487 FONTAINE, JAMES MAURY
A sermon preached by the Rev. James Maury Fountaine, at the funeral of Mrs. Francis Page . . . on the day of February 1787. Richmond, Thomas Nicolson [1787?]
16 p. 21 cm.
ViU mp. 45067

B6488 FREEMAN'S ORACLE
The following verses, on the commencement of the year 1787 are addressed to the customers of the *Freeman's Oracle*, by the lad who carries the same . . . [Exeter, 1787]
broadside 15.5 X 11 cm.
MH

B6489 FREEMASONS. SOUTH CAROLINA. GRAND LODGE
Preamble. Whereas, at a Grand annual communication . . . the following . . . duly elected Grand Officers . . . Circular, Charleston, South-Carolina, June 30th, A.D. 1787 . . . We the Grand Lodge of Ancient York Masons . . . announce to you our formation as such . . . [Charleston, 1787]
broadside 38 X 24.5 cm.
PPFM

B6490 FREEMASONS. SOUTH CAROLINA. LODGE NO. 190
Rules and orders, which are to be . . . kept by the . . . Fraternity of Free and Accepted Masons . . . In order to prevent all feuds . . . the members of our Lodge No. 190 . . . establish the following rules. Charleston, South-Carolina: Printed . . . in the year . . . 5787 [i.e. 1787]
13, [2] p. 19 cm.
NNFM

B6491 FRIENDS, countrymen and fellow-citizens! The present crisis demands . . . A constitutional mechanic. [Philadelphia, 1787]
broadside 56 X 35.5 cm.
DLC; NHi. Photostats: MHi; MWA mp. 45069

B6492 FRIENDS of America, Look at the insolence of Federalists. The St. George's Society . . . have the following toast . . . on Saturday . . . [New York? 1787?]
broadside 31.5 X 20.5 cm.
NHi mp. 45070

B6493 FRIENDS, SOCIETY OF. LONDON YEARLY MEETING
From our yearly-meeting held in London, by adjournments from the 28th day of the fifth month . . . 1787 . . . [Philadelphia, 1787]
2 p. fol.
CSmH mp. 45071

B6494 FRIENDS, SOCIETY OF. NEW ENGLAND YEARLY MEETING
To the General assembly of . . . Rhode-Island. Respectfully sheweth, The religious society of . . . Quakers . . . State of Rhode-Island . . . In General assembly, October session, A.D. 1787. An act to prevent the slave-trade . . . [Providence? J. Carter? 1787]
broadside 30.5 X 19.5 cm.
Alden 1073; Sabin 52604; Evans 20376?
Friends' Library, London. Photostats: MWA; RHi mp. 45072

B6495 GAINE, HUGH, 1726-1807
Catalogue of books and stationary, &c. Sold by Hugh Gaine . . . New-York, Hugh Gaine, 1787.
24 p.
About 480 titles
Brigham: Booksellers, p. 45
MWA mp. 45073

B6496 GEORGIA. LAWS
[Acts of the General Assembly, passed at Augusta in January and February, 1787. Augusta, John E. Smith, 1787]
48 p. A-M^2 caption title
24 acts, the first beginning: "An act for imposing a tax on the inhabitants . . . February 10, 1787."
De Renne p. 240
GU-De mp. 45074

B6497 GESSNER, SALOMON, 1730-1788
The death of Abel . . . The thirteenth edition. Philadelphia, Joseph Crukshank, 1787.
151 p. 15 cm.
MWA mp. 45075

B6498 HAMMON, JUPITER
An address to the Negroes in the state of New York . . . Philadelphia, David Humphreys, 1787.
15, [1] p. 20.5 cm.
Porter 110; Sabin 30085
MH; NHi; NN; PPL mp. 45078

B6499 HART, JOSEPH, 1712-1768
Hymns, &c. composed on various subjects . . . The tenth edition. Elizabeth Town, Shepard Kollock;—Likewise sold by R. Hodge, New-York [1787?]
[4], xx, [4], 231, [3] p. 16 cm.
Morsch 42; New York Public 869
DLC (2 copies); MWA; NN mp. 45079

B6500 HEALY, FRANCIS
The American calculator, or Countinghouse companion . . . By Francis Healy, accomptant . . . New-York, Thomas Greenleaf, 1787.
29 p. 18 cm.
Advertised in Greenleaf's *New-York Journal*, Sept. 6, 1787, as "next Monday will be published."

Huntington 535; New York Public 870; cf. Evans 20922
CSmH; NN mp. 45081

B6501 THE history of little Goody Two-Shoes. Philadelphia, Young and M. Culloch [sic] 1787.
158 p. illus. 12 cm.
Joseph T. Freeman, Philadelphia (1962) mp. 45077

B6502 HOPPIN, BENJAMIN
Lands for sale. Any person inclining to purchase lands in . . . Virginia . . . Terms by applying to Captain Benjamin Hoppin . . . in Providence . . . Providence, July 6, 1787.
broadside 26.5 X 19 cm.
Alden 1076
RHi mp. 45082

B6503 THE house that Jack built . . . The story of Little Red Riding Hood. Boston, Printed and sold by Nath'l Coverly [1787?]
31, [1] p. illus. 10.5 cm.
Dated from ownership inscription in MSaE copy
MSaE mp. 45083

B6504 INDEPENDENT GAZETTEER
Verses on the New Year. January 1, 1787 . . . [Philadelphia, 1787]
broadside
MWA mp. 45189

B6505 JAMES, JOSEPH
Proposals, for printing by subscription . . . an American edition of Barclay's Apology . . . "Meeting for sufferings, 17th day, 5th month, 1787 . . . [Philadelphia, 1787]
broadside 33.5 X 21 cm.
DLC mp. 45084

B6506 JARVES
Jarves, cabinet, chair and clock-case maker, from London, (No. 76) Newbury-Street, Boston: respectfully informs . . . that he makes . . . mahogany furniture . . . [Boston, 1787?]
broadside 8 X 10 cm.
Ford 2496
Photostat: MHi mp. 45085

B6507 JOHN STREET THEATRE, NEW YORK
John Street theatre. By the Old American company. On . . . the 20th of March . . . The Jealous Wife . . . [New York, 1787]
broadside
Reproduced in Ireland, Joseph H. *Records of the New York stage* (New York, 1866), 1:74
No copy traced mp. 45110

B6508 JOHN STREET THEATRE, NEW YORK
New-York, February 17, 1787. Theatre. By the Old American Company . . . The Gamester . . . The Agreeable Surprise . . . [New York, 1787]
broadside 42.5 X 26.5 cm.
DLC mp. 45111

B6509 JOHN STREET THEATRE. NEW YORK
New-York, March 17, 1787. Theatre. By the Old American Company. On Monday evening . . . a comedy, (by Shakespeare,) called, Much Ado about Nothing . . . [New York, H. Gaine? 1787]
broadside
Amer. Art Association cat., Dec. 6-7, 1921, item 214
New York Public 876
NN (reduced facsim.) mp. 45112

B6510 KEASE, JOHN, DEFENDANT
The trial of John Kease, Patrick Kinnon and John Campbell, for burglary and murder . . . At a court of oyer and terminer . . . of New-Jersey . . . Burlington, holden . . . the 18th of September, 1787 . . . Philadelphia, 1787.
24 p. 20.5 cm.
McDade 548
DLC mp. 45086

B6511 THE London cries . . . Philadelphia, Young and M'Culloch, 1787.
[3]-29, [1] p. 10.5 cm.
MWA mp. 45087

B6512 LOUDON'S New-York pocket almanac for . . . 1788. New-York, S. Loudon [1787]
[32] p.
Drake 5951
N

B6513 LUZERNE CO., PA.
Sales of forfeited estates in Pennsylvania . . . Philadelphia, Robert Aitken and Son [1787]
broadside 39 X 23 cm.
Sealock 104
PHi mp. 45088

B6514 MAGAW, SAMUEL, 1740-1812
An address, delivered in the Young Ladies Academy, at Philadelphia, on February 8th, 1787 . . . Philadelphia, Printed for Thomas Dobson, 1787.
15 p. 20 cm.
New York Public 872
MWA; NN; N; PPAmP mp. 45089

B6515 MAGAW, SAMUEL, 1740-1812
A prayer, delivered at the close of the quarterly examination, and after Mr. Swanwick's address . . . October 31, 1787 . . . Philadelphia, Printed for Thomas Dobson, 1787.
6 p. 22 cm.
RPJCB mp. 45090

B6516 MAGAW, SAMUEL, 1740-1812
A prayer, delivered in St. Paul's Church Philadelphia, on Wednesday, 27th December, 1786 . . . before the sermon to the . . . Masons of Pennsylvania. Philadelphia, Eleazer Oswald, 1787.
9, [1] p. 8vo
PPAmP; PPL mp. 45091

B6517 MARTIN'S North-Carolina gazette. Newbern [F. X. Martin] 1787.

Brigham p. 771
DLC (issues for July 11, Aug. 15, Dec. 19, 1787) (facsim.); MHi (facsim.)

B6518 MARYLAND. HOUSE OF DELEGATES
By the House of delegates, December 1, 1787. Ordered, That the printer to this state be directed to print . . . two thousand copies of the proceedings of the federal convention . . . [Baltimore, John Hayes, 1787]
[3] p. 40.5 cm.
Wheeler 432
MdBE mp. 45092

B6519 MARYLAND. HOUSE OF DELEGATES
[Present state of Maryland. By the delegates of the of the people. Annapolis, F. Green, 1787]

1800 copies ordered published Jan. 16, 1787
Brinley 3875; Sabin 45279; Wheeler 436
No copy known mp. 45093

B6520 MARYLAND. SENATE
By the Senate, January 20, 1787. Ordered, That the

printer be directed to print one thousand copies . . . [Annapolis, F. Green, 1787]
3 p. 43 cm. caption title
DLC mp. 45094

B6521 MARYLAND JOURNAL
The New-Year verses, of the flying mercuries . . . who carry the *Maryland Journal* . . . January 1, 1787 . . . [Baltimore, W. Goddard, 1787]
broadside 35.5 X 19 cm.
New York Public 873; Wheeler 446
MdBE. Photostat: NN mp. 45109

B6522 MASON, GEORGE, 1725-1792
The objections of the Hon. George Mason, to the proposed foederal constitution. Addressed to the citizens of Virginia. [Richmond] Thomas Nicolson [1787]
6 p. caption title
Davis 15; Swem 3515
Exists apparently only in Ford's *Pamphlets on the Constitution* (Brooklyn, 1888)
N (destroyed by fire 1911?) mp. 45095

B6523 MASSACHUSETTS. GENERAL COURT
Commonwealth of Massachusetts. In Senate, June 13, 1787, Whereas it appears to this Court, that a considerable number of persons concerned in this rebellion . . . enter into parts of the western counties . . . In the House of Representatives, June 13, 1787 . . . [Boston, 1787]
broadside 43.5 X 27.5 cm.
Ford 2472
MSaE mp. 45096

B6524 MASSACHUSETTS. GOVERNOR, 1787-1793
Commonwealth of Massachusetts. By . . . John Hancock . . . a proclamation. Whereas the legislature . . . [June 15, 1787] . . . Boston, Adams and Nourse [1787]
broadside 40 X 32.5 cm.
Ford 2477
DLC; MB; MHi; MSaE. Photostat: MWA mp. 45099

B6525 MASSACHUSETTS. HOUSE OF REPRESENTATIVES
Commonwealth of Massachusetts. In the House of Representatives, March 10, 1787. Ordered, That the Governor's objections . . . to the bill for establishing a salary . . . for the Governor . . . be published. [Boston, 1787]
broadside
Ford 2470
MBB; MHi; MWA mp. 45097

B6526 MASSACHUSETTS. HOUSE OF REPRESENTATIVES
Commonwealth of Massachusetts. In the House of representatives, March 10, 1787. Resolved, That the several . . . Boston, Edward Eveleth Powars, 1787.
broadside 42.5 X 19.5 cm.
Ford 2471; New York Public 874
DLC; MH; MHi; NN mp. 45103

B6527 MASSACHUSETTS. LAWS
Commonwealth of Massachusetts . . . An act for preventing persons serving as jurors . . . In Senate, February 26, 1787 . . . [Boston, 1787]
broadside 40 X 33 cm.
Ford 2467; New York Public 875
DLC; NN mp. 45100

B6528 MASSACHUSETTS. LAWS
Commonwealth of Massachusetts. In the year of Our Lord, one thousand seven hundred and eighty-seven. An act to incorporate certain persons, by the name of the Society, for propagating the Gospel among the Indians . . . November 19, 1787. [Boston, 1787]
broadside 44.5 X 28 cm.
Ford 2468
MH; MHi mp. 45101

B6529 MASSACHUSETTS. LAWS
For the information of importers, retailers, and others. Articles of impost and excise extracted from the two laws . . . passed . . . November 17, 1786, and took place the 1st of January 1787 . . . Boston, Sold by T. & J. Fleet [1787]
broadside 50 X 33 cm.
MHi mp. 45102

B6530 MASSACHUSETTS. MILITIA
Camp at 1787. A provision return for in the state of Massachusetts. [Boston? 1787]
broadside
Ford 2486
M-Ar

B6531 MASSACHUSETTS. MILITIA
Worcester, 1787. Received of the town of for the use of the troops of this Commonwealth, under the command of Major-General Lincoln . . . [n.p., 1787]
broadside
Ford 2490
M-Ar

B6532 MASSACHUSETTS. TREASURER
Commonwealth of Massachusetts. Alexander Hodgdon, Esq. Treasurer . . . November 6, 1787. [Boston, 1787]
broadside
Tax warrant
Ford 2480
M-Ar mp. 45104

B6533 MASSACHUSETTS CENTINEL
New Year's verses January 1, 1787 . . . [Boston, 1787]
broadside
MWA mp. 45119

B6534 MOORE, JAMES
A letter to Mr. John Stancliff, containing some remarks on his piece . . . "An account of the Murrinitish Plague" . . . [Philadelphia, 1787]
8 p. 8vo caption title
Not Evans 21265.—Edwin Wolf 2d
PHi

B6535 MORSE, JEDIDIAH, 1761-1826
To the friends of science . . . Philadelphia, Aug. 7, 1787 . . . Philadelphia, Robert Aitken & Son, 1787.
broadside 27.5 X 22 cm.
Prospectus for "an accurate Geographical and Topographical Grammar of the United States."
MB. Photostat: RPJCB mp. 45105

B6536 THE necessity of providing a house in . . . New-Brunswick, for . . . holding the courts in . . . the County of Middlesex . . . to accomodate the sitting of the Legislature, and the holding the Supreme Courts . . . is evident. The advantageous situation of . . . New-Brunswick . . . The payment of the sums subscribed, we . . . do promise shall be made . . . [New Brunswick? 1787]
broadside 33 X 21 cm.
Dated from cover letter in ms.
NjR

B6537 THE New-England primer improved . . . Boston, Printed and sold by the booksellers, 1787.
[64] p. [A]-D^8

Heartman 84; Rosenbach-Ch 122
MB mp. 45106

B6538 THE New-England primer, improved . . . Springfield, Mass., Printed and sold by Russell and Webster [1787]
[80] p.
Russell and Webster printed only in 1787
MWA mp. 45107

B6539 NEW HAMPSHIRE. GOVERNOR, 1786-1788
By his Excellency John Sullivan. A proclamation . . . 24th Oct. 1787. [n.p., 1787]
broadside
MWA

B6540 NEW HAMPSHIRE. SENATE
State of New-Hampshire. In Senate, September 24, 1787. Resolved . . . [Printed at Keene by J. A. Griffith, 1787]
broadside
Brackets printed in text
MWA

B6541 [THE New-Haven sheet almanack for 1788. New-Haven, Josiah Meigs, 1787]
broadside
Advertised in the *New-Haven Gazette*, Dec. 6, 1787, as "To be sold at this Office, a sheet almanack, for 1788."
Drake 423
No copy known

B6542 NEW JERSEY. LAWS
An act for laying an excise on sundry articles . . . Passed at Burlington, June 4, 1787. [Trenton, I. Collins, 1787]
8 p. 22 cm.
DLC mp. 45108

B6543 NEW YORK. GOVERNOR, 1777-1795
By His Excellency George Clinton . . . A proclamation [relating to Shays' Rebellion] New-York, S. and J. Loudon [1787]
broadside 36.5 X 23.5 cm.
Dated Feb. 24, 1787
New York Public 877
NN mp. 45114

B6544 NEW YORK. LAWS
[The ten pound act; an act for the more speedy recovery of debts to the value of ten pounds, enacted Apr. 7, 1787. Albany, 1787]

Title from N. Y. State Law Library catalog (1855)
McMurtrie: Albany 28
No copy known mp. 45115

B6545 NEWPORT MERCURY
Verses for the New-Year, 1787, by the boy who carries about the *Newport Mercury* . . . [Newport, S. Southwick, 1787]
broadside 17 X 11 cm.
Alden 1080; Winship p. 89
RHi. Photostat: MWA mp. 45187

B6546 NORTH CAROLINA. LAWS
State of North-Carolina. An act for appointing deputies . . . In General Assembly, January 6, 1787 . . . [Newbern, Hodge & Blanchard, 1787]
broadside 18.5 X15.5 cm.
McMurtrie: North Carolina 131
NN. Photostats: DLC; MHi; MWA; NHi mp. 45116

B6547 NORTHAMPTON CO., PA.
State of the accounts of James Pettigrew . . . till 20th June, 1786 . . . Philadelphia, Robert Aitken, 1787.
6 p. 22 cm.
DLC mp. 45124

B6548 NORTHAMPTON CO., PA.
State of the accounts of Samuel Rhea . . . from the time of his appointment April 1st, 1780, until his resignation June 1st, 1781. Philadelphia, Robert Aitken, 1787.
9 p. 22.5 cm.
Sealock 110
PHi mp. 45126

B6549 NURSE Truelove's New-Year's gift . . . Plymouth, Printed and sold by Nathaniel Coverly, 1787.
32 p. 10 cm.
MWA mp. 45117

B6550 OCCOM, SAMSON, 1723-1792
A choice collection of hymns and spiritual songs . . . Third edition. Hudson, Ashbel Stoddard, 1787.
109 p. 13 cm.
MWA mp. 45118

B6550a PATTILLO, HENRY, 1726-1801
The plain planter's family assistant . . . Wilmington, James Adams, 1787.
63 p.
Trinterud 311
PPPrHi

B6551 PENNSYLVANIA
Pennsylvania, ss. By the Supreme Executive Council of . . . Pennsylvania, a proclamation . . . [Sept. 26, 1787] . . . [Philadelphia] Francis Bailey [1787]
broadside 41 X 30.5 cm.
"Patents from Virginia since June 23, 1780 are not good titles to land."
Sealock 115
PHi mp. 45136

B6552 PENNSYLVANIA
Philadelphia, June 30, 1787. By virtue of a precept from the Trustees of the General Loan-Office of . . . Pennsylvania, to me directed, will be exposed for sale . . . Philadelphia, Charles Cist [1787]
broadside 34.5 X 21.5 cm.
Repeated in German
Sealock 116
PHi mp. 45135

B6553 PENNSYLVANIA. GENERAL ASSEMBLY
Minutes of the second session of the eleventh General Assembly . . . commenced . . . the twentieth day of February . . . [Colophon] Philadelphia, Hall and Sellers [1787]
p. [115]-198. 30.5 cm. caption title
PHi; PPL. Photostat: DLC mp. 45129

B6554 PENNSYLVANIA. GENERAL ASSEMBLY
Minutes of the third session of the eleventh General Assembly . . . commenced . . . the fourth day of September . . . [Colophon] Philadelphia, Hall and Sellers [1787]
p. [199]-250. 30.5 cm. caption title
PHi; PPL. Photostat: DLC mp. 45130

B6555 PENNSYLVANIA. GENERAL ASSEMBLY
Minutes of the first session of the twelfth General Assembly . . . commenced . . . the twenty-second day of October . . . Philadelphia, Hall and Sellers [1787]

97 p. 31.5 cm.
CSmH; DLC; PHi; PPL mp. 45131

B6556 PENNSYLVANIA. GENERAL ASSEMBLY
State of Pennsylvania. In General Assembly, Saturday, September 29th, 1787 . . . Philadelphia, Hall and Sellers [1787]
broadside
Extract of resolutions concerning the forthcoming Constitutional Convention
Adams: Pennsylvania 44
PU

B6557 PENNSYLVANIA. INDIAN COMMISSIONERS
State of the accounts of the Pennsylvania, Indian Commissioners . . . Philadelphia, Robert Aitken & Son, 1787.
11 p. 22 cm.
New York Public 879
NN mp. 45132

B6558 PENNSYLVANIA. LAWS
An act for the regulation of bankruptcy. [Philadelphia? 1787?]
15 p. caption title
Act dated 1785; amendment (p. 12-15) dated Mar. 15, 1787
RPJCB mp. 45133

B6559 PENNSYLVANIA. LAWS
State of Pennsylvania. In General Assembly, Wednesday, Nov. 14 . . . 1787. The bill, entitled, "An act to incorporate . . . bridge over the river Schuylkill . . . " was read the second time . . . [Philadelphia, 1787]
broadside 45 X 25.5 cm.
Text of bill in 3 columns, containing 13 articles
Sealock 117
PHi mp. 45127

B6560 PENNSYLVANIA. LAWS
A supplement to the bankrupt law and impost law . . . [Colophon] Philadelphia, Thomas Bradford [1787]
12 p. half-title
Separate printing of p. 237-246 of the laws passed by 11th General Assembly, 2nd sitting
PPL mp. 45134

B6561 PENNSYLVANIA. SUPREME EXECUTIVE COUNCIL
For £ In Council. Philadelphia, 178 Sir, Pay to invalid, or order . . . according to . . . an act of Assembly . . . September, 1785, To David Rittenhouse, Esq; Treasurer . . . [Philadelphia, 1787?]
broadside 20 X 16.5 cm.
Filled in for Nov. 1, 1787
DLC

B6562 PENNSYLVANIA. TREASURER
A state of the finances of the commonwealth of Pennsylvania. [Colophon] Philadelphia, Hall and Sellers [1787]
11 p. 32.5 cm. caption title
Dated at end: November 7th, 1787
DLC; MHi; NN; PPAmP; PPM; RPJCB mp. 45137

B6563 THE Pennsylvania almanac, for the year . . . 1788 . . . Pennsylvania: Printed by F. Bailey, J. Steele, and J. Bailey; and sold by F. Bailey, Philadelphia, J. Bailey, Lancaster, and J. Steele . . . Octorara [1787]
[36] p. illus. 17.5 cm.
PHi; WHi mp. 45138

B6564 POPE, ALEXANDER, 1688-1744
An essay on man . . . Boston, Re-printed by Thomas and John Fleet, 1787.
3 p.l., 48 p. 17.5 cm.
New York Public 880
MB; MWA; NN mp. 45141

B6565 POPE, ALEXANDER, 1688-1744
An essay on man . . . Philadelphia, Printed for Thomas Dobson, 1787.
48 p. 17 cm.
Sealock 121
PHi mp. 45142

B6566 PORTSMOUTH, N. H.
To your Continental, state and town tax, in silver money, in certificates . . . Joseph Akerman, Collector. June 1787. [Portsmouth, 1787]
broadside 12.5 X 10 cm.
Whittemore 435
MHi

B6567 POUGHKEEPSIE ADVERTISER
Verses of the post boy, January 1, 1787 . . . [Poughkeepsie, 1787]
broadside
Found in a volume of the newspaper
MWA mp. 45188

B6568 PRICES current, in Baltimore 178 Anchors . . . [Baltimore, W. Goddard? 1787]
broadside 23 X 19 cm.
This form in use from 1787 to 1790
Wheeler 450
RPJCB

B6569 PRIESTLEY, JOSEPH, 1733-1804
Extracts from Doctor Priestley's Catechism . . . Boston, Printed and sold by S. Hall [1787]
12 p. 16.5 cm.
Dated by Charles Evans in a letter to G. P. Winship Aug. 2, 1913, stating that the item was "Not in Evans."
RPJCB mp. 45144

B6570 PRINCETON UNIVERSTIY
Catalogus Collegii Neo-Caesariensis. Princeton, J. Tod, 1787.
12 p. 22 cm.
Morsch 53
DLC; NHi mp. 45145

B6571 THE prodigal daughter . . . Printed [by Isaiah Thomas] at Worcester, (Massachusetts) MDCCLXXXVII.
12 p. illus. 19 cm.
MWA. d'Alté A. Welch, Cleveland (p. [1]-2 wanting) mp. 45146

B6572 PROPOSALS for printing by subscription, A Geographical and Topographical History of America . . . [Philadelphia, Prichard and Hall, 1787.]
4 p. 16 cm. caption title
PHi mp. 45147

B6573 PROPOSALS for printing by subscription, The vision of Columbus . . . [New York? 1787?]
broadside 20 X 16 cm.
NHi mp. 45148

B6574 PROTESTANT EPISCOPAL CHURCH IN THE U. S. A. VIRGINIA (DIOCESE)
Journal of a convention . . . held . . . in . . . Richmond, May 16, 1787. Richmond, Thomas Nicolson, 1787.

9 p. 33.5 cm.
New York Public 881
NN mp. 45149

B6575 [RASPE, RUDOLPH ERICH] 1737-1794
Gullivcr revived . . . By Baron Muchausen. The fourth edition, considerably enlarged. Norfolk, Re-printed by John M'Lean, 1787.
iv, 139 p.
RPJCB (p. 3-4 wanting) mp. 45150

B6576 THE renowned history of Giles Gingerbread . . . Philadelphia, Young and M'Culloch, 1787.
32 p. 10 cm.
MWA mp. 45076

B6577 RHODE ISLAND. ELECTION PROX.
1787. Landholders. His Excellency William Bradford, Esq; Governor. The honourable John Malbone, Esq; Dep. Governor . . . [Providence? 1787]
broadside 18 X 14 cm.
Alden 1082; Chapin Proxies 40
RHi; RNHi; RPB mp. 45152

B6578 RHODE ISLAND. ELECTION PROX.
Perseverance. His Excellency John Collins, Esq; Governor. The honorable Daniel Owen, Esq; Deputy-Governor . . . [Providence? 1787]
broadside 21 X 12.5 cm.
Alden 1083; Chapin Proxies 39
RHi. Henry R. Drowne mp. 45151

B6579 RHODE ISLAND. GENERAL ASSEMBLY
State of Rhode-Island, &c. To the honorable the General assembly . . . Whereas the subscribers were . . . appointed a committee . . . March 16th, 1787 . . . Providence, Bennett Wheeler [1787]
broadside 28 X 18 cm.
On same sheet: An act for the more equal representation . . . (Evans 20687)
Alden 1084; Winship p. 52
DLC; R; RHi; RPJCB. Photostat: MWA mp. 45158

B6580 RHODE ISLAND. LAWS
State of Rhode-Island and Providence Plantations. In General assembly, December session, A.D. 1786. An act laying duties of excise . . . Providence, John Carter [1787?]
[2] p. 40 X 26 cm.
Bill submitted Jan. 14, 1787
Alden 1095; Winship p. 51
RHi; RNHi; RPJCB (mutilated); RWe. Photostat: MWA mp. 45153

B6581 RHODE ISLAND. LAWS
State of Rhode-Island and Providence Plantations. In General assembly, March session, A.D. 1787. An act for granting . . . a tax of twenty thousand pounds . . . [Providence, J. Carter, 1787]
broadside 38.5 X 26.5 cm.
Bill submitted Mar. 20, 1787
Alden 1096; Winship p. 52
RHi; RPB; RPJCB mp. 45154

B6582 RHODE ISLAND. LAWS
State of Rhode-Island, &c. In General assembly, March session, A.D. 1787. An act to prevent bribery . . . [Providence, J. Carter, 1787]
broadside 33 X 11 cm.
Bill submitted Mar. 31, 1787
Alden 1098; Winship p. 52
RHi; RWe mp. 45155

B6583 RHODE ISLAND. LAWS
State of Rhode-Island, &c. In General assembly, September session, A.D. 1787. An act for collecting . . . [Providence, J. Carter, 1787]
broadside 35.5 X 23 cm.
Alden 1099; Winship p. 52
DLC; MWA; RHi mp. 45156

B6584 RHODE ISLAND. LAWS
State of Rhode-Island, &c. In General Assembly, October session, 1787. An act for the more effectually punishing . . . [Providence, B. Wheeler, 1787]
broadside 27.5 X 21 cm.
Alden 1101; Winship p. 52
DLC; MWA; R; RHi; RPJCB mp. 45157

B6585 RIDGELY-CARNAN, CHARLES, 1762-1829
To Harry Dorsey Gouch, Esquire. Sir, It is impossible . . . August 8, 1787. Baltimore, John Hayes [1787]
[2] p. 43 X 26 cm.
Wheeler 451
MdHi (2 copies) mp. 45159

B6586 RUSH, BENJAMIN, 1745-1813
Syllabus of lectures, containing the application of the principles of natural philosophy . . . to domestic and culinary purposes . . . Philadelphia, Printed for Andrew Brown, 1787.
vi p. 8vo
PPL mp. 45160

B6586a SEARLE, JOHN, 1721-1787
Some observations on the doctrines of John Murray . . . Philadelphia, Francis Bailey, 1787.
16 p.
Trinterud 991
PPPrHi (imperfect)

B6587 [SERIOUS thoughts on sudden death. Bennington, Haswell & Russell, 1787]

Advertised in the *Vermont Gazette*, Mar. 19, 1787
McCorison 131
No copy known mp. 45161

B6588 [SERIOUS thoughts on the present troubles in Massachusetts. Bennington, Haswell & Russell, 1787]

Advertised in the *Vermont Gazette*, Mar. 19, 1787
McCorison 132
No copy known mp. 45162

B6589 A SHORT dialogue, between a learned divine and a beggard. Norwich, 1787.
8 p.
Trumbull: Supplement 2608
No copy located mp. 45163

B6590 SIMPLE division. Rule . . . Reduction.—Of money . . . Boston, Printed for James White, at Franklin's Head, Court-street [1787?]
broadside 24.5 X 20 cm.
Dated by MHi
Ford 2501
MHi mp. 45164

B6591 SMITH, ROBERT
Philadelphia, January 5th, 1787. Sir, The subscriber . . . Robert Smith. [Philadelphia, 1787]
broadside 23.5 X 18.5 cm.
DLC mp. 45165

B6592 [SMITH, WILLIAM] d. 1673
Joyful tidings to the begotten of God . . . Philadelphia, Joseph James, 1787.
1 p.l., 9 p. 18.5 cm.
CSmH; PHi mp. 45166

B6593 SOCIETY FOR THE RELIEF OF POOR AND DISTRESSED MASTERS OF SHIPS . . .
Rules of the Society . . . Philadelphia, Printed for the Society, by T. Bradford, 1787.
20 p. 20.5 cm.
MWA mp. 45167

B6594 SOCIETY OF THE CINCINNATI, NEW YORK
New-York, March 17, 1787. Sir, it not being convenient . . . Major-general Baron Steuben . . . begs leave to inform you . . . [New York, 1787]
broadside 19.5 X 16 cm.
p. [1] of a 4-page folder
MiU-C mp. 45168

B6595 SOUTH CAROLINA. COMMISSIONERS OF FORFEITED ESTATES
Will be sold, at public auction . . . 27th Feb. . . . tracts of land, also, a pew, and about ten Negroes . . . By order of the Commissioners of Forfeited Estates, Francis Gaultier, Auctioneer. Charleston, December 25, 1787.
broadside 43.5 X 26.5 cm.
Sc-Ar

B6596 STANCLIFF, JOHN
An account of the putrid Murrinitish plague, lately-broke out in . . . Philadelphia . . . with an infallible cure . . . Philadelphia [1787]
8 p. 20 cm. caption title
A tract against Antinomianism
Sabin 90147; Sealock 126
PHi; RPJCB mp. 45169

B6596a STEVENS, GEORGE ALEXANDER, 1710-1784
The celebrated lecture on heads . . . Philadelphia: Printed for Samuel Dellap, 1787.
28 p. 8vo
cf. Evans 20728 (without imprint date)
PPL

B6597 SWIFT, JONATHAN, 1667-1745
The adventures of Captain Gulliver . . . Philadelphia, Young and M'Culloch, 1787.
128 p. illus. 10 cm. A-D^{16}
Half the pages of sig. D printed twice, the other half not printed at all
Rosenbach-Ch 124
PP (p. 63-64 mostly wanting) mp. 45170

B6598 TEN minutes advice to every gentleman going to purchase a horse . . . Philadelphia, Printed and sold by Joseph Crukshank, 1787.
[6], 43, 70 p. 14.5 cm.
"The gentleman's pocket-farrier" (with same imprint): 70 p. at end, with continuous signatures (Evans 20222)
Austin 1867
MWA; PHi; RPJCB mp. 45171

B6599 THREE shillings and nine-pence per dozen . . . Just published, by John Hayes . . . The Maryland and Virginia almanac . . . for the year . . . 1788 . . . [Baltimore, John Hayes, 1787]
broadside 42.5 X 26 cm.
Wheeler 453
MdBE mp. 45080

B6600 TO the free, virtuous, and independent electors of Massachusetts. Freemen, attend!—The spirit of the present rebellion . . . seems to have subsided . . . [Boston, 1787?]
broadside 31.5 X 16.5 cm.
Against John Hancock
Ford 2502
MHi mp. 45172

B6601 TO the honourable the Legislative Council and General Assembly . . . of New-Jersey. The representation and petition of the subscribers, inhabitants of the Eastern Division of the said state. Humbly sheweth, That the Supreme Court . . . fixed at Trenton . . . [New Brunswick? 1787]
broadside 34 X 20 cm.
For date cf. Richard P. McCormick: *Experiment in independence* (1950), p. 125-6.—D. A. Sinclair
NjR

B6602 TO the voters of Baltimore County. If men of integrity . . . A friend to your welfare. September 25, 1787. [Baltimore, W. Goddard, 1787]
broadside 35.5 X 18 cm.
Wheeler 454
MdBE mp. 45173

B6603 TRINITY CHURCH, NEW YORK
Notice is hereby given, that in pursuance of an unanimous resolution of the Corporation of Trinity Church . . . the following lots of ground . . . will be sold at public auction . . . New-York, J. M'Lean [1787]
broadside 54 X 21 cm.
Dated May 23, 1787
New York Public 882
NN mp. 45113

B6604 U. S. CONSTITUTION
The Constitution of the United States . . . Philadelphia, Printed and sold by Young & McCulloch, 1787
12 p. 8vo A^6
NHi. Walter Trohan, Washington, D. C. mp. 45174

B6605 U. S. CONSTITUTION
The Constitution of the United States . . . Portsmouth, Printed by John Melcher, 1787.
16 p. 19 cm.
Whittemore 438; Evans 20797 textually, but with reset t.p., a cancel (F. Goff)
DLC; MB

B6606 U. S. CONSTITUTION
Constitution of the United States of America. [n.p., 1787?]
[2] p. 32 cm.
In double columns
New York Public 883
RHi. Photostats: MWA; NN mp. 45175

B6607 U. S. CONSTITUTION
New constitution of the United States of America . . . [Middletown, Woodward and Green, 1787]
broadsheet ([2] p.) 35.5 X 38.5 cm.
At end: triangular block of printers' ornaments
Dated by T. R. Harlow from corresponding material in *Middlesex Gazette*, Oct. 1, 1787
CtHi mp. 45684

B6608 U. S. CONSTITUTION
A plan of the new federal government. We, the people of the United States . . . [at end] Baltimore, William Goddard [1787]

2 p.
Text in 3 columns
RPJCB mp. 45176

B6609 U. S. CONSTITUTION
Verfahren der Vereinigten Convention, gehalten . . . in dem jahr 1787 . . . Auf verordnung der General assembly von Pennsylvanien aus dem englischen übersetzt. Germantaun, Michael Billmeyer [1787?]
16 p. 20.5 cm.
DLC mp. 45177

B6610 U. S. CONSTITUTION
We, the people of the United States, in order to form a more perfect union . . . do ordain and establish this constitution . . . [Colophon] [Philadelphia] Dunlap & Claypoole [1787]
4 p. 47 cm. caption title
Ford: Constitution 19
DLC; DS; MHi mp. 45178

B6611 U. S. CONSTITUTION
We, the people of the United States, in order to form a more perfect union . . . do ordain and establish this constitution . . . Wilmington, Frederick Craig & Co. [1787]
3 p. fol.
PPL mp. 45179

B6612 U. S. CONSTITUTIONAL CONVENTION, 1787
Proceedings of the Federal Convention. [Colophon on p. 16] Boston, Thomas and John Fleet [1787]
20 p. 18.5 cm. caption title
Ford: Constitution 8 and 14
DLC (imperfect: p. 17-20 wanting); MWA mp. 45180

B6613 U. S. CONSTITUTIONAL CONVENTION, 1787
Proceedings of the Federal Convention . . . [Colophon] [Providence] John Carter [1787]
[2] p. 34.5 X 23 cm.
Alden 1103; Winship p. 52
Ct; MH; RHi. Photostats: CSmH; MWA; NN; PHi
mp. 45182

B6614 U. S. CONTINENTAL CONGRESS, 1787
An ordinance for the government of the territory of the United States, northwest of the River Ohio. [Philadelphia, J. Dunlap, 1787]
[2] p. 33.5 X 21.5 cm.
Second reading of the bill
Ford: Bibliographical notes . . . 582
DLC mp. 45181

B6615 U. S. WAR DEPT. INSPECTOR-GENERAL'S OFFICE
Rules and articles for the better government of the troops . . . Richmond, Aug. Davis, 1787.
22 p. 22 cm.
DLC; ViHi mp. 45183

B6616 U. S. WAR DEPT. INSPECTOR-GENERAL'S OFFICE
Rules and articles for the government of the troops . . . as of May 31, 1786. [New York, John Swain, 1787]
42 p.
"Mr. Swain, by my direction, printed . . . one hundred and fifty copies . . . Given at the War Office the 31st March 1787. (s) H Knox"
Entry for 150 copies after Mar. 30, 1787, in Dunlap's accounts
Ford: Bibliographical notes . . . 570
NBuG mp. 45184

B6617 THE United States almanack for . . . 1788. By Eben W. Judd. New-York, Printed by and for Samuel Campbell [1787]
[32] p.
Drake 5953
WHi

B6618 VATTEL, EMMERICH DE, 1714-1767
The law of nations . . . New York, Printed for Berry and Rogers, 1787.
ixxiv [i.e., lxxiv], 728 p. 21 cm.
DLC; MWA; NN; NjP mp. 45185

B6619 VERMONT. LAWS
An act regulating the militia of the State of Vermont . . . [Windsor, Hough & Spooner, 1787]
16 p. 23 cm. caption title
Printer's bill dated May 23, 1787
McCorison 138; Sabin 99104
Vt mp. 45186

B6620 VIRGINIA. AUDITOR'S OFFICE
List of pensioners for the year 1786 . . . [Dated at end] January 30, 1787. [Richmond, 1787]
[2] p. 42.5 X 27 cm.
DLC (mutilated) mp. 45190

B6621 VIRGINIA. AUDITOR'S OFFICE
List of pensioners for the year 1787 . . . [Dated at end] 30th November, 1787. [Richmond, 1787]
[2] p. 44 X 27.5 cm.
DLC (2 copies) mp. 45191

B6622 VIRGINIA. COUNCIL
In Council, January 29, 1787. Gentlemen, The Executive having addressed . . . [Richmond, 1787]
broadside 33 X 21 cm.
DLC mp. 45192

B6623 VIRGINIA. COUNCIL
In Council, December 20, 1787. The Board proceeded to form a general rule for adjusting the precedency of captains and subalterns in the militia of the same county . . . A. Blair, C.C. [Richmond? 1787]
broadside 31.5 X 18 cm.
WHi mp. 45193

B6624 VIRGINIA. GENERAL ASSEMBLY
Resolved unanimously that the common right of navigating the Mississippi . . . That the delegates representing this state in Congress be instructed . . . to oppose . . . [Richmond, 1787]
broadside folio
James Lewis Hook Catalog 30, no. 305 (Sept. 1940)
No copy traced mp. 45194

B6625 VIRGINIA. GENERAL ASSEMBLY. SENATE
By the Senate, January 20, 1787. Ordered, that the printer be directed to print . . . the message on the . . . emission of paper money, sent to the House of Delegates the 5th instant . . . [Richmond, 1787]
[3] p. 53 cm.
Contains 4 messages of Jan. 1787
DLC mp. 45195

B6626 VIRGINIA. GOVERNOR, 1786-1788
Virginia, to wit: By His Excellency Edmund Randolph . . . A proclamation. Whereas it has been represented . . . that George Rogers Clarke . . . recruited a number of men for the support of the post at St. Vincent's . . . Given under my hand . . . [Feb. 28, 1787] Edmund Randolph. [Richmond, 1787]

broadside 32 X 21 cm.
WHi mp. 45196

B6627 VIRGINIA. TREASURER
State of the public taxes, payable for the year 1786, within the Commonwealth of Virginia. [Richmond, 1787]
broadside 42 X 34.5 cm.
Signed and dated: J. Ambler, Treasurer. Treasury-Office, January 1787
New York Public 886; Sabin 100415
NN mp. 45197

B6628 THE Virginia almanack for the year 1788 . . . by Robert Andrews . . . Petersburg, Hunter & Prentis [1787]
[48] p.
Bear 70; Wyatt 3
MWA mp. 45030

B6629 W., H.
A poem, descriptive of the terrible fire . . . in Boston, on the evening of Friday April 21, 1787 . . . Composed by H. W. [Boston] Sold at the Office next Liberty-Pole [1787]
broadside 37 X 24.5 cm.
Ford 2503
MHi mp. 45139

B6630 W., H.
A poem, descriptive of the terrible fire . . . Friday evening the twenty-first of April, 1787 . . . Composed by H. W. [at end] [Boston] Sold at the Printing-Office in Essex-Street [1787]
broadside 44 X 27 cm.
Variant of Ford 2503
RPJCB mp. 45140

B6631 WAIT, THOMAS B.
Proposals, for publishing by subscription, a large octavo volume, on husbandry . . . Thomas B. Wait. [at end] Portland, May 10, 1787.
broadside 33 X 21 cm.
List of subscribers in ms.
RPJCB mp. 45198

B6632 WEATHERWISE'S almanack for . . . 1788. By Abraham Weatherwise . . . Boston, Nathaniel Coverly [1787]
[24] p.
Drake 3402
MBC

B6633 WEBSTER, NOAH, 1758-1843
[The American spelling book. Bennington, Haswell & Russell, 1787]

Advertised in the *Vermont Gazette*, Aug. 27, 1787
McCorison 140; Skeel-Carpenter 12
No copy known mp. 45200

B6634 WEBSTER, NOAH, 1759-1843
A grammatical institute of the English language . . . The sixth edition .... Hartford, Hudson & Goodwin, 1787.
138 p. 16 cm.
cf. Evans 20868
DLC (p. i-vi wanting); NN mp. 45201

B6635 WEBSTER'S calendar; or the Albany, Columbia, Montgomery and Washington almanack for . . . 1788. By Eben W. Judd. The second edition. Albany, Charles R. Webster [1787]
[24] p.
Drake 5955
NRMA

B6636 WEBSTER'S New England almanack for . . . 1788 . . . By Copernicus . . . Springfield, Zephaniah Webster [1787]
[26] p.
MWA mp. 45202

B6637 WELD, EDMUND, 1631-1668
A dialogue between death, the soul, body, world and Jesus Christ. Composed by Edmond Weld . . . Boston, Printed by E. Russell for John Howe, of Ringe, (New-Hampshire) [1787]
broadside 33 X 33 cm.
MWA mp. 45203

B6638 WELD, EDMUND, 1631-1668
A funeral elegy by way of a dialogue . . . Springfield, Printed [by John Russell] at the Chronicle Printing-Office [1787?]
broadside 37 X 22.5 cm.
NHi mp. 45204

B6639 WHEATLEY, PHILLIS, 1754-1784
Poems on various subjects . . . Philadelphia, Joseph James, 1787.
55, [5] p. 16.5 cm.
Sabin 103139
DLC; MWA; NHi; PPL mp. 45205

B6640 WHEELER'S sheet almanac, for the year . . . 1788 . . . Providence, Bennett Wheeler [1787]
broadside 54 X 41.5 cm.
NHi mp. 45206

B6641 WHEREAS a certain congregation in Boston, calling themselves the first Episcopal Church in said town, have . . . introduced a liturgy . . . we the ministers of the Protestant Episcopal Church, whose names are underwritten . . . declare the proceedings . . . irregular . . . December 1787. [Boston, 1787]
broadside 32 X 20 cm.
MBAt; MHi mp. 45043

B6642 WILLCOCKS, HENRY
Proposals for printing by subscription, a weekly newspaper, intituled the *Virginia Gazette, and Hobb's Hole Advertiser*; . . . January 1, 1787. Henry Willcocks. [Winchester, 1787]
broadside 34.5 X 20.5 cm.
MWA mp. 45207

B6643 WILLOCK, THOMAS
For sale by the subscriber. Woollens. Linens. Hardware . . . Norfolk, 19th June, 1787. [Norfolk] John M'Lean [1787]
broadside 28 X 22 cm.
Huntington 541
CSmH mp. 45208

B6644 THE Wilmington pocket almanack, for the year 1788 . . . By Thomas Fox, Philom. Wilmington, James Adams [1787]
[28] p. 11 cm.
Drake 1375
DLC mp. 45068

B6645 THE Yarmouth tragedy; or, Jemmy and Nancy's garland. To which is added, Gay Damon. Worcester, Printed [by Isaiah Thomas], 1787.

8 p. 17 cm.
MWA mp. 45209

B6646 YORK CO., PA.
State of the account of Henry Miller and of Michael Hahn . . . Philadelphia, Robert Aitken, 1787.
6 p. 22 cm.
DLC mp. 45121

B6647 YORK CO., PA.
State of the accounts of John M'Clellan . . . from the time of his appointment, December 1785, till the 1st November 1786. Philadelphia, Robert Aitken, 1787.
6 p. 21.5 cm.
Sealock 134
PHi mp. 45125

B6648 ZION besieged. Just published, a new, humorous copperplate print . . . a few of which are left for sale at Mr. Poyntell's . . . [Philadelphia, 1787]
broadside 4to
cf. Evans 20908
PPL mp. 45143

1788

B6649 AN abstract of the cargo of the ship Hydra . . . of and for Newport, Rhode-Island . . . Salt-petre, 376,196 lbs. . . . [Newport, ca. 1788?]
broadside 24 X 37 cm.
Alden 1121
RHi; RNHi (2 copies) mp. 45210

B6650 AN act directing the mode of proceeding under certain executions . . . [n.p., 1788]
broadside 33 X 19.5 cm.
Dated Jan. 4, 1788: source indicated only by mention of "House of Delegates." Virginia? Maryland?
NcD mp. 45211

B6651 ADGATE, ANDREW, d. 1793
Rudiments of music . . . Philadelphia, Printed and sold by John M'Culloch, 1788.
22 p. 13.5 X 23.5 cm.
cf. Evans 20916
ICN; RPJCB mp. 45212

B6652 [ADGATE, ANDREW] d. 1793
A selection of sacred harmony . . . Philadelphia, W. Young, 1788.
1 p.l., [14], 84, [2] p. 11 X 23 cm.
Britton 658; cf. Evans 21453
CtHC; DLC mp. 45213

B6653 ADVICE to the fair sex, in a series of letters to a sister . . . Reading, Printed and sold by B. Johnson and T. Barton, 1788
p. cm.
Nolan p. 21, and 36-37
Louis J. Heizmann, Reading, Pa. (1930) mp. 45214

B6654 ALBANY, March 26, 1788. Sir, On the last Tuesday in April next, it becomes our duty to give our votes for members of the state convention . . . [Albany? 1788]
broadside 33 X 21 cm.
RPJCB mp. 45216

B6655 ALBANY, [ ] April, 1788. On the last Tuesday . . . [Albany, 1788]
broadside 47 X 36 cm.
WHi. Photostats: DLC; MHi; MWA mp. 45215

B6656 ALLEN, JOHN
A morning thought upon viewing the dawn of day . . . Exeter, Printed by Lamson and Ranlet, for John Allan, Stratham, 1788.
1 p.l., ii, 33 [i.e. 31], [1] p. 16 cm. $[A]-D^4E^{4?}$
MWA mp. 45217

B6657 AN almanack, for the year of the Christian aera, 1789; by Elijah Winslow. Exeter, Lamson and Ranlet [1788]
[24] p.
Nichols, p. 89
MWA ([22] p.).
E. S. Phelps (1928) mp. 45416

B6658 AN almanack, for the year . . . 1789 . . . By Samuel Bullard . . . Boston, Edes [1788]
[24] p. 17.5 cm.
Drake 3405; Huntington 545
CSmH (imperfect); DLC; MB; MHi (imperfect); MWA; MiGr (imperfect); MoS; NhD ([16] p.) mp. 45235

B6659 AMERICAN MERCURY, HARTFORD
The carrier of the *American Mercury* presents the following to his customers, wishing them a Happy New-Year . . . Hartford, January 1, 1788. [Hartford, Elisha Babcock, 1788]
broadside
1st line: From last year's mark we now aspire . . .
NHi mp. 45236

B6660 AMERICAN PHILOSOPHICAL SOCIETY
Philadelphia, 1788. At a meeting of the American Philosophical Society . . . [extract from the minutes] [Philadelphia, 1788]
2 p. 22.5 cm.
Brief report of the committee appointed to examine drawings of Rumsey's inventions
Sealock 137
DLC; RPJCB mp. 45218

B6661 ANALYSE des loix commerciales . . . des etates des deux Carolines, et de la Géorgie . . . Fayette-Ville, Bowen & Howard, 1788.
17 p. 21 cm.
Printed in France?
Turnbull p. 262 (v.1)
NN mp. 45219

B6662 ANTI-FEDERAL COMMITTEE, ALBANY, N.Y.
To the citizens of the city and county of Albany. Another publication of the Federal Committee, has at length . . . been obtained in this city . . . By order of the Anti-Federal Committee, Jer. V. Rensselaer, Chairman. Albany, Charles R. Webster [1788?]
broadside 33 X 21 cm.
NHi mp. 45221

B6663 ANTI-FEDERAL COMMITTEE, ALBANY, N.Y.
To the citizens of the city and county of Albany. At this late day, it is impossible to enter into a minute consideration of . . . a refutation of the objections offered by us to the New Constitution . . . By order of the Anti-Federal Federal Committee, Jer. V. Rensselaer, Chairman. [Albany? 1788?]
broadside 33 X 21 cm.
NHi mp. 45222

B6664 ARISTOTLE'S master piece completed . . . New York, 1788.
1 p.l., 7-103 p. front., illus. 16 cm.
DLC mp. 45223

B6665 ASH, JOHN, 1724?-1779
Grammatical institutes . . . A new edition, revised, corrected, and enlarged . . . Philadelphia, Re-printed and sold by Joseph Crukshank, 1788.
216 p. 13.5 cm.
cf. Evans 20936
DLC; MWA; P mp. 45224

B6666 AN astronomical diary . . . for the year . . . 1789 . . . By N. Strong . . . Hartford, Printed by Hudson & Goodwin [1788]
[24] p. 16.5 cm.
Bates: Connecticut almanacs p. 145; Trumbull 89
CtHi (imperfect); DLC; MB; MWA mp. 45369

B6667 AN astronomical diary . . . for the year . . . 1789 . . . By N. Strong . . . Hartford, Re-printed by Hudson & Goodwin [1788?]
[24] p. 16.5 cm.
Bates: Conn. almanacs p. 145
CtHi mp. 45370

B6668 BAPTISTS. CONNECTICUT. STONINGTON ASSOCIATION
Minutes of the Stonington Association, at their annual convention . . . in Colchester, 1788. [New London] T. Green, 1788.
8 p. 20.5 cm.
Trumbull: Supplement 2647
CtHi mp. 45225

B6669 BAPTISTS. PENNSYLVANIA. PHILADELPHIA ASSOCIATION
Minutes of the Baptist association, held in Philadelphia, October, 1788. [Philadelphia, 1788]
8 p. 20.5 cm. caption title
DLC; NHi mp. 45226

B6670 BENEZET, ANTHONY, 1713-1784
The mighty destroyer displayed . . . By a lover of mankind . . . Philadelphia, Joseph James, 1788.
39 p. 16.5 cm.
DLC; RPJCB mp. 45227

B6671 BIBLE. O.T. PSALMS
Psalms, carefully suited to the Christian worship . . . New York, Hugh Gaine, 1788.
xxiv, 282, [4] p. 14 cm.
DLC mp. 45228

B6672 BIBLE. N.T.
The New Testament of our Lord . . . Trenton, Printed and sold by Isaac Collins, 1788
12mo
Title from facsim. of t.p. of copy published in the catalogue of William Nelson library (American Art Galleries sale, Nov. 22-23, 1915)
Morsch 65
PU mp. 45229

B6673 BLÄSER, PETER, 1735-1813
Der besiegte Wiedertäufer, in Unterredungen über Kindertaufe und Untertauchung . . . Lancaster, Albrecht und Lahn, 1788.
[4], 92 p. 23 cm. [ ]^2[A]-L^{4}M^2
MWA; PPAmP; PPL mp. 45230

B6674 BOSTON
Your Commonwealth tax. Your town rate . . . Boston. September 1788. [Boston, 1788]
broadside
Ford 2505
MHi

B6675 [BOTTLER, JOHANN GEORG] 1754-1816
An die eingesegneten Kinder ein Väterlicher Nachruf . . . Ephrata, Gedruckt anno 1788.
31 p. 20 cm.
PGL

B6676 A BRIEF account of the execution of Elisha Thomas . . . Printed and sold at the Printing-Office in Market Street, Portsmouth [1788?]
broadside 34.5 X 22.5 cm.
Winslow 52
PHi

B6677 BROWN, ANDREW
To the public. The subscriber, having resigned the charge of the Young Ladies' Academy to its visitors, intends to establish a printing-office in this city . . . [Philadelphia, 1788]
[2] p. 30.5 X 20.5 cm.
MHi; MWA; PPL mp. 45231

B6678 BROWN, JOHN
Mr. John Brown requests the favour of company to a dance . . . on Friday evening next . . . January 2, 1788. [Providence, 1788]
broadside 6.5 X 9.5 cm.
Alden 1112; Winship Addenda p. 90
RPJCB. Photostat: MWA mp. 45233

B6679 BROWN, JOHN, 1722-1787
Dying advices to the associate congregation of Haddington . . . Philadelphia, Peter Stewart, 1788.
12 p. 18 cm.
MWA mp. 45232

B6680 BURNES, DANIEL, AND SON, firm
Burr mill-stones, made and sold at Daniel Burnes and Son's store . . . Philadelphia, August 11, 1788. Philadelphia, Joseph James [1788]
broadside 18.5 X 22.5 cm.
NHi mp. 45234

B6681 CHAMBERLAIN, THOMAS, d. 1784
The timely remembrancer, or the minister preaching his own funeral sermon . . . Hudson, Ashbel Stoddard, 1788.
12 p. 18 cm.
NN (p. 11-12 wanting); RPJCB mp. 45238

B6682 CHASE, SAMUEL, 1741-1811
To the Roman Catholic voters in Baltimore-Town. Gentlemen, The publication of the Rev. Mr. Sewall . . . Samuel Chase. Baltimore-town, October 4, 1788. [Baltimore, William Goddard, 1788]
broadside 40.5 X 21.5 cm.
Wheeler 460
MdHi mp. 45239

B6683 CHASE, SAMUEL, 1741-1811
To the voters of Baltimore-Town. Gentlemen, We take the liberty . . . Samuel Chase, David M'Mechen. Baltimore, Friday, 3d October, 1788 . . . [Baltimore, W. Goddard, 1788]
broadside ([2] p.) 28 X 23 cm.

Wheeler 461
MdHi mp. 45240

B6684 CLARK, JONAS, 1730-1805
A short and brief account of the shipwreck of Cap. Joshua Winslow . . . the 23d day of July, 1788. [and] Farewell hymn; on the death of Miss Polly Gould. [and] On the death of Uriah Brown. [Boston? 1788?]
broadside 26.5 X 44 cm.
Ford 2522
MWA mp. 45242

B6685 CLARK, JONAS, 1730-1805
A short and brief account of the shipwreck of Capt. Joshua Winslow . . . the 23rd day of July, 1788. [Boston? 1788?]
broadside 25.5 X 23.5 cm.
Author's name in text
Not Ford 2522; not Wegelin 769 or 1357
RPJCB mp. 45241

B6686 COMAN, WILLIAM
Five dollars reward. On Tuesday, the 3d instant, a person who said his name was Jacob Johnston . . . William Coman. Providence, June 4th, 1788. Providence, Bennett Wheeler [1788]
broadside 14 X 20 cm.
Alden 1115; Winship p. 53
RPTP mp. 45243

B6687 CONNECTICUT. TREASURER
State of Connecticut, in America. To Constable of and collector of the state tax for . . . 1789, Greeting . . . Hartford, the 1st day of November . . . 1788 . . . [Hartford? 1788]
broadside 33 X 20.5 cm.
CtHi mp. 45244

B6688 COXE AND FRAZIER, firm, Philadelphia
Es ist zu verkaufen . . . ein strich sehr köstlich bauland . . . Philadelphia, Melchior Steiner [1788] [Followed by] To be sold, or let on improving leases, a body of very valuable farming lands . . . Tench Coxe, N. Frazier . . . January the 8th, 1788. Philadelphia, Melchior Steiner [1788]
broadside 42.5 X 28 cm.
Sealock 130?
DLC mp. 45245

B6689 DAILY ADVERTISER
Supplement to the *Daily Advertiser.* Monday, November 10, 1788. Particulars of the general account published 3d instant . . . New-York, Francis Childs, 1788.
broadside 54 X 38 cm.
NHi mp. 45310

B6690 DAVIDSON, JOHN
To the public. Annapolis, July 18, 1788. Though nothing can be more disagreeable . . . John Davidson. [Annapolis, F. Green, 1788]
broadside 38.5 X 23 cm.
Wheeler 463
MdHi mp. 45246

B6691 DAVIDSON, JOHN
To the public. Annapolis, September 16, 1788. The turbulent and vindictive Mr. Petty, by his hand-bill of the 18th ultimo . . . John Davidson . . . [Annapolis, F. Green, 1788]
[2] p. 41.5 X 24 cm.
Wheeler 464
MdHi mp. 45247

B6692 DEBLOIS, GEORGE
George Deblois imports European and India goods for sale, at a reasonable rate for cash, at his store, No. 1, Cornhill, Boston . . . [Boston, 1788?]
broadside 19 X 15 cm.
MSaE mp. 45248

B6693 DEBLOIS, GILBERT
Gilbert Deblois, senior. At his store in Cornhill, No. 1 . . . Imports from Great-Britain, Ireland . . . and sells on the lowest terms . . . [at end] 1788. [Boston, 1788]
broadside 19 X14 cm.
"Gilbert" and "senior" struck out, and "George" substituted in ms. (MWA copy)
MSaE; MWA mp. 45249

B6694 DECALVES, ALONSO [pseud.]
New travels to the westward . . . Norwich, Printed and sold by John Trumbull, 1788.
34 p. 17 cm.
CtHi; ICN; MWA (wanting after p. 30) mp. 45250

B6695 DILWORTH, THOMAS, d. 1780
A new guide to the English tongue . . . The forty-sixth edition. Hartford, Printed and sold by Nathaniel Patten, 1788.
viii, [2], 154 p.
Trumbull: Supplement 2061
CtHi; CtY mp. 45251

B6696 DOBSON, THOMAS
Thomas Dobson, bookseller and stationer, at the new stone house, in Second street . . . has for sale, wholesale and retail . . . [Philadelphia, T. Dobson, 1788]
broadside 43 X 38 cm.
Sealock 147
PHi mp. 45252

B6697 EBERHARD, CASPAR
Kurze und einfältige Kinderlehr . . . aus dem Catechismo zusammen gezogen durch Casparum Eberhardi . . . Germantaun, Michael Billmeyer, 1788.
[95]-138 p. 15.5 cm.
MWA mp. 45253

B6698 ETLICHE liebliche und erbauliche Lieder . . . und zwey Lieder . . . von dem lieben Bruder Grumbacher . . . und . . . Christoph Saur . . . Nebst etliche . . . Liedern von Joh. Kelpius . . . Germantaun, Peter Leibert, 1788.
16 p. 17 cm.
PHi mp. 45254

B6699 F., P.
A few verses composed by P. F. on account of the sudden death of John Brown, and Huldy Brown . . . killed with lightning . . . the seventh day of June, 1788 . . . Worcester, Printed at D. Greenleaf's Office, for Richard Lee [1788]
broadside 44.5 X 20 cm.
MWA mp. 45258

B6700 FATHER Tammany's pocket almanac, for the year . . . 1789 . . . Philadelphia: Printed for W. Young [1788]
[36] p. illus. 17.5 cm.
Drake 10243
PHi mp. 45255

B6701 THE Federal almanac, for the year, 1789 . . . Wilmington, Frederick Craig [1788]

[36] p. 18.3 cm.
Drake 1378; Hawkins 24
DeWin; PHi (wanting after p. [26]) mp. 45256

B6702 THE Federal Catechism, agreeably to reason and revelation . . . By a Friend to Religion. Philadelphia: Printed and sold by John M'Culloch, 1788.
8 p. 8vo
PHi

B6703 FOSTER, BENJAMIN, 1750-1798
Primitive baptism defended . . . Second edition . . . New-York, J. Patterson, 1788.
1 p.l., 22 p. 21 cm.
Huntington 546; New York Public 889
CSmH; DLC; MWA; NN; RPJCB mp. 45259

B6704 FOUR excellent new songs, called, Yankee Doodle. Death of General Wolfe. Nancy Dawson. Guardian angels. New-York, Printed and sold by John Reid, 1788.
8 p. 15 cm.
New York Public 890; Wegelin 594
Oscar Wegelin. Photostat: NN mp. 45260

B6705 DER gantz neue verbesserte Nord-Americanische calender, auf das 1789ste jahr Christi . . . Zum dreyzehnten mal herausgegeben . . . von Anthony Sharp . . . Lancaster, Jacob Bailey [1788]
[32] p. 20.5 cm.
By David Rittenhouse
Drake 10245
DLC; DeWin; MWA; P mp. 45357

B6706 GARRISON, DAVID
Twenty dollars reward. Stolen out of a sloop . . . about 240 dollars . . . David Garrison. Newport, May 6, 1788.
broadside 15 X 18 cm.
Alden 1117A
RHi (bound with *Providence Gazette* for May 6, 1788) mp. 45261

B6707 GEISTLICHER Irrgarten, mit vier Gnadenbrunnen, dadurch kürzlich angedeutet werden . . . Ephrata, 1788.
broadside 43 X 34.5 cm.
MWA mp. 45262

B6708 A GENERAL description of the thirteen United States of America . . . Reading, Printed and sold by B. Johnson and T. Barton, 1788.
23 p. 17.5 cm. A-C[4]
New York Public 892; Rosenbach-Ch 129
PHi. Photostat: NN mp. 45263

B6709 GILL, JOHN, 1697-1771
Infant baptism, a part and pillar of Popery . . . Windsor, Hough and Spooner, 1788.
32 p. 17 cm.
Cooley 97
MWA; VtHi mp. 45264

B6710 GOODWIN, HEZEKIAH, 1739 or 40-1767
A vision. Shewing the sudden and surprizing appearance . . . of the departed spirit of Mr. Yeamans . . . to . . . Mr. H. Goodwin . . . New-Haven, Josiah Meigs [1788]
12 p. 18 cm.
Trumbull: Supplement 2194
CtY; DLC; MWA mp. 45265

B6711 GUILD, BENJAMIN
Addition to a catalogue of a large assortment of books . . . To be let or sold by Benjamin Guild . . . Boston. [Boston, 1788]
16 p.
Brigham: Booksellers, p. 50
MWA mp. 45266

B6712 HABERMANN, JOHANN, 1516-1590
Christliche morgen- und abend-gebäter . . . Germantaun, Peter Leibert, 1788.
62, 56, [1] p. 13.5 cm.
Seidensticker p. 122
DLC; PHi; PV mp. 45267

B6713 HABERMANN, JOHANN, 1516-1590
Christliche Morgen- und Abend-Gebäter . . . Philadelphia: Gedruckt und zu haben bey Carl Cist, 1788.
63, 65 p. port. 14.5 cm. A-E[12] F[4]
MWA; PHi mp. 45268

B6714 HAGUE, JOHN
American manufactures. The subscriber begs leave to inform the citizens . . . John Hague. Philadelphia, March 28, 1788 . . . [Philadelphia] B. Towne [1788]
broadside 27 X 22 cm.
DLC; RPJCB mp. 45269

B6715 HITCHCOCK, ENOS, 1744-1803
The parent's assistant. A short practical catechism . . . Providence, B. Wheeler, 1788.
16 p. 16.5 cm.
Alden 1120
MWA mp. 45272

B6716 HOCH-DEUTSCHES Reformirtes A B C und Namen Büchlein, für Kinder . . . Germantown, Michael Billmeyer, 1788.
[32] p. 17 cm.
Frontispiece and last leaf pasted to covers
MWA (sig. A lacking); PPL mp. 45273

B6717 HOCH-DEUTSCHES Reformirtes A B C- und Namen-Büchlein, für Kinder, welche anfangen zu lernen. Philadelphia, Carl Cist, 1788.
[28] p. incl. front. 16 cm.
Frontispiece and last leaf pasted to covers
New York Public 893
NN mp. 45724

B6718 HOPKINSON, FRANCIS, 1737-1791
Seven songs for the harpsichord or forte piano . . . Philadelphia: Publish'd & sold by T. Dobson [1788]
2 p.l., 11, [1] p. fol.
T.p. and music engraved
Adams: Pennsylvania 46
PU

B6719 [HUTCHINS, JOSEPH]
An abstract of the first principles of English grammar . . . Philadelphia, Printed for the editor, by T. Dobson and T. Lang, 1788.
72 p. 13.5 cm.
MWA mp. 45275

B6720 [IREDELL, JAMES] 1750-1799
Answers to Mr. Mason's Objections to the new constitution recommended by the late convention at Philadelphia. To which is added, An address to the freemen of North-Carolina. By Publicola . . . [at end] Newbern, Hodge and Wills [1788]
12 p. 35 cm.
"Answers" dated at end: January 1788
Publicola was Archibald Maclaine

McMurtrie: North Carolina 133 (appendix)
MH mp. 45276

B6721 JAY, JOHN, 1745-1829
Extract from an Address . . . [New York, 1788]
broadside 36 × 22 cm.
Photostats: CSmH; MWA mp. 45277

B6722 JENYNS, SOAME, 1704-1787
A view of the internal evidence of the Christian religion . . . The ninth edition, corrected. Philadelphia, Joseph Crukshank, 1788.
76 p. 19 cm.
MB; MWA; N; NN; NjP; PPL mp. 45278

B6723 LANCASTER CO., PA.
State of the accounts of the taxes in Lancaster County. Philadelphia, Robert Aitken, 1788.
83 p. 21.5 cm.
NN; PPl; PPiU; RPJCB mp. 45323

B6724 LAVATER, JOHANN CASPER, 1741-1801
J. C. Lavaters Erweckung zur Busse . . . Lancaster, Albrecht und Lahn, 1788.
36 p. 8vo
PPL mp. 45282

B6725 LEE, ARTHUR, 1740-1792
To the freeholders of the counties of Gloucester, Middlesex . . . When I offer myself, as a candidate . . . Arthur Lee. Fredericksburg, T. Green [1788]
broadside 32 × 19.5 cm.
ViU. Photostats: DLC; MHi; MWA; NHi; Vi
mp. 45283

B6726 [LOW, SAMUEL] b. 1765
Ode for the federal procession, upon the adoption of the new government. Composed by Mr. L**. [New York, 1788]
broadside 40 × 26 cm.
NHi. Photostats: DLC; MWA mp. 45284

B6727 MCALPINE, JOHN
Genuine narratives, and concise memoirs . . . of J. McAlpine . . . [n.p.] 1788.
72 p. 16.5 cm.
DLC; ICN mp. 45285

B6728 MACK, ALEXANDER, b. 1712
Anhang zur widerlegten Widertäufer, enthalt zwey Unterredungen, und den ganzlichen Abscheid Theophili . . . Ephrata, 1788.
25, [1] p. 8vo
PPL mp. 45286

B6729 MARY, JOHN
A speech on the government of good morals . . . [New York, 1788]
4 p. 21 cm. caption title
DLC mp. 45287

B6730 MARYLAND. CONVENTION, 1788
To the people of Maryland. The following facts . . . On Monday, the 21st of April, the convention met . . . [Annapolis, Frederick Green, 1788?]
[3] p. 31 cm. caption title
Wheeler 475
DLC; MdHi. Photostat: MWA mp. 45288

B6731 MARYLAND. ELECTION PROX.
Candidates to represent this state in Congress. Friends to amendments . . . [Baltimore, W. Goddard? 1788]
broadside 26 × 21.5 cm.
Wheeler 459
MdHi mp. 45289

B6732 MARYLAND. ELECTION PROX.
Representatives to Congress . . . Electors of President and Vice-President . . . [Baltimore, John Hayes, 1788]
broadside 18 × 10.5 cm.
Wheeler 484
MdBE; MdHi mp. 45290

B6733 MASSACHUSETTS. GENERAL COURT
Commonwealth of Massachusetts. In the House of Representatives, July 11, 1783 . . . In Senate, October 6, 1783 . . . In Senate, June 5, 1788 . . . Secretary's Office, Boston, June 11, 1788 . . . [Boston, 1788]
broadside 38 × 25 cm.
Resolutions concerning bounties for soldiers
NHi mp. 45293

B6734 MASSACHUSETTS. GOVERNOR, 1787-1793
Commonwealth of Massachusetts. By His Excellency John Hancock . . . A brief . . . [June 20, 1788] . . . [Boston, 1788]
broadside 50.5 × 39 cm.
Ford 2518
MBAt; MHi; MWA mp. 45291

B6735 MASSACHUSETTS. LAWS
[The following resolve passed the General Court, November 10, 1786.] . . . In the House of Representatives, March 25, 1788. This bill having had three several readings . . . In Senate, March 27, 1788. This bill . . . passed to be enacted . . . Boston, Adams and Nourse, 1788.
broadsheet 34 × 21 cm.
State treasurer to credit town of Northfield with back taxes
MHi mp. 45292

B6736 MASSACHUSETTS. TREASURER
Tax no. 6. Commonwealth of Massachusetts. Alexander Hodgdon, Esq. Treasurer . . . April 10, 1788. [Boston, 1788]
broadside
MWA

B6737 MASSACHUSETTS CENTINEL
New Year's verses January 1, 1788 . . . [Boston, 1788]
broadside
Found in a volume of the newspaper
MWA mp. 45237

B6738 MERCIER, LOUIS SÉBASTIEN, 1740-1814
The night cap . . . Philadelphia, W. Spotswood, M.DCC.LXXXIII [i.e. 1788]
2 v. ([4], 246, [2]; [4], 255 p.) 16 cm.
cf. Evans 21959
CSmH; MWA mp. 45295

B6739 METEOROLOGICAL observations, made at Springmill, 13 miles NNW. of Philadelphia . . . August, 1788. [Philadelphia? 1788]
broadside 30.5 × 19.5 cm.
Sealock 157
NN mp. 45296

B6740 METHODIST EPISCOPAL CHURCH
Minutes, taken at the several conferences of the Methodist Episcopal church, in America. For the year 1788. New-York, Wm. Ross, 1788.
12 p. 17.5 cm.
PHi; RPJCB mp. 45298

B6741 METHODIST EPISCOPAL CHURCH
The nature, design, and general rules, of the United Societies, of the Methodist Episcopal Church in America. The eighteenth edition . . . New-York, William Ross, 1788.
2 p.l., [3]-9 p. 16.5 cm.
New York Public 896
NN mp. 45297

B6742 METHODIST EPISCOPAL CHURCH
A pocket hymn book, designed as a constant companion for the pious . . . Eighth edition. Philadelphia, Prichard and Hall, 1788.
257, [1] p. 13 cm.
MWA mp. 45342

B6743 MONTEATH, WALTER
Brotherly-love. A sermon, preached in the Presbyterian Church of New-Brunswick, at a meeting of the Grand Lodge of Freemasons . . . of New-Jersey. On the 24th day of June, 1788 . . . New-Brunswick, Shelly Arnett, 1788.
20 p. 21.5 cm.
Morsch 74
NHi; NjP; NjR (p. 19-20 lacking); PPPrHi mp. 45299

B6744 MONTGOMERY CO., PA.
State of the accounts of Jacob Auld . . . till September 1787. Philadelphia, Robert Aitken, 1788.
7 p. 21.5 cm.
DLC; NN mp. 45324

B6745 MORAL songs composed to be sung August the 16th, 1788, at the celebration of the eleventh anniversary of the battle of Bennington . . . [n.p., 1788]
broadside 26.5 X 21 cm.
CtHi mp. 45300

B6746 MORRILL, JAMES
James Morrill, at his shop, No. 43, Newbury-Street, Boston, sells . . . [Boston, 1788?]
broadside
Ford 2521
MB mp. 45301

B6747 MUTUAL ASSURANCE COMPANY, NEW YORK
A sketch of the rates and conditions of insurance, of the Mutual Assurance Company . . . New-York, March 11, 1788. [New York] J. and A. M'Lean [1788]
broadside 40 X 24 cm.
NHi mp. 45303

B6748 THE New-England primer enlarged . . . Boston, Printed by E. Draper, for James White, 1788.
[80] p. [A]-E^8
Heartman 88
CSmH; CtSoP mp. 45304

B6749 THE New-England primer improved . . . Hartford, Hudson & Goodwin, 1788.
[80] p. 9.5 cm.
Trumbull: Supplement 2865 (1783)
Ct; DLC mp. 45305

B6750 THE New-England primer, improved . . . Hartford, Printed by Nath. Petten [sic], 1788.
[80] p. 10 cm.
Hamilton 123; Heartman 105 (1934 ed.)
CtHi; NjP ([64] p.) mp. 45306

B6751 THE New-England primer improved . . . New York, S. Loudon, 1788.
36 leaves. 12mo A-C^{12}
Rosenbach-Ch 133
A. S. W. Rosenbach (1933) mp. 45307

B6752 NEW HAMPSHIRE. GOVERNOR, 1788-1789
By . . . John Langdon . . . a proclamation for a general thanksgiving . . . [Oct. 10, 1788] . . . [Portsmouth, 1788]
broadside 38.5 X 32 cm.
DLC; NhHi mp. 45308

B6753 NEW HAMPSHIRE. LAWS
State of New-Hampshire. In the year . . . One Thousand seven Hundred and eighty-eight. An act, for carrying into effect . . . In the Senate, November 12, 1788 . . . [Portsmouth, 1788]
[2] p. 35.5 X 30 cm.
DLC; MWA; NhHi mp. 45309

B6754 NEW YORK. GENERAL ASSEMBLY
State of New-York. In Assembly, January 31st, 1788. Whereas the United States . . . [New York, 1788]
broadside 31 X 18 cm.
N. Photostats: DLC; NHi mp. 45311

B6755 NEW YORK. GOVERNOR, 1777-1795
By His Excellency George Clinton . . . A proclamation . . . Poughkeepsie, Nicholas Power [1788]
broadside 33 X 20 cm.
Declares John Livingston's leases invalid
Dated Mar. 1, 1788
New York Public 898
MHi; NN (facsim. of original formerly in collection of George M. B. Hawley) mp. 45312

B6756 NEW YORK PACKET
To the generous subscribers for the *New-York Packet.* [New York, S. and J. Loudon, 1788]
broadside 37 X 17.5 cm.
NHi mp. 45377

B6757 NEW-YORK, 12th of April, 1788. Friends and countrymen, From a sincere attachment . . . Your affectionate countrymen, Robert R. Livingston [et al.] [New York, 1788]
broadside 35 X 22.5 cm.
NHi mp. 45313

B6758 [NEWPORT HERALD]
A happy New Yera. The year's revolv'd . . . [Newport? Peter Edes? 1788?]
broadside 20.5 X 12.5 cm.
Imprint and date assigned from internal evidence
Alden 1124
NjHi. Photostat: RHi mp. 45270

B6759 NORTHAMPTON CO., PA.
Sale of a forfeited estate in Pennsylvania. Whereas the estate of Christian Hook . . . hath been forfeited . . . I, the subscriber . . . John M'Nair, jun. agent. September 16th, 1788. Philadelphia, Robert Aitken and Son [1788]
broadside 39.5 X 23.5 cm.
Sealock 155
DLC mp. 45314

B6760 NORTHAMPTON CO., PA.
State of the accounts of James Pettigrew . . . till the 20th June 1786 . . . Philadelphia, Francis Bailey, 1788.
5 p. 22.5 cm.
DLC mp. 45325

B6761 NORTHAMPTON CO., PA.
State of the accounts of Peter Burkholder . . . From

March 29th, 1780 till 1st April, 1783. Philadelphia, Robert Aitken, 1788.
8 p. 21.5 cm.
RPJCB mp. 45326

B6762 [OBSERVATIONS on a pamphlet, published in Philadelphia . . . inscribed to the Legislature of Maryland, by a citizen of Baltimore. Baltimore, John Hayes, 1788]

Advertised as "now in the press" Oct. 14, 1788
Wheeler 479a
No copy known mp. 45315

B6763 OCCOM, SAMSON, 1723-1792
A sermon at the execution of Moses Paul . . . To which is added a short account of the late spread of the Gospel; among the Indians. Also observation on the language of the Muhhekaneow Indians . . . by Jonathan Edwards, D.D. New-Haven, 1788.

cf. Sabin 56636
NhD (2 copies) mp. 45316

B6764 [ODELL, JONATHAN] 1737-1818, supposed author
On spring . . . [at end] Philadelphia: Printed in the year, 1788.
broadside 26.5 X 16.5 cm.
In verse
New York Public 899
PU. Photostat: NN mp. 45317

B6765 OLIPHANT, JAMES
A sacramental catechism, designed for communicants old and young . . . The fifth edition. Philadelphia, W. Young, 1788.
156 p. 16mo
Not used for Evans 24654 (microprint ed.)
PPL mp. 45318

B6766 ORDER of procession, in honor of the Constitution of the United States. At eight o'clock on Wednesday morning the 23d of July . . . Down Broadway to Great-Dock-Street . . . Richard Platt, Chairman. [New York, 1788]
broadside 46 X27 cm.
CtHi; DLC; NHi. Photostat: MWA mp. 45320

B6767 PENN, WILLIAM, 1644-1718
Fruits of a father's love . . . The seventh edition. Philadelphia, Printed and sold by Joseph Crukshank, 1788.
60 p. 16.5 cm.
Sealock 161; cf. Evans 20617
PHi mp. 45321

B6768 PENNSYLVANIA
Pennsylvania, ss. By the vice-president and the supreme executive council . . . a proclamation. [Philadelphia, 1788]
broadside 41.5 X 24 cm.
Issuing a reward for the kidnappers of Timothy Pickering
German translation on bottom half of sheet, dated 1788
MHi; RPJCB mp. 45335

B6769 PENNSYLVANIA. GENERAL ASSEMBLY
Minutes of the second session of the twelfth General Assembly . . . commenced . . . the nineteenth day of February . . . [Colophon] Philadelphia, Hall and Sellers [1788]
[99]-199 p. 31 cm. caption title
PHi; PPL. Photostat: DLC mp. 45238

B6770 PENNSYLVANIA. GENERAL ASSEMBLY
Minutes of the third session of the twelfth General Assembly . . . commenced . . . the second day of September . . . [Colophon] Philadelphia, Hall & Sellers [1788]
p. [201]-280. 31 cm. caption title
PHi; PPL. Photostat: DLC mp. 45329

B6771 PENNSYLVANIA. GENERAL ASSEMBLY
Minutes of the first session of the thirteenth General assembly . . . Philadelphia, Hall and Sellers, 1788.
49 p. 30.5 cm.
DLC; NN; PHi; PPL mp. 45330

B6772 PENNSYLVANIA. GENERAL ASSEMBLY
State of Pennsylvania. In General Assembly, Thursday, March 27, A.M. 1788. The bill, entitled, "A further act for quieting the disturbances at Wyoming . . ." . . . Philadelphia, Thomas Bradford [1788]
3 p. 34 cm.
Sealock 167
PHi mp. 45327

B6773 PENNSYLVANIA. LAWS
An act, relating to meadows, in Kingsessing and Tinicum townships. Philadelphia, Joseph James, 1788.
13 p. 20 cm.
Sealock 162
PHi mp. 45331

B6774 PENNSYLVANIA. LAWS
State of Pennsylvania. An act to explain and amend . . . "An act for the gradual abolition of slavery." . . . Enacted into a law . . . [Mar. 29, 1788]
broadside 33 X 20 cm.
MiU-C; NHi mp. 45332

B6775 PENNSYLVANIA. LAWS
State of Pennsylvania. An act to incorporate the Society for propagating . . . [Philadelphia, Charles Cist, 1788]
4 p. 18 cm. caption title
Sabin 86174
Second title of Stated rules of the Society . . .
DLC; MWA; PHi mp. 45333

B6776 PENNSYLVANIA. SUPREME COURT
Rules and orders for regulating the practice of the Supreme Court of . . . Pennsylvania . . . Philadelphia, Zachariah Poulson, 1788.
29 p. 17.5 cm. [A]-D^4 (D4 blank)
MWA; PPAmP mp. 45334

B6777 THE Pennsylvania sheet almanack for the year . . . 1789. Philadelphia, Printed and sold by B. Towne [1788]
broadside 52 X 65 cm.
Sealock 168
PHi mp. 45336

B6778 PETTY, JOHN
To the public. Annapolis, July 1, 1788. From a variety of circumstances . . . John Petty. [Annapolis, F. Green, 1788]
broadside 41.5 X 25.5 cm.
MdHi mp. 45337

B6779 PETTY, JOHN
To the public. Annapolis, August 18, 1788. It is with extreme pain . . . John Petty. [Annapolis, F. Green, 1788]
broadside ([2] p.) 41.5 X 25.5 cm.
Wheeler 482
MdHi mp. 45338

B6780 PHILADELPHIA. POST OFFICE
Establishment of the posts and post coaches for the year 1788 . . . Jan. 1, 1788. [Philadelphia, 1788]
broadside fol.
PPAmP mp. 45339

B6781 PHILADELPHIA. SHERIFF
Philadelphia, August 21, 1788. By virtue of a writ of venditioni exponas, to me directed, will be exposed for sale . . . a certain two story brick messuage or tenement, and lot . . . of ground . . . Joseph Cowperthwait, sheriff . . . Philadelphia, Charles Cist [1788]
broadside fol.
In English and German
PPL mp. 45340

B6782 PHILADELPHIA, 15th May, 1788. Inventory of the furniture and goods of . . . John Penn, Senr. which are to be exposed for sale on Monday the 19th instant . . . [Philadelphia] Dunlap and Claypoole [1788]
broadside 29 X 19 cm.
PHi (mutilated) mp. 45341

B6783 POOR Tom's almanack for . . . 1789 . . . Philadelphia, John Clark [1788]
[32] p. 15 cm.
MWA mp. 45343

B6784 POPE, ALEXANDER, 1688-1744
An essay on man . . . Philadelphia, William Spotswood, 1788.
42 p. 16.5 cm.
MWA mp. 45344

B6785 POPE, ALEXANDER, 1688-1744
The Messiah, a sacred eclogue . . . To which is added, A collection of poems, by several authors. Philadelphia, Joseph Crukshank, 1788.
2 p.l., 68 p. 12mo
Adams: Pennsylvania 48
PU

B6786 PORTSMOUTH, N.H.
South-Parish, in Portsmouth. To Your parish tax is Timothy Gerrish, Collector. October, 1788. [Portsmouth] J. Melcher [1788]
broadside 10.5 X 12 cm.
Whittemore 464
MHi

B6787 POWER of delusion! The following account of one of the most . . . powerful delusions of the human mind, is taken from the *Columbian Magazine*, for 1788 . . . and is re-published . . . may tend to check . . . a somewhat similar delusion in different parts of New-England . . . [n.p., 1788?]
broadside 44 X 23.5 cm.
MSaE mp. 45345

B6788 PROTESTANT EPISCOPAL CHURCH IN THE U. S. A. MARYLAND (DIOCESE)
At a meeting or convention of clergy and lay-delegates . . . May 29, 1788 . . . [Baltimore, W. Goddard, 1788]
7 p. 20 cm. caption title
Wheeler 483
DLC; MWA; MdBP mp. 45346

B6789 RAMSAY, ALLAN, 1686-1758
The gentle shepherd, a Scotch pastoral comedy . . . [n.p.] Printed in the year M.DCC.LXXXVIII.
60 p. 17 cm.
MWA mp. 45347

B6790 [RAMSAY, DAVID] 1749-1815
An oration, prepared for delivery before the inhabitants of Charleston, assembled on the 27th May, 1788 . . . [Charleston] Bowen, 1788.
12 p. 17 cm.
Sabin 87190; Turnbull p. 265 (v.1)
PHi mp. 45319

B6791 RAYMOND, GERSHOM
In what only true religion consist's . . . By Gershom Raymond, of Norwalk. Fairfield, Forgue and Bulkeley, 1788.
[2], 16 p.
Trumbull: Supplement 2529
CtHi mp. 45348

B6792 RHODE ISLAND. ELECTION PROX.
The Governor's prox. His Excellency John Collins, Esq; Governor. The honorable Daniel Owen, Esq; Deputy-Governor . . . [Providence? 1788]
broadside 19 X 12 cm.
Alden 1128; Chapin Proxies 41
RHi; RNHi; RPB mp. 45349

B6793 RHODE ISLAND. ELECTION PROX.
Liberty and property secured by perseverance. His Excellency John Collins, Esq; Governor . . . [Providence? 1788]
broadside 19.5 X 14 cm.
Alden 1129; Chapin Proxies 42a, 43b
RHi (2 variants) mp. 45350

B6794 RHODE ISLAND. LAWS
State of Rhode-Island and Providence-Plantations. In General assembly, June session, A. D. 1788. An act for granting . . . Providence, Bennett Wheeler [1788]
broadside 33.5 X 21.5 cm.
Alden 1132; Winship p. 53
DLC; RHi mp. 45351

B6795 RUMSEY, JAMES, 1743-1792
Proposals for forming a company, to enable James Rumsey to carry into execution . . . his steam-boat . . . In witness of the premises, we the subscribers, have hereunto set our names, this day of 1788. [Philadelphia? 1788]
broadside 34.5 X 28.5 cm.
DLC; WHi (mutilated) mp. 45352

B6796 RUMSEY, JAMES, 1743-1792
A short treatise on the application of steam . . . By James Rumsey, of Berkeley County, Virginia. Philadelphia, Joseph James, 1788.
25 p.
Not Evans 21442; t.p. and text reset
CSmH mp. 45353

B6797 RUTGERS UNIVERSITY
Rules and regulations for the government of Queen's College, in New-Jersey: enacted by a Board of the Trustees of said College, the 7th day of August, 1787. New-Brunswick: Printed by Shelly Arnett, 1788.
12 p. 17 cm.
NjR

B6798 [SANDS, BENJAMIN]
[Metamorphosis. Philadelphia, 1788?]
oblong leaf folded 3 times
Contains 8 woodcuts by James Poupard
Author's name first appears in Solomon Wieatt edition (Philadelphia, 1807)

Rosenbach-Ch 82 (dated [1775?])
PP mp. 45354

B6799 SARGEANT, SAMUEL, 1755-1818
A sermon, delivered at the introduction of . . . Nahum Sargeant, to the pastoral care of the church . . . Reading, November 23, 1787. By his brother Samuel Sargeant . . . Windsor, Hough and Spooner, 1788.
22 p. 20.5 cm.
Cooley 101
MBC; MH; MWA; RPJCB mp. 45355

B6800 A SCHOOL is opened in Perth-Amboy, in which boys will be taught . . . at . . . six pounds per annum . . . The school is under the direction of Mr. Joseph Bend . . . Trenton, Isaac Collins [1788?]
broadside 35 X 21.5 cm.
NjR

B6801 SCOTT, FRANCES
[A true and wonderful narrative of the surprising captivity and remarkable deliverance of Mrs. Frances Scott. The third edition. Boston, 1788]

Vail: Old frontier 787
MHi mp. 45356

B6802 [SEDAINE, MICHEL JEAN] 1719-1797
The deserter, a comic-opera . . . New-York: Printed for Samuel Campbell, MDCCLXXXVIII.
30, [1] p. 17 cm.
Attributed to Charles Dibdin
cf. Evans 20331 (dated 1787 in microprint)
NHi

B6803 [SHEET almanack for 1789. New-London, T. Green, 1788]
broadside
Advertised in the *Connecticut Gazette*, Dec. 19, 1788, as "Also the Sheet Almanack, to be sold at the Printing-Office, New-London."
Drake 441
No copy known

B6804 SMITH, WILLIAM, 1727-1803
An address to the General assembly . . . Philadelphia, R. Aitken, 1788.
32 p. 17.5 cm.
Signed on p. 31: William Smith
Sabin 84581
DLC; PHi; PPAmP mp. 45358

B6805 SMITH, WILLIAM LOUGHTON, 1752-1812
A dose for the doctor . . . William Smith. Charleston, November 25, 1788. [Charleston, 1788]
broadside 27.5 X 22 cm.
Sabin 84822
DLC; MH mp. 45359

B6806 SMITH, WILLIAM LOUGHTON, 1752-1812
To the citizens of Charleston district . . . William Smith. Charleston, Nov. 22. [Charleston, 1788]
broadside 54.5 X 40.5 cm.
Printed in five columns
Turnbull p. 267 (v.1)
DLC. Photostats: MWA; NHi mp. 45360

B6807 SOCIETY FOR THE ENCOURAGEMENT OF MANUFACTURES AND THE USEFUL ARTS IN AMERICA
Philadelphia, Sir, A respectable body . . . [Philadelphia, 1788]
broadside 38 X 23 cm.
Dated in manuscript: 1st. October 1788
DLC mp. 45361

B6808 SOCIETY OF THE CINCINNATI
Cincinnati. The members of this State Society of Cincinnatus will meet to-morrow morning . . . at the City Tavern, Broad-way . . . Tuesday morning, July 22, 1788. [New York? 1788]
broadside 16 X 15 cm.
MHi mp. 45362

B6809 SOCIETY OF THE UNITED BRETHREN
Stated rules of the Society of the United Brethren, for propagating the Gospel among the heathen. Philadelphia, Charles Cist [1788]
15, [1], 4 p. 18 cm.
4 p. at end: the act of incorporation of the Society
Sabin 86174; Sealock 176
DLC; MWA; NHi; PHi; PPL mp. 45363

B6810 SOUTH CAROLINA. CONSTITUTIONAL CONVENTION
Ratification. Charleston, May 26, 1788. [Charleston? 1788]
broadside 27 X 20 cm.
Sabin 87419
RPJCB mp. 45364

B6811 SOUTH CAROLINA. LEGISLATURE
In the House of Representatives, February 17th, 1788 . . . In the Senate, February 18, 1788. [Charleston, 1788]
[1], 2 p. 43 cm. caption title
Includes 8 resolutions
Sc-Ar

B6812 STANCLIFF, JOHN
[A letter to Mr. James Moore in answer to his letter containing some remarks on a late piece, entituled An account of the Murrinitish plague. Philadelphia, 1788?]

Sabin 90149; Sealock 178
No copy located mp. 45365

B6813 STERRY, CONSIDER
Proposals, for printing by subscription the *American Youth* . . . By Consider and John Sterry . . . [New London, 1788]
broadside 42 X 28 cm.
cf. *Conn. Gazette,* June 20, 1788
DLC mp. 45367

B6814 THE storekeeper's and mechanic's sheet almanac for the year . . . 1789. Wilmington, James Adams [1788]
broadside?
"Item 257 from Catalogue 576 (1926) of C. W. Unger (Pottsville."—Note on card in N. Y. Pub. Lib. imprint file
Hawkins: List C 16
No copy known mp. 45368

B6815 TAYLOR, JOSEPH
The revivification of young Joseph Taylor . . . Sixth edition. [Boston] America, Printed [by E. Russell] for, and sold by A. Nelson, traveling trader, Pownalboro' [1788?]
16 p. illus., port. 18 cm.
On illustrated cover: "The wonderful monitor . . ." Has same cuts and cover-title as the 1788 Boston ed. of *God's tender mercy*
cf. Evans 21488
MWA mp. 45371

B6816 TEMPLE PATRICK SOCIETY
A debate proposed in the Temple Patrick Society . . . Philadelphia, W. Young, 1788.
23, [1] p. 16 cm.
cf. Evans 24178
DLC; PHi mp. 45372

B6816a THIS indenture made the day of in the year . . . One Thousand Seven Hundred and between . . . Philadelphia, printed by Charles Cist [1788?]
broadside 18.5 X 45 cm.
All known copies found in or near the September 1788 issue of the *American Museum*.–Chester Hollenbeck
DLC; KyU; PP

B6817 THOMAS, ELISHA, d. 1788
The last words, and dying speech of Elisha Thomas . . . executed at Dover, on the 3d June, 1788 . . . for the murder of Captain Peter Drowne. [n.p., 1788]
broadside 44 X 34 cm.
Ford 2523
MWA mp. 45373

B6818 THOMAS, ELISHA, d. 1788
Life and dying speech of Elisha Thomas, who suffered at Dover, June 3, 1788, – for the murder of Capt. Peter Drowne. [Portsmouth? 1788]
broadside 34 X 21.5 cm.
Whittemore 466
NhHi mp. 45374

B6819 THOMPSON, JAMES, 1700-1748
The seasons . . . Philadelphia, Printed and sold by Prichard and Hall, 1788.
196 p. 14 cm.
New York Public 902
DGU; MWA; NN; PLB; RPJCB mp. 45375

B6820 TO Miss R****** M***. Please to read the following verses . . . MUM. Burlington, January 1, 1788. [New Brunswick? 1788]
broadside 19 X 11.5 cm.
Verses within elaborate floral ornaments
NjR (mutilated)

B6821 TO the citizens of New-York. A person who addresses you . . . is very angry . . . New-York, April 30, 1788 . . . [New York, 1788]
broadside 27 X 16.5 cm.
NHi. Photostats: DLC; MHi; MWA; NN mp. 45376

B6822 TO the independent electors, of the city and county of Albany. At a public and general meeting of the Federalists . . . a committee . . . was appointed . . . Robert M'Clallen . . . Albany, 16th March, 1788. [Albany] Charles R. Webster [1788]
broadside 33 X 20 cm.
Photostats: DLC; MHi; MWA mp. 45257

B6823 TO the independent electors, of the city and county of Albany. At a public . . . meeting of the Federalists . . . of Albany . . . March 14, 1788. Albany, Charles R. Webster [1788]
broadside 33 X 21 cm.
NHi mp. 45378

B6824 TO the independent electors of the City and County of Albany . . . Mat. Visscher, CLK. 15th March, 1788. Albany, Charles R. Webster [1788]
broadside 26 X 20 cm.
McMurtrie: Albany 29a
N; NHi mp. 45379

B6825 TO the inhabitants of King's County . . . Flatbush, 28th April, 1788. New-York, Francis Childs [1788]
broadside 29 X 16.5 cm.
DLC; NHi. Photostats: CSmH; NN mp. 45380

B6826 TO the inhabitants of the District of Schenectady. Our antient and respectable town, has long been famous . . . Schenectady Farmer. [n.p., ca. 1788]
broadside 20.5 X 16 cm.
NHi mp. 45381

B6827 TO the people of the district of Edenton. [Edenton? Hodge & Willis? 1788?]
13 p. 20.5 cm. caption title
Seven letters, of which I and VII are signed: A Citizen and Soldier
Dated at end: August, 1788
McMurtrie: North Carolina 132
MWiW-C; NcA-S; ViU. Photostat: NN mp. 45382

B6828 TO the people of the State of North-Carolina. Friends and fellow citizens . . . [at end] A Citizen of North-Carolina. August 18, 1788. [Newbern? Hodge & Willis? 1788]
3 p. 36.5 cm. caption title
Probably by James Iredell
McMurtrie: North Carolina 133a (appendix)
ViU mp. 45383

B6829 Deleted

B6830 U. S. CONSTITUTION
The Constitution of frame of government . . . [Colophon] Boston, Thomas and John Fleet [1788]
23 p. 18.5 cm. caption title
DLC mp. 45385

B6831 U. S. CONSTITUTION
The Constitution of the United States. We the people . . . [Hartford, 1788]
8 p. 29 cm. caption title
cf. Evans 21523 (slightly different printing)
DLC

B6832 U. S. CONSTITUTION
Die Constitution, so wie sie zur Regierung der Vereinigten Staaten . . . Albany, Carl R. Webster, 1788.
24 p. 15.5 cm.
McMurtrie: Albany 35
N mp. 45386

B6833 U. S. CONTINENTAL CONGRESS, 1788
By the United States in Congress assembled. February 12, 1788. On the report of a committee consisting of Mr. Dyre Kearny, Mr. John Kean and Mr. James Madison . . . [New York, 1788]
broadside?
Edition of 60 copies
Resolutions respecting sea letters
Ford: Bibliographical notes . . . 599
No copy known mp. 45387

B6834 U. S. CONTINENTAL CONGRESS, 1788
A supplement to an ordinance entitled, "An / ordinance for ascertaining the mode of disposing of lands / in the Western Territory./ [New York, 1788]
[2] p. 33.5 X 21 cm.
New York Public 906
NN

B6835 U. S. CONTINENTAL CONGRESS, 1788
A supplement to an ordinance entitled, "An ordinance

for ascertaining / the mode of disposing of lands in the Western Territory."/ [New York, 1788]
[2] p. 42 X 26 cm.
New York Public 907; cf. Evans 21533
NN (varies textually throughout from NYPL 906)
mp. 45388

B6836 U. S. DEPT. OF WAR
[The Secretary of the United States for the Department of War to whom was referred his letter to Congress of the 16 of April . . . New York, 1788]

Edition of 60 copies printed
Ford: Bibliographical notes . . . 574; not Evans 20786
No copy known mp. 45389

B6837 THE United States almanac, for . . . 1789 . . . By Eben. W. Judd . . . New-York, Printed for Samuel Campbell [1788]
[36] p.
Drake 5963
NHi mp. 45279

B6838 THE United States almanac, for . . . 1789 . . . By Eben. W. Judd . . . New-York, Printed for William and James Hays [1788]
[32] p.
Drake 5964
InU (imperfect); MWA mp. 45280

B6839 THE United States almanac, for . . . 1789. New York, James Reid [1788]
[36] p. 18 cm.
By Eben W. Judd
Does not contain the act called for on the t.p. of Evans 21182
CSmH (imperfect); MWA (lacks all beyond p. [30])
mp. 45281

B6840 THE Universal calendar, and the North-American almanack, for the year . . . 1789 . . . By Samuel Stearns . . . Boston, Edes [1788]
[24] p. 17.5 cm.
Nichols p. 69
DLC (p. [23-24] wanting; MHi; MWA mp. 45366

B6841 VERMONT. GOVERNOR, 1778-1789
By His Excellency, Thomas Chittenden . . . A proclamation . . . Thursday the 27th day of November next, to be observed as a day of public thanksgiving . . . [Bennington, Haswell and Russell, 1788]
broadside 33 X 22.5 cm.
McCorison 153; Sabin 99061
VtBrt mp. 45390

B6842 VERMONT. GOVERNOR, 1778-1789
[Fast day proclamation. Bennington, Haswell & Russell, 1788]
broadside?
Printer's bill for 140 copies dated Mar. 1788
McCorison 152
No copy known mp. 45391

B6843 VIRGINIA. AUDITOR'S OFFICE
A list of pensioners, for the year 1788 . . . Auditor's-Office, December 10, 1788. J. Pendleton. [Richmond, 1788]
broadside 51 X 39 cm.
DLC; MWA; NN mp. 45392

B6844 VIRGINIA. CONVENTION, 1788
Poghkeepsie [sic], July 2d, 1788. Just arrived by express, the ratification of the new Constitution by the Convention of the State of Virginia . . . [Poughkeepsie, 1788]
broadside 25 X 18.5 cm.
New York Public 901; Sabin 100031
NjP. Photostats: DLC; MHi; MWA; NHi; NN
mp. 45393

B6845 VIRGINIA. COUNCIL
In Council, May 20, 1788. Gentlemen, I beg leave to submit . . . Attest A. Blair, C. C. [Richmond, 1788]
broadside 24 X 19 cm.
DLC (2 copies); WHi mp. 45394

B6846 VIRGINIA. GENERAL ASSEMBLY
Virginia, to wit: In General assembly . . . the 20th November, 1788. Resolved, That an application . . . [Richmong, 1788]
broadside 23 X 19 cm.
DLC; MHi; PPRF; ViU. Photostats: MWA; NN
mp. 45395

B6847 VIRGINIA. GENERAL ASSEMBLY
Virginia, to wit: In General assembly . . . the 20th November, 1788. Sir, The freemen . . . [Richmond, 1788]
broadside 23 X 19 cm.
DLC; RPJCB. Photostats: MHi; MWA; NN mp. 45396

B6848 VIRGINIA. HOUSE OF DELEGATES
In the House of Delegates, Monday, the 7th of January, 1788. On a motion made, Ordered, that the . . . statement of the public revenue . . . be published . . . and that 2000 copies . . . printed . . . [Richmond, Thomas Nicolson, 1788]
[4] p. 36 cm.
New York Public 911; Sabin 100093
NN mp. 45397

B6849 VIRGINIA. HOUSE OF DELEGATES
In the House of delegates, the 25th of December, 1788. Resolved, That the executive . . . In Council, December 29, 1788. In pursuance of the above resolution . . . [Richmond, 1788]
broadside 17 X 21 cm.
DLC mp. 45402

B6850 VIRGINIA. LAWS
An act concerning the erection of Kentuckey [sic] into an independent state. [Passed the 29th of December 1788.] Whereas it is represented to the General Assembly . . . [Richmond, 1788]
broadside 26 X 21 cm.
In 2 columns
Imprint assigned by WHi
McMurtrie: Kentucky no. 11?
WHi mp. 45398

B6851 VIRGINIA. LAWS
An act directing the mode of proceeding under certain executions . . . [Richmond? 1788]
broadside 33 X 19.5 cm.
Dated at end: January 4, 1788. Passed the House of Delegates, John Beckley, C.H.D.
NcD mp. 45399

B6852 VIRGINIA. LAWS
An act to amend the several acts respecting the militia . . . [at end] A true copy from the enrollment, teste, John Beckley, C.H.D. In Council, January 1, 1788 . . . Attest, A. Blair, C.C. [Richmond, 1788]
broadside 22.5 X 19.5 cm.
WHi mp. 45400

B6853 THE Virginia almanack for the year . . . 1789 . . . By Robert Andrews . . . Richmond, John Dixon [1788]
[24] p. 15 cm.
Bear 72
ViU mp. 45220

B6854 [THE Virginia and North Carolina almanack for the year 1789. Petersburg? 1788?]

Title from advertisement in the *Virginia Gazette and Petersburg Intelligencer*, Nov. 27, 1788
Bear 74; Wyatt 7
No copy known mp. 45401

B6855 THE Virginia Gazette, and Independent Chronicle. Richmond, John Dixon [1788]

Brigham p. 1147
DLC (issues for Oct. 25, Nov. 1)

B6855a WARD, EDWARD, 1667-1731
Female policy detected; or, The arts of a designing woman laid open. By E. W. . . . [n.p.] Printed for the booksellers. M,DCC,LXXXVIII.
108 p. 15.5 cm.
Probably an American imprint. Judgment based on comparisons of type ornaments by R. G. Adams in 1932
MiU-C

B6856 WARD, RICHARD
Just imported, in the last ships from London and Bristol, and now selling by Richard Ward . . . Salem, an assortment of hard ware . . . [Salem, 1788?]
broadside 19 X 15 cm.
Blank verso used for a bill, dated Apr. 30, 1788
RPJCB mp. 45403

B6857 A WARNING to disobedient youth: being a relation concerning a certain Henry Webb, who was three days and nights in a trance . . . Carlisle: Printed for James Kiteley, living near Laird's-Mill, on Yellow-Breeches. 1788.
8 p. 21 cm.
MB mp. 45404

B6858 WASHINGTON, GEORGE, 1732-1799
Extract of a letter from His Excellency General Washington to the printer of the *American Museum*. Mount Vernon, June 25, 1788 . . . [Philadelphia, M. Carey, 1788?]
[2] p. 8vo
PPL mp. 45405

B6859 WATERHOUSE, BENJAMIN, 1754-1846
Heads of a course of lectures . . . By B. Waterhouse, M.D. Professor . . . of natural history in the College of Rhode-Island . . . Providence, Bennett Wheeler [ca. 1788?]
broadside 35 X 19.5 cm.
Alden 1135; New York Public 912; Winship p. 75
RHi. Photostat: NN mp. 45406

B6860 WATTS, ISAAC, 1674-1748
The child's catechism of the principles of religion . . . Norwich, J. Trumbull, 1788.
31 p.
Trumbull: Supplement 2716
No copy located mp. 45407

B6861 WATTS, ISAAC, 1674-1748
Divine songs; in easy language . . . Springfield, 1788.
31, [1] p.
Not Evans 22244
MWA mp. 45408

B6862 WAYNE, ANTHONY, 1745-1796
For sale, and may be taken possession of immediately . . . rice plantations, situate on the river Savannah . . . called Richmond and Kew . . . [32 lines] [Signed] Anthony Wayne. Charleston, January 21, 1788. [Charleston? 1788]
broadside 32.5 X 18 cm.
Enclosed in a letter from Wayne to Sharp Delany, 20 Feb. 1788
MiU-C

B6863 WEBSTER, NOAH, 1758-1843
[The American spelling book . . . Bennington, Haswell and Russell, 1788]

Advertised in the *Vermont Gazette* Aug. 4, 1788, as "This day published . . ."
Skeel-Carpenter 13
No copy known mp. 45409

B6864 WEBSTER, NOAH, 1758-1843
[The American spelling book . . . Boston, John Folsom, 1788]

Letter from Webster, Aug. 16, 1788: "I find Mr. Folsom has begun the Spelling Book . . . At his request . . . I write for your plates . . ."
Skeel-Carpenter 14
No copy known mp. 45410

B6865 WEBSTER, NOAH, 1758-1843
The American spelling book, or First part of the Grammatical institute of the English language . . . The eighth edition, with additional lessons. Philadelphia, W. Young, 1788.
p.
Skeel-Carpenter 8
CtY (t.p. only) mp. 45411

B6866 WEBSTER, NOAH, 1758-1843
[The American spelling book, or First part of the Grammatical institute of the English language . . . Ninth edition. New York, Samuel Campbell, 1788]

Advertised in the New York *Morning Post* July 1, 1788, as "a neat and accurate edition (being the ninth) . . ."
Skeel-Carpenter 9
No copy known mp. 45412

B6867 WEBSTER, NOAH, 1758-1843
The American spelling book: Containing, an easy standard of pronunciation . . . The eleventh edition. Hartford, Hudson and Goodwin [1788?]
153 p. illus. 17 cm.
Sabin 102337; Skeel-Carpenter 11
RPJCB mp. 45413

B6868 WEBSTER, NOAH, 1758-1843
An introduction to English grammar: being an abridgement . . . Philadelphia, W. Young, 1788.
36 p. 14.5 cm.
Huntington 554; Sabin 102359
CSmH; DLC; MWA; PHi; PPL mp. 45414

B6869 WILKINSON, EDWARD, 1727-1809
Wisdom, a poem. Philadelphia, Joseph James, 1788.
19 p. 8vo
PPL mp. 45415

B6870 THE Wilmington Centinel, and General Advertiser. Wilmington, N.C., Bowen and Howard [1788]

Brigham p. 780
DLC (photostat: June 18, 1788); MWA

B6871 YORK CO., PA.
State of the account of John M'Clellan . . . till 1st, August 1787 . . . Philadelphia, Robert Aitken, 1788.
7 p. 21 cm.
DLC mp. 45322

B6872 ZANE, ISAAC
Mühlen, and mühl platze und plantaschen, sind zu verkauffen oder verlehnen . . . Isaac Zahne. den 6 Junn 1788. Friederich-Stadt, Matthias Bärtgis [1788]
broadside 38 X 18 cm.
Wheeler 487
RPJCB mp. 45417

B6873 ZANE, ISAAC
To be sold or rented, Marbro' Iron-Works, situated about 12 miles from the borough of Winchester . . . Isaac Zane . . . [Frederick, M. Bartgis, 1788]
broadside 30.5 X 19.5 cm.
Wheeler 488
RPJCB mp. 45418

B6874 ZUM Neuen Jahr. Den 1sten Jenner, 1789. Seith Sekuln ist es eingefuhrt, Dass man zum Neuen Jahr sinander gratulirt . . . [Philadelphia, 1788?]
broadside 22.5 X 14.5 cm.
PHi mp. 45419

1789

B6875 ALBANY, Jan. 26, 1789. Extract of a letter from a gentleman in this city, to his friend in New York . . . Albany, Robert Barber [1789]
broadside 50 X 29.5 cm.
McMurtrie: Albany 38
N mp. 45420

B6876 ALBANY, February 14, 1789. At a meeting of a number of citizens from . . . the County of Albany . . . General Abraham Ten Broeck was unanimously nominated, as a candidate . . . [Albany? 1789]
broadside 29.5 X 42 cm.
NHi mp. 45421

B6877 ALBANY, 19th February, 1789. Gentlemen, One of the most important elections is soon to take place . . . Jacob C. Ten Eyck [and 32 others] [Albany, 178 1789]
broadside 34 X 19.5 cm.
New York Public 936
NAII. Photostat: NN mp. 45422

B6878 ALEXANDRIA
[Address of the mayor, with George Washington's response. Alexandria, George Richard, 1789]

Title from *Alexandria Gazette*, Sept. 24, 1858, which describes a copy
No copy known mp. 45423

B6879 AN almanack for the year . . . 1790 . . . By N. Strong . . . Hartford, Hudson and Goodwin [1789]
[24] p. 17.5 cm.
Bates: Connecticut almanacs p. 147; Morrison p. 20; Trumbull 114
CtHi; DLC; MWA; N mp. 45597

B6880 AN almanack, for the year . . . 1790. [Norwich, J. Trumbull? 1789]
broadside cut and stitched into 12 leaves. 17.5 cm.
Probably Bates: Connecticut almanacs . . . "Sheet almanack for 1790. Norwich: John Trumbull"
DLC mp. 45424

B6881 THE American museum: or repository of ancient and modern fugitive pieces . . . For August, 1787 . . . Vol. II. No. II. The second edition. Philadelphia, Mathew Carey, 1789.
1 p.l., [107]-207, [1] p. 21 cm.
Sealock 187
NN; NhD; OClW

B6882 THE American museum, or, Universal magazine: containing . . . for the year, 1789. [Volume 6] Second part from July to December. Philadelphia, Carey, Stewart, and Co., 1789.

CSmH; MHi; NhD; OClW

B6883 ANTHEM to be sung by the charity scholars, on Sunday, the 22d of November, at St. Paul's Church, after the charity sermon . . . [New York, 1789]
broadside 32 X 19.5 cm.
NHi mp. 45426

B6884 ARNAUD, FRANÇOIS THOMAS MARIE DE BACULARD D', 1718-1805
Fanny . . . The third American edition. Litchfield, Thomas Collier, 1789.
88 p. 16 cm.
MWA mp. 45427

B6885 ASSOCIATE PRESBYTERY OF PENNSYLVANIA
Act of the Associate Synod, explaining the connection of the Associate Presbytery . . . with the said Synod. Philadelphia, Printed and sold by John M'Culloch, 1789.
8, 4 p. 20.5 cm.
Sealock 188
P mp. 45428

B6886 AN astronomical diary, kalendar, or almanack, for . . . 1790 . . . Hartford, Elisha Babcock [1789]
[24] p. 18 cm.
By Isaac Bickerstaff
MWA mp. 45431

B6887 AN astronomical diary, kalendar, or almanack for . . . 1790. By N. Strong. Northampton, William Butler [1789]
[24] p.
Drake 3426
NjMoW

B6888 AN astronomical diary: or almanack for . . . 1790. By Nathanael Low. Boston, T. & J. Fleet. The only proprietors of Dr. Low's copy right. [1789]
[24] p.
Drake 3425
MHi; MWA

B6889 BAILEY, FRANCIS
Philadelphia, February 21, 1789. Proposals by Francis Bailey, for printing by subscription . . . True Christian Religion . . . by Emanuel Swedenborg . . . [Philadelphia, F. Bailey, 1789]
broadside 42 X 27.5 cm.
Sealock 189
NHi mp. 45429

B6890 BALTIMORE Assembly. Admittance for the season . . . November 10, 1789. [Baltimore, W. Goddard and J. Angell, 1789]

ticket 6.5 X 9 cm.
Wheeler 491
MdHi

B6891 BALTIMORE Assembly. As the most minute attention to every sentiment of politeness . . . is absolutely necessary . . . it is unnecessary to urge . . . observance of the following rules . . . Baltimore, W. Goddard and J. Angell [1789]
broadside 33.5 X 20.5 cm.
Wheeler 492
MdHi mp. 45430

B6892 THE Baltimore pocket almanack, for . . . 1790. By Thomas Fox. Baltimore, Samuel & John Adams [1789]
[25+] p. 12 cm.
MWA (lacking after p. 25) mp. 45479

B6893 BAPTISTS. VERMONT. WOODSTOCK ASSOCIATION
Minutes of the Woodstock Association, held at the Baptist meetinghouse in Marlow, 1789. Wednesday, September 30 . . . [Windsor? 1789?]
12 p. 18.5 cm.
McCorison 160
RPJCB; VtHi mp. 45432

B6894 BAPTISTS. VIRGINIA. ROANOKE DISTRICT ASSOCIATION
Minutes of the proceedings of the Roanoak district association, Virginia. Convened at Grassy Creek meeting house, May 1789. Hillsborough, R. Ferguson [1789]
15 p. 15.5 cm.
ViRU mp. 45433

B6895 BARBAULD, ANNA LETITIA (AIKIN), 1743-1825
Hymns in prose for children . . . The fifth edition. New-Haven, Abel Morse, 1789.
48 p. 12 cm.
Trumbull: Second supplement 2824
CtY mp. 45434

B6896 BARNES, JOSEPH
. . . As John Fitch has procured a number of handbills . . . [Philadelphia, 1789]
broadside 31 X 25 cm.
Dated: Philadelphia, Sept. 21, 1789
PHi mp. 45435

B6897 BARTON, BENJAMIN SMITH, 1766-1815
Proposals for printing, by subscription, An historical and philosophical inquiry into . . . various remains of antiquity . . . discovered in America . . . Philadelphia, December 22d. 1789.
broadside 30 X 19 cm.
New York Public 913
NN; PPAmP mp. 45436

B6898 BERQUIN, ARNAUD, 1749-1791
The friend of youth . . . Newburyport, Printed by John Mycall, for the proprietor of the Boston Bookstore, Boston [1789]
2 v. 18 cm.
Advertised in 1789 Benjamin Guild catalog
MWA mp. 45437

B6899 BEVERIDGE, THOMAS
The servants of the Lord, sustained by his mercy . . . A sermon preached at Philadelphia . . . October 31st, 1788, at the ordination of . . . David Goodwillie . . . Philadelphia, W. Young, 1789.
35, [1] p. 18 cm.
Sealock 194
NjP; P mp. 45438

B6900 BIBLE
A concise history of the Holy Bible . . . Philadelphia, Printed in the year 1789.
103, 17 p. 5.5 cm.
d'Alté A. Welch, Cleveland (1962) mp. 45439

B6901 BIBLE. O.T. PSALMS
The Psalms of David, imitated . . . By I. Watts, D.D. . . . Boston, John Norman [1789]
276, [8] p. 15.5 cm.
Second title (Hymns and spiritual songs) is Evans 22245
mp. 45741

B6902 BIBLE. N.T.
The New Testament . . . New York, Printed and sold by Hugh Gaine, 1789.
[336] p. 16 cm.
New York Public 914
NN mp. 45441

B6903 BIBLE. SELECTIONS
Translations and paraphrases of several passages of Sacred Scripture. Collected . . . by a committee appointed by the . . . Church of Scotland. Bennington, Haswell & Russell, 1789.
45 p. 16 cm.
Cooley 110
VtU-W mp. 45440

B6904 BOSTON
The following report is printed by order of the town, for the information of the inhabitants, to be considered at the adjournment, on Thursday, 21st instant . . . James Sullivan, Chairman. [Boston, 1789?]
broadside
Ford 2566
MB mp. 45442

B6905 BOSTON. COMMITTEE ON A PLAN OF PROCESSION
Boston, October 19, 1789. Sir, The committee appointed for the purpose of recommending a plan of procession, on the arrival of the President . . . [Boston, 1789]
broadside 34 X 21 cm.
Signed by Paul Revere and 13 others
cf. Evans 21701
MB; MWA

B6906 BOSTON. COMMITTEE ON PUBLIC EDUCATION
Recommendations to the schoolmasters, by the committee appointed to carry into execution the system of public education, adopted by the Town of Boston, the 15th of October 1789 . . . [Boston, 1789?]
broadside 29 X 20.5 cm.
MHi; MWA mp. 45443

B6907 BOUCHARD DE LA POTERIE, CLAUDE FLORENT
To the publick. On the fourth of February ult. 1789, a Frenchman . . . Louis Abraham Welsh, born and baptised in . . . Guadeloupe . . . resided in Dedham . . . [Boston, 1789]
[4] p. 25 cm.
Ford 2527
MHi; MWA mp. 45444

B6908 [BURKE, MRS.]
Ela: or The delusions of the heart . . . Wilmington, Printed and sold by Brynberg and Andrews, 1789.
140, ii p. 12mo
Huntington 557
CSmH mp. 45445

B6909 BUTLER, ANTHONY
Town of York & Manor of Springetsbury, in the County of York . . . Stadt York und Manor Springetsbury in York County. Philadelphia, Charles Cist [1789]
broadside 29 X 16.5 cm.
Dated: April 8, 1789
PHi mp. 45446

B6910 CAMPBELL, SAMUEL, OF NEW YORK
Samuel Campbell's Catalogue of books, for 1789 . . . [New York, 1789]
58 p. 8vo
1508 numbered titles
Brigham: Booksellers, p. 46
MWA mp. 45447

B6911 CAREY, JOHN
Sir, At the desire of my brother, Mathew Carey, Editor of the *American Museum* . . . John Carey . . . [Philadelphia, 1789]
[4] p. 14 cm.
Pages [2-4] blank
Circular dunning delinquent subscribers
Dated from ms. note on p. [4]: John Carey, June 1789
MHi mp. 44654

B6912 CAREY, MATHEW, 1760-1839
Philadelphia, August 15, 1789. To the Roman Catholics of America, Mathew Carey respectfully submits . . . proposals for printing by subscription . . . the Holy Bible . . . [Philadelphia, M. Carey, 1789]
4 p. 8vo
PPL mp. 45448

B6913 CHAMBERLAIN, R.
R. Chamberlain, No. 2, Newbury-Street, . . . Boston. European & India goods. [Boston, 1789?]
broadside 13.5 X 15 cm.
Ford 2530
MHi mp. 45449

B6914 CHESTERFIELD, PHILIP DORMER STANHOPE, EARL, 1694-1773
Lord Chesterfield's advice to his son . . . Wilmington, James Adams, 1789.
106, [2] p. 12mo
PPL mp. 45450

B6915 CHESTERFIELD, PHILIP DORMER STANHOPE, EARL, 1694-1773
Principles of politeness . . . with additions, by . . . John Trusler . . . New-Haven, A. Morse, 1789.
144 p. 14 cm.
CtHi; MWA mp. 45451

B6916 THE Christian oeconomy. Translated from the original Greek . . . Windsor, Alden Spooner, 1789.
48 p. 25 cm.
Cooley 112
MWA; VtHi mp. 45452

B6917 CITY GAZETTE, OR DAILY ADVERTISER, CHARLESTON, S.C.
New Year's verses for the lads that carry the *Daily Advertiser*, to the customers . . . Charleston, January 1, 1789.
broadside 29.5 X 14.5 cm.
New York Public 917
NN mp. 45534

B6918 CLARKE, ELIJAH, 1733-1799
Copy of a letter from Brigadier General Clarke to . . . the Governor, dated, Washington, May 29, 1789, 10 o'clock at night. Sir, Yesterday evening . . . information from the Creeks . . . instructions are, to fall on the frontiers of Georgia . . . E. Clarke . . . In Council, Augusta, May 31, 1789 . . . Meriwether, S.E.C. [Augusta? 1789]
broadside 31.5 X 20.5 cm.
NjR

B6919 CLINTON, JAMES, 1733-1812
To be sold, fine wheat, hemp and grass lands in the State of New-York . . . free from taxes for 5 or 6 years to come . . . For terms apply to General J. Clinton, New-York . . . [New York, 1789]
broadside 41.5 X 24.5 cm.
Includes certificates dated Feb. 12, 1789
New York Public 918
NHi. Photostat: NN mp. 45453

B6920 COLLINS, ISAAC, 1746-1817
Proposals, for printing by subscription, by Isaac Collins, in Trenton, the Holy Bible . . . Mr. Isaac Collins has . . . been . . . printer to the state . . . I have had abundant proof of the accuracy . . . of his publications . . . Trenton, 11 Sept. 1788. Wil Livingston. [Trenton, 1789]
[4] p. 4to
Huntington 556; Morsch 99
CSmH mp. 45454

B6921 THE Columbian almanac . . . for the year . . . 1790 . . . Wilmington, Peter Brynberg and Samuel Andrews [1789]
[48] p. 17.5 cm.
Hawkins 25
DeHi mp. 45455

B6922 A COMPANION for the counting house, or duties payable on goods imported into America . . . Philadelphia, Printed and sold by R. Aitken & Son, 1789.
16 p. 13.5 cm.
Sealock 195
P mp. 45456

B6923 CONNECTICUT. GOVERNOR, 1786-1796
By His Excellency Samuel Huntington . . . A proclamation tion. Whereas the . . . General Assembly . . . have thought fit . . . to lay an embargo . . . Hartford, the 22d day of May . . . 1789 . . . Samuel Huntington . . . Hartford, Hudson & Goodwin [1789]
broadside 33 X 20 cm.
CtHi (mutilated) mp. 45457

B6924 CONNECTICUT. TREASURER
State of Connecticut, in America. To Constable of and collector of the state tax for . . . 1790. Greeting . . . Hartford, August 1, 1789. [Hartford? 1789]
broadside 34 X 21.5 cm.
NHi mp. 45458

B6925 CONNECTICUT COURANT, HARTFORD
Verses for the New Year's Day, 1789. Addressed to the customers of the *Connecticut Courant*, by the lad who carries it . . . Hartford, Hudson and Goodwin [1789]
broadside 33 X 14 cm.
1st line: Since now we see the Constitution . . .
NHi mp. 45733

B6926 THE Connecticut, Massachusetts, New-York and

Vermont, almanack, for . . . 1790 . . . By Eben W. Judd. Litchfield, T. Collier [1789]

Trumbull: Supplement 1792
CtHi; MB mp. 45503

B6927 COWAN, JAMES
To the public. It is of infinite importance to every free people . . . James Cowan. Annapolis, June 3, 1789 . . . [Annapolis, F. Green? 1789]
broadside
Wheeler 496
MdHi. Photostat: MdBE mp. 45459

B6928 THE cruel murder or a mournful poem occasioned by sentence of death . . . upon William Brooks, James Buhannon, Ezra Ross . . . guilty of murdering Mr. Joshua Spooner . . . to be executed at Worcester . . . the 2d day of July next . . . Boston: Printed and sold by the gross or dozen at N. Coverly's Printing-Office. [1789]
broadside 33 X 20 cm.
88 lines in 2 columns
NHi mp. 45460

B6929 CRUKSHANK, JOSEPH
A catalogue of books to be sold by Joseph Crukshank, printer and stationer, in Market-Street . . . Philadelphia. [Philadelphia, J. Crukshank] 1789.
12 p. 12mo
PPL mp. 45461

B6930 DAILY ADVERTISER, NEW YORK
Supplement to the *Daily Advertiser*, Nov. 2, 1789. An account of cash paid . . . for the maintenance of the poor . . . New-York, October 6, 1789. [New-York, Francis Childs, 1789]
broadside 52 X 44.5 cm.
NHi; NN

B6931 DAILY ADVERTISER, NEW YORK
Verses for the year 1789, addressed to the subscribers for the *Daily Advertiser*. [New York, Francis Childs, 1789]
broadside 25 X 19.5 cm.
New York Public 919
NN mp. 45734

B6932 [THE death and burial of Cock Robin. Boston? Samuel Hall? ca. 1789?]
31 p. 10.5 cm.
Imprint and date assigned by d'Alté A. Welch
MWA (p. 5-26 only) mp. 45462

B6933 DEEKER, JOSEPH
Air balloon. The subscriber, who is the proprietor of the Speaking Image . . . is perfectly acquainted with the . . . construction of Air Balloons . . . Joseph Deeker. New-York, June 10, 1789. [New York, 1789]
broadside 34 X 20.5 cm.
NHi mp. 45463

B6934 DEFOE, DANIEL, 1659?-1731
Travels of Robinson Crusoe . . . The second Worcester edition. Worcester, Isaiah Thomas, 1789.
31 p.
Brigham: Robinson Crusoe 12
CtY (imperfect); MWA mp. 45464

B6935 [DEFOE, DANIEL] 1661-1731
Die wunderbare Lebensbeschreibung . . . Robinson Crusoe . . . Philadelphia, Carl Cist, 1789.
2 p.l., 154 p. 15 cm. [ ]^2 A-N^6
Rosenbach-Ch 138; cf. Evans 21045
MWA (all after p. 148 wanting). A. S. W. Rosenbach (1933) mp. 45465

B6936 THE Delaware pocket almanac for . . . 1790 . . . Wilmington, James Adams [1789]
[36] p.
By Thomas Fox
Drake 1381
DeWin

B6937 DOBSON, THOMAS
. . . Proposals, by Thomas Dobson, bookseller . . . Philadelphia, for printing by subscription, Encyclopedia Britannica: or, A dictionary of arts, sciences . . . [Philadelphia, 1789?]
4 p. 34 cm.
At head of title: A new edition, corrected, improved, and greatly enlarged
New York Public 920
NHi; NN; PHi mp. 45466

B6938 DODSLEY, ROBERT, 1703-1764
Select fables of Esop and other fabulists . . . Philadelphia, Peter Stewart, 1789.
215, [1] p. 14 cm.
Huntington 560
CSmH; MWA mp. 45467

B6939 THE duties, tonnage, discounts and drawbacks . . . to June 1st, 1796 . . . Gelston & Saltonstall. New-York, August 25, 1789. [New York, 1789]
broadside 31 X 20 cm.
DLC mp. 45469

B6940 F., P.
A few verses composed by P. F. on account of the sudden death of John Brown, and Huldy Brown, son and daughter, of Elder Eleazer Brown, of Stonington . . . killed with lightning . . . the seventh day of June 1788 . . . Norwich, 1789.
broadside 35 X 25 cm.
New York Public 922; Wegelin 134
PPRF. Wilberforce Eames (1926). Photostat: NN mp. 45472

B6941 THE Federal almanac for the year 1790 . . . Wilmington, F. Craig [1789]
[36] p.
By Jacobus Van Cuelen
Advertised in the *Delaware Gazette*, Oct. 31, 1789, as "just published and to be sold by the printers hereof."
Hawkins 26
MWA mp. 45792

B6942 FELLOW citizens, The man who, on this day of general joy . . . April 30, 1789. [New York, 1789]
broadside 17 X 19 cm.
Electioneering for Clinton
NHi mp. 45471

B6943 FELLOW citizens, you have this moment been witnesses to one of the noblest spectacles that the eyes of freemen ever beheld . . . [New York, 1789]
broadside 34 X 23 cm.
Signed and dated: Federalist. April 30, 1789
New York Public 921
NAll; NHi. Photostat: NN mp. 45470

B6944 [FENNING, DANIEL] d. 1767
Der geschwinde Rechner . . . Eine amerikanische Auflage . . . Reading, Gedruckt und zu verkaufen von Benjamin Johnson, 1789.

195 p. 17 cm.
Huntington 561; Karpinski p. 56; Nolan p. 22
CSmH; MWA; PPL mp. 45473

B6945 [FENNING, DANIEL] d. 1767
Der geschwinde Rechner . . . Eine amerikanische Auflage . . . Reading, Johnson, Barton and Jungmann, 1789.
195 p. 17 cm.
Karpinski p. 56
DAU; PHi mp. 45474

B6946 FITCH, JOHN, 1743-1798
The following petition and remonstrance was read in the House of assembly on the fifteenth instant . . . John Fitch. To the honorable the representatives . . . of Pennsylvania . . . [Dated at end] September 11, 1789. [n.p., 1789]
broadside 43.5 X 40.5 cm.
DLC (2 copies) mp. 45475

B6947 FITCH, JOHN, 1743-1798
To the honorable the representatives of the Commonwealth of Pennsylvania . . . Philadelphia, September 26, 1789. John Fitch. [Philadelphia, 1789]
broadside 34 X 21.5 cm.
DLC (2 copies) mp. 45476

B6948 FOR two nights only. A genteel entertainment of activity . . . Donegani . . . On the slack rope . . . walking on the wire . . . at Concert Hall, Salem, July 22, and 24, 1789. [Salem, 1789]
broadside 44 X 33 cm.
Tapley p. 347
MSaE mp. 45477

B6949 XIV SERMONS on the characters of Jacob's fourteen sons . . . Philadelphia: Printed for the author, by William Spotswood, 1789.
36 p.
Preface signed: Lycurgus III
RPJCB mp. 45478

B6950 FREEMASONS. VIRGINIA. GRAND LODGE
Regulations for the government of the Grand lodge . . . [Richmond, 1789]
broadside 33.5 X 20 cm.
CSmH mp. 45480

B6951 GERMAN FRIENDLY SOCIETY
Rules of the German Friendly Society; established at Charleston in South-Carolina, January 15, 1766. Revised . . . January 21, 1789. The second edition. Charleston: Printed for the Society, by William P. Young [1789?]
28 p. 19 cm.
Contains list of members 1766-1789
ScU

B6952 GILMAN, TRISTRAM, 1735-1809
The right education of children recommended, in a sermon, preached in a new school-house in North-Yarmouth, September 23, 1788 . . . Boston, Samuel Hall, 1789.
23 p.
RPJCB (half-title wanting) mp. 45482

B6953 THE glory of the heavenly city . . . manifested in a vision to a young lady of Bristol, on the 10th of October, 1781 . . . Wilmington, Brynberg and Andrews, 1789.
28 p. 12.5 cm.
Hawkins 27
DeHi mp. 45483

B6954 GOODRICH, CHARLES
Stop thief! Stolen from the subscriber, in Pittsfield, on Friday night last, a bay horse . . . Charles Goodrich. Pittsfield, June 29, 1789 . . . Also, Stolen the same night, from Zadock Hubbard . . . a dark roan horse . . . Zadock Hubbard. Pittsfield, June 29, 1789. [Windsor? A. Spooner? 1789]
broadside 21 X 18cm.
Shelburne Museum, Shelburne, Vt. mp. 45484

B6955 GRAHAM, RICHARD
Lands. Lands to be rented, or for sale . . . Richard Graham. Dumfries, August 22, 1789 . . . [n.p., 1789]
broadside 43.5 X 27 cm.
DLC mp. 45485

B6956 GRANT, MOSES
Imported and sold by Moses Grant, No. 6, Union-Street, a general assortment of upholstery, English goods . . . [Boston, 1789?]
broadside
Ford 2538
MHi mp. 45486

B6957 GRAY, GEORGE
Sir, The subscribers have spared no expence . . . A handsome stage waggon . . . will run twice a day . . . Gray's Ferry, May 20, 1789. [n.p., 1789]
broadside 25 X 20 cm.
NHi. Photostat: DLC mp. 45487

B6958 GREENWOOD, ISAAC, fl. 1789
Isaac Greenwood, dentist, no. 49 Marlborough-Street, acquaints the publick, that he continues to perform the necessary branches of that art . . . [Boston, 1789]
broadside 12 X 7.5 cm.
Ford 1161
MB; NNNAM mp. 45488

B6959 GREGORY, JOHN, 1724-1773
A father's legacy to his daughters . . . The first Bennington edition. Bennington, Haswell & Russell, 1789.
60 p. 16.5 cm.
Cooley 115; McCorison 165
VtHi mp. 45489

B6960 GUTHRIE, WILLIAM, 1620-1665
The Christian's great interest . . . Philadelphia, W. Young, 1789.
155, [1] p. 16 cm.
DLC mp. 45490

B6961 HARTFORD. MERCHANTS AND TRADERS
(Circular.) Hartford, December 15, 1789. Gentlemen, The critical and languishing state of our commerce . . . serious attention. There has been a meeting of . . . merchants and traders in this town . . . Committee of Ten . . . By order of the Committee, *Chas. Hopkins* To the merchants and traders of *Southbury* [Hartford, 1789]
[4] p. 34 cm.
Pages [2-4] blank
CtHi

B6962 HEIDELBERG CATECHISM
Catechismus, oder kurzer Unterricht . . . Germantown, Michael Billmeyer, 1789.
118 p.
PPL mp. 45492

B6963 THE history of little King Pippin . . . Hartford, Nathaniel Patten, 1789.

59 p. 10 cm.
MWA. Gillett Griffin, Princeton Univ. (1962)
mp. 45493

B6964 THE history of Master Jackey and Miss Harriot . . . Boston, Printed and sold by Samuel Hall [1789?]
30, [2] p. 10.5 cm.
Dated by d'Alté A. Welch
MWA mp. 45494

B6965 HITCHCOCK, ENOS, 1744-1803
The parent's assistant . . . The second edition. Providence, B. Wheeler, 1789.
16 p. 15.5 cm.
Advertised as "just published" Apr. 16, 1789
Alden 1148
MH; MSaE mp. 45495

B6966 HOPPIN AND SNOW, firm
To-morrow, (being the 12th of May) at nine in the morning, will be sold . . . at Hoppin and Snow's auction-office . . . in Providence, the following catalogue of books. [Providence, 1789?]
broadside 39.5 X 25 cm.
In contemporary ms. on back: . . . Auction May 12, 1789
RPJCB mp. 45497

B6967 HUMANE SOCIETY OF MASSACHUSETTS
Boston, July 21, 1789. Sir. It being now considered . . . This institution was stiled The Humane Society . . . [Boston, 1789]
[2] p. 32 X 20 cm.
Ford 2541; New York Public 924
DLC; MHi; MWA. Photostat: NN mp. 45499

B6968 HUMANE SOCIETY OF PHILADELPHIA
Directions for recovering persons, who are supposed to be dead, from drowning . . . Published by order of the Humane Society of Philadelphia . . . Philadelphia, Joseph James [1789]
broadside fol.
By Benjamin Rush
PPL mp. 45498

B6969 HYMNS, to be sung on Good Friday and Easter day; 1789. Albany, Charles R. Webster [1789]
broadside 25.5 X 19 cm.
McMurtrie: Albany 39; New York Public 925
NHi. Photostat: NN mp. 45500

B6970 JOHNSON, THOMAS, JR.
[The Kentucky miscellany . . . Lexington, John Bradford, 1789]

Advertised in the *Kentucky Gazette*, May 2, 1789, and later, as available "at Mr. Benjamin Beall's in Lexington, and at Gillespie Buney & Company, and Gen. Wilkinson's stores in Danville."
McMurtrie: Kentucky 3
No copy known mp. 45502

B6971 [JOHNSON, RICHARD] 1734-1793
Tea-table dialogues . . . Philadelphia, Joseph James, 1789.
123 p. illus. 12.5 cm.
For authorship cf. Weedon
Hamilton 127
MWA; MiU-C; NjP mp. 45501

B6972 LIBRARY COMPANY OF PHILADELPHIA
Be it remembered, in honor of the Philadelphia youth, (then chiefly artificers) that in MDCCXXXI they cheerfully instituted the Philadelphia Library . . . [Philadelphia, Zachariah Poulson, 1789]
broadside 8vo
PPL mp. 45502

B6973 LIBRARY COMPANY OF WILMINGTON
A catalogue of the books . . . Wilmington, Brynberg and Andrews, 1789.
19 p. lge. 12mo
Hawkins 29; Huntington 574
CSmH mp. 45750

B6974 LOW, SAMUEL, b. 1765
Ode to be sung on the arrival of the President . . . Composed by Mr. L** . . . [New York, 1789]
broadside 31 X 27.5 cm.
NHi mp. 45505

B6975 LOW, SAMUEL, b. 1765
Ode to charity: composed by Brother Low, of Holland-Lodge; and sung in St. Paul's Chapel, on the 24th day of June, 1789 . . . [New York, 1789]
broadside 33 X 19.5 cm.
NHi mp. 45506

B6976 LYMAN, GERSHOM CLARK, 1753-1813
A sermon, preached at Marlborough, September 1st, 1789; at the opening of the annual meeting of the freemen, for the choice of a governor . . . Windsor, Alden Spooner, 1789.
16 p. 17.5 cm.
McCorison 166
OCHP; VtHi mp. 45507

B6977 MARYLAND. GOVERNOR, 1788-1791
By . . . John Eager Howard . . . a proclamation. Whereas the General assembly . . . [Jan. 21, 1789] . . . [Annapolis, F. Green, 1789]
broadside 28 X 17 cm.
Wheeler 500a
DLC mp. 45508

B6978 MARYLAND. LAWS
An act directing the time, places and manner, of holding elections for representatives of this state in the Congress . . . [Annapolis, F. Green, 1789]
broadside 43.5 X 26 cm.
Wheeler 500
MdHi; RPJCB mp. 45509

B6979 MARYLAND. LAWS
An act for the benefit of Mary Cox . . . [Annapolis, F. Green, 1789]
broadside 5.5 X 15? cm.
Fragments assembled from a larger (?) broadside
PHi mp. 45510

B6980 MARYLAND. LAWS
An act to regulate the inspection of tobacco. Passed December 21, 1789. Annapolis, Frederick Green [1789]
28 p. 27.5 cm.
DLC mp. 45511

B6981 MARYLAND GAZETTE
The news-boy's verses, for January 1, 1790; respectfully inscribed to the friends and patrons of the *Maryland Gazette* . . . [Baltimore, John Hayes, 1789]

broadside 28 X 14 cm.
Wheeler 535
MdBE mp. 45542

B6982 MASSACHUSETTS
Commonwealth of Massachusetts. To the selectmen of the town of in the district of Greeting. These are in the name . . . [Feb. 9, 1789] . . . [Boston, 1789]
broadside 38 X 24 cm.
Ford 2548
Precept to elect a representative in the Congress of the United States
DLC mp. 45515

B6983 MASSACHUSETTS
Commonwealth of Massachusetts. To the selectmen of the town of in the district of These are in the name of the Commonwealth of Massachusetts . . . [Mar. 16, 1789] . . . [Boston, 1789]
broadside 37 X 23 cm.
Precept to elect a representative in the Congress of the United States
MHi mp. 45516

B6984 MASSACHUSETTS
Commonwealth of Massachusetts. To the selectmen of the town of in the district of Greeting. These are in the name . . . [Apr. 10, 1789] . . . [Boston, 1789]
broadside 37.5 X 24 cm.
Ford 2549
Precept to elect a representative in the Congress of the United States
DLC; MBB; MHi. Photostats: MWA; NHi mp. 45517

B6985 MASSACHUSETTS. GENERAL COURT
Commonwealth of Massachusetts. Extract of a resolve . . . passed 14th of February, 1789 . . . Treasury-office, Boston, July 29, 1789 . . . [Boston, Adams and Nourse, 1789]
broadside 33 X 19.5 cm.
Ford 2546
DLC (2 copies); M-Ar mp. 45518

B6986 MASSACHUSETTS. GOVERNOR, 1787-1793
Commonwealth of Massachusetts. These are in the name of the Commonwealth . . . to will and require you [to hold a town meeting to vote for a representative to Congress] . . . John Hancock . . . [Boston, 1789]
broadside 32.5 X 26 cm.
Dated Jan. 6, 1789
Ford 2547; New York Public 928
MWA; NN mp. 45514

B6987 MASSACHUSETTS. GOVERNOR, 1787-1793
The Governor and Council, present their respectful compliments to and request the favour of his company to dine on Tuesday next, at Faneuil-Hall, with the President . . . Sunday evening, October 25, 1789. [Boston, 1789]
broadside
Ford 2545
MHi mp. 45513

B6988 MASSACHUSETTS. MILITIA
[The following is a copy of the memorial presented by the officers of this State to Congress, and now on their table.] To the honourable the Senate and House . . . in Congress assembled, The officers of the Massachusetts line of the late American Army . . . [Boston, 1789?]
broadside 20 X 15.5 cm.
Signed in ms.: B. Lincoln
DLC. Photostat: MWA mp. 45621

B6989 MASSACHUSETTS. SENATE
Commonwealth of Massachusetts. In Senate, January 28, 1789. Whereas it appears . . . [Boston, 1789]
broadside 34 X 21 cm.
Dated in manuscript: Feby. 28th
Ford 2542
DLC mp. 45512

B6990 MASSACHUSETTS. TREASURER
Specie-tax, No. 7, granted Feb. 14, 1789. Commonwealth of Massachusetts. Alexander Hodgdon, Esq. Treasurer . . . To the selectmen or assessors . . . Boston, the tenth day of March . . . [1789] [Boston, 1789]
broadside 40 X 34.5 cm.
MHi; RPJCB mp. 45519

B6991 METHODIST EPISCOPAL CHURCH
Minutes, taken at the several conferences of the Methodist Episcopal Church, in America, for . . . 1789. New-York, Wm. Ross, 1789.
14 p. 16.5 cm.
New York Public 929
NN mp. 45520

B6992 MILITARY laboratory, at no. 34, Dock Street . . . Philadelphia: Where owners and commanders of armed vessels may be supplied . . . [Philadelphia] R. Aitken [1789]
broadside 41.5 X 24 cm.
DLC mp. 45521

B6993 MITFORD, JOHN
A treatise on the pleadings in suits in the Court of Chancery by English bill . . . Philadelphia, Rice and Co., 1789.
xv, 128 p. 17 cm.
James 67
MH-L mp. 45522

B6994 [MORSE, ABEL, firm, New Haven]
Proposals for printing by subscription, a book, entitled, "The doctrine of the endless punishment of the damned, argued and defended . . ." [New Haven, Abel Morse, 1789]
broadside 50 X 20 cm.
Prospectus for Jonathan Edwards' *The salvation of all men strictly examined* (New Haven, A. Morse, 1790), the preface of which is dated June 29, 1789
RPJCB

B6995 THE New-England primer enlarged . . . Boston, Printed by E. Draper for David West, 1789.
[80] p. [A]-E^8
Hurst sale, No. 691, Nov. 28, 1904
Heartman 98
No copy located mp. 45523

B6996 THE New-England primer enlarged . . . Boston, Printed by E. Draper, for James White, 1789.
[80] p. [A]-E^8
Heartman 93
CtSoP mp. 45524

B6996a THE New-England primer improved . . . New-Haven, A. Morse, 1789.
[72] p. 10.5 cm. [A]-C^{12}
MWA (p. 23-24, 47-48, 67-72 lacking) mp. 45527

B6997 THE New-England primer improved . . . New-Haven, Printed and sold by Abel Morse, 1789.
[72] p. 10.5 cm. [A]-C^{12}
Heartman 90
CtHi; MWA (mutilated) mp. 45526

B6998 THE New-England primer, Or, an easy and pleasant guide to the art of reading . . . Boston, Printed and sold by J. White and C. Cambridge, 1789.
[64] p. [A]-D^8
CSmH mp. 45525

B6999 THE New-England primer, or, An easy and pleasant guide to the art of reading. Adorn'd with cuts. To which is added, The Assembly of Divines' catechism. Boston: Printed and sold by J. White, near Charles-River Bridge. [1789]
[64] p. incl. front. (port.) 10.5 cm.
Heartman 404; Rosenbach-Ch 139
NRU; PP

B7000 NEW HAMPSHIRE
By his excellency John Pickering . . . A proclamation for a general fast . . . [Feb. 21, 1789] . . . Exeter, Lamson and Ranlet [1789]
broadside 36.5 X 31 cm.
Whittemore 480
NhHi mp. 45528

B7001 NEW HAMPSHIRE
The Committee appointed to re-examine and cast the votes . . . for Representatives . . . In Senate, January 2, 1789, read and concurred. J. Pearson, Sec'ry . . . [Exeter? 1789]
broadside 29 X 17.5 cm.
Whittemore 482
NhHi mp. 45529

B7002 NEW HAMPSHIRE. GOVERNOR, 1789-90
By his excellency John Sullivan . . . A proclamation for a general thanksgiving . . . [Sept. 28, 1789] . . . Exeter, Henry Ranlet [1789]
broadside 37.5 X 31 cm.
Whittemore 481
NhD; NhHi mp. 45530

B7003 NEW HAMPSHIRE. LAWS
State of New Hampshire. In the year . . . [1789] An act for the better observation of the Lord's Day . . . [Exeter, 1789]
4 p. 30 cm.
Passed the House Jan. 31, 1789, the Senate Feb 2
Whittemore 488
MWA mp. 45531

B7004 NEW JERSEY. GOVERNOR, 1776-1790
By His Excellency William Livingston . . . Proclamation . . . Perth Amboy, October 28, 1789. Wil. Livingston . . . [Trenton, Isaac Collins, 1789]
broadside 39 X 25.5 cm.
Appointing Nov. 26 a day of thanksgiving
Morsch 94
NHi; NjHi mp. 45532

B7005 NEW YORK (CITY) CITIZENS
At a meeting of a respectable number of freeholders held at Beekman's tavern . . . in the city of New-York . . . the 9th of March, 1789, Jonathan Lawrence . . . chosen chairman . . . Whereas . . . George Clinton . . . [New York, 1789]
12 p. 16 cm.
"To the independent electors of the state of New-York" (p. [3]-12)
Huntington 567
CSmH; MB; NHi mp. 45535

B7006 NEW YORK. ELECTION PROX.
The Federal Mechanic ticket. Robert Yates, esq. Governor. Pierre Van Cortlandt, esq. Lt. Governor . . . in behalf of the mechanics of the City of New-York . . . [New York, 1789?]
broadside 26.5 X 22.5 cm.
NHi mp. 45536

B7007 NEW YORK. LAWS
An act directing the times, places . . . electing representatives . . . Passed the 27th January, 1789. Albany, Samuel and John Loudon, 1789.
[2] p. 41.5 X 25.5 cm.
N. Photostats: DLC; MHi; MWA; NHi mp. 45538

B7008 NEW-YORK, March 24, 1789. Gentlemen, You will receive, with this, the proceedings of a meeting of the friends of Governor Clinton . . . to promote his re-election . . . [New York, 1789]
broadside 25 X 20.5 cm.
NHi mp. 45539

B7009 NEWARK, N. J.
Take notice. The trustees of the town of Newark think proper to inform the inhabitants . . . that on duly examining the ancient town records . . . By order of the board, John Peck, moderator. Newark, May 26, 1789. [Newark, 1789]
broadside 25.5 X 21 cm.
Morsch 97
NjHi mp. 45540

B7010 NEWBURYPORT, MASS.
Newbury-port, October 28, 1789. As this town is on Friday next to be honored with a visit from . . . the . . . President . . . [Newburyport, J. Mycall? 1789]
broadside 41 X 29 cm.
MB; MWA mp. 45541

B7011 NEWPORT HERALD
A New-Year's address, from the carrier of the *Newport Herald* to the generous . . . customers . . . [Newport, Peter Edes, ca. 1789]
broadside 24 X 12 cm.
Alden 1150
NjHi. Photostat: RHi mp. 45533

B7012 THE North-American pocket almanack, for . . . 1790 . . . Wilmington, Brynberg and Andrews [1789]
[32] p. 10.5 cm.
Drake 1382
MWA mp. 45543

B7013 NORTH CAROLINA. CONVENTION OF 1789
The ratification of the Constitution of the United States . . . State of North-Carolina. In convention, November 21, 1789 . . . [Edenton, Hodge & Wills, 1789?]
27 p. 18.5 cm. caption title
McMurtrie: North Carolina 146
NN; NcA-S mp. 45544

B7014 NORTHUMBERLAND CO., PA.
State of the account of Alexander Hunter . . . from 10th August 1784, till the 10th August 1785. Philadelphia, Francis Bailey, 1789.
6 p. 22 cm.
NHi; P; RPJCB mp. 45549

B7015 [NO. 1.] A circular letter from a Philadelphian to some members . . . Your well-wisher, Momoniensis. [To be continued.] Philadelphia [1789]
broadside 39 X 25 cm.
DLC mp. 45545

B7016 NURSE Truelove's Christmas box . . . Hartford, Nathaniel Patten, 1789.
26+ p. Illus. 10 cm.
CtHi (wanting beyond p. 26) mp. 45546

B7017 ODE on Washington, and Days of Absence. Ode sung on the arrival of President Washington, at the State House . . . October 24th, 1789. Great Washington's the hero's come . . . Days of Absence. Air Rosseau's dream . . . Sold wholesale and retail corner of Cross and Mercantile Streets, Boston. [1789]
broadside 22 X 20 cm.
RPB mp. 45547

B7018 ODE to the President . . . on his arrival at Boston . . . [Boston, 1789]
broadside 30 X 14 cm.
Sung at Kings Chapel Oct. 27, 1789
Ford 2551; Wegelin 693
DLC; MB; MHi; MWA. Photostats: CSmH; NN mp. 45496

B7019 A PACK of cards changed into a complete almanack, and prayer-book . . . The eleventh edition. Norwich, 1789.
6 leaves. 12mo A^4 B^2
Rosenbach-Ch 140; Trumbull: Supp. 2485
A. S. W. Rosenbach (1933) mp. 45548

B7020 PARKER, JAMES
To be sold at public vendue, on Thursday the 14th day of January next, the noted grist-mill in Alexandria . . . New-Jersey . . . December 19, 1789. New-Brunswick, Abraham Blauvelt [1789]
broadside 36 X 22.5 cm.
NjR

B7021 PENNSYLVANIA. CONSTITUTION
We, the people of the Commonwealth of Pennsylvania, ordain and establish this Constitution for its government. [Philadelphia] Zachariah Poulson [1789]
[3] p. 40.5 cm.
A partial report
Sealock 211
NHi mp. 45551

B7022 PENNSYLVANIA. GENERAL ASSEMBLY
Minutes of the thirteenth General Assembly . . . in their second session . . . [Colophon] Philadelphia, Hall & Sellers [1789]
p. 51-205. 30.5 cm. caption title
PHi; PPL. Photostat: DLC mp. 45554

B7023 PENNSYLVANIA. GENERAL ASSEMBLY
Minutes of the thirteenth General assembly . . . in their third session . . . [Colophon] Philadelphia, Hall & Sellers [1789]
p. 207-306. 30.5 cm. caption title
NN; PHi; PPL. Photostat: DLC mp. 45555

B7024 PENNSYLVANIA. GENERAL ASSEMBLY
Minutes of the first session of the fourteenth General Assembly . . . commenced . . . the twenty-sixth day of October . . . Philadelphia, Hall and Sellers, 1789.
113, [1] p. 32 cm.
CSmH; PHi; PPAmP; PPL. Photostat: DLC mp. 45556

B7025 PENNSYLVANIA. GENERAL ASSEMBLY
State of Pennsylvania. In General assembly, Tuesday, March 24th, 1789 . . . Extract from the minutes . . . Philadelphia, Hall & Sellers [1789]
broadside 27 X 21 cm.
PHi. Photostat: DLC mp. 45552

B7026 PENNSYLVANIA. GENERAL ASSEMBLY
State of Pennsylvania. In General Assembly, Tuesday, September 15, 1789. A.M. The report of the Committee of the Whole . . . was read the second time, and adopted . . . Philadelphia, Hall & Sellers [1789]
broadside 26.5 X 20.5 cm.
Concerns the Convention to amend the Pennsylvania constitution
Sealock 209
NHi mp. 45553

B7027 PENNSYLVANIA. LAWS
An act for incorporating the Methodist Episcopal Church, known by the name of Saint George's church, in . . . Philadelphia . . . Philadelphia, S. W. Neall, printer, 1789.
7 p. 23 cm. caption title
PHi mp. 45557

B7028 PENNSYLVANIA. REGISTER-GENERAL
Statement of the public accounts . . . from the first of January, 1788, to the thirtieth of September, 1789. Taken from the books of the Register-General's Office. [Philadelphia? 1789]
7 p. 33 cm.
Sealock 210
PHi mp. 45558

B7029 PENNSYLVANIA SOCIETY FOR PROMOTING THE ABOLITION OF SLAVERY
An address to the public . . . B. Franklin, President. Philadelphia, 9th of November, 1789 . . . [Colophon] Philadelphia, Francis Bailey [1789]
[2] 1. 35 cm.
Leaf 2 begins: Philadelphia, 26 October, 1789. At a meeting . . .
Sealock 212 & 214
CSmH; DLC (leaves disjoined); NHi; NjR; PHi (leaf 2 only); PPAmP; PPL mp. 45559

B7030 Deleted

B7031 PHILADELPHIA. POST OFFICE
Establishment of the post coaches, for . . . 1789 . . . James Bryson, P.M., Philadelphia, January 1st, 1789?]
broadside fol.
PPAmP mp. 45561

B7032 PHILADELPHIA CO., PA.
Philadelphia, May 15, 1789. By virtue of a writ of levari facias . . . will be exposed to sale . . . the 2d day of June next . . . a certain two story brick messuage or tenement . . . Philadelphia, Charles Cist [1789]
broadside 34.5 X 21.5 cm.
Repeated in German
Sealock 217
PHi mp. 45562

B7033 PHILADELPHIA DISPENSARY FOR THE MEDICAL RELIEF OF THE POOR
Rules of the Philadelphia Dispensary, for the Medical Relief of the Poor. Instituted April 12, 1786 . . . August 1st, 1789. [Philadelphia, 1789]
11 p.
Rogers 253; Sealock 219
DLC (not traced 1963) mp. 45563

B7034 THE Philadelphian magazine. Vol. II. [Jan.-Nov. 1789] [Philadelphia, 1789?]
416, 10, 447-448, [2], 51-88 p.
DGU (t.p. lacking)

B7035 PORTER, JOHN, 1716-1802
Superlative love to Christ a necessary qualification of a gospel-minister. A sermon, preached . . . Dec. 2, 1747. at the ordination of . . . Silas Brett . . . Newburyport, Reprinted and sold by John Mycall, 1789.
32 p. 20 cm.
MHi; MWA mp. 45564

B7036 PORTSMOUTH, N.H.
To Your Continental, state, county and town tax, in silver money, in certificates . . . Samuel Hutchings, Collector. August 1789. [Portsmouth, 1789]
broadside 11 X 14 cm.
Whittemore 404
MHi

B7037 PROTESTANT EPISCOPAL CHURCH IN THE U.S.A. CONNECTICUT (DIOCESE)
Proposals for instituting an Episcopal Academy in . . . Connecticut . . . New-Haven, January 16th, 1789 . . . Bela Hubbard, John Welton . . . [New Haven, 1789]
broadside 47 X 21 cm.
CtHi mp. 45565

B7038 PROTESTANT EPISCOPAL CHURCH IN THE U. S. A. MARYLAND (DIOCESE)
Journal of a convention . . . in the town of Baltimore . . . to Friday, June 5th, 1789. Baltimore, William Goddard, 1789.
2 p. 20 cm.
Wheeler 513
DLC; MWA; MdBP; MdHi; NN; RPJCB mp. 45566

B7039 PROTESTANT EPISCOPAL CHURCH IN THE U. S. A. NEW JERSEY (DIOCESE)
Proceedings of the sixth convention of the Protestant Episcopal Church . . . of New-Jersey . . . Elizabeth-Town, from the third to the fifth day of June, 1789, inclusive. [Trenton, Isaac Collins, 1789?]
[50]-57 p. 21 cm. caption title
Morsch 100; cf. Evans 21408
DLC; MWA; NjP mp. 45567

B7040 PROTESTANT EPISCOPAL CHURCH IN THE U. S. A. VIRGINIA (DIOCESE)
Journal of a convention . . . held in . . . Richmond from May 6, to May 9, 1789. Richmond, Thomas Nicolson [1789]
14 p. 21.5 cm.
New York Public 932
NN mp. 45568

B7041 PROVIDENCE SOCIETY FOR ABOLISHING THE SLAVE TRADE
Constitution of the Providence society . . . [Providence, 1789]
broadside 24 X 19 cm.
Alden 1153; New York Public 933
NHi; RHi. Photostat: NN mp. 45570

B7042 PROVIDENCE, Saturday afternoon, April 11, 1789. Gentlemen, I have in vain used every means . . . to procure a copy of the prox agreed upon at the convention in East-Greenwich, designing to reprint it . . . [Providence? 1789]
broadside 33 X 21 cm.
NHi mp. 45569

B7043 [PURDON, JOHN] d. 1835
At the ninth house above the drawbridge, in Front-street, is sold a general assortment of the following goods . . . Philadelphia, Daniel Humphreys [1789]
broadside 35 X 20.5 cm.
Sealock 220
PHi mp. 45571

B7044 REINAGLE, ALEXANDER, 1756-1809
A collection, of favorite songs arranged for the voice and piano forte . . . Philadelphia, Printed for A. Reinagle [1789?]
1 p.l., 22 p. 32.5 cm.
Sonneck-Upton p. 69; cf. Evans 21420
DLC; PU mp. 45572

B7045 REINAGLE, ALEXANDER, 1756-1809
Twelve favorite pieces . . . Philadelphia, Printed for A. Reinagle [1789?]
1 p.l., 24 p. 32.5 cm.
Sonneck-Upton p. 439
DLC mp. 45573

B7046 RHODE ISLAND. ELECTION PROX.
Convention prox, 1789. Landholders! Beware; be firm and persevere . . . His Excellency John Collins, Esquire, Governor . . . [Providence] B. Wheeler [1789]
broadside 22 X 14 cm.
Alden 1154; Chapin Proxies 44
RHi; RPB mp. 45574

B7047 RHODE ISLAND. ELECTION PROX.
His Excellency John Collins, Esquire, Governor. The Honorable Daniel Owens, Esq; Dep. Governor . . . [Providence] B. Wheeler [1789]
broadside 22 X 13.5 cm.
Alden 1155; Chapin Proxies 43
RNHi; RPB. Photostat: MWA mp. 45575

B7048 RHODE ISLAND. GOVERNOR, 1786-1790
[By . . . John Collins . . . A proclamation . . . [Nov. 2, 1789] . . . Providence, B. Wheeler, 1789]
[broadside?]
Bill submitted Nov. 2, 1789
Alden 1157
No copy known mp. 45576

B7049 RHODE ISLAND. LAWS
[An act laying an embargo on grain . . . Newport, Peter Edes, 1789]
[broadside?]
Bill submitted June 11, 1789
Alden 1178
No copy known; description conjectured from Schedules for June 1789 session mp. 45577

B7050 RHODE ISLAND. LAWS
State of Rhode-Island & Providence-Plantations. In General assembly, September session, A.D. 1789. An act for levying . . . certain duties . . . Providence, Bennett Wheeler [1789]
22 p. 35 cm. caption title
Bill submitted Oct. 5, 1789
Alden 1179; Winship p. 55; Winship Addenda p. 90
Ct; MHi; NN; RHi; RPB mp. 45578

B7051 RICE AND CO., firm, Philadelphia
Rice and Co. book-sellers and stationers . . . Philadelphia; have imported books . . . [Philadelphia, 1789?]
broadside 38 X 27.5 cm.
PHi mp. 45579

B7052 RUSH, BENJAMIN, 1745-1813
[An account of the climate of Pennsylvania. Philadelphia, 1789]

Goodman p. 382
No copy located mp. 45580

B7053 RUSH, BENJAMIN, 1745-1813
Observations on the duties of a physician . . . Philadelphia, Prichard & Hall, 1789.
11 p. 20 cm.
DLC; GU; MB; MnSRM; NjP; PHi; PPAN; PPAmP; PU
mp. 45581

B7054 RUSSEL, ROBERT
A sermon on the unpardonable sin . . . The seventeenth edition. Bennington, Haswell & Russell, 1789.
23 p. 16 cm.
McCorison 168
VtU-W mp. 45582

B7055 ST. JOHN'S COLLEGE, ANNAPOLIS
Annapolis, May 25, 1789. Sir, After a long suspension in the business of Saint John's College, the visitors and governors thereof . . . held a meeting . . . [Annapolis, F. Green, 1789]
broadside 33.5 X 21 cm.
Wheeler 514a
MdBE mp. 45583

B7056 SALEM, MASS.
By the Committee of Arrangements. As the President of the United States will honor this town with his presence next Thursday . . . Salem, October 27, 1789. [Salem, 1789]
broadside
Ford 2529; Tapley p. 347
MSaE mp. 45584

B7057 SAW ye my hero George . . . [Boston? 1789?]
broadside 25.5 X 20 cm.
Huntington 578
CSmH mp. 45575

B7058 SCHEME of a lottery authorized by Act of Assembly, for the sale of a real estate, and . . . paintings, engravings, &c. . . . of Mr. Robert Edge Pine, deceased . . . Philadelphia, November 21, 1789. [Philadelphia, 1789]
broadside 21.5 X 15.5 cm.
NHi mp. 45586

B7059 SCHEME of a lottery for assisting to pave the streets at Fell's-Point, etc. The following scheme . . . Baltimore, March 16, 1789. Baltimore, William Goddard [1789]
broadside 38 X 18 cm.
Wheeler 515
MdBMA mp. 45587

B7060 [SHEET almanack for 1790. Hartford, Nathaniel Patten, 1789]
broadside
Advertised in the *American Mercury*, Nov. 2, 1789, as "Just printed by said Patten, Bickerkerstaff's [sic], Strong's and Sheet Almanacs, for 1790."
Drake 459
No copy known

B7061 SHERIDAN, THOMAS, 1719-1788
A complete dictionary of the English language . . . The fifth edition, carefully revised and corrected by the Rev. John Andrews . . . Philadelphia, William Young, 1789.
vi, [2], [xiii]-liv [i.e. lii], [874] p. 23 cm.
Numbers xlv-xlvi omitted in paging
New York Public 934
MWA; NN; NjP; P; PHi; PPAmP; PU; RPJCB mp. 45588

B7062 SHERIDAN, THOMAS, 1719-1788
A rhetorical grammar of the English language . . . The third edition, carefully revised and corrected, by . . . John Andrews . . . Philadelphia, W. Young, 1789.
lxxiii, [2] p. 14.5 X 14 cm.
MWA mp. 45589

B7063 [SHERMAN, ROGER] 1721-1793
A short sermon on the duty of self examination . . . New-Haven, Printed and sold by Abel Morse, 1789.
20 p. 16.5 cm.
Trumbull: Supplement 2606
CtHi; CtY; MWA mp. 45590

B7064 SICARD, —
The President of the United States' march . . . Philadelphia, J. M'Culloch [1789?]
broadside 32.5 cm.
Sonneck-Upton p. 341
DLC; NN mp. 45591

B7065 SIR, You will readily discover, in the writing, which M. the Abbe de la Poterie has the honour to send you, here inclosed . . . Boston, 178 . [Boston, 1789]
broadside 33.5 X 21.5 cm.
Dated in ms.: Mar. 3, 1789, at Boston
Ford 2528
MHi mp. 45592

B7066 SOCIETY FOR THE RELIEF OF DISTRESSED AND DECAYED PILOTS, THEIR WIDOWS AND CHILDREN
Rules of the Society . . . An act for incorporating the Society . . . Philadelphia, Thomas Bradford [1789]
broadside 49 X 37 cm.
Dated: Nov. 10, 1788. Sept. 29, 1789
PHi mp. 45593

B7067 SOME account of John Burns, John Logan, John Ferguson, John Bennet, and Daniel Cronan, who were executed . . . Philadelphia, on Monday the 12th of October, 1789, for the murder . . . of John McFarland. [Philadelphia? 1789?]
broadside 37.5 X 18.5 cm.
In two columns, with execution cut at head
PHi mp. 45594

B7068 SOME queries intended to be put to the Rev. Dr. Witherspoon . . . on the trial in the Supreme Court of Pennsylvania, between Mr. Marshall and the Scots Presbyterian Church. [Philadelphia? 1789?]
4 p. 21 cm. caption title
MWA mp. 45595

B7069 SOUTH CAROLINA. TREASURY
No. I. Treasurers statement. The public of the State of South-Carolina, in general account of . . . monies loaned the public and for monies due sundry persons from 22d March 1783 to 31st December 1788 . . . 1789. January session report of the Committee of Ways and Means and statement – J. Read. [Charleston, 1789]
broadside 48 X 30.5 cm.
Sc-Ar

B7070 STATE of New-York. Letter from a committee, appointed at a meeting of a respectable number of persons, from different counties . . . to the hon. Robert Yates . . . Albany, 23d February, 1789. [Albany, 1789]
broadside 44.5 X 27 cm.
NHi mp. 45596

B7071 TAKE care!! By an act of the Legislature, passed

at Princeton . . . The power of choosing electors . . . A Friend to New-Jersey. [n.p., 1789]
broadside 37 X 24.5 cm.
Huntington 570; Morsch 102
CSmH. Photostats: DLC; MHi; MWA mp. 45599

B7072 THAYER, JOHN, 1755-1815
An account of the conversion of the Reverend Mr. John Thayer . . . who embraced the Roman Catholic religion . . . the 25th of May, 1783. Written by himself . . . The sixth edition. Wilmington, (North Carolina:) Reprinted by Bowen & Howard, 1789.
42 p. 22.5 cm.
McMurtrie: North Carolina 153
MHi (p. 41-42 wanting); NcA-S mp. 45600

B7073 THOMAS, ISAIAH, 1749-1831
Large family Bible. Search the Scriptures . . . Proposal of Isaiah Thomas . . . for printing . . . by subscription, an American edition . . . of the Holy Bible . . . Worcester, November, 1789. Isaiah Thomas . . . [Worcester, 1789]
[3] p. 44 cm.
MHi; MWA mp. 45601

B7074 THOMAS, ISAIAH, 1749-1831
Proposal for printing by subscription, Elements of general history. Translated from the French of the Abbe Millot . . . [Worcester, Isaiah Thomas, 1789?]
[4] p. 23 cm.
"Subscriptions are received by I. Thomas, the printer . . . of the work, at his bookstore in Worcester."
MWA mp. 45602

B7075 THOMAS, ISAIAH, 1749-1831
Worcester, January 12th, 1789. Proposal for printing by subscription A Disquisition on the Most Holy Deity . . . By the late Samuel Mather . . . [Worcester, Isaiah Thomas, 1789]
broadside
MB mp. 45603

B7076 THOMAS À KEMPIS, 1380-1471
An extract of the Christian's pattern . . . Philadelphia, Prichard & Hall, 1789.
306 p., 6? leaves. 10 cm.
NN (lacks final 3? leaves); RPJCB (p. 161-2, 191-2 wanting) mp. 45604

B7077 THOMAS AND ANDREWS, firm, Boston
Proposal, of Thomas and Andrews, for printing . . . an edition of the Book of Common Prayer . . . [Boston, Thomas and Andrews, 1789]
broadside 39 X 16.5 cm.
NHi mp. 45605

B7078 TO prevent mistakes, the fare of my carriage is established at the following prices . . . [New York, 1789?]
broadside 25.5 X 15.5 cm.
In contemporary ms. on back: Rate of Shas's hack coach in city N. York. Sept. 23 1789
RPJCB. Photostat: NN mp. 45606

B7079 TO the curious! To be seen at . . . Two camels, male and female, imported from Arabia . . . [Salem? 1789]
broadside 36.5 X 21.5 cm.
Dated Aug. 4, 1789
Tapley p. 348
MSaP. Photostat: MHi mp. 45607

B7080 TO the electors of the city and county of New-York. In an address of this day, signed by Alexander Hamilton . . . By order of the Committee, Jonathan Lawrence, Chairman. Tuesday, April 28, 1789. [New York, 1789]
broadside 25 X 26 cm.
New York Public 926
NAII. Photostat: NN mp. 45608

B7081 TO the electors of the city and county of New-York. This day commences the important election of a governor . . . By order of the Committee, Alexander Hamilton, Chairman. Tuesday, April 28, 1789. [New York, 1789]
broadside 26 X 21.5 cm.
MWA mp. 45491

B7082 TO the electors of the Southern District. In Mr. Child's paper of yesterday, a letter appeared, signed Candidus, directed to Cato . . . [New York, 1789]
broadside 45 X 26.5 cm.
Signed and dated: Brutus. April 27, 1789 [and] New-York, April 28, 1789
New York Public 915
NAII. Photostat: NN mp. 45609

B7083 TO the electors of the Southern District. In Mr. Child's paper of yesterday, a letter appeared, signed Candidus, directed to Cato . . . [New York, 1789]
broadside 45 X 26 cm.
Signed and dated: Brutus. April 28, 1789 [and] New-York, April 29, 1789
New York Public 916
NAII. Photostat: NN mp. 45610

B7084 TO the free and independent electors of the city and county of New-York. A number of your fellow citizens . . . New-York, April 28, 1789. [New York, 1789]
broadside 29.5 X 23.5 cm.
NHi mp. 45611

B7085 TO the freeholders of King's County, and the other counties in the Southern District [of New York. New York, 1789]
12 p. 16 cm. caption title
Signed at end: A freeholder of the Southern District. March 18, 1789
Concerns the election of George Clinton
MB mp. 45612

B7086 TO the freeholders of New-York. To-day, fellow-citizens, most of you have an important work to do . . . in rooting out Antifederalism . . . A Tried Friend. New-York, April 29, 1789. [New York, 1789]
broadside 25.5 X 18.5 cm.
New York Public 938
NAII. Photostat: NN mp. 45613

B7087 TO the freeholders of the Southern District. A writer, under the signature of A Citizen of New-York, has addressed you . . . [New York, 1789]
broadside 30.5 X 24 cm.
Signed and dated: An Independent Elector. New-York, April 28, 1789
New York Public 939
NAII. Photostat: NN mp. 45614

B7088 TO the inhabitants of the Southern District. Fellow citizens, The advocates for the reelection of Governor Clinton . . . A citizen of New-York. April 25, 1789. [New York, 1789]
broadside 31 X 20 cm.

New York Public 940
NAll. Photostat: NN mp. 45615

B7089 TO the mechanics of the city of New-York . . . A mechanic. April 28, 1789. [New York, 1789]
broadside 22 X 26 cm.
New York Public 941
N; NAll. Photostat: NN mp. 45616

B7090 TO the moderate and independent electors of Dutchess. At a meeting . . . Poughkeepsie, Nicholas Power [1789?]
broadside 34 X 21 cm.
DLC mp. 45617

B7091 TO the tenants of the manor of Rensselaerwyck . . . A tenant. [Albany? 1789]
broadside?
Referred to in Stephen Van Rensselaer's reply to a "publication . . . now distributing among you."
No copy known mp. 45618

B7092 TO the unbiassed & independent electors of the State of New-York. Since our last address to you, a publication . . . signed by Mr. Alexander Hamilton . . . By order of the Committee, Jonathan Lawrence, Chairman. New-York, April 7, 1789. [New York, 1789]
broadside 45 X 26 cm.
New York Public 927
NAll; NHi. Photostat: NN mp. 45619

B7093 TOM Thumb's folio: or, a new threepenny play thing for little giants . . . Hartford, Nathaniel Pattern, 1789.
29 p. illus. 9.5 cm.
Trumbull: Supplement 2680
CtHi (mutilated) mp. 45620

B7094 TRINITY CHURCH, NEW YORK
April 14, 1789. Church wardens Vestrymen [New York, 1789]
broadside 21 X 8.5 cm.
NHi mp. 45537

B7095 U. S. CONGRESS
Congress of the United States . . . Resolved . . . that it be recommended to . . . the several states to pass laws . . . the keepers of their gaols, to receive . . . prisoners . . . of the United States . . . Approved, September the 23d, 1789 . . . [New York, Childs and Swaine, 1789]
broadside 35.5 cm.
Printed certificate signed in ms. by Samuel A. Otis and John Beckley
New York Public 945 (19)
NN mp. 45721

B7096 U. S. CONGRESS
Congress of the United States . . . Resolved, That it shall be the duty of the Secretary of State, to procure . . . statutes of the several states . . . not . . . in his office . . . Approved, September the 23d, 1789 . . . [New York, Childs and Swaine, 1789]
broadside 35.5 cm.
Printed certificate signed in ms. by Samuel A. Otis and John Beckley
New York Public 945 (20)
NN mp. 45722

B7097 U. S. CONGRESS
Congress of the United States . . . Resolved . . . that John White . . . and his clerks, John Wright and Joshua Dawson, be considered as in office until the fourth day of February . . . Approved, September the 29th, 1789 . . . [New York, Childs and Swaine, 1789]
broadside 35.5 cm.
Printed certificate signed in ms. by Samuel A. Otis and John Beckley
New York Public 945 (31)
NN mp. 45720

B7098 U. S. CONGRESS
Congress of the United States . . . Resolved, That the survey directed by Congress in their act of June the sixth . . . be made and returned to the Secretary of the Treasury . . . Approved, August 26th, 1789 . . . [New York, Childs and Swaine, 1789]
broadside 35.5 cm.
Printed certificate signed in ms. by Samuel A. Otis and John Beckley
New York Public 945 (11)
NN mp. 45723

B7099 U. S. CONGRESS
The conventions of a number of the States having . . . expressed a desire . . . that restrictive clauses should be added . . . Resolved, by the Senate and House of Representative . . . [New-York, printed by Thomas Greenleaf] [1789]
2 p. 34 cm.
12 articles, the Bill of Rights as submitted to the states; 100 copies printed
Childs; Senate p. 190; cf. V. L. Eaton in *The New Colophon*, v. II, No. 7 (Sept. 1949) p. 281
DLC; DNA mp. 45717

B7100 U. S. CONGRESS
George Washington, Esquire, President of the United States. John Adams . . . Senators . . . Representatives . . . [New York, 1789]
[2] p. 33 X 18 cm.
North Carolina and Rhode Island omitted; New York senators (left blank) seated 25 and 27 July
Childs: House p. 105
DLC; NHi; NN; RPJCB (dated in ms.: May ye 15: 1789) mp. 45622

B7101 U. S. CONGRESS. HOUSE
Additional standing rules and orders of the House . . . [New York, 1789]
broadside 33.5 X 21 cm.
Childs: House p. 102
DLC mp. 45628

B7102 U. S. CONGRESS. HOUSE
In the House of Representatives of the United States, Tuesday, April 7, 1789. Resolved, That the rules and orders following, be establishing standing rules and orders of the House . . . Extract from the Journal, John Beckley, clerk. [New York, 1789]
3 p. 32 cm.
Childs: House p. 101
MHi mp. 45669

B7103 U.S. CONGRESS. JOINT COMMITTEE ON RULES
The Committee, appointed to confer with a committee of the Senate, in preparing proper rules . . . report . . . [New York, 1789]
broadside 33.5 X 21 cm.
100 copies ordered
Childs: House p. 105
DLC mp. 45670

B7104 U.S. CONGRESS. JOINT COMMITTEE ON RULES

[Joint rules for the enrollment, attestation, publication, and preservation of the acts of Congress . . . 1789, the 27th July. Resolved by the House of Representatives. New York, Thomas Greenleaf, 1789]

broadside

The resolve of the House on the report of a joint committee was read 5 Aug. and ordered to be printed for the Senate; 50 copies printed

Childs: Senate p. 187

No copy known mp. 45672

B7105 U.S. CONGRESS. JOINT COMMITTEE ON THE INAUGURATION

The Committees of both houses of Congress appointed to take order for conducting the ceremonies . . . have agreed to the following order thereon . . . April 29th, 1789. [New York, 1789]

broadside 34 X 21 cm.

Childs: House p. 103

DLC; NHi; NN. Photostats: CSmH; MWA mp. 45671

B7106 U.S. CONSTITUTION

The constitution of the United States, as recommended to Congress the 17th of September, 1787. By the Federal Convention. Portsmouth, Printed and sold by John Melcher, 1789.

40 p. 8vo

Huntington 571; Whittemore 497

CSmH. Photostat: NN mp. 45686

B7107 U.S. CONSTITUTION

The new constitution of the United States of America. Hartford, Nathaniel Patten, 1789.

[36] p. 15 cm.

Trumbull: Supplement 2424

CtHi mp. 45685

B7108 U.S. CONSTITUTION

[Plan of the federal government agreed to by a convention . . . 1787, and since ratified. Wilmington, F. Craig, 1789]

Advertised in the *Delaware Gazette,* Oct. 31, 1789, as "just published and to be sold by the printers hereof."

Hawkins 28

No copy known mp. 45687

B7109 U.S. LAWS

An act for establishing the salaries of the executive officers of government . . . [New-York, printed by Thomas Greenleaf] [1780]

broadside 34 cm.

House Bill [21] in the Senate

Read first time in Seante 31 Aug.; 50 copies printed on the first reading

Childs: Senate p. 189

DLC; DNA mp. 45673

B7110 U.S. LAWS

An act for laying a duty on goods, wares, and merchandize . . . 1789, May 16. Read the third time, and passed the House of Representatives. John Beckley, clerk. [New York, 1789]

[4] p. 34 cm. caption title

Read first time in Senate 18 May; 50 copies ordered on the first reading

Childs: Senate p. 183

DLC (2 copies) mp. 45674

B7111 U.S. LAWS

An act for the establishment and support of light-houses, beacons, and buoys. 1789, July 20th. Read the third time, and passed the House of Representatives. [New-York, Printed by Thomas Greenleaf.] [1789]

broadside 33.5 X 20 cm.

House bill [12] in Senate; 50 copies printed on first reading

Brackets in the original except for date

Information from James B. Childs

DLC; NhD mp. 45624

B7112 U.S. LAWS

An act for the establishment and support of light-houses, beacons, buoys and piers . . . [Colophon] [New-York, Printed by Thomas Greenleaf.] [1789]

broadside 33.5 X 20 cm.

Printing ordered by Senate July 24; 50 copies printed, as amended; sections numbered 1, 2, 3, 4, 5

Brackets in the original except for date

Childs: Senate p. 186

DLC (ms. corrections throughout); NhD (ms. corrections throughout) mp. 45678

B7113 U.S. LAWS

An act for the punishment of certain crimes against the United States . . . [New-York, Printed by Thomas Greenleaf.] [1789]

5 p. 41 cm. caption title

Senate bill no. [2] reported and read the first time 28 July; 120 copies printed on the first reading

Childs: Senate p. 186

DLC (dated [1790]) mp. 45679

B7114 U.S. LAWS

[An act for the punishment of certain crimes against the United States . . . New York, 1789]

12? p.

Senate Bill [2] in the House, read the first time 2 September; no order to print traced

Action postponed until the next session

Childs: House p. 118

No copy known mp. 45623

B7115 U.S. LAWS

[An act for the temporary establishment of the Post Office . . . New York]

broadside?

Senate Bill [3] in the House, read first time 16 September; no order to print traced

Not printed in the Senate

Childs: House p. 120

No copy known mp. 45625

B7116 U.S. LAWS

An act imposing duties on tonnage . . . 1789, May 29. Read the third time, and passed by the House of Representatives. John Beckley, clerk. [New-York, June 1789, Printed by Thomas Greenleaf.]

broadside 34 X 21 cm.

Read first time in Senate 9 June; 100 copies printed on the first reading

Childs: Senate p. 183

DLC mp. 45626

B7117 U.S. LAWS

An act providing for the actual enumeration . . . [Colophon] New-York, Thomas Greenleaf [1789]

4 p. 34 cm. caption title

DLC mp. 45702

B7118 U.S. LAWS
[An act to allow Baron de Glaubeck the pay of a Captain in the Army of the United States . . . New York, 1789]
broadside?
Senate Bill [5] in the House, read three times and passed by the House 29 September; no order to print traced
Not printed for the Senate
Childs: House p. 124
No copy known mp. 45627

B7119 U.S. LAWS
An act to establish an Executive Department to be denominated the Department of War . . . [at end] 1789, June 27. Read the third time and passed the House of Representatives. [New-York, Printed by Thomas Greenleaf.] [1789]
broadside 33 X 20 cm.
Brackets in the original except for date
House bill no. [7] in the Senate; read first time 6 July; read second time 21 July; 50 copies printed on the second reading
Childs: Senate p. 186
DLC; DNA. Photostats: MHi; MWA mp. 45629

B7120 U.S. LAWS
An act to establish the seat of government . . . 1789. September the 22d. [Passed the House] [New-York, Printed by Thomas Greenleaf.] [1789]
broadside 34 X 21 cm.
"On the banks of the . . . Susquehannah, in . . . Pennsylvania."
Brackets in original except for date
Read first time in Senate 22 Sept.; 50 copies printed on the first reading
Childs: Senate p. 190
DLC; DNA mp. 45630

B7121 U.S. LAWS
An act to establish the Treasury Department . . . 1789, July 2. [New-York, Printed by Thomas Greenleaf.] [1789]
[2] p. 33.5 X 21 cm.
Imprint bracketed in original
House bill no. [9] in the Senate; read first time 6 July; 80 copies printed on the first reading
Childs: Senate p. 185 (amended)
DLC (ms. corrections throughout); DNA mp. 45631

B7122 U.S. LAWS
An act to provide for the Government of the Territory, North-West of the River Ohio . . . [At end] 1789, July the 21st. [New-York, Printed by Thomas Greenleaf.] [1789]
broadside 33 X 20 cm.
Imprint bracketed in original
House bill no. [4] in the Senate. Read first time 21 July; 50 copies printed on the first reading
Childs: Senate p. 185 (amended)
DLC mp. 45632

B7123 U.S. LAWS
An act to provide for the safe keeping of the acts, records and seal . . . [New-York, Printed by Thomas Greenleaf.] [1789]
[2] p. 34.5 cm.
Imprint bracketed in original
Read first time in Senate 31 Aug.; 50 copies printed on first reading
Childs: Senate p. 189
DLC; DNA; NhD (numerous corrections) mp. 45675

B7124 U.S. LAWS
An act to regulate processes in the courts . . . In Senate of the United States, September 17, 1789. Read the first time. Samuel A. Otis, Sec. [Colophon] [New-York, Printed by Thomas Greenleaf.] [1789]
4 p. 34 cm. caption title
DLC; NhD mp. 45677

B7125 U.S. LAWS
[An act to regulate processes in the courts . . . New York, 1789]
4? p.
Senate Bill [4] in the House, read in House first and second times 19 September; no order to print traced.
Printed for the Senate
Childs: House p. 122
No copy known mp. 45676

B7126 U.S. LAWS
An act to regulate the collection of the duties imposed by law, on the tonnage of ships or vessels . . . 1789, July 14th. [Read the third time and passed the House of Representatives] [New-York, Printed by Thomas Greenleaf.] [1789]
20 p. 34 cm.
Bracketed in original except for date
Read in Senate first time 15 July; 80 copies printed on the first reading
Childs: Senate p. 185
DNA; NhD mp. 45633

B7127 U.S. LAWS
Be it enacted by the Senate and House of representatives . . . that at every session . . . 1789, August the 10th. [New York, 1789]
broadside 33.5 X 20 cm.
House Bill [19] to allow compensations to members of Senate and House; no order to print traced
Childs: House p. 116
DLC; DNA; NhD mp. 45634

B7128 U.S. LAWS
[A bill allowing certain compensation to the Judges of the Supreme and other Courts, and to the Attorney General . . . New York, 1789]
broadside?
House Bill [28], read first and second times 17 September; no order to print traced
Not printed in the Senate
Childs: House p. 121
No copy known mp. 45635

B7129 U.S. LAWS
[A bill concerning the importation of certain persons prior to the year 1808 . . . New York, 1789]
broadside?
House Bill [30], read in House first time 19 September; no order to print traced
Postponed in the House until the next session
Childs: House p. 122
No copy known mp. 45636

B7130 U.S. LAWS
[A bill establishing a Land Office in and for the Western Territory . . . New York, 1789]
broadside?
House Bill [17], read in House first time 31 July; 100 copies ordered to be printed
Never acted on
Childs: House p. 114
No copy known mp. 45637

B7131 U.S. LAWS
[A bill establishing the salaries of the Executive Officers of Government . . . New York, 1789]
broadside?
House Bill [21], read in House first time 24 August; no order to print traced
Printed in the Senate
Childs: House p. 117
No copy known mp. 45638

B7132 U.S. LAWS
[A bill for allowing a compensation to the President and Vice-President of the United States . . . New York, 1789]
broadside?
House Bill [15], read in House first time 22 July; no order to print traced
Printed in the Senate
Childs: House p. 113
No copy known mp. 45639

B7133 U.S. LAWS
[A bill for amending part of . . . "An act to regulate the collection of the duties imposed by law on the tonnage of ships or vessels . . ." New York, 1789]
broadside?
House Bill [26], read in House first time 17 September; no order to print traced
Not printed in the Senate
Childs: House p. 120
No copy known mp. 45640

B7134 U.S. LAWS
[A bill for collecting duties on goods, wares, and merchandizes, imported into the United States . . . New York, 1789]
broadside?
House Bill [3], read in House first time 8 May; 100 copies ordered to be printed
Childs: House p. 104
No copy known mp. 45641

B7135 U.S. LAWS
[A bill for laying a duty on goods, wares, and merchandizes, imported into the United States . . . New York, 1789]

House Bill [2], read in House first time 5 May; no order to print traced
Printed in the Senate
Childs: House p. 104
No copy known mp. 45642

B7136 U.S LAWS
[A bill for registering and clearing vessels, ascertaining their tonnage, and for regulating the coasting trade . . . New York, 1789]
14? p.
House Bill [16], read in House first time 24 July; 100 copies ordered to be printed
Childs: House p. 113
No copy known mp. 45643

B7137 U.S. LAWS
[A bill for registering and clearing vessels, ascertaining their tonnage, and for regulating the coasting trade . . . New York, 1789]
14? p.
House Bill [16], read in House third time 3 August; 100 copies ordered to be printed
Printed in the Senate
Childs: House p. 113
No copy known mp. 45644

B7138 U.S. LAWS
A bill for registering and clearing vessels, and regulating the coasting trade . . . 1789, August the 5th. [Passed the House of Representatives.] [New-York, Printed by Thomas Greenleaf.] [1789]
14 p. 33.5 cm. caption title
Read first time in Senate 6 Aug.; 50 copies printed on the first reading
Childs: Senate p. 187
Brackets in the original except for date
DLC; DNA mp. 45645

B7139 U.S. LAWS
A bill for registering and clearing vessels, and regulating the coasting trade . . . [Colophon] [New-York, Printed by Thomas Greenleaf.] [1789]
12 p. 33.5 cm. caption title
Contains 40 sections; apparently, 50 copies printed as passed with the 69 amendments 25 Aug.
Brackets in the original except for date
Childs: Senate p. 188
DLC; NhD mp. 45680

B7140 U.S. LAWS
[A bill for registering and clearing vessels, and regulating the coasting trade . . . Amendments sec. 25-29.] [New-York, Printed by Thomas Greenleaf.] [1789]
3 p. 34 cm.
Apparently the sundry amendments reported on 17 Aug. to Senate; 50 copies of supplements to the Coasting bill printed
Imprint bracketed in original
Childs: Senate p. 188
DLC mp. 45681

B7141 U. S. LAWS
[A bill for suspending the operations of part of . . . "An act imposing duties on tonnage . . . New York, 1789]
broadside?
House Bill [24], read in House first time 9 September; no order to print traced
Not printed in the Senate
Childs: House p. 118
No copy known mp. 45646

B7142 U. S. LAWS
[A bill for the establishment and support for light-houses, beacons and buoys, and for authorizing the several states to provide and regulate pilots . . . New York, 1789]
broadside?
House Bill [12], read in House first time 1 July; no order to print traced
Printed in the Senate
Childs: House p. 110
No copy known mp. 45647

B7143 U. S. LAWS
[A bill imposing duties on tonnage . . . New York, 1789]
broadside?
House Bill [5], read in House first time 25 May; no order to print traced
Printed in the Senate
Childs: House p. 106
No copy known mp. 45648

B7144 U. S. LAWS
[A bill making appropriations for the service of the present year . . . New York, 1789]

broadside?
House Bill [32], read in House first and second times 21 September; no order to print traced
Not printed for the Senate
Childs: House p. 122
No copy known mp. 45649

B7145 U. S. LAWS
[A bill making provision for the invalid pensioners of the United States . . . New York, 1789]
broadside?
House Bill [29], read in House first time 18 September; no order to print traced
Not printed in the Senate
Childs: House p. 121
No copy known mp. 45650

B7146 U. S. LAWS
[A bill providing for the establishment of hospitals for the relief of sick and disabled seamen, and prescribing regulations for the harbours of the United States . . . New York, 1789]

House Bill [22], read in House first time 27 August; no order to print traced
Action postponed until next session
Childs: House p. 117
No copy known mp. 45651

B7147 U. S. LAWS
[A bill providing for the expences which may attend negotiations or treaties with the Indian tribes, and the appointment of commissioners for managing the same . . . New York, 1789]
broadside?
House Bill [20], read in House first time 10 August; no order to print traced
Childs: House p. 117
No copy known mp. 45652

B7148 U. S. LAWS
[A bill to alter the time of the annual meeting of Congress . . . New York, 1789]
broadside?
House Bill [31], read in House first time 21 September; no order to print traced
Not printed for the Senate
Childs: House p. 122
No copy known mp. 45653

B7149 U. S. LAWS
[Bill to amend the Constitution of the United States with amendments . . . New York, 1789]
broadside?
The *Daily Advertiser* reported for the House proceedings on 14 September: "The Senate sent down the bill to amend the Constitution . . . Ordered, that it lie on the table and that copies of those amendments be printed . . ."
Childs: House p. 119
No copy known mp. 45682

B7150 U. S. LAWS
[A bill to establish an Executive Department to be denominated the Department of Foreign Affairs . . . New York, 1789]
broadside?
House Bill [8], read in House first time 2 June; 100 copies ordered to be printed
Childs: House p. 107
No copy known mp. 45654

B7151 U. S. LAWS
[A bill to establish an Executive Department to be denominated the Department of War . . . New York, 1789]
broadside
House Bill [7], read in House first time 2 June; 100 copies ordered to be printed
Printed in the Senate
Childs: House p. 107
No copy known mp. 45655

B7152 U. S. LAWS
[A bill to establish an Executive Department to be denominated the Treasury Department . . . New York, 1789]
[2]? p.
House Bill [9], read in House first time 2 June; no order to print traced
Printed in the Senate
Childs: House p. 107
No copy known mp. 45656

B7153 U. S. LAWS
A bill to establish the judicial courts of the United States . . . [Colophon] [New York, Printed by Thomas Greenleaf.] [1789]
16 p. 34 cm. caption title
Imprint bracketed in the original
Read the first time 12 June; 250 copies printed on the first reading
Childs: Senate p. 183; New York Public 942
DLC; MWiW-C; NN; NhD (32 sections numbered in ms.) mp. 45657

B7154 U. S. LAWS
[A bill to establish the judicial courts of the United States . . . New York, Thomas Greenleaf, 1789.]
16 p. 34 cm.
Read the third time with amendment 7–13 July; 120 copies printed, as amended on the third reading with sections numbered
Childs: Senate p. 184
No copy known mp. 45658

B7155 U. S. LAWS
A bill to establish the judicial courts of the United States . . . [Colophon] [New-York, Printed by Thomas Greenlead.] [1789]
12 p. 33.5 cm. caption title
Senate Bill [1] in the House
Childs: House p. 112
DLC; NhD mp. 45683

B7156 U. S. LAWS
[A bill to establish the seat of the government of the United States . . . New York]
broadside?
House Bill [25], read in House first time 14 September; no order to print traced
Printed in the Senate
Childs: House p. 119
No copy known mp. 45659

B7157 U. S. LAWS
[A bill to explain and amend . . . "An act for the registering and clearing vessels . . ." New York, 1789]
broadside?
House Bill [33], read in House first and second times 23 September; no order to print traced
Not printed for the Senate
Childs: House p. 124
No copy known mp. 45660

B7158 U. S. LAWS
[A bill to provide for the government of the territory Northwest of the river Ohio . . . New York, 1789]
broadside?
House Bill [14], read in House first time 16 July; no order to print traced
Printed in the Senate
Childs: House p. 112
No copy known mp. 45661

B7159 U. S. LAWS
[A bill to provide for the safe-keeping of the acts, records, and seal . . . New York, 1789]
[2]? p.
House Bill [18], read in House second time 3 August; 100 copies ordered to be printed
Printed in the Senate
Childs: House p. 115
No copy known mp. 45662

B7160 U. S. LAWS
A bill to provide for the settlement of the accounts between the United States . . . [New York] Francis Childs and John Swaine [1789]
broadside 34 X 21.5 cm.
Childs: House p. 111
DLC (2 copies) mp. 45663

B7161 U. S. LAWS
[A bill to recognize and adapt to the Constitution of the United States, the establishment of the troops . . . New York, 1789]
broadside?
House Bill [27], read in House first and second times 17 September; no order to print traced
Not printed in the Senate
Childs: House p. 120
No copy known mp. 45664

B7162 U. S. LAWS
[A bill to regulate the collection of duties imposed on goods, wares, and merchandizes, imported into the United States . . . New York, 1789]
20? p.
House Bill [6], read in House first and second time 27 May; 100 copies ordered to be printed
Replaced by House Bill [11] 29 June
Childs: House p. 106
No copy known mp. 45665

B7163 U. S. LAWS
[A bill to regulate the collection of duties imposed on goods, wares, and merchandizes, imported into the United States . . . New York, 1789]
20? p.
House Bill [11], read in House first time 29 June; 100 copies ordered to be printed
Replacing House Bill [6]
Printed in the Senate
Childs: House p. 109
No copy known mp. 45666

B7164 U. S. LAWS
[A bill to regulate the taking the oath or affirmation prescribed by the sixth article of the Constitution . . . New York, 1789]
broadside?
House Bill [1], read in House first time 14 April; no order to print traced
Childs: House p. 102
No copy known mp. 45667

B7165 U. S. LAWS
[A bill to suspend part of . . . "An act to regulate the collection of the duties imposed by law on the tonnage of ships or vessels . . ." New York, 1789]
broadside?
House Bill [23], read in House first time 28 August; no order to print traced
Not printed in the Senate
Childs: House p. 118
No copy known mp. 45668

B7166 U. S. LAWS
Congress of the United States . . . An act for allowing a compensation to the President and Vice-President of the United States . . . Approved, September the 24th, 1789 . . . [New York, Childs and Swaine, 1789]
broadside 35.5 cm.
Printed certificate signed in ms. by Samuel A. Otis and John Beckley
New York Public 945 (22)
NN mp. 45688

B7167 U. S. LAWS
Congress of the United States . . . An act for allowing certain compensation to the judges of the Supreme and other courts, and to the Attorney-General . . . Approved, September the 23d, 1789 . . . [New York, Childs and Swaine, 1789]
broadside 35.5 cm.
Printed certificate signed in ms. by Samuel A. Otis and John Beckley
New York Public 945 (21)
NN mp. 45689

B7168 U. S. LAWS
Congress of the United States . . . An act for allowing compensation to the members of the Senate and House of Representatives . . . Approved, September the 22d, 1789 . . . [New York, Childs and Swaine, 1789]
[2] p. 35.5 cm.
Printed certificate signed in ms. by Samuel A. Otis and John Beckley
New York Public 945 (18)
NN mp. 45690

B7169 U. S. LAWS
Congress of the United States . . . An act for establishing an executive department . . . the Department of Foreign Affairs . . . Approved, July 27, 1789 . . . [New York, Childs and Swaine, 1789]
broadside 35.5 cm.
Printed certificate signed in ms. by Samuel A. Otis and John Beckley
New York Public 945 (4)
NN mp. 45691

B7170 U. S. LAWS
Congress of the United States . . . An act for establishing the salaries of the executive officers . . . Approved September the 11th, 1789 . . . New-York, Francis Childs and John Swaine [1789]
broadside 33 X 21 cm.
New York Public 945 (14)
DLC; NN mp. 45692

B7171 U. S. LAWS
Congress of the United States . . . An act for laying a duty . . . Richmond, Aug. Davis [1789?]
broadside 33 X 20 cm.
List of articles taxed, with amounts
MWA mp. 45694

B7172 U. S. LAWS
Congress of the United States . . . An act for laying a duty on goods, wares and merchandizes . . . Approved, July 4, 1789 . . . [New York, Childs and Swaine, 1789]
[3] p. 35.5 cm.
New York Public 945 (2); cf. Evans 22193
Printed certificate signed in ms. by Samuel A. Otis and John Beckley
NN; NhD mp. 45693

B7173 U. S. LAWS
Congress of the United States . . . An act for registering and clearing vessels . . . and for other purposes . . . Approved, September the 1st, 1789 . . . [New York, Childs and Swaine, 1789]
12 p. 35.5 cm.
Printed certificate signed in ms. by Samuel A. Otis and John Beckley
New York Public 945 (12)
NN mp. 45696

B7174 U. S. LAWS
Congress of the United States . . . An act for registering and clearing vessels . . . [Colophon] [New York, Francis Childs and John Swaine] [1789]
12 p. 34 cm. caption title
New York Public 943
MiU-C; NN; PPL mp. 45695

B7175 U. S. LAWS
Congress of the United States . . . An act for settling the accounts between the United States and individual states . . . Approved, August the 5th, 1789 . . . [New York, Childs and Swaine, 1789]
21 p. 35.5 cm.
Printed certificate signed in ms. by Samuel A. Otis and John Beckley
New York Public 945 (6)
NN mp. 45697

B7176 U. S. LAWS
Congress of the United States . . . An act for the establishment and support of lighthouses, beacons, buoys, and public piers . . . Approved, August the 7th, 1789 . . . [New York, Childs and Swaine, 1789]
broadside 35.5 cm.
Printed certificate signed in ms. by Samuel A. Otis and John Beckley
New York Public 945 (9)
NN mp. 45698

B7177 U. S. LAWS
Congress of the United States . . . An act for the temporary establishment of the Post-Office . . . Approved, September the 22d, 1789 . . . [New York, Childs and Swaine, 1789]
broadside 35.5 cm.
Printed certificate signed in ms. by Samuel A. Otis and John Beckley
New York Public 945 (17)
NN mp. 45699

B7178 U. S. LAWS
Congress of the United States . . . An act imposing duties on tonnage . . . Approved, July 20, 1789 . . . [New York, Childs and Swaine, 1789]
broadside 35.5 cm.
New York Public 945 (3)
Printed certificate signed in ms. by Samuel A. Otis and John Beckley
NN mp. 45700

B7179 U. S. LAWS
Congress of the United States . . . An act making appropriation for the service of the present year . . . Approved September the 29th, 1789 . . . [New York, Childs and Swainc, 1789]
[2] p. 33.5 cm. caption title
Printed certificate signed in ms. by Samuel A. Otis and John Beckley
New York Public 945 (26)
MiU-C (2 copies); NN. Photostats: DLC; MWA mp. 45701

B7180 U. S. LAWS
Congress of the United States . . . An act providing for the expences which may attend negociations . . . with the Indian tribes . . . Approved, August the 20th, 1789 . . . [New York, Childs and Swaine, 1789]
broadside 35.5 cm.
Printed certificate signed in ms. by Samuel A. Otis and John Beckley
New York Public 945 (10); cf. Evans 22196
NN mp. 45703

B7181 U. S. LAWS
Congress of the United States . . . An act providing for the payment of the invalid pensioners of the United States . . . Approved, September the 29th, 1789 . . . [New York, Childs and Swaine, 1789]
broadside 35.5 cm.
Printed certificate signed in ms. by Samuel A. Otis and John Beckley
New York Public 945 (30); cf. Evans 22197
NN mp. 45704

B7182 U. S. LAWS
Congress of the United States . . . An act to allow the Baron de Glaubeck the pay of a captain in the Army of the United States . . . Approved September the 29th, 1789 . . . [New York, Childs and Swaine, 1789]
broadside 35.5 cm.
Printed certificate signed in ms. by Samuel A. Otis and John Beckley
New York Public 945 (27)
NN mp. 45705

B7183 U. S. LAWS
Congress of the United States . . . An act to alter the time for the next meeting of Congress . . . Approved, September the 29th, 1789 . . . [New York, Childs and Swaine, 1789]
broadside 35.5 cm.
Printed certificate signed in ms. by Samuel A. Otis and John Beckley
New York Public 945 (29)
NN mp. 45706

B7184 U. S. LAWS
Congress of the United States . . . An act to establish an executive department . . . the Department of War . . . Approved, August the 7th, 1789 . . . [New York, Childs and Swaine, 1789]
broadside 35.5 cm.
Printed certificate signed in ms. by Samuel A. Otis and John Beckley
New York Public 945 (7); cf. Evans 22194
NN; NhD

B7185 U. S. LAWS
Congress of the United States . . . An act to establish the judicial courts . . . Approved, September the 24th, 1789. [New York, F. Childs, 1789]

12 p. 34 cm.
New York Public 945 (23)
MWiW-C; NN mp. 45707

B7186 U. S. LAWS
Congress of the United States . . . An act to establish the Treasury Department . . . Approved, September the 2d, 1789 . . . [New York, Childs and Swaine, 1789]
[2] p. 35.5 cm.
Printed certificate signed in ms. by Samuel A. Otis and John Beckley
New York Public 945 (13)
NN mp. 45708

B7187 U. S. LAWS
Congress of the United States . . . An act to explain and amend an act . . . for registering . . . Approved, September the 29th, 1789 . . . New-York, Francis Childs and John Swaine [1789]
broadside 33.5 X 21.5 cm.
New York Public 945 (25)
DLC; NN; PPL mp. 45709

B7188 U. S. LAWS
Congress of the United States . . . An act to provide for the government of the territory north-west of the River Ohio . . . Approved, August the 7th, 1789 . . . [New York, Childs and Swaine, 1789]
broadside 35.5 cm.
Printed certificate signed in ms. by Samuel A. Otis and John Beckley
New York Public 945 (8); cf. Evans 22195
NN

B7189 U. S. LAWS
Congress of the United States . . . An act to provide for the safe-keeping of the acts, records, and seal of the United States . . . Approved, September the 11th, 1789 . . . [New York, Childs and Swaine, 1789]
[2] p. 35.5 cm.
Printed certificate signed in ms. by Samuel A. Otis and John Beckley
New York Public 945 (15)
NN mp. 45711

B7190 U. S. LAWS
Congress of the United States . . . An act to recognize and adapt to the Constitution . . . the establishment of the troops raised under the resolves of Congress assembled . . . Approved, September the 29th, 1789 . . . [New York, Childs and Swaine, 1789]
broadside 35.5 cm.
Printed certificate signed in ms. by Samuel A. Otis and John Beckley
New York Public 945 (24)
NN mp. 45712

B7191 U. S. LAWS
Congress of the United States . . . An act to regulate processess [sic] in the courts of the United States . . . Approved, September the 29th, 1789 . . . [New York, Childs and Swaine, 1789]
broadside 35.5 cm.
Printed certificate signed in ms. by Samuel A. Otis and John Beckley
New York Public 945 (28)
NN mp. 45714

B7192 U. S. LAWS
Congress of the United States . . . An act to regulate the collection of the duties . . . on the tonnage of ships . . . and on goods . . . Approved, July 31, 1789 . . . [New York, Childs and Swaine, 1789]
broadside 35.5 cm.
Printed certificate signed in ms. by Samuel A. Otis and John Beckley
New York Public 945 (5); cf. Evans 22198
NN mp. 45713

B7193 U. S. LAWS
Congress of the United States . . . An act to regulate the time and manner of administering certain oaths . . . Approved, June 1, 1789 . . . [New York, Childs and Swaine, 1789]
[2] p. 35.5 cm.
New York Public 945 (1)
Printed certificate signed in ms. by Samuel A. Otis and John Beckley
NN mp. 45715

B7194 U. S. LAWS
Congress of the United States . . . An act to suspend part of an act . . . to regulate the collection of the duties . . . Approved, September the 16th, 1789 . . . New-York, Francis Childs and John Swaine [1789]
broadside 33.5 X 21.5 cm.
DLC; NN mp. 45313

B7195 U. S. LAWS
Duties payable on goods imported into the United States of America, by act of Congress, of 4th July, 1789 . . . Mode of transacting business at the Custom-House . . . Philadelphia . . . Philadelphia, Printed by R. Aitken & Son, for Thomas Seddon [1789]
broadside 42 X 36 cm.
New York Public 944; Sealock 225
NN; PHi mp. 45468

B7196 U. S. LAWS
Impost and tonnage laws of the United States, and a table of fees . . . Approved, July 20, 1789. George Washington, President . . . Philadelphia, Daniel Humphreys [1789]
broadside fol.
PPL mp. 45718

B7197 U. S. LAWS
In Council, June 23, 1789. The Governor laid before the Board a letter from the President . . . inclosing . . . "An act to regulate the time . . ." . . . 200 copies . . . be struck, and . . . transmitted . . . A. Blair, C. C. Congress of the United States . . . An act to regulate the time and manner of administering certain oaths . . . Approved June 1, 1789 . . . [Richmond? 1789]
[2] p. 36 X 22 cm.
ViU mp. 45719

B7198 U. S. POST OFFICE
A table shewing the distance from one post town to another in the United States . . . May 1, 1789 . . . Philadelphia, Printed and sold by B. Towne [1789]
broadside 46.5 X 53.5 cm.
Sealock 224; cf. Evans 22922
MHi; PHi mp. 45598

B7199 U. S. PRESIDENT, 1789–1798
By the President . . . A proclamation . . . Whereas a treaty between the United States and . . . Indians . . . in the form and words following . . . [New York, 1789]
broadside 23.5 X 13.5 cm.
PHi mp. 45724

B7200 U. S. PRESIDENT, 1789–1797
By the President . . . A proclamation. Whereas by virtue of powers given . . . to Arthur St. Clair . . . [Sept. 29, 1789] . . . [n.p., 1789]
8 p. 33 cm. caption title
MHi; MWA (reduced facsim.); NhD. Photostats: DLC; NN mp. 45725

B7201 U. S. PRESIDENT, 1789–1797
Printing-office Lansingburgh, May 6, 1789. Since the close of Monday's paper, the editors have received . . . the following important proceeding . . . [Lansingburgh, John Babcock and Ezra Hickok, 1789]
broadside 43 X 27 cm.
An extra of the *Federal Herald*
MWiW-C

B7202 U. S. PRESIDENT, 1789–1797
Speech of His Excellency George Washington . . .delivered to . . . the Congress upon his introduction to office. [Newport, Henry Barber? 1789]
broadside 34.5 X 21 cm.
Alden 1188
RHi. Photostat: MWA mp. 45726

B7203 U. S. PRESIDENT, 1789–1797
Speech of His Excellency George Washington . . . upon his introduction to office. New York, May 1 [1789] [New York, 1789]
broadside 34.5 X 21.5 cm.
Not Alden 1188
NHi mp. 45727

B7204 USS, FRANCIS, 1761–1789
The narrative of the life of Francis Uss, who was executed at Poughkeepsie . . . the 31st of July, 1789. [Poughkeepsie?] Printed in August, 1789.
8 p. 21.5 cm.
". . . taken from a manuscript of the unhappy Francis Uss," p. [3]
New York Public 947; Sabin 98185
NN mp. 45728

B7205 VAN RENSSELAER, STEPHEN
To the inhabitants residing in the manor of Rensselaerwyck. Fellow citizens! A publication, directed *To the Tenants of the Manor of Rennselaerwyck*, and signed "A tenant," is now distributing among you . . . Stephen Van Rensselaer. Water-Vliet, April 27, 1789. [Albany? 1789]
broadside 31 X 19 cm.
Denying charges of oppression
N mp. 45730

B7206 VERMONT. GOVERNOR, 1778-1789
[Fast day proclamation. Bennington, Haswell & Russell, 1789]
broadside?
Printer's bill for 150 copies dated Apr. 6, 1789
McCorison 171
No copy known mp. 45732

B7207 VERMONT. GOVERNOR, 1789–1790
By his excellency Moses Robinson . . . A proclamation . . . Thursday the twenty-sixth of November next, to be observed as a day of public thanksgiving . . . [Oct. 17, 1789] . . . Moses Robinson . . . Joseph Fay, Secr'y . . . [Windsor, Alden Spooner, 1789]
broadside 33 X 23 cm.
Cooley 122
NHi mp. 45731

B7208 VIRGINIA. HOUSE OF DELEGATES
Extract from the journal of the House of Delegates, on Tuesday the 8th of December, 1789. The General Assembly, calling to mind the circumstances, under which the constitution of Virginia was formed . . . necessity of revising it . . . [Richmond, 1789]
[2] p. 35 X 19.5 cm.
DLC mp. 45736

B7209 VIRGINIA. HOUSE OF DELEGATES
In the House of delegates. December 15, 1789. Resolved, That the executive . . . [Richmond, 1789]
broadside 20.5 X 16.5 cm.
DLC mp. 45735

B7210 THE Virginia almanac; or the Winchester ephemeris . . . Calculated by the North Mountain philosopher. Winchester, Richard Bowen, [1789]
p.
Advertised in the *Winchester Centinal*, Nov. 11, 1789
No copy known mp. 45738

B7211 THE Virginia almanack for the year . . . 1790 . . . Petersburg, William Pleasants [1789]
[36?] p. 16 cm.
Vi mp. 45737

B7212 THE Virginia almanack for the year . . . 1790 . . . By Robert Andrews . . . Richmond, Printed and sold by John Dixon [1789]
[32] p.
Bear 76
PHi mp. 45425

B7213 WATTS, ISAAC, 1674–1748
Divine songs, attempted in easy language . . . New-Haven, J. Meigs, 1789.
8 p. 16 cm.
CtHi mp. 45739

B7214 WATTS, ISAAC, 1674–1748
Hymns and spiritual songs . . . New-York, Hugh Gaine, 1789.
1 p.l., 277, [4] p. 14 cm.
DLC mp. 45740

B7215 WEBSTER, NOAH, 1758–1843
[The American spelling book . . . Bennington, Haswell and Russell, 1789]

Advertised in the *Vermont Gazette*, Feb. 23, 1789, as "this day published, And in a few days will be bound, ready for sale."
Skeel-Carpenter 15
No copy known mp. 45742

B7216 WEBSTER, NOAH, 1758–1843
[The American spelling book . . . Twelfth edition. New York, Samuel Campbell, 1789]

Advertised by Campbell in the New York *Daily Advertiser*, May 8, 1789
Skeel-Carpenter 18
No copy known mp. 45743

B7217 WEBSTER, NOAH, 1758–1843
[The American spelling book . . . Twelfth edition. Philadelphia, William Young? 1789]

Baker, William S.: *Engraved portraits of Washington* (Philadelphia, 1880), no. 38; Skeel-Carpenter 19
No copy known mp. 45744

B7218 WEBSTER, NOAH, 1758–1843
The American spelling book . . . The twelfth edition, with additional lessons. Providence, John Carter, 1789.
146+ p. illus. 17 cm.
Alden 1190; Winship Addenda p. 90
MWA (imperfect) mp. 45745

B7219 WEBSTER, NOAH, 1758–1843
The New-England primer, amended and improved. By the author of The grammatical institute . . . New-York, J. Patterson, 1789.
[72] p. illus. 10 cm. [A]-C^{12}
Heartman (1934 ed.) 112; Skeel-Carpenter 773
CtHi; MWA (imperfect) mp. 45746

B7220 WEBSTER, NOAH, 1758–1843
A plain and comprehensive grammar of the English language: being the second part of Mr. Webster's Grammatical institute . . . Philadelphia, W. Young, 1789.
220 p. 15 cm.
Not used for Evans 22260 (microprint ed.)
MHi; MWA; N; NN; NRU mp. 45747

B7221 WHEATLEY, PHILLIS, 1754–1784
Poems on various subjects . . . Philadelphia, Joseph Crukshank, 1789.
66, [2] p. 16.5 cm.
Porter 274; Wegelin 434 (note)
DLC; MWA mp. 45748

B7222 WHITING, SAMUEL
Samuel Whiting, next door to the Court-House, Great-Barrington, has a handsome (little) assortment of dry goods . . . New York, W. Morton [1789?]
broadside 22.5 X 19 cm.
NHi mp. 45749

B7223 [WINCHELL, JOHN]
A few neglected scriptures recollected . . . Hudson: Printed by Ashbel Stoddard. 1789.
22 p.
MWA (photocopy) mp. 45751

B7224 THE witty and entertaining exploits of George Buchanan, who was commonly called The King's Fool . . . New-York, Printed for John Reid, 1789.
36 p. 17 cm.
MWA mp. 45752

B7225 YORK CO., PA.
State of the account of John Forsyth . . . till the 1st of August 1788. Philadelphia, Francis Bailey, 1789.
7 p. 22 cm.
DLC; MWA; NN mp. 45550

179-

B7226 AN authentic account of the conversion & experience of a Negro. Together with Christian experience: a poem. Printed at Portland [179-?]
8 p. 19.5 cm.
New York Public 951
NN mp. 45753

B7227 BACHE, BENJAMIN FRANKLIN, 1769-1798
A specimen of printing types belonging to Benjamin Franklin Bache's printing office, Philadelphia. [Philadelphia, 179-?]
[4] p. 46.5 cm.
Text includes date 1790
New York Public 952
CSmH (facsim.); MHi (facsim.) NN (facsim. and reduced photostat) mp. 45754

B7228 BAYARD, STEPHEN N.
Mohawk General Land-Office, held at Schenectady . . . by Stephen N. Bayard. Office rules, relative to proprietors of land . . . Rules relative to purchasers of land . . . [at end] Albany, Barber & Southwick [179-]
[2] p. 33.5 X 21 cm.
Vail: Old frontier 887
NHi mp. 45755

B7229 COLIZZI, JOHN A. K.
Six sonatinas . . . New York, Printed for F. Raush [179-]
14 p. 33 cm.
Sonneck-Upton p. 396
DLC; MB mp. 45756

B7230 A COLLECTION of easy and familiar dialogues for children. The fifth edition. Windsor, Alden Spooner [179-?]
56 p. 19 cm.
Cooley 113
Vt mp. 45757

B7231 COLLES, CHRISTOPHER, 1738-1821
Shortly will be published, An account of the astonishing beauties . . . of nature . . . now displayed at . . . New-York, by the solar microscope . . . By Christopher Colles . . . [New York, 179-?]
broadside 19 X 11.5 cm.
NHi mp. 45758

B7232 THE compleat tutor for the fife, with a choice collection of . . . marches . . . Philadelphia, Printed for and sold by George Willig No. 12 South Fourth street [179-?]
1 p.l., 21 p. 23 cm.
PHi mp. 45759

B7233 THE constant lovers: or, The valiant lady . . . Boston, Sold at the Bible & Heart in Cornhill [179-?]
broadside 34.5 X 22 cm.
Text in 2 columns
cf. Evans 26817
MSaE mp. 45760

B7234 COURIER DES DEUX MONDES
Prospectus du *Courier des Deux Mondes* . . . [Boston? 179-?]
broadside
Probably issued by Paul Joseph Guérard de Nancrède
Ford 2591
MSaE mp. 45761

B7235 THE crafty princess, or, golden bull. In four parts. [n.p., 179-?]
8 p.
In verse
"Probably pre-1800."--C. K. Shipton
MWA mp. 45761

B7236 CRAIGIE, WAINWRIGHT AND CO.
Craigie, Wainwright, and co. druggists . . . have imported . . . New-York, Samuel Loudon [179-]
broadside 42 X 24.5 cm.
DLC mp. 45762

B7237 DAGGETT, DAVID, 1764-1851
[The singular adventures, &c. n.p., 179-?]
32 p. 18.5 cm.

Concerns Joseph Mountain, executed Oct. 20, 1790, for rape
Probably the first edition
Porter 204
CtY (t.p. lacking) mp. 45763

B7238 DEATH and the blind man.—A dialogue. [n.p., 179-?]
broadside 52 X 44 cm.
Huntington 733
CSmH mp. 45765

B7239 THE death of General Wolfe. [n.p., 179-?]
broadside 24 X 20 cm.
Huntington 734
CSmH mp. 45766

B7240 A DIALOGUE between death and a lady . . . Sold [by John Byrne?] at the Printing-Office, Windham [179-?]
broadside 36 X 23 cm.
2 columns of verse
Woodcut in upper left corner
CtHi (reduced facsim.); RPJCB mp. 45767

B7241 [THE factor's garland. Sold at the Printing-office in Hartford] [179-?]
8 p. 15 cm.
Trumbull: Second supplement 2836
CtHi (t.p. wanting) mp. 45768

B7242 GEORGIA. Ships or vessels, of any burthen, may be laden at the first bluff, on the north side of St. Mary's River . . . For further particulars enquire at Mr. Wright's plantation . . . [Savannah? 179-?]
broadside 16 X 19 cm.
MB mp. 45769

B7243 THE golden bull: or, The crafty princess. In four parts. New York, Printed for the itinerant book-sellers [179-?]
8 p. 15 cm.
In verse
New York Public 959; cf. Evans 25550
NN (photostat) mp. 45770

B7244 GOLDTHWAIT, MISS
For sale, at Miss Goldthwait's shop, No. 18, Cornhill, a beautiful assortment . . . [Boston, 179-?]
broadside
Benjamin Goldthwaite, shopkeeper, was at 18, Cornhill in 1796, disappearing before 1800
Ford 2782
MB mp. 45771

B7245 HOPKINS, JOSEPH
A line to the modern ladies: found among the writings of Joseph Hopkins, late of Farmington, deceased. [n.p., 179-?]
broadside 33 X 20 cm.
In verse
Ford 3171; New York Public 962
Photostats: MHi; NN mp. 45772

B7246 JEFFERSON, THOMAS, PRES. U.S., 1743-1826
Th: Jefferson requests the favour of to dine with him at half after three. The favour of an answer is asked. [Philadelphia, 179-]
broadside 25.5 X 20.5 cm.
DLC; MB ([ca. 1800]); PPRF

B7247 [KOTZWARA, FRANZ] d. 1791
The battle of Prague . . . [Colophon] Philadelphia, Printed for A. Reinagle; J. Aitken sculpt. [179-?]
7 p. 32.5 cm.
Sonneck-Upton p. 39
DLC; MB; MiU-C mp. 45773

B7248 LADD, NATHANIEL
The dictates of right re[ason], or, A solemn warnin[g] to unfaithful ministers. By Nathaniel Ladd, of Sandbornton . . . [n.p., 179-]
broadside 46 X 29.5 cm.
cf. Evans 30597
MWA mp. 45774

B7249 LASS, mein Kind, den Hahnen dich früh aufwecken williglich . . . [Germantown, M. Billmeyer, 179-?]
broadside 33 X 33.5 cm.
PHi mp. 45775

B7250 [LEE, SAMUEL HOLDEN PARSONS] 1772-1863
Lee's genuine (Windham) bilious pills, or family physic . . . each bill of directions is signed by Samuel Lee, the patentee, in his own hand writing . . . The above . . . pills . . . prepared by the patentee at Windham, (Con.) . . . and sold wholesale, by Dr. Isaac Thompson, New-London, (Con.) joint proprietor . . . and by agents of his appointing . . . [n.p., 179-?]
broadside 20 X 17 cm.
MWA mp. 45776

B7251 [LEWIS, WILLIAM]
In the Supreme Court of the United States. To . . . John Jay . . . chief justice, and his associates . . . sitting in chancery. [at end] Philadelphia, D. Humphreys [179-?]
28 p. 35 cm.
Title from beginning of text
PHi mp. 45777

B7252 LIED von König von Preussen. [n.p., 179-]
broadside
Probably printed about 1795.—Edwin Wolf 2d
PPL mp. 45778

B7253 LOVE in a tub: or the merchant outwitted by a vintner.

Let every one who to mirth is inclin'd,
Come draw near, I pray, and listen a while . . .

[Boston? 179-?]
broadside
Ford 2577
MHi mp. 45779

B7254 MASSACHUSETTS
Town day of 179 To You are hereby notified and required to present me a list of your dwelling houses . . . [Boston? 179-]
broadside
Ford 2926
M-Ar

B7255 MASSACHUSETTS. TREASURER
ss. To the selectmen or assessors of the town of . . . Greeting. Whereas the General court . . . dated in the day of Anno Domini 179 . . . [Boston, 179-]
broadside 31 X 19 cm.
DLC

B7256 MASSACHUSETTS HISTORICAL SOCIETY
Boston 179 Sir, A meeting of the Massachusetts Historical Society is to be held at the Library-Room in Boston . . . [Boston, 179-]
broadside
Form used from 1796 on
Ford 2791
MHi

B7257 MILLER, SAMUEL
Medicine boxes, of every description with suitable directions . . . faithfully prepared, and put up, by Samuel Miller . . . West-Boston . . . [Boston, 179-?]
7 p.
MBCo mp. 45780

B7258 MILNS, WILLIAM, 1761-1801
A set of round hand copies for the use of schools by W. Milns. Engraved by S. Hill. Boston, Published by John West, No. 75 Cornhill [179-]
16 leaves. oblong
PPL copy purchase date (second hand) by old owner 1798
PPL mp. 45781

B7259 MONTH of 179 Town of County of State Prices. Flour, of wheat a barrel . . . Doll. Shil. Pen. . . . [n.p., 179-]
Questionnaire on prices of produce, labor, materials
[8] p. 32 cm.
NHi

B7260 A MOST bloody and cruel murder committed on the body of Mrs. Elizabeth Wood . . . Bennington, Anthony Haswell [179-?]
8 p.
Cooley 489
RPJCB mp. 45782

B7261 NEW YORK. GOVERNOR, 1795-1801
At a meeting of the Council of appointment, held . . . on the day of 179 . . . [Albany, 179-]
broadside 25.5 X 20 cm.
Dated Apr. 7, 1798
DLC

B7262 NEWBURYPORT, MASS.
First Parish in Newburyport. To Your tax for the year 179 [Newburyport, 179-]
broadside
Ford 2589
NHi

B7263 NEWBURYPORT, MASS.
Town of Newburyport, day of To You are hereby notified . . . to present me a list of your dwelling houses . . . possessed by you on the first day of October last. Assistant Assessor . . . [Newburyport, 179-?]
broadside 33 X 14.5 cm.
Filled in for Dec. 26, 1798
MWA mp. 45775

B7264 PARKYNS, G. I.
Proposals for engraving in aquatinta, four select views, three upon the River Shannandoah . . . and one upon the Schuylkill . . . From the painting of W. Winstanley; by G. J. Parkyns . . . Six dollars for the four views . . . [n.p., 179-]
broadside 26.5 X 21 cm.
DLC (photostat) mp. 45786

B7265 PENNSYLVANIA. LAWS
An act for more effectually securing the trade peace and safety of the port . . . [Colophon] [Philadelphia] Zachariah Poulson [179-]
4 p. 34 cm. caption title
DLC mp. 45787

B7266 PENNSYLVANIA. MILITIA
Cavalry. Form of a return for a troop of horse . . . Philadelphia, Zachariah Poulson [179-?]
broadside 37.5 X 33.5 cm.
Submitted Oct. 1795 according to endorsement
On same sheet are artillery and volunteer company returns
MiU-C

B7267 PENNSYLVANIA. MILITIA
Deserter. Whereas of having been duly engaged as a part of . . . the militia of Pennsylvania on the expedition against the western insurgents, did . . . last desert from his corp . . . Josiah Harmar, adjutant general of the militia . . . [n.p., 179-]
broadside 27.5 X 22.5 cm.
MiU-C (10 copies, each with manuscript letter on verso)

B7268 PENNSYLVANIA. MILITIA
General return of the militia of the state of Pennsylvania . . . Philadelphia: Printed by Zachariah Poulson, junior, number eighty, Chesnut-Street [179-]
broadside 46.5 X 37.5 cm. folded to 30 X 24 cm.
MiU-C (2 copies, dated Apr. 17, 1795, and Oct. 15, 1796)

B7269 PENNSYLVANIA. MILITIA
Return of an election held the day of 179 at in street, to fill up vacancies in . . . militia . . . of Philadelphia. [n.p., 179-]
broadside 20.5 X 17 cm.
At foot: "Directions" to judges
MiU-C

B7270 PENNSYLVANIA SOCIETY FOR MECHANICAL IMPROVEMENTS AND PHILOSOPHICAL INQUIRIES
The constitution and fundamental rules of the Pennsylvania Society . . . [Philadelphia, 179-?]
broadside 42 X 26 cm.
New York Public 969
NN (photostat) mp. 45788

B7271 A PENNY'S worth of wit . . . [n.p., 179-?]
broadside 30 X 20 cm.
3 columns of verse
CtHi mp. 45789

B7272 PERRY, WILLIAM
The only sure guide to the English tongue . . . Brookfield, E. Merriam [179-]
180 p. incl. front, illus. 16.5 cm.
DLC; MWA mp. 45790

B7273 PHILANDER and Rosabella . . . [229 lines]
Printed & sold in New-London [179-?]
broadside 35.5 X 20 cm.
Text in 3 columns
Dated by Edwin Wolf 2d
PHi

B7274 A PLAN calculated to facilitate the juridical studies of the State of New-York . . . [New York? 179-?]
8 p. 22.5 cm. caption title
Ms. note at end: Written by D. G. Blake
Inscribed in contemporary handwriting "The gift of Gulian C. Verplanck [d. 1799] to the New York Society Library" and bound with 5 other pamphlets with imprints from 1791 to 1797
NNS

B7275 RUDDOCK, SAMUEL A.
A geographical view of all the post towns in the United States of America and their distances from each other . . . By Samuel A. Ruddock accomptant. Boston. [Boston, 179-]
broadside 52.5 X 33 cm.
Engraved throughout
Printed after 1792 (internal evidence)
Ford 2761
MHi mp. 45792

B7276 THE seaman's journal: being an easy and correct method of keeping the daily reckoning of a ship . . . Sagg-Harbour, Printed and sold by David Frothingham [179-]
200 p. 33 cm.
Dated "1794" in ms.
NEh mp. 45793

B7277 SOCIETY FOR ESTABLISHING USEFUL MANUFACTURES
The establishment of manufactures in the United States, when maturely considered, will be found to be of the highest importance to their prosperity . . . [n.p., 179-?]
10 p. 22 cm. caption title
Last page refers to a New Jersey act of incorporation of such a society and ends: "In testimory whereof . . . in the year one thousand seven hundred and ninety-one."
cf. Evans 23609
NHi mp. 45794

B7278 THE Southern stages start from the Baltimore office . . . The Eastern Shore stage . . . starts on Monday, Wednesday, and Friday mornings . . . Philadelphia, Eleazer Oswald [179-]
broadside 26 X 22 cm.
DLC mp. 45795

B7279 TAYLOR, RAYNOR, 1747-1825
An easy and familiar lesson for two performers on one piano forte . . . Philadelphia, B. Carr; Baltimore, I. Carr [179-]
2-3 p. 33 cm.
Probably printed 1795-97
Sonneck-Upton p. 226
DLC mp. 45796

B7280 THOMPSON, ISAAC
Hinckley's infallible remedy for the haemorrhoids . . . Prepared . . . at New-London . . . and for sale . . . at the druggist store of Isaac Thompson. [New London, 179-?]
broadside 21.5 X 22 cm.
NHi

B7281 EINE Trauergeschichte oder ein neues Lied über eine grausame Mordthat. [n.p., 179-]
broadside
Probably printed about 1795.—Edwin Wolf 2d
PPL mp. 45798

B7282 DIE Tugende und Würkungen des Arzneymittels, genannt, Medicamentum Gratia Probatum. Diese Arzney . . . zu haben, bey Carl Heinitsch, in der Königs-Strasse zu Lancaster . . . [Lancaster, 179-?]
broadside 36 X 23 cm.
Dated between 1790 and 1810 by Edwin Wolf 2d
Text in 2 columns
PHi mp. 45799

B7283 U. S. CONGRESS. HOUSE. COMMITTEE ON COMMERCE
Resolved, as the opinion of this committee, That the interest of the United States would be promoted by further restrictions and higher duties . . . [Philadelphia? 179-]
broadside 33.5 X 21 cm.
DLC

B7284 THE vanity of the world, a poem. [n.p., 179-?]
broadside 35 X 17 cm.
New York Public 976
Photostats: MHi; NN mp. 45800

B7285 VARICK [woodcut] The worst card in the Federal Pack; black at heart as the ace of spades; infamous as Ruff him the King [Rufus King]. And as notorious as the Tory knave, [Samuel] Jones. Add the remainder of the Tory ticket pack . . . [New York, 179-]
broadside 33.5 X 24.5 cm.
Political cartoon, dated by NHi probably between 1791 and 1795
NHi mp. 45801

B7286 THE village wedding . . . Boston, Printed for W. Spotswood [179-]
22, 28 p. front. 10.5 cm.
Contains also The mocking bird's nest
cf. Evans 30311 [1796]
DLC mp. 45802

B7287 WASHINGTON, GEORGE, PRES. U.S., 1732–1799
The President and Mrs. Washington, request the pleasure of company to dine . . . [Philadelphia, 179–]
broadside 9.5 X 13.5 cm.
Engraved form, printed on a card
PPRF

B7288 WASHINGTON, GEORGE, PRES. U.S., 1732–1799
The President of the United States and Mrs. Washington, request the pleasure of company to dine, on next . . . [Philadelphia, 179–]
broadside 9.5 X 13.5 cm.
Engraved form, printed on paper
DLC; PPRF

B7289 WHEATON, HANNAH
A New Year's wish.
Now fair Aurora paints the east,
The Prince of day in crimson vest . . .
[Boston? 179–]
broadside
From reference to Washington and Adams, probably before 1797
Ford 2767
NHi mp. 45803

B7290 [WILLIAMS, REV.]
The prodigal daughter . . . [Boston] Printed and sold [by T. and J. Fleet] at the Bible & Heart [179–]
16 p. illus. 17 cm.
Dated by d'Alté A. Welch
d'Alté A. Welch, Cleveland (p. 13–16 wanting) mp. 45804

B7291 WILLIAMS, JOHN H.
John H. Williams, clock and watch-maker, corner of Albany and Peace Streets, opposite the White-Hall Tavern, New-Brunswick . . . offers for sale . . . the following goods . . . [New Brunswick? 179–?]
broadside 42.5 X 27.5 cm.
NjR

B7292 THE world turned upside down or the comical metamorphoses . . . Drawn and engraved [by John New-Brunswick . . . offers for sale . . . the following goods . . . [New Brunswick? 179–?]
2 p.l., 64 p. 10.5 cm.
Engraved throughout
MWA copy has inscription: Henry Mathewson's Book Stolen from a thief in the year 1797
CtHi; MWA (p. 49–62 wanting; [ca. 1794]) mp. 45805

1790

B7293 ADAMS, THOMAS
Printing-Office, Court-Street, Boston, May 1790 Sir, . . . a proposal for printing . . . the second volume of the Transactions of the American Academy of Arts and Sciences . . . Thos. Adams. [Boston, 1790]
broadside
PHi

B7294 AN address to a certain clergyman, on the subject of a late publication against the Methodists . . . York, Edies and Willcocks [1790]
8 p. 8vo
Huntington 580
CSmH mp. 45807

B7295 ALBEMARLE CO.
Address presented to the Hon. Thomas Jefferson . . . the 12th day of February, 1790 . . . [Richmond? 1790]
broadside 27.5 X 21 cm.
Davis 28
ViU mp. 45808

B7296 ALBRECHT, JOHANN, UND COMP.
Es ist so eben zum viertenmal im Druck heraus gekommen . . . bey Johann Albrecht und Comp. in der neuen Buchdruckerey zu Lancaster . . . der neue, gemeinnützige Landwirthschafte Calender, auf das Jahr Christi 1791 . . . [Lancaster, 1790]
broadside 44 X 28 cm.
MWA mp. 45809

B7297 ALEXANDRIA SOCIETY FOR THE PROMOTION OF USEFUL KNOWLEDGE
Alexandria, 179 . Sir, We take the liberty of enclosing you the constitution of a society . . . lately established in this town . . . [Alexandria, 1790]
broadside fol.
Copies dated 1790 in ms.
PHi; PPL mp. 45810

B7298 THE American almanack, for the year . . . 1791. By Nathan Ben Salomon . . . Calculated for the meridian of Litchfield . . . Litchfield, T. Collier [1790]

Trumbull: Supplement 1793
No copy located mp. 45823

B7299 ANDRÉ, JOHN, 1751–1780
The cow chace . . . Litchfield, Re-printed by Thomas Collier [1790]
12 p. 17 cm.
Page 8 misnumbered p. 9
Advertised in the *Litchfield Monitor*, Mar. 30, 1790, as "this day published."
MWA mp. 45811

B7300 ASSOCIATE PRESBYTERY OF PENNSYLVANIA
Act of the Associate Presbytery . . . for a public fast. Philadelphia, April 30th, 1790 . . . [Philadelphia, 1790]
4 p. 21 cm. caption title
MWA mp. 45813

B7301 ASSOCIATE REFORMED SYNOD
Extracts from the minutes of the acts, and proceedings of the Associate Reformed Synod, met at Philadelphia, May 19th, 1790 . . . Philadelphia, R. Aitken & Son, 1790.
16 p.
Sealock 232
PHi mp. 45812

B7302 AUSTIN, DAVID, 1760-1831
Elizabeth Town, April 1790. Reverend Sir, In behalf of the interests of the American Preacher, I take the liberty of enclosing to you a plan of the work . . . we hope for *three* of your manuscript sermons . . . your . . . fellow laborer in Jesus Christ, David Austin. [Elizabeth, Shepard Kollock? 1790]
broadside 23 X 19 cm.
Morsch 107
MHi. Photostat: NjR mp. 45814

B7303 B. FRANKLIN: Vir vixit integer, liber obiit . . . M. DCC. XC . . . [New York? 1790]
broadside 29.5 X 24 cm.
Obituary to the memory of Franklin
NHi mp. 45824

B7304 BACHE, BENJAMIN FRANKLIN, 1769–1798
Philadelphia, July 1790. Proposals for publishing a news-paper, to be entitled the *Daily Advertiser* . . . [Philadelphia, B. F. Bache, 1790]
broadside 33 X 21 cm.
Sealock 233
NHi mp. 45815

B7305 BAILEY, JOHN, d. 1790
Life, last words, and dying confession of John Bailey. A black man . . . executed at Boston this day . . . October 14, 1790, for burglary. Boston, E. Russell [1790]
broadside 45.5 X 31 cm.
Ford 2560a
MHi mp. 45816

B7306 BAILEY'S pocket almanac, for the year . . . 1791 . . . Philadelphia, Printed and sold by Francis Bailey [1790]
[32] p. 10 cm.
MWA; PHi ([28] p.) mp. 45817

B7307 BALTIMORE THEATRE
By authority. By the Old American Company. This present evening, Friday, October 29, 1790, by particular desire, being positively the last night of performing . . . The Father: or, American Shandyism . . . [Baltimore, John Hayes, 1790]
broadside 42 X 26 cm.
Wheeler 520
MdBE mp. 45818

B7308 BANK OF PENNSYLVANIA
A list of the stockholders in the Bank of Pennsylvania. [Philadelphia] E. Oswald [1790?]

broadside 37 X 26 cm.
PHi mp. 45819

B7309 BAPTISTS. VIRGINIA
Minutes of the Baptist General Committee, at their yearly meeting, held in the city of Richmond, May 8th, 1790. Richmond: Printed by T. Nicolson [1790?]
8 p. 18 cm.
NHi mp. 45820

B7310 Deleted

B7311 BARTRAM, JOHN, d. 1812
Catalogue of American trees . . . in John Bartram's garden, near Philadelphia . . . [Philadelphia, 1790?]
broadside 42.5 X 53 cm.
DLC mp. 45821

B7312 BEDFORD CO., PA.
State of the accounts of excise, Bedford County . . . Philadelphia, R. Aitken, 1790.
6 p. 22.5 cm.
cf. Evans 18098 for an earlier one
DLC; MWA; NN mp. 45946

B7313 BEDFORD CO., PA.
State of the accounts of the taxes of Bedford County. Philadelphia, Francis Bailey, 1790.
26 p. 23 cm.
MWA; PPL; PPiU mp. 45822

B7314 THE Berkshire lady. [Philadelphia?] Printed in the year 1790.
4 leaves. 12mo
Rosenbach-Ch 144
A. S. W. Rosenbach (1933) mp. 45825

B7315 BIBLE
The Bible in miniature . . . New York, A. Brower, Jun. [1790?]
128 leaves. illus. 5 cm.
Engraved title
A Thumb Bible
Dated from ownership inscription: "H Fortin her Book 1790 Born, 1782"
Rosenbach-Ch 145
PP. d'Alté A. Welch, Cleveland (1962) mp. 45828

B7316 BIBLE
The history of the Holy Bible, as contained in the Old and New Testament. Adorned with cuts . . . Boston, Printed and sold by J. White and C. Cambridge, 1790.
96 p. 10.5 cm.
MHi; MWA. d'Alté A. Welch, Cleveland (1962)
mp. 45827

B7317 BIBLE
The Holy Bible abridged, or, The history of the Old and New Testament . . . New-York, William Durell, 1790.
186 p. 10.5 cm.
Running title: The history of the Holy Bible
CtHi; MWA; PP mp. 45826

B7318 BIBLE. O.T. PSALMS
The Psalms of David, imitated . . . Norwich, Bushnell and Hubbard [1790]
309, [10], 246, [10] p. 13.5 cm.
DLC mp. 45829

B7319 BIBLE. N.T. APOCRYPHAL BOOKS. EPISTLE OF JESUS CHRIST
A copy of a letter written by . . . Jesus Christ . . . Norwich, 1790.
8 p. 17.5 cm.
Trumbull: Supplement 2022
CtHi mp. 45831

B7320 BIBLE. N.T. APOCRYPHAL BOOKS. EPISTLE OF JESUS CHRIST
Copy of a letter written by . . . Jesus Christ . . . Massachusetts [1790?]
8 p. 17.5 cm.
cf. Evans 19586, 30281, 31993–94
DLC mp. 45830

B7321 BICKERSTAFF'S genuine Boston almanack . . . for 1791 . . . By Benjamin West . . . [Boston] E. Russell [1790]
[24] p. 18 cm.
Drake 3448
CtY; InU; MHi; MWA (imperfect); N; NjMoW
mp. 45832

B7322 BICKERSTAFF'S genuine Boston almanack . . . for 1791 . . . By Benjamin West . . . Third edition. [Boston] E. Russell [1790]
[24] p. 18 cm.
Drake 3449; Huntington 596
CSmH; MHi (imperfect); MWA; N; NN mp. 45833

B7323 BICKERSTAFF'S genuine Boston almanack . . . for 1791 . . . By Benjamin West . . . Sixth edition. [Boston] E. Russell [1790]
[24] p. 18 cm.
MWA

B7324 [BORDLEY, JOHN BEALE] 1727–1804
National credit and character . . . [at end] Printed by Daniel Humphreys, Front-street, near the Drawbridge, Philadelphia - M.DCC.XC
4 p. 21 cm. caption title
Signed: B.
PHi; PPL mp. 45834

B7325 BOSTON, THOMAS, 1676–1732
Human nature in its fourfold state . . . A new edition . . . Philadelphia, Peter Stewart, 1790.
448 p. 20.5 cm.
MWA; MiU-C; N mp. 45835

B7326 BOSTON
Boston, ss. At a meeting of the selectmen, 179 ordered, that the assize of bread . . . be as follows . . . [Boston, 1790]
broadside 20.5 X 16.5 cm.
Ford 2565; Huntington 581
CSmH; MHi

B7327 BOSTON GAZETTE
The *Boston Gazette*. The news-boy: a New Year's wish . . . Boston, January 1, 1790. [Boston, Benjamin Edes, 1790]
broadside
MB mp. 45836

B7328 BOURNE, SYLVANUS
Mr. Sylvanus Bourne, consul from the United States, for the island of Hispaniola, hereby presents his respects to and begs leave . . . Boston, November, 1790. [Boston, 1790]
broadside 20.5 X 18 cm.
RPJCB (2 copies) mp. 45837

B7329 BRAYTON,____
Solemn hymns occasioned by the death of Molly

Brayton . . . written by her bereaved husband . . . Bennington, Haswell and Russell, 1790.
broadside 43 X 28 cm.
VtBennM mp. 45838

B7330 BRIDGE lottery. Scheme of a lottery to raise the sum of four hundred and seventy pounds ten shillings, for . . . a bridge over Conogocheague . . . Elizabeth-(Hager's) Town, Stewart Herbert [1790]
broadside 20.5 X 17 cm.
Wheeler 521
MdHi mp. 45853

B7331 BROOKS, SAMUEL
Medals, miniature and profile painting and shades . . . Samuel Brooks and Joseph Wright . . . Boston, September 23, 1790. [Boston] N. Coverly [1790]
broadside 22.5 X 19 cm.
Ford 2567
MHi mp. 45839

B7332 BROWN'S Self-interpreting folio family Bible, embellished with . . . copper-plates . . . New-York, March 1, 1790. [New York, 1790]
[4] p. 44.5 cm.
NHi mp. 45840

B7333 BUCKS CO., PA.
State of the account of William Harvey, Esq. Collector of Excise for Bucks County. From October 26th, 1786, till March 28th, 1789. Philadelphia, Francis Bailey, 1790.
4 p. 21 cm.
New York Public 954; Sealock 237
MH; NN mp. 45944

B7334 BUMSTEAD, JOSEPH
Boston, January, 1790. First American treatise of mensuration. Proposals for printing . . . A System of Mensuration . . . by William Croswell . . . Subscriptions taken by Joseph Bumstead, the publisher . . . [Boston, 1790]
broadside 39 X 31 cm.
MHi mp. 45841

B7335 [BURKE, MRS.]
Ela, or the delusions of the heart . . . Boston, Printed and sold by John W. Folsom, 1790.
141, 50 p. 17 cm. A-Q^6
MWA mp. 45842

B7336 [BURKE, MRS.]
Ela, or the delusions of the heart . . . Boston, Printed for and sold by Benj. Larkin, and John W. Folsom, 1790.
141, 50 p. 17 cm. A-Q^6
MWA mp. 45843

B7337 CAREY, STEWART, AND CO.
Address to the subscribers for the Doway translation of the Vulgate Bible . . . Carey, Stewart, and Co. Philadelphia, Sept. 24, 1790 . . . [Philadelphia, 1790]
4 p. 22 cm. caption title
MWA; NN; RPJCB mp. 45844

B7338 CARVER, JONATHAN, 1710-1780
[Travels through the interior parts of North-America, in the years 1766, 1767, and 1768 . . . Fayetteville, George Roulstone? 1790]

Referred to in the *North-Carolina Chronicle*, Sept. 27, 1790, as "Those gentlemen who had not an opportunity of subscribing for this paper . . . are hereby informed, that . . . part of the said history . . . printed separately."
McMurtrie: North Carolina 154
No copy known mp. 45846

B7339 CHAMBERLAIN, THOMAS, 1693–1748
The timely remembrancer, or the minister preaching his own funeral sermon . . . Bennington, Haswell and Russell, 1790.
12 p. 17 cm.
Cooley 126; Sabin 95838
MWA mp. 45847

B7340 CHAMPLIN, CHRISTOPHER
Just imported, by Christopher Champlin, from London . . . a neat assortment of goods . . . [Providence, ca. 1790?]
broadside 31 X 18.5 cm.
Alden 1197; Winship Addenda p. 91
RHi. Photostat: MHi mp. 45848

B7341 CHESTER CO., PA.
Account of the taxes of Chester County. Philadelphia, Francis Bailey, 1790.
8 p.
Andrew Boyd's account; cf. Evans 22771 (James Gibbons' account)
NHi; PPL mp. 45941

B7342 CHESTER CO., PA.
State of the accounts of Joseph Chapman, esq. Treasurer of Chester [i.e. Bucks] County, from 15th June, 1789 . . . until the 7th January, 1790. Philadelphia, R. Aitken & Son, 1790.
13, [1] p. 21.5 cm.
Sealock 238
PPL ("Chester" corrected to "Bucks" by hand throughout); PPiU mp. 45952

B7343 THE children in the woods: [Ballad] To a very mounrful tune . . . Sold at the Bible and Heart [by William Carleton?] in Salem [1790?]
broadside
Tapley p. 348; cf. Evans 19401
MSaE mp. 45849

B7344 COKE, THOMAS, 1747–1814
The substance of a sermon on the godhead of Christ, preached at Baltimore . . . Printed in New York; Reprinted in Danbury Connecticut, for Ebenezer Oakes, 1790.
23 p.
Trumbull: Supplement 1985
No copy located mp. 45851

B7345 CONNECTICUT. ELECTION PROX.
Nomination for 1791. State of Connecticut. At a General Assembly of the State . . . holden at New-Haven . . . October . . . 1790. The gentlemen nominated . . . to stand for election . . . New-Haven, Thomas and Samuel Green [1790]
broadside 31 X 18 cm.
CtHi mp. 45852

B7346 CUMBERLAND CO., N.J.
A tavern-bill, rated at the general Quarter-Sessions held at Bridgetown for the County of Cumberland . . . [Feb. 25, 1790] . . . By order of Court Giles, Clk. [n.p., 1790]
broadside 25 X 20.5 cm.
NHi mp. 45854

B7347 CUMBERLAND CO., PA.
State of the accounts of excise for Cumberland County . . . till June, 1789. Philadelphia, Francis Bailey, 1790.

4 p. 22 cm.
DLC; MiU-C
mp. 45947

B7348 CUMBERLAND CO., PA.
State of the accounts of Stephen Duncan . . . from June 1st, 1787, till he ceased to act, 1789. Philadelphia, Francis Bailey, 1790.
42, [1] p. 22 cm.
Sealock 242
PPL; PPiU
mp. 45953

B7349 DAGGETT, DAVID, 1764–1851
Sketches of the life of Joseph Mountain, a Negro . . . executed . . . the 20th day of October, 1790. . . Hartford, Printed and sold by Nathaniel Patten [1790]
14, [1] p. 20 cm.
Advertised in the *American mercury*, Oct. 25, 1790, as "Just printed by Nathaniel Patten."
Trumbull: Supplement 2613
MWA
mp. 45855

B7350 [DAGGETT, DAVID] 1764–1851
Sketches of the life of Joseph Mountain . . . executed at New-Haven, on the 20th day of October, 1790. For a rape . . . Norwich: Printed by john Trumbull [1790?]
16 p. 20 cm.
NHi
mp. 45856

B7351 DAILY ADVERTISER
The verses of the news-carrier, of the *Daily Advertiser*, to his customers, on the New Year, 1790 . . . [New York, Francis Childs and John Swaine, 1790]
broadside 33 X 20.5 cm.
NHi
mp. 46086

B7352 DAUPHIN CO., PA.
State of the account of Andrew Forrest, esq. collector of excise for Dauphin county. From September, 1786, till August, 1787. Philadelphia: Printed by Francis Bailey, M,DCC,XC.
5 p. 23 cm.
cf. Evans 22772
NHi
mp. 45943

B7353 DAUPHIN CO., PA.
State of the accounts of John Thome . . . from the time the County was erected until 24th September, 1789. Philadelphia, R. Aitken & Son, 1790.
8 p. 22 cm.
Sealock 244
PPL; PPiU
mp. 45951

B7354 DECALVES, ALONSO, pseud.
New travels to the westward . . . The third edition. Norwich, Printed and sold by John Trumbull, 1790.
34 p. 16.5 cm.
Vail: Old frontier 807
OClWHi
mp. 45857

B7355 DEFOE, DANIEL, 1661?–1731
Travels of Robinson Crusoe . . . Boston, J. White and C. Cambridge [1790?]
30 p.
Printed between 1789 and 1793
Brigham: Robinson Crusoe 16
MWA
mp. 45860

B7356 [DEFOE, DANIEL] 1661?–1731
Travels of Robinson Crusoe. Written by himself. Boston, Samuel Hall, 1790.
31 p. 10 cm.
DLC
mp. 45859

B7357 DEFOE, DANIEL, 1661?–1731
The wonderful life, and surprising adventures of . . . Robinson Crusoe . . . Albany, C. R. & G. Webster, 1790.
138 p. 12 cm.
Brigham: Robinson Crusoe 14
MWA
mp. 45858

B7358 A DIALOGUE between an assembly-man and a convention-man, on the subject of the state constitution of Pennsylvania . . . Philadelphia: Printed and sold for the author, by W. Spotswood [1790]
12 p. 2 plates. 21 cm.
PHi
mp. 45861

B7359 DILWORTH, THOMAS, d. 1780
A new guide to the English tongue . . . Boston, Printed and sold by J. White and C. Cambridge, 1790.
141 p. 17 cm.
MWA
mp. 45862

B7360 DILWORTH, THOMAS, d. 1780
A new guide to the English tongue . . . New-Haven, Printed and sold by A. Morse, 1790.
144 p.
Trumbull: Supplement 2062
CtY
mp. 45863

B7361 DILWORTH, THOMAS, d. 1780
A new guide to the English tongue . . . Philadelphia, Printed and sold by Prichard and Hall, 1790.
144 p.
MWA
mp. 45864

B7362 A DIVINE call to that highly favoured people the Jews . . . By the Watchman . . . Annapolis, Frederick Green [1790]
viii, 35 p. 19 cm.
Huntington 595; Rosenbach 82; Wheeler 547
CSmH; MdHi; NN
mp. 45865

B7363 DOBSON, THOMAS
A new edition, corrected, improved, and greatly enlarged. Proposals, by Thomas Dobson . . . for printing by subscription, Encyclopaedia Britannica . . . Philadelphia, Thomas Dobson [1790]
4 p. 34 cm.
Sealock 246
NN
mp. 45866

B7364 EDWARDS, JONATHAN, 1703-1758
A faithful narrative of the surprising work of God . . . And published with a large preface, by Dr. Watts and Dr. Guyse. A new American edition. Elizabeth-Town, Shepard Kollock, 1790.
125 p. 17 cm.
Without reference to *True grace* (sometimes bound with the *Faithful narrative*)
MWA; N
mp. 45867

B7365 ENCYCLOPAEDIA
A compendious system of anatomy. In six parts . . . Extracted from the American edition of the Encyclopaedia; now publishing. Philadelphia, Thomas Dobson, 1790.
105 p. 12 plates. 26 cm.
The plates are copies; 10 of them are signed; R. Scot, Philad[a]
CtY-M; DNLM; MWA; MWiW; NNU-M; P
mp. 45875

B7366 ESSENTIA hysterica. Hebammen- und Weiber-Tropfen . . . [Lancaster, 1790?]
broadside oblong 12mo
PPL
mp. 45868

B7367 ESSEX CO., MASS.
Essex, ss.—To either of the constables of the town of Salem . . . Greeting. You are . . . directed to warn . . . this day of 179 [Salem? 1790?]
broadside 18 X 14.5 cm.
Filled in for May 13, 1791
NHi

B7368 AN estimate of the residue on final settlements, not provided for by government, which Mr. Morris, from the Senate . . . [n.p., 1790?]
[2] p. 38 cm.
On the Funding Act
NHi mp. 45869

B7369 THE Federal almanac . . . for . . . 1791. By Father Abraham Hutchins . . . New Brunswick, Abraham Blauvelt [1790]
[40] p.
Drake 5146; Morsch 113
NjR mp. 45891

B7370 FILLMORE, JOHN, 1702-1777
A narration of the captivity of John Fillmore and his escape from the pirates. Bennington, Haswell and Russell, 1790.
24 p. 17 cm.
Cooley 127
Vt mp. 45870

B7371 FIRST CHURCH OF CHRIST, SUTTON, MASS.
The covenant, of the First Church of Christ in Sutton. Sutton, March 18, 1790 . . . [n.p., 1790?]
broadside 33.5 X 20.5 cm.
MWA mp. 45996

B7372 FIRST PRESBYTERIAN CHURCH, N.Y.C.
The address of the trustees of the First Presbyterian Church in . . . New-York, to their constituents . . . David Cation, Clerk. [New York, 1790]
broadside 33 X 24 cm.
NHi mp. 45926

B7373 FREEMASONS. PENNSYLVANIA. GRAND LODGE
Rules and regulations for the government of the Grand Lodge of Pennsylvania. Philadelphia, Carey, Stewart, & Co., 1790.
8 p. 19.5 cm.
MWA mp. 45871

B7374 FREEMASONS. VIRGINIA. GRAND LODGE
Grand Lodge of Virginia. Annual grand communication . . . (Richmond) the 28th of April, A. L. 5790, A.D. 1790 . . . [at end] Richmond, T. Nicolson [1790]
[3] p. 34 cm. caption title
Davis 38
CSmH mp. 45872

B7375 FREEMASONS. VIRGINIA. GRAND LODGE
Half yearly grand communication . . . Richmond, 28 October, A. L. 5790, A.D. 1790. [Richmond, 1790]
5 p. 29 cm. caption title
Davis 37
PPFM mp. 45873

B7376 FREEMASONS. VIRGINIA. GRAND LODGE
Regulations for the government of the Grand lodge of Virginia . . . April 28, 5790. [Richmond? 1790]
broadside 33.5 X 19.5 cm.
Davis 39
CSmH mp. 45874

B7377 GAINE'S universal register; or, Columbian kalendar, for . . . 1791 . . . New-York, Hugh Gaine, 1790.
214 p. 12.5 cm.
New York Public 957; Wall p. 27
CtY; NHi; NN mp. 45876

B7378 GAZETTE OF THE UNITED STATES
The carrier of the *Gazette of the United States*, among the congratulations of the season, presents the following . . . [New York, John Fenno, 1790]
broadside 20 X 20.5 cm.
NHi mp. 45845

B7379 EIN geistliches Lied . . . Hägers-Taun, Johann F. Koch [1790]
broadside 21.5 X 17.5 cm.
MWA mp. 45877

B7380 A GLORIOUS discovery; or The saint's eyes opened with new revelations . . . By a Presbyterian. [n.p.] Printed for the author, 1790.
14 p. 17 cm.
New York Public 958
NHi; NN mp. 45878

B7381 GREGOIRE, DE
Sir, You have probably been informed, by the public papers, that we were recommended by the French government, to claim as estate on one of our ancestors . . . Boston, September 26th, 1790. [Boston, 1790]
broadside 18 X 15 cm.
Ford 2570; New York Public 960
NN copy, signed in ms.: Mde et Mr De Gregoire, is addressed to Samuel Adams
NN mp. 45879

B7382 HAMMON, JUPITER
An evening's improvement . . . Hartford, Printed for the author, by the assistance of his friends [1790?]
sm. 4to
Huntington 583; cf. Evans 17969
CSmH (p. 25-28 reproduced in photostat) mp. 45880

B7383 HARVARD UNIVERSITY
The steward is directed by the immediate government of the University, at Cambridge, to send . . . the later part of Law 11 chap VIII, of the laws of the University. [Boston, 1790?]
broadside 20.5 X 16.5 cm.
Ford 2573; New York Public 961
MB. Photostat: NN mp. 45881

B7384 [HAYES, THOMAS]
Concise observations on the nature of our common food . . . Second edition. London printed; New-York, Re-printed by T. & J. Swords, for Berry and Rogers, 1790.
38 p. 17.5 cm.
Austin 512; cf. Evans 22563
DLC; NHi mp. 45882

B7385 HELLENBROEK, ABRAHAM, 1658-1731
Voorbeeld der godlyke waarheden . . . door A. Hellenbroek . . . Nieuw-Brunswick, Abraham Blauvelt, 1790.
62 p. 16.5 cm.
Morsch 115
George C. Rockefeller, Madison, N.J. (1969) mp. 45883

B7386 HERKIMER CO.
Advertisement.—County of Herkemer, By virtue of a writ of fieri facias . . . at the suit of Walter Livingston, against William Duer, I shall sell, at public vendue, on the day of next . . . the following lands . . .

Given . . . in the year One Thousand Seven Hundred Ninety. [n.p., 1790]
broadside 35 X 26.5 cm.
NHi mp. 45884

B7387 HERR, FRANZ
A short explication of the written word of God . . . Against the people called Quakers. [Lancaster] 1790.
43 p. 8vo
PPL mp. 45885

B7388 [HILLHOUSE, WILLIAM] 1757-1833
An essay on descents. [n.p., 1790?]
24 p. 23 cm.
Half-title only
DLC; NN; PPL mp. 45886

B7389 [THE history of Master Jackey and Miss Harriot . . . Boston, S. Hall, 1790?]
31, [1] p. illus. 10.5 cm.
Dated by d'Alté A. Welch from breaks in cut of man on horseback
d'Alté A. Welch, Cleveland (1964) (has only p. [5]-26) mp. 45887

B7390 HOLCOMBE, HENRY, 1762-1824
A discourse on the sovereignty and unchangeableness of the Deity . . . Charleston, Markland & M'Iver, 1790.
37 p. 16.5 cm.
"Erata" slip pasted on p. [4]
NRAB; NjR (final leaf wanting) mp. 45888

B7391 HULL, ELIZABETH
A relation of the religious experience of Miss Elizabeth Hull . . . Newburyport, John Mycall [1790?]
15, [1] p. 23 cm.
MWA mp. 45889

B7392 HUMPHREYS, DAVID, 1752-1818
A poem on the happiness of America . . . Albany, C. R. & G. Webster [1790?]
41 p.
Title from Brinley no. 6877
McMurtrie: Albany 49
No copy known mp. 45890

B7393 AN hymn to be sung by the Episcopal Charity-Children, at St. Paul's Church, on Sunday, December the 5th, 1790 . . . collection made for the benefit of that benevolent institution. [New York, 1790]
broadside 32.5 X 20 cm.
NHi mp. 45892

B7394 AN invitation to emigrate to the western country. Notice is hereby given, to such of the good people of Maryland . . . that a settlement is intended to be made, at the Chickasaw-Bluff . . . in the spring, 1792 . . . Frederick-Town, April 3, 1790. Frederick-Town, John Winter [1790]
broadside 42.5 X 27 cm.
CU mp. 45893

B7395 JACOBS Trauerlied, über die Reisse seines jüngsten Sohns Benjamin, nach Egypten. [Reading?] Gedruckt auf begehren Johannes Thaten, 1790.
8 p. 8vo
PPL mp. 45894

B7396 JENYNS, SOAME, 1704-1787
Disquisitions on several subjects . . . A new edition. Philadelphia, Thomas Dobson, 1790.
95 p. 23 cm.
ICN; MWA; PHi; PPL mp. 45895

B7397 [JOHNSON, RICHARD] 1734-1793
The history of a little boy, found under a haycock. Boston, Printed and sold by J. White, 1790.
30, [1] p. incl. covers. illus. 9 cm.
For authorship cf. Weedon
MWA (front cover and p. 21-28 wanting) mp. 45896

B7398 LANCASTER CO., PA.
State of the accounts of Jacob Krug . . . from the time of his appointment, until the 15th February, 1790. Philadelphia, R. Aitken & Son, 1790.
8 p. 22.5 cm.
Sealock 253
PPL; PPiU mp. 45948

B7399 LEE, LUDWELL, 1760-1836
An oration: delivered, Oct. 8th, 1790, before the Alexandria, Hanson and Bond, 1790.
8 p. 25 cm.
N mp. 45897

B7400 [LEE, RICHARD] b. 1747
Lines composed on the last and dying words of the Rev. Oliver Williams, pastor of the Baptist Church in Grafton, who died August 29th, 1790, aged 39 years. [Boston? 1790]
broadside
Appended is "An Acrostick" spelling Richard Lee—the author
Ford 2576
MH mp. 45898

B7401 LEITH AND SHEPHERD, DETROIT
Transport on Lakes Erie and Huron . . . [n.p., 1790]
broadside
McMurtrie: A printed broadside, dated at Detroit, Jan. 26, 1790; New York Public 964
N; NN (facsim.); MWA (facsim.) mp. 45899

B7402 [LESAGE, ALAIN RENÉ] 1668-1747
The comical adventures of Gil Blas . . . Philadelphia, Printed and sold by William Spotswood, 1790.
160 p.
cf. Evans 22619 (166 p.)
MWA

B7403 LINDSAY, OPIE
George-Town, November 6, 1790. Sir, Having established a post . . . Opie Lindsay . . . [Georgetown, 1790]
broadside 23 X 19 cm.
Goff: Georgetown 3; Wheeler 528a
DLC mp. 45900

B7404 LIST of state notes deposited in the Massachusetts Bank . . . Boston, 1790. [Boston? 1790]
broadside 19 X 22 cm.
RPJCB mp. 45909

B7405 MARINE SOCIETY, NEWPORT, R.I.
Charter of the Marine society . . . Newport, Peter Edes [ca. 1790?]
5 p. 16.5 cm.
Alden 1199A
RHi mp. 45933

B7406 MARTINET, JAN FORENS, 1735?-1796
The catechism of nature . . . Boston, Printed for David West, and E. Larkin [1790?]
108 p. 15 cm.
MWA mp. 45901

B7407 MARYLAND GAZETTE
The news-boy's verses, for January 1, 1790; respectfully inscribed to the friends and patrons of the *Maryland Gazette* . . . Verses, on George Washington . . . [Baltimore, John Hayes, 1790]
broadside 27.5 X 13.5 cm.
New York Public 965; Wheeler 535
MdBE. Photostat: NN mp. 45934

B7408 MASON, MARY
Sir, Mary Mason and family . . . solicit your friendly assistance . . . March 30, 1790. Mary Mason . . . [New York, 1790]
broadside 22 X 18 cm.
DLC mp. 45902

B7409 MASSACHUSETTS. LAWS
An act for the protection and security of the sheep and other stock on Tarpaulin-Cove-Island . . . and on Nennemessett Island . . . in the County of Dukes-County. Passed, January 30, 1790. [Boston, 1790]
broadside 36.5 X 22 cm.
Ford 2579
MHi; MWA mp. 45903

B7410 MASSACHUSETTS. LAWS
Commonwealth of Massachusetts. In the House of Representatives, June 14, 1790 . . . In Senate, June 18, 1790 . . . Boston, Thomas Adams [1790]
broadside
Concerns division of the state into eight Congressional districts
DLC; MB; MHi; MWA; MeHi mp. 45904

B7411 MASSACHUSETTS. MILITIA
General divisionary orders. . . . Newburyport, May 10, 1790. Jonathan Titcomb, Major General. [Newburyport? 1790]
broadside
Ford 2586
MSaE mp. 45905

B7412 MASSACHUSETTS. SUPREME COURT
Commonwealth of Massachusetts. Essex ss. At the Supreme Judicial Court . . . holden at Ipswich . . . the sixteenth day of said month . . . 1789 . . . [n.p., 1790?]
broadside
Concerns Daniel Foster, of Rowley
Dated from information from MSaE
Ford 2531
MSaE mp. 45906

B7413 MASSACHUSETTS. TREASURER
Commonwealth of Massachusetts. Alexander Hodgdon, Esq. Treasurer . . . to the selectmen or assessors of the town of [Boston, 1790]
broadside 43.5 X 35.5 cm.
Dated 1790 at end of text
Marginal note: Specie-tax, no. 8 granted March 3, 1790
RPJCB mp. 45907

B7414 MASSACHUSETTS. TREASURER
Specie tax, No. six, granted March, 1788. Commonwealth of Massachusetts. Alexander Hodgdon, Esq. Treasurer . . . 1790. [Boston, 1790]
broadside
Warrant to collect unpaid taxes
Ford 2583
M-Ar mp. 45908

B7415 MASSACHUSETTS STATE LOTTERY
Massachusetts State Lottery. More prizes than blanks . . . Scheme of the second class . . . 6000 tickets at four dollars each . . . Boston, April 10, 1790. Boston, Thomas Adams [1790]
broadside 53 X 31.5 cm.
Ford 2587
MHi mp. 45910

B7416 METHODIST EPISCOPAL CHURCH
Minutes; taken at a council of the bishop and delegated elders of the Methodist-Episcopal Church: held at Baltimore . . . December 1, 1790. Baltimore, W. Goddard and J. Angell, 1790.
8 p. 17 cm.
MWA mp. 45912

B7417 METHODIST EPISCOPAL CHURCH
Minutes, taken at the several conferences of the Methodist-Episcopal Church . . . for the year 1790. Philadelphia, Prichard & Hall, 1790.
12 p. 17.5 cm.
MWA; PHi mp. 45911

B7418 METHODIST EPISCOPAL CHURCH
A pocket hymn book, designed as a constant companion for the pious. Eighth edition. Wilmington, Andrews, Craig and Brynberg, 1790.
276, [10] p.
PPiPT mp. 45972

B7419 MONTGOMERY CO., PA.
State of the accounts of the taxes of Montgomery County. From March, 1785, till December 1789. Philadelphia, Eleazer Oswald, 1790.
30, [1] p. 22 cm.
Sealock 257
PPL; PPiU mp. 45954

B7420 [MOODY, ELEAZAR]
The school of good manners . . . Boston, Printed and sold by S. Hall, 1790.
55 p. 10 cm. A^7 B-C^8 D^4
Rosenbach-Ch 149
PP mp. 45914

B7421 MOORE, JOHN, 1729-1802
Zeluco. Various views of human nature . . . In two volumes. Vol. I[-II]. New-York, Hodge, Allen & Campbell, 1790.
230; 240 p. 12mo
MWA; PPL mp. 45915

B7422 DER Neue, gemeinnützige Landwirthschafts Calender auf . . . 1791 . . . [Lancaster, Johann Albrecht, 1790]
broadside
Sheet almanac issue; cf. Evans 22687
MWA

B4723 DER neueste und verbesserte Nord-Americanische Calender auf . . . 1791 . . . Lancaster, Jacob Bailey [1790]
[28?] p.
Drake 10286
PHi

B4724 THE New-England primer . . . Lancaster, J. Bailey, 1790.
[64] p.
MWA (p. 49-50 lacking) mp. 45919

B7425 THE New-England primer enlarged . . . Boston, Printed by E. Draper, for James White, 1790.
[80] p. [A]-E^8
Heartman 101
NN mp. 45917

B7426 THE New-England primer, Or, an easy and pleasant guide . . . Boston, Printed and sold by J. White and C. Cambridge, 1790.
[64] p. 10 cm. [A]-D^8
Heartman 100
CtSoP; DLC; MWA mp. 45918

B7427 NEW HAMPSHIRE. GOVERNOR, 1790-1794
By his excellency Josiah Bartlett . . . A proclamation for a public thanksgiving . . . [Oct. 13, 1790] . . . Exeter, Henry Ranlet [1790]
broadside 41 X 33 cm.
Whittemore 514
MB; NhD; NhHi mp. 45920

B7428 NEW HAMPSHIRE. GOVERNOR, 1790-1794
State of New-Hampshire. By his excellency the president of the state of New-Hampshire . . . A proclamation for a general fast . . . [Feb. 23, 1790] . . . Exeter, J. Lamson [1790]
broadside 36.5 X 30.5 cm.
Whittemore 520
NhHi mp. 45921

B7429 NEW HAMPSHIRE. TREASURER
Treasury-office, state of New-Hampshire. William Gardner, treasurer . . . to the selectmen . . . [Exeter? 1790]
broadside 30.5 X 19 cm.
Whittemore 522
NhD; NhHi mp. 45922

B7430 NEW JERSEY. GENERAL ASSEMBLY
Votes and proceedings of the fourteenth General Assembly . . . of New-Jersey . . . session begun . . . 27th day of October 1789 . . . the second sitting. New Brunswick, Abraham Blauvelt, 1790.
71 p. fol.
PHi mp. 45923

B7431 NEW JERSEY. GENERAL ASSEMBLY
Votes and proceedings of the fifteenth General Assembly . . . At a session begun at Burlington the 26th day of October, 1790 . . . Being the first sitting. Burlington, Neale and Lawrence, 1790.
100 p. 32.5 cm.
Huntington 587; New York Public 966
CSmH (p. 1-4 photostat); NN; Nj; NjHi (2 copies); PPL (p. 5-84) mp. 45924

B7432 NEW JERSEY. LAWS
Titles of the laws enacted by the Legislature of this state, during their late sitting . . . [Burlington, 1790]
broadside 35 X 10.5 cm. caption title
Reprinted from the *Burlington Advertiser*, Nov. 16, 1790, with same setting of text
NjR (photocopy)

B7433 NEW YORK. ADJUTANT GENERAL'S OFFICE
Extracts from the regulations for the order and discipline of the militia of the State of New-York. Albany, Charles R. & George Webster, 1790.
29 p. 13.5 cm.
New York Public 967
N. Photostat: NN mp. 45928

B7434 NEW YORK. COURT OF IMPEACHMENT AND ERRORS
In the Court for the Trial of Impeachment and the Correction of Errors. Peter Servis and others, respondents . . . Edward Livingston, Solicitor for respondents . . . [New York] T. Greenleaf, printer [1790?]
broadside 34 X 21 cm.
NHi mp. 45929

B7435 NEW YORK. LAWS
An act for taking a census of the electors and inhabitants in this state. Passed the 18th February, 1790 . . . [Colophon] New-York, Francis Childs and John Swaine, 1790.
2 p. 34 X 26.5 cm.
MWA; NHi mp. 45930

B7436 NEW-YORK JOURNAL
New-York Journal and Weekly Register. New-Year's verse, for 1790, presented by the carriers . . . News-Boy's Vision . . . January 1, 1790. [New York, 1790]
broadside 33 X 20 cm.
1st line: While slumb'ring on bed . . .
NHi (2 copies) mp. 45931

B7437 NEW YORK MORNING POST
Versus addressed by the carrier to the subscribers of the *New-York Morning Post, and Daily Advertiser*. January 1, 1790 . . . [New York, Francis Childs and John Swaine, 1790]
broadside 27.5 X 13.5 cm.
NHi mp. 46083

B7438 NEW-YORK WEEKLY MUSEUM
Verses for the year 1790. Addressed to the generous subscribers of the *New-York Weekly Museum* . . . [New York, Harrisson and Purdy, 1790]
broadside 26.5 X 23 cm.
New York Public 968
MWA; NHi. Photostat: NN mp. 46085

B7439 NEWBURYPORT, Sept. 3, 1790. The author of the following, about a twelvemonth since, exposed to public view a few imperfect lines, stamped with the appellation of "The Times" . . . The second number of the Times, a solemn elegy . . . [Newburyport? 1790]
broadside
Ford 2590
MSaE

B7440 NORTHAMPTON CO., PA.
State of the accounts of James Pettigrew . . . From June 20, 1786, till June 20, 1788. Philadelphia, Printed by Francis Bailey, 1790.
10 p. 21.5 cm.
Sealock 261
DLC; PPL mp. 45949

B7441 NORTHUMBERLAND CO., PA.
State of the accounts of Christopher Derring . . . until May 31st, 1789. Philadelphia, R. Aitken, 1790.
4 p. 22 cm.
DLC; MWA mp. 45945

B7442 NORTHUMBERLAND CO., PA.
State of the accounts of the taxes of Northumberland County. Philadelphia, Francis Bailey, 1790.
38, [1] p. 22 cm.
Sealock 263
P; PPiU mp. 45955

B7443 NORWICH PACKET
An address from the news-boy, to the customers of the *Norwich-packet*. For the year 1971. [Norwich, 1790]
broadside 30.5 X 10.5 cm.
Dated at end: December 31, 1790
RPJCB mp. 45806

B7444 NO. 1. A circular letter from a Philadelphian to some members of the Irish House of Commons, relative to the usage of servants; particularly describing Thomas Buckly . . . of Baltimore County . . . Philadelphia, Printed for the author [1790]
broadside 39.5 X 25 cm.
Signed: Momoniensis
Dated Jan. 7, 1790
Sealock 260
DLC mp. 45850

B7445 OGLEBY, RICHARD
Nebuchadnezzar, a full-bred dray horse, will stand the ensuing season . . . Richard Ogleby, Groom. March 19, 1790. Baltimore, W. Goddard and J. Angell, 1790.
broadside 33 X 17 cm.
Wheeler 538a
DLC mp. 45935

B7446 ORDER of procession, to be observed on the arrival of the President . . . [Providence] J. Carter [1790]
broadside 38.5 X 23.5 cm.
Alden 1200; Sabin 101869; cf. Evans 22824
CSmH mp. 45936

B7447 A PACK of cards changed into a compleat almanac and prayer-book . . . [Boston] Printed and sold at the printing-office in Marlborough-Street [1790?]
[8] p. 17 cm.
DLC mp. 45937

B7448 PENNSYLVANIA. CITIZENS
Memorial of the public creditors who are citizens of the commonwealth of Pennsylvania. Philadelphia, Zachariah Poulson, 1790.
28 p. 20.5 cm.
PHi mp. 45939

B7449 PENNSYLVANIA. CONSTITUTION
Die regierungsverfassung der republik Pennsylvanien . . . Germantaun, Michael Billmeyer, 1790.
28 p. 20 cm.
DLC mp. 45957

B7450 PENNSYLVANIA. GENERAL ASSEMBLY
Minutes of the second session of the fourteenth General Assembly of . . . Pennsylvania, which commenced . . . [Feb. 2, 1790] [Philadelphia, Hall & Sellers, 1790]
1 p.l., [115]-281 p. 32 cm.
Sealock 265
PHi; PPAmP; PPL. Photostat: DLC mp. 45958

B7451 PENNSYLVANIA. GENERAL ASSEMBLY
Minutes of the third session of the fourteenth General Assembly of . . . Pennsylvania, which commenced . . . [Aug. 24, 1790] [Philadelphia, Hall & Sellers, 1790]
[238]-302 p. 32 cm.
Sealock 266
PHi; PPAmP; PPL. Photostat: DLC mp. 45959

B7452 PENNSYLVANIA. LAWS
Acte donnant pouvoir aux Aubains . . . Passe en loi . . . le mercredi, onze de fevrier . . . Philadelphie, B. Franklin Bache [1790]
broadside 23 X 18.5 cm.
DLC (2 copies) mp. 45960

B7453 PENNSYLVANIA. LAWS
State of Pennsylvania. An act to repeal . . . "An act for ascertaining and confirming to . . . Connecticut Claimants, the lands by them claimed within the county of Luzerne . . ." . . . Enacted into a law at Philadelphia . . . [Apr. 1, 1790] . . . [Philadelphia, 1790]
broadside 21 X 16.5 cm.
NjR

B7454 PENNSYLVANIA. REGISTER GENERAL
David Rittenhouse, Esq. late Treasurer, account of balances as they stand on the books of the Register General's office . . . Examined, approved, and settled, the above . . . accounts . . . John Nicholson, Compt. Gens. Office, December 17th, 1790. [Philadelphia, 1790]
broadsheet ([2] p.) 33 X 20 cm.
PHi mp. 45942

B7455 PENNSYLVANIA. REGISTER-GENERAL
Report of the Register-General of public accounts to the . . . Committee of Ways and Means . . . Philadelphia, Hall & Sellers, 1790.
34 p. 23 cm.
Signed: John Donaldson
Sealock 267
MiU-C; NN (t.p. photostat only) mp. 45961

B7456 PENNSYLVANIA. SUPREME EXECUTIVE COUNCIL
The Supreme Executive Council met at Philadelphia, the 18th of December, 1790 . . . The Comptroller and Register General's reports . . . were read and approved . . . [Philadelphia, 1790]
broadside 32 X 20 cm.
PHi mp. 45962

B7457 PENNSYLVANIA. TREASURER
State of the finances of the Commonwealth of Pennsylvania, till October 1st, 1790. [Philadelphia, 1790?]
12+ p. caption title [A]-C^2
Page 12 ends: Carried forward, £10884 14 2
DLC

B7458 THE Pennsylvania almanac, for the year . . . 1791 . . . Lancaster: Printed and sold by Jacob Bailey [1790]
[36] p. $[A]^8$ B^8 C^4
Drake 10287
CtY

B7459 PENNSYLVANIA GAZETTE
New-Year verses, of those who carry the *Pennsylvania Gazette* to the customers, January 1, 1790 . . . . Philadelphia, Hall and Sellers [1790]
broadside 27 X 20.5 cm.
NHi mp. 45925

B7460 THE Pennsylvania pocket almanac, for the year . . . 1791 . . . Philadelphia: Printed by Thomas Lang, and sold at his house, and by Robert Campbell, bookseller [1790]
[24] p. 11 cm.
cf. Evans 22785
PHi mp. 45963

B7461 PHILADELPHIA. CORDWAINERS
A list of the prices of boots and shoes, &c. as agreed to

by the master cordwainers of the City and Liberties of Philadelphia, at a meeting held the 8th November, 1790. [Philadelphia, 1790]
broadside
PPL mp. 45964

B7462 PHILADELPHIA. ORDINANCES
By the Mayor, Aldermen, and citizens of Philadelphia: an ordinance for the regulation of the drivers of carriages and horses in . . . the streets of . . . Philadelphia. Philadelphia, James & Johnson [1790]
broadside 49 X 30.5 cm.
Sealock 268
PHi mp. 45965

B7463 PHILADELPHIA. ORDINANCES
By the Mayor, Aldermen, and citizens of Philadelphia. An ordinance for the suppression of nuisances . . . [Philadelphia, Peleg Hall, 1790]
broadside 48 X 43.5 cm.
Sealock 269
P (lower edge trimmed) mp. 45966

B7464 PHILADELPHIA. POST OFFICE
Post-Office, Philadelphia, December 30, 1790. Establishments of the mails for the year 1791. The Eastern Mail . . . The Mail for Pittsburg . . . [Philadelphia, Andrew Brown, 1790]
broadside 31 X 23 cm.
PHi (closely trimmed); PPAmP mp. 45967

B7465 PHILADELPHIA. SELECT COUNCIL
Rules and orders for the regulation of the Select Council. [Philadelphia, 1790]
3 p. 8vo
PPL mp. 45968

B7466 PHILADELPHIA. TREASURER
State of the accounts of John Baker . . . Treasurer of the City and County of Philadelphia. From the time of his appointment 1786, until the 1st of December, 1789. Philadelphia, Francis Bailey, 1790.
31 p. 21.5 cm.
Sealock 270
PPiU mp. 45950

B7467 PHILADELPHIA, September 6th, 1790. Gentlemen, Permit us to congratulate you upon the establishment of a constitution in Pennsylvania . . . [Philadelphia? 1790]
broadside 34.5 X 22 cm.
Autograph signatures of Robert Morris and others advocating Arthur St. Clair for governor
Sealock 258
PHi mp. 45969

B7468 PHILADELPHIA, September 14th, 1790. Sir, You are particularly requested to attend a meeting of General Mifflin's friends, at Mr. Epple's Tavern . . . on Thursday evening next . . . To Mr. [Philadelphia, 1790]
broadside 11 X 17.5 cm.
New York Public 970
NN mp. 45970

B7469 THE picture exhibition. Albany, Printed and sold by Charles R. & Geo. Webster, 1790.
broadside 53 X 42.5 cm.
McMurtrie: Albany 50; New York Public 971
N; NN mp. 45971

B7470 POEMS on different subjects: calculated to improve and edify young Christians. Albany, Charles R. and George Webster [1790?]
12 p. 12.5 cm.
RPB mp. 45973

B7471 POOR Robin's almanac, for . . . 1791 . . . Philadelphia: Printed and sold by John M'Culloch [1790]
[24] p. illus. 16.5 cm.
PHi mp. 45974

B7472 POPE, ALEXANDER, 1688-1744.
An essay on man . . . Concord, George Hough, 1790.
52 p. 18 cm.
Whittemore 529
MWA; NhHi mp. 45975

B7473 POTTER, JOHN
The words of the wise . . . Philadelphia, Joseph Crukshank, 1790.
75 p. 13 cm. A-F^6 G^2
Rosenbach-Ch 147
DeWI; MWA; PP. Mrs. Joseph Carson, Philadelphia (1962) mp. 45976

B7474 PRESBYTERIAN CHURCH IN THE U.S.A. PRESBYTERY OF LEXINGTON
A pastoral letter, from the Presbytery of Lexington, to the people under their care . . . [n.p., 1790?]
7 p. 17 cm. caption title
MWA mp. 45791

B7475 PRICES current, at Wilmington, North-Carolina, 179 the [Wilmington, 1790?]
broadside 15 X 18 cm.
Text in 2 columns
Earliest copy dated Dec. 14, 1790
RPJCB (3 copies)

B7476 A PRIMER: or, an easy and pleasant guide to the art of reading. Salem, Dabney and Cushing [1790]
[32] p. [A]-B^8
Heartman: Non-New-England 145; Tapley p. 349
MSaE; MWA mp. 45977

B7477 PROPOSALS for printing by subscription, the American Preacher; or, A collection of sermons, from the most eminent preachers in the United States . . . [Never before published.] It is proposed . . . in three volumes, octavo, of 400 pages each . . . [Elizabeth, 1790]
broadside 37 X 22.5 cm.
Enclosed with cover letter of David Austin dated Apr. 30, 1790
NjR

B7478 PROTESTANT EPISCOPAL CHURCH IN THE U.S.A.
Occasional offices of the Protestant Episcopal Church . . . Taken from the Book of Common Prayer. Philadelphia, Hall and Sellers, 1790.
[61] p. 8vo
Huntington 589; Sealock 272
CSmH; PPL mp. 45979

B7479 PROTESTANT EPISCOPAL CHURCH IN THE U.S.A.
Tables of lessons of Holy Scripture . . . [Philadelphia? 1790?]
[60] p.
Not Evans 26045; not octavo ed. of the alterations to the

Book of Common Prayer mentioned by McGarvey in *Liturgiae Americanae,* p. lxi
RPJCB mp. 45980

B7480 PROTESTANT EPISCOPAL CHURCH IN THE U.S.A. MARYLAND (DIOCESE)
Journal of the proceedings of a convention . . . held at Easton . . . [May 27-31, 1790] Wilmington, Andrews, Craig and Brynberg, 1790.
39 p. 20.5 cm.
Hawkins 30
MWA; NN mp. 45981

B7481 PROTESTANT EPISCOPAL CHURCH IN THE U.S.A. MASSACHUSETTS (DIOCESE)
Ecclesiastic constitution for the government of the Episcopal churches in the Commonwealth of Massachusetts, approved at a convention, holden at Salem, Mass., Oct. 5, and 6, 1790. [Salem? 1790]
broadside
Tapley p. 349
MSaE mp. 45982

B7482 PROTESTANT EPISCOPAL CHURCH IN THE U.S.A. NEW JERSEY (DIOCESE)
Proceedings of a convention . . . held . . . in Trenton, June second and third, 1790. Trenton, Isaac Collins, 1790.
22 p. 21 cm.
Morsch 125
DLC; MWA; NjHi; NjP; NjR mp. 45983

B7483 RAGUET, CLAUDIUS P.
Catalogue of French, and other books, for sale by Claudius P. Raguet, in Front-Street . . . Philadelphia. [Philadelphia, 1790]
8 p.
Printed in the advertising pages of the *American Museum* for March, 1790; also issued separately?
Brigham: Booksellers, p. 48
MWA; N mp. 45984

B7484 RHODE ISLAND. ELECTION PROX.
Coalition prox. His Excellency Arthur Fenner, Esq; Governor. The honourable Samuel J. Potter, Esq; Dep. Gov. . . . [Providence? 1790?]
broadside 19 X 12 cm.
Alden 1203A
RNHi mp. 45985

B7485 RHODE ISLAND. ELECTION PROX.
Country prox, 1790. The protectors of their country, and the supporters of the rights of mankind. His Excellency Arthur Fenner, Esquire, Governor . . . [Providence] Bennett Wheeler [1790]
broadside 22.5 X 14.5 cm.
Alden 1204
RHi mp. 45986

B7486 RHODE ISLAND. ELECTION PROX.
An opposer of land-taxes and high salaries. Benjamin Bourn, Representative in Congress. [Providence? 1790?]
broadside 8 X 10 cm.
Alden 1205; Chapin Proxies 54
RHi mp. 45987

B7487 RHODE ISLAND. ELECTION PROX.
A supporter of the rights of mankind. Job Comstock, Representative in Congress. [Providence? 1790]
broadside 7.5 X 11 cm.
Alden 1206; Chapin Proxies 55
RHi mp. 45988

B7488 RHODE ISLAND. ELECTION PROX.
Uninfluenced by party, the public good should be the only object. Benjamin Bourn, Representative in Congress. [Providence? 1790]
broadside 7.5 X 10 cm.
Alden 1207; Chapin Proxies 53
PHi; RNHi mp. 45989

B7489 RHODE ISLAND. GOVERNOR, 1790-1805
By his Excellency Arthur Fenner . . . A proclamation . . . [Nov. 1, 1790] . . . Providence, John Carter [1790]
broadside 39 X 32 cm.
Bill submitted Nov. 6, 1790
Alden 1209
RHi mp. 45990

B7490 RICHARDSON, JACOB, & CO.
Imported from London & Bristol, and to be sold cheap by Jacob Richardson & Company . . . [Newport, ca. 1790?]
broadside 28 X 22 cm.
Alden 1226; Winship p. 74
RHi mp. 45991

B7491 [SANDS, BENJAMIN]
[Metamorphosis. Philadelphia? ca. 1790]
[2-6] p. illus. 14.5 cm.
Each page has top and bottom flaps which form a picture over the underlying illustration
Imprint and date assigned by d'Alté A. Welch
Ludwig Ries, Forest Hills, N.Y. (1966)

B7492 [SHEET almanack for 1791. New-London, T. Green, 1790]
broadside
Advertised in the *Connecticut Gazette,* Nov. 26, 1790, as "Just published, and to be sold by the printers hereof, Freebetter's Almanack, for the year 1791. Also, Sheet Almanacks."
Drake 475
No copy known

B7493 THE sister's gift: or, The naughty boy reformed . . . New-York, 1790.
2 p.l., [7]-29 p. 10.5 cm.
CtY; MWA mp. 45992

B7494 SMITH, WILLIAM, 1717-1803
Discourse concerning the conversion of the heathen Americans . . . Philadelphia, John Dunlap, 1790.
iii, [1], 53 p. 12mo
PPAmP mp. 45993

B7495 SOME remarks on Mr. Worth's appeal to the public, &c. in a letter to a friend . . . Philadelphia, R. Aitken & Son, 1790.
10 p. 18.5 cm.
Sabin 86741; Sealock 277
NNUT mp. 45994

B7496 SOUTH CAROLINA. COMMITTEE TO CONSIDER THE PUBLIC DEBT.
The Committee to take into consideration the state of the debt, due from citizens of this state, and to report to this House, their opinion, as to . . . paying the same justly . . . and by what means . . . report . . . [Charleston, 1790?]
3 p. 43 cm. caption title
Latest date in broadside: Jan. 1, 1790
Sc-Ar

B7497 SOUTH CAROLINA. CONSTITUTION
The constitution of the state of South-Carolina. [Charleston, 1790]
8 p. 24 cm. caption title
On p. 8: Done in convention . . . the 3d day of June . . . 1790 . . .
Sabin 87415
DLC; RPJCB mp. 45995

B7498 SOUTH CAROLINA. CONSTITUTIONAL CONVENTION
Additional articles, ordained by the Convention, for framing a constitution for . . . South-Carolina. [Charleston, 1790]
broadside 20 X 16 cm.
Sc-Ar

B7499 T., J.
A moral reflection, on the sudden death of the two Miss Visschers . . . drowned in the River Hudson, March 15, 1790. Very respectfully inscribed to the . . . mourners, by . . . J. T. Albany, Printed and sold at Webster's Printing-Office [1790]
8 p. 19 cm.
MWA mp. 45916

B7500 TAMMANY SOCIETY
Constitutions of Tammany Society, or Columbian Order. [New York, 1790]
4 p. 22 cm. caption title
DLC mp. 45997

B7500a TAMMANY SOCIETY
1790. Brother, you are requested to attend a meeting of the Tammany Society . . . on next at the going down of the Sun . . . [New York, 1790]
broadside
PHi (4 copies)

B7501 TAYLOR, JOSEPH
Narrative of the revivication of Joseph Taylor, who was supposed to have been hanged to death, on Boston-Neck . . . the eighth day of May, 1788, for robbery. [n.p.] 1790.
12 p. 17 cm.
New York Public 973; Sabin 94519
MWA; NN mp. 45998

B7502 TAYLOR, JOSEPH
A remarkable and extraordinary narrative of the revivification of Joseph Taylor, who was supposed to have been hanged to death . . . the 8th of May, 1788 . . . Published by himself in a letter to . . . Phelim Donance . . . Baltimore: Re-Printed and sold by S. & J. Adams, for Isaiah Isaacs, 1790.
8 p. 17 cm.
MWA mp. 45999

B7503 THOMAS À KEMPIS, 1380-1471
An extract of the Christian's pattern . . . Published by John Wesley, M. A. Philadelphia: Printed by Prichard & Hall, and John Dickins, 1790.
vi, 7-306, [10] p. 10 cm.
cf. Evans 27179
MdBBC; NHi (imperfect) mp. 46000

B7504 THOMAS, ISAIAH, 1749-1831
Worcester, Massachusetts, Feb. 1, 1790. Rev. Sir, I . . . inclose you a proposal and subscription paper for printing an American edition of the Bible . . . Isaiah Thomas. P. S. Please to return the . . . paper . . . by the latter end of May next . . . [Worcester, 1790]
broadside 30 X 19.5 cm.
Printed in manuscript type
Ford 2597
MHi. Photostat: MWA mp. 46001

B7505 THOMAS AND ANDREWS, firm, Boston
Proposal, for printing by subscription the second and third volumes of the History of New-Hampshire. By Jeremy Belknap . . . Boston, December 21, 1790. [Boston, 1790]
broadside 27.5 X 22.5 cm.
NHi mp. 46002

B7506 THOMPSON, JOHN
The lost and undone son of perdition . . . Sold at No. 46, State-street, Albany . . . [1790?]
18 [i.e., 19] p. 16 cm.
Page 18 repeated in numbering
RPJCB

B7507 THOMPSON, WILLIAM, OF MASSACHUSETTS
To the respectable citizens of Boston. William Thompson, a native and freeholder . . . offers himself a candidate for . . . town-clerk . . . March 6, 1790. [Boston, 1790]
broadside 20 X 13.5 cm.
Ford 2599
MHi; MWA mp. 46003

B7508 THURBER AND CAHOON, firm, Providence
Just imported from London, and Bristol. And to be sold by Thurber and Cahoon . . . [Providence, ca. 1790?]
broadside 24 X 25 cm.
Alden 1230
CtY (mutilated) mp. 46004

B7509 THURBER AND CHANDLER, firm, Providence
Thurber & Chandler have for sale, on the most reasonable terms . . . Providence, Bennett Wheeler [ca. 1790?]
broadside 32 X 19 cm.
Alden 1231
Photostats: Ct; RHi mp. 46005

B7510 TO be sold, by public vendue, at the House of Mr. Daniel Barnitz at Hanover . . . a valuable tract of land . . . For further information apply . . . to John Steinmetz. October 27, 1790. Philadelphia, Melchior Steiner [1790]
broadside 30 X 16.5 cm.
In English and German
PHi mp. 46006

B7511 TO the public. It is a painful necessity only . . . A spectator. Baltimore, August 1, 1790. [Baltimore, John Hayes, 1790]
broadside 43 X 42 cm.
Wheeler 541
MdBE (2 copies) mp. 46007

B7512 TO the public. My silence for some time past . . . A spectator. Baltimore, July 21, 1790. [Baltimore, John Hayes? 1790]
broadside 43 X 25.5 cm.
Wheeler 542
MdBE mp. 46008

B7513 TRENCK, FRIEDRICH, FREIHERR VON DER, 1726-1794
The life of Baron Frederic Trenck . . . Philadelphia, William Spotswood, 1790.
2 p.l., 308 p. port. 15 cm.
Sealock 278

MWA (p. 291-292, 305-308 wanting); PHi; PLeB
mp. 46009

B7514 TRINITY CHURCH, NEW YORK
On Sunday the 1st of August, will be sung at Trinity Church, by . . . Benjamin Blagrove, the following anthems . . . [New York, 1790]
broadside 20 X 16.5 cm.
NHi mp. 45927

B7515 A TRUE account of a young lady . . . Bennington, Vt., Printed and sold by Haswell & Russell, 1790.
broadside
MWA mp. 46010

B7516 A TRUE and exact history of the Jesuits. By a Zealous partizan of the liberties of America. Albany, Printed and sold by Charles R. & George Webster, 1790.
24 p. 16 cm.
MWA mp. 46011

B7517 ULSTER CO., N. Y. CITIZENS
Ulster County, April 16th, 1790. Sir, We the subscribers, propose the following candidates . . . [Goshen? 1790]
broadside 27 X 21.5 cm.
[4] p., printed only on p. [1]
N mp. 46012

B7518 ULSTER CO., N.Y. COURT OF COMMON PLEAS
Rules . . . Goshen, Mandeville & Westcott [1790]
broadside 39 X 32.5 cm.
Rules drawn up July 6, 1790
New York Public 974
NHi. H. B. Bruyn (1931). Photostat: NN mp. 46013

B7519 UNITED SOCIETY OF HOUSE-CARPENTERS AND JOINERS
Lansingburgh, 19th June, 1790. Rules and regulations, formed by the United Society of House-Carpenters and Joiners of the towns of Lansingburgh and Troy . . . [Lansingburgh? 1790]
broadside 39 X 28.5 cm.
N. Photostat: MWA mp. 46014

B7520 U. S. CONGRESS
Congress of the United States: At the second session . . . Resolved by the Senate and House.. . . That all surveys . . . Approved, August the twelfth, 1790 . . . [New York, F. Childs and J. Swaine, 1790]
broadside 38.5 X 25 cm.
DLC; MiU-C; Sc-Ar mp. 46074

B7521 U. S. CONGRESS
Congress of the United States: At the second session . . . Resolved by the Senate and House . . . That the clerks in the office of the commissioner of army accounts . . . Approved, August the second, 1790 . . . [New York, F. Childs and J. Swaine, 1790]
broadside 37 X 24.5 cm.
DLC; Sc-Ar mp. 46075

B7522 U. S. CONGRESS
Congress of the United States. At the second session . . . Resolved by the Senate and House . . . That the expence of procuring seals for the supreme, circuit, and district courts . . . be defrayed . . . Approved, August the second, 1790 . . . [New York, F. Childs and J. Swaine, 1790]
broadside 38.5 X 25 cm.
Sc-Ar

B7523 U. S. CONGRESS. COMMITTEE APPOINTED TO REPORT A PLAN . . .
The committee appointed to report a plan, making provision for the payment of interest . . . [New York] Francis Childs and John Swaine [1790]
[2] p. 32.5 X 19.5 cm.
DLC mp. 46026

B7524 U. S. CONGRESS. SENATE
Congress of the United States. In Senate, July the 12th, 1790; The committee appointed July the 2d, 1790, reported . . . [Philadelphia] John Fenno [1790]
2 p. 33 X 21 cm.
DLC mp. 46029

B7525 U. S. CONGRESS. SENATE
Rules for conducting business in the Senate. [n.p., 1790?]
4 p. 31.5 cm.
Adopted at the first session
MiU-C mp. 46030

B7526 U. S. LAWS
An act declaring the consent of Congress . . . In Senate . . . January 5, 1790. [New York] John Fenno [1790]
broadside 34 X 20.5 cm.
DLC mp. 46031

B7527 U. S. LAWS
An act for establishing the temporary and permanent seat of the government of the United States . . . [New York] Printed by Francis Childs and John Swaine [1790?]
broadside 34 X 20 cm.
CtHi; MWA

B7528 U. S. LAWS
An act for regulating the military establishment . . . [Colophon] [New York] John Fenno [1790]
3 p. 34 cm.
DLC (2 copies); NhD mp. 46036

B7529 U. S. LAWS
An act for the encouragement of learning . . . [New York] John Fenno [1790]
2 p. 34.5 X 21 cm.
DLC (2 copies); NhD mp. 46037

B7530 U. S. LAWS
An act for the government of the territory . . . south of the River Ohio . . . [Philadelphia] John Fenno [1790]
broadside 34 X 20.5 cm.
DLC mp. 46040

B7531 U. S. LAWS
An act making further provision for the payment of the debts . . . 1790, July the 19th, Read the third time . . . [New York] John Fenno [1790]
2 p. 34 X 21 cm.
DLC mp. 46027

B7532 U. S. LAWS
An act making provision for the debt . . . [Colophon] [New York] John Fenno [1790]
4 p. 34 cm. caption title
DLC (3 copies) mp. 46049

B7533 U. S. LAWS
An act making provision for the debt . . . [New York, 1790]
4 p. 34.5 cm. caption title
Contains 14 sections; the Fenno imprint has 12 sections
DLC mp. 46047

B7534 U. S. LAWS
An act providing for the actual enumeration of the inhabitants . . . [Colophon] New-York, Thomas Greenleaf [1790]
4 p. 34.5 cm. caption title
DLC; NhD mp. 46052

B7535 U. S. LAWS
An act providing the means of intercourse . . . [New York] John Fenno [1790]
broadside 34 X 20.5 cm.
DLC; NhD mp. 46054

B7536 U. S. LAWS
An act, supplemental to the Act for establishing the salaries . . . [Philadelphia] John Fenno [1790]
broadside 34 X 20 cm.
DLC; NhD mp. 46057

B7537 U. S. LAWS
An act supplementary to the Act for the establishment and support of light-houses . . . [New York] John Fenno [1790]
broadside 33.5 X 21 cm.
DLC mp. 46058

B7538 U. S. LAWS
An act supplementory [sic] to . . . "An act making further provision for the payment of the debts of the United States." . . . Approved 27th December, 1790 . . . [n.p., 1790?]
broadside 28.5 X 19.5 cm.
MWA; NhD mp. 46059

B7539 U. S. LAWS
An act to allow compensation to John Ely . . . [Philadelphia] John Fenno [1790]
broadside 34 X 21 cm.
DLC; NhD mp. 46060

B7540 U. S. LAWS
An act to describe the mode in which the public acts . . . [Philadelphia] John Fenno [1790]
broadside 34 X 20 cm.
DLC (2 copies) mp. 46064

B7541 U. S. LAWS
An act to prevent bringing goods . . . [Philadelphia] John Fenno [1790]
2 p. 34 X 21 cm.
DLC (2 copies); NhD mp. 46066

B7542 U. S. LAWS
An act to promote the progress of useful arts. [Colophon] [Philadelphia] John Fenno [1790]
3 p. 34 cm. caption title
DLC; NhD mp. 46067

B7543 U. S. LAWS
An act to provide for mitigating . . . [Philadelphia] John Fenno [1790]
broadside 34 X 21 cm.
DLC; NhD mp. 46068

B7544 U. S. LAWS
An act to provide more effectually for the settlement of the accounts . . . 1790, June the 22d—Read the third time . . . [New York] John Fenno [1790]
2 p. 34 X 20 cm.
DLC mp. 46028

B7545 U. S. LAWS
An act to regulate trade and intercourse with the Indian tribes . . . 1790, June the 23d—Read the third time . . . [New York] John Fenno [1790]
2 p. 34 X 21 cm.
DLC; NhD mp. 46015

B7546 U. S. LAWS
Acts passed at the second session of the Congress . . . begun . . . the fourth of January . . . 1790 . . . Wilmington, Andrews, and Brynberg, 1790.
120 p. 34.5 cm.
Hawkins 31; cf. Evans 22952
DeHi mp. 46070

B7547 U. S. LAWS
A bill concerning the navigation and trade of the United States. [New York] Francis Childs and John Swaine [1790]
broadside 34 X 21 cm.
DLC mp. 46016

B7548 U. S. LAWS
A bill, declaring the officer, who, in case of vacancies . . . both of President and Vice-President . . . shall act as President . . . A bill declaring . . . when the electors . . . shall be appointed or chosen . . . A bill directing the mode in which . . . votes for a President shall be transmitted . . . [New York, 1790]
[2] p. 33 X 21.5 cm.
Presented in the House Dec. 20, 1790
New York Public 975
NN (photostat) mp. 46017

B7549 U. S. LAWS
A bill for the government and regulation of seamen . . . [Colophon] [New York] Francis Childs and John Swaine [1790]
4 p. 33.5 cm. caption title
DLC; NhD mp. 46018

B7550 U. S. LAWS
A bill making appropriations for the support of government. [New York] Francis Childs and John Swaine [1790]
[2] p. 33.5 X 21.5 cm.
DLC; NhD mp. 46019

B7551 U. S. LAWS
A bill making provision for the debt . . . [New York] Francis Childs and John Swaine [1790]
4 p. 34 cm. caption title
DLC mp. 46020

B7552 U. S. LAWS
A bill to establish an uniform rule of naturalization . . . New-York, Francis Childs and John Swaine [1790]
broadside 33.5 X 21 cm.
DLC; NhD mp. 46021

B7553 U. S. LAWS
A bill to establish an uniform rule of naturalization . . . New-York, Thomas Greenleaf [1790]
broadside 34 X 20.5 cm.
DLC (2 copies) mp. 46022

B7554 U. S. LAWS
A bill to promote the progress of useful arts. [Colophon] New-York, Francis Childs and John Swaine [1790]
4 p. 34 cm. caption title
DLC (2 copies) mp. 46023

B7555 U. S. LAWS
A bill, to regulate the collection of duties, imposed on

goods, wares . . . [Colophon] [New York] Francis Childs and John Swaine [1790]
14 p. 33.5 cm. caption title
DLC mp. 46024

B7556 U. S. LAWS
A bill to regulate the collection of duties on imposts and tonnage. [New York, Childs and Swaine, 1790]
68, [1] p. 34 cm. caption title
DLC mp. 46025

B7557 U. S. LAWS
[Certain laws interesting to gentlemen concerned in the revenue, navigation, and commerce. n.p., Goddard and Angell, 1790]

Announced in *Washington Spy* Dec. 23, 1790, as just published by Goddard and Angell
Wheeler 543
No copy known mp. 46071

B7558 U. S. LAWS
Congress of the United States: At the second session . . . An act declaring the assent of Congress to certain acts of . . . Maryland, Georgia, and Rhode-Island . . . Approved, August the eleventh, 1790 . . . [New York, F. Childs and J. Swaine, 1790]
broadside 39 X 25 cm.
Sc-Ar

B7559 U. S. LAWS
Congress of the United States: At the second session . . . An act for establishing the temporary and permanent seat of the government . . . [July 16, 1790] . . . [New York] Francis Childs and John Swaine [1790]
broadside 38 X 23 cm.
MWiW-C; NhD; Sc-Ar mp. 46032

B7560 U. S. LAWS
Congress of the United States: At the second session . . . An act for finally adjusting and satisfying the claims of . . . Steuben . . . Approved, June the 4th, 1790 . . . [New York] Francis Childs and John Swaine [1790]
broadside 34 X 21 cm.
DLC; PU; Sc-Ar mp. 46033

B7561 U. S. LAWS
Congress of the United States. At the second session . . . An act for giving effect to . . . "An act to establish the judicial courts . . ." within . . . Rhode-Island . . . Approved, June the twenty-third, 1790 . . . [New York, F. Childs and J. Swaine, 1790]
broadside 39 X 23.5 cm.
Sc-Ar

B7562 U. S. LAWS
Congress of the United States: At the second session . . . An act for giving effect to an act . . . providing for the enumeration . . . Approved, July the fifth, 1790 . . . [New York] Francis Childs and John Swaine [1790]
broadside 38.5 X 23 cm.
DLC; RHi; Sc-Ar. Photostat: MWA mp. 46034

B7563 U. S. LAWS
Congress of the United States, At the second session . . . An act for giving effect to the several acts . . . in respect to the state of North-Carolina . . . Approved, February the 8th, 1790 . . . New-York, Francis Childs and John Swaine [1790]
[2] p. 34 X 21 cm.
cf. Evans 22956
DLC; RPJCB mp. 46035

B7564 U. S. LAWS
Congress of the United States: At the second session . . . An act for the encouragement of learning . . . Approved, May the 31st, 1790 . . . [New York, F. Childs and J. Swaine, 1790]
[2] p. 34 X 20 cm.
DLC; MHi; Sc-Ar mp. 46038

B7565 U. S. LAWS
Congress of the United States: At the second session . . . An act for the government of the territory . . . Approved, May twenty-sixth, 1790 . . . [New York] Francis Childs and John Swaine [1790]
broadside 33.5 X 21.5 cm.
cf. Evans 22960
DLC mp. 46039

B7566 U. S. LAWS
Congress of the United States: At the second session . . . An act for the punishment . . . Approved, April the 30th, 1790 . . . [Colophon] [New York] Francis Childs and John Swaine [1790]
7 p. 34 cm.
DLC; Sc-Ar mp. 46041

B7567 U. S. LAWS
Congress of the United States: At the second session . . . An act for the relief of disabled soldiers . . . Approved, August the eleventh, 1790 . . . [New York, F. Childs and J. Swaine, 1790]
[2] p. 38 X 24.5 cm.
DLC; Sc-Ar mp. 46042

B7568 U. S. LAWS
Congress of the United States. At the second session . . . An act for the relief of Thomas Jenkins and Company . . . Approved, June the fourteenth, 1790 . . . [New York, F. Childs and J. Swaine, 1790]
broadside 38.5 X 23.5 cm.
Sc-Ar

B7569 U. S. LAWS
Congress of the United States: At the second session . . . An act further to provide for the payment . . . Approved, July the 16th, 1790 . . . [New York, F. Childs and J. Swaine, 1790]
broadside 36.5 X 23 cm.
DLC; Sc-Ar mp. 46043

B7570 U. S. LAWS
Congress of the United States: At the second session . . . An act making appropriations for the support of government . . . Approved, March 26th, 1790 . . . [New York, 1790]
broadside 38.5 X 24.5 cm.
MiU-C mp. 46044

B7571 U. S. LAWS
Congress of the United States: At the second session . . . An act making certain appropriations therein mentioned . . . Approved, August the twelfth, 1790. . . . [New York, 1790]
broadside 30 X 17.5 cm.
MH; Sc-Ar mp. 46045

B7572 U. S. LAWS
Congress of the United States: At the second session . . . An act making further provision for the payment . . . Approved, August the tenth, 1790 . . . [Colophon] [New York] Francis Childs and John Swaine [1790]
4 p. 34 cm.
DLC mp. 46046

B7573 U. S. LAWS
Congress of the United States: At the second session . . . An act making provision for the debt . . . Approved, August the fourth, 1790 . . . [New York, F. Childs and J. Swaine, 1790]
7 p. 35 cm.
DLC; Sc-Ar mp. 46048

B7574 U. S. LAWS
Congress of the United States: At the second session . . . An act making provision for the reduction . . . Approved, August the twelfth, 1790 . . . [New York, F. Childs and J. Swaine, 1790]
[2] p. 39 X 25 cm.
DLC; Sc-Ar mp. 46050

B7575 U. S. LAWS
Congress of the United States: At the second session . . . An act, providing for holding a treaty . . . Approved, July the twenty-second, 1790 . . . [New York] Francis Childs and John Swaine [1790]
broadside 34 X 21 cm.
cf. Evans 22966
DLC mp. 46051

B7576 U. S. LAWS
Congress of the United States: At the second session . . . An act providing for the enumeration of the inhabitants . . . [Mar. 1, 1790] . . . [New York, F. Childs and J. Swaine, 1790]
3 p. fol.
Huntington 592
CSmH mp. 46053

B7577 U. S. LAWS
Congress of the United States: At the second session . . . An act providing the means . . . Approved, July the first, 1790 . . . [New York, F. Childs and J. Swaine, 1790]
broadside 39 X 23.5 cm.
Huntington 593
CSmH (adjoining half of whole sheet blank and present); DLC; Sc-Ar mp. 46055

B7578 U. S. LAWS
Congress of the United States: At the second session . . . An act supplemental to the act for establishing the salaries . . . Approved June the fourth, 1790 . . . [New York, F. Childs and J. Swaine, 1790]
broadside 39.5 X 25.5 cm.
DLC; Sc-Ar mp. 46056

B7579 U. S. LAWS
Congress of the United States. At the second session . . . An act to accept a cession of the claims of the State of North-Carolina . . . Approved, April the second, 1790 . . . [New York, F. Childs and J. Swaine, 1790]
[3] p. 39 cm.
Sc-Ar

B7580 U. S. LAWS
Congress of the United States: At the second session . . . An act to alter the times . . . Approved, August the eleventh, 1790 . . . [New York, F. Childs and J. Swaine, 1790]
broadside 39.5 X 25 cm.
DLC; Sc-Ar mp. 46061

B7581 U. S. LAWS
Congress of the United States: At the second session . . . An act to authorize the purchase of . . . land [West Point] for the use of the United States . . . Approved, July the fifth, 1790 . . . [New York, Francis Childs and John Swaine, 1790]
broadside
MWA; NN (reduced facsim.); Sc-Ar mp. 46062

B7582 U. S. LAWS
Congress of the United States. At the second session . . . An act to continue in effect . . . "An act to regulate processes in the courts . . ." Approved, May twenty-sixth, 1790 . . . [New York, F. Childs and J. Swaine, 1790]
broadside 39 X 23.5 cm.
Sc-Ar

B7583 U. S. LAWS
Congress of the United States: At the second session . . . An act to continue . . . ". . . temporary establishment of the Post-Office" . . . Approved, August the fourth, 1790 . . . [New York, F. Childs and J. Swaine, 1790]
broadside 38 X 24 cm.
DLC; MWA; MWiW-C; Sc-Ar mp. 46063

B7584 U. S. LAWS
Congress of the United States: At the second session . . . An act to enable the officers . . . of the Virginia line . . . Approved, August the tenth, 1790 . . . [New York, F. Childs and J. Swaine, 1790]
[2] p. 38 X 25 cm.
DLC mp. 46065

B7585 U. S. LAWS
Congress of the United States. At the second session . . . An act to prevent the exportation of goods not duly inspected . . . Approved, April the 2d, 1790 . . . [New York, F. Childs and J. Swaine, 1790]
broadside 39 X 25 cm.
Sc-Ar

B7586 U. S. LAWS
Congress of the United States. At the second session . . . An act to provide for mitigating or remitting the . . . penalties, accruing under the revenue-laws . . . Approved, May twenty-sixth, 1790 . . . [New York, F. Childs and J. Swaine, 1790]
broadside 38.5 X 23 cm.
Sc-Ar

B7587 U. S. LAWS
Congress of the United States: At the second session . . . An act to satisfy the claims of John M'Cord . . . Approved, July the first, 1790 . . . [New York, F. Childs and J. Swaine, 1790]
broadside 37 X 23 cm.
DLC mp. 46074

B7588 U. S. LAWS
Extract from an act for regulating the military establishment of the United States, passed April 30, 1790. And be it further enacted, That the commissioned officers, shall receive . . . provisions, to wit: . . . [Philadelphia? 1790?]
broadside 34 X 20 cm.
NjR

B7589 U. S. LAWS
Laws of the United States, being a supplement to the Congressional Register. New-York, Hodge, Allen and Campbell, 1790.
cover-title, 145-185, [2], xiv, [2] p. 8vo
CSmH mp. 46072

B7590 U. S. LAWS
An ordinance for regulating the post-office . . . [New York, Childs and Swaine, 1790]

[4] p. 43 cm. caption title
DLC mp. 46073

B7591 U. S. PRESIDENT, 1789-1797
By the President of the United States of America, a proclamation. Whereas it hath . . . become . . . necessary to warn . . . against a violation of the treaties made at Hopewell . . . Cherokee, Choctaw, and Chickasaw nations . . . New-York, the twenty-sixth day of August . . . [1790] . . . G. Washington . . . [New York, Childs & Swaine? 1790]
4 p. 39.5 cm. caption title
MWA

B7592 U. S. PRESIDENT, 1789-1797
Speech of the President of the United States, to both houses of Congress, Wednesday, Dec. 8, 1790. [Philadelphia] John Fenno [1790]
broadside 41.5 X 32 cm.
NhD; NhHi; PHi; Vi mp. 46076

B7593 U. S. WAR DEPT.
War-Office, January 18, 1790. Sir, Having submitted to your consideration a plan for the arrangement of the militia . . . H. Knox, Secretary for the Department of War . . . [New York, 1790]
broadside 25.5 X 16.5 cm.
MWA mp. 46077

B7594 U. S. WAR DEPT.
War Office of the United States. Information is hereby given to all the invalid pensioners . . . [New York, Francis Childs and John Swaine, 1790]
broadside 21.5 X 7.5 cm.
Dated: January 28, 1790
PHi mp. 46078

B7595 VALUE of foreign gold, in dollars and cents, and in £. s. d. Salem, T. C. Cushing [1790?]
broadside 17 X 22 cm.
Ford 2601
MHi mp. 46079

B7596 VERMONT. CENSUS, 1ST
Schedule containing the number of inhabitants in each town and county in the state of Vermont, agreeable to the late enumeration. [n.p., 1790?]
broadside 30 cm.
Cooley 138
NhD; VtHi mp. 46080

B7597 VERMONT. TREASURER
State of Vermont. To constable of in the county of Windham. Greeting. Whereas the general assembly . . . in October, 1790, did grant a tax . . . Given at the treasurer's office in Tinmouth, this day of Oct. one thousand seven hundred and ninety. Treasurer. [n.p., 1790]
broadside 30 cm.
Cooley 139
VtHi mp. 46081

B7598 VERSCHIEDENE sympathetische und geheime Kunst-Stücke, welche nie zuvor im Druck erschienen. [Aus dem Spanischen übersezt.] Copy-right secured. Offenbach am Mayn [Reading, Pa.?]: Gedruckt in der Calender-Fabrike, auf Kosten eines Tyrolers, 1790.
16 p. 12mo
PPL (last leaf wanting) mp. 46082

B7599 VERSES composed on the death of eight young men, viz. William Noyes . . . of Newbury, who perished on Plumb-Island beach, April 28th, 1790 . . . [Newburyport? 1790]
broadside 43 X 25.5 cm.
28 4-line stanzas in double columns
MWA mp. 46084

B7600 A VERY surprising narrative, of a young woman, discovered in a rocky-cave . . . In a latter from a gentleman to his friend. Fifth edition. New-York [1790]
11 p. 17cm.
Signed at end: Abraham Panther
Sabin 93892
DLC; WHi mp. 45938

B7601 VIRGINIA. AUDITOR'S OFFICE
A list of pensioners . . . for the year 1789. [Dated at end] . . . January 1, 1790. [Richmond, J. Dixon, 1790]
broadside 52.5 X 21.5 cm.
DLC; NN mp. 46087

B7602 VIRGINIA. GOVERNOR, 1788-1791
In Council, January 21, 1790. Gentlemen, A list of the pensioners . . . has been forwarded to you . . . James Wood, Lieutenant-Governor. (The Governor being sick.) [Richmond, J. Dixon, 1790]
broadside 20.5 X 16.5 cm.
DLC (2 copies); NN mp. 46088

B7603 WALKER, JAMES
James Walker, at the sign of the Piece of Linen . . . is now selling off by the piece . . . a variety of seasonable . . . dry goods . . . New-York, Harrisson & Purdy [1790]
broadside 30.5 X 19.5 cm.
Form of receipt on verso dated in manuscript: March 30th 1790
DLC; N mp. 46089

B7604 WATTS, ISAAC, 1674-1748
Divine and moral songs, attempted in easy language, for the use of children. Revised and corrected. By Isaac Watts, D.D. Boston: Printed and sold by Samuel Hall, 1790.
71, [3] p. illus. 10 cm.
CtY mp. 46090

B7605 WATTS, ISAAC, 1674-1748
Divine songs attempted in easy language . . . Middletown, Moses H. Woodward, 1790.
32 p. 9 cm.
CtHi; MWA mp. 46091

B7606 WATTS, ISAAC, 1674-1748
Divine songs attempted in easy language . . . New-Haven, A. Morse, 1790.
66 p. illus. 13.5 cm.
Trumbull: Supplement 2724
MWA mp. 46092

B7607 WATTS, ISAAC, 1674-1748
Horae lyricae. Poems, chiefly of the lyric kind . . . Boston, Printed and sold by Samuel Hall, 1790.
xxxviii, 252 p. port. 18 cm.
cf. Evans 23041
MWA (p. 50-64, 69-72 wanting) mp. 46093

B7608 WATTS, ISAAC, 1674-1748
Horae lyricae. Poems, chiefly of the lyric kind . . . Boston, Printed by S. Hall, for I. Thomas in Worcester, 1790.
xxxviii, 252 p. 18 cm.
cf. Evans 23041
MWA

B7609 WATTS, ISAAC, 1674-1748
Hymns and spiritual songs . . . Boston, Joseph Bumstead, 1790.
276 p.
MB mp. 46094

B7610 WATTS, ISAAC, 1674-1748
A remarkable dream respecting eternal things . . . By Mr. W[atts] Benning[ton] [From the] Press [of Haswell and Russell? or A. Haswell?] [ca. 1790?]
12 p. 12.5 cm.
MWA (t.p. mutilated)

B7611 WATTS, ISAAC, 1674-1748
A wonderful dream . . . [at end] Sold at the Printing-Office Windham [1790?]
12 p. 16 cm. caption title
CtHi mp. 46095

B7612 [WEATHERWISE'S celebrated sheet almanack for 1791. n.p., 1790]
broadside
Advertised in the *Strafford Recorder*, Oct. 28, 1790
Nichols, p. 90
No copy known mp. 46096

B7613 WEATHERWISE'S town and country almanack for . . . 1791 . . . Boston, Printed for James D. Griffith [1790]
[24] p.
Drake 3464
CLU

B7614 WEBSTER, NOAH, 1758-1843
An American selection of lessons in reading and speaking . . . The sixth edition . . . Hartford, Hudson and Goodwin, 1790.
202 p. 17 cm.
New York Public 980; Skeel-Carpenter 460
Ct; CtHT-W (imperfect); CtHi; CtNhHi; NN mp. 46097

B7615 WEBSTER, NOAH, 1758-1843
The American spelling book . . . The fourth Vermont edition. Bennington, Anthony Haswell [1790?]
96+ p. 16 cm. A-H^6
Skeel-Carpenter 21
MWA (all after p. 96 wanting) mp. 46098

B7616 WEBSTER, NOAH, 1758-1843
[The American spelling book . . . Hartford, Hudson and Goodwin, 1790]

On Oct. 14, 1790, Webster wrote regarding deposit of a copy for copyright that he would submit one "as soon as an improved edition, now in the press, shall be finished."
Skeel-Carpenter 23
No copy known mp. 46099

B7617 WEBSTER, SAMUEL, 1719-1796
An elegy, [to the] memory of Mason and Alpheus, sons of Mr. Elisha Hale, of Douglas, who were drowned, July 3, 1790 . . . By Samuel Webster, Sutton . . . [n.p., 1790]
broadside
Ford 2569
MWA (fragment) mp. 46100

B7618 WEBSTER'S calendar: or, The Albany, Montgomery, Washington, Columbia & State of Vermont almanack, for . . . 1791 . . . By Eben W. Judd . . . Albany, Charles R. & George Webster [1790]
[24] p. 17.5 cm.
Drake 5986; New York Public 963; variant of Evans 22597
MWA ([16] p. only): NHi; NN (all after leaf 10 wanting)

B7619 WELD, EDMUND, 1631-1668
A funeral elegy by way of a dialogue; between Death, Soul, Body and Jesus Christ . . . Springfield, Printed at the Chronicle Printing-Office [1790]
broadside 37.5 X 22.5 cm.
Ford 2603
NHi. Photostat: MWA mp. 46101

B7620 WESTMORELAND CO., PA.
State of the accounts of William Perry . . . late Treasurer of Westmoreland County, till 20th March, 1788. Philadelphia, R. Aitken & Son, 1790.
8 p. 22 cm.
Sealock 281
P; PPL; PPiU mp. 45956

B7621 WILCOCKS, THOMAS, b. 1622
A choice drop of honey from the rock Christ . . . Carlisle, Re-printed and sold by Kline & Reynolds, 1790.
[2], 22 p. 18 cm.
MWA; PPL mp. 46103

B7622 [WILLIAMS, REV.]
The prodigal daughter . . . Boston, Printed and sold by E. Russell, 1790.
16 p. illus. 17.5 cm.
Author assigned by NhD
MB; NhD. Ruth Adomeit, Cleveland (p. 15-16 wanting) mp. 45978

B7623 [WILLIAMS, OTHO HOLLAND]
Congress. The residence law of Congress, and the late visit of our illustrious President, encourage the citizens of Washington county to hope . . . An inhabitant. October 26, 1790 . . . [Hagerstown? Stewart Herbert? 1790]
broadside 23.5 X 18.5 cm.
Wheeler 549
DLC mp. 46102

B7624 WINCHESTER ACADEMY
We the subscribers, do hereby promise . . . to pay . . . unto the trustees of the Winchester academy, the several sums of money, annexed to our several names . . . February 1790 . . . [Winchester? 1790]
broadside 31 X 19 cm.
DLC mp. 46104

B7625 [WOLCOT, JOHN] 1738-1819
Subjects for painters. By Peter Pindar . . . Philadelphia: Printed for W. Spotswood, Front-street; and Rice and co. Market-street. M DCC XC.
59 p. 16 cm.
PHi mp. 46105

B7626 YORK CO., PA.
The account of John Forsyth . . . until 1st October, 1789. Philadelphia, Francis Bailey, 1790.
7 p. 21 cm.
DLC; MWA mp. 45940

1791

B7627 AN acrostick . . . Newport, 1791.
broadside 20 X 17 cm.
A religious poem of 15 stanzas of 4 lines each, extolling the ministry of Gardner Thurston

Alden 1235
MWA; RNHi mp. 46106

B7628 ADAMS, EBENEZER
A true and wonderful relation of the appearance of three angels, (cloathed in white raiment) to a young man in Medford, near Boston, on the 4th of February, 1791, at night . . . as related by the young man himself to numbers of people . . . Ebenezer Adams . . . [Boston? 1791]
broadside 33.5 X 21 cm.
cf. Evans 23461
MWA mp. 46107

B7629 AN address to the manufacturers of pot and pearl ash, with an explanation of Samuel Hopkins's patent method of making the same . . . Also, copy of the patent granted to Samuel Hopkins. New-York, Childs and Swaine, 1791.
27 p. plate. 22 cm.
New York Public 982
NN (plate wanting) mp. 46109

B7630 ADGATE, ANDREW, d. 1793
Philadelphia harmony . . . Together with The rudiments of music . . . Philadelphia, Printed for the author, and sold by Westcott & Adgate [1791?]
[2], 20, 56, [2], 24 p. obl.
"The rudiments of music . . . The fourth edition" has separate t.p., with imprint: Philadelphia, John M'Culloch, 1791
MWA; PHi ("Rudiments" only); PPiW mp. 46110

B7631 AMERICAN MERCURY, HARTFORD
The carrier of the *American Mercury*, wishes his customers a happy New-Year, and presents the following . . . Hartford, January, 1st, 1791. [Hartford, Elisha Babcock, 1791]
broadside 34 X 20.5 cm.
NHi mp. 46132

B7632 AMICABLE SOCIETY, BALTIMORE
Amicable society, As the most minute attention to every sentiment of politeness . . . Baltimore, November 23, 1791. [Baltimore, W. Goddard and J. Angell? 1791]
broadside 33 X 31 cm.
Minick 1
MdHi mp. 46111

B7633 ARRANGEMENT of the performances, at Mr. St. Aivre's second exhibition, on Monday evening, March 14th . . . [New York] Childs and Swaine [1791]
broadside 33 X 21 cm.
New York Public 983
NHi. Photostat: NN mp. 46112; 46281

B7634 AN astronomical diary, kalendar, or almanack for 1792. By Isaac Bickerstaff. Hartford, Nathaniel Patten [1791]
[24] p.
Drake 477
CtHi

B7635 AT a meeting of the dealers in the public funds in the City of New-York . . . on the 21st September, 1791, it was agreed to be governed by the following rules . . . [New York] Childs and Swaine [1791]
broadside 33.5 X 21.5 cm.
New York Public 1001
NHi; NNMer (formerly). Photostat: NN mp. 46212

B7636 AUF das Fest der Menschwerdung Jesu. 1790 . . . [n.p., 1791]
broadside 8vo
PPL mp. 46113

B7637 AUSTIN, DAVID, 1760-1831
Proposals for printing by subscription, The American preacher . . . [ElizabethTown? Shepard Kollock? 1791?]
broadside 35.5 X 23.5 cm.
Morsch 132
MHi mp. 46114

B7638 THE babes in the wood. Their death and burial. Philadelphia, 1791.
4 leaves. 12mo
Rosenbach-Ch 151
A. S. W. Rosenbach (1933) mp. 46135

B7639 BALTIMORE, December 10. Further particulars of the late unfortunate conflict . . . Baltimore, W. Goddard and J. Angell, 1791.
broadside
Title from *Maryland Journal*, Dec. 13, 1791: "The following is a copy of a handbill, which we presented to our customers . . ."
Minick 3
No copy known mp. 46115

B7640 BANK OF THE U. S., 1791-1811
Report. The charter of incorporation granted to the Bank of the United States . . . [Colophon] Philadelphia, John Fenno [1791?]
[2] p. 33 cm.
New York Public 984
NN (photostat) mp. 46116

B7641 BANKS, GERARD
A sketch of the times . . . Fredericksburg, T. Green, 1791.
16 p. 4to
Parke-Bernet cat. 2310, p. 14 (Nov. 17, 1964)
No copy traced mp. 46117

B7642 A BAPTISM hymn, taken from third chapter of St. Matthew. [Boston] Sold at the Office next the stump of Liberty-tree, 1791.
broadside 29.5 X 20.5 cm.
Ford 2607
MSaE mp. 46119

B7643 BAPTISTS. VERMONT. SHAFTSBURY ASSOCIATION
Minutes of the Shaftsbury Association . . . Stockbridge, M DCC XCI. Bennington, Anthony Haswell [1791?]
14 p. 22 cm.
McCorison 191
MBC mp. 46120

B7644 BARBER'S Albany almanack . . . for . . . 1792. Albany, John Barber [1791]
[36] p.
MWA mp. 46121

B7645 BEERS, ISAAC, 1742?-1813
Catalogue of books sold by Isaac Beers at his bookstore in New-Haven. [New Haven] Thomas and Samuel Green, 1791.
24 p. 19.5 cm.
CtHi mp. 46123

B7646 BENJAMIN Bannicker's Pennsylvania, Delaware, Maryland and Virginia almanack . . . for the year . . . 1792 . . . Baltimore, William Goddard and James Angell; sold also by Joseph Crukshank and Daniel Humphreys in

Philadelphia, and by Hanson and Bond in Alexandria, 1791.
48 p. 17.5 cm.
Minick 5
MWA; PPL mp. 46118

B7647 BENNINGTON CO.
[Handbill for breach of jail, by order of Sheriff of Bennington. Bennington, A. Haswell, 1791]
broadside
Printer's bill dated Oct. 17, 1791
McCorison 195
No copy known mp. 46124

B7648 BIBLE
The Holy Bible abridged . . . Boston: Printed and sold by Samuel Hall, 1791.
173 p. illus. 10 cm.
MHi mp. 46126

B7649 BIBLE. O.T. PSALMS
Doctor Watts's Imitation of the Psalms of David, corrected and enlarged, by Joel Barlow . . . The fourth edition . . . Hartford, Hudson and Goodwin [1791?]
360 p.
Trumbull: Supplement 2720
MWA mp. 46122

B7650 BIBLE. O.T. PSALMS
The Psalms of David, imitated . . . Boston, John Norman, 1791.
232, [24] p. 15.5 cm.
MWA mp. 46347

B7651 BIBLE. O.T. PSALMS
The Psalms of David, imitated . . . Boston, John W. Folsom, 1791.
300, 276 p. 15.5 cm.
cf. Evans 23193
MWA; NN mp. 46346

B7652 BIBLE. O.T. PSALMS
The Psalms of David, imitated . . . Boston, Printed by Joseph Bumstead for D. West, and E. Larkin, 1791.
320 p. 16 cm.
CtHC; MB; MWA; NhD mp. 46345

B7653 BIBLE. O.T. PSALMS
The Psalms of David, in metre . . . Philadelphia, Peter Stewart, 1791.
364 p. 13.5 cm.
MWA mp. 46137

B7654 BIBLE. O.T. PSALMS
The Psalms of David, with hymns and spiritual songs . . . Albany, Charles R. and George Webster, 1791.
[6], 515, [3] p.
MWA; N mp. 46267

B7655 BIBLE. N.T.
The New Testament . . . Philadelphia, Hall and Sellers, 1791.
1 v. $A\text{-}Ee^{12}$
MWA mp. 46125

B7656 BICKERSTAFF'S almanack for . . . 1792 . . . [Portsmouth] Sold by the shopkeepers [1791]
[24] p.
Drake 4660
NHi

B7657 BICKERSTAFF'S astronomical diary; or almanack for . . . 1792 . . . Dover, Eliphalet Ladd, 1791.
[24] p. 17 cm.
Nichols, p. 90
MWA; NN (imperfect); NhD; NhHi mp. 46127

B7658 BOSTON
Notification. The freeholders and other inhabitants of the Town of Boston . . . August 3, 1791. [Boston, 1791]
broadside 9 X 11 cm.
Ford 2609; New York Public 987
NN mp. 46128

B7659 BROOK, MARY (BROTHERTON) 1726-1782
Reasons for the necessity of silent waiting . . . The fifth edition. Philadelphia, Re-printed by Joseph Crukshank, 1791.
32 p. 20 cm.
New York Public 988
MWA; N; NN mp. 46129

B7660 BROWN, JOHN, 1735-1788
The elements of medicine; or, A translation of the Elementa medicinae Brunonis . . . Philadelphia, William Spotswood, 1791.
2 v. in 1 (xv, 295, [8] p.) fold. plate. 22 cm.
cf. Evans 23226
CtY-M; MBCo; MBM; MdBJ-W; MdU-H; MnSRM; NNNAM (v.1); NhD; OCIM; PPC; PPL; RPJCB mp. 46130

B7661 CAREY, MATHEW, 1760-1839
Reverend Sir, The opportunity afforded by the present meeting is so favourable . . . Mathew Carey. Philadelphia, Nov. 7, 1791. [Philadelphia, M. Carey, 1791]
broadside 4to
PPL mp. 46132

B7662 CHARLESTON, S.C. ORDINANCES
Ordinances of the City Council of Charleston . . . passed since . . . August 1789 . . . Charleston, Markland & M'Iver, 1791.
106 p. 35 cm.
Mosimann 467
ScC

B7663 CHAUNCY, CHARLES, 1705-1787
"Breaking of bread," in remembrance of the dying love of Christ . . . Five sermons . . . Dover, Eliphalet Ladd, 1791.
114 p. 16 cm. $[A]\text{-}O^4\ [\ ]^1$
MWA (half-title wanting?); NhD mp. 46133

B7664 CHESTERTOWN SOCIETY
Constitution of the Chester-town Society, for promoting the abolition of slavery . . . Baltimore: Printed by William Goddard and James Angell. M.DCC.XCI.
7 p. 21 cm.
NHi mp. 46134

B7665 THE child's plain path-way to eternal life, or An heavenly messenger. Norwich, Printed by J. Trumbull, 1791.
15 p. 18 cm.
Trumbull: Second supplement 2829
NhD mp. 46136

B7666 CODMAN, JOHN
Boston, May 1791. Permit me to inform you that I have this day taken into copartnership, my brother, Mr. Richard Codman . . . [Boston, 1791]
3 p.
RPJCB mp. 46139

B7667 COKE, THOMAS, 1747-1814
An account of the great revival of the work of God in the city of Dublin . . . Richmond, Augustine Davis, 1791.

16 p. 17 cm.
Davis 50
MWA; PPL mp. 46140

B7668 COLLINS, ISAAC, 1746-1817
Holy Bible. Trenton, 9th month (Sept.) 1, 1791. Notice . . . to the subscribers to the edition of the Holy Scriptures now printing by Isaac Collins . . . finished by the first day of the tenth month (October) next. [Trenton, Isaac Collins, 1791]
broadside 45.5 X 28.5 cm.
Morsch 137
MB mp. 46141

B7669 COLLINS, ISAAC, 1746–1817
Proposals for printing by subscription by Isaac Collins, in Trenton. The Holy Bible . . . [Trenton, Isaac Collins, 1791]
[2] p.
MWA (photocopy)

B7670 THE Columbian almanack and ephemeris for . . . 1792 . . . by John Nathan Hutchins . . . New-York, Samuel Loudon [1791]
[36] p.
MWA; NHi

B7671 [TWO rows of coffins bearing names of 39 officers killed. 2 cuts flanking the title] The Columbian tragedy . . . bloody Indian battle . . . A funeral elegy on the occasion . . . Hartford: Printed, [Price Six Pence.] [1791?]
broadside 49 X 39 cm.
cf. Evans 23268
CtHi mp. 46142

B7672 CRAWFORD, DUGALD
Searmoin, chuaidh a liobhairt ag an Raft-Swamp, le D. Crauford, minister . . . Fayetteville, Sibley, Howard & Roulstone, 1791.
50 p. 18 cm.
McMurtrie: North Carolina 164
First Presb. Church, Fayetteville, N.C. mp. 46143

B7673 [CRISP, STEPHEN] 1628-1692
A short history of a long travel, from Babylon to Bethel . . . The tenth edition . . . Exeter, Re-[printed 1791?]
34+ p. 20.5 cm.
MWA mp. 46144

B7674 CUMBERLAND CO., PA.
List of dilinquent collectors. Carlisle, Kline & Reynolds [1791]
broadside 37 X 19 cm.
Signed by Alexander M'Keehen, Carlisle, March 28th, 1791
PHi mp. 46145

B7674a [DAGGETT, DAVID] 1764-1851
Das Leben und die Begebenheiten von Joseph Mountain, einem Neger, welcher zu Neu-Haven, an 20sten October, 1790 . . . hingerichtet worden . . . [Philadelphia, C. Cist, 1791]
16 p. 8vo caption title
PPL

B7675 [DAGGETT, DAVID] 1764-1851
The life and adventures of Joseph Mountain, a Negro highwayman . . . Bennington, Anthony Haswell, 1791.
28 p. 19 cm.
McCorison 198
VtBennM mp. 46146

B7676 THE death and burial of Cock Robin . . . Boston, Printed and sold by Samuel Hall, 1791.
[3]-30+ p. 10.5 cm.
CtHi; MWA (covers and all after p. 30 wanting) mp. 46138

B7677 DEFOE, DANIEL, 1661?-1731
Travels of Robinson Crusoe . . . Boston, Printed by J. White & C. Cambridge, near Charles' Rive [sic] Bridge. 1791.
29 p. illus. 10 cm.
MiU mp. 46147

B7678 DEFOE, DANIEL, 1661?-1731
The wonderful life, and surprising adventures of . . . Robinson Crusoe . . . Boston, J. White and C. Cambridge, 1791.
72 p. 13 cm.
Brigham; Robinson Crusoe 17
CtY; MWA; MiU; NjP. d'Alté A. Welch, Cleveland (1965) mp. 45148

B7679 DEIGENDESCH, JOHANNES
Nachrichters: oder nützliches und aufrichtiges Rossartzney-büchlein . . . Germantaun: Zum dritten mal gedruckt und zu finden bey Peter Leibert, 1791.
221, [7] p. 14.5 cm.
MBM; MWA; NNRT; NjR; PHi; PPL (final leaf wanting); RPJCB mp. 46149

B7680 DELAWARE. HOUSE OF ASSEMBLY
Votes and proceedings . . . at a session commenced . . . the twentieth day of October . . . Wilmington, James Adams, 1791.
13 p. 32.5 cm.
Covers session Oct. 20-26, 1791
Hawkins 34
De mp. 46151

B7681 DELAWARE. HOUSE OF ASSEMBLY
Votes of the Assembly . . . at a session commenced . . . the fifth day of September . . . Wilmington, Brynberg and Andrews [1791]
11 p. 32.5 cm.
Covers session Sept. 5-8, 1791
Hawkins 33
De mp. 46150

B7682 DELAWARE. LAWS
Laws of the Delaware state, passed at a session . . . commenced . . . the twentieth day of October, 1791. Wilmington, Brynberg and Andrews [1791?]
5 p. 30.5 cm.
Covers session Oct. 20-26, 1791
Hawkins 32
NNB mp. 46152

B7683 DESCRIPTION of a fête champêtre. [Baltimore? John Hayes? 1791]
broadside
Title from a notice in the *Maryland journal*, Dec. 9, 1791, addressed "to the despicable author of . . . 'Description of a fête champêtre'."
Minick 11
No copy known mp. 46153

B7684 DEWITT, PETER
A chance to gain twenty thousand dollars for one quarter of a dollar . . . Peter DeWitt. New-Haven, August 1st, 1791. [New Haven, 1791]
broadside 46 X 28 cm.
Concerns a New Haven wharf lottery
New York Public 989
NN mp. 46154

B7685 DICKINSON, JONATHAN, 1663-1722
God's protecting providence, man's surest help . . . The seventh edition. Philadelphia, Joseph Crukshank, 1791.
123 p. 14 cm.
New York Public 990; Vail: Old frontier 866
CtY; MWA; NN; PHi; PSC-Hi mp. 46155

B7686 DILWORTH, THOMAS, d. 1780
A new guide to the English tongue . . . Philadelphia, James & Johnson, 1791.
143, [1] p. 17.5 cm.
MWA mp. 46156

B7687 DILWORTH, THOMAS, d. 1780
A new guide to the English tongue . . . A new edition, with considerable alterations and additions. Philadelphia, Printed for Rice and Co., 1791.
136+ p. 12mo
PPL (all lacking after p. 136) mp. 46157

B7688 DILWORTH, THOMAS, d. 1780
A new guide to the English tongue . . . Wilmington, Brynberg & Andrews, 1791.
142+ p.
OClWHi mp. 46158

B7689 A DISCOURSE on popular magic: or Simon Magus delineated . . . [Litchfield?] Printed at the Asylum [by Thomas Collier?] 1791.
10 p.
Trumbull: Supplement 2068
No copy located mp. 46159

B7690 DOBSON, THOMAS
A new edition, corrected, improved, and greatly enlarged . . . Just published, by Thomas Dobson . . . Volume III. of Encyclopedia . . . Philadelphia, April 1791.
broadside 22.5 X 15 cm.
NHi mp. 46160

B7691 DODDRIDGE, PHILIP, 1702-1751
A plain and serious address to the master of a family . . . Sagg-Harbour, David Frothingham, 1791.
36 p. 18 cm.
McMurtrie: Sag Harbor 1; New York Public 990a
NEh; NShHi; NSmB. Photostat: NN mp. 46161

B7692 [DODSLEY, ROBERT] 1703-1764
Oeconomy of human life . . . Norwich, John Trumbull, 1791.
136 p. 16.5 cm.
CtHi; MWA mp. 46162

B7693 AN elegy on life, death and burial of Elder Nathaniel Green; late pastor . . . in Charlton. He . . . died greatly lamented March 21, 1791 in the 70th year of his age . . . Elegy [340 lines, verse] Taunton, A. Danforth, Printer, 1791.
broadside 45.5 X 42 cm.
Text in 5 columns
MAtt

B7694 ESSAYS on the subject of the slave-trade . . . Philadelphia, Eleazer Oswald, 1791.
22 p. 22 cm.
MWA mp. 46163

B7695 EVANS, OLIVER, 1755-1819
Improvements on the art of manufacturing grain into flour or meal. [Wilmington? Del., 1791?]
broadside 52.5 X 43 cm.
Includes certificates dated Aug. 4, 1790 and Mar. 28, 1791
New York Public 991
NN mp. 46164

B7696 EXPLANATIONS and instructions concerning the act . . . repealing . . . the duties . . . upon distilled spirits . . . Passed in the third session of Congress, on the second of March, 1791. Boston, S. Hall [1791?]
23 p. 20.5 cm.
cf. Evans 23897
DLC; ViU mp. 46165

B7697 THE famous history of Whittington and his cat . . . New-York, Printed & sold by William Durell, No. 19, Queen street [1791?]
[30] p. illus. 10 cm.
Durell was at 19 Queen street 1786-1789 and 1791-1793
Dated by d'Alté A. Welch
Mrs. Arthur M. Greenwood, Marlborough, Mass. (1962) mp. 46357

B7698 FATHER Hutchins revived; being an almanac for . . . 1792. By Father Abraham Hutchins. New-York, Printed for Thomas Allen [1791]
[36] p.
Drake 5990
Milton Drake, New York (1964)

B7699 THE federal almanac for . . . 1792 . . . Philadelphia, William Young [1791]
[36] p.
Drake 10303
MWA; PHC (16 l.)

B7700 [FIELDING, HENRY] 1707-1754
The remarkable history of Tom Jones, a foundling. Boston, Printed and sold by Samuel Hall, 1791.
28, [3] p. 10 cm.
MWA (p. [31] and rear cover wanting; N. d'Alté A. Welch, Cleveland (p. [31] and covers wanting) mp. 46166

B7701 FIELDING, HENRY, 1707-1754
The history of Tom Jones . . . Norwich (Connecticut) Printed and sold by Ebenezer Bushnell, 1791.
[2], 194 p. 12 cm.
Trumbull: Supplement 2132; cf. Evans 23371
CtHi mp. 46167

B7702 FORMAN, THOMAS M.
To the freemen of Caecil county. Gentlemen . . . I find my name introduced . . . Easton, 29th September, 1791, Thomas M. Forman. [Easton, Md.? James Cowan? 1791]
broadside 42 X 26 cm.
Minick 13
MdHi mp. 46168

B7703 FREDERICK, MD. THEATRE
Theatre, Frederick-Town. By Mr. M'Grath's Company . . . March the 10th. Frederick-Town, Winter [1791]
broadside
MWA

B7704 FREEMASONS. SOUTH CAROLINA. GRAND LODGE
General rules and regulations for the government of the Grand Lodge . . . of South-Carolina (Ancient York Masons) . . . Charleston, T. B. Bowen, 1791.
19, [1] p. 16.5 cm.
DSC

B7705 FREEMASONS. VIRGINIA
A list of the lodges . . . May 10, 1791. [Richmond, 1791]

broadside
CSmH mp. 46170

B7706 FREEMASONS. VIRGINIA. GRAND LODGE
Grand Lodge of Virginia. At an annual grand communication . . . Richmond. Wednesday, 13th April, A. L. MDCCXCI. A.D. MDCCXCI. [Richmond, 1791]
[3] p. fol.
CSmH mp. 46171

B7707 FREEMASONS. VIRGINIA. GRAND LODGE
Proceedings of the Grand lodge of Virginia . . . the twenty-eighth day of October, A.L. 5791, A.D. 1791. Richmond, John Dixon, 1791.
11 p. 17 cm.
Davis 51
DSC; IaCrM; Vi mp. 41672

B7708 FREEMASONS. VIRGINIA. GRAND LODGE
Proceedings of the Grand lodge of Virginia . . . the twenty third day of November, A.L. Five thousand seven hundred and ninety one. Richmond, John Dixon, 1791.
11 p. 17 cm.
Davis 52
DSC; IaCrM; MBFM; NNFM; Vi mp. 41673

B7709 FRESH and most interesting intelligence! Extract of a letter from Patrick Nailor to Richard Bellowsblower . . . Printed at P. Hassenclever's iron-works. [Baltimore? W. Goddard and J. Angell? 1791?]
broadside 27 X 19 cm.
Minick 31
Geo. C. Rockefeller suggests imprint: [n.p., n. d.]
MdBE mp. 46174

B7710 FRIENDS, SOCIETY OF
Advices of the yearly meeting, 1791, to be read at least once in the year, in each of the men's and women's quarterly and monthly meetings. [Philadelphia? 1791?]
broadside 23.5 X 18 cm.
RPJCB mp. 46175

B7711 FRIENDS, SOCIETY OF. LONDON MEETING FOR SUFFERINGS
Extract from the epistle of the Meeting for Sufferings in London, dated the sixth day of the seventh month, 1751 . . . Philadelphia, Joseph Crukshank [1791?]
broadside 53 X 47 cm.
DLC; MNBedf; MWA; RPJCB mp. 46176

B7712 FRIENDS, SOCIETY OF. PHILADELPHIA MEETING FOR SUFFERINGS
Meeting for Sufferings. Philadelphia, tenth month, 20th, 1791. The subscribers to "The history of our religious society . . . By John Gough," are notified . . . James Pemberton, clerk at this time . . . [Philadelphia, 1791]
broadside 4to
PPL mp. 46177

B7713 FURMAN, RICHARD, 1755-1825
A sermon on the constitution . . . of the Christian church . . . Charleston, Markland & M'Iver, 1791.
41 p. 17.5 cm.
Mosimann 469
NHi; NRAB (photocopy after p. 8); OClWHi; ScU

B7714 GAINE, HUGH, 1726-1807
Just published, and to be sold, wholesale and retail, by Hugh Gaine . . . Hutchins improved: being an almanack, for . . . 1792 . . . New-York, September 23, 1791. [New York, 1791]
broadside 41.5 X 26 cm.
N mp. 46178

B7715 GARDINER, JOHN
The widowed mourner. [Boston, 1791]
[8] p.
A poem, signed J. G.
Corrected ed. of Evans 23400, with advertisement on p. [8] instead of p. [1]
MWA; NBuG mp. 46179

B7716 GEORGETOWN WEEKLY LEDGER
The news-carrier's address to the subscribers of the *George-Town Weekly Ledger*. For January 1, 1792 . . . [Georgetown, Alexander Doyle, 1791]
broadside 30.5 X 20.5 cm.
Goff: Georgetown 5
DLC mp. 46243

B7717 GEORGIA. GOVERNOR, 1791-1793
Georgia. By his Excellency Edward Telfair, Governor . . . A proclamation . . . [Feb. 5, 1791] . . . [Augusta? 1791]
broadside 24.5 X 20.5 cm.
Concerns apprehension of forgers
De Renne p. 253
GU-De mp. 46180

B7718 GEORGIA. LAWS
An act to amend, explain and continue the "Act for regulating the judiciary departments . . ." . . . Concurred December 9, 1790. Edward Telfair, Governor. [Augusta, John E. Smith? 1791]
3 p. 4to caption title
De Renne p. 252
GU-De mp. 46181

B7719 GEORGIA. LAWS
[Acts of the General Assembly, passed at Augusta in December, 1790. Augusta, John E. Smith, 1791]
20 p. fol. A-E^2 caption title
10 acts, the first beginning: "An act for ascertaining the fees of public officers of this state."
De Renne p. 252
GU-De mp. 46182

B7720 GESSNER, SALOMON, 1730-1787
The death of Abel . . . New-York, Printed and sold by William Durell [1791]
133 p. incl. front. 15 cm.
MWA mp. 46183

B7721 [GOLDSMITH, OLIVER] 1728-1774
The vicar of Wakefield . . . Vol. I.[-Vol. II.] Norwich, Ebenezer Bushnell, 1791.
344 p. 16 cm.
Trumbull: Second supplement 2191
CtHi; DLC; MB; MWA; RPJCB mp. 46184

B7722 GORSUCH, ROBERT
[To the independent electors of Baltimore-Town and County, accusing William M'Laughlin of "having imposed upon the inhabitants of this county, when sheriff . . ."] [Baltimore? 1791]
broadside
Published about Aug. 1, 1791, preceding M'Laughlin's handbill
Minick 15
No copy known mp. 46185

B7723 H-----Y, F-----N
An elegiac poem. Composed by F-----n H-----y, a citizen of Boston . . . Bloody Indian battle at Miami, near Fort-Washington, in the Ohio-Country, Nov. 4, 1791 . . . [Boston, Esekiel Russell, 1791?]

broadside
Printer assigned from wood engraving of a military person used by Russell
MWA mp. 46186

B7724 HAMILTON, JOHN, of North Carolina
To the honorable the Speakers and Members of the General Assembly . . . of North-Carolina. The petition of John Hamilton . . . in behalf of himself and of Archibald Hamilton & Co. late merchants of Halifax County . . . North-Carolina. [Newbern, 1791]
[2] p. 34 X 21.5 cm.
4-page folder, printed on the inside pages
Dated at Newbern, Dec. 11, 1791
McMurtrie: North Carolina 165
NcD mp. 46187

B7725 THE happy man, and true gentleman . . . Danbury, Printed and sold by Douglas and Ely, 1791.
broadside 35 X 21 cm.
MWA mp. 46188

B7726 HARRIET: or, The vicar's tale . . . Hudson, Ashbel Stoddard, 1791.
23 p. 16 cm.
MWA mp. 46189

B7727 HEWES & ANTHONY, firm, Philadelphia
Philadelphia, 1st January, 1791. The partnership of Hewes & Anthony having expired with the year Ninety . . . [Philadelphia, 1791]
3 p.
RPJCB mp. 46190

B7728 THE history of Master Jackey and Miss Harriot . . . Boston: Printed and sold by Samuel Hall, 1791.
31 p. illus. 10.5 cm.
Mrs. Edgar S. Oppenheimer, New York City (1962)
mp. 46191

B7729 HOCH-DEUTSCHES Lutherisches A B C- und namen-büchlein . . . Verbesserte ausgabe. Philadelphia, Carl Cist, 1791.
[28] p. 16.5 cm.
DLC mp. 46192

B7730 HOLLINGSWORTH, HENRY, d. 1803
To the freemen of Caecil county. Gentlemen, When first I saw an address to you, signed William Matthews . . . H. Hollingsworth. Elkton, Sept. 23, 1791. [Baltimore? Goddard and Angell? 1791]
broadside 42.5 X 53 cm.
Minick 17
RPJCB mp. 46193

B7731 [HOLME, BENJAMIN] 1683-1749
A serious call in Christian love . . . New-York, Re-printed by Hugh Gaine, 1791.
55 p. 20.5 cm. [A]-G^4
MWA; NhD mp. 46194

B7732 HUMANE SOCIETY OF PHILADELPHIA
By the Humane Society of Philadelphia. Directions for preventing sudden death. [Philadelphia, 1791]
broadside fol.
By Benjamin Rush
PPL mp. 46195

B7733 HYMN for Easter Day, to be sung by the Episcopal charity children, April 24th, 1791 . . . [New York, 1791]
broadside 31 X 12.5 cm.
NHi mp. 46197

B7734 INDEPENDENT CHRONICLE
Supplement to the *Independent Chronicle.* Thursday, February 3, 1791. A brief account of the present state of the Society . . . Boston, Thomas Adams [1791]
[4] p. 36 cm.
Ford 2636
MHi mp. 46292

B7735 INDIANA COMPANY
In the Supreme Court of the United States. To the honorable John Jay, Esquire, Chief Justice . . . Philadelphia, D. Humphreys [1791]
28 p. fol.
Brief of the Indiana Company
PPL; Vi mp. 46198

B7736 JACKY Dandy's delight . . . Boston, Samuel Hall, 1791.
30, [1] p. 10.5 cm.
CLU; DLC (p. [31] wanting) mp. 46199

B7737 JANEWAY, JAMES, 1636?-1674
A token for children . . . Philadelphia, Printed and sold by R. Aitken & Son, 1791.
127 p. 13.5 cm.
MWA; PHi mp. 46200

B7738 KURZGEFASSTES Arzney-Büchlein, für Menschen und Vieh, darinnen 128 auserlesene Recepten . . . In Ephrata nachgedruckt, 1791.
24 p.
Not Evans 23483, which has CXXVIII instead of 128
PPL mp. 46202

B7739 KURZGEFASSTES Arzney-büchlein, für Menschen und Vieh, darinnen CXXVIII auslerlesene Recepten, einer prognostischen Tafel. In Wien gedruckt. In Ephrata nachgedruckt, 1791.
24 p. 12mo
No ( ) around page numbers
Not Evans 23483, which has ( ) around page numbers
PHi; PPL; PSt

B7740 THE London cries . . . Philadelphia, W. Spotswood, 1791.
31 p. 9.5 cm.
CLU mp. 46203

B7741 THE lovers instructor. Rendered plain and easy, with several other curious particulars. Norwich, 1791.
72 p.
Trumbull: Supplement 2356
No copy located mp. 46205

B7742 LUTTRELL, SIMON
To be sold, on the 30th inst. if fair, if not, the next fair day, all the perishable property belonging to the estate of William Carr, deceased . . . Simon Luttrell, Thomas Chapman, executors. Dumfries, March 1, 1791. Alexandria, Hanson & Bond [1791]
broadside 28.5 X 24 cm.
DLC mp. 46206

B7743 M'CALLA, DANIEL, 1748-1809
Two sermons to young men, preached . . . at Wappetaw, in Christ Church Parish . . . Charleston, Markland & M'Iver, 1791.
78 p. 17 cm.
New York Public 993
NN; NjP; PHi mp. 46207

B7744 M'CULLOCH'S pocket almanac, for the year 1792 ... Philadelphia, John M'Culloch [1791]
[32] p. 11 cm.
DLC; MWA (2 variants) mp. 46208

B7745 MACKLIN, CHARLES, 1697?-1747
Love a-la-mode ... Philadelphia, Printed and sold by Henry Taylor, 1791.
32 p. 17.5 cm.
MB; MWA; PHi mp. 46209

B7746 M'LAUGHLIN, WILLIAM
To the independent electors of Baltimore-Town and County. Gentlemen, After ten years spent in the public service ... I allude to handbills ... signed by Robert Gorsuch ... William M'Laughlin. Baltimore County, August 12, 1791. [Baltimore, William Goddard and James Angell? 1791]
broadside 43 X 26 cm.
Minick 19
MdBE mp. 46210

B7747 MADISON, JAMES, 1749-1812
An address to the convention ... Richmond, T. Nicolson [1791]
36 p. 19 cm.
Delivered May 4, 1791
Davis 56
DLC mp. 46211

B7748 MADISON, JAMES, 1749-1812
An address to the convention of the Protestant Episcopal Church in Virginia ... Shepherd's-Town, N. Willis [1791?]
22 p. 20 cm.
Norona 505; cf. Evans 24497
Maj. T. T. Perry, Jr., Charles Town, W. Va. (1958) mp. 46213

B7749 MAP of the middle states of North America with part of Canada ... [n.p., 1791]
map 41 X 32.5 cm.
Phillips p. 999
DLC mp. 46214

B7750 MARYLAND. ELECTION PROX.
The Chesapeak ticket. First district, Philip Key, Second district, Joshua Seney ... [Baltimore? W. Goddard and J. Angell? 1791?]
broadside 21.5 X 14 cm.
Minick 9
DLC mp. 46215

B7751 MARYLAND GAZETTE
New-Year's verses for 1791; respectfully inscribed to the ... patrons of the *Maryland Gazette* ... [Baltimore, John Hayes, 1791]
broadside 33.5 X 12.5 cm.
Minick 26; New York Public 994
MdBE. Photostat: NN mp. 46238

B7752 MASSACHUSETTS. LAWS
Commonwealth of Massachusetts. ... An act to suspend in certain cases, the operation of ... "An act for the limitation of personal actions ..." ... In Senate, February 23, 1791. This bill ... passed to be enacted ... Boston, Thomas Adams, 1791.
broadside 33 X 20 cm.
MBAt; MHi (closely trimmed); MWo mp. 46216

B7753 MASSACHUSETTS. SUPREME COURT
By order of the Supreme Judicial Court of Massachusetts ... October, 1790. On the 17th day of June next ... will be sold ... the residue ... of Waldo's Patent ... H. Knox, appointed agent ... by the legislature ... of Massachusetts. Philadelphia, March 21, 1791. [Philadelphia? 1791]
broadside 33.5 X 20.5 cm.
MHi mp. 46217

B7754 MASSACHUSETTS. TREASURER
Commonwealth of Massachusetts. Specie-tax. No 9, granted March 5, 1791. Alexander Hodgdon, Esq. Treasurer ... To the selectmen or assessors of the town of ... Boston ... [Apr. 11, 1791] [Boston, 1791]
broadside 43.5 X 35 cm.
MHi

B7755 MASSACHUSETTS HISTORICAL SOCIETY
Circular letter, of the Historical Society. ... Jeremy Belknap, November 1, 1791. [Boston, 1791]
[3] p.
Ford 2628
MHi mp. 46218

B7756 MELANCHOLY intelligence! Richmond, December 2. From the *Lexington* (Kentucky) *Gazette*. Copy of a circular-letter from Brigadier-general Scott ... Lexington, November 11, 1791 ... Baltimore, W. Goddard and J. Angell [1791]
broadside 31 X 10.5 cm.
Minick 29; New York Public 995
NN mp. 46219

B7757 METHODIST EPISCOPAL CHURCH
A pocket hymn book ... Ninth edition ... Baltimore, Printed for Rice and co., 1791.
1-256, 255[!], [258-259] p. 14 cm.
Minick 30; New York Public 996
MBNMHi; MdBS; NN mp. 46220

B7758 MILLER, ALEXANDER
The missionary's short catechism, for children ... Albany, Printed by C. R. & G. Webster [1791?]
19 p. 18 cm.
NHi mp. 46221

B7759 MOORE, EDWARD, 1712-1757
The gamester, a tragedy ... Philadelphia, Printed and sold by Henry Taylor, 1791.
80 p. 16 cm.
New York Public 997
MWA; NN mp. 46222

B7760 MOORE, RICHARD CHANNING, 1762-1841
A sermon delivered in Trinity Church, on the 11th day of October, 1791 ... New-York, T. and J. Swords, 1791.
15 p. 20.5 cm.
MWA mp. 46223

B7761 THE moralist: or, Young gentleman and lady's entertaining companion ... Boston, Printed and sold by John W. Folsom, 1791.
105 p. 15.5 cm.
MHi mp. 46224

B7762 MORGAN, GEORGE
Indiana business. Richmond, November 8, 1791. The following anonymous letter has been industriously circulated among ... the delegates of the General Assembly ... in order to prejudice them against the Indiana memorialists claim ... George Morgan. Agent for the Indiana Company. [Richmond, 1791]
broadside 34.5 X 22 cm.
WHi mp. 46225

B7763 MORTON, SARAH WENTWORTH (APTHORP) 1759-1846
Reanimation. A hymn for the Humane Society. [Boston, 1791?]
broadside
Ford 2629
NHi; PHi mp. 46226

B7764 MOUNT, THOMAS, 1764-1791
The confession, &c. of Thomas Mount . . . executed . . . the 27th day of May, 1791 . . . Portsmouth, Printed and sold by J. Melcher [1791?]
24 p. 17.5 cm.
cf. Evans 23773-74
MWA mp. 46227

B7765 THE New-England primer enlarged . . . Boston, Printed by E. Draper, for John Dabney, Salem, 1791.
[64] p. [A]-D^8
Heartman 104
MSaE mp. 46228

B7766 THE New-England primer (enlarged and much improved) . . . Philadelphia, Printed for Benjamin Johnson, 1791.
[78] p.
Heartman 105; Huntington 602
CSmH. Wm. H. Murray (1922) mp. 46231

B7767 THE New-England primer, improved . . . Middletown, Moses H. Woodward, 1791.
[80] p.
MWA (final leaf lacking) mp. 46229

B7768 THE New-England primer improved . . . New-York: Printed and sold by Samuel Campbell [1791]
70 p.
MWA mp. 46230

B7769 NEW HAMPSHIRE
. . . An act in addition to . . . An act for regulating schools in this State . . . [Portsmouth, 1791]
broadside 23 X 15 cm.
PHi mp. 46232

B7770 NEW HAMPSHIRE. COMMISSIONERS
State of New-Hampshire. Exeter, August 17, 1791. The commissioners . . . find themselves under the necessity . . . [Exeter, 1791]
8 p. 29 cm. caption title
DLC; NhHi mp. 46233

B7771 NEW HAMPSHIRE. HOUSE OF REPRESENTATIVES
A journal of the proceedings of the Hon. House . . . at a session . . . begun . . . the first day of June, 1791 . . . Portsmouth, J. Melcher. 1791.
96 p. 20.5 cm.
Huntington 603; New York Public 998
CSmH; MWA; NN; RPJCB mp. 46234

B7772 NEW HAMPSHIRE. LAWS
. . . An act in addition to . . . "An act to establish an equitable method of making rates and taxes . . . [Colophon] Portsmouth, George and John Osborne [1791]
[2] p. 31 X 19.5 cm.
Enacted Dec. 28, 1791
At head of title: State of New-Hampshire . . .
New York Public 999
DLC; MWA; NN; NhHi mp. 46235

B7773 NEW JERUSALEM CHURCH
A catechism for the use of the New Church. Philadelphia, Francis Bailey, 1791.
12 p. 17 cm.
MWA mp. 46236

B7774 THE new Pennsylvania almanac, for . . . 1792 . . . Philadelphia, Printed for Robert Campbell [1791]
[32] p. 18 cm.
New York Public 1000
NN mp. 46237

B7775 NEW YORK. ELECTION PROX.
Let every true Whig read this with attention. To the electors of the City and County of New-York . . . For Senators. Aaron Burr . . . The Republican Whig ticket . . . [New York, 1791]
broadside 47 X 26 cm.
NHi mp. 46239

B7776 NEW YORK. LAWS
State of New-York, in Senate, 16th. February, 1791 . . . An act for apportioning the representation in the legislature . . . Passed the 7th February, 1791 . . . [New York] Printed by Childs and Swaine, Printers to the State [1791]
broadside 33.5 X 21 cm.
N; NHi mp. 46240

B7777 NEW YORK DISPENSARY
Rules of the City Dispensary, for the medical relief of the poor. Instituted at New-York, February 1, 1791. [New York] Thomas Greenleaf [1791]
16 p. 18.5 cm.
Signed: Isaac Roosevelt, President, N-York December 16, 1791
Austin 1384; Rogers 303
NHi mp. 46241

B7778 NEW-YORK WEEKLY MUSEUM
Address to the generous subscribers of the *New-York Weekly Museum*, wishing them a Happy New-Year . . . [New York, 1791]
broadside 30 X 19.5 cm.
NHi mp. 46108

B7779 NEWPORT Trinity Church lottery . . . Newport . . . March 12, 1791.
broadside 25.5 X 18 cm.
Alden 1244
RNHi mp. 46242

B7780 NEWPORT MERCURY
January 1, 1791. New Year's verses humbly addressed to the customers of the *Newport Mercury* . . . [Newport, H. Barber, 1791]
broadside 18 X 9.5 cm.
Alden 1245
NjHi. Photostat: RHi mp. 46201

B7781 NORTH CAROLINA. LAWS
Laws of North-Carolina. At a General assembly, begun . . . at Newbern, on the fifth day of December . . . being the first session . . . [Colophon] Edenton, Hodge & Wills [1791]
32, [2] p. 34.5 cm. caption title
Huntington 621; McMurtrie: North Carolina 178
CSmH; DLC; MH; NNB; NcU; Nc-SC; PHi mp. 46244

B7782 [NORTH-Carolina almanack, for the year 1792. Newbern, F. X. Martin, 1791]

Advertised in the *North-Carolina Gazette*, Sept. 24, 1791, as "In the press . . ." and Nov. 5, 1791, as "just published."
McMurtrie: North Carolina 171
No copy known mp. 46245

B7783 NORTHAMPTON CO., PA.
State of the accounts of John Craig . . . Philadelphia, R. Aitken, 1791.
5 p. 21.5 cm.
DLC; NN mp. 46250

B7784 NUMBER FIVE FIRE CLUB
Toujours prêt. Articles of the No. 5 Fire-Club, associated in Salem, December 8, 1783 . . . Revised and corrected, 1791. Salem, Thomas C. Cushing [1791]
15 p.
Contains list of members
Tapley p. 350
MSaE mp. 46283

B7785 O'KEEFFE, JOHN, 1747-1833
The poor soldier . . . as performed . . . by the American Company. Written by John O'Keefe, Esq. Philadelphia, Printed and sold by Henry Taylor, 1791.
32 p. 17 cm.
MWA mp. 46246

B7786 [OSBORNE, GEORGE JERRY] 1761-1800
Printing-Office Portsmouth, January 1, 1791. Proposals for printing by subscription Four sermons . . . lately delivered by Benjamin Thurston . . . [Portsmouth, 1791]
broadside 29.5 X 19 cm.
Subscription form unfilled in
MWA mp. 46247

B7787 PECKHAM, THOMAS
To the members of the Hon. General assembly . . . Gentlemen, The clerk of the Court of common pleas . . . Thomas Peckham. Newport, May 3d, 1791. [Newport, 1791]
broadside 28.5 X 20 cm.
Alden 1246; Winship p. 58; NYPL 1003
RHi. Photostats: MWA; NN mp. 46248

B7788 PELOSI, VINCENT M.
Philadelphia 1791. At the request of several merchants . . . I have undertaken a weekly marine list . . . [Philadelphia, 1791]
broadside 23.5 X 20 cm.
RPJCB mp. 46249

B7789 PENNSYLVANIA. GOVERNOR, 1788-1799
Pennsylvania, ss. By Thomas Mifflin . . . A proclamation . . . Philadelphia, Hall and Sellers [1791]
broadside 46 X 24 cm.
Dated Nov. 14, 1791
Concerns members selected to serve in U.S. House of Representatives
PHi mp. 46252

B7790 PENNSYLVANIA. GOVERNOR, 1788-1799
Pennsylvania, ss. By Thomas Mifflin, . . . A proclamation . . . Given . . . this fourteenth day of November . . . Philadelphia, Hall and Sellers [1791]
broadside fol.
Certifying the election of sheriffs
PPL mp. 46253

B7791 PENNSYLVANIA. LAWS
In the House of Representatives, Tuesday, September 20, 1791, read the first time, An act to provide for compleating the repairs of the wharf . . . [Philadelphia, 1791]
broadside fol.
PPL mp. 46251

B7792 PENNSYLVANIA. SUPREME EXECUTIVE COUNCIL
The Supreme Executive Council met at Philadelphia . . . In Council . . . [Philadelphia, 1791]
broadside 14 X 16 cm.
Concerns treasurer's report
PHi mp. 46256

B7793 PENNSYLVANIA. TREASURER
Balance account. David Rittenhouse, Esq; late treasurer of Pennsylvania. [Philadelphia, 1791?]
broadside ([3] p.) 28 X 18 cm.
PHi mp. 46254

B7794 PENNSYLVANIA. TREASURER
List of diliquent [sic] collectors. Notice is hereby given to the following collectors, that unless they . . . discharge . . . balances by the first of August . . . Alexander M'Keehan, Esqr. Treasurer. Carlisle, March 28th, 1791 . . . Carlisle, Kline & Reynolds [1791]
broadside 41 X 22.5 cm.
Text in 2 columns
PHi mp. 46255

B7795 PERRY, PHILO, 1752-1798
A sermon, delivered at Danbury . . . June 24, 1791 . . . Danbury, Printed and sold by Douglas and Ely, 1791.
20 p. 17.5 cm.
MWA mp. 46257

B7796 [PETERSBURG church lottery. Petersburg? 1791?]
broadside
Parke-Bernet Catalogue 1570, 16 Feb. 1955, lot 203
Wyatt [8a]
Goodspeed's Bookstore mp. 46258

B7797 PHILADELPHIA. SHERIFF
By virtue of several writs of venditioni exponas . . . will be exposed to sale . . . Philadelphia, Hall and Sellers [1791]
broadside 16.5 X 14.5 cm.
Signed by Jacob Bennet, Sheriff
PHi mp. 46259

B7797a POPE, SAMUEL
Das Leben, Begebenheiten, und Bekänntniss von Samuel Pope, einem Mulatto; nebst einer Erzählung des Verfassers, welcher ihn von Zeit zu Zeit in seiner Gefangenschaft besuchet hat . . . [Reading, Barton and Jungmann, 1792]
16 p. 8vo
PPL

B7798 POST-ROAD LOTTERY
From the *United States Chronicle*. Post-Road lottery. The subscribers, being appointed managers . . . Cranston, March 9th, 1791. [Providence] Bennett Wheeler [1791]
broadside 20.5 X 14 cm.
Alden 1247
DLC; RPJCB. Photostat: MWA mp. 46261

B7799 PRICE-CURRENT. Charles-Town, 179
Dollars at 4s. 8d. [Charleston? S.C., 1791?]
3 p. 24 X 20 cm.

"Duties on goods imported . . . after 31st December, 1790," p. [2]-3
New York Public 1004; cf. Evans 23891-94
NN

B7800 PROPOSALS for a bank . . . Providence, September 6, 1791. [Providence, J. Carter? 1791]
broadside 27.5 X 16.5 cm.
Alden 1249
RNHi. Photostat: MWA mp. 46262

B7801 PROPOSALS for publishing . . . a dissertation [by John Churchman] on gravitation: containing conjectures concerning the cause of the several kinds of attraction . . . Baltimore, May 12, 1791. [Baltimore, 1791]
broadside fol.
PPL mp. 46263

B7802 PROTESTANT EPISCOPAL CHURCH IN THE U.S.A. VERMONT (DIOCESE)
[Minutes, &c. at a convention of the clergy and laity . . . Protestant Episcopal Church . . . Vermont, held in Sandgate, February 23, 1791 . . . Bennington? A. Haswell? 1791]
[3]-6+ p. 22.5 cm.
McCorison 203
NHi (t.p. and possibly p. 7-8 lacking) mp. 46264

B7803 PROTESTANT EPISCOPAL CHURCH IN THE U.S.A. VIRGINIA (DIOCESE)
Journal of a convention . . . held in . . . Richmond from May 3d to May 6th 1791 inclusive. Richmond, Thomas Nicolson [1791]
16 p. 20 cm.
New York Public 1005
NN mp. 46265

B7804 [RAMSAY, DAVID] 1749-1815
Observations on the impolicy of recommencing the importation of slaves . . . submitted to the . . . legislature of South-Carolina. By a Citizen of South-Calolina [sic]. [Charleston? 1791]
11 p. 21 cm.
Dated at end: Charleston, November 4, 1791
Authorship ascribed to Ramsay in ms. note in NcD copy
NcD

B7805 THE redeemer's work, or, Christ all in all . . . Albany, Charles R. and George Webster [1791?]
12 p. 17.5 cm.
MWA mp. 46266

B7806 RELIGIOUS instructions for children. The seventeenth edition. Philadelphia, Printed by Joseph Crukshank; sold by John Dickins, 1791.
72 p. 12 cm.
MWA mp. 46268

B7807 RELLY, JAMES, 1722?-1778
Union: or, A treatise of the consanguinity and affinity between Christ and His church . . . Boston, Re-printed by Edes & Son, 1791.
xxxiv, 174 p. 18 cm.
MWA mp. 46269

B7808 RELLY, JAMES, 1722?-1778
Union: or, A treatise of the consanguinity and affinity between Christ and His church . . . Boston, Printed by Edes & Son, for Benjamin Larkin [1791]
xxxiv, 174 p. 17.5 cm.
Advertised in the *Boston Gazette*, Sept. 5, 1791, as "This day published."
MWA mp. 46270

B7809 RHODE ISLAND. ELECTION PROX.
1791. His Excellency Arthur Fenner, Esq; Governor. The honorable Samuel J. Potter, Esquire, Deputy-Governor . . . [Providence] Bennett Wheeler [1791]
broadside 21 X 13 cm.
Alden 1251; Chapin 45a, 45b
RHi (2 variants) mp. 46271

B7810 RHODE ISLAND. GOVERNOR, 1790-1805
[By . . . Arthur Fenner . . . A proclamation . . . [Nov. 7, 1791] . . . Providence, J. Carter, 1791]
[broadside?]
Bill submitted by Carter Nov. 12, 1791
Alden 1252
No copy known mp. 46272

B7811 RICE, DAVID, 1733-1816
A lecture on the divine decrees. To which is annexed a few observations on a piece lately printed in Lexington, entitled "The Principles of the Methodists . . ." Lexington, John Bradford, 1791.
72 p. 15 cm.
McMurtrie: Kentucky 4a
MWA; PPPrHi mp. 46273

B7812 RICE AND CO., booksellers, Philadelphia
Rice and Co.'s Catalogue of books . . . [Philadelphia, 1791?]
60 p. 12mo.
Caption title on sig. A2; t.p. missing?
Brigham: Booksellers, p. 50
MWA mp. 46274

B7813 [RITCHIE, ELIZABETH]
A short account of the last sickness and death of the Rev. Mr. John Wesley. Baltimore, Samuel and John Adams, 1791.
12 p.
Signed E. R.
cf. Evans 23822, and Sabin 94539 note
RPJCB mp. 46275

B7814 ROWE, ELIZABETH SINGER, 1674-1737
Devout exercises of the heart . . . Abridged for the use of the Methodist Society. Philadelphia: Printed by Parry Hall; and sold by John Dickins, 1791.
214, [6] p. 16mo
PPL

B7815 [RUGGLES, SAMUEL]
To the free electors of the County of Suffolk. Fellow Citizens, The office of Register of Deeds being vacant . . . Boston, February 26, 1791. [Boston, 1791]
broadside 30.5 X 19.5 cm.
Signed in ms.: Samuel Ruggles
MHi mp. 46276

B7816 RUSH, BENJAMIN, 1745-1813
An enquiry into the effects of spirituous liquors upon the human body . . . The third edition, with additions. Philadelphia, John M'Culloch, 1791.
12 p. 18 cm.
Austin 1638
DNLM; PPC mp. 46277

B7817 RUSH, BENJAMIN, 1745-1813
The new method of inoculating for the small-pox. Delivered in a lecture . . . the 20th of February, 1781 . . . The third edition. Philadelphia, Printed and sold by Parry Hall, 1791.
26 p.
Rogers 306
DNLM; PPC mp. 46278

B7818 RUSSELL, ROBERT, of Wadhurst, Sussex
Sermons, on different important subjects . . . Baltimore, Samuel and John Adams, 1791.
112 p. 13.5 cm.
Minick 36
DLC; MWA; MdHi; OOC mp. 46279

B7819 RUSSELL, ROBERT, of Wadhurst, Sussex
Seven sermons . . . New-York, Re-printed and sold by William Durell, 1791.
156 p. 13.5 cm.
New York Public 1006
NN mp. 46280

B7820 S——A, MISS——
A letter from Miss S——a to Miss R——, who, on her way to Bath . . . Elizabeth-town [Md.], S. Herbert, 1791.
8 p. 20 cm.
Minick 37
PHi mp. 46204

B7821 Deleted

B7822 SAINT CLAIR'S DEFEAT
The fourth day of November,
In the year of ninety one,
We had a sore engagement
Near to Fort Jefferson.
[n.p., 1791?]
broadside 36.5 X 20.5 cm.
42 verses
CSmH mp. 46282

B7823 [SAUNDERS, EDWARD CLARK]
A collection of hymns, selected from sundry poets, together with a number of new poems, never before published . . . Windham, John Byrne, 1791.
34, [1] p. 17 cm.
Compiler's name in acrostic on p. 5
Huntington 605; Trumbull: Supplement 2590
CSmH; CtHC; CtY; DLC mp. 46285

B7824 SCOTT, WILLIAM, 1750-1804
Lessons in elocution . . . The third American edition, from the fifth British edition . . . Philadelphia, William Young, 1791.
1 p.l., vii-viii, [13]-436 p. 18 cm.
MWA mp. 46286

B7825 [SHEET almanack for 1792. New-London, T. Green, 1791]
broadside
Advertised in the *Connecticut Gazette*, Feb. 6, 1792, as "Sheet Almanacks, very convenient to paste up in public offices . . . may be had of the printers hereof."
Drake 489
No copy known

B7826 A SHORT account of the sickness and death, of the Rev. Mr. John Wesley . . . Philadelphia, S. Johnston, 1791.
12 p. 18.5 cm.
PHi mp. 46287

B7827 A SHORT account of the unhappy death of a profligate youth . . . Baltimore, Printed by David Graham for John Hagerty, 1791.
12 p. 17.5 cm.
Minick 38
MWA; MdHi mp. 46288

B7828 SIEMON, JOHN
John Siemon, No. 6, William-Street . . . manufactures and has for sale . . . muffs and tippets . . . John Siemon. New-York, October 31, 1791. [New York, 1791]
broadside 27 X 21 cm.
NjR

B7829 SOCIETY OF THE CINCINNATI
A list of the names of the members of the Cincinnati in the State of New-Jersey, with the rank they held in the army, made 1791 . . . [n.p., 1791]
broadside 27 X 37 cm.
MWA mp. 46290

B7830 SOCIETY OF THE CINCINNATI
Proceedings of the Cincinnati, by their delegates in an extra general-meeting convened at Philadelphia, the first Monday of May, 1791. Philadelphia, John Fenno, 1791.
6 p. 41.5 cm.
CtHi mp. 46289

B7831 SOUTH CAROLINA. GOVERNOR, 1789-1792
Sir, Whereas it has become essential to the peace and security of our citizens, that the law for prohibiting the importation of negro and other slaves . . . from Africa . . . should be strictly executed . . . Your most obedient servant . . . To [Charleston, 1791]
broadside 25 X 19.5 cm.
Signed in ms.: Charles Pinckney Charleston
Sc-Ar

B7832 SOUTH CAROLINA. LAWS
An act authorizing the inhabitants of the election districts, where county courts are not established, to choose Commissioners of the Poor . . . Feb. 19, 1791. [Charleston? 1791]
broadside 22 X 20.5 cm.
Sc-Ar

B7833 SOUTH CAROLINA. SENATE
In the Senate, February 2nd, 1791. The Committee appointed to confer with a committee of the House of Representatives, on the petition of James M'Douall . . . [Charleston? 1791]
[4] p. 32.5 cm.
Sc-Ar (3 copies)

B7834 THE strange and wonderful account of a Dutch hog. Who resides in New-York . . . [New York, 1791?]
broadside 44.5 X 28 cm.
Satire on Richard Varick, mayor of New York 1789-1801
Verse in 2 columns
N mp. 46291

B7835 SWEETING, WHITING, d. 1791
The narrative of Whiting Sweeting, who was executed at Albany, the 26th August, 1791 . . . Written by himself . . . [Albany? 1791?]
54 p. 18.5 cm. A-E^6 (E4-6 wanting)
MWA; RPJCB (47 p.) mp. 46293

B7836 SWIFT, JONATHAN, 1667–1745
The adventures of Captain Gulliver . . . Philadelphia, W. Young, 1791.
120 p. illus. 11 cm.
DeWin mp. 46294

B7837 TENNESSEE COMPANY
Notice is hereby given . . . that the subscriber intends to set out from Danville, on the tenth day of March next, for the settlement of the Muscle Shoals . . . John Gordon, Assistant Agent, Tennessee Co'y. Terms agreed on this first day of January 1791 by Zachariah Cox, Thomas Gil-

bert, and John S[t]rother proprietors of the Tennessee Company's Purchase . . . [n.p., 1791]
broadside 32.5 X 19.5 cm.
Sabin 94806; Vail: Old frontier 883
CU-B mp. 46295

B7838 THAYER, JOHN, 1755-1815
Controversy between the Reverend John Thayer . . . of Boston, and the Reverend George Lesslie . . . in Washington, New-Hampshire. George-Town, Alexander Doyle, 1791.
37 p. 17.5 cm. A-C^6 [D]^1
Goff: Georgetown 6; cf. Evans 26250
DGU

B7839 THOMAS, ISAIAH, 1749-1831
The friends of literature, who wish to encourage the art of printing in America, are respectfully informed that American editions of the following books . . . are now selling by Isaiah Thomas, in Worcester, and by said Thomas & Company, in Boston. [Worcester, 1791]
[4] p.
Dated in Isaiah Thomas's hand
Brigham: Booksellers, p. 50
MWA mp. 46296

B7840 THOMAS, ISAIAH, 1749-1831
To Christians of every denomination . . . [Worcester, I. Thomas, 1791]
[4] p. 28.5 cm.
Proposed new printing of the Bible, dated at Worcester December, 1791
NHi mp. 46297

B7841 THOSE veterans, whose services entitle them to lands in the Western Territory, are informed . . . April 22, 1971. [Boston? 1791]
broadside 39.5 X 26.5 cm.
Ford 2631
MHi mp. 46298

B7842 TO be sold, on the 30th inst. if fair . . . Dumfries, March 1, 1791. Alexandria, Hanson & Bond [1791]
broadside 28.5 X 24.5 cm.
DLC mp. 46299

B7843 TO the curious. A view of the ancient city of Jerusalem . . . At the house of Mr. John Woart . . . in Brattle-street . . . August 3, 1791. [Boston, 1791]
broadside 34.5 X 22 cm.
Ford 2638
MHi mp. 46300

B7844 TO the free & independent electors of the state of New-York. Fellow Citizens, A publication under the signature of Plain Truth . . . on . . . the ensuing elections . . . [New York? 1791]
broadside ([2] p.) 43.5 X 26.5 cm.
NHi mp. 46301

B7845 TO the freeholders of the Southern District of the State of New-York. Gentlemen, We have observed the names of several gentlemen . . . as candidates for the two vacant seats in the Senate . . . City of New-York, Many Electors, April 16, 1791. [New York, 1791]
broadside 25.5 X 19 cm.
Samuel Jones and Joshua Sands endorsed
N mp. 46302

B7846 TO the freeholders of the Southern District of the State of New York. Gentlemen, We the subscribers, freeholders in Kings-county, having nominated Joshua Sands . . . as a senator . . . Kings-county, March 10, 1791. [New York? 1791]
broadside 25.5 X 19.5 cm.
N mp. 46303

B7847 TO the voters of Baltimore Town and County, Charges . . . have been made to injure . . . William M'Laughlin, and to prevent his being elected your sheriff . . . Baltimore, August 31, 1791. Baltimore, W. Goddard and J. Angell [1791]
broadside 28 X 20 cm.
Minick 14
MdBE mp. 46304

B7848 TOM Thumb's folio: or, A new threepenny play thing for little giants . . . Boston, Printed and sold by Samuel Hall, 1791.
31 p. illus. 9 cm.
CtHi; MB (p. 31 wanting). Emerson Greenaway, Philadelphia (1962) mp. 46305

B7848a TWO hymns composed for the spiritual comfort . . . Sold next the stump of Liberty Tree [Boston] 1791.
broadside 30 X 20.5 cm.
NBuG

B7849 UNION FIRE CLUB, SALEM, MASS.
Rules and orders for the government of the Union Fire Club, instituted in Salem, on the 13th of September, 1770. Revised, corrected, and accepted . . . in December, 1791 . . . Salem, T. C. Cushing, 1791.
8 p. 14 cm.
Tapley p. 351
MSaE; MWA mp. 46284

B7850 U. S. CIRCUIT COURT FOR PENNSYLVANIA DISTRICT
A charge delivered to the Grand Jury [by James Wilson] at a special Circuit Court . . . Philadelphia, 1791 . . . Philadelphia: Printed by James & Johnson, 1791.
23 p. 8vo
PHi

B7851 U. S. CONGRESS. HOUSE
The Committee appointed to examine into and report what proceedings have been had under the act for . . . the protection of the frontiers . . . report . . . [Philadelphia? 1791]
broadside 34.5 X 21 cm.
NHi mp. 46306

B7852 U. S. CONGRESS. HOUSE
The Committee of Elections, to whom was referred the petition of Abraham Trigg, complaining of the undue election of Francis Preston, returned a member from . . . Virginia, report . . . [Philadelphia? 1791]
broadside ([2] p.) 34 X 20.5 cm.
NHi mp. 46307

B7853 U. S. LAWS
An act appointing representatives among the people . . . 1791, November the 24th—Read the third time . . . [Philadelphia] John Fenno [1791]
broadside 33.5 X 20.5 cm.
Photostats: DLC; NN mp. 46315

B7854 U. S. LAWS
An act concerning consuls and vice-consuls. [n.p., 1791]
[3] p. 32.5 cm. caption title
DLC mp. 46321

B7855 U. S. LAWS
An act concerning consuls and vice-consuls. [Colophon] Philadelphia, Andrew Brown [1791]
4 p. 32.5 cm. caption title
In manuscript on p. 4: Read the second time in the Senate . . . Jany. 12th 1791.
DLC (2 copies) mp. 46308

B7856 U. S. LAWS
An act for the relief of certain widows . . . 1791, December the 1st.—Read the third time . . . [Philadelphia] John Fenno [1791]
2 p. 33.5 X 20 cm.
DLC mp. 46316

B7857 U. S. LAWS
[An act repealing . . . the duties heretofore laid upon distilled spirits . . . Baltomore, W. Goddard and J. Angell, 1791]

Advertised in the *Maryland Journal,* June 24, 1791, as "Just published, and for sale, by the printers hereof."
Minick 41
No copy known mp. 46322

B7858 U. S. LAWS
An act repealing . . . the duties heretofore laid upon distilled spirits . . . [Philadelphia? 1791]
[3] p. 43.5 X 26.5 cm.
"Approved, March the third, 1791."
In triple columns
New York Public 1010; cf. Minick 41
MWA; NN mp. 46325

B7859 U. S. LAWS
An act repealing . . . the duties heretofore laid upon distilled spirits . . . [Philadelphia] John Fenno [1791]
24 p. 34 cm. caption title
DLC; NN; NhD mp. 46327

B7860 U. S. LAWS
An act to establish offices . . . 1791, February the 16th, —passed the House of representatives. [Colophon] [Philadelphia] John Fenno [1791]
4 p. 34 cm. caption title
DLC; MiU-C; NhD mp. 46310

B7861 U. S. LAWS
An act to incorporate the subscribers to the Bank of — [Colophon] [Philadelphia] John Fenno [1791]
7 p. 34 cm. caption title
DLC (2 copies) mp. 46323

B7862 U. S. LAWS
Acts passed at a Congress . . . held at . . . New-York . . . Being the acts passed at the first . . . session of the first Congress . . . Hartford, Hudson and Goodwin, 1791.
5 p.l., [3]-327 p. 23.5 cm.
CSmH; MiU-C (2 copies); NN mp. 46319

B7863 U. S. LAWS
Acts passed at the first session of the Congress . . . Philadelphia, Francis Childs and John Swaine, 1791.
157, [1] p. 20 cm.
DLC; NN (1st-3rd sessions in original boards, uncut); PPAmP mp. 46320

B7864 U. S. LAWS
Acts passed at the second session . . . Philadelphia, Francis Childs and John Swaine, 1791.
414 p. 20 cm.
DLC; NN; PPAmP mp. 46324

B7865 U. S. LAWS
Acts passed at the third session . . . Philadelphia, Francis Childs and John Swaine, 1791.
120, [1], [56] p. 20 cm.
DLC; NN; PPAmP mp. 46326

B7866 U. S. LAWS
Amendments to bill, entitled, "An act repealing . . . the duties heretofore laid upon distilled spirits . . . [Colophon] [Philadelphia] John Fenno [1791]
4 p. 34 cm.
DLC mp. 46309

B7867 U. S. LAWS
Amendments to the Act to establish the Post-Office and post roads . . . [Philadelphia] John Fenno [1791?]
[4] p. 33.5 cm.
Recites 67 amendments
NHi mp. 46311

B7868 U. S. LAWS
Amendments to the bill, entitled, "An act to encourage the recruiting service . . ." [Philadelphia? 1791?]
broadside 35 X 21 cm.
NHi mp. 46312

B7869 U. S. LAWS
A bill, repealing . . . the duties heretofore laid upon wines imported . . . [Colophon] [Philadelphia] Francis Childs and John Swaine [1791]
[3] p. 33.5 cm. caption title
DLC mp. 46313

B7870 U. S. LAWS
A bill respecting fugitives from justice and from the service of masters. [Philadelphia, 1791]
broadside 34 X 21 cm.
Presented in the House Nov. 15, 1791
New York Public 1013
NN (photostat) mp. 46318

B7871 U. S. LAWS
A bill to ascertain how far the owners of ships . . . [Philadelphia, 1791]
broadside 33.5 X 21 cm.
DLC mp. 46314

B7872 U. S. LAWS
Congress of the United States: At their third session . . . An act to continue an act . . . declaring the assent of Congress . . . Approved, February the 9th, 1791 . . . [Philadelphia, F. Childs and J. Swaine, 1791]
broadside 33 X 20.5 cm.
cf. Evans 23851; 23870
DLC mp. 46328

B7873 U. S. LAWS
Congress of the United States: At the third session . . . An act to provide for the unloading of ships . . . in cases of obstruction by ice . . . Approved, January the seventh, 1791 . . . [Philadelphia, 1791]
broadside 39 X 23.5 cm.
DLC mp. 46329

B7874 U. S. LAWS
Second Congress of the United States. At the first session . . . An act for the relief of David Cook and Thomas Campbell . . . Approved, December sixteenth, 1791 . . . [Philadelphia, Childs and Swaine, 1791]
broadside 41 X 25 cm.
New York Public 1008; cf. Evans 23884
DLC; NN mp. 46330

B7875 U. S. LAWS
Second Congress of the United States: At the first session . . . An act making appropriations for the support of government . . . [Philadelphia, 1791?]
[3] p. 40.5 cm.
"Approved, December twenty-third, 1791."
CSmH mp. 46331

B7876 U. S. PRESIDENT, 1789–1797
By the President . . . a proclamation . . . [Jan. 24, 1791] . . . [Philadelphia, 1791]
broadside 42 X 33 cm.
Proclamation defining the limits of District of Columbia
CSmH; DLC mp. 46332

B7877 U. S. PRESIDENT, 1789–1797
By the President . . . a proclamation . . . [Nov. 11, 1791] . . . [Philadelphia, 1791]
broadside 49 X 34.5 cm.
Proclamation of treaty with Cherokee Nation, with text of treaty
Huntington 609
CSmH; PHi mp. 46333

B7878 U. S. TREASURY DEPT.
Statement of the purchases of public stock by the agents to the trustees . . . [Philadelphia? 1791]
broadside 32.5 cm.
Signed: Nov. 4, 1791
MiU-C mp. 46334

B7879 U. S. TREASURY DEPT.
Treasury Department, May 13th, 1791. (Circular) Sir, I find instances . . . in some of the custom-houses . . . Secretary of the Treasury . . . [Philadelphia, 1791]
broadside ([4]) p.) 24 X 20.5 cm.
Pages [2–4] blank
MWA mp. 46335

B7880 U. S. TREASURY DEPT.
Treasury Department, September 21, 1791. (Circular) Sir, It being necessary to ascertain correctly the state of the public monies in the several custom-houses . . . Secretary of the Treasury. [Philadelphia, 1791]
broadside ([4] p.) 24 X 20 cm.
Pages [2–4] blank
MWA mp. 46336

B7881 UNITED States almanack for . . . 1792 . . . Sagg Harbour [1791]

Advertised in the *Long Island Herald*, Dec. 13, 1791
Drake 5996
No copy known

B7882 THE Universal Asylum and Columbian Magazine for 1791. Vol. I. [cut] Philadelphia, Printed for the proprietors by W. Young Bookseller [1791]
[2], 430, [2], 8 p. 8vo
Covers January-June 1791
cf. Evans 23930 ("Vol. II")
DGU

B7883 VALUE of foreign gold, in dollars and cents, and in £.s.d. . . . Salem, T. C. Cushing [1791]
broadside
Tapley, p. 351
MHi mp. 46337

B7884 VERMONT
[Handbills for apprehending a state prisoner. Windsor, James R. Hutchins, 1791]
broadside
Printer's bill dated Dec. 16, 1791
McCorison 200
No copy known mp. 46338

B7885 VERMONT. CENSUS
Schedule, containing the number of inhabitants in each town and county . . . of Vermont, agreeable to the late ennumeration . . . Total, 85,539. Windsor, Alden Spooner [1791]
broadside 30 X 20 cm.
In four columns
McCorison 204
NhD; VtHi mp. 46339

B7886 VERMONT. LAWS
An act regulating the choice of a council of censors . . . Windsor, Alden Spooner, 1791.
broadside 44.5 X 27.5 cm.
DLC mp. 46340

B7887 VIGILANT FIRE COMPANY
Rules of the Vigilant Fire Company. A list of members . . . January 26th, 1791. [Charleston? 1791?]
broadside 49 X 39.5 cm.
Sc-Ar

B7888 VIRGINIA. GOVERNOR, 1788–1791
By the Governor of the Commonwealth of Virginia . . . A proclamation. Whereas it is represented to me . . . Richmond . . . [May 3, 1791] Beverly Randolph. [Richmond, 1791]
broadside 37.5 X 31.5 cm.
$600 reward for apprehension of Samuel Brady and Francis McGuire for murder
Davis 57; New York Public 1014; Sabin 100219
NN (reduced photostat); PHi mp. 46341

B7889 THE Virginia almanack, for the year . . . 1792 . . . Petersburg, William Prentis [1791]
[32] p.
Advertisement of James Geddy and Sons on back cover
Wyatt 9
MWA mp. 46342

B7890 THE Virginia Gazette, and Agricultural Repository. Dumfries, Charles Fierer and Thomas U. Fosdick [1791]

Issues for Sept. 29, Oct. 13, Nov. 17, 24
Brigham p. 1113
DLC; MH; MWA (Oct. 13, 1791) mp. 46343

B7891 WATTS, ISAAC, 1674–1748
Hymns and spiritual songs . . . Boston, Printed by Joseph Bumstead for D. West, E. Larkin, and B. Larkin, 1791.
276 p. 16 cm.
MB mp. 46344

B7892 THE way to be happy in a miserable world . . . The sixth edition. New-York, S. Loudon, 1791.
23 p. 15 cm.
New York Public 1015
NN mp. 46348

B7893 WEATHERWISE'S almanack, for . . . 1792 . . . [n.p.] Printed for, and sold by most of the shopkeepers in town and country [1791]
[24] p.
Nichols, p. 90
NhHi mp. 46349

B7894 WEATHERWISE'S genuine almanack, for . . .

1792 . . . Keene, Printed and sold by James D. Griffith [1791]
[20] p.
MWA

B7895 WEBSTER, CHARLES R. AND GEORGE, firm, Albany
Printing-Office, State-street, Albany, July 20, 1791. Proposals . . . for printing by subscription, the writings on government, of . . . Thomas Paine . . . [Albany, Charles R. and George Webster, 1791]
broadside 35 X 17 cm.
CtHi mp. 46350

B7896 WEBSTER, NOAH, 1758–1843
The American spelling book . . . The tenth Connecticut edition. Hartford, Hudson and Goodwin [1791?]
153 p. illus. 16.5 cm.
cf. Skeel-Carpenter 23
CtHi mp. 46351

B7897 WESLEY, JOHN, 1703–1791
Explanatory notes upon the New Testament . . . Volume the second[-third]. The first American edition. Philadelphia, Printed by Charles Cist; sold by John Dickins, 1791.
348; 342 p. 17 cm.
Vol. 3 has imprint: Printed by Prichard and Hall: sold by John Dickins
Huntington 610; New York Public 1016; cf. Evans 23976 and 25011
CSmH (v.2); NN (v.3) mp. 46251–53

B7898 WESTMINSTER ASSEMBLY OF DIVINES
The shorter catechism . . . New-York, R. MacGill, 1791.
104+ p. 14 cm. A-E^9 F$^{9?}$
MWA mp. 46354

B7899 WETHERILL, SAMUEL, 1736–1816
The grounds and reason of the incarnation and process of Christ explained . . . In reply to several sermons preached by the Rev. Ashbel Green . . . By Samuel Wetherill. Philadelphia, Francis Bailey and Thomas Lang, 1791.
66 p, 1 l.
CSmH; NBuG mp. 46355

B7900 WHITEHEAD, JOHN, 1740–1804
A discourse delivered at the New Chapel . . . at the funeral of . . . John Wesley . . . The first American edition . . . Philadelphia, P. Hall, 1791.
69, [2] p. 17 cm.
cf. Evans 23999
PHi; PPL mp. 46356

B7901 WILL, WILLIAM
Philadelphia, October 26, 1791. By virtue of a writ . . . to me directed, will be exposed to public sale . . . the 9th of November next . . . six contiguous lots . . . on Province Island . . . [Philadelphia, 1791]
broadside 34 X 20.5 cm.
Signed: William Will, sheriff
New York Public 1017
NN mp. 46260

B7902 WILLIAM Story jun was married to Miss Bathseba Gray, December 6th, 1778 . . . The Fount. Eliza, on the death of her sister, who died August 12th, 1791 . . . Ipswich, May 14, 1791. [Salem? 1791]
broadside 26 X 16 cm.
Ford 2635
MSaE mp. 46358

B7903 WILLIAMS, RENWICK, defendant
Trial of . . . London, Printed. New-York: re-printed and sold by A. Marschalk, 1791.
v, [7]–55 p. port.
PHi (not traced 1966) mp. 46359

B7904 WILLIAMS, SIMON FINLEY, 1764–1800
Two sermons, delivered . . . in Methuen, August 21, 1791 . . . Newburyport, John Mycall, 1791.
54 p. 19 cm. [A]-G^4 (G^4 wanting)
MWA mp. 46360

B7905 WINCHESTER, ELHANAN, 1751–1797
[The face of Moses unveiled by the Gospel. Newbern? F. S. Martin, 1791]

Advertised in the *North-Carolina Gazette*, June 4, 1791, as "This day is published and for sale at the printing-office hereof."
McMurtrie: North Carolina 174
No copy known mp. 46361

B7906 WOODSTOCK, PA.
Charter of the town of Woodstock. Martinsburg, N. Willis [1791]
broadside 41.5 X 25 cm.
Historical records survey: *Check list of West Virginia imprints* 2; Sabin 105147
DLC. Photostat: NN mp. 46362

B7907 WOOLLEN MANUFACTORY LOTTERY
Scheme of a lottery, for the purpose of extending and improving the woollen manufactory in the City of Hartford . . . Class the second . . . Hartford, Feb. 17, 1791. [Hartford, 1791]
broadside 34.5 X 21 cm.
CtHi mp. 46363

B7908 WORCESTER, THOMAS, 1768–1831
A sacred ode, on the sudden death of Lieut. Emerson . . . [Boston?] Printed [by E. Russell] next Liberty Pole, 1791.
broadside 37 X 20.5 cm.
Huntington 612
CSmH mp. 46364

B7909 [YOUNG, EDWARD] 1683–1765
The complaint . . . A new edition . . . Philadelphia, Printed for William Young, 1791.
303 p. 17.5 cm.
MWA mp. 46365

B7910 ZANE, ISAAC
To be sold or rented, Marlbro' ironworks, situate about 12 miles from the borough of Winchester, in the state of Virginia . . . Isaac Zane . . . [Winchester? 1791]
broadside 30.5 X 19.5 cm.
Description of property in detail
MWA (place of publication given as [Philadelphia?]); PHi mp. 46366

1792

B7911 ACTS of Virginia, Maryland, and of the United States, respecting the District of Columbia. [Philadelphia?] Printed by order of the Senate of the United States. [1792?]
16 p.
Three acts dated 1789, 1790, 1791
cf. Evans 23847
RPJCB mp. 46614

B7912 THE adventure of the inn: or the affecting history of Emerton . . . Danbury, Printed and sold by Douglas and Ely, 1792.
22 p. 20.5 cm.
CtHi mp. 46369

B7913 AESOPUS
Fables of Aesop and others, translated into English, with instructive applications . . . By Samuel Croxall . . . The third American edition, carefully revised and improved. Philadelphia, Printed and sold by R. Aitken & Son, 1792.
[23], 316, [4] p. 17.5 cm.
DGU; MWA mp. 46370

B7914 ALBANY, 13th April, 1792. Sir, As the day of election is near . . . we . . . address you once more on that subject . . . [Albany, 1792]
broadside 30.5 X 20.5 cm.
Signed: James Caldwell [and 13 others], Committee of Correspondence
McMurtrie: Albany 63; New York Public 1020
N; NN mp. 46371

B7915 ALBANY, April 18, 1792. Sir, Our adversaries in the election . . . have descended to misrepresentations . . . to promote the reelection of Governor Clinton . . . [Albany, 1792]
broadside 30 X 18 cm.
Signed: James Caldwell [and 13 others], Committee of Correspondence
McMurtrie: Albany 64; New York Public 1021
NN mp. 46372

B7916 ALBANY Glass-House, September 12, 1792. The subscribers, proprietors of the Albany Glass-House . . . inform the public, that their works are completed, and that they have on hand an assortment of glass . . . [Albany, 1792]
broadside 19 X 27.5 cm.
McMurtrie: Albany 60; New York Public 1018
NHi; NN (reduced facsim.) mp. 46373

B7917 AN almanack and ephemeris for . . . 1793. New-Haven [1792]
[32] p.
Drake 491
MB (imprint imperfect)

B7918 AMERICAN MERCURY
Addressed by the carrier of the *American Mercury*, to the subscribers. Hartford, January 1, 1792 . . . [Hartford, Elisha Babcock, 1792]
broadside 34 X 20.5 cm.
MWA; NHi mp. 46368

B7919 THE American Museum . . . for June, 1788 . . . Vol. III. No. VI. The second edition. Philadelphia, Mathew Carey, 1792.
p. [497-499], 500-602. 21.5 cm.
DLC; NhHi mp. 46374

B7920 AMERICAN PHILOSOPHICAL SOCIETY
At a meeting of the committee appointed . . . for the purpose of collecting . . . Philadelphia, April 17th, 1792. [Philadelphia, 1792]
broadside 37 X 23 cm.
DLC; PPAmP mp. 46375

B7921 ANDERSON, SAMUEL
Philadelphia, February 28, 1792. Sales of stock, Tuesday noon . . . Samuel Anderson, stock-broker . . . [Philadelphia, 1792]
broadside 14 X 17 cm.
MWA; PHi mp. 46376

B7922 ANDERSON, SAMUEL
Philadelphia, March 6, 1792. Sales of stock, last evening . . . Samuel Anderson, Stock-broker, No. 104, Chestnut-street. [Philadelphia, 1792]
broadside 29 X 16 cm.
PHi mp. 46377

B7923 AUGUST 25, 1792. To the electors of the state of New-Jersey . . . A Continental soldier. [n.p., 1792]
broadside 42.5 X 26 cm.
DLC mp. 46379

B7924 AUSTIN, BENJAMIN, 1752–1820
Boston, January 30, 1792. Speech of the Hon. Benjamin Austin, jun. . . . on Thursday last . . . with respect to the police of the town . . . [Boston] B. Edes [1792]
broadside 36 X 26 cm.
MWA mp. 46380

B7925 THE balloon almanac for . . . 1793 . . . Lancaster, J. Bailey and W. Dickson [1792]
[36] p.
Drake 10323
NjP

B7926 BELL, JOHN
Animal electricity and magnetism demonstrated . . . Lancaster, J. Bailey and W. Dickson, 1792.
55 p. 17.5 cm.
Austin 188; Huntington 614
CSmH mp. 46381

B7927 BENNETT, JOHN, curate of St. Mary's, Manchester
Letters to a young lady, on a variety of useful and interesting subjects . . . Second Hartford edition. Hartford, Hudson and Goodwin, 1792.
2 v. in 1. 16 cm.
New York Public 1019; Trumbull: Supplement 1911–12
CtHi; MB; MWA; NN; NhD; PU mp. 46382

B7928 BIBLE
The Holy Bible abridged or, The history of the old and New Testament . . . New York, William Durell, 1792.
110, 60 p. 10.5 cm. $A\text{-}G^8$, A^{16} $B\text{-}C^8$
CtHi; NNC; NjP. Mrs. Arthur M. Greenwood, Marlborough, Mass. (1962) mp. 46386

B7929 BIBLE
The self-interpreting Bible . . . New-York, Printed for T. Allen, 1792.
3 v. in 1. 41.5 cm.
Apocrypha and N. T. have separate registers
CSmH; RPJCB mp. 46383

B7930 BIBLE. N.T.
The New Testament . . . newly translated out of the original Greek . . . Philadelphia, William Spotswood, 1792.
[280] p. 16.5 cm.
DLC mp. 46384

B7931 BIBLE. N.T. APOCRYPHAL BOOKS. EPISTLE OF JESUS CHRIST
A copy of a letter written by . . . Jesus Christ . . . Windham, Printed [by John Byrne], 1792.
8 p. 17 cm.
CtHi; MWA mp. 46385

B7932 BIBLE. O.T. PSALMS
The Psalms of David. Imitated . . . By I. Watts . . . Boston: Printed and sold by John West Folsom, M,DCC,XCII.
320 p. 16 cm.
NBuG

B7933 BICKERSTAFF'S genuine Boston almanack for . . . 1793. Third edition. [Boston] E. Russell [1792]
[24] p. 16.5 cm.
MWA mp. 46388

B7934 BLACK, JOHN, 1750-1802
The duty of Christians, in singing the praise of God . . . York, John and James Edie, 1792.
47 p. 17.5 cm.
MWA; PPL mp. 46389

B7935 [BORDLEY, JOHN BEALE] 1727-1804
Sketches on the rotation of crops. Printed for J. Cowan, in Talboton, 1792.
1 p.l., 47 p. 22.5 cm.
Errata slip included
Minick 54
MdHi mp. 46390

B7936 BOSTON. ASSESSORS
Assessors-Office, Boston, April 1792. [Ward, No.] You are requested to fill up this list as your valuation . . . [Boston, 1792]
broadside 38.5 X 32.5 cm.
Ford 2646
MHi; MWA (2 copies) mp. 46391

B7937 BOSTON. CITIZENS
At a meeting of the inhabitants of the Town of Boston, on Thursday, the 19th of January, 1792, it was voted, That ten of the clock . . . on Thursday next, be assigned for the inhabitants . . . to determine upon the report of their Committee on the police . . . [Boston, 1792]
broadside 27.5 X 23 cm.
Ford 2644
MHi mp. 46392

B7938 BOSTON. COLLECTOR OF TAXES
Ward, No. To Your town tax . . . Boston, October 1792. [Boston, 1792]
broadside 16 X 10 cm.
MB

B7939 BOSTON. YORK FIRE CLUB
Boston, 179 Sir, The Fire Club, whereof you are a member, is to meet on Wednesday next . . . [Boston, 1792?]
broadside 11 X 19 cm.
500 notifications ordered printed on 2 Nov. 1791; payment made 1 Feb. 1792
MB (7 copies) mp. 46394

B7940 BOWDEN, JOHN, 1751-1817
An address . . . To which is added, a letter to . . . James Sayre . . . New-Haven, T. and S. Green [1792]
23, [1] p. 18 cm.
cf. Evans 24139 (also at NHi)
NHi mp. 46395

B7941 BOWEN, MARY
A poem on the death of Mrs. Hannah Clossen . . . [Windsor? A. Spooner? 1792]
broadside 21 X 16.5 cm.
VtHi mp. 46396

B7942 BRADMAN, ARTHUR
A narrative of the extraordinary sufferings of Mr. Robert Forbes, his wife and five children . . . Exeter, Re-printed by Henry Ranlet, 1792.
23 p. 19 cm.
Vail: Old frontier 888
MWA; NHi; PPRF mp. 46397

B7943 [BRISSOT DE WARVILLE, JACQUES PIERRE] 1754-1793
Karakteristik der Quaker. Aus dem Französischen übersetzt. Boston, 1792.
2 p.l., 78 p. 18 cm.
Translation of his Nouveau voyage . . . en 1788
PHi mp. 46398

B7944 BRYDONE, PATRICK, 1741?-1818
A tour through Sicily and Malta . . . A new edition. Boston, Printed by Joseph Bumstead, for John Boyle, David West, and E. Larkin, jun. [1792?]
2 v. in 1. 18 cm.
cf. Evans 24150
MHi; MWA mp. 46399

B7945 BUNYAN, JOHN, 1628-1688
Solomon's temple spiritualized . . . A new edition . . . Philadelphia, Stewart & Cochran, 1792.
168 p. 13.5 cm.
CSmH (t.p. lacking); CtHi; DLC; MWA; PHi
mp. 46400

B7946 BURKE, EDMUND, 1729-1797
Reflections on the Revolution in France . . . Philadelphia, D. Humphreys, 1792.
256 p. 22.5 cm.
N; PHi mp. 46401

B7947 BURROUGHS, EDEN, 1738-1813
A faithful narrative of the wonderful dealings of God, towards Polly Davis . . . Boston, Printed for and sold by the booksellers [1792]
8 p. 19 cm.
NhD

B7948 BURROUGHS, EDEN, 1738-1813
A faithful narrative of the wonderful dealings of God, towards Polly Davis . . . Concord, Elijah Russell, 1792.
12 p. 18 cm.
MWA (poor); NhD mp. 46421

B7949 BURROUGHS, EDEN, 1738-1813
A faithful narrative of the wonderful dealings of God towards Polly Davis . . . [Windsor] Alden Spooner, 1792.
12 p. 15 cm.
Cooley 172
MWA; NhD mp. 46422

B7950 CAREY, MATHEW, 1760-1839
Mathew Carey's Catalogue of books, for September, 1792 . . . [Philadelphia, M. Carey, 1792]
12 p.
Brigham: Booksellers, p. 51
MWA; N (2 copies) mp. 46403

B7951 CARROLL, JOHN, 1735-1815
Pastoral letter. John, by Divine Permission . . . Bishop of Baltimore, to my dearly beloved brethren . . . in this diocese . . . The great extent of my diocese . . . [Baltimore, 1792]
6 p. 25 cm.
Pastoral on the First National Synod in the U. S.
DGU (p. 1-2 wanting) mp. 46408

B7952 CHAMBER OF COMMERCE, NEW YORK
To the farmers and traders in the state of New-York . . . New-York, April 7, 1792 . . . [New York, 1792]
broadside 32 X 26 cm.
DLC; N mp. 46523

B7953 CHESSELDEN, JOHN
Surprising account of the Devil's appearing to John Chesselden, and James Arkins, at a town near the Mississippi, on the 24th of May, 1784. Written with their own hands. [Natchez?] Printed in the year M,DCC,XCII.
16 p. 15.5 cm. [A]-B^4
MBCo

B7954 CHESTERFIELD, PHILIP DORMER STANHOPE, EARL, 1694-1773
The principles of politeness . . . To which are added, The oeconomy of human life . . . Moral maxims and reflexions. By . . . La Rochefoucauld. And Aphorisms on man. By . . . John Casper Lavater . . . Philadelphia, William Spotswood, 1792.
1 p.l., 155 p. 17 cm.
NNS

B7955 [CHETWOOD, WILLIAM RUFUS] d. 1766
The voyages and adventures of Captain Robert Boyle . . . the story of Mrs. Villars . . . the history of an Italian captive . . . Boston, Printed and sold by John W. Folsom, 1792.
249, [17] p. 17 cm.
MWA; N mp. 46409

B7956 THE children in the woods: being the true relations of the inhuman murder of two children of a deceased gentleman in Norfolk . . . [Salem] Sold at the Bible and Heart [by William Carleton?] [1792?]
broadside
Tapley p. 351; cf. Evans 19401
MSaE mp. 46410

B7957 THE Christian oeconomy. Translated from the original Greek of an old manuscript . . . The twenty-seventh edition. Windsor, Printed and sold by Alden Spooner, 1792.
43 p. 18 cm.
Cooley 173
MWA; VtHi mp. 46411

B7958 CITY of Albany, February 16, 1792. On the 13th instant, a letter was received . . . Albany, Charles R. & George Webster [1792]
broadside 32 X 19.5 cm.
DLC mp. 46412

B7959 A COLLECTION of contra dances . . . Printed and sold at Stockbridge, 1792.
16 p.
MWA mp. 46413

B7960 [COLLYER, MARY (MITCHELL)] d. 1763
The death of Cain . . . By a lady . . . New-York, Printed and sold by William Durell, 1792.
130 p. 14 cm.
MWA mp. 46414

B7961 COLUMBIA COUNTY, N.Y. CITIZENS
At a meeting of a number of respectable gentlemen, from the towns of Kinderhook, Canaan . . . in the county of Columbia, held at the City-Hall . . . the 19th day of June, 1792 . . . [Hudson? 1792]
broadside 45 X25 cm.
In three columns
New York Public 1022
NN mp. 46415

B7962 THE Columbian almanac for . . . 1793 . . . By James Login . . . Philadelphia, Printed for Robert Campbell [1792]
[40] p.
Drake 10326
NcD (17 l.)

B7963 COLUMBIAN CENTINEL
The carrier of Russell's *Columbian Centinel*, presents the following, to his respected patrons . . . Boston, January 1, 1792. [Boston, 1792]
broadside 26.5 X 11.5 cm.
Ford 2674
PHi. Photostat: MWA mp. 46404

B7964 THE conference, or Motley Assembly. A farce, Written by the Hon. Nehemiah Catch, and corrected by the Manager's Books. Georgia: Printed for Exekiel Scrape, and Jonathan Headstrong, 1792.
19 p. 8vo
PHi

B7965 CONNECTICUT COURANT
Supplement to the *Connecticut Courant*, December 17, 1792. List of the fortunate numbers in Enfield Falls-Lottery . . . [Hartford, Hudson and Goodwin, 1792]
broadside 41 X 22.5 cm.
NHi

B7966 COWPER, WILLIAM, 1731-1800
The diverting history of John Gilpin . . . [Salem?] Sold at the Bible and Heart [1792?]
broadside
Tapley p. 352
MSaE mp. 46416

B7967 COWPER, WILLIAM, 1731-1800
Poems . . . In two volumes. Salem, Printed by Thomas C. Cushing, for D. West, and E. Larkin, Jun., Boston, 1792.
2 v. 10.5 cm.
MWA (vol. 1 only, very imperfect); MSaE (vol. 1 only) mp. 46417

B7968 [CROUCH, NATHANIEL] 1632?-1752?
Eine Reise nach Jerusalem . . . Aus den Englischen übersetzt. Lancaster, Johann Albrecht, 1792.
72 p. 17 cm.
MWA; PHi mp. 46418

B7969 CULLEN, WILLIAM, 1710-1790
Synopsis and nosology, being an arrangement and definition of diseases . . . Hartford, Nathaniel Patten, 1792.
xxxix, 80 p. 16 cm.
An abridged translation of the author's *Genera morborum*
cf. Evans 24237
DNLM; N; NNNAM; NhD; OCIM mp. 46419

B7970 DAILY ADVERTISER
The carrier of the *Daily Advertiser*, presents the following lines to his customers . . . New-York, January 1, 1792. [New York, F. Childs and J. Swaine, 1792]
broadside 34 X 20.5 cm.
NHi mp. 46405

B7971 DAVIS, GEORGE
Law books. George Davis, in the Prothonotary's Office . . . has received the following . . . Philadelphia, September 25, 1792 . . . [Philadelphia, 1792]
broadside 28 X 21 cm.
Full border of type ornaments
PHi mp. 46420

B7972 DAY, THOMAS, 1749-1799
The history of Sandford and Merton . . . Printed for the booksellers, 1792.
107 p. 14 cm.
DLC mp. 46423

B7973 DEFOE, DANIEL, 1661?-1731
Travels of Robinson Crusoe . . . Windham, J. Byrne, 1792.
31 p. 10 cm.
Brigham: Robinson Crusoe 23
CtHi; PP mp. 46424

B7974 DEFOE, DANIEL, 1661?-1731
The wonderful life and most surprising adventures of Robinson Crusoe . . . Boston, Printed and sold at the Bible & Heart [1792?]
114+ p.
T. & J. Fleet were at this address from 1780 to 1797
Brigham: Robinson Crusoe 19
d'Alté A. Welch, Cleveland (imperfect) mp. 46425

B7975 DE MONTMOLLIN, S. AND F., firm, Quebec
To the public. As inhabitants of the state of Vermont . . . now feel ourselves injured and defeated . . . S. and F. De Montmollin. Middlebury, September 26, 1792. [Bennington? A. Haswell, 1792]
broadside 39.5 X 26 cm.
McCorison 225
MWA; VtU-W mp. 46426

B7976 DELAWARE. HOUSE OF REPRESENTATIVES
Journal of the House of representatives . . . at a session, commenced . . . the first day of November . . . Wilmington, Brynberg and Andrews [1792]
13 p. 27.5 cm.
Covers session Nov. 1-3, 1792
De; DeHi mp. 46427

B7977 DELAWARE. SENATE
Journal of the Senate . . . at a session . . . held at Dover . . . on Thursday the first day of November . . . Wilmington, James Adams [1792]
9 p. 26.5 cm.
Hawkins: List B 36
DLC; De; DeHi mp. 46428

B7978 A DESCRIPTION of the geographical clock . . . Philadelphia, [Printed] for Joseph Scott and sold by Francis Bailey and Peter Stewart, 1792.
12 leaves. 12mo. $A-B^6$
Rosenbach-Ch 156
A. S. W. Rosenbach (1933) mp. 46429

B7979 DILWORTH, THOMAS, d. 1780
A new guide to the English tongue . . . Philadelphia, Printed and sold by Joseph Crukshank, 1792.
158 p. 17.5 cm.
MWA mp. 46430

B7980 DILWORTH, THOMAS, d. 1780
The schoolmasters assistant . . . The latest edition . . . New-York, Printed and sold by William Durell, 1792.
xvi, [6], 114 [i.e. 214] p. 18 cm.
CtHi; MWA; N; NN (lacking after p. 118 mp. 46431

B7981 DIVINE service will begin with singing the CVIII Psalm. See Appendix, p. 121. A Thanksgiving Anthem . . . [New York? 1792?]
broadside 25 X 17 cm.
NHi mp. 46432

B7982 DODDRIDGE, PHILIP, 1702-1751
A sermon, urging the care of the soul . . . Newburyport, Reprinted by John Mycall, for Samuel White, of Haverhill [1792?]
24 p. 22 cm.
Dated by Charles Evans
MHi; MWA; N mp. 46433

B7983 DOW, HENDRICK, 1761-1814
A warning to little children, from the dying words of Jane Sumner, of Ashford, who died February 19th, 1783. AEtat. 12. Written nearly verbatim: to which is added an Acrostick by Hendrick Dow. New-London, T. Green and Son, 1792.
15 p. 13 cm.
CtHi mp. 46434

B7984 DUER, WILLIAM
To the holders of engagements under the signature of the subscriber. New-York Prison, March 24, 1792, It is with regret . . . his creditors . . . Wm. Duer. [New York, 1792]
broadside 21 X 17 cm.
CtHi

B7985 EASTON, MD. THEATRE
[For the benefit of Miss Kitely . . . on Wednesday evening, October 3d . . . The Roman Father . . . with other entertainments. Easton, James Cowan? 1792]
broadside
Advertised in the *Maryland Herald*, ending, "as will be expressed in the bills of the day."
Minick 59
No copy known mp. 46435

B7986 EDWARDS, JONATHAN, 1702-1758
The distinguishing marks of a work of the spirit of God. Extracted from Mr. Edwards . . . By John Wesley . . . Philadelphia, Printed by Parry Hall, and sold by John Dickins, 1792.
45, [2] p. 12mo
PPL mp. 46436

B7987 [ELLICOTT, ANDREW] 1754-1820
Plan of the city of Washington . . . Boston, Saml. Hill [1792]
map 43.5 X 52.5 cm.
Phillips, p. 1003
DLC; MWA mp. 46437

B7988 EMBLEMS, natural, historical, fabulous, moral, and divine . . . Philadelphia, Francis Bailey, 1792.

PHi mp. 46438

B7989 THE entertaining history of Polly Cherry . . . Philadelphia, F. Bailey, 1792.
30, [1] p. incl. covers. 11 cm.
MWA mp. 46439

B7990 EPICTETUS
The manual of Epictetus; being an abridgment of his philosophy. Translated . . . by George Stanhope, D.D. Philadelphia, Printed and sold by Thomas Lang, 1792.
iv, 67 p. 13 cm.
MWA; PHi mp. 46440

B7991 FATHER Tammany's almanac for . . . 1793 . . . Philadelphia, Printed for William Young [1792]
[36] p.
Drake 10329
MWA mp. 46668

B7992 FEDERAL PARTY. NEW YORK
Sir, we are directed by a joint resolution . . . to request your vote . . . in favour of John Jay, Esq. as governor . . . New-York, March 24, 1792. [New York, 1792]
broadside 21.5 X 18 cm.
Huntington 616
CSmH mp. 46441

B7993 FILLMORE, JOHN, 1702-1777
A narration of the captivity of John Fillmore, and his escape from the pirates. Portland, B. Titcomb, 1792.
16 p. 23 cm.
MWA mp. 46442

B7994 [FISH, SAMUEL]
An humble address to every Christian of every nation . . . Norwich, Printed by John Trumbull, for the author, 1792.
38 p. 22.5 cm. [A]-E^4 (E4 blank)
CtHi; MWA; RPJCB mp. 46443

B7995 FITZHUGH, PEREGRINE
[A lottery – Peregrine Fitzhugh. 1792 – December 9. Elizabethtown? 1792]
broadside?
Minick 61
DLC (copy not examined) mp. 46444

B7996 THE following New-Year's gift, was written a few years ago by a young woman in England . . . and is now republished . . . Philadelphia, 1st month 1st, 1792.
broadside 43 X 25 cm.
DLC mp. 46445

B7997 [FOX, WILLIAM]
An address to the people of Great Britain, on the propriety of abstaining from West-India sugar and rum . . . The ninth edition. Philadelphia, Benjamin Johnson, 1792.
12 p. 19 cm.
MWA; PHi; PPL mp. 46446

B7998 [FOX, WILLIAM]
An address to the people of Greatbritain, on the propriety of abstaining from Westindia sugar and rum . . . The tenth edition. Lancaster, J. Bailey and W. Dickson, 1792.
12 p. 17.5 cm.
MHi; MWA mp. 46447

B7999 FRASER, DONALD, 1755?-1820
[Young gentleman's and lady's assistant. Bennington, A. Haswell, 1792]

Advertised in the *Vermont Gazette*, Aug. 17, 1792, as "For sale by the printer."
McCorison 227
No copy known mp. 46448

B8000 FREEMASONS. MASSACHUSETTS
Instructions to all the lodges, under the jurisdiction of the Grand Lodge of Massachusetts . . . April 2d, 5792 . . . [Boston? 1792]
broadside
MWA

B8001 FREEMASONS. VIRGINIA
Sanction . . . [Richmond, 1792]
broadside 20.5 X 12.5 cm.
CSmH mp. 46449

B8002 FRIENDS, SOCIETY OF. LONDON YEARLY MEETING
From our yearly-meeting held in London . . . from the 21st of the Fifth Month, 1792 . . . [Philadelphia? 1792]
2 p. 33.5 X 20.5 cm.
DLC; PPL mp. 46450

B8003 FRIENDS, SOCIETY OF. NEW YORK MEETING FOR SUFFERINGS
At a Meeting for Sufferings in New-York, the 12th of the 6th month, 1792. This meeting on considering the deviations of divers among us . . . is concerned to remind Friends . . . [New York, 1792]
3 p. 32.5 cm.
New York Public 1025
NN mp. 46451

B8004 DAS fromme Mägdlein, uebersetzt aus dem Englischen. Ephrata, 1792.
8 p. 20.5 cm.
MWA mp. 46452

B8005 G., C.
C. G. of the City of New-York, to Titus Twitcher, of New-Paltz, in Ulster County . . . [New York, 1792]
broadside 44.5 X 27 cm.
Reply to an attack on Gov. Clinton in the 1792 gubernatorial election campaign
N mp. 46402

B8006 GEORGETOWN WEEKLY LEDGER
The news-carrier's address . . . for January 1, 1792. [Georgetown, A. Doyle, 1792]
broadside 31 X 20 cm.
DLC mp. 46530

B8007 GEORGIA. GOVERNOR, 1791-1793
Georgia. By his Excellency Edward Telfair, Governor . . . A proclamation. Whereas it has been officially represented . . . certain armed men . . . did . . . kill several amicable Indians . . . [Nov. 14, 1792] . . . [Augusta? 1792]
broadside 32.5 X 21 cm.
De Renne p. 256
GU-De mp. 46453

B8008 GOUGH, JOHN, 1721-1791
A treatise of arithmetic . . . To which are added, many valuable additions . . . by Benjamin Workman, A.M. Philadelphia, Printed for William Young, 1792.
vi, [2], [13]-370, [2] p. 18 cm.
MWA mp. 46454

B8009 GREENE, CALEB
Greene's fine American ink-powder for records . . . Sold wholesale and retail by Caleb Greene, New-Bedford, Massachusetts [1792?]
broadside 22 X 14 cm.
MWA mp. 46455

B8010 HALL, JONATHAN P.
Medicine boxes of all kinds, prepared . . . by Jonathan P. Hall, at the sign of the Golden Mortar, No. 1, Union-Street, Boston. [Boston] Thomas Adams, 1792.
7 p. 19 cm.
Pagination: t.p., 6, 7, 4, 5, 2, 3
MBCo mp. 46456

B8011 HAMILTON, ALEXANDER, 1757-1804
Philadelphia, September 26, 1792. Sir, I have . . . seen a publication . . . [Philadelphia, 1792]
broadside 30.5 X 19.5 cm.
DLC mp. 46457

B8012 [HAMMET, WILLIAM]
An impartial statement of the known inconsistencies of . . . Dr. Coke . . . superintendent of the Methodist

missionaries in the West-Indies . . . Charleston, W. P. Young, 1792.
16 p. 22 cm.
NHi mp. 46458

B8013 HARRISON, RALPH, 1748-1810
Rudiments of English grammar . . . The second American edition . . . Philadelphia, Printed and sold by Parry Hall, 1792.
[ii]-94 p. 14 cm. $A^{12}B^{6}C^{12}D^{6}E^{12}$
MWA (half title wanting?) mp. 46459

B8014 HART, JOSEPH, 1712-1808
Divine songs extracted from J. Hart's hymns . . . Boston, Wood & Co., 1792.
32 p. obl.
Edited by Abraham Wood
MH mp. 46460

B8015 HARTFORD. CABINETMAKERS
At a meeting of the cabinet makers, held in this city, the following resolutions were agreed upon by us . . . who have formed . . . a Society for the purposes of regulating the prices of our work . . . [Hartford, 1792]
8? p. 12mo
Dated: Hartford, August 1, 1792
Trumbull: Supplement 1879
CtHT-W mp. 46461

B8016 HEIDELBERG CATECHISM
Catechismus, oder kurzer Unterricht Christlicher Lehre . . . Germantaun, Gedruckt und zu finden bey Michael Billmeyer, 1792.
94 p., 1 leaf, [95]-118 p. 14 cm.
PHi mp. 46462

B8017 HIRTE, TOBIAS
Indianisch-French-Crieck-Seneca-Spring-Oel. Ein vortrefliches und bewährtes Medicament . . . Chesnuthill, Samuel Saur, 1792.
[2] p.
PPL mp. 46463

B8018 THE history of a schoolboy, with other pieces. New-York, Printed and sold by W. Durell, 1792.
74 p. illus. 13 cm.
NHi mp. 46464

B8019 THE history of Amelia . . . Boston: Printed and sold by N. Coverly, 1792.
32 p.
MWA mp. 46465

B8020 THE history of George Barnwell, of London . . . Norwich, John Trumbull, 1792.
21 p. 14.5 cm. $[A]^{4}B^{7}$
Rosenbach-Ch 158
PP mp. 46466

B8021 THE history of Joseph and his brethren . . . [at end] Philadelphia, Daniel Lawrence [1792?]
16 p. caption title
Rosenbach-Ch 159
PP mp. 46467

B8022 THE history of Master Jackey and Miss Harriot . . . Boston: Printed and sold by Samuel Hall [1792]
31 p. illus. 10.5 cm.
Dated by d'Alté A. Welch from 3 mm. breaks in border of cut on p. 24
RPB mp. 46468

B8023 HUBLEY, A
Catalogue of mezzotinto and copperplate prints, plate, and plated ware, &c. To be sold by public auction . . . the 26th inst. . . . A. Hubley, Auctioner. Dec. 20, 1792. [Philadelphia, 1792]
16 p. 20 cm.
RPJCB mp. 46469

B8024 THE hunting in Chevy Chase . . . Sold at the Bible & Heart in Salem [1792?]
broadside 40 X 26 cm.
Tapley p. 352
MSaE mp. 46470

B8025 HYMNS of praise, sung by the youth of the Evangelical . . . Hudson, Ashbel Stoddard, 1792.
46 p. 15.5 cm.
DLC mp. 46472

B8026 JARRATT, DEVEREUX, 1733-1801
Addresses to the . . . bishops . . . and lay members of the Protestant Episcopal church in the state of Virginia . . . Richmond, 1792.
31 p. 8vo
Davis 71
No copy known mp. 46473

B8027 JOHN STREET THEATRE, NEW YORK
New-York, April 14th, 1792. Theatre. Mrs. Gray's night. On . . . the 16th of April, will be presented, a comedy . . . The Beaux Stratagem . . . [New York, 1792]
broadside 41.5 X 24 cm.
NHi (trimmed) mp. 46524

B8028 [JOHNSON, RICHARD] 1734-1793
The hermit of the forest, and the wandering infants. A rural fragment . . . Boston, Printed and sold by Samuel Hall, 1792.
29, [2] p. incl. covers. 10.5 cm.
MWA; PP (p. [31] and rear cover wanting) mp. 46474

B8029 [JOHNSON, RICHARD] 1734-1793
The hermit of the forest, and the wandering infants, a rural fragment . . . New-York, William Durll [sic], 1792.
29 p. incl. front cover. 10 cm.
Hamilton 138
CtHi; CtY; MWA (front cover wanting); NjP mp. 46475

B8030 KENNEBEC-RIVER, price current for lumber delivered at Bath, Longreach. [Portland? 1792]
broadside 27 X 16.5 cm.
Text in 2 columns
Dated at bottom: Bath, August, 1792
RPJCB. Photostat: MWA mp. 46477

B8031 KENNEBECK PROPRIETORS
At a meeting of the Proprietors of the Kennebeck Purchase from the late Colony of New-Plymouth, held at Boston . . . July 2, 1792. Voted . . . [Boston, 1792]
broadside
Ford 2641
MHi mp. 46478

B8032 [KENRICK, WILLIAM] 1725?-1779
The whole duty of woman . . . By a lady . . . The thirteenth edition. Printed at Windsor, Vermont, by Alden Spooner, and for sale at his office. M,DCC.XCII.
48 p. 16 cm.
McCorison 229
VtHi. Brit. Mus. mp. 46479

B8033 KENTUCKY. CITIZENS
To the President and Congress . . . The remonstrance of

the subscribers, citizens of the commonwealth of Kentucky, sheweth . . . [Lexington, J. Bradford, 1792]
broadside 39 X 32 cm.
McMurtrie: Kentucky 6
DLC mp. 46480

B8034 KENTUCKY. GENERAL ASSEMBLY. HOUSE OF REPRESENTATIVES
Journal of the House of Representatives at the first session of the General Assembly . . . begun and held at . . . Lexington . . . [June 4, 1792] Lexington, John Bradford [1792]
35 p. 31 cm.
McMurtrie: Kentucky 8
ICU; KyLo (t.p. lacking) mp. 46483

B8035 KENTUCKY. GENERAL ASSEMBLY. HOUSE OF REPRESENTATIVES
[Rules and standing orders of the House of Representatives. Lexington, John Bradford, 1792]

On June 6, 1792, the House "Resolved, That the printer be directed to print forty copies of the rules and standing orders . . ."
McMurtrie: Kentucky 9
No copy known mp. 46481

B8036 KENTUCKY. GENERAL ASSEMBLY. SENATE
Journal of the Senate at the first session of the General Assembly . . . of Kentucky. Monday, June the 4th, 1792. [Lexington, John Bradford, 1792]
31 p. 31 cm. caption title
On June 7, 1792, the Senate "Ordered, That the public printer be directed to print twice a week . . . one hundred and twenty-two copies of the Journals of this house . . ."
McMurtrie: Kentucky 10
ICU; KyLo mp. 46485

B8037 KENTUCKY. GENERAL ASSEMBLY. SENATE
[Rules of the Senate. Lexington, John Bradford, 1792]

On June 8, 1792, the Senate "Ordered, That the public printer be directed to print twelve copies of the rules of this House . . ."
McMurtrie: Kentucky 12
No copy known mp. 46482

B8038 KENTUCKY. LAWS
[An act concerning the militia. Lexington, John Bradford, 1792]

On June 21, 1792, the Senate "Resolved, That the public printer . . . be directed to strike . . . also the act . . . entitled 'An act concerning the militia' and that 1000 copies . . . be deposited with the Governor . . ."
McMurtrie: Kentucky 16
No copy known mp. 46484

B8039 KENTUCKY. LAWS
Acts passed at the first session of the General assembly . . . of Kentucky . . . Lexington, John Bradford [1792]
52 p. 30 cm.
McMurtrie: Kentucky 14
DLC; ICU; KyU; MH-L; MWA; NNB mp. 46486

B8040 KENTUCKY. LAWS
Acts passed at the second session of the General assembly . . . of Kentucky . . . Lexington, John Bradford [1792]
58 p. 30.5 cm.
McMurtrie: Kentucky 15
DLC; ICU; KyU; MH-L; NNB mp. 46487

B8041 KENTUCKY. LAWS
[The revenue law as respects the collection of the land tax. Lexington, John Bradford, 1792]

On June 28, 1792, the Senate "Resolved, That the public printer be directed to print so much of the Revenue law as respects the land tax . . ."
McMurtrie: Kentucky 17
No copy known mp. 46488

B8042 KERR, DAVID
To the free and independent voters of Talbot county. Gentlemen, As my conduct seems to be disapproved of . . . David Kerr. Easton, 1st September, 1792 . . . [Easton? James Cowan? 1792]
broadside 42 X 26 cm.
Minick 63
MdHi mp. 46489

B8043 LEHIGH COALMINE COMPANY
Jacob Weiss, of Northampton County . . . having discovered a certain coal-mine . . . [Philadelphia, 1792]
broadside 28 X 15 cm.
Dated Feb. 13, 1792
PHi mp. 46490

B8044 LENGLET-DUFRESNOY, NICOLAS, 1674-1755
Du Fresnoy's Geography for youth . . . Translated from the French of Abbé Lenglet du Fresnoy, and now greatly augmented and improved . . . The thirteenth edition . . . Philadelphia, Printed for Rice and Co. [1792?]
156 [i.e. 164] p. front. (fold. map) 17 cm.
PHi. Forrest Bowe, N.Y.C. (microfilm)

B8045 THE life and death of Robin Hood, complete in twenty-four songs. Philadelphia, Stewart & Cochran [1792?]
54 leaves. 12mo A-F^{12,6}
Rosenbach-Ch 160
A. S. W. Rosenbach (1933) mp. 46563

B8046 LONDON REVIEW
Some remarks on silent worship, or devotion, seriously recommended to mankind universally . . . [From the *London Review* of December, 1791.] [Philadelphia? 1792?]
broadside 34 X 21 cm.
New York Public 1038
MWA; NN mp. 46576

B8047 MACGOWAN, JOHN, 1726-1780
The life of Joseph, the son of Israel . . . A new edition. Philadelphia, printed: Carlisle, Reprinted by George Kline, 1792.
144 p. 15 cm.
PHi mp. 46492

B8048 MACGOWAN, JOHN, 1726-1780
The life of Joseph, the son of Israel . . . A new edition. Sagg-Harbour, Printed and sold by David Frothingham [1792]
258 p. front. 15.5 cm.
McMurtrie: Sag Harbor 3
NEh; NSh mp. 46493

B8049 MCKNIGHT, ROBERT
The case of Robert McKnight, a bankrupt, written by himself in prison at Philadelphia, 1792. [Philadelphia, 1792]
24 p. 8vo caption title
PPL mp. 46494

B8050 MACPHERSON, JOHN, of Philadelphia
Vorlesungen über philosophische Sittenlehre . . . übersetzt durch G. F. Hoetz. Philadelphia, Melchior Steiner, 1792.
28 p.
Reproduced for microprint of Evans 24496 (Woodhouse)
PPL mp. 24496

B8051 MAGRUDER, NINIAN, d. 1823
An inaugural dissertation on the smallpox . . . Philadelphia, Zachariah Poulson, 1792.
24 p. 20.5 cm.
DLC (2 copies); DNLM; MBM; MdBJ; MdBJ-W; PPC; PPL; PPPH; PU mp. 46495

B8052 THE major's only son, and this true-love's overthrow. Being some lines composed by himself, on the occasion; He is a native of . . . Massachusetts, and is now alive the present year, 1792 . . . [Boston? 1792]
broadside 40 X 28 cm.
MWA mp. 46496

B8053 MARINE SOCIETY OF THE CITY OF NEW YORK
Charter of the Marine Society . . . to which are added, the bye-laws, and a list of the members . . . New-York, Francis Childs and John Swaine, 1792.
38 p. 19 X 16 cm.
New York Public 1026
NN mp. 46498

B8054 MARTIN, GEORG ADAM
Christliche Bibliothek . . . Ephrata, Gedruckt im Jahr M,DCC,XCII.
148 p. 8vo
Not Evans 24501 (MWA copy in microprint edition); extensively reset, and distinguishable by "Geschichte 17, 28" on p. 1 in place of "Act. 17, 28."
PPL

B8055 MARYLAND. CONSTITUTION
The constitution and form of government, as proposed to be amended . . . Annapolis, Frederick Green [1792]
25 p. 17.5 cm.
Huntington 620; Minick 66
CSmH; MdHi; NBLiHi. Photostat: NN mp. 46499

B8056 MARYLAND. LAWS
An act for the valuation of real and personal property . . . Annapolis, Frederick Green [1792]
23 p. 22 cm.
Minick 71
MdHi mp. 46500

B8057 MASSACHUSETTS
A list of the polls and of the estates real and personal, of the several proprietors and inhabitants of the Town of taken pursuant to an act . . . passed in . . . one thousand seven hundred and ninety-two . . . [Boston, 1792?]
broadside
Ford 2662
MB mp. 46501

B8058 MASSACHUSETTS. GOVERNOR, 1787-1793
By His Excellency John Hancock . . . A proclamation for removing the General Court from the Town of Boston to Concord . . . October 26, 1792. [Boston, 1792]
broadside
Ford 2660
M-Ar; MHi mp. 46502

B8059 MASSACHUSETTS. GOVERNOR, 1787-1793
Commonwealth of Massachusetts. To the selectmen of the town of in the second district . . . Given at the Council chamber . . . [Dec. 10, 1792] . . . [Boston, 1792]
broadside 37 X 22.5 cm.
Ford 2663; New York Public 1028
DLC; MB; MHi; MWA; NN mp. 46503

B8060 MASSACHUSETTS. HOUSE OF REPRESENTATIVES
Commonwealth of Massachusetts. In the House of representatives, June 6, 1792. Whereas in the Act for enquiring . . . [Boston, T. Adams, 1792]
broadside 34.5 X 21.5 cm.
Ford 2658; New York Public 1029
DLC; MBB; MHi; MWA; NN; RPJCB mp. 46505

B8061 MASSACHUSETTS. LAWS
Commonwealth of Massachusetts . . . An act providing for the payment of costs . . . March 6, 1792 . . . [Boston, T. Adams, 1792]
broadside 44 X 34.5 cm.
Ford 2657
DLC mp. 46504

B8062 MASSACHUSETTS. MILITIA
Circular letter from a committee appointed by the officers of the Massachusetts line of the Federal army, to the officers in the different states. Boston, (Massachusetts) February 28, 1792 . . . At a respectable meeting . . . on the 4th of July, 1792, in the city of New-York . . . Ebenezer Stevens, Chairman . . . [New York? 1792]
broadside 33.5 X 39.5 cm.
MWA mp. 46594

B8063 MASSACHUSETTS. TREASURER
[No. V.] An account of money and notes received for Eastern Lands, and paid into the Treasury, by the Committee . . . Boston, 7th March, 1791 . . . [No. VI.] The Commonwealth of Massachusetts in account . . . to the Committee on the Sale of Eastern Lands, —— Dr. . . . Boston, 7th March, 1792. [Boston, 1792]
broadsheet 41 X 21.5 cm.
Figures from 1785 to 1791
MSaE mp. 46506

B8064 MASSACHUSETTS MAGAZINE
The carrier, of the *Massachusetts Magazine*, to his patrons and friends, presents the best wishes of a good heart . . . Boston, Jan. 1792. [Boston, 1792]
broadside 25 X 13 cm.
Ford 2673
PHi. Photostat: MWA mp. 46406

B8065 MERCER, JOHN FRANCIS, 1759-1821
An off-hand reply to Voter . . . John F. Mercer. [Annapolis, F. and S. Green, 1792]
broadside 33.5 X 20 cm.
Minick 82
DLC; MdHi mp. 46507

B8066 MERCER, SILAS, 1745-1796
The doctrine of justification, by the righteousness of Christ, stated and maintained in an extract from . . . John Gill, D.D. By Silas Mercer . . . Charleston, Markland & M'Iver, 1792.
69 p. 17 cm.
Mosimann 485
NcD; NjPT

B8067 THE Middlesex almanack, or ladies and gentle-

mens' diary, for . . . 1793. Middletown, Moses H. Woodward [1792]
[24] p.
Advertised in the *Middlesex Gazette* Dec. 8, 1792
Drake 503; Trumbull: Supplement 1803
N (imperfect) mp. 46508

B8068 THE modern Quaker . . . Written in England by an observer, and presented to Friends' children. [Colophon] Philadelphia, Printed and sold by Daniel Lawrence [1792]
8 p. 17 cm. caption title
In verse
New York Public 1030; Sabin 49812
DLC; NN; PPL mp. 46509

B8069 MOORE, JOHN HAMILTON, d. 1807
The young gentleman and lady's monitor . . . The latest edition . . . New-York: Printed and sold by William Durell, 1792.
vi, 406 [8] p. 16.5 cm.
MWA; MiU-C; NN (plates I-II wanting); NjP; PPL (sig. S2 and S3 wanting) mp. 46510

B8070 MOORE, JOHN HAMILTON, d. 1807
The young gentleman and lady's monitor . . . The seventh edition . . . New-York, Hodge and Campbell, 1792.
324 p. 16 cm.
DLC; N (lacks p. 291-98, 301-24); NhHi mp. 46511

B8071 MORRELL, THOMAS
Truth discovered, or An answer to . . . Hammet's Appeal to truth and circumstances . . . Charleston, I. Silliman, 1792.
43 p. 20.5 cm. $[A-E]^4$ $[F]^2$
IEG

B8072 MORRELL, THOMAS
A vindication of Truth discovered . . . Philadelphia, Printed by Parry Hall and sold by John Dickins, 1792.
48 p. 17.5 cm.
IEG

B8073 NEUE UNPARTHEYISCHE LÄNCASTER ZEITUNG
Neujahrs-Verse, des Herumträgers der *Neuen Unpartheyische Läncaster Zeitung,* den lsten Januar, 1792 . . . [Lancaster, 1792]
broadside 29 X 18.5 cm.
PHi mp. 46512

B8074 THE New-England primer, improved . . . Boston, Printed by James Loring. Sold wholesale and retail at his bookstore, 1792.
[64] p. $[A]\text{-}D^8$
Heartman 109
MiU-C mp. 46513

B8075 THE New-England primer, improved . . . Hartford, Nath. Patten, 1792.
[64] p. $[A]\text{-}D^8$
Heartman 108; Rosenbach-Ch 161
CtSoP mp. 46514

B8076 THE New-England primer, improved . . . Litchfield, Collier and Buel, 1792.
29 p. 24mo
Trumbull: Second supplement 2866
CtY mp. 46515

B8077 THE New England primer improved . . . Middletown, Moses H. Woodward, 1792.
[30] p.
Trumbull: Supplement 2432; cf. C. F. Heartman auction catalog no. 56, June 23, 1916
Geo. D. Smith (1916) mp. 46516

B8078 THE New-England primer; much improved . . . Philadelphia, Johnston and Justice for [Robert] Campbell [1792]
36 leaves. 12mo $A\text{-}C^{12}$
On the flyleaf: Rebecca Carpenter her Book 1792
Heartman 322; Rosenbach-Ch 162
A. S. W. Rosenbach (1933) mp. 46517

B8079 NEW HAMPSHIRE. CONSTITUTION
Articles in addition to and amendment of the Constitution of . . . New Hampshire, agreed to by the Convention of said state . . . Dover, E. Ladd, 1792.
31 p.
Heartman: Cradle 39; Sabin 52802; cf. Evans 24578
MHi; NjP; RPJCB. Charles F. Heartman (1922)
mp. 46518

B8080 NEW HAMPSHIRE. GOVERNOR, 1790–1794
State of New-Hampshire. To the selectmen of Pursuant to an act of the legislature . . . passed June 20th, 1792 . . . you are hereby required to warn a meeting of the inhabitants of qualified to vote . . . Senators for the State Legislature . . . Given at the Council-Chamber, in Exeter, this 27th day of June, 1792. Josiah Bartlett, President. Exeter, Henry Ranlet [1792]
broadside 39 X 25 cm.
NjR

B8081 NEW HAMPSHIRE. HOUSE OF REPRESENTATIVES
State of New-Hampshire. In the House of Representatives, December the 11th, A.D. 1792 . . . [Portsmouth, J. Melcher, 1792]
broadside 38 X 31.5 cm.
DLC; NhHi mp. 46519

B8082 NEW HAMPSHIRE. LAWS
Acts of the state of New-Hampshire. An act directing the mode of ballotting . . . [Portsmouth, J. Melcher, 1792]
broadside 46 X 39 cm.
DLC; NhHi mp. 46520

B8083 THE New-Jersey and Pennsylvania almanac, for the year 1793 . . . Fitted to the latitude of 40 degrees . . . Burlington, Printed and sold by Isaac Neale [1792]
[48] p. 17.5 cm.
Morsch 173
MWA mp. 46521

B8084 THE new Pennsylvania almanac, for . . . 1793 . . . Philadelphia, Robert Campbell [1792]
[36] p. 18 cm.
By James Login
MWA mp. 46491

B8085 NEW YORK. LAWS
State of New-York. An act for establishing and opening lock navigations within this state, passed the 30th of March, 1792. [Colophon] [New York] Francis Childs and John Swaine, 1792.
4 p. 34 cm. caption title
In triple columns
New York Public 1033
NHi; NN mp. 46526

B8086 NEW YORK. LAWS
State of New-York, in Senate, March 21st, 1792. Re-

solved . . . That the Secretary of the state . . . [Colophon] [New York] Francis Childs and John Swaine, 1792.
4 p. 37 cm.
DLC mp. 46527

B8087 NEW YORK. SENATE
New-York, November 20th, 1792. Please to give the following extracts from the Journal of the Senate . . . a place in your paper, agreeably to the order of the Senate of the 17th instant thereto annexed . . . Abm. B. Bancker . . . [New York, 1792]
broadside 42.5 X 33.5 cm.
In four columns
New York Public 1032
NHi; NNMer (formerly). Photostat: NN mp. 46528

B8088 NEW YORK DAILY GAZETTE
The carrier of the *New-York Daily Gazette* begs leave to present the following address . . . with the compliments of the season . . . [New York, 1792]
broadside 25.5 X 24.5 cm.
NHi mp. 46407

B8089 NEW YORK MORNING POST
New-Year verses, humbly addressed to the patrons of the *Morning Post* . . . New-York, January 1, 1792 . . . [New York, W. Morton, 1792]
broadside 30 X 11.5 cm.
NHi mp. 46522

B8090 NEWBURYPORT, MASS.
To the assessors of Newburyport. A list of the polls and estate . . . of the subscriber . . . N.B. The law requires that the value of the estates . . . be made out, according to their real value on the first day of May, 1792. [Newburyport, 1792]
broadside 39.5 X 30.5 cm.
MWA mp. 46529

B8091 NO Mercer! No man for Congress who disregards the instructions . . . A farmer. September 28, 1792. [Annapolis? 1792?]
broadside 30 X 17 cm.
DLC mp. 46531

B8092 NORMAN, JOHN
The American pilot, containing the navigation of the sea coast of North America . . . Boston Printed and sold by John Norman at his Office N. 75 Newbury Street MDCCXCII.
2 p.l., 11 maps. 54 cm.
Phillips: Atlases 4474a; cf. Evans 23637
DLC mp. 46532

B8093 ODE for election-day, 1792. [24 lines of verse] [n.p., 1792]
broadside 16 X 10.5 cm.
CtHi mp. 46533

B8094 OHIO COMPANY
At a meeting of the Connecticut Proprietors in the Ohio Company's purchase, held at Hartford, on the 5th day of July, A.D. 1792 . . . [Hartford? 1792]
broadside 32.5 X 20.5 cm.
200 copies ordered printed
New York Public 1023
NN; RPJCB mp. 46534

B8095 OLD AMERICAN COMPANY
By authority. By the Old American Company, on Monday, December 17, (by particular desire) . . . The Road to Ruin . . . [Philadelphia, T. Bradford, 1792]
broadside fol.
PPL mp. 46544

B8096 OLD AMERICAN COMPANY
New-York, February 11th, 1792. Theatre. By the Old American Company. On . . . the 20th of February . . . a comedy . . . He Would Be a Soldier . . . Vivat Respublica. [New York, 1792]
broadside 42.5 X 25 cm.
Museum of the City of N.Y. (not traced) mp. 46525

B8097 A PACK of cards changed into a complete almanack, and prayer book . . . The eleventh edition. Stockbridge, 1792.
8 p. 17.5 cm.
MWA mp. 46535

B8098 PAINE, THOMAS, 1737–1809
The writings, of Thomas Paine . . . Containing, 1. Common Sense. 2. The Crisis. 3. Letter to Abbe Raynal. 4. Public Good. 5. Letter to the Earl of Shelburne. 6. Letter to Sir Guy Carlton. 7. Letter to Abbe Seyeys. 8. Letter to the Authors of the Republican. 9. Rights of man. Albany, Charles R. & George Webster [1792]
[517] p.
CSmH mp. 46536

B8099 THE paths of virtue, exemplified in the lives of eminent men and women . . . The first American edition. Philadelphia. Printed and sold by Daniel Lawrence, 1792.
167 p. 13.5 cm.
MWA mp. 46537

B8100 PEARL, STEPHEN
To the candid public. Having received information that a publication, signed S. & F. de Montmollin, is designed to be spread this morning . . . Stephen Pearl. Rutland, October 15, 1792. [Windsor? 1792]
broadside 12 X 13 cm.
McCorison 230
MWA mp. 46538

B8101 PENNSYLVANIA. COURT OF COMMON PLEAS
Rules and orders, for regulating the practice of the county courts of common pleas, in . . . Pennsylvania. Lancaster, J. Bailey and W. Dickson, 1792.
11 p. 17 cm.
MWA mp. 46539

B8102 PENNSYLVANIA. GENERAL ASSEMBLY
Report of the Committee on Ways and Means . . . [at end] [Philadelphia] Printed by Francis Bailey and Thomas Lang [1792]
6 p. fol.
PPL mp. 46540

B8103 PENNSYLVANIA MERCURY
Verses on the New-Year, January 2, 1792. Addressed to the subscribers to the *Pennsylvania Mercury* . . . [Philadelphia, D. Humphreys, 1792]
broadside 26.5 X 25 cm.
NHi mp. 46659

B8104 THE perplexity of poverty; or, A touch of the times . . . Concord [N.H.], 1792.
15 p. 15 cm.
MWA mp. 46541

B8105 PHILADELPHIA
Orders. For Wednesday, February 22, 1792. The Volunteer Company of Artillery and Infantry, are to march . . . it

being the anniversary of the President . . . Thomas Procter, Lieutenant of the City and Liberties. February 21, 1792. [Philadelphia, 1792]
broadside 38 X 22.5 cm.
MB mp. 46545

B8106 PHILADELPHIA. CITIZENS
Circular. Philadelphia, August 3d, 1792. Sir, By the enclosed . . . [Philadelphia, 1792]
broadside 33.5 X 21 cm.
DLC; PHi mp. 46542

B8107 PHILADELPHIA. CITIZENS
Extract from the minutes of the proceedings of a general meeting of the citizens of Philadelphia . . . the 30th of July, 1792 . . . Thomas M'Kean, Chairman . . . [Philadelphia, 1792]
broadside 17 X 8 cm.
PHi mp. 46543

B8108 PHILLIPS, CATHARINE (PAYTON) 1727–1794
Reasons why the people called Quakers cannot so fully unite with the Methodists, in their missions to the Negroes . . . Philadelphia, Printed and sold by Daniel Lawrence, 1792.
20 p. 16 cm.
DLC; NNMR; PGC; PPL; PSC-Hi mp. 46546

B8109 PIERSON, JOSIAH G.
New invented washing-mill, made by Josiah G. Pierson—No. 10 White-Hall-Street . . . The manufacturer lives at No. 11 Albany Pier. New-York, October 6, 1792. [New York] T. Greenleaf, print. [1792]
broadside 27.5 X 23 cm.
DLC mp. 46547

B8110 PIERSON, JOSIAH G.
New invented washing-mill . . . New-York, November 3, 1792. [New York] T. Greenleaf, print. [1792]
broadside 27.5 X 22.5 cm.
CSmH

B8111 POMEROY, JOSIAH
Doctor Pomeroy's affidavit . . . [n.p., 1792]
broadside 27.5 cm.
Signed and dated: Josiah Pomeroy. Sworn this 20th April, 1792. Before me, Israel Spencer, justice
New York Public 1035
NAll. Photostat: NN mp. 46548

B8112 THE poor orphans legacy . . . By a minister of the gospel . . . Richmond, John Dixon, 1792.
32 p. 21 cm.
Second edition
Davis 74; Huntington 623
CSmH; PHi mp. 46549

B8113 POPE, ALEXANDER, 1688–1744
An essay on man; in four epistles to H. St. John, Lord Bolingbroke . . . Boston, Printed and sold by John W. Folsom, 1792.
65 p. 18mo
Blank leaves instead of bookseller's advertisement at end; cf. Evans 24703
CSmH

B8114 PORTER, HUNTINGTON, 1755–1844
A discourse on resignation to the divine will . . . delivered at the funeral of . . . Martha Lock, February 3, 1792 . . . Portsmouth, John Melcher, 1792.
[3]–21 p. 21 cm. [A]-C^4 (A1 and C4 blank and genuine)
Huntington 624
CSmH; MWA mp. 46550

B8115 A PRESENT to children . . . Norwich, Ebenezer Bushnell, 1792.
14, [1] p. 11 cm.
CtY mp. 46551

B8116 PRIOR,
A funeral sermon, preached by the Rev. Mr. Prior . . . on the death of Miss Christiana Lane . . . October 5, 1792 . . . Baltimore, Samuel & John Adams, 1792.
12 p. 16.5 cm.
MWA mp. 46552

B8117 PROTESTANT EPISCOPAL CHURCH IN THE U.S.A. CONNECTICUT (DIOCESE)
The constitution of the Protestant Episcopal Church in . . . Connecticut, agreed upon . . . in convention . . . New-Haven, June 6, 1792. [New Haven, 1792]
broadside 33 X 21 cm.
NHi mp. 46553

B8118 PROTESTANT EPISCOPAL CHURCH IN THE U.S.A. VIRGINIA (DIOCESE)
Journal of a convention . . . Held in . . . Richmond, May 3, 1792. Rihmond [sic], Thomas Nicolson [1792]
8 p. 20 cm.
New York Public 1036
NN mp. 46554

B8119 PSALMS, hymns and spiritual songs . . . Philadelphia, Thomas Dobson, 1792.
1 p.l., 222 p., 1 leaf, viii p. 14.5 cm.
PHi mp. 46555

B8120 REMARKABLE account of Guy, who by strange enterprizes in war, obtained for his bride, Phelice . . . In a poem intirely new . . . Windsor, A. Spooner, 1792.
11 p. 18 cm.
"The fall of Dagon": p. 10–11
McCorison 231
MBAt mp. 46556

B8121 RHODE ISLAND. ELECTION PROX.
B. Bourn, First, Paul Mumford, Second, Representatives in Congress. [Providence? 1792]
broadside 6.5 X 13 cm.
Alden 1280; Chapin Proxies 57
RHi mp. 46557

B8122 RHODE ISLAND. ELECTION PROX.
[Benjamin Bourn. First Representative . . . Providence, 1792]
[broadside]
Alden 1281; Chapin Proxies 59
No copy found mp. 46558

B8123 RHODE ISLAND. ELECTION PROX.
A friend of the rights of man, Francis Malbone, Second Representative to the Congress of the United States. [Providence? 1792]
broadside 6.5 X 14 cm.
Alden 1283; Chapin Proxies 58
RHi mp. 46560

B8124 RHODE ISLAND. ELECTION PROX.
Friends to the rights of man. Benjamin Bourn, First, Francis Malbone, Second, Representative in Congress. [Providence? 1792]
broadside 6.5 X 13 cm.
Alden 1282; Chapin Proxies 56
RHi mp. 46559

B8125 RHODE ISLAND. GOVERNOR, 1790-1805
By His Excellency Arthur Fenner . . . A proclamation . . . [Nov. 5, 1792] . . . [Providence] J. Carter [1792]
broadside 40 X 31 cm.
Bill submitted by Carter Nov. 7, 1792
Alden 1284
RHi mp. 46561

B8126 THE Rhode-Island almanack, for the year . . . 1793 . . . Warren, Printed by Nathaniel Phillips, for Jacob Richardson, in Newport [1792]
[24] p. 17 cm.
Alden 1270; Winship Addenda p. 90
MWA; N; RHi; RNHi mp. 46582

B8127 THE Rhode-Island, Connecticut, Newhampshire, Massachusetts, and Vermont almanack, for . . . 1793 . . . Boston, Printed by Nathaniel Coverly, and sold by James Gardner . . . Providence [1792]
[24] p. 18 cm.
By Isaac Bickerstaff
MWA; N mp. 46387

B8128 RICHMOND THEATRE
By authority. The Virginia company. On Friday evening, August 3d, 1792 . . . [Richmond, 1792]
broadside 37 X 22 cm.
CSmH mp. 46562

B8129 ROSE, JOHANNES
Sassafras-oel. Lancaster Caunty. Canostogo Taunschip . . . N.B. Obengemeldetes Sassafras-oel ist zu haben bey Dr. Johannes Rose in Lancaster. [Lancaster, 1792]
broadside 4to
PPL mp. 46564

B8130 RUSH, BENJAMIN, 1745-1813
The new method of inoculating for the small-pox . . . The third edition. Philadelphia, Printed and sold by Parry Hall, 1792.
26, [1] p. 19 cm.
DLC; DeHi; PHi; PPC mp. 46565

B8131 RUSH, BENJAMIN, 1745-1813
A syllabus of a course of lectures on the institutes of medicine . . . Philadelphia, Parry Hall, 1792.
8 p. 22.5 cm.
DNLM; MWA; PPL mp. 46566

B8132 [RUSHTON, EDWARD] 1756-1814
[An expostulatory letter from Edward Rushton to George Washington, of Mount Vernon. Lexington, John Bradford, 1792]

Advertised in the *Kentucky Gazette*, Sept. 23, 1792, as "Just published at this office and for sale, price 9d."
cf. Evans 32785; McMurtrie: Kentucky 19
No copy located mp. 46567

B8133 RUSSELL AND CLAP, auctioneers
Tuesday morning, 16th October, at ten o'clock, will be sold by public vendue, at Russell and Clap's auction-room, the following collection of books . . . [Boston, 1792]
broadside
Ford 2672
MHi mp. 46568

B8134 [SANDS, BENJAMIN]
[Metamorphosis. Philadelphia, 1792?]
oblong leaf folded 3 times
Woodcuts by James Poupard
Dated by d'Alté A. Welch
Hamilton 1168 (1)
NjP mp. 46569

B8135 [SANDS, BENJAMIN]
Metamorphosis, oder eine Verwandlung von Bildern mit poetischen Erklärung zur Unterhaltung der Jugend. [Philadelphia, 1792?]
16 p.
Dated by d'Alté A. Welch
PP; PPL. d'Alté A. Welch, Cleveland (1962)
mp. 46570

B8136 SAY, THOMAS, 1709-1796
A true and wonderful account of Mr. Thomas Say . . . while in a trance . . . [Philadelphia?] 1792.
8 p. sm. 8vo
Huntington 625
CSmH mp. 46571

B8137 EINE schöne, anmuthige und lebenswürdige Historia, von der . . . Pfalzgräfin Genovefa . . . Zweyte Lancästersche Auflage. Lancaster, Jacob Bailey und Wilhelm Dickson, 1792.
52 p. 12mo
PPL mp. 46572

B8138 THE second edition. Poulson's town and country almanac, for the year . . . 1793 . . . Philadelphia, Zachariah Poulson, junior [1791]
[40] p. 12mo.
The astronomical calculations by William Waring
MWA; PPL mp. 46666

B8139 [SHEET almanack for the year 1793. Hartford, Nathaniel Patten, 1792]
broadside
Advertised in the *American Mercury*, Sept. 24, 1792, as "This day published, and selling as cheap as ever, by Nathaniel Patten, Bickerstaff's, Strong's, and Sheet Almanacks, for . . . 1793."
Drake 507
No copy known

B8140 [SMITH, EUNICE]
Practical language interpreted: in a dialogue between a believer and an unbeliever . . . Exeter, Printed by Henry Ranlet, for, and sold by Deacon Stephen Sleeper, of Poplin —sold also at this office—1792.
22 p. 18 cm.
MWA mp. 46574

B8141 SMITH, EUNICE
Some of the exercises of a believing soul described . . . Boston, Printed by E. Russell for Zadok King, in Conway, 1792.
24 p. 18 cm.
MWA mp. 46575

B8142 SONG, for the one hundred and fifty-third anniversary of the election of the officers of the Ancient and Honourable Artillery Company. June, 1792. [Boston, 1792]
broadside 16.5 X 9.5 cm.
Ford 2669
PHi mp. 46577

B8143 SOUTH CAROLINA. COMMISSIONERS TO SETTLE ACCOUNTS
To the honorable the Speaker, and the rest of the members of the House . . . The Commissioners appointed . . . to settle the accounts, of the former Commissioners of the

Treasury . . . submit the following report . . . Charleston, November 22, 1792. [Charleston? 1792]
broadside 41 X 33 cm.
Sc-Ar

B8144 SOUTH CAROLINA. LAWS
An act prescribing on the part of this State, the . . . manner of holding elections for the representatives in the Congress . . . Dec. 21, 1792. [Charleston? 1792]
broadside 40.5 X 32.5 cm.
Sc-Ar

B8145 [STERNE, LAURENCE] 1713–1768
Letters from Yorick to Eliza. Burlington, Isaac Neale, 1792.
63 p. 13.5 cm. A-E^6 D^2
MWA mp. 46678

B8146 [STORY, ISAAC] 1774–1803
Yarico to Inkle, an epistle . . . Hartford, Elisha Babcock, 1792.
19 p. 18.5 cm.
Sabin 105982; Trumbull: Supplement 2812
CtHi; DLC; MH; MWA mp. 46677

B8147 [THE story of Amelia; or the Treacherous brother, in a series of letters. Selected from the *Morning Ray*. Windsor, Printed by James Reed Hutchins, and to be sold at this office, by W. H., 1792]

Advertised in the *Morning Ray*, May 15, 1792
McCorison 235
No copy known mp. 46579

B8148 SWIFT, JONATHAN, 1667–1745
A sermon, on the Trinity . . . Portland, Benjamin Titcomb, Jun., 1792.
21 p. 8vo
Huntington 627
CSmH mp. 46580

B8149 TEN BROEK, ABRAHAM
On the 13th instant, a letter was received by Abraham Ten Broeck . . . inclosing the following proceedings of a meeting convened at New-York, for the purpose of nominating candidates for . . . Governor . . . Abraham Ten Broeck, Chairman. City of Albany, February 16, 1792. Albany, Charles R. George Webster [1792]
broadside 29 X 18 cm.
NHi mp. 46581

B8150 Deleted

B8151 TO the freemen of Pennsylvania. [Philadelphia, 1792]
broadside 35.5 X 20.5 cm.
Signed: Mentor
PHi mp. 46584

B8152 TO the freemen of the city of Philadelphia. [Philadelphia, 1792]
broadside 28 X 15.5 cm.
Dated Oct. 9, 1792
Signed: Hambden
PHi mp. 46585

B8153 TO the independent electors of Pennsylvania. Citizens and friends to the Federal government! [Philadelphia, 1792]
broadside 21.5 X 16.5 cm.
Signed: A Federalist
PHi mp. 46586

B8154 TO the inhabitants of South-Carolina. As there is no established rule for regulating medical charges, we the subscribers, practitioners of physic . . . James Clitherall, chairman . . . Charleston, July 9, 1792. [Charleston, 1792]
broadside 38 X 24.5 cm.
MBCo; PPL mp. 46587

B8155 TO the people. Friends and Fellow-Citizens, When partial mischiefs . . . Monday, 18th June, 1792. Brutus . . . [New York? 1792]
broadside
NHi mp. 46588

B8156 TO the public . . . By the Editor of the *Gazette* we are accused with beginning a dispute in his paper . . . April 23, 1792. Z. The following is the piece which the Editor . . . refused to publish. For the *Providence Gazette* . . . Abraham Mathewson! poor dupe! . . . Z. [Providence, 1792]
2 p. 27.5 cm.
Not Evans 26265
MWA mp. 46589

B8157 TO the voters of Anne-Arundel . . . A voter. September 26, 1792. [Annapolis? 1792]
broadside 32 X 21 cm.
DLC (2 copies) mp. 46590

B8158 A TRAGICAL account of the defeat of Gen. St. Clair by the savages . . .
November the Fourth in the year of Ninety one,
We had a sore engagement near to Fort Jefferson . . .
[Boston? 1792?]
broadside 33.5 X 26 cm.
Includes also: Battle of Bunker's Hill
Ford 2614; Vail: Old frontier 897
NHi mp. 46591

B8159 A TRUE and particular narrative of the late tremendous tornado . . . July 1, 1792 . . . Boston, E. Russell [1792]
broadside 56.5 X 44 cm.
Variant of Evans 24864; Ford 2671; Wegelin 814 (added line after imprint, and 10 additional coffins at the top)
DLC

B8160 . . . TUMBLING feats, by the two surprising youths . . . Don Peter will walk round the room on . . . a moving ladder . . . hornpipe by Master Hearn . . . [New York] Printed by Louis Jones, No. 54 King-Street [1792]
broadside 23.5 X 20 cm.
NHi (top of broadside lacking) mp. 46592

B8161 TWITCHER, TITUS
Copy of a letter from the New-Paltz . . . Your's, &c. Titus Twitcher. 11th April, 1792. [New York, 1792]
broadside 31.5 X 20.5 cm.
DLC mp. 46593

B8162 UNION FIRE SOCIETY
Laws of the Union fire society, instituted at Boston, November 25, 1792. Boston, Benjamin Edes [1792]
8 p. 15.5 cm.
DLC mp. 46393

B8163 U. S.
Commissioner's Office. Redeived of Nathaniel Appleton, Commissioner of Loans in the State of Massachusetts . . . interest on stock . . . United States to the 31st of March 1792. [Philadelphia? 1792]
broadside 15 X 17 cm.
Pierce W. Gaines, Fairfield, Conn. (1963) mp. 46595

B8164 U. S.
Manual exercise and evolutions of the cavalry. As practised in the late American army. Norwich, J. Trumbull, 1792.
46 p.
Trumbull: Second supplement 2858
Ct; RPJCB mp. 46497

B8165 U. S. ARMY. CONTINENTAL ARMY
Circular letter from a committee appointed by the officers of the Massachusetts Line . . . February 28, 1792. [New York? 1792]
broadside
MWA mp. 46594

B8166 U. S. ARMY. CONTINENTAL ARMY
[The following is a copy of the memorial presented by the officers of this state to Congress, and now on their table.] To the honourable the Senate and House of Representatives . . . The officers of the Massachusetts line of the late American Army . . . [New York? 1792]
broadside 20 X 16 cm.
Signed by B. Lincoln
Ford 2650
MB; NHi; NN

B8167 U. S. CONGRESS
An alphabetical list of the senators . . . first session of the second Congress . . . An alphabetical list of the members of the House . . . [Philadelphia? 1792]
broadside 40 X 33.5 cm.
CtHi (much annotated) mp. 46598

B8168 U. S. CONGRESS
George Washington, President . . . John Adams, Vice President . . . Senators . . . Representatives . . . [Philadelphia? 1792?]
broadside 40 X 34 cm.
Dated from presence of name of Sen. John Taylor (Va.), who served from Oct. 18, 1792 to May 11, 1794
CtHi mp. 46611

B8169 U. S. CONGRESS
Members of Congress. [2d Congress, 1792–1793] [Philadelphia, 1792]
broadside 49.5 X 15.5 cm.
DLC mp. 46612

B8170 U. S. CONGRESS
Members of the Second Congress. Senate House of Representatives . . . [Philadelphia, 1792]
broadside 40.5 X 33.5 cm.
In 3 columns, by states
CtHi; MWA mp. 46317

B8171 U. S. CONGRESS. HOUSE
Resolved, That a loan to the amount of the balances . . . found due . . . to the individual states, be opened at the Treasury . . . [Philadelphia? 1792]
broadside 34 X 21 cm.
2d Cong., 2d sess. House, Dec. 12, 1792
Lines separately numbered
MiU-C mp. 46618

B8172 U. S. CONGRESS. HOUSE. COMMITTEE ON ALTERATIONS IN THE ACTS ESTABLISHING THE TREASURY AND WAR DEPARTMENTS
The committee appointed to consider and report whether any and what alterations are necessary . . . the acts establishing the Treasury and War Departments, submit . . . the following resolutions . . . [Philadelphia, 1792]
[2] p. 34 cm.
Presented in the House Feb. 29, 1792
New York Public 1039
NN (photostat) mp. 46614

B8173 U. S. CONGRESS. HOUSE. COMMITTEE ON COMMERCE
The Committee to whom was referred the message of the President . . . of the 14th instant, report as follows: [Philadelphia, 1792]
broadside 32.5 X 19.5 cm.
DLC mp. 46616

B8174 U. S. CONGRESS. HOUSE. COMMITTEE ON POST-OFFICE AND POST-ROADS
The Committee appointed to take into consideration, the act for establishing the post-office . . . report: [Philadelphia, 1792]
[2] p. 33.5 X 20 cm.
DLC mp. 46615

B8175 U. S. CONGRESS. HOUSE. COMMITTEE ON THE PETITION OF JAMES WARINGTON
The Committee, to whom was referred the petition of James Warington . . . report . . . [Philadelphia, Childs and Swaine, 1792]
3 p. 32.5 cm. caption title
DLC mp. 46617

B8176 U. S. CONGRESS. SENATE
Congress of the United States. In Senate, May the 7th, 1792, Ordered, That the Secretary of the Treasury do lay before the Senate . . . a statement of the salaries . . . [New York? 1792]
broadside 23.5 X 14 cm.
NHi mp. 46620

B8177 U. S. CONSTITUTION
Congress of the United States . . . The conventions of a number of the states . . . expressed a desire . . . Resolved . . . That the following articles be proposed to the legislatures . . . as amendments to the Constitution . . . [Philadelphia, Childs and Swaine, 1792]
11 p. 34 cm.
The edition with the ratifications
Childs and Swaine paid July 18, 1792, for 135 copies (James B. Childs)
Parke-Bernet sale 11/25/1952, item 50
DLC; MWA (t.p. photostat) mp. 46596

B8178 U. S. INSPECTOR-GENERAL'S OFFICE
Rules and articles for the better government of the troops, raised . . . by, and at the expence of the United States of America. [n.p., 1792?]
2 p.l., 64 p. 21 cm. $[\ ]^2$ B-I^4
"An act for making farther . . . provisions for the protection of the frontiers" (p. 59) dated at end: Approved, March the fifth, 1792
Ownership statement dated in ms.: 1794
ViU mp. 46621

B8179 U. S. LAWS
An act concerning the duties on spirits distilled within the United States . . . 1792, May the 2d—Passed the House of representatives. [Colophon] [Philadelphia] John Fenno [1792]
5 p. 34 cm. caption title
DLC mp. 46623

B8180 U. S. LAWS
An act concerning the duties on spirits distilled within

the United States . . . Approved, May eighth, 1792. [Philadelphia, 1792]
5 p. 8vo
cf. Evans 24894
PPL mp. 46624

B8181 U. S. LAWS
An act for regulating processes in the courts . . . [Colophon] [Philadelphia] John Fenno [1792]
3 p. 34 cm. caption title
Photostats: DLC; MWA; NN mp. 46630

B8182 U. S. LAWS
An act more effectually to provide for the national defence . . . 1792, March the 6th–Passed the House . . . [Colophon] [Philadelphia] John Fenno [1792]
7 p. 33.5 cm. caption title
DLC (photostat) mp. 46634

B8183 U. S. LAWS
[An act more effectually to provide for the national defence by establishing an uniform militia. Lexington, John Bradford, 1792]

On June 21, 1792, the Senate of Kentucky "Resolved, That the public printer . . . be directed to strike . . . 'An act more effectually [etc.]' . . . 1000 copies . . ."
McMurtrie: Kentucky 20
No copy known mp. 46632

B8184 U. S. LAWS
An act relative to the compensations to certain officers . . . 1792, May the 2d . . . [Philadelphia] John Fenno [1792]
2 p. 34 X 20.5 cm.
DLC mp. 46633

B8185 U. S. LAWS
An act to ascertain and regulate the claims to half pay . . . 26th of January, 1792 . . . [Colophon] [Philadelphia] John Fenno [1792]
3 p. 33.5 cm. caption title
Photostats: DLC; NN mp. 46635

B8186 U. S. LAWS
An act to erect a light-house on Montaugh Point . . . [Philadelphia] John Fenno [1792]
broadside 33.5 X 21 cm.
DLC; NhD mp. 46638

B8187 U. S. LAWS
An act to establish the post-office and post-roads . . . Passed the House . . . and sent to the Senate for concurrence. [Colophon] [Philadelphia] John Fenno [1792]
7 p. 34 cm. caption title
This printing ends with Sec. 32
DLC mp. 46613

B8188 U. S. LAWS
[An act to provide for calling forth the militia to execute the laws of the Union. Lexington, John Bradford, 1792]

On June 21, 1792, the Senate of Kentucky "Resolved, That the public printer . . . be directed to strike . . . 'An act to provide [etc.]' . . . 1000 copies . . ."
McMurtrie: Kentucky 21
No copy known mp. 46641

B8189 U. S. LAWS
Amendments to the bill, entitled, "An act for regulating processes . . ." [Colophon] [Philadelphia] John Fenno [1792]
3 p. 33.5 cm. caption title
DLC mp. 46599

B8190 U. S. LAWS
Amendments to the bill, entitled, "An act more effectually to provide for the national defence . . ." [Philadelphia] John Fenno [1792]
2 p. 34 X 20.5 cm.
DLC mp. 46600

B8191 U. S. LAWS
Amendments to the bill, entitled, "An act to ascertain and regulate the claims . . ." [Philadelphia] John Fenno [1792]
broadside 26 X 21 cm.
Photostats: DLC; NN mp. 46601

B8192 U. S. LAWS
A bill, declaring the officer, who . . . shall act as President . . . [Philadelphia, 1792]
[2] p. 33 X 21.5 cm.
DLC (photostat) mp. 46602

B8193 U. S. LAWS
A bill directing the mode in which the evidences of the debt . . . [Philadelphia, 1792]
broadside 34 X 21 cm.
DLC mp. 46603

B8194 U. S. LAWS
[A bill for making farther and more effectual provision for the protection of the frontiers of the United States.] [Colophon] [Philadelphia] John Fenno [1792]
4 p. 33 cm.
Title from House Journal, 2 Cong., 1st sess., p. 498
Lines separately numbered; printed act differs textually from this bill.–L. M. Stark
Presented Jan. 25, 1792
New York Public 1055; cf. Evans 24880 (also at NN)
NN (photostat of p. 3–4 only)

B8195 U. S. LAWS
A bill for regulating the post-office . . . [Colophon] New-York, Francis Childs and John Swaine [1792]
6 p. 33.5 cm. caption title
DLC mp. 46604

B8196 U. S. LAWS
A bill more effectually to provide for the national defence . . . [Colophon] [Philadelphia] Francis Childs and John Swaine [1792]
7 p. 33 cm. caption title
DLC mp. 46605

B8197 U. S. LAWS
A bill providing for the sale of land . . . north-west of the River Ohio . . . [Philadelphia, 1792]
broadside 34 X 20.5 cm.
DLC mp. 46606

B8198 U. S. LAWS
A bill providing for the settlement of the claims of persons . . . barred by the limitations heretofore established . . . [New York] Childs and Swaine [1792?]
broadside 33.5 X 21.5 cm.
MiU-C. Photostat: NN mp. 46607

B8199 U. S. LAWS
A bill to authorize a loan in the certificates . . . of such states as shall have balances due to them . . . [n.p., 1792]
broadside 33.7 X 21 cm.

Bill introduced in House Dec., 1792, passed Jan. 26, 1793, rejected by the Senate Feb. 4, 1793
MiU-C mp. 46608

B8200 U. S. LAWS
A bill to establish the post-office and post-roads . . . [Colophon] [Philadelphia] Francis Childs and John Swaine [1792]
7 p. 33.5 cm. caption title
This printing ends with Sec. 30
DLC mp. 46609

B8201 U. S. LAWS
A bill to indemnify the estate of the late Major-general Nathaniel Greene, for a certain bond entered into by him for the public service, during the late war . . . [Philadelphia, 1792]
broadside fol.
PPL mp. 46610

B8202 U. S. LAWS
Duties payable on goods, wares . . . imported into the United States . . . New-York, Printed for Thomas Allen, 1792.
1 p.l., 26 p. 19 cm.
DLC mp. 46642

B8203 U. S. LAWS
Extract from an act of the President of the United States, dated the fourth day of August 1792 . . . Extract from an act . . . dated the twenty ninth day of October 1792 . . . [Philadelphia? 1792?]
broadside 26.5 X 17 cm.
Concerns duties on distilled spirits
New York Public 1057
NN mp. 46644

B8204 U. S. LAWS
Second Congress of the United States: At the first session . . . An act authorizing the grant . . . of certain lands to the Ohio Company of Associates . . . Approved, April twenty-first, 1792. [Philadelphia, Childs and Swaine, 1792]
[2] p. 31 X 19.5 cm.
New York Public 1041
NN mp. 46621

B8205 U. S. LAWS
Second Congress of the United States: At the first session . . . An act, concerning consuls and vice consuls . . . [Apr. 14, 1792] . . . [Philadelphia, Childs and Swaine, 1792]
[4] p. 31 cm. caption title
New York Public 1042
MiU-C; NN mp. 46622

B8206 U. S. LAWS
Second Congress of the United States: At the first session . . . An act for altering the times of holding the circuit courts . . . and for other purposes . . . [Apr. 13, 1792] . . . [Philadelphia, Childs and Swaine, 1792]
[2] p. 31 X 19.5 cm.
New York Public 1043
NN mp. 46625

B8207 U. S. LAWS
Second Congress of the United States: At the first session . . . An act for apportioning representatives among the several states . . . [Apr. 14, 1792] . . . [Philadelphia, 1792]
broadside 31 X 19.5 cm.
Huntington 629; New York Public 1044
CSmH; NN mp. 46626

B8208 U. S. LAWS
Second Congress of the United States: At the first session . . . An act for ascertaining the bounds of a tract of land purchased by John Cleves Symmes . . . [Apr. 12, 1792] . . . [Philadelphia, Childs and Swaine, 1792]
broadside 31 X 19.5 cm.
New York Public 1045
NN mp. 46627

B8209 U. S. LAWS
Second Congress of the United States: At the first session . . . An act for finishing the light-house . . . at the mouth of Cape Fear river in . . . North-Carolina . . . [Apr. 2, 1792] . . . [Philadelphia, Childs and Swaine, 1792]
broadside 31 X 19.5 cm.
New York Public 1046
NN mp. 46628

B8210 U. S. LAWS
Second Congress of the United States: At the first session . . . An act for fixing the compensations of the doorkeepers of the Senate and House . . . [Apr. 12, 1792] . . . [Philadelphia, Childs and Swaine, 1792]
broadside 31 X 19.5 cm.
New York Public 1047
NN mp. 46629

B8211 U. S. LAWS
Second Congress of the United States: At the first session . . . An act for the relief of persons imprisoned for debt . . . [May 5, 1792] . . . [Philadelphia, Childs and Swaine, 1792]
broadside fol.
PPL

B8212 U. S. LAWS
Second Congress of the United States: At the first session . . . An act supplemental to the Act for making . . . more effectual provision for the protection of the frontiers . . . [Mar. 28, 1792] . . . [Philadelphia, Childs and Swaine, 1792]
broadside 41 X 24.5 cm.
New York Pub. 1049; cf. Evans 24885, which lacks "Deposited among the Rolls in the office of the Secretary of State . . ."
NN

B8213 U. S. LAWS
Second Congress of the United States: At the first session . . . An act supplementary to the act for the establishment and support of light-houses . . . and public piers . . . [Apr. 12, 1792] . . . [Philadelphia, Childs and Swaine, 1792]
broadside 31 X 19.5 cm.
New York Public 1050
NN mp. 46634

B8214 U. S. LAWS
Second Congress of the United States: At the first session . . . An act to compensate the Corporation of Trustees of the . . . Academy of Wilmington . . . for . . . damages done . . . during the late war . . . [Apr. 13, 1792] . . . [Philadelphia, Childs and Swaine, 1792]
broadside 31 X 19.5 cm.
New York Public 1052
NN mp. 46636

B8215 U. S. LAWS
Second Congress of the United States: At the first session . . . An act to compensate the services of the late

Colonel George Gibson . . . Approved, May eighth, 1792 . . . [Philadelphia, Childs and Swaine, 1792]
broadside 34.5 X 22.5 cm.
cf. Evans 24902
DLC mp. 46637

B8216 U. S. LAWS
Second Congress of the United States: At the first session . . . An act to erect a light-house on Montok point . . . New-York . . . [Apr. 12, 1792] . . . [Philadelphia, Childs and Swaine, 1792]
broadside 31 X 19.5 cm.
New York Public 1053
NN mp. 46639

B8217 U. S. LAWS
Second Congress of the United States: At the first session . . . An act to establish the post-office and post-roads . . . Approved, February the twentieth, 1792 . . . [Philadelphia, Childs and Swaine, 1792]
6 p. 33.5 cm.
cf. Evans 24876
DLC mp. 46640

B8218 U. S. PRESIDENT, 1789-1797
By the President of the United States. A proclamation. Whereas certain violent . . . proceedings have lately taken place . . . [Philadelphia, 1792]
broadside
Dated Sept. 15, 1792
Stan V. Henkels cat. 1463, Apr. 26, 1932, item 253
New York Public 1040
NN (reduced facsim.) mp. 46643

B8219 U. S. PRESIDENT, 1789–1797
Terms and conditions declared by the President . . . [Oct. 17, 1791] for regulating the materials and manner of the buildings . . . of Washington . . . George Washington. Terms of sale of lots in . . . Washington, the eighth day of October, 1792 . . . [Philadelphia? 1792]
broadside 42.5 X 25.5 cm.
DLC mp. 46645

B8220 U. S. PRESIDENT, 1789–1797
United States. To all to whom these presents come—Greetings. Whereas John Bailey of Boston . . . hath presented a petition . . . I have caused these letters to be patent . . . City of Philadelphia February 23d, 1792 . . . [Philadelphia, 1792]
broadside 37.5 X 66 cm.
Mass. Bar Association mp. 46646

B8221 U. S. TREASURY DEPT.
Abstract of goods, wares and merchandize exported . . . from 1st October 1790, to the 31st September, 1791. [n.p., April 12, 1792]
[5] p. 41.5 cm. caption title
Signed: Treasury department, April 12th, 1792
MiU-C. Pierce W. Gaines, Fairfield, Conn. (1963) mp. 46647

B8222 U. S. TREASURY DEPT.
(Circular to the collectors of the customs.) Treasury Department, October 25, 1792. Sir, Pursuant to the discretion vested in me . . . immediate superintendance of the collection of the duties . . . to the Comptroller of the Treasury . . . [Philadelphia, 1792]
broadside 23 X 19 cm.
MWA mp. 46648

B8223 U. S. TREASURY DEPT.
(Circular.) Treasury Department, July 20, 1792. Sir, It is with great satisfaction . . . [Philadelphia, 1792]
[2] p. 23.5 X 19 cm.
MWA mp. 46650

B8224 U. S. TREASURY DEPT.
(Circular.) Treasury Department, August 6, 1792. Sir, It is the opinion of the Attorney General . . . [Philadelphia, 1792]
broadside 23.5 X 19 cm.
MWA mp. 46651

B8225 U. S. TREASURY DEPT.
(Circular.) Treasury Department, August 27th, 1792. Sir, It would be of use in regard to the return of exports . . . if the expected articles were . . . in alphabetic order . . . [Philadelphia, 1792]
[2] p. 16.5 X 19 cm.
New York Public 1058
NN mp. 46652

B8226 U. S. TREASURY DEPT.
(Circular.) Treasury Department, August 31st, 1792. Sir, Agreeably to an order of the Senate . . . [Philadelphia, 1792]
[2] p. 23.5 X 19 cm.
MWA mp. 46653

B8227 U. S. TREASURY DEPT.
(Circular.) Treasury Department, October 12, 1792. Sir, I request that . . . at the close of every quarter . . . [Philadelphia, 1792]
broadside 23.5 X 19 cm.
MWA mp. 46654

B8228 U. S. TREASURY DEPT.
Treasury Department, February 6, 1792. (Circular.) Sir, It is my wish that you transmit to this office a return of the public property . . . [Philadelphia, 1792]
broadside 23.5 X 20 cm.
MWA mp. 46649

B8229 U. S. TREASURY DEPT.
Treasury Department, September 15th, 1792. Sir, A letter directed to William Gardner, Commissioner of Loans for New-Hampshire . . . [Philadelphia, 1792]
broadside 23 X 19 cm.
MWA mp. 46655

B8230 UNIVERSAL TONTINE
Philadelphia, 1792, Received of one dollar, as a deposit on one share in the Universal Tontine . . . [Philadelphia, 1792]
broadside 40 X 23.5 cm.
PHi (4 copies)

B8231 VERMONT. GOVERNOR, 1790-1797
[Fast day proclamation. Bennington, A. Haswell, 1792]
broadside?
Printer's bill for 200 copies dated May 15, 1792
McCorison 240
No copy known mp. 46656

B8232 VERMONT. GOVERNOR, 1790-1797
[Thanksgiving day proclamation. Bennington, A. Haswell, 1792]
broadside?
Printer's bill for 200 copies dated Oct. 20, 1792

McCorison 241
No copy known mp. 46657

B8233 VERMONT. TREASURER
State of Vermont To first constable in the county of Greeting. Whereas the Legislature . . . Rutland this day of 1792. Treasurer. [Rutland? 1792]
broadside fol.
Cooley 189
No copy located

B8234 VERMONT almanack, for the year . . . 1793 . . . Vermont: Printed by Anthony Haswell, and sold at his offices in Bennington and Rutland [1792]
[24] p. 18 cm.
MWA mp. 46658

B8235 VIRGINIA. CITIZENS
To the honorable the Legislature of Virginia. The memorial of sundery merchants, traders, farmers, and other citizens of this Commonwealth, sheweth: That whereas the public voice has called for the establishment of a bank . . . your memorialists . . . entreat, that an act may pass . . . establishing an independent bank at the city of Richmond . . . [Richmond? 1792?]
broadside 37 X 24 cm.
MSaE mp. 46660

B8236 VIRGINIA. GOVERNOR, 1791-1794
By the Governor . . . a proclamation. Whereas the public interest demands . . . the 7th day of June, 1792. Henry Lee. [Richmond, A. Davis, 1792]
broadside 33.5 X 20.5 cm.
Sabin 100220
DLC mp. 46661

B8237 VIRGINIA. GOVERNOR, 1791-1794
Richmond, July 6, 1792. Gentlemen, I beg leave to transmit to you a copy of a letter of the 21st of January, 1790 . . . [Richmond, A. Davis, 1792]
broadside 20.5 X 17 cm.
Sabin 100221
DLC (2 copies) mp. 46662

B8238 VIRGINIA. LAWS
An act concerning the erection of the district of Kentucky into an independent state . . . Constitution of the United States. [Lexington, John Bradford, 1792]
broadside 26 X 21 cm.
On June 8, 1792, the Kentucky Senate "Ordered, That the public printer . . . strike eleven copies of the act of seperation [sic] of Virginia, and the Constitution of the United States."
McMurtrie: Kentucky 11
WHi mp. 46663

B8239 THE Virginia almanack, for the year . . . 1793 . . . By Robert Andrews . . . Richmond, John Dixon [1792]
[36] p. 14 cm.
Bear 90; Huntington 613
CSmH ([35] p.); MWA mp. 46378

B8240 THE Virginia Gazette, and Agricultural Repository. Dumfries, Charles Fierer and Thomas U. Fosdick [1792]

Brigham p. 1113
MWA (issues for June 14, July 12, Dec. 13). Photostat: DLC mp. 46664

B8241 VIRTUE and vice: or, the history of Charles Careful and Harry Heedless . . . Boston, Printed and sold by Samuel Hall, 1792.
61, [2] p. incl. covers. 10 cm.
MWA mp. 46665

B8242 WATSON, CHARLES C.
Charles C. Watson, Taylor and Habitmaker . . . March 28, 1792. [Philadelphia] Johnston and Justice [1792]
broadside 6.5 X 9 cm.
DLC mp. 46667

B8243 WATTS, ISAAC, 1674-1748
Divine songs, attempted in easy language . . . Boston, Printed and sold by Samuel Hall, 1792.
71, [3] p. front., illus. 16mo
[3] p. at end are advertisements for other children's books printed by Hall
MB mp. 46669

B8244 WATTS, ISAAC, 1674-1748
Hymns and spiritual songs . . . Boston: Printed and sold by John West Folsom, M,DCC,XCII.
276 p. 16 cm.
Bound with: Bible. O.T. Psalms. The Psalms of David. Boston, Folsom, 1792
NBuG

B8245 WATTS, ISAAC, 1674-1748
Hymns and spiritual songs . . . A new edition . . . New-York, Printed by Hodge & Campbell, and sold at their respective book-stores, 1792.
286, [2] p. 15.5 cm.
New York Public 1060
MWA; NN mp. 46670

B8246 WATTS, ISAAC, 1674-1748
A wonderful dream . . . Middletown: Printed for and sold by Amos Bow, jun., 1792.
[16] p.
Trumbull: Second supplement 2894
CtY mp. 46671

B8247 WATTS, ISAAC, 1674-1748
A wonderful dream, or the flight of the soul . . . New-Haven, Abel Morse, MDCCXKII [sic] [1792]
11 p. 15.5 cm.
MWA; RPJCB mp. 46672

B8248 WEATHERWISE'S genuine almanack, for the year . . . 1793; calculated for the meridian of Portsmouth, N. H. . . . [Portsmouth] Printed for, and sold by the shopkeepers in the town and country [1792]
[24] p. 16 cm.
DLC mp. 46673

B8249 WEBSTER, NOAH, 1758-1843
The American spelling book . . . The eleventh Connecticut edition. Hartford, Hudson and Goodwin [1792?]
153 p. illus. 16 cm.
Skeel-Carpenter 26
CSt mp. 46674

B8250 WEBSTER'S calendar: or the Albany almanack, for . . . 1793 . . . By Eben W. Judd . . . Albany, Charles R. & George Webster [1792]
[24] p.

Second edition
Drake 6007; McMurtrie: Albany 82; Wall p. 28
MWA; N; NHi mp. 46476

B8251 WEEKLY MUSEUM, NEW YORK
Address to the generous subscribers of the *Weekly Museum.* Wishing them a Happy New-Year . . . New-York, January 2, 1792. [New York, 1792]
broadside
1st line: Once more your humble votary . . .
NHi mp. 46367

B8252 [WILKINSON, EDWARD] 1727?–1809
Wisdom, a poem . . . Litchfield, Collier and Buel, 1792.
20 p. 16 cm.
CtHi; MWA mp. 46675

B8253 WINDSOR CAUSEY LOTTERY
Windsor Causey Lottery. Granted by the Legislature . . . of Connecticut in May last, for . . . building a causey in Windsor . . . Scheme. 7000 tickets at 2 dollars . . . Windsor, June 30, 1792. [Hartford? 1792]
broadside 35 X 21 cm.
CtHi mp. 46676

B8254 . . . WOODS'S Town and country almanac, for . . . 1793. New York, Durell [1792]
[36] p. 18 cm.
By John Nathan Hutchins
cf. Evans 25058
MWA mp. 46471

B8255 YOUNG, WILLIAM, of Philadelphia
Brown's Dictionary of the Bible. Proposals, by William Young . . . for printing by subscription, a Dictionary of the Holy Bible . . . [Philadelphia, W. Young, 1792]
broadside 22.5 X 14 cm.
RPJCB mp. 46678

1793

B8256 ALBANY, N. Y. LIBRARY
A catalogue of the books belonging to the Albany Library: with . . . the bye-laws of the corporation . . . Albany, Barber and Southwick, 1793.
38 p. 17.5 cm.
McMurtrie: Albany 80
N mp. 46680

B8257 ALEXANDRIA, September 3d, 1793. To the honorable the speakers and gentlemen of the two houses of the General assembly . . . of Virginia . . . [Alexandria? 1793]
2 leaves. 37.5 cm.
Printed on recto on leaf 1 only
Vi mp. 46681

B8258 ALL able bodied seamen who are willing to engage in the cause of Liberty, and in the service of the French Republic, will please to apply to the French Consul . . . Philadelphia, August, 1793.
broadside 27 X 23 cm.
DLC

B8259 ALLEN, IRA, 1751-1814
General Allen's address. To the Hon. the Legislature of the State of Vermont, convened in Windsor . . . Windsor, October 30th, 1793. [Windsor? A. Spooner? 1793]
broadside 24.5 X 19.5 cm.
McCorison 246
VtU-W mp. 46682

B8260 AN almanack, and register, for the State of Vermont: for . . . 1794 . . . Walpole, Newhampshire, I. Thomas and D. Carlisle, jun. for the author [1793]
[14], 32, [4] p.
Drake 4668; Nichols, p. 91
DLC; MB; MHi; MWA; MiD-B. Brit. Mus. mp. 46683

B8261 AMBITIOUS of cementing, the many respectable connections, the House of Jacques & Theodore Rocheteau & Co., of Surinam, has on this continent . . . [n.p., 1793?]
broadside
Dated from ms. note at end: Jh.[?] d'Happart Baltimore 12th. Sept. 1793
PHi

B8262 AMERICAN MERCURY, HARTFORD, CONN.
Addressed by the boy who carries the *American Mercury*, to the subscribers. Hartford, January 1, 1793. [Hartford, Elisha Babcock, 1793]
broadside 44 X 26 cm.
By Richard Alsop
1st lines: In ancient days, in England's court . . .
NHi mp. 46684

B8263 AMERICAN ticket, patriotic Americans, and honest foreigners. No Genet–No Emmet–No Clinton . . . No governed Governor . . . Republicanism and our country for ever . . . [New York? 1793?]
broadside 28.5 X 20.5 cm.
NHi mp. 46685

B8264 AN answer to the Rev. Joseph Lathrop . . . In his two discourses on Matthew vii. 15, 16 . . . By Z. P. . . . Windham, John Byrne, 1793.
12 p.
By Zaphnath Paaneah?
Trumbull: Supplement 2817
CtHi mp. 46686

B8265 ARTILLERY COMPANY OF NEWPORT
The charter and regulations of the artillery company of the town of Newport . . . Warren, Nathaniel Phillips, 1793.
19 p. 15.5 cm.
Alden 1316
DLC; RNHi mp. 46838

B8266 ASPLUND, JOHN, d. 1807
[New collection . . . Baltimore, 1793]

Title from Metcalf: *American psalmody*, p. 11
Probably collection of sacred music
Minick 101
No copy known mp. 46687

B8267 BÄRTGIS'S General Staatsbothe mit den Neusten . . . Nachrichten an die Deutsche Nation in Amerika. Frederick, Md., Jan. 5-Dec. 21, 1793.

BSA *Papers* 55 (1961): 133-137
William Bartgis Storm, Frederick, Md. (1961)

B8268 A BAG of nuts, ready cracked . . . By the celebrated and facetious Thomas Thumb, Esq. . . . Philadelphia, W. Young, 1793.
52+ p. 10 cm.
d'Alté A. Welch, Cleveland (all wanting after p. 52)
mp. 46688

B8269 BANK OF PENNSYLVANIA
Bank of Pennsylvania. The following resolutions of the Board of Directors . . . Edward Fox, cashier. June 29, 1793. [Philadelphia, 1793]

broadside 43 X 33 cm.
MB mp. 46689

B8270 BANKS, GERALD
The right of suffrage: addressed to the friends of liberty . . . [Fredericksburg? 1793]

Title from the *Virginia Herald*, Mar. 21, 1793, as "Just published and for sale."
No copy known mp. 46690

B8271 BANNEKER'S almanack . . . for the year . . . 1794 . . . Philadelphia, Joseph Crukshank [1793]
[48] p. 19 cm.
Porter 31
MHi; MWA; NjP mp. 46691

B8272 BAPTISTS. SOUTH CAROLINA. CHARLESTON ASSOCIATION
Rules of the General Committee, for Forming . . . a Fund amongst the Baptist churches united in the Charleston Association, South-Carolina. Finally ratified the 7th November, 1792. Charleston, Markland & M'Iver, 1793.
14 p. 15.5 cm.
LNB; ScGF (lacking after p. 9)

B8273 [BARBAULD, ANNA LETITIA (AIKIN)] 1743-1825
Lessons for children, from two to four years old. Part I. Portland, Thomas B. Wait, 1793.
95 p. 9.5 cm.
PP mp. 46693

B8274 [BARBAULD, ANNA LETITIA (AIKIN)] 1743-1825
Lessons for children from four to five years old. Part III. Portland, Thomas B. Wait, 1793.
107 p. 9 cm.
PP mp. 46694

B8275 [BARBAULD, ANNA LETITIA (AIKIN)] 1743-1825
Lessons for children of four years old. Part II. Portland, Thomas B. Wait, 1793.
96 p. 9 cm.
PP mp. 46695

B8276 BARTON, BENJAMIN SMITH, 1766-1815
An inquiry into the question, Whether the apis mellifica . . . is a native of America . . . [Philadelphia, Robert Aitken, 1793]
21 p.
Offprint from Amer. Phil. Soc. *Transactions*, vol. III, with new pagination
PPL

B8277 BERKSHIRE REPUBLICAN LIBRARY
The property of the Berkshire Republican Library . . . [Stockbridge, 1793]
broadside 15 X 10 cm.
Bookplate with regulations for loan of books to shareholders; dated: Stockbridge, June 1, 1793
New York Public 1062
NN (photostat)

B8278 BERQUIN, ARNAUD, 1749-1791
The children's friend . . . Newburyport, Printed by J. Mycall, for Benjamin Larkin, Cornhill, Boston [1793?]
341, iii p. 16.5 cm.
Vol. I only
MH mp. 46696

B8279 BEVERIDGE, WILLIAM, 1637-1708
Resolutions on the most interesting and important subjects . . . Philadelphia, Printed for and sold by Henry Willis, 1793.
144 p. 13.5 cm.
MB; MWA mp. 46697

B8280 BIBLE
An abridgement of the history of the Holy Bible . . . Hudson, Ashbel Stoddard, 1793.
16 leaves. 16 mo. A^4B^{12}
Rosenbach-Ch 164
A. S. W. Rosenbach (1933) mp. 46698

B8281 BIBLE. O.T. PSALMS
Psalms carefully suited . . . Wilmington, Brynberg and Andrews, 1793.
315 p. 13.5 cm.
MWA mp. 46699

B8282 BIBLE. O.T. PSALMS
The Psalms of David, imitated . . . Boston, From the press of J. Bumstead, for James White and E. Larkin, 1793.
574 p. 13.5 cm.
MWA mp. 46937

B8283 BIBLE. O.T. PSALMS
The Psalms of David, imitated . . . Norwich, Printed by Bushnell and Hubbard, for B. Larkin [1793]
309, [11], 246, [8] p. 14 cm.
MWA; NN mp. 46938

B8284 BIBLE. O.T. PSALMS
The Psalter: or, Psalms of David . . . Boston, Peter Edes, 1793.
204 p.
MWA mp. 46700

B8285 BICKERSTAFF'S genuine New-England almanack for . . . 1794 . . . Springfield, Edward Gray [1793]
[24] p.
Drake 3509
MS

B8286 THE Book of Knowledge . . . By Abraham Weatherwise, Esq. London, Printed: New-York, Reprinted, in the year 1793.
34 p. 13 cm.
MWA mp. 46939

B8287 THE Book of Knowledge . . . Written by Erra Pater . . . Made English by W. Lilly . . . Exeter, Printed and sold by Henry Ranlet, 1793.
82 p. 15 cm.
MWA (lacks front.); N (not traced 1967) mp. 46745

B8288 THE Book of Knowledge . . . Written by Erra Pater . . . Made English by W. Lilly . . . New-London: Printed by Samuel Green, for James Harrison [sic], New-York, M,DCC,XCIII.
120 p. 13 cm.
CtHi

B8289 THE Book of Knowledge . . . Written by Erra Pater . . . Made English by W. Lilly . . . Philadelphia, 1793.
[4], 144, [6] p. 13 cm.
Rogers 367
MH mp. 46746

B8290 BOSTON. CITIZENS
At a very full and respectable meeting of the merchants

and others . . . residing in Boston, and convened at Faneuil Hall . . . July 22, 1793 . . . [Boston, 1793]
broadside 23 X 18 cm.
RPJCB mp. 46701

B8291 BRADMAN, ARTHUR
A narrative of the extraordinary sufferings of Mr. Robert Forbes, his wife and five children . . . in the year 1784 . . . Taken partly from their own mouths . . . and published at their request. By Arthur Bradman. Windsor, Printed and sold by Alden Spooner, 1793.
15 p. 16mo
Ever published?
cf. McCorison 222n; Vail: Old frontier 931
No copy known mp. 46702

B8292 BROADDUS, ANDREW, 1770-1848
The doctrine of justification . . . Fredericksburg, T. Green, 1793.
24 p. 18.5 cm.
MAnP; MWA mp. 46703

B8293 BUNYAN, JOHN, 1628-1688
Grace abounding to the chief of sinners . . . Exeter, J. Lamson, and T. Odiorne, 1793.
[2], iv, 106 p. 16 cm.
MWA; RPJCB mp. 46704

B8294 BUNYAN, JOHN, 1628-1688
The riches of Christ, and glorious treasure of heavenly jobs . . . Danbury, Re-printed by E. Ely, for James Crawford, 1793.
8 p. 23 cm.
MWA mp. 46705

B8295 BUNYAN, JOHN, 1628-1688
The visions of John Bunyan . . . giving an account of the glories of Heaven . . . New York, Printed by John Harrisson for Benjamin Gomez, 1793.
144 p. 13.5 cm.
Hamilton 147
MWA; N; NjP mp. 46706

B8296 BURLINGTON, N. J.
At a meeting of the Corporation of the City of Burlington, August 30th, 1793, the following recommendations . . . Whereas there is a great reason for caution against the malignant fever . . . in Philadelphia . . . [Burlington? 1793]
broadside 33.5 cm.
NNNAM mp. 46707

B8297 BURROUGHS, EDEN, 1738-1813
A faithful narrative of the wonderful dealings of God, towards Polly Davis . . . Printed at Norwich (Connecticut) by J. Trumbull, 1793.
1 p.l., 2-12 p. 19 cm.
NHi; NhD mp. 46700

B8298 CAREY, JOHN, 1756-1826
To be published by subscription, The American Remembrancer, or, Proceedings of the Old Congress . . . to March 1789 . . . Subscriptions will be received . . . by the editor, John Carey. No. 26, Pear-Street, Philadelphia. [Philadelphia, 1793]
broadside 19 X 15.5 cm.
"As soon as 500 Cpoies are subscribed for, the work will be put to press."
MHi mp. 46708

B8299 CAREY, MATHEW, 1760-1839
Carey's [ ] A n[ew] sys[tem of] modern ge[ography,] or geographical, historical . . . By William G[uthrie] . . . [Philadelphia, M. Carey, 1793]
[4] p. 27.5 cm.
A catalog of Carey's offerings, with Guthrie's work given prominence
cf. Evans 25574
Photocopy: NjR (p. [1-2] defective)

B8300 CAREY, MATTHEW, 1760-1839
A desultory account of the yellow fever, prevalent in Philadelphia . . . [Philadelphia, M. Carey, 1793]
12 p. 12mo caption title
Austin 401; Rogers 350; Sabin 10865
MHi; PPC; PPL mp. 46709

B8301 CATHOLIC CHURCH
A short abridgement of Christian doctrine, newly revised for the use of the Catholic Church in the United States . . . The twelfth edition, with approbation. Georgetown, James Doyle, 1793.
22 l. 13 cm. ? B^8 C^6
Goff: Georgetown 10; Parsons 116
DGU (lacks t.p. and half-title [?]); MdBS (not traced 1958) mp. 46711

B8302 [CHALLONER, RICHARD] 1691-1781
The garden of the soul . . . Philadelphia, Mathew Carey, 1793.
357, [3] p. 13.5 cm. $[-]^4$ $B\text{-}X^{12,6}$ Y^2
DGU mp. 46712

B8303 THE Christian oeconomy . . . Litchfield, Collier and Buel [1793]
34 p.
Trumbull: Supplement 1980
No copy located mp. 46714

B8304 CISH, JANE
Die Endzückung und wunderbare Erfahrung der Johanna Cish . . . Reading, Jungmann und Gruber, 1793.
1 p.l., ii, 28 p.
CSmH; MWA; PPL mp. 46715

B8305 LES citoyens francois, habitans des Etats-unis . . . à leur patrie, à ses réprésentans. [New York? 1793?]
17 p. 22 cm.
New York Public 1063
NN mp. 46716

B8306 CLAY, ELEAZAR, d. 1836
Hymns and spiritual songs selected from several approved authors . . . Richmond, John Dixon, 1793.
265 p. 11.5 cm.
Davis 86
NN (microfilm); ViRU mp. 46717

B8307 CLENDININ, JOHN
The practical surveyor's assistant. Calculated by John Clendinin. Philadelphia, Printed for the author, by Benjamin Johnson, 1793.
v [i.e. iv], 20, 10 p. 12.5 cm.
New York Public 1064
DGU; MWA; NN; RPJCB mp. 46718

B8308 CONNECTICUT COURANT
The address of the carrier of the *Connecticut Courant,* to his customers. Hartford, January 1, 1793 . . . [Hartford, 1793]

broadside 35 X 20.5 cm.
CtHi mp. 46679

B8309 COWPER, WILLIAM, 1731-1800
The diverting history of John Gilpin . . . Printed at Osborne's Press, Market-Square, Newburyport, 1793.
12 p. 15 cm.
cf. Evans 25354
OClWHi mp. 46719

B8310 [CRISP, STEPHEN] 1628-1692
A short history of a long travel from Babylon to Bethel . . . Bennington, Printed by Anthony Haswell, for Thomas Spencer, and sold at his book store, Albany, 1793.
35 p. 13 cm.
Cooley 208
MWA mp. 46720

B8311 A CURIOUS piece of antiquity of the crucifixion of our Saviour and the two thieves. [Philadelphia] Samuel Sower [1793?]
broadside 38 X 30.5 cm.
In verse
PHi mp. 46721

B8312 DAYS drawing, arrived from Washington, Enquire No. 192, Water Street. Examining tickets will be 6d. per number . . . When the heavy expence of postage is considered . . . the above will not be thought unreasonable . . . if it is, Cole and Goodluck must . . . retire to Washington . . . [New York] Printed by Louis Jones, No. 24, Smith Street [1793]
broadside 22.5 X 19.5 cm.
Jones at this address in 1793 only
NHi mp. 46722

B8313 [DEFOE, DANIEL] 1661?-1731
The most surprising adventures, and wonderful life of Robinson Crusoe . . . Newburyport, Osborne's Office, 1793.
118 p. 14 cm.
Brigham: Robinson Crusoe 24; New York Public 1065
MSaE; MWA (imperfect); NN mp. 46724

B8314 DELAWARE. HOUSE OF REPRESENTATIVES
Journal of the House of representatives . . . at a session commenced . . . the first day of January . . . Wilmington, Adams's Press, 1793.
82 p. 27.5 cm.
Covers session Jan. 1-Feb. 2, 1793
Hawkins 38
De; DeHi mp. 46725

B8315 DELAWARE. HOUSE OF REPRESENTATIVES
Journal of the House of representatives . . . at a session commenced . . . the twenty-seventh day of May . . . Wilmington, Samuel and John Adams, 1793.
55 p. 27.5 cm.
Covers session May 27-June 19, 1793
Hawkins 39
De; DeHi mp. 46726

B8316 DELAWARE. SENATE
Journal of the Senate . . . at a session commenced . . . the first day of January . . . Wilmington, Adams's Press, 1793.
41 p. 27.5 cm.
Covers session Jan. 1-Feb. 2, 1793
Hawkins 40
DLC; De; DeHi mp. 46727

B8317 DELAWARE. SENATE
Journal of the Senate . . . at a session . . . commenced . . . the twenty-seventh day of May . . . Wilmington, Samuel and John Adams, 1793.
40 p. 27.5 cm.
Covers session May 27-June 19, 1793
Hawkins 41
DLC; De; DeHi mp. 46728

B8318 DEMOCRATIC SOCIETY OF KENTUCKY
Fellow-citizens. The Democratic society of Kentucky have directed us . . . December 31, 1793 . . . [Lexington, John Bradford, 1793]
broadside 34 X 20 cm.
McMurtrie: Kentucky 25
DLC mp. 46729

B8319 DEMOCRATIC SOCIETY OF KENTUCKY
To the inhabitants of the United States west of the Allegany . . . December 13, 1793. [Lexington, John Bradford, 1793]
broadside 39.5 X 31.5 cm.
McMurtrie: Kentucky 26
DLC mp. 46730

B8320 DEMOCRATIC SOCIETY OF KENTUCKY
To the President and Congress . . . The remonstrance of the citizens west of the Allegany Mountains . . . [Lexington, John Bradford, 1793]
broadside 55.5 X 22 cn,
McMurtrie: Kentucky 27
DLC mp. 46731

B8321 A DIALOGUE between death and a lady . . . Exeter, Printed and sold at H. Ranlet's Office, 1793.
8 p. 17.5 cm.
MWA mp. 46732

B8322 DILWORTH, THOMAS, d. 1780
The Schoolmaster's assistant . . . The latest edition. New York, Printed and sold by John Buel, 1793.
114 [i.e. 214] p. plate
Karpinski p. 75
MiU-C; NHi mp. 46733

B8323 DILWORTH, W H
The complete letter writer, or young secretary's instructor . . . New-York, Benjamin Gomez, 1793.
120 p.
Brit. Mus. mp. 46734

B8324 DOD, JOHN, 1549?-1645
Moral reflections, or flowers selected from the garden of Mr. Dodd . . . Exeter, Printed by J. Lamson, and T. Odiorne, and sold at their book store, 1793.
31 p., 1 leaf. 13.5 cm. [A]-C^6 (Al, C6 blank)
MWA mp. 46735

B8325 DODDRIDGE, PHILIP, 1702-1751
Sermons to young persons . . . The sixth edition. Philadelphia, William Young, 1793.
viii, [13]-196 p. 15 cm.
CL; DLC; MWA; Nc; NjP; OCl; PP; PPL; PPLT; PSt; RNHi; Sc mp. 46736

B8326 DODSLEY, ROBERT, 1703-1764
The toy-shop . . . Exeter, Henry Ranlet, 1793.
46 p. 15 cm.
DLC; MWA mp. 46737

B8327 A DREAM dreamed by one in the year 1757, concerning Philadelphia, and repeated again, in the same manner, about eleven years after, by the same person. Germantown, Peter Leibert [1793]
broadside
Docketed on back: "Publish'd 10Mo:1793"
PPL mp. 46738

B8328 DER durch Europa und America aufmerksame Reisende, in Abischt zu suchen wahre Kinder Gottes . . . zum drittenmale gedruckt . . . Reading [Barton & Jungmann] 1793.

Nolan p. 25
C. W. Unger, Pottsville, Pa. (1930) mp. 46739

B8329 AN easy method of working by the plain and sliding rules . . . Lansingburgh, Silvester Tiffany, and sold at Spencer's book-store, Albany, 1793.
24 p. fold. table
RPJCB mp. 46740

B8330 EDWARDS, JONATHAN, 1703-1758
President Edward's Whole Works. Proposals for printing by subscription, The whole works of the late . . . President Edwards . . . [New York? 1793?]
broadside 45 X 28 cm.
1794 is given as the deadline for accepting proposals
NHi mp. 46741

B8331 ELLICOTT'S New-Jersey, Pennsylvania, Delaware, Maryland and Virginia almanac . . . for the year . . . 1793 . . . Baltimore, Samuel and John Adams [1793?]
[36] p. 18 cm.
"Preface" dated: Printing-Office, Baltimore, September 5, 1793. Misprint for 1792? cf. Evans 24295
MdBP mp. 46742

B8332 ELLIOTT, SIR JOHN, 1736-1786
A medical pocket-book . . . The third edition, with additions and corrections. New-York, T. Allen, 1793.
[6], 169, [4] p. 14.5 cm.
CtY-M; MBCo; MWA; PPC mp. 46743

B8333 [ELY, JOHN] 1758-1847
The child's instructor . . . By a teacher of little children in Philadelphia. Volume I. The second edition . . . Philadelphia, John M'Culloch, 1793.
108 p. 17 cm. A^8 B-H^6 I^4
No more published?
New York Public 1066; Rosenbach-Ch 168
NN. A. S. W. Rosenbach (1933) mp. 46744

B8333a AN examination of the late proceedings in Congress, respecting the official conduct of the secretary of the treasury. Printed within the United States, 1793.
28 p. 8vo
Attributed to John Taylor, 1750-1824
Dated on p. [3]: 20th October, 1793
NN

B8334 EXTRACTS from the records of antiquity. Windsor, Alden Spooner, 1793.
13 p. 19 cm.
MWA mp. 46747

B8335 FAIRFAX, FERDINANDO, 1766-1820
Ten dollars. The above reward will be given to any one who . . . shall give . . . information of the person . . . who lately set fire to that part of the Blue Ridge which was the property of the late George William Fairfax . . . Ferdinando Fairfax . . . [May 4th] 1793. Winchester, Richard Bowen [1793]
broadside 19.5 X 16 cm.
ViU mp. 46748

B8336 THE famous history of Doctor John Faustus . . . Exeter, 1793.
40 p. 19 cm.
DLC mp. 46749

B8337 FESSENDEN, THOMAS, 1739-1813
A discourse, occasioned by the death, and delivered at the interment of, the Rev. Bulkley Olcott . . . Springfield, James Reed Hutchins, 1793.
15 p. 18 cm.
New York Public 1067
MWA; NN (p. 11-14 wanting) mp. 46750

B8338 FOOTE, EBENEZER
Fellow Citizens of Ulster County. Once more I address you on the subject matter of dispute between Mr. Tappen and myself . . . Ebenezer Foote. Marlborough, March 26, 1793. Kingston, Power & Copp [1793]
broadside 40.5 X 34 cm.
NHi mp. 46751

B8339 A FORM of prayer to be used at St. Philip's and St. Michael's, Charleston. On Wednesday the 23d day of October . . . a general fast . . . Charleston, Timothy and Mason, 1793.
8 p. 18.5 cm.
New York Public 1068
NN mp. 46713

B8340 THE fortune-teller . . . By the renowned Dr. Hurlo Thrumbo . . . Philadelphia, Francis Bailey, 1793.
63 p. illus. 10.5 cm. A-B^{16}
PP mp. 46752

B8341 THE forty-fifth aerial flight of the universally celebrated Mr. Blanchard, at Philadelphia . . . [Philadelphia? 1793?]
7 p. 17 cm.
The flight took place Jan. 9, 1793
Huntington 634
CSmH mp. 46753

B8342 FOUR excellent modern songs. Jocking to the fair . . . Roslin Castle . . . Guardian angels . . . Force of musick . . . [n.p., 1793?]
broadside 28.5 X 26 cm.
In 3 columns with lines of type ornaments between
Ms. note: Kingston February 12 day year 1793. These a B D
Ford 3113
MSaE mp. 46754

B8343 FREEMASONS. VIRGINIA. GRAND LODGE
Proceedings of the Grand lodge of Virginia, held . . . the twenty-eighth day of October, A.L. 5793. Richmond, John Dixon [1793]
13 p. 21 cm.
Davis 87
DSC mp. 46755

B8344 FRIENDS, SOCIETY OF. PHILADELPHIA YEARLY MEETING
Philadelphia, 6th of 12th mo. 1793. A Committee of Friends this day attended . . . the legislature of this state, with the following address and petition . . . Signed . . . on behalf of a meeting appointed to represent our religious society . . . by John Drinker, Clerk. [Philadelphia, 1793]
broadsheet ([2] p.) 27 X 20 cm.
PHi mp. 46756

B8345 FROST, SAMUEL, 1765–1793
The confession and dying words of Samuel Frost, who was executed at Worcester, the 31st day of October, 1793, for . . . murder . . . Keene, Printed and sold by Henry Blake & Co. [1793]
broadside 44.5 X 27.5 cm.
MWA mp. 46757

B8346 [GENÊT, EDMOND CHARLES] 1763-1834
Les français libres à leurs freres les canadiens. [Philadelphia, 1793]
8 p. 17 cm. caption title
DLC (8 copies); PPL; RPJCB mp. 46758

B8347 [GENÊT, EDMOND CHARLES] 1763–1834
Liberte Egalite Les français libres à leurs freres de la Louisiane. [Philadelphia, 1793]
8 p. 17 cm. caption title
PPL; RPJCB mp. 46759

B8348 GENÊT, EDMOND CHARLES, 1793–1834
Proclamation. Liberté Egalité. Au nom de la République Française nous Edmond-Charles Genêt . . . New-York, ce 28 août 1793 . . . A l'Imprimerie de Louis Jones, No. 24, Rue de Smith [1793]
broadside 39 X 32 cm.
Advertising the arrival of the vessel Jupiter in New York
NHi mp. 46760

B8349 GIORANDI, GIUSEPPE, 1744–1798
A concerto for the piano forte . . . Op: XIV . . . Philadelphia, Printed for I. C. Moller [1793–94]
p. [29]–35. 34 cm.
Sonneck-Upton p. 86
DLC; NN

B8350 GODINEAU,
Oration upon religious worship, delivered by Citizen Godineau . . . on the 20th of November, 1793. [Colophon] Philadelphia [1793]
8 p. 20 cm. caption title
Sowerby 2679
DLC; PHi (2 copies); PPL mp. 46762

B8351 GRANYE, an excellent patriotic Irish song. Lord Conway's contest in in [sic] the British Parliament against the American war . . . Boston, Printed for and sold by Richard Lee, 1793.
broadside 38 X 19.5 cm.
MWA (imperfect) mp. 46765

B8352 [GREEN, JACOB] 1722–1790
A vision of Hell . . . By Theodorus Van Shermain . . . Springfield [Mass.], E. Gray, 1793.
23 p. 18 cm.
MWA mp. 46766

B8353 GREENWOOD, ISAAC
Sublime entertainment. This evening will commence at the Court-House, a brilliant electrical exhibition . . . Providence, February 1793. [Providence, 1793]
broadside 32.5 X 19.5 cm.
RPJCB mp. 46767

B8354 GREGORY, JOHN, 1724–1773
A father's legacy to his daughters . . . A new edition. New-York, T. Allen, 1793.
viii, [2], 68, [4] p. 15 cm. A-G^6 (Al blank)
MWA mp. 46768

B8355 GROS,
Recit historique sur les evenemens . . . dans les camps . . . depuis le 26 octobre 1791 jusqu'au 24 decembre . . . Par m. Gros . . . Baltimore, S. et J. Adams, 1793.
83, [1] p. 18.5 cm.
Minick 119
MdHi mp. 46769

B8356 HACKER, ISAAC
A catalogue of books sold by James Phillips, George Yard, Lombard Street, London: and sold also by Isaac Hacker, Salem: of whom may be had Bibles, Testaments, and stationary wares in general. [Salem] 1793.
16 p.
Tapley p. 354
MSaE mp. 46770

B8357 HARBAUGH, LEONARD
[Publication against Christopher Hughes. Baltimore, W. Goddard and J. Angell, 1793?]

An indictment against Goddard and Angell was mentioned in the *Maryland Journal*, Mar. 21, 1794, "as the printers of a publication of Leonard Harbaugh against Christopher Hughes."
Minick 120
No copy known mp. 46771

B8358 HARVARD UNIVERSITY
Extracts from the laws of Harvard College . . . Cambridge, August 13, 1793. [Boston? 1793?]
[3] p.
MWA mp. 46772

B8359 [HASWELL, ANTHONY] 1756–1816
Hymn of Masonry, presented to Temple Lodge, by a brother, to be sung at the installation of their officers . . . Bennington, July 29, 1793. [Bennington, A. Haswell]
broadside 23 X 10 cm.
By Anthony Haswell?
MWA mp. 46773

B8360 [HASWELL, ANTHONY] 1756–1816
Masonry universal . . . [Bennington] A. Haswell, print. [1793]
broadside 15 X 8 cm.
cf. Spargo: *A. Haswell*, p. 186, 292
On greenish-blue paper
MWA mp. 46774

B8361 [HASWELL, ANTHONY] 1756–1816
Ode sacred to Masonry . . . [Bennington, A. Haswell, 1793]
broadside 14.5 X 7 cm.
cf. Spargo: *A. Haswell*, p. 293
On greenish-blue paper
MWA mp. 46775

B8362 HEIDELBERG CATECHISM
Catechismus, oder kurzer Unterricht . . . Germantaun, Gedruckt und zu finden bey Michael Billmeyer, 1793.
94 p., 1 leaf, [95]–118 p. 17 cm. A-E^{12}
MWA; PPL mp. 46776

B8363 [HELMUTH, JUSTUS HEINRICH CHRISTIAN] 1745–1825
Nachempfindungen bey dem Grabe . . . Johann Hermann Winkhauses . . . den 7ten October, 1793, begraben . . . [Philadelphia, 1793]
4 p. 12mo caption title
PPL mp. 46777

B8364 HIBERNIAN SOCIETY, PHILADELPHIA
The incorporation, bye-laws, &c. of the Hibernian Society for the relief of emigrants from Ireland. Philadelphia, Daniel Humphreys, 1793.

15, [1] p. 18.5 cm.
PHi; PU mp. 46778

B8365 HIRTE, TOBIAS
Dr. Van Swieten's, late physician to his Imperial Majesty, renowned pills . . . [Philadelphia, 1793]
broadside
Advertised for sale by Tobias Hirte
PPL mp. 46779

B8366 HIRTE, TOBIAS
Hochberühmte und bewährte Familien-Pillen. [Philadelphia, 1793?]
broadside
Mrs. Marion Carson (1960) mp. 46780

B8367 HIRTE, TOBIAS
Verzeichnis der Matärien des neuen, auserlesenen, gemeinnützigen Handbüchleins welches soeben zum Druck befördert wurde. [Philadelphia, 1793?]
broadside
cf. Evans 24396
Mrs. Marion Carson (1960) mp. 46781

B8368 THE history of Amelia . . . Boston, Printed and sold by N. Coverly, 1793.
32 p. illus. 10.5 cm.
CtHi; MWA (covers wanting, and all after p. 26)
mp. 46782

B8369 THE history of Little Dick. Written by Little John. Philadelphia, Francis Bailey, 1793.
60, [2] p. illus. 10 cm.
Welch 712.1
d'Alté A. Welch, Cleveland (1963) mp. 46783

B8370 THE history of little Goody Two-Shoes . . . Philadelphia, W. Young, 1793.
136 p. illus. 10.5 cm.
MWA (p. 95–96 wanting). Mrs. Edgar S. Oppenheimer, New York City (1962) mp. 46763

B8371 THE history of little Goody Two-Shoes . . . Wilmington, Brynberg and Andrews, 1793.
127 p. illus. 10 cm.
DeWI mp. 46764

B8372 THE history of the Holy Jesus . . . By a Lover of their precious souls. New York, John Bull for Wm. Durell [1793?]
31 p. 11 illus. 9.5 cm.
Rosenbach-Ch 193
PP. Emerson Greenaway, Philadelphia (p. [31] wanting); d'Alté A. Welch, Cleveland (p. [2]-6, 29–[31] wanting)
mp. 46784

B8373 HOUGH, SIMON
A true gospel church organized and disciplined . . . Stockbridge, Printed [by Loring Andrews] for the author, MDCCCXCIII [i.e. 1793]
15 p. 20.5 cm.
"On hirelings and priest craft" (poem): p. 14–15
MWA mp. 46785

B8374 AN hour's amusement . . . Printed at Hudson (New-York) by Ashbel Stoddard, and sold wholesale and retail, at his Printing-Office, 1793.
23 p. illus. 8 cm.
CtHi mp. 46786

B8375 HUNTER, GEORGE, AND CO.
Catalogue of books, to be sold by George Hunter, and Co. at their store in Queen-Street, on Monday afternoon, the twenty-seventh day of May, instant . . . [New York, 1793]
broadside 32.5 X 27 cm.
MWA; NIIi mp. 46788

B8376 HUTCHIN'S New-York alamanack for . . . 1794 . . . By Andrew Beers . . . [New York? 1793]
[24] p.
Drake 6017
Ct

B8377 [JOHNSON, RICHARD] 1734–1793
The hermit of the forest . . . A rural fragment . . . New-York, William Durell, 1793.
29, [1] p. illus. 10 cm.
MiD (front cover wanting). Ruth Adomeit, Cleveland (p. 29–[30] wanting) mp. 46789

B8378 [JOHNSON, RICHARD] 1734–1793
The hermit of the forest, and the wandering infants, a rural fragment . . . Philadelphia, Benjamin Johnson, 1793.
31, [1] p. 10 cm.
MWA. d'Alté A. Welch mp. 46790

B8379 [JOHNSON, RICHARD] 1734–1793
The history of Tommy Careless . . . Wew-York [sic]: Printed and sold by William Durell [1793?]
31 p. illus. 10 cm.
Page 29 misprinted 23
Dated by d'Alté A. Welch
For authorship cf. Weedon
CtHi mp. 46791

B8380 [JOHNSON, RICHARD] 1734–1793
Rural felicity or, the history of Tommy and Sally . . . Philadelphia, Francis Bailey, 1793.
31 p. 9 cm.
Facsim. of t.p. and front. in *American clipper* [American Autograph Shop] v.9 (September 1939), no. 4, item 109
No copy located mp. 46792

B8381 KENDALL, JAMES, 1769–1859
Some principles and precepts of the Christian religion explained . . . The first Salem edition. Salem: Printed by T. C. Cushing; and sold by W. Carlton, at the Bible and Heart.—1793.
35; [1] p. 13.5 cm.
Not used for microprint ed. of Evans 28923
MWA mp. 46793

B8382 [KENRICK, WILLIAM] 1725?–1779
The whole duty of woman . . . By a lady. The ninth edition. Newburyport: Printed and sold by Blunt and Robinson, 1793.
47 p. 17 cm.
MB mp. 46796

B8383 [KENRICK, WILLIAM] 1725?–1779
The whole duty of woman . . . By a lady . . . The fourteenth edition. Concord, George Hough, 1793.
35 p. 16 cm.
MWA mp. 46794

B8384 [KENRICK, WILLIAM] 1725–1779
The whole duty of a woman . . . By a lady . . . Fourteenth edition. Danbury, Printed and sold by N. Douglas, 1793.
33 p. 17.5 cm.
CtHi mp. 46795

B8385 KENTUCKY. GENERAL ASSEMBLY. HOUSE OF REPRESENTATIVES
Journal of the House of Representatives, at the first session of the second General Assembly . . . held, at . . . Frankfort . . . [Nov. 4, 1793] . . . Lexington, John Bradford [1793?]
92 p. 31.5 cm.
Session adjourned Dec. 21, 1793
McMurtrie: Kentucky 28
ICU mp. 46797

B8386 KENTUCKY. GENERAL ASSEMBLY. SENATE
Journal of the Senate, at the third session of the General Assembly . . . held, at . . . Frankfort . . . [Nov. 4, 1793] . . . Lexington, John Bradford [1793?]
14 p. 32 cm.
Incomplete: acc. to a ms. note on p. 14, smallpox prevented printing the remainder
McMurtrie: Kentucky 29
ICU mp. 46798

B8387 KENTUCKY. LAWS
Acts passed at the first session of the second General assembly . . . begun . . . the fourth of November . . . Lexington, John Bradford [1793]
56 p. 30.5 cm.
McMurtrie: Kentucky 30
DLC; ICU; KyU; MH-L; NNB mp. 46799

B8388 LADD, JOSEPH BROWN, 1764–1786
[An essay on primitive, latent, and regenerated light. Newport? 1793]

Entered for copyright Dec. 23, 1793, by Ladd. Advertised in the *Newport Mercury* Jan. 7, 1794
Alden 1314; cf. Evans 19746
No copy known mp. 46800

B8389 LADD, JOSEPH BROWN, 1764–1786
[The poems of Arouet. Newport? 1793]

Entered for copyright by Ladd Dec. 23, 1793
Alden 1315; cf. Evans 19747
No copy known mp. 46801

B8390 LANCASTER, PA. CITIZENS
At a meeting of the inhabitants of the borough of Lancaster, held . . . Thursday, September 19th, 1793 . . . to take into consideration . . . the malignant fever . . . in . . . Philadelphia. Jasper Yeates, in the chair . . . [Philadelphia, 1793]
broadside 42.5 cm.
Text in English and German
NNNAM; PPC mp. 46802

B8391 LARKIN, EBENEZER
Ebenezer Larkin's Catalogue of books . . . Boston, Printed for Ebenezer Larkin, MDCCLXCIII [1793?]
60 p. 16 cm.
MiU-C; N (60 p. but no t.p.); NN (imperfect)
mp. 46803

B8392 LA ROCHEFOUCAULD, FRANÇOIS VI, DUC DE, 1613–1680
Maxims and moral reflections . . . A new edition, revised and improved. Boston, Printed by Isaac Larkin, for Ebenezer Larkin, 1793.
141 p., 1 l. 13 cm.
Publisher's advertisement, 1 leaf at end
New York Public 1070
MWA; N; NN mp. 46804

B8393 LAUGH and be fat; or, The wit's merry medley . . . New-York, Printed and sold by John Harrisson, 1793.
143 p. incl. front. 14 cm.
MWA mp. 46805

B8394 LAW, ANDREW, 1748–1821
The rudiments of music . . . Fourth edition . . . Cheshire, Printed and sold by William Law, 1793.
v, [1], 76 p. oblong 12 X 21 cm.
Trumbull: Second supplement 2857
Ct; CtHi; MWA; PPiPT mp. 46806

B8395 [LELAND, JOHN] 1754–1841
The history of Jack Nips . . . Printed in Massachusetts, 1793.
16 p. 19 cm.
MWA (torn) mp. 46807

B8396 LELAND, JOHN, 1754–1841
A true account, how Matthew Womble murdered his wife, (who was pregnant) and his four sons on June 19th, 1784 . . . by John Leland, V.D.M. Stockbridge, Printed for Richard Lee, 1793.
8 p. 17 cm.
MH-L (not traced); MWA (t.p. wanting); NBuG
mp. 46808

B8397 [A LIBERAL plea for impartial liberty: being a brief dissertation concerning the parish glebes of Virginia . . . by a Blue-Mountaineer. Published by a friend to impartiality. [Fredericksburg? 1793]

Title from an advertisement in the *Virginia Herald*, June 20, 1793, as "Just published and for sale at the Herald Office."
No copy known mp. 46809

B8398 LILLO, GEORGE, 1693–1739
The London merchant, or, The history of George Barnwell . . . Boston, Belknap and Hall, 1793.
60 p. 17.5 cm.
New York Public 1071
MWA; NN mp. 46810

B8399 [LOGAN, GEORGE] 1753–1821
Excise, the favorite system of aristocrats . . . The pimping eye of the exciseman is already authorized . . . to watch the motions of the farmer, the sugar-refiner, tobacconist . . . if not checked . . . greedy hand of government . . . thrust into every crevice of industry . . . We . . .call upon . . . the Democratic Societies . . . [Philadelphia, 1793]
broadside 42 X 26 cm.
PHi. Pierce W. Gaines, Fairfield, Conn. (1964)
mp. 48115

B8400 LOUIS XVI, KING OF FRANCE, 1754–1793, defendant
The trial of Louis the XVIth, King of France, before the National Convention . . . Translated from the original French. New-York: Printed in the year 1793.
12 p. 17 cm.
cf. Evans 25499
NHi mp. 46811

B8401 LOVE, CHRISTOPHER, 1618–1651
Prophecies of the Rev. Christopher Love: who was be-

headed . . . August, 1651 . . . Boston: Printed and sold at the Bible and Heart, in Cornhill, 1793.
11 p. 17 cm.
cf. Evans 25725 mp. 46812
NHi

B8402 LOVE, CHRISTOPHER, 1618–1651
The strange and wonderful predictions of Mr. Christopher Love . . . To which are added, Two letters from his wife to him . . . Philadelphia, Printed by Johnston & Justice, for William Glendinning, 1793.
12 p. 12mo
PPL mp. 46813

B8403 LUTHER, MARTIN, 1483–1536
Der kleine Catechismus . . . Vierte Auflage. Germantown, Michael Billmeyer, 1793.
[4], 127, [1] p. 12mo
PPL mp. 46814

B8404 MACKLIN, CHARLES, 1697?–1797
Love a-la-mode . . . New-York, Printed by J. Harrisson, for R. Macgill, 1793.
32 p. 14.5 cm.
MiU-C mp. 46815

B8405 MACWHORTER, ALEXANDER, 1734–1807
A few observations, in reference to the character of the Rev. Mr. Aaron Richards of Rahway; father to William Richards, Esq. of Middletown. Delivered at his funeral . . . Middletown, Moses H. Woodward, 1793.
8 p. 18 cm.
NHi mp. 46816

B8406 MADISON, JAMES, 1749–1812
An address to the convention . . . by Bishop Madison.–May 1793 . . . [Richmond, T. Nicolson, 1793]
16, [1] p. 19 cm.
DLC; MWA mp. 46817

B8407 THE MAIL
The news-carrier's verses to the subscribers of the *Mail or Daily Advertiser*. January 1st, 1793 . . . [New York, Childs and Swaine, 1793]
broadside 30 X 13.5 cm.
NHi mp. 46840

B8408 THE major's only son, and his true-loves overthrow. Being some lines composed by himself and on the occasion. [He is . . . now alive in 1793] . . . [n.p., 1793]
broadside 33 X 15 cm.
MWA mp. 46818

B8409 MASSACHUSETTS. GOVERNOR, 1787–1793
Commonwealth of Massachusetts. By His Excellency John Hancock . . . A proclamation. Whereas the Governor . . . has this day been served . . . with the following writ . . . [July 9, 1793] . . . [Boston, Adams & Larkin, 1793]
broadside 41 X 34 cm.
William Vassall vs. Comm. of Mass.
MB mp. 46819

B8410 MECHANIC LIBRARY SOCIETY, NEW HAVEN
The constitution and bye-laws of the Mechanic Library Society of New Haven, with a catalogue of books and list of the proprietors. New-Haven, Abel Morse, 1793.
17 p. 19.5 cm.
Trumbull: Second supplement 2831
CtY mp. 46831

B8411 MEDICAL SOCIETY IN THE STATE OF CONNECTICUT
The act incorporating a Medical Society, in the State of Connecticut; together with the bye-laws . . . and a list of the Fellows and officers, for the years 1792, and 1793. . . . New-Haven, T. and S. Green [1793]
16 p. 19.5 cm.
Rogers 379
NNNAM mp. 46820

B8412 MEMOIRS of the life of Mrs. Sarah Demick . . . Danbury, Printed by N. Douglas for James Crawford [1793?]
12 p. 16 cm.
CtHi mp. 46821

B8413 [THE mermaid, or nautical songster. New York, Sold by John Harrisson, 1793]

Advertised Apr. 20, 1793, as "for sale."
Sonneck-Upton, p. 258
No copy known mp. 46822

B8414 MOORE, EDWARD, 1712–1757
Fables for the ladies. To which are added, Fables of flora. By Dr. Langhorne. Philadelphia, Printed and sold by W. Gibbons, 1793.
[7]–144 p. 13 cm.
DGU; MWA mp. 46823

B8415 MOORE, JOHN, V.D.M.
[The Christian religion tried by the standard of truth . . . Halifax, Abraham Hodge, 1793]

Advertised in the *North-Carolina Journal*, June 5, 1793, as "Just published, and for sale at the Printing-Office."
McMurtrie: North Carolina 183
No copy known mp. 46824

B8416 MORRIS, DEBORAH
Abstract of special legacies in the will of Deborah Morris, deceased. [Philadelphia, 1793]
[2] p. fol. caption title
PPL mp. 46825

B8417 MORTON, JOHN AND JAMES, firm
John and James Morton, have just imported . . . from London & Bristol, via New-York, the following goods . . . Likewise at their store in New-york, in Queen-Street . . . all sorts of English and India goods . . . [New York, 1793]
broadside 26 X 16.5 cm.
NHi mp. 46826

B8418 A MOST bloody and cruel murder, committed on the body of Mrs. Elizabeth Wood, by her own son . . . Bennington, Anthony Haswell [1793?]
8 p. 17.5 cm.
McCorison 272
RPJCB mp. 46827

B8419 MUIR, JAMES, 1757–1820
A funeral sermon (on Zach. i.5, in memory of the Rev. James Hunt). Alexandria, Hanson and Bond [1793]
20 p.
Brit. Mus. mp. 46828

B8420 Deleted

B8421 NATIONAL GAZETTE
Supplement to the *National Gazette*, no. 153. Advertisement. Whereas it appears unto us . . . the commissioners of Bedford County . . . 9th day of February, A.D. 1793 . . . [Philadelphia? 1793]
broadsheet 35 X 27 cm.
Text in 3 columns
NHi

B8422 THE New-England primer . . . Hartford, Elisha Babcock, 1793.
80 p. 11.5 cm.
cf. Evans 25866; Heartman 133; Trumbull 1149
DLC; NRU mp. 46829

B8423 NEW HAMPSHIRE. GOVERNOR, 1790–1794
By His Excellency Josiah Bartlett . . . A proclamation for a day of public fasting, humiliation and prayer. Portsmouth, John Melcher, 1793.
broadside 36 X 29 cm.
Dated Feb. 9, 1793
New York Public 1072
Lewis M. Stark (1960). Photostat: NN mp. 46830

B8424 NEW JERSEY. MILITIA
Brigade orders. August 26, 1793. The enrolled militia in the Counties of Gloucester and Burlington . . . Joseph Bloomfield, Brigadier-General, of the said first brigade. [n.p., 1793]
broadside 34 X 20.5 cm.
NjR

B8425 NEW-JERSEY and Pennsylvania almanac for . . . 1794. By Eben W. Judd. Trenton, Day and Hopkins [1793]
[32] p.
Drake 5160
NjT (15 l.)

B8426 NEW YORK. COMMITTEE APPOINTED TO PREVENT THE INTRODUCTION AND SPREADING OF INFECTIOUS DISEASES
As it is a point agreed on by all writers on infectious diseases . . . it becomes a matter of great importance to the safety of this city in regulating the intercourse with Philadelphia . . . New-York, September 30, 1793. [New York, 1793]
broadside 31 X 21 cm.
NHi mp. 46832

B8427 NEW YORK. COMMITTEE APPOINTED TO PREVENT THE INTRODUCTION AND SPREADING OF INFECTIOUS DISEASES
To the inhabitants of the State of New-York; and those of the neighboring states. Friends . . . the citizens of New-York appointed a committee of seven, to take measures . . . New-York, September 30, 1793. [New York, 1793]
broadside 30.5 X 21 cm.
NHi mp. 46833

B8428 NEW YORK. GOVERNOR, 1777–1793
By George Clinton . . . a proclamation, Whereas a proclamation of the President . . . [May 9, 1793] . . . [New York, 1793]
broadside 35.5 X 19.5 cm.
DLC; NAll. Photostat: NN mp. 46834

B8429 NEW YORK. GOVERNOR, 1777–1793
By George Clinton. A proclamation. Whereas by the statute entitled "An act to prevent bringing in . . . infectious distempers . . .," it is enacted "that all vessels . . . having on board any person . . . infected . . ." [New-York, 1793]
broadside 34 X 21.5 cm.
Austin 1409
NHi. Photocopy: NNNAM mp. 46835

B8430 NEW-YORK, 24th January, 1793. Sir, A number of gentlemen . . . propose . . . giving a subscription ball at Belvedere-House . . . William Armstrong, John Oaks Hardy [and 4 others] An answer is requested at No. 24, Water-street. [New York, 1793]
broadside 25 X 20 cm.
NHi mp. 46836

B8431 NEWARK ACADEMY LOTTERY
Scheme of the Newark Academy Lottery . . . to finish . . . an academy in the town of Newark . . . Newark, July 3, 1793. [Newark? John Woods? 1793]
broadside 20 X 16.5 cm.
Morsch 207
NjHi mp. 46837

B8432 NEWPORT. THEATRE
[. . . Theatre. Newport. This evening will be presented . . . Barnaby Brittle . . .] After which, dancing on the tight rope . . . [Newport, 1793]
broadside 17 X 27.5 cm.
Probably advertised in the *Newport Mercury* for July 23, 1793
Alden 1315A; Winship p. 75
RHi (mutilated). Photostat: NN mp. 46839

B8433 NICCOLAI, VALENTINO
Six sonatas, for the piano forte, or harpsichord. Op. XI. Philadelphia, I. C. Moller [1793?]
31 p.
NBuG

B8434 NICHOLS, THOMAS, of Coventry
Hymns, and anthems . . . Albany, Charles R. & George Webster, 1793.
204 p. 13 cm.
DLC mp. 46841

B8435 NICHOLSON, WILLIAM, 1753–1815
An introduction to natural philosophy . . . A new edition, with improvements . . . In two volumes . . . Philadelphia, T. Dobson, 1793.
2 v. 21.5 cm.
DGU (v. 2 only); MWA (v. 2 only); N (v. 2 only) mp. 46842

B8436 NIXON, WILLIAM
A sermon, preached in St. Michael's Church . . . Grand Lodge of South-Carolina . . . 1792. Charleston, Markland & M'Iver, 1793.
16 p. 19 cm.
Mosimann 495
MBFM

B8437 NORTH CAROLINA. GOVERNOR, 1792–1795
State of North-Carolina, by . . . Richard Dobbs Spaight . . . A proclamation . . . [Newbern, F. X. Martin? 1793]
broadside 22 X 19 cm.
Proclamation designed to prevent "a pestilential fever" through contact with vessels from Philadelphia
Nc-Ar mp. 46843

B8438 NORTH CAROLINA. LAWS
Laws of North-Carolina. At a General assembly, begun . . . on the fifteenth day of November . . . being the first session . . . [Halifax, Hodge and Wills, 1793]
20 p. 33 cm. caption title
McMurtrie: North Carolina 187
DLC; MH-L; NcU

B8439 PEIRCE, JOHN, JR.
The new American spelling-book . . . The sixth edition. Philadelphia, Printed and sold by Joseph Crukshank, 1793.
[6], 198 p. 12mo
PPL mp. 46844

B8440 PEMBERTON, THOMAS, 1728–1807
An historical journal of the American war, 1765–1784 . . . Printed by Samuel Hall, No. 53 Cornhill, Boston. 1793.
1 p.l., 206 p. 21 cm.
NHi mp. 46845

B8441 PENNSYLVANIA. HOUSE OF REPRESENTATIVES
Journal of the second session of the third House of Representatives . . . Philadelphia, Francis Bailey [1793]
35, [22] p. fol.
PPL mp. 46848

B8442 PENNSYLVANIA. LAWS
In General Assembly, Monday, March 25, 1793. An act for the better preventing of crimes . . . [Colophon] Philadelphia, T. Bradford [1793]
10 p. 35 cm. caption title
Printed as a bill, with the lines of each section separately numbered
New York Public 1077
NN mp. 46846

B8443 PENNSYLVANIA. LAWS
In General Assembly, Saturday, December 21, 1793. A supplement to . . . "An act to enable the Governor . . . to incorporate a company for . . . promoting the cultivation of vines . . ." [at end] Philadelphia, T. Bradford [1793]
2 p. 34.5 cm. caption title
Printed as a bill, with the lines of each section separately numbered
MWA mp. 46847

B8444 [THE Pennsylvania, Maryland and Virginia almanack, for the year 1794. Frederick-Town, M. Bartgis, 1793]

Advertised in *Bartgis's Maryland Gazette*, Dec. 19, 1793, as "In the press, and speedily will be published, almanacks for . . . 1794."
Minick 132
No copy known mp. 46849

B8445 A PERPETUAL calendar, or pocket almanack . . . Boston, Nathaniel Coverly, 1793.
[16] p. 16 cm.
By Timothy Carter
MWA mp. 46710

B8446 PERRY, PHILO
A sermon delivered at New-Milford . . . December 27, 1792; at the request . . . of St. Peter's Lodge, in New-Milford . . . Danbury, Douglas and Ely, 1793.
23 p. 16.5 cm.
Trumbull: Supplement 2497
CtHi mp. 46850

B8447 PHILADELPHIA
Order of the procession . . . Philadelphia, Zachariah Poulson [1793?]
broadside
PPL mp. 46851

B8448 PHILADELPHIA. POST OFFICE
Post-Office, Philadelphia, January 1st, 1793. Establishment of the mails from the 1st of January, 1793, to the 1st of June, 1794 . . . Robert Patton, Post-master. Philadelphia, Charles Cist [1793]
broadside 47.5 × 29 cm.
MB mp. 46852

B8449 PHILADELPHIA COMPANY OF PRINTERS AND BOOKSELLERS
The constitution and proceedings, &c. of the Philadelphia Company of Printers and Booksellers. [Philadelphia] Printed by Daniel Humphreys, 1793.
12 p. 8vo
PPL

B8450 PHILADELPHIA COMPANY OF PRINTERS AND BOOKSELLERS
Monday, April 1, 1793. A quorum met . . . [Philadelphia, Daniel Humphreys, 1793]
p. 13–14
In accordance with the rules, the proceedings were to be printed after each meeting
Printed on one side of the leaf only
PPL

B8451 PHILADELPHIA COMPANY OF PRINTERS AND BOOKSELLERS
Monday, July 1, 1793. At a meeting of the Philadelphia Company of Printers and Booksellers . . . [Philadelphia, D. Humphreys, 1793]
p. 15
In accordance with the rules, the proceedings were to be printed after each meeting
PPL

B8452 PIKE, NICHOLAS, 1743–1819
Abridgment of the new and complete system of arithmetick . . . Worcester, Printed for Isaiah Thomas [1793?]
371 p. 17.5 cm.
cf. Evans 26002
MWA mp. 46853

B8453 EINE Predigt, über I. Joh. Cap. 2, V. 28 zum Abschied, gehalten in Bern Taunschip den 6ten October, 1793. Reading, Jungmann & Gruber, 1793.

Nolan p. 26
C. W. Unger, Pottsville, Pa. (1930) mp. 46854

B8454 PRIESTLEY, JOSEPH, 1733–1804
Extracts from Doctor Priestley's catechism. Salem, Thomas C. Cushing, 1793.
12 p. 15.5 cm.
MSaE mp. 46855

B8455 PROTESTANT EPISCOPAL CHURCH IN THE U.S.A. NORTH CAROLINA (DIOCESE)
Circular. Dearly beloved, the convention . . . at their meeting held at Tarborough on the 21st day of November, 1793, Resolved . . . [Edenton? Hodge & Wills? 1793]
broadside 25.5 × 20 cm.
McMurtrie: North Carolina 188
Nc-Ar mp. 46856

B8456 PROTESTANT EPISCOPAL CHURCH IN THE U.S.A. VIRGINIA (DIOCESE)
Journal of a convention . . . Richmond, May 2, 1793 . . . Richmond, T. Nicolson [1793]
31 p.
MWA mp. 46857

B8457 RANKIN, ADAM, 1755–1827
A process in the Transilvania presbytery . . . Lexington, Maxwell & Cooch [1793]
96 p. 16 cm.
McMurtrie: Kentucky 32
DLC; ICU; KyLx; KyU; MiU-C; OClW mp. 46858

B8458 REESE, THOMAS, 1742–1796
Steadfastness in religion, recommended . . . Philadelphia, William Young, 1793.
36 p. 20 cm.
Huntington 640
CSmH; NHi; NjP mp. 46859

B8459 REFLECTIONS on the present state government of Virginia; and a variety of good causes shewn for altering the same . . . By a native. [Richmond?] 1793.
34 p. 18 cm.
New York Public 1078; Sabin 100518
NN mp. 46860

B8460 RELLY, JAMES, 1722?–1778
The salt of the sacrifice . . . Concord, Reprinted by E. Russell, 1793.
viii, 112 p. 16.5 cm. A-C^8 D^4 E-H^8
MWA mp. 46861

B8461 REPARATION LOTTERY
Reparation Lottery: Class the first . . . Rutland, October 31, 1792. [Windsor? A. Spooner? 1793]
broadside 30.5 X 20 cm.
Lottery scheme with list of prizes
Signatures of Samuel Miller, Timothy Olcott, Martin Chittenden, managers of the lottery
McCorison 275; New York Public 1037
NhD; VtHi. Photostat: NN mp. 46862

B8462 THE reprobate's reward, or, A looking-glass for disobedient children, being a full . . . account of the . . . murder of one Elizabeth Wood . . . by her own son . . . Philadelphia, 1793.
8 p. 18.5 cm.
In verse
New York Public 1079; cf. Evans 25849
NN mp. 46863

B8463 REPUBLICAN SOCIETY OF SOUTH CAROLINA
Charleston, August, 1793. Fellow citizens, The present state of Europe . . . [Charleston, 1793]
[2] p. 39 X 25 cm. caption title
DLC; MB; RPJCB mp. 46864

B8464 RHODE ISLAND. ELECTION PROX.
1793. His Excellency Arthur Fenner, Esq. Governor. The honorable Samuel J. Potter, Esquire, Deputy-governor . . . [Providence] B. Wheeler [1793]
broadside 20 X 13 cm.
Alden 1322; Chapin Proxies 46
RHi mp. 46865

B8465 RHODE ISLAND. GOVERNOR, 1790–1805
By His Excellency Arthur Fenner, Esq; Governor . . . A proclamation . . . [Nov. 4, 1793] . . . [Providence] Carter and Wilkinson [1793]
broadside 42 X 34 cm.
Bill submitted Nov. 6, 1793
Alden 1323; Sabin 70559
MH; RHi mp. 46866

B8466 THE Rhode-Island almanack . . . for the year . . . 1794 . . . Warren, Nathaniel Phillips [1793]
[24] p. 17.5 cm.
Alden 1303; Winship p. 61; cf. Evans 26257
RHi; RNHi mp. 46867

B8467 [RICHARDSON,]
The history of two good boys and girls . . . Boston, Printed and sold by N. Coverly, 1793.
30, [2?] p. illus. 8 cm.
MWA (p. [1–2], 7–8, [31–32] wanting) mp. 46868

B8468 [RICHARDSON,]
The history of two good boys and girls, To which is added, The story of three naughty girls and boys . . . Boston: Printed and sold by N. Coverly, 1793.
16 p. 10 cm.
"From the works of Mr. Richardson": p. 4
MWA mp. 46869

B8469 THE royal alphabet . . . Boston, Printed for and sold by Samuel Hall, 1793.
30, [1] p. illus. 10 cm.
NNC mp. 46870

B8470 RUSH, BENJAMIN, 1745–1813
[An account of the causes and indications of longevity, and of the state of the body and mind in old age . . . Philadelphia, 1793]

Goodman p. 382
No copy known mp. 46871

B8471 RUSH, BENJAMIN, 1745–1813
Directions. As soon as you are affected [with yellow fever] . . . September 10, 1793. B.R. [Philadelphia, 1793]
broadside 19.5 X 11.5 cm.
PPL mp. 46872

B8472 RYER, JOHN, 1759–1793
Narrative of the life, and dying speech, of John Ryer . . . executed at White-Plains . . . the seond day of October, 1793, for the murder of Dr. Isaac Smith, deputy sheriff . . . Printed by E. Ely, in Danbury: for the publisher.—1793.—
15 p.
PP

B8473 RYER, JOHN, 1759–1793
Narrative of the life, and dying speech, of John Ryer . . . executed at White-Plains . . . the second day of October, 1793, for the murder of Dr. Isaac Smith, deputy sheriff . . . Danbury, Nathan Douglas, 1793.
15 p. 21.5 cm.
McDade 841
MWA; NHi mp. 46873

B8474 SCHUYLER, PHILIP JOHN, 1733–1804
To the stockholders in the Northern and Western Inland-Lock-Navigation Companies . . . Stillwater, on Hudson's river, June 7, 1793 . . . Your obedient servant, Ph: Schuyler. [Albany? 1793]
broadside 52 X 44.5 cm.
In three columns
McMurtrie: Albany 91; New York Public 1080
NN. Photostat: DLC mp. 46874

B8475 SMITH, JOSHUA, d. 1795
Divine hymns, or spiritual songs . . . being a collection by Joshua Smith and Samuel Sleeper. The fifth Exeter edition . . . Exeter, Printed by Henry Ranlet for Samuel Sleeper, 1793.
192 p. 13.5 cm.
MWA mp. 46875

B8476 SOCIETY FOR PROMOTING THE MANUFACTURE OF SUGAR
Constitution of the Society for Promoting the Manufacture of Sugar from the Sugar Maple-tree and furthering the interests of agriculture in . . . Pennsylvania . . . Philadelphia, Robert Aitken, 1793.
8 p.
PPAmP mp. 46876

B8477 SOME account of the life and death of Matthew Lee, executed . . . October 11, 1752 . . . Philadelphia, Johnston & Justice, 1793.
23 p. 15.5 cm.
DLC mp. 46877

B8478 SOUTH CAROLINA. GOVERNOR, 1792–1793
The State of South Carolina. By his Excellency William Moultrie . . . Proclamation . . . this 9th day of December . . . [1793] . . . William Moultrie. By the Governor's command, Peter Freneau, Secretary of State. [Charleston, 1793]
broadside 21.5 × 33.5 cm.
Prohibiting enlistment not sanctioned by the U.S. or by South Carolina
Sc-Ar

B8479 SOUTH CAROLINA. HOUSE OF REPRESENTATIVES
In the House of Representatives, December 20, 1793 . . . [Charleston? 1793].
4 p. 33 cm.
House proceedings for the day
Sc-Ar (2 copies)

B8480 STANFORD, JOHN, 1754–1834
An address delivered at the interment of Mrs. Sarah Burger . . . who departed this life June 10, 1793, aged 49 years . . . New-York, Printed for Mr. Burger—by T. and J. Swords, 1793.
10 p. 17 cm.
MWA; NHi mp. 46878

B8481 STANFORD, JOHN, 1754–1834
A collection of evangelical hymns . . . New-York, T, and J. Swords, 1793.
180 p. 13.5 cm.
CtHC; MH-AH; MWA mp. 46879

B8482 STERNE, LAURENCE, 1713–1768
The whole story of the sorrows of Maria, of Moulines. Selected from various works of . . . Sterne . . . Second edition. Boston, 1793.
23 p. 16 cm.
"Maria" (poem): p. 23
MWA mp. 46880

B8483 STORY, THOMAS, 1670?–1742
The means, nature, properties and effects of true faith considered. A discourse . . . Philadelphia, Re-printed and sold by William Gibbons, 1793.
35, [1] p. 17 cm.
MWA mp. 46881

B8484 STRONG, CYPRIAN, 1743–1811
A discourse, delivered at the interment of Mrs. Ruth Sage, consort of Mr. Abner Sage, of Chatham; who died . . . Dec. 3d, A.D. 1793, aetat. 28 . . . Middletown, Moses H. Woodward [1793?]
16 p. 18.5 cm.
Trumbull: Supplement 2653
MWA; NHi mp. 46882

B8485 STRONG'S Connecticut and New-York almanack, for . . . 1794 . . . By Nehemiah Strong . . . Litchfield, Collier and Buel [1793]
[24] p.
Drake 522; Trumbull: Supplement 1794
Ct (imperfect); CtHi; CtLHi; CtNhHi; CtY; KHi; MB
mp. 46883

B8486 [SWAN, TIMOTHY] 1758–1842
The federal harmony . . . Boston, John Norman, 1793.
130 p. 13 × 23 cm.
DLC mp. 46884

B8487 TAMMANY SOCIETY
Constitutions of Tammany Society or Columbian Order. [New York] John Harrisson [1793?]
8 p. 19.5 cm.
Sabin 94294
MWA; NHi mp. 46885

B8488 TAPPEN, CHRISTOPHER
To the inhabitants of Ulster County. The public prints . . . Christopher Tappen, Kingston, April 16, 1793 . . . Kingston, Power & Copp [1793]
broadside 45.5 × 24 cm.
NAII; NHI. Photostats: DLC; NN mp. 46886

B8489 TESTAMENT de mort d'Ogé, et adresse de Pinchiant aux hommes de couleur, en date du 13 décembre dernier . . . par un habitant de Saint-Domingue . . . Philadelphia, Parent [1793?]
[2], 28 p.
RPJCB mp. 46887

B8490 THOMSON, J.
Modern practice of farriery; or, Complete horse-doctor . . . New York, Printed for Berry, Rogers and Berry [1793]

cf. R. W. Henderson: *Early American sport* (N.Y., 1937), p. 15–16
NNRT mp. 46888

B8491 TO the public . . . A Friend to truth. Shawangunk, April 24th, 1793. [n.p., 1793]
broadside 32 × 21 cm.
In two columns
New York Public 1082
NN mp. 46889

B8492 TOM Thumb's folio: or, A new play-thing for little giants . . . New-York, William Durrell, 1793.
30 p. illus. 9.5 cm.
d'Alté A. Welch, Cleveland (1962). Photocopy: MWA
mp. 46890

B8493 TRENCK, FRIEDRICH, FREIHERR VON DER, 1726–1794
The life of Baron Frederic Trenck . . . translated from the Germany, by Thomas Holcroft. Boston, William Greenough, 1793.
4 v. (107; 100; 92; 120 p.) 12mo
Vol. II–III have added imprint: For E. Larkin, Jun., and E. & S. Larkin
cf. Evans 26279
MWA (v. III–IV only); PPL mp. 46891

B8494 A TRUE and particular account of the cruel massacre . . . at Cape-Francois, which began on the 17th of June, 1793 . . . and increased until the 23d . . . 14 or 15,000 lives . . . Printed for and sold by J. Plummer, Jun., Trader, of Newbury-Port [1793?]
broadside 54 × 44 cm.
NHi

B8495 A TRUE narrative of a most stupendous trance and vision, which happened at Sharon, in Connecticut. in January, 1789. Written by an impartial hand. [n.p.] Printed for the book-sellers, 1793.

12 p. 18 cm.
Ct; CtHi; MWA mp. 46892

B8496 TUCKER, ST. GEORGE, 1752–1827
To the public. My connection with Mr. Richard Randolph . . . S. G. Tucker. Fredericksburg, May 5, 1793. [Fredericksburg? 1793]
[4] p. 34 cm.
Page [1] only printed
ViW mp. 46893

B8497 U.S. BOARD OF COMMISSIONERS OF THE SINKING FUND
The Vice-President of the United States . . . the chief Justice, the secretary of state . . . and the Attorney general, respectfully report to Congress . . . [Philadelphia? 1793?]
4 p. 21 cm. caption title
Signed: 16th December, 1793
MiU-C (imperfect) mp. 46894

B8498 U.S. COMMISSIONERS FOR THE SETTLEMENT OF THE ACCOUNTS
The commissioners appointed to execute the several acts of Congress . . . Philadelphia, June 29th, 1793 . . . [Philadelphia, 1793]
broadside 32.5 X 19 cm.
CtHi; NHi. Photostats: DLC; NN mp. 46895

B8499 U.S. CONGRESS
Resolved, that a loan to the amount of the balances . . . due from the United States to the individual states, be opened at the Treasury . . . [Philadelphia, 1793?]
broadside 34 X 21 cm.
Lines of each section separately numbered
New York Public 1093
NN (photostat) mp. 46903

B8500 U.S. CONGRESS. HOUSE. COMMITTEE ON SUNDRY PETITIONS OF PERSONS THAT HAVE BEEN RENDERED INVALIDS
The Committee to whom were referred sundry petitions . . . and also a letter from the judges of the circuit court for . . . North-Carolina . . . [Philadelphia? 1793]
broadside 32.5 cm.
Reported to House Dec. 14, 1793.—cf. Greely, p. 113
MiU-C mp. 46902

B8501 U.S. CONGRESS. HOUSE. COMMITTEE ON THE MEMORIAL OF ARTHUR ST. CLAIR
The Committee to whom was referred the memorial of Arthur St. Clair, Report . . . [Philadelphia, 1793]
broadside 33.5 X 20.5 cm.
Submitted Mar. 1, 1793
New York Public 1085
NN mp. 46898

B8502 U.S. CONGRESS. HOUSE. COMMITTEE ON THE TRANSPORTATION OF NEWSPAPERS
The Committee to whom was referred that part of the President's speech which relates to the transportation of newspapers, Report . . . [Philadelphia, 1793]
[2] p. 32.5 cm.
Submitted Feb. 18, 1793
New York Public 1086
NN mp. 46899

B8503 U.S. DEPT. OF STATE
Philadelphia, January 8th, 1793. Sir, I have the honor . . . Th: Jefferson. January 8, 1793. [Philadelphia, Childs and Swaine, 1793]
2 leaves. 33 cm.
DLC (2 copies); MiU-C; RPJCB mp. 46905

B8504 U.S. LAWS
An act to authorize the settlement of the accounts of Lewis Garanger . . . 1793, January 2d . . . [Philadelphia] John Fenno [1793]
broadside 33.5 X 21 cm.
DLC mp. 46906

B8505 U.S. LAWS
An act to continue in force . . . and to amend the act . . . providing the means of intercourse . . . 1793, January the 18th . . . [Philadelphia] John Fenno [1793]
broadside 34 X 20 cm.
DLC mp. 46907

B8506 U.S. LAWS
Acts passed at the first[-third] session of the Congress of the United States . . . M,DCC,LXXXIX[-M,DCC,XC] . . . Volume I. Philadelphia, E. Oswald, 1793.
375, [46] p. 20.5 cm.
2nd-3rd sessions have half title only
New York Public 1088
MiU-C; NN; PPL mp. 46908

B8507 U.S. LAWS
Acts passed at the first[-second] session of the Second Congress of the United States . . . M,DCC,XCI [-M,DCC,XCII] . . . Volume II. Philadelphia, E. Oswald, 1793.
380, [26] p. 20.5 cm.
Second session has half-title only
New York Public 1089
DLC; MiU-C; NN; PPL mp. 46909

B8508 U.S. LAWS
A bill for placing on the pension list, such officers and privates . . . as may be wounded and disabled . . . [Philadelphia? 1793]
broadside 34.5 X 21 cm.
Presented in the House Feb. 15, 1793
New York Public 1090
NN (photostat) mp. 46900

B8509 U.S. LAWS
A bill providing for destroyed certificates of certain descriptions. [Philadelphia, 1793]
broadside 33.5 X 21 cm.
Presented in the House Dec. 27, 1793
New York Public 1091
NN (photostat) mp. 46904

B8510 U.S. LAWS
A bill to authorize a loan in the . . . notes of such states as shall have balances due to them . . . [Philadelphia, 1793]
broadside 33.5 X 21 cm.
Presented in the House Jan 15, 1793
New York Public 1092
NN (photostat) mp. 46901

B8511 U.S. LAWS
Second Congress of the United States: At the second session . . . An act to provide for the allowance of interest. Approved, January fourteenth, 1793 . . . [Philadelphia, Childs and Swaine, 1793]
broadside 39 X 25 cm.
cf. Evans 26300, which lacks deposit statement
DLC

B8512 U.S. LAWS
Second Congress of the United States: At the second session . . . An act in addition to . . . "An act to extend the time . . ." Approved, February twenty seventh, 1793 . . . [Philadelphia, Childs and Swaine, 1793]
broadside 39 X 25.5 cm.
cf. Evans 26314, which lacks deposit statement
DLC

B8513 U.S. LAWS
Second Congress of the United States: At the second session . . . An act supplementary to the act . . . to provide more effectually . . . Approved, March second 1793 . . . [Philadelphia, Childs and Swaine, 1793]
[2] p. 38.5 X 25.5 cm.
cf. Evans 26327, which lacks deposit statement
DLC

B8514 U.S. LAWS
Second Congress of the United States: At the second session . . . An act to ascertain the fees in admiralty proceedings . . . Approved, March first 1793 . . . [Philadelphia, Childs and Swaine, 1793]
[2] p. 38.5 X 25 cm.
cf. Evans 26318, which lacks statement of deposition
DLC

B8515 U.S. LAWS
Second Congress of the United States: At the second session . . . An act to authorize the adjustment of a claim . . . [Philadelphia, Childs and Swaine, 1793]
broadside 38.5 X 25.5 cm.
cf. Evans 26311 and 26312, which lack statement of deposition
DLC

B8516 U.S. LAWS
Second Congress of the United States: At the second session . . . An act to continue in force . . . Approved, February 9th, 1793 . . . [Philadelphia, Childs and Swaine, 1793]
broadside 38.5 X 24.5 cm.
cf. Evans 26304, which lacks statement of deposition
DLC

B8517 U.S. LAWS
Second Congress of the United States: At the second session . . . An act to regulate the claims to invalid pensions . . . Approved, February twenty eighth 1793 . . . [Philadelphia, Childs and Swaine, 1793]
[2] p. 28.5 X 25 cm.
cf. Evans 26317, which lacks statement of deposition
DLC

B8518 U.S. PRESIDENT, 1789–1797
Fellow Citizens of the Senate, and of the House of Representatives . . . Philadelphia, December 3, 1793 . . . [Philadelphia, 1793]
broadside 40 X 35.5 cm.
NHi mp. 46910

B8519 U.S. PRESIDENT, 1789–1797
Speech of the President . . . to both houses of Congress, December 3, 1793. [Philadelphia, Childs and Swaine, 1793]
broadside 50 X 40.5 cm.
RPJCB. Photostat: DLC mp. 46911

B8520 U.S. PRESIDENT, 1789–1797
Speech of the President . . . to both houses of Congress. Fellow-citizens of the Senate, and of the House . . . Philadelphia, December 3d, 1793. [Philadelphia? 1793]
[4] p. 33.5 cm.
MiU-C mp. 46912

B8521 U.S. TREASURY DEPT.
[Circular.] Treasury Department, *June 25*, 1793. Sir, It appears that the summary of the amount of duties on imposts and tonnage . . . [Philadelphia, 1793]
broadside 23.5 X 20 cm.
Italicized portion in manuscript
Pierce W. Gaines, Fairfield, Conn. (1964) mp. 46916

B8522 U.S. TREASURY DEPT.
[(Circular.)] Treasury Department, January 22d, 1793. [Sir,] Enclosed is an act, entitled, "An act concerning the registering and recording . . . [Philadelphia, 1793]
broadside 23.5
MWA (left side wanting) mp. 46917

B8523 U.S. TREASURY DEPT.
(Circular.) Treasury Department, March 13, 1793. Sir, Proof has been filed in the office of the Collector of Newbury Port . . . [Philadelphia, 1793]
broadside 23.5 X 20 cm.
MWA mp. 46918

B8524 U.S. TREASURY DEPT.
(Circular.) Treasury Department, March 29th 1793. Sir, A question has been made . . . [Philadelphia, 1793]
broadside 23.5 X 20 cm.
MWA mp. 46919

B8525 U.S. TREASURY DEPT.
(Circular) Treasury Department, April 12, 1793. Sir, The collectors stand charged with the sealed blank certificates . . . [Philadelphia, 1793]
broadside 23.5 X 19.5 cm.
Pierce Gaines, Fairfield, Conn. (1964) mp. 46920

B8526 U.S. TREASURY DEPT.
(Circular.) Treasury Department, April 29th, 1793. Sir, It having been deemed expedient . . . [Philadelphia, 1793]
broadside 24 X 20 cm.
MWA mp. 46921

B8527 U.S. TREASURY DEPT.
(Circular.) Treasury Deparrment, May 30, 1793. Sir, It being the opinion of the Executive . . . [Philadelphia, 1793]
broadside 23.5 X 20 cm.
MWA mp. 46922

B8528 U.S. TREASURY DEPT.
(Circular.) Treasury Department, August 22, 1793. Sir, Though it was not expressly said . . . clearly implied in the instruction contained in my circular of the 4th instant . . . [Philadelphia, 1793]
broadside 23.5 X 20 cm.
MWA mp. 46923

B8529 U.S. TREASURY DEPT.
[Circular] Treasury department, Comptroller's office, April 27d, 1793 . . . [Philadelphia, 1793]
broadside 24 X 20 cm.
PPRF mp. 46896

B8530 U.S. TREASURY DEPT.
Explanations and forms of official documents in relation to the acts concerning . . . ships and vessels. Sir, As various questions have been stated to this office . . . [Dec. 28, 1793[[Philadelphia, 1793]
15, [1]+ p. fol.
MWA mp. 46897

B8531 U.S. TREASURY DEPT.
Statement of the purchases of the public stock by the agents to the trustees named in the act of the reduction of the public debt to the 1st of August, 1793 . . . Register's Office, December 13, 1793. [Philadelphia, 1793]
broadside 23.5 X 27 cm.
NHi mp. 46913

B8532 U.S. TREASURY DEPT.
Statement of the purchases of public stock by the agents to the trustees named in the act for the reduction of the public debt to the 16th December, 1793 . . . Treasury Dpt. John Nourse, Register . . . [Philadelphia, 1793]
broadside 21 X 27 cm.
NHi mp. 46914

B8533 U.S. TREASURY DEPT.
Sundry statements made by the Secretary of the treasury . . . 23d of January, 1793 . . . [Philadelphia, Childs and Swaine, 1793]
[4] p. 3 fold. tables. 31.5 cm.
Half-title only
DLC; MiU-C; NN; RPJCB mp. 46924

B8534 U.S. TREASURY DEPT.
The Treasurer of the United States' accounts of payments and receipts of public monies . . . to the thirty-first day of December, 1792 . . . [Philadelphia] Childs & Swaine, 1793.
23 p.
MBAt mp. 46915

B8535 U.S. TREASURY DEPT.
Treasury department, January 10th, 1793. Sir, The resolution . . . [Philadelphia, Childs and Swaine, 1793]
[2] p. 34.5 X 21 cm.
DLC (3 copies); NN; RPJCB mp. 46925

B8536 U.S. TREASURY DEPT.
Treasury department. February 1793. Sir, In obedience to an order . . . [Philadelphia, Childs and Swaine, 1793]
6 p. 32 cm. caption title
Huntington 641
CSmH; DLC (2 copies); MiU-C mp. 46926

B8537 U.S. TREASURY DEPT.
Treasury Department, February 14th, 1793. Sir, I have the honor to transmit . . . three several statements marked A. B. C. . . . [adddressed to] The Vice President of the United States, and President of the Senate. [Philadelphia, 1793]
[2] p. 29 X 21 cm.
MWA mp. 46927

B8538 U.S. TREATIES
Extract from the treaty of amity and commerce between the United States . . . and His Most Christian Majesty . . . Article 25 . . . [Philadelphia, 1793]
broadside 23 X 19.5 cm.
Includes a similar paragraph from the treaty with the Netherlands, Oct. 8, 1782
Enclosed in a circular from the Comptroller of the Treasury, May 23, 1793
PPRF mp. 46928

B8539 A USEFUL essay: being a concise account of the excellency of the Common Prayer, in the Episcopal Church. By a clergyman. Hanover, Printed and sold by Josiah Dunham, 1793.
11 p. 19.5 cm.
Probably by John Cosens Ogden
Advertised in the Rutland *Farmer's Library*, July 8, 1794
CtHi; MH mp. 46929

B8540 VERMONT. LAWS
Acts and laws of the state of Vermont, passed by the Legislature of Rutland, 1792. [Bennington, A. Haswell, 1793]
40 p. 27 cm. caption title
McCorison 282; Sabin 99113
MWA; Vt; VtU (2 copies)

B8541 VERMONT. LAWS
Acts and laws. Passed by the Legislature of the State of Vermont, at their session at Windsor, October, 1793 . . . [Bennington, A. Haswell, 1793]
p. 41–84. 19 cm. caption title
McCorison 282; Sabin 99116
MWA; Vt; VtU-W

B8542 VIRGINIA. GOVERNOR, 1791–1794
By the Governor . . . a proclamation. The President . . . having been pleased . . . [May 13, 1793] . . . [Richmond, A. Davis, 1793]
broadside 33 X 20 cm.
MHi. Photostat: DLC mp. 46930

B8543 VIRGINIA. GOVERNOR, 1791–1794
By the Governor of the Commonwealth of Virginia: A proclamation. Whereas. . . the plague . . . quarantine . . . 17th day of September . . . 1793. [Richmond, 1793]
broadside 34 X 26.5 cm.
CSmH mp. 46931

B8544 VIRGINIA. LAWS
Richmond, January *19th* 1793. Gentlemen, I do myself the honor to transmit to you . . . certains acts passed the last session . . . Among them you will find . . . "An act for the regulating the militia of this Commonwealth." . . . [Richmond, 1793]
broadside 33.5 X 19.5 cm.
Signed in ms.: Ach. B. L. Lee
PHi mp. 46932

B8545 THE Virginia almanac for the year . . . 1794 . . . Likewise, a variety of essays . . . By the North Mountain Philosopher. Winchester, Richard Bowen [1793]
[36?] p. 17 cm.
Bear 94
MWA ([34] p.) mp. 46933

B8546 THE Virginia almanack for the year . . . 1794 . . . Calculated by Benjamin Banneker . . . Petersburg, William Prentis [1793]
[36] p. 16 cm.
Advertised in the *Virginia Gazette and Petersburg Intelligencer*, Nov. 19, 1793
Bear 95; Wyatt 12
MWA [16] p.; t.p. missing); NN mp. 46692

B8547 THE Virginia Gazette & Agricultural Repository. Dumfries, Charles Fierer [1793]

Brigham p. 1113
DLC (photostat: issues for Apr. 11, Dec. 19); MWA
mp. 46692

B8548 THE wandering young gentlewoman, or cat-skin's garland. [n.p.] Printed in the year . . . M,DDC,XCIII [i.e. 1793]
[8] p. 13.5 cm.
MWA mp. 46934

B8549 WATTS, ISAAC, 1674–1748
Hymns and spiritual songs . . . Philadelphia, Wm. Spotswood, 1793.
246, x p.
MB mp. 46935

B8550 WATTS, ISAAC, 1674–1748
Hymns and spiritual songs . . . Wilmington, Brynberg and Andrews, 1793.
284 p.
No copy located mp. 46936

B8551 WEBSTER, NOAH, 1758–1843
The American spelling book . . . Thomas & Andrews's fifth edition . . . Boston, 1793.
144 p. illus. 17 cm.
Rosenbach-Ch 170; Skeel-Carpenter 29
ICHi; PP mp. 46940

B8552 WEBSTER, NOAH, 1758–1843
The American spelling book . . . Thomas & Andrews's sixth edition . . . Boston, 1793.
144 p. illus. 17 cm.
New York Public 1097; Skeel-Carpenter 30
MWA; NN mp. 46941

B8553 WEBSTER, NOAH, 1758–1843
The American spelling book . . . Thomas & Andrews's eighth edition . . . Boston, 1793.
144 p. illus. 17 cm.
Skeel-Carpenter 31
NN mp. 46942

B8554 WEBSTER, NOAH, 1758–1843
[The American spelling book . . . Fifteenth edition. New York, Samuel Campbell, 1793]

In a letter to Webster, Sept. 22, 1792, Campbell refers to his 15th edition's being in preparation
Skeel-Carpenter 33
No copy known mp. 46943

B8555 WEIHNACHTS-LIEDER, Gebäter . . . für die Kinder in der Stadt und auf dem Lande . . . Reading, Jungmann & Gruber, 1793.

Nolan p. 25
J. Bennett Nolan, Reading, Pa. (1930); C. W. Unger, Pottsville, Pa. (1930) mp. 46944

B8556 WHEATON, HANNAH
A New Year's wish. The author's being absent by reason of the small-pox, prevented her addressing her Friends the last year . . . Hannah Wheaton, December, 1793. [Philadelphia? 1793]
broadside 34 X 14 cm.
MWA mp. 46945

B8557 [WILCOCKS, THOMAS] 1549?–1608
A choice drop of honey . . . The forty-fifth edition. Baltimore, Samuel and John Adams, 1793.
24 p. 15.5 cm.
Minick 140; cf. Evans 28085
PHi mp. 46946

B8558 WILLIAMS, JOHN FOSTER, 1743–1814
Capt. J. F. Williams' apparatus for extracting fresh water from salt water. Boston, Benj. Russell [1793]
[2] p. illus. 39.5 X 32 cm.
Printed on verso of a "Shipping Paper" made out for the Schooner Polly
New York Public 1098
NN mp. 46947

B8559 WILSON, SAMUEL, 1703–1750
A scripture-manuel . . . Tenth edition . . . Elizabeth-Town, Reprinted by Shepard Kollock, 1793.
22 p. 18.5 cm. [A]-B^6 (B6 blank)
MWA mp. 46948

B8560 WINTER, JOHN, d. 1821
[Address to the inhabitants of Frederick-Town and County. Baltimore? John Winter? 1793]
broadside?
Title from a notice in *Bartgis's Maryland Gazette*, Aug. 15 1793; "John Winter, the pretended printer of Frederick-Town, has . . . published an address in Baltimore . . ."
Minick 142
No copy known mp. 46949

B8561 [WOLCOT, JOHN] 1738–1819
The works of Peter Pindar . . . A new edition. In three volumes . . . New York, Printed for L. Wayland, 1793.
3 v. 17 cm.
Huntington 642
CSmH (vol. 3 lacking) mp. 46950

B8562 WOOLWORTH, AARON, 1763–1821
The evil of lying: a sermon, delivered at Bridgehampton, January 13, 1793 . . . Sagg-Harbour, David Frothingham, 1793.
15 p. 21 cm.
McMurtrie: Sag Harbor 4; New York Public 1099; Sabin 105219
NEh; NSmB; PPPrHi. Photostat: NN mp. 46951

B8563 ZANCHI, GIROLAMO, 1516?–1590
The doctrine of absolute predestination . . . Translated . . . by Augustus Toplady . . . York, John Edie, 1793.
155 p. 18 cm.
MWA mp. 46952

1794

B8564 ACCOUNT of a horrid murder, committed by Captain William Corran of the brig Falmouth, on the body of Mr. Joseph Porter, his passenger. With the particulars of his trial and execution at Halifax, July 17-21, 1794. New-York: Printed by Citizens Loudon and Cock [1794?]
12 p. 19 cm.
Dated tentatively by CtHi
CtHi

B8565 AN account of the remarkable conversion of a little boy and girl . . . Bennington, Anthony Haswell, 1794.
18 p. 15.5 cm.
Cooley 236
MWA mp. 46954

B8566 ADAMS, PHINEAS, 1741-1801
A sermon, preached at the ordination of . . . Nathan Bradstreet . . . Exeter, John Lamson, 1794.
35 p. 19.5 cm.
DLC mp. 46955

B8567 AERZNEY Büchlein für Menschen und Vieh . . . Reading, Jungmann & Gruber, 1794.

Nolan p. 26
Historical Society of Berks County
mp. 46958

B8568 AMERICAN APOLLO
The carrier of the *American Apollo* wishes all his kind

patrons, a Happy New Year. Boston, January 1, 1794 . . . [Boston, 1794]
broadside
MWA mp. 47002

B8569 AMERICAN STAR
Supplement to the *American Star*, No. 5. Culture of the vine . . . J. Swanwick . . . Philadelphia, January 21, 1794. Plan of a subscription . . . N.B. The shares are at 20 dollars each . . . [Philadelphia, 1794]
broadside 25.5 X 20 cm.
Text in 2 columns, English in left, French in right
MHi mp. 47223

B8570 THE American tutor's assistant; or a compendious system of practical arithmetic . . . Third edition. Philadelphia, Zachariah Poulson, 1794.
[4], 200 p.
Karpinski p. 98
PHi mp. 46959

B8571 AMOUREUX, M.
A short and practical treatise on the culture of the wine-grapes in the United States of America . . . Georgetown, Hanson & Briggs [1794]
broadsheet 38 X 22 cm.
A copy was enclosed by the author in a letter to George Washington, dated 10 November 1794
Goff: Georgetown II
DLC (2 copies) mp. 46960

B8572 ARABIAN NIGHTS
The history of Sindbad the sailor . . . Boston, Printed and sold by S. Hall, 1794.
121, [1] p. 11 cm.
MWA mp. 46963

B8573 ARABIAN NIGHTS
The seven voyages of Sinbad the Sailor . . . Philadelphia, Printed and sold by H. and P. Rice, 1794.
96 p. 16 cm. B^{12} C^{8} $D\text{-}E^{12}$ F^{4}
Rosenbach-Ch 184
MB; PP. Mrs. Joseph Carson, Philadelphia (1962)
mp. 46964

B8574 ARISTOTLE'S master-piece . . . [n.p.] Printed in the year 1794.
132 p. 14.5 cm. $A\text{-}E^{12}F^{6}$
MWA mp. 46965

B8575 [ARNOLD, SAMUEL] 1740-1802
Pauvre Madelon, a favorite dialogue and duett in The surrender of Calais. New^{k}., Printed for G. Gilfert & co., No. 191 Broadway [1794-95]
[2] p. 36 cm. caption title
Sonneck Upton p. 328
MiU-C

B8576 AT a meeting of a number of inhabitants of the territory of Columbia, on the 4th of February, 1794, Robert Peter in the chair . . . Resolved, That a seminary . . . be established in . . . Washington . . . [Georgetown, Samuel Hanson, 1794]
broadside 29.5 X 37.5 cm.
Goff: Georgetown 12
DLC mp. 46966

B8577 BAKER, GARDINER
Natural history. At a menagerie of living animals and birds, the corner of Pearl-street . . . viz. A young female panther from Kentucky . . . Gardiner Baker. Museum, in the Exchange, New-York, Sept. 25, 1794. [New York, 1794]
broadside 27 X 22.5 cm.
NHi mp. 46967

B8578 BAKER, GARDINER
New Museum, contained in the front rooms of the Exchange, opposite the entrance of the Museum and Wax-Work . . . Gardiner Baker . . . September 29, 1794. New-York, John Buel [1794]
broadside 39.5 X 33 cm.
NHi mp. 46968

B8579 BALCH, HEZEKIAH
[Sermon on Psalmody, preached at Salem Church at the opening of the Presbytery of Abingdon, October 12, 1786. Knoxville? George Roulstone? 1794]

Advertised in the *Knoxville Gazette*, Feb. 13, 1794, as "Just published and for sale . . . in Jonesborough . . . in Greenville . . . in Knoxville."
McMurtrie: Tennessee 3
No copy known mp. 46969

B8580 BALTIMORE. NEW THEATRE
[The last week of performance. New theatre . . . Seignior Falconi will introduce an automaton . . . Baltimore, 1794]
broadside
Title from the *Baltimore Daily Intelligencer*, Feb. 17, 1794, which states: "Handbills being put up . . ."
Minick 143
No copy known mp. 46970

B8581 BALTIMORE DAILY INTELLIGENCER
New-Year's verses, addressed to the patrons of the *Baltimore Daily Intelligencer* . . . January 1, 1794 . . . [Baltimore, Yundt and Patton, 1794]
broadside 24.5 X 21.5 cm.
Minick 145
MdBP mp. 47132

B8582 BALTIMORE EQUITABLE SOCIETY
[Constitution or deed of settlement of the Baltimore Equitable Society . . . Baltimore, John Hayes, 1794]
16 p. 8vo
Minick 146
MdBP (not traced) mp. 46971

B8583 BALTIMORE, September 27. By two gentlemen . . . from Kentucky we have been favored . . . Lexington, September 8, 1794 . . . Baltimore, Yundt and Patton [1794]
broadside 23 X 17.5 cm.
Minick 148
MdHi; PHi; WHi. Photostat: MdBE mp. 46972

B8584 BANNAKER'S Wilmington almanac . . . for 1795. Wilmington, S. & J. Adams [1794]
[36] p.
Drake 1395; cf. Evans 26613
DeWin; MdBP

B8585 BANNEKER'S almanack, for the year 1795 . . . Philadelphia, Printed for William Young [1794]
[36] p. 17 cm.
Porter 35
DLC (2 copies); NN; PPL mp. 46973

B8586 BAPTISTS. CONNECTICUT. DANBURY ASSOCIATION
Minutes of the Danbury Baptist Association, holden at Suffield, Sept. 17th and 18th, 1794. [n.p., 1794]
7 p.

Trumbull: Second supplement 2862
Photocopy: MWA mp. 46975

B8587 BAPTISTS. NORTH CAROLINA. NEUSE BAPTIST ASSOCIATION
Minutes of the Neuse Baptist Association. Holden at Bear-Marsh Meeting-House, Duplin County, North-Carolina, October, 1794 . . . [Wilmington? 1794]
4 p. 27 cm. caption title
McMurtrie: North Carolina 189
NcWsW mp. 46976

B8588 BAPTISTS. SOUTH CAROLINA. CHARLESTON BAPTIST ASSOCIATION
A summary of church-discipline . . . By the Baptist Association, in Charleston, South-Carolina. The second edition . . . Charleston, Markland, M'Iver, & co., 1794.
28 p. 21 cm.
Sabin 93597a
NRAB

B8589 BAPTISTS. VIRGINIA. PORTSMOUTH ASSOCIATION
Minutes of the Virginia Portsmouth Baptist Association, holden . . . May 24, 25 and 26, 1794. Richmond, Thomas Nicolson, 1794.
14 p. 18 cm.
Davis 99
NRAB mp. 46977

B8590 BARRELL AND HOSKINS, firm, Boston
Boston Joseph Barrell . . . having retired from business, has resigned it to us . . . [Boston, 1794]
broadside 23 X 19 cm.
Filled in for Aug. 1, 1794
RPJCB (2 copies) mp. 46978

B8591 BAYLEY, DANIEL
The Psalm singer's assistant. Newbury-Port [1794]
16 p.
RPB mp. 46979

B8592 BECKER, CHRISTIAN LUDWIG, 1756–1818
Die Absicht Gottes . . . Philadelphia, Carl Cist, 1794.
22 p. 21 cm.
MWA mp. 46980

B8593 BENJAMIN Bannaker's [sic] Pennsylvania, Delaware, Maryland, and Virginia almanac, for the year . . . 1795 . . . Philadelphia, Printed for Jacob Johnson [1794]
[36] p. 18.5 cm.
Porter 37
NHi mp. 46974

B8594 [BERQUIN, ARNAUD] 1750–1791
The mountain piper; or, The history of Edgar and Matilda . . . The first Worcester edition. Worcester, Printed and sold by Isaiah Thomas, 1794.
96 p. 11 cm.
MWA (t.p. and back cover wanting) mp. 46981

B8595 BIBLE
An abridgement of the history of the Holy Bible. New-York, H. Gaine, 1794.
30, [1] p. illus. 10 cm.
First and last pages pasted to covers
NN mp. 46984

B8595a BIBLE. N.T.
The New Testament . . . Philadelphia, William Young, 1794.
[193] p.
MWA mp. 46982

B8596 BIBLE. N.T.
The New Testament . . . Wilmington, Peter Brynberg and Samuel Andrews [1794?]
[306] p. 18 cm.
Suggested date from DeWI card
Hawkins 42
DeWI mp. 46983

B8597 BICHENO, JAMES, d. 1831
The signs of the times . . . Baltimore, John Hayes, 1794.
2 p. l., 40 p. 18 cm.
Minick 154
MdBE mp. 46985

B8598 BICKERSTAFF'S almanack for . . . 1795 . . . Boston, Printed for, and sold by the booksellers [1794]
[16] p. 17.5 cm.
MWA mp. 46986

B8599 BOSTON. COLLECTOR OF TAXES
Ward, No. To Your commonwealth tax. Your town and county tax . . . Boston, October 1794. [Boston, 1794]
broadside 13 X 16 cm.
MB

B8600 BOSTON. SELECTMEN
Boston, August 5, 1794. Gentlemen, Short, but fervent, is the request of the really distressed. You, probably, before this, have heard of the vast devastation lately made in this town by fire . . . [Boston, 1794]
broadside 32 X 19.5 cm.
M-Ar

B8601 BOSTON THEATRE
Boston Theatre. On Monday, February Third, will be performed . . . Gustavus Vasa . . . To which will be added, a farce . . . Modern antiques . . . [Boston, 1794]
broadside 20.5 X 17 cm.
MH; MHi (photostat) mp. 46987

B8602 BRADLEY, WILLIAM CZAR, 1782–1867
The rights of youth, composed, revised, and submitted to the candid reader . . . Westminster, John Goold, 1794.

Cooley 242
No copy known mp. 46988

B8603 BRISTOL. ARTILLERY COMPANY
The charter and regulations of the artillery company . . . of Bristol . . . Warren, Nathaniel Phillips, 1794.
19 p. 15.5 cm.
Alden 1356
RHi mp. 46989

B8604 BROOKE, HENRY, 1703?–1783
Gustavus Vasa . . . As performed at the New Theatre in Boston. Boston, Printed for David West [1794]
62 p. 17 cm.
cf. Evans 26704
DLC mp. 46970

B8605 BROOKE, HENRY, 1703?–1783
The history of a reprobate . . . First American edition. Philadelphia, Printed for Robert Campbell, 1794.
71 p. 16 cm.
RPJCB (p. [1–2] wanting) mp. 46991

B8606 BROWN UNIVERSITY
Exhibition. The honour of company is requested at the exhibition in the College chapel . . . Rhode-Island college, December 29, 1794. [Providence, 1794]
broadside 10.5 X 11 cm.

Alden 1385
RHi. Photostats: DLC; MHi; MWA mp. 46992

B8607 BRUCE, GEORGE, & CO., publishers
To the public. It is a subject of general complaint . . . To accommodate country readers, the publishers of the *Minerva* propose to print . . . *The Herald*, (*A Country Gazette*.) . . . Noah Webster Jun. compiler. George Bunce, & Co. Publishers. New-York, May 7th, 1794 . . . [New York, 1794]
broadside 39 X 32 cm.
CtHi mp. 46943

B8608 BUNYAN, JOHN, 1628–1688
The pilgrim's progress . . . By John Bunyan. New York, H. Gaine, 1794.
396 p. 12mo
Hamilton 209
NjP (2 copies) mp. 46994

B8609 BURTON, JOHN, 1746–1806
Lectures on female education and manners . . . The first American edition. New-York, Printed [by Samuel Campbell] for Berry, Rogers and Berry, 1794.
334 p. 17 cm.
cf. Evans 26723
NNS

B8610 EIN Busslied von einem Gesichte welches einer Person in Lancäster Caunty in der neunten Nacht erschienen ist . . . [Lancaster?] 1794.
8 p. 17.5 cm.
MWA mp. 46995

B8611 CAREY, MATHEW, 1760–1839
Eine kurze Nachricht von dem bösartigen Fieber welches kürzlich in Philadelphia grassiret . . . Nach der vierten verbesserten Auflage aus dem Englischen übersetzt von Carl Erdmann. [Chestnut Hill] Gedruckt für den Verfasser, bey Samuel Saur, 1794.
176 p. 21 cm.
Evans 26739 has list of deaths at end in English; in this issue the list and other translatable matter is rendered into German
DLC; DNLM; PHi; PP; PPC; PPL mp. 46996

B8612 LA CARMAGNOLE Price 25 cents Philadelphia, Carr [1794]
2 p. 33 cm.
Sonneck-Upton p. 56
DLC; PU mp. 46997

B8613 CARR, BENJAMIN, 1768/69–1831
Four ballads, three from Shakespear, and one by Harwood . . . Philadelphia, Carr [1794]
9 p. 30.5 cm.
Sonneck-Upton p. 145
DLC mp. 46998

B8614 CARR, BENJAMIN, 1768/69–1831
When nights were cold . . . Philadelphia, Carr [1794]
p. 8–9. 32.5 cm.
Sonneck-Upton p. 463
DLC; MWA mp. 46999

B8615 CARRÉ, CHARLES
[Supplement aux Grammaires anglaises. Baltimore? 1794]

Title from advertisement in the *Baltimore Daily Gezette*, May 15, 1794; "Cet ouvrage se trouve chez l'auteur."
Minick 156
No copy known mp. 47000

B8616 CARRICK, SAMUEL
[Sermon given at Knoxville, February 25, 1794, in the presence of the governor, William Blount, and Assembly. Knoxville, George Roulstone, 1794]

Advertised in the *Knoxville Gazette*, Apr. 10, 1794, as "Just published and for sale for one shilling, by George Roulstone and Company."
McMurtrie: Tennessee 4
No copy known mp. 47001

B8617 CATHOLIC CHURCH. LITURGY AND RITUAL
Ordo divini officii recitandi . . . pro Anno Domini M, DCC, XCV . . . Baltimori, J. Hayes [1794]
35 p. 15.5 cm.
Minick 157; Parsons 127
DLC mp. 47005

B8618 CHAMBERLAIN, THOMAS, d. 1784
America's timely remembrancer . . . Frederick-Town, M. Bartgis, 1794.
11 p. 17.5 cm.
Minick 158
MdBP. Alden E. Fisher (Frederick, Md.) mp. 47006

B8619 THE Chester garland . . . Keene, Printed [by Henry Blake & Co.], 1794.
8 p. 17.5 cm.
MWA (torn) mp. 47007

B8620 CHRISTMAS tales, for the amusement . . . of young ladies & gentlemen . . . By Solomon Sobersides . . . Hudson, Printed and sold by Ashbel Stoddard, 1794.
159, [1] p. 10.5 cm.
MWA (p. 127–128 wanting); N (p. 29–32 mutilated) mp. 47217

B8621 CLARK, EDWARD
Letters to a friend: containing thoughts on the beginning of the New Testament dispensation . . . Stockbridge, Loring Andrews, 1794.
47 p. 18.5 cm.
Huntington 644
CSmH mp. 47008

B8622 CLARK, WILLIAM
A new mode of legislation, lately invented by Matthew Clay . . . [who] did present . . . petition, foı clearing Banister River to Pittsylvania County . . . The subscriber submits to the public . . . whether any person . . . be permitted to imitate his invention . . . William Clark. [Lynchburg? 1794?]
broadside 28 X 45 cm.
Vi. Photostat: ViU mp. 47009

B8623 CLINTON ACADEMY, EAST HAMPTON, N.Y.
Rules and regulations, for the government of the Academy, in East-Hampton. Sagg-Harbour, David Frothingham, 1794.
12 p. 16 cm.
McMurtrie: Sag Harbor 6; New York Public 1101
NEh; NSmB. Photostat: NN mp. 47010

B8624 THE Columbian almanac, for . . . 1795. By James Login. Philadelphia, Robert Campbell [1794]
[40] p. 18.5 cm.
MWA mp. 47099

B8625 COLUMBIAN CENTINEL
Dedication. To the liberal and right worthy patrons of the *Columbian Centinel*, this tenth anniversary ode, is . . . dedicated, by . . . The Carrier . . . January 1, 1794. [Boston, 1794]

broadside 47 X 15 cm.
MSaE; MWA mp. 47022

B8626 COLUMBIAN SOCIETY
City of Washington. The advantageous situation . . . prospects of its prosperity . . . induce the subscribers . . . to form themselves . . . into . . . the "Columbian Society." . . . Philadelphia, January 15th, 1794. [on verso] An estimated statement to shew what the subscribers . . . may . . . expect . . . [Philadelphia, 1794]
[2] p. 24 X 19 cm.
Earnings predicted through 1808 on verso
cf. Evans 27068
MHi; MWA mp. 47012

B8627 THE complete family book-keeper . . . for the year 1794 . . . Philadelphia, Printed by Jones, Hoff & Derrick, for John Curtis, 1794.
54 p. 20 cm.
MB

B8628 CONDEMNATION of the slave-trade; being an investigation of the origin and continuation of that inhuman traffic . . . By a friend to humanity. New York, Printed for the author, 1794.
20 p. 16 cm.
MWA; PPL mp. 47013

B8629 CONNECTICUT. GENERAL ASSEMBLY
At a General Assembly . . . holden at Hartford . . . May, A.D. 1794. To the honorable General Assembly, now sitting. The Committee appointed . . . to receive, sort and count the votes . . . for gentlemen to stand in nomination . . . in the Congress . . . report . . . Hartford, Hudson and Goodwin [1794]
broadside 33 X 20.5 cm.
MWA mp. 47014

B8630 CONNECTICUT. GOVERNOR, 1786-1796
By His Excellency Samuel Huntington . . . A proclamation . . . Hartford, March 12, 1794. Hartford, Hudson & Goodwin [1794]
broadside 39 X 32 cm.
Concerns support of missionaries by various religious bodies
CtHi; NHi mp. 47015

B8631 CONNECTICUT COURANT
To all Christian people; more especially those who take the *Connecticut Courant* . . . Hartford, January 1, 1794. [Hartford, Hudson and Goodwin, 1794]
broadside 45 X 26.5 cm.
CtHi; NHi mp. 47233

B8632 CONNECTICUT MEDICAL SOCIETY
The act, incorporating a Medical Society, in . . . Connecticut; together with the byelaws and regulations of said Society, and a list of the fellows and officers, for . . . 1792, and 1793 . . . New-Haven, T. and S. Green [1794]
16 p. 19 cm.
NNAM mp. 47016

B8633 COWLEY, HANNAH (PARKHOUSE) 1743-1809
The belle's stratagem . . . Boston, Printed for John West, 1794.
73 p. 18 cm.
cf. Evans 26824
DLC; MWA; NjP mp. 47017

B8634 CRISP, STEPHEN, 1628-1692
A short history of a long travel . . . The tenth edition. Danbury, N. Douglas, 1794.
23 p. 17.5 cm.
CtHi mp. 47018

B8635 [CROUCH, NATHANIEL] 1632?-1725?
A journey to Jerusalem . . . Poughkeepsie, Printed and sold by Nicholas Power, 1794.
34 p. 17 cm.
MWA mp. 47019

B8636 DABNEY, JOHN, 1752-1819
Additional catalogue of books, for sale or circulation . . . at the Salem Bookstore . . . [Newburyport] At Osborne's Office, Printed for J. Dabney, at Salem, 1794.
34 p.
Tapley p. 355
MHi; MSaE; RPJCB mp. 47020

B8637 THE danger of excessive drinking. A poem . . . [n.p.] Printed for the author, 1794.
8 p. 18.5 cm.
MH; MWA. Bernard L. Gordon, Boston (1965) mp. 47021

B8638 THE death and burial of Cock Robin . . . The second Worcester edition. Worcester, Printed and sold by Isaiah Thomas, 1794.
31 p. incl. covers. 10.5 cm.
MWA mp. 47011

B8639 DECALVES. ALONSO, pseud.
Travels to the westward . . . By Alonso Decavles [sic]. Windsor, Alden Spooner, 1794.
36 p. 17 cm.
Vail: Old frontier 981
ICN mp. 47023

B8640 DEFOE, DANIEL, 1661?-1731
The life and most surprising adventures of Robinson Crusoe . . . Boston, I. Thomas and E. T. Andrews, 1794.
231 p. 18 cm.
Brigham: Robinson Crusoe 27
CtY; MWA; MiU-C. Dr. Edgar S. Oppenheimer mp. 47024

B8641 [DEFOE, DANIEL] 1661?-1731
Religious courtship . . . New-York, Printed and sold by J. Harrisson, 1794.
143 p. 14 cm. A^{12} B^{6} C^{12} D^{6} E^{12} F^{6} G^{12} H^{6}
MWA (p. 11-14 wanting) mp. 47025

B8642 [DEFOE, DANIEL] 1661?-1731
[Travels of Robinson Crusoe. Written by himself. Boston, Printed and sold by Samuel Hall, 1794?]
31 p. incl. covers. 11 cm.
Imprint and date assigned by Clarence S. Brigham by comparison with Hall's 1790 and 1798 editions
MWA (t.p. and p. 29-30 wanting) mp. 47026

B8643 DEFOE, DANIEL, 1661?-1731
Travels of Robinson Crusoe . . . The third Worcester edition. Worcester, I. Thomas, 1794.
31 p. 10 cm.
Brigham: Robinson Crusoe 29; Rosenbach-Ch 171
MWA; PP mp. 47027

B8644 DEFOE, DANIEL, 1661?-1731
The wonderful life and adventures of Robinson Crusoe . . . Philadelphia: Printed and sold by John M'Culloch, 1794.
144 p. illus. 13.5 cm.
d'Alté A. Welch, Cleveland (1965)

B8645 [DELAIRE, JAS.]
Au citoyen Rochambeau fils. A New-Port Rhode-Island,

Citoyen, Comme vous pourriez avoir perdu la copie de la lettre que vous écrivîtes le 1 Janvier 1793 . . . Ja^s. Delaire. Charleston, ce premier Septembre . . . 1794. [Philadelphia? 1794]
6 p. 27.5 X 21.5 cm.
NN copy removed from *Courrier Français*, Philadelphia, following Nov. 27, 1794 issue
New York Public 1103
NN; RPJCB mp. 47028

B8646 [DELANO, STEPHEN] 1747?–1822
Elegiac poems; also, a small collection of hymns. By a country farmer, in Woodstock, (Vermont). Windsor, Alden Spooner, 1794.
47 p. 19 cm.
Cooley 243
MWA mp. 47029

B8647 DELAWARE
Attention, Light Infantry. Saturday 20th inst. being appointed as a Field day for the first Regiment of Delaware Militia . . . Wilmington, Brynberg and Andrews [1794]
broadside 25.5 X 18 cm.
Signed: David Bush, Capt.
PHi mp. 47030

B8648 DIBDIN, CHARLES, 1745–1814
[Songs in the Deserter. Baltimore, P. Edwards, 1794]

Advertised in the *Maryland Journal*, Oct. 28, 1794, as "Books of the songs in the comic opera of the Deserter . . . performed this evening . . . price twelve cents."
Libretto only?
Minick 166
No copy known mp. 47031

B8649 DODDRIDGE, PHILIP, 1702–1751
The rise and progress of religion in the soul . . . Exeter, Printed by Henry Ranlet, for Thomas & Andrews, Boston, 1794.
390, [5] p. 18.5 cm.
cf. Evans 26901
MWA; NhD mp. 47032

B8650 DODDRIDGE, PHILIP, 1702–1751
The rise and progress of religion in the soul . . . Bradford's second edition. Philadelphia, Thomas & William Bradford [1794]
311 p. 17.5 cm.
cf. Evans 26902
CtY; DLC; MdW; MoSpD; NBuG; PPPrHi; WyHi mp. 47033

B8651 [DODSLEY, ROBERT] 1703–1764
The economy of human life . . . New-York, T. Allen, 1794.
131 p. 14.5 cm.
MWA (p. 61–62 wanting) mp. 47034

B8652 DORCHESTER LIBRARY
Rules and orders of the Dorchester Library, with a catalogue of the books, August, MDCCXCIV. Boston, I. Thomas and E. T. Andrews, 1794.
12 p. 18 cm.
MWA ([14] p. of additional books, in ms.); RPJCB mp. 47035

B8653 DUTCHESS CO., N. Y. CITIZENS
(Circular) Sir, We were appointed a committee to communicate to you the result of a . . . meeting of the electors . . . Senator—Peter Cantine, Junior. For Assembly. David Brooks . . . [n.p., 1794?]
broadside 33 X 20.5 cm.
NHi mp. 47036

B8654 EASY lessons for young children. Philadelphia, W. Young, 1794.
108, [3] p. 10.5 cm.
Rosenbach-Ch 172
PP mp. 47037

B8655 THE entertaining history of honest Peter, by Miss D______ y . . . Boston, Printed and sold by Samuel Hall, 1794.
48, [3] p. 10.5 cm.
RPB mp. 47038

B8656 AN exposition of the church catechism. Hagerstown, Stewart Herbert [1794?]
35 p. 16 cm.
Advertised in the *Washington Spy*, Jan. 31, 1794, as "For sale at the printing office, in Hagerstown."
Minick 169
MdBE mp. 47039

B8657 THE famous history of Sir Richard Whittington, and his cat . . . Printed [by Philip Edwards?] for, and sold by John Fisher, Stationer, in Market-Street, Baltimore —1794.
31 p. illus. 10 cm.
Minick 170
MWA. d'Alté A. Welch, Cleveland (1962) mp. 47328

B8658 THE Farmer's American almanack for . . . 1795. By Andrew Beers. Danbury, Edwards Ely [1794]
[24] p.
Drake 531
CtHi

B8659 THE father's gift . . . Boston, Printed and sold by Samuel Hall, 1794.
30, [1] p. 10 cm.
Pages [1] and [31] pasted to covers
CtHi mp. 47040

B8660 THE father's gift . . . Third Worcester edition. Worcester, Isaiah Thomas, 1794.
30 p. 10 cm.
MWA (imperfect). Emerson Greenaway, Philadelphia (1961) mp. 47041

B8661 [FIELDING, HENRY] 1707–1754
The remarkable history of Tom Jones, a foundling. Boston, Printed and sold by Samuel Hall, 1794.
28, [3] p. 10 cm.
Mrs. Edgar S. Oppenheimer, N.Y.C. (1961) (pages [2] and [31] wanting) mp. 47042

B8662 [FIELDING, HENRY] 1707–1754
The remarkable history of Tom Jones . . . The third Worcester edition. Worcester, Printed and sold by Isaiah Thomas, 1794.
31 p. incl. covers. 10 cm.
MWA mp. 47043

B8663 FISH, SAMUEL
An humble address to every Christian . . . Norwich, Printed by John Trumbull, for the author, 1794.
39 p.
Trumbull: Supplement 2145
CtHi mp. 47044

B8664 THE following lines were compos'd by the desire of a friend upon the death of Mr. Timothy Bacon, who died 24th of May, A.D. 1794, in the 23d year of his age . . . [n.p., 1794?]
broadside 30 X 16 cm.
NHi. Photostat: MWA mp. 47045

B8665 FOLSOM, JOHN WEST
John W. Folsom's Catalogue of books for sale and circulation . . . [Boston, J. W. Folsom, 1794?]
[48] p. 20 cm.
Advertisement dated "December 24, 1794" on p. [48]
MB mp. 47046

B8666 FOSTER, ISAAC, d. 1807
Divine righteousness in the salvation, and damnation of sinners exhibited . . . Norwich, Printed by John Trumbull, and sold by James Springer, New London, 1794.
90 p.
Trumbull: Supplement 2155; cf. Evans 26990
No copy located mp. 47047

B8667 FOWLER, B.
An elegy. On the death of a virtuous young lady. Miss Betsey Waterman, Smithfield . . . Rhode Island . . . [Providence?] Printed for the author, B. Fowler, 1794.
broadside 30.5 X 16 cm.
Alden 1363
MWA mp. 47048

B8668 FOX, WILLIAM
Thoughts on the death of the King of France . . . Elizabethtown [Md.], Stewart Herbert, 1794.
22, [2] p. 19.5 cm.
Minick 172
MWA mp. 47049

B8669 THE Franklin almanack, for . . . 1795 . . . Boston, Joseph Bumstead [1794]
[24] p. 17.5 cm.
Drake 3529
MB; MHi; MWA; N mp. 47050

B8670 FREEMASONS. VIRGINIA. GRAND LODGE
Proceedings, &c. at a Grand communication held in . . . Richmond, on Tuesday 28th day of October, A.L. 5794–A.D. 1794. [Richmond? 1794]
14 p. 20 cm.
Davis 101
NNFM mp. 47051

B8671 FREEMASONS. VIRGINIA. GRAND LODGE
Proceedings of the Grand lodge of Virginia. Held . . . the twenty-eighth day of October; and . . . the twenty-fifth day of November, A. L. 5794–A.D. 1794. Richmond, John Dixon, 1794.
16 p. 21 cm.
Davis 102
DSC; IaCrM; MBFM; Vi mp. 47052

B8672 FREEMASONS. VIRGINIA. SAGESSE LODGE
Tableau des F. F. qui composent la loge provinciale Francaise . . . la Sagesse . . . en Virginie . . . 5794. Norfolk, Baxter & Wilson [1794]
8 p.
McCoy 13
DSC mp. 47053

B8673 A FRIENDLY address to the inhabitants of the town of Providence. Friends, brethren, and fellow-citizens . . . Providence, December 19, 1794. [Providence] B. Wheeler [1794]
broadside 27 X 22.5 cm.
Alden 1372; cf. Evans 27580
RHi mp. 47194

B8674 FRIENDS, SOCIETY OF. LONDON YEARLY MEETING
From our Yearly Meeting held . . . in London, from the 19th to the 28th of the fifth month, 1794 . . . to the Yearly Meeting in Philadelphia . . . [Philadelphia, 1794]
2 p. 33 cm. caption title
Not Evans 27022
CSmH; MB mp. 47054

B8675 GAIFER
A letter from Gaifer, in London, to Aly-Ben-Hayton . . . Exeter, Printed and sold by W. Stearns and S. Winslow, 1794.
23 p. 8vo
MB mp. 47055

B8676 GENÊT, EDMOND CHARLES, 1763–1834
The correspondence between Citizen Genet . . . and the officers of the federal government . . . [Philadelphia, 1794?]
11 p. 20.5 cm. caption title
DLC mp 47056

B8677 GEORGIA. GOVERNOR, 1794–1795
Georgia. By His Excellency George Mathews, Governor . . . A proclamation. Whereas I have received official information, that Elijah Clarke . . . with intent . . . to establish . . . independent government . . . [July 28, 1794] . . . [Augusta? 1794]
broadside
De Renne p. 262
GU-De mp. 47057

B8678 GEORGIA. LAWS
An act for appropriating a part of the unlocated territory of this State, for payment of the late state troops . . . December 28th, 1794. [Savannah, 1794]
broadside 34 X 20 cm.
cf. Evans 28736
NHi mp. 47058

B8679 GESSNER, SALOMON, 1730–1787
The death of Abel . . . The twelfth edition. New-Haven, Abel Morse, 1794.
251 p. 14.5 cm.
Trumbull: Supplement 2185
CtHi; CtY; DLC; MH; MWA; RPJCB mp. 47059

B8680 GESSNER, SALOMON, 1730–1787
The death of Abel . . . New-York, Printed for, and sold by Evert Duyckinck, from Mott & Hurtin's Press, 1794.
144 p. 13.5 cm.
MWA (half-title wanting?) mp. 47061

B8681 GESSNER, SALOMON, 1730–1787
The death of Abel . . . To which is added, The death of Cain . . . Newburyport, Edmund M. Blunt, 1794.
184, 84 p. 14 cm. A-X^5 Y^2
"The death of Cain" (p. [185]) has imprint: Newburyport, Printed for E. Larkin, Boston
MWA; N mp. 47062

B8682 GLENDINNING, WILLIAM
A sermon containing some observations . . . on Lot's flight out of Sodom . . . Philadelphia, Printed for William Glendinning by William W. Woodward, 1794.
28 p. 16 cm.
CSmH mp. 47064

B8683 GLENDINNING, WILLIAM
A sermon on the unity of the Christian church . . . Philadelphia, Printed for William Glendinning by W. W. Woodward, 1794.
33 p. 19 cm.
DLC mp. 47065

B8684 GODINEAU, HENRI FRANÇOIS
Oration upon religious worship, delivered by Citizen Godineau . . . before the representatives of the people Tallien and Yzabeau, on the 20th of November, 1793 . . . [at end] Philadelphia, Printed and sold [by B. F. Bache] at No. 112, Market-Street [1794]
8 p. 8vo caption title
Adams: Pennsylvania 58
PHi; PPL; PU

B8685 GRAM, HANS
Bind kings with chains. [Boston? 1794?]
8 p. 12.5 X 22.5 cm. caption title
First sung in October 1794
CtY mp. 47066

B8686 GRAM, HANS
Resurrection, an anthem for Easter Sunday. Charlestown, 1794.
8 p.
CtY; MHi mp. 47067

B8687 HABERMANN, JOHANN, 1516–1590
Christliche Morgen- und Abend-Gebäter . . . wie auch D. Neumanns Kern aller Gebäter . . . Philadelphia, Gedruckt und zu haben bey Carl Cist, 1794.
[2], 63, [2] p. front. 14 cm.
PHi mp. 47068

B8688 HALLAM & HODGKINSON
Hallam & Hodgkinson having purchas'd the entire theatrical property belonging to the Old American Company and being persuaded that the citizens of New-York are desirous of . . . a New Theatre . . . [New York, 1794]
broadside 33 X 21 cm.
NHi mp. 47069

B8689 HENRY, MATTHEW, 1662–1714
[A church in the house.] A sermon, preached in London, April 16th, 1704, concerning family religion . . . The second American edition. Philadelphia, Printed and sold by John M'Culloch, 1794.
36 p. 12mo
PPL mp. 47070

B8690 THE HERALD; A GAZETTE FOR THE COUNTRY
To the public . . . To accommodate country readers, the publishers of the *Minerva* propose to print a distinct paper . . . *The Herald, (A Country Gazette.)* . . . Noah Webster, Jun. Compiler . . . [New York, 1794]
broadside 40 X 33 cm.
New York Public 1107; Skeel-Carpenter 790
NN mp. 47326

B8691 HIRTE, TOBIAS
. . . Sclaven-Handel . . . Verfahrungs-Art um Sclaven zu bekommen, und ihre Behandlung in West-Indien . . . Philadelphia, Samuel Saur, 1794.
broadside 46 X 39 cm.
Ornamental borders
PHi mp. 47071

B8692 HIRTE, TOBIAS
Warnung, vor falschen Seneca-Oel. Indianisch-French-Crieck-Seneca-Oel. Ein vortrefliches . . . Medicament, ist zu haben in Philadelphia, bey Tobias Hirte . . . Kurze Nachricht von dessen Nutzen und Gebrauch . . . [Philadelphia, 1794?]
broadside 36 X 23 cm.
10 testimonial letters dated from 1792 to 1794
PPL. Photostat: MWA. Mrs. Marion Carson (1960)
mp. 47072

B8693 THE history of a school boy . . . Philadelphia, Benjamin Johnson, 1794.
124 p. 10 cm.
d'Alté A. Welch (1960) mp. 47073

B8694 THE history of Constantius & Pulchera, or Constancy rewarded . . . Boston, 1794.
99 p. 12.5 cm.
Wright 1197
MWA (has p. 9, 93–99) (Xerox copy). Howard S. Mott (1948); Wm. F. Kock, Haverhill, N. H. (1964).
mp. 47074

B8695 THE history of Master Jackey and Miss Harriot . . . The second Worcester edition. Worcester, Printed and sold by Isaiah Thomas, 1794.
31 p. incl. covers. 10.5 cm.
MWA (mutilated) mp. 47075

B8696 HOOK, JAMES, 1746–1827
Ma belle coquette . . . New York, G. Gilfert [1794–95]
[2] p. 34 cm.
Sonneck-Upton p. 245
DLC; RPJCB mp. 47076

B8697 HOOK, JAMES, 1746–1827
Sweet lillies of the Valley . . . New-York, Printed and sold by G. Gilfert [1794–96]
[2] p. 28 cm. caption title
First line: O'er barren hills . . .
Sonneck-Upton p. 416
MiU–C

B8698 HOTCHKIN, BERIAH
The mysteries of providence; a funeral sermon, delivered in Catskill, at the funeral of Mrs. Sarah Graham, who died February 5th, 1793 . . . Catskill: Printed by Mackay Croswell, & co. M,DCC,XCIV.
22 p. 17 cm.
NHi mp. 47077

B8699 HOUGH, SIMON
Letters to a son, and others . . . Stockbridge: Printed by Loring Andrews. M.DCC.XCIV
30 p. 21 cm.
NHi mp. 47078

B8700 THE house that Jack built . . . New York, W. Durell [1794?]
30 p. illus. 10 cm.
"Alphabet" on p. 4 misspelled "alphaaet."
Dated by d'Alté A. Welch
MWA ([1793?]). d'Alté A. Welch, Cleveland (1962)
mp. 46787

B8701 HUMANE SOCIETY OF THE STATE OF NEW YORK
To the public. With a view of promoting the interests of humanity . . . citizens have associated under the name of "The Humane Society . . . of New-York," and have agreed to the following constitution . . . New-York, July 12, 1794. At a special meeting . . . the following . . . were elected to . . . offices . . . [New York, 1794]

[2] p. 33 cm.
2 p. of four-page folder printed
MHi mp. 47079

B8702 AN important case argued: in three dialogues . . . The first American edition. New-York, Nathaniel Birdsall and Walter W. Hyer, 1794.
16 p. 20.5 cm.
DLC mp. 47080

B8703 INTERESTING intelligence! Boston, March 27, 1794 . . . Reprinted in Salem [1794]
broadside 44.5 X 21 cm.
Concerns detaining of American ships
Tapley p. 356
MSaE mp. 47081

B8704 JACHIN and Boaz; or, an authentic key to the door of free-masonry . . . to which are added, a select collection of songs. Boston, Printed by J. Bumstead for E. Larkin, 1794.

BSA *Papers*, 54(1960): 64
MH (imperfect) mp. 47082

B8705 JERMENT, GEORGE
Parental duty . . . Philadelphia, Printed and sold by Stewart & Cochran, 1794.
91, 206 p. 17 cm. A-H^6 A-R^6
"Early piety, illustrated and recommended" (with same imprint as above) has separate pagination and signatures, but t.p. is at sig. H6 of "Parental duty."
MWA; NjP mp. 47083

B8706 JOHN STREET THEATRE
New York, April 1, 1794. Theatre. By the Old American Company. On Wednesday evening, the 2d of April, will be presented . . . PERCY . . . To which will be added . . . Don Juan . . . Vivat Respublica. [New York, 1794]
broadside 41 X 23 cm.
NHi mp. 47134

B8707 [JOHNSON, RICHARD] 1734-1793
The hermit of the forest, and the wandering infants. A rural fragment. Boston, Printed and sold by Samuel Hall, 1794.
29, [2] p. incl. covers. 11 cm.
Hamilton 149b
MSaE; MWA; NjP; PP (p. [31] mutilated). d'Alté A. Welch, Cleveland (1962) mp. 47084

B8708 [JOHNSON, RICHARD] 1734-1793
The history of a little child, found under a haycock . . . Boston, Printed and sold by N. Coverly, 1794.
16 p. illus. 9.5 cm.
d'Alté A. Welch, Cleveland (1962) mp. 47085

B8709 [JOHNSON, RICHARD] 1734-1793
Tea-table dialogues . . . Philadelphia, Francis Bailey, 1794.
144 p. illus. 10.5 cm.
CLU mp. 47086

B8710 [JONES, STEPHEN] 1763-1827
The life and adventures of a fly . . . Boston, Printed and sold by John Norman [1794?]
96 p. incl. covers. illus. 11 cm. A-C^{16}
Preface signed: S. J.
MSaE; MWA (p. [1-2], 29-32, 65-66, 95-96 wanting). Martens Museum, Marietta, O.; d'Alté A. Welch, Cleveland (1962) mp. 47087

B8710a JUVENILE extracts in prose and verse . . . Vol. I. Philadelphia, Jones, Hoff & Derrick, 1794.

Ruth Adomeit, Cleveland (1969)

B8711 KEATE, GEORGE, 1729-1797
[An account of the Pelew islands . . . Baltimore, George Keatinge, 1794]

Advertised in the *Baltimore Daily Advertiser*, Apr. 2, 1794, as "This day is published."
Minick 178; cf. Evans 27177
No copy known

B8712 KEATINGE, GEORGE, d. 1811
[Catalogue of books. Baltimore, 1794]

Title from advertisement in the *Maryland Journal*, May 23, 1794, which states: "His catalogue of books . . . may be had at either of the above stores."
Minick 179
No copy known mp. 47088

B8713 KEDDIE, JAMES
James Keddie, bookseller and stationer . . . has opened store in Market-Street, Baltimore . . . Baltimore, *2 September* 1794. [Baltimore, 1794]
broadside
Italicized portion in ms.
PHi

B8714 KENTUCKY. GENERAL ASSEMBLY. HOUSE OF REPRESENTATIVES
Journal of the House of Representatives at the first session of the third General Assembly . . . in . . . Frankfort . . . [Nov. 3, 1794] . . . Frankfort, John Bradford, 1794.
84 p. 31.5 cm.
Session adjourned Dec. 20, 1794
McMurtrie: Kentucky 36
ICU; KyU mp. 47089

B8715 KENTUCKY. GENERAL ASSEMBLY. SENATE
Journal of the Senate at the fourth session of the General Assembly . . . in . . . Frankfort . . . [Nov. 3, 1794] . . . Frankfort, John Bradford, 1794.
56 p. 32 cm.
McMurtrie: Kentucky 37
ICU mp. 47091

B8716 KENTUCKY. LAWS
Acts passed at the first session of the third General assembly . . . begun . . . the third day of November . . . Lexington, John Bradford [1794?]
51, [1] p. 31 cm.
McMurtrie: Kentucky 38
DLC; ICU; KyU; MH-L; NNB mp. 47090

B8717 [KILNER, DOROTHY] 1755-1836
Short conversations; or, An easy road to the temple of fame . . . Boston, Printed and sold by Samuel Hall, 1794.
70 p. 12.5 cm.
MWA (t.p., front. and last leaf mutilated) mp. 47092

B8718 KRUMPHOLTZ, JOHANN BAPTIST, 1745-1790
Louisa's complaint . . . the music by Krumpholtz . . . New York, Printed for G. Gilfert [1794-95]
[2] p. 32.5 cm.
Sonneck-Upton p. 237
DLC; NN; NRU-Mus; RPJCB mp. 47093

B8719 LAMBERT, ANNE THÉRÈSE DE MARGUENAT DE COURCELLES, MARQUISE DE, 1647-1733
The fair solitary; or, The female hermit . . . Boston,

Printed and sold by S. Hall, 1794.
[2], 57 p. 15.5 cm.
MWA mp. 47094

B8720 LAROCQUE, A. J.
Suite de l'article intitulé Economie politique. Inseré dans le numero premier du *Niveau de l'Europe* . . . Philadelphie, T. Bradford, 1794.
37 p.
French on verso; English on recto
RPJCB mp. 47095

B8721 LEE, CHAUNCEY, 1763–1842
The spiritual temple. A sermon delivered . . . June 25th, 1793; before . . . the North Star Lodge . . . Bennington, Anthony Haswell, 1794.
20 p. 18 cm.
MWA; NhD mp. 47096

B8722 [LELAND, JOHN] 1754–1841
The history of Jack Nips . . . Exeter, Printed and sold at Stearns & Winslow's Office, 1794.
12 p. 16.5 cm.
New York Public 1108
MWA; NN (t.p. photostat); NhD (t.p. mutilated)
mp. 47097

B8723 LETTER from a gentleman in Philadelphia, to his friend in Alexandria. Philadelphia, Printed for Mathew Carey, by R. Folwell, 1794.
16 p. 8vo
PPL mp. 47098

B8724 LOUIS XVI, KING OF FRANCE, 1754–1793, defendant
The trial, &c. of Louis XVI . . . and Marie Antoinette . . . Lansingburgh, Printed by Silvester Tiffany, for, and sold by, Thomas Spencer, Albany, 1794.
2 p.l., 36 p. 18 cm.
MWA mp. 47100

B8725 LOVE, CHRISTOPHER, 1618–1651
Prophecies of the Reverend Christopher Love: and his last words on the scaffold . . . Windsor, Alden Spooner, 1794.
12 p. 19 cm.
Cooley 252
MWA mp. 47101

B8726 LOWNES, CALEB
An account of the alteration and present state of the penal laws of Pennsylvania . . . Lexington, J. Bradford, 1794.
20 p. incl. table. 20 cm.
McMurtrie: Kentucky 39; New York Public 1110
MH-L. Photostat: NN mp. 47102

B8727 [MACGOWAN, JOHN] 1726–1780
Infernal conference: or, Dialogues of devils. By the listener. Worcester, Leonard Worcester, 1794
419 p. 21.5 cm.
Huntington 648; cf. Evans 29005
CSmH; MWA mp. 47103

B8728 [MACGOWAN, JOHN] 1726–1780
The life of Joseph, the son of Israel . . . Danbury, Printed and sold by N. Douglas, 1794.
131 p. 16.5 cm.
CSmH; MWA mp. 47104

B8729 MAHY, GUILLAUME FRANÇOIS, BARON DE CORMERÉ
Histoire de la revolution . . . Baltimore, Samuel et John Adams, 1794.
110, 79 p. 23.5 cm.
DLC mp. 47105

B8730 MARINE SOCIETY, SALEM, MASS.
Laws of the Marine Society, at Salem . . . Massachusetts, as amended . . . Nov. 4, 1790. To which are annexed, The several acts of the General Court, relating to the Society . . . Salem, T. C. Cushing, 1794.
24 p. 15 cm.
Contains list of members
Tapley p. 356; cf. Evans 22868 (20 p.)
MB; MSaE mp. 47847

B8731 MARTIN and James; or the reward of integrity . . . Philadelphia, Printed for H. & P. Rice, 1794.
64 p. 10.5 cm.
MWA (t.p. wanting); NNC mp. 47106

B8732 MARTINET, JOHANNES FLORENTIUS, 1729–1795
The catechism of nature; for the use of children . . . Philadelphia, Hoff & Derrick, 1794.
54 leaves. 12 mo A–C^{18}
Rosenbach-Ch 178
A. S. W. Rosenbach (1933) mp. 47107

B8733 MARYLAND. LAWS
For consideration. An act for incorporating Baltimore-town . . . passed in November sesion, 1793 . . . Baltimore, Philip Edwards, 1794.
ix, 11 p. 21 cm.
"To the citizens of Baltimore town:" p. [iii]–ix
Minick 188
MdHi mp. 47108

B8734 MARYLAND. LAWS
[The militia law of Maryland. Hagerstown, Stewart Herbert, 1794]

Title from advertisement in the *Washington Spy*, Feb. 28, 1794, which states: "The militia law . . . is just published and for sale at the printing-office."
Minick 186
No copy known mp. 47110

B8735 MARYLAND. LAWS
State of Maryland. An act supplementary to an act . . . for the more effectual paving the streets of Baltimore-town . . . [Baltimore, Yundt and Patton, 1794]
broadside 41 X 34 cm.
Minick 187
MdBE mp. 47109

B8736 MARYLAND JOURNAL AND BALTIMORE ADVERTISER
New-Year's verses, addressed to the . . . patrons of the *Maryland Journal* . . . January 1, 1794 . . . [Baltimore, James Angell & Paul J. Sullivan, 1794]
broadside 25.5 X 20 cm.
Minick 192; New York Public 1111
MdBE. Photostat: NN mp. 47133

B8737 MASSACHUSETTS
These certify, that the returns from the several towns within the Third Southern District, for a representative . . . in the Congress, have been examined agreably to an act of

the General Court, passed the 27th of June, 1794 . . . [Boston? 1794?]
broadside 11.5 X 17 cm.
Signed in ms.: John Avery Sec[y]
MWA mp. 47112

B8738 MASSACHUSETTS. HOUSE OF REPRESENTATIVES
Commonwealth of Massachusetts. In the House of Representatives, June 7, 1794. The Committee to whom was referred . . . dividing the Commonwealth into districts . . . [Colophon] Boston, 1794.
7 p. 31.5 cm. caption title
Pierce W. Gaines, Fairfield, Conn. (1964) mp. 47111

B8739 MASSACHUSETTS CHARITABLE FIRE SOCIETY
The constitution of the Massachusetts Charitable Fire Society. [Boston, 1794]
15 p. 22.5 cm.
Page 10: The government for the year 1794
MWA; NHi; RPJCB (t.p. and p. 15 wanting)
mp. 47113

B8740 MASSACHUSETTS HISTORICAL SOCIETY
Circular letter of the Massachusetts Historical Society, respectfully addressed, in 1794, by Rev. Jeremy Belknap . . . to every gentleman of science . . . [Boston, 1794]
[3] p.
Ford 2726
MHi; MSaE mp. 47114

B8741 MASSACHUSETTS MAGAZINE
The carrier of the *Massachusetts Magazine*, to every patron . . . Jan. 1, 1794. [Boston, 1794]
broadside
PHi mp. 47003

B8742 MERCURY
The carrier of the *Mercury*. To his liberal and generous patrons . . . January 1, 1794. [Boston, 1794]
broadside
MWA

B8743 [THE Middlesex almanac for 1795. Middletown, Moses H. Woodward, 1794]

Advertised in the *Middlesex Gazette*, Dec. 13, 1794, as "Just Published and for Sale at the Printing-Office . . . The Middlesex Almanack for 1795."
No copy known

B8744 MILNS, WILLIAM, 1761–1801
Plan of instruction by private classes . . . New York, Samuel Loudon, 1794.
16 p. 20 cm.
MiU–C mp. 47115

B8745 MONTAGU, EDWARD WORTLEY, 1713–1776
The life, travels and adventures of Edward Wortley Montague . . . In two volumes . . . Boston: Printed by John West Folsom, for Daniel Brewer of Taunton. [1794?]
2 v. (144 p.) 15.5 cm.
cf. Evans 27335 (microprint)
MHi mp. 47216

B8746 [MOODY, ELEAZAR]
The school of good manners . . . Boston, Printed by B. Edes & Son, sold by them, and also by W. T. Clap, 1794.
92 p. 12 cm.
cf. Evans 27337
MWA (p. 57–58 mutilated) mp. 47116

B8747 MOORE, JOHN, 1729–1802
A journal during a residence in France . . . In two volumes. Vol. II . . . New-York, Re-printed by Thomas and James Swords, for Berry, Rogers and Berry, F. Childs and Co. and Thomas Allen, 1794.
354 p. fold. map. 18 cm.
MWA; N mp. 47117

B8748 MORE, HANNAH, 1745–1833
The search after happiness, a pastoral drama. From the poetry of Miss More. By a Lady in Connecticut. Catskill, M. Croswell & Co., 1794.
30 p.
Hill 259
MH mp. 47118

B8749 MORRILL, JAMES
James Morrill, No. 21, Cornhill, Boston, imports and sells, English, India and other goods . . . [Boston] N. Coverly [1794?]
broadside 10 X 12.5 cm.
Huntington 651
CSmH mp. 47119

B8750 MUIR, JAMES, 1757–1820
Proposals for printing by subscription. An examination of . . . "The Age of Reason," in ten sermons, by James Muir . . . Alexandria, October 28, 1794. [Alexandria? 1794]
broadside 34 X 23 cm.
New York Public 1112
NN (photostat) mp. 47120

B8751 MUTUAL ASSURANCE COMPANY
Deed of settlement of the Mutual Assurance Company, for insuring houses from loss by fire. Norwich, Thomas Hubbard, 1794.
8 p. 8vo [A]^4
Trumbull: Second supplement 2833
MHi; RPJCB

B8752 THE New England primer improved . . . Concord, Printed and sold by Nathaniel Coverly, 1794.
unpaged
MWA mp. 47121

B8753 THE New-England primer, improved . . . New-London, Thomas C. Green, 1794.
[78+] p. front. 9.5 cm.
DLC mp. 47122

B8754 THE New-England primer, with the shorter catechism. Wilmington: Printed by Brynberg & Andrews. M,DCC,XCIV.
72 p. 10 cm.
Mrs. A. Ward France, Wyncote, Pa. (1963). Facsim: d'Alté A. Welch, Cleveland (1963) mp. 47123

B8755 NEW HAMPSHIRE. GOVERNOR, 1790–1794
By . . . Josiah Bartlett . . . a proclamation for a day of public fasting, humiliation and prayer . . . [Mar. 27, 1794] . . . [Portsmouth? 1794]
broadside
Dated 6 Feb. 1794
MWA mp. 47125

B8756 NEW HAMPSHIRE. GOVERNOR, 1794–1805
By . . . John Taylor Gilman . . . a proclamation for a public thanksgiving . . . [Sept. 29, 1794] . . . Portsmouth, John Melcher, 1794.
broadside 39 X 32.5 cm.
DLC mp. 47124

B8757 NEW JERSEY
An estimate of the rateables in the State of New-Jersey, taken by the Legislature, January 25, 1794. Names of counties . . . [n.p., 1794]
broadside 33.5 X 41 cm.
NjR

B8758 NEW JERSEY. ADJUTANT GENERAL'S OFFICE
Cavalry orders, Bedford, December 5, 1794. The dismission and sudden departure of the cavalry . . . from Pittsburg to their respective states . . . prevented the General . . . from conveying . . . the thanks . . . Anthony W. White, Brig. Gen. commanding the cavalry ordered on the Western Expedition. [Trenton? 1794]
broadside
In two columns
NjR

B8759 NEW JERSEY. ADJUTANT GENERAL'S OFFICE
General orders. Trenton, June 27, 1794. The requisition of the President . . . directing a detachment of the militia . . . A. W. White, Adj. Gen. [Trenton, 1794]
broadside
In four columns
NjR

B8760 NEW JERSEY. ADJUTANT GENERAL'S OFFICE
General orders. Trenton, August 23, 1794. As the Commander in Chief has recently received information . . . *Anthy W. White* Adj. Gen. . . . [Trenton, 1794]
broadside 26.5 X 18 cm.
NjR

B8761 NEW JERSEY. CITIZENS
To the honourable Senate and House of Representatives of the United States . . . The petition . . . of the subscribers, inhabitants of . . . New-Jersey . . . [n.p., 1794]
broadside 33.5 X 20 cm.
Ms. note: "This petition was circulated first in Morris County in November 1794."
Morsch 246
NHi mp. 47126

B8762 NEW JERSEY. GENERAL ASSEMBLY
Votes and proceedings of the eighteenth General Assembly of . . . New-Jersey. At a session begun . . . [Oct. 22, 1793] . . . Being the third sitting. Burlington, Isaac Neale, 1794.
17 p. fold. table. 32.5 cm.
Morsch 248; cf. Evans 27390
NN; Nj; NjHi; NjR; PPL

B8763 NEW JERSEY. LAWS
Laws for regulating the militia of . . . New-Jersey. Philadelphia, Charles Cist, 1794.
39 p. 16 cm.
Huntington 652
CSmH; DLC mp. 47131

B8764 NEW JERSEY. LAWS
State of New-Jersey. An act more effectually to prevent the waste of timber in this state, and to repeal the former act . . . Passed June 13, 1783. An act to prevent the burning of woods, marshes and meadows . . . Passed at Trenton, November 24, 1794. [Trenton, 1794]
broadside 48.5 X 30 cm.
Morsch 243
NjHi mp. 47127

B8765 NEW JERSEY, LAWS
State of New-Jersey. An act to alter the mode of collecting militia fines from delinquents . . . Passed at Trenton, June 20, 1794. [Trenton, 1794]
broadside 34 X 20 cm.
Morsch 244; New York Public 1114
NN (imperfect): NjR mp. 47128

B8766 NEW JERSEY. LAWS
State of New-Jersey. An act to authorize the commander in chief . . . Passed at Trenton, June 20, 1794. [Trenton, 1794]
4 p. 18 cm. caption title
DLC mp. 47129

B8767 NEW JERSEY. LAWS
[State of New Jersey. An act to prevent persons . . . from cutting timber on the unlocated lands in this state . . . Passed at Trenton, February 10, 1794. Trenton, 1794]
braodside
Title from Nelson
Morsch 237
No copy known mp. 47130

B8768 NEW JERSEY. MILITIA
Detachment orders. Elizabeth Town, September 5, 1794. Major General Dayton . . . to the troops under his command the General Orders . . . subjoined . . . Marching Orders for the corps of 1500 men last detailed . . . Matthias Williamson, Aid-de-camp. [Elizabeth? 1794]
broadside 27.5 X 21.5 cm.
NjR

B8769 THE new Pennsylvania almanac for . . . 1795. By James Login . . . Philadelphia, Robert Campbell [1794]
[36] p.
Drake 10381
NjP

B8770 NEW YORK. LAWS
The ten pound act: . . . enacted into a law . . . the 17th day of April . . . 1787 . . . Albany, Charles R. and George Webster, 1794.
24 p. π^4 B–C^4
McMurtrie: Albany 103
NHi. Erwin G. Radley, Marion, N. Y. (1966) mp. 47135

B8771 NEW YORK. SENATE
State of New-York. In Senate, January 10, 1794. Resolved . . . that the printer to the State . . . publish . . . a copy of . . . "An act for registering deeds . . ." [New York, 1794]
broadside 40 X 32.5 cm.
NHi (mutilated) mp. 47136

B8772 NEWARK, New-Jersey, January 1, 1794. Proposals, for publishing by subscription, a periodical work . . . the United States Magazine . . . [New York, 1794]
broadside 32 X 20 cm.
NHi mp. 47137

B8773 NEWBURYPORT, Sept. 3, 1794. The author of the following, about a twelve month since, exposed to public view a few imperfect lines, stamped with the appellation of "The Times" . . . The second number of the Times, a solemn elegy . . . [Newburyport?1794]
broadside 36 X 22.5 cm.
Ford 2590
MSaE; MWA mp. 47138

B8774 NEWPORT THEATRE
(For the benefit of the unfortunate Americans . . . in Algiers.) . . . Theatre. Newport. This evening, May 29th. will be presented . . . Barbarossa, Tyrant of Algiers . . . [Newport, Henry Barber? 1794]
broadside 42 X 28 cm.
Advertised May 27, 1794, in the *Newport Mercury*
Alden 1369A
RNHi mp. 47139

B8775 NEWPORT GUARDS
The charter and by-laws of the Newport Guards . . . Newport, Henry C. Southwick, 1794.
23, [1] p. 18 cm.
Alden 1370
RHi mp. 47140

B8776 NORTH CAROLINA. LAWS
Laws of North-Carolina. At a General Assembly, begun and held at Newbern, on the seventh of July . . . [1794] . . . Being the second session of the said Assembly. [Halifax, Hodge and Wills, 1794]
8 p. 32.5 cm. caption title
Supplement to Iredell's *Revision*
McMurtrie: North Carolina 198
MH-L mp. 47142

B8777 [NURSE Truelove's Christmas box . . . Boston, Printed and sold by S. Hall, 1794]
31? p. 11 cm.
Title-page made up by Wilbur M. Stone
MWA (t.p. and all beyond p. 26 wanting) mp. 47143

B8778 OGDEN, ABRAHAM
[To be sold.] At public vendue, on Monday the 18th of August next, at the house of William Willis . . . All the estate of Henry Cuyler the elder, and Henry Cuyler the younger, deceased . . . Abraham Ogden and James Parker, Trustees to the said estates. July 16, 1794. New-Brunswick--Printed by A. Blauvelt [1794]
broadside 30 X 22.5 cm.
Top line supplied from simultaneous newspaper advertisement
Hunterdon County Historical Society. Photocopy: NjR

B8779 EIN päcklein von diesem pulver thut man in ein peint . . . [Frederick, Md., M. Bartgis, 1794]
broadside 11.5 X 15.5 cm.
Had been laid in: Neuer erfahrner . . . Frederichstadt, 1794
MiU-C mp. 47144

B8780 PAINE, ROBERT TREAT, 1773-1811
Boston, September 1794. Sir. The editor of the *Federal Orrery* has published his proposals . . . and . . . he esteems it his duty to present them . . . [Boston, 1794]
broadside 19 X 15 cm.
Addressed to W. W. P. White and signed Thos. Paine
RPJCB mp. 47145

B8781 PAINE, THOMAS, 1737-1809
The age of reason . . . New-York: Printed for J. Fellows. 1794.
69 p. 17 cm.
"Books lately published . . . J. Fellows": p. 67-69
cf. Evans 27460
NHi mp. 47146

B8782 PAINE, THOMAS, 1737-1809
The age of reason . . . New-York, Re-printed by Birdsall and Hyer, 1794.
69 p.
RPJCB (t.p. imperfect) mp. 47147

B8783 PAINE, THOMAS, 1737-1809
Rights of man. Part the second . . . Albany, C. R. & G. Webster, 1794.
vii, [8]-96, 10 p. 19.5 cm.
MiU-C; N mp. 47148

B8784 PAINE, THOMAS, 1737-1809
The writings of Thomas Paine . . . Albany, Printed by Charles R. and George Webster; sold by Webster & Steel and T. Spencer, Albany: W. W. Wands, Lansingburgh: A. Stoddard, Hudson: N. Power, Poughkeepsie: T. Allen, S. Campbell, T. Greenleaf, J. Fellows, W. Durell, and T. & J. Swords, New York [etc., etc.] 1794.
xii, 60, 186, 41, 70, 24, 124, 96, 10 p. 20 cm.
cf. Evans 27466
MWA; MiU-C; PPL mp. 47149

B8785 PATTERSON, ROBERT, 1743-1824
A new table of latitude and departure, for every degree and five minutes of the quadrant . . . [Philadelphia] Stewart & Cochran, 1794.
30 [i.e. 36] p. incl. tables. 16 cm.
Double tables, p. 2-6, paged in duplicate; "Explanation of the foregoing table," one unnumbered page between p. 7 and 8
New York Public 1115
NN; PHi mp. 47152

B8786 PENNSYLVANIA. GOVERNOR, 1790-1799
Pennsylvania, ss. In the name and by the authority of the commonwealth of Pennsylvania, by Thomas Mifflin . . . a proclamation. Whereas it appears . . . [Aug. 7, 1794] . . . [Philadelphia, 1794]
broadside 37 X 23 cm.
DLC mp. 47170

B8787 PENNSYLVANIA. LAWS
. . . An act for more effectually securing the trade, peace and safety of . . . Philadelphia . . . [at end] [Philadelphia] Zachariah Poulson, junr. [1794?]
4 p. 34 cm. caption title
At head of title: GG
Printed as a bill, with separately numbered lines for each section
Ms. annotation: Approved Febry 28th. 1794
MB mp. 47153

B8788 PENNSYLVANIA. LAWS
An act for the better preventing of crimes and for abolishing the punishment of death in certain cases . . . [at end] [Philadelphia] Zachariah Poulson [1794]
9 p. fol. caption title
PHi

B8789 PENNSYLVANIA. LAWS
An act to enable the governor of this commonwealth to incorporate a company for making an artificial road . . . Lancaster to . . . Susquehanna . . . [at end] [Philadelphia] Zachariah Poulson [1794]
20 p. fol. caption title
PHi

B8790 PENNSYLVANIA. LAWS
. . . An act to exonerate the late Proprietaries from the payment of certain taxes . . . [Philadelphia, Z. Poulson, 1794]
2 p. 34.5 cm. caption title
At head of title: O
Printed as a bill, with separately numbered lines for each section

Read the third time in the Senate Mar. 20, 1794
MWA mp. 47154

B8791 PENNSYLVANIA. LAWS
An act to fix the number of senators, form the state into districts and determine the portion to be allotted to each . . . [at end] [Philadelphia] Zachariah Poulson [1794]
4 p. fol. caption title
PHi

B8792 PENNSYLVANIA. LAWS
. . . An act to prevent the damages which may happen by firing of woods . . . [at end] [Philadelphia] Zachariah Poulson, junr. [1794]
3 p. 35 cm. caption title
At head of title: QQ
Printed as a bill, with separately numbered lines for each section, and incorporating ms. changes in the similar bill printed by Humphreys
MWA mp. 47155

B8793 PENNSYLVANIA. LAWS
. . . An act to repeal an act entitled "An act for erecting a loan-office . . ." enacted the eleventh day of April last . . . [at end] [Philadelphia] Zachariah Poulson [1794?]
2 p. 35 cm. caption title
At head of title: P
Printed as a bill, with each section having separately numbered lines
MWA mp. 47156

B8794 PENNSYLVANIA. LAWS
In General Assembly, February 22, 1794. An act to incorporate the Insurance Company of the State of Pennsylvania . . . [at end] Philadelphia, T. Bradford [1794]
10 p. fol. caption title
PHi

B8795 PENNSYLVANIA. LAWS
In General Assembly, Friday, January 17, 1794. An act to provide for the safe keeping of the records . . . of this Commonwealth . . . [Philadelphia, T. Bradford, 1794]
2 p. 34.5 cm. caption title
Printed as a bill, with the lines of each section separately numbered
MWA mp. 47158

B8796 PENNSYLVANIA. LAWS
In General Assembly, Friday, February 21, 1794. An act for the relief of Grizel Robinson . . . [Philadelphia, T. Bradford, 1794]
3 p. 35 cm. caption title
Printed as a bill, with the lines of each section separately numbered
MWA mp. 47157

B8797 PENNSYLVANIA. LAWS
In General Assembly, Friday, March 7, 1794. An act to prescribe the times places and manner of choosing senators . . . United States . . . [at end] Philadelphia, T. Bradford [1794]
4 p. fol. caption title
PHi

B8798 PENNSYLVANIA. LAWS
In General Assembly, Monday, January 20, 1794. An act for the relief of Blackall William Ball . . . [at end] Philadelphia, T. Bradford [1794]
2 p. 35 cm. caption title
Printed as a bill, with the lines of each section separately numbered
MWA mp. 47160

B8799 PENNSYLVANIA. LAWS
In General Assembly, Monday, February 17, 1794. An act to prevent the damages which may happen by firing of woods . . . [Philadelphia, T. Bradford, 1794]
3 p. 35 cm. caption title
Printed as a bill, with the lines of each section separately numbered
MWA mp. 47159

B8800 PENNSYLVANIA. LAWS
In General Assembly, Monday, February 23, 1794. An act for more effectually securing . . . safety of the port of Philadelphia . . . [at end] Philadelphia, T. Bradford [1794]
4 p. fol. caption title
PHi

B8801 PENNSYLVANIA. LAWS
In General Assembly, Monday March 24, 1794. An act to regulate the practice of physic and surgery within this Commonwealth . . . Philadelphia, T. Bradford [1794]
4 p.
Page 4 misnumbered 10
PPC mp. 47161

B8802 PENNSYLVANIA. LAWS
In General Assembly, Saturday, February 15, 1794. An act to authorize the admission of certain persons as witnesses . . . [Philadelphia, T. Bradford, 1794]
broadside 35 X 21 cm.
Printed as a bill, with the lines separately numbered
MWA mp. 47162

B8803 PENNSYLVANIA. LAWS
In General Assembly, Saturday, February 22, 1794. An act for the prevention of vice and immorality and of unlawful gaming . . . [Colophon] Philadelphia, T. Bradford [1794]
13 p. 35 cm. caption title
Printed as a bill, with lines numbered and spaces left blank
New York Public 1116
NN mp. 47163

B8804 PENNSYLVANIA. LAWS
In General Assembly, Saturday, February 22, 1794. An act to incorporate the . . . Insurance Company of North America . . . [at end] Philadelphia, T. Bradford [1794]
10 p. 34.5 cm. caption title
Printed as a bill, with the lines of each section separately numbered
RPJCB mp. 47164

B8805 PENNSYLVANIA. LAWS
In General Assembly, Thursday, March 20, 1794. An act to authorise the Governor . . . incorporate a company . . . bridge over the . . . Delaware at . . . Easton . . . [at end] Philadelphia, T. Bradford [1794]
16 p. fol. caption title
PHi

B8806 PENNSYLVANIA. LAWS
In General Assembly, Tuesday, January 21, 1794. An act to regulate the exportation of pot and pearl ash . . . [at end] Philadelphia, T. Bradford [1794]
6 p. 35 cm. caption title
Printed as a bill, with the lines of each section separately numbered
MWA mp. 47165

B8807 PENNSYLVANIA. LAWS
In General Assembly, Tuesday, March 25, 1794. An act for the better preventing of crimes and for abolishing the

punishment of death in certain cases. [Colophon] Philadelphia, T. Bradford [1794]
10 p. 35.5 cm. caption title
Printed as a bill, with the lines separately numbered
New York Public 1117
NN mp. 47166

B8808 PENNSYLVANIA. LAWS
. . . In General Assembly. Wednesday, December 17, 1794. A supplement to the . . . "Act for the regulation of bankruptcy . . ." [at end] [Philadelphia] D. Humphreys [1794]
2 p. 35 cm. caption title
Printed as a bill, with the lines of each section separately numbered
At head of title: No. II
MWA mp. 47168

B8809 PENNSYLVANIA. LAWS
Laws of . . . Pennsylvania, regulating the general elections . . . Philadelphia, Zachariah Poulson, 1794.
55 p. 19 cm.
DLC mp. 47171

B8810 PENNSYLVANIA. LAWS
. . . A supplement to the Act entitled "An act to enable the Governor . . . to incorporate a company for opening a canal and lock navigation on . . . Brandywine Creek." [at end] [Philadelphia] Zachariah Poulson, junr. [1794]
2 p. 24.5 cm. caption title
At head of title: EE
Printed as a bill, with separate numbering for the lines of each section
Signed into law by the Governor Mar. 19, 1794
MWA mp. 47169

B8811 PENNSYLVANIA. MILITIA
(Circular.) General orders. Philadelphia May 21st, 1794. Sir, In consequence of the orders herewith transmitted . . . you will without delay draft from your brigade . . . To Brigade Inspector of the brigade of the militia of Pennsylvania [n.p., 1794]
[2] 1. 33.5 X 20.5 cm.
In script type
MiU-C

B8812 PENNSYLVANIA. MILITIA
Gentlemen, The Governor having received information, that a . . . cruel outrage has been committed in the county of Allegheny . . . [at end] Your . . . humble servant, Secretary's Office, Philadelphia, 25th July, 1794. To [Philadelphia, 1794]
[4] p. 23 cm.
Pages [2-4] blank
Addressed to the brigade inspector of the Ninth Division
WHi mp. 47173

B8813 PENNSYLVANIA. MILITIA
Roll designating the quota of the several brigadiers of Pennsylvania . . . 10,768 militia, officers included, agreeably to . . . a letter from the Secretary at War, dated the 19th day of May, 1794 . . . [Philadelphia? 1794?]
broadside 41 X 34 cm.
DLC mp. 47172

B8814 PENNSYLVANIA. MILITIA
Sir, As a confidential communication, you will receive inclosed, a copy of a letter from the Governor . . . Philadelphia, 21st May, 1794. To Brigade inspector of the brigade . . . [n.p., 1794]
[2] p. 41.5 X 26 cm.
Page [2]: Gov. Mifflin's letter dated 19th May, 1794
Both documents in script types
MiU-C

B8815 PENNSYLVANIA. SENATE. SPECIAL COMMITTEE ON BILL Q
. . . Report of a special committee on bill Q . . . [at head of title] [Philadelphia] Zachariah Poulson [1794]
broadside 34 X 20.5 cm.
MWA mp. 47549

B8816 PENNSYLVANIA GAZETTE
Address to the customers . . . January 1st, 1794. [Philadelphia, 1794]
broadside
MWA mp. 46957

B8817 PERRY, WILLIAM
The only sure guide to the English tongue . . . S. Hall's Second Boston edition. Boston, S. Hall, 1794.
180 p.
Hamilton 154
NjP mp. 47174

B8818 PERRY, WILLIAM
The only sure guide to the English tongue . . . By W. Perry. Ninth Worcester edition. Worcester, Isaiah Thomas, 1794.
180 p.
Hamilton 154a
NjP mp. 47175

B8819 PHILADELPHIA. MERCHANTS
The committee having been notified by the Secretary of State, that the agent of claims . . . is to embark . . . for London . . . Nov. 6, 1794. Thomas Fitzsimons . . . Notice is hereby given . . . the merchants of Philadelphia . . . have appointed a committee, consisting of Thomas Fitzsimons, James Yard, Stephen Girard . . . Nov. 8, 1794 . . . [Philadelphia, 1794]
broadside 35 X 21 cm.
CtHi mp. 47176

B8820 PHILADELPHIA. MERCHANTS
—From Thomas Fitzsimons to the Secretary of State.—Philadelphia, 22d October, 1794. Sir, At a meeting of the merchants yesterday, they instructed their committee . . . In behalf and by order of the Committee . . . Thos: Fitzsimons . . . Department of State, to wit: I hereby certify the foregoing letter of 22d Oct. . . . true copies . . . 7th November 1794. [Philadelphia, 1794]
[2] p. 24.5 cm.
CtHi mp. 47177

B8821 PHILADELPHIA. ORDINANCES
Carters, porters, and others . . . are requested to take notice, that . . . an ordinance for the regulation of the drivers of carriages . . . enacted the 22d day of September, 1794, will be put in force . . . William Pidgeon, Superintendent. [Philadelphia, D. Humphreys] [1794]
broadside 37.5 X 28.5 cm.
PHi mp. 47178

B8822 PHILADELPHIA. ORDINANCES
A supplement to an ordinance, passed the 22d day of September, 1794, for regulating the cording of wood . . . [Philadelphia, 1794?]
broadside 30 X 15 cm.
Signed by Wm. Linnard, president
PHi mp. 47179

B8823 PHILADELPHIA COMPANY OF PRINTERS AND BOOKSELLERS
A catalogue of books, published by the different members of the Philadelphia Company . . . now for sale at Mathew Carey's . . . Philadelphia, D. Humphreys, 1794.
24 p. 12 mo
MH; PHi

B8824 PHILADELPHIA COMPANY OF PRINTERS AND BOOKSELLERS
The constitution, proceedings, &c., of the Philadelphia Company of Printer & Booksellers . . . [Philadelphia] Printed by Daniel Humphreys, 1793 [i.e. 1794]
17 p.
Includes minutes of meetings through that of Apr. 7, 1794, which appears on p. 17
PPL

B8825 PHILADELPHIA COMPANY OF PRINTERS AND BOOKSELLERS
Monday, October 7, 1793. [no meeting] . . . Monday, January 6, 1794. A quorum met . . . [Philadelphia, D. Humphreys, 1794]
p. 16
Printed on one side of the leaf only
According to the rules, the proceedings were to be printed after each meeting
PPL

B8826 PHILADELPHIA COMPANY OF PRINTERS AND BOOKSELLERS
Monday, April 7, 1794. A quorum met . . . [Philadelphia, D. Humphreys, 1794]
p. 17
Printed on one side of the leaf only
According to the rules, the proceedings were to be printed after each meeting
PPL

B8827 PHILLIP'S United States Diary; or an almanack, for the year . . . 1795 . . . From Creation, according to the Scriptures, 5798. Calculated for the meridian of Rhode-Island . . . Warren, Nathaniel Phillips [1794]
[24] p. 18 cm.
Alden 1348A; cf. Evans 27521 (corrected ed.)
RHi; RPJCB (lacks [B]4)

B8828 PHILOLOGICAL SOCIETY, PHILADELPHIA
The constitution, laws and rules of the Philological Society. Philadelphia, William W. Woodward, 1794.
13 p. 21 cm.
Huntington 655
CSmH mp. 47181

B8829 PLAN of an association in honor of Jesus Christ . . . Baltimore, John Hayes, 1794.
12 p. 16.5 cm.
Minick 197; Parsons 130
MdW (copy not traced) mp. 47182

B8830 [PLEYEL, IGNAZ JOSEPH] 1757-1831
Come blushing rose. [New York] G. Willig [1794-95]
broadside 32.5 cm.
Sonneck-Upton p. 81
DLC; MWA; PHi mp. 47183

B8831 PLEYEL, IGNAZ JOSEPH, 1757-1831
Henry's cottage maid . . . Philadelphia, Printed at Carr & Co[s] Musical Repository [1794]
[2] p. 33 cm. caption title
First line: Ah! where can fly . . .
Sonneck-Upton p. 184
MiU-C

B8832 POPE, ALEXANDER, 1688-1744
An essay on man . . . Exeter, Thomas Odiorne, 1794.
63 p. 13 cm.
MWA mp. 47184

B8833 PORTER, SAMUEL
An address to the Rev. John Jamison . . . Hagerstown, Stewart Herbert, 1794.
24 p. 21.5 cm.
Minick 198
OMC; PHi (p. 19-24 lacking) mp. 47185

B8834 A PRESENT to children . . . Norwich, Thomas Hubbard, 1794.
[16] p. 12 cm.
DLC mp. 47186

B8835 A PRETTY ptay-thing [sic], for children of all denominations . . . Philadelphia, Benjamin Johnson, 1794.
62+ p. 10.5 cm.
MWA (first and last leaves wanting) d'Alté A. Welch, Cleveland (first and last leaves wanting) mp. 47187

B8836 PRINCETON UNIVERSITY
Catalogus Collegii Naeo-Caesariensis. Trenton, E typis Isaaci Collins, 1794.
15 p. 23 cm.
MWA; NHi; NjP mp. 47188

B8837 PROCÈS verbal de célébration de la fête du 23 thermidor . . . [Colophon] Philadelphia, Parent [1794]
8 p.
Last "discours" dated: Philadelphia, le 2 vendemiaire, l'an 3e. de la République . . .
RPJCB mp. 47189

B8838 PROPHETIC conjectures on the French Revolution . . . Baltimore, Printed by John Hayes for the Rev. Mr. Lewis Richards, 1794.
1 p.l., 63 p. 17 cm.
Huntington 656; Minick 199
CSmH; MdBE; NN mp. 47190

B8839 PROPHETIC conjectures on the French Revolution . . . The third edition. Northampton, William Butler, 1794.
96 p. 16 cm.
DLC mp. 47191

B8840 THE prophet's disguise, or Baptist's complaint . . . Baltimore, Philip Edwards, 1794.
55, [2] p. 16.5 cm.
Minick 176
PWW mp. 47192

B8841 PROTESTANT EPISCOPAL CHURCH IN THE U.S.A.
The A, B, C. with the shorter catechism, appointed by the General Assembly of Divines at Westminster . . . Philadelphia, William Young, 1794.
24 p. 12mo
PPL mp. 46953

B8842 PROTESTANT EPISCOPAL CHURCH IN THE U.S.A. VIRGINIA (DIOCESE)
Journal of a convention . . . Held in . . . Richmond, May 6, 1794. Ricmond [sic] T. Nicolson [1794]
8 p. 20 cm.
New York Public 1118
NN mp. 47193

B8843 PUBLIC notice is hereby given that a general inoculation is to take place within this city . . . Richmond, 1794.
broadside oblong 4to
Title from Heartman cat. 287 (June 1939), no. 182
No copy known mp. 47195

B8844 [REEVE, WILLIAM] 1757-1815
The galley slave . . . Philadelphia, Carr [1794]
[2] p. 32.5 cm.
Sonneck-Upton p. 153
DLC; MB; MWA; NN; RPJCB mp. 47196

B8845 REMARKABLE curiosities . . . To which is subjoined, a remakable [sic] prophesy. The whole compose a genteel & expert compendium. [n.p.] 1794.
16 p. 13.5 cm.
New York Public 1119
MWA. Photostat: NN mp. 47197

B8846 THE renowned history of Valentine and Orson . . . New-York, Printed by G. Forman for B. Gomez, 1794.
142 p. front. 13.5 cm.
Mrs. R. L. Gruen, East Hampton, L. I. (1957). Microfilm: Forrest Bowe mp. 47309

B8847 REVEREND Mr. Sir. It having pleased the great head of the church, so far to smile on the attempts expressed in the first circular letter . . . plan of general union . . . Walter King David Austin . . . cordial acquiescence in the same. Jonathan Edwards. New-Haven December 5th. 1794. [Norwich? 1794]
[4] p. 32.5 cm.
CtHi; NHi mp. 47198

B8848 REV. Mr. ——— Sir, We have taken the liberty of forwarding for your perusal an invitation to the ministers and churches of every Christian denomination . . . Walter King. David Austin. Norwich, (Connecticut,) Sept. 1794. [Norwich, 1794]
broadside ([2] p.) 32 X 19.5 cm.
Trumbull: Supplement 2563; cf. Evans 26595
CtHi mp. 47199

B8849 RHODE ISLAND. ELECTION PROX.
Peleg Arnold, Esq; 1st Representative to the 4th Congress . . . [Providence? 1794]
broadside 4 X 11 cm.
Alden 1374; Chapin Proxies 60
RHi mp. 47200

B8850 RHODE ISLAND. GOVERNOR, 1790-1805
[By . . . Arthur Fenner . . . A proclamation . . . [Apr. 7, 1794] . . . Providence, Carter and Wilkinson, 1794]
[broadside?]
Bill submitted by Carter and Wilkinson Apr. 7, 1794
Alden 1376
No copy known mp. 47201

B8851 RHODE ISLAND. GOVERNOR, 1790-1805
By His Excellency Arthur Fenner . . . A proclamation . . . [Nov. 3, 1794] . . . Warren, Nathaniel Phillips [1794]
broadside 36 X 26 cm.
Bill submitted Nov. 6, 1794
Alden 1377
RHi mp. 47202

B8852 RICHARDSON, SAMUEL, 1689-1761
The history of Pamela . . . Philadelphia, Printed and sold by William Gibbons, 1794.
107 p. 17 cm.
MWA (imperfect) mp. 47203

B8852a RICHARDSON, SAMUEL, 1689-1761
The history of Sir Charles Grandison, abridged from the works of Samuel Richardson, Esq. . . . Eleventh edition. Philadelphia: Printed for Mathew Carey, by R. Folwell. M.DCC.XCIV.
160 p. 10 cm.
CtY; MWA

B8853 RICHARDSON & WALKER, firm, Boston
A general assortment European & India goods, sold, wholesale and retail . . . by Richardson & Walker, No. 66, Cornhill, Boston. [Boston, 1794?]
broadside 10 X 11 cm.
Dated from ms. note: Jany. 1-1795
Receipted bill on verso
MSaE mp. 47204

B8854 [ROBERTSON, JAMES]
An account of the trial of Thomas Muir . . . for sedition . . . New-York, Printed by W. Durell, 1794.
142 p. 19 cm.
cf. Evans 27635
CtHi; MWA

B8855 ROSANNA, or the cruel lover. To which is added A toast. Danbury, Nathan Douglas, 1794.
8 p.
Trumbull: Supplement 2578
RPB mp. 47205

B8856 ROUGET DE LISLE, CLAUDE JOSEPH, 1760-1836
The Marseilles hymn. In French and English . . . Philadelphia, Printed for Carr & Co. at their Musical Repository, No. 136 High St. [1794?]
[3] p. 33.5 cm.
DLC

B8857 Deleted

B8858 ROWE, ELIZABETH (SINGER) 1674-1737
Devout exercises of the heart . . . New-York, Printed by Tiebout & O'Brien, for V. Nutter, 1794.
233 p. 11 cm.
MWA (p. 153-157, 167-176 wanting) mp. 47206

B8859 ROWLANDSON, MARY (WHITE) 1635?-1678?
A narrative of the captivity, sufferings, and removes . . . [Leominster] Printed [by Charles Prentiss] for Chapman Whitcomb [1794]
6 p. 18.5 cm.
Sabin 73588; Vail: Old frontier 1003
ICN; Lancaster Town Library; Leominster Public Library; MHi (t.p. wanting); MWA; N (imperfect); NN; RPJCB mp. 47207

B8860 ROXBURY CHARITABLE SOCIETY
Whereas in a state of civil society, the bounties of providence are variously disposed . . . we the subscribers do hereby agree . . . to form ourselves into . . . the "Roxbury Charitable Society," under . . . regulations following . . . Boston, E. Russell, 1794.
broadside 42 X 26 cm.
MHi mp. 47208

B8861 ST. ANDREW'S SOCIETY
At a quarterly meeting of the St. Andrew's Society . . .

the 15th day of May, 1794. Mr. Vice-President Lenox proposed . . . [New York, 1794]
broadside 47.5 X 38 cm.
In four columns
NHi mp. 47209

B8862 SCHUYLKILL AND SUSQUEHANNA CANAL
Plan for raising by loan a sum of money . . . till the end of the present year 1794. [Philadelphia, 1794]
broadside 41 X 33.5 cm.
DLC mp. 47210

B8863 SCITUATE, August 27, 1794. Whereas the honorable the General assembly . . . passed an act empowering the several towns . . . At a town-meeting held in Scituate . . . on the 26th day of August, A.D. 1794 . . . Providence, Bennett Wheeler [1794]
broadside 42.5 X 28.5 cm.
Alden 1390; Winship Addenda p. 90
RNHi mp. 47211

B8864 A SELECTION of sacred harmony . . . Fourth edition . . . Philadelphia, Printed by John M'Culloch, for William Young, 1794.
[4], 132 p. oblong
CtHC; MWA mp. 47212

B8865 THE shepherd's contemplation . . . By Pastor Americanus, a patriot . . . Philadelphia, W. W. Woodward, 1794.
8 p. 20.5 cm.
DLC; NNC mp. 47213

B8866 SMITH, JOSHUA, d. 1795
Divine hymns, or spiritual songs . . . by Joshua Smith [and others] Fifth edition, corrected. Danbury, Nathan Douglas, 1794.
180 p. 13.5 cm.
CtHi mp. 47214

B8867 SMITH, JOSHUA, d. 1795
Divine hymns, or spiritual songs . . . being a collection by Joshua Smith and Samuel Sleeper. The sixth Exeter edition, enlarged and corrected. Exeter, Printed and sold by Stearns & Winslow, 1794.
192 p. 13.5 cm.
MWA mp. 47215

B8868 SOCIETY FOR THE INFORMATION AND ADVICE OF IMMIGRANTS
Society for the Information and Advice of Immigrants. Boston, December 30, 1793 . . . Articles . . . Officers . . . Members . . . [Boston, 1794?]
broadside 39 X 23 cm.
MB; MH mp. 47218

B8869 SOUTH CAROLINA. FREEMEN
State of South-Carolina. The memorial of the freemen residing in the six upper districts of the said state. To . . . the Senate and House of Representatives thereof . . . [n.p., 1794?]
broadside 41 X 31 cm.
Turnbull p. 305 (v. 1)
NHi

B8870 SOUTH CAROLINA. LAWS
An act for raising supplies for the year one thousand seven hundred and ninety-four . . . Dec. 20, 1794. Charleston, Young & Faust [1794]
broadside 51.5 X 38 cm.
Sc-Ar

B8871 SOUTH CAROLINA. SENATE
. . . In the Senate. December 16, 1794. The committee, to whom were referred the several petitions [for reform of representation] . . . By order of the Senate, Felix Warley, C. S. [at top] Columbia: Printed by Young & Faust [1794]
broadside 30 X 13 cm.
ScU

B8872 SOUTH CAROLINA. TREASURER
L. An abstract of the general tax for the state of South Carolina for the year 1794. As settled at the Treasury at Charleston. [Charleston? 1794]
broadside fol.
Sabin 87730; Turnbull p. 298 (v. 1)
CtY

B8873 SOUTH CAROLINA. TREASURER
M. An abstract of the general tax for the State of South Carolina for the year 1794; as settled at the Treasury at Columbia. [Columbia? 1794]
broadside fol.
Sabin 87731; Turnbull p. 298 (v. 1)
CtY

B8874 SOUTH CAROLINA. TREASURER
Sale of lands mortgaged for the paper medium . . . The Treasurer in Charleston will . . . the eleventh day of June next, expose to the public sale . . . the following lands . . . June 11, 1794. [Charleston? 1794]
broadside 44 X 34 cm.
Sc-Ar

B8875 STEPHEN Van Rensselaer and John Frey . . . have been nominated by our friends in this city, candidates for the Senate . . . Albany, March 31st, 1794. [Albany? 1794]
broadside 23 X 18.5 cm.
NHi mp. 47219

B8876 STEPHENS, THOMAS, bookseller
A catalogue of prints and paintings: for sale by Thomas Stephens, No. 57, South Second Street. Philadelphia, W. W. Woodward, 1794.
8 p. 8vo
Apparently incomplete; cf. H. P. Kraus Catalogue 89, item 481
No copy traced mp. 47220

B8877 STODDARD, ASA, 1771?-1794
Composition of Asa Stoddard, of Guilford, who departed this life . . . aged twenty-two years. Middletown, M. H. Woodward [1794?]
11 p.
Trumbull: Supplement 2645
CtY mp. 47221

B8878 STRONG, CYPRIAN, 1743-1811
A discourse delivered at the interment of Mrs. Ruth Sage, consort of Mr. Abner Sage . . . containing also . . . the awful circumstances of her death . . . Middletown, Moses H. Woodward [1794]
16 p. 16.5 cm.
CtHi mp. 47222

B8879 THE subscribers, animated by a warm attachment to the principles of liberty and equality . . . offer . . . a voluntary testimonial of our . . . esteem for Edmund Charles Genet, late Minister Plenipotentiary of the French Republic . . . [n.p., 1794]
broadside 41 X 34 cm.
DLC

B8880 SWIFT, JONATHAN, 1667–1745
The adventures of Captain Gulliver . . . Abridged from the works of . . . Dean Swift. Philadelphia, W. Young, 1794.
159, [1] p. 10.5 cm. A-E^{16}
NjP mp. 47224

B8881 SWORDS, T. AND J., firm
New-York, October 14, 1794. Proposals by T. and J. Swords, for printing by subscription, in one large octavo volume, Zoonomia . . . [New York, 1794]
broadside 45 X 18 cm.
NHi mp. 47225

B8882 TATHAM, WILLIAM, 1752–1819
Address to the shareholders and others interested in the canals of Virginia. Richmond, 1794.
8vo
Title from a clipping from an unidentified catalogue
Davis 105; Sabin 94406
No copy known mp. 47226

B8883 TAYLOR, AMOS, 1748–fl. 1813
[The genuine experience, and dying address, of Mrs. Dolly Taylor. 2nd ed. Windsor, 1794?]

Referred to by Taylor on p. 52 of his *Bookseller's legacy*
McCorison: Taylor 11
No copy known mp. 47227

B8884 TAYLOR, AMOS, 1748–fl. 1813
[Poetical specimens of a new, beautiful, and religious system of English education. Windsor, 1794?]

Referred to by Taylor on p. 52 of his *Bookseller's legacy*
McCorison: Taylor 13
No copy known mp. 47228

B8885 TENNESSEE (TERRITORY). HOUSE OF REPRESENTATIVES
[Journal of the proceedings of the House of Representatives of the Territory . . . south of the River Ohio; begun . . . Knoxville, the 25th day of August, 1794. Knoxville, George Roulstone, 1794]

Title from Nashville 1852 reprint
On Sept. 30, 1794, it was "Resolved, that George Roulstone & Co. . . . ten dollars . . . fifty copies of the act . . . what property shall be deemed taxable . . ."
McMurtrie: Tennessee 6
No copy known mp. 47229

B8886 TESTART FRÈRES & CIE.
A Philadelphie, 15 mai, 1794. M Conformement à la lettre ci-jointe . . . nous venons de contracter une nouvelle société . . . Testart frères & Compagnie. Notre maison sera rétablie au Cap . . . [Philadelphia, 1794]
2 leaves. 23 cm.
Signed in type: François Testart . . . Alexandre Testart
NN mp. 47230

B8887 THOMAS'S Massachusetts, Connecticut, Rhode-Island, Newhampshire and Vermont almanack . . . for the year . . . 1795. Worcester, Isaiah Thomas Jun. [1794]
[48] p. 19 cm.
CSmH; MWA (wanting after p. 44) mp. 47063

B8888 THOMPSON, JOHN
The lost and undone son of perdition: or, The birth, life and character of Judas Iscariot . . . [n.p.] 1794.
13 p. 18 cm.
New York Public 1120
NN mp. 47231

B8889 [THORNTON'S sheet almanack for 1794. Providence? 1794]
[broadside]
Alden 1351; Chapin p. 44
No copy known mp. 47232

B8890 TO the electors of the County of Dutchess . . . Rhinebeck, April 7, 1794. [Poughkeepsie? 1794]
broadside 18 X 15 cm.
Concerns false electioneering
NHi mp. 47234

B8891 TO the electors of the district of Long-Island. Fellow-Citizens, The election for a Representative to Congress commences on Tuesday next . . . December 6, 1794. An Elector. [New York, 1794]
broadside 30.5 X 24.5 cm.
NHi mp. 47235

B8892 TO the free and independent citizens of Ulster County, and more particularly those of . . . Woodstock and Stamford. I call you free and independent . . . Cincinnatus. April, 1794. [n.p., 1794]
broadside 40.5 X 33.5 cm.
NHi mp. 47236

B8893 TO the free electors of the City of New-York. Fellow-Citizens . . . New-York, April 30, 1794. A Federal Democrat. [New York, 1794]
broadside 24 X 21.5 cm.
NHi mp. 47237

B8894 TOM Thumb's folio: or, A new threepenny plaything for little giants . . . Boston, John Norman [1794?]
29 p. illus. 9 cm.
Inscription in Welch copy: Saley Smith her book 1795
Dated by d'Alté A. Welch
Rosenbach-Ch 150
MWA; PP. d'Alté A. Welch, Cleveland mp. 47238

B8895 TOM Thumb's folio: or, A new threepenny plaything for little giants . . . Boston, Printed and sold by Samuel Hall, 1794.
28, [3] p. illus. 10 cm.
Hamilton 155; Rosenbach-Ch 185
MH; NjP; PP mp. 47239

B8896 TOM Thumb's play-book . . . Worcester, Printed and sold by Isaiah Thomas, 1794.
30, [1] p. incl. covers. 7.5 cm.
MWA (closely trimmed). d'Alté A. Welch, Cleveland (p. [2]–4 wanting) mp. 47240

B8897 TOMMY Thumb's song book . . . By Nurse Love-Child . . . The second Worcester edition. Worcester, Printed and sold by Isaiah Thomas, 1794.
59, [4] p. incl. covers. 10 cm.
MWA mp. 47241

B8898 TRANSYLVANIA SEMINARY
We the subscribers, for the purpose of promoting learning and useful knowledge, do subscribe the following sums . . . for . . . a public seminary, as agreed on by the Transylvania Presbytery . . . Witness our hands . . . May, one thousand, seven hundred and ninety four. [Lexington, Ky., 1794]

broadside 20 X 32 cm.
PPPrHi mp. 47244

B8899 [THE trooper's pocket companion . . . Rutland, J. Lyon, 1794]

Advertised in the *Farmer's Library*, Aug. 12, 1794
McCorison 313
No copy known mp. 47243

B8900 TYLER, ROYALL, 1757–1826
A Christmas hymn . . . sung at Claremont, N.H. 1793. [Windsor? 1794]
broadside 24.5 X 20 cm.
New York Public 1083
NN (reduced facsim.); NhD. Photostats: MWA; VtHi mp. 47244

B8901 UNION FIRE COMPANY, PHILADELPHIA
Articles of the Union Fire-Company, of Philadelphia. [Philadelphia, 1794]
broadside 34.5 X 31 cm.
PHi mp. 47180

B8902 U. S.
Abstract of goods, wares and merchandize, exported . . . in the years . . . [from 1st Oct. 1793 to 30th Sept. 1794] [n.p., 1794]
broadside 54 X 37 cm.
DLC mp. 47245

B8903 U.S. ARMY
Recruiting instructions for in the service of the United States. Sir, If you accept the appointment of which I have informed you, by my letter of you are immediately to commence the recruiting service in the State of . . . Each recruit is to receive a bounty of eight dollars . . . [Philadelphia? 1794?]
[4] p. 34 cm.
NjR

B8904 U.S. COMMISSIONERS FOR THE SETTLEMENT OF THE ACCOUNTS . . .
Report of the Commissioners . . . stating balances. Read 5th December, 1793. [Philadelphia? 1794?]
4 p. 20.5 cm.
MiU-C mp. 47246

B8905 U.S. CONGRESS
In Congress, March 26, 1794. Resolved by the Senate and House . . . That an embargo be laid on all ships . . . Approved—March the twenty-sixth, 1794 . . . [Philadelphia, Childs and Swaine, 1794]
broadside 17.4 X 20.5 cm.
DLC mp. 47291

B8906 U.S. CONGRESS
In Congress, March 26, 1794. Resolved by the Senate and House . . . That an embargo be laid on all ships . . . Approved—March the twenty-sixth, 1794 . . . By direction of the President . . . all armed vessels . . . are considered as not liable to the embargo. [Philadelphia, Childs and Swaine, 1794]
broadside 20 X 21.5 cm.
MiU-C; ViU. Photostat: DLC mp. 47295

B8907 U.S. CONGRESS
In Congress, March 26, 1794. Resolved by the Senate and House . . . That an embargo be laid on all ships . . . Approved—March the twenty-sixth, 1794 . . . Reprinted in Salem, March 30, 1794.
broadside 35 X 22.5 cm.
Tapley p. 356
MSaE mp. 47292

B8908 U.S. CONGRESS
A list of the names, and places of abode, of the members of the Senate and House . . . [Dated at end] Philadelphia, Nov. 19, 1794. [Philadelphia, 1794]
broadside 40.5 X 35 cm.
NHi; RPJCB. Photostat: DLC mp. 47253

B8909 U.S. CONGRESS
Resolved, that provision ought to be made . . . for the sequestration of all the debts due . . . to the subjects of the king . . . [n.p., 1794?]
broadside 33.5 X 20.5 cm.
MiU-C mp. 47255

B8910 U.S. CONGRESS
Third Congress of the United States: At the first session . . . Resolved by the Senate and House . . . That during the continuance of the present embargo . . . Approved—April the second 1794 . . . [Philadelphia, Childs and Swaine, 1794]
broadside 32.5 X 20.5 cm.
DLC; MiU-C; NhD mp. 47293

B8911 U.S. CONGRESS
Third Congress of the United States: At the first session . . . Resolved by the Senate and House . . . that the following article be proposed . . . as an amendment to the Constitution . . . viz: The judicial power . . . shall not be construed to extend to any suit in law or equity . . . [Philadelphia, Childs and Swaine, 1794]
broadside 32 X 19.5 cm.
Motion made Jan. 2, 1794
New York Public 1121
NN; RPJCB mp. 47254

B8912 U.S. CONGRESS
Third Congress of the United States: At the first session . . . Resolved by the Senate and House . . . That the present embargo be continued . . . Approved—April the eighteenth, 1794 . . . [Philadelphia, Childs and Swaine, 1794]
broadside 33.5 X 21 cm.
Without statement of deposition; filmed for E27881
New York Public 1128; cf. Evans 27881
NN

B8913 U.S. CONGRESS
Whereas, the injuries which have been suffered . . . from violations . . . by Great Britain on their neutral rights . . . Resolved, that . . . all commercial intercourse . . . be prohibited. [n.p., 1794?]
broadside 33.5 X 20 cm.
MiU-C mp. 47294

B8914 U.S. CONGRESS. HOUSE. COMMITTEE ON ELECTIONS
The Committee of Elections, to whom was referred the petition of Henry Latimer . . . complaining of the undue election of John Patterson . . . Report . . . [Philadelphia, 1794?]
[2] p. 33.5 X 20.5 cm.
New York Public 1122
NN (photostat) mp. 47264

B8915 U.S. CONGRESS. HOUSE. COMMITTEE ON INVALID PENSIONS
The Committee appointed to enquire if any or what alterations ought to be made to the act, passed the 7th day of June 1794 . . . report . . . [n.p., 1794]

broadside 33.5 X 21 cm.
Report by Mr. Greenup Dec. 23, 1794
MiU-C mp. 47260

B8916 U.S. CONGRESS. HOUSE. COMMITTEE ON INVALID PENSIONS
The committee to whom were referred two reports of the Secretary for the Department of War, respecting the return of invalids report, That by a report . . . dated 25th April, 1794 . . . [Philadelphia, Childs and Swaine, 1794 or 1795]
[2] p. 33.5 X 20.5 cm.
DLC mp. 47274

B8917 U.S. CONGRESS. HOUSE. COMMITTEE ON LIGHT HOUSES
The committee to whom it was referred to consider and report on the expediency . . . report: . . . [Philadelphia, Childs and Swaine, 1794 or 1795]
broadside 34 X 20.5 cm.
DLC mp. 47265

B8918 U.S. CONGRESS. HOUSE. COMMITTEE ON MILITIA
The committee, to whom it was referred, to report the means of rendering the force . . . have unanimously agreed . . . [Philadelphia, Childs and Swaine, 1794]
broadside 33.5 X 20.5 cm.
DLC mp. 47266

B8919 U.S. CONGRESS. HOUSE. COMMITTEE ON THE NAVAL FORCE
The Committee, to whom it was referred to report, "The naval force necessary . . . " report: that . . . the naval force of the Algerines, consists of eight vessels . . . [Philadelphia? 1794]
7 p. 32 cm.
Report given Jan. 20, 1794.—cf. Greely
MiU-C mp. 47267

B8920 U.S. CONGRESS. HOUSE. COMMITTEE ON THE PETITION OF COLONEL LEWIS DUBOIS
The committee to whom was referred the petition of Colonel Lewis Dubois, report . . . [Philadelphia, Childs and Swaine, 1794]
broadside 33.5 X 20.5 cm.
Printed on a sheet conjugate with the report of the Committee on the Virginia Line
DLC mp. 47271

B8920a U.S. CONGRESS. HOUSE. COMMITTEE ON THE PETITION OF SUNDRY INHABITANTS
The Committee, to whom was referred a petition of sundry inhabitants from the County of Washington . . . Maryland, and . . . petitions . . . Counties of Chester and Lancaster . . . report . . . [n.p., 1794]
[2] p. 3 tables (2 fold.) 34 cm.
Report by Andrew Moore, May 16, 1794
Pierce W. Gaines, Fairfield, Conn. (1969)

B8921 U.S. CONGRESS. HOUSE. COMMITTEE ON THE PETITION OF WILLIAM DENNING
The Committee to whom was referred the petition of William Denning and others . . . report . . . [n.p., 1794]
broadside 33.5 X 20.5 cm.
Greely 151?
MiU-C; NHi mp. 47272

B8922 U.S. CONGRESS. HOUSE. COMMITTEE ON THE PRESIDENT'S MESSAGE
The committee to whom was referred that part of the President's speech, which relates to the improvement . . . [Philadelphia, Childs and Swaine, 1794]
broadside 33.5 X 20.5 cm.
DLC; PPRF mp. 47268

B8923 U.S. CONGRESS. HOUSE. COMMITTEE ON THE PRESIDENT'S MESSAGE
The Committee to whom was referred the message from the President . . . inclosing . . . letter from the Governor of North-Carolina . . . report: That, in the cession of a certain district . . . by the state . . . to the United States . . . [Philadelphia, 1794]
broadside 33 X 20 cm.
Dated from penciled notation on the verso: Feb. 19, 1794
MWA (not traced 1965) mp. 47270

B8924 U.S. CONGRESS. HOUSE. COMMITTEE ON THE PRESIDENT'S MESSAGE
The committee to whom was referred the President's message of the 30th of January last, report . . . the present situation of the south-western frontier . . . [Philadelphia, Childs and Swaine, 1794]
broadside 33.5 X 20.5 cm.
cf. Greely p. 123 Senate; p. 136 House
DLC; MiU-C. Pierce W. Gaines, Fairfield, Conn. (1963) mp. 47269

B8925 U. S. CONGRESS. HOUSE. COMMITTEE ON THE REDUCTION OF THE PUBLIC DEBT
The committee appointed to prepare and report a plan for the reduction . . . report: . . . [Philadelphia, Childs and Swaine, 1794]
[4] p. 33.5 cm. caption title
DLC; NHi mp. 47263

B8926 U.S. CONGRESS. HOUSE. COMMITTEE ON THE REMONSTRANCE OF THE PEOPLE . . .
The Committee to whom was referred, the remonstrance of the people west of the Allegany mountain, relative to the navigation of the river Mississippi, report . . . [Philadelphia, Childs and Swaine, 1794]
broadside 34 X 20.5 cm.
cf. Greely p. 149
MiU-C mp. 47273

B8927 U.S. CONGRESS. HOUSE. COMMITTEE ON THE SUPPORT OF PUBLIC CREDIT
The Committee appointed to enquire whether any, or what further or other revenues are necessary for the support of public credit . . . report . . . [n.p., 1794]
[4] p. 33.5 cm.
Report by William Smith, Apr. 17, 1794
MiU-C mp. 47264

B8928 U.S. CONGRESS. HOUSE. COMMITTEE ON THE VIRGINIA LINE
The committee appointed to enquire, whether any and what alterations . . . [Followed by] The committee to whom was referred the consideration of a remission . . . [Philadelphia, Childs and Swaine, 1794]
broadside 33.5 X 20.5 cm.
DLC mp. 47261

B8929 U.S. CONGRESS. HOUSE. COMMITTEE TO INQUIRE INTO THE STATE OF THE TREASURY DEPARTMENT
In the House of representatives, Monday, February 24, 1794. Resolved, That a committee be appointed . . . [Colophon] [Philadelphia] Francis Childs and John Swaine [1794]

6 p. 32.5 cm. caption title
DLC mp. 47276

B8930 U.S. CONGRESS. SENATE. COMMITTEE OF ELECTIONS
Congress of the United States. In Senate, February 10th, 1794. The Committee of elections to whom was referred the petition of Conrad Laub . . . [Philadelphia] John Fenno [1794]
[4] p. 35 cm.
NHi mp. 47275

B8931 U.S. DEPT. OF JUSTICE
No. I. Philadelphia, February 7th, 1794. Sir, I have considered the letter from the Collector of Newport inclosed in yours . . . Wm. Bradford . . . [Philadelphia, 1794]
broadside 22.5 X 18.5 cm.
Letter from the Attorney General, enclosed in a circular from the Comptroller of the Treasury, 24 April 1794
DLC; PPRF mp. 47281

B8932 U.S. DEPT. OF JUSTICE
No. II. Philadelphia, March 14th, 1794. Sir, I have the honor of acknowledging . . . W. Bradford. [Philadelphia, 1794]
broadside 22.5 X 18.5 cm.
Letter from the Attorney General, enclosed in a circular from the Comptroller of the Treasury, 24 April 1794
DLC; PPRF mp. 47282

B8933 U.S. DEPT. OF STATE
Letter of instructions from Sir William Scott and Doctor John Nicholl, prepared at the instance of Mr. Jay . . . Department of State, 22d Nov. 1794 . . . [Philadelphia, Childs and Swaine, 1794]
8 p. 8vo
PPL mp. 47283

B8934 U. S. DEPT. OF WAR
Department of War, December 10, 1794. Sir, In obedience to the orders of the President . . . I . . . submit . . . a statement of such difficulties . . . [Philadelphia, 1794?]
4 p.
RPJCB mp. 47308

B8935 U.S. DEPT. OF WAR
War Department, Philadelphia 8 o'clock P.M. 26 March 1794. Sir. I am instructed by the President . . . to transmit . . . resolve . . . laying an embargo for thirty days . . . [Philadelphia, 1794]
broadside 21 X 18.5 cm.
Pierce W. Gaines, Fairfield, Conn. (1962)

B8936 U.S. INSPECTOR-GENERAL'S OFFICE
Regulations for the order and discipline of the troops of the United States . . . and the militia act of Massachusetts . . . 1793. A new edition . . . Boston, Printed for David West, and John West, 1794.
153, [3], 34 p. 8 plates. 17 cm.
CSmH; MHi mp. 47284

B8937 U.S. INSPECTOR-GENERAL'S OFFICE
Regulations for the order and discipline of the volunteer army . . . Baltimore, Printed by S. &. J. Adams, for George Keatinge, 1794.
36 p. 15 cm.
Minick 208; cf. Evans 27957 (note)
NHi; PHi; PPAmP mp. 47285

B8938 U.S. LAWS
An act directing a detachment from the militia of the United States . . . Passed the House of Representatives, April 23d, 1794. [Philadelphia, 1794]
broadside 35 X 20.5 cm.
Printed as a bill, with the lines separately numbered
New York Public 1123; cf. Evans 27852
NN mp. 47277

B8939 U.S. LAWS
An act in addition to the Act for the punishment of certain crimes against the United States. [Colophon] [Philadelphia] John Fenno [1794]
[4] p. 33.5 cm.
Lines separately numbered
Presented in the House Mar. 14, 1794
New York Public 1124; cf. Evans 27869
NN (photostat) mp. 47278

B8940 U.S. LAWS
An act in addition to the Act for the punishment of certain crimes against the United States. [Colophon] [Philadelphia] John Fenno [1794]
[4] p. 34.5 cm.
Lines separately numbered
Presented in the House June 2, 1794
New York Public 1125
NN (photostat) mp. 47279

B8941 U.S. LAWS
An act in alteration of the Act establishing a mint . . . [Philadelphia] John Fenno [1794]
broadside 34.5 X 20.5 cm.
Lines separately numbered
Presented in the House Feb. 18, 1794
New York Public 1126
NN (photostat) mp. 47280

B8942 U.S. LAWS
An act laying additional duties on goods, wares, and merchandize . . . and on the tonnage of ships . . . [Philadelphia, 1794]
broadside 35.5 X 20.5 cm.
"Passed the House of Representatives, May 17th, 1794."
NHi mp. 47256

B8943 U.S. LAWS
An act prohibiting for a limited time the exportation of arms . . . [Philadelphia, Childs and Swaine, 1794]
broadside 35 X 21 cm.
DLC mp. 47289

B8944 U.S. LAWS
An act to regulate the pay of the noncommissioned officers, musicians and privates of the militia of the United States . . . December 12th, 1794, Passed the House of Representatives. [Philadelphia, 1794]
broadside 30.5 X 21 cm.
NHi mp. 47257

B8945 U.S. LAWS
Acts passed at the Third Congress . . . begun . . . the second of December, 1793 . . . Third Congress . . . first session . . . [Hartford, 1794]
[1], 488–570 p. lge. 8vo
Huntington 661
CSmH mp. 47290

B8946 U.S. LAWS
A bill authorizing the President . . . to lay, regulate, and revoke embargoes. [Philadelphia, Childs and Swaine, 1794]

broadside 33.5 X 20 cm.
DLC mp. 47251

B8947 U.S. LAWS
A bill laying duties upon carriages . . . [Philadelphia, Childs and Swaine, 1794]
[4] p. 33.5 cm. caption title
DLC mp. 47258

B8948 U.S. LAWS
A bill making further provision for securing . . . [Philadelphia] Childs and Swaine [1794]
[2] p. 35 X 20.5 cm.
DLC mp. 47259

B8949 U.S. LAWS
A bill to establish an uniform system of bankruptcy . . . [Philadelphia] Childs and Swaine [1794?]
13 p. 34.5 cm. caption title
MiU-C mp. 47252

B8950 U. S. LAWS
Third Congress of the United States: At the first session . . . An act authorizing a loan of one million of dollars . . . Resolved . . . That the President . . . be authorized to employ . . . such of the revenue-cutters . . . Approved—March the twentieth, 1794 . . . [Philadelphia, Childs and Swaine, 1794]
broadside 33.5 X 21 cm.
Without statement of deposition; filmed for E27836
New York Public 1128; cf. Evans 27836
CSmH; NN; NhD

B8951 U.S. LAWS
Third Congress of the United States: At the first session . . . An act directing a detachment . . . Approved—May the ninth 1794 . . . [Philadelphia, Childs and Swaine, 1794]
broadside 35 X 21 cm.
DLC; NjR mp. 47286

B8952 U.S. LAWS
Third Congress of the United States: At the first session . . . An act for the remission of the duties arising on the tonnage of sundry French vessels which have taken refuge . . . Approved—March the seventh 1794 . . . [Philadelphia, Childs and Swaine, 1794]
broadside 33.5 X 21 cm.
Without statement of deposition; filmed for E27833
New York Public 1128; cf. Evans 27833
NN

B8953 U.S. LAWS
Third Congress of the United States: At the first session . . . An act laying duties upon carriages . . . Approved—June the fifth 1794 . . . [Philadelphia, Childs and Swaine, 1794]
37 p. 19 cm. A-E^4
Five 1794 acts; cf. Evans 27864; 27867; 27868; 27878; 27870
RPJCB mp. 47287

B8954 U.S. LAWS
Third Congress of the United States: At the first session . . . An act making appropriations . . . Approved—March the fourteenth 1794 .... [Philadelphia, Childs and Swaine, 1794]
3 p. 33.5 cm.
DLC; NhD mp. 47288

B8955 U.S. LAWS
Third Congress of the United States: At the first session . . . An act making further provision for the expenses attending the intercourse of the United States with foreign nations . . . Approved—March the twentieth, 1794 . . . [Philadelphia, Childs and Swaine, 1794]
broadside 33.5 X 21 cm.
Without statement of deposition; filmed for E27835
New York Public 1128; cf. Evans 27835
NN; NhD

B8956 U.S. LAWS
Third Congress of the United States: At the first session . . . An act providing for the relief of such of the inhabitants of Santo Domingo, resident within the United States . . . Approved, February the twelfth, 1794. [Philadelphia, Childs and Swaine, 1794]
broadside 31 X 18.5 cm.
New York Public 1127; cf. Evans 27829, with two lines added: Deposited among the rolls . . .
NN

B8957 U.S. LAWS
Third Congress of the United States: At the second session . . . An act extending the privilege of franking to James White . . . Approved, December the third, 1794 . . . [Philadelphia, F. Childs, 1794]
broadside 33.5 X 21 cm.
Without statement of deposition; filmed for E27887
New York Public 1128; cf. Evans 27887
NN; NhD

B8958 U.S. LAWS
Third Congress of the United States: At the second session . . . An act to amend and explain the twenty-second section of "The Act establishing the judicial courts . . ." . . . Approved, December the twelfth, 1794 . . . [Philadelphia, Francis Childs, 1794]
broadside 33.5 X 21 cm.
Without statement of deposition; filmed for E27888
New York Public 1128; cf. Evans 27888
NN; NhD

B8959 U.S. LAWS
Third Congress of the United States: At the second session . . . An act to authorize the officers of the Treasury to audit and pass the account of the late Edward Blanchard . . . Approved, December the eighteenth, 1794 . . . [Philadelphia, Childs and Swaine, 1794]
broadside 33.5 X 21 cm.
Without statement of deposition; filmed for E27889
New York Public 1128; cf. Evans 27889
DLC; NN; PHi

B8960 U.S. LAWS
Third Congress of the United States: At the second session . . . An act to authorize the President to call out and station a corps of militia, in . . . Pennsylvania . . . Approved, November the twenty-ninth, 1794 . . . [Philadelphia, Francis Childs, 1794]
broadside 33.5 X 21 cm.
Without statement of deposition; filmed for E27889
New York Public 1128; cf. Evans 27886
NN; NhD

B8961 U.S. TREASURY DEPT.
(Circular to the collectors.) Treasury department. Comptroller's office, April 1794. Sir, I herewith transmit . . . [Philadelphia, 1794]
broadside 22.5 X 18.5 cm.
PPRF mp. 47249

B8962 U.S. TREASURY DEPT.
Circular to the collectors and naval officers. Treasury

department, Comptroller's office, June 19, 1794. Sir, You will receive . . . [Philadelphia, 1794]
broadside 23 X 18.5 cm.
PPRF mp. 47248

B8963 U.S. TREASURY DEPT.
Circular to the collectors and naval officers. Treasury department, Comptroller's office, Aug. 1794. Sir, I enclose . . . [Philadelphia, 1794]
broadside 24 X 20.5 cm.
PPRF mp. 47247

B8964 U.S. TREASURY DEPT.
(Circular.) Treasury Department, *21 March* 1794. Sir, The monthly schedule of bonds to be returned to this office were originally stated . . . of importance . . . [Philadelphia, 1794]
broadside 23 X 18.5 cm.
Signed in ms. by A Hamilton and Jedediah Huntington
MHi

B8965 U.S. TREASURY DEPT.
(Circular) Treasury Department April 18, 1794. Sir, You will herewith receive for your government a resolve of Congress . . . relatively to the embargo . . . [Philadelphia, 1794]
broadside 23 X 18.5 cm.
MWA mp. 47298

B8966 U.S. TREASURY DEPT.
(Circular) Treasury Department, April 23d, 1794. Sir, it is understood that by virtue . . . of our treaty with Sweden, vessles of that nation are exempted . . . [Philadelphia? 1794]
broadside 22.5 X 18.5 cm.
MiU-C mp. 47299

B8967 U.S. TREASURY DEPT.
(Circular) Treasury Department, Nov. 29, 1794. Sir, I have to request that you will retain in your hands a sufficient sum . . . for the purpose of discharging the allowances to fishing vessels . . . With a form of the draft . . . [Philadelphia? 1794]
broadside
MWA mp. 47300

B8968 U.S. TREASURY DEPT.
Principles and course of proceeding, with regard to the disposition of monies . . . Philadelphia, April 1, 1794. [Philadelphia, Childs and Swaine, 1794]
broadside 33 X 20 cm.
DLC; MWA mp. 47301

B8969 U.S. TREASURY DEPT.
Query, stated by the Secretary of the treasury . . . 24th March, 1794. [Philadelphia, Childs and Swaine, 1794]
broadside 33 X 20.5 cm.
DLC mp. 47302

B8970 U.S. TREASURY DEPT.
Statements exhibiting the periods at which monies were received for the sale of bills on Amsterdam . . . [Philadelphia] Childs and Swaine [1794]
[7] l. 32 X 40 cm. A-F[2]
Sowerby 3037
DLC; MWA (sewed with Evans 27950); MWiW; MiU-C; RPJCB mp. 47303

B8971 U.S. TREASURY DEPT.
The treasurer of the United States' accounts of payments and receipts of public monies . . . also, the War department accounts . . . to the thirty-first day of December, 1793 . . . [Philadelphia] Francis Childs and John Swaine [1794]
60 p. 34 cm.
DLC (2 copies); NN mp. 47296

B8972 U.S. TREASURY DEPT.
The treasurer of the United States' accounts of payments and receipts of public monies . . . ending the thirty-first of March 1794. Also the War department accounts . . . to the thirty-first day of March 1794 . . . [Philadelphia] Francis Childs and John Swaine [1794]
51 p. 32 cm.
Dated: May 8, 1794
MiU-C; NN mp. 47297

B8973 U.S. TREASURY DEPT.
Treasury Department, Comptroller's Office June 26th, 1794. Circular to the collectors . . . [Philadelphia, 1794]
broadside 24 X 20.5 cm.
PPRF mp. 47250

B8974 U.S. TREASURY DEPT.
Treasury Department, February 5th, 1794. Sir, I have the honor to transmit . . . [Philadelphia, Childs and Swaine, 1794]
[3] p. 33.5 cm. caption title
DLC; NN; RPJCB mp. 47305

B8975 U.S. TREASURY DEPT.
Treasury Department, April 25, 1794. Sir, I have the honor to transmit . . . [Philadelphia, Childs and Swaine, 1794]
[4] p. 32 cm.
DLC; NN; RPJCB mp. 47304

B8976 U.S. TREASURY DEPT.
Treasury Department. Revenue office, 1794. A note of the general dimensions of the heavy cannon . . . [Philadelphia, 1794]
broadside 41.5 X 35.5 cm.
DLC mp. 47306

B8977 U.S. TREATIES
Treaty with Great Britain. Mercury-Office, Saturday, July 4. As great anxiety . . . for a perusal of the treaty . . . the following epitomy of that instrument as published in Philadelphia, and received by this day's mails.] . . . The following, from the *Philadelphia Aurora* . . . [Boston, Young and Minns, 1794]
broadside 30 X 22 cm.
MWA mp. 47307

B8978 VAN LIEW, FREDERICK
To be sold at public vendue, on Tuesday the 25th day of this instant, at the late dwelling house of John Van Liew . . . estate of said deceased . . . Frederick Van Liew, Garrit Voorheese. Executors. November 11, 1794. New-Brunswick, A. Blauvelt [1794]
broadside 21.5 X 16.5 cm.
Photostat: NjR

B8979 VERMONT. GOVERNOR, 1790–1797
General orders. State of Vermont, Rutland, June 21st 1794 . . . [Bennington? A. Haswell? 1794]
broadside 34 X 20.5 cm.
Appointing David Fay Adjutant General
McCorison 316
VtU-W mp. 47310

B8980 VERMONT. GOVERNOR, 1790–1797
[Thanksgiving day proclamation. Windsor, A. Spooner, 1794]

Printer's bill for 200 copies dated Oct. 20, 1794
McCorison 317
No copy known mp. 47311

B8981 VERMONT. TREASURER
State of Vermont. To first constable in the county of Greeting. Whereas the legislature . . . Rutland, this day of 1794. Treasurer. [Rutland? 1794]
broadside fol.
Cooley 264
VtHi mp. 47312

B8982 VERY surprising narrative of a young woman, who was discovered in a rocky cave . . . In a letter from a gentleman to his friend. Second Windsor edition. [Windsor] Alden Spooner, 1794.
12 p. 14 cm.
Cooley 268; Sabin 93894; Vail: Old frontier 996
ICN; MWA mp. 47150

B8983 [A VERY surprising narrative of a young woman, who was discovered in a rocky cave . . . Third edition. Springfield, 1794]

Edition reported by Edward Eberstadt and Sons
Vail: Old frontier 997
No copy known mp. 47151

B8984 VIRGINIA. GOVERNOR, 1791–1794
By the Governor of the Commonwealth of Virginia, a proclamation. Whereas . . . banditti from the Western parts of Pennsylvania, have in defiance of law and order . . . [Aug. 20, 1794] . . . Henry Lee. [Richmond, 1794]
broadside 28 X 19.5 cm.
Concerns the Whiskey Rebellion
WHi mp. 47313

B8985 VIRGINIA. GOVERNOR, 1791–1794
By the Lieutenant Governor of . . . Virginia, a proclamation. Whereas I have received information . . . contagious disease . . . may be brought . . . by vessels arriving from . . . New-Orleans . . . [Richmond, 1794]
broadside 34 X 20.5 cm.
Dated Aug. 2, 1794
CSmH mp. 47314

B8986 VIRGINIA. GOVERNOR, 1791–1794
(Circular.) Richmond, January 25, 1794. Gentlemen, It is essentially necessary that all vacancies in the office of Escheator . . . be filled up . . . [Richmond, 1794]
broadside 21 X 17 cm.
DLC mp. 47315

B8987 VIRGINIA, GOVERNOR, 1791–1794
General orders . . . July 19, 1794 . . . [Richmond, 1794]
broadside 18 X 17 cm.
CSmH mp. 47316

B8988 VIRGINIA. GOVERNOR, 1791–1794
Militia orders . . . [Richmond, 1794]
broadside 18.5 X 17 cm.
CSmH mp. 47317

B8989 VIRGINIA. GOVERNOR, 1794–1796
Richmond, December 16, 1794. Sir, When the citizens of the United States are mutually congratulating each other . . . every Virginian . . . must feel highly gratified . . . R. Brooke. [Richmond, 1794]
broadside 20.5 X 17 cm.
WHi mp. 47318

B8990 THE Virginia almanack for the year . . . 1795 . . . By Robert Andrews. Lynchburg, Printed and sold by Robert M. Bransford [1794]
[20] p.
Title from Amer. Art Assn., American galleries, sale of May 9–10, 1935. Catalogue 4180, lot 341
Bear 100
No copy known mp. 46961

B8991 THE Virginia almanack, for the year . . . 1795 . . . By Robert Andrews . . . Petersburg, William Prentis [1794]
[32?] p. 17 cm.
Bear 104; Wyatt 13
MWA (8 leaves only); NcD ([22] p.) mp. 46962

B8992 WARING, THOMAS
Charleston, October 14, 1794. Dear Sir, As I propose to offer myself a candidate at the next general election, for the Surveyor General's Office . . . [Charleston, 1794]
broadside 18 X 15 cm.
"Surveyor General's" struck out and "Secretary's" substituted
MWA mp. 47319

B8993 WATTS, ISAAC, 1674–1748
Divine songs, attempted in easy language . . . (The sixty fourth edition.) Boston, Printed and sold by N. Coverly, 1794.
48 p. 16 cm.
MWA (p. [i]–vi, 41–48 wanting). Gillett Griffin, Princeton Univ. (1962) mp. 47320

B8994 WATTS, ISAAC, 1674–1748
Divine songs attempted . . . Canaan, Printed and sold by E. Phinney, 1794.
36 p. 12.5 cm.
CSmH mp. 47321

B8995 WATTS, ISAAC, 1674–1748
Select songs for children . . . New-York, J. Harrisson, 1794.
68, [3] p. 13 cm.
DLC mp. 47323

B8996 WATTS, ISAAC, 1674–1748
A wonderful dream . . . Danbury, Printed by Nathan Douglas, for James Crawford, 1794.
12 p. 16 cm.
CtHi mp. 47322

B8997 WEBSTER, NOAH, 1758–1843
The American spelling book . . . The eighth Vermont edition. Bennington, Anthony Haswell, 1794.
156 p. illus. 17 cm.
Skeel-Carpenter 35
OClWHi (lacks all before p. [5]) mp. 47324

B8998 WEBSTER, NOAH, 1758–1843
To the public. It is a subject . . . Noah Webster, Jun. compiler. New-York, George Bunce, May 7th, 1794.
broadside 40 X 33 cm.
Skeel-Carpenter 790
NN mp. 47325

B8999 WEEKLY MUSEUM
Address to the generous subscribers of the *Weekly Museum* . . . Upon the stage your news-boy comes once more, To speak a prologue—to Young Ninety-Four . . . [New York, 1794]
broadside 24 X 19 cm.
In 2 columns
NHi mp. 46956

B9000 WESTCOTT, JAMES D
An oration, commemorative of the Declaration of American Independence; delivered before the Ciceronian Society, on the fourth of July, M,DCC,XCIV . . . Philadelphia, William Young, 1794.
16 p. 20.5 cm.
Sabin 102958
NjP; PHi (18 p.) mp. 47327

B9001 [WILLIAMS, THOMAS]
The age of infidelity: in answer to Thomas Paine's Age of reason. By a Layman . . . London printed: New-York, re-printed by J. Buel, M,DCC,XCIV.
59, [1] p. 20 cm.
Pierce W. Gaines, Fairfield, Conn. (1964) mp. 47329

B9002 [WILLIAMS, THOMAS]
The age of infidelity: in answer to Thomas Paine's Age of reason. By a Layman . . . London printed: New-York, re-printed by J. Buel, for J. Fellows, M,DCC,XCIV.
59 p. 20 cm.
NHi mp. 47330

B9003 WOODS'S NEWARK GAZETTE
The newsboys address to the generous subscribers of *Woods's Newark Gazette* . . . January 1, 1794. [Newark, 1794]
broadside 33 X 14 cm.
Morsch 260
NHi mp. 47141

B9004 WOODS'S NEWARK GATETTE
Supplementary to *Woods's Newark Gazette*, No. 141. [Newark, 1794]
broadside 34 X 20 cm.
Proposals for publishing the paper semi-weekly, signed Public Good
Morsch 261
NHi; NN

B9005 YALE UNIVERSITY
Catalogue of the Junior class . . . M,DCC,XCIV. New-Haven, A. Morse [1794]
broadside
CtY mp. 47331

B9006 YALE UNIVERSITY
Catalogus classis Sophimorum MDCCXCIV. [New Haven, 1794]
broadside
CtY mp. 47332

B9007 YOUNG (ALEXANDER) AND THOMAS MINNS, BOSTON
Proposal, for printing by subscription, in one volume octavo, Gospel news: being the writings of Shippie Townsend . . . [Boston, Young and Minns, 1794?]
broadside 37.5 X 15.5 cm.
Townsend's work was published in 1794 by Young and Minns; the broadside was detached from MWA copy
MWA mp. 47333

1795

B9008 THE A, B, C; with the shorter catechism . . . Carlisle, Printed for Archibald Loudon . . . by Steel & M'Clean, 1795.
24 p. 19.5 cm.
MWA mp. 47334

B9009 ADAMS, JOSEPH
A Poetical dialogue between two dead bodies . . . composed by Joseph Adams . . . with the remarkable conversion of a little boy . . . Windsor, Alden Spooner, 1795.
12 p. 17 cm.
McCorison 324
NhHi mp. 47335

B9010 AH well a day poor Anna . . . New York, G. Gilfert [1795]
[2] p. 33.5 cm.
Sonneck-Upton p. 10
DLC mp. 47340

B9011 ALMY AND BROWN, firm, Providence
Cotton goods. Almy and Brown has for sale . . . Providence, a variety of cotton goods . . . Providence, 4th mo. 15th, 1795. [Providence] B. Wheeler [1795]
broadside 32.5 X 21 cm.
Alden 1405
RHi. Photostat: MWA mp. 47341

B9012 AMERICAN DAILY ADVERTISER
The carriers of the *American Daily Advertiser* to their customers, on the commencement of the year 1795 . . . [Philadelphia, 1795]
broadside 23 X 17.5 cm.
In two columns
MWA mp. 47373

B9013 ASH, JOHN
Grammatical institutes . . . A new edition, revised and corrected. Charleston, W. P. Young, 1795.
141 p. 12.5 cm.
Mosimann 531
ScU

B9014 ASYLUM COMPANY
Articles of agreement . . . [Colophon] Philadelphia, Zachariah Poulson [1795]
[4] p. 38.5 cm.
Extract of minutes of meeting, Feb. 21, 1795, p. [4]
New York Public 1134; cf. Evans 26586
NN mp. 47342

B9015 [ATTWOOD, THOMAS?] 1765-1838
The convent bell . . . New York, G. Gilfert [1795?]
1 leaf 33 X 23 cm.
Sonneck-Upton p. 88
DLC; MWA mp. 47343

B9016 BAILEY AND WALLER, firm, Charleston, S.C.
A new catalogue of books, of the latest publications, newest editions, & in elegant bindings, just imported from Europe, by Bailey and Waller, No. 27, Elliott street . . . Charleston. [Charleston, 1795?]
33 p. 17.5 cm.
Latest imprint date 1794; Peter Pindar's Works (3 v.) perhaps 1795 Charleston ed.
ScU

B9017 BALTIMORE. NEW THEATRE
The last night but one. On Wednesday, December 2, 1795 . . . a celebrated comedy . . . called The Rage. . . [Baltimore, Clayland, Dobbin? 1795]
broadside 33.5 X 20.5 cm.
Minick 216
MdBE mp. 47344

B9018 BALTIMORE. NEW THEATRE
New theatre. On Monday, August 24, 1795 . . . The

Merchant of Venice . . . Baltimore, Clayland, Dobbin [1795]
broadside 33.5 X 21 cm.
Minick 214
MdBE mp. 47345

B9019 BALTIMORE. NEW THEATRE
New theatre. The last night but two. On Tuesday, December 1, 1795 . . . a tragedy, called Fontainville Forest . . . [Baltimore, Clayland, Dobbin? 1795]
broadside 32.5 X 21 cm.
Minick 215
MdBE mp. 47346

B9020 BALTIMORE. NEW THEATRE
New theatre. The last night. On Thursday, December 3, 1795 . . . The School for Scandal . . . [Baltimore, Clayland, Dobbin? 1795]
broadside 33 X 21.5 cm.
Minick 217
MdBE mp. 47347

B9021 BAPTISTS. CONNECTICUT. DANBURY ASSOCIATION
Minutes of the Danbury Baptist Association, holden at Pawlingstown, September 16th and 17th, 1795 . . . Newfield, Beach & Jones [1795]
8 p.
Trumbull: Supplement 2043
Ct. Photocopy: MWA mp. 47348

B9022 BAPTISTS. KENTUCKY. ELKHORN ASSOCIATION
Minutes of the Elkhorn Association of Baptists, held at Cooper's Run, August 8, 1795, and continued . . . until the 10th. [Lexington? 1795]
4 p. 21 cm. caption title
McMurtrie: Kentucky 43
OClWHi. Photocopy: MWA mp. 47349

B9023 BAPTISTS. NEW HAMPSHIRE. NEW HAMPSHIRE ASSOCIATION
Minutes of the New-Hampshire Association, held . . . in Salisbury . . . June 10th and 11th, 1795. Portsmouth, Charles Peirce, 1795.
8 p. 18.5 cm.
Huntington 666
CSmH (p. 3–6 lacking) mp. 47350

B9024 BAPTISTS. VERMONT. WOODSTOCK ASSOCIATION
Minutes . . . Windsor, Alden Spooner, 1795.
8 p. 20.5 cm.
NRAB; VtHi mp. 47351

B9025 BAPTISTS. VIRGINIA. DOVER DISTRICT ASSOCIATION
Minutes of the Baptist Dover Association, holden . . . October 20, 1795. Richmond, Thomas Nicolson, 1795.
[4], 14 p. 18 cm.
Davis 108
ViRU mp. 47353

B9026 BAPTISTS. VIRGINIA. DOVER DISTRICT ASSOCIATION
Minutes of the Dover Baptist Association, holden . . . October 11th, 1794. Richmond, Thomas Nicolson, 1795.
[3], 11 p. 16.5 cm.
Davis 109
ViRU mp. 47352

B9027 BAPTISTS. VIRGINIA. GOSHEN DISTRICT ASSOCIATION
Minutes of the Goshen Baptist Association, holden . . . in Orange county. Begun third Saturday in October, 1795, and continued to Monday inclusive. Richmond, John Dixon [1795?]
[2], 8 p. 17 cm.
Davis 110
ViRU mp. 47354

B9028 BAPTISTS. VIRGINIA. KETOCTON ASSOCIATION
Minutes of the Ketocton Baptist Association . . . at Goose Creek . . . August 1975. Dumfries [Va.], Thornton [1795]
[8] p.
NRAB. Photostat: MWA mp. 47355

B9029 BAPTISTS. VIRGINIA. ROANOKE DISTRICT ASSOCIATION
Minutes of the Roaroak [sic] District Association, held at Banister meeting-house, Pittsylvania County, Virginia. May 2d, 3d, 4th, 1795. Lynchburg, Robert M. Bransford [1795]
8 p.
MNtcA mp. 47356

B9030 BARBAULD, ANNA LETITIA AIKIN, 1743-1825
Evening tales, consisting of miscellaneous pieces for . . . children. Extracted from the works of Mrs. Barbauld and Mr. Aiken. Philadelphia, W. Young, 1795.
160 p. 16mo
PPL mp. 47357

B9031 BELL, ABIGAIL, b. 1779?
Lines, composed by Miss Abigail Bell, jun. aged sixteen years, daughter of Benjamin Bell, Esq. of Hebron. On the death of Miss Lucy Dutton and Miss Sally Olcott . . . [Hartford?] Printed in the year 1795.
broadside 29 X 15 cm.
In 2 columns
CtHi mp. 47359

B9032 BELLAMY, JOSEPH, 1719-1790
An essay, on the nature and glory of the gospel of Jesus Christ . . . Worcester, Leonard Worcester, 1795.
307 p. 18 cm.
MWA mp. 47360

B9033 BELLE LETTRE CLUB
Regulations for the Belle Lettre Club. [New York, 1795]
broadside 36.5 X 22 cm.
dated in manuscript at end: Feb[y]. 24. 1795
NAII. Photostats: DLC; MWA; NN mp. 47361

B9034 [BERQUIN, ARNAUD] 1750-1791
The looking-glass for the mind . . . A new edition, with thirty-six cuts . . . New York, Printed by W. Durell, 1795.
[4], 259 p. 17 cm.
Hamilton 210
DGU; MWA (poor); NjP mp. 47362

B9035 [BERQUIN, ARNAUD] 1750-1791
The looking-glass for the mind . . . A new edition with 36 cuts, elegantly engraved. New York, Printed by W. Durell for Edward Mitchell, 1795.
[4], 259 p. 17 cm.
Hamilton 210
NN; NjP mp. 47363

B9036 [BERQUIN, ARNAUD] 1750-1791
The looking-glass for the mind . . . A new edition, with thirty-six cuts . . . New-York, Printed by W. Durell for Robert M'Gill, 1795.
[4], 259 p. 17 cm.
RPJCB mp. 47364

B9037 BIBLE. O.T. PSALMS
Doctor Watts's Imitation of the Psalms . . . Corrected and enlarged. By Joel Barlow . . . New-York, Samuel Campbell, 1795.
372 p. 13.5 cm.
Huntington 667
CSmH; MWA mp. 47358

B9038 BICKERSTAFF'S Boston almanack for . . . 1796 . . . Boston, Printed for the booksellers [1795]
[24] p.
Drake 2545
CLU

B9039 BINGHAM, CALEB, 1757-1817
The child's companion; being a concise spelling-book . . . The fourth edition . . . Boston, Manning & Loring, 1795.
84 p. 16 cm.
MWA mp. 47365

B9040 BROWN, JOHN, 1722-1787
Two short catechisms, mutually connected . . . Carlisle, Printed for Abraham Craig, student, by George Kline, 1795.
53 p. 20.5 cm.
MWA mp. 47367

B9041 BROWN, MOSES, 1738-1836
In memory of Moses, second son of Mr. Nicholas Brown . . . He died July 17, 1794 . . . In memory of Mrs. Mary Vanderlight . . . She deceased at the house of her brother, Mr. Moses Brown . . . May, 1795 . . . [Providence? 1795?]
broadside 26.5 X 14 cm.
Alden 1408
RPJCB. Photostat: MWA mp. 47368

B9042 CANAL BRIDGE PROPRIETORS
To the members of the Massachusetts Legislature. Equal justice and protection . . . the petition of A. Craigie, as President of the Proprietors of the Canal Bridge; now before the Legislature . . . [Boston, 1795?]
broadside 28.5 X 23 cm.
NHi mp. 47369

B9043 CAREY, MATHEW, 1760–1839
The general atlas for Carey's edition of Guthrie's Geography improved . . . Philadelphia, Mathew Carey, May 1, 1795.
1 p.l., 45 maps (part fold.) 37.5 cm.
cf. Evans 30162 ("May 1, 1796")
MB; MiU–C; PPAmP mp. 47370

B9044 CAREY, MATHEW, 1760–1839
Philadelphia, March 17, 1795. Proposals by Mathew Carey, for publishing by subscription, The history of the earth and animated nature. By Oliver Goldsmith . . . [Philadelphia, 1795]
broadside 25.5 X 19 cm.
MWA mp. 47371

B9045 CARPENTERS' SOCIETY OF BALTIMORE
Additional rules . . . [Baltimore, 1795?]
21 p. 20.5 cm.
PPAmP. Photostat: MWA mp. 47372

B9046 CATHOLIC CHURCH
A short abridgment of Christian doctrine . . . The thirteenth edition . . . Baltimore, Samuel Sower, 1795.
54 p. 11 cm.
Minick 224; Parsons 138
MdW mp. 47374

B9047 CATHOLIC CHURCH. LITURGY
Catholisches Gebät-Buch. Ba[ltimore:] Gedruckt bey [Samuel Saur, 1795.]
269, [1] p. 18mo
PPL copy has defective t.p., but includes a ms. note giving a bibliographical description
PPL mp. 47375

B9048 CATHOLIC CHURCH. LITURGY
Ordo divini officii recitandi . . . Pro anno Domini MDCCXCVI. Baltimori, Typis Johannis Hayes [1795]

Minick 225; Parsons 145
No copy known mp. 47376

B9049 [CERACCHI, GIUSEPPE] 1760–1801
A description of a monument designed to perpetuate the memory of American liberty . . . [Philadelphia? 1795?]
broadside 38 X 29 cm.
"Mr. Ceracchia Feby 9th [17]95"—contemporary ms. endorsement on verso of sheet
Not Evans 28403.—John E. Alden
MB

B9050 CHAPIN, PELATIAH, 1746–1837
A dialogue between Jamy and Hervey . . . Windsor, Alden Spooner, 1795.
11 p. 15 cm.
MDeeP mp. 47378

B9051 CHAPIN, PELATIAH, 1746–1837
Jamy and Hervey's second dialogue . . . Windsor, Alden Spooner, 1795.
12 p. 15 cm.
Emerson Greenaway (1961) mp. 47379

B9052 CHARLESTON, S. C. CITIZENS
Report of the select committee, chosen by ballot of the citizens of the United States, in Charleston, South-Carolina, in pursuance of a resolution . . . of the citizens . . . the sixteenth of July, 1795 . . . Charleston, W. P. Young [1795]
broadside 41 X 24.5 cm.
DLC mp. 47380

B9053 THE cheap and famous farrier. Ephrata, 1795.
64 p. illus. 12 cm.
PHi; PU–V mp. 47381

B9054 [CHETWOOD, WILLIAM RUFUS] d. 1766
The remarkable history of Miss Villars . . . Keene, Printed & sold by C. Sturtevant, Jun. & Co., 1795.
17 p. 18 cm.
MWA (torn); RPJCB (p. 17 wanting) mp. 47383

B9055 THE Christian oeconomy . . . Printed by Thomas Dickman, and sold at his Book Store, Greenfield, Mass., 1795.
59 p.
MWA mp. 47384

B9056 (CIRCULAR) Reverend Sir, I am directed by the Secretary of State, to promulge, throughout this district, the President's proclamation for a public thanks-

giving . . . District of New-York, January 18, 1795. [New York, 1795]
broadside 23 X 18 cm.
NHi mp. 47385

B9057 [CLARKE'S Charleston directory, with large and elegant plan of the city engraved by Ralph. Charleston, Printed by S. J. Elliott, and sold at Bailley & Waller's bookstore, 1795]
46 p.
Elias Ball, Charleston, S.C. (map wanting) Microfilm: ScC mp. 47386

B9058 COLE, JAMES
Ten dollars reward. Ran away . . . a Negro man named Harry . . . speaks good English and Low Dutch . . . James Cole. New-Brunswick . . . Sept. 30, 1795. New-Brunswick, Abraham Blauvelt [1795]
broadside 25.5 X 21.5 cm.
NjR

B9059 COLLOT, GEORGES HENRI VICTOR
Réponse aux inculpations que Hugues a voulu faire résulter de la publication d'une de mes lettres, en date du 20 mai 1794: adressée aux comités de salut public, des colonies et de marine. [Philadelphia, 1795]
28 p. 8vo caption title
PPL mp. 47387

B9060 COLUMBIAN CENTINEL
Dedication. To the ever liberal and right worthy patrons of the *Columbian Centinel*, this eleventh anniversary ode, is . . . dedicated, by . . . The Carrier. . . . Boston Jan. 1, 1795. [Boston, 1795]
broadside 47.5 X 15.5 cm.
MWA mp. 47399

B9061 COLUMBIANUM, PHILADELPHIA
The exhibition of the Columbianum . . . established at Philadelphia, 1795 . . . Philadelphia, Francis & Robert Bailey, 1795.
1 p.l., [6] p. 19.5 cm.
NNFr; PHi; PPAmP. Photostat: DLC mp. 47388

B9062 CONNECTICUT. GOVERNOR, 1786-1796
By His Excellency Samuel Huntington . . . A proclamation . . Norwich, March 11, 1795 . . . Hartford, Hudson and Goodwin [1795]
broadside 40 X 33.5 cm.
CtHi; MHi; NHi mp. 47389

B9063 CONNECTICUT COURANT
To all Christian people; more especially those who take the *Connecticut Courant* . . . Hartford, January 1, 1795. [Hartford, 1795]
broadside 44 X 27 cm.
CtHi; MSaE; NHi mp. 47623

B9064 CONNECTICUT GORE LAND COMPANY
Articles of agreement for conducting the business respecting . . . the Gore . . . Hartford, Sept. 17, 1795. [Hartford, 1795]
broadside 41 X 21.5 cm.
Vail: Old frontier 1015; cf. Evans 30272
CtY; DLC; ICN; MH; PPiU mp. 47390

B9065 CONNECTICUT LAND COMPANY
[Votes of the Connecticut Land Company. Hartford, September 5, 1795.] [Hartford, 1795]
broadside?
400 copies printed; original ms. in OClWHi
Trumbull: Supplement 2002; Vail: Old frontier 1018
No copy known mp. 47391

B9066 THE consociational court of inquisition. [n.p.] 1795.
7 p. 23 cm.
MiU-C mp. 47392

B9067 A CONSTITUTION of the Consociation of the Southern District in Litchfield County. [Litchfield, Thomas Collier, 1795]
8 p. 15 cm.
Trumbull: Supplement 2010
CtHi mp. 47393

B9068 COTTON, ROWLAND
Cain's lamentations over Abel . . . The second edition . . . New-York, Wayland and Davis, 1795.
239 p. 12mo
MWA; N; PPL mp. 47394

B9069 COUNT Roderic's castle; or, Gothic times, a tale. In two volumes . . . Philadelphia, Thomas Bradford, 1795.
2 v. in 1 (112; 122, [6] p.) 18 cm.
cf. Evans 28486
ICN; MWA; PHi; PU

B9070 DAILY ADVERTISER
Address of the carrier of the *Daily Advertiser*, to his customers . . . New-York, January 1, 1795. [New York, Francis Childs, 1795]
broadside 30.5 X 18.5 cm.
NHi mp. 47336

B9071 DAVIS, GEORGE
Law books—Latest Irish editions. George Davis . . . informs his friends . . . No. 313, High-Street, Philadelphia, November 16, 1795. [Philadelphia, 1795]
broadside 33 X 20.5 cm.
RPJCB mp. 47395

B9072 [DAY, THOMAS] 1748-1789
The history of little Jack . . . Philadelphia, Printed and sold by H. and P. Rice and Co. Baltimore, 1795.
1 p.l., 94 p. illus. 16 cm.
New York Public 1138
NN (imperfect) mp. 47396

B9073 [DEBRAHM, JOHN WILLIAM GERAR] 1718-1799
Sum of testimonies of truth. [Philadelphia? 1795]
7 p. 8vo
Signed at end: 1st. day of the year (vulgarly 20th. March) 1795
De Renne p. 265
CSmH; GU-De mp. 47397

B9074 DECALVES, ALONSO, pseud.
New travels to the westward . . . By Don Alonso Decalves . . . [n.p.] Printed in the year 1795.
1 p.l., iii, [5]-58 p. 13 cm.
Sabin 98447; Vail 1023
NHi mp. 47398

B9075 [DEFOE, DANIEL] 1661?-1731
The family instructor . . . An American edition. New-York, Printed by Hurtin & Commardinger for Evert Duyckinck, 1795.
319 p. 18 cm.
cf. Evans 28550
MWA mp. 47400

B9076 DEFOE, DANIEL, 1661?-1731
The wonderful life and most surprising adventures of . . . Robinson Crusoe . . . New York, Hurtin & Commardinger, for Benjamin Gomez, 1795.

143 p. 13.5 cm.
Brigham 32; Rosenbach–Ch 190
MWA; PP mp. 47401

B9077 DERRICK,
Cynthia's cottage . . . Philadelphia, G. Willig [1795]
broadside 31 cm.
"The words by Mr Derrick."
Sonneck-Upton p. 96
DLC; MWA; PP; PU mp. 47402

B9078 [DIALOGUE between a young convert, a minister, and a Christian brother . . . Windsor, A. Spooner, ca. 1795]

Advertised in J. MacGowan's *Life of Joseph* (Windsor, 1795)
McCorison 334
No copy known mp. 47403

B9079 THE DIARY
Address presented by the carriers of the *Diary*, to their numerous and respectable patrons, January 1, 1795. [New York, Samuel Loudon, 1795]
broadside 32 X 14.5 cm.
NHi mp. 47339

B9080 DIBDIN, CHARLES, 1745–1814
Mad Peg . . . New York & Philadelphia, B. Carr; Baltimore, J. Carr [1795–96]
Sonneck-Upton p. 245
[2] p. 31 cm.
DLC; NN mp. 47404

B9081 DIBDIN, CHARLES, 1745–1814
Peggy Perkins . . . [Philadelphia] G. Willig [1795–97]
broadside 33 cm.
Sonneck-Upton p. 329
DLC; MWA mp. 47405

B9082 DILWORTH, THOMAS, d. 1780
A new guide to the English tongue . . . A new edition . . . Philadelphia, Printed and sold by Stewart & Cochran, 1795.
120+ p. 17 cm. A–K^{6}
MWA (all wanting after p. 120) mp. 47406

B9083 DILWORTH, W. H.
The complete letter-writer . . . By H. W. Dilworth, A. M. New-York, Samuel Campbell, 1795.
81 [i.e. 108] p. 14 cm. A–I^{6}
Final page misnumbered
MWA mp. 47407

B9084 [DODSLEY, ROBERT] 1703–1764
The economy of human life . . . New-York, Printed for Evert Duyckinck, 1795.
122 p. 13.5 cm.
New York Public 1139; Sabin 90280
NN mp. 47408

B9085 DODSLEY, ROBERT, 1703–1764
The economy of human life . . . New York, Printed for Robert Hodge, & Co., 1795.
122 p. 12mo
PPL mp. 47409

B9086 DONALD of Dundee . . . New York, Printed for G. Gilfert [1795]
p. 12–13. 33.5 cm.
Sonneck-Upton p. 111
DLC mp. 47410

B9087 [DOW, HENDRICUS] 1761–1814
[A warning to little children. Windsor, A. Spooner, ca. 1795]

Advertised in J. MacGowan's *Life of Joseph* (Windsor, 1975)
McCorison 336
No copy known mp. 47411

B9088 [ELLICOTT, ANDREW] 1754–1820
Plan of the city of Washington . . . Rollinson sculp^{t}. N. York, I. Reid, L. Wayland and C. Smith [1795?]
map 41.5 X 57.5 cm.
Huntington 670; cf. Phillips: Atlases 1216, 1366
CSmH mp. 47413

B9089 FAIR Lucretia: being a sorrowful history of a rich merchant . . . To which is added, Edwin and Angelina . . . Danbury, Printed and sold by N. Douglas [1795?]
12 p. 16 cm.
Huntington 671; Trumbull: Supplement 2121
CSmH; NHi mp. 47414

B9090 THE famous history of Whittington and his cat . . . Newfield, Printed by Beach and Jones [1795?]
27 p. illus. 10 cm.
Dated by d'Alté A. Welch
MWA mp. 47684

B9091 FATAL effects of jealousy: a Spanish novel. Founded on facts. New-York, J. Harrisson, 1795.
47 p. 15.5 cm.
MH (uncut in orig. wrappers); MWA mp. 47415

B9092 FATHER Abraham's almanac, for . . . 1796 . . . Philadelphia: Printed for H. & P. Rice [1795]
[40] p. 18 cm.
cf. Evans 28786
By David Hale
MB mp. 47442

B9093 FATHER Hutchins revived: being an almanack . . . for . . . 1796 . . . New-York, Printed and sold by Samuel Campbell [1795]
[36] p. 18 cm.
New York Public 1143
MWA; NN mp. 47461

B9094 [FÉNELON, FRANÇOIS DE SALIGNAC DE LA MOTHE-] 1651–1715
Some advice to governesses and teachers. Written by the author of The evidence of the existence of God. Supposed to be translated by Bishop Barclay. Litchfield, Re-printed by Coll[ier & Buel], M,DC[CXCV?]
8 p. 14.5 cm.
Trumbull: Supplement 2625
Dated by Forrest Bowe
Forrest Bowe, New York City (defective) mp. 47417

B9095 [FENNING, DANIEL]
Federal money. [Dover, N.H., Samuel Bragg jun., 1795]
7, [1] p. 12mo caption title
PPL mp. 47419

B9096 [FESSENDEN, THOMAS GREEN] 1771–1837
Jonathan's courthip . . . [New Haven? 1795?]
broadside 28 X 21 cm.
MWA (imperfect) mp. 47420

B9097 Fête civique célébrée par les patriotes francais, américains et hollandais . . . [Colophon] Philadelphia, Parent [1795]
4 p.

Begins: L'an troisième de la République . . . le 17 germinal . . .
RPJCB (2 copies) mp. 47421

B9098 FLAVEL, JOHN, 1639?–1691
A token for mourners . . . Exeter, Printed by Henry Ranlet, for Ozias Silsby, 1795.
168 p. 14.5 cm.
cf. Evans 28677
MWA; N mp. 47422

B9099 . . . THE following are the established prices of printing . . . [New York, 1795]
broadside 33 X 20 cm.
Reproduced in *Established prices of printing.* Meriden, Conn., Meriden gravure company, 1937
No copy known mp. 47423

B9100 THE following lines were composed on the melancholly state of the family of Mr. Benjamin Sandborn, of Sandbornton, who departed this life October 20, 1794 . . . [n.p., 1795]
broadside
Reprinted (1909) by The Tuttle, Morehouse & Taylor Company, New Haven
MWA (reproduction) mp. 47424

B9101 FORTIS, EDMUND, d. 1794
The last words and dying speech of Edmund Fortis, a Negro man . . . executed . . . the twenty-fifth day of September, 1794, for . . . murder . . . of Pamela Tilton . . . fourteen years of age . . . Printed and sold at Exeter, 1795.
12 p. 16 cm.
McDade 312
MWA mp. 47425

B9102 FREEMASONS. MASSACHUSETTS. GRAND LODGE
At a meeting of the Grand Lodge of Massachusetts, on the evening of the 13th of September, A. L. 5795 . . . The following vote was passed unanimously . . . [Boston, 1795]
broadside
MWA mp. 47426

B9103 FREEMASONS. PENNSYLVANIA. GRAND LODGE
Account of Grand Lodge dues, due from Lodge No. 2 Ancient York Masons held in . . . Philadelphia . . . to St. Johns Day December 1795 . . . [Philadelphia, 1795]
broadside 25 X 21.5 cm.
PPL mp. 47427

B9104 FREEMASONS. PENNSYLVANIA. LODGE NO. 2
Return of the members of Lodge No. 2, Ancient York Masons held in . . . Philadelphia . . . to St. John's Day December 1795 . . . [Philadelphia, 1795]
broadside 41 X 22 cm.
PPL mp. 47428

B9105 FREEMASONS. VIRGINIA. SAGESSE LODGE
Tableau des F. F. qui composent la loge provinciale Francaise . . . la Sagesse . . . en Virginie . . . 5795. Norfolk, Willett and O'Connor [1795]
8 p.
McCoy 15
DSC mp. 47429

B9106 FRIENDLY FIRE SOCIETY, PORTSMOUTH, N.H.
Friendly Fire Society, established at Portsmouth . . . We whose names are hereunto subscribed . . . Portsmouth, November, 1795. [Portsmouth] J. Melcher [1795]
broadside 45 X 32 cm.
MWA mp. 47553

B9107 FRIENDS, SOCIETY OF. LONDON YEARLY MEETING
Abstract of the epistle from the yearly meeting held in London . . . from the 18th to the 27th of the fifth month, 1795 . . . [Philadelphia? 1795?]
3, [1] p.
MWA mp. 47430

B9108 FRIENDS, SOCIETY OF. PHILADELPHIA MONTHLY MEETING
A further salutation of brotherly love, from the Monthly-Meeting of Friends of Philadelphia . . . Philadelphia: Printed by Jacob Johnson & Co., 1795.
8 p. 8vo
Printer's name in imprint in Roman caps; cf. Evans 28714 (printer's name in microprint in italic caps)
PHi

B9109 FURMAN AND HUNT, firm
New ferry to Long Island, to commence Saturday 1st August, 1795 . . . Furman and Hunt. [New York, 1795]
broadside 28 X 18 cm.
NHi mp. 47431

B9110 GAZETTE OF THE UNITED STATES
Address of the carrier of the *Gazette of the United States* January 1st, 1795. [New York, 1795]
broadside 41 X 35 cm.
In two columns
MWA mp. 47337

B9111 [THE gentleman's political almanac for . . . 1796. Alexandria, Ellis Price [1795]]

Advertised in the *Columbian Mirror*, Dec. 19, 1795
Drake 13848
No copy known

B9112 THE gentleman's political pocket almanac for . . . 1796. By Charles Smith . . . New-York, Printed by J. Buel, for C. Smith, No. 51, Maiden-Lane [1795]
112 p.
Wall p. 29
NjP; WHi mp. 47603

B9113 GILLISS, JOHN
To be sold . . . on Saturday the first day of August next . . . John Gilliss. July 13th, 1795. Baltimore, Clayland, Dobbin [1795]
broadside 18 X 21.5 cm.
Minick 232
MdHi mp. 47433

B9114 GIORDANI, GIUSEPPE, 1744–1798
Loose were her tresses . . . [Philadelphia] G. Willig [1795-97]
[2] p. 33.5 cm.
Sonneck-Upton p. 236
DLC; MWA mp. 47434

B9115 GIRAL DEL PINO, HIPPOLYTO SAN JOSÉ
. . . A new Spanish grammar, or the elements of the Spanish language . . . Philadelphia, Printed by and for Colerick and Hunter, 1795.
iv, 399 p. 17 cm.
At head of title: First American edition
Huntington 673; New York Public 1141
CSmH; MWA; N; NN; PPL (lacking after p. 394)
mp. 47435

B9116 GOODWIN, HEZEKIAH, 1740–1767
A remarkable vision! Shewing the sudden and surprising appearance . . . of the departed spirit of Mr. Yeamans . . . to and with Mr. H. Goodwin . . . The second edition, carefully revised and corrected by James Treadway . . . Amherst, N. H., Printed and sold, by Nathaniel Coverly and Son [1795]
15, [1] p. 20 cm.
cf. Evans 28762
MWA mp. 47436

B9117 [GREENE, ROBERT]
The history of Dorastus and Faunia . . . Boston, J. White, 1795.
24 p. 16.5 cm.
CSmH; MB; MWA mp. 47438

B9118 GREENLEAF, THOMAS, 1755–1798
New-York, Feb. 10, 1795. Proposals for printing by subscription a magazine, entitled, *The United States Christian Magazine* . . . [New York, 1795]
broadside 44 X 20 cm.
NHi mp. 47439

B9119 GREGORY, JOHN, 1724–1773
A father's legacy to his daughters . . . Worcester, Printed and sold by Isaiah Thomas [1795]
120 p. 15 cm. [A]–K^6
Advertised as "for sale" in the *Massachusetts Spy*, Worcester, Aug. 12, 1795
MWA mp. 47440

B9120 GROSIER, JEAN BAPTISTE GABRIEL ALEXANDRE, 1742–1828
A general description of China . . . Vol. I. Translated from the French . . . Philadelphia, Printed by Dunning and Hyer for Robertson and Palmer, 1795.
v, xxv, 1–32 p. only. 23 cm.
No more published?
DLC mp. 47441

B9121 [HAMILTON, ADAM]
The confession and lamentation of a leper . . . New-London, Printed and sold by J. Springer, 1795.
26 p. 19 cm.
T.p. contains acrostic on author's name
Colophon: Printed at Norwich, by John Trumbull, and sold by James Springer, New-London.
New York Public 1142; Trumbull: Supplement 2231
CtHi; NN mp. 47443

B9122 HANCOCK, THOMAS AND JOHN, firm, Boston
[Business card, printed from copper plate engraving by Joseph Callender. Boston, 1795]
broadside
Bill for 100 copies rendered the firm by Callender Apr. 24, 1795.–Boston Pub. Library
No copy known

B9123 HANCOCK, THOMAS AND JOHN, firm, Boston
[Business card, printed in red, blue and black. Boston, Joseph Callender, 1795]
broadside
Bill for 200 copies rendered the firm by Callender May 9, 1795.–Boston Pub. Library
No copy known

B9124 HART, JOHN
100 dollars reward. Benedict Madden . . . committed . . . by John Palmer . . . for courterfeiting bank bills . . . escaped from gaol . . . John Hart, Sheffiff C. T. D. . . . September 18, 1795. Charleston, Markland & M'Iver [1795]
broadside 28 X 22 cm.
Sc-Ar

B9125 HARVARD UNIVERSITY
Harvard College lottery . . . Scheme of the 4th class . . . [Boston, 1795]
broadside 15 X 10.5 cm.
CSmH (facsim.) mp. 47444

B9126 HELLENBROEK, ABRAHAM, 1658–1731
A specimen of divine truths . . . Translated from the Dutch. New-Brunswick, Abraham Blauvelt, 1795.
60 p. 16.5 cm.
MWA mp. 47445

B9127 HENDEL, WILHELM, 1730?–1798
Wohlmeynende Warnung vor dem abscheulichen Fluchen . . . Philadelphia, Steiner und Kämmerer, 1795.
8 p. 16 cm.
MWA mp. 47446

B9128 HERVEY, JAMES, 1714–1758
Meditations and contemplations . . . Philadelphia, Jacob Johnson, 1795.
2 v. in 1. (151 [i.e. 351], [3] p.) 18 cm.
Paged continuously
Huntington 674
CSmH; MB; MWA; MiU-C; NhD; PPL mp. 47447

B9129 HERVEY, NATHAN
[Hymns. Windsor, A. Spooner, ca. 1795]

Advertised in J. MacGowan's *Life of Joseph* (Windsor, 1795)
McCorison 340
No copy known mp. 47448

B9130 HEWITT, JAMES, 1770–1827
Three sonatas for the piano forte . . . Op. 5 . . . New York, Printed for the author and sold at Carr's Musical Repository and at Gilfert & Co's Musical Magazine [1795–97]
17 p. 33.5 cm.
Sonneck-Upton p. 395
DLC (3 copies, variant) mp. 47449

B9131 HEWITT, JAMES, 1770–1827
Time. A favorite rondo . . . New York & Philadelphia, B. Carr; Baltimore, I. Carr [1795–96]
[2] p. 31 cm.
Sonneck-Upton p. 432
DLC; NN mp. 47450

B9132 HISTORY of the wicked life and horrid death of Doctor John Faustus . . . Norwich: Printed in the year 1795.
22 p. 16.5 cm.
CtHi mp. 47416

B9133 THE hive: or a collection of thoughts on civil, moral, sentimental and religious subjects . . . Worcester, From the press of Isaiah Thomas, jun. for Isaiah Thomas, and sold at their respective bookstores, 1795.
252 p. plate. 18 cm.
cf. Evans 28841 (also at MWA)
MWA; NhD; NjP

B9134 HOCH-DEUTSCHES Lutherisches ABC und Namen Büchlein . . . Reading, Johann Gruber, 1795.
[32] p.
MWA

B9135 HOOK, JAMES, 1746–1827
I'll die for no shepherd not I . . . New York, G. Gilfert [1795]
[2] p. 34 cm.
Sonneck-Upton p. 203
DLC; MWA mp. 47451

B9136 [HOOK, JAMES] 1746–1827
Keep your distance . . . New York, G. Gilfert [1795]
[2] p. 31.5 cm.
Sonneck-Upton p. 219
DLC; MWA; RPJCB mp. 47452

B9137 [HOOK, JAMES] 1746–1827
The lass of Richmond Hill. Sung by Mr. Incledon. New York, Printed & sold by G. Gilfert & Co. No. 209 Broadway [1795]
1 leaf. 35.5 cm. caption title
Sonneck Upton p. 225
MiU–C

B9138 [HOOK, JAMES] 1746–1827
Listen listen to the voice of love . . . New York, G. Gilfert [1795]
broadside 33 cm.
Sonneck-Upton p. 232
DLC (2 copies); MWA; NN mp. 47453

B9139 HOOK, JAMES, 1746–1827
Love shall be my guide . . . New York, G. Gilfert [1795]
[2] p. 33.5 cm.
Sonneck-Upton p. 238
DLC (2 copies); RPJCB mp. 47454

B9140 HOOK, JAMES, 1746–1827
The silver moon . . . New York, Printed for G. Gilfert [1795]
[2] p. 34 cm.
Sonneck-Upton p. 382
DLC (2 copies); MWA; NN; RPJCB mp. 47455

B9141 HOOK, JAMES, 1746–1827
Willy of the dale . . . New York, G. Gilfert [1795]
[2] p. 33.5 cm.
Sonneck-Upton p. 472
DLC; RPJCB mp. 47456

B9142 [HOOK, JAMES] 1746–1827
Within a mile of Edinburgh . . . New York, Printed for G. Gilfert [1795]
[2] p. 34 cm.
Sonneck-Upton p. 475
DLC mp. 47457

B9143 HOPPIN, BENJAMIN
[A catalogue of a most valuable collection of books . . . To be sold at auction at the office of Benjamin Hoppin . . . Providence, 1795]

Dated from an advertisement of Aug. 22, 1795
Alden 1418; McKay 138E
No copy known mp. 47458

B9144 HOSACK, DAVID, 1769–1835
Plan for collecting the grasses and other plants of the state of New York into an herbarium–in a communication from Doctor David Hosack . . . [New York, 1795]
broadside
PPAmP mp. 47459

B9145 [HOWARD, THOMAS]
The history of the Seven wise mistresses of Rome . . . Philadelphia: Printed and sold by H. & P. Rice, also by J. Rice and Co., Baltimore, 1795.
114, [2] p. 14 cm.
Preface by Thomas Howard
PHi. Mrs. Joseph Carson, Philadelphia (1962) mp. 47460

B9146 IN General Committee, Albany, April 9, 1795.
Sir, We transmit you nominations for Governor and Lieutenant Governor . . . [Albany? 1795]
broadside 33 X 20 cm.
NHi mp. 47464

B9147 INDEED young man I must deny . . . New York, G. Gilfert [1795]
p. 12–13. 32.5 cm.
Sonneck-Upton p. 207
DLC; MWA mp. 47465

B9148 INSTRUCTIVE and entertaining emblems . . . By Miss Thoughtful. Hartford, J. Babcock, 1795.
31 p. incl. covers. 10.5 cm.
MWA; CLU; CtHi. d'Alté A. Welch (covers wanting) mp. 47466

B9149 JAY, FREDERICK
Catalogue of books, for sale by Frederick Jay, on Friday the 8th of May . . . at his auction-room, No. 167 Pearl-street . . . New-York, May 7, 1795–Printed by T. & J. Swords . . .
broadside 42 X 27 cm.
182 items in 4 columns
CtHi mp. 47467

B9150 JOHN STREET THEATRE
Benefit of Mr. Hallam, jun. On Monday evening, the 25th of May . . . The Rage . . . [New York, 1795]
broadside 42 X 23.5 cm.
Original in Ireland 1:24–25. Extra-illustrated
CSmH mp. 47514

B9151 JOHN STREET THEATRE
. . . Benefit of Mr. Humphreys . . . [New York, 1795]
broadside 41 X 24.5 cm.
Original in Ireland 1:126–27
CSmH (mutilated) mp. 47515

B9152 JOHN STREET THEATRE
Mr. Carr's night. On Wednesday evening, the 22d of April . . . The Highland reel . . . [New York, 1795]
broadside 42 X 24.5 cm.
Original in Ireland 1:122–23
CSmH mp. 47516

B9153 [JOHNSON, RICHARD] 1734–1793
The blossoms of morality . . . By the editor of The looking-glass for the mind. First American edition. 1795. Philadelphia, Printed by and for William W. Woodward.
4 p.l., 212p. 16 cm.
Has been wrongly attributed to Arnaud Berquin
New York Public 1136; cf. Evans 28479
CtY; ICU; MWA; NN. Forrest Bowe, New York City (1962) mp. 47468

B9154 JOHONNET, JACKSON
The remarkable adventures of Jackson Johonnet, of Massachusetts . . . Written by himself . . . Exeter, Printed by and for J. Lamson [1795]
15, [1] p. 19 cm.
Vail: Old frontier 1030
ICN mp. 47469

B9155 JOSEPHUS, FLAVIUS
The whole genuine and complete works of Flavius Josephus . . . Baltimore, Pechin and co., 1795.
723, [4] p. illus., maps. 42 cm.
Minick 236; New York Public 1144
MdBE; MdBG; NN; OCo mp. 47470

B9156 [THE jovial songster . . . Baltimore, 1795]

Advertised in the *Baltimore Telegraphe*, Mar. 26, 1795, among "New publications, printed in Baltimore for Keatinge's bookstore."
Minick 237
No copy known mp. 47472

B9157 JULIA; or, The penitent daughter . . . Philadelphia, Stewart & Cochran, 1795.
108 p. 13.5 cm.
DLC mp. 47473

B9158 THE juvenile miscellany, in prose and verse . . . Philadelphia, Printed for the compiler, by Mordecai Jones, 1795.
108 p. 17 cm.
New York Public 1145
NN; PHi mp. 47474

B9159 KELBURN, SINCLAIR, 1754–1802
The divinity of our Lord Jesus Christ asserted . . . Philadelphia, Printed by and for W. W. Woodward, 1795.
2 p.l., 127 p. 25.5 cm.
Huntington 675
CSmH; DLC; MB; MWA; NhD; NjP; PHi; PPL
mp. 47475

B9160 KENTUCKY. GENERAL ASSEMBLY. HOUSE OF REPRESENTATIVES
Journal of the House of Representatives, at the first session of the fourth General Assembly . . . held . . . in . . . Frankfort . . . [Nov. 2, 1795] . . . Lexington, John Bradford [1795?]
76 p. 30.5 cm.
Session adjourned Dec. 21, 1795
McMurtrie: Kentucky 45
ICU; Ky mp. 47476

B9161 KENTUCKY. GENERAL ASSEMBLY. SENATE
Journal of the Senate at the fifth session of the General Assembly . . . held . . . in . . . Frankfort . . . [Nov. 2, 1795] . . . Lexington, John Bradford [1795?]
47 p. 32 cm.
McMurtrie: Kentucky 46
ICU; Ky mp. 47477

B9162 [KILNER, DOROTHY] 1755–1836
The good child's delight . . . Philadelphia, W. Young, 1795.
64 p. illus. 10.5 cm.
cf. Evans 28760
DLC (p. 45–52 wanting) mp. 47478

B9163 LANGHORNE, JOHN, 1735–1779
The fables of Flora . . . New-York: Printed by Brewer & Lang. M,DCC,XCV.
99 p. front., plates.
MWA; RPJCB mp. 47479

B9164 LANSINGBURGH RECORDER
The news-boy's address to the subscribers of the *Lansingburgh Recorder*. Lansingburgh, January 1, 1795. [Lansingburgh, N. Y., George Gardner and James Hill, 1795]
broadside 31 X 18 cm.
NHi mp. 47521

B9165 LARKIN, EBENEZER
Eben. Larkin's exchange catalogue, Boston. [Boston, 1795?]
broadside
Dated from ms. note from Larkin to Mathew Carey: Oct. 20, 1795
36 book titles listed
PHi

B9166 LEAR & CO., WASHINGTON, D.C.
Washington, January 1st, 1795. Having established ourselves in this place, for the purpose of transacting business . . . [Washington, 1795]
folder [1] p. 22 X 19 cm.
Signed in ms.
MB mp. 47480

B9167 [LEE, RICHARD]? 1747–1823
A story about Mary's conversion. Rutland, Printed [by James Kirkaldie] for the Flying Stationers [1795?]
4 p. 19.5 cm.
"Printed for Richard Lee:" p. 4
McCorison 343
MWA mp. 47481

B9168 LEE, SAMUEL HOLDEN PARSONS, 1771–1863
Medical advice to seamen; with directions for a medicine chest. New-London, Samuel Green, 1795.
16 p. 19 cm.
Signed at end: Auctori [sic] S. H. P. Lee, Physician
DNLM mp. 47482

B9169 LETTER from doctors Taylor and Hansford. [Account of the fever in Norfolk, Va., in 1795] [Norfolk? 1795?]

McCoy
PU mp. 47483

B9170 [LETTER from the Man in the Moon, to the Rev. Messrs. Hopkins and Hemminway. Windsor, A. Spooner, ca. 1795]

Advertised in J. MacGowan's *Life of Joseph* (Windsor, 1795)
McCorison 344
No copy known mp. 47484

B9171 LEWIS, SAMUEL
The state of New York . . . [Philadelphia, M. Carey, 1795]
map 41.5 X 52.5 cm.
CSmH mp. 47485

B9172 THE little gipsey . . . New York, B. Carr; Baltimore, J. Carr [1795–96]
broadside 32.5 cm.
Sonneck-Upton p. 233
DLC mp. 47486

B9173 LOTTERY, for raising six thousand six hundred and sixty-seven dollars and fifty cents . . . Paterson, November 24, 1795. [Newark] John Woods [1795]
broadside 33.5 X 20 cm.
Held for the Society for Establishing Useful Manufactures
Morsch 279
DLC mp. 47607

B9174 LOUISIANA. GOVERNOR, 1791–1797
Reglement concernant la police génèrale . . . Par permission & privilège de Mr. le Gouverneur. [at end] Nouvelle Orléans. ce. ler. Juin, 1795. Le Baron de Carondelet. [New Orleans, 1795]
27 p. 17 cm.
In French throughout
Two pages numbered 25
McMurtrie: New Orleans 36
CU–B mp. 47487

B9175 MACDONALD, PHILIP
A surprising account of the captivity and escape of Philip MacDonald, and Alexander M'Leod, both of Virginia, from the Chickkemogga Indians . . . Written by themselves. Windsor, Re-printed by Alden Spooner, and sold to the peddlers [1795]
12 p. 17 cm.
Advertised in the Windsor *Vermont journal*, June 15, 1795, as "just published."
McCorison 348; Vail: Old frontier 1034
CtY mp. 47488

B9176 MASSACHUSETTS
[No. XXIV] An account of lands belonging to the Commonwealth, in the District of Maine . . . June 19th, 1795. Approved, *Samuel Adams* . . . [Boston? 1795?]
[4] p. folder 40 X 25 cm.
Printed on first page only
MSaE

B9177 MASSACHUSETTS. GENERAL COURT
Commonwealth of Massachusetts. To the selectmen of the town of Whereas by the tenth article . . . Given . . . at Boston, the sixteenth day of February . . . One thousand seven hundred and ninety-five . . . President of the Senate. Speaker of the House . . . [Boston, 1795]
broadside 39 X 23 cm.
Directing a vote on amendments to the constitution
MWA mp. 47489

B9178 MASSACHUSETTS. GOVERNOR, 1794–1797
Commonwealth of Massachusetts. By the Governor . . . Samuel Adams . . . By the President of the United States. A proclamation . . . [Jan. 1, 1795] . . . [Boston] Adams and Larkin [1795]
broadside 50 X 42 cm.
Dated Jan. 16, 1795 and designating Feb. 19, 1795 a day of thanksgiving
MB; MWA mp. 47490

B9179 MILES, SMITH
The mourner. The following, written by the Rev. Smith Miles, upon the death of Mr. Joseph Sherwood, who died in the West-Indies, on the 25th February, 1795, was spoken at a public exhibition in Derby, in April following by Hannah Sherwood . . . [n.p., 1795?]
broadside 46 X 14.5 cm.
MWA mp. 47491

B9180 [MILES, WILLIAM AUGUSTUS]
A letter to the Prince of Wales . . . First American, from the sixth London edition. From the Apollo Press in Boston. For the proprietor of the Boston Bookstore, 1795.
58 p. 18 cm.
cf. Evans 28968
CSmH mp. 47492

B9181 THE MIRROUR
A New Year. The carrier of the *Mirrour*, to his customers . . . Concord, January 1795 . . . [Concord, 1795]
broadside
Signed: Good-News-Boy
1st line: Custom has, long since . . .
NHi mp. 47510

B9182 MOORE, JOHN HAMILTON, d. 1807
The young gentleman and lady's monitor, and English teacher's assistant . . . New York, Printed and sold by Samuel Campbell, 1795.
406, [2] p. 4 plates. 17.5 cm.
MWA mp. 47493

B9183 MORSE, WILLIAM
Mechanical arts, in thirty-two receipts . . . Hartford, Elisha Babcock, 1795.
14 p. 17 cm.
Trumbull: Supplement 2419
CtHi mp. 47494

B9184 MOULDS, JOHN, fl. 1785–1800
The Caledonian maid . . . Philadelphia, B. Carr; New-York; Baltimore, I. Carr [ca. 1795]
[2] p. 32.5 cm.
Sonneck-Upton p. 30
DLC; ICN; MWA; RPJCB mp. 47495

B9185 MOULDS, JOHN, fl. 1785–1800
She dropt a tear and cried be true . . . New York, George Gilfert [1795]
[2] p. 32.5 cm.
Sonneck-Upton p. 378
DLC; RPJCB mp. 47496

B9186 MOZART, WOLFGANG AMADEUS, 1756–1791
The fowler . . . Philadelphia, G. Willig [1795–97]
[2] p. 33 cm.
Sonneck-Upton p. 146
DLC; RPJCB mp. 47497

B9187 THE much admired song of Arabella the Caledonian maid, with an harp accompaniment. New York, Printed for G. Gilfert [1795]
[2] p. 33.5 cm.
Sonneck-Upton p. 30
DLC; NN; RPJCB mp. 47498

B9188 MUCKARSIE, JOHN
The children's catechism . . . The twelfth edition. Harrisburgh, Printed for Archibald Loudon, of Carlisle, by John Wyeth, 1795.
36 p. 18 cm.
MWA; MiU–C mp. 47499

B9189 MUTUAL ASSURANCE COMPANY
Deed of settlement of the Mutual Assurance Company . . . Norwich, Thomas Hubbard, M,DCC,XCV.
12, [2] p. 12mo $A^6[B]^2$
RPJCB

B9190 NEW Amphitheatre. This evening, January 6th, 1795, will be presented, surprising feats of horsemanship . . . [New York, 1795]
broadside 45 X 16 cm.
New York Public 1146
NN mp. 47500

B9191 A NEW collection of hymns and spiritual songs, from various authors. Printed . . . by Nathaniel Heaton Jun., Wrentham, Mass., 1795.
46 p.
MWA mp. 47501

B9192 THE New-England primer, enlarged and improved

. . . Boston, Printed for and sold by the booksellers, 1795.
[64] p.
MWA (p. 11–12 mutilated) mp. 47503

B9193 THE New-England primer enlarged and improved . . . Boston, Thomas Fleet, 1795.
[96] p.
Heartman 122; cf. Evans 29149 (64 p.)
MB mp. 47502

B9194 THE New England primer, improved . . . Elizabeth-Town: printed and published by Shepard Kollock, 1795.
68 p. 10 cm.
NjP. W. H. Lowdermilk & Co., Washington (1962) mp. 47504

B9195 THE New-England primer improved . . . Norwich, John Sterry and Co., 1795.
66+ p. 12 cm.
Trumbull: Second supplement 2867
CtHi mp. 47505

B9196 NEW HAMPSHIRE. GOVERNOR, 1794–1805
By His Excellency John Taylor Gilman . . . A proclamation [appointing Apr. 2 a day of fasting and prayer] [Concord? 1795]
broadside 29 X 18.5 cm.
Dated at Concord, Jan. 13, 1795
New York Public 1147
Lewis M. Stark (1960). Photostat: NN mp. 47506

B9197 NEW-HAVEN, May 20. On the evening of Tuesday the 12th instant . . . departed this life . . . Ezra Stiles, in the 68th year of his age . . . [n.p., 1795]
broadside 32 X 9 cm.
MWA mp. 47507

B9198 NEW JERSEY. CITIZENS
To George Washington, President of the United States of America. The petition and remonstrance of the subscribers, citizens of . . . New-Jersey . . . have read with attention the treaty . . . at London on the 19th day of November last . . . [n.p., 1795?]
broadside 35 X 17.5 cm.
Jay's Treaty was signed Nov. 19, 1794
NjR (photocopy)

B9199 NEW JERSEY. COUNCIL OF PROPRIETORS OF THE WESTERN DIVISION
An address, from the Council of Proprietors . . . to the occupiers of lands within the angle. [Burlington? 1795?]
3 p. fol.
cf. Evans 28773 (without "Remarks . . . ")
Dated in ms.: May 7th 1795
CSmH mp. 47366

B9200 NEW JERSEY. LEGISLATIVE COUNCIL
Journal of the proceedings of the Legislative-Council of . . . New-Jersey . . . convened at Trenton . . . the 11th day of June . . . Being the third sitting of the eighteenth session. Trenton, Isaac Collins, 1795.
12 p. 32.5 cm.
Morsch 285
Nj; NjHi; PPL. Photostat: NN mp. 47508

B9201 THE New-Jersey, Pennsylvania and Maryland almanac, for . . . 1796 . . . Philadelphia, Jacob Johnson & Co. [1795]
[36] p. 18 cm.
MWA mp. 47509

B9202 A NEW-YEAR'S warning. Another year has roll'd its round . . . Providence, January 1, 1795.
broadside 21 X 13 cm.
Alden 1424
NHi mp. 47511

B9203 NEW YORK
A general account of the number of electors in . . . New-York, made from the returns . . . of the State . . . pursuant to . . . "An act for taking a census . . . " passed the third of March, 1795 . . . [New York? 1795?]
[2] p. 34 cm.
NHi mp. 47518

B9204 NEW YORK. ELECTION PROX.
Albany, February 23, 1795. Gentlemen, Agreeable to the . . . constitution . . . an election for governor and lieutenant-governor is to be held . . . Robert Yates . . . for governor, and William Floyd for lieutenant-governor . . . [Albany, 1795]
broadside 35 X 23 cm.
McMurtrie: Albany 114
NHi mp. 47519

B9205 NEW YORK. GENERAL ASSEMBLY
Extract from the Journals of Assembly, March 19, 1795 . . . [New York? 1795]
broadside 34 X 21 cm.
NHi mp. 47517

B9206 NEW YORK (CITY) COMMITTEE APPOINTED TO PREVENT THE INTRODUCTION AND SPREADING OF INFECTIOUS DISEASES
Health Committee.—Information having been received, that fevers . . . prevail in . . . the West-India Islands . . . New-York, April 3, 1795. [New York, 1795]
broadside 29.5 X 19 cm.
NHi mp. 47513

B9207 NEW YORK. LAWS
The Ten Pound act: that is to say, an act for the more speedy recovery of debts . . . Albany, Charles R. and George Webster [1795]
23, [1] p. 18.5 cm.
cf. Evans 29193; does not call for nor contain "the amendment."
CSmH; N

B9208 THE New-York almanack, for the year . . . 1796 . . . By Abm. Weatherwise, Gent. Albany, Charles R. and George Webster [1795]
[36] p. 18.5 cm.
DLC mp. 47674

B9209 THE New-York almanack, for the year . . . 1796 . . . By Abm. Weatherwise, Gent. Whitestown, Oliver P. Easton [1795]
[24] p. 16.5 cm.
Drake 6046
MWA; N mp. 47675

B9210 NEW YORK CHAMBER OF COMMERCE
I. That the members of the New-York Chamber of Commerce, shall meet at their chamber on the first Tuesday in every month . . . [New York? 1795?]
broadside 49.5 X 38 cm.
Upper margin bears ms. heading: Regulations of New York Chamber of Commerce, 1795
N mp. 47512

B9211 NEW YORK JOURNAL
Address, of the carrier to the patrons of the *New-York*

Journal, and Patriotic Register, with the compliments of the season . . . [New York, 1795]
broadside 32 X 20 cm.
NHi mp. 47338

B9212 NEWPORT long-wharf, hotel and public school lottery . . . Newport . . . March 20th, 1795. Warren, Nathaniel Phillips [1795]
broadside 37.5 X 27.5 cm.
Alden 1425
RNHi. Photostat: MWA mp. 47520

B9213 NORTH CAROLINA. LAWS
An act to authorize the secretary to issue grants for military lands . . . [Halifax, Hodge & Wills, 1795?]
broadside 42 X 25 cm.
McMurtrie: North Carolina 212
NcD mp. 47523

B9214 NORTH CAROLINA. LAWS
A bill to authorize the secretary to issue grants for military lands . . . [Halifax, Hodge & Wills, 1795?]
broadside 44 X 25 cm.
Dated November 1795 in manuscript
Nc-Ar (2 copies) mp. 47522

B9215 NORTH CAROLINA. LAWS
Laws of North-Carolina. At a General Assembly, begun and held at . . . Raleigh [Dec. 30, 1794] . . . Being the first session of the said Assembly . . . [Halifax, Hodge & Wills, 1795]
20 p. 32.5 cm. caption title
Supplement to Iredell's *Revision*
McMurtrie: North Carolina 211
MH-L mp. 47524

B9216 OVIDIUS NASO, PUBLIUS
Ovid's Art of love . . . To which are added, The court of love, The history of love, and Armstrong's Oeconomy of love. New-York, Printed and sold by Samuel Campbell, 1795.
216 p. 14 cm.
MWA; N mp. 47526

B9217 PAINE, THOMAS, 1737-1809
The age of reason . . . Philadelphia, Richard Folwell, 1795.
82, [1] p. 12mo
PPL mp. 47527

B9218 PEAKE, THOMAS
Cases determined at nisi prius, in the Court of King's Bench . . . [1790-94] . . . By Thomas Peake . . . A new edition, with improvements. By Thomas Day . . . Hartford, Hudson and Goodwin [1795?]
iv, 241, [36] p.
Preface by Peake dated April, 1795
RPJCB mp. 47528

B9219 PELOSI, VINCENT M.
Sir, The wish of respectable citizens, and the advice of my clients, have induced me to publish proposals for opening a coffee-house . . . Philadelphia, 10th November, 1795. *Vincent M. Pelosi.* [Philadelphia, 1795]
broadside
PHi

B9220 PENNSYLVANIA. HOUSE OF REPRESENTATIVES
Journal of the second session of the fourth House of Representatives . . . of Pennsylvania . . . Philadelphia, Francis Bailey, M,DCC,XCIV [1795]
65 p. fol.
PPL

B9221 PENNSYLVANIA. LAWS
An act for establishing an health office . . . Approved April 17, 1795. [Philadelphia? 1795?]
44 p.
cf. Evans 27474 (1794)
MWA mp. 47550

B9222 PENNSYLVANIA. LAWS
. . . An act relative to donation lands . . . [at head of title] [Philadelphia] Zachariah Poulson [1795?]
5 p. 34.5 cm. caption title
At head of title: NNN
Printed as a bill, with the lines of each section separately numbered
MWA (p. 3-4 wanting) mp. 47529

B9223 PENNSYLVANIA. LAWS
. . . An act to amend an act entitled "An act to regulate the trails of contested elections . . ." [at head of title] [Philadelphia] Zachariah Poulson [1795?]
2 p. 34 cm. caption title
At head of title: JJ
Printed as a bill, with the lines of each section separately numbered
MWA mp. 47530

B9224 PENNSYLVANIA. LAWS
. . . An act to enable the president and managers of the Schuylkill and Susquehanna Navigation and the president and managers of the Delaware and Schuylkill Canal Navigation to raise by . . . lottery . . . four hundred thousands dollars . . . Approved, April 17. 1795 . . . [Philadelphia] Zachariah Poulson [1795]
2 p. 4to
PPL mp. 47554

B9225 PENNSYLVANIA. LAWS
An act to enable the president, managers and company of the Philadelphia and Lancaster Turnpike Road to increase the width of the said road . . . [Philadelphia, 1795]
broadside 23.5 X 16.5 cm.
PHi mp. 47551

B9226 PENNSYLVANIA. LAWS
. . . An act to erect an additional election district in Washington County . . . [at end] [Philadelphia] Zachariah Poulson [1795?]
broadside 34 X 21 cm.
At head of title: GGG
Printed as a bill, with the lines separately numbered
MWA mp. 47531

B9227 PENNSYLVANIA. LAWS
. . . An act to erect the township of Heidelberg . . . into a separate election district . . . [at head of title] [Philadelphia] Zachariah Poulson [1795?]
broadside 34.5 X 20.5 cm.
At head of title: KK
Printed as a bill, with the lines separately numbered
MWA mp. 47532

B9228 PENNSYLVANIA. LAWS
. . . An act to establish [the permanent] seat of the government [of Pennsylvania . . . [at head of title] [Philadelphia] Zachariah Poulson [1795]
3 p. 35 cm. caption title
At head of title: HHH
Printed as a bill, the lines of each section separately

numbered; incorporates the ms. corrections in the earlier Humphreys' printing
MWA (mutilated) mp. 47533

B9229 PENNSYLVANIA. LAWS
[Act to incorporate the President, Managers and Company of the Wissahickon Toll Road. Philadelphia, 1795?]
6+ p. 35.5 cm.
Page 3 begins with line 7 of sect. 2
Printed as a bill, with the lines of each section separately numbered
MWA (p. 3–6 only) mp. 47534

B9230 PENNSYLVANIA. LAWS
... An act to supply the deficiencies in former appropriations and for other purposes ... [at head of title] [Philadelphia] Zachariah Poulson [1795?]
2 p. 35 cm. caption title
At head of title: RR
Printed as a bill, with the lines of each section separately numbered
MWA mp. 47535

B9231 PENNSYLVANIA. LAWS
... In General Assembly. Friday, March 6, 1795. An act to alter certain election districts in the County of Chester ... [at end] [Philadelphia] D. Humphreys [1795]
2 p. 34.5 cm.
At head of title: No. LIX
Printed as a bill, with separately numbered lines for each section
MWA mp. 47540

B9232 PENNSYLVANIA. LAWS
... In General Assembly. Friday, March 6, 1795. An act to repeal so much of ... "An act for raising and collecting of money ..." as imposes a tax on the owners ... of any coach chariot or post-chaise phaeton ... [Philadelphia] D. Humphreys [1795]
broadside 35 × 20.5 cm.
At head of title: No. LX
Printed as a bill, with separately numbered lines
MWA mp. 47541

B9233 PENNSYLVANIA. LAWS
... In General Assembly. Monday, March 16, 1795. An act to reimburse the guardians of certain orphan children ... [Philadelphia, D. Humphreys, 1795]
broadside 34.5 × 20.5 cm.
At head of title: No. LXX
Printed as a bill, with the lines of each section separately numbered
MWA mp. 47542

B9234 PENNSYLVANIA. LAWS
... In General Assembly. Monday, March 23, 1795. A supplement to the laws for preventing the exportation of flour not merchantable ... [at end] [Philadelphia] D. Humphreys [1795]
2 p. 34.5 cm.
At head of title: No. LXXXIV
Printed as a bill, with the lines of each section separately numbered
MWA mp. 47545

B9235 PENNSYLVANIA. LAWS
... In General Assembly. Saturday, February 28, 1795. An act for reviving suits and process which have been discontinued in the courts of oyer and terminer ... [at end] [Philadelphia] D. Humphreys [1795]
2 p. 34 cm.
At head of title: No. XLIX
Printed as a bill, with separately numbered lines for each section
MWA mp. 47538

B9236 PENNSYLVANIA. LAWS
... In General Assembly. Thursday, March 19, 1795. An act to erect the townships of Cocalico and Elizabeth ... into a separate election district ... [Philadelphia] D. Humphreys [1795]
broadside 34.5 × 20.5 cm.
At head of title: No. LXXVII
Printed as a bill, with the lines separately numbered
MWA mp. 47544

B9237 PENNSYLVANIA. LAWS
... In General Assembly. Thursday, March 19, 1795. An act to establish the permanent seat of the government of Pennsylvania ... [at end] [Philadelphia] D. Humphreys [1795]
3 p. 34.5 cm. caption title
At head of title: No. LXXV
Printed as a bill, with the lines of each section separately numbered
MWA (with ms. corrections) mp. 47543

B9238 PENNSYLVANIA. LAWS
... In General Assembly. Tuesday, February 10, 1795. An act for the relief of Anne Russel ... [at end] [Philadelphia] D. Humphreys [1795]
2 p. 34 cm.
At head of title: No. XXXIX
Printed as a bill, with numbered lines for each section
MWA mp. 47536

B9239 PENNSYLVANIA. LAWS
... In General Assembly. Tuesday, February 17, 1795. An act declaring Lacoming Creek a highway ... [Philadelphia] D. Humphreys [1795]
broadside 34 × 20.5 cm.
At head of title: No. XLIV
Printed as a bill, with numbered lines for each section
MWA (mutilated) mp. 47537

B9240 PENNSYLVANIA. LAWS
... In General Assembly. Tuesday, March 3, 1795. An act for the relief of John Kline ... [at end] [Philadelphia] D. Humphreys [1795]
2 p. 34 cm.
At head of title: No. LIII
Printed as a bill, with separately numbered lines for each section
MWA mp. 47539

B9241 PENNSYLVANIA. LAWS
... In General Assembly. Wednesday, March 25, 1795. An act for erecting part of the county of Northumberland into a separate county ... [at end] [Philadelphia] D. Humphreys [1795]
4 p. 34.5 cm. caption title
At head of title: No. XC
Printed as a bill, with the lines of each section separately numbered
MWA mp. 47546

B9242 PENNSYLVANIA. LAWS
... A supplement to an act entitled An act making provision for ... orphan children ... [at head of title] [Philadelphia] Zachariah Poulson [1795]
broadside 34 × 20.5 cm.

At head of title: II
Printed as a bill, with each section having separately numbered lines
MWA (mutilated) mp. 47547

B9243 PENNSYLVANIA. LAWS
. . . A supplement [to] the act entitled "An act to appoint trustees to purchase . . . land . . . and . . . erect a court-house and prison for the . . . county of Westmoreland." . . . [at head of title] [Philadelphia] Zachariah Poulson [1795]
broadside 34 X 20.5 cm.
Passed Mar. 31, 1795
Printed as a bill, with separately numbered lines
MWA (mutilated) mp. 47548

B9244 PENNSYLVANIA. TREASURY
Accounts of the Treasury of Pennsylvania . . . Philadelphia, Hall and Sellers, 1795.
8 p. 33.5 cm.
DLC mp. 47552

B9245 THE Pennsylvania almanac, for the year . . . 1796. . . . By Joshua Sharp. Philadelphia; Printed for Mathew Carey [1795]
[36] p. 17 cm.
PHi mp. 47598

B9246 Deleted

B9247 PHILANTHROPIC COMPANY, WARREN, R.I.
By-laws for the regulation of the Philanthropic company . . . Warren, Nathaniel Phillips, 1795.
16 p. 17 cm.
Alden 1452
Bradford Swan, Providence, R.I. mp. 47557

B9248 PIKE, NICHOLAS, 1743–1819
Abridgment of the new and complete system of arithmetick . . . By Nicolas Pike . . . The second edition. Worcester, Printed by Isaiah Thomas. Sold by him in Worcester. Sold also by said Thomas and Andrews, D. West, and E. Larkin, in Boston; and by said Thomas and Carlisle, in Walpole, New-hampshire; and by the booksellers in the United States, 1795.
348 p. 17.5 cm.
cf. Evans 29324 (note)
MWA; NhD mp. 47558

B9249 [PINCHARD, MRS.]
The blind child . . . By a lady. Philadelphia, Printed and sold by H. & P. Rice, and J. Rice & Co., Baltimore, 1795.
191, [1] p. 10.5 cm.
MWA; PHC mp. 47559

B9250 [PLAN of the review for July 4, 1795. Baltimore, Clayland and Dobbin, 1795]

Advertised in the *Federal Intelligencer*, June 5, 1795: "Plan of the review . . . just printed, and to be sold at the office . . ."
Minick 247
No copy known mp. 47560

B9251 [PLAN of the review for October 29, 1795. Baltimore, Clayland and Dobbin, 1795]

Mentioned in a notice in the *Federal Intelligencer*, Oct. 27, 1795: "Plans of the review are ready to be delivered at the *Telegraphe* office, to the several captains . . ."
Minick 248
No copy known mp. 47561

B9252 THE political register . . . [Philadelphia, 1795]
p. 249–549. 8vo
Continues Evans 28382, covering Nov. 28, 1794–Jan. 13, 1795
PPAmP

B9253 POWER, NICHOLAS
Books and stationary, a handsome collection, just received and for sald by N. Power . . . in Poughkeepsie . . . [Poughkeepsie, 1795]
broadside 43.5 X 26 cm.
Includes "Hutchin's Almanacks for 1796."
New York Public 1150
NN mp. 47563

B9254 A PRECISE journal of General Wayne's last campaign in the year 1794 . . . taken down in the course of the campaign . . . Hagers-Town, John Gruber, 1795.
36 p. 18 cm.
MWA mp. 47564

B9255 PRESBYTERIAN CHURCH
An act of the Reformed Presbytery in North America for a day of public fasting . . . W. King, Moderator. J. M. M'Kinney, Clerk. Rocky Creek (South Carolina) August 5, 1795. [Charleston? 1795]
12 p. 16 cm.
NNHuC

B9256 PROCÈS verbal de la fête qui a eu lieu le 2 pluviose . . . [Colophon] Philadelphie, Parent [1795?]
7 p.
RPJCB mp. 47565

B9257 PROCÈS verbaux de l'Assemblée tenue par les colons réfugiés à Philadelphie . . . [Colophon] Philadelphie, Parent [1795]
7 p.
Begins: L'an troisième . . . le vingt-six ventose
RPJCB (3 copies) mp. 47556

B9258 THE prodigal daughter . . . Printed and sold at the Bible & Heart . . . Boston [1795?]
12+ p.
MWA mp. 47566

B9259 [THE prodigal daughter. Windsor, A. Spooner, ca. 1795]

Advertised in J. MacGowan's *Life of Joseph* (Windsor, 1795)
McCorison 352
No copy known mp. 47567

B9260 PROPOSALS for a subscription, to build a Cathedral church at Baltimore . . . [Baltimore] Pechin & co. [1795]
2 folio leaves, with smaller leaf inserted
Minick 223; Parsons 137
MdW (not traced) mp. 47568

B9261 PROPOSALS for printing by subscription, a magazine entitled the Christian Herald, or the Union Magazine . . . [New York? 1795?]
broadside 34.5 X 20.5 cm.
CtHi; NHi mp. 47569

B9262 PROTESTANT EPISCOPAL CHURCH IN THE U.S.A. MARYLAND (DIOCESE)
Journal of a convention . . . held in Baltimore-Town, from May 28, to May 30 1795 . . . Baltimore, P. Edwards and J. W. Allen, 1795.
15 p. 17 cm.

Minick 256; New York Public 1151
DLC; MWA; MdBP; NN mp. 47570

B9263 PROTESTANT EPISCOPAL CHURCH IN THE U.S.A. PENNSYLVANIA (DIOCESE)
An act of association of the clergy and congregations of the Protestant Episcopal Church, in the State of Pennsylvania . . . [Philadelphia? 1795?]
3 p. 33 cm.
Dated by MHi
MHi mp. 47571

B9264 PROTESTANT EPISCOPAL CHURCH IN THE U.S.A. PENNSYLVANIA (DIOCESE)
Canons of the Protestant Episcopal Church in the Commonwealth of Pennsylvania passed in convention of the said Church . . . Philadelphia, Ormrod & Conrad, 1795.
7 p. 19.5 cm.
MWA; NHi; PPL mp. 47572

B9265 PROVIDENCE STREET LOTTERY
List of the fortunate numbers in the third class of Providence Street Lottery . . . June 8th, 1795. [Providence, 1795]
broadside 40 X 22 cm.
Alden 1430; Winship Addenda p. 90
RHi. Photostat: MWA mp. 47573

B9266 PUBLIC notice is hereby given, that a certain quantity of flour, pork and peas are wanted at Kingston and Niagara, for the supply of His Majesty's forces in Upper Canada . . . [New York, 1795]
broadside 32.5 X 20 cm.
NHi mp. 47437

B9267 RELATION de l'anniversaire de la Fédération du 14 juillet 1789, célébrée . . . 14 juillet 1795 . . . [Colophon] Charleston, Béleurgey, 1795.
4 p. caption title
RPJCB mp. 47574

B9268 RHODE ISLAND. ELECTION PROX.
1795. His Excellency Arthur Fenner, Esq; Governor. The honourable Samuel J. Potter, Esq; Deputy-governor . . . [Providence] Carter and Wilkinson [1795]
broadside 23.5 X 16 cm.
Alden 1431; Chapin Proxies 48
RHi mp. 47575

B9269 RHODE ISLAND. GOVERNOR, 1790–1805
By His Excellency Arthur Fenner . . . A proclamation . . . [Nov. 6, 1795] . . . Providence, Carter and Wilkinson [1795]
broadside 38 X 31 cm.
Bill submitted Nov. 7, 1795
Alden 1433
RHi mp. 47576

B9270 RHODE ISLAND. LAWS
Charter of the Rhode-Island Bank . . . October session, A.D. 1795. An act to incorporate the stockholders . . . [Newport? Henry Barber? 1795?]
8 p. 23.5 X 19 cm. caption title
Alden 1441; Winship Addenda p. 90
RNHi mp. 47577

B9271 RHODE ISLAND. LAWS
State of Rhode-Island, &c. In General assembly. June session, A.D. 1795. An act for taking a general estimate . . . Warren, Nathaniel Phillips, 1795.
broadside 31.5 X 18.5 cm.
Bill submitted Aug. 10, 1795
Alden 1439; Winship p. 65
RHi mp. 47578

B9272 RICARD, N X
Précis du compte rendu à la convention nationale, par le général N. X. Ricard. De sa conduite publique son départ de France . . . Philadelphie, Parent, 1795.
29 p. 23.5 cm.
PHi; PPAmP mp. 47579

B9273 RICE, H. & P., firm, Philadelphia
Henry & Patrick Rice's catalogue of a large and valuable collection of books . . . for 1795 . . . Philadelphia, Printed for H. & P. Rice, 1795.
72, [2] p. 17 cm.
PHi mp. 47580

B9274 [ROUGET DE L'ISLE, CLAUDE JOSEPH] 1760–1836
The Marseilles hymn. Philadelphia, Printed for G. Willig [1795–97]
[2] p. 33 cm.
Sonneck-Upton p. 252
DLC; PU mp. 47581

B9275 ROWE, ELIZABETH (SINGER) 1674-1737
Devout exercises of the heart . . . Abridged for the use of the pious. New-York, Printed by Tiebout & O'Brien for E. Mitchell [1795?]
233, [8] p. port. 9.5 cm.
Engraved t.p.
New York Public 1153; Rosenbach-Ch 200
NN; NjP. A. S. W. Rosenbach (1933) mp. 47583

B9276 ROWE, ELIZABETH (SINGER) 1674-1737
Devout exercises of the heart . . . Reviewed and published at her request by Isaac Watts, D.D. New York, Printed and sold by William Durell, 1795.
6 p.l., [25]-178, [2] p. 14 cm.
DLC; MB; MWA; NN mp. 47582

B9277 ROWSON, SUSANNA (HASWELL) 1762-1824
The fille de chambre, a novel . . . Baltimore, Printed by S. & J. Adams, for Keatinge's book-store, 1794.
256 p. 17.5 cm.
Minick 258
ICU; MWA (poor) mp. 47584

B9278 ROWSON, SUSANNA (HASWELL) 1762-1824
The fille de chambre, a novel . . . Baltimore, Printed [by S. & J. Adams] for Thomas E. Clayland, 1795.
256 p. 16.5 cm.
Minick 259
MH; WMMD mp. 47585

B9279 [RUDDOCK, SAMUEL A.]
Valuable tables. No. 1. A table shewing the value of any number of cents . . . No. II. [–III.] Tables for receiving and paying gold coins . . . No. IV. A table of simple interest . . . Keene, Newhampshire, Printed by Cornelius Sturtevant, jun. & Co., 1795.
broadside 27.5 X 22.5 cm.
cf. Evans 29444-449
MWA (2 copies) mp. 47586

B9280 RUSH, BENJAMIN, 1745-1813
A syllabus of a course of lectures on the institutes of medicine . . . Philadelphia, Printed & Sold by Thomas Bradford, 1795.
15 p. 16 cm.
PPL; PPPH; PU mp. 47587

B9281 RUSSEL, ROBERT, of Wadhurst, Sussex
Seven sermons . . . By Robert Russel, at Wadhurst, in Sussex. Philadelphia, Printed for H. & P. Rice, 1795.
144 p. 14 cm.
MWA: NN mp. 47588

B9282 RUSSEL, ROBERT, of Wadhurst, Sussex
Seven sermons . . . By Robert Russel, at Wadhurst, in Sussex. Philadelphia, Printed for Mathew Carey, 1795.
144 p. 14 cm.
MWA; N mp. 47589

B9283 RUSSELL, JOHN AND JOSEPH N., firm
A useful publication. Boston, Oct. 13, 1795. Mess: John and Jos: N: Russell respectfully address the public . . . [Boston, 1795]
broadside
PHi

B9284 RUSSELL, SAMUEL
Statement of snuff and tobacco manufactures . . . Samuel Russell, agent for the snuff and tobacco manufacturers . . . of New-York. The general facts . . . in the above . . . apply . . . in . . . Pennsylvania. Thomas Leiper, Tobacconist. [Philadelphia, Dec. 7, 1795]
broadside 39 X 24 cm.
NHi mp. 47590

B9285 S., L.
The porcupine, alias the hedge-hog . . . Written after the manner of Ignatius Irony . . . By L. S. living in Fox Island . . . Canaan, Printed and sold by E. Phinney, and by the author, at his house opposite Subtilty and a ton of Stimulators . . . January, 1795
48 p. 18 cm.
NHi. Cedric L. Robinson, Windsor, Conn. (1964)
mp. 47562

B9286 SANDERS, DANIEL CLARKE, 1768-1850
[A sermon on the death of the wife of Dr. Hoyt, New Haven, Vt., 1795]

McCorison 354
No copy known mp. 47591

B9287 SCHRÖTER, JOHANN SAMUEL
The conquest of Belgrade. A sonata for the harpsichord or piano forte . . . New York, Printed for G. Gilfert & Co. [1795]
11 p. 31.5 cm.
Sonneck-Upton p. 87
MB mp. 47592

B9288 SCHULTZ, BENJAMIN
Oration delivered before the Mosheimian Society, on July 23d, 1795 . . . Philadelphia, Thomas Dobson, 1795.
14 p.
PPAmP mp. 47593

B9289 SCOTT, WILLIAM, 1750-1804
Lessons in elocution . . . New-Haven, Abel Morse, 1795.
427 p. 17.5 cm.
CtHi mp. 47594

B9290 [SEABURY, SAMUEL] 1729-1796
Prayers. A prayer for the Courts of Justice. O Almighty . . . [n.p., 1795?]
[4] p. 16 cm. caption title
Dated from Goodspeed's reference to Beardsley's *Life of Samuel Seabury*, and Beardsley's *History of the Episcopal Church in Connecticut*
Pierce W. Gaines (Fairfield, Conn., 1964) mp. 47595

B9291 THE seaman's journal-book . . . Providence, Carter and Wilkinson, 1795.
[157] p. 33 cm.
Printed forms, to be filled out in manuscript
Alden 1446
MWA mp. 47596

B9292 SELECT pamphlets. Second volume. Containing, I. Raynal's Revolution of America . . . IV. Masonic sermon; preached by the Rev. William Smith . . . IX. Letter to the Belfast Company of Irish Volunteers. Philadelphia: Sold by Mathew Carey, 1795.
1 v. 8vo
Not Evans 29484
PPL

B9293 SEVEN SAGES
History of the seven wise masters of Rome . . . Philadelphia, Printed and sold by H. & P. Rice, also by J. Rice & Co., Baltimore, 1795.
100 p. 14 cm.
MWA mp. 47597

B9293a A SHOCKING narrative of the murder of Mr. Joseph Porter, by Captain William Corran . . . the 27th day of May, 1794 . . . Walpole, N.H., I. Thomas and D. Carlisle, 1795.
10 p. 19 cm.
MWA (mutilated) mp. 47599

B9294 A SHORT dialogue, between a learned divine and a beggar; to which is added a selection of poetry. Norwich, 1795.
11 p. 16.5 cm.
Trumbull: Supplement 2609
CtHi mp. 47600

B9295 SIR, At a late meeting of the General Committee appointed in this city to promote the election of Robert Yates as governor . . . we were appointed . . . to communicate with our republican friends . . . [New York? 1795]
broadside 35.5 X 20.5 cm.
New York Public 1154
NAII. Photostats: NN; NHi mp. 47601

B9296 THE sister's gift . . . The third Worcester edition. Worcester, Printed by Isaiah Thomas jun. for Isaiah Thomas. Sold at their respective bookstores, and by Thomas and Andrews in Boston, 1795.
31 p. incl. covers. 10.5 cm.
MWA mp. 47602

B9297 [SMITH, EUNICE]
Some arguments against worldly-mindedness . . . Rutland, Printed [by James Kirkaldie] for Richard Lee, 1795.
15 p. 21.5 cm.
Cooley 288; Sabin 86600
MBC; RPJCB; WHi mp. 47604

B9298 [SMITH, WILLIAM] 1727-1803
An historical account of the rise, progress and present state of the canal navigation in Pennsylvania . . . Philadelphia, Zachariah Poulson, 1795.
xvi, 77 p. map. 21 X 17 cm.
An earlier issue of Evans 29472
New York Public 1155; Sabin 84620
MWA; NHi; NN; RPJCB mp. 47605

B9299 SOME advice to governesses and teachers. Written by the author of The evidence of the existence of God

. . . New-York, Printed for Daniel Lawrence, by Samuel Campbell, 1795.
8 p. 15 cm.
By F. de Salignac de La Mothe Fénelon?—cf. Brit. Mus. cat. (under Advice)
New York Public 1156; Sabin 86591
NN mp. 47418

B9300 [SOME] remarkable cities and towns, when founded, with their present number of inhabitants . . . The longitude . . . from the meridian of Philadelphia . . . The city Philadelphia . . . In 1794, the houses had increased to about 9000 . . . For . . . the plan of the city Washington, see Guthrie's *Geography*, improved by Mr. Carey, volume II. page 471. [Philadelphia? M. Carey? 1795?]
[2] p. 45.5 X 24.5 cm.
Carey published Guthrie's *Geography* in 1795
MWA mp. 47608

B9301 SOUTH CAROLINA. COMMISSIONERS TO SETTLE THE ACCOUNTS
The Commissioner, to settle the accounts of the former Commissioners of the Treasury . . . submit the following report . . . Nov. 9, 1795. [Charleston] Young & Faust [1795]
[2] p. 42 cm.
Sc-Ar

B9302 SOUTH CAROLINA. GOVERNOR, 1794-1796
Notice to all masters of vessels. Whereas it has become too common a practice for masters of vessels, to hire . . . negroes . . . as mariners . . . By order of the Governor. Arnoldus Vander Horst, Jun. Secretary to the Governor. Charleston, July 31, 1795. Charleston, W. P. Young [1795]
broadside 28 X 20.5 cm.
Sc-Ar

B9303 SOUTH CAROLINA. HOUSE OF REPRESENTATIVES
In the House of Representatives, December 12, 1795 . . . Charleston, Young and Faust [1795]
3 p. 45 cm.
Sc-Ar (2 copies)

B9304 SOUTH CAROLINA. LAWS
An act for raising supplies for the year one thousand seven hundred and ninety-five . . . Dec. 19, 1795. [Charleston? 1795]
[3] p. 33 cm.
Sc-Ar

B9305 SPOTSWOOD, WILLIAM, 1753?-1805
Boston, 20th April, 1795. To the public . . . Prospectus of a Belles Lettres Paper . . . The *Farrago* . . . [Boston, W. Spotswood, 1795]
broadside
MWA mp. 47606

B9306 STANFORD, JOHN, 1754-1834
The convert instructed in the origin, signification, and advantages of baptism . . . New-York, T. & J. Swords, 1795.
65, [1] p., 1 leaf
MWA; NNS; NjR mp. 47604

B9307 STEPHENS, THOMAS
Stephens's Catalogue of books, &c. for 1795. The whole . . . sold on the most reasonable terms, at Thomas Stephens's Book and Stationary Store . . . [Colophon] [Philadelphia] W. W. Woodward [1795]
84, [1] p. 12mo
1876 entries
Brigham: Booksellers, p. 57
MWA mp. 47610

B9308 [STERNE, LAURENCE] 1713-1768
A sentimental journey . . . By Mr. Yorick. New York, Printed by Tiebout and O'Brien for Charles Smith and John Reid, 1795.
316 p. front. 17 cm.
cf. Evans 29565
MiU-C mp. 47611

B9309 [STORACE, STEPHEN] 1763-1796
Lullaby, a favorite song in *The pirates*. New York, G. Gilfert [1795]
broadside 33.5 cm.
Sonneck-Upton p. 243
DLC; MiU-C; PU; RPJCB mp. 47612

B9310 STORACE, STEPHEN, 1763-1796
No more his fears alarming . . . [Philadelphia] G. Willig [1795-97]
[2] p. 33 cm.
Sonneck-Upton p. 299
DLC mp. 47613

B9311 STORACE, STEPHEN, 1763-1796
Spirit of my sainted sire . . . New York & Philadelphia, B. Carr; Baltimore, J. Carr [1795-96]
[2] p. 34 cm.
Sonneck-Upton p. 407
DLC; NN mp. 47614

B9312 STUART, JAMES
Directions for medicine chests, prepared by Bankson & Stuart . . . Philadelphia. With a short treatise, of the diseases most incident to seamen. By Dr. Stuart. Philadelphia, Ormrod and Conrad, May 9, 1795.
8 p. 22.5 cm.
Austin 112; Rogers 517; Sabin 93166
DLC; PPC (not traced 1960) mp. 47615

B9313 TABLES, shewing in three different views, the comparative value of the currency of . . . New-York . . . also, of French crowns . . . New-York, Printed for Francis Childs and Co., 1795.
[2], 33 p. 17 cm.
MWA mp. 47616

B9314 TAYLOR, RAYNOR, 1747-1825
Amyntor a pastoral song . . . Philadelphia, New York, Carr; Baltimore, I. Carr [1795]
[2] p. 33.5 cm.
Sonneck-Upton p. 23
DLC; MWA; PP mp. 47617

B9315 TAYLOR, RAYNOR, 1747-1825
Citizen soldiers. A new patriotic song, words by Amyntor—music by Mr. R. Taylor . . . [Philadelphia, 1795?]
broadside 33 cm.
PPL mp. 47618

B9316 TAYLOR, RAYNOR, 1747-1825
Nancy of the vale a pastoral ballad . . . Philadelphia, New York, B. Carr; Baltimore, I. Carr [1795]
[2] p. 32.5 cm.
Sonneck-Upton p. 286
DLC; PP mp. 47619

B9317 TENNESSEE (TERRITORY) HOUSE OF REPRESENTATIVES
[Journal of the proceedings of the House of Representa-

tives of the Territory . . . south of the River Ohio; begun . . . Knoxville, the 29th of June, 1795. Knoxville, George Roulstone, 1795]
Title from Nashville 1852 reprint
McMurtrie: Tennessee 10
No copy known mp. 47620

B9318 TENNEY, JOSEPH
The gamut, or scale of music; containing . . . the rules of singing, and amended . . . By Joseph Tenney. [Windsor] Alden Spooner, 1795.
5 p. 20 X 8 cm.
Includes blank leaves
Cooley 298
VtHi mp. 47621

B9319 THEN I fly to meet my love a favorite song. New York, G. Gilfert [1795]
p. [6]-7. 32.5 cm.
Sonneck-Upton p. 426
DLC; RPJCB mp. 47622

B9320 TO all people to whom these presents shall come: Greeting. Whereas the General Assembly . . . of Connecticut, at their session holden . . . [May 1795] . . . lands belonging to this State lying west of the west line of Pennsylvania . . . This Assembly do appoint John Treadwell, James Wadsworth . . . our hands and seals the second day of September . . . [1795] . . . [Hartford? 1795]
broadside 43.5 X 28 cm.
CtHi mp. 47624

B9321 TO be sold at publick vendue, on Wednesday the 13th day of May next . . . in Trenton, the following books, belonging to . . . the late William-Churchill Houston . . . [Trenton, I. Collins, 1795]
broadside narrow fol.
Dated from ms. accounting of the auction.–Edwin Wolf, 2d
PPL

B9322 TO the citizens of New-York. The inhabitants of this city . . . New-York, July 18. 1795. [New York, 1795]
broadside 23 X 19 cm.
DLC mp. 47625

B9323 TO the editor of the *Providence Gazette*. The enemies of Governor Fenner . . . South-Kingstown, November 6, 1785 . . . Fair Play . . . [Providence, cas. 1795?]
broadside 40 X 21 cm.
The latest date in the text is June, 1794
Alden 1416; Winship Addenda p. 89
RHi; RPB mp. 47626

B9324 TO the electors of the State of New-York. Friends and fellow citizens, . . . a report has been circulated . . . that Mr. Jay cannot return to America, this spring . . . New-York, April 17, 1795. [New York, 1795]
broadside 24.5 X 26 cm.
Signed: Nicholas Cruger, Robert Troup, Josiah Ogden Hoffman
New York Public 1137
NAll. Photostat: NN mp. 47627

B9325 TO the electors of the State of New-York. Friends and fellow-citizens, The impropriety of electing any man . . . governor, who is absent, in Europe . . . New-York, April 23, 1795. [New York, 1795]
broadside 27.5 X 21.5 cm.
Signed: William W. Gilbert [and 6 others]
New York Public 1140
NAll. Photostats: DLC; NN mp. 47628

B9326 TO the free electors of the State of New-York. Friends and fellow-citizens . . . New-York, February 23, 1795 . . . [New York, 1795]
broadside 40 X 26 cm.
Recommending Yates for governor
MWA; N mp. 47629

B9327 TO the honourable the speakers and members of both houses of the General assembly of Virginia . . . [Fredericksburg? 1795?]
broadside 39 X 25 cm.
A petition with manuscript signatures, for Spotsylvania County, concerning the passage of a law adding to the capital of the Bank of Alexandria; presented Nov. 21, 1795
Vi (2 copies; copy 2 from Fairfax County) mp. 47630

B9328 TOM Thumb's play-book, to teach children their letters . . . Norwich, T. Hubbard, 1795.
32 p. 7 cm.
Trumbull: Supplement 2681
CtHi mp. 47631

B9329 THE town and country almanack, for the year . . . 1796 . . . By Joseph Osgood. Boston, J. White [1795]
[24] p. 16 cm.
DLC; MWA mp. 47525

B9330 [TOWNSEND, BARKLEY]
The restoration of the Church, is promised by a branch out of the root of Jesse. [Wilmington?] Printed in the year 1795
8 p. 8vo
At end: State of Delaware, Sussex County, October 27, 1795
PHi

B9331 TRIMMER, SARAH (KIRBY) 1741–1810
Fabulous histories . . . Baltimore, Printed for Keating's book-store [by Samuel Sower?], 1795.
214 p. 17 cm.
Minick 263
MdBP; MdHi mp. 47632

B9332 TRIMMER, SARAH (KIRBY) 1741–1810
Fabulous histories . . . Philadelphia, Jacob Johnson & Co., 1795.
214 p. 17 cm.
RPJCB mp. 47633

B9333 TRUE ASSISTANT SOCIETY OF HATTERS
Rules & regulations, adopted by the True Assistant Society of Hatters in New-York: and ordered to be printed for their government. [New York, 1795]
14 p. 16 cm. caption title
Dated from internal evidence
MWA mp. 47635

B9334 TUCKER, THOMAS TUDOR, 1754–1828
To the honorable the President and Senate . . . the petition of Thomas Tuder Tucker . . . [n.p., 1795]
3 p. 31.5 cm. caption title
Dated in manuscript: 1795 Nov. 18th
DLC; Sc-Ar mp. 47634

B9335 THE two babes in the wood . . . New-York: Printed for the United Company of Flying Stationers [1795?]

8 p. 16 cm.
Dated by d'Alté A. Welch
d'Alté A. Welch, Cleveland (1962) mp. 47382

B9336 ULSTER COUNTY, N.Y.
Circular. Sir, A number of your fellow-citizens . . . Kingston, April 13, 1795. [Kingston, 1795]
broadside
NAll. Photostats: DLC; NN mp. 47636

B9337 UNION COLLEGE, SCHENECTADY, N.Y.
[Catalogue of the officers. Schenectady, 1795]

Reported to National Union Catalog by NjP, but not found in that library (1938)
cf. McMurtrie: Schenectady 2
No copy located mp. 47637

B9338 UNITARIANISM; or, The doctrine of the trinity confuted . . . Philadelphia, 1795.
46 p. 19.5 cm.
Sabin 97836
CtY; DLC; MH; MWA; MiU-C; NjR mp. 47638

B9339 U.S. CONGRESS. HOUSE
Mr. Hillhouse's motion. 16th February, 1795 . . . Published by order of the House of Representatives. [Philadelphia, 1795]
[4] p. 20.5 cm.
Regarding deposition of a witness in the trial of a contested election
New York Public 1158
NN mp. 47646

B9340 U.S. CONGRESS. HOUSE. COMMITTEE ON CLAIMS
The Committee of claims, to whom was referred the petition of Joab Stafford, report . . . [Philadelphia, F. Childs and J. Swaine, 1795]
[2] p. 34 X 20.5 cm.
DLC mp. 47644

B9341 U.S. CONGRESS. HOUSE. COMMITTEE ON FINANCE
The committee appointed to enquire and report what progress . . . [Philadelphia, 1795]
[2] p. 34 X 20 cm.
DLC; MiU-C mp. 47642

B9342 U.S. CONGRESS. HOUSE. COMMITTEE ON PROTECTION OF THE FRONTIERS
The Committee appointed to examine into and report what proceedings have been had . . . for the protection of the frontiers . . . report . . . [Philadelphia, 1795]
broadside 34.5 X 21.5 cm.
Report by Mr. Cobb, Feb. 2, 1795
Greely p. 169?
MiU-C mp. 47643

B9343 U.S. CONGRESS. HOUSE. COMMITTEE ON THE MEMORIAL OF ARTHUR ST. CLAIR
The committee to whom was referred the memorial of Arthur St. Clair, report: . . . [Philadelphia, Childs and Swaine, 1795]
broadside 33.5 X 20 cm.
DLC mp. 47645

B9344 U.S. LAWS
An act authorizing the transfer of the stock standing to the credit of certain states. Be it enacted by the Senate and House . . . Approved, January the second, 1795. Go. Washington, President . . . Deposited among the rolls . . . [Philadelphia, 1795]
broadside 20.5 X 19 cm.
cf. Evans 29712, 29683
DLC mp. 47649

B9345 U.S. LAWS
An act of the President . . . making provision for the compensation of the officers of the revenue in . . . Ohio and Tennessee . . . [Jan. 28, 1795] . . . [Philadelphia, 1795]
broadside 33.5 X 20.5 cm.
Huntington 683
CSmH mp. 47652

B9346 U.S. LAWS
An act to regulate proceedings in cases of outlawry . . . [Philadelphia, 1795]
[4] p. 33 cm.
Read in the Senate, Feb. 6, 1795
Printed as a bill, with the lines of each section separately numbered
New York Public 1162
NN mp. 47647

B9347 U.S. LAWS
Acts passed at the second session of the Third Congress of the United States . . . begun . . . [Nov. 3, 1794] Philadelphia, Francis Childs, 1795.
1 p.l., [145]-260, iv p. 22 cm.
cf. Evans 29677
CSmH mp. 47653

B9348 U.S. LAWS
Acts passed at the Second Session of the Third Congress . . . begun . . . November, 1794 . . . [Philadelphia, F. Childs, 1795]
[570]-640 p.
NBuG

B9349 U.S. LAWS
A bill relative to cessions of jurisdiction in places where . . . erected . . . lighthouses, beacons, buoys, and public piers . . . [Philadelphia, 1795]
broadside 34.5 X 21 cm.
Presented in the House Jan. 26, 1795
Lines of each section separately numbered
New York Public 1163; cf. Evans 29685
MiU-C. Photostat: NN mp. 47641

B9350 U.S. LAWS
A bill to alter and amend the act . . . laying certain duties upon snuff and refined sugar. [Philadelphia, 1795]
[4] p. 34 cm. caption title
DLC mp. 47639

B9351 U.S. LAWS
A bill to establish an uniform rule of naturalization, and to repeal the act heretofore passed on that subject . . . [Philadelphia, 1795]
[2] p. 34.5 X 20.5 cm.
Lines of each section separately numbered
MWA mp. 47640

B9352 U.S. LAWS
Duties payable by law on all goods . . . imported . . . after the last day of March 1795 . . . [Philadelphia, 1795]
15 p. 19 cm. caption title
DLC mp. 47654

B9353 U.S. LAWS
Third Congress of the United States: At the second session . . . An act authorizing the payment of four thousand dollars for the use of the daughters of the late Count

de Grasse . . . Approved, February the twenty seventh, 1795 . . . [Philadelphia, Francis Childs, 1795]
broadside 30 X 19 cm.
Huntington 681; New York Public 1159
CSmH; NN; PPRF mp. 47648

B9354 U.S. LAWS
Third Congress of the United States: At the second session . . . An act for continuing and regulating the military establishment . . . Approved, March the third, 1795 . . . [Philadelphia, Francis Childs, 1795]
[4] p. 30 cm.
Without statement of deposition
New York Public 1164; cf. Evans 29680
NN

B9355 U.S. LAWS
Third Congress of the United States: At the second session . . . An act for reviving certain suits and process . . . Approved, January the twenty-eighth, 1795 . . . [Philadelphia, Francis Childs, 1795]
broadside 30 X 19 cm.
Without statement of deposition
New York Public 1164; cf. Evans 29681
NN; NhD

B9356 U.S. LAWS
Third Congress of the United States: At the second session . . . An act for the more effectual recovery of debts due from individuals to the United States . . . Approved, March the third, 1795 . . . [Philadelphia, Francis Childs, 1795[
[2] p. 30 X 19 cm.
Without statement of deposition
New York Public 1164; cf. Evans 29682
NN

B9357 U.S. LAWS
Third Congress of the United States: At the second session . . . An act for the more general promulgation of the laws . . . An act making provision for . . . trade with the Indians . . . [Philadelphia, Francis Childs, 1795]
broadside 30 X 19 cm.
New York Public 1160
NN; PPRF mp. 47650

B9358 U.S. LAWS
Third Congress of the United States: At the second session . . . An act for the reimbursement of a loan authorized by an Act of the last session of Congress . . . Approved, February the twenty first, 1795 . . . [Philadelphia, Francis Childs, 1795]
broadside 30 X 19 cm.
Without statement of deposition
New York Public 1164; cf. Evans 29686
NN; NhD

B9359 U.S. LAWS
Third Congress of the United States: At the second session . . . An act for the relief of Peter Covenhoven . . . Approved, January the second, 1795 . . . [Philadelphia, Francis Childs, 1795]
broadside 30 X 19 cm.
Without statement of deposition
New York Public 1164; cf. Evans 29683
NN; NhD

B9360 U.S. LAWS
Third Congress of the United States: At the second session . . . An act for the relief of William Seymour . . . Approved, March the second, 1795 . . . [Philadelphia, Francis Childs, 1795]
broadside 30 X 19 cm.
Without statement of deposition
New York Public 1164; cf. Evans 29685
NN

B9361 U.S. LAWS
Third Congress of the United States: At the second session . . . An act for the remission of the tonnage duties on certain French vessels . . . Approved, January the twenty eighth, 1795 . . . [Philadelphia, 1795]
broadside 30 X 19 cm.
Without statement of deposition
New York Public 1164; cf. Evans 29684
NN; NhD

B9362 U.S. LAWS
Third Congress of the United States: At the second session . . . An act further extending the time for receiving on loan the domestic debt . . . Approved January the twenty eighth, 1795 . . . [Philadelphia, Francis Childs, 1795]
broadside 30 X 19 cm.
Without statement of deposition
New York Public 1164; cf. Evans 29687
DLC; NN; NhD

B9363 U.S. LAWS
Third Congress of the United States: At the second session . . . An act in addition to the act, entitled, "An act to regulate the pay of the non-commissioned officers, musicians and privates . . ." Approved, January the twenty-ninth, 1795 . . . [Philadelphia, Francis Childs, 1795]
broadside 30 X 19 cm.
New York Public 1161
NN; NhD; PPRF mp. 47651

B9364 U.S. LAWS
Third Congress of the United States: At the second session . . . An act making appropriations for the support of government . . . Approved, January the second, 1795 . . . [Philadelphia, Francis Childs, 1795]
[3] p. 30 cm.
Without statement of deposition
New York Public 1164; cf. Evans 29688
NN

B9365 U.S. LAWS
Third Congress of the United States: At the second session . . . An act making appropriations for the support of the military establishment . . . and for the expences of the militia . . . Approved, thirty first Decr. 1794 . . . [Philadelphia, Francis Childs, 1795]
broadside 30 X 19 cm.
Without statement of deposition
New York Public 1164; cf. Evans 29689
NN; NhD

B9366 U.S. LAWS
Third Congress of the United States: At the second session . . . An act making further appropriations for the military and naval establishments . . . March the third, 1795 . . . [Philadelphia, Francis Childs, 1795]
[2] p. 30 X 19 cm.
Without statement of deposition
New York Public 1164; cf. Evans 29690
NN

B9367 U.S. LAWS
Third Congress of the United States: At the second session . . . An act making further provision for the support

of public credit . . . Approved, March the third 1795 . . . [Philadelphia] John Fenno [1795]
[6] p. 30 cm.
Without statement of deposition
New York Public 1164; cf. Evans 29691
NN

B9368 U.S. LAWS
Third Congress of the United States: At the second session . . . An act making futher provision in cases of drawbacks . . . Approved, January the twenty ninth, 1795 . . . [Philadelphia, Francis Childs, 1795]
[3] p. 30 cm.
Without statement of deposition
New York Public 1164; cf. Evans 29692
NN; NhD

B9369 U.S. LAWS
Third Congress of the United States: At the second session . . . An act providing for the payment of certain instalments of foreign debts . . . Approved, January the eighth, 1795 . . . [Philadelphia, Francis Childs, 1795]
broadside 30 X 19 cm.
Without statement of deposition
New York Public 1164; cf. Evans 29693
NN; NhD

B9370 U.S. LAWS
Third Congress of the United States: At the second session . . . An act relative to the compensations of certain officers employed in the collection of the duties of imports and tonnage . . . Approved, February the fourteenth, 1795 . . . [Philadelphia, Francis Childs, 1795]
[2] p. 30 X 19 cm.
Without statement of deposition
New York Public 1164; cf. Evans 29694
NN; NhD

B9371 U.S. LAWS
Third Congress of the United States: At the second session . . . An act relative to the passing of coasting vessels between Long Island and Rhode Island . . . Approved, March the second, 1795 . . . [Philadelphia, Francis Childs, 1795]
broadside 30 X 19 cm.
Without statement of deposition
New York Public 1164; cf. Evans 29695
NN

B9372 U.S. LAWS
Third Congress of the United States: At the second session . . . An act supplementary to the Act concerning invalids . . . Approved, February the twenty first, 1795 . . . [Philadelphia, Francis Childs, 1795]
broadside 30 X 19 cm.
Without statement of deposition
New York Public 1164; cf. Evans 29696
NN; NhD

B9373 U.S. LAWS
Third Congress of the United States: At the second session . . . An act supplementary to the Act, intituled "An act establishing a mint . . ." Approved, March the third, 1795 . . . [Philadelphia, Francis Childs, 1795]
[2] p. 30 X 19 cm.
Without statement of deposition
New York Public 1164; cf. Evans 29697
NN

B9374 U.S. LAWS
Third Congress of the United States: At the second session . . . An act supplementary to the Act, intituled "An act to provide more effectually for the collection of the duties on goods . . ." Approved, February the twenty sixth, 1795 . . . [Philadelphia, Francis Childs, 1795]
[4] p. 30 cm.
Without statement of deposition
New York Public 1164; cf. Evans 29698
NN; NhD

B9375 U.S. LAWS
Third Congress of the United States: At the second session . . . An act supplementary to the several acts imposing duties on goods . . . Approved, January the twenty ninth, 1795 . . . [Philadelphia, Francis Childs, 1795]
[2] p. 30 X 19 cm.
Without statement of deposition
New York Public 1164; cf. Evans 29699
NN; NhD

B9376 U.S. LAWS
Third Congress of the United States: At the second session . . . An act to alter and amend the Act, intituled "An act laying certain duties upon snuff and refined sugar." . . . Approved, March the third, 1795 . . . [Philadelphia, Francis Childs, 1795]
[4] p. 30 cm.
Without statement of deposition
New York Public 1164; cf. Evans 29700
NN

B9377 U.S. LAWS
Third Congress of the United States: At the second session . . . An act to amend the Act, entitled, "An act to establish the post-office and post-roads within the United States." . . . Approved, February the twenty fifth, 1795 . . . [Philadelphia, Francis Childs, 1795]
[2] p. 30 X 19 cm.
Without statement of deposition
New York Public 1164; cf. Evans 29701
NN

B9378 U.S. LAWS
Third Congress of the United States: At the second session . . . An act to authorize a grant of lands to the French inhabitants of Gallipolis . . . Approved, March the third, 1795 . . . [Philadelphia, Francis Childs, 1795]
[2] p. 30 X 19 cm.
Without statement of deposition
New York Public 1164; cf. Evans 29702
NN

B9379 U.S. LAWS
Third Congress of the United States: At the second session . . . An act to authorize the allowance of drawback on part of the cargo of the ship Enterprize . . . Approved, February the thirteenth, 1795 . . . [Philadelphia, Francis Childs, 1795]
broadside 30 X 19 cm.
Without statement of deposition
New York Public 1164; cf. Evans 29703
NN

B9380 U.S. LAWS
Third Congress of the United States: At the second session . . . An act to continue in force for a limited time the Acts therein mentioned . . . Approved, March the second, 1795 . . . [Philadelphia, Francis Childs, 1795]
broadside 30 X 19 cm.
Without statement of deposition
New York Public 1164; cf. Evans 29704
DLC; NN

B9381 U.S. LAWS
Third Congress of the United States: At the second session . . . An act to continue in force the Act "for ascertaining the fees in admiralty proceedings . . ." . . . Approved, February the twenty-fifth, 1795 . . . [Philadelphia, Francis Childs, 1795]
broadside 30 X 19 cm.
Without statement of deposition
New York Public 1164; cf. Evans 29705
NN

B9382 U.S. LAWS
Third Congress of the United States: At the second session . . . An act to establish an uniform rule of naturalization . . . Approved, January the twenty ninth, 1795 . . . [Philadelphia, Francis Childs, 1795]
[2] p. 30 X 19 cm.
Without statement of deposition
New York Public 1164; cf. Evans 29706
NN; NhD

B9383 U.S. LAWS
Third Congress of the United States: At the second session . . . An act to establish the office of purveyor of public supplies . . . Approved, February the twenty-third, 1795 . . . [Philadelphia, Francis Childs, 1795]
broadside 30 X 19 cm.
Without statement of deposition
New York Public 1164; cf. Evans 29707
NN

B9384 U.S. LAWS
Third Congress of the United States: At the second session . . . An act to provide for calling forth the militia to execute the laws of the Union . . . Approved, February the twenty-eighth, 1795 . . . [Philadelphia, Francis Childs, 1795]
[2] p. 30 X 19 cm.
Without statement of deposition
New York Public 1164; cf. Evans 29708
NN

B9385 U.S. LAWS
Third Congress of the United States: At the second session . . . An act to provide some present relief to the . . . citizens who have suffered . . . by the insurgents in the western counties of Pennsylvania . . . Approved, February the twenty seventh, 1795 . . . [Philadelphia, Francis Childs, 1795]
broadside 30 X 19 cm.
Without statement of deposition
New York Public 1164; cf. Evans 29709
NN

B9386 U. S. LAWS
Third Congress of the United States: At the second session . . . An act to regulate the compensation of clerks . . . Approved, March the third, 1795 . . . [Philadelphia, Francis Childs, 1795]
broadside 30 X 19 cm.
Without statement of deposition
New York Public 1164; cf. Evans 29710
NN

B9387 U.S. LAWS
Third Congress of the United States: At the second session . . . An act to regulate the pay of the non-commissioned officers, musicians and privates . . . Approved, January the second, 1795 . . . [Philadelphia, Francis Childs, 1795]
[2] p. 30 X 19 cm.
Without statement of deposition
New York Public 1164; cf. Evans 29711
NN

B9388 U.S. PRESIDENT, 1789–1797
George Washington, President . . . [Commission issued to Thomas H. Cushing, dated Aug. 27, 1795] Philada. Drawn & engrav'd by Thackara & Vallance [1795?]
broadside 47.5 X 38 cm.
CSmH

B9389 U.S. PRESIDENT, 1789–1797
George Washington, President . . . [ship's clearance paper in French, English, and Dutch in parallel columns] [Philadelphia, 1795?]
broadside 39.5 X 33 cm.
CSmH

B9390 U.S. PRESIDENT, 1789–1797
President's message. Philadelphia, March 31.—The following is a copy of the message from the President . . . Geo. Washington. United States, January 30. [Newport? Henry Barber? 1795]
broadside 39 X 22 cm.
Alden 1450
RHi mp. 47655

B9391 U.S. TREASURY DEPT.
Accounts of the treasurer of the United States, of payments and receipts . . . ending the thirtieth day of September, 1794. [Philadelphia] F. Childs [1795]
31, 16 p. 33.5 cm.
DLC; MiU-C; NN mp. 47656

B9392 U.S. TREASURY DEPT.
(Circular) To the collectors and naval-officers. Treasury department, March, 1795. Sir, You will receive herewith . . . [Philadelphia, 1795]
1 p.l., [6] p. 25 cm.
Contains various forms
PPRF mp. 47657

B9393 U. S. TREASURY DEPT.
Circular to the collectors and naval officers. Treasury department, March 18th, 1795. Sir, You will receive herewith . . . [Philadelphia, 1795]
broadside 24.5 X 20 cm.
PPRF mp. 47658

B9394 U.S. TREASURY DEPT.
[Received the 17th of December, 1795] Treasury of the United States, December 16, 1795. Sir, my specie accounts . . . Samuel Meredith, Treasurer . . . [n.p., 1795?]
16 p. 32 cm.
MiU-C mp. 47659

B9395 U.S. TREASURY DEPT.
Sir, It is necessary that I should inform you that John Kean . . . has resigned the office of cashier of the Bank of the United States . . . and that George Simpson . . . has been appointed . . . [Philadelphia, 1795]
broadside 24 X 19.5 cm.
PPRF mp. 47660

B9396 U.S. TREASURY DEPT.
Treasury Department. January 21, 1795. Sir, In consequence of the resolution of the House . . . of the 16th instant . . . a statement, shewing the amount of goods on which the duties . . . were paid in . . . the year 1793 . . . [Philadelphia, 1795]

broadsheet
RPJCB mp. 47661

B9397 U.S. TREATIES
(Authentic.) Treaty of amity, commerce & navigation . . . Albany, Printed and sold by Charles R. and George Webster, 1795.
32, [4] p. 16 cm.
McMurtrie: Albany 121
N mp. 47662

B9398 U.S. TREATIES
George Washington, President of the United States of America. To all to whom these presents shall come: Greeting . . . "Articles with the Cherokee Indians . . . "A treaty . . . the Six Nations . . . "A treaty . . . the Oneida, Tuscorora and Stockbridge Indians . . . [Philadelphia, 1795]
7 p. 30 cm.
Treaties ratified Jan. 21, 1795
De Renne p. 271; New York Public 1167
GU-De; PHi; NN mp. 47663

B9399 U.S. TREATIES
[Treaty of amity, commerce & navigation . . . Ordered printed in comfidence for the Senate. Washington, John Fenno? 1795]
The order to print appears in the *Executive Journal*, June 1795. In July B. F. Bache printed an unauthorized edition from a copy presumably "leaked" to him by Sen. Thomas Mason. (Information from James B. Childs)
No copy known

B9400 U.S. WAR DEPT.
Department of War, January 26th, 1795. Sir, In pursuance of a resolution of the House . . . of the 21st instant . . . [Philadelphia, 1795]
[2] p. 32 X 19.5 cm.
MWA; PPRF; RPJCB mp. 47664

B9401 THE United States almanac, for the year . . . 1796 . . . By Gabriel Hutchins . . . New-York, Printed for Naphtali Judah [1795]
[36] p. 17.5 cm.
CSmH (upper part of t.p. and all after p. [26] wanting); CU mp. 47463

B9402 THE United States almanac, for the year . . . 1796 . . . By Gabriel Hutchins . . . New-York, Printed for Thomas Allen [1795]
[36] p. 18 cm.
DLC mp. 47462

B9403 [THE United States' almanac . . . for 1796 . . . Wilmington, J. Adams and H. Niles [1795]]
[40] p.
By Thomas Fox
Drake 1401
PHi (t.p. and 1 leaf lacking)

B9404 [UNITED States and New Hampshire register for the year 1796. Dover, Samuel Bragg, 1795]

Stickney sale, Mar. 22, 1910
Nichols p. 92
No copy known mp. 47665

B9405 UNIVERSALISTS
Circular. The ministers, elders, and messengers . . . in General Convention, at Bennington, Vermont, September 16th, 1795. [Bennington? A. Haswell? 1795]

MMeT (not found, 1961) mp. 47666

B9406 UNIVERSITY OF PENNSYLVANIA
The rport of the Committee for the Arrangement of the schools in the University of Pennsylvania. Philadelphia, Samuel H. Smith, 1795.
32 p. 19.5 cm.
Adams: Pennsylvania 61
DLC; PPAmP; PU mp. 47555

B9407 USEFUL tables. 1st. A table shewing the value of any number of dollars & cents . . . 2d. A table shewing the value of foreign gold . . . 3d. A table shewing the value of silver coins . . . Worcester, Printed by James R. Hutchins, for Samuel Brazer, April 27th, 1795.
broadside 27 X 23.5 cm.
MWA mp. 47667

B9408 VIRGINIA. GOVERNOR, 1795-1796
By the governor . . . a proclamation . . . May 21, 1795. [Richmond, 1795]
broadside 46 X 27 cm.
CSmH (mutilated); Vi mp. 47668

B9409 VIRTUE in a cottage, or, A mirror for children, displayed in the history of Sally Bark and her family . . . Hartford, J. Babcock, 1795.
31 p. 10.5 cm.
MWA mp. 47669

B9410 VOGLER, GEORG JOSEPH, 1749-1814
The request. Composed by l'Abé Vogler. New York, Printed & sold by G. Gilfert & Co. [1795]
1 leaf. 35 cm. caption title
Sonneck-Upton p. 353
MiU-C

B9411 WATTS, ISAAC, 1674-1748
A catechism for children . . . Windham, John Byrne, 1795.
47 p. incl covers. 11 cm.
MWA mp. 47670

B9412 WATTS, ISAAC, 1674-1748
Christmas anthem: the hymn being in commemoration of the birth of Our Divine Saviour . . . Set to musick, by Isaac Lane. Worcester, Isaiah Thomas, Jun., 1795.
8 p. 8vo
MWA mp. 47671

B9413 WATTS, ISAAC, 1674-1748
Divine songs, attempted in easy language . . . Hartford, J. Babcock, 1795.
31 p. illus. 10.5 cm.
Rosenbach-Ch 201; Trumbull: Supplement 2726
CtHi; MWA; PP mp. 47672

B9414 WATTS, ISAAC, 1674-1748
Hymns and spiritual songs . . . New-York, Samuel Campbell, 1795.
312 p.
Second title of his *Imitation of the Psalms* (see above under Bible)
MWA

B9415 WATTS, ISAAC, 1674-1748
Hymns and spiritual songs . . . Newburyport: Printed and sold by John Mycall, sold also by Thomas and Co., E. Larkin, and D. West, in Boston [ca. 1795]
26+ p. 12mo
PPL (wanting after p. 26) mp. 47673

B9416 WATTS, ISAAC, 1674-1748
The second set of catechisms and prayers . . . First Charleston edition. [Charleston] W. P. Young, 1795.

vi, 41 p. 16.5 cm.
Mosimann 552
ScC

B9417 WEBSTER, NOAH, 1758–1843
(Circular.) To the physicians of Philadelphia, New-York, Baltimore, Norfolk and Newhaven . . . Noah Webster, Jun. New-York, Oct. 31, 1795.
2 leaves (printed only on the recto of the 1st) 33 X 20 cm.
Austin 2024; Skeel-Carpenter 782
PPL mp. 47676

B9418 [WEBSTER, NOAH] 1758–1843
The prompter . . . New-York, Printed and sold by Samuel Campbell, 1795.
108 p. 14 cm.
New York Public 1168; Skeel-Carpenter 666
MWA; NN mp. 47677

B9419 WEEKLY REGISTER
The news-boy's address, to the customers of the *Weekly Register* . . . Norwich, January 1st, 1795. [Norwich, Conn., 1795]
broadside 33 X 20 cm.
MHi

B9420 THE Western ephemeris, for . . . 1796 . . . Pittsbrugh, John Scull [1795]
[44] p. 18 cm.
MWA mp. 47678

B9421 DIE Westliche Correspondenz, und Hägerstauner Wochenschrift. Hägerstaun, Johann Gruber, 1795.

Minick 266
Description from no. 68 (Sept. 28, 1796)
No copy known

B9422 WHEATON, HANNAH
A New-Year's ode . . . [New York? 1795]
broadside 28 X 10.5 cm.
Ford 2768
NHi mp. 47679

B9423 WHEN rural lads and lasses gay . . . New York, G. Gilfert [1795]
[2] p. 23 cm.
Sonneck-Upton p. 464
DLC mp. 47680

B9424 WHITCOMB, CHAPMAN, 1765–1833
Miscellaneous poems . . . Rutland, Printed [by James Kirkaldie] for the author, 1795.
12 p. 22.5 cm.
cf. Evans 29884
MH (mutilated) mp. 47681

B9425 [WHITCOMB, CHAPMAN] 1765–1833
A poem, on religious ignorance, pride & avarice . . . To which is added the Gospel minister . . . [n.p.] Printed [by Chapman Whitcomb] for the purchasers, 1795.
broadside 45 X 20 cm.
cf. Evans 29332
MWA mp. 47682

B9426 WHITTEMORE, JOSEPH
To his friends and customers . . . January 1, 1795. [Boston, 1795]
broadside
MWA mp. 47683

B9427 WILCOCKS, THOMAS, b. 1622
A choice drop of honey . . . Walpole, New-hampshire, Printed for Richard Lee, travelling bookseller, 1795.
20 p. 22.5 cm.
Huntington 687
CSmH (wanting after p. 16); CtHi; MWA (t.p. photostat only) mp. 47685

B9428 [WILKINSON, REBECCA]
Sermons to children . . . By a lady. Philadelphia, W. Young, 1795.
159, [1] p. 10.5 cm.
MWA; PHi mp. 47686

B9429 WILLIAMS, NATHAN, 1735–1829
Circumspection in our walk distinguishes the wise from the foolish . . . Norwich, John Sterry, 1795.
16 p. 23.5 cm.
MWA mp. 47687

B9430 WILLIAMS, SIMON FINLEY, 1764–1800
A sermon delivered at the interment of Miss Sally Philbrick, who departed this life June 10, 1795 . . . Concord, Printed by Russell and Davis for the author, 1795.
23 p. 19 cm.
MWA (top half of t.p. wanting); NhHi mp. 47688

B9431 WINCHESTER, ELHANAN, 1751–1797
The universal restoration . . . First American edition . . . Boston, Printed and sold by John W. Folsom, 1795.
250, [1] p. 18 cm. A-X^6
MWA mp. 47689

B9432 THE winter evenings amusement, or, Jovial companion. Boston, Printed and sold by J. White and W. T. Clap, 1795.

Sonneck-Upton p.473
RPB (imperfect) mp. 47690

B9433 [WOLCOT, JOHN] 1738–1819
The poetical works of Peter Pindar . . . Charleston, W. P. Young. 1795.
3 v. 18 cm.
Mosimann 553
ScU

B9434 YALE UNIVERSITY
Catalogue of the Sophimore class . . . 1795. [New Haven, 1795]
broadside
CtY mp. 47691

B9435 ZANCHI, GIROLAMO, 1516–1590
[Toplady's Translation of Zanchius on predestination. Knoxville? George Roulstone? 1795]

Advertised in the *Knoxville Gazette*, Feb. 3, 1795: "The subscribers . . . are informed that the work is now published and ready for delivery. All subscribers are requested to send for their books – at the Printing Office – four shillings per copy."
McMurtrie: Tennessee 8
No copy known mp. 47692

1796

B9436 ABOLITION SOCIETIES
Philadelphia, December 12th, 1796 . . . the convention of the different abolition societies . . . directed us . . . to notify . . . [Philadelphia, 1796]

broadside 24.5 X 20.5 cm.
DLC mp. 47883

B9437 AN accrostick. Washington. [n.p., 1796?]
broadside 26.5 X 11.5 cm.
CSmH mp. 47693

B9438 ADDISON, ALEXANDER, 1759-1807
A discussion of the question lately agitated . . . with regard to the obligation of treaties . . . Pittsburgh, John Scull [1796]
24 p. 16 cm.
"Introduction by the publisher" signed: H. H. Brackenridge. Pittsburgh, May 20, 1796
MiU-C mp. 47694

B9439 ADDRESS to the inhabitants of Philadelphia . . . Bishop Carroll, Bishop of Baltimore . . . has recommended to the Reverend Mr. Carr, superior of the Augustinian Order in Dublin [to settle in Philadelphia] . . . Willing's Alley, May 29th, 1796. [Philadelphia? 1796]
broadside
There is a Willing's Alley in Philadelphia
PHi

B9440 ADGATE, ANDREW, d. 1793
Rudiments of music . . . The fourth edition. Philadelphia, Printed for, and sold by Mathew Carey, 1796.
76 p. 21.5 cm.
OClWHi; PPiPT

B9441 THE adventures of an illnatured boy, and store [story?] of ants and flies. Boston: Printed by J. Wh[ite], 1796.
[3-5] 6-[31?] p. 8.5 cm.
PP (imperfect)

B9442 Deleted

B9443 ALBANY REGISTER
Jan. 1, 1796. Indep. XX. The humble address of the carriers of the *Albany Register*, to their generous customers . . . [Albany, 1796]
broadside 37 X 24.5 cm.
New York Public 1169
NN mp. 47817

B9444 ALLEN, JEREMIAH
United States of America, December 23d, 1796. To the . . . Senate and the House . . . in Congress assembled. The memorial and petition of the subscribers [Jeremiah Allen and 4 others], for themselves and others . . . [Philadelphia? 1796?]
[3] p. 23 cm. caption title
Concerns redemption of bills issued by the U. S. Mar. 18, 1780
cf. Evans 28153 for an earlier petition
MB mp. 47947

B9445 ALLINE, HENRY, 1748-1784
Hymns and spiritual songs . . . Windsor, Alden Spooner, 1796.
22 p. 17 cm.
First Windsor edition
VtHi mp. 47697

B9446 AN almanack for . . . 1797 . . . Washington [Pa.], Colerick, Hunter and Beaumont, [1796]
[36] p.
Drake 10416
MiU-C (15 l.); NjP; OCHP

B9447 THE American academy of compliments; or, The complete American secretary . . . With a collection of the newest songs. Philadelphia, Godfrey Deshong, and Richard Folwell, 1796.
106 p. 13.5 cm.
New York Public 1170
MWA; NN mp. 47698

B9448 THE American jest-book . . . Part I. Boston, 1796.
240 p. 14.5 cm.
p. [123]-240: The merry fellow's companion
cf. Evans 29970
DLC; MWA mp. 47699

B9449 THE American jest book: containing a choice selection of jests, anecdotes, bon mots, stories, &c. Harrisburgh: Printed by John Wyeth, 1796.
116 p. 12mo
cf. Evans 29971
PPL

B9450 AMERICAN MERCURY
The carrier of the *American Mercury*, wishes his customers a Happy New Year . . . Hartford, January 1, 1796. [Hartford, 1796]
broadside 34 X 14 cm.
CtHi; NHi mp. 47748

B9451 [AMERICAN songs, with a variety of small matters for pedlars . . . Fairhaven, J. P. Spooner, ca. 1796]

Advertised in Defoe's *Wonderful life . . . Robinson Crusoe* (Fairhaven, 1796)
McCorison 376A
No copy known mp. 47700

B9452 AMES, FISHER, 1758-1808
The speech of Mr. Ames, in the House of Representatives . . . April 28, 1796 . . . Philadelphia, William Young, 1796.
[4], 59 p. 8vo
cf. Evans 29985, with variant imprint
PPL mp. 47701

B9453 AN approved collection of entertaining stories . . . By Solomon Winlove, Esq. Boston, Printed and sold by Samuel Hall, 1796.
128 p. illus. 10 cm.
Hamilton 166
MB; MWA (imperfect); NjP. Gillett Griffin, Princeton Univ. (1962); d'Alté A. Welch, Cleveland (1962)
mp. 48029

B9454 ARISTOTLE'S complete masterpiece, in three parts . . . The thirtieth edition. [New York?] Printed and sold by the booksellers, 1796.
162 p. front.
Austin 54; Hamilton 167; Rogers 525
NjP; PPC; PPL mp. 47702

B9455 ARISTOTLE'S master-piece, or, the secrets of nature displayed: complete in two parts . . . Philadelphia, Printed for the purchasers, 1796.
94 p. 16.5 cm.
NNS mp. 47703

B9456 ARNE, THOMAS AUGUSTINE, 1710-1778
A celebrated duett in Artaxerxes Fair Aurora composed by Dr. Arne and published by Mr. Trifobio. [Philadelphia, 1796-99]
[2] p. 34 cm.

Sonneck-Upton p. 131
DLC; NN mp. 47704

B9457 [ARNOLD, SAMUEL] 1740–1802
The way worn traveller . . . Philadelphia, Carr [1796?]
4 p. 32.5 cm.
p. 4 (numbered 72) identical with p. 72 of *The gentleman's amusement*
Sonneck-Upton p. 456; cf. Evans 26783 (1794)
CtY; DLC; MWA; NN mp. 47705

B9458 AN astronomical diary, calendar, or almanack for . . . 1797 . . . By N. Strong . . . Litchfield, T. Collier [1796]
[24] p.
Drake 554; Trumbull: Supplement 1795
Ct; CtLHi; CtY mp. 47925

B9459 [ATTWOOD, THOMAS] 1765–1838
The favorite carol sung in *The Adopted Child*, a muscal [sic] drama. New York, Printed for G. Gilfert & co. at their Musical Magazine, No. 177 Broadway [1796]
1 leaf. 33 cm. caption title
Sonneck Upton p. 56
MiU-C

B9460 AYLETT, PHILIP, plaintiff
Report of the case between Aylett and Aylett determined by the High Court of Chancery, in which the decree was reversed by the Court of Appeals. Richmond, Printed and sold at T. Nicolson, 1796.
31 p. 20 cm.
By George Wythe
MHi; ViU mp. 47706

B9461 BALTIMORE. NEW THEATRE
New theatre. On Monday evening, October 24, 1796 . . . Love's Frailties . . . [Baltimore, Clayland, Dobbin? 1796]
broadside 31 X 18.5 cm.
Minick 269
MdBE mp. 47707

B9462 BALTIMORE. NEW THEATRE
New theatre. On Wednesday evening, October 12, 1796 . . . Othello . . . [Baltimore, Clayland, Dobbin? 1796]
broadside 32 X 19.5 cm.
Minick 268
MdBE mp. 47708

B9463 BALTIMORE COUNTY
Notic [!] is hereby given, that the commissioners of the tax, for Baltimore county . . . May 22, 1796. [Baltimore, Philip Edwards? 1796]
broadside 19.5 X 21 cm.
Minick 270
MdHi mp. 47709

B9464 BANNAKER'S Maryland and Virginia almanack . . . for the year . . . 1797 . . . Baltimore, Printed by Christopher Jackson for George Keatinge's book store [1796]
[36] p. illus. 16.5 cm.
Minick 272
MdHi mp. 47710

B9465 BANNAKER'S Virginia and North Carolina almanac and ephemeris, for the year . . . 1797 . . . Petersburg, William Prentis and William T. Murray [1796]
[36?] p. 16.5 cm.
Bear 109; Porter 43; Wyatt 15
MWA mp. 47711

B9466 BAPTISTS. CONNECTICUT. DANBURY ASSOCIATION
Minutes of the Danbury Baptist Association, holden at Stratfield, September 21st, and 22d, M,DCC,XCVI. Hartford, Hudson & Goodwin, 1796.
8 p.
Trumbull: Supplement 2044
Ct. Photocopy: MWA mp. 47712

B9467 BAPTISTS. KENTUCKY. ELKHORN ASSOCIATION
Minutes of the Elkhorn Association of Baptists, held at Town Fork August 13, 1796. [n.p., 1796]
5 p. 20 cm. caption title
McMurtrie: Kentucky 52
NRAB; OClWHi. Photocopy: MWA
mp. 47713

B9468 BAPTISTS. NEW HAMPSHIRE. MEREDITH BAPTIST ASSOCIATION
Minutes of the Meredith Baptist Association held at Sandbornton . . . Sept. 9th and 10th, 1795. Concord, George Hough, 1796.
7 p.
British Museum mp. 47714

B9469 BAPTISTS. NORTH CAROLINA. KEHUKEE BAPTIST ASSOCIATION
Minutes of the Kehukee Baptist Association, holden at Parker's Meeting-House, on Meherrin, Hertford County, North-Carolina, September, 1796 . . . [at end] Halifax, Abraham Hodge [1796]
8 p. 20 cm. caption title
McMurtrie: North Carolina 215
RPJCB mp. 47715

B9470 BAPTISTS. NORTH CAROLINA. NEUSE BAPTIST ASSOCIATION
Minutes of the Neuse Baptist Association; held at Chechquamin Chapel . . . October 1796. [Newbern, F.-X. Martin, 1796]
[4] p. 25.5 cm. caption title
NcWsW mp. 47716

B9471 BAPTISTS. VERMONT. VERMONT ASSOCIATION
The constitution of the Vermont Association. 1796. Rutland, 1796.
12 p. 18 cm.
Cooley 347
DLC; NRAB; VtHi mp. 47717

B9472 [BARLOW, JOEL] 1754–1812
The hasty-pudding: a poem . . . [New Haven? 1796?]
12 p. 20 cm.
NHi; PPRF mp. 47718

B9473 BARRINGTON, GEORGE, 1755–1804
Voyage to New South Wales . . . New-York: Printed by John Swaine [1796?]
184 p. 20.5 cm.
CtHi; NhD ([1801?]) mp. 47719

B9474 [BARTHOLOMEW, SAMUEL] 1762–1842
[A rake exhibited: or A plain narrative of the life and death of Will Witling . . . Fairhaven, J. P. Spooner, 1796]
80 p. 18mo
Advertised in the *Farmer's Library*, May 30, 1796
McCorison 380
No copy known mp. 47720

B9475 BERQUIN, ARNAUD, 1750–1791
The children's friend . . . Wilmington [Del.], Joseph Johnson, 1796.
108 p. 15.5 cm.
MWA mp. 47721

B9476 [BERQUIN, ARNAUD] 1750–1791
The friend of youth . . . Philadelphia, Printed by Budd and Bartram for Benjamin & Jacob Johnson, 1796.
120 p. 11 X 10 cm.
MWA (lacks p. 35–38) mp. 47722

B9477 BIBLE
An abridgement of the History of the Holy Bible . . . Hudson, Printed by Ashbel Stoddard and sold at his printing-office & book-store, 1796.
29, [2] p. illus. 9.5 cm.
First and last pages pasted to covers
CtHi mp. 47723

B9478 BIBLE
The Bible in miniature . . . Philadelphia: for John Dickins [1796]
96 leaves. 5.5 cm. A–F^{16}
Rosenbach–Ch 204
PP; PPL mp. 47725

B9479 BIBLE
A concise history of the Holy Bible . . . Lansingburgh, Luther Pratt, 1796.

Julia Wightman, New York City (1962) mp. 47724

B9480 BIBLE
A new hieroglyphical Bible . . . Boston, W. Norman [1796?]
144 p.
cf. Evans 30068
MWA mp. 47726

B9481 BIBLE. O. T. PSALMS
The Psalms of David, in metre . . . Philadelphia, John M'Culloch, 1796.
303 p. 10.5 cm.
MWA mp. 47727

B9482 BIBLE. O.T. PSALMS
The Psalms of David, with hymns and spiritual songs . . . For the use of the Reformed Dutch Church in North-America. Albany, Charles R. and George Webster, 1796.
530, [10] p. 14 cm.
DLC mp. 47728

B9483 BIBLE. O.T. PSALMS
The Psalms of David, with hymns and spiritual songs . . . For the use of the Reformed Dutch Church in North America. New-York: Printed and sold by C. Forman, 1796.
xvi, 488 p.
MWA mp. 47729

B9484 BIBLE. N.T. ENGLISH
The New Testament . . . New-Haven, Printed and sold by Tiebout & O'Brien, also sold . . . at their Printing-Office . . . New-York [1796?]
[336] p. 16 cm.
Trumbull: Supplement 2454
DLC mp. 47730

B9485 BICKERSTAFF'S genuine New-England almanack for . . . 1797 . . . By Isaac Bickerstaff. West Springfield, Edward Gray [1796]
[24] p.
Drake 3563
MWA

B9486 BLAUVELT, ABRAHAM
New-Brunswick, August 29, 1796. A. Blauvelt, proposes printing by subscription, An Apology for the Bible . . . addressed to Thomas Paine . . . By R. Watson . . . [New Brunswick, A. Blauvelt, 1796]
broadside 33 X 13.5 cm.
NjR

B9487 BLOOMFIELD, JOSEPH
To the public. I beg leave to call the attention of the public . . . in vindication of myself, against . . . persons, who . . . blast my character with anti-Federalism . . . Joseph Bloomfield. Burlington, December, 1796 . . . [Burlington? 1796?]
broadside 28 X 22 cm.
Morsch 306
NjHi mp. 47333

B9488 BOSTON. ORDINANCES
By-law relative to bulls and cows . . . Boston, April 1796. [Boston, 1796]
broadside 31 X 12 cm.
DLC mp. 47734

B9489 BOSTON DISPENSARY
Certificate of recommendation, and rules to be observed by the patients. [Adopted Sept. 21, 1796] [Boston, 1796]
broadside
Entry from *Index Cat.* (S.G.O.) ser. 1, v. 2, p. 278
Austin 234
No copy located mp. 47736

B9490 BOSTON EVENING COURIER
The carrier of the *Boston Evening Courier*, to his generous patrons . . . January 1, 1796. [Boston, 1796]
broadside
MWA mp. 47749

B9491 BOSTON THEATRE (FEDERAL STREET)
Boston Theatre. Federal Street. On Friday evening, Sept. 30th, '96. Will be presented . . . Know Your Own Mind . . . To which will be added . . . Rosina . . . [Boston, 1796]
broadside 45.5 X 29 cm.
NHi mp. 47737

B9492 BOSTON THEATRE (FEDERAL STREET)
Boston Theatre. On Friday evening, December 16, 1796, will be presented . . . The Mountaineers . . . To which will be added . . . My Grandmother . . . [Boston, Young and Minns, 1796]
broadside 45 X 30 cm.
MB mp. 47738

B9493 BOSTON THEATRE (FEDERAL STREET)
Boston Theatre. This evening, Wednesday, February 17th, will be presented, the celebrated tragedy of George Barnwell . . . [Boston, Young and Minns, 1796]
broadside 32 X 18 cm.
MB mp. 47739

B9494 BOSTON THEATRE (FEDERAL STREET)
Mr. Jones's benefit. Boston Theatre. Friday evening, November 4, 1796, will be presented, for the first time this season . . . Inkle & Yarico . . . To which will be added, a new farce . . . The First Floor . . . [Boston, 1796]

broadside 46.5 X 30.5 cm.
MHi mp. 47740

B9495 BOSTWICK, DAVID, 1720-1763
Self disclaimed and Christ exalted: a sermon, preached at Philadelphia, before the . . . synod of New-York, May 25th, 1758 . . . Richmond, T. Nicolson, 1796.
42 p. 8vo
PPL

B9496 BOYD, WILLIAM, 1776-1800
Beauty, a poem. Delivered at Cambridge, on the anniversary commencement, July 20, 1796 . . . [Boston? 1796?]
8 p. 16 cm.
MWA mp. 47741

B9497 BRADFORD, THOMAS, 1745-1838
Bradford's Catalogue of books and stationary . . . for 1796. Philadelphia, Thomas Bradford, 1796.
[2], 73, [4] p. 8vo
Not Evans 30121; Supplement, p. [67]-73; advertisements, p. [74-77]
PHi

B9498 BUCHAN, WILLIAM, 1729-1805
A letter to the patentee concerning the medical properties of the fleecy hosiery . . . The third American edition, with additional notes and observations, by the editor. London, Printed: Newark, New-Jersey, Re-printed by John Woods, for M. Trappal, 1796.
23, [1] p. 19 cm.
Austin 342; Morsch 307; Rogers 529
MHi mp. 47742

B9499 BUEL, ELIAS, 1768-1808
[An oration, delivered to the First Democratic Society in Rutland County, on the 4th of July 1796, by their late president. Fairhaven, J. P. Spooner, 1796]

Advertised in the *Farmer's Library*, Aug. 22, 1796; text of the address printed in Aug. 8, 1796, issue
McCorison 382
No copy known mp. 47743

B9500 BUNN, MATTHEW, 1772-
A journal of the adventures of Matthew Bunn . . . taken by the savages, and made his excape . . . the 30th of April, 1792 . . . Walpole, New Hampshire, David Carlisle, Jun., 1796.
22+ p. 22.5 cm.
Vail: Old frontier 1054
OClWHi mp. 47744

B9501 BURGESS,
Extracts from Rev. Mr. Burgess, on the divinity of Christ, in answer to Dr. Priestley. Philadelphia, Francis & Robert Bailey, 1796.
20 p. 18 cm.
NHi mp. 47745

B9502 CABOT, SAMUEL
Boston, 7th July, 1796. Sir, In consequence of a representation made by . . . principal merchants . . . that some commercial character might be employed . . . to aid the business of the Commissioners in London, the President . . . has been pleased to honor me with this appointment . . . Sam. Cabot. [Boston, 1796]
broadside 23 X 19 cm.
RPJCB mp. 47746

B9503 CAMBRIAN COMPANY
Impelled by motives of mutual advantage, we . . . have agreed to form an actual settlement, in the most eligible situation . . . within the United States of America . . . [Signed] Morgan J. Rhees, president, Thomas Cumpston, treasurer . . . Philadelphia. [Philadelphia] Lang and Ustick, printers. [1796?]
[4] p. 34.5 cm.
Printed on p. [1] only.
MiU-C

B9504 [CARLTON, WILLIAM]
Proposal for publishing by subscription, More Wonders of the Invisible World . . . Collected by Robert Calef . . . It will contain about 350 duodecemo [sic] pages . . . [Salem, 1796?]
broadside 37 X 16 cm.
Ford 2839; cf. Evans 30149 (pub. 1797)
MSaE mp. 47747

B9505 CARTER AND WILKINSON, firm, Providence
[Catalogue of the books in the circulating library. Providence, Carter & Wilkinson, 1796]
[broadside?]
Advertised July 2, 1796, as "This day published."
Alden 1463
No copy known mp. 47750

B9506 [CECIL, RICHARD] 1748-1810
A friendly visit to the house of mourning . . . Boston, Printed by Manning & Loring, for Rev. J. Morse, and J. Dennison; sold by said Dennison, at his bookstore in Charlestown, and by Thomas & Andrews, J. White, S. Hall, E. Larkin, and D. & J. West, in Boston, 1796.
72 p. 14 cm.
MWA mp. 47751

B9507 CHARLESTON, S. C. ORDINANCES
Ordinances of the City Council of Charleston . . . collected and revised . . . by Dominick Augustin Hall . . . Charleston, John M'Iver, 1796.
[3], 163 p. 30.5 cm.
Mosimann 563
ScC

B9508 CHARLESTON, S.C. ORDINANCES
Ordinances, rules, and bye-laws for the Poor House of Charleston . . . [Charleston] 1796.
broadside 52 X 34.5 cm.
MH

B9509 A CHOICE collection of new and approved country dances. Northampton, 1796.
8 leaves. 8vo
Rosenbach-Ch 206
A. S. W. Rosenbach (1933) mp. 47752

B9510 CHRISTIANITY contrasted with Deism . . . By Peter Porcupine. Philadelphia: Printed for the author. 1796.
64 p. 18 cm.
Not by Wm. Cobbett, who denounced an impostor for using his pseudonym (cf. Evans 33523, p. 52).—Pierce W. Gaines
cf. Evans 30192
NHi mp. 47754

B9511 CHURCH, JAMES
For the cure of coughs, colds, asthma and consumptions, Church's cough drops . . . prepared (only) by Dr. James

Church, sold at his medicine store . . . Philadelphia, and at his home, New-York. [Philadelphia? 1796?]
broadside
cf. Evans 35305
NHi mp. 47753

B9512 COLLEY, THOMAS, d. 1812
A tender salutation in gospel love . . . Philadelphia, D. Humphreys, 1796.
16 p. 20 cm.
PHi mp. 47755

B9513 THE Columbian almanac, for . . . 1797. Lancaster, Printed by William & Robert Dickson, for John Wyeth, Harrisburg [1796]
[40] p. 17.5 cm.
MWA mp. 47756

B9514 THE Columbian calendar, or New-England almanack for . . . 1797 . . . Dedham, Minerva Press [1796]
[24] p. 18.5 cm.
By John Newman
MWA (2 copies, varying imprints) mp. 47866

B9515 CONGREGATIONAL CHURCHES IN MASSACHUSETTS. CAMBRIDGE ASSOCIATION
To the public. An address from the ministers of the association in and about Cambridge, at their stated meeting . . . October, 1796. Fellow-citizens . . . [at end] Jonathan Homer [and 10 others] . . . Boston, Printed and sold by S. Hall [1796]
broadside 44 X 27 cm.
MWA mp. 47757

B9516 CONNECTICUT GORE LAND CO.
Supplementary articles of agreement. [Hartford, 1796]
7 p. 17.5 cm.
Dated at end: Hartford, April 8, 1796
ICN; MWA; PPiU mp. 47758

B9517 COOK, JAMES, 1728–1779
Captain Cook's third and last voyage to the Pacific Ocean . . . New York, Printed for, and sold by B. Gomez, 1796.
144 p. 13.5 cm.
NjP (not traced 1965) mp. 47759

B9518 CORREY, MOLLESTON
The Traveling Millenarian to the people of America . . . [n.p.] Printed for the author, Molleston Correy, 1796.
36 p.
MWA mp. 47760

B9519 COSTELOW, THOMAS
The cherry girl . . . New York & Philadelphia, B. Carr; Baltimore, I Carr [1796]
[2] p. 33 cm.
Sonneck-Upton p. 61
DLC; MWA mp. 47761

B9519a COWPER, WILLIAM, 1731–1800
The diverting history of John Gilpin . . . Boston, Printed and sold by William Spotswood, 1796.
10+ p. illus. 19 cm.
DLC (all after p. 10 wanting)

B9520 CULVER, NATHAN, d. 1791
A very remarkable account of the vision of Nathan Culver . . . Jan. 10, 1791 . . . Fifth edition . . . Portsmouth, Printed at the *Oracle* Office [by Charles Peirce], 1796.
16 p. 20.5 cm.
MWA mp. 47762

B9521 CYNTHIA, with the account of the unfortunate loves of Almerin and Desdemona . . . Boston: Printed by J. White, 1796.
59+ p. 8vo
PPL

B9522 DAVENPORT, RUFUS
Having established myself in this place, for the purpose of transacting the business of all those . . . Boston . . . [Boston, 1796?]
broadside 23 X 18.5 cm.
Filled in for Dec. 1, 1796; signed at bottom: Rufus Davenport
RPJCB mp. 47763

B9523 [DAY, THOMAS] 1748–1789
The grateful Turk, or the advantages of friendship. Boston, J. White, 1796.
30, [1] p. illus. 9 cm.
Cut of Crusoe on rear paper cover
Gillett Griffin, Princeton Univ. (1961) mp. 47764

B9524 DEFOE, DANIEL, 1661?–1731
Travels of Robinson Crusoe . . . Windham, J. Byrne, 1796.
31 p. 10 cm.
Brigham: Robinson Crusoe 36; Rosenbach–Ch 207
CtHi; MWA; PP mp. 47765

B9525 DEFOE, DANIEL, 1661?–1731
The wonderful life, and most surprising adventures of . . . Robinson Crusoe . . . Fairhaven, J. P. Spooner [1796]
46, [1] p. 13 cm.
Brigham: Robinson Crusoe 34; Rosenbach–Ch 208
PP. d'Alté A. Welch, Cleveland (1963) mp. 47766

B9526 DELAWARE. SUPREME COURT
Causes for trial and argument, at the April term . . . before the . . . Supreme Court, at New-Castle. First class of trials, commencing Tuesday April 5th, 1796 . . . [Wilmington? 1796]
broadside 33 X 20.5 cm.
NjR

B9527 DICKSON'S Balloon almanac for . . . 1797 . . . Lancaster, W. and R. Dickson [1796]

Drake 10429, from Bausman
No copy known

B9528 THE disobedient son, and cruel husband . . . To which are added, The wild rover. And The humours of whiskey. Dublin [Philadelphia]: Printed by W. Jones, January, 1796.
8 p. 12mo
PPL mp. 47767

B9529 DODDRIDGE, PHILIP, 1702–1751
Three sermons . . . Chambersburg, Dover & Harper, 1796.
viii, 76 p. 17.5 cm.
DLC; MWA mp. 47768

B9529a DODSLEY, ROBERT, 1703–1764
Select fables of Esop and other fabulists . . . By Robert Dodsley . . . A new edition. Philadelphia: Printed for, and sold by, Joseph and James Crukshank, 1798.
208, [20] p. 17.5 cm.
ViU

B9530 DOW, HENDRICK, 1761–1814
A warning to little children, from the dying words of

Jane Sumner . . . New-London, Printed and sold by James Springer, 1796.
16 p. 15.5 cm.
cf. Evans 30362
CtHi mp. 47769

B9530a DUTTON, TIMOTHY
Verses, &c. The following verses were written . . . August 8th, 1796, by the desire of Mr. Oliver Wright and his wife . . . [n.p., 1796?]
12 p. 18 cm. caption title A^6
Stoddard 77
RPB

B9531 [ELLICOTT, ANDREW] 1754–1820
Plan of the city of Washington . . . Rollinson sculp^t N. York. [New York] Publish'd by I. Reid [1796?]
map 40.5 X 56 cm.
First issued with imprint: Publish'd by I. Reid, L. Wayland and C. Smith, 1795
MB (bound with Evans 31078 (American atlas, New York, 1796)

B9532 ELLIS, LUTHER
Luther Ellis, (No.) Market-Street, Portsmouth, imports and sells European and India goods . . . [Portsmouth, 1796]
broadside 18.5 X 14 cm.
Huntington 692
CSmH mp. 47771

B9533 THE entertaining history of Tommy Gingerbread . . . New-York, James Oram, 1796.
31 p. incl. covers. 10 cm.
MWA mp. 47772

B9534 FAIR Maria of the dale . . . New York, Printed for G. Gilfert [1796]
broadside 33.5 cm.
Sonneck-Upton p. 131
DLC; NBuG mp. 47773

B9535 FAIRBANKS, JASON, d. 1796.
Price nine pence. For some time past the public have been anxiously waiting to be informed of the . . . last dying words of Jason Fairbanks . . . Boston: Printed and sold in Russell-street, near West Boston bridge [1796?]
broadside 63 X 50 cm.
Ford 3110
PPRF mp. 47774

B9536 [THE family almanac for 1797. Portsmouth, C. Peirce [1796]]
[24] p.
Drake 4697
MWA (t. p. and last leaf lacking)

B9537 FARMER'S BROTHER
Speech of Farmer's Brother. The following speech was delivered in a public council . . . November 21, 1796, by Ho-na-ya-wus, . . . called Farmer's Brother . . . Boston, N. Coverly, Jr. [1796?]
broadside 26 X 20.5 cm.
On verso: The Projectors . . . and . . . Empire travelling westward
Ford 2795, 2800
MHi; N mp. 47775

B9538 FATHER Hutchins revived . . . for . . . 1797. New-York, Printed for John Reid [1796]

Drake 6054
IU

B9539 FATHER Tammany's almanac, for the year 1797 . . . Philadelphia, Printed for W. Young [1796]
[36] p. illus. 19 cm.
PHi mp. 47776

B9540 FEDERAL tables, useful and necessary to every person who is or is not acquainted with federal money. Printed and sold by S. Trumbull, Norwich, August 26th, 1796.
[2] p.
MWA mp. 47777

B9541 FELLOWS, JOHN
Supplement to John Fellows's circulating library . . . [New York, 1796?]
24 p. 18 cm. caption title
cf. Evans 30412
NHi mp. 47778

B9542 FISH, ELISHA, 1719–1795
The baptism of Jesus Christ not to be imitated by Christians . . . By the Rev. Elisha Fish . . . and the Rev. John Crane . . . Warren, Nathaniel Phillips [ca. 1796?]
24 p. 18 cm.
Alden 1466
MWA; RHi; RPJCB mp. 47779

B9543 FISHER, JONATHAN, 1768–1847
Two elegies, on the deaths of Mrs. Marianne Burr . . . Jan. 2, 1795; and of Mrs. Rebekah Walker . . . Jan. 27, 1795 . . . Hanover, Dunham and True. January 1st, 1796.
11 p. 16.5 cm.
New York Public 1173
Lewis M. Stark (1960). Photostat: NN mp. 47780

B9544 FORM of an entry to be made by every person having or keeping a carriage, or carriages, as required by the 4th section of the act of May 28, 1796. [Boston, 1796?]
broadside
Ford 2789
MHi mp. 47781

B9545 FORTIS, EDMUND, d. 1794
The last words and dying speech of Edmund Fortes . . . executed at Dresden . . . the 25th of September 1794 . . . Exeter, 1796.
8 p. 17.5 cm.
Porter 85
Arthur B. Spingarn, New York City mp. 47782

B9546 FOUR new songs, viz. The Shipwreck'd Sailors, on the Rocks of Scylla . . . Also the Sorrowful Gaol Groans, of Sarah Delany; with The Sweet Little Girl that I Love; and the American Independence. Philadelphia, William Jones, 1796.
8 p. 12mo
PPL mp. 47783

B9547 FRANCE
Authentic translation of a note from the Minister of the French Republic, to the Secretary of State . . . Bennington, Anthony Haswell, 1796.
67 p. 14 cm.
Cooley 338
VtBennM mp. 47784

B9548 FRANCE
[Citizen Adet's note to the secretary of the United States. Baltimore, Christopher Jackson, 1796]

Title from advertisement in the *Maryland Journal* Nov. 26, 1796: "Stolen out of the printing office . . . 500 of the first half sheet of Citizen Adet's note."

Minick 284
No copy known mp. 47785

B9549 FRANCE
Maryland Journal, extra. Note of P. A. Adet . . . to the secretary of state . . . Baltimore, Philip Edwards, 1796.
18 p. 22.5 cm.
Minick 285
MdHi; RPJCB mp. 47786

B9550 FREEMASONS. MASSACHUSETTS. GRAND LODGE
Complaint having been received . . . that the Harmonic Lodge . . . contrary to the directions . . . of the 13th June, 5796 . . . [Boston, 1796?]
broadside
MWA mp. 47787

B9551 FREEMASONS. VERMONT. AURORA LODGE
Hampton: Aurora Lodge opened in due form, the 24th June . . . 5796. Resolved . . . to return the thanks of this body to Brother Lyon, for his address delivered this day to this lodge; and that he be requested to favor them with a copy thereof, to be printed . . . [Fairhaven, J. P. Spooner, 1796]
16 p.
Cooley 323; McCorison 393
VtHi (t.p., 7–8 missing) mp. 47788

B9552 FRIENDS, SOCIETY OF
The following vindication of the character of George Fox, from the account given of him in the Encyclopaedia, Vol. XV. page 734, was drawn up by the Society called Quakers . . . [Philadelphia, 1796]
4 p. 4to
PPL

B9553 [FRITH, EDWARD]
The contented cottager . . . New York, G. Gilfert [1796]
[2] p. 32.5 cm.
Sonneck-Upton p. 88
DLC; NN; RPJCB mp. 47789

B9554 A GAMUT, or scale of music, adapted to the use of beginners in psalmody . . . Lansingburgh, L. Pratt & Co., 1796.
[60] p.
N mp. 47432

B9555 GAZETTE OF THE UNITED STATES
Address of the carrier of the *Gazette of the United States* . . . January 1st, 1796. [Philadelphia, 1796]
broadside 35 X 21 cm.
MWA mp. 47695

B9556 GIBSON, ROBERT
A treatise of practical surveying . . . Philadelphia, Printed for Joseph Crukshank, 1796.
viii, 288, [1], 90 p., 1 leaf, 56 p. XIII fold. plates. 20 cm.
Second title: Tables of difference of latitude . . .
Third Title: A table of logarithms . . .
DLC; MWA; MiU; MnU; NjP; OSW; P; PBL; PPL; PSC; PU; TKL mp. 47790

B9557 GOD'S dreadful judgment on false swearing . . . [at end] 1796. [Ephrata? 1796]
12 p. 15.5 cm.
Cut on t.p. and page numerals identical with those used in "Gottes schreckliches Bericht . . ." (see below)
MWA mp. 47791

B9558 GORDON, PETER
A catalogue of books & stationary, for sale, at Peter Gordon's Store, in Trenton . . . [Trenton, 1796?]
broadside 45 X 29 cm.
Photostat: NjR

B9559 GOTTES schreckliches Bericht an William Burn, wegen einem falschen Eyd . . . [at end] 1796. [Ephrata? 1796]
12 p. 16.5 cm.
Cut on t.p. and page numerals identical with "God's dreadful judgment . . ."
MWA mp. 47793

B9560 GREENLEAF, JAMES
Philadelphia, December 16th, 1796. Gentlemen, I have given you the trouble of meeting me . . . James Greenleaf. To the gentlemen creditors of James Greenleaf. [Philadelphia, 1796]
broadside 34.5 X 21 cm.
NHi mp. 47794

B9561 GREENWOOD, ISAAC
An exposition of the emblems contained in a certificate for the members of the Providence Association of Mechanics and Manufacturers . . . The above concise explanation . . . submitted to the members . . . by . . . Isaac Greenwood, delineator. [Providence] Carter and Wilkinson [ca. 1796?]
broadside 25 X 34 cm.
Alden 1482; Winship Addenda p. 92
RHi. Carleton R. Richmond, Milton, Mass. (1949)
Photostat: MWA mp. 47795

B9562 GRIMKE, JOHN FAUCHERAND, 1752–1819
Letter from Judge Grimke to the House of Representatives . . . Columbia, Young & Faust [1796]
broadside 27 X 21.5 cm.
Concerns William Shaw's remarks about Grimke
Sc-Ar (4 copies)

B9563 HAMPSHIRE CO. CITIZENS
At a meeting of a respectable number of freeholders . . . of the County of Hampshire, holden at Northampton . . . the 27th of April 1796 . . . Voted, That . . . the Treaty . . . with Great-Britain, ought to be carried into immediate effect . . . Voted, That the Grand Jury be requested to forward to each Town . . . a copy of the petition . . . [Northampton? 1796]
[2] p. 19 cm.
M–Ar

B9564 HARPER, ROBERT GOODLOE, 1765–1825
An address from Robert Goodloe Harper . . . to his constituents . . . New-York, Printed by T. & J. Swords for J. Rivington, 1796.
[2], [37] p. 23 cm.
cf. Evans 30539
CSmH mp. 47796

B9565 HARTFORD. CITIZENS
Notice. From the present state of things in the House of Representatives of the United States, there are strong reasons to fear, that the appropriations necessary to carry into effect the treaty lately concluded . . . will not be made . . . a number of the inhabitants . . . met . . . request an universal meeting . . . this day . . . Hartford, April 21, 1796. [Hartford, 1796]
broadside 27 X 21.5 cm.
CtHi mp. 47797

B9566 HARTFORD. CITIZENS
The petition of the freemen of the town of Hartford in the State of Connecticut, sheweth, that the present situation . . . fervent wishes, that measures may be taken . . . to carry the treaty between the United States and Great-Britain into complete effect. Dated at Hartford the 21st day of April, 1796 . . . Thomas Seymour, Chairman. [Hartford, 1796]
broadside 33 X 19.5 cm.
CtHi mp. 47798

B9567 HARVARD UNIVERSITY
Harvard College Lottery. The managers of Harvard College Lottery, assure the public . . . commence drawing the fourth class of said Lottery . . . the fifteenth of September next . . . Boston, April 7, 1796. Benjamin Austin, jun. [and 4 others] Managers. [Boston, 1796]
broadside 34.5 X 22 cm.
MHi mp. 47799

B9568 HAVERHILL LIBRARY, HAVERHILL, MASS.
Haverhill Library. Newburyport, Blunt and March [1796?]
22 p. 19 cm.
"Rules and regulations of Haverhill Library. Made and accepted April 12, 1796:" p. [5]
MWA (all after p. 16 wanting) mp. 47800

B9569 HEIDELBERG CATECHISM
Catechismus, oder kurzer Unterricht . . . Germantaun, Gedruckt und zu finden bey Michael Billmeyer, 1796.
118 p. 14 cm.
MWA mp. 47802

B9570 HERVEY, JAMES, 1714–1758
Meditations and contemplations . . . Wilmington, Printed by P. Brynberg for John Boggs, 1796.
62, [lxiii]–lxxii p. 17 cm.
Hawkins 65
DeWI; PHi mp. 47803

B9571 HERZLICHE Bitte an die Kinder und Jugend. Reading, Gottlob Jungmann [1796?]
[8] p. 10.5 cm.
Owner's name dated in ms.: 1797
MWA mp. 47804

B9572 HEWITT, JAMES, 1770–1827
The wish . . . New York and Philadelphia, B. Carr; Baltimore, J. Carr [1796]
[2] p. 33.5 cm.
Sonneck-Upton p. 474
DLC; MWA mp. 47805

B9573 THE history of little King Pippin . . . Philadelphia, Neal & Kammerer, 1796.
63 p. illus. 10.5 cm.
PP mp. 47807

B9574 THE history of Master Jackey and Miss Harriot . . . Boston, Printed and sold by S. Hall [1796?]
31 p. incl. covers. 11 cm.
Dated by d'Alté A. Welch
MWA

B9575 THE Hive: or a collection of thoughts . . . Second edition. From the press of Thomas, Son and Thomas . . . Worcester, Mass., 1796.
227 p. front. 12mo
"Second edition" engraved on frontispiece; otherwise Evans 30567
MWA mp. 47806

B9576 HOOK, JAMES, 1746–1827
Jem of Aberdeen, a favorite Scotch song. Composed by Mr. Hook. [Boston, 1796–97]
p. 40–41. 30.5 cm. caption title
Extracted from *The musical repertory*. Boston. No. III, p. 40-41. cf. Sonneck-Upton p.216
With this is Storace, Stephen. The jealous Don. p. 41–43
MiU–C

B9577 HUDSON & GOODWIN, firm, Hartford
Proposals for printing . . . a volume of sermons . . . May 12, 1796. [Hartford, 1796]
broadside
MWA mp. 47808

B9578 HUGHLETT, WILLIAM
Delaware State Mills. [Sir] Being desirous of driving my mills to the extent, it requires a great deal of wheat, corn, and rye, to keep them in operation: . . . [Wm Hughlett February 18th 1796] [Wilmington? 1796]
broadside 4to
Salutation, signature, and date in autograph
PPL mp. 47810

B9579 HUMANE SOCIETY OF MASSACHUSETTS
Summary of the method of treatment to be used with persons apparently dead from drowning . . . one or two assistants, are to be employed in blowing up tobacco smoke, into the fundament . . . The trustees of the Humane Society of . . . Massachusetts, have procured five sets of tobacco machines . . . deposited . . . in several parts of . . . Boston . . . [Boston, 1796?]
broadside 20.5 X 16.5 cm.
MWA mp. 47811

B9580 I NEVER would be married . . . New York, G. Gilfert [1796]
[2] p. 33.5 cm.
Sonneck-Upton p. 201
DLC; NN mp. 47813

B9581 INSTRUCTIVE and entertaining emblems on various subjects. By Miss Thoughtful. Hartford, J. Babcock, 1796.
30 p., 1 leaf. illus. 10 cm.
MiU–C. d'Alté A. Welch (1960) mp. 47814

B9582 THE instructive story of industry and sloth . . . Hartford, J. Babcock, 1796.
29, [1] p. illus. 10 cm.
DLC; MWA mp. 47815

B9583 THE Italien mock trio . . . New York, G. Gilfert [1796]
broadside 33.5 cm.
Sonneck-Upton p. 264
DLC mp. 47816

B9584 JOHN STREET THEATRE
New-York, February 27, 1796. Theatre. By the Old American Company. On . . . the 29th of February . . . a tragedy, called, The Carmelite . . . [New York, 1796]
broadside 41 X 22.5 cm.
New York Public 1174
NN mp. 47858

B9585 JOHN STREET THEATRE
New-York, March 7, 1796. Theatre. (By particular desire.) On Wednesday evening, the 9th of March, will be presented, a comedy, called, The Deserted Daughter . . . [New York, 1796]

broadside 42 X 24.5 cm.
NHi (mutilated) mp. 47859

B9586 JOHN STREET THEATRE
New-York, May 18, 1796. Mrs. Johnson's benefit. On Friday evening, the 20th of May, will be presented, a favorite comedy . . . First Love . . . [New York, 1796]
broadside 42 X 26 cm.
NHi mp. 47860

B9587 JOHN STREET THEATRE
New-York, September 26, 1796. Theatre. On Wednesday evening, the 28th of September, will be presented . . . The Carmelite . . . To which will be added . . . The Romp . . . [New York, 1796]
broadside 44.5 X 31 cm.
NHi mp. 47861

B9588 [JOHNSON, RICHARD] 1734–1793
The hermit of the forest . . . Philadelphia, Budd & Bartram, 1796.
31 p. incl. covers. illus. 10 cm.
PP mp. 47818

B9589 [JOHNSON, RICHARD] 1734–1793
Rural felicity; or, the history of Tommy and Sally. Embellished with cuts. New-York, J. Oram, 1796.
31 p. illus. 9.5 cm.
Rosenbach–Ch 218
PP. d'Alté A. Welch, Cleveland (1962) mp. 47819

B9590 KENTUCKY ACADEMY
We the subscribers do severally promise to pay . . . the trustees of the Kentucky Academy . . . December, one thousand seven hundred and ninety-six, the sums annexed . . . [Lexington? 1796]
broadside 21 X 23 cm.
PPPrHi mp. 47820

B9591 [LEE, SAMUEL HOLDEN PARSONS] 1772–1863
Lee's genuine Windham bilious . . . pills, prepared by Samuel Lee, jun. of Windham . . . Connecticut . . . obtained a patent April 30, 1796 . . . (n.p., 1796?]
broadside
MWA mp. 47821

B9592 LELAND, JOHN, 1754–1841
An oration delivered to a numerous audience; at the request of the Free and Accepted Masons, in Cheshire, Massachusetts, August 18, 1794. On the day of the incorporation of the Franklin Lodge . . . Hanover, Printed [by Dunham & True] for John Asplund, July, 1796.
30, [3] p. 17.5 cm.
CtHi

B9593 LE SAGE, ALAIN RENÉ, 1668–1747
Le diable boiteux. En français et en anglais . . . Londres, Ches [!] T. Boosey, No. 4, Old Broad-street, Royal Exchange [i.e. New York, Chez J. Rivington; Imprimerie de T. et J. Swords], 1796.
2 v. in 1. 15.5 cm.
Vol. 2 has t.p. in French and English, and imprint: New York, 1796. Rivington or Swords may have bound up remainders of N. Y. 1795 cd., with Londres imprint for vol. 1.—Forrest Bowe
Forrest Bowe, New York City (1967)

B9594 LESLIE, CHARLES, 1650–1722
A short and easy method with the deists . . . Chambersburg, Dover & Harper, 1796.
35 p. 12mo
PPL mp. 47822

B9595 LINLEY, FRANCIS, 1774–1800
Linley's Assistant, for the piano-forte . . . A new edition . . . Baltimore, I. Carr [1796]
4 leaves, 5–32 p. 31.5 cm.
Advertised Sept. 30, 1796 as printed and sold by J. Carr, Baltimore
Minick 291
MdHi mp. 47823

B9596 [A LOOKING glass for children. Fairhaven, J. P. Spooner, ca. 1796]

Advertised in Defoe's *Wonderful life . . . Robinson Crusoe* (Fairhaven, 1796)
McCorison 391A
No copy known mp. 47824

B9597 LOUISIANA
[Tarifa acordada para el comercio de la provincia de la Luisiana . . . Nueva Orleans, 27 de agosto de 1796.]
41 p.
Title from Luis Martino Pérez: *Guide to the materials for American history in Cuban archives* (Washington, 1907), no. 406
McMurtrie: Louisiana 15
Archivo Nacional, Havana mp. 47825

B9598 LOW, NICHOLAS, 1739–1826
New-York, 3d May, 1796. Sir, The state of public affairs being essentially changed . . . the two companies . . . have determined . . . to subscribe policies on the usual terms . . . [New York, 1796]
broadside 23.5 X 18 cm.
Signed (names in ms.) [Nich. Low] President of the United Insurance Company. [Arch: Gracie] . . . [Gulian Verplanck] . . .
New York Public 1175
NN mp. 47826

B9599 LOWER CANADA. EXECUTIVE COUNCIL
[The order of the Governor and Council of Lower Canada, for regulating the trade between that Province and the United States. Fairhaven, J. P. Spooner, 1796]
11 p. 8vo
Advertised in the *Farmer's Library*, Aug. 22, 1796
McCorison 392
No copy known mp. 47827

B9600 LYON, MATTHEW, 1746–1822
[Address, delivered before Aurora Lodge, Hampton, N. Y., June 24th, 1796. Fairhaven? J. P. Spooner? 1796]
16 p.
McCorison 393
VtHi (t.p., p. 7–8 wanting; not located 1961)
mp. 47828

B9601 [MACGOWAN, JOHN]
The life of Joseph, the son of Israel . . . New-York: MDCCXCVI.
160 p. 12.5 cm.
MWA mp. 47829

B9602 MARTIN, FRANÇOIS XAVIER, 1764–1846
[A few cases determined in the Superior Courts of North-Carolina. Newbern, F. X. Martin, 1796]

Advertised in the *North-Carolina Gazette*, Newbern, Oct. 1, 1796, as "This day is published . . . These cases,

twenty-six in number . . . copied from the notes of the most respectable law characters."
Possibly the basis of Evans 32426
McMurtrie: North Carolina 220
No copy known

B9603 MASSACHUSETTS. LAWS
Fee bill. Law of Massachusetts. Published by authority . . . An act, establishing and regulating the fees of the several officers . . . By the Governor approved Feb. 13 . . . [Boston, 1796]
broadside 48.5 X 30 cm.
Found in file of [Boston] *Columbian Centinel*, between issues of Mar. 16 and 19, 1796
MWA mp. 47830

B9604 MEDITATIONS on death and the grave . . . Windham, John Byrne, 1796.
8, 4 p. 18 cm.
"An answer to the Universalists": 4 p. at end
Trumbull: Second supplement 2860
CtHi; NHi; RPB mp. 47831

B9605 MERRICK, JOHN
A friendly retort in behalf of truth; or, an alarm to the Universalists . . . By John Merrick . . . Trenton, Matthias Day, 1796.
79 p. 17 cm.
NHi mp. 47832

B9606 MILLER, FRIEDERICH
Doctor Benjamin Godfrey's Cordial. Dieses ist eine Medicin . . . zu haben bey Friederich Miller, Drogist und Apotheker, in Hägerstaun . . . [Hagerstown, Johann Gruber, 1796]
broadside 27.5 X 19.5 cm.
PPL mp. 47833

B9607 MINERVA
New-Year verses, or circular epistle from the carrier, to the patrons of the *Minerva*. January 1, 1796 . . . [Dedham, Mass., Nathaniel and Benjamin Heaton, 1796]
broadside 32 X 20 cm.
In 2 columns
NHi mp. 47855

B9608 MITCHILL, SAMUEL LATHAM, 1764–1831
Address & c. [New York, 1796]
8 p. 21 cm.
Prospectus of the *Medical Repository*
Signed at end by S. L. Mitchill, Edward Miller, and E. H. Smith, and dated Nov. 15, 1796
Austin 1317
NNNAM mp. 47834

B9609 MOLLER, JOHN CHRISTOPHER, d. 1803
Meddley with the most favorite airs . . . Philadelphia, G. Willig [1796]
2–6 p. 33.5 cm.
Sonneck-Upton p. 257
DLC; NN; PPL; RPJCB mp. 47835

B9610 MOORE, JOHN HAMILTON, d. 1807
The young gentleman and lady's monitor, and English teacher's assistant . . . The tenth edition . . . New-York, Reprinted by Hugh Gaine, 1796.
[4], 368, [32] p. illus. 16.5 cm.
NN mp. 47836

B9611 MOSELEY, BENJAMIN, 1742–1819
A treatise concerning the properties and effects of coffee. First American edition . . . Philadelphia, Samuel H. Smith, 1796.
45 p. 18.5 cm.
DLC; NNNAM; PHi; PPC mp. 47837

B9612 MUCKARSIE, JOHN
The children's catechism . . . Philadelphia: Printed and sold by John M'Culloch, 1796.
24 p. 17.5 cm.
NN

B9613 MULLALLA, JAMES
An essay on the origin of Masonry . . . First American edition. Baltimore, Printed by Christopher Jackson for George Keatinge's bookstore, 1796.
15 p. 15.5 cm.
Minick 307
PPFM mp. 47838

B9614 MUTUAL ASSURANCE SOCIETY AGAINST FIRE
Instructions . . . form of the declaration for assurance . . . The foregoing valuation . . . Given . . . in the year 179 [n.p., 1796]
[2] p. 31.5 X 20 cm.
Established Dec. 26, 1795
DLC (2 copies) mp. 47839

B9615 NEALE, ISAAC
(Circular) Burlington, April 28, 1796 Sir, The subscriber having just published . . . one thousand copies of the Miscellanies of Mrs. Moore . . . Isaac Neale. [Burlington, I. Neale, 1796]
broadside
PHi

B9616 [NETLY Abbey, a Gothic story. Baltimore, 1796]

Advertised in the *Maryland Journal*, Aug. 23, 1796, as "This day is published and for sale, at George Keatinge's . . . book-store . . . Netly abbey . . ."
Minick 308
No copy known mp. 47840

B9617 DER neue Nord-Americanische Stadt und Land Calender, auf das Jahr . . . 1797 . . . Zum erstenmal herausgegeben. Hägerstaun, Johann Gruber [1796]
[28] p. 4to.
Cover-title: Neuer Hägerstauner Calendar
Advertised in the *Westliche Correspondenz*, Sept. 28, 1796
Minick 310
PPL. F. L. Recher, Hagerstown mp. 47841

B9618 THE New-England almanac, and gentlemen and ladies' diary for . . . 1797. By Nathan Daboll. New-London, Samuel Green [1796]
[16] p.
Second edition
Drake 563
NHi

B9619 THE New-England almanack . . . for the year . . . 1797 . . . By Isaac Bickerstaff, Esq; Philom. Providence, Carter and Wilkinson [1796]
[24] p. 18 cm.
Alden 1455; Winship p. 66
DLC; MB; MWA; MiD-B; MiU-C; MoU; NBuHi; NN (imperfect); OCl; RHi; RPB mp. 47731

B9620 THE New-England primer, enlarged and improved . . . Boston: Printed by Thomas Fleet junior. MDCCXCVI.
[64] p.

MWA (lacks last leaf and 4 leaves of sig. A) mp. 47842

B9621 THE New-England primer, enlarged and improved . . . Boston: Printed by Thomas Fleet junior for David West. MDCCXCVI.
[64] p.
MWA (t.p. and 3 leaves of sig. A only) mp. 47843

B9622 THE New-England primer; much improved . . . Germantown, 1796.
[20] p.
Heartman 127
An abridged issue
Hetrich (1922) mp. 47844

B9623 THE new Federal primer, or, An easy and pleasant guide to the art of reading . . . Wilmington: Printed by Brynberg & Andrews, M,DCC,XCVI.
72 p. illus. 10 cm.
NN mp. 47845

B9624 NEW HAMPSHIRE. GOVERNOR, 1794–1805
State of New-Hampshire. To the Selectmen of Greeting. . . . You are hereby required to . . . warn a meeting . . . on the first Monday of November next . . . voting . . . for . . . Jonathan Freeman . . . or Peleg Sprague . . . for . . . Congress . . . Exeter, H. Ranlet [1796]
broadside 34.5 X 22 cm.
Dated Sept. 24, 1796
New York Public 1176
NhD. Lewis M. Stark. Photostat: NN mp. 47846

B9625 NEW HAMPSHIRE. HOUSE OF REPRESENTATIVES
A journal of the proceedings . . . at their session begun . . . December, 1795. Portsmouth, John Melcher, 1796.
152 p. 20 cm.
DLC; MWA; NN mp. 47847

B9626 NEW HAMPSHIRE. LAWS
Laws passed by the Honorable Legislature of . . . Newhampshire, Concord session, 1796. Concord, Moses Davis [1796]
7 p. 23.5 cm.
New York Public 1180
NN mp. 47850

B9627 NEW HAMPSHIRE. SENATE
A journal of the proceedings . . . at a session . . . holden at Concord, December, 1795. Portsmouth, John Melcher, 1796.
72 p. 19.5 cm.
DLC; MWA; NN mp. 47848

B9628 NEW HAMPSHIRE. SENATE
A journal of the proceedings . . . at a session . . . holden at Exeter, June, 1796. Portsmouth, John Melcher, 1796.
57 p. 16.5 cm.
DLC; MWA; NN mp. 47849

B9629 NEW JERSEY. GENERAL ASSEMBLY
Votes and proceedings of the twentieth General Assembly . . . of New-Jersey . . . second sitting. [Feb. 3-Mar. 18, 1796] Trenton, Isaac Collins, 1796.
66 p. 32 cm.
Morsch 318; New York Public 1181
NN; Nj; NjHi mp. 47851

B9630 NEW JERSEY. GENERAL ASSEMBLY
Votes and proceedings of the twenty-first General Assembly of . . . New-Jersey . . . Being the first sitting. Trenton, Matthias Day, 1796.
95 p. 32 cm.
Oct. 25–Nov. 17, 1796
Morsch 319
NN; Nj; NjHi; PPL mp. 47852

B9631 NEW JERSEY. LAWS
State of New-Jersey. A bill, intitled, An act concerning sheriffs. [Trenton? 1796?]
16 p. 32 cm.
Morsch 317
Nj mp. 47853

B9632 NEW JERSEY. LAWS
State of New-Jersey. An act directing the time and mode of electing representatives . . . of the Congress of the United States, for this state . . . Passed at Trenton, November 14, 1796. [Trenton? 1796?]
broadside 46 X 22.5 cm.
NjR (photocopy)

B9633 NEW JERSEY. LEGISLATIVE COUNCIL
Journal of the proceedings of the Legislative-Council . . . Trenton, Matthias Day, 1796.
[2], 69 p. fol.
1st–2nd sittings of the twentieth session
PPL

B9634 NEW JERSEY. MILITIA
Brigade orders. August 1st, 1796. The muster and exercises of the militia of . . . Burlington and Gloucester . . . the first brigade, in the first division of the militia of New-Jersey . . . Joseph Bloomfield, Brigadier general of said brigade. [n.p., 1796]
broadside 34 X 21 cm.
Morsch 315
NjHi mp. 47854

B9635 NEW YORK
City of New-York, ss. Be it remembered, that . . . in the year . . . One Thousand Seven Hundred and Ninety-six . . . [New York, 1796]
broadside 33.5 X 21.5 cm.
DLC mp. 47856

B9636 NEW YORK. ASSEMBLY
Journal of the Assembly of the State of New-York. At their nineteenth session, begun . . . the sixth of January . . . New-York, Printed by John Childs, for the printer to the State, 1796.
193 p., 61. 33 cm.
New York Public 1183
NN (t.p. in photostat) mp. 47862

B9637 NEW YORK. COMMISSIONERS OF THE ALMS-HOUSE
At a meeting of the Commissioners of the Alms-House and Bridewell of the City of New-York, on Monday, the first of February, 1796. To the Mayor, Aldermen . . . John Stagg, Chairman . . . 200 copies thereof be printed in hand-bills . . . February 8, 1796. New-York, George Forman [1796]
broadside 24.5 X 15.5 cm.
NHi (photostat) mp. 47857

B9638 NEW YORK. ELECTION PROX.
To the electors of the Southern District Fellow-citizens, At a very numerous and respectable meeting . . . the 8th day of April . . . agreed, to support the following candidates for Senators . . . Aaron Burr . . . Abel Smith . . . New-York, April 19, 1796 . . . [New York, 1796]
broadside 34 X 20 cm.
N mp. 47863

B9639 NEW YORK. LAWS
An act for the more effectual prevention of crimes. Whereas, the experience . . . Be it enacted by the people . . . of New-York . . . murder in the second degree . . . imprisonment . . . for any time not less than nor more than years . . . [Albany? 1796?]
7 p. 30 cm.
Possibly a preliminary version of the act passed Mar. 26, 1796 ". . . making alterations in the criminal law of this State . . ."
NNS

B9640 NEW YORK. LAWS
The following is a copy of an act of Assembly of our neighbours of Newyork; in consequence of which no intruders attempt to settle on their lands . . . An act to prevent intrusions . . . under pretence of title from . . . Connecticut. Passed 11th March, 1796 . . . [n.p., 1796?]
broadside 34 X 20.5 cm.
MWA mp. 47864

B9641 NEW YORK. LAWS
New-York. An act to prevent intrusions on lands . . . under pretence of title from . . . Connecticut, passed 11th March, 1796 . . . [n.p., 1796?]
broadside 21 X 17 cm.
CtHi

B9642 NEW YORK. SECRETARY OF STATE
A general account of the number of electors in the State of New-York, made from the returns delivered into the Secretary's Office . . . [Albany? 1796]
[4] p. 34 cm.
Dated Jan. 20, 1796
NHi mp. 47865

B9643 NEWPORT, Aug. 3, 1796. Francis Malbone, Esq; one of our Representatives . . ., having declined . . . Mr. Christopher Grant Champlin . . . is proposed as a candidate for that office . . . [Newport, 1796]
broadside 33.5 X 21 cm.
Alden 1476
RNHi. Photostat: MWA mp. 47867

B9644 NEWTON, JOHN
A letter, on the doctrines of election and final perseverance . . . Martinsburg, N. Willis [1796?]
8 p. 19 cm.
Norona 599
Boyd B. Stutler, Charleston, W. Va. (1958) mp. 47868

B9645 THE North-Carolina almanack, for the year . . . 1797 . . . Calculated for the meridian of Raleigh . . . Newbern, Francois X. Martin [1796]
[36] p. 16.5 cm.
McMurtrie: North Carolina 225
NcU mp. 47869

B9646 NORWICH, CONN.
To Mr. Benjamin Tracy. By virtue of a special statute . . . respecting the support of schools, you are . . . directed to warn all the inhabitants within the limits of the first society in Norwich, legal voters . . . for school purposes, to meet . . . the 31st instant . . . Norwich the 24th of Oct. 1796. Andrew Huntington, Justice of Peace . . . The above is a true copy of the original warrant. Test. *Benj*[n] *Tracy*
broadside 13.5 X 21 cm.
CtHi mp. 47870

B9647 NORWICH LIBRARY COMPANY
A catalogue of books belonging to Norwich Library Company . . . Norwich, J. Trumbull [1796?]
12 p. 18.5 cm.
CtHi

B9648 NOTICE. The citizens of New-York, who are determined to support the Constitution . . . New-York, April 21, 1796. [New York, 1796]
broadside 26 X 20.5 cm.
Meeting to be held April 22, 1796
NHi mp. 47871

B9649 NURSE Truelove's New-Year's gift: or, The book of books for children. Boston, Printed and sold by Samuel Hall [1796?]
58, [5] p. incl. covers. 11 cm.
Dated by d'Alté A. Welch
MWA (t.p. and [5] p. at end wanting); NN (imperfect). d'Alté A. Welch, Cleveland (lower 2/3 of t.p. and p. [63] wanting) mp. 47872

B9650 [PAISIELLO, GIOVANNI] 1773–1836
How can I forget . . . New York & Philadelphia, B. Carr [1796]
[2] p. 30.5 cm.
Sonneck-Upton p. 191
DLC; MWA mp. 47873

B9651 THE parent's best gift: containing the church catechism . . . New-York, J. Harrisson, 1796.
23 p. 12 cm.
MWA mp. 47874

B9652 PEIRCE, LEVI
Levi Peirce, No. 20, Cornhill, Boston, imports and has for sale, a general assortment of European goods, on the lowest terms for cash. [Boston] Young and Minns, Printers [1796?]
broadside 9 X 15.5 cm.
Receipted bill on verso dated Oct. 13, '96
MSaE mp. 47875

B9653 PENNSYLVANIA. LAWS
An act for the government and regulation of seamen . . . In pursuance of an act of the Congress of the United States . . . Philadelphia, William Young [1796]
broadside 34.5 X 29.5 cm.
PHi mp. 47876

B9654 [THE Pennsylvania, Maryland and Virginia almanack, for the year 1797. Frederick-Town, M. Bartgis, 1796]

Advertised in *Bartgis's Federal Gazette*, Dec. 22, 1796, as "Just published and to be sold by M. Bartgis . . . English and German almanacs, for the year 1797."
Minick 315
No copy known mp. 47877

B9655 PENNSYLVANISCHER Kalender, auf das 1797ste Jahr Christi . . . York: Gedruckt und zu haben bey Salomon Mäyer [1796]
[44] p.
Drake 10439
MWA; PHi mp. 47878

B9656 [PERKINS, ELISHA] 1741–1799
Certificates of the efficacy of Doctor Perkins's patent metallic instruments. New-London, From S. Green's Press [1796]
16 p. 22 cm.
Dated: Plainfield, August 12, 1796
DNLM; MBCo; MH; MWA; NNNAM; RPJCB mp. 47879

B9657 PERKINS, ELISHA, 1741–1799
To all people to whom these presents shall come, greeting; whereas, I, Elisha Perkins . . . obtained a patent . . . [Philadelphia? 1796?]
broadside 31 X 17 cm.
License form granting the right to use Perkins' metallic tractors, including a copy of letters patent dated Feb. 19, 1796
Austin 1498
CtHi; MBCo; MSaE; NNNAM; PPL. Photocopy; DNLM mp. 47880

B9658 PHILADELPHIA. POST OFFICE
Post-office, Philadelphia, 19th. September, 1796. Establishment of the mails . . . Robert Patton, Post-master. [Philadelphia, F. Childs, 1796]
broadside 47.5 X 27 cm.
DLC mp. 47881

B9659 PHILADELPHIA. SHERIFF
Philadelphia, June 27, 1796. By virtue of a writ of plurios venditioni exponas, to me directed, will be exposed at public sale . . . all those three lots of ground . . . John Baker, Sheriff. [Philadelphia, 1796]
broadside
In English and German
PPL mp. 47882

B9660 PICTURES of seventy-two beasts & birds . . . Boston, Printed and sold by Samuel Hall, 1796.
118 p. incl. front. 11cm.
MWA. d'Alté A. Welch (1960) (p. 115–118 wanting) mp. 47884

B9661 THE power of grace illustrated, in six letters . . . Philadelphia, Printed by Neale & Kammerer, Jun., 1796.
142 p. 17 cm.
The letters are signed: Christodulus [i.e. Van Lier]
MWA; NjP mp. 48000

B9662 THE power of grace illustrated, in six letters . . . Philadelphia, Printed by Neale & Kammerer, Jun. for Thomas Condie, 1796.
142 p. 17 cm.
The letters are signed: Christodulus [i.e. Van Lier]
MWA mp. 48001

B9663 THE power of grace illustrated, in six letters . . . Philadelphia, Printed for James J. Denoon, 1796.
142 p. 17 cm.
The letters are signed: Christodulus [i.e. Van Lier]
cf. Evans 30194, with publisher's name
PPL mp. 47999

B9664 PRESIDENT II. Being observations on the late official address of George Washington . . . Philadelphia printed; Baltimore reprinted [by Clayland & Dobbin?] 1796.
16 p. 16 cm.
Advocating Jefferson for President
Minick 317; Sabin 101873
WHi. Photostat: MdBE mp. 47885

B9665 PROPOSAL for printing by subscription, The doctrine of eternal punishment, stated and proved . . . By Nathan Strong . . . Hartford, Sept. 5, 1796. [Hartford, 1796]
broadside 40 X 17.5 cm.
NHi mp. 47809

B9666 PROPOSALS for establishing an association for working mines . . . Philadelphia, Samuel H. Smith, 1796.
22 p. 21 cm.
DLC mp. 47886

B9667 PROPOSALS for publishing a periodical work . . . entitled *The American Library or Universal Magazine* . . . By a Society of Literary Gentlemen . . . Subscriptions received by William Y. Birch . . . by Richard Lee . . . likewise by John Low . . . New-York. [Philadelphia, 1796]
broadside 26.5 X 20.5 cm.
Dated by NHi
NHi mp. 47887

B9668 PROVIDENCE. THEATRE
By desire of the . . . Society of Free and Accepted Masons. Theatre, Providence. This evening, June 24, 1796, will be presented . . . The Benevolent Hebrew . . . [Providence] B. Wheeler [1796]
broadside 28 X 23 cm.
Alden 1480
RHi mp. 47888

B9669 RATE of dockage of vessels and wharfage of goods, on and after January 1, 1796. Dockage . . . Wharfage . . . Storage . . . [Boston] Young & Minns, printers. [1796?]
broadside 29 X 22.5 cm.
NjR

B9670 REID, JOHN
The American atlas: containing the following maps . . . New York: Published by John Reid [1796?]
[2] p., 20 maps. fol.
cf. Sabin 104830n
NN; PPL

B9671 RELIEF FIRE SOCIETY, BOSTON
The rules and articles of the new Relief Fire Society . . . Boston, John W. Folsom, 1796.
23 p. 15 cm.
Huntington 690
CSmH mp. 47735

B9672 RELLY, JAMES, 1722?–1778
[Christian hymns, poems, and spiritual songs . . . Fairhaven, Judah P. Spooner, 1796]
40, 47 p. 16.5 cm.
McCorison 397A
MWA (t.p. lacking) mp. 47889

B9673 REMARKS on the Bill of rights . . . 3d art. of the Bill of rights of Virginia—[n.p.] 1796.
35 p. 17 cm.
Signed: A Virginian born and bred
Sabin 100519; cf. Evans 30549
DLC mp. 47801

B9674 REPUBLICAN prayers. Precepts of reason. Maxims. National festivals, and Principles of morality. New York, Printed from the Paris edition, 1796.
[24] p. 16.5 cm. [A]-B^6

Translations from various republican sources
Forrest Bowe, NYC (1967) mp. 47892

B9675 REVEALED mistery of Nature . . . how to beget children of the sex desired . . . New-York, August 22, 1796. [New York, 1796]
4 p. folder (first page printed)
On p. [3] ms. signature: *Charles Smith*, explaining that he is to print the work if there are enough subscribers
PHi

B9676 RHODE ISLAND. ELECTION PROX.
James Burrill, jun. Esq. 1st Representative to the 5th Congress . . . [Providence? 1796]
broadside 4.5 X 12 cm.
Alden 1486; Chapin Proxies 62
RHi mp. 47893

B9677 RHODE ISLAND. ELECTION PROX.
Peleg Arnold, Esq; 1st Representative to the 5th Congress . . . [Providence? 1796]
broadside 4 X 11.5 cm.
Alden 1487; Chapin Proxies 64
RHi mp. 47894

B9678 RHODE ISLAND. ELECTION PROX.
Representatives in Congress. Benjamin Bourn, First Representative. Christopher Grant Champlin, Second Representative. [Providence? 1796]
broadside 7 X 15 cm.
Alden 1488; Chapin Proxies 61
RHi (2 variants) mp. 47895

B9679 RHODE ISLAND. ELECTION PROX.
1796. His Excellency Arthur Fenner, Esq; Governor. The honorable Samuel J. Potter, Esq; Deputy-governor . . . [Providence] Carter and Wilkinson [1796]
broadside 23 X 14 cm.
Alden 1489
MWA (not traced 1965); RHi mp. 47896

B9680 RHODE ISLAND. ELECTION PROX.
Thomas Tillinghast, Esq. of East-Greenwich, 1st Representatives to the 5th Congress . . . [Providence? 1796]
broadside 5.5 X 11.5 cm.
Alden 1490; Chapin Proxies 63
RHi mp. 47897

B9681 RHODE ISLAND. GOVERNOR, 1790–1805
By His Excellency Arthur Fenner . . . A proclamation . . . [Nov. 7, 1796] . . . Warren, Nathaniel Phillips [1796]
broadside 40 X 32 cm.
Bill submitted Nov. 24, 1796
Alden 1492
RHi (mutilated) mp. 47898

B9682 RHODE ISLAND. LAWS
[State of Rhode-Island, &c. In General assembly. October session, A.D. 1796. An act directing the mode of choosing a Representative to Congress in the room of Benjamin Bourn . . . Providence, Carter and Wilkinson, 1796]
[broadside]
Bill submitted by Carter and Wilkinson Nov. 5, 1796
Alden 1500; Winship p. 66
Maximillian Zigler (N.Y.C.) mp. 47899

B9683 RICE, H. & P., booksellers, Philadelphia
Henry & Patrick Rice's Catalogue of a large and valuable collection of books . . . for 1796 . . . Philadelphia, Printed for H. & P. Rice [1796]
82 p. 12mo
Brigham: Booksellers, p. 58
MWA (p. 81–82 mutilated) mp. 47900

B9684 RICHARDSON, SAMUEL, 1689–1761
The history of Pamela . . . Lansingburgh, Printed and sold by Luther Pratt, 1796.
146 p. 13 cm.
MWA mp. 47901

B9685 RICHARDSON, SAMUEL, 1689–1761
The history of Pamela . . . New York, Printed and sold, by Tiebout & O'Brien, 1796.

H. J. Snyder, New York City (1935) mp. 47902

B9686 RICHARDSON, SAMUEL, 1689–1761
The history of Sir Charles Grandison . . . Boston, Printed for John West, 1796.
176 p. 14.5 cm.
MWA; MHi mp. 47903

B9687 RISE Columbia! An occasional song written by Mr. Thomas Paine of Boston. The air . . . adapted from . . . Rule Britannia. [Boston? ca. 1796]
18–19 p. 30.5 cm. caption title
Appears to be a separate issue from *The musical repertory* (Boston, 1796)
Sonneck-Upton p. 354
MiU-C

B9688 ROGERS, JAMES
An address delivered at the instalment of the Rev. John Hemphill, as pastor of Hopewell . . . September 19, 1796 . . . Charleston: Printed by J. M'Iver, MDCCXCVI.
16 p. 21.5 cm.
NcMHi

B9689 ROGERS, JAMES
A vindication of some important truths . . . the difference between the Associate Reformed Presbytery, and the Synod of the Carolinas and Georgia . . . By the Rev. James Rogers . . . Charleston: Printed by J. M'Iver, MDCCXCVI.
40 p. 31.5 cm.
NcMHi

B9690 [ROUGET DE L'ISLE, CLAUDE JOSEPH] 1760–1836
The Marseilles hymn in French and English. New York, G. Gilfert [1796]
3 p. 32.5 cm.
Sonneck-Upton p. 252
DLC mp. 47904

B9691 SALEM, April 22, 1796. To the selectmen of the town of . . . In behalf of the inhabitants of Salem, we are induced to address you upon the present alarming crisis. [Salem, 1796]
broadside 38.5 X 23.5 cm.
Concerns the treaty with Great Britain
Ford 2798
MSaE mp. 47905

B9692 SALENKA, GABRIEL
Gabriel Salenka, lately arrived from Europe . . . brought with him a dog . . . who performs the most surprizing feats of sagacity . . . [Philadelphia] W. W. Woodward [1796]
broadside 39 X 22.5 cm.
Found in file of *Claypoole's American Daily Advertiser* after issue of Jan. 27, 1796
MWA mp. 47906

B9693 SCHUYLER, PHILIP JOHN, 1733–1804
Friends and fellow-citizens! Your attention is called to a subject involving your interest, your happiness, and your peace . . . [Albany, 1796]
broadside
Signed and dated: By order, Ph: Schuyler, chairman. Albany, April 23, 1796
New York Public 1184.
NN (reduced (?) facsim.) mp. 47907

B9694 SCOTT, JOSEPH
An atlas of the United States . . . Philadelphia, Francis and Robert Bailey; B. Davis; and H. and P. Rice, 1796.
cover title, 19 maps. 16.5 cm.
DLC mp. 47908

B9695 SCOTT, WILLIAM, 1750–1804
Lessons in elocution; or, A selection of pieces in prose and verse, for . . . reading and speaking . . . The fourth American edition . . . New-York, George Forman, 1796.
400 p. 18.5 cm.
MWA mp. 47909

B9696 SCOTT, WILLIAM, 1750–1804
Lessons in elocution: or a selection of pieces, in prose and verse, for . . . reading and speaking . . . The sixth American, from the fifth British edition . . . Philadelphia, William Young, 1796.
viii, [13]-436. 17 cm.
MWA; PPL mp. 47910

B9697 A SERIES of letters on courtship and marriage . . . Elizabeth-Town, Shepard Kollock, 1796.
152 p. 14.5 cm.
MWA; NjP mp. 47911

B9698 A SERIES of letters on courtship and marriage . . . Elizabeth-Town, Printed by Shepard Kollock, for Cornelius Davis, 1796.
152 p. 14 cm.
MWA mp. 47912

B9699 SEVEN SAGES
Roman histories; or, The history of the Seven Wise Masters of Rome . . . The fiftieth edition. [Wilmington?] Printed for, and sold by James Wilson, Book binder, Wilmington, 1796.
103 p. 13 cm.
DeHi mp. 47913

B9700 SEVEN SAGES
Roman stories: or, The history of the Seven Wise Masters of Rome . . . Fiftieth edition. Wilmington, Peter Brynberg, 1796.
103 p.
Ludwig Ries, Forest Hills, N.Y. (1966)

B9701 SHERIDAN, THOMAS, 1719–1788
A complete dictionary of the English language . . . The sixth edition. Philadelphia, Printed for W. Young, Mills & Son, 1796.
104, [887] p. 18 cm.
Printed one column to the page
cf. Evans 31185
MB; MWA; PPL mp. 47914

B9702 SHIELD, WILLIAM, 1748–1829
Old Towler, a favorite hunting song . . . New York, G. Gilfert [1796]
[2] p. 31.5 cm.
Sonneck-Upton p. 314
DLC; NN mp. 47915

B9703 SLATER AND LORD, firm
Public auction. On Tuesday next, the 16th instant, will be sold, at the vendue-house, at XI o'clock . . . Nassau, February 13, 1796 . . . [New York? 1796]
broadside 35 × 31.5 cm.
NHi mp. 47916

B9704 SMALL, ABRAHAM
Sir, We have taken the liberty to leave for your perusal our proposals for proposals for printing . . . an edition of the Holy Scriptures . . . Abraham Small, John Thompson. Philadelphia, June, 1796. [Philadelphia, 1796]
broadside 27.5 × 22.5 cm.
NHi mp. 47917

B9705 SMALL, ABRAHAM
Superb family Bible. Proposals for printing and publishing . . . folio edition of the Sacred Scriptures . . . Philadelphia, June, 1796. Conditions of publication . . . Subscriptions received by Abm. Small . . . and by John Thompson, at his Printing-Office in Carter's Alley, Philadelphia. [Philadelphia, 1796]
broadsheet ([2] p.) 41.5 × 25 cm.
NHi mp. 47918

B9706 SMALL, JACOB
[The prices of carpenters' work, stipulated by the Carpenters' association, as a standard for Baltimore town. Baltimore, 1796?]

Copyrighted Dec. 16, 1795 (*Federal Gazette*, Jan. 6, 1796)
Minick 319
No copy known mp. 47919

B9707 SO dearly I love Johnny O . . . New York, G. Gilfert [1796]
[2] p. 32.5 cm.
Sonneck-Upton p. 388
DLC; RPJCB mp. 47920

B9708 SOCIETY FOR THE INSTITUTION AND SUPPORT OF FIRST DAY OR SUNDAY SCHOOLS
Sunday schools. Whereas the good education of youth is of the utmost importance . . . Constitution. [Philadelphia, 1796]
broadside
PPL mp. 47921

B9709 SOUTH CAROLINA. SURVEYOR-GENERAL'S OFFICE
Account of plats, for lands granted before the late war . . . now in the Surveyor-general's Office, but . . . never recorded. Columbia, Young & Faust, June, 1796.
96 p. 19.5 cm.
ScU

B9710 [SPOONER'S almanac and Vermont register for 1797. Fairhaven, J. P. Spooner, 1796]

Advertised in the *Farmer's Library*, Dec. 14, 1796
McCorison 372
No copy known mp. 47922

B9711 [SPOONER'S sheet almanac and register, for the year 1797. Fairhaven, J. P. Spooner, 1796]

Announced in the *Farmer's Library*, Dec. 14, 1796, as "ready for sale at this office, next week."
McCorison 373
No copy known mp. 47923

B9712 STANFORD, JOHN, 1754–1834
Collection of tracts . . . New-York, T. and J. Swords, 1796.
1 v. 17 cm.
Contents: Evans 23789; 23768; 24811; 25201; 27734; and 48406
NNS

B9713 [STERNE, LAURENCE] 1713–1768
A sentimental journey through France and Italy. By Mr. Yorick. New-York, Printed for John Reid, 1796.
316 p. front. 17 cm.
Consists of the same sheets, except t.p. and plates, as the New York, 1795 edition (Evans 29565)
New York Public 1185; Sabin 91351
MWA; NN mp. 47924

B9714 STORACE, STEPHEN, 1763–1796
The jealous Don. A comie [!] duet in the opera of *The Pirates*. Composed by Sr. Storace. [Boston, 1796–97]
p. 41–43. 30.5 cm. caption title
Appears to be a separate issue from *The musical repertory* (Boston, 1796)
Sonneck-Upton p. 215
MiU-C

B9715 SWEETING, WHITING, d. 1791
A remarkable narrative of Whiting Sweeting; who was executed at Albany . . .for murder . . . The fourth edition. Dover, Samuel Bragg, 1796.
70 p. 16.5 cm.
PHi mp. 47926

B9716 SWIFT, JONATHAN, 1667–1745
The adventures of Capt. Gulliver, in a voyage to . . . Lilliput . . . Fairhaven [J. P. Spooner, 1796?]
47 p. 12.5 cm.
Rosenbach-Ch 221
PP mp. 47927

B9717 TAYLOR, AMOS
Inestimable lines of poetry . . . occasioned by the oppression of a cruel brother in law . . . [Keene, N.H., 1796]
broadside
MWA (photostat) mp. 47928

B9718 TAYLOR, RAYNOR, 1747–1825
Independent and free . . . [Philadelphia] Carr [1796]
broadside 32.5 cm.
Sonneck-Upton p. 207
DLC; NRU-Mus mp. 47929

B9719 TENNESSEE. CONSTITUTION
The constitution of the State of Tennessee . . . [Knoxville? 1796]
[3]-17 p. 23 cm. caption title $[A]-B^4$
McMurtrie: Tennessee 13
CSmH; NHi mp. 47930

B9720 TENNESSEE. GOVERNOR, 1796–1801
State of Tennessee John Sevier, Governor . . . a proclamation . . . Knoxville, this 10th day of August, 1796. John Sevier. By the Governor, Wm. Maclin, Sec'y. [Knoxville, George Roulstone, 1796]
broadside
McMurtrie: Tennessee 22
T mp. 47931

B9721 TENNESSEE. HOUSE OF REPRESENTATIVES
[Journal of the House of Representatives of the State of Tennessee, begun . . . Knoxville . . . [July 30, 1796] Knoxville, George Roulstone, 1796]
Title from Nashville 1852 reprint
McMurtrie: Tennessee 20
No copy known mp. 47932

B9722 TENNESSEE. LAWS
Acts passed at the second session of the first General Assembly of . . . Tennessee, begun . . . Knoxville . . . [July 30, 1796] Knoxville, George Roulstone, 1796.
13 p. 20 cm.
McMurtrie: Tennessee 21
MH-L mp. 47935

B9723 TENNESSEE. SENATE
[Journal of the Senate of the State of Tennessee, begun . . . Knoxville . . . [Mar. 28, 1796] Knoxville, George Roulstone, 1796]

Title from Nashville 1852 reprint
On April 23rd it was "Resolved, that George Roulstone . . . print five hundred copies of the acts, and one hundred copies of the journals. . ."
McMurtrie: Tennessee 15
No copy known mp. 47933

B9724 TENNESSEE. SENATE
[Journal of the Senate of the State of Tennessee, begun . . . Knoxville . . . [July 30, 1796] Knoxville, George Roulstone, 1796]

Title from Nashville reprint of 1852
McMurtrie: Tennessee 19
No copy known mp. 47934

B9725 THANKSGIVING poem . . . Newtown, October 28th. 1796. [n.p., 1796]
broadside 34 X 20 cm.
NHi

B9725a THOMAS, ANDREWS & PENNIMAN
Thomas, Andrews & Penniman List of books for exchange. [65 titles in 2 columns] [Albany, Thomas, Andrews & Penniman, 1796]
4-page folder printed on p. [3] 22 X 17 cm.
Ms. note on p. [1]: To Mathew Carey from Thomas, Andrews & Penniman, Albany, September 25, 1796 . . .
Information from Chester Hollenbeck
PHi

B9726 THOMPSON, ANDREW
Andrew Thompson born February 2, 1770 . . . Andrew Thompson, jun. born July 23, 1794 . . . The property of Andrew Thompson. Providence, March 20, 1796. [Providence, J. Carter? 1796]
broadside 30 X 24 cm.
Alden 1505
RPB mp. 47936

B9727 TO the citizens of Philadelphia. Fellow-citizens, It is at all times the duty of a people who wish to preserve their freedom . . . A Mechanick. October 11th, 1796. [Philadelphia, 1796]
broadside 37 X 26 cm.
MWA mp. 47937

B9728 TO the freeholders of Prince William, Stafford, and Fairfax. Fellow-citizens . . . [Fredericksburg? 1796]
[4] p. 31.5 cm.
A presidential campaign document
DLC (imperfect) (Jefferson Papers, v. 7, p. 1178)
mp. 47938

B9729 TO the memory of the late Dr. Rittenhouse, this

poetical effusion of his sincere admirer is inscribed, by the author. [Philadelphia] Ormrod & Conrad [1796]
4 p. 8vo caption title
PPL mp. 47939

B9730 TOM Thumb's folio or a new penny plaything for little giants . . . New-York: Printed by J. Oram, for the Society of Bookbinder's 1796.
30 p. illus. 10 cm.
NB mp. 47940

B9731 TOWNSEND, ROBERT
For sale, the following houses and tracts of land, latebly belonging to Samuel Townsend, of Oyster Bay, deceased . . . Robert Townsend. [New York, 1796]
broadside 31.5 X 25.5 cm.
Dated: Oyster-Bay, February 1, 1796
NHi mp. 47941

B9732 TRUTH exploded; or, The art of lying and swearing, made easy . . . Hartford, 1796.
16 p.
Trumbull: Supplement 2694
CtHi mp. 47942

B9733 TWO unfortunate concubines: or the history of Fair Rosamond . . . Boston, J. White, 1796.
56+ p. 17.5 cm. A-D^6 E^6?
MWA (all wanting after p. 56) mp. 47943

B9734 THE unfortunate concubines; or, The history of Fair Rosamond . . . and Jane Shore . . . Wilmington, Printed and sold by Peter Brynberg, 1796.
140 p. 13.5 cm.
MWA mp. 47944

B9735 UNION COLLEGE, SCHENECTADY, N.Y.
Laws & regulations for the government of Union-College . . . Schenectady, Cornelius P. Wyckoff, 1796.
20 p. 17.5 cm.
Huntington 699
CSmH; NSchU mp. 47945

B9736 UNITED INSURANCE COMPANY
We the subscribers hereby agree each with the others, to form an insurance company, the stile and title of which shall be The United Insurance Company . . . [New York, 1796]
broadside 37.5 X 32 cm.
Dated February 1, 1796
NHi mp. 47946

B9737 U.S.
Duties payable on goods, wares, and merchandize, imported into the United States . . . after the last day of March, 1796 . . . With extracts from the revenue acts, and sundry forms . . . New-York: Printed for T. Allen, 1796.
32 p. 20 cm.
cf. Evans 27936–37
NHi mp. 47770

B9738 U.S. ARMY. CONTINENTAL ARMY
Official letters to the honorable American Congress, written during the war . . . by . . . George Washington, commander-in-chief of the continental forces . . . Vol. II. New-York, Printed and sold by James Rivington and Samuel Campbell, 1796.
[2], 311 p. 20 cm.
MWA mp. 48017

B9739 U.S. CONGRESS. HOUSE
Alexander White, one of the commissioners appointed by the President . . . respectfully states to the committee, to whom the memorial of the said commissioners, and the President's message [Evans 31406] . . . were referred . . . [Philadelphia, 1796?]
3 p. 34 cm. caption title
Dated 21st January 1796; but cf. Greely p. 241
MiU-C. Pierce W. Gaines, Fairfield, Conn. (1964)

B9740 U.S. CONGRESS. HOUSE
Reports of committees, on the petition of sundry refugees . . . [Feb. 17, 1796] . . . Published by order of the House. [Philadelphia, 1796]
8 p.
MWA mp. 47952

B9741 U.S. CONGRESS. HOUSE. COMMITTEE ON CLAIMS
Report of the Committee of Claims, on the petition of Henry Hill. 26th May, 1796. Committed to a committee of the whole House, tomorrow . . . [Philadelphia, 1796]
3 [i.e. 4] p. 20.5 cm.
New York Public 1186; cf. Evans 32990
MWA; NN. Photostat: DLC mp. 47950

B9742 U.S. CONGRESS. HOUSE. COMMITTEE ON CLAIMS
Report of the Committee of claims, on the petition of John Gibbons. 29th April 1796, committed to a committee of the whole House, on Monday next . . . [n.p., 1796?]
9 p. 31.5 cm.
MiU-C mp. 47951

B9743 U.S. CONGRESS. SENATE
In Senate of the United States, May 5, 1796. The following message and papers from the President . . . were read . . . [Philadelphia, 1796]
8 p. 8vo
Concerns an explanatory article proposed to be added to the treaty of amity with Great Britain
Pierce W. Gaines, Fairfield, Conn. (1964) mp. 47953

B9744 U.S. DEPT. OF STATE
Department of State, April 16, 1796. The Secretary of State requests the ____________ to permit any person interested, and inquiring for the statement below, to see the same. A statement of the claims of citizens of the United States . . . settled with the French Government, by Fulwar Skipwith . . . [Washington? 1796]
13 p. 35 cm.
NHi mp. 47954

B9745 U.S. LAWS
An act for establishing trading houses with the Indian tribes . . . 1796, February the 1st, read the third time . . . [Philadelphia, F. Childs, 1796]
4 p. 34.5 cm. caption title
DLC mp. 47948

B9746 U.S. LAWS
An act for the government and regulation of seamen in the merchants service . . . New-London, (Beach-Street) Printed and sold by James Springer [1796?]
broadside ([2] p.) 41 X 35 cm.
On verso: Seamen's articles, dated 1797
Springer was at Beach Street from 1796
CtHi mp. 47961

B9747 U.S. LAWS
An act for the relief of persons imprisoned for debt. Sec. 1. Be it enacted by the Senate and . . . Approved—

May the twenty-eighth 1796 . . . [Philadelphia, F. Childs, 1796]
broadside 35 X 20.5 cm.
DLC mp. 47965

B9748 U. S. LAWS
An act for the relief of Israel Loring . . . Approved–March the tenth 1796 . . . [Philadelphia, F. Childs, 1796]
broadside 34.5 X 20 cm.
DLC mp. 47964

B9749 U.S. LAWS
An act laying duties on carriages for the conveyance of persons, and repealing the former act for that purpose . . . Passed the House of Representatives, May 9, 1796 . . . [Colophon] [Philadelphia] John Fenno [1796]
8 p. caption title
RPJCB mp. 47949

B9750 U.S. LAWS
An act passed at the first session of the fourth Congress . . . begun . . . Monday, the seventh of December, 1795 . . . Detroit, John M'Call, 1796.
1 p.l., 16 p. 19 cm.
Regulating trade with Indian tribes. Approved May 17, 1796
McMurtrie: Michigan 1
MiD-B. Facsims.: CSmH; DLC; MWA mp. 47972

B9751 U.S. LAWS
Extract from an act, for the relief and protection of American seamen. Section 5. . . . Section 6. . . . [n.p., 1796]
broadside 20 X 11 cm.
Act passed May 28, 1796
MWA mp. 47979

B9752 U.S. LAWS
Fourth Congress of the United States: At the first session . . . An act authorising and directing the Secretary at war to place certain persons . . . on the pension list . . . [Philadelphia, F. Childs, 1796]
5 p. 34 cm. caption title
Approved Apr. 20, 1796
PPRF mp. 47955

B9753 U.S. LAWS
Fourth Congress of the United States: At the first session . . . An act authorizing the erection of a light-house on Baker's island . . . [Philadelphia, 1796?]
broadside 34 X 20.5 cm.
MiU-C; PPRF; RPJCB mp. 47956

B9754 U.S. LAWS
Fourth Congress of the United States: At the first session . . . An act authorizing the erection of a light-house on Cape Cod . . . [n.p., 1796?]
2 p. 32 cm.
MiU-C; PPRF; RPJCB mp. 47957

B9755 U.S. LAWS
Fourth Congress of the United States: At the first session . . . An act for allowing compensation to the members of the Senate, and House of Representatives . . . Approved, March the tenth 1796. Go. Washington, President . . . [Philadelphia, 1796]
broadsheet 34 X 20.5 cm.
DLC mp. 47958

B9756 U.S. LAWS
Fourth Congress of the United States: At the first session . . . An act for establishing trading houses with the Indian tribes . . . [Apr. 18, 1796] . . . [Philadelphia, 1796]
3 p. 33.5 cm.
Without statement of deposition
Huntington 701
CSmH; PPRF; RPJCB mp. 47959

B9757 U.S. LAWS
Fourth Congress of the United States: At the first session . . . An act for laying duties on carriages for the conveyance of persons . . . Approved–May the twenty-eighth, 1796 . . . [Philadelphia, F. Childs, 1796]
4 p. 34 cm.
cf. Evans 31335 (8 p.)
Pierce W. Gaines, Fairfield, Conn. (1964) mp. 47960

B9758 U.S. LAWS
Fourth Congress of the United States: At the first session . . . An act for the relief of Benjamin Strother . . . [Philadelphia, F. Childs, 1796]
broadside 34 X 20 cm.
Approved Feb. 26, 1796
PPRF mp. 47962

B9759 U.S. LAWS
Fourth Congress of the United States: At the first session . . . An act for the relief of certain officers and soldiers . . . Approved–March the twenty-third 1796 . . . [Philadelphia, F. Childs, 1796]
2 p. 26 X 20.5 cm.
DLC; MiU-C; PPRF; RPJCB; WHi mp. 47963

B9760 U.S. LAWS
Fourth Congress of the United States: At the first session . . . An act further extending the time for receiving on loan the domestic debt . . . [Feb. 19, 1796] . . . [Philadelphia, F. Childs, 1796]
broadside 34 X 20 cm.
PPRF mp. 47966

B9761 U.S. LAWS
Fourth Congress of the United States: at the first session . . . An act in addition to . . . "An act making futher provision for the . . . redemption of the public debt." . . . [Apr. 28, 1796] . . . [Philadelphia, F. Childs, 1796]
2 p. 34 cm.
MiU-C; PPRF; RPJCB mp. 47967

B9762 U.S. LAWS
Fourth Congress of the United States: At the first session . . . An act in addition to . . . "An act making further provision for the support of public credit, and for the redemption of the public debt." Approved–April the twenty-eighth, 1796 . . . Deposited among the rolls, in the office of the Department of State . . . [Philadelphia, 1796]
2 p. 32.5 cm.
New York Public 1187
NN

B9763 U.S. LAWS
Fourth Congress of the United States: At the first session . . . An act making an appropriation towards defraying . . . Approved–May the sixth 1796 . . . [Philadelphia, 1796]
4 p. 34 cm.
CSmH; DLC (2 p.); PPRF mp. 47969

B9764 U.S. LAWS
Fourth Congress of the United States: At the first session . . . An act making appropriations . . . Approved–February the fifth, 1796 . . . [Philadelphia, F. Childs, 1796]

4 p. 34.5 cm. caption title
DLC; PPRF mp. 47968

B9765 U.S. LAWS
Fourth Congress of the United States: At the first session . . . An act making certain provisions in regard to the Circuit court for the district of North-Carolina . . . [Philadelphia, Francis Childs, 1796]
2 p. 34 X 20 cm.
Approved: 31 March 1796
MiU-C; PPRF; RPJCB mp. 47970

B9766 U.S. LAWS
Fourth Congress of the United States: At the first session . . . An act making further provision for the expenses attending the intercourse of the United States with foreign nations . . . Approved–May the thirtieth 1796 . . . [Philadelphia, 1796]
2 p. 32 cm. caption title
MiU-C; PPRF; RPJCB mp. 47971

B9767 U.S. LAWS
Fourth Congress of the United States: At the first session . . . An act providing for the sale of the lands . . . north-west of the river Ohio . . . [Philadelphia, Francis Childs, 1796]
4 p. 34.5 cm. caption title
Approved: 18 May 1796
MiU-C; PPRF; RPJCB mp. 47973

B9768 U.S. LAWS
Fourth Congress of the United States: At the first session . . . An act providing for the sale of lands . . . north-west of the river Ohio . . . [Philadelphia, Francis Childs, 1796]
4 p. 34.5 cm. caption title
Approved: 18 May 1796
Without notice of deposition among the rolls
PPRF

B9769 U.S. LAWS
Fourth Congress of the United States: At the first session . . . An act regulating the grants of land . . . Approved–June the first 1796 . . . [Philadelphia, F. Childs, 1796]
4 p. 34 cm. caption title
DLC; MiU-C; PPRF; RPJCB mp. 47974

B9770 U.S. LAWS
Fourth Congress of the United States: At the first session . . . An act supplementary to . . . "An act to provide a naval armament." Approved, April the twentieth 1796. [Philadelphia, 1796]
broadside 32 X 20.5 cm.
CSmH; MiU-C; PPRF; RPJCB mp. 47975

B9771 U.S. LAWS
Fourth Congress of the United States: At the first session . . . An act to ascertain and fix the military establishment of the United States . . . Approved–May the thirtieth 1796. [Philadelphia, 1796]
4 p. 34.5 cm. caption title
PPRF; RPJCB mp. 47976

B9772 U.S. LAWS
Fourth Congress of the United States: At the first session . . . An act to continue in force . . . for the appointment of a health officer . . . [Philadelphia, F. Childs, 1796]
3 p. 34 cm.
Approved May 12, 1796
Contains 3 other acts
PPRF mp. 47977

B9773 U. S. LAWS
Fourth Congress of the United States: At the first session . . . An act to regulate the compensation of clerks . . . Approved–May the thirtieth 1796 . . . [Philadelphia, F. Childs, 1796]
4 p. 34.5 cm.
DLC; MiU–C; PPRF; RPJCB mp. 47978

B9774 U. S. POST OFFICE
Table of post-offices in the United States, with distance from the post-office at Philadelphia . . . Philadelphia, November 15, 1796 . . . [Philadelphia, 1796]
broadside 70.5 X 59.5 cm.
Signed: Joseph Habersham Post-Master-General
MHi mp. 47980

B9775 U. S. PRESIDENT, 1789–1797
The address, and resignation of His Excellency Geo. Washington . . . Lansingburgh, Luther Pratt, 1796.
26 p., 1 leaf. 17 cm.
New York Public 1193
MiU; NNS. Photostat: NN mp. 48010

B9776 U. S. PRESIDENT, 1789–1797
The address, and resignation of His Excellency Geo. Washington . . . Second Lansingburgh edition. Lansingburgh, Luther Pratt, 1796.
24 p. 16 cm.
MWA mp. 48011

B9777 U. S. PRESIDENT, 1789–1797
Address from the President to the people of the United States, announcing his intention of retiring . . . Petersburg, William Prentis [1797]
[3]–16 p. 17 cm.
Imprint on p. 16
Sabin 101576; Wyatt 17
ViL mp. 48012

B9778 U. S. PRESIDENT, 1789–1797
Address of George Washington . . . preparatory to his declination. Wilmington, Printed for James Wilson's bookstore, 1796.
23 p. 19 cm.
Hawkins 68
DeWI mp. 48013

B9779 U. S. PRESIDENT, 1789–1797
Address of George Washington, President . . . to the people of the United States . . . Baltimore, Printed by Christopher Jackson for George and Henry S. Keatinge, booksellers, 1796.
36 p. 16 cm.
Minick 329
MdBJ mp. 48014

B9780 U. S. PRESIDENT, 1789–1797
An address to the people of the United States . . . [Sept. 17, 1796] . . . Exeter, Printed and sold by Henry Ranlet, 1796.
1 p.l., 8p. 22.5 cm.
Huntington 705
CSmH mp. 48015

B9781 U. S. PRESIDENT, 1789–1797
From the office of the *Pennsylvania Daily Advertiser*, Philadelphia . . . April 1. The following . . . message from the President . . . [Mar. 30, 1796] . . . [Philadelphia? 1796]
broadside 27 X 21.5 cm.

Huntington 702
CSmH mp. 47981

B9782 U. S. PRESIDENT, 1789–1797
The legacy of the Father of his Country. Address of George Washington, on declining being considered a candidate . . . [n.p., 1796?]
4, 25–40 p. 22 cm. caption title
Apparently complete
Title on blue cartridge-paper wrapper: General Washington's address
Dated by Victor H. Paltsits
MWA mp. 48016

B9783 U. S. PRESIDENT, 1789–1797
The President's address to the citizens of the United States in consequence of his resignation . . . [Richmond, 1796]
[20] p. 18mo caption title
Without t.p.
Advertisement on last leaf dated: Richmond, Sept. 14th, 1796
Davis 126; Sabin 101584
MB mp. 48018

B9784 U. S. PRESIDENT, 1789–1797
[The President's address to the people of the United States . . . Elizabeth (Hager's) Town, 1796]
8vo
Advertised in the *Washington Spy*, Oct. 12, 1796, as "Just published, in a handsome octavo pamphlet."
Minick 330; Sabin 101562
No copy known mp. 48019

B9785 U. S. PRESIDENT, 1789–1797
The President's address, to the people of the United States . . . [Reading, Pa.] From the press of J. Schneider [1796]
18 p. 22 cm.
New York Public 1194; Sabin 101583
NN mp. 48020

B9786 U. S. PRESIDENT, 1789–1797
The President's message, on the treaty papers. Herald-office, April 8, 1796. A gentleman . . . from Boston, has favored us with the following . . . communication . . . to the House of Representatives . . . the 30th ult. . . . [Newburyport? Blunt and March? 1796]
broadside 40 X 24 cm.
cf. Ford 3804
MB mp. 47982

B9787 U. S. PRESIDENT, 1789–1797
Talk of the President of the United States, to his beloved men of the Cherokee Nation . . . Given at . . . Philadelphia, the twenty-ninth day of August . . . one thousand seven hundred and ninety-six . . . [Philadelphia, 1796]
broadside 51 X 41 cm.
DLC (2 copies); MHi; MWA (reduced facsim.)
mp. 47983

B9788 U. S. TREASURY DEPT.
. . . Account of fines, penalties, and forfeitures . . . paid in the quarter ending December 31, 1795, without the institution of suits for their recovery. Cr. . . . Collector's Office, January 1, 1796. John Hall, Collector of the Revenue for the 1st Division . . . [Boston? 1796]
broadside 20 X 32 cm.
MHi mp. 47984

B9789 U. S. TREASURY DEPT.
Circular to the collectors and naval officers. Treasury department, June 3rd, 1796 . . . [Philadelphia, 1796]
[2] p. 23 X 19 cm.
PPRF mp. 47985

B9790 U. S. TREASURY DEPT.
(Circular.) Supervisor's Office, District of New-York, June 30th, 1796. Gentlemen, Since my last circular letter . . . the "Act of the 28th May, laying duties on carriages, &c:" has been received . . . [New York, 1796]
[2] p. 24 X 19.5 cm.
New York Public 1188
NN mp. 47986

B9791 U. S. TREASURY DEPT.
(Circular) Supervisor's-Office, New-York, June 1, 1796. Sir, A letter recently received from the Treasury contains the following paragraphs . . . [New York, 1796]
[2] p. 25 X 20.5 cm.
New York Public 1189
NN mp. 47987

B9792 U. S. TREASURY DEPT.
District of Rhode-Island. Duties on carriages, and on licences for retailing wines and . . . spirits . . . Notice . . . receiving the entries and duties in the County of in said district, required by . . . "An act laying duties on carriages . . . " . . . Collector of the Revenue, for said County of [Providence? 1796?]
broadside 31.5 X 21.5 cm.
Act passed May 28, 1796
MWA mp. 47988

B9793 U. S. TREASURY DEPT.
Extracts from circular letters . . . to the collectors, naval-officers, and surveyors. Selected June 1796. Philadelphia, John Fenno [1796]
69 p. 20 cm.
DLC mp. 47989

B9794 U. S. TREASURY DEPT.
Letter from the Secretary of the Treasury, accompanying a plan for . . . collecting direct taxes, by apportionment . . . in pursuance of a resolution of the House, of the fourth of April, 1796. 14th December 1796,—ordered to lie on the table. Published by order of the House of Representatives. [Philadelphia, 1796?]
68, [1] p. 11 tables (8 fold.) 32.5 cm.
cf. Evans 33076
CSmH mp. 47990

B9795 U. S. TREASURY DEPT.
Letter from the Secretary of the treasury to the chairman of the Committee of ways and means accompanying an estimate of the probable receipts . . . 18th May, 1796 . . . [n.p., 1796?]
[7] p. 32 cm.
MiU–C mp. 47991

B9796 U. S. TREASURY DEPT.
[Presented to the House the 3d of February, 1796.] Letter from the Secretary of the treasury to the chairman of the Committee of ways and means relative to certain additional provisions . . . [Philadelphia, F. Childs, 1796]
6 p. 33.5 cm.
DLC (2 copies); MiU–C mp. 47992

B9797 U. S. TREASURY DEPT.
A statement of the aggregate of the appropriations . . .

and the actual expenditures . . . for the War department . . . to the 1st January, 1796. [n.p., 1796]
19 p. 20.5 cm.
MiU–C mp. 47993

B9798 U. S. TREASURY DEPT.
Treasury Department, August 8, 1796. Public notice is hereby given, In pursuance of an act . . . for the sale of the lands . . . north west of the river Ohio . . . Given under my hand at Philadelphia the day and year aforementioned. Oliver Wolcott, Secretary of the Treasury. [Philadelphia, 1796]
broadside (2 p.) 40 X 25.5 cm.
On verso: Schedule of quarter townships . . .
MWA mp. 47994

B9799 U. S. TREATIES
At a treaty, held at the City of New-York, with the nations or tribes of Indians denominating themselves "The Seven Nations of Canada." [New York? 1796?]
3 p. 21.5 cm. caption title
Signed at New-York, May 31, 1796
New York Public 1190
NN mp. 47996

B9800 U. S. TREATIES
By George Washington, President . . . a Proclamation. Whereas a Treaty of Amity, Commerce and Navigation . . . Go: Washington. By the President Timothy Pickering, Secretary of State. Deposited among the rolls in the office of the department of State . . . [Philadelphia, Francis Childs, 1796]
[30] p. 22.5 cm.
Pierce W. Gaines, Fairfield, Conn. (1964) mp. 47995

B9801 U. S. TREATIES
George Washington, President of the United States of America. To all to whom these presents shall come,—Greeting: Whereas a treaty . . . Algiers . . . [Mar. 7, 1796] . . . By the President, Timothy Pickering, Secretary of State. Deposited among the rolls in . . . the Department of State . . . [Philadelphia, 1796]
8 p. 22 cm.
Huntington 703; cf. Evans 31409
CSmH

B9802 U. S. TREATIES
A treaty of peace and friendship, made and concluded between the President . . . and the undersigned kings, chiefs and warriors of the Creek Nation of Indians . . . [New York? 1796]
4 p. 21.5 cm. caption title
Dated June 29, 1796
New York Public 1191
NN mp. 47997

B9803 THE United States almanac, for the year . . . 1797 . . . By Gabriel Hutchins . . . New-York, Printed for Samuel Campbell [1796]
[36] p. 17 cm.
Wall p. 30
CtY; DLC; MWA; NHi; WHi mp. 47812

B9804 VANDEN BROEK, REINIER JOHN
Address delivered at the consecration of the room, accommodated for the meetings of Independent Royal-Arch Lodge, No. 2, the 23d day of June, 1796 . . . New-York, James Oram, 1796.
19 p. 20 cm.
MWA mp. 47998

B9805 VERGER & RENAULT, firm, Philadelphia
Prospectus of an allegorical picture, of the triumph of Liberty . . . Renault & Verger. December 1, 1796 . . . [Philadelphia? 1796]
broadside 32 X 20 cm.
In 2 columns, separated by type ornaments, the second column in French
CtHi; RPJCB mp. 47890

B9806 VERGER & RENAULT, firm, Philadelphia
Sir, Conscious of your taste for the arts and sciences . . . we thought it our duty to present you with a view of a work . . . [New York, 1796]
broadside 24 X 19.5 cm.
Both known copies corrected in ink to May 1797
RPJCB (copy 1 printed Sept. 20, 1796; copy 2 printed Dec. 15, 1796) mp. 47891

B9807 VERMONT. ATTORNEY GENERAL
The several states' attorneys in account for civil and criminal prosecutions with the State of Vermont . . . Isaac Tichenor, David Wing, jun. Rutland, October 25th, 1796. [Rutland, John S. Hutchins for S. Williams & Co., 1796]
broadside 40 X 32.5 cm.
McCorison 405
VtHi mp. 48004

B9808 VERMONT. LAWS
An act dividing the state into districts, for electing representatives . . . Rutland, 1796.
15 p. 14 cm.
Cooley 339; Sabin 99120
MH–L; Vt mp. 48002

B9809 VERMONT. LAWS
Acts and laws, passed by the General Assembly of . . . Vermont, at their session in Windsor, October 1795. [Bennington, A. Haswell, 1796]
77, [5] p. 19 cm. caption title
Certificate of accuracy at end dated: Bennington, 27th May, 1796
Cooley 300; New York Public 1192; Sabin 9919
MH–L; MWA; Vt; VtU–W. Photostat: NN
mp. 48003

B9810 THE Vermont almanac for the year . . . 1797 . . . Fitted to the latitude and longitude of Rutland . . . Printed at Rutland, (Vermont) [by John S. Hutchins] and sold . . . at the printing office [1796]
[24] p. 18.5 cm.
McCorison 375
MWA (fragment of t.p. only); VtU–W mp. 48005

B9811 VERSES composed by a young lady, on the death of Miss Clarissa Huntington, who died in East-Hartford, July 11th, 1796 . . . [Hartford, 1796]
broadside 37 X 15 cm.
CtHi mp. 48006

B9812 VIRGINIA. LAWS
An act to amend the penal laws of this Commonwealth. [Richmond, Augustine Davis, 1796?]
16 p. 20.5 cm. caption title
Sabin 100063?
PPRF mp. 48007

B9813 [VOGLER, GERARD]
The request. Philadelphia & New York, B. Carr; Baltimore, J. Carr [1796]

broadside 32 cm.
Sonneck-Upton p. 353
DLC; MWA mp. 48008

B9814 WANDS'S Lansingburgh almanack, for the year . . . 1797 . . . By Isaac Bickerstaff . . . Lansingburgh, William W. Wands [1796]
36 p. 18 cm.
DLC mp. 47732

B9815 [WARREN, JOHN] 1753–1815
A monody on the death of . . . Thomas Russell, Esq. sung after the eulogy delivered by Doctor John Warren, in the church in Brattle-Street . . . May 4, 1796 . . . [Boston, 1796]
broadside 39 X 16 cm.
Ford 2807; Wegelin 416
DLC; MHi. Photostat: MWA mp. 48009

B9816 WATTS, ISAAC, 1674–1748
Divine songs, attempted in easy language . . . Third Dover edition. [Dover, N.H.] Samuel Bragg, Jr., 1796.
32+ p. 12.5 cm.
MH (all after p. 32 wanting) mp. 48021

B9817 WATTS, ISAAC, 1674–1748
Divine songs: in easy language, for the use of children . . . New-London, Printed and sold by James Springer, 1796.
28 p. illus. 9.5 cm.
Rosenbach–Ch 223; Trumbull: Supplement 2732
CtHi; PP mp. 48022

B9818 WATTS, ISAAC, 1674–1748
The first catechism of the principals [sic] of religion . . . Davison, printer. W. Springfield, Mass. [1796?]
[24] p.
MWA mp. 48023

B9819 WATTS, ISAAC, 1674–1748
Hymns and spiritual songs . . . Wilmington: Printed and sold by Peter Brynberg, 1796.
242, [10] p.
MWA (bound with his *Psalms carefully suited* . . . Wilmington. 1805) mp. 48024

B9820 WATTS, ISAAC, 1674–1748
Preservation from the sins and follies of childhood and youth . . . First Charleston edition. [Charleston] W. P. Young, 1796
v, 96 p. 16.5 cm.
Mosimann 575
ScC

B9821 WEBSTER, NOAH, 1758–1843
The American spelling book . . . The IXth Vermont edition. Bennington, Anthony Haswell, 1796.
167 p. illus. 16 cm.
Skeel-Carpenter 44
VtMiS mp. 48025

B9822 DIE Westliche Correspondenz, und Hägerstauner Wochenschrift. Hägerstaun, Johann Gruber, 1796.
41 cm. weekly
Minick 332; Seidensticker p. 144
PRHi

B9823 WESTMINSTER ASSEMBLY OF DIVINES
The larger catechism, ratified and adopted by the Synod of New-York and Philadelphia; held at Philadelphia, May the 16th, 1788 . . . New-Brunswick, Abraham Blauvelt, 1796.
52 p. 16 cm.
NjR

B9824 WILLIAMS COLLEGE
Catalogue of students . . . October, 1796. Stockbridge [1796]
broadside
Photocopy: MWA mp. 48020

B9825 WILLIAMSON, PETER, 1730–1799
Sufferings of Peter Williamson, one of the settlers in the back parts of Pennsylvania. Written by himself. Stockbridge, 1796.
15 p. 22.5 cm.
MWA mp. 48027

B9826 THE wonderful escape, or sagacity outwitted: a curious story. Boston, J. White, 1796.
12 leaves. 12mo
Rosenbach–Ch 226
NjP. A. S. W. Rosenbach (1933) mp. 48028

B9827 ZIMMERMANN, JOHANN GEORG, RITTER VON, 1728–1795
Solitude considered . . . Translated from the French of J. B. Mercier . . . First New-York edition. [New-York] Printed by Mott & Lyon, for Evert Duyckinck & Co., C. Davis, J. Harrisson, J. Fellows, and J. Lyon [1796]
v, 328 p. front. 17 cm.
Advertised in *The Weekly Museum*, Oct. 15, 1796, as "just published."
New York Public 1195; Shaw-Shoemaker 1702; cf. Evans 31685
MH; NN mp. 48030

1797

B9828 ABOLITION SOCIETIES
To the free Africans and other free people of color in the United States . . . Philadelphia, Zachariah Poulson [1797]
broadside 39 X 26 cm.
Dated at Philadelphia, May 9, 1797
NHi mp. 48270

B9829 ADAM and Eve. A favorite new song, much in vogue among the young ladies and gentlemen . . . Boston: Printed near Liberty Pole. 1797.
broadside 30 X 21 cm.
Verse in 2 columns
MHi mp. 48031

B9830 ADGATE, ANDREW, d. 1793
Rudiments of music . . . The fifth edition. Philadelphia: Printed for, and sold by Mathew Carey, 1797.
2, 102 p. 21 cm.
CtY

B9831 ALBANY LIBRARY
Albany Library. Additional catalogue. 1797. [Albany] Charles R. and George Webster [1797]
7 p. 17 cm.
Half-title only
McMurtrie: Albany 142
N mp. 48036

B9832 ALEXANDRIA. CITIZENS
The petition of the freeholders and other inhabitants of the town of Alexandria, to the General assembly . . . of Virginia . . . [Alexandria? 1797?]
2 leaves. 32 cm.
Presented Dec. 22, 1797
Vi mp. 48037

B9833 AN almanack for . . . 1798 . . . Washington [Pa.], Colerick, Hunter and Beaumont [1797]
[24] p.
Drake 10445
NjP (imperfect)

B9834 THE American union, and the birth of General Washington. [n.p., 1797?]
broadside 33.5 X 23 cm.
Wegelin 490
MWA. Photostat: CSmH mp. 48038

B9835 AMERICANISCHER Calender auf . . . 1798 . . . Ephrata, Benjamin Mayer [1797]
[44] p.
Drake 10448
MWA (t.p. lacking); PLHi

B9836 AMUSEMENT Hall; or An easy introduction to the attainment of useful knowledge. By a Lady . . . Elizabeth-Town, Printed by Shepard Kollock, for Cornelius Davis, New-York, 1797.
103 p. 13.5 cm.
Morsch 334
CtHi; NjP mp. 48039

B9837 ARGUS
The carrier of the *Argus*, presents the following address . . . New-York, January 2, 1797. [New York, 1797]
broadside 33.5 X 19 cm.
NHi mp. 48086

B9838 ARGUS
Greenleaf's Argus extraordinary. The public anxiety to be acquainted with the important subject . . . at this special session of Congress, has induced the editor . . . [New York, Thomas Greenleaf, 1797]
broadside 49.5 X 30 cm.
Speech by John Adams, May 16, 1797
NN

B9839 ARGUS
Supplement to *Greenleaf's Argus*. Friday, August 4, 1797. [Colophon] New-York, Thomas Greenleaf [1797]
2 leaves. 49.5 cm.
Speech by Charles James Fox, May 26, 1797
NN

B9840 ARMSTRONG, JAMES
Es wird öffentlich versteigert werden, Freytags, den 6ten October nächstfolgend, an Peter Maurers Wirthshaus . . . beynahe 2 Meilen von der Stadt Lancaster . . . ein gesunder Neger, ehemals das Eigenthum der verstorbenen James M'Elheny . . . James Armstrong, Executor. Den 26sten September, 1797. [Lancaster? 1797]
broadside 16 X 20.5 cm.
NjR

B9841 [ARNOLD, SAMUEL] 1740–1802
At the dead of the night . . . Philadelphia & New York, Carr; Baltimore, B. Carr [1797]
broadside 33.5 cm.
Sonneck-Upton p. 34
DLC mp. 48040

B9842 ARNOULD,
The American heroine, a pantomine in three acts. By M. Arnould . . . Translated from the French, by Samuel Chandler . . . Printed at Paris: and re-printed and sold by Parent, Philadelphia, 1797.
20 p. 22 cm.
PHi mp. 48041

B9843 AS the question whether the House of representatives have a right to impeach . . . Constitutionalist. December 10, 1797. [n.p., 1797]
broadside 24 X 19.5 cm.
DLC mp. 48042

B9844 [ASTRONOMICAL diary, kalendar or almanack for 1798. By N. Strong. West Springfield, Printed by Edward Gray; sold by N. Patten, Hartford, 1797]

Information from T. R. Harlow, improving Drake 569
No copy known

B9845 BAKER, GARDINER
February 1, 1797 New panorama. Belonging to G. Baker. On Monday next, the 6th inst. will be opened in Greenwich-Street . . . [Boston, 1797]
broadside 52.5 X 39.5 cm.
NHi mp. 48052

B9846 BALTIMORE. NEW THEATRE
New theatre. For four weeks only. This evening . . . May 17, 1797 . . . The Child of Nature . . . [Baltimore, Clayland, Dobbin? 1797]
broadside 30 X 20.5 cm.
Minick 337
MdBE (mutilated) mp. 48045

B9847 BALTIMORE. NEW THEATRE
New theatre. For four weeks only. This evening . . . May 18, 1797 . . . Venice Preserv'd . . . [Baltimore] Clayland, Dobbin [1797]
broadside 30 X 21 cm.
Minick 338
MdBE mp. 48046

B9848 BALTIMORE. NEW THEATRE
New theatre. For four weeks only. This evening . . . May 22, 1797 . . . The Fair Penitent . . . [Baltimore] Clayland, Dobbin [1797]
broadside 31 X 21 cm.
Minick 339
MdBE mp. 48047

B9849 BALTIMORE. ORDINANCES
Ordinances of the corporation of the city of Baltimore: passed at their first session, held February, 1797 . . . Baltimore, Philip Edwards, 1797.
150 p. 20.5 cm.
Minick 340; cf. Evans 31768
MdHi mp. 48044

B9850 BAPTISTS. CONNECTICUT. DANBURY ASSOCIATION
Minutes of the Danbury Baptist Association, holden at Wallingford, October 4th and 5th, M,DCC,XCVII . . . Hartford, Elisha Babcock, 1797.
8 p.
Trumbull: Supplement 2045
Ct. Photocopy: MWA mp. 48048

B9851 BAPTISTS. KENTUCKY. ELKHORN ASSOCIATION
Minutes of the Elkhorn Association of Baptists, held at Clear Creek, August 12, 1797. [n.p., 1797]
7 p. 20 cm. caption title
McMurtrie: Kentucky 58
OClWHi. Photocopy: MWA mp. 48049

B9852 BAPTISTS. NORTH CAROLINA. NEUSE BAPTIST ASSOCIATION
Minutes of the North-Carolina Neuse Baptist Associa-

tion holden at Naughunty meeting house . . . Newbern, Francois-X. Martin [1797?]
[4] p. 18 cm. caption title
First reported meeting Oct. 7, 1797
NcWsW mp. 48050

B9853 BAPTISTS. SOUTH CAROLINA. BETHEL ASSOCIATION
Minutes of the Bethel Association. Met at the Baptist Church on Jamey's Creek, Spartanburgh County, South-Carolina, 11th August, 1797 . . . [Charleston, 1797]
8 p. 21 cm. caption title
ScGF

B9854 BAPTISTS. VERMONT. LEYDEN ASSOCIATION
Minutes of the Leyden Association . . . Putney, Cornelius Sturtevant, 1797.
10 p. 18.5 cm.
NRAB mp. 48051

B9855 BAPTISTS. VERMONT. RICHMOND ASSOCIATION
Minutes of the Richmond Association, for 1797 . . . [at end] Printed by Judah P. Spooner, Fairhaven. [1797?]
8 p. 18 cm. caption title
Meeting held in Fairfax, Vt., Aug. 30–31, 1797
VtBaHi mp. 48052

B9856 BAPTISTS. VIRGINIA. DOVER DISTRICT ASSOCIATION
Minutes of the Baptist Dover Association, held . . . October 14, 1797. Richmond, John Dixon, 1797.
[3], 8 p. 17 cm.
Davis 127
ViRU mp. 48054

B9857 BAPTISTS. VIRGINIA. DOVER DISTRICT ASSOCIATION
Minutes of the Baptist Dover Association, holden . . . October 8, 1796. Richmond, Thomas Nicolson, 1797.
[3], 12 p. 18 cm.
Davis 128
ViRU mp. 48053

B9858 BAPTISTS. VIRGINIA. KETOCTON ASSOCIATION
Minutes of the Ketockton Baptist Association, held at Frying-Pan, Loudoun county, August 1797. [n.p., 1797]
8 p. 20.5 cm.
Half-title only
DLC. Photocopy: MWA mp. 48055

B9859 BAZIN, ABRAHAM
Abraham Bazin. No. 16, Cornhill, Boston: Imports and sells at the lowest price for cash, a general assortment of hard-ware, goods, looking-glasses, &c. [Boston] S. Etheridge, Print. No. 9, Newbury-Street [1797?]
broadside 11 × 13.5 cm.
Dated by MHi
MHi mp. 48056

B9860 BEACH, JESSE
A sermon at a Masonic installation in Harmony Lodge in Derby. Litchfield, T. Collier, 1797.
16 p. 18 cm.
Trumbull: Supplement 1899
CtHi mp. 48057

B9861 BIBLE. O.T. PSALMS
Psalms carefully suited to the Christian worship . . . Elizabeth-Town, Printed and sold by Shepard Kollock, 1797.
314, [10] p. 13.5 cm.
cf. Evans 31811
RPJCB mp. 48058

B9862 BIBLE. O.T. PSALMS
Psalms carefully suited to the Christian worship . . . Elizabeth-Town, Printed by Shepard Kollock for Naphtali Judah, 1797.
314, [10]; [2], 286 p.
Second title: Hymns and spiritual songs . . . By I. Watts.
cf. Evans 31811
MWA mp. 48059

B9863 BIBLE. O.T. PSALMS
The Psalms of David in metre . . . Allowed by the authority of the General Assembly of the Kirk of Scotland. Carlisle, Kline, 1797.
312 p. 13 cm.
cf. Evans 31813
MWA (lacks p. 35–36) mp. 48060

B9864 BIBLE. N.T.
The New Testament . . . Wilmington, Peter Brynberg, 1797.
336 p. 12mo
DeWI; KU mp. 48061

B9865 BIBLE. N.T. APOCRYPHAL BOOKS. TESTAMENT OF THE TWELVE PATRIARCHS
Testament und Abschrift . . . Hagerstaun, Johann Gruber, 1797.
116 p.
MWA mp. 30089

B9866 BICKERSTAFF'S genuine almanack for . . . 1798 . . . Boston, Sold by B. Larkin, E. Larkin, S. Hall, C. Bingham [etc.] [1797]
[24] p.
Drake 3578; cf. Evans 33169
PHi (lacks 1 leaf)

B9867 BIRD, JOHN
An oration; delivered in Troy, July 4th, 1797; being the twenty-second anniversary of American Independence . . . Troy: Printed by Luther Pratt [1797?]
11 p. 16 cm.
NHi mp. 48062

B9868 BLUNT, EDMUND MARCH
New catalogue of books, for sale by Edmund M. Blunt, at the Newburyport Bookstore . . . [Newburyport] October 1797.
broadside
460 titles in 6 columns
Brigham: Booksellers, p. 59
MWA mp. 48063

B9869 [BORDLEY, JOHN BEALE] 1727–1804
Intending to retire . . . B. July, 1797. [Philadelphia, Charles Cist, 1797]
8 p. fold. table. 8vo
At head of title: Commerce feeds the passions; agriculture calms them
PPL mp. 48064

B9870 BOSTON. COLLECTOR OF TAXES
Ward, No. To Your commonwealth tax. Your town and county tax . . . Boston, October 1797. [Boston, 1797]
broadside 14 × 15 cm.
MB

B9871 BOSTON. FEDERAL STREET SCHOOL
The constitution of the school in Federal-street. By the proprietors. [Boston] 1797.
15 p. 15.5 cm.
MiU-C

B9872 BOSTON LIBRARY SOCIETY
Catalogue of books in the Boston Library, May 1, 1797 . . . [Boston, 1797]
27 p. 24 cm.
MWA (final leaf mutilated) mp. 48065

B9873 BOSTON THEATRE (FEDERAL STREET)
Notice. Proprietors of the Boston Theatre. To Samuel Cooper . . . We the subscribers . . . request you to authorize one of us to call a meeting of the Proprietors . . . Nathan Frazier, John Gardner, Simon Elliot, Henry Newman, Samuel Parkman . . . Boston, 10th June, .97 . . . [Boston, Young and Minns, 1797]
broadside 20 × 11 cm.
MB mp. 48067

B9874 BRIGGS, ISAAC
Sharon, [Penna.?] 25th of the 2d Month, 1797. My friend This little production . . . Isaac Briggs. [Philadelphia? 1797]
broadside
Sends materials for an almanac to Mathew Carey (probably among other publishers) to use if he wishes
PHi

B9875 BRIGGS' Virginia & Maryland almanac; or Washington ephemeris for the year . . . 1798 . . . Alexandria, Printed by Thomas & Westcott for F. V. Thomas, bookseller [1797]
[36] p. 16 cm.
NNC mp. 48068

B9876 BROTHERS, RICHARD, 1757–1824
Eine Offenbahrung der Erkentniss von den Weissagungen und Zeiten. Das erste Buch . . . Harrisburg, Johannes Wyeth, 1797.
100 p. 12mo
PPL mp. 48069

B9877 THE brother's gift . . . New-York, W. Durell & Co. No. 15, Little Dock-Street. [1797?]
30, [1] p. illus. 9.5 cm.
First and last pages pasted to covers
Dated by d'Alté A. Welch
cf. Evans 37051–52
NRU mp. 48070

B9878 BROWN UNIVERSITY
Exhibition in College chapel, on Wednesday, the 23d of August, 1797 . . . [Providence] Carter and Wilkinson [1797]
broadside 24 × 15.5 cm.
Alden 1548
RPB mp. 48071

B9879 BUCHAN, WILLIAM, 1729–1805
Domestic medicine . . . Adapted to the climate and diseases of America, by Isaac Cathrall. Philadelphia, Printed [by Richard Folwell] for H. & P. Rice, and sold by James Rice, Baltimore, 1797.
512 p. 21 cm.
DNLM (incomplete) mp. 48078

B9880 BUCHAN, WILLIAM, 1729–1805
Domestic medicine . . . Adapted to the climate and diseases of America, by Isaac Cathrall. Philadelphia, Printed by Richard Folwell, for Henry Sweitzer, 1797.
512 p. 21 cm.
CtY-M; DNLM mp. 48079

B9881 BUCHAN, WILLIAM, 1729–1805
Domestic medicine . . . Adapted to the climate and diseases of America, by Isaac Cathrall. Philadelphia, Printed by Richard Folwell, for Joseph & James Crukshank, 1797.
512 p. 21 cm.
Rogers 591
CLM; DLC; NNC mp. 48077

B9882 BUCHAN, WILLIAM, 1729–1805
Domestic medicine . . . Adapted to the climate and diseases of America, by Isaac Cathrall. Philadelphia, Printed by Richard Folwell, for Mathew Carey, 1797.
512 p. 21 cm.
KyU; MoSMed mp. 48076

B9883 BUCHAN, WILLIAM, 1729–1805
Domestic medicine . . . Adapted to the climate and diseases of America, by Isaac Cathrall. Philadelphia, Printed by Richard Folwell, for Robert Campbell & Co., 1797.
512 p. 21 cm.
cf. Evans 31887
DLC; MBCo; MdU-H; NNNAM mp. 48075

B9884 BUCHAN, WILLIAM, 1729–1805
Domestic medicine . . . Adapted to the climate and diseases of America, by Isaac Cathrall. Philadelphia, Printed by Richard Folwell, for T. Allen, New-York, 1797.
512 p. 21 cm.
NN mp. 48073

B9885 BUCHAN, WILLIAM, 1729–1805
Domestic medicine . . . Adapted to the climate and diseases of America, by Isaac Cathrall. Philadelphia, Printed by Richard Folwell, for Thomas Bradford, 1797.
512 p. 21 cm.
Vi mp. 48074

B9886 BUCHAN, WILLIAM, 1729–1805
Domestic medicine . . . Adapted to the climate and diseases of America, by Isaac Cathrall. Philadelphia, Printed by Richard Folwell, for William W. Woodward, 1797.
512 p. 22 cm.
ScCM mp. 48080

B9887 BUNYAN, JOHN, 1628–1688
The visions of John Bunyan; being his last remains . . . New-York, Printed by John Tiebout, for B. Gomez, 1797.
144 p. 14.5 cm.
MWA; NRU mp. 48081

B9888 THE burden of Issachar: a politico-theological sermon; containing hints for the people of Virginia, &c. By their sincere friend, Republicanus; author of the notes on Episcopalius's sermon . . . Richmond: Printed (for the author) by Samuel Pleasants, Jun. December, 1797.
8 p. 20 cm.
NHi mp. 48082

B9889 [BURGH, JAMES] 1714–1775
Youth's friendly monitor: or The affectionate school master . . . The fourth American edition . . . Worcester, Isaiah Thomas, Jun., 1797.
84 p. 13.5 cm.
New York Public 1197
MWA; NN mp. 48083

B9890 BURR, JONATHAN, 1757–1842
A compendium of religion, in questions and answers . . . Boston, Printed and sold by Samuel Hall [1797?]
24 p. 15 cm.
Preface dated June 19, 1797
MB; MWA mp. 48084

B9891 BUTLER, THOMAS, b. 1748
To the settlers within the Cherokee Boundary, as established by the Treaty of Holston, on the second day of July, one thousand seven hundred and ninety-one. [Knoxville, George Roulstone, 1797]
broadside 39 X 32 cm.
McMurtrie: Tennessee 23; New York Public 1198
RPJCB. Photostat: NN mp. 48085

B9892 CARROLL, JOHN, 1735–1815
John, by the grace of God . . . bishop of Baltimore, to my beloved brethren . . . of Trinity church, Philadelphia . . . [Colophon] Baltimore, Feb. 22, 1797. Printed by J. Hayes [1797]
8 p. 24.5 cm.
Minick 348; Parsons 170
DGU; PHi mp. 48087

B9893 CATHOLIC CHURCH. LITURGY
The burial service, according to the Roman ritual. Baltimore, John Hayes, 1797.
1 p.l., 21 p. 16 cm.
Latin and English
Minick 350; Parsons 169
MdW mp. 48089

B9894 CATHOLIC CHURCH. LITURGY
Ordo divini officii recitandi . . . pro anno Domini MDCCXCVIII. Baltimori, typis Johannis Hayes [1797]

Minick 349; Parsons 181
No copy known mp. 48088

B9895 CENTINEL OF FREEDOM
Address, presented by the carrier to the patrons of the *Centinel of Freedom*, with the compliments of the season . . . [Newark, Daniel Dodge & Co., 1797]
broadside 32.5 X 20.5 cm.
Dated by NHi
NHi mp. 48035

B9896 CLEATOR, JAMES
The Charleston directory, and stranger's guide, for . . . 1797. With a map of the city . . . Charleston, W. P. Young [1797]
vi, 78 p. map. 17.5 cm.
MHi

B9897 [COBBETT, WILLIAM] 1762–1835
The life of Thomas Paine, interspersed with remarks and reflections, by Peter Porcupine. Philadelphia, 1797.
60 p. 12mo
Sabin 13894
No copy traced mp. 48090

B9898 [COBBETT, WILLIAM] 1762–1835
Part II. A bone to gnaw, for the Democrats; containing, 1st, Observations on a patriotic pamphlet . . . 2dly, Democratic memoirs . . . By Peter Porcupine. Philadelphia, Printed by William Young, for William Cobbett, 1797.
[2], 66 p. 8vo
Probably a separate edition, differing from Evans 31948 in spelling "memoirs" and in 5 lines for section starting "2dly."
PPL mp. 48984

B9899 [COLLINS, ISAAC]
Proposals for printing by subscription . . . the Journal of . . . Job Scott. [New York, Isaac Collins, 1797]
broadside 38 X 23 cm.
PHi mp. 48091

B9900 COLLINS, JOEL
An object worthy the attention of families emigrating to Kentucky . . . [at end] Lexington, James H. Stewart [1797]
broadside 18.5 X 15 cm.
Announcement of 35,000 acres of land for sale
Signed: Joel Collins, Richland Creek, July 10, 1797
McMurtrie: Kentucky 60
OCHP mp. 48092

B9901 [COLLYER, MARY (MITCHELL)] d. 1763
The death of Cain . . . By a Lady. New-Haven, Bunce and Spencer, 1797.
107 p. 13.5 cm.
Trumbull: Supplement 2053
CtHi; MWA mp. 48093

B9902 THE comical sayings of Paddy from Cork . . . The seventeenth edition. Leominster, 1797.
24 p. 17 cm.
MWA mp. 48094

B9903 A COMPLETE collection of the most remarkable voyages . . . Vol. I[-VIII] Baltimore, Printed for George and Henry Keatinge, 1797.
8 v. 14 cm.
Minick 354
DLC mp. 48096

B9904 CONNECTICUT. GENERAL ASSEMBLY
At a General Assembly of the State of Connecticut holden at New-Haven on the second Thursday of October 1797. Resolved by this Assembly, That Jonathan Bull, Elizur Goodrich . . . appointed . . . to receive and count the votes . . . for six persons to . . . stand in the nomination . . . as representatives . . . Congress . . . [New Haven, T. & S. Green, 1797]
broadside 20.5 X 17 cm.
NHi. Stan Henkels (1931). Photostat: MWA
mp. 48097

B9905 CONNECTICUT. GENERAL ASSEMBLY
At a General Assembly of the State of Connecticut, holden at New-Haven on the second Thursday of October 1797. The persons returned by the votes . . . to stand in nomination for election . . . are as follows . . . New-Haven, T. & S. Green [1797]
broadside 34.5 X 20.5 cm.
MWA mp. 48098

B9906 COOPER, W. D.
The history of North America . . . New-Brunswick, Abraham Blauvelt, 1797.
6 p.l., 160 p. 14 cm.
New York Public 1199
MB; NN mp. 48099

B9907 THE cottage boy a favorite song . . . New York, G. Gilfert [1797?]
[2] p. 33.5 cm.
Sonneck-Upton p. 91
DLC; MWA mp. 48100

B9908 CROADE, NATHANIEL
Nathaniel Croade, in Pawtucket . . . respectfully informs his customers . . . that he has on hand . . . Warren, N. Phillips [1797?]

broadside 33 X 20 cm.
Alden 1528; Winship Addenda p. 92
RHi. Photostat: MWA mp. 48101

B9909 CROSWELL'S diary, or the Catskill almanac for . . . 1798. Catskill, M. Croswell [1797]

Advertised in the *Catskill Packet*, Jan. 6, 1798
Drake 6066
No copy known

B9910 DAILY ADVERTISER
Address of Robbin the carrier of the *Daily Advertiser*, to his kind customers . . . Jan. 1, 1797. [New York, 1797]
broadside 33.5 X 20.5 cm.
NHi mp. 48032

B9911 DAILY ADVERTISER
Supplement to the *Daily Advertiser.* New York, Monday, November 6, 1797 . . . We the subscribers . . . Richard Varick, Mayor, James Kent, Recorder . . . Aldermen. [New-York, 1797]
broadside 54 X 33 cm.
City treasurer's accounts, in tabular form
MH

B9912 THE day of marriage, sung by Mrs. Jones. Baltimore, J. Carr [1797?]
2 leaves. 31 cm. caption title
MiU-C mp. 48102

B9913 THE devout Christian's vade mecum . . . Philadelphia, Printed for Mathew Carey by S. C. Ustick, 1797.
285, [3] p. 9.5 cm.
CSmH; DLC mp. 48103

B9914 A DIALOGUE between the Devil and George Third . . . Augusta (Kennebeck) Re-printed by Peter Edes. 1797.
32 p. 19 cm. A–B^6 C^4
PPRF mp. 48104

B9915 DIANA of the Ephesians, a type of the confession of faith: a sermon, preached at the opening of the Synod of Wogselt and Rya . . . By the late Reverend John Mistyfigo . . . New-London, Charles Holt, 1797.
34 p. 16 cm.
NBuG

B9916 DIBDIN, CHARLES, 1745–1814
Father and mother and Suke . . . Baltimore, C. Hupfeld and F. Hammer [1797?]
4 p. 33 cm.
Sonneck-Upton p. 135
DLC mp. 48105

B9917 DIBDIN, CHARLES, 1745–1814
Nancy or The sailors journal. Composed by Mr. Dibdin. Pr. 25 ct. [Boston, 1797–98?]
56–57 p. 30.5 cm. caption title
"Apparently a reprint from No. [IV] of *The musical repertory*, Boston, 1797–99." Sonneck-Upton p. 286
cf. Evans 32040
MiU-C

B9918 DIBDIN, CHARLES, 1745–1814
The patent coffin . . . New York, J. Hewitt; Philadelphia, B. Carr; Baltimore, J. Carr [1797]
[2] p. 34 cm.
Sonneck-Upton p. 326
DLC mp. 48106

B9919 DIBDIN, CHARLES, 1745–1814
The sailor's journal . . . New York & Philadelphia, B. Carr; Baltimore, J. Carr [1797]
[2] p. 32.5 cm.
Sonneck-Upton p. 287
DLC; MWA; NN mp. 48107

B9920 DILWORTH, THOMAS, d. 1780
A new guide to the English tongue . . . A new edition . . . Philadelphia, Printed and sold by Stewart & Cochran, 1797.
131, [1] p. 17.5 cm.
MWA (port. and p. 3–8 wanting) mp. 48108

B9921 A DISCOURSE on baptism, published with a view to remove the scruple of those, who . . . doubt . . . its validity by sprinkling . . . Lexington, John Bradford, 1797.
43 p. 21 cm.
McMurtrie: Kentucky 61
PPiU mp. 48109

B9922 A DISH of all sorts, or the novelist's companion . . . Compiled from the works of curious men, by the Hon. Secretary of the company of flying booksellers. [Norwich?] Printed in the year 1797.
1 p.l., [20] p. 17 cm.
NHi (closely trimmed) mp. 48110

B9923 DODSLEY, ROBERT, 1703-1764
The toy-shop . . . Troy, Printed and sold by Luther Pratt [1797]
36 p. 15.5 cm.
MWA mp. 48111

B9923a DOROTHY, an heroic pantomime, in three acts. Preceded by The Valiant Knights . . . in one act. Performed . . . at Paris . . . in 1786, and presented under the direction of Mr. Jaymond . . . in Philadelphia in July 1797 . . . Philadelphia: Printed by C. Parent, 1797.
16 p. 19.5 cm.
Translated by J. Parker
NNS

B9924 EDENTON THEATRE
The last night of performance at Edenton, this season. On Thursday evening, the 20th of July, 1797 . . . [Edenton, Hodge & Willis? 1797]
broadside 32 X 20 cm.
"Tickets for admittance . . . at the Printing Office . . ."
ViWC mp. 48112

B9925 EDGAR,
Mr. Edgar most respectfully informs the ladies and gentlemen of Trenton that he will open his theatre for one night only . . . the 9th of April . . . scenes from . . . George Barnwell. [Trenton, Matthias Day? 1797]
broadside
Title from Nelson
Morsch 353
No copy located mp. 48113

B9926 [AN elegiac poem, on the death of Mrs. Clark, who died in this town April 3, 1796; addressed to her surviving consort. Bennington, Benjamin Smead, 1797]

Freedom Clark was the wife of Joseph Clark, selectman of Brattleboro
Advertised in the *Federal Galaxy*, Apr. 28, 1797
McCorison 433
No copy known mp. 48114

B9927 ERSKINE, THOMAS, 1750-1823
A view of the causes and consequences of the present

war with France . . . Philadelphia:/Printed by William Cobbett, opposite/Christ Church./1797.
73 p. 8vo
cf. Evans 32097 (3-line imprint)
PHi

B9928 FATHER Abraham's almanac for . . . 1798 . . . Philadelphia, Stewart and Cochran [1797]
[40] p.
Drake 10460
NjR (16 l.)

B9929 FEDERAL GAZETTEER
Address, presented by the carrier of the *Federal Gazetteer*, to his generous and respectable patrons. January 1, 1797 . . . [New-Haven, Edward O'Brien & Co., 1797]
broadside 22.5 X 15.5 cm.
NHi mp. 48034

B9930 FÉNELON, FRANÇOIS DE SALIGNAC DE LA MOTHE, 1651-1715
The adventures of Telemachus . . . A new edition . . . Two volumes in one. Boston, Printed for J. Nancrede, 1797.
2 p.l., 372, [4] p. 18 cm.
cf. Evans 32124
MWA; OU mp. 48116

B9931 FLEMING, JOSEPH H
The following was the speech of Joseph H. Fleming, of . . . Philadelphia, in the Lyceum . . . at Mr. Poor's schoolhouse, on Wednesday evening, Feb. 8, 1797 . . . [Philadelphia, 1797]
8 p. 21 cm.
DLC; PHi; PPL mp. 48117

B9932 [FRASER, DONALD] fl. 1797
The recantation: being an anticipated valedictory address, of Thomas Paine to the French Directory. New-York: Printed for the author. Re-printed in North-Carolina, 1797.
13 p. 23 cm.
New York Public 1200
NN mp. 48118

B9933 FREEMASONS. CONNECTICUT. GRAND LODGE
Proceedings of the Grand Lodge of Connecticut, holden at . . . Hartford . . . the 17th of May . . . A.D. 1797. Hartford, Elisha Babcock, 1797.
8 p. 17 cm.
Trumbull: Supplement 2524
CtHi mp. 48119

B9934 FREEMASONS. CONNECTICUT. GRAND ROYAL ARCH CHAPTER
The constitution of the Grand Royal Arch chapter of the state of Connecticut, formed . . . A.L. 5797. Middletown, T. Dunning, 1797.
10 p. 18 cm.
Trumbull: Supplement 2013
CtHi mp. 48120

B9935 FREEMASONS. MARYLAND. GRAND LODGE
Grand lodge of the state of Maryland, at Baltimore. Lodge of Sir and brethren . . . M. Ducatel W. M. . . . [Baltimore? Clayland, Dobbin? 1797]
broadside 33 X 42 cm.
Minick 358
PPFM

B9936 FREEMASONS. MARYLAND. GRAND LODGE
Minutes of the proceedings of the . . . Grand Lodge . . . for the state of Maryland . . . Baltimore, Thomas Dobbin, 5797 [i.e. 1797]
8 p. 24 cm.
Minick 360
MdBFM mp. 48121

B9937 FREEMASONS. MARYLAND. GRAND LODGE
Proceedings of the Grand lodge . . . of Maryland . . . Baltimore, Clayland & Dobbin [1797]
8 p. 17 cm.
Minick 361
MBFM; MdBFM; PPFM mp. 48122

B9938 FREEMASONS. NORTH CAROLINA. GRAND LODGE
[Circular . . . July 19, 1797. Halifax, 1797]

4-page folder printed on first page only
McMurtrie: North Carolina 229
NNFM; PPFM mp. 48123

B9939 FREEMASONS. VIRGINIA. GRAND LODGE
Proceedings of the Grand Lodge of Virginia . . . Richmond, 1797.
8 p. 20 cm.
Davis 130
DSC; IaCrM; Vi mp. 48124

B9940 FREEMASONS. VIRGINIA. GRAND LODGE
Richmond, Virginia, 1st March 5797. Most worshipful sir and brother . . . I . . . inclose you the proceedings of their last Grand annual communication . . . [Richmond? 1797]
2 p. 39.5 cm. caption title
Davis 131
PPFM mp. 48125

B9941 FREEMASONS. VIRGINIA. RICHMOND LODGE
Richmond Lodge, no. 10. Richmond, March 9, 5797. Brother, You are requested to attend . . . [Richmond, 1797]
broadside 20.5 X 16.5 cm.
CSmH mp. 48126

B9942 FRIENDS, SOCIETY OF
To the Quarterly and Monthly Meetings of Friends. [Philadelphia, 1797]
broadside 10 X 13.5 cm.
PHi mp. 48127

B9943 FRIENDSHIP FIRE COMPANY, PHILADELPHIA
The Friendship Fire-Company. A meeting . . . will be held at the City Tavern, at six o'clock tomorrow evening . . . Monday, Nov. 20th, 1797. . . [Philadelphia] Zachariah Poulson, Jr. [1797]
oblong broadside
PPL mp. 48229

B9944 FRUMMANN, HANS
Büchlein des Hans Frummann, welcher von Himmel und Hölle zeuget . . . York, Salomon Mäyer, 1797.
53 p. 16.5 cm. [A]-C^8 $[D]^4$ (D4 blank)
MWA; PPL (wanting after p. 51) mp. 48128

B9945 FUNNY stories: or the American jester . . . New-Haven, Printed for, and sold by Edward O'Brien, 1797.
108 p. 14.5 cm.
Trumbull: Supplement 2176
CtHi mp. 48130

B9946 GAIFER
The conversion of a Mahometan to the Christian religion . . . The tenth edition. Charlestown [Mass.], 1797.
16 p. 16 cm.
MWA mp. 48131

B9947 GAZETTE OF THE UNITED STATES
Address of the carrier of the *Gazette of the United States*. January - 1797 . . . [Philadelphia, 1797]
broadside 34.5 X 20.5 cm.
MWA mp. 48033

B9948 GENERAL statement of the contracts for opening and improving roads and rivers . . . Philadelphia, Zachariah Poulson, 1797.
19 p. incl. tables. 33.5 X 18.5 cm.
New York Public 1201
NN mp. 48133

B9949 GEORGIA. LAWS
An act to extend the time for the pretended purchasers of the western territory of this state, to receive the sums they deposited . . . Jared Irvin, Governor . . . February 13, 1797 . . . [Augusta, Ga., 1797]
broadside 39 X 24 cm.
MiU-C; NN (reduced facsim.) mp. 48134

B9950 GERALD, GABRIEL
[Pamphlet in the defence of his sentiment regarding the Sabbath . . . Charleston? 1797?]

Mentioned in a letter to Gerald from Richard Furman, dated Dec. 11, 1797.--Richard P. Morgan
Starr G692
No copy known

B9951 GRANGER, GIDEON, 1767-1822
Oration spoken on Tuesday, the Fourth of July, 1797 . . . in Suffield. Suffield: Printed by Havila & Oliver Farnsworth for Oliver D. & J. Cooke, booksellers, Hartford, 1797.
24 p.
Trumbull: Second supplement 2845; cf. Evans 32203
No copy traced mp. 48135

B9952 GREEN, WILLIAM
The trial of John Young for the murder of Robert Barwick . . . taken by means of short-hand for the benefit of the citizens of New-York by William Green. [New York? 1797]
16 p.
NIC-L

B9952a GRIFFING, AUGUSTUS
Soliloquy on the death of Miss Deziah Griffing, who died December 11, 1794, aged 24 years . . . New-York: Printed at the office of John Harrisson [1797?]
8 p. 15.5 cm.
Stoddard 105
N (cropped at foot, possibly removing imprint date)

B9953 GRIFFITH, BENJAMIN
To the editor of *Porcupines Gazette* . . . Benjamin Griffith. November 6th, 1797. [n.p., 1797?]
[5] p. 20.5 cm. caption title
DLC mp. 48136

B9954 GRISWOLD, ALEXANDER VIETS, 1766-1843
A short sketch, of the life of Mr. Lent Munson . . . Litchfield: Printed by Thomas Collier. M,DCC,XCVII.
8 p. 21.5 cm.
Sabin 28881 note; Trumbull: Supplement 2224
MiU-C (bound with Evans 32215)

B9955 HABERMAN, JOHANN, 1516-1590
Christliche Morgen und Abend-gebäter . . . Ephrata, Benj. Mayer, 1797.
160 p. 16mo
PPL mp. 48137

B9956 [HARPER, ROBERT GOODLOE] 1765-1825
The case of the Georgia sales on the Mississippi considered . . . Philadelphia, 1797.
[4], 109 p. 23.5 cm.
Brinley 3930; Gaines 151
PHi mp. 48138

B9957 HARTFORD. THEATRE
Theatre. On Monday evening, August 14th, 1797, will be presented . . . Jane Shore . . . To which will be added . . . The Lyar . . . The ladies and gentlemen of East-Hartford . . . the ferrymen . . . attend . . . every evening after the performance . . . [Hartford, 1797]
broadside 44 X 27 cm.
CtHi

B9958 HAYMARKET THEATRE, BOSTON
Hay-Market Theatre. On Friday evening, September 15th, '97. Will be presented . . . The Young Quaker . . . To which will be added . . . Don Juan . . . [Boston, 1797]
broadside 28 X 23 cm.
MHi mp. 48066

B9959 HEIDELBERG CATECHISM
A compendium of the Christian religion: taken from the Heidelberg Catechism . . . Frederick-Town, Matthias Bartgis, 1797.
16 p. 16 cm.
Minick 353
MdHi mp. 48139

B9960 HEIDELBERG CATECHISM
The Heidelbergh shorter catechism or a compendium of the Christian religion . . . Philadelphia, Henry Sweitzer, 1797.
35 p. 16mo
PPL mp. 48140

B9961 HERVEY, JAMES, 1714-1758
The beauties of Hervey . . . Philadelphia, Robert Campbell, 1797.
226, [6] p. 18 cm.
MWA; NhD mp. 48141

B9962 [HILLARD, ISAAC] b. 1737
To the honourable General Assembly of . . . Connecticut . . . The memorial of Harry, Cuff, and Cato, blackmen now in slavery in Connecticut . . . [n.p., 1797]
12 p. 21 cm. caption title
Trumbull: Supplement 2246
DLC. Photostat: CSmH mp. 48142

B9963 HILLARD, ISAAC, b. 1737
To the public. Whereas numbers . . . [n.p., 1797]
16 p.
CtHi mp. 48143

B9964 THE history of Jack Nips. Walpole, David Carlisle, 1797.
15 p. 17 cm.
NhHi mp. 48165

B9965 THE history of the blind beggar of Bethnal Green; shewing his birth and parentage. New-Haven, 1797.
45 p. illus. 9.5 cm.
Trumbull: Supplement 2253
CtHi mp. 48144

B9966 HOCHDEUTSCHES Lutherisches ABC und Namenbüchlein . . . Verbesserte Ausgabe. Hannover, Wilhelm Lepper und Endredy Stettinius, 1797.
14 leaves
Mrs. Augustus P. Loring, Boston (1944). Photostat: MWA (t.p. only) mp. 48145

B9967 [HONEYWOOD, ST. JOHN] 1763-1798
A poem on the President's farewell address, with a sketch of the character of his successor. Second edition. Philadelphia, Printed for John Ormrod by Ormrod & Conrad [1797?]
8 p. 21.5 cm.
Huntington 711; cf. Evans 30580
CSmH; PU mp. 48146

B9968 HOOK, JAMES, 1746-1827
Anna; or, The adieu . . . New York, Printed for and sold at I C Moller^s musical store [1797]
[2] p. 32 cm.
Sonneck-Upton p. 26
DLC; MB; MWA; NN mp. 48147

B9969 HOOK, JAMES, 1746-1827
Bright Phoebus, a favorite hunting song . . . New York, J. Hewitt; Philadelphia, B. Carr; Baltimore, J. Carr [1797-99]
[2] p. 34 cm.
Sonneck-Upton p. 49
DLC; MB; MH; NN mp. 48148

B9970 HOOK, JAMES, 1746-1827
The flower of yarrow . . . [New York] Printed for Hewitt & Rausch [1797]
broadside 32.5 cm.
Sonneck-Upton p. 143
DLC mp. 48149

B9971 [HOOK, JAMES] 1746-1827
The kiss . . . New York, B. Carr; Baltimore, J. Carr [1797?]
[2] p. 31.5 cm.
Sonneck-Upton p. 220
DLC; MB mp. 48150

B9972 [HOOK, JAMES] 1746-1827
Lash'd to the helm . . . New York and Philadelphia, B. Carr; Baltimore, J. Carr [1797]
[2] p. 33 cm.
Sonneck-Upton p. 224
DLC; MdHi; NN mp. 48151

B9973 HOOK, JAMES, 1746-1827
May Day morn, a favorite sonnett . . . [New York] Printed for and sold by James Hewitt; Philadelphia, B. Carr; Baltimore, J. Carr [1797-99]
[2] p. 34 cm.
Sonneck-Upton p. 257
DLC; MB mp. 48152

B9974 HOOK, JAMES, 1746-1827
Now's the time to sing and play . . . New York, J. Hewitt [1797-99]
[2] p. 31.5 cm.
Sonneck-Upton p. 302
DLC mp. 48153

B9975 HUDSON & GOODWIN, firm, Hartford
Hudson & Goodwin, have for sale at their store opposite the North Meeting-House, Hartford, the following books . . . [Hartford, 1797?]
broadside 42.5 × 37.5 cm.
Similar advt. in *Connecticut Courant*, Dec. 9, 1799, contains titles not on this list and apparently published in 1798
CtHi; NHi mp. 48154

B9975a HUMBERT, JONAS
Thoughts on the nature of civil government . . . New York, Wilson & Kirk, 1797.
69 p. 12mo
PHi

B9976 HUNTINGTON, WILLIAM, 1745-1813
God, the poor man's guardian . . . Newburyport: Printed and sold by William Barrett, Market-Square. 1797.
xi, [13]-124 p., 2 l. (the first blank), 24 p.
cf. Evans 32295
NN

B9977 AN hymn to be sung by the Episcopal charity-children, at St. Paul's Church, on Sunday, December the 3d, 1797, when a sermon will be preached . . . [New York, 1797]
broadside 33 × 20.5 cm.
NHi (2 copies) mp. 48156

B9978 I LOVE them all . . . Philadelphia, B. Carr; Baltimore, J. Carr; New York, J. Hewitt [1797]
2 p. 32.5 cm.
Sonneck-Upton p. 200
DLC; NN mp. 48157

B9979 ILLINOIS AND WABASH COMPANY
No. 1. To the committees of the Senate and House . . . on the Illinois and Wabash Companies . . . [Philadelphia, 1797]
8 p. 8vo caption title
cf. Sabin 84577n; not included in Evans 30618
PHi

B9980 ILLINOIS AND WABASH COMPANY
No. II. Additional statements by the agents of the Illinois and Wabash Land Companies . . . [Philadelphia, 1797]
7 p. 8vo caption title
PHi

B9981 ILLINOIS AND WABASH COMPANY
No. III. To the honourable committees of the Senate and House . . . on the Illinois and Wabash land purchases . . . [Philadelphia, 1797]
7 p. 8vo caption title
PHi

B9982 [JAMES, WILLIAM]
The letters of Charlotte, during her connexion with Werter . . . Vol. I. [-II.] New York, Printed by William A. Davis, for Napthali Judah, 1797.
2 v. in 1 (240 p. front.) 16.5 cm.
Variant of Evans 32313-14

Huntington 713
CSmH; MWA; MWiW-C mp. 48167

B9983 JOHNSON, JOHN, 1706-1791
The advantages and disadvantages of the marriage state . . . New-Haven, 1797.
22 p. 18.5 cm.
Trumbull: Supplement 2295
CtHi mp. 48159

B9984 [JONES, STEPHEN] 1763-1827
The life and adventures of a fly . . . Boston, Printed and sold by Samuel Etheridge, 1797.
95 p. 11.5 cm.
First and last leaves pasted to covers
MWA mp. 48160

B9985 JONES, THOMAS
Funeral sermon, sacred to the memory of . . . Elhanan Winchester . . . Sunday, May 7th, 1797. Philadelphia, Richard Folwell, 1797.
14, [1] p. 21 cm.
MWA; PPL mp. 48161

B9986 KATECHETISCHER unterricht für die Christl. Katholische Jugend. Herausgegeben von Fridericus Caesarius Reuter . . . [Baltimore] Samuel Saur, 1797.
4 p.l., 112 p. 15 cm.
Minick 363; Parsons 184
MdW mp. 48162

B9987 KENDAL, DAVID, d. 1853
The young lady's arithmetic . . . Leominster, Charles Prentiss, 1797.
44 p. 12mo
Without errata
Huntington 715; cf. Evans 32333
CSmH

B9988 LARKIN, EBENEZER, 1769?-1813
Boston, Feb. 20, 1797. Proposals, for printing by subscription, A gazetteer of America . . . by . . . Jedidiah Morse . . . A specimen of the work accompanies these proposals . . . Subscription papers be returned to E. Larkin, the publisher . . . [Boston, 1797]
[4] p. (enclosing p. [1]-32 of *The American gazetteer*, sig. B-E^4). 20.5 cm.
"Subscribers' names:" p. [3-4]
MWA mp. 48163

B9989 [LEE, RICHARD] 1747-1823
Fifty four acrostic, on the names of Richard Lee, and his four sons . . . [Rutland? Richard Fay? 1797?]
24 p. 17.5 cm.
Cooley 382; Huntington 716
CSmH (lower part of t.p. wanting, including imprint) mp. 48164

B9989a LELAND, JOHN, 1754–1841
A true account, how Matthew Womble murdered his wife . . . June the 19th, 1784 . . . Norwich: Printed for Richard Lee. 1797.
8 p.
Stoddard 142
N. D. Scotti, Providence, R.I. (1970)

B9990 LESLIE, CHARLES, 1650-1722
A short and easy method with the Deists . . . From the seventh London edition. Lexington [Ky.], John Bradford, 1797.
86 p. 21.5 cm.
MiU-C mp. 48166

B9991 LOUISIANA. GOVERNOR, 1792-1797
Proclamation. Le gouvernment ayant été informé . . . Nll. Orléans ce 31 Mai 1797. [New Orleans, 1797]
broadside 29 X 20.5 cm.
Signed in manuscript: Le Baron de Carondelet
McMurtrie: New Orleans 40; New York Public 1203
CU-B. Photostats: DLC; NN mp. 48168

B9992 MCCORKLE, SAMUEL EUSEBIUS, 1746-1811
Four discourses on the general first principles of deism and revelation contrasted; delivered . . . in April and May 1797 . . . Discourse I. Salisbury, Francis Coupee, 1797.
56 p. 17 cm.
Discourse II was printed in 1798; see below
McMurtrie: North Carolina 231
NcU. Bruce Cotten, Baltimore (1938) mp. 48169

B9993 MADAN, MARTIN, 1726-1790
An account of the triumphant death of F---- S---- . . . Concord, Printed by George Hough, for Francis Mitchel, of Hopkinton, N. Hampshire, 1797.
12 p. 17.5 cm.
MWA mp. 48171

B9994 MARSH, WILLIAM
A few select poems, composed on various subjects . . . To which is added an elegy, on the death of his two sons . . . Bennington, Anthony Haswell, 1797.
47 p. 18 cm.
Cooley 385
MWA; VtHi mp. 48172

B9995 [MARTIN, FRANÇOIS-XAVIER] 1746-1846
Notes of a few decisions in the Superior Courts of the State of North-Carolina, and in the Circuit Court of the U. States, for North-Carolina District. Newbern, Francois-Xavier Martin, 1797.
[8], 78, 83, [8] p. 20 cm.
Title page does not mention the Latch's cases sometimes included. cf. Evans 32426
McMurtrie: North Carolina 232
MH-L; NcA-S. Bruce Cotten, Baltimore (1938) mp. 48173

B9996 MARTINET, JOANNES FLORENTIUS, 1729-1795
The catechism of nature . . . New-Haven, Geo. Bunce, 1797.
107, [1] p. 13.5 cm.
Huntington 717
CSmH; CtHi; PPL mp. 48174

B9997 MARYLAND. AGENT
To the honourable the General assembly of Maryland. William Marbury, agent . . . begs leave to report . . . Nov. 8, 1797. [Annapolis, F. Green? 1797]
[2] p. 34 X 21.5 cm.
Minick 373
MdHi mp. 48175

B9998 MARYLAND. AUDITOR'S OFFICE
To the honourable the General assembly of Maryland. The auditor begs leave to lay before your honours the following accounts . . . Robert Denny, aud. gen. Auditor's office, Annapolis, Nov. 22, 1797. [Annapolis, F. Green? 1797]
broadside 17 X 21 cm.

Minick 374
MdHi mp. 48176

B9999 MARYLAND. LAWS
Act of incorporation of the city of Baltimore. An act to erect Baltimore Town . . . Baltimore, D. Finchet Freebairn, 1797.
broadside 48.5 X 32 cm.
Minick 334; New York Public 1196
MdHi; NN mp. 48177

B10000 MARYLAND. LAWS
[An act to establish a bank, and incorporate the subscribers thereto. Baltimore, John Hayes, 1797]

Advertised in the *Maryland Journal*, June 9, 1797, as "Published and for sale by John Hayes."
Minick 342
No copy known mp. 48178

B10001 MARYLAND, Virginia and Kentucky almanack, for the year . . . 1798 . . . Baltimore, Printed for G. Keating's book store [1797]
[36] p. 17 cm.
Drake 2258; Minick 362
DeWin (imperfect); MdHi (17 l.) mp. 48179

B10002 MASSACHUSETTS
Commonwealth of Massachusetts. To the selectmen of the town of . . . March 23, 1797. [Boston, 1797]
broadside
Precept to elect a representative to Congress
Ford 2830; cf. Evans 25781
M-Ar mp. 48180

B10003 MASSACHUSETTS. GENERAL COURT
Commonwealth of Massachusetts. In Senate, Feb. 27, 1797. On the petitions of Thomas Rice and others . . . Resolved, That it shall be the duty of the selectmen . . . In the House . . . Feb. 28, 1797. Read and concurred . . . March 2d, 1797–Approved, Samuel Adams . . . Boston, Young and Minns [1797]
broadside 34 X 22 cm.
Ordering a vote on the separation of Maine from Massachusetts
MWA mp. 48181

B10004 MASSACHUSETTS. TREASURER
Tax, for the year 1797 . . . In obedience to a law . . . passed the 22d day of February, 1797 . . . [Boston, 1797]
broadside 43.5 X 34 cm.
Tax warrant dated in manuscript March 15
Ford 2828
DLC; MB mp. 48182

B10005 MERCIER, LOUIS SÉBASTIEN, 1740-1814
Seraphina: a novel . . . To which is added Auguste & Madelaine . . . By Miss Helen Maria Williams. Charlestown, John Lamson, 1797.
102 p. 10.5 cm. A-C^{16} D^{4}
MWA mp. 48183

B10006 MOORE, JOHN HAMILTON, d. 1807
The young gentleman and lady's monitor . . . New Haven, Printed by George Bunce for Spencer, 1797.
322, [30] p.
cf. Evans 32494
MWA mp. 48184

B10007 MORE, HANNAH, 1745-1833
The search after happiness: a pastoral drama. A new edition . . . Boston, Printed and sold by William Spotswood, 1797.
33, [3] p. 16mo
MWA; PPL mp. 48185

B10008 MOULTRIE, ALEXANDER [ET AL.] VS. GEORGIA
United States, in equity, to wit, in the Supreme Court. To the honourable Oliver Ellsworth . . . Alexander Moultrie, Isaac Huger . . . complaints . . . [p. 18] . . . filed in the Supreme Court [June 24, 1796] . . . I Wagner . . . [Philadelphia? 1797?]
18 p. 33 cm. caption title
Accompanied by ms. map and reply certified by I. Wagner Aug. 30, 1797
Probably a copy of the original complaint (summer of 1796) prepared after 1797 decree
MiU-C

B10009 [NÄGELI, HANS GEORG] 1773-1836
The favorite German song Freut euch des Lebens, in German and English. New York, Printed & sold by G. Gilfert [1797-1801]
[2] p. 33.5 cm. caption title
Sonneck-Upton p. 229
MiU-C

B10010 NANCREDE, PAUL JOSEPH GUÉRARD DE, 1760-1841
Books published by Joseph Nancrede, No. 49, Marlborough Street, Boston . . . [Boston, 1797?]
[4] p. 20.5 cm.
Dated from publication dates of six titles in the list published by Nancrede
DLC mp. 48186

B10011 NEAL, JAMES A.
Philadelphia, December 18th, 1797. Hitherto my zealous exertions . . . James A. Neal. [Philadelphia, 1797]
[2] p.
Increasing the tuition of his school one dollar
PHi

B10012 NEW ENGLAND MISSISSIPPI LAND COMPANY
Articles of association and agreement, constituting the New-England Mississippi Land Company. [Boston, 1797?]
7 p. 8vo
De Renne p. 281; Vail: Old frontier 1134
GU-De mp. 48187

B10013 THE new game of cards . . . Printed and sold at Northampton, 1797.
8 p.
MWA mp. 48188

B10014 NEW HAMPSHIRE. GOVERNOR, 1794-1805
State of New-Hampshire. To the selectmen of Greeting. The Hon. Jeremiah Smith having resigned his office as a representative . . . in the Congress . . . John Taylor Gilman, governor . . . Exeter, Henry Ranlet [1797]
broadside 29.5 X 20.5 cm.
Dated Sept. 23, 1797
Calls for the election of Peleg Sprague or Woodbury Langdon to replace Smith
MiU-C

B10015 NEW HAMPSHIRE. HOUSE OF REPRESENTATIVES
State of New-Hampshire. In the House of Representatives, Dec. 7th, 1797. Resolved, that the selectmen . . . shall take an inventory of the polls and rateable estates . . . [Portsmouth] J. Melcher, printer [1797?]
broadside 30 X 38 cm.

"Approved, December 9th, 1797."
MiU-C

B10016 NEW HAMPSHIRE. LAWS
The laws of the State of New-Hampshire, passed . . . at Portsmouth, November, 1797 . . . Portsmouth, John Melcher, 1797.
1 p.l., 499-512 p. 23 cm.
New York Public 1205
NN mp. 48190

B10017 NEW HAMPSHIRE. SENATE
A journal of the proceedings of the Honorable Senate . . . of New-Hampshire . . . June, 1797. Portsmouth, John Melcher, 1797.
58 p. 19.5 cm.
New York Public 1204
MWA; NN mp. 48189

B10018 [A NEW introduction to reading . . . The fourth edition, with additions, compiled by the publisher. Baltimore, Joseph Townsend, 1797]

Title from the *Federal Gazette*, Feb. 18, 1797, as "Just published, and for sale by Joseph Townsend."
Minick 387
Bordeaux Public Lib. mp. 48191

B10019 NEW JERSEY
State of New-Jersey. sitting of legislature. This is to certify, that has attended days of this present sitting . . . Given . . . this day of 1797 . . . [n.p., 1797?]
broadside 17 X 21 cm.
MiU-C

B10020 NEW JERSEY. ADJUTANT GENERAL'S OFFICE
Adjutant General's Office. The adjutant general having reported the dates . . . Ant. W. White, Adjutant General. November 14, 1797. [Trenton? 1797]
broadside 17.5 X 10.5 cm.
NjR

B10021 NEW JERSEY. ADJUTANT GENERAL'S OFFICE
Adjutant General's Office. September 16, 1797. In order that the following resolve of the Legislature . . . may be immediately complied with . . . name, rank and date of commissions of the officers . . . Anth. W. White . . . [Trenton? 1797]
broadside 19 X 11.5 cm.
NjR

B10022 NEW JERSEY. ADJUTANT GENERAL'S OFFICE
General orders. Trenton, August 16, 1797. The commander in chief of New-Jersey having received direction from . . . the President . . . to organize, arm and equip . . . Anthony W. White, Adjutant General. [Trenton? 1797]
broadside 24.5 X 15.5 cm.
NjR

B10023 NEW JERSEY. GENERAL ASSEMBLY
Votes and proceedings of the twenty second General Assembly of the state of New-Jersey . . . Being the first sitting. Trenton, Matthias Day, 1797.
73 p. 32 cm.
Session Oct. 24-Nov. 10, 1797
Huntington 720; New York Public 1206
CSmH; NN; Nj; NjHi; PPL mp. 48192

B10024 NEW JERSEY. LAWS
An additional supplement to an act . . . for organizing and training the militia . . . [Mar. 9, 1797] . . . [Trenton, 1797]
23 p. 17.5 cm.
Huntington 719; Morsch 356
CSmH; NjP mp. 48193

B10025 NEW JERSEY. LEGISLATIVE COUNCIL
Journal of the proceedings of the Legislative Council of the State of New-Jersey . . . Trenton, Matthias Day, 1797.
93 p. 32 cm.
1st-2nd sittings of the twenty-first session
NN; Nj; NjHi; NjR; PPL mp. 48194

B10026 [THE New-Jersey and New-York almanack for . . . 1798. Newark, Jacob Halsey [1797]]

Drake 5179
No copy known

B10027 NEW YORK. COURT FOR THE TRIAL OF IMPEACHMENTS AND THE CORRECTION OF ERRORS
State of the case and argument on the part of Gouverneur and Kemble, in their controversy with Louis Le Guen. 1797. New-York, Printed at the Argus Office, 1797.
99 p. 20 cm.
NNC-L

B10028 NEW YORK. NEW THEATRE
New-York, October 2, 1797. New Theatre, Greenwich-Street . . . On Wednesday evening, the 4th of October . . . The way to get married . . . To which will be added . . . The death of Captain Cook . . . [New York, 1797]
broadside
New York Public 1208
NN (reduced facsim.) mp. 48195

B10029 NEW YORK. SUPREME COURT
Rules reflecting the admission of attornies and counsellors in the Supreme Court of Judicature . . . of New-York. At a Supreme Court . . . held for the State . . . at the City-Hall of the City . . . the 28th day of October, 1797, Ordered, 1st. . . . Jas. Fairlie, Clk. [New York, 1797]
broadside 33.5 X 20 cm.
MH mp. 48196

B10030 NEW YORK. SURVEYOR GENERAL
Gentlemen, By an act of the legislature . . . in addition . . . to . . . "An act for the further direction of the Commissioners of the Land-Office . . ." passed the 28th of March, 1797 . . . Albany, 20th May, 1797 . . . [Albany, 1797]
broadside 42 X 27 cm.
Concerns directions for making local maps
McMurtrie: Albany 156
MH mp. 48197

B10031 NEW YORK HOSPITAL
No. 1. Charity extended to all. State of New-York Hospital for . . . 1797. Governors. Gerald Walton, President. Matthew Clarkson, Vice-President . . . This Institution was undertaken by private subscriptions . . . in the year 1770, and . . . incorporated . . . 1771 . . . [New York, 1797]
[4] p. 38 cm.
MH mp. 48198

B10032 NEW YORK MISSIONARY SOCIETY
Thoughts on the plan for social prayer, proposed by

the directors of the New-York Missionary Society . . . New-York, T. & J. Swords, 1797.
10 p. 16 cm.
CtHi mp. 48199

B10033 NEWARK GAZETTE
Proposals for publishing (by the proprietors of the *Newark Gazette*) by subscription, a weekly paper . . . the *Rural Magazine* . . . [Newark, 1797?]
broadside 54 X 21.5 cm.
Not mentioned by Brigham
NHi mp. 48321

B10034 NEWBERN THEATRE
Newbern Theatre. Dr. Llewellyn Lechmere Wall . . . will on . . . the 16th of May, 1797, administer . . . wholesome physic to the mind . . . [Newbern, J. Pasteur, 1797]
broadside 20 X 16.5 cm.
"Tickets may be had . . . at the Printing-Office of J. Pasteur . . ."
ViWC mp. 48200

B10035 NEWBERN THEATRE
New theatre, Newbern. This evening, Friday March the 31st, 1797, will be presented, a variety of entertainments . . . [Newbern, J. Pasteur, 1797]
broadside 37 X 16 cm.
"Tickets to be had . . . at the Printing-Office, of J. Pasteur . . ."
ViWC mp. 48201

B10036 NEWBERN THEATRE
To all lovers of wit, satire . . . and sentiment. At the Newbern Theatre. Llewellyn L. Wall . . . will exhibit on . . . the 13th of May, 1797: an antidote for the spleen . . . [Newbern, J. Pasteur, 1797]
broadside 20 X 16 cm.
ViWC mp. 48202

B10037 NEWBURYPORT, MASS. ORDINANCES
Bye-laws of Newburyport . . . Newburyport, July, 1797 . . . [Newburyport, 1797]
broadside 45 X 43 cm.
In four columns
DLC mp. 48203

B10038 NEWCASTLE COUNTY, DEL.
List of rates, for innkeepers in the County of New-Castle, as settled by the justices of the Court of General Sessions . . . in the May sessions, one thousand seven hundred and ninety-seven . . . Newcastle, S. & J. Adams [1797]
broadside 14 cm.
Hawkins: List C 18
DeHi mp. 48204

B10039 NEWS carrier's address to his customers. For January 1, 1797 . . . [n.p., 1797]
broadside
1st line: As custom directs me, once more I appear . . .
NHi mp. 48205

B10040 NEWTON, JOHN, 1725-1807
A review of ecclesiastical history . . . Whitehall: Printed by William Young, Philadelphia, 1797.
xviii, 320 p. 12mo
PPL mp. 48206

B10041 THE nightingale. Amherst, Samuel Preston, 1797.

BSA *Papers*, 54(1960):65
MWA (imperfect) mp. 48207

B10042 NORTH ASSOCIATION OF HARTFORD COUNTY
The North Association of Hartford County, To the piously and benevolently disposed within our limits . . . Farmington October 4, 1797 . . . [n.p., 1797]
broadside 17 X 16 cm.
DLC; NHi mp. 48095

B10043 O'KEEFFE, JOHN, 1747-1833
The Highland Reel: a comic opera, in three acts. As performed . . . at the Theatre–Federal-street . . . Boston, Printed for Wm. P. and L. Blake, 1797.
68, [3] p. 15.5 cm.
CSmH mp. 48208

B10044 ON Joseph's making himself known to his brethren . . . [Boston? 1797?]
broadside 35 X 12 cm.
cf. Evans 32613
MWA mp. 48209

B10045 PAINE, THOMAS, 1737-1809
Agrarian justice, opposed to agrarian law, and to agrarian monopoly . . . Albany, Printed and sold by Barber & Southwick, 1797.
31, [1] p. 20.5 cm.
McMurtrie: Albany 157
N mp. 48210

B10046 PAINE, THOMAS, 1737-1809
The rights of man, for the benefit of all mankind . . . Philadelphia: Printed and sold by D. Webster, a British exile. 1797.
iv, 56 p. 20.5 cm.
Adams: Pennsylvania 69
PU. Pierce W. Gaines, Fairfield, Conn. (1964)
mp. 48211

B10047 PAISIELLO, GIOVANNI, 1741-1816
Recitative e rondo . . . Filadelfia, Trisobio [1797]
8 p. 34.5 cm.
Sonneck-Upton p. 351
DLC mp. 48212

B10048 PAPERS respecting intrusions by Connecticut claimants. [Colophon] [Philadelphia] Hall & Sellers [1797?]
6 p. 34 cm. caption title
Latest date in text: Jan. 3, 1797
In double columns
New York Public 1209; cf. Evans 30958
NN (p. 3-4 wanting) mp. 48213

B10049 PARKER, RICHARD, d. 1797
The tryal. Last dying words, speech and confession of Richard Parker, (alias Admiral Parker) late president of the mutinous fleet . . . executed . . . the 30th of June, 1797 . . . [New York? 1797?]
broadside 44 X 27 cm.
NHi mp. 48214

B10050 PAUL, WILLIAM
A treatise on prayer . . . West Springfield, Edward Gray [1797?]
44 p.
Gray published in West Springfield Oct. 4, 1796 to Nov. 28, 1797
MWA mp. 48215

B10051 PENNSYLVANIA. HOUSE OF REPRESENTATIVES
Journal of the second session of the seventh House of

Representatives of . . . Pennsylvania . . . Philadelphia, Hall and Seller, 1797.
18 p. fol.
Session Aug. 28-29, 1797
PPL mp. 48218

B10052 PENNSYLVANIA. HOUSE OF REPRESENTATIVES
A list of the members and offieers of the House of Representatives of . . . Pennsylvania, with the places of their residence in . . . Philadelphia. [Philadelphia, 1797?]
broadside 45 X 28 cm.
The names correspond with the membership of the 1st session of the 7th House (Dec. 1796-Apr. 1797)
DLC

B10053 PENNSYLVANIA. LAWS
No. XXXVIII. In General Assembly. Friday, January 27, 1797. An act for affording relief to persons who have paid money into the Land Office . . . [Philadelphia] Thomas Bradford [1797]
4 p. fol.
PPL mp. 48216

B10054 PENNSYLVANIA. LAWS
No. LXXV. In General assembly Friday, March 3, 1797. An act to prevent and punish . . . [Philadelphia, 1797]
16 p. 34 cm. caption title
DLC mp. 48217

B10055 PENNSYLVANIA. MILITIA
Huntingdon 21 Oct. 1797. In conformity to the commands of the governor . . . [marching orders of brigade inspector to each field officer]. [signed] John Cadwallader, brigade inspector. [n.p., 1797]
broadside 21.5 X 19 cm.
Not filled in
MiU-C

B10056 PENNSYLVANIA. MILITIA
Sir, In obedience to brigade orders, to draft men from my company, you are hereby notified that you . . . appear . . . in readiness to march at a moment's warning. Given . . . this day of Oct. A.D. 1797. Captain. To Mr. [n.p., 1797]
broadside 7 X 19 cm.
MiU-C (not filled in)

B10057 PENNSYLVANIA. REGISTER-GENERAL
Report of the Register-general of the state of the finances of Pennsylvania, for the year 1796. Philadelphia, Hall and Sellers, 1797.
16 p. fol.
Not Evans 32657 (also in PPL)
PPL

B10058 THE Pennsylvania almanack for . . . 1798 . . . By Joshua Sharp . . . Philadelphia, Printed for Robert Campbell [1797]
[32] p.
Drake 10467
PDoBHi

B10059 PENNSYLVANIA HOSPITAL
The committee appointed to prepare an account of the monies received from the Legislature . . . report . . . [Philadelphia, 1797]
broadside
PPL

B10060 PENNSYLVANIA HOSPITAL
To the Senate and House of Representatives, of the Commonwealth of Pennsylvania. The memorial of the managers of the Pennsylvania Hospital . . . 12th month, 28th, 1797. [Philadelphia, 1797]
[2] p. fol.
PPAmP; PPL mp. 48219

B10061 PENNSYLVANIA LAND COMPANY
A schedule of the property of the Pennsylvania Land Company . . . [Philadelphia? 1797?]
12 p. 22 cm. caption title
NHi mp. 48220

B10062 PENNSYLVANIA LAND COMPANY
Statement of the incumbrances at present on the property of the Pennsylvania Land Company. [Philadelphia, 1797]
3 p. 22 cm.
Sabin 60341; Vail: Old frontier 1138
DLC; NHi; PPAmP mp. 48221

B10063 PENNSYLVANISCHER Calender auf das 1798ste Jahr . . . York, Salomon Mäyer [1797]
[44] p. 20 cm.
Drake 10470
MWA; PAtM (20 l.); PHi; PPG mp. 48222

B10064 [PERCY, JOHN] 1749-1797
The captive. New York, I. C. Moller [1797]
[2] p. 32.5 cm.
Sonneck-Upton p. 55
DLC mp. 48223

B10065 PERKINS, DANIEL
An oration, pronounced before the Western Star Lodge, in Bridgewater . . . June 24, A.L. 5797 . . . Whitestown, William M'Lean, 1797.
16 p. 17 cm.
N. Photostats: DLC; MWA; NN mp. 48224

B10066 PERKINS, ELISHA, 1741-1799
Evidences of the efficacy of Doctor Perkins's patent metallic instruments. Richmond, John Dixon [1797]
40 p. 16 cm.
Austin 1497; Huntington 722
CSmH mp. 48225

B10067 [PERRAULT, CHARLES] 1628-1703
Little Red Riding-Hood, The fairy, and Blue Beard; with morals. Philadelphia, Printed and sold by John M'Culloch, 1797.
31 p. 10 cm.
d'Alté A. Welch, Cleveland (1962) mp. 48226

B10068 PHILADELPHIA
. . . Information relative to the title of the Corporation to the North-east Public-square . . . Alexander Wilcocks, Recorder. Philadelphia, June 5th, 1797. [Philadelphia] Zachariah Poulson, junior, June 13th, 1797.
broadsheet ([2] p.) 35.5 X 21 cm.
Plan of Philadelphia, by Thomas Holmes
Imprint at head of title
PHi mp. 48227

B10068a PHILADELPHIA. POST OFFICE
Post-office, Philadelphia, 30th. March, 1797 . . . Robert Patton, post-master. [Philadelphia, 1797]
broadside 43 X 25.5 cm.
DLC; MWA mp. 48230

B10069 PHILADELPHIA DISPENSARY
To the attending physician of the Philadelphia Dispensary. I recommend . . . to the care of the Dispensary,

believing to be a proper object of this charity . . . [Philadelphia, 1797]
broadside 20 X 15.5 cm.
Includes 6 rules to observed by patients
PU mp. 48228

B10070 PHILADELPHIA GAZETTE
Brown's Gazette extra. Symptoms of treason! . . . Col. King's Iron-Works, April 21, 1797. Dear Carey . . . William Blount . . . Office of the *Philadelphia Gazette*. Wednesday evening, July 5. [Philadelphia, 1797]
broadside 28.5 X 33.5 cm.
MWA mp. 48072

B10071 PHILADELPHIA SOCIETY FOR THE INFORMATION AND ASSISTANCE OF PERSONS EMIGRATING FROM FOREIGN COUNTRIES
The act of incorporation, constitution and by-laws of the Philadelphia Society . . . with a compilation of the laws of the United States and . . . Pennsylvania, relative to mariners and persons . . . from foreign countries. Philadelphia, Joseph Gales, 1797.
72 p. 20 cm.
In contemporary ms.: by W. F.
MWA mp. 48232

B10072 PHINNEY'S calendar: or, Western almanack for . . . 1798. By Gabriel Goodweather. Cooperstown, Elihu Phinney [1797]

Drake 6073
NBuHi (7.1): NCooHi (t.p. only); NSchU (9.1)

B10073 [PLAN of Baltimore. Baltimore, Published by George Keatinge, 1797]

Advertised in the *Telegraphe and Daily Advertiser*, Dec. 9, 1797, as "This day is published, and for sale at George Keatinge's . . . the plan of Baltimore . . . elegantly engraved by Galland, from actual survey."
Minick 364
No copy known mp. 48132

B10074 PLEASANT stories and lessons for children. Fairhaven, J. P. Spooner, 1797.
30, [1] p. incl. covers. 10 cm.
Cooley 390
VtHi mp. 48233

B10075 POLE, EDWARD
Large folio Bible. On Thursday the twenty-ninth of June . . . at public auction . . . folio edition (in sheets) of the Holy Bible . . . Edward Pole. Philadelphia, June 22, 1797. [Philadelphia, 1797]
broadside
PHi

B10076 POOR Richard improved: being an almanack . . . for the year . . . 1798 . . . Philadelphia, Printed and sold by Hall & Sellers [1797]
[44] p. 17.5 cm.
Drake 10471
MB; PDoBHi; PHi (imperfect) mp. 48234

B10077 POUGHKEEPSIE JOURNAL
To the worthy supporters of the *Poughkeepsie Journal* . . . Wet from the types and scarcely born . . . January 1, 1797. [Poughkeepsie, 1797]
broadside 36 X 16.5 cm.
Within ornamental border
NHi mp. 48273

B10078 PRINCETON UNIVERSITY
Catalogus Collegii Naeo-Caesariensis. Trenton, Matthias Day [1797]
16 p. 22 cm.
Morsch 363
MWA; NjHi; NjP mp. 48235

B10079 THE prodigal daughter . . . Boston, Printed and sold at Russell's Office, 1797.
16 p. 22 cm.
MWA (poor) mp. 48236

B10080 PROTESTANT EPISCOPAL CHURCH IN THE U.S.A. MARYLAND (DIOCESE)
Journal of a convention . . . held at Easton, from May 19, to May 21, 1797 . . . Baltimore, John Hayes, 1797.
24 p. 18 cm.
Minick 391; New York Public 1210
DLC; MWA; MdBP; MdHi; NN mp. 48237

B10081 PROTESTANT EPISCOPAL CHURCH IN THE U.S.A. SOUTH CAROLINA (DIOCESE)
Constitutional rules for the order, good government and discipline of the Protestant Episcopal Church, in . . . South-Carolina. Charleston, Timothy & Mason, 1797.
8 p. 19.5 cm.
MH-AH

B10082 READING THEATRE, READING, PA.
Reading Theatre, (under the direction of Mr. M'Grath.) on Thursday evening, February 7, will be acted . . . George Barnwell . . . After the play, Brother M'Grath will have the honor of delivering a Masonic address . . . [Reading, Jacob Schneider? 1797]
broadside
Nolan p. 30
J. Bennett Nolan, Reading, Pa. (1930) mp. 48238

B10083 [REEVE, WILLIAM] 1757–1815
The galley slave. New York, Printed & sold by J. Hewitt. Sold also by B. Carr, Philadelphia & J. Carr, Baltimore [1797–99]
[2] p. 33.5 cm.
Sonneck–Upton p. 153
MiU–C

B10084 [REEVE, WILLIAM] 1757–1815
The witch . . . New York, G. Gilfert [1797]
[2] p. 34 cm.
Sonneck-Upton p. 474
DLC; MWA mp. 48239

B10085 [REINAGLE, ALEXANDER] 1756–1809
Indian march of the much admeired [!] American play caled [sic] Columbus. Philadelphia, C. Hupfeld [ca. 1797]
broadside 33 cm.
Sonneck-Upton p. 207
One Charles Hupfeld was listed as a grocer in the 1799 Philadelphia directory
ICN mp. 48240

B10086 REINAGLE, ALEXANDER, 1756–1809
. . . Song in The stranger . . . The words by R. B. Sheridan, the air by A. Reinagle. Philadelphia, B. Carr [etc.] [1797–1799]
2 leaves. 31 cm. caption title
MiU–C mp. 48250

B10087 RHODE ISLAND. ELECTION PROX.
1797. His Excellency Arthur Fenner, Esq; Governor. The honourable Samuel J. Potter, Esq; Deputy-governor . . . [Providence] Carter and Wilkinson [1797]

broadside 23 X 14 cm.
Alden 1536; Chapin Proxies 49a, 49b
RHi (2 variants) mp. 48241

B10088 RICHARDSON, SAMUEL, 1689–1761
The history of Sir Charles Grandison . . . Twelfth edition. New-London, James Springer, 1797.
156 p. 24 mo
Trumbull: Supplement 2567
No copy located mp. 48242

B10089 RICKETTS, JOHN BILL
Ricketts's Circus, lower end of Greene-Street. On Friday, August the 4th, 1797, a great variety of equestrian exercises . . . [Albany, 1797]
broadside 44 X 27.5 cm.
New York Public 1212
American Autograph Shop, Merion Station, Pa. (1940).
NN (reduced facsim.) mp. 48243

B10090 [ROBSON, JOHN C]
A scriptural view of the rise of the heathen, Jewish, and Christian monarchies . . . New-York, Printed and sold by J. Buel, 1797.
99, [1] p. 22.5 cm.
MWA mp. 48244

B10091 ROSS, AARON
Stone cutting. The subscriber begs leave to inform the public . . . he proposes carrying on the stone cutting business . . . Aaron Ross. New-Brunswick, May 13, 1797. New-Brunswick, A. Blauvelt [1797]
broadside 19 X 23.5 cm.
NjR

B10092 [S., R.]
Jachin and Boaz; or, An authentic key to the door of Free Masonry . . . A new edition, greatly enlarged and improved. Albany, Charles R. & George Webster, 1797.
75, [1] p. front. 16 cm. $A–I^4 K^2$
IaCrM (2 copies); MBFM; MWA; NNFM; RPJCB
mp. 48158

B10093 ST. CECILIA SOCIETY
Constitution and bye laws of the New-York St. Cecilia Society, adopted 7th January 1797. New-York, John Harrisson, 1797.
8 p. 17 cm.
NHi mp. 48245

B10094 ST. PIERRE, JACQUES HENRI BERNARDIN DE, 1737–1814
A vindication of Divine Providence . . . Translated by Henry Hunter . . . First American edition. Worcester, Printed [by Thomas, Son & Thomas] for J. Nancrede, 1797.
[2], 331, [4] p. front. 20.5 cm.
Ends with the words: The end
cf. Evans 32797
MWA; NhD; RPJCB

B10095 ST. THOMAS'S AFRICAN CHURCH, PHILADELPHIA
Constitutions and rules to be observed and kept by the Friendly society of St. Thomas's African church . . . Philadelphia, W. W. Woodward, 1797.
8 p. 19.5 cm.
Porter 229
PPAmP; PPL mp. 48231

B10096 SAMMLUNG von erbaulichen gesängen . . . für die deutschen gemeinen in Nord-Carolina. Die erste Auflage . . . Salisbury, F. Coupee und J. M. Schlump, 1797.
[2], 30 p. 17 cm.
NcWsM mp. 48246

B10097 SCOTT, SARAH ROBINSON, d. 1795
The man of sensibility . . . Philadelphia, John Johnson, 1797.
92 p. 16.5 cm.
cf. Evans 32812
ViU mp. 48247

B10098 THE seaman's journal-book . . . Providence, Carter and Wilkinson, 1797.
[48] p. 32.5 cm.
Alden 1550
RPJCB mp. 48248

B10099 SEVEN SAGES
The history of the Seven Wise Masters of Rome . . . New-York, Printed and sold by John Tiebout, 1797.
95 p. 12 cm.
MH (imperfect) mp. 48249

B10100 [SHEET almanack for 1798. New-London, S. Green, 1797]
broadside
Advertised in the *Connecticut Gazette*, Jan. 10, 1798, as "Sheet Almanacks, for 1798, for sale by S. Green."
Drake 579
No copy known

B10101 [SHIELD, WILLIAM] 1748–1829
The streamlet . . . New York, J. Hewitt; Philadelphia, B. Carr; Baltimore, J. Carr [1797–99]
broadside 32 cm.
Sonneck-Upton p. 411
DLC; NN; PP; RPJCB mp. 48251

B10102 [SHIELD, WILLIAM] 1748–1829
Whilst with village maids I stray. New York, I. C. Moller [1797]
[2] p. 33 cm.
Sonneck-Upton p. 470
DLC mp. 48252

B10103 SIBBES, RICHARD, 1577–1635
Divine meditations and holy contemplations . . . on the Philadelphia plague . . . Wilmington, Printed by Bonsal & Niles, for Molleston Correy, 1797.
60 p. 12mo
PPL mp. 48253

B10104 [SMITH, DANIEL] 1740–1818
A short description of the state of Tennessee . . . New-York, J. S. Mott, 1797.
47 p. 17 cm.
Huntington 724
CSmH mp. 48254

B10104a A SOLEMN call to the citizens of the United States. By a citizen of Newburyport . . . Newburyport: Printed and sold by Angier March [1797?]
11 p. 18.5 cm.
Sabin 86361; Stoddard 229
RPB

B10105 SOUTH CAROLINA. CITIZENS
The petition of the subscribers, inhabitants of Orange, Richland . . . Union, York and Spartanburgh Counties . . . sheweth . . . greatly advanced by clearing . . . the Congaree, Broad and Pacolet rivers . . . [Charleston? 1797]

broadside 51 × 41 cm.
In ms.: 10th November 1797
Sc–Ar

B10106 SOUTH CAROLINA. COMMISSIONERS OF THE TOBACCO INSPECTION
Rules, to be observed, agreeable to law, by the tobacco inspectors . . . Commissioners of the Tobacco Inspection. Charleston, January 6, 1797. [Charleston] W. P. Young [1797]
broadside 27 × 21 cm.
Sc–Ar

B10107 SOUTH CAROLINA. GOVERNOR
State of South-Carolina, by His Excellency Charles Pinckney, Governor . . . a proclamation [against illegal enlistments for improper purposes] . . . [Aug. 24, 1797] . . . Stephen Ravenel, Secretary of the State. [Charleston, 1797]
broadside 31.5 × 19 cm.
Mosimann 591
DNA

B10108 SOUTH CAROLINA. HOUSE OF REPRESENTATIVES
In the House of Representatives, December 6, 1797. The committee, to whom it was referred, to ascertain the debts due by the state . . . report . . . Columbia, Young & Faust [1797]
broadside 43 × 33.5 cm.
Sc–Ar

B10109 SOUTH CAROLINA. HOUSE OF REPRESENTATIVES
In the House of Representatives, December 9, 1797 . . . [at end] [Charleston] Printed by Daniel Faust & Co. [1797]
[2] p. 44.5 cm. caption title
Sc–Ar

B10110 SOUTH CAROLINA SOCIETY FOR PROMOTING AND IMPROVING AGRICULTURE
Agricultural Society, Monday, October, 1797. On motion, received, That all members who are in arrers . . . be . . . wrote to . . . P. Bounetheau, Secretary . . . [Charleston, 1797]
broadside 23 × 19 cm.
On folded sheet for addressing
Signed by John Champneys as treasurer
ScU

B10111 SOWER, SAMUEL, 1767–1820
Printing and binding done with neatness and dispatch, by Samuel Sower, Fayette-street. [Baltimore, S. Sower, 1797?]
broadside 6 × 9.5 cm.
Minick 395
NN mp. 48255

B10112 [SPOFFORD, REGINALD] 1770–1827
Ellen, the Richmond primrose girl . . . Philadelphia and New York, B. Carr; Baltimore, J. Carr [1797?]
[2] p. 32.5 cm.
Sonneck-Upton p. 123
DLC; MB; MWA; MdHi mp. 48256

B10113 [SPOFFORD, REGINALD] 1770–1827
Hark the goddess Diana . . . New York, J. Hewitt; Philadelphia, B. Carr; Baltimore, J. Carr [1797–99]
3 p. 32.5 cm.
Sonneck-Upton p. 178
DLC; MB; MWA; MdHi; MiU–C; NN; PP–K
mp. 48257

B10114 STEWART, JESSE
Genuine French Creek Seneca oil, an excellent and approved medicine, may be had in Springfield, of Mr. Jesse Stewart, nigh Mr. Roll's tavern. A short account of this oil, its virtucs and uses . . . [Springfield, N. J.? 1797?]
broadside
NNNAM. Photocopy: NjR mp. 48258

B10115 [STORACE, STEPHEN] 1763–1796
Fal lal la the favorite Welch air . . . New York, G. Gilfert [1797]
[2] p. 33 cm.
Sonneck-Upton p. 133
DLC mp. 48259

B10116 [STORACE, STEPHEN] 1763–1796
Tho' you think by this to vex me . . . New York, James Hewitt; Philadelphia, B. Carr; Baltimore, J. Carr [1797–99]
[2] p. 32.5 cm.
Sonneck-Upton p. 430
DLC; MdHi; NN mp. 48260

B10117 THE story of Joseph. Philadelphia, Printed for Joseph Crukshank, 1797.
48 p. 10.5 cm.
MWA mp. 48261

B10118 TAMMANY SOCIETY
Jany 1 1797 Brother, you are requested to attend a meeting of the Tammany Society, or Columbian Order, to be held on next . . . Secretary. [New York, 1797]
broadside
PHi

B10119 TAPLIN, WILLIAM, d. 1807
A compendium of practical and experimental farriery . . . Philadelphia, Printed for Robert Cambell [sic] & Co., 1797.
2 p.l. (2nd blank), [iii]–viii, 290, [6] p. fold. front. 17.5 cm.
DLC; MWA; RPJCB mp. 48262

B10120 TAYLOR, AMOS, 1748–fl. 1813
[Poetical specimens of a new, beautiful and religious system of English education. Putney, C. Sturtevant jun. & Co., 1797]

Possibly advertised in the *Argus*, May 4, 1797, as "The Christian art of teaching the rules of reading and singing."
McCorison 454
No copy known mp. 48263

B10121 [TAYLOR, RAYNOR] 1747–1825
While the morn is inviting to love . . . Philadelphia, B. Carr; Baltimore, J. Carr; New York, J. Hewitt [1797–99]
[2] p. 33 cm.
Sonneck-Upton p. 469
DLC; MdHi; MiU–C; NN; PP mp. 48264

B10122 THE tea-drinking wife. To which are added, The tempest, and Pretty Nancy. New-York: Printed for the hawkers.—1797.
8 p. 16.5 cm.
In verse
RPB (p. 3–6 lacking); MWA (Xerox copy) mp. 48265

B10123 [THE tenets of Union discipline. Baltimore? 1797]

Title from advertisement in the *Federal Gazette*, which states, "On Sabbath, the 4th day of June, 1797 . . . there

will also be a number of pamphlets distributed, entitled, 'The tenets of Union discipline'."
Minick 397
No copy known mp. 48266

B10124 THOMAS & ANDREWS, firm
Proposal for printing by subscription, The life of Ezra Stiles . . . by Abiel Holmes. Cambridge, July 18, 1797. [Boston, 1797]
broadside
cf. Evans 33889
MB mp. 48267

B10125 THREE sweet hearts I boast . . . New York, G. Gilfert [1797]
[2] p. 33.5 cm.
Sonneck-Upton p. 431
DLC; MWA mp. 48268

B10126 TO MR. You being one of the train band in the foot company of militia in this town . . . [n.p., 1797]
broadside 12 X 11.5 cm.
Call for appearance at parade, dated at Salisbury, October 1797
NHi

B10127 TO the citizens of America, and especially those of Philadelphia . . . Spring-Mill . . . August 18, 1797. [Philadelphia, 1797]
broadside 20 X 16 cm.
DLC mp. 48269

B10128 TO the honourable the Senate and House of Representatives of . . . Pennsylvania . . . The memorial of the subscribers . . . to promote . . . a company for erecting a permanent bridge over the . . . Schuylkill . . . Philadelphia, January 25, 1797. [Philadelphia, 1797]
broadside 28 X 20 cm.
PHi mp. 48271

B10129 TO the public. As the election for members to represent this state in Congress . . . January 4th, 1797. [New Jersey, 1797]
broadside 45 X 28 cm.
DLC mp. 48272

B10130 TODD, AMBROSE
Death and mortality. A sermon preached at the interment of Mrs. Abiah Griswold, late consort of Solomon Griswold . . . January 31st, A.D. 1797 . . . Hartford, Hudson & Goodwin, 1797.
16 p. 20 cm.
CtHi; MWA; PPL mp. 48274

B10131 TODD, JOSEPH J.
[Catalogue of books in the Circulating Library in Joseph J. Todd's bookstore . . . Providence. Providence, 1797]

Advertisement July 15, 1797, states "Catalogues delivered gratis."
Alden 1553
No copy known mp. 48275

B10132 THE town and country almanac, for the year . . . 1798 . . . By J. N. Hutchings [sic], Philom. Newark, Printed for Naphtali Judah, New-York [1797]
[36] p. 17.5 cm.
CSmH mp. 48155

B10133 THE trial, condemnation and horrid execution of David M'Lean, formerly of Pennsylvania, for high treason . . . at . . . Quebec, on the 21st of July last . . . Windham, Printed [by John Byrne] 1797.
12 p.
Trumbull: Supplement 2683
CtHi mp. 48170

B10134 [TRISOBIO, FILIPPO]
La marmotte. Avec accompagnement de harpe . . . Philadelphia, Trisobio [1797–98]
[2] p. 34 cm.
Sonneck-Upton p. 251
DLC; NN mp. 48276

B10135 U. S. CONGRESS. HOUSE
Mr. Harper's motion. 24th November 1797, committed to a Committee of the whole House on Wednesday next. [Philadelphia, 1797]
2 p. 21.5 cm.
Concerns taking evidence in the trial of contested elections
New York Public 1215
NN mp. 48284

B10136 U.S. CONGRESS. HOUSE. COMMITTEE APPOINTED TO INQUIRE INTO THE OPERATION OF THE ACT FOR THE RELIEF AND PROTECTION OF AMERICAN SEAMEN
Report of the Committee appointed to inquire into the operation of the act . . . 28th February, 1797 . . . 22d November 1797, committed to a committee of the whole House . . . [Philadelphia, W. Ross, 1797]
1 p.l., [19]–41 [i.e. 43] p. 20.5 cm.
DLC (3 copies); MWA; MiU–C; NN mp. 48285

B10137 U. S. CONGRESS. HOUSE. COMMITTEE ON CLAIMS
Report of the Committee of claims, on the petition of Comfort Sands . . . 9th February, 1797 . . . 20th December, 1797, committed to a committee of the whole House, on Friday next . . . [Philadelphia? 1797?]
1 p.l., [153]–156 p. 20.5 cm.
MiU–C mp. 48286

B10138 U. S. CONGRESS. HOUSE. COMMITTEE ON CLAIMS
Report of the Committee of claims, on the petition of Edward St. Loe Livermore . . . 8th December, 1797, committed to a committee of the whole House . . . [Philadelphia, 1797]
1 p.l., [73]–74 p. 20 cm.
cf. Evans 33000
DLC; MWA; MiU–C; PPL mp. 48287

B10139 U. S. CONGRESS. HOUSE. COMMITTEE ON CLAIMS
Report of the Committee of claims, on the petitions of Samuel Abbot and others . . . 27th November 1797, committed to a committee of the whole House . . . [Philadelphia, 1797]
[43]–46 p. 20.5 cm.
DLC; MiU–C mp. 48288

B10140 U. S. CONGRESS. HOUSE. COMMITTEE ON CLAIMS
Report of the Committee of claims, to whom were recommitted the petition of Henry Hill . . . 22d November 1797, committed to a committee of the whole House . . . [Philadelphia, 1797]
1 p.l., [45]–48 p. 20.5 cm.
DLC; MiU–C; NN mp. 48289

B10141 U. S. CONGRESS. HOUSE. COMMITTEE ON THE SALE OF LANDS NORTH-WEST OF THE RIVER OHIO
Committee appointed to enquire into the progress made in . . . sale of the lands . . . north-west of the river Ohio . . . [Philadelphia, 1797]
7 p. 20.5 cm.
Includes (p. [5]-7) a letter from Oliver Wolcott to John Nicholas
PPRF mp. 48283

B10142 U. S. CONGRESS. SENATE. COMMITTEE ON CLAIMS
The Committee, to whom was referred the memorial and petition of Margaret Lapsley . . . report . . . [Philadelphia, 1797]
broadside
PHi

B10143 U. S. CONGRESS. SENATE. COMMITTEE ON THE IMPEACHMENT OF WILLIAM BLOUNT
In Senate of the United States, July 6th, 1797. The Committee to whom was referred that part of the President's message . . . [Philadelphia, 1797]
5 p. 20.5 cm.
DLC mp. 48290

B10144 U. S. LAWS
17th June, 1797 . . . A bill to prohibit citizens of the United States from entering into the military . . . service of any foreign prince or state. [Philadelphia, 1797]
3 p. 35 cm.
Lines separately numbered
New York Public 1218
NN mp. 48278

B10145 U. S. LAWS
22d November 1797. A bill for the relief of refugees from . . . Nova-Scotia . . . [n.p., 1797]
broadside 34.5 X 21 cm.
MiU-C mp. 48280

B10146 U. S. LAWS
19th December 1797 . . . A bill to prescribe the mode of taking evidence in cases of contested elections . . . [n.p., 1797]
3 p. 34.5 cm.
MiU-C mp. 48281

B10147 U. S. LAWS
26th December, 1797 . . . A bill supplementary to the . . . act in addition to the act for the punishment of certain crimes against the United States." [n.p., 1797]
4 p. 34.5 cm.
MiU-C mp. 48282

B10148 U. S. LAWS
An act laying duties on stamped vellum, parchment and paper . . . Approved July 6, 1797. John Adams, President . . . [Philadelphia, 1797]
14 p. 8vo
PHi mp. 48292

B10149 U. S. LAWS
An act passed at the second session of the Fourth Congress . . . concerning the circuit-courts of the United States . . . Approved, March third, 1797 . . . Philadelphia, Richard Folwell [1797]
broadside
PPL

B10150 U. S. LAWS
An act to provide for the further defence of the ports and harbours of the United States . . . June 23d, 1797. Approved: John Adams . . . Deposited among the rolls . . . [Philadelphia, 1797]
broadside 23 X 19 cm.
CtHi mp. 48293

B10151 U. S. LAWS
Acts passed at the first [-second] session of the Fourth Congress . . . Philadelphia, Thomas Dobson, 1797.
1 p.l., [263]-316, 325-455, [495]-566 p., 60 l. 21 cm.
New York Public 1217
NN mp. 48291

B10152 U. S. LAWS
A bill for an apportionment of representatives . . . to compose the House . . . after the 3d day of March, 1797. [Colophon] [Philadelphia] Childs and Swaine [1797]
[3] p. 34 cm. caption title
DLC mp. 48277

B10153 U. S. LAWS
. . . Cap. XCVII. An act for carrying into execution the treaty of amity . . . concluded between His Majesty and the United States of America. [4th of July, 1797.] [Philadelphia] Duane, printer [1797]
24 p. 35 cm.
Printer's imprint at head of title
Lines separately numbered
New York Public 1219
NN mp. 48279

B10154 U. S. LAWS
Duties payable by law, on all goods, wares & merchandize, imported . . . after the last day of June, 1797. The inward column exhibiting the rates . . . [Philadelphia, 1797]
20 p. 18.5 cm. caption title
Minick 398?
DLC mp. 48294

B10155 U. S. LAWS
Information to distillers. District of Maryland, Supervisor's office, May 1st, 1797. Abstract of the act . . . repealing in part, the act 'concerning the duties on spirits . . .' and imposing certain duties on the capacities of stills . . . John Kilty, supervisor of the revenue for the district of Maryland. Baltimore, Clayland, Dobbin [1797]
broadside 39.5 X 48 cm.
Minick 365
MdBE mp. 48304

B10156 U. S. LAWS
Third Congress of the United States: At the first session . . . An act to establish the post-office . . . [Philadelphia, 1797]
41, [8], 13, [1], 14-16, [1], 17-20 p. 19 cm. caption title
p. 17-20: Additional post-roads, 1797
DLC

B10157 U. S. MINT
Letter from the Secretary of State, inclosing a report of the Director of the Mint . . . 20th December, 1796, referred to Mr. Page, Mr. Havens, and Mr. Goodrich. [Philadelphia, 1797]
19 p. 23 cm.
DLC (2 copies); PHi mp. 48298

B10158 U. S. PRESIDENT, 1789–1797
The President's message of January 19, 1797, and the letter to the secretary of state, to Mr. Pinckney, our ambassador . . . on . . . notes presented . . . by Citizen Adet . . . 1796. Albany, Charles R. and George Webster, 1797.
44 p. 8vo
McMurtrie: Albany 159
MB; N mp. 48296

B10159 U. S. TREASURY DEPT.
An account of the receipts and expenditures of the United States, for the year 1796 . . . Philadelphia, John Fenno [1797]
2 p.l., 11–85, [13] p. 6 fold. charts. 35 cm.
Pages 81–82 repeated; p. 83–84 wanting
DLC; MWA; MWiW; NN. Pierce W. Gaines, Fairfield, Conn. (1964) mp. 48297

B10160 U. S. TREASURY DEPT.
Circular to collectors, naval officers and surveyors. Treasury department, comptroller's office, July 4, 1797. Sir, I transmit . . . [Philadelphia, 1797]
broadside 23.5 cm.
MiU–C mp. 48298

B10161 U. S. TREASURY DEPT.
Circular to the collectors of the customs and supervisors of the revenue. Treasury department, November 28th, 1797 . . . [Philadelphia, 1797]
broadside 23.5 X 19 cm.
PPRF mp. 48300

B10162 U. S. TREASURY DEPT.
(Circular to the collectors of the customs.) Treasury department, April 8th, 1797 . . . [Philadelphia, 1797]
broadside 23 X 19 cm.
PPRF mp. 48299

B10163 U. S. TREASURY DEPT.
(Circular.) Treasury department, June 16th, 1797. Sir, Herewith you will receive . . . "An act prohibiting . . . the exportation of arms and munitions . . . " [Philadelphia, 1797]
broadside 23.5 X 19 cm.
PPRF mp. 48302

B10164 U. S. TREASURY DEPT.
(Circular.) Treasury department, July 6th, 1797. Sir, I hereto subjoin the form of a bond to be taken on the transportation of military stores . . . [Philadelphia, 1797]
broadside 23.5 X 19 cm.
PPRF mp. 48303

B10165 U. S. TREASURY DEPT.
(Circular.) Treasury department, March 1797. Sir, Herewith you will receive sea letters and Mediterranean passports . . . [Philadelphia, 1797]
broadside 23 X 19 cm.
PPRF mp. 48301

B10166 U. S. TREASURY DEPT.
Proceedings of the accounting officers of the Treasury, upon certain claims not admitted to be valid . . . 29th December 1796, committed to a committee of the whole House, to-morrow . . . [Philadelphia? 1797?]
31 p. 20.5 cm.
MiU–C mp. 48305

B10167 U. S. TREATIES
Treaty of peace and friendship between the United States of America and the bey and subjects of Tripoli . . . Signed . . . the 3d day of January 1797 . . . [Philadelphia, 1797]
7 p. 20.5 cm. caption title
DLC; MiU–C mp. 48306

B10168 THE universal interpreter of dreams and visions . . . Philadelphia, Printed and sold by Stewart & Cochran, 1797.
120 p. 14 cm.
MWA mp. 48307

B10169 [EIN wahrhafter und besonderer Bericht von dem Zustand des Richard Merrels. Reading, Gottlob Jungmann, 1797]

Advertised in the *Neue Unpartheyische Readinger Zeitung*, Dec. 27, 1797
Nolan p. 30
No copy known mp. 48308

B10170 WALLIS, JAMES
The Bible defended; being an investigation of . . . Thomas Paine's Age of reason, part the second . . . By James Wallis, pastor . . . in New-Providence . . . North-Carolina. Halifax, Abraham Hodge, 1797.
115 p. 23 cm.
McMurtrie: North Carolina 239
PPPrHi mp. 48309

B10171 WALTERS, JAMES
A new periodical publication. Proposal of James Walters, for publishing by subscription . . . *The Weekly Magazine* . . . Philadelphia, 13th of December, 1797. Subscriptions received by the publisher in Willing's Alley . . . [Philadelphia, 1797]
broadside 28 X 21 cm.
PHi mp. 48310

B10172 WATSON, RICHARD, 1737–1816
An apology for the Bible . . . Newbern, Francois-X. Martin, for Joseph Shute and Durant Hatch, 1797.
77 p. 22 cm.
McMurtrie: North Carolina 240
NcU mp. 48311

B10173 WATTS, ISAAC, 1674–1748
Divine songs, attempted in easy language . . . To which are added The principles of The Christian religion . . . By P. Doddridge . . . New-Haven, Re-printed by George Bunce, 1797.
72 p. 12 cm.
CtY mp. 48312

B10174 WATTS, ISAAC, 1674–1748
Divine and moral songs for children . . . Second Leominster edition. [Leominster] Charles Prentiss, 1797.
48 p. 13 cm.
MWA mp. 48313

B10175 WATTS, ISAAC, 1674–1748
The historical catechism for children and youth . . . Windham, John Byrne, 1797.
70 p. 10 cm.
Trumbull: Supplement 2734
CtHi mp. 48314

B10176 WATTS, ISAAC, 1674–1748
Hymns and spiritual songs . . . Elizabeth-town, S. Kollock, 1797.
[2], 286 p.
MWA mp. 48315

B10177 WAY & GROFF, firm, Philadelphia
Proposals by Way & Groff, for printing, by subscription, Count Rumford's essays . . . [Philadelphia, Zachariah Poulson, Jr., 1797]
broadside
PPL mp. 48316

B10178 WEATHERWISE'S almanac for 1798. By Benjamin Fry. [Portsmouth] Charles Peirce [1797]
[24] p.
Nichols p. 34
NhHi mp. 48129

B10179 WEBBE, SAMUEL, 1740–1816
The mansion of peace . . . Philadelphia, G. Willig [1797–99]
[2] p. 32.5 cm.
Sonneck-Upton 246
DLC; MB; NN mp. 48318

B10180 WEBBE, SAMUEL, 1740–1816
The mansion of peace . . . New York, J. Hewitt [1797–99]
[2] p. 34 cm.
Sonneck-Upton p. 246
DLC; MB; NN mp. 48317

B10181 THE western calendar: or, an almanack for . . . 1798 . . . Washington, (Penn.), John Colerick [1797]
[34] p. 17 cm.
Drake 10478
OCHP

B10182 DIE Westliche Correspondenz, und Hägerstauner Wochenschrift. Hägerstaun, Johann Gruber [1797]
41 cm.
Minick 402
No copy known

B10183 WETMORE, ROBERT GRIFFITH, 1774–1803
An oration on the festival of St. John . . . twenty-seventh December, 5797 . . . Printed in Catskill, by M. Croswell [1797]
22 p. 17 cm.
NjR

B10184 [WILKINSON, EDWARD] 1727–1809
Wisdom, a poem . . . New-York, Isaac Collins, 1797.
21 p. 18.5 cm.
cf. Evans 35029
MWA; RPJCB mp. 48319

B10185 WILLIAMS COLLEGE
Catalogue of students in Williams College, October, 1797. Stockbridge, Rosseter & Willard [1797]
broadside
MWiW-C. Photocopy: MWA mp. 48320

B10186 WOODWARD, JOHN
The noted stud horse [cut] Favorite, will be let to mares at five dollars the season . . . John & Amos Woodward. New-London, May, 1797. [New London] Green's Press [1797]
broadside 25 × 20 cm.
CtHi mp. 48322

B10187 YALE UNIVERSITY
Catalogue of the members of Yale-College, 1797. [New Haven] Thomas and Samuel Green [1797]
broadside
CtY mp. 48324

B10188 YALE UNIVERSITY
Scheme of the exercises at the public commencement; Yale-College, September 13th, 1797 . . . [New Haven] T. & S. Green [1797]
broadside 27.5 × 21.5 cm.
CtHi mp. 48323

B10189 YOUNG, EDWARD, 1683–1765
The last day. A poem. In three books . . . Elizabeth-Town, Printed by Shepard Kollock, for Cornelius Davis, New-York, 1797.
39 p. 16 cm.
cf. Evans 31953 (second title); separately signatured and issued in contemporary binding
CSmH; MWA mp. 48325

B10190 THE zealous churchman: a politico-theological sermon; to be preached before the . . . Senate of the state of Virginia, by their devoted servant, Episcopalius . . . Richmond: Printed (for the author) by Samuel Pleasants, Jun. December, 1797.
12 p. 20 cm.
NHi mp. 48326

1798

B10191 ADAMS & LORING, firm, Boston
Boston, May 2d, 1798. This will serve to inform you, that we . . . dissolved the copartnership of Adams & Loring . . . [Boston, 1798]
broadside 23 × 19 cm.
RPJCB mp. 48327

B10192 ADDISON, ALEXANDER, 1759–1807
Liberty of speech and of the press. Charge to the grand juries of the county courts of the fifth circuit,.of the state of Pennsylvania. [n.p., 1798]
16 p. 8vo caption title
PPL mp. 48328

B10193 THE affecting history of the children in the wood . . . Hartford, John Babcock, 1798.
29, [2] p. 11 cm.
Pages [1] and [31] pasted to covers
David McKell, Chillicothe, O. (1961) mp. 48389

B10194 [THE affecting history of the dreadful distresses of Frederic Manheim's family . . . Newport, H. & O. Farnsworth, 1798]
[square 12mo]
Advertised Aug. 11, 1798, as "Now in the press and shortly will be published."
Alden 1554
No copy known; description from Terry catalogue, pt. 3, no. 180 mp. 48331

B10195 ALBANY. CITIZENS
Albany, 28th March, 1798. Gentlemen At a very large . . . meeting of the citizens of Albany . . . the following nomination of candidates . . . unanimously made. John Jay, for Governor . . . [Albany, 1798]
broadside 32 × 20 cm.
N mp. 48332

B10196 THE Albany almanack for . . . 1799. By Andrew Beers. Albany, Printed for the booksellers [1798]
[2] p.
Drake 6077
N; NCooHi (9 1.)

B10197 ALBEMARLE CO., VA. CITIZENS
To the Senate and House of representatives of the United States. We whose names are hereunto subscribed ... are urged ... to remonstrate ... [n.p., 1798]
broadside 47.5 X 24 cm.
A protest against the alien and sedition laws
DLC (2 copies) mp. 48333

B10198 ALERT FIRE SOCIETY, BOSTON
Afflictis consolatio. Rules and regulations of the Alert Fire-Society, instituted at Boston, November 19, 1787. Boston, Samuel Hall, 1798.
28 p. 15.5 cm.
MB mp. 48373

B10199 ALEXANDRIA CORPORATION
1797, Alexandria corporation. Dr. in account with Summers, deceased ... [Alexandria, Thomas and Westcott, 1798]
broadside 42 X 25 cm.
Bound after the Feb. 8, 1798, issue of the *Alexandria Advertiser*
DLC mp. 48334

B10200 AN alphabet in prose ... First American edition. Worcester, Printed and sold by Isaiah Thomas, Jun., 1798
31 p. incl. covers. 10.5 cm.
MWA. d'Alté A. Welch (1961) mp. 48335

B10201 AMBROSE and Eleanor, or The adventures of two children deserted on an uninhabited island ... Baltimore, Printed for Thomas, Andrews, and Butler, by Warner and Hanna, 1798.
215 p. 17 cm.
Minick 404
CSmH; MdHi. Forrest Bowe (1951) mp. 48336

B10202 THE American jest book; or, Merry fellow's companion ... Philadelphia, Printed and sold by John M'Culloch, 1798.
108 p. 13.5 cm.
PHi mp. 48337

B10203 THE American ladies pocket book, for the year 1799 ... Philadelphia, Published by William Y. Birch [1798]
143 p. ports. 12 cm.
New York Public 1223
MWA; NN mp. 48338

B10204 AMERICAN MERCURY
The news-boy's address to the readers of the *American Mercury* ... Hartford, January 1, 1798 ... [Hartford, Elisha Babcock, 1798]
broadside 29.5 X 16 cm.
NHi mp. 48550

B10205 THE American Museum, or, universal magazine ... volume X. Philadelphia, Mathew Carey, 1798.
308, 36, 48, 44 p. 20.5 cm.
CSmH; RPJCB

B10206 ARGUS
Greenleaf's Argus, Extra. New-York, Thursday, April 12, 1798. Message of the President ... April 3, 1798 ... [New York, Thomas Greenleaf, 1798]
2 leaves. 51 cm.
NN

B10207 ARISTOTLE'S master-piece, completed: in two parts. The first containing the secrets of generation ... The second part being a private looking glass for the female sex ... New-York, 1798.
102 p. 16 cm.
Austin 63; New York Public 1224
NHi; NN; RPJCB mp. 48339

B10208 [ARNE, THOMAS AUGUSTINE] 1710–1778
The soldier tired ... New York, J. Hewitt; Philadelphia, B. Carr; Baltimore, J. Carr [1798?]
[3] p. 32 cm.
Sonneck-Upton p. 388
DLC mp. 48340

B10209 [ARNOLD, SAMUEL] 1740–1802
Oh the moment was sad ... New York, J. Hewitt [1798?]
broadside 31.5 cm.
Sonneck-Upton p. 308
DLC; ICN; NN mp. 48341

B10210 ASH, JOHN, 1724–1779
Grammatical institutes: or, An easy introduction to Dr. Lowth's English grammar ... Second Charleston edition, improved. [Charleston] Printed by W. P. Young, 1798.
142 p.
ScC

B10211 ASH, JOHN, 1724–1779
Grammatical institutes: or, An easy introduction to Dr. Lowth's English grammar ... Second Charleston edition, improved. [Charleston] Printed by W. P. Young, and sold by him, and by Bailey, Waller, & Bailey, 1798.
142 p.
CtSoP

B10212 AN astronomical diary, calendar, or almanack for ... 1799. By N. Strong. Litchfield [1798]
[24] p.
Drake 587
CtLHi (mutilated; imprint torn)

B10213 [AUBORN, A. D']
The French convert ... Catskill, M. Croswell [1798?]
114 p. 13.5 cm.
MWA mp. 48343

B10214 BAILEY, BENJAMIN, d. 1798
The confession of Benjn. Bailey, who was executed at Reading, Pennsylvania, the sixth day of January, 1798; for the murder of ... Jost Follaber ... August, 1797 ... concluding with his favorite prayer. Reading, J. Schneider & Comp., 1798.
20 p. 16.5 cm.
NCooHi. Roger Butterfield, New York City (1960)
mp. 48344

B10215 BALTIMORE. LIBRARY COMPANY
A catalogue of the books, &c. belonging to the Library Company of Baltimore ... Baltimore, John Hayes, 1798.
xviii, 62 p. 20 cm.
Minick 406
MdHi; PHi; PPAmP mp. 48345

B10216 BALTIMORE CHARITABLE MARINE SOCIETY
Rules and bye-laws of the Baltimore Charitable Marine Society; also, a list of the members ... Baltimore, W. Pechin, 1798.
25 p. 19 cm.
MdBE; RPJCB mp. 48347

B10217 BAPTISTS. CONNECTICUT. DANBURY ASSOCIATION
Minutes of the Danbury Baptist Association, held at Bristol, October 3d and 4th, 1798 . . . [Colophon] [Suffield] H. & O. Farnsworth [1798]
8 p. 21 cm.
Ct; CtHi; MWA (pagination removed by trimming)
mp. 48348

B10218 BAPTISTS. KENTUCKY. ELKHORN ASSOCIATION
Minutes of the Elkhorn Association . . . at The Forks of Elkhorn . . . August, 1798. Lexington, John Bradford [1798]
7 p. 21 cm.
McMurtrie: Kentucky 69
OClWHi. Photocopy: MWA mp. 48349

B10219 BAPTISTS. MARYLAND. BALTIMORE ASSOCIATION
[Minutes of the sixth meeting of the Baltimore Association, Tuscarora Valley, Aug. 3, 1798. Frederick? 1798]

cf. Jones, J. H.: *History of the Baltimore Baptist association*, p. 6: "The circular for 98 was the reprint of the circular of the Warwick association for 1795."
Minick 412
No copy known mp. 48350

B10220 BAPTISTS. NEW HAMPSHIRE. NEW HAMPSHIRE ASSOCIATION
Minutes of the New-Hampshire Association . . . Berwick . . . June 13th and 14th, 1798. Portsmouth, Charles Peirce, 1798.
12 p. 18.5 cm.
CSmH mp. 48351

B10221 BAPTISTS. NORTH CAROLINA. KEHUKEE ASSOCIATION
Minutes of the Kehukee Baptist Association holden at Caskie Meeting-House, Bertie County, N. Carolina. Thursday, September 20, 1798. [Edenton? 1798]
9 p. 22 cm. caption title
McMurtrie: North Carolina 242
PHi mp. 48352

B10222 BAPTISTS. NORTH CAROLINA. NEUSE BAPTIST ASSOCIATION
Minutes of the North-Carolina Neuse Baptist association, holden at Falling-Creek meeting house . . . [Newbern, John C. Osborn. 1798?]
[4] p. 28 cm. caption title
First reported meeting Oct. 20, 1798
NcWsW mp. 48353

B10223 BAPTISTS. SOUTH CAROLINA. BETHEL ASSOCIATION
Minutes of the Bethel Association, convened at the Bethlehem Church, in Spartanburgh County, South-Carolina, August 11, 1798 . . . [Charleston, 1798]
4, 4 p. 20.5 cm. caption title
KyLoS

B10224 BAPTISTS. VERMONT. LEYDEN ASSOCIATION
Minutes of the Leyden Association, held at the Baptist-Meeting House, in Leyden: M,DCC,XC,VIII. Printed at Brattleboro', Vermont: By Benjamin Smead. 1798.
11 p. 19 cm.
VtHi mp. 48354

B10225 BAPTISTS. VERMONT. WOODSTOCK ASSOCIATION
Minutes of the Woodstock Association, held at Newport . . . Newhampshire, Sept. 26, 1798 . . . [Windsor? A. Spooner? 1798?]
8 p. 21 cm. caption title
NhD (p. 5–6 wanting); VtHi mp. 48355

B10226 BAPTISTS. VIRGINIA. DOVER ASSOCIATION
Minutes of the Baptist Dover association held at Kingston meeting-house . . . October 13th, 1798. Richmond, Samuel Pleasants [1798]
8 p. 20 cm.
DLC (mutilated); ViRU mp. 48356

B10227 BARLOW, JOEL, 1754–1812
Barlow's Letter. From the *Connecticut Courant*. Messrs. Hudson & Goodwin, The inclosed pamphlet was printed at . . . [Hartford, 1798]
broadside
BAL 896
CtY; MSaE; RPB mp. 48357

B10228 BARLOW, JOEL, 1754–1812
[Copy of a Letter from an American Diplomatic Character in France to a Member of Congress in Philadelphia. 1st March, 1798 . . .] [Constitution Hill, 1798 (i.e., Fairhaven, Vt., Printed by James Lyon for Matthew Lyon, 1798.)]
pamphlet
Ascribed to Lyon's press by *Newhampshire and Vermont Journal: Or, The Farmer's Weekly Museum,* Walpole, N.H., October 22, 1798, and by preliminary matter at the head of a broadside reprinting of the text in Hartford, Conn. entitled *Barlow's Letter. From the Connecticut Courant.* [Hartford, 1798] (BAL 896).
Matthew Lyon denied "that he printed said letter . . . but . . . that he used his endeavors to suppress it, by destroying the copies that came into his possession." Cf. Annals of Congress, 16th Cong., 2d sess., col. 478
Title from the broadside version; imprint from the *Farmer's Weekly Museum*
NNS mp. 48358

B10229 [BARROW, DAVID] 1753–1819
Circular letter. Southampton county, Virginia; February 14, 1798 . . . Norfolk, Willett & O'Connor [1798]
14 p. 20 cm.
McCoy 27; New York Public 1225
ViRU. Photostats: NN (author's autograph on blank leaf at end); Vi mp. 48359

B10230 BATCHELDER, WILLIAM, 1768–1818
A sermon, delivered June 7th 1798, at the ordination of Otis Robinson . . . Dover, Samuel Bragg [1798]
23 p. 23 cm.
MB; MWA mp. 48360

B10231 THE battle of the wooden sword. Or, the modern pugilists. A new song—in 2 parts . . . [n.p., 1798?]
8 p. 18 cm. caption title
Concerns the Lyon-Griswold confrontations in Congress.
Stoddard 16a
CtHi. Photocopy: MWA mp. 48361

B10231a THE battle of the wooden sword! Or, the modern pugilists. A new song. In two parts . . . [n.p., 1798?]

8 p. 18 cm. caption title
Stoddard 16b
PHi

B10232 BAYNON, ELIAM
Der barmherzige Samariter . . . Hannover, Samuel Endredy Stettinius, 1798.
184 p. 16 cm.
Historical Soc. of York County; RPJCB mp. 48362

B10233 THE beggar and no beggar: or Every man a king if he will . . . Philadelphia, F. & R. Bailey, 1798.
21 p. 14.5 cm.
PHi mp. 48363

B10234 BEND, JOSEPH GROVE JOHN, 1762–1812
A discourse delivered in Christ-Church, Baltimore . . . the twenty-fifth of March, 1798; on occasion of the death of Mr. Charles Henry Wilmans . . . Baltimore, Thomas Dobbin, 1798.
22 p. 16.5 cm.
Minick 414
MWA; MdBP; MdHi mp. 48364

B10235 BERQUIN, ARNAUD, 1750–1791
The children's friend, and youth's monitor . . . New-Haven, George Bunce, 1798.
143 p. 14 cm.
CtHi; MWA mp. 48365

B10236 BERQUIN, ARNAUD, 1750–1791
The children's friend, and youth's monitor . . . New-Haven; Printed by George Bunce, for C. Davis, New-York, 1798.
143 p. 14 cm.
MWA mp. 48366

B10237 BERQUIN, ARNAUD. 1750–1791
The looking-glass for the mind, or the juvenile friend . . . In prose and verse . . . Philadelphia, Printed for John Ormrod, by Ormrod & Conrad, 1798.
[4], 271, [1] p. front. 17.5 cm.
MWA; PHi; PPL mp. 48367

B10238 BEVERLY, MASS.
Your taxes for 1798. State tax. Town & County tax. Parish tax. [Salem? 1798]
broadside
Ford 2854
MHi

B10239 BIBLE
History of the Holy Bible. Adorned with cuts. The fifth edition. Philadelphia, Printed for John Wigglesworth, at his hardware, toy and brush-shop, in Second Street [1798?]
23, [1] p. 4 plates. 8 cm.
Dated from notes by Wilberforce Eames on Philadelphia directories
MWA mp. 48369

B10240 BINGHAM, CALEB, 1757–1817
The child's companion . . . The sixth edition . . . Boston, Manning & Loring, 1798.
84 p. illus. 15.5 cm.
DLC (mutilated); MWA; NjP mp. 48370

B10241 THE black-bird. Being a collection of favorite Scots, English and Irish songs, to which is added, The adventure of John Gilpin . . . New-York, Printed for Benjamin Gomez, No. 97, Maiden-Lane [1798?]
NN (photostat of t.p. only, in Pennypacker collection) mp. 48371

B10242 [BORDLEY, JOHN BEALE] 1727–1804
Cattle pastured and soiled in summer: kept and fattened in winter . . . [Philadelphia, Charles Cist, 1798]
12 p. 8vo caption title
PPL mp. 48372

B10243 BOSTON. YORK FIRE CLUB
Sir, A meeting of the Fire Club, of which you are a member . . . [Boston, Young & Minns, 1798]
broadside 8 X 20 cm.
500 copies ordered printed 2 May 1798; payment recorded in November, 1798
MB (3 copies) mp. 48376

B10244 THE Boston collection: containing, I. An introduction to the grounds of music . . . II. A large collection . . . Psalm and hymn tunes . . . together with several new ones . . . Boston, William Norman [1798?]
10, 15–16, [2], 17–112 p. obl.
DLC; MWA mp. 48377

B10245 BOSTON THEATRE (FEDERAL STREET)
Never performed in Boston. On Wednesday evening, Nov. 28, will be presented a drama . . . the Castle Spectre . . . To which will be added . . . the Double Disguise . . . [Boston, 1798]
broadside 45 X 29 cm.
Nov. 28 fell on Wednesday in 1798
MHi mp. 48375

B10246 [BRACKENRIDGE, HUGH HENRY] 1748–1816
Narrative of a late expedition against the Indians . . . barbarous execution of Col. Crawford . . . escape of Dr. Knight & John Glover . . . 1782 . . . escape of Mrs. Frances Scott, an inhabitant of Washington County, Virginia. Andover, Ames & Parker [1798?]
46 p. 14.5 cm. $A–D^6$
ICN; MWA (t.p. photostat) mp. 48378

B10247 BRIGGS, ENOS
The Salem frigate. Take notice! [Salem, 1798]
broadside
Signed and dated: Enos Briggs. Salem, Nov. 23, 1798
New York Public 1226
NN (reduced facsim.) mp. 48379

B10248 BRYDONE, PATRICK, 1743–1818
A tour through Sicily and Malta . . . Printed at Greenfield, Massachusetts, by Thomas Dickman, for Isaiah Thomas, and sold at his bookstore in Worcester, and by the printer in Greenfield, 1798.
2 v. in 1 (2 p.l., viii, 339 p.) 17 cm.
New York Public 1227; cf. Evans 33467
CSmH; MWA; NN; NhD (2 copies) mp. 48380

B10249 THE buck's pocket companion; or, Merry fellow, a choice collection of songs . . . New-Haven, George Bunce, 1798.
71 p. 12mo
BSA *Papers* 54(1960): 65; Trumbull: Supplement 1947
CtY (imperfect) mp. 48381

B10250 BURRELL, WILLIAM
Medical advice; chiefly for the consideration of seamen . . . By William Burrell; who prepares medicine chests . . . New-York, Printed for the author by R. Wilson, 1798.
53, [4] p. 20 cm.

Austin 368; Rogers 649
NNNAM mp. 48383

B10251 BURROUGHS, STEPHEN, 1765–1840
Stephen Burrough's Sermon, delivered at Rutland, on a hay-mow, to his auditory the Pelhamites . . . [n.p., 1798?]
7, [1] p. 18 cm. caption title
cf. Evans 33479
MWA mp. 48384

B10252 BURROUGHS, STEPHEN, 1765–1840
Stephen Burroughs' Sermon. Delivered in Rutland on a hay-mow. To his auditory the Pelhamites . . . [Hanover? Benjamin True? 1798?]
9, [1] p. 17.5 cm. caption title
MWA; NhD (imperfect) mp. 48385

B10253 CALENDER für . . . 1799 . . . Philadelphia, Henrich Schweitzer [1798]
[40] p.
Drake 10486
MWA (no t.p.): N; PHi; PPG

B10254 [CAPRON, HENRY] fl. 18th cent., supposed author
Come genius of our happy land . . . Philadelphia, B. Carr; Baltimore, J. Carr; New-York, J. Hewitt [1798?]
broadside 33 cm.
Sonneck-Upton p. 82
DLC mp. 48386

B10255 CARR, BENJAMIN, 1769–1831
The little sailor boy, a favourite ballad. Written by Mrs. Rowson—composed by B. Carr. Price 25 cents . . . Sold at B. Carr's Musical repository Philadelphia, J. Carr's Baltimore, & J. Hewitt's New York [1798]
[2] p. 33 cm. caption title
Sonneck-Upton p. 234
MiU–C

B10256 CATHOLIC CHURCH. LITURGY
[Ordo divini officii recitandi . . . pro anno Domini MDCCXCIX. Baltimori, Typis Johannis Hayes, 1798]

Minick 421; Parsons 194
No copy known mp. 48387

B10257 CENTINEL OF FREEDOM
From the office of the *Centinel of Freedom*. Newark, August 30, 1798. To lay in a degree the anxiety of our readers . . . this Extra. Sheet, the following correspondence between Mr. Talleyrand . . . and Mr. Gerry . . . [Newark, 1798]
broadside 27 X 22.5 cm.
NjR

B10258 CHARITY rewarded, or the history of the charitable farmer . . . (The first American edition.) Suffield, H. & O. Farnsworth, 1798.
119 p.
Trumbull: Supplement 1971
Kent Library mp. 48388

B10259 CHATEAUDUN, R., fl. 1796–1799
Adieu sweet girl, taken from the Children of the Abbey by Maria Regina Roche. The music by R: Chateaudun. Philadelphia, Printed & sold by G. Willig, No. 185 Market St. [1798–99]
[2] p. 34.5 cm. caption title
Sonneck-Upton p. 6
MiU–C

B10260 CHILDREN in the wood . . . Newport, H. & O. Farnsworth [1798?]
broadside 31.5 X 24 cm.
Alden 1560; Winship p. 74
RHi; RNHi mp. 48390

B10261 [A CHOICE collection of songs. Suffield, 1798]

Advertised May 30, 1798, as "first published."
BSA *Papers*, 54(1960):66
No copy known mp. 48392

B10262 (CIRCULAR.) To the officers of the 5th and 6th brigades . . . Gentlemen, A continued system of tyranny . . . Halifax, June 25th, 1798 . . . [Halifax? Abraham Hodge? 1798]
[4] p. 30 cm.
Pages 2–4 blank; manuscript letter on p. 3, address on p. 4
Nc–Ar; NcU mp. 48393

B10263 THE citizen and farmer's almanac for . . . 1799 . . . Philadelphia, Printed for John M'Culloch [1798]
[36] p.
Drake 10486
ViLxV (17 l.)

B10264 [COBBETT, WILLIAM] 1762–1835
Detection of a conspiracy, formed by the United Irishmen, with the evident intention of aiding the tyrants of France . . . by Peter Porcupine. Philadelphia, Published by William Cobbett, May 6, 1798.
29 p. 8vo
Probably Sabin 13881
PPL mp. 48395

B10265 COCHRAN, JAMES
Land-office. For sale, by the subscribers . . . the following lots . . . Apply to James Cochran and Charles Walton. September 27, 1798. Albany, L. Andrews [1798]
broadside 34.5 X 21 cm.
DLC mp. 48396

B10266 COFFIN, EBENEZER, 1769–1816
An oration, delivered in the Meeting House of the Second Parish in Portland . . . June 25th, 5798, at the request . . . of the Portland Lodge of . . . Masons . . . By the Rev. Brother Ebenezer Coffin. Portland, Baker and George, 1798.
14 p. 18.5 cm.
McMurtrie: Maine 2
MBFM mp. 48397

B10267 COLLINS, ISAAC
Proposals for printing by subscription, by Isaac Collins, in New-York, a Journal or historical account of the life . . . George Fox . . . Meeting for sufferings in Philadelphia, 1st mo. 19th, 1798. A letter from the clerk of the meeting . . . in New-York . . . informs us, that meeting approves of the printer's proposals . . . [New York, Isaac Collins, 1798]
broadside 45.5 X 29 cm.
NjR

B10268 COMMISSION UNDER ARTICLE VI OF JAY'S TREATY, 1797
Commissioner's Office, Philadelphia, May 21, 1798. In the case of . . . Charles Inglis. [Philadelphia, 1798]
[2] p. 23 X 19 cm.
New York Public 1228
NN mp. 48648

B10269 CONNECTICUT
A list of the officers who have been appointed in Connecticut, pursuant to the acts of Congress, passed on the 9th . . . of August 1798. [n.p., 1798]
broadside 31.5 × 18.5 cm.
DLC (2 copies) mp. 48505

B10270 CONNECTICUT. COMMISSIONERS
Circular. State of Connectict, Hartford, September 28th, 1798. We enclose you an act . . . Sir, Your very humble servants . . . [Hartford, 1798]
broadside 33 × 39 cm.
DLC mp. 48399

B10271 CONNECTICUT. GENERAL ASSEMBLY
At a General Assembly of the State of Connecticut, holden at New-Haven . . . October, A. D. 1798. The persons returned by the votes of the freemen . . . to stand in nomination for election . . . are as follow, viz. . . . New-Haven, Thomas and Samuel Green [1798]
broadside 33 × 20.5 cm.
CtHi mp. 48400

B10272 CONNECTICUT. GOVERNOR, 1798–1809
By the honorable Jonathan Trumbull . . . A proclamation. It being an acknowledged duty, highly becoming a sinful people . . . Lebanon . . . this first day of March, 1798 . . . Hartford, Elisha Babcock [1798]
broadside 33.5 × 27 cm.
CtHi mp. 48401

B10273 CONNECTICUT. GOVERNOR, 1798–1809
By the honorable Jonathan Trumbull . . . a proclamation. It having pleased . . . [Oct. 22, 1798] . . . New-Haven, Thomas & Samuel Green [1798]
broadside 41 × 34 cm.
cf. Evans 33559
CtHi; DLC

B10274 CONNECTICUT COURANT
Guillotina, for the year 1798 . . . Hartford, 1798.
broadside
In three columns
New York Public Library 1229
NN

B10275 CONNECTICUT GAZETTE
Bulletina. An humble imitation. The address of the lad who carries the *Connecticut Gazette*, to his customers . . . New-London, January 1, 1798. [New London, Samuel Green, 1798]
broadside 46 × 26 cm.
NHi mp. 48382

B10276 COOPER, W. D.
The history of North America . . . By the Rev. Mr. Cooper. Philadelphia, Printed and sold by Stewart & Cochran, 1798.
161 p. 13 cm.
CSmH; PHi; PU mp. 48402

B10277 COXE, TENCH, 1755–1824
Gentlemen, Several weeks have elapsed since my application . . . Walnut Street, January 25, 1798. To the members of the Senate and . . . the House of Representatives . . . [Philadelphia, 1798]
[4] p. fol.
PPL mp. 48403

B10278 CRADDOCK, JOHN
[Sale of the lands of Doctor John Craddock, near Reister's Town, to be at half past two o'clock, on Monday the 23d July. Baltimore, 1798]
broadside
Title from the *Telegraphe*, June 28, 1798, which states, "Hand bills having . . . through mistake, appeared, mentioning the sale . . . to be at half past two o'clock . . ."
Minick 424
No copy known mp. 48404

B10279 CRAMMER, J. B.
March Turque par Crammer. New York, J. Paff [1798?]
[2] p. 32.5 cm.
Sonneck-Upton p. 249
DLC mp. 48405

B10280 CRISIS. To the people of the State of New-York. War! War! War! [n.p., 1798]
broadside 30 × 22 cm.
Advocates the candidacy of Robert R. Livingston for governor
New York Public 1230; cf. Evans 33277
NAII. Photostat: NN mp. 48406

B10281 DAVIS, THOMAS TERRY, d. 1807
Philadelphia, 20th, March, 1798. Dear Sir, I have been sometime waiting for something important to communicate to you . . . [Philadelphia? 1798]
[4] p. 26 × 21 cm.
Includes text of Adams' message to Congress, Mar. 19, 1798
New York Public 1231
MHi; NN. Photostat: DLC mp. 48407

B10282 DEVONSHIRE, GEORGIANA SPENCER CAVENDISH, DUCHESS OF, 1757–1806
I have a silent sorrow here . . . New York, J. Hewitt; Philadelphia, B. Carr; Baltimore, J. Carr [1798–99]
[2] p. 33 cm.
Sonneck-Upton p. 199
DLC; NRU–Mus mp. 48410

B10283 A DIALOGUE, between a fond father and his little son. Designed to amuse and instruct children. Norwich, John Trumbull, 1798.
36 p. 13 cm.
Trumbull: Supplement 2057
CtHi; NBuG mp. 48411

B10284 DICKSON'S Columbian almanac, for . . . 1799. Lancaster, W. & R. Dickson [1798]
[40] p. 18 cm.
MWA mp. 48412

B10285 DILWORTH, THOMAS, d. 1780
The schoolmaster's assistant . . . The latest edition. New London, Printed by Samuel Green for Nathaniel Patten, Hartford, 1798.
xvi, [6], 192 p.
Karpinski p. 75
NHi mp. 48413

B10286 DILWORTH, THOMAS, d. 1780
The schoolmaster's assistant . . . with many additions . . . by James Gibbons. Wilmington [Del.], Peter Brynberg, 1798.
xvi, 288 p. plate. 17 cm.
Karpinski p. 75
DAU; MiU-C (lacks p. i-viii) mp. 48413a

B10287 DUANE, WILLIAM, 1760-1835
A history of the French Revolution, from its commence-

ment to the complete establishment of the Republic . . . By William Duane . . . Philadelphia, Stewart and Rowson, 1798.
[2], 589 [i.e. 590] p. map, 8 plates. 24.5 cm.
ICN; MBAt; PHi; PPL. Forrest Bowe, New York City (1967) mp. 48414

B10288 DUNHAM, JOSIAH, 1769-1844
An oration, for the Fourth of July, 1798 . . . The second edition. Hanover, Benjamin True [1798]
16 p. 20 cm.
CSmH; NhD mp. 48415

B10288a [DUPON, J. M.]
Address to the French merchants, trading with the United States . . . By a French Citizen. Philadelphia: 1798.
15 p. 8 vo
Signed at end
PHi

B10289 THE effects of obedience & disobedience: or the history of a good boy & bad girl . . . New-York, 1798.
60 p. 10.5 cm.
First leaf pasted to cover
MWA (t.p. and front cover slightly mutilated) mp. 48416

B10290 ENCYCLOPAEDIA
A compendious system of mineralogy and metallurgy: extracted from the Encyclopaedia. Philadelphia, Published by A. Bartram, 1798.
iv, 505 p. 18.5 cm.
cf. Evans 26801
NBuG; PPL mp. 48398

B10291 THE entertaining history of Tommy Gingerbread . . . Boston: Printed and sold by John W. Folsom, 1798.
31 p. illus. 10 cm.
MSaE mp. 48417

B10292 EPISCOPAL CHURCH OF ST. PHILIP
The by-laws or constitutional form of government of the Episcopal Church of St. Philip . . . Charleston . . . South Carolina. Charleston, William Mason, 1798.
49 p. 16mo
Turnbull p. 347
ScCC (imperfect)

B10293 THE farmer's calendar . . . for . . . 1799 . . . By Benjamin Fry. Albany, J. Fry; sold at Thomas Spencer's Book Store [1798]
[32] p.
Drake 6079
N; NRMA mp. 48449

B10294 FARMER'S ORACLE, TROY, N.Y.
Troy, Jan. 1, 1798. Ind. xxii. The news-lad's address, to the readers of the *Farmer's Oracle*, wishing them a happy New Year . . . [Troy, 1798]
broadside 30 X 20.5 cm.
By Freneau; first printed as the carrier's address of the *Freeman's Journal*, Jan. 7, 1784
1st line: Accept the address I humbly bring
NHi mp. 48444

B10295 FAYETTE CO., KY. CITIZENS
At a meeting of a large number of the farmers and planters . . . John Roe, clk. April 28, 1798. [Lexington, 1798]
broadside 17 X 21 cm.
McMurtrie Kentucky 71
DLC (2 copies) mp. 48418

B10296 FELLOW citizens. Among the principal objects of the ensuing general election . . . [Philadelphia, 1798?]
broadside 21.5 X 15.5 cm.
Signed: A Mechanic
PHi mp. 48419

B10297 FENNELL, JAMES, 1766-1816
An address to the young men, of Philadelphia, who first offered their services to their country. Philadelphia, 1798.
14 p. 16 cm.
MH; PPL mp. 48420

B10298 FENNELL, JAMES, 1766-1816
Philadelphia, July 6th, 1798. To Mr. William Corbet. Sir, I shall ever . . . James Fennell 129 Chestnut Street. [Philadelphia, 1798]
broadside 45 X 31 cm.
Concerns Fennell's plan for extracting salt from sea water
In four columns
PHi mp. 48421

B10299 [FENNING, DANIEL] d. 1767
Der geschwinde Rechner . . . York, Gedruckt und zu finden bey Salomon Mäyer, 1798.
191 p. 17 cm.
MWA. Historical Soc. of York Co., Pa. mp. 48422

B10300 FIELDING, HENRY, 1707-1754
The remarkable history of Tom Jones, a foundling. Boston, Printed and sold by S. Hall, 1798.
28, [3] p. 10 cm.
MHi. Ruth Adomeit, Cleveland (1961) mp. 48423

B10301 FIFTH Ward. The Independent Republican electors of the Fifth Ward, are particularly requested to meet . . . the 16th inst. at 8 o'clock . . . June 15. By order of the Ward Committee. [New York, 1798]
broadside 46 X 28 cm.
NHi mp. 48409

B10302 FONERDEN, ADAM
A valedictory address to the people called Methodists . . . The address of Adam Fonerden and John Hargrove . . . Baltimore, 5th June, 1798. [Baltimore, 1798]
broadside 22 X 32.5 cm.
Minick 429
DLC (not traced) mp. 48424

B10303 FOOD for the mind: or, A new riddle book . . . By John-the-Giant-Killer, Esq. . . . Boston, Printed and sold by S. Hall, 1798.
63 p. illus. 10 cm.
RPB mp. 48425

B10304 THE fortunate discovery: or, The history of Henry Villars. By a lady of the State of New-York . . . Stockbridge, Re-printed by Rosseter & Willard, 1798.
148 p. 15 cm.
New York Public 1233
NN (all after p. 144 wanting); NjP mp. 48426

B10305 FOSTER, JOHN, 1763?-1829
A discourse, delivered at Norton April 16, 1798 . . . Providence, Bennett Wheeler, 1798.
20 p. 22 cm.
Alden 1564
MH mp. 48427

B10306 [FOWLER, JOHN] of Fairfax Co., Va.
Strictures upon strictures; containing a reply to Bishop Watson's Apology for the Bible . . . Alexandria, Henry Gird, 1798.
140 p. 23.5 cm.
NjP mp. 48428

B10307 FRANCE. DIRECTOIRE
Translation of the message of the Executive Directory to the Council of Five Hundred, of the 15th Nivôse, 6th year, (4th January, 1798). [Philadelphia, 1798]
3 p. 8vo caption title
PPL mp. 48429

B10308 FRANCE. LAWS
A law prohibiting the importation and sale into France, of English merchandize . . . Extract of an arret of the French Directory, dated . . . November 21st, 1796 . . . Published by the French consul, resident at Boston. [Boston? 1798?]
4 p. 32 cm.
MWA mp. 48430

B10309 FREEMASONS. CONNECTICUT. GRAND LODGE
Proceedings of the Grand Lodge of Connecticut, holden . . . New-Haven, on Wednesday the 18th of October . . . 1797. Hartford, Elisha Babcock, 1798.
8 p. 17 cm.
Trumbull: Second supplement 2875
CtHi; CtHFM mp. 48431

B10310 FREEMASONS. MARYLAND. GRAND LODGE
Grand Lodge of Maryland. At the regular half-yearly communication . . . [Baltimore? Thomas Dobbin? 1798]
4 p. 22 cm. caption title
Minick 430
MdBFM mp. 48432

B10311 FREEMASONS. MARYLAND. GRAND LODGE
Proceedings of the Grand Lodge of Maryland, in committee of the whole . . . [Baltimore? Thomas Dobbin? 1798]
8 p. 26 cm. caption title
Minick 431
PPFM mp. 48433

B10312 FREEMASONS. NEW YORK. GRAND LODGE
Regulations of the Deputy Grand Royal Arch Chapter of the state of New-York. Albany, J. Fry, 5798 [1798]
12 p. 18 cm.
McMurtrie: Albany 177a
PPFM mp. 48434

B10313 FREEMASONS. NORTH CAROLINA. GRAND LODGE
An abstract from the proceedings of the Grand Lodge of North-Carolina . . . [at end] Halifax, A. Hodge, 1798.
16 p. 20.5 cm. caption title
". . . convened in . . . Raleigh . . . the 30th of November, A.L. 5797, A.D. 1797."
McMurtrie: North Carolina 246
DSC; IaCrM; NNFM; PPFM mp. 48435

B10314 FREEMASONS. NORTH CAROLINA. GRAND LODGE
An abstract of the proceedings of the Grand Lodge of North-Carolina, in the year A.L. 5798. A.D. 1798 . . . [at end] Halifax, A. Hodge [1798]
24 p. 20 cm. caption title
McMurtrie: North Carolina 247
NNFM; PPFM mp. 48436

B10315 FREEMASONS. NORTH CAROLINA. GRAND LODGE
The constitution of the Grand Lodge of North-Carolina. Halifax, A. Hodge, 1798.
12 p. 18 cm.
McMurtrie: North Carolina 245
NNFM; PPFM mp. 48437

B10316 FREEMASONS. NORTH CAROLINA. GRAND LODGE
Halifax, (N.C.) January 20 A.L. 5798— A.D. 1798. The most worshipful the Grand Lodge of Right worshipful and most respected brethren . . . transmit to you a copy of the constitution of our Grand Lodge, and an abstract from the proceedings of our last grand annual communication, holden in . . . Raleigh . . . [Halifax? 1798]
4-page folder printed on first page only. 32 cm.
McMurtrie: North Carolina 244
NNFM mp. 48438

B10317 FREEMASONS. PENNSYLVANIA. PARFAITE UNION LODGE
Tableau des membres qui composent la A. L. francaise de Saint-Jean de Jerusalem, sous le titre distinctif, La Parfaite Union, Orient de Philadelphia . . . a l'époque de la St. Jean, 5798. Philadelphia, F. Parent [1798]
16 p. 8vo
PPL mp. 48439

B10318 FREEMASONS. SOUTH CAROLINA. LODGE LA CANDEUR
[enclosure of type ornaments] Loge Française de La Candeur. No. 12. Tableau de la T. . . R. . . Loge de St.-Jean, sous le titre distinctif de La Candeur, No. 12, etablie a Charleston . . . 5796 . . . 27eme. jour du 10eme. mois de l'an 5798 . . . Charleston: Imprimé par J. A. d'Acqueny, Imprimeur. [1798]
8 p. 18 cm.
Shearer 11
DSC

B10319 FREEMASONS. VIRGINIA. AMITIE LODGE
Tableau des F . . . F . . . qui composent la r . . . l . . . francaise . . . l'Amitie. A l'o. . . de Petersburg, en Virginie 1798. [Petersburg? 1798?]
7 p.
Wyatt 20
PHi mp. 48440

B10320 FREEMASONS. VIRGINIA. GRAND LODGE
Account of the Grand treasurer of the Grand Lodge of Virginia for the years 1794, 1795, 1796, and 1797. Richmond, John Dixon [1798?]
8 p.
Davis 129
IaCrM mp. 48441

B10321 FREEMASONS. VIRGINIA. GRAND LODGE
Proceedings of the Grand Lodge of Virginia. Held . . . the twenty-seventh day of November, A.L. 5797–A.D. 1797. Richmond, John Dixon, 1798.
21, [2] p. 17.5 cm.
Davis 138
CSmH; DSC; IaCrM; MBFM; Vi mp. 48442

B10322 FREEMASONS. VIRGINIA. GRAND LODGE
Richmond, Virginia, Jan. 28, A.D. 1798, A.L. 5798. Most worshipful sir and brother! . . . In behalf of the Grand Lodge of Virginia . . . *W. H. Fitzwhylsonn G. S.* [Richmond? 1798]
3 p. 39 cm. caption title
List of officers of the Grand lodge
Italicized portion in ms.
Davis 140
CSmH; PPFM mp. 48443

B10323 FREEMASONS. VIRGINIA. LA SAGESSE LODGE
Table of the brethren who compose the Provincial French Lodge, under the distinctive title of Wisdom. In the east of Portsmouth, in Virginia . . . 5798. Norfolk, Willett and O'Connor [1798]
10 p. 12mo
MBFM (so located by Amer. Impr. Inventory; not found)

B10324 FREUHERTZIGE Erinnerung und Warnung bestehend in vielen Klagreden vom Bersall des Christenthums in ausserlichen Gottesdienst. Hannover, Samuel E. Stettinius, 1798.
110 p. 15.5 cm.
Historical Society of York Co., Pa. mp. 48445

B10325 FRIENDS, SOCIETY OF. LONDON YEARLY MEETING
From our Yearly Meeting of Friends held in London, by adjournments from the 21st of the fifth month to the 29th of the same inclusive, 1798. To the Yearly Meeting of Pennsylvania, &c. [Philadelphia, 1798]
broadside 34 X 21 cm.
CSmH; PPL mp. 48446

B10326 FRIENDS, SOCIETY OF. PYRMONT MONTHLY MEETING
A testimony of the Monthly Meeting of Friends, at Pyrmont in Westphalia, Germany, concerning John Pemberton . . . with his epistle to the inhabitants of Amsterdam . . . Philadelphia, Henry Tuckniss, 1798.
24 p. 21 cm.
cf. Evans 35768 (also PPL)
CSmH; PPL mp. 48447

B10327 [FROM the *Philadelphia Gazette*. New York, Jan. 2. Important intelligence. The brig Rosetta is just arrived . . . Peace is made with the emperor . . . Baltimore, Yundt and Brown, 1798]
broadside
Title from the *Federal Gazette*, Jan. 6, 1798: "The following intelligence having been struck off in hand-bills, this morning . . . is now republished."
Minick 432
No copy known mp. 48448

B10328 GAFFER Goose's golden plaything; being a new collection of entertaining fables . . . Boston, Printed and sold by John W. Folsom, 1798.
28, [3] p. illus. 10 cm.
DLC (poor) mp. 48450

B10329 GAIFER
Conversion of a Mahometan . . . described in a letter from Gaifer . . . to Aly-Ben-Hayton . . . The seventh edition. London: Printed, New-London: Re-printed, and sold by S. Green, 1798.
16 p. 20.5 cm.
CtHi mp. 48451

B10330 GARNETT, JAMES MERCER, 1770-1843
Essex, March 29th, 1798. To the freeholders of Essex, Gentlemen . . . James M. Garnett. [Fredericksburg? 1798]
broadside 37 X 23 cm.
ViU mp. 48452

B10331 GAULINE, J. B.
So sweet her face, her form divine. Music by J. B. Gauline. Philadelphia, G. Willig [1798?]
2 leaves. 31 cm. caption title
MiU-C mp. 48453

B10332 GEORGETOWN UNIVERSITY
[Colegio de George-Town, (Potomack) en el estado de Maryland . . .] [At end] George-Town, 1° de enero, 1798. [Georgetown, 1798]
3 p. 25 cm. caption title
Goff: Georgetown 21
DGU (known only from a surviving fragment, a small portion of the lower half of page 3) mp. 48454

B10333 GEORGETOWN UNIVERSITY
College of George-Town, (Potomack) in the state of Ma Maryland . . . [At end] George-Town, January 1st, 1798. Wm. Du Bourg, President of the College. [Georgetown, 1798]
3 p. 25 cm. caption title
Prospectus of the College
Goff; Georgetown 20; Parsons 189
DGU (2 copies; in copy 2 the name of Leonard Neale replaces the crossed-out name of DuBourg) mp. 48455

B10334 GILL, JOHN, 1697-1771
Infant-baptism, a part and pillar of popery . . . Fourth edition. Boston, Manning and Loring [1798?]
36 p.
RPJCB mp. 48456

B10335 THE good old Virginia almanack for the year . . . 1799 . . . The astronomical part only, by Isaac Briggs . . . Richmond, T. Nicolson [1798]
[24] p. 14 cm.
ViU mp. 48457

B10336 THE good old Virginia almanack for the year . . . 1799 . . . The astronomical part only, by Isaac Briggs . . . Richmond, Printed [by T. Nicolson?] for M. L. Weems [1798]
[21], 23 p. 13 cm.
CSmH; PHi mp. 48458

B10337 GT. BRIT.
Official account of Admiral Nelson's destruction of the French fleet . . . The following was received in a hand bill by a gentleman from Portsmouth, on Saturday . . . [Concord, George Hough, 1798]
broadside 35 X 21 cm.
PPRF mp. 48460

B10338 GRIFFITH, BENJAMIN
To the editor of *Porcupine's Gazette* . . . Benjamin Griffith. [n.p., 1798]
8 p. 19.5 cm. caption title
DLC mp. 48461

B10339 [GRIFFITH, JOHN]
The gentleman & lady's companion . . . Norwich, J. Trumbull, 1798.
24 p. 12 cm.
Damon, S. F.: History of square dancing (AAS *Proceedings* v. 62, p. 77); Trumbull: Supplement 2183
CtHT-W; DLC. Photostat: RPJCB mp. 48462

B10340 THE happy child. You parents who have children dear . . . Newport, H. & O. Farnsworth [1798?]
broadside 29 X 24 cm.
Alden 1564A; Winship p. 74
RNHi. Photostat: MWA mp. 48463

B10341 HARRIS, HEMAN
A dream of Mr. Heman Harris, in his last sickness . . . Worcester, Printed [by Leonard Worcester], 1798.
12 p. 17 cm.
Advertised in the *Massachusetts Spy*, Dec. 19, 1798, as "just published."
MWA mp. 48464

B10342 HAVEN, SAMUEL, 1727-1806
An ode, occasioned by the repairing of the South Church, and providing a convenient seat for the singers . . . [Portsmouth] Printed by C. Peirce [1798]
broadside 28 X 11 cm.
Dated by New-York Historical Society
NHi mp. 48465

B10343 HAWLES, SIR JOHN, 1645-1716
The Englishman's right . . . Philadelphia, Printed by James Thompson, for A Brodie, 1798.
70 p. 8vo
PPL (p. 9-16 lacking; PPL has also Evans 33862) mp. 48466

B10344 HAYMARKET THEATRE, BOSTON
Hay Market Theatre. Mr. Villiers' night . . . On Wednesday evening, April 25, 1798 . . . The Married Man . . . [Boston, 1798]
broadside 33 X 22 cm.
MB mp. 48374

B10345 HEIDELBERG CATECHISM
The Heidelbergh catechism, or method of instruction . . . The eighth edition. New-York; Printed and sold by T. Greenleaf, M,DCC,LXXXVIII.
48 p. 20 cm.
NjR

B10346 HAYNES, LEMUEL, 1753-1833
The important concerns of ministers, and the people of their charge . . . Illustrated in a sermon, delivered at Rutland . . . August 22d, 1797, at the interment of the Rev. Abraham Carpenter . . . Rutland, 1798.
23 p. 19 cm.
Cooley 437; Porter 120
CSmH; NHi mp. 48467

B10347 HEMMENWAY, MOSES, 1735-1811
A discourse on the divine institution of water baptism . . . Portsmouth, William & Daniel Treadwell [1798?]
17 p.
RPJCB mp. 48468

B10348 HERALD Office, Monday morning, [June] 1798. 1798. Anxious to gratify our patrons . . . Norfolk, Willett & O'Connor [1798]
broadside
McCoy 29
ViW mp. 48469

B10349 THE history of Goody Two-Shoes . . . Litchfield, T. Collier, 1798.
112 p. illus. 12 cm.
CtHi (t.p. and many pages wanting). Mrs. Edgar S. Oppenheimer, New York City (1962) mp. 48459

B10350 THE history of little Goody Goosecap, and her brother little Charles. To which is added, The story of Johnny Bad-boy. Boston, Printed and sold by John W. Folsom, 1798.
29, [2] p. 10.5 cm.
MH (imperfect); MSaE; MWA (covers and p. 13-20 wanting) mp. 48470

B10351 THE history of Tommy Titmouse. A little boy, who became a great man by minding his learning . . . Boston, Printed and sold by John W. Folsom, 1798.
58+ p. illus. 10 cm.
Gillett Griffin, Princeton Univ. (all after p. 58 wanting) mp. 48471

B10352 HOCH-DEUTSCHES Lutherisches A, B, C, und Names Büchlein, für Kinder, welche anfangen zu lernen. Elisabeth (Hägers) Taun: Gedruckt und zu haben bey Johann Gruber, 1798.
31 p. 12 mo
End leaves pasted down
PPL mp. 48472

B10353 HOCH-DEUTSCHES Reformirtes A B C- und Namen-Büchlein . . . Verbesserte Ausgabe. Philadelphia, Carl Cist, 1798.
[32] p. incl. end leaves. 16 cm.
MWA mp. 48473

B10354 HOOK, JAMES, 1746-1827
O whither can my William stray . . . New York, J. Hewitt; Philadelphia, B. Carr; Baltimore, J. Carr [1798]
[2] p. 33 cm.
Sonneck-Upton p. 308
DLC; NN; NRU-Mus mp. 48474

B10355 [HOOK, JAMES] 1746-1827
The silver moon. Boston, P. A. von Hagen [1798-99]
[2] p. 30 cm.
Sonneck-Upton p. 382
DLC; RPJCB mp. 48475

B10356 HOOK, JAMES, 1746-1827
The silver moon . . . Philadelphia, C. Hupfeld; Baltimore, H. S. Keating [1798]
[2] p. 33 cm.
Sonneck-Upton p. 382
DLC; MWA; NN; PU mp. 48476

B10357 [HOPKINSON, JOSEPH] 1770-1842
Hail Columbia. [and] A Federal ode. Boston, Sold by J. White [1798?]
broadside 33 X 20.5 cm.
New York Public 1234
NN (reduced facsim.). Photostat: MWA mp. 48477

B10358 AN hymn to be sung by the Episcopal Charity-Children at St. George's Chapel, on Sunday, December 2, 1798 . . . [New York, 1798]
broadside 33 X 21 cm.
NHi mp. 48480

B10359 [IMPORTANT! Extract of a letter from a respectable gentleman in Norfolk . . . dated January 5, 1798 . . . Extract of another letter from a gentleman in Richmond . . . dated January 9, 1798 . . . Baltimore, Thomas Dobbin, 1798]
broadside
Title from the *Telegraphe*, Jan. 17, 1798: "The following intelligence, we yesterday published in a hand bill."
Minick 434
No copy known mp. 48481

B10360 [HOWARD, THOMAS]
The history of the Seven Wise Mistresses of Rome . . . Philadelphia, Printed for the booksellers, 1798.
[iii]-vi [i.e. iv], [5]-132 p. 14 cm.
"To the reader" signed: Tho. Howard
MWA mp. 48478

B10361 INSTRUCTIVE and entertaining emblems on various subjects. By Miss Thoughtful. Hartford, John Babcock, 1798.
30 p. 12 cm.
New York Public 1250; Trumbull: Supplement 2286
CtHi; NN (imperfect) mp. 48482

B10362 IVERNOIS, SIR FRANCIS D', 1757–1842
Reflections on war. In answer to reflections on peace . . . Philadelphia: Published by Francis C. King, 1798.
1 p.l., 135, [1] p. 22 cm.
cf. Evans 33928
NHi mp. 48483

B10363 JACKY Dandy's delight: or, The history of birds and beasts, in verse and prose . . . Boston, Printed and sold by S. Hall, 1798.
30, [2] p. incl. covers. 11 cm.
MWA mp. 48484

B10364 JEFFERSON, THOMAS, 1743-1826
Philadelphia, December 31st, 1797. Dear Sir, Mr. Tazewell has communicated to me . . . [Philadelphia, 1798]
4 p.
Letter to Gov. Henry
cf. JCB *Annual report,* 1949/50: 43-48
RPJCB mp. 48485

B10365 JOHNSON, NATHANIEL, fl. 1796-1805
Nathaniel Johnson, at his shop in Court-street . . . has for sale crockery and glass ware . . . [Boston, 1798?]
broadside 18.5 X 15.5 cm.
On verso is a receipted bill to the Boston (Federal St.) Theatre, dated Sept. 5, 1798
MB mp. 48486

B10366 [JOHNSON, RICHARD] 1734-1793
The hermit of the forest, and the wandering infants. A rural fragment . . . Boston, Printed and sold by S. Hall, 1798.
29, [3] p. incl. covers. 10.5 cm.
Rosenbach-Ch 236
MWA; PP mp. 48487

B10367 [JOHNSON, RICHARD] 1734-1793
The hermit of the forest, and the wandering infants, a rural fragment . . . Charlestown, Printed and sold by J. Lamson, 1798.
31, [1] p. incl. covers. 10.5 cm.
MB; MWA mp. 48488

B10368 [JOHNSON, RICHARD] 1734-1793
Rural felicity . . . Charlestown: Printed and sold by J. Lamson, 1798.
31 p. illus. 10 cm.
d'Alté A. Welch, Cleveland (1962) mp. 48489

B10369 JOHNSON, THOMAS, fl. 1773 (ca.)-1798
Every man his own doctor; or the poor man's family physician . . . By Thomas Johnson. Salisbury, Printed for the author, 1798.
v, 50 p. 17 cm.
Austin 1076; McMurtrie: North Carolina 249
NcD; NcU. Bruce Cotten, Baltimore (1938) mp. 48490

B10370 [THE jovial songster. 4th edition, with additors. New York, Printed and sold by John Harrison [sic], 1798

Listed in a book catalogue issued by H. V. Button of Waterford, N. Y.
BSA *Papers* 54(1960): 66
No copy known mp. 48491

B10371 KEILING,
A convention if you please. Mr. Sidney . . . I expected prudence would have directed you . . . Keiling. [Lexington? 1798]
[2] p. 27.5 X 22 cm.
McMurtrie; Kentucky 76
DLC mp. 48492

B10372 [KEMPER, HEINRICH]
Treuhertzige Erinnerung und Warnung bestehend in vielen Klagreden von Verfall des Christethums [sic] . . . Hannover, Samuel F. Stettinius, 1798.
110 p. 8vo
PPL mp. 48493

B10373 KENTUCKY. GENERAL ASSEMBLY. HOUSE OF REPRESENTATIVES
[Journal of the House . . . at the second session of the sixth General Assembly . . . [Jan. 1, 1798] . . . Frankfort, John Bradford [1798]]
46+ p. 31 cm.
Title page assumed from ms. copy in Kentucky State Library in above form
McMurtrie: Kentucky 77
ICU (has only p. 11-46) mp. 48496

B10374 KENTUCKY. GENERAL ASSEMBLY. HOUSE OF REPRESENTATIVES
Journal of the House of Representatives. [Frankfort? Hunter & Beaumont? 1798?]
94+ p. 32 cm. caption title
Session Nov. 5-Dec. 22, 1798
Acts of this session printed by Hunter & Beaumont
McMurtrie: Kentucky 78
ICU (p. 5-6, 9-21, and all after 94 wanting); Ky (all after p. 94 wanting) mp. 48497

B10375 KENTUCKY. GENERAL ASSEMBLY. HOUSE OF REPRESENTATIVES
Legislature of Kentucky. House of Representatives. Wednesday, Nov. 7, 1798 . . . [at end] Frankfort, Hunter & Beaumont [1798]
broadside 44.5 X 28 cm.
The famous Kentucky Resolutions
McMurtrie: Kentucky 80
DLC mp. 48494

B10376 KENTUCKY. GENERAL ASSEMBLY. HOUSE OF REPRESENTATIVES
Rules and regulations of the House of Representatives. [Lexington? John Bradford? 1798?]
4 p. 33.5 cm. caption title
Certain classes of petitions not to be considered "unless three times inserted in the *Kentucky Gazette*" (p. 4)
McMurtrie: Kentucky 79
DLC; ICU mp. 48495

B10377 KENTUCKY. GENERAL ASSEMBLY. SENATE
Journal of the Senate at the second session of the sixth General Assembly . . . held . . . Frankfort . . . [Jan. 1, 1798]
70 p. 30.5 cm.

McMurtrie: Kentucky 83
KyU mp. 48498

B10378 KENTUCKY. LAWS
Acts (of a general nature,) passed at the second session of the sixth General Assembly . . . held . . . Frankfort . . . [Jan. 1, 1798] . . . Lexington, John Bradford [1798]
170 p. 20 cm.
Advertised in the *Kentucky Gazette*, May 9, 1798, as "This day is published by the printer hereof."
McMurtrie; Kentucky 85
MH-L; NNB mp. 48499

B10379 KURZGEFASSTES Arzney-Büchlein, für Menschen und Vieh . . . Ephrata, zum siebentenmal gedruckt, von Benjamin Mayer, 1798.
32 p. 13 X 10 cm.
DNLM (imperfect); MWA mp. 48500

B10380 THE launch, a Federal song . . . [Boston? 1798?]
broadside 44.5 X 25.5 cm.
12 4-line stanzas
The Launch, or, Huzza! for the Constitution, a "musical piece," opened in Boston Sept. 20, 1797
MWA mp. 48501

B10381 LEIGH, EDWARD, 1602-1671
The history of the twelve Caesars . . . Philadelphia, Printed for Robert Johnson, & Co., 1798.
105 p. 14.5 cm.
MWA; NjP mp. 48502

B10382 LESSONS for youth, selected for the use of Ackworth, and other schools . . . New-York, Re-printed and sold by Isaac Collins, 1798.
201, [3] p. 17.5 cm.
PHi mp. 48504

B10383 LEWIS, MATTHEW GREGORY, 1775-1818
Ambrosio, or The monk: a romance . . . Three volumes in two . . . The first American, from the fourth British edition . . . Philadelphia: Printed for W. Cobbett, 1798.
2 v. (323, 325 p.) 12mo
Adams: Pennsylvania 71
PU

B10384 THE little riddle-book . . . By John-the-Giant Killer, Esq. Boston: Printed and sold by S. Hall, 1798.
30 p. illus. 10 cm.
RPB (mutilated) mp. 48506

B10385 LOUISIANA. GOVERNOR, 1797-1799
Dn. Manuel Gayoso de Lemos . . . Gobernador general . . . de la Luisiana, y Florida Occidental . . . Bando de buen gobierno . . . [at end] Nueva Orleans . . . Enero de 1798. [New Orleans, 1798]
[11] p. 22 cm.
McMurtrie: New Orleans 42
CU-B mp. 48507

B10386 LOVE preferred to fortune: or the history of Colin & Mira . . . Portsmouth, N.H. Printed at the Oracle-Press, 1798.
14+ p. 11 cm.
MWA (lacking after p. 14) mp. 48508

B10387 MCCORKLE, SAMUEL EUSEBIUS, 1746-1811
Four discourses, on the general first principles of deism and revelation contrasted; delivered in Salisbury . . . April & May, 1797 . . . Discourse II. Salisbury, Francis Coupee, & John M. Slump, 1798.
42 p. 18.5 cm.
Discourse I appeared in 1797 (above). No record of Discourses III-IV
McMurtrie: North Carolina 251
NcA-S; NcU; PPPrHi. Bruce Cotten (1938) mp. 48509

B10388 MCCORKLE, SAMUEL EUSEBIUS, 1746-1811
Three discourses on the terms of Christian communion . . . Discourse I. Salisbury, Francis Coupee & John M. Slump, 1798.
50 p. 18.5 cm.
No record of Discourses II-III
McMurtrie: North Carolina 252
NcC; NcU. Bruce Cotten, Baltimore (1938) mp. 48510

B10389 MCLAUGHLIN, MARTIN
[Last words of Martin McLaughlin. Reading, Gottlob Jungmann, 1799]

Advertised in the *Neue Unpartheyische Readinger Zeitung*
Nolan p. 31
No copy located mp. 48511

B10390 MCMANUS, CHARLES
Die lezten worte und sterbende bĕkanthnus von . . . Charles M'Manus . . . Im gefängnis . . . den 12ten Julius, 1798. Harrisburg, John Wyeth [1798]
broadside 41 X 34.5 cm.
DLC mp. 48512

B10391 THE marriage of a deceased wife's sister incestuous. In answer to "A letter from a citizen to his friend." . . . New-York: Printed by T. & J. Swords, 1798.
61 p. 22 cm.
Signed: Eudoxius
NNS

B10392 MARYLAND. LAWS
An act for the better preservation of last wills and testaments disposing of real estates . . . [Annapolis, F. Green, 1798]
broadside ([2] p.) 34 X 21.5 cm.
Minick 440
MdHi

B10393 MARYLAND. LAWS
An act to alter, abolish and repeal, such parts . . . of the constitution and forms of government . . . [Annapolis, F. Green, 1798]
broadside ([4] p.) 34 X 42 cm., folded
Not the form of the act which became law
Minick 441
MdHi mp. 48513

B10394 MASSACHUSETTS. GENERAL COURT
Commonwealth of Massachusetts. Boston, July 12, 1798. Sir, The two branches of the Legislature . . . barrier should be opposed to the introduction of foreign influence . . . [Boston, 1798]
[3] p. 35 cm.
Evans 34066 on p. [2-3]
MHi mp. 48514

B10395 Deleted

B10395a METAMORPHOSIS. A satirical poem . . . [n.p., 1798?]
8 p. 20.5 cm. caption title
At end of text: This done at Eagle-Hall . . . in the most enlightened year of the eighteenth century . . . By the scribe to the President.

Concerns the Lyon-Griswold fracas
Stoddard 160
RPB

B10396 MINERVA
Address of the carrier of the *Minerva*, to his patrons. Winter appears – the hoary monarch . . . January 1st, 1798. [New York, 1798]
broadside 32 X 15.5 cm.
NHi mp. 48329

B10397 THE misfortunes of anger. A drama in two parts. Boston, Printed for W. Spotswood, 1798.
42 p. 32mo
"The writer does not . . . intend her dramatic dialogues to be performed."--Preface
Hill 190
MH mp. 48516

B10398 MOELLER, HEINRICH
Eine ernstliche Warnung gegen die Sünde . . . Lancaster, Johann Albrecht, 1798.
16 p. 19 cm.
MWA; PPL mp. 48517

B10399 THE MONITOR, LITCHFIELD, CONN.
The news-boy's New-Year jingle, for 1798. Scowl'd from the presence of the epic bard, your news-boy deems his case most despit hard . . . Litchfield, January 1, 1798. [Litchfield, 1798]
broadside 30 X 24 cm.
NHi mp. 48551

B10400 MOORE, JOHN, 1730-1802
Edward. Various views of human nature . . . In two volumes. Vol. I[-II] Mount-Pleasant, Printed by W. Durell, for J. Harrison, C. Davis, W. Milns, A. Somerville, R. Macgill, Gaine & Teneyck, & T. Allen, 1798.
2 v. 12mo
Variant imprint of Evans 34129; vol. II agrees with Evans
MWiW

B10401 MORTON, THOMAS, 1764-1838
A cure for the heart-ache . . . First American edition. New-York, Printed by R. Wilson, for Evert Duyckinck, 1798.
61, [3] p. 17.5 cm.
MWA mp. 48518

B10402 MOULTRIE, ALEXANDER [ET AL.] VS. GEORGIA
In thr [sic] Supreme Court of the United States. Moultrie, et al. versus state of Georgia, et al. In equity, complainants brief. The bill . . . in year 1789, complainants with one Thomas Washington, now dead . . . [Philadelphia? 1798?]
7 p. 29 cm. caption title
Imprint date assigned by MiU-C from internal evidence
MiU-C

B10403 THE mountain piper, or, The history of Edgar and Matilda . . . Hartford, John Babcock, 1798.
29, [2] p. incl. covers. 12 cm.
MWA mp. 48368

B10404 [A NARRATIVE of the life of Zilpha Smith, alias Sylva Wood . . . She hung herself in Herkemer Gaol . . . Providence, Bennett Wheeler, 1798]
Advertised July 26, 1798, as "In the press and next week will be published."
Alden 1567
No copy known mp. 48519

B10405 THE New-England primer improved . . . Baltimore: Printed by W. Pechin, No. 15, for Thomas, Andrews & Butler, No. 184, Market-street. [1798?]
72 p. illus. 9.5 cm.
Without second title on p. 49
cf. Evans 34181; cf. Minick 448
d'Alté A. Welch, Cleveland (1963) mp. 48520

B10406 THE New-England primer, improved . . . Boston, James Loring [1798]
[62] p. illus. 10 cm.
CtHi mp. 48521

B10407 THE New-England primer, improved . . . Litchfield, Thomas Collier, 1798.
[72] p.
Trumbull: Second supplement 2868
No copy located mp. 48522

B10408 THE New-England primer improved . . . New-London, Printed by S. Green, for John W. Green [1798?]
[72] p.
Trumbull: Supplement 2443
No copy located mp. 48523

B10409 THE New-England primer, improved . . . Troy: Printed by R. Moffitt & Co., 1798.

Fox Book Co., Tacoma, Wash. (1966)

B10410 NEW HAMPSHIRE. LAWS
The laws of the state of New-Hampshire, passed at a session . . . begun . . . June, 1798 . . . Portsmouth, John Melcher, 1798.
2 p.l., p. 515-516. 23 cm.
DLC; MWA; NhD mp. 48524

B10411 NEW JERSEY. GENERAL ASSEMBLY
Votes and proceedings of the twenty-third General Assembly of . . . New-Jersey . . . Being the first sitting. Trenton, Matthias Day, 1798.
64 p. fold. table. 32.5 cm.
Session Oct. 23-Nov. 8, 1798
Morsch 399
NN; Nj; NjHi; PPL mp. 48525

B10412 NEW JERSEY. LAWS
An act of the Legislature of . . . New-Jersey, passed at Trenton, the 15th of March, 1798, authorizing justices of the peace to take cognizance in civil actions . . . for sixty dollars or under . . . Morristown, Jacob Mann, 1798.
[2], 23 p. 20.5 cm.
Morsch 387
CSmH; NjR mp. 48526

B10413 NEW JERSEY. LAWS
Acts of the twenty-third General assembly . . . At a session begun at Trenton . . . Being the first sitting. Trenton, Gershom Craft, 1798.
1 p.l., 415-421 p. 30.5 cm.
Morsch 389; New York Public 1237
DLC; NN; Nj; NjHi mp. 48533

B10414 NEW JERSEY. LAWS
State of New-Jersey. A bill, intitled, "An act concerning fines and common recoveries." . . . [Colophon] Trenton,

Matthias Day, 1798.
11 p. 34.5 cm.
NjR

B10415 NEW JERSEY. LAWS
State of New-Jersey. A bill, intitled, An act concerning sheriffs . . . [Trenton, Matthias Day, 1798]
8+ p. fol. caption title
PHi (lacking after p. 8)

B10416 NEW JERSEY. LAWS
State of New-Jersey. A bill, intitled, "An act constituting courts for the trial of small causes . . ." [Trenton, 1798]
15 p. 35 cm. caption title
Passed at Trenton, Mar. 15, 1798
Lines separately numbered
Morsch 395; New York Public 1238
NN mp. 48529

B10417 NEW JERSEY. LAWS
State of New-Jersey. A bill, intitled, "An act granting relief . . . against collusive judgments . . ." [Trenton, 1798]
4 p. 34.5 cm. caption title
Passed at Trenton, Mar. 2, 1798
Lines separately numbered
Morsch 396; New York Public 1239
NN mp. 48530

B10418 NEW JERSEY. LAWS
State of New-Jersey. A bill, intitled, "An act making provision for carrying into effect the act for the punishment of crimes . . ." [Trenton, 1798]
7 p. 35 cm. caption title
Title from Nelson
Morsch 390
No copy located mp. 48531

B10419 NEW JERSEY. LAWS
State of New-Jersey. A bill, intitled, "An act making provision for working . . . the highways . . ." [Trenton, 1798]
6 p. 35 cm. caption title
Passed at Trenton, Mar. 16, 1798
Lines separately numbered
Morsch 397; New York Public 1240
NN; Nj mp. 48532

B10420 NEW JERSEY. LAWS
State of New-Jersey. An act to incorporate the chosen freeholders in respective counties of the state . . . [Trenton, 1798]
9 p. 32.5 cm.
Passed at Trenton, Feb. 13, 1798
Morsch 394
NNC-L mp. 48527

B10421 NEW JERSEY. LEGISLATIVE COUNCIL
Journal of the proceedings of the Legislative-Council of . . . New-Jersey . . . convened . . . [Oct. 24, 1797]. Being the first and second sittings of the twenty-second session. Trenton, Matthias Day, 1798.
83 p. 32 cm.
Morsch 391
NN; Nj; PPL mp. 48528

B10422 THE New-Jersey and New-York almanac, for the year 1799. Being the third after leap-year . . . By Abraham Shoemaker. Newark, Printed and sold by Jacob Halsey, & co. [1798]
[36] p. 17 cm.
Morsch 400
CSmH; DLC; NHi mp. 48614

B10423 NEW Presidents march. Philadelphia, Printed and sold by G. Willig [ca. 1798]
1 leaf. 33.5 cm. caption title
"Published possibly as early as 1798."—Sonneck-Upton p. 454. cf. Evans 35638
MiU-C

B10424 [A NEW song, witty and satirical, containing a faithful abridgement of the proceedings of six days of a very great legislative body. By a citizen of Baltimore. Baltimore? 1798]

Advertised in the *Telegraphe*, Mar. 8, 1798, as "This day is published."
Minick 422
No copy known mp. 48534

B10425 NEW Yankee Doodle sung with great applause at the theatre by Mr. Hodgkinson. New York, Printed & sold at J. Hewitt's music repository; sold also by B. Carr, Philadelphia, & J. Carr, Baltimore [1798]
[4] p. 32.5 cm.
CSmH mp. 48535

B10426 NEW YORK. ADJUTANT GENERAL
Adjutant General's office. July 20, 1798. General orders . . . Aug. 19, 1798. General orders . . . Albany, Charles R. and George Webster [1798]
broadside 27.5 X 13.5 cm.
McMurtrie: Albany 183
N mp. 48539

B10427 NEW YORK. BOARD OF COMMISSIONERS TO SETTLE DISPUTES ON TITLES TO LANDS
Military lots; the claims to which are to be heard and determined by the Board of Commissioners at Albany. The Board . . . will . . . commence the first Tuesday in August next . . . examine the claims . . . mentioned in their advertisement of 7th October, 1797 . . . Albany, Printed by Charles R. and George Webster, and sold at their bookstore [1798]
broadside 26.5 X 15 cm.
NjR

B10428 NEW YORK. COMMISSIONERS FOR ERECTING STATE PRISONS
To the honorable the legislature of the state of New-York. The commissioners appointed by the statute . . . ". . . for erecting state prisons," report . . . [Albany] Loring Andrews [1798]
broadside 35 X 22 cm.
Progress report over the name of John Watts, chairman, dated Jan. 13, 1798
McMurtrie: Albany 189
MH mp. 48540

B10429 NEW YORK. COMMISSIONERS OF THE ALMS-HOUSE
City of New-York, ss. At a Common Council held on Monday, the 15th day of January, 1798 — The following representation of the Commissioners of the Alms-House, was read . . . and it was ordered, . . . printed in hand-bills . . . also in the newspapers . . . [New York, 1798]
broadside 41.5 X 26 cm.
MH; NHi mp. 48537

B10430 NEW YORK. COMPTROLLER
To the honourable the Legislature of . . . New-York

. . . Comptroller. Albany, August 15, 1798. [Albany, 1798]
[3] p. 35 cm.
NHi mp. 48541

B10431 NEW YORK. COURT FOR THE TRIAL OF IMPEACHMENTS AND THE CORRECTION OF ERRORS
Court for the Correction of Errors. Gouverneur and Kemble, vs. Louis Le Guen. Reasons assigned by Mr. Chief Justice Lansing, and Mr. Justice Benson, for the judgment, in the Court below. Albany, Charles R. and George Webster [1798]
[1], 17 p. 19 cm.
Dated from ms. notes in NNC-L copy, which is appended to Evans 32369
NNC-L

B10432 NEW YORK. COURT FOR THE TRIAL OF IMPEACHMENTS AND THE CORRECTION OF ERRORS
Court for the Trial of Impeachments and the Correction of Errors: Isaac Gouverneur and Peter Kemble, appellants; and Louis LeGuen, respondent: Case, on the part of Louis LeGuen . . . [Albany] Charles R. & George Webster [1798?]
[2], 25 p. 19 cm. [A]-C^4 D^2
MWA has also photocopy of variant issue
MWA; N mp. 48502

B10433 NEW YORK. GOVERNOR, 1795-1801
By . . . John Jay . . . A proclamation. Whereas it is the duty and the interest . . . [Mar. 1, 1798] . . . [Albany? 1798]
broadside 34 X 30.5 cm.
MiU-C mp. 48542

B10434 NEW YORK. GOVERNOR, 1795-1801
Governor's Speech. Gentlemen of the Senate and Assembly, Perceiving the various objections . . . [Colophon] [Albany] Loring Andrews & Co. [1798]
[2] p. 33.5 X 20.5 cm.
Singed and dated: John Jay. Albany, August 9th, 1798
New York Public 1242
NN mp. 48543

B10435 NEW YORK. HOUSE OF ASSEMBLY
Members of the House of Assembly, the counties they represent, and places of lodging. Albany, January 2, 1798. [Albany] Charles P. & George Webster [1798]
broadside 46.5 X 20.5 cm.
McMurtrie: Albany 186
N mp. 48546

B10436 NEW YORK. HOUSE OF ASSEMBLY
Rules and orders . . . [Albany] Loring Andrews [1798]
broadside 38 X 25 cm.
Loring Andrews was printer to the state only in 1798
McMurtrie: Albany 187
MH mp. 48547

B10437 NEW YORK. INSPECTORS OF THE STATE PRISON
The inspectors of the state-prison respectfully report . . . [Albany] Loring Andrews [1798]
[3] p. 4to
Dated: New-York, first month 1798
McMurtrie: Albany 194
N mp. 48544

B10438 NEW YORK. LAWS
Laws of the state of New-York . . . from the first to the twentieth session . . . Volume II. Second edition . . . New-York, Thomas Greenleaf, 1798.
1 p.l., 520 p. 20.5 cm.
cf. Evans 34214 (v. 1 only)
DLC mp. 48545

B10439 NEW YORK. MILITIA
Sir, Pursuant to the act of the Legislature of . . . New-York . . . you are hereby summoned . . . before the Court Martial of the First Regiment of Militia . . . at Hunter's Hotel . . . in Broadway . . . to shew cause why the fine incurred by you . . . should not be levied. Dated this day of in the year . . . one thousand seven hundred and ninety-eight . . . [New York, 1798]
broadside 29 X 21.5 cm.
NHi (photostat)

B10440 NEW YORK. NEW THEATRE
New-York, May 14, 1798. For the benefit of Mr. Milns . . . May 16, will be presented . . . Wives pleased, and maids happy . . . N.B. The box-office is removed to the New Theatre. [New York, 1798]
broadside
New York Public 1241
NN (reduced facsim.) mp. 48538

B10441 NEW YORK. SENATE
Members composing the Senate of the state of New-York; with their respective districts, classes and places of lodging. Albany, January 2d, 1798. [Albany] Charles R. & George Webster [1798]
broadside 34.5 X 15 cm.
McMurtrie: Albany 201
N mp. 48549

B10442 NEW YORK. SENATE
State of New-York, in Senate, August 17th, 1798. Ordered, That Mr. Foote . . . [Albany] Loring Andrews [1798]
broadside 33 X 21 cm.
DLC; N mp. 48548

B10443 NICHOLAS, GEORGE, 1754-1799
To the citizens of Kentucky . . . [at end] George Nicholas, Lexington, October 15, 1798. [Lexington? 1798]
42 p. 17 cm. caption title
McMurtrie: Kentucky 90
CSmH mp. 48552

B10444 THE noble slaves. Being an entertaining history of the surprising adventures, and remarkable deliverances, from Algerine slavery, of several Spanish noblemen and ladies of quality. New-Haven, George Bunce, 1798.
216 p. 14.5 cm.
Trumbull: Second supplement 2869
Ct; CtHi mp. 48342

B10445 NORMAN, WILLIAM
The American pilot, containing the navigation of the sea coast of North America . . . Boston, Wm. Norman, 1798.
3 p.l., 11 maps. 54 cm.
Phillips p. 595; Phillips: Atlases 1217; cf. Evans 34239 (variant title)
DLC mp. 48553

B10446 NORTH CAROLINA. LAWS
Laws of North-Carolina. At a General Assembly, begun . . . [Nov. 20, 1797] . . . being the first session . . . [Halifax, A. Hodge, 1798]
15 p. 33 cm. caption title

McMurtrie: North Carolina 257
DLC; MH-L; NcU

B10447 NORTON, ELIJAH
The impossibility of sinners' coming to Christ . . . a discourse preached at Royalton . . . Printed at Suffield, by H. & O. Farnsworth, for Mr. S. Shepherd, M,DCC,XCVIII.
[48] p. 19.5 cm.
Entirely different setting of type from Evans 34258
CtHi

B10448 O'DONNEL, CHARLES, d. 1797
The life and confession of Charles O'Donnel . . . executed at Morgantown, June 19, 1797, for the wilful murder of his son; though he had murdered a woman about 27 years before . . . not discovered . . . As related by himself, to the Rev. Simon Cochrun . . . Lancaster, Printed and sold by W. & R. Dickson, 1798.
14 p. 21 cm.
NHi mp. 48554

B10449 [O'KELLY, JAMES] 1735-1826
The author's apology for protesting against the Methodist Episcopal government. Richmond, John Dixon, 1798.
120 p. 17 cm.
Signed: Christicola
Davis 144
IEG mp. 48555

B10450 ON the decrees, or The Arminian attacked. By a gentleman of Dutchess County . . . Poughkeepsie, John Woods, 1798.
19 p. 19 cm.
New York Public 1243
NN mp. 48556

B10451 [PAINE, ROBERT TREAT] 1773-1811
Adams and liberty. [n.p., 1798?]
broadside 33 X 13 cm.
No cut at head of caption, unlike Ford 2878
CSmH

B10452 [PAINE, ROBERT TREAT] 1773-1811
Adams and liberty. New York, Printed and sold by G. Gilfert [1798?]
2 leaves. 4to
With the music
CSmH mp. 48557

B10453 PAINE, ROBERT TREAT, 1773-1811
Adams and liberty, a new patriotic song . . . Baltimore, Printed by Hanna and Greene, for Thomas, Andrews, & Butler, and Solomon Cotton [1798]
7 p. 23 cm.
Without music
Advertised as "Just published and for sale" in the *Telegraphe*, June 2, 1798
Minick 450
MdHi mp. 48559

B10454 PAINE, ROBERT TREAT, 1773-1811
Adams and liberty. The Boston patriotic song. Written by Thomas Paine, A.M. [n.p., 1798?]
broadside ([2] p.)
Ford 2883
With the music
MSaE

B10454a [PAINE, ROBERT TREAT] 1773-1811
Adams and liberty. Ye sons of Columbus . . . [Worcester? 1798]
broadside
MWA mp. 48558

B10455 [A PAMPHLET for the information of merchants concerned in the export of merchandize entitled to a drawback of duties. Baltimore, John Hayes, 1798]

Advertised in the *Federal Gazette*, Jan. 13, 1798, as "Just published, by John Hayes."
Minick 451
No copy known mp. 48560

B10456 PAR sa legereté. [Philadelphia, Filippo Trisobio, 1798?]
broadside 32.5 X 23 cm.
CSmH mp. 48561

B10457 [PAWTUCKET cannon factory 5 December 1798. Providence, 1798]
broadside
Alden 1568; Winship Addenda p. 91
No copy known mp. 48562

B10458 [PENN, JAMES] 1727-1800
The farmer's daughter of Essex . . . New-York, John Tiebout, 1798.
96 p. 17.5 cm.
MWA mp. 48564

B10459 PENNSYLVANIA. LAWS
No. LV. In General Assembly. Tuesday, February 6, 1798. An act to provide for unsatisfied warrants for cases where lands have been surveyed out of the state . . . [Philadelphia, 1798]
2 p. fol.
PPL mp. 48565

B10460 PENNSYLVANIA. REGISTER-GENERAL
(Appendix.) Report of the register-general of the state of finances of Pennsylvania, for the year M,DCC,XCVII. Philadelphia, Francis & Robert Bailey [1798]
19 p. fol.
cf. Evans 34334
PPL mp. 48566

B10461 PENNSYLVANIA. TREASURY
(Appendix.) Receipts and expenditures in the treasury of Pennsylvania, from the first of January to the thirty-first of December, 1797, both days inclusive. Philadelphia, F. & R. Bailey, 1798.
62 p. fol.
cf. Evans 34333
PPL mp. 48567

B10462 PENNSYLVANIA GAZETTE
The *Gazette*. Philadelphia, Monday evening, November 19 . . . Remonstrance, addressed to the Executive Directory of the French Republic . . . By John Caspar Lavater . . . Zurich, the 10th of May, 1798 . . . [Philadelphia, 1798]
broadside 56 X 34.5 cm.
Issued as a supplement
MSaE

B10463 THE Pennsylvania, New-Jersey, Delaware, Maryland and Virginia almanac, for . . . 1799 . . . By Tom Tattle. Philadelphia: Printed for H. & P. Rice [1798]
[40] p.
Drake 10497; cf. Evans 34631
NjR; PHi (imperfect mp. 48568

B10464 [PERRAULT, CHARLES] 1628-1703
Fairy tales, or Histories of past times . . . New-York, Printed by John Harrisson and sold at his book store, 1798.

107 p. illus. 11.5 cm.
d'Alté A. Welch, Cleveland (1964) (p. 19-30 wanting)
mp. 48569

B10465 PERTH AMBOY, N. J. CITIZENS
To the Legislative-Council and General Assembly of . . . New-Jersey. The petition of the inhabitants of . . . Perth-Amboy, in the Count of Middlesex. Presented the 27th day of January, 1798 . . . [Trenton, 1798]
broadside
Title from Nelson
Morsch 386
No copy located mp. 48570

B10466 PHILADELPHIA. CITIZENS
At a meeting of a number of the citizens of Philadelphia . . . for the purpose of nominating a candidate to be supported at the ensuing election . . . [Philadelphia, 1798]
broadside 21 X 13.5 cm.
PHi mp. 48571

B10467 PHILADELPHIA, March 20, 1798. Dear Sir,
After fourteen days delay . . . the President sent to us . . . With esteem, Your friend and servant, [Philadelphia, 1798]
broadside 25 X 20.5 cm.
DLC mp. 48574

B10468 PHILADELPHIA, August 9, 1798. By virtue of a writ of fieri facias . . . [Philadelphia] D. Humphreys [1798]
broadside 28.5 X 23 cm.
DLC mp. 48575

B10469 PHILADELPHIA, December 1798.
The late distress, occasioned by . . . an infectious malignant fever . . . [Philadelphia, 1798]
broadside 38.5 X 23.5 cm.
Petition for quarantine law, with 10 signatures
RPJCB mp. 48576

B10470 PHILADELPHIA CAVALRY
Bye-laws of the first troop of Philadelphia Cavalry. [Philadelphia, 1798]
12 p. 16 cm. caption title
DLC; PPL mp. 48572

B10471 [PHILE, PHILIP]
Presidents march. Philadelphia, Printed and sold by G. Willig, Mark [!] Street No. 185 [ca. 1798]
1 leaf. 33.5 cm. caption title
Includes arrangement for the flute
Sonneck-Upton p. 343, 4th item
MiU-C

B10472 PHINNEY'S calendar; or, Western almanack for . . . 1799. Cooperstown, Elihu Phinney [1798]

Advertised in the *Otsego Herald*, Dec. 6, 1798
Drake 6085
No copy known

B10473 PHOENOMENON. That beautiful full blooded stallion . . . March 28, 1798. [Portsmouth] J. Melcher [1798]
broadside 28 X 23.5 cm.
DLC mp. 48577

B10474 PICTURE exhibition, or, The ladder to learning . . . First Worcester edition. Worcester, Isaiah Thomas, Jun. Sold at his Book-Store - September, 1798.
30, [1] p. illus. 10.5 cm.
Wilbur M. Stone (present location unknown); d'Alté A. Welch, Cleveland (microfilm) mp. 48578

B10475 [PINCHARD, MRS.]
The misfortune of anger . . . Boston, Printed for William Spotswood, 1798.
42 p. front. 11 cm.
Separate issue of one story from Dramatic dialogues (Evans 34381)
MWA mp. 48579

B10476 PLAN of the French invasion of England and Ireland, &c. Extract of a letter, dated London, April 16, 1798 . . . Philadelphia, James Carey [1798]
broadside 46 X 27.5 cm.
cf. Evans 33753
DLC mp. 48580

B10477 PLAN of the town of Alexandria . . . 1798. Alexandria. Published by I. V. Thomas. Engrav'd by T. Clarke New York [1798]
map 62.5 X 50 cm.
Phillips p. 97
DLC mp. 48394

B10478 THE plea of Erin, or the case of the natives of Ireland in the United States, Fairly displayed . . . in the respectful memorial of the republican Irish . . . addressed . . . to the Congress of the year 1798 . . . Philadelphia, Printed at the office of the *Freeman's Journal*, No. 21, Walnut-street [1798?]
[4] p. 30.5 cm.
DLC mp. 48581

B10479 A POEM on the untimely deaths of the unfortunate Mr. Rufus Randall and Mr. Hopkins Hudson, both of Cranston . . . the cause of each other's death, in the year 1798 . . . [Providence? B. Wheeler? 1798?]
broadside
RPB (all text wanting after quatrain 13, line 2)
mp. 48582

B10480 A POLITICAL creed. I believe that the proceedings of the Senate . . . [Lexington? 1798]
broadside 27.5 X 20.5 cm.
McMurtrie: Kentucky 93
DLC mp. 48583

B10481 PROCEEDINGS in different parts of Virginia, on the subject of the late conduct of the general government. [n.p., 1798]
[2] p. 43.5 cm. X 26 cm.
Contains three sets of resolutions, dated from Aug. 20 to Sept. 24, 1798
DLC mp. 48584

B01482 PROTESTANT EPISCOPAL CHURCH IN THE U.S.A. MARYLAND (DIOCESE)
Journal of a convention . . . held in Baltimore, from . . . the 31st of May, to . . . the 2d of June . . . Baltimore, Samuel Sower, 1798.
12 p. 17 cm.
Minick 455; New York Public 1244
DLC; MWA; MdBE; MdBP; MdHi; NN mp. 48585

B10483 PROTESTANT EPISCOPAL CHURCH IN THE U.S.A. PENNSYLVANIA (DIOCESE)
Journal of the twelfth[-fourteenth] convention of the Protestant Episcopal Church, in . . . Pennsylvania . . . May 24th, 1796 [-June 6, 1798] . . . [Philadelphia, 1798?]
[10] p. 20 cm. [ ]^4 B^1
MWA mp. 48586

B10484 PROVIDENCE GAZETTE
New-Year verses of the carrier of the *Gazette* . . . Providence, January 1, 1798. [Providence, Carter and Wilkinson, 1798]
broadside 20.5 X 10.5 cm.
Alden 1571; Winship Addenda p. 91
RHi mp. 48536

B10485 QUESTIONS to be put to the electors. [Philadelphia] John Ormrod [1798?]
broadside 26.5 X 18 cm.
PHi mp. 48587

B10486 RAMSAY, DAVID, 1749-1815
Sir, Having made some progress in collecting materials for a General History of South-Carolina . . . I beg . . . answers to all or any of the following enquiries . . . Charleston, November 19, 1798. . . . [Charleston, 1798]
broadside 25.5 X 20.5 cm.
NcU

B10487 [READ, JACOB] 1751-1816
Resolved, that the duty or trust imposed by the Constitution . . . is not of such a nature as to render a Senator impeachable . . . [Philadelphia] John Fenno [1798]
1 leaf. 32.5 cm.
Motion was made by Mr. Read Feb. 14, 1798. cf. 5 Cong. 2 sess. Senate. Journal
MiU-C mp. 48715

B10488 REEVE, WILLIAM
[The galley slave: a ballad. Walnut Hills, Miss., Andrew Marschalk; 1798?]

Mentioned in a letter from Marschalk, Sept. 2, 1837 as follows: ". . . in the year '97-'98, I . . . obtained a small font of type . . . and while at the Walnut Hills, printed a ballad, 'The Galley Slave.'. . ."
McMurtrie: Mississippi 1
No copy known mp. 48588

B10489 A REMARKABLE prophecy, supposed to have laid six hundred years under a stone in Paris . . . Boston, J. White, 1798.
11 p.
cf. Evans 34438
RPB mp. 48589

B10490 THE reprobate's reward . . . Philadelphia, 1798.
8 p. 12.5 cm.
In verse
Rosenbach-Ch 240
PP mp. 48590

B10491 THE reward of avarice: or, Abdalla and the iron candlestick. A Turkish tale . . . Hartford, John Babcock, 1798.
29, [2] p. 11.5 cm.
PP mp. 48591

B10492 RHODE ISLAND. ELECTION PROX.
Christopher Grant Champlin, Second Representative for the state of Rhode-Island, &c. in the Sixth Congress . . . [Providence? 1798]
broadside 5.5 X 15 cm.
Alden 1573; Chapin Proxies 65
RHi mp. 48592

B10493 RHODE ISLAND. ELECTION PROX.
John Brown, Esq; 1st Representative to the 6th Congress . . . Christopher G. Champlin, Esq; 2d Representative . . . [Providence? 1798]
broadside 5.5 X 11.5 cm.
Alden 1574; Chapin Proxies 66
RHi mp. 48593

B10494 RHODE ISLAND. GOVERNOR, 1790-1805
[By His Excellency Arthur Fenner . . . A proclamation . . . [Nov. 5, 1798] . . . Newport, Oliver Farnsworth, 1798] [broadside?]
Bill submitted by Farnsworth Dec. 29, 1798
Alden 1576
No copy known mp. 48594

B10495 RICHARDSON, SAMUEL, 1689-1761
The history of Pamela . . . New-York, Printed by T. Kirk, for Cornelius Davis, 1798.
90, [2] p. 16.5 cm.
MWA mp. 48595

B10496 RICHARDSON, SAMUEL, 1689-1761
The history of Pamela . . . New-York, Printed by T. Kirk, for John Tiebout, 1798.
90, [2] p. 16.5 cm.
MWA (lacks front.) mp. 48598

B10497 RICHARDSON, SAMUEL, 1689-1761
The history of Pamela . . . New-York, Printed for T. Kirk, for Naphtali Judah, 1798.
90, [2] p. 16 cm.
CtY mp. 48596

B10498 RICHARDSON, SAMUEL, 1689-1761
The history of Pamela . . . New-York, Printed by T. Kirk, for Stephen Stephens, 1798.
90, [2] p. 16 cm.
d'Alté A. Welch, Cleveland (1964) mp. 48597

B10499 ROBISON, JOHN, 1739-1805
Proofs of a conspiracy . . . The fourth edition . . . New-York, Printed and sold by George Forman, 1798.
399 p. 21.5 cm.
New York Public 1246; cf. Evans 34478
DGU; NHi; NN; NjP; OClW; OU

B10500 ROCHE, REGINA MARIE (DALTON) 1764?-1845
The children of the abbey, a tale . . . First American, from the second London, edition . . . New York, Printed by M. L. & W. A. Davis, for H. Caritat, 1798.
4 v. in 2. 16.5 cm.
New York Public 1247
NN mp. 48599

B10501 ROOT, ERASTUS, 1773-1846
An introduction to arithmetic . . . Portsmouth, N.H., 1798.
105 p.
Karpinski p. 111
Not in MWA mp. 48600

B10502 ROSS, JAMES, 1744-1827
A practical, new vocabulary Latin and English . . . Chambersburg, Snowden and M'Corkle, Nov. 10, 1798.
[iii]-vi, 68 p. 16 cm. $[A]^2$ $B\text{-}E^6$ G^6 H^4
MWA mp. 48601

B10503 THE royal alphabet . . . Boston, S. Hall, 1798.

Mrs. Arthur M. Greenwood, Marlborough, Mass. (1962) mp. 48602

B10504 THE rural casket. Vol. I. No. 1[-15] June 5[-September 11] 1798. [Colophon] Poughkeepsie, Power & Southwick [1798]

242 p. 21 cm.
New York Public 1248
NN

B10505 RUTGERS, HARMAN G.
Catalogue of books, for sale by H. G. Rutgers . . . December 1st, at 6 o'clock. New York, Isaac Collins [1798]
broadside 40 X 26.5 cm.
McKay 141; New York Public 1249
NN mp. 48603

B10506 SACRED to the memory of Mrs. Ann Brown . . . She departed this transitory life June 16, 1798 . . . [Providence, John Carter, 1798]
broadside 31 X 19 cm.
Alden 1559
RPJCB. Photostat: MWA mp. 48604

B10507 THE sailor, who had served in the slave trade. New Bedford, Sold at the Printing-Office [1798?]
broadside
Ford 2887
MWA; NHi mp. 48605

B10508 ST. PAUL'S P. E. CHURCH, BALTIMORE
A form of prayer, compiled for the use of the congregations of St. Paul's and Christ-Church, Baltimore . . . Baltimore, John Hayes, 1798.
8 p. 21 cm.
Minick 408
MWA mp. 48346

B10509 ST. PIERRE, JACQUES HENRI BERNARDIN DE, 1737-1814
The beautiful history of Paul and Virginia, an Indian story. Translated . . . by H. Hunter . . . Exeter, Printed and sold by Henry Ranlet, 1798.
163, [3] p. 14.5 cm.
MWA mp. 48606

B10510 SALEM HOSPITAL
The following regulations are to be observed at Salem Hospital . . . Salem, June 25, 1798. [Salem, 1798]
broadside 34 X 24 cm.
MSaE mp. 48607

B10511 [SANDS, BENJAMIN]
[Metamorphosis. Philadelphia, 1798?]
oblong leaf folded 3 times
Verses 1-21 numbered in Arabic
Author's name first appeared in Solomon Wieatt edition (Philadelphia, 1807)
Dated by d'Alté A. Welch
Hamilton 1168 (2)
NjP mp. 48608

B10512 THE seaman's journal . . . New London: Printed by James Springer for Thomas C. Green, 1798.
[90] p. fol.
MWA (filled in with record of voyage of ship "Commerce" of New London, to West Indies, 1799) mp. 48609

B10513 THE seaman's log book . . . Providence, Carter and Wilkinson, 1798.
96 leaves. 45 cm.
Alden 1591
RPJCB mp. 48610

B10514 SEVEN SAGES
The history of the Seven Wise Masters of Rome . . . Philadelphia: Printed for the booksellers, 1798.
96 p. 14.5 cm.
d'Alté A. Welch, Cleveland (1962) mp. 48611

B10515 SHALL the free men of Kentucky secure their rights? . . . A Republican. [Lexington? 1798]
broadside 32 X 27 cm.
McMurtrie: Kentucky 94
DLC mp. 48612

B10516 SHALL we have a convention. Citizens of Kentucky . . . Your conduct at the approaching general election . . . Gracchus. [Lexington, 1798]
[2] p. 28 X 22 cm.
McMurtrie: Kentucky 74
DLC mp. 48613

B10517 SHAW, JOSIAH CROCKER, d. 1847
An oration, delivered July 4th, 1798 . . . By Josiah C. Shan [sic], M.A. . . . Newport, H. & O. Farnsworth, 1798.
20 p. 18 cm.
Page 20 ends with the correction of an error
Alden 1592; Winship p. 68; cf. Evans 34536
RHi (imperfect)

B10518 [SHIELD, WILLIAM] 1748-1829
When bidden to the wake or fair. A favorite song in Rosina. New York, Printed and sold at J. Hewitt's Musical repository. [ca. 1798]
1 leaf. 31.5 cm. caption title
Sonneck-Upton p. 459
MiU-C

B10519 [A SHORT account of the plague . . . in the city of London in the year 1665 . . . Newport, H. & O. Farnsworth, 1798]

Advertised Oct. 13, 1798, as "This day from the press."
Probably by Defoe
Alden 1594
No copy known mp. 48408

B10520 SIDNEY, ALGERNON, pseud.
No convention. Friends, fellow-citizens and countrymen . . . Algernon Sidney. [Lexington? 1798]
2 p. 43.5 X 28.5 cm.
DLC mp. 48615

B10521 SINCE then I'm doom'd . . . Philadelphia, C. Hupfeld; Baltimore, H. S. Keating [1798?]
broadside 33 cm.
Sonneck-Upton p. 383
DLC; PHi mp. 48616

B10522 SMITH, F
Mr. F. Smith respectfully informs the admirers of the polite arts . . . his exhibition of paintings, in vitrified stained glass . . . the people of Philadelphia . . . [Philadelphia? 1798]
broadside
Dated 1798 because originally in bound volume of 1798 letters to M. Carey in Lea & Febiger collection
PHi

B10523 SMITH, JAMES, 1738-1812
A concise economical plan of the family medical institution for administring [sic] advice and medicines . . . intended to operate as a security from dangerous delays, unscientific bewildered practice and injudicious prescription . . . New-York, T. Kirk [1798?]
16 p. 18 cm.
DNLM mp. 48167

B10524 SMITH, JAMES, 1738-1812
Yellow fever. As the yellow fever has again made its appearance in this city, the opinion of a physician . . .

[signed] James Smith, M. D. No. 10, Lombard-Street, New York, Sept. 10, 1798. [New York, 1798]
broadside 37 X 22.5 cm.
NHi mp. 48618

B10525 SOCIETY OF VICTUALLERS, PHILADELPHIA
Rules and orders of the Society of Victuallers, . . . of Philadelphia, instituted . . . Novbmeer [sic] 7, 1793. Philadelphia, Henry Sweitzer, 1798.
21 p. 8vo
PPL mp. 48573

B10526 THE South-Carolina & Georgia almanac for . . . 1799 . . . Charleston, Freneau & Paine [1798]
[48] p.
Second edition
Drake 13163
ScC (imperfect)

B10527 SOUTHEY, ROBERT, 1774–1843
The triumph of woman, a poem . . . Now first published from manuscript. Philadelphia, John Ormrod, 1798.
19 p. 8vo
PPL mp. 48619

B10528 [SPOFFORD, REGINALD] 1770–1827
Ellen the Richmond primrose girl. Boston, P. A. von Hagen [1798–99]
[2] p. 30.5 cm.
Sonneck-Upton p. 123
DLC mp. 48620

B10529 STATE GAZETTE
State Gazette, Extra. Printed by Matthias Day, Trenton. Trenton, October 30, 1798. This day . . . the Corporation of this city . . . waited on . . . Charles Cotesworth Pinckney . . . and presented him with the following address, to which he returned the annexed answer . . . [Trenton, 1798]
broadside 41 X 16 cm.
Text in 2 columns
PHi

B10530 STRONG'S astronomical diary, calendar or almanac for . . . 1799 . . . West-Springfield, Edward Gray [1798]
[24] p.
Drake 3604
M

B10531 TAYLOR, RAYNOR, 1742–1825
Nobody . . . [Philadelphia] Printed and sold at B. Carrs Musical repository [1798?]
[4] p. 32 X 22.5 cm.
CSmH mp. 48621

B10532 TAYLOR, RAYNOR, 1742–1825
Silvan the shepherd swain . . . Philadelphia, B. Carr; Baltimore, J. Carr; New York, J. Hewitt [1798]
[2] p. 33 cm.
Sonneck-Upton p. 382; cf. Evans 33786
DLC; MWA mp. 48622

B10533 TEMPLE, SAMUEL
A concise introduction to practical arithmetic . . . By Samuel Temple. Second edition. Boston, Printed and sold by Samuel Hall, 1798.
118 p.
Karpinski p. 115
MH; NNC mp. 48623

B10534 TENNESSEE. GOVERNOR, 1796–1801
Knoxville, 23d April, 1798. Sir, So various and critical . . . our American affairs, for three or four months past . . . I have the honor to be . . . Your friend and humble servant, John Sevier. [Knoxville, George Roulstone? 1798]
broadside 19.5 X 20.5 cm.
McMurtrie: Tennessee 25
WHi (trimmed) mp. 48624

B10535 THAYER, JOHN, 1758–1815
A discourse, delivered at the Roman Catholic church, in Boston, on the 9th of May, 1798 . . . The second edition. Baltimore, A. Hanna, 1798.
31 p. 20.5 cm.
Minick 458; Parsons 197
DGU; MdBJ-G; MdHi mp. 48625

B10536 THOMAS À KEMPIS
An extract of the Christian's pattern . . . Philadelphia, Printed by Henry Tuckniss, sold by John Dickins, 1798.
160 leaves. 16mo A-K^{16}
Rosenbach-Ch 242
A. S. W. Rosenbach (1933) mp. 48626

B10537 THOMPSON AND SMALL, firm, Philadelphia
Superb hot-pressed family Bible. Plan and conditions of the . . . grand folio edition of the Sacred Scriptures, now publishing by a general subscription . . . published by John Thompson, and Abraham Small, of Philadelphia . . . Philadelphia, January, 1798.
broadside 39.5 X 24.5 cm.
MH mp. 48627

B10538 TITFORD, ISAAC
Wholesale silk ware-house, &c. &c. &c. Isaac Titford, . . . late De Launey's store . . . Shew-days of silks, on Tuesday and Fridays, from 10 till 2 o'clock. [New York] M'Lean & Lang [1798?]
broadside 38 X 23 cm.
M'Lean & Lang were in partnership from 1797 to 1799; M'Lean died in 1798
MHi. Photostat: MWA mp. 48628

B10539 TO Jacob Gibson. I cannot but consider your silence with respect to Brutus . . . Brutus. Sept. 22, 1798 . . . [n.p., 1798]
broadside 38.5 X 46 cm.
DLC mp. 48629

B10540 TO Messrs. Voter, Gracchus, Scaevola, Keiling . . . We, the people of Kentucky . . . The people. April 30, 1798. [Lexington, 1798]
broadside 16 X 28.5 cm.
McMurtrie: Kentucky 97
DLC mp. 48630

B10541 TO the electors of Franklin county. Fellow-citizens . . . Junius. May 1, 1798. [Frankfort, 1798]
broadside 34.5 X 21 cm.
McMurtrie: Kentucky 75
DLC mp. 48631

B10542 TO the electors of the Eastern District. Fellow Citizens! The period will soon arrive when you . . . exercise . . . the right of election . . . three men . . . to represent the Eastern District in the Senate of this state . . . Philip S. Van Rensselaer, Chairman. [New York? 1798]
broadside 26 X 21.5 cm.
NHi mp. 48632

B10543 TO the electors of the Upper Districts of South-Carolina. [Charleston, 1798]
23 p. 8vo
Half-title only
PHi

B10544 TO the farmers and others, who bring wheat to the City of New-York for sale. We the subscribers, residing in the said city, engaged in the manufactory of flour . . . interested . . . in improving the quality . . . address you . . . New-York, June 1st, 1798 . . . New-York, Isaac Collins [1798]
broadside 44 X 27.5 cm.
N mp. 48633

B10545 TO the free and independent electors of the state of New-York. Fellow-citizens! In the present truly alarming situation . . . Junius. April 19th, 1798. [New York, 1798]
broadside 42 X 23 cm.
DLC mp. 48634

B10546 TO the free and independent electors of the State of New-York. Fellow-citizens! The important election for governor is fast approaching . . . [n.p., 1798]
broadside 45.5 X 16.5 cm.
Signed: The Voice of Thousands
Advocates candidacy of Robert R. Livingston
New York Public 1251
NAll; NHi. Photostat: NN mp. 48635

B10547 TO the freeholders of the congressional district of Henrico, &c. [Richmond, T. Nicolson, 1798]
6 p. 16 cm. caption title
Signed at end: Another freeholder
A campaign tract opposing John Marshall for Congress in April 1799 elections
Sowerby 3247
DLC mp. 48636

B10548 TO the honorable the legislators of the United States. Being informed . . . All which is . . . offered by the creditors. February, 1798 . . . [n.p., 1798]
[2] p. 34 X 20.5 cm.
DLC mp. 48637

B10549 TO the honorable the speaker and House of delegates, for the state of Virginia, the petition of sundry inhabitants of the Federal district, and of the state of Virginia . . . [Alexandria? 1798]
broadside 38 X 31 cm.
Vi mp. 48638

B10550 TO the independent electors of the City of New-York. To support the British nomination, abuse . . . is resorted to . . . New-York, April 24th, 1798. [New York, 1798]
broadside 33 X 20.5 cm.
NHi mp. 48639

B10551 TO the inhabitants of Germantown. Look before you leap! [Philadelphia, 1798]
broadside 19 X 21.5 cm.
Signed: Another of the people
PHi mp. 48640

B10552 TO the inhabitants of the county of Philadelphia . . . [Philadelphia, 1798]
broadside 27.5 X 14.5 cm.
Signed: A Dutch Man
PHi mp. 48641

B10553 TO the Senate and House of Representatives of the United States . . . Providence, December 31, 1798. [Providence, 1798?]
3 p.
Unsigned petition, for procuring continued government aid in prosecuting claims for American property captured by European powers
RPJCB mp. 48642

B10554 TO the voters of the City and County of Baltimore. Gentlemen, When the extract of colonel Howard's letter was first printed, general Smith denied the whole . . . Baltimore, Yundt and Brown [1798]
broadside 51.5 X 23 cm.
Includes letters dated Aug.–Sept. 1798
New York Public 1253
NN mp. 48643

B10555 TOM Thumb's new riddle book; containing a variety of entertaining riddles for . . . young masters and misses . . . Boston, Printed and sold by John W. Folsom, 1798.
31 p. illus. 10 cm.
MSaE mp. 48644

B10556 [TOM Thumb's play-book. n.p., 1798?]
30, [1] p. 9 cm.
Tentatively dated ca. 1798 by d'Alté A. Welch
MWA (t.p., p. 4–6, 29–30 wanting) mp. 48645

B10557 THE trifle-hunter: or, The adventures of Prince Bonbennin. A Chinese tale. Hartford, John Babcock, 1798.
28, [3] p. incl. covers. 12 cm.
MWA. Gillett Griffin, Princeton Univ. (1962)
mp. 48646

B10558 THE two babes in the wood . . . Poughkeepsie, Printed for the travelling booksellers [1798?]
12 p. 20 cm.
Printed on blue-gray paper
Dated by d'Alté A. Welch
cf. Evans 31326
CtHi mp. 48391

B10559 TYLER, JOHN, 1742–1823
A discourse, delivered in the Meeting House . . . before an assembly of . . . Masons . . . the 27th of June . . . 5798 . . . Norwich, J. Trumbull, 1798.
27 p. 23 cm.
CSmH; MWA mp. 48647

B10560 U. S. CONGRESS
The committee to whom was referred the bill "to define more particularly the crime of treason . . . [Philadelphia] Way & Groff [1798]
2 p. 32 X 20 cm.
DLC mp. 48655

B10561 U. S. CONGRESS
Resolved by the Senate and House . . . two thirds of both Houses concurring, that the following articles be proposed . . . as amendments to the Constitution . . . [Philadelphia] John Fenno [1798]
broadside 34.5 X 21.5 cm.
MiU–C mp. 48657

B10562 U. S. CONGRESS. HOUSE
In the House of Representatives, Columbia, November 28, 1798. The Committee, appointed to draw up rules and orders for the government of the House, reported . . . [Philadelphia, 1798]
broadside 21.5 X 20.5 cm.
NHi

B10563 U. S. CONGRESS. HOUSE. COMMITTEE APPOINTED TO CONSIDER THE AMENDMENTS TO THE BILL FOR THE RELIEF OF THE REFUGEES
Report from the Committee Appointed to Consider . . . 27th February, 1798 . . . Philadelphia, Joseph Gales [1798?]
1 p.l., 429–434 p. 20.5 cm.
MiU–C mp. 48662

B10564 U. S. CONGRESS. HOUSE. COMMITTEE ON A REPRESENTATION AND REMONSTRANCE OF . . . GEORGIA
Report of the committee to whom was referred, on the 30th of November last . . . 3d May, 1798, committed to a committee of the whole House . . . [Philadelphia, 1798]
[527]–530 p. 20.5 cm.
cf. Evans 34784
DLC (2 copies); PPL mp. 48669

B10565 U. S. CONGRESS. HOUSE. COMMITTEE ON CLAIMS
Report of the Committee of Claims, to whom was referred, on the 20th of December last, a motion relative to the amendments . . . 26th March, 1798, committee to a committee of the whole House . . . [Philadelphia, 1798]
[463]–472 p. 23 cm.
DLC (3 copies) mp. 48663

B10566 U. S. CONGRESS. HOUSE. COMMITTEE ON CLAIMS
Report of the Committee of Claims, to whom was referred, on the 22d of December last, the memorial of James Swan. 28th March, 1798, committee to a committee of the whole House . . . [Philadelphia, 1798]
[475]–482 p. 21 cm.
DLC (2 copies); MiU–C; PPL mp. 48664

B10567 U. S. CONGRESS. HOUSE. COMMITTEE ON CLAIMS
Report of the Committee of Claims, to whom was referred, on the 30th of March last, the petition of Jonathan Haskell. 16th April, 1798, committed to a committee of the whole House, to-morrow . . . [n.p., 1798?]
1 p.l., 501–502 p. 20.5 cm.
MiU–C; NN; PPL mp. 48665

B10568 U. S. CONGRESS. HOUSE. COMMITTEE ON COMMERCE AND MANUFACTURES
Report of the Committee of Commerce & Manufactures, to whom was referred the petition of Reuben Smith . . . presented the twenty-third of February, 1797. 15th February, 1798, committed to a committee of the whole House . . . [Philadelphia, 1798]
[411]–414 p. 20.5 cm.
DLC; MWA; NN; PPL mp. 48666

B10569 U. S. CONGRESS. HOUSE. COMMITTEE ON THE BILL REGULATING IMPEACHMENT
In committee, to whom was referred the bill, regulating certain proceedings . . . The following amendments thereto ordered to be reported . . . [Philadelphia, John Fenno, 1798]
3 p. 34.5 cm.
MiU–C mp. 48660

B10570 U. S. CONGRESS. HOUSE. COMMITTEE ON THE MEMORIAL OF THE PEOPLE CALLED QUAKERS
Report of the Committee, to whom was referred, on the 30th of November last . . . 28th January, 1798, committee to a committee of the whole House . . . [Philadelphia, 1798]
[295]–310 p. 22.5 cm.
CSmH; DLC (2 copies); NN; PPL mp. 48670

B10571 U. S. CONGRESS. HOUSE. COMMITTEE ON THE PRESIDENT'S MESSAGE
Report, in part, from the Committee appointed on so much . . . 1st May, 1798. Referred to the committee of the whole House . . . Philadelphia, Joseph Gales [1798]
[515]–518 p. 21 cm.
DLC; MiU–C; PPL mp. 48661

B10572 U. S. CONGRESS. HOUSE. COMMITTEE ON THE PRESIDENT'S MESSAGE
Report of the Committee to whom was referred, on the 23d ultimo . . . 8th March, 1798, committed to a committee of the whole House . . . [Philadelphia, 1798]
[447]–454 p. 20.5 cm.
DLC; MiU–C mp. 48672

B10573 U. S. CONGRESS. HOUSE. COMMITTEE ON THE PRESIDENT'S MESSAGE
Report of the Committee, to whom was referred, on the 29th of November . . . 16th January, 1798, committed to a committee of the whole House . . . [Philadelphia, 1798]
[263]–272 p. 22 cm.
DLC (2 copies); MiU–C; NN; PPL mp. 48673

B10574 U. S. CONGRESS. HOUSE. COMMITTEE ON THE PROTECTION OF COMMERCE
Report of the Committee on the Protection of Commerce . . . to whom was referred, the memorial of the New-York Chamber of commerce. 2d April, 1798, referred to the committee of the whole House . . . [Philadelphia, 1798]
[483]–486 p. 21 cm.
DLC (2 copies); MiU–C; NN; PPL mp. 48667

B10575 U. S. CONGRESS. HOUSE. COMMITTEE ON WAYS AND MEANS
Report in part, of the Committee of ways and means, to whom was referred, on the 11th of December last . . . 1st January, 1798, committed to a committee of the whole House . . . [Philadelphia, 1798]
[235]–238 p. 20.5 cm.
DLC; MiU–C; NN; PPL mp. 48656

B10576 U. S. CONGRESS. HOUSE. COMMITTEE TO WHOM WAS REFERRED THE BILL ENTITLED "AN ACT, AUTHORIZING THE PRESIDENT . . ."
Report of the Committee to whom was referred, on the 30th ultimo . . . 4th May, 1798, committed to a committee of the whole House . . . [Philadelphia, 1798]
[531]–534 p. 21 cm.
DLC; MiU–C; NN; PPL mp. 48671

B10577 U. S. CONGRESS. HOUSE. COMMITTEE TO WHOM WAS REFERRED THE BILL INTITULED "AN ACT, IN ADDITION TO THE ACT . . ."
Report of the Committee to whom was referred, on the nineteenth instant . . . 22d June, 1798, committed to a Committee of the whole House . . . [Philadelphia, 1798]
4 p. 21 cm.
DLC mp. 48668

B10578 U. S. CONGRESS. SENATE
Congress of the United States. In Senate, March the 26th, 1798. A motion was made . . . [Philadelphia, 1798]

broadside 32 X 20.5 cm.
Five resolutions
DLC (20.5 X 20.5 cm.); MiU–C mp. 48706

B10579 U. S. CONGRESS. SENATE
Congress of the United States. In Senate, April the 25th, 1798. A motion was made . . . that a committee be appointed to consider . . . removing from . . . the United States, such aliens . . . as may be dangerous . . . [Philadelphia] John Fenno [1798]
broadside 35 X 22 cm.
MiU–C mp. 48712

B10580 U. S. CONGRESS. SENATE
Congress of the United States. In Senate, April the 26th, 1798. A motion was made . . . that instead of the three existing circuits, the several districts . . . be divided . . . into four circuits . . . [Philadelphia] John Fenno [1798]
broadside 34.5 X 21 cm.
MiU–C mp. 48713

B10581 U. S. CONGRESS. SENATE. COMMITTEE APPOINTED TO CONFER WITH THE HOUSE COMMITTEE ON THE REFUGEE BILL
Congress of the United States. In Senate, March 28th, 1798. The Committee appointed . . . to confer . . . on the subjects of difference . . . report . . . [Philadelphia] Way & Groff [1798]
broadside 34 X 20.5 cm.
MiU–C mp. 48707

B10582 U. S. CONGRESS. SENATE. COMMITTEE ON APPROPRIATIONS
Congress of the United States. In Senate, April 11th, 1798. The Committee to whom was referred the bill . . . for completing the buildings . . . report . . . with an amendment . . . [Philadelphia] John Fenno [1798]
broadside 35 X 21.5 cm.
MiU–C mp. 48709

B10583 U. S. SENATE. COMMITTEE ON FOREIGN AFFAIRS
The Committee, to whom was referred the consideration of the treaty . . . [New York] John Fenno [1798]
broadside 32 X 20 cm.
Peace with the Bey of Tunis
MiU–C mp. 48716

B10584 U. S. CONGRESS. SENATE. COMMITTEE ON FOREIGN AFFAIRS
The Committee, to whom was referred the consideration of the treaty . . . [Philadelphia, 1798]
broadside 20.5 X 20 cm.
DLC mp. 48717

B10585 U. S. CONGRESS. SENATE. COMMITTEE ON THE ARTICLES OF IMPEACHMENT AGAINST WILLIAM BLOUNT
Report of the committee appointed to report the proper measures to be adopted relative to the articles of impeachment against William Blount . . . [Philadelphia] William Ross [1798]
6 p. 22 cm.
Dated Feb. 22, 1798
New York Public 1260
NN mp. 48714

B10586 U. S. CONGRESS. SENATE. COMMITTEE ON THE JUDICIARY
Congress of the United States. In Senate March the 28th, 1798. The Committee on the bill supplementary to . . . "An act to establish the judicial courts . . ." report that the bill ought to pass . . . [Philadelphia] John Fenno [1798]
[2] p. 34.5 cm.
CtHi; MiU–C mp. 48708

B10587 U. S. CONGRESS. SENATE. COMMITTEE ON THE PETITION OF JOSEPH NOURSE
Congress of the United States. In Senate, March 23d, 1798. The Committee, to whom was referred the petition . . . [Philadelphia] John Fenno [1798]
2 p. 33.5 cm.
DLC; MiU–C mp. 48705

B10588 U. S. CONGRESS. SENATE. COMMITTEE TO WHOM WAS REFERRED A BILL TO AUTHORIZE CERTAIN OFFICERS TO ADMINISTER OATHS
Congress of the United States. In Senate, April the 20th, 1798. The Committee to whom was referred a bill, sent from the House . . . report, that . . . the said bill ought to be amended . . . [Philadelphia] John Fenno [1798]
broadside 35 X 21.5 cm.
MiU–C mp. 48710

B10589 U. S. CONGRESS. SENATE. COMMITTEE TO WHOM WAS REFERRED THE ACT TO ALTER THE TIME OF MAKING ENTRY OF STILLS
Congress of the United States. In Senate, April 20th, 1798. The Committee to whom was referred the act . . . beg leave to report sundry amendments . . . [Philadelphia] John Fenno [1798]
broadside 35 X 21.5 cm.
MiU–C mp. 48711

B10590 U. S. DEPT. OF STATE
Department of State, 1st September, 1798. Sir, Annexed is a copy of a letter from William Fawkener, Esq. communicating to the Commissioners of his Britannic Majesty's Treasury . . . [Philadelphia? 1798]
broadside 33 X 20.5 cm.
Dated at Perth Amboy
NHi mp. 48718

B10591 U. S. DEPT. OF STATE
Instructions to Charles Cotesworth Pinckney, John Marshall and Elbridge Gerry, envoys extraordinary . . . to the French Republic, referred to in the message of the President . . . of the third instant. Philadelphia, William Cobbett, 1798.
15 p. 20.5 cm.
cf. Evans 34837
MWA mp. 48719

B10592 U. S. INSPECTOR-GENERAL
Scheme of the review, for the 13th November, 1798, in pursuance of orders . . . The inspector does himself the honor to enclose . . . [Philadelphia, 1798]
broadside 36.5 X 24 cm.
DLC mp. 48720

B10593 U. S. LAWS
3d January, 1798, read the first and second time . . . A bill providing for the payment of the interest on a certificate due to General Kosciusko . . . [n.p., 1798]
broadside 34.5 X 21.5 cm.
MiU–C mp. 48674

B10594 U. S. LAWS
4th January, 1798 . . . A bill to prescribe the mode of taking evidence in cases of contested elections . . . and to compel the attendance of witnesses . . . [n.p., 1798]
4 p. 34 cm.
MiU–C mp. 48675

B10595 U. S. LAWS
8th January, 1798 . . . A bill in addition to the act . . . for the relief . . . of American seamen." [n.p., 1798]
3 p. 33.5 cm.
MiU–C mp. 48676

B10596 U. S. LAWS
10th January, 1798. A bill for the relief of the refugees from . . . Nova-Scotia . . . [n.p., 1798]
broadside 33.5 X 20 cm.
MiU–C mp. 48677

B10597 U. S. LAWS
15th January, 1798 . . . A bill providing for the means of intercourse between the United States and foreign nations. [n.p., 1798]
broadside 33.5 X 20.5 cm.
MiU–C mp. 48678

B10598 U. S. LAWS
13th February, 1798 . . . A bill for the erection of a light-house, and placing buoys . . . [Philadelphia? 1798]
broadside 34 X 21 cm.
The lighthouse to be erected on "Eaton's Neck, on Nassau Island," and the buoys "near Sandy Hook."
NHi. Pierce W. Gaines, Fairfield, Conn. (1964)
mp. 48679

B10599 U. S. LAWS
13 February, 1798. A bill in addition to, and alteration of an act ". . . to promote the progress of useful arts . . . " [n.p., 1798]
broadside 33.5 X 21 cm.
MiU–C mp. 48680

B10600 U. S. LAWS
14th February, 1798 . . . A bill to amend the . . . act laying duties on stamped vellum . . . [Philadelphia] J. Gales [1798]
3 p. 31 cm.
MiU–C mp. 48681

B10601 U. S. LAWS
28th February, 1798. A bill for the relief of sick and disabled seamen . . . [n.p., 1798]
3 p. 33.5 cm.
MiU–C; NjR mp. 48682

B10602 U. S. LAWS
7th March, 1798 . . . A bill to continue in force . . . "An act prohibiting . . . the exportation of arms and ammunition . . . [n.p., 1798]
broadside 33.5 X 20.5 cm.
MiU–C mp. 48683

B10603 U. S. LAWS
14th March, 1798. A bill for an additional appropriation to provide . . . a naval armament . . . [n.p., 1798]
broadside 34.5 X 21 cm.
MiU–C mp. 48684

B10604 U. S. LAWS
15th March, 1798 . . . A bill making an appropriation for completing the buildings . . . of the government . . . at the city of Washington. [n.p., 1798]
broadside 34 X 20.5 cm.
MiU–C mp. 48685

B10605 U. S. LAWS
19th March, 1798 . . . A bill to revive and continue in force, the act respecting the compensation of clerks . . . [n.p., 1798]
broadside 34.5 X 21.5 cm.
MiU–C mp. 48686

B10606 U. S. LAWS
23d March, 1798. A bill authorizing an expenditure . . . for the reimbursement of monies advanced by the consuls . . . [n.p., 1798]
broadside 34 X 20.5 cm.
MiU–C mp. 48687

B10607 U. S. LAWS
30th March, 1798 . . . A bill making appropriations for the military establishment, for the year one thousand seven hundred and ninety-eight . . . [n.p., 1798]
3 p. 34 cm.
MiU–C mp. 48688

B10608 U. S. LAWS
3d April, 1798 . . . A bill for providing compensation for the marshals, clerks . . . [Philadelphia, 1798]
9 p. 34.5 cm. caption title
DLC; MiU–C mp. 48689

B10609 U. S. LAWS
6th April, 1798. A bill for the relief of sick and disabled seamen . . . [n.p., 1798]
3 p. 34 cm.
MiU–C mp. 48690

B10610 U. S. LAWS
10th April, 1798 . . . A bill supplementary to the act providing for the further defence . . . [Philadelphia, 1798]
2 p. 34 X 20.5 cm.
DLC; MiU–C mp. 48691

B10611 U. S. LAWS
15th April, 1798 . . . A bill to provide an additional regiment of artillerists and engineers . . . [n.p., 1798]
broadside 34 X 20.5 cm.
MiU–C mp. 48692

B10612 U. S. LAWS
16th April, 1798 . . . A bill to enable the President . . . to procure cannon . . . [n.p., 1798]
broadside 34 X 20 cm.
MiU–C mp. 48693

B10613 U. S. LAWS
23d April, 1798. An act, to establish an executive department . . . the department of the Navy. [n.p., 1798]
broadside 34 X 20.5 cm.
MiU–C mp. 48721

B10614 U. S. LAWS
25th April, 1798 . . . A bill supplementary to . . . "An act for the relief of persons imprisoned for debt." [n.p., 1798]
broadside 34 X 20.5 cm.
MiU–C mp. 48694

B10615 U. S. LAWS
30th April, 1798. An act, to authorize the President . . . to cause to be purchased . . . a number of small vessels . . . [n.p., 1798]
broadside 34 X 20 cm.
MiU–C mp. 48722

B10616 U. S. LAWS
6th July, 1798 . . . A bill to augment the army . . . [Philadelphia, 1798]
[3] p. 36 cm.
DLC mp. 48695

B10617 U. S. LAWS
An act laying duties on stamped vellum, parchment and paper [with other acts] . . . Approved – February 28, 1798. [Philadelphia, 1798]
20 p. 8vo
PPL mp. 48723

B10618 U. S. LAWS
An act making an appropriation for completing the buildings . . . for the . . . government . . . at the city of Washington. [n.p., 1798]
broadside 34 X 20.5 cm.
MiU–C mp. 48724

B10619 U. S. LAWS
An act, to lay and collect a direct-tax within the United States. [Philadelphia, 1798]
15 p. 20.5 cm. caption title
DLC mp. 48725

B10620 U. S. LAWS
An act to provide for the valuation of lands and dwelling-houses . . . [Hartford, Hudson and Goodwin, 1798]
19 p. 19.5 cm. caption title
MWA. Photostat: DLC mp. 48726

B10621 U. S. LAWS
An act to regulate and fix the compensation of the officers employed in collecting the internal revenues of the United States . . . Approved, April 11, 1798. [Philadelphia, 1798]
7 p. 8vo
PPL mp. 48727

B10622 U. S. LAWS
Amendments of the Senate to the bill, intituled "An act to suspend the commercial intercourse . . . " [Published by order of the House of representatives.] [n.p., 1798?]
2 leaves. 20.5 cm.
MiU–C mp. 48696

B10623 U. S. LAWS
A bill authorizing the President . . . to raise a provisional army . . . [Philadelphia, John Fenno, 1798]
broadside 35 X 21 cm.
MiU–C mp. 48697

B10624 U. S. LAWS
A bill authorizing the President . . . to raise a provisional army . . . [Philadelphia, Way & Groff, 1798]
4 p. 34 cm.
MiU–C mp. 48658

B10625 U. S. LAWS
A bill concerning aliens. [n.p., 1798]
3 p. 33 cm.
MiU–C mp. 48649

B10626 U. S. LAWS
A bill regulating certain proceedings in cases of impeachment. [Philadelphia, John Fenno, 1798]
broadside 34.5 X 21.5 cm.
MiU–C mp. 48698

B10627 U. S. LAWS
A bill supplementary to the act, entitled, "An act to establish the judicial courts . . ." [n.p., 1798]
broadside 33.5 X 20.5 cm.
MiU–C mp. 48650

B10628 U. S. LAWS
A bill to alter and amend the act, entitled, "An act to establish the judicial courts . . ." [Philadelphia, Way & Groff, 1798]
7 p. 34.5 cm.
MiU–C mp. 48659

B10629 U. S. LAWS
A bill to alter and extend the provisions of the act entitled "An act to establish the judicial courts . . ." [n.p., 1798]
broadside 33.5 X 20 cm.
MiU–C mp. 48651

B10630 U. S. LAWS
A bill to amend the act . . . to amend and repeal . . . "An act to ascertain and fix the military establishment . . ." [Philadelphia] John Fenno [1798?]
broadside 33.5 X 20.5 cm.
MiU–C mp. 48699

B10631 U. S. LAWS
A bill to authorize the President . . . to cause to be purchased . . . a number of small vessels . . . [Philadelphia] John Fenno [1798]
broadside 35 X 21.5 cm.
MiU–C mp. 48700

B10632 U. S. LAWS
A bill to declare the treaties betwixt the United States and . . . France, void and of no effect . . . [Philadelphia, Way & Groff, 1798]
4 p. 33.5 cm.
In manuscript: In Senate . . . laid on the table June 22d 1798
MiU–C mp. 48701

B10633 U. S. LAWS
A bill to enable the President . . . to purchase or lease one or more foundries. [Philadelphia] John Fenno [1798]
broadside 34.5 X 21 cm.
MiU–C mp. 48702

B10634 U. S. LAWS
A bill to establish an executive department . . . the department of the Navy. [Philadelphia] John Fenno [1798]
broadside 35 X 21.5 cm.
MiU–C mp. 48703

B10635 U. S. LAWS
A bill to establish an uniform system of bankruptcy . . . [Philadelphia, Childs and Swaine, 1798]
13 p. 33.5 cm. caption title
DLC mp. 48652

B10636 U. S. LAWS
A bill to establish an uniform system of bankruptcy . . . [Colophon] [Philadelphia] Childs and Swaine [1798]
13 p. 32 cm. caption title
DLC mp. 48653

B10637 U. S. LAWS
A bill to extend to the District of Tennessee, the exception contained in . . . "An act to provide . . . for the collection of the duties . . ." [Philadelphia] John Fenno [1798]
broadside 34.5 X 21.5 cm.
MiU–C mp. 48704

B10638 U. S. LAWS
A bill to provide an additional armament for the . . . protection of the trade . . . [Philadelphia, Way & Groff, 1798]
3 p. 33 cm.
MiU–C mp. 48654

B10639 U. S. LAWS
Duties, imposed, by an act of Congress, on all stamped vellum, parchment and paper, for . . . five years from the 31st day of December, 1797 . . . [New-York] G. F. Hopkins, Printer [1798?]
broadside 44.5 X 27.5 cm.
NHi mp. 48728

B10639a U. S. LAWS
Heads of the most important acts passed by Congress . . . session . . . November, 1797 . . . July, 1798 . . . [Philadelphia? 1798]
28 p.
PHi

B10640 U. S. LAWS
Notice to mariners. We publish for the information . . . coasting trade, the following extracts from the Act of 16th July, 1798 . . . Hogan & Thompson, Stationers, 108 Chestnut Street. [Philadelphia, 1798?]
broadside 31 X 23.5 cm.
PHi mp. 48729

B10641 U. S. PRESIDENT, 1797–1801
Message of the President . . . to both houses of Congress. June 18th, 1798. [Philadelphia, 1798]
72 p. 20.5 cm.
Transmitting instructions to and dispatches from the envoys extraordinary to France
Not Evans 34824 (also PPL)
CSmH; MiU–C; PPL; RPJCB mp. 48730

B10642 U. S. PRESIDENT, 1797–1801
Message of the President . . . to both houses of Congress . . . The first despatches from our envoys . . . at Paris, were received at the secretary of state's office . . . last evening . . . [Philadelphia? 1798]
[5] p. 21 cm.
Message dated: Mar. 5, 1798
MiU–C mp. 48731

B10643 U. S. PRESIDENT, 1797–1801
The President's address, to both houses of Congress. Philadelphia, Dec. 8 . . . [Richmond] A. Davis [1798]
broadside 34.5 X 20.5 cm.
DLC mp. 48732

B10644 U. S. PRESIDENT, 1797–1801
President's speech. By an arrival this morning from New-York, we have been favored with the President's address to both Houses . . . John Adams. [Newport] H. & O. Farnsworth [1798]
broadside 45 X 22.5 cm.
Alden 1600; Winship Addenda p. 91
NjR; RHi. Photostat: MWA mp. 48733

B10645 U. S. TREASURY DEPT.
The following schedule and estimate, are referred to the Committee of the whole House, to whom is committed, the "Bill to regulate and fix the compensations . . . in collecting the internal revenues . . ." [Philadelphia, 1798]
2 p. 22 cm.
Dated: Treasury Department, May 1798
New York Public 1261
NN mp. 48734

B10646 U. S. TREASURY DEPT.
(N.) Form of a collector's half-yearly abstract of duties on country stills . . . using the produce of the United States . . . Collector's Office, January 20th, 1798. Samuel Overton, Collector of the Revenue, 2d Division, 4th Survey, of Virginia, [n.p., 1798]
broadside 60 X 24 cm.
MHi mp. 48735

B10647 U. S. TREASURY DEPT.
Received 30th May, 1798 . . . I am, Sir . . . your very humble servant, Samuel Meredith, Treasurer . . . [Philadelphia, 1798]
17–40 p. 22.5 cm.
DLC

B10648 U. S. TREASURY DEPT.
Statement of the purchases of public stock, by the agents to the trustees . . . [Philadelphia? 1798]
fold. table 20 cm.
Signed: Dec. 10, 1798
MiU–C mp. 48736

B10649 U. S. TREASURY DEPT.
Treasury department, February 15, 1798. (Circular.) Sir, I have been directed by . . . the Senate . . . to obtain from the collectors of the customs . . . the number and tonnage of the vessels . . . captured or detained . . . [Philadelphia, 1798]
broadside 22.5 X 19 cm.
PPRF mp. 48737

B10650 U. S. TREASURY DEPT.
Treasury department, February 24, 1798. Circular. Sir, I have been directed by . . . the House of representatives . . . to obtain from the collectors of the customs . . . a statement of the vessels . . . captured or detained . . . [Philadelphia, 1798]
broadside 23 X 19 cm.
PPRF mp. 48738

B10651 U. S. TREASURY DEPT.
Treasury Department, March 1, 1798. Public notice is hereby given . . . the several stamped duties . . . will be levied and collected . . . Given under my hand, at Philadelphia . . . Secretary of the Treasury. [Philadelphia, 1798]
broadside 48 X 38 cm.
N; NHi mp. 48739

B10652 U. S. TREATIES
Treaty of peace and friendship, between the United States . . . and the kingdom of Tunis. [Philadelphia, 1798]
11 p. 20.5 cm.
DLC; MiU–C mp. 48740

B10653 U. S. WAR DEPT.
M
Regulations respecting extra-allowances to officers . . . [at end] December 19, 1798. [Philadelphia? 1798?]
broadside 30.5 X 20 cm.
Pierce W. Gaines, Fairfield, Conn. (1964) mp. 48741

B10654 U. S. WAR DEPT.
To volunteer companies, who have associated . . . War Office . . . November 1st, 1798. [Philadelphia, 1798]
broadside 34 X 21 cm.
DLC mp. 48742

B10655 THE United States almanac for . . . 1799. By Abraham Shoemaker: Elizabeth-Town, Printed by Shepard Kollock, for Samuel Campbell [1798]
[36] p.
Drake 5192
NHi

B10656 VERMONT. GOVERNOR, 1797–1807
General orders. In pursuance of a requisition of the

President of the United States . . . the Commander in Chief directs that 2150 of the militia . . . be organized, armed, and equipt . . . Isaac Tichenor . . . Bennington, January 2, 1798. Rutland, J. Fay [1798]
broadside 35.5 X 29 cm.
McCorison 505
VtU–W. George A. Russell, Arlington, Vt. (1963)
mp. 48743

B10657 VERMONT. GOVERNOR, 1797–1807
Speech of his Excellency Governor Tichenor to the Council and House . . . of Vermont . . . City of Vergennes, October 12, 1798. [Vergennes, G. & R. Waite, 1798]
broadside 44 X 25.5 cm.
McCorison 506
NhD mp. 48744

B10658 VERMONT GAZETTE
[Supplement, June 1, 1798; containing Col. Matthew Lyon's Address. Bennington, A. Haswell, 1798]

Announced in the May 25, 1798, issue
McCorison 491
No copy known

B10659 VERSES made on the sudden death of six young women . . . who were drowned at Jamestown, Rhode-Island, July 13, 1782 . . . [Newport] H. & O. Farnsworth [1798?]
broadside 16 X 10 cm.
Alden 1602; Wegelin 820; Winship p. 74; Winship Addenda p. 93
RHi; RNHi. Photostat: MWA mp. 48745

B10660 DIE Verstossung der französischen Freyheit und Gleichheit, aus Himmel, Fegfeuer und Hölle . . . Lancaster, Johann Albrecht, 1798.
36 p. 8vo
PPL mp. 48746

B10661 VIRGINIA. HOUSE OF DELEGATES
Virginia resolutions of 1798 . . . In the Virginia House of delegates. Drawn by Mr. Madison. [Richmond? 1798?]
39 p. 21.5 cm. caption title
Dated Dec. 21, 1798
After 1800?–F. R. Goff
Davis 147
KHi; MH mp. 48747

B10662 THE Virginia almanack for the year . . . 1799 . . . Leesburg, Bartgis and Silliman [1798]
[36] p.
Bear 120; Drake 13863
ICU. Photostat: ViU mp. 48748

B10663 THE Virginia almanack . . . for the year . . . 1799 . . . Petersburg, William Prentis [1798]
[32] p.
Bear 124; Wyatt 21
MWA (imperfect: lacks t.p. and Jan.–Feb.; has [v]-xvii, 23+ p.) mp. 48749

B10664 VOLNEY, CONSTANTIN FRANÇOIS CHASSEBOEUF, COMTE DE, 1757–1820
Travels through Egypt and Syria . . . Vol. I[-II]. New-York, Printed and sold by John Tiebout, 1798.
2 v. (256, [3]; 297, [4] p.) port. 19.5 cm.
DLC; MWA (imperfect); NBuG; OU; PPL mp. 48750

B10665 [WALKER, PATRICK]
The life and prophecies of the Reverend Mr. Alexander Peden . . . Re-printed at Newburyport, for Alexander Walker, 1798.
59 p. 18 cm.
Also published under title: "The great Scots prophet" (cf. Evans 8279)
MB mp. 48751

B10666 WASHINGTON, GEORGE, 1732–1799
Interesting. By Capt. Earl, arrived this morning . . . we are favored with the most pleasing news . . . Go. Washington . . . [Newport] From the *Companion* Office [1798]
broadside 31 X 25 cm.
Alden 1602A
RHi (mutilated) mp. 48752

B10667 WASHINGTON, GEORGE, 1732–1799
Senate of the United States, July 18, 1798. Gentlemen . . . , believing that the letter received this morning from General Washington will give high satisfaction . . . , I transmit them a copy of it . . . John Adams . . . [Philadelphia, 1798]
4 p. 20.5 cm. caption title
CSmH; MiU–C mp. 48753

B10668 WATTS, ISAAC, 1674–1748
Divine songs, attempted in easy language . . . Hartford, John Babcock, 1798.
60 p. 16.5 cm.
CtHi mp. 48754

B10669 [WEBSTER, NOAH] 1758–1843
The prompter . . . [n.p.] 1798.
44 leaves. 12mo A–F^6 G^8
Rosenback–Ch 243; Trumbull; Sec. suppl. 2896
A. S. W. Rosenbach (1933) mp. 48755

B10670 WEBSTER, NOAH, 1758–1843
The prompter . . . Chambersburg, Robert Harper for Mathew Carey, 1798.
85 p. 16 cm.
Sabin 102390; Skeel-Carpenter 675
DLC; NN mp. 48756

B10671 WEEKLY MUSEUM
Address of the carrier of the *Weekly Museum* to his patrons . . . January 1, 1798. [New York, 1798]
broadside 31 X 15 cm.
NHi mp. 48330

B10672 WEST, JOHN
Boston, *11th April* 1798. Subjoined is a list of publications which I offer you in exchange. Be so kind as to forward me a list of yours . . . John West. [Boston, 1798]
broadside
25 titles of books for exchange
PHi

B10673 THE Western calendar: or, an almanack for the year . . . 1799. Washington [Pa.], John Colerick [1798]
[36] p.
MWA (final 2 leaves lacking) mp. 48757

B10674 DIE Westliche Correspondenz, und Hägerstauner Wochenschrift. Hägerstaun, Johann Gruber [1798]
44 cm. weekly
Minick 463; Seidensticker p. 149
PHi (no. 153 only, May 17)

B10675 WILLIAM Reily's courtship, trial, and marriage . . . [Baltimore? Michael Duffey? 1798?]
12 p. 18 cm. caption title
"The Baltimore volunteers. A new song, composed on the grand review . . . October 29, 1798:" p. 9–12
Minick 464
MdHi mp. 48758

B10676 WILLIAMS COLLEGE
Catalogue of students in Williams college, Nov. 1798. Pittsfield, Holly & Smith [1798]
broadside 40.5 X 34 cm.
MWiW mp. 48760

B10677 WILLIAMS COLLEGE
Commencement at Williams-College, September 5, 1798. The order of the exercises. Stockbridge, Benjamin Rosseter [1798]
broadside
MWiW (photostat) mp. 48759

B10678 WILLOCK, JOHN
The voyages and adventures of John Willock, mariner . . . Philadelphia, Printed and sold by Hogan & M'Elroy, 1798.
2 p.l., [ix]-xi, [13]-283, 8 p. 16 cm.
New York Public 1264; Sabin 104534; cf. Evans 35033 (wrongly credited to NN)
ICN; NN; NhD; RPJCB mp. 48761

B10679 YOUNG, WILLIAM, of Philadelphia
Current price of paper for sale by William Young, bookseller and stationer Philadelphia . . . [Philadelphia, 1798]
broadside 41 X 24.5 cm.
Dated assigned from ms. note on verso: William Young's . . . prices . . . 19th Feby 1798
MWA mp. 48762

B10680 ZU verkaufen eine anzahl kostbarer landesstriche . . . im staat Virginien . . . Philadelphia, den 26sten December 1798. [Philadelphia, 1798]
broadside 27 X 22.5 cm.
DLC mp. 48763

B10681 ZUM Grossen Sabbath, den 7ten April 1798. [Salisbury, Francis Coupee, 1798]
4 p. 8vo caption title
PPL mp. 48764

B10682 ZUR Christnacht, 1798, in Salem . . . [Salisbury, F. Coupee? 1798]
[4] p. 16 cm.
Records of the Moravians, VI:2613: December 11, 1798: "We have received a proof of the hymns for Christmas, printed in Salisbury . . ."
NcWsM mp. 48765

1799

B10683 ADDISON, ALEXANDER, 1756-1807
Liberty of speech and of the press. A charge to the grand juries . . . Albany, C. R. and G. Webster [1799?]
27 p.
MWA mp. 48766

B10684 [AIKIN, JOHN] 1747-1822
Evenings at home . . . An abridgement of the London edition. Philadelphia, R. Davison, 1799.
143, [1] p. 14.5 cm.
MWA mp. 48770

B10685 ALEXANDRIA. MERCHANTS
To the honourable the General assembly of Virginia. The petition of the merchants, tradesmen . . . of Alexandria, humbly sheweth . . . [Alexandria? 1799?]
2 leaves. 38 cm.
Presented Dec. 16, 1799
Vi mp. 48772

B10686 ALONE beside a stream. Boston, Printed & sold by P. A. von Hagen & Cos. Musical Magazine, No. 3 Cornhill. And to be had at G. Gilfert, No. 177 Broadway, New York [ca. 1799]
[2] p. 36 cm. caption title
Sonneck-Upton p. 14
MiU-C; RPJCB

B10687 THE American primer; or young child's hornbook . . . Newfield, Printed and sold by Lazarus Beach, 1799.
72 p. 32mo
Heartman: Non-New-England 14; Trumbull: Supplement 1866
MWA (lacks p. 10-14, 35-38) mp. 48773

B10688 AMERICAN TELEGRAPHE, BRIDGEPORT, CONN.
Address of the carrier of the *American Telegraphe* to its patrons. January 1, 1799 . . . [Bridgeport, 1799]
broadside
1st line: Ye friends of good order . . .
NHi mp. 48768

B10689 AMERICANISCHER Calender aufs Jahr . . . 1800. Harrisburg, Benjamin Mayer [1799]
[36] p. 20.5 cm.
DeWin; MWA (imperfect); P mp. 48774

B10690 [ARNOLD, SAMUEL] 1740-1802
In dear little Ireland . . . New York, George Gilfert [1799?]
[2] p. 33 cm.
Sonneck-Upton p. 205
DLC mp. 48775

B10691 [ARNOLD, SAMUEL] 1740-1802
Little Sally . . . New York, George Gilfert [1799?]
1 leaf. 32 cm. caption title
MiU-C mp. 48776

B10692 [ARNOLD, SAMUEL] 1740-1802
When on the ocean . . . New York, George Gilfert [1799?]
[2] p. 32.5 cm.
Sonneck-Upton p. 463
DLC; MWA mp. 48777

B10693 BABCOCK, JOHN, 1752?-1843
Hartford, July 4, 1799. Proposals. The present religious state of many towns in New-England . . . great demand for hymns and spiritual songs . . . [Hartford] Printing executed by John Babcock: Correct and Fair. [1799]
broadside 37 X 23.5 cm.
NHi mp. 48778

B10694 THE babes in the wood. To which is added The Bonney Sailor. Sold at the printing office in State-street, Albany [1799?]
8 p.
MWA (mutilated) mp. 48819

B10695 BAILEY, EBENEZER
A token of love . . . by Elder E. Bailey . . . Putney, Cornelius Sturtevant, 1799.
24 p. 17.5 cm.
VtHi mp. 48779

B10696 [BALDWIN, THOMAS] 1753-1825
A brief account of the late revivals of religion in a number of towns in the New-England states . . . Norwich, Printed and sold by John Sterry, July, 1799.
8 p.

Trumbull: Second supplement 2826; cf. Evans (35139-42)
CtHi mp. 48780

B10697 BALTIMORE. NEW THEATRE
[Mr. L'Estrange (prompter) & Miss L'Estrange's night. January 21 . . . Baltimore, 1799]
broadside
The *Telegraphe*, Jan. 23, 1799, states: "Mr. and Miss l'Estrange . . . apologise for having omitted the dance (mentioned in the bills)."
Minick 471
No copy known mp. 48783

B10698 BALTIMORE. ORDINANCES
Ordinances of the corporation of the city of Baltimore, passed at their second session, held February 1798. Baltimore, Thomas Dobbin, 1799.
89 p. 20 cm.
Half-title (p. [19]): Ordinances . . . passed at their third session . . . February 1799
Minick 472
MdBE mp. 48783

B10699 BALTIMORE CIRCULATING LIBRARY
[Catalogue. Baltimore? 1799]

Title from advertisement in the *American*, Aug. 6, 1799, which states, "Now received a large . . . addition to the library, a catalogue of which is now in readiness."
Minick 469
No copy known mp. 48784

B10700 THE Baltimore repository, for the year 1800: containing an almanac . . . Baltimore, Printed [by Bonsal and Niles] for Thomas and Caldcleugh [1799]
[159] p. 13.5 cm.
Minick 475; cf. Evans 35150
PPiU (imperfect). J. R. Harman, Baltimore
mp. 48785

B10701 BANK OF THE MANHATTAN COMPANY, NEW YORK
Manhattan Company. The Office of Discount and Deposit will open . . . at 10 o'clock . . . and continue open until 3 o'clock in the afternoon . . . Henry Remsen, cashier. September 24, 1799. [New York, 1799]
broadside 9.5 X 5.5 cm.
New York Public 1265
NN (facsim.) mp. 48786

B10702 BAPTISTS. CONNECTICUT. DANBURY ASSOCIATION
Minutes of the Danbury Baptist Association, held at Paulingstown, October 2d and 3d, 1799. Together with their circular and corresponding letters. [n.p., 1799?]
8 p.
Trumbull: Supplement 2047
NRAB. Photocopy: MWA (p. 6–7 lacking)
mp. 48787

B10703 BAPTISTS. KENTUCKY. ELKHORN ASSOCIATION
Minutes of the Elkhorn Association of Babtists [sic], held at the Great Crossing, August 10th, 11th and 12th, 1799. [Colophon] Lexington, J. H. Stewart [1799]
4 p. 22 cm. caption title
McMurtrie: Kentucky 104
OClWHi. Photocopy: MWA mp. 48788

B10704 BAPTISTS. MARYLAND. BALTIMORE ASSOCIATION
[Minutes of the Baptist Association, met at the meeting house near Reister's-Town, May 24 to 28, 1799. Baltimore? 1799]
Title from Address from the dissenting brethren (p. 5)
Minick 476
No copy known mp. 48789

B10705 BAPTISTS. NEW YORK. NEW YORK ASSOCIATION
Minutes of the New-York Baptist Association, holden in the City of New-York, May 22d and 23d, 1799. [New York, 1799]
8 p. 21.5 X 18 cm. caption title
New York Public 1266
NN mp. 48790

B10706 BAPTISTS. NEW YORK. WARWICK ASSOCIATION
Minutes of the Warwick Baptist Association . . . Clinton, Dutchess County, May the 28th and 29th, 1799. [n.p., 1799?]
7 p.
NRAB mp. 48791

B10707 BAPTISTS. SOUTH CAROLINA. BETHEL ASSOCIATION
Minutes of the Bethel Association, convened at the Bethel Church, in Spartanburgh County, South-Carolina, August 10th, 1799 . . . [Charleston, 1799]
8 p. 21 cm. caption title
ScGF

B10708 BAPTISTS. VERMONT. LEYDEN ASSOCIATION
Minutes of the Leyden Association, held at the Baptist Meeting House, in Colrain: M,DCC,XCIX. Printed at Brattleboro', Vermont, by Benjamin Smead: For the Association. 1799.
12 p. 19.5 cm.
VtHi mp. 48792

B10709 BAPTISTS. VERMONT. VERMONT ASSOCIATION
Minutes . . . Clarendon, 1796, Middletown, 1797, and Salem, (N.Y.), 1798. Rutland, Herald Press, 1799.
12 p. 22 cm.
MNtcA; NRAB mp. 48793

B10710 BAPTISTS. VERMONT. WOODSTOCK ASSOCIATION
Minutes . . . Dublin, Newhampshire, Sept. 18th and 19th, 1799. [Windsor? A. Spooner? 1799?]
6 p. 21 cm. caption title
VtHi mp. 48794

B10711 BARBAULD, ANNA LETITIA (AIKIN) 1743–1825
Hymns in prose, for children . . . Dedham, Printed and sold by H. Mann, 1799.
[4], 32 p. 14 cm. A–B^8 C^2
MWA mp. 48795

B10712 BARKER, FRANCIS, publisher
Proposals for printing by subscription, a sermon, entitled The Advantages . . . of wisdom: delivered at Deerfield; –Jan. 1st. 1799. At the opening of the Academy . . . By the Rev. Joseph Lyman . . . Francis Barker, the

intended publisher . . . Greenfield, Jan. 8th, 1799 . . . [Greenfield, 1799]
broadside 37 X 14.5 cm.
MWA mp. 48796

B10713 BENSON, JOSEPH, 1749-1821
Four sermons on the second coming of Christ . . . New York, T. Kirk, 1799.
119 p.
MWA mp. 48799

B10714 BERQUIN, ARNAUD, 1749–1791
The children's friend, and youth's monitor . . . Philadelphia, David Hogan, 1799.
120 p. 12.5 cm.
Page 74 misnumbered 64
MWA mp. 48800

B10715 BETHLEHEM, N. Y. FREEHOLDERS
At a meeting . . . freeholders of the town of Bethlehem . . . 18th day of April, 1799 . . . [Albany? 1799]
broadside 31 X 19 cm.
Bethlehem is now a part of Albany; the meeting was at the home of James Wands, in New Scotland, just outside Albany
McMurtrie: Albany 217; cf. Evans 36672
NHi mp. 48801

B10716 BIBLE. N.T. PSALMS
Psalms carefully suited to the Christian worship . . . Harrisburg, John Wyeth, 1799.
351 p. 14.5 cm.
MWA mp. 48802

B10717 [BICKERSTAFFE, ISAAC] 1735?–1812?
The life and adventures of Ambrose Gwinett . . . Fairhaven: Re-printed and sold by J. P. Spooner [1799?]
46 p. illus. 12 cm.
McCorison 520
VtHi (p. 15–18 lacking) mp. 48803

B10718 [BLODGET, SAMUEL] 1724–1807
The subscriber has begun, and nearly accomplished a suit of locks on Amoskeig Falls in Merrimack River . . . [Boston? 1799?]
broadside 18 X 17 cm.
Subscription form for shares in Amoskeag Canal Company
MB (trimmed) mp. 48804

B10719 [BLODGET, SAMUEL] 1724–1807
To the public. The cutting a canal at Amoskeig Falls, is of very great importance . . . [Concord, N. H.? 1799?]
broadside 42 X 33 cm.
Includes text of letter of Loammi Baldwin to Blodget, dated Sept. 3, 1799, and forms for subscription of shares in the Amoskeag Canal Company
MB mp. 48805

B10720 BOSTON. COLLECTOR OF TAXES
Ward, No. To Mr. Your commonwealth tax. Your town and county tax. . . . Boston, October 1799. [Boston, 1799]
broadside 14 X 15 cm.
MB

B10721 BOSTON CAVALRY
Dr. Boston Cavalry, in account with John Marston, Cr. . . . Boston, December 27, 1798 . . . John Marston, Treasurer . . . The Committee appointed . . . to examine and pass the accounts of John Marston . . . report . . . Josiah Quincy. John T. Apthorp. Gorham Parsons. [Boston, 1799?]
broadsheet 30 X 40.5 cm.
NjR

B10722 BOSTON THEATRE (FEDERAL STREET)
The last night for this week. Mr. S. Powell's benefit. On Wednesday evening, March 20, will be presented . . . the Stranger . . . To which will be added . . . Inkle & Yarico . . . [Boston, 1799]
broadside 50 X 30 cm.
MHi mp. 48807

B10723 BOSTON THEATRE (FEDERAL STREET)
On Wednesday evening, 1st January, will be presented . . . The Roman Father . . . [Boston, Young and Minns, 1799]
broadside 30 X 23 cm.
MB mp. 48808

B10724 BOSTON THEATRE (FEDERAL STREET)
[2d time ever performed in America.] On Wednesday evening, 11th December, will be present . . . Pizarro: or, The Death of Rolla . . . [Boston, Young and Minns, 1799]
broadside 30 X 23 cm.
MB mp. 48809

B10725 [BOWEN, DANIEL] 1760–1856
Columbian Museum, head of the mall, Boston. Paintings . . . Boston: Printed at the Columbian Museum Press [1799]
broadside
Cuts of bear, clock, and porcupine at top
PPL

B10726 [BRACKENRIDGE, HUGH HENRY] 1748-1816
A remarkable narrative of an expedition against the Indians with an account of the barbarous execution of Col. Crawford and Dr. Knight's escape from captivity. [Leominster, Mass.] Printed for Chapman Whitcomb [1799?]
23, [1] p.
Huntington 735; Sabin 38110; Vail: Old frontier 1202; cf. Evans 35689
CSmH; Leominster Public Library; MWA mp. 48810

B10727 A BRIEF exhibition of the right of jurisdiction and soil of the state of Pennsylvania. [Philadelphia, 1799?]
8 p. caption title
Relates to the Connecticut Gore
MB mp. 48811

B10728 BRISTOL, ME. CONGREGATIONAL CHURCH
A summary of doctrines, taken from the Westminster confession of faith, adopted as the creed of the Church in Bristol . . . Wiscasset, Henry Hoskins, 1799.
10 p. 16.5 cm.
MWA (mutilated) mp. 48812

B10729 THE Bucanshire tragedy. To which is prefixed the new game of cards, or, A pack of cards changed into a complete . . . almanack . . . [n.p.] Printed for the travelling booksellers, 1799.
12 p. 20.5 cm.
MWA mp. 48813

B10730 BURBANK, JOHN
A new collection of country dances. For the year 1799 . . . Brookfield, 1799.

12 p. 14 cm.
MWA mp. 48814

B01731 CAPTAIN James, who was hung and gibbeted in England, for starving to death his cabbin-boy. Boston, Nathaniel Coverly, Jun. [1799?]
broadside
Ford 2920
MH mp. 48896

B10732 CAPTAIN James, who was hung and gibbeted in England, for starving to death his cabbin-boy. Boston, Wholesale and retail on Cross Street, near Mercantile Wharf [1799?]
broadside
MSaE

B10733 CAPTAIN James, who was hung and gibbeted in England, for starving to death his cabbin-boy. [n.p., 1799?]
broadside
Ford 2922a
MHi mp. 48895

B10734 CAPTAIN James, who was hung and gibbeted in England for starving to death his cabin Boy . . . [n.p., 1799?]
broadside 27 X 22 cm.
In two columns. Not Evans 37094
CtHi

B10735 CAREY, MATHEW, 1760-1839
Just published, by Mathew Carey . . . A plumb pudding for the humane, valiant, chaste, enlightened, Peter Porcupine. To the public . . . [Philadelphia, 1799]
broadside 22.5 X 14 cm.
New York Public 1267
NN mp. 18815

B10736 [CAREY, MATHEW] 1760-1839
To the public. It is difficult to account for the rancour which the weak and wicked John Ward Fenno displays . . . [Philadelphia, 1799]
broadside
Not Evans 35274
PPL mp. 48816

B10737 CENTINEL OF FREEDOM
From the office of the *Centinel*. Saturday morning, December 14, 1799. Important. Office of the *New-York Gazette* . . . December 13. At a late hour last night, we met the ship Argus, Capt. Main . . . [Newark, Pennington and Dodge, 1799]
broadside 23 X 19 cm.
Morsch 424
NjHi mp. 48856

B10738 CHAPTAL, JEAN ANTOINE CLAUDE, COMTE DE CHANTELOUP, 1756-1832
Elements of chemistry . . . Translated from the French, by William Nicholson. Three volumes in one. Philadelphia, John Ormrod, 1799.
L, 673, [3], [1] p. 8vo
PPL mp. 48817

B10739 CHESTERFIELD, PHILIP DORMER STANHOPE, 4TH EARL, 1694-1773
Principles of politeness . . . To which is annexed A father's legacy to his daughters, by . . . Dr. Gregory . . . Newburyport, Edmund M. Blunt, 1799.
118 p. 17.5 cm.
MWA mp. 48818

B10740 A CHOICE collection of riddles . . . Worcester, Isaiah Thomas, 1799.
31 p. 10.5 cm.
First and last pages pasted to covers
CtHi. d'Alté A. Welch (1961) mp. 48820

B10741 [CIRCULAR] Lancaster, May 30th, 1799. Sir, [31 lines] By order of the Committee, *Edw! Hind* Chairman. [Lancaster, 1799]
broadside 30 X 20 cm.
Chairman's name in ms.
Invitation to Lancaster on June 19 to vote on nominating James Ross for governor
PHi (3 copies) mp. 48821

B10742 A COLLECTION of contradances containing newest, most approved and fashionable figures. Printed and sold at Stockbridge, 1799.
16 p.
MWA

B10743 COLUMBIAN CENTINEL
A card. The carrier of the *Columbian Centinel*. Presents his respects to his friends and patrons . . . January 1, 1799. [Boston, 1799]
broadside 40.5 X 14 cm.
Printed on silk
MBB (torn); MWA mp. 48899

B10744 COMMISSION UNDER ARTICLE VI OF JAY'S TREATY, 1794
Commissioners' Office, 19th February, 1799 . . . In the case of the Right Reverend Charles Inglis . . . [Philadelphia? 1799]
63 p. 25 cm.
"In the case of Samuel Brailsford," p. 60; "In the case of Joseph Anderson," p. 62; "In the case of Daniel Dulany," p. 63
RPJCB mp. 48822

B10745 THE companion: being a selection of the beauties of the most celebrated authors . . . [Wrentham] Printed by Nathaniel and Banjamin Heaton, for Joseph J. Todd, Providence, 1799.
280 p. 14.5 cm.
Distinguishable from Evans 35333 (microprint) by lack of ornamental border on t.p.
RPJCB

B10746 THE complete fortune teller . . . New York: Printed for the booksellers, 1799.
128 p.
MWA (lacks p. 77-80) mp. 48823

B10747 CONDIE, THOMAS
Philadelphia, Sir, I take the liberty to inform you , that I have lately commenced the manufacture of printing ink . . . Thomas Condie, stationer No. 20, Carter's Alley, Philadelphia. [From Thompson's hot-press.] Printed, September, 1799.
broadside
Brackets in original
PHi

B10748 CONGREGATIONAL CHURCHES. VERMONT
Articles of consociation revised, and, with some additions, recommended to a number of churches in the Western District of Vermont . . . by their representatives met at Pawlet, June 7th, A.D. 1798. Fairhaven, Judah P. Spooner, 1799.

16 p.
CtHi

B10749 CONNECTICUT. GENERAL ASSEMBLY
At a General Assembly of the State of Connecticut, holden at New-Haven on the second Thursday of October . . . 1799. The persons returned by the votes of the freemen . . . in nomination for election . . . to this Assembly . . . New-Haven, Thomas Green and Son [1799]
broadside 33.5 X 20.5 cm.
MWA mp. 48824

B10750 CONNECTICUT. GOVERNOR, 1798-1809
By His Excellency Jonathan Trumbull . . . A proclamation. That the people of this state may have an opportunity of presenting to Almighty God . . . gratitude and praise . . . New-Haven, this 21st day of October . . . [1799] . . . New-Haven, Thomas Green and Son [1799]
broadside 41 X 32 cm.
CtHi; CtY; NHi mp. 48825

B10751 CONNECTICUT. GOVERNOR, 1798-1809
By His Excellency Jonathan Trumbull . . . A proclamation. Whereas the General Assembly . . . in October last, passed a resolution . . . Lebanon . . . this second day of April . . . 1799 . . . Hartford, Hudson & Goodwin [1799]
broadside 37 X 29.5 cm.
CtHi; CtY; NHi mp. 48826

B10752 CONNECTICUT. GOVERNOR, 1798-1809
To the sheriff of the County of . . . Greeting . . . Given under my hand, at Hartford . . . this 3th day of August . . . 1799 . . . Gov'r . . . [Hartford, 1799]
broadside ([2] p.) 33 X 20 cm.
Page [2]: At a General Assembly of the state . . . holden at Hart-ford . . . the second Thursday of May, A.D. 1798. [List of nominees]
Orders for calling a freemen's meeting
Trumbull: Supplement 2677
CtHi mp. 48827

B10753 CONNECTICUT. LAWS
At a General Assembly of the State of Connecticut, holden at Hartford . . . May, A. D. 1799. An act for appointing, regulating and encouraging schools . . . [Hartford, 1799]
3 p. 34.5 cm.
CtHi mp. 48828

B10754 CONNECTICUT COURANT
Guillotina, for the year 1799. Addressed to the readers of the *Connecticut Courant* . . . [Hartford, 1799]
broadside 47 X 28 cm.
By Lemuel Hopkins.—P. W. Gaines
CtHi; MSaE. Pierce W. Gaines, Fairfield, Conn. (1964) mp. 48866

B10755 CONNECTICUT LAND COMPANY
For sale and settlement in Connecticut Reserve . . . March 27, 1799. [New Haven? 1799]
broadside 32.5 X 20.5 cm.
Vail: Old frontier 1187
CtY mp. 48829

B10756 CONNECTICUT SOCIETY FOR THE PROMOTION OF FREEDOM
The constitution of the Connecticut society . . . [New-Haven, 1799]
[2] p. 20 cm.
MiU-C mp. 48830

B10757 CONRAD, M. & J., booksellers, Philadelphia
[Catalogue of books. Philadelphia, 1799?]
76 p.
Date assigned from title printed in Philadelphia in 1799, "lately published."
Brigham: Booksellers, p. 63
MWA (p. 11-76 only) mp. 48831

B10758 CYNTHIA and Orsamus, with a tragical account of the unfortunate loves of Almerin and Desdemona . . . Hudson, Printed and sold by A. Stoddard, 1799.
101 p. 14 cm. [A]-$Q^{4,2}$ R^4
MWA mp. 48832

B10758a DALLAS, ALEXANDER JAMES, 1759–1817
Reports of cases in the Supreme Court of the United States . . . Volume I. Philadelphia: Printed for the Reporter by J. Ormrod, 1799.
[2], iv, 480, xix p. 8vo
Evans 33598, with cancel title.—Edwin Wolf 2d
PHi

B10759 DAVIS, GEORGE
Davis's law catalogue, for 1799. [Philadelphia] Zachariah Poulson [1799]
4 p. 34 cm. caption title
Imprint at top of first page
DLC mp. 48833

B10760 DELAWARE. LAWS
Laws of the state of Delaware, passed at a session . . . begun . . . the first day of January . . . New-Castle, Samuel and John Adams, 1799.
1 p.l., 47-113 p. 23 cm.
Hawkins: List B 105
CSmH; DLC; NNB; RPJCB mp. 48834

B10761 DESAUSSURE, HENRY WILLIAM, 1763-1839
Statement, &c. [n.p., 1799?]
23 p. 20 cm. caption title
Concerns dispute over John Cattell's will
Turnbull, p. 364 (v.1)
NHi mp. 48835

B10762 DESSERT TO THE TRUE AMERICAN
Address of the carrier of the *Dessert to the True American* to his patrons, for the year 1799 . . . [New York, 1799]
broadside 30 X 19.5 cm.
NHi mp. 48769

B10763 A DIALOGUE on the subject of the Sabbath, between a Baptist, Rogerene, Roman Catholic, Episcopalian or Churchman. New-Brunswick, Printed for the author, by Abraham Blauvelt, 1799.
23 p. 15.5 cm.
NjR

B10764 DUSSEK, JAN LADISLAV, 1761?-1812
Good night. A favorite song in . . . the Captive of Spilberg . . . By I. L. Dussek. Baltimore, R. Shaw [1799]
broadside 27 cm.
Minick 485
NN mp. 48836

B10765 DUSSEK, JAN LADISLAV, 1761?-1812
Heigho! In the new opera of the Captive of Spilberg . . . by I: L: Dussek. Baltimore, R. Shaw [1799]
broadside 32.5 cm.
Minick 486
DLC mp. 48837

B10766 EASTON, MD. THEATRE
[August 27, 1799. The comic opera of Love in a village . . . Easton, James Cowan? 1799]
broadside
Advertised in the *Maryland Herald*, Aug. 27, 1799; the issue for Aug. 20, 1799, states: "Bills will be published announcing the entertainment of that evening."
Minick 487
No copy known mp. 48839

B10767 EASTON, MD. THEATRE
[On the race-ground. Tuesday, September 3. A favourite comedy . . . The country girl . . . Easton, James Cowan? 1799]
broadside
Advertised in the *Maryland Herald*, Sept. 3, 1799
Minick 488
No copy known mp. 48840

B10768 ELECTORS of New-York, To preserve the rights, maintain the liberty, and support the Constitution . . . are the most sacred . . . duties of American freemen . . . Marcus Junius. [n.p., 1799]
broadside 28 X 23.5 cm.
Refers to the flogging, "a few days since," of Jacob Schneider, printer, of Reading, Pa. This took place in April 1799
New York Public 1270
NAll. Photostat: NN mp. 48841

B10769 ELEGANT seat and valuable lots for sale. On Tuesday, the 24th September . . . public sale, on the premises. [31 lines] Lavenir. September 3d, 1799. Germantown: Printed by Michael Billmeyer. Saturday - once. [1799]
broadside 28 X 20 cm.
PHi mp. 48842

B10770 ELEGY on the death of General George Washington. [Philadelphia? 1799]
broadside 30.5 X 18.5 cm.
Headpiece composed of Masonic symbols
PHi mp. 48843

B10771 ELY, HENRY, 1755-1835
A sermon, on the death of Capt. Aaron Kelsey . . . March 25th, A.D. 1799, in the 65th year of his age . . . Middletown, Tertius Dunning, 1799.
16 p. 23 cm.
CtHi; MWA mp. 48844

B10772 EQUAL to Hutchins, An almanack and ephemeris, for . . . 1800 . . . Poughkeepsie, Printed and sold by Power and Southwick [1799]
[36] p. 18.5 cm.
Drake 6091; New York Public 1268; cf. Evans 35166
CLU; N; NN mp. 48846

B10773 ESSAYS on political science. [n.p., 1799?]
194 p. 22.5 cm.
Half-title: Political society
DLC mp. 48847

B10774 FACTS respecting the Bank of North America . . . [Colophon] [Harrisburg] John Wyeth, printer [1799?]
8 p. 21 cm.
CSmH; MWA mp. 48848

B10775 FACTS, respecting the Bank of North-America. [Colophon] [Lancaster] William Dickson [1799]
8 p. 21 cm. caption title
DLC mp. 48849

B10776 THE farmers almanac, for the year . . . 1800 . . . By Andrew Beers, Philom. [Manchester, Vt.] Printed for & sold by Archibald Pritchard [1799]
[18] p. 14.5 cm.
McCorison 513A
Ct; CtLHi mp. 48797

B10777 FOR sale, at public auction, on the first day of March next, at the Tontine Coffee-House, in . . . New-York . . . [New York] Printed by John Tiebout, No. 358 Pearl-Street. [1799]
broadside 32 X 25.5 cm.
NHi mp. 48850

B10778 FOX, JOSEPH
Proposals of Joseph Fox, Jun. for printing by subscription, the Friends Monthly Magazine . . . each number to contain EIGHTY pages . . . octavo, stiched [!] in a coloured paper . . . Philadelphia, March 13, 1799. Susscribers names. Places of abode. [Philadelphia, 1799]
broadside 35 X 21 cm.
NjR

B10779 FRASER, DONALD
Mental flower-garden . . . Danbury, Douglas & Nichols, 1799.
208, [4] p. 17.5 cm.
CtHi mp. 48851

B10780 FREEMASONS. MARYLAND. GRAND LODGE
Extract of proceedings of the Grand Lodge . . . of the state of Maryland . . . [Baltimore, Thomas Dobbin? 1799]
[4] p. 25 cm. caption title
Minick 490
MdBFM mp. 48852

B10781 FREEMASONS. MARYLAND. GRAND LODGE
Proceedings of the Grand Lodge, of the state of Maryland, held the 22d day of June, A. L. 5799, A. D. 1799. Baltimore, John Hayes, 1799.
19 p. 20 cm.
Minick 491
MdBFM mp. 48853

B10782 FREEMASONS. MASSACHUSETTS. KING SOLOMON'S LODGE
Charlestown, December 28, 1799. The master, wardens and brethren . . . present their affectionate respects . . . in memory of George Washington. [Charlestown, Mass., 1799]
folder ([1] p.) 23.5 X 18.5 cm.
MB mp. 48854

B10783 FREEMASONS. SOUTH CAROLINA. GRAND LODGE
Circular. Charleston 24th of June, 5799. Brothers, the Grand Lodge . . . having received letters . . . induced to appoint a standing committee of correspondence . . . [Charleston, 1799]
3 p. 23 cm. caption title
Mosimann 622
PPFM

B10784 FREEMASONS. VIRGINIA. RICHMOND LODGE
Richmond Lodge, No. 10. Brother, You are requested to meet your brethren, at their lodge room, on [Sunday morning next . . .] [Richmond, 1799]
broadside 20.5 X 16.5 cm.
CSmH mp. 48855

B10785 GALLATIN, ALBERT, 1761-1849
The substance of two speeches of Mr. Gallatin, on the bill for augmenting the Navy establishment . . . Philadelphia, Joseph Gales, 1799.
12, 16 p. 21 cm.
cf. Evans 35531 (also at NHi)
NHi mp. 48857

B10786 THE gentleman & lady's companion; containing, the newest cotillions and country dances . . . Newport, Oliver Farnsworth, 1799.
23 p. 16 cm.
Alden 1619
RNHi mp. 48865

B10787 THE gentleman's annual pocket remembrancer, for . . . 1800. Philadelphia, John Bioren [1799]
160 p. 11.5 cm.
MWA mp. 48858

B10788 GENTLEMEN, At a very large . . . meeting of the citizens of Albany . . . the 17th of March . . . Albany, March 28, 1799. [Albany, 1799]
broadside 31 X 19 cm.
McMurtrie: Albany 178a
N mp. 48771

B10789 [DER general staatsbote. Friedrichstadt, M. Bärtgis, 1799]

Bartgis's Federal Gazette, Aug. 28, 1799, states, "Advertisements for the English and German newspapers . . . duly inserted in either or both."
Minick 492
No copy known

B10790 GERMAN SOCIETY IN THE STATE OF NEW YORK
Rules and orders of the German Society . . . established the 9th of October . . . 1784. New-York, T. & J. Swords, 1799.
20 [i.e. 31] p. 20 cm.
German half-title on prelim. leaf; duplicate pagination for German and English text, p. [2]-12; p. 13 omitted
NHi. Photostat (t.p. only): MWA mp. 48859

B10791 GIN ye can loo me lass . . . New York, Sold by S. Howe [1799-1800]
2 leaves. 32 cm. caption title
MiU-C mp. 48860

B10792 GIRAUD, JEAN JACQUES, 1759-1839
Doctor Giraud's specific and universal salt, for the venereal disease . . . [at end] The deposite of the . . . salt is, viz. At Philadelphia, at Mr. Parent, a printer . . . New-York, at Mr. Pariset, a printer . . . Baltimore, at the author's store in Market-Street No. 40 [1799?]
7 p. 20.5 cm.
Austin 822
NNNAM mp. 48861

B10793 GLORIOUS news! A brief account of the late revivals of religion . . . [Mount Holly] Printed by S. C. Ustick, and sold at Philadelphia, 1799.
24 p. 18 cm.
cf. Evans 37523
DLC; MWA mp. 48781

B10794 THE good old Virginia almanack for the year . . . 1800 . . . Richmond, Thos. Nicolson [1799]
[64] p. 13 cm.
Bear 127; Swem 5910
MWA; Vi ([62] p.); ViHi ([36] p.); ViU mp. 48862

B10795 GREEN, SAMUEL
Appeal to the public. In private disputes, to be compelled to appeal to the public, is a disagreeable alternative . . . S. Green. New-London, Nov. 19, 1799 . . . [New London, 1799]
broadside 34.5 X 21 cm.
CtHi mp. 48863

B10796 . . . GREENLEAF'S New-York, Connecticut, & New-Jersey almanack . . . for . . . 1800. Brooklyn, Printed by T. Kirk, for Ann Greenleaf [1799]
[36] p. 18 cm.
MWA (imperfect) mp. 48798

B10796a GREGORY, JOHN, 1724-1773
A father's legacy to his daughters . . . Philadelphia, John Bioren, 1799.
72 p. 14 cm.
MWA mp. 48864

B10797 HAMPTON. CITIZENS
To the public. When an individual, in his personal quarrels with his fellow-citizen, has the effrontery to appeal to the community . . . we the inhabitants of the town of Hampton, have thought proper to publish a few remarks, respecting the conduct of Mr. Samuel Green towards Mr. Thomas Farnham . . . Hampton, November 2d, 1799. [n.p., 1799]
broadside 29.5 X 22 cm.
CtHi mp. 48867

B10798 HANOVER BOOKSTORE, HANOVER, N. H.
Catalogue of books, for sale at the Bookstore in Hanover . . . [Hanover] Printed for the Hanover Bookstore, 1799.
35 p. 16.5 cm.
New York Public 1269
NN; NhD mp. 48868

B10799 HARPER, ROBERT GOODLOE, 1765-1825
Philadelphia, March 20th, 1799. My dear sir . . . your very humble servant, Robert G. Harper. [Philadelphia, 1799]
3 p. 39 X 24 cm.
DLC mp. 48870

B10800 HARTFORD. THEATRE
. . . Theatre, Hartford, For the benefit of Mr. Hallam. On Friday evening, Oct. 25, 179[9] will be presented a comedy never performed here, written by Miss Lee . . . called The, New Peerage; or, [ ]ves may deceive us. Mr. Hodgkinson. Mr. Hallam, jun. . . . [Hartford, 1799]
broadside
At the head of title: [ ] of the season the doors will open at 5 and the curtain rise precisely at 6 o'clock
CtHi (mutilated) mp. 48871

B10801 HARTFORD. THEATRE
. . . Theatre, Hartford. For the benefit of Mrs. Hodgkinson. On Wednesday evening, Oct. 23, 1799, will be presented . . . Love & Liberty . . . Tickets . . . to be had as usual, and of Mess. Hudson & Goodwin. [Hartford, Hudson & Goodwin, 1799]
broadside 51.5 X 28 cm.
At head of title: The public are respectfully informed, that for the rest of the season the doors will open at 5 . . .
CtHi

B10802 HAYDN, FRANZ JOSEPH, 1732-1809
Favorite easy sonata. Haydn. [New York] P. Erben [1799-1800?]
5 p. 32 cm. caption title
MiU-C mp. 48872

B10803 HAYMARKET THEATRE, BOSTON.
Hay-Market Theatre. On Monday evening, May 27th, 1799, will be presented (for the last time) the . . . Stranger . . . To which will be added . . . the Wandering Jew . . . [Boston, 1799]
broadside 51 X 32 cm.
MH. Photostat: MHi mp. 48806

B10804 HAYNES, SYLVANUS, 1768-1826
A brief, and scriptural defence of believers in baptism, by immersion . . . Fairhaven, Judah P. Spooner, 1799.
27 p. 17 cm.
VtHi mp. 48873

B10805 HELLENBROEK, ABRAHAM, 1658-1731
A specimen of divine truths . . . Translated from the Dutch. New-Brunswick, Abraham Blauvelt, 1799.
60 p. 17 cm.
MWA mp. 48874

B10806 HELMUTH, JUSTUS HEINRICH CHRISTIAN, 1745-1826
Geliebte Mitbrüder und Glaubens Genossen in Northampton Caunty . . . Philadelphia den 28sten März, 1799. [Philadelphia, 1799]
broadside 28 X 16 cm.
PHi mp. 48875

B10807 [HENDERSON, JOHN] 1755-1841
[Paine detected . . . Natchez, Andrew Marschalk, 1799]
ii, 53 p. 17.5 cm.
McMurtrie: Mississippi 2
DLC (photostat; t.p. wanting) mp. 48876

B10808 HERTY, THOMAS
Conveyancer's office. Thomas Herty has opened an office . . . for the purpose of drawing conveyances of land . . . Baltimore, July 28th, 1799. Baltimore, T. Dobbin [1799]
broadside 8 X 13 cm.
Minick 494
MH mp. 48877

B10809 HOCH-deutsches Lutherisches A, B, C, und namen büchlein . . . Elisabeth (Hägers) Taun, Johann Gruber, 1799.
[32] p. 17.5 cm.
Minick 497
J. McC. Zimmerman, Hagerstown mp. 48880

B10810 THE honest landlord, truth swearing judge, and the real genuine patent Republican; or, the patriot of '75, Whig of '76, and soldier of '77 . . . Shubael Gorham, of Lansingburgh in the county of Rensselaer . . . Sworn before me this eleventh day of October, 1799, John Van Rensselaer . . . [Lansingburgh? 1799?]
broadside 40 X 32 cm.
Concerns a land dispute
MWA mp. 48882

B10811 [HONEY comb. Baltimore, 1799]
4to.
Announced in the *American*, Aug. 14, 1799: "To compensate my subscribers for the deficiency in size of the *American* I shall . . . present them with a literary paper . . . on a quarto size . . . every Monday, to be entitled '*The Honey comb*'."
Minick 498
No copy known mp. 48883

B10812 [HOOK, JAMES] 1746-1827
Lillies and roses . . . Boston, P. A. von Hagen; New York, G. Gilfert [1799]
[2] p. 32.5 cm.
Sonneck-Upton p. 230
DLC; NRU-Mus; RPB mp. 48884

B10813 [HOOK, JAMES] 1746-1827
The little singing girl . . . Boston, P. A. von Hagen; New York, G. Gilfert [1799]
[2] p. 32.5 cm.
Sonneck-Upton p. 235
DLC; MWA; N; NN mp. 48885

B10814 HOOK, JAMES, 1746-1827
She lives in the valley below . . . New York, S. Howe [1799-1800]
2 leaves. 32 cm. caption title
MiU-C mp. 48886

B10815 HOOK, JAMES, 1746-1827
The unfortunate sailor . . . New York, J. Hewitt [1799-1800]
2 leaves. 32 cm. caption title
MiU-C mp. 48887

B10816 [HOOK, JAMES] 1746-1827
The wedding day. Boston, P. A. von Hagen; N. York, G. Gilfert [1799?]
[2] p. 32.5 cm.
Sonneck-Upton p. 457
DLC; MWA; N; NN; RPJCB mp. 48888

B10817 THE house that Jack built. To which are added. The history of Miss Kitty Pride. And The virtue of a rod. Second Worcester edition. Worcester, Printed by Isaiah Thomas, Jun., 1799.
27, [1] p. 11 cm.
MWA mp. 48889

B10818 HUNT, GARNER A
A discourse occasioned by the death of Jacob Anderson . . . delivered . . . at the house of the deceased, Amwell, New-Jersey . . . Trenton, Sherman, Mershon & Thomas, 1799.
11 p. 19 cm.
NHi mp. 48890

B10819 HYMNS and an anthem, to be performed at the ordination in Federal-Street . . . [Boston, 1799]
broadside 28.5 X 23.5 cm.
"Sung at the ordination of the Rev. Mr. Popkin. 10 July 1799."
MWA mp. 48891

B10820 IDLE SOCIETY, LEOMINSTER, MASS.
United States of America. By his high and mighty laziness Ephraim Eager, Captain General . . . of the Idle Society . . . To Gentleman, Greeting. You . . . are constantly to refrain from all necessary labor . . . Given . . . at Leominster, the day of first year of the Idle Society . . . [Leominster? 1799]
broadside 39.5 X 32 cm.
Filled in for Nov. 1, 1799
MWA mp. 48892

B10821 IN committee, Albany, 8th April, 1799. The annexed ticket will announce to you the candidates . . . Philip S. Van Rensselaer, chairman . . . [Albany, 1799]
broadside 44 X 27 cm.
DLC; NHi mp. 48893

B10822 IN the press, and shortly will be published, instructions . . . for the formation . . . of the cavalry . . . [Halifax, Abraham Hodge, 1799]
[4] p. 33 cm. caption title

Pages 2-4 blank, for insertion of names of advance subscribers. Dated Apr. 29, 1799
Nc-Ar mp. 48881

B10823 INFORMATION is requested on the following subjects, viz. . . . The convention of delegates from several states at Annapolis . . . The state of the national debt . . . at the commencement of the Federal Government, and at the close of . . . 1798 . . . The situation . . . as it respects the states of Barbary . . . Discoveries and improvements in philosophy, physic, &c. . . . [n.p., 1799?]
broadside ([2] p.) 32.5 X 20 cm.
CtHi mp. 48894

B10824 JACKSON, GEORGE K 1745-1822
One kind kiss. Boston, Printed & sold by P. A. Von Hagen. And to be had of G. Gilfert, New York [1799?]
1 leaf. 28.5 cm. caption title
cf. Evans 30931; Sonneck-Upton p. 315
MiU-C

B10825 JAMES, ROBERT, defendant
The case of Robert James, with the particulars of the trial, observations and depositions . . . New York, Printed for the author, 1799.
26 p.
DLC mp. 48898

B10826 JEMMY and Nancy. A tragical relation of the death of five persons . . . Sold at the Printing-Office, New-London [1799?]
broadside 32 X 23 cm.
3 columns of verse
cf. Evans 35661
CtHi mp. 48900

B10827 [KELLY, MICHAEL] 1764?-1826
The favorite duett of Tink a Tink. New York, G. Gilfert [1799?]
3 p. 31.5 cm.
Sonneck-Upton p. 432
DLC; MWA mp. 48901

B10828 [KELLY, MICHAEL] 1764?-1826
My honor's guardian far away . . . New York, G. Gilfert [1799]
[2] p. 32.5 cm.
Sonneck-Upton p. 283
DLC mp. 48902

B10829 KELLY, MICHAEL, 1764?-1826
Young Henry lov'd his Emma well . . . New York, J. Hewitt [1799-1800]
1 leaf. 32 cm. caption title
MiU-C mp. 48903

B10830 KENTUCKY. CONSTITUTION
The constitution, or form of government for the state of Kentucky . . . Frankfort, Hunter and Beaumont, 1799.
48 p. 18 cm.
In larger type and more widely spaced than the 30-page issue (Evans 35681)
McMurtrie: Kentucky 107
DLC; ICU; KyLx (imperfect after p. 38) mp. 48904

B10831 KENTUCKY. CONSTITUTION
The constitution, or form of government for . . . Kentucky. Lexington, James H. Stewart, 1799.
26 p. 19 cm.
McMurtrie: Kentucky 108
PHi mp. 48905

B10832 KENTUCKY. CONSTITUTIONAL CONVENTION
Journal of the Convention begun . . . [July 22, 1799] . . . Frankfort, Hunter & Beaumont, 1799.
50 p. 36 cm.
McMurtrie: Kentucky 110
KyU (t.p. wanting). William M. Bullitt, Louisville (1939) mp. 48906

B10833 KENTUCKY. CONSTITUTIONAL CONVENTION
Resolutions and proceedings in committee of the whole, on the 30th day of July, 1799. [Frankfort, Hunter and Beaumont, 1799]
broadside 28.5 X 22.5 cm.
McMurtrie: Kentucky 113 a
DLC mp. 48907

B10834 KENTUCKY. CONSTITUTIONAL CONVENTION
Resolutions and proceedings in committee of the whole, on the 31st day of July, 1799. [Frankfort, Hunter and Beaumont, 1799]
broadside 14 X 22 cm.
McMurtrie: Kentucky 111 b
DLC mp. 48908

B10835 KENTUCKY. CONSTITUTIONAL CONVENTION
Resolutions and proceedings in committee of the whole, on the 2d day of August, 1799. [Frankfort, Hunter and Beaumont, 1799]
broadside 28.5 X 23 cm.
McMurtrie: Kentucky 113 d
DLC (2 copies) mp. 48909

B10836 KENTUCKY. CONSTITUTIONAL CONVENTION
Resolutions and proceedings in committee of the whole, on the 3d day of August, 1799. [Frankfort, Hunter and Beaumont, 1799]
broadside 28 X 22 cm.
McMurtrie: Kentucky 113 e
DLC (2 copies) mp. 48910

B10837 KENTUCKY. CONSTITUTIONAL CONVENTION
Resolutions and proceedings in committee of the whole, on the 5th day of August, 1799. [Frankfort, Hunter and Beaumont, 1799]
broadside 14 X 22.5 cm.
McMurtrie: Kentucky 113 f
DLC mp. 48911

B10838 KENTUCKY. CONSTITUTIONAL CONVENTION
Resolutions and proceedings in committee of the whole, on the 6th day of August, 1799. [Frankfort, Hunter and Beaumont, 1799]
broadside 28.5 X 22.5 cm.
McMurtrie: Kentucky 113 g
DLC mp. 48912

B10839 KENTUCKY. CONSTITUTIONAL CONVENTION
Resolutions and proceedings in committee of the whole, on the 7th day of August, 1799. [Frankfort, Hunter and Beaumont, 1799]
broadside 16 X 25 cm.
McMurtrie: Kentucky 113 h
DLC (not traced 1964) mp. 48913

B10840 KENTUCKY. CONSTITUTIONAL CONVENTION
Resolutions and proceedings in committee of the whole, on the 8th day of August, 1799. [Frankfort, Hunter and Beaumont, 1799]
broadside 14 X 22 cm.
McMurtrie: Kentucky 113 i
DLC mp. 48914

B10841 KENTUCKY. CONSTITUTIONAL CONVENTION
Resolutions and proceedings in committee of the whole, on the 9th day of August, 1799. [Frankfort, Hunter & Beaumont, 1799]
broadside 14 X 16 cm.
McMurtrie: Kentucky 113 j
DLC (not traced 1964) mp. 48915

B10842 KENTUCKY. GENERAL ASSEMBLY. HOUSE OF REPRESENTATIVES
[Jonrnal of the House . . . at the first session of the eighth General Assembly . . . held . . . [Nov. 4, 1799] . . . Frankfort, William Hunter [1799?]]
136 p. 27.5 cm.
Title page assumed from other sessions
McMurtrie: Kentucky 114
M (t.p. and p. 1-4 wanting) mp. 48916

B10843 [KILNER, MARY JANE (MAYE)] b. 1753
The happy family or memoirs of Mr. & Mrs. Norton . . . Philadelphia, S. C. Ustick, 1799.
2 p.l., 90 p. front. 10.5 cm.
Welch 676
d'Alté A. Welch, Cleveland (1963) mp. 48917

B10844 KURZGEFASSTES Weiber-Büchlein. Enthält Aristotels und Albert Magni Hebammen-kunst, mit den darzu gehörigen Recepten. Die zehente Auflage. [Ephrata, G. Baumann] 1799.
64 p. 13.5 cm.
Austin 1109
MWA; PPL; RPJCB mp. 48918

B10845 [LATHOM, FRANCIS] 1777-1832
The midnight bell. A German story . . . Philadelphia, James Carey, 1799.
3 v. in 1. 17 cm.
Wrongly attributed to George Walker, 1772-1847
New York Public 1271
NN (imperfect) mp. 48919

B10846 [LEE, RICHARD] b. 1747
Lines composed on the last and dying words of the Rev. Oliver Williams . . . who died August 29th, 1790, aged 39 years. Worcester, D. Greenleaf [1799?]
broadside
MWA

B10847 THE lover's almanac, No. I . . . Fredericksburg, Printed by T. Green, for M. L. Weems [1799]

Skeel 155; also 161 note 3; 172 note 1; 174 note 2; 186 note 2
ViWC mp. 48920

B10848 LOVE'S pilgrimage: a story founded on facts . . . Philadelphia, Printed by John Bioren, for Robert Campbell, 1799.
vi, 274 p. 18 cm.
MWA mp. 48921

B10849 LYON, JOSEPH
Miscellaneous essays, written at different periods, on moral and religious subjects. By Joseph Lyon, Sen. of Lyon's Farms. Elizabeth-Town, Printed by Shepard Kollock for the author, 1799.
36 p. 17.5 cm.
CSmH; NjR; PPL mp. 48922

B10850 LYON, MATTHEW, 1746-1822
Colonel Lyon's address to his constituents. To the freemen of the Western District of Vermont. Vergennes Gaol, January 10th, 1799 . . . [n.p., 1799]
broadside 34.5 X 20 cm.
CtHi mp. 48923

B10851 MARYLAND. GENERAL ASSEMBLY
Resolved, that the treasurer of the Western Shore be . . . empowered to subscribe . . . for one hundred and thirty shares . . . of the Patowmack company . . . [Annapolis, F. Green, 1799]
broadside 17 X 20 cm.
Read before the House, Nov. 22, 1799; before the Senate, Dec. 4
Minick 503
MdHi mp. 48925

B10852 MARYLAND. HOUSE OF DELEGATES
By the committee of claims. Your committee begs leave to report, that they have examined the accounts . . . of Thomas Harwood . . . [Annapolis, F. Green, 1799]
[2] p. 34 X 20 cm.
Read before the House, Nov. 14, 1799
Minick 507
MdHi mp. 48926

B10853 MARYLAND. HOUSE OF DELEGATES
The committee appointed to inquire whether any and what alterations are necessary in superintending the revenue . . . [Annapolis, F. Green, 1799]
broadside 34 X 21 cm.
Read before the House, Dec. 26, 1799
Minick 506
MdHi mp. 48927

B10854 MARYLAND. HOUSE OF DELEGATES
The committee to whom was referred the agent's report, have considered the same . . . By order, Richard Key Watts, clk. [Annapolis, F. Green, 1799]
[2] p. 33.5 X 21 cm.
Read before the House, Nov. 25, 1799
Minick 508
MdHi mp. 48928

B10855 MARYLAND. LAWS
An act to regulate elections . . . [46 lines on p. [2]] . . . [Annapolis, F. Green, 1799]
[4?] p. 33.5 cm.
Not the form of the act which became law
Minick 516
MdHi (p. [1-2] only)

B10856 MARYLAND. LAWS
An act to regulate elections . . . [54 lines on p. [2]; 56 on p. [3]; 51 on p. [4]] . . . [Annapolis, F. Green, 1799]
[4] p. 33.5 cm.
Not the form of the act which became law
Minick 517
MdHi mp. 48924

B10857 MARYLAND. LAWS
An act to regulate elections . . . [Annapolis, F. Green, 1799]
[6?] p. 34 cm.
The form of the act which became law

Minick 518
MdHi (lacks p. [3-4]) mp. 48929

B10858 MARYLAND. LAWS
A further supplement to the act . . . for making the river Susquehanna navigable . . . [Annapolis, F. Green, 1799]
broadside 34 X 21 cm.
Minick 519
MdHi mp. 48930

B10859 MARYLAND. LAWS
Laws of Maryland, made and passed at a session . . . begun and held . . . the fifth of November . . . Annapolis, Frederick Green [1799]
104 p. 32 cm.
Minick 511
DLC (t.p. lacking); Md; MdBP; MdHi mp. 48931

B10860 MARYLAND. LAWS
A supplement to an act . . . to direct descents . . . [Annapolis, F. Green, 1799]
[2] p. 33.5 cm.
Minick 520
MdHi mp. 48932

B10861 MARYLAND. LAWS
[A supplement to the act . . . to regulate and discipline the militia of this state. Annapolis? 1799]
22, [1] p. 8vo
Minick 514
MB (not traced) mp. 48933

B10862 MARYLAND. SENATE
Votes and proceedings of the Senate . . . November session, 1798. Being the third session of the fifth senate . . . [Annapolis, F. Green, 1799]
74 p. 34 cm. caption title
Minick 509
CSmH; Md; MdBP; MdHi mp. 48934

B10863 MARYLAND. TREASURER
Dr. the state of Maryland, in account current with Thomas Harwood, treasurer of the Western Shore . . . Annapolis, November 1st, 1799 . . . [Annapolis, F. Green 1799]
broadside 33.5 X 41 cm.
Minick 521
MdHi

B10864 MARY'S bower. Boston, Printed & sold at P. A. von Hagen & c°s imported piano forte warehouse, and to be had at G. Gilfert, New York. [Boston, ca. 1799]
[2] p. 33 cm. caption title
First line: To Mary's bower haste away
Sonneck-Upton p. 253
MiU-C

B10865 MASON, JOHN, 1646?-1694
Select remains of the Rev. John Mason . . . Salem, Printed by Joshua Cushing, for Stephen Youngs, 1799.
1 p.l., [3]-5, [vi]-xiii, [2], [15]-189 p. 18 cm.
[ ]^1 B^6 [ ]^1 C-Q^6 R^4
MWA mp. 48935

B10866 MASSACHUSETTS
Circular. Boston, November 9, 1799. Sir, Agreeable to the opinion of the Secretary of the Treasury of the United States, and a vote of the Board of Commissioners, for the valuation of lands . . . [Boston, 1799]
broadside 32.5 X 20 cm.
Ford 2931
M-Ar; MHi mp. 48971

B10867 MASSACHUSETTS. MILITIA
(Circular.) Stockbridge, September 14, 1798. At a court martial . . . [Stockbridge, 1799]
[3] p. 23 cm.
Dated on p. [3]: June 5, 1799
On p. [2]: Lenox, Oct. 4, 1798. At a meeting of a general committee of officers . . . of the militia . . .
DLC (p. [3] lacking); MWA mp. 48515; 48936

B10868 MERRILL, DAVID
The psalmodist's best companion . . . Exeter, N.H., Printed by Henry Ranlet for the author, 1799.
71, [1] p. 13 X 22.5 cm.
MiU-C mp. 48937

B10869 MILITARY CLUB, CHARLESTON, S.C.
Rules of the Military Club of Charleston. Charleston, Freneau & Paine, 1799.
8 p. 16 cm.
ScU

B10870 MILLENIAL orders, from the throne of God and of the Lamb; promulgated, at the hand of the man whose name is the Branch . . . Hartford, State of Connecticut, April 23d, 1799.
broadside 33.5 X 21 cm.
NHi mp. 48938

B10871 MISSISSIPPI. LAWS
[Laws of the Mississippi Territory; published at a session . . . begun in . . . Natchez upon the 22nd day of January . . . 1799 . . . to the 25th day of October . . . Fort McHenry (Walnut Hills), Andrew Marschalk, 1799]
16 p. 19 cm.
Printed without t.p.; t.p. supplied from t.p. of the laws of Feb.-May 1799
McMurtrie: Mississippi 4
M. Photostat: Ms-Ar mp. 48940

B10872 MISSISSIPPI. LAWS
Mississippi Territory. A law in aid of, and in addition to, the regulations of the governor, for the permanent establishment of the militia . . . [Natchez? A. Marschalk, 1799]
11 p. 18 cm. caption title
Dated Feb. 28, 1799
New York Public 1272
Archivo general de Indias, Seville. NN (facsim.)
mp. 48939

B10873 THE MONITOR, LITCHFIELD, CONN.
The address of Little Jack, the carrier of the *Monitor*, to his old friends and customers, for the 1st of January, 1799 . . . [Litchfield, 1799]
broadside
1st line: Since Fortune first . . .
NHi mp. 48767

B10874 DER neue unpartheyische Baltimore Bote und Märyländer Staats-register. Baltimore, Samuel Saur, 1799.

Minick 528; Seidensticker p. 151
No copy known

B10875 A NEW academy of compliments: or, complete secretary . . . [New York?] Printed for B. Gomez, Maiden Lane [1799?]
1 p.l., [5]-144 p. front. 14 cm.
cf. Evans 29145
NHi mp. 48941

B10876 NEW HAMPSHIRE. LAWS
An act for the better observing of the Lord's Day, and for

repealing all the laws heretofore made for that purpose. [Portsmouth, John Melcher, 1799]
7 p. 8vo caption title
Dated at end: December 24, 1799
PHi

B10877 NEW HAMPSHIRE. LAWS
State of Newhampshire. In the year . . . [1798] An act to incorporate Samuel Blodget, esquire, and others . . . with the exclusive right . . . of cutting a canal by Amoskeag Falls . . . and locking the same. [Portsmouth, N.H.? John Melcher? 1799?]
3 p. 31 cm. caption title
"Approved December 24th, 1798."
MB mp. 48492

B10878 NEW JERSEY. LAWS
The practice of the courts of law and equity, in . . . New-Jersey. As comprised in the act relative to the Supreme and Circuit Courts [and three other acts] Printed . . . for the convenience of the judges . . . Trenton, G. Craft [1799]
1 p.l., 20, 25 p. 22 cm. $*^1$ [A]-B^4 C^2 [A]-C^4 D^1
Apparently 4 items (incl. Evans 35901) published in 1799 and brought together with a title leaf.--D. A. Sinclair
NjR

B10878a NEW JERSEY. MILITIA
General orders. Trenton, December 18, 1799. The Commander in Chief of the Militia . . . announcing to his brother officers, the death of . . . General George Washington . . . By order of His Excellency, the Commander in Chief, J. Rhea, Aid-de-camp. [Trenton, 1799]
broadside 30 X 24 cm.
Middendorf Collection, New York City (1970)

B10879 THE New-Jersey and New-York almanac for . . . 1800. Newark, Jacob Halsey & Co. [1799]
[36] p.
Drake 5195; probably Evans 36304, declared "ghost" in microprint edition
DLC

B10880 NEW YORK. ADJUTANT-GENERAL
The Adjutant-General's report: to the honorable the House of Assembly. [Albany? 1799?]
28 p. 20 cm.
Signed: D. Van Horne, Adjutant-General
NHi mp. 48944

B10881 NEW YORK. ELECTION PROX.
In Committee, Albany, 8th April, 1799. The annexed ticket . . . Philip S. Van Rensselaer, Chairman . . . Senators. Moses Vail . . . Assemblymen. Dirck Ten Broeck . . . [Albany, 1799]
broadside 44.5 X 26.5 cm.
DLC; NHi mp. 48945

B10882 NEW YORK. FIRE DEPT.
Constitution of the Fire Department for the City of New-York . . . New-York, J. Harrisson, 1799.
15 p. 21 cm.
Title vignette
NNS

B10883 NEW YORK. LAWS
An act for regulating and governing the militia of the state of New-York. [n.p., 1799?]
80 p. 20 cm. caption title
cf. Evans 35919
NHi mp. 48946

B10884 NEW YORK. LAWS
An act for the benefit of insolvent debtors and their creditors. [Albany, L. Andrews, 1799?]
15 p. 20 cm. caption title
cf. Evans 34205 (also at NHi)
NHi mp. 48947

B10885 NEWBURYPORT, MASS.
Arrangements made for paying a tribute of public respect to the memory of . . . Washington . . . Order of procession . . . Newbury-Port, December 31, 1799. [Newburyport] E. M. Blunt, print. [1799]
broadside 39.5 X 23 cm.
MWA mp. 48948

B10886 NEWTON LIBRARY SOCIETY
Constitution of the Newton Library Society. [Newton, Mass.? ca. 1799]
8 p. 21.5 cm. caption title
MiU-C mp. 48949

B10887 [THE North-Carolina Register, and Almanac for 1800. Wilmington, Gazette Office [1799]]

Advertised in the *Wilmington Gazette*, Mar. 3, 1799
Drake 8882
No copy known

B10888 ORDER of procession . . . Philadelphia, T. Bradford [1799]
broadside 28 X 16.5 cm.
After the death of Washington
PHi mp. 48950

B10889 PARISMAS, THOMAS
The history of Captain Thomas Parismas . . . to which is added, The remarkable and entertaining story of Alcander & Rosilla. Medford, Printed and sold by Nathaniel Coverly, 1799.
31, 19, 4 p. 18.5 cm.
4 p. at end: The fatal effects of seduction, by Thomas Bellamy
MWA mp. 48879

B10890 PARKYNS, G. I.
No. 1. Sketches of select American scenery, by G. I. Parkyns. Philadelphia, John Ormrod, 1799.
[6] p. 2 plates
RPJCB mp. 48951

B10891 PARKYNS, G. I.
Proposals for publishing in aquatint, a series of views . . . [Philadelphia, John Ormrod, 1799]
broadside 30.5 X 24 cm.
Bound with his *Sketches of select American scenery*
RPJCB mp. 48952

B10892 PENNSYLVANIA. LAWS
An act to extend . . . "a further supplement to the act, entitled an act for making an artificial road from . . . Philadelphia to . . . Lancaster . . ." [Philadelphia, 1799]
broadside 24 X 16.5 cm.
PHi mp. 48953

B10893 PENNSYLVANIA. PROTHONOTARY
[Arden & Harrington] Second period, 9th December, 1799. [Philadelphia, 1799]
broadside fol.
Jury list
PPL

B10894 [THE Pennsylvania, Maryland, and Virginia

almanack, for the year 1799. Frederick-Town, M. Bartgis, 1799?]

Advertised in *Bartgis's Federal Gazette*, June 19, 1799, as "Just published, and for sale."
Minick 529
No copy known mp. 48954

B10895 PHILADELPHIA, May 27th, 1799. Sir, Deeply interested in the approaching election of governor . . . Levi Hollingsworth, Samuel Morris [and 11 others]. [Philadelphia, 1799]
broadside
Recommending the election of James Ross
PPL mp. 48956

B10896 PHINNEY'S calendar; or, Western almanack for . . . 1800. Cooperstown, Elihu Phinney [1799]

Drake 6100
NCooHi (10 l., t.p. lacking)

B10897 PHIPPS, JOSEPH, 1700-1787
An address to the youth of Norwich . . . Hudson, Ashbel Stoddard, 1799.
12 p. 15 cm.
NHi mp. 48955

B10898 [DER Readinger Magazin. Reading, Jacob Schneider, 1799]

Advertised in the *Readinger Adler*, Jan. 8, 1799, as "beynahe zur Presse fertig," and issued on Feb. 1, 1799
Nolan p. 14-15, and 32 (where it is put under 1800)
No copy known

B10899 REDFIELD, LEVI, 1745-1838
A true account of some memorable events . . . in the life of Levi Redfield . . . Written by himself . . . Norwich, Printed for Ezra White, a flying bookseller [1799]
24 p. 19 cm.
Advertised in the Stonington *Journal of the Times*, Feb. 27, 1799
New York Public 1245; Trumbull: Supplement 2879
MWA; NN mp. 48957

B10900 ROSLINE Castle, a favorite Scots song, the words by Rd. Hewit. New York, J. Hewitt [1799-1800]
2 leaves. 32 cm. caption title
MiU-C mp. 48878

B10901 RUSSEL, ROBERT, of Wadhurst, Sussex
Seven sermons . . . Suffield, Printed by Edward Gray for Henry Dwier, and sold by said Dwier . . . Hartford [1799?]
144 p. 14 cm.
Trumbull: Second supplement 2883
CtHi mp. 48958

B10902 RUTH, WILLIAM
Twenty-five dollars reward . . . William Ruth, gaoler. New-Castle, Aug. 19, 1799. New-Castle, S. & Jno. Adams [1799]
broadside
Concerns three escaped prisoners
PPL mp. 48959

B10903 SCHEME of a lottery, for the purpose of completing the building of the Roman Catholic Church of St. Augustine . . . [Philadelphia, 1799]
broadside 33.5 × 21.5 cm.
Approved by T. Mifflin, May 15, 1799
PHi mp. 48960

B10904 EIN schön Jesus = Lied . . . [Reading? 1799?]
broadside
9 stanzas of verse
Dated from ms. note: Elizabeth Kunsman her song June 22th 1799
Adams: Pennsylvania 72
PU

B10905 SCHUBART, CHRISTIAN FRIEDRICH DANIEL
Schubart's Klaglied: ich habe viel gelitten, in Musik gesetzt von Dr. Haydn. [Philadelphia] Gedruckt bey Carl Cist, und zu haben in Hrn. G. Willig's, in Hrn. G. Gilfert's, zu Neu-York, und bey Hrn. C. J. Hütter, zu Lancaster [1799?]
[2] p. fol.
PPL mp. 48961

B10906 SELECTION for St. John's Day, 5799. A favourite Masonic song . . . The Mason's prayer . . . Anthem . . . [Hartford? 1799]
broadside 28 × 22 cm.
CtHi

B10907 SELECTION of prayers and hymns from various authors . . . Middletown, Tertius Dunning, 1799.
30 p. 17 cm.
CtHi mp. 48962

B10908 SMITH, CHARLOTTE (TURNER) 1749-1806
The romance of real life . . . Baltimore: Printed for Campbell, Conrad & Co. 1799.
333, [1] p. 15 cm.
Table of contents on verso of [1] p. at end
Edward G. Howard, Baltimore (1965)

B10909 [SONG from the Jew and the doctor. Baltimore, R. Shaw, 1799]

Advertised in the *Telegraphe*, Dec. 4, 1799, as "Just published at the above place [No. 92, Market-street] . . . a much admired song, sung by Mr. Bernard."
Minick 540
No copy known mp. 48963

B10910 SPOONER'S Vermont and New York almanack, for the year . . . 1800 . . . By a lover of science . . . Bennington, Printed and sold by Judah P. Spooner Fairhaven [1799]
[24] p.
McCorison 514A
CtY mp. 48964

B10911 TAMMANY MUSEUM
Tammany Museum, belonging to Gardiner Baker. Extract from the resolution of the Tammany Society, passed the 16th of March, 1795 . . . New-York: Printed by John Harrisson, Yorick's Head, No. 3 Peck-slip [1799?]
broadside 29 × 24.5 cm.
Dated by MHi
MHi mp. 48943

B10912 TO the citizens of New York. Your attention and curiosity having been much excited, by an act . . . incorporating . . . the "Manhattan Company" . . . [New York, 1799]
broadside 33 × 26 cm.
Signed and dated: A Citizen. April 30, 1799

New York Public 1274
NHi. Photostat: NN mp. 48965

B10913 TO the electors of a Representative to Congress, for the First District . . . A Republican elector. [New York? 1799]
broadside 34 X 23.5 cm.
Advocates the election of Gen. John Smith to succeed J. N. Havens, who died July 7, 1799
New York Public 1275
NAll. Photostat: NN mp. 48966

B10914 TO the electros of the State of New-York. Poor Behrens! The discreet . . . citizen, will be cautious in confiding . . . to a man [Aaron Burr] . . . marked with suspicion . . . solicits . . . the governmental chair . . . A Young German. [New York, 1799?]
broadside 41.5 X 38 cm.
Albreight Behrens died in 1797 in NYC. A nephew met only with discouragement in dealing with Burr, who filed an inventory of the large estate.--NHi
Dated 1804 by Shaw-Shoemaker
NHi

B10915 TO the General Assembly of Virginia . . . [Alexandria? 1799?]
broadside 32 cm.
A petition filled in in manuscript for Fairfax County, with manuscript signatures, respecting the formation of a district court in Centerville; presented Dec. 19, 1799
Vi mp. 48967

B10916 TO the honorable the General Assembly of the Commonwealth of Virginia. The petition of sundry freeholders and farmers of the county of humbly sheweth . . . [Alexandria? 1799?]
broadside 37 cm.
A petition with manuscript signatures, presented Dec. 11, 1799
Vi mp. 48968

B10917 TO the Republicans of Pennsylvania. [Philadelphia, 1799]
7 p. caption title
Dated "August 7th, 1799."
Text begins on verso of first leaf, and the odd page numbers appear on the versos throughout
cf. Evans 36435 (dated "31st of August, 1799")
MB mp. 48969

B10918 TYLER, ROYALL, 1757-1826
Convivial song, sung at Windsor, on the evening of the fourth of July . . . [Walpole, N.H.? David Carlisle? 1799]
broadside?
VtU. Photostat: MWA mp. 48970

B10919 U. S.
Duties payable on goods, wares and merchandize imported . . . after the 30th Sept. 1797 . . . also, rates of coins . . . also the mode of transacting business at the Custon-House . . . New-York . . . New York. Prinded [sic] by James Oram, 1799.
43 p. 23 cm.
Pierce W. Gaines, Fairfield, Conn. (1964) mp. 48838

B10920 U. S. CONGRESS
The committee to whom was recommitted the report of the committee appointed to report what further provisions are necessary . . . Philadelphia, W. Ross, 1799.
broadside 33.5 X 20.5 cm.
DLC mp. 48973

B10921 U. S. CONGRESS
Fifth Congress, third session. A list of acts passed during the session. [Philadelphia? 1799]
[2] p. 34 X 20.5 cm.
New York Public 1276
NN mp. 48974

B10922 U. S. CONSTITUTION
The Constitution of the United States. Lexington, John Bradford, 1799.
lxvi p. 19.5 cm.
T.p. supplied in ms. in copy described
McMurtrie: Kentucky 124
ICU mp. 48976

B10923 U. S. CONTINENTAL CONGRESS
Journals of Congress: containing the proceedings from January 1, 1776, to December 31, 1776 . . . Volume II. Philadelphia: From Folwell's Press, 1799.
480, [22] p.
cf. Evans 38750 (dated 1800 in microprint)
PHi

B10924 U. S. DEPT. OF STATE
Standing instructions to consuls and vice-consuls of the United States. Department of State. *24 Jany. 1800* Sir, In addition to the special duties pointed out in the act . . . 14th of April, 1792 . . . [Philadelphia, 1799?]
broadside 22.5 X 17 cm.
Signed: T. P. [Timothy Pickering]
MHi mp. 48977

B10925 U. S. LAWS
An act to regulate the collection of duties on imports and tonnage. Passed at the third session of the Fifth Congress, begun . . . the third of December, 1798. New-London: Printed by Samuel Green. 1799.
[2], 23-123 p. 20.5 cm.
cf. Evans 36482, with part of p. 22 reset on verso of new t.p.
Pierce W. Gaines, Fairfield, Conn. (1964)

B10926 U. S. LAWS
A bill, giving eventual authority to the President . . . to augment the army . . . [n.p., 1799]
4 p. 34 cm.
MiU-C mp. 48972

B10927 U. S. TREASURY DEPT.
Circular to collectors, naval officers and surveyors. Treasury department, comptroller's office. 23d February, 1799. Sir, from information . . . [Philadelphia, 1799]
[3] p. 23.5 cm.
M iU-C mp. 48978

B10928 U. S. TREASURY DEPT.
(Circular to the Commissioners of Loans.) Treasury Department. Comptroller's office, June 1st, 1799. [Philadelphia, 1799]
[2] p. 4to
PPL mp. 48979

B10929 U. S. TREASURY DEPT.
District of Connecticut. To Surveyor of the Revenue for the Assessment District . . . of Connecticut. In pursuance of an act passed on the 14th July 1798 . . . you are required forthwith to make out lists to furnish the quota . . . apportioned to . . . Connecticut . . . Supervisor's Office at Wethersfield . . . [n.p., 1799?]
[3] leaves. 33 X 20.5 cm.
Dated October 31, 1799 in ms.
CtHi mp. 48980

B10930 U. S. TREASURY DEPT.
Supervisor's office, Massachusetts District, Boston. December 1799. . . . [Boston? 1799]
broadside 37 X 23 cm.
Concerns surveyors of the revenue
Ford 2928
MWA mp. 48981

B10931 U. S. TREASURY DEPT.
To the inhabitants of the Collection District, State of Connecticut. You are hereby notified . . . by virtue of an act . . . 14 July 1798 . . . becomes due . . . [Dec. 17, 1799] . . . [n.p., 1799]
broadside 20 X 16.5 cm.
Filled in for fourth district
Pierce W. Gaines, Fairfield, Conn. (1964) mp. 48982

B10932 U. S. TREASURY DEPT.
Treasury Department, February 12th, 1799. Circular to the collectors, naval officers and surveyors of the customs. [Philadelphia, 1799]
[2] p. 22.5 cm.
PPL; PPRF mp. 48983

B10933 U. S. TREASURY DEPT.
Treasury department, June 26th, 1799. Circular to the collectors of the customs. Sir, I herewith transmit a copy of a proclamation . . . by the President . . . [Philadelphia, 1799]
broadside 24.5 X 19.5 cm.
PPRF mp. 48984

B10934 U. S. TREASURY DEPT.
Treasury department. August 1, 1799. Circular to the collectors of the customs. Sir, In pursuance of authority . . . I have to inform you . . . that the cutters and other vessels . . . are hereafter to be distinguished from other vessels . . . [Philadelphia, 1799]
broadside 22.5 X 19 cm.
PPRF mp. 48985

B10935 U. S. WAR DEPT.
Articles of agreement, made on the day of Anno Domini, one thousand seven hundred and ninety-nine, between James M'Henry, secretary for the department of war . . . of the one part, and of the other part. This agreement . . . supply rations . . . [Philadelphia, 1799]
[3] p. 38 cm.
NjR

B10936 THE United States almanac, for the year . . . 1800 . . . By Abraham Shoemaker. Elizabeth-Town, Printed and sold by Shepard Kollock [1799]
[36] p. 17 cm.
Drake 5203
CtY (imperfect); NHi

B10937 THE United States almanack for . . . 1800 . . . By Eliab Wilkinson . . . Warren, Nathaniel Phillips [1799]
[24?] p.
Drake 12968
RWa

B10938 [UNITED States repository and New Hampshire register for 1800. By J. A. Harper. Portsmouth, Wm. Treadwell, 1799]

Brinley, no. 2466; Nichols p. 96
No copy traced mp. 48869

B10939 [DER verbesserte hoch-deutsche americanische Land und Staats Calender, auf das Jahr 1800. Friedrichstadt, M. Bärtgis, 1799?]
Bartgis's Federal Gazette, Feb. 5, 1800, announces "almanacs for the year 1800 for sale at this office."
Minick 546; Seidensticker p. 151
No copy known

B10940 VERMONT. GOVERNOR, 1797-1807
[Fast day proclamation, 1799]

McCorison 548
No copy known mp. 48986

B10941 VERMONT. TREASURER
State of Vermont, treasurer's office, June 2, 1799. To the sheriff of the county of Greeting . . . Middlebury, this day of June . . . 1799. [Rutland? 1799]
broadside 32 cm.
Cooley 504
VtHi mp. 48987

B10942 THE Virginia almanack, for the year . . . 1800 . . . Lynchburg, John Carter [1799]
[32] p. 16 cm.
Bear 129
ViL (2 leaves wanting at end) mp. 48988

B10943 [VON HAGEN, PETER ALBRECHT] 1781-1837
How tedious alas! are the hours . . . Boston, Printed & sold at P. A. von Hagen & cos. musical magazine; also by G. Gilfert, New York [1799]
[2] p. 30.5 cm. caption title
Below imprint: For the piano forte, German flute, or violin
Sonneck-Upton p. 194
MiU-C

B10944 WEATHERWISE'S almanac for 1800 . . . [Boston] Printed for the booksellers in Boston, and the country traders [1799]
[24] p.
Drake 3617
N

B10945 WEBSTER, NOAH, 1758-1843
An American selection of lessons in reading and speaking . . . Being the third part of A grammatical institute of the English language. The twelvth [sic] edition. New-York, Printed for E. Duyckinck, R. Magill, N. Judah, P. A. Mesier, C. Davis, J. Harrisson, and B. Gomez, 1799.
261, [2] p. 17 cm.
Skeel-Carpenter 487
Ct; N mp. 48989

B10946 WEBSTER, NOAH, 1758-1843
The American spelling book . . . The XVth Vermont edition. Bennington, Printed by [Anthony Haswell] the proprietor, for Ralph M. Pomeroy, 1799.
164 p. 17 cm. A-N^6 O^4
MWA mp. 48990

B10947 THE Western calendar, or, an almanack for . . . 1800 . . . Washington, John Colerick [1799]
[34] p.
Drake 10540
OHi

B10948 WHEATON,
Wheaton's jaundice bitters, secured to him by letters patent . . . Sold, wholesale and retail, by the patentee, Dedham . . . [n.p., 1799?]
broadside 29.5 X 22.5 cm.
5 testimonials, all dated 1799
MWA mp. 48991

B10949 WILBERFORCE, WILLIAM, 1759-1833
A practical view of the prevailing religious system of professed Christians . . . Boston, Printed by Manning & Loring, for Ebenezer Larkin, 1799.
300 p. 18 cm.
cf. Evans 36716
MWA; NhD mp. 48992

B10950 [WILKINSON, REBECCA]
Sermons to children. To which are added short hymns, suited to the subjects. By A Lady. Pittsfield: reprinted by Chester Smith. May, 1799.
96 p. 13 cm.
CtHi mp. 48993

B10951 WILLICH, ANTHONY FLORIAN MADINGER
Proposals for printing by subscription Lectures on diet and regimen . . . [Boston, Joseph Nancrede, 1799?]
7 p.
MBM mp. 48994

B10952 YARROW, THOMAS, 1778?-1841
An oration, delivered at Port-Elizabeth . . . New-Jersey, on the fourth of July, 1799 . . . Philadelphia, John Bioren [1799]
15 p. 21 cm.
NjR

B10953 A YEARLY tax of 140,000 dollars! A few plain facts, for the consideration of the electors of New-York! The Corporation of your City . . . framed a petition . . . [New York, 1799]
broadside 28 X 22.5 cm.
Dated April 30, 1799
NHi. Photostat: NN mp. 48995

1800

B10954 ABRAMS, HARRIET, 1760-1825
Crazy Jane . . . set to music by Miss Abrams. Philadelphia, G. Willig [1800?]
2 leaves. 32 cm. caption title
MiU-C mp. 48996

B10955 AN address to the citizens of North-Carolina, on the subject of the approaching elections. July, 1800. [Raleigh? Hodge & Boylan? 1800]
[2], 14 p. 21.5 cm.
Signed at end: A North-Carolina planter
NcU mp. 48997

B10956 ADVICE against swearing. [Philadelphia, 1800?]
4 p. 12mo
PPL mp. 48998

B10957 AESOPUS
Fables of Aesop and others . . . By Samuel Croxall . . . New-York, Printed by William Durell, for T. B. Jansen and Co., 1800.
63 p. illus. 10 cm.
PP mp. 48999

B10958 AFFECTING history of the dreadful distresses of Frederick Manheim's family . . . [Leominster?] Printed [by Adams & Wilder?] for Chapman Whitcomb [1800?]
39 p. 17 cm.
MWA mp. 49000

B10958a AKIN & HARRISON, firm, Philadelphia
Akin & Harrison, junr. No. 1, Johnson's Court, North Eighth-street, Philadelphia, having taken considerable pains to engrave an elegant design in remembrance of the late illustrious General Washington . . . January 24th, 1800. Philadelphia, Henry Tuckniss [1800]
broadside 4to
PPL mp. 49001

B10959 ALMANACK for 1801 . . . [Hartford] Printed by John Babcock [1800]
broadside
Drake 610
NHi

B10960 AN almanack, for the year . . . 1801 . . . By Joseph Osgood, Philom. Portsmouth, William Treadwell [1800]
[24] p. 16 cm.
DLC mp. 49128

B10961 AMBLER, JACQUELIN
A treatise on the culture of lucerne . . . Richmond, T. Nicolson [1800?]
9 p. 13 cm.
Davis 163
DLC mp. 49002

B10962 THE American ladies pocket book for the year 1800. Philadelphia, William Y. Birch, 1800.

BSA *Papers*, 54(1960): 66
No copy located mp. 49003

B10963 AMOSKEAG CANAL LOTTERY
Amoskeag Canal-lottery. The managers . . . present . . . the following scheme of the fouth [sic] class of said lottery . . . Exeter, New-Hampshire, August 5, 1800. Ephraim Robinson, Samuel Tinney, Nathan'l Parker, managers. [Exeter, N.H.? 1800]
broadside 30 X 18 cm.
MB mp. 49004

B10964 AN appeal to the temperance voters of this city: I have waited long . . . A temperance man and voter. [Providence, 1800]
broadside 38 X 25.5 cm.
In pencil on margin: "Nov. 1800 Providence R.I."
Alden 1655
RPB mp. 49005

B10965 ARABIAN NIGHTS
Arabian nights entertainments . . . Translated into French from the Arabian MSS. by Mr. Galland . . . and now into English from the Paris edition. Wilmington, Printed and sold by Bonsal & Niles.—also sold at their Book-store, Baltimore, 1800.
156 p. 14 cm.
New York Public 1277
NN mp. 49006

B10966 ARGUMENTS in favor of the ladies . . . [Leominster?] Printed [by Adams & Wilder?] for Chapman Whitcomb [1800?]
12 p. 20 cm.
MWA mp. 49007

B10967 [ARNE, MICHAEL] 1741-1784
Fresh and strong the breeze is blowing . . . Baltimore, Carr's Music store [1800?]
[2] p. 29 cm. caption title
Minick 553; Sonneck-Upton p. 54
DLC mp. 49008

B10968 AN astronomical diary . . . for the year . . . 1801 . . . Boston [1800]
[24] p. 8vo
By Seth Chandler
DLC mp. 49009

B10969 AN astronomical diary, calendar, or almanack for . . . 1801. By N. Strong. Hartford [1800]

Bates: Conn. almanacs p. 73
CtY (imperfect)

B10970 BALTIMORE. BOARD OF HEALTH
Resolved, That the following extracts . . . April 7, 1800. [Baltimore] John Hayes [1800]
broadside
MSaE. Photocopy: MWA mp. 49010

B10971 BAPTISTS. NEW HAMPSHIRE. NEW HAMPSHIRE ASSOCIATION
Minutes of the New-Hampshire Association, held . . . in Brentwood. Wednesday and Thursday, June 11th and 12th. 1800. Portsmouth, Charles Peirce, 1800.
12 p. 18 cm.
New York Public 1278
NN mp. 49011

B10972 BAPTISTS. NEW YORK. WARWICK ASSOCIATION
Minutes . . . May 27 & 28, 1800 . . . [n.p., 1800]
8 p.
Photocopy: MWA mp. 49012

B10973 BAPTISTS. NORTH CAROLINA. NEUSE BAPTIST ASSOCIATION
Minutes of the North-Carolina Neuse Baptist Association, holden at Meadow meeting-house, Green County. Raleigh, Joseph Gales [1800]
11 p. 23.5 cm. caption title
First reported meeting Oct. 11, 1800
NcWsW mp. 49013

B10974 BAPTISTS. VERMONT. SHAFTSBURY ASSOCIATION
Minutes of the Shaftsbury Association . . . June Fifth and Sixth, 1800. Troy, Robert Moffitt, 1800.
16 p.
NRAB. Photocopy: MWA mp. 49014

B10975 BARBAULD, ANNA LETITIA (AIKIN) 1743-1825
Evening tales . . . extracted from the works of Mrs. Barbauld and Mr. Aiken. Wilmington, Printed and sold by Peter Brynberg [1800?]
106, [1] p. 10.5 cm. $A-C^8$ $E-G^8$ H^6
Rosenbach-Ch 251
MWA; PP. Mrs. Edgar S. Oppenheimer, New York City (1962) mp. 49015

B10976 BARBAULD, ANNA LETITIA (AIKIN) 1743-1825
Hymns in prose for children . . . Bennington: Reprinted for Collier and Stockwell. M,CCC [i.e. 1800]
36 p.
MWA

B10977 BARRETT, MICHAEL
The reply of a Friend to justice, to a Friend to propriety, on the fate of the unfortunate Robbins . . . recommended to the perusal of American seamen. [Charleston, 1800]
16 p. caption title
Author mentioned on p. 1
Advertised in the *State Gazette and Daily Advertiser*, May 9, 1800
ScSp

B10978 BARTHELEMAW, —
Three favorite duetts for two performers on one piano forte . . . New York, Peter Erben [1800?]
9, [2] p. 32 cm.
MiU-C mp. 49016

B10979 BENNEVILLE, GEORGE DE, 1703–1793
A true and remarkable account of the life and trance of Dr. George de Benneville, late of Germantown . . . translated from the French of his own manuscript, to which is prefixed a recommendatory preface by the Rev. E. Winchester. Norristown, Printed and sold by David Sower, 1800.
35 p. 18.5 cm.
PHi mp. 49018

B10979a BENNEVILLE, GEORGE DE, 1703–1793
A true and remarkable account of the life and trance of Dr. George de Benneville . . . Norristown, Printed and sold by David Sower, 1800.
39 p.
Title and imprint identical with B10979, but completely different printing.—Edwin Wolf 2d
PPL

B10980 BIBLE
The Holy Bible abridged. New-York: Printed by W. Durell, for Evert Duyckinck, 1800.
108 p. illus. 14 cm.
cf. Evans 36953
NjP mp. 49020

B10981 BIBLE. O.T. PSALMS
Der Psalter des Königs . . . Lancaster, Christian Jacob Hütter [1800?]
376 p.
MWA mp. 49019

B10982 BIRCH, WILLIAM RUSSELL, 1755-1834
Philadelphia and New-York. William Birch thus informs the Public of his intentions to picture the two principal cities of North America . . . We the underneath subscribers, do agree to take . . . what we have named in this Subscription Paper . . . [Philadelphia? 1800?]
broadside 42 X 26.5 cm.
Only known copy bound with Evans 38259
RPJCB mp. 49021

B10983 BISHOP, ABRAHAM, 1763-1844
Connecticut Republicanism. An oration on the extent and power of political delusion. Delivered in New-Haven, on the evening preceding the public commencement, September 1800 . . . [New Haven?] 1800.
68, vii p. 23 cm. $[A]-I^4$ K^2
MWA; NjP (2 copies) mp. 49022

B10984 BLUMEN-Gärtlein inniger Seelen . . . Germantown, Michael Billmeyer, 1800.
576 p. 14 cm.
Historical Soc. of York Co. mp. 49023

B10985 BOSTON THEATRE (FEDERAL STREET)
By particular desire, and for the last time this season. Federal-Street Theatre. On Friday evening Nov. 14th. will be presented . . . Speed the Plough . . . [Boston, Young and Minns, 1800]

broadside 30 X 23 cm.
MB mp. 49024

B10986 BOSTON THEATRE (FEDERAL STREET)
Federal-Street-Theatre. Never acted in Boston. C. E. Whitlock respectfully informs the public that . . . he has postponed the theatrical entertainments, untill Thursday, January 1st, 1801. When a new comedy . . . Indiscretion . . . [Boston, Young and Minns, 1800]
broadside 30 X 24 cm.
MB mp. 49025

B10987 BOSTON THEATRE (FEDERAL STREET)
Federal-Street Theatre. On Friday evening, Nov. 28th. will be presented for the last time this season . . . The Castle Spectre . . . [Boston, Young and Minns, 1800]
broadside 30 X 23 cm.
MB mp. 49026

B10988 BOSTON THEATRE (FEDERAL STREET)
Federal-Street Theatre. On Monday evening, Dec. 8th. (For that night only) will be performed . . . the Mountaineers . . . [Boston, Young and Minns, 1800]
broadside 30 X 23 cm.
MB mp. 49027

B10989 BOSTON THEATRE (FEDERAL STREET)
Federal-Street-Theatre. On Monday evening, Dec. 22d. will be presented . . . The Grecian Daughter: or Liberty restored . . . [Boston, Young and Minns, 1800]
broadside 30 X 24 cm.
MB mp. 49028

B10990 BOSTON THEATRE (FEDERAL STREET)
Federal-Street Theatre. The unfavourable weather on the last representation . . . of Kotzebue's Stranger, having deprived a number . . . of seeing it, C. Whitlock, is induced to repeat it . . . Wednesday evening Nov. 26th . . . [Boston, Young and Minns, 1800]
broadside 30 X 23 cm.
MB mp. 49029

B10991 BOSTON THEATRE (FEDERAL STREET)
The last time of performing Bunker Hill, in Boston. On Friday evening, 7th February, will be performed . . . Bunker Hill; or, Death of Gen. Warren . . . [Boston, Young and Minns, 1800]
broadside 30 X 24 cm.
MB mp. 49030

B10992 BOSTON THEATRE (FEDERAL STREET)
Mr. S. Powell's benefit. On Friday evening, 14th March, will be presented . . . The Rival Queens; or, Alexander the Great . . . [Boston, Young and Minns, 1800]
broadside 30 X 24 cm.
MB mp. 49031

B10993 BOSTON THEATRE (FEDERAL STREET)
Mr. Villier's benefit. On Wednesday evening, March 26, 1800, will be presented . . . Next Door Neighbors . . . [Boston, Young and Minns, 1800]
broadside 30 X 23 cm.
MB mp. 49032

B10994 BOSTON THEATRE (FEDERAL STREET)
Never performed in America. Federal-Street Theatre. On Wednesday evening, 22d January, will be presented . . . Five Thousand a Year . . . [Boston, Young and Minns, 1800]
broadside 30 X 23 cm.
MB mp. 49033

B10995 BOSTON THEATRE (FEDERAL STREET)
Never performed in Boston and for this night only. For the benefit of Mr. Barrett. On Monday evening March 10th will be presented Shakespears . . . Henry the Eighth . . . [Boston, Young and Minns, 1800]
broadside 62 X 26 cm.
MB mp. 49034

B10996 BOSTON THEATRE (FEDERAL STREET)
Never performed in Boston. Federal-Street Theatre. On Wednesday evening, 19th February, will be presented . . . The Secret; or Partnership Dissolved . . . [Boston, Young and Minns, 1800]
broadside 30 X 24 cm.
MB mp. 49035

B10997 BOSTON THEATRE (FEDERAL STREET)
Not acted here this 4 years. On Wednesday evening, 8th January, will be presented . . . Wild Oats . . . [Boston, Young and Minns, 1800]
broadside 30 X 23 cm.
MB mp. 49036

B10998 BOSTON THEATRE (FEDERAL STREET)
Positively the last night for this season. For the benefit of Mr. Simpson & Miss Westray. On Wednesday next, Oct. 22d, 1800 will be presented . . . The Rivals . . . [Boston, Young and Minns, 1800]
broadside 30 X 23 cm.
MB mp. 49037

B10999 EIN B[rief] so von Gott selb[sten geschrieben, und zu] Magdeburg niedergelassen w[orden ist.] [n.p., 1800?]
broadside
PPL mp. 49038

B11000 THE brother's gift . . . The first Hudson edition. Hudson, Printed and sold by Ashbel Stoddard, 1800.
31 p. 9.5 cm.
NB mp. 49039

B11001 [BUCKLAND, JAMES]
Wonderful discovery of a hermit . . . Suffield: Printed [by Edward Gray] 1800.
11 p. 19.5 cm.
CtHi mp. 49040

B11002 [BUCK'S delight; or a pill to purge melancholy. New York, 1800?]

BSA *Papers*, 54(1960):66
No copy located mp. 49041

B11003 BY the arrival at Philadelphia of the ship Active, M'Dougal, in 29 days . . . operations of the . . . armies . . . present campaign . . . [New York, 1800]
broadside
Evidence for printing in B11046 (*infra*)
No copy known

B11004 CAREY, MATHEW, 1760-1839
Philadelphia, November 5, 1800. Sir, As you probably have to decide . . . our proposed edition of the laws of the State . . . request your attention to the following address . . . To the public . . . Jan. 17, 1800. Lancaster, Printed by W. & R. Dickson for Mathew Carey and John Bioren, 1800.
2 p. 25 cm.
First portion in script type
PHi; PPL

B11005 CAREY, MATHEW, 1760-1839
To the public. A proposition has been made to the Legislature . . . for a new edition of the laws . . . Mathew Carey. Philadelphia. Jan. 17, 1800. Philadelphia, Printed for Mathew Carey, 1800.
4 p. 21 cm.
PHi

B11006 CARMEN pro Americani incolumitate imperii, aliquantulum more carminis secularis Horatiani. [Philadelphia, 1800?]
3 p. 8vo caption title
PPL mp. 49042

B11007 CARPENTER, JOSIAH, 1762-1851
The importance of right views in matrimony, set forth in a sermon . . . March 19, 1800 . . . at the . . . marriage between Samuel G. Bishop . . . and Abigail Tuck . . . Gilmanton, 1800.
16 p. 17.5 cm.
New York Public 1279
NN mp. 49043

B11008 [CATALOGUE of a choice collection of well bound new books to be sold at auction . . . May 23, 1800, at Mr. David Fulton's. Baltimore, Thomas Dobbin? 1800]

Title from advertisement in the *Telegraphe*, May 23, 1800, which states, "Catalogues . . . may be had at this office."
Minick 564
No copy known mp. 49044

B11009 [THE celebrated tragedy, called the Regent . . . The profits . . . are to be applied toward . . . the erection of an academy in Hagers-Town. Tuesday, February 25, 1800, at Mr. Ragan's ball-room. Elizabeth (Hager's) Town, Thomas Grieves? 1800]
broadside
Advertised in the *Maryland Herald*, Feb. 20, 1800: "Playbills will be issued on Monday morning next."
Minick 621
No copy known

B11010 THE child's first primer; or, A new and easy guide to the invaluable science of A. B. C. Philadelphia, Printed for W. Jones, stationer, 1800.
28 p.
Heartman: Non-New-England 38
CtSoP mp. 49045

B11011 CHRISTLICHER Ha[us-see]gen, nebst der zwölf Stunden Ge[däch]tniss. [n.p., 1800?]
broadside
PPL mp. 49046

B11012 CLAIBORNE, WILLIAM CHARLES COLE, 1775-1817
(Circular). Philadelphia, April 21st. 1800. Dear Sir. Since my circular letter of the 23d of January . . . William Charles Cole Claiborne. [Philadelphia, 1800]
2 p. 19 X 23 cm.
DLC mp. 49047

B11013 CLAP, WILLIAM T
Catalogue of books, &c. for sale . . . at his bookstore, Fish-street, corner Proctor's Lane, Boston. [Boston, 1800?]
broadside 55 X 44 cm.
MB

B11014 CLARK, WILLIAM
A new mode of legislation . . . invented by Matthew Clay . . . [who] did present . . . a counterfeit petition, for clearing Banister river to Pittsylvania county . . . The subscriber submits to the public . . . whether any person . . . should be permitted to imitate his invention . . . William Clark. [Lynchburg? 1800?]
broadside 28 X 45 cm.
Vi. Photostat: ViU mp. 49048

B11015 COLE, JOHN, 1774-1855
[Episcopalian harmony. Baltimore, 1800]

Title from Metcalf: *American psalmody* p. 20
Probably advertised in the *Federal Gazette*, July 26, 1800, as "Now in the press . . . a new collection of church music . . . adapted to the service of the Protestant Episcopal church . . . By John Cole."
Minick 570
No copy known mp. 49049

B11016 CONNECTICUT. GENERAL ASSEMBLY
At a General Assembly of the State of Connecticut, holden at Hartford . . . May, 1800. The follwoing gentleman are chosen by the freemen, to stand in nomination . . . as Representatives in Congress . . . [Hartford, 1800]
broadside 34 X 20.5 cm.
CtHi mp. 49050

B11017 CONNECTICUT. GENERAL ASSEMBLY
At a General Assembly of the State of Connecticut, holden at New-Haven . . . October . . . 1800. The persons returned by the votes of the freemen . . . to stand in nomination for election . . . to this Assembly, are as follow . . . New-Haven, Thomas Green and Son [1800]
broadside 34 X 21 cm.
CtHi mp. 49051

B11018 CONNECTICUT. GOVERNOR, 1798-1809
By His Excellency Jonathan Trumbull . . . A proclamation. To call the attention of the people of this state to a . . . review of their moral and religious conduct . . . Given . . . at Lebanon . . . [Mar. 1, 1800] . . . Hartford, Hudson & Goodwin [1800]
broadside 47 X 27 cm.
CtHi mp. 49052

B11019 CONNECTICUT. GOVERNOR, 1798-1809
To the sheriff of the County of . . . Greeting . . . Given under my hand at Hartford . . . this 5th day of August . . . 1800 . . . Governor. [Hartford, 1800]
broadside ([2] p.) 33 X 20 cm.
Page [2]: At a General Assembly of the state . . . holden at Hartford . . . the second Thursday of May, 1798. [List of nominees]
Orders for calling a freemen's meeting
CtHi mp. 49053

B11020 CONNECTICUT EVANGELICAL MAGAZINE
[Circular.] Hartford, 180 Sir, The subscribers, editors of the *Connecticut Evangelical Magazine* . . . Nathan Strong, Nathan Perkins, Abel Flint. [Hartford, 1800]
broadside 33 X 19.5 cm.
Filled in for Apr. 12, 1800
RPJCB. Photostat: MWA

B11021 CONNECTICUT EVANGELICAL MAGAZINE
[Private.] Hartford, 180 Sir, Herwith are inclosed proposals for publishing monthly . . . *Connecticut*

Evangelical Magazine . . . Nathan Strong, Nathan Perkins, Abel Flint. [Hartford, 1800]
broadside 20 X 16.5 cm.
Filled in for Apr. 12, 1800
RPJCB. Photostat: MWA mp. 49054

B11022 CONNECTICUT GORE LAND COMPANY
To the honorable General Assembly, now in session, at New-Haven. The present claimants, and proprietors of the lands . . . commonly called the Gore . . . [at end] Dated at Hartford, October 10th, 1800. [Hartford, 1800]
[3] p. 33.5 cm.
CtHi mp. 49055

B11023 COURIER
Extra. Courier-office. Monday morning. Nov. 10. By an arrival at Philadelphia . . . The *Courier* of the 6th Oct. 1800 contains the following paragraph . . . [Philadelphia, 1800]
broadside 11 X 29.5 cm.
DLC

B11024 CROSWELL'S diary: or, The Catskill almanac for . . . 1801 . . . By Andrew Beers, Philom. Catskill, Printed and sold by M. & H. Croswell [1800]
[34+] p. 16.5 cm. [B-C]^4 D-E^4 F$^{2?}$
Probably 36 p., like almanacs of 1803, 1806, and 1808
ViU (wanting after p. [34]) mp. 49017

B11025 [DAVIDSON, ROBERT] 1750-1812
Geography epitomized . . . in verse . . . [Leominster?] Printed [by Adams & Wilder?] for Chapman Whitcomb [1800?]
60 p. 20 cm. A-E^6
Rosenbach-Ch 255; Wegelin 448
MWA. A. S. W. Rosenbach (1933) mp. 49056

B11026 [DEFOE, DANIEL] 1661?-1731
The life of Poll Flanders . . . [Leominster?] Printed [by Adams & Wilder?] for Chapman Whitcomb [1800?]
63 p. 19.5 cm. [A]^2 B-F^6
MWA; Leominster Public Lib. (final leaf wanting)
mp. 49057

B11027 DEM lieben und würdigen Bruder Friedrich Wilhelm von Marschall . . . Salisbury, Francis Coupee [1800?]
8 p. 18.5 cm.
Words for solo and choral music in honor of the pastor's 80th birthday; probably printed near end of 1800 to enable singers to prepare for the Feb. 5, 1801, lovefeast
NcWsM mp. 49058

B11028 DES blinden Rosshandlers Arzeney-Mittel. [Frederick, Md.] M. Märtgis [sic] [1800?]
broadside
PPL mp. 49061

B11029 DILWORTH, W. H.
The life of Alexander Pope . . . [Leominster?] Printed [by Adams & Wilder?] for Chapman Whitcomb [1800?]
76 p. 20 cm. A-F^6 G^2
MWA mp. 49064

B11030 EDWARDS, JONATHAN, 1703-1758
The justice of God in the damnation of sinners . . . Northampton, Printed by Daniel Wright & Co. for Simeon Butler [1800?]
143, [1] p. 15 cm.
Dated by Charles Evans
DLC; MNF; MWA; NNS mp. 49067

B11031 FAHRNY, PETER
Blutreinigung. Diese wird mit Quart kochend Wasser . . . [Hagerstown, 1800?]
broadside
PPL mp. 49068

B11032 THE famous history of Whittington and his cat . . . New-York, Printed by W. Durell, for Evert Duyckinck, 1800.
31 p. illus. 10 cm.
cf. Evans 37395
NB mp. 49193

B11033 THE famous history of Whittington and his cat . . . New-York, Printed by W. Durell, for Stephen Stephens, 1800.

cf. Amer. Art Auction cat. 4079 (1934) item 190; cf. Evans 37395
No copy traced mp. 49194

B11034 A FAREWELL to General Washington. [n.p., 1800?]
broadside 28.5 X 23.5 cm.
12 stanzas in double columns beginning: Farewell, great chief
MWiW-C mp. 49069

B11035 [FATHER Tammany's almanac for . . . 1801 . . . By Joshua Sharp . . . Philadelphia, Printed for John M'Culloch [1800]]
[36] p.
Drake 10548; imprint assumed from advertisements at end
PDoBHi (t.p. lacking)

B11036 FEDERAL meeting. At a large and respectable meeting of the inhabitants of the County of Cumberland, held . . . in Bridgetown, this day . . . preparatory to the ensuing Congress election--Joel Fithian, Esq. was chosen Chairman . . . Eli Elmer, Secretary . . . December 17, 1800. Address to the voters of the County of Cumberland . . . [at end] Philadelphia, C. P. Wayne [1800]
broadside 41 X 26 cm.
NjR

B11037 FLEET'S pocket almanack for the year . . . 1801 . . . Boston, Printed and sold by J. & T. Fleet [1800]
36 p. 14 cm.
Drake 3624
MB; MHi mp. 49070

B11038 FREEMASONS. VIRGINIA. NAPHTALI LODGE
Bye-laws of the Lodge of Naphtali, no. 56, Norfolk, Virginia. Norfolk, A. C. Jordan [1800]
[18] p. 18.5 cm.
McCoy 32
DSC; IaCrM mp. 49072

B11039 FREEMASONS. VIRGINIA. ROYAL ARCH CHAPTER
. . . Constitution and proceedings of the M. E. S. G. Royal Arch Chapter of Virginia: from its establishment in MMDCCC. Collated . . . by W. G. Lyford, 1800. [Norfolk? 1800?]
64 p. 18 cm.
McCoy 33
PPFM mp. 49073

B11040 [DER general Staatsbote. Friedrichstadt, M. Bartgis, 1800]

Bartgis's Federal Gazette, Feb. 5, 1800, carries this notice: "Advertisements for the English and German newspapers . . . duly inserted in either or both."
Minick 579
No copy known

B11041 A GIFT for children. Norwich: Printed and sold by John Sterry, 1800.
29 p. 12 cm.
d'Alté A. Welch, Cleveland (1962) mp. 49075

B11042 [DAS Glücks-rad in Frag und Antwort. Baltimore, S. Saur, 1800?]

Advertised on p. 96 of Das hundertjahrige calender, as "wird in wenigen Tagen in diesiger Buchdruckerey zu haben seyn."
Minick 581
No copy known mp. 49076

B11043 GUEST, HENRY
New-Brunswick, New-Jersey, February, 1800. Sir, Your very obliging letter of 25th November . . . to the superintendants of the constructions of vessels of war . . . [New Brunswick, 1800]
[2] p. fol.
PPL mp. 49077

B11044 HALL, JOHN
Philadelphia, May 20th, 1800. Sir, You are hereby summoned to attend at the Philadelphia gaol . . . [Philadelphia, 1800]
broadside
PPL mp. 49078

B11045 HARRISON, RALPH, 1748-1810
Rudiments of English grammar. A new edition, with additions and improvements by an eminent hand. Wilmington, James Wilson [1800?]
107, [1] p. 14 cm.
Hawkins 63; Huntington 547
Dated by Evald Rink
CSmH; DLC; DeWI mp. 45271

B11046 HARTFORD COURANT
Courant Office, Hartford, June 9, 1800. After our paper went to press last evening, we received a hand-bill printed in New-York last Friday . . . [Hartford, 1800]
25.5 X 22 cm.
CtHi

B11047 [HASWELL, ANTHONY] 1756-1816
[Elegiac poems. Bennington, A. Haswell, 1800?]
30+ p. 16 cm.
Four of the poems concern friends who died in 1790, 1797, 1800, and 1800
MWA (p. 1-8, and all after p. 30 wanting); VtBennM (p. 5-30 only) mp. 49080

B11048 HAY, JOHN, of York
An das Publicum. Geliebte Mitbürger. Ihr werdet ein Stück . . . John Hay, York, den 4ten October, 1800. [n.p., 1800]
broadside 20 X 34 cm.
DLC mp. 49081

B11049 HEATON, BENJAMIN, 1775-1800
The Columbian spelling-book . . . The second edition . . . Wrentham, Printed for the author: sold by E. Larkin, Boston, 1800.
144 p.
RPJCB mp. 49082

B11050 HERRICK, CLAUDIUS, 1775-1831
An oration, delivered at Deerfield, on the Fourth of July, 1800 . . . Greenfield, Thomas Dickman, 1800.
40 p. 21 cm.
cf. Evans 37612 (19 p.)
Pierce W. Gaines, Fairfield, Conn. (1964) mp. 49083

B11051 THE history of little Jack . . . Hartford, Printed by John Babcock [1800?]
31 p. incl. covers. 11.5 cm.
CtY; MWA mp. 49085

B11052 THE history of little King Pippin . . . New-York, Printed by Wm. Durell, for Cornelius Davis, 1800.
63 p. 10.5 cm.
d'Alté A. Welch, Cleveland (p. 31-63 wanting) mp. 49086

B11053 HOCH-DEUTSCHES Lutherisches ABC-und Namen-Büchlein, für Kinder . . . Philadelphia, Henrich Schweizer, 1800.
[30] p.
Ray Trautman (1960) mp. 49087

B11054 HOLMES, DAVID, 1770-1832
Dear Sir The indisposition with which I was afflicted during the last summer and fall . . . Your fellow citizen, D. Holmes. Philadelphia, 13th May, 1800. [Philadelphia, 1800]
[2] p., blank leaf. 23 cm.
Pierce W. Gaines, Fairfield, Conn. (1964) mp. 49088

B11055 THE house that Jack built . . . New-York, Printed by W. Durell, for Thomas B. Jansen & Co., 1800.
31 p. incl. covers. 10.5 cm.
MWA (poor) mp. 49090

B11056 HUNT, AUGUSTINE
Hunt's mite at the eleventh hour, corrected and somewhat improved by Brundydge. [New York?] Printed for the author. 1800.
27 p. 23 cm.
Signed by Augustine Hunt, p. [3]
Introductory note by author (p. [2]) ends: Union Society, State of New-York
NjR

B11057 HURLBURT, OZIAS
Poetical pieces, religious & descriptive . . . Stockbridge, Printed for the author, by H. Willard [1800?]
23 p. 24 cm.
MWA mp. 49091

B11058 HUTCHINS improved: being an almanack and ephemeris . . . for . . . 1801. By Andrew Beers . . . New-York, Printed for and sold by John Tiebout [1800]
[36] p.
Drake 6119
MnU

B11059 HUTCHINS improved: being an almanack and ephemeris . . . for . . . 1801. By Andrew Beers. Poughkeepsie, Printed for Nicholas Power [1800]
[36] p.
Drake 6120
NN

B11060 HUTCHINS improved: being an almanack and ephemeris . . . for . . . 1801. By Andrew Beers. Poughkeepsie, Printed for Power & Southwick [1800]
[36] p.
Drake 6121
CtY; MWA; N; NP; NPV

B11061 DER im Walde sitzende schlafende Böhmische Bauer . . . Trauergesang . . . [n.p., 1800?]
broadside
PPL mp. 49092

B11062 JEMMY and Nancy . . . [New York? ca. 1800?]
broadside 21.5 X 54 cm.
Dated from typography
N

B11063 JESS, ZACHARIAH
The American tutor's assistant . . . Second edition corrected and revised . . . Wilmington, Printed and sold by Bonsal and Niles. Also sold at their bookstore . . . Baltimore, 1800.
[4], 204 p. 17 cm.
Hawkins 126; Karpinski p. 123
DeWI; MWA (very imperfect); PHi mp. 49093

B11064 JOHNSON, GERSHOM
[Circular.] To the owners of landed property, bounded by, or near the Wissahickon Road. Gentlemen, The present impossibility of assistance . . . for turnpiking the roads . . . Philadelphia, June 20, 1800 . . . [Philadelphia, 1800]
broadside
PPL mp. 49094

B11065 [JOHNSON, RICHARD] 1734-1793
The history of Tommy Careless . . . New-York, Printed by W. Durell, for Evert Duyckinck, 1800.
31 p. illus. 10 cm.
NB (covers wanting) mp. 49095

B11066 [JOHNSON, RICHARD] 1734-1793
The history of Tommy Careless . . . New-York, Printed by W. Durell, for J. Harrisson, 1800.
31 p. illus. 10 cm.
Miss Elizabeth Ball, Muncie, Ind. (1964) mp. 49096

B11067 [JOHNSON, RICHARD] 1734-1793
The history of Tommy Careless . . . New-York, Printed by W. Durell, for Thomas B. Jansen, 1800.
31 p. illus. 10 cm.
d'Alté A. Welch, Cleveland (front. and p. 31 wanting) mp. 49097

B11068 THE jolly fisherman. To which is added, The honest fellow. The request. The frizure; or the jolly barber. Dermot and Shelah. The Carlow lass. [Philadelphia] Printed for the Flying Stationers, 1800.
8 p. 12mo
PPL mp. 49098

B11069 JUVENAL poems; or the alphabet in verse . . . Hartford, John Babcock, 1800.
28, [3] p. incl. covers. 11.5 cm.
CtHi (covers wanting); MWA. d'Alté A. Welch, Cleveland (p. [3-4] wanting) mp. 49099

B11070 KIDD, WILLIAM, 1645?-1701
The dying words of Captain Kidd, a noted pirate . . . Printed & sold at New-London [1800?]
broadside 37 X 18.5 cm.
NHi mp. 49100

B11071 LADY Washington's lamentation . . . When my country's sad millions in sorrow are drowned, let me mingle the current . . . [n.p., 1800?]
broadside 29 X 14 cm.
CtHi mp. 49101

B11072 LADY Wasington's [!] lamentation . . . Providence [ca. 1800]
broadside 4to
A doggerel poem on Washington's death
Robert K. Black, Montclair, N. J. (1964) mp. 49102

B11073 [LA NEUVILLE, J]
Le dernier cri de St. Domingue, et des colonies . . . Philadelphie, Thomas & William Bradford, 1800.
[4], 38, [1] p. 30 cm.
Dedication signed: M. J. La Neuville
DeGE; PHi mp. 49103

B11074 LANG, EDWARD S
Medicine chests: with suitable directions: Prepared by Edward S. Lang at his shop in Essex-Street . . . [Salem, 1800?]
[24] p. 18 cm.
Not Evans 38455, also at MSaE
MSaE mp. 49105

B11075 LAW, ANDREW, 1748-1821
The musical primer . . . newly revised and improved . . . Third edition. [Cheshire, 1800?]
iv, [7]-48 p. obl.
MWA mp. 49106

B11076 LENEGAN THEATRE, LANCASTER, PA.
By desire of Governor M'Kean, who means to honor the theatre with his presence, this evening, January 2, 1800 . . . Lancaster, William Hamilton [1800]
broadside 19.5 X 16 cm.
PPRF mp. 49104

B11077 THE life and death of Tom Thumb, the little giant. Together with some curious anecdotes respecting Grumbo . . . Hartford, John Babcock, 1800.
31 p. illus. 11 cm.
Hamilton 190
Ct (1st and last pages wanting); NjP mp. 49107

B11078 LINES, sung at Haverhill, on the twenty second day of February, 1800: in memory of . . . George Washington . . . [Haverhill, Mass.? 1800?]
broadside 25 X 20 cm.
Printed on silk
MB; MWA (not traced 1966) mp. 49108

B11079 LINLEY, THOMAS, 1732-1795
The woodman, written by Wm. Pearce . . . music by Mr. Linley . . . Philadelphia, Printed and sold by R. Shaw [1800?]
[2] p. 30.5 cm. caption title
Sonneck-Upton p. 477
MiU-C

B11080 THE little innocent porcupine hornet's nest. United States of America: Printed for the author [1800]
35 p. 8vo
PHi

B11081 [LOUVET DE COUVRAY, JEAN BAPTISTE] 1760-1797
Interesting history of Baron de Lovzinski . . . Hudson, Printed and sold by Ashbel Stoddard [1800?]

117 p. 14 cm.
MWA mp. 49109

B11082 MAGDALEN SOCIETY, PHILADELPHIA
Advice to a Magdalen. [Philadelphia, 1800]
broadside
PPL mp. 49110

B11083 MALL, THOMAS
A short collection of the history of the martyrs . . . [Leominster?] Printed [by Adams & Wilder?] for Chapman Whitcomb [1800?]
47 p. 20 cm.
MWA mp. 49111

B11084 MARTIN and James; or, The reward of integrity . . . Philadelphia, Printed for Mathew Carey, 1800.
64 p. illus. 10 cm.
Mrs. A. Ward France, Wyncote, Pa. (1962) mp. 49112

B11085 MASSACHUSETTS. GOVERNOR, 1800-1807
Commonwealth of Massachusetts. To the selectmen of the town of in the fourth western district: Greeting: Whereas the Constitution . . . vacancies in Congress . . . Given . . . at Boston . . . [Sept. 18, 1800] . . . These certify, that the returns from the several towns . . . [Boston, 1800]
broadside 38 X 23.5 cm.
MWA mp. 49114

B11086 MASSACHUSETTS. GOVERNOR, 1800-1807
Commonwealth of Massachusetts. To the selectmen of the town of in the third middle district: Greeting: Whereas the Constitution . . . vacancies in Congress . . . Given . . . at Boston . . . [July 10, 1800] . . . [Boston, 1800]
broadside 39.5 X 24.5 cm.
MWA mp. 49113

B11087 MASSACHUSETTS. LAWS
. . . Acts and laws. Passed by the General Court . . . November . . . 1800. [Boston, Young and Minns, 1800]
p. 439-141 [i.e. 441] 35 cm.
New York Public 1280
NN mp. 49115

B11088 MASSACHUSETTS. MILITIA
Mr. You are hereby notified and warned to appear at the Meeting House, West Parish; – on Tuesday the 6th day of May next . . . with your gun . . . for the express purpose of examination . . . Isaac How, Captain. Haverhill, April 22d, 1800. [Haverhill, 1800]
broadside 11 X 9.5 cm.
MHaHi

B11089 MATHER, COTTON, 1662-1728
The Gospel of justification . . . Wilmington: Printed by Bonsal & Niles, for Molleston Correy [1800?]
60 p.
Holmes: Cotton Mather 115-C
MB mp. 49116

B11089a [MATHIAS, THOMAS JAMES] 1754?-1835
Pursuits of literature. Philadelphia: Printed by H. Maxwell, for J. Nancrede, Boston; and A. Dickins, and J. Ormrod, Philadelphia, 1800.
481 p. 8vo
cf. Evans 37939
DLC; PHi

B11090 MOORE, EDWARD, 1712-1757
Fables for the female sex . . . Printed in Bennington, by Anthony Haswell, for the booksellers in Albany, New York, &c. [1800?]
48 p. 15 cm.
McCorison 575
MH mp. 49117

B11091 MOTHER Goose's melody . . . Boston, Printed by S. Hall, 1800.
95 p. illus. 10 cm.
CtHi; MB (imperfect) mp. 49118

B11092 [THE New-England calendar and ephemeris for 1801 . . . Newport, Printed by Oliver Farnsworth for Jacob Richardson, 1800]

Alden 1652; Hammett p. 14
No copy known; description conjectured from Hammett mp. 49119

B11093 THE New-England primer improved . . . Boston, John W. Folsom [1800?]
[64] p. 19.5 cm.
Dated by MHi
Huntington 736
CSmH; MHi (imperfect) mp. 45784

B11094 NEW YORK. COURT FOR THE TRIAL OF IMPEACHMENTS AND THE CORRECTION OF ERRORS
In the Court for the Trial of Impeachments, and the Correction of Errors, by appeal from the Court of Chancery. Louis Le Guen vs. Isaac Gouverneur and Peter Kemble. Case on the part of the appellant . . . [New York? 1800?]
13 p. 21 cm.
cf. Evans 38080
NNU-L

B11095 THE nightingale; or Rural songster: in two parts . . . sentimental songs . . . patriotic songs . . . Dedham, H. Mann, 1800.
125, [3] p. 14 cm.
MB; MWA mp. 49123

B11096 [THE North-Carolina almanack, for the year . . . 1801 . . . Salisbury, F. Coupee, 1800]
[44] p. 16 cm.
DLC (t.p. wanting) mp. 49124

B11097 A NUMBER OF CITIZENS OF THE FOURTH DISTRICT
[Hand bill. Hagerstown? 1800?]
broadside
To the freemen of the Fourth district, by Thomas Johnson (Evans 37711), is a reply to "the piece under the signature of 'A number of citizens of the Fourth district' . . . circulated in hand bills."
Minick 618
No copy known mp. 49125

B11098 NURSE Truelove's New Year's gift . . . Third Worcester edition. Worcester, Printed and sold by Isaiah Thomas, 1800.
60 p. illus. 10 cm.
d'Alté A. Welch, Cleveland (1962) mp. 49126

B11099 OSGOOD, DAVID, 1747-1822
A discourse delivered December 29, 1799 . . . Samuel Hall, No. 53 Cornhill, Boston. 1800.
19 p. 23 cm.
Tailpiece "Finis": p. 19
cf. Evans 38170, without the address
Pierce W. Gaines, Fairfield, Conn. (1964) (uncut) mp. 49127

B11100 PAISIELLO, GIOVANNI, 1741-1816
For tenderness form'd . . . For the piano forte or harp. Composed by Paesiello. Philadelphia, Printed & sold by R. Shaw [ca. 1800]
[2] p. 30.5 cm. caption title
Includes an arrangement for German flute
Sonneck-Upton p. 144; cf. Evans 26720
MiU-C

B11101 PARISMAS, THOMAS
The history of Capt. Thomas Parismas . . . [Leominster?] Printed [by Adams & Wilder?] for Chapman Whitcomb [1800?]
33 p. 20 cm.
MWA mp. 49084

B11102 [PENN, JAMES] 1727-1800
The farmer's daughter, of Essex . . . By William Pen [i.e., James Penn]. [Leominster?] Printed [by Adams & Wilder?] for Chapman Whitcomb [1800?]
18 p. 19 cm.
Shaw-Shoemaker 9112
MWA mp. 49130

B11103 PENNSYLVANIA
Report. The Committee to whom was referred the statements of the Comptroller-general and Register-general, on Mr. Dallas's accounts . . . March 8, 1800. [Lancaster, 1800]
2 p.
PPL mp. 49131

B11104 PENNSYLVANIA. RECEIVER-GENERAL
The Receiver-general most respectfully begs leave to submit the following report to the Governor of the Commonwealth . . . January 6th, 1800. [Lancaster, 1800]
3 p. fol.
PPL mp. 49132

B11105 PENNSYLVANIA. REGISTER-GENERAL'S OFFICE
Report of the Register-general of the state of finances of Pennsylvania, from the first of January to the thirtieth of November, 1800 . . . Lancaster, Francis Bailey, 1800.
21 p. 34 cm.
Signed: Samuel Bryan; and dated December 8, 1800
Included in 1801 by Shaw-Shoemaker
MiU-C

B11106 PENNSYLVANISCHER Calender auf . . . 1801 . . . York, Salomon Mayer [1800]
[40] p.
Drake 10561
PPi

B11107 PERCY, JOHN
The schedule referred to in these letters patent . . . containing a description, in the words of the said John Percy himself, of his improvement, being a new mode of dying a blue colour . . . John Percy. March 1, A.D. 1800. [n.p., 1800]
broadside 17 X 22 cm.
New York Public 1282
NN mp. 49133

B11108 [PERRAULT, CHARLES] 1628-1703
Cinderella or the little glass slipper. Litchfield, T. Collier [1800?]
29 p. illus. 9 cm.
Trumbull: Supplement 1981
MiU-C mp. 49134

B11109 PETITION to the Senate and House of Representatives of the United States, in Congress assembled . . . [Philadelphia] Z. Poulson [1800?]
8 p. 22 cm.
PHi mp. 49135

B11110 PLEYEL, IGNAZ JOSEPH, 1757-1831
Pleyel's German hymn, with variations. New York, P. Erben [1800?]
4 p. 32 cm. caption title
MiU-C mp. 49136

B11111 A PRESENT to children . . . [Leominster?] Printed [by Adams & Wilder?] for Chapman Whitcomb [1800?]
12 p. 17.5 cm.
ICN; MWA mp. 49138

B11112 PRICE, LAURENCE, 1628-1680
A key to open Heaven's gate: or A ready path way to lead to Heaven . . . Springfield (Massachusetts), T. Ashley, 1800.
10 p. 18.5 cm.
New York Public 1283
NN mp. 49139

B11113 PRIESTLEY, JOSEPH, 1733-1804
The doctrine of phlogiston established, and that of the composition of water refuted . . . Northumberland, Printed for the author by A. Kennedy, 1800.
xv, 90, [2] p. 8vo
NjP; PPL mp. 49140

B11114 PROSPECTUS of a new weekly paper submitted to men of affluence, men of liberality, and men of letters . . . The Port Folio. [Philadelphia, Asbury Dickins, 1800]
Issued by Joseph Dennie
broadside 26.5 X 23 cm.
MWA; PHi mp. 49060

B11115 THE puzzling cap: a choice collection of riddles, in familiar verse. By Master Billy Wiseman . . . New-York, Printed by William Durell for Thomas B. Jansen & Co., 1800.
31 p. illus. 10 cm.
d'Alté A. Welch, Cleveland (p. 23-24, 27-31 wanting)
mp. 49141

B11116 RELIEF FIRE SOCIETY, NEWBURYPORT, MASS.
Articles and regulations of the Relief Fire-Society, in Newburyport; formed . . . 1775 . . . [p. 8] 1800, June. Present member's names . . . [Newburyport, 1800]
8 p. 16 cm.
MWA mp. 49121

B11117 THE remarkable history of Augi; or, A picture of true happiness . . . [Boston?] Massachusetts, Printed for the Booksellers [1800?]
31 p. front. 10 cm.
"The dreamer": p. 28-31
Text same as Worcester, 1796 ed.
MWA (p. 1-6 wanting). Microfilm: Forest Bowe (NYC)

B11118 A REMARKABLE narrative of the captivity and escape of Mrs. Frances Scott . . . of Washington County, Virginia. [Leominster?] Printed [by Adams & Wilder?] for Chapman Whitcomb [1800?]
16 p. 12 cm.
ICN; MWA mp. 49143

B11119 ROSE, JOHANNES
Mineralisches Pferde-Pulver. [Lancaster, 1800?]
broadside
PPL mp. 49144

B11120 [SCOTT, SARAH (ROBINSON)] 1723-1795
The man of real sensibility . . . [Leominster, Mass.?] Printed [by Adams & Wilder] for Chapman Whitcomb [1800?]
42 p.
MWA mp. 49145

B11121 SHIELD, WILLIAM, 1748-1829
Distress me with these tears no more . . . Philadelphia, Printed and sold by R. Shaw [ca. 1800]
[2] p. 30.5 cm. caption title
Includes an arrangement for German flute
Sonneck-Upton p. 110
MiU-C

B11122 A SHORT address to the voters of Delaware . . . Kent County, Sept. 24, 1800. A Christian Federalist. [Dover? W. Black? 1800]
7 p. 23 cm.
Hawkins 138
DLC mp. 49147

B11123 SOLOMON, SAMUEL, 1780-1818
A guide to health; or, Advice to both sexes: with an essay on a certain disease, seminal weakness . . . Fifty-second edition. Stockport, Printed, for the author, by J. Clarke . . . and sold by Robert Bach, New-York [1800]
270 p. port. 12mo
PPL mp. 49148

B11123a SOME account of a remarkable vision which a gentleman had in Germany, and who is now an inhabitant of Pennsylvania . . . [n.p., 1800?]
8 p. 8vo
PHi

B11124 THE spendthrift clapt into limbo. To which are added, Love in my pocket. The modern beau. One bottle more. [Philadelphia] 1800.
8 p. 12mo
PPL mp. 49149

B11125 SPICER, -----
Spicer's pocket companion; or, The young Mason's monitor . . . To which is annexed, a collection of Masonic songs, and others, with notes. Part Second. Printed at Northampton, by Andrew Wright.—For the compiler. [1800]
31, [1] p.
Sabin 89428
CtHi; CtY

B11126 [STORACE, STEPHEN] 1763-1796
No more I'll heave the tender sigh. Sung by Mrs. Crouch . . . Philadelphia, Printed by R. Shaw [ca. 1800]
[2] p. 30.5 cm. caption title
Sonneck-Upton p. 299
MiU-C

B11127 SURR, THOMAS SKINNER, 1770-1847
George Barnwell, a novel, in two volumes. Phila.: Printed at the Office of "The True American." 1800.
2 v. in 1 ([2], 167; [2], 185 p.)
Norman Kane, Lansdowne, Pa. (1962)
mp. 49150

B11128 TAYLOR, JEREMY, 1613-1667
The lives, travels & sufferings of the holy Evangelists . . . [Leominster?] Printed [by Adams & Wilder] for Chapman Whitcomb [1800?]
48 p. 18 cm.
MWA mp. 49151

B11129 THIS Bible, was presented to the pulpit of the second Presbyterian Church, in Newbury-Port, on the 1st of January, 1800, by the following young gentlemen and ladies . . . [Newburyport, 1800]
broadside 33.5 X 19 cm.
MWA mp. 49122

B11130 THOMPSON, JOHN
The lost and undone son of perdition . . . Judas Iscariot . . . [Leominster?] Printed [by Adams & Wilder?] for Chapman Whitcomb [1800?]
12 p. 19.5 cm.
MWA; RPJCB mp. 49152

B11131 THURBER, BENJAMIN
Benjamin Thurber, at his store . . . keeps . . . for sale, a large assortment of broadcloths . . . Providence. [1800?]
broadside 14 X 11.5 cm.
Alden 1706
NN mp. 49153

B11132 TO the electors of Pennsylvania. And particularly of those counties in which senators for the State Legislature are to be voted for . . . A Native Pennsylvanian. [Carlisle? 1800]
7 p. 8vo
PHi

B11133 TO the honorable speaker, and the rest of the honorable members of the House of delegates of Virginia. The petition of sundry inhabitants of the county of sheweth . . . [Alexandria? 1800?]
broadside 31 cm.
A petition respecting the opening of a road from Alexandria to Norman's Ford
Vi mp. 49180

B11134 TO the honorable the President, and the other Members of the Senate, of . . . South-Carolina. The memorial . . . [Columbia? 1800?]
fold. sheet 36 X 15 cm.
Petitions for legislation against duelling
ScU

B11135 TOMMY Trip's history of beasts in verse and prose . . . To which is added, The story of little Pheebe [sic] and her lamb . . . New-York, Printed and sold by Wm. Durell, 1800.
31 p. illus. 10.5 cm.
PP mp. 49154

B11136 THE town and country almanac calculated for Pennsylvania, Delaware, Maryland . . . for the year . . . 1801 . . . Baltimore Printed for Thomas, Andrews & Butler [1800]
[48] p. 16.5 cm.
Drake 2293
KyHi

B11137 THE town and country almanac, for . . . 1801 . . . Calculated to the meridian of the Middle States . . . [Baltimore?] Printed for and sold by Michael & John Conrad, Market-Street, Baltimore [1800]
[48] p.
Drake 2292
NHi

B11138 THE town and country almanack for . . . 1801. By Abraham Weatherwise. Boston, Printed for the booksellers [1800]
[24] p.
Drake 3628
DLC; MB; MHi; MWA (2 varieties); NN; WHi

B11139 TRACY'S New-York and Vermont almanack for . . . 1801. By Andrew Beers. Lansingburgh, Gardiner Tracy [1800]
[36] p.
Drake 6128
NIC

B11140 A TRIBUTE to the memory of George Washington. [filet] My friends attend while I unfold . . . [n.p., 1800?]
broadside 31 X 17.5 cm.
NjR (glued onto a board)

B11141 THE trifle-hunter; or, The adventures of Prince Bonbennin. A Chinese tale . . . Printed at Providence [ca. 1800]
32 p. illus. 10.5 cm.
Dated by d'Alté A. Welch on the basis of comparison of breaks in the rule borders of various cuts; a "First Newport edition" (Alden 1647a) appeared in 1799
Ruth E. Adomeit, Cleveland (1966)

B11142 TUCKER & THAYER, firm, Boston
Tucker & Thayer, No. 19 Cornhill, Boston import and sell wholesale & retail . . . English & India goods. [Boston, ca. 1800?]
broadside 19 X 11.5 cm.
Lower half of a handwritten bill
Dated by John Alden
MSaE mp. 49155

B11143 TULLOH, ANDREW
To farmers. Large tracts of land in Loyalsock Township, Lycoming County, are now parcelled off in lots for settlement . . . Williamsport, September 23, 1800. [Northumberland, 1800]
broadside
PPL mp. 49156

B11144 U. S. COMMISSIONERS FOR THE RELIEF OF THE REFUGEES FROM THE BRITISH PROVINCES
Letter from the commissioners appointed pursuant to the act entitled "An act for the relief of the refugees from the British provinces of Canada and Nova Scotia." 8th May, 1800 . . . [Philadelphia, 1800]
15 p. 8vo
PPL mp. 49157

B11145 U. S. CONGRESS. SENATE. COMMITTEE TO WHOM WAS REFERRED THE BILL PROVIDING FOR THE SALE OF LANDS NORTHWEST OF THE OHIO
Report of the committee, to whom was referred the bill, entitled "An act . . . providing for the sale of the lands of the United States . . ." Printed by order of the Senate . . . April 19th, 1800. [Philadelphia, 1800]
8 p. 23 cm.
New York Public 1284
NN mp. 49164

B11146 U. S. LAWS
3d March, 1800. Read the first and second time, and committed to a Committee fo the whole House, On Wednesday next. A bill to enable the President . . . to borrow money . . . [Philadelphia? 1800]
2 p. 34.5 cm.
RPJCB mp. 49159

B11147 U. S. LAWS
21st March, 1800, read the first and second time . . . A bill to authorize the President . . . to accept for the United States, a cession of jurisdiction of the Territory . . . commonly called the Western Reserve of Connecticut . . . [Philadelphia, 1800]
3 p. fol.
PPL

B11148 U. S. LAWS
26th March, 1800. Read the first and second time, and committed to a Committee of the whole House on Monday next. A bill making appropriation for the support of government for the year 1800 . . . [Philadelphia, 1800]
9 p. 34 cm.
NHi mp. 49161

B11149 U. S. LAWS
31st March, 1800. Read the first and second time, and committed to a Committee of the whole House tomorrow. An act prescribing the mode of deciding disputed elections of President and Vice-President . . . [Philadelphia, 1800]
6 p. 34.5 cm.
Printed as a bill, with the lines of each section separately numbered
New York Public 1288
NN mp. 49162

B11150 U. S. LAWS
15th April, 1800. Read the first and second time, and committed to a Committee of the whole House, on Thursday next. A bill in addition to the act intituled "An act to prohibit . . . the slave trade . . ." . . . [Philadelphia, 1800]
4 p. 34 cm.
NHi mp. 49160

B11151 U. S. LAWS
An act to establish a General Stamp-Office. [Colophon] City of Washington, Way & Groff [1800]
8 p. 20 cm. caption title
"Approved, April 23, A.D. 1800."
New York Public 1285
NN mp. 49165

B11152 U. S. LAWS
Acts passed at the second session of the Fifth Congress . . . Philadelphia, Printed by John Bioren, for Thomas Dobson, 1800.
1 p.l., [51]-240, vii p. 20 cm.
New York Public 1286
NN mp. 49166

B11153 U. S. LAWS
Amendments of the Senate to the bill intituled "An act providing for the enumeration of the inhabitants . . ." 6th February, 1800. Referred to the Committee of Ways and Means. [Published by order of the House of Representatives.] [Philadelphia, 1800]
4 p. 23 cm.
New York Public 1287
NN mp. 49163

B11154 U. S. LAWS
A bill to provide for the execution of the twenty-seventh article of the Treaty of Amity . . . with Great Britain.

[As amended in Committee of the whole House, on the 2d of April 1800.] . . . [Philadelphia, 1800]
3 p. 33.5 cm.
NHi mp. 49158

B11155 U. S. LAWS
Law to establish an uniform system of bankruptcy, throughout the United States. Passed the fifth day of April, 1800. New-York: Printed for Samuel Campbell [1800]
44 p. 13 cm.
CtHi mp. 49167

B11156 U. S. TREASURY DEPT.
[Circular.] District of Connecticut, Supervisor's-Office, August 26th, 1800. Sir, Whenever any collector of the direct tax . . . To Surveyors of the Revenue. [Hartford? 1800]
broadside 33 X 20 cm.
CtHi mp. 49168

B11157 U. S. TREASURY DEPT.
(Circular.) Supervisor's Office, Providence, May 5th, 1800. Gentlemen, A variety of causes . . . [Providence? 1800]
[3] p. 39 cm.
RNHi. Photostat: MWA mp. 49169

B11158 U. S. TREASURY DEPT.
Circular to the collectors of the customs, Treasury Department, Washington, Sept. 27, 1800 . . . By John Adams . . . a proclamation . . . [Washington, 1800]
2 p.
PPL mp. 49170

B11159 U. S. TREASURY DEPT.
Connecticut, Supervisor's-Office, March 1800. [Circular to Surveyors.] Sir, The following Treasury instructions . . . received . . . from William Miller, Esquire, Commissioner of the revenue . . . [Hartford? 1800]
broadside 33 X 20.5 cm.
CtHi mp. 49171

B11160 U. S. TREASURY DEPT.
Exports of the United States, from the first of October 1798, to the thirtieth of September 1799 . . . February 7th. 1800. Joseph Nourse, Register. [Philadelphia? 1800]
fold. table 44 cm.
MiU-C mp. 49172

B11161 U. S. TREASURY DEPT.
Form C. District of Massachusetts. To Surveyor of the Revenue In pursuance of an act . . . 14th July, 1798 . . . Given under my hand at the day of [Boston? 1800?]
broadside ([2] p.) 39 X 24 cm.
Filled in for Boston, March 24, 1800
MWA mp. 49173

B11162 U. S. TREASURY DEPT.
A statement exhibiting the amount of drawback on the sundry articles exported . . . in the years 1796, 1797, 1798 . . . [Philadelphia? 1800]
fold. table 24 cm.
Signed: February 5th, 1800
MiU-C mp. 49174

B11163 U. S. TREASURY DEPT.
Supervosor's Office, Massachusetts District, Boston, March 24, 1800. Sir, Sundry papers and books . . . [Boston, 1800]
[3] p. 39 cm.
MWA (3 copies) mp. 49175

B11164 U. S. TREASURY DEPT.
Supervisor's Office, Massachusetts District, Boston, October 24, 1800. Sir, I some months since wrote to the Treasury Department for final directions . . . [Boston, 1800]
[4] p. 39 cm.
Page [3]: Copies and extracts of letters received by J. Jackson . . .
Pages [2] and [4] blank
MWA (2 copies) mp. 49176

B11165 U. S. TREATIES
[Treaty between the French Republic and the United States. Baltimore, Yundt and Brown, 1800]
broadside
Title from notice in the *Telegraphe*, Dec. 25, 1800: "The intimation given yesterday in the handbill from . . . the *Federal Gazette*, that an incorrect copy of the treaty . . . had come to hand . . ."
Minick 586
No copy known mp. 49177

B11166 THE United States almanac for . . . 1801. Harrisburg, Printed for John Wyeth [1800]
[36] p.
Drake 10567
PHi (17 l.)

B11167 [THE United States almanac for . . . 1801. Wilmington [1800]]

Drake 1411
No copy known

B11168 UNITED STATES THEATRE, WASHINGTON, D. C.
. . . On Monday evening, Sept. 1st 1800 will be presented a new comedy . . . The Secret; or, Partnership Dissolved . . . To which will be added, a favourite farce, called The Positive Man; or, Sailors on Shore . . . [Washington, Way & Groff, 1800]
broadside 44 X 27 cm.
DLC mp. 49183

B11169 UNIVERSITY OF PENNSYLVANIA
List of the estate and property of the University of Pennsylvania. December 31st, 1799 . . . [Philadelphia? 1800?]
4 p. 8vo caption title
Signed at end: Edward Fox, Treasurer. December 31st, 1799
Adams: Pennsylvania 73
PU

B11170 [DER verbesserte hoch deutsche americanische Land-und Staats Calendar, auf das Jahr 1801. Friedrich-Stadt, M. Bärtgis, 1800]

Minick 628; Seidensticker p. 154
No copy known

B11171 VERMONT GAZETTE
Bennington, March 24, 1800. Sir, The establishment of the press is progressing desirably, and the first payment . . . is now wanting, to put the office on a respectable footing . . . Treasurer. Received of [Bennington, A. Haswell, 1800]
broadside 15.5 X 13 cm.

McCorison 587
VtU-W mp. 49178

B11172 VERMONT GAZETTE
To the Republicans of the western districts of Vermont. Gentlemen, Impelled from principle to wish for a perpetuation of a Republican vehicle of intelligence in our part of the union . . . Anthony Haswell. Bennington, Vermont, Feb. 13, 1800. [Bennington, A. Haswell, 1800]
broadside 55 X 15 cm.
Appeal to investors to buy shares
McCorison 586
VtU-W mp. 49179

B11173 W., N., of the County of Worcester
Remarkable dreams, &c. . . . By N. W. of the County of Worcester . . . [Worcester?] Printed in the year . . . 1800.
36 p. 21 cm. [ ]^6 A-B^6
MWA mp. 49142

B11174 WASHINGTON, GEORGE, 1732-1799
The legacy of the Father of his Country. Address of George Washington, on declining being considered a candidate for the President . . . [Charlestown? Samuel Etheridge? 1800]
22 p. 20 cm.
Not Evans 38986, nor part of 37332
RPJCB (bound with a copy of Evans 37581) mp. 49181

B11175 WASHINGTON, GEORGE, 1732-1799
[The will of General George Washington . . . Elisabeth (Hager's) Town, Thomas Grieves, 1800]

Advertised in the *Maryland Herald*, Feb. 27, 1800, as "In the press;" and Mar. 27, 1800, as "Just published, and for sale."
Minick 629
No copy known mp. 49182

B11176 WATERHOUSE, BENJAMIN, 1754-1846
Heads of a course of lectures on natural history (given annually since 1788) . . . [Printed at the University Press in Cambridge, by W. Hilliard] [1800?]
broadside
Hilliard began printing in 1800
MWA

B11177 WATTS, ISAAC, 1674-1748
Divine and moral songs in easy language for the use of children . . . Printed in Catskill, by M. & H. Croswell, for Geo. Chittenden, sign of the Bible, Hudson. [1800?]
36 p. 13.5 cm.
Dated by d'Alté A. Welch
d'Alté A. Welch, Cleveland (1962) mp. 49185

B11178 WATTS, ISAAC, 1674-1748
Divine songs, attempted in easy language . . . (The ninety-fifth edition) Boston: Printed & sold by N. Coverly [1800?]
36 p.
MWA (2 copies) mp. 49184

B11179 WATTS, ISAAC, 1674-1748
Divine songs, attempted in easy language . . . Philadelphia, Printed and sold by John M'Culloch, 1800.
31 p. 10.5 cm.
Mrs. Joseph Carson, Philadelphia (1962) mp. 49186

B11180 WAYNE, CALEB P
Philadelphia, July 28 1800 Sir, Having purchased of Mr. J. W. Fenno . . . title to the *Gazette of the United States* . . . C. P. Wayne. [Philadelphia, 1800]
broadside
PHi

B11181 WEBSTER, NOAH, 1758-1843
An American selection of lessions in reading and speaking . . . Being the third part of A grammatical institute of the English language. The fifteenth edition. Hartford, Hudson and Goodwin [1800?]
240 p. 16 cm.
Skeel-Carpenter 492
Ct; CtHT-W (imperfect); MWA (imperfect) mp. 49187

B11182 WEBSTER, NOAH, 1758-1843
An American selection of lessons in reading and speaking . . . Being the third part of A grammatical institute of the English language. New-York, Printed by G. and R. Waite, for Evert Duyckinck, 1800.
261, [3] p. 17 cm.
Skeel-Carpenter 493; New York Public 1289
CtY; MH; MWA; NN; NhD mp. 49188

B11183 WESTERN calendar: or, an almanack for the year . . . 1801 . . . Washington [Pa.], John Colerick [1800]
[36] p.
MWA

B11184 [WHITCOMB, CHAPMAN] 1765-1833
A concise view of antient and modern religion . . . [Leominster?] Printed [by Adams & Wilder?] for Chapman Whitcomb [1800?]
12 p. 18.5 cm.
Same wording as Whitcomb's "Comparative View of Religion" printed in his "Miscellaneous Poems."
MWA mp. 49190

B11185 [WHITCOMB, CHAPMAN] 1765-1833
A poem, on religious ignorance, pride and avarice;--- or the modern priest . . . [Leominster? Adams & Wilder? 1800?]
broadside 26.5 X 19 cm.
Practically the same wording as his "Concise view of antient and modern religion."
MWA mp. 49191

B11186 WHITE, JAMES
For sale, by James White, at Franklin's Head, opposite the Prison, Court-Street, Boston, A large collection of books . . . [Boston, J. White, ca. 1800?]
broadside 39.5 X 31.5 cm.
Dated by John Alden
MH (2 copies) mp. 49192

B11187 WILKINS, WILLIAM
Take notice. To be sold at auction in Billerica . . . Billerica, May 27th, 1800. [Boston? 1800]
broadside 18 X 20 cm.
MB mp. 49195

B11188 THE wood robin. Boston, Printed & sold at P. A. von Hagens Musical Magazine No. 3 Cornhill [1800?]
broadside 33 X 23.5 cm.
Words and music
Von Hagen was at this address in July 1800
RPJCB mp. 49196

B11189 ZUM 13ten November, 1800, in Salem. [Salisbury, N. C., Francis Coupee, 1800]
4 p. 12mo caption title
PPL mp. 49187

NO DATE

B11190 A DIALOGUE between a noble lord, and a poor woodman . . . [n.p., 17–]
broadside 35.5 X 24.5 cm.
3 columns of verse
From typography, probably about 1770
CtHi mp. 49062

B11191 A DIALOGUE between a noble lord, and a poor woodman . . . Sold at the Printing-Office in Hartford [17--]
broadside 31 X 21 cm.
From typography, probably about 1790
CtHi mp. 49063

B11192 THE doctor and squire. You lovers of England, whoever you be . . . Sold at the Bible & Heart, Cornhill, Boston. [n.d.]
broadside 34.5 X 23.5 cm.
MHaHi mp. 49065

B11193 THE drunken husband and tea-drinking wife, &c. . . . [col. 2] The hounds are all out, &c. . . . [n.p., n.d.]
broadside 34 X 23 cm.
Columns separated by vertical row of rosette printers' ornaments
CtHi mp. 49066

B11194 [THE fortunate] lovers: [o] r [Sweet William] of Plymouth . . . Because they appeared so gallant and gay With musick and dancing finish's the day. FINIS. Printed and sold in New-London. [n.d.]
broadside 34.5 X 23.5 cm.
18th century typography
3 columns of verse
Wording supplied by Roger E. Stoddard
CtHi (upper left quadrant lacking) mp. 49071

B11195 FÜR den Fünften May. Un Einige meiner vertrautesten Freunde und theilnehmenden Brüder . . . [n.p., 17--]
4 p. 21 cm.
Postscript dated 1766; Abbots-Creek [Pa.] mentioned
"Probably pre-1800."--C. K. Shipton
MWA mp. 49074

B11196 HAMMON, JUPITER
An evening thought. Salvation by Christ with penetential cries: composed by Jupiter Hammon . . . the 25th of December, 1760 . . . [n.p., n.d.]
broadside 26 X 20 cm.
Porter 113
NHi mp. 49079

B11197 HOOK, JAMES, 1746-1827
Rondo. Hook. [n.p., n.d.]
11 p. 32 cm. caption title
MiU-C mp. 49089

B11198 NEW song. My dearest life, were you my wife, How happy should I be . . . When up and down, from town to town, We jolly soldiers rove, Then you, my queen, in Chase Marine, Shall more like queen of love . . . [n.p., n.d.]
broadside 23 X 12 cm.
18th century typography
5 stanzas
CtHi mp. 49120

B11199 THE parable of the one talent, expounded according to Scripture and Reason: Matthew XXV . . . [n.p., n.d.]
broadside
4 columns of verse
CtHi mp. 49129

B11200 THE poor man's wealth described, in an epitome of a contented mind . . . Printed and sold in New-London [17--]
broadside 35 X 20 cm.
2 columns of verse
From typography, probably about 1770
CtHi mp. 49137

B11201 [SECCOMB, JOHN] 1708-1792
Cambridge, December 1731. Some time since died here Mr. Mathew Abbey . . . his last will and testament . . . New-Haven, January, 1731-2. Our sweeper having lately buried his spouse . . . [n.p., 17–]
broadside 35.5 X 21.5 cm.
In verse
Ford 611; New York Public 171
MHi (imperfect). Photostat: NN

B11202 A SHORT account of a dreadful thunder storm in Goshen in Connecticut, and elsewhere . . . [n.p., n.d.]
broadside
Refers to the deaths of Martin Wilcox, James Rich, Sarah Larkin, Joseph Young
3 columns of verse
CtHi (reduced facsim.) mp. 49146

B11203 A SORROWFUL history of a rich merchant and Lucretia . . . [Hartford] [Printed near Hartford Bridge.] [17--]
broadside 40 X 25 cm.
Date assigned from typography
CtHi

B11204 WHEATLEY, PHYLLIS, 1754-1784
An ode, on the birth day of Pompey Stockbridge. [n.p., n.d.]
broadside 10.5 X 9.5 cm.
Probably written by Phyllis Wheatley
Porter 267
Arthur B. Spingarn, New York City mp. 49189

Addenda

The items which follow came to light in early 1970. They are chiefly the result of the zealous efforts of C. William Miller. Mr. Miller visited the Science Press, saw the page proofs, and speedily communicated corrigenda, delenda, and addenda.

B11025 [CA'N yn dangos Truenus hanes, Ma'b a Merch . . . Philadelphia, B. Franklin, 1730]
broadside?
Translation from the Welsh begins: A song giving the sad story of a youth and a maid . . .
Advertised in the *Pennsylvania Gazette*, Feb. 19, 1729/30, as just published and for sale at the New Printing-Office.—C. William Miller
No copy known

B11206 MANUEL, DAVID, d. 1726
[Cyfraith yr Iâr a'r Mynawyd . . . Philadelphia, B. Franklin, 1730]
broadside?
Advertised in Welsh in the *Pennsylvania Gazette*, Feb. 19, 1729/30, as just published and for sale
No copy known

B11207 SYNOD OF PHILADELPHIA
[Agreement to adopt Westminster Confession of Faith. Philadelphia, B. Franklin, 1730]
broadside?
Ascribed to Franklin's press by C. William Miller on the basis of a payment record to Franklin "1730-31 Jany 7th . . . for printing ye Synods Agreement, £1.13.4."
No copy known

B11208 GRAY, THOMAS, OF DELAWARE
Advertisement. To be sold by way of publick vendue, by Thomas Gray, executor of the estate of Mr. John Henzey . . . New-Castle County, dated the day of 1731 . . . [Philadelphia, B. Franklin, 1731]
broadside 21 × 16 cm.
Imprint assigned by C. William Miller
DeHi

B11209 PENNSYLVANIA. GOVERNOR, 1726-1736
[Proclamation for the regulation of traffic with the Indians, Aug. 20, 1731. Philadelphia, B. Franklin, 1731]
broadside
On Aug. 27, 1731, Franklin charged the Province "for printing a proclamation 1 sheet, £1.5.0."
No copy known

B11210 PENNSYLVANIA. LAWS, STATUTES
Anno Regni Georgii II . . . octavo. At a General Assembly of . . . Pennsylvania, begun . . . the fourteenth day of October . . . continued . . . to the seventeenth day of March, 1734. Philadelphia: Printed and sold by B. Franklin, M,DCC,XXXIV [i.e. 1735]
5p. 33 cm. A^4
Text: "An act for enabling diverse inhabitants . . . to hold lands," a resetting of p. 152-154 of the session laws
CtY

B11211 PENNSYLVANIA
[By the Proprietaries. Notice calling for payment of consideration money, Nov. 23, 1738. Philadelphia, B. Franklin, 1738]
broadside?
Text in German, parallel to Evans 4297
Franklin charged Thomas Penn on Nov. 22, 1738, 15s. "for 200 Dutch Advertisements."—C. William Miller
No copy known

B11212 PENNSYLVANIA. RECEIVER-GENERAL
[By the Proprietaries. Quit-rent notice, Feb. 15, 1737/38. James Steel, Rec. Gen. Philadelphia, B. Franklin, 1738]
broadside
On Feb. 27 Franklin charged Thomas Penn for "500 Advertisements Receiver General—£1.5.0."—C. William Miller
No copy known

B11213 PENNSYLVANIA. RECEIVER-GENERAL
[By the Proprietaries. Quit-rent notice, Feb. 15, 1737/38. James Steel, Rec. Gen. Philadelphia, B. Franklin, 1738]
broadside
German text, parallel to B11212
On Feb. 27 Franklin charged Thomas Penn for "500 Advertisements Dutch, £1.5.0."—C. William Miller
No copy known

B11214 PHILADELPHIA. ORDINANCES
[Ordinance for preventing frauds and abuses in the measuring of salt, flax seed, wheat and other grains . . . Philadelphia, B. Franklin, 1738]
broadside?
Ordered published Apr. 29, 1738; Franklin charged the Commonalty £4.5.0. "for printing the act . . . relating to measuring salt, flour etc."—C. William Miller
No copy located

B11215 PENNSYLVANIA. RECEIVER-GENERAL
[By the Proprietaries. Quit-rent notice, Feb. 8, 1738/39. James Steel, Rec. Gen. Philadelphia, B. Franklin, 1739]
broadside?
On Feb. 11 Franklin charged Thomas Penn for "800 advertisements English, £1.12.6."—C. William Miller
The advertisement ran in the *Pennsylvania Gazette* Feb. 8 to Mar. 15
No copy known

B11216 PENNSYLVANIA. RECEIVER-GENERAL
[By the Proprietaries. Quit-rent notice, Feb. 8, 1738/39. James Steel, Rec. Gen. Philadelphia, B. Franklin, 1739]
broadside?

German text, parallel to B11215
On Feb. 11 Franklin charged Thomas Penn for "500 advertisements Dutch, £1.5.0."—C. William Miller
No copy known

B11217 PENNSYLVANIA. RECEIVER-GENERAL
[By the Proprietaries. Quit-rent notice, June 25, 1739. Philadelphia, B. Franklin, 1739]
broadside
On June 28 Franklin charged Thomas Penn for "200 folio advts English" and for "200 d[itt]o Dutch."—C. William Miller
Text in German; the English notice is Evans 4410
No copy known

B11218 [SHEET almanack for the year 1740. Philadelphia, B. Franklin, 1739?]
broadside
On Jan. 3, 1739/40, Franklin charged "Capt. Spicer Soldier" for "printing 520 sheet almanacks at 4d.—£8.13.4."—C. William Miller
No copy known

B11219 SOME necessary precautions, worthy to be considered . . . [Philadelphia, B. Franklin, 174–]
broadside 29.5 X 16.5 cm.
Ascribed to Franklin's press by C. William Miller on the basis of type; cf. Evans 2964
Nj

B11220 EVANS, DAVID, 1688-1751
A short, plain help for parents . . . to feed their babes with the sincere milk of God's word . . . The second edition. Philadelphia, B. Franklin, 1740.
46 p. 14 cm.
PPF

B11221 PENNSYLVANIA. RECEIVER-GENERAL
[By the Proprietaries. Quit-rent notice, Feb. 15, 1739/40. James Steel, Rec. Gen. Philadelphia, B. Franklin, 1740]
broadside
On Feb. 15 Franklin charged Thomas Penn "for 300 advts quitrents, 10s."—C. William Miller
No copy known

B11222 DELAWARE. LAWS, STATUTES
[Act for establishing a militia within this government. Philadelphia, B. Franklin, 1741]
broadside
On Sept. 18, 1741, Franklin charged Joseph Wharton £3.10.6. for "282 New-Castle militia laws at 3d."—C. William Miller
No copy known

B11223 [ALMANACK for the year 1742. Philadelphia, B. Franklin, 1742]

In March 1741/42 Franklin charged Joseph Grover, a merchant of Spanish Town, Jamaica, "Printing & paper 1200 alm^{s}—£20, 350 book ditto—£8.15.0."—C. William Miller
No copy known

B11224 HAND-IN-HAND FIRE COMPANY
[Articles of agreement. Philadelphia, B. Franklin, 1742]

In March 1742 Franklin charged the Company the sum of £5 for "printing their articles & list [of members?]."—C. William Miller
No copy known

B11225 [CREAGHEAD, ALEXANDER] d. 1766
[A renewal of the covenants . . . and engagement to duties . . . as they were carried on at Middle Octorara, Nov. 11, 1743. Philadelphia, B. Franklin and D. Hall, 1743?]
1 leaf, 104 p. 16.5 cm.
Title-page reconstructed from 2d ed. (B11233)
PHi (t.p. and sig. A-B in ms.) mp. 40475

B11226 STAR FIRE COMPANY
[Articles of agreement. Philadelphia, B. Franklin, 1743]

On July 5, 1743, Franklin charged the Company with "printing their articles & names, £2.17.6."—C. William Miller
No copy known

B11227 UNION FIRE COMPANY
Articles of the Union Fire-Company in Philadelphia . . . [Philadelphia, B. Franklin, 1743]
broadside 55.5 X 42 cm.
In two columns
Ascribed to the Franklin press by C. William Miller on the evidence of the type and the recording of a bill tendered to the Company for printing these articles and a list of the members, dated Oct. 31, 1743
PHC

B11228 NEW JERSEY. GOVERNOR, 1738
[By Lewis Morris, Governor of New Jersey, proclamation, June 14, 1744, announcing the declaration of war with France. Philadelphia, B. Franklin, 1744]
broadside?
Franklin charged the Province £1.15.0. for printing on June 14, 1744, "Declat^{n} of War—35s."—C. William Miller
No copy known

B11229 NEW JERSEY. GOVERNOR, 1738
[By Lewis Morris, Governor of New Jersey, a proclamation, June 14, 1744, encouraging citizens to state of readiness. Philadelphia, B. Franklin, 1744]
broadside?
On June 14, 1744, Franklin charged the Province £1.15.0. for printing "Encouragmt &c. . . . 35s."—C. William Miller
No copy known

B11230 BIBLE. N.T.
[New Testament. Philadelphia, B. Franklin, 1745?]

Evidence for printing by Franklin supplied by C. William Miller
No copy known

B11231 HASLAM, JOHN, 1690-1773
Handsworth Woodhouse, in Yorkshire, 6th month, 12th, 1746. To Friends in Pennsylvania and New-Jersey, in America . . . [Philadelphia, B. Franklin, and D. Hall, 1746]
2 p. 31 cm.
1000 copies ordered printed in November 1746; distributed to the Philadelphia Meeting on Dec. 26, 1746. Payment itemized Sept. 5, 1753, as follows: "To cash pd Franklin and Hall for printing 1000 copies J. Haslam's Epistles . . . in 1746, £4.3.4."—C. William Miller
PHi. Archives, Society of Friends, Philadelphia

B11232 NEW JERSEY. COUNCIL
[Proclamation concerning tumultuous and riotous assemblies, Dec. 10, 1746. Philadelphia, B. Franklin and D. Hall, 1746]
broadside

The Council ordered the proclamation to be sent to Franklin "with directions to him to make one hundred copys," to be distributed in packets of ten to every sheriff. —C. William Miller
No copy known

B11233 [CREAGHEAD, ALEXANDER] d. 1766
A renewal of the covenants, national and solemn league; a confession of sins, and engagement to duties . . . at Middle Octorara . . . November 11, 1743 . . . [Philadelphia?] Re-printed in the year, MDCCXLVIII.
66 p. 16.5 cm.
Second edition of B11225.—C. William Miller
MHi; PPPrHi

B11234 CASE between Hugh Boyle and Joseph Jones, with sundry affidavits and certificates; being a full answer to . . . malicious calumnies and aspersions thrown on the character of Peter Worrall . . . Witness our hands at Philadelphia, this twelfth day of September, 1750. Israel Pemberton, Thomas Leech . . . [Philadelphia, 1750]
4 p. 29 cm.
PHi

B11235 POOR Richard improved: being an almanack . . . for . . . 1751. By Richard Saunders . . . Philadelphia, B. Franklin [1750]
[36] p.
On p. 34: "Superior Courts of New-England"; cf. Evans 6502
CSmH; CtY; DLC; MB; NjHi

B11236 [A CATALOGUE of curious and valuable books sold at auction, Feb. 12, 1750/51. Philadelphia, B. Franklin and D. Hall, 1751]

Ascribed by C. William Miller to Franklin's press on the basis of a lengthy entry charging Thomas Osborne, a London bookseller, for having sold at auction a group of books, "including all charges of cataloguing and numbering, printing & dispersing of catalogues . . ." The auction was advertised repeatedly; ". . . Catalogues . . . given gratis at the Post-Office, and at the place of sale."
No copy known

B11237 PHILADELPHISCHER Wiederschall des hertzlichen Wunsches der Evangelischen Brüder in Teutschland . . . Philadelphia, Benjamin Franklin, und Johann Böhm [1751]
5 p. 33 cm.
Printed by Böhm for use in dedicating on May 12, 1751, the first organ acquired by a Colonial German congregation.—C. William Miller
MBMu

B11238 A DESCRIPTION of the covenant of grace . . . Boston: Printed and sold by S. Kneeland in Queen-Street. 1752.
broadside
MB

B11239 GT. BRIT. POST OFFICE
Directions to the deputy post-masters, for keeping their accounts . . . B. Franklin. [Philadelphia? B. Franklin and D. Hall? 1753?]
broadside 56 X 43.5 cm.
C. William Miller suggests a slightly later date for this and B1604
CtY

B11240 DELAWARE. LAWS, STATUTES
. . . At an Assembly held at New-Castle, the twentieth day of October, 1753. Philadelphia: Printed and sold by B. Franklin, and D. Hall, MDCCLIV.
9 p. 28.5 cm. A-B^2
An act concerning written and nuncupative wills
MH-L

B11241 GERMANTOWN LIBRARY
[Instrument of partnership. Philadelphia, B. Franklin and D. Hall, 1754]

On May 6, 1754, Hall charged the Library £3.11.6. "for printing their instrument of partnership."—C. William Miller
No copy known

B11242 GT. BRIT. POST OFFICE
Benjamin Franklin, and William Hunter, Esquires, Post-Masters-General of all . . . dominions on the Continent of North-America. To all to whom these presents . . . Dated the day of 175 . . . [Philadelphia, B. Franklin and D. Hall, 1754?]
broadside 23 X 37.5 cm.
Certificate of appointment to deputy postmaster
Earliest date inserted by hand: Dec. 24, 1754; latest date July 11, 1760
NN (2 copies); PPAmP

B11243 PHILADELPHIA. NEW THEATRE
For the benefit of Mr. Lewis Hallam, by a company of comedians from London, at the New Theatre . . . this present evening (being the twenty-seventh of May, 1754) will be presented . . . Tunbridge Walks . . . [Philadelphia, B. Franklin and D. Hall, 1754]
broadside 36.5 X 21.5 cm.
In April and May 1754 Hall charged the company on 12 separate occasions for a total of 4300 playbills and almost 5000 tickets; at least 10 printed playbills are missing from the series.—C. William Miller
PHi

B11244 PENNSYLVANIA. GOVERNOR, 1756-1769
[By . . . William Denny, Esq; Lieutenant-governor . . . a proclamation, Dec. 11, 1758, appointing December 28 as day of public thanksgiving . . . Philadelphia, B. Franklin and D. Hall, 1758]
broadside?
Hall charged the Province £2.10.0. for printing 200 copies.—C. William Miller
No copy known

B11245 PENNSYLVANIA. GOVERNOR, 1756-1759
[By . . . William Denny, Esq; Lieutenant-governor . . . a proclamation appointing October 31 as day of public thanksgiving . . . Oct. 17, 1759 . . . Philadelphia, B. Franklin and D. Hall, 1759]
broadside?
Hall charged the Province on Oct. 19, 1759, £2.10.0 for printing 200 copies—C. William Miller
No copy known

B11246 PENNSYLVANIA. GOVERNOR, 1756-1759
[By . . . William Denny, Esq; Lieutenant-governor . . . a proclamation for preventing sickly vessels coming up to the City . . . July 21, 1759. Philadelphia, B. Franklin and D. Hall, 1759]
broadside?
Hall charged the Province £1.15.0 on July 26, 1759, for printing this proclamation.—C. William Miller
No copy known

B11247 PENNSYLVANIA. GOVERNOR, 1756-1759
[By . . . William Denny, Esq; Lieutenant-governor . . . a proclamation for raising men for his Majesty's service . . . Apr. 21, 1759. Philadelphia, B. Franklin and D. Hall, 1759]
broadside?
Hall charged the Province £2.10.0. on Apr. 21, 1759, for printing this proclamation (200 copies?).–C. William Miller
No copy known

B11248 GT. BRIT. ARMY
[Advertisement for wagons for the King's service. B. Franklin and D. Hall, 1760]
broadside?
Hall charged General Monckton £2.0.0. for carrying this advertisement in *Pennsylvania Gazette* May 22, 1760, and for printing 300 single copies.–C. William Miller
No copy known

B11249 HALL, DAVID, 1714-1772
Books imported in the last vessel from London, and to be sold by David Hall . . . Philadelphia . . . [Philadelphia, B. Franklin and D. Hall, 1760?]
broadside 33? × 17.5 cm.
In two columns
Bound after the Feb. 7, 1760, issue of the MWA copy of the *Pennsylvania Gazette*; caption wording the same, but textually unlike the three-column broadside (at PHi) described by Hildeburn 1620 and Evans 8362.–C. William Miller
MWA mp. 8632

B11250 PENNSYLVANIA. GOVERNOR, 1759-1763
[By the honourable James Hamilton, Esq.; Lieutenant-Governor . . . Proclamation, Feb. 21, 1760, offering a reward for the murderers of some Indians in Cumberland County . . . Philadelphia, B. Franklin and D. Hall, 1760]
broadside?
Hall charged £2.1.0. for 200 copies, Feb. 22, 1760
No copy known

B11251 PENNSYLVANIA. GOVERNOR, 1759-1763
[By the honourable James Hamilton, Esq.; Lieutenant-Governor . . . Proclamation, Apr. 15, 1760, for raising men . . . Philadelphia, B. Franklin and D. Hall, 1760]
broadside?
Hall charged £2.10.0 for 200 copies, Apr. 15, 1760
No copy known

B11252 PENNSYLVANIA. GOVERNOR, 1759-1763
[Notice for officers and soldiers of the Pennsylvania Regiment to be at Carlisle by June 10, 1760 . . . Philadelphia, B. Franklin and D. Hall, 1760]
broadside?
Hall charged 10s. for 100 copies, May 24, 1760
No copy known

B11253 PHILADELPHIA CONTRIBUTIONSHIP
[Deed of Settlement, including rules and orders . . . Philadelphia, B. Franklin and D. Hall, 1760]
The Directors ordered 1500 copies to be printed, and directed the clerk to extract from the minutes rules and orders to be noted in the new printing. Hall charged £8 for printing 1000 copies, Jan. 18, 1760.–C. William Miller
No copy known

B11254 SAYRE, MCLEAN, AND STEWART, firm
[List of medicines. Philadelphia, B. Franklin and D. Hall, 1760]
broadside?
On Oct. 3, 1760, Hall charged these merchants £6.10.0. for printing 1200 copies.–C. William Miller
No copy known

B11255 WADE, FRANCIS
[Advertisement relating to John White. Philadelphia, B. Franklin and D. Hall, 1760]
broadside?
On Nov. 18, 1760 Hall charged Wade £2 for printing 1000 single copies.–C. William Miller
No copy known

B11256 FRIENDSHIP FIRE COMPANY
[Articles of agreement and list of members . . . Philadelphia, B. Franklin and D. Hall, 1761]
broadside?
Hall charged on Feb. 14, 1761, for 60 copies of their Articles and 60 lists of names.–C. William Miller
No copy known

B11257 AMERICAN FIRE COMPANY
[Articles of agreement . . . Philadelphia, B. Franklin and D. Hall, 1762]
broadside?
Hall charged the Company £2.10.0 on Apr. 19, 1762, for printing 100 copies.–C. William Miller
No copy known

B11258 PENNSYLVANIA. GOVERNOR, 1759-1763
By the honourable James Hamilton, Esq; Lieutenant-Governor . . . a proclamation. Whereas divers persons . . . made several attempts . . . to possess themselves of . . . tract of land . . . not yet purchased from the Indians . . . [June 2, 1763] . . . Philadelphia, B. Franklin and D. Hall [1763]
broadside 35 × 24 cm.
Hall charged the Province £2.10.0. for printing 200 copies.–C. William Miller
CtY

B11259 PENNSYLVANIA. GENERAL ASSEMBLY
Proceedings of the Assembly of the Province of Pennsylvania, on the supply bill . . . [Philadelphia, B. Franklin and D. Hall, 1764]
broadside 40 × 26.5 cm.
In three columns
Latest date in text: March 24, 1764
Hall charged the Province on Apr. 12, 1764, for 3000 copies.–C. William Miller
PPAmP. Archives, Society of Friends, Phila.

B11260 BURROUGHS, EDEN, 1738-1813
A faithful narrative of the wonderful dealings of God, towards Polly Davis . . . By the Reverend Mr. Burroughs . . . and the Reverend Mr. Easterbrooks . . . Exeter: Printed and sold by Henry Ranlet–1793.
8 p.
ICN

B11261 ST. MICHAEL'S AND ZION LUTHERAN CHURCH, PHILADELPHIA
Ein Geschenk für die Kinder, von den Gliedern des Kirchenraths der St. Michaelis- und Zions-Gemeinde in Philadelphia. Philadelphia, Gedruckt bey Steiner und Kämmerer, 1793.
[8] p. 17 cm.
PGL

B11262 [HERVEY, ELIZABETH.] fl. 1788-1814
The history of Ned Evans. Interspersed with moral and critical remarks . . . and incidental strictures on the present state of Ireland . . . Dublin: Printed by John Rice . . . and sold by H. and P. Rice, Philadelphia, 1796.
2 v. 17.5 cm. 12mo
In part, set in America during the later stages of the Revolutionary War.–Roger Stoddard
MH

Analysis of Items Located

In the *Supplement* there are 11,262 numbered items. Thirty-nine of these have been deleted, and fifty-nine have been added with an "a." The actual total, then, is 11,282.

No copy is known of 694 out of these 11,282. The entries are included because the compiler feels that the evidence submitted by the relevant bibliographers is convincing. On the other hand, very likely actual copies of items which the compiler is excluding will some day come to light, thus adding embarrassment to his sins of omission.

Checking a large number of items for their pagination produces some interesting findings. It might have been predicted that items supplementary to a work as comprehensive as the original Evans would turn up a large number of broadsides, and this did in fact happen. Broadsides make up about 45% of all entries. If to these are added the pamphlets of two to four pages, the percentage of items with four pages or fewer rises to 54%. The pagination of an additional 5.5% is unknown, though in many instances it can be surmised. This leaves 40.5% as the percentage of entries which contain five or more pages.

A count has been made of unique items held by individual libraries. Excluding 268 items owned by private collectors at the time of their recording in someone's bibliography, we find an amazing number of entries that describe unique copies – 7155 out of 11,282. If a photocopy or facsimile is held by only one library, and if the location of the original is unknown, the item is credited to that library as unique; but if the original also is located, the library owning the original is credited with the unique item, and the library owning the photocopy is not considered.

Unique items held outside the United States total 130, distributed as follows:

Sweden	1	
Cuba	2	
France	4	
Spain	11	
Gt. Brit.	112	(94 in the Public Record Office)

Unique items are to be found in 27 states, distributed as follows:

Massachusetts	1996	New Jersey	144	Ohio	13
New York	1187	South Carolina	80	Louisiana	5
Pennsylvania	955	Virginia	65	Maine	4
Dist. of Col.	866	Vermont	48	Kentucky	3
Rhode Island	519	North Carolina	46	Indiana	1
Connecticut	346	Georgia	36	Iowa	1
California	321	Illinois	25	Minnesota	1
Michigan	195	Wisconsin	22	Missouri	1
Maryland	171	Delaware	17	Tennessee	1

Libraries owning 30 or more uniques are listed below, in order of rank. Among them they account for 6366 items. At the same time it is interesting to observe that 83 libraries have only a single unique item each, and that 55 others have only two to four items. In all, unique items are held by 218 libraries.

American Antiquarian Society	921
Library of Congress	846
New-York Historical Society	571
Massachusetts Historical Society	498
Historical Society of Pennsylvania	497
New York Public Library	472
John Carter Brown Library	279
Library Company of Philadelphia	275
Connecticut Historical Society	270
Boston Public Library	220
Henry E. Huntington Library	202
William L. Clements Library	193
Rhode Island Historical Society	163
Harvard University (including 13 in departmental libraries)	107
Essex Institute	102
Maryland Historical Society	99
Public Record Office	94
Rutgers–The State University	83
Archives Division (Massachusetts)	63
Rosenbach Foundation	57
Yale University	55
New York State Library	49
New Hampshire Historical Society	48
South Carolina Archives	39
Enoch Pratt Free Library	38
Brown University	34
University of Pennsylvania	31
De Renne Georgia Library	30
Princeton University	30

20–29 unique

MBAt	29
RNHi	28
PP	24
NNS	22
WHi	22
PPAmP	20
VtHi	20

10–19 unique

Vi	19
ViU	17
NAII	16
MWiW-C	16
NcU	15
ScU	15
VtU	14
CU-B	12
ICN	12
Nj	12
NjHi	11
Archivo general (Seville)	11
NBUG	10
NcD	10
NhD	10
ScC	10

5-9 unique	**2-4 unique**	**1 unique only**
28 libraries	55 libraries	83 libraries

Items listed in the Addenda are included in the above distribution.

The preëminence of the well-known collections of American imprints is again demonstrated. The leading six libraries account for 3805 of the unique items and are heavily represented among the items not unique.

A second glance at the top twenty libraries reveals certain libraries which even yet have not received the scholarly attention that is their due for their holdings of early Americana. Among these are Rutgers, the Connecticut Historical Society, the Essex Institute, and the former Ridgeway Branch of the Library Company of Philadelphia.

It is interesting to speculate how much the distribution of library holdings as shown in the main body of Evans resembles that of the *Supplement*, and how much it was skewed by Evans' limitations of time, money, and strength. His travels forty to sixty years ago admittedly did not cover even all the imprint collections he knew of, nor did he have access to most of the regional and subject bibliographies available today, nor to modern copying devices. The present supplementarian, surrounded by modern bibliographic conveniences, can only bow in awe before the magnitude of Evans' accomplishment.